THE KOVELS'
COMPLETE
ANTIQUES PRICE LIST

BOOKS BY RALPH AND TERRY KOVEL

Dictionary of Marks—Pottery and Porcelain.

A Directory of American Silver, Pewter and Silver Plate

American Country Furniture, 1780–1875

Know Your Antiques,® Revised

The Kovels' Complete Antiques Price List

The Kovels' Complete Bottle Price List

The Kovels' Collector's Guide to American Art Pottery

Kovels' Organizer for Collectors

The Kovels' Price Guide for Collector Plates, Figurines, Paperweights, and Other Limited Editions

ELEVENTH EDITION

THE KOVELS'
COMPLETE
ANTIQUES PRICE LIST

A guide to the 1978–1979 market for professionals, dealers, and collectors

by Ralph and Terry Kovel

ILLUSTRATED

Crown Publishers, Inc., New York

Inquiries should be addressed to Crown Publishers, Inc.,
One Park Avenue, New York, N.Y. 10016

Printed in the United States of America

Published simultaneously in Canada by General Publishing Company Limited

Library of Congress Catalog Card Number: 72-84290

ISBN: 0-517-534681

INTRODUCTION

The past year of sales for antiques has been a time of rising prices, record-breaking sales, and increased involvement by buyers who had never before considered antiques as part of an investment plan. Once again Chinese porcelains, signed French furniture, and Oriental rugs were among the most popular items in the worldwide market. In the high-priced prestige auction houses of the United States, American antiques did well, especially top-quality furniture, nineteenth-century still-life paintings, Southern antiques, eighteenth- and nineteenth-century jewelry, Tiffany lamps, and a new area called "International Victorian style." Investors disenchanted with both the stock market and the American dollar turned to objects of value, and the antiques market boomed on all levels.

Prices on very few types of antiques listed in *Kovels' Complete Antiques Price List* seem lower this year. Carnival glass, Heisey glass, a few types of art glass, and eighteenth-century English porcelains were at the same or lower levels. Advertising antiques, Hummel Goebel pieces, Royal Doulton figures and jugs, Fiesta ware, depression glass, art pottery, folk art, baskets, country furniture, and paper memorabilia rose in price.

Record prices were set for many types of antiques. A cardboard advertising sign for Bull Durham tobacco sold for $1,900, a tin sign for Sharples Cream Separator picturing an art nouveau lady and little girl brought $1,775.

A glazed pottery figure of a lion by John Bell of Waynesboro, Pennsylvania, astounded bidders with a record $18,000. A salt-glazed punchbowl, 15½ in., cobalt-blue decoration, inscribed "1811" brought $12,500. Even the small Goss China models hit new heights as a model of Sulgrave Manor brought $1,326. A Meissen cockatoo by Johann Kaendler sold for $60,000, another record, while a Staffordshire naval jug showing Perry's victory sold for $4,500. The Sevres milk pail made for Marie Antoinette sold in England for $102,600, a record for a piece of Sevres at auction and certainly the world's most expensive milk pail.

American furniture broke records. A block-front chest of drawers, Massachusetts, 1760–1780 brought $57,000; a miniature Philadelphia highboy brought $65,000, a record for both miniature furniture and Queen Anne style furniture. Interest in southern furniture hit a new high with $40,000 for a Chippendale walnut and cherry-wood secretary by John Shearer of Martinsburg, West Virginia.

Foreign furniture set new records: $11,735 for a German lacquered bureau, $42,857 for an ormolu-decorated desk and chair by Louis Marjorelle, and $11,224 for a 1904 Koloman Moser chair.

Top price ever for a piece of carnival glass was realized at a midwestern auction when $9,400 was paid for a red Regal Iris Gone with the Wind lamp. A Johnstown, Pennsylvania, bottle, dark green Engrees squat soda, sold for a reported $210. A Clichy convolvulus bouquet paperweight brought $51,000.

An art nouveau corsage ornament by Alphonse Mucha and Georges Fouquet brought $44,844, and a Faberge 1913 Easter egg sold for $220,000.

Paul Revere's autograph attached to the expense account for his famous ride brought $70,000 at auction; a Lincoln letter sold for $31,000. John F. Kennedy's check set a record at $5,250.

Three Gutenberg bibles were sold during the past year, the record auction price being two million dollars, although the private sale price for another copy is reported at two million four hundred thousand dollars.

Collectibles had a few startling sales: a 78 RPM record of "Stormy Weather" by the Five Sharps brought $3,866; a wax cylinder phonograph, $2,275; a carte de visite photograph of Abraham Lincoln, $750; a firemark, $1,400; a woven coverlet with a Hempfield railroad design, $5,500; a tinplate Mickey Mouse organ-grinder toy, $3,105; a set of toy soldiers of the Royal Marine Light Infantry, $1,400; a mid-nineteenth century bronze corkscrew, $1,795; and a Honus Wagner baseball card, $3,876.

Record prices for silver included the world record for any art object other than a painting: $1,135,575 for a pair of Meissonier soup tureens. An American silver teapot, Peter Van Dyck, 1720–1740, fetched $47,000; a marked American copper coffeepot, eighteenth century, $14,000; and a pewter tankard by Henry Will, 1761–1793, $8,250.

Tiffany price records included $60,500 for a 1914 stained-glass window and $60,000 for a lotus lamp, 25 in. high.

The record sale of the year was probably the Von Hirsch collection sold in Europe for thirty-four million dollars, with dozens of record prices for fine arts, paintings, ivories, drawings, and textiles.

The general trend of the antique and collectible market is still up. Golden-oak furniture, mission furniture, even the hotel reproduction furniture of the 1920s are up. Twentieth-century glass and pottery, and ephemera, such as paper items, comic books, and political items, continue to rise.

All the prices included in this book are reports, not estimates. This means that at some sale in the United States the antique described was *offered for sale* at the price we have listed. A few of the prices are from auctions, but most are from shops and shows. We feel this is as accurate a method of reporting as is possible, although there are many regional variations in pricing. We have tried to avoid prices from auctions where it is apparent that "auction fever" has taken hold and the prices paid include the buyer's interest in the fame of the original owner.

Ralph M. Kovel, American Society of Appraisers, Senior Member

Terry H. Kovel, American Society of Appraisers, Senior Member
July, 1978

KOVELS' COMPLETE ANTIQUES PRICE LIST 11TH EDITION—PICTURE ACKNOWLEDGMENTS

Able Auctioneering Co.; Americana Auction Co.; Richard A. Bourne Co., Inc.; Joe Buberger; Christie; Manson & Woods; Douglas Galleries; Early's Antiques & Auction Co.; Robert C. Eldred Co., Inc.; Fleetville Auctions; Clarence B. Froman; Garths Auctions, Inc.; O. Rundle Gilbert; Hake's Americana & Collectibles; Donald Hall; Jordan-Volpe Galleries; Kaleidoscope; Conestoga Auction Co.; Kruse Auction Co.; Milwaukee Auction Galleries; Morton's Auction Exchange; Pacific Label Archives; Arthur Paholke; S. J. Phillips, LTD.; Arnold Schack Country Fare Auctions; Sotheby Parke Bernet, Inc.; Nancy Stolzenbach & Jack Kieffer; Tepper Galleries; Clyde R. Terry; Ward-Price Ltd.; Richard Withington Co.; Woody Auction Co.

OLD STURBRIDGE VILLAGE COLOR PICTURES

Old Sturbridge Village in Sturbridge, Massachusetts is a re-created New England town representing the fifty years following the Revolution. Buildings, objects, animals, farmlands, and working exhibits show the life of the times. A visit to a restored country store, printing office, meeting house, cooper shop, carding mill, grist mill, blacksmith shop, or saw mill is possible at the Village. Period homes, a law office, a tavern, a bank, covered bridge, school, and other buildings are furnished and open for inspection. Old Sturbridge is a working museum designed for the enjoyment of the whole family. Even the animals and farm products are as close to the nineteenth century as possible, with special breeds of sheep and varieties of fruit.

There are many special collections included in the museum buildings, such as lighting devices, woodenware, pottery, glass, textiles, firearms, folk art, paperweights, toys, and tinware.

The objects in the color pictures included in this book are representative of the collections of Old Sturbridge. The cover is a view of the dining room of the General Salem Towne House. On the table is a set of Japan pattern Mason's Patent Ironstone dishes. The Chippendale-type chairs are in a transitional form of the 1770s.

Old Sturbridge Village is open year round, in the summer from 9:30 to 5:30, in the winter from 10:00 to 4:00. It is on Rte. 20 west near the junction of Interstate 86 and exit 9 on the Massachusetts Turnpike. Remember it is an outdoor museum so dress comfortably and be prepared to walk.

Our special thanks to: John O. Curtis, Director, Curatorial Department; Henry J. Harlow, Chief Curator; Larry Morrison, Director of Public Information; Donald F. Eaton, Museum Photographer; Elaine Bushnell; Etta Falkner; and Sally Kesseli.

GUIDE TO USE

There are just a few simple rules to follow in using this book. Each listing is arranged in the following manner: CATEGORY (such as pressed glass, silver, or furniture); OBJECT (such as vase, spoon, table); DESCRIPTION (which includes as much information as possible about size, age, color, and pattern). Pressed glass is the only exception to this rule, and it is listed CATEGORY, PATTERN, OBJECT, DESCRIPTION. All items are presumed to be in good condition, undamaged, unless otherwise noted. Leaf through the book and examine the various category headings. Most of them are exactly as one would expect.

Several special categories were formed to make a more sensible listing of items possible. "Fire" includes fire-fighting equipment, fireplace equipment, and related pieces. "Kitchen" and "tool" include special equipment. As it would be unreasonable to expect the casual collector to know the proper name for each variety of tool, such as an "adze" or a "trephine," we have lumped them together in the special categories. Other special categories are "commemorative," "coronation," "store," "nautical," "weapon," and "railroad."

This book has several idiosyncrasies of style that must be noted before it can be used properly. The prices are compiled by computer, and the machine has dictated several strange rules. Everything in the book is listed alphabetically according to the IBM alphabetic system. This means that words such as "mt." are alphabetized as "M-T," not as "M-O-U-N-T." Another peculiarity of the machine alphabetizing is that all numerals come after all letters, thus 2 comes after z. A quick glance at a listing will make this clear, as the alphabetizing is consistent throughout the book.

No price over $9,999 can be listed.

We have made several editorial decisions that affect the use of the book. A bowl is a bowl and not a dish unless it is a special type of dish, such as a sauce dish. A butter dish is a "butter" and a celery dish is a "celery." A salt dish is called a "salt" to differentiate it from a saltshaker. A toothpick holder is called a "toothpick." It is always a "sugar and creamer," never a "creamer and sugar." Where one dimension is given, it is the height of the piece, or if the object is round, the dimension is the diameter. Height of a picture is listed before width. Glass is clear unless a color is indicated.

This book does not include price listings of fine-art paintings, books, comic books, stamps, coins, and a few other categories that are covered in specialized books. Prices for collector's editions and bottles are included, although both are more completely reported in *Kovels' Price Guide for Collector Plates, Figurines, Paperweights, and Other Limited Editions* and *Kovels' Complete Bottle Price List.*

Several categories such as "milk glass" and "bottles" include special reference numbers. These numbers refer the reader to the most widely known books about the category. When these numbers appear, the name of the special book is given in the paragraph heading. All of these numbers take the form "B-22," "Mck-G-11," and so forth. The letter is the author's initial; the number refers to a picture in the author's book.

All black-and-white pictures in *Kovels' Complete Antiques Price List* are of antiques sold during the past year. The prices are as reported by the seller. Each piece pictured is listed with the word "illus." as part of the description. Pictures are placed as close to the price listing as is possible. Color pictures are all from the collections of Old Sturbridge Village, and no prices are given for these antiques.

All prices listed in this book were recorded from antique shows, sales, flea markets, and auctions between June 1977 and June 1978. The prices have been taken from sales in all parts of the country, and variations are sometimes due to the geographic differences in pricing. Antiques of top quality tend to be most expensive near the town where they originated because the local collectors are informed about them. We have tried to be accurate in all of the prices reported, but we cannot be responsible for any errors that may have occurred. We welcome any suggestions for future editions of this book, but cannot answer letters asking for advice or appraisals.

THE KOVELS'
COMPLETE
ANTIQUES PRICE LIST

ABC plates, or children's alphabet plates, were popular from 1780 to 1860. The letters on the plate were meant as teaching aids for the children who were learning to read. The plates were made of pottery, porcelain, metal, or glass.

ABC, Book, Linen, 1884, 5 1/2 X 4 In.	5.00
ABC, Cup & Saucer, Toys & Pets, Germany	20.00
ABC, Cup, Letters & Animals	18.00
ABC, Dish, Baby, Jack & Jill, Verse & Pictures, Germany Mark, 7 1/2 In.	30.00
ABC, Mold, Turkey Ready For Oven, Tin, 3 1/2 In.	4.00
ABC, Mug, Handled, Simple Simon, Child's, C.1850	18.00
ABC, Mug, 4 Children In Cycle Scene, Pink, Leaf Handle, Staffordshire	46.00
ABC, Plate, Aluminum, 7 In.	9.00
ABC, Plate, Black Children, Riddle	42.00
ABC, Plate, Blue Transfer, F's For The Fowls	27.00
ABC, Plate, Boy & Girl Rolling Hoops, Tin, 3 In.	27.00
ABC, Plate, Boy Selling Newspapers, Girl Watching Rabbits, 7 In.	18.00
ABC, Plate, Brownies, Tin, 8 In.	35.00
ABC, Plate, Bulldog Center, Green, 6 1/2 In.	18.00
ABC, Plate, Carnival Glass, Stork	40.00
ABC, Plate, Child's, Frosted Center, Rabbit	25.00
ABC, Plate, Cinderella, Tunstall, England	35.00
ABC, Plate, Clear Glass, Scalloped Edge, Star Center, 6 In.	15.00
ABC, Plate, Clock, 7 In.	30.00
ABC, Plate, Cock Robin, Tin	32.00 To 50.00
ABC, Plate, Crusoe And Pets, 8 In.	38.00
ABC, Plate, Crusoe At Work, Multicolor Center Transfer, 7 1/4 In.	75.00
ABC, Plate, Crusoe Viewing The Island	60.00
ABC, Plate, Dog In Center, 6 1/2 In.	35.00
ABC, Plate, Ducks & Ducklings, Raised Letters On Stippled Rim, Amber, 6 In.	27.00
ABC, Plate, Elephant In Center	31.00
ABC, Plate, Farmyard, Black Transfer Child On Pony, Staffordshire, 7 In.	45.00
ABC, Plate, Fisherman Falling In Pond, 8 3/8 In.	39.50
ABC, Plate, Floral Center, 6 1/2 In.	16.00
ABC, Plate, George Washington, Tin	45.00
ABC, Plate, Girl With Rabbits, Malkin China, 6 In.	37.50
ABC, Plate, Glass, Frosted Floral Center, 6 In.	21.00
ABC, Plate, Man & Dog Sliding Down Cliff, Couple In Front, Blue Green	40.00
ABC, Plate, Mary & Lamb, Verse, Raised Border & Design, 7 1/2 In.	42.00
ABC, Plate, Mulberry, Water Hen, Set Of 6, 5 1/2 In.	36.00
ABC, Plate, Nations Of The World, Turkey, English, December 14, 1883, 7 In.	38.00
ABC, Plate, Organ Grinder & Children, Allerton	36.00
ABC, Plate, Our Donkey & Foal, Staffordshire	29.00
ABC, Plate, Raised Letters, Multicolored Hunting Scene, 8 1/2 In.	39.00
ABC, Plate, Silks & Satins, Franklin Proverb, Meakin	60.00
ABC, Plate, Simple Simon, Silver Plate, Oneida, 6 In.	40.00
ABC, Plate, Star In Center, Glass	28.00
ABC, Plate, The Graces, Transfer Scene Of 3 Girls, 6 In.	46.00
ABC, Plate, The Guardian, Child & Dog, Elsemore & Sons, England, 8 In.	46.00
ABC, Plate, This Little Pig Went To Market, Clear Glass, 6 1/4 In.	38.50
ABC, Plate, Tin, Boy & Girl Rolling Hoops, 3 In.	27.00
ABC, Plate, Tin, Eagle In Middle, Alphabet & Numbers, 3 In.	22.50
ABC, Plate, Tin, Washington, 6 1/4 In.	25.00
ABC, Plate, Tin, Who Killed Cock Robin, 7 1/8 In.	35.00
ABC, Plate, Titmouse, Milk Glass, 7 In.	29.50
ABC, Plate, Toddy, Franklin's Proverbs, A Sheep & A Cow, Black, Enamel	48.00
ABC, Plate, Tom The Piper's Son, Alphabet Border, Ceramic, 6 3/4 In.	28.00
ABC, Plate, Who Killed Cock Robin, Tin, 8 In.	27.00
ABC, Plate, 1876 Centennial	45.00
ABC, Teapot, A To Z Around Top, Animals Between, White, Marked Germany	48.00
ABC, Teapot, White Animals, Marked Germany	48.00
ABC, Tray, Brewery, Brass	100.00
ABC, Trivet, Brass, Marked China	8.00
Abingdon, Vase, High Glass, Handled, No.180, 10 In.	15.00

Adams china was made by William Adams and Sons of Staffordshire, England. The firm was founded in 1769 and is still working.

Adams, see also Flow Blue

Adams, Barrel, Biscuit, Dark Blue, White Figs, Cover, Handle 145.00
Adams, Bowl, Blue, Green, Red, 1881 .... 50.00
Adams, Bowl, Columbia, 11 X 9 In. 65.00
Adams, Bowl, Dr.Syntax, 9 1/2 In. 25.00
Adams, Bowl, Pink, 5 3/4 In., Set Of 5 .... 6.50
Adams, Cookie Jar, Jasperware, Signed 95.00
Adams, Cup & Saucer, Cries Of London 25.00
Adams, Cup & Saucer, English Rural Scene, Deep Blue Transfer 85.00
Adams, Dish, Cheese, Dark Blue & White Jasper, 8 1/2 In. 145.00
Adams, Dish, Cheese, Dark Blue, White Jasper, Horses, Huntsmen, Hounds, 8 In. 175.00
Adams, Jar, Biscuit, Classical Figures, Blue 125.00
Adams, Jardiniere, Hunting Scene, Dark Blue, White Bas Relief, 8 In. 175.00
Adams, Jug, Milk, Dr.Syntax, 4 1/2 In. 17.50
Adams, Pitcher, Classical Figures, White Trim, Blue, Signed, 17 In. 90.00
Adams, Pitcher, Gravy, Dark Blue On White 15.00
Adams, Plate, Columbus, Pink, 10 1/2 In. 55.00
Adams, Plate, Cries Of London, Octagonal, 8 In. 18.00
Adams, Plate, Cries Of London, 10 1/2 In. 20.00
Adams, Plate, Currier & Ives, Floral Border, Woodcock Shooting 25.00
Adams, Plate, Dickensware, Old Curiosity Shop, Pierced, 12 In. .... 30.00 To 40.00
Adams, Plate, Dr. Syntax, 10 1/2 In. 35.00
Adams, Plate, Gracefield, Queen's County, Ireland, 10 1/4 In. 75.00
Adams, Plate, Montevideo, Connecticut, Pink, 7 In. 60.00
Adams, Plate, Palestine, Deep Pink, 7 1/2 In. 98.00
Adams, Plate, Palestine, Pink, 8 1/2 In. 50.00
Adams, Plate, Palestine, Pink, 9 1/2 In. 30.00
Adams, Plate, Soup, Headwaters Of The Juniata, U.S., Pink 120.00
Adams, Plate, Soup, Rose, Soft Paste, C.1820-40, 9 In. 120.00
Adams, Plate, Soup, Rose, 10 In. 80.00
Adams, Plate, White Windmill Scene, A Cape Cod Windmill, Blue, 7 3/4 In. 12.50
Adams, Platter, Columbus, Pink, 17 In. 150.00
Adams, Platter, Rose Staffordshire, 14 1/2 X 17 1/2 In. 225.00
Adams, Platter, Royal Ivory, Oblong, 12 X 15 In. 20.00
Adams, Sugar & Creamer, Cries Of London 25.00
Adams, Sugar, Blue Applied Figures & Horses, Pewter Cover & Bail, Tunstall 62.00
Adams, Teapot, Dr.Syntax 30.00
Adams, Tureen, Covered Vegetable, Bologna, Medium Blue 68.00
Advertising, see Store

*Agata glass was made by Joseph Locke of the New England Glass
Company of Cambridge, Massachusetts, after 1885. A metallic stain was
applied to New England Peachblow and the mottled design characteristic of
agata appeared.*
Agata, Bowl, Finger, Gold Veining, Blue Mottling, Fluted 1195.00
Agata, Bowl, Green Opaque, 8 X 4 In. 850.00
Agata, Celery, Mottled Effect And Color, 6 1/2 In. 1250.00
Agata, Celery, 4 1/2 In. 1650.00
Agata, Celery, 6 In. 125.00
Agata, Cruet, Without Stopper 350.00
Agata, Cup, Punch 600.00
Agata, Pitcher, Water 1850.00
Agata, Spooner, 6 In. 1250.00
Agata, Sugar 1600.00
Agata, Toothpick, Square Mouth 450.00
Agata, Tumbler, Gold Tracery, Blue, Black Spots, Glossy 695.00
Agata, Tumbler, Mottled, Peachblow Coloring 650.00
Agata, Vase, Green, 6 1/4 In. 850.00
Agate, Figurine, Chimpanzee, Sitting, Rose Diamond Eyes, 2 3/8 In. 485.00
Agate, Figurine, Dormouse, Gold, Sapphire Eyes, Wheat Strands In Paws, 3 In. 600.00
Agate, Figurine, Swan Alighting Upon Rock, Silver Feet, 7 1/2 X 11 In. 1450.00
Agate, Horse, Walking, Gray, 2 X 4 In. 80.00
Agate, Seal, Letter, King's Crown 75.00

*Akro agate glass was made in Clarksburg, West Virginia, from 1932 to
1951. Before that time the firm made children's glass marbles. Most of the
glass is marked with a crow flying through the letter A.*

Akro Agate, **Ashtray**, Marbleized Green & White	2.00
Akro Agate, **Ashtray**, Shell, Opaque White, Marbleized Orange Swirls, Pair	9.50
Akro Agate, **Bowl**, Footed, Darts, Pumpkin, 5 1/2 In.	8.00
Akro Agate, **Box**, Powder, Colonial Lady, White	28.00
Akro Agate, **Box**, Powder, Pink Scottie Dog	35.00
Akro Agate, **Child's Set**, Black & White, Original Box	37.50
Akro Agate, **Cigarette Set**, Green, Urn & 4 Ashtrays	8.00
Akro Agate, **Creamer & 4 Plates**, Child's, Green	9.50
Akro Agate, **Creamer**, Child's, Concentric Ring Pattern, Cobalt Blue	4.50
Akro Agate, **Creamer**, Child's, Green, Marble Interior, Large	25.00
Akro Agate, **Cup & Saucer**, Blue Slag	10.00
Akro Agate, **Cup & Saucer**, Child's, Green, Marble Interior, Large	35.00
Akro Agate, **Cup & Saucer**, Demitasse, Marbleized Pumpkin & White	10.00
Akro Agate, **Cup**, Red Swirls In Opaque White, 3 In.	8.25
Akro Agate, **Dish**, Amber Swirls In Opaque White, Rectangular, 5 1/2 X 3 In.	8.25
Akro Agate, **Figurine**, Colonial Lady, Cobalt	97.50
Akro Agate, **Flower Pot**, Miniature, 1 1/2 In.	3.00
Akro Agate, **Jar**, Apothecary, Black	25.00
Akro Agate, **Jar**, Apothecary, White	12.50
Akro Agate, **Jar**, Blue & White, Mexicali	18.00
Akro Agate, **Jar**, Scotty Dog, Pink	48.00
Akro Agate, **Jar**, 3 Footed	13.00
Akro Agate, **Knobs**, Gear Shift, Swirls, 14 Pieces	225.00
Akro Agate, **Lamp**, Ivory, 7 In., Pair	35.00
Akro Agate, **Lemonade Set**, Stacked Disc & Panel, Green, 5 Piece	35.00
Akro Agate, **Lemonade Set**, 7 Piece	38.00
Akro Agate, **Luncheon Set**, Green & White, Box, 16 Piece	42.00
Akro Agate, **Match Holder**, Blue Swirls In Opaque White	10.00
Akro Agate, **Match Holder**, Cornucopia, Blue Swirl	6.00
Akro Agate, **Mortar & Pestel**, Black	15.00
Akro Agate, **Planter**, Green, Marbleized, 6 In.	9.00
Akro Agate, **Planter**, Raised Flowers	10.00
Akro Agate, **Plate**, Child's, Green, 4 1/2 In.	4.00
Akro Agate, **Plate**, 8 Sided, Child's, Green	3.00
Akro Agate, **Pot**, Custard, Darts	10.00
Akro Agate, **Pot**, Flower, 2 1/2 In.	7.00
Akro Agate, **Set Of Dishes**, Child's, Chiquita, Green	39.95
Akro Agate, **Tea Set**, Child's, Raised Daisy, 15 Piece	175.00
Akro Agate, **Teapot**, Child's, Red, Small	20.00
Akro Agate, **Tray**, Shell	6.00
Akro Agate, **Tumbler**, 2 In.	5.50
Akro Agate, **Vase**, Daffodil, Green Slag	6.00
Akro Agate, **Vase**, Molded Lilies, Marbleized Orange Swirls, 4 1/2 In.	15.00
Akro Agate, **Vase**, Orange Swirls In Opaque White, 4 1/2 In.	15.00
Akro Agate, **Water Set**, Child's, Cube Pattern, 7 Piece	33.00
Akro Agate, **Water Set**, Green Pitcher, White Glasses, Original Box	24.50
Akro Agate, **Water Set**, Green, Cube Pattern, Miniature, 7 Piece	33.00
Akro Agate, **Water Set**, Opaque, Blue Pitcher, 6 White Stacked Disc Tumblers	42.50
Alabaster, Box, Jewelry, Puffy, Pink, Hinged, Large	30.00
Alabaster, Figurine, Sphinx	20.00
Alabaster, Torchere, Lady Holding Lamb, Onyx Pedestal, Italian, 54 In.	300.00

Albums were popular in Victorian times to hold the myriad pictures and cutouts favored by the collectors. All sorts of scrapbooks and albums can still be found.

Album, Photograph, see Photography, Album

Alexandrite glass was first made by Thomas Webb & Sons at the beginning of the 20th century. It is a transparent glass shading from pale yellow to rose to blue. Stevens & Williams later produced alexandrite glassware by plating a transparent yellow body with rose and blue glass.

Alexandrite, see also Moser

Alexandrite, Plate, Pink, 8 In. 75.00

Amber glass is the name of any glassware with the proper yellow-brown shade. It was a popular color after the Civil War.

Amber Glass, Basket, Fluted Edges, 6 In.	20.00
Amber Glass, Basket, Maltese Cross	28.00
Amber Glass, Basket, Ruffled, Applied Handle, 8 X 8 In.	18.00
Amber Glass, Bottle, Bohemian, Deer & Pine, Paneled Sides, 4 1/2 In.	60.00
Amber Glass, Bottle, Perfume, Green Leaves, Red Berries, Blue Floral, 7 In.	45.00
Amber Glass, Bowl, Maple Leaf, Log Feet, Oval, 10 X 6 In.	28.00
Amber Glass, Bowl, Multicolor Enameled Flowers, Green Leaves, 7 3/4 X 3 In.	65.00
Amber Glass, Bowl, Sugar, Diamond-Quilted	15.00
Amber Glass, Bowl, Waste, 2 Panels	24.00
Amber Glass, Box, Paneled Sides, 4 Brass Feet, Blue Birds On Top, 3 1/2 In.	225.00
Amber Glass, Candlestick, Center Of Stick Is Twisted, 3 Mold, 9 1/2 In.	35.00
Amber Glass, Castor Set, Daisy & Button, Yellow, Blue, 5 Piece	120.00
Amber Glass, Creamer, Ground Pontil, Reeded Handle	17.50
Amber Glass, Cruet, Blue Applied Handle, Blue Faceted Stopper, 7 1/2 In.	35.00
Amber Glass, Cruet, Melon Ribbed, Blue Handle, Stopper, Blown, 8 X 4 In.	95.00
Amber Glass, Cruet, Stars & Bars	43.00
Amber Glass, Cruet, 1,000-Eye, 3 Ball Stopper	65.00
Amber Glass, Dish, Hen Cover, 5 In.	50.00
Amber Glass, Figurine, Standing Horse, Paden City	90.00
Amber Glass, Goblet Set, Trees, Dog, Moose Etched On Base, 4 Piece	65.00
Amber Glass, Jam, Covered, Footed, Wildflower, 7 1/2 In.	55.00
Amber Glass, Liqueur Set, Enameled Flowers & Leaves, 8 Piece	145.00
Amber Glass, Match Holder, Boot, Victorian	30.00
Amber Glass, Mug, Child's, Lighthouse, Sailboat	15.00
Amber Glass, Mug, Robin On Side, 2 In.	20.00
Amber Glass, Pitcher, Applied Handle, Crimped Top, 9 1/2 In.	190.00
Amber Glass, Pitcher, Cream, Applied Blue Reeded Shell Handle, 5 In.	65.00
Amber Glass, Pitcher, Water, Inverted Thumbprint, Enameled Floral, 8 3/4 In.	135.00
Amber Glass, Pitcher, Water, Threaded	22.50
Amber Glass, Plate, Mary Gregory Style, Courting Couple, 10 1/2 In.	45.00
Amber Glass, Plate, Silver Overlay, 10 In.	25.00
Amber Glass, Platter, Rectangular, Wildflower, 10 In.	30.00
Amber Glass, Rose Bowl, Flowered Scroll, Large	48.50
Amber Glass, Salt, Christmas, Pewter Top, Dated, Pair	85.00
Amber Glass, Shaker, Sugar, Hobnail	58.00
Amber Glass, Spooner, Swirl, Petticoat Pedestal Base, C.1865	49.00
Amber Glass, Stein, Munich Maid Enamel Decoration, Pewter Lid, 7 In.	95.00
Amber Glass, Sugar, Covered, Wildflower	43.00
Amber Glass, Syrup, Rope & Thumbprint, Lid	40.00
Amber Glass, Syrup, Wild Flower, Dated Top	115.00
Amber Glass, Tumbler, Threaded, Pansy Decoration	165.00
Amber Glass, Vase, Blown, Diamond Swirl, Ruffled, Victorian Edging, 7 In.	32.50
Amber Glass, Vase, Paneled, Scalloped Top, Hand Holding Vase, 12 In.	24.50
Amber Glass, Vase, Tapered Form, 12 In.	105.00
Amber Glass, Vase, White Overlay, Clear Handle, 4 1/2 In.	25.00
Amber, Glass, Wine, Fine Cut And Block	35.00

Amberette, see Pressed Glass, Klondike

Amberina is a two-toned glassware made from 1883 to about 1900. It was patented by Joseph Locke of the New England Glass Company. The glass shades from red to amber.

Amberina, see also Baccarat, Bluerina, Plated Amberina

Amberina, Boat, Daisy & Button, 14 In.	175.00
Amberina, Bookend, Horses Rearing, Pair	58.00
Amberina, Bottle, Swirled, Cranberry To Amber, Stopper, 9 1/4 In.	145.00
Amberina, Bowl, Cranberry To Olive Amber, Coin Gold Floral, Oval, 8 In. High	395.00
Amberina, Bowl, Daisy & Button, Deep Color, 8 1/2 In. Square	225.00
Amberina, Bowl, Diamond-Quilted, Blown, 9 In.	295.00
Amberina, Bowl, Dragon & Lotus, Red, 5 In.	185.00
Amberina, Bowl, Finger, Baby Inverted, Diamond Pattern, Ground Pontil	130.00
Amberina, Bowl, Finger, Fuchsia, Diamond-Quilted, Venetian, 5 In.	125.00
Amberina, Bowl, Finger, Inverted Thumbprint	79.00
Amberina, Bowl, Finger, Round Base, Square Shape At Rim, 5 In.	65.00
Amberina, Bowl, Finger, Venetian Double-Quilted, Fuchsia, 2 X 5 In.	125.00
Amberina, Bowl, Flared, Libbey, 5 In.	12.00

Amberina, Bowl, Hobnail, Ruffled, Fuchsia Red Top To Amber, 3 1/4 In.	65.00
Amberina, Bowl, Inverted Thumbprint, 6 1/4 In.	50.00
Amberina, Bowl, Pedestaled, Cambridge, 10 In.	35.00
Amberina, Bowl, Scalloped Top, Inverted Thumbprint, 8 In.	165.00
Amberina, Carafe, Inverted Thumbprint	170.00
Amberina, Carafe, Inverted Thumbprint, 7 In.	160.00
Amberina, Castor, Pickle, Inverted Baby Thumbprint, Footed Frame	400.00
Amberina, Castor, Pickle, Inverted Thumbprint, New England Glass Co.	375.00
Amberina, Celery, Diamond-Quilted, Deep Fuchsia, 6 1/2 In.	265.00
Amberina, Celery, Diamond-Quilted, Square Top	265.00
Amberina, Celery, Fuchsia At Square Top, Diamond-Quilted	265.00
Amberina, Celery, Inverted Ribbing, Cranberry To Amber, Scalloped Rim, 4 In.	140.00
Amberina, Console Set, Honeycomb, Emerald Stems, 4 Piece	95.00
Amberina, Creamer, Bulbous, Inverted Thumbprint, Cranberry To Amber	134.50
Amberina, Creamer, Inverted Thumbprint, Applied Handle	145.00
Amberina, Creamer, Inverted Thumbprint, Polished Pontil, 4 1/4 In.	65.00
Amberina, Creamer, Thumbprint, Fuchsia, 5 3/4 In.	84.00
Amberina, Cruet, Amber Handle & Faceted Stopper, Inverted Thumbprint	225.00
Amberina, Cruet, Applied Amber Handle, Stopper, 6 In.	235.00
Amberina, Cruet, Bulbous, Cranberry To Amber, Gold Flowers, 8 1/4 In.	195.00
Amberina, Cruet, Clear Handled, Stopper	200.00
Amberina, Cruet, Inverted Thumbprint, Amber Handle, Cut Stopper	235.00
Amberina, Cruet, Inverted Thumbprint, Clear Applied Ribbed Handle, 7 In.	65.00
Amberina, Cruet, Original Amber Stopper	225.00
Amberina, Cruets & Salt & Pepper, Silver Plated Holder	685.00
Amberina, Cup & Saucer, Inverted Thumbprint	90.00
Amberina, Cup, Punch, Applied Clear Handle, Fuchsia	84.50
Amberina, Cup, Punch, Inverted Thumbprint, Amber Handle, Polished Pontil	95.00
Amberina, Cup, Punch, Inverted Thumbprint, Fuchsia, Applied Reeded Handle	125.00
Amberina, Cup, Punch, Plated, Nice Color	2250.00
Amberina, Dish, Sauce, Daisy & Button, Red To Amber, Square, Flint, 5 In.	88.00
Amberina, Flip, Reeded Handle, Tumbler	125.00
Amberina, Jug, Water, Inverted Thumbprint, 7 1/2 In.	100.00
Amberina, Mug, Baby Thumbprint, 3 In.	110.00
Amberina, Mug, Child's, Sandwich Flint	80.00
Amberina, Pepper, Baby Thumbprint, Fuchsia, Round, Plated Cap, 2 1/2 In.	75.00
Amberina, Pitcher, Cream, Clear Applied Handle, 4 1/2 In.	85.00
Amberina, Pitcher, Cream, Inverted Baby Thumbprint, Reeded Handle, 4 1/2 In.	95.00
Amberina, Pitcher, Deep Red To Light Amber, Clear Ribbed Handle, 4 1/2 In.	85.00
Amberina, Pitcher, Inverted Coin Spot, Amber Reeded Handle, 8 1/2 In.	245.00
Amberina, Pitcher, Inverted Thumbprint, Amber Handle, 5 In.	250.00
Amberina, Pitcher, Inverted Thumbprint, Amber Reed Handle, Square Top, 6 In.	250.00
Amberina, Pitcher, Inverted Thumbprint, Amber Reeded Handle, Miniature	165.00
Amberina, Pitcher, Syrup, Ruffled Top, 6 In.	265.00
Amberina, Pitcher, Tree Bark Pattern	250.00
Amberina, Pitcher, Tricorner Pinch Spout, Applied Handle	79.00
Amberina, Pitcher, Water, Almond Thumbprint, Handle	195.00
Amberina, Pitcher, Water, Bulbous, Melon Ribbed, Inverted Thumbprint, Ruffled	310.00
Amberina, Pitcher, Water, Hexagonal Block, Pleated Rim	125.00
Amberina, Pitcher, Water, Inverted Thumbprint, Applied Reeded Handle	250.00
Amberina, Pitcher, Water, Inverted Thumbprint, Rufffled Top	235.00
Amberina, Pitcher, Water, Optic Honeycomb, Applied Handle, Pleated Rim	135.00
Amberina, Pitcher, Water, Swirl, Cranberry Shaded To Golden Amber, 7 1/8 In.	195.00
Amberina, Rose Bowl, Fluted, Plated, 6 In.	2800.00
Amberina, Salt & Pepper, Enameled Strawberries, Pewter Tops	135.00
Amberina, Salt & Pepper, New England, Ruby To Amber, Pewter Top, 3 7/8 In.	175.00
Amberina, Sauce, Swirl Pattern	4.00
Amberina, Shade, Diamond-Quilted, Blossom Shape, Crimped Edge, 5 1/2 X 8 In.	250.00
Amberina, Shade, Diamond-Quilted, 5 In. Fitter	455.00
Amberina, Spittoon, Lady's	195.00
Amberina, Spooner, Inverted Thumbprint, Scalloped Top	35.00
Amberina, Spoonholder, Swirled	120.00
Amberina, Sugar & Creamer, Inverted Thumbprint, Reeded Handles, Square Tops	250.00
Amberina, Syrup, Hobnail, Silver Plated Lid, Collar, & Handle, 6 In.	525.00
Amberina, Syrup, Ruffled Top, 6 In.	265.00

Amberina, Tankard, Inverted Thumbprint, Amber Reeded Handle, 9 1/4 In. 350.00
Amberina, Toothpick, Daisy & Button Footed 145.00
Amberina, Toothpick, Diamond-Quilted, Pair 145.00
Amberina, Toothpick, Fuchsia Color At Top, 2 5/8 In. 175.00
Amberina, Toothpick, Fuchsia, Square Top, 2 1/4 In. 125.00
Amberina, Toothpick, Fuchsia, Tricorner Top, 2 1/4 In. 150.00
Amberina, Toothpick, Prescut Daisy & Button 135.00
Amberina, Toothpick, Venetian Diamond, Tricornered, Amber To Fuchsia Base 250.00
Amberina, Tumbler 75.00
Amberina, Tumbler, Diamond-Quilted .... 95.00 To 142.50
Amberina, Tumbler, Expanded Diamond, Fuchsia Upper Part 85.00
Amberina, Tumbler, Fuchsia 32.00
Amberina, Tumbler, Inverted Baby Thumbprint, Red To Amber, 4 In. 35.00
Amberina, Tumbler, Inverted Diamond, Deep Fuchsia 95.00
Amberina, Tumbler, Inverted Diamond, Ground Pontil, 4 In. 80.00
Amberina, Tumbler, Inverted Thumbprint, 4 1/2 In. 68.00
Amberina, Tumbler, Swirl, Gold Decorated, Cranberry To Amber, 5 1/8 In. 60.00
Amberina, Tumbler, Swirled, Polished Pontil, 5 1/4 In. 85.00
Amberina, Vase, Applied Amber Rigaree, Enameled Flower Sprays, 9 In., Pair 445.00
Amberina, Vase, Basket Weave, Fuchsia, Amber Scalloped Rim, 9 3/4 In. 195.00
Amberina, Vase, Basket Weave, Ruffled, Cranberry To Amber, Pontil, 10 X 5 In. 145.00
Amberina, Vase, Blown, Inverted Thumbprint, 6 In. 65.00
Amberina, Vase, Celery, Diamond-Quilted 200.00
Amberina, Vase, Cranberry To Amber, Melon Sectioned, Footed, 4 1/2 In. 85.00
Amberina, Vase, Cranberry, Amber Swirl Base, Bulbous, 10 In. 500.00
Amberina, Vase, Deep Fuchsia To Amber, Applied Rim & Base, 12 In. 295.00
Amberina, Vase, Diamond-Quilted, Applied Rigaree, 5 1/4 In. 380.00
Amberina, Vase, Double, Amber Middle, Deep Ruby Top & Bottom, 10 X 6 1/8 In. 275.00
Amberina, Vase, Fuchsia, Round Base, Square Top, 6 In. 235.00
Amberina, Vase, Hobnail, Crimped Top 24.00
Amberina, Vase, Inverted Thumbprint, Cranberry To Gold, Leaves, 6 5/8 In. 295.00
Amberina, Vase, Inverted Thumbprint, Fuschia, 6 1/2 X 3 1/2 In. 250.00
Amberina, Vase, Inverted Thumbprint, Jack-In-The-Pulpit, Asters, Gold Leaves 235.00
Amberina, Vase, Jack-In-The-Pulpit, Expanded Inverted Thumbprint, 13 In. 225.00
Amberina, Vase, Lily Form, Ribbed, Libbey, 8 In. 325.00
Amberina, Vase, Lily, Fuchsia, Ribbed, 10 In. 375.00
Amberina, Vase, Lily, Ribbed, 8 In. .... 350.00 To 375.00
Amberina, Vase, Reverse Coloring, Diamond-Quilted, Applied Feet, 6 In. 325.00
Amberina, Vase, Scalloped Rim, 4 1/8 X 6 3/4 In. 125.00
Amberina, Vase, Swirl, Cranberry To Amber, Enameled Flowers, 8 1/4 In., Pair 395.00
Amberina, Vase, Swirl, Floral, Leaves, Ruffled, Footed, Cranberry To Amber 195.00
Amberina, Vase, Swirl, Gold Leaves, Berries, Fan Shape, Amber Rim, Footed 185.00
Amberina, Vase, Swirled, Victorian Shape, Polished Pontil, 11 1/4 X 7 In. 225.00
Amberina, Vase, Trumpet, 20 In. 210.00
Amberina, Vase, Victorian Shape, Honey Colored Rim, Polished Pontil 225.00
Amberina, Water Set, Inverted Thumbprint, Applied Handle, 5 Piece 250.00
Amberina, Water Set, Inverted Thumbprint, 7 Piece 485.00
Amelung Type Glass, Bottle, Soda Lime, Gilt Decoration, Flint, 7 In. 35.00
Amelung Type, Decanter, Engraved Florals, Facet-Cut Stopper, Quart 125.00
Amelung Type, Decanter, Soda Lime, Flint, Quart 40.00
Amelung Type, Decanter, Tapered, Soda Lime, Flint, 1 Quart 40.00
American Art Clay, Bowl, Open, Green To Sang De Boeuf, Signed, 3 X 5 In. 145.00
American Art Clay, Vase, Art Deco, Incised, Indianapolis, 9 1/2 In. 28.00
American Art Clay, Vase, Matte Glaze, Signed Rhead, 4 1/2 X 3 1/2 In. 195.00

*American Encaustic Tiling Co. of Zanesville, Ohio, worked from 1879
to 1935. Decorative glazed, embossed, and faience tiles were made.*
American Encaustic Tiling Co., Pastoral Scene, Hand-Painted, 1905, 6 In. 20.00
American Encaustic Tiling Co., Tile, Boy In Ruffled Collar, Framed, 6 In. 63.00
American Encaustic Tiling Co., Tile, Brown Glazed, Thistle Pattern, Set, 17 .... 135.00
American Encaustic Tiling Co., Tile, Dedication, April 19, 1892 .... 50.00
American Encaustic Tiling Co., Tile, Fall Scene, Trees, Stream, 3 X 6 In. 60.00
American Encaustic Tiling Co., Tile, Portrait, Young Boy, Dark Green, 6 In. 50.00
American Encaustic Tiling Co., Tile, Presidential, Bryan, 1896, High Glaze 30.00
American Encaustic Tiling Co., Tile, Wm.Jennings Bryan, Blue & White, 3 In. 55.00

Amethyst glass is any of the many glasswares made in the proper dark purple shade. It was a color popular after the Civil War.

Amethyst Glass, Ashtray, Coal Bucket, Black	7.00
Amethyst Glass, Ball, Witch, Blown, Pontil	17.50
Amethyst Glass, Basket, Black, 12 In.	40.00
Amethyst Glass, Basket, Quilted, Enamel Flowers, Clear Bamboo Handle, 6 In.	45.00
Amethyst Glass, Bottle, Barber, Enameled Decoration, Pair	110.00
Amethyst Glass, Bottle, Collar & Rim Colored, 7 5/8 In.	75.00
Amethyst Glass, Bottle, Cologne, Inside Swirl Ribbing, Pontil, Blown, 7 In.	45.00
Amethyst Glass, Bottle, Violin, Hanging Holder	35.00
Amethyst Glass, Bowl, Scalloped Open Work Edge, 10 In.	35.00
Amethyst Glass, Box, Powder, Amber, Fawn On Cover	20.00
Amethyst Glass, Candleholder, Copper Wheel Edge, Leaf & Flower, 14 In.	225.00
Amethyst Glass, Candlestick, Pair	18.00
Amethyst Glass, Candlestick, Silver Overlay, 9 In., Pair	40.00
Amethyst Glass, Celery, Diamond-Quilted	45.00
Amethyst Glass, Compote, Farber Nude Stem	26.00
Amethyst Glass, Condiment Set, Farber Holders, 5 Piece	35.00
Amethyst Glass, Condiment Set, 4 Piece & Tray	30.00
Amethyst Glass, Console Set, 6 1/4 In.Candleholders, 3 Piece	50.00
Amethyst Glass, Cordial Set, Floral, Gold Overlay, 7 Piece	65.00
Amethyst Glass, Cruet, Tiny Optic	68.00
Amethyst Glass, Decanter, Paneled, Pittsburgh Glass, 2 Quart	450.00
Amethyst Glass, Dish, Candy, Purple, Swirl, Covered, 12 In.	15.00
Amethyst Glass, Dish, Hen, Covered, White Head	20.00
Amethyst Glass, Jar, Biscuit, Silver Plated Cover, Bail Handle, 4 1/2 X 6 In.	85.00
Amethyst Glass, Lamp Base, Miniature, Twinkle	45.00
Amethyst Glass, Pitcher, Blue Enamel, Daisy Design	95.00
Amethyst Glass, Pitcher, Bulbous, Pouring Spout On Side, Large	45.00
Amethyst Glass, Pitcher, Inverted Baby Thumbprint, Pontil Mark	80.00
Amethyst Glass, Pitcher, Ruffled Top, Bulbous Bottom, Gold Applied Flowers	110.00
Amethyst Glass, Plate, Black, Reticulated, 9 In.	22.00
Amethyst Glass, Plate, Copper Wheel Edge, Leaf & Flower, 8 In., Set Of 8	600.00
Amethyst Glass, Rose Bowl, Diamond Pattern, Large	45.00
Amethyst Glass, Spooner, Leaf Medallion	85.00
Amethyst Glass, Tie Back, Curtain, Pair	75.00
Amethyst Glass, Tumbler, Inverted Strawberry, Gold, Marked Near Cut	35.00
Amethyst Glass, Tumbler, Whirlpool, Set Of 6	35.00
Amethyst Glass, Vase, Black, Raised Heart With Dancing Girls	20.00
Amethyst Glass, Vase, Black, 9 In.	15.00
Amethyst Glass, Vase, Bud, Blown, Paneled, 12 1/4 In.	22.50
Amethyst Glass, Vase, Dancers In Heart Shapes, Footed, Handled, 7 1/4 In.	30.00
Amethyst Glass, Vase, Diamond-Quilted, Squat, Ruffled, Turned Edging, 6 In.	50.00
Amethyst Glass, Vase, Paneled, White & Gold Decoration, Blown, Pontil	31.50
Amethyst Glass, Vase, Punty, Plain Rim, Hexagonal Base, 10 In.	625.00
Amethyst Glass, Vase, Tricornered, Nude On Each Panel, Art Nouveau, 8 In.	35.00
Amethyst Glass, Vase, Trumpet, Polished Pontil, 12 In.	36.00
Amethyst Glass, Water Set, Enameled Dotted Decoration, Gold Trim, 5 Piece	225.00
Amethyst Glass, Water Set, Iris With Meander, Gold, 5 Piece	265.00
Amethyst Glass, Water Set, Swag & Bracket, Gold, 7 Piece	165.00
Amethyst Glass, Whiskey, Flint, Handled, Miniature	95.00
Amethyst Glass, Wine, Iridescent Exterior, Hand Blown, Italian, Set Of 5	150.00
Amos & Andy, Car, Fresh Air Taxi	110.00
Amos & Andy, Smoking Stand, Figural, Plaster, I'se Regusted, 8 In.	38.00
Amos & Andy, Toy, Fresh Air Taxi, Windup, Original Box	275.00
Amphora, see Teplitz	
Andiron, many related fireplace items, see, Fire	
Ansbach, Plate, Soup, 10 In. *Illus*	850.00
Apothecary jar, see Bottle, Apothecary	
Apple Peeler, see Kitchen, Peeler, Apple	
Arequipa, Vase, Molded Trees, Blue Over Speckled White, 3 1/2 In.	95.00
Argy-Rousseau, see G. Argy-Rousseau	
Arita, Plate, Scalloped, Pair	65.00
Arita, Teapot, Birds, Crane, 12 Sides	60.00
Arita, Vase, Fish, Birds & Geometrics On Reverse Side, 7 In.	145.00

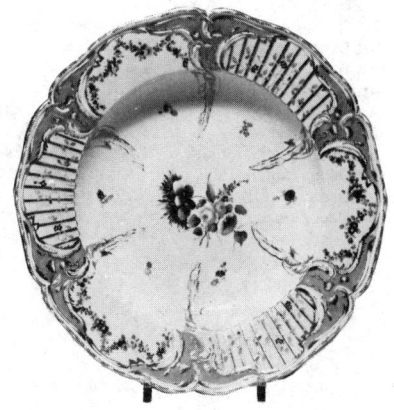

Ansbach, Plate, Soup, 10 In.

Art Deco, or Art Moderne, is a style started at the Paris Exposition of 1925, characterized by linear, geometric designs. All types of furniture and decorative arts, jewelry, bookbindings, and even games, were designed in this style.

Art Deco, Ashtray, Green Marble, Brown Veins, Bronze Bird, Bizette, 7 In.	45.00
Art Deco, Ashtray, Greyhound, Germany	14.00
Art Deco, Ashtray, Nude Girl, Full Figure, Bronzed, Signed, 20 In.	55.00
Art Deco, Atomizer, Black & Blue, 22K Gold Decoration, 7 1/2 In.	27.50
Art Deco, Beads, Crystal, 30 In.	45.00
Art Deco, Bookend, Nudes Sitting On Cubelike Blocks, Pot Metal, Washed, Pair	20.00
Art Deco, Bookholder, Expandable, Brass & Iron, Openwork, Lady, 2 Dogs	17.00
Art Deco, Bottle, Perfume, Black Glass, Gold Relief Decoration, Arrow Stopper	12.00
Art Deco, Bottle, Perfume, Cone Shape, 10 In., 7 In. Pointed Crystal Stopper	45.00
Art Deco, Bottle, Perfume, Figure Draped Nude, Large Flowers, Stopper, Green	77.00
Art Deco, Bottle, Perfume, Hand-Painted Flowers, Bulb Squeezer	18.50
Art Deco, Box, Covered, Reclining Partially Nude On Top, Metal, 6 X 6 In.	65.00
Art Deco, Box, Elephant Cover, Green Frosted Glass	26.00
Art Deco, Box, Powder, Kneeling Nudes Holding Box On Backs, Pink Frosted	45.00
Art Deco, Box, Powder, Raised Lovebirds, Frosted, 3 In.	9.00
Art Deco, Box, Powder, Shell-Shaped, Lid	6.00
Art Deco, Box, Powder, Toussant Glass, Green	25.00
Art Deco, Box, Puff, Pink Frosted, Lady Sitting On Cover, Large	35.00
Art Deco, Bust, Black, Young Lady Wearing Off-White Turban, 11 1/2 In. High	25.00
Art Deco, Cigarette Holder, Bakelite And Chrome, Opens To 14 In.	10.00
Art Deco, Coffee Set, Royal Rochester, 1924, 4 Piece	275.00
Art Deco, Compact, Geometric, Silver On Orange	13.00
Art Deco, Dresser Box, Silver Plate Cover, Diamond Shape, 9 In.	28.00
Art Deco, Dresser Set, Geometric Design, Brown & Gold	65.00
Art Deco, Dresser Set, Monogram, Sterling Silver, 19 Piece	325.00
Art Deco, Emerald Green, Leaf Design, Gold Band, 9 1/4 In.	58.00
Art Deco, Figurine, Child Sitting On Watermelon, Porcelain, German, 9 In.	55.00
Art Deco, Figurine, Girl Holding Amber Ball, Signed, 8 In.	150.00 To 275.00
Art Deco, Figurine, Nude, Blue Drapery, Band Of White Flowers, 6 In.	165.00
Art Deco, Figurine, Prancing Pony, Clear & Frosted, Embossed VW, Pair	85.00
Art Deco, Flower Frog, Light Blue Glass Sitting Nude, 6 1/2 In.	24.00
Art Deco, Flower Frog, Pink Pottery Nude In Flower, 6 1/2 In.	24.00
Art Deco, Flower Frog, White Porcelain, Nude Lady, 6 In.	12.00
Art Deco, Inkwell, Glass, Horse Head, Cover	16.00
Art Deco, Jar, Amber Camphor, Jewels, Lace, Pedestal	19.00
Art Deco, Jar, Powder, Figural, Lady In Mopcap, Germany	20.00
Art Deco, Jar, Powder, Metal Base With Enameling, Glass Girl & Boy Top	26.00
Art Deco, Lamp Base, Alabaster, 15 In.	20.00
Art Deco, Lamp, 2 Dancing Maidens	125.00
Art Deco, Mirror, Hand, Pearl Finish	15.00

Art Deco, Mirror, Makeup	15.00
Art Deco, Picture, Sexy Lady Litho, Framed, Signed, 15 X 9 1/2 In.	22.00
Art Deco, Pitcher, Orange, Brown, Red, & Green Fused Colors, G.De Feure, 7 In.	95.00
Art Deco, Salt & Pepper, Orange & Blue, Crown Austria, Pair	12.50
Art Deco, Smoking Stand, Steel, Jadite Trim, 26 1/2 In.	10.00
Art Deco, Tea Set, Mottled Light Green, Low Luster Glaze, 3 Piece	42.00
Art Deco, Tumbler, Amethyst, Footed, Set Of 3	10.00
Art Deco, Tumbler, Black Clear Top, Green Opaque Base	5.00
Art Deco, Tumbler, Milk Glass, Yellow & Blue, Raspberries	29.00
Art Deco, Vase, Draped Nude, Mori Yama Japan, 8 3/4 In.	20.00
Art Deco, Vase, Egyptian, Partly Nude Women, Blue, 9 In.	45.00
Art Deco, Vase, Red Interior, Mauve & Purple Swirls, Cased Outside, 11 In.	70.00
Art Deco, Vase, Signed Mehatch, 9 In.	45.00

Art glass means any of the many forms of glassware made during the late nineteenth century or early twentieth century. These wares were expensive and made in limited production. Art glass is not the typical commercial glass that was made in large quantities, and most of the art glass was produced by hand methods.

Art Glass, see also separate headings such as Burmese, Nash, Schneider, etc.

Art Glass, Atomizer, Crystal, Beveled Edges, 2 1/2 In.	22.00
Art Glass, Atomizer, Red, Threaded	75.00
Art Glass, Basket, Blue, Applied Handle With Rosettes, 7 1/2 X 4 In.	22.50
Art Glass, Basket, Blue, Chartreuse Flecks, Cased, Ruffled Rim, 7 In.	125.00
Art Glass, Basket, Green Bubble Design, Applied Leaves & Cherries, 9 1/2 In.	120.00
Art Glass, Basket, Pink & White Spatter, Cased In White, Thorn Handle, 7 In.	65.00
Art Glass, Basket, Quilted, Green, Applied Orange Petal Rim, 6 In.	135.00
Art Glass, Bookend, Hollow Glass, Horsehead, 5 1/2 In., Pair	8.00
Art Glass, Bowl, Bride's, Light Blue, Ruffled & Scalloped, Footed, 5 X 9 In.	37.50
Art Glass, Bowl, Centerpiece, Floral, Bronze Trim, Molded Blue	175.00
Art Glass, Bowl, Dorflinger, Etched, Kalana Pansy Intaglio Cut, 7 X 3 In.	115.00
Art Glass, Bowl, Fruit, Opaque Bed, Black Rim & Pedestal, Flare Rim, 11 In.	65.00
Art Glass, Bowl, Opalescent, Raised Florals, R.D.Avesn, France, Shallow, 9 In.	100.00
Art Glass, Bowl, Ruby Cut To Clear, Cameo Scenic, Oval, 8 X 4 In.	150.00
Art Glass, Bowl, S Shaped, Honeycomb Pattern, Caramel Color, 13 X 8 X 3 In.	175.00
Art Glass, Bowl, Sandwich, Lemon Shading To Orange, Crimped, Fluted, 7 1/2 In.	95.00
Art Glass, Box, Hinged, 3 Ormolu Feet, Red Flash, Gold Beading, 4 In.Diameter	58.00
Art Glass, Box, Sapphire Blue, White Enameled Floral, Pink Buds, Hinged, 3 In.	210.00
Art Glass, Bride's Bowl, Pink, On Ornate Silver Plated Stand	175.00
Art Glass, Candlestick, Applied Blue Glass, Ornate Decoration, 7 In., Pair	45.00
Art Glass, Celery, Etched Garlands On Center Band, Ribbed, Ruffled, 9 In.	40.00
Art Glass, Centerpiece, Opalescent, Fish Fin Handles, Swirl Pattern, 18 In.	300.00
Art Glass, Compote, Green Iridescent, Silver Plated Stand, With Trees & Deer	165.00
Art Glass, Compote, Green With Gold, 7 1/2 X 6 1/2 In.	52.00
Art Glass, Cracker Jar, Pink Cased, Florette, Silver Bail Handle	195.00
Art Glass, Cruet, The Summit, Ruby Flashed, Clear Faceted Stopper	65.00
Art Glass, Decanter, Emerald Green, Enameled Floral, Applied Handle, 13 In.	58.00
Art Glass, Dish, Fox Cover, Basket Weave Base, 7 X 6 X 6 In.	28.50
Art Glass, Dish, Reclining Cow, Frosted, Pattern In Base, Covered	50.00
Art Glass, Dish, Relish, Oval, Holly Amber	375.00
Art Glass, Egg, Enameled Floral & Leaves, Brass Pedestal, French, 10 1/2 In.	395.00
Art Glass, Ewer, 4 Butterflies, Clear Applied Handle, English, 11 1/2 In.	275.00
Art Glass, Flower Frog, Penguin, Frosted	32.00
Art Glass, Goblet, Black, White Rim, Ground Pontil, 6 In.	17.50
Art Glass, Jar, Cracker, Frosted To Pink, Enameled Grapes, Metal Lid	85.00
Art Glass, Jug, Frosted, Enameled Church Scene, Signed Vessiere, 2 1/2 In.	95.00
Art Glass, Jug, Green, Bulbous, White Enamel Decoration, 2 1/8 In.	32.00
Art Glass, Jug, Orange, Bulbous, Gold Enamel Flowers, 2 1/4 In.	50.00
Art Glass, Jug, Tankard, Green, White & Blue Enameled Flowers, 2 3/8 In.	50.00
Art Glass, Knife Rest, Clear & Frosted Poodle	18.00
Art Glass, Pitcher, Frosted Green To Rust, Signed G.De Faure	65.00
Art Glass, Pitcher, Rust Color, 5 1/2 X 7 In.	65.00
Art Glass, Pitcher, Silver Deposit, Ovoid X-Section, Floral, Applied Handle	48.00
Art Glass, Rose Bowl, Amber Applied Decoration, Overlay, Ivory	80.00

Art Glass, Rose Bowl, Iridescent, Puffed Panels, Brass Top, 5 1/2 In.	45.00
Art Glass, Rose Bowl, Molded Flowers & Leaves, 6 X 6 In.	150.00
Art Glass, Rose Bowl, Oriental Butterfly, Floral, White & Gold Enameling	22.00
Art Glass, Rose Bowl, Shell & Seaweed, Yellow Cased With White, Enamel, 4 In.	95.00
Art Glass, Rose Bowl, Topaz, Iridescent, Melon Shape, 5 In.	65.00
Art Glass, Shade, Gold Iridescent, Purple Highlights, 5 In.	15.00
Art Glass, Shade, Gold, Ribbed & Bell Shaped, Pair	95.00
Art Glass, Shade, Green Drape, Gold Hooked Border On Calcite, Gold Lined	100.00
Art Glass, Shade, Rose, Apricot Luster, Opal, Green Threading, 4 X 4 In.	45.00
Art Glass, Shade, Shades Of Yellow & Blue, Set Of 6	120.00
Art Glass, Shade, Threaded Vines, Leaves, Pair	190.00
Art Glass, Shade, White, Gold Lined, Leaves, Gold Webbing, Lustre Art, 6 In.	95.00
Art Glass, Tumbler, Frosted, Blue, Slightly Iridescent	30.00
Art Glass, Vase, Amethyst Paneled, Enameled Roses, Gold Leaf, 14 1/4 In.	1150.00
Art Glass, Vase, Amethyst Shading To Clear, Cut Flowers & Stems, 11 In.	225.00
Art Glass, Vase, Amethyst, Green, Pink, Rose Enameled Floral, 14 1/4 In.	1150.00
Art Glass, Vase, Blue, Orange, & Gold On Oyster Background, French, 6 1/2 In.	75.00
Art Glass, Vase, Bright Blue, Yellow Hearts, 5 In.	100.00
Art Glass, Vase, Browns, Green, & Rust, Trees & Woods, French, Leune, 16 In.	175.00
Art Glass, Vase, Cinnamon, White Enamel Flowers, 10 1/4 In.	350.00
Art Glass, Vase, Corset Shape, Clear, Gold Enamel, Pinched-In Top, 12 In.	45.00
Art Glass, Vase, Cut Amethyst To Clear, Gold Enameled Florals, 14 In.	35.00
Art Glass, Vase, Dark Blue & Green Iridescence, Spider Web Design, 9 In.	160.00
Art Glass, Vase, Embossed Fish, Sea-Horse Handles, French, 7 1/2 In.	50.00
Art Glass, Vase, English, Cream, Pink Flowers, Green Leaves, 16 In.	80.00
Art Glass, Vase, Flower Form, Silver Plated Deer Holder, Iridescent	150.00

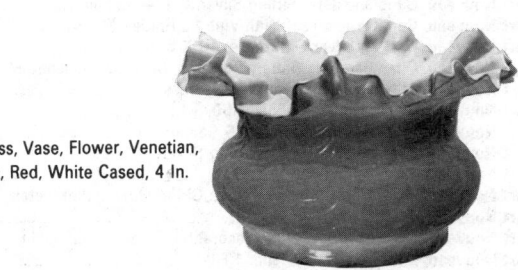

Art Glass, Vase, Flower, Venetian,
Cream, Red, White Cased, 4 In.

Art Glass, Vase, Flower, Venetian, Cream, Red, White Cased, 4 In. *Illus*	45.00
Art Glass, Vase, Frosted Blue & White Decoration, Fluted, Blown, 7 In.	37.50
Art Glass, Vase, Gold Thistle, White Beading, Iridescent, French, 11 1/2 In.	125.00
Art Glass, Vase, Goldstone In Red Glass, Clear Glass Overlay, 5 X 9 3/4 In.	95.00
Art Glass, Vase, Gourd Shape, Green, Iridescent, Applied Green Handle, 4 In.	125.00
Art Glass, Vase, Gourd Shape, Lavender, Aqua, Green, Rust Tracings, 7 In.	80.00
Art Glass, Vase, Green Enamel, Gold Overlay, 5 3/4 X 2 1/2 In.	50.00
Art Glass, Vase, Green Iridescent, Ground Pontil, Pair, 4 In.High, 6 In.Diam.	125.00
Art Glass, Vase, Green Malachite, 6 Nude Females, 5 In.	75.00
Art Glass, Vase, Green, Acid Cut, Gold, L.Cie, St.Denis, Paris, 18 In.	650.00
Art Glass, Vase, Green, Silver Overlay, 14 In.	175.00
Art Glass, Vase, Iridescent Green, Threaded, Gourd Shape, 31 In.	150.00
Art Glass, Vase, Iridescent Red To Green, Texture, 9 In.	149.00
Art Glass, Vase, Iridescent, Applied Flower & Leaves, Blown	395.00
Art Glass, Vase, Iridescent, Pleated Top, Spiral Design, 13 In., Pair	100.00
Art Glass, Vase, Lorraine, Chimney Neck, Orange, Blue, Brown, Signed, 9 X 7 In.	85.00
Art Glass, Vase, Milk Glass Exterior, Swirl Bulbous Body, Ruffled, Fluted	65.00
Art Glass, Vase, Mother-Of-Pearl, Iridescent Applied Feet, Cased, 5 1/2 In.	345.00
Art Glass, Vase, Opalescent, Raised & Cut-Out Diamond Shapes, Etling, 8 In.	200.00
Art Glass, Vase, Oranges To Purples To Greens, Iridescent, 13 In.	160.00
Art Glass, Vase, Pink, Opaque, Roses, Vines, Leaves, Gold, 6 1/2 X 4 3/4 In.	47.50
Art Glass, Vase, Pulled Loop, Domed Bottom, 11 In.	48.00
Art Glass, Vase, Red, Brown, Green, White, Smoke, Arabs Outside Mosque, 9 In.	75.00
Art Glass, Vase, Ribbed, Green, 6 1/2 In.	38.00

Art Glass, Vase, Rigaree Sides On Yellow Crystal, Polished Top, 8 In. 30.00
Art Glass, Vase, Silvered Design, Multicolored Leaves & Flowers, 13 In. 180.00
Art Glass, Vase, Stick, Gold Iridescent, Bronze Holder, 12 1/2 In. 95.00
Art Glass, Vase, Swirl, Iris, Leaves, Sterling Overlay, Blue, Art Nouveau, 8 In. 225.00
Art Glass, Vase, Swirl, Ruffled Ribbon Rim, Pontil, 6 1/2 In. 60.00
Art Glass, Vase, Tree Bark, Green, Opalescent, 11 In. 48.00
Art Glass, Vase, Trumpet, Gold Fleur-De-Lis, Fluted, 14 1/4 X 7 1/2 In. 58.00
Art Glass, Vase, Turquoise & Black Enamel, Hand-Painted Peasant Girls, Pair 275.00
Art Glass, Vase, Victorian, Pink Swirl, Clear Applied Feet 23.00
Art Glass, Vase, White With Pink, Green, & Gold Iridescence, 4 In., Pair 1250.00
Art Glass, Vase, Yellow, Gold Enameling Applied To Clear Base, 5 In., Pair 90.00

Art Nouveau, a style characterized by free-flowing organic design, reached
its zenith between 1895 and 1905. The style encompassed all decorative and
functional arts from architecture to furniture and posters.

Art Nouveau, Barber Brush, Lady In Orchid Gown, Germany, 7 1/2 In. 45.00
Art Nouveau, Basket, Swing Handle, Embossed Iris, Pierced Openings, Hallmark 70.00
Art Nouveau, Bookend, Nudes With Flowers, Bronzed, Pair 40.00
Art Nouveau, Bottle, Cologne, Irises, Leaves, Sterling Silver Overlay, Footed 70.00
Art Nouveau, Bowl, Legs Terminate Over Top In Griffins, 10 In. 120.00
Art Nouveau, Box, Collar Button, 1904 .... 13.00
Art Nouveau, Box, Jewel, Copper, Emblem, Footed, 4 X 3 In. 18.50
Art Nouveau, Box, Jewel, Embossed Floral, Pink Lining, 4 In. 12.00
Art Nouveau, Box, Ring, Heavy Glass, Silver Cover, 3 1/2 X 1 1/2 In. 10.00
Art Nouveau, Box, Treasure, For Rings, Footed, Gilted, Metal, 2 X 4 In. 12.50
Art Nouveau, Buttonhook, Draped Lady, Sterling Silver 25.00
Art Nouveau, Buttonhook, Woman With Long Flowing Hair, Silver 22.00
Art Nouveau, Candleholder, Sterling Silver, 6 1/4 In., Pair 90.00
Art Nouveau, Candlestick, Leaf With Vine As Holder, Metal 48.00
Art Nouveau, Casket, Silver On Bronze, 10 X 5 In. 250.00
Art Nouveau, Chamberstick, Battery Powered, Brownish Finished Metal, 6 In. 28.00
Art Nouveau, Cleaner Set, Inkwell & Pen, Brass 18.00
Art Nouveau, Clock, Figural, Cupid, 1890, 14 In. 20.00
Art Nouveau, Comport, Brass, Jewels & Cameo 145.00
Art Nouveau, Dresser Set, Floral, Sterling Silver, 12 Piece 250.00
Art Nouveau, File, Sterling 10.00
Art Nouveau, Flower Frog, German, Nude Girl In Flower, Pink Petals 35.00
Art Nouveau, Glove Stretcher 35.00
Art Nouveau, Jar, Peacock Feather Decoration, Cream Ground, Lid 35.00
Art Nouveau, Knife, Round, 1 Blade, 1 File 25.00
Art Nouveau, Lamp, Basket, Blue & White Beading, Blown Fruits, 11 In. 95.00
Art Nouveau, Lamp, Brass & Tole, Green, Yellow, Leaves, Floral 450.00
Art Nouveau, Lamp, Circular Shaped, Quezal Shade, White Opalescent, Signed 180.00
Art Nouveau, Lamp, Jeweled Brass Shade, 27 1/2 In. 300.00
Art Nouveau, Letter Opener, Mother-Of-Pearl Blade 15.00
Art Nouveau, Match Safe, Embossed Florals, German Silver 26.50
Art Nouveau, Match Safe, Man-In-The-Moon, Stars, Silver Plate 40.00
Art Nouveau, Mirror, Brass, Cameo Medallion Lady 8.00
Art Nouveau, Mirror, Shaving, Bronze, Beveled Glass, 18 In. ....*Illus* 37.50

Art Nouveau, Mirror, Shaving, Bronze, Beveled Glass, 18 In.

Art Nouveau, **Mirror**, Vanity, Free Standing, Solid Brass	45.00
Art Nouveau, **Mirror**, Woman In Dress At Side, Beveled, Gilded Brass Frame	37.00
Art Nouveau, **Pendant**, Girl, Full Figure, HW.999 Silver	115.00
Art Nouveau, **Pitcher**, Cream, Gold Nude Handles, Floral, 4 1/2 In., Pair	50.00
Art Nouveau, **Pitcher**, Urn Shaped, Pastel Coloring, 6 X 5 1/2 In.	60.00
Art Nouveau, **Pitcher**, Urn, Hand-Painted Busts Of Women On Gold, Vienna, 6 In.	60.00
Art Nouveau, **Plaque**, Lady's Head, Birds, Green, Marked Germany, 16 In.	200.00
Art Nouveau, **Plaque**, Porcelain, Raised Work, Marked Cico, Germany, 16 In.	450.00
Art Nouveau, **Plate**, Pond Lilies, Silver, Unger Bros., 5 In.	95.00
Art Nouveau, **Pot**, Inkwell, Gilded Metal Base	75.00
Art Nouveau, **Purse**, Raised Flowers, Silk Lined, Hallmarked, 3 1/4 X 3 In.	45.00
Art Nouveau, **Shade**, Gold, 6 In.High	50.00
Art Nouveau, **Shoehorn**, Loves Dream, Sterling Silver, Unger Bros.	45.00
Art Nouveau, **Surround**, Serpentine, Relief & Leafage On Panel, Cornice, Marked	225.00
Art Nouveau, **Table Set**, Clear, Gold, 4 Piece	185.00
Art Nouveau, **Tankard**, Brown To Yellow Pottery, Flowers, 12 1/2 In.	100.00
Art Nouveau, **Tea Set**, Dark Blue, Silver Overlay, 3 Piece	150.00 To 200.00
Art Nouveau, **Tea Strainer**, Sterling Silver	20.00
Art Nouveau, **Torchere**, Satin Glass Shade, Signed Roby, Paris, Tulip Base, Pair	325.00
Art Nouveau, **Tray**, Blue, Gold Bird Figure, Artist's Palette Shape, 13 X 18 In.	24.00
Art Nouveau, **Tray**, Brass, 2 Girls Looking At A Crane, Sunset, 14 X 8 In.	200.00
Art Nouveau, **Tray**, Bread, Floral, Resilvered, 13 In.	12.00
Art Nouveau, **Tulipery**, 4 Branches, Tall Center Tulip, Silver, 8 In.	50.00
Art Nouveau, **Vase**, Black & Red, 9 In., Pair	245.00
Art Nouveau, **Vase**, Bronze Patina Over Spatter, Scenic, J.Cardinier, 15 In.	215.00
Art Nouveau, **Vase**, Cream, Gold Nude Form Handles, Florals, 4 1/2 In., Pair	50.00
Art Nouveau, **Vase**, Denbec, 4 In.	55.00
Art Nouveau, **Vase**, Florals In Enamel, Patin, TSV & Co., France, 18 In.	310.00
Art Nouveau, **Vase**, J.Garnier, 15 In., Pair	225.00
Art Nouveau, **Vase**, Molded Green Glass, Six Maidens On Base, 5 In.	80.00
Art Nouveau, **Vase**, Molded Green Glass, 3 Maidens Supporting Vase, 8 3/4 In.	90.00
Art Nouveau, **Vase**, Ormolu Green Swirl, 15 X 7 In.	195.00
Art Nouveau, **Vase**, Portrait, Girl With Doves, German, 13 In.	220.00
Art Nouveau, **Vase**, Snowdrops, Silver On Bronze, Stippled Emblem, 6 In.	25.00
Art Nouveau, **Vase**, White Poppies On Chocolate Band, Signed, 10 1/2 In.	95.00
Art Nouveau, **Wine**, Crystal, Silver Overlay, Silver Stopper, 2 Matching	95.00
Arthur Osborne, see Ivorex	

AURENE *Aurene glass was made by Frederick Carder of New York about 1904. It is an iridescent gold glass, usually marked Aurene or Steuben.*

Aurene, see also Tiffany Glass

Aurene, **Atomizer**, Blue, Unsigned, 7 In.	200.00
Aurene, **Basket**, Flared, Ribbed, Iridescent, Handle Comes To Point, 7 1/2 In.	825.00
Aurene, **Bottle**, Perfume, Blue, Pair, 7 3/4 In.	402.00
Aurene, **Bottle**, Perfume, Mushroom Shape, Blue, Silver Luster, Stopper, Signed	150.00
Aurene, **Bottle**, Perfume, Steuben, Gold, Teardrop Stopper, 5 In.	175.00
Aurene, **Bottle**, Steuben, Gold, Blue Highlights, Teardrop Stopper, 5 In.	175.00
Aurene, **Bowl & Underplate**, Steuben, Calcite, Gold, 5 1/2 X 2 1/2 In.	215.00
Aurene, **Bowl**, Blue, Urn Shape, Iridescence, Signed Aurene, 2687, 10 X 5 1/2 In.	750.00
Aurene, **Bowl**, Bonbon, Gold Iridescent, 2 3/8 In.	135.00
Aurene, **Bowl**, Centerpiece, Gold & Calcite, 15 In.	225.00
Aurene, **Bowl**, Deep Bluish Purple To Light Blue Stretched Edge, 11 3/4 In.	600.00
Aurene, **Bowl**, Red Highlights On Gold, Calcite, 10 In.	195.00
Aurene, **Bowl**, Steuben, Blue, Signed & Numbered, 9 In.	395.00
Aurene, **Candlestick**, Blue, Twisted Stem, Iridescent, Aurene No.680, 8 In.	350.00
Aurene, **Candlestick**, Gold Iridescence, Twisted Stem, Signed, 8 In., Pair	155.00
Aurene, **Compote**, Footed Base, Blue, Signed, 12 In.	475.00
Aurene, **Compote**, No.5604, Blue, Signed, 6 In.	495.00
Aurene, **Compote**, Pinwheel Ribbing, Gold Iridescent, Paper Label, 5 In.	230.00
Aurene, **Compote**, Steuben, Blue, Ruffled Bowl, Twisted Stem, 8 X 7 In.	575.00
Aurene, **Compote**, Steuben, Gold, Paper Label, 5 1/4 X 2 1/2 In.	265.00
Aurene, **Dish**, Steuben, Ruffled, Swirled Ribs, Gold, 7 1/4 X 1 7/8 In.	125.00
Aurene, **Goblet**, Gold, Iridescent, Bell Shaped, Twisted Stem, Signed	145.00
Aurene, **Lamp**, Steuben, Rainbow Iridescence, Acanthus Leaf Trim, Urn Shape	525.00
Aurene, **Nappy**, Gold, Triangular, Elevated Handle, Signed, 5 1/2 In.	295.00

Aurene, Salt, Fancy Base, Signed	125.00
Aurene, Salt, Gold, Attached Pedestal Base, Signed & Numbered	135.00
Aurene, Shade, Brown, Applied Zigzag Border, 10 In.	850.00
Aurene, Shade, Gold, Ribbed, Signed Steuben, 5 In.	135.00
Aurene, Sherbet, Steuben, Oriental Poppy, Pink Opalescent, Green Base	295.00
Aurene, Sugar & Creamer, Belmont's Royal, Signed	50.00
Aurene, Vase, Barrel Shape, Blue, Signed, 5 1/2 In.	350.00
Aurene, Vase, Blue Iridescent, Tree Stump, Signed, 6 1/4 In.	335.00
Aurene, Vase, Blue, Barrel Shape, Signed, 5 1/2 In.	350.00
Aurene, Vase, Bud, Gold, Signed & Numbered, 10 In.	160.00 To 175.00
Aurene, Vase, Classic Shape, Gold Iridescent, Signed, 5 In.	275.00
Aurene, Vase, Finger, Gold, Fan Shape, Pair	475.00
Aurene, Vase, Flower Form, Green Drape Over Gold Iridescence, 10 1/2 In.	975.00
Aurene, Vase, Gold Iridescent Turning Red In Light, Ruffled, 3 1/2 In.	165.00
Aurene, Vase, Gold Iridescent, Applied Decorative Handles, Signed, 12 In.	275.00
Aurene, Vase, Gold Iridescent, Flower Form, 10 In.	325.00
Aurene, Vase, Gold Iridescent, Free Form Pattern On Opalescent, 10 1/2 In.	750.00
Aurene, Vase, Gold Iridescent, 5 1/2 In.	185.00
Aurene, Vase, Gold, Signed, 6 1/8 In.	225.00
Aurene, Vase, Gold, Trumpet, Signed, Tall	270.00
Aurene, Vase, Green Decoration On Gold, Ruffled Top, 3 1/2 In.	125.00
Aurene, Vase, Green Drape, Gold Iridescent, Flower Form, No.195b, 10 1/2 In.	975.00
Aurene, Vase, Green Iridescent, Applied Flower, 7 In.	85.00
Aurene, Vase, Iridescent, Peacock Blue, Signed, 5 1/2 In.	285.00
Aurene, Vase, Lily, Steuben, Calcite & Gold, Ivorene Foot, 8 In.	295.00
Aurene, Vase, No.1789, Gold Iridescent, Blue Highlights, 4 1/4 In.	175.00
Aurene, Vase, Platinum, Gold, Iridescent, No.154	235.00
Aurene, Vase, Steuben, Baluster Shape, Signed, 8 In.	425.00
Aurene, Vase, Steuben, Blue, Classical Shape, Iridescent, 11 1/2 In.	375.00
Aurene, Vase, Steuben, Blue, Platinum Iridescence, 6 1/4 In.	625.00
Aurene, Vase, Steuben, Finger, Blue, No.2762, Signed, 9 1/4 X 7 1/4 In.	425.00
Aurene, Vase, Steuben, Flower Form, Green Drag Loops On Gold, 10 In.	1050.00
Aurene, Vase, Steuben, Gold Iridescent, Red Highlights, 4 3/4 X 2 1/2 In.	200.00
Aurene, Vase, Steuben, Gold, Blue Base, 9 X 9 In.	265.00
Aurene, Vase, Steuben, Gold, 7 X 8 1/2 In.	550.00
Aurene, Vase, Steuben, Gold, 10 In.	325.00
Aurene, Vase, Steuben, Light Gold, No.140, 8 1/2 In.	395.00
Aurene, Vase, Steuben, No.2556, Blue, Stick, 10 1/4 In.	275.00
Aurene, Vase, Steuben, No.6031, Purple-Blue To Gold, Spiral Ribbed, 7 X 6 In.	875.00
Aurene, Vase, Stick, Steuben, Gold, Signed & Numbered, 10 1/2 In.	185.00
Aurene, Water Set, Bedside, Gold, Red, & Silver, Signed & Numbered, 2 Piece	490.00
Aurene, Wine, Gold, Twisted Stem, Signed	125.00
Aurene, Wine, Steuben, Gold, Twisted Stem, Blue Iridescence, 4 1/4 In.	130.00
Aurene, Wine, Steuben, No.2361, Twisted Stem, 4 1/2 In.	145.00
Austria, see Royal Dux, Kauffmann, Porcelain	
Auto, Ornament, Hood, see also Lalique	

Auto parts and accessories are collectors' items today.

Auto, Emblem, Plymouth, Wings, Pictured Ship	15.00
Auto, Headlight, Brass, Solar, C.1909, 13 1/2 In.	85.00
Auto, Horn, London Taxi, 1920s, Brass, Lucas, King Of The Road	23.50
Auto, Hub Cap, Buick	5.00
Auto, Key, Nash, Uncut In Box	9.00
Auto, Knob, Gearshift, Agate, Blue, Flat	18.50
Auto, Knob, Gearshift, Blue Swirl Marble	14.00
Auto, Knob, Gearshift, Green & White	15.00
Auto, Knob, Gearshift, Red & White Swirl Marble	18.00
Auto, License Attachment, Goodrich Silvertown Safety League, Reflector	8.50
Auto, License Plate, Massachusetts, 1914	3.00
Auto, License Plate, Michigan, 1917	7.00
Auto, License Plate, Michigan, 1939	22.00
Auto, License Plate, Nebraska, 1918	135.00
Auto, License Plate, Ohio, 1916	10.00
Auto, License Plate, Pennsylvania, 1906, First Year, Porcelain	125.00
Auto, License Plate, Vermont, 1949	1.00

Auto, License Plate, Yukon, 1971, Home Of The Klondike	4.00
Auto, Luggage Rack, Model T Ford, Metal	10.50
Auto, Moto-Meter, Durant	15.00
Auto, Nameplate, Hood, Studebaker, 8 3/4 In., Set Of 2	7.50
Auto, Ornament, Hood, Chrome Wheel, Copper Bell Center, Auto Club, California	30.00
Auto, Ornament, Hood, Dodge Ram, Chromed, 17 In.	15.00
Auto, Ornament, Hood, Hudson	5.00
Auto, Ornament, Hood, Mercury, 1951	15.00
Auto, Ornament, Hood, Rising Swan, Uplifted Wings	10.00
Auto, Pump Globe, American	65.00
Auto, Pump Globe, Amoco	65.00
Auto, Pump Globe, Ashland Flying Octane	60.00
Auto, Pump Globe, Bell Regular	60.00
Auto, Pump Globe, Blue Sunoco	90.00
Auto, Pump Globe, Boron DX	50.00
Auto, Pump Globe, Cadillac Service	80.00
Auto, Pump Globe, Chevrolet Sales Service	65.00
Auto, Pump Globe, Chrysler Sales	65.00
Auto, Pump Globe, Cities Service	60.00
Auto, Pump Globe, Clark's	60.00
Auto, Pump Globe, Dodge Bros.	80.00
Auto, Pump Globe, Flying A Ethyl	65.00
Auto, Pump Globe, Ford Sales	65.00
Auto, Pump Globe, Gulf	65.00
Auto, Pump Globe, Kan O Tex	80.00
Auto, Pump Globe, Kendall Gasoline	50.00
Auto, Pump Globe, Musgo, Michigan's Mile Maker	225.00
Auto, Pump Globe, Oriental	60.00
Auto, Pump Globe, Packard Sales Service	80.00
Auto, Pump Globe, Pontiac Service	65.00
Auto, Pump Globe, Richfield Ethyl	85.00
Auto, Pump Globe, Richfield Hi Octane	85.00
Auto, Pump Globe, Rock Island Anti Knock Gasoline	60.00
Auto, Pump Globe, Save More Ethyl	65.00
Auto, Pump Globe, Save More Regular	65.00
Auto, Pump Globe, Save X	65.00
Auto, Pump Globe, Shell	70.00
Auto, Pump Globe, Sinclair Dino	35.00
Auto, Pump Globe, Sinclair Gasoline	90.00
Auto, Pump Globe, Sinclair HC	65.00
Auto, Pump Globe, Sinclair Power X	50.00
Auto, Pump Globe, Sinclair Power X Over 100 Octane	55.00
Auto, Pump Globe, Skelly Fortified	60.00
Auto, Pump Globe, Skelly Gasoline	60.00
Auto, Pump Globe, Skelly Supreme	50.00
Auto, Pump Globe, Standard Red Crown	70.00
Auto, Pump Globe, Studebaker	80.00
Auto, Pump Globe, Stutz, The Car That Made Good In A Day	80.00
Auto, Pump Globe, Texaco Sky Chief	70.00
Auto, Pump Globe, Texaco Star	70.00
Auto, Pump Globe, Zephyr Gasoline	65.00
Auto, Radiator Cap, Emblem, Star, Head & Sword, White Metal, 4 In.	85.00
Auto, Radiator Cap, Esso Man .... *Illus*	130.00
Auto, Steering Wheel Fan, Dodge Bros., 1936	9.50
Auto, Vase, Clear, Etched Design, Metal Holder	15.00

Autumn Leaf pattern china was made by the Hall China Co., from 1936.

Autumn Leaf, Bowl, Mixing, Jewel Tea, 3 Piece	20.00
Autumn Leaf, Bowl, Salad, Jewel Tea	7.00
Autumn Leaf, Bowl, Vegetable, Jewel Tea	8.00
Autumn Leaf, Cake Carrier, Jewel Tea	10.00
Autumn Leaf, Coffee Pot, Jewel Tea	18.50
Autumn Leaf, Cup & Saucer, Jewel Tea	4.50
Autumn Leaf, Gravy Boat, Jewel Tea	8.50

Auto, Radiator Cap, Esso Man
(See Page 15)

Baby Carriage, Canopy Top

Autumn Leaf, Lamp, 5-Sided	350.00
Autumn Leaf, Pitcher, Milk, Jewel Tea	6.50
Autumn Leaf, Pitcher, Water, Jewel Tea	12.00
Autumn Leaf, Plate, Cake, Jewel Tea	8.50 To 9.00
Autumn Leaf, Plate, Pie, Jewel Tea	6.50
Autumn Leaf, Plate, 9 In.	2.50
Autumn Leaf, Platter, Jewel Tea, 13 1/2 In.	8.50
Autumn Leaf, Range Set, Jewel Tea	15.00
Autumn Leaf, Teapot, Aladdin, Jewel Tea	17.50
Aventurine, Finger Bowl, With Plate, Gold & Rust Swirled Ribbon, 6-Sided	167.00
Aventurine, Pitcher, Bulbous, Waffle Pattern, Goldstone, 4 1/2 In.	73.00
Aventurine, Vase, Raised Coil, Gold Dust, Dark Spatter, 9 1/2 In.	185.00
Avon, see Bottle, Avon	
Aynsley, see also Chelsea Grape	
Aynsley, Breakfast Set, Green & Cream Pastel, Service For One, 15 Piece	95.00
Aynsley, Cup & Saucer, Demitasse, Yellow, Gold Trim	15.00
Aynsley, Sugar & Creamer, Green & Cream, Embossed Scroll Design	15.00
Aynsley, Teapot, Green & Cream, Embossed Scroll Design, Covered	25.00
Baby Carriage, Canopy Top .... *Illus*	415.00
Baby Carriage, The Gendron, Wicker	175.00

*Baccarat glass was made in France by La Compagnie des Cristalleries
de Baccarat, located about 150 miles from Paris. The factory was started
in 1765. The firm went bankrupt and began operating again about 1822.
Famous cane and millefiori paperweights were made there during the 1860-1880
period. The firm is still working near Paris making paperweights and
glasswares.*

Baccarat, Atomizer, Rose Tiente, Pinwheel, Bulb	55.00
Baccarat, Bobeche, Blue, Square, Signed	27.50
Baccarat, Bottle, Amberina, Perfume, Swirl, Matching Tops, 6 In.	65.00
Baccarat, Bottle, Amberina, Perfume, Swirl, Matching Tops, 7 1/2 In.	75.00
Baccarat, Bottle, Cologne, Guerlain, 4 In.	20.00
Baccarat, Bottle, Perfume, Amberina Swirl, Ground Stopper, Signed, Pair, 7 In.	129.00
Baccarat, Bottle, Perfume, Crystal, Gold Trim, Diamond Pressed Pattern, Pair	45.00
Baccarat, Bottle, Perfume, Gold Hand Holding Satin Glass Bottle, 5 In.	35.00
Baccarat, Bottle, Perfume, Guerlain Mitsouko, Signed	20.00
Baccarat, Bottle, Perfume, Hold Lion Heads, Signed	35.00
Baccarat, Bottle, Perfume, Open Heart Stopper	20.00
Baccarat, Bottle, Perfume, Surrender, Ciro, Paris, Art Deco, Velvet Cover	35.00
Baccarat, Bottle, Underplate, Amberine Swirl, Numbered Stopper, 9 1/2 In.	150.00
Baccarat, Box, Etched Gold On Amber To Blue Ground, Covered, Signed, 6 In.	175.00
Baccarat, Bucket, Ice, Rose Tiente, Signed, 6 1/4 In.	150.00
Baccarat, Cake Stand, Clear, Diamond Pattern Scalloped Edge, Footed, 11 In.	70.00
Baccarat, Candelabra, 5-Branch, Comes Apart	360.00
Baccarat, Candleholder, Rose Tiente Swirl, 6 In., Pair	35.00
Baccarat, Candlestick, Cherub In Frosted Glass Supports Torch, 12 In.	175.00
Baccarat, Carafe Set, Amberina, Embossed Swirl, 3 Piece	145.00
Baccarat, Celery, Amberina	35.00

Baccarat, Compote, Frosted Ribbon Pattern, Signed, 9 1/2 In. 160.00
Baccarat, Compote, Swirled, Scalloped, Gold Rim, Aqua, Marked, 7 X 3 1/2 In. 25.00
Baccarat, Cordial Tantalus, Ormolu & Beveled Crystal Case, C.1860, 16 Piece 2400.00
Baccarat, Cordial, Hobstar, Star, Square, Faceted Stopper, Signed 275.00
Baccarat, Decanter, Flower Petal Stopper, Ruby, 9 In. 65.00
Baccarat, Dish, Relish, Rubina, 3 1/2 X 10 In. 38.00
Baccarat, Dish, Rose Tiente, Swirl, Baccarat-Depose, Covered, 5 In. 125.00
Baccarat, Dresser Set, 5 Graduated Bottles, 8 Piece 125.00
Baccarat, Inkwell, Swirl, Clear, Lidded, 2 1/2 X 2 In., Pair 48.00
Baccarat, Jar, Powder, Blue Opaline, Ball Finial, Covered 45.00
Baccarat, Jar, Powder, Gilt Ruby On Crystal, Cameo, Sterling Lid, 2 1/2 In. 250.00
Baccarat, Knife Rest, Camphor Satin Baby Head At End, 4 In. 40.00
Baccarat, Knife Rest, Crystal Bars, Camphor Satin Baby Head End, 4 In., Pair 45.00
Baccarat, Lamp, Oil, Swirl, Chimney, Square Base, Blue, Kosmos-Brenner, 12 In. 80.00
Baccarat, Liquor Set, Amberina, Embossed Swirl, 6 Piece 245.00
Baccarat, Paperweight, Church, Zodiac Silhouettes, Domed Millefiori, 1967 .... 150.00
Baccarat, Paperweight, Jackson, Andrew, Green Ground 60.00
Baccarat, Paperweight, Kennedy, John F., Sulfide 95.00
Baccarat, Paperweight, Monroe, President, Star Cut Base 125.00
Baccarat, Paperweight, Napoleon, Sulfide, 1974 .... 70.00
Baccarat, Paperweight, Paine, Thomas, Sulfide, 1976 .... 75.00
Baccarat, Paperweight, Persian Blue, 2000 Anniversary Of Persia 80.00
Baccarat, Paperweight, Pope John, Sulfide, 1963 .... 100.00
Baccarat, Paperweight, Rogers, Will, Sulfide 10.00
Baccarat, Paperweight, Roosevelt, Eleanor, Star Cut Base 95.00
Baccarat, Paperweight, Roosevelt, Eleanor, Sulfide 75.00
Baccarat, Paperweight, Roosevelt, Eleanor, Sulfide, 1971 .... 85.00
Baccarat, Paperweight, Roosevelt, Theodore, Sulfide 125.00
Baccarat, Paperweight, Rubina Swirl, 4 In.Diameter 22.00
Baccarat, Pitcher, All Over Etching, Signed 85.00
Baccarat, Pitcher, Cameo, Cranberry & Crystal Acid, Florals, Floral & Leaves 425.00
Baccarat, Salt, Amberina Swirl 35.00
Baccarat, Toothpick, Swirl 25.00
Baccarat, Tray, Rubena Swirl, Round, 11 In. 85.00
Baccarat, Tumble-Up, Matching Underplate, Swirl Pattern, Blue, Signed 165.00
Baccarat, Tumbler, Amberina Swirl, Footed, 4 1/2 In. 35.00
Baccarat, Tumbler, Green Swirl, Footed, Signed, 5 In. 20.00
Baccarat, Tumbler, Vaseline Swirl, Signed 25.00
Baccarat, Vase, Bird, Butterfly, Floral, Signed, 12 In. 245.00
Baccarat, Vase, Birds, Pink, Red, Signed, 6 X 3 1/4 In. 70.00
Baccarat, Vase, Clear Crystal, Pedestal, 6 X 12 In. 75.00
Baccarat, Vase, Fluted, Art Nouveau, Signed, C.1900, 15 1/2 In. 135.00
Baccarat, Vase, Ruby Crystal, Etched & Gilt, Dore Bronze Base, 9 1/2 In., Pair 275.00
Baccarat, Vase, Ruby, Etched, Gilt, Dore Bronze, Sea & Fish, 9 1/2 In., Pair 275.00
Badge, A.C.C., Figural Spread Winged Eagle & Ladies, Justice, Prudence 15.00
Badge, Board Of Health Inspector, Winthrop, Massachusetts, Raised Seal 15.00
Badge, Building Inspector, Littleton, Massachusetts, Commonwealth 15.00
Badge, Consultant Dept.Of Public Works, Gold Plated, Massachusetts 16.50
Badge, Junior Air Warden, Gilded 12.50
Badge, Junior G-Man, Tin 50.00
Badge, Massachusetts Governor's Commission, Boating Advisory, Lettered 18.00
Badge, Massachusetts State Senate For Legislature, Gold Plated, Crest 20.00
Badge, Mayor's Office, Somerville, Massachusetts, City Seal, Gold Plate 16.00
Badge, Natural Resource Officer, Division Of Law Enforcement, Shield 17.50
Badge, Railroad, Railroad Men Tickets, Lettered 17.50
Badge, Round Deputy Forest Fire Warden, C.1870 .... 20.00
Badge, School Crossing Guard No.20, Atlantic City, N.J., Raised Seal 14.00
Badge, Security Guard, Seal Of North Carolina, Butler Bros. 15.00
Badge, Trustee For Peoria Heights, Illinois, Raised Eagle, Gold Plated 15.00
Badge, Western Union, Brass, Keystone Shape 17.00
    Bag, Beaded, see Beaded Bag

*Metal banks have been made since 1868. There are still banks, mechanical
banks, and registering banks (those which total money deposited on the face of
the bank). Many old banks have been reproduced since the 1950s in iron*

or plastic. The Whiting numbers refer to the book "Old Iron Still Banks" by Hubert B. Whiting.

Bank, A & P Coffee, Tin	5.00
Bank, Abraham Lincoln Log Cabin, Van Dyke Teas, Pottery	27.00
Bank, American Can Company, Historical American Figures, Tin	10.00
Bank, Apollo 8, Iron, Figural Red Rocket On Moon	35.00
Bank, Arabian Safe, Brass	38.00
Bank, Aunt Jemima, Ceramic, 6 1/2 In.	8.00
Bank, Auto, Wh-157	425.00
Bank, Bank Building, Iron, 5 In.	28.00
Bank, Bank Building, Wh-366	40.00
Bank, Barrel, Clear Glass, Embossed Staves And Bands	6.00
Bank, Barrel, Clear Glass, 4 1/2 In.	7.95
Bank, Barrel, Happy Days, Tin	6.50
Bank, Barrel, Iron, Wh-283	80.00
Bank, Baseball Batter, Cast Iron	63.00
Bank, Baseball Player, Wh-10	65.00 To 95.00
Bank, Baseball, Camphor Glass	14.00
Bank, Baseball, Custard Glass, Tin Closure & Base	35.00
Bank, Baseball, Glass	8.50
Bank, Battleship Oregon	140.00
Bank, Bear With Teddy On Side, Wh-331, 2 1/2 X 4 In.	61.50
Bank, Bear, Standing, Glass, 7 1/4 In.	5.00
Bank, Bear, Standing, Metal	14.50
Bank, Bear, Wh-330	35.00
Bank, Bear, 5 1/2 In.	95.00
Bank, Beehive, Iron	45.00
Bank, Beehive, Tin	12.50
Bank, Ben Franklin Bust, Wh-313	35.00
Bank, Bennington, Reclining Horned Sheep	24.50
Bank, Billikin, Cast Iron	25.00
Bank, Black Beauty, Horse Shaped, Cast Iron, C.1888, 5 X 4 1/4 In.	58.00
Bank, Bokar Coffee, Tin	7.00
Bank, Bosco Clown, Glass	15.00
Bank, Boston Bull Dog, Standing, Cast Iron	45.00
Bank, Boy Scout, Cast Iron	55.00
Bank, Brass, Victorian, 12 In.	145.00
Bank, Budget, Key, Tin	8.50
Bank, Building Form, Tin, 4 3/4 X 3 1/2 X 3 In.	48.00
Bank, Building, Square, 3 1/4 In.	34.00
Bank, Building, Wh-366	36.00
Bank, Building, 12 Stories, 5 1/2 In.	39.50
Bank, Building, 4 Turrets, Cast Iron, 4 1/2 In.	15.00
Bank, Bulldog Pup, Cast Iron, Fly On Dog's Back	35.00
Bank, Bulldog, Seated, Cast Iron	38.00
Bank, Bust Of Ben Franklin, Bronze Finish, Wh-313	6.95
Bank, Buster Brown	50.00 To 150.00
Bank, Cab, Yellow, Wh-158	375.00
Bank, Camel, Small, Wh-202	60.00
Bank, Captain Kid, Wh-38	225.00
Bank, Captain Marvel, Dime Register	45.00
Bank, Cash Register, Aster, 5 In.	10.00
Bank, Cash Register, Barrel	85.00
Bank, Cash Register, Benjamin Franklin	50.00
Bank, Cash Register, Bucket	60.00
Bank, Cash Register, Tin, Chein	15.00
Bank, Cash Register, Tom Thumb	5.00
Bank, Cash Register, Uncle Sam, Metal	40.00
Bank, Cash Register, Uncle Sam, 1930, Tin	35.00
Bank, Cash Register, 9 Keys, Ornate, Tin, Benjamin Franklin, 7 1/2 In.	65.00
Bank, Charlie Chaplin, Wh-393	85.00
Bank, Chinaman, Seated, Fat, Enameled, C.1900	135.00
Bank, Clown Head, Tin, Chein	20.00
Bank, Clown Standing, Cast Iron	38.00

Bank, Clown, Cast Iron, C.1880	62.00
Bank, Combination Lock, Cast Iron, 4 1/2 X 3 1/2 In.	15.00
Bank, Combination, Security Safe Deposit, Dated 1887, 5 In.	45.00
Bank, Cow, Penny, Brass	10.00
Bank, Cow, Small, Wh-188	165.00
Bank, Cow, Wh-188	95.00
Bank, Cow, Wh-200	45.00
Bank, Cracker Jack	4.00
Bank, Deer	75.00
Bank, Deposit, Safe, Cast Iron	28.00
Bank, Dime Register, Shape Of Beehive, Iron	125.00
Bank, Dime, Round, Eagle Pencil Company, 2 1/2 In.	9.00
Bank, Dog With Bee	60.00
Bank, Dog With Pack	25.00 To 58.00
Bank, Dog With Pack, 3 1/2 In.	40.00
Bank, Dog With Pack, 6 In.	60.00
Bank, Dog, Cast Iron, 5 X 3 1/2 In.	25.00
Bank, Dog, White & Black, Fido On Collar, Cast Iron	95.00
Bank, Donkey With Saddle, Metal	50.00
Bank, Donkey, Small, Wh-198	36.00
Bank, Doughboy, Iron	25.00
Bank, Duck On Tub, Save For A Rainy Day, Iron	65.00
Bank, Electrolux Refrigerator	6.00
Bank, Electrolux Refrigerator, Cast Iron	10.00
Bank, Elephant On Tub, Wh-59	125.00
Bank, Elephant On Wheels, Cast Iron	95.00
Bank, Elephant, Bisque, C.1885, 3 3/4 X 5 In.	20.00
Bank, Elephant, Grayish White, 3 X 5 1/2 In.	35.00
Bank, Elephant, Large	65.00
Bank, Elephant, Standing, 3 X 4 In.	45.00
Bank, Elephant, Wh-67	17.00
Bank, Elephant, 5 In.	175.00
Bank, Esso Man, Plastic	9.00
Bank, Fireman, Wh-9	195.00
Bank, Foxy Grandpa, Cast Iron	60.00
Bank, Frigidaire, Pot Metal, Original Paint	7.00
Bank, Furnace, Mellow, Wh-129	100.00
Bank, Gas Parlor Stove, Wh-133	100.00
Bank, Gasoline Pump	325.00
Bank, General Pershing	120.00 To 150.00
Bank, Glass, Snowcrest Bear, 7 In.	6.00
Bank, Globe On Arc	125.00
Bank, Globe, Tin	3.50
Bank, Goose, Wh-211	75.00
Bank, Grapette, Clown	7.50
Bank, Gray Cat With Ball	145.00
Bank, Happy Days, Barrel Shaped, Chein, Tin	7.50
Bank, Home Safe, Iron	26.00
Bank, Home Savings Bank, Bank Building Shape	35.00
Bank, Horse Beauty, Wh-82	36.00 To 45.00
Bank, Horse On Oval Base, Cast Iron	50.00
Bank, Horse On Tub, Wh-56	85.00
Bank, Horse On Wheels, Cast Iron	60.00
Bank, Horse, Standing, Bronze	10.00
Bank, Horse, Standing, Good Luck	35.00
Bank, Horseshoe With Buster Brown, Tige, Wh-83	100.00
Bank, Horseshoe, Roy Rogers	18.00
Bank, Independence Hall, Gold Paint, Cast Iron	185.00
Bank, Indian Boy In War Bonnet Holding Rifle, Post World War II	27.50
Bank, Jester's Head, White Glazed Pottery	10.00
Bank, John Wanamaker Founder, 1st Penny Savings, Phila., Bronze, 4 In.	11.50
Bank, Kitten, White, Blue Ribbon & Bow, Cast Iron	42.50
Bank, Large Dog With Pack, Wh-113	45.00
Bank, Liberty Bell, Brown Metal, 10 In.	10.00
Bank, Liberty Bell, Cast Iron	10.00

Bank, Liberty Bell, Clear	15.00
Bank, Liberty Bell, Marigold, Carnival	14.00
Bank, Liberty Bell, Steel, Attached Brass Plaque, 1919	25.00
Bank, Liberty Bell, 3 1/2 In.	85.00
Bank, Lion On Tub, Cast Iron	45.00
Bank, Lion On Wheels, Cast Iron	60.00
Bank, Lion, Cast Iron, Gold Paint Tracery, 5 1/2 X 4 1/4 In.	35.00
Bank, Lion, Cast Iron, Gold Paint, 4 X 5 In.	35.00
Bank, Lion, Cast Iron, Gold Paint, 5 X 6 1/2 In.	50.00
Bank, Lion, Enclosed Feet	55.00
Bank, Lion, Standing, 4 In.	38.00
Bank, Lucky Jumbo, Glass Elephant	15.00
Bank, Mail Box, Cast Iron	35.00
Bank, Mail Box, Ohio Art	5.00
Bank, Mail Box, United States	75.00
Bank, Mailbox, Wh-122	21.00 To 24.00
Bank, Mammy With Spoon, Iron, Wh-17	75.00
Bank, Mammy, Cast Iron	45.00
Bank, Mason Jar, 4 In.	3.50
Bank, McCoy, Cookie Jar	30.00

Mechanical banks were first made about 1870. Any bank with moving parts is considered mechanical, although those most collected are the metal banks made before World War I. Reproductions are being made.

Bank, Mechanical, Artillery	260.00
Bank, Mechanical, Atlas	160.00 To 1600.00
Bank, Mechanical, Baseball Player, Wh-10	95.00
Bank, Mechanical, Bear And Tree Stump	550.00
Bank, Mechanical, Bulldog Standing	600.00
Bank, Mechanical, Butting Buffalo	1850.00
Bank, Mechanical, Cabin, Man Flips Upside Down, Kicks Coin Into Cabin	145.00
Bank, Mechanical, Calumet Type II	350.00
Bank, Mechanical, Chief Big Moon	370.00
Bank, Mechanical, Chimpanzee	1700.00
Bank, Mechanical, Circus	3900.00
Bank, Mechanical, Clown, Chein	12.00
Bank, Mechanical, Columbian Magic	375.00
Bank, Mechanical, Creedmoor	250.00
Bank, Mechanical, Cupola Bank	780.00
Bank, Mechanical, Darkey In Cabin, Cranmer's No.65	100.00
Bank, Mechanical, Dime Registering Chest	100.00
Bank, Mechanical, Dinah, Aluminum	450.00
Bank, Mechanical, Dog, I Hear A Call	140.00 To 275.00
Bank, Mechanical, Elephant, Man In Howdah	350.00
Bank, Mechanical, Elephant, 1930	25.00
Bank, Mechanical, Elephant, 3 Clowns On Tub	495.00
Bank, Mechanical, Father Christmas	400.00
Bank, Mechanical, Feed The Kitty	800.00
Bank, Mechanical, Frog On Round Base *Illus*	200.00
Bank, Mechanical, Gem	290.00
Bank, Mechanical, Globe On Arc	125.00
Bank, Mechanical, Haunted House, Box	40.00
Bank, Mechanical, Home Bank I	650.00
Bank, Mechanical, Humpty Dumpty	300.00
Bank, Mechanical, Initiating	5500.00

Bank, Mechanical, Frog On Round Base

Bank, Mechanical, Joe Socko 350.00
Bank, Mechanical, Jolly Nigger With High Hat 100.00
Bank, Mechanical, Jonah And The Whale 375.00
Bank, Mechanical, Jukebox, 1920s, Coin Activated, Musical Mechanism 165.00
Bank, Mechanical, Kick-Inn 650.00
Bank, Mechanical, Kiltie 950.00
Bank, Mechanical, Magician 425.00
Bank, Mechanical, Miniature Coffee Grinder, Daisy, 1910 .... 45.00
Bank, Mechanical, Minstrel, Tin 450.00
Bank, Mechanical, Monkey & Parrot, Tin 550.00
Bank, Mechanical, Monkey On Organ, Painted 225.00
Bank, Mechanical, Mule Entering Barn 210.00
Bank, Mechanical, National Recording 125.00
Bank, Mechanical, Negro In Shack 130.00
Bank, Mechanical, New Bank, Type II 425.00
Bank, Mechanical, Organ Cat And Dog 250.00
Bank, Mechanical, Organ Monkey 190.00
Bank, Mechanical, Owl 190.00
Bank, Mechanical, Owl, Slot In Beak 200.00
Bank, Mechanical, Owl, Slot In Book 160.00
Bank, Mechanical, Owl, Slot In Head 525.00
Bank, Mechanical, Owl, Turns Head 225.00
Bank, Mechanical, Paddy And The Pig 85.00
Bank, Mechanical, Pelican, Man Thumbs Nose 750.00
Bank, Mechanical, Picture Gallery 1950.00
Bank, Mechanical, Pig In Chair 340.00
Bank, Mechanical, Pineapple, Penny Pineapple, Hawaii, July 4, 1960 .... 38.50
Bank, Mechanical, Pistol Bank 750.00
Bank, Mechanical, Popeye Knockout, Tin 475.00
Bank, Mechanical, Presto Building 275.00
Bank, Mechanical, Public Telephone 55.00
Bank, Mechanical, Pump And Bucket 950.00
Bank, Mechanical, Punch And Judy 375.00
Bank, Mechanical, Rabbit In Cabbage Patch 225.00
Bank, Mechanical, Rabbit, Small .... 280.00 To 325.00
Bank, Mechanical, Reclining Chinaman 850.00
Bank, Mechanical, Rocket, 1957 .... 12.50
Bank, Mechanical, Rooster .... 105.00 To 275.00
Bank, Mechanical, Safety Locomotive 1100.00
Bank, Mechanical, Scotchman, Tin 650.00
Bank, Mechanical, Snap-It 275.00
Bank, Mechanical, Southern Comfort, Shoots Into Bottle .... 45.00 To 65.00
Bank, Mechanical, Speaking Dog 375.00
Bank, Mechanical, Squirrel & Tree Stump 950.00
Bank, Mechanical, Swift Thrift, Tin 300.00
Bank, Mechanical, Tammany, Cast Iron 105.00
Bank, Mechanical, Tank, Cannon, Aluminum 700.00
Bank, Mechanical, Tank, Cannon, Cast Iron .... 345.00 To 700.00
Bank, Mechanical, Teddy And The Bear .... 275.00 To 450.00
Bank, Mechanical, Trick Dog 160.00

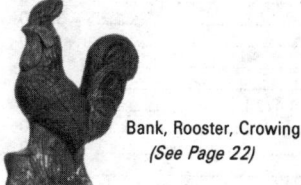

Bank, Rooster, Crowing
(See Page 22)

Bank, Mechanical, Uncle Sam
(See Page 22)

Bank, Mechanical, U.S.Bank Safe 1750.00
Bank, Mechanical, Uncle Sam .... *Illus* 400.00
Bank, Mechanical, Uncle Tom 260.00
Bank, Mechanical, Watch Dog Safe .... 260.00 To 275.00
Bank, Mechanical, Wild West 14.00
Bank, Mechanical, William Tell, Dated 1875 .... 184.00
Bank, Mechanical, Windmill .... 45.00 To 125.00
Bank, Mechanical, Wooden Chest Of Drawers, Coin Disappears From Top Drawer 65.00
Bank, Mechanical, World's Fair 400.00
Bank, Mechanical, Zoo 650.00
Bank, Mermaid 240.00
Bank, Merry-Go-Round, Semimechanical .... 75.00 To 225.00
Bank, Monkey & Coconut, Lacking Trap 550.00
Bank, Monkey Tips Hat, Tin, Lithographed, Chein 22.50
Bank, Mutt & Jeff 75.00
Bank, Negro Bust, Two-Faced 60.00
Bank, Oak Barrel, Monarch Teenie Weenie Sweet Pickles, Lion's Head 37.00
Bank, Owl, Iron, Wh-203 .... 65.00
Bank, Owl, Turns Head, Lacking Trap 80.00
Bank, Pabst Blue Ribbon Beer Can, Miniature, 8 X 2 3/4 In. 22.50
Bank, Penny, Brass, Sheep 10.00
Bank, Pig In Tuxedo, Bank On Republic Pig Iron, Cast Iron, 7 In. 30.00
Bank, Pig Seated, Wh-179 .... 25.00
Bank, Pig, Iron, Gold Paint, Circa 1890, 4 1/2 X 3 In. 25.00
Bank, Pig, Long Snout, Black Cast Iron, 7 In. 60.00
Bank, Pig, Slipware, Pink Clay, 5 X 3 In. 30.00
Bank, Pig, Solid Brass, 7 X 3 1/4 In. 35.00
Bank, Pig, Spongeware, Gray & Green 65.00
Bank, Piggy, Ohio Oil Co., Small 15.00
Bank, Piggy, Spongeware, Green & Brown, 3 1/2 In. 55.00
Bank, Policeman, Round, Tin 35.00
Bank, Poll-Parrot, Shoes Pictured On Tin Bank 45.00
Bank, Post Office, Tin 18.00
Bank, Prancing Horse, Iron .... 29.00 To 65.00
Bank, Presto, Bank Building, 3 1/4 X 2 1/2 In. 22.00
Bank, Queen's Doll House, Tin With Key 75.00
Bank, Radio, 3 Dials 90.00
Bank, Red Circle Coffee, Tin, Yellow 10.00
Bank, Red Goose Shoes, Iron 69.00
Bank, Refrigerator, G.E., Red Paint 62.00
Bank, Register, Uncle Sam, 3 Coin 20.00
Bank, Rhino, Wh-252 .... 275.00
Bank, Rival Dog Food, Tin .... 5.00 To 7.00
Bank, Rolltop Desk, Carved Pine, Dark Red Paint, 5 1/2 X 4 1/4 In. 95.00
Bank, Rooster, Crowing .... *Illus* 150.00
Bank, Rooster, Wh-187 .... 32.00 To 45.00
Bank, Safe With Combination, Moon & Stars, Cast Iron, 2 1/2 X 4 In. 35.00
Bank, Safe, Arabian 100.00
Bank, Safe, Coin Deposit, Ornate Iron 19.50
Bank, Safe, Combination, Steel, 5 1/2 X 4 1/4 In. 35.00
Bank, Safe, Ideal Safe Deposit, Cast Iron, Combination, Brass Handle, 4 In. 38.50
Bank, Safe, Treasure 100.00
Bank, Santa, 1910 .... 32.00
Bank, Schlitz Beer Can, Tin 2.00
Bank, Scotty Dog, Seated, Cast Iron 60.00
Bank, Scotty Dogs In Basket 45.00
Bank, Security Safe Deposit, Gold Decoration, Dial On Doors, Iron, 4 1/2 In. 55.00
Bank, Sheep, Penny, Brass 10.00
Bank, Simple Simon, Tin, Lithographed 49.00
Bank, Sitting Cat, Wh-248 .... 55.00
Bank, Sniffles The Mouse 28.00
Bank, Souvenir, Centennial, Glass, 4-Way Base, 5 1/4 In. 95.00
Bank, Spaceman, Glass 5.00
Bank, Sport's Safe, Wh-374 .... 35.00
Bank, Stagecoach, Tin, Lithographed 8.00

Bank, State, Cast Iron, Square Cupola, 3 In.	15.00
Bank, Statue Of Liberty, Wh-269	55.00
Bank, Stick Horse, Papier-Mache, C.1900	25.00
Bank, Stove, Cast Iron	40.00
Bank, Stovepipe Beaver Hat, Pass Around The Hat, Cast Iron	55.00
Bank, Sunny South, Negro Wearing Floppy Hat, Two-Faced	65.00
Bank, Tank, Large, Wh-161	75.00
Bank, Tank, World War 1, 6 In.	125.00
Bank, Telephone, Cradle Pay Phone, Tin	45.00
Bank, Three Little Pigs, Green	25.00
Bank, Three Monkeys, Wh-236	145.00
Bank, Ticker Tape, Metal	4.00
Bank, Time Safe, Iron, Decorated, Wh-397	125.00
Bank, Tin, National Dim	12.00
Bank, Tin, Tea, Betsy Ross, Slot Top, 930, 3 1/2 In.	2.25
Bank, Top Hat	45.00
Bank, Tower Tank	150.00
Bank, Trunk, 5 In.	75.00
Bank, Turkey, Iron, 4 In.	43.00
Bank, Turtle, Bronzed	9.00
Bank, Two-Faced Negro	75.00
Bank, Two-Faced Woman	45.00
Bank, U.S.Mail Letter Box, Iron	32.50
Bank, Uncle Sam In Shape Of Hat, Chein	25.00
Bank, Uncle Sam, 3 Coin, Tin	10.00
Bank, Wall Hanger, Smile And Save	550.00
Bank, Watch Me Grow Tall, Tin	52.00
Bank, Windmill	80.00
Bank, Windup Monkey Holding Balloons, Dances Around	25.00
Bank, Wooden Box, Lithograph Of 3 Large Wheel Bicycles And Black Man	39.00
Bank, Wooden Shoe, Dutch Boy, 5 In.	15.00
Bank, Woolworth Building, 8 In.	55.00
Banko, Cup & Saucer, 3 Women, 3 Men, Korean, Signed	175.00
Banko, Elephant, 2 Heads, Joined-Trunks Handle, Humorous	100.00
Banko, Teapot, 6 Blown Out Faces, Lid Is Face, Moustache Is Lift Knob, Marked	285.00
Banko, Vase, 5 Apes, Signed, 12 1/2 In.	175.00
Barometer, Desk Model, Silver, Gilt, Translucent Enamel Case, Cartier, C.1910	300.00
Barometer, Desk, French, Gold Blackamoor Woman Holding Drum, 9 1/8 In.	195.00
Barometer, Figural, Banjo, Wall, Silvered Metal, Marked Dressler, N.Y.	9.50
Barometer, Mahogany, Flame Grain Veneer, Kendall Bros., N.Y., 35 In.	475.00
Barometer, Mahogany, Stick, Adams, Fleet Street, London, Late 18th Century	500.00
Barometer, Mahogany, Stick, Swan's Neck Crest, Aiano, Canterbury, C.1790	500.00
Barometer, Mahogany, Wheel, Swan's Neck Pediment, C.Botta, Poole, C.1850	275.00
Barometer, Mahogany, Wheel, Swan's Neck Pediment, Joseph Solcha, Hull, C.1775	250.00
Barometer, Wheel, Carved Gilt Wood Frame, Louis XV, C.1750, 43 1/2 In.	1700.00
Barumware, Bowl, Egyptian Design, Cobalt, England, 1905, 12 1/4 In.	95.00

*Basalt is a black stoneware made by mixing iron and oxides into a basic clay.
It is very hard and can be finished on a lathe. Wedgwood developed his
famous black basalt in 1769, which was an improvement on a similar ware made in
Staffordshire, England, as early as 1740. Basalt is still being made in
England and on the Continent.*

Basalt, Coffe Pot, Enameled Flowers, 5 In.	275.00
Basalt, Creamer, Black, English	48.00
Basalt, Lamp, Figure Holding Book	750.00
Basalt, Sugar, Oval, Covered, Swan Finial, Black, P Mark, 5 5/8 X 3 3/8 In.	75.00
Basalt, Teapot, Oriental Scene In Relief, Widow's Peak Finial, Square	115.00
Basket, Archback, Miniature, Pennsylvania, 5 1/2 In. *Illus*	75.00
Basket, Armadillo, Miniature, Splint Handle, Pennsylvania, 7 In. *Illus*	75.00
Basket, Cheese, Round, Hexagonal Base, Shaker, 12 In.	230.00
Basket, Chinee, Miniature, Painted, 3 3/4 In. *Illus*	40.00
Basket, Covered, Green Bands	28.00
Basket, Honeysuckle, Green Paint	60.00
Basket, Kidney, Rib-Type Splint, C.1850, 16 X 8 X 14 In.	55.00
Basket, Melon Shape, Rib Type, Pennsylvania, 10 1/2 In. *Illus*	45.00

Basket, Nantucket, Early, 8 In.	85.00
Basket, Rye Straw, Dough, Coiled, German, 11 1/2 In. .... *Illus*	32.50
Basket, Splint Basket & Handle, Pennsylvania, 11 In. .... *Illus*	30.00
Basket, Splint Buttocks, Handled, 6 X 6 1/2 X 7 In.	45.00
Basket, Wicker, Bilateral Handles, 14 X 3 1/2 In.	10.00
Basket, Woven Indian Head Design, Central America, 9 1/2 X 4 3/4 In.	35.00
Basket, Woven, Nantucket Lightship, Cherry Bottom, Label, 10 In. .... *Illus*	160.00
Basket, Woven, Nantucket Lightship, 8 In. .... *Illus*	230.00
Batman, Alligator, Stuffed, Dressed In Batman Costume, 9 In.	19.50
Batman, Radio, Wrist	8.00

Battersea enamels are enamels painted on copper and made in the Battersea District of London from about 1750 to 1756. Many similar enamels are mistakenly called Battersea.

Battersea, Box, A Pinch Of This Deserves A Kiss	140.00
Battersea, Box, Birds & Flowers, Peace & Plenty	125.00
Battersea, Box, Forget-Me-Not, Blue Enamel, Bilston	37.00
Battersea, Box, Hand-Painted Rose Bouquet On White, 1 3/16 X 3/4 In.	75.00
Battersea, Box, May You Be Happy, Green Emperor Butterfly Lid, Bilston	37.00
Battersea, Box, Men In Top Hats Driving Bicycles	140.00
Battersea, Box, Partridge Shooting, Enamel, 1 1/2 X 1 1/4 X 2 In.	345.00
Battersea, Box, Peacock On Branch	125.00
Battersea, Box, Roses, Oval, Covered, 2 1/2 In.	127.00
Battersea, Box, Stamp, Enameled, 2 Bronze Ink Wells, Cobalt, Florals, Miniature	225.00

Bavaria was a district where many types of pottery and porcelain were made for centuries. The words Bavaria, Germany, appeared after 1871.

Basket, Melon Shape, Rib Type, Pennsylvania, 10 1/2 In.
(See Page 23)

Basket, Splint Basket & Handle,
Pennsylvania, 11 In.

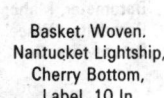

Basket, Chinee, Miniature,
Painted, 3 3/4 In.
(See Page 23)

Basket, Rye Straw, Dough,
Coiled, German, 11 1/2 In.

Basket. Woven.
Nantucket Lightship,
Cherry Bottom,
Label, 10 In.

Basket, Woven,
Nantucket Lightship, 8 In.

Basket, Armadillo, Miniature,
Splint Handle. Pennsylvania, 7 In.
(See Page 23)

Basket, Archback, Miniature,
Pennsylvania, 5 1/2 In.
(See Page 23)

Bavarian, see also Rosenthal

Bavarian, Basket, Floral & Gold Trim, Signed, 7 1/2 X 4 In.	13.50
Bavarian, Bowl, Chantilly Shaped Rim, Lavender Flowers, Gold Edge, 11 In.	30.00
Bavarian, Bowl, Flowers, Scalloped Rim, White, Pink, 9 In.	37.50
Bavarian, Bowl, Fruit, Open Lattice Sides, Multicolor Floral Interior, Gold	65.00
Bavarian, Bowl, Light Green, Water Lilies, Gold, Green Wreath Signed, 10 In.	79.00
Bavarian, Bowl, Opalescent, Flowered, Marked, 8 1/2 In.	18.00
Bavarian, Bowl, Pheasants, Dark Scenery Background, Crown Bavaria	39.50
Bavarian, Bowl, Versailles, Scalloped, Gold Trim, White, Floral	47.50
Bavarian, Box, Cufflink, Hand-Painted, Round	9.00
Bavarian, Butter, The Queen's Rose, Covered, Tirchenreuth	35.00
Bavarian, Cake Set, Orchid Background, Man & Lady Center, Victorian Dress	85.00
Bavarian, Charger, Teal Blue Edge, Gold Rim, Roses, Wreath-Crown Mark, 12 In.	35.00
Bavarian, Chocolate Pot, High Glaze White, Undecorated	25.00
Bavarian, Chocolate Set, White, Lavender & White Violets, Gold Trim, 9 Piece	75.00
Bavarian, Coffee Set, Pale Green, Apple Blossoms, 9 Piece	60.00
Bavarian, Coffee Set, Pink Roses, Gold Trim, 4 Piece	195.00
Bavarian, Creamer, Floral, Band Of Pink Luster, Lion Mark, 4 In.	6.50
Bavarian, Cup & Saucer, Blue, White, Gold, Artist Signed	9.00
Bavarian, Cup & Saucer, Gold & Cream, Stouffer	10.00
Bavarian, Hair Receiver, Pink Roses, Lion Mark	20.00
Bavarian, Holder, Hatpin, Swirl, Roses, Ives, Scalloped, Signed, 4 3/4 In.	48.00
Bavarian, Mug, Eastern Bluebirds, Bareuther	12.00
Bavarian, Mug, Western Tanagers, Bareuther	12.00
Bavarian, Pitcher, Tankard, Grapes, Leaves, Vines, Helmet Spout, Handled, 14 In.	195.00
Bavarian, Plate, Blue & Pink, Roses, Crown RC, 9 1/2 In.	25.00
Bavarian, Plate, Cake, Open Gold Handle, Yellow, Open Flowers, Gold Rim, 9 In.	40.00
Bavarian, Plate, Chautauqua, New York, Hand-Painted, 7 1/2 In.	10.00
Bavarian, Plate, Forest Scene, Stag And Deer, 11 1/2 In.	75.00
Bavarian, Plate, Game, Long-Billed Bird, Pierced, Z.S. & Co., 9 In.	34.00
Bavarian, Plate, Gold Rim, Pink Rose Border, 7 1/2 In.	10.00
Bavarian, Plate, Green & Gold Trim, 10 1/2 In.	30.00
Bavarian, Plate, Hand-Painted Red Cherries & Green Leaves, 8 1/2 In.	12.00
Bavarian, Plate, Hand-Painted, Blue & Gold Border, Signed, 7 1/2 In.	10.00
Bavarian, Plate, Iris, Tulips, Lily-Of-The-Valley, Scalloped Rim, Lang, 12 In.	55.00
Bavarian, Plate, Little Nell, Z.S.& Co., 9 In.	18.00
Bavarian, Plate, Longpere, Autumn Leaves, Berries, Daisies, Signed, 6 In.	8.00
Bavarian, Plate, Orchids, Ivy, Gold Border, Green, Signed Raoul	30.00
Bavarian, Plate, Pink Roses, Scalloped Gold Rim, R.C.Versailles, 7 3/4 In.	8.00
Bavarian, Plate, Violets, Hand-Painted, Signed Hawk, 5 1/2 In.	12.00
Bavarian, Plate, Yellow, Purple Violets, Hand-Painted, 6 In.	8.00
Bavarian, Receiver, Hair, Roses, Monogram B, Pink	45.00
Bavarian, Relish, Roses, Hand-Painted, Z.S. & Co., 13 In.	18.50
Bavarian, Salt, Footed, Gilt Edge	3.50
Bavarian, Sauce Boat, Roses, Pearlized Inside, Sides Fold Inward, Gold, 10 In.	37.50
Bavarian, Server & Underplate, Lemon & Butter, Blue & White Rose, Marked	25.00
Bavarian, Sugar & Creamer, Gold & Cream, Stouffer	17.00
Bavarian, Sugar & Creamer, Medium Large	10.00
Bavarian, Sugar Shaker, Art Deco, Gold Trim, 4 1/2 In.	20.00
Bavarian, Tea Set, Pink Flowers, Scalloped Bottoms, 7 Piece	155.00
Bavarian, Tea Set, Silver Luster, Demitasse, RW, 15 Piece	85.00
Bavarian, Tureen, Wild Rose, Two-Handled, Miniature	18.00
Bavarian, Urn, Pink & Lavender Chrysanthemums, Gold Trim, 6 1/2 X 11 In.	125.00
Bavarian, Vase, Pearlized, Cylinder Shape, 8 In.	15.00

Bayonet, see Weapon, Bayonet

Beaded Bag, Amber Glass, Gold Color Thread, Peppercorn Size, 7 1/4 X 5 In.	26.50
Beaded Bag, Child's, Whimsey, 1904	10.00
Beaded Bag, Dark Beads, Brass Frame	25.00
Beaded Bag, French, Gold, Fringe, 7 1/2 In.	30.00
Beaded Bag, Orchid & Lavender, Draped Beads, Draw Strings	28.00
Beaded Bag, Silver Plate, Art Nouveau Clasp, Victorian	35.00
Beaded Bag, White Iridescent Beads, Silver Frame	18.00
Beatles, Album, John Lennon's Wedding, Complete	50.00
Beatles, Book, Paperback, 1964, Autographed Pullout Pinup	10.00
Beatles, Book, Quiz, London, 1964, 32 Pages	6.00

Beatles, Brass Token, Commemorating Visit To United States In 1964	1.00
Beatles, Button, Paul, Flasher	5.00
Beatles, Button, Yellow & Red With Pictures Of Group	1.50
Beatles, Card, Gum, Set Of 19	10.00
Beatles, Coin, Commemorative, 1964	2.00
Beatles, Diary, 1965, 32 Pages	6.50
Beatles, Doll, Ringo, 1964, Box	15.00
Beatles, Game, Flip Your Wig, 1964	10.00
Beatles, Penholder, Figural	12.00
Beatles, Pillow, Figural, C.1964	18.00
Beatles, Pin, Fan, Official, Pictures	.75
Beatles, Pin, Lapel, Sergeant Pepper, Set Of 4	12.00
Beatles, Poster, Colored, 5 X 4 Ft.	20.00
Beatles, Poster, Hard Day's Night, 27 X 41 In.	35.00
Beatles, Poster, Help, 41 X 81 In.	45.00
Beatles, Poster, Let It Be	45.00
Beatles, Poster, Yellow Submarine, 41 X 81 In.	45.00
Beatles, Print On Canvas, Color, C.1960, 17 X 14 In.	6.00
Beatles, Record Holder, 1966	25.00
Beatles, Ring, Flasher, Set Of Four	1.50
Beatles, Scarf, White & Red, Faces & Signatures	6.00
Beatles, Tray, Metal	7.00
Beatles, Tray, Tin, Pictures Of Beatles, Made In England	7.50
Beatles, Tray, 4 Faces	11.00
Beck, see also Buffalo Pottery	
Beck, Corn Set, Vari-Hued Corn Decoration, Platter, 4 Plates	125.00
Beck, Fish Set, Fish Decoration, Sauceboat, Underplate, 11 X 9 In. Plates	145.00
Beck, Plate, Deer, 9 In., Set Of 6	120.00
Beck, Plate, Game, Wild Geese In Flight, Pierced For Hanging	26.00
Beck, Plate, Hunters In Field, Sky, Foliage	29.00

Beehive, Austria, or Beehive, Vienna, china includes all the many types of decorated porcelain marked with the famous beehive mark. The mark has been used since the eighteenth century.

Beehive, see also Royal Vienna	
Beehive, Chocolate Pot, Portrait	250.00
Beehive, Cup & Saucer, Chocolate, Marked	30.00
Beehive, Cup & Saucer, Lovers In Garden, Footed Cup, Pedestaled Saucer	65.00
Beehive, Figurine, Cleopatra Holding Asp Over Head, Vienna, 8 1/2 In.	80.00
Beehive, Jar, Lemon Yellow, Flowers, Gilding, Lidded, 4 1/2 In., Pair	285.00
Beehive, Plate, Austrian, Marie Antoinette, Blue Border, Gold, Signed, 7 In.	28.00
Beehive, Plate, German, Portrait Of Woman, Cherub, Carlsbad, 8 In.	65.00
Beehive, Plate, Othello Scene, Walter Paget	30.00
Beehive, Plate, Trout Swimming In Water, Green & Gold Border, Marked, 10 In.	22.00
Beehive, Vase, Austrian, People Both Sides, Rose On Neck, Greens, Reds, Ivory	165.00
Beehive, Vase, Lemon Yellow, Blooming Flowers, Gilding, Lidded, 4 1/2 In., Pair	285.00
Beer Can, Amana	10.00
Beer Can, Ballantine Draught Beer, Gallon	12.50
Beer Can, Billy Beer By Cold Spring Brewery	1.00
Beer Can, Black Label, Canadian	.75
Beer Can, Chippewa Pure Water	2.00
Beer Can, Labatt's Ale, Canadian	.75
Beer Can, Old German	2.50
Beer Can, Point View	2.50
Beer Can, Pure Water Days By Leinenkugel Farm Fest, Schell's Mistake Can	4.00
Beer Can, Robin Hood	2.50
Beer Can, Schell Multi, 12 Oz.	2.00
Beer Can, Schell's, White Background	5.00
Beer Can, Schmidt, Scenic, Punch, Flat Top	2.75

Bells have been made of china, glass, or metal. All types are collected.

Bell, Brass, Car, Wall Bracket, Pull Cord, Hand Grip, Dated 1909, 11 X 5 In.	85.00
Bell, Brass, Cow, Hung From Strap, 3 X 3 1/2 In.	7.50
Bell, Brass, Cow, Iron Clapper, 4 1/2 In.	16.50
Bell, Brass, Dinner, Negro Mammy Leaning On A Stick	38.00

Bell, Brass, Dutch Girl, 9 In.	25.00
Bell, Brass, Eagle Handle, 4 3/4 X 2 7/8 In.	60.00
Bell, Brass, English, Elizabeth Regina, June, 1953, Relief Handle, 3 1/2 In.	15.00
Bell, Brass, Figural, Lady, Oriental	40.00
Bell, Brass, Figural, Stork Sitting On Bell, Clapper, 4 In.	25.00
Bell, Brass, Flank, 6 On Strap	97.50
Bell, Brass, Hand, Teacher's, 11 X 5 3/4 In.	45.00
Bell, Brass, Hotel, Fancy Ironwork	25.00
Bell, Brass, Lady In Victorian Dress, Carrying Umbrella, 5 1/2 X 3 1/4 In.	68.00
Bell, Brass, Lady, Petticoat Style, 4 In.	15.00
Bell, Brass, Ornate, Embossed, Dated 1878, 4 X 3 1/2 In.	30.00
Bell, Brass, Railroad, Brass Knob, Marked Frisco, 17 X 13 In.	875.00
Bell, Brass, School, Teacher's, Nickel Over Top	38.00
Bell, Brass, School, Walnut Handle, C.19th Century, 8 In.	57.50
Bell, Brass, School, Wooden Handle, 12 In.	65.00
Bell, Brass, School, Wooden Handle, 6 In.Diameter, 3 1/2 In.	45.00
Bell, Brass, School, Wooden Handle, 7 In.	25.00
Bell, Brass, Sleigh, Graduated, Leather Strap, 40 In., 12 Bells	67.50
Bell, Brass, Sleigh, Riveted, Cotter Keys, 59 On 92 In.Leather Strap	650.00
Bell, Brass, Sleigh, Set Of 29, Leather Strap	29.00
Bell, Brass, Sleigh, 10, On Partial Leather Strap	30.00
Bell, Brass, Sleigh, 24 Graduated On Leather Strap	125.00
Bell, Brass, Sleigh, 26 On Strap	95.00
Bell, Brass, Sleigh, 32 Graduated On Strap, Small	125.00
Bell, Brass, Square Iron Base, Thumb Side Strike, 5 In.	22.50
Bell, Brass, Strap Hook For Hanging, 3 X 2 1/2 In.	18.50
Bell, Brass, Trolley Car, Pull Chain Operated, Wood Base, 8 In.	62.00
Bell, Brass, Wooden Handle, 6 In.	15.00
Bell, Brass, 120 Bells, Nickel Plated, Strap, 80 In.	325.00
Bell, Bronze, Lighthouse, 17 X 20 In.	395.00
Bell, Cow, Iron	9.50
Bell, Cow, Strap & Buckle, 6 1/4 X 7 1/2 In.	9.50
Bell, Cow, Swiss, 1898	7.50
Bell, Delft, Shape Of Cowbell, Windmill, Water Scene, Crossed Pipes Mark	39.00
Bell, Desk, Steel, 5 In.	9.00
Bell, Dinner, Negro Mammy, Pottery	10.00
Bell, Encased In Original Oak Frame, Dated 1773, 50 X 32 X 48 In.	4200.00
Bell, Fire Engine, Brass, Cast-Iron Clapper, 5 In.	40.00
Bell, Fire Engine, Brass, 20 Pounds, 10 X 7 1/2 In.	325.00
Bell, Hand, Dearing's Bread	6.50
Bell, Hand, School Marm's, Brass, Wooden Handle, 7 1/4 X 3 3/4 In.	19.95
Bell, Harness, Wood, Hames With Brass Balls	7.00
Bell, Liberty, Cast Iron	10.00
Bell, Locomotive, Brass, Copper Clapper, Cast-Iron Frame, 7 X 9 3/4 In.	150.00
Bell, Milk Glass, Smoke, Applied Ring, Fluted Rim, 6 In.	14.00
Bell, Porcelain, New Brunswick Scene, Pink Luster, 2 1/2 X 2 1/4 In.	22.50
Bell, Porcelain, Smoke, White, Fluted Rim, Brass Ring, 4 1/4 X 3 1/2 In.	20.00
Bell, School, Wooden Handle, 7 1/2 In.	22.00
Bell, Servants Call Box, Electric, 9 Room Signals, Edinburgh, 1893	70.00
Bell, Silver Plated, Wooden Handle, 11 In.	20.00
Bell, Sleigh, Nickel On Brass, Swedish, Set Of 3	85.00
Bell, Sleigh, Six On Leather Strap	15.00
Bell, Smoke, Scalloped Rim, Vaseline, Opalescent, 6 1/2 In.	35.00
Bell, Sterling Silver, Woman In Balloon Skirt, Vermeil, 3 1/2 In.	125.00
Bell, Tap, White Marble Base, Pewter Platform, 7 X 4 3/4 In.	32.50
Bell, Teacher, Hand, Turned Handle, 9 3/4 In.	40.00
Bell, Town Crier's, Maple Handle, Iron Clapper	140.00

*Belle Ware was made in 1903 by Carl V. Helmschmied. In 1904 he
started a corporation known as the Helschmied Manufacturing Company.
His factory closed in 1908 and he worked on his own until his death in 1934.*

Belle Ware, Box, Jewel, Overshot Granulated Crystal, Bouquet Of Roses, Hinged	250.00
Belle Ware, Box, Pastel Roses On White, Pebbled, Frosted, 3 X 4 In.	350.00
Belle Ware, Dish, Pin, Lined, Enameled Violets	65.00

Belleek china is made in Ireland, other European countries, and the United States. The glaze is creamy yellow and appears wet. The first Belleek was made in 1857.

Belleek, see also Ceramic Art Co., Haviland, Lenox, Matt Morgan, Ott & Brewer

Belleek, Ashtray, Horseshoe Shape	27.00
Belleek, Basket, Bird's Nest, Colored Flowers On Rim, 3 3/4 In.	70.00
Belleek, Basket, Heart Shape, Flowered, Ribbon Mark, No.464	170.00
Belleek, Basket, Irish, Basketware, 3 Strand, 1st Mark, 11 In.	550.00
Belleek, Basket, Irish, 4 Strand, Floral, Leaves On Rim, Green Heart Inside	145.00
Belleek, Basket, Pierced Rim, Signature Impressed, 10 1/2 In.	275.00
Belleek, Basket, Shamrock Shape, Applied Flowers, 5 In.	145.00
Belleek, Basket, 3 Strand, Glazed, 1st Period, 6 1/2 In.	525.00
Belleek, Basket, 3 Strand, Oval, 1st Period, Large, 12 1/2 In.	690.00
Belleek, Bowl, Applied Flowers, No Color, 2nd Black Mark	165.00
Belleek, Bowl, Diamond Pattern, Pearl Essence, 2nd Black Mark, 4 X 4 1/2 In.	85.00
Belleek, Bowl, Grasses Pattern, Covered, 1st Black Mark	95.00
Belleek, Bowl, Heart Shape, Fluted & Ruffled, 2nd Black Mark, 8 X 6 In.	59.00
Belleek, Bowl, Irish, Shell, 2nd Black Mark, 5 In.	55.00
Belleek, Bowl, Ivory, Willet, 4 1/4 X 3 In.	25.00
Belleek, Bowl, Lotus Form, Enameled Yellow, Green, Gold Florals, Ott & Brewer	150.00
Belleek, Bowl, Oval, Green Trim, 2nd Black Mark	150.00
Belleek, Bowl, Peacock Feathers, Willet, 8 In.	85.00
Belleek, Bowl, Punch, Gold Serpent Handles, Floral, Willet, 13 1/2 In.	120.00
Belleek, Bowl, Willet, Yellow Roses Around Edge, Brown Body, 8 1/4 In.	50.00
Belleek, Box, Dresser, Willet, Scalloped Lid, Ivory	22.00
Belleek, Box, Trinket, Shamrock, 2nd Black Mark	55.00
Belleek, Coffeepot, Limpet, 3rd Mark, 8 In.	250.00
Belleek, Coffeepot, Sterling Silver Overlay, Palette Mark	85.00
Belleek, Compote, Art Nouveau, Factory Decorated, Palette	52.50
Belleek, Compote, Dolphin Pedestal, 1st Black Mark, 10 X 3 3/4 In.	325.00
Belleek, Compote, Ruffled, Rustic Legs, 9 In.	225.00
Belleek, Compote, Shell On Coral Stem, Columbian Art Co., 3 3/4 X 5 1/2 In.	65.00
Belleek, Cornucopia, Rock Form Base, 2nd Black Mark, 9 1/2 In.	210.00
Belleek, Cream, Double Shell, Toy, Green Mark	50.00
Belleek, Creamer & Sugar, Green Mark, Bows, Set	37.50
Belleek, Creamer, Echinus, Gilt Border, Pink Trim	95.00
Belleek, Creamer, Floral, 3 X 2 1/2 In.	30.00
Belleek, Creamer, Grasses Pattern, 1st Black Mark	185.00
Belleek, Creamer, Harp & Shamrock, 2nd Black Mark, 3 1/2 In.	65.00
Belleek, Creamer, Irish, Basket Weave, Numbered	38.00
Belleek, Creamer, Ivy, 1st Black Mark	100.00
Belleek, Creamer, Lotus, 1891 Black Mark	45.00
Belleek, Creamer, Plateaux, Small, Black Mark	100.00
Belleek, Creamer, Rathmore, 1st Black Mark, Pink Handle, 4 In.	75.00
Belleek, Creamer, Shamrock, Basket Weave, 3rd Black Mark	34.00
Belleek, Creamer, Shamrock, 2nd Black Mark, Twig Handle, 4 1/2 In.	45.00
Belleek, Creamer, Shamrock, 3rd Black Mark, Twig Handle, 4 1/2 In.	38.00
Belleek, Creamer, Shamrocks & Basket Weave, 4 In., Black Mark	36.00
Belleek, Creamer, Shell Pattern, 3rd Black Mark	75.00
Belleek, Creamer, Shell, 2nd Black Mark, 4 In.	58.00
Belleek, Creamer, Thistle, No Color, 2nd Black Mark	65.00
Belleek, Creamer, Toy Shell, 1891 Black Mark, White, Green Trim	45.00
Belleek, Creamer, Tridacna, Green Trim, 2nd Black Mark, 5 In.	45.00
Belleek, Creamer, Tridacna, Pink Trimmed, 1st Black Mark, 2 1/2 X 3 1/2 In.	45.00
Belleek, Creamer, White, Basket Weave Bottom & Flowers, Green Harp & Crown	45.00
Belleek, Cup & Saucer, Artichoke, 1st Black Mark	75.00
Belleek, Cup & Saucer, Basket Weave, Shamrock, 3rd Black Mark	25.00
Belleek, Cup & Saucer, Cake Plate, Mark In Red, C.1861, Black & Gold	200.00
Belleek, Cup & Saucer, Celtic, Black Mark	100.00
Belleek, Cup & Saucer, Cloverleaf, Harp, 3rd Black Mark	24.95
Belleek, Cup & Saucer, Coffee	25.00
Belleek, Cup & Saucer, Coxon, Floral Transfers	75.00
Belleek, Cup & Saucer, Demitasse, Fluted, Scalloped, Gold Trim, Ott & Brewer	55.00
Belleek, Cup & Saucer, Demitasse, Pink, Gold Trim, 1st Black Mark	65.00

Belleek, Cup & Saucer, Demitasse, Ribbed, Gold Dragon Handle, Willet	78.00
Belleek, Cup & Saucer, Dragon, Gilt Trim, 1st Black Mark, 1880	85.00
Belleek, Cup & Saucer, Farmer's, Artichoke, 1st Mark	75.00
Belleek, Cup & Saucer, Flowers, Square Handle, 2nd Black Mark	75.00
Belleek, Cup & Saucer, Gold Interior, Violet Blossoms	165.00
Belleek, Cup & Saucer, Grapes & Leaves, Gold Decorated, Willet	145.00
Belleek, Cup & Saucer, Grass Pattern, Demitasse, 2nd Black Mark	75.00
Belleek, Cup & Saucer, Harp Shamrock, 3rd Black Mark	37.50
Belleek, Cup & Saucer, Limpet, Pink & Gold Trim, 3rd Black Mark	45.00
Belleek, Cup & Saucer, Neptune, Pink Trim, 2nd Black Mark	42.00
Belleek, Cup & Saucer, Pink & Gold	48.00
Belleek, Cup & Saucer, Seashell Form, Gold Rim, Ott & Brewer	50.00
Belleek, Cup & Saucer, Shamrock, Harp Handled, 2nd Black Mark	25.00
Belleek, Cup & Saucer, Shamrock, 2nd Black Mark	45.00
Belleek, Cup & Saucer, Shamrock, 3rd Black Mark	32.00
Belleek, Cup & Saucer, Shell, 2nd Black Mark	65.00
Belleek, Cup & Saucer, Tridacna, Enameled, God Speed Greenock, Black Mark	150.00
Belleek, Cup & Saucer, Tridacna, Pink Trim, 2nd Black Mark	47.00 To 49.00
Belleek, Cup & Saucer, Willet, Cactus	75.00
Belleek, Cup & Saucer, Willet, Floral, Gold Decoration, Demi-Size	65.00
Belleek, Cup & Saucer, Willet, Flowers, Gold Medallion, Embossed, Multicolor	60.00
Belleek, Cup & Saucer, Willet, Gold Grape & Leaf Design, Footed	48.00
Belleek, Cup & Saucer, Willet, Hand-Painted Florals	70.00
Belleek, Cup & Saucer, Willet, Heavy Gold Grapes & Leaves	65.00
Belleek, Cup & Saucer, 6 In.Plate, Sydney, Green Trim, 2nd Black Mark	75.00
Belleek, Cup & Saucer, 7 In.Plate, Celtic, Brown Decoration, 3rd Black Mark	75.00
Belleek, Cup, Hawthorne Pattern, Coral Legs & Handle	75.00
Belleek, Dish, Bonbon, Willet, Button Feet, Hand-Painted, 5 In.	39.00
Belleek, Dish, Dessert, Primrose, 3rd Black Mark, Blossom Shape, Yellow, 5 In.	20.00
Belleek, Dish, Salt, Willet, Roses, 3 Gold Feet	6.00
Belleek, Ewer, Applied Floral, GM, 7 1/2 In.	125.00
Belleek, Ewer, Applied Flowers, Green Mark, 7 In.	85.00
Belleek, Ewer, Green, White, Purple Berries, Flowers, Willet, 4 1/2 In.	92.00
Belleek, Ewer, Twig Handles, Gold Thistles & Leaves, Gold Rim & Foot, 5 In.	285.00
Belleek, Figurine, Belgian Hawkers, 1st Black Mark, Signed, 7 In., Pair	1600.00
Belleek, Figurine, Frog, 1st Black Mark, 4 1/2 In.	320.00
Belleek, Figurine, Leprechaun, 3rd Black Mark, 5 1/2 In.	200.00
Belleek, Figurine, Meditation, High Glaze Gown, 2nd Black Mark, 15 In.	775.00
Belleek, Figurine, Meditation, Polychrome Glaze, 1st Black Mark, 14 1/2 In.	1050.00
Belleek, Figurine, Pig Sitting, Green Mark, 3 X 2 In.	20.00
Belleek, Figurine, Pig Sitting, White, 4 X 2 1/2 In.	25.00
Belleek, Figurine, Swan, 1st Black Mark, Lease No.329	85.00
Belleek, Figurine, The Crouching Venus, 2nd Black Mark, 18 In.	2000.00
Belleek, Flowerpot, Diamond Point, 2nd Black Mark, 4 In.	85.00
Belleek, Flowerpot, Flared, 2nd Black Mark	110.00
Belleek, Flowerpot, White, Basket Weave, 2nd Black Mark, 3 1/2 In.	60.00
Belleek, Frame, Oval, Lilac Luster, 1st Black Mark, 6 1/2 X 5 1/2 In.	690.00
Belleek, Frame, Oval, 1st Black Mark, 16 1/2 In.	1400.00
Belleek, Jar, Cracker, Herringbone, Covered, 2nd Black Mark, 5 1/2 In.	225.00
Belleek, Jar, Marmalade, Shamrock, Basket Weave, 3rd Black Mark, 4 1/2 In.	52.00
Belleek, Jar, Puff, Willet, Scalloped Edge On Lid, Ivory, 4 In.	32.00
Belleek, Jug, Cider, Dark Green, Band Of White Flowers, Palette Mark, 6 In.	85.00
Belleek, Jug, Cream, Neptune, Green Trim, 2nd Black Mark	40.00
Belleek, Lamp Base, Pink & Turquoise, Brown & Black On Hoofs, 1st Black Mark	525.00
Belleek, Luncheon Set, Green Banded, 2nd Black Mark, 42 Piece	675.00
Belleek, Marmalade Jar, Irish, Barrel, Numbered, 3rd Black Mark, Shamrock	50.00
Belleek, Mirror, Oval, Applied Flowers, 1st Black Mark, 5 1/4 X 6 1/4 In.	250.00
Belleek, Mug, Brown High Glaze, Yellow Enameled Lemons & Floral, 7 1/4 In.	73.00
Belleek, Mug, Colonial Boys Dancing, Trees & Sky Background, Willet, 6 In.	110.00
Belleek, Mug, Hand-Painted Purple, Green & Red Grapes, Willet, L.A.S., 5 In.	105.00
Belleek, Mug, Hawthorne Pattern, No Color, 2nd Black Mark	75.00
Belleek, Mug, Monk Drinking, Willet, 5 1/2 In.	65.00
Belleek, Mug, Portrait Of Man With Drinking Vessel, Rust & Green, 6 1/2 In.	95.00
Belleek, Mug, Red Poppies, Blue Flowers, Gold Ornate Handle, Willet	75.00
Belleek, Mug, Shamrock, 2nd Black Mark	35.00

Belleek, Mug, Willet, Bust Portrait Of Indian On Dark Brown	40.00
Belleek, Mug, Willet, Hand-Painted Grape Clusters, Signed L.A.S., 5 In.	95.00
Belleek, Mug, Willet, Purple, Green & Red Cluster Of Grapes, Handled	95.00
Belleek, Mug, Willet, Red, Blue & White Grapes, Gilt & Green Handle, Signed	95.00
Belleek, Mush Set, Bacchus Pattern, Black Mark	90.00
Belleek, Mustard Pot, Irish, Shell, Numbered	50.00
Belleek, Pitcher, Cider, Floral & Fruit, Signed	145.00
Belleek, Pitcher, Cream, Deep Swirls & Beading, Green Mark, 6 X 4 3/4 In.	25.00
Belleek, Pitcher, Cream, Irish, Black Mark, Cream & Yellow	24.00
Belleek, Pitcher, Cream, Rope Twist Handle, Double Mark, C.1876, 4 5/8 In.	125.00
Belleek, Pitcher, Cream, Silver Overlay, Palette Signed, 5 X 5 In.	197.50
Belleek, Pitcher, Double Spout & Handle, 1st Black Mark	150.00
Belleek, Pitcher, Helmet, Ivory, Gold Trim, Handle, Square Base, Willet, 7 In.	28.00
Belleek, Pitcher, Lemonade, Art Nouveau Design, Willet	75.00
Belleek, Pitcher, Lemonade, Lenox	75.00
Belleek, Pitcher, Shell Pattern, Green Mark, 4 1/2 In.	30.00
Belleek, Pitcher, Willet, Cherries, Leafy Vines, Gold Trim Russet To Green	58.00
Belleek, Pitcher, Willet, Dragon Handle, Hand-Painted Florals, 11 In.	105.00
Belleek, Planter, Irish, Flowers, Birds, Vines, 2nd Black Mark, 8 X 10 1/2 In.	550.00
Belleek, Plate, Basket Weave, Black Mark, 10 1/2 In.	40.00
Belleek, Plate, Bread, Shamrock, 2nd Black Mark	45.00
Belleek, Plate, Cake, Basket Weave Shamrock, 3rd Black Mark, 7 In.	15.00
Belleek, Plate, Cake, Shamrock, 2nd Black Mark	30.00
Belleek, Plate, Cake, Sydney, Green Trim, 2nd Black Mark	75.00
Belleek, Plate, Christmas, 1970	100.00
Belleek, Plate, Coal Island, Flowers, 7 In.	125.00
Belleek, Plate, Irish, Limpet, Pink & Gold Trim, 3rd Black Mark, 6 1/4 In.	160.00
Belleek, Plate, Limpet Cog, 3rd Black Mark, 7 In.	22.00
Belleek, Plate, Limpet, Pink & Gold Trim, 3rd Black Mark, 6 1/4 In.	16.00
Belleek, Plate, Pink & Gold Trim, 6 1/4 In.	16.00
Belleek, Plate, Shamrock, 2nd Black Mark, 6 In.	16.50
Belleek, Plate, Tridacna, Black Mark, 6 3/4 In.	20.00
Belleek, Plate, Tridacna, Black Mark, 8 In.	15.00
Belleek, Pot, Honey, Grass	250.00
Belleek, Pot, Mustard, Flying Goose, Fir Trees, Silver Overlay, Mark, 5 In.	80.00
Belleek, Pot, Mustard, Shamrock	22.00
Belleek, Pot, Mustard, 3rd Black Mark	55.00
Belleek, Pot, Waterlily, Pink & Brown Trim, 2nd Black Mark	140.00
Belleek, Ring Tree, Dragon, Black Mark	188.00
Belleek, Rose Bowl, Applied Flowers & Leaves, 1st Black Mark, 3 In.	129.00
Belleek, Salt Set, Willet, Ivory, Wide Gold Band, Set Of 6	42.00
Belleek, Salt, Gold Wash Lining, Yellow, Purple, Pink, Blue, Gold, Open	12.50
Belleek, Salt, Individual, Willet, Ruffled, Crimped Edge, Luster Inside	10.00
Belleek, Salt, Irish, Shell, Open, Numbered	22.00
Belleek, Salt, Lenox, Footed, Cream Gold Trim, Set Of 6	65.00
Belleek, Salt, Open, Shamrock, Shell Surface, 3rd Black Mark, 2 X 3 1/4 In.	25.00
Belleek, Salt, Pink Trim Shell, 2nd Black Mark	75.00
Belleek, Salt, Shamrock, 2nd Black Mark	28.00
Belleek, Salt, Willet, Heart Shape, Ruffled, Gold Trim, Floral Center, Sides	17.00
Belleek, Saltshaker, Tridacna, 3 In.	25.00
Belleek, Saucer, Tinted Pink, Hexagon, Black Mark	25.00
Belleek, Shell, Coral Base, Pink Coral & Edging, 1st Black Mark, 4 1/2 In.	250.00
Belleek, Sucrier, Echinus, First Period, Black Mark	145.00
Belleek, Sugar & Creamer, Applied Gold Twig Handles, Blue Opalescent, Ribbed	200.00
Belleek, Sugar & Creamer, Clovers, 3rd Black Mark	66.00
Belleek, Sugar & Creamer, Harp Shamrock, 3rd Black Mark	68.00
Belleek, Sugar & Creamer, Hexagon, Green Trim, 2nd Black Mark	85.00
Belleek, Sugar & Creamer, Irish, Shamrock, Black Mark	75.00
Belleek, Sugar & Creamer, Irish, Shamrock, Green Mark	45.00
Belleek, Sugar & Creamer, Irish, Shell, Black Mark	50.00
Belleek, Sugar & Creamer, Ivy, Black Mark	35.00
Belleek, Sugar & Creamer, Lily, Green Trim Top & Handle, 3rd Black Mark	68.00
Belleek, Sugar & Creamer, Lily, Pink Trim, 2nd Black Mark	75.00
Belleek, Sugar & Creamer, Lotus Blossom, Green Mark	35.00
Belleek, Sugar & Creamer, Lotus, Yellow Trim, 3rd Black Mark	60.00

Belleek, Sugar & Creamer, Lotus, 3rd Black Mark, Pair 60.00
Belleek, Sugar & Creamer, Neptune, Green Trim, 2nd Black Mark 85.00
Belleek, Sugar & Creamer, Pink Ribbon, 2nd Black Mark 95.00
Belleek, Sugar & Creamer, Shamrock, 2nd Black Mark 62.00
Belleek, Sugar & Creamer, Shell, Black Mark 50.00
Belleek, Sugar & Creamer, Twig Handles 32.00
Belleek, Sugar & Creamer, Twig, Cream, Pink Edge & Handle, 3rd Black Mark 100.00
Belleek, Sugar & Creamer, Willet, White, Gold Lizard Handles, CPK In Gold 115.00
Belleek, Sugar, Covered, Grasses Pattern, 1st Black Mark, 5 In. 185.00
Belleek, Sugar, Gold Handle, Fleur-De-Lis On Lid, 4 In. 42.00
Belleek, Sugar, Grasses, Covered, Luster, Black Mark 90.00
Belleek, Sugar, Hexagon, Green Trim, 2nd Black Mark, 2 1/4 In. 35.00
Belleek, Sugar, Irish, Basket Weave, Numbered 30.00
Belleek, Swan, Open, 2nd Black Mark, 4 1/2 In. 90.00
Belleek, Swan, Second Period, Black Mark, 4 In. 190.00
Belleek, Swan, Willet, White, 4 1/4 X 5 In. 75.00
Belleek, Tea Caddy, Willet, Geisha Girls & Lanterns, Covered 95.00
Belleek, Tea Set, Basket Weave & Shamrock, Green Mark, 4 Pieces 50.00
Belleek, Tea Set, Cream, Gold Designs, Handles, Lenox Palette Mark 125.00
Belleek, Tea Set, Echinus, Orange Coral Handles & Base, 1st Black Mark, 3 Piece ... 550.00
Belleek, Tea Set, Echinus, 1st Mark, 5 Piece 600.00
Belleek, Tea Set, Fan, Cream, Yellow Panels, 2nd Black Mark, 7 Piece 395.00
Belleek, Tea Set, Harp Shamrock, 2nd Black Mark, 6 Piece 265.00
Belleek, Tea Set, Hexagon, Second Period, Black Mark, Teapot 5 1/2 In. 395.00
Belleek, Tea Set, Irish, Neptune, Pink Trim, 2nd Black Mark, 8 Piece 800.00
Belleek, Tea Set, Irish, Teapot, Sugar, Creamer, 2nd Mark 75.00
Belleek, Tea Set, Neptune, Green Trim, 1891, Black Mark, 12 Piece 375.00
Belleek, Tea Set, Neptune, Green Trim, 2nd Black Mark, 7 Piece 325.00
Belleek, Tea Set, Neptune, Pink Trim, 2nd Black Mark, 7 Piece 350.00
Belleek, Tea Set, Shamrock, Basket Weave, 3rd Green Mark, 1946-55, 12 Piece ... 225.00
Belleek, Tea Set, Shamrock, 2nd Black Mark, 7 Piece 225.00
Belleek, Tea Set, Tridacna, Green Trim, 2nd Black Mark, 7 Piece 255.00
Belleek, Tea Set, Tridacna, Pink Trim, 1st Mark, 12 Piece 575.00
Belleek, Tea Set, Tridacna, Pink, 2nd Black Mark, 28 Piece 700.00
Belleek, Tea Set, White Neptune, 2nd Black Mark, 10 Piece 375.00
Belleek, Tea Set, Willet, House & Windmill, Silver Overlay, 3 Piece 275.00
Belleek, Teakettle, Echinus, Overhead Handle, 1st Black Mark 145.00
Belleek, Teapot, Celtic 150.00
Belleek, Teapot, Dragon, Gilded Handle, Griffin, 1st Black Mark, 10 X 5 In. ... 740.00
Belleek, Teapot, Echinus, Gilt Trim, Small, 1st Black Mark 225.00
Belleek, Teapot, Echinus, Irish, White With Gold Trim, 1st Black Mark 195.00
Belleek, Teapot, Grass, 1st Black Mark .... 225.00 To 235.00
Belleek, Teapot, Irish, Lease No.905, 2nd Blue Mark 135.00
Belleek, Teapot, Neptune, Pink Trim, 2nd Black Mark 125.00
Belleek, Teapot, Pink & Gilded Tridacna, 1st Black Mark, 7 In. 390.00
Belleek, Teapot, Shamrock, Basket Weave, Green Handle, 2nd Black Mark, 8 In. ... 165.00
Belleek, Teapot, Sugar & Creamer, Neptune, 2nd Black Mark 350.00
Belleek, Teapot, Tridacna, Green Mark, 7 X 6 In. 85.00
Belleek, Teapot, Willet, Cobalt, Silver Overlay 85.00
Belleek, Tray & 6 Serving Plates 260.00
Belleek, Tray, Echinus, Pink Trim, 1st Black Mark 300.00
Belleek, Tray, Echinus, Plain, 1st Black Mark 225.00
Belleek, Tray, Echinus, 1st Black Mark, 15 1/2 X 12 1/2 In. 275.00
Belleek, Tray, Tea, Grasses Pattern, 1st Black Mark, 17 X 14 In. 375.00
Belleek, Tub, Small, Shamrock, Black Mark 22.00
Belleek, Vase, Bird Stump, Dragon Ring Tree, 1st Black Mark, 12 In., Pair 950.00
Belleek, Vase, Bud, Creamy White, Sterling Silver Overlay, 6 In. 55.00
Belleek, Vase, Cobalt, Daffodils & Narcissus, Willet, 12 1/2 In. 175.00
Belleek, Vase, Corn, Green Color, 1st Black Mark 350.00
Belleek, Vase, Fish, Applied Butterflies, 1st Black Mark, 12 In. 445.00
Belleek, Vase, Geranium, Green & Red Ground, Palette Green Mark, 11 1/2 In. ... 75.00
Belleek, Vase, Green Bullrushes, 2nd Black Mark 125.00
Belleek, Vase, Green, Red & Pink Roses, Gold Scroll Top, Willet, 16 In. 225.00
Belleek, Vase, Irish, Lilac Luster Leaves, 1st Black Mark, 6 In. 240.00
Belleek, Vase, Irish, Rockspill, 2nd Black Mark, Lease No.453 .... 65.00

Belleek, Vase, Irish, Tree Stump, 1st Mark, Pair	150.00
Belleek, Vase, Lemon Tree, Gold Designs, Willet, 11 1/2 In.	95.00
Belleek, Vase, Lily, 3rd Black Mark, High Glaze Yellow Accents, 6 3/4 In.	70.00
Belleek, Vase, Nautilus, Coral Base, White, 1st Blue Mark, 8 1/2 In.	250.00
Belleek, Vase, Nile, Calla Lily, Yellow Luster Trim, Green Mark, 7 1/4 In.	19.00
Belleek, Vase, Nile, 1st Black Mark, 9 1/2 In.	210.00
Belleek, Vase, Pink Luster Interior, 8 1/2 In.	55.00
Belleek, Vase, Portrait, Arabs On Horseback, Signed, 10 1/2 In.	375.00
Belleek, Vase, Quiver, White, Musical Designs On Base, 1st Black Mark	790.00
Belleek, Vase, Red, Gold, & Black Designs, Gold Grapes, Art Nouveau, 6 In.	75.00
Belleek, Vase, Ribbed Corset Shape, High Glaze Yellow, 2nd Black Mark, 3 In.	45.00
Belleek, Vase, Roses, Red, Pink, Round, Small	60.00
Belleek, Vase, Roses, Willet, Signed & Dated, 12 In.	100.00
Belleek, Vase, Scalloped Leaf Top, Gold Band, 1st Green Mark, 6 1/2 In.	65.00
Belleek, Vase, Scenic, Willet, 16 In.	125.00
Belleek, Vase, Shamrocks, Scalloped Top, Harp Handle, 3rd Black Mark, 7 In.	108.50
Belleek, Vase, Shell, Coral Base, Pink Tinge, 1st Black Mark, 7 X 6 In.	190.00
Belleek, Vase, Shell, Dolphin, 1st Black Mark, 4 1/2 In.	240.00
Belleek, Vase, Tree Trunk, Flowers, Two Birds	325.00
Belleek, Vase, Trunk Stump, Ivy Trim, 1st Black Mark	94.00
Belleek, Vase, White & Green, Roses, Gold Scrollwork, Willet, 15 3/4 In.	195.00
Belleek, Vase, White Roses, Green Leaves On White, 10 In.	275.00
Belleek, Vase, Willet, Gold Nasturtiums On Orange, 1903, 7 In.	185.00
Belleek, Vase, Willet, Hand-Painted, Flared Top, 15 1/2 X 4 In.	195.00
Belleek, Vase, Willet, Lemon Tree Decoration, 11 1/2 In.	115.00
Belleek, Vase, Willet, Pink, Yellow, Red Roses, Gold Rim, Green, 16 1/2 In.	265.00
Belleek, Vase, Willet, Scenic, Sunset, Trees, Blue & Green Ground, 16 In.	150.00
Belleek, Vase, Willet, White & Green, Roses, Gold Scrollwork, 15 3/4 In.	195.00
Belleek, Water Set, Cream Color, Hand-Painted Trim, Palette Signed	137.00
Belleek, Willet, Hand-Painted, Lavender To Pink Iris, Artist Signed, 8 In.	60.00

Bennett, see Edwin Bennett

 *Bennington ware was the product of two factories working in Bennington, Vermont. Both firms were out of business by 1896. The wares include brown and yellow mottled pottery, Parian, scroddled ware, stoneware, graniteware, yellowware, and Staffordshire-like vases.*

Bennington, see also Rockingham

Bennington Type, Bowl, Mixing, Brown & Cream Mottling, 3 1/4 X 10 1/2 In.	65.00
Bennington Type, Pitcher, Greek Column, Picture Each Side, 2 Quart	60.00
Bennington, Bowl, Low, 11 X 8 In.	47.00
Bennington, Bowl, Mixing, Brown, Mottled, Flat Bottom, 10 1/2 In.	60.00
Bennington, Bowl, 1849, Signed, 13 X 3 1/2 In.	165.00
Bennington, Box, Grapes In Relief Cover, Parian, 4 1/4 In.	40.00
Bennington, Box, Salt	65.00
Bennington, Box, Trinket, Blue And White	60.00
Bennington, Bust, Juliet, Parian, Jones & Thos.Bennington, C.1865	75.00
Bennington, Bust, Parian, Girl, 7 In.	125.00
Bennington, Creamer, Figural, Cow, Brown	50.00
Bennington, Creamer, Hearts, Flint, Enamel, Signed	370.00
Bennington, Crock, E.Norton & Co., 5 Gallon	70.00
Bennington, Crock, Floral, Signed, C.1869, 7 In.	30.00
Bennington, Crock, Jug Ears, Signed, 1823-28	40.00
Bennington, Dish & Underplate, Covered, Parian, 6 In. Bowl	115.00
Bennington, Dish, Parian, Wheat, Underplate, Lid	100.00
Bennington, Dish, Pudding, Flared Sides, Mottled Brown & Yellow, 12 X 4 In.	68.00
Bennington, Figurine, Cat And Urn, Parian, 4 1/2 In.	195.00
Bennington, Figurine, Parian, Blond Hair, Black Shoes, 11 In., Pair	475.00
Bennington, Flask, Book	250.00
Bennington, Jar, Rockingham Glaze, Cover	225.00
Bennington, Jug, Blue Floral, E.& L.P.Norton, 1861-81	58.00
Bennington, Jug, Brown Slip Glazed, E.& L.P.Norton, Pinched Spout	85.00
Bennington, Jug, E. & L.P.Norton, Flower, 2 Gallon	50.00
Bennington, Jug, E. & L.P.Norton, Leaf Design, 1 Gallon	40.00
Bennington, Jug, E.Norton & Co., Brown, Pouring Lip, 2 Gallon	40.00
Bennington, Jug, Embossed Busts Of Man, 8 In.	68.00

Bennington, Jug, Squatty, Dark Brown, Flared Pouring Spout, Norton, 2 Gallon	45.00
Bennington, Jug, 2 Gallon, Julius Norton, Blue & Gray	65.00
Bennington, Pitcher, Batter, Norton	45.00
Bennington, Pitcher, Blue, Yellow, 6 1/2 X 3 In.	65.00
Bennington, Pitcher, Caramel, Raised Swan & Lily Pad Decoration, 7 1/4 In.	125.00
Bennington, Pitcher, Cream, Parian, Cupid & Psyche, 4 In.	29.00
Bennington, Pitcher, Embossed Leaves, Nuts, 9 In.	43.00
Bennington, Pitcher, Embossed, Bust Of Man, 8 In.	88.00
Bennington, Pitcher, Floral Decoration, Salt Glaze, 8 In.	70.00
Bennington, Pitcher, Hunt Scene, 7 1/2 In.	90.00
Bennington, Pitcher, Hunter & Dog, Brown Glaze, 6 In.	45.00
Bennington, Pitcher, Medallion With Ladies Head Both Sides	45.00
Bennington, Pitcher, Milk, Green, 8 3/4 In.	150.00
Bennington, Pitcher, Sponge, Brown	75.00
Bennington, Pitcher, Water, Hunting Scene, Branch Handle, Rockingham Glaze	155.00
Bennington, Plate, Pie, Mottled Brown & Cream Glaze, 8 In.	50.00
Bennington, Plate, Pie, 9 In.	45.00
Bennington, Spittoon, Flint Glaze, Signed, 1849	160.00

Bicycle, Black Painted Iron Velocipede, 37 In.

Bicycle, High Wheeled, Red Painted

Bennington, Spittoon, Mottled Green, Blue, Brown & Beige, 4 1/4 X 7 3/4 In.	55.00
Bennington, Spittoon, Scallop Rim, Shells Impressed	45.00
Bennington, Teapot, Streaked Brown & Green, Hinged Pewter Top	110.00
Bennington, Teapot, 6 Cup Size, Mandarin	50.00
Bennington, Toby Jug, Ben Franklin Seated, Bone Spackled Brown, 6 1/4 In.	40.00
Bennington, Vase, Parian, Grapes & Tendrils, 9 In.	55.00
Bennington, Vase, Parian, Sparrow & Crocus, 4 In.	26.00
Beswick, Figurine, Bald Eagle, 7 1/4 In.	38.00
Beswick, Figurine, Fell Pony, Champ Mare, Dene Dauntless, 6 3/4 In.	24.00
Beswick, Figurine, Highland Pony, Champion Stallion Jenty, 7 1/4 In.	24.00
Beswick, Figurine, Mare & Colt, 7 1/2 X 9 In.	60.00
Beswick, Figurine, Quarter Horse, 8 1/4 In.	22.50
Beswick, Figurine, Siamese Kitten	12.00
Beswick, Salt & Pepper, Laurel & Hardy, Holder	30.00
Bicycle, Black Painted Iron Velocipede, 37 In. .... *Illus*	150.00
Bicycle, High Wheeled, Red Painted .... *Illus*	1200.00
Bicycle, Tricycle, Rubber Tire, 22 In.Rear Wheels	500.00

*Bing and Grondahl is a famous Danish factory making fine porcelains from
1853 to the present. Their Christmas plates are especially well known.*

Bing & Grondahl, see also Collector, Plate

Bing & Grondahl, Beaker, Stork Nest	15.00
Bing & Grondahl, Figurine, Baby Sparrow With Beak Open, 2 1/2 In.	30.00
Bing & Grondahl, Figurine, Boy Dancing With Girl, 2 X 5 X 8 1/4 In.	90.00
Bing & Grondahl, Figurine, Boy In Undershirt Fastening Blue Pants, 6 In.	50.00
Bing & Grondahl, Figurine, Boy, No.2258, 5 In.	20.00
Bing & Grondahl, Figurine, Boy, One Shoe On, One Off, Early Mark, 5 1/4 In.	65.00
Bing & Grondahl, Figurine, Boy, Tan Overalls, 5 1/4 In.	65.00
Bing & Grondahl, Figurine, Brown & White Cocker Spaniel Standing, 8 In.	65.00
Bing & Grondahl, Figurine, Child In Tan Overalls, White Shirt, One Shoe On	75.00

Bing & Grondahl, Figurine, Cocker Spaniel, Brown & White, Standing, 8 X 6 In.	65.00
Bing & Grondahl, Figurine, Girl Feeding Geese, Axel Locher	140.00
Bing & Grondahl, Figurine, Girl Holding Boy, No.1668, 4 In.	20.00
Bing & Grondahl, Figurine, Little Boy Sitting & Drinking, 6 In.	50.00
Bing & Grondahl, Figurine, Man Kissing Girl, 7 In.	105.00
Bing & Grondahl, Figurine, Old Fisherman, No.2370, Seated On Rock	125.00
Bing & Grondahl, Figurine, Owl, Brown, White Mottled Face, No.1800, 4 1/2 In.	45.00
Bing & Grondahl, Figurine, Tall Boy Dancing With Shorter Girl, 8 1/4 In.	85.00
Bing & Grondahl, Figurine, Young Boy In Short Pants Holding Dog	66.00
Bing & Grondahl, Group, Youthful Boldness, Young Man Kissing Girl, 7 In.	105.00
Bing & Grondahl, Jug, Cherry Heering, Stopper	25.00
Bing & Grondahl, Mug, The Old Inn, 5 In.	35.00
Bing & Grondahl, Plate, Mary Had A Little Lamb	55.00
Bing & Grondahl, Vase, Flowers, Bulbous, 6 1/2 In.	27.00
Bing & Grondahl, Vase, Miniature, Scenic Design, Blues And Grays, Pair	52.00
Bing & Grondahl, Vase, Scenic, Light Blue & Green, Miniature, 3 1/2 In.Pair	50.00
Birdcage, Wicker	55.00

*Bisque is an unglazed baked porcelain. Finished bisque has a slightly sandy
texture with a dull finish. Some of it may be decorated with various colors.
Bisque gained favor during the late Victorian era when thousands of bisque
figurines were made.*

Bisque, see also Disneyana

Bisque, Basket, Young Girl Figurine, 12 3/4 In.	150.00
Bisque, Bootie, White, Blue Bow, Gold Laces, 3 1/2 In.	15.00
Bisque, Bust, Girl, White On Cobalt, Gold Base, 6 In.	12.00
Bisque, Bust, Mozart, Germany, No.1392/10, 4 In.	15.00
Bisque, Creamer, Mother Goose, German	35.00
Bisque, Fairy Lamp, Pastel Colors, Light Shines Through, 3 3/4 In.	225.00
Bisque, Figurine, Angel & Horn, 3 In.	10.00
Bisque, Figurine, Bathing Beauty Lying Down, Germany, 3 In.	55.00
Bisque, Figurine, Bathing Beauty Standing	35.00
Bisque, Figurine, Bathing Beauty, Reclining, German, 7 In.	95.00
Bisque, Figurine, Bearded Elf Shoemaker, High-Button Shoe To Waist, Numbered	60.00
Bisque, Figurine, Boy & Girl, Glazed, 12 1/2 In., Pair *Illus*	150.00

Bisque, Figurine, Boy & Girl, Glazed, 12 1/2 In., Pair

Bisque, Figurine, Boy & Girl, Pet Animals, French, 18 In., Pair	130.00
Bisque, Figurine, Boy & Girl, Sitting, Boy Is Fishing While Girl Watches	6.50
Bisque, Figurine, Boy Carrying Goose, Girl With Carrots, German, 12 In., Pair	110.00
Bisque, Figurine, Boy On Skis, 2 In.	8.75
Bisque, Figurine, Boy, Googly Eyes, German, 6 In.	58.00
Bisque, Figurine, Boy, Smoking A Pipe, Captioned Gee I Feel Good Now, 4 In.	18.00
Bisque, Figurine, Boy, Snowballer, Intaglio Eyes, Yellow, Pink, 3 In.	70.00
Bisque, Figurine, Bride & Groom Doll In Wedding Attire, Wooden Box, Caption	3.00
Bisque, Figurine, Bulldog, Standing, Stone	7.50
Bisque, Figurine, Cavalier, Peach, Cream, Green, French, 12 3/8 In.	89.00
Bisque, Figurine, Couple Arm In Arm, Victorian Dress, C.1800, German	150.00
Bisque, Figurine, Elephant On Tub, German, 3 1/2 X 1 3/4 X 4 In.	25.00
Bisque, Figurine, Elizabethan Lady In Waiting, Lime, Lavender, 8 In.	29.00
Bisque, Figurine, French, Girl With Basket, Blue Dress, Floral Trim, 12 3/4 In	165.00
Bisque, Figurine, German, Crawling Baby, 3 1/8 X 2 3/4 X 7 In.	68.00

Bisque, Figurine, German, Girl With Basket On Wheelbarrow, 5 1/2 X 3 X 7 In. 60.00
Bisque, Figurine, Girl By Tree Stump, Bare Feet, Apron, Pastel, 12 In. 100.00
Bisque, Figurine, Girl In Nightgown, Praying, 10 X 2 1/2 In. 110.00
Bisque, Figurine, Girl On Cornucopia, 3 1/2 In. 20.00
Bisque, Figurine, Girl On Dove, 3 1/2 In. 20.00
Bisque, Figurine, Girl On Skates, 2 In. 8.75
Bisque, Figurine, Girl With Doll, German, 6 1/2 In. 75.00
Bisque, Figurine, Girl, Blonde Hair, Yellow, White, & Gold Dress, 9 In. 45.00
Bisque, Figurine, Girl, Golden Haired, Pinks, Whites, 5 In. 31.00
Bisque, Figurine, Grandmother With Boy, Flowers, Basket Of Vegetables, 13 In. 225.00
Bisque, Figurine, Lady, Victorian, Elizabethan Dress, Pastels, 8 In. 35.00
Bisque, Figurine, Little Boy Playing A Drum, Miniature, Marked, 3 In. 6.00
Bisque, Figurine, Mermaid On Seahorse, Boy Mermaid On Dolphin, Pink, German 45.00
Bisque, Figurine, Monk, Pair, German, 5 3/8 In. 95.00
Bisque, Figurine, Nude Girl Dancing On Toes, 6 1/2 In. 68.00
Bisque, Figurine, Nude Seated Woman, Signed TC 65.00
Bisque, Figurine, Orphan Annie Standing Beside Basket, 3 In. 10.00
Bisque, Figurine, Pig In Tub Holding Baby With Bunny 27.50
Bisque, Figurine, Pug Dog 27.50
Bisque, Figurine, Rabbits Having Tea At Table, Green & Gold, 3 Piece Set 65.00
Bisque, Figurine, Santa On Sled, 2 In. 11.00
Bisque, Figurine, Seated Children, German, Pair, 3 1/4 In. 80.00
Bisque, Figurine, Seated Maiden, Pastels, Victorian, Germany, 6 1/2 In. 45.00
Bisque, Figurine, Swan With Cupid, White, Pastel Colors, 8 In. 50.00
Bisque, Figurine, Victorian Lady, 11 In. 65.00
Bisque, Figurine, White & Black, Blue Ribbon, Gold Bell, 3 X 3 1/2 In. 22.50
Bisque, Figurine, Young Napoleon, Signed, 15 In. 2000.00
Bisque, Group, Apache Dancers, Painted, 6 In. 30.00
Bisque, Group, Boy & Girl On Seesaw, Italian, Dipietro, 8 In. 50.00
Bisque, Group, Polka Dancers & French Poodle 80.00
Bisque, Jar, Tobacco, White, Monkey Smoking Pipe, 5 1/2 In. 49.50
Bisque, Match Holder With Striker, Figural, Boy Hunting Rabbit 30.00
Bisque, Match Holder, Collie Dog's Head, Pewter Rim 32.00
Bisque, Match Striker, German, Dog & Umbrella, 2 5/8 X 4 In. 25.00
Bisque, Muffineer, Cinderella & Prince, Hallmarked Sterling Top 75.00
Bisque, Planter, Figural, Rams, Gray, Embossed, Fur, Pink Horns, No.C6323, Pair 35.00
Bisque, Planter, Figurine, Girl With Seashell, Marked Germany, 5 X 5 In. 35.00
Bisque, Sailor, Mouth Moves, Nodder, Hat Is Ashtray, 4 1/2 In. 35.00
Bisque, Shade Pull, Baby In Basket 36.00
Bisque, Slipper, Pink, Blue Bow, Green Lining, 2 Cupids, 9 In. 165.00
Bisque, Toothpick, Little Boy In Farmer Hat Holding Basket, Gold Dot Trim 45.00
Bisque, Vase, Figural, Lorelei, White, Green, Gold Decoration, 7 X 6 In., Pair 27.00
Bisque, Vase, Girl With Goose, German 25.00

Black amethyst glass appears black until it is held to the light, then a dark purple can be seen. It was made in many factories from 1860 to the present time.

Black Amethyst, Bottle, Pinch, Silver Overlay Design, Sterling, 10 1/2 In. 100.00
Black Amethyst, Bowl, Thorn, 11 1/2 In. 35.00
Black Amethyst, Console Set, Low Pedestaled Bowl, Pair Of Candlesticks 45.00
Black Amethyst, Dish, Shaving, Covered 8.00
Black Amethyst, Hat, Blown, Turned Up Rim 48.00
Black Amethyst, Lamp, Fancy Base, Ornate Shade Holder, Amber Prisms, 21 In. 18.00
Black Amethyst, Lamp, Purple, Milk Glass Pedestal Base 45.00
Black Amethyst, Pitcher, Ivy Pattern, Footed, 4 1/2 In. 18.00
Black Amethyst, Plate, Cake, Ornate Brass Base, 9 In. X 5 3/4 In. 20.00
Black Amethyst, Plate, Handles, Silver Overlay, 7 In. 7.00
Black Amethyst, Plate, Scalloped Rim, Square, Fry, 8 In., Set Of 4 .... 40.00
Black Amethyst, Vase, Applied Clear Handle, 9 1/2 In. 50.00
Black Amethyst, Vase, Art Nouveau Dancers & Musicians, 7 In. 18.00
Black Amethyst, Vase, Girl And Boy On Side, 2 Handled, 8 1/2 In. 15.00
Black Amethyst, Vase, Gold, White Enameling, 6 In. 10.00
Black Amethyst, Vase, 6 Sided, 9 In. 15.00
Black Amethyst, Vase, 7 In. 25.00
Black Amethyst, Vase, 10 In. 30.00

Blanc De Chine, Burner, Incense, Squatty, 4 Footed, 4 1/2 X 3 In. 15.00
Bloor Derby, Dish, View Of North Wales, Gilt & Cobalt, 1820-40 .... 150.00

> *Blown glass was formed by forcing air through a rod into molten glass.*
> *Early glass and some forms of art glass were hand blown. Other types of*
> *glass were molded or pressed. The McKearin numbers refer to the book*
> *"American Glass" by George and Helen McKearin.*

Blown Glass, Atomizer, Perfume, Sapphire Blue, Etched Brass Fittings, 6 In. 20.00
Blown Glass, Basket, Bride's, Rose To Light Pink, White Cased, 12 In. 150.00
Blown Glass, Bottle, Scent, Sandwich, Fiery Opalescent, Flint, McK 241 .... 32.00
Blown Glass, Bottle, Snuff, Amber, Rectangular, Sheared Lip 25.00
Blown Glass, Bottle, Toilet, McK G 1-7, Blue 150.00
Blown Glass, Bottle, Toilet, Stopper, McK G 1-7, Flint 190.00
Blown Glass, Bottle, Toilet, 3 Mold, McK G 1-3, Stopper, 1/2 Pint, Flint 50.00
Blown Glass, Bottle, Toilet, 3 Mold, Purple, Blue, McK G I-7 .... 135.00
Blown Glass, Bottle, 3 Mold, 12 Flat Panels 40.00
Blown Glass, Bowl, Air Twist Trumpet, 20 In. 300.00
Blown Glass, Bowl, Clear, Amber Rim, 4 X 7 In. 22.00
Blown Glass, Bowl, McK G II-21, Flint, 5 In. 120.00
Blown Glass, Bowl, Ruby, Smoothed Pontil, Footed, 7 In. 25.00
Blown Glass, Bowl, 3 Mold, Clear, Pink Flowers 85.00
Blown Glass, Castor Set, 4 Bottles, Pewter Stand, Rufus Dunham 170.00
Blown Glass, Castor Set, 5 Bottles, McK G 1-13, Trask Pewter Stand 250.00
Blown Glass, Cologne, Ruby, Frosted, Stopper, 7 In., Pair 45.00
Blown Glass, Compote, Clear Top, Blue Base, 11 In. 75.00
Blown Glass, Compote, Folded Rim, Pittsburgh, 7 X 7 In. 100.00
Blown Glass, Compote, Pressed Base, Copper Wheel Engraved, Pittsburg 250.00
Blown Glass, Cordial, 9 Cut Panels, Flint, 3 In. 10.00
Blown Glass, Cruet, Clear, Steeple Stopper, 6 In. 45.00
Blown Glass, Cruet, Vinegar, Emerald Green, Crystal Stopper 57.00
Blown Glass, Cruet, Wheel Cut Flowers, Cut Stopper, 7 1/2 In. 20.00
Blown Glass, Cup, Punch, Blue, Applied Amber Handle, Flint 14.00
Blown Glass, Decanter, Cut Flint, Mushroom Stopper, Polished Pontil 30.00
Blown Glass, Decanter, Flint, Fluted Base, 18th Century, 1/2 Pint 40.00
Blown Glass, Decanter, Flint, Folded Lip, Rough Pontil, 6 In. 35.00
Blown Glass, Decanter, Folded Lip, Flint, 1/2 Pint, 6 In. 35.00
Blown Glass, Decanter, McK G I-29, Quart 100.00
Blown Glass, Decanter, McK G II-33, Triple Neck Rings, Blown Stopper, Quart 110.00
Blown Glass, Decanter, McK G II, Rigaree Neck Ring, Stopper, 18 Qt. 95.00
Blown Glass, Decanter, Riverboat, Matching Stopper, 8 Rib, Quart, Flint 120.00
Blown Glass, Decanter, Stopper, Geometric And Sunburst, Keene, 11 In. 265.00
Blown Glass, Decanter, 3 Mold, Baroque Pattern, Matching Stopper, 11 In. 195.00
Blown Glass, Decanter, 3 Mold, McK GIII-2 .... 100.00
Blown Glass, Decanter, 3 Mold, Stopper, Quart, McK G 222-15 .... 125.00
Blown Glass, Decanter, 4 Compartments, Brandy, Rum, Gin, Whiskey, Etch, 13 In. 65.00
Blown Glass, Dome, 11 1/2 X 5 1/2 In. 21.00
Blown Glass, Egg, Milk Glass, Brown Rabbit, Easter Joy, 5 1/2 In. 25.00
Blown Glass, Egg, Ostrich 15.00
Blown Glass, Epergne, Crystal, Miniature, 6 In. 15.00
Blown Glass, Flask, Historical, McK G VIII-20 .... 800.00
Blown Glass, Flask, McK G III-6, 1/4 Pint 350.00
Blown Glass, Flip, Enameled Scene, Windmill, People, Trees, 5 1/2 In. 50.00
Blown Glass, Flip, Molded, 4 1/2 X 3 3/4 In. 155.00
Blown Glass, Flip, 3 Mold, McK G I-6, 6 In. 90.00
Blown Glass, Glass, Flip, Enameled Windmill Scene, Flint, 5 In. 50.00
Blown Glass, Goblet, Amber, Swirled Ribbing, Air Bubbles, 8 In. 58.00
Blown Glass, Hat, Amber, Ellenville, 3 X 2 In. 145.00
Blown Glass, Hat, McK G III-3 .... 110.00
Blown Glass, Hat, McK G III-7, Light Deposit 40.00
Blown Glass, Hat, Victorian Novelty, Red Amber, Stoddard 75.00
Blown Glass, Jar, Apothecary, Covered, Flint, 6 In. 25.00
Blown Glass, Lamp, Oil, Marble & Brass Base 75.00
Blown Glass, Mug, Amber, Applied Handle, Ellenville, New York, 4 In. 120.00
Blown Glass, Mug, Geometric, Clear, Enameled Remember Me, Applied Handle 60.00
Blown Glass, Pan, Milk, Clear, Sapphire Blue Flint Rim 150.00

Blown Glass, Pitcher, Amber Hobnail, Square Mouth, Applied Handle, 9 In. 85.00
Blown Glass, Pitcher, Claret, Polished Pontil, Applied Handle, Irish, 7 In. 22.00
Blown Glass, Pitcher, Clear Flower & Leaf Design, 9 In. 135.00
Blown Glass, Pitcher, Lemonade, Ruffled Edge, Enameled Flowers, Green 65.00
Blown Glass, Pitcher, Thumbprint, Amber, Applied Handle, Fluted Rim, 8 In. 85.00
Blown Glass, Rose Bowl, Victorian, Green, Gold & Cream Decoration 20.00
Blown Glass, Salt, McK G III-20 .... 130.00
Blown Glass, Salt, Pinched, McK G I-6, Flint 65.00
Blown Glass, Stein, For Your Birthday In German, Porcelain Insert, 1/2 Liter 75.00
Blown Glass, Tankard, Hand-Painted Flowers, German, Zum Hockzeitz, 15 In. 75.00
Blown Glass, Tumbler, Aqua, 20 Rib Mold, Gallatin Kramer, Small 250.00
Blown Glass, Tumbler, Corset Shape, Clear With White Ribbons, 4 1/2 In. 30.00
Blown Glass, Tumbler, Swirl, Green 6.00
Blown Glass, Tumbler, Venetian Type, Latticinio & Prunts 30.00
Blown Glass, Vase, Amber, Flared Top, Superimposed Glass Swirls, 9 1/2 In. 75.00
Blown Glass, Vase, Engraved Floral, Cut Stem & Star Base, 3 3/4 X 8 3/4 In. 50.00
Blown Glass, Vase, Green, Gold & Floral Trim, Stemmed, 10 In. 14.00
Blown Glass, Vase, Jack-In-The-Pulpit, Diamond Point, Green To Clear, 6 In. 45.00
Blown Glass, Vase, Pink & White Loopings, Pittsburgh Glass, 11 In. 450.00
Blown Glass, Vase, Pittsburgh Pillar, Clear Flint, McK 53-6, 11 In., Pair 250.00
Blown Glass, Vase, Ruby, 3 1/2 In. 22.00
Blown Glass, Vase, Spangled Glass, Sandwich, Flint, 10 1/2 In. 60.00
Blown Glass, Wine, Engraved, Knop Stem, C.1800, 4 In. 30.00
   Blue Amberina, see Bluerina
   Blue Glass, see Cobalt Blue
   Blue Onion, see Onion

*Blue Willow pattern has been made in England since 1780. The pattern
has been copied by factories in many countries, including Germany, Japan, and
the United States. It is still being made. Willow was named for a
pattern that pictures a bridge, birds, willow trees, and a Chinese landscape.*

Blue Willow, Bowl, Vegetable, Covered, Finial, Large 50.00
Blue Willow, Bowl, Vegetable, Round Open, Allerton, 9 In. 12.00
Blue Willow, Creamer, Ridgway 7.00
Blue Willow, Cup & Saucer, Demitasse, Ridgway 15.00
Blue Willow, Cup & Saucer, Ridgway 12.00
Blue Willow, Dish, Oval, Maddock 8.00
Blue Willow, Pitcher, Milk, Large, Shenango 20.00
Blue Willow, Plate, Divided, Staffordshire 6.50
Blue Willow, Plate, Hommage, Moulin, France, 9 In. 8.00
Blue Willow, Plate, Royal Sometuke Nippon, 9 3/4 In. 5.00
Blue Willow, Plate, 6 1/2 In. 4.50
Blue Willow, Platter, Allerton, England, 9 X 11 In. 10.00
Blue Willow, Platter, Bacon, Burslem 2.50
Blue Willow, Platter, Davenport, Gold Trim, C.1810, 10 1/4 X 9 1/4 In. 48.00
Blue Willow, Platter, Wedgwood, 11 In. 15.00
Blue Willow, Punch Bowl, Pedestal Base, Doulton, 9 X 16 In. 400.00
Blue Willow, Set Of Dishes, 16 Piece, Child's 36.00
Blue Willow, Tea Set, Anchor Emblem, Signed Bridgwood, 33 Piece 300.00
Blue Willow, Tea Set, Child's, Japan, Setting For 6 .... 48.00
Blue Willow, Tea Set, 14 Piece 35.00
Blue Willow, Tumbler, Water, Frosted, Enameled 5.75
Blue Willow, Vase, Burleigh Ware Willow, Burslem, England, 9 In. 40.00
Blue Willow, Vase, Rington Tea Merchant, 6 X 4 In. 30.00
Blue Willow, Vegetable, Allerton, 9 In. 14.00
Blue Willow, Vegetable, Ridgway, Lid 45.00
Blue Willow, Washstand Set, Ridgway Tower 125.00

*Bluerina is a type of art glass which shades from light blue to ruby. It is
often called blue amberina.*

Bluerina, Bowl, Medallions, 5 In. 110.00
Bluerina, Pitcher, Milk, Wheeling, C.1880 .... 250.00
Bluerina, Tumbler, Water 125.00
Bluerina, Vase, Cranberry Flash To Blue, Rigaree Base, Gold, 5 1/2 In. 70.00
Boch Freres, Urn, Art Deco, Deer, Black, Handled 115.00

Boch, Vase, Enamel Glazed, Citron To Cobalt, Ormolu Rims, Belgium, 8 1/2 In. 75.00

Bohemian glass is an ornate, overlay, or flashed glass made during the Victorian era. It has been reproduced in Bohemia, which is now a part of Czechoslovakia. Glass made from 1875 to 1900 is preferred by collectors.

Bohemian Glass, Bottle, Barber, Deer & Castle, Red To Clear, 9 1/2 In.	95.00
Bohemian Glass, Bottle, Perfume, Ruby & Clear Panels, Steeple Stopper, 7 In.	85.00
Bohemian Glass, Bottle, Wine, Red & Frosted, Pair, 15 In.	250.00
Bohemian Glass, Bowl & Underplate, Clear Diagonal Ovals Bordered By Ruby	85.00
Bohemian Glass, Case, Castle & Deer, Ruby Glass, 15 1/2 In.	175.00
Bohemian Glass, Compote, Deer & Castle, Ruby & Clear, 8 X 7 In.	35.00
Bohemian Glass, Console Set, Ruby, Faceted Knobs, Cut Forest Scenes, 3 Piece	650.00
Bohemian Glass, Cordial Set, Bird & Castle, Ruby, 6 Footed Glasses	185.00
Bohemian Glass, Creamer, Floradora, Cranberry & Gold, Miniature	65.00
Bohemian Glass, Cruet, Deer & Castle, Ruby	75.00
Bohemian Glass, Decanter, Birds, Cattails, Cut, 14 In.	65.00
Bohemian Glass, Decanter, Cobalt Cut To Crystal, Stopper, 16 In.	100.00
Bohemian Glass, Decanter, Deer & Castle, 14 In.	115.00
Bohemian Glass, Decanter, Ruby Cut To Clear, 15 In.	119.00
Bohemian Glass, Decanter, Ruby To Clear, English Silverplated Cart, Pair	150.00
Bohemian Glass, Decanter, Ruby, Trailing Vine	65.00
Bohemian Glass, Decanter, Trees & Deer, Castle, With Stopper, Square, 8 In.	75.00
Bohemian Glass, Decanter, Vintage Design On Ruby Flash, 13 1/2 In.	70.00
Bohemian Glass, Decanter, Vintage Grape, Matching Stopper, 12 In.	95.00
Bohemian Glass, Dish, Candy, Grape Clusters & Ives, Footed, 9 In.	38.00
Bohemian Glass, Dish, Candy, Ruby Clear Grape Clusters, Leaves, Cover, 9 In.	35.00
Bohemian Glass, Goblet, Gold Decorated, Scallops, Paneled, 1847, Signed, 7 In.	100.00
Bohemian Glass, Goblet, Vintage, Long Stem	25.00
Bohemian Glass, Pitcher, Cobalt Blue, Thumbprint Handle, 11 X 5 1/2 In.	75.00
Bohemian Glass, Stein, Clear Circles Bordered By Ruby	85.00
Bohemian Glass, Stein, Ruby Cut To Clear, 15 Square Panels, Palaces, 1831	70.00
Bohemian Glass, Sugar Shaker, Rose Cutting	35.00
Bohemian Glass, Tankard, Crest Of Archbishop Of Salzburg, 9 1/2 In.	65.00
Bohemian Glass, Tankard, Enameled Crest, Green, Pewter Top, 9 1/2 In.	95.00
Bohemian Glass, Toothpick, Cranberry With Gold	80.00
Bohemian Glass, Toothpick, Etched Deer, Trees, Mushroom Base, 3 3/4 In.	25.00
Bohemian Glass, Toothpick, Red Cut To Clear, Deer, Bird, 2 3/4 In.	25.00
Bohemian Glass, Tumbler, Cut Glass, Honey Amber, C.1850	65.00
Bohemian Glass, Tumbler, Etched Bird, Floral, & Castle, 4 1/4 In.	35.00
Bohemian Glass, Tumbler, Floral, Scroll Top & Bottom, Red Flower, 4 In.	60.00
Bohemian Glass, Tumbler, Purple, Blue, & Yellow, Birds In Flight, 6 In.	40.00
Bohemian Glass, Tumbler, Ruby Cut To Clear	25.00
Bohemian Glass, Vase, Amber, Deer & Castle, Footed	37.50
Bohemian Glass, Vase, Amber, Deer & Pine, 12 In.	140.00
Bohemian Glass, Vase, Amber, Footed, Deer & Castle Pattern, 8 In.	65.00
Bohemian Glass, Vase, Amber, Grape & Leaf	175.00
Bohemian Glass, Vase, Bird, Castle, Amber	48.00
Bohemian Glass, Vase, Blue Cut To Clear, 5 X 4 In.	75.00
Bohemian Glass, Vase, Bottle Shaped, Flared Mouth, 10 1/2 In.	35.00
Bohemian Glass, Vase, Bulbous, Ruby Bird On Bough, Opening, 4 In.	38.00
Bohemian Glass, Vase, Butterflies & Flowers Medallion, 14 In.	85.00
Bohemian Glass, Vase, Castle & Bird, Ruby Overlay, 10 1/4 In.	115.00
Bohemian Glass, Vase, Castle & Deer, Ruby Glass Overlay, 9 1/2 In.	125.00
Bohemian Glass, Vase, Cranberry Overlay, Gold Trim, 6 1/2 In.	95.00
Bohemian Glass, Vase, Deer & Cattle, Clear & Ruby, 8 In.	35.00
Bohemian Glass, Vase, Engraved Castle, Swallow, Punties, Ruby To Clear, 8 In.	100.00
Bohemian Glass, Vase, Frosted Design, Stag, Scrolls, Trees, Birds, Castle	45.00
Bohemian Glass, Vase, Frosted Red Leaf & Bird, Gold Trim, 11 In.	75.00
Bohemian Glass, Vase, Gold Applique, Tapered, 10 In.	75.00
Bohemian Glass, Vase, Grape & Vine Leaf Decoration, Ruby, 10 1/4 In., Pair	125.00
Bohemian Glass, Vase, Red To Clear, Deeply Etched, 21 1/2 In.	120.00
Bohemian Glass, Vase, Ruby Cut To Clear, Flowers & Vines, Geometrics, 12 In.	100.00
Bohemian Glass, Vase, Ruby Cut To Clear, 9 3/4 In.	65.00
Bohemian Glass, Vase, Ruby, Acid Cut To Clear, Floral & Vines, Bulbous, 12 In.	125.00
Bohemian Glass, Vase, Ruby, Birds, Trees, & Castle, 8 1/2 In., Pair	135.00

Bohemian Glass, Vase, Ruby, 5 In. 35.00
Bohemian Glass, Vase, Spill, Red Floral On Opaque Glass, 8 1/4 In. 40.00
Bohemian Glass, Vase, Vintage, Ruby, Heavy Engraving, 10 1/4 In., Pair 150.00
Bohemian Glass, Water Set, Etched Flowers, Applied Handle, 7 Piece 95.00
Bohemian Glass, Wine Set, Cranberry Cut To Clear, 3 Piece 95.00
Bohemian Glass, Wine, Amber, Cut Stems, Intaglio Cut Stag, Doe & Landscape 26.00
Bone, Letter Opener, Vertical Etched Stripes, 10 In. 10.00
Bone, Spoon, Fiddleback Handle, C.1850, 5 1/2 In. 12.50
    Book, see Hopalong Cassidy, Book; Paper, Book Shirley Temple;
    Book, and others.
    Boston & Sandwich Co., see Sandwich, Fireglow, Lutz

*Bottle collecting has become a major American hobby. There are several
general categories of bottles such as historic flasks, bitters, household,
figural, and others. The McK numbers refer to the book "American
Glass" by George and Helen McKearin.*

Bottle, A.L.Murdock Liquid Food, Boston, Amber, 7 1/2 In. 7.50
Bottle, Amber, Cork Top, Pennzoil Motor Oil 3.00
Bottle, Apothecary, Cobalt Blue, Label Bordered In Gold, 9 In. 22.50
Bottle, Apothecary, Elixir, Clear, Round, Mushroom Stopper, Gold Label 25.00
Bottle, Apothecary, Finger Grip Stopper, Wide Mouth, Pint Size, 7 1/2 In. 24.00
Bottle, Apothecary, Fluid Extract Nux Vomica, Emerald Green, 7 1/2 In. 25.00
Bottle, Apothecary, Linim Saponis, Clear, Ground Stoppers, 10 1/2 In. 18.00
Bottle, Apothecary, Straight Sided, Ground Glass Stopper, Round, 20 In. 49.00
Bottle, Atomizer, Tasseled Bulb, Yellow Glass 16.00

*Avon started in 1886 as the California Perfume Company. It was not
until 1929 that the name Avon was used. In 1939 it became Avon
Products, Inc. Each year Avon sells many figural bottles filled with
cosmetic products. Ceramic, plastic, and glass bottles are made in limited
editions.*

Bottle, Avon, Apple Blossom Toilet Water, 1941 .... 22.00
Bottle, Avon, Chess Set, Numbered Board, 18 .... 125.00
Bottle, Avon, Cologne, Nearness, C.1955, 4 Oz. 12.50
Bottle, Avon, Pitcher, Transfer Of Medieval Troubador, 10 In. 65.00
Bottle, Avon, Pitcher, Utility, Tulips, Castle Mark Stamped In Blue 34.00
Bottle, Baby, Large Rabbit Emblem With 3 Small Rabbits 7.50
Bottle, Bar, Diamond Thumbprint, Flint, Pint 95.00
Bottle, Barber, Amber, Enameled Floral, Pewter Stopper, Bulging Neck 68.00
Bottle, Barber, Amethyst, Blown, Enameled Flowers, 8 In. 75.00
Bottle, Barber, Amethyst, Decorated, Pontil 58.00
Bottle, Barber, Amethyst, Enamel Decoration, Spout, Pontil 62.00
Bottle, Barber, Amethyst, Multicolor Enamel Florals, Bulbous, 6 3/4 In. 68.00
Bottle, Barber, Blown Cranberry Opalescent, Hobnail, 8 1/2 X 16 In. 95.00
Bottle, Barber, Blown, Sapphire Blue, Corset Shape, Enameled, 8 In. 45.00
Bottle, Barber, Blue Cased Over White, Satin Finish, Spout 65.00
Bottle, Barber, Blue Opal, Seaweed 85.00
Bottle, Barber, Bohemian, Pair 165.00
Bottle, Barber, Brown & White Spatter 75.00
Bottle, Barber, Clambroth, Bay Rum, Porcelain & Cork Stopper, 7 In. 22.50
Bottle, Barber, Clambroth, Stopper, Marked T.Noonan, Boston 25.00
Bottle, Barber, Clambroth, Witch Hazel, Stopper 38.00
Bottle, Barber, Cobalt Blue, Enameled Decoration 50.00
Bottle, Barber, Cobalt Blue, Melon Rib, Ceramic Stopper 25.00
Bottle, Barber, Cranberry Cased Glass, Smooth Outside, Inverted Thumbprint 85.00
Bottle, Barber, Cranberry, Opalescent, 8 1/4 In. 69.00
Bottle, Barber, Cranberry, White Opalescent Stripes, 7 In. 70.00
Bottle, Barber, Emerald Green, Molded, Signed M In Diamond, Screw Top, 7 In. 55.00
Bottle, Barber, Enameled Decoration On Amethyst Glass, Pewter Stopper 50.00
Bottle, Barber, Green Opalescent Glass, 12 1/2 In. 65.00
Bottle, Barber, Lime Green, Black Enamel Trim, Pewter Stopper 56.00
Bottle, Barber, Mary Gregory Type, Child Picking Flowers, White Enamel 95.00
Bottle, Barber, Melon Ribbed, Satin Vaseline, Opalescent Stripe, 7 1/4 In. 65.00
Bottle, Barber, Milk Glass, Hand-Painted Rose, Bay Rum, Koken, St.Louis, 9 In. 60.00
Bottle, Barber, Opal, Cranberry, Hobbs Brockunier 110.00

Bottle, Barber, Purple, Burgundy Band, Gold Trim, Enameled Floral, Pair	110.00
Bottle, Barber, Sapphire Blue, Blown Glass, Corset Shape, 8 In.	45.00
Bottle, Barber, Smoky White, 8-Sided, Porcelain Stopper, 8 In., Pair	43.00
Bottle, Barber, Spanish Lace Pattern, Opalescent Cranberry Glass	85.00
Bottle, Barber, Vitalis, Metal Top	1.50
Bottle, Battery Jar, Aqua Glass, Marked E.C.L. & Co., Boston, Massachusetts	15.00

Beam bottles are made to hold Kentucky Straight Bourbon made by the
James B.Beam Distilling Company. The Beam series of ceramic
bottles began in 1953.

Bottle, Beer, Blatz, Miniature, 4 In.	5.00
Bottle, Beer, Blob Top, Chattanooga Brewing Co., Wings, Amber, Quart	10.00
Bottle, Beer, Blob Top, Embossed, 1904 N Elson G. Van Dyke, Manchester	3.00
Bottle, Beer, Blue Dotted Letters, J.C., 11 In.	75.00
Bottle, Beer, Carling, Miniature, 4 In.	5.00
Bottle, Beer, Pre-Prohibition Washington, Brewery, Quart	10.00
Bottle, Beer, Ruppert, Miniature, 4 In.	5.00
Bottle, Beer, Schlitz, Royal Ruby, 7 Oz.	14.00
Bottle, Bitters, Atwood's Genuine, Round, Aqua, 1/2 Pint	10.00
Bottle, Bitters, Caldwell's Herb, Iron Pontil	145.00
Bottle, Bitters, Cooper's New Discovery, Aqua, Rectangular, 9 In.	7.50
Bottle, Bitters, Dr.Baxter's Mandrake, Aqua	7.00
Bottle, Bitters, Dr.J.Hostetter's Stomach, Amber, 18 Oz.	18.00
Bottle, Bitters, Greeley's, Bourbon Bitters, Green	350.00
Bottle, Bitters, Holtzerman's Patent Stomach, Cabin Shape, Amber	138.50
Bottle, Bitters, Langley's Root And Herb, Aqua	25.00
Bottle, Bitters, Mishler's, Herb, Yellow Amber	38.00
Bottle, Bitters, National Bitters, Ear Of Corn	210.00
Bottle, Bitters, Sazerac Aromatic, Milk Glass, Lady's Leg	375.00
Bottle, Bitters, Van Dunck's Genever, Figural, Amber, 8 3/4 In.	145.00
Bottle, Bitters, Vermo Stomach, Amber	12.00
Bottle, Bitters, West India, Amber	47.50
Bottle, Blob Top, Bubbly, Whittling, Green, Half Gallon	22.00
Bottle, Boot On Hassock, Clear	65.00
Bottle, Castor Set, Blown Stoppers, C.1870, 6 Matching Bottles	87.00
Bottle, Chestnut, Pontil, Green	78.00
Bottle, Coca-Cola, see Coca-Cola, Bottle	
Bottle, Cologne, Clear Glass, Cranberry, 8 3/8 X 3 In.	110.00
Bottle, Cologne, Opaline, Aqua, Stopper	60.00
Bottle, Cologne, Ruby Stained, Matching Stopper, 8 In.	28.00
Bottle, Crown, Tripure & Emblem In Circle, Tripure Water Co., 3 Sided, Green	6.00
Bottle, Cut Crystal, Carved, Hinged Sterling Lid, 3 1/4 In.	20.00
Bottle, Decanter, Blown, Bell Shape, Floral, Faceted Stopper, 12 In.	20.00
Bottle, Decanter, Cinzano Vermouth, Picture, Glass	15.00
Bottle, Decanter, Claret, Triple Cut Handle, Stopper, Strawberries, Diamond	175.00
Bottle, Decanter, Clown, Handstand, Bischoff	8.00
Bottle, Decanter, Cut To Cranberry, Overlay, 15 X 6 In.	185.00
Bottle, Decanter, Etched, Ruby Stain, Stopper	70.00
Bottle, Decanter, Overlay, Decorated, Cut To Green, 15 X 7 In., Pair	395.00
Bottle, Decanter, Wine Set, French, Original Carrying Box, 18th Century, 1780	750.00
Bottle, Decanter, Wine, Grape Clusters, Spigot, Crystal, Brass Holder, 6 Cups	595.00
Bottle, Decanter, Wine, Green Crystal, Brass Holder, Grape Clusters, 6 Glasses	595.00
Bottle, Eiffel Tower, American, 1889, 18 In.	39.50
Bottle, Figural, Apple, Clear Glass, Branch Handles	15.00
Bottle, Figural, Bear, Hamms Beer, Dated 1973	18.00
Bottle, Figural, Bell, Clear, 9 In.	15.00
Bottle, Figural, Cabin, Tobacco Brown, Whitney Glass Works, 7 3/4 In.	500.00
Bottle, Figural, Child's, Perfume, Pig, W.Germany, Emblem On Bottom	3.00
Bottle, Figural, Chinaman, Sprinkling	6.50
Bottle, Figural, Cigar, Tobacco Leaf Concentrics, Amber, 5 1/2 In.	37.50
Bottle, Figural, Clam, Marked Patent Applied For	24.00
Bottle, Figural, Double American Eagle, Shield Above Laurel Wreath	225.00
Bottle, Figural, Fish, Amber	10.00
Bottle, Figural, Flask, Pretzel, Cork Stopper, 6 X 4 1/4 In.	36.00
Bottle, Figural, French Sailor With Rifle, Camphor Glass, Signed Depose	30.00

Bottle, Figural, George Washington, Purple, 10 In.	8.00
Bottle, Figural, Kummel Bear, Black Amethyst	60.00
Bottle, Figural, Santa Claus, BIMAL, German, Creme De Menthe Label, 13 In.	75.00
Bottle, Figural, Santa Claus, Husted, 12 In.	35.00
Bottle, Figural, Shoe, Revenue Stamp On Sole, 4 1/2 In.	21.00
Bottle, Figural, Soldier, Hessian, 7 1/4 In.	50.00
Bottle, Figural, Statue Of Liberty	66.00
Bottle, Figural, Teddy Roosevelt With Dog & Rifle In Safari Dress, 14 In.	55.00
Bottle, Figural, Violin, Clear, 8 In.	6.00
Bottle, Flask, Colburn Company, Pumpkin Seed	12.00
Bottle, Flask, Double Eagle, Amber, Pontiled, Pint	115.00
Bottle, Flask, Eagle Cornucopia, Aqua, 1/2 Pint	225.00
Bottle, Flask, Emerald Green, Baltimore Monument, 6 In.	950.00
Bottle, Flask, McK GX-I9, Aqua, Historical, Quart	65.00
Bottle, Flask, Pocket, Pewter Cup & Cap, Olry, Phila.C.1860, Flint, 4 In.	18.00
Bottle, Flask, Success To The Railroad, Set Of 3, 19th Century, 1 Pint	675.00
Bottle, Flask, Zanesville, Amethyst, 18 Vertical Ribs, 5 1/2 In.	175.00
Bottle, Food, Armour Co., Chicago, Crockery, Handle, Long Neck	22.50
Bottle, Food, E.F.Griswold Co., Horseradish, Deep Aqua, 4 1/2 In.	3.25
Bottle, Food, Nash's Mustard, Clock	32.00
Bottle, Food, S.S.Pierce, Boston, Emerald Green, Oval	10.50
Bottle, Fruit Jar, Aqua Lafayette Canning Jar, 1 Quart, Glass Top, Inscribed	35.00
Bottle, Fruit Jar, Aqua, Applied Lip, 3 Part Mold, 11 In. *Illus*	35.00
Bottle, Fruit Jar, Atlas-EZ Seal, Amber, Quart	27.50
Bottle, Fruit Jar, Ball Perfect Mason, Amber, 1/2 Gallon	22.00
Bottle, Fruit Jar, Cohansey Glass Mfg.Co., Aqua, Barrel Form *Illus*	92.50
Bottle, Fruit Jar, Flaccus Bros., Green, Glass Cap, 6 In.	550.00
Bottle, Fruit Jar, Flaccus Bros., Threaded Lid Marked Simplex *Illus*	25.00
Bottle, Fruit Jar, J & B, Aqua, Zinc Lid	42.50
Bottle, Fruit Jar, Kerr Self-Sealing Mason, Amber, Quart	9.50
Bottle, Fruit Jar, Lightning, Amber, 1/2 Gallon	35.00
Bottle, Fruit Jar, Magic Fruit Jar Wm.McCully & Co., Aqua *Illus*	305.00
Bottle, Fruit Jar, Mason's Patent 11-30-1858, Citron, Zinc Lid *Illus*	72.50
Bottle, Fruit Jar, The Van Vliet Jar, 1881, Aqua, Lid, Fastener *Illus*	305.00
Bottle, Fruit Jar, Whitall, Tatum & Co., Blown, Lip, Lid, Fastener *Illus*	45.00
Bottle, Fruit Jar, Whitmore's Patent, Rochester, N.Y., Aqua, Lid *Illus*	225.00

Bottle, Fruit Jar, Aqua, Applied Lip, 3 Part Mold, 11 In.

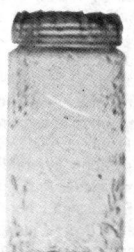
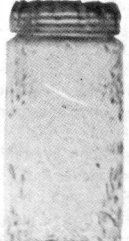

Bottle, Fruit Jar, Magic Fruit Jar Wm. McCully & Co., Aqua

Bottle, Fruit Jar, Cohansey Glass Mfg.Co., Aqua, Barrel Form

Bottle, Fruit Jar, Flaccus Bros., Threaded Lid Marked Simplex

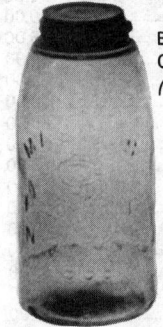

Bottle, Fruit Jar, Mason's Patent 11-30-1858,
Citron, Zinc Lid
(See Page 41)

Bottle, Fruit Jar, Whitall, Tatum & Co.,
Blown, Lip, Lid, Fastener
(See Page 41)

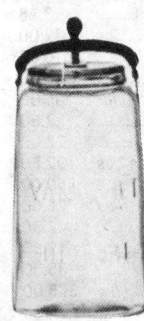

Bottle, Fruit Jar, The Van Vliet Jar,
1881, Aqua, Lid, Fastener
(See Page 41)

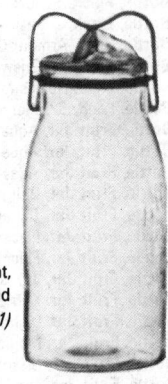

Bottle, Fruit Jar, Whitmore's Patent,
Rochester, N.Y., Aqua, Lid
(See Page 41)

Bottle, Gemel, Pink & White Loops On Clear Glass, Blown, 9 1/2 In.	95.00
Bottle, Germicide Co., Raised Script	3.00
Bottle, Gin, Free-Blown, Olive Amber, Squashed Lip, Pontil	35.00
Bottle, Humphrey's Homeopathic No.1, Woman Sitting Astride A Lion Label	3.50
Bottle, Hutchinson, Alabama Bottling Co., Clear, Eagle In Circle	4.00
Bottle, Hutchinson, Chattanooga Bottling Co., Light Green	17.50
Bottle, Hutchinson, Geneva Bottling Works, William Dunn & Co.Proprieters	6.00
Bottle, Hutchinson, Round Bottom, Green	3.50
Bottle, Hutchinson, Slug Plate Center, Renfro Manufacturing Co., Green	8.00
Bottle, Hutchinson, 8 Panels, Please Return When Empty To The Owner, Amber	10.00
Bottle, Hutchinson, 8 Panels, The Best What Gives T.M., Amber	10.00
Bottle, Ink, Bixby, Cone, Blue Green, Patented, 4 1/4 In.	16.75
Bottle, Ink, Blown, Pontiled, Umbrella, Aqua, Whittling Marks	25.00
Bottle, Ink, Brown, Darker Mottling Effect	18.50
Bottle, Ink, Carter's Ink, Male Figure, Colored Porcelain, C.1918, 3 5/8 In.	48.00
Bottle, Ink, Carter's, Cathedral, Cobalt, Quart	45.00
Bottle, Ink, Mr.And Mrs.Carter, Pair	85.00
Bottle, Ink, Sanford's, One Quart, Amber, 9 5/8 X 3 3/4 In.	3.75
Bottle, Ink, Umbrella Shape, 8-Sided Coning Upward, Blob Top, Pontil	25.00
Bottle, Ink, Umbrella, Clear, Open Pontil	18.00
Bottle, Kerosene, Blown-In-Mold, Aqua, Encased With Tin, 1/2 Gallon	22.50
Bottle, Leak's Fancy Inks, Schoolhouse Shape	25.00
Bottle, Medicine, August Flower, Green's Great Dyspeptic Panacea, 7 1/2 In.	5.00
Bottle, Medicine, Bartine's Lotion, Emerald Green, Whittled, 2 X 6 In.	400.00
Bottle, Medicine, Bonpland's Fever And Ague Remedy, New York, 5 In.	32.00
Bottle, Medicine, Bryo's, Embossed, Emerald Green, 3 1/2 In.	5.00
Bottle, Medicine, Campbell & Lyon Umatilla Indian Hogah, Detroit, Blue, 9 In.	28.00
Bottle, Medicine, Chamberlain's Colic, Cholera & Diarrhea Remedy, 5 1/4 In.	8.00
Bottle, Medicine, Chlorodyne Cough Syrup, H.D. Godfrey, 5 1/2 In.	6.00
Bottle, Medicine, Citrate Of Magnesia, Clear	25.00

Bottle, Medicine, Dr.Clocum's Coltsfoote Compound Expectorant, 6 1/4 In. 6.50
Bottle, Medicine, Dr.D.Jayne's, Carminative, Philadelphia, Aqua, Round, 5 In. 8.50
Bottle, Medicine, Dr.Harter's Wild Cherry Bitters, St.Louis 22.50
Bottle, Medicine, Dr.Kauffman's Rheumatism Cure, Clear 17.50
Bottle, Medicine, Dr.Kilmer's Swamp Root, Aqua 15.00
Bottle, Medicine, Dr.N.Wilson, Amber, Half Barrel 55.00
Bottle, Medicine, Dr.Shiloh's System Vitalizer, New York, 7 In. 12.50
Bottle, Medicine, Dr.Townsend's Sarsaparilla, Black, Amber 250.00
Bottle, Medicine, Dr.Townsend's Sarsaparilla, Emerald Green 55.00
Bottle, Medicine, Dr.Townsend's Sarsaparilla, Light Blue, Green 75.00
Bottle, Medicine, Dr.Van Wert's Balsam, Whooping Cough, Aqua Blue, 8 In. 12.00
Bottle, Medicine, Dr.Wistar's Wild Cherry Balsam, 8-Sided, Aqua 60.00
Bottle, Medicine, Edwards & Son Embrocation For The Whooping Cough 12.00
Bottle, Medicine, Fluid Extract Of Triticum, Sharp & Dohme, Amber, 4 Ozs. 5.00
Bottle, Medicine, Gouleys Fountain Of Health, Aqua, Tumbled 100.00
Bottle, Medicine, Grover Imperial Mange Remedy, Amber 16.00
Bottle, Medicine, Hill's Dys-Pep-Gu Cure, Amber 19.00
Bottle, Medicine, John Bull Extract Of Sarsaparilla, Louisville, Ky., Aqua 100.00
Bottle, Medicine, Kickapoo Indian Sagwa, Healy & Bigelow Indian Label, Aqua 50.00
Bottle, Medicine, Kilmer's Oceanweed Heart Remedy, Aqua 25.00
Bottle, Medicine, Kimbell's Tonic Herb Bitters, 8 In. 17.50
Bottle, Medicine, Loxol Pain Expeller, F.A.Richter & Co., 5 In. 6.00
Bottle, Medicine, Lydia E.Pinkham's Pills, Full Contents 6.50
Bottle, Medicine, Lyman's Dandelion Bitters, Ice Blue, 10 1/2 In. 19.00
Bottle, Medicine, Magic Mosquito Bite Cure, Sallade & Co., Aqua 25.00
Bottle, Medicine, Mexican Mustang Liniment, Aqua, 4 X 1 3/4 In. 17.00
Bottle, Medicine, Munyon's Inhaler Cure, Emerald Green 16.00
Bottle, Medicine, Paine's Celery Compound, Square, Amber, 10 In. 13.50
Bottle, Medicine, Pratt's Distemper And Pink Eye Cure, Amber, 7 In. 30.00
Bottle, Medicine, Robin's Elixir, Embossed, Lion On Label 12.00
Bottle, Medicine, Roche's Embrocation For The Hooping Cough, 4 7/8 In. 8.50
Bottle, Medicine, Rohrer's Cherry Pectoral, Amber, Pontil 145.00
Bottle, Medicine, Sagwa Indian, Full Dress Indian On Front, Embossed 11.50
Bottle, Medicine, Smelling Salts, Green Larkin Co., Buffalo 10.00
Bottle, Medicine, Smith & Shakman's Universal Cough Syrup, Aqua, 5 3/4 In. 4.50
Bottle, Medicine, The East India Nerve Specific, Washington, D.C., 5 1/2 In. 7.50
Bottle, Medicine, Warner's Safe Cure, London, Light Amber, Pint 70.00
Bottle, Medicine, Warner's Safe Nervine, London, Yellow, Amber, 1/2 Pint 140.00
Bottle, Medicine, White's Hair Restorative, Aqua, Pontil, 6 1/2 In. 85.00
Bottle, Medicine, Wyeth & Bro., Phila.Liquid Malt, Amber, 9 1/4 In. 18.00
Bottle, Milk, Baby Face, Pint 12.50
Bottle, Milk, Farmer's Dairy, Mishawaka, Indiana, MFD Co., Quart 3.00
Bottle, Milk, Idlenot, Amber 3.00
Bottle, Milk, Tin Handles, Smalleys, Quart 37.00
Bottle, Mineral Water, Buffalo Water, Lithia Springs, Woman On Stool 25.00
Bottle, Mineral Water, Saratoga, Green, Pint 27.00
Bottle, Nu-Grape, Pinched Middle, Light Green, July 20, 1920 .... 4.00
Bottle, Orange Crush, Clear, July 20, 1920 .... 3.50
Bottle, Orange Crush, Emerald Green, July 20, 1920 .... 7.50
Bottle, Pepsi-Cola, Block Letters, Pepsi-Cola Knoxville, Tennessee, Green 4.50
Bottle, Pepsi-Cola, In Script, Green, 12 Oz. 10.00
Bottle, Pepsi-Cola, Script Slug, Plate Base, 1 Charlotte, North Carolina, Tall 8.00
Bottle, Pepsi-Cola, Slug Plate, Middle Like Hobble Skirt, 6 1/2 Oz. 8.50
Bottle, Pepsi-Slug Around Albany Pepsi-Cola, Albany, Georgia, Clear 8.00
Bottle, Perfume, Apothecary, Label, Stopper, 10 In. 24.00
Bottle, Perfume, Apple Green, Nude On Glass Stopper, 4 1/2 In. 10.00
Bottle, Perfume, Blown, Vaseline, Matched Stopper With Dabber, 6 In. 35.00
Bottle, Perfume, Crystal, Eve And Snake Engraving 185.00
Bottle, Perfume, Crystal, Pyramid Shape, Frosted Leaves & Floral, 7 1/2 In. 25.00
Bottle, Perfume, Diamond, Emerald & Ruby, Victorian 300.00
Bottle, Perfume, Dresser Type, Pair, 5 In. 26.00
Bottle, Perfume, Ed Pinaud, Paris, Basket Of Flowers Embossed, 10 3/4 In. 5.75
Bottle, Perfume, Embossed In Circle, Adolph Spiehler, Stopper, 7 1/2 In. 5.00
Bottle, Perfume, Frosted Amethyst, Cabbage Rose Base, Butterfly Stopper 65.00
Bottle, Perfume, Golliwogs, Afro Hair & Face, France, 4 In. 25.00

Bottle, Perfume, Houbigant, Gold Inlaid, Baccarat Signed Stopper, 8 In.	25.00
Bottle, Perfume, Lime Green, Gold Leaves & Branches, Silver Floral, 4 In.	58.00
Bottle, Perfume, Miniature Schiaparelli Torso, Dome Case	18.00
Bottle, Perfume, Mt.Vernon, Crystal, Stopper	18.00
Bottle, Perfume, Pink Cased, Melon Ribbed, Ruffled Collar, Stopper	30.00
Bottle, Perfume, Pressed Glass, Sandwich, Clear With Gold, Stopper, 7 In.	85.00
Bottle, Perfume, Purple Stained Glass, Enameled Floral, Gold Leaves, 5 In.	36.00
Bottle, Perfume, Roger & Gallet, Paris, Acid Etched, Shaker Top, 6 1/2 In.	6.25
Bottle, Perfume, Ruby Stained, Decorated, Matching Stopper, 8 In.	22.00
Bottle, Perfume, Silver On Glass, Matched Stopper, 5 In.	25.00
Bottle, Perfume, Silver Overlay On Clear, Louise Monogram, Bulbous, 3 1/4 In.	29.00
Bottle, Perfume, Silver Overlay, Green Glass, Stopper, Marked Sterling, 3 In.	46.50
Bottle, Perfume, Steuben, Floral Engraving, 4 1/2 In.	75.00
Bottle, Perfume, Yardley, Wrapped In Wicker, 5 1/2 In.	5.00
Bottle, Perfume, 6 Rounded Panels, Signed, Czechoslovakia, 7 1/2 In.	25.00
Bottle, Poison, Amber, Oval, Ribbed	2.50
Bottle, Rockingham, Boot	150.00
Bottle, Roman, Pale Olive Green, 4 1/8 In.	145.00
Bottle, Roman, Pear-Shaped Lower End, Iridescent, 4 3/4 In.	145.00
Bottle, Roman, Spherical Lower Part, 4 In.	135.00
Bottle, Rose Jar, Blue Florals On Ivory, Foliage, Gold, Covered, Kosterle, T.K.	25.00
Bottle, Sarsaparilla, Greens, Aqua	8.00
Bottle, Scent, Sandwich, South Jersey, Pattern Molded, 19th Century, Set Of 6	325.00
Bottle, Schlitz, Quart, Red, Marked Duraglass Royal Ruby, Textured	14.50
Bottle, Sherry, Zorro, Black Sandman, A Mark, Royal Doulton	45.00
Bottle, Snuff, Amber, Painted Horned Animal, 19th Century, Chinese, 2 1/2 In.	145.00
Bottle, Snuff, Blue Chinese Enamel On Silver, Teakwood Stand, 3 3/4 In.	60.00
Bottle, Snuff, Blue, White, Pine Tree, Flat Oval, Dipper, Chinese, 18th Century	30.00
Bottle, Snuff, Hollowed Inside, Polished Exterior, Agate	250.00
Bottle, Snuff, Man & Child, Ovoid, 3 In.	45.00
Bottle, Snuff, Monkey Holding A Tigereye Turtle, Rock Crystal, 3 1/2 In.	210.00
Bottle, Snuff, Multicolor Chinese Enamel On Silver, Floral, 2 1/2 In.	60.00
Bottle, Snuff, Olive Green, 3 3/4 In.	70.00
Bottle, Snuff, Painted Oriental Scene, Red Wood Cap & Spoon, Large, 11 In.	225.00
Bottle, Snuff, Painting Under Glass, Signed	18.00
Bottle, Snuff, Porcelain, Oriental Scenes, Mid-1800s, Bone Scoop, 2 1/2 In.	45.00
Bottle, Snuff, Rock Crystal, Shape Of Sitting Monkey, Tigereye Turtle, 6 In.	190.00
Bottle, Snuff, Waffle, Tin Screw Top, Blue Opaque, 7 In.	45.00
Bottle, Soda, Casey, P, Drogheda, Torpedo Shape, Emerald Green, 8 1/2 In.	30.00
Bottle, Soda, Dennis, C.Manuf.Soda, Geneva N.Y., Blob Top, Aqua	25.00
Bottle, Soda, Dr.Pepper For Life, Clock	3.50
Bottle, Soda, E.W.& Co., Embossed Eagle With Banner	80.00
Bottle, Soda, Eagle, Vestry, Varwick & Canal Sts., Premium Soda, Pontil, Green	75.00
Bottle, Soda, Gemenden Eagle Soda, Pontil, Green	71.00
Bottle, Soda, Gillette, T.W.Soda, New Haven, Octagonal, Blob Top, Iron Pontil	171.00
Bottle, Soda, Grone & Co.Soda, St.Louis, Mo., Pontil, Aqua	8.00
Bottle, Soda, Harvey & Co.Soda, Norwich, Conn.Collared Mouth, Aqua, 1/2 Pint	30.00
Bottle, Soda, Harvey, J.& 4.W. Soda, Norwich Conn.Medium Green, 1/2 Pint	130.00
Bottle, Soda, Henry Kuck, Savannah, Apple Green	43.00
Bottle, Soda, Kensington Glass Works, Green	40.00
Bottle, Soda, Lancaster Glass Works, N.Y., Pontil, Green	38.00
Bottle, Soda, Luke Beard, Howard St.Boston, This Bottle Is Never Sold, Pint	50.00
Bottle, Soda, Moxie, With Man, 6 1/2 In.	4.50
Bottle, Soda, Premium Mineral Waters, Octagonal, Green, 1/2 Pint	90.00
Bottle, Soda, Reynolds & Co.Bottles, Philadelphia, Iron Pontil, Green	60.00
Bottle, Soda, Royal Crown Cola, 1936	6.50
Bottle, Soda, Ryan Soda, Augusta & Savannah, Squat	90.00
Bottle, Soda, Schille Soda, Columbus, Ohio, Blob Top, Aqua	12.00
Bottle, Talcum, China, Cork In Bottom, 4 5/8 In.	30.00
Bottle, Tear, Blown, Dimpled, Given To Sailor's Sweetheart Before Sail	7.50
Bottle, The Original 3 Centa Drink, Green Emblem	4.00
Bottle, Toilet, Hobnail, Green, 6 In., Pair	50.00
Bottle, Whiskey, Bennett & Carrol, Barrel, Yellow Amber, Iron Pontil	175.00
Bottle, Whiskey, Display, Rose Valley, 17 In.	360.00
Bottle, Whiskey, E.G. Booz's Blue Log Cabin, C.1930	38.00

Bottle, Whiskey, Embossed Head Of Horse, P.J.McDonald & Co. 5.00
Bottle, Whiskey, Meridith's Diamond Club, Quart 43.00
Bottle, Whiskey, Miniature, Henry Boaquets, Louisville, Kentucky 35.00
Bottle, Whiskey, Sam Thompson Old Pure Rye, Prohibition, 1917, Unbroken Seal 22.00
Bottle, Whiskey, Spider & Fly, Web, Amber, Set Of 5 .... 48.00
Bottle, Wine, Frosted, Bohemian Red, 15 Inch, Pair 250.00
Bottle, Wine, Royal Silver Wedding, Elizabeth II, Certificate 75.00
Bottle, Wine, Swirl Glass, Cranberry, Amber, 8 7/8 X 8 3/8 In. 135.00
Bottle, Wine, Vaseline Glass, Diamond Quilted, 14 7/8 In. 118.00
Bottle, Zanesville, Aqua, 24 Rib, Broken Swirl 280.00

Box, Candle, Dovetailed, Carved Slide Lid,
Walnut, Molded Edge

*Boxes of all kinds are collected. They were made of thin strips of inlaid
wood, metal, tortoiseshell, embroidery, or other material.*
Box, see also Ivory, Box; Porcelain, Box; Shaker, Box; Store
Box; Tin, Box; and various porcelain categories.
Box, Ballot, Oak, Dovetailed Edges, Black & White Balls, Handled, 10 1/2 In. 56.00
  Box, Battersea, see Battersea, Box
Box, Burnt Wood, Painting On Lid, Oval, 7 X 5 X 4 In. 28.00
Box, Button, Round, Walnut, 4 X 5 In. 18.00
Box, Candle, Dovetailed, Carved Slide Lid, Walnut, Molded Edge .... *Illus* 130.00
Box, Candle, Red And Black Graining 25.00
Box, Chinese, Famille Rose Colors, 3 X 5 In. 85.00
Box, Decoupage, Woodcut Prints, C.1825 .... 110.00
Box, Document, Black Tin, Round Top, Brass Handle, Lock, Hallmark, 10 X 15 In. 55.00
Box, Document, Pine, C.1830, 16 1/4 X 9 1/2 X 4 1/2 In. 65.00
Box, Document, Revolutionary Period, C.1802, 9 X 4 1/2 X 3 1/2 In. 75.00
Box, Document, Tole 28.00
Box, Fluted Silver Plate Lid, Finial, Signed Rogers Bro., 5 X 4 In. 16.00
Box, French Cameo, Cover, Etched Background, Yellow Floral, White 195.00
Box, Heart Shape, Scroll & Shield, Velvet Lining, Hinged Lid 15.00
Box, Jewelry, Dark Green, Satin Finish, Enameling, Hinged 160.00
Box, Jewelry, Ivory Inlaid, Mercury, 8 1/2 X 6 X 4 In. 50.00
Box, Knife, Chippendale, Inlay, Mahogany, C.1760 .... 485.00
Box, Knife, Georgian Mahogany 70.00
Box, Leather, Oriental, Women On Cover, Fruit On Side, C.1900, 10 In. 65.00
Box, Moss, Green 65.00
Box, Music, 2 Figures That Play Bells 695.00
Box, Pine, Brass Handle, Iron Lock, Key, C.1830, 11 X 8 X 7 In. 85.00
Box, Pipe, 18th Century 525.00
Box, Portrait, China, Lady, Court Dress, Burgundy, Gold Leaves, Signed, Lid 58.00
Box, Powder, Flowers, Overlay, Gold, White Cut To Cranberry, 2 X 4 In. 135.00
Box, Powder, Gold Decoration, Lacy Dotting, Brass Fittings, Hinged, Round 55.00
Box, Red, Tan, Cream, & Black, Name Sabina In Design On Lid, Wooden, 11 In. 65.00
Box, Regina, Mahogany, 21 X 18 1/2 X 15 1/2 In. 1250.00
Box, Silver Snowflakes Decoration, Cobalt, Glass, Lid, C.1950, Sweden 12.00
Box, Snuff, Damascene, French Tortoise Shell, Silver, Mother-Of-Pearl 85.00
Box, Snuff, G.W.Gail & Ax Tobacco Company, 2 1/2 X 1 1/4 X 1/2 In. 30.00
Box, Snuff, Hand-Carved, Mahogany, Boat Shape, Lid Opens, 3 X 1 1/2 In. 20.00
Box, Snuff, Lacquer, English 25.00
Box, Snuff, Mahogany, Hand Carved, Trick Lid, 1 1/2 X 3 X 1 In. 20.00
Box, Snuff, Tortoiseshell, Hinged Lid, 1 X 1 1/2 X 3/4 In. 22.00
Box, Spice, Knobs, Molding 165.00

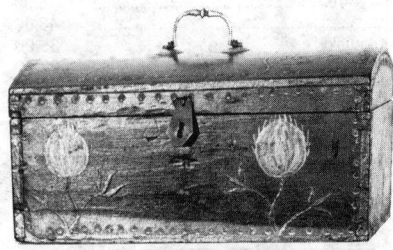

Box, Trinket, Dovetailed Dome Lid,
Brass Bail, Rosette Handle

Box, Spice, 8 Drawer	125.00
Box, Tapestry Cover, Blue Coloring, 3 X 5 In.	45.00
Box, Trinket, Dogwood Florals, Leafage, Gold Vines, Pink Frosted, Brass, Lid	18.50
Box, Trinket, Dovetailed Dome Lid, Brass Bail, Rosette Handle *Illus*	425.00
Box, Trinket, Florals, Blue, Rust, Round, White Porcelain, 2 In.	4.00
Box, Wall, Dovetailed Corners, Red Paint, Divider Inside, C.1830-40, 13 In.	125.00
Box, Wooden, Roll Top Of Tiny Slats, Intricate Decorations, 3 X 8 In.	18.00
Box, Writing, English Regency, Mother-Of-Pearl Inlay, Rosewood, 1820	225.00
Box, Writing, 3 Inkwell Inserts, Hinged Doors, Brass Knobs, Handle, Wood	350.00
Boy Scout, Binoculars, Marked Paris, Brass	18.00
Boy Scout, Book, Book Of Scouting, 1959	3.50
Boy Scout, Catalogue, Equipment, 1918	6.00
Boy Scout, Diary, Pocket, Of Useful Information, C.1917	12.00
Boy Scout, Drum, Tin, Lithograph With Eagle, Flat, 1908	25.00
Boy Scout, Handbook, 1944	4.00
Boy Scout, Hat, Felt, Campaign	22.00
Boy Scout, Hatchet	18.00
Boy Scout, Knife	8.00
Boy Scout, Knife, Three Blades, Cub Scout, 1940, 3 1/2 In.	12.00
Boy Scout, Master's Hat, Holder	18.50
Boy Scout, Paperweight, Brass, Emblem, Swingout Magnifying Glass, Late 1920s	22.50
Boy Scout, Pin, Fifth Roundup	5.00
Boy Scout, Scrapbook, 1928	18.00
Boy Scout, Tin, Campfire	24.00
Bradley & Hubbard, Bookend, Stalking Lion, Pair	25.00
Bradley & Hubbard, Candlestick, Brass, Saucer Type, Finger Handle, 5 1/2 In.	35.00
Bradley & Hubbard, Clock, Iron Front, 8 Day, Strike	120.00
Bradley & Hubbard, Clock, Nude Girl, Art Nouveau, Copper Finish, 8 In.	115.00
Bradley & Hubbard, Desk Set, Brass, 3 Piece	65.00
Bradley & Hubbard, Desk Set, Bronze, Green Enameled Border, Art Deco, 5 Piece	85.00
Bradley & Hubbard, Desk Set, 4 Piece, Brass	125.00
Bradley & Hubbard, Frame, Picture, Brass	75.00
Bradley & Hubbard, Inkstand, Bronzed Metal, Pressed Flint Swirl Pattern, Lid	45.00
Bradley & Hubbard, Inkwell, Pen Tray Attached, Glass Insert, Bronze, Green	35.00
Bradley & Hubbard, Lamp, Banquet, Hand-Painted Globe, Miniature, 1896	225.00
Bradley & Hubbard, Lamp, Banquet, 19 In.	80.00
Bradley & Hubbard, Lamp, Brass Base, Green Domed Shade, Signed	225.00
Bradley & Hubbard, Lamp, Brass Base, Signed, 15 X 19 In.	175.00
Bradley & Hubbard, Lamp, Brass, 8 Glass Panels	125.00
Bradley & Hubbard, Lamp, Caramel Slag, Filigree Floral, Glass Shade, Signed	225.00
Bradley & Hubbard, Lamp, Double Student Turtleback, Brass, Bronze, Beading	1500.00
Bradley & Hubbard, Lamp, Floor, Signed, Adjustable Bronze Shade	575.00
Bradley & Hubbard, Lamp, Gone With The Wind, Dogs Hunting, Ducks, 25 In.	395.00
Bradley & Hubbard, Lamp, Gone With The Wind, Floral On Rust, 25 In.	225.00
Bradley & Hubbard, Lamp, Green Geometric Shade, Bronze Base, 18 In.	1250.00
Bradley & Hubbard, Lamp, Hanging, Up-Down Mechanism, Blue Morning Glories	225.00
Bradley & Hubbard, Lamp, Leaded Green & Yellow Glass, Lily Pad Base, 18 In.	425.00
Bradley & Hubbard, Lamp, Leaded, Base Signed	475.00
Bradley & Hubbard, Lamp, Library, Bristol Shade, Pull Down Canopy, 1889	395.00
Bradley & Hubbard, Lamp, Maroon Shade, Signed, 10 X 17 In.	165.00
Bradley & Hubbard, Lamp, Parlor, Aladdin Type, Signed	600.00
Bradley & Hubbard, Lamp, Reverse Painting, Shade, Signed Base & Shade, 21 In.	450.00

Bradley & Hubbard, Lamp, Table, Brass Base, 10 In.Green-Domed Shade	225.00
Bradley & Hubbard, Lamp, Table, Brass, Frosted Shade, Signed, 21 In.	325.00
Bradley & Hubbard, Lamp, Table, Caramel Slag, 23 X 18 In.	250.00
Bradley & Hubbard, Lamp, Table, Green Slag Shade, Red Slag Border, Square	275.00
Bradley & Hubbard, Letter Holder, Victorian	48.00
Bradley & Hubbard, Smoking Stand, Figural Dolphin, Trefoil Base	190.00
Bradley & Hubbard, Table, Bronze Figural Dolphins, 28 In.	275.00
Bradley & Hubbard, Tray, Nude Maiden Blowing Bubbles, Iron, Signed, 7 3/4 In.	22.50

Brass has been used for decorative pieces and useful tablewares since ancient times. It is an alloy of copper, zinc, and other metals.

Brass, see also Bell, Tool, Trivet, etc.

Brass, Anvil, Miniature, Embossed, Philadelphia 1876, 3 1/2 In.	12.00
Brass, Ashtray, Attached Shoes, Enameled Decoration, China, 4 1/2 In.	15.00
Brass, Ashtray, Figural, Camel	15.00
Brass, Ashtray, Lookout Mountain, Colorado, Embossed Indian's Head	90.00
Brass, Badge, Chauffeur's, 1915	10.00
Brass, Badge, Chauffeur's, 1947	8.50
Brass, Badge, Willys Marrow	10.00
Brass, Basket, Handled, 8 1/2 In.	25.00
Brass, Bed, Baby's	800.00
Brass, Bed, Doll Size	110.00
Brass, Bedwarmer, Bottom Copper	125.00
Brass, Bookend, Figural, Resting Camels, Pair	28.50
Brass, Bookend, Oriental Man & Woman, High Relief, 4 1/2 In., Pair	35.00
Brass, Bookend, Owls, Pair	28.00
Brass, Bottle, Hot Water, Gillette, 1914	45.00
Brass, Bowl, Centerpiece, Footed, Art Nouveau, 10 X 14 In.	115.00
Brass, Bowl, Fruit, Oval, 8 In.	20.00
Brass, Bowl, Marked China, Wood Base, 11 X 6 In.	50.00
Brass, Bowl, Oriental, Dragons, 10 In.	55.00
Brass, Box, Chinese, Hinged, 3 3/4 X 7 1/4 X 2 In.	20.00
Brass, Box, Chinese, Wood Lined, Oriental Designs, 7 1/4 X 5 X 3 In.	35.00
Brass, Box, Cricket, Footed, Square, Hinged Strap, Handle, Pillar Posts, 4 In.	58.00
Brass, Box, Jewel, French, Hinged, Applied Filigree, Lady On Ivory	125.00
Brass, Box, Letter, Art Nouveau	75.00
Brass, Box, Musket, Persian, Uncut Emerald In Medallion, 4 X 4 In.	95.00
Brass, Box, Patch, Blue Stones On 4 Corners, Round, 2 1/2 In.	100.00
Brass, Box, Round, Hinged, Signed Oil On Ivory Lady On Cover, 3 1/2 In.	95.00
Brass, Box, Stamp, Art Nouveau, Owl Face Lid, 4 1/2 X 3 1/4 In.	25.00
Brass, Box, Stamp, Chinese, Enameled, Flowers In Relief	30.00
Brass, Bucket, Handle, Small	35.00
Brass, Bucket, Iron Bail Handle, Dated 1866, 8 1/2 X 12 3/4 In.	85.00
Brass, Bucket, Polished, Spun, 13 In.	65.00
Brass, Bucket, Wrought Iron Bail, Signed, Dated, 9 X 12 1/2 In.	65.00
Brass, Bulldog, John Merriam Company, 3 1/2 X 2 1/2 In.	9.00
Brass, Burner, Incense, Turtle, 4 3/4 In.	15.00
Brass, Burner, Incense, Vine, Flower, 2 Open Handles, 3 Legs, Marked, 6 X 6 In.	115.00
Brass, Button, Lapel, Izaak Walton League Lettered	2.00
Brass, Buttonhook, Fancy, Chinese, Large	35.00
Brass, Cage, Bird, 1920s	45.00
Brass, Cage, Cricket, 2 1/2 X 2 3/4 In.	20.00
Brass, Can, Cream, 5 Gallon	45.00
Brass, Candelabra, 3 Light, Flowers, 12 3/4 In., Pair	65.00
Brass, Candelabra, 4 Arm, Mercury Head, Ram's Head, Empire, Pair, 18 In.	400.00
Brass, Candelabrum, Dogs Consuming Tendrils, Openwork, 3 Candles	20.00
Brass, Candelabrum, Floral, Scrolls & 4 Faces, Art Nouveau, 6 Holders, 16 In.	225.00
Brass, Candelabrum, Patina, Bell Tone, 7 Light Sockets, 15 In.	75.00
Brass, Candelabrum, 3 Light, Held By 2 Lions, 11 1/2 In.	30.00
Brass, Candelabrum, 5 Arm, China	26.00
Brass, Candelabrum, 7 Holders, Adjustable Arms, China, 12 In.	35.00
Brass, Candleholder, Elephant, Heavy	45.00
Brass, Candleholder, Pusher, Beehive & Diamond, England, 9 In., Pair	70.00
Brass, Candlesnuffer, Scissors Type, 6 1/2 In.	27.50
Brass, Candlestick, Adjustable Swinging Arms, Five, 10 1/2 In.	90.00

Brass, Candlestick, Altar, Spooled, 3 Sections, 37 X 2 3/4 X 7 In.	225.00
Brass, Candlestick, Art Deco, 11 In.	45.00
Brass, Candlestick, Baluster Shape, C.1840, 8 3/4 In., Pair	85.00
Brass, Candlestick, Baluster Turned, Push-Up, 19th Century, Pair	90.00
Brass, Candlestick, Double Twisted Spiral, Bell, Metal, Pair	115.00
Brass, Candlestick, English, Hand-Forged, Pair	130.00
Brass, Candlestick, Louis XVI, Chased, C.1790, 10 1/2 In., Pair	248.00
Brass, Candlestick, Marked SB With Crown, 8 In., Pair	35.00
Brass, Candlestick, Matched Plate, Handle & Pull, C.1810, Pair	100.00
Brass, Candlestick, Octagonal Base, Plunger Type, C.1820, 10 In., Pair	70.00
Brass, Candlestick, Persian Hurricane Shade, Ruby & Gilt, Prisms, 19 In., Pair	110.00
Brass, Candlestick, Push-Up, English, 12 In., Pair	90.00
Brass, Candlestick, Push-Up, Rectangular Base, 7 In., Pair	70.00
Brass, Candlestick, Queen Anne, 8 In.	175.00
Brass, Candlestick, Queen Of Diamonds, English, 11 1/2 In., Pair	115.00
Brass, Candlestick, Raised Flowers, Saucer Base, C.1880, Pair	50.00
Brass, Candlestick, Round Saucer Base, 19th Century, 7 In., Pair	45.00
Brass, Candlestick, Saucer, C.1915, 7 In., Pair	22.50
Brass, Candlestick, Square Base, Cut Corners, 11 3/4 In.	45.00
Brass, Candlestick, Stepped Hexagon Base, 19 In., Pair	85.00
Brass, Candlestick, Turned, Miniature, 1 1/2 In.	22.00
Brass, Candlestick, Twist Stems, Round Base, India 2545, 7 1/4 In., Pair	25.00
Brass, Candlestick, With Ring, China, Pair	19.95
Brass, Candlestick, 12 Sided, 8 Sides On Knobs & Cup, 11 1/2 In., Pair	88.00
Brass, Candlestick, 17th Century, Capstan, Pair	425.00
Brass, Candlestick, 8 X 4 In., Pair	90.00
Brass, Cannon, Miniature, Dark Wood Base, 19 X 8 In.	375.00
Brass, Chafing Dish, Copper Bottom, 3 Part, S.Sternau & Co., Dated 1893	33.00
Brass, Chamberstick, Saucer, Handle, Thumbrest, Push-Up Type, 4 1/2 In.	15.00
Brass, Chandelier, 4 Arm, 36 In.	325.00
Brass, Cigar Cutter, Desk Type, Cone Handles, Ornate, 8 In.	38.00
Brass, Cigar Cutter, With Match Holder, Table Model	40.00
Brass, Cigarette Set, Underplate With Holders For Cigarettes, Matches	27.50
Brass, Clock, Car, 8 Day, Stem Wind	7.50
Brass, Coffeepot, Reticulated Brass Trivet, Bedouin	75.00
Brass, Coffeepot, Straight Spout, Slant Sided, Handled, C.1830, 7 1/4 In.	60.00
Brass, Compact, Red Enamel Top Design	8.00
Brass, Container, Oil, Handled Porous Stone Torch, Fireplace Cover, Hammered	35.00
Brass, Corkscrew, Shape Of Dog, Tail Is Screw	15.00
Brass, Crimper, Pie, Fluted End	12.00
Brass, Cup, Communion, Traveling, C.1800	48.00
Brass, Cuspidor, Enamel Liner, 8 1/2 In.	50.00
Brass, Desk Set, Engraved Flowers & Vines, Marked China, 4 Piece	55.00
Brass, Desk Set, Letter Rack, Inkwell, Stamp Box, Roller Blotter, Utility Box	145.00
Brass, Desk Set, Village Scenes In Relief, JB, 5 Piece	145.00
Brass, Desk Set, 2 Turned Handles, 2 Cut Crystal Wells	225.00
Brass, Dish, Candy, 3 Sectional Depression Glass Inserts	10.00
Brass, Dish, Chafing, Manning-Bowman Co., 1901	100.00
Brass, Dish, Dragon Design, China, 4 5/8 In.	4.95
Brass, Door Knocker, American Eagle, 1800s, 8 3/4 X 4 3/4 In.	100.00
Brass, Door Knocker, Bust Of Churchill, His Name, November 1879-January 1965	50.00
Brass, Door Knocker, Bust Of William Wordsworth, England, 2 1/2 X 3 3/8 In.	24.00
Brass, Door Knocker, Horseshoe, Head Of Horse In Center	8.00
Brass, Door Knocker, Shape Of Lady's Hand, 4 3/4 In.	16.75
Brass, Doorbell, Ornate, Handcrank	18.00
Brass, Doorknob, Egg-Shaped End, Iron Connecting Shank, 19th Century, Pair	9.00
Brass, Doorknob, 1904 .... *Illus*	5.00
Brass, Doorstop, Elizabeth I Figure	15.00
Brass, Doorstop, Figural, Pirate, 7 In.	55.00
Brass, Doorstop, Figure Of Prancing Horse, Forge Mark, 7 1/2 X 10 In.	75.00
Brass, Doorstop, Pirate, Sword & Dagger, 7 In.	50.00
Brass, Doorstop, Shape Of Ship, 11 3/4 X 10 1/2 In.	25.00
Brass, Epergne, Applied Strawberries & Leaves, 10 1/2 In.	275.00
Brass, Ewer, Raised Inverted Feather, Bronze, C.1842, 10 Pounds, 18 1/2 In.	150.00
Brass, Figurine, Ferocious Sitting Bulldog, JB-2922, 4 X 5 In.	65.00

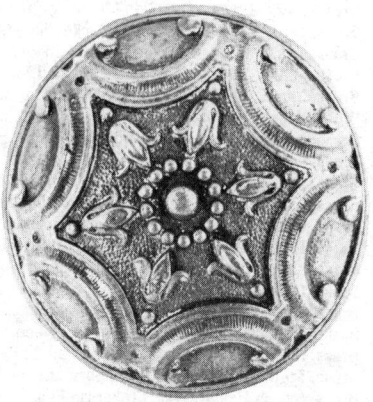

Brass, Doorknob, 1904

Brass, Figurine, Lady's Hand, Cuff Closing On Shield, Marked	60.00
Brass, Finial, Eagle With Wood Screw Mount, 7 3/4 X 6 1/2 In.	75.00
Brass, Fireplace Set, Stand, Shovel, Poker, & Brush	50.00
Brass, Foot Warmer, Pierced, English, C.1820	140.00
Brass, Footman, Pierced Design, Heart-Shaped Feet	285.00
Brass, Footscraper, Prancing Horses Swag Between, 12 X 4 In.	15.00
Brass, Frame, Easel, Lacy, Oval Opening, Mirror, 12 X 17 In.	55.00
Brass, Frame, Picture, Boy In W.W.II Uniform, Cherub Design, 9 X 12 In.	95.00
Brass, Frame, Picture, Cherubs, Snails, Bumblebees, Art Nouveau	75.00
Brass, Frame, Victorian, Easel Type, Ornate, 2 3/4 X 3 1/2 In.	29.00
Brass, Gas Fixture, Double Arm	25.00
Brass, Glasses, Sliding Bows, Metal Case, 18th Century	12.00
Brass, Glove Stand, 3 Gloved Hands, 12 In.	15.00
Brass, Goblet, Turned, Miniature, 7/8 In.	15.00
Brass, Gondola, Removable Oars, Patina, 11 3/4 In.	75.00
Brass, Gong, Dinner, Female Nude Holds Up Cross Bar Of Stand, 6 1/2 X 8 In.	35.00
Brass, Grinder, Pepper, 1860, 6 1/4 In.	37.00
Brass, Handle, Air Brake Control, From Railroad Steam Engine	30.00
Brass, Hook, Clothes, Horsehead, 6 In.	5.00
Brass, Hook, Snap, Navy Anchor	6.00
Brass, Humidifier, Finial For Coal Burning Stove, 3 Open Handles, 8 X 5 In.	50.00
Brass, Humidor, La Palissa Senators, Embossed On Removable Brass Top	25.00
Brass, Humidor, 3 Indian Faces In Relief	32.50
Brass, Ice Box, Mansion, Golden Oak, 4 Door, 50 X 36 1/2 In.	400.00
Brass, Incense Burner, Butterfly Base Candleholders, 5 In.	25.00
Brass, Ink Set, Impressed Scroll Work, 4 Piece	37.00
Brass, Inkstand, Rococo Floral Scrolls, Butterflies, Footed, Covered, Signed	65.00
Brass, Inkstand, Rococo Floral Scrolls, Butterflies, Signed VM, 8 1/2 In.	95.00
Brass, Inkwell, Covered, Hinged Top, 2 Part Glass Insert	10.00
Brass, Inkwell, Double Wells, Leaves, & Flowers, Art Nouveau, 7 X 8 In.	75.00
Brass, Inkwell, Figural, Fox's Head, Pottery Insert, 4 X 5 1/2 In.	110.00
Brass, Inkwell, Glass Insert, Swivel Cover, 6 In.	30.00
Brass, Inkwell, Hinged Cover Glass Insert, 4 1/4 In.	8.95
Brass, Inkwell, Violin Shape, Black & Gilt, Calf-Skin Cover, 4 In.	19.00
Brass, Iron, Chinese Charcoal, Birds, Flowers, Green, Blue, Yellow, Purple, Pink	65.00
Brass, Jar, Tobacco, Domed, Knobbed Cover, 6 1/2 X 4 In.	25.00
Brass, Jar, Tobacco, Man Feeding Chickens, Relief Men, Enameled Sides, Signed	145.00
Brass, Jardiniere, Copper Coat Of Arms & Trim, C.1860, 3 Paw Feet, 15 1/2 In.	248.00
Brass, Kettle, Bail Handle, 10 In.	75.00
Brass, Kettle, Candy, Iron Handles, 8 1/2 X 3 In.	39.00
Brass, Kettle, Dragon Spout, Burner Stand, C.1880	150.00
Brass, Kettle, Tea, Kerosene Burn, Blue Wood Handle & Finial	95.00
Brass, Lamp Frame, With Prisms, Hanging	115.00
Brass, Lamp, Bicycle, 1899, Nickel Plated, Carbide, Clamp, 6 1/2 In.	16.00
Brass, Lamp, Candle, Opaque, Green Bend Shade, Unmarked	80.00

Brass, Lamp, Driving, Left Side Mounting Bracket, Red & Clear Lenses	75.00
Brass, Lamp, Mechanical Burner, Nickel Plated, Patent Hitchcock, Dated 1873	140.00
Brass, Lamp, Student, Double Original Shades	350.00
Brass, Lamp, Student, Pink Shade, Marked American Student Lamp, C.1877	510.00
Brass, Lamp, Whale Oil, 11 In.	65.00
Brass, Lantern, Gem	75.00
Brass, Lantern, Porch, 6 Frosted Glass Panes, Hinged Door, 25 In.	120.00
Brass, Letter Caddy, Israel	10.00
Brass, Letter Opener, Eagle Handle, Old American Insurance Co.	12.50
Brass, Letter Opener, German Insurance Co., Freeport, Illinois	12.50
Brass, Letter Opener, Pan American Exposition, C.1901	14.00
Brass, Letter Opener, Thompson Derr, Wilkes Barre, Pa., Transportation	25.00
Brass, Lighter, Table, Figural, Snapdragon, 3 In.	20.00
Brass, Lock & Key, Animal Shape	35.00
Brass, Lock, Horseshoe Shaped, Good Luck	50.00
Brass, Lock, Star Shaped Lock, No Key, Keen Kutter	20.00
Brass, Match Holder, Little Girl With Pail By Well, 6 X 5 In.	135.00
Brass, Match Holder, Pair Of Slippers, Looped Wire Hanger	22.00
Brass, Match Holder, Wall, Striker On Front, 4 X 2 1/4 In.	6.95
Brass, Match Safe, Pocket, Brass, Rochester Brewing Co.	14.95
Brass, Matchbox Holder, Aladdin	15.00
Brass, Matchbox, Vestas, Cylindrical, Patterned, Lid With Hole, 2 1/2 In.	22.00
Brass, Measure, 3 Nested Chinese	7.00
Brass, Microscope, Black, Bausch And Lomb Optical Co.	55.00
Brass, Mirror, Chinese, Teak Stand, 19th Century, 23 In.	350.00
Brass, Mold, Bullet, Marked Colt	35.00
Brass, Mold, Spoon, Rattail, 8 In.	225.00 To 325.00
Brass, Mortar & Pestle, Mortar 4 In.Diameter, Pestle 6 1/4 In.	60.00
Brass, Nozzle, Firehose, 10 In.	12.50
Brass, Nutcracker, Alligator, 7 1/2 In.	9.00
Brass, Nutcracker, Bill Sikes, Fagin	39.00
Brass, Nutcracker, Knight In Armor	29.00
Brass, Nutcracker, Lady's Legs, 4 1/2 In.	15.00
Brass, Nutcracker, Parrot, 5 1/2 In.	30.00
Brass, Nutcracker, Punch & Judy	25.00
Brass, Nutcracker, Rooster Head, 6 In.	15.00
Brass, Nutcracker, Shakespeare	11.00
Brass, Nutcracker, Squirrel	30.00
Brass, Opener, Bottle Cap, Fish Shape, 5 1/2 In.	10.00
Brass, Opener, Bottle, Rooster, 3 In.	18.00
Brass, Opener, Letter, Attorney, Patent	5.00
Brass, Opener, Letter, Chinese, Ornate Handle	5.00
Brass, Opener, Letter, Crowned Head, Old Man With Beard, 1910, 10 In.	15.00
Brass, Opener, Letter, Dragon Figure Handle, China, 7 1/2 In.	15.00
Brass, Opener, Letter, William Jennings Bryan, 9 In.	25.00
Brass, Pail, Jelly, Polished & Lacquered, Handled, 5 X 12 In.	125.00
Brass, Pan, Iron Handle, 3 X 6 In.	75.00
Brass, Pan, Iron Handle, 8 X 4 In.	95.00
Brass, Pan, Scale Computer, Decorated Plaques & Brass, 14 1/2 X 18 In.	115.00
Brass, Paper Clip, Art Nouveau, Four-Leaf Clover, Numbered	35.00
Brass, Paper Clip, Duck Head & Ruff, Glass Eyes	45.00
Brass, Paper Clip, Figural, Owl	25.00
Brass, Paper Clip, Good Luck, R.C.Cola	6.00
Brass, Paper Clip, Hand With Card	34.00
Brass, Paper Clip, Shoe, Laced, Registry Mark	50.00
Brass, Paperweight, Fireman's, Eagle, Two Horns, 3 1/2 X 4 In.	30.00
Brass, Paperweight, Submarine, W.W.II, 11 In.	25.00
Brass, Pin, Rabbit Shaped, Blanket	25.00
Brass, Pitcher, 4 1/2 In.	15.00
Brass, Planter, Dovetailed Bottom & Sides, German, 10 X 7 In.	60.00
Brass, Pump, Brass Funnel End, Wooden Plunger, T-Handle, 27 In.	45.00
Brass, Pump, Wooden Plunger, Rubber Hose, Copper Nozzle, August 5, 1884, 31 In.	45.00
Brass, Rack, Letter, Ornate, Victorian	50.00
Brass, Razor, Gillette, Aristocrat, In Brass Plus Lined Case, Blade Holder	15.00
Brass, Roaster, Chestnut	95.00

Brass, Roasting Jack, Willard Type, Marked Salter No.40 .... 125.00
Brass, Rose Bowl, Dragons, Foliage, 5 Pounds, 6 X 4 In. 65.00
Brass, Rosette, Bridle, Plain Design, Pair 4.95
Brass, Samovar, With Tray & Waste Bowl, Russian Mark, 11 In. .... 250.00 To 335.00
Brass, Samovar, 12 Paneled, Urn Shape, Russian, 16 In. 295.00
Brass, Scale, Postal Letter 45.00
Brass, Scale, Rope Turned Standard & Adjustment Lever, 19 1/2 In. 125.00
Brass, Scale, Tubular, 1 X 8 1/2 In. 16.00
Brass, Scale, Winchester Grain, Brass Bucket 45.00
Brass, Scale, 6 Weights, 14 In. 75.00
Brass, Sconce, Leaves & Vines Frame Mirrors, Head Of Woman At Top, Pair 275.00
Brass, Sconce, 2 Light, Dolphins, Beveled Mirror, English, 23 In., Pair 110.00
Brass, Scoop, Country Store Type, 9 1/2 X 3 3/4 In. 25.00
Brass, Screen, Spatter, Ebony Handle, Wall Piece, 9 1/4 In. 45.00
Brass, Seal, Carved Bone Handle, 2 1/2 In. 12.00
Brass, Shaft Bells, On Metal Strap, Burnished, Set Of Three 22.50
Brass, Skimmer, Pierced, 9 In. 75.00
Brass, Snuff, Candle, Scissors Type, 6 1/2 In. 27.50
Brass, Spittoon, Large, Tavern Size 65.00
Brass, Spittoon, Redskin Brand Chewing Tobacco Cut Plug, Indian Chief Head 150.00
Brass, Spoon, Tasting, American, Hand Wrought Iron Handle & Hook, 12 In. 50.00
Brass, Spur, Single Cock 7.00
Brass, Stand, Bible, Handmade, 14 X 7 X 13 1/2 In. 250.00
Brass, Stand, Missal, IHS Engraved, 11 X 8 X 5 In. 22.00
Brass, Stand, Pitcher, Easel Type, 11 In. 12.00
Brass, Stirrup, Spanish, 10 1/2 In., Pair 50.00
Brass, Table, Tilt Top, Miniature, 1840, 5 In. 135.00
Brass, Taper Stick, Bell Metal, Square Base, 3 In. 12.50
Brass, Taper Stick, Incised Flowers, Swedish, C.1925 .... 50.00
Brass, Teakettle & Burner, Iron Standard 90.00
Brass, Teakettle On Stand, Dated 1892 .... 48.00
Brass, Teakettle, With Bail, American, Dated 75.00
Brass, Teapot, Footed, Amber Handle 60.00
Brass, Teapot, Raised Sprig Design, Hard-Stone Floral, Oriental, China, 5 In. 20.00
Brass, Teapot, S & Co. 39.50
Brass, Teapot, Squat Shape, Burner, Stand 46.00
Brass, Teapot, Stand With Alcohol Burner 55.00
Brass, Telescope, One Pull, Pocket, 3 In.Closed 25.00
Brass, Thermometer, Shape Of Castle, C.1900, 12 In. 30.00
Brass, Thermometer, Wall, Mercury, Fever Heat, Blood Heat, Spirit Boils, Water 30.00
Brass, Tieback, Cast Pattern, Brass Plated Shank, 4 1/2 In., Pair 19.50
Brass, Tieback, Floral Design, C.1840, 2 Pairs 10.00
Brass, Tieback, Rosette, Pair, 3 5/8 In. 30.00
Brass, Tongs, Candy, Jensen's 7.00
Brass, Tongs, Pipe, 10 In. 58.00
Brass, Toothbrush Holder, Wall Mount, Victorian, C.1890, 6 In. 22.50
Brass, Tray, Calling Card, Black Marble Base, Cherub In Chariot Holding Top 125.00
Brass, Tray, Card, Reclining Devil Holding Draped Spread, 6 In. 40.00
Brass, Tray, Raised Design, Raised Rim, 15 1/2 In. 18.00
Brass, Tray, Rim Guard All-Over Decoration, Round, 15 1/2 In. 32.00
Brass, Tray, Round, Russian, 6 1/2 In. 12.00
Brass, Tray, Russian, Double Handle, Marked, 12 In. 30.00
Brass, Tree, Hall, Miniature, 15 In. 65.00
Brass, Trivet, Claw Feet, England 28.00
Brass, Trivet, Footed & Handled, George Washinton Bust, 9 1/2 In. 60.00
Brass, Trivet, Good Luck, Horseshoe 22.00
Brass, Trivet, Inverted Heart Handle, Footed, Ornate, 9 1/2 X 5 In. 25.00
Brass, Trumpet, Fireman's, Inscription, Home Company No.7, Pair 125.00
Brass, Umbrella Stand, Claw Feet, Separate Drip Pan 55.00
Brass, Vase, Applied Salamanders, Dore Look, France, 14 In. 145.00
Brass, Vase, Quilted, Flowers, Band Of Persian Characters In Center, Handles 750.00
Brass, Warmer, Hand, Chinese 120.00
Brass, Warming Pan 190.00
Brass, Weight, Brass Cup, Nested Set Of 8, C.1895, Largest 8 Oz. 59.00
Brass, Whistle, Backup, Passenger Car 35.00

Brass, Whistle, Hunting, Engraved Bird, 15 In.Brass Chain, Initialed 15.00
Brass, Whistle, Locomotive, 3 Tone, 12 In. 125.00
Brass, Whistle, Steam, Buckeye Brass Works, 8 X 13 In. 95.00
Brass, Whistle, Steam, Cylinder, Powell's Improved Whistle, 19 1/2 In. 82.00
Brass, Whistle, Steamboat, S Shaped Iron Lever Cord, Finial, 14 1/2 X 3 In. 65.00
Brass, Window, Bank 75.00
    Bread Plate, see various Pressed Glass patterns.
Bretby, Jar, 3 Relief Cameos Of Women's Heads, Flowers, Bird, Covered, 4 In. ... 110.00
Bretby, Vase, Art Nouveau Flowers, Gold Beading, C.1880, Rising Sun Mark 67.50
Bretby, Vase, Figural, Relief, Mr.Pickwick, 8 1/4 In. 55.00

Brides' baskets of glass were usually one-of-a-kind novelties made in
American and European glass factories. They were especially popular about
1880 when the decorated basket was often given as a wedding gift. Cut-glass
baskets were popular after 1890. All brides' baskets lost favor about 1905.
Bride's Basket, Cased, Diamond-Quilted, Mother-Of-Pearl, Blue, Silver Border 1250.00
Bride's Basket, Cased, Fluted, Clear Edge 45.00
Bride's Basket, Cranberry Inside, White Outside, Ruffled, 10 In. 75.00
Bride's Basket, Cranberry Quilted Opalescent, Fluted, Plated Frame, 7 In. 100.00
Bride's Basket, Cranberry, Opalescent Poinsettia, Ruffled Edge 175.00
Bride's Basket, Crimson To Pink, Enameled, Silverplate Figural Stand 175.00
Bride's Basket, Green To Pink Overshot Glass, Silver Plated Frame 148.00
Bride's Basket, Ice Blue Shaded To Cobalt, Ruffled, Milk Glass Base, 9 In. 90.00
Bride's Basket, Miniature, Vaseline To Blue, Silver-Plated Frame 65.00
Bride's Basket, Pink To Opalscent Inside, Ruffled, Victorian, 11 In. 65.00
Bride's Basket, Red, Silver Frame, Ruffled, Footed, 11 In. 235.00
Bride's Basket, Rose To Pink, Ruffled, Silver Plate Frame, 11 1/2 In. 225.00
Bride's Basket, Turquoise To Vaseline, Blown Petals, Deer Head Handles 195.00
Bride's Basket, White & Pink, Ruffled, Silver Plated Frame, Enameled, 10 In. 145.00
Bride's Basket, White Casing, White To Red Interior, Glossy, Gold Flakes 325.00
Bride's Bowl, Cased, White Outside, Pink Inside, Floral Enamel, Beaded, 11 In. ... 200.00
Bride's Bowl, Enamel On Milk Glass, Reed & Barton Holder 150.00
Bride's Bowl, Hobnail, Pink, Scalloped, Ruffled, 4 X 10 In. 27.50

Bristol glass was made in Bristol, England, after the 1700s. The
Bristol glass most often seen today is a Victorian, lightweight opaque glass
that is often blue. Some of the glass was decorated with enamels.
Bristol, Bottle, Barber, White Floral 28.00
Bristol, Bottle, Dresser, Enameled Flowers, Blue, Pair 45.00
Bristol, Bowl, Bride's, White, Light To Dark Cranberry Inside, Enamel, 10 In. 95.00
Bristol, Bowl, Finger, Floral, Raised Painting 55.00
Bristol, Box, Cherub Kissing Roses On Lid, Hinged, Round, 6 In. 58.00
Bristol, Box, Hinged Cover, Pink & White With Cupid Scene, 3 3/4 In. 50.00
Bristol, Butter, Covered, Gold & White Enamel On Blue 85.00
Bristol, Butter, Gold & White Enamel Decoration On Blue, Covered 85.00
Bristol, Castor, Pickle, Blue, Lilies Of The Valley 275.00
Bristol, Castor, Pickle, Pink, Decorated, Signed Boucher 325.00
Bristol, Creamer, Enameled Teardrops & Flowers On Blue 45.00
Bristol, Dresser Set, Black, Hand-Painted White Florals, Gold Trim, 3 Piece 90.00
Bristol, Dresser Set, Covered Bottle & Jar, Portrait Medallion On Tan, Pair 30.00
Bristol, Dresser Set, Green Band Decoration On Tan, Bottle & Jar, Covered 30.00
Bristol, Epergne, Blue, Ruffled Rims, Enameled Flowers, 10 X 7 In. 125.00
Bristol, Jar, Cookie, Victorian Lovers In Garden, Yellow To Pink Ground 85.00
Bristol, Jar, Covered, Rose Decoration, 7 X 20 1/2 In., Pair 75.00
Bristol, Jar, Cracker, Green, Glossy Decoration, Gold Trim, 7 1/4 X 5 1/4 In. 88.00
Bristol, Jar, Tobacco, Cabbage Roses, Ives, Floral, Bulbous, Green, Blue, 21 In. ... 48.00
Bristol, Jar, Victorian Lovers, Garden, Shaded Pastel Yellow To Pink 45.00
Bristol, Lamp Base, Red Carnations Hand-Painted On White, Metal Base 195.00
Bristol, Lamp Base, Red Carnations, White, Turquoise Borders, Top & Bottom 100.00
Bristol, Lamp, Oil, Flower Band 100.00
Bristol, Luster, Enameled In White & Gold, Prisms, Cased, Pink, 15 In., Pair 400.00
Bristol, Luster, White To Cranberry, Clear Faceted Prisms, England, Pair 200.00
Bristol, Lustres, Blue, 5 Prisms, Floral Decoration, 7 1/2 In., Pair 195.00
Bristol, Lustres, Green, Clear Faceted Prism Drops, English, 13 1/2 In., Pair 75.00
Bristol, Pitcher, Ewer Shape, Tan Florals, Blown, Applied Handles, 8 In., Pair ... 95.00

Bristol, Plate, Flowers, White, 8 In. 10.00
Bristol, Plate, Ruffled Edge, Deep Rose, Enameled, 8 1/2 In. 48.00
Bristol, Plate, White, Flowers, Green Leaves, Hand-Painted, 8 In. 25.00
Bristol, Rose Bowl, Enameled Florals, Light Blue 53.00
Bristol, Rose Bowl, Enameled Gold & Jeweling On Turquoise Blue, 3 Ball Feet 135.00
Bristol, Rose Bowl, Light Blue, Floral Patterns, Enameled 53.00
Bristol, Salt & Pepper, Pink, Hand-Decorated 40.00
Bristol, Shade, Gas, White, 5 In.High, Set Of 5 .... 33.00
Bristol, Shoe, Pink Over White, Milk Glass 110.00
Bristol, Smoke Bell, White With Blue Piping, Lily Shape, Crimped, 8 1/2 In. 23.00
Bristol, Tumble-Up, Opaque Green, Pink & Beige Enamel Flowers 50.00
Bristol, Urn, Portrait Of Lady, Greens, Blue & Gold, 19 In. 135.00
Bristol, Vase, Aqua, Lavender Floral, Green Fern, Gold Beading, 9 In. 34.50
Bristol, Vase, Beige, Red & Gold Geometric Designs, Footed, 10 1/4 In., Pair 50.00
Bristol, Vase, Bird Decoration, 8 In., Pair 38.50
Bristol, Vase, Blown Decoration, Fiery, Purple, 11 1/2 In., Pair 75.00
Bristol, Vase, Blue, Birds, Flowers, & Leaves, Enameled, 11 1/2 In. 65.00
Bristol, Vase, Blue, Butterfly & Flowers, Hand-Painted, 11 1/2 In. 59.50
Bristol, Vase, Blue, Floral, 7 In. 12.00
Bristol, Vase, Blue, White Enameled Grapes & Bees, Gold Trim, 7 1/2 In. 17.50
Bristol, Vase, Bright Blue, Enameled Birds, Flowers, & Leaves, 11 1/2 In. 65.00
Bristol, Vase, Cased Pink, Enameled Birds, Flowers, 13 In., Pair 190.00
Bristol, Vase, Clambroth, Enameled Flowers, Leaves, Butterfly, 8 In. 55.00
Bristol, Vase, Cobalt Blue Color, Enamel Floral, 10 In. 22.00
Bristol, Vase, Fireglow, Flowers, Footed, Bulbous, 11 1/4 In. 65.00
Bristol, Vase, Floral Sprays, Urn Shape, Ruby, 14 In. 35.00
Bristol, Vase, Floral, Baluster-Shaped, White, Pink, Green, 12 1/4 X 4 In. 45.00
Bristol, Vase, Floral, Enameled, Green, 10 In., Pair 68.00
Bristol, Vase, Green, Hand Painted, 12 In., Pair 97.50
Bristol, Vase, Hand Blown, Blue, 6 1/2 In. 60.00
Bristol, Vase, Hand-Painted Birch Trees, 7 In. 14.00
Bristol, Vase, Hand-Painted Florals & Leaves On Pink, 9 In. 60.00
Bristol, Vase, Hand-Painted, Ruffled Rim, White, Pair 25.00
Bristol, Vase, Hand-Painted, Smoky, 12 In. 60.00
Bristol, Vase, Medallion Portrait, Victorian Ladies, Gold Trim, 10 In., Pair 75.00
Bristol, Vase, Multicolored Enamel & Gold On Frosted White, 8 1/2 In. 35.00
Bristol, Vase, Pale Green, Enameled Floral & Leaves, Orange Trailings, 12 In. 40.00
Bristol, Vase, Pink, Enameled Birds & Flowers, 10 In. 45.00
Bristol, Vase, Pink, Enameled Birds & Flowers, 13 In. 45.00
Bristol, Vase, Pink, Enameled Butterflies & Florals, Urn Shape, 14 In., Pair 120.00
Bristol, Vase, Pink, Hand-Painted Flowers, 12 In., Pair 60.00
Bristol, Vase, Portrait, Medallion Bust Of European Woman, Cream, 1870, 12 In. 65.00
Bristol, Vase, Roman Portrait Medallions, Metal Bases, Tan, 12 In., Pair 150.00
Bristol, Vase, Ruffled Edge, White, Pontil, 6 1/2 In. 12.00
Bristol, Vase, Ruffled Top, Pontil, Hand-Painted, 7 In. 18.00
Bristol, Vase, Seminude & Cherubs, 11 In. 18.00
Bristol, Vase, Smoky, 7 In. 45.00
Bristol, Vase, Water Lily, Foliage, Bulbous, Tapers, Satin Finish, 8 In. 235.00
Bristol, Vase, Wheat Sprays, Enameled, Off White, 8 In., Pair 85.00
Bristol, Vase, White, Enameled Leaves & Butterfly, 12 1/2 In. 35.00
Bristol, Vase, White, Enameled Roses, Lily Of The Valley, Gold, 15 In. 32.00
Bristol, Vase, White, Opalescent, Floral Decoration, 10 3/4 In. 25.00
Bristol, Vase, Young Girl Looking At Parrot, Pedestal, Gold Rim, 10 In. 80.00
Bristol, Water Set, Enameled Flowers On Transparent Light Pink, 5 Piece 150.00
Britannia, see Pewter
Bronze, Ashtray, Arab Sitting On Sitting Camel, 4 X 4 In. 18.00
Bronze, Ashtray, Compote, Riding Crop, Goat Head, 2 In. 22.00
Bronze, Ashtray, Fisherman, Wife, Fishing Net, 4 1/2 X 6 In. 35.00
Bronze, Bell, Church, Troy, N.Y.1871, 22 In.Diameter 1450.00
Bronze, Bell, Figural, Girl, 2 1/2 X 2 X 1 1/2 In. 30.00
Bronze, Bird Bath, Lotus & Buds With Crabs, 19th Century, 10 X 16 In. 225.00
Bronze, Blotter, Rocker, Top Inlaid With Silver 22.00
Bronze, Bookend, Abe Lincoln, 6 1/2 In., Pair 50.00
Bronze, Bookend, Bust Of Indian, Brass Back, Wood Base, Signed, Pair 55.00
Bronze, Bookend, Ear Of Corn, 4 Pounds, 6 1/2 In., Pair 30.00

Bronze, Bookend, Elephant With Ivory Tusks, 4 1/2 X 5 1/2 In.	65.00
Bronze, Bookend, J.L.Lambert, Indian In Worship Position, 8 1/4 In.	85.00
Bronze, Bookend, Jennings Brothers, Indian On Horse, 7 X 6 In., Pair	275.00
Bronze, Bookend, Pompeian Bronze Co., Elephant, Ivory Tusks, C.1920, Pair	45.00
Bronze, Bookend, Santa Maria Ship, 2 1/2 Pounds, Marked 5 1/2 In., Pair	30.00
Bronze, Bookend, Sculptured Sail Ships, Pair	18.00
Bronze, Bowl, Art Nouveau, Holder & 2 Handles	75.00
Bronze, Box, Dark Blue & Gold, Bronze Figures In Center, 3 X 5 In.	190.00
Bronze, Box, Jewelry, Bas Relief, Gothic, 8 X 9 In.	195.00
Bronze, Box, Receipt, National Cash Register, Glass In 2 Slides, Hinged, Slot	75.00
Bronze, Box, Sailing Ship Design On Cover, Art Deco, 4 X 3 1/2 In.	25.00
Bronze, Box, Shaggy Dog, Oblong, Lid	57.00
Bronze, Box, Silver Inlay, Hinge Top, 4 Compartment, Middle East, 9 In.	90.00
Bronze, Box, Stoeving, Girl Portrait, Art Nouveau, 4 In.	275.00
Bronze, Burner, Incense, Nude, Gilded, Art Nouveau, C.1920, Marked	35.00
Bronze, Bust, Barbedienne, Small Child, 3 1/4 In.	85.00
Bronze, Bust, Beautiful Maiden, Marble Base, 27 In.	950.00
Bronze, Bust, Carl Kauba, Winged Putti On Pedestal, 1800s, Signed, 9 In., Pair	450.00
Bronze, Bust, Duchoiselle, Elderly Couple Strolling, Turtle Doves, 12 In.	650.00
Bronze, Bust, Falguiere, Diana, Old Paris Porcelain Base, RG 3 1816, 7 In.	250.00
Bronze, Bust, Goethe & Schiller, 2 1/2 In., Pair	178.00
Bronze, Bust, H.Muller, Schiller, Foundry Mark, 6 In.	189.00
Bronze, Bust, Hawthorne, Foundry Mark, 1897, 6 In.	189.00
Bronze, Bust, Napoleon, 2 3/4 In.	75.00
Bronze, Bust, Remington, American Indian Savage, 13 In.	950.00
Bronze, Bust, Remington, Sergeant, Green Patina, 11 In.	1050.00
Bronze, Bust, Spanish Woman, Dore Comb In Hair, Lace Shawl, Patina, 8 In.	195.00
Bronze, Bust, Villanis, Ida, 6 In.	175.00
Bronze, Card Holder, P.Gailhard, Nude, Art Nouveau, 9 1/2 X 6 In.	295.00
Bronze, Coach, Cinderella, Gilded Cast Iron, Signed, Numbered, 9 X 6 In.	150.00
Bronze, Compote, Oriental, Lily, Frog Resting On Tipping, 7 In.	225.00
Bronze, Cooler, Wine, Chinese, Chinese Character Signature	350.00
Bronze, Cross, Blue Enameled, 19th Century, Russian, 3 In.	75.00

Bronze Figurines

Bronze, Figurine, A.Bordiga, Bust Of Lady, Roma, 1884, 31 In.	1150.00
Bronze, Figurine, A.Carrier, Mandolin Player, 3 Ft., 6 In.	2000.00
Bronze, Figurine, A.Jungbluth, Gibson Girl, 13 1/2 In.	475.00
Bronze, Figurine, A.Varnier, Dogs Chained To Post, Marble Base, 15 X 11 In.	1650.00
Bronze, Figurine, A.Vetu, Warrior Stringing Bow, 12 1/2 In.	600.00
Bronze, Figurine, Air, Parcel Gilt, Inscribed Auguste Moreau & L'air, 26 In.	1300.00
Bronze, Figurine, Airedale Terrier, Bronze Base, Signed, 8 X 8 In.	95.00
Bronze, Figurine, Alice Morgan Wright, Athlete, Art Deco, 11 In.	832.00
Bronze, Figurine, Anchorman, Naked Athlete, 15 In.Long X 15 In.Tall	1450.00
Bronze, Figurine, Athlete On Rocky Plinth, Italian, 19th Century, 20 In.	650.00
Bronze, Figurine, Auguste DeWever, Mephistopheles, Gold Wash, 11 1/2 In.	1375.00
Bronze, Figurine, Austria, Springer Spaniel, 3 In.	60.00
Bronze, Figurine, Avenging Angel, 20 In.Wingspan, 2 In.Tall	350.00
Bronze, Figurine, Bacchus, Green Black Patina, 19th Century, 25 In.	300.00
Bronze, Figurine, Ballas, Polar Bear With Fish In Mouth, 5 X 5 In.	195.00
Bronze, Figurine, Barrias, Joan Of Arc, Gold Finish, 2 1/2 In.	950.00
Bronze, Figurine, Bayre, Lion, 8 1/2 In.	850.00
Bronze, Figurine, Bayre, Mule, 9 In.	950.00
Bronze, Figurine, Bayre, Tiger, 5 In.	650.00
Bronze, Figurine, Bearded Worker, Marble Base, French, 12 In.	475.00
Bronze, Figurine, Bloodhound, Head Down, Dark Patina, 5 X 2 1/2 In.	125.00
Bronze, Figurine, Bonheur, Calf Walking Over Log, 6 X 9 In.	800.00
Bronze, Figurine, Bonheur, Hound, 12 1/4 In.	850.00
Bronze, Figurine, Bouraine, Girl Playing Court Tennis, Art Deco, 16 In.	1050.00
Bronze, Figurine, Boy Chasing Geese, Camille, 10 X 10 X 6 In.	495.00
Bronze, Figurine, Boy With Sword, Dore Case, R.Larche, 10 In.	425.00
Bronze, Figurine, Boy, Seated, Pulling Thorn From Foot, Marble Base, Signed	100.00
Bronze, Figurine, Brochette, Selenius & Dionysus, 20 In.	875.00
Bronze, Figurine, Brose, German, Miner, C.1905, 14 1/2 In.	495.00
Bronze, Figurine, Buddha, Indo-Chinese, C.1880, 9 1/2 In.	65.00

Bronze, Figurine, Bull, Bone Horns, 4 1/4 X 2 1/2 In. 125.00
Bronze, Figurine, Bull, J.Clesinger, 1859, 7 X 6 In. 425.00
Bronze, Figurine, Bulldog Sitting In Lady's Glove, 3 X 1 1/2 In. 75.00
Bronze, Figurine, C.Kauba, Doe, Warrior On Horse, 16 X 12 In. 2250.00
Bronze, Figurine, Cain, Pheasant On Wood Base, 7 1/2 In. 225.00
Bronze, Figurine, Cambodian, Monks Kneeling On 3 Tiered Platform, 9 3/4 In. 425.00
Bronze, Figurine, Camel, Attached Hinged Baskets On Saddle, 3 1/2 X 7 In. 95.00
Bronze, Figurine, Cat, Miniature, Black Patina, Hagenauer Austria, 2 In. 75.00
Bronze, Figurine, Charles Humphriss, Indian On Horse, Brown Patina, 16 In. 2900.00
Bronze, Figurine, Chicken, Polychrome, Russian, 2 1/2 In. 69.00
Bronze, Figurine, Chinese, Foo Dog, 2 1/4 X 4 1/2 In., Pair 650.00
Bronze, Figurine, Chinese, Seated Figure, Polychrome, 17th Century, 17 In. 490.00
Bronze, Figurine, Chinese, Stalking Lion, Glass Eyes, Signed, 8 X 11 3/4 In. 650.00
Bronze, Figurine, Cleopatra Reclining, France, 19th Century, 11 In. 225.00
Bronze, Figurine, Cleopatra, Reclining, Gilt, 19th Century, 16 1/4 In. 400.00
Bronze, Figurine, Clodion, Cherub Riding Ram, 11 X 20 In. 1095.00
Bronze, Figurine, Clown, Playing Instrument, 3 1/2 In. 22.00
Bronze, Figurine, Costeau, Man Trying To Restrain Rearing Horse, 12 In. 395.00
Bronze, Figurine, Cyrus Dallin, Standing Indian Brave, 37 1/2 In. 1800.00
Bronze, Figurine, Daillion, Nude Woman, Art Nouveau, Dark Patina, 24 In. 975.00
Bronze, Figurine, Dancing Satyr, 12 In. 125.00
Bronze, Figurine, De Bologne, Mercury, Marble Base, 27 In. 1250.00
Bronze, Figurine, Dog, Retriever, Russian, 4 1/2 In. 69.00
Bronze, Figurine, Donkey, Austria, 2 3/4 X 2 In. 50.00
Bronze, Figurine, Dubucand, Persian Hunter On Horse, Lion In Check, 17 In. 1950.00
Bronze, Figurine, Duck, Polychrome, Russian, 2 1/2 In. 69.00
Bronze, Figurine, Dying Captive, Brown, Black, Collas Stamp, 19th Century 550.00
Bronze, Figurine, Dying Gaul, Brown Patina, Collas Stamp, 19th Century, 16 In. 450.00
Bronze, Figurine, E.Fremiet, Knight In Armor, Marble Plinth, France, 16 In. 325.00
Bronze, Figurine, E.Fremiet, Medieval Knight In Armor, 1924, 15 In. 1250.00
Bronze, Figurine, Eagle, Wingspan, 24 In. 575.00
Bronze, Figurine, Eagle, 8 In.Wingspread 65.00
Bronze, Figurine, Edwin Dallin, Horse And Cart, Both Pieces Signed 875.00
Bronze, Figurine, Elephant, Paul Herzel, Signed 225.00
Bronze, Figurine, Equestrian Group Of A Knight, Marble Base, 12 In. 200.00
Bronze, Figurine, Erzgiesser, Beethoven, Austria, Black Marble Base, 13 In. 30.00
Bronze, Figurine, F.Barbedienne, Alligator, 7 1/2 In. 650.00
Bronze, Figurine, F.Barbedienne, Fondeur, Male Athlete, 19th Century, 12 In. 250.00
Bronze, Figurine, F.Barbedienne, 2 Kissing Parakeets 375.00
Bronze, Figurine, F.Gornik, Bedouin Tribesman On Camel, Marble Base, 12 In. 850.00
Bronze, Figurine, F.Iffland, Young Boy Sculpturing, Marble Base, 9 In. 450.00
Bronze, Figurine, Faun, Minor Roman Deity, 5 In. 80.00
Bronze, Figurine, Female Dancer, Thomasch, Art Deco, 17 In. 615.00
Bronze, Figurine, Fiedler, Nude Dancer, Signed, C.1935 .... 350.00
Bronze, Figurine, Flamenco Dancer, Full Costume, Tambourine, Patina, 16 In. 1200.00
Bronze, Figurine, Flamingo On Back Of Tortoise, Dore, 17 In. 225.00
Bronze, Figurine, Flamingo Standing On Turtle, Dore, 14 In. 275.00
Bronze, Figurine, Foo Dog, Open Mouth, C.1850, 6 X 4 1/2 In. 95.00
Bronze, Figurine, Foundry Worker, Marble Base, Stamped & Signed, 7 1/2 In. 245.00
Bronze, Figurine, Francois Thomas Cartier, Stag, 19 X 17 In. 850.00
Bronze, Figurine, Fratin, Goat, Signed, Small 155.00
Bronze, Figurine, Fratin, Stag, 6 In. 1250.00
Bronze, Figurine, Fremiet, Knight In Medieval Armor, Signed, 12 In. 1400.00
Bronze, Figurine, Fremiet, Setter, 6 1/4 In. 325.00
Bronze, Figurine, Fremiet, Young Troubadour With Harp, Silvered, 11 1/2 In. 700.00
Bronze, Figurine, French, Hermes, Marble Base, C.1870, Signed, 24 In. 495.00
Bronze, Figurine, French, Napoleon Standing, Folded Arms, Wood Base, 12 In. 175.00
Bronze, Figurine, French, Pheasant, Signed Cubucand, 11 1/2 X 7 1/2 In. 400.00
Bronze, Figurine, Gayrard, Reclining Wolf Hound, Dated 1848, France, 6 In. 150.00
Bronze, Figurine, Geschutz, Indian On Horse, Polychromed, Vienna, Numbered 600.00
Bronze, Figurine, Girl, Reading Musical Score, Ivory Face & Hands, 10 In. 375.00
Bronze, Figurine, Goose, Oriental, 8 In., Pair 175.00
Bronze, Figurine, Gornik, Basketball Player, 13 1/4 In. .... 350.00 To 425.00
Bronze, Figurine, Gratcheff, Farewell Kiss, 8 1/2 In. 2225.00
Bronze, Figurine, Gratcheff, Troika, 4 1/2 X 8 In. 1950.00

Bronze, Figurine, Heinz Muller, Shouldering The Scythe, 17 In. 750.00
Bronze, Figurine, Hoffman, Boy From Java, Black Italian Marble Base, 8 In. 1000.00
Bronze, Figurine, Humphriss, Indian On Horse, 15 In. 1600.00
Bronze, Figurine, Hunting Dog On The Point, Signed, 5 X 2 1/2 In. 295.00
Bronze, Figurine, I.Bonheur, Calf Walking Over Tree Log, 6 X 9 In. 900.00
Bronze, Figurine, I.Bonheur, Hound, 12 1/4 In. 925.00
Bronze, Figurine, I.Pilar, Wien, C.1890, Viennese, 12 In. 600.00
Bronze, Figurine, Ibex, Wood Mounted, Hand-Carved, 8 X 8 In. 125.00
Bronze, Figurine, J.Csadek, Spread-Winged Eagle, Austria, 12 1/2 In. 675.00
Bronze, Figurine, J.Guillot, Cavalier, France, 19th Century, 6 1/2 In. 125.00
Bronze, Figurine, J.Moigniez, Retriever Standing On Foliage, 12 1/2 X 8 In. 925.00
Bronze, Figurine, J.Moigniez, Stag, Running, Head To One Side, 7 X 7 In. 750.00
Bronze, Figurine, Jacquemart, Hyena, 5 1/4 In. 190.00
Bronze, Figurine, Japanese, Samurai Warrior, Stand, C.1880, Signed, 16 1/2 In. 850.00
Bronze, Figurine, Juan Clara, Child Climbing On Chair, 4 1/2 In. 495.00
Bronze, Figurine, Jules Moigniez, Mountain Sheep, 8 1/2 In. 595.00
Bronze, Figurine, Jules Moigniez, Pur Sang, Green Marble Plinth, 1900s, 8 In. 550.00
Bronze, Figurine, Kauba, Big Eagle, Indian Chief, 6 1/8 In. 950.00
Bronze, Figurine, Kauba, Great Dane In Standing Show Position, 14 X 14 In. 1050.00
Bronze, Figurine, Kauba, Indian, Big Eagle, Chief Presidential Medal, 6 In. 950.00
Bronze, Figurine, Kauba, Nude Female, Florals, Art Nouveau, 5 1/4 In. 375.00
Bronze, Figurine, Kauba, Turtle, Signed, 6 X 2 In. 195.00
Bronze, Figurine, Kauba, Warrior On Running Stallion, Signed, Dore, 26 In. 2200.00
Bronze, Figurine, Kitten Pushing Boot, Dark Gold Patina, 3 1/2 X 2 1/2 In. 125.00
Bronze, Figurine, L.C.Busch, Berlin, Presentation Piece, 17 1/2 In. 1250.00
Bronze, Figurine, L.Pilet, Mozart, Opera Don Juan, 13 In. 475.00
Bronze, Figurine, Lady Feeding Grapes To Goats, Art Deco, Marble Base 1200.00
Bronze, Figurine, Lady Holding Swivel Mirror, Art Nouveau, 1913, 17 In. 125.00
Bronze, Figurine, Lady, Bowl Of Fruit In Hand, Ivory Head & Arms, Art Deco 650.00
Bronze, Figurine, Lady, Ivory Head & Arms, Open Book In Hand, Art Deco, Signed 750.00
Bronze, Figurine, Lanceray, Cossack On Horse, 14 In. 4100.00
Bronze, Figurine, Lanceray, Tolstoy, 7 In. 500.00
Bronze, Figurine, Lapointe, Discus Thrower, Signed, 7 In. 350.00
Bronze, Figurine, Le Coup De Vent, Ivory, Onyx Base, Gilt, 20th Century, 12 In. 2300.00
Bronze, Figurine, Lugerth, Triumph Of Labor, Marble Base, 22 In. 1950.00
Bronze, Figurine, M.Krimse, Scottie, Gorham Co., 3 1/4 In. 90.00
Bronze, Figurine, M.M.Y., Girl, Art Deco, 6 In. 20.00
Bronze, Figurine, Miniature, 3 Great Danes, 2 X 1 1/2 In. 75.00
Bronze, Figurine, Moigniez, Pointer Dog & Partridge, Patina, 8 X 11 In. 795.00
Bronze, Figurine, Moigniez, Retriever, Marble Base, 12 1/2 X 8 In. 850.00
Bronze, Figurine, Morise, Equestrian Group Of Napoleon, Signed .... *Illus* 1600.00
Bronze, Figurine, Muller, Girl With Flowing Hair, Signed, 5 1/4 X 5 1/2 In. 275.00

Bronze, Figurine, Morise, Equestrian Group Of Napoleon, Signed

Bronze, Figurine, Muller, Girl With Flowing Hair, Signed, 7 1/2 In. 250.00
Bronze, Figurine, Night Watchman, Holding Lantern & Holding Horn, 3 1/4 In. 145.00
Bronze, Figurine, Nude Boy On Stomach, Talking To Frog, 6 X 13 1/2 In. 500.00
Bronze, Figurine, Nude Boy, Sitting On Rock, Bubble Pipe, Bowl, Signed RBS 550.00
Bronze, Figurine, Nude Male After Antique Bacchus, 25 In. 450.00
Bronze, Figurine, Nude Male, Bronze Base, 17 In. 450.00
Bronze, Figurine, Nude Male, Patina, 17 X 6 In. 450.00
Bronze, Figurine, Nude, Dying Warrior, Marble Base, Russian, 3 X 5 In. 69.00
Bronze, Figurine, Nude, Snake Entwined On Arm, Patina, Double Marble Platform 1150.00

Bronze, Figurine, Onyx & Marble Base, 7 In. 95.00
Bronze, Figurine, Oriental Figure In Sitting Position, China, 7 In. 135.00
Bronze, Figurine, P.Herzel, Dog, Shepherd Type, Sitting Up On Base, 8 1/2 In. 70.00
Bronze, Figurine, P.J.Mene, Arabian Stallion, 12 In. 1750.00
Bronze, Figurine, P.J.Mene, Cow Nursing Calf, 13 In. 1250.00
Bronze, Figurine, P.J.Mene, Cow Nursing Infant Calf, Signed, 13 X 9 1/4 In. 1400.00
Bronze, Figurine, P.J.Mene, Derby Winner, Marble Base, 13 1/4 In. 1450.00
Bronze, Figurine, P.J.Mene, Derby Winner, On Horse, Marble Base, 13 1/4 In. 1325.00
Bronze, Figurine, P.J.Mene, Fox, Dark Patina, Brass Highlights, 6 X 2 1/2 In. 350.00
Bronze, Figurine, P.J.Mene, Goat, 7 In. 550.00
Bronze, Figurine, P.J.Mene, Group Of Stag Attacked By Hounds, 12 X 17 In. 1650.00
Bronze, Figurine, P.J.Mene, King Charles Cavalier & Spaniel, 5 1/2 In. 275.00
Bronze, Figurine, P.J.Mene, Mare & Stallion 5700.00
Bronze, Figurine, P.J.Mene, Nymphenburg Whippet, Crouching, 3 1/2 X 4 In. 85.00
Bronze, Figurine, P.J.Mene, Ram, 8 1/4 In. 650.00
Bronze, Figurine, P.J.Mene, Scottish Huntsman & Hound, 19 In. 3700.00
Bronze, Figurine, P.J.Mene, Scottish Huntsman & Hound, 20 In. 4900.00
Bronze, Figurine, P.J.Mene, Stag, 3 1/2 In. 195.00
Bronze, Figurine, P.J.Mene, Three Dogs Burrowing, Dark Brown, 15 X 9 In. 2200.00
Bronze, Figurine, Pautrout, 2 Woodcocks, Silver Finish, 5 X 5 1/4 In. 350.00
Bronze, Figurine, Phillipe, Dancing Girl, Ivory, Signed, 18 In. 16.00
Bronze, Figurine, Phoenix Bird, Marble Base, 5 In. 60.00
Bronze, Figurine, Polish, Huntress With Dog, 13 In. 750.00
Bronze, Figurine, Rabbit, Signed R, 2 1/4 In. 45.00
Bronze, Figurine, Reclining Deer, Thailand, 20 In., Pair 225.00
Bronze, Figurine, Remington, Man On Horse Descending Mountain, 28 1/2 In. 7500.00
Bronze, Figurine, Remington, Mountain Man, 28 1/2 In. 7500.00
Bronze, Figurine, Remington, Rattlesnake, 23 1/2 In, High 4900.00
Bronze, Figurine, Remington, Savage, Roman Bronze Works, 13 In. 950.00
Bronze, Figurine, Remington, The Savage, Signed, C.1908, 13 In. 980.00
Bronze, Figurine, Rosa Bonheur, Reclining Ewe, 8 1/2 In. 895.00
Bronze, Figurine, Sargentor-Wein, Buffalo, 5 In. 350.00
Bronze, Figurine, Savioress Syamatara, Nepal, Gilt, 18th Century, 33 In. 2700.00
Bronze, Figurine, Schmidt-Cassel, Ivory Face, Arms, & Feet, Onyx Base, 12 In. 475.00
Bronze, Figurine, Sea Horse, Gondola Fitting, 8 In., Pair 50.00
Bronze, Figurine, Seated Buddha, Thailand, Gilded, 19th Century, 11 In. 125.00
Bronze, Figurine, Seated Buddha, Thailand, Gilded, 19th Century, 4 In. 40.00
Bronze, Figurine, Shrady, Elk Buffalo, 23 In. 24000.00
Bronze, Figurine, Slaves Bear Lady In Sedan, Shields, Drapes, Fretwork, 15 In. 2450.00
Bronze, Figurine, Smitty, Marble Base, Stamped & Signed, 7 In. 240.00
Bronze, Figurine, Snake Charmer, Muscular, Dancing, Fife, Copper Patina, 22 In. 1550.00
Bronze, Figurine, Soccerist: Position IV, Player In Uniform, Patina, 9 In. 750.00
Bronze, Figurine, Soldier, Battle Dress, Crawling, Rifle In Hand, Signed, 4 In. 750.00
Bronze, Figurine, Srivichai, Buddha, Thailand, Gilt, 19th Century, 8 1/2 In. 100.00
Bronze, Figurine, Stag & Doe, Dubacond, 6 1/2 X 5 1/2 In. 375.00
Bronze, Figurine, Stalking Lion, T.Cartier, 16 X 10 1/2 In. 575.00
Bronze, Figurine, Stalking Lion, Vidal, 1874, 28 X 14 In. 1295.00
Bronze, Figurine, Standing Lady, China, 9 In. 425.00
Bronze, Figurine, Standing Pointer, 9 X 9 1/2 In. 475.00
Bronze, Figurine, Sword Dancer, Nude Girl Holding 2 Swords, Dance Posture 1275.00
Bronze, Figurine, Thomas, Lion, 16 1/2 X 9 3/4 In. 565.00
Bronze, Figurine, Tiger Attacking An Antelope, Group, 19th Century, 23 In. 2600.00
Bronze, Figurine, Turkey, Polychrome, Russian, 2 1/2 In. 69.00
Bronze, Figurine, Vienna, Antlered Stag, 2 1/4 X 1 1/4 In. 75.00
Bronze, Figurine, Vienna, Black Warrior With Spear & Shield, 7 1/2 In. 225.00
Bronze, Figurine, Vienna, Cardinal, Geschutz, 7 In. 195.00
Bronze, Figurine, Vienna, Carpet Seller, 9 In. 200.00
Bronze, Figurine, Vienna, Dancing Cats, 1 1/2 In. 45.00
Bronze, Figurine, Vienna, Doe, Geschutz, 3 X 3 In. 95.00
Bronze, Figurine, Vienna, Dog, 2 1/2 In. 48.00
Bronze, Figurine, Vienna, Mallard Duck, 3 1/4 In. 50.00
Bronze, Figurine, Vienna, Parrot, Green, Red Topped Head, Geschutz, 5 1/2 In. 125.00
Bronze, Figurine, Vienna, Seated Laughing Chimp, 2 1/4 In. 85.00
Bronze, Figurine, Vienna, St.Michael & Dragon, Marble Base, C.1870, 6 In. 250.00
Bronze, Figurine, Whippet Dog Looking At Ball, 3 1/2 In. 125.00

Bronze, Figurine, Wolf, Cossack & Woman On Horse Going Down Mountain, 9 In. 1950.00
Bronze, Figurine, Wounded Gladiator, 6 X 3 X 3 1/4 In. 225.00
Bronze, Flower Holder, Flamond, Full-Length Girl, Art Nouveau, 15 1/2 In. 650.00
Bronze, Frame, Picture, Easel Back, Dore, Double, 4 1/2 X 6 In. 70.00
Bronze, Gorham, Figurine, 40th Anniversary Consolidated Edison, 1922 .... 135.00
Bronze, Groefner, Boy Smoking, Marble Base, Signed, 7 1/2 In. 175.00

Bronze Group

Bronze, Group, A.Mercie, Gloria Victis, Inscribed, 28 In. .... *Illus* 1500.00
Bronze, Group, A.Waagen, Stag And Doe, German, 19th Century, 25 X 20 In. 800.00
Bronze, Group, Barye, Soldier & Rabbit, 19th Century, 6 1/2 X 7 In. 300.00
Bronze, Group, Bayre, Turkeys, 3 1/2 In. 250.00
Bronze, Group, Edouard Henri DeLaSalle, Cleopatra On Sphinx, 22 In. 800.00
Bronze, Group, Eugene Lanceray, Peasant & Mules, Russian, 1800s, 10 1/2 In. 1800.00
Bronze, Group, Eugene Lanceray, Troika, Russian, 1800s, 7 X 12 1/2 In. 3300.00
Bronze, Group, F.Laugier, Wrestlers, Signed, France, 26 X 10 1/2 In. 725.00
Bronze, Group, Fremiet, Equestrian, Chef Galois, 14 X 12 In. 950.00
Bronze, Group, Leon Pilet, Classical Mother & Child, Marble Base, 17 In. 475.00
Bronze, Group, Mene, Arabian Stallion And Mare, 13 In. 2250.00
Bronze, Group, Moreau, 2 Form Maidens, Inscribed .... *Illus* 1800.00
Bronze, Group, Rochard, Deer At Pool, Art Deco, Pewter Finish, 25 X 5 1/2 In. 300.00
Bronze, Holder, Pipe, Figural, Scotty Dog 35.00
Bronze, Holder, Snuff, Eagle Feather, Talon, Vienna, 12 In. 125.00
Bronze, Inkwell, Bouval, Frogs On Lily Pad 94.00
Bronze, Inkwell, Bulldog Perched On Top Of Inkwell, 11 In. 225.00
Bronze, Inkwell, Devil's Head, Ear Pen Rests, 2 1/2 X 3 In. 85.00
Bronze, Inkwell, Egyptian Temple Dogs On Side Of Mausoleum, 4 X 2 In. 125.00
Bronze, Inkwell, Fisherman, Boat, Splashing Waves, Signed LeBlanc A Paris 685.00
Bronze, Inkwell, Plein Omaha, The Vanishing Race 850.00
Bronze, Jardiniere, Cactus, Umbrella Stand 175.00
Bronze, Jardiniere, Gilt Ormolu Mounts, C.1820, Japanese, , 9 1/2 X 13 In. 850.00
Bronze, Kettle, Animal Shape, Chinese, Late 19th Century, 7 In. 220.00

Bronze, Group, A.Mercie, Gloria Victis, Inscribed, 28 In.

Bronze, Group, Moreau, 2 Form Maidens, Inscribed

Bronze, Knife Rest, Figural, Fox, 4 1/2 In. 35.00
Bronze, Knife, Letter, Girl In Deep Relief, Bouchardon, French, Signed, 11 In. 49.00
Bronze, Lamp, Table, Dragons, Medallions, 15 1/2 In. 135.00
Bronze, Lamp, Wick, Bird Ornament 25.00
Bronze, Letter Opener, Indian On Handle, Grand Canyon, Arizona 14.00
Bronze, Lighter, Cigar, Figural, Elephant, Trunk Up, Flint Device, 5 X 3 In. 20.00
Bronze, Lighter, Cigarette, Figural, Elephant, 5 1/2 X 3 In. 20.00
Bronze, Match Holder, Figural, Bacchus Bust, Boy Begging For Wine On Base 38.00
Bronze, Medal, Abraham Lincoln, 1909, Centennial, Signed 35.00
Bronze, Medal, Abundance, America, C.1930, Society Of Medalists, Signed 20.00
Bronze, Medal, Agriculture, French-American, 1930, Signed 25.00
Bronze, Medal, Cathedral Of Rheims, 1914, Signed 30.00
Bronze, Medal, Credit, Industrial, Commercial, Cornucopia, Nude, 1959, Signed 25.00
Bronze, Medal, Dr.G.Angell, Memorial, 1918, Signed 40.00
Bronze, Medal, G.A.R., Lincoln's Birthday, 1909, Signed 35.00
Bronze, Medal, Hannover, 1913, Signed 35.00
Bronze, Medal, Health, Great Central Fair Sanitary Commission, 1864, Signed 45.00

Bronze, Medal, Indo Chine, Lion Head, Girl, C.1930, Signed	20.00
Bronze, Medal, James Jerome Hill, Memorial, 1916, Signed	25.00
Bronze, Medal, John W. Snyder, Secretary Of Treasury, C.1935, Signed	25.00
Bronze, Medal, LaVapeur, French Train, C.1930, Signed	35.00
Bronze, Medal, Lindbergh, 1927, Signed	45.00
Bronze, Medal, Los Angeles, California, Xth Olympiad, Signed, 1932	35.00
Bronze, Medal, Lyre, Wreath, Oblong, Signed	15.00
Bronze, Medal, Mechanical Engineers, 1930, Signed	25.00
Bronze, Medal, New Jersey-New York, 1931, Signed	35.00
Bronze, Medal, New York City Medical Art, C.1935, Signed	30.00
Bronze, Medal, Pan-Pacific International Exposition, 1955, Signed	40.00
Bronze, Medal, Port Of New York Authority, Bus Terminal, 1950, Signed	30.00
Bronze, Medal, The New World, 1939, Signed	30.00
Bronze, Medal, World Unity, 1945, Signed	25.00
Bronze, Medallion, George IV, Mounted Roman Horseman, 1825	20.00
Bronze, Mirror, Japanese, Raised Decoration, Seashell Leaves, 3 1/2 In.	65.00
Bronze, Mirror, Japanese, Tree-Like Design, Seashell Leaves, 8 In.Diameter	65.00
Bronze, Paperweight, Bust Of Lincoln, Capitol Dome & Log Cabin, Marked	30.00
Bronze, Paperweight, Girl, Signed A.Forster, Art Nouveau, 3 3/4 X 6 1/4 In.	175.00
Bronze, Pedestal, Fizel Aine Depose, Champleve Enameled, Onyx, 42 In.	950.00
Bronze, Pipe Holder, Lincoln In Relief, Hanging	52.00
Bronze, Planter, Oriental, Silver Enamel Bird Scenes, 8 X 10 In.	175.00
Bronze, Plaque, Abraham Lincoln	65.00
Bronze, Plaque, Castle, Knight On Horse, 7 1/2 In., Pair	95.00
Bronze, Plaque, Flight Of The Cupids, Mahogany Frame, Signed, Square, 6 In.	250.00
Bronze, Plaque, General Boulanger In Full Regalia, 5 In.	42.00
Bronze, Plaque, Have Suit Case, Will Travel, Map In Center, Letters On Edge	24.00
Bronze, Plaque, Launt Thompson, Lifesize Profile Of Daniel Webster, 1833-94	395.00
Bronze, Plaque, Linot, Liberation Of Lorraine, World War I, C.1919, 3 X 3 In.	40.00
Bronze, Plaque, R.Plaght, Heads Of Great Dane, St.Bernard & Bloodhound, 4 In.	75.00
Bronze, Plaque, Relief Head Of Man & Lady, Art Nouveau, J.A.Carles, 12 In.	145.00
Bronze, Plaque, Seminude With Flowing Veil, 18 X 11 In.	150.00
Bronze, Plaque, Teddy Roosevelt, Bas-Relief, Signed James Earle Fraser, 1919	95.00
Bronze, Plaque, Water Lilies, Cattails, 2 Swans, Flowers, Raised Relief, Mark	750.00
Bronze, Plaque, World War I Soldier & Sailor, 7 X 5 1/2 In.	20.00
Bronze, Ruler, The Gold Medal Scaffold Advertisement, 12 In.	6.00
Bronze, Sconce, Wall, English, Pair	375.00
Bronze, Shaving Cup, Russian, Brass Liner, Carved, Signed	75.00
Bronze, Skull, On Base, 6 3/4 X 4 1/2 In.	95.00
Bronze, Snuffer, Cigar, Figural, Voodoo King Of Haiti, Chicken Foot Base	450.00
Bronze, Statue, Octavius Caesar Augustus, Emblem Of Roman State, 12 X 31 In.	1200.00
Bronze, Stirrup, Conquistador, 17th Century, Pair	150.00
Bronze, Sundial, 10 In.Diameter	52.00
Bronze, Toothpick, Figural, Dog On Hind Legs Holding Hat In Mouth	85.00
Bronze, Tray, Christofle, Dore, Copper Cockfight Plaque, C.1800, 17 1/2 In.	450.00
Bronze, Tray, Figural, Face Of Man Smoking Pipe, 4 1/2 X 6 In.	55.00
Bronze, Tray, Kauba, American Indian Smoking Peace Pipe, 7 1/2 X 5 In.	75.00
Bronze, Tray, Pin, Figural, Inscribed S.Gonzalez & Epreuve Unique, Brown	350.00
Bronze, Tray, Tricornered, Boar's Head	25.00
Bronze, Urn, Champleve, 10 X 6 In.	79.00
Bronze, Urn, Champleve, 18th Century, 15 X 8 In.	259.00
Bronze, Urn, Chinese, Drum Form, 3-Monkey Base, Wooden Stand, 4 1/2 In.	45.00
Bronze, Urn, Grecian Frieze On Center, Double Handles, Pair	390.00
Bronze, Vase, Champleve Enamel, Palace, Floral Design, 10 In.	125.00
Bronze, Vase, Chinese Temple, Entertainers In Clouds, C.1850, 14 1/2 In.	150.00
Bronze, Vase, Chinese, Double Elephant Handles, 12 In.High	310.00
Bronze, Vase, Chinese, Woman & Child In Relief, Brass Finish	32.00
Bronze, Vase, Double Elephant Handles, C.1830, 12 In.	380.00
Bronze, Vase, Flowers, Birds, Oriental, Signed, 10 In., Pair	265.00
Bronze, Vase, Handled, Japanese, 4 3/4 In.	35.00
Bronze, Vase, Heintz Co., Sterling Inserts Of Leaves, 1912, 10 1/2 In.	35.00
Bronze, Vase, Leda And The Swan, Art Nouveau, C.1900	525.00
Bronze, Vase, Octagonal, Applied Elephant On Green Patina, Chinese, 12 In.	260.00
Bronze, Vase, Oriental, Detailed Dragon Wrapped Around, 12 1/4 In.	250.00
Bronze, Vase, Oriental, Reptilian Handles, Animal Decorated, 7 In., Pair	125.00

Bronze, Vase, Palace, Champleve, Dragon Design, 11 In.	150.00
Bronze, Vase, Silver Crest, Hammered, Silver, Green, Sterling Overlay, 11 In.	75.00
Bronze, Vase, Silver Geometrics, Signed Pomone, Art Deco, 11 1/2 In.	550.00
Bronze, Vase, Trumpet Shape, Gold Dore Panels, Brown Patina, 7 In.	95.00
Bronze, Vase, Urn Shape, Sterling Silver Tree, Silvered, 4 In.	45.00
Bronze, Vase, 2 Catfish Standing On Tails, Japanese, 14 In.	395.00
Bronze, Weight, Figural, Duck, Opium	38.00
Bronze, Whistle, Steam, 6 3/4 In.	25.00
Brown Ware, Pitcher, Small Mouth, Handle, 8 3/4 In.High X 6 1/2 In.Diameter	20.00
Brown Ware, Teapot, Rebecca At The Well, 9 X 10 In.	82.00
Brownie, Box, Palmer Cox, Brownies In Relief, Nickel Plated Brass, 3 1/2 In.	35.00
Brownie, Box, Stamp, Palmer Cox, Brownie On Sled, Silver Plate, Pairpoint Co.	95.00
Brownie, Humidor, Brownie Head, No Cover, 3 3/4 In.	17.00
Brownie, Plate, Palmer Cox, Ripple Edge, 16 Portraits, Marked Germany, 9 In.	29.00
Brownie, Puzzle, Blind Man's Bluff, The Dance, Mounted, 1891, McLoughlin	100.00
Brownie, Puzzle, Palmer Cox, Blind Man's Bluff, The Dance, 1891, 11 X 13 In.	75.00
Brownie, Record, Wonder Record, C.1906	2.50
Brownie, Rolling Pin, Palmer Cox, Early 1900s, Picture Of All The Brownies	18.00
Brownie, Rubber Stamp Blocks, C.1881, One Dozen	49.50
Brownie, Sketch, Cowboy, Swimming Across River To People, Gun In Mouth, Cox	125.00
Buck Rogers, Badge, Solar Scouts	19.00
Buck Rogers, Box, Pencil	25.00
Buck Rogers, Gun, Sonic Ray, Box	30.00
Buck Rogers, Gun, 21st Century	95.00
Buck Rogers, Painting Set, Large With Box	195.00
Buck Rogers, Pen, Brass	20.00
Buck Rogers, Rocket Police Patrol, Marx, 1927, Original Box	250.00
Buck Rogers, Ship, Space, Heavy Metal	10.00
Buck Rogers, Venus Duo-Destroyer, 2 Battlecruisers, 3 Piece	130.00

Buffalo pottery was made in Buffalo, New York, after 1902. The company was established by the Larkin Company, famous manufacturers of soap. The wares are marked with a picture of a buffalo and the date of manufacture. Deldare ware is the most famous pottery made at the factory. It is a khaki-colored transfer-decorated ware.

Buffalo Pottery, Bowl, Blue Willow, 1908, 8 1/2 X 2 1/4 In.	14.00
Buffalo Pottery, Bowl, Gaudy Willow, 9 1/4 In.	28.00
Buffalo Pottery, Butter, Blue Willow, 1909	5.00
Buffalo Pottery, Chamber Pot, Blue Willow, 1910	65.00
Buffalo Pottery, Creamer, Blue Willow	12.00
Buffalo Pottery, Creamer, White, Dated 1919, 5 In.	17.00
Buffalo Pottery, Cup & Saucer, Cup Marked, Blue Willow	12.50
Buffalo Pottery, Deldare, Bowl, Fallowfield Hunt, W.Foster, 9 X 4 In.	175.00
Buffalo Pottery, Deldare, Candlestick, Village Scene, 9 In., Pair	465.00
Buffalo Pottery, Deldare, Candlestick, Village Scenes, Shieldback	490.00
Buffalo Pottery, Deldare, Charger, The Fallowfield Hunt, 14 In.	285.00
Buffalo Pottery, Deldare, Creamer, Scenes Of Village Life In Ye Olden Days	95.00
Buffalo Pottery, Deldare, Fruit Bowl, Emerald, Dr.Syntax Reading His Tour	450.00
Buffalo Pottery, Deldare, Mug, Ye Lion Inn, 3 1/2 In.	165.00
Buffalo Pottery, Deldare, Pitcher, Annual Rent, 8 In.	260.00 To 297.50
Buffalo Pottery, Deldare, Pitcher, Fallowfield Hunt, 8 In.	325.00
Buffalo Pottery, Deldare, Pitcher, Fox Hunt, Whirl Of The Town, 1906	300.00
Buffalo Pottery, Deldare, Pitcher, He Returned With Curtsy, A.Delaney, 6 In.	195.00
Buffalo Pottery, Deldare, Pitcher, Octagonal, 8 In.	240.00
Buffalo Pottery, Deldare, Pitcher, Their Manner Telling Story	175.00 To 210.00
Buffalo Pottery, Deldare, Pitcher, Whirl Of The Town & Fox Hunt, 1906	300.00
Buffalo Pottery, Deldare, Plate, An Evening At Ye Lion Inn, 13 1/2 In.	295.00
Buffalo Pottery, Deldare, Plate, Bread & Butter, At Ye Lion Inn, G.R., 6 In.	38.00
Buffalo Pottery, Deldare, Plate, Chop, Evening At Ye Lion Inn, E.Broel, 14 In.	350.00
Buffalo Pottery, Deldare, Plate, Deer Hunt, 1907, 6 1/2 In.	200.00
Buffalo Pottery, Deldare, Plate, Dr.Syntax Makes A Discovery	350.00
Buffalo Pottery, Deldare, Plate, Fallowfield Hunt, The Death, 8 1/2 In.	110.00
Buffalo Pottery, Deldare, Plate, Fallowfield Hunt, The Start, 1908, 9 1/2 In.	450.00
Buffalo Pottery, Deldare, Plate, Fallowfield Hunt, 6 1/2 In.	105.00
Buffalo Pottery, Deldare, Plate, Fallowfield Hunt, 7 1/2 In.	115.00

Buffalo Pottery, Deldare, Plate, Hanging, Ye Lion Inn, 12 In. 250.00
Buffalo Pottery, Deldare, Plate, Multicolor Geranium, 1906, 10 In. 100.00
Buffalo Pottery, Deldare, Plate, Ye Lion Inn, 6 1/4 In. 100.00
Buffalo Pottery, Deldare, Plate, Ye Town Crier, 1908, 8 1/2 In. .... 99.50 To 150.00
Buffalo Pottery, Deldare, Plate, Ye Village Gossips, 10 In. 185.00
Buffalo Pottery, Deldare, Saucer, Art Nouveau Decoration, Emerald 35.00
Buffalo Pottery, Deldare, Saucer, Dr.Syntax, Signed Ford 65.00
Buffalo Pottery, Deldare, Saucer, Ye Village Street, Ford 55.00
Buffalo Pottery, Deldare, Tankard, The Hunt Supper, M.Gerhardt, 12 In. 390.00
Buffalo Pottery, Deldare, Tea Set, Scenes Of Village Life, 3 Piece 115.00
Buffalo Pottery, Deldare, Teapot, Scenes Of Village Life, 4 1/2 In. 200.00
Buffalo Pottery, Deldare, Teapot, Village Life In Ye Olden Times, 9 X 6 In. 295.00
Buffalo Pottery, Deldare, Tile, Traveling In Ye Olden Days, Round, 6 1/4 In. 118.00
Buffalo Pottery, Deldare, Tray, Card, Ye Lion Inn, L.Newman, 1908 .... 200.00
Buffalo Pottery, Deldare, Tray, Dr.Syntax Robbed Of His Property, 8 In. 220.00
Buffalo Pottery, Deldare, Tray, Relish 295.00
Buffalo Pottery, Deldare, Tray, Tea, Heirlooms, 13 1/2 X 10 1/2 In. 375.00
Buffalo Pottery, Deldare, Tray, Tea, Heirlooms, 13 3/4 X 10 1/2 In. 400.00
Buffalo Pottery, Deldare, Tray, Ye Lion Inn, 1909, Signed, 9 X 12 In. 425.00
Buffalo Pottery, Deldare, Vase, Emerald Pattern, Tall 425.00
Buffalo Pottery, Dish Set, Blue Willow, 65 Pieces 750.00
Buffalo Pottery, Dish, Feeding, Campbell Kids' Drayton 32.50
Buffalo Pottery, Dish, Gravy, Willow Pattern, 1916 .... 15.00
Buffalo Pottery, Game Set, Seven Piece, Artist Beck 200.00
Buffalo Pottery, Pitcher, Blue & White, 5 X 5 1/2 In. 40.00
Buffalo Pottery, Pitcher, Blue Background, White Flowers, Marked, 6 In. 45.00
Buffalo Pottery, Pitcher, Blue Willow, 1917, 5 1/4 In. 36.00
Buffalo Pottery, Pitcher, Blue, White, Chrysanthemum Pattern, 7 In. 25.00
Buffalo Pottery, Pitcher, Cover, Blue Willow, 5 In. 45.00
Buffalo Pottery, Pitcher, Dutch Jug, 1907, 6 1/4 In. 125.00
Buffalo Pottery, Pitcher, George Washington 295.00
Buffalo Pottery, Pitcher, Indian Tree, Blue, 7 In. 140.00
Buffalo Pottery, Pitcher, Landing Of Roger Williams, 1906 .... 325.00
Buffalo Pottery, Pitcher, Multicolor Geranium, 4 1/2 In. 145.00
Buffalo Pottery, Pitcher, Oriental Scene, Cobalt Blue Trim, 1907, 7 In. 75.00
Buffalo Pottery, Pitcher, Robin Hood 275.00
Buffalo Pottery, Pitcher, Roosevelt Bears, 8 In. 115.00
Buffalo Pottery, Pitcher, Whirl Of Town & Fox Hunt, 6 In. 150.00
Buffalo Pottery, Plate, Bedford Harbor, Sepia & White 65.00
Buffalo Pottery, Plate, Cake, Hand-Painted Roses, 10 1/2 In. 28.00
Buffalo Pottery, Plate, Capitol, Washington, D.C., 10 In. 23.00
Buffalo Pottery, Plate, Caribou Deer, 9 In. 36.00
Buffalo Pottery, Plate, Dedham, Iris, 8 1/2 In. 95.00
Buffalo Pottery, Plate, Fallow Deer, 9 In. 36.00
Buffalo Pottery, Plate, Faneuil Hall, Boston, 10 In. 31.00
Buffalo Pottery, Plate, Gaudy Willow, C.1908, 10 1/4 In. 58.00
Buffalo Pottery, Plate, Gaudy Willow, 9 1/4 In. 25.00
Buffalo Pottery, Plate, Green Rim Decorated, 2 In. 5.00
Buffalo Pottery, Plate, Hamilton College Chapel 28.00
Buffalo Pottery, Plate, Independence Hall, Blue Green Decoration, 13 In. 22.00
Buffalo Pottery, Plate, Independence Hall, Blue Green, 10 In. .... 30.00 To 45.00
Buffalo Pottery, Plate, Lafayette Square 130.00
Buffalo Pottery, Plate, Landlocked Salmon, 9 In. 35.00
Buffalo Pottery, Plate, Main Street, Hamburg Fair 110.00
Buffalo Pottery, Plate, Moose, 9 In. 36.00
Buffalo Pottery, Plate, Mt.Vernon, Blue & White, 10 1/2 In. 35.00
Buffalo Pottery, Plate, Niagara Falls, 7 1/2 In. .... 32.00 To 35.00
Buffalo Pottery, Plate, Roosevelt Bears, Scenes Around Edge.C.1906, 10 In. 115.00
Buffalo Pottery, Plate, Roosevelt Bears, 7 1/4 In. .... 59.00 To 65.00
Buffalo Pottery, Plate, Sike Deer, 9 In. 30.00
Buffalo Pottery, Plate, Trinity Church, New York City 70.00
Buffalo Pottery, Plate, U.S.Capitol, Blue, 10 In. 15.00
Buffalo Pottery, Plate, Wanamaker, 4 1/2 In. 75.00
Buffalo Pottery, Plate, White House, Green 30.00
Buffalo Pottery, Plate, Wild Ducks, Green Tones 30.00

Buffalo Pottery, Plate, Willow Ware, Dated 1915, 10 1/4 In. 16.00
Buffalo Pottery, Plate, Ye Olde Ivory, The Fallowfield Hunt, 6 1/4 In. 200.00
Buffalo Pottery, Platter, Blue Willow, 1909, 10 1/2 X 8 1/2 In. 20.00
Buffalo Pottery, Platter, Blue Willow, 1909, 14 1/4 X 11 1/2 In. 25.00
Buffalo Pottery, Platter, Buffalo Hunt, 1905 .... 80.00
Buffalo Pottery, Platter, Deer Hunt, Rectangular, 11 X 14 In. 125.00
Buffalo Pottery, Platter, Fish, 11 X 15 In. 75.00
Buffalo Pottery, Platter, Flowers, Ironstone, Brown, White, 12 In. 6.00
Buffalo Pottery, Platter, Willow, 12 In. 16.00
Buffalo Pottery, Sugar & Creamer, 1920 .... 6.00
Buffalo Pottery, Teapot, Argyle, Blue, White, Fully Signed, 1914 .... 67.50 To 85.00
Buffalo Pottery, Teapot, White With Blue Florals Decoration, Marked 68.00
Buggy, Wooden, Two Horse 600.00

Burmese glass was developed by Frederick Shirley at the Mt.Washington
Glass Works in New Bedford, Massachusetts, in 1885. It is a two-toned
glass, shading from peach to yellow. Some have a pattern mold design. A few
Burmese pieces were decorated with pictures or applied glass flowers of
colored Burmese glass.

Burmese, see also Gunderson

Burmese, Atomizer, Flowers, Leaves, Acid Finish, 3 1/4 In. 200.00
Burmese, Bell, Mt.Washington, 5 1/2 In. 245.00
Burmese, Bowl, Berry, Acid Finish, 5 In. 89.00
Burmese, Bowl, Epergne, Single Lily, Pink To Yellow, Acid Finish, 9 In. 265.00
Burmese, Bowl, Finger, 5 In. 79.00
Burmese, Bowl, Fluted Edge, 3 X 6 In. 375.00
Burmese, Bowl, Glossy Rose, 2 1/2 X 2 1/2 In. 275.00
Burmese, Bowl, Mt.Washington, Glossy Finish, 8 In. 800.00
Burmese, Bowl, Nut, 4 In. 140.00
Burmese, Bowl, Rose, 5-Petal Rose Decoration, 3 In. 195.00
Burmese, Candleholder, Black Heads, Pair 120.00
Burmese, Condiment Set, Mt.Washington, Signed Pairpoint Holder, 5 Piece 850.00
Burmese, Condiment Set, Ribbed In Silver Frame, 3 Piece 450.00
Burmese, Cruet, Mt.Washington, Ribbed Body And Stopper, No.157 On Bottom 1025.00
Burmese, Epergne, Set In Sculptured Brass, 5 In. 100.00
Burmese, Glass, Juice, Berry, Pontil, Yellow To Salmon, 2 3/4 In. 200.00
Burmese, Lamp, Fairy, Base, Base & Candle Holder Both Signed S.Clarke 495.00
Burmese, Lamp, Fairy, Clarke Base, 3 3/4 In. 295.00
Burmese, Lamp, Fairy, Decorated, Rose To Yellow 650.00
Burmese, Lamp, Fairy, Pink, Clarke Holder, 5 1/4 In. 225.00
Burmese, Lamp, Pink, Yellow, Matte Finish, Base Crystal, Signed, 3 3/4 X 3 In. 400.00
Burmese, Pear, Shiny, Stem 135.00
Burmese, Pitcher, Acid Finish, Mt.Washington, Yellow, Pink, Bulbous, 3 1/4 In. 475.00
Burmese, Pitcher, Hobnail, Applied Yellow Reeded Handle, 5 In. 175.00
Burmese, Pitcher, Lemonade, Pink 1/3 Down, 8 1/2 In. .... 360.00 To 425.00
Burmese, Pitcher, Mt.Washington, Acid Finish, 7 1/2 In. 450.00
Burmese, Plate, Mt.Washington, 10 In. 475.00
Burmese, Powder Box, White To Pink, Decorated Silver Cap 295.00
Burmese, Rose Bowl, Crimped Rim, Satin 175.00
Burmese, Rose Bowl, Glossy, Hexagon Top, 2 1/2 X 2 1/2 In. 275.00
Burmese, Rose Bowl, Salmon To Yellow Base, Scalloped Rim, Miniature 275.00
Burmese, Salt & Pepper, Holder 325.00
Burmese, Salt & Pepper, Mt.Washington, Ribbed 65.00
Burmese, Salt, Peach To Yellow, Enameled Yellow & Wine Daisies, Melon Shape 145.00
Burmese, Saltshaker, Melon Shape, Peach To Yellow, Enameled Daisies 115.00
Burmese, Shade, Ruffled Top, Soft Coloring, 5 In. 300.00
Burmese, Toothpick, Mt.Washington, Bulbous, Square Top, 2 3/4 In. 215.00
Burmese, Toothpick, Mt.Washington, Diamond-Quilted, Ruffled Top, 2 1/2 In. 215.00
Burmese, Toothpick, Mt.Washington, Enameled Flowers, Square Top, 2 3/4 In. 235.00
Burmese, Toothpick, Mt.Washington, Venetian Diamond, Square Mouth 325.00
Burmese, Toothpick, Mt.Washington, Yellow To Pink To Yellow, Flowers 215.00
Burmese, Toothpick, Tricornered, Hand-Decorated, Acid Finish 325.00
Burmese, Toothpick, 6 Sided Top, 2 5/8 In. 225.00
Burmese, Tumbler, Glossy Finish, 4 In. 120.00
Burmese, Tumbler, Mt.Washington, Pink Shaded To Yellow, Glossy, 4 X 2 3/4 In. 165.00

Burmese, Vase, Corset Shape, 5 Point Rolled Stained Top, Satin, 3 1/2 In. 150.00
Burmese, Vase, Double Gourd, 12 1/2 In. 600.00
Burmese, Vase, Hat, Glossy, 6 X 6 1/2 In. 375.00
Burmese, Vase, Lily, Acid Finish, Bled-Out Yellow Edge, 13 X 4 3/4 In. 1250.00
Burmese, Vase, Lily, Acid Finish, Bled-Out Yellow Edge, 6 1/2 In. 350.00
Burmese, Vase, Lily, Acid Finish, Bled-Out Yellow Edge, 8 7/8 X 3 3/4 In. 850.00
Burmese, Vase, Lily, Footed, 12 In. 290.00
Burmese, Vase, Mt.Washington, Acid Yellow, Pink Band, Wood Peg Base, 7 1/2 In. 210.00
Burmese, Vase, Mt.Washington, Applied Rigaree Ribbon At Neck, 5 1/2 In. 255.00
Burmese, Vase, Mt.Washington, Jack-In-The-Pulpit, Yellow To Pink, 17 In. 875.00
Burmese, Vase, Mt.Washington, Lemon To Pink, 14 In. 350.00
Burmese, Vase, Mt.Washington, Rigaree Ribbon On Neck, 5 1/2 In. 255.00
Burmese, Vase, Mt.Washington, Satin Finish, Jack-In-The-Pulpit, 17 In. 600.00
Burmese, Vase, Stick Neck, Bulbous Base, 8 In. 325.00
Burmese, Vase, Stick, Acid Finish, 4-Sided Dimpled Base, 6 1/8 In. 295.00
Burmese, Vase, Stick, Ivy Decoration, 7 1/4 In. 385.00
Burmese, Vase, Trumpet Shape, Silver-Plated Figural Boy Holder, 8 3/4 In. 250.00
Burmese, Vase, Trumpet, 19 In. 875.00
     Burmese, Webb, see Webb Burmese
Buster Brown, Baby's Set, Brown, Lithographed Buster & Tige, Cup, Dish, Plate 125.00
Buster Brown, Bank, 5 In. 45.00
Buster Brown, Blotter 3.50
Buster Brown, Book, Comic 5.00
Buster Brown, Clicker 5.00
Buster Brown, Creamer, Buster & Tige 12.50
Buster Brown, Cup & Saucer 35.00
Buster Brown, Doll, Paper, 4 Outfits 30.00
Buster Brown, Figurine, Buster, Bisque, Advertising, 2 3/4 In. 25.00
Buster Brown, Figurine, Lead, 1915 .... 8.50
Buster Brown, Fork, C.1910 .... 10.00
Buster Brown, Game, Pin The Tie On Buster, Oilcloth, 12 Ties, 26 X 30 In. 68.00
Buster Brown, Hatchet, Iron, Buster Brown Shoes, Embossed Buster & Tige 50.00
Buster Brown, Knife, Hunting, Marble 45.00
Buster Brown, Mannequin, Doll, Original Clothes, 23 In. 85.00
Buster Brown, Mirror, Pocket, Buster & Tige, C.1946 .... 3.00 To 8.50
Buster Brown, Mug, Buster Brown & Tige 85.00
Buster Brown, Mug, Tige Balancing Teapot On Nose 29.50
Buster Brown, Pencil, Metal 8.00
Buster Brown, Pencil, 1914 .... 10.00
Buster Brown, Pin, Advertising, Buster Brown Shoes, 1 In. 8.50
Buster Brown, Pin, Hose Supporter 15.00
Buster Brown, Plate, Buster Pouring Tea For Tige, 6 1/4 In. 27.00
Buster Brown, Print, Goes Swimming, Leon & Cupples, 1907 .... 25.00
Buster Brown, Sign, Brass, Buster & Tige, Chain Hanger, 5 X 13 In. 32.00
Buster Brown, Sign, Tin, Wood Frame, 1920s, 22 X 30 In. 125.00
Buster Brown, Tea Set, Child's, Buster & Tige, 15 Piece 120.00
Buster Brown, Tray, China, Small 27.50
Buster Brown, Valentine, Mechanical, Die-Cut, Embossed 20.00
Buster Brown, Whistle, Lithographed Tin, Buster & Tige, Germany 14.00
     Buttermilk Glass, see Custard Glass

Buttons have been known throughout the centuries, and there are millions of
styles. Only a few of the most common types are listed for comparison.
Button, Brass, Figures Of Boy & Girl On Blue Steel Ground, Kate Greenaway 28.00
Button, Carved Ivory, Floral, 1 1/16 In. 15.00
Button, Cleopatra In Hammock, Brass On Black, Ornate Trim, 1 1/2 In. 5.00
Button, Copper, Ivory Cameo Center 25.00
Button, Cupid Shooting Arrow, Bronze Finished Brass, 1 1/2 In. 6.00
Button, German Silver, Emperor Frederick III, Imperial Eagle, Set Of 3 .... 25.00
Button, Gutta-Percha, Shore Bird, Brass Setting, Nov.12, 1846, 1 1/4 In. 12.00
Button, Les Incroyables, French Dandy With Cane, Brass On Black, 1 1/8 In. 7.00
Button, Reverse Painting On Glass, Prong Set In Gilt Metal 5.00
Button, Satsuma, Geisha Girl, Gold Trim, Kyoto, Japan, 1940s, 1 In. 6.00
     Buttonhook, see Silver, Sterling Buttonhook, Store Buttonhook
Bybee, Vase, Matte Green, 8 1/2 In. 16.00

Bybee, Vase, Three Looped Handles, Metallic Green Glaze, Selden, 10 1/2 In. 35.00
    Calcite, see also Steuben
Calcite, Bowl, Flared, Red Highlights, 2 X 10 1/2 In. 95.00
Calcite, Bowl, Gold Lining, 10 X 2 3/4 In. 180.00
Calcite, Bowl, Gold, 2 X 8 1/2 In. 100.00
Calcite, Compote, Gold, 6 X 4 In. 90.00
Calcite, Sherbet, Gold Lining, Purplish Iridescence, Steuben, 3 7/8 In. 100.00

Calendar plates were very popular in the United States from 1906 to 1929.
Since then plates have been made every year. A calendar, the name of a
store, a picture of flowers, a girl, or a scene was featured on the plate.
Calendar, Paper, 1925, Peters Cartridge Co., Ducks Flying Over Marsh 200.00
Calendar, Paper, 1928, Hunting Dog In Field, Peters Ammo 125.00
Calendar, Paper, 1938, West End Brewing Co., Utica Club, 50th Anniversary, 32 In. 85.00
Calendar, Paper, 1942, Dupont, Hunting Dog 50.00
Calendar, Paper, 1953, Marilyn Monroe 4.00
Calendar, Paper, 1974, Elvis Presley, RCA Pocket 1.50
Calendar, Plate, 1907, Santa Claus & Sleigh 45.00
Calendar, Plate, 1908, Crossed Flags, Oyster Bay 25.00
Calendar, Plate, 1908, Crossed Flags, Wahpeton, N.D. 14.00
Calendar, Plate, 1908, English Cottage Scene 13.50
Calendar, Plate, 1908, Indian With Headdress, Months On Feathers, Meyercord 35.00
Calendar, Plate, 1908, Roses, Horse Bluffs, Nebraska, 8 In. 34.50
Calendar, Plate, 1908, Vacation Home Scene, 9 In. 24.00
Calendar, Plate, 1909, Bird With Ribbon In Mouth 30.00
Calendar, Plate, 1909, Dog Head, Chicago, 7 3/4 In. 14.00
Calendar, Plate, 1909, Gibson Girl, Galesville, Wisconsin 32.50
Calendar, Plate, 1909, Rural Scene 35.00
Calendar, Plate, 1909, Waterlilies, Spear Drug Co., Diller, Nebraska, 9 In. 22.50
Calendar, Plate, 1910, Angels Ringing Bell, 8 In. 18.00
Calendar, Plate, 1910, Archie Gunn Portrait 35.00
Calendar, Plate, 1910, Bell 15.00
Calendar, Plate, 1910, Cherubs Ringing In New Year 25.00
Calendar, Plate, 1910, Cupids Striking New Year's Bell 20.00
Calendar, Plate, 1910, Flowers On Border, Cupids In Center 11.50
Calendar, Plate, 1910, Four Seasons, Compliments J.B.Foatz, Bethany, Penna. 20.00
Calendar, Plate, 1910, Gibson Type Girl And Horse's Head 19.00
Calendar, Plate, 1910, Girl With Horse .... 16.00 To 30.00
Calendar, Plate, 1910, Gold Rim, Holly Center, 7 1/2 In. 9.00
Calendar, Plate, 1910, Lady Driving Antique Auto 35.00
Calendar, Plate, 1910, Ocean Scene, Walnut Grove, Maine 45.00
Calendar, Plate, 1910, Roses, 9 In. .... *Illus*   24.50
Calendar, Plate, 1910, Spring Valley 22.00
Calendar, Plate, 1911, Clipper Ship, Blue Sea 15.00
Calendar, Plate, 1911, Cupids & Pink Roses 15.00
Calendar, Plate, 1911, Farm Scene 29.00
Calendar, Plate, 1911, Heads Of White & Brown Horses In Horseshoe 26.00

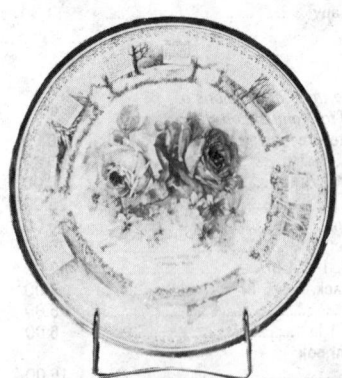

Calendar, Plate, 1910, Roses, 9 In.

Calendar, Plate, 1911, Months On Ship Sails, 8 In. 16.00
Calendar, Plate, 1911, Rabbits .... 18.50 To 25.00
Calendar, Plate, 1911, Should Auld Acquaintances, Gibson Girl & Date 29.00
Calendar, Plate, 1911, Wild Ducks & Rushes, 7 1/2 In. 24.50
Calendar, Plate, 1911, 1912, Arapahoe, Nebraska 30.00
Calendar, Plate, 1912, Benner, Jeweler, Optometrist, Waldoboro, Maine 25.00
Calendar, Plate, 1912, Farm Scene, Fall Leaves 18.00
Calendar, Plate, 1912, Fish Creek, Wisconsin, Owl 18.00
Calendar, Plate, 1912, Indian Maiden 34.00
Calendar, Plate, 1912, Owl On Open Book, R.W.Shawl, Druggist, Sandy Creek, N.Y. 17.00
Calendar, Plate, 1912, Plums & Compliments Of Medford Co-Op Co, Medford, Wis. 14.00
Calendar, Plate, 1912, President Martyrs, Lincoln, Garfield, McKinley 50.00
Calendar, Plate, 1913, Fruit & Flowers Border, Roses In Center 12.50
Calendar, Plate, 1913, Ragged Urchin In Arch, Hopple, North Dakota, 7 In. 24.50
Calendar, Plate, 1914, Browntone Christmas Scene 18.00
Calendar, Plate, 1915, Panama Canal, Flow Blue Style Border 29.00
Calendar, Plate, 1915, Young Boy & Father Time 22.00
Calendar, Plate, 1916, Dutch Children Cartoon 18.00
Calendar, Plate, 1917, Deer Grazing 25.00
Calendar, Plate, 1919, Mayflower Center, Yacht 25.00
Calendar, Plate, 1920, Eagle, Victory, Flags Of 4 Countries, War's End, , 9 In. 50.00
Calendar, Plate, 1920, Peace, Flags, Dove, 8 1/4 In. 17.00
Calendar, Plate, 1920, World War Globe, Dove 15.00
Calendar, Plate, 1954, Fiesta, Ivory 12.00
Calendar, Plate, 1956, Dutch Harbor Scene 15.00
Calendar, Plate, 1972, Girl, Striped Pajamas, Holding Teddy Bear 10.00
Camark, Bowl, Flying Fish, Paper Label, 10 In. 8.00
Camark, Cookie Jar, Dutch Boy, White, Black Trim, 12 X 21 In. 16.50
Camark, Sign, Dealer's, Matte Green, 6 1/4 X 6 3/4 In. 35.00

Cambridge art pottery was made in Cambridge, Ohio, from about 1895 until World War I. The factory made brown glazed decorated wares marked with a variety of marks including an acorn, the name Cambridge, the name Oakwood, or the name Terrhea.

Cambridge Pottery, Vase, Brownish Green Glaze, Signed, 4 1/2 X 5 In. 28.00

The Cambridge Glass Company made pressed glass in Cambridge, Ohio. The words "near-cut" were used after 1906. It was marked with a C in a triangle about 1916.

Cambridge, Ashtray, Amethyst Insert, Farberware Holder 8.00
Cambridge, Ashtray, Caprice, Green-Yellow, 3 Toed, 3 In. 8.00
Cambridge, Ashtray, Cobalt, Nude Stem 90.00
Cambridge, Ashtray, Crown Tuscan, Round, 7 In. 17.50
Cambridge, Ashtray, Footed Shell, Crown Tuscan 14.00
Cambridge, Ashtray, Ruby, Square, 6 In. 35.00
Cambridge, Basket, Near-Cut, 7 In. 22.00
Cambridge, Basket, Rosepoint, 11 X 7 In. 85.00
Cambridge, Berry Set, Lacy Daisy, 7 Piece 50.00
Cambridge, Bonbon, Ball Finial, Gold & Black, Triangle C Mark 55.00
Cambridge, Bonbon, Pink, Turned-Up Sides, Signed 17.50
Cambridge, Bookend, Eagle, Pair 110.00
Cambridge, Bookend, Pouter Pigeons, Crystal, Pair 140.00
Cambridge, Bottle, Oil & Vinegar, Etched Oil & Vinegar & Leaves 24.00
Cambridge, Bottle, Water, Near-Cut, Marked 45.00
Cambridge, Bowl With Underplate, Mayonnaise, Caprice, Crystal 7.00
Cambridge, Bowl, Amber, Gold-Encrusted Etched Diane, Pierced Handles, 8 In. 45.00
Cambridge, Bowl, Amber, Light Floral & Line Cutting, 11 3/4 X 4 1/2 In. 35.00
Cambridge, Bowl, Amber, Nude Farber Stem, 8 In. 24.50
Cambridge, Bowl, Azurite, Blue, 1920-1930, Signed, 11 In. 40.00
Cambridge, Bowl, Azurite, 8 In. 45.00
Cambridge, Bowl, Banana, Everglades, Moonlight Blue 78.00
Cambridge, Bowl, Blue, Caprice, 13 In. 30.00
Cambridge, Bowl, Buffalo, Amber, Flared Rim, 16 In. 430.00
Cambridge, Bowl, Candy, Mandarin, Gold, Gold Etched Gloria, 4 Footed 39.00
Cambridge, Bowl, Caprice Alpine, Blue, Flat, Footed, 12 1/2 In. 15.00

Cambridge, Bowl, Caprice, Blue, 14 X 3 In. 15.00
Cambridge, Bowl, Caprice, Yellow 25.00
Cambridge, Bowl, Centerpiece, Crown Tuscan, Flying Nude 125.00
Cambridge, Bowl, Chantilly, Amber, Gold-Encrusted, Etched Floral, 8 X 12 In. 50.00
Cambridge, Bowl, Chantilly, 3 Ft.3 1/2 In. 22.00
Cambridge, Bowl, Console, Caprice, Crystal 15.00
Cambridge, Bowl, Console, Ebony, Blue, Melon Section, Handled, 16 X 8 In. 62.50
Cambridge, Bowl, Console, Etched, Gold, Footed, Signed, 12 In. 27.50
Cambridge, Bowl, Creamer, Cherry Blossom, Pink 6.50
Cambridge, Bowl, Crown Tuscan, Footed & Flared 60.00
Cambridge, Bowl, Crown Tuscan, Mandarin Gold 75.00
Cambridge, Bowl, Crown Tuscan, Seashell, 3 Footed, 10 In. 65.00
Cambridge, Bowl, Crown Tuscan, 3 Toed, Seashell, Rose, Gold 75.00
Cambridge, Bowl, Cup & Saucer, Cloverleaf, Pink 4.50
Cambridge, Bowl, Diane, Etch, Gold-Encrusted, Amber, Scalloped, 8 X 12 X 3 In. 45.00
Cambridge, Bowl, Emerald Green, 4-Toed, C In Triangle 16.00
Cambridge, Bowl, Etched Decoration, Green, 8 1/2 X 4 In. 14.00
Cambridge, Bowl, Etched Diane, 4 Toed, Flared, 12 In. 20.00
Cambridge, Bowl, Etched Floral, Yellow, Footed, 11 In. 35.00
Cambridge, Bowl, Everglades, Blue, Caprice, Oval, Pedestal, 12 X 8 In. 35.00
Cambridge, Bowl, Everglades, Emerald Green, 12 In. 55.00
Cambridge, Bowl, Feather, Signed, Near-Cut, 6 X 2 1/2 In. 22.00
Cambridge, Bowl, Flying Nude, Dolphin Fitted Candleholders Inside 260.00
Cambridge, Bowl, Footed, Peachblow, 8-Sided, Etched Florals, Pink, 12 In. 48.00
Cambridge, Bowl, Footed, Rosepoint, 11 In. 37.00
Cambridge, Bowl, Forest Green, Collared Base, Scalloped Edge, 11 In. 15.00
Cambridge, Bowl, Fruit, Ivy Cut, Peachblow, 11 In. 75.00
Cambridge, Bowl, Green With Gold, Inverted Thistle, Near-Cut, 9 1/2 In. 48.00
Cambridge, Bowl, Green, Etched, Handled, 8 1/2 X 4 In. 14.00
Cambridge, Bowl, Heliotrope Acid Cut Back, Daisy Design, 7 1/2 X 3 3/4 In. 32.00
Cambridge, Bowl, Heliotrope, Opaque, 9 In. 35.00
Cambridge, Bowl, Heliotrope, 12 In. 30.00
Cambridge, Bowl, Honeycomb, Amberina, Pedestal 75.00
Cambridge, Bowl, Inverted Thistle, Green With Gold, 9 1/2 In. 48.00
Cambridge, Bowl, Ivy, Cobalt With Clear Keyhole Stem, 8 In. 25.00
Cambridge, Bowl, Ivy, Green Top, Nude Stem 50.00
Cambridge, Bowl, Mayonnaise, Underplate, Chantilly 22.50
Cambridge, Bowl, Nappy, Cherry Blossom, Green, Small 6.00
Cambridge, Bowl, Nude Stem Wine, Amber 45.00
Cambridge, Bowl, Opaque Azurite, 12 In. 40.00
Cambridge, Bowl, Opaque Black Ebony, 12 In. 30.00
Cambridge, Bowl, Pink Caprice, 12 1/2 In.Diameter 75.00
Cambridge, Bowl, Pink, Gold Dore Holder 85.00
Cambridge, Bowl, Primrose Yellow, Honeycomb, Footed, 9 3/4 In. 27.50
Cambridge, Bowl, Primrose, 8 In. 27.00
Cambridge, Bowl, Rosepoint, Crown Tuscan, Gold Etched, 12 In. 110.00
Cambridge, Bowl, Rosepoint, Deep Scallops, 12 In. 28.00
Cambridge, Bowl, Rosepoint, Handled, 6 In. 40.00
Cambridge, Bowl, Rosepoint, 4 Footed, 11 In. 37.00
Cambridge, Bowl, Rubina, Footed, 9 1/2 In. 225.00
Cambridge, Bowl, Rubina, Signed, 10 In. 150.00
Cambridge, Bowl, Salad, Alpine, Crystal 20.00
Cambridge, Bowl, Seashell Pattern, 3 Toed, Crown Tuscan, Signed, 10 In. 65.00
Cambridge, Bowl, Shell, Crown Tuscan, 10 1/2 In. 50.00
Cambridge, Bowl, Sherbet, Swirl, Ultramarine 3.00
Cambridge, Bowl, Vaseline, Honeycomb, Footed Flared, 9 3/4 In. 20.00
Cambridge, Bowl, Wheatsheaf, 9 In. 15.00
Cambridge, Bowl, Willow Blue, Ivory, 10 In. 285.00
Cambridge, Bowl, 2 Handled, No.3500, 10 In. 35.00
Cambridge, Bowl, 4 Toed, Cross-Like Shape, Crown Tuscan, 12 1/4 To 7 In. 47.50
Cambridge, Box, Candy, Carmen, Square Pattern, Covered, 7 In. 58.00
Cambridge, Box, Candy, 3 Compartment, Covered, Crown Tuscan, 8 In. 49.00
Cambridge, Box, Cigarette, Caprice Alpine, Blue 46.50
Cambridge, Box, Cigarette, Crown Tuscan, Dolphin Feet 28.00
Cambridge, Box, Covered, Crown Tuscan, Seashell Pattern, Floral, 2 1/2 X 3 1/2 ...... 45.00

Cambridge, Box, Crown Tuscan, Cover, Dolphin Feet, Pink, 2 X 5 In. 37.50
Cambridge, Box, Crown Tuscan, Seashell, Dolphin Feet, 4 X 5 In. 45.00
Cambridge, Brandy, Amethyst, Nude Stem, 1 Oz. 45.00
Cambridge, Brandy, Nude Stem, Carmen Top 45.00
Cambridge, Brandy, Nude Stem, Green Top 45.00
Cambridge, Bucket, Ice, Green, Etched Florals 22.00
Cambridge, Bucket, Ice, Rosepoint 35.00
Cambridge, Butter, Diane, No.3400 .... 45.00
Cambridge, Butter, Fernland, Green 40.00
Cambridge, Candleholder, Crown Tuscan, Nude 75.00
Cambridge, Candleholder, Dolphin, Emerald, 9 1/2 In., Pair 145.00
Cambridge, Candleholder, Dolphin, Mount Vernon, 9 1/2 In., Pair 95.00
Cambridge, Candleholder, Double, Emerald Green, Pair 45.00
Cambridge, Candleholder, Double, Primrose, Ruby Flashed, Pair 35.00
Cambridge, Candleholder, Moonlight Blue, 2 Light, 6 In., Pair 20.00
Cambridge, Candleholder, Moonlight Blue, 3-Arm 38.00
Cambridge, Candleholder, Nude Stem, 9 In. 80.00
Cambridge, Candleholder, Pristine, Double 18.00
Cambridge, Candleholder, Ramshead Bowl, Peach Blow 180.00
Cambridge, Candleholder, 2 Light, Etched Rosepoint, Crystal, Pair 35.00
Cambridge, Candlestick, Amber Ring, Single 25.00
Cambridge, Candlestick, Caprice Alpine, Single, Clear, Pair 38.00
Cambridge, Candlestick, Caprice, 3 Light, Crystal 17.50
Cambridge, Candlestick, Chantilly, Short 15.00
Cambridge, Candlestick, Crown Tuscan, Nude Lady, 9 In. 140.00
Cambridge, Candlestick, Crown Tuscan, Ram's Head, 4 1/2 In., Pair 250.00
Cambridge, Candlestick, Crown Tuscan, 3 1/4 In., Pair 32.00
Cambridge, Candlestick, Crucifix, Clear, 10 In., Pair 40.00
Cambridge, Candlestick, Dolphin, Mt.Vernon, Dark Amber 48.00
Cambridge, Candlestick, Ebony, Doric Column, Pair 100.00
Cambridge, Candlestick, Gadroon, Carmen, 6 In., Pair 42.00
Cambridge, Candlestick, Ivory 30.00
Cambridge, Candlestick, Jade Twisted, Pair 40.00
Cambridge, Candlestick, Removable Bobeches Base, Etched, Prisms, Pair 125.00
Cambridge, Candlestick, Ritz, Blue, 9 1/2 In., Pair 40.00
Cambridge, Candlestick, Rosepoint, Separate Ring & Prism Inserts, 7 In., Pair 65.00
Cambridge, Candlestick, Rubina, 7 In., Pair 135.00
Cambridge, Candlestick, Twist Stem, Amber, 8 1/2 In., Pair 25.00
Cambridge, Candlestick, 2 Light, Crown Tuscan 32.50
Cambridge, Candlestick, 3 Light, Pair 25.00
Cambridge, Candy, Caprice, Lid 15.00
Cambridge, Centerpiece, Amber, Decagon, Etched Cleo, Signed 30.00
Cambridge, Champagne, Cobalt, Nudes Banquet 45.00
Cambridge, Champagne, Long Stem, No.3500 .... 18.00
Cambridge, Champagne, Rosepoint 14.00
Cambridge, Cheese Set, Plate 12 In., Pedestal Dish, Rosepoint 35.00
Cambridge, Cigarette Set, Caprice, Clear, Covered Box, 4 Footed Ashtrays 30.00
Cambridge, Coaster, Rosepoint 23.75
Cambridge, Cocktail Set, Farber Chrome Shaker, 6 Green Cocktails 30.00
Cambridge, Cocktail Shaker, Diane 47.50
Cambridge, Cocktail, Carmen, Nude Stem, 3 Ounce 65.00
Cambridge, Cocktail, Crystal Nude Stem, Blue Flared Top 49.00
Cambridge, Cocktail, Ebony Nude Stem, Crystal Top 49.00
Cambridge, Compote, Amber, Chrome Holder, 5 In. 25.00
Cambridge, Compote, Azurite, Decorated 37.50
Cambridge, Compote, Candy, Nude Stem, Farber, Amethyst Insert 42.00
Cambridge, Compote, Carmen Top, Nude Stem 75.00
Cambridge, Compote, Crown Tuscan, Flying Nude, 12 X 9 In. 175.00
Cambridge, Compote, Crown Tuscan, Footed, Seashell, 7 In. 30.00
Cambridge, Compote, Crown Tuscan, Nude Stem, Shell Top, Gold, Roses, 5 1/2 In. 79.00
Cambridge, Compote, Crown Tuscan, Roses, Gold, Ship Scene, 7 1/2 In. 70.00
Cambridge, Compote, Crown Tuscan, Shell Footed, 9 In. 55.00
Cambridge, Compote, Crown Tuscan, Shell, Nude Stem, Gold Trim .... 120.00 To 125.00
Cambridge, Compote, Crystal Nude Stem 65.00
Cambridge, Compote, Diane, Etched, 5 1/2 In. 20.00

Cambridge, Compote, Diane, 4 Feet, 6 In.	12.00
Cambridge, Compote, Emerald Green, Clear Nude Stem, 8 1/4 X 7 In.	74.00
Cambridge, Compote, Etched Diane, Sterling Silver Holder	30.00
Cambridge, Compote, Etched Gloria, Clear Stem, Green Bowl	25.00
Cambridge, Compote, Etched, Gold, Ebony, No.532, 6 1/2 In., Pair	65.00
Cambridge, Compote, Gilded Rosepoint, 5 1/4 X 3 In.	30.00
Cambridge, Compote, Glass Covered, Red, Pagoda Shape, 8 1/2 In.	75.00
Cambridge, Compote, Helio, 6 1/2 In.	48.50
Cambridge, Compote, Honeycomb Pattern, Rolled Edge, Rubena, 7 X 3 1/2 In.	75.00
Cambridge, Compote, Mandarin, Gold Nude, 8 In.	150.00
Cambridge, Compote, Metal Nude Stem, Green, Signed Farber	42.50
Cambridge, Compote, Moonlight Blue, Gadroon, Tall	19.50
Cambridge, Compote, Nude Stem, Gold Hair & Trim, 8 In.	125.00
Cambridge, Compote, Nude Stem, Shell Top, 8 In.	120.00
Cambridge, Compote, Nude, Seashell Top, Rose Decoration, Crown Tuscan, 8 In.	125.00
Cambridge, Compote, Orchid, Plume Stem, 5 1/4 In.	45.00
Cambridge, Compote, Portia, Footed, 3 X 5 1/2 In.	25.00
Cambridge, Compote, Primrose, Gold Stripe On Rim, 10 3/4 In.	25.00
Cambridge, Compote, Red Amberina, Farber	35.00
Cambridge, Compote, Rosepoint, Amber	22.00
Cambridge, Compote, Rosepoint, No.3121, 5 1/4 In.	19.90
Cambridge, Compote, Rosepoint, Tall Ring Stem	45.00
Cambridge, Compote, Rubena, Honeycomb Pattern	69.00
Cambridge, Compote, Seashell, Footed, Crown Tuscan, 6 1/4 In.	37.50
Cambridge, Compote, Tricolor, Rubena	115.00
Cambridge, Condiment Set, Amethyst, No.3400, Farber Chrome, 5 Piece	24.00
Cambridge, Console Set, Apple Blossom, Amber, 3 Piece	32.00
Cambridge, Console Set, Black, Heavy Gold Trim, 3 Piece	75.00
Cambridge, Console Set, Bowl & Pair Of Candleholders, Crown Tuscan	250.00
Cambridge, Console Set, Caprice, Alpine Blue, Prism Candlesticks	40.00
Cambridge, Console Set, Etched Bowl, Keyhole Candlesticks, Yellow, 3 Piece	37.00
Cambridge, Console Set, Pair Candlesticks & Center Bowl, Jade	69.00 To 95.00
Cambridge, Console Set, Rosepoint, Footed Bowl, 2 Arm Candleholders	80.00
Cambridge, Cordial Set, Amethyst Ball Shape, Farberware Holder, 7 Piece	55.00
Cambridge, Cordial, Honey Top, Nude Stem	65.00
Cambridge, Cornucopia, Crown Tuscan, 3 In.	15.00 To 24.00
Cambridge, Creamer, Caprice	6.00
Cambridge, Creamer, Child's, Colonial Green	22.00
Cambridge, Creamer, Colonial	9.00
Cambridge, Creamer, Fernland, Child's Green	30.00
Cambridge, Creamer, Fernland, Cobalt Blue	30.00
Cambridge, Creamer, Fernland, Green	18.00
Cambridge, Creamer, Rosepoint, Individual, No.3500-15	12.00
Cambridge, Cruet Set, Ball Shape, Farber Holders & Tray, Set	32.00
Cambridge, Cruet Set, Crystal, Caprice, 3 Piece	12.50
Cambridge, Cruet, Caprice, Clear, Original Stopper	18.00
Cambridge, Cup & Saucer, Clear Cup, Black Saucer	150.00
Cambridge, Cup & Saucer, Pink, Square Saucer	5.50
Cambridge, Cup & Saucer, Rosepoint, Gold Decoration, Miniature	30.00
Cambridge, Cup, Tea, Portia, Etched	12.95
Cambridge, Decanter Set, Barrel & Mugs, Amber, Black Amethyst Tray, 14 Piece	75.00
Cambridge, Decanter Set, Melon Rib, Amber, No.1369, 7 Piece	55.00
Cambridge, Decanter, Amethyst, Farberware Holder	20.00
Cambridge, Dish, Candy, Cover, Cleo, Green	47.50
Cambridge, Dish, Candy, Crown Tuscan, Covered, Sectional	45.00
Cambridge, Dish, Candy, Crown Tuscan, Seashell, Covered, 6 In.	50.00
Cambridge, Dish, Candy, Crown Tuscan, 3 Sided, 3 Handled, Gold Etching	75.00
Cambridge, Dish, Candy, Mt.Vernon, Amber, Lidded	22.00
Cambridge, Dish, Candy, Rosepoint, Gold Encrusted, Covered, 7 In.	30.00
Cambridge, Dish, Candy, Rosepoint, Three Part, Gold Encrusted, Covered, 8 In.	55.00
Cambridge, Dish, Candy, Triplex, Lid	45.00
Cambridge, Dish, Footed, Etched Pattern, 7 1/2 In.	18.00
Cambridge, Dish, Footed, Seashell, Hand-Painted Roses, Crown Tuscan, 7 1/2 In.	35.00
Cambridge, Dish, Mayonnaise, Rosepoint	19.00
Cambridge, Dish, Nut, Caprice, Crystal, 2 1/2 In.	3.50

Cambridge, Dish, Nut, Footed, Crown Tuscan, 3 In. 18.00
Cambridge, Dish, Ornate Handles, Green, 11 In. 12.00
Cambridge, Dish, Pin, Floral, Crown Tuscan, 5 In. 20.00
Cambridge, Dish, Pink, Crown Tuscan, Scallop Shell, 7 1/2 In. 25.00
Cambridge, Dish, Pink, Floral Decoration, Crown Tuscan, 5 In. 17.00
Cambridge, Dish, Relish, Rosepoint, 3 Section, Handles, Footed, 12 X 8 X 2 In. 32.00
Cambridge, Dish, Royal Blue, 3 Handled, 3 Sections 14.00
Cambridge, Dish, Sweetmeat, Turkey Cover, Pink, Dianthus, 8 In. 225.00
Cambridge, Dish, Turkey Cover, 7 1/2 In. .... 45.00 To 68.00
Cambridge, Dish, 3-Handled, 3 Sections, Signed, Royal Blue 14.00
Cambridge, Figurine, Crown Tuscan Dolphin, 5 In., Pair 100.00
Cambridge, Figurine, Geisha, Amber, Different Hair Style, 11 In., Pair 300.00
Cambridge, Figurine, Goose Girl, Large 37.00
Cambridge, Figurine, Swan, Clear, Marked, 5 1/2 In. 20.00
Cambridge, Figurine, Swan, Crown Tuscan, Bent Over Neck, Paper Label, 4 In. 42.00
Cambridge, Figurine, Swan, Pink, 3 X 2 In. 18.00
Cambridge, Figurine, Swan, Signed Ebony, 3 In. 32.00
Cambridge, Figurine, Swan, Signed, 3 1/2 In. 16.00
Cambridge, Flower Holder & Bowl, Pink, Bashful Charlotte, 12 1/2 In. 145.00
Cambridge, Flower Holder, Amber, Two Children, 9 In. 145.00
Cambridge, Flower Holder, Bashful Charlotte, Apple Green, 9 In. 75.00
Cambridge, Flower Holder, Bashful Charlotte, Clear, 6 In. 38.00
Cambridge, Flower Holder, Bashful Charlotte, Clear, 6 1/2 In. 35.00
Cambridge, Flower Holder, Bashful Charlotte, Clear, 6 3/4 In. 35.00
Cambridge, Flower Holder, Bashful Charlotte, Pink, 8 1/2 In. 50.00
Cambridge, Flower Holder, Bashful Charlotte, 11 In. 65.00
Cambridge, Flower Holder, Bashful Maiden, Mandarin Gold, 13 In. 175.00
Cambridge, Flower Holder, Draped Lady, 13 In. 47.00
Cambridge, Flower Holder, Full Figure Girl In Clear Glass, 8 3/4 In. 45.00
Cambridge, Flower Holder, Green, Bashful Charlotte, 9 In. 85.00
Cambridge, Flower Holder, Green, September Morn, 11 In. 100.00
Cambridge, Flower Holder, Gull, 9 1/2 In. 28.00
Cambridge, Flower Holder, Heron 65.00
Cambridge, Flower Holder, Lady With Roses, Custard, 9 3/4 In. 175.00
Cambridge, Flower Holder, Pink, Bashful Charlotte, Marked, 9 In. 50.00
Cambridge, Flower Holder, Seagull, 9 3/4 In. 35.00
Cambridge, Flower Holder, Two Children, Amber, 9 In. 145.00
Cambridge, Flower Holder, Two Children, Green, 9 In. 125.00
Cambridge, Glass, Ice Tea, Rosepoint, Footed 21.50
Cambridge, Goblet, Banquet, Nude Stem, Carmen Top 120.00
Cambridge, Goblet, Caprice, Blue, Stemmed, 7 3/4 In. 12.00
Cambridge, Goblet, Caprice, Pink Bowl, Green Stem 16.00
Cambridge, Goblet, Cobalt, Nudes Banquet 65.00
Cambridge, Goblet, Etched Rosepoint 20.00
Cambridge, Goblet, Gold Encrusted, Diane Carmen 16.00
Cambridge, Goblet, Gold Encrusted, Portia Carmen 16.00
Cambridge, Goblet, Rosepoint Etching, Long Stem, 10 Oz. 16.00
Cambridge, Goblet, Stem, Rosepoint, 5 1/4 In. 16.00
Cambridge, Goblet, Tempo 12.50
Cambridge, Ice Bucket, Rosepoint 75.00
Cambridge, Ivy Ball, Amber, Clear Keyhole Stem 25.00
Cambridge, Ivy Ball, Amethyst, Crystal Keyhole Stem 33.00
Cambridge, Ivy Ball, Amethyst, Farberware Nude Lady Stem 40.00
Cambridge, Ivy Ball, Black, Clear Keyhole Stem 45.00
Cambridge, Ivy Ball, Carmen, Nude Lady Stem 65.00
Cambridge, Ivy Ball, Clear, Nude Stem 70.00
Cambridge, Ivy Ball, Cobalt Ring Stem 30.00
Cambridge, Ivy Ball, Crown Tuscan, Ring Stem, 8 1/4 In. 30.00
Cambridge, Ivy Ball, Crown Tuscan, 8 3/4 In., Pair 120.00
Cambridge, Ivy Ball, Mandarin Gold, Ring Stem 22.00
Cambridge, Ivy Ball, Melon, Ebony, Clear Key Stem 47.50
Cambridge, Ivy Ball, Nude Lady, Royal Blue, 9 1/2 In. 85.00
Cambridge, Ivy Ball, Nude Stem, Clear 70.00
Cambridge, Ivy Ball, Optic, Ring Stem, Apple Green, 8 1/2 In. 22.00
Cambridge, Ivy Ball, Royal Blue, Ring Stem, 8 1/2 In. 35.00

Cambridge, **Ivy,** Ball, Purple Ring Stem 35.00
Cambridge, **Jug,** Ale, Rosso Antiqua, Gold Coat-Of-Arms, 7 In. 225.00
Cambridge, **Jug,** Ball, Amethyst, Ice Lip, 80 Ounce 25.00
Cambridge, **Jug,** Ball, Apple Green, 80 Ounces 22.00
Cambridge, **Jug,** Ball, Carmen 35.00
Cambridge, **Jug,** Ball, Royal Blue, Crystal Handle, Ice-Lipped, 80 Ounces 75.00
Cambridge, **Jug,** Elaine, 80 Ounce 50.00
Cambridge, **Jug,** Ice, Tilt, Ebony, No.5400 .... 38.00
Cambridge, **Jug,** Tilt, Amber, 80 Oz., No.3400 .... 20.00
Cambridge, **Lamp,** Buddha, Topaz 150.00
Cambridge, **Lamp,** Dresser, Orange & Black, Signed Sterling, Pair 65.00
Cambridge, **Lamp,** Wildflower Vase, No.278, 11 In. 150.00
Cambridge, **Luncheon Set,** Tally Ho, Carmen, 23 Piece 110.00
Cambridge, **Mayonnaise Set,** Caprice, 3 Piece 12.00
Cambridge, **Mayonnaise Set,** Decagon, Clear, 2 Piece 12.00
Cambridge, **Mayonnaise Set,** Rosepoint, 3 Piece 38.00
Cambridge, **Mug,** Carmen, Tally Ho, 14 Oz. 22.00
Cambridge, **Pail,** Ice, Etched Chrysanthemum, Bail Handle, No.1121 .... 18.00
Cambridge, **Parfait,** Rosepoint 16.00
Cambridge, **Pencil Holder,** Dog, Green, Original Label 19.00
Cambridge, **Pencil Holder,** Dog, Yellow 24.00
Cambridge, **Pencil Holder,** Figural, Dog, Amber 14.00
Cambridge, **Pitcher,** Cobalt, Clear Handle, Ice Lip 45.00
Cambridge, **Pitcher,** Ice Lip, Carmen, Red 40.00
Cambridge, **Pitcher,** Ruby With Clear Handle 65.00
Cambridge, **Pitcher,** Tankard, Snowflake, Quart 16.75
Cambridge, **Pitcher,** Water, Nautilus, Clear Applied Handle 50.00
Cambridge, **Pitcher,** Water, Snowflake 16.75
Cambridge, **Pitcher,** 80 Oz., Amber 18.00
Cambridge, **Plate,** Amber, Etched, Marked, 8 In. 7.50
Cambridge, **Plate,** Apple Blossom, 12 In. 15.00
Cambridge, **Plate,** Blue Caprice, 8 1/2 In. 5.00
Cambridge, **Plate,** Cake, Blue Caprice, Footed 12.00
Cambridge, **Plate,** Cake, Rosepoint 26.75
Cambridge, **Plate,** Carmen, 8 In. 8.00
Cambridge, **Plate,** Carmen, 13 In. 45.00
Cambridge, **Plate,** Caprice, Torte, Black, 14 In. 28.00
Cambridge, **Plate,** Caprice, Torte, Footed, 12 In. 7.00
Cambridge, **Plate,** Cobalt, Signed, 8 In. 25.00
Cambridge, **Plate,** Ebony, Etched, 2 Handles, 7 In. 18.00
Cambridge, **Plate,** Ebony, 8 In. 5.00
Cambridge, **Plate,** Everglades, Blue, Oval, Footed, 14 1/2 In. 20.00
Cambridge, **Plate,** Everglades, Water Lilies, Crystal, 13 1/2 In. 27.50
Cambridge, **Plate,** Red Square, 11 In. 17.00
Cambridge, **Plate,** Rosepoint, 2 Handled, 8 In. 21.00
Cambridge, **Plate,** Rosepoint, 7 1/2 In. 10.00
Cambridge, **Plate,** Salad, Rosepoint, Encrusted Gold, 8 1/2 In. 18.00
Cambridge, **Plate,** Shell, Crown Tuscan, Roses, Gold Trim, 14 In. 120.00
Cambridge, **Plate,** Torte, Caprice, Blue, 14 In. 14.00
Cambridge, **Plate,** 10 Sided, Light Blue 4.00
Cambridge, **Platter,** 2 Handled, No.3400/35, 11 In. 32.00
Cambridge, **Punch Set,** Feather Pattern, Bowl, Eight Cups, Signed Near-Cut 110.00
Cambridge, **Relish,** Caprice, Oval 12.00
Cambridge, **Relish,** Diane, Divided, Sterling Silver Pedestal 22.00
Cambridge, **Relish,** Divided, Apple Blossoms Etched, Keyhole Handle 15.00
Cambridge, **Relish,** Red, Divided, 12 In. 36.00
Cambridge, **Relish,** Rosepoint, Gadroon Border, 3 Sections, Footed, 12 In. 33.00
Cambridge, **Relish,** Rosepoint, 2 Part, 6 In. 20.00
Cambridge, **Relish,** Rosepoint, 3 Sections, Handled, 8 In. 25.00
Cambridge, **Relish,** Seashell, Footed, 3 Sections, Crown Tuscan, 9 In. 62.50
Cambridge, **Rose Bowl,** Caprice, Moonlight Blue, 8 In. 50.00
Cambridge, **Salt & Pepper,** Amber, Ball Shape 22.00
Cambridge, **Salt & Pepper,** Amethyst, Farber Holders 7.00
Cambridge, **Salt & Pepper,** Chantilly 20.00
Cambridge, **Salt & Pepper,** Rosepoint .... 14.50 To 40.00

Cambridge, Saltshaker, Chantilly, Handled 10.00
Cambridge, Saltshaker, Crystal, Footed, Marked 5.00
Cambridge, Saltshaker, Rosepoint 13.00
Cambridge, Seashell, Crown Tuscan, Decorated, Oval, 8 In. 40.00
Cambridge, Seashell, Crown Tuscan, Roses, Seaside Scene, Pedestal, 9 X 6 In. 50.00
Cambridge, Seashell, 5 3/4 In., Pair 75.00
Cambridge, Shaker, Cocktail, Farber Chrome, 6 Green Cocktails, Set 26.00
Cambridge, Sherbet, Caprice 9.00
Cambridge, Sherbet, Etched Portia, Regency Stem 15.00
Cambridge, Sherbet, Rosepoint, No.3500, 4 3/4 In. 14.00
Cambridge, Soup Set, Carmen, 6 Soups & Underplates, 12 Piece 60.00
Cambridge, Spooner, Child's, Colonial, Cobalt 20.00
Cambridge, Spooner, Child's, Colonial, Green 22.00
Cambridge, Spooner, Child's, Fernland, Green 30.00
Cambridge, Spooner, Cobalt 30.00
Cambridge, Spooner, Colonial, Miniature 12.50
Cambridge, Stein, Dark Green, 14 Ounces, Tally Ho 15.00
Cambridge, Sugar & Creamer, Amethyst Nautilus 34.00
Cambridge, Sugar & Creamer, Caprice, Clear 12.00
Cambridge, Sugar & Creamer, Chantilly 20.00
Cambridge, Sugar & Creamer, Chantilly, Sterling Footed, Individual 27.50
Cambridge, Sugar & Creamer, Child's, Tappan, Green 24.00
Cambridge, Sugar & Creamer, Daffodil 18.00
Cambridge, Sugar & Creamer, Decagon, Ebony 16.00
Cambridge, Sugar & Creamer, King Edward, Sterling Silver Bases 42.50
Cambridge, Sugar & Creamer, Portia 30.00
Cambridge, Sugar & Creamer, Portia, Individual 30.00
Cambridge, Sugar & Creamer, With Tray, Individual, Caprice 15.00
Cambridge, Sugar & Creamer, With Tray, Pink, Cambridge, Signed 25.00
Cambridge, Sugar, Caprice, Crystal 6.00
Cambridge, Sugar, Caprice, Individual, Footed, Blue 5.00
Cambridge, Swan, Amberina, Signed, 3 In. 65.00
Cambridge, Swan, Apple Green, Signed, 8 In. 60.00
Cambridge, Swan, Apple Green, Triangle C Mark, 3 1/2 In. 25.00
Cambridge, Swan, Black Amethyst, 10 3/4 In. 185.00
Cambridge, Swan, Black, Signed, 10 In. 195.00
Cambridge, Swan, Black, 6 1/2 In. 105.00
Cambridge, Swan, Carmen, 3 1/2 In. 100.00
Cambridge, Swan, Clear, Frosted, Signed, 8 In. 79.00
Cambridge, Swan, Clear, Marked, 3 1/2 X 2 In. 10.00
Cambridge, Swan, Clear, 6 In. 30.00
Cambridge, Swan, Clear, 9 In. 40.00
Cambridge, Swan, Crown Tuscan, Gold Trim, 8 3/4 In. 122.00
Cambridge, Swan, Crown Tuscan, 3 1/2 In. 28.00
Cambridge, Swan, Crystal, Painted Roses, Leaves Trimmed In Gold, 13 1/2 In. 175.00
Cambridge, Swan, Crystal, Satin Finish, Triangle C Mark, 9 In. 75.00
Cambridge, Swan, Crystal, Signed, 3 In. .... 15.00 To 16.00
Cambridge, Swan, Crystal, 4 1/2 In. 15.00
Cambridge, Swan, Diane, Apple Green, 4 1/2 In. 42.00
Cambridge, Swan, Ebony, 3 In. 45.00
Cambridge, Swan, Ebony, 3 1/2 In. 45.00
Cambridge, Swan, Ebony, 8 1/2 In. 35.00
Cambridge, Swan, Emerald Green, Signed, 12 In. 135.00
Cambridge, Swan, Mandarin Gold, 3 In. 22.00
Cambridge, Swan, Peachblow, 2 1/2 In. 22.00
Cambridge, Swan, Peachblow, 6 1/2 In. 41.00
Cambridge, Swan, Pink, Signed, 3 1/2 In. 24.00
Cambridge, Swan, White Milk Glass, Paper Label, 4 1/2 In. 45.00
Cambridge, Syrup, Rosepoint 38.50
Cambridge, Tile, Ribbon & Shell, Mottled Green, 8 In. 20.00
Cambridge, Tile, Rose Pattern In Relief, Glossy Wine Color, 6 In., Square 35.00
Cambridge, Toothpick, Crown Tuscan, Coney Island, 1905 .... 25.00
Cambridge, Toothpick, Feather 12.00
Cambridge, Tray, Clover Shaped, Black, Handled, Signed 11.00
Cambridge, Tray, Oval, Handled 25.00

Cambridge, Tray, Playing Card Design, Pink, Keyhole Handle 15.00
Cambridge, Tray, Relish, Etched Apple Blossom, Keyhole Handle, Divided 15.00
Cambridge, Tray, Sandwich, Clear, Etched, Gold Encrusted Portia 30.00
Cambridge, Tray, Sandwich, Green, Handled, No.732, 10 In. 12.00
Cambridge, Tray, Sandwich, Handled, Green, No.732, 10 In. 12.00
Cambridge, Tumbler Set, Rosepoint, Footed, 10 Oz., 7 In., Set Of 3 .... 20.00
Cambridge, Tumbler, Caprice, Footed 11.50
Cambridge, Tumbler, Cordial, Cut & Engraved, Carmen Foot, 3 3/4 In. 6.00
Cambridge, Tumbler, Everglades, Footed, 5 1/2 In. 6.00
Cambridge, Tumbler, Georgian, Light Green, C In Triangle 6.50
Cambridge, Tumbler, Imperial Hunt, Tally-Ho Blanks, Green, Footed 35.00
Cambridge, Tumbler, Mt.Vernon 6.50
Cambridge, Tumbler, No.9403 .... 16.00
Cambridge, Tumbler, Rosepoint, Footed, 5 Oz. 22.00
Cambridge, Tumbler, Tally Ho, Cobalt, 1 1/2 In. 9.95
Cambridge, Urn, Cobalt, Mt.Vernon, 8 In. 30.00
Cambridge, Vase, Apple Green, Ring Stem, 10 In., Pair 39.00
Cambridge, Vase, Berry Decoration, Handled, Artist Signed M.S., 8 In. 175.00
Cambridge, Vase, Bud, Chantilly 30.00
Cambridge, Vase, Bud, Clear, Pedestal, 10 In. 10.00
Cambridge, Vase, Bud, Crown Tuscan, Roses, Gold Decoration, 10 In. 50.00
Cambridge, Vase, Bud, Etched Primrose, Footed, Pink, Pair 17.50
Cambridge, Vase, Bud, Red, Nude Stem 135.00
Cambridge, Vase, Caprice, Moonlight, Pastel Blue, 4 In. 15.00
Cambridge, Vase, Chantilly, 8 In. .... 45.00 To 50.00
Cambridge, Vase, Chantilly, 10 In. 32.00
Cambridge, Vase, Cobalt, Clear Foot, 8 In. 7.00
Cambridge, Vase, Cobalt, Globe, 6 1/2 In. 45.00
Cambridge, Vase, Cornucopia, Crown Tuscan, 10 In. 40.00
Cambridge, Vase, Cornucopia, Shell Foot, Crown Tuscan, Pair 85.00
Cambridge, Vase, Crown Tuscan, Conch Shell 75.00
Cambridge, Vase, Crown Tuscan, Diamond Peg, Fan Shape, 8 1/2 In. 25.00
Cambridge, Vase, Crown Tuscan, Gold, Hand-Painted Flowers, 12 In. 90.00
Cambridge, Vase, Crown Tuscan, Rosepoint Pattern, 10 In. 85.00
Cambridge, Vase, Crown Tuscan, 4-Shell Pebble Base, 10 In. 125.00
Cambridge, Vase, Crystal, Gold Encrusted, Footed 12.50
Cambridge, Vase, Diane, 11 In. 55.00
Cambridge, Vase, Festoon Drape, Cobalt Blue, 9 In. 37.00
Cambridge, Vase, Horn Of Plenty, Signed, Pair 19.00
Cambridge, Vase, Japonica, B.23-2-3, 11 In. 260.00
Cambridge, Vase, Keyhole Base, Forest Green 25.00
Cambridge, Vase, Morning Glory, Etched, 11 In. 23.00
Cambridge, Vase, Optic Ring, Stemmed, Amber, 10 In. 20.00
Cambridge, Vase, Optic Ring, Stemmed, Belled, Crystal, 10 In. 15.00
Cambridge, Vase, Peacock Etching, Ebony, No.736, 9 In. 50.00
Cambridge, Vase, Pearl Green, 6 In. 12.50
Cambridge, Vase, Portia, Green, No.1308, 6 In. 20.00
Cambridge, Vase, Primrose, Gold Encrusted Band, 8 In. 68.00
Cambridge, Vase, Rosepoint, 13 1/2 X 6 1/4 In. 50.00
Cambridge, Vase, Satin Finish, Crystal, 4 1/2 In. 13.50
Cambridge, Vase, Stick, Pair, 10 In. 40.00
Cambridge, Vase, Trumpet, Red, 10 In. 135.00
Cambridge, Vase, Wildflower, Gold Encrusted, No.279, 13 1/2 In. 60.00
Cambridge, Vinegar & Oil, Amethyst, With Tray, Farber 20.00
Cambridge, Vinegar & Oil, Pepper & Salt With Tray, Amethyst 30.00
Cambridge, Water Set, Cobalt, 6 Piece 68.00
Cambridge, Water Set, Pattee Cross, 6 Piece 75.00
Cambridge, Wine Set, Amethyst, Farberware Decanter 45.00
Cambridge, Wine, Black Nude Stem, Clear Bowl, 6 1/2 In. 40.00
Cambridge, Wine, Tally Ho, 1 Dozen 95.00

Cameo glass was made in layers in much the same manner as a cameo in jewelry.
Part of the top layer of glass was cut away to reveal a different colored

glass beneath. The most famous cameo glass was made during the nineteenth century.

Cameo, Bottle, Perfume, English, Lay-Down, Citron & Gold, 7 In.	950.00
Cameo, Bottle, Perfume, English, Lay-Down, 9 In.	1150.00
Cameo, Box, French, Lidded, Cranberry, Frosted White & Gold, 3 1/8 In.At Base	192.00
Cameo, Bucket, Ice, Leaves, Frosted White, Lavender, Purple, Gold, 5 X 8 In.	450.00
Cameo, Flask, English, Lay-Down, Lid, Floral, Intaglio Cut Insect, Marked	895.00
Cameo, Goblet, French, Green, 6 In.	39.00
Cameo, Lamp Base, Floral & Leaf Pattern, Dark & Light Orange, 9 5/8 In.	225.00
Cameo, Tumbler, Orange Translucent, Brown Trees, Acid Cuttings, Lamiral	175.00
Cameo, Vase, Acid Cut, Green & Dark Yellow, Pear Shaped, 11 In.	175.00
Cameo, Vase, Acid Cutback, L.Cie St.Denis, France, 7 1/2 In.	125.00
Cameo, Vase, Baulster Shape, Water Scene, Blue On Frosted Ground, 5 3/4 In.	650.00
Cameo, Vase, Blue Deco Design On White Frosted Background, 19 1/2 In.	350.00
Cameo, Vase, Blue Frosted, Foliage & Pine Cone Cameo, Oval, 7 In.	875.00
Cameo, Vase, Cabinet, Ivy & Tendrils, Pebbly Surface, Brown, Orange, Yellow	175.00
Cameo, Vase, Chateau On Cove, Mountains, Vines, Acid Cutting, Pink, Blue, Yellow	645.00
Cameo, Vase, Clipper Ship, Rocks, Flying Birds, Layered Over 4 Colors, 16 In.	325.00
Cameo, Vase, Enameled Sunflowers, Frosted Finish, Gilting, 13 In.	195.00
Cameo, Vase, English, Acorns & Oak Leaves, Double Bands, Green, Signed, 5 In.	650.00
Cameo, Vase, English, Carved Acorn & Oak Leaves, Signed Cameo, 4 1/2 In.	650.00
Cameo, Vase, English, Floral, Vines, Leaves, Red, Chartreuse, 4 1/2 In.	675.00
Cameo, Vase, English, Raspberry Red, White Carving, Ovoid Shape, 6 In.	2500.00
Cameo, Vase, Flask Shape, Frosted Blue, Purple Flowers, 3 1/4 In.	450.00
Cameo, Vase, Floral Vine Over Pond, Carmel Color, 12 In.	675.00
Cameo, Vase, Florentine, Bridge, Trees, Gold, Pinched, 8 1/2 In.	150.00
Cameo, Vase, French, Fish Scene, Frosted, Seaweed Decoration, Nancea, 5 1/8 In.	350.00
Cameo, Vase, French, Windmill Scene, Signed, 6 In.	275.00
Cameo, Vase, Frosted Green, Allover Green Leaf, 5 3/4 In.	290.00
Cameo, Vase, Frosted Mottled Pink, Landscape, Acid Cutting, 16 1/2 In.	645.00
Cameo, Vase, Frosted Turquoise, Purple Leaves & Boughs, 3 1/4 In.	475.00
Cameo, Vase, Geometric Candy Cane, Mottled Camphor, Orange, Signed, 18 1/2 In.	450.00
Cameo, Vase, Gold Ducks & Cattails On Amber Ground, 6 In.	150.00
Cameo, Vase, Gold Ducks, Cattails, Bulbous With Gold, Flared Neck, 6 X 4 In.	150.00
Cameo, Vase, Lilac Flowers On Frosted Amethyst, 3 In.	325.00
Cameo, Vase, Maroon Over Blue, Two-Colored Cameo, 6 In.	650.00
Cameo, Vase, Orange & Brown Floral, Signed	425.00
Cameo, Vase, Oval, Blue Frosted, Foliage & Pine Cones In Amber, 7 In.	875.00
Cameo, Vase, Purple Berries, Acid-Finished White Ground, Ovoid, Signed, 12 In.	325.00
Cameo, Vase, Rabbits In Snow, 3 Colors, Arsall, 8 In.	650.00
Cameo, Vase, Roses, Leaves, Branches, Mottled Green To Chartreuse, D'aurys	235.00
Cameo, Vase, Sailboats, Translucent Frosted Green Ground, T.Michel, 3 1/4 In.	265.00
Cameo, Vase, Wheel Cut, Green To Frosted To Clear, Tulips, Erlebach, 6 In.	250.00
Cameo, Vase, Yellow, Orange Frosted, Carved Florals, Signed Peynaud, 2 1/2 In.	185.00
Cameo, Vase, Yellow, Purple Blossoms Overlaid & Cut, 5 1/4 In.	490.00
Campaign, see Political Campaign	
Campbell Kid, see also Buffalo Pottery	
Campbell Kid, Bowl, Silver Over Copper, Pair	9.00
Campbell Kid, Cup	2.50
Campbell Kid, Doll, Girl, Original Clothing	12.50
Campbell Kid, Doll, Girl, Rag	15.00
Campbell Kid, Doll, Rubber, 10 In.	7.00
Campbell Kid, Potholder	4.00
Campbell Kid, Spoon, Boy & Girl, Silverplate, Pair	12.00
Campbell Kid, Spoon, Set Of 2	14.00
Campbell Kid, Trivet	5.00

Camphor glass is a cloudy white glass that has been blown or pressed. It was made by many factories in the Midwest during the mid-nineteenth century.

Camphor Glass, Bowl, Scalloped Top, Gold Trim, 10 In.	12.00
Camphor Glass, Box, Powder, Girl, 2 Dogs, Pink, Art Deco	10.00
Camphor Glass, Box, Trinket, Lidded, Scrolls	12.50
Camphor Glass, Candleholder, 3 Light, 7 In., Pair	18.50

Camphor Glass, Candlestick, Figural Nude On Geometric Base, 4 1/2 In.	48.00
Camphor Glass, Cup, Niagara Falls, Clear, 2 3/4 In.	11.00
Camphor Glass, Dish, Hairpin, Gold Cherub	25.00
Camphor Glass, Dish, Hen Cover, 2 1/4 In.	10.00
Camphor Glass, Dish, Shell Finial Cover, Dolphin Feet, Portieux, 5 In.	85.00
Camphor Glass, Figurine, Dog, Pug, Findley, 2 3/4 X 3 1/4 In.	35.00
Camphor Glass, Flower Frog, Seminude Maiden On Stump, Amber, 5 1/2 In.	25.00
Camphor Glass, Jar, Powder, Fluted Bowl, Round Finial On Lid, 3 In.	3.50
Camphor Glass, Jar, Powder, Green Lid Finial, Girl With 2 Dogs	16.50
Camphor Glass, Mug, Cherokee Rose & Clematis, Tennessee, 16 Stars	45.00
Camphor Glass, Plate, Three Kittens, 7 1/4 In.	17.00
Camphor Glass, Salt & Pepper, Hand Holding Torch, C.1876, 3 1/4 In.High	75.00
Camphor Glass, Salt, Cat, Metal Head, Collar, & Bow	35.00
Camphor Glass, Vase, Bud, Blue Base, Green Stem, 10 1/2 In.	14.00
Camphor Glass, Vase, Handled, 1876	45.00
Canary Glass, see Vaseline Glass	
Candleholder, Bronze, 10 Lusters, Marble Plinths, 15 In., Pair	98.00
Candlestick, see also Brass, Candlestick; Pewter, Candlestick;	
Sandwich Glass, Candlestick; Silver, Sterling, Candlestick;	
Vaseline Glass, Candlestick; and various porcelain categories.	
Candlestick, Bronze, Art Nouveau, 4 1/2 In., Pair	85.00
Candlestick, Bronze, Frog Standing On Turtle, 4 3/4 In., Pair	135.00
Candlestick, Bronze, Gorham Co., Corinthian Pillars, C.1904, 9 3/4 In., Pair	275.00
Candlestick, George III, Cut Glass, Pair, 19th Century, 10 In.	150.00
Candlestick, Hog Scraper, Iron, Push-Up Marked Shaw, 7 1/4 In.	48.00
Candlestick, Hog Scraper, Iron, Push-Up With Chair Hook, 5 3/4 In.	48.00
Candlestick, Hog Scraper, Pine Handle	5.00
Candlestick, Hog Scraper, Tin, Push-Up	35.00
Candlestick, Miner, Wrought Iron	25.00
Candlestick, Saucer, Finger Loop, Tin, 5 In.Diameter, 2 In.Tall	18.50
Candlestick, Sheffield, Pair, 9 In.	50.00
Candlestick, Winged Dragon, Cast Iron	20.00
Candlestick, Wooden Spiral, Brass Drip Tray, 8 In., Pair	25.00

Candy containers, especially those made of glass, were popular during the late Victorian era.

Candy Container, see also Kewpie, Candy Container	
Candy Container, Airplane, Army Bomber-15-P-7	10.00
Candy Container, Airplane, Tin Wings, Marked S In Shield	15.00
Candy Container, Airplane, U.S., P-51	18.00
Candy Container, Apple Green, Pink Rose On Lid, Footed, Signed, 8 1/2 In.	27.50
Candy Container, Army Bomber	10.00
Candy Container, Auto, Bevel Windows, 4 In.	75.00
Candy Container, Auto, Miniature, Streamlined	10.00
Candy Container, Automobile, Hearse No.2, 4 Windows, Tassels, Closure, 5 In.	65.00
Candy Container, Automobile, Streamlined Touring	18.00
Candy Container, Baby Chick, Standing	15.00 To 30.00
Candy Container, Baseball, Clear	16.50
Candy Container, Battleship Oregon, Lid	35.00
Candy Container, Bottle, Cigar Shape, Amber, 5 1/2 In.	37.50
Candy Container, Bugle, With Cover	44.00
Candy Container, Building Shape, C.1914, 2 3/4 X 1 3/4 X 3 In.	22.50
Candy Container, Bulldog, Black Paint And Gold Collar	39.00
Candy Container, Bulldog, Sitting	10.00 To 29.00
Candy Container, Buster Brown's Dog Tige, 3 In.	28.00
Candy Container, Candlestick Telephone, Whistle At Top	9.00
Candy Container, Chamber Pot, Flash Red	17.50
Candy Container, Charles Lindbergh's Spirit Of Goodwill, 1927	65.00
Candy Container, Charlie Chaplin	45.00 To 65.00
Candy Container, Chicken	20.00
Candy Container, Chicken On Nest	12.00 To 15.00
Candy Container, Cincinnati Reds Signatures	20.00
Candy Container, Clarinet, Glass	10.95
Candy Container, Clear, Metal Cap, Sugar Starch Corn Syrup, 2 1/2 In.	8.00

Candy Container, Clown On Rocking Horse, Glass	45.00
Candy Container, Cruiser	7.50
Candy Container, Dog, Blue, No Cover	40.00
Candy Container, Dog, By Barrel	75.00
Candy Container, Duck Family Swimming	50.00
Candy Container, Fire Engine With Large Boiler & Driver, 15 In.	10.00
Candy Container, Fire Engine, Hose On Back	25.00
Candy Container, Gas Pump, Gas Written On Both Sides Of Globe	25.00
Candy Container, Gas 23 Cents Today	75.00
Candy Container, Gun, Metal Closure, Large Size	8.50
Candy Container, Happy Hooligan	18.00
Candy Container, Hat With Tin Brim, Milk Glass	17.50
Candy Container, Hat, Military, Amber	15.00
Candy Container, Hearse With Fringe & Spare Tire, Green Closure	40.00
Candy Container, Hen On Basket, Jeanette Glass	18.00
Candy Container, Hen On Nest	15.00
Candy Container, Hen On Oval Nest, 4 5/8 In.	12.50
Candy Container, Hobnail, OK, Trade Mark Marked On Side, 1 1/2 In.	9.50
Candy Container, Hound Pup Without Hat	8.00
Candy Container, Hound Pup, Metal Screw Top	10.00
Candy Container, Independence Hall	155.00
Candy Container, Jeep	16.00
Candy Container, Kitten, Tan Papier-Mache, Glass Eyes	10.00
Candy Container, Lamp With Flint Globe	20.00
Candy Container, Lantern	10.00 To 12.00
Candy Container, Lantern, Black Metal, 3 1/2 In.	20.00
Candy Container, Lantern, Flashed Cranberry Globe, Tin Base & Top, Bail	14.00
Candy Container, Lantern, Large, Red Metal, 4 1/2 In.	25.00
Candy Container, Lantern, Paneled Globe, Tin Base & Top, Bail Handle, 4 In.	8.00
Candy Container, Lantern, Twins	15.00
Candy Container, Lantern, V.G.Co., 3 5/8 In.	9.00
Candy Container, Lantern, 3 1/8 In.	6.00
Candy Container, Learned Fox	35.00
Candy Container, Liberty Bell, Amber Glass, Tin Base, 3 1/2 In.	40.00
Candy Container, Limousine, Metal Wheel	25.00
Candy Container, Lion, Seated	20.00
Candy Container, Locomotive 888	12.50
Candy Container, Locomotive, Brainard's, 1923	30.00
Candy Container, Mail Box, Blue, No Cover	12.00
Candy Container, Man On Barrel	35.00
Candy Container, Man On Motorcycle	150.00
Candy Container, Military Hat, Large	32.50
Candy Container, Millstein's Horn, Red	25.00
Candy Container, Mug	10.00
Candy Container, Mutt, Sugar Starch Corn Syrup, 2 1/2 In.	10.00
Candy Container, Nurser	12.00
Candy Container, Opera Glasses, Original Gold Cover, Milk Glass	75.00
Candy Container, Opera Glasses, Plain Panels, Milk White	65.00
Candy Container, Owl, Screw Top	7.50
Candy Container, Peter Rabbit	30.00
Candy Container, Phonograph	25.00 To 50.00
Candy Container, Pistol, Amber, 6 3/4 In.	18.00
Candy Container, Pistol, Amber, 8 In.	45.00
Candy Container, Powder Horn, Cambridge Glass Co.	30.00
Candy Container, Pup, Heavy Glass, Open Base	12.00
Candy Container, Puppy, Sitting, 3 In.	5.00
Candy Container, Rabbit Coming Out Of Shell	35.00 To 40.00
Candy Container, Rabbit Family, Gilt, Marked V.G.Co., Jeannette, Pa., 14 In.	65.00
Candy Container, Rabbit With Basket On Right Arm, Screw Base, Emblem, 2 In.	16.00
Candy Container, Rabbit, Basket On Arm	50.00
Candy Container, Rabbit, Feet Together, Round Note	35.00
Candy Container, Rabbit, Legs Apart	15.00
Candy Container, Rabbit, Sitting, Jeannette Glass	18.00
Candy Container, Railroad Lantern, Tin Top & Handle	10.00
Candy Container, Revolver, Amethyst Glass, Old Cap, 8 In.	28.00

Candy Container, Revolver, Amethyst Glass, Screw Cap, 7 In.	28.00
Candy Container, Revolver, With Closure, 7 7/8 In.	10.00
Candy Container, Santa Boot, 2 1/2 In.	9.00
Candy Container, Santa Claus Entering Chimney	34.00
Candy Container, Santa Claus, Original Closure, Long Coat, No.671	40.00
Candy Container, Santa Claus, Papier-Mache	4.00
Candy Container, Santa Claus, Plastic Head	25.00
Candy Container, Scotty Dog, Head Right Side	8.50
Candy Container, Scotty Dog, Open Bottom	6.00
Candy Container, Scotty Dog, Open Top	5.00
Candy Container, Snowman, German	12.00
Candy Container, Soldier, Plastic Screw Base	8.00
Candy Container, Spark Plug	50.00 To 60.00
Candy Container, Spark Plug, 80 Percent Paint	45.00
Candy Container, Spirit Of Goodwill	50.00
Candy Container, Suitcase, Stippled	30.00
Candy Container, Suitcase, Tin Sliding Bottom, Pat.Appl.For	15.00 To 35.00
Candy Container, Tank, Victory Glass, Toy Division	12.00
Candy Container, Telephone, Heavy Cardboard, Wooden Receiver, Bells, 10 In.	48.00
Candy Container, Tin Building	10.00
Candy Container, Trunk With Closure, Milk Glass	40.00
Candy Container, Trunk With Original Tin Closure, Milk Glass	37.00
Candy Container, Turkey Gobbler	75.00
Candy Container, Turkey Gobbler, Pressed Glass	75.00
Candy Container, Village Building, Lithographic Tin, Used Over Glass, 1914	22.50
Candy Container, Windmill	25.00 To 65.00
Cane, Blown Glass, Clear, 33 In.	55.00
Cane, Carved Bird, Polychrome Wings	165.00
Cane, Carved Ivory Boar's Head Handle, Sterling Silver Bands On Cane	65.00
Cane, Clear Stripings, Blue, White, Glass	150.00
Cane, Glass, Feathered, 57 In.	110.00
Cane, Hand-Carved, Monkey	75.00
Cane, Irish Shilling	6.00
Cane, Opaque Amber Celluloid Bird's Head, Glass Eyes, Curved Neck Handle	12.50
Cane, Pairpoint, Black Glass, Brass Tip	45.00
Cane, Peacock, Carved Bamboo	15.00
Cane, Swagger Stick, Sterling Top, Bullet End, Marked 326th	23.00
Cane, Sword, Gold Handle	47.50
Cane, Whale Tooth Handle, Eagle, Compass, Carved, 1975, Initialed, 37 In.	325.00
Cane, Wood Dog's Head With Glass Eyes Handle	15.00
Caneware, Teapot, Blue Floral Relief, Early 19th Century	85.00

Canton china is a blue-and-white ware made near Canton, China, from about 1785 to 1895. It is hand-decorated with Chinese scenes.

Canton, Bottle, Water, 8 In., Pair	250.00
Canton, Bowl & Dish, Leaf Shaped Dish, Underglaze Blue Willow Pattern, Pair	650.00
Canton, Bowl, Blue & White, Slash Border, 4 1/4 In.	25.00
Canton, Bowl, Blue Pagodas, Pavilions, Notched Corners, 19th Century, 10 In.	375.00
Canton, Bowl, Cut-Corner Salad	450.00
Canton, Bowl, Soup, Blue & White, 8 1/2 In.	48.00
Canton, Coffeepot, Lighthouse, Twist Handle, Blue & White, 7 In.	475.00
Canton, Cup & Saucer, Willow, Wishbone Handle	40.00
Canton, Dish, Flat Leaf, 7 In.	135.00
Canton, Dish, Hot Water, Oblong, Covered, 19th Century	400.00
Canton, Dish, Leaf, Willow	135.00
Canton, Dish, Oval Sweetmeat And Tray	220.00
Canton, Dish, Pickle, Leaf, Blue & White	65.00
Canton, Dish, Serving, Blue, Oval, C.1820, 11 1/2 X 9 X 1 3/4 In.	130.00
Canton, Dish, Serving, Open, Square, 9 In.	185.00
Canton, Dish, Shrimp, Tin	225.00 To 298.00
Canton, Dish, Vegetable, Strawberry Finial, Cover, 11 1/2 In.	190.00
Canton, Flower Pot, Blue & White, Hexagonal, Footed, 2 1/2 In.	22.00
Canton, Flower Pot, Blue & White, Hexagonal, Footed, 4 1/4 In.	38.00
Canton, Jar, Foo Dog Finial, Pretzel Handles, 4 Feet, Blue, White, 7 X 6 In.	155.00
Canton, Jar, Ginger, Stand, 7 In.	50.00

Canton, Jar, Tea, Decoration, Dark Blue, Lid 45.00
Canton, Plate, Blue & White, C.1800, 9 In. 45.00
Canton, Plate, Blue & White, Reticulated, 9 1/4 In. 120.00
Canton, Plate, Blue & White, River Scene, 6 1/4 In.Diameter 20.00
Canton, Plate, Blue & White, 10 In. 35.00
Canton, Plate, Blue & White, 8 In. 28.00
Canton, Plate, Blue, White, & Orange, Butterflies, Gold Trim, 8 1/2 In. 68.00
Canton, Plate, Scenic, Blue & White, Unglazed Underside Rim, 10 In. 48.00
Canton, Plate, Soup, Blue & White 48.00
Canton, Platter, Blue & White, 10 In. 115.00
Canton, Platter, Blue & White, 13 1/2 In. 140.00
Canton, Platter, Clipped Corners, Orange Peel Bottom, 19 X 16 In. 228.00
Canton, Sauceboat, Leaf, Blue & White 140.00
Canton, Teapot, Ball Form, Round, Blue & White 190.00
Canton, Teapot, Blue & White, China Insert Strainer, 5 X 6 1/2 In. 50.00
Canton, Teapot, Blue & White, 6 In. 140.00
Canton, Teapot, Cylinder Form, Gooseneck Spout 125.00
Canton, Teapot, Deep Blue, Straight-Sided, Button Finial, 6 In. 175.00
Canton, Teapot, Drum, 4 1/2 In. 250.00
Canton, Tureen, Sauce, Blue & White, Mid-19th Century, 9 In. 225.00
Canton, Urn, Baluster, 13 In. 870.00

N *Capo-Di-Monte porcelain was first made in Naples, Italy, from 1743 to 1759. The factory moved near Madrid, Spain, and reopened in 1771 and worked to 1834. Since that time the Doccia factory of Italy acquired the molds and style, even using the N and crown mark, which was made famous by the factory.*

Capo-Di-Monte, Basket Of Flowers, Miniature, Signed 37.50
Capo-Di-Monte, Box, Glove, 13 X 6 In. 400.00
Capo-Di-Monte, Box, Heavy Relief Mermaid, Cherub, Dolphins, 8 X 3 1/2 In. 175.00
Capo-Di-Monte, Box, Jewel, Set In Brass, Hinged, Footed, Blue Mark Crown & N 145.00
Capo-Di-Monte, Box, Life Of Christ Scenes, Wildflower Sprays, Gilt Mount 600.00
Capo-Di-Monte, Box, Oval, Hinged, C.1900, 4 1/2 X 3 In.Diameter 125.00
Capo-Di-Monte, Box, Patch, Clover Shape, Cupid & Flowers, 2 1/4 X 4 In. 115.00
Capo-Di-Monte, Box, Patch, Cupid & Garlands Of Flowers, Clover Shape, 4 In. 115.00
Capo-Di-Monte, Box, Powder, Hinged Top, Woman & Child On Top, C.1771, 4 In. 210.00
Capo-Di-Monte, Casket, 17 Children, Jewel, Polychrome, Oblong, Signed, 6 In. 185.00
Capo-Di-Monte, Chair, Arm, Miniature, High-Back, Upholstery & Gilt, 4 1/2 In. 45.00
Capo-Di-Monte, Compote, Cherub, Relief On 4 Panels Of Lid & Compote, Footed 265.00
Capo-Di-Monte, Cup & Saucer, Women, Children, Animals, Sun, Blue Crown 62.00
Capo-Di-Monte, Cup, Cover, Handle, People Walking In Gardens, Demitasse 80.00
Capo-Di-Monte, Figurine, Bearded Man With Violin, Blue Crown N, 6 1/2 In. 125.00
Capo-Di-Monte, Figurine, British Soldier, C.1880, 11 In. 325.00
Capo-Di-Monte, Figurine, Double, 2 Cherubs On Bench, Sharing Fruit 125.00
Capo-Di-Monte, Figurine, Female Flower Seller, Signed, 8 1/2 In. 135.00
Capo-Di-Monte, Figurine, Girl Selling Flowers, 8 3/4 In. 175.00
Capo-Di-Monte, Figurine, Girl, Blue Crown & N Signature, 8 1/2 In. 125.00
Capo-Di-Monte, Figurine, Lady In 18th Century Dress, Male Escort, 9 In., Pair 225.00
Capo-Di-Monte, Figurine, Lady, Pink, Brown, & Lavender Ruffled Dress, 10 In. 150.00
Capo-Di-Monte, Figurine, Man Leaning On Stump, Basket Of Grapes, 10 1/2 In. 75.00
Capo-Di-Monte, Figurine, Man, Violin In Hand, Hat In Other Hand, 6 1/2 In. 135.00
Capo-Di-Monte, Figurine, Monkey Band, Six Pieces 210.00
Capo-Di-Monte, Figurine, 18th Century Male On Bridge, Gray Mark, 9 In. 120.00
Capo-Di-Monte, Jardinere, Man Hunting Boar, Woman In Garden, 6 X 8 1/2 In. 180.00
Capo-Di-Monte, Jardiniere, Biblical Figure Of Man, Cherub & Animals, 5 In. 150.00
Capo-Di-Monte, Jardiniere, Cherubs Dancing, Crowned N Mark, 9 3/4 In. 395.00
Capo-Di-Monte, Jardiniere, Men Hunting Wild Boar, Women In Garden Reverse 180.00
Capo-Di-Monte, Lamp, Children Design, Signed 175.00
Capo-Di-Monte, Planter, Women In Garden, Men Hunting Boars, 6 X 8 1/2 In. 195.00
Capo-Di-Monte, Planter, Women Of Pleasure, Men Hunting On Other Side, 6 In. 195.00
Capo-Di-Monte, Plaque, Infant Bacchus, Napoleon's Head, White, N With Wreath 4995.00
Capo-Di-Monte, Plate, Armorial, Coat Of Arms Center, Figs On Rim, Set Of 8 .... 2500.00
Capo-Di-Monte, Plate, Miniature, Portraits Of Nude Children, Signed, Pair 35.00
Capo-Di-Monte, Stein, Beer, Horsemen Battling Lions, Lion Cover, 10 1/4 In. 250.00
Capo-Di-Monte, Stein, C.1820, 10 1/2 In. 650.00

Capo-Di-Monte, Table, Oval, Miniature, Louis XVI, Blue Crown Over N, 4 In.	45.00
Capo-Di-Monte, Tankard, Elephant Handle	300.00
Capo-Di-Monte, Urn, Miniature, 2 Handled, Pedestaled, Crowned N Mark, Pair	225.00
Capo-Di-Monte, Urn, Panoramic Battle Scene, Ram's Head Handles, 7 1/4 In.	325.00
Capo-Di-Monte, Vase, Raised Cupids, Gold Crown & Blue N Mark, 3 In.	9.00
Captain Midnight, Badge, 1946	40.00
Captain Midnight, Mug	12.00
Card, see also Postcard	
Card, Advertising, Adams Pepsin Tutti Frutti Gum, 1893 Calendar, 2 X 3 In.	6.00
Card, Advertising, Mother's Cookies, 63 Movie Stars	37.50
Card, Advertising, Pepsin Child With Dog, 5 1/2 X 4 In.	12.00
Card, Advertising, Star Wars, Was A Wonder Bread Give-A-Way, Set Of 16	2.00
Card, Baseball, John Honus Wagner, Chewing Tobacco	100.00
Card, Playing, Beatle Arcade, Set Of Four	2.00
Card, Playing, Brandywine Button Mushrooms	4.75
Card, Playing, Miniature Size, Sturdy Box, U.S.Playing Card Co., 2 Decks	12.00
Card, Playing, Miniature, Double Deck, Box	12.00
Card, Playing, Noah's Ark, Litho Animals, Boxed	25.00
Card, Playing, NYNH & H., Deck	16.50
Card, Playing, Pennsylvania Railroad, Deck	7.50
Card, Playing, Railroad, Southern Pacific Lines	20.00
Card, Playing, Schaffhouse, Switzerland	5.00
Card, Playing, Sights Of Boston, Deck	18.00
Card, Playing, Silent Movie Stars, C.1920	45.00
Card, Playing, South Pacific, Train On Front	7.50
Card, Playing, Southern Pacific Lines	10.00
Card, Playing, Southern Railway, Boxed	14.00
Card, Trade, Currier & Ives, High Toned, Tobacco, Lithographic Color, 1880	28.00
Card, Trade, Depicting Negro In Early Advertising, Set Of 6	20.00
Card, Trade, Gold Dust Twins	7.00
Card, Valentine, Dan Cupid Stands Among 4 Layers Of Florals, Die Cut, Opens	6.50
Card, Valentine, Dutch Boy & Girl, Basket Of Florals, Stand-Up, 3 Layer, Opens	6.50
Card, Valentine, Figural, Bonneted Girl Next To Wheelbarrow, Cargo Of Hearts	5.00
Card, Valentine, Figural, Boy & Girl, Stand-Up, 2 Layers, Die Cut, Opens	5.00
Card, Valentine, Figural, Embossed Cupid On Stick Telephone, Stand-Up	6.50
Card, Valentine, Figural, Victorian Boy & Girl, Carrying Basket Of Florals	17.50
Card, Valentine, Figural, Victorian Girl, Bonneted, 2 Baskets of Flowers, Opens	17.50
Card, Valentine, Figural, 2 Victorian Children, Basket Of Florals, Stand-Up	5.00
Card, Valentine, Pop-Up, German, C.1910	20.00
Card, Valentine, The Queen Of Hearts, Stand-Up, Signed Ernest Nister	5.00

Carlsbad, Germany, is a mark found on china made by several factories in Germany. Most of the pieces available today were made after 1891.

Carlsbad, Berry Set, Floral Border, Gold Trim, Marked Austria, Signed, 7 Piece	33.00
Carlsbad, Coffee Set, Wild Roses, Pot And 8 Cups & Saucers	60.00
Carlsbad, Compote, Candy, Flower Form, Raised Relief, Vine, Footed, Pedestaled	35.00
Carlsbad, Jar, Cracker, Ornate Rim, Lid Finial, Floral Decoration	35.00
Carlsbad, Jar, Underplate, Gold Side Handles, Pink Flowers, Covered, Victoria	40.00
Carlsbad, Match Holder, Head Of Bulldog	24.00
Carlsbad, Pitcher, Flowers, Gold Twisted Handle, Bulbous, Yellow, Ivory, 7 In.	80.00
Carlsbad, Plate, Irving College, 1895, Hand-Painted	18.50
Carlsbad, Plate, Oyster, Gold-Leaf Flowers, Dark Green Borders	25.00
Carlsbad, Plate, Portrait, Man, Green, Gold, Signed Darphin, 8 1/2 In.	40.00
Carlsbad, Shaker, Sugar, Floral, Bird, Egg Shape, Marked Victoria	65.00
Carlsbad, Shot Glass, Blue, Green, Cranberry, Yellow, Sterling Silver Overlay	125.00
Carlsbad, Tray, Celery, Green, Floral, 14 1/2 In.	22.50
Carlsbad, Tray, Serving, Violets, Handled, Austria, 15 X 13 In.	42.00
Carlsbad, Vase, Cream Satin, Raised Gold Cattails, Leaves, & Stems, 8 1/2 In.	55.00
Carlsbad, Vase, Hand-Painted Flowers, Twig Handle, Powder Horn Shape, 6 In.	36.00
Carlton Ware, Dish, Baby's, Jack & Jill	29.00
Carlton Ware, Dish, Oriental Dragon, Red, Black, Gold, Handle, Footed, 10 In.	30.00
Carlton Ware, Pitcher, Rouge Flambe, 6 In.	25.00
Carlton Ware, Plate, Baby's, Jack & Jill Scene	24.00
Carlton Ware, Vase, Fairyland Luster, Oriental Scene, Iridescent Colors	145.00

Carlton Ware, Vase, Red Flambe, 4 In. 16.00
Carnelian, Figurine, Eagle, Translucent, 3 3/4 In. 150.00

*Carnival, or taffeta, glass was an inexpensive, pressed, iridescent glass made
from about 1900 to 1920. Over 200 different patterns are known.
Carnival glass is currently being reproduced.*

Carnival Glass, see also Northwood
Carnival Glass, Banana Boat, Grape & Cable 215.00
Carnival Glass, Banana Boat, Grape & Cable, Marigold, Footed 135.00
Carnival Glass, Banana Boat, Grape & Cable, Purple 150.00
Carnival Glass, Banana Boat, Grape & Cable, Purple, Iridescent, Oval 185.00
Carnival Glass, Banana Boat, Grape & Cable, Stippled, Green 220.00
Carnival Glass, Banana Boat, Imperial, Marigold, Iridescent 85.00
Carnival Glass, Banana Boat, Kittens 85.00
Carnival Glass, Banana Boat, Peach & Pear, Marigold .... 45.00 To 61.00
Carnival Glass, Banana Boat, Stippled Rays, Green 22.00
Carnival Glass, Banana Boat, Thistle, Footed, Marigold, Fenton 65.00
Carnival Glass, Banana Boat, Wreathed Cherry, Marigold 54.00
Carnival Glass, Banana Boat, Wreathed Cherry, Purple 95.00
Carnival Glass, Banana Boat, Wreathed Cherry, Purple, 12 X 9 1/2 In. 100.00
Carnival Glass, Banana Boat, Wreathed Cherry, White 140.00
Carnival Glass, Base, Punch Bowl, Grape & Cable, Purple 24.00
Carnival Glass, Basket, Basketweave, Marigold, Clear Applied Handle, 7 In. 40.00
Carnival Glass, Basket, Bride's, Horseshoe Curve, Marigold 85.00
Carnival Glass, Basket, Bushel, Aqua Opalescent, N 95.00
Carnival Glass, Basket, Bushel, Blue, Northwood 52.00
Carnival Glass, Basket, Bushel, Ice Green 95.00
Carnival Glass, Basket, Bushel, White, N 60.00
Carnival Glass, Basket, Electric Blue, N, Straight Sides 65.00
Carnival Glass, Basket, Footed, Ice Green, Northwood 90.00
Carnival Glass, Basket, Imperial Grape, Marigold, 10 In. 45.00
Carnival Glass, Berry Bowl, Master, Drapery, White Opalescent, N, 9 In. 75.00
Carnival Glass, Berry Set, Acorn Burr, 7 Piece 175.00
Carnival Glass, Berry Set, Butterfly & Berry, Marigold 125.00
Carnival Glass, Berry Set, Flute, Purple, 7 Piece .... 85.00 To 195.00
Carnival Glass, Berry Set, Garden Path, Peach Opalescent, 5 Piece 110.00
Carnival Glass, Berry Set, Grape & Cable, Iridescent, N, 7 Piece 195.00
Carnival Glass, Berry Set, Grape & Cable, Purple, Northwood, 5 Piece 175.00
Carnival Glass, Berry Set, Grape & Gothic Arches, Green, 5 Piece 65.00
Carnival Glass, Berry Set, Open Rose, Marigold, 7 Piece 70.00
Carnival Glass, Beverage Set, Oriental Poppy, Purple, 7 Piece, Northwood 750.00
Carnival Glass, Bonbon, Butterflies, Purple, N 35.00
Carnival Glass, Bonbon, Butterfly, Blue, Northwood 50.00
Carnival Glass, Bonbon, Fruits & Flowers, Electric Blue 47.00
Carnival Glass, Bonbon, Fruits & Flowers, Ice Green Pastel 65.00
Carnival Glass, Bonbon, Grape & Cable, Purple 45.00
Carnival Glass, Bonbon, Grape, Blue, 2 Handles, Northwood, 7 1/2 X 2 In. 25.00
Carnival Glass, Bonbon, Holly, Amethyst, 2 Handled, Millersburg 27.50
Carnival Glass, Bonbon, Honeycomb & Clover, Marigold 19.00
Carnival Glass, Bonbon, Pond Lily, Amethyst, 2 Handled 38.00
Carnival Glass, Bonbon, Pond Lily, Marigold 18.00
Carnival Glass, Bonbon, Question Mark, Marigold, 6 In. 20.00
Carnival Glass, Bonbon, Question Marks, Marigold, Footed, 6 In. 25.00
Carnival Glass, Bonbon, Strawberry, Marigold 20.00
Carnival Glass, Bonbon, Vintage, Blue 25.00
Carnival Glass, Bottle, Cologne, Grape & Cable, Purple 95.00
Carnival Glass, Bottle, Cologne, Grape & Cable, Purple Base, Green Stopper 147.00
Carnival Glass, Bottle, Corn, Smoky 145.00
Carnival Glass, Bottle, Little Barrel, Marigold 55.00
Carnival Glass, Bottle, Perfume, Grape & Cable, Marigold 365.00
Carnival Glass, Bottle, Whiskey, Jackman, Marigold, Pint 9.95
Carnival Glass, Bowl & Stand, Punch, Acorn Burrs, Amethyst, Northwood 455.00
Carnival Glass, Bowl & Stand, Whirling Star, Marigold 25.00
Carnival Glass, Bowl Base, Punch, Memphis, Purple, N 25.00
Carnival Glass, Bowl, Acorn Pattern, Green, 7 In. 37.00

Carnival Glass, Bowl, Autumn Acorns, Cobalt, Ruffled, 9 In.	38.00
Carnival Glass, Bowl, Autumn Acorns, Red, 7 In.	145.00
Carnival Glass, Bowl, Berry, Fluted, Panther, Marigold, Large	75.00
Carnival Glass, Bowl, Berry, Fluted, Panther, Marigold, Small	25.00
Carnival Glass, Bowl, Berry, Open Rose, Iridescent, Blue Bottom, 10 1/2 In.	35.00
Carnival Glass, Bowl, Berry, Panther, Marigold, Footed	50.00
Carnival Glass, Bowl, Berry, Peacock At The Fountain, Marigold	18.00 To 22.00
Carnival Glass, Bowl, Berry, Peacock At The Fountain, Small, Purple	22.00
Carnival Glass, Bowl, Berry, Peacock At The Fountain, Small, White	32.00
Carnival Glass, Bowl, Blackberry Spray, Blue, Hat Shape, 6 1/2 In.	22.00
Carnival Glass, Bowl, Bull's-Eye & Leaves, Green, N, 8 1/2 In.	30.00
Carnival Glass, Bowl, Butterfly & Berry, Dark Green, Claw Footed, 9 In.	70.00
Carnival Glass, Bowl, Captive Rose, Marigold, Ruffled Edge, 8 In.	45.00
Carnival Glass, Bowl, Centerpiece, Grape & Cable, Marigold, Footed	225.00
Carnival Glass, Bowl, Centerpiece, Persian Medallion, Grape & Cable, Cobalt	150.00
Carnival Glass, Bowl, Cereal, Bouquet & Lattice, Marigold, 6 1/2 In.	2.75
Carnival Glass, Bowl, Cherry Circle	33.00
Carnival Glass, Bowl, Cherry, Marigold, 3 Footed, 9 In.	22.00
Carnival Glass, Bowl, Chrysanthemum, Marigold, Fluted, 9 In.	25.00
Carnival Glass, Bowl, Chrysanthemum, Windmills, Marigold, Footed, 10 1/2 In.	36.00
Carnival Glass, Bowl, Coin Dot, Marigold, Ruffled Rim, 8 In.	12.00
Carnival Glass, Bowl, Coin Spot, Green, Crimped Edge, 9 In.	45.00
Carnival Glass, Bowl, Comet, Green	28.00
Carnival Glass, Bowl, Comet, Purple, Low, Millersburg	60.00
Carnival Glass, Bowl, Coral, Marigold, 9 In.	29.00
Carnival Glass, Bowl, Dragon & Lotus, Amethyst, 9 In.	29.00
Carnival Glass, Bowl, Dragon & Lotus, Blue	29.50 To 50.00
Carnival Glass, Bowl, Dragon & Lotus, Blue, Ruffled, 9 In.	30.00
Carnival Glass, Bowl, Dragon & Lotus, Cobalt, Iridescent, Shallow, 9 In.	47.50
Carnival Glass, Bowl, Dragon & Lotus, Fluted, Blue, 9 1/4 In.	30.00
Carnival Glass, Bowl, Dragon & Lotus, Fluted, Purple, 9 In.	35.00
Carnival Glass, Bowl, Dragon & Lotus, Green, Footed, 8 In.	43.00
Carnival Glass, Bowl, Dragon & Lotus, Green, Ruffled, 9 In.	33.00
Carnival Glass, Bowl, Dragon & Lotus, Marigold, 8 1/2 In.	22.50
Carnival Glass, Bowl, Dragon & Lotus, Marigold, 9 In.	22.00
Carnival Glass, Bowl, Dragon & Lotus, Marigold, 10 In.	55.00
Carnival Glass, Bowl, Dragon & Lotus, Ruffled, 8 3/4 In.	28.00
Carnival Glass, Bowl, Drapery, Marigold, Fluted, 9 In.	20.00
Carnival Glass, Bowl, Fanciful, Fluted, White, 8 3/4 In.	60.00
Carnival Glass, Bowl, Feathered Serpent, Green, Ruffled, 10 1/2 In.	32.00
Carnival Glass, Bowl, File, Purple, 5 1/2 In.	20.00
Carnival Glass, Bowl, Fishscale & Beads, Marigold To Pearl Scallop, 7 In.	25.00
Carnival Glass, Bowl, Fishscale & Beads, Marigold, 6 3/4 In.	16.00
Carnival Glass, Bowl, Flowers & Frames, Purple, Dome Footed, 8 3/4 In.	35.00
Carnival Glass, Bowl, Flowers & Water Lilies, Marigold, 3 Footed, 10 In.	55.00
Carnival Glass, Bowl, Fluted, Grape And Cable, Purple, 8 3/4 In.	37.50
Carnival Glass, Bowl, Fluted, Grape Leaves, Purple, 8 3/4 In.	37.50
Carnival Glass, Bowl, Fluted, Green, 9 In.	35.00
Carnival Glass, Bowl, Four Flowers, Peach, Crimped, 9 1/2 In.	30.00
Carnival Glass, Bowl, Fruit, Fashion, Marigold, 11 1/2 In.	20.00
Carnival Glass, Bowl, Fruit, Orange Tree, Marigold, Footed, Ruffled, 10 In.	50.00
Carnival Glass, Bowl, Good Luck, Amethyst, Ruffled, Iridescent, 9 In.	80.00
Carnival Glass, Bowl, Good Luck, Aqua Opalescent, 8 3/4 In.	225.00
Carnival Glass, Bowl, Good Luck, Blue, Low, 9 In.	80.00 To 85.00
Carnival Glass, Bowl, Good Luck, Blue, Ruffled, 9 In.	89.00
Carnival Glass, Bowl, Good Luck, Electric Blue	129.00
Carnival Glass, Bowl, Good Luck, Marigold, 9 In.	55.00
Carnival Glass, Bowl, Grape & Cable, Amethyst & Green, N, 7 3/4 In.	45.00
Carnival Glass, Bowl, Grape & Cable, Amethyst, M, 7 3/4 In.	35.00 To 60.00
Carnival Glass, Bowl, Grape & Cable, Amethyst, Shallow, N, 8 1/4 In.	45.00
Carnival Glass, Bowl, Grape & Cable, Amethyst, 8 In.	45.00
Carnival Glass, Bowl, Grape & Cable, Green, Northwood	50.00
Carnival Glass, Bowl, Grape & Cable, Green, Shallow, N, 8 1/4 In.	45.00
Carnival Glass, Bowl, Grape & Cable, Persian Medallion Inside, Orange, 10 In.	79.00
Carnival Glass, Bowl, Grape & Cable, Persian Medallion, Marigold	64.00

Carnival Glass, Bowl, Grape & Cable, Purple, Iridescent, Northwood 245.00
Carnival Glass, Bowl, Grape, Blue, Millersburg 35.00
Carnival Glass, Bowl, Grape, Purple, Fluted Rim, 10 X 4 In. 45.00
Carnival Glass, Bowl, Greek Key, Green, Northwood, 8 1/2 In. 50.00
Carnival Glass, Bowl, Hattie, Marigold, 9 In. 25.00
Carnival Glass, Bowl, Hearts & Flowers, Amethyst, Gold Iridescence, 9 In. 30.00
Carnival Glass, Bowl, Hearts & Flowers, Ruffled Edge, Collared Base, Ice Blue 95.00
Carnival Glass, Bowl, Hearts & Flowers, White, N, Low 95.00
Carnival Glass, Bowl, Holly, Blue, Fluted, 6 In. 25.00
Carnival Glass, Bowl, Holly, Blue, 9 In. .... 30.00 To 48.00
Carnival Glass, Bowl, Holly, Fluted, Blue, 8 3/4 In. 30.00
Carnival Glass, Bowl, Holly, Marigold, Footed, Ruffled, 8 3/4 In. 28.00
Carnival Glass, Bowl, Horses' Heads, Blue, Footed, 7 1/2 In. 55.00
Carnival Glass, Bowl, Horses' Heads, Blue, 3 Footed 75.00
Carnival Glass, Bowl, Horses' Heads, Green, 7 In. 45.00
Carnival Glass, Bowl, Ice Cream, Grape & Cable, Marigold 210.00
Carnival Glass, Bowl, Ice Cream, Grape & Cable, Marigold, Large 90.00
Carnival Glass, Bowl, Ice Cream, Grape & Cable, Purple, Stemmed 30.00
Carnival Glass, Bowl, Ice Cream, Peacock And Urn, Blue, 10 In. 225.00
Carnival Glass, Bowl, Ice Cream, Peacock And Urn, Dark Marigold 100.00
Carnival Glass, Bowl, Ice Cream, Persian Garden, White, 11 1/4 In. 110.00
Carnival Glass, Bowl, Imperial Pansy, Green, 8 1/2 In. 22.50
Carnival Glass, Bowl, Leaf & Beads, N, 3 Log Feet, Purple, 7 1/2 In. 65.00
Carnival Glass, Bowl, Leaf And Chain, White, 9 In. 79.00
Carnival Glass, Bowl, Lion, Blue, 6 In. 140.00
Carnival Glass, Bowl, Lion, Grape Exterior, Marigold Iridescent, 7 In. 95.00
Carnival Glass, Bowl, Little Fishes, Blue, Large 125.00
Carnival Glass, Bowl, Little Fishes, Marigold, 9 In. 100.00
Carnival Glass, Bowl, Luster Rose, Marigold, 3 Footed, 9 In. 14.00
Carnival Glass, Bowl, Marigold, Persian, Medallion, 8 1/2 In. 28.00
Carnival Glass, Bowl, Nesting Swan, Millersburg, Purple 175.00
Carnival Glass, Bowl, Open Rose, Green, 7 In. 18.00
Carnival Glass, Bowl, Orange Tree, Blue, 3 Footed, 9 1/2 In. 145.00
Carnival Glass, Bowl, Orange Tree, Marigold, Iridescent, 3 Feet, 10 In. 55.00
Carnival Glass, Bowl, Pansy, Amethyst 35.00
Carnival Glass, Bowl, Pansy, Marigold, Stippled, Fluted, 9 In. 30.00
Carnival Glass, Bowl, Panther, Cobalt, Footed, 9 In. 150.00
Carnival Glass, Bowl, Peach, Opalescent, 8 1/2 In. 43.00
Carnival Glass, Bowl, Peacock & Dahlia, Marigold, 7 In. 25.00
Carnival Glass, Bowl, Peacock & Grape, Blue, 9 In. 45.00
Carnival Glass, Bowl, Peacock & Grape, Geeen, 7 1/2 In. 50.00
Carnival Glass, Bowl, Peacock & Grape, Smoky, 3 Footed, 8 In. 28.00
Carnival Glass, Bowl, Peacock And Urn, Beaded Berries, Marigold, 9 In. 45.00
Carnival Glass, Bowl, Peacock And Urn, Blue, 8 1/2 In. 49.00
Carnival Glass, Bowl, Peacock And Urn, Marigold, Beaded Berry, 8 In. 42.00
Carnival Glass, Bowl, Peacock And Urn, Marigold, Millersburg, 10 1/2 In. 65.00
Carnival Glass, Bowl, Peacock At Fountain, Purple, Fluted Top 175.00
Carnival Glass, Bowl, Peacock On Fence, Electric Blue 139.00
Carnival Glass, Bowl, Peacock On Fence, Marigold, 9 In. 45.00
Carnival Glass, Bowl, Peacock, Amethyst, Northwood, 9 In. 85.00
Carnival Glass, Bowl, Peacock, Blue, Northwood, 9 In. 80.00
Carnival Glass, Bowl, Peacock, Blue, 9 In. 95.00
Carnival Glass, Bowl, Pine Cone, Marigold, 6 1/2 In. 30.00
Carnival Glass, Bowl, Plaid, Marigold, 8 1/2 In. 30.00
Carnival Glass, Bowl, Poinsettia & Lotus, Marigold, 3 Footed, 9 1/2 In. 28.00
Carnival Glass, Bowl, Pony, Marigold, 8 In. 38.00
Carnival Glass, Bowl, Pony, Pale Blue, 8 1/2 In. 90.00
Carnival Glass, Bowl, Poppy, Green, Marked Northwood N., 7 In. 37.50
Carnival Glass, Bowl, Primrose, Marigold, Millersburg, 10 In. 42.50
Carnival Glass, Bowl, Prism, Fluted, Green, Iridescent, 8 1/4 In. 26.00
Carnival Glass, Bowl, Rays & Ribbon, Amethyst, Millersburg, 10 In. 35.00
Carnival Glass, Bowl, Ribbed Swirl, Marigold, Fluted, 9 In. 20.00
Carnival Glass, Bowl, Ribbon Tie, Amethyst, 9 In. 27.50
Carnival Glass, Bowl, Ribbon Tie, Marigold, 9 In. 20.00
Carnival Glass, Bowl, Rose Petal, White, Flared, Footed, 9 1/2 In. 45.00

Carnival Glass, Bowl, Rose, Horses' Heads, Turquoise, Stands 3 Feet 175.00
Carnival Glass, Bowl, Rosettes, Footed, Marigold, M, 7 In. 20.00
Carnival Glass, Bowl, Sailboats, Blue, Crimped, 6 In. 30.00
Carnival Glass, Bowl, Scroll, Amethyst, 7 1/2 In. 28.00
Carnival Glass, Bowl, Single Flower, Peach, Opalescent, Pattern On Back, 9 In. 39.00
Carnival Glass, Bowl, Six Petals, Marigold, Crimped, 7 1/2 In. 22.00
Carnival Glass, Bowl, Ski Star, Opalescent Peach, 10 1/2 In. .... 42.00 To 55.00
Carnival Glass, Bowl, Stag & Holly, Amethyst, Footed 50.00
Carnival Glass, Bowl, Stag & Holly, Cobalt, Ruffled, Footed, 8 1/2 In. 75.00
Carnival Glass, Bowl, Stag & Holly, Marigold, Footed, 8 In. 42.00
Carnival Glass, Bowl, Stag & Holly, Marigold, Footed, 10 1/2 In. .... 59.00 To 75.00
Carnival Glass, Bowl, Star Of David & Bows, Amethyst, Ruffled, 8 In. 25.00
Carnival Glass, Bowl, Stippled Grape & Cable, Blue, 8 3/4 In. 40.00
Carnival Glass, Bowl, Stippled Grape & Cable, Pastel Blue, 8 1/2 In. 65.00
Carnival Glass, Bowl, Stippled Rays, Amethyst 30.00
Carnival Glass, Bowl, Stippled Rays, Amethyst, Northwood, 9 In. 30.00
Carnival Glass, Bowl, Stippled Rays, Amethyst, Ruffled Edge, N, 8 In. 30.00
Carnival Glass, Bowl, Stippled Rays, Green, 6 In. 20.00
Carnival Glass, Bowl, Stippled Rays, Purple, 8 1/2 In. 20.00
Carnival Glass, Bowl, Strawberry Pattern, Green, 8 1/2 In. 60.00
Carnival Glass, Bowl, Strawberry, Amethyst, Northwood, 9 In. 62.00
Carnival Glass, Bowl, Strawberry, Basket Weave, Amethyst, 9 1/2 In. 55.00
Carnival Glass, Bowl, Strawberry, Green, Northwood, 9 In. 67.00
Carnival Glass, Bowl, Sunburst, Bowl, Amethyst, 8 In. 35.00
Carnival Glass, Bowl, Sunflower, Greek Key Band, Collared Foot, Green, 8 In. 50.00
Carnival Glass, Bowl, Sunflower, Green, Footed, Northwood, 9 In. 47.50
Carnival Glass, Bowl, Sunflower, Marigold, 3 Footed, 9 In. 28.00
Carnival Glass, Bowl, Thistle, Fluted, Blue, 9 In. 30.00
Carnival Glass, Bowl, Thistle, Green, Crimped Edge, 8 1/2 In. 38.00
Carnival Glass, Bowl, Thistle, Marigold, 4 Feet, 8 In. 29.00
Carnival Glass, Bowl, Three Fruits, Amethyst, Northwood, 8 3/4 In. 58.00
Carnival Glass, Bowl, Three Fruits, Amethyst, 8 1/2 In. 30.00
Carnival Glass, Bowl, Three Fruits, Purple, Footed, 8 3/4 In. 35.00
Carnival Glass, Bowl, Three Fruits, White, Dome, Footed, N, 9 In. 65.00
Carnival Glass, Bowl, Thunderbird, Dark Purple, Berries, 9 3/4 In. 150.00
Carnival Glass, Bowl, Tree Of Life, Orange, Marigold, 10 In. 40.00
Carnival Glass, Bowl, Trout & Fly, Marigold, 8 1/2 In. 30.00
Carnival Glass, Bowl, Two Flowers, Blue, Footed, 11 1/2 In. 40.00
Carnival Glass, Bowl, Two Flowers, Cobalt Blue, Footed, 9 In. 60.00
Carnival Glass, Bowl, Vintage, Green, 9 In. 18.00
Carnival Glass, Bowl, Vintage, Marigold, Ruffled, 8 In. 19.00
Carnival Glass, Bowl, Water Lily, Marigold, Footed, 6 In. 13.00
Carnival Glass, Bowl, Windflower, Marigold, 8 In. 25.00
Carnival Glass, Bowl, Windmill, Marigold, Fluted, 8 In. 38.00
Carnival Glass, Bowl, Windmill, Smoky, 8 In. 25.00
Carnival Glass, Bowl, Wishbone, Northwood, Footed, Fluted, Green, Luster, 8 In. 45.00
Carnival Glass, Butter, Cabbage Rose, Marigold 30.00
Carnival Glass, Butter, Grape & Cable, Green, N, Covered 175.00
Carnival Glass, Butter, Grape & Cable, Purple 185.00
Carnival Glass, Butter, Grape & Gothic Arches, Marigold 70.00
Carnival Glass, Butter, Luster Rose, Marigold, Covered 42.00
Carnival Glass, Butter, Maple Leaf, Amethyst 135.00
Carnival Glass, Button, Dog, Purple 11.00
Carnival Glass, Candlestick Holder, Florentine, Blue, 11 In., Pair 50.00
Carnival Glass, Candlestick, Colonial, Marigold, Hexagonal, 8 1/2 In. .... 135.00 To 140.00
Carnival Glass, Candlestick, Grape & Cable, Green 65.00
Carnival Glass, Candlestick, Grape & Cable, Purple, N, 8 In. 18.00
Carnival Glass, Candlestick, Grape, Marigold, Squatty, Pair 15.00
Carnival Glass, Candlestick, Thin Rib, Ice Green, Pair 59.00
Carnival Glass, Candlestick, Tree Of Life, Marigold, 7 In. 15.00
Carnival Glass, Carafe, Imperial Grape, Amethyst 80.00
Carnival Glass, Carafe, Water, Grapes, Green 75.00
Carnival Glass, Chain With Star, Compote, Scalloped Rim, Low Standard, 8 In. 20.00
Carnival Glass, Compote, Blackberry & Leaf, Amethyst, Ruffled, 6 1/2 X 5 In. 40.00
Carnival Glass, Compote, Blackberry, Blue, Miniature 29.00

Carnival Glass, Compote, Blackberry, Ruffled, Amethyst, 3 In.Stem, 7 X 5 In. 27.00
Carnival Glass, Compote, Butterflies & Bells, Dark Purple, 7 1/4 In. 100.00
Carnival Glass, Compote, Cherry Mikado, Blue, Large 160.00
Carnival Glass, Compote, Hearts & Flowers, Aqua, Opalescent 135.00
Carnival Glass, Compote, Hearts & Flowers, Marigold .... 20.00 To 35.00
Carnival Glass, Compote, Hobstar, Marigold, Tall 25.00
Carnival Glass, Compote, Honeycomb, Clear, Low Standard 18.00
Carnival Glass, Compote, Marigold, Ruffled, Northwood, 6 In., Pair 110.00
Carnival Glass, Compote, Starfish, Purple, 2 Handled, Sides Pulled Up, 6 In. 30.00
Carnival Glass, Compote, Vintage, Blue, 5 3/4 In. 40.00
Carnival Glass, Compote, Wreath Of Roses, Blue, 6 1/2 In. 25.00
Carnival Glass, Console Set, Ram's Head, Purple, 3 Piece 50.00
Carnival Glass, Creamer, Acorn Burr, Green, N 70.00
Carnival Glass, Creamer, Butterfly And Berry, Marigold 25.00
Carnival Glass, Creamer, Curved Star, Marigold 20.00
Carnival Glass, Creamer, Grape & Cable, Marigold, Large 75.00
Carnival Glass, Creamer, Grape & Gothic Arches, Marigold 22.50
Carnival Glass, Creamer, Hanging Cherries, Marigold, Millersburg 38.00
Carnival Glass, Creamer, Hobstar, Marigold 15.00
Carnival Glass, Creamer, Luster Flute, Green, Northwood 35.00
Carnival Glass, Creamer, Luster Rose, Green 39.00
Carnival Glass, Creamer, Luster Rose, Marigold 29.00
Carnival Glass, Creamer, Luster Rose, Purple, Iridescent 68.00
Carnival Glass, Creamer, Orange Tree, Amethyst 20.00
Carnival Glass, Creamer, Pansy, Marigold 15.00
Carnival Glass, Creamer, Peacock At The Fountain, Blue 89.00
Carnival Glass, Creamer, Pineapple, Blue 42.00
Carnival Glass, Creamer, S Repeat, Purple, Small 55.00
Carnival Glass, Creamer, Singing Birds, Marigold 200.00
Carnival Glass, Creamer, Singing Birds, Purple, N 30.00
Carnival Glass, Creamer, Springtime, Marigold, Table Size 38.00
Carnival Glass, Creamer, Thistle, Purple, Millersburg 13.00
Carnival Glass, Creamer, Wreathed Cherry, Purple 75.00
Carnival Glass, Cruet, Buzz Saw, Green, 3 3/4 In. 150.00
Carnival Glass, Cup & Saucer, Bouquet & Lattice, Marigold 3.50
Carnival Glass, Cup & Saucer, Grape & Cable, Marigold 40.00
Carnival Glass, Cup & Saucer, Kittens, Dark Marigold 175.00
Carnival Glass, Cup & Saucer, Kittens, Marigold .... 90.00 To 100.00
Carnival Glass, Cup, Orange Tree, Marigold 10.00
Carnival Glass, Cup, Punch, Acorn Burr, Iced Blue 80.00
Carnival Glass, Cup, Punch, Acorn Burr, Marigold 16.50
Carnival Glass, Cup, Punch, Fashion, Marigold 7.50
Carnival Glass, Cup, Punch, Fruit Salad, Marigold 28.50
Carnival Glass, Cup, Punch, Fruit Salad, Peach Opalescent 45.00
Carnival Glass, Cup, Punch, Grape & Cable, Amethyst 18.00
Carnival Glass, Cup, Punch, Grape & Cable, Iridescent, Marigold 15.00
Carnival Glass, Cup, Punch, Hobstar & Feather, Marigold 15.00
Carnival Glass, Cup, Punch, Hobstar & Feather, Marigold, Millersburg 20.00
Carnival Glass, Cup, Punch, Memphis, Green 25.00
Carnival Glass, Cup, Punch, Memphis, Marigold 16.50
Carnival Glass, Cup, Punch, Stork And Rushes, Amethyst 25.00
Carnival Glass, Cup, Punch, Stork And Rushes, Purple 15.00
Carnival Glass, Cup, Punch, Vintage, Purple 20.00
Carnival Glass, Cup, Punch, Wreath Of Roses, Blue 14.00
Carnival Glass, Cup, Punch, Wreath Of Roses, Grapes Inside, Blue 16.00
Carnival Glass, Cup, Punch, 474, Marigold 7.00
Carnival Glass, Decanter & 4 Wine, Harvest, Marigold 165.00
Carnival Glass, Decanter, Diamond & Lace, Marigold 75.00
Carnival Glass, Decanter, Diamond & Sunburst, Purple 145.00
Carnival Glass, Decanter, Grapes & Leaves, Purple, Blown Out, 12 In. 40.00
Carnival Glass, Decanter, Imperial Grape, Blue 47.50
Carnival Glass, Decanter, Octagon, Marigold 38.00
Carnival Glass, Decanter, Whiskey, Grape & Cable, Marigold, Stopper 350.00
Carnival Glass, Decanter, Wine, Imperial Grape, Marigold 40.00
Carnival Glass, Dish, Acorn, Red, 8 In. 175.00

Carnival Glass, Dish, Bellflower, Amethyst, Arlington, Iowa, 6 In. 32.00
Carnival Glass, Dish, Candy, Three Fruits, Green, Northwood, 6 1/2 In. 40.00
Carnival Glass, Dish, Dragon & Lotus, Red, Scalloped Edge, 8 1/2 In. 250.00
Carnival Glass, Dish, Fishscale & Beads, Purple, 7 1/4 In. 19.00
Carnival Glass, Dish, Goodluck, Fluted, Blue, 8 3/4 In. 90.00
Carnival Glass, Dish, Ice Cream, Orange Tree, Marigold, Base Clear 15.00
Carnival Glass, Dish, Kittens, Ruffled Edge, Marigold 45.00
Carnival Glass, Dish, Pickle, Pansy, Marigold 22.50
Carnival Glass, Dish, Pinecone, Blue, 5 In. 20.00
Carnival Glass, Dish, Ruffled, Peacock Tail, Amethyst, 7 In. 20.00
Carnival Glass, Dish, Scales, Peach Opalescent, Tricornered 45.00
Carnival Glass, Dish, Shell, Purple, Footed, 6 3/8 In. 30.00
Carnival Glass, Dish, Stemmed, Beaded Stars, Marigold, 6 In. 16.50
Carnival Glass, Dresser Set, Concave Diamond, Marigold, 6 Piece 350.00
Carnival Glass, Dresser Tray, Grape & Cable, Purple 275.00
Carnival Glass, Fernery, Butterfly & Berry, Blue 225.00
Carnival Glass, Fernery, Open Rose, Marigold, 3 Footed 14.00
Carnival Glass, Goblet, Buttermilk, Iris, Marigold 60.00
Carnival Glass, Goblet, Buttermilk, Iris, Millersburg, Green 120.00
Carnival Glass, Goblet, Flute, Marigold 17.50
Carnival Glass, Goblet, Grape, Purple 12.00
Carnival Glass, Goblet, Imperial Grape, Marigold 35.00
Carnival Glass, Goblet, Imperial Grape, Purple, Iridescent 90.00
Carnival Glass, Goblet, Octagon, Marigold 45.00
Carnival Glass, Goblet, Old Imperial Grape, Marigold 15.00
Carnival Glass, Goblet, Paneled Thistle, Clear To Marigold 5.00
Carnival Glass, Goblet, Peacock At Urn, Marigold 55.00
Carnival Glass, Goblet, Wide Panel, Dark Marigold 14.00
Carnival Glass, Gravy Boat, Holly, Purple, Millersburg 35.00
Carnival Glass, Hatpin Holder, Grape & Cable, Marigold 120.00
Carnival Glass, Hatpin Holder, Grape & Cable, Purple .... 130.00 To 140.00
Carnival Glass, Hatpin Holder, Grape, Green, N 150.00
Carnival Glass, Hatpin Holder, Orange Tree, Marigold 125.00
Carnival Glass, Hatpin, Butterfly, Iridescent, Art Deco 10.00
Carnival Glass, Ice Cream Set, Peacock At Urn, Iced Blue, 5 Piece 425.00
Carnival Glass, Ice Cream Set, Peacock At Urn, Purple, 5 Piece 500.00
Carnival Glass, Jar, Cracker, Inverted Feather, Covered, Green 117.00
Carnival Glass, Jar, Powder, Grape & Cable, Dark Amethyst, Northwood 95.00
Carnival Glass, Jar, Powder, Orange Tree, Blue, Lidded 70.00
Carnival Glass, Jar, Powder, Orange Tree, Marigold .... 27.50 To 35.00
Carnival Glass, Jar, Powder, Scotty 6.00
Carnival Glass, Jar, Powder, Vintage, Marigold, Covered 30.00
Carnival Glass, Jar, Tobacco, Grape & Cable, Marigold 275.00
Carnival Glass, Jar, Tree Bark, Marigold, Novelty, 1/2 Pint 9.00
Carnival Glass, Jewelry, Beads, Strung, Orange, 8 In. 18.00
Carnival Glass, Lamp, Base, Peacock, Marigold 80.00
Carnival Glass, Lamp, Gone With The Wind, Regal Iris, Red ....Illus 9400.00
Carnival Glass, Mug, Beaded Shell, Cobalt 50.00
Carnival Glass, Mug, Dandelion, Aqua, Opalescent & Butterscotch Iridescent, N 225.00
Carnival Glass, Mug, Fisherman's, Grape & Cable, Purple, Iridescent 70.00

Carnival Glass, Lamp, Gone With The Wind, Regal Iris, Red

Carnival Glass, Mug, Orange Tree, Blue .... 25.00 To 42.50
Carnival Glass, Mug, Orange Tree, Marigold 15.00
Carnival Glass, Mug, Orange Tree, Red 95.00
Carnival Glass, Mug, Singing Bird, Marigold 22.50
Carnival Glass, Mug, Singing Birds, Amethyst .... 42.00 To 50.00
Carnival Glass, Mug, Singing Birds, Amethyst, N .... 45.00 To 85.00
Carnival Glass, Mug, Singing Birds, Green 110.00
Carnival Glass, Mug, Stork & Rushes, Marigold 20.00
Carnival Glass, Mug, Vintage Banded, Marigold 15.00
Carnival Glass, Nappy, Butterfly, Amethyst, 2 Handles 38.00
Carnival Glass, Nappy, Butterfly, Green, N 49.00
Carnival Glass, Nappy, Butterly, Marigold 27.50
Carnival Glass, Nappy, Grape & Cable, Blue .... 63.00 To 68.00
Carnival Glass, Nappy, Grape & Cable, Marigold 45.00
Carnival Glass, Nappy, Grape & Lattice, One Handle, Imperial, Marigold 21.00
Carnival Glass, Nappy, Holly Berry, Green, N 39.00
Carnival Glass, Nappy, Holly Spray, Dark Purple 35.00
Carnival Glass, Nappy, Illusion, Blue 48.00
Carnival Glass, Nappy, Leaf Luster, Amethyst 20.00
Carnival Glass, Nappy, Leaf Rays, White, 1 Handle 39.00
Carnival Glass, Nappy, Pansy, Marigold, Imperial 18.00
Carnival Glass, Nappy, Persian Medallion, Marigold, 2 Handles 16.00
Carnival Glass, Nappy, Rose Panel, Marigold 15.00
Carnival Glass, Pintray, Seacoast, Iridescent, Deep Green 95.00
Carnival Glass, Pitcher & Tumbler, Marigold, Grape, Arbor, Tankard, Set 215.00
Carnival Glass, Pitcher, Butterfly & Fern, Amethyst 350.00
Carnival Glass, Pitcher, Cherries & Blossoms, Blue 105.00
Carnival Glass, Pitcher, Cherries & Blossoms, Blue, Hand Decoration 115.00
Carnival Glass, Pitcher, Cherries & Blossoms, Hand Decorated, Black 110.00
Carnival Glass, Pitcher, Dandelion, Paneled, Iridescent, Blue, Tankard 315.00
Carnival Glass, Pitcher, Floral & Grape, Purple 175.00
Carnival Glass, Pitcher, Frosted Windmill, Marigold, Imperial 30.00
Carnival Glass, Pitcher, Grape & Cable, Marigold 29.00
Carnival Glass, Pitcher, Grape & Lattice, Marigold 130.00
Carnival Glass, Pitcher, Grapes, Marigold, Imperial 48.00
Carnival Glass, Pitcher, Milk, Cherry, Green, Red Cherries, Millersburg 450.00
Carnival Glass, Pitcher, Milk, Grape, White 20.00
Carnival Glass, Pitcher, Milk, Mayflower, Smoke Green 125.00
Carnival Glass, Pitcher, Milk, Raspberry Luster, Iced Blue 875.00
Carnival Glass, Pitcher, Milk, Raspberry, Purple 90.00
Carnival Glass, Pitcher, Milk, Star Medallion, Marigold .... 18.00 To 22.00
Carnival Glass, Pitcher, Pastel, Poinsettia Pattern, 5 1/2 In.High 95.00
Carnival Glass, Pitcher, Rose Marie, Cobalt Blue & Green 1550.00
Carnival Glass, Pitcher, Rose, Marigold, Imperial 48.00
Carnival Glass, Pitcher, Strawberry, Scroll, Iridescent, Blue 395.00
Carnival Glass, Pitcher, Tankard, Lattice And Grape, Marigold, Set Of 4 .... 95.00
Carnival Glass, Pitcher, Treebark, Marigold, 8 1/2 In. 30.00
Carnival Glass, Pitcher, Water, Acorn Burr, Purple 495.00
Carnival Glass, Pitcher, Water, Apple Tree, Marigold 138.00
Carnival Glass, Pitcher, Water, Blueberry, Cobalt Blue 250.00
Carnival Glass, Pitcher, Water, Bouquet, Marigold 110.00
Carnival Glass, Pitcher, Water, Diamond Lace, Purple 175.00
Carnival Glass, Pitcher, Water, Fashion, Marigold 69.00
Carnival Glass, Pitcher, Water, Floral & Grape, Marigold 75.00
Carnival Glass, Pitcher, Water, Grape & Cable, Marigold, N 140.00
Carnival Glass, Pitcher, Water, Grape, Marigold, Ruffled Top, Bulbous 75.00
Carnival Glass, Pitcher, Water, Iris & Herringbone, Marigold 25.00
Carnival Glass, Pitcher, Water, Luster Rose, Marigold 30.00
Carnival Glass, Pitcher, Water, Peacock At Fountain, Marigold, N 140.00
Carnival Glass, Pitcher, Water, Robin, Marigold 80.00
Carnival Glass, Pitcher, Water, Vineyard, Marigold 45.00
Carnival Glass, Plate, Apple Blossom & Twigs, Amethyst, 8 In. 65.00
Carnival Glass, Plate, Basketweave Back, Purple, Ruffled, Nippon, 9 In. 33.00
Carnival Glass, Plate, Cherry Chain, Marigold, 6 1/2 In. 27.50
Carnival Glass, Plate, Chop, Four Flowers, Purple 350.00

Carnival Glass, Plate, Chop, Hattie, Green, 10 1/2 In.	245.00
Carnival Glass, Plate, Chop, Heavy Grape, Marigold	95.00
Carnival Glass, Plate, Chop, Heavy Grape, Marigold, 12 In.	150.00
Carnival Glass, Plate, Chop, Little Flowers & Crab Claw, Cobalt Blue	400.00
Carnival Glass, Plate, Chop, Little Flowers, Marigold, 10 In.	135.00
Carnival Glass, Plate, Chop, Persian Garden, Purple, Iridescent, 15 In.	1950.00
Carnival Glass, Plate, Chop, Stag & Holly, Marigold, Large, Footed	425.00
Carnival Glass, Plate, Chop, Wishbone, Marigold	250.00
Carnival Glass, Plate, Chrysanthemum, Green, Nuart, 10 In.	985.00
Carnival Glass, Plate, Fish Scale & Beads, Purple, 7 1/2 In.	39.00
Carnival Glass, Plate, Floral & Optic, White, Flat, Footed, 10 In.	65.00
Carnival Glass, Plate, Four Flowers, Purple, 9 1/2 In.	125.00
Carnival Glass, Plate, Frosted Block, 9 In.	6.00
Carnival Glass, Plate, Good Luck, Marigold, Flat, 9 In.	125.00
Carnival Glass, Plate, Good Luck, Silver Iridescent, Purple	135.00
Carnival Glass, Plate, Grape & Cable, Amethyst, 9 In.	48.00
Carnival Glass, Plate, Grape & Cable, Flat, Hand Grip, Green, N, 7 3/4 In.	50.00
Carnival Glass, Plate, Grape & Cable, Marigold	45.00
Carnival Glass, Plate, Grape, Ice Blue, 9 In.	95.00
Carnival Glass, Plate, Heavy Grape, Amber, 8 In.	45.00
Carnival Glass, Plate, Holly, Blue, Iridescent, 9 1/2 In.	82.00
Carnival Glass, Plate, Holly, Blue, 10 In.	95.00
Carnival Glass, Plate, Imperial Grape, Marigold, 9 In.	28.00
Carnival Glass, Plate, Imperial Jewel, Red, 8 1/2 In.	55.00
Carnival Glass, Plate, Leaf Chain, Marigold, 7 3/4 In.	18.00
Carnival Glass, Plate, Orange Tree, Marigold, 9 In.	79.00
Carnival Glass, Plate, Pastel, Grapevine Lattice, 7 In.	35.00
Carnival Glass, Plate, Peacock Eye, 9 In.	95.00
Carnival Glass, Plate, Persian Medallion, Marigold, 6 In.	19.00
Carnival Glass, Plate, Petal & Fan, Purple, 6 In.	20.00
Carnival Glass, Plate, Pine Cone, Marigold, 6 In.	24.00
Carnival Glass, Plate, Poppy, White, 9 1/2 In.	250.00
Carnival Glass, Plate, Purple Grape & Cable, Iridescent, Northwood, 9 In.	85.00
Carnival Glass, Plate, Show, Poppy, Pastel Blue, 9 1/4 In.	230.00
Carnival Glass, Plate, Strawberry, Purple, Flat, 9 In.	70.00
Carnival Glass, Plate, Strawberry, Purple, Hand Grip, N, 7 1/2 In.	60.00
Carnival Glass, Plate, Strawberry, Purple, N, 9 In.	69.00
Carnival Glass, Plate, Thistle & Thorn, Footed, Marigold, 8 1/2 In.	25.00
Carnival Glass, Plate, Three Fruits, Marigold, 9 In.	40.00
Carnival Glass, Plate, Vintage, Purple, 6 In.	30.00
Carnival Glass, Plate, Wishbone, Amethyst, Footed, 8 1/2 In.	125.00
Carnival Glass, Punch Bowl & Base, Flute, Millersburg	155.00
Carnival Glass, Punch Bowl & Stand, Acorn Burrs, Amethyst, N	460.00
Carnival Glass, Punch Bowl Set, Grape & Vine, Gold Iridescent, 13 Piece	175.00
Carnival Glass, Punch Bowl Set, Marigold, 8 Piece	180.00
Carnival Glass, Punch Bowl, Grape & Cable, Purple, N	45.00
Carnival Glass, Punch Bowl, Stork In Rushes, Marigold	38.00
Carnival Glass, Punch Cup, Grape & Cable, Amethyst, Northwood	18.00
Carnival Glass, Punch Cup, Grape & Cable, Purple	15.00
Carnival Glass, Punch Cup, Persian Medallion, Fenton's Rose, Amethyst, Signed	25.00
Carnival Glass, Punch Set, Broken Arches, Marigold, 13 Piece	175.00
Carnival Glass, Punch Set, Grape & Cable, Purple, Northwood, 2 Piece	390.00
Carnival Glass, Punch Set, Grape & Vine, Gold Iridescent, 13 Piece	175.00
Carnival Glass, Punch Set, Imperial Grape, Green	500.00
Carnival Glass, Punch Set, Marigold, Bowl, Stand, 6 Cups	150.00
Carnival Glass, Punch Set, Memphis, Amethyst, Northwood, 5 Piece	400.00
Carnival Glass, Punch Set, Memphis, Purple, 8 Piece	250.00
Carnival Glass, Punch Set, Orange Tree, Marigold, 8 Piece	110.00
Carnival Glass, Punch Set, S Repeat, Purple, 12 Piece	1250.00
Carnival Glass, Punch Set, Two-Piece Bowl, 6 Handled Cups, Green, Marked	500.00
Carnival Glass, Relish, Poppy, Green	22.00
Carnival Glass, Relish, Poppy, Purple, Oval, Northwood	45.00
Carnival Glass, Rose Bowl, Amethyst, Leaf & Beads, 3-Footed	50.00
Carnival Glass, Rose Bowl, Beaded Cable, Green	55.00
Carnival Glass, Rose Bowl, Beaded Cable, Marigold, Northwood	42.50

Carnival Glass, Rose Bowl, Beaded Grape, Purple 40.00
Carnival Glass, Rose Bowl, Daisy & Plume, Green, Northwood 35.00
Carnival Glass, Rose Bowl, Drapery, Aqua Opalescent 90.00
Carnival Glass, Rose Bowl, Garland, Blue 55.00
Carnival Glass, Rose Bowl, Grape Delight, White 85.00
Carnival Glass, Rose Bowl, Grape, Purple, 6-Footed 50.00
Carnival Glass, Rose Bowl, Horse's Head, Marigold 135.00
Carnival Glass, Rose Bowl, Leaf & Beads, Marigold .... 30.00 To 35.00
Carnival Glass, Rose Bowl, Persian Medallions, Marigold 40.00
Carnival Glass, Rose Bowl, Two Flowers, Blue, Large 175.00
Carnival Glass, Rose Bowl, Vintage, Marigold 15.00
Carnival Glass, Rose Bowl, Vintage, Purple, 6-Footed .... 40.00 To 55.00
Carnival Glass, Saltshaker, Horseshoe, Purple 75.00
Carnival Glass, Sauce, Dahlia, White 32.00
Carnival Glass, Sauce, Panther, Marigold 18.00
Carnival Glass, Sauce, Peacock At Fountain, Marigold, Northwood 12.00
Carnival Glass, Sauce, Singing Bird, Green 39.00
Carnival Glass, Sauce, Wreathed Cherry, Amethyst 16.00
Carnival Glass, Sauce, 4 Feathered Scroll, Green 14.00
Carnival Glass, Shade, White, Northwood 60.00
Carnival Glass, Sherbet, Bouquet & Lattice, Marigold, Footed 2.95
Carnival Glass, Sherbet, Maple Leaf, Stemmed, Iridescent, Northwood 45.00
Carnival Glass, Spittoon, Swirled Hobnail, Marigold 325.00
Carnival Glass, Spooner, Beaded Shell, Marigold 20.00
Carnival Glass, Spooner, Butterfly & Berry, Marigold 20.00
Carnival Glass, Spooner, Grape & Cable, Purple 95.00
Carnival Glass, Spooner, Kitten, Marigold 75.00
Carnival Glass, Spooner, Luster Rose, Green 39.00
Carnival Glass, Spooner, Maple Leaf, Amethyst 50.00
Carnival Glass, Spooner, Palm Beach, White 60.00
Carnival Glass, Spooner, Peach, White, N 60.00
Carnival Glass, Spooner, Peacock At Fountain, Blue 89.00
Carnival Glass, Sugar & Creamer, Flute, Marigold 14.00
Carnival Glass, Sugar & Creamer, Flute, Purple 85.00
Carnival Glass, Sugar & Creamer, Grape & Gothic Arches, Green 55.00
Carnival Glass, Sugar & Creamer, Grape, Marigold, On Pedestal 20.00
Carnival Glass, Sugar & Creamer, Orange Tree, White 68.00
Carnival Glass, Sugar & Creamer, Raised Rose, Amber, Large 35.00
Carnival Glass, Sugar & Creamer, Stippled Ray, Blue 25.00
Carnival Glass, Sugar & Creamer, Strutting Peacock, Amethyst .... 70.00 To 90.00
Carnival Glass, Sugar & Creamer, Vintage, Marigold, Old Northwood Mark 35.00
Carnival Glass, Sugar & Creamer, With Candlesticks, Marigold, 4 Piece 50.00
Carnival Glass, Sugar, Basketweave & Cable, Marigold, Covered 35.00
Carnival Glass, Sugar, Butterfly & Berry, Marigold, Covered 35.00
Carnival Glass, Sugar, Colonial, Aqua Opalescent 45.00
Carnival Glass, Sugar, Grape & Cable, Green, Covered 175.00
Carnival Glass, Sugar, Grape & Gothic Arches, Marigold, Covered 27.50
Carnival Glass, Sugar, Grape & Thumbprint, Marigold, Covered 40.00
Carnival Glass, Sugar, Luster Flute, Green 20.00
Carnival Glass, Sugar, Luster Flute, Marigold, Northwood 18.50
Carnival Glass, Sugar, Peacock At Fountain, Blue 110.00
Carnival Glass, Sugar, Star & File, Marigold 15.00
Carnival Glass, Sweetmeat, Grape & Cable, Purple 195.00
Carnival Glass, Syrup, Etched Daisy, Marigold 175.00
Carnival Glass, Table Set, Cherry Wreath, Marigold, 4 Piece 175.00
Carnival Glass, Table Set, Flute, Marigold, N, 4 Piece 100.00
Carnival Glass, Table Set, Singing Birds, Marigold, N, 3 Piece 135.00
Carnival Glass, Tankard, Grape & Cable, Marigold 35.00
Carnival Glass, Tankard, Star Medallion, Marigold 15.00
Carnival Glass, Toothpick, Flute, Marigold 35.00
Carnival Glass, Toothpick, Kitten, Marigold 55.00
Carnival Glass, Toothpick, Miter Panel, Dark Marigold 150.00
Carnival Glass, Toothpick, 3 Kittens Drinking Milk, Marigold 115.00
Carnival Glass, Tray, Card, Grape & Cable, Green, N, 7 3/4 In. 45.00
Carnival Glass, Tray, Card, Three Fruits, Purple, 7 1/2 In. 50.00

Carnival Glass, Tray, Dresser, Grape & Cable, Marigold 165.00
Carnival Glass, Tray, Iris Herringbone, Marigold, 11 3/4 In. 6.00
Carnival Glass, Tray, Pin, Grape & Cable, Dark Amethyst, Northwood, 5 3/4 In. 195.00
Carnival Glass, Tray, Pin, Seacoast, Green 180.00
Carnival Glass, Tray, Pin, Seacoast, Marigold 225.00
Carnival Glass, Tray, Pin, Seacoast, Purple 175.00
Carnival Glass, Tray, Pin, Sunflower, Marigold 175.00
Carnival Glass, Tray, Pin, Sunflower, Purple 140.00
Carnival Glass, Tray, Sandwich, Vintage, Marigold, Center Handle 22.00
Carnival Glass, Tumbler, Acorn Burr, Amethyst 40.00
Carnival Glass, Tumbler, Acorn Burr, Green 45.00
Carnival Glass, Tumbler, Amethyst, Wreathed Cherry 30.00
Carnival Glass, Tumbler, Apple Tree, Marigold 15.00
Carnival Glass, Tumbler, Beaded Shell, Purple 48.00
Carnival Glass, Tumbler, Blackberry Block, Purple 20.00
Carnival Glass, Tumbler, Blueberry, Blue 65.00
Carnival Glass, Tumbler, Butterfly & Berry, Blue 27.00
Carnival Glass, Tumbler, Butterfly & Berry, Marigold .... 13.00 To 20.00
Carnival Glass, Tumbler, Butterfly & Fern, Marigold 25.00
Carnival Glass, Tumbler, Butterfly & Plume, Amethyst 29.00
Carnival Glass, Tumbler, Daisy & Lattice, Marigold 15.00
Carnival Glass, Tumbler, Dandelion, Marigold 39.00
Carnival Glass, Tumbler, Dandelion, Purple, N .... 38.00 To 39.00
Carnival Glass, Tumbler, Diamond Lace, Purple 30.00
Carnival Glass, Tumbler, Double Star, Green 45.00
Carnival Glass, Tumbler, Feather & Heart, Marigold 75.00
Carnival Glass, Tumbler, Field Flower, Marigold 26.00
Carnival Glass, Tumbler, Floral & Grape, Iridescent, Amethyst 22.00
Carnival Glass, Tumbler, Floral & Grape, White 35.00
Carnival Glass, Tumbler, Fluffy Peacock, Blue 60.00
Carnival Glass, Tumbler, Flute, Purple 40.00
Carnival Glass, Tumbler, Grape & Cable, Amethyst, Northwood 29.75
Carnival Glass, Tumbler, Grape & Cable, Marigold 18.00
Carnival Glass, Tumbler, Grape & Cable, Purple .... 22.00 To 45.00
Carnival Glass, Tumbler, Grape & Gothic Arches, Marigold 18.00
Carnival Glass, Tumbler, Grape & Lattice, Blue 15.00
Carnival Glass, Tumbler, Grape Arbor, Iced Blue 80.00
Carnival Glass, Tumbler, Grape Arbor, Marigold 27.00
Carnival Glass, Tumbler, Grape, Iridescent, Marigold 16.00
Carnival Glass, Tumbler, Harvest Flower, Marigold 95.00
Carnival Glass, Tumbler, Imperial Grape, Amber, Stippled 32.50
Carnival Glass, Tumbler, Imperial Grape, Marigold 12.00
Carnival Glass, Tumbler, Inverted Strawberry, Amethyst, Near-Cut 145.00
Carnival Glass, Tumbler, Jeweled Heart, Marigold 65.00
Carnival Glass, Tumbler, Lattice & Grape, Marigold 15.00
Carnival Glass, Tumbler, Luster Rose, Marigold .... 8.00 To 15.00
Carnival Glass, Tumbler, Millersburg Diamond, Green 18.00
Carnival Glass, Tumbler, Orange Tree, Footed, Gold, White 85.00
Carnival Glass, Tumbler, Oriental Poppy, Blue 85.00
Carnival Glass, Tumbler, Oriental Poppy, Marigold .... 25.00 To 35.00
Carnival Glass, Tumbler, Oriental Poppy, Purple 45.00
Carnival Glass, Tumbler, Paneled Dandelion, Amethyst, Iridescent 35.00
Carnival Glass, Tumbler, Paneled Dandelion, Marigold 35.00
Carnival Glass, Tumbler, Peach, Blue, N 39.00
Carnival Glass, Tumbler, Peach, Green 35.00
Carnival Glass, Tumbler, Peacock At Fountain, Dark Purple 25.00
Carnival Glass, Tumbler, Peacock At Fountain, Marigold 32.00
Carnival Glass, Tumbler, Rambler Rose, Blue 32.00
Carnival Glass, Tumbler, Rambler Rose, Marigold .... 17.00 To 20.00
Carnival Glass, Tumbler, Raspberry Luster, Green 38.00
Carnival Glass, Tumbler, Raspberry, Green, Basket Weave Border, N, 4 1/2 In. 25.00
Carnival Glass, Tumbler, Raspberry, Green, Northwood 25.00
Carnival Glass, Tumbler, Raspberry, Marigold 17.00
Carnival Glass, Tumbler, Singing Bird, Green 35.00
Carnival Glass, Tumbler, Singing Bird, Purple, Marked N 25.00

Carnival Glass, Tumbler, Springtime, Marigold 40.00
Carnival Glass, Tumbler, Stork & Rushes, Blue 22.00
Carnival Glass, Tumbler, Stork & Rushes, Purple 20.00
Carnival Glass, Tumbler, Ten Mums, Blue 39.00
Carnival Glass, Tumbler, Tiger Lily, Purple .... 37.00 To 55.00
Carnival Glass, Tumbler, Treebark, Marigold, 4 1/4 In. 10.00
Carnival Glass, Tumbler, Vineyard, Marigold 22.00
Carnival Glass, Tumbler, Vintage, Marigold 22.00
Carnival Glass, Tumbler, Waterlily & Cattails, Marigold 22.00
Carnival Glass, Tumbler, Windmill, Marigold, Set Of 6 .... 35.00
Carnival Glass, Tumbler, Wreathed Cherry, Marigold .... 35.00 To 45.00
Carnival Glass, Tumbler, Wreathed Cherry, Purple 65.00
Carnival Glass, Vase, April Showers, Green, 11 In. 15.00
Carnival Glass, Vase, Blackberry Spray, Red, Hat Shaped 110.00
Carnival Glass, Vase, Car, Marigold, Pair 20.00
Carnival Glass, Vase, Car, Scroll, Marigold, Fittings, 7 In. 12.00
Carnival Glass, Vase, Corn, Green 165.00
Carnival Glass, Vase, Corn, Ice Blue 900.00
Carnival Glass, Vase, Corn, Iced White 150.00
Carnival Glass, Vase, Diamond & Rib, Marigold, 11 In. 15.00
Carnival Glass, Vase, Diamond Point, Amethyst, N, 11 In. 30.00
Carnival Glass, Vase, Fine Rib, Green, Ruffled Rim, 10 In. 18.00
Carnival Glass, Vase, Fine Rib, Marigold, 10 In. 12.50
Carnival Glass, Vase, Grape & Cable, Purple, Ribbed, 7 In. 20.00
Carnival Glass, Vase, Hat, Jack-In-The-Pulpit, Holly, Red 229.00
Carnival Glass, Vase, Hobnail, White, 6 1/4 In. 30.00
Carnival Glass, Vase, Horse Chestnut, White, Iridescent, 9 In. 125.00
Carnival Glass, Vase, Mary Ann, Marigold 48.00
Carnival Glass, Vase, Poppy Delight, Dark Marigold, 18 In. 225.00
Carnival Glass, Vase, Poppy, Mirrored Bottom, Purple, Large 1200.00
Carnival Glass, Vase, Ripple, Scalloped Edge, Purple, 12 1/2 In. 32.00
Carnival Glass, Vase, Tadpole, Green, Ruffled Top, 4 X 6 In. 10.00
Carnival Glass, Vase, Thorn, Amethyst, Northwood, 10 3/4 In. 50.00
Carnival Glass, Vase, Thorn, Marigold, 9 1/2 In. 30.00
Carnival Glass, Vase, Tree Bark, Green 22.00
Carnival Glass, Water Set, Beaded Shell, Purple, 6 Piece 666.50
Carnival Glass, Water Set, Butterfly & Berry, Marigold, 4 Piece 130.00
Carnival Glass, Water Set, Butterfly & Plume, Cobalt Blue, 6 Piece 425.00
Carnival Glass, Water Set, Diamond Lace, Purple, Iridescent, 7 Piece 425.00
Carnival Glass, Water Set, Diamond Lace, Purple, 7 Piece .... 325.00 To 475.00
Carnival Glass, Water Set, Fashion, Marigold, 5 Piece 200.00
Carnival Glass, Water Set, Fashion, Marigold, 7 Pieces 225.00
Carnival Glass, Water Set, Floral & Grape Variant, Marigold, 7 Piece 150.00
Carnival Glass, Water Set, Frosted Windmill Panels, Marigold, 7 Piece 65.00
Carnival Glass, Water Set, Grape & Cable, Amethyst, N, 7 Piece .... 350.00 To 500.00
Carnival Glass, Water Set, Grape & Cable, Thumbprint Pitcher, Amethyst, N 485.00
Carnival Glass, Water Set, Grape & Cable, 5 Pieces, Marigold 275.00
Carnival Glass, Water Set, Greek Key, Green, 5 Piece 1100.00
Carnival Glass, Water Set, Imperial Grape, Green, 7 Piece 160.00
Carnival Glass, Water Set, Imperial Grape, Marigold, 7 Piece 120.00
Carnival Glass, Water Set, Imperial Grape, Smoky Purple, 7 Piece 54.00
Carnival Glass, Water Set, Inverted Coin Dot, Marigold, 7 Piece 300.00
Carnival Glass, Water Set, Inverted Strawberry, Purple, 7 Piece 1600.00
Carnival Glass, Water Set, Lattice & Daisy, Marigold, 7 Piece .... 80.00 To 165.00
Carnival Glass, Water Set, Lattice & Grape, Cobalt Blue, 7 Piece 475.00
Carnival Glass, Water Set, Lattice & Grape, Marigold, 7 Piece 150.00
Carnival Glass, Water Set, Luster Rose, Marigold, 5 Piece 99.00
Carnival Glass, Water Set, Luster Rose, Marigold, 7 Piece 120.00
Carnival Glass, Water Set, Luster Rose, Pastel Marigold, 7 Piece 98.00
Carnival Glass, Water Set, Orange Tree Orchard, Marigold, 6 Piece 350.00
Carnival Glass, Water Set, Paneled Dandelion, Blue, 6 Piece 595.00
Carnival Glass, Water Set, Paneled Dandelion, Marigold, 7 Piece 465.00
Carnival Glass, Water Set, Peach, Blue, Northwood, 7 Piece 550.00
Carnival Glass, Water Set, Peacock At Fountain, Cobalt, 7 Piece 385.00
Carnival Glass, Water Set, Rambler Rose, Blue, 5 Piece 395.00

Carnival Glass, Water Set, Singing Bird, Green, N, 9 Piece 525.00
Carnival Glass, Water Set, Singing Bird, Purple, Northwood, 7 Piece 475.00
Carnival Glass, Water Set, Tankard, Grapevine, Lattice, Purple 600.00
Carnival Glass, Water Set, Ten Mums, Marigold, 7 Piece 435.00
Carnival Glass, Water Set, Tiger Lily, Marigold, 6 Piece 110.00
Carnival Glass, Water Set, Tree Bark, Marigold, 7 Piece 125.00
Carnival Glass, Water Set, Vineyard, Marigold, 7 Piece .... 160.00 To 195.00
Carnival Glass, Water Set, Windmill, Marigold, Frosted, 7 Piece 98.00
Carnival Glass, Water Set, Windmill, Purple, 7 Piece 125.00
Carnival Glass, Whiskey, Golden Wedding 5.00
Carnival Glass, Whiskey, Grape & Cable, Purple .... 75.00 To 170.00
Carnival Glass, Wine Set, Imperial Grape, Marigold, 5 Piece 125.00
Carnival Glass, Wine, Imperial Grape, Marigold 14.00
Carnival Glass, Wine, Octagon, Marigold, 4 In. .... 10.00 To 15.00
Carnival Glass, Wine, Orange Tree, Marigold 20.00
Carnival Glass, Wine, Purple Imperial Grape, Iridescent 28.00
Carnival Glass, Wine, Vintage, Amethyst 25.00
Carousel, Deer, Dentzel, Jumping 2500.00
Carousel, Horse, Velvet Seat & Glass Eyes, American, C.1870 .... 950.00
Carousel, Horse, Wooden, Armitage Herchell, 1900 .... 300.00
Carousel, Horse, Wooden, Prancing, Glass Eyes, Life Size, C.1870 .... 2500.00

Cased glass is made with one thin layer of glass over another layer or layers
of colored glass. Many types of art glass were cased. Cased glass is
usually a well-made piece by a reputable factory.

Cased Glass, Basket, Apricot To Opalescent, Applied Clear Handle, 7 1/2 In. 110.00
Cased Glass, Basket, Blue Over White, Clear Flat Handle 45.00
Cased Glass, Basket, Butterscotch, Gold Metallics, Rosettes, 8 1/2 In. 175.00
Cased Glass, Basket, Dimpled Sides, Scalloped Round Top, Butterscotch, 7 In. 95.00
Cased Glass, Basket, Pink Inside, White Outside, Ruffled, Rope Handle, 6 In. 78.00
Cased Glass, Basket, Thorn Handle, Pink & White Stripe 85.00
Cased Glass, Basket, White & Blue, Twisted Crystal Handle, 6 In. 85.00
Cased Glass, Bowl, Ruffled Top, Pink, 5 1/2 X 6 In. 200.00
Cased Glass, Bowl, White Cut To Cranberry, Enameled Overlay, 9 X 5 1/2 In. 150.00
Cased Glass, Box, Sweetmeat, Cranberry, Enameled Overlay, 7 1/2 In. 150.00
Cased Glass, Butterscotch, White, Clear Reeded Handle, 6 In. 45.00
Cased Glass, Compote, Cut To Cranberry, Covered, Footed, 8 X 6 In. 170.00
Cased Glass, Cruet, Cranberry Spatter, Leaf Mold 225.00
Cased Glass, Jar, Cracker, Florette, Pink, Silver Bail Handle 195.00
Cased Glass, Pepper, Quilted Phlox, Green 25.00
Cased Glass, Pitcher, Ruffled Top, White And Pink, 9 In. 200.00
Cased Glass, Pitcher, Water, Guttate, Glossy Pink 225.00
Cased Glass, Salt & Pepper, Flower Pattern 45.00
Cased Glass, Saltshaker, Paneled Shell, Pink 23.00
Cased Glass, Saltshaker, Pink, Lapped Leaf 25.00
Cased Glass, Spooner, Cut To Cranberry, Enameled Decoration, 6 In. 95.00
Cased Glass, Sugar Shaker, Glossy Pink Cone 48.00
Cased Glass, Sugar Shaker, Glossy Pink Guttate 92.00
Cased Glass, Sugar Shaker, Pink, Cone Pattern 60.00
Cased Glass, Syrup, Cranberry Spatter, Leaf Mold 250.00
Cased Glass, Vase, Blue Over White, Melon Shape, Ruffled Top, 8 1/4 In. 25.00
Cased Glass, Vase, Clear Ruffled Trim On Top, Pink Inside, 9 In., Pair 35.00
Cased Glass, Vase, Marshmallow, Bluish Cast, Swirled, Flared Ribbon Edge 85.00
Cased Glass, Vase, Melon Shape, Ruffled Top, Blue Over White, 8 1/4 In. 25.00
Cased Glass, Vase, Owl, 12 In. 30.00
Cased Glass, Vase, Pink On White, Ruffled Rim, Applied Decoration, 8 In. 18.00
Cased Glass, Vase, Yellow, Spangled, Gold Decoration, Butterflies, Leaves 25.00
Cash Register, see Store, Cash Register

Castor sets have been known as early as 1705. Most of those that have been
found today date from Victorian times. A castor set usually consists of a
silver-plated frame that holds three to seven condiment bottles. The pickle
castor was a single glass jar about six inches high and held in a silver frame.
A cover and tongs were kept with the jar. They were popular from 1890 to

1900. The McK numbers refer to the book "American Glass" by George and Helen McKearin.

Castor Set, see also various porcelain and glass categories

Castor Set, 3 Bottles, Gothic Pattern, All Glass	55.00
Castor Set, 3 Bottles, Leaves, Medallions, Garlands, Reed & Barton, C.1867	58.00
Castor Set, 3 Bottles, Miniature, 2 In.	35.00
Castor Set, 4 Bottles, Blown Glass, 3 Mold, McK G 1-14, Eben Smith Pewter	160.00
Castor Set, 4 Bottles, Breakfast, Silver Plated Holder & Tops, E.P.N.S.	30.00
Castor Set, 4 Bottles, Cranberry, Amber, Blue And White Opalescent	45.00
Castor Set, 4 Bottles, English Hallmark Base, P.G.S., 8 In.	75.00
Castor Set, 4 Bottles, Etched, Pewter Stand	110.00
Castor Set, 4 Bottles, Geometric, Clear, Eben Smith Pewter Stand	160.00
Castor Set, 4 Bottles, Glass Stoppers, Revolving Metal Stand, Miniature	65.00
Castor Set, 4 Bottles, Leaf & Lattice Pattern, Child's	59.00
Castor Set, 4 Bottles, Opalescent, Cranberry, Canary, Clear	195.00
Castor Set, 4 Bottles, Pewter Stand, Rufus Dunham	170.00
Castor Set, 4 Bottles, Silver Plate Holder, Handled, 9 In.	32.00
Castor Set, 5 Bottles, Bellflower, Flint, Pewter Stand	275.00
Castor Set, 5 Bottles, Cranberry, Silver Plated Stand	158.00
Castor Set, 5 Bottles, Cranberry, Thumbprint, Meriden Silver Frame	149.00
Castor Set, 5 Bottles, Dove & Flowers On Wm.Rogers Base, 16 1/2 In.	135.00
Castor Set, 5 Bottles, Flint Gothic Arch, Pewter Stand, C.1860	60.00
Castor Set, 5 Bottles, Floral Decorated Silver Plate Frame, Wilcox, 16 In.	75.00
Castor Set, 5 Bottles, Pedestal Base, Loop Bail, Silver Plate	72.00
Castor Set, 5 Bottles, Pewter	50.00
Castor Set, 5 Bottles, Sandwich Glass Bottles, Victorian, 16 1/2 In.	120.00
Castor Set, 5 Bottles, Tiered Pedestal, Ornate Bail	135.00
Castor Set, 5 Bottles, Trimmed Frame And Bail, Resilvered	110.00
Castor Set, 5 Bottles, With Bell	90.00
Castor Set, 6 Bottles, Blown Glass, 3 Mold, McK G I-7, Rectangular Stand	120.00
Castor Set, 6 Bottles, Clear Glass, Silver Plate Mustard Spoon & Stand	170.00
Castor Set, 6 Bottles, Etched, Wilcox	120.00
Castor Set, 6 Bottles, Rectangular, Silver Plate Frame	100.00

Castor, Pickle, see also Amberina, Castor, Pickle, Pomona, Castor, Pickle, and various glass categories

Castor, Pickle, Amber Cane Insert, Silver Plated Frame & Tongs	90.00
Castor, Pickle, Amberina Glass, Inverted Thumbprint, Insert, Marked Tongs	475.00
Castor, Pickle, Amethyst Glass, Flowers, Deep Color	200.00
Castor, Pickle, Amethyst, Etched, Adelphi Silver Plate Frame	55.00
Castor, Pickle, Apple Blossom, Decorated Green, Plain Frame	175.00
Castor, Pickle, Apple Green Insert, Enameling	200.00
Castor, Pickle, Block Pattern, Tongs	55.00
Castor, Pickle, Blue Cane Insert, Tongs & Silver Plated Holder, Mid-1800s	125.00
Castor, Pickle, Blue Insert, Enamel Florals, Silver Frame & Tongs	195.00
Castor, Pickle, Blue Insert, Inverted Thumbprint Enameled In Flowers	265.00
Castor, Pickle, Blue Opalescent Swirl, Pear-Shaped Insert	175.00
Castor, Pickle, Blue, Beatty Rib, Opalescent Stripe, Footed Frame	275.00
Castor, Pickle, Buttons & Bars, Silver Plate Frame & Cover, Reed & Barton	75.00
Castor, Pickle, Cane & Rosette Insert, Silver Plated Frame Marked Meriden	72.00
Castor, Pickle, Cathedral, Aqua, 3 Latticed Windows, Door, 14 1/2 In.	65.00
Castor, Pickle, Child In Garden, Clear Paneled Insert, Berry Finial On Lid	65.00
Castor, Pickle, Clear Cupid & Venus Insert, Silver Plate Frame, Cover, Tongs	95.00
Castor, Pickle, Clear Octagonal Insert, Silver Plate Holder, Fancy Finial	45.00
Castor, Pickle, Clear Opalescent Swirled, Windows Pattern	175.00
Castor, Pickle, Clear Panel Insert, Silver Plated Stand, Dog Finial, Cover	57.50
Castor, Pickle, Clear Patterned Glass Insert, Silver Ornate Frames & Tongs	85.00
Castor, Pickle, Clear Prism Insert, Silver Plate Frame, Cover & Tongs	45.00
Castor, Pickle, Clear Swirl Glass, Pairpoint Frame	60.00
Castor, Pickle, Clear Threaded, Engraved Insert, Wilcox Silver Cover, 11 In.	145.00
Castor, Pickle, Cone Pattern, Ruby Stained, Footed Frame	175.00
Castor, Pickle, Cranberrry, Signed N In Circle	150.00
Castor, Pickle, Cranberry Insert, Enameled Florals	195.00
Castor, Pickle, Cranberry Inverted Thumbprint, Enameled, Pairpoint Holder	225.00
Castor, Pickle, Cranberry, Inverted Thumbprint, Enameled Daisies Insert	185.00

Castor, Pickle, Daisy & Button With V Ornament, Apple Green 175.00
Castor, Pickle, Daisy & Button, Cross Bar Insert, Square Bail 40.00
Castor, Pickle, Daisy & Button, With V Ornament, Vaseline, Footed Frame 175.00
Castor, Pickle, Decorated Amber, Pear-Shaped Insert 200.00
Castor, Pickle, Decorated Pink Satin, Lined, Bail On Jar 400.00
Castor, Pickle, Diamond & Sawtooth, Knickerbocker Silver Plate Frame 55.00
Castor, Pickle, Diamond-Quilted Mother-Of-Pearl, Rose, Grooves On Rim 425.00
Castor, Pickle, Diamond-Quilted, Enameled, Silver Plate Frame, Cover, & Tongs 100.00
Castor, Pickle, Diamond-Quilted, Mother-Of-Pearl Satin Glass, Green, Gold 300.00
Castor, Pickle, Double, Amethyst, Bulbous Inserts With Gold Flecks 275.00
Castor, Pickle, Double, Finger Flute, Blazes, Gray Floral, Bird Finial, Lid 150.00
Castor, Pickle, Embossed Band, Bird Finial, Clear, Hand Tongs, Resilver 110.00
Castor, Pickle, Fine Cut, Ornate Meriden Frame & Tongs 68.00
Castor, Pickle, Floral Spray On Base & Bail, Silver Plate 85.00
Castor, Pickle, Flowers On Insert, Plain Frame, Tongs 200.00
Castor, Pickle, Geometric, Bulbous, 1895, Ground Stopper, 5 1/2 In. 40.00
Castor, Pickle, In Frame, Complete, Apollo 75.00
Castor, Pickle, Inverted Thumbprint, Amethyst, Corset-Shaped Insert 225.00
Castor, Pickle, Inverted Thumbprint, Cranberry, 4 1/8 In. 47.00
Castor, Pickle, Milk Glass, Coreopsis, Green & White 175.00
Castor, Pickle, Ornamented, Frame & Lid, Signed Webster 33.00
Castor, Pickle, Paneled Dewdrop 28.00
Castor, Pickle, Rose In Snow, Double 50.00
Castor, Pickle, Ruby Stained Overlay Insert, Daisy Medallion, Metal Frame 40.00
Castor, Pickle, Sapphire, Blue Inverted Thumbprint, 11 1/4 X 4 In. 245.00
Castor, Pickle, Satin Finish Insert, Painting 280.00
Castor, Pickle, Silver Frame, Footed, Tongs, 12 1/2 In. 135.00
Castor, Pickle, Tongs, Diamond & Fan, Aurora Triple Plate Holder 40.00
Castor, Pickle, Tongs, Lid With Finial 47.00
Castor, Pickle, Tongs, Round Insert 65.00
Castor, Pickle, Unlined Satin Glass, Raspberry Decoration 175.00
Castor, Pickle, Utopia Optic, Blue, Plain Frame 200.00
Castor, Pickle, Vaseline, Daisy & Button, Pairpoint Holder, Tongs 15.00
Castor, Pickle, Vaseline, Fine Cut, Pairpoint Silver Stand, Tongs 125.00
Castor, Pickle, Windows Pattern, Decorated Cobalt Blue 225.00
Castor, Pickle, With Fork, Quadruple Silver Plate Frame, Middletown Plate Co. 57.00
Castor, Pickle, Zipper Pattern, Green, Plain Frame 125.00
Catalina, Vase, Blue Matte, 9 In. 14.00
    Catalogue, see Paper, Catalogue
    Caughley, see also Salopian
Caughley, Tray, Chinese Junk In Water, Blue & White, Salopian, 6 X 3 1/2 In. 75.00

Cauldon is an English pottery factory working after 1905.
    Cauldon, see also Indian Tree
Cauldon, Plate, Floral Border, Made For C.A.Selzer, 10 1/2 In., Set Of 12 .... 175.00
Cauldon, Plate, Flower, 9 3/4 In. 10.00
Cauldon, Platter, Scenic, Blue & White, Plaid Border, Pair 110.00
Cauldon, Stand, Umbrella, Chinoiserie, Hexagonal Sides To Flare Top, Cobalt 250.00

Celadon is a Chinese porcelain having a velvet-textured green-gray glaze.
Japanese and Korean factories also made a celadon-colored glaze.
Celadon, Bowl, Covered, Small 13.00
Celadon, Dish, Jade, Lacy Border, Chrysanthemum Centers, 4 1/2 In. 325.00
Celadon, Figurine, Duck, Base 3 1/2 In.Wide, 10 In.High 75.00
Celadon, Figurine, Foo Dog, Unglazed Paws, 6 1/2 X 7 1/2 In. 300.00
Celadon, Ginger Jar, Chinese 89.00
Celadon, Ginger Jar, Chinese, Old 89.00
Celadon, Jar, Biscuit, Lid Has Sugar Cane Finial 75.00
Celadon, Jar, Oil, South China Yuan, Ming, 2 1/2 In., Pair 45.00
Celadon, Jardiniere, Green, Blue, White, Footed, Square, 8 1/2 In. 120.00
Celadon, Pitcher, C.1910, Oriental Signature, 4 In. 25.00
Celadon, Pitcher, Pale Green, 6 In. 6.00
Celadon, Plate, Bird & Butterflies, 6 In. 75.00
Celadon, Plate, Birds & Butterflies Over Flowers, 7 1/2 In. 85.00

Celadon, Plate, Birds, Butterflies & Flowers, Cloud Motif, C.1785	85.00
Celadon, Plate, Salad, Bird & Butterfly Design	50.00
Celadon, Teapot, Dome Top	395.00
Celadon, Teapot, Pink & White Flowers, Green Bushes, Raffia Handle	42.00
Celadon, Vase, Blue Phoenix Bird, Floral, Foo Dog Handles, Flared, 17 In.	150.00
Celadon, Vase, Bulbous, Elephant Heads For Handles, Pair, 9 In.	265.00
Celadon, Vase, Cobalt Design, 9 In.	65.00
Celadon, Vase, Paneled, Light Green, Embossed Pink Floral, Gold Birds, 7 In.	85.00
Celadon, Vase, Temple, Chinese, 23 In.	350.00
Celadon, Vase, Urn, Grape & Leaf Underglaze, Korean, C.1850, 10 1/2 In.	50.00
Celadon, Vase, Wall, Oriental, Blue & White Flower, Green Leaves, 10 In.	35.00
Celluloid, Badge, Chauffeur, 1945	8.50
Celluloid, Blotter, Santa Claus, 1905	20.00
Celluloid, Box, Collar, Dark, 6 1/2 In.	10.00
Celluloid, Box, Dresser, Large Green, With Roses	8.50
Celluloid, Box, Satin Lining, Girl Feeding Chickens	16.00
Celluloid, Brush, Cothes, Fabric Fire Hose Co., N.Y., Lion Center	16.00
Celluloid, Buckle, Best, Carved, 1920s, 3 1/2 In.	15.00
Celluloid, Buffer, Nail	2.50
Celluloid, Case, Cigarette, Over Metal, Scenic Top, Signed, German	7.00
Celluloid, Comb, Baby, 2 Sided, Ornate Embossed Sterling Handle	20.00
Celluloid, Dresser Set, Amber, Occupied Japan, 8 Pieces	12.00
Celluloid, Dresser Set, Blue, Caramel & Pink Designs, 5 Piece	250.00
Celluloid, Dresser Set, Trunk Shape Box, Victorian Lady, 9 Pieces	110.00
Celluloid, Fan, Pierced With Celluloid Link Chain	7.00
Celluloid, Figurine, Felix The Cat, Pacing, 2 In.	20.00
Celluloid, Frame, Oval, 5 1/2 X 4 1/4 In.	2.50
Celluloid, Glove Stretcher	8.00
Celluloid, Hair Receiver & Powder Box	15.00
Celluloid, Letter Opener, Folding Knife	15.00
Celluloid, Match Holder, KKK, Hooded Rider On Horse With Caption	38.00
Celluloid, Match Safe, Black Shoe	18.00
Celluloid, Mirror, Picture Of Old Fashioned Lady	8.50
Celluloid, Napkin Ring, Rabbit, Yellow, Green Eyes	7.00
Celluloid, Notebook, Austin-Western Machinery, Seminude Picture, 1915	22.00
Celluloid, Pin, Santa Shape	5.00
Celluloid, Tea Set, Pink, Teapot, Creamer, 2 Cups	20.00
Centennial, Figurine, Ruth The Gleaner, Frosted, Gillinder & Sons, 4 In.	80.00
Centennial, Kerchief, Silk, Liberty Bell, Signed, 10 X 18 X 12 1/2 In.	29.00
Centennial, Vase, Hand Holding Torch, Camphor, Marked Centennial 1876, 7 In.	36.50

The Ceramic Art Company of Trenton, New Jersey, was established
in 1889 by J. Coxon and W. Lenox, and was an early producer of
American Belleek porcelain. Some lines are still being manufactured.

Ceramic Art Co., Bowl, Green, Flowers, Sterling Silver Holder, 4 In.	65.00
Ceramic Art Co., Box, Swirls, Flowers, Portrait Of Page, Heart Shape, 6 In.	135.00
Ceramic Art Co., Cider Pitcher, Belleek, Beaded Handle, Hand-Painted Fruits	110.00
Ceramic Art Co., Compote, Cream, Gold Design, Twig Handle, Pedestal, 6 In.	98.00
Ceramic Art Co., Cup, Friendly Sons Of St.Patrick, 2-Handled, Gold	135.00
Ceramic Art Co., Cup, Loving, Hand-Painted, Dated 1904	78.00
Ceramic Art Co., Jug, Hand-Painted Currants In Red, Green, Violet, 5 3/4 In.	105.00
Ceramic Art Co., Mug, Belleek, Berries, Peach & Pink Background, Palette Mark	87.00
Ceramic Art Co., Mug, Belleek, Hand-Painted Shore Scene, 3-Handled, 5 In.	215.00
Ceramic Art Co., Mug, Belleek, Painting Of Lighthouse & Water, K.S.initial	145.00
Ceramic Art Co., Mug, Brown & Green Pinecones, Hand-Painted, 5 In.	35.00
Ceramic Art Co., Mug, Cream, Grapes, Green, Gray Leaves, Hand-Painted	95.00
Ceramic Art Co., Mug, Hand-Painted Portrait Of A Monk, 5 1/2 In.	110.00
Ceramic Art Co., Mug, Ladies, Allover Silver Florals, White Ground	135.00
Ceramic Art Co., Mug, Lenox, Indoor Tavern, Sepia Colors, C.1900	175.00
Ceramic Art Co., Mug, Monk Playing Violin, 1903, 5 1/2 In.	95.00
Ceramic Art Co., Mug, Orange, Berries, Hand-Painted, Phipps, 4 3/4 In.	95.00
Ceramic Art Co., Mug, Portrait, Girl In Native Costume, Gold Outline, 5 In.	75.00
Ceramic Art Co., Mug, Shaded Lavender, Yellow, Purple Grapes, 5 3/4 In.	72.00
Ceramic Art Co., Mug, Shaving, Belleek, 3 Robins, Wooded Forest, Footed, 4 In.	145.00
Ceramic Art Co., Mug, Storks Decoration, 6 In.	140.00

Ceramic Art Co., Picture, Tankard, Standing Monk, Monochrome, C.1895, Marked 325.00
Ceramic Art Co., Pitcher, Cider, Belleek, Floral, Dark Green, 6 In. 75.00
Ceramic Art Co., Pitcher, Cider, Blackberries, Floral, Leaves, 6 In. 135.00
Ceramic Art Co., Pitcher, Hand-Painted Yellow & Purple Indian Corn, 13 In. 225.00
Ceramic Art Co., Pitcher, Lemonade, Belleek, Grapes & Leaves, Beaded 57.00
Ceramic Art Co., Pitcher, Lenox Belleek, Blackberries & Floral, 6 In. 135.00
Ceramic Art Co., Plate, Canadian Geese Flying Over Lake, Pine Trees, 7 In. 75.00
Ceramic Art Co., Sherbet, Belleek, Gold Trim, Palette Mark 60.00
Ceramic Art Co., Sugar & Creamer, Gold & Lavender, 1935, Signed 75.00
Ceramic Art Co., Tankard, Belleek, Grapes, Artist Signed, C.1897-98 .... 295.00
Ceramic Art Co., Tankard, Belleek, Peacocks, Pastel, J.Lubbin, 1916, 7 1/2 In. 145.00
Ceramic Art Co., Teapot, Mauser Silver, Three Piece 80.00
Ceramic Art Co., Tobacco Jar, Lenox, Monk, Smiling, Monochromatic, Green, 1899 .... 48.00
Ceramic Art Co., Vase, Allover Silver Florals, Art Nouveau, 6 In. 150.00
Ceramic Art Co., Vase, Belleek, Bird On Tree Stump, A.Williams 135.00
Ceramic Art Co., Vase, Belleek, Black Boy Playing Banjo, M.B.P., 1901, 11 In. 165.00
Ceramic Art Co., Vase, Gray Crackle Glaze, Gold Rim, 9 1/2 In. 75.00
Ceramic Art Co., Vase, Hand-Painted, 10 X 28 In. 225.00
Ceramic Art Co., Vase, Lenox Belleek, Pink Roses & Leaves, 19 In. 250.00
Ceramic Art Co., Vase, Lenox, Cobalt, Sterling Overlay, 4 In. 75.00
Ceramic Art Co., Vase, Lenox, Floral Silver Work, Silver Overlay, Brown, 5 In. 150.00
Ceramic Art Co., Vase, Lenox, Silver Overlay, Blue Ground, Electrolite, 4 In. 98.00
Ceramic Art Co., Vase, Lenox, Silver Overlays, Blue Background, 10 In. 110.00
Ceramic Art Co., Vase, Magpie On Black, Gold Insert, C.1897, 7 1/2 In. 115.00
Ceramic Art Co., Vase, Metallic Crackle, Art Nouveau, Artist Signed, 9 1/2 In 75.00
Ceramic Art Co., Vase, Metallic Gray & Gold Crackle, Art Nouveau, 9 1/2 In. 65.00
Ceramic Art Co., Vase, Orange To Brown, Portrait, Palette, 1901, 11 In. 165.00
Ceramic Art Co., Vase, Pink Roses, Green Leaves, Palette, 19 In. 195.00

*Chalkware is really plaster of Paris decorated with watercolors. The
pieces were molded from known Staffordshire and other porcelain models and
painted and sold as inexpensive decorations. Most of this type of chalkware
was made from about 1820 to 1870.*

Chalkware, Figurine, see also Kewpie

Chalkware, Bookend, Seminole Indian, Artist Signed, Orange, Brown, Pair 12.50
Chalkware, Figurine, Cat, Gray, Blue Eyes, 4 In. 22.00
Chalkware, Figurine, Cat, 6 In. 20.00
Chalkware, Figurine, Dog, 8 1/2 In. 100.00
Chalkware, Figurine, German Shepherd, Tall, Red Set Eyes, Base, 17 1/2 In. 35.00
Chalkware, Figurine, Girl Clutching Boy As Crab Crawls Up Toward The Base 55.00
Chalkware, Figurine, Man, Japanese, Sitting 20.00
Chalkware, Figurine, Squirrel, Sitting & Eating, Brown & Yellow, 6 In. 145.00
Chalkware, Figurine, 3 Little Pigs, Pink & Blue Bonnets & Diapers, 2 In. 3.00
Chalkware, Humidor, Black Man, Dark Green Cap Lid, Cigarette In Teeth, 9 In. 150.00
Chalkware, Statue, Carnival, Circus Horse, Riverview Park 10.00
Chantilly, Figurine, Oriental Male, European Lady, Open Baskets On Backs 1000.00
Chantilly, Plate, Sprig, Basketwork Rims, Outlines In Blue, 1760, Set Of 11 .... 650.00
Chantilly, Swan, French Bisque, Hissing, Numbered, 5 In. 100.00
Charlie Chaplin, Box, Handkerchief 25.00
Charlie Chaplin, Box, Pencil, Red, Tin 25.00
Charlie Chaplin, Film, 16MM, 100 Feet 6.00
Charlie Chaplin, Glass, Candy Container, Original Paint 65.00
Charlie Chaplin, Knife, Pocket, 2 1/2 In. 22.00
Charlie Chaplin, Tin, Windup, Shuffles With Cane, Iron Feet 350.00
Charlie McCarthy, Doll, Chalkware Carnival, 15 In. 15.00
Charlie McCarthy, Doll, Chalkware, Red Suit, 9 In. 11.50
Charlie MCcarthy, Doll, Effanbee, 19 In. 65.00
Charlie McCarthy, Game, Bingo 8.00
Charlie McCarthy, Game, Board 7.00
Charlie MCcarthy, Game, Radio Party, 1938 .... 32.00
Charlie McCarthy, Locket, Raised Figure, 1 3/4 In. 7.00
Charlie McCarthy, Spoon .... 5.50 To 6.00

*Chelsea grape pattern was made before 1840. A small bunch of grapes in a
raised design, colored with purple or blue luster, is on the border of the white*

plate. Most of the pieces are unmarked. The pattern is sometimes called Aynsley or Grandmother.

Chelsea Grape, Beaker, Covered, No Mark	25.00
Chelsea Grape, Creamer, Ribbed, Embossed Leaf Trim, Leaf Handle	22.00
Chelsea Grape, Plate, 12 Panels, Purple, 7 In., Pair	12.00
Chelsea Grape, Tea Set, Early 1800s, 24 Piece	798.00

Chelsea Keramic Art Works, see Dedham

Chelsea porcelain was made in the Chelsea area of London from about 1745 to 1784. Recent copies of this work have been made from the original molds.

Chelsea Sprig, Cup & Saucer, Purple Luster	25.00
Chelsea Sprig, Plate, Handled, 9 1/2 In.	15.00
Chelsea, Candlestick, Birds, Floral, Scrollwork Nozzles, 10 3/4 In., Pair	1600.00
Chelsea, Cup & Saucer, Pink, Pale Green, & Gold, Wheat, Vines, Ribbons, C.1770	100.00
Chelsea, Dish, Sunflower, Red Anchor Period, 8 7/8 In.	250.00
Chelsea, Dish, 2 Cucumbers, Cherries, Purple Berries Centered, Oval, 8 3/4 In.	175.00
Chelsea, Ewer, Trefoil Lip, Branch, Apple Blossom, Brown, Gray, 1880, 9 1/2 In.	425.00
Chelsea, Figurine, Boy Spading Garden, Girl Digging With Hoe, Marked, Pair	175.00
Chelsea, Figurine, Drunken Peasant, Lavender Hat, Red Anchor Period, 5 In.	2600.00
Chelsea, Figurine, Pantaloon, White Costume, Red Anchor Period, 4 3/8 In.	1300.00
Chelsea, Figurine, Parrot Perched On Tree Trunk, Gold Anchor, 9 In.	100.00
Chelsea, Pitcher, Blue Design, R & E Lever 1842 In Gold	75.00
Chelsea, Pitcher, Greek Key, High Gloss Green-Brown Glaze, 8 X 6 1/2 In.	265.00
Chelsea, Plate, Cake, Tab Handled, Thistle, Unmarked	35.00
Chelsea, Tankard, English Garden Flowers, Red Anchor Period, 5 3/4 In.	325.00
Chelsea, Vase, Inset Of Exotic Birds, Apple Green Background, 19th Century	185.00

Chinese export porcelain is all the many kinds of porcelain made in China for export to America and Europe in the eighteenth and nineteenth centuries. Included in the category are Nanking, Canton, Chinese Lowestoft, Armorial, Jesuit, and other types of the ware.

Chinese Export, see also Canton, Celadon, Nanking

Chinese Export, Basin, Famille Rose, 3 Figures, Flowering Tree, C.1880, 5 In.	85.00
Chinese Export, Basket, With Undertray, Florals, C.1800, 10 1/2 In.	425.00
Chinese Export, Bottle, Flask Shape, Blanc De Chine, Strap Handles, 12 In.	80.00
Chinese Export, Bottle, Flower Encrusted, C.1830, Pair, 15 1/4 In.	700.00
Chinese Export, Bowl, Blue & Gold Decoration, 16 In.	600.00
Chinese Export, Bowl, Covered, Round, Animal Finial, Rope Handles, 6 In.	80.00
Chinese Export, Bowl, Footed, Family Life Scenes, C.1800, 4 In.	250.00
Chinese Export, Bowl, Green Interior, Florals In Wraparound Panorama, 5 In.	32.50
Chinese Export, Bowl, Grisaille Swag & Florals, C.1800, 10 In.	200.00
Chinese Export, Bowl, Lotus Quatrefoil Panels, C.1768, 11 In.Diameter	1000.00
Chinese Export, Bowl, Scalloped Edge, Raised Pedestal Base, C.1840, 8 In.	275.00
Chinese Export, Box, Jewelry, Jade Trim, China, 11 In.	175.00
Chinese Export, Cachepot & Saucer, Yellow Ground, 9 In., Pair	300.00
Chinese Export, Charger, Famille Rose, Octagonal, C.1840, 13 In. *Illus*	300.00
Chinese Export, Creamer, Figural, Helmet	150.00

Chinese Export, Charger, Famille Rose, Octagonal, C.1840, 13 In.

Chinese Export, Cup, Scalloped Rim, Blue Gilt Handle, Coat Of Arms In Wreath 55.00
Chinese Export, Dish, Enamel Decorated, Fruit Form, 4 1/2 X 5 In. 32.50
Chinese Export, Dish, Hot Water, Octagonal, C.1780, 11 1/8 In. 250.00
Chinese Export, Dish, Oval Serving, Famille Rose, Floral, Bamboo, 10 In., Pair 70.00
Chinese Export, Dish, Serving, Famille Rose, C.1770, 16 1/2 In. 325.00
Chinese Export, Dish, Vegetable, Green Bird & Butterfly, Oval, Covered, 10 In. 350.00
Chinese Export, Figurine, Flying Buddhist Angel, Inset Eyes, 16 In. 125.00
Chinese Export, Figurine, Sage Holding Child, Enameled, C.1840, 24 In. 200.00
Chinese Export, Figurine, Seated Buddha, Lotus Blossom Base, C.1880, 16 In. 130.00
Chinese Export, Figurine, Seated Deity, Blanc De Chine, 19th Century, 4 In. 85.00
Chinese Export, Garden Seat, Famille Rose, C.1850, Pair 4200.00
Chinese Export, Jar, Food, Covered, Blue & White, 9 In. 155.00
Chinese Export, Jar, Ginger, Blue & White, Calligraphy Panels, 19th Century 120.00
Chinese Export, Jar, Ginger, Blue & White, Wood Top, C.1850, 9 In., Pair 150.00
Chinese Export, Jar, Ginger, Chinese Children At Play, Dome Lid, Marks, 4 In. 32.00
Chinese Export, Jar, Ginger, Enamel Floral 210.00
Chinese Export, Jar, Ginger, Famille Rose, Early 19th Century, 9 1/8 In. 300.00
Chinese Export, Jardiniere, Famille Noir, Floral & Birds, C.1880, Pair 275.00
Chinese Export, Jardiniere, White Flowers, Blue Decoration, 9 1/2 In., Pair 185.00
Chinese Export, Jardiniere, 19th Century, 14 X 15 In., Pair 850.00
Chinese Export, Jug, Milk, Helmet Shaped, Green Floral, Bamboo Shaped Handle 145.00
Chinese Export, Jug, Milk, Helmet Shaped, Green Floral, Handle, C.1790 .... 145.00
Chinese Export, Mug & Plate, Famille Rose, C.1750, 4 X 9 1/8 In. 275.00
Chinese Export, Mug, Fish, Flowers, Birds, Pastel Coloring, 2 1/4 In. 30.00
Chinese Export, Mug, White & Blue Borders, Armorial Crest, 6 In. 275.00
Chinese Export, Planter, Enameled, Bell Form, Peking, 14 In., Pair 500.00
Chinese Export, Plaque, Famille Rose, Men Trapping Bats, Signed, 16 1/2 In. 75.00
Chinese Export, Plate, Blue Fish Design On White, Fishscale Border, 12 In. 85.00
Chinese Export, Plate, Famille Rose, C.1730, Pair, 8 7/8 In. 200.00
Chinese Export, Platter, Orange Peel, Enameled, 18th Century, 11 In. 155.00
Chinese Export, Platter, Well-In-Tree, Green Bird & Butterfly, 16 1/2 In. 500.00
Chinese Export, Pot, Cosmetic, Celadon Glaze, Grisaille Shield, Pair 85.00
Chinese Export, Pot, Crocus, Dragon, Floral Decoration, 10 In. 275.00
Chinese Export, Rose Bowl, Flowers & Dragons, Teak Stand, China, 5 1/2 In. 185.00
Chinese Export, Salt, Open, Blue & White, Traces Of Gold, C.1800 .... 125.00
Chinese Export, Sauce, Shaped As Fruit, Enamel Pastel Colored, 4 X 5 In. 12.50
Chinese Export, Saucer, New York State Seal, C.1800, 5 1/2 In. 95.00
Chinese Export, Tea Bowl & Saucer, Grisaille Decorations, C.1800, 5 Sets 225.00
Chinese Export, Tea Caddy, Pewter Liner & Lid, Gold Leaf Flower, Black, 6 In. 125.00
Chinese Export, Tea Caddy, Rectangular 75.00
Chinese Export, Tea Set, Heavy Enamel, Brown & Gold, 5 Faces 200.00
Chinese Export, Tea Set, Thousand Flower, 19th Century, 13 Piece 110.00
Chinese Export, Teacup, Armorial Decoration, Applied Handles, 2 X 2 In. 60.00
Chinese Export, Teapot, Blue, White Rice Pattern, Bamboo Handle & Spout 55.00
Chinese Export, Teapot, Fruit Finial, Blue Decoration, C.1800, 5 1/2 In. 275.00
Chinese Export, Teapot, Genre Scenes, People In Oriental Dress 95.00
Chinese Export, Teapot, Strawberry & Leaves Cover, Hand-Painted 135.00
Chinese Export, Tureen & Cover, Blue & White, C.1775, 13 3/8 In. 375.00
Chinese Export, Tureen, Blue & White, Octagonal, Covered 550.00
Chinese Export, Tureen, Blue & White, Rabbit Handles, C.1760, 13 X 8 1/2 In. 950.00
Chinese Export, Tureen, Chicken 2600.00
Chinese Export, Tureen, Duck 2400.00
Chinese Export, Tureen, Flower & Leaf Design, Berry Knob, C.1800, 5 1/4 In. 125.00
Chinese Export, Urn, Figural Finial, Warrior Scene, Famille Verte, 17 1/2 In. 300.00
Chinese Export, Vase, Baluster Shape, Covered, C.1800, 11 In., Pair 325.00
Chinese Export, Vase, Baluster Shape, Famille Rose, Lions, 10 In. 200.00
Chinese Export, Vase, Blue Speckled Glaze, Baluster Shape, C.1850, 12 In. 60.00
Chinese Export, Vase, Dragon Handles & Medallions, 8 1/2 In., Pair 60.00
Chinese Export, Vase, Dragon Handles, Squirrel, Florals, C.1780, 12 In., Pair 2500.00
Chinese Export, Vase, Famille Rose, Florals, 20th Century, 11 In., Pair 65.00
Chinese Export, Vase, Famille Rose, Polychrome Florals, 9 In. 50.00
Chinese Export, Vase, Famille Rose, Polychrome Landscape, Signed, 9 In. 50.00
Chinese Export, Vase, Famille Verte, Court Scenes, 11 In. 400.00
Chinese Export, Vase, Floral Centers, Circles, Florals Allover, Rectangular 135.00
Chinese Export, Vase, Miniature, Floral, Cobalt Blue, Multicolor, 19th Century 40.00

Chinese Export, Vase, Temple, Family Scene, 19th Century, 17 In.	100.00
Chinese Export, Vase, Trumpet, Enameled Archaic Vessels, C.1820, Pair	300.00
Chinese Export, Vase, Yellow, White Flowers, Early 19th Century, 12 In., Pair	750.00

Chocolate glass, sometimes mistakenly called caramel slag, was made by the Indiana Tumbler and Goblet Company of Greentown, Indiana, from 1900 to 1903.

Chocolate Glass, Berry Set, Greentown, Leaf Pattern, 7 Piece	175.00
Chocolate Glass, Bowl, Marbleized, Hobnail & Fan, 8 X 3 In.	125.00
Chocolate Glass, Box, Rooster Cover	35.00
Chocolate Glass, Butter, Cactus, Footed And Covered	435.00
Chocolate Glass, Butter, Leaf Bracket, Greentown	175.00
Chocolate Glass, Compote, Cactus, Scalloped, Greentown	150.00
Chocolate Glass, Compote, Scalloped Top, Covered, 8 1/2 X 4 1/2 In.	200.00
Chocolate Glass, Cruet, Cactus, Clear Stopper, Greentown	95.00
Chocolate Glass, Cruet, Cactus, Greentown	35.00
Chocolate Glass, Cruet, Leaf Bracket	150.00
Chocolate Glass, Cruet, Wild Rose & Bowknot, Original Stopper, Greentown	210.00
Chocolate Glass, Cup, Punch, Shuttle, Greentown	45.00
Chocolate Glass, Dish, Dolphin, Fish Cover, Greentown	235.00
Chocolate Glass, Dish, Leaf & Bracket, 5 1/2 X 11 In.	75.00
Chocolate Glass, Dish, Rabbit Cover, Greentown	200.00
Chocolate Glass, Dish, Sweetmeat, Cactus, Footed & Covered	375.00
Chocolate Glass, Figurine, Dolphin, Fish Finial	28.00
Chocolate Glass, Match Holder, Rooster	20.00
Chocolate Glass, Mug, Cactus, Greentown	42.00
Chocolate Glass, Mug, Elephant, Handled	12.00
Chocolate Glass, Mug, Herringbone Buttress, Greentown	50.00
Chocolate Glass, Mug, Herringbone, Paneled	20.00
Chocolate Glass, Mug, Shuttle, Greentown	50.00
Chocolate Glass, Nappy, Cactus, Greentown	60.00
Chocolate Glass, Nappy, Cactus, Handled	55.00
Chocolate Glass, Nappy, Leaf Bracket, Tricornered, Greentown	32.00 To 45.00
Chocolate Glass, Nappy, Masonic, Greentown	105.00
Chocolate Glass, Nappy, Ruffled, 6 Points, Greentown	75.00
Chocolate Glass, Pitcher, Bamboo Base	55.00
Chocolate Glass, Pitcher, Cactus	200.00
Chocolate Glass, Pitcher, Syrup, Cactus, Lid	95.00
Chocolate Glass, Pitcher, Windmill	22.00
Chocolate Glass, Plate, Cactus	35.00
Chocolate Glass, Plate, Serenade, Greentown, 8 In.	120.00
Chocolate Glass, Powder Box, Orange Tree	50.00
Chocolate Glass, Salt, Master, Swan	22.00
Chocolate Glass, Sauce, Cactus, Footed	20.00
Chocolate Glass, Sauce, Geneva, Oval	39.00 To 49.00
Chocolate Glass, Sauce, Leaf Bracket	35.00 To 42.00
Chocolate Glass, Spooner, Leaf Bracket, Greentown	45.00 To 95.00
Chocolate Glass, Sugar & Creamer, Dewey Flower Flange, Greentown	100.00
Chocolate Glass, Sugar, Cactus, Covered, Greentown	65.00 To 145.00
Chocolate Glass, Sugar, Covered, Daisy	82.00
Chocolate Glass, Sugar, Dewey, Greentown	25.00
Chocolate Glass, Sugar, Leaf Bracket, Covered	70.00 To 75.00
Chocolate Glass, Syrup, Cactus, Lift Cover	155.00
Chocolate Glass, Syrup, Hearts Of Loch Laven, Greentown	50.00
Chocolate Glass, Syrup, Shuttle, Greentown	40.00 To 95.00
Chocolate Glass, Table Set, Leaf Bracket, Greentown, 4 Piece	285.00
Chocolate Glass, Toothpick, Cactus	45.00
Chocolate Glass, Toothpick, Greentown	30.00 To 45.00
Chocolate Glass, Toothpick, Witch's Head, Greentown	100.00
Chocolate Glass, Tumbler, Cactus Pattern	32.50
Chocolate Glass, Tumbler, Cactus, Greentown	12.00 To 42.00
Chocolate Glass, Tumbler, Greentown, Uneeda Biscuit	68.00
Chocolate Glass, Tumbler, Leaf Bracket	65.00
Chocolate Glass, Tumbler, Sawtooth Band	45.00 To 58.00
Chocolate Glass, Tumbler, Shuttle, Hearts Of Loch Laven	40.00

Chocolate Glass, Vase, Scalloped Flange	35.00
Chocolate Pot, Wine Luster Bands, Embossed Gold, 9 1/2 In.	12.50
Christmas Plate, see Collector, Plate	
Christmas Tree Ornament, see also Disneyana, Light	
Christmas Tree, Light Bulb, Bear With Guitar	10.00
Christmas Tree, Light Bulb, Bird, 4 In.	5.00
Christmas Tree, Light Bulb, Clown	10.00
Christmas Tree, Light Bulb, Diamond Point, Amethyst	22.00
Christmas Tree, Light Bulb, Diamond-Quilted, Amber	7.50
Christmas Tree, Light Bulb, Figural, Snowman	5.00
Christmas Tree, Light Bulb, Fish, Milk Glass, 2 1/2 In.	4.00
Christmas Tree, Light Bulb, Frog, 2 1/2 In.	5.00
Christmas Tree, Light Bulb, Fruit, Milk Glass, 1 1/2 In.	2.00
Christmas Tree, Light Bulb, Humpty Dumpty, Milk Glass, 3 In.	6.00
Christmas Tree, Light Bulb, Puss In Boots, 3 In.	60.00
Christmas Tree, Light Bulb, Santa Painted	9.00
Christmas Tree, Light Bulb, Santa With Pack, 2 1/2 In.	5.00
Christmas Tree, Light Bulb, Santa, Double Face, 3 In.	40.00
Christmas Tree, Light Bulb, Santa, Milk Glass	10.00
Christmas Tree, Light Bulb, Snowman, Milk Glass	10.00
Christmas Tree, Light Bulb, Star	5.00
Christmas Tree, Light Bulb, Zeppelin, 2 1/2 In.	70.00
Christmas Tree, Ornament, Boat, Paper, Candy Container, 2 In.	8.50
Christmas Tree, Ornament, Boot, Trimmed Cloth Candy Container, 4 In.	17.50
Christmas Tree, Ornament, Cardboard Tree, Santa & Toys Inside, C.1906, 6 In.	25.00
Christmas Tree, Ornament, Celluloid Animal	2.50
Christmas Tree, Ornament, Corn, Blown Glass, Pale Pink, 4 1/2 In.	22.00
Christmas Tree, Ornament, Fish	20.00
Christmas Tree, Ornament, Flying Angel, Bisque, Gold Garment, German, 4 In.	22.00
Christmas Tree, Ornament, Horn	7.00
Christmas Tree, Ornament, Large Grape Cluster	9.00
Christmas Tree, Ornament, Lion Head	35.00
Christmas Tree, Ornament, Paper, Victorian	2.50
Christmas Tree, Ornament, Paper, Victorian, Set Of 15	25.00
Christmas Tree, Ornament, Santa Claus, Hand-Sewn, Vivid Colors, 8 In.	10.00
Christmas Tree, Ornament, Santa, Cloth, On Skis, Plaster Face	8.75
Christmas Tree, Ornament, Santa, Plaster Face, 5 In.	8.00
Christmas Tree, Ornament, Santa, Plaster, 3 In.	10.00
Christmas Tree, Ornament, Wax Angel	35.00
Christmas, Tree, Light Bulb, Diamond Point, Amethyst, Wire Bail Hanger	22.00
Cigar Cutter, see Brass, Cutter, Cigar; Store, Cutter,	
Cigar	
Cigar Store Indian, see Wooden, Cigar Store Indian	

Cinnabar is a vermilion or red lacquer. Some pieces are made with hundreds of thicknesses of the lacquer that is later carved.

Cinnabar, Box, Red, 1 1/2 X 5 1/2 X 4 In.	25.00
Cinnabar, Plaque, Oriental Figures, Landscape, Framed, 8 1/4 X 10 In.	40.00
Cinnabar, Vase, China, Marked, 9 In.	85.00

Civil War mementos are important collectors' items. Most of the pieces are military items used from 1861 to 1865.

Civil War, Ammunition Kit, Carried On Belt	10.00
Civil War, Bayonet, Union, Triangular	12.00
Civil War, Book, Life & Campaigns Of General Robert E.Lee, 1870	15.00
Civil War, Box, Cap, Union Navy, Marked & Dated	30.00
Civil War, Box, Cartridge, Lead-Backed Brass, Union Insignia	28.00
Civil War, Buckle, Belt, Confederate Navy, Anchor & Crossed Cannons	45.00
Civil War, Bugle, Brass	45.00
Civil War, Bugle, Horstman Co., Phila., Burnished Brass, Ribbon & Pummel	35.00
Civil War, Bullet, Virginia Battlefields	1.00
Civil War, Canteen, Bull's-Eye	44.00
Civil War, Canteen, Confederate, Concentric Ring Type, Strap, Cover, Stopper	35.00
Civil War, Chest, Personal, Union Surgeon's, Silver Lid, Surgeon H.Janes	90.00
Civil War, Cup, Collapsible, Pewter	16.00

Civil War, Diary, Joseph S.C.Taber, Co.B, 23, Leather Bound, 4 X 6 In. 150.00
Civil War, Discharge Certificate, Battery L, 1st Regiment, N.Y.Infantry 12.50
Civil War, Discharge, Framed 28.00
Civil War, Drum, Infantry Marching, Painted American Eagle & Shield, 11 In. 225.00
Civil War, Form, Blank Inventory Of Personal Effects Of Deceased 3.50
Civil War, Knife, Bowie, Confederate, Wood Grips, Clip Blade, 1st Va.Cavalry 300.00
Civil War, Knife, Surgeon's, Probe To Remove Pellets, Tortoise Handle 35.00
Civil War, Mold, Bullet, For Shell & Ball, Confederate, Augusta, Ga. 35.00
Civil War, Revolver, Percussion, Adams Patent, Engraved Frame 275.00
Civil War, Sword, Belt, Buckle, Iron Scabbard, Brass Spread Eagle Buckle 175.00
Civil War, Sword, Brass Hilt 76.00
Civil War, Sword, Cavalry 125.00
Civil War, Sword, Leather Scabbard, Etched U.S.& Eagle, 30 1/4 In. 55.00
Civil War, Sword, Nashville Plow Works 475.00
Civil War, Telescope 50.00
Civil War, Tin, Black Powder Can For Pistol Or Percussion Priming, 4 In. 35.00
Civil War, Tintype, Officer, Case, 2 X 2 1/2 In. 28.00

Clambroth glass, popular in the Victorian era, is a grayish color and is semiopaque like clambroth

Clambroth, Candlestick, Dolphin, Turquoise Cup, 9 In. 250.00
Clambroth, Candlestick, Petal Socket, Pair 275.00
Clambroth, Candlestick, Petal Top, 9 1/2 In., Pair 90.00
Clambroth, Mug, Swan On 2 Sides, Rushes On Other, Gray Opaque 37.50
Clambroth, Pipe, Souvenir, Garretson, S.D., Painted Florals, 6 In. 25.00
Clambroth, Spill, Turquoise, Diamond Point, 3 Narrow Panels 375.00
Clambroth, Tumbler, Souvenir, Meadville, Mo. 16.00

Clewell ware was made in limited quantities by Charles Walter Clewell of Canton, Ohio, from 1902 to 1955. Pottery was covered with a thin coating of bronze, then treated to make the bronze turn different colors. Pieces covered with copper, brass, or silver were also made. Mr. Clewell's secret formula for blue patina bronze was burned when he died in 1965.

Clewell, Punch Set, Nail Head Pattern, Pedestaled Cups, 13 Piece 775.00
Clewell, Vase, Green Wash On Bronze, 9 In. 120.00

Clews pottery was made by George Clews & Co.of Brownhill Pottery, Tunstall, England, from 1806 to 1861.

Clews, see also Flow Blue

Clews, Bowl, Children & Dog, Dark Blue 75.00
Clews, Box, Floral Decoration, Hand-Painted, Matching Lid, 6 X 3 In. 48.00
Clews, Compote, Windsor Castle, Square Footed, Blue Transfer, 9 1/2 In. 215.00
Clews, Cup & Saucer, Dark Blue, Christmas Eve, Handleless Cup 175.00
Clews, Cup & Saucer, Deep Blue, American Eagle On Urn 265.00
Clews, Cup & Saucer, Jessamine, Mulberry 65.00
Clews, Cup Plate, Sandy Hill, Hudson River, Pink, 3 7/8 In. 55.00
Clews, Dish, Serving, Covered, Samuel Howitt, 1807, Field Sports, 12 1/2 In. 125.00
Clews, Dish, Vegetable, Blue, Hudson River, 9 3/4 X 7 3/4 In. 67.50
Clews, Dish, Vegetable, Zoological Gardens, London, Pink, 9 5/8 In. 63.00
Clews, Plate, Baker's Falls, Hudson River, Sepia, 9 In. 75.00
Clews, Plate, Dinner, Romantic Views, C.1820, 9 3/4 In. 56.00
Clews, Plate, Double Print River Scene, Blue 70.00
Clews, Plate, Escape Of The Mouse, 10 In. 155.00
Clews, Plate, Lafayette La Grange 250.00
Clews, Plate, Landing Of Lafayette At Castle Gardens, Dark Blue, 9 In. 225.00
Clews, Plate, Landing Of Lafayette, C.1840, 10 In. .... 150.00 To 225.00
Clews, Plate, Near Ft.Miller, Hudson River, Black, 9 In. 75.00
Clews, Plate, Peace & Plenty, Dark Blue, 9 In. 210.00
Clews, Plate, Peace & Plenty, 10 1/4 In. .... 175.00 To 200.00
Clews, Plate, Soup, Don Quixote, Deep Blue, 9 In. 150.00
Clews, Plate, States, Blue, 10 1/2 In. .... 225.00 To 275.00
Clews, Plate, Winter View Of Pittsfield, Mass., Dark Blue, 8 3/4 In. 200.00
Clews, Platter, Landing Of Lafayette, Blue, 15 1/4 X 11 3/4 In. 395.00
Clews, Platter, Landing Of Lafayette, Blue, 19 X 14 1/2 In. 995.00
Clews, Platter, Newburgh, Hudson River, Black, 15 1/2 In. 125.00

Clews, Tureen, Sauce, Dr.Syntax Series, 4 Scenes, Deep Blue Transfer 325.00

The Clifton Pottery was founded by William Long in Clifton,
New Jersey, in 1905. He worked there until 1908 making a line
called Crystal Patina.

Clifton, Bowl, Twist Handled, GFB, 4 X 5 In.	80.00
Clifton, Teapot, Crystal Patina, Green, Numbered, 3 1/2 In.	60.00
Clifton, Teapot, Indianware, Red With Black Indian, No.274, No Lid, 3 3/4 In.	35.00
Clifton, Vase, Crystalline, Shaded Greens, 6 In.	75.00
Clifton, Vase, Crystalline, Signed, 7 X 3 In.	55.00
Clock, see also Coca-Cola, Clock; Disneyana, Clock;	
Store, Clock	
Clock, Alabaster Base, French Statue, 8 Day, Time & Strike, Porcelain Dial	265.00
Clock, Alarm, Double Top, Bell, Brass	4.00
Clock, Alarm, Pictures Members Of McKinley's Cabinet, 1899	95.00
Clock, Alarm, Spinning Wheel, Lux	55.00
Clock, Alarm, Tin Can, Double Brass Bells On Top	25.00
Clock, Alex T.Willard, Grandfather, Cherry, Painted Face, C.1800, 8 Ft.3 In.	4500.00
Clock, Amber Glass, Octagonal, C.1881, 3 1/4 In.Diameter	85.00
Clock, Animated, Alarm, 2 Soldiers Striking Bell	28.50
Clock, Ansonia, Ardita, Marble, Porcelain Dial, 8 Day, 11 1/2 X 8 In.	110.00
Clock, Ansonia, Carriage, Silver Plated, Alarm, 6 1/4 X 4 1/2 In.	165.00
Clock, Ansonia, Chime, Brass Case	185.00
Clock, Ansonia, China, Visible Escapement, Signed Tide	200.00
Clock, Ansonia, Figural, Shakespeare Statue, 1881, Open Escapement	495.00
Clock, Ansonia, Figure 8, Wall, 21 1/2 In.	350.00
Clock, Ansonia, Gingerbread, Ornate, 24 In.	180.00
Clock, Ansonia, Gingerbread, Walnut, 30 Hour	110.00
Clock, Ansonia, Green China	150.00
Clock, Ansonia, Huntress & Fisher Double Statue Outside Escapement	550.00
Clock, Ansonia, Iron, Gilt Columns, Corinthian Capitals, 8 Day, 14 In.High	85.00
Clock, Ansonia, Iron, Ornamental Ring Ends, Marbleized Molding, 14 1/8 In.	95.00
Clock, Ansonia, Long Drop, Time & Strike	275.00
Clock, Ansonia, Mantel, Brass & Iron, Gilded Dial, 13 1/2 X 9 In.	410.00
Clock, Ansonia, Miniature Grandfather, Brass & Wood, 10 1/2 In.	200.00
Clock, Ansonia, Miniature, White Porcelain, Pink & Yellow Flowers, 5 3/4 In.	65.00
Clock, Ansonia, Outside Escapement Statue, Shakespeare	250.00
Clock, Ansonia, Outside Escapement, Metal Case, Roman Sculpture, 1892	350.00
Clock, Ansonia, Porcelain Dial, Visible Escapement	200.00
Clock, Ansonia, Porcelain, Hour & 1/2 Hour Strike, Floral, 13 X 14 In.	320.00
Clock, Ansonia, Porcelain, Pink, Yellow Roses, Blue Scrolled, 11 X 14 1/2 In.	395.00
Clock, Ansonia, Regulator, Long Drop, 31 1/2 In.	290.00
Clock, Ansonia, School, Long Drop, Walnut, 8 Day, Time & Strike	300.00
Clock, Ansonia, School, Oak, Long Drop, Time & Calendar	250.00
Clock, Ansonia, School, Walnut Dew Drop, 8 Day, Time & Strike	275.00
Clock, Ansonia, Short Drop, Ebony Case, 24 In.	280.00
Clock, Ansonia, Tear Drop, 8 Day, Approximately Dated 1878	450.00
Clock, Ansonia, Visible Escapement, Marble, 8 Day, 11 1/2 X 9 In.	110.00
Clock, Ansonia, Wall, Mahogany Case, 30 Day, 16 In.	150.00
Clock, Ansonia, Wall, 30 Hour, Strike, C.1840, 15 1/2 X 25 X 4 1/2 In.	325.00
Clock, Ansonia, Walnut Case, Bagdad Model, 8 Day, 50 In.	650.00
Clock, Ashwin Co., Walnut Case, 7 In.	2000.00
Clock, Atkins & Porter, Empire, 8 Day, Time & Strike, Weight Driven	450.00
Clock, Atlas, Desk, Brass, Standing Atlas Supporting Orb, European, 10 1/2 In.	75.00
Clock, Atmos, Perpetual, Brass & Glass, C.1940	185.00
Clock, Banjo, Simon Willard	3250.00
Clock, Becker, Vienna Regulator, 3 Weight	875.00
Clock, Beehive Waterbury Striker, 8 Day, Regulator .... *Illus*	175.00
Clock, Birge & Mallory, Triple Decker	445.00
Clock, Box, Brass Bezel, Pendulum, 8 Day, Strikes Hourly, C.1885-1900	50.00
Clock, Bracket, English, Gothic Style, Inlaid Mahogany Case, Double Fusee	450.00
Clock, Brass, Bicycle & Man, Clock In Wheel	240.00
Clock, Brass, Girl With Bonnet, Glass Case, Seth Thomas .... *Illus*	875.00
Clock, Brass, Wag-On-Wall, French, Time & Double Strike, Signed Dial	525.00

Clock, Beehive Waterbury Striker, 8 Day, Regulator

Clock, Brass, Girl With Bonnet,
Glass Case, Seth Thomas

Clock, Calendar, Maranville, Pat.3-5-81

Clock, French, Boulle, Base, C.1760, 42 In.
(See Page 102)

Clock, Ithaca, Calendar,
Pat.1866. Strikes
(See Page 103)

Clock. Kitchen. Calendar,
Strikes Rooster, Oak
(See Page 103)

Clock, Bronze, Figural, Athena On Her Chariot, 2 Stags, Draws Arrow, 22 In.	2300.00
Clock, Bronze, With Alarm, Carriage, French	275.00
Clock, Burwell Carter, Weight Driven, Double Dial	835.00
Clock, Calendar, Gilbert Grocery	275.00
Clock, Calendar, Maranville, Pat.3-5-81 .... *Illus*	700.00
Clock, Carriage, Black Iron, Side Glasses, Bottom Alarm	75.00
Clock, Carriage, Brass Repeater, Beveled Glass Sides, Porcelain Dial, Handle	675.00
Clock, Carriage, French, Brass, Black, Starr & Frost, 2 1/4 X 1 9/16 In.	500.00
Clock, Carriage, French, Brass, Porcelain Dial, Beveled Glass, 4 1/2 In.	225.00
Clock, Carriage, French, Repeater, Time, Strike, Alarm, Travel Case	900.00
Clock, Carriage, New Haven, 1920	18.00
Clock, Carriage, Repeating, Brass Case, Waterbury, Conn., C.1901	425.00

Clock, Chauncey Jerome, Mahogany, 8-Day Shelf, Eglomise Painting, 30 In.	150.00
Clock, Chauncey Jerome, School, Mahogany, 23 In.	325.00
Clock, Chelsea, Bronze Tambour Case, Ship's Bell Strike	260.00
Clock, Chelsea, Ship, Bell, Brass Case, 5 In.Face	250.00
Clock, Cherry, C.1889, Walter H.Durfee, Providence	2900.00
Clock, China, Ansonia Movement, Royal Bonn	225.00
Clock, China, Tall Hand Painted Floral Design, 9 1/2 In.	65.00
Clock, Chippendale, Bonnet Hood, Swan's Neck, Arched Dial, Moon, Date	3000.00
Clock, Cobalt Blue Glass, Octagonal, 4 3/4 In.	65.00
Clock, Cuckoo, Black Forest, 15 3/4 In.	50.00
Clock, Cuckoo, 3 Weight	225.00
Clock, D.Pratt, Empire, Shelf, 8 Day	210.00
Clock, Double Fussee, Carved Mahogany, C.1840	850.00
Clock, E.& S.W.Bartholmew, Shelf, Transparent Case	400.00
Clock, E.Currier, Wall, Mahogany & Giltwood, Lyreform, C.1830, 39 1/2 In.	3500.00
Clock, E.Howard, Oak Case, Skeleton Movement, Weight Driven, 42 X 18 In.	600.00
Clock, Edwardian, Mahogany, German, 1925	90.00
Clock, Electric Time Co., Master Clock, Floor Model, Oak, One Slave	500.00
Clock, Electric, Seagram VO	5.00
Clock, F.Kroeber, Wall, Walnut, Regulator No.31, Small	340.00
Clock, Formal Regulator, Mahogany, 1915	130.00
Clock, Forrestville, Electric, Heavy Brass Balance Wheel, Glass Dome	160.00
Clock, Francis Marshall, Durham, Tall Case, Mahogany, 18th Century, 7 Ft.3 In.	1750.00
Clock, French, Black Marble Base, Bronze Warrior Top, Porcelain Face, 20 In.	625.00
Clock, French, Black Marble, Bronze Mounts, C.1810	525.00
Clock, French, Boulle, Base, C.1760, 42 In. *Illus*	7100.00
Clock, French, Boulle, Tortoise Shell & Brass Inlay, Cherub Finial	3500.00
Clock, French, Cloisonne On Dial & Case	375.00
Clock, French, Crystal Regulator, Green Onyx Roof & Floor, Porcelain Dial	475.00
Clock, French, Crystal, Bow Front, Porcelain Dial, Mercury Pendulum	300.00
Clock, French, Enamel, With Candelabra, Colors On Bronze, Japy Freres	2000.00
Clock, French, Green Marble, 24K Gold Ormolu, Warrior Figure, 13 X 21 In.	595.00
Clock, French, Hall, Heavily Carved, Double Bell, C.1870	1300.00
Clock, French, Mantel, Bronzed Figural, Time Only, 11 In.	110.00
Clock, French, Mantel, Gilded Figures, Trees, Animals, Porcelain Face, 20 In.	340.00
Clock, French, Mercury, Brass Encasement, Beveled Glass Sides, 10 1/2 In.	295.00
Clock, French, Statue, Signed	655.00
Clock, French, Victorian, Walnut Case, 8 Day, Barometer, Chimes	575.00
Clock, French, Wall, 8 Day, Time & Strike, French, 8 In.	230.00
Clock, French, White Metal, Gold Dore, Cupid Leaning On Clock, 10 1/4 In.	225.00
Clock, Gaslight, American Waltham Watch Co., Leather Case	195.00
Clock, German, Box, Beveled Glass	215.00
Clock, German, Lenzkirch, Free Swinger, 7 Ft, 5 In.	225.00
Clock, German, Statue Swinger, Female Figure	300.00
Clock, German, Wag-On-Wall, C.1825	325.00
Clock, Gilbert Bancroft, Wall, Cherry Parlor, Time & Strike	265.00
Clock, Gilbert, Banjo, Eagle Finial, 8 Day, 9 1/4 X 30 1/2 In.	45.00
Clock, Gilbert, Banjo, Hampshire Model Pendulum, 22 In.	115.00
Clock, Gilbert, Banjo, Time & Strike, 32 In.	250.00
Clock, Gilbert, Celluloid Alarm	26.50
Clock, Gilbert, Curfew, Top Bell Strike, 8 Day, 16 X 18 In.	145.00
Clock, Gilbert, Frame Scenery, Winsted, Connecticut	22.50
Clock, Gilbert, Kitchen, Oak, 8 Day, Time & Strike, Alarm, 15 1/4 X 22 In.	110.00
Clock, Gilbert, Kitchen, Walnut	155.00
Clock, Gilbert, Winsted Clock Co., 8 Day, Time & Strike, 10 1/2 X 9 5/8 In.	45.00
Clock, Granddaughter, English, C.1920	125.00
Clock, Grandfather, Burl Walnut, Brass Face, Signed, 8 Ft.	6900.00
Clock, Grandfather, Calendar Movement, Mahogany, Silaw & London	1200.00
Clock, Grandfather, English, Bell Strike, C.1831	600.00
Clock, Grandfather, Sheraton Style, Curly Maple & Cherry	1450.00
Clock, Gustav Becker, Mantel, Westminster Chime, Mahogany, 9 X 12 In.	150.00
Clock, Gustav Becker, Silesia, Regulator, 4 Chime Rods, 27 In.	200.00
Clock, Gustav Becker, Vienna, 2 Weight, 40 In.	325.00
Clock, Gustav Becker, 3 Weight, Vienna Regulator, Repeater, Blind Man's Pull	795.00
Clock, H.B.Horton, Calendar, Ithaca Clock Company	850.00

Clock, Haddon, Electric, Children On Teeter-Totter 65.00
Clock, Howard, Banjo, Brass Works, Weight Driven, Crank, C.1830 .... 1575.00
Clock, Hula Girl, Animated 100.00
Clock, Ingraham, Banjo 75.00
Clock, Ingraham, Banjo, Treasure Island, Mahogany, Reverse Painting 335.00
Clock, Ingraham, Calendar, 8 Day Time, Oak Case, 36 X 16 In. 295.00
Clock, Ingraham, Kitchen, Gingerbread, 8 Day, Time & Strike, Oak, 23 In. 85.00
Clock, Ingraham, Kitchen, Oak, Fancy, Calendar 190.00
Clock, Ingraham, Kitchen, Oak, Globe, 8 Days 110.00
Clock, Ingraham, Kitchen, Oak, Shelf, Time & Strike, Pat.1885 .... 110.00
Clock, Ingraham, Long Drop, Outside Bell, 30 In. 325.00
Clock, Ingraham, Mantel, Lion Heads On Ends, Ebony Finish, 8 Day, Hour Strike 95.00
Clock, Ingraham, Schoolhouse, Walnut Dew-Drop, 8 Day, Time & Calendar 275.00
Clock, Ingraham, Wall, Oak, Landau Model, 8 Day 225.00
Clock, Ingraham, 8-Sided, Swinging Pendulum Enclosed 100.00
Clock, Ithaca, Calendar, Pat.1866, Strikes .... Illus 700.00
Clock, Ithaca, Double Dial Calendar, Farmers No.10, Walnut, 1866 .... 595.00
Clock, Ithaca, Granger, Double Dial 700.00
Clock, Ithaca, Hanging New Library, Double Dial 950.00
Clock, Ithaca, No.11, Octagon, Double Dial .... 485.00 To 550.00
Clock, J.C.Brown, Ripple Steeple 950.00
Clock, Jerome & Co., Alarm, C.1850, 8 X 13 In. 100.00
Clock, Jerome & Co., Venetian Model, Doric, Shelf, 8 Day, Rosewood 190.00
Clock, Jerome & Co., Walnut, Mantel, Time & Alarm, 30 Hour, 15 In. 90.00
Clock, Jerome & Co., Steeple, Large 110.00
Clock, John Finney, Mantel, Silver Mounted, Ebony, C.1730, Irish, 21 1/2 In. 1600.00
Clock, John Rogers, Tall Case, Cherrywood, C.1790, 7 Feet 4 In. X 19 In. 3200.00
Clock, Junghans, Mantel, Oak, German, 8 Day, Time & Strike, 15 In. 375.00
Clock, Junghans, Oak Mantel, Brass Face, Gong, 15 1/2 In. 235.00
Clock, Kitchen, Calendar, Strikes Rooster, Oak .... Illus 245.00
Clock, Kitchen, Walnut, Time & Strike, Alarm 145.00
Clock, Lantern, Thomas Hicks, London, Short Pendulum, 17th Century 1500.00
Clock, Lenzkirch, German, Walnut, Mantel, Time Only, 10 In. 190.00
Clock, Lux, Animated Wall, Dog Standing, Head Moves 65.00
Clock, Lux, Animated, Old Man & Woman, Spinning Wheel 35.00
Clock, Mantel, Black, 4 Columns Lions' Heads, Lad With Trumpet 95.00
Clock, Mantel, Carved Feet, Stenciled Pediment & Columns, Reverse Painting 550.00
Clock, Mantel, Carved Walnut, Double Fusee, C.1840 .... 900.00
Clock, Mantel, Columned, Seth Thomas 85.00
Clock, Mantel, French Dore Bronze & Crystal, Enameled Dial, 10 1/2 In. 175.00
Clock, Mantel, French Empire, Dore Bronze, Neo-Egyptian, 16 X 9 In. 950.00
Clock, Mantel, Gilbert, Black, Brass, Dated 1912 .... 85.00
Clock, Mantel, Jn.Baptiste Helye, Paris, Louis XVI, Bronze & Dore, 14 In. 725.00
Clock, Mantel, Pressed Oak, 19th Century, 14 1/2 X 14 In. 168.00
Clock, Mantel, Victorian, Crackle Ceramic, Gilt, Floral, Bone, Hour Strike 49.95
Clock, New England, Butternut Case, Moon Dial, C.1820, 7 Ft.6 In. 2850.00
Clock, New Haven, Banjo, Time & Strike, Pendulum, Ship Scene 200.00
Clock, New Haven, Banjo, Time & Strike, Walnut, 42 In. 325.00
Clock, New Haven, Banjo, Whitney, 8 Day, Time & Strike 135.00
Clock, New Haven, Carriage, Ornate Spelter Case 250.00
Clock, New Haven, Crystal Regulator, Mercury Pendulum, Exposed Escapement 195.00
Clock, New Haven, Gingerbread, Oak 13.00
Clock, New Haven, Gold, Cherub On Top, Porcelain Face, 8 Day, 7 X 11 In. 135.00
Clock, New Haven, Mother & Baby On Top, White Metal, Gold Dore Case, 7 In. 95.00
Clock, New Haven, Parlor, 30 Day, Columbia, Chestnut Case 375.00
Clock, New Haven, School, Round, Mahogany, 25 In. 250.00
Clock, New Haven, School, 8 Day, Time & Strike, 28 In. 295.00
Clock, New Haven, Shelf, Art Nouveau, Bronze Case, Bust Of Woman, 10 In. 85.00
Clock, New Haven, Statue Front Escapement 525.00
Clock, New Haven, Time & Strike, Bim Bam, 29 In. 195.00
Clock, New Haven, Two-Toned Strike Tambour, 20 X 9 1/2 In. 40.00
Clock, Oak, Grandfather, Miniature Mission, C.1890 .... 75.00
Clock, Ogee, Chauncey Jerome 100.00
Clock, Pennsylvania, Cherry Case, Curtis Lewis, Reading, C.1790, 7 Ft.10 In. 4200.00
Clock, Pillar & Scroll, Seth Thomas, C.1920, 23 In. 165.00

Clock, Pillar, French, C.1800 .... 1750.00
Clock, Plymouth, Banjo, Washington & Mt.Vernon, 8 Day, Time & Strike, 28 In. 140.00
Clock, Porcelain, Figure Of Lady In Full Evening Dress On Top, 9 In. 65.00
Clock, Porcelain, Pink, Yellow Floral, Blue & Gold Scrolls, 11 X 14 1/2 In. 395.00
Clock, Pottery, Art Nouveau, 11 1/2 X 9 In. 450.00
Clock, R.Whiting, Curly Birch Case, 1813-1835, 94 In. 1350.00
Clock, Rodeo, Animated Bartender 200.00
Clock, Roosevelt, Animated Dial 125.00
Clock, Roxbury, Tall Case, Massachusetts, 8 Ft.2 In. 3650.00
Clock, Royal Bonn, Green & Cream, Floral Decoration, 8 X 10 1/2 In. 295.00
Clock, School, Brass Bezel, Pendulum, 8 Day, Strikes Hourly, C.1885-1900 .... 65.00
Clock, School, Oak, C.1905 .... 125.00
Clock, Sessions, Bronze, Nude 105.00
Clock, Sessions, Mantel, Pillar, Black, Keywind 60.00
Clock, Sessions, Porcelain Face, 8 Day, Time & Strike, 18 1/2 X 10 In. 35.00
Clock, Sessions, Star Pointer, Long Drop 295.00
Clock, Seth Thomas, Adamantine, 8 Day, Time & Strike, 16 1/2 X 11 In. 60.00
Clock, Seth Thomas, Atlas, Cherry Case, Bell & Strike 500.00
Clock, Seth Thomas, Banjo, Mt.Vernon Picture, 8 Day, Time & Strike, 29 In. 225.00
Clock, Seth Thomas, Banjo, 4 Jewel, Eagle Top, Wood Case, 18 X 5 In. 75.00
Clock, Seth Thomas, Brass, Locomotive, Roman Numberals, 7 In. 200.00
Clock, Seth Thomas, Cherry Wood, Gong, Overhand Top 70.00
Clock, Seth Thomas, Delft China, Key Wind 100.00
Clock, Seth Thomas, Full Column Bull's-Eye, 30 Hour, Time & Strike, 16 In. 45.00
Clock, Seth Thomas, Kitchen Shelf, Oak, Alarm & Strike, Lion Head Pendulum 195.00
Clock, Seth Thomas, Kitchen, Walnut, 8 Day, Alarm, Lever On Top Of Case 225.00
Clock, Seth Thomas, Lyre, 8 Day 400.00
Clock, Seth Thomas, Mahogany, Westminster Chime, Beehive Shape, 8 Day 150.00
Clock, Seth Thomas, Mantel, Black, Green, Marbleized Finish 55.00
Clock, Seth Thomas, Mantel, Red, Columned, Time & Strike 95.00
Clock, Seth Thomas, Mantel, Simulated Rosewood Case, Small, Square 75.00
Clock, Seth Thomas, Miniature .... *Illus* 375.00
Clock, Seth Thomas, Miniature Round Top Cottage 90.00
Clock, Seth Thomas, No.4, Hanging, Double Dial 745.00
Clock, Seth Thomas, No.20, Mahogany Case, Jeweled Panels, Regulator 1300.00
Clock, Seth Thomas, Oak, Wall, Rectangular, 8 Day, Label 100.00
Clock, Seth Thomas, Octagonal Calendar 425.00
Clock, Seth Thomas, Office, Rosewood Case 320.00
Clock, Seth Thomas, Omber Wall, 30 Day 650.00
Clock, Seth Thomas, Shelf, Mahogany Veneers, Reverse Painting, 8 Day 160.00
Clock, Seth Thomas, Ship's Bell, Brass Case 250.00
Clock, Seth Thomas, Sonora, Adamtine Case 195.00
Clock, Seth Thomas, Wall, Oak, Level & Alarm 225.00
Clock, Sexton, Brass, New York, Small 310.00
Clock, Shelf, Oak, 22 X 7 In. 38.00
Clock, Shelf, Pillar, Scroll, Inlaid Mahogany, 1841-45, 31 1/4 In. .... *Illus* 650.00
Clock, Shelf, Wafer Thin, Art Nouveau, Battery Operated, 12 X 15 In. 95.00
Clock, Steeple, Brewster & Ingraham, Time Strike & Alarm, 1886 .... 225.00
Clock, T.Thurber Co., Providence, R.I., Regulator, Enamel & Onyx, 18 In. 1800.00
Clock, Tall Case, Dickson & Harper, Mahogany, Sheraton, C.1830, 86 In. 1050.00
Clock, Tall Case, Humphrey Williams, Conway Tower & Tubular, C.1790, Oak 975.00
Clock, Tall Case, Inlaid Mahogany, English Chippendale, Dore Bronze, C.1800 .... 1500.00
Clock, Tall Case, Jeweler's Regulator, Silver 3 Track Dial, C.1850, 9 1/2 Ft. 750.00
Clock, Tall Case, Jon Clowes, C.1670, Bell Strike, Marquetry Case, English 7500.00
Clock, Tall Case, Mahogany, Colonial Clock Co., Michigan, Straight Sides 975.00
Clock, Tall Case, Weinberger, 2 Part, Carved Walnut, 94 In. 900.00
Clock, Tall Case, 8 Day, Dial Hand, Painted, Scottish Mahogany, Signed, 1815 .... 2700.00
Clock, Taylor, Whitehaven, Rocking Ship, Steel, & Brass Dial, C.1775, 93 In. 4800.00
Clock, Thomas Hicks, London, Lantern, Strike, Alarm, Short Pendulum, 1600s 1500.00
    Clock, Tiffany, see Tiffany, Clock
Clock, Tiffany Bronze, Mantel, Grapevine, Mottled Green, Signed, 1899, 11 In. 2100.00
Clock, Tiffany, Alarm, With Case, Gold Squares 50.00
Clock, Tiffany, Bronze, Dore, 4 X 4 1/4 In. 150.00
Clock, Tiffany, Dresser, Brass, Onyx 85.00
Clock, Tiffany, Never-Wind, Under Glass Dome 85.00

Clock, Seth Thomas, Miniature

Clock, Shelf, Pillar, Scroll,
Inlaid Mahogany, 1841–45, 31 1/4 In.

Clock, Wall, Animated Wag On Wall, French
(See Page 106)

Clock, Wall, Shamrocks On Pendulum,
Strikes, 8 Day, German
(See Page 106)

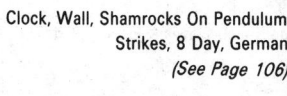

Clock, U.S.Clock Co., N.Y., Shelf, Curly Maple, Rosewood & Mahogany Inlay	165.00
Clock, United Clock Co., Office, Large Oak, Electric Chronometer, C.1902	225.00
Clock, Vienna, Gustave Becker, 8 Day, Time & Strike, Spring Driven, 40 In.	575.00
Clock, Vienna, 2 Weight	425.00
Clock, W & H, Oak Bracket, English, Time & Strike, 18 X 12 In.	490.00

Clock, W.N. Welsh, School, 8 Day, Calendar, Time & Strike, C.1880	295.00
Clock, Walford, English Fusee, C.1810, Round Mahogany, Time Only, 18 In.	290.00
Clock, Wall, Animated Wag On Wall, French ....*Illus*	550.00
Clock, Wall, French Acorn, C.1854	375.00
Clock, Wall, French Picture Frame, Mother-Of-Pearl, 8 Day, Time & Strike	235.00
Clock, Wall, Long Drop, Oak, Welch Mfg., Co., Calendar	400.00
Clock, Wall, Self-Wind, 3 Window Calendar In Bottom	975.00
Clock, Wall, Shamrocks On Pendulum, Strikes, 8 Day, German ....*Illus*	700.00
Clock, Wall, Tiffany, French Brass, Triband Decoration, Case, 15 X 10 In.	950.00
Clock, Wall, Weight Driven, 30 Hours, Brass, Veneered Case, C.1840	265.00
Clock, Waterbury, Beehive, Mahogany, 8 Day, Time & Strike, 18 In.	135.00
Clock, Waterbury, Brass Bound, Short Drop, 21 In.	290.00
Clock, Waterbury, Carriage, Nickel, Brass	95.00
Clock, Waterbury, Figural Statue, Porcelain Dial	295.00
Clock, Waterbury, Gallery, Brass Case, Time & Strike, 8 Day	240.00
Clock, Waterbury, Gallery, Metal, Lever, 30 Hour	90.00
Clock, Waterbury, Kitchen, Oak, 8 Day, Time & Strike, 14 1/2 X 21 1/4 In.	85.00
Clock, Waterbury, Mantel, 17 X 11 In.	50.00
Clock, Waterbury, Pillar And Scroll Mantel, C.1835, 31 1/2 X 16 1/2 In.	1100.00
Clock, Waterbury, Regulator Wall, 7 Ft.	1700.00
Clock, Waterbury, School, Short Drop, Brass Bottom Door, Time & Strike	135.00
Clock, Waterbury, Ship's Bell, Brass	275.00
Clock, Waterbury, Wall, Double Weight	950.00
Clock, Waterbury, Wall, Ingraham Mosaic, Double Dial	900.00
Clock, Wedgwood, Dark Blue, White Cameos, 12 In.	440.00
Clock, Welch, Figure 8, Wall, Carved Throat, 30 Day	395.00
Clock, Welch, Gingerbread, Walnut	14.00
Clock, Welch, Kitchen, Walnut, 8 Day, Time & Strike	125.00
Clock, Welch, School, Rosewood, Long Drop, 15 Day	290.00
Clock, Welch, Schoolhouse, Rosewood, Time, Strike, Calendar, Short Drop	250.00
Clock, Welch, Shelf, Grecian, Carved Throat	225.00
Clock, Welch, Shelf, Rosewood, Venetian With Gold Columns, 30 Hour	125.00
Clock, Welch, Shelf, Time & Strike With Alarm	75.00
Clock, Welch, Spring Driven, 30 Hour, 18 X 11 1/2 In.	145.00
Clock, Welch, Steeple, Small	95.00
Clock, Westclox, Big Ben, Alarm	32.50
Clock, Westminster, German Mahogany, Mantel, 13 1/2 In.	150.00
Clock, Willard, Boston, Banjo Presentation, Ornate Gold Leaf Trim	1475.00

*Cloisonne Enamel was developed during the nineteenth century. A glass
enamel was applied between small ribbonlike pieces of metal on a metal base.
Most Cloisonne is Chinese or Japanese.*

Cloisonne, Ashtray With Lid	65.00
Cloisonne, Ashtray, Field With Flowers & Bird, Blue, Square, 3 In.	44.00
Cloisonne, Ashtray, Flowered Design On White, 3 1/2 In.	25.00

Cloisonne, Bowl, Waves & Flowers, Lid, Blue, White, 5 In.

Cloisonne, Box, Chinese, Polychrome Floral, Blue, Lid, 3 In.

Cloisonne, Ashtray, Flowers, 3 1/2 In.	7.00
Cloisonne, Bottle, Snuff, Birds & Flowers, Double Gourd Shape	375.00
Cloisonne, Bottle, Snuff, Blue, Floral, 2 1/2 In.	150.00
Cloisonne, Bottle, Snuff, Double, Yellow, Floral	295.00
Cloisonne, Bowl, Black, Fishscale, Dragon, Flaming Pearl, 7 1/2 In., Pair	175.00
Cloisonne, Bowl, Bulb, Black Ground, Dragon, Verse, Wood Stand, C.1880, 8 In.	110.00
Cloisonne, Bowl, Dragon, Blue & Gold, 6 1/2 In.	195.00
Cloisonne, Bowl, Dragon, Dark Blue, Green Edged, Brass Trim, 6 1/2 In.	175.00
Cloisonne, Bowl, Green, Yellow Plum Blossoms, 6 X 3 1/4 In.	475.00
Cloisonne, Bowl, Intricate Design, Blue-Black, Enamel On Brass, 8 In.	175.00
Cloisonne, Bowl, Nut, Blue Inside, Blue With Flowers Outside, 3 3/4 In.	85.00
Cloisonne, Bowl, Polychrome Floral On Light Blue, 1 1/4 In.	15.00
Cloisonne, Bowl, Waves & Flowers, Lid, Blue, White, 5 In. *Illus*	65.00
Cloisonne, Bowl, 5-Toed Dragons, C.1880, 9 In.	190.00
Cloisonne, Box, Barrel Shape, Animal Design On Blue, Covered, 3 3/4 In.	75.00
Cloisonne, Box, Black Ground, Flowers, Butterfly, China, 4 1/2 X 3 1/2 In.	50.00
Cloisonne, Box, Blue, Gold Network With Flowers, Foo Dog Finial, Round, 5 In.	50.00
Cloisonne, Box, Chinese, Polychrome Floral, Blue, Lid, 3 In. *Illus*	25.00
Cloisonne, Box, Cigarette	38.00
Cloisonne, Box, Cigarette, Ashtray, Blue Flowers On White, 2 1/2 In.Tray	65.00
Cloisonne, Box, Cylindrical, Covered, Floral, Stars, Blue Ground, 2 1/2 X 3 In.	38.00
Cloisonne, Box, Cylindrical, Raised Cameo Cutouts, Green, Blue, White, 3 In.	60.00
Cloisonne, Box, Field & Flowers, White, 5 X 4 In.	88.00
Cloisonne, Box, Floral On Blue, Foo Dog Finial, Round, Lid, China, 5 1/4 In.	75.00
Cloisonne, Box, Floral On Terra Cotta, Knobbed Legs, Hinged, 6 X 4 1/2 In.	75.00
Cloisonne, Box, Floral, Hinged Dome Lid, Footed, Black Background, Marked	45.00
Cloisonne, Box, Flowers, Leaves On Black & Gold, Covered, 3 1/4 In.	175.00
Cloisonne, Box, Flowers, White Background, Hinged, 5 1/2 X 4 X 1 3/4 In.	125.00
Cloisonne, Box, Flowers, 3 Compartments, Ball Feet, Hinged, Blue, White, 8 In.	95.00
Cloisonne, Box, Girls On Cover, Enameled, Hinged, 3 In.	135.00
Cloisonne, Box, Green Ground, Flowers & Leaves, Footed, 6 X 4 1/2 In.	50.00
Cloisonne, Box, Green, Floral, Footed, 4 Compartments, 6 X 4 1/2 X 1 1/2 In.	75.00
Cloisonne, Box, Green, Multifloral China, Covered, 4 X 5 In.	30.00
Cloisonne, Box, Jade Insert, Cameo Cutout Design, Cylindrical, 3 1/4 In.	60.00
Cloisonne, Box, Japanese, Birds, Flowers, Duck, Water, Oval, Hinged, Footed, 5 In.	475.00
Cloisonne, Box, Multicolored Flowers On Black, Foo Dog Finial, 6 1/2 In.	130.00
Cloisonne, Box, Ornate Flowers On Black, Silver, Square	95.00
Cloisonne, Box, Oval Jade Insert On Top, Rust, Intricate Design, 5 In.	125.00
Cloisonne, Box, Red, Green Floral, Round, Covered, 3 In.	110.00
Cloisonne, Box, Round, Dark Blue, Yellow On Turquoise, 3 1/4 X 3 1/4 In.	125.00
Cloisonne, Box, Water Fowls, Fishscale, Wavy Lines Depicting Water, Lid, 4 In.	70.00
Cloisonne, Box, White Jade Carved Insert, Blue Arabesque Design, 2 X 2 In.	150.00
Cloisonne, Box, White, Multicolored Flowers, 6 Sided, 3 In.	95.00
Cloisonne, Burner, Incense, Cobalt Blue Enamel, Temple Dog Finial, 7 1/4 In.	685.00
Cloisonne, Burner, Incense, Floral On Black, 4 In.	125.00
Cloisonne, Burner, Incense, Foo Dog Finial, Blue Enamel, 3 Footed, 6 In.	40.00
Cloisonne, Candlestick, Vines Wind Around Stem, Imperial Yellow, 8 In., Pair	250.00
Cloisonne, Chalice, Rust Brown, Pink, White & Blue Pompon Flowers, 9 In.	225.00
Cloisonne, Charger, Blues, Blacks, Rust, Pink & White, Gold Speckled, 13 In.	555.00

Cloisonne, Charger, Gold, Green, Black, 3 Cranes Flying, 12 In. 185.00
Cloisonne, Charger, Intricate Floral, Scalloped, 12 In. 295.00
Cloisonne, Charger, Medallion, Dragons, & Birds On Border, Goldstone, 12 In. 395.00
Cloisonne, Charger, Multicolored, Square, 13 In. 415.00
Cloisonne, Charger, Ornate Gold, Green, & Black Edge, 3 Cranes Flying, 12 In. 185.00
Cloisonne, Charger, Pink & White Floral, Detailed Medallion Border, 24 In. 1500.00
Cloisonne, Compote, Blue Peacock Center, Flowers Allover, Signed, 6 1/2 In. 89.00
Cloisonne, Compote, Brown Orange, Pink, White, & Blue Mums, Covered, 9 In. 225.00
Cloisonne, Compote, Burnt Orange, Pink, White, & Blue Flowers, Covered, 9 In. 225.00
Cloisonne, Cup & Saucer, Commemorates Trade Of U.S.& Orient, 2 Flags, 2 In. 125.00
Cloisonne, Cup, Saki, Reddish Brown, Various Flowers 50.00
Cloisonne, Desk Set, Red Enamel On Bronze, 4 Piece 375.00
Cloisonne, Desk Set, Yellow Dragon, Cloud Scroll & Green, 3 Piece 150.00
Cloisonne, Dish, Candy, Foo Finial, China Mark, 5 In. 68.00
Cloisonne, Dish, Rust & White, 3 1/2 In. 12.00

Cloisonne, Jar, Ginger, Multicolor Floral, Green, 4 3/4 In.

Cloisonne, Figurine, Double Headed Ram, Removable Urn, 7 1/2 X 8 1/2 In. 780.00
Cloisonne, Figurine, Hen & Rooster, Blue, Green, Yellow, Pink, Brown, 9 1/2 In. 995.00
Cloisonne, Figurine, Turtle, Lidded Backs, Pale Blue, Scroll Work, 6 In., Pair 650.00
Cloisonne, Ginger Jar, Black & Yellow, Covered, 6 1/2 In. 230.00
Cloisonne, Hair Brush, Silver Filigree Border, Multicolored Bird In Flight 110.00
Cloisonne, Holder, Cigarette, With Ivory 20.00
Cloisonne, Incense Burner, Champleve, Korean 1200.00
Cloisonne, Inkwell, Pen Rest, Triangle, Japan 40.00
Cloisonne, Inkwell, Yellow, Bronze Cover, Multicolor Enameling, Floral, 6 In. 225.00
Cloisonne, Jar, Blue With Red, Pink, Yellow, 6 X 8 In. 325.00
Cloisonne, Jar, Cover, Flowers & Butterflies, 7 1/2 In. 215.00
Cloisonne, Jar, Covered, Black Background, Floral Design, 5 1/2 X 6 In. 40.00
Cloisonne, Jar, Ginger, Black, White Floral, Covered, 7 In. 95.00
Cloisonne, Jar, Ginger, Blue Blossoms, 8 1/2 In., Pair 250.00
Cloisonne, Jar, Ginger, Blue On Sterling Silver Background, 7 1/2 In. 165.00
Cloisonne, Jar, Ginger, Bulbous, Black, Blue, Florals, Chinese, 7 In., Pair 130.00
Cloisonne, Jar, Ginger, Floral On Pearlized Mosaic, Footed, Lid, 3 3/4 In. 115.00
Cloisonne, Jar, Ginger, Floral On Terra Cotta Background, 5 X 7 In. 125.00
Cloisonne, Jar, Ginger, Floral On Yellow Ground, China, 4 In. 50.00
Cloisonne, Jar, Ginger, Floral, Terra Cotta Background, Lid, 7 X 5 In. 100.00
Cloisonne, Jar, Ginger, Green Background, Marked China, Pair 395.00
Cloisonne, Jar, Ginger, Green, Flowers, 15 In. 225.00
Cloisonne, Jar, Ginger, Intricate Design, Mid-19th Century, Covered, 6 1/2 In. 230.00
Cloisonne, Jar, Ginger, Lilac & White Dragon On Black, 6 1/2 In. 230.00
Cloisonne, Jar, Ginger, Miniature, Three Ball Feet, Lid 85.00
Cloisonne, Jar, Ginger, Miniature, 2 1/2 In. 125.00
Cloisonne, Jar, Ginger, Multicolor Floral, Green, 4 3/4 In. ....Illus   75.00
Cloisonne, Jar, Ginger, Pink Floral Sprays, Blue Ground, Pair ....Illus   250.00
Cloisonne, Jar, Ginger, Yellow Background, Blue, Pink & Red Flowers, 9 In. 145.00
Cloisonne, Jar, Ginger, Yellow, Multicolored Leaves & Flowers, Pheasant, Pair 450.00
Cloisonne, Jar, Intricate Decoration, Blue On Black, Lid, Whooping Crane Mark 85.00
Cloisonne, Jar, One Thousand Flowers, 10 In. 175.00

Cloisonne, Jar, Red, Florals, 9 In.	150.00
Cloisonne, Lamp, Hurricane, Miniature, 3 1/2 In.	48.00
Cloisonne, Lamp, 28 In.	145.00
Cloisonne, Match Safe, Blue, Flowers, 2 X 2 1/2 In.	40.00
Cloisonne, Matchbook Holder, China	8.50
Cloisonne, Matchbox Holder, Black Ground, Flowers	15.00
Cloisonne, Matchbox Holder, Jade Insert, Footed	35.00
Cloisonne, Napkin Ring, Dragon	25.00
Cloisonne, Pin Tray, Floral Each Corner, Tricornered, Goldstone One Corner	24.00
Cloisonne, Pipe, Water	125.00
Cloisonne, Planter, Blue, Black, Red, Brown, & Yellow, Enameled, 4 1/2 X 9 In.	310.00
Cloisonne, Planter, Multicolor Flowers, Birds, 9 In.Square, 4 1/2 In.High	375.00
Cloisonne, Plaque, Multicolor On Green, Square, 19th Century, 13 In.	425.00
Cloisonne, Plate, Blue & White Bird, 12 In.	250.00
Cloisonne, Plate, Charger, Fans, Flowers, Birds, Speckled, Black, Gold, 14 In.	525.00
Cloisonne, Plate, Chinese, Floral, Brass Rim, Cloisons, 4 1/8 In. ....Illus	85.00
Cloisonne, Plate, Red, Pink, & Yellow Floral, Blue Background, 6 In.	150.00
Cloisonne, Plate, 2 Plaques, Turquoise Ground, Flowers, Birds, Bamboo, Scroll	175.00
Cloisonne, Pot, Flower, 3 Ceramic Feet, Turquoise, 9 In.	475.00
Cloisonne, Pot, Jewel Tree, 19th Century, 21 In.	285.00
Cloisonne, Rose Bowl, Blue, Flowers, Stand, 4 X 4 In.	58.00
Cloisonne, Rose Bowl, Footed, Flowers & Butterflies	75.00
Cloisonne, Rose Bowl, Goldstone All Over, Footed	60.00
Cloisonne, Rose Bowl, Multicolored Decorations, Dark Blue, Footed	105.00
Cloisonne, Salt & Pepper, Fishscale, Green, Squat Pepper Can Sit In Salt	45.00
Cloisonne, Salt & Pepper, Gold Trim, Pair	40.00
Cloisonne, Salt & Pepper, Green & Gold, 1 3/4 In., Pair	75.00

Cloisonne, Jar, Ginger, Pink Floral Sprays,
Blue Ground, Pair

Cloisonne, Salt, Black, Flower Decoration	35.00
Cloisonne, Salt, Floral, Blue, Metal Lid, 2 1/4 In.	25.00
Cloisonne, Salt, Individual, Black & Yellow Design, Set Of 4	50.00
Cloisonne, Salt, Round, Metal Top, Blue Ground, Florals, 2 1/4 In.	35.00
Cloisonne, Saltshaker, Floral, Blue Ground, Metal Lid, 2 1/4 In.	30.00
Cloisonne, Saltshaker, Pink, White, & Green Floral On Blue, 2 1/4 In.	30.00
Cloisonne, Tazza, Multicolor Flowers, Green, Lid, 8 1/4 In. ....Illus	95.00
Cloisonne, Teapot, Birds, Butterflies, Goldstone, Handle	165.00
Cloisonne, Teapot, Blue, Metallic, Butterflies & Flowers, 5 1/2 In.	235.00
Cloisonne, Teapot, Miniature, Flowers & Butterflies, Paneled, 3 1/2 In.	145.00
Cloisonne, Teapot, Miniature, Flying Butterflies & Diaper Pattern, 3 1/2 In.	145.00
Cloisonne, Teapot, Miniature, Foil Background, Blue & Green Panels, Covered	225.00
Cloisonne, Teapot, Miniature, Spring Scroll, Green, Bulbous, 6 In.	160.00
Cloisonne, Teapot, White, Blue, Green, Fishscale Handle & Spout, 4 X 5 In.	150.00
Cloisonne, Toothpick, Multicolor Flowers On Aqua, Royal Scallops	23.00
Cloisonne, Tray, Bird Center, Marked China, 3 1/4 In., Square, Pair	55.00
Cloisonne, Tray, Floral Decoration, Mutton Fat Jade Center, 4 1/2 In.	55.00
Cloisonne, Tray, Pierced Brass Gallery, Greek Key, 10, 000 Flowers, 15 In.	295.00
Cloisonne, Tray, Pin, Blossoms & Bird, 4 3/4 In.	46.00
Cloisonne, Tray, Pin, Floral, Three Cornered, Goldstone, 3 X 4 In.	30.00
Cloisonne, Tumbler, Dragons, Colored, Chinese, 3 1/2 In.	65.00

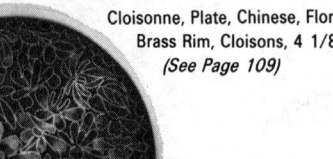

Cloisonne, Plate, Chinese, Floral,
Brass Rim, Cloisons, 4 1/8 In.
(See Page 109)

Cloisonne, Tazza. Multicolor Flowers,
Green. Lid. 8 1/4 In.
(See Page 109)

Cloisonne, Urn, Red Parakeets,
Multicolor Chrysanthemums,
One Of A Pair

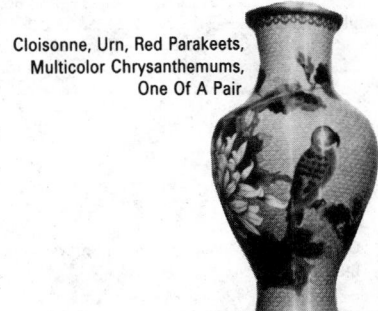

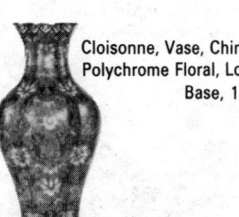

Cloisonne, Vase, Chinese,
Polychrome Floral, Lobed,
Base, 19 In.

Cloisonne, Urn, Black, Goldstone Leaves & Flowers, Covered, 10 1/2 In., Pair	500.00
Cloisonne, Urn, Pink, Yellow, & Blue Floral On Green, Pedestaled, 8 In.	145.00
Cloisonne, Urn, Red Parakeets, Multicolor Chrysanthemums, Pair .... *Illus*	600.00
Cloisonne, Vase, Alternating Blue & Gold Speckled Panels, Butterflies, 7 In.	150.00
Cloisonne, Vase, Baluster Shape, Blue, Multicolored Leaves, 10 In., Pair	225.00
Cloisonne, Vase, Baluster Shape, Cobalt Ground, Dragon, Wood Stand, 9 1/2 In.	70.00
Cloisonne, Vase, Bird Form, Chinese, 9 1/2 In.	500.00
Cloisonne, Vase, Bird, Floral, Butterfly, Landscape, Turquoise Ground, 12 In.	500.00
Cloisonne, Vase, Birds, Pink Rose On Blue, 9 1/2 X 6 In.	195.00
Cloisonne, Vase, Black With Apple Blossoms, 5 In.	45.00
Cloisonne, Vase, Blue & Gold Speckled Panels, Flower, Bird, Butterfly Design	150.00
Cloisonne, Vase, Blue Dragon On Red, 4 1/4 In.	40.00
Cloisonne, Vase, Blue Floral, Silver Wire, 8 1/2 In.	590.00
Cloisonne, Vase, Blue Foil Band In Center, 19th Century, Japanese, 5 In.	95.00
Cloisonne, Vase, Blue With Flowers, 6 In.	75.00
Cloisonne, Vase, Blue, Apple Blossoms, Teak Base, 9 1/2 In., Pair	155.00
Cloisonne, Vase, Blue, Bird On Branch, Lavender & White Floral, 5 3/4 In.	125.00
Cloisonne, Vase, Blue, Flowers, Japanese, 7 In.	195.00
Cloisonne, Vase, Bright Green, Red & White Flowers, Enameled, 9 1/2 In., Pair	150.00
Cloisonne, Vase, Bulbous, Melon-Ribbed Bottom, Brass Bands, Red, Peonies, 9 In.	250.00
Cloisonne, Vase, Butterflies, Iridescent Green, 9 In.	165.00
Cloisonne, Vase, Butterfly & Floral, Turquoise Background, 6 In., Pair	300.00
Cloisonne, Vase, China, Burgundy Background, Signed, 10 In.	125.00
Cloisonne, Vase, Chinese, Polychrome Floral, Lobed, Base, 19 In. .... *Illus*	1750.00
Cloisonne, Vase, Cobalt Blue, Cherry Trees, Birds On Branches, 7 In., Pair	385.00

Cloisonne, Vase, Cobalt Florals, Green, Goldstone Medallions, 4 1/2 In. 165.00
Cloisonne, Vase, Desert Scene, Fish Scale, 4 3/4 In. 110.00
Cloisonne, Vase, Dragon, 8 1/2 In. 175.00
Cloisonne, Vase, Fishscale, White To Red, White & Blue Flowers, 9 1/2 In. 175.00
Cloisonne, Vase, Fishscale, Wisteria Blossoms, Light Blue, 7 1/2 In. 175.00
Cloisonne, Vase, Floral Geometrical Pattern, Pearlized Green, 6 1/4 In. 125.00
Cloisonne, Vase, Floral On Midnight Blue, Enameled & Glazed, Covered, 6 In. 225.00
Cloisonne, Vase, Floral On Turquoise, 3 3/4 In. 40.00
Cloisonne, Vase, Floral, Blue Inserts, Pearlized Green Background, 6 In. 125.00
Cloisonne, Vase, Flower Tree, 5 In. 90.00
Cloisonne, Vase, Flowers & Butterflies On Gold, Blue, Green, Black, 4 In. 80.00
Cloisonne, Vase, Flowers, Butterfly, Silver Flakes, Blue, 6 In. 95.00
Cloisonne, Vase, Foil, Green To Red, Flowers, Silver, 9 3/4 In. 300.00
Cloisonne, Vase, Gold Speckled On Dark Green, Butterflies, Flowers, 5 In. 175.00
Cloisonne, Vase, Gold, Blue, Green, & Black Enamel, 4 In. 80.00
Cloisonne, Vase, Gold, Green Leaves, White Flowers, 4 In. 80.00
Cloisonne, Vase, Gold, Red Rose, White Tipped Petals, Green Foliage, 5 1/2 In. 125.00
Cloisonne, Vase, Goldstone, Butterflies, Small 45.00
Cloisonne, Vase, Green, Black, Flowers, C.1900, 6 In., Pair 175.00
Cloisonne, Vase, Inlaid Floral Design, Enameled, 5 In., Pair 200.00
Cloisonne, Vase, Iridescent Green & Blue, Enameled, Covered, 4 1/2 In. 250.00
Cloisonne, Vase, Japanese, Butterflies, Metallic Luster, 8 In. .... *Illus* 100.00
Cloisonne, Vase, Japanese, Yellow, Floral, 6 In. 125.00
Cloisonne, Vase, Long Neck, 3 Medallions, Blue Ground, 5 In. .... *Illus* 190.00
Cloisonne, Vase, Lotus Flowers, Green Leaves, White To Rose, 11 In. 225.00
Cloisonne, Vase, Multicolor Dragons, Enamel, Gold Speckled, 5 1/8 X 2 1/2 In. 125.00
Cloisonne, Vase, Multicolor Foil Designs, 6 1/8 X 3 In. 135.00
Cloisonne, Vase, Multicolor, Dragons, Bulbous, C.1900, 9 In., Pair 275.00
Cloisonne, Vase, Multicolored Birds & Flowers On Blue & Black, 8 1/2 In. 300.00
Cloisonne, Vase, Mustard Color Fish Scale Design, 8 In. 75.00
Cloisonne, Vase, On Pottery, C.1860s, Japanese, 5 In. 250.00
Cloisonne, Vase, Panels Of Multicolored Flowers, 8 In. 145.00
Cloisonne, Vase, Pink Flowers, Green Leaves, Black, Pair .... *Illus* 385.00
Cloisonne, Vase, Purple, Green Stems, White & Red Orchids, Japanese, 2 3/4 In. 175.00
Cloisonne, Vase, Red Ground, Green, Yellow, Pink Flowers, 9 1/2 In. 125.00
Cloisonne, Vase, Red Pink Floral Sprays, Gold, Miniature, Pair .... *Illus* 200.00
Cloisonne, Vase, Red, Birds In Reeds, Leaves, Pink, White Roses, 7 1/4 In. 275.00
Cloisonne, Vase, Red, Blue, Yellow, 10 In., Pair 150.00
Cloisonne, Vase, Red, Roses, Bamboo On Back, Silver Top, C.1920, 8 In. 125.00
Cloisonne, Vase, Rust Background, Cream Flowers, 4 In. 45.00
Cloisonne, Vase, Rust, Blue Flowers, With Stand, 2 3/4 In. 35.00
Cloisonne, Vase, Rust, 4 In. X 2 1/2 In. 43.50
Cloisonne, Vase, Sang De Boeuf Ground, Floral, 5 1/2 In., Pair .... *Illus* 90.00
Cloisonne, Vase, Scroll Wire Work, Cloud Diaper, Green, 9 X 12 In., Pair 150.00
Cloisonne, Vase, Star Cloisonnes, Peonies, Geometric Design, Brown, 10 In. 250.00
Cloisonne, Vase, Stylized Floral, Birds, Pearlized Green & Purple, 6 In., Pair 450.00
Cloisonne, Vase, Thousand Flower, Gilt, Brown Tones, China Mark, 8 In. 95.00
Cloisonne, Vase, Translucent Enameled Flowers, Silver Foil, 7 1/4 In. 75.00
Cloisonne, Vase, Translucent Green, Goldstone, Phoenix Bird, 6 In. 250.00
Cloisonne, Vase, Tree Bark, Water Scene, Crane, 10 In. 585.00
Cloisonne, Vase, Turquoise Blue, Flowers On Fretwork Background, 10 1/2 In. 375.00
Cloisonne, Vase, Turquoise, Gold Arabesque Forms, Art Nouveau, Covered, 7 In. 65.00
Cloisonne, Vase, Two 5-Toed Dragons, Flowers On Yellow, 9 In. 210.00
Cloisonne, Vase, Wall, Butterflies, Floral, Goldstone, Black Background, 11 In. 250.00
Cloisonne, Vase, White, Blue & Turquoise Foil Flowers, 7 1/4 X 3 1/4 In. 145.00
Cloisonne, Vase, White, Florals, 5 1/2 In. 55.00
Cloisonne, Vase, 5-Toed Dragon, Black Background, 6 In. 185.00
Cloisonne, Vase, 5-Toed Yellow Dragon, Black & Turquoise, Pair, 6 1/2 In. 375.00
    Clothing, see Textile

*Cluthra glass is a two-layered glass with small air pockets that form white
spots. The Steuben Glass Works of Corning, New York, made it after
1903. Kimball Glass Company of Vineland, New Jersey, made Cluthra
from about 1925.*

Cluthra, see also Steuben
Cluthra, Vase, Blue Green, Gold Flecks, 8 1/2 In. 85.00
Cluthra, Vase, Light Blue & Gray, Signed Kimball, 4 1/2 X 3 1/2 In. 85.00
Cluthra, Vase, Urn Top, Robin's-Egg Blue, 9 3/4 In. 85.00

Coalbrookdale was made by the Coalport porcelain factory of England during the Victorian period. The pieces are heavily decorated with floral encrustations.

Coalport ware has been made by the Coalport Porcelain Works of England from 1795 to the present time.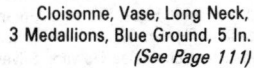

Coalport, see also Indian Tree
Coalport, Bottle, Perfume, Turquoise And Red Jewels, 1891, 3 1/2 In. 425.00
Coalport, Bowl, Miniature, Raised Gold Sea Plants, 3 White Panels With Fish 135.00
Coalport, Buffet Service, Broseley Dragon, C.1900, 46 Piece 950.00
Coalport, Cachepot, 350th Anniversary Landing Of Pilgrims, 5 1/2 In. 40.00
Coalport, Cake Set, Yellow & Gold, Square, 4 Dishes, 6 In. 125.00
Coalport, Coffeepot, Flowers, Bird On Limb, White Ground, Marked, 5 1/2 In. 67.50
Coalport, Cup & Saucer, Demitasse, Blue, White, Gold Trim, Birds & Foliage 22.50
Coalport, Dish, Ruffled, Square, 4 1/4 In. 20.00
Coalport, Ewer, Blue, White Decoration, 11 1/2 In. 45.00
Coalport, Ewer, Flowers, Serpent Entwined Handle, Blue, White, 11 1/2 In. 45.00
Coalport, Finger Bowl, Apple Green, Pair, 4 1/2 X 2 1/4 In. 60.00
Coalport, Plate, Admiral Dewey, Blue & White 40.00
Coalport, Plate, Scalloped, Oriental Design, C.1850 .... 19.00
Coalport, Urn, Blue, Gold Gilding, Hand-Painted Scene, Lidded, 5 3/4 In. 95.00
Coalport, Vase, Floral Sprays, Fully Marked, 2 3/4 X 1 5/8 In., Pair 45.00
Coalport, Vase, Oyster Color, Shell Shaped, 4 1/2 X 8 In., Pair 68.00

Cobalt blue glass was made using oxide of cobalt. The characteristic bright dark blue identifies it for the collector. Most cobalt glass found today was made after the Civil War.

Cobalt Blue, see also Shirley Temple
Cobalt Blue, Bottle, Perfume, Beige Scrolls, Gold, Steeple Stopper, 6 1/2 In. 20.00

Cloisonne, Vase, Japanese,
Butterflies, Metallic Luster, 8 In.
(See Page 111)

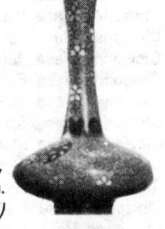

Cloisonne, Vase, Long Neck,
3 Medallions, Blue Ground, 5 In.
(See Page 111)

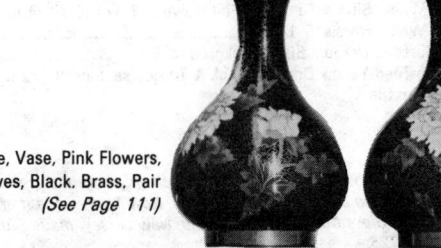

Cloisonne, Vase, Pink Flowers,
Green Leaves, Black. Brass. Pair
(See Page 111)

Cobalt Blue, Bottle, Perfume, Gold & White Petitpoint, 4 Ruby Jewels	75.00
Cobalt Blue, Bottle, Poison, Quilted Design, Stopper, 3 3/4 In.	24.00
Cobalt Blue, Bottle, Poison, Round, Mushroom Style Stopper, 12 1/4 In.	39.00
Cobalt Blue, Bottle, Poison, Triangular, Embossed, 3 1/4 In.	9.00
Cobalt Blue, Bottle, Quilted, Label Space, Stopper, Sharp Points, Embossed	22.00
Cobalt Blue, Bottle, 2 Plain Sides, 2 Horizonal Ribbing Sides, Poison Emblem	8.00
Cobalt Blue, Bowl, Finger, 4 1/2 In.	15.00
Cobalt Blue, Bowl, Gold Top With Raised Sculptured Wheat Stalks, 8 1/4 In.	150.00
Cobalt Blue, Box, Beveled, Gold Molded Nudes In Relief, Round, Covered, 3 In.	65.00
Cobalt Blue, Box, Covered, 3 Scotties	60.00
Cobalt Blue, Box, Patch, Enameled White Florals, 1 1/8 X 2 In.	65.00
Cobalt Blue, Box, Puff, Geometric Cutting On Top & Bottom, Clear, 6 1/2 In.	160.00
Cobalt Blue, Bucket, Ice, Metal Handle And Tongs	75.00
Cobalt Blue, Candlestick, Hand Etched, 10 In., Pair	150.00
Cobalt Blue, Candlestick, Swirled, 7 1/2 In., Pair	24.00
Cobalt Blue, Carafe, Blown, Panel, Bulbous Bottom, Pontil, Quart, 7 1/2 In.	45.00
Cobalt Blue, Celery, Raised Lily Of The Valley, Gold Decoration	45.00
Cobalt Blue, Cordial Set, Silver Decoration, 7 Piece	65.00
Cobalt Blue, Cruet, Swirl, Clear Ball Stopper, Applied Handle	28.50
Cobalt Blue, Eye Cup	4.00 To 6.50
Cobalt Blue, Hat, Blown, Diamond-Quilted, Alexandrite Ground, 3 In.	45.00
Cobalt Blue, Hatpin Holder, Flowers, White, Pink, & Gold, 5 1/2 X 3 1/4 In.	22.50
Cobalt Blue, Jar, Apothecary, Ground Stopper, 7 3/4 X 4 3/4 In.	15.00
Cobalt Blue, Jar, Biscuit, Enameled Foliage & Scrolls, Gold Trim, 10 In.	135.00
Cobalt Blue, Jar, Biscuit, Enameled Lilies Of The Valley & Cupid, 8 In.	145.00
Cobalt Blue, Jar, Ginger, 2 Ring Mark On Bottom	37.50
Cobalt Blue, Lamp, Hand, Miniature, Worded Little Buttercup, 7 1/2 In.	65.00
Cobalt Blue, Lamp, Miniature, Manila, Smith No.30	75.00
Cobalt Blue, Lamp, Miniature, Nutmeg, Smith No.29	65.00
Cobalt Blue, Match Safe, Blue, Enameled, Footed, 2 X 2 1/2 In.	40.00

Cloisonne, Vase,
Red Pink Floral Sprays,
Gold, Miniature, Pair
(See Page 111)

Cloisonne, Vase,
Sang De Boeuf Ground,
Floral, 5 1/2 In., One Of A Pair
(See Page 111)

Cobalt Blue, Mug, Flip, Handblown, Silver Border Top, Ring Bottom, 8 X 6 In.	100.00
Cobalt Blue, Mug, Flip, Silver Bank Top, Silver Line At Bottom, Blown	100.00
Cobalt Blue, Nappy, Pond Lily, Handled	25.00
Cobalt Blue, Pitcher, Clear Applied Handle, 10 In.	40.00
Cobalt Blue, Pitcher, Milk, High Glaze, 8 1/2 In.	32.00
Cobalt Blue, Pitcher, Pear Shaped, Metal Rim & Handle & Lid, 6 X 10 In.	47.50
Cobalt Blue, Pitcher, Water, Bulbous, Ribbed Handle, 8 In.	35.00
Cobalt Blue, Plate, Wild Rose, Scenic Center, C.1860, 9 1/4 In.	29.00
Cobalt Blue, Punch Set, Blown, 14 Piece	135.00
Cobalt Blue, Ring Tree, Gold & White Enameled Flowers & Leaves, 2 1/2 In.	32.00
Cobalt Blue, Salt Dip, Cambridge, Footed	17.50
Cobalt Blue, Salt, Sterling Silver Stand And Spoon	18.50
Cobalt Blue, Salt, Stiegel Type, Blown, Expanded Diamond, Flint	225.00

Cobalt Blue, Soup, Cream, Royal Lace 14.00
Cobalt Blue, Spooner, Log Cabin 225.00
Cobalt Blue, Table Set, Child's, Miniature, 4 Piece Set, Cambridge Colonial 130.00
Cobalt Blue, Toothpick, Small Boot 28.00
Cobalt Blue, Vase, Applied Handles, Czechoslovakia, 5 1/2 In. 35.00
Cobalt Blue, Vase, Blue, Ruffled Edge, Victorian, 9 In. 95.00
Cobalt Blue, Vase, Flowers & Leaves, Gourd Shaped, 17 1/2 In., Pair 350.00
Cobalt Blue, Vase, Gold Decoration, 6 1/2 In. 28.00
Cobalt Blue, Vase, Raised Enamel Scene, Foo Dog Handles, Gold Trim, 8 In. 30.00
Cobalt Blue, Vase, Silver Overlay Tulips, 6 In. 50.00
Cobalt Blue, Vase, Top Hat, Stippled Band 15.50
Cobalt Blue, Vase, Trumpet, 7 In. 18.00
Cobalt Blue, Water Set, Clear Reeded Handled Pitcher, 7 Piece 50.00
Cobalt Blue, Water Set, Duck Bill Pouring Spout Pitcher, 7 Piece 175.00
Cobalt Blue, Witches' Ball, Blown, Swirl Ribbed, Closed Pontil, 6 In. 145.00

Coca-Cola advertising items have become a special field for collectors.
Coca-Cola, Ashtray, Things Go Better With Coke, Metal, 4 X 4 In. 3.50
Coca-Cola, Billfold, 1915 .... 40.00
Coca-Cola, Blotter, Lithographed In Color, 1956 .... 4.50
Coca-Cola, Blotter, 1939 .... 4.00
Coca-Cola, Book, Alphabet, 1928 .... 40.00
Coca-Cola, Bottle, Amber, 1910 .... 20.00
Coca-Cola, Bottle, Dec.25, 1923, 20 In. 100.00
Coca-Cola, Bottle, Dispenser, Ten-Sided, Green, Sharon, Pa., 12 In. 60.00
Coca-Cola, Bottle, Script In Hebrew With Star Of David, 6 1/2 Oz. 5.60
Coca-Cola, Bottle, Straight Sides, C.1905 .... 8.00
Coca-Cola, Bottle, Straight Sides, Coca-Cola Co., Canada, Blue, C.1910 .... 10.00
Coca-Cola, Bottle, Straight Sides, With Arrow On Side, Amber, 1909 .... 25.00
Coca-Cola, Bottle, Straight, Clear, Embossed, 24 Oz. 18.50
Coca-Cola, Bottle, 1931, 36 In. 90.00
Coca-Cola, Bottle, 50th Anniversary, Gold, Base 45.00
Coca-Cola, Bowl, Pretzel, Aluminum, 3 Bottles For Legs, 1935 .... 35.00
Coca-Cola, Box, Gum, Wooden Packing, 12 X 6 X 6 In. 47.00
Coca-Cola, Calendar, C.1972 .... 2.50
Coca-Cola, Calendar, Framed, 1921 .... 30.00
Coca-Cola, Calendar, 1918, June Caprice 75.00
Coca-Cola, Calendar, 1922, Framed, 29 X 14 In. 175.00
Coca-Cola, Calendar, 1923 .... 95.00
Coca-Cola, Card, Trade, Nature Studies, C.1930 .... 1.00
Coca-Cola, Carrier, Holds 6 Bottles, Metal 7.50
Coca-Cola, Carton, Aluminum, 1940s .... 4.50 To 8.00
Coca-Cola, Case, Thimble, Marked 5.00
Coca-Cola, Cases, Wooden Bottles, Miniature 5.00
Coca-Cola, Clock, Brown & Red, Electric, 1930s 40.00
Coca-Cola, Clock, Illuminated, Swinging Pendulum, Electric, 16 X 16 In. 125.00
Coca-Cola, Clock, Metal, Logo On Glass 38.00
Coca-Cola, Clock, Round, Internal Pendulum, C.1900 .... 325.00
Coca-Cola, Clock, Square, 1930s 120.00
Coca-Cola, Clock, Things Go Better With Coke, Electric 60.00
Coca-Cola, Clock, 1950 .... 28.00
Coca-Cola, Cooler, Bottle 325.00
Coca-Cola, Cooler, Oak Boards, Zinc Liner, Red Coke Logo 495.00
Coca-Cola, Dish, Pretzel, 1935 .... 60.00
Coca-Cola, Doll, Santa With Bottle In Hand .... 30.00 To 48.00
Coca-Cola, Door Push, Figural, Bottle, Porcelain 29.00
Coca-Cola, Fan, C.1940s 13.00
Coca-Cola, Fan, Cardboard, 1930s 14.00
Coca-Cola, Festoon, 5 Piece 175.00
Coca-Cola, Knife, 2 Blades, Pearl Finish, Coke Ad In Red 2.50
Coca-Cola, Letter Opener, Coca-Cola One Side, Coca-Cola Bottler On Other 8.00
Coca-Cola, Lock, 1967 .... 18.00
Coca-Cola, Machine, 1950s 150.00
Coca-Cola, Match Safe, Celluloid Design, Tin,C. 1925 .... 29.50
Coca-Cola, Mirror, Fleet Of Old Cars, Rectangular, C.1973 .... 2.75

American empire sofa, c. 1830.

American Empire-style chest of drawers. Label, Bancroft Furniture. Warerooms, Worcester, Mass., 1841.

Tin teapot with cast pewter cover, handle, and spout. Cheshire, Conn., c. 1850–1860.

Pressed tin chamberstick, c. 1840.

Lard-tin lamp, Drummond's pattern. Berlin, Conn., c. 1840–1860.

Dark green sunburst. Keene, N.H., c. 1835. Half-pint Coventry, Conn., piece. Profile of Lafayette, c. 1825.

Tin-domed document box. Freehand decoration, c. 1840.

Octagonal pressed glass preserve bottle, c. 1840–1850. Pressed glass colorless bottle. Label, Dr. Hartshorn's Lemon Extract, c. 1850.

Paperweight, Mt. Washington Rose, c. 1860.

Homemade baby's rattle and homemade spinning top, early nineteenth century.

Cased glass apple paperweight. New England Glass Co., c. 1850.

Wooden flour scoop, late eighteenth century.

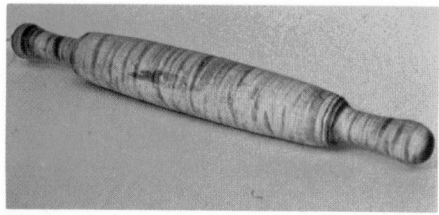

Curly maple rolling pin, early nineteenth century.

Lacemaker's lamp. Water-filled globes magnify the light, c. 1800.

Glass whale-oil lamp. Base made in a cup-plate mold. Sandwich, Mass., c. 1825.

Half-pint molded flask. Cornucopia and urn motifs. Keene, N.H., c. 1830.

Two-part mirror. Upper glass and frame stenciled in gold leaf, c. 1835.

Pressed clear glass candlestick in the form of a dolphin. Sandwich, Mass., c. 1835.

Free-blown lily pad glass pitcher. Olive green. Stoddard, N.H., c. 1943.

Large pressed glass low bowl. Lacy Sandwich Princess Feather pattern. Sandwich, Mass., c. 1830.

Three-mold pressed glass sugar bowl. Keene, N.H., or Sandwich, Mass., c. 1830.

Footed pewter baptismal bowl. Israel Trask. Beverly, Mass., 1830–1840.

Country Sheraton-style washstand, c. 1830.

Pewter porringer. Eagle mark of Josiah Danforth. Middletown, Conn., 1825–1837.

Daguerreotype of Mr. and Mrs. Henry Harrington. Southbridge, Mass., c. 1860.

Pair of watercolor miniatures on paper. Artist unknown, c. 1812.

Tortoiseshell comb box with comb. Label, Cary, Boynton and Woodford. Boston, Mass., c. 1836.

Hatbox and patriotic covering. Label, John and Charles Cook. Boston, Mass., c. 1830.

Pack of playing cards. Patriotic figures are used instead of usual hearts, diamonds, etc. New York City, c. 1839–1842.

Coin silver tea set. Bristol, Conn., area, c. 1810.

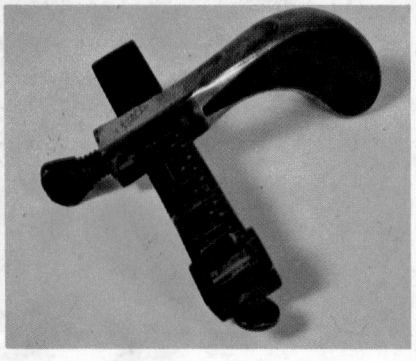

Pistol grip leather cutter. Philadelphia, c. 1800.

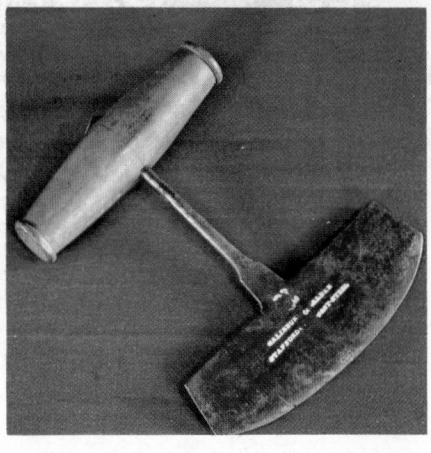

Hand-forged food chopper. Stafford, Conn., c. 1800.

Needlework garden scene taken from a French engraving, c. 1820.

Needlework memorial scene done by Abigail Mason. Granby, Mass., c. 1802–1805.

Coca-Cola, Mirror, Pocket, Girl, C.1909	55.00
Coca-Cola, Mirror, Pocket, 1911	95.00
Coca-Cola, Mirror, Surf Girl, Rectangular	1.50
Coca-Cola, Napkin, Paper, Girl Holding Bottle, 1910	32.00
Coca-Cola, Paperweight, Glass, 3 1/2 In.	9.50
Coca-Cola, Paperweight, Pink & Blue	50.00
Coca-Cola, Paperweight, Red & White	50.00
Coca-Cola, Paperweight, Red, White, & Blue, Glass, 1916, 2 3/4 X 4 1/4 In.	14.00
Coca-Cola, Paperweight, Red, 3 1/2 In.	9.50
Coca-Cola, Pin, Copper, Porcelain, Shape Coke Lid	5.00
Coca-Cola, Pinback, Coca-Cola Club	15.00
Coca-Cola, Plaque, Pyramid, Number Of Gallons Of Coke Sold Since 1886, 1901	45.00
Coca-Cola, Poster, Chinese Girl, Chinese Calligraphy, 1936	150.00
Coca-Cola, Radio, Crystal	90.00
Coca-Cola, Radio, Transistor	18.00
Coca-Cola, Server, Oblong, 13 X 11 In.	12.50
Coca-Cola, Sharpener, Knife, 1950	5.00
Coca-Cola, Sharpener, Pencil, Miniature Red Metal Bottle, 1940s	16.00
Coca-Cola, Shorts, Lady's, Approximately Size 9, C.1973	6.00
Coca-Cola, Sign, Bottle Shape, Porcelain, 16 In.	30.00
Coca-Cola, Sign, Bottle, Tin, 36 In.	80.00
Coca-Cola, Sign, C.1937, 27 X 19 In.	30.00
Coca-Cola, Sign, Cardboard, Metal Frame, 40 1/2 In.	22.00
Coca-Cola, Sign, Christmas Bottle, Tin, 1923, 19 X 27 In.	65.00
Coca-Cola, Sign, Fountain Service, Porcelain, 1930s, 25 X 23 In.	65.00
Coca-Cola, Sign, Lollipop	125.00
Coca-Cola, Sign, Menu Board, Tin, C.1932, 19 X 28 In.	75.00
Coca-Cola, Sign, Porcelain, 17 In.	20.00
Coca-Cola, Sign, Santa With Elves, Cardboard, Stand-Up	28.00
Coca-Cola, Sign, Tin, C.1937, 27 X 19 In.	65.00
Coca-Cola, Sign, 36 In.Bottle, Dated 1931	90.00
Coca-Cola, Slacks, Lady's, Approximately Size 9, New, C.1973	6.00
Coca-Cola, Suit, Bathing, Yellow, 1932	210.00
Coca-Cola, Thermometer, Bottle Shaped	22.50
Coca-Cola, Thermometer, Bottle Shaped, 15 In.	15.50
Coca-Cola, Thermometer, Bottle, 29 In.	35.00
Coca-Cola, Thermometer, Gold Bottle, 7 In.	20.00
Coca-Cola, Thermometer, Markon Robertson, Tin, 15 In.	10.00
Coca-Cola, Thermometer, 1923, 16 In.	16.50
Coca-Cola, Thimble, Drink Coca-Cola In Bottles	4.50
Coca-Cola, Token, Brass, Good For One Bottle, Embossed Picture, C.1919	4.50
Coca-Cola, Tray, Picture Of Old 6-Pack, Wooden Handle, Serve Coke At Home	17.50
Coca-Cola, Tray, Tip, Woman With Bonnet, Pink	47.00
Coca-Cola, Tray, Tip, 1905, Juanita	125.00
Coca-Cola, Tray, Tip, 1906, Relieves Fatigue, Oval	185.00
Coca-Cola, Tray, Tip, 1909, Coca-Cola Girl, Oval	125.00
Coca-Cola, Tray, Tip, 1912, Girl With Rose In Hat	65.00
Coca-Cola, Tray, Tip, 1917	45.00
Coca-Cola, Tray, 1904, Lillian Russell, With A Glass	125.00
Coca-Cola, Tray, 1914, Betty, Oval, 12 1/2 X 15 1/2 In. ....Illus	180.00
Coca-Cola, Tray, 1914, Betty, Rectangular	85.00
Coca-Cola, Tray, 1917, Elaine	60.00 To 85.00
Coca-Cola, Tray, 1921, Summer Girl	135.00
Coca-Cola, Tray, 1923, Flapper In Blue & White On Brown Ground	125.00
Coca-Cola, Tray, 1924, Smiling Girl	65.00
Coca-Cola, Tray, 1927, Bobbed Hair	85.00
Coca-Cola, Tray, 1927, Soda Fountain Clerk	125.00
Coca-Cola, Tray, 1930, Bathing Beauty	52.00 To 80.00
Coca-Cola, Tray, 1930, Girl With Telephone	50.00
Coca-Cola, Tray, 1934, Maureen O'Sullivan & Johnny Weissmuller	275.00 To 315.00
Coca-Cola, Tray, 1935, Madge Evans	40.00 To 45.00
Coca-Cola, Tray, 1936, Hostess	40.00 To 65.00
Coca-Cola, Tray, 1937, Running Girl	42.50
Coca-Cola, Tray, 1938, Girl In The Afternoon, Tin, 11 X 17 In.	22.50 To 35.00
Coca-Cola, Tray, 1939, Springboard Girl	38.00

Coca-Cola, Tray, 1940, Sailor Girl .... 35.00 To 60.00
Coca-Cola, Tray, 1941, Girl Ice Skater .... 30.00 To 35.00
Coca-Cola, Tray, 1943, Girl With Wind In Her Hair 35.00
Coca-Cola, Tray, 1950, Girl With Menu 20.00
Coca-Cola, Tray, 1958, Picnic Basket 6.00
Coca-Cola, Tray, 1961, Pansy Garden, Be Really Refreshed 8.50
Coca-Cola, Tray, 1973, Santa 10.00
Coca-Cola, Wall Hanger, Bottle Shape, Heavy Metal, 12 1/2 In. 15.00

Coffee grinders, home size, were first made about 1894. They lost favor by
the 1930s.
Coffee Grinder, Arcade, Wall, Glass, Signed 100.00
Coffee Grinder, Brass, Small Handle 65.00
Coffee Grinder, Electric, Holwick, Green, Small 85.00
Coffee Grinder, Enterprise No.7, Original Stenciling, 17 In.Wheels, 23 In. 325.00
Coffee Grinder, Enterprise, Floor Model 1400.00
Coffee Grinder, Fairbanks Morse, Two-Wheel, 1887, 24 In. 275.00
Coffee Grinder, Golden Rule 95.00
Coffee Grinder, Lap Type, Tin Hopper, Hardwood, 6 X 6 X 4 In. 25.00
Coffee Grinder, Wall Mount, Golden Rule Blend Coffee 75.00
Coffee Grinder, Wall, Increase Wilson's, Connecticut 25.00
Coffee Grinder, Wall, Iron & China, Blue & White, German 50.00
Coffee Grinder, Wall, Telephone Mill, Brass Front, Oak, C.1893 .... 125.00
Coffee Grinder, Wooden, Dovetailed, 7 1/2 In. 48.50
Coin Spot, Banana Stand, Blue Opalescent 55.00
Coin Spot, Basket, White, Ruffled, Opalescent, 6 1/4 In. 18.50
Coin Spot, Bowl, Blue Opalescent, Ruffled Edge 27.50
Coin Spot, Bowl, Finger, Opalescent 15.00
Coin Spot, Dish, Clear, Footed, Opalescent 21.50
Coin Spot, Pitcher, Fluted Top, Green, 10 In. 95.00
Coin Spot, Pitcher, Water, Blue, Opalescent, 4 Glasses 165.00
Coin Spot, Pitcher, Water, Cranberry, Opalescent, Large 120.00
Coin Spot, Pitcher, Water, Green, Opalescent 95.00
Coin Spot, Sugar Shaker, Blue 58.00
Coin Spot, Syrup, Blue, Bulbous Base, Opalescent .... 95.00 To 125.00
Coin Spot, Syrup, Bulbous Base, Metal Top, Green, Opalescent 70.00
Coin Spot, Syrup, Sugar Shaker, Ring Neck, Rubena, Opalescent 98.00
Coin Spot, Syrup, White On White, Ring Neck, Opalescent 69.00
Coin Spot, Tumbler, Cranberry, Opalescent 38.00
Coin Spot, Vase, White, Ruffled Top, Opalescent, 8 1/4 In. 45.00
Coin Spot, Water Set, Opalescent, Blue, 5 Piece 200.00

Coca-Cola, Tray, 1914, Betty, Oval, 12 1/2 X 15 1/2 In.
(See Page 115)

Collector plates are any of the plates produced in limited editions.
The most famous were made by the Bing & Grondahl Factory of Denmark,
after 1895, and the Royal Copenhagen Factory, after 1908.
Collector, Plate, Belleek, Christmas, 1970 .... 65.00 To 130.00
Collector, Plate, Belleek, 1971 .... 15.00 To 30.00
Collector, Plate, Belleek, 1972 .... 22.50 To 30.00

Collector, Plate, Belleek, 1974 .... 39.00 To 125.00
Collector, Plate, Berlin, Christmas, 1970 .... 29.95 To 150.00
Collector, Plate, Berlin, Christmas, 1972 .... 10.00 To 25.00
Collector, Plate, Berlin, Christmas, 1974 .... 8.00 To 25.00
Collector, Plate, Bing & Grondahl, Christmas, 1897 .... 600.00 To 1050.00
Collector, Plate, Bing & Grondahl, Christmas, 1903 .... 119.00 To 270.00
Collector, Plate, Bing & Grondahl, Christmas, 1905 .... 74.00 To 120.00
Collector, Plate, Bing & Grondahl, Christmas, 1908 .... 49.00 To 62.00
Collector, Plate, Bing & Grondahl, Christmas, 1909 .... 55.00 To 96.00
Collector, Plate, Bing & Grondahl, Christmas, 1911 .... 56.00 To 81.00
Collector, Plate, Bing & Grondahl, Christmas, 1912 .... 56.00 To 80.00
Collector, Plate, Bing & Grondahl, Christmas, 1913 .... 56.00 To 80.00
Collector, Plate, Bing & Grondahl, Christmas, 1914 .... 45.00 To 72.00
Collector, Plate, Bing & Grondahl, Christmas, 1917 .... 46.00 To 75.00
Collector, Plate, Bing & Grondahl, Christmas, 1919 .... 45.00 To 84.00
Collector, Plate, Bing & Grondahl, Christmas, 1921 .... 45.00 To 75.00
Collector, Plate, Bing & Grondahl, Christmas, 1925 .... 45.00 To 67.50
Collector, Plate, Bing & Grondahl, Christmas, 1927 .... 45.00 To 60.00
Collector, Plate, Bing & Grondahl, Christmas, 1931 .... 49.00 To 84.00
Collector, Plate, Bing & Grondahl, Christmas, 1932 .... 50.00 To 78.00
Collector, Plate, Bing & Grondahl, Christmas, 1934 .... 45.00 To 75.00
Collector, Plate, Bing & Grondahl, Christmas, 1935 .... 40.00 To 85.00
Collector, Plate, Bing & Grondahl, Christmas, 1938 .... 72.00 To 108.00
Collector, Plate, Bing & Grondahl, Christmas, 1940 .... 87.00 To 139.00
Collector, Plate, Bing & Grondahl, Christmas, 1942 .... 89.00 To 165.00
Collector, Plate, Bing & Grondahl, Christmas, 1944 .... 59.00 To 105.00
Collector, Plate, Bing & Grondahl, Christmas, 1945 .... 71.00 To 135.00
Collector, Plate, Bing & Grondahl, Christmas, 1947 .... 45.00 To 81.00
Collector, Plate, Bing & Grondahl, Christmas, 1949 .... 59.00 To 135.00
Collector, Plate, Bing & Grondahl, Christmas, 1951 .... 50.00 To 90.00
Collector, Plate, Bing & Grondahl, Christmas, 1953 .... 45.00 To 81.00
Collector, Plate, Bing & Grondahl, Christmas, 1955 .... 56.00 To 75.00
Collector, Plate, Bing & Grondahl, Christmas, 1957 .... 67.00 To 137.50
Collector, Plate, Bing & Grondahl, Christmas, 1959 .... 75.00 To 149.00
Collector, Plate, Bing & Grondahl, Christmas, 1961 .... 60.00 To 135.00
Collector, Plate, Bing & Grondahl, Christmas, 1963 .... 68.00 To 139.00
Collector, Plate, Bing & Grondahl, Christmas, 1964 .... 34.00
Collector, Plate, Bing & Grondahl, Christmas, 1965 .... 34.00
Collector, Plate, Bing & Grondahl, Christmas, 1966 .... 28.00 To 49.95
Collector, Plate, Bing & Grondahl, Christmas, 1969 .... 12.00 To 25.00
Collector, Plate, Bing & Grondahl, Christmas, 1970 .... 9.00 To 22.50
Collector, Plate, Bing & Grondahl, Christmas, 1971 .... 7.50 To 21.95
Collector, Plate, Bing & Grondahl, Christmas, 1972 .... 8.50 To 21.95
Collector, Plate, Bing & Grondahl, Christmas, 1973 .... 7.50 To 27.50
Collector, Plate, Buffalo Pottery, Christmas, 1950 .... 35.00 To 45.00
Collector, Plate, Buffalo Pottery, Christmas, 1952 .... 35.00 To 40.00
Collector, Plate, Buffalo Pottery, Christmas, 1958 .... 25.00 To 30.00
Collector, Plate, Buffalo Pottery, Christmas, 1962 .... 125.00 To 150.00
Collector, Plate, Fenton, Christmas, 1971, Blue Satin .... 10.00 To 25.00
Collector, Plate, Fenton, Christmas, 1971, White Satin .... 12.00 To 30.00
Collector, Plate, Fenton, Christmas, 1972, White Satin .... 10.00 To 12.50
Collector, Plate, Fontana, Christmas, 1972 .... 59.00 To 35.00
Collector, Plate, Fontana, Christmas, 1973 .... 10.00 To 37.00
Collector, Plate, Fontana, Mother's Day, 1973 .... 5.00 To 35.00
Collector, Plate, Furstenberg, Christmas, 1971 .... 8.00 To 28.00
Collector, Plate, Furstenberg, Christmas, 1972 .... 8.00 To 27.50
Collector, Plate, Furstenberg, Christmas, 1973 .... 12.00 To 24.00
Collector, Plate, Furstenberg, Christmas, 1974 .... 15.00 To 30.00
Collector, Plate, Goebel Hummel, Annual, 1971 .... 925.00 To 1000.00
Collector, Plate, Goebel Hummel, Annual, 1973 .... 200.00 To 225.00
Collector, Plate, Goebel Hummel, Annual, 1974 .... 75.00 To 115.00
Collector, Plate, Kaiser, Christmas, 1970 .... 20.00 To 48.00
Collector, Plate, Kaiser, Christmas, 1972 .... 21.00 To 42.00
Collector, Plate, Kaiser, Christmas, 1973 .... 20.00 To 39.00

Collector, Plate, Lenox, Boehm, Meadowlarks, 1973 .... 45.00
Collector, Plate, Porsgrund, Christmas, 1970 .... 11.00 To 20.00
Collector, Plate, Porsgrund, Christmas, 1971 .... 7.00 To 20.00
Collector, Plate, Porsgrund, Christmas, 1974 .... 16.00 To 30.00
Collector, Plate, Reed & Barton, Christmas, 1970 .... 125.00 To 175.00
Collector, Plate, Reed & Barton, Christmas, 1971 .... 37.50 To 75.00
Collector, Plate, Reed & Barton, Christmas, 1972 .... 40.00 To 70.00
Collector, Plate, Reed & Barton, Christmas, 1973 .... 50.00 To 65.00
Collector, Plate, Rorstrand, Christmas, 1968 .... 300.00 To 520.00
Collector, Plate, Rorstrand, Christmas, 1970 .... 15.00 To 25.00
Collector, Plate, Rorstrand, Christmas, 1971 .... 18.00 To 20.00
Collector, Plate, Rorstrand, Christmas, 1973 .... 60.00 To 100.00
Collector, Plate, Royal Bayreuth, Christmas, 1967 .... 50.00 To 100.00
Collector, Plate, Royal Bayreuth, Father's Day, 1969 .... 25.00 To 75.00
Collector, Plate, Royal Bayreuth, Father's Day, 1971 .... 8.00 To 22.00
Collector, Plate, Royal Bayreuth, Mother's Day, 1969 .... 17.50 To 75.00
Collector, Plate, Royal Bayreuth, Mother's Day, 1970 .... 7.00 To 25.00
Collector, Plate, Royal Bayreuth, 1970 .... 16.00
Collector, Plate, Royal Copenhagen, Christmas, 1909 .... 75.00 To 106.00
Collector, Plate, Royal Copenhagen, Christmas, 1911 .... 80.00 To 135.00
Collector, Plate, Royal Copenhagen, Christmas, 1914 .... 75.00 To 115.00
Collector, Plate, Royal Copenhagen, Christmas, 1916 .... 40.00 To 90.00
Collector, Plate, Royal Copenhagen, Christmas, 1917 .... 40.00 To 85.00
Collector, Plate, Royal Copenhagen, Christmas, 1919 .... 57.00 To 75.00
Collector, Plate, Royal Copenhagen, Christmas, 1920 .... 52.00 To 75.00
Collector, Plate, Royal Copenhagen, Christmas, 1921 .... 47.00 To 72.00
Collector, Plate, Royal Copenhagen, Christmas, 1922 .... 47.00 To 75.00
Collector, Plate, Royal Copenhagen, Christmas, 1923 .... 46.00 To 75.00
Collector, Plate, Royal Copenhagen, Christmas, 1924 .... 59.00 To 75.00
Collector, Plate, Royal Copenhagen, Christmas, 1926 .... 53.00 To 70.00
Collector, Plate, Royal Copenhagen, Christmas, 1927 .... 72.00 To 95.00
Collector, Plate, Royal Copenhagen, Christmas, 1930 .... 55.00 To 75.00
Collector, Plate, Royal Copenhagen, Christmas, 1931 .... 55.00 To 84.00
Collector, Plate, Royal Copenhagen, Christmas, 1933 .... 72.00 To 90.00
Collector, Plate, Royal Copenhagen, Christmas, 1934 .... 67.00 To 112.00
Collector, Plate, Royal Copenhagen, Christmas, 1936 .... 76.00 To 120.00
Collector, Plate, Royal Copenhagen, Christmas, 1938 .... 142.00 To 240.00
Collector, Plate, Royal Copenhagen, Christmas, 1939 .... 142.00 To 240.00
Collector, Plate, Royal Copenhagen, Christmas, 1941 .... 200.00 To 375.00
Collector, Plate, Royal Copenhagen, Christmas, 1943 .... 300.00 To 540.00
Collector, Plate, Royal Copenhagen, Christmas, 1944 .... 84.00 To 150.00
Collector, Plate, Royal Copenhagen, Christmas, 1946 .... 81.00 To 135.00
Collector, Plate, Royal Copenhagen, Christmas, 1949 .... 79.00 To 130.00
Collector, Plate, Royal Copenhagen, Christmas, 1952 .... 43.00 To 96.00
Collector, Plate, Royal Copenhagen, Christmas, 1954 .... 74.00 To 135.00
Collector, Plate, Royal Copenhagen, Christmas, 1956 .... 75.00 To 150.00
Collector, Plate, Royal Copenhagen, Christmas, 1959 .... 70.00 To 135.00
Collector, Plate, Royal Copenhagen, Christmas, 1961 .... 81.00 To 135.00
Collector, Plate, Royal Copenhagen, Christmas, 1962 .... 98.00 To 180.00
Collector, Plate, Royal Copenhagen, Christmas, 1964 .... 40.00 To 60.00
Collector, Plate, Royal Copenhagen, Christmas, 1967 .... 18.00 To 35.00
Collector, Plate, Royal Copenhagen, Christmas, 1968 .... 15.00 To 31.00
Collector, Plate, Royal Copenhagen, Christmas, 1970 .... 10.00 To 25.00
Collector, Plate, Royal Copenhagen, Christmas, 1971 .... 10.00 To 22.00
Collector, Plate, Royal Copenhagen, Christmas, 1972 .... 12.00 To 22.00
Collector, Plate, Royal Copenhagen, Christmas, 1973 .... 11.00 To 25.00
Collector, Plate, Royal Copenhagen, Christmas, 1974 .... 12.00 To 22.00
Collector, Plate, Royal Doulton, Christmas, 1972 .... 35.00 To 40.00
Collector, Plate, Royal Doulton, Mother's Day, 1973 .... 400.00 To 500.00
Collector, Plate, Royal Doulton, Mother's Day, 1974 .... 105.00 To 140.00
Collector, Plate, Svend Jensen, Christmas, 1970 .... 100.00 To 200.00
Collector, Plate, Svend Jensen, Christmas, 1972 .... 30.00 To 39.00
Collector, Plate, Svend Jensen, Christmas, 1973 .... 30.00 To 37.00
Collector, Plate, Svend Jensen, Christmas, 1974 .... 30.00 To 38.00
Collector, Plate, Veneto Flair, Christmas, 1971 .... 45.00 To 60.00

Collector, Plate, Veneto Flair, Christmas, 1972 .... 8.00 To 20.00
Collector, Plate, Veneto Flair, Christmas, 1973 .... 10.00 To 35.00
Collector, Plate, Veneto Flair, Christmas, 1974 .... 16.00 To 22.00
Collector, Plate, Wedgwood, Christmas, FE, 1969 .... 185.00
Collector, Plate, Wedgwood, Christmas, 1969 .... 122.00 To 250.00
Collector, Plate, Wedgwood, Christmas, 1971 .... 10.00 To 45.00
Collector, Plate, Wedgwood, Christmas, 1973 .... 20.00 To 45.00
Collector, Plate, Wedgwood, Christmas, 1974 .... 20.00 To 45.00

*Commemoration items have been made to honor members of royalty and those of
great national fame. World's fairs and important historical events are also
remembered with commemoration pieces.*

Commemoration, see also Coronation, World's Fair
Commemoration, Basket, Pink, Florals, Queen Victoria, Jubilee, 1887, 5 1/4 In. 135.00
Commemoration, Beaker, Queen Victoria, 1837-1897, Enameled 50.00
Commemoration, Dish, Fluted, Coronation, King George VI, Queen Elizabeth 16.00
Commemoration, Dish, Maple Leaf, Queen Alexandra, King Edward VII, 5 In. 18.00
Commemoration, Jug, Victoria, 1897, Portraits On Tan, Doulton Lambeth, 7 In. 75.00
Commemoration, Mug, Edward VIII, Signed Laura Knight 24.00
Commemoration, Mug, Peace, 1919, Beatty & Haig, 3 In. 20.00
Commemoration, Mug, 60th Year Of Queen Mary's Reign, 6 1/4 In. 40.00
Commemoration, Needlebook, Victoria Jubilee, Fold-Out, Engravings 55.00
Commemoration, Pitcher, King George V & Queen Mary, 1911, Royal Doulton 140.00
Commemoration, Pitcher, Longfellow & Bryant, Salt Glaze, 7 1/2 In. 150.00
Commemoration, Pitcher, Queen Victoria, Heads In Relief, Royal Doulton, 5 In. 85.00
Commemoration, Plate, Cup, Landing Of The Fathers At Plymouth, Scrolls, 4 In. 230.00
Commemoration, Plate, Gladstone For The Million, 9 1/2 In. 40.00
Commemoration, Plate, J.F.Kennedy Center 8.50
Commemoration, Plate, Lindbergh, Plane, Statue Of Liberty, Limoges 22.00
Commemoration, Plate, New York To Paris Flight, Dated May 20, 1927 .... 75.00
Commemoration, Plate, Park Theater, New York, Acorn, Oak Leaves, Blue, 10 In. 220.00
Commemoration, Plate, Queen Elizabeth's Silver Jubilee, Wedgwood 800.00
Commemoration, Plate, Queen Victoria, 60 Year, Foley China, 8 In. 15.00
Commemoration, Plate, Rear Admiral George Dewey, Marked, 10 In. 25.00
Commemoration, Plate, Washington, Newburgh, Ny, Johnson Brothers, Eng., 8 In. 18.00
Commemoration, Platter, Declaration Of Independence, 1776-1876, Glass 95.00
Commemoration, Teapot, Edward VII, Creamware, Wedgwood 125.00
Commemoration, Tin, George V, Queen Mary, Silver Jubilee, 3 1/2 X 5 1/2 In. 22.00
Commemoration, Trivet, Embossed Crown, Elizabeth R., 1953, 6 In. 18.00
Commemoration, Tumbler, Edward VII & Queen Alexandra, 1902, 4 In. 20.00
Commemoration, Tumbler, Louisiana Purchase, 1803-1904, Victor Art Co. 18.50

*Coors ware was made by a pottery in Golden, Colorado, owned by the
Coors Beverage Company. It was produced from the turn of the
century until the pottery was destroyed by fire in the 1930s. It
resembles Homer Laughlin lines such as Fiesta. The name Coors
is marked on the back.*

Coors, Ashtray, 6 In. 4.00
Coors, Bowl, 3-Legged, Shallow, Orange 12.50
Coors, Pitcher, Water, Rosebud, Pottery Stopper 10.00
Coors, Vase, Blue, 8 In. 7.00
Coors, Vase, Brown Matte, Handled 18.00
Coors, Vase, Porcelain, Bulbous, 6 In. 12.50
Coors, Vase, Yellow, Handled 20.00

*W.T.Copeland & Sons, Ltd., ran the Spode Works in Staffordshire,
England, from 1847 to the present. Copeland & Garrett was the firm name
from 1833 to 1847.*

Copeland Spode, see also Flow Blue
Copeland Spode, Butter, Wicker Lane 4.50
Copeland Spode, Compote, Pedestal Base, Agate Ware, C.1843 .... 175.00
Copeland Spode, Cup & Saucer, Bouillon, Blue & White, Handled Saucer, Marked 18.00
Copeland Spode, Cup & Saucer, Bouillon, 2-Handled, Blue & White 18.00
Copeland Spode, Cup & Saucer, Willow, Demitasse 20.00

Copeland Spode, Pitcher, Country Scene, Blue, White, C.1850, 7 In.	45.00
Copeland Spode, Pitcher, Pastoral Scene, Blue Underglaze	39.00
Copeland Spode, Pitcher, White Men On Horses On Fox Chase, Blue, 8 In.	95.00
Copeland Spode, Plate, Byron Series No.2, Sectioned, 10 In.	18.00
Copeland Spode, Plate, Chinese Rose, 7 1/4 In., Pair	15.00
Copeland Spode, Plate, Rosedale, Basket Weave Border, 7 3/4 In., Set Of 6	50.00
Copeland Spode, Plate, Shanghai, 9 1/2 In.	25.00
Copeland Spode, Plate, Soup, Spode Tower, Pink, 9 1/2 In., Set Of Six	66.00
Copeland Spode, Service, Countryside Scene, For Six, Red Mark, 37 Pieces	275.00
Copeland Spode, Sugar & Creamer, Jasperware, Blue & Tan, Hunt Scene, Signed	65.00
Copeland Spode, Table Set, Cups & Saucers, Creamer, Sugar, Set Of 4	35.00
Copeland Spode, Tray, Tower, 7 3/4 In.	15.00
Copeland Spode, Tureen & Underplate, Blue On White, Tower, Covered, 13 In.	140.00
Copeland Spode, Tureen, Vegetable, Tower Cover, Cobalt Decoration	50.00
Copeland, see also Spode	
Copeland, Bust, Sir Walter Scott, Parian, 16 1/2 In.	225.00
Copeland, Jug Pitcher, England, White Classic Figures, Flower Garlands, 5 In.	22.00
Copeland, Pitcher, White Glazed, Chinese Personage, Pigtail Handle, 4 1/4 In.	60.00
Copeland, Plate, Peacock Center, C.1843, 8 In.	46.50
Copeland, Plate, Spode's Italian, Blue, White, 9 In.	15.00
Copeland, Plate, The Statue Of Jupiter Olympus	24.00
Copeland, Platter, Light Mauve, Yanina Pattern, C.1833-1847	35.50
Copeland, Pot, Chocolate, Gold & Blue Decorations, Marked	65.00
Copeland, Sugar & Creamer, Coral, Shell Shape, 5 1/4 In.	80.00
Copeland, Tile, Pastoral Scene, W.Yale, C.1880, 16 1/2 X 8 1/2 In., Pair	350.00
Copeland, Vase, Coral, Shell Shape, 1865, 6 1/4 In.	80.00
Copeland, Vegetable, Chrysanthemums, Raised Grapes & Leaves, Cover, Footed	35.00
Copper Luster, see Luster, Copper	
Copper, Ashtray, Embossed, Sailor In Marine Setting, Navy Player's Mixture	20.00
Copper, Ashtray, Navy Sailor, 5 In.	20.00
Copper, Bedwarmer, Turned Wooden Handle, Large	225.00
Copper, Bottle, Hot Water, Everready Hot Bottle Co., Chicago, Kansas City	20.00
Copper, Box, Enameled Garden Scene, Cover Has Cut-In Corners	195.00
Copper, Box, Tinder With Strike, Wrought Iron Ram's Head Curls, 6 1/4 In.	150.00
Copper, Bucket, Bail, Tip Handle, 10 1/2 X 14 In.	65.00
Copper, Bucket, Brass Bail, 5 In.	20.00
Copper, Bucket, Coal, Helmet, Brass Handle	150.00
Copper, Candlestick, Shape, Marked Warsaw, 5 1/2 In.	25.00
Copper, Chafing Dish, 1902	38.50
Copper, Coffee Set, Turkish, Brass Handled Pop, Intricate Designs, 7 Piece	23.00
Copper, Coffeepot, Burnished	37.00
Copper, Coffeepot, Gooseneck Spout	17.00 To 18.00
Copper, Coffeepot, 1/2 Gallon, Burnished, Lacquered	38.00
Copper, Flask, Powder, Shell Design, 8 In.	32.50
Copper, Foot Warmer, Oval, 14 X 9 In.	35.00
Copper, Funnel, 9 X 26 In.	19.00
Copper, Holder, Whetstone, Cone Shape, Iron Belt Loop, 18th Century, 8 X 2 In.	140.00
Copper, Horn, Coaching, Mid-19th Century, 43 In.	75.00
Copper, Humidor, Crossed Pipes On Front, 6 In.	12.50
Copper, Jardiniere, 3 Brass Feet, Rolled Edge, Russian Mark, 23 1/2 In.	36.50
Copper, Jug, Water, Iron Foot Ring, Italian, 15 In.	75.00
Copper, Kettle, Apple Butter, Handled, 18 In.	148.00
Copper, Kettle, Apple Butter, Iron Handle & Burner, 19 In.	108.00
Copper, Kettle, Apple Butter, Wrought Iron Bail, 25 In.	200.00
Copper, Kettle, Brass Braised Joints, C.1800, 13 1/2 In.	95.00
Copper, Kettle, Dovetailed Decorations, Riveted Edging At Base, 17 X 22 In.	250.00
Copper, Kettle, Gooseneck, Dovetailed, American, 6 1/2 X 6 In.	120.00
Copper, Kettle, Hand Hammered, Dovetailed, Rolled Edges, Hand-Forged Handles	95.00
Copper, Kettle, Stewing, Dovetailed	95.00
Copper, Kettle, Tea, Dovetailed, 5 Quart	65.00
Copper, Kettle, Tea, Miniature, Beveled Sides, Brass Handle, 2 1/2 X 2 3/4 In.	65.00
Copper, Kettle, Tea, Pewter Bird On Pouring Spout	36.00
Copper, Lamp, Kerosene, Miniature	14.00
Copper, Letter Opener, Municipal Auditorium, St.Louis	12.50
Copper, Measure, Beer, 6 1/2 In.	75.00

Copper, Mold, Domed Geometric Design, 7 In. 30.00
Copper, Mold, Geometric Design, Fluted, 10 In. 40.00
Copper, Pitcher, Beer, Disc Pedestal Base, Contoured Spout, Handle, 8 In. 28.00
Copper, Pitcher, Chinese, Mums, Symbols, Steps On Lid, Fat Body, Brass Collar 85.00
Copper, Pitcher, Hammered, Urn Shaped, Double Lipped, Bail Handle, 19 In.High 55.00
Copper, Plaque, Lincoln, Head In High Relief, 10 In. 59.00
Copper, Pot, Glue, Bail Handle, Wooden Grip, Rolled Edges, 6 1/2 In. 75.00
Copper, Print Block, Side View Horse, 1906, 5 X 6 In. 14.00
Copper, Server, Coffee, Burnished, Lacquered 26.00
Copper, Steamer, Dome Top, Grip Handles, Rectangular, Drainer, 12 1/4 X 10 In. 150.00
Copper, Still, 15 Gallon 75.00
Copper, Syrup, Brass Lid Stripped & Polished 24.00
Copper, Teakettle, Gooseneck Spout, Brass Hinge, Wooden Handle 37.50
Copper, Teakettle, 3 Queen Anne Legs, Dovetailed, Gooseneck Spout 65.00
Copper, Teapot, Dovetailed, Scandinavian 50.00
Copper, Teapot, Swing Handle, Gooseneck Spout, Hammered, Covered 175.00
Copper, Thermometer, Candy, Reads Blood Heat, Summer Heat, Temple Rate, Freeze 26.00
Copper, Vase, Dirk VanErp, 5 X 4 1/2 In. 60.00
Copper, Vase, Enameled Lady In Garden, Basket Of Flowers, French, 2 1/2 In. 150.00
Copper, Warmer, Bed, Pierced Decorative Top, Wooden Handle, French, 12 In. 125.00
Copper, Warmer, Foot, Round 27.50

*Coralene glass was made by firing many small colored beads on the outside of
glassware. It was made in many patterns in the United States and
Europe in the 1880s. Reproductions are made today.*
Coralene, Japanese Pottery, see Japanese Coralene
Coralene, Basket, White & Green Floral On Green, Gold, 1909, 4 1/2 In. 95.00
Coralene, Cup, Mustache, Pink Flower, Raised Gold, Think Of Me 37.00
Coralene, Ewer, Brown Shade To Tans & Pink, Green Floral Beading, 1909, 8 In. 140.00
Coralene, Vase, Allover Floral, Handled, Signed, 7 In. 185.00
Coralene, Vase, Ball Shape, Raised Work, Gold, Floral, 4 1/2 X 3 1/4 In. 55.00
Coralene, Vase, Beading With Gold, Signed, Kinran Patent, 1909, 8 1/2 In. 94.00
Coralene, Vase, Branched Beading, Cylinder Collar, Creamy Lower Part, Blue 319.00
Coralene, Vase, Cased, White & Cranberry, Victorian, 5 In. 235.00
Coralene, Vase, Clear, Blue, Ruffled, Daisies & Goldenrod, Footed, 8 1/2 In. 150.00
Coralene, Vase, Cocoa, Pink Flowers, Handled, Bulbous, 1909, 8 1/2 In. 110.00
Coralene, Vase, Cranberry To Clear, Bulbous, Flanged Top, 4 3/8 In. 200.00
Coralene, Vase, Cranberry, Flower & Leaf Decoration 275.00
Coralene, Vase, Florals, 2 Handles, 7 In. 185.00
Coralene, Vase, Green, Pink & Green Beading, 2-Handled, 1909, 5 1/2 In. 75.00
Coralene, Vase, Green, Pink Decoration, 1909, 5 1/2 In. 85.00
Coralene, Vase, Heart Shape, Seaweed Design, Gold Coral, White To Pink, 7 In. 650.00
Coralene, Vase, Mother-Of-Pearl, Herringbone, Yellow To White, 3 1/2 In. 375.00
Coralene, Vase, Narcissus, Leaves, Shaded, Gold Decorated & Beading, 4 3/4 In. 90.00
Coralene, Vase, Pansies On Green, Gold Beading & Trim, Japanese, 7 In. 160.00
Coralene, Vase, Rainbow, Blue, Yellow, Rose, Yellow Seaweed Coralene, 7 In. 775.00
Coralene, Vase, Scenic, Gold Outlines, RS Japan, 7 1/4 In. 55.00
Coralene, Vase, Sky Blue To Peach, Floral Beading, 1909, 8 In. 125.00
Coralene, Vase, Yellow To Green & Blues, Purple & Yellow Flowers, Marked 135.00
Coralene, Vase, 2 Shades Of Green, Stylized Greens & Pink, 1909, 12 1/2 In. 225.00

*Coronation cups have been made since the 1800s. Pieces of pottery or glass
with a picture of the monarch and the date have been made as souvenirs for many
coronations.*
Coronation, see also Commemoration
Coronation, Beaker, King Edward VII, 1902, Royal Doulton 18.00
Coronation, Bell, Elizabeth II, 1953, Brass, Queen's Head Handle, 6 In. 15.00
Coronation, Book, Coloring, Queen Elizabeth II, Her Young Family, Uncut 25.00
Coronation, Bottle, Scent, 2nd June 1953 Coronation 10.00
Coronation, Bowl, Diamond Jubilee, Victoria, Center Portrait, 9 In. 45.00
Coronation, Cup & Saucer, Elizabeth II, Hand-Painted, Radford Bone China 15.00
Coronation, Cup & Saucer, Elizabeth II, Queen Anne China 15.00
Coronation, Cup & Saucer, Queen Elizabeth II, C.1953 .... 27.50
Coronation, Cup & Saucer, Queen Elizabeth Jubilee, 1897 .... 35.00
Coronation, Dish, Sweet, Elizabeth II, June 5, 1953 .... 6.00

Coronation, Mug Set, Portraits Of Edward VIII & George & Elizabeth, Pair	45.00
Coronation, Mug, Edward VIII, 2 1/2 In.	12.00
Coronation, Mug, Elizabeth II, June 5, 1953	6.00
Coronation, Mug, Elizabeth II, Portrait And Coat-Of-Arms	10.00
Coronation, Mug, Elizabeth II, 1953, Blue & White, Wedgwood	7.95
Coronation, Mug, George V & Queen Mary, Dated June 30th, 1911, Royal Doulton	25.00
Coronation, Mug, George VI, C.1937	32.50
Coronation, Mug, King Edward VIII, May 1937	12.75
Coronation, Mug, King George & Queen Elizabeth, Laura Knight	28.00
Coronation, Mug, King George V And Queen Mary, 1911	55.00
Coronation, Mug, Queen Elizabeth, Raised Face, White	12.00
Coronation, Paperweight, Queen Elizabeth, Red Jasper, Millefiori Canes, 1953	375.00
Coronation, Pitcher, Elizabeth II, 1953, Pink, White Relief, Johnson, 5 In.	15.00
Coronation, Plate, Edward VIII, Cream Petal, Grindley England, 7 3/4 In.	10.00
Coronation, Plate, Edward VIII, Cream Petal, Grindley England, 9 3/4 In.	15.00
Coronation, Plate, Edward VIII, 5 In.	8.00
Coronation, Plate, George VI, May 12, 1937, God Save The King, 10 In.	35.00
Coronation, Plate, King George V And Queen Mary	20.00
Coronation, Plate, Queen Elizabeth, 1953, Mayer China	11.00
Coronation, Plate, Queen Victoria Jubilee, Octagon, 1887	55.00
Coronation, Sauce, Edward VIII, Cream Petal, Grindley England	10.00
Coronation, Spoon, Elizabeth, 1953, Set Of 3	16.50
Coronation, Tea Set, Edward VIII, Dark Blue Jasper, Wedgwood, 3 Piece	475.00
Coronation, Tray, George VI, Elizabeth, Sterling Silver, English, 3 1/4 In.	50.00
Coronation, Tray, Pin, Edward VII, June 26, 1902, Sterling, 2 In.	38.00
Coronation, Tumbler, Edward VII's Coronation Dinner, Large, Royal Doulton	35.00
Coronation, Tumbler, Elizabeth II, June 5, 1953	6.00
Coronation, Tumbler, George V & Mary, Portraits, 1911, Crest Of Kendal Mayor	20.00
Coronation, Tumbler, H.M.George V & Queen Mary's Silver Jubilee, 1910-35	20.00
Coronation, Mug, Edward VIII, 1937, 3 X 4 In.	25.00

Cosmos pattern glass is a pressed milk glass pattern with colored flowers.

Cosmos, Butter, Pink Band, Covered	178.00 To 200.00
Cosmos, Castor, Pickle, Pink, Frame & Lid	425.00
Cosmos, Lamp Base, Pink Band Decorated, Miniature	42.50
Cosmos, Lamp, Kerosene, Umbrella Shade, Clear, Miniature	55.00
Cosmos, Lamp, Miniature, Pink Band	185.00 To 200.00
Cosmos, Lamp, Pink Band	275.00
Cosmos, Pitcher, Water, Pink Neck, Pink & Blue Floral, 10 1/4 In.	200.00
Cosmos, Salt & Pepper, Pink, Blue & Yellow Flowers	50.00
Cosmos, Sugar, Pink Band, Flowers, Covered	100.00 To 185.00

Country Store, see Store

Cowan pottery was made in Cleveland, Ohio, from 1913 to 1920. Most pieces of the art pottery were marked with the name of the firm in various ways.

Cowan, Ashtray, Duck Shape, Green Glaze, Signed	10.00
Cowan, Bowl, Blue Gray, Iridescent Luster, 12 In.	30.00
Cowan, Bowl, Blue Luster, Footed, 4 1/2 X 12 In.	32.00
Cowan, Bowl, Cobalt Blue, Multicolored Floral Border, 6 In.	35.00
Cowan, Breakfast Set, Turquoise, Setting For One	75.00
Cowan, Candelabra, 3 Light, Brass, Pair	22.00
Cowan, Candlestick, Blue Luster, 4 3/4 In.	15.00
Cowan, Candlestick, Light Green, 5 1/2 In.	8.50
Cowan, Candlestick, Low, Green	6.00
Cowan, Candlestick, Matte White, Signed, Set Of 4	20.00
Cowan, Compote, Ivory, Rose Interior, Seahorse Stem, 4 X 6 In.	18.00
Cowan, Compote, Seahorse Stem, Ivory, Marked	15.00
Cowan, Console Set, Creamy White, Turquoise Interior, 5 Piece	38.00
Cowan, Flower Holder, Art Nouveau, Nude Figurine, Ivory Glaze, 6 1/2 In.	15.00
Cowan, Vase, Blue Iridescent, 6 1/4 In., Pair	40.00
Cowan, Vase, Blue Luster, 8 In.	30.00
Cowan, Vase, Dragonflies On Orange Luster Ground, 13 In.	99.00
Cowan, Vase, Jade Green, 5 In.	25.00
Cowan, Vase, Orange Luster, 5 In.	18.50
Cowan, Vase, Turquoise & Wine Coloring, Semigloss, 7 In.	18.00

Cowan, Vase, 4 In.Band Of Berries, Royal Blue, 8 In., Pair 100.00

Crackle glass was originally made by the Venetians, but most of the ware found today dates from the 1800s. The glass was heated, cooled, and refired so that many small lines appeared inside the glass. It was made in many factories in the United States and Europe.

Crackle Glass, see also Fry
Crackle Glass, Celery, Corset Shaped, Marked 18.00
Crackle Glass, Pitcher, Amethyst Applied Handle, 5 1/2 In. 38.00
Crackle Glass, Pitcher, Lemonade, Lid, Clear, Amber Handle 50.00
Crackle Glass, Pitcher, Water, Clear, Blue Handle, 8 In. 34.00
Crackle Glass, Vase, Applied Handles, Ground Pontil, 5 In. 30.00
Crackle Glass, Vase, Clear With Bluish Tin, Applied Gold Trim, 8 1/2 In. 35.00
Crackle Glass, Vase, Clear, 3 Applied Blue Flowers, 8 1/2 In. 42.00
Crackle Glass, Vase, Emerald Green, Pontil Base, 8 3/4 In. 25.00
Crackle Glass, Vase, Fish Swimming Among Seaweed, 7 1/2 In. 130.00
Crackle Glass, Vase, Grays, Reds, Greens, Browns, Glazed, Cheng Hua, 3 X 5 In. 95.00
Crackle Glass, Vase, Smoke Color, Applied Rings Around Center, 11 In. 45.00

Cranberry glass is an almost transparent yellow red glass. It resembles the color of cranberry juice.

Cranberry Glass, see also Northwood, Rubena Verde, etc.
Cranberry Glass, , Vase, Applied Feet, Matsu-No-Ke Decoration, 10 In. 85.00
Cranberry Glass, Argus Swirl, Saltshaker 17.00
Cranberry Glass, Basket, Blown Crimped Top, Applied White Crossed Handle 82.00
Cranberry Glass, Basket, Clear Handle With Faces 50.00
Cranberry Glass, Basket, Clear Loop Handle, 6 In. 125.00
Cranberry Glass, Basket, Hobnail, Opalescent, Clear Thorn Handle, 7 In. 38.00
Cranberry Glass, Bell, Clear Handle, Double Knob Finial, 10 3/4 In. 125.00
Cranberry Glass, Bell, Clear Handle, Large, 10 In. 165.00
Cranberry Glass, Bell, Opaque Cream-Colored Handle, Clear Clapper, 9 1/4 In. 135.00
Cranberry Glass, Bell, 12 In. 115.00
Cranberry Glass, Bottle, Barber, Diamond & Melon Slice Design, 10 In. 95.00
Cranberry Glass, Bottle, Barber, Panel Pattern, Enameled Flowers 110.00
Cranberry Glass, Bottle, Barber, Striped Square Shape 95.00
Cranberry Glass, Bottle, Barber, Swirl, Opalescent 115.00
Cranberry Glass, Bottle, Cranberry Stopper, 10 In. 85.00
Cranberry Glass, Bottle, Perfume, Enameled Flowers, Sprays, & Leaves, Gold 80.00
Cranberry Glass, Bottle, Perfume, Gold & Multicolor Enameled Florals, 5 In. 32.00
Cranberry Glass, Bowl & Underplate, Finger, Applied Clear Rigaree, 7 In. 95.00
Cranberry Glass, Bowl & Underplate, Finger, Blown, Star Cut Center 38.00
Cranberry Glass, Bowl, Applied Crystal Ruffled Skirt Near Top, 4 1/2 In. 60.00
Cranberry Glass, Bowl, Bride's, Ruffled 35.00
Cranberry Glass, Bowl, Clear Applied Feet, Ruffled Edge, 6 In. 75.00
Cranberry Glass, Bowl, Criss-Cross Quilted Design Inside, Fluted, 4 In. 85.00
Cranberry Glass, Bowl, Diamond-Quilted, Crystal Base, 4 1/2 In. 45.00
Cranberry Glass, Bowl, Finger, Fluted, Enameled Berries, Butterfly, Gold 60.00
Cranberry Glass, Bowl, Finger, Strawberry Diamond Cut, Cut To Clear, 5 In. 175.00
Cranberry Glass, Bowl, Hobnail, Square, Victorian 185.00
Cranberry Glass, Bowl, In Silver Holder, 4 In. 88.00
Cranberry Glass, Bowl, Shaded To Clear Base, Enameled Flowers, Quilted, 6 In. 165.00
Cranberry Glass, Bowl, Sweetmeat, Applied Threaded Feet, 5 1/4 In.Diameter 75.00
Cranberry Glass, Bowl, Thumbprint, Triangular 45.00
Cranberry Glass, Box, Applied Feet, Round, Cover, English, 4 3/4 X 3 3/4 In. 65.00
Cranberry Glass, Box, Butterfly, Floral, Bronze Bands, Footed, Rings, Round 125.00
Cranberry Glass, Box, Enameled Flowers, Brass Hinged Collar 55.00
Cranberry Glass, Box, Flowers, Brass Fittings, Hinged, Enamel & Gold, 5 In. 175.00
Cranberry Glass, Box, Patch, Enameled Flowers, 3 X 2 1/2 In. 52.00
Cranberry Glass, Box, Patch, Jewel Decorations 95.00
Cranberry Glass, Box, White Floral, Brass Hinged Cover, 2 1/2 X 1 1/2 In. 65.00
Cranberry Glass, Butter, Flint, Cleared Applied Ruffled Trim, Applied Finial 295.00
Cranberry Glass, Cased, White, Enamel Birds, Trees, Marked Middletown, Conn. 150.00
Cranberry Glass, Castor Set, Inverted Thumbprint, Crystal Stopper 150.00
Cranberry Glass, Castor, Pickle, Decorated, Frosted 275.00
Cranberry Glass, Castor, Pickle, Enameled Insert, Silver Holder, Tufts 175.00

Cranberry Glass, Castor, Pickle, Enameled, Footed Frame, Lid, Tongs	175.00
Cranberry Glass, Castor, Pickle, Inverted Thumbprint, Frame & Tongs	175.00
Cranberry Glass, Celery, Hobnail, Square Top, 7 1/8 In.	175.00 To 195.00
Cranberry Glass, Celery, Opalescent, Ribbed Lattice	110.00
Cranberry Glass, Celery, Ruffled Edge, Clear Applied Feet, 7 1/4 In.	68.00
Cranberry Glass, Celery, Seaweed, Opalescent, 6 1/2 In.	95.00
Cranberry Glass, Chalice, Double Teardrop, Stem, 11 1/4 In.	140.00
Cranberry Glass, Compote, Crystal Pedestal Foot, Covered, 9 In.	85.00
Cranberry Glass, Compote, Diamond-Quilted, Ormolu Mountings, Brass Handles	195.00
Cranberry Glass, Compote, Ruffled, Clear Stem & Base, 3 1/4 X 5 3/4 In.	85.00
Cranberry Glass, Compote, Threaded, Clear, 8 1/4 X 6 1/2 In.	75.00
Cranberry Glass, Condiment Set, Paneled, Silver-Plated Tops, 2 Piece	65.00
Cranberry Glass, Creamer, Applied Reed Handle, 3 1/2 In.	46.00
Cranberry Glass, Creamer, Diamond, Clear Handle, 4 1/4 In.	45.00
Cranberry Glass, Cruet, Blown Optic Rib, Clear Handle & Stopper, 8 1/4 In.	165.00
Cranberry Glass, Cruet, Clear Applied Handle, Clear Stopper, 8 In.	55.00
Cranberry Glass, Cruet, Clear Handle, Hollow Stopper, Blown Glass, 7 In.	85.00
Cranberry Glass, Cruet, Diamond-Quilted	145.00
Cranberry Glass, Cruet, Pristine, Tricornered Spout, Bulge Body, Stopper	72.00
Cranberry Glass, Cruet, Vinegar, Cut Glass Stopper	50.00
Cranberry Glass, Cruet, Vinegar, Inverted Thumbprint, Teardrop Stopper	85.00
Cranberry Glass, Cruet, Vinegar, Lacy Pattern, Dots, Flowers, Gold Trim, 7 In.	115.00
Cranberry Glass, Cruet, White Enameled Daisies, Clear Stopper, 14 In.	195.00
Cranberry Glass, Cruet, 12 Rows Of Hobstars, Cut Stopper, Bulge Type	152.00
Cranberry Glass, Cruet, 14 Rows Of Hobstars, Cut Stopper	83.00
Cranberry Glass, Cup, Loving, Sterling Silver Rim, English Hallmark	50.00
Cranberry Glass, Cup, Miniature, Applied Handle	40.00
Cranberry Glass, Cup, Punch, Blown, Clear Applied Handle, Polished Base	19.00
Cranberry Glass, Cup, Punch, Raised Daisies & Oak Leaves, Gold Trim, Handle	65.00
Cranberry Glass, Decanter, Crystal Steeple Shape Stopper, Hand Blown, 10 In.	55.00
Cranberry Glass, Decanter, Cut Frosted Stripes, 10 In.	40.00
Cranberry Glass, Decanter, Hobnail, Opalescent, Bulbous, 8 In.	125.00
Cranberry Glass, Decanter, Paneled, Crystal Applied Handle & Stopper, 8 In.	175.00
Cranberry Glass, Decanter, Ribbed, Hexagon Finial, Handle, Bulbous, 8 In.	175.00
Cranberry Glass, Dish, Candy, Applied Clear Shells Under Rim	32.00
Cranberry Glass, Dish, Candy, Silver-Plated Holder, 5 3/8 X 5 3/4 In.	68.00
Cranberry Glass, Dish, Nut, Hand Blown, Applied Base, 3 1/2 In.	35.00
Cranberry Glass, Dish, Sweetmeat, Applied Threaded Feet, 4 1/4 In.	75.00
Cranberry Glass, Dish, Sweetmeat, Cranberry Cut To Clear, 5 In.	135.00
Cranberry Glass, Epergne, Opalescent, Swirl, Ruffled Edge, 16 In.	75.00
Cranberry Glass, Epergne, Single Lily, Daisy & Fern, 13 1/4 In.	175.00
Cranberry Glass, Epergne, Swirl, 3 Horns With Applied Glass Designs, 16 In.	295.00
Cranberry Glass, Epergne, 3 Lilies, Spiral Trim, 5 Petal Tops, Ruffled Base	325.00
Cranberry Glass, Epergne, 4 Trumpets, 19 In.High X 10 In.Diameter	350.00
Cranberry Glass, Ewer, Clear Rippled Applied Handles, 8 In., Pair	150.00
Cranberry Glass, Glass, Juice	20.00
Cranberry Glass, Goblet, Ribbed, Clear Reeded Stem	12.50
Cranberry Glass, Hat, Cased, Crimped Top, Opalescent Polka Dot Pattern, 3 In.	48.00
Cranberry Glass, Hat, Hobnail, Blown, 2 3/4 X 4 1/2 In.	14.00
Cranberry Glass, Hat, Opalescent Polka Dots, Crimped Top, Cased Glass, 3 In.	48.00
Cranberry Glass, Inkwell, Loetz Type	165.00
Cranberry Glass, Jar, Biscuit, Coralene Flowers, Squatty, Swirled, Gold Washed	195.00
Cranberry Glass, Jar, Jam, Lid, Applied Crystal, Handle, 6 In.	138.00
Cranberry Glass, Jar, Pickle, Thumbprint, Hourglass Shape, Lid, 7 X 4 In.	90.00
Cranberry Glass, Jug, Claret, White Enameling, 9 X 6 In.	85.00
Cranberry Glass, Jug, Clear Handle, 4 3/4 In.	60.00
Cranberry Glass, Jug, Ribbed, Clear Applied Handle, 8 In.	75.00
Cranberry Glass, Lamp Base, Pattern Font, Brass Column, Marble Base, European	60.00
Cranberry Glass, Lamp Shade For Banquet Lamp, Embossed With Flowers, 9 In.	85.00
Cranberry Glass, Lamp, Brass Base, Handled, 8 1/2 In.Diameter	345.00
Cranberry Glass, Lamp, Miniature Hanging Candle	175.00
Cranberry Glass, Lamp, Oil, Brass, Pull Down Shade	225.00
Cranberry Glass, Lamp, Oil, Coin Spot Font, Footed, Divider Removes, 9 In.	135.00
Cranberry Glass, Lamp, Peg, Font	58.00
Cranberry Glass, Muffineer, Faceted Panels, Dome Top	57.50

Cranberry Glass, Muffineer, Leaf Umbrella, Original Top 155.00
Cranberry Glass, Muffineer, Paneled, Silver Lid 45.00
Cranberry Glass, Mug, Diamond-Quilted, Bulbous, Clear Applied Handle 60.00
Cranberry Glass, Perfume Set, Clear, Etched, 3 Piece 68.00
Cranberry Glass, Perfume Set, Etched To Clear, 3 Piece 48.00
Cranberry Glass, Pipe, 18 In. .... 185.00 To 250.00
Cranberry Glass, Pitcher, Applied Clear Handle, 29 X 3 1/2 In. 75.00
Cranberry Glass, Pitcher, Applied Reeded Handle, 8 X 4 In. 110.00
Cranberry Glass, Pitcher, Bulbous, Blown Cascades, Opalescent, 9 In. 235.00
Cranberry Glass, Pitcher, Bulbous, Fluted Top, 13 1/2 In. 140.00
Cranberry Glass, Pitcher, Bulbous, Inverted Thumbprint, Enamel Floral 175.00
Cranberry Glass, Pitcher, Clear Applied Handle, Enameled Flowers, 8 1/2 In. 100.00
Cranberry Glass, Pitcher, Clear Applied Handle, 7 5/8 In. 120.00
Cranberry Glass, Pitcher, Clear Handle, Ruffled Edge, Quilted, 5 Glasses 140.00
Cranberry Glass, Pitcher, Crimped Top, Ribbed Body, Applied Handle, 7 In. 98.00
Cranberry Glass, Pitcher, Floral Decoration, Clear Applied Handle, 8 In. 95.00
Cranberry Glass, Pitcher, Floral, Handle & Top Into Body, Gold, Blue, 11 In. 68.00
Cranberry Glass, Pitcher, Inverted Thumbprint, Applied Clear Handle, 6 In. 70.00
Cranberry Glass, Pitcher, Inverted Thumbprint, Bulbous, Ribbed Handle, 5 In. 75.00
Cranberry Glass, Pitcher, Inverted Thumbprint, Bulbous, 7 7/8 In. 98.00
Cranberry Glass, Pitcher, Milk, Diamond-Quilted, Applied Clear Handle 55.00
Cranberry Glass, Pitcher, Milk, Hobnail, Crystal Applied Handle, Reeded, 5 In. 75.00
Cranberry Glass, Pitcher, Opalescent, Coin Spot, 4 In. 45.00
Cranberry Glass, Pitcher, Plain, Clear Applied Handle, Milk Size 69.00
Cranberry Glass, Pitcher, Ribbed, Fluted, Pinched Sides, Applied Handle, 6 In. 125.00
Cranberry Glass, Pitcher, Scalloped Top, Cut Rayed Base, Clear Handle, 7 In. 88.00
Cranberry Glass, Pitcher, Swirl, Clear Applied Handle, Bulbous, 3 1/2 In. 18.00
Cranberry Glass, Pitcher, Swirl, Opalescent, Applied Clear Handle, 2 Quart 69.00
Cranberry Glass, Pitcher, Tankard Shape, Applied Handle, 6 3/8 In. 115.00
Cranberry Glass, Pitcher, Tankard Shape, Applied Handle, 7 5/8 X 4 3/4 In. 120.00
Cranberry Glass, Pitcher, Tankard Shape, Crystal Clear Handle, 4 3/4 In. 60.00
Cranberry Glass, Pitcher, Thumbprint, Clear Applied Handle, 6 1/2 In. 90.00
Cranberry Glass, Pitcher, Water, Blue & White Forget-Me-Nots, 7 1/8 In. 145.00
Cranberry Glass, Pitcher, Water, Coin Spot, Opalescent 110.00
Cranberry Glass, Pitcher, Water, Enameled Flowers, 11 1/2 In. 135.00
Cranberry Glass, Pitcher, Water, Enameled Swallow, Gold Thistle, 11 3/4 In. 175.00
Cranberry Glass, Pitcher, Water, Enameled, Applied Handle, 12 1/2 In. 115.00
Cranberry Glass, Pitcher, Water, Hobnail, Opalescent, Polished Pontil 200.00
Cranberry Glass, Pitcher, Water, Inverted Thumbprint, 7 1/2 In. 110.00
Cranberry Glass, Pitcher, Water, Opalescent Swirl, Applied Handle, 9 1/2 In 110.00
Cranberry Glass, Pitcher, Water, Opalescent, Christmas Snowflake 250.00
Cranberry Glass, Pitcher, Water, White Enameled Flowers, Gold Trim, 7 1/4 In. 145.00
Cranberry Glass, Pitcher, White Opalescent Coin Spot, 7 In. 42.00
Cranberry Glass, Plate, Cut To Clear, 6 1/2 In., Set Of 8 .... 95.00
Cranberry Glass, Punch Bowl Set, Inverted Thumbprint, 7 Piece 350.00
Cranberry Glass, Punch Set, Inverted Thumbprint, 7 Piece 350.00
Cranberry Glass, Rose Bowl, Clear To Cranberry Paneling, 5 3/4 In. 55.00
Cranberry Glass, Rose Bowl, Crystal Cut, Notched Top, 2 5/8 In. 100.00
Cranberry Glass, Rose Bowl, Ruffled Top, 3 1/2 In. 22.00
Cranberry Glass, Salt & Pepper, Baby Thumbprint With Holder 65.00
Cranberry Glass, Salt & Pepper, Painted Flowers 50.00
Cranberry Glass, Salt & Pepper, Panel Pattern, Decorated Holder 95.00
Cranberry Glass, Salt, Clear Applied Feet, 1 1/2 In. 30.00
Cranberry Glass, Salt, Master, Cut, 3 5/8 In. 55.00
Cranberry Glass, Salt, Pedestaled, Hand Blown, Applied Clear Handle, Pair 45.00
Cranberry Glass, Salt, 3 Reeded Feet, Berry Pontil 34.50
Cranberry Glass, Saltshaker, Honeycomb, Pewter Top, 2 5/8 In. 23.00
Cranberry Glass, Saltshaker, Inverted Thumbprint, Enameled Flowers 65.00
Cranberry Glass, Saltshaker, Molded Swirl, Pewter Top, 3 In. 28.00
Cranberry Glass, Saltshaker, Pillar, Sixteen, White Spatter 45.00
Cranberry Glass, Server, Pancake, Covered, Ornate Gold & Floral Design, Gold 75.00
Cranberry Glass, Shade, Hanging, Ribbed, Bell Shape, Rings, 13 In. 65.00
Cranberry Glass, Shade, Hobnail, Fluted, 7 1/2 X 5 In. 85.00
Cranberry Glass, Shade, Hobnail, Ruffled, 8 In.Diameter 57.00
Cranberry Glass, Shade, Opalescent Swirl, Ruffled Top, 6 3/4 In., Pair 110.00

Cranberry Glass, Shaker, Sugar, Cut Panels, 5 3/4 In.	68.00
Cranberry Glass, Shaker, Sugar, Venetian Diamond	90.00
Cranberry Glass, Spooner, Delaware	45.00
Cranberry Glass, Sugar & Creamer, Enameled Yellow & Blue Flowers, Gold Trim	95.00
Cranberry Glass, Sugar & Creamer, Victorian, White Thread Decoration	85.00
Cranberry Glass, Sugar & Creamer, White Threaded Top, Applied Ruffle & Feet	150.00
Cranberry Glass, Sugar Castor, Ribbed, Silver Plated Fitting	42.00
Cranberry Glass, Sugar Shaker, Flower Mold	120.00
Cranberry Glass, Sugar Shaker, Inverted Thumbprint, Nine Panel	80.00
Cranberry Glass, Sugar Shaker, Leaf, Umbrella	165.00
Cranberry Glass, Sugar Shaker, Opalescent, Vertical Stripes	87.50
Cranberry Glass, Sugar Shaker, Reverse Swirl, Opalescent	100.00
Cranberry Glass, Sugar Shaker, Ribbed, Opal Lattice	75.00
Cranberry Glass, Sugar Shaker, Ring Neck, Optic	65.00
Cranberry Glass, Tankard, Enameled Flowers, Clear Applied Handle	95.00
Cranberry Glass, Tankard, Thumbprint, Clear Handle	125.00
Cranberry Glass, Tankard, Water, Clear Handle, 8 In.	88.00
Cranberry Glass, Toothpick, Sprig, Paneled	40.00
Cranberry Glass, Tumbler, Daisy And Fern	35.00
Cranberry Glass, Tumbler, Delaware, Gold, Proof, Set Of 6	100.00
Cranberry Glass, Tumbler, Inverted Thumbprint, Blown, 4 1/2 In.	23.00
Cranberry Glass, Tumbler, Panel Of Vintage Pattern, Engraving Around Top	35.00
Cranberry Glass, Tumbler, Paneled Optic, 4 In.	17.50
Cranberry Glass, Tumbler, Swirl, Opalescent	24.00
Cranberry Glass, Tumbler, Thumbprint, Enameled	45.00
Cranberry Glass, Tumbler, Twist, Opalescent	47.00
Cranberry Glass, Tumbler, Windows	31.00
Cranberry Glass, Tumbler, 10-Row Hobnail, Opalescent	125.00
Cranberry Glass, Vase, Applied Crystal Spiraling, Paneled, 9 1/2 In.	75.00
Cranberry Glass, Vase, Bronze Fitting	85.00
Cranberry Glass, Vase, Bud, Bulbous Bottom, Overlay	75.00
Cranberry Glass, Vase, Bud, Thorny, Clear Applied Rosette Foot, 7 1/8 In.	55.00
Cranberry Glass, Vase, Bud, White Enamel Figures, 10 In.	275.00
Cranberry Glass, Vase, Bud, 3 3/4 In.	22.00
Cranberry Glass, Vase, Bulbous, Enameled Flowers, Paneled Look, 7 In.	125.00
Cranberry Glass, Vase, Celery, White Stripes	35.00
Cranberry Glass, Vase, Clear Applied Crimped Edge, 7 In., Pair	95.00
Cranberry Glass, Vase, Clear Applied Top, 4 1/2 In.	85.00
Cranberry Glass, Vase, Corset Shape, Quatrefoil	72.50
Cranberry Glass, Vase, Corset Shape, Thumbprint, Scalloped Rim, 7 1/2 In.	110.00
Cranberry Glass, Vase, Cranberry Cut To Clear, 10 X 8 1/2 In.	125.00
Cranberry Glass, Vase, Crystal Applied Spiral Shell Trim, 6 3/4 X 4 1/2 In.	75.00
Cranberry Glass, Vase, Crystal Top & Foot, Swirled, 4 5/8 In., Pair	150.00
Cranberry Glass, Vase, Crystal Trim & Feet, Applied Rigaree, 10 3/4 In.	200.00
Cranberry Glass, Vase, Diamond-Quilted, Hand Blown, 4 1/2 X 3 1/4 In.	55.00
Cranberry Glass, Vase, Enameled Flowers & Butterfly, Ribbed, 5 X 4 In., Pair	110.00
Cranberry Glass, Vase, Fence & Daisies, 10 1/2 In.	185.00
Cranberry Glass, Vase, Flashed, 10 In.	9.50
Cranberry Glass, Vase, Flask Shaped, Clear Applied Rigaree	45.00
Cranberry Glass, Vase, Flower Form, Gold Vine Stand, 12 In.	85.00
Cranberry Glass, Vase, Fluted, Enameled, 8 In.	115.00
Cranberry Glass, Vase, Grape Pattern, 10 In., Pair	30.00
Cranberry Glass, Vase, Hand-Engraved, Crystal Foot, 10 In., Pair	100.00
Cranberry Glass, Vase, Hobnail, Fluted Top, 3 1/2 In.	10.00
Cranberry Glass, Vase, Hobnail, Opalescent, Ruffled, 7 1/2 In.	40.00
Cranberry Glass, Vase, Hobnail, Ruffled Rim, Opalescent, 7 1/2 X 5 In.	275.00
Cranberry Glass, Vase, Jack-In-The-Pulpit, Crystal Base, 8 3/4 In.	84.00
Cranberry Glass, Vase, Jack-In-The-Pulpit, Petal Shaped Feet, 9 In.	95.00
Cranberry Glass, Vase, Jack-In-The-Pulpit, Scalloped Top, 10 1/4 In.	85.00
Cranberry Glass, Vase, Jack-In-The-Pulpit, White Loopings, 7 3/4 In.	158.00
Cranberry Glass, Vase, Jack-In-The-Pulpit, 9 1/2 In.	78.00
Cranberry Glass, Vase, Lily, Opalescent, Silver-Plated Holder, 7 1/2 In., Pair	175.00
Cranberry Glass, Vase, Melon Ribbed, Scalloped & Fluted Top, 8 1/2 In.	37.50
Cranberry Glass, Vase, Ribbed Rustic, Crimped Edge, 6 In., Pair	95.00
Cranberry Glass, Vase, Ruff Top, Clear Applied Feet, 7 1/2 In.	55.00

Cranberry Glass, Vase, Silver Plated Holder, Signed & Dated, 9 In. 225.00
Cranberry Glass, Vase, Stick, Thorn Imprints, Clear Applied Feet, 12 In. 42.00
Cranberry Glass, Vase, Swirl Pattern, Opalescent, 10 In. 75.00
Cranberry Glass, Vase, Swirl, Clear Applied Ruffled Top & Base, 7 In. 60.00
Cranberry Glass, Vase, Threaded, Clear Applied Handles, 3 In. 45.00
Cranberry Glass, Vase, Trumpet, Applied Crystal, 10 3/4 In. 160.00
Cranberry Glass, Vase, White Enamel Floral & Leaves, Footed & Fluted, 6 In. 85.00
Cranberry Glass, Vase, White Enameled Flowers, 3 In. 35.00
Cranberry Glass, Water Pitcher, Opalescent, Diamonds 135.00
Cranberry Glass, Water Set, Daisy & Fern, 6 Piece 250.00
Cranberry Glass, Water Set, Enameled Honeycombs, 5 Piece 400.00
Cranberry Glass, Water Set, Gold Enameled Decoration, Hand Blown, 6 Piece 210.00
Cranberry Glass, Water Set, Melon Pattern, Ruffled Top, 7 Piece 160.00
Cranberry Glass, Water Set, Thumbprint 115.00
Cranberry Glass, Wine, Cameo Floral Bowl, St.Louis, Tall, Stemmed, Signed 125.00
Cranberry Glass, Wine, Clear Foot & Stem, 5 In. 29.00
Cranberry Glass, Wine, Clear Stem, Flint, C.1900 .... 75.00
Cranberry Glass, Wine, Cut To Clear, Set Of 8 .... 90.00
Cranberry Glass, Wine, Gold Scrolls & Trim, Baluster Stem, 6 5/8 In. 68.00
Cranberry Glass, Wine, Hollow-Cut Clear Stems, Allover Gold, 6 3/4 In., Pair 145.00
Cranberry Glass, Wine, Russian Cut To Clear, Honeycomb Stem 85.00

Creamware, or queensware, was developed by Josiah Wedgwood about 1765. It
is a cream-colored earthenware that has been copied by many factories.

Creamware, see also Wedgwood
Creamware, Basket, Pierced Handle, Brown Buildings On Yellow, 11 X 8 In. 135.00
Creamware, Basket, Twig, C.1810-1820, 11 X 3 In. 75.00
Creamware, Bowl, 3 White Center Bands, 7 1/2 In. 20.00
Creamware, Creamer, Yellow Glaze, Bulbous, High-Domed Lid, C.1800, 5 3/4 In. 125.00
Creamware, Cup, Tea, Wishbone, Handled 18.00
Creamware, Jug, Lafayette's Visit To U.S., 1824, Rich.Hall & Son, 6 1/2 In. 175.00
Creamware, Jug, Liverpool, Transfer Printed, C.1800, 8 1/2 In. 450.00
Creamware, Jug, Liverpool, Transfer Printed, Enameled, C.1805, 8 3/4 In. 375.00
Creamware, Jug, 6-Color Cartoon, Fighting Bull, Spanish Patriot, 7 3/4 In. 40.00
Creamware, Mug, Decal, Dutch, 5 In. 36.50
Creamware, Plate, Toddy, Brown Edge, Parrot & Peacock In Center, 4 1/2 In. 32.00
Creamware, Pot, High Relief Of Sacrifice, Embossed, C.1850, 10 In. 265.00
Creamware, Tankard, Dutch, 11 1/2 In. 135.00
Creil, Box, Round, Covered, Montereux 20.00
Croesus, see Pressed Glass, Croesus

Crown Derby is the nickname given to the works of the Royal Crown
Derby Factory which began working in England in 1859. An earlier and
more famous English Derby factory existed from 1750 to 1848. The two
factories were not related. Most of the porcelain found today with the
Derby mark is the work of the later Derby factory.

Crown Derby, see also Royal Crown Derby
Crown Derby, Bowl, Gold Gilding & Filigree Work, 9 1/4 In.Diameter 395.00
Crown Derby, Cachepot, White, Blue, Orange & Gold Curvilinear Design, Footed 200.00
Crown Derby, Ewer, Raised Gold Leaf Design, Bluish Black Background, 1886 .... 195.00
Crown Derby, Figurine, Adam & Eve, Dated 1940, 5 In., Pair 195.00
Crown Derby, Vase, Banjo, Miniature, Raised Floral, Gold, Dated 1885, 3 1/4 In. 125.00
Crown Derby, Vase, Blooming Flowers, Geometric Work Around Neck, 9 In. 165.00
Crown Derby, Vase, Cobalt Blue, White, Gold & Red Trim, Pedestal, C.1893 .... 235.00
Crown Derby, Vase, Repousse, Pastel Florals, Gold Trim, Signed, 5 In. 200.00
Crown Derby, Vase, Yellow Cream, Jeweled Flowers, Gold Gilded Relief, 10 In. 155.00

Crown Ducal is the name used on some pieces of porcelain made by the
A. G. Richardson and Co., Ltd., England. The name has been
used since 1916.
Crown Ducal, Plate, Tabby Cat Center, Green & Gold Border, 10 In. 15.00

Crown Milano glass was made by Frederick Shirley about 1890. It had a
plain biscuit color with a satin finish. It was decorated with flowers, and
often had large gold scrolls.

Crown Milano, Basket, Bride's, Floral, Silver Plated Stand, 6 X 7 1/2 In.	1500.00
Crown Milano, Biscuit Barrel, 4 Sided, Swirls, Milano Sticker On Back	595.00
Crown Milano, Bowl, Violets, Pansies, Tricorn Shape, Signed	460.00
Crown Milano, Box, Hand-Painted, Signed, 9 In.	550.00
Crown Milano, Cookie Jar, Acorns, Silver Handle & Lid	425.00
Crown Milano, Ewer, Cream, Fall Colored Leaves & Acorns, Handled, 12 In.	1350.00
Crown Milano, Ewer, Cream, Leaves & Acorns, Rusts, Tans, & Browns, Gold, 12 In.	105.00
Crown Milano, Ewer, Floral Decoration, Glossy, 5 1/4 In.	750.00
Crown Milano, Jar, Biscuit, Jeweled, Silver	395.00
Crown Milano, Jar, Cookie, Jeweled Decoration, Signed M.W.	395.00
Crown Milano, Jar, Cookie, Jeweled Octopus & Seaweed, Pebbled Ground, 8 In.	1350.00
Crown Milano, Jar, Cookie, Silver Lid & Handle, Signed P	480.00
Crown Milano, Jar, Cookie, Silverplate Cover, Pansies & Gold On Beige	385.00
Crown Milano, Jar, Cookie, Water Lilies & Pads, Gold Outlined, 5 X 7 In.	575.00
Crown Milano, Jar, Covered, Jeweled Decoration, Cover Signed M.W.	395.00
Crown Milano, Jar, Covered, Jeweled Octopus & Seaweed, Pebbled Ground, 8 In.	1350.00
Crown Milano, Jar, Cracker, Maidenhair Fern Pattern, Gilt, Silverplated Rim	350.00
Crown Milano, Jar, Cracker, Oak Leaves & Acorn, Pairpoint Mark	250.00
Crown Milano, Jar, Gold Enameled Roses, Covered, Signed, 3 1/2 In.	475.00
Crown Milano, Jar, Jam, Cactus Flowers	525.00
Crown Milano, Jardiniere, Orange, Red & Gold, Signed, 11 1/4 X 8 1/4 In.	695.00
Crown Milano, Jardiniere, Signed In Pontil, 8 X 7 In.	675.00
Crown Milano, Rose Bowl, Pink To White, Oak Leaf & Acorn Decoration, 5 In.	375.00
Crown Milano, Rose Bowl, Yellow To White, Green & Pink Floral, Gold, 5 In.	350.00
Crown Milano, Salt & Pepper, Reclining Egg Shapes	100.00
Crown Milano, Saltshaker, Peach To Pale Yellow, Enameled Daisies, Flowers	90.00
Crown Milano, Saltshaker, Peach, Yellow Daisies, 1 1/2 X 2 1/2 In.	90.00
Crown Milano, Sugar & Creamer, Gold Mums, Sterling Silver Top, Melon Shape	750.00
Crown Milano, Sugar & Creamer, Melon Shape, Gold Flowers, Sterling, Pair	650.00
Crown Milano, Sugar & Creamer, Shell Design, Pink To White, Enameled, M.W.	275.00
Crown Milano, Tumbler, Heavy Gold Decorated Swags, Glossy Finish	225.00
Crown Milano, Vase, Bulbous Rib, Brown & Gold Oak Leaves, Signed C/599, 5 In.	150.00
Crown Milano, Vase, Chrysanthemums Trimmed In Gold, Gold Beaded, Cream, 5 In.	275.00
Crown Milano, Vase, Enameled Leaf & Vine, Wired For Lamp, 9 In.	140.00
Crown Milano, Vase, Encrusted Gold & Enamel Decoration, Bulbous Base, 16 In.	1950.00
Crown Milano, Vase, Floral Design, 15 1/2 In.	1650.00
Crown Milano, Vase, Gold & Silver, Duck On Red	200.00
Crown Milano, Vase, Melon Ribbed, Gold Decorated, Green To Peach, 7 In.	275.00
Crown Milano, Vase, Pastel Roses On Cream, Bulbous Bottom, 12 In.	575.00
Crown Milano, Vase, Ruffled Rim, Gold Chrysanthemums On Cream, 5 X 5 In.	275.00
Crown Tuscan, see Cambridge	
Crown Tuscan, Candleholder, Nude Stem, 9 In.	75.00
Crown Tuscan, Comport, Decorated Nude Stem, 6 In.	80.00
Crown Tuscan, Comport, Shell, Flowers, Gold Trim, Nude Stem, 8 X 7 1/4 In.	115.00
Crown Tuscan, Compote, Nude Stem, Shell, Roses & Gold, 6 In.	55.00
Crown Tuscan, Relish, Flowers, Divided, Cambridge	30.00
Crown Tuscan, Tray, Leaf Shaped, Shell Border, Roses, 5 In.	40.00

Cruets of glass or porcelain were made to hold vinegar or oil. They were especially popular during Victorian times.

Cruet, see also Amber Glass, and other glass sections	
Cruet, Amber With Blue Stopper & Handle	135.00
Cruet, Amber, Trefoil Lip, Clear Applied Ribbed Handle, 7 In.	65.00
Cruet, Cranberry Glass, Pewter, Raised Gargoyle, Winged Angel, 11 In.	185.00
Cruet, Double Lip, Floral Engraved, Sterling Silver Lid	75.00
Cruet, Light Blue, Amber Reeded Handle, Enamel Flowers, Stopper, 8 3/4 In.	75.00
Cruet, Salt, Pepper, Mustard, Victorian, Silver Plate	18.00
CT Altwasser, Cup & Saucer, Set Of 9	50.00
CT Altwasser, Dish, 4 Section, Hand-Painted, Gold, Luster, 4 1/2 In.	135.00
CT Germany, Cake Plate, Portrait, Lady With Flowers, Pearls In Hair, Open	42.50
CT Germany, Chocolate Set, Roses, Gilt, Marked, Green Eagle, 7 Piece	55.00
CT Germany, Plate, Portrait, White Persian Green-Eyed Pussycat, Gold Rim	35.00

Cup plates are small glass or china plates that held the cup, while a gentleman of the mid-nineteenth century drank his coffee or tea from the

saucer. The most famous cup plates were made of glass at the Boston and
Sandwich Factory located in Massachusetts. The L numbers refer to
the book "American Glass Cup Plates" by R. W. Lee and J. H. Rose.

Cup Plate, Ben Franklin, Ship, Sandwich	35.00
Cup Plate, Bunker Hill, McK 186 No.2	58.00
Cup Plate, Eagle, Dated 1831, Lacy, Sandwich Glass	22.50
Cup Plate, Eagle, Sandwich Glass	35.00
Cup Plate, Fiery Opalescent, 13 Heart, Lacy, Sandwich Glass	55.00
Cup Plate, Foliage, Flow Mulberry, C.1835, J.Walley Ironstone, 3 3/4 In.	22.00
Cup Plate, Fort Meigs, Sandwich Glass	35.00
Cup Plate, General Harrison, Sandwich Glass	35.00
Cup Plate, Lacy, Hearts, Opalescent, Sandwich Glass	125.00
Cup Plate, Lacy, Henry Clay, Sandwich Glass	35.00 To 95.00
Cup Plate, Log Cabin & Cider Barrel, Sandwich Glass	35.00
Cup Plate, Scenic Rim & Center, Purple Mulberry, E.Mayer Ironstone, 5 In.	25.00
Cup Plate, Steamboat Center, Shields On Border, Lacy, Sandwich Glass	95.00
Cup Plate, The Wedding Day & 3 Weeks After, Lacy Sandwich	40.00

Currier & Ives made the famous American lithographs marked with their
name from 1857 to 1907.

Currier & Ives, Central Park, Dated 1863	85.00
Currier & Ives, Hebe, Original Gilt Frame, 7 1/4 X 9 1/4 In.	20.00
Currier & Ives, Lower Lakes Of Killarney	38.00
Currier & Ives, Luke Blackburn	145.00
Currier & Ives, Moonlight In The Tropics	72.00
Currier & Ives, Nellie, Medium Folio, Color, 13 3/4 X 18 In.	65.00
Currier & Ives, No You Don't	45.00
Currier & Ives, Old Oaken Bucket, Framed, 12 X 13 In.	175.00
Currier & Ives, Pocahontas Saving The Life Of Captain John Smith	110.00
Currier & Ives, Political Campaign Cartoon, The Chicago Platform, 1864	85.00
Currier & Ives, Providence & Stovington Steamship Co.Steamers, Folio, Large	650.00
Currier & Ives, Scene, Central Park, Dated 1863	185.00
Currier & Ives, The Bridge At The Outlet, Lake Memphremagog, Framed	55.00
Currier & Ives, The Old Manse	120.00
Currier & Ives, The Sea Of Tiberias, Unframed	32.00
Currier & Ives, Winter In The Country, Maple Frame, 14 X 11 In.	25.00
Currier & Ives, Woodcock Shooting, Framed, 11 1/2 X 15 1/2 In.	105.00
Currier & Ives, Wound Up & Run Down, 1884, Hand-Colored, Signed, Pair	200.00

Custard glass is an opaque glass sometimes known as buttermilk glass. It
was first made after 1886 at the La Belle Glass Works, Bridgeport, Ohio.
Custard Glass, see also Maize

Custard Glass, Banana Boat, Chrysanthemum Sprig, Blue, Gold Trim, Northwood	325.00
Custard Glass, Banana Boat, Chrysanthemum Sprig, Gold, Footed, 11 X 7 In.	125.00
Custard Glass, Banana Boat, Louis XV, Gold Trim, 10 1/2 X 7 3/4 In.	145.00
Custard Glass, Banana Boat, Louis XV, 10 1/2 X 7 3/4 In.	135.00 To 160.00
Custard Glass, Bell, Beaver Falls, Pennyslvania, May 1, 1911, 6 1/4 In.	95.00
Custard Glass, Bell, Rockaway Beach, L.I., Roses, Gold	135.00
Custard Glass, Berry Set, Geneva, Oval, 5 Piece	250.00
Custard Glass, Berry Set, Geneva, Red & Green Trim, 5 Piece	180.00
Custard Glass, Berry Set, Intaglio Green, 7 Piece	395.00
Custard Glass, Berry Set, Louis XV, Gold, Northwood, 5 Piece	340.00
Custard Glass, Bonbon, Green, Grape & Thistle, Crimped Edges, Handled	39.00
Custard Glass, Bonbon, Notched Handles, Scalloped, Serated Rim, Basketweave	45.00
Custard Glass, Bonbon, Prayer Rug, Footed	19.00
Custard Glass, Bonbon, 2 Handles, 7 1/4 In.	32.00
Custard Glass, Bowl, Berry, Argonaut Shell, Master	155.00
Custard Glass, Bowl, Berry, Beaded Circle, Gold, Enamel	65.00
Custard Glass, Bowl, Berry, Chrysanthemum Sprig, Blue, Gold Trim	225.00 To 400.00
Custard Glass, Bowl, Berry, Chrysanthemum Sprig, Oval, Gold, Large	195.00
Custard Glass, Bowl, Berry, Diamond Maple Leaf, Silver Deposit	185.00
Custard Glass, Bowl, Berry, Diamond Peg, Rose Decoration	32.00
Custard Glass, Bowl, Berry, Geneva, Green & Red Decorations, Oval	35.00

Custard Glass, Bowl, Berry, Grape & Gothic Arches, Pearl Finish, Gold Trim	75.00
Custard Glass, Bowl, Berry, Intaglio	135.00
Custard Glass, Bowl, Berry, Little Gem, Pink Flowers	85.00
Custard Glass, Bowl, Berry, Louis XV, Gold, Oval, Large	140.00
Custard Glass, Bowl, Berry, Louis XV, Small	30.00
Custard Glass, Bowl, Berry, Oval, Footed, Louis XV, Large	90.00
Custard Glass, Bowl, Flower Border, McKee, 11 In.	33.00
Custard Glass, Bowl, Fruit, Argonaut Shell, 5 X 10 1/2 In.	97.50
Custard Glass, Bowl, Fruit, Peacock At Urn, Northwood, 10 In.	95.00
Custard Glass, Bowl, Ice Cream, Nutmeg Coloring, Fiery Opalescence	200.00
Custard Glass, Bowl, Inverted Fan & Feather, Gold, Pink, 10 X 5 1/2 In.	275.00
Custard Glass, Bowl, King Pattern, Cobalt & Gold	29.50
Custard Glass, Bowl, Pier And Wave	25.00
Custard Glass, Bowl, Rope & Lattice, Wright, Northwood, 5 1/2 In.	15.00
Custard Glass, Bowl, Stalking Lion	65.00
Custard Glass, Bowl, Three Fruits, 10 1/2 X 4 1/2 In.	55.00
Custard Glass, Butter, Argonaut Shell	100.00
Custard Glass, Butter, Beaded Circle, Cream, Covered	75.00
Custard Glass, Butter, Chrysanthemum Sprig, Covered, Blue, Signed Northwood	675.00
Custard Glass, Butter, Chrysanthemum Sprig, Lid	275.00
Custard Glass, Butter, Fan, Gold Decorated, Covered	135.00
Custard Glass, Butter, Geneva, Covered	49.00 To 105.00
Custard Glass, Butter, Georgia Gem, Enameled Flowers, Cover	95.00 To 175.00
Custard Glass, Butter, Intaglio Cut, Gold & Green Trim	185.00
Custard Glass, Butter, Intaglio, Blue Trim	47.50
Custard Glass, Butter, Intaglio, Green, Gold Decorated	68.00
Custard Glass, Butter, Little Gem, Flowers	135.00
Custard Glass, Butter, Louis XV, Cover	110.00 To 185.00
Custard Glass, Butter, Maple Leaf, Gold & Green Trim	175.00
Custard Glass, Butter, Maple Leaf, Gold Trim, Covered, Northwood	265.00
Custard Glass, Butter, Ribbed Drape	155.00
Custard Glass, Butter, Winged Scroll, Cover	175.00
Custard Glass, Cake Stand, Peacock & Dahlia, Low Standard, Northwood, 12 In.	85.00
Custard Glass, Candleholder, Jeweled Vermont, Handled	48.00
Custard Glass, Candy Dish, Prayer Rug, Ruffled, Satin, Impressed, 6 In.	30.00
Custard Glass, Celery, Chrysanthemum Sprig, Signed	450.00
Custard Glass, Compote, Argonaut Shell, Stemmed, 5 X 3 1/4 In.	175.00
Custard Glass, Compote, Chrysanthemum Sprig, Gold	45.00
Custard Glass, Compote, Fruit, Flowers & Leaves, Pink Inside, Pedestal, 9 In.	375.00
Custard Glass, Compote, Jelly, Argonaut Shell, Gold & Green	75.00 To 135.00
Custard Glass, Compote, Jelly, Chrysanthemum Sprig	100.00
Custard Glass, Compote, Jelly, Geneva, Green & Gold Decoration	105.00
Custard Glass, Compote, Jelly, Intaglio, Blue And Gold	47.00
Custard Glass, Compote, Jelly, Intaglio, Green And Gold	95.00 To 110.00
Custard Glass, Compote, Jelly, Intaglio, Green Decoration, Northwood	95.00
Custard Glass, Creamer, Argonaut Shell, Gold, Signed Northwood In Script	150.00
Custard Glass, Creamer, Delaware, Blue Design	45.00 To 55.00
Custard Glass, Creamer, Delaware, Pink Decoration, Individual	65.00
Custard Glass, Creamer, Intaglio, Opalescent	40.00
Custard Glass, Creamer, Iris, Gold Trim	115.00
Custard Glass, Creamer, Jackson	95.00
Custard Glass, Creamer, Limb & Leaf Pattern, Green, Brown, Orange	47.00
Custard Glass, Creamer, Louis XV	40.00 To 85.00
Custard Glass, Creamer, Louis XV, Fiery Opalescent, Northwood	75.00
Custard Glass, Creamer, Louis XV, Gold	80.00 To 95.00
Custard Glass, Creamer, Maple Leaf	95.00
Custard Glass, Creamer, Wild Bouquet	115.00
Custard Glass, Cruet Set, Chrysanthemum Sprig	945.00
Custard Glass, Cruet, Chrysanthemum Sprig	85.00 To 250.00
Custard Glass, Cruet, Chrysanthemum Sprig, Gold, Blue, Stopper	500.00
Custard Glass, Cruet, Clear Stopper, Fluted Scroll With Flower Band	90.00
Custard Glass, Cruet, Jackson, No Decoration Or Stopper	95.00
Custard Glass, Cruet, Louis XV, Stopper	275.00
Custard Glass, Cruet, Winged Scroll	225.00
Custard Glass, Dish, Berry, Argonaut Shell	55.00

Custard Glass, Dish, Berry, Peacock & Urn, Nutmeg Coloring	60.00
Custard Glass, Dish, Butter, Covered, Louis XV	150.00
Custard Glass, Dish, Chrysanthemum, Footed, Northwood, 4 X 5 In.	55.00
Custard Glass, Dish, Diamond Peg, Berry, Rose Decoration	32.00
Custard Glass, Dish, Mustard, Corning Swan Song	35.00
Custard Glass, Dish, Mustard, Horse's Heads	35.00
Custard Glass, Dresser Set, Ring Band, Gilded Finial, Gold, 5 Piece	325.00
Custard Glass, Globe, Ceiling Light, Hand-Painted, Round, 4 1/2 In.	25.00
Custard Glass, Hair Receiver, Georgia Gem, Marshall, Michigan	55.00
Custard Glass, Hat, Berry, 5 In.Brim	34.00
Custard Glass, Hat, Grape Arbor, Nutmeg Stain, Northwood	65.00
Custard Glass, Hat, Sailor, Pink Band Decoration	58.00
Custard Glass, Heisey, Butter, Ring Band, Lid	100.00
Custard Glass, Ice Cream, Peacock At Urn	75.00
Custard Glass, Lamp Shade, 2 In.Top Diameter, 5 1/4 In.Bottom	15.00
Custard Glass, Light Globe, Hand-Painted, Round, 4 1/2 In.	25.00
Custard Glass, Match Holder, Souvenir, Pennsylvania	35.00
Custard Glass, Match Holder, Winged Scroll, 2 1/4 X 2 1/2 In.	135.00
Custard Glass, Mug, Diamond Peg, Souvenir, 3 Oz.	55.00
Custard Glass, Mug, Singing Bird, Brown Stain	75.00
Custard Glass, Mug, Souvenir, Abrams, Wis., Miniature	12.00
Custard Glass, Mug, Washington, Band Around Base, Souvenir	25.00
Custard Glass, Nappy, Peacock At Fountain, 5 1/2 In.	25.00
Custard Glass, Pitcher, Diamond Peg, Coney Island, Floral, 7 1/2 In.	135.00
Custard Glass, Pitcher, Georgia Gem, 6 1/2 X 5 1/2 In.	250.00
Custard Glass, Pitcher, Hand Enamel Decorating, Beading At Base, 3 7/8 In.	35.00
Custard Glass, Pitcher, Maple Leaf, 6 Tumblers	595.00
Custard Glass, Pitcher, Milk, Amber Applied Handle, Pontil, 5 In.	77.00
Custard Glass, Pitcher, Rose Design, Gold Band	47.00
Custard Glass, Pitcher, Souvenir, Woodstock, Ill.	45.00
Custard Glass, Pitcher, Water, Argonaut Shell, Northwood In Script	285.00
Custard Glass, Pitcher, Water, Chrysanthemum Sprig	195.00
Custard Glass, Pitcher, Water, Controlled Bubbles, Applied Handle	95.00
Custard Glass, Pitcher, Water, Intaglio, Green Trim	250.00
Custard Glass, Pitcher, Water, Inverted Fan & Feather	365.00
Custard Glass, Pitcher, Water, Jackson, No Decoration	135.00
Custard Glass, Pitcher, Water, Louis XV, 8 In.	135.00
Custard Glass, Plate, Flower & Leaf Border, McKee, 9 In.	40.00
Custard Glass, Plate, Grape & Cable, Nutmeg Ground	48.00
Custard Glass, Plate, Stalking Lion, Staining, Green	100.00
Custard Glass, Plate, Three Fruits, Signed N In Circle, 7 In.	28.50 To 85.00
Custard Glass, Rose Bowl, Beaded Cable	75.00
Custard Glass, Rose Bowl, Finecut And Roses	65.00 To 85.00
Custard Glass, Salt & Pepper, Chrysanthemum Sprig, Blue	400.00
Custard Glass, Salt & Pepper, Chrysanthemum Sprig, Original Lids	200.00
Custard Glass, Salt & Pepper, Corn	95.00
Custard Glass, Salt & Pepper, Georgia Pattern, Little Gem	35.00
Custard Glass, Salt & Pepper, Twist	85.00
Custard Glass, Salt & Pepper, Winged Scroll, Pair	100.00
Custard Glass, Salt, Fleur-De-Lis In Wreath	20.00
Custard Glass, Salt, Winged Scroll, Gold, Singleton	65.00
Custard Glass, Saltshaker, Diamond Peg, Rose Decoration, Souvenir, Pair	135.00
Custard Glass, Saltshaker, Diamond Peg, Souvenir, Pair	95.00
Custard Glass, Saltshaker, Intaglio, Gold & Green Decoration	45.00
Custard Glass, Sauce, Argonaut Shell, Gold	50.00
Custard Glass, Sauce, Blue Delaware	60.00
Custard Glass, Sauce, Chrysanthemum Sprig	65.00
Custard Glass, Sauce, Chrysanthemum Sprig, Blue	125.00 To 145.00
Custard Glass, Sauce, Diamond Peg, Kokomo, Indiana, 4 1/2 In.	25.00
Custard Glass, Sauce, Intaglio, Blue Trim	55.00
Custard Glass, Sauce, Intaglio, Gold & Green, Footed, Northwood	55.00
Custard Glass, Sauce, Inverted Fan & Feather	55.00
Custard Glass, Sauce, Louis XV, Footed, Oval, Northwood, 5 In.	50.00
Custard Glass, Sauce, Winged Scroll, Gold, 4 In.	25.00
Custard Glass, Shaker, Beaded Circle, Lid	150.00

Custard Glass, Sherbet, Grape & Cable, Stemmed 55.00
Custard Glass, Shot Glass, Octagonal 11.00
Custard Glass, Shot Glass, Souvenir, Damariscotta Mills, Maine 17.00
Custard Glass, Shot Glass, Souvenir, East Tilton, New Hampshire 15.00
Custard Glass, Spooner, Argonaut Shell, Gold, Signed Northwood 150.00
Custard Glass, Spooner, Beaded Circle, Gold 172.50
Custard Glass, Spooner, Chrysanthemum Sprig, Gold, Green, & Pink 125.00
Custard Glass, Spooner, Geneva, Green, Red Decoration 65.00
Custard Glass, Spooner, Georgia Gem, Enameled Flowers 65.00
Custard Glass, Spooner, Georgia Gem, Floral 55.00
Custard Glass, Spooner, Intaglio, Gold & Green Decoration .... 70.00 To 85.00
Custard Glass, Spooner, Iris, Gold Trim 115.00
Custard Glass, Spooner, Louis XV .... 40.00 To 85.00
Custard Glass, Spooner, Maple Leaf, Gold Trim, Northwood .... 75.00 To 150.00
Custard Glass, Spooner, Ruffled Edge, 5 In. 35.00
Custard Glass, Spooner, Vermont, Blue Trim 65.00
Custard Glass, Spooner, Wild Bouquet .... 60.00 To 125.00
Custard Glass, Spooner, 4 Footed, 4 Sides Painted, Beaded Around Top, Green 20.00
Custard Glass, Sugar & Creamer, Chrysanthemum Sprig, Gold, Covered Sugar 75.00
Custard Glass, Sugar & Creamer, Geneva 140.00
Custard Glass, Sugar & Creamer, Louis XV .... 135.00 To 150.00
Custard Glass, Sugar & Creamer, Miniature, Austrian, Greentown 120.00
Custard Glass, Sugar, Argonaut Shell, Gold, Match, Signed Northwood 100.00
Custard Glass, Sugar, Chrysanthemum Sprig, Blue 100.00
Custard Glass, Sugar, Covered, Chrysanthemum Sprig .... 95.00 To 165.00
Custard Glass, Sugar, Fluted Scrolls, Open .... 7.00 To 12.00
Custard Glass, Sugar, Georgia Gem, Enameled Flowers, Cover 95.00
Custard Glass, Sugar, Intaglio, Blue & Gold 150.00
Custard Glass, Sugar, Louis XV, Gold Trim, Covered .... 85.00 To 115.00
Custard Glass, Sugar, Maple Leaf, Covered, Northwood 185.00
Custard Glass, Table Set, Chrysanthemum Sprig, Yellow, Northwood, 4 Piece 1500.00
Custard Glass, Table Set, Geneva, 4 Piece 495.00
Custard Glass, Table Set, Georgia Gem, Green Opaque, 4 Piece 585.00
Custard Glass, Table Set, Intaglio, Green With Gold, 4 Piece 495.00
Custard Glass, Table Set, Leaf & Flower Band, 3 Piece 40.00
Custard Glass, Table Set, Louis XV, Gold Trim, 4 Piece .... 450.00 To 595.00
Custard Glass, Table Set, Louis XV, 4 Piece 410.00
Custard Glass, Table Set, Maple Leaf, Gold, Northwood, 4 Piece .... 425.00 To 550.00
Custard Glass, Table Set, Nautilus 555.00
Custard Glass, Table Set, Winged Scroll, Gold, 3 Piece 350.00
Custard Glass, Tankard, Winged Scroll 150.00
Custard Glass, Toothpick, Cherry 3.50
Custard Glass, Toothpick, Chrysanthemum Sprig, Blue, Northwood 395.00
Custard Glass, Toothpick, Chrysanthemum Sprig, Gold 170.00
Custard Glass, Toothpick, Colorado, Green 30.00
Custard Glass, Toothpick, Coney Island, Diamond With Peg, Roses, Gold 35.00
Custard Glass, Toothpick, Diamond Peg 48.00
Custard Glass, Toothpick, Diamond Peg, Rose Decoration, Souvenir 75.00
Custard Glass, Toothpick, Florette, Pink, Cased 45.00
Custard Glass, Toothpick, Geneva, Northwood 55.00
Custard Glass, Toothpick, Georgia Gem 45.00
Custard Glass, Toothpick, Green, Footed, Beaded, Souvenir Eau Claire 35.00
Custard Glass, Toothpick, Harvard 35.00
Custard Glass, Toothpick, Harvard, Sebago Lake, Maine 38.00
Custard Glass, Toothpick, Honeycomb With Flower Rim 65.00
Custard Glass, Toothpick, Inverted Fan & Feather .... 375.00 To 485.00
Custard Glass, Toothpick, Iris Meander, Green 42.00
Custard Glass, Toothpick, Jefferson, Colonial, Blue 42.00
Custard Glass, Toothpick, Maiden Blush Banded, Portland 32.00
Custard Glass, Toothpick, Ribbed Drape, Roses With Gold Trim 150.00
Custard Glass, Toothpick, Ring Band, Floral Spray 65.00
Custard Glass, Toothpick, Ring Band, Roses 75.00
Custard Glass, Toothpick, Tarentum Thumbprint, Orange Floral, Souvenir 42.00
Custard Glass, Toothpick, Winged Scroll, Gold Decoration 35.00
Custard Glass, Tumbler, Argonaut Shell .... 47.00 To 65.00

Custard Glass, Tumbler, Beaded Circle	65.00
Custard Glass, Tumbler, Chrysanthemum Sprig, Blue	150.00 To 195.00
Custard Glass, Tumbler, Chrysanthemum Sprig, Decoration	40.00
Custard Glass, Tumbler, Chrysanthemum Sprig, Gold, Green, Pink Trim	70.00
Custard Glass, Tumbler, Diamond & Peg, Red Roses, Gold, York, N.D.	28.00
Custard Glass, Tumbler, Diamond Peg	30.00 To 35.00
Custard Glass, Tumbler, Diamond Peg, Souvenir	35.00
Custard Glass, Tumbler, Fan & Feather, Gold	132.00
Custard Glass, Tumbler, Geneva	35.00
Custard Glass, Tumbler, Geneva, Gold	60.00
Custard Glass, Tumbler, Geneva, Red & Green Decoration	40.00
Custard Glass, Tumbler, Grape & Gothic Arches, Nutmeg Decoration	38.00
Custard Glass, Tumbler, Grape & Gothic Arches, Pearl Finish, Gold	50.00
Custard Glass, Tumbler, Intaglio	65.00
Custard Glass, Tumbler, Intaglio Blue Decoration	45.00
Custard Glass, Tumbler, Intaglio Green Decoration	45.00
Custard Glass, Tumbler, Intaglio, Green, Gold, Set Of 6	185.00
Custard Glass, Tumbler, Ivorina Verde	55.00
Custard Glass, Tumbler, Louis XV	55.00
Custard Glass, Tumbler, Red & Gold Wheat Design, Heisey, 4 1/4 In.	40.00
Custard Glass, Tumbler, Ribbed Thumbprint, Rose Decoration	35.00
Custard Glass, Tumbler, Rose Decoration, Heisey	40.00
Custard Glass, Tumbler, Roses, Overbrook, Kansas Souvenir	75.00
Custard Glass, Tumbler, Souvenir, Catholic Church Doylestown, Wisconsin	24.00
Custard Glass, Tumbler, Souvenir, Sandwich, Ill., Red Rose	27.50
Custard Glass, Tumbler, Souvenir, State Penitentiary, Anamosa, Iowa	75.00
Custard Glass, Tumbler, Wild Rose	28.50
Custard Glass, Tumbler, Winged Scroll	45.00 To 50.00
Custard Glass, Vase, Celery, Winged Scroll, Gold, Heisey	225.00
Custard Glass, Vase, Curtain, 9 In., Pair	75.00
Custard Glass, Vase, Diamond & Peg, Flowers, Coney Island, 6 In.	35.00
Custard Glass, Vase, Diamond & Peg, 10 In.	75.00
Custard Glass, Vase, Grape & Gothic Arches	85.00
Custard Glass, Vase, Grape & Lattice Pattern, Crimped Top, Northwood, 4 In.	69.00
Custard Glass, Vase, Grape, Lattice, Top Hat Shape	43.00
Custard Glass, Vase, Grasshopper, 8 1/4 In.	67.00
Custard Glass, Vase, Jack-In-The-Pulpit, 6 In., Pair	85.00
Custard Glass, Vase, Roses, Panel Bottom, Brewster, Minnesota	32.50
Custard Glass, Vase, Roses, 8 In.	60.00
Custard Glass, Water Set, Apple Blossom, 7 Piece	375.00
Custard Glass, Water Set, Argonaut Shell, 7 Piece	850.00
Custard Glass, Water Set, Blue Chrysanthemum Sprig, 7 Piece	1200.00
Custard Glass, Water Set, Chrysanthemum Sprig, 7 Piece	595.00 To 800.00
Custard Glass, Water Set, Geneva, Green & Red Decorations, 6 Piece	495.00
Custard Glass, Water Set, Georgia Gem, 5 Piece	295.00
Custard Glass, Water Set, Louis XV, Gold Trim, 7 Piece	385.00 To 800.00
Custard Glass, Water Set, Louis XV, 6 Piece	445.00
Custard Glass, Whiskey, Diamond Peg, Souvenir	45.00
Custard Glass, Wine, Berry Vine Inside, Medallions & Sailboat Outside	55.00
Custard Glass, Wine, Diamond Peg, Paynesville, Minnesota	35.00
Custard Glass, Wine, Honeycomb	45.00
Custard Glass, Winged Scroll, Dish, Olive, Custard, 6 In.	42.00

Cut glass has been made since ancient times, but the large majority of the pieces now for sale date from the brilliant period of glass design, 1880 to 1905. These pieces had elaborate geometric designs with a deep miter cut.

Cut Glass, see also Vaupel

Cut Glass, Atomizer, Crystal, Sterling Silver Top, Collar, & Button	75.00
Cut Glass, Atomizer, Notched Prism Cut, Silver Metal Top	17.50
Cut Glass, Banana Boat, Cut Pears, Crosshatching, Fans, Signed Hawkes, 12 In.	155.00
Cut Glass, Banana Boat, Hobstars, Brilliant, 7 1/2 X 5 1/4 In.	110.00
Cut Glass, Banana Boat, Pedestal, German Cobalt Overlay Cut To Clear, 9 In.	225.00
Cut Glass, Banana Boat, Rose Combination, Irving Cut Glass Co., 11 1/4 In.	190.00
Cut Glass, Banana Bowl, Harvard Pattern, Large, High Pinched-In Sides	390.00

Cut Glass, Banana Bowl, Hobstars, Stars, Diamond, Fan, Large 175.00
Cut Glass, Banana Bowl, Pears & Leaves, Pinwheels, 12 X 7 5/8 In. 110.00
Cut Glass, Banana Bowl, Pinwheels, Fans, Bars Of Zipper Cut, 9 3/4 In. 40.00
Cut Glass, Barrel, Spout, Etched Gin, Irish, 2 Gallon 225.00
Cut Glass, Basket, Allover Cut, Notched Handle, 14-Point Star Base, 6 X 8 In. 95.00
Cut Glass, Basket, Harvard & Morgan Floral, Swirled, Applied Notched Handle 295.00
Cut Glass, Basket, Harvard, Cosmos, Notched Handles, Base, 8 In. 195.00
Cut Glass, Basket, Laurel Cut Glass Co., 1907, 5 In.High 30.00
Cut Glass, Basket, Notched Handle, Signed Fry, 7 In. 195.00
Cut Glass, Basket, Pinwheel, 8 X 6 In. 45.00
Cut Glass, Basket, St.Louis Handle, Hobstar, Buzz Diamond, Fan, Fry, 7 In. 195.00
Cut Glass, Basket, Sterling Rim & Handle, Etched, Signed Hawkes, 7 In. 35.00
Cut Glass, Basket, Triple Notched Handle, Allover Cut, Signed Fry, 7 In. 225.00
Cut Glass, Bell, Intaglio Daisies & Leaves, 5 1/4 In. 30.00
Cut Glass, Berry Bowl, Hobnails, Fans & Diamonds, 8 In. 100.00
Cut Glass, Berry Bowl, Hobstar, Beaded Vesicas, Maltese Cross Center, 8 In. 95.00
Cut Glass, Berry Bowl, Hobstars, 5 In. 60.00
Cut Glass, Biscuit Barrel, Sterling Silver Rim & Handle, 9 X 5 1/2 In. 130.00
Cut Glass, Bottle, Barber, Diamond & Fan, 7 1/2 In. 135.00
Cut Glass, Bottle, Bell Shape, Pinwheels, Crosshatching, Fans, Stopper, 7 In. 65.00
Cut Glass, Bottle, Cologne, Cane, Silver Necks, Stoppers, 7 1/2 In., Pair 125.00
Cut Glass, Bottle, Cologne, Crosscut Diamond, Hawkes, 9 In. 125.00
Cut Glass, Bottle, Cologne, Faceted Stopper, Russian, 7 In. 350.00
Cut Glass, Bottle, Cologne, St.Louis Diamond, Gorham Sterling Top 95.00
Cut Glass, Bottle, Comet With Caning, 16 Point Star Base, Stopper, 6 1/2 In. 50.00
Cut Glass, Bottle, Dresser, Square Cut, Sterling Top, 4 3/4 X 11 1/2 In. 125.00
Cut Glass, Bottle, Hobstars, Diamond, Matching Stopper, 12 In. 195.00
Cut Glass, Bottle, Multifaceted Crystal Stopper, 6 1/4 In. 80.00
Cut Glass, Bottle, Pefume, Globular, Pinwheels, Faceted Stopper, 5 1/2 In. 35.00
Cut Glass, Bottle, Perfume, Blue & White To Clear, Triple Overlay, 4 1/2 In. 125.00
Cut Glass, Bottle, Perfume, Cubes, 5 In. 12.00
Cut Glass, Bottle, Perfume, Deep Spiral Cut, Silver Top, 10 3/4 In. 50.00
Cut Glass, Bottle, Perfume, Diamond Cut, Repousse English Hallmark Top, Pair 175.00
Cut Glass, Bottle, Perfume, Fan, Pinwheel & Triangle, Brass Screw Top, 5 In. 35.00
Cut Glass, Bottle, Perfume, Flattened Diamond, Embossed Sterling Flip, 4 In. 35.00
Cut Glass, Bottle, Perfume, Harvard, Sterling Silver Top, 7 In. 95.00
Cut Glass, Bottle, Perfume, Intaglio Cutting Matching Stopper, 4 In. 35.00
Cut Glass, Bottle, Perfume, Pear Shape, Hallmarked & Enameled Stopper, 4 In. 120.00
Cut Glass, Bottle, Perfume, Pinwheels, Flat Star Centers, X-Split Vesicas 85.00
Cut Glass, Bottle, Perfume, Rib & Diamond Cut, Green To Clear, 2 1/2 In. 25.00
Cut Glass, Bottle, Perfume, Russian Cut, Sterling Collar, Screw Top, 2 3/4 In. 45.00
Cut Glass, Bottle, Sachet, Allover Cut, Stopper, Lid 155.00
Cut Glass, Bottle, Sauce, Flute Neck, Engraved Floral Cutting, 8 In. 40.00
Cut Glass, Bowl & Underplate, Mayonnaise, Hobstar & Cross Cut, Libbey 145.00
Cut Glass, Bowl & Underplate, Mayonnaise, Hobstars, Diamond Point, 7 In. 195.00
Cut Glass, Bowl, Ambrosia, Harvard, 2 Piece 795.00
Cut Glass, Bowl, Bishop's Hat, Intaglio, 10 In. 195.00
Cut Glass, Bowl, Bread, Harvard & Floral Cut, 11 X 6 X 4 In. 80.00
Cut Glass, Bowl, Brunswick Pattern, Signed Hawkes, 9 1/4 In. 225.00
Cut Glass, Bowl, Bull's-Eye & Fan, Scalloped Top, 8 1/2 In. 35.00
Cut Glass, Bowl, Clear, Intaglio Cut, Etched Pansies, Dorflinger, 7 X 3 In. 115.00
Cut Glass, Bowl, Comet, 8 X 4 In. 450.00
Cut Glass, Bowl, Copper Wheel Cut Flowers, Leaves & Punties, 11 3/4 In. 135.00
Cut Glass, Bowl, Cosmos & Hobstars, 8 X 3 In. 55.00
Cut Glass, Bowl, Cut Floral, Birds, Mold Blown, 8 Sided, Signed Fry 32.50
Cut Glass, Bowl, Deep Sharp Cutting, Low, Signed Hoare, 9 X 3 In. 173.00
Cut Glass, Bowl, Dessert, Clear, Straight Sides, Intaglio Stars, Hawkes, 4 In. 30.00
Cut Glass, Bowl, Dessert, Intaglio Cut Stars, Amber-Stained Comets, Hawkes 30.00
Cut Glass, Bowl, Double Knopped Stems, Leaded Quartz 30.00
Cut Glass, Bowl, European Cut, Trifid Scroll Feet, 12 In. 50.00
Cut Glass, Bowl, Fern, Brilliant Hobstars Alternating With Flashed Hobs 135.00
Cut Glass, Bowl, Fern, 3 Applied Feet, Hobstar, Hobnail & Fan, 7 1/2 In. 145.00
Cut Glass, Bowl, Finger, Ellsmere Design, Libbey, 4 1/2 In. 35.00
Cut Glass, Bowl, Finger, Strawberry, Diamond & Fan 25.00
Cut Glass, Bowl, Finger, Underplate, Old Colony, Dorflinger 125.00

Cut Glass, Bowl, Florals, Butterfly, Leaves, Rayed Base, Sawtooth Rim, Rolling 91.00
Cut Glass, Bowl, Flower, Hobstars On Sides, Star Base, Lip Rim, 8 In. 95.00
Cut Glass, Bowl, Fruit, Pinwheel & Fan, 9 In. 65.00
Cut Glass, Bowl, Fruit, Signed, 9 X 3 3/4 In. 100.00
Cut Glass, Bowl, Giant Hobstar Center, Oblong, 9 In. 73.00
Cut Glass, Bowl, Harvard Top & Bottom, Flowers, Leaves, 8 X 4 In. 145.00
Cut Glass, Bowl, Harvard, Flowers, Footed, 7 X 3 1/2 In. 125.00
Cut Glass, Bowl, Hobs & Cut Flowers, Signed, 3 3/4 X 6 1/2 In. 140.00
Cut Glass, Bowl, Hobs, Cluster Of Small Hobs, Signed, 20 X 4 In. 190.00
Cut Glass, Bowl, Hobs, Notched Prisms, Sterling Rim, 3 Compartment, 6 In. 100.00
Cut Glass, Bowl, Hobstar & Cane, Signed, 7 In.. .... 100.00
Cut Glass, Bowl, Hobstar & Fan, American, 4 X 8 In. 75.00
Cut Glass, Bowl, Hobstar Bottom, Points, Fans, Parisian, 8 1/4 X 2 3/4 In. 165.00
Cut Glass, Bowl, Hobstar Bottom, 9 1/4 X 3 In., 7 1/2 In.Diameter 115.00
Cut Glass, Bowl, Hobstar Chain, Cane, Orange, 8 X 5 In. 110.00
Cut Glass, Bowl, Hobstar In Base, Pinwheels, Deep Cutting, 8 X 3 In. 75.00
Cut Glass, Bowl, Hobstar, Chair Bottom, Deep Miter, 9 In. 85.00
Cut Glass, Bowl, Hobstar, Fans, Large, 9 In. 89.00
Cut Glass, Bowl, Hobstar, Flower, Rodin Can & Stars In Base, Signed, 8 In. 100.00
Cut Glass, Bowl, Hobstar, Signed Tuthill, 8 In. 250.00
Cut Glass, Bowl, Hobstar, Strawberry Diamond, Diamond Field, 8 In. 85.00
Cut Glass, Bowl, Hobstars & Fan, 8 X 2 3/4 In. 155.00
Cut Glass, Bowl, Hobstars & Fans, Notched Scalloped Top, 8 X 3 In. 155.00
Cut Glass, Bowl, Hobstars, Brilliant, 7 1/2 X 10 1/2 In. 100.00
Cut Glass, Bowl, Hobstars, Canes, Miniature, 6 X 3 1/2 X 2 In. 78.00
Cut Glass, Bowl, Hobstars, Daisy Center, Brilliant Period, 8 1/4 In. 90.00
Cut Glass, Bowl, Hobstars, Fan & Strawberry Diamonds, 8 X 2 1/2 In. 60.00
Cut Glass, Bowl, Hobstars, Fan, 8 In. 100.00
Cut Glass, Bowl, Hobstars, Fans & Diamonds, 8 X 3 1/4 In. 65.00
Cut Glass, Bowl, Hobstars, Harvard, American, Brilliant, Deep, 9 In. 165.00
Cut Glass, Bowl, Hobstars, Single Stars, Fans, Scalloped, 8 In. 85.00
Cut Glass, Bowl, Hobstars, Strawberry Diamonds, Crosshatching, Square, 6 In. 70.00
Cut Glass, Bowl, Houston, Hobstars & Fans, 8 In. 100.00
Cut Glass, Bowl, Houston, Hobstars, Fans 90.00
Cut Glass, Bowl, Hunter Pattern, Huntley Co.1913, 8 1/2 In. 80.00
Cut Glass, Bowl, Hunt's Royal Pattern, 11 In. 225.00
Cut Glass, Bowl, Hunt's Royal, 8 In., Deep, 2 1/4 In.Tall 165.00
Cut Glass, Bowl, Ice Cream, Hobstars, Diamonds, Caning, Sawtooth Edge, 7 In. 135.00
Cut Glass, Bowl, Iris, Gravic Glass, Signed, 8 X 3 1/2 In. 275.00
Cut Glass, Bowl, Kalana Daisy, Intaglio Cut, Flared Rim, Dorflinger, 7 In. 115.00
Cut Glass, Bowl, Kalana Pansy, Flaring Rim, Dorflinger, 7 X 3 1/2 In. 115.00
Cut Glass, Bowl, Kalana Pansy, Intaglio Cut, Etched Pansies, Dorflinger, 7 In. 115.00
Cut Glass, Bowl, Lace, Hunt, 9 X 2 In. 350.00
Cut Glass, Bowl, Like A Diamond, Allover Strawberry Hobnail, 8 X 4 In. 275.00
Cut Glass, Bowl, Low Trefoil, Buzz, 9 In. 85.00
Cut Glass, Bowl, Marsella, Hobstar Bottom, Libbey, 9 1/2 X 2 1/2 In. 225.00
Cut Glass, Bowl, Mayonnaise With Underplate, 7 In. 75.00
Cut Glass, Bowl, Nut, Openwork Sterling Silver Rim, Miniature, 4 In. 35.00
Cut Glass, Bowl, Octagon, Harvard, Mitered Flowers & Leaves, 9 X 2 3/4 In. 150.00
Cut Glass, Bowl, Oval, Sawtooth Edge, Hobstar Base, 11 3/4 X 7 In. 95.00
Cut Glass, Bowl, Parisian, 10 X 2 3/4 In. 160.00
Cut Glass, Bowl, Pedestal Base, Berry & Leaf Design, Hawkes, 7 1/2 In. 65.00
Cut Glass, Bowl, Pinwheel, Hobstars, Notched Scalloped Top, 9 X 3 1/2 In. 210.00
Cut Glass, Bowl, Punch, Allover Cut, Original Standard, 30 In. 285.00
Cut Glass, Bowl, Punch, Large Hobstars, Cane & Fan, 12 X 12 In., 2 Piece 575.00
Cut Glass, Bowl, Punch, Signed Hawkes, 2 Piece, 12 X 11 In. 1000.00
Cut Glass, Bowl, Punch, Strawberry, Diamond, & Fan 550.00
Cut Glass, Bowl, Punch, Tulip-Shaped, Sawtoothed Edge, Base, 8 X 8 In. 700.00
Cut Glass, Bowl, Queen Lace, Scalloped Rim, 4 1/8 X 2 1/8 In. 20.00
Cut Glass, Bowl, Rose Floral, Triangle Concentrics, Sawtooth Rim, 8 X 3 In. 69.50
Cut Glass, Bowl, Rose, Cornflower, Flat, 8 In. 75.00
Cut Glass, Bowl, Roses Around Base, Sawtooth, 10 X 4 In. 110.00
Cut Glass, Bowl, Rosettes, Oval Loop, Rolling Edge, Sawtooth, Flint, Belltone 85.00
Cut Glass, Bowl, Royal, Hunt, 9 X 4 In. 275.00
Cut Glass, Bowl, Russian Cut Panels, 8 X 4 In. 200.00

Cut Glass, Bowl, Russian Cut, Repousse Silver Rim, 3 X 5 1/2 In., Pair	225.00
Cut Glass, Bowl, Russian Cut, Rolled-Over Sides, Triangular, 8 In.	115.00
Cut Glass, Bowl, Russian, Repousse Silver Rims, C.1900, 5 1/2 X 3 In., Pair	225.00
Cut Glass, Bowl, Salad, Allover Sharp Cut, 3 Feet, 3 1/2 X 9 In.	130.00
Cut Glass, Bowl, Sawtooth Edge, Leaded, 8 X 4 In.	90.00
Cut Glass, Bowl, Scalloped Rim, Entire Surface Cut, 2 1/2 X 8 In.	225.00
Cut Glass, Bowl, Senora Pattern, Signed Libbey, 9 In.	150.00
Cut Glass, Bowl, Single Stars & Fans, Hobstars, Signed Clark, 7 X 3 In.	100.00
Cut Glass, Bowl, Six Vesicas, Alternating Hobstars, Fans, 9 X 2 In.	95.00
Cut Glass, Bowl, Snowflake Bottom, Libbey, 8 X 4 In.	150.00
Cut Glass, Bowl, Snowflake, Hobstars & Crosshatching, 6 1/2 X 1 3/4 In.	75.00
Cut Glass, Bowl, Sterling Silver Rim, 1868, 10 In.	410.00
Cut Glass, Bowl, Strawberry, Diamond & Fan, 8 1/2 In.	45.00
Cut Glass, Bowl, Strawberry, 7 In.	125.00
Cut Glass, Bowl, Three Corner, 3 1/2 X 9 In.	185.00
Cut Glass, Bowl, Toddy, Separate Pedestal, 9 In.Diameter	250.00
Cut Glass, Bowl, Tulip & Butterfly Design, 8 In.	225.00
Cut Glass, Bowl, Turned Down 4 In.Rim, Leaves & Flowers, 15 In.Diameter	47.50
Cut Glass, Bowl, Undulating Sawtooth Edge, Hobstars, Rectangular, 11 1/2 In.	130.00
Cut Glass, Bowl, Water Lily , Signed Verlys, 13 1/2 In.	75.00
Cut Glass, Bowl, 3 Oval Pointed Strawberry Vesicas, Hobstars, 6 In.	50.00
Cut Glass, Bowl, 5-Pointed Star With Cane Patterns, Clark, 8 In.	165.00
Cut Glass, Box & Underplate, Dresser, Round, Button & Fan	48.00
Cut Glass, Box, Boudoir, Intaglio Cut Flower & Cane, Covered, 3 1/2 X 3 In.	75.00
Cut Glass, Box, Cigar, Russian, Lid Fits Inside Box, Allover Cut, 4 1/2 In.	400.00
Cut Glass, Box, Covered, Footed, Harvard Cut, Oval, 6 1/2 X 4 In.	175.00
Cut Glass, Box, Feathers, Fans, Vesicas, Zipper, Strawberry Diamond, Maple City	50.00
Cut Glass, Box, Glove, Hobstars & Strawberry Diamond	115.00
Cut Glass, Box, Heart Shaped, Clover Leaf Design, Hobstars, Lid, 6 In.	225.00
Cut Glass, Box, Hobstar & Fan, Round, Covered, Hinged Lid, 8 In.	195.00
Cut Glass, Box, Hobstars, Hinged, Round, 5 1/2 X 17 In.	155.00
Cut Glass, Box, Jewel, Heart Shaped, Flowers, & Leaves, 5 1/2 X 3 In.	165.00
Cut Glass, Box, Jewel, Lapidary Knob On Cover, Round, 11 1/4 In.	50.00
Cut Glass, Box, Ointment, Raised Diamond & Fan, Scene On Porcelain Top, 2 In.	55.00
Cut Glass, Box, Powder, Crystal, Cobalt Cut To Clear, 5 In.	115.00
Cut Glass, Box, Powder, Crystal, 32 Point Star, Hinged, 5 X 3 In.	135.00
Cut Glass, Box, Powder, Etched Flower On Lid, Star Bottom, Round	50.00
Cut Glass, Box, Powder, Matching Hair Receiver, Pair	180.00
Cut Glass, Box, Yellow Basse Taille Enamel, Sterling Lid, 6 In.Diameter	68.00
Cut Glass, Bucket, Ice, Brilliant Deep Cut, Corning, N.Y., 5 1/4 X 5 1/2 In.	75.00
Cut Glass, Bucket, Ice, Diamond & Fan, Rayed Bottom, 2 1/4 X 1 3/4 In.	49.00
Cut Glass, Bucket, Ice, French Lace	150.00
Cut Glass, Bucket, Ice, Hobstars, American, 7 X 6 In.	185.00
Cut Glass, Bucket, Ice, Tabs, Serrated Edge, Hobstar Base, Fans, Stars, 5 In.	165.00
Cut Glass, Bucket, Ice, 24 Point Hobstar Base	295.00
Cut Glass, Butter Dish, Hobstar, Crosshatch .... *Illus*	275.00
Cut Glass, Butter Pat, Hobstars, Fans	19.00
Cut Glass, Butter, Corinthian, Straus	240.00
Cut Glass, Butter, Covered, Clusters Of Hobs, Brilliant	295.00
Cut Glass, Butter, Covered, Snail, Brilliant, C.1892	45.00

Cut Glass, Butter Dish, Hobstar, Crosshatch

Cut Glass, Butter, Dome, American, Diamond & Sharp Fan 78.50
Cut Glass, Butter, Dome, Buzz, Stars, Fans, Hobnail, Proof, 8 X 6 In. 295.00
Cut Glass, Butter, Floral, Russian 195.00
Cut Glass, Butter, Good Luck Underplate, Harvard Edge, Dome, 7 In. 350.00
Cut Glass, Butter, Harvard & Cosmos, Signed, 24 Star Base 60.00
Cut Glass, Butter, Hobstars, Diamond, Fan, Covered 225.00
Cut Glass, Butter, Pinwheel & Diamond 175.00
Cut Glass, Butter, Russian, Cornflower & Leaves, Dome 195.00
Cut Glass, Candelabrum, Prisms, 4 Silver Plated Arms & Base, 21 In. 295.00
Cut Glass, Candlestick, Brunswick Pattern, Signed Hawkes, 10 In., Pair 675.00
Cut Glass, Candlestick, C.1850, Flint, 9 3/4 In., Pair 95.00
Cut Glass, Candlestick, Copper Wheel Engraving, Intaglio Beaded Stem, Pair 175.00
Cut Glass, Candlestick, Daisy & Geometric, Swirl Stem, 10 1/4 In., Pair 150.00
Cut Glass, Candlestick, Elongated Punty, 7 In.Teardrop, 11 In., Set Of 4 .... 275.00
Cut Glass, Candlestick, Elongated Teardrop In Cut Knob, Hobstars, 5 In. 115.00
Cut Glass, Candlestick, Hollow Stem, Paneled & Etched, Star Base, 11 In., Pair 325.00
Cut Glass, Candlestick, Teardrop Center, Signed Bergen, 10 In. 185.00
Cut Glass, Canoe, Cane Cut, Clarke, 12 1/2 X 4 1/2 In. 260.00
Cut Glass, Canoe, Flat Bottomed, 12 1/2 X 4 In. 125.00
Cut Glass, Canoe, Harvard Pattern, 11 In. 145.00
Cut Glass, Canoe, Harvard, Large 110.00
Cut Glass, Canoe, Harvard, 11 1/2 X 5 In. 235.00
Cut Glass, Canoe, Hobstars, Fans, Tooth Rim, 11 X 5 In. 160.00
Cut Glass, Carafe, Comet, Fluted Neck, Signed Hoare 200.00
Cut Glass, Carafe, Corinthian Pattern, Libbey, 8 In. 125.00
Cut Glass, Carafe, Fluted & Notched Neck, Crosscut Diamonds & Fans, 6 In. 90.00
Cut Glass, Carafe, Hobstar, Fans, Splits, 20 Point Hobstar Base, Brilliant Cut 75.00
Cut Glass, Carafe, Hobstars, Fans, Rayed Base, Panel, & Notched Neck 50.00
Cut Glass, Carafe, Notched Prisms 38.00
Cut Glass, Carafe, Parisian, Dorflinger 100.00
Cut Glass, Carafe, Pinwheel & Pineapple, Rayed Base, 7 1/2 In. 50.00
Cut Glass, Carafe, Split Vesica & Bead, 8 1/4 In. .... 110.00 To 155.00
Cut Glass, Carafe, Water, Strawberry, Fan 50.00
Cut Glass, Celery, Allover Cut, 1/2 In.Thick 88.00
Cut Glass, Celery, Allover Hobstars, Checkered Diamond, 11 1/2 X 4 3/4 In. 85.00
Cut Glass, Celery, Allover Hobstars, Strawberry Diamond, 11 1/2 In. 110.00
Cut Glass, Celery, Buzz Stars & Bars Of Cane, Signed, 11 3/4 X 5 1/2 In. 300.00
Cut Glass, Celery, Diamond Thumbprint, Scalloped Top, Flint, 9 1/4 In. 175.00
Cut Glass, Celery, Fan & Crosshatch, Brilliant, 12 1/2 In. 55.00
Cut Glass, Celery, Harvard Pattern 135.00
Cut Glass, Celery, Hobstar & Fan, 11 3/4 In. 110.00
Cut Glass, Celery, Hobstar & Fan, 12 X 4 1/2 In. 75.00
Cut Glass, Celery, Hobstars Each End, Cross Vesicas, Beading, 11 X 5 In. 65.00
Cut Glass, Celery, Hobstars, Crosshatching, Beading, 11 1/2 X 4 In. 80.00
Cut Glass, Celery, Hobstars, Fans, Strawberry Diamonds 37.50
Cut Glass, Celery, Hobstars, Single Stars, Strawberry Diamond, Fan, 11 In. 45.00
Cut Glass, Celery, Hobstars, Zipper, 11 1/2 X 4 1/2 In. 49.00
Cut Glass, Celery, Hobstars, 12 In. 120.00
Cut Glass, Celery, Lotus, Eggington, 11 In., Pair 160.00
Cut Glass, Celery, Modified Hobstars, Fan, Turned-In Sides, 12 X 5 1/2 In. 100.00
Cut Glass, Celery, Signed Tuthill, 6 1/2 X 10 In. 150.00
Cut Glass, Celery, 4 Hobstar Clusters, 2 Strawberry Diamond Cross Panels 145.00
Cut Glass, Chalice, Engraved, Sterling Silver Base, Signed 135.00
Cut Glass, Champagne, Bellflower, 5 In. 235.00
Cut Glass, Champagne, Fluted, Diamond, Wide Bowl, Set Of 8 .... 150.00
Cut Glass, Champagne, Hexagonal Cut Panels, Double Teardrop Stem, 4 3/4 In. 25.00
Cut Glass, Champagne, Russian Cut, Long Teardrop In Stem 65.00
Cut Glass, Champagne, Russian Pattern 69.00
Cut Glass, Champagne, Signed, Hawkes 30.00
Cut Glass, Cheese, Domed Lid, Hoare, Hindoo, 10 In. 525.00
Cut Glass, Claret, Encore, Straus, Hand Polished, 12 In. 245.00
Cut Glass, Clock, Boudoir, Profusely Cut In Harvard Runs 200.00
Cut Glass, Coffeepot, Florence .... Illus 4500.00
Cut Glass, Cologne, Cut & Band Of Single Star, Faceted Stopper, 5 1/2 In. 30.00
Cut Glass, Compote, American, Bevel Cut Prismatic Stem, Hobstars, 8 In. 250.00

Cut Glass, Compote, Bishops' Hat Shape, Rolled Rim, 9 1/4 In. 500.00
Cut Glass, Compote, Corinthian, Teardrop, Hobstars, Cane, J.Hoare, 10 1/2 In. 190.00
Cut Glass, Compote, Diamond Point, Scalloped Edge, Open, 7 1/2 In. 26.00
Cut Glass, Compote, Engraved Flowers & Leaves, Twisted Stem, Libbey, 7 In. 65.00
Cut Glass, Compote, Fans & Block Design, Triangular Form, 6 1/2 In. 30.00
Cut Glass, Compote, Fans, Hobs, Strawberry Diamond, Zipper Stem & Scallops 110.00
Cut Glass, Compote, Fans, Hobstars, Serrated Stem, Cuts On Pedestal, 14 In. 490.00
Cut Glass, Compote, Floral Engraving, Fluted Top, Hawkes, 8 X 7 1/4 In. 85.00
Cut Glass, Compote, Floral Wreathes & Garlands, Signed Libbey, 6 X 7 In., Pair 95.00
Cut Glass, Compote, Flutes & Panel Border, Signed, Pair, 4 In. 395.00
Cut Glass, Compote, Harvard & Floral, 8 X 6 In. 65.00
Cut Glass, Compote, Harvard, 6 1/2 X 3 1/2 In. 75.00
Cut Glass, Compote, Hobstar & Leaf, Lattice, Teardrop Stem ....*Illus* 200.00
Cut Glass, Compote, Hobstars Cut, 8 X 11 1/2 In. 195.00
Cut Glass, Compote, Hobstars With Strawberry Diamond, Hoare, 7 X 6 In. 95.00
Cut Glass, Compote, Hobstars, Cane, Teardrop In Faceted Ball Stem, 8 In. 375.00
Cut Glass, Compote, Hobstars, Crosshatch, 24 Point Hobstar Base 210.00
Cut Glass, Compote, Hobstars, Epergne Base, 8 X 8 1/2 In. 135.00
Cut Glass, Compote, Hobstars, Fan, Square, Teardrop Stem, 7 3/4 In. 175.00
Cut Glass, Compote, Hobstars, Fans & Strawberry Diamonds, Paisley, 7 1/2 In. 225.00
Cut Glass, Compote, Hobstars, Fans, Notched Panels, 10 Sections, 7 X 8 In. 125.00
Cut Glass, Compote, Hobstars, Fans, Teardrop Stem, Clarke, 8 X 6 In. 150.00
Cut Glass, Compote, Hobstars, Strawberry & Fan, Teardrop Stem, 6 In. 110.00
Cut Glass, Compote, Hobstars, Strawberry Diamond & Hobstar Center, 8 In. 140.00
Cut Glass, Compote, Honeycomb, Hawkes, 7 X 7 1/4 In., Pair 175.00
Cut Glass, Compote, Intaglio Cut, Libbey, 6 1/4 In. 95.00
Cut Glass, Compote, Intaglio, 6 1/2 X 4 3/4 In. 35.00
Cut Glass, Compote, Jelly, Boat Shaped, Hobstars, Standard 185.00
Cut Glass, Compote, Jelly, Chain Of Hobstars, Cane, & Fan, Notched Stem, Pair 165.00
Cut Glass, Compote, Kalana Lily, Dorflinger, Footed, 6 X 4 In. 150.00
Cut Glass, Compote, Kalana Lily, Footed, Dorflinger, 6 In. 150.00
Cut Glass, Compote, Lily Of The Valley, Libbey, 5 X 6 1/4 In. 45.00
Cut Glass, Compote, Prismatic, Shaped Stem, Serrated Bowl, 9 In. 120.00
Cut Glass, Compote, Rose Pattern, Hawkes, 9 In. 285.00
Cut Glass, Compote, Soft Green Cut To Clear, Engraved Floral Band, Sinclaire 60.00
Cut Glass, Compote, St.Louis, Greek Key, Cranberry Rim, 6 3/8 X 8 3/8 In. 100.00
Cut Glass, Compote, Strawberry, Diamond, Fan, 9 1/4 X 7 1/2 In. 175.00
Cut Glass, Compote, Strawberry, Serrated Top, Rayed Base, Clark, 7 In. 195.00
Cut Glass, Compote, Tazza, 8 X 8 1/4 In. 225.00
Cut Glass, Compote, Teardrop Center, Hobstars, Strawberry Diamonds, 8 In. 140.00
Cut Glass, Compote, Teardrop Stem, Clark, 7 1/2 X 6 In. 250.00
Cut Glass, Compote, Teardrop Stem, 7 1/2 In. 110.00
Cut Glass, Compote, Thumbprint Edge, Feathered Fan & Star, Miter Cuts 40.00
Cut Glass, Compote, Tuthill, 6 X 3 In. 235.00
Cut Glass, Conoe, Hobstars, Stars, 11 1/2 X 4 1/2 In. 145.00
Cut Glass, Cookie Jar, S Stop Zipper, Crossed Vesicas, Crosshatch, Fan, 6 In. 350.00
Cut Glass, Cooler, Champagne, Hobstars & Cane, Silver Liner 550.00
Cut Glass, Cooler, Wine, 4 Cranberry Floral Etched Panels 65.00
Cut Glass, Cordial, Paneled Bowl, Herringbone Cutting, Signed Libbey 15.00
Cut Glass, Cordial, Straw & Fan, 3 1/4 In. 95.00
Cut Glass, Cracker Jar, Intaglio Flowers & Leaves, Covered, 6 X 9 In. 135.00
Cut Glass, Cracker Jar, Strawberry Diamond, Single Star Bottom, 7 In. 385.00

Cut Glass, Coffeepot, Florence *(See Page 137)*

Cut Glass, Compote, Hobstar & Leaf, Lattice, Teardrop Stem

Cut Glass, Creamer, Child's, Hobnail With Thumbprint Base, Dark Amber	23.00
Cut Glass, Creamer, Diamond Point, Footed, Applied Handle, Pontil Mark	75.00
Cut Glass, Creamer, Footed, Hobstars, Pinwheels, 16 Star Base, 5 1/4 In.	45.00
Cut Glass, Creamer, Gothic, Flint	60.00
Cut Glass, Cruet, Allover Cut, Bulge Body, Cut Stopper, Tricorn Spout	62.00
Cut Glass, Cruet, Bulbous, Middlesex Pattern	55.00
Cut Glass, Cruet, Flowers, Harvard Base, Faceted Stopper, 9 1/4 In.	38.00
Cut Glass, Cruet, Hobstar Chain & Strawberry Diamond, 5 In., Pair	225.00
Cut Glass, Cruet, Hobstars, Notched Prism & Handle, 6 In.	59.00
Cut Glass, Cruet, Pinwheel, Diamond Cut Stopper, 3 Lips, 7 In.	80.00
Cut Glass, Cruet, Renaissance, 5 In.	46.00
Cut Glass, Cruet, Ruby Cut To Clear Pinwheel, 5 In.	65.00
Cut Glass, Cruet, Shallow Cut, Faceted Stopper, 6 1/2 In.	17.00
Cut Glass, Cruet, Sterling Silver Stopper, Floral Sprays, Hawkes, 7 1/2 In.	65.00
Cut Glass, Cruet, Straight Sides, Tapered, Flute Cut, Lapidary Stopper, 9 In.	50.00
Cut Glass, Cruet, Vinegar, Flowers, Star Centers, Notched Handle, 6 1/2 In.	75.00
Cut Glass, Cruet, Vinegar, Original Stopper, Renaissance, 5 1/2 In.	47.50
Cut Glass, Cruet, 24 Point Star, Steeple Top Stopper, 6 1/2 In.	85.00
Cut Glass, Cup, Fan & Diamond, Pedestaled & Handled, Set Of 3	65.00
Cut Glass, Cup, Punch, Hob, Fan, Cane & Crosshatch	35.00
Cut Glass, Cup, Punch, Hobstars, Set Of Six	130.00
Cut Glass, Cup, Punch, Royal Pattern, Handled, Signed Hunt	35.00
Cut Glass, Cuspidor, Signed Fry	88.00
Cut Glass, Decanter, Allover Hobstars, Strawberry, Diamond, Handled, 11 In.	135.00
Cut Glass, Decanter, Bands Of Bull's-Eyes, Band Of Vintage, Teardrop Stopper	77.50
Cut Glass, Decanter, Brilliant Cut, Faceted Stopper	265.00
Cut Glass, Decanter, Bulbous, Original Stopper, 1 Quart	125.00
Cut Glass, Decanter, Cranberry To Clear, Thumbprint, Grapes, 13 1/2 In.	110.00
Cut Glass, Decanter, Deer, Castle, Dog, Rabbit, Scrolls, Amber, Mushroom Stopper	145.00
Cut Glass, Decanter, Emerald Green Cut To Clear, Pyramid Shape, 13 In.	575.00
Cut Glass, Decanter, Flange Lip, 3 Ringed Neck, Pointed Steeple Stopper	97.00
Cut Glass, Decanter, Gooseneck, Step Cutting, Cane, Cornflower, Leaves, Stopper	110.00
Cut Glass, Decanter, Greek Key, Double Lips, Large Honeycomb, Faceted, Stopper	65.00
Cut Glass, Decanter, Harvard, Triple-Notched Handle	195.00
Cut Glass, Decanter, Hobstar Cutting, 11 1/2 In.	150.00
Cut Glass, Decanter, Hobstars, Fan, Stopper, Almay & Thomas	275.00
Cut Glass, Decanter, Hobstars, Notched Prism Neck, Cut Stopper, Brilliant	74.00
Cut Glass, Decanter, Inverted Thistle Shaped, 8 3/4 In.	250.00
Cut Glass, Decanter, Multipaneled Faceting, 3 Ring Neck, Steeple Stopper	97.00
Cut Glass, Decanter, Mushroom Faceted Stopper, Engraved Deer, Castle, 13 In.	145.00
Cut Glass, Decanter, Rayed Base, Stars, Fluted Notched Neck, Stopper, 20 In.	300.00
Cut Glass, Decanter, Russian, Honeycomb Neck, Cut Faceted Stopper, 10 1/2 In.	75.00
Cut Glass, Decanter, Stopper & Decanter Signed Signet	350.00
Cut Glass, Decanter, Strawberry Diamond, Gorham Sterling Flip Top, 10 In.	295.00
Cut Glass, Decanter, Swirl Star, Canes, Pineapple, Fan, Fluted Stopper, 13 In.	110.00
Cut Glass, Decanter, Teardrop Stopper, Honeycomb Pattern, Greek Key Design	130.00
Cut Glass, Decanter, Whiskey, Squares, Cane Bottom, Cane Stopper, 10 In.	250.00

Cut Glass, Decanter, Whiskey, Strawberry Diamonds, Fan, Lapidary Cut Stopper 78.00
Cut Glass, Decanter, Wine Urn, Pedestaled, Red Spout, Crystal Stopper, 14 In. 200.00
Cut Glass, Decanter, Wine, Buzz, Fan, Cane Bottom, Mushroom Stopper, 11 1/4 In. 200.00
Cut Glass, Decanter, Wine, Grape & Leaf, Stopper, Blue To Clear, 15 1/2 In. 200.00
Cut Glass, Decanter, Wine, Hobstars, Prism, Narrow Neck, Applied Handle, 12 In. 185.00
Cut Glass, Desk Set, Engraved Flowers And Trailing Vines, 3 Piece 195.00
Cut Glass, Desk Set, Garlands & Wreaths, Hawkes, 3 Piece 210.00
Cut Glass, Dessert Set, Pinwheel, Hobstar, Strawberry, Set Of 8 Dishes, 6 In. 150.00
Cut Glass, Dish, Banana, Hobstars, Hobnail & Fan, Hawkes, 11 X 4 1/2 In. 245.00
Cut Glass, Dish, Brazilian, Hawkes, 1890, 10 In. 225.00
Cut Glass, Dish, Candy, Hobstar, Flower On Bottom, 2 Handles, 6 In. 32.00
Cut Glass, Dish, Candy, Hobstar, Signed Fry, 7 In. 55.00
Cut Glass, Dish, Candy, Hobstars, Diamond, Handled, Pedestaled, 8 1/4 In. 95.00
Cut Glass, Dish, Candy, Pedestaled, Hobstar, Cane, Diamond, Fan, 8 In. 150.00
Cut Glass, Dish, Cheese & Cracker, Flowers With Crosshatched Centers 85.00
Cut Glass, Dish, Cheese & Cracker, Flowers, Crosshatch, Pedestal 125.00
Cut Glass, Dish, Cheese & Cracker, Pineapple & Fan, 10 1/4 In. 185.00
Cut Glass, Dish, Cheese, Covered, Rambler Rose, Enterprise Cut Glass Co. 120.00
Cut Glass, Dish, Cheese, Hobstar & Comet, Scalloped Edge, Cut Finial, 9 In. 375.00
Cut Glass, Dish, Cheese, Lid, Hobstars, Cane, Knob Cut In Hobstar, Cane & Fan 375.00
Cut Glass, Dish, Cheese, Sharp Hobstars, 9 In. 95.00
Cut Glass, Dish, Covered Sweetmeat, Intaglio Engraved, Domed Finial, Hawkes 95.00
Cut Glass, Dish, Creswick, Signed Hoare, 7 In. 80.00
Cut Glass, Dish, Double 8 Vesicas, Hobstars, Fan & Strawberry Diamond, 8 In. 75.00
Cut Glass, Dish, Flashed Hobstars, Strawberry, Diamond & Fans, 8 In. 85.00
Cut Glass, Dish, Four Sections, 2 Handles, 9 1/2 In. 85.00
Cut Glass, Dish, Fruit, Crosshatch & Fan, 20 Point Star Bottom, 8 In. 75.00
Cut Glass, Dish, Fruit, 4 Brass Claw Feet On Marble & Brass Base, 10 In. 135.00
Cut Glass, Dish, Hobstars, Notch Cutting, Fan, Heart Shaped, 5 1/2 X 5 In. 65.00
Cut Glass, Dish, Hobstars, 8 Point Star, Notched Handles, 4 Section, 7 In. 100.00
Cut Glass, Dish, Ice Cream, Cosmos Star, Handled, Signed Tuthill 250.00
Cut Glass, Dish, Ice Cream, Fans, Stars, 6 In. 10.00
Cut Glass, Dish, Ice Cream, Hobstars, Strawberry Diamond, & Fan, 7 In. 50.00
Cut Glass, Dish, Mayonnaise, Underplate, Hobstars & Hobnail, Irregular Rim 150.00
Cut Glass, Dish, Miter Cut, Pedestal, 8 In. 95.00
Cut Glass, Dish, Nut, Fans, Pinwheels, Oval, 2 3/4 X 4 3/4 In. 25.00
Cut Glass, Dish, Oblong Relish, Intaglio Feathered Stars, Hoare, 7 1/4 In. 55.00
Cut Glass, Dish, Olive, Hobstar, Cherries, Hawkes, Signed 170.00
Cut Glass, Dish, Pickle, Hobstar & Diamond, 7 1/2 In. 55.00
Cut Glass, Dish, Pickle, Russian Cut, Turned-In Sides, 7 1/4 X 2 1/2 In. 135.00
Cut Glass, Dish, Powder, Covered, Hobstars, 4 In. 75.00
Cut Glass, Dish, Powder, Intaglio, Covered 42.50
Cut Glass, Dish, Russian Cut Center, Covered, 5 1/8 X 3 In. 125.00
Cut Glass, Dish, Serving, Expanding Star, 8 In. 155.00
Cut Glass, Dresser Set, Floral Center, Cut Stripes Each Side, 3 Piece 165.00
Cut Glass, Dresser Tray, Hobstar Border, Engraved Flowers In Center 95.00
Cut Glass, Ferner, Footed, Brilliant Cut, 4 1/2 X 7 3/4 In. 200.00
Cut Glass, Ferner, Hobstar & Fan, 8 In. 90.00
Cut Glass, Ferner, Hobstars, 3 Footed, Brilliant, 7 3/4 In. 61.00
Cut Glass, Ferner, Sterling Rim, 10 In. 130.00
Cut Glass, Flask, Lady's, Russian Pattern, Set In Silver, Silver Cap 150.00
Cut Glass, Frame, Picture, Engraved Floral Decoration, 9 X 11 In. 95.00
Cut Glass, Glass Set, Juice, Dorflinger's Middlesex, Set Of 10 .... 275.00
Cut Glass, Goblet, Bellflower, 6 1/4 In. .... 225.00 To 250.00
Cut Glass, Goblet, Cable, Flint 52.00
Cut Glass, Goblet, Crosshatch, Strawberry Diamond & Fans 22.00
Cut Glass, Goblet, Diamond Cut, Anglo-Irish, C.1810 .... 45.00
Cut Glass, Goblet, Flowers & Leaves, Punties, Signed Hawkes, 7 In., Set Of 6 .... 190.00
Cut Glass, Goblet, Intaglio Cut Roses, Panel Cut Stems, 6 1/4 In., Pair 40.00
Cut Glass, Goblet, Kalana Lily, Dorflinger 70.00
Cut Glass, Goblet, Stemmed, Hand Engraved, Signed Hawkes, Set Of 4, 7 In. 85.00
Cut Glass, Goblet, Strawberry & Diamond, Set Of 8 .... 575.00
Cut Glass, Goblet, Stylized Fern & Floral, Notched Cutting On Stem, Hawkes 27.00
Cut Glass, Goblet, Tulip Pattern, 6-Footed 95.00
Cut Glass, Hair Receiver & Box, Hobstars, Diamond Cuts 180.00

Cut Glass, Ice Bucket, Hobstar, Crosshatch, Hobnail, Fan, 11 In.

Cut Glass, Hair Receiver, Pinwheels, Crosshatching, Fans, Lid	50.00
Cut Glass, Hobnail, Tray, Water, Blue, 11 1/2 In.	40.00
Cut Glass, Hobstars, Diamond, & Fan, 12 In.	225.00
Cut Glass, Hobstars, Fans, 9 In.	89.00
Cut Glass, Humidor, Bull's-Eyes, Sterling Silver Cover	150.00
Cut Glass, Ice Bucket, Hobstar, Crosshatch, Hobnail, Fan, 11 In. .... *Illus*	1300.00
Cut Glass, Ice Tub, 5 1/2 In.	75.00
Cut Glass, Inkwell, Cane Bottom, Beveled Edges, 1 7/8 In.Square	45.00
Cut Glass, Inkwell, Fluted & Notched, Sterling Silver Hinged Top	55.00
Cut Glass, Inkwell, Frosted Cut To Clear, Enameled White Forest, Tan Deer	75.00
Cut Glass, Inkwell, Hobstars, Strawberry Diamond, Split Vesicas & Fans	35.00
Cut Glass, Inkwell, Sterling Silver Top, Square, Russian, 3 X 3 In.	55.00
Cut Glass, Inkwell, 2 Wells, Sterling Rims & Covers, Harvard Cut Base	60.00
Cut Glass, Jar, Candy, Chased Sterling Silver Top, Hobstars, Fans, Fern, 5 In.	200.00
Cut Glass, Jar, Cracker, Allover Strawberry, Diamond, 7 3/4 X 7 In.	385.00
Cut Glass, Jar, Cracker, Frosted, Metal Bail & Lid, 8 In.	28.00
Cut Glass, Jar, Cracker, Silver Lid & Bail, Marked Straus	85.00
Cut Glass, Jar, Dresser, Sterling Cover, Notched Prism Pattern	40.00
Cut Glass, Jar, Jam, Etched Daisy, Blue Enamel, Sterling Finial	13.00
Cut Glass, Jar, Jam, Poinsettia Flower, Sterling Lid, Signed Tuthill	135.00
Cut Glass, Jar, Jam, Sterling Monogrammed Lid, Stars & Cross Hatching	50.00
Cut Glass, Jar, Jam, Sterling Spoon And Cover, Hawkes	30.00
Cut Glass, Jar, Jam, Thistle, Diamond & Fan, Crosshatching, Cut Finial	45.00
Cut Glass, Jar, Mustard, Silver Top And Handle	35.00
Cut Glass, Jar, Pickle, Silver Frame, Silver Fork To Match, 9 In.	60.00
Cut Glass, Jar, Pomade, Zipper, Footed, Lid, Dometop Brass Lid	20.00
Cut Glass, Jar, Pomade, Zipper, Turtle, Cobalt Blue Faceted Stone On Shell	14.00
Cut Glass, Jar, Powder, Sterling, Angel Kissing Woman, 5 X 3 3/4 In.	95.00
Cut Glass, Jug, Whiskey, Flute Design, Signed Hawkes	130.00
Cut Glass, Jug, Whiskey, Pinwheel, Stopper, Vertical Prism, Crosshatch, Handle	485.00
Cut Glass, Jug, Whiskey, Pinwheels, Small, 5 In.	110.00
Cut Glass, Knife Rest, Allover Cut, Heavy	43.00
Cut Glass, Knife Rest, Ball Shaped, Facet-Cut Ends, 4 1/2 In.	35.00
Cut Glass, Knife Rest, Daisy & Button Ends, Ornate, Large	38.00
Cut Glass, Knife Rest, Faceted Ball Ends, 3 1/2 In.	21.00
Cut Glass, Knife Rest, Lapidary Ball Ends, Panel Cut Bar, 4 In.	25.00
Cut Glass, Knife Rest, Large Faceted Ball Ends With Stars	22.50
Cut Glass, Knife Rest, 6-Sided Shank, Ball Ends	35.00
Cut Glass, Ladle, Teardrop, Hobstars, Straw, Fan, Cut Handle, 10 In.	135.00
Cut Glass, Lamp, see Lamp	
Cut Glass, Match Holder, Daisy & Button, Shoe On Toboggan, Victorian	24.50
Cut Glass, Mayonnaise Bowl & Plate, Matches, Hobstars, Prism Cut	95.00
Cut Glass, Mayonnaise Bowl, Hobstars, Sawtooth Rim, 2 Piece	12.00
Cut Glass, Mayonnaise Bowl, Hunt's Royal Pattern, 2 3/4 X 6 1/4 In.	165.00
Cut Glass, Mayonnaise Set, Oval Top & Underplate, Harvard Pattern	255.00
Cut Glass, Muffineer, Clear, 6 In.	35.00
Cut Glass, Muffineer, Cranberry, 5 1/2 In.	65.00
Cut Glass, Muffineer, Diamond Point, Green, Silver Lid, 6 In.	185.00
Cut Glass, Muffineer, Nailhead Diamonds, 8 Point Star Base, 5 1/2 In.	55.00
Cut Glass, Muffineer, Red Cut To Clear, Diamond Point, Silver Lid, 6 In.	185.00
Cut Glass, Muffineer, Silver Plated Top Stands, 4 3/4 In.	90.00

Cut Glass, Mustard, Waffle Block, Silver Top	38.00
Cut Glass, Napkin Ring, see Napkin Ring	
Cut Glass, Nappy, American Beauty, Handled, Averbeck, 5 In.	40.00
Cut Glass, Nappy, Athens Pattern, Handle, Dorflinger Greek Key	48.00
Cut Glass, Nappy, Corinthian, Handled, Hawkes, 5 In.	65.00
Cut Glass, Nappy, Cosmos Flowers, Leaves, Serrated Edge, 7 1/2 In.	49.50
Cut Glass, Nappy, Double Knotched Handled, 11 X 8 In.	90.00
Cut Glass, Nappy, Fan & Diamond, Handled, 6 In.	47.50
Cut Glass, Nappy, Feathered Fan, Strawberry Diamond, Handleless, Unger Bros.	75.00
Cut Glass, Nappy, Feathered Fan, Strawberry, Diamond, Crosshatching, Signed	65.00
Cut Glass, Nappy, Flowers, Leaves, Sawtooth Scalloped Edge, 5 In.	20.00
Cut Glass, Nappy, Handled, Hunt's Royal Pattern, 6 In.	185.00
Cut Glass, Nappy, Harvard & Cornflowers, Handled, 8 In.	24.00
Cut Glass, Nappy, Hobstars, Cane, & Fan, 4 Compartment, 2 Handled, 7 In.	135.00
Cut Glass, Nappy, Hobstars, Crosscut Diamond, Ring Handle, Libbey, 6 1/2 In.	65.00
Cut Glass, Nappy, Hobstars, Fans, Strawberry Diamond, Applied Handle, 7 In.	40.00
Cut Glass, Nappy, Hunt's Royal, Handleless, 6 In.	45.00
Cut Glass, Nappy, Lacy Hobstars, Loop Handle	45.00
Cut Glass, Nappy, Nassau, Signed J.Hoare & Co., 6 In.	55.00
Cut Glass, Nappy, One Handle, Hob & Cane, 6 In.Diameter	55.00
Cut Glass, Nappy, Pinwheel, Hobstar, Scalloped Edge, Sections, 8 X 11 In.	95.00
Cut Glass, Nappy, Russian Pattern, Unstarred Hobnail, 6 In.	60.00
Cut Glass, Nappy, Strawberry & Pinwheel, Sawtooth Edging, 6 X 5 1/2 In.	55.00
Cut Glass, Nut Set, Master, 6 5/8 In., Six Servers, 3 3/4 In.	225.00
Cut Glass, Oil Bottle, Whiting Sterling Top, 3 1/4 In.	50.00
Cut Glass, Parfait, Harvard Pattern	50.00
Cut Glass, Parfait, Hobstars, Set Of 5	155.00
Cut Glass, Perfume, Hobstars, Vesicas, Faceted Knob Stopper, 4 In., Pair	250.00
Cut Glass, Perfume, Ruby, Star In Base, Hinged, Silver Cover	35.00
Cut Glass, Perfume, Zipper Pattern, Sterling Top, Ring For Chain, 6 1/2 In.	12.00
Cut Glass, Pitcher, Allover Hobstars, 10 1/2 In.	85.00
Cut Glass, Pitcher, Brunswick Pattern, Hawkes, 9 In.	295.00
Cut Glass, Pitcher, Champagne, Fans & Strawberry Diamond, 12 1/2 In.	225.00
Cut Glass, Pitcher, Cider, Hobstar, Prism & Bull's-Eye, Notched Handle, 8 In.	150.00
Cut Glass, Pitcher, Cider, Hobstars, Cane, Strawberry Diamond & Fan, 8 In.	225.00
Cut Glass, Pitcher, Claret, Encore Pattern, 12 In.	245.00
Cut Glass, Pitcher, Claret, Hobstars On Front, Buzz-Cane Bottom, Prism, 12 In.	250.00
Cut Glass, Pitcher, Claret, Sterling Silver Rim & Spout, Prism, Averbeck	175.00
Cut Glass, Pitcher, Crystal, 3 Deep Cut Stars, Polished Pontil, 8 1/4 In.	45.00
Cut Glass, Pitcher, Daisy Swirls, Star In Squares, 16 Rayed Star Base, 10 In.	125.00
Cut Glass, Pitcher, Double Bull's-Eye Handle, Caning Frames Roses, 10 In.	150.00
Cut Glass, Pitcher, Harvard & Cornflower, Hobstar Centers, 9 1/2 In.	95.00
Cut Glass, Pitcher, Hawkes Devonshire, Triple Notch Handle, Star Bottom	215.00
Cut Glass, Pitcher, Hawkes, Gravic Cut Flowers & Vines, Serrated Edge	225.00
Cut Glass, Pitcher, Hobstar Fan & Diamond, 18-Point Star Base, Hoare, 7 In.	210.00
Cut Glass, Pitcher, Hobstars & Vesicas, Brilliant, 8 In.	96.00
Cut Glass, Pitcher, Hobstars, Diamond, Fan, 9 3/4 In.	85.00
Cut Glass, Pitcher, Hobstars, Fans, Beading, Beveled Handle, Clarke, 9 1/2 In.	175.00
Cut Glass, Pitcher, Hobstars, Oval Patches Of Diamonds, Fans, 11 1/2 In.	125.00
Cut Glass, Pitcher, Hobstars, Pinwheel, Cane, Fan, Notched Handle, 9 1/2 In.	90.00
Cut Glass, Pitcher, Hobstars, Pinwheels, 16 Rayed Star On Base, V Handle	95.00
Cut Glass, Pitcher, Lemonade, Silver Stirrer, Leaves & Vines, Hawkes, 16 In.	180.00
Cut Glass, Pitcher, Lemonade, Zipper & Hobstars, Brilliant, 11 X 6 In.	239.00
Cut Glass, Pitcher, Milk, Celtic, 6 1/2 In.Tall, 6 In.Wide	195.00
Cut Glass, Pitcher, Milk, Handle Cut, Hawkes, 8 1/2 In.	195.00
Cut Glass, Pitcher, Milk, Hobstars, Brilliant, 7 In.	175.00
Cut Glass, Pitcher, Milk, Kalana Lily, Dorflinger, 7 In.	230.00
Cut Glass, Pitcher, Milk, Russian, Starred Buttons, 5 In.	375.00
Cut Glass, Pitcher, Millicent, Hawkes, 8 1/2 X 6 In.	195.00
Cut Glass, Pitcher, Napoleon, Higgins & Seiter, 2 Quart	340.00
Cut Glass, Pitcher, Notched Prism, Hobstars, Diamond Fan, Sterling Top, Beaded	110.00
Cut Glass, Pitcher, Overall Hobstars & Fans, Notched Handle, 7 In.	48.50
Cut Glass, Pitcher, Pinwheel & Strawberry Diamond, 10 In.	15.00
Cut Glass, Pitcher, Pinwheels, Thistles, 9 1/2 In.	95.00
Cut Glass, Pitcher, Pinwheels, 16 Point Rayed Base, 9 1/2 In.	95.00

Cut Glass, Pitcher, Pinwheels, 7 1/2 In. 55.00
Cut Glass, Pitcher, Signed Tuthill, 10 In. 350.00
Cut Glass, Pitcher, Spangled, Bulbous Bottom, Gold & Silver Mica 145.00
Cut Glass, Pitcher, Starred Base, Hobstars, Diamonds, Lip & Handle Cut 90.00
Cut Glass, Pitcher, Strawberries, Diamond, Fan, Dorflinger 225.00
Cut Glass, Pitcher, Sunburst, Notching, Fan, Thumbprints, 3 Notch Handle, 8 In. 95.00
Cut Glass, Pitcher, Syrup, Strawberry Diamond, Fan, 4 In. 55.00
Cut Glass, Pitcher, Tankard, Hobstars, 11 1/4 In. 175.00
Cut Glass, Pitcher, Triple Notch Handle, 32 Point Star Bottom, 8 In. 175.00
Cut Glass, Pitcher, Vintage, Engraved Sterling Overlay, 4 1/2 X 9 1/2 In. 165.00
Cut Glass, Pitcher, Water, Fans, Honeycomb Handle, Bulbous, 8 1/2 In. 150.00
Cut Glass, Pitcher, Water, Fern & Star, Hobstars, 9 1/2 In. 125.00
Cut Glass, Pitcher, Water, Grapes, Libbey 85.00
Cut Glass, Pitcher, Water, Gravic Fruits Band On Middle, Pear Shape, Marked 325.00
Cut Glass, Pitcher, Water, Harvard Cut Flowers, Hobstar Base, Notched Handle 375.00
Cut Glass, Pitcher, Water, Hobstars, Fans, 10 In. 125.00
Cut Glass, Pitcher, Water, Hobstars, Vesicas, Diamond, 8 In. 98.00
Cut Glass, Pitcher, Water, Intaglio Florals, Silverplate Handle, 10 1/2 In. 80.00
Cut Glass, Pitcher, Water, Lid, Glass Insert For Ice, U.S.Zone Germany 48.00
Cut Glass, Pitcher, Water, Notched Handle, Tuthill, 8 1/2 In. 195.00
Cut Glass, Pitcher, Water, Star & Sunburst, 9 1/4 In. 35.00
Cut Glass, Pitcher, Water, Stars & Diamond, 10 In. 95.00
Cut Glass, Pitcher, Water, Thistle & Leaves, 12 In. 95.00
Cut Glass, Pitcher, 24 Point Hobstar, 8 1/2 In. 125.00
Cut Glass, Pitcher, 32 Point Hobstar, Prism & Bull's-Eye, 8 In. 150.00
Cut Glass, Plate, Cake, Basket Weave, Intaglio Center, Pedestal, 10 In. 110.00
Cut Glass, Plate, Cake, Clusters Of Hobstars, Pinwheels On 4 Edges, 12 In. 225.00
Cut Glass, Plate, Cake, Scalloped Edge, Brilliant Cut, 12 In. 275.00
Cut Glass, Plate, Carnation, Hawkes Gravic, 7 In. 110.00
Cut Glass, Plate, Dessert, Signed Hawkes, 6 1/2 In., Set Of 8 .... 110.00
Cut Glass, Plate, Dinner, Signed Unger Bros., 10 1/2 In. 265.00
Cut Glass, Plate, Fans, 11 In. 150.00
Cut Glass, Plate, Roland, Pitkin & Brooks, 12 In. 300.00
Cut Glass, Plate, Russian, 7 In. 125.00
Cut Glass, Plate, Sandwich, Hobstar, Pinwheels, Deep Cutting, 9 In. 90.00
Cut Glass, Plate, Soup, Rock Crystal, Engraved Floral, 9 In., Set Of 12 .... 410.00
Cut Glass, Plate, Tuthill, 5 In. 45.00
Cut Glass, Pot, Flower, Florence Hobstar, Vertical Hobstar Chain, 5 In. 160.00
Cut Glass, Pudding Set, Strawberry Diamond & Fan, Set Of 12 .... 300.00
Cut Glass, Punch Bowl & Base, Crosscut, Scalloped Rim & Base, 12 3/4 In. 300.00
Cut Glass, Punch Bowl, Carnations, Harvard Cut Bands, 2 Pieces, 12 In. 295.00
Cut Glass, Punch Bowl, Hobstar, Bell Tone, Two Piece, 14 X 9 In. 345.00
Cut Glass, Punch Bowl, Strawberry Diamond & Fans, English, C.1800, 11 3/4 In. 150.00
Cut Glass, Punch Bowl, 12 Cups, Pinwheel, 10 1/2 In. 600.00
Cut Glass, Punch Set, 6 Glasses, Bowl, Ladle, Crystal, 14 X 6 1/2 In. 775.00
Cut Glass, Relish, Boat Shaped, Heavily Cut, Pitkin & Brooks, 4 X 6 In. 55.00
Cut Glass, Relish, Central Hobstar, Stars & Diamond Point, 4 1/2 X 12 In. 55.00
Cut Glass, Relish, Fans, Hobstar On Bottom, Crosshatching, Stars, 4 X 11 In. 38.00
Cut Glass, Relish, Feathered Pinwheels, Center Cut, Oval, 6 1/2 X 4 1/2 In. 45.00
Cut Glass, Relish, Harvard Cut, 8 X 4 In. 65.00
Cut Glass, Relish, Hobstar, Chair Bottom, Signed Taylor, 7 1/4 X 6 In. 50.00
Cut Glass, Relish, Mars Pattern, Serrated Edge, 10 1/2 In. 85.00
Cut Glass, Relish, Scalloped Sawtooth Edge, Brilliant Period, 12 In. 65.00
Cut Glass, Rose Bowl, Bleeding Heart, 4 X 19 In. 90.00
Cut Glass, Rose Bowl, Clear Buttons, Russian, 7 X 8 In. 350.00
Cut Glass, Rose Bowl, Harvard And Cornflower, 3 Legs, 7 1/2 X 8 1/2 In. 95.00
Cut Glass, Rose Bowl, Hobnail With Fans Top, Large Hob On Bottom, 8 X 7 In. 120.00
Cut Glass, Rose Bowl, Soft Green, Fleur-De-Lis, Floral Band, Hawkes, 6 X 6 In. 95.00
Cut Glass, Rose Bowl, Strawberry, Diamond, Fan, Stars, Hobstar Bottom, Pedestal 150.00
Cut Glass, Rose Bowl, Thumbprint And X, Blue Cut To Clear 65.00
Cut Glass, Salt & Pepper, Glass Screw On Lids, Faceted Base, 7 In. 22.50
Cut Glass, Salt & Pepper, Ivory Tops 15.00
Cut Glass, Salt & Pepper, Stars, Pair 10.00
Cut Glass, Salt, Amber, Fan Shape, 2 In. 15.00
Cut Glass, Salt, Brilliant, Signed With Maple Leaf 14.00

Cut Glass, Salt, Diamond & Fan, 2 In.	18.00
Cut Glass, Salt, Honeycomb	8.00
Cut Glass, Salt, Round, Pinwheel, Notched Prisms	4.00
Cut Glass, Saltshaker, Mt.Washington, Pansy Decoration, Pair	125.00
Cut Glass, Serving Set, Ray Cut Ends, Silverplated Handles, 10 In., 2 Piece	85.00
Cut Glass, Shade, Mushroom Dome, Hobstar, Pinwheels, Sawtooth, 6 1/2 In.	95.00
Cut Glass, Shaker, Cocktail, Hawkes Type Cut, 18 In.	70.00
Cut Glass, Shaker, Cocktail, Sterling Lid, Signed Hawkes, 13 In.	185.00
Cut Glass, Sherbet, Edged With Silver At Top & Bottom, 3 3/4 In., Set Of 3	27.50
Cut Glass, Sherbet, Kalana Lily, Dorflinger	60.00
Cut Glass, Sherbet, Stemmed, 9 Piece	22.50
Cut Glass, Spittoon, Lady's, Cut & Shaped	170.00
Cut Glass, Spittoon, Lady's, Devonshire, Flowers & Leaves, 8 1/2 In.	145.00
Cut Glass, Spittoon, Lady's, Stars, Diamond & Fan	325.00
Cut Glass, Spooner, Corset Shape, Bull's Eye, Strawberry Diamond & Fan	95.00
Cut Glass, Spooner, Crosscut Diamond-Tooth Rim, 24 Point Rayed Base, 5 In.	45.00
Cut Glass, Spooner, Crosscut Diamonds, Tooth Rim, 4 3/4 X 3 1/4 In.	55.00
Cut Glass, Spooner, Hobstar, Strawberry, Diamond Fans, 4 1/2 In.	65.00
Cut Glass, Spooner, Middlesex, 5 In.	70.00
Cut Glass, Spooner, Pinwheel, 2 Handled, 4 1/2 In.	125.00
Cut Glass, Spooner, Signed Unger Bros., 4 In.	150.00
Cut Glass, Spooner, Thumbprint, Handled, 4 1/2 In.	40.00
Cut Glass, Spooner, 2 Handles, Hobstars	125.00
Cut Glass, Stein, Russian Cut, Pewter Lid, 8 X 4 In.	130.00
Cut Glass, Stickpin Holder, Sterling Base	34.00
Cut Glass, String Holder, Zipper & Prism, Lacy Gorham Sterling Top	85.00
Cut Glass, Sugar & Creamer, Basketweave, Flowers & Leaves, Pedestaled, Hawkes	185.00
Cut Glass, Sugar & Creamer, Bergen's Newport	85.00
Cut Glass, Sugar & Creamer, Boatshape, Allover Cutting, Flint	82.00
Cut Glass, Sugar & Creamer, Deeply Cut & Serrated, Thumb Handles, Libbey	90.00
Cut Glass, Sugar & Creamer, Diamond Motif, Intaglio Daisy Design, Heavy	125.00
Cut Glass, Sugar & Creamer, Diamond Point, Concave Centers Of Flower Design	160.00
Cut Glass, Sugar & Creamer, Feathered Pinwheels, Vesicas, Notching, Fan, Large	65.00
Cut Glass, Sugar & Creamer, Flowers On Each Side, Intaglio, Signed Hunt	60.00
Cut Glass, Sugar & Creamer, Geometric, Hobstars, Brilliant Period	55.00
Cut Glass, Sugar & Creamer, Heart Pattern, Oval	185.00
Cut Glass, Sugar & Creamer, Hobstar, Scalloped Top, Star Base	75.00
Cut Glass, Sugar & Creamer, Hobstars Zipper & Fans, Libbey	90.00
Cut Glass, Sugar & Creamer, Hobstars, Crosshatching & Fans	35.00
Cut Glass, Sugar & Creamer, Hobstars, Diamond & Fan, Scalloped Border	72.00
Cut Glass, Sugar & Creamer, Hobstars, Fans & Hobnails, 2 1/4 In.	145.00
Cut Glass, Sugar & Creamer, Kalana Lily, Dorflinger, Pedestaled	250.00
Cut Glass, Sugar & Creamer, Large Hobstars	65.00
Cut Glass, Sugar & Creamer, Marked Maple Leaf Elite	87.50
Cut Glass, Sugar & Creamer, Miniature, Vesicas, Cane, Fan, St.Louis Handles	85.00
Cut Glass, Sugar & Creamer, Pedestal, Chains Of Hobstars	125.00
Cut Glass, Sugar & Creamer, Pedestal, Harvard Pattern	450.00
Cut Glass, Sugar & Creamer, Pinwheel	88.00
Cut Glass, Sugar & Creamer, Pinwheels, Stars, Fans, Hobstar On Base	57.00
Cut Glass, Sugar & Creamer, Russian At Top, One Inch Band	135.00
Cut Glass, Sugar & Creamer, Sawtooth Top, Flowers, Allover Cut	60.00
Cut Glass, Sugar & Creamer, Signed Eggington, 3 In.	150.00
Cut Glass, Sugar & Creamer, Star & Leaf Design	25.00
Cut Glass, Sugar & Creamer, Star With Variations, Notched Handles	89.00
Cut Glass, Sugar & Creamer, Starflower Decoration	69.00
Cut Glass, Sugar & Creamer, Sunburst, Signed Pitkin & Brooks	195.00
Cut Glass, Sugar & Creamer, Swirling Stars, Hobstars, Fans, Notched Handles	60.00
Cut Glass, Sugar Shaker, Chair Bottom, Silver Plate Top	35.00
Cut Glass, Sugar, Cross Split Vesica, Hobstar Base, Triple Cut Handles	65.00
Cut Glass, Syrup, Light Cut Flowers & Leaves, Silver Hinged Top, 1916, 4 In.	40.00
Cut Glass, Syrup, Prism Cut, American	50.00
Cut Glass, Syrup, Silver Plated Cover	110.00
Cut Glass, Syrup, Strawberry Diamond & Fan, Allover Cut, Lid & Handle	65.00
Cut Glass, Tankard, Allover Floral, Thumbprint Helmet Top, 1910, 10 1/2 In.	135.00
Cut Glass, Tankard, Flashed Hobstars, Crosscut Diamonds, 9 1/2 In.	90.00

Cut Glass, Tankard, Hobstar, Cane, Strawberry, 10 In. 95.00
Cut Glass, Tankard, Hobstars, Deep Cutting, 8 In. 115.00
Cut Glass, Tankard, Hobstars, Fans, Crosshatching, Punty Notched Handle 135.00
Cut Glass, Tankard, Hobstars, Fish, Brilliant Period 85.00
Cut Glass, Tankard, Notched Handle, Alternating Panels Of Cane, Hobstars 185.00
Cut Glass, Tankard, Notched Prisms, Beehive On Sterling Silver Top, 12 In. 164.00
Cut Glass, Tankard, Sterling Silver Scrolled Rim, Brunswick 97.00
Cut Glass, Tankard, Swirl & Ribbon, Double Notched Handle, 10 1/2 In. 105.00
Cut Glass, Tazza, Intaglio Fruit & Leaves, Libbey, 7 1/2 In. 450.00
Cut Glass, Tooth Powder, Russian Cut, Starred Button, Sterling Cap, 7 In. 110.00
Cut Glass, Toothpick, Cane Pattern, Cradle 30.00
Cut Glass, Toothpick, Deep Intaglio Cut Poppies 35.00
Cut Glass, Toothpick, Floral, Pedestal, Pair 20.00
Cut Glass, Toothpick, Footed, Signed Fry 28.00
Cut Glass, Toothpick, Geometric Cutting, Pedestaled 42.00
Cut Glass, Toothpick, Intaglio, 8 Sided 45.00
Cut Glass, Toothpick, Pinwheels, Notched Prisms 20.00
Cut Glass, Toothpick, Swirling Hobstar 25.00
Cut Glass, Tray, Bread, Flowers, Fan, Crosshatching, 13 In. 90.00
Cut Glass, Tray, Bun, Notched Prisms, 11 1/2 X 8 1/2 In. 160.00
Cut Glass, Tray, Celery, Russian Cut Pattern, Rectangular, 4 X 9 In. 125.00
Cut Glass, Tray, Celery, Russian Pattern, Rectangular, 4 X 9 In. 120.00
Cut Glass, Tray, Cranberry Cut To Clear, Stars, Notched Edge, 13 1/4 In. 225.00
Cut Glass, Tray, Gloria Pattern, Libbey, Round, 7 3/4 In. 150.00
Cut Glass, Tray, Hobstar Center With Radiants Around, 11 1/2 In. 110.00
Cut Glass, Tray, Ice Cream, Bontemps Pattern, 14 X 9 In. 310.00
Cut Glass, Tray, Ice Cream, Bontemps, Straus, Hand Polished, 14 X 9 In. 310.00
Cut Glass, Tray, Ice Cream, Deep Vesicas, 14 1/2 In. 145.00
Cut Glass, Tray, Ice Cream, Fishtail Ends, 16 1/2 X 9 1/2 X 2 1/4 In. 895.00
Cut Glass, Tray, Ice Cream, Harvard Cut, 8 X 14 In. 350.00
Cut Glass, Tray, Ice Cream, Hobstar & Diamond, Oval, 10 X 7 In. 85.00
Cut Glass, Tray, Ice Cream, Hobstar Center, Floral & Mixer Cut, 13 1/4 In. 195.00
Cut Glass, Tray, Ice Cream, Hobstar, Diamond, Fans, Flakes, 16 1/2 In. 135.00
Cut Glass, Tray, Ice Cream, Hobstars & Crosscut Vesicas, 22 X 7 1/2 In. 160.00
Cut Glass, Tray, Ice Cream, Hobstars, Fans & Pin Wheels, 14 X 7 1/2 In. 150.00
Cut Glass, Tray, Ice Cream, Kimberly, 14 X 7 1/2 In. 175.00
Cut Glass, Tray, Ice Cream, Large Vesicas, 14 1/2 In. 145.00
Cut Glass, Tray, Ice Cream, Oval, Hobstars, 14 X 7 1/2 In. 245.00
Cut Glass, Tray, Ice Cream, Strawberries, Diamond, Hobstars, Fans, 14 1/2 In. 152.00
Cut Glass, Tray, Pin, Prisms & Strawberry Diamond, Bow Shaped, 7 In. 40.00
Cut Glass, Tub, Ice, Cane Bottom, 4 Cane Panels, 4 Cornflowers Panels, Octagon 145.00
Cut Glass, Tub, Ice, High Tabs, Harvard Pattern 295.00
Cut Glass, Tub, Ice, Hobstars, Strawberry Diamonds & Fans, 7 In. 175.00
Cut Glass, Tub, Ice, Strawberry, Hobstar Base, Russian, 5 1/4 X 6 1/2 In. 285.00
Cut Glass, Tumbler Set, Blanks, 16 Point Star Base, Set Of 6 .... 135.00
Cut Glass, Tumbler, Cordial, Cut From Amethyst To Clear In Pineapple Fan 35.00
Cut Glass, Tumbler, Cut Floral Designs, Hawkes 20.00
Cut Glass, Tumbler, Fans, Strawberry, Crosshatch 20.00
Cut Glass, Tumbler, Floral And Leaf Pattern, Rayed Base, Set Of Four 67.50
Cut Glass, Tumbler, Hobstar & Panel, Hawkes 20.00
Cut Glass, Tumbler, Hobstars, Diamond, Fan 25.00
Cut Glass, Tumbler, Intaglio Ferns & Cattails, Libbey 30.00
Cut Glass, Tumbler, Intaglio Leaves, Star Shaped Flowers 55.00
Cut Glass, Tumbler, Kalana Lily, Dorflinger, 4 In. 45.00
Cut Glass, Tumbler, Miniature, Deep Stars, Octagons, Set Of 6 .... 35.00
Cut Glass, Tumbler, Russian Pattern .... 69.00 To 70.00
Cut Glass, Tumbler, Straw & Fan 55.00
Cut Glass, Tumbler, Whiskey, Pinwheel & Fan 20.00
Cut Glass, Urn, Wine Decanter, 14 In. 200.00
Cut Glass, Vase, American, Signed Bergen, 12 3/4 In. 575.00
Cut Glass, Vase, Apple Green Shading, Dorflinger, 17 3/4 X 6 1/2 In. 295.00
Cut Glass, Vase, Bands Of Hobstars, Bull's-Eyes, Notched Prism, 24 Point Base 175.00
Cut Glass, Vase, Blue, Cut To Clear, Bull's-Eye & Thumbprint, 6 1/2 In. 45.00
Cut Glass, Vase, Brilliant, Overall Cut, 10 In. 70.00
Cut Glass, Vase, Bull's-Eye & Prism, Hawkes, 14 In. 250.00

Cut Glass, Vase, Buzz Star, 10 In. 35.00
Cut Glass, Vase, Buzz Star, 4 X 4 X 2 1/2 In. 35.00
Cut Glass, Vase, Cane, Intaglio Leaf Band, Roden Bros., Ltd., Toronto, 10 In. 110.00
Cut Glass, Vase, Corset Shape, Deep Cut Roses & Buds, Notched Rim, 12 In. 75.00
Cut Glass, Vase, Covered With Hobstars & Variants, 18 In. 325.00
Cut Glass, Vase, Cranberry Cut To Clear, Corset Shape, 10 X 9 In. 125.00
Cut Glass, Vase, Devonshire Variant, 8 In. 75.00
Cut Glass, Vase, Diamond Cut Velvet, Red, Pink, 5 1/2 In., Pair 450.00
Cut Glass, Vase, Diamond, Star, Vesicas, 4 1/4 In. 69.00
Cut Glass, Vase, Emerald Green To Clear, 7 X 11 1/2 In. 500.00
Cut Glass, Vase, Engraved Flowers, Double Triform Handles, Hawkes, 5 3/4 In. 110.00
Cut Glass, Vase, Engraved Scene, Artist Signed, 10 In. 575.00
Cut Glass, Vase, European Cut Amethyst To Clear, Gold Floral, 14 In. 35.00
Cut Glass, Vase, Fan, Harvard, Daisy, Pedestaled, 8 1/4 X 6 1/4 In. 95.00
Cut Glass, Vase, Fern, Flower & Butterfly Scalloped Top, Star Base, 12 In. 45.00
Cut Glass, Vase, Hobstar & Deeply Carved Flowers, Panels, 10 In. 110.00
Cut Glass, Vase, Hobstar & Intaglio, Silver Thread, 8 In. 350.00
Cut Glass, Vase, Hobstars & Cane, 12 In. 85.00
Cut Glass, Vase, Hobstars Around Middle, Ruffled Top, Hawkes, 9 3/4 In. 65.00
Cut Glass, Vase, Hobstars In Vesicas, Tricornered, 2 1/4 X 2 1/4 In. 45.00
Cut Glass, Vase, Hobstars, Diamond Points, Lozenges, Fans, 17 3/4 In. 185.00
Cut Glass, Vase, Hobstars, Diamond, & Fan, Trumpet Shape, 10 In. 65.00
Cut Glass, Vase, Hobstars, Raised Centers, Flashed Fans, Cross Cut, 16 In. 175.00
Cut Glass, Vase, Hobstars, Strawberry & Crosscut Diamonds, 10 In. 150.00
Cut Glass, Vase, Horse Show Pattern, Cutout Top & Bottom, Good Luck, 12 In. 255.00
Cut Glass, Vase, Hour Glass Shape, Can & Daisy Pattern, Large, 12 In. 130.00
Cut Glass, Vase, Intaglio Flowers & Ivy, Signed Sinclaire, 5 In. 95.00
Cut Glass, Vase, Intaglio Grapes & Leaves In Heart, Crosshatch ....*Illus* 475.00
Cut Glass, Vase, Intaglio, Engraved Deer & Tree, 4 3/4 X 10 1/2 In. 110.00
Cut Glass, Vase, Iris & Leaves, Shaded Yellow To Clear, 11 1/2 In. 175.00
Cut Glass, Vase, Pinwheels, Fans, 16 Point Star In Base, 10 1/2 In. 95.00
Cut Glass, Vase, Scalloped Top, Brilliant Cut, 12 X 5 In. 110.00
Cut Glass, Vase, Split Vesica & Thumbprint Flower, Daisy 225.00
Cut Glass, Vase, Strawberry Diamond, Hobstars, Cane, Pedestal, J.Hoare, 13 In. 295.00
Cut Glass, Vase, Strawberry, Diamond & Fan, 8 1/2 In. 45.00
Cut Glass, Vase, Strawberry, Diamond, Fan, Slender, 8 1/2 X 1 3/4 X 2 3/4 In. 45.00
Cut Glass, Vase, Sunbursts Around Top, 12 In. 185.00
Cut Glass, Vase, Swag, Oval & Star, Art Nouveau, Hawkes, 12 In. 150.00
Cut Glass, Vase, Sweet Pea, Kalana Pansy, Dorflinger, 12 In. 135.00
Cut Glass, Vase, Teardrop Engraved Knob, Libbey, 10 In. 95.00
Cut Glass, Vase, Triple Square, Clark, 10 In. 250.00
Cut Glass, Vase, Trumpet Shape, Signed Hawkes, 11 1/2 In. 130.00
Cut Glass, Vase, Trumpet Top, Pedestal Foot, In Panels, 18 1/4 X 7 1/4 In. 275.00
Cut Glass, Vase, Trumpet, Brunswick Pattern, Hawkes, 10 In. 165.00
Cut Glass, Vase, Trumpet, Brunswick Pattern, Signed Hawkes, 13 3/4 In. 250.00
Cut Glass, Vase, Trumpet, Fan, Strawberry Diamond, 6-Sided Zipper Stem, 12 In. 85.00
Cut Glass, Vase, Trumpet, Heavy Allover Cut, Including Base, 12 1/2 In. 90.00
Cut Glass, Vase, Trumpet, Rayed Base, Diamond Cut, Stem, Stars, Fans, 14 In. 145.00
Cut Glass, Vase, Trumpet, Strawberry, Fan, Hobstar, Scalloped Base, 10 In. 85.00

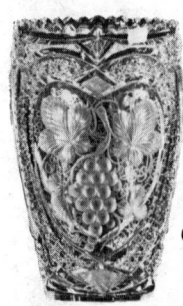

Cut Glass, Vase, Intaglio Grapes & Leaves In Heart, Crosshatch

Cut Glass, Wine Ewer,
Intaglio In Baroque French Frame, Pair

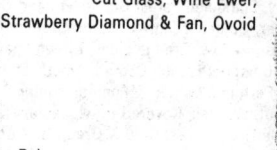

Cut Glass, Wine Ewer,
Strawberry Diamond & Fan, Ovoid

Cut Glass, Vase, Tube Shape, Crosshatching On Panels, 12 In.	30.00
Cut Glass, Vase, Violet, 3 1/4 X 3 1/4 In.	70.00
Cut Glass, Vase, Yellow To Clear, Floral, Thumbprint Base, 4 1/4 X 5 In.	90.00
Cut Glass, Vase, 2 Panels Roses & Leaves, Crosshatch Around Panels, 12 In.	40.00
Cut Glass, Vase, 20 Point Hobstar Base, Hawkes, 14 In.	250.00
Cut Glass, Water Set, Buzz, Finecuts, Fans, 11 Piece	245.00
Cut Glass, Water Set, Flowers, Leaves, 7 Piece	250.00
Cut Glass, Water Set, Hobstars, Strawberry, Notch Prisms, 7 Piece	285.00
Cut Glass, Water Set, Pinwheels, 7 Piece	425.00
Cut Glass, Water Set, Red Block, Squat Pitcher & 6 Tumblers	245.00
Cut Glass, Whiskey, Colored, Set In Farberware Castor Frame	65.00
Cut Glass, Wine Ewer, Intaglio In Baroque French Frame, Pair *Illus*	475.00
Cut Glass, Wine Ewer, Strawberry Diamond & Fan, Ovoid *Illus*	65.00
Cut Glass, Wine, Double Knob, Prism Stem, 6 1/2 In.	25.00
Cut Glass, Wine, Kalana Lily, Dorflinger, Small	25.00
Cut Glass, Wine, Roses, Diamond Hatch, Ruby Cut To Clear Stemmed, Set Of 12	150.00
Cut Glass, Wine, Russian, Cranberry Cut To Clear, Flint, Honeycomb Stem	85.00
Cut Glass, Wine, Straw & Fan	55.00
Cut Glass, Wine, Three Fruits Gravic Pattern, Tall, Hawkes, 6 1/2 In.	55.00

Cut velvet is a special type of art glass made with two layers of blown glass, which shows a raised pattern. It usually had an acid finish or velvetlike texture. It was made by many glass factories during the late Victorian years.

Cut Velvet, Pale Blue, Dark Blue Ribbing, Ruffled Top, Cased In White, 4 In.	130.00
Cut Velvet, Vase, Green, 4 3/4 In.	60.00
Cut Velvet, Vase, Pink & White, 9 In.	225.00
Cut Velvet, Vase, Pink On White, Ruffled Top, 9 In.	275.00
D'Albret, Paperweight, see Paperweight, D'Albret	

D'Argental was a French cameo glassmaker of the late Victorian period. The D'Argental factory made multilayered, acid-cut cameo glass in France in the late nineteenth century. The glass is decorated with floral or scenic designs.

D'Argental, Box, Powder, Flowers & Leaves, Brown & Orange Cut To Amber	395.00
D'Argental, Box, Powder, Red Roses Cut On Gold, Covered	295.00
D'Argental, Cachepot, Band Of Butterflies, Magenta, 4 1/2 In.	395.00
D'Argental, Vase, Bleeding Hearts, 8 In.	375.00
D'Argental, Vase, Blue Lilies, Cameo, 5 In.	275.00
D'Argental, Vase, Cameo, Frosted Aqua Foilage Cameo In Wine Red, 4 1/2 In.	290.00
D'Argental, Vase, Cameo, Gourd, Pine Branches, Needles, Cones, Green, Signed	525.00
D'Argental, Vase, Frosted Aqua Ground, Foliage Cames In Red, RC-R, 4 In.	290.00
D'Argental, Vase, Leaves & Blackberries, 3 Colors, Cameo, 8 X 3 In.	545.00
D'Argental, Vase, Roses, Deep Cut, Slender, Dark Red	350.00
D'Argental, Vase, Trees, Chateau On Hill, Frosted Gold Background, 11 In.	495.00
Daguerreotype, see Photography, Daguerreotype	
Danish Christmas Plate, see Collector, Plate, Bing & Grondahl, Collector, Plate, Royal Copenhagen	

Daum
Nancy

Daum Nancy is the mark used by Auguste and Antonin Daum on pieces of French cameo glass made after 1875.

Daum Nancy, Ashtray, Enameled Forest Scene, Frosted Ground, Square, 5 1/4 In.	365.00
Daum Nancy, Atomizer, Golden Yellow Stippled Ground, Orange Lilies, Leaves	250.00
Daum Nancy, Atomizer, Yellow, Orange Lilies, Brown Leaves, 7 1/2 In.	265.00
Daum Nancy, Bottle, Cologne, French Cameo, Amethyst, Irises, 8 1/8 In.	365.00
Daum Nancy, Bottle, Perfume, Cameo & Enamel Winter Scene, Signed, 9 In.	575.00
Daum Nancy, Bowl Set, Wassail, Covered Bowl, Ladle, Tray, 10 Cups	450.00
Daum Nancy, Bowl, Berries, Leaves, Gold & Green Ground, Oval, 11 1/2 In.	475.00
Daum Nancy, Bowl, Cameo, Green, Leaves, Berries, Signed, 5 X 2 1/4 In.	200.00
Daum Nancy, Bowl, Cameo, Scenic, Three Colors, 8 X 4 In.	525.00
Daum Nancy, Bowl, Camphor, Purple & Green Flowers, Oval, 7 1/2 X 11 1/2 In.	550.00
Daum Nancy, Bowl, Carved Sweet Peas, Leaves & Vines, Acid Finish, 8 In.	275.00
Daum Nancy, Bowl, Carved Winter Scene, Yellow Ground, 3 1/2 X 1 3/4 In.	190.00
Daum Nancy, Bowl, Gold Foil, Spatterings, Silveria, Orange Layers, 3 In.	150.00
Daum Nancy, Bowl, Mottled Green & Royal Blue, Signed, 6 X 3 In.	95.00
Daum Nancy, Bowl, Mottled, Metallic Inclusions, C.1930, 8 3/4 In.	200.00
Daum Nancy, Bowl, Rose, French Cameo, Pastel Colors, 3 1/4 X 2 3/4 In.	225.00
Daum Nancy, Bowl, Silveria, Gold Foil Spatterings, Mottled Orange, 4 In.	225.00
Daum Nancy, Bowl, Smoke, Tiers, Signed, 12 In.	450.00
Daum Nancy, Bowl, Sweet Peas Carved In Gloss, Leaves, Vines, Round, 8 In.	285.00
Daum Nancy, Bowl, White, Lavender, Brown, Shoreline, Pine Cones, 2 3/8 In.	194.00
Daum Nancy, Bowl, Yellow To Purple Pebbly Ground, Cornflowers, 6 In.	255.00
Daum Nancy, Box, Cameo, Bees, Stalks Of Wheat, Gold Enamel Trim	1050.00
Daum Nancy, Box, Covered, Orange, Red, Yellow, 8 In.	250.00
Daum Nancy, Box, Frosty Pink To Light Green, Cut Flowers, Gold Tracery	450.00
Daum Nancy, Box, Powder, Flowers, Red & Brown, Gold Background, Square Base	595.00
Daum Nancy, Box, Powder, Pink To Frosty Green, Cameo Floral, Gold Tracery	395.00
Daum Nancy, Bud Vase, Winter Landscape, Gray, Pink, Green, Black, C.1900, 8 In.	1600.00
Daum Nancy, Chandelier, Peonies, Leafage, Lobed Bowl, Chevrons, Carved, C.1925	1400.00
Daum Nancy, Cruet, Apricot, Frosted Stopper & Handle, Gold Trim, 4 1/2 In.	450.00
Daum Nancy, Cup, Intaglio Thistle, Gold Trim, Reeded Handles, Pair	125.00
Daum Nancy, Flask, Lady's, Carved Lavender To White, Silver Top & Cup	248.00
Daum Nancy, Holder, Card, Carved Trees, Sailboat Scene, 1 1/2 X 5 X 3 3/4 In.	265.00
Daum Nancy, Lamp, Bright Green Geometrics On Orange & Yellow, 13 In.	575.00
Daum Nancy, Lamp, Night, Dragonfly, Soft Pastel, 20 1/2 In.	2500.00
Daum Nancy, Lamp, Nightlight, Scenic, Black Amethyst, Acid Cut, 6 1/8 In.	365.00
Daum Nancy, Lamp, Serpent, Mottled, C.1925, Edgar Brandt, 41 In. .... *Illus*	5000.00
Daum Nancy, Pitcher, Enameled Leaves, Orange Flowers, White Ground, 12 In	395.00
Daum Nancy, Planter, Purple & Green Laurel, 7 1/2 X 11 1/2 X 3 1/2 In.	550.00
Daum Nancy, Plate, French Cameo, Triangular, Gold, Magenta Floral, 12 In.	950.00
Daum Nancy, Plate, 2 Corners Turned Up, Floral, Colorful, 6 X 4 1/2 In.	450.00
Daum Nancy, Rose Bowl, Blue Bachelor's Buttons, Small, Signed	256.00
Daum Nancy, Salt Dip, Carved & Enameled Black Tree Scene, Tab Handles	135.00
Daum Nancy, Salt Dip, Carved & Enameled Snow Scene, 1 1/4 X 2 In.	225.00
Daum Nancy, Salt Dip, Enameled Black Forest On Frosted White, Green, 1 In.	395.00
Daum Nancy, Salt, Oval, Frosted, Cameo Floral Enameled Gold, Black, 2 In.	145.00
Daum Nancy, Shot Glass, Pink, Gold Flowers, Nothing Without Love	215.00
Daum Nancy, Shot Glass, Scenic Work, Blue Background, Gold Signed	275.00
Daum Nancy, Toothpick, Barrel Shape, Enameled Forest On Mottled Gilt, 2 In.	185.00
Daum Nancy, Tumbler, Carved Gold Leaves & White Berries, Cranberry Ground	195.00

Daum Nancy, Lamp, Serpent, Mottled, C.1925, Edgar Brandt, 41 In.

Daum Nancy, Tumbler, Carved Purple Grapes, Magenta & White Leaves, 5 In. 240.00
Daum Nancy, Tumbler, Cranberry, Cameo Cut Mistletoe, White Berries, 3 1/2 In. 125.00
Daum Nancy, Tumbler, Forest Scene, Carved & Enameled, Barrel Shaped, 5 In. 425.00
Daum Nancy, Tumbler, French Cameo, Barrel Shaped, Enameled Floral, 5 In. 350.00
Daum Nancy, Tumbler, Frosted Mistletoe, Blue Highlights, Gold Rim, 5 In. 150.00
Daum Nancy, Tumbler, Intaglio Pattern Of Fruit, C.1910, Deep Blue 95.00
Daum Nancy, Tumbler, Lady Slippers, Frosted, White To Gold, Barrel Shape 245.00
Daum Nancy, Vase, Acid Cut, Gold Ground, Ivy Leaves Band, Footed, 7 1/4 In. 150.00
Daum Nancy, Vase, Acid-Etched Green Glass, Cross Of Lorraine, 7 1/2 In. 235.00
Daum Nancy, Vase, Allover Raised Floral, Lilac, 6 In. 110.00
Daum Nancy, Vase, Art Deco Dancing Girls, Blue Crystal, C.1930, 11 In. 650.00
Daum Nancy, Vase, Autumn Leaves, Molted Colors, 12 In. 375.00
Daum Nancy, Vase, Autumn Scene, 8 1/2 In. 598.00
Daum Nancy, Vase, Blossoms, Veining, Yellow & Red, Signed, 6 3/4 In. 1150.00
Daum Nancy, Vase, Blue Mottling, Blue & White Flowers, Cut Leaves, 11 In. 525.00
Daum Nancy, Vase, Blue, Ovoid, Clear Lines & Dots, 10 In. 150.00
Daum Nancy, Vase, Blue, Yellow, & Green, Square Bottom, 24 1/2 In. 350.00
Daum Nancy, Vase, Boughs & Applied Cones On Yellow & Pink, C.1900, 8 In. 300.00
Daum Nancy, Vase, Brown & Russet, Metal Holder, L.Majorelle, 5 X 4 1/2 In. 310.00
Daum Nancy, Vase, Brown Vegetation On Pink, Incised Signature, 16 1/2 In. 675.00
Daum Nancy, Vase, Brown, Orange, Yellow, Hammered Effect, Signed, 12 In. 700.00
Daum Nancy, Vase, Bud, Green & Violet Floral, Lt.Blue Background, 7 In. 295.00
Daum Nancy, Vase, Bud, 1 Acid Cutting, Enameled Violets, 9 In. 350.00
Daum Nancy, Vase, Carved & Enameled Leaves On Yellow, 4 1/4 In. 275.00
Daum Nancy, Vase, Carved Floral & Leaves Spider Web, Frosted, 3 3/4 In. 165.00
Daum Nancy, Vase, Carved Leaves & Berries, Frosted Cream, 3 1/8 X 2 1/4 In. 225.00
Daum Nancy, Vase, Carved Rose, Pink Florals, Pale Green & Lavender, 16 In. 375.00
Daum Nancy, Vase, Carved Roses, 5 In. 195.00
Daum Nancy, Vase, Chartreuse, Green And Deep Blue, 6 In. 260.00
Daum Nancy, Vase, Cluthra-Like Mottled, Purple Base, Cylindrical, 15 3/4 In. 150.00
Daum Nancy, Vase, Daisy Leaf Pattern, Green & Lilac, Coralene, 6 X 12 1/2 In. 290.00
Daum Nancy, Vase, Diamond Shape, Winter Scene, 4 X 6 3/4 In. 375.00
Daum Nancy, Vase, Dutch Scene, Black Enamel, Opaque Frosted Ground, 8 In. 395.00
Daum Nancy, Vase, Edelweiss, White, Green, Blue & Yellow Center, Signed, 7 In. 475.00
Daum Nancy, Vase, Emerald Green, Wine Red Foliage, Stippled, 2 1/2 X 6 In. 275.00
Daum Nancy, Vase, Enameled Black Forest, Green Pedestal, Frosted, 4 1/4 In. 425.00
Daum Nancy, Vase, Enameled Sweet Peas & Leaves, Cameo, 12 1/2 In. 595.00
Daum Nancy, Vase, Enameled Violets On Mottled White To Purple, 1 5/8 In. 300.00
Daum Nancy, Vase, Floral, Stems, Rectangular, Signed, 9 In. 485.00
Daum Nancy, Vase, Flower Form, Olive Green & Chocolate Brown, 22 1/4 In. 650.00
Daum Nancy, Vase, Flower Form, Signed Degue, Blue On White, 19 1/2 In. 350.00
Daum Nancy, Vase, Forest Scene, Carved & Enameled, Frosted Ground, 14 In. 395.00
Daum Nancy, Vase, Frosted Green, Leaves, Berries, Acid Cut, Enameled, 1 3/8 In. 175.00
Daum Nancy, Vase, Frosted Yellow Translucent Satin, Boat Scene, 11 7/8 In. 425.00
Daum Nancy, Vase, Frosted, Green & Gold Leaves & Berries, Enameled, 13 In. 650.00
Daum Nancy, Vase, Gold, Band Of Ivy Leaves, Footed, ACB, 7 1/4 In. 150.00
Daum Nancy, Vase, Golden-Brown, Signed, France, 4 1/2 In. 325.00
Daum Nancy, Vase, Green Frosted, Brown Matte, Copper Leaves, 18 In. 525.00
Daum Nancy, Vase, Green, Gold Trim, Cylindrical, 13 3/4 X 4 1/4 In. 280.00
Daum Nancy, Vase, Horn Shape, Acid Etched Signature, 14 1/2 In. 250.00
Daum Nancy, Vase, Ice Green, Deep Cutting, 17 In. 600.00
Daum Nancy, Vase, Inverted Bell Shape, Lake, Trees, Rushes, Purple, Blue, 4 In. 325.00
Daum Nancy, Vase, Iris On Frosted Blue To Black, 7 1/4 In. 250.00
Daum Nancy, Vase, Light Blue Mottled, Flowers In Blue & White Cameo, 11 In. 650.00
Daum Nancy, Vase, Light Blue, Signed, 10 1/4 X 5 1/4 In. 150.00
Daum Nancy, Vase, Lorraine Cross, Jade Green, Applied Leaves, Signed, 5 In. 195.00
Daum Nancy, Vase, Mimosa, Square, Acid Cut, Enameled, 3 7/8 In. 210.00
Daum Nancy, Vase, Miniature, Swan Scene, 2 In. 250.00
Daum Nancy, Vase, Mottled Blue Green, 5 X 7 In. 175.00
Daum Nancy, Vase, Mottled Leaves, Stems, Padded Bleeding Hearts, Green, 5 In. 325.00
Daum Nancy, Vase, Mottled Red & Blue Splatter, 4 Crimpings, 4 1/2 In. 99.00
Daum Nancy, Vase, Opalescent Peach, Green Cameo Floral, 7 In. 475.00
Daum Nancy, Vase, Oval, Enameled Florals, Mottled Green & Rose, 3 7/8 In. 300.00
Daum Nancy, Vase, Padded Orange Flowers, Signed, 12 1/2 In. 725.00
Daum Nancy, Vase, Pale Amber, Translucent Body, Leaves, Bulbous, 9 1/4 In. 750.00

Daum Nancy, Vase, Pale Amber, 9 1/4 In. 750.00
Daum Nancy, Vase, Pastel Colors, Signed, 4 X 1 1/2 In. 150.00
Daum Nancy, Vase, Peach To Purple, Enameled Berries, Signed, 21 1/4 In. 975.00
Daum Nancy, Vase, Pink, Red, Flowers & Leaves, Ovoid Conical Shape, 8 1/2 In. 895.00
Daum Nancy, Vase, River, Pine Trees, Gray, Black, Green, Signed, C.1900, 5 In. 100.00
Daum Nancy, Vase, Rooster, Lion, Goat, & Deer, Gold Mottled Frosted, 3 3/4 In. 325.00
Daum Nancy, Vase, Sailboat & Mountain On Pink Frosted Ground, 8 1/2 In. 425.00
Daum Nancy, Vase, Sailboats, Rocks, Gold Satin, Black, Signed, 12 In. 450.00
Daum Nancy, Vase, Snow Laden Trees, Diamond Shape, 4 X 3 1/4 In. 375.00
Daum Nancy, Vase, Snow Scene, Miniature, 2 3/4 In. 450.00
Daum Nancy, Vase, Stems & Raspberry Garlands, Red Brown Leaves, 8 In. 450.00
Daum Nancy, Vase, Sylveria, Metallic Inclusions In Amber, 25 3/4 In. 1200.00
Daum Nancy, Vase, Top & Bottom, Triangular, Signed, 30 3/4 In. 800.00
Daum Nancy, Vase, Translucent Amber Body, Dark Green May Apple Leaves, 4 In. 750.00
Daum Nancy, Vase, Translucent Off-White, Trees, Leaves, Pink Clouds, 6 1/4 In. 375.00
Daum Nancy, Vase, Trees, Bat In Flight, Black, 3 Sided, 3 1/2 In. 165.00
Daum Nancy, Vase, Winter Scene, Cameo, Barren Forest Trees, Snow, Acid Cut 750.00
Daum Nancy, Vase, Winter Scene, Diamond Shape, 4 X 3 1/4 In. 375.00
Daum Nancy, Vase, 6 Boats, Intaglio Cut Clouds, Orange, Green, Yellow, Brown 575.00

Davenport pottery and porcelain were made at the Davenport Factory in Longport, Staffordshire, England, from 1793 to 1887. Earthenwares, creamwares, porcelains, ironstone wares, and other products were made. Most of the pieces are marked with a form of the word Davenport.

Davenport, Creamer, Nankin, C.1862 .... 15.00
Davenport, Dessert Set, Gilded, Green Border, Florals, C.1820, 12 Piece 250.00
Davenport, Plate, Blue & White, Marked Oxburgh Hall, C.1810 .... 55.00
Davenport, Plate, Blue Embossed Basket Weave, Rural View, Shepherd's Family 28.00
Davenport, Plate, Flow Blue, Anchor Mark 35.00
Davenport, Plate, Gold Trim, C.1850 .... 37.50
Davy Crockett, Game, Harett, 1955 .... 6.00
Davy Crockett, Mug, Shaker 7.00
Davy Crockett, Tumbler 2.50

De Vez is a name found on special pieces of French cameo glass made by the Cristallerie de Pantin about 1890. Monsieur de Varreux was the art director of the glassworks and he signed pieces "De Vez."

De Vez, Vase, French Cameo, Scenic, Wine On Beige, Signed, 4 1/4 In. 360.00
De Vez, Vase, French, Maritime Scene, Signed, 8 In. 515.00
De Vez, Vase, Frosted, Scenic, French, Signed, 7 3/4 X 5 In. 445.00
De Vez, Vase, Gray, Black & Amber Cameo Of Butterflies & Leaves, 8 1/4 In. 475.00
De Vez, Vase, Landscape, Cameo Glass, Signed, 3 7/8 X 3 In. 375.00
De Vez, Vase, Maritime Scene, Sailboats, Rocks, Reflections In Water, 8 In. 487.00
De Vez, Vase, Pink, Blue, White, Robin On Branch, 7 1/8 In. 510.00
De Vez, Vase, Scenic, 2 Cuttings On 3 Layers, Blue Pink & Yellow, Boats, 8 In. 590.00
De Vez, Vase, Soft Frosted Gold, Navy Cut To Deep Rose Scene, 7 7/8 In. 495.00
De Vez, Vase, Soft Translucent Green To Pale Blue, Sailboat & House, 10 In. 475.00
De Vez, Vase, Translucent Frosted Pink, Navy Blue Scene, Signed Cameo, 10 In. 495.00
De Vez, Vase, Woodland Scene, Brown & Tan Shades Cut To Yellow, 5 3/4 In. 400.00
De Vez, Vase, 3 Cuttings, Mountains, Water, Trees, Pink, Blue, White, 4 In. 295.00

Decoys are carved or turned wooden copies of birds. The decoy was placed in the water to lure flying birds to the pond for hunters.

Decoy, August Mock Drake, Canvasback, C.1900 .... 140.00
Decoy, Black, Feathered Bodies, Pair, 3 X 5 1/2 X 12 In. 35.00
Decoy, Canada Goose, Polished Wood, Life-Size 100.00
Decoy, Canada Goose, Ward Brothers 2000.00
Decoy, Canada Goose, Wooden, Hand-Painted, Life Size 150.00
Decoy, Canada Goose, 42 In. 125.00
Decoy, Drake, Butterball, Handmade, Painted 33.00
Decoy, Duck, Composition 115.00
Decoy, Duck, Pacific Northwest 22.00
Decoy, Duck, Papier-Mache, 5 In. 15.00
Decoy, Duck, Ringnecked, Herter, Signed 55.00
Decoy, Duck, Wooden, Glass Eyes 5.75

Decoy, Duck, Wooden, Mustard Highlights, 14 In.	42.50
Decoy, Goose, Paul Emile Lacombe, Three Rivers, Quebec, 1950s	300.00
Decoy, Hen & Drake, Ken Harris, Woodville, New York, 14 In., Pair	165.00
Decoy, Mallard Drake, Ward Brothers, Crisfield, Maryland, C.1930	4000.00
Decoy, Owl, Stuffed Cloth, Used To Decoy Crows, 19th Century, 21 In.Tall	175.00
Decoy, Pintail Duck, Green Beak	35.00
Decoy, Shore Bird, Wooden, Glass Eyes, Carved, 10 1/4 X 6 In.	45.00
Decoy, Shore, Heron	275.00
Decoy, St.Lawrence River Black Duck, Scratch-Type Feather Painting	65.00

 *The Dedham Pottery Company of Dedham, Massachusetts, started making pottery in 1866. It was reorganized as the Chelsea Pottery Company in 1891, and became the Dedham Pottery Company in 1895. The factory was famous for its crackleware dishes, which picture blue outlines of animals, flowers, and other natural motifs.*

Dedham, Bowl, Cereal, Rabbit	55.00
Dedham, Bowl, Full Face Rabbit Alternates With Full Rabbit, 4 1/4 In.	180.00
Dedham, Bowl, Grape, 8 1/2 In.	245.00
Dedham, Bowl, Lotus, Blue Trim, 5 In.	95.00 To 110.00
Dedham, Bread & Butter, Pond Lilies, 6 In.	50.00
Dedham, Charger, One-Eared Rabbit, 12 In.	225.00
Dedham, Cup & Saucer, Elephant Pattern, One Small Baby Elephant	145.00
Dedham, Cup & Saucer, Rabbit	68.00 To 80.00
Dedham, Cup Plate, Swan Pattern, 4 In.	195.00
Dedham, Dish, Rabbit Cover, 9 In.	275.00
Dedham, Eggcup, Double, Rabbit	120.00
Dedham, Knife Rest, Rabbit	175.00
Dedham, Lamp, Oil, Pottery Section, 8 X 4 In., Opening, CKAW	465.00
Dedham, Pitcher, Horsechestnut	195.00
Dedham, Pitcher, Rabbit, 7 In.	185.00
Dedham, Plate, Bird In Orange Tree, Blue & Rose, 6 In.	75.00
Dedham, Plate, Crab Off Center, Blue On White, Crackle, 8 1/2 In.	160.00
Dedham, Plate, Duck, Signed M.Davenport, 8 In.	85.00
Dedham, Plate, Grapes, 6 In.	40.00
Dedham, Plate, Grapes, 7 1/2 In.	68.00
Dedham, Plate, Horse Chestnut, Raised, 8 In.	80.00
Dedham, Plate, Horse Chestnut, 6 In.	40.00 To 65.00
Dedham, Plate, Horse Chestnut, 7 1/2 In.	72.00
Dedham, Plate, Horse Chestnut, 8 In.	85.00
Dedham, Plate, Iris, 8 1/2 In.	65.00 To 95.00
Dedham, Plate, Magnolia, 6 In.	48.00 To 60.00
Dedham, Plate, Magnolia, 8 In.	110.00
Dedham, Plate, Magnolia, 8 1/2 In.	55.00 To 68.00
Dedham, Plate, Moth, 10 In.	175.00
Dedham, Plate, Polar Bear	128.00
Dedham, Plate, Pond Lily Variant, 6 In.	85.00
Dedham, Plate, Pond Lily, 6 In.	40.00 To 85.00
Dedham, Plate, Pond Lily, 8 1/2 In.	70.00
Dedham, Plate, Pond Lily, 10 In.	130.00
Dedham, Plate, Rabbit, One Ear, 8 1/2 In.	75.00 To 95.00
Dedham, Plate, Rabbit, 6 In.	32.50
Dedham, Plate, Rabbit, 6 1/4 In.	37.50
Dedham, Plate, Rabbit, 8 In.	85.00
Dedham, Plate, Rabbit, 8 1/2 In.	55.00 To 68.00
Dedham, Plate, Rabbit, 8 1/2 In., C.1897	85.00
Dedham, Plate, Snowtree, 8 In.	65.00
Dedham, Plate, Turkey, 8 1/2 In.	75.00
Dedham, Plate, Turtles, 10 In.	175.00
Dedham, Plate, Water Lily, 6 In.	65.00
Dedham, Plate, Water Lily, 8 1/2 In.	65.00 To 70.00
Dedham, Salt & Pepper, Globular, 3 1/2 In.	115.00
Dedham, Salt & Pepper, Rabbits	135.00
Dedham, Sugar & Creamer, Rabbit	200.00
Dedham, Sugar, Rabbit, Handled, Covered	90.00
Dedham, Tile, Relief Bust Of Man, High Glaze, 1882, Chelsea, 6 7/8 In.	200.00

Dedham, Tray, Bacon, Pond Lilies 110.00
Dedham, Tray, Bacon, Rabbit 145.00
Dedham, Tray, Bacon, Swan Border, 9 X 5 In. 140.00
Dedham, Vase, Pale Ivory To Honey Brown, Streaked Gloss Glaze, 8 1/4 X 8 In. 350.00
Dedham, Vase, Volcanic Glaze, Glossy Dark Green Over Light, HCR, 7 In. 300.00
DeGue, Vase, Arab & Camel Sunset Scene, Acid Cuttings, 5 1/2 X 3 In. 325.00
DeGue, Vase, Caramel Leaves On Light Amethyst, Cameo, Signed, 6 X 5 In. 95.00
DeGue, Vase, Wine Cameo, Polished Rose On Frosted Amber, 5 1/2 In. 375.00

*Delatte glass is a French cameo glass made by Andre Delatte. It was
first made in Nancy, France, in 1921. Lighting fixtures and opaque
glassware in imitation of Bohemian opaline were made.*

Delatte, Pitcher, Carved Purple Sweet Peas On White, 6 1/2 In. 395.00
Delatte, Vase, Brown Floral Carved On Mottled Yellow, Ovoid, 4 1/2 In. 170.00
Delatte, Vase, Carved Landscape, Translucent Aqua Ground, 3 1/2 In. 145.00
Delatte, Vase, Maroon Leaves & Vine Carved On Frosted Pink, 7 1/2 In. 295.00
Delatte, Vase, Red, Geometric Band, Green & Purple Enamel, Urn Shape, 4 In. 115.00
Delatte, Vase, Red, Green, Purple, Geometric Design, Black Rim, Signed, 4 In. 115.00
Delatte, Vase, Scenic Cameo, Frosted Translucent Gold, Trees, Water, 5 1/4 In. 395.00
Delatte, Vase, Translucent Gold Satin, Village Scene, Bulbous, Signed, 5 1/4 In. 395.00
   Delaware, see Pressed Glass, Custard Glass
   Deldare, see Buffalo Pottery, Deldare

*Delft is a tin-glazed pottery that has been made since the seventeenth
century. It is decorated with blue on white or with colored decorations.
Most of the pieces sold today were made after 1891, and the name Holland
appears with the Delft factory marks.*

Delft, Ashtray, Pair Of Shoes Applied, Scene Of Windmill, Blum 12.50
Delft, Bowl, Children Playing Ring Around Rosie, Windmill, Lake, Boat, Marked 49.50
Delft, Canister Set, 5 Piece 50.00
Delft, Chocolate Pot, Blue, Windmill 85.00
Delft, Creamer, Reclining Cow, Blue & White 45.00
Delft, Creamer, Standing Cow 135.00
Delft, Dish, Bird, Polychrome, Yellow, Green, Blue, Red, 18th Century, 9 In. 500.00
Delft, Dish, Pin, Pedestal, Handled, German, 3 1/2 In. 18.00
Delft, Figurine, Dutch Boy, 4 In. 25.00
Delft, Humidor, Van Rossens Toback, Anno 1750, Man In Stocks, Brass Lid 30.00
Delft, Inkwell, Heart Shaped, 3 Quill Holders, 4 In. 40.00
Delft, Inkwell, Mulberry, 16th Century Dressed Man, Shell-Shaped Back 65.00
Delft, Inkwell, 3 Quill Holders, Heart Shaped 35.00
Delft, Pitcher, Blue & White Cat Handle, Windmill Design, 5 In. 30.00
Delft, Pitcher, Scenic, Maroon Floral, Bulbous, 6 In. 28.00
Delft, Plaque, Children & Mother, 15 3/4 In. 150.00
Delft, Plaque, Mother Fixing Girl's Doll, Blue & White, M.Bloomers, 13 In. 275.00
Delft, Plaque, Roadway Scene, Blue On White, 8 In. 39.00
Delft, Plate, Blue Sponged Border, Polychrome Griffin Center, Pierced, 9 In. 34.00
Delft, Plate, English, Blue & White, Pair, C.1750, 11 3/4 In.Diameter 375.00
Delft, Plate, Hanging, Blue & White Floral, 1880, Signed, 14 In. 95.00
Delft, Platter, Blue Windmill, Church, Signed, 10 X 14 In. 34.00
Delft, Platter, Irish, 12 5/8 X 9 1/2 In. 248.00
Delft, Shoe, Dutch, Windmill & House Scene, Signed, 2 In. 20.00
Delft, Tile, Polychrome, Warrior With Sword 32.50
Delft, Tile, Purple On White, Brass Frame, Ball Feet, 5 1/4 In. 30.00
Delft, Vase, Covered, Blue, Heart Shape, Sailboats 28.00
Delft, Vase, Straight Sides, Scalloped, Gold Trim, Dutch Canal Scene, Pair 100.00
Delft, Vase, Windmill Scene With Gold On Front, 11 In., Pair 125.00
   Dentist, see Doctor

*Depression glass was an inexpensive glass manufactured in large quantities
during the 1920s and early 1930s. It was made in many colors and patterns by
dozens of factories in the United States. The name depression glass is a
modern one.*

Depression Glass, Ashtray, Adam, Pink 7.50
Depression Glass, Ashtray, Coaster, Louisa, Flora Gold 5.00
Depression Glass, Ashtray, English Hobnail, Blue 10.00

Depression Glass, Ashtray, Homespun, Pink 5.00
Depression Glass, Ashtray, Sunflower, Pink 2.50
Depression Glass, Ashtray, Windsor Diamond, Green 24.00
Depression Glass, Basket, Hobnail, 7 1/2 In. 25.00
Depression Glass, Berry Set, Coronation, Ruby Red, 7 Piece 35.00
Depression Glass, Berry Set, Waterford, Pink, 7 Piece 30.00
Depression Glass, Bowl, Adam, Green 6.50
Depression Glass, Bowl, American Sweetheart, Pink, 9 In. 8.00
Depression Glass, Bowl, Beaded Block, 2 Handled, Blue, 4 1/2 In. 10.00
Depression Glass, Bowl, Boat, Windsor, Pink, 3/4 In. 9.00
Depression Glass, Bowl, Cabbage Rose, Amber, 8 1/2 In. 2.50
Depression Glass, Bowl, Cherry, Green, Footed, 10 1/2 In. 27.50
Depression Glass, Bowl, Console, Madrid, Amber 3.50
Depression Glass, Bowl, Coronation, Pink, 8 In. 4.50
Depression Glass, Bowl, Doric, Handled, 9 In. 7.25
Depression Glass, Bowl, Fiesta, Rose, 5 1/2 In. 3.50
Depression Glass, Bowl, Flared, Mayfair, Pink 12.00
Depression Glass, Bowl, Florentine No.1, Pink, 8 In. 13.00
Depression Glass, Bowl, Lace Edge, Crystal, 9 1/2 In. 3.00
Depression Glass, Bowl, Lace Edge, Pink, 9 1/2 In. .... 4.25 To 5.00
Depression Glass, Bowl, Madrid, Amber, 5 In. 2.25
Depression Glass, Bowl, Madrid, Crystal, 8 1/4 In. 4.50
Depression Glass, Bowl, Madrid, Green, 10 In. 6.00
Depression Glass, Bowl, Madrid, Yellow, Oval, 10 In. 4.00
Depression Glass, Bowl, Madrid, Yellow, 5 In. 1.00
Depression Glass, Bowl, Manhattan, Crystal, Handled, 9 1/2 In. 4.00
Depression Glass, Bowl, Mayfair, Blue, Oval 10.00
Depression Glass, Bowl, Mayfair, Pink, Oval, 10 In. 2.00
Depression Glass, Bowl, Mayfair, Pink, 10 1/2 In. 5.00
Depression Glass, Bowl, Open Lace, Ribbed, Pink, 9 1/2 In. 8.00
Depression Glass, Bowl, Open Rose, Pink, 10 In. 7.00
Depression Glass, Bowl, Parrot, Green, 8 In. 25.00
Depression Glass, Bowl, Queen Mary, Pink, 5 In. 1.00
Depression Glass, Bowl, Royal Lace, Blue, Footed, 10 In. 35.00
Depression Glass, Bowl, Sandwich, Red 14.00
Depression Glass, Bowl, Sandwich, Ruby, Anchor Hocking, 9 In. 20.00
Depression Glass, Bowl, Sharon, Green, 10 1/2 In. 14.00
Depression Glass, Bowl, Sharon, Pink, 5 In. 2.50
Depression Glass, Bowl, Soup, American Sweetheart, Monax 17.50
Depression Glass, Bowl, Soup, Sharon, Pink, 7 1/2 In. 8.00
Depression Glass, Bowl, Ultramarine Swirl, Handled, Footed 7.50
Depression Glass, Bowl, Vegetable, Adam, Pink, Covered, 9 In. 12.50
Depression Glass, Bowl, Vegetable, Royal Lace, Oval, Green 10.00
Depression Glass, Bowl, Vegetable, Sharon, Oval, Pink 3.50
Depression Glass, Bowl, Vegetable, Sharon, Pink, 9 1/2 In. 5.00
Depression Glass, Box, Cigarette, Candlewick, Covered 12.75
Depression Glass, Box, Powder, Donkey On Cover, Jeanette Glass Co. 18.50
Depression Glass, Bucket, Ice, Tea Room, Green, Metal Bail, 6 3/4 In. 15.00
Depression Glass, Butter And Cover, Queen Mary, Pink 65.00
Depression Glass, Butter, Adam, Pink 50.00
Depression Glass, Butter, Cameo, Green, Covered 95.00
Depression Glass, Butter, Colonial, Crystal, Covered 9.00
Depression Glass, Butter, Doric, Green 47.00
Depression Glass, Butter, Floragold, Lidded, Round 25.00
Depression Glass, Butter, Floral, Pink, Covered 65.00
Depression Glass, Butter, Florentine, Topaz 75.00
Depression Glass, Butter, Georgian, Green, Covered 40.00
Depression Glass, Butter, Homespun, Clear, Covered 60.00
Depression Glass, Butter, Homespun, Pink, Covered 35.00
Depression Glass, Butter, Princess, Pink 52.50
Depression Glass, Butter, Sharon, Amber, Covered 20.00
Depression Glass, Butter, Sharon, Pink .... 27.00 To 32.50
Depression Glass, Butter, Sharon, Pink, Covered 30.00
Depression Glass, Butter, Sierra, Green 40.00
Depression Glass, Butter, Windsor Diamond, Green 55.00

Depression Glass, Butter, Windsor Diamond, Pink	27.00
Depression Glass, Candleholder, Iris, Marigold, Pair	17.00
Depression Glass, Candleholder, Oyster & Pearl, Pink	10.00
Depression Glass, Candleholder, Queen Mary, Clear, Pair	6.50
Depression Glass, Candleholder, Royal Lace, Cobalt, Ruffled Edge	15.00
Depression Glass, Candlestick, Della Robbia, 3 1/2 In., Pair	10.00
Depression Glass, Candlestick, English Hobnail, Crystal, 9 In., Pair	25.00
Depression Glass, Candlestick, Floral, Pink, Pair	15.00
Depression Glass, Candlestick, Moonstone, Opalescent, Pair	7.00
Depression Glass, Candlestick, Oyster & Pearl, Red, Pair	8.00
Depression Glass, Casserole, Mayfair, Pink, Covered	25.00
Depression Glass, Coaster, Adam, Green, 3 3/4 In.	3.50
Depression Glass, Compote, Florentine, Cobalt, Ruffled, 3 1/2 In.	28.00
Depression Glass, Console Set, Madrid, Amber, 3 Piece	18.00
Depression Glass, Console Set, Madrid, Iridescent, 3 Piece	20.00
Depression Glass, Cookie Jar, Madrid, Amber, Covered	20.00
Depression Glass, Cookie Jar, Royal Lace, Pink	15.00
Depression Glass, Creamer, American Sweetheart, Monax	4.00
Depression Glass, Creamer, Cherry Blossom, Pink	19.00
Depression Glass, Creamer, Dogwood, Green	25.00
Depression Glass, Creamer, Madrid, Amber	2.50
Depression Glass, Creamer, Moderntone, Blue	2.50
Depression Glass, Creamer, Royal Lace, Blue	13.25
Depression Glass, Creamer, Sharon, Green	4.50
Depression Glass, Creamer, Tea Room, Pink	6.00
Depression Glass, Creamer, Thumbprint, Pink	5.00
Depression Glass, Cup & Saucer, Cherry Blossom, Pink, Child's	14.00
Depression Glass, Cup & Saucer, Cloverleaf, Green	4.00
Depression Glass, Cup & Saucer, Dogwood, Green	7.00
Depression Glass, Cup & Saucer, Lace Edge, Blue	12.00
Depression Glass, Cup & Saucer, Laurel, Jade	6.00
Depression Glass, Cup & Saucer, Madrid, Green	5.50
Depression Glass, Cup & Saucer, Miss America, Pink	12.50
Depression Glass, Cup & Saucer, Normandie, Pink	5.00
Depression Glass, Cup & Saucer, Normandie, Sunburst	3.25
Depression Glass, Cup, American Sweetheart, Monax	5.00
Depression Glass, Cup, Child's, White Opalescent, Rose Decal, Hazel Atlas	3.00
Depression Glass, Cup, Cubist, Pink	1.00
Depression Glass, Cup, Mayfair, Blue	15.00
Depression Glass, Cup, Mayfair, Pink	6.00
Depression Glass, Cup, Measuring, Ultramarine, Set Of Four	19.00
Depression Glass, Cup, Moonstone	2.50
Depression Glass, Cup, Punch, Royal Ruby	1.50
Depression Glass, Cup, Queen Mary, Pink	2.00
Depression Glass, Cup, Royal Lace, Pink	4.00
Depression Glass, Cup, Royal Ruby	2.50
Depression Glass, Cup, Sharon, Green	5.50
Depression Glass, Decanter, Mayfair, Pink, With Stopper	3.00 To 50.00
Depression Glass, Dish, Candy & Lid, Sharon, Pink	15.00
Depression Glass, Dish, Candy With Lid, Mayfair	16.50
Depression Glass, Dish, Candy With Lid, Miss America, Pink	70.00
Depression Glass, Dish, Candy, Block, Pink, Low, Covered	12.00
Depression Glass, Dish, Candy, Cameo, Yellow, Low	35.00
Depression Glass, Dish, Candy, Clover Leaf, Green, Covered	23.50
Depression Glass, Dish, Candy, Doric, Covered, Pink	15.00
Depression Glass, Dish, Candy, Iris, Clear, Covered	35.00
Depression Glass, Dish, Candy, Iris, Crystal	30.00
Depression Glass, Dish, Candy, Mayfair, Open Rose, Pink, Covered	10.00
Depression Glass, Dish, Candy, Mayfair, Pink, Covered	16.50
Depression Glass, Dish, Candy, Miss America, Pink, Lidded	58.00
Depression Glass, Dish, Candy, Princess, Green, Covered	18.00
Depression Glass, Dish, Candy, Sharon, Amber	18.00
Depression Glass, Dish, Candy, Sharon, Pink, Cover	18.00
Depression Glass, Dish, Cheese And Cover, Sharon, Amber	125.00
Depression Glass, Dish, Fire King, Blue, Covered	40.00

Depression Glass, **Dish,** Pickle, Aunt Polly, Blue	8.00
Depression Glass, **Dish,** Vegetable, Daisy, Amber, Oval	5.00
Depression Glass, **Dish,** Vegetable, Mayfair, Oval, Blue	19.00
Depression Glass, **Glass,** Florentine No.2, Pink, 4 In.	7.00
Depression Glass, **Glass,** Nursery Rhyme, Hazel Atlas	3.50
Depression Glass, **Goblet,** Colonial, Clear	10.00
Depression Glass, **Goblet,** Colonial, Green, Footed, 1 Oz.	10.00
Depression Glass, **Goblet,** Iris, Clear, 4 Oz.	5.00
Depression Glass, **Goblet,** Miss America, Pink, 5 1/2 In.	25.00
Depression Glass, **Goblet,** Waterford, Clear, 5 1/4 In.	3.50
Depression Glass, **Jar,** Candy, Cube, Green, Covered	9.50
Depression Glass, **Jar,** Candy, Cube, Pink, Covered, 7 1/2 In.	9.00
Depression Glass, **Jar,** Cookie, Madrid, Amber, Covered	18.50
Depression Glass, **Jar,** Cookie, Mayfair, Blue	50.00
Depression Glass, **Jar,** Cookie, Mayfair, Open Rose, Pink Covered	18.50
Depression Glass, **Jar,** Cookie, Patrician, Green	150.00
Depression Glass, **Jar,** Cookie, Princess, Green	14.00
Depression Glass, **Jug,** English Hobnail, Crystal, Quart	20.00
Depression Glass, **Jug,** Florentine, Pink, 36 Oz.	30.00
Depression Glass, **Lemonade Set,** Grape, 8 In.Pitcher, 6 Glasses	125.00
Depression Glass, **Mold,** Jello, Madrid, Amber, 2 In., Set Of 6	21.00
Depression Glass, **Pitcher,** Adam, Pink	15.00 To 97.50
Depression Glass, **Pitcher,** Adam, Pink, Square Base	18.50
Depression Glass, **Pitcher,** American Sweetheart, 8 In.	148.50
Depression Glass, **Pitcher,** Cameo, Green, Rope	22.90
Depression Glass, **Pitcher,** Cherry Blossom, Green	50.00
Depression Glass, **Pitcher,** Cherry, Pink, Footed	22.50
Depression Glass, **Pitcher,** Fiesta, Orange	18.00
Depression Glass, **Pitcher,** Fiesta, Red, 2 Quart	15.00
Depression Glass, **Pitcher,** Florentine No.2, Footed, 30 Oz.	20.00
Depression Glass, **Pitcher,** Florentine, Green	24.00
Depression Glass, **Pitcher,** Hobnail, Hocking, 18 Oz.	7.50
Depression Glass, **Pitcher,** Holiday, Six Tumblers	50.00
Depression Glass, **Pitcher,** Lemonade, Floral, Pink	125.00
Depression Glass, **Pitcher,** Lemonade, Mayfair, Open Rose, Clear	10.00
Depression Glass, **Pitcher,** Madrid, Amber	18.00
Depression Glass, **Pitcher,** Mayfair, Pink, 6 In.	17.50
Depression Glass, **Pitcher,** Mayfair, Pink, 8 In.	10.00 To 15.00
Depression Glass, **Pitcher,** Mayfair, Pink, 8 1/2 In.	20.00 To 25.00
Depression Glass, **Pitcher,** Mayfair, Pink, 80 Oz.	22.00
Depression Glass, **Pitcher,** Milk, Poppy, Yellow	14.00
Depression Glass, **Pitcher,** Miss America, Clear, 8 3/4 In.	27.50
Depression Glass, **Pitcher,** Miss America, Crystal, 8 In.	32.00
Depression Glass, **Pitcher,** Patrician, Amber, 8 In.	40.00
Depression Glass, **Pitcher,** Princess, Green	18.00
Depression Glass, **Pitcher,** Princess, Yellow, 8 In.	31.50 To 36.00
Depression Glass, **Pitcher,** Royal Lace, Blue, 54 Ounce	45.00
Depression Glass, **Pitcher,** Royal Lace, Blue, 7 In.	60.00
Depression Glass, **Pitcher,** Royal Lace, Clear, 8 1/2 In.	21.90
Depression Glass, **Pitcher,** Royal Ruby, Hobnail	15.00
Depression Glass, **Pitcher,** Sandwich, Green, Hocking, 1/2 Gallon	149.50
Depression Glass, **Pitcher,** Sandwich, Green, 36 Oz.	50.00
Depression Glass, **Pitcher,** Sharon, Amber, Ice Lip	40.00
Depression Glass, **Pitcher,** Tea Room, Green	55.00
Depression Glass, **Pitcher,** Water, Sharon, Amber, Ice Lip	35.00
Depression Glass, **Pitcher,** Windsor Diamond, Green, 9 In.	14.50
Depression Glass, **Plate,** Adam, Pink, 7 3/4 In. .....*Illus*	4.50
Depression Glass, **Plate,** Bread, American Sweetheart, 10 In. .....*Illus*	6.00
Depression Glass, **Plate,** Bubble, 6 3/4 In. .....*Illus*	1.00
Depression Glass, **Plate,** Cake, Adam, Footed	5.00
Depression Glass, **Plate,** Cake, Adam, Green	10.00
Depression Glass, **Plate,** Cake, Adam, Pink	6.50
Depression Glass, **Plate,** Cake, Cherry Blossom, Green, Open Handles, 10 In.	20.00
Depression Glass, **Plate,** Cake, Dogwood, Pink	37.50
Depression Glass, **Plate,** Cake, Doric, Green	10.50

Depression Glass, Plate,
Adam, Pink, 7 3/4 In.
(See Page 155)

Depression Glass, Plate,
Bread, American Sweetheart, 10 In.
(See Page 155)

Depression Glass, Plate,
Cameo, Green, 8 In.

Depression Glass, Plate,
Bubble, 6 3/4 In.
(See Page 155)

Depression Glass, Plate, Cake, Octagonal, Handle, Copper Wheel, Pink	12.00
Depression Glass, Plate, Cake, Sharon, Amber, Footed	8.00
Depression Glass, Plate, Cake, Sharon, Pink	9.00
Depression Glass, Plate, Cake, Wildflower, Clear, 11 In.	8.00
Depression Glass, Plate, Cameo, Green, 8 In. *Illus*	2.00
Depression Glass, Plate, Candlewick, Round, 14 In.	13.00
Depression Glass, Plate, Cheese, Custard Cover	31.50
Depression Glass, Plate, Cherry Blossom, Green, 9 In.	9.00
Depression Glass, Plate, Cherry Blossom, Pink, 7 In.	7.00
Depression Glass, Plate, Cloverleaf, Black, 8 In.	7.50
Depression Glass, Plate, Cubist, Green, 8 In. *Illus*	2.50
Depression Glass, Plate, Dinner, Cherry Blossom, Pink	6.00
Depression Glass, Plate, Dinner, Lace Edge	3.50
Depression Glass, Plate, Dinner, Miss America, Pink	8.00
Depression Glass, Plate, Dinner, Rosemary, Amber	3.75
Depression Glass, Plate, Dogwood, Pink, 6 In.	2.00
Depression Glass, Plate, Dogwood, Pink, 8 In.	1.50
Depression Glass, Plate, Dogwood, Pink, 9 1/4 In. *Illus*	7.95
Depression Glass, Plate, Doric & Pansy, Pink, 6 In.	4.00
Depression Glass, Plate, Doric, Green, 7 In.	2.25
Depression Glass, Plate, Floral, Pink, 9 In. *Illus*	3.75
Depression Glass, Plate, Florentine No.I, Green, 8 1/2 In. *Illus*	3.50
Depression Glass, Plate, Florentine No.2, Yellow, 8 1/2 In. *Illus*	3.00
Depression Glass, Plate, Georgian Lovebirds, Green, 6 In.	1.00
Depression Glass, Plate, Georgian, Green, 6 In.	2.00
Depression Glass, Plate, Grill, Normandie, Iridescent	3.00
Depression Glass, Plate, Grill, Princess, Green, Handled, 11 1/2 In.	4.50
Depression Glass, Plate, Lace Edge, Blue, 10 In.	1.00
Depression Glass, Plate, Madrid, Amber, 7 1/2 In.	3.60
Depression Glass, Plate, Madrid, Amber, 10 1/2 In.	13.00
Depression Glass, Plate, Madrid, Green, 9 In. *Illus*	5.00
Depression Glass, Plate, Mayfair, Pink, 6 In. *Illus*	3.00
Depression Glass, Plate, Miss America, Pink, 8 1/2 In. *Illus*	2.00
Depression Glass, Plate, Moderntone, Blue, 8 In. *Illus*	2.00

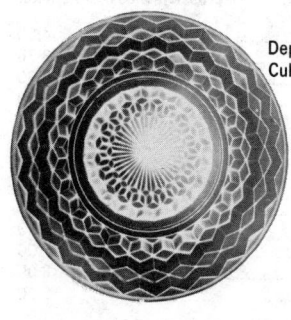

Depression Glass, Plate,
Cubist, Green, 8 In.

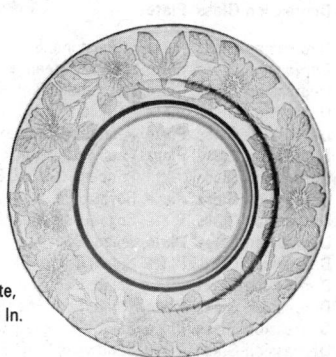

Depression Glass, Plate,
Dogwood Pink, 9 1/4 In.

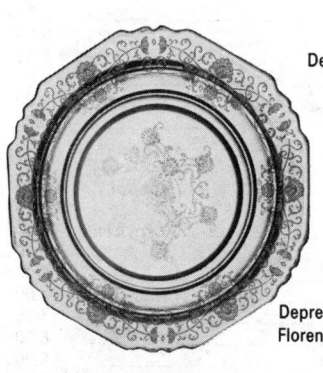

Depression Glass, Plate,
Floral, Pink, 9 In.

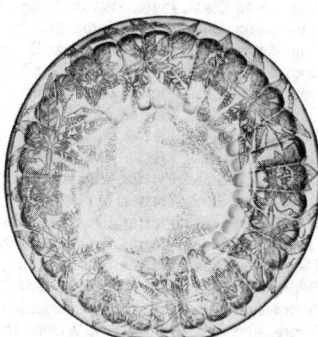

Depression Glass, Plate,
Florentine No.I, Green, 8 1/2 In.

Depression Glass, Plate,
Florentine No.2, Yellow, 8 1/2 In.

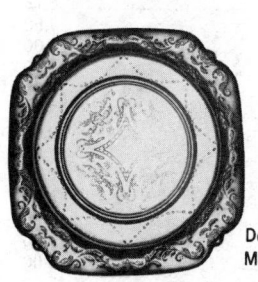

Depression Glass, Plate,
Madrid, Green, 9 In.

Depression Glass, Plate,
Mayfair, Pink, 6 In.

Depression Glass, Plate,
Miss America, Pink, 8 1/2 In.

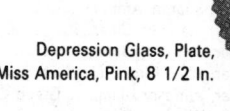

Depression Glass, Plate, Moonstone, 8 In.	4.00
Depression Glass, Plate, No.612, Green, 8 1/2 In. *Illus*	3.75
Depression Glass, Plate, Normandie, Pink, 8 In. *Illus*	5.00
Depression Glass, Plate, Patrician, Green, 7 1/2 In. *Illus*	4.50
Depression Glass, Plate, Petalware, Cremax, 8 In.	2.75
Depression Glass, Plate, Petalware, Monax, 6 In.	2.50
Depression Glass, Plate, Princess, Yellow, 8 In. *Illus*	4.50
Depression Glass, Plate, Royal Lace, Blue	8.00
Depression Glass, Plate, Royal Lace, Blue, 6 In.	2.85
Depression Glass, Plate, Salad, Cabbage Rose, Pink	1.50
Depression Glass, Plate, Salad, Cherry Blossom, Pink, 7 In. *Illus*	7.00
Depression Glass, Plate, Salad, Cherry, Pink	8.00
Depression Glass, Plate, Salad, Lace Edge	2.50
Depression Glass, Plate, Salad, Rosemary-Dutch Rose, 6 3/4 In.	1.00
Depression Glass, Plate, Sandwich, Doric Pansy, Ultramarine, 2-Handled	9.00
Depression Glass, Plate, Sandwich, Oyster & Pearl, Ruby	12.00
Depression Glass, Plate, Sharon, Amber, 9 1/2 In. *Illus*	3.50
Depression Glass, Plate, Sharon, Pink, 9 In.	3.50
Depression Glass, Plate, Waterford, Crystal, 3/4 In.	3.00
Depression Glass, Plate, Windsor Diamond, Pink, 9 In. *Illus*	4.00
Depression Glass, Platter, Adam, Pink	7.00
Depression Glass, Platter, American Sweetheart, Monax	20.00 To 21.90
Depression Glass, Platter, Bubble, Blue	6.50
Depression Glass, Platter, Cabbage Rose, Pink, 12 1/2 In.	5.00
Depression Glass, Platter, Miss America, Clear	5.00
Depression Glass, Platter, Moderntone, Blue	5.00
Depression Glass, Platter, Royal Lace, Blue	20.00
Depression Glass, Platter, Royal Lace, Pink	8.00
Depression Glass, Platter, Sharon, Pink	5.00
Depression Glass, Punch Bowl & Pedestal, Circular Saw	35.00
Depression Glass, Punch Bowl, Royal Ruby	20.00
Depression Glass, Punch Set, Moderntone, Blue, Metal Holder	42.00
Depression Glass, Punch Set, Royal Ruby	45.00
Depression Glass, Punch Stand, Royal Ruby	10.00
Depression Glass, Relish, Lace Edge	5.00
Depression Glass, Relish, Lace Edge, Partitioned	4.00
Depression Glass, Relish, Lace Edge, Pink, 3 Part, 10 1/2 In.	4.75
Depression Glass, Relish, Mayfair, Pink, 4 Section	6.50
Depression Glass, Relish, Miss America, Clear, Divided, 8 1/2 In.	8.00
Depression Glass, Relish, Miss America, Pink, 4 Part	6.75
Depression Glass, Relish, Miss America, 4 Part	7.50
Depression Glass, Salt & Pepper, Adam, Pink	20.00
Depression Glass, Salt & Pepper, American Sweetheart, Monax	110.00
Depression Glass, Salt & Pepper, American Sweetheart, Pink	125.00
Depression Glass, Salt & Pepper, Cabbage Rose, Amber	23.50
Depression Glass, Salt & Pepper, Cameo, Green, Footed	40.00
Depression Glass, Salt & Pepper, Cloverleaf, Green	17.50
Depression Glass, Salt & Pepper, Cubist, Green	10.00
Depression Glass, Salt & Pepper, Della Robbia, Crystal, Colored Fruit	18.00
Depression Glass, Salt & Pepper, Floral, Pink	14.00 To 15.50
Depression Glass, Salt & Pepper, Florentine, Topaz	23.00
Depression Glass, Salt & Pepper, Mayfair, Pink	25.00
Depression Glass, Salt & Pepper, Miss America, Crystal	15.00
Depression Glass, Salt & Pepper, Moderntone, Blue	10.00
Depression Glass, Salt & Pepper, Moderntone, Cobalt	12.00
Depression Glass, Salt & Pepper, New Century, Green	15.00
Depression Glass, Salt & Pepper, Royal Lace, Cobalt	100.00
Depression Glass, Salt & Pepper, Royal Lace, Pink	22.00
Depression Glass, Salt & Pepper, Sharon, Amber	18.00
Depression Glass, Salt & Pepper, Starlight, Clear	6.00
Depression Glass, Salt & Pepper, Swirl, Ultramarine	17.50
Depression Glass, Salt & Pepper, Waterford, Clear, Aluminum Lids	2.50
Depression Glass, Salt & Pepper, Windsor Diamond, Green	28.00
Depression Glass, Salt & Pepper, Windsor, Pink	9.00
Depression Glass, Saltshaker, Cloverleaf, Green	15.00

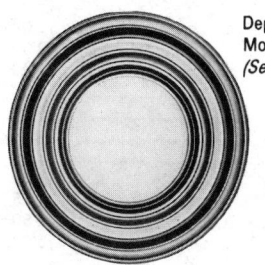

Depression Glass, Plate,
Moderntone, Blue, 8 In.
(See Page 156)

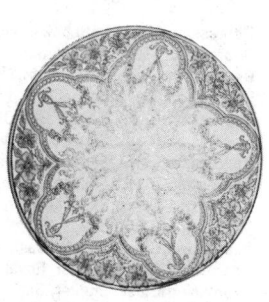

Depression Glass, Plate,
No.612, Green, 8 1/2 In.

Depression Glass, Plate,
Normandie, Pink, 8 In.

Depression Glass, Plate,
Patrician, Green, 7 1/2 In.

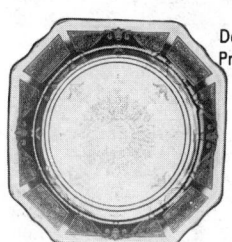

Depression Glass, Plate,
Princess, Yellow, 8 In.

Depression Glass, Plate,
Windsor, Diamond, Pink, 9 In.

Depression Glass, Plate,
Salad, Cherry Blossom, Pink, 7 In.

Depression Glass, Plate,
Sharon, Amber, 9 1/2 In.

Depression Glass, **Saltshaker**, Floral, Green 10.00
Depression Glass, **Saltshaker**, Sharon, Green 19.00
Depression Glass, **Saltshaker**, Sharon, Pink 10.00
Depression Glass, **Sauce Boat**, Fiesta, Gray 4.50
Depression Glass, **Sauce**, Tree Of Life, Clear, Footed, 4 In. 15.00
Depression Glass, **Saucer**, Cabbage Rose, Pink 1.00
Depression Glass, **Saucer**, Cherry Blossom, Blue Delphite, Child's 7.00
Depression Glass, **Saucer**, Cloverleaf, Yellow 3.00
Depression Glass, **Saucer**, Holiday, Pink .... *Illus* 1.75
Depression Glass, **Saucer**, Royal Lace, Green .... *Illus* 2.50
Depression Glass, **Server**, Mayfair, Green, Center Handle 15.00
Depression Glass, **Shaker**, Royal Lace, Pink 10.90
Depression Glass, **Shaker**, Sharon, Amber 10.00
Depression Glass, **Sherbet & Plate**, Cherry Blossom, Pink, 3 Sets 24.00
Depression Glass, **Sherbet**, American Sweetheart, Monax 8.00
Depression Glass, **Sherbet**, Block, Green, 5 1/2 In. 3.50
Depression Glass, **Sherbet**, Cherry, Green 7.00
Depression Glass, **Sherbet**, Crackle, Pink, Stemmed 1.50
Depression Glass, **Sherbet**, Dogwood, Pink 5.50
Depression Glass, **Sherbet**, Iris, Iridescent, 5 3/4 In. .... *Illus* 3.00
Depression Glass, **Sherbet**, Mayfair, Pink, Footed, 3 In. 4.50
Depression Glass, **Sherbet**, Mayfair, Pink, Set Of 4 .... 4.50
Depression Glass, **Sherbet**, Miss America, Pin, Set Of 2 .... 4.50
Depression Glass, **Sherbet**, Patrician, Amber Foot 2.00
Depression Glass, **Sherbet**, Petalware, Monax 2.50
Depression Glass, **Sherbet**, Spiral, Green .... .75
Depression Glass, **Sugar & Creamer**, Cameo, Green, Open 9.00
Depression Glass, **Sugar & Creamer**, Cameo, Yellow 12.50
Depression Glass, **Sugar & Creamer**, Colonial, Green 15.00
Depression Glass, **Sugar & Creamer**, Delphite Swirl, Green 9.00
Depression Glass, **Sugar & Creamer**, Dogwood, Pink 7.50
Depression Glass, **Sugar & Creamer**, Holiday, Pink 15.00
Depression Glass, **Sugar & Creamer**, Laurel, Jade, Tall 16.00
Depression Glass, **Sugar & Creamer**, Lovebird, Green, 3 In. 8.50
Depression Glass, **Sugar & Creamer**, Royal Lace, Pink, Opalescent 9.00
Depression Glass, **Sugar & Creamer**, Royal Ruby, Open 6.00
Depression Glass, **Sugar & Creamer**, Sandwich, Green 10.00
Depression Glass, **Sugar & Creamer**, Tea Room, Pink 10.00
Depression Glass, **Sugar**, American Sweetheart, Monax 4.00
Depression Glass, **Sugar**, Cherry Blossom, Pink, Covered 5.00
Depression Glass, **Sugar**, Covered, Moderntone, Blue 15.00
Depression Glass, **Sugar**, Dogwood, Green 20.00
Depression Glass, **Sugar**, Florentine, Round, Open, Pink 4.00
Depression Glass, **Sugar**, Holiday, Pink 1.00
Depression Glass, **Sugar**, Horseshoe, Yellow 5.75
Depression Glass, **Sugar**, Ribbon Candy, Crystal, Stemmed 5.00
Depression Glass, **Sugar**, Sandwich, Green 6.00
Depression Glass, **Sugar**, Sharon, Pink, Lidded 7.00
Depression Glass, **Tea Set**, Diane, 12 Pieces With Holder, Child's 45.00
Depression Glass, **Teapot**, Chiquita, Cobalt, Lid, Child's 12.00
Depression Glass, **Tray**, Tid-Bit, Dogwood, Pink 75.00
Depression Glass, **Tumbler**, Adam, Pink, Footed 6.75
Depression Glass, **Tumbler**, Diamond Panel, Pink 4.00
Depression Glass, **Tumbler**, Doric & Pansy, Teal Green, 9 Oz. 15.00
Depression Glass, **Tumbler**, Fine Rib, Blue, 5 Ounce 3.50
Depression Glass, **Tumbler**, Floral, Green, 7 Oz. 5.00
Depression Glass, **Tumbler**, Florentine, Footed, Yellow, 12 Oz. 15.00
Depression Glass, **Tumbler**, Homespun, Pink, Footed, 4 In. 3.00
Depression Glass, **Tumbler**, Mayfair, Pink, Footed 15.00
Depression Glass, **Tumbler**, Mayfair, Pink, Footed, 3 1/4 In., Set Of 3 .... 75.00
Depression Glass, **Tumbler**, Mayfair, Pink, Footed, 6 1/2 In. 12.50
Depression Glass, **Tumbler**, Royal Lace, Blue 14.00
Depression Glass, **Tumbler**, Royal Lace, Blue, 9 Oz. 14.50
Depression Glass, **Tumbler**, Sharon, Pink, Flat, 5 In. 14.00
Depression Glass, **Vase**, Cameo, Green, 8 In. 15.00

Depression Glass, Vase, Royal Ruby, Round, Ball Shape, 4 In.	4.00
Depression Glass, Vase, Sweet Pear, Mayfair, Blue	30.00
Depression Glass, Vase, Swirl, Ultramarine, 8 In.	7.50
Depression Glass, Water Set, Iris, Crystal, 7 Piece	35.00
Depression Glass, Water Set, Old English, Clear With Orange & Black Paint	35.00
Depression Glass, Whiskey Set, Cranberrry, 7 Piece	15.00
Depression Glass, Whiskey, Colonial, Green	10.00
Depression Glass, Wine, English Hobnail, Crystal Stem	5.00
Depression Glass, Wine, Iris & Herringbone, Clear	5.00

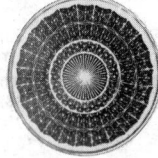  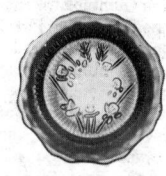

Depression Glass, Saucer,
Holiday, Pink

Depression Glass, Saucer,
Royal Lace, Green

Depression Glass, Sherbet,
Iris, Iridescent, 5 3/4 In.

*Derby porcelain was made in Derby, England, from 1756 to the present.
The factory changed names and marks several times. Chelsea Derby (1770-
1784), Crown Derby (1784-1811), and the modern Royal Crown Derby are
some of the most famous periods of the factory.*

Derby, see also Chelsea, Crown Derby, Royal Crown Derby

Derby, Cream Jug, Floor, 5 1/2 In., 1825-40	40.00
Derby, Cup & Saucer, Floral Design, Gold Leaves, On White, Red Mark, C.1815-30	90.00
DeVilbiss, Atomizer, Black & Gold Rings, Clear Crystal, Steuben, 6 1/2 In.	85.00
DeVilbiss, Atomizer, Black & Gold Rings, Crystal, Mesh Bulb, 6 1/2 In.	60.00
DeVilbiss, Atomizer, Blue Aurene, Signed	190.00
DeVilbiss, Atomizer, Cranberry, Signed	95.00
DeVilbiss, Atomizer, Enameled Glass, Allover Gold, Raised Roses, Signed, Pai	75.00
DeVilbiss, Atomizer, Gold Encrusted, Cranberry Bulbous Base, 7 In.	20.00
DeVilbiss, Atomizer, Gold Middle, Black Design, Paper Label, Signed, 7 In.	40.00
DeVilbiss, Atomizer, Gold, Vaseline Ovals	25.00
DeVilbiss, Atomizer, Hand Blown, Pink, Original Stickers	37.50
DeVilbiss, Atomizer, Iridescent Honey, Mesh Bulb, 7 In.	235.00
DeVilbiss, Atomizer, Orange Opaque, Marked, 6 In.	50.00
DeVilbiss, Atomizer, Orange, Gold Decoration, Art Deco	32.50
DeVilbiss, Atomizer, Sapphire Blue, Pressed Glass, 5 1/2 In.	27.50
DeVilbiss, Atomizer, Satin Glass, Signed, 5 1/2 In.High	45.00
DeVilbiss, Atomizer, Signed Steuben, Aurene, Complete	165.00
DeVilbiss, Atomizer, Swirl, Opalescent Yellow	22.00
DeVilbiss, Atomizer, Swirled Feather, Gold Plated Lid, Sticker	15.00
Dick Tracy, Badge, Detective Club, Brass, Nostalgia	12.50
Dick Tracy, Badge, Detective Club, Leather Pouch On Back	48.00
Dick Tracy, Badge, Red, Blue, & Gold Bust Of Tracy, Brass, Republic Pictures	10.00
Dick Tracy, Car, Battery Powered, Painted Metal, Red Light, 11 X 4 1/4 In.	30.00
Dick Tracy, Car, Marx, Key Wind, B.O. And Light On Roof, 10 1/2 In.	15.00
Dick Tracy, Car, Squad No.1, Tin, Windup	18.00
Dick Tracy, Car, Squad, Friction, Siren & Lights, Marx, 1949	30.00
Dick Tracy, Doll, Bonnie Braids, 1951	70.00
Dick Tracy, Doll, Comic	9.00
Dick Tracy, Game, Junior Detective Set	20.00
Dick Tracy, Game, Master Detective	25.00
Dick Tracy, Gun Clacker, Metal	7.00
Dick Tracy, Knife, Pocket, 1940s	15.00
Dick Tracy, Poster, Dick Tracy Versus Phantom Empire, 41 X 27 In.	30.00
Dick Tracy, Wristwatch, New Haven Clock & Watch Co., Leather Strap	35.00
Dionne Quintuplet, Book, Doctor & Early Life Of Babies	14.50
Dionne Quintuplet, Book, Paper Doll Cut-Out, C.1937	50.00

Dionne Quintuplet, **Book**, We're Two Years Old, Going On Three	8.50
Dionne Quintuplet, **Book**, Whitman, Story Of Dionnes, We're Two Years Old	12.00
Dionne Quintuplet, **Bowl**, Cereal, Chrome, 6 In.	10.00
Dionne Quintuplet, **Calendar**, 1940	18.00
Dionne Quintuplet, **Calendar**, 1950	18.00
Dionne Quintuplet, **Dish**, Baby, Aluminum	12.00
Dionne Quintuplet, **Doll**, Madame Alexander, 7 In.	80.00
Dionne Quintuplet, **Fan**, Playing In The Sand, 1930s	35.00
Dionne Quintuplet, **Life Magazine**, May, 1940, First Communion Cover Story	5.00
Dionne Quintuplet, **Magazine Cover**, Liberty Magazine, March 29, 1941	9.00
Dionne Quintuplet, **Paper Dolls**, Merrill, 1935, Uncut	50.00
Dionne Quintuplet, **Postcard**, Birthplace	2.50
Dionne Quintuplet, **Radio**	55.00
Dionne Quintuplet, **Spoon**, Annette	10.00
Dionne Quintuplet, **Spoon**, Cecile	12.50
Dionne Quintuplet, **Spoon**, Set Of 5	65.00 To 95.00
Disneyana, **Ashtray**, Figural, Mickey Mouse, Wooden, 29 In.	75.00
Disneyana, **Bank**, Donald Duck Nodder	125.00
Disneyana, **Bank**, Dumbo Elephant	5.00
Disneyana, **Bank**, Jam Jar, 1935, Embossed With Mickey & Minnie Mouse	15.00
Disneyana, **Bank**, Little Pigs, Leather Covered Treasure Chest, 1930s	35.00
Disneyana, **Book**, Alice In Wonderland, Punch Out	12.00
Disneyana, **Book**, Mickey Mouse & Pluto	25.00
Disneyana, **Book**, Mickey Mouse Story, Soft Cover, 1931	45.00
Disneyana, **Book**, Mickey Mouse, 1938	17.00
Disneyana, **Book**, Nutcracker Suite, Fantasia Colored Dust Jacket	15.00
Disneyana, **Book**, Pinocchio, 1939	6.00
Disneyana, **Book**, Pop-Up Minnie Mouse, 1933	110.00
Disneyana, **Book**, Sheriff Of Nugget Gulch, 1938	11.00
Disneyana, **Book**, Story Of Donald Duck, C.1938, Whitman Publishing Co.	6.50
Disneyana, **Book**, Story Of Mickey Mouse, C.1938, Whitman Publishing Co.	6.50
Disneyana, **Book**, Story Of Minnie Mouse, C.1938, Whitman Publishing Co.	6.50
Disneyana, **Bookend**, Mickey Mouse, China, Pair	10.00
Disneyana, **Bottle**, Figural, Snow White	3.50
Disneyana, **Bottle**, Hot Water, Donald Duck, Italy	15.00
Disneyana, **Box**, Paint, Tin, Donald Duck	7.00
Disneyana, **Box**, Pencil, Mickey Mouse Parade, Dixon, 5 3/4 X 10 1/2 In.	15.00
Disneyana, **Box**, Watch, Mickey Mouse, Ingersoll	10.00
Disneyana, **Bubble Gum Machine**, Mickey Mouse, Plastic	10.00
Disneyana, **Button**, Mickey Mouse Club, 1950s, 3 1/2 In.	3.00
Disneyana, **Camera**, Donald & His Nephews On Back, 1940s	38.00
Disneyana, **Camera**, Donald Duck, In Box	20.00
Disneyana, **Can**, Watering	8.00
Disneyana, **Card**, Christmas, Mickey Mouse, 1937	19.00
Disneyana, **Card**, Playing, 40 Cards To A Box, 4 Boxes	25.00
Disneyana, **Cards**, Playing, 3 Little Pigs	11.00
Disneyana, **Chair**, Beach, Mickey Mouse, Canvas, W.D.E. On Back	95.00
Disneyana, **Charm**, Celluloid, Donald Duck, Long Bill, 1 In.	12.00
Disneyana, **Christmas Tree Lights**, Mickey Mouse, Noma	90.00
Disneyana, **Clock**, Alarm, Mickey Mouse	5.00
Disneyana, **Clock**, Animated Pluto, Eyes Roll, Tongue Moves, Box, Electric	125.00
Disneyana, **Clock**, Ingersoll Alarm, Celluloid Case, Mickey Mouse On Face	325.00
Disneyana, **Clock**, Mickey Mouse, Electric, Ingersoll *Illus*	310.00
Disneyana, **Clock**, Wall, Mickey Mouse, Electric, Blue Enamel On Metal	20.00
Disneyana, **Comic**, Walt Disney's Donald Duck Comic Book, 1948 *Illus*	25.00
Disneyana, **Cookie Jar**, Turnabout, Mickey & Minnie, 13 In.	15.00
Disneyana, **Costume**, Jimmy Dodd, Chief Mouseketeer	10.00
Disneyana, **Cup & Saucer**, Mickey Mouse, Tan & White	7.00
Disneyana, **Dish**, Betty Boop & Mickey Mouse, Japan, 5 In. *Illus*	48.00
Disneyana, **Disneyland Express**, Casey Jr., Key Wind	20.00
Disneyana, **Doll**, Celluloid, Jointed, Walt E. Disney, 4 In.	46.50
Disneyana, **Doll**, Doc, Hard Rubber, 5 1/2 In.	30.00
Disneyana, **Doll**, Donald Duck, Bisque	12.50
Disneyana, **Doll**, Dopey, Composition, 1930	75.00
Disneyana, **Doll**, Dopey, Rubber Face, Original Clothes, 13 In.	20.00

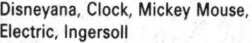

Disneyana, Comic, Walt Disney's
Donald Duck Comic Book, 1948

Disneyana, Clock, Mickey Mouse,
Electric, Ingersoll

Disneyana, Dish, Betty Boop &
Mickey Mouse, Japan, 5 In.

Disneyana, Doll, Grumpy, Composition, 11 In.	55.00
Disneyana, Doll, Long-Bill Donald Duck, Stuffed Cloth	85.00
Disneyana, Doll, Mickey Mouse Holding Gun On Shoulder	15.00
Disneyana, Doll, Mickey Mouse, Corduroy, 1940s, 13 In.	45.00
Disneyana, Doll, Mickey Mouse, English, 1932, 6 1/2 In.	200.00
Disneyana, Doll, Mickey Mouse, Stuffed, Walt Disney Tag, 13 In.	35.00
Disneyana, Doll, Mickey Mouse, Sun Rubber Co., 10 1/2 In.	18.00
Disneyana, Doll, Minnie Mouse Playing Mandolin, Bisque, 1930, Japan, 3 1/2 In.	22.00
Disneyana, Doll, Minnie Mouse, Bisque, With Umbrella, 1930s, 4 In.	20.00
Disneyana, Doll, Minnie Mouse, Wood, Jointed, Cloth Skirt, Walt E.Disney, 3 In.	42.50
Disneyana, Doll, Paper, Seven Dwarfs, Uncut Book	10.00
Disneyana, Doll, Rag, Minnie Mouse, Cloth Body, Vinyl Face, 17 In.	26.00
Disneyana, Doll, Small World, Greece	10.00
Disneyana, Doll, Small World, India	10.00
Disneyana, Doll, Small World, Spain	10.00
Disneyana, Doll, Snow White & Seven Dwarfs, Lithographed Cloth, C.1930	95.00
Disneyana, Donald Duck Wind Up, Chein	15.00
Disneyana, Donald Duck, Duet, Original Box	195.00
Disneyana, Dwarf, Dopey, Bisque, 4 In.	16.00
Disneyana, Figurine, Bashful, Goebel, 3 In.	50.00
Disneyana, Figurine, Dumbo, Ceramic, 1941, 5 X 6 In.	40.00
Disneyana, Figurine, Dwarf, Grumpy, 4 In.	16.00
Disneyana, Figurine, Minnie Mouse Holding Umbrella & Purse, Bisque, 1930s	20.00
Disneyana, Figurine, Pig Playing Fiddle, 3 1/2 In.	10.00
Disneyana, Fork & Spoon, Baby's, Mickey & Minnie	17.50
Disneyana, Game, Mickey Mouse Club Magic Adder, Jacmar, Battery	7.50
Disneyana, Game, Mickey Mouse Magic Slate, Easel, Box	12.00
Disneyana, Game, Mickey Mouse Magic Subtractor, Jacmar, Battery	7.50
Disneyana, Game, Mouseketeers	6.50
Disneyana, Game, Target, Mickey Mouse, 18 In.	25.00
Disneyana, Game, Wolverine Pin Ball, Mickey Mouse Club	28.00
Disneyana, Handcar, Mickey Mouse, 27 In.Circle Track	1500.00

Disneyana, **Holder,** Toothbrush, Bisque, Donald With Arms Around Mickey, Minnie 98.00
Disneyana, **Holder,** Toothbrush, Bisque, Mickey, Minnie, Donald, Long Bill 65.00
Disneyana, **Jack-In-The-Box,** Musical 5.00
Disneyana, **Jar,** Cookie, Mickey & Minnie Double Faced 35.00
Disneyana, **Jar,** Lollipop, Raised Mickey, Donald, & Ludwig Von Drake, 8 In. 20.00
Disneyana, **Jeep,** Mickey Mouse, Lithographed Tin, 9 In. 12.00
Disneyana, **Lamp Base,** Pie-Eyed Mickey Mouse, Tin 25.00
Disneyana, **Lamp,** Figural Snow White 7.00
Disneyana, **Library Of Games,** Mickey Mouse 25.00
Disneyana, **Lunch Box,** Mickey Mouse Club 7.00
Disneyana, **Lunch Box,** Mickey Mouse, School Bus, Thermos 12.50
Disneyana, **Lunch Pail,** Aladdin, Disney On Parade Characters 8.00
Disneyana, **Lunch Pail,** Firefighters 10.00
Disneyana, **Magazine,** Comic, Mickey Mouse Weekly, 1937, 12 Pages 20.00
Disneyana, **Magazine,** Mickey Mouse, Vol.4, No.1, 1938 .... 14.00
Disneyana, **Marionette,** Mickey & Minnie, Wooden Body, Box, 1940s, Pair 90.00
Disneyana, **Mask,** Mickey Mouse, Early 1930s 14.00
Disneyana, **Mickey Mouse Washer,** Lithographed Tin, 6 In. .... *Illus* 150.00
Disneyana, **Mickey Mouse,** Bell, Bicycle, Chrome 12.00
Disneyana, **Mickey Mouse,** Book, Scrap, 1935 .... 22.00
Disneyana, **Mickey Mouse,** Book, 1931 .... 50.00
Disneyana, **Mickey Mouse,** Clock, Alarm, 1940 .... 75.00
Disneyana, **Mickey Mouse,** Doll, Rubber, Marked Walt Disney Productions, 7 In. 12.50
Disneyana, **Mickey Mouse,** Figurine, Playing The Saxophone, 5 1/2 In. 45.00
Disneyana, **Mickey Mouse,** Film, 16mm, 100 Feet 9.00
Disneyana, **Mickey Mouse,** Newsreel Sound Projector, Film, Slides, 4 Records 28.00
Disneyana, **Mickey Mouse,** Pocketbook, Plastic Zipper, Blinks Eyes 12.50
Disneyana, **Mickey Mouse,** Puzzle, Wood Inlaid Clock 18.00
Disneyana, **Mickey Mouse,** Ring, 1941 .... 8.00
Disneyana, **Mickey Mouse,** Spoon, Branford, Silver Plate 7.50
Disneyana, **Mickey Mouse,** Tea Set, Child's, Japan, 1929, 11 Piece 50.00
Disneyana, **Mickey Mouse,** Teaspoon 5.00
Disneyana, **Mickey Mouse,** Trivet, Cast Iron, 3 Feet 30.00
Disneyana, **Mickey Mouse,** Watch Fob, Disney 17.00
Disneyana, **Mickey Mouse,** Watch, Pocket, Ingersoll, Reverse 1939 .... 200.00 To 400.00
Disneyana, **Necklace,** Mickey Mouse, Silver Chain, Enameled Mickey & Minnie 50.00
Disneyana, **Nodder,** Pluto, JVZ Co. 8.00
Disneyana, **Pail,** Sand, Mickey Mouse, Atlantic City, Tin, 6 In. .... *Illus* 92.00
Disneyana, **Paper Doll,** Silly Symphonies, 3 Little Pigs, Uncut 60.00
Disneyana, **Picture,** Dopey, Walt Disney Productions, Framed, 8 X 10 In. 15.00
Disneyana, **Picture,** Gun, Automagic, Mickey Mouse Club, 1946 .... 30.00
Disneyana, **Pillow,** Mickey Mouse Series, Vogue Needlecraft, N.Y. 27.50
Disneyana, **Planter,** Bambi, 9 1/2 X 7 In. 12.00
Disneyana, **Planter,** Mickey Mouse 10.00
Disneyana, **Projector,** Mickey Mouse Club, Slides, Screen, Box 12.00
Disneyana, **Projector,** Mickey Mouse, 9 Rolls, 1 Record, 1929 .... 150.00
Disneyana, **Pull Toy,** Donald Duck, Choo-Choo, 1940 .... 12.50
Disneyana, **Puppet,** Hand, Donald Duck 7.00
Disneyana, **Puppet,** Minnie Mouse, Walt Disney Productions 9.00
Disneyana, **Purse,** Mesh, Mickey Mouse Minnie, C.1930 .... 27.50
Disneyana, **Radio,** Emerson, Mickey Mouse, Wood, C.1935 .... *Illus* 330.00
Disneyana, **Radio,** Mickey Mouse, Emerson, C.1935 .... 325.00
Disneyana, **Ring,** Mickey Mouse, Sterling Silver 9.00
Disneyana, **Rug,** Mickey & Donald, Worn, C.1930, 26 X 32 In. .... *Illus* 52.00
Disneyana, **Rug,** Scatter, Silly Symphony, Mickey, Donald, & Pig, 1930s, 42 In. 38.00
Disneyana, **Salt & Pepper,** Mickey & Minnie, Ceramic, Seated On Wood Bench 19.00
Disneyana, **Set Of Dishes,** Child's, Mickey Mouse, Service For 4 .... 125.00
Disneyana, **Sharpener,** Pencil, Figural, Donald Duck 10.00
Disneyana, **Sharpener,** Pencil, Figural, Mickey Mouse 11.00
Disneyana, **Sharpener,** Pencil, Figural, Pinocchio 9.00
Disneyana, **Sharpener,** Pencil, Mickey Mouse 4.75
Disneyana, **Sled,** Mickey & Minnie Sledding 100.00
Disneyana, **Snow White & The 7 Dwarfs,** Porcelain Figures, Goebel's, VBee 640.00
Disneyana, **Spoon,** Mary Poppins, Silver Plate 5.50
Disneyana, **Spoon,** Mickey Mouse 8.00

Disneyana, Mickey Mouse Washer, Lithographed Tin, 6 In.

Disneyana, Pail, Sand, Mickey Mouse, Atlantic City, Tin, 6 In.

Disneyana, Rug, Mickey & Donald, Worn, C.1930, 26 X 32 In.

Disneyana, Radio, Emerson, Mickey Mouse, Wood, C.1935

Disneyana, Toy, Donald Duck, Seiberling Rubber, 6 In.

Disneyana, Spoon, Mickey Mouse, Silver Plated	5.00
Disneyana, Spoon, Pinocchio, Silver Plate	5.50
Disneyana, Spoon, Pluto, Stainless Steel	4.00
Disneyana, Straw, Mickey Mouse	5.00
Disneyana, String Holder, Mickey Mouse, Decals On Painted Tin	25.00
Disneyana, Tea Set, Child's, Mickey Mouse, C.1929, Japan, 11 Piece	50.00
Disneyana, Tea Set, China, Luster, Mickey Mouse With Long Tail, 10 Piece	28.00
Disneyana, Tea Set, Mickey & Minnie Mouse, Box, 21 Piece	65.00
Disneyana, Tea Set, Mickey, Minnie, Porcelain, 9 Piece, Original Box, 1930s	87.00
Disneyana, Tie Bar, Mickey Mouse, 1930s, 2 In.	24.50
Disneyana, Toothbrush Holder, Minnie & Mickey Mouse	38.00
Disneyana, Toy, Acrobatic Pinocchio, 1939, Marx	135.00
Disneyana, Toy, Donald Duck In Car, Sun Rubber Co.	20.00
Disneyana, Toy, Donald Duck Pushing Wheelbarrow, Celluloid, 1930s	12.00
Disneyana, Toy, Donald Duck, Seiberling Rubber, 6 In. .... *Illus*	60.00
Disneyana, Toy, Fire Truck, Mickey Mouse, Donald Duck Riding, 6 1/2 In.	16.00
Disneyana, Toy, Mickey Mouse Jazz Drummer	65.00
Disneyana, Toy, Mickey Mouse Magician, Battery Operated, Original Box	150.00
Disneyana, Toy, Mickey Mouse Pushing Wheel Barrel, 2 In.Feet	15.00
Disneyana, Toy, Mickey Playing Xylophone, Windup, Walt Disney Productions	75.00
Disneyana, Toy, Mickey, Tin Windup, Linemar, Original Box	32.00
Disneyana, Toy, Minnie Mouse Knits In Rocking Chair, Tin, Windup, 1950s	59.00
Disneyana, Toy, Pinocchio The Acrobat, 1939	75.00
Disneyana, Toy, Pinocchio, Windup, Tin, Marx	48.00
Disneyana, Toy, Pull, Donald Duck, Fisher Price, 1940	8.00

Disneyana, Toy, Xylophone, Donald Duck, Pull Toy	18.00
Disneyana, Tractor, Mickey Mouse, Hard Rubber, Sun Rubber Co.	12.50
Disneyana, Tractor, Mickey Mouse, Red, 6 In.	15.00
Disneyana, Train, 3 Cars, Part Wood, Wheels Wind, Disney Pictures	25.00
Disneyana, Tumbler Set, Figural Snow White & 7 Dwarfs, 8 Piece	15.00
Disneyana, Tumbler, Figural Daisy & Donald Duck	3.50
Disneyana, Tumbler, Mickey Mouse, 1939	7.50
Disneyana, Tumbler, Sleeping Beauty	2.00
Disneyana, Umbrella, Mickey Mouse, Rayon	10.00
Disneyana, Valentine, Pluto, Walt Disney Productions, 1939	3.00
Disneyana, Vase, Bambi, China, 3 1/2 In.	4.00
Disneyana, Watch, Cinderella	15.00
Disneyana, Watch, Mickey Mouse, Ingersoll	95.00
Disneyana, Watch, Mickey Mouse, Oblong Case By Ingersoll, Walt Disney	65.00
Disneyana, Watch, Mickey Mouse, 3 Mice Second Hands, 1930	140.00
Disneyana, Watch, Pinocchio, Red Strap	80.00
Disneyana, Watch, Pocket, Ingersoll, Mickey Mouse, 1934	210.00
Disneyana, Watch, Pocket, Mickey Mouse, 1935	175.00 To 185.00
Disneyana, Watch, Rectangular, U.S.Time, 1947	70.00
Disneyana, Watch, Wrist, Animated Second Dial, Leather Band, 1930, Ingersoll	145.00
Disneyana, Watch, Wrist, Mickey Mouse, Ingersoll, 1940s	50.00 To 85.00
Doctor, Bag, Country Doctor, Black Leather, Brass Lock, Hardware	7.50
Doctor, Bag, Hard Saddle Leather, Telescope, 4 Sections, 46 Bottles, C.1875	35.00
Doctor, Bag, Medicine, Black Leather, Rectangular Case On Bottom	35.00
Doctor, Bleeder, Bone Handle, Hand-Forged Blades, C.1840	51.00
Doctor, Bleeder, Bone Over Brass Case, 3 Blades, 3 In.	45.00
Doctor, Bleeder, Brass, 3 Heavy Blades, 3 1/2 In.	52.00
Doctor, Cabinet, Dental, Twenty Drawer, Black Amethyst Pulls, Maple	275.00
Doctor, Cabinet, Dentist's, Walnut, 20 Drawers, 3 Doors	100.00
Doctor, Case, Optometrist Eye Glass, With Lenses	85.00
Doctor, Crutch For Wooden Leg, Cradle For Leg Stump, Civil War, 25 1/4 In.	75.00
Doctor, Drill, Dentist's, Treadle	100.00
Doctor, Fleam, Brass, Steel, Spring Operated, Velvet Lined Calfskin Case	44.00
Doctor, Kit, Renulife Violet Ray Cure	22.50
Doctor, Kit, Roll Up, 14 Instruments, 13 1/2 X 6 In.	70.00
Doctor, Kit, Surgery, 1836	108.00
Doctor, Knife, Blood, Tortoise Shell Handle, C.1890	24.00
Doctor, Lamp, Spirit, Chrome, Case, Basin, Pioneer, N.Y., U.S.A.	27.50
Doctor, Lens Set, Optometrist's, Leather Case, Oculist's Trial Frame, C.1900	160.00
Doctor, Machine, Double Cell Faradic Cure-All	24.00
Doctor, Machine, Electro-Galvanic Generator Belt, Brochure	19.00
Doctor, Machine, Medical, Electric-Shocking	28.00
Doctor, Machine, Renulife Shocking, 7 Elements	4.00
Doctor, Microscope, Brass, 1880s	165.00
Doctor, Microscope, Mahogany Case & Accessories, Signed, 1850s	335.00
Doctor, Pump, Breast, Ground Glass, 4 7/8 In.	45.00
Doctor, Satchel, Cowhide, Black, Key	10.00
Doctor, Saw, Surgical, Stainless Steel, Small Handle, 12 In.	7.50
Doctor, Sign, Dentist, Pine, Iron Bracket, Side Mount, 2 Names, 20 X 15 In.	38.00
Doctor, Sign, Outdoor, Wood & Tin	50.00
Doctor, Stool, Swivel, Dentist's	30.00
Doctor, Syringe, Aluminum Case, Stainless Steel With 4 Vials	15.00

Doll entries are listed by marks printed or incised on doll, if possible.
If there are no marks, the doll is listed by name of subject or country.
Doll, see also Campbell Kid, Doll; Charlie Chaplin, Doll;
Doll, Paper, see Paper, Doll)
Dionne Quintuplet, Doll; Disneyana, Doll; Kewpie, Doll;
Political Campaign, Doll; Popeye, Doll; Shirley Temple Doll
Doll, Paper, see Paper, Doll
Doll, A.M., see also Doll, Armand Marseille

Doll, A.M., Bisque Head Baby, Sleep Eyes, Composition Body, Dressed, 13 In.	140.00
Doll, A.M., Bisque, Glass Eyes, Mohair Wig, Straw Hat, Pressed Mark, 3 In.	95.00
Doll, A.M., Brown Eyes, Leather Body, 24 In.	145.00
Doll, A.M., Campbell Kid, Toddler Body, Intaglio Eyes To Side, Bisque, 9 In.	185.00

Doll, A.M., Girl, Bisque, Brown Eyes, Ball-Jointed Body, 29 In.	295.00
Doll, A.M., Rockabye, Life Style, 26 In.	550.00
Doll, A.M.253, Googly, Sleep Eyes, Melon Mouth, Baby Body .... *Illus*	475.00
Doll, A.M.323, Googly Eyes, 9 In.	595.00
Doll, A.M.323, Googly, Blue Sleep Eyes, Closed Smiling Mouth, 6 1/2 In.	295.00
Doll, A.M.327-GBbaby, Blue Sleep Eyes, Human Hair Wig, 13 In.	265.00
Doll, A.M.329, Character Baby, Sleep Blue Paperweight Eyes, Bisque, 15 In.	245.00
Doll, A.M.370, Bisque Head & Shoulder, Leather Body, Dressed	100.00
Doll, A.M.370, Kid Body, 20 In.	145.00
Doll, A.M.390, Bisque Head, Sleep Eyes, Joint Composition Body, 35 In.	350.00
Doll, A.M.390, Blue Gray Sleep Eyes, Horsehair Wig, 29 In.	290.00
Doll, A.M.390, Blue Sleep Eyes, Ball-Jointed Body, 20 In.	125.00
Doll, A.M.390, Boy, 11 In.	65.00
Doll, A.M.390, Jointed Body, Blonde Mohair Wig, Open Mouth, 10 In.	100.00
Doll, A.M.390, Turned Head, Hinged Legs & Arms, Kid Body, 18 In.	125.00
Doll, A.M.390, Walking, Talking, Kissing, Bisque, Brown Sleep Eyes, 21 In.	325.00
Doll, A.M.765, Baby, Bent Limb, Kid Body, 15 In.	300.00
Doll, A.M.985, Character Baby, 2 Upper Teeth, Dimples, 10 In.	160.00
Doll, A.M.990, Baby, Blue Sleep Eyes, 2 Upper Teeth, 14 In.	145.00
Doll, Alexander, see Doll, Madame Alexander	
Doll, American Character Co., Betsy McCall, 36 In.	55.00
Doll, Annie Rooney, Bisque, Dressed, 3 In.	125.00
Doll, Armand Marseille, see also Doll, A.M.	
Doll, Aunt Jemima, Stuffed Rag Doll	20.00
Doll, Baby Gloria, Bisque Head, Open Mouth, Brown Eyes, Cloth Body, 15 In.	325.00
Doll, Baby Topsy, 3 Pigtails, Composition, 13 In.	25.00
Doll, Bahr & Prothchild, Toddler, Pinafore, 9 In.	210.00
Doll, Barbie, Vinyl, Movable Head, Arms, Legs, 11 1/2 In, 1959	100.00
Doll, Belton Type, Bisque Head, Paperweight Eyes, Jointed, French, 16 In.	350.00
Doll, Betty, Wind Up, Walking, Tin	55.00
Doll, Bisque Head, Brown Sleeping Eyes, Original Brown Wig, Open Mouth, Teeth	150.00
Doll, Bisque Head, Scottish Clothing, Composition Eyes, 6 In. .... *Illus*	70.00
Doll, Bisque, L 15/0, Kid Body, Set Eyes, Dressed, 11 In.	80.00
Doll, Bisque, Leaf Bonnet-Head, Cloth Body, Bisque Limbs, Dressed, 8 In.	100.00
Doll, Bisque, Moving Eyes, Kid Body, Composition Limbs, Bonnet	329.00
Doll, Bisque, Paperweight Eyes, 5 Teeth, Bisque Hands, Kid Body, R63 3 DEP	300.00
Doll, Bisque, Turban Bonnet Head, Cloth Body, Bisque Limbs, 7 In.	75.00
Doll, Black, Knitted, Red, Blue, Gold Clothes, C.1900, 15 In.	60.00
Doll, Bonnet Head, Bonnet Molded With Flowers, No Feet, 10 In. .... *Illus*	50.00

Doll, Bisque Head,
Scottish Clothing,
Composition Eyes, 6 In.

Doll, Lady, Blonde Hair With Top Knot,
4 1/2 In. *(See Page 170)*

Doll, Man, Black Suit,
Bow Tie, Mustache,
6 1/4 In.
(See Page 171)

Doll, Doll House Lady,
One Leg Separated,
Molded Hair, Top Knot
(See Page 168)

Doll, F.G., Bisque Head,
Stationary Eyes, No Wig,
5 1/2 In. *(See Page 169)*

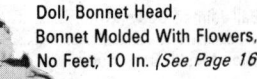

Doll, Bonnet Head,
Bonnet Molded With Flowers,
No Feet, 10 In. *(See Page 167)*

Doll, Stone Bisque, Cloth Body,
China Arms & Legs, 11 In.
(See Page 172)

Doll, Sailor Boy, Bisque Head,
Sleep Eyes, Wool Suit, Cap, 8 In.
(See Page 171)

Doll, A.M.253, Googly, Sleep Eyes,
Melon Mouth, Baby Body
(See Page 167)

Doll, Bonnie Braids, Box	27.00
Doll, Boy, Schoenhut, Green Checked Suit & Cap, Marked, 14 In.	350.00
Doll, Breather Baby, 28 In.	350.00
Doll, Bru Jne 1, Bisque Head, Pierced Earrings, Velvet Outfit, 15 In.	1500.00
Doll, Bru Jne 8, Leather Gusseted Body, Glass Eyes, 24 In.	250.00
Doll, Bruno Schmidt, Tommy Tucker, Jointed Composition Body, Dressed, 22 In.	772.50
Doll, Buddy Lee, H.D.Lee Co., Composition, Striped Overall & Cap	79.00
Doll, Bye-Lo Baby, Bisque Head, Grace S.Putman, Blue Sleep Eyes 250.00 To	350.00
Doll, Bye-Lo, Biskaloid, Blue Eyes, Circular Head, Celluloid Hands	175.00
Doll, C.M.Bergmann, see also Doll, S.&H., Doll, Simon & Halbig	
Doll, C.M.Bergmann, Composition Body, Pierced Ears, 24 In.	175.00
Doll, Century, Baby, Bisque Head, Sleep Eyes, 2 Upper Teeth, 13 In.	300.00
Doll, Charlie McCarthy, Composition, Original Outfit, 19 In.	45.00
Doll, Chase, Stockinette, Painted Eyes, Brown Molded Hair, 1922, 15 1/2 In.	285.00
Doll, China, Head, Arms, Legs, Molded Black Hair, Cloth Body, 17 In.	135.00
Doll, Cloth, Hug Me Tight, Grace Drayton	38.00
Doll, Compostion Head, Straw Body, Wig, Original Clothes, 15 In.	25.00
Doll, Cream Of Wheat, Black Man, Rag	50.00
Doll, Cuno & Otto Dressel, Girl, Bisque Shoulder & Head, Blue Eyes	145.00
Doll, Cuno & Otto Dressel, Girl, Black Eyes, Open Mouth, Oily Bisque, 13 In.	140.00
Doll, Curly Top, Blonde China Head, China Limbs, 22 In.	400.00
Doll, Deanna Durbin, Green Sleep Eyes, Signed Head & Body, 17 In.	225.00
Doll, Doll House Lady, One Leg Separated, Molded Hair, Top Knot *Illus*	90.00
Doll, Dream Baby, Blue Sleep Eyes, Composition Body, 13 In.	295.00
Doll, Dream Baby, Closed Mouth	400.00
Doll, Dutch Rolly Dolly, Schoenhut, Marked, 11 In.	225.00
Doll, Eden Bebe, Girl, Brown, Paperweight Eyes, 21 In.	495.00
Doll, Ee-Gee, Lil Debutante, 15 In.	15.00

Doll, Effanbee, Anne Shirley, Original Clothes & Bracelet, 21 In.	48.00
Doll, Effanbee, Anne Shirley, 15 In.	45.00
Doll, Effanbee, Grumpy Boy, Composition Body, 12 In.	85.00
Doll, F.G., Bisque Head, Stationary Eyes, No Wig, 5 1/2 In.	90.00
Doll, F S.& Co., Baby, Breather, Blue Sleep Eyes, 15 In.	250.00
Doll, Floradora, Kid Body, Dressed, 21 In.	175.00
Doll, Floradora, Wood Body, 16 In.	95.00
Doll, French, Child, Ball-Jointed, Closed Mouth, Sleep Brown Eyes, 7 1/2 In.	375.00
Doll, French, Girl, Cloth, 1920, 17 In.	125.00
Doll, Frozen Charlie, 12 3/4 Inch	150.00
Doll, Fulper, Baby, Blue Sleep Eyes, Brown Human Hair Wig, 18 In.	295.00
Doll, Fulper, Bisque Head, Jointed Toddler Body, Celluloid Blue Eyes, 26 In.	325.00
Doll, Fulper, Kid Body, Blue Sleep Eyes, 23 In.	225.00
Doll, Fulper, Sleep Eyes, Bisque Head, Kid Body, 17 In.	148.00
Doll, Georgine Averill, Baby, Wet Bisque, Christening Dress & Slip, 15 In.	800.00
Doll, German, Baby, Bisque, Jointed At Shoulders, Dressed, 3 In.	30.00
Doll, German, Bisque Baby, Jointed Limbs, Painted Eyes, 3 1/2 In.	22.00
Doll, German, Bisque, Molded Petticoat, Movable, 6 In.	50.00
Doll, German, Boy, Fat Tummy, Painted, Frightened Look, Arms Move, 6 In.	95.00
Doll, German, Boy, Molded Hair, Painted Features, Arms & Legs Move, Nude, 8 In.	135.00
Doll, German, Brown Inset Eyes, Closed Mouth, Incised S/5, 16 In.	400.00
Doll, German, Girl, Blue Sleep Eyes, Lashes, Composition Body, 20 In.	135.00
Doll, German, Girl, Brown Wig, Blue Glass Sleep Eyes, Arms & Legs Move, 8 In.	135.00
Doll, Grace Putnam, Baby, Composion Head, Celluloid Hands, Dressed, 15 In.	85.00
Doll, Handwerck HK, Ball-Jointed Body, Sleep Eyes, 4 Teeth, 26 In.	175.00
Doll, Handwerck 109-B.J., Sleep Eyes, Blue Velvet Dress, 21 In.	225.00
Doll, Handwerck 119, Bisque Body, Sleep Eyes, Pierced Ears, 19 In.	195.00
Doll, Happifat, Bisque, Borgfeldt, C In Circle Mark, Pair	550.00
Doll, Happifat, Bisque, Girl, Blonde Hair, D In Circle Mark	275.00
Doll, Happifat, German, Bisque, 3 1/2 In.	95.00
Doll, Happy Hooligan, Schoenhut, 1924	295.00
Doll, Heubach, Koppelsdorf, 267, Boy, Toddler, Composition & Wood, 13 In.	395.00
Doll, Heubach Koppelsdorf 320, Baby, Breather, Sleep Eyes, 17 1/2 In.	210.00
Doll, Heubach Koppelsdorf, 342, Baby, 7 In.	65.00
Doll, Heubach Koppelsdorf, Baby, Composition Limb Body, 10 In.	160.00
Doll, Heubach Koppelsdorf, Jointed, Blue Sleep Eyes, 27 In.	250.00
Doll, Heubach, Boy, Laughing, Original Kid Body, Bisque & Color, 12 In.	260.00
Doll, Heubach, Boy, Swivel Neck, Character Face, Painted Features, 8 In.	350.00
Doll, Heubach, Dancing Girl, Bisque, Graceful Pose	395.00
Doll, Heubach, Piano Baby, White Dress, Pink Bow, Dimples, 10 In.	120.00
Doll, Hopalong Cassidy, 1940s, 23 In.	175.00
Doll, Howdy Doody, Wood, Smith, Marked, 12 In.	85.00
Doll, Indian, see Indian, Doll	
Doll, Irwin, Creeping Baby, Composition, Key Wind, 7 In.	50.00
Doll, J.D.K., see also Doll, Kestner	
Doll, J.D.K.211, Baby, 2 Lower Teeth, Composition Limb Body, 14 In.	295.00
Doll, J.Verlingue, Bisque Head, Blue Sleep Eyes, French, 24 In.	350.00
Doll, Jackie Coogan, Bisque, 6 1/2 In.	55.00
Doll, Japan, Bisque Head, Arms & Feet, Cloth Body, Brown, 6 In.	25.00
Doll, Jenny Lind Type, China Head, Velvet Clothes, Wood Arms, Legs Painted	185.00
Doll, Jerry Mahoney, 32 In.	70.00
Doll, Jumeau, Closed Mouth, Blue Eyes, 21 In.	1200.00

Doll, Bisque, Moving Eyes, Kid Body, Composition Limbs, Bonnet *(See Page 167)*

Doll, Jumeau, Clothed, Extra Silk Dress, Marked, 24 In. .... *Illus* 1500.00
Doll, Jumeau, Fashion, Swivel Head, Paperweight Eyes, Kid Body, 13 In. 625.00
Doll, Jumeau, Girl, Brown Sleep Eyes, 1907, 23 In. 695.00
Doll, Just Me, Painted Bisque, 15 In. 525.00
Doll, Jutta, 1912, Baby, Blue Sleep Eyes, 14 In. 375.00
Doll, K & H 167, Baby Boy, Brown Eyes, 13 In. 225.00
Doll, K * R SH 121, Toddler, 14 In. 325.00
Doll, K * R Simon & Halbig 43, Composition Body, Pierced Ears, 19 In. 150.00
Doll, K * R 101, Character Baby, Jointed Composition Body, 8 1/2 In. 60.00
Doll, K * R 114, Pouty, Bisque, 13 In. 100.00
Doll, K * R 126, Brown Sleep Eyes, Composition Body, Blonde Mohair Wig, 20 In. 275.00
Doll, K * R 21, Stationary Eyes, Teeth, Molded Socks & Shoes, Wig, 8 1/2 In. 75.00
Doll, K * R, Character Baby, No.1000, Bisque, 11 In. 300.00
Doll, K * R, 126, Baby, 25 In. 475.00
Doll, Kaiser, Baby, Expressive, Coloring, 11 In. 325.00
Doll, Kallus, Pete The Pup, Wooden-Jointed Body, 12 In. 30.00
Doll, Kathe Kruse, Boy, Early 300.00
Doll, Kellogg's Alligator 30.00
Doll, Kellogg's Duck 30.00
Doll, Kelloggs, Goldilocks, Mama, Papa, Baby Bear, Rag 175.00
     Doll, Kestner, see also Doll, J.D.K.
Doll, Kestner 148, Bisque Head, Brown Sleep Eyes, Kid Body, 20 In. 165.00
Doll, Kestner 149, Brown Sleep Eyes, Ball-Jointed, 17 In. 185.00
Doll, Kestner 152, Gray Sleep Eyes, Composition Baby Body, 10 In. 225.00
Doll, Kestner 154, Bisque Head & Arms, Sleep Eyes, Kid Body, Wig, 26 In. 225.00
Doll, Kestner 154, Kid Body, 18 In. 185.00
Doll, Kestner 162, Lady, Blue Sleep Eyes, Open Mouth, Adult Body, 21 1/2 In. 395.00
Doll, Kestner 167, Blue Sleep Eyes, Ball-Jointed Body, 18 In. 185.00
Doll, Kestner 167, Brown Eyes, Molded Brow, 16 In. 210.00
Doll, Kestner 171, Bisque Jointed Body, 21 In. 395.00
Doll, Kestner 171, Daisy, Ball-Jointed Body, 21 In. 195.00
Doll, Kestner 171, Girl, Brown Sleep Eyes, Ball-Jointed Body, 33 In. 395.00
Doll, Kestner 192, Girl, Composition Body, 8 1/2 In. 125.00
Doll, Kestner, Blonde Hair, Brown Sleep Eyes, 32 In. 300.00
Doll, Kestner, Gibson Girl, Sleep Eyes, Bisque Hands, Cloth Body, 10 In. 750.00
Doll, Kestner, Hilda, Jointed Composition Body, 19 In. 140.00
Doll, Kestner, Kid Body, Bisque Hands, French Curls, Brown Sleep Eyes, 16 In. 165.00
Doll, Kestner, Kid Body, Blue Eyes, Wig, Gold Satin Dress, 13-147 Mark, 29 In. 325.00
Doll, Kestner, Kid Body, Closed Mouth, 12 In. 235.00
     Doll, Kewpie, see Kewpie, Doll
Doll, Kewpie, Rose O'Neill, 8 In. 165.00
Doll, Kewty, Metal Sleep Eyes, Composition, 13 1/2 In. 45.00
Doll, Key Wind Walker, R.D.French Body, Flirty Eyes, Cork Pate & Wig, 20 In. 850.00
Doll, Klay & Hahn, Character No.167, Bisque Head, Baby Body, 16 In. 295.00
Doll, Knickerbocker, Dino The Dinosaur, Plush, 17 In. 22.50
Doll, Knickerbocker, Dwarf, Happy, Composition, Original Outfit, 9 In. 50.00
Doll, Knickerbocker, Fred Flintstone, Vinyl, 12 In. 15.00
Doll, Knickerbocker, Huckleberry Hound, Plush, 18 In. 22.50
Doll, L.W. & Co.152, Bisque, 4 Upper Teeth, Sleep Eyes, Brown Wig, 19 In. 285.00
Doll, Lady, Blonde Hair With Top Knot, 4 1/2 In. .... *Illus* 110.00
Doll, Lily, Kid Body, Fancy Dress & Plumed Hat 175.00

Doll, Jumeau, Clothed, Extra Silk Dress, Marked, 24 In.

Doll, **Lily**, 6/0, Brown Eyes, Kid Body, 17 In.	118.50
Doll, **Limoges**, Paperweight Brown Eyes, 22 In.	395.00
Doll, **Little Wide Awake**, Boy, Big Eyes To Right, Laughing, Nude, German, Signed	250.00
Doll, **Little Women**, Hand-Painted, Vinyl Heads, 1963, Set	210.00
Doll, **M.B.Japan**, Fat Baby, 25 In.	250.00
Doll, **M.3/12/210**, Dream Baby, Bisque Head, Blue Eyes, Cloth Body, 10 1/4 In.	150.00
Doll, **Madame Alexander**, Alice In Wonderland, Composition, 14 In.	40.00
Doll, **Madame Alexander**, Barbara Jane, 1952, 29 In.	95.00
Doll, **Madame Alexander**, Brenda Starr, 14 In.	75.00
Doll, **Madame Alexander**, Bride, Vinyl Bendable Knee, With Stand, 7 In.	35.00
Doll, **Madame Alexander**, Dionne, Sleep Eyes, 10 1/2 In.	67.50
Doll, **Madame Alexander**, Jeannie Walker, Labeled Dress, 14 In.	95.00
Doll, **Madame Alexander**, Jo, Little Women, 14 In.	85.00
Doll, **Madame Alexander**, Lissy, 13 In.	45.00
Doll, **Madame Alexander**, Little Butch, Composition Body, 13 In.	45.00
Doll, **Madame Alexander**, Princess Elizabeth, Composition, 16 In.	85.00
Doll, **Madame Alexander**, Sonja Henie, Composition Body, Swivel Waist, 13 In.	125.00
Doll, **Madame Alexander**, Sonja Henie, 15 In.	125.00
Doll, **Madame Alexander**, Swiss, 8 In.	16.00
Doll, **Madame Alexander**, Timmy, 23 In.	40.00
Doll, **Majestic**, Kid & Cloth Body, Sleep Eyes, 4 Upper Teeth, 15 In.	160.00
Doll, **Mama**, Latex Limbs, Composition Head, Looks Like Magic Skin, 6 In.	15.00
Doll, **Man**, Black Suit, Bow Tie, Mustache, 6 1/4 In. *Illus*	110.00
Doll, **Mickey Mouse**, Hard Rubber, Signed Disney	25.00
Doll, **Miss Millionaire**, Bisque, Kid Body, 22 In.	120.00
Doll, **Moa Welsch**, Bisque Face, Composition Body, Swiss Costume, 14 In.	128.00
Doll, **Mr.Peanut**	10.00
Doll, **Mr.Peanut**, All Wood, Jointed, Kallas, Ideal, 1936	65.00
Doll, **Negro**, Composition, Red Felt Suit, Cloth Body, C.1910, 15 In.	65.00
Doll, **Nippon**, Baby, Bisque, With Bottle, 4 In.	25.00
Doll, **Nippon**, Baby, Character Face, Bald Head, Open Mouth, 2 Teeth, 13 In.	150.00
Doll, **Nippon**, Boy, Bisque, Painted Features, Clothes, Fat Tummy, Marked, 3 In.	55.00
Doll, **Nippon**, Girl, Bisque, Jointed, Painted Eyes, Wig, 6 In.	25.00
Doll, **Nippon**, Girl, Bisque, Painted Features, Clothes, Fat Tummy, Marked, 4 In.	55.00
Doll, **Occupied Japan**, Celluloid, Movable Arms, Bathing Suit, 6 1/2 In.	8.00
Doll, **Orphan Annie**, Original Dress, Marked, 18 In.	48.00
Doll, **P.M.914**, Toddler, Blue Sleep Eyes, 5 Piece Body, Dressed, 12 In.	210.00
Doll, **Paper**, In Original Box With Clothes, Mary Hayes Huber	22.00
Doll, **Papier-Mache**, Cloth Body, P.M.Arms, Boots On Feet, German, 50 In.	650.00
Doll, **Pincushion, see Pincushion Doll**	
Doll, **Planters Mr.Peanut**, All Wooden, Jointed, 1930	40.00
Doll, **Prince Edward**, Blue Glass Eyes, Felt, England	55.00
Doll, **Quaker Girl**, Bisque, Painted Eyes, Jointed, 6 In.	23.00
Doll, **Queen Louise**, Brown Sleep Eyes, 23 In.	175.00
Doll, **Queen Louise**, Open Mouth, Ball-Jointed, 24 In.	225.00
Doll, **Revlon**, Jointed Body, High Heel Shoes, Ideal Label	50.00
Doll, **Russian Boys**, Cloth, Marked, 12 In.	22.50
Doll **S & H, see Doll, C. M. Bergmann, Doll, Simon & Halbig**	
Doll, **S & H 3**, Solid Dome, Ball-Jointed Body, Closed Mouth, 7 1/2 In.	375.00
Doll, **S & H 739**, Brown Bisque Moroccan, Jointed Body, Costumed, 19 In.	495.00
Doll, **S & H 940**, Bisque, Closed Mouth, Inset Eyes, Kid Body, 15 In.	450.00
Doll, **S & H 1009**, Brown Eyes, 21 In.	235.00
Doll, **S & H 1079**, Blue Sleep Eyes, Jointed, 23 In.	250.00
Doll, **S & H 1079**, Pierced Earrings, Wood-Jointed Composition Body, 22 In.	180.00
Doll, **S & H 1160**, Pink Cloth Body, Bisque Limbs, Closed Mouth, 6 In.	200.00
Doll, **S & H 1269**, Jointed Wood & Composition Body, 11 In.	195.00
Doll, **S & H, Girl**, Smiling, Brown Eyes, Kid Body, 20 In.	200.00
Doll, **S & H, Santa**, 18 In.	350.00
Doll, **S.F.B.J.60**, Closed Mouth, Painted Eyes, 13 In.	295.00
Doll, **S.F.B.J.227**, Boy Toddler, Painted Hair, Jewel Eyes, Old Suit, 14 In.	900.00
Doll, **S.F.B.J.235**, Boy, Blue Glass Eyes, Composition Body, Upper Teeth, 14 In.	450.00
Doll, **S.F.B.J.236**, Baby, Dark Eyes, 12 In.	525.00
Doll, **S.F.B.J.252**, Pouty, Jointed Composition Body, 19 In.	140.00
Doll, **Sailor Boy**, Bisque Head, Sleep Eyes, Wool Suit, Cap, 8 In. *Illus*	120.00
Doll, **Santa Claus**, Felt, White Fur On Jacket, Plaster Face, C.1870, 8 1/2 In.	65.00

Doll, Scarlett O'Hara, Green Dress, 16 In. 160.00
Doll, Schmidt, Closed Mouth, Brown Eyes, Painted Body, No.18 On Crown, 30 In. 1700.00
Doll, Schoenhut, Boy, Brown Eyes, Open Mouth, Molded Teeth, 19 In. 275.00
Doll, Schoenhut, Circus Lady, Bisque Head, Original Clothes, 8 In. 200.00
Doll, Schoenhut, Girl, Dolly Face, Open Mouth 325.00
Doll, Schoenhut, Jointed, Original Wig 250.00
Doll, Schoenhut, Painted Eyes, Teeth, Shoes & Dress, 21 In. 375.00
Doll, Schoenhut, Pouty, 16 In. 195.00
Doll, Schoenhut, Wood-Jointed Body, 18 In. 195.00
Doll, Scootles, Dressed, 12 1/2 In. 195.00
   Doll, Simon & Halbig, see also Doll, C.M.Bergmann; Doll, S.&H.
Doll, Simon & Halbig 62, Human Hair, Blue Sleep Eyes, Jointed, 24 In. 245.00
Doll, Simon & Halbig 949, Brown Paperweight Eyes, Ball-Jointed Body, 30 In. 695.00
Doll, Simon & Halbig 1249, Santa, Blue Sleep Eyes, 27 In. 450.00
   Doll, Shirley Temple, see Shirley Temple
Doll, Simon & Halbig, Blue Sleep Eyes, Ball-Jointed Body, 24 In. 245.00
Doll, Simon & Halbig, Child, Flapper Type, Blue Sleep Eyes, Dressed, 7 1/4 In. 190.00
Doll, Simon & Halbig, PB In Star, Kid Body, Dressed 175.00
Doll, Skookum, With Papoose 40.00
Doll, Snow Baby, Cloth Body, Bisque Hands & Feet, Shoulder Head, 6 In. 395.00
Doll, Snow White, Original Dress, Composition, 15 In. 70.00
Doll, Sound Of Music, Brigitta, Large 80.00
Doll, Sound Of Music, Friedrich, Large 85.00
Doll, Sound Of Music, Gretl, Small 40.00
Doll, Sound Of Music, Maria, Large 80.00
Doll, Sound Of Music, Marta, Large 65.00
Doll, Spanish Lady In Orange & Black Costume, 1920s, 18 In. 40.00
Doll, Squeeze Toy, Bisque Headed Boy, Blue Eyes, Wooden Feet & Hands, 10 In. 70.00
Doll, Stone Bisque, Cloth Body, China Arms & Legs, 11 In. .... *Illus* 40.00
Doll, Terra Cotta, Creche, Glass Eyes 165.00
Doll, Tete Jumeau, Blue Paperweight Eyes, Applied Ears, 30 In. 1250.00
Doll, Tete Jumeau, Flirty Blue Eyes, 1938, 18 In. 350.00
Doll, Tete Jumeau, Paperweight Eyes, Applied Ears, Closed Mouth, 13 In. 1495.00
Doll, Turtle, Boy, Celluloid, Blue Glass Eyes, Molded Hair, 10 In. 35.00
Doll, Turtle, Girl, Celluloid, Sleep Eyes, 15 In. 37.50
Doll, Unis, France, 5-Piece Jointed Body, Painted Eyes, Composition Body, 8 In 35.00
Doll, Vogue, Angel Baby, Puppet, Blue Sleep Eyes, Molded Hair, 1964 .... 24.00
Doll, Vogue, Ginny Baby, Sleep Eyes, Platinum Hair, Hard Plastic, 12 In. 20.00
Doll, Vogue, Ginny, 7 1/2 In. 12.00
Doll, Wagner & Zetzche, Paperweight Sleep Eyes, Kid Body, 28 In. 550.00
Doll, Wax, Glass Eyes, C.1700, Glass Dome, Pair 195.00
Doll, Wimpy, Rubber, 8 1/2 In. 12.50
Doll, 5 & 5, Baby, Brown Eyes, Cloth Body, Composition Arms & Legs, 15 In. 200.00
   Donald Duck, see Disneyana
   Doorstop, see Iron, Doorstop
Dorchester, Cereal, Blueberry 28.00
Dorchester, Cereal, Pinecone 28.00
Dorchester, Cream & Sugar, Scroll Design 32.50
Dorchester, Crock, Covered, 10 In. 48.00
Dorchester, Cup, Coffee, Grape 20.00
Dorchester, Cup, Coffee, Scroll 20.00
Dorchester, Decanter, Waffle And Thumbprint, Flint 85.00
Dorchester, Demitasse, Blueberry 22.50
Dorchester, Demitasse, Pinecone 22.50
Dorchester, Demitasse, Pussywillow 27.50
Dorchester, Dish, Pinecone 40.00
Dorchester, Foot Warmer 55.00
Dorchester, Mug, Pear, 4 In. 35.00
Dorchester, Mug, Sacred Cod, 4 In. 30.00
Dorchester, Pitcher, Batter, 9 In. 65.00
Dorchester, Plate, Blueberry, 10 In. 125.00
Dorchester, Shell, 3 Feet, Scalloped, Blue, 5 1/2 X 13 X 11 In. 135.00
Dorchester, Sugar & Creamer, White & Blue Scrolling, Signed, C.1957 .... 32.50

Doulton pottery and porcelain were made by Doulton and Co.of Burslem,
England, after 1882. The name Royal Doulton appeared on their wares after 1902.

Doulton, see also Royal Doulton

Doulton, Barrel, Biscuit, C.1891, Blue & White, Silver Plated Lid	55.00
Doulton, Barrel, Biscuit, Impasto, Dated 1881, Signed, Lid, Twisted Handle	55.00
Doulton, Beaker, Sterling Silver Rim, Leather Ware, C.1891, 4 3/4 In.	50.00
Doulton, Bottle, Pilgrim, Donkeys, Buff, Blue Slip Border, Lambeth, 1875, 7 In.	400.00
Doulton, Bowl, Blue Willow, 9 X 4 In.	45.00
Doulton, Bowl, Here's To Charlie, Bobby Burns, C.1926, 9 1/2 In.	37.50
Doulton, Bowl, Kew Pattern, Square, Round Silver Plated Rim, Artist Signed	75.00
Doulton, Bowl, Punch, Blue Willow, Pedestal Base, 9 X 13 In.	400.00
Doulton, Bowl, Punch, Hand-Painted Florals, Pink, Blue, Gold, Burslem, 14 In.	200.00
Doulton, Candlestick, Eliza Simmance, Stoneware, Designs, Mosaic, Lambeth, Pair	175.00
Doulton, Candlestick, Mottled Brown Glaze, Flowered Fern Base & Top, 9 In.	150.00
Doulton, Creamer, Dark Brown With Stars, Lambeth, 5 1/2 In.	40.00
Doulton, Creamer, Raised Decoration, Ruffled Top, Braided Handles, Lambeth	48.00
Doulton, Cup, Loving, D'ye Ken John Peel, 9 In.	325.00
Doulton, Decanter, Art Deco, Flowers & Leaves, Artist Signed, Lambeth	85.00
Doulton, Dresser Set, Burslem, 5 Pieces, Tango Pattern	100.00
Doulton, Ewer, Art Deco Shape & Decoration, Lambeth, 6 1/2 In.	37.50
Doulton, Ewer, Browns, Blues, Rosette Decorated, Lambeth, Frank Butler, 1876	195.00
Doulton, Ewer, Cats & Dogs, Lambeth, Hannah B. Barlow, 10 In.	425.00
Doulton, Ewer, Cobalt Blue Irises Outlined In Gold, Burslem, 8 1/2 In.	65.00
Doulton, Ewer, Flowers, Gold Trim, Pre-1890, Burslem	95.00
Doulton, Ewer, White & Aqua Enameled Flowers, Gold, 1890, Slater, 6 1/2 In.	69.00
Doulton, Holder, Toothbrush, Flow Blue, Lily	48.00
Doulton, Jar, Tobacco, Covered, Artist Anne Partridge, 5 1/2 In.	125.00
Doulton, Jar, Tobacco, Tan, Tree, Windmill, 3 Figures Of Men, Dog, Lambeth	50.00
Doulton, Jar, Tobacco, With Match Holder, Blue, Brown, Frank Butler, Lambeth	275.00
Doulton, Jardiniere, Cobalt, Tapestry Floral Bank, Doulton & Slater, C.1905	100.00
Doulton, Jug, Blue Flowers, Sterling Silver Cover, Dated 1874, Lambeth, 12 In.	250.00
Doulton, Jug, Hunt, Irish Silver Covered Top, Edward Power, Dublin, 1832	188.00
Doulton, Jug, Whiskey, Portrait Of Robert Burns, Lambeth Abbotsford, 9 In.	45.00
Doulton, Jug, White, Herons & Bulrushes In Water, Lambeth, Barlow, 1874, 7 In.	350.00
Doulton, Lamp, Oil, Lambeth Stoneware, Brown, Blue, Pink Flower, C.1885, Pair	188.00
Doulton, Mug, 2-Handled, Brown & Tan, Man, Bird Dog, Doulton, 3 1/2 In.	68.00
Doulton, Pitcher, Blue & White, Burslem, 7 1/2 In.	90.00
Doulton, Pitcher, Brown To Rust, Beading, Lambeth, C.1872, 8 In.	185.00
Doulton, Pitcher, Cream Bottom, Beige Top, Flowers, Gold Spout, Burslem, 8 In.	155.00
Doulton, Pitcher, Embossed Hunt Scene, Buff & Brown, C.1903, Lambeth, 7 In.	68.00
Doulton, Pitcher, Lambeth, Columbian Exposition 1893, No.8386c, 7 1/2 In.	200.00
Doulton, Pitcher, Metal Lid & Thumb Piece, Brown Stoneware, Lambeth, 7 In.	75.00
Doulton, Pitcher, Milk, Hand-Painted, Florals, Gold, C.1885, Burslem, 6 3/4 In.	75.00
Doulton, Pitcher, Raised Figures, Brown & Tan, Lambeth, 6 3/4 In.	30.00
Doulton, Pitcher, Raised Hunting Dogs, Hunter, Brown & White, 7 In.	85.00
Doulton, Plaque, Babes In Woods, Burslem, 11 X 14 In., Pair	675.00
Doulton, Plaque, Christ Healing Sick Man, Lambeth, George Tinworth, 9 In.	175.00
Doulton, Plaque, Pandora, Gold Edge, Burslem, W.T.Thomas, 17 1/2 In.	225.00
Doulton, Plate, Floral, Purple, Blue, & Rose, Scalloped, Burslem, 9 In.	18.00
Doulton, Plate, Madras, Flow Blue, 10 1/2 In.	25.00
Doulton, Plate, Mother & Child, Burslem, 14 In.	175.00
Doulton, Plate, Turkey, White, Blue Birds, 10 In.	48.00
Doulton, Plate, Watteau, 10 In.	22.00
Doulton, Pot, Mustard, Brown, White Hounds Scene, Silverplated Collar	40.00
Doulton, Rose Bowl, Blue Flowers On Speckled Tan Ground, Artist V.H.	65.00
Doulton, Tankard, Character On Cobbled Street, 4 1/2 X 5 1/2 In.	65.00
Doulton, Teapot, Flow Blue, Persian Spray, Burslem, 1882-1891 Mark	89.50
Doulton, Teapot, Gold & Turquoise Enameling, Lambeth	225.00
Doulton, Teapot, Raised Designs, Gold & Turquoise Enameling, Lambeth	225.00
Doulton, Toby Jug, Jolly Fat Man, Lambeth, 3 X 3 In.	185.00
Doulton, Tureen, Raised Blue, Pink Flowers On White, Handles, Burslem, 7 In.	55.00
Doulton, Vase, Brown, Green, Floral, Slater's Patent, 1887, 4 3/4 In.	65.00
Doulton, Vase, Burslem, Beige, Flowers, Gold Edged Top & Trim, U.S.Patent, Pair	95.00
Doulton, Vase, Burslem, Flow Blue Roses, Cobalt & Gold Trim, Dijon, 9 In.	75.00

Doulton, Vase, Cobalt, Tapestry Band, Gold, Blue, Doulton & Slater, 9 In. 125.00
Doulton, Vase, Floral, Lambeth, Slater's Patent, 1887, Artist Signed, 4 1/2 In. 85.00
Doulton, Vase, Lambeth Faience, Stylized Floral, 1880, 10 In. 90.00
Doulton, Vase, Lambeth Faience, 4 Sided Daisy & Buttercups, 1880, 8 In. 80.00
Doulton, Vase, Lambeth, Floral, Green, Yellow, Blue, Artist Signed, 9 In., Pair 110.00
Doulton, Vase, Mottled, Tapestry Border, Slater's Patent, 7 In. 48.00
Doulton, Vase, Pigs & Foxes, H.B.Barlow, Doulton, 10 1/2 In., Pair 455.00
Doulton, Vase, Red Clay, Blue Snake Skin, Stars, Medallion Of Woman, Slater's 165.00
Doulton, Vase, Red Floral, Gold Gilding, Handled, Burslem, 9 In. 95.00
Doulton, Vase, Scenic, Lobsterman, Girl, Lady, Holbein, 14 1/2 In. 575.00
Doulton, Vase, Scroll Work, Pate-Sur-Pate Scenic Panels, Barlow, 10 In., Pair 575.00
Doulton, Vase, Stoneware, Blue, Horses, Florence Barlow, Lambeth, 14 In. 350.00
Doulton, Vase, Stoneware, 5 Incised Blue Horses Grazing, Lambeth, 14 In. 295.00
Doulton, Vase, Symmetrical Incised Design, Lambeth, Edith Lupton, 14 1/2 In. 275.00
Doulton, Vase, Tapestry, Bulbous, Floral & Gold Trim, Burslem, 6 In. 48.00
    Dr.Syntax, see Adams, Staffordshire

Dresden china is any china made in the town of Dresden, Germany. The
most famous factory in Dresden is the Meissen Factory.
Dresden, see also Meissen
Dresden, Basket, Candy, Cabbage Rose, Brass Trimming & Handle, 7 X 7 In. 53.00
Dresden, Basket, Flower Decoration, 1 1/2 X 4 In. 38.00
Dresden, Blotter, Rocking, Floral Pattern, 5 1/2 In. 45.00
Dresden, Bowl, Candy, Cabbage Rose, Pierced Handles, AVR, 3 X 6 In. 65.00
Dresden, Bowl, Candy, Cabbage Rose, Pierced Handles, Open Lace, AVR, 9 In. 65.00
Dresden, Bowl, Floral Lattice Border, Cupids, Gold Rim, Signed, 9 1/2 X 2 In. 185.00
Dresden, Bowl, Floral Lattice, Applied Flowers, Pedestal, 9 1/2 X 7 1/2 In. 120.00
Dresden, Bowl, Shaded Yellow, White, & Pink, Tulips, Gold Leaves, 12 1/4 In. 65.00
Dresden, Box, Triangular, Lidded 30.00
Dresden, Butter Pat, Floral, Hand-Painted 6.50
Dresden, Chocolate Pot, Floral Design, Yellow Band At Top, 7 3/4 In. 125.00
Dresden, Clock, Mantel, 2 Matching Vases, Victorian 110.00
Dresden, Coffee Set, Blue Flowers, Gold, Blue Eagle, CT, 23 Piece 375.00
Dresden, Compote, Footed, Multicolor Floral, Scalloped Gold Edge, C.1880 .... 75.00
Dresden, Compote, Hand-Painted Floral, Pierced Rim, C.1880, Blue Mark, 5 In. 75.00
Dresden, Compote, Hand-Painted Flowers, Gold Trim, Pierced Edge, 3 X 7 In. 65.00
Dresden, Compote, Multicolor Floral, Scalloped Gold Rim, Pierced, Footed, Mark 75.00
Dresden, Creamer, Flowers, Robin's Egg Ground, Rococo Handle, Tiefenfurth 50.00
Dresden, Cup & Saucer, Bouillon, Lamb Mark, Signed, No.347, Set Of 2 .... 15.00
Dresden, Cup & Saucer, Demitasse, Crossed Swords 75.00
Dresden, Cup & Saucer, Gold, Floral 22.00
Dresden, Cup & Saucer, Harbor Scenes, 4 Panels, Hand-Painted, AR 110.00
Dresden, Cup & Saucer, Round Panels, White & Gold Flowers 33.00
Dresden, Cup & Saucer, White, Colorful Flowers, Gold Trim, Footed, Marked 45.00
Dresden, Dessert Set, Hand Painted, Floral & Coin Gold Decorated, 26 Pieces 350.00
Dresden, Ewer, Cobalt, Bird, Branches, Gold, Handle, Cross Swords, 13 1/2 In. 150.00
Dresden, Figurine, Ballerina, Lacy, Applied Flowers On Skirt, 4 1/2 In. 45.00
Dresden, Figurine, Ballerina, 7 In. 55.00
Dresden, Figurine, Jackdaws Perched On Tree Stump, 11 1/2 In., Pair 290.00
Dresden, Figurine, Macaws Perched On Tree Stump, Green & Yellow, 7 In. 225.00
Dresden, Figurine, Parrot Perched On Tree Trunk, Potschappel, 12 In. 80.00
Dresden, Figurine, Parrot, Green Yellow & Blue Yellow, 7 In., Pair 215.00
Dresden, Figurine, Parrot, Red, Yellow, Green Blue, On Tree Stump, 16 In., Pair 395.00
Dresden, Figurine, Pug Puppy Playing Under Mother, 9 1/2 In. 275.00
Dresden, Figurine, Sitting Pug Wearing Collar With Gold Bells, 9 In., Pair 315.00
Dresden, Figurine, Young Pug Playing Under Mother, 9 1/2 In. 215.00
Dresden, Frame, Photo, Rococo Gold Scrolls, Forget-Me-Nots, 9 X 6 1/2 In. 65.00
Dresden, Group, Cavalier & Lady, 18 X 9 1/2 In. 225.00
Dresden, Group, Cavalier & Lady, 20 X 11 In. 200.00
Dresden, Group, Lady In Sedan Chair, 20th Century, 9 1/2 In. 300.00
Dresden, Hatpin Holder, Augustus RK 65.00
Dresden, Inkwell, Floral, Insert & Lid, 3 X 2 1/2 In. 45.00
Dresden, Lamp, Bowl Held By 3 Cupids, Miniature, Pair 60.00
Dresden, Pen, Straight, Floral, 6 1/2 In. 60.00
Dresden, Place Card, Pink Roses, Footed, Set Of 12, 1 1/2 In. 45.00

Dresden, Plaque, Raised Figures Of Man & Woman, Pastels, 9 X 7 1/2 In., Pair 135.00
Dresden, Plate, Buildings Near Stream In Mountains, Cobalt, Gilt, Leaf Mark 35.00
Dresden, Plate, Chop, Two Deer At A Drinking Stream, Signed, 13 In. 50.00
Dresden, Plate, Floral, Gold Trim, 8 1/2 In. 15.00
Dresden, Plate, Flowers & Gold Work, Scalloped, 5 3/4 In., Set Of 3 .... 37.50
Dresden, Plate, Flowers, Open Lattice Border, Cobalt, Gold, Signed 40.00
Dresden, Plate, Fruits, Nuts, & Berries Center, Gold Rim, 10 1/2 In. 35.00
Dresden, Plate, Gold & Flowers, Blue Trim, Scalloped, Crossed Swords, 8 In. 57.50
Dresden, Plate, Scalloped Pierced Borders, Hand-Painted, 8 1/4 In., Pair 45.00
Dresden, Plateau, Cabbage Rose, Open Lace, AVR, 11 1/2 In. 45.00
Dresden, Platter, Floral Pattern, Deep, 18 1/2 X 14 1/2 In. 98.00
Dresden, Ramekin & Underplate, Floral 18.00
Dresden, Salt Set, Portrait Scenes, Flowers On Pierced Rims, Marked, 6 Piece 110.00
Dresden, Salt, Double, Floral, Center Handle, Lamb Mark 45.00
Dresden, Stand, Cake, Floral, Reticulated Base & Top Border, Signed, 4 X 9 In. 95.00
Dresden, Sugar & Creamer, Gold, Green Band With Cherub Scenes, Marked 165.00
Dresden, Swan, Elfinware, 3 In. 85.00
Dresden, Tazza, Two-Piece, Multicolor Flowers, Schumann, 7 X 3 1/2 In. 65.00
Dresden, Teapot, Elfinware 85.00
Dresden, Tile, Tea, Floral & Gold, Round, Marked Crown, Dresden, 6 1/2 In. 30.00
Dresden, Toddy, Tower Of London, Covered, 4 1/2 X 3 1/2 In. 195.00
Dresden, Tray, Pin, Floral Design, Scene In Center, 9 1/4 In. 60.00
Dresden, Vase, Bird Of Paradise, Floral, Lizard Handles, Pierced, 9 1/2 In. 165.00
Dresden, Vase, Pink, Yellow, Green, & Blue, Bird Of Paradise, Temple Dog Finial 190.00
Dresden, Vase, Portrait, Nude Woman, Gold, Blue Jeweling, Wagner, 8 1/2 In. 350.00
Dresden, Vase, Portrait, Turquoise Jewels, Gold, Peach, & Burgundy, 7 1/2 In. 350.00
Dresden, Vase, Temple Dog Finial Top, Oriental, Lizard Handles, 9 1/2 In. 165.00

*Duncan & Miller glass was made at the George A. Duncan and Sons
Company in Washington, Pennsylvania. The company was started in 1894,
with James E. Duncan, president, and Edwin C. Miller, secretary.*

Duncan & Miller, Ashtray, Canterbury 3.00
Duncan & Miller, Ashtray, Crystal, Duck 12.00
Duncan & Miller, Ashtray, Duck, Large 20.00
Duncan & Miller, Ashtray, Duck, Small 10.00
Duncan & Miller, Banana Boat, Mardi Gras, 9 3/4 X 5 3/4 In. 20.00
Duncan & Miller, Basket, Canterbury, Chartreuse, 9 1/2 X 10 In. .... 38.00 To 55.00
Duncan & Miller, Basket, Canterbury, Pink Opalescent, 6 1/2 X 10 In. 60.00
Duncan & Miller, Basket, Canterbury, Pink Opalescent, 10 X 9 1/2 In. 85.00
Duncan & Miller, Basket, Canterbury, 10 In. 23.00
Duncan & Miller, Basket, Clear, Silver Overlay, Tannersville, N.Y., 5 In. 28.00
Duncan & Miller, Basket, Sandwich, Clear, Handle, 12 In. .... 25.00 To 35.00
Duncan & Miller, Basket, Sandwich, 11 In. 32.50
Duncan & Miller, Basket, Sandwich, 6 X 6 In. 30.00
Duncan & Miller, Basket, Tavern, Floral Cutting, 7 1/2 In. 15.00
Duncan & Miller, Bowl With Underplate, Mayonnaise, Etched Floral, Gold Edge 22.00
Duncan & Miller, Bowl, Amber Panels To Clear Top, Canterbury, 5 X 10 1/2 In. 20.00
Duncan & Miller, Bowl, Berry, Sylvan, Divided, 11 1/2 In. 32.00
Duncan & Miller, Bowl, Canterbury, Scalloped, 11 In. 27.00
Duncan & Miller, Bowl, Centerpiece, Sanibel, Pink, 13 1/4 X 14 1/8 In. 65.00
Duncan & Miller, Bowl, Clear, Canterbury, Star Shape, 11 1/2 In. 12.00
Duncan & Miller, Bowl, Console, Large, Flower Etched, Gold Trim 15.00
Duncan & Miller, Bowl, Console, Oval, 10 In. 20.00
Duncan & Miller, Bowl, Crystal Hobnail, Oval, 12 In. 20.00
Duncan & Miller, Bowl, Crystal, Flared, Flat Scallops, 3 X 12 In. 16.00
Duncan & Miller, Bowl, Lacy, Clear, Oblong, 11 1/2 X 7 X 4 In. 48.00
Duncan & Miller, Bowl, Lacy, Scalloped Edge, 10 In. 42.50
Duncan & Miller, Bowl, Murano, Crimped, Pink Opalescent, 11 1/2 X 4 1/2 In. 45.00
Duncan & Miller, Bowl, Murano, Pink Opalescent, 10 In. 45.00
Duncan & Miller, Bowl, No.42, 4 1/2 X 2 1/2 In. 9.00
Duncan & Miller, Bowl, Punch & Base, Mardi Gras 110.00
Duncan & Miller, Bowl, Scalloped, Canterbury, 11 In. 27.00
Duncan & Miller, Bowl, Swirl, Pink Opalescent, 12 In. 48.00
Duncan & Miller, Bowl, Tepee, 8 In. 15.00
Duncan & Miller, Bowl, Tulip, Candlesticks, First Love, Etched 42.50

Duncan & Miller, Box, Candy, Canterbury No.115, Lid	18.00
Duncan & Miller, Box, Cigarette, Sitting Duck Cover	47.50
Duncan & Miller, Bucket, Ice, No.44	35.00
Duncan & Miller, Butter, Dome-Top Cover, Mardi Gras	19.00
Duncan & Miller, Candleholder, Blue Opal, Pair	28.00
Duncan & Miller, Candleholder, Petal Shape, Opalescent Blue, 2 In., Pair	27.50
Duncan & Miller, Candlestick, Green, Handled, Pair	30.00
Duncan & Miller, Celery, Canterbury Lovelace	15.00
Duncan & Miller, Celery, Snail	37.00
Duncan & Miller, Celery, Tepee, Tall	20.00
Duncan & Miller, Champagne, Block-Rosette	22.00
Duncan & Miller, Comport, Mardi Gras, 5 1/4 In.	20.00
Duncan & Miller, Comport, Mardi Gras, 6 1/2 X 9 1/4 In.	45.00
Duncan & Miller, Compote, Jelly With Underplate, Teardrop	15.00 To 20.00
Duncan & Miller, Compote, Tepee, 5 X 5 In.	22.00
Duncan & Miller, Compote, Tree Of Life, Silver Standard, Electric Blue, 8 In.	67.00
Duncan & Miller, Cordial, Mardi Gras	20.00
Duncan & Miller, Cornucopia, Blue, Opalescent, 14 In.	75.00
Duncan & Miller, Cornucopia, Cape Cod, Blue Opalescent, 3 Feather, 12 In.	68.00
Duncan & Miller, Cornucopia, First Love, 12 In.	45.00
Duncan & Miller, Cornucopia, Footed, Clear, Heavy, 12 In.	25.00
Duncan & Miller, Cornucopia, Lay-Down, Clear, 13 In.	29.00
Duncan & Miller, Cornucopia, Pink, Opalescent, 13 In.	65.00
Duncan & Miller, Creamer, Teardrop	12.00
Duncan & Miller, Cup & Saucer, With Tray, First Love, Miniature	30.00
Duncan & Miller, Cup, Punch, Mardi Gras	8.00
Duncan & Miller, Dish, Candy, Canterbury, Chartreuse	20.00
Duncan & Miller, Dish, Candy, Pink Opalescent, 5 Cornered	25.00
Duncan & Miller, Dish, Candy, 3-Part, Lidded, Ruby Canterbury	92.50
Duncan & Miller, Dish, Canterbury, Pink Opalescent, 2 Handles, 8 In.	26.00
Duncan & Miller, Dish, Cheese, Tepee Covered	75.00
Duncan & Miller, Dish, Honey, White, Blackberry Pattern, 4 In.	24.00
Duncan & Miller, Dish, Sanibel, Blue Opalescent, Flat Shell	28.00
Duncan & Miller, Duck, Solid, 4 In.	60.00
Duncan & Miller, Duck, 2 1/2 In.	17.00
Duncan & Miller, Duck, 4 In.	45.00
Duncan & Miller, Duck, 5 In.	30.00
Duncan & Miller, Epergne, 4 Flower Holders, Crystal Bowl, Pink Opalescent	125.00
Duncan & Miller, Flower Holder, Pink & Blue, 4 In.	18.00
Duncan & Miller, Flower Holder, Pink, 5 1/2 In.	28.00
Duncan & Miller, Glass, Shot, Frosted	18.00
Duncan & Miller, Goblet, First Love, Terrace Stem	12.50
Duncan & Miller, Goblet, Teardrop	8.00
Duncan & Miller, Hat, Pink, 3 In.	22.50
Duncan & Miller, Heron	75.00
Duncan & Miller, Jar, Cookie, Mardi Gras, 8 1/2 In.	55.00
Duncan & Miller, Jar, Cracker, Covered	42.50
Duncan & Miller, Jug, Honey, No.42	30.00
Duncan & Miller, Jug, Tepee, Squat, 1/2 Gallon	35.00
Duncan & Miller, Match Holder, Crystal Boot	15.00
Duncan & Miller, Mayonnaise Set, Canterbury, Etched Flowers, Gold Edge	22.00
Duncan & Miller, Nappy, Diamond Ridge, Round Scalloped Edge, 5 In.	14.50
Duncan & Miller, Nappy, Gold	16.00
Duncan & Miller, Nappy, No.42	13.50
Duncan & Miller, Pitcher, Milk, Button Arches, Ruby Stained, Souvenir, 1920	28.50
Duncan & Miller, Pitcher, Tankard, Mardi Gras	50.00
Duncan & Miller, Plate, Caribbean, Blue, Tab Handled, 13 In.	12.00
Duncan & Miller, Plate, No.42, 5 In.	10.00
Duncan & Miller, Plate, Ruby, Teardrop, Handles, 10 1/4 In.	30.00
Duncan & Miller, Plate, Sanibel, Pink Opalescent, 7 1/2 In.	25.00
Duncan & Miller, Platter, Sylvan, Yellow Opalescent, 13 In.	38.00
Duncan & Miller, Punch Set, Crystal, Red-Handled Cups, 14 Piece	115.00
Duncan & Miller, Punch Set, 12 Cups, Ladle, Underplate, Hobnail	95.00
Duncan & Miller, Relish, Canterbury, Blue Opalescent, 2-Handled, Divided	25.95
Duncan & Miller, Relish, Canterbury, First Love, 3 Compartments, 3 Handled	18.00

Duncan & Miller, **Relish**, Divided, Blue Opalescent Shell	24.00
Duncan & Miller, **Relish**, First Love, Canterbury	15.00
Duncan & Miller, **Relish**, Mardi Gras, 8 In.	15.00
Duncan & Miller, **Relish**, No.130, Jasmine, Opalescent, 13 X 9 1/4 In.	49.00
Duncan & Miller, **Relish**, Sanibel, Blue Opalescent, 2-Compartment, 8 1/2 In.	20.00
Duncan & Miller, **Relish**, Sanibel, Blue Opalescent, 3 Sections, 13 In.	39.00
Duncan & Miller, **Relish**, Shell Shape, Divided, Pink Opalescent, 8 1/2 In.	20.00
Duncan & Miller, **Relish**, Sylvan, Blue Opalescent, Divided, 8 1/2 In.	20.00
Duncan & Miller, **Relish**, Sylvan, Ruby Handle, 3 Part, 11 1/2 In.	22.50
Duncan & Miller, **Relish**, 3 Compartment, Green Handles, Teardrop, 8 In.	12.00
Duncan & Miller, **Rose Bowl**, Blue Opalescent	23.00 To 35.00
Duncan & Miller, **Rose Bowl**, Grated Diamond & Sunburst, No.158	25.00
Duncan & Miller, **Salt**, Mardi Gras	3.00
Duncan & Miller, **Salt**, Single With Top, Tepee	8.00
Duncan & Miller, **Salt**, Snail	18.00
Duncan & Miller, **Sauce**, Heavy Paneled Finecut, Footed, Square	7.00
Duncan & Miller, **Shade**, Tepee	22.00
Duncan & Miller, **Sherbet**, Crystal, Canterbury	5.00
Duncan & Miller, **Sherbet**, Plaza, Pink	7.00
Duncan & Miller, **Shoe**, Daisy & Button, Victorian Novelty	20.00
Duncan & Miller, **Spooner**, Block	25.00
Duncan & Miller, **Spooner**, Mardi Gras, Gold, Child's	30.00
Duncan & Miller, **Spooner**, Snail	35.00
Duncan & Miller, **Sugar & Creamer**, Block, Yellow Flashed, Etched	50.00
Duncan & Miller, **Sugar & Creamer**, Blue Opalescent, Canterbury	45.00
Duncan & Miller, **Sugar & Creamer**, Pink Opalescent, Canterbury	32.00
Duncan & Miller, **Sugar**, Caribbean, Crystal	7.00
Duncan & Miller, **Sugar**, Diamond	3.00
Duncan & Miller, **Sugar**, Mardi Gras	9.00
Duncan & Miller, **Sugar**, Teardrop	12.00
Duncan & Miller, **Swan**, Blue Opalescent, 12 In.	95.00
Duncan & Miller, **Swan**, Chartreuse, 7 1/2 In.	39.00
Duncan & Miller, **Swan**, Chartreuse, 10 1/2 In.	57.00
Duncan & Miller, **Swan**, Clear, Ming, 12 X 10 In.	37.50
Duncan & Miller, **Swan**, Clear, 7 In.	12.00
Duncan & Miller, **Swan**, Clear, 7 1/2 In.	9.00
Duncan & Miller, **Swan**, Clear, 10 1/2 X 8 1/2 In.	16.50
Duncan & Miller, **Swan**, Clear, 11 In.	24.00
Duncan & Miller, **Swan**, Crystal, 3 1/2 In.	15.00
Duncan & Miller, **Swan**, Crystal, 7 in.	9.50
Duncan & Miller, **Swan**, Crystal, 14 In.	35.00
Duncan & Miller, **Swan**, Emerald Green, 14 In.	52.00
Duncan & Miller, **Swan**, Green Body, Clear Neck, 10 In.	40.00
Duncan & Miller, **Swan**, Green Body, Clear Neck, 11 In.	35.00
Duncan & Miller, **Swan**, Green, 10 In.	40.00
Duncan & Miller, **Swan**, Opalescent Pink Spread Wing, 12 In.	65.00
Duncan & Miller, **Swan**, Pall Mall, 3 In.	25.00
Duncan & Miller, **Swan**, Pall Mall, 12 In.	49.00
Duncan & Miller, **Swan**, Red Body, Clear Neck, 6 In.	18.00
Duncan & Miller, **Swan**, Red Body, Clear Neck, 7 1/4 In.	25.00
Duncan & Miller, **Swan**, Red Body, Clear Neck, 12 In.	60.00
Duncan & Miller, **Swan**, Red, Clear Neck & Head, 5 In.	47.50
Duncan & Miller, **Swan**, Red, Clear Neck, 7 In.	18.00
Duncan & Miller, **Swan**, Red, Factory Sticker, 10 In.	54.00
Duncan & Miller, **Swan**, Red, 4 In.	75.00
Duncan & Miller, **Swan**, Red, 4 1/2 In.	50.00
Duncan & Miller, **Swan**, Red, 6 1/2 In.	38.00
Duncan & Miller, **Swan**, Red, 11 In.	62.00
Duncan & Miller, **Swan**, Red, 7 1/2 In.	30.00
Duncan & Miller, **Swan**, Smoky Avocado, 10 1/2 In	60.00 To 68.00
Duncan & Miller, **Swan**, Solid Crystal, 3 X 5 In., Pair	55.00
Duncan & Miller, **Swan**, Sterling Overlay, 6 1/2 In.	48.00
Duncan & Miller, **Swan**, Sylvan Blue Opalescent, 7 1/2 In.	75.00
Duncan & Miller, **Swan**, Sylvan Pink Opalescent, 5 1/2 In.	42.50
Duncan & Miller, **Swan**, Sylvan, Blue Opalescent, 5 In.	47.50

Duncan & Miller, Swan, Sylvan, Blue Opalescent, 7 In. 65.00
Duncan & Miller, Swan, Sylvan, Pink Opalescent, 8 In. 65.00
Duncan & Miller, Swan, Sylvan, 3 In. 25.00
Duncan & Miller, Swan, Sylvan, 7 1/2 In. 30.00
Duncan & Miller, Swan, Vaseline, 7 In. 35.00
Duncan & Miller, Swan, Vaseline, 8 In. 25.00
Duncan & Miller, Swan, Wings Spread, Large 30.00
Duncan & Miller, Sweetmeat, Sanibel, Opalescent, Blue, 8 In. 22.50
Duncan & Miller, Tankard, No.20 .... 57.00
Duncan & Miller, Toothpick, Mardi Gras 30.00
Duncan & Miller, Toothpick, Tepee .... 25.00 To 30.00
Duncan & Miller, Tray, Mint, Sylvan, 7 1/2 In. 12.00
Duncan & Miller, Tray, Sanibel, Blue Opalescent, 7 In. 18.00
Duncan & Miller, Tray, Sanibel, Pink Opalescent, 13 In. .... 32.00 To 55.00
Duncan & Miller, Tray, Sanibel, Pink Opalescent, 3 Compartment, 12 In. 45.00
Duncan & Miller, Tray, Sweetmeat, Pink Opalescent, Sanibel, 6 1/2 In. 12.50
Duncan & Miller, Tumbler, Cocktail, Dover, Red, 4 In. 15.00
Duncan & Miller, Tumbler, Footed, 12 Ounces 4.00
Duncan & Miller, Tumbler, Ice Tea, Laurel Wreath, Touraine Stem, 12 Oz. 12.00
Duncan & Miller, Urn, Ruby, Covered, Label, 10 In. 40.00
Duncan & Miller, Vase, Blue Opalescent, Crimped, 3 1/2 In. 18.00
Duncan & Miller, Vase, Blue Opalescent, 4 In. 15.00
Duncan & Miller, Vase, Canterbury, Blue Opalescent, Violet 12.00
Duncan & Miller, Vase, Canterbury, Blue Opalescent, 5 X 4 In. 25.00
Duncan & Miller, Vase, Canterbury, Blue Opalescent, 5 1/2 In. 30.00
Duncan & Miller, Vase, Canterbury, Clear, 5 In. 8.50
Duncan & Miller, Vase, Canterbury, Pink, Opalescent, 6 In. 30.00
Duncan & Miller, Vase, Canterbury, Sterling Overlay Of Flowers, 9 In. 30.00
Duncan & Miller, Vase, Cyrstal, Handled, Urn Shape 11.00
Duncan & Miller, Vase, Hat, Blue Opalescent 25.00
Duncan & Miller, Vase, Hobnail, Amber, 7 1/2 In., Pair 12.50
Duncan & Miller, Vase, Hobnail, Blue Opalescent, 8 In. 65.00
Duncan & Miller, Vase, Hobnail, Pink Opalescent, Crimped Top, 8 1/2 In. 30.00
Duncan & Miller, Vase, Intaglio Cut Garlands & Fern Shapes, 3 Feet, 9 In. 45.00
Duncan & Miller, Vase, Mardi Gras, Tapered, 6 3/4 In. 30.00
Duncan & Miller, Vase, Mardi Gras, 13 In. 20.00
Duncan & Miller, Vase, No.42, 6 1/2 In. 12.00
Duncan & Miller, Vase, Opalescent, Canterbury, 3 In. 12.50
Duncan & Miller, Vase, Opalescent, Canterbury, 4 1/2 In. 15.00
Duncan & Miller, Vase, Teardrop, Copper Wheel Cut Florals, 9 In. 36.00
Duncan & Miller, Vase, Trumpet, Caribbean, Blue, 7 1/4 In. 20.00
Duncan & Miller, Vase, Violet, Crimped, 4 1/2 In. 15.95
Duncan & Miller, Vase, Violet, Pair 10.00
Duncan & Miller, Viking Ship, Clear, 12 In. 38.00
Duncan & Miller, Wine, Mardi Gras 14.00
Duncan & Miller, Wine, No.42 .... 15.00

*Durand glass was made by Victor Durand from 1879 to 1935 at several
factories. Most of the iridescent Durand glass was made by Victor
Durand, Jr., from 1912 to 1924 at the Durand Art Glass Works in
Vineland, New Jersey.*

Durand, Atomizer, Orange Iridescent 120.00
Durand, Bowl, Amber Luster, Opalescent Pull-Ups, 4 1/4 X 8 1/2 In. 225.00
Durand, Bowl, Rose, Applied Iridescent Threading 110.00
Durand, Candlestick, Orange Iridescent, Signed, 10 In. 185.00
Durand, Compote, Feather, 13 In. 800.00
Durand, Compote, Iridescent Gold, 7 1/2 X 8 In. 325.00
Durand, Decanter, Bull's-Eyes, Stars, Arches, Faceted Stopper 110.00
Durand, Dish, Scalloped Rim, Footed, Yellow, Green, 5 1/4 X 2 1/2 In. 55.00
Durand, Jar, Iridescent Pumpkin Over White, 10 1/2 In. 225.00
Durand, Lamp Base, Egyptian Crackle & Brass 300.00
Durand, Lamp, Iridescent Gold, Spider Web Threading, 14 1/2 In. 450.00
Durand, Lamp, Luster, Spider Web Threading, Original Fittings, 12 In. 350.00
Durand, Lamp, Table, Threading, Blue Iridescent 200.00

Durand, Liquor, Blue & White Feather Pattern, Canary Round Base, 4 1/2 In.	185.00
Durand, Pitcher, Hand Wrought, Green, Emil Larsen	325.00
Durand, Rose Bowl, Green & Blue Iridescent, Spider Webbing	110.00
Durand, Rose Bowl, Pulled Green Feather On Butterscotch, Threading, Footed	475.00
Durand, Shade, Lily Shape, Iridized And Threaded, 8 In.	185.00
Durand, Stem Liquor, Blue & White Feather Pattern, 4 1/2 In.	185.00
Durand, Tumbler, Liquor, Blue & White, Feather, Stemmed, 4 1/2 In.	185.00
Durand, Vase, Beige, Random Gold Threading, Polished Pontil, 8 In.	365.00
Durand, Vase, Blue Feathering, Platinum Iridescence On White, Gold, 6 In.	875.00
Durand, Vase, Blue Flowers, Gold Iridescent Background, 6 1/2 In.	425.00
Durand, Vase, Blue Iridescence, Applied Blue Threads, White Hearts, 7 In.	475.00
Durand, Vase, Blue Iridescent Glass, Signed & Numbered, 10 In.	850.00
Durand, Vase, Blue Iridescent, Applied Threading, No.1710, Signed, 7 In.	525.00
Durand, Vase, Blue Iridescent, Ruffled Rim, 9 In.	375.00
Durand, Vase, Blue Iridescent, White Heart & Vines, Gold Base, 8 In.	625.00
Durand, Vase, Blue Luster, Spider Webbing, 8 1/2 In.	975.00
Durand, Vase, Blue Threading, Iridescent, Blue, Signed, 7 In.	525.00
Durand, Vase, Blue, Signed, Numbered, 10 In.	450.00
Durand, Vase, Butterscotch Iridescent, White Decoration, 12 In.	435.00
Durand, Vase, Crackle, Red & Clear, 12 In.	475.00
Durand, Vase, Fluorescent Blue, Signed & Numbered, 7 In.	295.00
Durand, Vase, Gold & Apricot Threaded, Bulbous, 8 X 6 1/2 In.	550.00
Durand, Vase, Gold & Green, King Tut Design, Everted Rim, 6 In.	900.00
Durand, Vase, Gold Iridescence, 10 X 7 In.	550.00
Durand, Vase, Gold Iridescent, White King Tut Pattern, Signed, 6 1/2 In.	475.00
Durand, Vase, Gold Threaded & Decorated, Signed, 10 In.	1000.00
Durand, Vase, Gold, White, & Red, Egyptian Crackle, Bulbous, 7 In.	600.00
Durand, Vase, Hearts & Vine, Blue, Opalescent Decoration, 10 In.	850.00
Durand, Vase, Iridescent Blue Ground, Silver Thread, 8 X 7 1/2 In.	125.00
Durand, Vase, Iridescent Blue, No.1710-6, Signed, 6 1/2 In.	595.00
Durand, Vase, Iridescent Blue, Signed, 6 In.	290.00
Durand, Vase, Iridescent Emerald Green, Signed, 5 In., Pair	140.00
Durand, Vase, Iridescent Gold, Blue Highlights, Paperweight Base, 8 1/2 In.	150.00
Durand, Vase, King Tut On Cobalt, 3 In.	185.00
Durand, Vase, King Tut, Green, Gold Decorated & Lined, 9 1/2 In.	1150.00
Durand, Vase, Overlay, Silvery Threading, Iridescent, Blue, 7 1/2 In., Pair	950.00
Durand, Vase, Peacock Blue, Random Threading, Signed, 5 In.	525.00
Durand, Vase, Platinum, Iridescent, 10 1/4 In.	445.00
Durand, Vase, Sapphire Blue, Silver Feathering, Maroon Interior, 10 1/2 In.	750.00
Durand, Vase, Threading, Orange Iridescent, No.1710, Signed, 6 1/2 In.	450.00
Durand, Vase, Turquoise Blue, Spider Webbing, 7 In.	575.00
Durand, Vase, White Opal Glass With Raised Gold Threading, 7 1/2 In.	325.00
Durand, Vase, White, Signed, 10 In.High	275.00
Durand, Wine, Feather Pattern, Ruby Top, Stemmed, Applied Base, 5 3/4 In.	195.00
Durand, Wine, Gold Iridescent, Unsigned	90.00
Edwin Bennett, Syrup, Gray, Vertical Markings, Pewter Lid, 6 In.	75.00
Edwin Bennett, Syrup, Raised Floral & Geometrics, Pewter Lid, 7 In.	75.00
Edwin Bennett, Syrup, Vertical Markings, Pewter Lid, Gray Glaze, 7 In.	65.00
Elvis Presley, Album, Roustabout	8.50
Elvis Presley, Autograph	35.00
Elvis Presley, Bracelet, Dog Tag, 1956	20.00
Elvis Presley, Button, Fan Club, Dated 1956	8.50
Elvis Presley, Button, Flasher, Dated 1956, 2 1/2 In.	3.00
Elvis Presley, Button, Photo, Late 1950s	3.00
Elvis Presley, Calendar, RCA, 1970	3.00
Elvis Presley, Card, Lobby, Elvis On Tour	7.50
Elvis Presley, Flasher Pin, Love Me Tender, 1956	2.50
Elvis Presley, Hat, Black & White Cotton, Dated 1956	20.00
Elvis Presley, Hat, Tag With Picture, Dated 1956	65.00
Elvis Presley, Knife, Portrait, Name, Dates, King Of Rock-N-Roll, 3 1/2 In.	10.00
Elvis Presley, Matches, Las Vegas	8.00
Elvis Presley, Matches, Memphis	8.00
Elvis Presley, Mirror, Pocket, Elvis & Parents 1956 Lettered, 2 X 3 In.	3.50
Elvis Presley, Movie Still, Blue Hawaii	5.00
Elvis Presley, Necklace, Dog Tag	3.50

Elvis Presley, **Necklace**, Picture, Oval Pendant	3.50
Elvis Presley, **Photograph**, Glossy, 4 X 5 In.	5.00
Elvis Presley, **Picture**, Signed, Easter Greetings, Elvis Presley, 1967	15.00
Elvis Presley, **Pin**, Flasher, Love Me Tender, C.1956	3.00
Elvis Presley, **Poster**, Clambake, 50 X 90 In.	75.00
Elvis Presley, **Poster**, Follow That Dream, 50 X 90 In.	75.00
Elvis Presley, **Poster**, Frankie & Johnny, 50 X 96 In.	75.00
Elvis Presley, **Poster**, Las Vegas, 24 X 36 In.	8.50
Elvis Presley, **Record**, Elvis Sun, No.210	400.00
Elvis Presley, **Record**, Sun Label, Baby Let's Play House	250.00
Elvis Presley, **Record**, Vol.1, 1956, 4 Songs In Jacket	20.00
Elvis Presley, **Scarf**, Signed	35.00 To 45.00
Elvis Presley, **Sheet Music**	20.00
Elvis Presley, **Spoon**, Gold Plated, C.1960, Palladium Appearance	5.00
Elvis Presley, **Tape Measure**, Figural, Heart, Love Me Tender	3.00
Elvis Presley, **Wristwatch**	25.00
Enamel Ware, see Graniteware	
Enamel, **Austrian**, Vase, Emerald Green, 2 Panels, 16 1/2 In.	110.00
Enamel, **Bell**, 14K Gold Chain, Diamond Clapper	50.00
Enamel, **Box**, Chinese Design, 3 X 3 1/2 In.	23.00
Enamel, **French**, Plaque, Portrait	255.00
Enamel, **Plaque**, Viennese, Blind Man's Bluff, Brass Frame, 6 In.	225.00
Enamel, Russian, see also Faberge	
Enamel, **Russian**, Case, Cigarette, Turquoise & White, Gustav Klingert	1200.00
Enamel, **Russian**, Fork, Turquoise, White Border, Gustav Klingert	145.00
Enamel, **Russian**, Salt Cellar, Shaded Enamel	445.00
Enamel, **Russian**, Scoop, Sugar, Foliated Design, Champleve, Anton Kuzmichev	700.00
Enamel, **Russian**, Silver & Enamel Cigar Box, Sazikov, 5 1/2 In. ....*Illus*	5500.00
Enamel, **Russian**, Spoon, Demitasse, Fitted Case, Gustav Klingert, Set Of 12	3000.00
Enamel, **Russian**, Spoon, Karelian Birch, Fine Detail, CK	375.00
Enamel, **Russian**, Spoon, Serving, Champleve, Anton Kuzmichev	575.00
Enamel, **Russian**, Sugar Basket, Silver-Gilt, Plique-A-Jour, 4 In. ....*Illus*	9500.00
Enamel, **Russian**, Sugar Tongs, Ivan Saltykov	625.00
Enamel, **Russian**, Sword & Scabbard, Miniature, Marked, 84 Moveable Parts	275.00
Enamel, **Vase**, Dark Blue, Pastel Colored Floral & Scroll Work, 8 3/4 In.	215.00

End-of-day glass is now an out-of-fashion name for spattered glass. The glass was made of many bits and pieces of colored glass. Traditionally, the glass was made by workmen from the odds and ends left from the glass used during the day. Actually it was a deliberately manufactured product popular about 1880 to 1900, and some of it is still being made.

End-Of-Day, **Atomizer**, Bulbous Top, Slim Body, Flared Base, 6 1/2 In.	47.50
End-Of-Day, **Basket**, Cased White Inside, 5 1/2 In.	85.00
End-Of-Day, **Basket**, Green, Blue, & Pink, Chartreuse Lining, 8 1/4 X 3 5/8 In.	85.00
End-Of-Day, **Basket**, Ruffled, Cobalt Applied Handle, Pontil, Blue, Chartreuse	65.00
End-Of-Day, **Bottle**, Cologne, Ricksecker, Applied Clear Handles, Gold Letters	150.00

Enamel, Russian, Silver & Enamel
Cigar Box, Sazikov, 5 1/2 In.

Enamel, Russian, Sugar Basket, Silver-Gilt,

Plique-A-Jour, 4 In.

End-Of-Day, Bowl, Red, Blue, Pink, Yellow, & Orange, Flared Sides, 8 1/2 In. 38.00
End-Of-Day, Bowl, Scalloped, Multicolored, 12 X 3 1/2 In. 45.00
End-Of-Day, Candlestick, Spatter Glass Cased In Clear, Pair, 9 1/4 In. 145.00
End-Of-Day, Creamer, Cased, Tortoise 45.00
End-Of-Day, Rose Bowl, Cased, Shells Form Cupped Base, Shell Feet, Clear Stem 57.50
End-Of-Day, Shoe, Clear Decoration, Reds, Cased White 65.00
End-Of-Day, Shoe, High Top, Cased, Yellow, Orange, & White, Clear Applied Leaf 85.00
End-Of-Day, Syrup, Cranberry & Opalescent, Dated Top 100.00
End-Of-Day, Vase, Amber, Green & Burgundy Colors, Fluted Top, White Interior 55.00
End-Of-Day, Vase, Applied Decoration & Handle, Squatty, White Initial, 3 In. 45.00
End-Of-Day, Vase, Aventurine, Pinched Base, Fluted Top, Cased, Pontil, Pair 85.00
End-Of-Day, Vase, Cased Glass, Applied Glass Base, 6 1/4 In. 68.00
End-Of-Day, Vase, Cobalt Interior, Overshot Multicolors Outside, 6 1/2 In. 12.00
End-Of-Day, Vase, Fluted Lip, Yellow, Burgundy, Bulbous, 6 In. 55.00
End-Of-Day, Vase, Jack-In-The-Pulpit, Crimped, 7 1/2 In. 35.00
End-Of-Day, Vase, Melon Shape, Ruffled Top, Cased In White, Blue, Green, 9 In. 48.00
End-Of-Day, Vase, Red, White, & Blue, Yellow Pontil, 6 X 5 1/2 In. 45.00
End-Of-Day, Vase, Ruffled Top, Triangular, Pink, Green, White, 7 1/2 In. 48.00
End-Of-Day, Vase, Six-Sided, Red, White, Blue, 6 In. 20.00
End-Of-Day, Vase, 2 Applied Cobalt Handles, 4 1/2 In. 65.00
End-Of-Day, Vase, 5 Clear Feet, White, Pink, Brown, 5 In. 50.00
ES Germany, Basket, Handled, Bird 58.00
ES Germany, Berry Set, Four Seasons, Portraits Of Ladies, 10 Piece 235.00
ES Germany, Berry Set, Tapestry, Cloverleaf, Wild Rose On Beige, 11 Piece 650.00
ES Germany, Bowl, Grecian Scenes Each Section, Divided, Handle, Gold, 10 In. 40.00
ES Germany, Bowl, Green, Luster, Gold Scrolls, Maidens, Crown Mark, 13 1/2 In. 75.00
ES Germany, Bowl, Handled, Ships Docked, Windmill, Lighthouse, GROV SXEmark 55.00
ES Germany, Bowl, Pale Green Luster, Gold Scrolls, Maiden Center, 13 1/2 In. 75.00
ES Germany, Bowl, Portrait, Royal Saxe, 9 In. 125.00
ES Germany, Bowl, Raised Floral, Luster Panels, Gold Handle, 11 In. 45.00
ES Germany, Box, Dresser, Emerald Green Glass, Gold Cover, Footed 17.50
ES Germany, Chocolate Set, Floral, Provsaxe Mark, 9 Piece 95.00
ES Germany, Cup & Saucer, Chocolate, Yellow Roses 20.00
ES Germany, Cup & Saucer, Classic Scene, 2 Women, Angel, Blue, Green, Orange 55.00
ES Germany, Dish, Bird On Branch, Handled, No.1 Mark 55.00
ES Germany, Dish, Divided Serving, Twig Handle, Hand-Painted Florals, 10 In. 64.00
ES Germany, Dish, Luster, Oblong, Silver Deposit Trim, 9 In. 20.00
ES Germany, Dish, Robin On Tree Branch, Clover Shape, 12 In. 75.00
ES Germany, Dish, Scalloped Pink & White Roses, Handled, 14 1/2 X 9 1/2 In. 40.00
ES Germany, Ewer, Jeweled Brunette Woman Holding Rose, Gold Trim, 16 1/2 In. 375.00
ES Germany, Figurine, Pheasant, Plumage, 8 In. 38.00
ES Germany, Mayonnaise Dish, Flowers, Underplate Attached, Green 18.00
ES Germany, Nappy, Scenic, Handled, 7 In. 50.00
ES Germany, Plate, Bird On Tree Limb, Rusts & Browns, Square, 7 X 8 In. 68.00
ES Germany, Plate, Cake, White Flowers, Gold Trim, Hand-Painted, 10 In. 18.00
ES Germany, Plate, Classical Scene, A.Kaufmann, Marked, 10 In. 95.00
ES Germany, Plate, Classical Scene, Puffed Medallion Border 15.00
ES Germany, Plate, Game, Woodland Scene, Embossed Scrolls, 10 In. 115.00
ES Germany, Plate, Portrait, Hanging, 10 In. 90.00
ES Germany, Plate, Portrait, Ladies, Iridescent Pearl Ground, Gold Frame, Pair 92.00
ES Germany, Plate, Portrait, Maid Harvesting Wheat, Blue With Gold, 10 In. 65.00
ES Germany, Plate, 3 Maidens Dancing, No.36 Mark, Signed A.Kauffmann 60.00
ES Germany, Plate, 4 Grecian Woman, 1 Mark, 6 1/2 In. 20.00
ES Germany, Relish, Bird On Limb, Blue Sky, Green Grass, 7 X 5 In. 39.00
ES Germany, Toothpick, 2 Handle, Red Mark 35.00
ES Germany, Tray, Dresser, Grosbeak Bird On Flowered Branch, 7 X 14 In. 75.00
ES Germany, Tray, Dresser, Peaches 40.00
ES Germany, Vase, Butterfly & Portrait, 7 In. 45.00
ES Germany, Vase, Classical Scene, Red, Royal Saxe, 9 In. 89.00
ES Germany, Vase, Double Handled, Portrait Of Girl, 7 1/2 In. 160.00
ES Germany, Vase, Handled, Pink Roses, Shaded White To Charcoal, 8 In. 70.00
ES Germany, Vase, Jeweled Portrait, 2-Handled, 15 3/4 In. 250.00
ES Germany, Vase, Lady & Peacock, 2-Handled, 11 In. 285.00
ES Germany, Vase, Portrait, Lady & Peacock, Double Gold Handles, 5 In. 98.50
ES Germany, Vase, Portrait, Royal Saxe, 6 X 6 In. 89.00

ES Germany, Vase, Queen Louise Portrait, 7 1/2 In. 80.00
ES Germany, Vase, Scenic, Patrician Lady, Gold Double Handles, 16 In. 185.00
ES Germany, Vase, White To Dark Charcoal Ground, Pink Roses, Handled, 8 In. 70.00
ES Germany, Vase, 2-Handled, Young Girl & Birds, 15 In. 125.00
ES Prussia, Bowl, Yellow Roses, Rust To Cream Background, 10 In. 65.00
ES Prussia, Chocolate Set, Violet Decoration, 13 Piece 285.00
ES Prussia, Teapot, White Roses, Pastel Apricot Ground, Marked 65.00
ES Saxe, Plate, Game, Hanging, Bird On Cliff, Woodland Scene, Embossed, 10 In. 100.00
Eskimo, Walrus Tusk, 21 In. 175.00
Eskimo, Walrus Tusk, 29 In. 375.00
  Etruscan Majolica, see Majolica

  Faberge was a firm of jewelers and goldsmiths founded in St.
  Petersburg, Russia, in 1842, by Gustav Faberge. Peter Carl
  Faberge, his son, was jeweler to the Russian Imperial Court from
  about 1870 to 1914.
Faberge, Cufflink, Gold, Diamond And Pearl, C.1900, Pair, 1/2 In.Diameter 1200.00
Faberge, Figurine, Chimpanzee, Agate, Rose-Diamond Eyes, 2 3/8 In. 485.00
Faberge, Fork, Silver, Neo-Egyptian, C.1910, Set Of 12 .... 700.00
Faberge, Hand Mirror, Silver, Parcel-Gilt, C.1900, 9 3/4 In. 750.00
Faberge, Jewel Casket, Silver And Enamel, C.1910, 6 3/8 In. 9000.00
Faberge, Knife, Paper, Ivory, Mounted In Gold & Enamel, C.1900, 6 In. 1600.00
Faberge, Mug, Silver, Cylindrical Shape, Frieze Of Swans, C.1910, 3 1/2 In. 1200.00
Faberge, Salver, Silver, Reeded Edge, C.1890, 9 1/2 In.Diameter 1500.00
Faberge, Toilet Set, Silver And Cut Glass, C.1910, 8 Piece 2500.00
Faberge, Vase, Silver, Tapered Cylindrical Body, C.1900, 9 1/8 In. 1000.00
Faience, Box, Woman Gathering Wheat, Trefoil, Joseph Olery, Moustiers, C.1745 .... 200.00
Faience, Charger, Birds, Vines, Cupid Head Flower Centers, Nove ZA, 13 In. 125.00
Faience, Inkwell, Florals, Enamel Work, Rouen, 1780, Blue, Red, Rust, Yellow 75.00
Faience, Mush Set, Cream, Mulberry Leave & Berry, Gold, Avalon 115.00
Faience, Planter, Hanging Hat, 5 1/2 X 7 3/4 In. 68.00
Faience, Plate, Rural Scene, Tournai, Dated 1760, Pair 90.00
Faience, Porringer, Yellow Bird, White Glaze, Handled, 5 1/4 In. 18.00
Faience, Tile, Galleon At Sea, Marked, 5 1/2 In.Square 55.00
Faience, Vase, Covered, Purple Wisteria, Gold, Tortoise Shell, 16 In. 495.00
Faience, Vase, Floral, Leaves, Foliage, Barbotine Painted, 7 In. 55.00
Faience, Vase, French, Drip Glaze, 8 1/2 In. 20.00
Faience, Vase, High-Gloss Brown, 5 3/4 In. 65.00

  Fairings are small souvenir china boxes sold at country fairs during the
  nineteenth century.
Fairing, Box, Trinket, Boy And Rooster 65.00
Fairing, Box, Trinket, Boy With Dog, Polychrome Decoration, Oval 30.00
Fairing, Box, Trinket, Chest Of Drawers With Cover, Open Mirror Frame 45.00
Fairing, Box, Trinket, Child & Dog Atop Mirrored Chest, 4 1/4 In. 45.00
Fairing, Box, Trinket, Child Rowing In Round Basin 40.00
Fairing, Box, Trinket, Fireplace With Mantel, Boy With Hoop & Stick 48.00
Fairing, Box, Trinket, Jester & Dog, Conta & Boehm, 9 1/2 In. 175.00
Fairing, Box, Trinket, Lady Holding Spaniel Dog 95.00
Fairing, Box, Trinket, Lid Form Of King's Bust, 3 3/4 X 3 3/4 In. 70.00
Fairing, Box, Trinket, Man With Turban On Horse 24.00
Fairing, Box, Trinket, Mirror Frame Lid, Crown, Orb, Scepter, Sword 32.00
Fairing, Box, Trinket, Napoleon Seated In Chair Holding Cane, 10 In. 175.00
Fairing, Box, Trinket, Patch, White & Gold, Boy, Tree Stump, Basket Of Fruit 48.00
Fairing, Box, Trinket, Ring & Watch On The Lid 47.00
Fairing, Box, Trinket, Saltglaze Lion On Cover, Small 24.00
Fairing, Box, Trinket, Swan On Nest, White & Gold, 3 In. 25.00
Fairing, Box, Trinket, Violin On Lid, Oval 18.00
Fairing, Box, Trinket, Washington And Horse, 4 In. 57.50
Fairing, Box, Trinket, Watch On Cover, Ring, Mirror 45.00
Fairing, Box, Trinket, White & Gold, Basket Weave, Pear Finial, 3 1/4 In. 24.50
Fairing, Couple On Horseback, Captioned Going To Market 66.00
Fairing, Last To Bed 48.00
Fairing, Marriage Bed, Last To Bed To Put Out The Lights, Small 35.00
Fairing, Married For Money 52.00

Fairing, To Be Taken In Cold Water, Tipsy Man Sitting In Bathtub	65.00
Fairing, Welsh Tea Party, 3 Ladies In Steeple Hats At Table	20.00
Famille Rose, see Chinese Export	
Fan, see also Store, Fan	
Fan, Batiste, Silver & White Florals, White Stick, Silver Decoration	18.00
Fan, Black Ostrich Feather, 20 In.Across	22.00
Fan, Black Silk & Lace, Blue & Purple Flowers	16.50
Fan, Carved Ivory, Hand-Painted, Satin Florals	45.00
Fan, Celluloid With Birds	12.50
Fan, Courting Couple, Art Nouveau, Mother-Of-Pearl Frame	195.00
Fan, Figural, Cigar Shaped When Closed	25.00
Fan, Folding, Lady's	5.00
Fan, Ivory Inlay Of Silver, Sequined Silk	25.00
Fan, Japan, Paper	6.00
Fan, Lace, Amber Sticks, In Satin Box, Paris, Large	250.00
Fan, Miniature, Etched Mother-Of-Pearl, Ivory Leaves Dance Card, Gold	58.00
Fan, Ostrich Feather, L.C.Monogram Outlined In Diamonds, Boxed, Signed	300.00
Fan, Ostrich Feather, Marquise De Gennaro	35.00
Fan, Ostrich, Tortoise Shell Ribs, Turquoise, 24 X 20 In.	55.00
Fan, Parchment, Violets & Green Leaves, Blue Sticks, Tassel	18.00
Fan, Pretty Lady, Funeral Home, 1927	3.50
Fan, Wood & Red Silk, Hand-Painted Roses, 14 In.	35.00
Fan, Wood & Silk, Scenic, Cloth Insets, 17 In.	50.00
Fan, Wooden, Portrait Of Senorita, Handpainted, Scenic, 38 Sections, 10 In.	30.00
Fan, 1893 Columbian Exposition, Parchment Over Bamboo, Signed	10.00

*Fenton Art Glass Company, founded in Martins Ferry, Ohio, by
Frank L.Fenton, is now located in Williamstown, West Virginia. It
is noted for early carnival glass produced between 1907 and 1920. Many other
types of glass were also made.*

Fenton, Basket, Red Slag, C.1932, 9 X 6 X 4 1/2 In.	90.00
Fenton, Bowl, Console, Mongolian, Green, Fluted Edge, Dome Foot, 12 1/4 In.	42.50
Fenton, Bowl, Red Slag	35.00
Fenton, Centerpiece Set, Ruby With Amber Dolphin, 3 Piece	25.00
Fenton, Compote, Dolphin Handles, Jade	18.00
Fenton, Figurine, Bird, 7 In.	22.00
Fenton, Jar, Jam, Black Base & Lid	28.00
Fenton, Jar, Powder, Opalescent	12.00
Fenton, Mug, Bull's-Eye, Red	9.50
Fenton, Nappy, Pale Blue Slag, Hobnail, Heart Shaped, Handled	12.00
Fenton, Paperweight, Eagle, Bicentennial	15.00
Fenton, Plate, Orange Tree, Blue, Iridescent, 9 1/2 In.	42.50
Fenton, Rose Bowl, Burmese	18.00
Fenton, Rose Bowl, Custard Glass, Persian Medallion, Green Staining	65.00
Fenton, Vase, Caramel Green, 2 Harem Ladies, Art Deco, 9 In.	75.00 To 85.00
Fenton, Vase, Cranberry Opalescent, Hobnail, 5 In.	65.00
Fenton, Vase, Diamond-Quilted, Lavender, 8 In.	20.00
Fenton, Vase, Honey Amber, Overlay, 8 In.	15.00

fiesta

*Fiesta dinnerware was introduced in 1936 by the Homer Laughlin China
Co., redesigned in 1969, and withdrawn in 1973. The simple design was
characterized by a band of concentric circles, beginning at the rim. Cups
had full-circle handles until 1969, when partial-circle handles were made.
Harlequin and Riviera were related wares.*

Fiesta Ware, Ashtray, Old Green	12.00
Fiesta Ware, Bowl, Cream Soup, Turquoise	8.00
Fiesta Ware, Bowl, Dessert, Aqua, 6 In.	6.00
Fiesta Ware, Bowl, Fruit, Cobalt	40.00
Fiesta Ware, Bowl, Salad, Ivory, Large	12.50
Fiesta Ware, Candleholder, Bulb Type, Ivory, Pair	14.50
Fiesta Ware, Candleholder, Bulb Type, Red, Pair	25.00
Fiesta Ware, Candleholder, Tripod, Pair	52.50
Fiesta Ware, Candlestick, Bulb, Green, Pair	18.00
Fiesta Ware, Candlestick, Light Blue, Pair	10.00
Fiesta Ware, Carafe, Cobalt, 10 In.	25.00 To 38.50

Fiesta Ware, Casserole, Aqua, Covered, Handled 27.00
Fiesta Ware, Casserole, Covered, Forest Green 20.90
Fiesta Ware, Coffeepot, Amberstone 18.00
Fiesta Ware, Coffeepot, Blue 36.50
Fiesta Ware, Coffeepot, Gray 24.00
Fiesta Ware, Compote, Fruit, Bone, 12 In. 35.00
Fiesta Ware, Creamer, Red, Stick Handle 5.00
Fiesta Ware, Creamer, Rose 4.00
Fiesta Ware, Creamer, Scotty, Harlequin, Green 7.00
Fiesta Ware, Cup & Saucer, After Dinner, Red 14.50
Fiesta Ware, Cup, Nut, Harlequin, Red 3.00
Fiesta Ware, Demitasse, Navy 15.00
Fiesta Ware, Eggcup, Dark Green 18.00
Fiesta Ware, Eggcup, Yellow .... 9.00 To 15.00
Fiesta Ware, Gravy Boat, Aqua 7.00
Fiesta Ware, Gravy Boat, Chartreuse 8.00
Fiesta Ware, Gravy Boat, Cobalt 13.00
Fiesta Ware, Gravy Boat, Gray 9.00
Fiesta Ware, Gravy Boat, Navy 8.00
Fiesta Ware, Gravy Boat, Turquoise 8.00
Fiesta Ware, Jar, Kitchen Kraft, Red, 3 Piece 180.00
Fiesta Ware, Jug, Ivory, 2 Pint 12.00
Fiesta Ware, Jug, Yellow, 2 Pint 15.00
Fiesta Ware, Juice Set, Multicolor, 6 Piece 50.00
Fiesta Ware, Mug, Turquoise .... 15.00 To 20.00
Fiesta Ware, Nappy, Old Ivory, 8 1/2 In. 6.00
Fiesta Ware, Nappy, Yellow 6.00
Fiesta Ware, Pitcher, Disk, Red 12.00
Fiesta Ware, Pitcher, Juice, Gray 25.00
Fiesta Ware, Pitcher, Juice, Red, Small 25.00
Fiesta Ware, Plate, Chop, Navy, 12 In. 12.00
Fiesta Ware, Plate, Chop, Red, 14 In. 20.00
Fiesta Ware, Plate, Chop, Rose, 12 In. 15.00
Fiesta Ware, Plate, Chop, Yellow 15.00
Fiesta Ware, Plate, Compartment, Ivory, 10 1/2 In. 5.00
Fiesta Ware, Plate, Pie, Gray 3.00
Fiesta Ware, Plate, Pie, Turquoise 1.25
Fiesta Ware, Plate, Yellow, 9 In. 2.50
Fiesta Ware, Platter, Turquoise, 12 In. 8.00
Fiesta Ware, Pot & Lid, After Dinner, Turquoise 35.00
Fiesta Ware, Saltshaker, Red 5.00
Fiesta Ware, Saltshaker, Yellow 3.00
Fiesta Ware, Saucer, After Dinner, Red 3.50
Fiesta Ware, Server, Cake, Green 15.00
Fiesta Ware, Spoon, Salad, Blue 15.00
Fiesta Ware, Teapot, Turquoise, Large 20.00
Fiesta Ware, Teapot, Yellow, Small 25.00
Fiesta Ware, Tray, Utility, Turquoise 6.00
Fiesta Ware, Vase, Bud, Green, 6 In. 37.50
Fiesta Ware, Vase, Bud, Red 20.00

*Findlay, or onyx, glass was made using three layers of glass. It was
manufactured by the Dalzell Gilmore Leighton Company about 1889 in
Findlay, Ohio. The silver, ruby, or black pattern was molded into the glass.
The glass came in several colors, but was usually white or ruby.*

Findlay Onyx, Bowl, Creamy Ivory With Silver, 8 In. 275.00
Findlay Onyx, Butter, Raspberry, Silver, Covered 700.00
Findlay Onyx, Celery, Creamy Ivory With Silver 325.00
Findlay Onyx, Celery, 6 1/2 In. 425.00
Findlay Onyx, Creamer, Cinnamon 800.00
Findlay Onyx, Creamer, Ivory, Applied Handle With Silver, 4 1/2 In. 400.00
Findlay Onyx, Muffineer, Platinum Decoration, 5 1/4 X 3 In. 400.00
Findlay Onyx, Muffineer, Platinum On Cream, Original Cover 260.00
Findlay Onyx, Sugar Shaker 275.00
Findlay Onyx, Toothpick, Raspberry & White 505.00

Findlay Onyx, Toothpick, Silver Overlay	150.00
Findlay Onyx, Tumbler, Barrel Shape, Creamy Ivory, Silver	220.00
Findlay Onyx, Vase, Becomes Wider At Bottom, 4 X 3 1/4 In.	175.00
Fire, Andiron, Brass Cannon Ball Finials, Iron	85.00
Fire, Andiron, Brass, Adam Design	64.00
Fire, Andiron, Brass, C.1800, 16 1/2 In., Pair	185.00
Fire, Andiron, Brass, C.1860, 16 In., Pair	198.00
Fire, Andiron, Brass, Chippendale, C.1800, Spool Finials, 26 In.	350.00
Fire, Andiron, Brass, Chippendale, Urn Standard, C.1830, Pair	275.00
Fire, Andiron, Brass, Miniature, 1 3/4 In., Pair	20.00
Fire, Andiron, Footed Gooseneck, 18 In., Pair	140.00
Fire, Andiron, Gooseneck Style, 19 X 19 In.	65.00
Fire, Andiron, Gooseneck, Faceted Head, 13 In., Pair	90.00
Fire, Andiron, Gooseneck, Hand-Forged, C.1850, 19 In.	55.00
Fire, Andiron, Gooseneck, Iron, 18th Century, 13 X 24 In., Pair	128.00
Fire, Andiron, Iron, Figures Of George Washington, ESC DB VA15 In., Pair	200.00
Fire, Andiron, Iron, Large, Pair	200.00
Fire, Andiron, Owl, Cast Iron, Glass Eyes	42.00
Fire, Andiron, Queen Anne, Brass, Pair	70.00
Fire, Andiron, Steeple Top, Brass, C.19th Century, 22 X 18 In.	85.00
Fire, Andiron, Victorian Bronze, Cupids, Italian, C.1850, 3 Ft.High, Pair	1850.00
Fire, Ax, Black Paint, Wooden, Blade Points, Pick End, 20 In.	23.00
Fire, Badge, Gold Plated Deputy Chief Department, Red Lettering	29.00
Fire, Bag, Handwoven Material, C.Burr Printed In Black, 4 1/2 X 2 In., Pair	165.00
Fire, Bellows, Brass, Harlech Castle Gatenhouse, Leather & Hobnails	45.00
Fire, Bellows, Wood & Leather	25.00
Fire, Belt, Fireman's, Leather, Red & White, Embossed Salem	95.00

Fire, Helmet, Fireman's, Plumed,
Brass, Pompier D'Annency

Fire, Stove, Caboose,
Southern Pacific Railroad, Rim, 38 In.

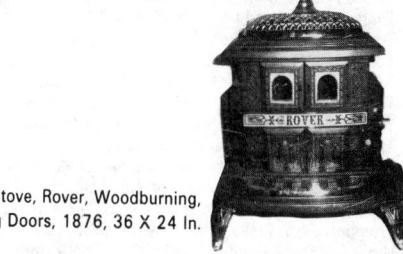

Fire, Stove, Parlor Favorite, 57 X 26 In.

Fire, Stove, Red Cross,
Base Burner, 9-17-1889, 62 X 44 In.

Fire, Stove, Rover, Woodburning,
Sliding Doors, 1876, 36 X 24 In.

Fire, Broiler, Upright, Braced, 18th Century, 11 X 11 In.	145.00
Fire, Broiler, Whirling, Rotating, Iron, Hand Forged, C.1740, 8 In.	230.00
Fire, Bucket, Leather, A.Sturtevant, No.2	70.00
Fire, Bucket, Leather, Clasped Handles, Dated 1807, 14 In.	350.00
Fire, Button, Fireman's, Ribbon, Pin, Terryville, Connecticut, 1936, 1 1/2 In.	15.00
Fire, Crane, Fireplace, 23 In.	38.00
Fire, Crane, Fireplace, 42 In.Post, 44 In.Arm	200.00
Fire, Crane, Hand Forged, For Deep Fireplace, 18th Century, 38 In.	75.00
Fire, Ember Tongs, Wrought Iron, 17 In.	65.00
Fire, Extinguisher, Brass, Kidde, 24 In.	20.00
Fire, Extinguisher, Fuse Melts, Hanging Type	10.00
Fire, Extinguisher, Fyr-Fyter, Junior Firefighters Picture, Brass, 18 In.	22.50
Fire, Extinguisher, Hand, Brass, 14 In.	17.00
Fire, Extinguisher, Hose, Copper & Brass, 2 1/2 Gallon	27.50
Fire, Fan, Louis XVI Ormolu, 28 In.	275.00
Fire, Fender, Brass & Iron, Copper Rosettes, 1 X 4 Ft.	145.00
Fire, Fender, Brass, C.1860, 54 X 14 X 7 1/4 In.	228.00
Fire, Fender, Federal, Pierced & Engraved Brass, C.1825, 6 X 60 In.	375.00
Fire, Fender, Pierced Brass, English, C.1820, 41 X 11 In.	230.00
Fire, Fender, Pierced Iron, Brass Top Rail, 27 3/4 In.	95.00
Fire, Fender, Wire, American, C.1800, 37 In.	80.00
Fire, Fireplace Shield, Ships, Handle, Legs, Brass	45.00
Fire, Fork, 2-Tine, Hand-Forged Iron, Shaped Handle, 19 In.	67.00
Fire, Grill, Iron, Handle, 4 Footed Legs, 19 1/2 In.	65.00
Fire, Guard, For Fireplace, Solid Brass Finials, C.1800	200.00
Fire, Helmet, Eagle, C.1880	125.00
Fire, Helmet, Fireman's, French, Pigeon On Top	85.00
Fire, Helmet, Fireman's, Gloucester, Massachusetts, Fire Department No.1	57.50
Fire, Helmet, Fireman's, Plumed, Brass, Pompier D'Annency .... *Illus*	70.00
Fire, Hod, Coal, Grecian Design In Relief On Cover	248.00
Fire, Lighter, Cast Iron, 4 Clasped Hands, Hole For Hanging	18.00
Fire, Nozzle, Brass, Hose, 7 In.	8.50
Fire, Nozzle, Brass, Hose, 13 In.	35.00
Fire, Poker, Loop Handle, Hand-Forged, 23 In.	14.50
Fire, Screen, Louis XV, Carved, Gessoed, Gilt, 3-Fold Boudoir, C.1880, 43 In.	250.00
Fire, Screen, Rosewood, Needlework, Early 19th Century	450.00
Fire, Scuttle, Coal, American, Brass, Shield On Handle, 15 In.	228.00
Fire, Stove, Bonnie Sunshine, Eisenglass Parlor, Sears, 1895, 4 Ft.	650.00
Fire, Stove, Bonnie Sunshine, Ornate Parlor	675.00
Fire, Stove, Caboose, Southern Pacific Railroad, Rim, 38 In. .... *Illus*	695.00
Fire, Stove, Gas, Graniteware, Blue & White, 1920s, Apartment Size	275.00
Fire, Stove, Iron, 1848	125.00
Fire, Stove, Parlor Favorite, 57 X 26 In. .... *Illus*	895.00
Fire, Stove, Potbelly, 26 In.	80.00
Fire, Stove, Radiant Estate, No.517, Hard Coal	2100.00
Fire, Stove, Red Cross, Base Burner, 9-17-1889, 62 X 44 In. .... *Illus*	4750.00
Fire, Stove, Rover, Woodburning, Sliding Doors, 1876, 36 X 24 In. .... *Illus*	795.00
Fire, Stove, Wood Burning, Parlor, Nickel Trim, 4 1/2 Ft.	850.00
Fire, Stove, Wood Burning, 3 Panel, Shaker	300.00
Fire, Tongs, Hand-Forged Iron, Pipe Tongs, 11 In.	95.00
Fire, Tongs, Hand-Forged Iron, 13 In.	45.00
Fire, Tongs, Hand-Forged Iron, 17 In.	65.00
Fire, Tool Set, Figural Owls On Handles, 3 Piece	75.00
Fire, Tool Set, Shovel, Poker, Tongs, Brass	65.00
Fire, Tool Set, Stand, Brush, Shovel, Poker, 14 In.	35.00
Fire, Trivet, Brass & Iron, Cabriole Leg, English, Late 18th Century	175.00
Fire, Trivet, Brass, Queen Anne Legs, Home Sweet Home On Front	228.00
Fire, Trivet, Fireplace, Square, Footed, Handled, Iron, 19th Century	55.00
Fire, Trivet, Hand-Forged, 3 Bars, C.1700, 1 1/2 X 5 1/2 X 6 In.	45.00
Fire, Trumpet, Silver Presentation, Dated 1892	400.00
Fire, Urn, Coal, Black Granite, 2 Handles At Top & Bottom, 24 In.	34.00

*Fireglow glass resembles English Bristol glass. But a reddish-brown
color can be seen when the piece is held to the light. It is a form of art*

glass made by the Boston and Sandwich Glass Co.of Massachusetts, and other companies.

Fireglow, Ewer, Diamond-Quilted, Mother-Of-Pearl Handle, Apricot, 8 In.	75.00
Fireglow, Ewer, Enamel Woodland Scene, 7 1/2 In.	225.00
Fireglow, Pitcher, Gold Enameling, Webb, 2 In.	125.00
Fireglow, Tumbler, Water, Peach To Pink, Enameled Floral, Acid Finish	130.00
Fireglow, Vase, Autumn Colored Leaves, Edged In Gold, 9 In.	100.00
Fireglow, Vase, Brown & Red Orange Sprays, Shells, Scrolls, Feathery, 7 In.	110.00
Fireglow, Vase, Coralene & Enameling, 14 In.	60.00
Fireglow, Vase, Enameled Flowers, Ruffled Top, 3 1/4 In.	90.00
Fireglow, Vase, Geraniums, Green Ives, Banded Top, Long Neck, Bulbous, 15 In.	160.00
Fireglow, Vase, Hand-Enameled Floral Spray, 7 In., Pair	280.00
Fireglow, Vase, Ruffled, Sandwich, 3 1/4 In.	90.00
Fireplace Tools, see Fire, Tongs, etc.	

Fischer porcelain was made in Herend, Hungary. The factory was founded in 1839, and has continued working into the twentieth century. The wares are sometimes referred to as Herend porcelain.

Fischer, Bowl, Budapest, Flowers & Gold Decoration, Upturned Ends, Footed	250.00
Fischer, Cake Plate, Birds, Hand-Painted, 9 1/2 X 11 In.	110.00
Fischer, Figurine, Nude Kneeling, Looking In Mirror, 4 In.	65.00 To 145.00
Fischer, Pitcher, Milk, Raised Enamel Florals, Paneled, Gold Base, 5 1/2 In.	32.00
Fischer, Sugar, Raised Enamel Florals, Paneled, Reticulated Gold Base, Cover	50.00
Fischer, Vase, Birds, Butterflies, 4 Footed, Square Gold Stand, 8 In.	95.00
Fischer, Vase, Reticulated Body, Blue Florals, Gold Handles, 7 3/4 In.	95.00
Fish Set, Hand Painted, Fish Jumping Over Waves, Art Nouveau	165.00
Fish Set, Platter, 9 Dishes, Haviland, Artist Signed, 10 Piece	450.00
Flag, see Textile, Flag	
Flash Gordon, Book, Paint, 1936	18.00
Flash Gordon, Jacket, Costume	8.00
Flash Gordon, Toy, Windup Rocket Fighter No.5, Mint	90.00
Flatiron, see Kitchen, Flatiron	

Flow blue, or flo blue, was made in England about 1830 to 1900. The plates were printed with designs using a cobalt blue coloring. The color flowed from the design to the white plate so the finished plate had a smeared blue design. The plates were usually made of ironstone china.

Flow Blue, Basin, Wash, Kan-Su, Mulberry, T.Walker, C.1850, 13 1/2 In.	120.00
Flow Blue, Bone Dish, Adderleys, Laurier	10.00
Flow Blue, Bone Dish, Duchess, Grindley	14.00
Flow Blue, Bone Dish, Idris, Grindley	12.50
Flow Blue, Bone Dish, Le Pavot, Grindley, Set Of 3	25.00
Flow Blue, Bone Dish, Lorne	14.00
Flow Blue, Bone Dish, Marked England	17.00
Flow Blue, Bone Dish, Osborne, Ridgway	16.00
Flow Blue, Bone Dish, Portman	15.00
Flow Blue, Bowl, Albany, Embossed Flange Around, Tab Handles, Grindley, 17 In.	145.00
Flow Blue, Bowl, Berry, Clarence	15.00
Flow Blue, Bowl, Celtic, Grindley, Oblong, 10 1/4 X 7 1/4 In.	30.00
Flow Blue, Bowl, Cereal, Fairy Villas, 6 3/4 In.	18.50
Flow Blue, Bowl, Cereal, Normandy, Johnson, 6 1/4 In.	18.50
Flow Blue, Bowl, Clyde, F & Sons, 12 In.	20.00
Flow Blue, Bowl, Coup, Argyle, Grindley, 10 In.	22.50
Flow Blue, Bowl, Covered, Blue Danube, 2 Handles, Oblong, 12 1/2 In.	75.00
Flow Blue, Bowl, Covered, Melbourne, Grindley, Oblong, 12 X 7 1/2 In.	95.00
Flow Blue, Bowl, Covered, Osborne, Ridgway, 5 1/2 In.	45.00
Flow Blue, Bowl, Covered, Osborne, Ridgway, 10 1/2 X 9 1/2 In.	60.00
Flow Blue, Bowl, Covered, Osborne, 2 Handled, 5 1/2 In.	45.00
Flow Blue, Bowl, Covered, Tonquin, 9 In.	150.00
Flow Blue, Bowl, Covered, Touraine, Alcock, Oblong, 12 1/2 X 7 1/2 In.	100.00
Flow Blue, Bowl, Dark Flowers & Bird, Blue Inside, 3 X 6 In.	85.00
Flow Blue, Bowl, Deep River Scene Sailing Boats, 9 X 4 In.	55.00
Flow Blue, Bowl, Fairy Villas, 10 In.	45.00
Flow Blue, Bowl, Gravy, Alaska, 6 In.	30.00
Flow Blue, Bowl, Hanley, 10 In.	35.00

Flow Blue, Bowl, Indian, Pratt, C.1840, 10 3/4 In.	65.00
Flow Blue, Bowl, Jenny Lind, C.1895, 3 1/4 X 7 1/2 In.	39.50 To 55.00
Flow Blue, Bowl, Jenny Lind, Royal Staffordshire, Burslem, England, 7 1/2 In.	47.00
Flow Blue, Bowl, Melbourne, Grindley, Oblong, 8 X 6 1/2 In.	35.00
Flow Blue, Bowl, Middleport Scenes & People, Nonpareil, Burgess Leigh	20.00
Flow Blue, Bowl, Ning Po, R.Hall, C.1845, 10 3/4 In.	65.00
Flow Blue, Bowl, Rose, Ridgway, 8 1/2 In.	25.00
Flow Blue, Bowl, Round, Melbourne, Grindley, 11 In.	70.00
Flow Blue, Bowl, Round, Touraine, Stanley, 9 1/4 In.	40.00
Flow Blue, Bowl, Scalloped, Oval, Low, Keswick, 12 1/4 X 9 1/4 In.	40.00
Flow Blue, Bowl, Serving, Fairy Villa, 10 In.	55.00
Flow Blue, Bowl, Serving, Round, Conway, New Wharf Pottery, 9 In.	30.00
Flow Blue, Bowl, Serving, Round, Melbourne, 9 1/4 In.	40.00
Flow Blue, Bowl, Serving, Round, Shanghai, Grindley, 8 1/4 In.	30.00
Flow Blue, Bowl, Serving, Round, Waldorf, New Wharf Pottery, 9 In.	30.00
Flow Blue, Bowl, Shanghai, Findley Co., 7 1/2 In.	27.00
Flow Blue, Bowl, Shell Shape, Unmarked, 8 1/2 In.	35.00
Flow Blue, Bowl, Shusan, Clementson, 12 X 12 In.	225.00
Flow Blue, Bowl, Soup, Belmont, 8 3/4 In.	7.95
Flow Blue, Bowl, Soup, Belmont, 9 1/2 In.	8.95
Flow Blue, Bowl, Soup, Flange Edge, Nonpareil, Burgess & Leigh, 8 3/4 In.	37.50
Flow Blue, Bowl, Soup, Flange Edge, Watteau, Doulton, 9 3/4 In.	25.00
Flow Blue, Bowl, Soup, Monarch, Myott	20.00
Flow Blue, Bowl, Soup, Nonpareil, Burgess & Leigh, 7 3/4 In.	25.00
Flow Blue, Bowl, Soup, Shanghai, Grindley, 7 3/4 In.	15.00
Flow Blue, Bowl, Touraine, Round, H.Alcock, 9 1/4 In.	30.00
Flow Blue, Bowl, Touraine, Stanley Co., 8 3/4 In.	27.00
Flow Blue, Bowl, Touraine, Stanley, Oblong, 9 3/4 X 7 In.	40.00
Flow Blue, Bowl, Vegetable & Stand, Covered, Oval, Norberry	100.00
Flow Blue, Bowl, Vegetable, Benjapore, G.Phillips, Longport, C.1836, 10 In.	210.00
Flow Blue, Bowl, Vegetable, Covered, Del Monte, Johnson Brothers, 13 In.	60.00
Flow Blue, Bowl, Vegetable, Covered, Idris, C.1890	60.00
Flow Blue, Bowl, Vegetable, Covered, Oval, With Stand, Josephine Ridgway	100.00
Flow Blue, Bowl, Vegetable, Covered, Peach Royal	35.00
Flow Blue, Bowl, Vegetable, Covered, Pekin, Wood & Son	75.00
Flow Blue, Bowl, Vegetable, Covered, Scinde, Alcock, 10 X 13 In.	235.00
Flow Blue, Bowl, Vegetable, Covered, Shanghai, J.F.& Co., C.1890, 11 1/2 In.	285.00
Flow Blue, Bowl, Vegetable, Melbourne	95.00
Flow Blue, Bowl, Vegetable, Nonpareil, Flower Finial, Covered, 8 X 11 3/4 In.	125.00
Flow Blue, Bowl, Vegetable, Normandy, Oval, Johnson	60.00
Flow Blue, Bowl, Vegetable, Normandy, Red, Johnson, 9 In.	65.00
Flow Blue, Bowl, Vegetable, Open, Round, W.H.Grindley, 9 1/4 In.Diameter	28.00
Flow Blue, Bowl, Vegetable, Osborne, Grindley, C.1842, 10 X 7 1/2 In.	40.00
Flow Blue, Bowl, Vegetable, Oval, Handles, Waldorf, New Wharf	95.00
Flow Blue, Bowl, Vegetable, Round, Covered, Handles, Watteau, Doulton	100.00
Flow Blue, Bowl, Vegetable, Touraine, H.Alcock, 9 1/4 In.	30.00
Flow Blue, Bowl, Vegetable, Vermont, Oval, 5 1/2 X 7 1/4 X 12 1/4 In.	48.00
Flow Blue, Bowl, Vegetable, Waldorf, 9 In.	20.00
Flow Blue, Bowl, Vegetable, Yeddo, Royal Staffordshire, 10 In.	35.00
Flow Blue, Bowl, Waste, Normandy, Johnson, 6 In.	55.00
Flow Blue, Bowl, Waste, Stafford, W In Diamond Mark	25.00
Flow Blue, Bowl, Waste, Touraine	40.00
Flow Blue, Bowl, Watteau, F.Morley & Co., 1845	36.00
Flow Blue, Butter Pat, Gironde	4.25
Flow Blue, Butter Pat, Linda	6.00
Flow Blue, Butter Pat, Normandy, Set Of 6	95.00
Flow Blue, Butter Pat, Portsmouth, Gilt Edge	8.50
Flow Blue, Butter Pat, Princess, Booth	12.00
Flow Blue, Butter Pat, W.H.Grindley	10.00
Flow Blue, Butter Pat, Windflower, Burgess & Leigh, C.1895	10.00
Flow Blue, Butter Pat, With Gold, Set Of 6	78.00
Flow Blue, Butter, Dakota, Covered	25.00
Flow Blue, Butter, Florida, Three Pieces, Johnson Bros.	80.00
Flow Blue, Butter, La Francaise, Covered	28.00
Flow Blue, Butter, Lancaster, Covered	75.00

Flow Blue, Butter, Lorne, Covered 80.00
Flow Blue, Butter, Melbourne, Grindley 17.50
Flow Blue, Cachepot, Cattle Scenery, Adams, Footed, 6 5/8 X 5 1/2 In. 135.00
Flow Blue, Celery, Osborne, Ridgway 15.00
Flow Blue, Chamber Pot, Floral, W.H.Grindley 50.00
Flow Blue, Chocolate Pot, Gladiolus, Doulton, 10 1/2 In. 150.00
Flow Blue, Cracker Jar, La Belle 55.00
Flow Blue, Creamer, Amoy, Davenport 60.00
Flow Blue, Creamer, California, C.1849, 5 1/2 In. 95.00
Flow Blue, Creamer, Eglington Tournament 20.00
Flow Blue, Creamer, Grape 30.00
Flow Blue, Creamer, Holland, Johnson Bros. 55.00
Flow Blue, Creamer, Indian, Pratt, C.1840 .... 125.00
Flow Blue, Creamer, Kyber, W.Adams & Sons, C.1891 .... 110.00
Flow Blue, Creamer, La Belle .... 40.00 To 45.00
Flow Blue, Creamer, La Francaise 18.00
Flow Blue, Creamer, Lorne, Grindley 75.00
Flow Blue, Creamer, Marchael Neil, Grindley 75.00
Flow Blue, Creamer, Milk, Nanking, Doulton 50.00
Flow Blue, Creamer, Monarch, Myott 60.00
Flow Blue, Creamer, Normandy, Johnson 85.00
Flow Blue, Creamer, Osborne, Ridgway 50.00
Flow Blue, Creamer, Paris, New Wharf 50.00
Flow Blue, Creamer, Portman, Grindley, 5 1/2 X 6 In. 75.00
Flow Blue, Creamer, Stanley, With Gold, 4 1/2 In. 60.00
Flow Blue, Creamer, Touraine .... 52.00 To 95.00
Flow Blue, Creamer, Waldorf, New Wharf Pottery, 3 1/2 X 5 In. 75.00
Flow Blue, Cup & Saucer, Amoy, Gold Edged, Handled Cup 55.00
Flow Blue, Cup & Saucer, Amoy, Handleless Cup 60.00
Flow Blue, Cup & Saucer, Beaufort, Grindley 20.00
Flow Blue, Cup & Saucer, Bolingbroke Ridge 40.00
Flow Blue, Cup & Saucer, Brunswick, Wood 30.00
Flow Blue, Cup & Saucer, Cauldon, Flowers, Gold Borders 25.00
Flow Blue, Cup & Saucer, Clarence, Demitasse 25.00
Flow Blue, Cup & Saucer, Duchess, Grindley 26.00
Flow Blue, Cup & Saucer, Florida, Johnson Bros. .... 32.00 To 36.00
Flow Blue, Cup & Saucer, Formosa, T & J Mayer 65.00
Flow Blue, Cup & Saucer, Gironde, Grindley 25.00
Flow Blue, Cup & Saucer, Hindustan, Maddock 35.00
Flow Blue, Cup & Saucer, Hong Kong 42.00
Flow Blue, Cup & Saucer, Indian Bridge, Handleless Cup, Red Accents 70.00
Flow Blue, Cup & Saucer, Kaolin, Handleless Cup, C.1850 .... 65.00
Flow Blue, Cup & Saucer, Lancaster, New Wharf 27.50
Flow Blue, Cup & Saucer, Leaf & Berry, Luneville, France 35.00
Flow Blue, Cup & Saucer, Martha Washington, State's, Shawmut Furniture Co. 71.00
Flow Blue, Cup & Saucer, Milan 29.00
Flow Blue, Cup & Saucer, Monarch, Myott 40.00
Flow Blue, Cup & Saucer, Nonpareil, B & L 50.00
Flow Blue, Cup & Saucer, Nonpareil, Jones 95.00
Flow Blue, Cup & Saucer, Normandy, Johnson 35.00
Flow Blue, Cup & Saucer, Oriental, Demitasse 42.00
Flow Blue, Cup & Saucer, Paris, New Wharf Pottery 26.00
Flow Blue, Cup & Saucer, Penshurst, Ridgeway Mark 28.00
Flow Blue, Cup & Saucer, Portsmouth 29.00
Flow Blue, Cup & Saucer, Rhone, Furnival 60.00
Flow Blue, Cup & Saucer, Richmond, Meakin 40.00
Flow Blue, Cup & Saucer, Scinde, Large 60.00
Flow Blue, Cup & Saucer, Temple Podmore Walker, Handleless 85.00
Flow Blue, Cup & Saucer, Tonquin, Handleless 55.00
Flow Blue, Cup & Saucer, Touraine, Alcock .... 35.00 To 37.00
Flow Blue, Cup & Saucer, Touraine, Stanley .... 22.00 To 44.00
Flow Blue, Cup & Saucer, Turkey Feather 37.50
Flow Blue, Cup & Saucer, Versailles, Furnival 28.00
Flow Blue, Cup Plate, Amoy, Davenport, C.1844, 4 1/4 In. 50.00
Flow Blue, Cup Plate, Tonquin, Adams & Son, C.1845 .... 40.00

Flow Blue, Cup, Bouillon, Shanghai, Grindley, Double Handled	32.00
Flow Blue, Cup, Canton, John Maddock, C.1850	55.00
Flow Blue, Cup, Posset, Manilla, C.1845	60.00
Flow Blue, Dish, Cheese, Cavendish, Lid, Keeling & Co., Burslem, England	50.00
Flow Blue, Dish, Cheese, Flowered Design, Staffordshire	45.00
Flow Blue, Dish, Honey, Scinde, Alcock, 5 In.	40.00
Flow Blue, Dish, Serving, Oblong, Nonpareil, Burgess & Leigh, 9 3/4 In.	60.00
Flow Blue, Eggcup, Madras, Set Of 6, Each	15.00
Flow Blue, Gravy Boat & Underplate, Belmont	32.00 To 35.00
Flow Blue, Gravy Boat & Underplate, Del Monte, Johnson Bros., C.1890-1900	50.00
Flow Blue, Gravy Boat & Underplate, Mentone, Johnson Bros.	65.00
Flow Blue, Gravy Boat & Underplate, Norberry	50.00
Flow Blue, Gravy Boat, Davenport, Wood & Sons	22.50
Flow Blue, Gravy Boat, Denton, Grindley	25.00
Flow Blue, Gravy Boat, Devon	25.00
Flow Blue, Gravy Boat, Fairy Villa	60.00
Flow Blue, Gravy Boat, Fairy Villas, Footed, Adams & Co.	45.00
Flow Blue, Gravy Boat, Floral, Tray, Hughes	65.00
Flow Blue, Gravy Boat, Indian Jar, Thos.Furnival, C.1843	100.00
Flow Blue, Gravy Boat, La Francaise	12.00
Flow Blue, Gravy Boat, Melbourne, Grindley	50.00
Flow Blue, Gravy Boat, Royal Blue, Burgess	35.00
Flow Blue, Gravy Boat, Royston, Johnson Bros.Mark	35.00
Flow Blue, Gravy Boat, Togo, Winkle	50.00
Flow Blue, Gravy Boat, Tokio, Tray, Johnson Bros.	52.00
Flow Blue, Gravy Boat, Touraine, Alcock	45.00
Flow Blue, Gravy Boat, Virginia	35.00
Flow Blue, Hatpin Holder, 5 In.	35.00
Flow Blue, Holder, Toothbrush, 3 Sections, 5 1/2 X 4 1/2 In.	55.00
Flow Blue, Inkwell, Brass Foot, Hinged Brass Lid, 5 X 4 In.	100.00
Flow Blue, Jardiniere, Gadroon Edge, Gold Accent, 8 1/2 X 10 3/4 In.	110.00
Flow Blue, Jardiniere, Gloire De Dijon, Doulton, Large	190.00
Flow Blue, Knife Rest, Floral, Marked Rogers, Burslem Co., 4 X 1 In., Pair	12.00
Flow Blue, Mug, Singa, 2 Handled, Cork, Edge & Malkin, C.1865	125.00
Flow Blue, Nappy, Oval, Princess, Booth	15.00
Flow Blue, Nappy, Watteau, Staffordshire, Set Of 3	25.00
Flow Blue, Pitcher & Bowl Set, Garland	235.00
Flow Blue, Pitcher, Fairy Villas, William Adams & Co., 9 1/2 X 10 In.	125.00
Flow Blue, Pitcher, Flowers, Trent, B & S, 8 3/4 In.	75.00
Flow Blue, Pitcher, Hofburg, W.H.Grindley, C.1890, 1 1/2 Quart	85.00
Flow Blue, Pitcher, Milk, Dane, TR & Co., Octagonal, Gold Tracery	30.00
Flow Blue, Pitcher, Milk, La Belle, 2 Quart	75.00 To 125.00
Flow Blue, Pitcher, Milk, La Francaise	18.00
Flow Blue, Pitcher, Milk, Madras, Doulton, 6 1/2 In.	55.00
Flow Blue, Pitcher, Milk, Portman, Grindley, 5 3/4 X 6 1/2 In.	85.00
Flow Blue, Pitcher, Milk, Scinde, Alcock, 3 Quart	350.00
Flow Blue, Pitcher, Octagon Base, Cobra Handle	100.00
Flow Blue, Pitcher, Oyama, 7 In.	55.00
Flow Blue, Pitcher, Persian Moss, 7 1/2 In.	26.00
Flow Blue, Pitcher, Snowflower, 9 In.	95.00
Flow Blue, Pitcher, Syria	45.00
Flow Blue, Pitcher, Tankard, Medallion Center, S.Johnson Ltd., Burslem	30.00
Flow Blue, Pitcher, Village Scene, Cauldon, England, 7 1/2 In.	25.00
Flow Blue, Pitcher, Virginia, Maddock, 8 1/2 In.	60.00
Flow Blue, Plate, Alhambra, 8 In.	17.00 To 20.00
Flow Blue, Plate, Amoy, Davenport, 7 1/4 In.	30.00
Flow Blue, Plate, Amoy, Davenport, 7 1/2 In.	35.00 To 50.00
Flow Blue, Plate, Amoy, Davenport, 9 In.	36.00
Flow Blue, Plate, Amoy, Davenport, 9 1/2 In.	50.00 To 55.00
Flow Blue, Plate, Amoy, Davenport, 10 3/8 In.	40.00
Flow Blue, Plate, Amoy, Davenport, 10 1/2 In.	60.00
Flow Blue, Plate, Arabesque, Mayer, 10 1/2 In.	35.00 To 45.00
Flow Blue, Plate, Arabesque, Mayer, 10 3/4 In.	48.00
Flow Blue, Plate, Argyle, 10 In.	26.00
Flow Blue, Plate, Ashton, Crossed Swords, Pountney & Brist Ltd., 10 In.	10.00

Flow Blue, Plate, Astoria, Johnson, 8 In. 20.00
Flow Blue, Plate, Astoria, Johnson, 10 In. 22.00
Flow Blue, Plate, Athens, Meigh, 10 In. 45.00
Flow Blue, Plate, Baltic, W.H.Grindley, 9 7/8 In. 20.00
Flow Blue, Plate, Beaufort, Grindley, 6 In. 7.50
Flow Blue, Plate, Beaufort, Grindley, 9 In. 12.50
Flow Blue, Plate, Belmont, 8 In. 6.95
Flow Blue, Plate, Belmont, 9 In. 16.00
Flow Blue, Plate, Belmont, 10 1/2 In. 9.95
Flow Blue, Plate, Blue Danube, 9 In. 25.00
Flow Blue, Plate, Blue Danube, 10 In. 25.00
Flow Blue, Plate, Blue Rose, Grindley, 8 In. 18.00
Flow Blue, Plate, Bread & Butter, Monarch, Myott 20.00
Flow Blue, Plate, Bread & Butter, Touraine, Stanley, 6 1/2 In. 15.00
Flow Blue, Plate, Brooklyn, Johnson Bros., England, 8 In. 16.00
Flow Blue, Plate, Cake, Nonpareil, Burgess & Leigh, 11 In. .... 35.00 To 67.00
Flow Blue, Plate, Cake, Osborne, Ridgway, 10 In. 35.00
Flow Blue, Plate, Canton, 7 In. 35.00
Flow Blue, Plate, Cashmere, Morley, 9 In. 55.00
Flow Blue, Plate, Cashmere, Morley, 10 1/2 In. 75.00
Flow Blue, Plate, Cattle Decoration, Wedgwood, 10 In. 25.00
Flow Blue, Plate, Chatsworth, Ford & Son, 9 In. 18.00
Flow Blue, Plate, Chen-Si, John Meir, 7 1/2 In. 38.50
Flow Blue, Plate, Chen-Si, John Meir, 8 In. 35.00
Flow Blue, Plate, Chinese, Kaolin Ware, C.1845, 8 In. 23.50
Flow Blue, Plate, Chinese, Wedgwood, 8 In. 22.00
Flow Blue, Plate, Chusan, Morley, C.1850, 10 1/2 In. 50.00
Flow Blue, Plate, Chusan, S & H, 10 In. 28.50
Flow Blue, Plate, Clarence, 8 In. 25.00
Flow Blue, Plate, Clarence, 10 In. 30.00
Flow Blue, Plate, Coburg, C.1860, John Edwards, 7 1/2 In. 38.50
Flow Blue, Plate, Conway, 8 1/2 In. 25.00
Flow Blue, Plate, Conway, 9 In. 20.00
Flow Blue, Plate, Conway, Grindley, 10 In. 30.00
Flow Blue, Plate, Conway, New Wharf, 10 In. 25.00
Flow Blue, Plate, Coral, Johnson Bros., 9 In. .... 20.00 To 25.00
Flow Blue, Plate, Coral, 8 In., Set Of 6 .... 60.00
Flow Blue, Plate, Countess, Henna Flowers Overlay, 9 3/4 In. 15.00
Flow Blue, Plate, Crawford Cooking Range, 10 In. 30.00
Flow Blue, Plate, Eton College, 7 1/2 In. 19.50
Flow Blue, Plate, Etruria, Wedgwood, Spirit Of '76, 9 In. 45.00
Flow Blue, Plate, Fairy Villas, 9 In. 22.00
Flow Blue, Plate, Fairy Villas, 10 In. 30.00
Flow Blue, Plate, Festoon, W.Adams, 1879 Mark 35.00
Flow Blue, Plate, Florida, Johnson Bros., England, 10 In. 20.00
Flow Blue, Plate, Formosa, Ridgway, C.1834, 9 1/2 In. 50.00
Flow Blue, Plate, Formosa, T.J.& J.Mayer, C.1850, 10 1/2 In.Diameter 62.00
Flow Blue, Plate, Gironde, Grindley, 10 In. 15.00
Flow Blue, Plate, Gironde, 6 In. 12.00
Flow Blue, Plate, Gironde, 9 In. 25.00
Flow Blue, Plate, Gothic, J.F.& Co., C.1850, 9 In. 39.00
Flow Blue, Plate, Hong Kong, C.Meigh, C.1845, 10 1/4 In. 55.00
Flow Blue, Plate, Hudson, 9 In. 25.00
Flow Blue, Plate, Hudson, 10 In. 25.00
Flow Blue, Plate, Idris, 10 In. 11.00
Flow Blue, Plate, Indian, Pratt, C.1840, 9 1/2 In. 50.00
Flow Blue, Plate, Iris, A.Wilkinson, 8 In. 12.50
Flow Blue, Plate, Japan, Thos.Fell & Co., C.1860, 9 1/2 In. 40.00
Flow Blue, Plate, Jeddo, W.Adams & Sons, C.1845, 9 In. 30.00
Flow Blue, Plate, Jeddo, W.Adams & Sons, 9 1/4 In. 25.00
Flow Blue, Plate, Kin Shan, Challinor, C.1855, 8 3/4 In. 35.00
Flow Blue, Plate, Kin Shan, Challinor, 8 3/4 In. 45.00
Flow Blue, Plate, Kyber, Adams, 10 In. .... 28.00 To 35.00
Flow Blue, Plate, Kyber, 9 In. 32.00
Flow Blue, Plate, Kyber, 9 1/4 In. 25.00

Flow Blue, Plate, La Belle, Gold Trim, Scalloped, 7 1/4 In. 35.00
Flow Blue, Plate, La Belle, 9 In. 22.00
Flow Blue, Plate, Leicester, S.Hancock, 10 In. 22.50
Flow Blue, Plate, Lorne, 10 In. 25.00
Flow Blue, Plate, Lugano, 9 In. 22.00
Flow Blue, Plate, Luster Band, 10 1/2 In. 12.00
Flow Blue, Plate, Madras, Doulton, 9 1/2 In. 35.00
Flow Blue, Plate, Manilla, P.W. & Co., 7 1/2 In. 32.00
Flow Blue, Plate, Manilla, P.W. & Co., 9 In. 29.00
Flow Blue, Plate, Martha Washington, 9 In. 25.00
Flow Blue, Plate, Melbourne, 10 In. 30.00
Flow Blue, Plate, Milan, Grindley, 8 In. 20.00
Flow Blue, Plate, Milan, Grindley, 10 In. 25.00
Flow Blue, Plate, Moorish Palace, 10 In. .... 30.00 To 35.00
Flow Blue, Plate, Morea, J.Goodwin, 10 1/4 In. 42.00
Flow Blue, Plate, Myott, Crumlin, 9 In. 20.00
Flow Blue, Plate, Nelson, 9 In. 20.00
Flow Blue, Plate, Ning Po, 9 In. 42.00
Flow Blue, Plate, Nonpareil, Burgess & Leigh, 9 In. 37.50
Flow Blue, Plate, Nonpareil, Burgess & Leigh, 10 In. 40.00
Flow Blue, Plate, Nonpareil, 8 1/2 In. 30.00
Flow Blue, Plate, Normandy, Johnson, 6 In. 15.00
Flow Blue, Plate, Normandy, Johnson, 7 In. 20.00
Flow Blue, Plate, Normandy, Johnson, 9 In. .... 16.00 To 25.00
Flow Blue, Plate, Normandy, Johnson, 10 In. 35.00
Flow Blue, Plate, Oriental, Alcock, 8 1/4 In. 25.00
Flow Blue, Plate, Oriental, Alcock, 9 In. 35.00
Flow Blue, Plate, Persian, 9 In. 25.00
Flow Blue, Plate, Pie, Clarence 20.00
Flow Blue, Plate, Poppy, 8 1/2 In. 22.00
Flow Blue, Plate, Rhoda, Johnson Bros., 9 In. 15.00
Flow Blue, Plate, Rose, 9 In. 25.00
Flow Blue, Plate, Roxberry, 10 In. 45.00
Flow Blue, Plate, Scinde, Alcock, C.1840, 7 In. 40.00
Flow Blue, Plate, Scinde, Alcock, C.1840, 8 1/2 In. .... 42.00 To 45.00
Flow Blue, Plate, Scroll, 8 1/4 In. 22.00
Flow Blue, Plate, Shanghai, W In Diamond, England, 9 3/4 In. 110.00
Flow Blue, Plate, Shanghai, 8 1/2 In. 30.00
Flow Blue, Plate, Soup, Amoy, 10 1/2 In. 45.00
Flow Blue, Plate, Soup, Hong Kong, 9 1/4 In. 35.00
Flow Blue, Plate, Soup, Kyber, Adams, 9 In. 35.00
Flow Blue, Plate, Soup, Linda, Maddock, 9 In. 15.00
Flow Blue, Plate, Soup, Scinde, Alcock, 10 In. 75.00
Flow Blue, Plate, Soup, Touraine, Alcock, 10 In. 40.00
Flow Blue, Plate, Soup, Touraine, 9 In. 25.00
Flow Blue, Plate, Souvenir, Garden Of Gods, Colorado, England, 9 In. 17.00
Flow Blue, Plate, Souvenir, Regent Spring, Excelsior Springs, Mo., 7 3/4 In. 17.00
Flow Blue, Plate, Souvenir, San Jose, California, 7 3/4 In. 16.00
Flow Blue, Plate, Spinach With Circled Flower, 7 In. 15.00
Flow Blue, Plate, Spinach, 7 3/8 In. 24.00
Flow Blue, Plate, Stanley, Johnson Bros., 10 In. 18.00
Flow Blue, Plate, Tillenberg, J., Clementson, 9 In. 28.50
Flow Blue, Plate, Togo, F.Winkle, 9 1/2 In. 20.00
Flow Blue, Plate, Tonquin, 10 In. 55.00
Flow Blue, Plate, Touraine, Gold Trim, 8 3/4 In. 13.00
Flow Blue, Plate, Touraine, H.Alcock & Sons, 8 1/2 In. 16.00
Flow Blue, Plate, Touraine, H.Alcock, 8 3/4 In. 17.00
Flow Blue, Plate, Touraine, H.Alcock, 9 In. 20.00
Flow Blue, Plate, Touraine, Stanley, 9 In. .... 20.00 To 28.00
Flow Blue, Plate, Touraine, Stanley, 10 In. .... 23.00 To 35.00
Flow Blue, Plate, Touraine, 6 1/2 In. 170.00
Flow Blue, Plate, Touraine, 7 In. 14.50
Flow Blue, Plate, Touraine, 8 In. .... 10.00 To 20.00
Flow Blue, Plate, Touraine, 9 In. 25.00
Flow Blue, Plate, Trilby, 9 1/2 In., Pair 22.00

Flow Blue, Plate, Turkey, Blue & White, Ridgway, 10 1/2 In.	39.00
Flow Blue, Plate, Turkey, La Belle, China, Ornate	40.00
Flow Blue, Plate, Turkey, Wedgwood, 9 In.	45.00
Flow Blue, Plate, Waldorf, New Wharf, 8 In.	25.00
Flow Blue, Plate, Waldorf, 9 1/2 In.	18.00
Flow Blue, Plate, Watteau, Doulton, 1890, 10 In.	28.00
Flow Blue, Plate, Watteau, Doulton, 7 1/2 In.	13.00
Flow Blue, Plate, Watteau, Doulton, 9 1/2 In.	19.00
Flow Blue, Plate, Watteau, Doulton, 10 In.	20.00
Flow Blue, Plate, Willow, 7 1/2 In.	20.00
Flow Blue, Platter, Bacon, Normandy, Johnson, 5 1/2 X 8 In.	45.00
Flow Blue, Platter, Bamboo, Peony, 17 In.	150.00
Flow Blue, Platter, Belmont, 11 3/4 In.	25.00
Flow Blue, Platter, Chaplet, Oval, 12 1/2 X 9 In.	22.00
Flow Blue, Platter, Chen-Si, 14 X 17 1/2 In.	165.00
Flow Blue, Platter, Conway, New Wharf, 8 X 11 In.	36.00
Flow Blue, Platter, Conway, New Wharf, 10 1/2 In.	30.00
Flow Blue, Platter, Conway, New Wharf, 11 In.	40.00
Flow Blue, Platter, Duchess, Oval, Grindley, 16 In.	40.00
Flow Blue, Platter, Duchess, W.H.Grindley, 14 X 10 In.	48.00
Flow Blue, Platter, Floral, 12 In.	16.00
Flow Blue, Platter, Florida, Grindley, C.1889, 14 In.	55.00
Flow Blue, Platter, Florida, Grindley, 18 In.	65.00
Flow Blue, Platter, Gestic, Findley Co., 15 In.	65.00
Flow Blue, Platter, Gothic, JF & Co., C.1850, 16 1/4 X 12 1/2 In.	125.00
Flow Blue, Platter, Gothic, 11 X 8 1/2 In.	55.00
Flow Blue, Platter, Indian, Pratt, C.1840, 15 1/4 X 11 3/4 In.	125.00
Flow Blue, Platter, Iris, Oval, 9 1/4 X 13 In.	29.00
Flow Blue, Platter, Jeddo, Adam & Son, 12 X 9 1/2 In.	40.00
Flow Blue, Platter, Kyber, Adams, 7 1/2 X 10 In.	35.00
Flow Blue, Platter, Kyber, W.Adams, 15 In.	50.00
Flow Blue, Platter, La Francaise, 8 X 11 In.	20.00
Flow Blue, Platter, Linda, J.Maddock, 17 X 12 In.	45.00
Flow Blue, Platter, Lois, 8 X 11 1/2 In.	45.00
Flow Blue, Platter, Lois, 11 In.	35.00
Flow Blue, Platter, Lugano, Ridgway, C.1910, 13 1/2 In.	55.00
Flow Blue, Platter, M.Neil, Grindley, 12 1/4 X 9 1/4 In.	40.00
Flow Blue, Platter, M.Neil, Grindley, 16 In.	65.00
Flow Blue, Platter, Malo, 17 In.	30.00
Flow Blue, Platter, Manilla, PW & Co., 15 1/2 X 12 In.	175.00
Flow Blue, Platter, Melbourne, Grindley, 18 1/4 X 13 In.	85.00
Flow Blue, Platter, Melbourne, 14 In.	60.00
Flow Blue, Platter, Melbourne, 16 In.	65.00
Flow Blue, Platter, Milan, Rectangular, C.1890, 13 X 10 In.	45.00
Flow Blue, Platter, Moorish Palace, 14 In.	55.00
Flow Blue, Platter, Normandy, Johnson, 14 In.	55.00
Flow Blue, Platter, Normandy, Johnson, 16 In.	65.00
Flow Blue, Platter, Oregon, Johnson, 14 1/2 X 10 3/4 In.	40.00
Flow Blue, Platter, Oriental, 9 In.	30.00
Flow Blue, Platter, Osborne, Ridgway, 12 1/4 X 9 1/4 In.	35.00
Flow Blue, Platter, Osborne, Ridgway, 14 1/4 X 10 1/2 In.	45.00
Flow Blue, Platter, Osborne, Ridgway, 17 1/4 X 13 In.	60.00
Flow Blue, Platter, Peach, Johnson, 9 1/2 In.	40.00
Flow Blue, Platter, Peach, Johnson, 10 X 8 In.	30.00
Flow Blue, Platter, Phil Lahore, 17 In.	165.00
Flow Blue, Platter, Poppy, Meigh, 17 In.	75.00
Flow Blue, Platter, Shanghai, J.F.& Co., C.1860, 10 1/2 In.	115.00
Flow Blue, Platter, Tonquin, Adams, 13 1/2 X 10 1/4 In.	75.00
Flow Blue, Platter, Touraine, Alcock, 15 1/2 X 10 3/4 In.	60.00
Flow Blue, Platter, Touraine, Oval, 13 X 8 In.	45.00
Flow Blue, Platter, Touraine, Stanley, Oval, 12 1/2 In.	48.00
Flow Blue, Platter, Touraine, Stanley, 12 1/2 X 8 1/2 In.	39.00
Flow Blue, Platter, Touraine, Stanley, 15 1/4 X 10 1/2 In.	60.00
Flow Blue, Platter, Touraine, Stanley, 15 1/2 X 10 3/4 In.	60.00
Flow Blue, Platter, Touraine, 15 1/2 In.	20.00

Flow Blue, Platter, Turkey, Royal Doulton, Burslem, 22 1/2 X 18 In.	250.00
Flow Blue, Platter, Waldorf, New Wharf, Oval, 10 In.	35.00
Flow Blue, Platter, Waldorf, New Wharf, 11 In.	31.00
Flow Blue, Platter, Waldorf, 8 X 10 1/2 In.	35.00
Flow Blue, Punch Bowl, Amherst, Footed, 7 X 12 In.	175.00
Flow Blue, Punch Bowl, Gold Overglaze & Rim, Floral, 14 In.	225.00
Flow Blue, Relish, Geisha, Upper Hanley	10.00
Flow Blue, Sauce, Amoy, Davenport, C.1844	20.00 To 25.00
Flow Blue, Sauce, Astoria, Johnson	15.00
Flow Blue, Sauce, Athens, Charles Meigh, C.1840, 5 In.	32.00
Flow Blue, Sauce, Columbia, Clemenston & Young, 5 In.	15.00
Flow Blue, Sauce, Gothic, Jacob Furnival & Co., 6 1/2 In.	24.00
Flow Blue, Sauce, Melbourne	12.00
Flow Blue, Sauce, Peach, Johnson	5.00
Flow Blue, Sauce, Persian Moss, Utzschneider & Co., C.1891, 4 3/4 In.	12.50
Flow Blue, Sauce, Touraine, H.Alcock, 5 1/2 In.	15.00
Flow Blue, Sauce, Turkey Feather	10.00
Flow Blue, Saucer, Amoy, Davenport	40.00
Flow Blue, Saucer, Chapoo, Wedgwood	18.00
Flow Blue, Saucer, Countess, Demitasse, Red Flowers, W.H.Grindley	26.00
Flow Blue, Saucer, Florida, Johnson Bros., England	8.00
Flow Blue, Saucer, Formosa, Mayer	15.00
Flow Blue, Saucer, Kyber, Deep, J.Meir & Son, C.1870	15.00
Flow Blue, Saucer, Lorne	4.00
Flow Blue, Saucer, Martha Washington	6.00
Flow Blue, Saucer, Oregon, Johnson Bros., 6 In.	5.00
Flow Blue, Saucer, Pelew	18.00
Flow Blue, Saucer, Regout's Flower	6.00
Flow Blue, Saucer, Waldorf	15.00
Flow Blue, Server, Vegetable, Kin-Shan, E.Challinor, C.1855, 11 X 8 1/2 In.	65.00
Flow Blue, Soup, Bombay	15.00
Flow Blue, Soup, Coral, Johnson Bros.Mark	20.00
Flow Blue, Soup, Flange	20.00
Flow Blue, Soup, Melrose, Marked Doulton	28.00
Flow Blue, Soup, Normandy, Johnson, 5 In.	10.00
Flow Blue, Soup, Ochis, 9 In.	12.00
Flow Blue, Soup, Versailles	7.00
Flow Blue, Soup, Waldorf, Set Of Ten	350.00
Flow Blue, Sugar & Creamer, Del Monte, Johnson Bros., Covered	95.00
Flow Blue, Sugar & Creamer, Oriental, Ridgway	125.00
Flow Blue, Sugar & Creamer, Persian Moss	50.00
Flow Blue, Sugar, Amoy, Octagonal, Open	12.00
Flow Blue, Sugar, Covered, Gladys, New Wharf	50.00
Flow Blue, Sugar, Covered, Oregon, Johnson Bros.	50.00
Flow Blue, Sugar, Lorne, Grindley	75.00
Flow Blue, Sugar, Manilla, P.Walker, 1845	125.00
Flow Blue, Sugar, Open, Jones, Formosa	75.00
Flow Blue, Sugar, Oregon, TJ & J Mayer, C.1845	175.00
Flow Blue, Sugar, Osborne, Ridgway	50.00
Flow Blue, Sugar, Touraine, Alcock	95.00
Flow Blue, Teapot, Persian Moss , Utzschneider & Co.	100.00 To 110.00
Flow Blue, Teapot, Arabesque, Mayer, 9 1/2 In.	275.00
Flow Blue, Teapot, Argyle, Grindley	175.00
Flow Blue, Teapot, Chapoo	270.00
Flow Blue, Teapot, Oregon, 1840	250.00
Flow Blue, Teapot, Segapore, Ca.1864	175.00
Flow Blue, Tile, Tea, Warwick	25.00
Flow Blue, Tray, La Belle, 12 X 7 1/2 In.	40.00
Flow Blue, Tub, Butter, Underplate & Cover, Whampoa, S.Wales Pottery	200.00
Flow Blue, Tureen & Tray, Morning Glory, Lilies, Daisies	100.00
Flow Blue, Tureen & Underplate, Sauce, Chusan, Covered, Wedgwood, 7 1/2 In.	105.00
Flow Blue, Tureen, Agra, Covered, 9 In.	160.00
Flow Blue, Tureen, Belmont, Covered	42.00
Flow Blue, Tureen, Clarence, 10 In.	175.00

Flow Blue, Tureen, Cover, Oval, Bolingbroke	95.00
Flow Blue, Tureen, Covered, Normandy, 2 Handles, Oblong, 11 In.	95.00
Flow Blue, Tureen, Fern, Cover, Adams, C.1870	85.00
Flow Blue, Tureen, La Belle, Green & White, Lilac Flowers, 3 1/2 X 8 In.	40.00
Flow Blue, Tureen, Normandy, Red, Cover, Johnson	110.00
Flow Blue, Tureen, Pansy, Oval, Covered, 12 In.	95.00
Flow Blue, Tureen, Regal, 9 In.	30.00
Flow Blue, Tureen, Sauceboat, Underplate, Sobraon, 1850	215.00
Flow Blue, Tureen, Sauceboat, Underplate, Lid, Scinde, J.& G.Alcock, C.1840	235.00
Flow Blue, Tureen, Soup, Athol	125.00
Flow Blue, Tureen, Soup, Covered, J.Maddock & Sons, Co., 1896, 12 In.	115.00
Flow Blue, Tureen, Soup, Willow, Green	125.00
Flow Blue, Tureen, Vegetable, Jeddo, Covered, Footed, Octagonal	225.00
Flow Blue, Urn, Covered, White Enameled Flowers, 29 In., Pair	350.00
Flow Blue, Vase, Babes In Woods, Doulton, Burslem, 11 1/4 In.	195.00
Flow Blue, Vase, Jonquil, Middleport, Footed, Gold Side Handles, 8 1/2 In.	45.00
Flow Blue, Vegetable, Conway, 9 X 2 1/2 In.	35.00
Flow Blue, Vegetable, Cover, Castle, Small Boats In Foreground, Floral, 12 In.	100.00
Flow Blue, Vegetable, Cover, Luster Band, Tulip	75.00
Flow Blue, Vegetable, Cover, Pansy, Wood	95.00
Flow Blue, Vegetable, Devon Pattern, Burslem, England, 11 In.	85.00
Flow Blue, Vegetable, Florida, Handled, Large, Open, Grindley	38.00
Flow Blue, Vegetable, Geisha, Open, Upper Hanley, 10 In.	26.00
Flow Blue, Vegetable, Lois, Open, Round, New Wharf Mark	30.00
Flow Blue, Vegetable, Oriental Stone, Open, Signed, Scinde, 9 1/4 X 7 In.	65.00
Flow Blue, Vegetable, Watteau, Open, Red, New Wharf Mark	32.00
Flow Blue, Washstand Set, Burslem Argyle Pattern, 4 Piece	450.00
Flow Blue, Washstand Set, Ewer, Togo, Winkle	125.00
Flow Blue, Washstand Set, Syrian, Grindley, 3 Piece	354.00
Flow Blue, Waste, Container, China, La Belle	25.00
Folk Art, Sign, Haberdasher's, Tin, Iron, Early 19th Century _____ Illus_	650.00

Foo dogs are mythical Chinese figures, part dog and part lion. They were made of pottery, porcelain, carved stone, and wood.

Foo Dog, Figurine, Yellow, Green, Brown Glaze, Mouth Open, 9 3/4 In.	35.00
Foo Dog, Gold Pearls, Black Mane, Imari Coloring, 5 X 8 In.	100.00

FOSTORIA   *Fostoria glass was made in Fostoria, Ohio, from 1887 to 1891. The factory was moved to Moundsville, West Virginia, and most of the glass seen in shops today is a twentieth-century product.*

Fostoria, see also Milk Glass

Fostoria, Bookend, Lyre, Clear	15.00
Fostoria, Bookend, Rearing Horse, Pair	25.00 To 32.00
Fostoria, Bowl, Baroque, 10 1/2 In.	17.00
Fostoria, Bowl, Berry, Victorian	20.00
Fostoria, Bowl, Blue, Opalescent, Crimped, 9 In.	25.00
Fostoria, Bowl, Leaf Spray, Ruby, Signed, 10 In.	85.00
Fostoria, Bowl, Nut, 3 Toe, Baroque Topaz	6.00
Fostoria, Bowl, Pink, Lace Edge, 5 In.	20.00
Fostoria, Bowl, Ruby, Leaf Tree, 10 In.	100.00

Folk Art, Sign, Haberdasher's, Tin, Iron, Early 19th Century

Fostoria, Bowl, Victoria, Frosted, 8 In.	24.00
Fostoria, Cake Stand, Salver, 9 1/2 X 6 In.	35.00
Fostoria, Candelabra, Amber, 7 X 8 1/2 In., Pair	43.00
Fostoria, Candelabra, 3 Bay, Amber, 7 In., Pair	43.00
Fostoria, Candelabrum, Baroque, Double Holder	15.00
Fostoria, Candleholder, Baroque Meadow Rose, Double, 1930s, Pair	24.00
Fostoria, Candleholder, Evangeline, Yellow, Double, Pair	25.00
Fostoria, Candleholder, Middle Dish, Pink Opalescent, Points	95.00
Fostoria, Candlestick, Ebony Scroll, Pair	13.00
Fostoria, Candlestick, No.1963, Amber, 9 In.	16.00
Fostoria, Castor Set, Raleigh Pattern, 5 Piece	96.00
Fostoria, Celery, Wedding Bells, Clear, Cranberry Flashed	35.00
Fostoria, Champagne, Beacon	7.00
Fostoria, Champagne, Rainbow, 1920s, Set Of 8	32.00
Fostoria, Compote, Etched Flowers, Scalloped, 5 X 7 In.	10.00
Fostoria, Compote, Shirley, Crystal, 5 1/2 In.	12.50
Fostoria, Console Set, Trojan, Topaz	48.00
Fostoria, Console Set, Versailles, Green, 3 Piece	25.00
Fostoria, Cordial, Alexis	8.00
Fostoria, Cruet, American	25.00
Fostoria, Cup & Saucer, June, Blue	17.50
Fostoria, Cup & Saucer, June, Pink	11.00
Fostoria, Cup & Saucer, Victoria	35.00
Fostoria, Cup, Punch, Priscilla, Etched, 1899	16.00
Fostoria, Dish, Heirloom, Pink, Opalescent, Oval, 13 In.	28.00
Fostoria, Figurine, Chanticleer	125.00
Fostoria, Figurine, Penguin	38.00
Fostoria, Figurine, Sitting Horse	24.00
Fostoria, Figurine, Squirrel, Amber, Pair	25.00
Fostoria, Figurine, Standing Colt, 4 In.	22.00
Fostoria, Figurine, Standing Deer, 4 In.	22.00
Fostoria, Goblet, Christiana, Set Of 3	10.00
Fostoria, Goblet, Holly, Set Of 4	55.00
Fostoria, Goblet, June, Clear	12.00
Fostoria, Goblet, June, Yellow	20.00
Fostoria, Goblet, Lavender, No.5299	17.00
Fostoria, Hat, Clear, American Pattern, 4 X 6 In.	16.50
Fostoria, Mayonnaise Set, American Pattern, Pink	10.00
Fostoria, Pail, Whip Cream, Green, Oakwood Brocade	17.50
Fostoria, Plate, Etched Floral, Pink, 9 In.	48.00
Fostoria, Platter, Emerald Green, 18 In.	25.00
Fostoria, Shade, Clinging Hearts & Vines	125.00
Fostoria, Shade, Gold Zipper, Green Pulled Decoration, Gold Lined, 4 1/2 In.	95.00
Fostoria, Shade, Green Drag Loop, Gold Lined, 7 3/4 In.	145.00
Fostoria, Shade, Vertical Gold Heart & Vine, Gold Lined, 5 In.	90.00
Fostoria, Shade, White Feather, Gold Iridescent Glass, Corset Waist	120.00
Fostoria, Sherbet, June, Clear	12.00
Fostoria, Sugar & Creamer, American Pattern, Covered Sugar	28.00
Fostoria, Sugar & Creamer, Buttercup	17.00
Fostoria, Sugar & Creamer, Colony	6.00
Fostoria, Sugar & Creamer, Shirley	30.00
Fostoria, Sugar & Creamer, Wild Rose, Amber	15.00
Fostoria, Sugar, Versailles, Green	8.50
Fostoria, Tray, Sandwich, Gold Buttercup	18.00
Fostoria, Tumbler, Double Scroll	10.00
Fostoria, Tumbler, Priscilla, Green	12.50
Fostoria, Tumbler, Wedding Bells, Cranberry Flashed	18.50
Fostoria, Urn, Cigarette, Etched Sterling Base, 3 1/2 In., Pair	12.00
Fostoria, Vase, American, 8 In.	10.00
Fostoria, Vase, Green, Opalescent, 8 In.	20.00
Fostoria, Vase, Navarre, 10 In.	20.00
Fostoria, Vase, Rose Amber, Polished Pontil, 8 In.	15.00

Foval, see Fry Foval
Frame, see Furniture, Frame

Francisware is an amber hobnail glassware made by Hobbs Brockunier and Company, Wheeling, West Virginia, in the 1880s.

Francisware, Berry Set, 13 Piece	189.00 To 295.00
Francisware, Bonbon, Finial On Lid, 6 In.	115.00
Francisware, Bowl, Berry, Frosted Swirl, Fluted Amber Rim, Dated, 1 1/2 In.	55.00
Francisware, Bowl, Berry, Tricornered, Four Sauces, Blocks & Flowers Pattern	160.00
Francisware, Bowl, Berry, 8 1/4 In.	45.00
Francisware, Bowl, Frosted Swirl, Amber Rim, 7 1/2 In.	60.00
Francisware, Bowl, Frosted, Square, Ruffled, 7 1/2 In.	75.00
Francisware, Bowl, Master Berry	45.00
Francisware, Castor, Pickle, Frosted, Gold-Plated Holder	285.00
Francisware, Celery Tray, Swirl Frosted, 12 1/2 X 4 In.	30.00 To 38.00
Francisware, Celery, Swirl, 8 In.	70.00
Francisware, Creamer	35.00
Francisware, Lemonade Set, Frosted, 5 Piece	450.00
Francisware, Pitcher, Applied Clear & Frosted Handle	110.00 To 158.00
Francisware, Pitcher, Water, Bulbous	140.00 To 200.00
Francisware, Sugar & Creamer	95.00
Francisware, Sugar, Frosted Hobnail, Open	29.00
Francisware, Toothpick	22.00 To 60.00
Francisware, Toothpick, Amber Stained Rim	32.00
Francisware, Tray, Swirl, Frosted, Amber Stain, Oval, 12 In.	55.00
Francisware, Water Set, Swirl Frosted, Amber, 5 Piece	295.00
Francisware, Water Set, 6 Piece	345.00
Frankenthal, Figurine, Hurdy-Gurdy Player, C.1760, 6 In. *Illus*	1600.00
Frankoma, Ashtray, Cream & Brown, Four-Leaf Clover	10.00
Frankoma, Bowl, Brown & Green Tones, 5 In.	10.00
Frankoma, Bowl, Oval, Green, Silver Overlay, 6 In.	25.00
Frankoma, Console Set, Green, Brown Trim, 3 Piece	22.00
Frankoma, Figurine, Indian Maid	7.50
Frankoma, Mug, Elephant	6.75 To 8.50
Frankoma, Plate, Methodist, 1966, 8 In.	15.00
Frankoma, Sugar & Creamer, Art Deco, Green, Brown, C.1920, Marked	28.00
Frankoma, Sugar & Creamer, Wagon Wheel, Brown & Green, 2 1/2 In.	7.00
Frankoma, Tea Set, Wagon Wheel Design, 3 Pieces	18.00
Frankoma, Vase, Bud, Snail, Green & Aqua Tones	10.00
Fraunfelter, Bowl, Florals All Around, Signed Lessell, 3 X 9 In.	70.00

Fry glass was made by the famous H.C.Fry Glass Company of Rochester, Pennsylvania. It includes cut glass, but the famous Fry glass today is the foval, or pearl, art glass. This is an opal ware decorated with colored trim. It was made from 1922 to 1933.

Fry, see also Cut Glass

Fry Foval, Beaker, Ice Tea, Applied Jade Green Handles, Pair	90.00
Fry Foval, Bowl, Berry, Jade Standard, 8 In.	125.00
Fry Foval, Bowl, Blue Stem & Rim, 9 1/2 X 4 1/2 In.	145.00
Fry Foval, Bowl, Cereal, Pearl, 7 1/2 In.	25.00
Fry Foval, Candleholder, Cobalt Trim, Swirled	195.00

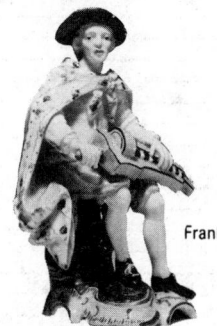

Frankenthal, Figurine, Hurdy-Gurdy Player, C.1790, 6 In.

Fry Foval, **Candlestick**, Blue Spiral Threading & Wafers, Opaline, 16 In., Pair	345.00
Fry Foval, **Candlestick**, Opalescent Swirled, 2 Blue Rings, 10 In.	250.00
Fry Foval, **Candlestick**, Opalescent Threading, Jade Green, 16 In., Pair	295.00
Fry Foval, **Champagne**, Tall	45.00
Fry Foval, **Compote**, Blue Stem, 7 X 6 In.	225.00
Fry Foval, **Compote**, Blue Trim & Wafer, Opaline, 10 1/4 X 10 In.	180.00
Fry Foval, **Compote**, Blue With Gold, Fruit, 11 1/2 In.Diameter	225.00
Fry Foval, **Compote**, Green Jade Finial & Stem, Covered, 6 X 8 In.	160.00
Fry Foval, **Cup & Saucer**, Cup 3 1/4 In.	35.00
Fry Foval, **Cup & Saucer**, Green Handle	85.00 To 92.50
Fry Foval, **Cup & Saucer**, Jade Handle, Engraved	65.00
Fry Foval, **Cup**, Blue	35.00
Fry Foval, **Glass**, Lemonade, Green Opaque Handle, 5 1/2 In.	55.00
Fry Foval, **Goblet**, Jade Stem	40.00
Fry Foval, **Lemonade Set**, Applied Blue Handle, Five Pieces	350.00
Fry Foval, **Lemonade Set**, Covered Pitcher & 6 Handled Glasses	395.00
Fry Foval, **Pitcher**, Opalescent, 9 In.	125.00
Fry Foval, **Rose Bowl**, Pale Green & White, Signed	95.00
Fry Foval, **Sugar**, Jade Handles, Lid	39.00
Fry Foval, **Tea Set**, Opalescent, Green Applied Handles & Spout, 11 Piece	375.00
Fry Foval, **Teapot**, Jade Green Finial, Spout, & Handle	65.00
Fry Foval, **Tray**, Sandwich, Handle In Center, Pearl Opalescent	25.00
Fry Foval, **Tumbler**, Footed, Clear, Black Petal Shaped Foot	12.00
Fry Foval, **Vase**, Bud, Milky, Applied Blue Rim, 8 1/2 In.	75.00
Fry Foval, **Vase**, Jade Green Wafer, 6 In.	85.00
Fry Foval, **Water Set**, Yellow, Cobalt Handled Pitcher, 6 Piece	350.00
Fry Foval, **Wine**, Blue Stem	75.00
Fry, **Bowl**, Bishop's Hat, Signed, 10 In.	95.00
Fry, **Bowl**, Finger, Cobalt Rim, Pair	40.00
Fry, **Bowl**, Hobstars, Beading, Fans, Serrated Edge, 8 In.	165.00
Fry, **Candlestick**, Blue Spiral Threading & Wafers, 10 1/2 In., Pair	200.00
Fry, **Candlestick**, Blue With Gold, Fruit Band, 10 In., Pair	270.00
Fry, **Casserole**, Opalescent, Covered, 1951	6.00
Fry, **Casserole**, Ovenware, Metal Holder, Lid, Marked, Dated, 1 Quart	30.00
Fry, **Champagne**, Opalescent, Twisted Stem	35.00
Fry, **Compote**, Green Stem, 7 1/2 X 6 1/2 In.	95.00
Fry, **Creamer**, Opal, Blue Spout & Handle	55.00
Fry, **Juice Reamer**, Opalescent	12.00
Fry, **Lemonade Set**, Opalescent Striped Pitcher, 5 Tumblers, Blue Handles	200.00
Fry, **Vase**, Blue Applied Leaves, Crackle Glaze, 14 In.	48.00 To 85.00
Fry, **Vase**, Opalescent, Ribbon, 6 In., Pair	75.00
Fry, **Water Set**, Fredrick Pattern, Scalloped Top Pitcher, 7 Piece	375.00

Fulper is the mark used by the American Pottery Company of Flemington, New Jersey. The art pottery was made from 1910 to 1929. The firm had been making bottles, jugs, and housewares from 1805. Doll heads were made about 1928. The firm became Stangl Pottery in 1929.

Fulper, see also Doll

Fulper, **Bowl**, Black Luster, Scalloped Rim, 7 1/2 In.	39.00
Fulper, **Bowl**, Blue Crystalline, 16 1/2 In.	60.00
Fulper, **Bowl**, Blue Flambe Interior, Dark Blue Exterior, 10 1/4 In.	40.00
Fulper, **Bowl**, Blue, Iridescent, Footed, 9 3/4 In.	31.00
Fulper, **Bowl**, Centerpiece, Turquoise & Cream, Paneled, 15 In.	55.00
Fulper, **Bowl**, Crystalline, Green, 11 In.	30.00
Fulper, **Bowl**, Dark Streaked Gloss, 1 3/4 X 6 In.	12.00
Fulper, **Bowl**, Flower, Effigy, Monkey Base, 7 1/4 X 10 1/2 In.	200.00
Fulper, **Bowl**, Lavender Matte Glaze, Art Deco, 4 In.	18.00
Fulper, **Bowl**, Shallow, Yellow To Green, 7 1/2 In.	30.00
Fulper, **Bowl**, Tan, Blue Brush Strokes, 5 3/4 In.	16.50
Fulper, **Box**, Dresser, Spanish Girl, Open Fan Covers Box, Artist Initial	65.00
Fulper, **Box**, Powder, Figural, Art Decoration, Lady In Pink Dress	55.00
Fulper, **Candlestick**, Matte Green Glaze, Handled, Marked, 2 1/2 In.	20.00
Fulper, **Case**, Posey, Pointed Oval, Green, Brown, 3 1/2 In.	38.00
Fulper, **Compote**, Geese Holding Bowl, High Glaze Blue	80.00
Fulper, **Compote**, Grotesque Figures Holding Bowl, Light Blue	85.00

Fulper, Flower Bowl, 12-Holed Leaping Fish Frog, Blue, Crystalline Glaze	75.00
Fulper, Flower Frog, Nude Lady On Lily Pad	22.50
Fulper, Jar, Powder, Figural, Girl In Pink, Art Deco, Signed	125.00
Fulper, Lamp, Ballerina Perfume, Azure Blue	95.00 To 125.00
Fulper, Lamp, Perfume, Ballerina, Orange To Natural	100.00
Fulper, Night Light, Salmon & White Ballerina, Salmon Colored Base, Marked	65.00
Fulper, Pitcher, Bennington Type, Signed, 6 In.	15.00
Fulper, Pitcher, Crystalline Glaze, Spotted Green Glaze, Vertical Ink Mark	50.00
Fulper, Pitcher, Green, Brown & Black Mottled, 6 X 6 1/2 In.	25.00
Fulper, Pitcher, Mottled Brown Flambe, Applied Handle, Signed, 6 X 6 In.	29.00
Fulper, Pitcher, Mottled Green Matte Glaze Over Brown, 5 1/2 In.	35.00
Fulper, Pocket, Wall, Triangle Shape, Blue Green, High Glaze	34.00
Fulper, Shade, Blue & White Slag Panels, Cone Shaped, Signed, 15 In.	1095.00
Fulper, Vase, Art Deco Design, Blue Flambe, Signed, 16 In.	50.00
Fulper, Vase, Art Deco Design, Fan Shape, 3 1/2 X 6 X 2 3/4 In.	55.00
Fulper, Vase, Blue Drip Over Brown, 4 1/2 In.	16.00
Fulper, Vase, Blue To Deep Pink Semigloss Glaze, Marked, 4 In.	16.00
Fulper, Vase, Boat Shape, Blue Mottled, Raised Art Deco, 4 X 6 In.	22.00
Fulper, Vase, Brown Mottled, Bulbous, 4 In.	24.00
Fulper, Vase, Bud, Blue & Rose Drip Glaze, 8 In.	12.00
Fulper, Vase, Bulbous, 3 3/4 In.	28.00
Fulper, Vase, Cucumber Green, 2 Handled, Paper Label, 7 3/4 X 5 In.	24.00
Fulper, Vase, Dark Brown High Glass, No.826, 4 1/2 In.	24.00
Fulper, Vase, Drip High Glaze In Blues, Marked, 4 1/2 In.	17.50
Fulper, Vase, Dusty Rose, Semigloss Finish, 7 In.	32.00
Fulper, Vase, Flambe, Crystalline Blue Glazes, Glossy, Matte, 8 In.	32.00
Fulper, Vase, Green & Pink, Bulbous, 2 Handles, 7 1/2 In.	50.00
Fulper, Vase, Green Crystalline Glaze, 7 3/4 In.	32.00
Fulper, Vase, Green Crystalline High Gloss, No.825, 4 1/4 In.	24.00
Fulper, Vase, Green Glaze, Handled, Vertical Ink Mark & D643, 7 In.	30.00
Fulper, Vase, Lavender Matte Glaze, Bulbous, Oriental Handles, 5 X 5 In.	22.00
Fulper, Vase, Luster Drip Over Green, 3 1/2 In.	24.00
Fulper, Vase, Maroon, 3 1/2 In.	14.00
Fulper, Vase, Medium & Light Blues, Beehive Shape, Handled, 9 1/2 In.	60.00
Fulper, Vase, Single Flower, Blue Shades, Side Handle, 5 In.	12.00
Furniture, Armchair, Arched Crest, Closed Wings, Scroll Arms, Serpentine	4000.00
Furniture, Armchair, High Backed, Regency Mahogany, Yellow Velvet, C.1820	800.00
Furniture, Armchair, Lolling, Carved, Martha Washington	875.00
Furniture, Armchair, Louis XV, Painted, Carved, C.1750, Damask, Pair	2900.00
Furniture, Armchair, Mahogany, Hepplewhite, C.1780	530.00
Furniture, Armchair, Mahogany, Hepplewhite, England, 22 X 36 1/2 In.	975.00
Furniture, Armchair, Rococo Chinoiserie, 18th Century, Decorated	600.00
Furniture, Armchair, Wicker	100.00
Furniture, Armchair, Wing, English, Queen Anne, Late 18th Century, New York	325.00
Furniture, Armchair, Wing, English, Queen Anne, Striped Floral, C.1820	275.00
Furniture, Armoire, French Provencale, Pine, 18th Century	3200.00
Furniture, Armoire, Grain Painted, Mustard And Ochre	295.00
Furniture, Armoire, Jacobean Style, Carved Oak, Plinth Base, 1890, 7 Ft.2 In.	750.00
Furniture, Armoire, Louis XV Style, Walnut Parquetry, Marquetry, 7 Ft.3 In.	2200.00
Furniture, Armoire, Louis XV Style, Walnut, Molded Cornice, 8 Ft.	1000.00
Furniture, Armoire, Louis XVI Style, 3 Doors, Beveled Glass Mirror	2900.00
Furniture, Armoire, Miniature, Mirror Front On Door, Turned Trim, 8 In.	58.00
Furniture, Armoire, Victorian Cottage Style, Chestnut, Single Long Door	550.00
Furniture, Armoire, Victorian Cottage Style, Walnut, Single Long Drawer	225.00
Furniture, Armoire, Victorian, Ormolu Mounted Marquetry, Ebony & Brass, 7 Ft.	650.00
Furniture, Armoire, Walnut, Early 1900s, 57 In.X 7 Ft.	800.00
Furniture, Bed, Brass, Queen Mountain Top	2200.00
Furniture, Bed, Brass, 57 X 54 In.	545.00
Furniture, Bed, Cannonball, Half Spindle & Scroll Headboard, Maple, Pa.	350.00
Furniture, Bed, Carved Walnut, Full Size, Canopy, 7 Ft.8 In., C.1830	3000.00
Furniture, Bed, Child's, Rope, Cherry, 18th Century	145.00
Furniture, Bed, Four-Poster, Rope, Birch Wood, Canopy Frame	1350.00
Furniture, Bed, French Victorian, Mahogany ......*Illus*	1600.00
Furniture, Bed, High Post Double, Cherry, Sheraton	450.00
Furniture, Bed, Maple, High Poster, Canopy, 3/4 Size, Cherry Headboard, C.1820	1500.00

Furniture, Bed, French Victorian, Mahogany

Furniture, Buffet, Claw Feet

Furniture, Cabinet, Chinese, Lacquer, Softstone, Brass, Pair

Furniture, **Bed,** Murphy, Oak, Buffet Shape	250.00
Furniture, **Bed,** Oak High Headboard, Double Size, 70 In.	250.00
Furniture, **Bed,** Sheraton, Canopy Style	900.00
Furniture, **Bed,** Single, Cast Iron, Brass Ball Trim, Canopy, C.1890	225.00
Furniture, **Bed,** Single, Venetian, Hand Decorated And Gilded, C.1800	500.00
Furniture, **Bed,** Spool Turned, Walnut	510.00
Furniture, **Bed,** Steel, French Campaign, Alors	750.00
Furniture, **Bed,** Walnut, Half Size Tester, Carved On Bed & Tester	1950.00
Furniture, **Bed,** Youth, Victorian, Walnut	175.00
Furniture, **Bedroom Set,** 5 Piece, Oak, Cherry, Carved Dogwood	2000.00
Furniture, **Bench,** Blacksmith's, Wooden, Drawer	35.00
Furniture, **Bench,** Bucket, Molded Shelves & Sides, Pennsylvania, C.1780	395.00
Furniture, **Bench,** Bucket, Shelves, Tombstone Shaped Ends, Pine, C.1840, 42 In.	165.00
Furniture, **Bench,** Meeting House, 7 Ft.	95.00
Furniture, **Bench,** Pine, Green, New York, 19th Century, 10 Ft.	85.00
Furniture, **Bench,** Vanity, Louis XV, Carved & Painted, Floral Needlepoint	200.00
Furniture, **Bin,** Bean, Lift-Forward Top Forms Bin Into Desk	295.00
Furniture, **Blanket Box,** 3-Drawer, C.1818, Pennsylvania, Lock, Hinges	675.00
Furniture, **Bookcase,** American Empire Classical Revival, Mahogany, 91 In.	1800.00
Furniture, **Bookcase,** Breakfront, Mahogany, Georgian, Glazed Doors, C.1800	3100.00
Furniture, **Bookcase,** Butler's Secretary, Mahogany, American Hepplewhite	1500.00
Furniture, **Bookcase,** Ebonized, 3 Glass Doors, Metal Beading, 41 X 56 In.	210.00
Furniture, **Bookcase,** Golden Oak, 4 Shelves, 4 Lifting Glazed Doors	175.00
Furniture, **Bookcase,** Mahogany, English Hepplewhite, C.1790, 50 X 23 1/4 In.	2950.00
Furniture, **Bookcase,** Mahogany, English Hepplewhite, 2-Part, Carved, C.1810	1800.00
Furniture, **Bookcase,** Mahogany, Georgian Secretaire, C.1785, 40 X 85 1/2 In.	8750.00
Furniture, **Bookcase,** Oak, Breakfront, Chippendale, 3 Drawer, C.1875, 77 In.	1300.00
Furniture, **Bookcase,** Oak, Cylinder Roll, Side By Side, 56 X 6 Ft.6 In.	1250.00
Furniture, **Bookcase,** Secretary, Mahogany, American Hepplewhite, C.1810, 77 In.	1200.00
Furniture, **Bookcase,** Stackable, Mahogany, Pair, 34 X 60 In.	575.00
Furniture, **Bookcase,** Walnut, Queen Anne, Mirrored Doors, C.1700, 41 X 78 In.	2500.00
Furniture, **Box,** Blanket, Hudson Valley Shoefoot, Six Board, Blue, Green	85.00
Furniture, **Box,** Blanket, Oak, Pine, Paneled, C.17th Century	1500.00
Furniture, **Box,** Handkerchief, Walnut	185.00
Furniture, **Box,** Ice, Brass Handles, Three Door, Oak	350.00
Furniture, **Box,** Knife, English Hepplewhite, Mahogany, C.1800, 15 In.	350.00
Furniture, **Box,** Quebec, Clay Benson Of Port Hope, Ontario, 19th Century	265.00

Furniture, Box, Shawl, Gold Lacquer, Chinese Black, 19 1/4 In. 475.00
Furniture, Bracket, Mirrored Back, Chinese Chippendale, Carved, Gilt, Pair 1700.00
Furniture, Buffet, A Deux Corps, Bleached Elm, French Provencale, 1800 .... 1500.00
Furniture, Buffet, Claw Feet .... *Illus* 150.00
Furniture, Buffet, Golden Oak, Lead Glass 230.00
Furniture, Buffet, Rosewood, Burl, Mirror Back, Marble Top, Louis XVI, C.1890. .... 700.00
Furniture, Buffet, Rosewood, Regency, C.1820 .... 770.00
Furniture, Bureau, George I, Walnut, C.1720, Small 3080.00
Furniture, Bureau, Golden Oak, Princess 150.00
Furniture, Bureau, Writing, Chippendale, Mahogany, C.1770 .... 1650.00
Furniture, Bureau, Writing, Slant Top, Chippendale Mahogany, C.1790 .... 1250.00
Furniture, Cabinet, Barber's, Wall Hanging, Folk Art Carving, 1850s, 19 In. 100.00
Furniture, Cabinet, Black Lacquer, Mirror-Backed Shelves, Chinese, 6 Ft. 700.00
Furniture, Cabinet, Boulle, Marble Top, Double Doors, Ormolu Cherubs, 3 Feet 900.00
Furniture, Cabinet, China, Curved Glass 535.00
Furniture, Cabinet, China, Curved Glass, Oak, 4 Shelves, 60 X 35 X 13 In. 375.00
Furniture, Cabinet, China, French Provincial, 3 Compartment, 52 In. 495.00
Furniture, Cabinet, China, Golden Oak, Curved Glazed Doors & Sides, C.1900 .... 1400.00
Furniture, Cabinet, China, Molding, 2 Shelves, Curved Glass Sides, 23 In. 47.50
Furniture, Cabinet, China, Oak, Curved Glass Sides, Straight Door, 60 In.Long 550.00
Furniture, Cabinet, Chinese, Lacquer, Softstone, Brass, Pair .... *Illus* 1500.00
Furniture, Cabinet, Corner, Cherry & Maple, 2-Part, C.1830, American, 86 In. 1555.00
Furniture, Cabinet, Corner, Pine, American, C.1820, 55 X 93 In. 450.00
Furniture, Cabinet, Corner, Pine, 2 Part, Doors & Shelves, Canadian, C.1820 .... 250.00
Furniture, Cabinet, Corner, Walnut, American Chippendale, C.1800, 88 In. 1900.00
Furniture, Cabinet, Fruit, Parquet Inlay, Louis XVI, Beveled Glass, 84 In. 550.00
Furniture, Cabinet, George I, Black Japanned, Gilt, Early 1700s, 5 Ft. 1700.00
Furniture, Cabinet, Hoosier, 3 Drawers, Bin, Cabinet, Enamel Surface 450.00
Furniture, Cabinet, Hutch, Walnut, Victorian, Two-Part, C.1875, 64 X 89 In. 750.00
Furniture, Cabinet, Kitchen, Bootjack End, Glazed Doors, C.1820 .... 160.00
Furniture, Cabinet, Kitchen, Pine, Glass Doors, 6 1/2 X 7 Ft. 400.00
Furniture, Cabinet, Louis XV, Vitrine, Double Glass Doors.C.1750, 93 In. 2600.00
Furniture, Cabinet, Mahogany, Glass Top Section, Drawer, Art Nouveau, 6 Ft. 300.00
Furniture, Cabinet, Oak, Curved Glass, Claw Feet, Lion's Head 900.00
Furniture, Cabinet, Oak, Curved Glass, Mirrored Top Piece 400.00
Furniture, Cabinet, Soft Maple, Pennsylvania, Pegged, Large 795.00
Furniture, Cabinet, Spice, Oak, Wooden Knobs, Scalloped Back, 8 Drawers 83.00
Furniture, Cabinet, Spice, Pine, 8 Drawer 50.00
Furniture, Cabinet, Victorian Side, Ormolu Mounted Boulle Marquetry, 43 In. 425.00
Furniture, Cabinet, 2 Piece, 2 Doors, 2 Drawers, 2 Doors With Arched Inserts 275.00
Furniture, Candlestand, Cherry, Circular Top, Tripod Base, Stenciled 35.00
Furniture, Candlestand, Cherry, Cut Corners, Snake Feet, Small .... ? J.00
Furniture, Candlestand, Cherry, Square Top, C.1790, American, 27 In. 200.00
Furniture, Candlestand, Cross Base, Wallace Nutting 90.00
Furniture, Candlestand, Dunlap Style 275.00
Furniture, Candlestand, Spider Leg, Octagonal Top, Maine, Early 19th Century 575.00
Furniture, Candlestand, Tilt Top, Cherry, New England, C.1790, 24 X 28 In. 325.00
Furniture, Candlestand, Walnut, Sheraton, One Drawer, American, 29 In. 110.00
Furniture, Candlestand, 2 Light, Cherry, William & Mary, C.1720, 51 3/4 In. 1200.00
Furniture, Cellarette, Inlaid Satinwood, C.1795 .... 635.00
Furniture, Chair & Love Seat, Lion Head Armrests, Claw Feet, Mahogany 625.00
Furniture, Chair, Arch Slat, Maple & Curly Maple, C.1760-1800, 44 In., Pair 2900.00
Furniture, Chair, Arrowback, Plank Seat, C.1830, American 75.00
Furniture, Chair, Arrowback, Unusual Pink Color, Arm 185.00
Furniture, Chair, Bannister, C.1750, Signed L.W. 250.00
Furniture, Chair, Bentwood, High Back, Cane Seat & Back, Arms 175.00
Furniture, Chair, Bishop's, Italian Baroque, Walnut, Late 17th Century 200.00
Furniture, Chair, Bow Back Windsor, Pine 135.00
Furniture, Chair, Brewster, Ash & Oak, Arms, Pilgrim Century Style 550.00
Furniture, Chair, Carved Dragon & Peacock 750.00
Furniture, Chair, Child's Wicker 50.00
Furniture, Chair, Child's, Country, Irish, 18th Century 125.00
Furniture, Chair, Child's, Slat Back, Rush Seat 150.00
Furniture, Chair, Child's, Swivel, Maple 50.00
Furniture, Chair, Child's, Yellow & Brown Paint, Continuous Arm 975.00

Furniture, Chair, Chinese, Hardwood, Set Of 8 .... *Illus* 1600.00
Furniture, Chair, Continuous Arm Brace Back, Red Surface 2900.00
Furniture, Chair, Corner, Chippendale, Mahogany, C.1760 .... 850.00
Furniture, Chair, Corner, Commode, Walnut, Geo.II 280.00
Furniture, Chair, Corner, Maple, Ash, Nutting 700.00
Furniture, Chair, Corner, Queen Anne, Maple 750.00
Furniture, Chair, Corner, Stretcher Base, Maple Queen Anne, Circa 1750 .... 1350.00
Furniture, Chair, Country Chippendale, Cherry, Rush Seat, C.1760-80 .... 375.00
Furniture, Chair, Dining Room, English Chippendale, C.1750, Mahogany, 7 Piece 5500.00
Furniture, Chair, Directoire, C.1800, Set Of 4 .... 80.00
Furniture, Chair, Eastlake, Set Of 4 .... 325.00
Furniture, Chair, Empire, Gentleman & Lady's, Mahogany, Carved, C.1820, Pair 1600.00
Furniture, Chair, English, Yew Wood, Arms, Mid-19th Century 70.00
Furniture, Chair, Flemish, Arms, 17th Century, 58 In. 375.00
Furniture, Chair, Folding, Child's, Carpet Seat 85.00
Furniture, Chair, Hinoki, Carved Phoenix Bird Crestrail, C.1880 .... 275.00
Furniture, Chair, Hitchcock, Set Of 6 .... 1100.00
Furniture, Chair, Ice Cream, Nickel Plated, Set Of 6 .... 510.00
Furniture, Chair, Jacobean, Miniature, Oak, 9 3/4 X 6 In. 140.00
Furniture, Chair, Jeffersonian Library, Converts To Steps 900.00
Furniture, Chair, Ladder Back, Child's 60.00
Furniture, Chair, Ladder Back, New England, Maple, C.1780 .... 875.00
Furniture, Chair, Ladder Back, Rush Seat, Curly Sycamore, Set Of 4 .... 295.00
Furniture, Chair, Ladder Back, Shaker, Child's 60.00
Furniture, Chair, Ladder Back, Shaker, Red Paint, Canterbury, Early 1800s 275.00
Furniture, Chair, Ladder Back, Shaker, Sausage Turnings, Arms, Splint Seat 410.00
Furniture, Chair, Ladder Back, 5 Slat, Arms 495.00
Furniture, Chair, Ladder Back, 5 Slat, Delaware Valley 1050.00
Furniture, Chair, Lady's, Walnut, Victorian 295.00
Furniture, Chair, Louis XVI Slipper, Balloon Seat, Carved Pediment, C.1890 .... 200.00
Furniture, Chair, Mahogany, Arms, Empire, C.1825 .... 225.00
Furniture, Chair, Mahogany, Carved, Inlaid Splines, Silk Fabric, C.1800 .... 485.00
Furniture, Chair, Mahogany, Chippendale, C.1760, Upholstered Back & Seat 730.00
Furniture, Chair, Man's, Walnut, Victorian 295.00
Furniture, Chair, Maple, Rush Seat, Arms, New England, C.1760 .... 250.00
Furniture, Chair, Miniature, Oak, Jacobean, Carved Back & Front, 9 3/4 X 6 In. 100.00
Furniture, Chair, Morris, Child's 45.00
Furniture, Chair, Musical, Carved, Key Wind, Child's, 27 In. 295.00
Furniture, Chair, New England Writing, Arm, C.1760-70 .... 4750.00
Furniture, Chair, Oak, Jacobean, Two With Full Figure Carving, Set Of 8 .... 1500.00
Furniture, Chair, Potty, Oak, Captain's 37.50
Furniture, Chair, Pressed Back, Oak, Set Of 6 .... 250.00 To 325.00
Furniture, Chair, Quaker, Sycamore, C.1690, Chester County, Pennsylvania, Pair 500.00
Furniture, Chair, Reclining, Oak, Leather Upholstery, Stickley .... *Illus* 1200.00
Furniture, Chair, Red Walnut, George II, C.1740, Pair 895.00
Furniture, Chair, Rocker, Comb Back, Windsor 395.00
Furniture, Chair, Rush Seat, Arms, C.1680-1700, Ball Feet 550.00
Furniture, Chair, Shaker, Rocker Number 3, Mustard Paint, Tape Seat 275.00
Furniture, Chair, Shaker, Rocker, Label, No.3 .... 225.00
Furniture, Chair, Shaker, Watervliet, Replaced Seats, Set Of 6 .... *Illus* 1080.00
Furniture, Chair, Sheraton, Rush Seat, Arms, English, C.1810, Set Of 6 .... 3500.00

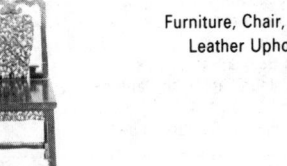

Furniture, Chair, Reclining, Oak,
Leather Upholstery, Stickley

Furniture, Chair, Chinese, Hardwood, Set Of 8

Furniture, Chair, Side, American Hepplewhite, Cherry, Pair 695.00
Furniture, Chair, Side, American Queen Anne, Walnut, Philadelphia, C.1750 .... 2200.00
Furniture, Chair, Side, Ballroom, Painted And Gilt, Tufted Upholstered, Pair 100.00
Furniture, Chair, Side, Chippendale, Carved Mahogany, Pair, C.1760 .... 350.00
Furniture, Chair, Side, Chippendale, Mahogany, Massachusetts, 1763-80 .... 900.00
Furniture, Chair, Side, English Sheraton, Mahogany, Oak Turned Support 400.00
Furniture, Chair, Side, Federal Painted & Decorated, 1820s, Pair 335.00
Furniture, Chair, Side, High Back, Carved Walnut, Irish, Upholstered 300.00
Furniture, Chair, Side, Hitchcock, Decorated, C.1830, Pair 130.00
Furniture, Chair, Side, Lacquer & Partial Gild, Spanish Rococo, C.1780, Pair 800.00
Furniture, Chair, Side, Louis XV, Balloon Seat, Fluted Legs, Pair 300.00
Furniture, Chair, Side, Louis XV, Carved & Painted Frame, 19th Century, Pair 125.00
Furniture, Chair, Side, Mahogany, American Chippendale, Crewel Seat, Carved 350.00
Furniture, Chair, Side, New York, C.1760, Pair 7650.00
Furniture, Chair, Side, Oak, Leather Seats, Stickley, Set Of 11 .... *Illus* 450.00
Furniture, Chair, Side, Original Red Under Old Black, 1780-1800, New England 250.00
Furniture, Chair, Side, Plank Seat, Flared Back, Yellow & Black Paint, Pair 585.00
Furniture, Chair, Side, Queen Anne, Pad Foot, C.1790 .... 135.00
Furniture, Chair, Side, Rhode Island Queen Anne, Balloon Seat, Walnut, 7 Piece 32500.00
Furniture, Chair, Side, Signed, Shaker 400.00
Furniture, Chair, Side, Spanish Toe, Chippendale, Carved Ears 300.00
Furniture, Chair, Side, Square Back, Mahogany, Carved, Four 2250.00
Furniture, Chair, Side, Walnut, Carved, Upholstered, C.1880, Pair 70.00
Furniture, Chair, Side, Walnut, Italian Renaissance, 17th Century, Rococo, Pair 170.00
Furniture, Chair, Side, Walnut, Rococo, Carved, English 35.00
Furniture, Chair, Slipper, New York, C.1760, 36 X 22 X 15 In., Pair 4850.00
Furniture, Chair, Slipper, Windsor, Hoop Back, C.1770-1800 .... 175.00
Furniture, Chair, Stencil, Light Green, Windsor, Pair 165.00
Furniture, Chair, Swivel, Pressed-Back Spindle 95.00
Furniture, Chair, Tilting, Buttons, Shaker 250.00
Furniture, Chair, Upholstered Step-Down Windsor, One Armchair, Set Of Four 2500.00
Furniture, Chair, Wainscot, Stylized Tulip Crest, Arms, 1690, Small 850.00
Furniture, Chair, Walnut, Arms, Caned, Flemish, Carved, C.1790 .... 90.00
Furniture, Chair, Wicker, Fan Back, Matching Table, White 200.00
Furniture, Chair, Window Seat, Mahogany, Sheraton, C.1800 .... 550.00
Furniture, Chair, Windsor, Arm, Brace Back, B.Green 1250.00
Furniture, Chair, Windsor, Birdcage, Black Paint 250.00

Furniture, Chair, Side, Oak, Leather Seats, Stickley, Set Of 11

Furniture, Chair, Shaker, Watervliet,
Replaced Seats, Set Of 6

Furniture, Chair, Windsor, Bow Back, 18th Century	295.00
Furniture, Chair, Windsor, Child's, Bow Back, Arms	468.00
Furniture, Chair, Windsor, Comb Back	1300.00
Furniture, Chair, Windsor, Double Comb Back	2600.00
Furniture, Chair, Windsor, Fanback	265.00
Furniture, Chair, Windsor, Fanback, Old Red Paint, Early 19th Century	285.00
Furniture, Chair, Windsor, Hoop Back, Arms, Late 18th Century	525.00
Furniture, Chair, Windsor, Knuckle Arm, American	675.00
Furniture, Chair, Windsor, Nine Spindle Brace Back	575.00
Furniture, Chair, Windsor, Rhode Island, Arms	1600.00
Furniture, Chair, Windsor, Step-Down, Black Paint, Pair	425.00
Furniture, Chair, Windsor, Step-Down, 7 Spindle	360.00
Furniture, Chair, Wing, Sheraton, Mahogany With Pine & Chestnut, New York	850.00
Furniture, Chair, Wingback, Mahogany, Georgian, C.1880, Carved Cabriole Legs	170.00
Furniture, Chair, 4-Slat, New England, Arms, C.1800	375.00
Furniture, Chest-On-Chest, Chippendale, English Red Walnut, 1790	800.00
Furniture, Chest-On-Chest, Mahogany, C.1790, Small	1200.00
Furniture, Chest-On-Chest, Mahogany, English Chippendale, C.1800, 74 In.	1150.00
Furniture, Chest-On-Chest, Oak, Small	1100.00
Furniture, Chest On Frame, Queen Anne, New England, Cherry & Tulipwood	1900.00
Furniture, Chest, American Federal, Cherry & Birdseye Maple, 46 X 46 In.	250.00
Furniture, Chest, Apothecary, Mahogany & Pine, 30 Drawer, Glass Knobs, C.1860	340.00
Furniture, Chest, Apothecary, Mahogany, Glass Labels & Knobs, 10 Drawer	230.00
Furniture, Chest, Apothecary, Mahogany, 16 1/2 X 12 In.	168.00
Furniture, Chest, Apothecary, 12 Drawers, Brown Paint	775.00
Furniture, Chest, Black Lacquered, Gilt, Soft Stone Inlay, Korean, 23 In., Pair	700.00
Furniture, Chest, Blanket, Butternut, 2 Drawer, Bootjack End	325.00
Furniture, Chest, Blanket, Chippendale, Painted Poplar, Hinged Lid, 4 X 28 In.	700.00
Furniture, Chest, Blanket, Continental, Forged Escutcheon, Hinges, Carved, Oak	375.00
Furniture, Chest, Blanket, Curly Maple, Sheraton, 1810	850.00
Furniture, Chest, Blanket, Fruitwood, Late 18th Century, 62 X 39 In.	1200.00
Furniture, Chest, Blanket, Miniature, Dovetailed, C.1860	100.00
Furniture, Chest, Blanket, One Drawer, Lift Top, Pine, 39 X 35 In.	225.00
Furniture, Chest, Blanket, Painted & Decorated, Pennsylvania, C.1840, 19 In.	600.00
Furniture, Chest, Blanket, Pine, Hinged Lid, American, C.1720-50, 43 1/2 In.	375.00
Furniture, Chest, Blanket, Pine, Iron Handles, Elisha Richardson, 1803, 15 In.	165.00
Furniture, Chest, Blanket, Pine, Red, Mid-18th Century, 27 X 11 X 14 In.	240.00
Furniture, Chest, Blanket, Sheraton, Crotch Curly Maple, C.1810	1500.00
Furniture, Chest, Blanket, Sheraton, Walnut & Cherry, Child's Size	425.00
Furniture, Chest, Blanket, Stippled And Panel Decorated	2900.00
Furniture, Chest, Blanket, Two Drawer, Dovetailed Bracket Base, 18th Century	145.00
Furniture, Chest, Blanket, Two Drawer, Pine, Connecticut	350.00
Furniture, Chest, Blanket, Walnut, Cedar Lined, C.1860, 37 X 22 In.	120.00
Furniture, Chest, Blanket, Yellow, Pine, Orange Stippled Tree	575.00
Furniture, Chest, Bonnet, Reeded Leg, Sheraton	160.00
Furniture, Chest, Bow Front, Cherry, Original Brasses	1400.00
Furniture, Chest, Bow Front, English Sheraton, Mahogany, Brass Feet, 34 In.	325.00
Furniture, Chest, Bow Front, Mahogany, English Sheraton, 5 Drawers, 29 In.	175.00
Furniture, Chest, Burl Wood, Korean, 4 Drawers, C.1880, 42 X 55 In.	300.00
Furniture, Chest, Burl Wood, 2 Sections, Korean, C.1880, 34 X 54 In.	500.00
Furniture, Chest, Campaign, Cedar, Brass Bindings, Handles, & Lock, 34 3/4 In.	525.00
Furniture, Chest, Carved Oak, Carved Crests, English, 40 X 17 In.	250.00
Furniture, Chest, Chart, Dovetailed Pine	125.00
Furniture, Chest, Cherry, Bird's-Eye Maple, Bow Front, Salem, 44 X 42 In.	475.00
Furniture, Chest, Cherry, Brass Handles, Locking Drawers, Key, 1780-1800	1200.00
Furniture, Chest, Child's, Cedar, 21 X 9 1/2 In.	45.00
Furniture, Chest, Chippendale, Cherry, Connecticut, C.1775, 34 In.	2450.00
Furniture, Chest, Chippendale, Mahogany, American, 18th Century, 35 In.High	600.00
Furniture, Chest, Chippendale, Maple, 5 Drawer, 36 X 42 In.	1275.00
Furniture, Chest, Chippendale, Pinwheel Carved Base, Cherry	1400.00
Furniture, Chest, Clothes, 2-Story, Elm Root Panels, Mountain Design, Korean	2195.00
Furniture, Chest, Dome Top, Red On Yellow Graining, Maine, C.1840	250.00
Furniture, Chest, Dovetailed Drawers, Brass Pulls, Marble Top	295.00
Furniture, Chest, Dower, Pennsylvania Dutch, Decorated, C.1820, Signed	1625.00
Furniture, Chest, Drawers, Attached Wishbone Mirror, Empire, Large	400.00

Furniture, Chest, Drawers, Birch, Bird's-Eye Maple	450.00
Furniture, Chest, Eastlake, Brown Marble, 3 Drawers	285.00
Furniture, Chest, Empire, Tiger Maple & Veneer, 52 X 46 X 23 In.	450.00
Furniture, Chest, English Mahogany, 4 Drawer, Oval Inlay, C.1760, 32 1/2 In.	3000.00
Furniture, Chest, Fall Front, Maple, Hand-Carved Ivory Escutcheon, 43 In.	385.00
Furniture, Chest, Fall Front, Rice Storage, Korean, C.1880, 36 1/2 X 32 In.	150.00
Furniture, Chest, Hepplewhite, Bow Front, Red Paint	775.00
Furniture, Chest, Korean Burl Root, 4 Drawers, Storage Compartment, 32 In.	300.00
Furniture, Chest, Korean Wood, Fall Front, Wrought Iron Mounts, 32 X 17 In.	200.00
Furniture, Chest, Korean Wood, Rice, Fall Front, Brass Mounts, 29 X 27 In.	375.00
Furniture, Chest, Mahogany, Bachelor's, Federal, 4 Drawer, 47 X 43 In.	450.00
Furniture, Chest, Mahogany, Bowfront, Sheraton, C.1810, 41 In.	325.00
Furniture, Chest, Mahogany, Chippendale, Beau Brummel, C.1800, 24 X 33 In.	750.00
Furniture, Chest, Mahogany, Chippendale, English, C.1800, 48 In.	600.00
Furniture, Chest, Mahogany, Hepplewhite, C.1810, 37 X 36 In.	700.00
Furniture, Chest, Mahogany, With Drawers, 39 1/2 X 22 1/2 X 35 In.	600.00
Furniture, Chest, Mahogany, 4 Drawer, 14 X 7 X 14 1/2 In.	225.00
Furniture, Chest, Medicine, Korean Wood, 30 Drawer, Brass Ring, 25 X 30 In.	240.00
Furniture, Chest, Military, Mahogany, C.1850	860.00
Furniture, Chest, Miniature, Bracket Foot, Dovetailed *Illus*	45.00
Furniture, Chest, Miniature, Drawers, Feather-Grained Veneer, Paneled Sides	395.00
Furniture, Chest, Oak, Bun Feet, 3 Ft.	700.00
Furniture, Chest, Oak, German, 4 Carved Relief Panels, C.1714, 22 In.	425.00
Furniture, Chest, Oak, 4 Drawer, C.1800, 34 X 34 In.	575.00
Furniture, Chest, Pennsylvania, 18th Century, 29 1/2 X 49 1/2 X 21 1/2 In.	850.00
Furniture, Chest, Pine, Built-In Tray, 13 X 9 X 9 In.	65.00
Furniture, Chest, Pine, Drawers, C.1800, 3 Ft.	300.00
Furniture, Chest, Pine, William & Mary, 4 Drawer, 36 In.	2500.00
Furniture, Chest, Sample, Drawers, Mahogany, Empire, Signed Harry Clay NYC	175.00
Furniture, Chest, Sea Captain's, China Trade Piece, C.1870, Mixed Woods	1400.00
Furniture, Chest, Sea, Old Paint, Plain Rope Beckets	75.00
Furniture, Chest, Secretaire, Mahogany, Sheraton, C.1790	1130.00
Furniture, Chest, Shaker, South Union, Cherry, Burl Knobs, 45 In. *Illus*	625.00
Furniture, Chest, Sheraton, 4 Drawer	350.00

Furniture, Chest, Shaker, South Union, Cherry, Burl Knobs, 45 In.

Furniture, Chest, Miniature, Bracket Foot, Dovetailed

Furniture, Chest, Sheraton, 4 Large, 2 Small Drawers, Bowfront	650.00
Furniture, Chest, Storage, 4 Drawers, C.1880, Korean, 36 X 39 In.	250.00
Furniture, Chest, Sword, Oak, Small	250.00
Furniture, Chest, Tiger Maple And Cherry, Empire, 7 Drawers	450.00
Furniture, Chest, Tiger Maple, Beading On Drawer Fronts, C.1840	1350.00
Furniture, Chest, Tiger Maple, New England, Ogee Feet, C.1770, 6 Ft.8 In.	8500.00
Furniture, Chest, Walnut, Pine, Sycamore, American, Handmade, 37 1/2 X 49 In.	350.00
Furniture, Chest, William & Mary, Escutcheon, Brass, Walnut, 18th Century	3500.00
Furniture, Chest, 3 Drawers, Turned Legs, Pegged Construction, Mixed Woods	185.00
Furniture, Chest, 5 Drawers, Apron, Stepped Base, Painted Grain, Red, C.1800	625.00
Furniture, Chest, 5 Drawers, Maple, C.1710, Old Red Paint	6500.00
Furniture, Chest, 6 Drawers, Cherry, Inlay Base, C.1790, 5 Ft. 8 In.	3250.00

Furniture, China Cabinet, Oak .... *Illus* 650.00
Furniture, China Cabinet, Oak, Curved Sides, 42 In. 350.00
Furniture, Commode, Fruitwood, Bowfront, European, Mid-1700s, 49 X 36 In. 1700.00
Furniture, Commode, Louis XV, Carved Walnut, C.1880, Marble Insert, 34 In. 140.00
Furniture, Commode, Mahogany, Georgian, C.1790 .... 635.00
Furniture, Commode, Mahogany, Serpentine Front, English, C.1800, 25 In. 1100.00
Furniture, Commode, Marble Top, Pine, Ash, Walnut, Salesman's Sample 145.00
Furniture, Commode, Oak, Marble Top, Back Splash, One Drawer, Double Doors 195.00
Furniture, Commode, Victorian, Salesman's Sample, Pine, Oak, Walnut, 16 In. 145.00
Furniture, Couch, Carved, Walnut, Victorian, 7 Feet 625.00
Furniture, Couch, Empire, Country Version 550.00
Furniture, Couch, Fainting, Walnut, Carved Back, Victorian 195.00
Furniture, Cradle, Baby, Solid Sides, Dark Brown Paint, 22 In. 115.00
Furniture, Cradle, Bentwood 75.00
Furniture, Cradle, Square Nails, Pine, 3 1/2 Feet 195.00
Furniture, Cradle, Walnut, American Sheraton, Stationary Stand, 41 In. 90.00
Furniture, Cradle, Wicker, Pink 8.00
Furniture, Credenza, Italian Renaissance, 2 Panel Doors, C.1600, 43 In. 625.00
Furniture, Credenza, Walnut, Continental Renaissance, C.1740, 51 In. 1400.00
Furniture, Cupboard, Bedside, Georgian, Mahogany, Tambour Door, C.1790 .... 690.00
Furniture, Cupboard, Butternut, 12 Panel 1150.00
Furniture, Cupboard, Butternut, 2 Pieces 275.00
Furniture, Cupboard, Carved Oak, English Renaissance, 19th Century, 46 In. 400.00
Furniture, Cupboard, Corner, Cherry, 2-Piece, C.1800, Pennsylvania 3750.00
Furniture, Cupboard, Corner, Chippendale Barrel Back, Painted Interior, Pine 3900.00
Furniture, Cupboard, Corner, Open Door, Poplar, Blue Paint 750.00
Furniture, Cupboard, Corner, Original Paint, Rockland County 1400.00
Furniture, Cupboard, Corner, Pennsylvania, Decorated, C.1840, 86 X 47 In. 2250.00
Furniture, Cupboard, Corner, Poplar, Paneled Doors, 3 Dovetailed Drawers 650.00
Furniture, Cupboard, Corner, 4 Pierced Tin Panels, Grained 1500.00
Furniture, Cupboard, Double Corner, Oak, Mahogany Crossbanded 1100.00
Furniture, Cupboard, Double Glass Door, Wooden Counter, 2 Bins 475.00
Furniture, Cupboard, French Provincial, Louis XV, 4 Doors, 2 Sections 1400.00
Furniture, Cupboard, Jam, 2 Doors, 2 Drawers, Pine, C.1840 .... 300.00
Furniture, Cupboard, Jam, 2 Doors, 2 Drawers, High Back, Shelf, Victorian 245.00
Furniture, Cupboard, Jelly, Poplar, Large, 19th Century 350.00
Furniture, Cupboard, Jelly, Shaker, Mt.Lebanon, Red Satin 550.00
Furniture, Cupboard, Mahogany, Georgian, 4 Sliding Trays, 2 Drawers, C.1800 .... 730.00
Furniture, Cupboard, Oak Spice, Paneled Door, C.1710, 17 X 23 In. 500.00
Furniture, Cupboard, Open, Original Brown Paint, Small 425.00
Furniture, Cupboard, Paneled, Pine, Rosehead Nails, C.1790 .... 995.00
Furniture, Cupboard, Pine, Arched Detail On Doors, Pierced Tin Insets 400.00
Furniture, Cupboard, Pine, Glass Doors, 3 Drawers, 1900, 82 X 45 In. 350.00
Furniture, Cupboard, Pine, Open Pewter Top, 18th Century, 35 X 81 In. 2250.00
Furniture, Cupboard, Pine, Wood Doors, 4 Drawers, C.1880, 47 X 76 In. 375.00
Furniture, Cupboard, Pine, 46 1/2 X 37 1/2 In. 20.00
Furniture, Cupboard, Raised Panels, 6 Above, 2 Below, C.1820, Red, 7 X 43 In. 495.00
Furniture, Cupboard, Shaker Pharmaceutical 2500.00
Furniture, Cupboard, Step-Back, Cherry Finish, C.1820, 70 X 36 X 19 In. 1475.00
Furniture, Cupboard, Step-Back, 2 Top & Bottom One-Board Doors, Pine 445.00
Furniture, Cupboard, 1726, Documented 12000.00
Furniture, Cupboard, 3 Shelf Corner, Solid Door, Cupboard, C.1800 .... 750.00
Furniture, Cupboard, 8 Doors, Carved Crossed Stems With Leaves On Panels 495.00
Furniture, Desk, Accountant's, Lift Top, Dovetailed, Cubbies, Pine 85.00
Furniture, Desk, Accountant's, Walnut, Slant Top, Book Shelf, C.1850, 58 In. 200.00
Furniture, Desk, Butler's, Mahogany, Hepplewhite, French Feet 650.00
Furniture, Desk, Butler's, 7 Drawers In Desk, 3 Below, Carved Columns, Wood 475.00
Furniture, Desk, Campaign, Portable, Mahogany, Morocco Leather Top 300.00
Furniture, Desk, Canadian Butler's, Maple & Walnut, C.1830 .... 975.00
Furniture, Desk, Captain's, Walnut .... *Illus* 450.00
Furniture, Desk, Cherry Raised Panel, S Curve Roll Top, Many Pigeon Holes 1725.00
Furniture, Desk, Cherry, Brass Handles, Open Compartments On Top 2250.00
Furniture, Desk, Child's, Roll Top, Comes With Chair 150.00
Furniture, Desk, Child's, Slant Front, Inlaid Escutcheons 3950.00
Furniture, Desk, Chippendale Fall Front, Cherry, 36 In. 2750.00

Furniture, Desk, Chippendale Slant Front 3800.00
Furniture, Desk, Cylinder Roll Secretary, Walnut, Refinished, 40 X 7 Ft. 950.00
Furniture, Desk, Cylinder Top, Walnut & Burl Inlay, Victorian, 4 Drawers 400.00
Furniture, Desk, Drop Front Secretary, Chippendale, Mahogany, 1800 .... 1500.00
Furniture, Desk, Fall Front, Cherry, New England Chippendale, C.1780, 42 In. 1050.00
Furniture, Desk, Fall Front, Mahogany, English Chippendale, C.1800, 43 In. 1700.00
Furniture, Desk, Fall Front, Walnut, Chippendale, American, 41 X 41 In. 200.00
Furniture, Desk, George I, Mahogany Secretary, Mirrored Door, C.1730, 79 In. 16500.00
Furniture, Desk, Governor Winthrop, Cherry, C.1750 .... 2300.00
Furniture, Desk, Kneehole, Mahogany, Chippendale, Block Front, 31 In. 225.00
Furniture, Desk, Lady's, Inlaid Mahogany, C.1810, 53 1/2 In. .... *Illus* 1300.00
Furniture, Desk, Lap, Brass Edges, Mahogany, 14 X 9 1/2 X 6 1/2 In. 125.00
Furniture, Desk, Lap, Burled Walnut, 11 1/2 X 7 1/4 In. 45.00
Furniture, Desk, Lap, Compartmented, C.1860, 8 X 12 X 4 1/8 In. 35.00
Furniture, Desk, Lap, Pine, Slant Top, Lock & Key 65.00
Furniture, Desk, Lap, Walnut, Brass Trim, 12 X 4 1/2 X 9 Inch 120.00
Furniture, Desk, Larkin, Oak, Mirror 135.00
Furniture, Desk, Mahogany, French Empire, Tooled Leather Drawers, C.1850 .... 500.00
Furniture, Desk, Mahogany, Mock Partners', C.1800, 55 X 30 In. 3800.00
Furniture, Desk, Mahogany, Roll Top, C Design, 48 In.High 475.00
Furniture, Desk, Mahogany, Roll Top, 60 In. 375.00
Furniture, Desk, Man's, Cherry, Connecticut, Signed, C.1800 .... 2800.00
Furniture, Desk, Maple, Slant Front, High Bracket Feet, 36 In.Wide 4500.00
Furniture, Desk, Maple, Slant Front, 4 Drawers, Tiger Maple Pattern 1500.00
Furniture, Desk, Oak, Side-By-Side, 40 In. 425.00
Furniture, Desk, Paneled, 5 In.Slide, Oak 650.00
Furniture, Desk, Pedestal, Paneled Sides, Ball & Claw Footed, Mahogany, 1860 .... 2250.00
Furniture, Desk, Plantation, Cherry, Red Paint Inside, 38 X 67 X 26 In. 495.00

Furniture, China Cabinet, Oak

Furniture, Desk, Lady's, Inlaid Mahogany, C.1810, 53 1/2 In.

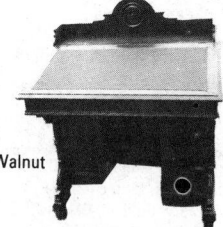

Furniture, Desk, Captain's, Walnut

Furniture, Desk, Queen Anne, Tiger Maple, 37 X 25 In. 1500.00
Furniture, Desk, Roll Top, C Design, Mahogany, 48 In. 475.00
Furniture, Desk, Roll Top, Oak, Large 750.00
Furniture, Desk, Roll Top, Oak, S Roll, 60 In. 595.00
Furniture, Desk, Roll Top, Youth Size 45.00
Furniture, Desk, S Roll Top, Double Pedestal, Oak, 50 In. 550.00
Furniture, Desk, S Roll, Oak, Double Pedestal, 50 X 32 X 51 In. 1200.00
Furniture, Desk, School, Original Conditon 19.95
Furniture, Desk, Schoolmaster's, Leather Top, Pencil-Shelf 350.00
Furniture, Desk, Schoolmaster's, Pine, Mid-19th Century, 26 1/2 X 38 1/2 In. 195.00

Furniture, Desk, Schoolmaster's, Walnut, Lift Top	375.00
Furniture, Desk, Schoolmaster's, Walnut, Slant Top, 1 Drawer, C.1860, 34 In.	150.00
Furniture, Desk, Secretary, Cherry, 4 Drawer, 42 In.	2350.00
Furniture, Desk, Sewing, Shaker, From Pleasant Hill, Kentucky	450.00
Furniture, Desk, Slant Front, Carved Mahogany, Chippendale .... Illus	2800.00
Furniture, Desk, Slant Front, Maple, Bracket Base, C.1790	1600.00
Furniture, Desk, Slant Front, Ogee Feet, Cherry And Chestnut, C.1740	3400.00
Furniture, Desk, Slant Front, Pine, Painted, C.1800, 36 3/4 In. .... Illus	2750.00
Furniture, Desk, Slant Top, Cherry, Ogee Feet, 3 Drawers	975.00
Furniture, Desk, Slant Top, Walnut	1250.00
Furniture, Desk, Stand-Up, Pine, 17 X 17 X 37 In.	275.00
Furniture, Desk, Table, George III, Mahogany, Leather Top, 44 X 30 In.	1500.00
Furniture, Desk, Walnut & Ormolu, French Empire, C.1815, 45 X 51 In.	1100.00
Furniture, Desk, Walnut, Burl Walnut, Fall Front, Italian, C.1790, 39 In.	425.00
Furniture, Desk, Walnut, Italian, Ebonized, Bone Inlaid Scenes, C.1850, 44 In.	700.00
Furniture, Desk, Walnut, Roll Top, Oak Inlay On Top, 51 X 44 In.	150.00
Furniture, Desk, Walnut, William & Mary, Ball Foot, 44 In. .... Illus	3500.00
Furniture, Desk, Walnut, William & Mary, Slant Front, 17th Century, 33 In.	3750.00
Furniture, Desk, Wells Fargo, Iron Label, Wooten Desk Co., C.1874, 46 X 58 In.	7500.00
Furniture, Desk, Writing, Satinwood, Mother-Of-Pearl Inlay, Crossbanding	625.00
Furniture, Dining Room Set, Walnut, Hand-Carved, Art Nouveau, 10 Piece	450.00
Furniture, Door, Cupboard, Checkerboard Painted In Red & Gray, Pine, 26 In.	85.00
Furniture, Dough Box, Legs, Elm, Color	450.00
Furniture, Dresser, Burl Cherry, 4-Drawer	375.00
Furniture, Dresser, Child's Toy, Oak	22.50
Furniture, Dresser, Cottage, Drop Front, Drawers, 4 Small, 2 Wide, Mirror	125.00
Furniture, Dresser, Country Oak, Shaped Apron, C.1720, 78 X 34 In.	3400.00
Furniture, Dresser, Welsh, Oak & Mahogany, C.1845	1600.00
Furniture, Dresser, Welsh, Oak, Open Pot Board Below, C.1790, 5 Ft.	2900.00
Furniture, Dry Sink, Chestnut, Drawer On Top, Cupboard Doors Below, 47 In.	300.00
Furniture, Dry Sink, Comb-Grained Decoration	325.00
Furniture, Dry Sink, Pine & Poplar, High Back, Small Drawers, Refinished	500.00
Furniture, Dry Sink, Pine, Cupboard Doors Flanked By Smaller Doors, 36 In.	600.00
Furniture, Dry Sink, Pine, 2 Drawers, Cupboard Door Below, 54 In.	350.00
Furniture, Dry Sink, Pine, 74 In.	345.00
Furniture, Dry Sink, Poplar, Hutchback, Drawers, Cupboard Doors, 52 In.	385.00
Furniture, Easel, Eastlake, Adjustable Supports, Burl Walnut, C.1870	525.00
Furniture, English, Pub Armchairs, Set Of 8	325.00
Furniture, Foot Warmer, Carpet Covered, Briquettes In Drawer	16.00
Furniture, Footstool, Louis XVI, Carved And Painted, Upholstered, C.1850	125.00
Furniture, Frame, Quilting, Cherry Legs & Brackets, Pine Rails .... Illus	100.00
Furniture, Hall Tree & Umbrella Stand, Iron, Oriental, Mirrored Top, 6 Ft.	1450.00
Furniture, Hall Tree, Oak	300.00
Furniture, Hall Tree, Walnut, Marble Top, Early Victorian	500.00
Furniture, Hamper, Wicker	45.00
Furniture, Hat Rack, Walnut, Folding, Black, 13 Porcelain Buttons	26.00
Furniture, High Chair, Stroller, Convertible .... Illus	200.00
Furniture, Highboy, Chippendale, Mahogany, Bonnet Top, 7 Ft.4 3/4 In.	2600.00
Furniture, Highboy, Curly Maple, Original Brass, C.1760, 36 X 72 In.	7500.00
Furniture, Highboy, Mahogany, Sheraton, Bowfront, C.1780	1200.00
Furniture, Highboy, Maple, Connecticut Queen Anne, C.1770, Two-Part, 75 In.	1700.00
Furniture, Highboy, New England, Queen Anne, Pine & Maple, 65 1/2 In.	5800.00
Furniture, Highboy, Two-Part, William & Mary, English, C.1740, 39 X 57 In.	2200.00
Furniture, Highchair, Child's, Windsor, Comb Back, C.1760	1500.00
Furniture, Huntboard, Mahogany, Hepplewhite, English, C.1820, 38 In.	750.00
Furniture, Huntboard, Pine, 19th Century	2100.00
Furniture, Hutch, Valley Forge, Glass Doors, 2 Drawers, Cabinet Doors, C.1800	1500.00
Furniture, Ice Cream Parlor Set, Chairs, Oak, Round Table	350.00
Furniture, Ice Cream Parlor Set, Child's, 5 Piece	85.00 To 175.00
Furniture, Ice Cream Set, Round Table, Cane Type Top, Wooden, Table & Chair	38.00
Furniture, Kitchen-Secretary, 2 Shelf Bookcase, Glass Doors, 2 Keys, Oak	475.00
Furniture, Library File, 72 Drawer, Oak, 68 In.Tall, 31 In.Wide, 26 In.Deep	275.00
Furniture, Linen Press, Mahogany, Satinwood Inlaid	3000.00
Furniture, Love Seat & Chair, Lady's, Nuts & Fruit Pattern, Victorian	750.00
Furniture, Love Seat, Grape Carved Crest, Victorian, 5 1/2 Feet	350.00

Furniture, Desk, Slant Front,
Carved Mahogany, Chippendale

Furniture, Desk, Slant Front, Pine,
Painted, C.1800, 36 3/4 In.

Furniture, Desk, Walnut, William & Mary, Ball Foot, 44 In.

Furniture, High Chair, Stroller, Convertible

Furniture, Frame, Quilting, Cherry Legs & Brackets, Pine Rails

Furniture, Love Seat, Hand-Carved Walnut, Early Victorian	1450.00
Furniture, Love Seat, Oak, Wingback, Carved Two's Company, 43 X 47 In.	650.00
Furniture, Love Seat, Serpent Arms, Eagle Motif On Back, Gold Padded Seat	2500.00
Furniture, Love Seat, Wicker, Red Velvet Seat	375.00
Furniture, Lowboy, Centennial, Queen Anne, Maple, 1876	525.00
Furniture, Lowboy, Cherry, Original Brass	16000.00
Furniture, Lowboy, Cottage Oak, 3 Drawer, C.1740, 28 X 32 In.	750.00
Furniture, Lowboy, George II, Mahogany, Single Drawer, C.1765	1250.00
Furniture, Lowboy, Mahogany, Ball & Claw Feet, English, C.1760, 29 X 31 In.	2400.00
Furniture, Lowboy, Oak, Pad Feet Mahogany Crossbanded	900.00
Furniture, Lowboy, Queen Anne, Cherry, American, C.1730	1200.00
Furniture, Lowboy, Queen Anne, Walnut, English, 18th Century, 32 X 29 In.	1150.00
Furniture, Lowboy, Queen Anne, 30 In.	9000.00
Furniture, Lowboy, William & Mary, Inlaid Mahogany, 3 Drawers, 32 X 29 In.	500.00
Furniture, Mirror, American Federal, Eglomise Panel, C.1830, 35 X 17 In.	200.00
Furniture, Mirror, Beveled, Gold Leaf Frame, Oval, 7 Ft.	300.00
Furniture, Mirror, Cherubs On Rock Scenery, French Enamel	115.00
Furniture, Mirror, Cheval, Mahogany, George III, C.1780	300.00
Furniture, Mirror, Chippendale, Gold Protruded Bird Near Top, 21 In.	320.00
Furniture, Mirror, Chippendale, Inlaid Walnut, Parcel-Gilded, 54 In.	3000.00
Furniture, Mirror, Convex, Gold Leafed, Eagle On Top, 6 In.	17.50
Furniture, Mirror, Embossed Bird At Top, Chippendale, 2 Ft.High	290.00

Furniture, Mirror, George II, Walnut, C.1740, 23 3/4 X 42 In.	3250.00
Furniture, Mirror, Gilt Pier, Eglomise Landscape, Carved, Gesso, C.1850	250.00
Furniture, Mirror, Gilt, Reverse Painting Of Ballerina, 13 1/2 X 25 In.	110.00
Furniture, Mirror, Girandole, Eagle, Candle Sconces, C.1810, 32 In., Pair	3000.00
Furniture, Mirror, Louis XV, Carved And Gilt, 29 X 41 In.	85.00
Furniture, Mirror, Mahogany Veneer, 1840, 17 X 20 In.	24.00
Furniture, Mirror, Mahogany, Gilt, Chippendale, Carved Pediment, C.1780, 22 In.	1150.00
Furniture, Mirror, Marriage, Triptych Form, Birds & Floral Doors, Persian	200.00
Furniture, Mirror, Pier, Federal, Gilt, Eglomise Of Mt.Vernon, C.1880, 28 In.	170.00
Furniture, Mirror, Pier, Louis XVI, Carved, Gessoed, Gilt, C.1800, 77 In.	600.00
Furniture, Mirror, Pier, Louis XVI, Carved, Gessoed, 19th Century, 59 In.	145.00
Furniture, Mirror, Pier, Painted & Gilt, Gessoed, Late 19th Century, 47 In.	65.00
Furniture, Mirror, Pier, Walnut And Partial Gilt, Queen Anne, C.1730, 50 In.	750.00
Furniture, Mirror, Plateau, Fleur-De-Lis Silver Border, Ornate, 14 1/2 In.	32.00
Furniture, Mirror, Plateau, Ornate, Beveled, 14 1/2 In.	35.00
Furniture, Mirror, Queen Anne, Mahogany, 18th Century, 11 X 14 In.	190.00
Furniture, Mirror, Reverse Painting Of Side-Wheeler Washington, 11 X 21 In.	50.00
Furniture, Mirror, Shaving, Chippendale, Mahogany, 2 Drawers, C.1810, 16 In.	125.00
Furniture, Mirror, Shaving, Empire, 18 1/2 X 23 1/4 In.	65.00
Furniture, Mirror, Shaving, 2 Drawers In Base, Bracket Feet, Frame, 25 In.	100.00
Furniture, Mirror, Toilet, Mahogany, Chippendale, Drawer, C.1800, 20 In.	100.00
Furniture, Mirror, Toilet, Mahogany, 3 Drawers, Hepplewhite, English, 27 In.	80.00
Furniture, Mirror, Traveling, Walnut, Oval, Brass Rivet, Sliding Cover, 7 In.	75.00
Furniture, Mirror, Victorian, Brass Plated, Easel Scrolled, 2 Cherub Heads	45.00
Furniture, Mirror, Wall, Giltwood & Gesso, C.1815, 32 3/4 X 19 In.	375.00
Furniture, Mirror, Wall, Giltwood, Gesso, C.1800, 5 Feet 1 In. *Illus*	750.00
Furniture, Panel, Chinese Teak, Carved Dragon, Sea, Clouds, C.1850, Pair	1100.00
Furniture, Pantry, Kitchen, Narrow Strips Of Wood, L Feet	265.00
Furniture, Pedestal, Cherry, Victorian, Carved, C.1890, 42 In.	100.00
Furniture, Pedestal, Mahogany, Corinthian Column On Step Base, C.1890, 63 In.	100.00
Furniture, Pie Safe, Pine, Ornate Tins, C.1820	450.00
Furniture, Pie Safe, Raised Panel Doors, Scrolled Gallery, Drawer, Pierced	295.00
Furniture, Pie Safe, Screening	235.00
Furniture, Pie Safe, Walnut Front, Pierced Tin Doors, Latches	495.00
Furniture, Platform Rocker *Illus*	230.00
Furniture, Potty, Child's, Oak, Pattern Back	48.50
Furniture, Press, China, Walnut, Louis XV, Two-Part, Beveled Glass, C.1880	1100.00
Furniture, Rack, Hall, Walnut, Oval Mirror, Iron Umbrella Drips, C.1870, 80 In.	175.00
Furniture, Rack, Hat, Oak, 12 Wire Hooks, Center Mirror Insert, 30 X 17 In.	24.00
Furniture, Rack, Magazine, Victorian, 30 1/2 X 17 1/2 In.	90.00
Furniture, Rack, Magazine, Wall Type, Bamboo, Decorative, 17 X 22 In.	28.00
Furniture, Rack, Towel & Comb, Hanging, 36 In.	125.00
Furniture, Rocker, Adjustable Writing Arm, Sliding Headrest	400.00
Furniture, Rocker, Arrowback, Country, Yellow Paint, Green Striping, C.1810	650.00
Furniture, Rocker, Arrowback, Mammy	425.00
Furniture, Rocker, Boston, Curves, Arched Spindle Back, Stained, C.1840	130.00
Furniture, Rocker, Child's, Bentwood Back & Arms, 22 In.	45.00

Furniture, Platform Rocker

Furniture, Mirror, Wall, Giltwood, Gesso, C.1800, 5 Feet 1 In.

Furniture, Rocker, Oak

Furniture, Settee, Chinese, Mother-Of-Pearl, Hardwood, 6 Feet

Furniture, Rocker, Child's, Boston, C.1830	135.00
Furniture, Rocker, Child's, Cherrywood, Brass Button Top, Cane Bottom Seat	125.00
Furniture, Rocker, Child's, Happy Days, Floral Head Rest	95.00
Furniture, Rocker, Child's, Oak, Hepplewhite, C.1800, 15 In.Wide	200.00
Furniture, Rocker, Child's, Oak, 29 In.	37.50
Furniture, Rocker, Child's, Platform, Caned Seat & Back	150.00
Furniture, Rocker, Child's, Spindle, Pine	85.00
Furniture, Rocker, Child's, Wicker	25.00
Furniture, Rocker, Comstock & Son, Maine, New York, C.1860	325.00
Furniture, Rocker, Hitchcock, Signed	300.00
Furniture, Rocker, Nursing, Demi-Arms, Caned Seat & Back	55.00
Furniture, Rocker, Oak *Illus*	135.00
Furniture, Rocker, Pressed Back, Oak	100.00
Furniture, Rocker, Shaker	300.00
Furniture, Rocker, Victorian, Wicker, Arms	145.00
Furniture, Rocker, Wicker, Child's, 1920s	48.50
Furniture, Rocker, Wicker, Victorian	250.00
Furniture, Rocker, Windsor, Arrow Back	190.00
Furniture, Rocker, Windsor, Arrow Comb Back, Early 19th Century, American	180.00
Furniture, Sconce, Adam, Gessoed & Gilt, Mirror, Shelves, C.1800, 21 In.	110.00
Furniture, Screen, Chinese Coraline Lacquer, 8 Fold Panel, 16 X 72 In.	3000.00
Furniture, Screen, Chinese Coromandel, Three-Fold, Lakeside Dwellings, 57 In.	1100.00
Furniture, Screen, Fireplace, French Provincial, Fruitwood, C.1800, 36 In.	150.00
Furniture, Screen, Gold-Figured Damask, 3 Fold, 72 X 63 In.	100.00
Furniture, Screen, Oriental, 4 Panels, Embroidered On Pink Silk, 14 X 5 In.	65.00
Furniture, Screen, Table, Four-Panel, Mother-Of-Pearl Chinese Figures	250.00
Furniture, Secretary Bookcase, 3 Drawer, Burled Cylinder Roll Desk Top	1800.00
Furniture, Secretary, Chippendale, Mahogany, C.1770, 6 Drawers, 8 1/2 Ft.	9700.00
Furniture, Secretary, Cylinder, Walnut, 8 Feet	750.00
Furniture, Secretary, Mahogany, American Federal, Glass Doors, C.1850	425.00
Furniture, Secretary, Pine, 85 X 37 X 27 In.	925.00
Furniture, Secretary, Roll Top, Walnut, 8 Feet	950.00
Furniture, Secretary, Sheraton, Mahogany, American, C.1800	795.00
Furniture, Secretary, Slant Front, Walnut	575.00
Furniture, Secretary, Victorian, Cylinder Front, C.1860	1095.00
Furniture, Secretary, Walnut, Fall Front, Pigeonholes, Drawers, C.1870, 64 In.	375.00
Furniture, Server, Country Sheraton, Marbleized Top	495.00
Furniture, Server, Mahogany, N.Y.State, C.1830, Small	700.00
Furniture, Settee, Chinese, Mother-Of-Pearl, Hardwood, 6 Feet *Illus*	850.00
Furniture, Settee, Louis XV, Carved, Upholstered, C.1775, 58 In.	700.00
Furniture, Settee, Louis XVI, Carved Frame, Upholstery, C.1750, 64 In.	1500.00
Furniture, Settee, Mahogany, Queen Anne, English, C.1750, Double Chair, 54 In.	600.00
Furniture, Settee, Medallion Back, Walnut	495.00
Furniture, Settee, Oak & Walnut, Wingback, English, Rococo, 18th Century	75.00
Furniture, Settee, Oak, Stickley, Stamped, 6 Feet 6 In. *Illus*	1500.00
Furniture, Settee, Satinwood, Triple-Back, Painted, C.1860	1850.00

Furniture, **Settee,** Windsor Step-Down, Rhode Island, C.1800 .... 1500.00
Furniture, **Settee,** Windsor, 3 Separate Chair Bases, C.1810, 7 Ft.6 In. 1075.00
Furniture, **Settle,** Child's, Hinged Seat, Green, 19th Century, 42 X 30 X 15 In. 485.00
Furniture, **Shelf,** Wall Hanging Corner, Chinoiserie, English, C.1700, 41 In. 200.00
Furniture, **Showcase,** Rose Marble Base, Oak Frame, 26 X 42 X 132 In. 525.00
Furniture, **Side Chairs,** Square Back, Mahogany, Carved, Set Of 4 .... *Illus* 2250.00
Furniture, **Sideboard,** Baltimore, Demilune, C.1790, 24 X 32 1/2 In. 9600.00
Furniture, **Sideboard,** Chinese, Lien-San, Brass, 38 X 8 Feet .... *Illus* 850.00
Furniture, **Sideboard,** Demilune, Satinwood Inlay, Sheraton, English, C.1840 .... 600.00
Furniture, **Sideboard,** Georgian, Mahogany, C.1800 .... 1010.00
Furniture, **Sideboard,** Hepplewhite, Inlay Of Satinwood 2500.00
Furniture, **Sideboard,** Inlaid Mahogany, 1790-1810, 40 1/4 In. .... *Illus* 1900.00
Furniture, **Sideboard,** Mahogany, American Federal, 4 Panel Doors, C.1840 .... 120.00
Furniture, **Sideboard,** Mahogany, Double Serpentine, C.1780, 85 X 40 3/4 In. 7980.00
Furniture, **Sideboard,** Mahogany, Georgian, Serpentine Front, C.1790, 57 In. 6500.00
Furniture, **Sideboard,** Mahogany, Hepplewhite, American, C.1790, 64 X 45 In. 2200.00
Furniture, **Sideboard,** Mahogany, Sheraton, Bowfront, Small Proportions, C.1790 .... 2100.00
Furniture, **Sideboard,** Mahogany, Sheraton, 3 Drawers, C.1800, 40 X 21 In. 950.00
Furniture, **Sideboard,** Sheraton, Mahogany, C.1800, 4 Ft., 2 1/2 In. 1450.00
Furniture, **Sideboard,** Victorian Oak, Miniature, Scalloped Shelf, 7 1/2 In. 55.00
Furniture, **Sideboard,** Victorian, Marble Top, Walnut Trim, Signed 2500.00
Furniture, **Sink,** Dry, Red, Poplar, Dovetailed Base, Amish 400.00
Furniture, **Sofa,** American Empire, Mahogany Veneer Crest, Winged Scroll Feet 825.00
Furniture, **Sofa,** Camelback, Chippendale-Federal, Mahogany Legs, C.1795, 17 In. 3600.00
Furniture, **Sofa,** Empire, Rose Tapestry Cover, 1840, 7 Ft.Long 850.00
Furniture, **Sofa,** Mahogany, American Federal, C.1870, 80 In. 275.00
Furniture, **Sofa,** Mahogany, American Federal, Cornucopia Arms, C.1835, 79 In. 210.00
Furniture, **Sofa,** Mahogany, Art Nouveau, C.1900, 73 In. .... *Illus* 700.00
Furniture, **Sofa,** Mahogany, Satinwood Inlay, 6-Leg, Sheraton, Upholstery, 70 In. 500.00
Furniture, **Sofa,** Rosewood, Victorian, Soft Blue Velvet, 36 X 78 In. 800.00
Furniture, **Sofa,** Victorian, Carved & Pierced, Walnut Frame, 65 X 28 In. 1000.00
Furniture, **Spice Shelf,** Hanging, Pine, 6 Drawer 140.00
Furniture, **Stand,** Chinese Carved Teak, Rose Marble Insert, 19 In. 325.00
Furniture, **Stand,** Fern, Brass, Onyx, Barley Twist Legs, 13 In.Square 350.00
Furniture, **Stand,** Library, Mounted With Smith Globe, C.1868, 24 In., Pair 300.00
Furniture, **Stand,** Serving, Walnut, Inlaid Marquetry, English, C.1880, 28 In. 225.00
Furniture, **Stand,** Sheraton, Mahoganized Pine, Bird's-Eye Drawer 225.00
Furniture, **Stand,** Tiger Maple, 2-Drawer, C.1820, New York 395.00
Furniture, **Stepstool,** Shaker, Red Paint, Two Sisters, Enfield, Connecticut 155.00
Furniture, **Stool,** American Pine And White Oak, Joined 6700.00
Furniture, **Stool,** Button Terminations On Legs In Black Paint 175.00
Furniture, **Stool,** Dressing, George I, Walnut, Cabriole Legs, C.1725 .... 1000.00
Furniture, **Stool,** Foot, Green Paint, Cutout Base, 8 X 15 In. 35.00
Furniture, **Stool,** Foot, Hand-Hooked Wool Top, Maple Legs, Round, 13 In. 15.00
Furniture, **Stool,** Joint, Oak, English, 20 1/2 X 12 1/2 X 19 1/4 In. 275.00
Furniture, **Stool,** Milking, 12 X 8 In. 45.00
Furniture, **Stool,** Mortised, Green 35.00
Furniture, **Stool,** Organ, Horsechair Adjustable Set, Victorian 49.00
Furniture, **Stool,** Piano, Turn Up, Ball & Claw Feet 59.50

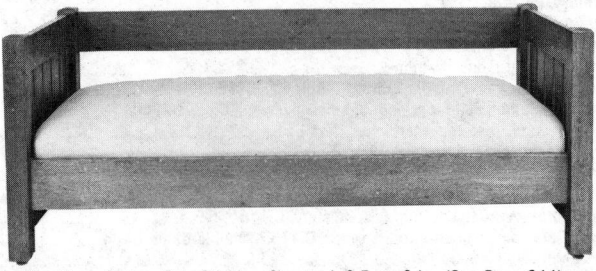

Furniture, Settee, Oak, Stickley, Stamped, 6 Feet 6 In. *(See Page 211)*

Furniture, Sideboard, Chinese, Lien-San, Brass, 38 X 8 Feet

Furniture, Side Chairs, Square Back, Mahogany, Carved, Set Of 4

Furniture, Sideboard, Inlaid Mahogany, 1790-1810, 40 1/4 In.

Furniture, Table, Altar, Chinese, Carved Hardwood, 36 X 41 In.

Furniture, Sofa, Mahogany, Art Nouveau, C.1900, 73 In.

Furniture, Stool, Shaker, Old Blue Paint	48.00
Furniture, Stool, Weaving, Windsor	1100.00
Furniture, Table & Two Chairs, Child's, Wicker, 1920s	145.00
Furniture, Table, Altar, Chinese, Carved Hardwood, 36 X 41 In. .... *Illus*	500.00
Furniture, Table, American Empire, Cherrywood, Round Top, 4 Double Paw Legs	250.00
Furniture, Table, Banquet, Sheraton, 3 Part, Reeded Legs, Virginia	2800.00
Furniture, Table, Banquet, 2 Part, Mahogany, Hepplewhite, Biggs, Va., 30 In.	750.00
Furniture, Table, Banquet, 24 In.Leaf, Mahogany, American Sheraton, 8 Seats	750.00
Furniture, Table, Black Lacquer, Mother-Of-Pearl, Chinese, C.1880, 31 In.	350.00
Furniture, Table, Breadboard Ends, 2-Board Top, Red Base	370.00
Furniture, Table, Breakfast, Regency, Mahogany, Circular, C.1810	1550.00
Furniture, Table, Candlestand, Oval Tilt, Mahogany Top, 18th Century	475.00
Furniture, Table, Card, Boston, C.1790	1400.00
Furniture, Table, Card, Federal, Serpentine, C.1790-1810, 28 1/4 X 35 1/4 In.	1300.00
Furniture, Table, Card, Greek Key & Segmented Banding, Mahogany, C.1800-1810	1000.00
Furniture, Table, Card, Hepplewhite, C.1810, Baltimore	800.00
Furniture, Table, Card, Hepplewhite, Inlaid, Cherry, American, C.1780-1800	750.00
Furniture, Table, Card, Mahogany With Pine, Signed W.I.Price, Salem, C.1810	800.00

Furniture, Table, Card, Mahogany, Satinwood, C.1810, 28 3/4 In. .... *Illus*	1400.00
Furniture, Table, Card, Marquetry, Walnut, C.18th Century	750.00
Furniture, Table, Card, Sheraton, C.1810, 36 In.Side	750.00
Furniture, Table, Card, Sheraton, Mahogany & Satinwood Inlays, C.1790	1400.00
Furniture, Table, Card, Sheraton, Mahogany, Flip Over Swing Leg, C.1780, 36 In.	350.00
Furniture, Table, Carved Teakwood, Folding Legs, Square, 19 1/2 In.	195.00
Furniture, Table, Carved Walnut, 18th Century, 25 X 19 In.	210.00
Furniture, Table, Cherry Base, 2-Board Top, 27 X 47 In.	125.00
Furniture, Table, China Brass Top & Tray, 26 X 30 In.	150.00
Furniture, Table, Claw Feet, Red .... *Illus*	100.00
Furniture, Table, Claw Feet, 4 Leaves, Ribbon Style Pedestal, Oak, 54 In.	650.00
Furniture, Table, Conference, Hand-Carved Walnut, French	1695.00
Furniture, Table, Console, Chinese, Mother-Of-Pearl, Hardwood .... *Illus*	550.00
Furniture, Table, Console, Pier Mirror, Italian Baroque, Carved, Gesso, Gold	4500.00
Furniture, Table, Console, 19th Century, Duncan Phyfe	850.00
Furniture, Table, Corner, Bird's-Eye Maple, Undershelf, C.1820-30, 27 In.High	200.00
Furniture, Table, Corner, Bird's-Eye, Turned Legs, Wedge Top, Shelf, Maple	185.00
Furniture, Table, Country Pine, Mellow Dark Graining, C.1830, 30 In.	180.00
Furniture, Table, Curly Sycamore, C.1800, Oblong, Single Board	450.00
Furniture, Table, Dining & Library, Oak, Draw Leaf, Carved Base, 44 X 66 In.	575.00
Furniture, Table, Dining, Cherry Drop, Leaf, C.1815, Sheraton	650.00
Furniture, Table, Dining, Chinese, Carved Hardwood, 4 X 5 Feet .... *Illus*	550.00
Furniture, Table, Dining, Drop Leaf, Mahogany, American Federal, 1820	450.00
Furniture, Table, Dining, Swing Leg, Walnut, Georgian, C.1730, Seats 8	4700.00
Furniture, Table, Dining, 2 Pedestals, Extends To 9 Feet, English Sheraton	4500.00
Furniture, Table, Dining, 6 Leaves, Oak, 29 1/2 X 53 3/4 In. .... *Illus*	700.00
Furniture, Table, Dish Top Queen Anne, Walnut, Pennsylvania, C.1780	350.00
Furniture, Table, Dish Top Tea, William & Mary, C.1760, 38 X 30 In.	225.00
Furniture, Table, Dish Top Tripod, Philadelphia Chippendale, C.1700, 29 In.	4500.00
Furniture, Table, Double Pedestal Base, Acanthus Leaf & Claw Feet, Mahogany	2800.00
Furniture, Table, Dressing, Gentleman's, 18th Century, 17 X 16 X 33 1/2 In.	750.00
Furniture, Table, Dressing, Mahogany, Chippendale, C.1765	1250.00
Furniture, Table, Dressing, Moon-Shaped, Transitional, Empire	225.00
Furniture, Table, Dressing, Sheraton, J.P.Caffey, Cabinetmaker, Maine, 2 Drawer	145.00
Furniture, Table, Dressing, Walnut, Queen Anne, English, C.1850, 31 In.	600.00
Furniture, Table, Dressing, 4-Drawer, Sheraton, Black Paint, Graining	300.00
Furniture, Table, Drop Leaf Breakfast, Cherry, Sheraton, American, 28 In.	300.00
Furniture, Table, Drop Leaf Dining, Honduras Mahogany, Pedestal, C.1830	600.00
Furniture, Table, Drop Leaf Dining, Mahogany, Sheraton, C.1840, 29 In.	150.00
Furniture, Table, Drop Leaf, Cherry & Maple, Sheraton, C.1820, 36 X 30 In.	325.00
Furniture, Table, Drop Leaf, Cherry, Sheraton	395.00
Furniture, Table, Drop Leaf, Chippendale, Inlaid, One Drawer	450.00
Furniture, Table, Drop Leaf, Country Hepplewhite, Tiger Maple	775.00
Furniture, Table, Drop Leaf, Country Style, Hepplewhite, Birch, C.1800	225.00
Furniture, Table, Drop Leaf, Dark Wood, 24 In.	65.00
Furniture, Table, Drop Leaf, Flame Grained Top & Leaves, Red Base	335.00
Furniture, Table, Drop Leaf, Gate Leg, English, Mid-17th Century, 52 X 29 In.	250.00
Furniture, Table, Drop Leaf, Hepplewhite, Red Base, N.Y.State	450.00
Furniture, Table, Drop Leaf, Mahogany, Spindle Leg, Chippendale, C.1770	1050.00
Furniture, Table, Drop Leaf, Oak, Dutch, Demilune, Molded Edge Top, C.1800	130.00
Furniture, Table, Drop Leaf, Walnut, C.1850, 30 X 32 1/2 In.	175.00
Furniture, Table, Drop Leaf, Walnut, Chippendale, C.1770, 48 X 28 In.	900.00
Furniture, Table, Drop Leaf, Walnut, Sheraton, One Drawer, C.1860, 29 In.	100.00
Furniture, Table, Drum, Coromandel, Wood, Small, C.1780	2390.00
Furniture, Table, Drum, Regency Rosewood, Green Tooled Leather Top, C.1810	3090.00
Furniture, Table, End, Wicker, 27 3/4 X 22 3/4 In.	75.00
Furniture, Table, Fall Front, American Queen Anne, Ball Feet, C.1790, 41 In.	600.00
Furniture, Table, Farm, Walnut, One-Board Top	1150.00
Furniture, Table, Fold-Over Tea, Mahogany, Chippendale, Cabriole Legs, C.1750	915.00
Furniture, Table, French Marquetry, Floral Inlay, Ormolu Mounts	650.00
Furniture, Table, Game, Demilune, Biedermeier, Rosewood Inlaid, C.1820, 29 In.	350.00
Furniture, Table, Game, Fold Top, Mahogany, Chippendale, English, C.1770	425.00
Furniture, Table, Game, Fold Top, Mahogany, Hepplewhite, American, C.1810	525.00
Furniture, Table, Game, Fold Top, Oak, English, 18th Century, 31 In.	150.00
Furniture, Table, Game, Foldout Sides, Poker Chip Compartments	85.00

Furniture, Table, Card, Mahogany, Satinwood, C.1810, 28 3/4 In.

Furniture, Table, Claw Feet, Red

Furniture, Table, Console, Chinese, Mother-Of-Pearl, Hardwood

Furniture, Table, Dining, Chinese, Carved Hardwood, 4 X 5 Feet

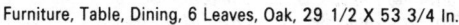

Furniture, Table, Dining, 6 Leaves, Oak, 29 1/2 X 53 3/4 In.

Furniture, Table, Library, Oak, Stickley, 5 Ft. X 31 X 6 1/4 In.
(See Page 216)

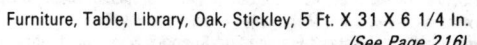

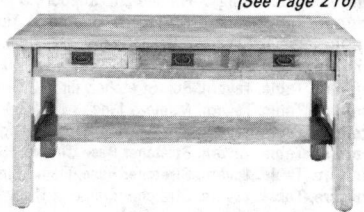

Furniture, Table, Game, Marquetry, Dutch, 30 X 30 In.	650.00
Furniture, Table, Game, Queen Anne, Fold Top, Green Suede Inset, 30 In.	275.00
Furniture, Table, Game, Queen Anne, Slide Top, 44 X 29 1/2 In.	300.00
Furniture, Table, Game, Triple-Top, George II, Mahogany, C.1750, 29 1/2 In.	3900.00
Furniture, Table, Gateleg, Maple, 18th Century, 26 X 42 In.	3500.00
Furniture, Table, Gateleg, Walnut, With Drawer, C.1720, 5 Ft.	1300.00
Furniture, Table, Golden Oak, 34 In.	50.00
Furniture, Table, Harvest, 15 X 3 In.	75.00
Furniture, Table, Hepplewhite, Cherry	195.00
Furniture, Table, Hunt, Inlaid Mahogany, Irish Hepplewhite, C.1800, 36 In.	1400.00
Furniture, Table, Hutch, Scrub Top And Original Paint	1250.00
Furniture, Table, Irish Wake, Mahogany, 8 1/2 Ft.Long	4500.00
Furniture, Table, Library, Louis XV Style, Carved Oak, C.1880, 46 X 36 In.	500.00
Furniture, Table, Library, Oak, Stickley, 5 Ft. X 31 X 6 1/4 In. *Illus*	1600.00
Furniture, Table, Library, Oak, 2-Drawer, 58 X 36 In.	250.00
Furniture, Table, Louis XV, Parquetry Inlay, 3 Drawers, 29 In., Pair	350.00
Furniture, Table, Louis XVI Console, Marble Top, 30 X 36 In.	100.00
Furniture, Table, Mahogany, D-Shape Card, Inlaid, Salem Hepplewhite, C.1790	3000.00
Furniture, Table, Mahogany, Drop Leaf, English, C.1740, Carved, Leaves, 29 In.	3500.00
Furniture, Table, Mahogany, Marble Top, Carved Eagle Legs, C.1830, 28 1/2 In.	850.00
Furniture, Table, Mahogany, Phyfe Quality, New York, C.1815, 28 1/2 In.	2850.00
Furniture, Table, Nest, Black Lacquer, Chinese, 19th Century, 28 X 20 In.	400.00
Furniture, Table, New England Maple, Drop Leaf, 8 Legs, C.1740, 25 In.High	275.00
Furniture, Table, Oak, Round, Claw Feet	375.00
Furniture, Table, Oak, Tilt Top, Pedestaled, 5 Leaves, 1920, 45 In.	240.00
Furniture, Table, Octagon Shaped, Oak, Folding	28.00
Furniture, Table, Oval, Marbletop, Victorian, 22 In.	175.00
Furniture, Table, Pedestal, Italian, Carved, Gesso & Gilt, C.1860, 31 In.	160.00
Furniture, Table, Pedestal, Solid Walnut, 3-12 In.Leaves, Carved Legs	500.00
Furniture, Table, Pembroke, Birch, C.1790	700.00
Furniture, Table, Pembroke, Mahogany & Satinwood, Salem, C.1820, 28 In.	550.00
Furniture, Table, Pembroke, Mahogany, English, C.1790, 48 In.	825.00
Furniture, Table, Pembroke, Mahogany, Hepplewhite, Tooled Leather, 28 In.	125.00
Furniture, Table, Pembroke, Mahogany, Sheraton, C.1790	765.00
Furniture, Table, Pier, Marble Top, Mahogany Columns, Black Paw Feet	2000.00
Furniture, Table, Pier, Pier Mirror, Louis XVI, Paint & Gilt, C.1880, 51 In.	1350.00
Furniture, Table, Pilgrim Chair, Feet Extended, 45 In.	1400.00
Furniture, Table, Pine Sawbuck, Early 19th Century, 7 Feet X 26 X 28 In.	700.00
Furniture, Table, Pub, Floral & Grape, Marble Top, Cast Iron, C.1800, 28 In.	325.00
Furniture, Table, Queen Anne, Breadboard Ends, Molded Apron, Ring Turn Legs	950.00
Furniture, Table, Red Paint, One-Board Top, 27 3/4 X 43 1/2 X 25 3/4 In.	445.00
Furniture, Table, Sawbuck, Pine, 6 1/2 In.	600.00
Furniture, Table, Sawbuck, Scrubbed Top, Red On Base	550.00
Furniture, Table, Sewing, Drop Leaf, Mahogany, American Federal, C.1840, 27 In.	325.00
Furniture, Table, Shaker, One-Board Scrubbed Top, Red Paint, 27 X 43 1/2 In.	445.00
Furniture, Table, Sheraton, Mahogany, C.1930, Oval, 21 X 30 X 30 In.	225.00
Furniture, Table, Ship's, Pine, Signed Brasses, 19th Century	350.00
Furniture, Table, Side, Italian Renaissance, 18th Century, 14 In.	310.00
Furniture, Table, Side, Louis XVI, Carved Walnut, C.1880, Marble Inset	70.00
Furniture, Table, Side, Mahogany, Hepplewhite, C.1815, 27 In.	120.00
Furniture, Table, Side, One Drawer, Library Step, Mahogany, Chippendale, 29 In.	100.00
Furniture, Table, Side, Rococo, Octagonal Top, Italian, Moorish Design, 19 In.	450.00
Furniture, Table, Sofa, Mahogany, William IV, Paw Feet	985.00
Furniture, Table, Sofa, X-Framed End Support, Sheraton, Mahogany, C.1790	2200.00
Furniture, Table, Square, Mahogany, George III, Tip Up, C.1800, 44 X 36 In.	800.00
Furniture, Table, Stretcher Base, Cherry, 1 Drawer	425.00
Furniture, Table, Tapered Legs, Drawer, Maple, 40 X 29 In.	425.00
Furniture, Table, Tavern, Box Stretcher, Pine, 2 Drawers	1000.00
Furniture, Table, Tavern, Maple & Pine, 36 X 23 1/2 X 25 In.	585.00
Furniture, Table, Tavern, One Drawer, Tapered Leg, Stretcher Base, Pine, Maple	950.00
Furniture, Table, Tavern, Stretcher Base, Drawer, Sturbridge, Mass., C.1800	750.00
Furniture, Table, Tavern, Stretcher Base, Flame Birch Top	625.00
Furniture, Table, Tavern, Stretcher Frame, 2 Drawers, C.1800	850.00
Furniture, Table, Tavern, Wallace Nutting	200.00
Furniture, Table, Tea, Gallery Top, Chinese Chippendale, English, C.1880	125.00

Furniture, Table, Tea, Mahogany, Turnover Top, C.1815 .... 744.00
Furniture, Table, Tea, New England Queen Anne, Maple, 18th Century, 27 In. 650.00
Furniture, Table, Tea, Porringer Top, Queen Anne, Wallace Nutting, Maple 450.00
Furniture, Table, Tea, Queen Anne, Red, 3 Ft. 800.00
Furniture, Table, Tea, Regency Mahogany, Turnover Top, C.1815 .... 750.00
Furniture, Table, Tea, Tiger Maple, Queen Anne, Porringer Top, Wallace Nutting 450.00
Furniture, Table, Tea, Tray-Top, Queen Anne, 27 X 30 1/4 In. 1300.00
Furniture, Table, Teak, Carved, Marble Insert, Chinese 650.00
Furniture, Table, Teakwood, Marble Insert, Chinese 225.00
Furniture, Table, Tiger Maple, Skirt, Button Feet 3200.00
Furniture, Table, Tilt Top, Breakfast, Mahogany, English Regency, 1850, 29 In. 225.00
Furniture, Table, Tilt Top, Cherry & Mahogany, New York, C.1825 .... 350.00
Furniture, Table, Tilt Top, Cherry & Pine, New England, C.1800, 27 In. 350.00
Furniture, Table, Tilt Top, Maple Birdcage 585.00
Furniture, Table, Tilt Top, Tea, Mahogany, English Chippendale, C.1780, 29 In. 900.00
Furniture, Table, Trestle, Walnut & Satinwood, German, Rococo, 1695, 29 In. 475.00
Furniture, Table, Tric-Trac Writing, Walnut, Pullout, C.1780, English, 31 In. 400.00
Furniture, Table, Tripod, Mahogany, Candlestand Top, Carved Feet, 21 X 14 In. 250.00
Furniture, Table, Tripod, Mahogany, Carved Feet, Candlestand Top, 21 In. 250.00
Furniture, Table, Turtle Shape Center, Mahogany, Victorian, C.1855, 31 In. 250.00
Furniture, Table, Work, Serpentine Top, Molded Edge, 19th Century, 20 In. 175.00
Furniture, Table, Writing, Walnut Parquetry, Inlaid, Louis XV, 30 In. 900.00
Furniture, Table, Writing, Walnut, Marble Top, Louis XV, C.1850, 28 In. 450.00
Furniture, Table, 2 Leaves, Split Pedestal, Oak, Round, 54 In. 425.00
Furniture, Tabouret, Bronze, Phoenix Birds, Eagle, Dragons, 1860, Vienna, 14 In. 525.00
Furniture, Washstand, Corner, Mahogany, American, C.1800, 38 In. 160.00
Furniture, Washstand, Mahogany, English Sheraton, Bowl Niche, C.1800, 34 In. 110.00
Furniture, Washstand, Pine, C.1825 .... 145.00
Furniture, Washstand, Towel Bars, Drawer, 2 Doors Below, Mahogany 175.00
Furniture, Welsh Dresser, Oak, Pot Shelf And Apron, C.1780, 57 1/2 In. 2400.00
Furniture, Wine Container, Wicker, 3 Compartments, Lid 22.00
Furniture, Wine Cooler, Mahogany, Lead Lined, C.1780 .... 750.00
Furniture, Wine Cooler, Mahogany, Sheraton, Brass Bound, C.1800, 17 In. 2500.00
Furniture, Workbench, 4 Paneled Drawers, Dovetailed, 47 X 42 X 22 In. 475.00

*Gabriel Argy-Rousseau, born in 1885, was a French glass artist
who produced a variety of objects in Art Deco style. his mark,
G. Argy-Rousseau, was usually impressed.*

G.Argy-Rousseau, Bowl, Pate De Verre, Green & Purple Leaves & Floral, 2 In. 350.00
G.Argy-Rousseau, Vase, Pate De Verre, Gray, Purple & Blue Zinnias, 5 3/4 In. 700.00

*Galle glass was made by the Galle Factory founded in 1874 by Emile
Galle of France. The firm made cameo glass, furniture, and other
Art Nouveau items, including some pottery. After Galle's
death in 1904, the firm continued in production until 1935.*

Galle, Atomizer, Cameo Carved Amethyst Flowers On Gold, Signed 300.00
Galle, Atomizer, No Bulb, Maroon Flowers On Frosted Gold Background, Signed 220.00
Galle, Bottle, Perfume, Cuttings Of Foliage, Brown & Green On Pink, 8 In. 395.00
Galle, Bowl, Cameo, Fish, C.1900, 5 1/2 In. .... Illus 2200.00
Galle, Bowl, Enameled, Cameo, C.1900, 7 In. .... Illus 500.00
Galle, Bowl, Scrolls, Leaves, Blossoms, Wide Mouth, Gray, Purple, C.1904, 5 In. 150.00

Galle, Bowl, Cameo, Fish, C.1900, 5 1/2 In.

Galle, Bowl, Enameled, Cameo, C.1900, 7 In.

Galle, Bowl, White, Trees, Grass In 3 Shades, 3 1/2 In.	354.00
Galle, Box, Cameo, Raised Leaves, Pale Green, Purple Flower, Round, 6 1/2 In.	1150.00
Galle, Box, Powder, Cameo, Orange, Yellow, & Green Jonquils, Star, 4 1/2 In.	450.00
Galle, Box, Powder, Leaves & Vines In Purple To Frosted Ground, 2 1/4 In.	395.00
Galle, Box, Powder, Orange, Yellow, & Green Jonquils On Camphor, 4 1/2 In.	425.00
Galle, Candelabrum, Figural, Royal Lion, Holds Bronze Candle Supports, 24 In.	850.00
Galle, Creamer, Frosted Handle, Red Berries & Leaves, Frosted Handle, 3 In.	245.00
Galle, Dish, Clover Shape, Blue & White Irises On Purple-Blue, 5 X 7 In.	260.00
Galle, Ewer, Folk Scene On Front, Birds & Butterflies On Back, Gold, 12 In.	450.00
Galle, Glass, Flowers, Leaves, Orange On Frost Satin, 2 1/2 In.	160.00
Galle, Lamp, Cameo Shade, Maroon & Gold, Silver Base, Bat Designs, 6 1/2 In.	950.00
Galle, Lamp, Cameo, Glossy Shade, Medallion, Scene, Art Nouveau Base, 8 In.	2250.00
Galle, Lamp, Cameo, Ocean Scene On Base, Eagles On Shade, 23 1/2 In.	3950.00
Galle, Lamp, Cameo, Signed, C.1900.22 In. *Illus*	5250.00
Galle, Lamp, Table, Forest Scene On Base, Butterflies In Flight On Shade	4000.00
Galle, Pitcher, Handled, Ornate, Blue Glaze, Signed, 8 In.	685.00
Galle, Plate, Light Blue, Gold Dragon, Art Nouveau, Signed, 10 1/4 In.	125.00
Galle, Pottery, Bowl, Floral Interior, Woven Wicker Design Underside, 5 In.	265.00
Galle, Scenic, Brown Tones On Orange, 5 In.	575.00
Galle, Toothpick, Multicolor Floral Enamel On Topaz, Signed, 2 In.	125.00
Galle, Tray, Wood, Thistle & Vines, Cross Of Lorraine, 14 1/2 X 11 In.	350.00
Galle, Tumbler, Shepherdess In The Rain, Poem, 4 1/4 In.	295.00
Galle, Vase, Amber, Enameled Cross Of Lorraine, Signed, 9 1/2 In.	525.00
Galle, Vase, Amethyst Trees, Blue Mountains, Cut To Frosted, 14 In.	950.00
Galle, Vase, Autumn Colors, Cut-Polished Layer, Cameo, 6 X 5 In.	460.00
Galle, Vase, Baluster Shape, Frosted Blue, Amethyst, Green Cameos, 11 3/4 In.	750.00
Galle, Vase, Baluster Shape, Orange Fruit & Leaves On Camphor, 3 In.	150.00
Galle, Vase, Banjo Shape, Amethyst Florals, Orchid To Yellow Base, 9 1/2 In.	675.00
Galle, Vase, Banjo Shape, 3-Layer Green Leaf Design, Cameo, Signed, 5 1/2 In.	200.00
Galle, Vase, Berries, Lavender Cut To Yellow, Signed, 5 1/2 In.	345.00
Galle, Vase, Birch Decoration, Cameo, 3 In.	265.00
Galle, Vase, Birch Tree, 2 Shades Of Green, Signed, 2 1/2 In.	250.00
Galle, Vase, Brown & Golden Beige, Pinched-In Neck, 4 In.	275.00
Galle, Vase, Brown Cameo Flowers On Yellow, Signed, 5 1/4 In.	225.00
Galle, Vase, Brown Cameo On Cut Crystal, Cradle Shape, 1st Period, 3 X 5 In.	550.00
Galle, Vase, Brown Crocuses On Yellow, Purple Base, Footed, 5 In.	475.00
Galle, Vase, Brown Flowers & Leaves On Yellow, 2 Cuttings, 5 In.	275.00
Galle, Vase, Brown Flowers, Yellow Ground, 5 1/4 In.	225.00
Galle, Vase, Brown On Orange, Yellow, White & Clear, 5 Layers, 3 In.	375.00
Galle, Vase, Brown Wild Flowers On Yellow, Signed, 5 1/2 In.	315.00
Galle, Vase, Bud, Apricot Daisies, Camphor Ground, 4 1/2 In.	160.00
Galle, Vase, Bud, Crystal & Enamel, Autumn Colored Floral, 5 In.	200.00
Galle, Vase, Bud, Five Colors, 4 1/2 In.	248.00
Galle, Vase, Bud, Purple Foliage, Silver Base, 7 In.	160.00
Galle, Vase, Cabinet, Frosted Turquoise, Deep Purple Cameo, 3 1/4 In.	475.00
Galle, Vase, Cameo, Amethyst, Floral, 3 In.	250.00 To 275.00
Galle, Vase, Cameo, Baluster Shape, Frosted Pink, Taupe Green, 4 3/4 In.	390.00
Galle, Vase, Cameo, Blossoms, Leaves, Footed, Orange, Gray, Green, Signed, 4 In.	550.00
Galle, Vase, Cameo, Blue Frosted, Purple Cameo Of 5-Leafed Flower, 3 1/2 In.	450.00
Galle, Vase, Cameo, Blue Green Base To Blue Top, Leaves & Berries, 14 In.	950.00

Galle, Vase, Cameo, Fern, Palm Leaves, Footed, Amber, Green, C.1904-15, 4 In. 375.00
Galle, Vase, Cameo, Floral, Mauve, Signed, 5 1/4 In. 250.00
Galle, Vase, Cameo, Flowers, Leaves, Stems, Maroon, Frosted Peach, Signed, 6 In. 245.00
Galle, Vase, Cameo, Green Fern, Palm Leaves, Indentation, Pedestal Style, 4 In. 375.00
Galle, Vase, Cameo, Maroon & Yellow Floral, Signed, 4 In. 275.00
Galle, Vase, Cameo, Mountains, Trees, Blue, Green, Clear, Wheel Polished, 8 In. 695.00
Galle, Vase, Cameo, Peach & White, Purple Leaves, 14 1/2 In. 595.00
Galle, Vase, Cameo, Red, Magenta, & Yellow, Polished Flowers, Footed, 6 1/2 In. 495.00
Galle, Vase, Cameo, Sea Ferns, Sea Weeds, Maroon On Green To Clear, 10 1/2 In. 475.00
Galle, Vase, Cameo, Shades Of Green, Wine Colored Flowers, 15 In. 750.00
Galle, Vase, Cameo, 3 Layers, Amethyst, Green, Gray, Polished Floral, 11 3/4 In. 995.00
Galle, Vase, Cameo, 3 Layers, Stylus & Wheel Cutting, Acid Finish, 6 1/4 In. 350.00
Galle, Vase, Camphor Ground, Orange Fruit & Leaves, Signed, 3 In. 150.00
Galle, Vase, Cranberry Fruit On Greens To Gold, Signed, 5 In. 250.00
Galle, Vase, Crystal Cone Shape, Matching Jar, Florals & Mosquitos, Set 650.00
Galle, Vase, Cut Lace Background, Brown To Amber, 5 1/4 In. 1950.00
Galle, Vase, Deep Maroon Over Blue Base, 2 Acid Cuttings, 6 In. 650.00
Galle, Vase, Deep Sable Colored Cameo On Honey Tones, 5 3/4 In. 240.00
Galle, Vase, Enameled Florals, Pink, Orchid, Gold On Amber, 15 1/2 In. 950.00
Galle, Vase, Ferns In Green, Yellow Background, 4 X 2 3/4 In. 325.00
Galle, Vase, Floral, 4 Color, Signed, 16 1/2 In. 1750.00
Galle, Vase, Flower Form Shape, Signed, 9 1/2 In. 425.00
Galle, Vase, Flowers & Leaves, Green & Satin, 6 1/2 In. 295.00
Galle, Vase, Flowers, Acid Etched, Enamel, 3 Layers Of Colors, 13 1/2 In. 725.00
Galle, Vase, Flowers, Branches, Water Lilies, Intaglio, Cameo, 11 In. 135.00
Galle, Vase, Flowers, Lily Pads, Purple, Blue, Frosted, Signed, 5 In. 495.00
Galle, Vase, French Cameo, Pale Green, Pink, Signed, 4 In. 205.00
Galle, Vase, Frosted & Lemon, Purple Berries & Leaves, 5 3/4 In. 475.00
Galle, Vase, Frosted Blue, 2 Cameo Flowers In Amethyst & Green, 11 3/4 In. 750.00
Galle, Vase, Frosted, Deep Purple Flowers, Galle With Star, 4 In. 200.00
Galle, Vase, Globular, Green Fern Designs, 2 1/2 In. 245.00
Galle, Vase, Glossy Pink, Gold Shades, Honey & Orange Flowers, 3 3/4 In. 275.00
Galle, Vase, Gold Acid Mottled, Gray Enameled Leaves & Vines, 6 1/2 In. 150.00
Galle, Vase, Gold To White, Trees & Mountains Reflecting On Lake, 15 In. 1195.00
Galle, Vase, Gold, Magenta, Carved, Ovoid, 10 X 8 In. 1350.00
Galle, Vase, Grapes, Leaves, Trailing Vines, Ribbed, Milky Glass, 13 In. 975.00
Galle, Vase, Green & Lavender Flowers, Frosted Star Galle Signed, 8 In. 495.00
Galle, Vase, Green Cut On Shaded Apricot, Moon Flash Shape, 7 In. 485.00
Galle, Vase, Green Leaves, Flowers, Pink Ground, 4 1/4 In. 175.00
Galle, Vase, Green River, Trees, Pink Sky, 6 1/2 In. 430.00
Galle, Vase, Green, Birch Tree Decoration, 3 1/2 In. 275.00
Galle, Vase, Green, Cut Aubergine Leaves & Berries, 4 1/2 In. 450.00
Galle, Vase, Green, Pink, Lavender, White Leaves & Flowers, Signed, 8 1/4 In. 325.00
Galle, Vase, Landscape, French Cameo, Signed, 5 5/8 X 2 1/4 In. 235.00
Galle, Vase, Lavender, Green, Peach, & White Flowers Cut In Layers, 17 1/2 In. 850.00
Galle, Vase, Lemon Frosty Ground, Purple Flowers & Leaves, 6 X 6 In. 450.00
Galle, Vase, Lemon Yellow, Brown Leaves, Blue Fuchsia, Cameo, 5 1/2 In. 375.00
Galle, Vase, Lilies Of The Valley, Gray, Lilac, Amethyst, Signed With Star 295.00
Galle, Vase, Lily Pond, Violet, Blue, Green & Clear, Signed, 9 5/8 In. 495.00

Galle, Lamp, Cameo, Signed, C.1900, 22 In.

Galle, Vase, Lime Green Ferns, Pink & Amber Highlights, Cameo, 6 3/4 In.	325.00
Galle, Vase, Medallion Of Fruits & Leaves, Signed, 9 In.	385.00
Galle, Vase, Multicolored Enameled Floral, Gold Trim, Amber, 12 3/4 In.	1250.00
Galle, Vase, Nancy, Art Nouveau, Floral, Gold, Crystal, Amber, 3 In.	125.00
Galle, Vase, Orange Poppies On Camphor Ground, Signed, 12 1/4 X 5 In.	545.00
Galle, Vase, Pale Cream, Rose, & Green, Oak Leaves & Acorns, 3 Layers, 16 In.	900.00
Galle, Vase, Pale To Deep Amber Flowers & Leaves, Wheel Polished, 10 1/2 In.	1975.00
Galle, Vase, Paneled, Buds, Floral, Fretwork, Angular Oval Flare, Signed, 7 In.	1300.00
Galle, Vase, Pink & Frosted, Green Thistles, Footed, 4 In.	175.00
Galle, Vase, Purple Maple Leaves & Flowers, 4 In.	200.00
Galle, Vase, Purple Maple Leaves On Yellow Green Ground, Minature, 4 In.	250.00
Galle, Vase, Red & Yellow Floral, 6 In.	375.00
Galle, Vase, Red Cameo Work Against Amber Background, Signed, 4 X 7 In.	285.00
Galle, Vase, Sculptured Purple Over Yellow, Water Lilies, 5 1/4 In.	375.00
Galle, Vase, Shades Of Brown, 6 1/2 In.	485.00
Galle, Vase, Spider Berries On Rust Tones Of Coral, Smoke Background, 9 In.	275.00
Galle, Vase, Squat, Double Gourd, Lilies, Leaves, Red, Etched Name, C.1900, 6 In.	1100.00
Galle, Vase, Three-Color Floral Vine & Leaf Decoration, 24 In.	950.00
Galle, Vase, Three Layers On Yellow Frosted Sky, 5 In.	575.00
Galle, Vase, Two-Tone Purple Violets, Signed, 2 1/2 In.	225.00
Galle, Vase, Wheel & Acid Cut, Burgundy Yellow & Frosted, Foliage, 2 7/8 In.	385.00
Galle, Vase, White Frosted, Green Vines On Gold, Deep Cut, Purple Base, 26 In.	975.00
Galle, Vase, Yellow & Orange, Brown Trees & Fence, Lake Scene, 5 In.	575.00
Galle, Vase, Yellow & Orange, To Shades Of Red Berries & Leaves, 4 1/4 In.	265.00

Game plates are any type of plate decorated with pictures of birds, animals, or fish. The game plates usually came in sets consisting of twelve dishes and a serving platter. These game plates were most popular during the 1880s.

Game, see also Disneyana, Game; Lone Ranger, Game; Popeye, Game.

Game Plate, Set, 6 Plates 9 1/2 In., Platter 16 In., Haviland	150.00
Game Plate, Snipe, White, Gold Detail, 11 In.	8.00
Game Plate, Wild Turkeys, Tan & Lavender Luster, Leuchtenbia, Germany, 8 In.	12.00
Game, Airplane Shoot Target, Lindstrom, Windup	14.00
Game, Assembly Line	4.00
Game, Auction Letters, Rabbit Design Cover On Box, Parker Bros., Dated 1900	15.00
Game, Bagatelle Set, Mahogany, English Victorian, 9 Ivory Balls	250.00
Game, Baseball, Autographed, 15 Signatures From 1968 All Star Game	22.00
Game, Bat Masterson, C.1958, Gene Barry On Box	10.00
Game, Bing Crosby	8.00
Game, Board, Backgammon, Red, Black, Mustard, C.1880	70.00
Game, Captain Kangaroo, C.1956	8.00
Game, Card, Complete, Original Box, Cincinnati Game Co., Dated 1896	25.00
Game, Card, The Boys In Blue, Man In Military Uniform, McLoughlin	25.00
Game, Checkerboard, Pine, Original Paint, 19th Century, 24 X 20 X 2 In.	40.00
Game, Checkerboard, Plaid Pattern, Pottery Carpet Balls, Colorful, Leeds	36.00
Game, Checkerboard, Wood, C.1875	30.00
Game, Chess Set, Black Basalt & Blue Jasper, Marked Wedgwood, Arnold Machin	1500.00
Game, Chess Set, Ivory, Red & White, Complete	122.00
Game, Chinese Checkers, Woodhaven, Metal, Glass Marbles	6.50
Game, Counter, Penny Arcade, What Should I Be Ashamed Of, 1 Cent	95.00
Game, Cribbage Board, Metal Top, Walnut	25.00
Game, Croquet, Victorian, Boxed	34.50
Game, Dart, Felix The Cat, In Package	15.00
Game, Dominoes, Brass Pegged Bone & Ebony, 55 Piece	40.00
Game, Dominoes, Brass Pegged Bone & Rosewood	35.00
Game, Dominoes, Brass Pegged Bone, Ebony, Set Through 6's, Wood Box, 28 Pieces	28.00
Game, Dominoes, Ivory & Ebony In Wooden Box	17.50
Game, Dominoes, Miniature, Wood & Ivory, 28 Pieces	30.00
Game, Eddie Cantor, Parker Brothers	8.00
Game, Gambling, French Horse Race	45.00
Game, Gem Puzzle Map Of The United States, Boxed, Milton Bradley	25.00
Game, Groucho Marx TV Quiz Game, 3-Dimensional Groucho Figure	16.50
Game, Jackie Gleason Honeymooner	18.00
Game, Lindstrom's Rocket Shot	12.00

Game, Lindy, The New Flying Game, Parker Bros. 15.00
Game, Lotto, Milton Bradley, 1920s 5.00
Game, Mah-Jongg Set, Alligator, Covered Box, C.1940s 45.00
Game, Mah-Jongg, Complete Set, Original Box .... 57.00 To 72.00
Game, Mah-Jongg, Wood, Dated 1922 .... 18.00
Game, Mysterious Woodpecker, Knot Hole Game, Marx, C.1952, Original Box 8.00
Game, Peg Board, Popeye's, King Features, C.1934, Complete 30.00
Game, Phoebe Snow, Scenes Of Train & Major Cities, Board, Can Be Hung, C.1910 ... 15.00
Game, Pike's Peak Or Bust, Board, Boxed, Parker Bros., Dated 1895, 8 X 8 In. 25.00
Game, Pin Ball, Poll Parrot, Wood Case, 11 1/2 X 18 In. 65.00
Game, Pit 1919 .... 6.00
Game, Punch Board, BlueBelle, 12 X 12 In. 5.00
Game, Puzzle, In Box, C.1907, Parker Bros., Pair 18.00
Game, Puzzle, Jig Of Jigs, Maxfield Parrish, In Box, 9 1/2 X 12 In. 75.00
Game, Puzzle, Jigsaw, Hood's Sarsaparilla, Factory, Hansom Cab, 2 Horses 50.00
Game, Puzzle, Jigsaw, Sliced Birds, C.1910, Selchow & Righter 22.00
Game, Puzzle, Jigsaw, Uncle Sam, Sand In Foreground, Naval Ship, C.1908, Box 50.00
Game, Puzzle, Jigsaw, Walnut, Carved, 2 X 2 1/2 X 5 1/4 In. 95.00
Game, Rodeo Bagatelle 9.00
Game, Roulette Wheel, Jeu De Roulette, 23 X 16 In.Felt, 6 In.Chips, 1920 .... 125.00
Game, Round The World, Durable Toys 14.00
Game, Scarlett O'Hara, Marble, 8 2/3 X 5 3/4 In. 25.00
Game, Scouting, For Boys, Milton Bradley 18.00
Game, Space Satellite Target, Battery Operated, Tin Gun 8.00
Game, Spot-A-Plane Game, 2nd Series, C.1942 .... 15.00
Game, Stock Exchange, Gavitts, 1904 .... 8.50
Game, Target, Wyandotte Duck 12.00
Game, Uncle Wiggily, 1920s 10.00
Game, Vita Life 2.50
Game, Winnie Winkle, Board, Comic Character, Branner 32.00
Game, Wizard Of Oz, 1921, Original Box 55.00

*Gaudy Dutch pottery was made in England for America from about 1810 to
1820. It is a white earthenware with Imari style decorations of red, blue,
green, yellow, and black. Only sixteen patterns of Gaudy Dutch were made—
Butterfly, Carnation, Dahlia, Double Rose, Dove, Grape, Leaf,
Oyster, Primrose, Single Rose, Strawflower, Sunflower, Urn,
War Bonnet, Zinnia, and No Name. Other similar wares are called
Soft Paste, Gaudy Ironstone, or Gaudy Welsh.*

Gaudy Dutch, Bowl & Saucer, Tea, Dove 275.00
Gaudy Dutch, Bowl, Dove, 6 X 11 In. 200.00
Gaudy Dutch, Cup & Saucer, War Bonnet 475.00
Gaudy Dutch, Pitcher, Oyster Pattern, 4 In. 39.00
Gaudy Dutch, Plate, Carnation, 9 3/4 In. 650.00
Gaudy Dutch, Plate, Single Rose, 10 In. 500.00
Gaudy Ironstone, Bowl, Blue, Rust, Gold Pagoda, C.1800, 7 1/2 In. 35.00
Gaudy Ironstone, Cup & Saucer, Blinking Eye Pattern, Handleless 125.00
Gaudy Ironstone, Cup & Saucer, Oriental Scenes In Imari Color, Japan 45.00
Gaudy Ironstone, Pitcher, Floral & Butterfly, Iron Red, Magenta, & Gold, 6 In. 110.00
Gaudy Ironstone, Pitcher, Serpent Handle, 5 In. 75.00
Gaudy Ironstone, Plate, Cobalt, Pink Flowers, 8 1/2 In. 45.00
Gaudy Ironstone, Plate, Hand-Painted, Geometric Borders, 8 1/2 In. 25.00
Gaudy Ironstone, Plate, Indian, 6 In. 22.00
Gaudy Ironstone, Plate, Leaf, Cobalt Blue, Gold, Red, 1845, 10 1/2 In. 50.00
Gaudy Ironstone, Plate, Orange Cobalt, Coalport, 7 In. 10.00
Gaudy Ironstone, Vase, Orange, Cobalt, Handled, 4 1/2 In. 20.00

*Gaudy Welsh is an Imari decorated earthenware with red, blue, green, and
gold decorations. It was made after 1820.*

Gaudy Welsh, Bowl, Oyster Pattern, 8 X 4 1/2 In. 45.00
Gaudy Welsh, Bowl, Round, Pedestal, Oyster Pattern, Allerton, 2 X 2 3/4 In. 44.00
Gaudy Welsh, Bowl, Waste, Tulip Pattern, Footed 39.00
Gaudy Welsh, Chocolate Set, Blue & Gold, Medallion Of Flowers 110.00
Gaudy Welsh, Coffeepot, Oyster Pattern, Allerton, 5 1/2 In. 88.00
Gaudy Welsh, Creamer, Oyster, C.1850, 4 1/2 In. 38.00
Gaudy Welsh, Creamer, Pink & Copper Luster With Orange & Blue, 3 1/4 In. 38.00

Gaudy Welsh, Creamer, Tulip Pattern	35.00
Gaudy Welsh, Cup & Saucer, Cobalt Blue Triangles, Rust Floral, C.1850	50.00
Gaudy Welsh, Cup & Saucer, Coffee, Oyster Pattern, Allerton	57.00
Gaudy Welsh, Cup & Saucer, Handleless Cup, Deep Saucer	65.00 To 95.00
Gaudy Welsh, Cup & Saucer, Imari Type Decoration	29.00
Gaudy Welsh, Cup & Saucer, Oyster Pattern, Allerton	59.00
Gaudy Welsh, Cup & Saucer, Oyster Pattern, Pink Luster Trim	35.00
Gaudy Welsh, Cup & Saucer, Tulip Pattern	30.00
Gaudy Welsh, Cup & Saucer, Wagon Wheel, Blue, Gilt Trim	45.00
Gaudy Welsh, Jar, Cookie, Tulip Pattern	82.00
Gaudy Welsh, Jug, Pewter Lid, 7 In.	45.00
Gaudy Welsh, Mug, Wagon Wheel	40.00
Gaudy Welsh, Mush Set, Tulip Pattern, 3 Piece	75.00
Gaudy Welsh, Pitcher, Cobalt, Orange & Green On White, 4 3/4 In.	55.50
Gaudy Welsh, Pitcher, Copper Luster With Blue, Orange, Green, Squatty, 6 In.	45.00
Gaudy Welsh, Pitcher, Milk, Cobalt Blue Glazing On White Porcelain, 5 In.	45.00
Gaudy Welsh, Pitcher, Milk, Green Snake Handle, Octagonal Sides	75.00
Gaudy Welsh, Pitcher, Oyster, 4 3/4 In.	31.00
Gaudy Welsh, Plate, Deep, Oyster, 9 1/2 In.	68.00
Gaudy Welsh, Plate, Oyster, Allerton, 6 3/4 In.	45.00
Gaudy Welsh, Plate, Oyster, 5 1/2 In.	20.00
Gaudy Welsh, Plate, Oyster, 7 In.	18.00
Gaudy Welsh, Plate, Oyster, 9 In.	17.50
Gaudy Welsh, Plate, Tulip, 6 In.	8.00
Gaudy Welsh, Plate, Tulip, 10 In.	35.00
Gaudy Welsh, Plate, Wagon Wheel, 4 1/2 In.	23.00
Gaudy Welsh, Plate, Wagon Wheel, 7 In.	55.00
Gaudy Welsh, Plate, Wagon Wheel, 7 In., Set Of 4	135.00
Gaudy Welsh, Sugar, Footed, Covered, Tulip Pattern	135.00
Gaudy Welsh, Sugar, Handled, No Cover, Oyster Pattern, Allerton	33.00
Gaudy Welsh, Sugar, Tulip Pattern	75.00
Gaudy Welsh, Syrup, Silverplated Top, 5 3/4 In.	58.00
Gaudy Welsh, Tea Set, Tulip Pattern, 19 Piece	250.00
Gaudy Welsh, Tea Set, Tulip Pattern, 26 Piece	500.00
Gaudy Welsh, Teapot, Single Rose Pattern, Pedestal Base, 4 Feet, 7 1/2 In.	95.00
Gaudy Welsh, Teapot, Tulip Pattern	85.00
Gaudy Welsh, Vase, Imperial, Free Hand, Blue, 12 In.	125.00
Gene Autry, Belt	3.00
Gene Autry, Figurine, Ceramic, Signed	16.00
Gene Autry, Souvenir Program, C.1957	8.00

Gibson Girl plates were made in the early 1900s by the Royal Doulton
Pottery at Lambeth, England. There are twenty-four different plates
featuring a picture of the Gibson Girl by the artist Charles Dana
Gibson.

Gibson Girl, Plate, Failing To Find Rest, She Returns Home	55.00 To 75.00
Gibson Girl, Plate, Fancy Dress Ball As Juliet	60.00
Gibson Girl, Plate, Head In Profile, Bows & Hearts Border	55.00
Gibson Girl, Plate, Hostile Criticism	48.00
Gibson Girl, Plate, Message From Outside World, Royal Doulton	55.00
Gibson Girl, Plate, Miss Babbles Reads	75.00
Gibson Girl, Plate, Miss Babbles The Authoress	57.50 To 65.00
Gibson Girl, Plate, Mrs.Waddles Arrives Late	60.00
Gibson Girl, Plate, Quiet Dinner With Dr. Bottles	55.00
Gibson Girl, Plate, She Finds That Exercise Doesn't Improve Spirits	65.00
Gibson Girl, Plate, Skating	55.00
Gibson Girl, Plate, Winning New Friends	60.00

GILLINDER   Gillinder pressed glass was first made by William T. Gillinder of
Philadelphia in 1863. Many pressed glass items were made for the
Centennial.

Gillinder, Bust, Abraham Lincoln, Centennial Exhibition, 6 In.	335.00
Gillinder, Compote, Open, Frosted Figural, Hand Holding Torch, 8 1/8 X 9 In.	275.00
Gillinder, Figurine, Buddha, Golden Amber, Signed, 5 3/4 In.	80.00
Gillinder, Figurine, Chick & Egg, Centennial Frosted Glass, Opaque On Head	62.00
Gillinder, Figurine, Shakespeare, Frosted, Signed	125.00

Gillinder, Paperweight, Frosted Lion's Head, 1886	56.00
Gillinder, Shoe, Centennial Exposition, 1876, 5 1/2 X 2 3/4 In.	25.00 To 32.50
Gillinder, Sugar Shaker, White Satin, Tea Roses, Hand-Painted	85.00
Girl Scout, Handbook, 1924	5.00
Girl Scout, Tin, Lunch, Scenes Of Girl Scouts, 1920s	15.50
Gold, Cutter, Cigar, 14K	50.00
Gold, Handle, Umbrella, Heart Shape, Dated 1911	25.00
Gold, Toothpick, Retractable	25.00
Goldscheider, Figurine, Bust Of Oriental Women	20.00
Goldscheider, Figurine, Girl In Victorian Costume, Bonnet, Parasol, Marked	42.00
Goldscheider, Figurine, Miss Siddons, 6 1/2 In.	38.00
Goldscheider, Figurine, Prince Of Wales, 7 In.	50.00
Goldscheider, Figurine, Temple Dancer, 8 In.	30.00
Golf Club, see Toy, Golf Club	
Gonder, Cornucopia, Dark Green	4.50
Gonder, Teapot, Purple	6.50

*Goofus glass was made from about 1900 to 1920 by many American factories.
It was originally painted gold, red, green, bronze, pink, purple, and other
bright colors.*

Goofus Glass, Berry Set, Bird & Strawberry, 6 Piece	150.00
Goofus Glass, Bowl, Gold & Red, 9 In.	15.00
Goofus Glass, Bowl, Gold With Red Poinsettia & Holly, 9 1/4 X 3 1/4 In.	16.00
Goofus Glass, Bowl, Gold With Red Roses, 8 1/2 X 3 In.	12.00
Goofus Glass, Bowl, Gold, Red Carnations & Pansies, 9 In.	10.50 To 15.00
Goofus Glass, Bowl, Gold, Red Flowers, 9 In.	15.00
Goofus Glass, Bowl, Gold, Red Strawberries, Scalloped Rim, 10 In.	20.00
Goofus Glass, Bowl, Grape Pattern, Scalloped, 9 1/4 In.	12.00
Goofus Glass, Bowl, Red & Gold Holly & Poinsettias, Ruffled, 11 In.	35.00
Goofus Glass, Bowl, Red Carnations, 9 In.	15.00
Goofus Glass, Bowl, Red Roses, 9 In.	12.00
Goofus Glass, Bowl, Scalloped, Marked Northwood	25.00
Goofus Glass, Bowl, Vegetable, No Paint, 8 1/2 In.	8.00
Goofus Glass, Jar, Apple Green, Floral Embossing, 2 1/2 In.	40.00
Goofus Glass, Jar, Pickle, Amber, 15 1/2 In.	45.00
Goofus Glass, Jar, Powder, Roses	18.50
Goofus Glass, Lamp, Table, Birds, Grapes	22.00
Goofus Glass, Nappy, Red Cherries, Gold Leaves, Heart Shaped, Ruffled Edge	9.00
Goofus Glass, Plate, Gold & Red, Blue Grapes In Center, 12 1/2 In.	15.00
Goofus Glass, Plate, Gold With Red Poppies, Scalloped Edge, 10 1/2 In.	16.00
Goofus Glass, Plate, Gold, Red Roses, 10 In.	14.50
Goofus Glass, Plate, Hey Diddle Diddle, 6 1/2 In.	15.00
Goofus Glass, Plate, Rabbit, Easter Greeting Center, 6 In.	12.00
Goofus Glass, Red & Gold, Pinecones, 10 1/2 In.	14.50
Goofus Glass, Tray, Bureau, Red Roses, Chrysanthemum Pattern, 8 X 11 In.	27.50
Goofus Glass, Vase, Blue, Gold, & Red, 9 In.	10.00
Goofus Glass, Vase, Grape	8.00
Goofus Glass, Vase, Lovebirds On Branch, Trees, Shrubs, 2 1/2 In.	16.00

*Goss china has been made since 1858. English potter William Henry
Goss first made it at the Falcon Pottery in Stoke-on-Trent. In 1934
the factory name was changed to Goss China Company when it was taken over
by Cauldon Potteries. Goss china resembles Irish Belleek in both body
and glaze. The company also made popular souvenir china.*

W.H. COSS

Goss, Carafe, Wimborne Crest	10.00 To 18.00
Goss, Cup & Saucer, Trinity College, Dublin, Falcon Mark	20.00
Goss, Figurine, Model Of Roman Vessel, Woodbridge Crest	18.00
Goss, Goblet, Libation, Woodbridge, Impressed W.H.Goss	15.00
Goss, Jug, Cream, White, Turquoise Rope Handle, Trim, Impressed Mark, 4 1/2 In.	40.00
Goss, Mug, Child's, The Dancing Lesson, 1922	22.00
Goss, Pitcher, Grasmere, Falcon Mark	15.00
Goss, Toby, Seated, Model Of Stratford Toby Jug, 3 In.	110.00
Goss, Vase, Model Of Ostend Vase, Lowestoft Crest	18.00

*Gouda is a district in Holland famous for tin-glazed pottery and tiles.
Gouda pottery has been made by many factories in the district since the*

seventeenth century and is still being made. Most of the pieces found today are from the nineteenth and twentieth centuries.

Gouda, Ashtray, Plazuid, Flowers, Black, 4 1/2 X 1 3/4 In.	38.00 To 45.00
Gouda, Bottle, Wine, Top & Handle, House Mark, 10 In.	90.00
Gouda, Bowl, Blanca, Decorated, Green Interior, Handled, House Mark, 12 X 5 In.	75.00
Gouda, Bowl, Flat, High Glaze, 3 1/2 In.	45.00
Gouda, Bowl, Floral On White, Art Nouveau, Hand-Painted, Signed, 6 X 4 In.	150.00
Gouda, Bowl, Windmill, Boat, Signed Zuid Holland, House Mark, 4 X 3 In.	65.00
Gouda, Box, Regina, Covered With Paper Label, 2 X 4 1/2 X 3 1/2 In.	58.00
Gouda, Box, White, Red, Yellow, Blue, Green, High Glaze, Covered, 3 3/4 In.	30.00
Gouda, Candleshelf, Blue, House Mark, 7 In.	55.00
Gouda, Candlestick, Art Deco Designs, 4 In., Pair	50.00
Gouda, Candlestick, Floral, Black Top & Base, Zomer, 8 In.	55.00
Gouda, Candlestick, Multicolor Glaze, Regina Gouda Holland, 4 1/2 In.	30.00
Gouda, Candlestick, Orange, Yellow, White, & Black, Art Nouveau, 8 1/2 In., Pair	175.00
Gouda, Candlestick, Waxy Green, Blue, Yellow, 12 In.	65.00
Gouda, Chamberstick, Floral Interior, Black Exterior, Matte, 1911, 6 1/2 In.	95.00
Gouda, Chamberstick, Handled Shieldback Style, 8 In.	90.00
Gouda, Chamberstick, Iridescent Green, Paisley Design	75.00
Gouda, Charger, House Mark, Pierced For Hanging, 12 In.Diameter	165.00
Gouda, Cigarette Set, Tray, Holder, Ashtray, Signed	40.00
Gouda, Compote, Multicolored Decoration On Green, Handled, Zuid, 10 X 3 In.	35.00
Gouda, Creamer, Art Nouveau Design	32.00
Gouda, Creamer, Pastel Flowers, High Glaze, 3 In.	40.00
Gouda, Cruet Set, High Glaze, Art Nouveau, Fatma, 3 Piece	325.00
Gouda, Decanter, Regina, 3 Pinched Sides, Stopper, 9 1/2 In.	160.00
Gouda, Dish, Paris Pattern, Footed, 5 1/2 X 3 In.	35.00
Gouda, Dish, Salt	13.00
Gouda, Humidor, Stylized Sunbursts On Royal Blue, Gouda, Melvin	125.00
Gouda, Jar, Covered, Cream, Blue Windmill, 5 1/2 X 6 1/2 In.	85.00
Gouda, Jar, Floral, Full Mark	90.00
Gouda, Jar, Tobacco, High Glaze, Covered	115.00
Gouda, Jug, Matte Finish, Handled, Marked Holland, 7 1/2 In.	75.00
Gouda, Jug, Stylized Decoration, Cobalt Blue, Marked, 6 In., Pair	110.00
Gouda, Lamp Base, Dark High Glaze Art Nouveau Design, Hexagonal, 7 3/8 In.	105.00
Gouda, Mug, Osiris On Black Matte, Regina Gouda, Holland, 4 1/2 X 4 1/2 In.	80.00
Gouda, Pitcher, Floral, Black Matte & Art Deco, Tosca, 6 In.	28.00
Gouda, Pitcher, Floral, Strap Handle, Royal Zuid, 9 1/2 In.	35.00
Gouda, Pitcher, Handle, Lip, Blue, Brown, Beige, Blossoms, Yellow Ground, 10 In.	75.00
Gouda, Pitcher, House Mark, 2 1/2 In.	30.00
Gouda, Pitcher, Miniature, Long Lip, Signed Zwaro	22.00
Gouda, Pitcher, Tulip Design, 5 In.	50.00
Gouda, Plate, Dessert, Crown & Royal Goedewaagen, Set Of 6, 8 1/4 In.	48.00
Gouda, Plate, Tropical Bird, 10 1/2 In.	125.00
Gouda, Platter, Allover Floral, Arnheim, Signed, 7 1/2 In.	135.00
Gouda, Platter, Dark Brown Edging, House Mark, 12 In.Diameter	95.00
Gouda, Rose Bowl, Cutout Rim	68.00
Gouda, Salt Dip, Splash Luster, Rust Floral, Leaves, Glazed, Marked, 2 1/2 In.	12.50
Gouda, Shoe, Crocus, 5 1/2 In.	45.00
Gouda, Tile, Dutch Man And Woman, Dutch Scenes, Pair	35.00
Gouda, Tray, Flambe, High Glaze, 17 X 12 In.	165.00
Gouda, Tray, Glazed, Zuid Holland, 8 1/2 X 4 1/2 In.	95.00
Gouda, Tray, Heart-Shaped Leaf With Stem, Lavender, Florals, 7 1/2 X 6 1/2 In	30.00
Gouda, Tray, Zenith Gouda Ruby, Round, Two Handles, Black, Green, Yellow, Blue	35.00
Gouda, Urn, Glossy, 2 Handled, 3 In.	37.00
Gouda, Urn, 2-Eared, Traditional Design, Blue, Rust, White, 8 1/2 X 7 In.	85.00
Gouda, Vase, Art Deco, Orange, Gold, Blue, Hexagonal, Goedewaagen, 9 In.	135.00
Gouda, Vase, Beige, Tulip Floral, Irene, 1930, 7 In.	47.00
Gouda, Vase, Black, Orange, Red, Yellow, & Blue Flowers, Marked, 6 In.	45.00
Gouda, Vase, Brown, Rust, Blue, Cream, Art Nouveau, 14 X 8 3/4 In.	260.00
Gouda, Vase, Cream, Pastel Florals, High Glaze, 3 In.	40.00
Gouda, Vase, Damascus, Art Deco, 6 1/2 X 5 In.	45.00
Gouda, Vase, Dark Mottled Green, Rust, Blue, & Green Flowers, 4 1/2 In.	42.00
Gouda, Vase, Flared Top, Marked Gouda Holland, 7 In.	60.00
Gouda, Vase, Floral, Art Nouveau, Holland Mark, C.1900, 7 In.	45.00

Gouda, Vase, Floral, 2 Colorful Fish, Royal Blue & White, Art Nouveau, 8 In.	225.00
Gouda, Vase, Miniature Scenic, High Glaze, Fully Marked, 2 In.	36.00
Gouda, Vase, Multicolored Floral, House Mark, 4 X 7 In.	35.00
Gouda, Vase, Multicolored, Art Nouveau, House Mark, 6 X 5 In.	45.00
Gouda, Vase, Nova, Holland, 6 1/2 In.	60.00
Gouda, Vase, Regina, Art Nouveau In Red & Black, 6 1/4 In.	35.00
Gouda, Vase, Regina, Handled, 4 1/2 In.	35.00
Gouda, Vase, Shiny Tulip, 8 1/2 In.	95.00
Gouda, Vase, Wall, Marked Anger, Thick Enameled Colors, 4 1/2 X 11 In.	60.00
Gouda, Vase, Yellow, Blue, & Aqua, Art Nouveau, Regina Verona, 8 In., Pair	150.00
Gouda, Vase, Yellow, Orange, & Blue, A.K., 2 1/2 In.	25.00
Gouda, Vase, Zuid, Cone Shape, Footed, 6 1/2 In.	45.00

Graniteware is an enameled tinware that has been used in the kitchen from the late nineteenth century to the present. Earlier graniteware was green or turquoise blue, with white spatters. The later ware was gray with white spatters. Reproductions are being made in all colors.

Graniteware, Board, Scrub, Blue Scrub Surface, Wood Frame, Soap Shelf At Top	46.00
Graniteware, Bowl, Blue, Mottled, 8 In.	10.00
Graniteware, Can, Cream, Lidless, Strap Handle	14.00
Graniteware, Candleholder, Child's, White, Blue Rims, Ring Handle	11.50
Graniteware, Coffeepot, Blue & White, Wooden Handle, Gooseneck Spout, 10 In.	28.00
Graniteware, Coffeepot, Blue, 7 In.	4.50
Graniteware, Coffeepot, Gray, Tin Lid	20.00
Graniteware, Coffeepot, Gray, 11 In.	12.50 To 17.50
Graniteware, Colander, Gray, Handled, 8 In.	6.50
Graniteware, Compote, Miniature, White With Violets, 1 1/2 In.	8.00
Graniteware, Dipper, Gray	13.00
Graniteware, Funnel, Bottle	4.00
Graniteware, Kettle, Gray, Bail Handle, 5 X 10 1/4 In.	5.00
Graniteware, Mug, Gray	4.00
Graniteware, Pan, Muffin, Gray	10.00
Graniteware, Pan, Pudding, Fluted	15.00
Graniteware, Pan, Tube, Swirled Rib, Reddish Brown Exterior, 10 X 5 In.	38.00
Graniteware, Pie Pan, Blue Gray, 9 3/4 In.	2.50
Graniteware, Pie Pan, Mottled Green & White	21.00
Graniteware, Pie Plate, Gray, Mottled, 11 In.	6.00
Graniteware, Pitcher, Blue Splash, 9 1/2 In.	24.00
Graniteware, Pitcher, Gray, 1 Gallon	22.50
Graniteware, Plate, Gray, 8 1/2 In., Pair	15.00
Graniteware, Pot, Blue & White Splash, Wire Bail, Square Handle, 15 X 7 In.	35.00
Graniteware, Pot, Chamber, Gray	26.00
Graniteware, Shredder, Gray Mottled, Ornate Iron Table Clamp, Large	42.00
Graniteware, Teakettle, Gray And White	25.00
Graniteware, Teapot, Tin Lid	20.00
Graniteware, Washbasin, Gray, Mottled, 11 In.	8.50
Graniteware, Washbasin, Hole For Hanging, 3 X 8 1/2 In.	5.00
Graniteware, Washbasin, 7 In.	1.00

Greentown glass was made by the Indiana Tumbler and Goblet Company of Greentown, Indiana, from 1894 to 1903. In 1899, the factory name was changed to National Glass Company. A variety of pressed, milk, and chocolate glass was made.

Greentown, see also Chocolate Glass, Custard Glass, Holly Amber, Milk Glass, Pressed Glass

Greentown, Bowl, Berry, Teardrop & Tassel, Green	30.00
Greentown, Bowl, Cactus, Canary	20.00
Greentown, Bowl, Canary Yellow, Dewey, 3 1/2 X 8 In.	20.00
Greentown, Bust, Witch Head, Nile Green	45.00
Greentown, Butter, Amber, Dewey	30.00
Greentown, Butter, Dewey, Clear, Covered	30.00
Greentown, Cakestand, No.11, 9 In.	27.00
Greentown, Compote, Teardrop & Tassle Cover, Clear, 11 1/2 X 7 In.	85.00
Greentown, Creamer, Dewey, Amber, Large	45.00
Greentown, Creamer, Overall Lattice	22.00 To 30.00

Greentown, Creamer, Shuttle 28.00
Greentown, Cruet, Dewey, Nile Green 600.00
Greentown, Cup, Punch, Ruby Stained, Lattice, Souvenir 18.00
Greentown, Cup, Punch, Shuttle 15.00
Greentown, Dish, Domed Rabbit Cover, Translucent Blue 200.00
Greentown, Dish, Rabbit Cover, Green 150.00
Greentown, Dish, Rabbit-On-Nest Cover, Fat Mold, Blue 85.00
Greentown, Dish, Robin-On-Nest Cover, White Milk Glass 150.00
Greentown, Dish, Sauce, Cord Drapery, Amber, Footed 10.50
Greentown, Dustpan, Blue 55.00
Greentown, Figurine, Dolphin, Chocolate 135.00
Greentown, Figurine, Dolphin, Red Agate 325.00
Greentown, Figurine, Fat Rabbit On Nest, Blue 125.00
Greentown, Mug, Custard Serenade 35.00
Greentown, Mug, Elves, Green, No.299 .... 15.00 To 28.00
Greentown, Mug, Elves, White Opaque 25.00
Greentown, Mug, Knights, Blue 8.00
Greentown, Mug, Knights, Green .... 22.00 To 40.00
Greentown, Mug, Serenade, Blue, Opaque .... 24.00 To 35.00
Greentown, Mug, Serenade, Nile Green 30.00
Greentown, Mug, Shuttle, Red Agate 60.00
Greentown, Pitcher, Water, Pleat Band .... 30.00 To 33.00
Greentown, Pitcher, Water, Squirrel 145.00
Greentown, Plate, Cake, No.11 .... 21.00
Greentown, Plate, Serenade, 6 1/2 In. 55.00
Greentown, Spooner, Clear With Gold, No.11 .... 20.00
Greentown, Sugar, Cactus, Canary Opalescent, Cover, 6 In. .... 39.00 To 50.00
Greentown, Sugar, Clear With Gold, Lidded, No.11 .... 25.00
Greentown, Toothpick, Hand Holding Vase, Nile Green 75.00
Greentown, Toothpick, Picture Frame, Original Mirror 125.00
Greentown, Tumbler, Brazen Shield, Blue 35.00
Greentown, Vase, Green With Gold, No.11, 6 In. 20.00
Greentown, Wheelbarrow, Nile Green 145.00
Greentown, Wine, Beehive 38.00

Grueby Faience Company of Boston, Massachusetts, was incorporated in 1897 by William H. Grueby. Garden statuary, art pottery, and architectural tiles were made until 1920.

Grueby, Bowl, Green, 4 In. 95.00
Grueby, Bowl, Rolled In Rim, Green Matte Glaze, 3 In. 135.00
Grueby, Candlestick, Blue, 5 1/2 In. 150.00
Grueby, Lamp, Green, Raised Buds, 16 X 8 In. 350.00
Grueby, Paperweight, Scarab, Green, 3 1/2 In. 110.00
Grueby, Paperweight, Scarab, Yellow, Clear Mark, 4 In. 115.00
Grueby, Scarab, Blue, Miniature 200.00
Grueby, Tile, Green, 2 X 6 In. 30.00
Grueby, Vase, Blue Crawling Glaze Revealing Tan Clay Body, 6 In. 285.00
Grueby, Vase, Cucumber Green, 7 In. 225.00
Grueby, Vase, Dark Green, 8 In. 160.00
Grueby, Vase, Green Stippled Glaze, Bulbous Bottom, Tapered Neck, 7 In. 175.00
Grueby, Vase, Mottled Green, Signed, 4 In. 125.00
Grueby, Vase, Mustard Glaze, Bulbous, 4 X 6 In. 250.00
Grueby, Vase, Yellow, Signed, 4 In. 125.00
Grueby, Vase, 3 Green Tooled Leaves, 3 White Buds On Green Ground, 4 1/2 In. 395.00
Gum Ball Machine, see Store, Machine
Gun, see Weapon, Handgun; Weapon, Rifle; Weapon, Shotgun; etc.

Gunderson glass was made at the Gunderson Pairpoint Works of New Bedford, Massachusetts, from 1952 to 1957. Gunderson Peachblow is especially famous.

Gunderson, Cup & Saucer, White & Fuchsia, Applied Ribbed Handle, Pontil 130.00
Gunderson, Peachblow, Bowl, Footed, 10 X 4 In. 200.00
Gunderson, Peachblow, Compote, White To Deep Raspberry, 3 X 5 1/2 In. 195.00
Gunderson, Peachblow, Creamer, White Applied Handle, 4 1/2 In. 135.00
Gunderson, Peachblow, Cruet 300.00

Gunderson, Peachblow, Cup & Saucer .... 160.00 To 250.00
Gunderson, Peachblow, Sherbet, White To Raspberry, Acid Finish, 4 7/8 In. 100.00
Gunderson, Plate, Fuchsia & White, Pontil, 8 In. 125.00
Gunderson, Vase, Raspberry Shading, Bulbous, Scalloped Top, 8 In. 250.00
    Gutta-Percha, see also Photography, Daguerreotype Case
Gutta-Percha, Box, Hinged Scenic Lid, 4 3/4 X 4 3/4 X 3 1/4 In. 32.00
Gutta-Percha, Buckle, George & Martha Washington, C.1850 .... 65.00
Gutta-Percha, Mirror, Hand, Woodland Scene & House, Dated 1872 .... 27.00
Halcyon, Vase, Lizard On Side, 13 1/4 X 9 X 3 1/2 .... 1750.00
    Hall, see also Autumn Leaf
Hall, Bowl, Cereal, Green, No.545, 8 Pieces 12.00
Hall, Casserole, Rose Parade, Covered 9.50
Hall, Casserole, Royal Rose 8.00
Hall, Coffeepot, Dripolator, Poppy 20.00
Hall, Cracker Jar, Blue Pansies, Satin Finish, Bail & Lid, A.J.Hall 145.00
Hall, Cup & Saucer, Castle Toward, Deep Blue 95.00
Hall, Dispenser, Coffee, Wild Rose 10.00
Hall, Pitcher, Water, Cobalt, Aristocrat, Lidded 16.00
Hall, Punch Set, Tom & Jerry, Gold Lettering, 13 Piece 60.00
Hall, Teapot, Aladdin, Jewel Tea 15.95

    Hampshire pottery was made in Keene, New Hampshire, between 1871 and
    1923. Hampshire developed a popular line of colored glazed works as early as
    1883, which included a Royal Worcester-type pink, olive green, blue, and
    mahogany.
Hampshire, Bowl, Flower, Heavy Matte Dark Blue Textured Glaze, 8 7/8 In. 28.00
Hampshire, Chocolate Pot, Green Leaves, Gold Trimmed, Pale Yellow 75.00
Hampshire, Mug, Blownout Leaves & Bottom Scenic, Portrait 90.00
Hampshire, Nappy, Violets, Ivory Ground, Signed, 9 In. 35.00
Hampshire, Pitcher, Bulbous Tree-Bark Body, Tan, Green, Gold Handle, 6 In. 75.00
Hampshire, Planter, Green, Raised Cat-O'-Nine-Tails Design, 4 X 6 1/2 In. 25.00
Hampshire, Relish, Finger Loop, Thayer Memorial Building, 7 1/2 In. 18.00
Hampshire, Tankard, Green, JST Co. 60.00
Hampshire, Vase, Blue Mottled, 12 In. 56.00
Hampshire, Vase, Cylinder, Mottled Blue, 7 In. 28.00
Hampshire, Vase, Green, Greek Key Design, 5 1/4 In. 45.00
Hampshire, Vase, Green, 6 In., Pair 60.00
Hampshire, Vase, Green, 7 3/4 In. 14.00
Hampshire, Vase, Mottled Blue, Artist Initialed, 7 3/4 In. 39.00
Hampshire, Vase, Mottled Blue, Cylindrical, 7 In. 30.00
Hampshire, Vase, Mottled Blue, Designed Band, Initialed, 7 3/4 In. 46.00
Hampshire, Vase, Pinch Sided, Green Squared Top, 3 3/4 In. 7.00
Hampshire, Vase, Relief Stylized Dandelions, Green Matte, M In Circle, 6 In. 37.00
Hampshire, Vase, Squatty, Dark Green, Raised Cat O'nine Tail, 4 X 6 1/2 In. 65.00
Hampshire, Vase, White Arched Concentrics, Blue Matte, 7 1/2 In. 250.00

    Philip Handel worked in Meriden, Connecticut, about 1885 and in New
    York City from about 1900 to the 1930s. His firm made art glass and other
    types of lamps.
Handel, Ashtray, Full Figure Of Brown Bull Dog On Ivory, Kalsey, 4 1/2 In. 115.00
Handel, Candlestick, Copper, Mission, Pair 275.00
Handel, Humidor, Brown & Gold Scenic, Signed, 6 X 8 In. 225.00
Handel, Humidor, Chipped Ice, Brass Hinges, Green 225.00
Handel, Humidor, Green & Brown Opalescent, Horse On Tan Ground 170.00
Handel, Humidor, Hunting Dogs On Brown & Green, Signed Bauer, 6 In. 225.00
Handel, Humidor, Opal Green Glass, Melon Shape, 7 In. 255.00
Handel, Jar, Tobacco, Hunting Dog, Brass Trim, Signed 85.00
Handel, Lamp Base, Bronze, Cloth Label, 20 In. 145.00
Handel, Lamp, Bird Of Paradise, Artist Signed, 27 X 18 In. 2450.00
Handel, Lamp, Cherry Blossoms, Leaves, Bronze, Leaf Molded Base, 25 X 18 In. 4500.00
Handel, Lamp, Desk, Leaded, Pink Flowered Shade, 10 In. 450.00
Handel, Lamp, Desk, Palm Trees, 4 Panels, Chocolate Brown Patina, Red, Signed 525.00
Handel, Lamp, Floral Leaded Shade, Morning Glories, 28 In. 2285.00
Handel, Lamp, Gone With The Wind, Kerosene, Floral On Pink Glass, 19 1/2 In. 1500.00
Handel, Lamp, Gone With The Wind, Kerosene, Pink, Signed, 19 1/2 In. 850.00

Handel, Lamp, Green Filigree Shade, Tan Panels, Signed, 17 In.	500.00
Handel, Lamp, Handel Hook Inside Shade, Signed Base, 16 X 22 In.	750.00
Handel, Lamp, Kerosene, Wide Floral Border, Pond Lilies, Leaded Shade, 20 In.	875.00
Handel, Lamp, Leaded Table, Green Top, Yellow Roses, Signed, 21 In.	650.00
Handel, Lamp, Leaded, Green Top, Yellow Roses, 21 In.	350.00
Handel, Lamp, Leaded, Spider Web Design, 23 In.	875.00
Handel, Lamp, Lily Pad & Fern Decorated, Signed B.S.	1050.00
Handel, Lamp, Mantel, Etched Globe, Prisms, Brass Base	45.00
Handel, Lamp, Mushroom Cap, Flowers, Ice Finish, Footed Base, 18 In.	395.00
Handel, Lamp, Mushroom Shade, 18 In.	1250.00
Handel, Lamp, Orange, Blue, Green, 18 Jewels, Filigree Wings, 20 In.	4750.00
Handel, Lamp, Palm Tree Design Over Tones Of Red Slag Glass, Paneled, Signed	525.00
Handel, Lamp, Reverse Painted Clusters Of Roses, B & S, 12 In., Shade	675.00
Handel, Lamp, Scenic Painted On Inside & Out, Signed, 18 In.	435.00
Handel, Lamp, Scenic Reverse Painted Woodlands, Sunset Colors, Signed, 18 In.	1475.00
Handel, Lamp, Scenic, Bronze Tree Trunk Base, Forest, Orange Sunset, 15 In.	725.00
Handel, Lamp, Slag Panel, 4-Sided, Red Berry & Green Leaf, Signed, Pair	385.00
Handel, Lamp, Sunset Palm Tree Overlay, 26 In.	1375.00
Handel, Lamp, Triple Acorn Pulls, Finial, Forest And Water Scenes, Signed	1500.00
Handel, Shade, Bronze, Variegated Tan, Marbleized, Palm Trees, 6 X 7 X 2 In.	200.00
Handel, Shade, Leaded, Green & Gold, Signed, Set Of 5	300.00
Handel, Shade, Student Type, Chipped Ice Top Finish, Light Ochre, 10 In., Pair	225.00
Handel, Vase, Mint Green, Brass Rim, Hand-Painted Florals, 12 In.	165.00
Harker, Casserole, Pink, Covered	6.50
Harker, Creamer, Pink, Cameo Pattern	5.00

*Harlequin dinnerware was produced by the Homer Laughlin Company
from 1938 to 1964, and sold without trademark by the F. W. Woolworth
Co. It had a concentric ring design like Fiesta, but the rings were
separated from the rim by a plain margin and cup handles were angular in
shape*

Harlequin Ware, Casserole, Green, Covered	18.00
Harlequin Ware, Cat, Green	45.00
Harlequin Ware, Cup & Saucer, Maroon, Set Of 3	5.00
Harlequin Ware, Donkey, Yellow	45.00
Harlequin Ware, Duck, Green	45.00
Harlequin Ware, Duck, White & Silver	45.00
Harlequin Ware, Lamb, Green	45.00
Harlequin Ware, Lamb, Yellow	45.00
Harlequin Ware, Penguin, Green	45.00
Harlequin Ware, Penguin, Yellow	45.00
Harlequin Ware, Pitcher, Water, Yellow	9.00
Hatpin Holder, see also Porcelain and various porcelain categories	
Hatpin Holder, Austrian China, Hand Painted, Signed, 1909	24.00
Hatpin Holder, Cushion, Beaded, Bird & Floral Design, 11 X 9 In.	38.00
Hatpin Holder, Gold Beading, White Background	24.00
Hatpin Holder, Hand-Painted Violets, Gold Trim, Artist Signed	12.00
Hatpin Holder, Hand-Painted, Gold Decorated Handle, 1912, Signed	45.00
Hatpin Holder, Hot Pink, Crown Ducal Ware, England, 5 1/2 In.	12.50
Hatpin Holder, Nippon, Red & Gold	57.00
Hatpin Holder, Nippon, Scenic Panels, Beading, 4 3/4 In.	38.00
Hatpin Holder, Poppy, Roayl Bayreuth	110.00
Hatpin, Brass Sailor Hat, Red Bow, 9 1/2 In.	12.50
Hatpin, Brass Snake, Blue Grids, 6 1/2 In.	8.00
Hatpin, Cluster Of Purple Stones, 2 In. Diameter, Victorian	25.00
Hatpin, Fancy Dome, Topped With Large Green And 6 Small Stones, 9 7/8 In.	8.00
Hatpin, Fluttering Hummingbird, Rhinestones	26.00
Hatpin, Iridescent China Bell	20.00
Hatpin, Large Topaz Color Set In Frame Of Fancy Brass, 12 1/2 In.	12.50
Hatpin, Octagon Brass Top, Bee Etching, 9 1/4 In.	9.00
Hatpin, Porcelain Portrait, Gold Paint Border, 10 1/2 In.	22.00
Hatpin, Rippled Square, Large Green Stone, 4 Brilliants, 10 3/8 In.	10.00
Hatpin, Sterling, Lady Golfer & Landscape, Art Nouveau	29.50

Haviland china has been made in Limoges, France, since 1846. The factory was started by the Haviland Brothers of New York City. Other factories worked in the town of Limoges making a similar chinaware.

Haviland, Bone Dish, Lavender Floral, French	3.00
Haviland, Bowl, Fruit, Short Pedestal, Autumn Browns & Tans, 9 1/2 In.	45.00
Haviland, Bowl, Pastel Florals, Gold Trim, Fluted, Scalloped, Footed, 9 1/4 In.	45.00
Haviland, Bowl, Strawberries Hand-Painted Inside & Out, 5 1/2 X 2 1/2 In.	12.50
Haviland, Butter Pat Set, Waterfall Pattern, Set Of 6	22.00
Haviland, Butter Pat, Gold Band, Marked	4.00
Haviland, Butter, Floral Cover, Insert	20.00
Haviland, Butter, Limoges, Roses, Leaves, Ruffled, Gold Border, Pink, Green, Lid	35.00
Haviland, Butter, Limoges, Tea Roses, Blue Scrolls, Gold Trim, Insert	25.00
Haviland, Celery, Black-Eyed Susan, Hand-Painted, 11 1/2 In.	25.00
Haviland, China Set, Limoges, Autumn Leaf, No.60, 52 Piece Set	650.00
Haviland, Chocolate Pot, Ivory, Pink, Blue, & Yellow Flowers, 10 In.	42.00
Haviland, Chocolate Pot, Limoges, Princess Pattern	85.00
Haviland, Chocolate Pot, No.66	65.00
Haviland, Chocolate Pot, Pink Flowers, Gold Trim	65.00
Haviland, Chocolate Set, Pink Spray, 13 Piece	88.00
Haviland, Coffeepot, Limoges, Blue Floral, Gold Bow, 8 In.	25.00
Haviland, Creamer, Pink & Yellow Roses	20.00
Haviland, Creamer, Rose Garland	15.00
Haviland, Cup & Saucer, Bouillon, Pale Yellow, Gold Decorated, CFH	8.00
Haviland, Cup & Saucer, Bouillon, Ransom	20.00
Haviland, Cup & Saucer, Demitasse, Pink & Blue Flowers	20.00
Haviland, Cup & Saucer, Demitasse, Wilton, Beige, Pink Roses	15.00
Haviland, Cup & Saucer, Limoges, Pink Carnations, White Porcelain	12.50
Haviland, Cup & Saucer, Marquis	18.00
Haviland, Cup & Saucer, Moss Rose, Green Trim	25.00
Haviland, Cup & Saucer, Pedestal, Hand-Painted, Green Mark	20.00
Haviland, Cup & Saucer, Pink Cabbage Roses With Gold	14.00
Haviland, Cup & Saucer, Ransom, White	22.00
Haviland, Cup & Saucer, Silver Pattern	20.00
Haviland, Cup, Demitasse, Paradise	3.50
Haviland, Cuspidor, White, Rose Upper Body, Yellow Floral, Gilt Edging, 7 In.	71.00
Haviland, Dinner Set, Limoges, White, Gold Band, Service For 8, 72 Piece	600.00
Haviland, Dish & Tray, Cover, Multicolored Flowers, 7 In.	45.00
Haviland, Dish Set, Pink Florals, Blue Green Ribbons, Gold, Signed, 56 Piece	450.00
Haviland, Dish, Cheese, Cover, Green Trim, Pink Roses, Limoges, 7 In.	30.00
Haviland, Dish, Pancake, Roses, Forget-Me-Nots, Gold Handles, 10 1/2 In.	57.50
Haviland, Dish, Vegetable, Covered, Red & Green Mark, Oval, 8 1/2 X 12 In.	39.00
Haviland, Dish, Vegetable, Gold Encrusted Band, Lid, No.1106	22.50
Haviland, Dish, Vegetable, Open, Red & Green Mark, 8 1/2 X 12 In.	22.00
Haviland, Figurine, Hearth, Sleeping Cat, Blue Body, White Head, 10 X 8 In.	175.00
Haviland, Gravy Boat & Underplate, Yellow & Brown, Gold	18.00
Haviland, Ice Cream Set, Flowers, Vines, Pink, Gray Green, 13 Piece	100.00
Haviland, Jar, Biscuit, Lily Of The Valley	75.00
Haviland, Jar, Biscuit, Pink Flowers, Gold Trim, With Lid & Plate	20.00
Haviland, Jar, Cracker, Hand-Painted, Ring Finial	30.00
Haviland, Match Holder, Green & White, Mounted On Saucer	35.00
Haviland, Nappy, Princess	25.00
Haviland, Plate, Amber, Basket Weave, 7 In.	6.50
Haviland, Plate, Cake, Green Leaf Decoration, Gold Trim, 12 In.	25.00
Haviland, Plate, Chop, White Flying Geese On Gold & Blue, Signed L.King	48.50
Haviland, Plate, Clover, Scallops, Gold Edge, Blank No.1, 8 3/4 In.	9.00
Haviland, Plate, Cobalt, Angel Head, Gold Pine Cones & Needles, 7 In.	27.00
Haviland, Plate, Dinner, Ransom	8.00
Haviland, Plate, Fish, Fish Swimming Against Blue, Floral, J.Martin, C.1899	35.00
Haviland, Plate, Fish, Hand-Painted Catfish On Green Ocean, C.1890	27.50
Haviland, Plate, Floral, Butterfly, Chateau St.Germain, Signed, 9 In., Set Of 6	125.00
Haviland, Plate, Lavender Mums, Hand-Painted, 7 1/2 In.	12.50
Haviland, Plate, Oyster, White, Gold Fluted Edge, 8 1/2 In., Set Of 12	335.00
Haviland, Plate, Pink Roses, Hand-Painted, Signed Cuthbertson, 8 3/4 In.	35.00
Haviland, Plate, Two Fish Swimming, Gold Rim, Artist Signature, 1913, 10 In.	30.00

Haviland, Plate, Wall, Pink Floral Motif, Scalloped Rim, Gold Trim, Limoges	6.50
Haviland, Plate, White Background, Bouquets Of Flowers, 12 In.	48.00
Haviland, Plate, Yellow Roses, Scallop Edge, 8 1/2 In.	22.50
Haviland, Platter, Baltimore Rose, 21 In.	85.00
Haviland, Platter, Cornflower, 12 1/2 X 8 1/4 In.	18.00
Haviland, Platter, Trianon, 16 In.	15.00
Haviland, Platter, Well & Tree, 19 In.	36.00
Haviland, Sauce Boat With Undertray, Painted Flowers, Butterfly	55.00
Haviland, Saucer, Red, Drop Rose	15.00
Haviland, Sugar & Creamer, Cover, Autumn Leaves, Gold Handles	52.00 To 60.00
Haviland, Sugar & Creamer, 24K Gold Trim	29.00
Haviland, Tea Set, All White With Gold Band, 3 Piece	75.00
Haviland, Tea Set, Limoges, Butterfly & Gold Spider Webbing, 3 Piece	125.00
Haviland, Tureen, Soup, White, Pink & Gray, Floral, Charles Field, 11 1/2 In.	95.00
Haviland, Tureen, Soup, White, Pink & Gray Floral, Charles Field, 14 1/2 In.	95.00
Haviland, Tureen, 2-Handled, Lidded, No.72, 11 3/4 In.	80.00

  T.G.Hawkes & Company of Corning, New York, was founded in 1880. The firm cut glass made at other firms until 1962. Many pieces are marked with the trademark, a trefoil ring enclosing a fleur-de-lis and two hawks.

Hawkes, see also Cut Glass

Hawkes, Atomizer, Green, Engraved, Gold Trim, Stemmed	28.00
Hawkes, Bottle, Oil & Vinegar, Signed	65.00
Hawkes, Bottle, Oil & Vinegar, Silver Stopper, C.1914	135.00
Hawkes, Bottle, Vinegar, Sterling Silver Top, Signed	40.00
Hawkes, Bowl, Brazilian Pattern, Signed, 8 3/4 X 2 1/2 In.	115.00
Hawkes, Bowl, Dessert, Cut Stars, Lines, Amber Comets, Signed, 4 X 2 1/4 In.	55.00
Hawkes, Bowl, Dessert, Intaglio Cut Stars, Lines, Amber Stained Comet Shapes	55.00
Hawkes, Bowl, Fans, Zippers, Squares, Middlesex, 8 X 1/2 X 3 In.	185.00
Hawkes, Bowl, Footed, Leaded Crystal, 5 X 5 In.	38.50
Hawkes, Bowl, Later Panel Pattern, Long, Low Ring, Signed Hawkes, 9 In.	130.00
Hawkes, Bowl, Punch, Brunswick Pattern, Hobstars, Vertical Prisms, 7 1/2 In.	650.00
Hawkes, Bowl, Salad, Vesica, Hobstars, 8 In.	145.00
Hawkes, Bowl, 4 Partitioned, Two Handled, Queen's Pattern, Signed, 11 In.	425.00
Hawkes, Candy, Cover, Engraved Flower, Swag, Signed	85.00
Hawkes, Cologne, Middlesex, Signed	95.00
Hawkes, Compote, Covered, Pedestal, Ruby Glass, Signed, 10 1/2 In.	425.00
Hawkes, Compote, Crystal, Etched Flower Designs, Gold Rims, 3 1/2 In.	35.00
Hawkes, Compote, Diamond Pattern, Teardrop Stem, Rayed Bottom, Signed, Pair	250.00
Hawkes, Compote, Diamond, Teardrop Stem, Rayed Bottom, Roll Rim, 6 In., Pair	250.00
Hawkes, Compote, Rock Crystal Cutting, Signed, 5 X 6 In.	60.00
Hawkes, Cup & Saucer, Frosted Bands, Punties, Stars, Notched Rim, Signed	160.00
Hawkes, Decanter, Allover Cut, Signed, Large	95.00
Hawkes, Decanter, Engraved Birds & Marsh, Sterling Silver Top & Lock	75.00
Hawkes, Decanter, Paneled Sides, Slender, Signed	125.00
Hawkes, Dish, Bonbon, Crystal, Floral Engraving, Footed, 5 1/4 In.	48.00
Hawkes, Dish, Ice Cream, , Set Of 4, 6 1/4 In.	120.00
Hawkes, Frame, Picture, Silver Trim, 12 X 14 In.	325.00
Hawkes, Glass, Flip, Signed	125.00
Hawkes, Glass, Wine, Engraved, Sterling Silver Stem, Set Of 8	275.00
Hawkes, Goblet, Floral & Leaf, Reeded, Green, Signed, 6 In.	60.00
Hawkes, Goblet, Water, Intaglio Carved, Set Of 12	160.00
Hawkes, Ice Bucket, Silver Rim & Bale Handle, Signed	40.00
Hawkes, Nappy, Cut Glass, Intaglio & Miter Cut, 6 In.	55.00
Hawkes, Nappy, Gravic, Iris Decoration, Handled, Signed	110.00
Hawkes, Pitcher, Hobstar, Fluted Panels, Handle, Signed, 7 In.	265.00
Hawkes, Plate, Dessert, Diamond Shapes Chain, Crosshatching Rim, 3 Feet, Pair	45.00
Hawkes, Plate, Dessert, Fancy Cut, Pressed Heavy Crystal, 5 1/4 In., Pair	125.00
Hawkes, Relish, Band Of Hobstars, Center Star, Spokes, Notched Rim, 7 X 5 In.	68.50
Hawkes, Table Set, Cut Salt, Pepper, Tray, Signed	60.00
Hawkes, Tray, Sandwich, Rock Crystal, Sterling Center Handle, 9 X 6 In.	95.00
Hawkes, Tumbler Set, Devonshire, 6 Piece	270.00
Hawkes, Vase, Art Deco, Square Base, Signed, 10 In.	60.00
Hawkes, Vase, Art Nouveau, Resembles Stylistic Blown Out Floral, Footed	90.00

Hawkes, Vase, Cut Glass, Signed, 14 In. 135.00
Hawkes, Vase, Engraved Chain & Leaf, 2 Hawkes In Trefoil Mark, 11 1/4 In. 65.00
Hawkes, Vase, Etched Floral, 8 In. 87.00
Hawkes, Vase, Flowers, Swag, Signed, 11 1/4 In. 38.00
Hawkes, Vase, Rayed Bottom, Gravic Glass, Signed, 10 In. 175.00
Hawkes, Vase, Square Base, Art Deco, 10 In. 50.00
Hawkes, Vase, Tiger Lily, Signed, 16 1/2 In. 210.00
Hawkes, Wine, Cranberry To Clear 39.00

Heisey glass was made from 1895 to 1958 in Newark, Ohio, by A.H.
Heisey and Co., Inc.
Heisey, see also Custard Glass

Heisey, Ashtray, Crystal, General's Cap 28.00
Heisey, Ashtray, Down Lodestar 50.00
Heisey, Ashtray, Hat 25.00
Heisey, Basket, Bowtie, Moonglo, Gold Trim 35.00
Heisey, Basket, Bowtie, Moonglo, 4 In. 21.50
Heisey, Basket, Butterfly & Floral, Etched, 11 In. 55.00
Heisey, Basket, Cut Roses On 2 Panels, Buds On 4 Panels, Applied Handle 90.00
Heisey, Basket, Etched, Flowers, Leaves, Signed, No.462 .... 65.00
Heisey, Basket, Flamingo Bowtie, 8 1/2 In. 35.00
Heisey, Basket, Flamingo, Octagon, 5 In. 35.00
Heisey, Basket, Flamingo, Pleat & Panel, 8 In. 37.50
Heisey, Basket, Flowers, Stars, Leaves, Fan Shaped, 15 In. 150.00
Heisey, Basket, Fruit, Leaf & Flower Cut Design 55.00
Heisey, Basket, Pink, Handled, Large 25.00
Heisey, Berry Bowl, Winged Scroll 95.00
Heisey, Berry Set, Beaded Swag, 7 Piece 360.00
Heisey, Berry Set, Colonial Pattern, Signed, 5 Piece 35.00
Heisey, Berry Set, Cross-Lined Flute, Patented, 5 Piece 35.00
Heisey, Berry Set, Custard Ring Band, Roses & Gold Trim 395.00
Heisey, Berry Set, Custard, Winged Scroll, No Gold, 7 Piece 225.00
Heisey, Berry Set, Ivorene Verde 550.00
Heisey, Berry Set, Prison Stripe, Gilt Trim, 7 Piece 195.00
Heisey, Berry Set, Sunburst 70.00
Heisey, Bonbon, Lariat, 8 In. 12.00
Heisey, Bookend, Fish .... 70.00 To 75.00
Heisey, Bookend, Fish, Pair 150.00
Heisey, Bookend, Horse Head, Pair 200.00
Heisey, Bottle, French Dressing, Puritan, Original Stopper 30.00
Heisey, Bottle, Oil, Pleat & Panel Moonglo 47.50
Heisey, Bottle, Oil, Yeoman, 2 Ozs. 22.00
Heisey, Bottle, Perfume, Crystal, 8 In. 50.00
Heisey, Bottle, Perfume, Etched Cut, Pedestal 12.00
Heisey, Bottle, Perfume, Wheel Cut, Flowers In Gold Basket, Applicator, 6 In. 80.00
Heisey, Bottle, Perfume, 8 In. 45.00
Heisey, Bottle, Water, Puritan 35.00
Heisey, Bowl & Base, Punch, Puritan, 13 In. 90.00
Heisey, Bowl & Plate, Finger, Ipswich 25.00
Heisey, Bowl & Stand, Punch, Crystal, Prison Stripe, 12 In. 295.00
Heisey, Bowl & Underplate, Crystolite, Signed 50.00
Heisey, Bowl & Underplate, Mayonnaise, Grapevine, Etched, 5 X 5 In. 40.00
Heisey, Bowl & Underplate, Queen Anne 95.00
Heisey, Bowl & Underplate, Zodiac, Limelight 50.00
Heisey, Bowl Set, Clear, Marked, Set Of 8, 5 In. 33.00
Heisey, Bowl, Berry, Custard Ring Band 125.00
Heisey, Bowl, Berry, Locket On Chain 77.50
Heisey, Bowl, Berry, Pinwheel & Fan 30.00
Heisey, Bowl, Bouillon, Plain Pattern, Wide Rim, Vaseline, 9 In. 75.00
Heisey, Bowl, Centerpiece, 8 Sided, 11 1/2 In. 40.00
Heisey, Bowl, Clear, Etched Flowers, Square, 8 1/2 In. 25.00
Heisey, Bowl, Clear, 5 In., Set Of 8 .... 32.00
Heisey, Bowl, Colonial, Marked, 9 1/2 In. 20.00
Heisey, Bowl, Colonial, 9 1/2 In. 12.00

Heisey, Bowl, Crystal, Oblong, 12 In.	20.00
Heisey, Bowl, Diamond Optic, Signed, 12 In.	35.00
Heisey, Bowl, Diamond Optic, 4 In.	55.00
Heisey, Bowl, Dolphin Footed, Etched Flowers, Large	38.00
Heisey, Bowl, Dolphin Footed, 6 In.	11.95
Heisey, Bowl, Empress, Lion's Head	295.00
Heisey, Bowl, Empress, Orchid Etched, 6 In.	30.00
Heisey, Bowl, Empressed Dolphin Footed, 11 In.	25.00
Heisey, Bowl, Etched Baskets & Flowers, 3 Dolphin Feet, 10 In.	18.00
Heisey, Bowl, Etched Orchid, Flared, 12 In.	25.00
Heisey, Bowl, Finger, Fancy Loop	8.00
Heisey, Bowl, Finger, Rib & Panel	6.00
Heisey, Bowl, Fish, Signed, 9 In.	450.00
Heisey, Bowl, Flamingo, Footed, 11 In.	30.00
Heisey, Bowl, Floral, Ipswich, 11 In.	32.00
Heisey, Bowl, Flower, Arctic, Dolphin Feet, 11 In.	67.50
Heisey, Bowl, Footed, Empress, Orchid Etched, 7 In.	30.00
Heisey, Bowl, Footed, Empress, 11 In.	40.00
Heisey, Bowl, Footed, Meander, Opal To Green, 9 In.	23.00
Heisey, Bowl, Fruit, Dawn Lodestar, 12 In.	90.00
Heisey, Bowl, Fruit, Marked, 9 In.	18.00
Heisey, Bowl, Fruit, Plunger Cut	60.00
Heisey, Bowl, Fruit, Ridgeleigh Pattern, Swan Handles, 14 In.Long	65.00
Heisey, Bowl, Fruit, Ridgeleigh, 9 X 4 In.	30.00
Heisey, Bowl, Greek Key, Flat Rim, Large	40.00
Heisey, Bowl, Green Floral, Octagon, Base, 11 In.	22.50
Heisey, Bowl, Horn Of Plenty, Footed, Ribbed And Scalloped, 11 X 5 In.	50.00
Heisey, Bowl, Larger Underplate, Signed, 12 In.	75.00
Heisey, Bowl, Lariat, 10 X 4 In.	25.00
Heisey, Bowl, Lariat, 12 X 3 In.	30.00
Heisey, Bowl, Lariat, 3 Section, 10 In.	30.00
Heisey, Bowl, Lariat, 7 X 3 In.	15.00
Heisey, Bowl, Limelight Saturn, Optic, 6 1/4 X 1 3/4 In.	20.00
Heisey, Bowl, Lion Headed, Sahara, Empress, Lion Footed, 4 Sculptured Heads	300.00
Heisey, Bowl, Orchid Etched, 12 In.	35.00
Heisey, Bowl, Orchid, 9 In.	21.75
Heisey, Bowl, Oval Floral, Sahara	52.50
Heisey, Bowl, Oval, Zircon, Signed, 6 1/2 In.	29.00
Heisey, Bowl, Pineapple & Fan, 8 In.	55.00
Heisey, Bowl, Pleat & Panel, Pink, Set Of 12	75.00
Heisey, Bowl, Punch, Footed, Greek Key, No.433	195.00
Heisey, Bowl, Punch, Greek Key, 15 X 15 In.	200.00
Heisey, Bowl, Punch, Prince Of Wales Plume, Base	175.00
Heisey, Bowl, Punch, Punty & Diamond Point, No.305	95.00
Heisey, Bowl, Punch, Tulip Shape, Base, 11 1/4 X 13 1/2 In.	175.00
Heisey, Bowl, Queen Anne, Dolphin Feet, Flowers, Butterfly Bird, Large	35.00
Heisey, Bowl, Sahara, Dolphin Footed, 6 In.	18.95
Heisey, Bowl, Sahara, Queen Anne, Dolphin Foot, 5 1/4 In.	21.50
Heisey, Bowl, Salad, Crystolite, Clear, 12 In.	14.00
Heisey, Bowl, Sea Horse, Footed	25.00
Heisey, Bowl, Silver Plate Band, Etched Festoons, Silver Trim, 10 X 3 In.	49.00
Heisey, Bowl, Waverly Orchid, Etched, 12 In.	32.00
Heisey, Bowl, Waverly, Floral, Orchid Etching, 13 In.	22.00
Heisey, Bowl, Waverly, Floral, Rose Etching, 13 In.	25.00
Heisey, Bowl, 3 Dolphin Feet, Etched Flowers & Baskets, 10 In.	18.00
Heisey, Box, Candy, Gold Metal Engraved Cover, Wreath Pattern	42.00
Heisey, Box, Cigarette, Covered, Crystolite, 4 In.	18.00
Heisey, Box, Cigarette, Crystolite	12.00
Heisey, Box, Cigarette, Horse Head	45.00
Heisey, Box, Cigarette, Puritan, Horse Head Finial, 4 In.	39.00
Heisey, Box, Cigarette, Ribbed	18.00
Heisey, Box, Covered, Round, Finial Top, 7 X 4 1/2 In.	38.00
Heisey, Box, Crystal, Victorian, Covered, 4 1/4 In.	23.50
Heisey, Box, Trinket, Emerald, Winged Scroll, Souvenir, 1910	65.00
Heisey, Box, Trinket, Opalescent, Winged Scroll, Souvenir, Coldwater, Mich.	50.00

Heisey, Bucket, Ice, Fancy Loop	75.00
Heisey, Bucket, Ice, Greek Key, 6 1/2 In.	50.00
Heisey, Bucket, Ice, Oceanic, Flamingo Color, Oval, 8 3/4 X 5 1/2 X 5 In.	43.00
Heisey, Bucket, Ice, Swirl, Hammered Silver Bail	45.00
Heisey, Butter Lid, Flowers, Beaded Swag, Opalescent	65.00
Heisey, Butter Pat, Old Sandwich, Etched Flower	6.00
Heisey, Butter Pat, Panel, Set Of 4	16.00
Heisey, Butter, Covered, Beaded Swag	130.00
Heisey, Butter, Covered, Beaded Swag, Etched	125.00
Heisey, Butter, Covered, Winged Scroll, Custard & Gold	195.00
Heisey, Butter, Heisey Rose, Covered	57.00
Heisey, Butter, Pineapple & Fan, Green	75.00
Heisey, Butter, Puritan, Covered	45.00
Heisey, Cake Stand, Etched, 11 3/4 In.Diameter, 2 1/4 In.High	60.00
Heisey, Candelabra, Orchid Etched, Single Light, Queen Anne, Pair	55.00
Heisey, Candelabra, Single Light, Orchid Etched, Queen Anne, Pair	85.00
Heisey, Candelabra, Two Branch, Orchid, Pair	47.00
Heisey, Candelbra, Single Light, Colonial, 9 1/2 In.	65.00
Heisey, Candleblock, Crystolite, Flamingo, Pair	40.00
Heisey, Candleblock, Crystolite, Pair	9.50
Heisey, Candleblock, Flamingo, No.99, Pair	15.00
Heisey, Candleblock, Whirlpool, Pair	35.00
Heisey, Candleholder, Crystal, Pair	18.00
Heisey, Candleholder, Handled, 4 1/2 In.	12.50
Heisey, Candleholder, Regency, 2 Candle, Colonial Bobeches, Signed	40.00
Heisey, Candleholder, 2 Light, Crystolite, Pair	35.00
Heisey, Candlestick, Chamber, Banded Flute	35.00
Heisey, Candlestick, Cornucopia, Single Holder, Pair	20.00
Heisey, Candlestick, Crystolite Swirl, Pair	18.00
Heisey, Candlestick, Dolphin, Flamingo, 10 1/2 In., Pair	200.00
Heisey, Candlestick, Emerald Green, No.110, 10 In.	175.00
Heisey, Candlestick, Flamingo Dolphin, One-Light Petticoat, Pair	245.00
Heisey, Candlestick, Flamingo, No.113, 3 1/2 In., Pair	15.00
Heisey, Candlestick, Grape, Double M, Pair, 10 In.	185.00
Heisey, Candlestick, Moonglo, No.116, Pair	15.00
Heisey, Candlestick, Old Sandwich, 6 In.	20.00
Heisey, Candlestick, Orchid	27.50
Heisey, Candlestick, Ring Handle, Miniature	15.00
Heisey, Candlestick, Sahara Empress, Dolphin Footed, Signed, Pair	185.00
Heisey, Candlestick, Toy, No.31, Pair	40.00
Heisey, Candlestick, Toy, No.5	40.00
Heisey, Candlestick, Toy, No.5, Pair	75.00
Heisey, Candlestick, Triple, No.136, Flamingo, Signed, 6 1/4 In., Pair	85.00
Heisey, Candlestick, 8 Sided, Clear, Pair, 7 1/2 In.	45.00
Heisey, Candy Dish, Etched, Ribbed, Signed, 10 In.	45.00
Heisey, Candy Dish, Ipswich, Purple, Lid, 10 In.	75.00
Heisey, Celery, Amber Satin, 12 In.	47.50
Heisey, Celery, Block Pattern, Star Rayed Bottom, 12 In.	13.00
Heisey, Celery, Fancy Loop	38.00
Heisey, Celery, Flamingo, Marked, 12 X 5 In.	25.00
Heisey, Celery, Flamingo, 12 In.	15.00
Heisey, Celery, Lodestar, 10 In.	47.50
Heisey, Celery, Metal Frame, Yellow, 9 In.	26.00
Heisey, Celery, Paneled Insert, Silver Plated Frame, C.1900	45.00
Heisey, Celery, Rib & Panel, 12 In.	20.00
Heisey, Celery, Star, Rayed Center, Oblong, Pink	25.00
Heisey, Celery, Sunburst, 12 In.	40.00
Heisey, Chamberstick, Signed, Pair	40.00
Heisey, Champagne, African Stem, Moonglo Foot	45.00
Heisey, Champagne, Banded Flute	6.00 To 15.00
Heisey, Champagne, Cobalt, Spanish Stem	50.00
Heisey, Champagne, Danish Princess, Saucer, 6 1/4 In.	15.00
Heisey, Champagne, Duquesne, Sahara	20.00
Heisey, Champagne, Orchid	16.50
Heisey, Champagne, Sahara, Sandwich	11.50

Heisey, Champagne, Saucer Base, Kalarama, Monte Cristo Stem, 6 Ozs.	35.00
Heisey, Champagne, Symphone, Danish Princess	11.00
Heisey, Champagne, Tangerine, Spanish Stem	170.00
Heisey, Cigarette Box, Ribbed, Marked	18.00
Heisey, Claret, Kalarama, Monte Cristo Stem, 4 Ozs.	35.00
Heisey, Coaster, Lariat	4.00
Heisey, Coaster, Rib & Panel, Set Of 6	18.00
Heisey, Cocktail Shaker, Strainer & Rooster Head Stopper, 1 1/2 Quart	45.00
Heisey, Cocktail, Oyster, Sahara, Queen Anne, Old Colony Etching	11.50
Heisey, Cocktail, Rooster Head, 4 1/4 In.	32.00
Heisey, Cocktail, Rooster Stem, 5 5/8 In.	35.00
Heisey, Cocktail, Tyrolean Stem, No.5025	22.00
Heisey, Comport, Greek Key, 5 X 5 1/2 In.	38.00
Heisey, Comport, Jelly, Narrow Flute, 5 X 5 1/4 In.	15.00
Heisey, Compote, Charter Oak, Moonglo	45.00
Heisey, Compote, Colonial Style, Signed, 5 1/2 In.	20.00
Heisey, Compote, Colonial, Signed, 4 X 5 In.	25.00
Heisey, Compote, Crimped Bowl, No.1225, 8 1/2 X 8 In.	50.00
Heisey, Compote, Diamond Optic, Footed, 6 1/2 In.	12.00
Heisey, Compote, Empress, Oval, Cut	50.00
Heisey, Compote, Etched Orchid, Scalloped, 6 In.	18.00
Heisey, Compote, Gold Trimmed, 10 1/2 In.	38.00
Heisey, Compote, Jelly, Course Rib, 5 In.	12.00
Heisey, Compote, Locket & Chain, 7 1/4 In.	75.00
Heisey, Compote, Moonglo, Rib & Panel, 5 In.	15.00
Heisey, Compote, Orchid Etched, Scalloped, 6 In.	18.00
Heisey, Compote, Orchid, Waverly	24.95
Heisey, Compote, Pleat & Panel, Pedestal, Lid, Signed	35.00
Heisey, Compote, Twist Green, Signed, 5 In.	17.50
Heisey, Condiment Set, Gold Decorated, 5 Piece	70.00
Heisey, Cordial Set, Rooster Decanter, 8 Moonglo Wines	325.00
Heisey, Cordial, Jamestown, 1 Oz.	42.50
Heisey, Cordial, Narrow Flute, 1 Oz., Set Of 4	75.00
Heisey, Creamer, Diamond Shape, Cut Leaves & Flowers, Dated 1917	75.00
Heisey, Creamer, Diamond, Pedestal	12.00
Heisey, Creamer, Etched Orchid	17.50
Heisey, Creamer, Individual, Beaded Swag, Ruby Stained	50.00
Heisey, Creamer, Prince Of Wales	35.00
Heisey, Creamer, Queen Anne, Etched	20.00
Heisey, Creamer, Rose Decoration, Ring Band	75.00
Heisey, Creamer, Souvenir, Belgrade Lakes, Maine, Punty Band	35.00
Heisey, Creamer, With Sugar Cube Tray, Lavender, 4 In.	50.00
Heisey, Cruet, Clear, Fancy Loop, Stopper	45.00
Heisey, Cruet, Colonial, Flower Cutting	45.00
Heisey, Cruet, Crystolite	25.00 To 28.00
Heisey, Cruet, Custard, Ring Band	135.00
Heisey, Cruet, Empress, Cut	45.00
Heisey, Cruet, Flowers, Beaded, Swag, Emerald Green, White, Stopper	135.00
Heisey, Cruet, Moonglo, Twist	45.00
Heisey, Cruet, Orchard Etched, Waverly	95.00
Heisey, Cruet, Saturn Optic, Stopper	25.00
Heisey, Cruet, Saturn, Sterling Stopper	30.00
Heisey, Cruet, With Stopper, Old Sandwich	27.00
Heisey, Cup & Saucer, Beaded Swag, Ruby Stained, Souvenir, Mother	35.00
Heisey, Cup & Saucer, Deep Etching, Save America-Elect London	190.00
Heisey, Cup & Saucer, Greek Key, Gold Trim	45.00
Heisey, Cup & Saucer, Oceanic, Moonglo	15.00
Heisey, Cup & Saucer, Orchid Etching, No.1401	22.00
Heisey, Cup & Saucer, Pink	12.00
Heisey, Cup, Nut, Alexandrite, Dolphin Footed	50.00
Heisey, Cup, Nut, Colonial	60.00
Heisey, Cup, Nut, Moonglo, Octagon	7.00
Heisey, Cup, Punch, Banded Panel, Signed, Dozen	40.00
Heisey, Cup, Punch, Beaded Panel & Sunburst	20.00
Heisey, Cup, Punch, Colonial, Star Base	5.00

Heisey, Cup, Punch, Continental	15.00
Heisey, Cup, Punch, Fancy Loop, Crystal	10.00
Heisey, Cup, Punch, Greek Key	12.00 To 16.00
Heisey, Cup, Punch, Marked	3.50
Heisey, Cup, Punch, Pinwheel & Fan, Numbered	9.00
Heisey, Cup, Punch, Prince Of Wales Plumes, Clear	15.00
Heisey, Cup, Punch, Prince Of Wales Plumes, Numbered	12.00
Heisey, Cup, Punch, Raised Loop	20.00
Heisey, Cup, Punch, Rib & Panel	15.00
Heisey, Cup, Punch, Victorian, Marked	9.00
Heisey, Decanter, Alexandrite, No Stopper	100.00
Heisey, Decanter, Moonglo	130.00
Heisey, Dish & Underplate, Ribbed, Enameled	40.00
Heisey, Dish, Baked Apple, Engraved Narrow Flute With Rim, No.473	25.00
Heisey, Dish, Banana Split, Greek Key, Pedestal	15.00
Heisey, Dish, Banana, Greek Key, Signed	55.00
Heisey, Dish, Bonbon, Fern, 6 In.	12.00
Heisey, Dish, Candy, Blue & Pink Enameled Floral Band On Cobalt, 11 1/4 In.	35.00
Heisey, Dish, Candy, Covered, Gold Trim, 8 In.	22.50
Heisey, Dish, Candy, Covered, Pleat & Panel, Pink	30.00
Heisey, Dish, Candy, Covered, Sea Horse Handles, Rose Etching, 2 In.Finial	45.00
Heisey, Dish, Candy, Etched, 6 In.	12.00
Heisey, Dish, Candy, Glass Flower On Brass Lid, Marked	34.00
Heisey, Dish, Candy, Heart Shaped, 5 In.	20.00
Heisey, Dish, Candy, Imperial Slag, Waverly, Signed	45.00
Heisey, Dish, Candy, Silver Leaves, Handled, 8 X 3 1/4 In.	22.00
Heisey, Dish, Cheese & Cracker, Colonial	25.00
Heisey, Dish, Cheese & Cracker, Silver Trim, Engraved Floral Design	35.00
Heisey, Dish, Divided, Handled, Signed, 10 3/4 In.	28.00
Heisey, Dish, Empress Flamingo, 2 Handled, Diagonal, 13 In.	18.00
Heisey, Dish, Glass Flower, Metal Lid	40.00
Heisey, Dish, Greek Key, Clear, 2 Handles, 5 1/2 In.	21.00
Heisey, Dish, Individual Jelly, Diamond Point	6.50
Heisey, Dish, Jelly, 2 Handled, Marigold, Signed	25.00
Heisey, Dish, Lemon, Dolphin Finial, Queen Anne, Farberware Holder	35.00
Heisey, Dish, Nut & Mint, Divided, Etched Sterling Base	48.00
Heisey, Dish, Nut, Greek Key	15.00
Heisey, Dish, Nut, Moonglo, Octagon	10.00
Heisey, Dish, Nut, Queen Anne Sahara	15.00
Heisey, Dish, Nut, Swan	15.00
Heisey, Dish, Pickle, Fandango, 6 1/4 In.	15.00
Heisey, Dish, Pickle, Greek Key, 9 In.	25.00
Heisey, Dish, Plantation, Divided, 5 1/2 X 3 1/2 In.	32.00
Heisey, Dish, Relish, Compartmented, Molded Handle Pattern, 11 In.	25.00
Heisey, Dish, Relish, Flamingo, 6 In.	22.00
Heisey, Dish, Rib & Panel, No.411, 2-Handled, Hawthorne	24.00
Heisey, Dish, Serving, Lariat, Oval, 2 X 12 In.	8.00 To 12.00
Heisey, Dish, Wide Rib Turned Up At Sides, Handles, Star Bottom, 6 1/4 In.	12.50
Heisey, Dish, 4 Sections, Handle, Ridgeleigh, 10 1/2 In.	40.00
Heisey, Eggcup, Puritan	10.00
Heisey, Figurine, , Mallard, Wing Up	135.00
Heisey, Figurine, Bunnies	85.00
Heisey, Figurine, Chick	35.00
Heisey, Figurine, Colt, Free Standing, Signed	65.00
Heisey, Figurine, Dog, Clydesdales	195.00
Heisey, Figurine, Fighting Rooster	85.00
Heisey, Figurine, Floating Duckling	95.00
Heisey, Figurine, Giraffe, Head Back	135.00
Heisey, Figurine, Giraffe, Head Backward	100.00
Heisey, Figurine, Giraffe, Head Sideways	110.00
Heisey, Figurine, Goose, Wings Down	210.00
Heisey, Figurine, Goose, Wings Halfway, 4 1/2 X 8 1/2 In.	47.50 To 80.00
Heisey, Figurine, Goose, Wings Up	45.00 To 80.00
Heisey, Figurine, Horse, Fillies, Head Turned	1750.00
Heisey, Figurine, Horse, Frosted Head, 1 1/2 In.	20.00

Heisey, Figurine, Horse, Head Straight	1600.00
Heisey, Figurine, Horse, Kicking Colt	145.00
Heisey, Figurine, Horse, Show	750.00
Heisey, Figurine, Horse, Sparky	95.00
Heisey, Figurine, Horse, Standing Colt	65.00
Heisey, Figurine, Madonna	40.00
Heisey, Figurine, Madonna, Frosted, 9 In.	35.00
Heisey, Figurine, Mallard, Wing Down	165.00
Heisey, Figurine, Plug Horse	75.00
Heisey, Figurine, Pony, Standing	55.00
Heisey, Figurine, Scotty	75.00
Heisey, Figurine, Signet, Signed	100.00
Heisey, Figurine, Sitting Duckling, Signed	85.00
Heisey, Figurine, Sparky, Plug Horse	75.00
Heisey, Figurine, Sparrow	60.00 To 75.00
Heisey, Figurine, Wren, Frosted	90.00
Heisey, Glass, Cocktail, Stanhope	15.00
Heisey, Glass, Iced Tea, Duquesne, Normandy Etched	10.00
Heisey, Glass, Iced Tea, Moonglo, Old Sandwich	17.50
Heisey, Glass, Shot, Double, Moonglo, Fancy Loop Variant	75.00
Heisey, Glass, Shot, Plain	6.00
Heisey, Glass, Shot, Rib & Panel	9.50
Heisey, Glass, Soda, Ipswich, Marked, 5 3/4 In.	12.00
Heisey, Glass, Soda, Provincial, 12 Oz.	35.00
Heisey, Goblet, Bead Swag, Custard, Souvenir, Theresa, Wisc.	55.00
Heisey, Goblet, Bead Swag, Red Roses, Custard	65.00
Heisey, Goblet, Beaded Swag, Custard, Souvenir	70.00
Heisey, Goblet, Carcassonne, Short Stem, No.3390, 7 In.	18.00
Heisey, Goblet, Cocktail, Rooster	45.00
Heisey, Goblet, Colonial	10.00
Heisey, Goblet, Comet	15.00
Heisey, Goblet, Crystal, Etched, Tyrolean Stems, Set Of 8	160.00
Heisey, Goblet, Custard, Beaded, Souvenir, Churchs Ferry, N.D.	60.00
Heisey, Goblet, Etched Belle La Rose, No.5009	25.00
Heisey, Goblet, Greek Key, Marked	85.00
Heisey, Goblet, Kalarama, Monte Cristo Stem, 9 Ozs.	35.00
Heisey, Goblet, Minuet Etching, Symphone Stem, 9 Ounces	17.00
Heisey, Goblet, Orchid Etched, 6 In.	15.00
Heisey, Goblet, Pied Piper	24.00
Heisey, Goblet, Pied Piper, Etched, Tall	14.00
Heisey, Goblet, Pied Piper, Tall Stemmed, Signed	13.00
Heisey, Goblet, Renaissance Etch	15.00
Heisey, Goblet, Rose	27.00
Heisey, Goblet, Rose Decoration, Beaded, Swag, Custard	48.00
Heisey, Goblet, Sahara, Diamond Optic, No.3368 Stem	15.00
Heisey, Goblet, Sahara, Diamond Optic, Yeoman Stem	18.50
Heisey, Goblet, Saturn Optic, Tall Stem	22.00
Heisey, Goblet, Symphone With Minuet Etching	25.00
Heisey, Goblet, Tall Stemmed, Olympiad	17.00
Heisey, Goblet, Toddy, Sahara, Optic, Pair	22.00
Heisey, Goblet, Water, Ipswich, Set Of 6	14.00
Heisey, Goblet, Waverly, Signed	10.00
Heisey, Goblet, Zircon Saturn, Stanhope	39.00
Heisey, Hair Receiver, Silver Overlay	20.00
Heisey, Hair Receiver, Squared Fan, Silver Top	45.00
Heisey, Hair Receiver, Star Base, Silver Overlay	45.00
Heisey, Holder, Cigarette, Moonglo, Rib & Panel, Covered	47.50
Heisey, Holder, Cigarette, Signed, Pair	15.00
Heisey, Humidor, Colonial Pattern, Marked	68.00
Heisey, Ice Bucket, Dolphin Footed, Sterling Overlay	35.00
Heisey, Jar, Candy, Covered, Narrow Flute, Enameled & Gold Decorated, No.393	42.00
Heisey, Jar, Candy, Gold Enameled Flowers, Lid, 11 In.	50.00
Heisey, Jar, Candy, Steeple Cover, 9 1/2 In.	20.00
Heisey, Jar, Covered, Notched Prism, 2 1/4 In.	5.00
Heisey, Jar, Cracker, Covered, Beaded Panel & Sunburst	135.00

Heisey, Jar, Flat Panel, No.352, Signed & Dated, 2 Quart	95.00
Heisey, Jar, Footed, Allover Panels Of Gold, Gold Finial, Signed, 9 1/2 In.	45.00
Heisey, Jar, Jam, Floral, Frosted Etching, Lid, Signed	22.50
Heisey, Jar, Lavender, Williamsburg, 6 In.	15.00
Heisey, Jar, Powder, Embossed Silver Plate Cover	15.00
Heisey, Jar, Powder, Gold Jeweled Cover	35.00
Heisey, Jar, Powder, Sterling Raised Flower Cover, Large, Signed	25.00
Heisey, Jar, Ridgeleigh, Ribbed, Floral Overlay, Lid, Heisey Mark In Diamond	45.00
Heisey, Jar, Silver Deposit Apothecary, Silver Scrolling, Stopper, Signed	75.00
Heisey, Jelly, Greek Key, Footed, 5 In.	32.50
Heisey, Jug, Puritan, 1/2 Gallon	45.00 To 55.00
Heisey, Jug, Sahara	67.00
Heisey, Match Holder, Winged Scroll, Green & Gold	85.00
Heisey, Mayonnaise Bowl & Ladle, Flamingo, Empress, Dolphin Foot, Signed	28.00
Heisey, Mayonnaise Set, Jeannette, Blue	25.00
Heisey, Mayonnaise, Etched Poppies, 3 Piece	20.00
Heisey, Mayonnaise, Underplate, Signed, 6 X 3 In.	25.00
Heisey, Muffineer, Plantation	35.00
Heisey, Mug, Beaded Swag, Ruby Stained	35.00
Heisey, Mug, Pineapple & Fan, Emerald With Gold, Souvenir	30.00
Heisey, Mug, Sand-Etched Sporting Subject, 16 Oz.	100.00
Heisey, Nappy, Beaded Swag, Custard, Souvenir	30.00
Heisey, Nappy, Crisscross, 4 In.	15.00
Heisey, Nappy, Hawthorne, Rib & Panel, Curved	25.00
Heisey, Nappy, Hawthorne, Rib & Panel, 2 Handled	25.00
Heisey, Nappy, Milk Glass, Beaded Swag, Metal Base	15.00
Heisey, Nappy, Opalescent, Pink Bottom, 4 In.	45.00
Heisey, Nappy, Prison Stripe, Clear, 5 In.	18.00
Heisey, Nappy, Puritan, 8 In.	22.00
Heisey, Nappy, Sunburst, Crimped, 10 In.	40.00
Heisey, Nappy, 2 Handled, Crystolite, 5 In.	15.00
Heisey, Nut Server, Rectangular, Pink, 3 X 5 In., Set Of 4	25.00
Heisey, Parfait, Moonglo, Footed, Etched	16.00
Heisey, Perfume, Clear Dauber, Stopper, Signed	30.00
Heisey, Pitcher, Colonial, Large, Squatty	29.50
Heisey, Pitcher, Flamingo Empress, Dolphin Footed, Signed	90.00
Heisey, Pitcher, Lodestar, Dawn, 8 In.	40.00
Heisey, Pitcher, Milk, Greek Key	50.00
Heisey, Pitcher, Milk, Pressed Panels Outside, Scalloped Lip, Signed, 8 In.	65.00
Heisey, Pitcher, Pinwheel & Fan, Large	18.00
Heisey, Pitcher, Raised Panel, Signed & Dated, 6 1/2 In.	45.00
Heisey, Pitcher, Ribbed, Applied Handle, 6 1/8 X 5 In.	42.00
Heisey, Pitcher, Single Row & Slash, 3 Pint	40.00
Heisey, Pitcher, Squatty, Bulbous, 7 In.	45.00
Heisey, Pitcher, Tankard, Winged Scroll	175.00
Heisey, Pitcher, Tomato Juice, Sahara, Gascony	55.00
Heisey, Pitcher, Water, Greek Key	75.00
Heisey, Pitcher, Water, Moonglo, 1/2 Gallon	65.00
Heisey, Pitcher, Water, Moonglo, 6 In.	55.00
Heisey, Pitcher, Water, Paneled, Applied Handle, Star Bottom, 9 In.	25.00
Heisey, Pitcher, Water, Plain Panel, No.429, Quart	45.00
Heisey, Pitcher, Water, Royal Oak, Frosted & Cranberry	265.00
Heisey, Pitcher, Water, Signed 5-10-10	75.00
Heisey, Pitcher, Water, Williamsburg, Clear, Signed	25.00
Heisey, Plate Set, Empress, Sahara Color, 6 In., Set Of 12	50.00
Heisey, Plate, Alexandrite, Empress, 8 In.Square	35.00 To 38.00
Heisey, Plate, Beehive, Clear, 4 In.	10.00
Heisey, Plate, Beehive, Clear, 8 In.	15.00
Heisey, Plate, Beehive, Clear, 14 In.	80.00
Heisey, Plate, Beehive, Flamingo, 8 In.	20.00
Heisey, Plate, Beehive, Flamingo, 14 In.	100.00
Heisey, Plate, Beehive, Moonglo, 8 In.	25.00
Heisey, Plate, Cake, Black & Gold Band On Edge, Marked, 11 3/4 X 2 1/4 In.	47.50
Heisey, Plate, Cake, Etched Flowers, Signed, 14 In.	20.00
Heisey, Plate, Coarse Rib, No.407, 6 In.	6.75

Heisey, Plate, Colonial, Set Of Eight, 7 1/2 In.	30.00
Heisey, Plate, Colonial, 6 In., Twelve	66.00
Heisey, Plate, Colonial, 6 1/2 In.	4.00
Heisey, Plate, Colonial, 7 1/2 In.	5.00
Heisey, Plate, Cracker & Cheese, Signed, Grecian Border, 10 In.	25.00
Heisey, Plate, Empress, Chintz Etching, 6 In.Square	12.50
Heisey, Plate, Etched Flower, 13 In.	24.00
Heisey, Plate, Flamingo, Beehive, 8 In.	12.50
Heisey, Plate, Flamingo, Twist, Signed, 7 In.	5.00
Heisey, Plate, Hors D'oeuvre, Moonglo, Empress, Handled, 13 1/2 In.	18.00
Heisey, Plate, Lariat, 7 1/2 In.	5.50
Heisey, Plate, Lariat, 8 In.	5.50
Heisey, Plate, Lariat, 9 In.	20.00
Heisey, Plate, Luncheon, No.1401, 8 1/2 In.	14.00
Heisey, Plate, Marigold, 6 In.	12.00
Heisey, Plate, Moonglo, Beehive, 8 In.	30.00
Heisey, Plate, Moonglo, Beehive, 13 In.	115.00
Heisey, Plate, Moonglo, Empress, 6 In.	6.00
Heisey, Plate, Muffin, Old Colony, Etched, Handled	32.00
Heisey, Plate, Oceanic, Moonglo, 7 In.	10.00
Heisey, Plate, Oyster, Old Dominion, Etched In Sahara	18.00
Heisey, Plate, Paneled, Deep, Signed, 9 1/4 In.	12.00
Heisey, Plate, Queen Anne, Tangerine, 8 In.	170.00
Heisey, Plate, Rib, Narrow, Star Bottom, 7 1/4 In.	11.50
Heisey, Plate, Ribbed Pattern, Pink, Signed, 7 1/2 In., Set Of 11	40.00
Heisey, Plate, Sahara, Set Of 13, 6 In.	50.00
Heisey, Plate, Sandwich Pattern, Clear, 12 Pieces, 7 In.	60.00
Heisey, Plate, Sandwich, Center Handle, Cut Flowers	32.00
Heisey, Plate, Sandwich, Clear, Heavy Silver Overlay, Lariat, Unmarked, 14 In.	37.50
Heisey, Plate, Sandwich, Handled, Pink	32.00
Heisey, Plate, Serving, Center Handle, Marked, 11 In.Diameter	25.00
Heisey, Plate, Square, Ipswich Sahara, 8 In.	15.00
Heisey, Plate, Tangerine, Marked, 6 In.	100.00
Heisey, Platter, Alexandrite, 2 Handled, Round, 12 In.	125.00
Heisey, Platter, Alexandrite, 14 In.	30.00
Heisey, Platter, Oval Dish Insert, 13 1/2 In.	45.00
Heisey, Plumes, Prince Of Wales	65.00
Heisey, Punch Bowl & Base, Greek Key	185.00
Heisey, Punch Bowl Set, Lariat, 15 Piece, 21 In.Diameter	275.00
Heisey, Punch Bowl, Fancy Loop, Footed, Crimped	90.00
Heisey, Punch Bowl, Greek Key, Green	75.00
Heisey, Punch Set, Greek Key, 14 Piece	400.00
Heisey, Punch Set, Lariat, 8 Piece	99.00
Heisey, Relish, Crystolite	20.00
Heisey, Relish, Divided, 9 In.	15.00
Heisey, Relish, Lariat, Three Part, Signed, 10 1/4 In.	20.00
Heisey, Relish, Lariat, 3 Sectioned, 10 In.Diameter	27.50
Heisey, Relish, Lariat, 8 1/2 In.	14.00
Heisey, Relish, Oceanic Twist, Marigold, 7 In.	32.00
Heisey, Relish, Puritan, No.341	14.00
Heisey, Relish, Rose, 3 Compartment, 11 In.	27.00
Heisey, Relish, Sahara, Queen Anne, 10 1/2 In.	12.00
Heisey, Relish, Sahara, Queen Anne, 13 In.	15.00
Heisey, Relish, Triplex, 7 In.	25.00
Heisey, Rose Bowl, Pineapple & Fan, Green, Gold, 4 In.	53.00
Heisey, Salt & Pepper, Beaded Swag	50.00
Heisey, Salt & Pepper, Individual, Oval Tray	25.00
Heisey, Salt & Pepper, Orchid, Etched, Waverly	20.00
Heisey, Salt & Pepper, Pineapple & Fan, Sterling Tops	35.00
Heisey, Salt & Pepper, Ruby Stained, Wagoner Street Fair, 1901	45.00
Heisey, Salt Dip, Sawtooth, Signed	8.00
Heisey, Salt Set, Diamond Cut, Polished Star Bottoms, 12 Piece	75.00
Heisey, Salt Set, Rippled Rim, Sunburst Bottom, 2 1/2 In., 12 Pieces	60.00
Heisey, Salt, Fancy Loop	12.00
Heisey, Salt, Figural, Swan	11.00

Heisey, Salt, Ring Band, Souvenir, Stark, Maine	28.00
Heisey, Salt, Single, With Top, Turquoise, Little Gem	50.00
Heisey, Salt, Swan, Small	11.00
Heisey, Saltshaker, Beaded Swag, Gold Band Trim	22.00
Heisey, Sauce Boat, Narrow Flute, Crystal, Footed	12.00
Heisey, Sauce, Empress Sahara, Dolphin Footed, 7 1/2 In.	18.50
Heisey, Sauce, Plain, Star Bottom, 4 1/8 In.	4.50
Heisey, Saucer, Champaign Plantation, 5 1/2 Oz.	15.00
Heisey, Server, Moonglo, Center Handle, Signed, 11 In.	35.00
Heisey, Shade, Crystal, Punty & Diamond Point, 8 In.	52.50
Heisey, Shaker Set, Rose, Punty Band, Custard, Oxford, Wisconsin, Pair	65.00
Heisey, Shaker, Cocktail, Cut Antelope, One Quart	55.00
Heisey, Shaker, Cocktail, Rooster Head, Engraved, 10 1/2 In. .... 50.00 To 58.00	
Heisey, Shaker, Cocktail, Rooster Stopper	60.00
Heisey, Sherbert Set, Fluted, Footed, Marked On Stem, Set Of 12	7.50
Heisey, Sherbet, Flamingo, Egyptian Pattern	8.50
Heisey, Sherbet, Flute, Set Of 8	40.00
Heisey, Sherbet, Frontenac, Etched, Signed	13.00
Heisey, Sherbet, Greek Key, Footed, 4 1/2 In.	5.00
Heisey, Sherbet, Kalarama, Monte Cristo Stem, 6 Ozs.	30.00
Heisey, Sherbet, Moonglo, Lariat Stem	14.00
Heisey, Sherbet, Old Colony	10.00
Heisey, Sherbet, Paneled, Fluted Rims	6.25
Heisey, Sherbet, Plantation	14.00
Heisey, Sherbet, Saturn Optic, Kohinoor, Tall Stem	22.00
Heisey, Sherbet, 4-Footed, Continental	10.00
Heisey, Sign, Diamond H, Glass	185.00
Heisey, Soda Glass, 12 Ounce	17.00
Heisey, Spittoon, Marigold, Small	155.00
Heisey, Spooner, Beaded Swag	95.00
Heisey, Spooner, Custard, Winged Scroll	65.00
Heisey, Spooner, Etched Floral, 6 In.	21.00
Heisey, Spooner, Ring Band, White Custard, Signed	79.50
Heisey, Spooner, Rose Decoration, Ring Band	75.00
Heisey, Spooner, Winged Scroll	75.00
Heisey, Sugar & Creamer With Tray, Ribbed, Miniature	36.00
Heisey, Sugar & Creamer, Clear, Paneled	35.00
Heisey, Sugar & Creamer, Colonial Pattern, Applied Handle, 5 In.	39.00
Heisey, Sugar & Creamer, Crystolite	20.00
Heisey, Sugar & Creamer, Crystolite, Flamingo	30.00
Heisey, Sugar & Creamer, Crystolite, Oval	27.00
Heisey, Sugar & Creamer, Crystolite, Signed, With Tray	35.00
Heisey, Sugar & Creamer, Cut Flower, Dated July 9, 1912	69.50
Heisey, Sugar & Creamer, Engraved Flat Panel, No.352	75.00
Heisey, Sugar & Creamer, Fluted, Scalloped Top, 4 3/4 In.	26.00
Heisey, Sugar & Creamer, Hotel Pattern, Pink, No.1231	32.50
Heisey, Sugar & Creamer, Individual, Crystolite, Flamingo	40.00
Heisey, Sugar & Creamer, Lariat	20.00
Heisey, Sugar & Creamer, Lariat, Crystal, Flower Etching	25.00
Heisey, Sugar & Creamer, Miniature, Ribbed	15.00
Heisey, Sugar & Creamer, Miniature, Sahara, Queen Anne	38.50
Heisey, Sugar & Creamer, Orchid	32.00
Heisey, Sugar & Creamer, Orchid, Etched	29.00
Heisey, Sugar & Creamer, Orchid, Miniature	30.00
Heisey, Sugar & Creamer, Oval, Gold & Blue Decoration	25.00
Heisey, Sugar & Creamer, Pattern No.42752, Octagon, Marked	40.00
Heisey, Sugar & Creamer, Pineapple & Fan, Emerald	55.00
Heisey, Sugar & Creamer, Plain Round Shape, Pink	25.00
Heisey, Sugar & Creamer, Pleat & Panel	25.00
Heisey, Sugar & Creamer, Provincial, Deep Amethyst	35.00
Heisey, Sugar & Creamer, Quator Hotel, Cut Flowers	40.00
Heisey, Sugar & Creamer, Quator, Diamond Shape, Marked	30.00
Heisey, Sugar & Creamer, Quator, Footed	35.00
Heisey, Sugar & Creamer, Ridgeleigh	29.50
Heisey, Sugar & Creamer, Rose Etched, Waverly	30.00

Heisey, Sugar & Creamer, Sahara, Octagon	25.00 To 40.00
Heisey, Sugar & Creamer, Silver Overlay, Signed	50.00
Heisey, Sugar, Beaded Swag	90.00
Heisey, Sugar, Domino	25.00
Heisey, Sugar, Lariat, 3 In.	9.00
Heisey, Sugar, Rosalie	9.75
Heisey, Syrup, Beaded Swag, Pewter Snap Top	165.00
Heisey, Syrup, Butterfly Etched, Metal Cap, 1910 Patent	20.00
Heisey, Syrup, Custard, Ring Band, No.1245	145.00
Heisey, Syrup, Flamingo	30.00
Heisey, Table Set, Beaded Swag, 4 Piece	375.00
Heisey, Tankard, Beaded Swag	360.00
Heisey, Toothpick, Colonial	35.00 To 90.00
Heisey, Toothpick, Opal, Beaded Swag, Pink Floral	58.00
Heisey, Toothpick, Oval Diamond Pattern, Flashed Ruby	28.50
Heisey, Toothpick, Prince Of Wales Plumes, Gold Trim	75.00
Heisey, Toothpick, Prince Of Wales Plumes, Ruby Stained	200.00
Heisey, Toothpick, Ring Band, Custard, Roses, Signed	45.00
Heisey, Toothpick, Souvenir, Founded 1896, Oval Diamond, Ruby Stained	28.50
Heisey, Tray, Banded Flute, 10 In.	20.00
Heisey, Tray, Diamond Shape, Etching, Divided In Four, Signed	25.00
Heisey, Tray, Greek Key	35.00
Heisey, Tray, Nut, Revere, 5 Piece	35.00
Heisey, Tray, Pickle, Moonglo, 7 In.	18.00
Heisey, Tray, Sandwich, Crystal, 2-Handled, Copper Wheel Engraving, Signed	35.00
Heisey, Tray, Star, Ridgeleigh, 5 Compartment	28.00
Heisey, Tray, Twist, Pink, 14 In.	18.00
Heisey, Tumbler, Beaded Swag	70.00
Heisey, Tumbler, Custard, Enid, Oklahoma, Punty Band	46.00
Heisey, Tumbler, Custard, St.Ignace, Michigan	48.00
Heisey, Tumbler, Dark Red, Signed	98.00
Heisey, Tumbler, Dawn, Signed	35.00
Heisey, Tumbler, Donna, Orchid Etched	25.00
Heisey, Tumbler, Fancy Loop	12.00
Heisey, Tumbler, Iced Tea, Limelight	35.00
Heisey, Tumbler, Iced Tea, Oxford, Maryland, 12 Ozs.	14.00
Heisey, Tumbler, Moonglo, Fancy Loop	45.00
Heisey, Tumbler, Moonglo, Fancy Loop Variant	125.00
Heisey, Tumbler, No.154, 8 Ozs.	15.00
Heisey, Tumbler, Opalescent, Ring Band, Kneipp Sanitarium, Rome City, Ind.	100.00
Heisey, Tumbler, Pineapple & Fan, Emerald, Miami 1899	45.00
Heisey, Tumbler, Prince Of Wales Plumes, Clear	20.00
Heisey, Tumbler, Ring Band, Custard, Souvenir, Fairfield, Maine	28.00
Heisey, Tumbler, Sahara	29.50
Heisey, Tumbler, Scroll Decoration, Footed, Set Of 5	55.00
Heisey, Tumbler, Soda, Empress, Etched, Footed	20.00
Heisey, Tumbler, Twist, Green, Footed	15.00
Heisey, Tumbler, Whirlpool, Tangerine, Signed, 5 1/2 In.	35.00
Heisey, Tumbler, Winged Scroll	45.00
Heisey, Tumbler, Winged Scroll, Pan Am 1901, Green	36.00
Heisey, Vase, Candle, Zircon, Ridgeleigh, 4 5/8 In.	32.00
Heisey, Vase, Cobalt Ball, 6 In.	150.00
Heisey, Vase, Colonial, Signed, 8 In.	30.00
Heisey, Vase, Cornucopia, Warwick, 9 In., Pair	40.00
Heisey, Vase, Cornucopia, 7 In.	27.50 To 28.50
Heisey, Vase, Cornucopia, 9 In.	32.00
Heisey, Vase, Crystolite, Signed, 9 1/4 In.	35.00
Heisey, Vase, Flat Panel, Medium Flare	65.00
Heisey, Vase, Lariat, Cranberry Flashed, Fan Shaped	20.00
Heisey, Vase, Lariat, Fan, Clear	15.00
Heisey, Vase, Orchid, Lariat, 6 In.	22.95
Heisey, Vase, Pineapple & Fan, Gold, 6 1/2 In.	20.00
Heisey, Vase, Pineapple & Fan, 10 In.	40.00
Heisey, Vase, Prison Stripe, 8 Sided, 9 1/2 In.	45.00
Heisey, Vase, Ridgeleigh, 6 In.	18.00

Heisey, Vase, Ridgeleigh, 8 In.	30.00
Heisey, Vase, Sahara, Empress, Old Colony Etching, Dolphin Foot, 9 1/2 In.	48.00
Heisey, Vase, Sahara, Queen Anne	55.00
Heisey, Vase, Victorian, Flared, Footed, 8 1/2 In.	30.00
Heisey, Vase, Warwick, 9 In.	25.00
Heisey, Vase, Zircon, Ridgeleigh, 4 1/2 In.	28.00
Heisey, Wine, Dewdrop, 11 Paneled	14.00
Heisey, Wine, Kalarama, Monte Cristo Stem, 2 1/2 Ozs.	35.00
Heisey, Wine, Renaissance, Signed	22.00
Heisey, Wine, Saturn, Set Of 12	95.00
Herend, see Fischer	
Herend, Cup & Saucer, Demitasse, Raised Enamel Florals, Paneled, Gold Base	35.00
Herend, Figurine, Bird, Orange & Blue, Long Tailed, 8 1/2 In.	80.00
Herend, Figurine, Cat, Sitting, Green Eyes, Pink Mouth, Ears, White	35.00
Herend, Figurine, Nude Kneeling On Leg Admiring Herself In Mirror, 9 In.	145.00
Heubach, Figurine, Boy With Bucket, Bisque, Pastel Colors, 9 1/4 In.	95.00
Heubach, Figurine, Boy With Glasses, Sitting On Chair, Bisque, 7 1/2 In.	85.00
Heubach, Figurine, Boy, Left Hand In Pocket, Other Hand On Glasses, On Tree	95.00
Heubach, Figurine, Bunny, Glazed, Gray & White, 4 3/4 In.	45.00
Heubach, Figurine, Dancing Girl, Bisque, 6 1/2 X 3 5/8 In.	60.00
Heubach, Figurine, Dog, Glazed, White, Gray, Marked, 5 In.	65.00
Heubach, Figurine, Dog, High Glaze, Early Impressed Mark	65.00
Heubach, Figurine, Dutch Girl, Blue & White, Holding 2 Broken Eggs, 4 1/2 In.	125.00
Heubach, Figurine, Farmer With Scythe, Bisque, 12 3/4 In.	145.00
Heubach, Figurine, Girl Holding Bucket, Boy Smoking, 4 In.Base, 11 In., Pair	195.00
Heubach, Figurine, Girl Holding Sides Of Dress, Bisque, 7 In.	85.00
Heubach, Figurine, Girl, Blue Shoes, Trim On Dress & Bonnet, Sunburst Mark	120.00
Heubach, Figurine, Guinea Pig, 3 X 4 In., Set Of 3	35.00
Heubach, Figurine, Lady At Ship's Wheel, Pink & Blue With Cream, 12 1/2 In.	165.00
Heubach, Figurine, Seated Dutch Boy, Gray Cap, Intaglio Eyes, Wooden Shoes	70.00
Heubach, Lamp, Fairy, Boy, Bisque, Brown Hair, Blue Eyes, Ruffle Collar, Bow	115.00
Heubach, Vase, Birds & Boat Decoration, 5 In.	60.00
Heubach, Vase, Dusty Rose Pate-Sur-Pate Art Nouveau, Woman, Marked, 3 1/2 In.	65.00
Heubach, Vase, Gray & White Bird, Boat, High Glaze, 5 1/2 In.	62.00
Heubach, Vase, Gull, Boat, High Glaze, Sunburst Mark, Artist Signed, 5 1/2 In.	40.00

Higbee glass was made by the J.B.Higbee Company of Bridgeville, Pennsylvania, about 1900.

H I G

Higbee, see also Pressed Glass	
Higbee, Cake Stand, Pineapple, Signed	18.00
Higbee, Plate, Cake, Pedestal, 9 In.Wide	22.00
Higbee, Plate, Square, Amberina, H.I.G. On Bee, Floral Oval & Cane	60.00
Historic Blue, see Adams, Clews, Ridgway, Staffordshire	

Hobnail glass is a pattern of pressed glass with bumps in an allover pattern. Dozens of hobnail patterns and variants have been made. Reproductions of many types of hobnail glass can be found.

Hobnail, see also Francisware	
Hobnail, Basket, Clear To White, Fluted, Opalescent, 5 3/4 In.	13.00
Hobnail, Basket, Crimped & Flared, Applied Handle, Opalescent, 5 In.	35.00
Hobnail, Basket, White Opal, 7 1/2 In.	20.00
Hobnail, Bottle, Perfume, Ball Bottom, 7 In.	8.00
Hobnail, Bottle, Perfume, Blue, Opalescent, 4 1/2 In.	10.00
Hobnail, Bottle, Perfume, Cranberry, White, Opalescent, 4 In., Pair	25.00
Hobnail, Bowl, Berry, White, Large, Opalescent	85.00
Hobnail, Box, Cigarette, Opalescent, Blue & White, Covered, 5 X 3 1/2 In.	15.00
Hobnail, Candleholder, Blue White, Opalescent, 2 X 4 In., Pair	15.00
Hobnail, Compote, Blue White, Opalescent, Ruffled, Pedestal, 11 X 7 1/2 In.	75.00
Hobnail, Creamer, Blue, Opalescent	49.00
Hobnail, Dish, Candy, Covered, White, Opalescent	25.00
Hobnail, Gas Shade, White Opalescent, Lemon Yellow Rim, 8 X 5 In.	135.00
Hobnail, Jar, Powder, Covered, White, Opalescent	15.00
Hobnail, Pitcher, Clear With Clear Handle	75.00

Hobnail, Pitcher, Milk, Blue, Bull's-Eye, Clear Feet, Opalescent	67.50
Hobnail, Pitcher, Water, Pink, Applied Handle, Crimped Rim, 8 In.	92.00
Hobnail, Shade, Gas, White Opalescent, Crimped Rim, 8 In.	125.00
Hobnail, Shade, Lamp, Ruffled, Ruby, 8 1/4 X 5 In.	55.00
Hobnail, Spooner, Ruffled	18.00
Hobnail, Spooner, Umbilicated, Leaf, Berry Etching	25.00
Hobnail, Tumbler, 10-Row, Opalescent	50.00
Hobnail, Vase, Blue, Ruffled Cone, Footed, Opalescent, 5 1/2 In.	18.75
Hobnail, Vase, Deep Blue, Plain Top, Opalescent, 3 1/2 In.	8.75
Hobnail, Vase, Fan, Blue, Opalescent, 8 X 11 In.	32.00
Hobnail, Vase, Pale Blue, Ruffled, Opalescent, 3 1/2 In.	8.75

 Hochst, or Hoechst, porcelain was made in Germany from 1746 to 1796. It was marked with a six-spoke wheel.

Holly amber, or golden agate, glass was made by the Indiana Tumbler and Goblet Company from January 1, 1903, to June 13, 1903. It is a pressed glass pattern featuring holly leaves in the amber shaded glass.

Holly Amber, Relish, Oval, 7 1/2 X 4 1/2 In.	495.00
Holly Amber, Sugar, Covered	285.00
Holly Amber, Syrup	850.00
Holly Amber, Tumbler	247.50 To 275.00
Honesdale, Jar, Seaweed Acid Cut Back Design, Butterscotch To Clear, Lid	145.00
Honesdale, Vase, Blue & Yellow Enamel Bands, Iridized Surface, 7 X 9 In.	250.00
Honesdale, Vase, Cameo, Blue & Gold Decoration, Frosted, Signed, 7 In.	500.00
Honesdale, Vase, Trumpet, Gold On Frost, Footed, 12 In.	189.00
Hopalong Cassidy, Binoculars, Cast Metal	12.00
Hopalong Cassidy, Blotter, Picture Of Hopalong & Friends	6.00
Hopalong Cassidy, Book, Coloring	5.00
Hopalong Cassidy, Book, Pop-Up	10.00
Hopalong Cassidy, Camera, Flash	65.00
Hopalong Cassidy, Cereal	18.00
Hopalong Cassidy, Chair, Folding, Wood, C.1950, 12 X 24 In. *Illus*	115.00
Hopalong Cassidy, Drum, Tom-Tom, Cardboard With Rubberoid Pictures, 1950	32.00
Hopalong Cassidy, Glass, Milk, Picture Of Hopalong	7.00 To 8.50
Hopalong Cassidy, Knife, Pocket, Pictorial	15.00 To 22.00
Hopalong Cassidy, Look Magazine Cover, 1950	5.00
Hopalong Cassidy, Mug	4.00 To 5.50
Hopalong Cassidy, Night-Light, Glass	35.00
Hopalong Cassidy, Photo, Lobby, Set Of 4	10.00
Hopalong Cassidy, Plate, Milk Glass, 7 In.	8.50
Hopalong Cassidy, Postcard	1.75
Hopalong Cassidy, Radio, Arvin	90.00
Hopalong Cassidy, Roller Skates, Box	100.00
Hopalong Cassidy, Spoon & Fork	17.00
Hopalong Cassidy, Spoon, Full Figure Of Hoppy	6.00
Hopalong Cassidy, Suit, Boy	13.00
Hopalong Cassidy, Target Set, Bear & Outlaw & Eagle Targets, Metal	20.00
Hopalong Cassidy, Thermos	4.50
Hopalong Cassidy, Tumbler, Milk Glass, 4 3/4 In.	6.00 To 12.50

Hopalong Cassidy, Chair, Folding, Wood, C.1950, 12 X 24 In.

Hopalong Cassidy, Tumbler, Picture And Saying	9.00
Hopalong Cassidy, Twin Holster Set	25.00
Hopalong Cassidy, Watch, U.S. Time	30.00
Hopalong Cassidy, Wristwatch, Leather Band, Black Case	47.50
Hopalong Cassidy, Wristwatch, Lucky Hoppy	45.00
Hopalong Cassidy, Wristwatch, 1950	12.50
Horn, Longhorns, Texas, Leather Inset, Over 6 Feet Tip To Tip	250.00
Howdy Doody, Doll, Composition, Cloth Body, 21 In.	70.00
Howdy Doody, Doll, In Cowboy Suit	15.00
Howdy Doody, Doll, Sleep Eyes, Cloth Body, Composition Head, 17 In.	30.00
Howdy Doody, Marionette, Boxed	17.00
Howdy Doody, Marionette, 17 In.	20.00
Howdy Doody, Puppet, Marionette, 16 In.	35.00
Howdy Doody, Puppet, No.180, Kohner Push Button	15.00
Howdy Doody, Record, Illustrated Sleeve	25.00

*Hull pottery is made in Crooksville, Ohio. The factory started in 1903
as the Acme Pottery Company. Art pottery was first made in 1917.*

Hull, Ashtray, Butterfly, Heart Shape, 7 In.	12.00
Hull, Basket, Bowknot, Beige, Pink, 6 1/2 In.	17.50
Hull, Basket, Bowknot, Blue, 6 In.	24.50
Hull, Basket, Bowknot, 10 1/2 In.	35.00
Hull, Basket, Tokay, Moon, 11 In.	28.00
Hull, Basket, Tokay, 8 In.	18.00
Hull, Basket, Woodland, Chartreuse, 12 In.	30.00
Hull, Bowl, Bowknot, Matte Finish, 10 1/2 In.	30.00
Hull, Bowl, Console, Wildflower, Pink & Blue, Numbered	25.00
Hull, Bowl, Rose, Pink & Yellow Poppies, Pink To Blue, 4 X 3 In.	14.50
Hull, Bowl, Sunflower, 7 1/4 In.	8.00
Hull, Box, Clear, Embossed Basket Weave, Flower On Cover, Footed, 2 1/2 In.	7.75
Hull, Butter, Red Riding Hood	35.00
Hull, Casserole, Yellow, Covered, Divided, 9 X 3 1/2 In.	8.00
Hull, Centerpiece, Glossy Pink, 13 In.	22.00
Hull, Centerpiece, Pink, Marked USA Hull Art H23, 13 In.	21.00
Hull, Compote, Tree Of Life With Hand, 8 1/2 In.	75.00
Hull, Console Set, Woodland, Glossy Blue, 3 Piece	25.00
Hull, Console Set, Woodland, Green & Pink, 3 Piece	27.50
Hull, Cookie Jar, Duck, Script Mark	20.00
Hull, Cookie Jar, Goldilocks	30.00
Hull, Cookie Jar, Red Riding Hood	17.50 To 30.00
Hull, Cornucopia, Blue-Green, Pink Lined, High Glaze, No.64, 4 1/2 In.	20.00
Hull, Cornucopia, Bowknot, Pink, Blue, 7 1/2 In.	22.50
Hull, Cornucopia, Double, Magnolia, Brown & Yellow	25.00
Hull, Cornucopia, Floral, Pink, Blue, 6 In., Pair	8.50
Hull, Cornucopia, No.19, 8 1/2 In.	18.50
Hull, Cornucopia, Parchment & Pine, 11 3/4 In.	32.50
Hull, Cornucopia, Pink, No.W64, 11 X 6 In.	15.00
Hull, Cornucopia, W-7, 7 1/2 In.	13.50
Hull, Cornucopia, Woodland, W-2, 5 1/2 In.	10.00
Hull, Creamer, Magnolia, Blue To Yellow To Pink	6.00
Hull, Double Cornucopia, Pink & Blue	18.00
Hull, Ewer, Creamy White, Rose Butterflies, Flowers	15.00
Hull, Ewer, Orchid, 13 In.	27.50
Hull, Ewer, Parchment, Pine	36.00
Hull, Ewer, Salmon, White Dogwood, Small	10.00
Hull, Ewer, Serenade, Yellow, 8 1/2 In.	22.50
Hull, Ewer, Woodland, 6 1/2 In.	8.00
Hull, Ewer, Yellow, Pink, & Green Floral	14.00
Hull, Jardiniere, Orchid, Miniature	18.00
Hull, Jardiniere, Tulip	25.00
Hull, Pitcher, Blue To Ivory, Rose, Florals, Pair, 6 In.	15.00
Hull, Pitcher, Chartreuse Glossy, 13 1/2 In.	35.00
Hull, Pitcher, Milk, Red Riding Hood	20.00 To 25.00
Hull, Pitcher, Milk, 8 In.	17.50
Hull, Pitcher, Water Lily, Pink, Blue, 15 1/2 In.	13.50

Hull, Pitcher, Woodland, High Glaze Chartreuse, No.W24, 13 1/2 In.	33.00
Hull, Pitcher, Woodland, Pink, 6 1/2 In.	15.00
Hull, Planter, Duck	10.00
Hull, Planter, Mother & Baby, White, Pair	17.50
Hull, Planter, Wall Pocket, Ivy & Berries, Gold Trim, Maroon, Greenhull 112	25.00
Hull, Pocket, Wall, Broom	18.00
Hull, Pot With Attached Saucer, Woodland, W11, 5 3/4 In.	25.00
Hull, Pot, Parchment, Pine, Demipot, Lid	30.00
Hull, Salt & Pepper, Red Riding Hood, Pair	9.00
Hull, Swan, White, Large	10.00
Hull, Tea Set, Cream & Pink, 3 Piece	35.00
Hull, Tea Set, Ebbtide, 3 Piece	47.00
Hull, Tea Set, Woodland, Glossy, 3 Piece	30.00 To 35.00
Hull, Teapot, Magnolia, Blue To Yellow To Pink	32.50 To 40.00
Hull, Teapot, Red Riding Hood	24.00
Hull, Vase, Bowknot, Blue Green, 6 1/2 In.	24.50
Hull, Vase, Bowknot, Blue Green, 8 1/2 In.	22.50
Hull, Vase, Bowknot, Blue, B9, 8 1/2 In.	18.00 To 25.00
Hull, Vase, Bowknot, Pink And Turquoise, 12 1/2 In.	35.00
Hull, Vase, Bud, Tulip, Pink, 7 In.	9.50
Hull, Vase, Fan Shape, 2 Handles, 10 3/4 In.	25.00
Hull, Vase, Flat, Floral, Pink, Blue, 9 In.	18.00
Hull, Vase, Floral, Cream Color, 5 3/4 In.	12.00
Hull, Vase, Floral, Leaves, Gold Outline, Lined Top & Spout, Handle, Pink, 6 In.	22.50
Hull, Vase, Footed, Parchment & Pine, 10 1/2 In.	28.00
Hull, Vase, Glossy Dark Green, Tulip Shaped, 6 In.	9.00
Hull, Vase, Green To Pink, Embossed Water Lilies, 8 1/2 In.	17.50
Hull, Vase, Jack-In-The-Pulpit, No.560-33, 10 In.	35.00
Hull, Vase, Jack-In-The-Pulpit, 13 In.	48.00
Hull, Vase, Lavender, Pink, & Green, 7 X 3 3/4 In.	55.00
Hull, Vase, Madonna & Child, Pink, U.S.A., 5 1/2 X 7 In.	22.50
Hull, Vase, Magnolia, Blue To Pink, 10 1/2 X 8 1/2 In.	22.00
Hull, Vase, Magnolia, Pink To Black Base, Handled, 10 1/2 In.	25.00 To 35.00
Hull, Vase, Magnolia, Tan To Beige, U.S.A., 15 In.	65.00
Hull, Vase, Morning Glory, 7 1/2 In.	7.00
Hull, Vase, Narcissus, Pink, Blue, Original Seal, 403, 8 1/2 In.	22.00
Hull, Vase, Parchment & Pine, Spout, Footed, 14 In.	35.00
Hull, Vase, Parchment & Pine, 10 1/2 In.	30.00
Hull, Vase, Pastel, Iris, 6 1/4 In.	8.00
Hull, Vase, Pinecone, Turquoise Fitted, Handled, 6 1/2 In.	24.00
Hull, Vase, Pink & Blue Flowers Running Up Sides, Pitcher Shaped	14.00
Hull, Vase, Pink & Green, Butterfly-Wing Handles, Pink & Yellow Roses	14.00
Hull, Vase, Pink & Yellow, 2 Handles, Hull Art, 8 In.	20.00
Hull, Vase, Pink Glaze, Deeper Pink Flowers, Green Leaves, 11 In.	15.00
Hull, Vase, Pink, Gray Feet, Swan Handles, Flowers, 12 1/4 In.	20.00
Hull, Vase, Pink, Wild Rose, 6 1/2 In.	15.00
Hull, Vase, Poppy, No.611, 6 1/2 In.	18.00
Hull, Vase, Snail Shaped, Fish Figures At Base, 7 In.	45.00
Hull, Vase, Thistle Blue, Handled, 6 1/4 In.	25.00
Hull, Vase, Thistle, Pink, 6 1/2 In.	15.00
Hull, Vase, Wall, Green, Pink Flowers	11.00
Hull, Vase, Water Lily, Pink And Green	12.00
Hull, Vase, Wildflower, L-3, 5 1/2 In.	10.00
Hull, Vase, Wildflower, Pink & Blue, W-8, 7 1/2 In.	16.00
Hull, Vase, Wildflower, W-2, 5 1/2 In.	12.00
Hull, Vase, Woodland Glazed, White, Pink Flower, 5 1/2 X 6 1/2 In., Set Of 3	25.00
Hull, Wall Pocket, Whisk Broom, Pink Glaze, 8 In.	10.00

Hummel figurines, based on the drawings of Berta Hummel, are made by the W.Goebel Porzellanfabrik of Oeslau, Germany. They were first made in 1934.

Hummel, Ashtray, Singing Lesson, Stylized Bee Mark	40.00
Hummel, Candleholder, Little Boy Holding Horse, No.117, 1950s Mark, 3 3/4 In.	50.00
Hummel, Candlestick, Art Deco, Crown Mark, Pair	22.00
Hummel, Creamer, Cow, Impressed Bee & Crown Mark, 7 1/2 In.	30.00

Hummel, Figurine, Adoration, Full Bee, 6 1/4 In. 210.00
Hummel, Figurine, Angel Duet, 1950-60, 5 In. 117.50
Hummel, Figurine, Apple Tree Boy, Life-size 7000.00
Hummel, Figurine, Apple Tree Boy, No.142, Incised Bee, 6 1/2 In. 210.00
Hummel, Figurine, Apple Tree Boy, Stylized Bee, West Germany, 4 In. 40.00
Hummel, Figurine, Apple Tree Girl & Apple Tree Boy, 10 1/4 In., Pair 419.00
Hummel, Figurine, Apple Tree Girl, No.141, Incised Bee, 6 1/2 In. 210.00
Hummel, Figurine, Apple Tree Girl, No.141, Incised Bee, 6 1/4 In. 210.00
Hummel, Figurine, Auf Weidersehen, Boy Wearing Hat, No.153, Full Bee, 5 In. 2200.00
Hummel, Figurine, Band Leader, Full Bee, Germany, 5 In. 95.00
Hummel, Figurine, Barnyard Hero, No.195, Crown Mark, 5 3/4 In. 250.00
Hummel, Figurine, Barnyard Hero, 5 1/2 In. 95.00
Hummel, Figurine, Begging His Share, Hole In Cake, Crown Mark, 6 In. 390.00
Hummel, Figurine, Big Housecleaning, 4 In. .... *Illus* 50.00
Hummel, Figurine, Bird Duet, 4 In. 95.00
Hummel, Figurine, Birthday Serenade, Incised Bee, 4 1/4 In. 450.00
Hummel, Figurine, Blessed Event, No.333, 3 Line Mark, 1965, 5 1/2 In. 95.00
Hummel, Figurine, Bookworm, Impressed Crown Mark, 5 1/2 In. 110.00
Hummel, Figurine, Bugle Boy, Full Bee Mark, 5 In. 60.00
Hummel, Figurine, Chimney Sweep, Full Bee Mark, 4 In. 50.00
Hummel, Figurine, Chimney Sweep, Full Bee, Germany, No.12, 5 1/2 In. 95.00
Hummel, Figurine, Coquettes, No.179, Full Bee, 5 In. 175.00
Hummel, Figurine, Culprits, No.58, Incised Bee, 6 3/4 In. 130.00
Hummel, Figurine, Doctor, Full Bee, Black, Western Germany, 4 In. 70.00
Hummel, Figurine, Farm Boy, No.66, Full Bee, 5 In. 80.00
Hummel, Figurine, Flower Madonna, Doughnut Halo, Full Bee, 10 X 9 1/2 In. 350.00
Hummel, Figurine, Flower Madonna, 9 1/4 In. 110.00
Hummel, Figurine, Flower Vendor, 5 1/2 In. .... *Illus* 40.00
Hummel, Figurine, Friends, Full Bee, Black Mark, Germany, 5 1/2 In. 85.00
Hummel, Figurine, Going To Grandma's, Stylized Bee, No.52/1, 6 1/4 In. 450.00
Hummel, Figurine, Goose Girl, Full Bee, 7 1/2 In. 165.00
Hummel, Figurine, Happy Pastime, Stylized Bee, West Germany, 3 1/2 In. 40.00
Hummel, Figurine, Hear Ye, Hear Ye, Stylized Bee, West Germany Mark, 5 1/4 In. 39.00
Hummel, Figurine, Hello, No.124/0, Green Pants, Pink Vest, Full Bee, 6 1/2 In. 190.00
Hummel, Figurine, Hello, No.124/1, White Vest, Stylized Bee, 6 3/4 In. 375.00
Hummel, Figurine, Joyous News, 2 3/4 In. 35.00
Hummel, Figurine, Keeper Of The Flock, 8 1/2 In. 75.00
Hummel, Figurine, Little Cellist, 6 In. 35.00
Hummel, Figurine, Little Shopper, 5 1/2 In. 75.00
Hummel, Figurine, Madonna & Child, White, Artist Signed R.Unger, 11 In. 196.00
Hummel, Figurine, Madonna & Child, White, Full Bee, Black Mark, 9 1/4 In. 130.00
Hummel, Figurine, Madonna Without Halo, Full Bee Mark, Pair 40.00
Hummel, Figurine, Madonna, Color, Doughnut Halo, Full Bee, No.10/3, 13 In. 485.00
Hummel, Figurine, Madonna, Standing, Halo, 1950-55, 16 3/4 In. 250.00
Hummel, Figurine, March Winds, Boy, Scarf, Crown Mark, 5 1/2 In. .... 125.00 To 145.00
Hummel, Figurine, Mother's Darling, Full Bee, 6 In. .... 70.00 To 150.00
Hummel, Figurine, Retreat To Safety, Full Bee, 6 3/4 In. 113.50
Hummel, Figurine, Ring Round Rosie, W.Goebel, Oeslau, 1957, 6 3/4 In. 600.00
Hummel, Figurine, Singing Lesson, Full Bee, 2 3/4 In. 36.50
Hummel, Figurine, Sister, 5 1/2 In. 36.00

Hummel, Figurine, Big Housecleaning, 4 In.

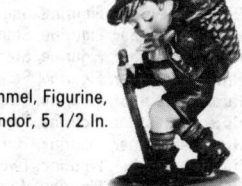

Hummel, Figurine,
Flower Vendor, 5 1/2 In.

Hummel, Figurine, Stormy Weather, Full Bee, Germany, 6 1/2 In. .... 90.00 To 300.00
Hummel, Figurine, Stormy Weather, No.71, Incised Bee, 6 1/4 In. 290.00
Hummel, Figurine, Telling Her Secret, No.196/O, Three Line Mark, 5 1/2 In. 70.00
Hummel, Figurine, Telling Her Secret, No.196, Incised Bee, 6 1/2 In. 650.00
Hummel, Figurine, To Market, 5 1/2 In. 105.00
Hummel, Figurine, Trumpet Boy, 4 1/2 In. 22.00
Hummel, Figurine, Umbrella Boy, Stylized Bee, W.Germany, In Black, 8 In. 425.00
Hummel, Figurine, Village Boy, Stylized Bee, W.Germany, No.51/0, 6 In. 85.00
Hummel, Figurine, Village Boy, 6 1/2 In. 110.00
Hummel, Figurine, Weary Wanderer, Impressed 1949, Full Bee 80.00
Hummel, Figurine, X-Max & Moritz, Bee Mark, 5 In. 100.00
Hummel, Lamp Base, Culprits, Full Bee Mark, 9 1/2 In. 145.00
Hummel, Plaque, Dealer's, Crown & Full Bee 750.00
Hummel, Plaque, Happy Bugler 750.00
Hummel, Plaque, Madonna, No.222 .... 650.00
Hummel, Plaque, Retreat To Safety, No.126, Stylized Bee, 4 3/4 X 4 In. 50.00
Hummel, Salt & Pepper, Pig 50.00
Hummel, Sugar, Figural, Monk, Pre-World War II, Goebel, Blue Underglaze Mark 28.00
Hummel, Table Set, Sugar, Creamer, Silver Plated Mustard, Full Bee, Monk 65.00
Hummel, Toby Mug, Monk, Bee Mark, S747 S-O 15.00
Hummel, Vase, Art Deco, Full Bee, 4 In. 10.00
Hummel, Vase, High Glaze, Multicolors, Crown Mark, Goebel, 4 3/4 In. 20.00
Hutschenreuther, Bowl & Underplate, Gold & Pink Floral, Hand-Painted 13.50
Hutschenreuther, Bowl, Bavarian Favorite, Roses, Gold Trim, 9 3/4 In. 65.00
Hutschenreuther, Cat, Siamese, Sitting, Signed Granget, 6 1/2 In. 68.00
Hutschenreuther, Cup & Saucer, Cameo Of Man On Blue, 1915, Gelb 150.00
Hutschenreuther, Figurine, Bird On Tree Stump, Signed Tutter, 6 In. 45.00
Hutschenreuther, Figurine, Boxer Dog, Stands, Fawn, 5 X 4 1/2 In. 42.00
Hutschenreuther, Figurine, Boxer, 6 1/4 In. 50.00
Hutschenreuther, Figurine, Cat, Matte Finish, Artist Signed, 7 In. 120.00
Hutschenreuther, Figurine, Cat, Signed, 3 1/2 X 5 In. 90.00
Hutschenreuther, Figurine, Cat, Sitting, U.S.Zone, 6 1/2 In. 110.00
Hutschenreuther, Figurine, Chubby Child Pursued By Goose, Signed Tutter 48.00
Hutschenreuther, Figurine, Clown, Holding Red Flower, Art Deco, 11 In. 275.00
Hutschenreuther, Figurine, Condor, C.1920, 12 1/2 In. 85.00
Hutschenreuther, Figurine, Courtier, 1814, Marked, 6 In., Pair 195.00
Hutschenreuther, Figurine, Dachshund Standing, 5 X 9 In. 10.00
Hutschenreuther, Figurine, Dalmatian, 6 1/2 In. 24.00
Hutschenreuther, Figurine, Donkey, Gray, Standing, 5 X 4 In. 38.00
Hutschenreuther, Figurine, Elephant With Trunk In Air, Porcelain, 8 X 9 In. 100.00
Hutschenreuther, Figurine, Fish Leaping Above Rolling Wave, Signed, 4 In. 60.00
Hutschenreuther, Figurine, Gazelle, Granget, 5 1/2 In. 85.00
Hutschenreuther, Figurine, Goldfinch, Green Mark, Signed K.Tutter, 6 1/2 In. 55.00
Hutschenreuther, Figurine, Great Dane, Harlequin, 8 X 8 In. .... 115.00 To 125.00
Hutschenreuther, Figurine, Hummingbird, Nest With Eggs, 3 In. 67.00
Hutschenreuther, Figurine, Lady In Bat-Wing Costume, Dancing, 6 1/4 In. 110.00
Hutschenreuther, Figurine, Lady Seated, Playing Flute, U.S.Zone Germany Mark 85.00
Hutschenreuther, Figurine, Lady, Dancing, Turquoise, Art Deco, K.Tutter 110.00
Hutschenreuther, Figurine, Lizard On Rock, Green Foliage, 1 1/2 X 4 In. 40.00
Hutschenreuther, Figurine, Marlin Leaping Over Rolling Wave, 4 In. 55.00
Hutschenreuther, Figurine, Owl, Perch, 6 1/2 In. 85.00
Hutschenreuther, Figurine, Siamese Cat, Sitting, Granget, 6 1/2 .... 68.00 To 70.00
Hutschenreuther, Figurine, Sitting Bulldog, 4 In. 45.00
Hutschenreuther, Figurine, Squirrel On Acorn Leaf, Holding Acorn, 3 In. 35.00
Hutschenreuther, Figurine, Standing Collie, Tan & White, 4 1/2 X 6 1/4 In. 50.00
Hutschenreuther, Figurine, Standing Dachshund, 5 X 9 In. 100.00
Hutschenreuther, Figurine, Standing Pekinese, Brown, 3 1/2 X 4 1/2 In. 44.00
Hutschenreuther, Figurine, Striped Tammy Cat, Matte Finish, Signed, 7 In. 120.00
Hutschenreuther, Figurine, Tan & White Collie, Standing, 4 1/2 X 6 1/4 In. 50.00
Hutschenreuther, Figurine, Turbaned Youth, Dog, Friedrich Heuler, 14 In. 125.00
Hutschenreuther, Figurine, Two Cats Sitting Side By Side, 7 X 7 In. 200.00
Hutschenreuther, Figurine, Woman & Boy, White, 10 In. 95.00
Hutschenreuther, Figurine, Yellow Tammy Cat, Matt Finish, 7 In. 120.00
Hutschenreuther, Figurine, Yellow Warbler, Worm In Beak, Granget, 5 In. 125.00
Hutschenreuther, Figurine, 2 Foxes Standing Side By Side, 7 X 11 In. 195.00

Hutschenreuther, Plaque, Girl Holding Bouquet, Signed Bock, Gold Leaf Frame 1250.00
Hutschenreuther, Plate, Dresden Pattern, 10 1/2 In. 15.00
Hutschenreuther, Plate, Hand-Painted Roses, Gold Trim, 8 In. 9.50
Hutschenreuther, Plate, Plums, Blackberries, Hand-Painted, 7 3/4 In. 25.00
Hutschenreuther, Platter, Melon Boys Shooting Dice, Round 125.00
Hutschenteuther, Figurine, Swimming Fish, Granget, 3 1/4 X 4 1/2 In. 55.00
    Icebox, see Kitchen, Icebox
Icon, Russian, Our Lady Of The Sign, Silver Riza, 19th Century, 12 X 10 In. 595.00
Icon, Russian, St.Catherine, Metal Riza, 19th Century, 8 X 10 In. 500.00

    Imari patterns are named for the Japanese ware decorated with orange and
    blue stylized flowers. The design on the Japanese ware became so
    characteristic that the name Imari has come to mean any pattern of this type.
    It was copied by the European factories of the eighteenth and early
    nineteenth centuries.

Imari, Bowl, Blue Basket Center, Flowers, Teakwood Stand, 8 1/2 X 3 1/2 In. 95.00
Imari, Bowl, Blue, Orange, White, 10 In. 90.00
Imari, Bowl, Blues, Greens, 8 1/2 X 2 3/4 In. 50.00
Imari, Bowl, C.1840, 12 X 5 1/2 In. 495.00
Imari, Bowl, Fluted, Scalloped Rim, 12 1/2 X 5 1/2 In. 450.00
Imari, Bowl, Red & Blue Panels, Scalloped Top, 10 In. 100.00
Imari, Bowl, Red, Gold, & Blue, 6 In. 45.00
Imari, Bowl, Rice, Imari Decoration, Lid, C.1900 .... 49.00
Imari, Bowl, Rice, Multicolored Flying Phoenix Medallions, C.1850, 5 In. 58.00
Imari, Bowl, Scalloped Border, C.1800, 8 3/4 In. 175.00
Imari, Bowl, Scalloped Rim, Dark Blue, Red & Green, 7 1/4 In. 45.00
Imari, Bowl, Scalloped Rim, Panels Of Fish & Rabbits, Peonies, 9 3/4 In. 135.00
Imari, Bowl, Scalloped Rim, Scroll Designs, Water Scene, Blue & White, 6 In. 16.50
Imari, Bowl, Scalloped Rim, 6 Colors, Gold Trim, 9 3/4 X 3 1/2 In. 110.00
Imari, Bowl, 9 1/2 In.Diameter 80.00
Imari, Case, Flying Squirrel On Grapevine, Diamond Shape, 12 In. 135.00
Imari, Charger, Bird On Rockery, Flowers, Blue & White Underglaze, 14 3/4 In. 150.00
Imari, Charger, Blue & White River Scene, Red Cherries At Random, 14 1/2 In. 165.00
Imari, Charger, Blue & White, Birds In Flowering Tree, C.1800, 15 In. 85.00
Imari, Charger, Chrysanthemum Pattern, 4 Colors 160.00
Imari, Charger, Cobalt, Orange & Gold, 15 3/4 In. 238.00
Imari, Charger, Crane, Floral, C.1850, 14 1/2 In. 225.00
Imari, Charger, Scalloped Edge, Vase Of Flowers Decoration, 11 In. 55.00
Imari, Charger, Scenic Figures, Butterfly, Bridge, Gold Tracery, 16 In. 385.00
Imari, Charger, 12 In. 100.00
Imari, Compote, Boat Shape, Center Medallions Of Painted Scenes, 9 1/2 In. 185.00
Imari, Cracker Jar, Mums & Prunus, Covered, Signed, 6 In. 89.00
Imari, Cup & Saucer, Longevity Symbol Center, Overglaze Enamels 95.00
Imari, Cup & Saucer, Scenic Reserves, Red, Blue, Gold, C.1880 .... 60.00
Imari, Cup, Handleless 25.00
Imari, Dish, Scallop Rim, Multicolor, Gold, 4 3/4 In. 12.00
Imari, Dish, Square, Rounded Corners, Blue, C.1860 .... 90.00
Imari, Dish, Sweetmeat, Blue & White, 6 3/4 In. 11.00
Imari, Jar, Foo Dog Finial, Blue, Gold On White, 9 1/2 In. 130.00
Imari, Jar, Foo Dog Finial, Cover, C.1850, 8 1/2 In. 125.00
Imari, Plaque, Lake & Mountain Scene, Cobalt, Red, & Gold, 16 In.Diameter 200.00
Imari, Plate, Basket Of Flowers Center, 8 1/4 In. 37.50
Imari, Plate, Bird Design, Blue, Brown Scalloped Edge, C.1850, 12 In. 75.00
Imari, Plate, Blue & White, Bird, Square Cut Corners, 10 X 10 In. 65.00
Imari, Plate, Blue Floral Center, Floral & Fish Around Edge, 8 1/2 In. 40.00
Imari, Plate, Bluebird Decoration, Brown Scalloped Edge, C.1850, 12 In. 75.00
Imari, Plate, Chop, Cobalt, Red, Green, Decorated, 13 In. 95.00
Imari, Plate, Cobalt Blue, Deep Red, Oriental Red Mark, 9 In. 70.00
Imari, Plate, Cobalt Orange, Green Panels, 8 1/2 In. 30.00
Imari, Plate, Deep Blue, Brown Scalloped Edge, Glazed Enamel, 11 1/2 In. 45.00
Imari, Plate, Dragons & Scorpions Decoration, Blue, 12 In. 80.00
Imari, Plate, Fan Shape, Small 45.00
Imari, Plate, Fish & Floral, 8 In. 45.00
Imari, Plate, Floral Scene, Semienclosed Medallions, Signed, 18 In. 200.00
Imari, Plate, Japanese Transfer, C.1850, 9 In., Pair 65.00

Imari, Plate, Octagon, 7 1/2 In.	110.00
Imari, Plate, Ornate Blue On White, 1800s	90.00
Imari, Plate, Red & Green Floral, Calligraphy On Edge, 9 In.	40.00
Imari, Plate, Scalloped Rim, Blue, Red & Green Decoration, 8 1/2 In.	45.00
Imari, Plate, Scalloped, 19th Century, 8 1/2 In.	48.00
Imari, Plate, 12 Panel, Tree Branches, Blossoms, Cobalt Blue, Red, Green, 12 In.	110.00
Imari, Platter, Blue & White Floral, 14 In.	65.00
Imari, Saki Set, Peacocks, Peonies, Gold & Rust On White, 5 In.Bottle, 6 Piece	49.00
Imari, Seat, Garden, Red & Blue Ground, Floral & Birds, Pair	300.00
Imari, Tureen, Blue & Orange Fans & Hearts On White, C.1800, Covered, 10 In.	950.00
Imari, Vase, Cobalt, Orange, Red, & Green Floral, Medallion, 9 In.	56.00
Imari, Vase, Diamond Shape, Flying Squirrel, Brown, Green, Gold, Black, 12 In.	135.00
Imari, Vase, Floral, 8 1/2 In.	165.00
Imari, Vase, Gold & Orange, Bulbous, 5 In.	9.00
Imari, Vase, Miniature, Multicolor, 3 3/4 In.	18.00
Imari, Vase, Slender Neck, Overglaze Red, Gold, Cobalt Medallions, 5 1/8 In.	35.00
Imari, Vase, Temple, C.1850, 10 In.	170.00
Imari, Vase, Temple, Covered, C.1850, 10 In.	170.00
Imari, Vase, Unusual Flare Crimp Top, 5 In.	29.00
Imari, Vase, 6 1/2 In.	85.00

Imperial Glass Corporation was founded in Bellaire, Ohio, in 1902.
Stretch glass and art glass are two of the many kinds of glass made.

Imperial, Bowl, Amethyst, Iridescent, Signed, 2 1/2 X 10 3/4 In.	60.00
Imperial, Bowl, Console, Paper Sticker	10.00
Imperial, Bowl, High Relief Roses, Vines, & Leaves In & Out, Alabaster, 9 In.	75.00
Imperial, Bowl, Iridescent Amethyst Stretch, Signed, 10 3/4 X 2 1/2 In.	60.00
Imperial, Bowl, Iridescent, Signed, 5 1/2 In.	65.00
Imperial, Bowl, Orange, Nucut, 7 1/2 Lbs.	75.00
Imperial, Bowl, Ram's Head, Blue Carnival	37.50
Imperial, Bowl, Red Slag, Raised Rose Pattern	18.00
Imperial, Bowl, Roses, Caramel Slag, 20 Year	21.00
Imperial, Bowl, Stretch, 5 X 2 In.	15.00
Imperial, Candlestick, Gold Iridescent, 11 In.	35.00
Imperial, Centerpiece, Hand-Painted Orchids, 10 X 6 1/2 In.	55.00
Imperial, Compote, Gold Iridescent, Ribbed, Clear Pedestal Base, 5 In.	18.00
Imperial, Dish, Butter, Amethyst	35.00
Imperial, Figurine, Scolding Bird, Frosted, Virginia B. Evans	35.00
Imperial, Figurine, Standing Colts, Ultra-Blue, Signed	50.00
Imperial, Mallard, Wing Halfway, Caramel Slag	20.00
Imperial, Mallard, Wing Up, Caramel Slag	20.00
Imperial, Plate, Iridescent, Jewels, 9 3/8 In.	55.00
Imperial, Plug Horse, Caramel Slag	20.00
Imperial, Relish, Grape	15.00
Imperial, Sugar & Creamer	25.00
Imperial, Swan, Blue, Opalescent, 4 1/2 In.	16.50
Imperial, Swan, Emerald, 4 1/2 In.	12.50
Imperial, Swan, Large	36.00
Imperial, Vase, Blue Pull-Ups On Dark Blue, 10 1/4 In.	225.00
Imperial, Vase, Blue Pulled Feather On Orange Luster, Cobalt Rim, Pedestal	285.00
Imperial, Vase, Bronze Luster Over Clear, Rainbow Shading, 10/ 1/2 In.	95.00
Imperial, Vase, Flared, Stretched Top, Iridescent, Signed, 5 1/2 In.	80.00
Imperial, Vase, Flower Bowl, Iridescent Green, Red, Pink, And Blue, Small	85.00
Imperial, Vase, Gold Amber, Greek Shape, Signed, 5 1/4 In.	75.00
Imperial, Vase, Green Iridescent, White Decoration, 10 3/4 In.	275.00
Imperial, Vase, Jewels, Purple, Highlights, Cross Mark, 4 1/2 In.	68.00
Imperial, Vase, Orange & Black Mirror Finish, 10 1/2 In.	125.00
Imperial, Vase, Orange Luster Over Opaque Body, 9 1/2 In.	85.00
Imperial, Vase, Orange Luster, Bronze Pulls, 8 3/4 In.	145.00
Imperial, Vase, Pedestaled, Mirror, Orange & Black, 10 1/2 In.	110.00
Imperial, Vase, Solid Orange, 11 1/2 In.	115.00
Imperial, Water Set, Grapes, Purple Carnival, IG Mark	150.00
Imperial, Wine Set, Green, Frosted, 7 Piece	60.00

Indian Tree is a china pattern that was popular during the last half of
the nineteenth century. It was copied from earlier patterns of English

*china that were very similar. The pattern includes the crooked branch of a
tree and a partial landscape with exotic flowers and leaves. It is colored
green, blue, pink, and orange.*

Indian Tree, Bowl, Coalport, Oval, 7 In.	30.00
Indian Tree, Bowl, Soup, 7 1/4 In.	8.00
Indian Tree, Cup & Saucer, Demitasse, Coalport	22.00
Indian Tree, Dish, Oval, Open	35.00
Indian Tree, Luncheon Set, Coalport, 12 Place Setting	395.00
Indian Tree, Plate, Coalport, Fluted Edge, 7 In., Set Of 8	90.00
Indian Tree, Plate, Swirl, Myott, 6 In.	5.00
Indian Tree, Plate, 6 1/4 In.	5.00
Indian Tree, Plate, 8 In.	8.00
Indian Tree, Platter, Burgess & Leigh, Gold Rim, 15 1/2 In.	45.00
Indian Tree, Platter, Davison & Son, England, 16 1/2 In.	35.00
Indian Tree, Platter, Spode, 13 X 10 In.	35.00
Indian Tree, Platter, 14 In.	19.00

*Indian art from North America has attracted the collector for many years.
Each tribe has its own distinctive designs and techniques. Baskets, jewelry,
and leatherwork are of greatest collector interest.*

Indian, Ax, War, Apache, Iron, Wm.T.Wood & Co., 13 In.	68.50
Indian, Baby Carrier, Willow, Eastern Woodland, C.1880, 20 In.	125.00
Indian, Back Rest, Crow, Beaded Medallion Trade Cloth, C.1890	200.00
Indian, Bag, Chickawa, Heavy Beaded Flowers	65.00
Indian, Bag, Cornhusk, Nez Perce, Geometric Design, 16 X 18 In.	200.00
Indian, Bag, Leather, Heavily Beaded, Sioux	135.00
Indian, Bag, Nez Perce, Beaded, Buckskin Back, 7 X 10 In.	100.00
Indian, Bag, Pipe, White Leather, Beads, Quills, Sioux	250.00
Indian, Bag, Sioux, Tepee, Canvas Lined With American Flag, 24 X 16 In.	375.00
Indian, Bag, Tepee, Crow, Beaded On One Side, Tin Dangles, 12 X 16 In.	275.00
Indian, Bag, Tepee, Crow, Fully Beaded, 12 X 16 In.	150.00
Indian, Bag, War, Made From Cavalry Uniform, Small Envelope Type, Apache	300.00
Indian, Ball, Puberty, Plains, Beaded, C.1920	75.00
Indian, Basket Tray, Beige & Brown, 16 In.	55.00
Indian, Basket, Coiled, Pima, Figure And Maze Decoration, 9 1/2 In.	250.00
Indian, Basket, Coiled, Rattlesnake Decoration, South Calif., 12 1/2 In.	500.00
Indian, Basket, Eskimo, Carved Stone Handle, Carved Stone Polar Bear Lid	75.00
Indian, Basket, Gift, Shell & Feather Ornaments, Pomo Indians, Calif, 4 In.	375.00
Indian, Basket, Klikitat, Imbricated Design, 6 X 7 In.	150.00
Indian, Basket, Maine, C.1900, 13 X 8 1/2 In.	85.00
Indian, Basket, Micmac, Reverse Birch Bark, Goose On Each Side, 1890	150.00
Indian, Basket, Northern Maine Potato Stenciling, 9 X 6 X 6 In.	40.00
Indian, Basket, Pack, Conical, Yurok-Karok, Northwest Coast, 17 In.	800.00
Indian, Basket, Papago, Dogs In Devil's Claw, 4 X 6 In.	65.00
Indian, Basket, Papago, Southwestern Tribe, Devil's Claw, C.1930, 11 X 5 In.	85.00
Indian, Basket, Papago, Woven Black & Natural, 7 1/4 X 2 3/4 In.	45.00
Indian, Bell, Sleigh, 6 On Leather Strap, Crow Indian, Montana, Dance Bells	150.00
Indian, Belt, Chickawa, Beaded In Flower Pattern, Blue, Red, Yellow Beads	165.00
Indian, Belt, Comanche, Leather, Needlework, C.1900, 44 1/2 In.	32.00
Indian, Belt, Leather, Needlework Designs, C.1900s, 3 X 44 In.	25.00
Indian, Blanket, Navajo, Red Germantown Yarn, Blue Tipped White Crosses	2200.00
Indian, Blanket, Navajo, Wool, C.1880, 84 X 63 In.	550.00
Indian, Blanket, Saddle, Sioux, Reservation Period, 5 X 2 Ft.	1500.00
Indian, Bookend, Seminole, Chalk, Orange, Yellow, & Brown, 6 1/2 In., Pair	12.50
Indian, Bowl, Acoma, 4 1/4 In.	32.00
Indian, Bracelet, Bird In Flight	75.00
Indian, Bull Whip, Braided Leather	22.00
Indian, Case, Awl, Sioux, Fully Beaded, Tin Dangles	60.00
Indian, Choker, Bird Bone, Sioux	95.00
Indian, Collar, Ceremonial, Blue & White Bugle Beads, Diamond Pattern	85.00
Indian, Doll, Mohave, Pottery Body, Cradle Board, 1800s, 12 In.	275.00
Indian, Doll, Skookum, 14 In.	47.50
Indian, Game, Nez Perce, Deer Bone & Stick, Carrying Pouch	50.00
Indian, Gauntlet Gloves, Beadwork, Birds, Pair	75.00
Indian, Gauntlet, Nez Perce, Fully Beaded	150.00

Indian, Hair Rosette, Scalp Lock Braid, Beaver Tooth, Trade Beads, C.1880	200.00
Indian, Jar, Pueblo, Pottery	110.00
Indian, Jar, Squat, Hopu	600.00
Indian, Knife, Fighting, South Carolina, Horn Grip, Handmade, 10 In.	18.50
Indian, Leggings, Crow, Fully Beaded, Red Trade Cloth, C.1920	150.00
Indian, Letter Opener, American, Turquoise Setting, 7 In.	40.00
Indian, Loom, Bead, Wood, Apache	10.00
Indian, Mask, Cornhusk, Eastern Woodland, C.1930-40, 15 In.	65.00
Indian, Mask, Tongass, Cape Fox, South Alaska	32500.00
Indian, Mask, Wooden, Tongass, South Alaska	58000.00
Indian, Medal, Crow Reservation, Strung On Hair Pipe Necklace, 1910	150.00
Indian, Moccasin, Apache, Man's, Beaded, 1900	375.00
Indian, Moccasin, Flathead, Beaded	90.00
Indian, Moccasin, Fully Beaded, Sioux, 1920, Red, White, Blue, Pair	125.00
Indian, Moccasin, Huron, Pair	4600.00
Indian, Moccasin, Lady's, Sioux, Fully Beaded, Sinew Sewn	110.00
Indian, Moccasin, Man's, Cheyenne, Fully Beaded, Sinew Sewn	100.00
Indian, Moccasin, Stitched In Red, White, Blue Pony Beads, Northern Plains	800.00
Indian, Moccasins, Arapaho, Sinew Sewn, Yellow Clay Dyes	85.00
Indian, Moccasins, Child's, Sioux, Leather Sole, Beaded Geometrics, C.1890	85.00
Indian, Necklace, Northern Plains, Reservation Period	750.00
Indian, Necklace, Tennessee, Made Of Buckeyes & Berries	22.00
Indian, Paddle, Canoe, Painted, Northwest Coast, C.1880, 48 In.	75.00
Indian, Pipe, Peace, Tomahawk, Brass, Omaha 1895, Sioux	275.00
Indian, Pipe, Peace, Tomahawk, Solid Brass Head, Omaha 1895 Outlined, Sioux	275.00
Indian, Plate, Marie Pottery	2500.00
Indian, Pouch, Fringed, Beaded, Bird In Flight	90.00
Indian, Pouch, Medicine, Sioux, Beaded, Fully Quilled Center, C.1860, 9 In.	300.00
Indian, Pouch, Quill Work, Northern Woodlands Indians	6190.00
Indian, Purse, Chippewa, Cree, Beaded, 1900	68.00
Indian, Quiver, Sioux, Beaded Top & Bottom, Sinew Sewn, C.1860	150.00
Indian, Rattle, Haida, Carved With Animal Forms, For Ritual Dances	53000.00
Indian, Rug, Natural, Red, Blue, Black, Gray, Navajo, C.1910	165.00
Indian, Rug, Navajo, Burgundy, Black, Gray, Geometric, 31 X 51 In.	175.00
Indian, Rug, Navajo, Eagle Center, 18 X 20 In.	20.00
Indian, Rug, Navajo, Fringe Ties, C.1880, 23 X 37 1/2 In.	275.00
Indian, Rug, Navajo, Geometric Centers, 18 X 20 In.	20.00
Indian, Rug, Navajo, Red, Black, White, & Gray, 31 1/2 X 56 In.	85.00
Indian, Rug, Navajo, Wool, C.1880, 65 X 40 In.	350.00
Indian, Rug, Navajo, 1916 Woven Into Gray, Red, Black Design, 48 X 82 In.	275.00
Indian, Sash, Maternity, Navajo, Wool, Long, 1920	95.00
Indian, Sheath, Knife, Canadian Kamsack, Beaded, Attached Metal Cones	125.00
Indian, Sheath, Knife, Fully Beaded, Moosehide Dangles, 13 In.	150.00
Indian, Sheath, Sioux, Fully Beaded, C.1920	50.00
Indian, Shirt, Beaded Hide, Chief Moses, North Plains Indian	9250.00
Indian, Shirt, Deerskin, Colored Beads, Teton Dakota	8000.00
Indian, Teapot, Corn Pattern, Shawnee	25.00
Indian, Totem Pole, Thunderbird On Top, Late 1800s, 6 1/4 In.	25.00
Indian, Vase, Cherokee, Stoneware, Green, 2 Handled, 8 1/2 In.	45.00
Indian, Vase, Pine Ridge Sioux, Rust & Beige, Bulbous, 4 1/2 X 11 In.	14.00
Indian, Wall Pocket, Moccasin Shape, Beadwork, 4 In.	9.50
Inkstand, Bamboo Design, Leaves, Mythical Creatures, Cut Crystal Well, 1835	325.00
Inkstand, Brass Oriental Design, Cut Glass Inkwell, Black Lacquered Wood	125.00
Inkstand, Brass, Covered Sander, Inkwell, 2 Pen Holders, Butter Bell, 7 In.	225.00
Inkstand, Bronze Holder, Colonnade Relief, Raised Arches, Vertical Holders	85.00
Inkstand, Bronze, 2 Square Inkwells, Art Nouveau Design, Pierced Handles	225.00
Inkstand, Cut Crystal Inkwell Attached With Brass Beaded Collar, Embossed	310.00
Inkstand, Desk Set, Double Inkwell, Oblong Stand, Glass Insert, Floral	235.00
Inkstand, Desk Set, Signed, Marcus & Company, New York, Silver, C.1910	350.00
Inkstand, Double, Iron Well Covers Attached To Stand, 2 Pressed Glass Wells	175.00
Inkstand, Marble, Tray, Pen, Hinged Lid, Inkwell, Brass, Dutch Girl, 10 In.	125.00
Inkstand, Metal, Arc De Triomphe Center, Brass-Lidded Wells	50.00
Inkstand, Mythological Figures, Brass, 14 In.	150.00
Inkstand, Porcelain, Flower Garland, Eagles & Flame Torch, German	125.00
Inkstand, Porcelain, Seated Cupid, Well & Sander, Schlaggenwald, C.1835	80.00

Inkstand, Raised Cupids On Mythical Stallions, Scrolls, Leaf, Dolphins, Brass	145.00
Inkstand, Sea Green Onyx, Pen Supports In Onyx, Leaf Detailed, Acorn Finial	275.00
Inkwell, see also Brass, Inkwell; Pewter, Inkwell; and various porcelain	
categories	
Inkwell, Ball Shaped, Allover Sterling Silver Overlay, Top Removes, 3 In.	110.00
Inkwell, Blown Glass, 3-Mold, Amber, Keene	95.00
Inkwell, Blown Glass, 3-Mold, Olive Amber, McK G III-18	140.00
Inkwell, Blown Glass, 9 Panels To Lower Half, Round Dome Top, 2 In.	10.00
Inkwell, Blue Boot	55.00
Inkwell, Bonzo Dog, Painted Black Eyes, Nose, Red Tongue, 3 1/2 In.	35.00
Inkwell, Brass, Deer Head Antler Pen Rest With Glass Inkwell	82.00
Inkwell, Brass, Floral Design, 4 Feet	41.00
Inkwell, Brass, Mephistopheles, 2 Wells	30.00
Inkwell, Bronze Bear	18.00
Inkwell, Bronze, Art Nouveau, Oval, 4 X 2 In.	85.00
Inkwell, Bronze, Insert Of Crystal, Embossed Design On Panels, Acid Etched	135.00
Inkwell, Bronze, 4 Leaf Clover, Lady In Bonnet Cover, Gold Edging, 5 1/4 In.	55.00
Inkwell, Bull's-Eye Carving, Faceted Corners, Round Lid, Square, Soapstone	45.00
Inkwell, Cane On Bottom, Monogrammed, Sterling Silver Hinged Lid, Square	110.00
Inkwell, Cast Iron, 4 Feet, Pen Rest, Bone Handle, Gold Pen	90.00
Inkwell, Chair Shape, Blue, Pressed Glass, Daisy & Button	38.00
Inkwell, Champleve, Enamel, Brass Well, Grooved Onyx Base	100.00
Inkwell, Clear Vesicas, Tiffany Sterling Hinged Top, Footed	110.00
Inkwell, Coffin Shape, Molded Edges, Hinged, Pewter, 2 X 4 1/2 In.	75.00
Inkwell, Crystal & Brass, Blown Glass, British Made	33.00
Inkwell, Crystal, Painted Front & Top, 1 3/8 X 2 3/8 In.	24.00
Inkwell, Cut Crystal, Enamel Design, Cover Attached With Brass Collars	175.00
Inkwell, Cut Glass, Hinged Lid, Large	62.00
Inkwell, Deer, Double, Signed, Hubley & Bradley	145.00
Inkwell, Dome Shape, Brown Plastic Screw Top, Amber, Marked, 12-7-09	17.00
Inkwell, Donkey, Saddle Opens Up To Display Inkwell	110.00
Inkwell, Embossed Metal, 3 Glass Wells, Pen Rack, 3 X 4 X 2 In.	15.00
Inkwell, Figural, Deer's Hoof, Glass Insert, Metal Cover	22.50
Inkwell, Floral Enameled, Brass Hinged Lid & Saucer, Fischer	85.00
Inkwell, Glass, Self-Closing, Hard Rubber Top, 1914	14.00
Inkwell, Holly, Iridescent Blue, Green, Purple, Art Glass, 5 In.	125.00
Inkwell, Lacquer Box, Japanese, Rust, Gold, Gray Scenes, 2 1/2 X 2 1/4 In.	25.00
Inkwell, Laughing Woman, Porcelain, 3 In.	30.00
Inkwell, Metal, Figural, Bird, Branch, Nest, Eggs, Hinged Lid, 5 1/2 X 2 3/4 In.	50.00
Inkwell, Metal, Sterling, Red Wolf	45.00
Inkwell, Owl On Tree Trunk, Potmetal, Enameled Glass Insert, 6 1/4 In.	68.00
Inkwell, Owl, Glass Eyes, White Metal	38.00
Inkwell, Owl, Pewter	65.00
Inkwell, Paperweight, Bubbles, Open Top, 2 X 3 In.	20.00
Inkwell, Pewter, Bulldog With Pipe In Mouth	75.00
Inkwell, Pewter, Fox Head	45.00
Inkwell, Pewter, Hinge Cover, Small	53.00
Inkwell, Pewter, Saucer Based	60.00
Inkwell, Porcelain Bowl, Floral, Brass Top, 5 Pen Holders, 1 Well, Green, Red	140.00
Inkwell, Porcelain Bowl, Gold Chinoiserie Design, Brass Top, 5 Pen Holders	125.00
Inkwell, Porcelain, Benedictine Liqueur Bottle On Tray, Advertising	225.00
Inkwell, Porcelain, Commemorates U.S.Centenary Year, Uncle Sam, Lucy Liberty	550.00
Inkwell, Porcelain, Double Wells, Penholders, Rope Handles, Serpent Heads	525.00
Inkwell, Porcelain, 2 Rooster Design, Royal Copenhagen, 9 X 5 In.	250.00
Inkwell, Revolving Inks, Tatum Cinti, Cast Iron, 3 3/4 X 4 1/4 X 3 3/4 In.	95.00
Inkwell, Ribbed Glass, Pierced Sheffield Stand & Lid	65.00
Inkwell, Round, Cane Pattern, Hinged Sterling Silver Top, 3 In.	75.00
Inkwell, Round, Olive Green, White, Wedgwood	375.00
Inkwell, Sapphire Blue Glass, Hinged Glass Top, Ball Shaped & Feet, 4 In.	75.00
Inkwell, Scroll Over Tortoise Shell, 3 Quill Holder, Gilt, Signed, 4 In.	58.00
Inkwell, Sgraffito Carving, Soapstone, 2 X 1/2 In.	60.00
Inkwell, Tiffany, see Tiffany, Inkwell	
Inkwell, Traveling, Figural, Man's Shoe, Leather On Metal, 3 3/4 X 2 In.	60.00
Inkwell, Walnut, Corset Shaped, Inlaid Rim, Kinney Bros., Boston, 3 In.	15.00
Inkwell, White Metal, Double Bottle	42.00

Insulator, Aqua, F.M.Locke & Co.Victor, N.Y., 5-22-1894, 4 In.

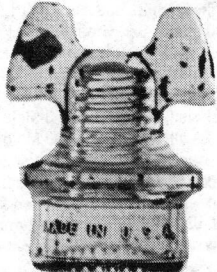

Insulator, Lynchburg, Aqua, 12-19-1871, 3 3/4 X 4 In.

Insulator, Hemingray-60, Pale Green, 5 In.

Inkwell, White, Pink & White Roses, Gold & Green Leaves, 4 Feet, 3 In.	19.50

Insulators of glass or pottery have been made for use on telegraph or telephone poles since 1844.

Insulator, Aqua, F.M.Locke & Co.Victor, N.Y., 5-22-1894, 4 In. ......*Illus*	3.00
Insulator, Armstrong, 14, Clear	12.00
Insulator, Brookfield, Aqua	2.00
Insulator, Brookfield, Aqua, Frosted Glass	3.00
Insulator, Brookfield, Aqua, Skirt-Shaped Dome	1.00
Insulator, Cable, Aqua	5.00
Insulator, California, Sage	4.00
Insulator, Castle, Straw, Mint	75.00
Insulator, CD 130, Light Aqua	130.00
Insulator, City Fire Alarm, Light Blue	25.00
Insulator, Cook, Brown Porcelain, U-295	3.00
Insulator, Dominion 42, Yellow, Mint	25.00
Insulator, Dominion, Amber	5.00
Insulator, Gayner, 530, Aqua	6.00
Insulator, Hemingray-60, Pale Green, 5 In. ......*Illus*	2.50
Insulator, Hemingray, E-14B, Opalescent	10.00
Insulator, Hemingray, No.12, Aqua	.25
Insulator, Hemingray, No.55, Aqua	2.00
Insulator, Hemingray, Patent Date, Columbia, Drips	47.00
Insulator, Insulator, Am.Ins.Co., Smooth Dome	75.00
Insulator, K.C.G.W., Green	8.00 To 25.00
Insulator, Knowles 6, Boston, Blue	70.00
Insulator, Lynchburg, Aqua, 12-19-1871, 3 3/4 X 4 In. ......*Illus*	5.00
Insulator, Lynchburg, No.44	.75
Insulator, Lynchburg, 53, Light Aqua	5.00
Insulator, Manhattan, Green	20.00
Insulator, Maydell, Milk Glass	7.00
Insulator, McLaughlin, No.62, Emerald Green	33.00
Insulator, McLaughlin, No.9, Emerald Green	6.00
Insulator, Mershon, Aqua, 3 Ridge Style	50.00
Insulator, Mulford & Biddle, Light Aqua	75.00
Insulator, Muncie, Hemingray, Blue, Mint	60.00
Insulator, N.E.G.M.Co., Aqua, Straight Sided	35.00
Insulator, No.4 Cable, Crisp Aqua, Good Embossing	70.00
Insulator, Oakman, Aqua, Embossed Base	15.00
Insulator, Pettingell Andrews Co.Boston, Aqua	65.00
Insulator, Prism, Blue, Mint	25.00
Insulator, Pyrex 661, Brilliant Carnival, Mint	35.00
Insulator, Pyrex, No.131, Yellow	8.00
Insulator, Pyrex, 171, Carnival Glass	19.00

Insulator, Pyrex, 233, Carnival Glass 45.00
Insulator, S.S. & Company, Lime Green 55.00
Insulator, Sombrero, Aqua, 7 In. 4.00
Insulator, Southern Massachusetts Telephone Company, Aqua 38.00
Insulator, Star, Aqua, Pointed Dome 2.00
Insulator, Star, Green, High Wire Groove 4.00
Insulator, T-H-B-9200, Aqua 80.00
Insulator, Unembossed Paisley, Light Blue With Amber Swirl 40.00
Insulator, U223a, White, 2 Piece Transposition 200.00
Insulator, V.G.Converse, Aqua 24.00
Insulator, Viking Helmet, Aqua 32.50
Insulator, Western Electric, Candlestick Phone, Battery Box, 1913 Patent 165.00
Insulator, Westinghouse, No.2, Blue, l/s/c 165.00
Insulator, Westinghouse, No.4, Yellow 30.00
Insulator, Westinghouse, No.6, Green 175.00
    Iron, see also Kitchen, Tool, Store
Iron, Ashtray, Stylized Black Scotty Dog, Art Deco, Marked Hubley 15.00
Iron, Auto Dray, 1911 Kenton, 9 In. 375.00
Iron, Boiler, Ham, Oval Shape, 24 1/4 In 55.00
Iron, Bookend, Art Deco, The Thinker, Original Paint 20.00
Iron, Bookend, Bronze Finish, Shape Of Ship, 4 1/2 In., Pair 5.95
Iron, Bookend, Dutch Girl Holding 2 Pails Over Shoulder, 6 In., Pair 10.00
Iron, Bookend, Figural, Lion, Standing, 4 X 6 In. 15.00
Iron, Bookend, Mayflower Ship, Pair 8.00
Iron, Bookend, Nude Sitting Inside Arch, Green Enamel, Pair 35.00
Iron, Bookend, Parrot, Pair 25.00
Iron, Bookend, Stagecoach, 4 X 7 In. 15.00
Iron, Bookend, The Thinker, Gilded, Pair 25.00
Iron, Bootjack, American Bulldog, Pistol Shape .... 30.00 To 37.50
Iron, Bootjack, Beetle Shaped, 1 Piece 22.50
Iron, Bootjack, Double-Ended 12.00
Iron, Bootjack, Geometrical Designs, 11 1/2 In. 22.50
Iron, Bootjack, Heart Design, 13 In. 30.00
Iron, Bootjack, Pitts Novelty Works, Buggy Wrench On One End, 13 In. 50.00
Iron, Bootjack, Reclining Nude, C.1860, 10 In. 25.00
Iron, Bottle Opener, Figural, Nude Girl 15.00
Iron, Bottle Opener, Wall Type, 5 In.Man's Face, Top Hat 24.00
Iron, Box, Mail, Wall, C.1900, 12 X 5 3/4 In. 12.00
Iron, Bracket, Lamp, Cast, Lacy Type, 20 X 11 In. 25.00
Iron, Bracket, Shelf, Cook Hook Buttons, Holds Shelf, Cast, Pair 9.50
Iron, Bracket, Shelf, Lacy, 9 X 7 In. 7.95
Iron, Bracket, Snake Protruding With Loop In Mouth, Vergennes, Vt., Pair 495.00
Iron, Bucket & Shovel, Coal, Miniature, No.200 On Bottom, 2 X 3 In. 12.00
Iron, Candleholder, Black, Floral Design, Brass Connectors, 6 1/2 In., Pair 37.50
Iron, Candleholder, Hogscraper, Push-Up, Lip Hanger, 7 1/2 In. 110.00
Iron, Candlestick, Hogscraper With Push-Up, Shaw, 7 In. 55.00
Iron, Candlestick, Spiral, Push-Up, Wood Base .... 125.00 To 155.00
Iron, Cat, Painted, 9 X 7 In. 65.00
Iron, Cauldron, Knob Handles, Rounded Bottom, D., 31 1/2 X 20 1/4 In. 125.00
Iron, Cauldron, 3 Triangular Feet, Convex Bottom, Diameter 39 In. 55.00
Iron, Chandelier, With Crystal, 8 Light, 24 X 23 In. 150.00
Iron, Chopper, Sugar, Peacock Head 400.00
    Iron, Coffee Grinder, see Coffee Grinder
Iron, Coffee Mill, Wood Base & Drawer, Wheel 10 In., Fairbanks Morse, Chicago 65.00
Iron, Colored Boy, Fishing, Sitting, White & Red Paint, 18 In. 45.00
Iron, Cork Presser, Apothecary, C.1870 .... 35.00
Iron, Corkscrew, Lignum Vitae, Handle-Brush 16.00
Iron, Cowbell, Large 10.00
Iron, Curling Iron, Scissor Style, 11 3/4 In. 38.00
Iron, Cuspidor, Cast 18.00
Iron, Dipper, Hand-Wrought, Handle Stamped 1859, 12 3/4 In. 20.00
Iron, Dispenser, Cigarette, With Ashtray, Elephant With Howdah 48.50
Iron, Dog, Black Scotty, 2 1/2 X 1 1/2 In. 12.00
Iron, Dog, White Sealyham, 2 X 1 3/8 In. 10.00
Iron, Dog, Wirehair Terrier, 3 X 3 In. 18.00

Iron, Door Knocker, Eagle 22.00

Iron doorstops have been made in all types of designs. The vast majority of the doorstops sold today are cast iron and were made from about 1890 to 1930. Most of them are shaped like people, animals, flowers, or ships.

Iron, Doorstop, Basket Of 8 Tulips, 10 In.	29.00
Iron, Doorstop, Boot, 11 1/4 In.	25.00
Iron, Doorstop, Cat, Flat Side	17.00
Iron, Doorstop, Cockatoo, 7 In.	15.00
Iron, Doorstop, Cottage	18.00
Iron, Doorstop, Frog, 5 1/2 In.	40.00
Iron, Doorstop, Full-Bodied Scotty Dog, Cat With Green Eyes	43.00
Iron, Doorstop, Goat	16.00
Iron, Doorstop, Horse	25.00 To 65.00
Iron, Doorstop, Kittens, Female & Male, 7 1/2 In.	30.00
Iron, Doorstop, Parrot Perched On Tree Trunk, 6 1/2 In.	14.00 To 45.00
Iron, Doorstop, Ship	22.00
Iron, Doorstop, Spaniel	12.00
Iron, Doorstop, Terrier, Large	30.00
Iron, Doorstop, Uncle Wiggily Rabbit, 10 In.	19.75
Iron, Doorstop, Windmill	19.00
Iron, Doorstop, Woman	20.00
Iron, Dumbbell, Miniature, 5 3/4 In.	10.00
Iron, Footscraper, Full Bodied, Dachshund Dog, 21 X 6 In.	60.00
Iron, Frame, Folding Stand, Design, 7 3/4 X 11 In.	42.50
Iron, Gate, Decorated, Early 20th Century, 67 X 54 In.	60.00
Iron, Gate, 8 Foot Section	100.00
Iron, Grinder, Food, Clamp-On, Signed Mt.Joy, 7 In.	20.00
Iron, Hinge, Ram's Horns, Hand-Wrought, Pair	50.00
Iron, Holder, Bill, Dated, 1889, 5 In.	16.00
Iron, Holder, Bill, Wall Hanging, Spike Type, Case, Ornate Scrollwork, 6 In.	10.00
Iron, Holder, Candle, Rush Saucer Base	275.00
Iron, Holder, Horsewhip	12.00
Iron, Holder, String, Beehive Shape, Cast	22.00
Iron, Holder, Tool, Fireplace, Ornate, Bradley & Hubbard	60.00
Iron, Holder, Twine, Round, Fancy	15.00
Iron, Holder, Whip, Buggy, With Hanger, Dated 1898	55.00
Iron, Hook, Meat, Hand-Wrought, 4 Prong, Ring Top, 18th Century, 8 1/2 In.	20.00
Iron, Horse, Prancing, Floral Base, 8 X 8 In.	35.00
Iron, Ice Tongs, 18 In.	12.00
Iron, Kettle, Bail Handle, Blue Porcelain, 6 X 10 In.	26.00
Iron, Kettle, Black, 3 Foot Bail, 2 X 1 In.	8.50
Iron, Kettle, Gooseneck, No.2 Size, Shaped Handle, 5 1/2 X 6 1/2 In.	365.00
Iron, Kettle, Tipping, Brass Finial Cover, C.1800	125.00
Iron, Kettle, Wire Bail, Iron Footed Ring To Sit On, Miniature	12.00
Iron, Kettle, 3 Footed, Bail Handle	52.00
Iron, Latch & Thumbpiece, Wrought, Suffolk, 18th Century, Pennsylvania, 15 In.	85.00
Iron, Lifter, Stove Plate	5.00
Iron, Lion, Reclining, Life Size, 1870	550.00
Iron, Lock & Key, Door, Handmade	35.00
Iron, Lock, Smokehouse	35.00
Iron, Lock, With Key, Trapezoid, 18th Century, 5 3/4 X 8 3/4 In.	120.00
Iron, Mailbox, Round, Century 1890	10.00
Iron, Match Holder, see also Match Holder	
Iron, Match Holder, Double, Rabbit, Bird, Gun, Wall Type, 10 1/2 In.	48.50
Iron, Match Holder, Lady's High-Button Shoe, Pedestal, 5 X 4 X 3 3/4 In.	30.00
Iron, Match Holder, Mechanical, Hinged Bird Picks Up Matches, 4 1/2 X 3 In.	35.00
Iron, Match Holder, Wall, Hunting Dog On Lid	27.50
Iron, Match Holder, Wall, Self-Closing, Dec.20, 1864, DM & Co., New Haven	18.00
Iron, Match Safe, 2 Pouch, Game Decoration, Hanging, Ring Top, 9 In.	36.00
Iron, Mold, Bullet, For Mini Balls, Two Cavity	15.00
Iron, Mold, Bullet, Pincers	15.00
Iron, Mold, Cookie, Floral, Oval	48.00
Iron, Mold, Cookie, 3 Tulips, Cast, Albany, New York, 4 X 6 In.	65.00

Iron, Mold, Doorstop, Wood Burner Locomotive, 27 Lbs., 10 1/4 X 7 X 4 In.	175.00
Iron, Nipper, Sugar, Spring Release, Hand Wrought, 9 In.	70.00
Iron, Nutcracker, Alligator, Green	15.00
Iron, Nutcracker, Figural, Dog, Brown Paint	22.00
Iron, Nutcracker, Figural, Squirrel	12.00
Iron, Nutcracker, Figural, St.Bernard Dog, 10 X 4 1/4 In.	35.00
Iron, Nutcracker, Lever Action, Marked, C.1913	25.00
Iron, Nutcracker, Lion Head & Crown	20.00
Iron, Nutcracker, Rooster Head, Brass	10.00
Iron, Nutcracker, Squirrel, Pennsylvania, C.1880	50.00
Iron, Nutcracker, Table Clamp-On Model, 1909 Patent	11.75
Iron, Opener, Bottle, Cast Model Of Bulldog's Head, 3 X 4 In.	10.50
Iron, Opener, Bottle, Cast, Model Of Pelican	8.00
Iron, Opener, Bottle, Parrot	15.00
Iron, Opener, Corkscrew & Bottle, , Mr.Snifter, 7 In.	38.50
Iron, Padlock, Bulldog On Front	20.00
Iron, Pail, Milk, Handle, Lid, 1 Gallon	7.50
Iron, Pail, Rock Island Lines, Lid, Handle, 6 Quart	22.50
Iron, Pan, Cornstick, 7 Ear Mold, Cast	15.00
Iron, Pan, Fry, Cast, Hand-Wrought Handle, Curved Rattail Hook, 11 1/2 In.	89.00
Iron, Pan, Fry, Long Handled, C.1880	125.00
Iron, Pan, Muffin, Scalloped Cups, Cast, 12 1/4 X 9 1/2 In.	32.50
Iron, Pan, Muffin, 3-Cup, Cast, 7 1/2 X 9 In.	8.00
Iron, Paperweight, Duck, C.1870, 2 1/2 In.	40.00
Iron, Paperweight, Eagle, 3 1/4 In.	12.00
Iron, Paperweight, Figural, Rat, 2 1/4 X 2 In.	10.00
Iron, Paperweight, Sitting Cat, 2 3/4 In.	12.00
Iron, Peeler, Apple, Clamp, Reading Hardware Co., 1872-76, 8 X 12 In.	50.00
Iron, Peeler, Wooden Knob Handle, June 10, 1873, 8 In.	25.00
Iron, Pipe Tongs, 18th Century	250.00
Iron, Pistol, Cap, The Big Noise, 5/16/22	32.00
Iron, Pitcher, Straight Sides, 3 1/4 X 5 In.	285.00
Iron, Plant Stand, Victorian	100.00
Iron, Planter, Hawk, Cutout, 12 In.	18.00
Iron, Pointer Dog, Gold Color, 6 1/2 X 11 In.	25.00
Iron, Porringer, Handled, Hand-Wrought, Signed Kenrick, 5 1/2 In.	65.00
Iron, Pot, Bean, With Cover, Cast, 10 X 6 1/2 In.	15.00
Iron, Pot, Rendering, Pot Within Pot, 4 In.	9.00
Iron, Pot, 19th Century, T. & C.Clark, 1 1/2 Pint	65.00
Iron, Pot, 3-Legged, Bean	18.00
Iron, Press, Lard	48.50
Iron, Print, Cookie, Bird On Branch, Oval	8.00
Iron, Pulley, Well	15.00
Iron, Pump, Pitcher, Old Red	25.00 To 35.00
Iron, Ricer, Potato, Dated 1887, 11 X 4 1/2 In.	15.00
Iron, Safe, Match, Double Urn, Hanging, Dated 1869	29.00
Iron, Scale, Blue Paint & Gold Leaf Borders, Brass Scoop, Early 19th Century	72.00
Iron, Scale, Table, Curved Legs, Brass Arm Across Front, 9 X 15 In.	40.00
Iron, Scissors, Candlewick, Civil War Era	17.50
Iron, Scissors, Hand-Forged, Signed Atkin	30.00
Iron, Scraper, Foot, Scotty Dog, 10 1/2 In.	35.00 To 50.00
Iron, Scraper, Ice, No.12	10.00
Iron, Sheller, Corn	45.00
Iron, Shovel, Hearth, Loop Handle, C.1860, 23 In.	20.00
Iron, Skate, Ice, Upturned Toepieces, Brass Acorn Tips, 19th Century, Pair	50.00
Iron, Skewer, Twisted Shank, 11 In.	18.00
Iron, Skillet, Miniature, Advertising On Back	7.00
Iron, Skillet, White Enameled Lining, 12 1/2 X 9 In.	15.00
Iron, Skillet, Wrought Iron Range Co.Home Comfort St.Louis, 2 1/2 In.	7.00
Iron, Skillet, 3-Footed, Handled, Cast	12.00
Iron, Snow Eagles, Cast In Form Of Spread-Winged American Eagle, 4 In.	325.00
Iron, Snow Eagles, 6 In., Pair	20.00
Iron, Spatula, Hand-Wrought	28.00
Iron, Spittoon, Tin Cover, Enameled Flange, 4 Pounds	45.00
Iron, Spittoon, Figural, Tortoise, Step-On Head, C.1880	125.00

Iron, Spoon, Hand-Wrought, 18th Century	24.00
Iron, Spoon, Marrow, Hand-Wrought, Folding, Open Handled	20.00
Iron, Steamboat, Gray, 8 In.	39.00
Iron, Stove, Miniature, American Comfort Woodburning, Includes Case	250.00
Iron, String Holder, Beehive Shape	15.00 To 22.00
Iron, Teakettle, Decoration On Spout, G.W.Ball & Co., Cincinnati, Ohio, 1866	125.00
Iron, Teakettle, Gooseneck Spout & Lid, Cast	25.00
Iron, Teakettle, Gooseneck, Ball Shape, 18th Century	160.00
Iron, Teakettle, Star With 7 On Sliding Cover	22.00
Iron, Teakettle, Twisted Bail Handle, Sliding Lid, Tip Ring, 13 X 13 In.	45.00
Iron, Toaster, Hand-Wrought, Design On Rack, 18 In.	85.00
Iron, Toaster, 22 In.	55.00
Iron, Tongs, Ember, Hand-Wrought, 18th Century, 13 In.	70.00
Iron, Torchere, Carved Bas Relief Alabaster Panel, Quatrefoil Shape, 68 In.	75.00
Iron, Toy, Fire Wagon, Driver, 2 Horses, 12 In.	175.00
Iron, Trap, Bear, Newhouse, No.5	220.00
Iron, Trimmer, Candlewick, Scissors Type, Hand-Wrought	24.00
Iron, Trimmer, Wick, Scissors, Dated 1864	11.00
Iron, Trivet, Embossed Richmond, Virginia, C.1922, 10 X 4 1/2 In.	14.00
Iron, Trivet, Figural, Turtle	12.50
Iron, Trivet, Heart	6.95
Iron, Trivet, Horseshoe Shape, Eagle At Top, Good Luck	11.95
Iron, Trivet, Horseshoe Shape, Good Luck, Star Center	9.00
Iron, Trivet, Mephistopheles, 13 1/4 In.	32.50
Iron, Trivet, Mrs. Streeters Magic Wier & Polisher, 4 Footed, Rectangular	25.00
Iron, Trivet, Openwork Center, Enterprise Manufacturing Co., 3 Footed, 6 In.	12.00
Iron, Trivet, The Cleveland Foundry Co., Star, Fan, Footed, 6 In.	12.00
Iron, Trivet, Tree, Cleveland Foundry	6.50
Iron, Trough, Watering, Horse	185.00
Iron, Waffle Iron, Heart Pattern, Turn Over, In Stand	22.50
Iron, Warmer, Boot, H.W.Hescock, Patented 1877	90.00
Iron, Warmer, Handle, Pan, Brass Lid, C.1800	195.00
Iron, Wheel, Circus Wagon, Set Of 4	90.00

Ironstone china was first made in 1813. It gained its greatest popularity during the mid-nineteenth century. The heavy, durable, off-white pottery was made in white or was colored with any of hundreds of patterns. Much flow blue pottery was made of ironstone. Some of the pieces had raised decorations.

Ironstone, see also Chelsea Grape, Gaudy Ironstone, Moss Rose, Wedgwood

Ironstone, Bone Dish, Bishop Stonier	5.00
Ironstone, Bowl & Pitcher, Blue Dragons, Octagon, White, Mason's, 14 X 5 In.	175.00
Ironstone, Bowl, Covered, Figural Handles, Faces	6.50
Ironstone, Bowl, Meakin, Essex, Brown Transfer, Lid, 9 X 6 In.	32.00
Ironstone, Bowl, White & Blue, Multicolor Floral, Ashworth, 10 In.	25.00
Ironstone, Box, Toothbrush, Floral, Luster Trim, Flower Finial, Covered, 9 In.	22.00
Ironstone, Butter Keeper, High Glaze, 19th Century, 9 X 9 In.	25.00
Ironstone, Can & Saucer, Coffee, Willow Pattern, Miles Mason, C.1800-1816	35.50
Ironstone, Chamber Pot With Lid, Wild Roses, C.1885, Wilkinson	45.00
Ironstone, Coffee Server, Rose Trim, Royal	35.00
Ironstone, Coffee Set, Child's, White, Pink Bands, Girl With Fan, Boys, 7 Piece	110.00
Ironstone, Coffeepot, Flowers & Leaves, Brown & White, 8 1/2 In.	35.00
Ironstone, Compote, Raised Grape Relief, Marked J & E Mayer, 10 X 6 In.	15.00
Ironstone, Compote, Ribbed, Footed, Bridgwood & Clarke, 4 In.	45.00
Ironstone, Compote, White, Blue & Brown Flowers Inside, Scalloped, 8 1/2 In.	35.00
Ironstone, Cup & Saucer, Demitasse, Oriental Scene, Raised Acorn, Mason	12.00
Ironstone, Cup & Saucer, Green, Grape Clusters, Hand-Painted	15.00
Ironstone, Cup & Saucer, Handleless, Luster Band, Livesley, Powell	16.00
Ironstone, Cup & Saucer, Handleless, Strawberry	135.00
Ironstone, Dish, Soap, Built-In Drain, F & T Co.	8.50
Ironstone, Dish, Soap, Maidenhair Fern, Gold, Soap Deck, Victorian	15.00
Ironstone, Dish, Vegetable, Covered, Chinese Pattern	90.00
Ironstone, Dish, Vegetable, Fruit Finial, Oval, J.Edwards	45.00

Ironstone, Dish, Vegetable, W.Baker Co., Blackberry, Ovoid, Covered	45.00
Ironstone, Dish, Vegetable, White, Covered, Matching Ladle, 6 X 5 X 3 In.	125.00
Ironstone, Foot Warmer, Oblong, Leytonstone	35.00
Ironstone, Gravy Boat, Tureen Shape, Spoon Opening In Lid, Acorn Finial	35.00
Ironstone, Gravy Boat, White Embossed Wheat, Robert Cohran & Co.Glasgow	19.00
Ironstone, Invalid Feeder	5.50
Ironstone, Jar, Black & Ocher Boar Hunting Scene On Blue Glaze, 4 In.	38.00
Ironstone, Jar, Mustard, Lid, Germany	4.00
Ironstone, Jug, Octagonal, Serpent Handle, Blue Willow, C.1850, 4 In.	58.00
Ironstone, Lid, Tureen, White, 9 1/2 In.	5.00
Ironstone, Match Holder, Geometric Symbol	10.00
Ironstone, Match Holder, White, Bell Shaped, 3 1/4 In.Base, 1 1/4 In.Top	30.00
Ironstone, Mold, Pudding, White	24.00
Ironstone, Pitcher, Brown Velvet, Mason, Octagonal, 5 In.	28.00
Ironstone, Pitcher, Chamber, Lily Of The Valley, Mellor & Co., 11 3/4 In.	35.00
Ironstone, Pitcher, Fleur-De-Lis, Molded, Beaded Edge, Meakin, 6 In.	20.00
Ironstone, Pitcher, Mason's, Oriental, Snake Handle	65.00
Ironstone, Pitcher, Milk, Alfred Meakin, 6 In.	40.00
Ironstone, Pitcher, Vista, Octagonal, Mason, 6 In.	25.00
Ironstone, Pitcher, White, 2 Quart	40.00
Ironstone, Plate, Blue Coat-Of-Arms Framed In Florals, 1868, 10 In.	30.00
Ironstone, Plate, Florals In Black, Gold, Brown, Ashworth, 9 In.	35.00
Ironstone, Plate, Flow Mulberry, 8 3/4 In.	30.00
Ironstone, Plate, Metallic Blue, Coat Of Arms, Floral Frame, Scalloped Edge	30.00
Ironstone, Plate, Oriental Scene, Multicolor, Pair, 10 1/4 In.	88.00
Ironstone, Plate, Pie, High Glaze, 19th Century, 10 X 1 1/2 In.	15.00
Ironstone, Plate, Pink & White, Roselle On Bottom, 8 1/2 In.	25.00
Ironstone, Plate, Pink, Fuchsia, Blue Floral, Glaze, Reticulated, C.1850, 10 In.	40.00
Ironstone, Plate, Salad, Teaberry Luster, Marked EXF, 7 1/2 In.	70.00
Ironstone, Plate, White, Blue & Red Border, John Maddock, 9 In.	5.00
Ironstone, Plate, White, Blue Grape Bunches On Border, 9 1/2 In.	9.00
Ironstone, Plate, White, Meakin, 10 In.	3.00
Ironstone, Plate, White, 7 1/2 In.	8.00
Ironstone, Platter, Blue & White, Oval, Ashworth Brothers, 10 In.	25.00
Ironstone, Platter, Jenny Lind, 4 Colors, Scenic Transfer, 10 X 13 In.	75.00
Ironstone, Platter, Meakin, Essex, Brown Transfer, 16 X 11 In.	25.00
Ironstone, Platter, Moss Rose, Meakin, 14 X 10 In.	24.00
Ironstone, Platter, Mulberry, Oblong, Corean, J.Clemonson, 10 X 7 1/2 In.	22.00
Ironstone, Platter, Tureen, Crazing, Marked, 10 1/4 X 15 In.	8.00
Ironstone, Platter, Vincennes, Red, Alcock, C.1853, 18 1/2 In.	124.00
Ironstone, Platter, White, Johnson Brothers, 11 1/2 X 16 In.	35.00
Ironstone, Platter, White, 12 X 18 In., Pair	18.00
Ironstone, Server, Cheese, Mason, Center Pedestal Early 1900s, Blue, Orange	23.00
Ironstone, Stamp, Butter, Carved Wheat, 3 In.	37.00
Ironstone, Sugar, Forget-Me-Nots, Meakin, 6 In.	28.00
Ironstone, Sugar, Scenic, Child Dog, River, English Mark	35.00
Ironstone, Syrup, Beige, Hand-Painted Floral, W & W Co., English	95.00
Ironstone, Tea Leaf, Bowl, Footed, Covered, Anthony Shaw, 10 1/2 In.	58.00
Ironstone, Tea Leaf, Bowl, Paneled, 5 1/4 X 3 1/2 In.	34.00
Ironstone, Tea Leaf, Butter Pat, Fluted, Square, M.Taylor, 2 1/2 In.	12.50
Ironstone, Tea Leaf, Butter Pat, Square, Meakin, 2 3/4 In., Set Of 4	40.00
Ironstone, Tea Leaf, Coffee Set, Child's, Mellnor Taylor, 3 Piece	135.00
Ironstone, Tea Leaf, Coffeepot	85.00
Ironstone, Tea Leaf, Coffeepot, Meakin	95.00
Ironstone, Tea Leaf, Cup & Saucer, A.J.Wilkinson	24.00
Ironstone, Tea Leaf, Cup & Saucer, Demitasse	24.00
Ironstone, Tea Leaf, Dish, Covered, Royal Ironstone China, A.J.Wilkinson	75.00
Ironstone, Tea Leaf, Dish, Vegetable, Covered, A.J.Wilkinson, 9 X 6 1/4 In.	30.00
Ironstone, Tea Leaf, Dish, Vegetable, Rectangular, Covered, 8 1/2 In.	65.00
Ironstone, Tea Leaf, Dish, Vegetable, Square, Covered, 7 In.	50.00
Ironstone, Tea Leaf, Gravy Boat	27.00
Ironstone, Tea Leaf, Gravy Boat With Underplate, Alfred Meakin	45.00
Ironstone, Tea Leaf, Pitcher, J. & E.M., 6 In.	35.00
Ironstone, Tea Leaf, Pitcher, Thomas Furnival & Sons, 7 3/4 In.	60.00
Ironstone, Tea Leaf, Plate, A.J.Wilkinson, 8 3/4 In.	90.00

Ironstone, Tea Leaf, Plate, A.Meakin, 8 1/2 In. 14.50
Ironstone, Tea Leaf, Plate, Cake, 9 1/2 In. 18.00
Ironstone, Tea Leaf, Plate, Davenport Impressed Anchor, C.1800, 7 In. 14.00
Ironstone, Tea Leaf, Plate, H.Burgess, 7 3/4 In. 19.50
Ironstone, Tea Leaf, Plate, Luster, Shaw, 9 1/2 In. 14.00
Ironstone, Tea Leaf, Plate, Soup, E.Malkin & Co., Set Of 5 .... 25.00
Ironstone, Tea Leaf, Plate, Soup, Edwards Co. 15.00
Ironstone, Tea Leaf, Plate, Wedgwood, 8 1/2 In. 17.00
Ironstone, Tea Leaf, Platter, A.J.Wilkinson, 12 X 8 In. 22.00
Ironstone, Tea Leaf, Platter, Alfred Meakin, 10 X 14 In. 25.00
Ironstone, Tea Leaf, Platter, Alfred Meakin, 16 In. 30.00
Ironstone, Tea Leaf, Platter, Alfred Meakin, 8 1/2 X 12 In. 22.00
Ironstone, Tea Leaf, Platter, Anthony Shaw, 19 X 13 1/2 In. 35.00
Ironstone, Tea Leaf, Platter, Copper Luster, Alfred Meakin, 16 X 11 In. 40.00
Ironstone, Tea Leaf, Platter, Curved Ends, Grindley, 10 X 14 In. 45.00
Ironstone, Tea Leaf, Platter, Impressed Burgess, 10 X 14 In. 28.00
Ironstone, Tea Leaf, Platter, Ridged Edge, Wedgwood, 10 X 14 In. 45.00
Ironstone, Tea Leaf, Platter, 12 X 17 In. 22.50
Ironstone, Tea Leaf, Relish, Grindley, 5 X 8 1/4 In. 24.00
Ironstone, Tea Leaf, Sauce, Oval, M.Taylor, 4 X 5 1/2 In. 30.00
Ironstone, Tea Leaf, Saucer, Anthony Shaw 6.00
Ironstone, Tea Leaf, Soup, Wedgwood, 8 3/4 In. 18.00
Ironstone, Tea Leaf, Sugar, Alfred Meakin, Covered, 7 X 7 1/2 In. 48.00
Ironstone, Tea Leaf, Sugar, Covered, Tall, Alfred Meakin, England 50.00
Ironstone, Tea Leaf, Teapot, Royal Ironstone, Alfred Meakin, England, 9 In. 75.00
Ironstone, Tea Leaf, Tray, Serving, 12 In. 12.00
Ironstone, Tea Leaf, Tureen, Royal Ironstone China, A.J.Wilkinson, England 100.00
Ironstone, Tea Set, Child's, Gold Luster Tea Leaf, Mellor & Taylor, 23 Piece 1000.00
Ironstone, Tea Set, Child's, Scenes, Blue Trim, 9 Piece 58.00
Ironstone, Tea Set, Child's, 20 Piece 25.00
Ironstone, Teapot, Gold Trim, White, England, Meakin, 11 In. 35.00
Ironstone, Tile, Scenic, Blue & White, Wooden Footed Frame, 8 In. 30.00
Ironstone, Toast Rack, Mason, Pawsley 18.00
Ironstone, Tumble-Up Set, Red Floral Decoration, 2 Piece 32.50
Ironstone, Tureen & Ladle, White, J & S Meakin, 10 1/2 X 7 In. 105.00
Ironstone, Tureen, Soup, White, Bar Handles, 13 X 7 1/2 In. 60.00
Ironstone, Tureen, White, Johnson Bros. 40.00
Ironstone, Vase, Cameo, Bird & Flower, Green Satin 25.00
Ironstone, Vegetable Bowl, Covered, Wheat & Clover, Meakin 55.00
Ironstone, Vegetable, Copper Luster Trim, Cover, Handles, Registered, 12 In. 95.00
Ironstone, Washbowl & Pitcher, Octagonal, Gaudy, Flow Blue, Burnt Orange 85.00
Ironstone, Washbowl Set, Pink & Yellow Flowers, Gold Trim, 10 Piece 180.00
Ironstone, Washbowl, Pitcher, White, Royal Crown 16.00
Ironstone, Washbowl, Wheat 30.00
Ironstone, Washstand Service, C.1850, Mason's Of England, 4 Piece 350.00
Ironstone, Washstand Set, Birds & Flowers, C.1845, Mason 265.00
Ivorex, Plaque, Niagara Falls, Wax, 1908, Signed 30.00
    Ivory, see also Napkin Ring, Netsuke
    Ivory, Netsuke see Netsuke
Ivory, Ball, Billiard, Oak Box, Pair 75.00
Ivory, Box, Patch, Inlaid Gold & Silver, 18th Century, 1 7/8 X 3 5/8 In. 785.00
Ivory, Box, Pin, Screw On Lid 15.00
Ivory, Box, Vesta, In Form Of Book, 1 X 1 1/2 In. 22.00
Ivory, Buddha, On Carved Amber Base, 1 1/2 X 1 In. 30.00
Ivory, Bust, Head Of Woman, Bronze Pedestal, Signed Bernoud, 4 1/4 In. 125.00
Ivory, Buttonhook, French 2.00
Ivory, Candlestick, Engraved Dragon & Floral, Wood Base, 19th Century, 12 In. 100.00
Ivory, Card Case, Heavily Carved 195.00
Ivory, Charm, Figural, Foo Dog, Chinese, Gold Loop 18.50
Ivory, Chess Set, Marble Board, Elephant Ivory 750.00
Ivory, Chime, Carved, Figure, 2 In. 27.00
Ivory, Cigarette Holder, Dragon Claw, 3 In. 8.75
Ivory, Cigarette Holder, Intricately Carved 10.00
Ivory, Dominos, Handmade, Wood Backs, Full Set 35.00
Ivory, Ear Spoon, Carved 4.00

Ivory, Elephant, Attached To Wood, Carved, 7 Elephants	47.00
Ivory, Etui, Fitted, 9 Silver Sewing Articles, French	335.00
Ivory, Figurine, African, 10 Elephants On Bridge, 30 In.	875.00
Ivory, Figurine, Buddha On Carved Amber Base, 1 1/2 X 1 In.	30.00
Ivory, Figurine, Camel, 1 1/2 X 1 1/2 In.	25.00
Ivory, Figurine, Carved Figure Of Sitting Hoeti, 2 1/2 In.	38.00 To 55.00
Ivory, Figurine, Dark Haired Man, Papier-Mache Frame, 1840's	125.00
Ivory, Figurine, Diety Of Thousand Hands, Chinese Carving, 8 1/2 In.	195.00
Ivory, Figurine, Doctor's Lady, Figure Lying On Rosewood Stand, 9 In.	175.00
Ivory, Figurine, Emperor & Empress, Carved, Teakwood Stand, 12 In.	650.00
Ivory, Figurine, Emperor & Empress, Pierced Wood Stand, 21 1/2 In., Pair	1500.00
Ivory, Figurine, Foo Dog, Wood Stand, 5 In., Pair	340.00
Ivory, Figurine, Hoeti With Hands Over Head, 2 1/2 In.	38.00
Ivory, Figurine, Horses, Semiprecious Stones, 4 X 4 1/2 In.	300.00
Ivory, Figurine, Immortals, Chinese, 4 1/2 In.Set Of Eight	355.00
Ivory, Figurine, Japanese Fisherman, Signed, 6 1/4 X 1 1/2 In.	95.00
Ivory, Figurine, Lady Seated Holding Book, Oriental Carving, 6 In.	250.00
Ivory, Figurine, Maiden, China, 19th Century, 7 1/2 In., Pair	350.00
Ivory, Figurine, Man Carrying Net Filled With Fish, Japanese, 6 In.	230.00
Ivory, Figurine, Man Drumming On Drum, 8 In.	150.00
Ivory, Figurine, Man Holding Basket Of Turtles, Japanese, 5 3/4 In.	260.00
Ivory, Figurine, Man With Son, C.1850, Chinese, 4 1/4 In.	95.00
Ivory, Figurine, Man With Staff, 6 3/4 In.	175.00
Ivory, Figurine, Man, Monkey On Back, Japanese, Signed, 4 In.	60.00
Ivory, Figurine, Medicine Doll On Pierced Wood Settee, 19 In.	550.00
Ivory, Figurine, Nude Oriental Woman Standing In Clamshell, Sea Life, 8 In.	215.00
Ivory, Figurine, Phoenix Bird, 10 In., Pair	400.00
Ivory, Figurine, Rabbi, 6 Standing, Long Robes & Skull Caps, 4 In.	550.00
Ivory, Figurine, Reclining Doctor's Lady, Movable Bracelets, 8 In.	115.00
Ivory, Figurine, Sea Goddess Holding Basket Of Fish, Chinese, 9 1/2 In.	260.00
Ivory, Figurine, Sitting Queen, 4 In.	95.00
Ivory, Figurine, Standing Buddha Holding Lotus Blossom, 16 In.	950.00
Ivory, Figurine, Standing Hoeti, Arms Raised Over Head, Carved, 4 1/4 In.	42.00
Ivory, Figurine, Standing Loham, Chinese, Carved, 1368-1644, 9 In.	600.00
Ivory, Figurine, Standing Longevity, 11 In.	225.00
Ivory, Figurine, Standing Pig, 2 3/4 In.	15.00
Ivory, Group, Bearded Sage On Horse With Attendant, China, 9 In.	300.00
Ivory, Group, Four Men, Deep Carving, Teak Stand, China, 10 In.	485.00
Ivory, Group, Man & Two Children, Actors, Chinese, Carved, 7 In.	200.00
Ivory, Group, Two Men & Boy, Japanese, 6 In.	225.00
Ivory, Holder, Cigar & Cigarette In Leather Carrying Case	15.00
Ivory, Holder, Pen, Hand Carved, Open Work, Horse-Head Top, 7 1/2 In.	10.00
Ivory, Knife Rest, Elephant Detail	16.00
Ivory, Knife, Ceremonial, Ebony Head, African, C.1900, 18 In.	150.00
Ivory, Knife, Encased Hara-Kiri, 12 In.Holder	295.00
Ivory, Mask Set, Emperor & Empress, Carved, Wood Stand, 4 In., Pair	130.00
Ivory, Match Holder, Pig, Well On Back, Striker On Belly, 5 X 2 1/4 In.	58.00
Ivory, Napkin Ring, Carved Scene, Deer In Woodland	32.00
Ivory, Pin, Carved, Brass Framed	25.00
Ivory, Pipe, Carved, Inked, Oriental Gods, Sterling Insert, Gold Band	125.00
Ivory, Rattle, Baby, Miniature, Hand-Painted, 2 1/2 In.	19.00
Ivory, Shoehorn, Carved Fish Handle, Oriental, 4 1/4 In.	30.00
Ivory, Spoon, Salt, Carved, C.1850, 2 1/2 In.	12.50
Ivory, Statue, Dragon, Carved, Stand, 52 In.	3500.00
Ivory, Stickpin, Owl	10.00
Ivory, Stretcher, Glove, Carved	45.00
Ivory, Stretcher, Glove, 7 In.	20.00
Ivory, Triptych, Judaic, Carved Ivory Ball, Judaic Scenes On Inside	140.00
Ivory, Tusks, Walrus, Female, 30 X 23 In.	785.00
Ivory, Tusks, Walrus, Mounted, Male, 29 1/2 X 22 In.	800.00
Ivory, Urn, Charcoal, Carved Dragons, Handled, Wood Platform, Chinese, 6 In.	490.00
Ivory, Urn, Covered, Tree & Foo Dog Finials, Carved Panels, 20 In.	650.00
Ivory, Urn, Hanging, Salamander Panels, Kylin Mask Handles, 27 1/2 In.	1400.00
Ivory, Vase, Dragon Finial, Clouds, Wood Stand, Oriental, Covered, 9 In.	175.00
Ivory, 10 Layer Carved Ball On Stand	95.00

Jack Armstrong, Flashlight, Bullet, Black 12.50
Jack Armstrong, Pedometer 10.00
Jack Armstrong, Telescope 10.00

*Jack-In-The-Pulpit vases were named for their odd trumpetlike shape
that resembles the wild plant called jack-in-the-pulpit. The design
originated in the late Victorian years.*

Jack-In-The-Pulpit, Vase, Amber & White Striped, 5 Applied Pink Feet, Pair 60.00
Jack-In-The-Pulpit, Vase, Cobalt Stripes, 11 In. 125.00
Jack-In-The-Pulpit, Vase, Cranberry To Clear, Applied Glass On Body, 9 In. 65.00
Jack-In-The-Pulpit, Vase, Cranberry, Scalloped, Flower Shape Top, 8 In. 85.00
Jack-In-The-Pulpit, Vase, Diamond-Quilted, Clear To Red Edge, 5 3/4 In. 75.00
Jack-In-The-Pulpit, Vase, End-Of-Day, 7 1/2 In. 33.00
Jack-In-The-Pulpit, Vase, Fiery Opalescent, 5 1/4 In, Pair 110.00
Jack-In-The-Pulpit, Vase, Footed, Maroon To Cream Overlay, Scalloped, 7 In. 118.00
Jack-In-The-Pulpit, Vase, Green, White, Yellow, Orange Enamel Design, 7 In. 24.50
Jack-In-The-Pulpit, Vase, Ground Bottom, 6 1/2 In. 20.00
Jack-In-The-Pulpit, Vase, Opalescent Cranberry Swirl, 9 In. 65.00
Jack-In-The-Pulpit, Vase, Pink To Clear, Gold & Enameled Floral, 6 1/2 In. 45.00
Jack-In-The-Pulpit, Vase, Pink, Opalescent, Shading Down To Clear, 9 1/4 In. 60.00
Jack-In-The-Pulpit, Vase, Prayer Rug, Custard, Pair 60.00
Jack-In-The-Pulpit, Vase, Ruffled, Spatter Glass Top, Pink, White, 14 In. 35.00
Jack-In-The-Pulpit, Vase, Threaded, In Ornate Metal Stand, 8 In. 35.00
Jack-In-The-Pulpit, Vase, Vaseline, Opalescent, Cranberry, 6 5/8 In. 125.00
Jack-In-The-Pulpit, Vase, White, Blue, Ruffled Edge, Pair, 4 In. 25.00

*Jackfield ware was originally a black glazed pottery made in Jackfield,
England, from 1750 to 1775. A yellow glazed ware has also been called
Jackfield ware. Most of the pieces referred to as Jackfield are black
pieces made during the Victorian era.*

Jackfield, Creamer, Cow, 7 In. 40.00
Jackfield, Pitcher, Black, 6 In. 15.00
Jade, Bottle, Snuff, Tulip, Green, Teakwood Stand, 6 X 2 X 1 In. 200.00
Jade, Bowl, Bronze Form, Horned Dragon-Head Handles, 19th Century, 8 In. 900.00
Jade, Bowl, Drum Shape On 3 Ogre Mask, Stump Feet, Carved, Handled, 7 In. 1250.00
Jade, Bowl, Flaring, Footed, Black Flecks, Wooden Stand, 4 7/8 In., Pair 350.00
Jade, Box, Carved Top Set In 3-Compartment Brass Box 125.00
Jade, Buckle, Recumbent Horse Form, Monkey On Back, Wooden Stand, 4 In. 250.00
Jade, Cricket Cage, 2-Part, Purse Form, Carved, Scrolled, 2 1/2 In. 325.00
Jade, Cup, Half-Melon Form, Carved Handle, Leaf Forming Foot, 4 1/4 In. 425.00
Jade, Cup, Handleless, Bell Shape, Ring Foot, Wooden Stand, 2 1/2 In., Pair 200.00
Jade, Cup, Interwined With Flowers & Vines, 5 1/2 X 4 1/2 X 2 1/2 In. 375.00
Jade, Cup, Teakwood Stand In Nailhead Decoration, 2 1/2 X 4 3/4 In. 275.00
Jade, Dish, Lotus Leaf Form, Carved Handles, Wooden Stand, 9 1/4 In. 700.00
Jade, Figurine, Birds Perched On Branch, Flowers, Teakwood Stand, 10 In. 1800.00
Jade, Figurine, Carnelian Eagle, 3 3/4 X 2 X 1 1/2 In. 150.00
Jade, Figurine, Elephant Striding, Wooden Stand, 4 3/4 In., Pair 250.00
Jade, Figurine, Elephant, White, Teak Base, 4 In., Pair 159.00
Jade, Figurine, Fantail Goldfish Swimming, Teak Base, Plum, 1 3/4 X 2 In. 200.00
Jade, Figurine, Foo Dog, Brown Jade Spots, Oval Teakwood Stand, 2 X 5 In. 425.00
Jade, Figurine, Foo Dog, Brown Spots, Green, Teakwood Stand, Oval, 2 X 5 In. 425.00
Jade, Figurine, Foo Lion, Crouching, Incised Mane & Tail, 18th Century, 4 In. 1100.00
Jade, Figurine, Horse, Green, Teakwood Stand, Miniature, 2 1/2 X 3 In., Pair 150.00
Jade, Figurine, Horse, Spinach Green With Black Mottlings, 23 X 15 1/2 In. 12000.00
Jade, Figurine, Horse, Teakwood Stand, 2 1/2 X 3 In., Pair 150.00
Jade, Figurine, Rhino, Green, Teakwood Stand, Miniature, 3 X 3 In., Pair 150.00
Jade, Figurine, Rhino, Teakwood Stand, 2 1/2 In., Pair 150.00
Jade, Figurine, Turtle Sitting On Pedestal, Green & Black Veining, 3 In. 80.00
Jade, Incense Burner, Lion Masks, Dragon-Head Handles, 3 Feet, 4 3/4 In. 750.00
Jade, Screen, Carved Teakwood Frame And Stand 75.00
Jade, Vase, Pale Green, Circular, Fluted Sides, 2 1/8 In., Pair 400.00

*Japanese Coralene is a pottery decorated with small raised beads and dots.
It was first made in the nineteenth century. Later wares made to imitate
coralene had dots of enamel.*

Japanese Coralene, Box, Cover	98.00
Japanese Coralene, Box, Victorian Lady & Man On Cover, Hand-Painted	98.00
Japanese Coralene, Lamp Base, 13 In.	139.00
Japanese Coralene, Urn, Stars, Geometric, Green Shades, Art Deco, 12 In.	150.00
Japanese Coralene, Vase, Beaded Roses, Cobalt, Gold Trim, 1909, 5 In.	95.00
Japanese Coralene, Vase, Coral, 2 Handles, Footed, Gold Jeweling, 7 In.	175.00
Japanese Coralene, Vase, Cream To Brown, Dandelion, Gold Trim, 10 1/4 In.	150.00
Japanese Coralene, Vase, Gold Leaf Trim, 1909, 5 In.	225.00
Japanese Coralene, Vase, Moriage, Blue & White Flowers On Yellow, 6 1/2 In.	125.00
Japanese Coralene, Vase, Pale Green, Pastel Floral, Jeweled Handles, 7 In.	175.00
Japanese Coralene, Vase, Two Handled, Slender, Gilded Handles & Borders, 7 In	135.00
Japanese Coralene, Vase, Yellow Roses With Shades Of Green On Pink, 5 In.	60.00

Jasperware is a fine-grained pottery developed by Josiah Wedgwood in 1755. The jasper was made in many colors including the most famous, a light blue. It is still being made.

Jasperware, see also Various Art Potteries, Wedgwood

Jasperware, Bowl, Pipe, Dark Blue, White	325.00
Jasperware, Box, Heart Form, Raised Art Nouveau Nymphs, Green, White, No.1259b	41.50
Jasperware, Box, Light Green, Cherubs, 2 1/4 X 3 X 4 1/2 In.	35.00
Jasperware, Chamberstick, Blue & White, Heart Shaped	22.00
Jasperware, Cheese Keeper, Christmas Trees, Knotted Rope Handle On Bell	425.00
Jasperware, Cigar Holder, 3 Classical Motifs Inside, Blue, White	145.00
Jasperware, Figurine, Rhinoceros, Ruby Eyes, 2 1/4 X 4 1/2 In.	485.00
Jasperware, Hair Receiver, Blue & White, Heart Shape, 4 In.	40.00
Jasperware, Hair Receiver, Green	65.00
Jasperware, Hatpin Holder, Art Nouveau	40.00
Jasperware, Hatpin Holder, Cameo Of Lady, Gilded Frame, 6 Sided, 5 1/2 In.	75.00
Jasperware, Jar, Cracker, Dark Blue, Adams, Tunstall, England, 9 1/2 In.	135.00
Jasperware, Jar, Dancing Maidens, Blue, Covered, 3 In.	30.00
Jasperware, Jug, Wedgwood, White Relief Classical Ladies, Blue Border, Marked	125.00
Jasperware, Pitcher, Cameo Lady, 5 1/8 In.	78.00
Jasperware, Pitcher, Classical Figures, Vintage, Rope Handle, Marked, 7 In.	95.00
Jasperware, Plaque, Cupid & Venus, Green, 6 In.	85.00
Jasperware, Plaque, Green, Raised Cupids, 5 In.	42.50
Jasperware, Plaque, Lady In Hammock, Cherub, Charcoal, 8 X 11 In.	300.00
Jasperware, Sugar & Creamer, White Cherubs On Green	20.00 To 29.00
Jasperware, Sugar Shaker, Wedgwood, White Relief Classical Figures On Blue	135.00
Jasperware, Sugar Shaker, 2 Molded Reliefs Of Classical Figures, Blue, White	165.00
Jasperware, Teapot, Dark Blue, 10 X 6 In.	195.00
Jasperware, Urn, Miniature, Dancing Hours Motif, Satyr Heads On Sides, Black	550.00
Jasperware, Water Set, Copeland Spode, 7 Piece	375.00
Jervis, Bowl, Molded Seashells, 1 3/4 X 2 1/4 In.	175.00
Jervis, Vase, Bud, Brown-Pepper Yellow Matte Glaze, Green Top, 7 In.	150.00

Jewel Tea, see Autumn Leaf
Jewelery, Ring, see also Disneyana, Ring; Hopalong Cassidy, Ring
Jewelry, see also Coronation, Faberge, Gutta-Percha

Jewelry, Beads, Amber, Uncut, 40 Inch Strand	90.00
Jewelry, Beads, Cherry Amber, 33 In.	65.00
Jewelry, Beads, Cherry Amber, 35 In.	85.00
Jewelry, Beads, Coral, Small, Round, 30 In.	35.00
Jewelry, Beads, Gold-Filled, Graduated, Round, 15 In.	20.00
Jewelry, Beads, Graduated Marble Glass	30.00
Jewelry, Beads, Jet & Crystal, Art Deco, 30 In.	45.00
Jewelry, Beads, Rock Crystal, Faceted, 50 In.	85.00
Jewelry, Beads, Teardrop, Oval & Round Camphor Glass	25.00
Jewelry, Beads, With Earrings, Honey Amber, 26 In.	95.00
Jewelry, Beads, 120 14K Gold Beads, 27 In.	495.00
Jewelry, Beads, 93 Graduated Opals, Cut Crystal Rondels	300.00
Jewelry, Bib Clip, Sterling Silver, Pink & White Underglaze, Enamel, Chain	22.00
Jewelry, Box, Trinket, General Lee & White Horse, Gold Trim	55.00
Jewelry, Bracelet & Earrings, Silver & Jade, Mexican	30.00
Jewelry, Bracelet, Antique, 7 Small Charms, 18K Gold	75.00
Jewelry, Bracelet, Bangle, Sterling, Tiffany	35.00
Jewelry, Bracelet, Cloisonne, Silver Lion Heads On Copper, Blue, Flowers	100.00

Jewelry, Bracelet, Cuff, Chinese, Carved Apricot Jade, 3 1/2 In. 250.00
Jewelry, Bracelet, Enameled, Garnets & Turquoises, Hungary, 5 Links 225.00
Jewelry, Bracelet, Lava, 9 Carved Cameos, Victorian 285.00
Jewelry, Bracelet, Link, 5 Apple Jade Stones, 14K Gold 75.00
Jewelry, Bracelet, Links, Flat, Gold, Pearl, 14K 96.00
Jewelry, Bracelet, Pearl & Sapphire, Triple Strand, 3 Sapphires 800.00
Jewelry, Bracelet, Pinchbeck & Enamel, Victorian 195.00
Jewelry, Bracelet, Snake, Stone Inset Eyes, Scales, Carved, Ivory, India 85.00
Jewelry, Bracelet, Tortoiseshell 25.00
Jewelry, Bracelet, Victorian, Wide Goldtone, One Carved, Lady's, C.1890 .... 15.00
Jewelry, Bracelet, 18K Gold, Faceted & Chased Links 495.00
Jewelry, Bracelet, 18K Heavy Gold Estate, Faceted, Chased Links 495.00
Jewelry, Bracelet, 3 Ivory Panels, Oriental Lady's, 5 Link, Safety Chain 150.00
Jewelry, Brooch, Amethyst Crystal & Baroque Pearl, Yellow Gold Mount 225.00
Jewelry, Brooch, Black & White Medallion In Victorian Sterling, 1 7/8 In. 175.00
Jewelry, Brooch, Black Onyx, Opal And Pearl Center, Gold Frame, Victorian 4.00
Jewelry, Brooch, Bohemian Garnet, Set In Low-Carat Gold, 2 In. 55.00
Jewelry, Brooch, Courtier Playing Lute, Brass, Limoges 25.00
Jewelry, Brooch, Floral, Sterling Silver 7.00
Jewelry, Brooch, Gold Hair, Black Enamel Border, Glass Window, 19th Century 35.00
Jewelry, Brooch, Shell Cameo, 3 Muses, Gold Frame, Peter Stephenson, 2 1/8 In. 225.00
Jewelry, Brooch, Victorian, Enameled, Floral 40.00
Jewelry, Brooch, 14K Gold, Victorian, Enamel, Pearls, Turquoises 105.00
Jewelry, Brooch, 54 Cut Garnets, Large Garnet On Top, Gold, Oval 90.00
Jewelry, Buckle, Marcasite, Oval, French, 1 1/2 In. 18.00
Jewelry, Case, Cigarette, Champleve, Dragon's Head, Silver Over Copper 85.00
Jewelry, Chain, Chinese, 5 Graduated Lapis Lazuli Balls, Silver, 16 In. 68.00
Jewelry, Chain, Italian Box Neck, 14K, 16 In. 66.00
Jewelry, Chain, Link Design, Sterling Silver, 23 In. 22.50
Jewelry, Chain, Lorgnette, 14K Gold, Waldemere, Linked With Swivel 95.00
Jewelry, Chain, Watch, Braided Hair 18.00
Jewelry, Chain, Watch, Lady's Amethyst Stone, Slide 80.00
Jewelry, Chain, Watch, Lady's, Gold, Fan Fob, Leaves Of Gold, Mother-Of-Pearl 29.50
Jewelry, Chain, Watch, 14K, Yellow Gold, Swivel Hook, 24 In. 140.00
Jewelry, Chain, 14K, White Gold, 18 In. 22.00
Jewelry, Chain, 14K, Yellow Gold, Curb Link, 22 In. 78.00
Jewelry, Charm, Sterling Silver Miniature World War II Tank 14.00
Jewelry, Charm, 14K Gold Thimble 45.00
Jewelry, Chatelaine, Pin, Bar, Black Onyx, Black Enamel 65.00
Jewelry, Cuff Links, Steamship, Blue & White Enamel On Silver 10.00
Jewelry, Cutter, Cigar, 14K Gold 55.00
Jewelry, Cutter, Cigar, 14K Gold, Scissors Shape, 2 3/4 X 1 3/4 In. 250.00
Jewelry, Earring, Lapis & Gold Nugget, Pierced, Shape Of Small Leaves 160.00
Jewelry, Earrings, Art Deco, Stud, Moonstones, 3 Rubies, 14k Gold 50.00
Jewelry, Earrings, Carved Ivory, Crystal Drop, Pierced, 1 3/4 In. 30.00
Jewelry, Earrings, Chinese Ivory Face, Clip-On 22.00
Jewelry, Earrings, Double Drop Garnets, 2 Large Garnets, Pierced 32.50
Jewelry, Earrings, Enameled Pansy, Pearl Each Center, 14K 175.00
Jewelry, Earrings, Garnet Cluster, Gold Setting, Screw Back, Pair 125.00
Jewelry, Earrings, Garnet, Surrounded By 9 Small Stones, Screw Backs, Pair 48.50
Jewelry, Earrings, Gold Victorian, Etruscan Work, European Backs 45.00
Jewelry, Earrings, Gold-Filled Victorian, Hand-Painted Cupids 195.00
Jewelry, Earrings, Jade With Pearls, Pierced, 14k Yellow Gold 145.00
Jewelry, Earrings, Nautilus Shell On Seaweed, Sterling Silver, Jensen, Pair 42.00
Jewelry, Earrings, Oval Bohemian Garnet Carbuncle, 14K 90.00
Jewelry, Earrings, Victorian Gold Flower, Diamond Center 65.00
Jewelry, Earrings, 14K Gold, Oval Tiger's Eye 48.00
Jewelry, Hatpin, Brass, Sailor's Hat, Blue Bow, 9 1/2 In. 12.50
Jewelry, Hatpin, Porcelain, Hand-Painted Portrait, Gilt Border, 10 1/2 In. 22.00
Jewelry, Hatpin, Sterling Silver, Pennsylvania State College, 1855 .... 25.00
Jewelry, Indian, see Indian
Jewelry, Lavaliere, Almondine Garnet, 14k Yellow Gold 225.00
Jewelry, Lavaliere, Bohemian Garnet 195.00
Jewelry, Lavaliere, Oriental Seed Pearls, Marquise Ruby Center 65.00
Jewelry, Lavaliere, Rubies, Seed Pearls, Enamel, Silver, Hungarian Hallmark 75.00

Jewelry, Lavaliere, Shell Cameo, 14K Gold Frame, Oval, 1 1/4 X 1 In.	48.00
Jewelry, Lavaliere, 14K Gold, 6 Diamonds, Pearl Surrounded By 12 Diamonds	145.00
Jewelry, Locket, Baby, Gold, Initial B	17.50
Jewelry, Locket, Heavy Gold, Raised Gold Flowers With Diamonds & Enamel	250.00
Jewelry, Locket, Perfume, Fine Cut Glass, Loop For Chain, 1 In.	55.00
Jewelry, Locket, Victorian, Etched Center, Carved Sardonyx Center, Opens	48.00
Jewelry, Lorgnette & Chain, 14K Gold	135.00
Jewelry, Lorgnette, Gold Over Sterling, Art Nouveau, Dated 1914, 4 1/2 In.	200.00
Jewelry, Necklace, Clowns Head, Blue, Green & Black, Art Deco, Sterling Silver	32.00
Jewelry, Necklace, Squash Blossom, Cabochon Cut Turquoise, Navajo	1500.00
Jewelry, Necklace, Turquoise, 3 Strand, Santo Domingo, Joclas, C.1915	1200.00
Jewelry, Necklace, 5 Diamonds Set Into Chain, 3 In Front, 1 On Each Side	210.00
Jewelry, Pencil, Gold Shell, Engraved, Topaz Stone On Top, C.1870	35.00
Jewelry, Pendant, Amethyst Set In Lacy Gold Frame, 18 In.Gold Chain	35.00
Jewelry, Pendant, Art Deco, Gold Etched, Frosted Crystal, 5 Pt.Diamond	175.00
Jewelry, Pendant, Art Glass Owl, Sterling Silver Mounting	25.00
Jewelry, Pendant, Cameo, Set In Gold Filigree, 19 In. Chain	130.00
Jewelry, Pendant, Entwined Double Rattlesnakes, C.1750-1820, Marked, 2 In.	200.00
Jewelry, Pendant, Floral Setting, Sapphire, Sterling Silver, China, 34 In.	450.00
Jewelry, Pendant, Floral, Blue Opalescent, Lalique	160.00
Jewelry, Pendant, Malachite Heart, 1 1/2 In.	25.00
Jewelry, Pendant, Victorian, 9K Gold, Pearls, 1 1/4 In.Diameter	75.00
Jewelry, Pendant, Watercolor Of A Black Man, Oval, Back Holds Mementos	150.00
Jewelry, Pin Pendant, Limoges, Pink Roses, Silver Frame	15.00
Jewelry, Pin Set, 3 Piece, Black Enamel On Gold	200.00
Jewelry, Pin, Art Deco, Carnelian Center, Georg Jensen	125.00
Jewelry, Pin, Art Nouveau, Gold, Pearl, Pink & Green Enamel, Flower Form, 1 In.	300.00
Jewelry, Pin, Bar, 15K Gold, 3 Turquoise	60.00
Jewelry, Pin, Barber's, Figural Comb & Shears, Silver Plated	2.50
Jewelry, Pin, Bohemian Garnet Carbuncle, Pearl Crescent, 14K	240.00
Jewelry, Pin, Bohemian Garnet, Gold Filled, 1 In., Diamond	60.00
Jewelry, Pin, Breast, Heart, 2 Pearls, 4 Rubies, C.1835	34.00
Jewelry, Pin, Butterfly, Open Filigree, Silver	8.00
Jewelry, Pin, Butterfly, 21 Large Garnets Set In Gold, Bohemian, 1 1/2 In.	275.00
Jewelry, Pin, Crescent, 14K Gold, Raised Blue Enameled Forget-Me-Nots	22.00
Jewelry, Pin, Elk's Tooth, Ruby Eyes	30.00
Jewelry, Pin, Florentine, Rabbit, Ruby Eye, Gold Work, 1 3/4 In.	150.00
Jewelry, Pin, Fox, Diamond On Nose, 10 Teardrop Sapphires, Gold	350.00
Jewelry, Pin, Gold Acorn, Faceted Citrine, Pearl, 1 1/4 In.Long	125.00
Jewelry, Pin, Gold Filled Enameled Cornucopia, Victorian, 1 1/2 In.	18.00
Jewelry, Pin, Gypsy Coin, 7 Mexican Coins, Pure Gold	375.00
Jewelry, Pin, Heart Shape, Georg Jensen, Denmark, 1 X 1 1/8 In.	55.00
Jewelry, Pin, Horseshoe Arch, Georg Jensen, Denmark, 1 1/4 X 7/8 In.	55.00
Jewelry, Pin, Initial C, 18K Gold, Round, Victorian	35.00
Jewelry, Pin, Lapel, BPOE, Elk Head, 14K, Tiny Diamond Eyes	22.50
Jewelry, Pin, Lapel, Elk, Ruby Eyes	25.00
Jewelry, Pin, Limoges Porcelain, Hand-Painted Portrait, Gold Roped Frame	30.00
Jewelry, Pin, Marcasite & Black Onyx, Sterling, Germany	185.00
Jewelry, Pin, Mosaic, Canes Of Flowers	15.00
Jewelry, Pin, Opaque Yellow & Clear Amber, Polish	12.00
Jewelry, Pin, Owl On Branch, Silver & Gold, Rubies, 2 1/4 In.	125.00
Jewelry, Pin, Portrait Of Woman Painted On Porcelain, Gold Frame, Oval, 2 In.	150.00
Jewelry, Pin, Scotch Kilt, Sterling, Topaz, Stone, Malachite, 2 1/4 In.	48.00
Jewelry, Pin, Silver, Triple Horse Head, Gold Filled Fittings, 2 1/8 In.	125.00
Jewelry, Pin, Solid Gold Spray, Umbrella Shaped Floral, 2 Diamond Centers	65.00
Jewelry, Pin, Thistle, Gold, Pearl, & Faceted Citrine, 1 1/4 In.	125.00
Jewelry, Pin, Tulips & Fruit, Georg Jensen, Denmark, 1 3/4 X 1 1/8 In.	60.00
Jewelry, Pin, Violet Shape, 5 Rose Cut Diamonds On 5 Petals, Diamond Center	425.00
Jewelry, Pin, White Gold Filigree, Faceted Amethyst, 1 1/8 In.	175.00
Jewelry, Pin, 3 Baroque Pearls, 10 Tiny Black Pearls, 14k Gold	95.00
Jewelry, Ring, Amethyst, Oval, 3 Diamonds Each Side, 14K Gold	76.00
Jewelry, Ring, Art Deco, Fan Shaped, 6 Rubies & 4 Diamonds, 14K Pink Gold	65.00
Jewelry, Ring, Art Nouveau, Openwork, Garnet At Lady's Forehead	14.00
Jewelry, Ring, Art Nouveau, Wraparound, Woman's, 5 Marcasites	19.00
Jewelry, Ring, Baby, 14K, Pearl	7.00

Jewelry, Ring, Band, Dated 1916, 14K Yellow Gold	32.00
Jewelry, Ring, Black Onyx, Diamonds & Emeralds, Gold Trim, 14K Gold	110.00
Jewelry, Ring, Bohemian Garnet, Dragonfly In Gold Filled Setting	225.00
Jewelry, Ring, Cameo, Oval Black Stone, 14S Gold, Ornate Floral Work	64.00
Jewelry, Ring, Cluster, 17 Garnets, 14K Gold	50.00
Jewelry, Ring, Domed, 5 Diamonds Pavee Set Into Dome, 14K	185.00
Jewelry, Ring, Dragon, Ruby Eye, 14K Yellow Gold	85.00
Jewelry, Ring, Floral Carved Spinach Jade, Sterling, Raised Floral Side	95.00
Jewelry, Ring, Gold Filigree, Fire Opal	39.00
Jewelry, Ring, Gold, White Enamel Dome, 5 Turquoise Stones Around Diamond	150.00
Jewelry, Ring, Lady's, Garnet, 28 Faceted Stones, One Large Center, Gold	73.50
Jewelry, Ring, Lady's, 14K Gold Set, Cameo, Shell Carved, Lady's Profile	39.00
Jewelry, Ring, Lapis Lazuli, Oval, 1 1/2 Ct.	14.00
Jewelry, Ring, Light Topaz & 2 Red Stones, Art Deco, 14K Gold	22.00
Jewelry, Ring, Lion, Ruby Eyes, Open Mouth, Curly Tail	75.00
Jewelry, Ring, Love, 4 1/2 In., 14K Gold	15.00
Jewelry, Ring, Man's, Platinum, Heavy, Oval Ruby Center, 2 Side Diamonds	210.00
Jewelry, Ring, Mourning, Black & White Enamel, Urn, Dated 1779	295.00
Jewelry, Ring, Opal, Set In Black Onyx, Sterling Silver, Man's	49.50
Jewelry, Ring, Oval Cameo Of Man, Victorian, 14K Gold	64.00
Jewelry, Ring, Pear Shaped Amethyst, 24K Gold	25.00
Jewelry, Ring, Pear Shaped Fire Opal, 12 Full Cut Diamonds	265.00
Jewelry, Ring, Pear Shaped Opal, 7 Diamond Around It, 14K Gold Setting	175.00
Jewelry, Ring, Pearl, Twin, 14K Gold, Size 5 1/2	25.00
Jewelry, Ring, Snakes On Shank, Unusual Agate	75.00
Jewelry, Ring, Sterling & Gold Sailor At Helm, Art Nouveau	20.00
Jewelry, Ring, Sterling, Art Nouveau, Woman, Face, Garnet	12.00
Jewelry, Ring, Sterling, Art Nouveau, Wraparound, Woman's, Printemps	14.00
Jewelry, Ring, Sterling, Butterfly, 3 Garnets	10.00
Jewelry, Ring, Sterling, Face, Bulldog, Pouting	12.00
Jewelry, Ring, Sterling, Long Dinner, 3 Garnets, Set	15.00
Jewelry, Ring, Sterling, Mask, Comedy & Tragedy	10.00
Jewelry, Ring, Sterling, Onyx, Black, Oval, Serpent	17.00
Jewelry, Ring, Stone Cameo, White Chalcedony Woman's Head, Black Onyx Slab	65.00
Jewelry, Ring, Turquoise Stone, Indian Sterling Silver	15.00
Jewelry, Ring, Warrior Head On Hematite Stone, Sterling	25.00
Jewelry, Ring, Wide Band, Carved Amethyst, 18K Gold	28.00
Jewelry, Ring, Yellow Gold Bloodstone, 2 Diamonds, Art Deco	20.00
Jewelry, Ring, Yellow Green Leaf, Veins In Blue Sapphires & Diamonds	225.00
Jewelry, Ring, 3 Diamonds, Tiffany Set, 3 Smaller Ones Each Side, 14K Gold	345.00
Jewelry, Ring, 9 Diamonds, Synthetic Ruby, Platinum Top, 18K Yellow Gold	225.00
Jewelry, Stickpin, Baroque Pearl	30.00
Jewelry, Stickpin, Black Jasper, White Domed Bust, Sterling Bezel, Small	20.00
Jewelry, Stickpin, Do-Wah-Jack Indian's Head On Top Sword, Round, Oak	17.50
Jewelry, Stickpin, Egyptian Sarcophagus, Enameled Silver Gilt, C.1900	28.00
Jewelry, Stickpin, Gold Nugget Attached	150.00
Jewelry, Stickpin, Gold, 3 Opals In Clover Leaf Formation	28.00
Jewelry, Stickpin, Indian Good Luck Sign, Swastika At Top, Sterling Silver	5.00
Jewelry, Stickpin, Jeweled Flower, Diamond Center, Sapphire & Ruby Buds, Gold	65.00
Jewelry, Stickpin, Love Knot Diamond, 15K Gold	22.50
Jewelry, Stickpin, Natural Gold Nugget	100.00
Jewelry, Stickpin, Scarab, 14K	28.00
Jewelry, Stickpin, Shell Cameo, Classic Head On Tan, Rose Gold Frame	38.00
Jewelry, Stickpin, Topaz, 14K White Gold Filigree, 5/8 X 1/4 In.Stone	39.00
Jewelry, Watch, see Watch	
Jewelry, Watch Bracelet, Black Enamel, Western Germany	35.00
Jewelry, Watch Bracelet, Round Cover, 11 Diamonds Around Sides, 14K Gold	110.00
Jewelry, Watch Chain, Lady's, Gold Filled Links, Slide, Pearl, 25 1/2 In.	45.00
Jewelry, Watch Chain, Man's, Pink Gold, 9k-375 Stamped On Every Link	225.00
Jewelry, Watch Chain, 14K Gold, Dated 1917	295.00
Jewelry, Watchband, Stretch, Pink Gold, 14k	30.00

John Rogers statues were made from 1859 to 1892. The originals were bronze, but the thousands of copies made by the Rogers Factory were of painted plaster. Eighty different figures were made.

John Rogers, Group, Rip Van Winkle
At Home, 1871, 18 1/2 In.

Judaica, Candelabrum, Hanukkah
Menorah, Oil Pitcher, 20 3/4 In.

Judaica, Box, Bridal, Vienna,
Silver, 1847, 5 3/8 In.

Judaica, Spice Box,
Tower Form, Silver,
10 5/8 In.

Judaica, Spice Box,
Windmill, Silver, 4 1/4 In.

Judaica, Spice Box, Portuguese,
Silver, 5 3/4 In.

Judaica, Spice Holder, Fish,
Silver, Enameled Eyes, 18 In.

Judaica, Torah Crown, Silver, Parcel-Gilt, Glass Jewel, 5 1/4 In.

John Rogers, Group, Is It So Nominated In The Bond		450.00
John Rogers, Group, Neighboring Pews		550.00
John Rogers, Group, Parting Promise		310.00
John Rogers, Group, Rip Van Winkle At Home, 1871, 18 1/2 In.	Illus	250.00
John Rogers, Group, Shaughraun & Tatters, March 2, 1875		350.00
John Rogers, Group, The Favored Scholar, April 1878		475.00
John Rogers, Group, The School Examination		375.00
John Rogers, Group, Weighing The Baby, November 21, 1876		450.00
John Rogers, Group, Wounded To The Rear, One More Shot		275.00
Judaica, Box, Bridal, Vienna, Silver, 1847, 5 3/8 In.	Illus	1000.00
Judaica, Candelabrum, Hanukkah Menorah, Oil Pitcher, 20 3/4 In.	Illus	2400.00
Judaica, Goblet, Silver, Covered Ceremonial, Repousse Grapes, 7 In.		200.00
Judaica, Pointer, Torah, Silver, Hand, Cuffrod, Hebraic Inscription		150.00
Judaica, Spice Box, Portuguese, Silver, 5 3/4 In.	Illus	350.00
Judaica, Spice Box, Tower Form, Silver, 10 5/8 In.	Illus	175.00
Judaica, Spice Box, Windmill, Silver, 4 1/4 In.	Illus	325.00
Judaica, Spice Container, Repousse, Wagon Form, 19th Century, Silver		325.00
Judaica, Spice Container, Silver, Flower Form, C.1880, 5 1/2 In.		150.00
Judaica, Spice Holder, Fish, Silver, Enameled Eyes, 18 In.	Illus	425.00
Judaica, Torah Crown, Silver, Parcel-Gilt, Glass Jewel, 5 1/4 In	Illus	500.00

Jugtown pottery refers to pottery made in North Carolina as far back as the 1750s. In 1915 Juliana and Jacques Busbee set up a training and sales organization for what they named Jugtown Pottery. In 1921 they built a shop at Jugtown, North Carolina, and hired Ben Owen as a potter in 1923. The Busbees moved the Village Store where the pottery was sold and promoted to 37 East Sixtieth Street in New York City. Juliana Busbee sold the New York store in 1926 and moved into a log cabin near the Jugtown Pottery. The pottery ended production in 1958.

Jugtown, Creamer, Blue	10.00
Jugtown, Dish, Oriental-Style, Mottled Blue, Footed	45.00

Kate Greenaway, who was a famous illustrator of children's books, drew pictures of children in high-waisted Empire dresses. She lived from about 1846 to 1901. Her designs appear on china, glass, and other pieces.

Kate Greenaway, Almanac, 1888	45.00
Kate Greenaway, Book, Almanac For 1886	60.00
Kate Greenaway, Book, Birthday, Original Dust Jacket	22.75
Kate Greenaway, Book, The Birthday Book, Color Plates, 3 3/4 X 4 In.	45.00
Kate Greenaway, Book, Under The Window	28.00
Kate Greenaway, Bowl, Children Having Tea Party, Footed	15.00
Kate Greenaway, Box, Tin, Spring Design, 3 1/2 X 4 X 7 In.	65.00
Kate Greenaway, Dish, Form Of Bonneted Girl's Face, Round, 4 1/2 In.	22.00
Kate Greenaway, Figurine, China Boy, Girl, 6 1/4 In., Pair	65.00
Kate Greenaway, Figurine, Girl In Blue Dress Holding Yellow Purse	18.00
Kate Greenaway, Figurine, Greenaway Girls, Porcelain, 6 1/4 In., Pair	65.00
Kate Greenaway, Foot Bath, Baby's, Divided, 11 X 15 X 4 1/2 In.	95.00
Kate Greenaway, Holder, Flower, Figural, Silver Plate, Amber Glass	96.00
Kate Greenaway, Match Holder & Ashtray, Milk Maid, Silver Plate, Signed	95.00
Kate Greenaway, Napkin Ring, Figural, Boy	90.00
Kate Greenaway, Napkin Ring, Figural, Cherub	80.00
Kate Greenaway, Napkin Ring, Figural, Dog Sitting Up, Boy Holds Object	190.00
Kate Greenaway, Plate, Boy & Girl, Marked Wedgwood, 10 In.	65.00
Kate Greenaway, Plate, Flow Blue, February, Boy & Girl, Wedgwood, 10 1/4 In.	65.00
Kate Greenaway, Salt & Pepper, Boy & Girl, 3 In.	110.00
Kate Greenaway, Saltshaker, Boy In Basket	23.00
Kate Greenaway, Set, 6 Plates & Butter Dish, Nursery Poem, Custard	225.00
Kate Greenaway, Tea Set, Varied Children's Scenes, 22 Piece	150.00
Kate Greenaway, Tile, Spring, Autumn, Blue Decoration, Registration Mark, Pr.	150.00
Kate Greenaway, Toothpick, Blue, 2 Bonneted Girls Sitting Each Side	75.00
Kate Greenaway, Toothpick, Boy In Long Coat & Top Hat, Silver Plated	145.00
Kate Greenaway, Toothpick, Little Girl Dressed In Pink, Holding Umbrella	125.00
Kate Greenaway, Whistle, Figural, Girl, China	35.00

Kauffmann refers to the type work done by Angelica Kauffmann, a painter and decorative artist for Adam Brothers in England between 1766 and 1781. Porcelains signed Kauffmann were made in the nineteenth century.

Kauffmann, Case, Trinket, Cylindrical, Hinged, Covered, 1 X 3 1/2 In.	45.00
Kauffmann, Chocolate Set, Mythological Scenes, Cherubs, Figures, Gold, 7 Piece	135.00
Kauffmann, Cup & Saucer, Demitasse, Portrait, Cobalt & Gold, Signed	37.50
Kauffmann, Mug, Blue, Carlsbad	25.00
Kauffmann, Plate, Classical Scene, Signed, 8 1/2 In., Pair	37.50
Kauffmann, Plate, 3 Figures, Gold Tracery, Beehive Under Glaze, Signed, 8 In.	49.00
Kauffmann, Vase, Classical Figures, 4 Footed, 2 Handles, Signed, 5 In.	25.00
Kauffmann, Vase, Classical Scene, Gold Tracery, Reticulated Handles, 16 In.	58.00
Kauffmann, Vase, Urn Shaped, Lid, Prussia, Signed	275.00
Kauffmann, Vase, Victoria Carlsbad, Austria, Signed	75.00
Kauffmann, Vase, 4 Classic Figures, Green, Gold, Signed, 10 In.	70.00

Kayserzinn, see Pewter
Kaziun, see Paperweight, Kaziun

KELVA *Kelva glassware was made by the C.F.Monroe Company of Meriden, Connecticut, about 1904. It is a pale pastel painted glass decorated with flowers, designs, or scenes.*

Kelva, Basket, Enameled White Shasta Daisy, Pink Ground, Brass Collar, Signed	88.00
Kelva, Box Powder, Blue & Pink Flowers	275.00
Kelva, Box, Covered, Mottled Blue, Flowered Top, Silver Collar, 3 X 3 1/2 In.	200.00

Kelva, Box, Green & White, Pink & White Floral, Beading, 4 1/2 X 3 1/2 In. 275.00
Kelva, Box, Hinged, Dark Green, Brown Beige Leaf, 4 In. 225.00
Kelva, Box, Maple Leaf On Top, Signed, 3 X 4 In. 275.00
Kelva, Box, Mauve, Floral, Covered, Signed, 4 In. 195.00
Kelva, Box, Mottled Green, Apricot Blossoms, Silver Collar, Hinged, 4 1/4 In. 300.00
Kelva, Box, Pink Florals On Mottled Gray, Ormolu Handles, Signed, 5 In. 45.00
Kelva, Box, Powder, Blue, Pink Floral, Ormolu Rim, Swivel Mirror, Signed 275.00
Kelva, Box, Silver Collar, Mottled Blue & Green, Flowered Top, Signed, 3 In. 200.00
Kelva, Box, Trinket, Pink, White Daisies, Brass Fittings, Square, Signed 295.00
Kelva, Dish, Dresser, Olive Green Foliage, Pink Flowers, Silver Collar, 6 In. 165.00
Kelva, Jar, Powder, Mottled Orange, Signed 50.00
Kelva, Shade, Pink, Berries & Leaves 70.00
Kelva, Vase, Enameled Spray Of Apricot-Pink Florals, Signed, 13 In. 260.00
Kelva, Vase, Mottled Peach, Orange, Red Carnations, Green Leaves, Silver Rim 175.00

> Kemple glass was made by John Kemple of East Palestine, Ohio, and
> Kenova, West Virginia, from 1945 to 1970. The glass was made from old
> molds. Many designs and colors were made. Kemple pieces are usually
> marked with a K on the bottom.

Kemple, Compote, Aztec, Amberina, 5 1/4 In. 20.00
Kemple, Dish, Football Cover, Milk Glass 55.00
Kemple, Dish, Lion Cover, Milk Glass 35.00
Kemple, Plate, Openwork Border, 18 In. 20.00

> Kew blas is the name used by the Union Glass Company of Somerville,
> Massachusetts. The name refers to an iridescent golden glass made from the
> 1890s to 1924.

Kew Blas, Candlestick, Iridescent Gold, Blue, & Green, Twisted Stem, 8 In. 250.00
Kew Blas, Candlestick, Swirled Rib Pattern, Rainbow Gold Iridescence, Pair 550.00
Kew Blas, Compote, Iridescent Gold, Rayed Pattern, Signed, 5 In. 550.00
Kew Blas, Tumbler, Iridescent Gold, Flared Rim, Dimpled Sides, 5 In. 295.00
Kew Blas, Vase, Apricot, Pulled, Feathers, Gold Filagree, Signed, 7 In. 695.00
Kew Blas, Vase, Feathered, Apricot, 6 In. 695.00
Kew Blas, Vase, Gold Iridescent, Pulled-Up Light Green Loopings, 6 1/2 In. 300.00
Kew Blas, Vase, Gold With Pink Highlights, Signed, 10 In. 550.00
Kew Blas, Vase, Gold, Gold Luster Lining, Signed, 3 3/4 X 5 1/2 In. 675.00
Kew Blas, Vase, Green & Gold Feather Embossed Decoration, 4 In. 425.00
Kew Blas, Vase, Iridescent Gold Fishscale, Green Swirl, Signed, 8 In. 725.00
Kew Blas, Vase, Jack-In-The-Pulpit, Gold Iridescent, Blue Green, 11 1/2 In. 750.00
Kew Blas, Vase, Pulled Feather, Apricot, Gilt Filigree, Signed 695.00

> Kewpies were first pictured in the 'Ladies' Home Journal' by Rose
> O'Neill. The pixielike figures became an immediate success, and Kewpie
> dolls started appearing in 1911. Kewpie pictures and other items soon
> followed.

Kewpie, Bank, Glass, Original Cover 35.00
Kewpie, Bank, Glass, Original Paint, 3 In. 75.00
Kewpie, Bisque, No.605, Made In Japan, 4 3/4 In. 15.00
Kewpie, Box, Covered, Bisque 3.50
Kewpie, Camera, Kamera No.3a, Sears Roebuck, Box & Booklet 28.00
Kewpie, Candy Container, Borgfeldt 37.50
Kewpie, Candy Container, Clear Glass 55.00
Kewpie, Candy Container, Glass, Metal Bank Closure 35.00
Kewpie, Child's Set, Mug, Bowl, Divided Plate 102.00
Kewpie, Container, Candy, Standing Next To Barrel, Signed .... 38.00 To 60.00
Kewpie, Creamer, Action Kewpies, Royal Rudolstadt, 3 In. .... 56.00 To 98.00
Kewpie, Creamer, Jasper, Signed 175.00
Kewpie, Creamer, Kewpie Figures, Blue, White, Signed Rose O'Neill 135.00
Kewpie, Cup & Saucer, Rose O'Neill, Royal Rudolstadt 125.00
Kewpie, Cup, Miniature, Rose O'Neill 85.00
Kewpie, Cup, Royal Rudolstadt, Rose O'Neill, 2 1/2 In. 110.00
Kewpie, Dish, Covered, Blue Jasperware, 7 Action Kewpies In Relief, 3 In. 250.00
Kewpie, Dish, Feeding, Divided, C.1920 .... 45.00
Kewpie, Dish, Wag The Chief Center, 4 In. 60.00

Kewpie, Doll, Baby On Scale, Hanging, Bisque, 5 1/4 In. 85.00
Kewpie, Doll, Bisque, Blue Wings, 4 1/2 In. 3.40
Kewpie, Doll, Bisque, Germany, 4 1/2 In. 28.00
Kewpie, Doll, Bisque, Original, Signed O'Neill On Feet, 5 In. .... 70.00 To 90.00
Kewpie, Doll, Bisque, Signed Heart Label, 10 1/2 In. 350.00
Kewpie, Doll, Bisque, Signed On Foot, 9 In. 225.00
Kewpie, Doll, Bisque, With Umbrella And Bulldog, Signed 235.00
Kewpie, Doll, Black Cat In Lap, C In Circle 185.00
Kewpie, Doll, Black Celluloid, Miniature, Original Label, 1913, 3 In. 48.00
Kewpie, Doll, Blue Wings, Movable Arms, Rose O'Neill On Feet, Germany 65.00
Kewpie, Doll, Bridal, Bisque, 4 1/2 In., Pair 175.00
Kewpie, Doll, Bride & Groom, Rose O'Neill, Bisque, 2 1/2 In. 65.00
Kewpie, Doll, Bride & Groom, 4 1/2 In., Pair 135.00
Kewpie, Doll, Buttonhole, Arms Out, 2 In. 110.00
Kewpie, Doll, Celluloid, Movable Arms, Marked Japan, 7 In. 12.00
Kewpie, Doll, Chalkware, Red Dress, 12 In. 25.00
Kewpie, Doll, Christ Child, Lying On Back, Brown Hair, Blue Cover, Bisque 35.00
Kewpie, Doll, Composition, Rose O'Neill, 1913, 12 In. 55.00
Kewpie, Doll, Head, 2 In. 120.00
Kewpie, Doll, Huggers, Bisque, 3 In. 125.00
Kewpie, Doll, Huggers, German, 3 1/2 In. 135.00
Kewpie, Doll, Jointed Arms & Legs, Sleep Eyes, Hard Plastic, C.1940, 13 In. 85.00
Kewpie, Doll, Nippon, Bathing Suit, Movable Arms, 3 1/2 In. 35.00
Kewpie, Doll, Piano Baby, Blue Cap, 4 1/4 In. 65.00
Kewpie, Doll, Seated, Holding Purple Flower, 1 3/4 In. 135.00
Kewpie, Doll, Soldier, Red Cap, Gun & Sword, 4 3/4 In. 225.00
Kewpie, Doll, Standing, Arms Extended In Air, 2 1/2 In. 85.00
Kewpie, Doll, Standing, Jointed Arms, 4 1/2 In. 880.00
Kewpie, Doll, The Huggers, Original Label, 3 1/2 In. 120.00
Kewpie, Doll, Traveler 185.00
Kewpie, Doll, Vinyl, The Thinker, Signed 3.00
Kewpie, Doll, With Doodle Dog 165.00
Kewpie, Figurine, Glazed Kewpie Sitting On Mushroom, 2 1/2 In. 30.00
Kewpie, Figurine, Reading Book, On Chair, Paper Label, 4871, C In Circle, 5 In. 62.00
Kewpie, Flask, Talcum Powder, Nippon 150.00
Kewpie, Hair Receiver, Jasperware, Rose O'Neill, Pink Action Kewpies, Green 175.00
Kewpie, Hatpin 35.00
Kewpie, Hatpin Holder, Blue Jasperware, Signed Rose O'Neill 165.00
Kewpie, Hatpin Holder, Rose O'Neill, Green, Jasper, 3 Kewpies .... 215.00 To 250.00
Kewpie, Holder, Place Card, Books Behind With Mandolin, C In Circle 165.00
Kewpie, Hot Plate 45.00
Kewpie, Jar, Mayonnaise, Kewpie On Lid & Label, Pint 18.50
Kewpie, Jar, Talc, Red Hearts, Hand-Painted 45.00
Kewpie, Lamp 35.00
Kewpie, Mold, Candy, Tin, 10 1/2 In. 35.00
Kewpie, Mug, Child's, Pearlized Finish, Rose O'Neill, Germany 65.00
Kewpie, Mug, Rose O'Neill Wilson, 4 Kewpies, Royal Rudolstadt, 2 1/2 In. 59.50
Kewpie, Mug, White, 2 Kewpies, Handled, 3 1/2 In. 36.00
Kewpie, Night-Light, Bisque 65.00
Kewpie, Planter, Blue Eyes, White 18.00
Kewpie, Plate, Christmas, Santa, 10 Kewpies 15.00
Kewpie, Plate, Kewpies & Santa Design In Center, 9 In. 10.00
Kewpie, Plate, 2 Action Kewpies, Marked Rose O'Neill, Germany, 5 1/4 In. 45.00
Kewpie, Plate, 3 Kewpies On Blue, Austria, 6 1/2 In. 16.00
Kewpie, Postcard, Valentine, Rose O'Neill 14.50
Kewpie, Salt & Pepper, Silver Plated, 3 In. 45.00
Kewpie, Salt & Pepper, Silver, Signed, 2 3/4 In. 185.00
Kewpie, Scrapbook, 50 Kewpie Pages, All Signed Rose O'Neill, C.1920 .... 80.00
Kewpie, Sheet Music, 1915, Kewpies On Cover 2.00
Kewpie, Shoulder Head, Marked, Germany, 2 1/2 In. 225.00
Kewpie, Snow Baby, Arms Stretched Out, 2 In. 60.00
Kewpie, Soap, Kewpie Doll With Heart, Rose O'Neill 22.50
Kewpie, Teapot, 2 Gesturing Kewpies On Side, Dancing Kewpie On Lid, Signed 97.50
Kewpie, Tin, Two Kewpies Swinging 17.50
Kewpie, Tray, Dresser, 5 Kewpies, Clover Shape, Green, White Jasperware, Signed 250.00

Kewpie, Tray, Trefoil, Jasper, Heubach, 5 Kewpies & Flowers	190.00
Kewpie, Valentine, Mechanical, Cats, Girl Holding Kewpie, 5 1/2 X 3 In.	11.50
Kimball, see also Cluthra	
Kimball, Vase, Cluthra, Black & White, Peacock Feather Pattern, 6 In.	175.00
Kimball, Vase, Cluthra, Green, 6 In.	145.00
Kimball, Vase, Cluthra, Light Green, 7 In.	198.00
Kimball, Vase, Cluthra, Sea Green, 8 In.	200.00
Kimball, Vase, Cluthra, White, Signed K, 6 In.	150.00
Kimball, Vase, Cluthra, White, Signed, 10 In.	150.00
King's Rose, see Soft Paste	
Kitchen, see also Iron, Store, Tool, Wooden	
Kitchen Popcorn Popper, Wooden Handle, Wire Basket	9.00
Kitchen Tool, Slicer, Vegetable, Iron, Landers, Frary & Clark	20.00
Kitchen, Apple, Peeler, see Kitchen, Peeler, Apple	
Kitchen, Butter, Mold, see Kitchen, Mold, Butter	
Kitchen, Cherry, Pitter, see Kitchen, Pitter, Cherry	
Kitchen, Match Safe, see Match Safe	
Kitchen, Beater, Carpet, Wicker	12.00
Kitchen, Board, Cookie, Pine, Oblong, Pierced Handle For Hanging	26.00
Kitchen, Board, Cookie, Wooden	45.00
Kitchen, Board, Cutting, Pine, Handled, Hole For Hanging, 13 X 7 In.	15.00
Kitchen, Board, Cutting, Shield Shape, Extended Oval Handle, Hole, 7 1/4 In.	28.00
Kitchen, Board, Cutting, Wooden, Coffin Shaped, Iron Ring End, 17 X 9 In.	32.00
Kitchen, Board, Cutting, Yew-Wood, Hole For Hanging, 17 In.	58.00
Kitchen, Board, Pie, Oblong, Arched Tab, Dovetailed Maple Spline, 16 X 23 In.	60.00
Kitchen, Board, Springerle, 2 Rows Of 4, 8 Patterns, Animals, Flowers	60.00
Kitchen, Bowl, Butter, Burly Maple, Hand-Carved, 19th Century	75.00
Kitchen, Bowl, Green, Bleached, Footed, 5 X 4 In.	32.00
Kitchen, Bowl, Salt, Blue & Gray Crockery	39.00
Kitchen, Bowl, Serving, Maple, Hand-Hewn Inside, Gilt Paint Outside, 13 In.	20.00
Kitchen, Bowl, Serving, Turned, Round, Wooden, 10 In.	9.00
Kitchen, Box, Bread, Cover, Pottery, Putti In Bamboo, Brown Glaze, 1800s, 15 In.	400.00
Kitchen, Box, Dough, Mustard Paint, 10 X 25 In.	65.00
Kitchen, Box, Knife & Fork Inlay, Inlaid Scrimshaw Pillars	925.00
Kitchen, Box, Knife, Dovetailed, Slanted Sides, Handle At Top	22.00
Kitchen, Box, Pantry, Green Paint, 8 3/4 In.	30.00
Kitchen, Box, Pantry, Green, Lapped, Oval, 5 3/4 In.	68.00
Kitchen, Box, Pantry, Lapped In Natural Finish, I.Whiton, 3 3/4 In.	35.00
Kitchen, Box, Pantry, Oval, Laps In Natural Finish, Copper Nails, 6 1/8 In.	50.00
Kitchen, Box, Pantry, Oval, Laps In Natural Finish, 5 1/2 In.	45.00
Kitchen, Box, Pantry, Red Paint, 8 1/4 In.	24.00
Kitchen, Box, Pepper, Deep Red	22.00
Kitchen, Box, Salt, Double Compartment, Wooden, 12 In.	32.00
Kitchen, Box, Salt, Pine, Scalloped Back, Wall Type	23.00
Kitchen, Box, Shaker, Oval, Natural Finish, 12 In.	125.00
Kitchen, Box, Wall, Cream, Lollipops For Good Little Girls & Boys, 10 1/2 In.	28.00
Kitchen, Bread Maker, Universal, Embossed Tin	25.00
Kitchen, Breadboard, Carved Bread On Border, 9 1/2 In., Round	35.00
Kitchen, Breadboard, Hand-Carved, Maple, 12 In.Round	45.00
Kitchen, Breadboard, Lotus Flower Edge, 11 1/2 In.	28.00
Kitchen, Breadboard, Round, Bread Carved On Wood, 9 1/2 X 9 3/4 In.	36.00
Kitchen, Breadboard, Wheat Design Border, Word Bread, 11 1/2 In.	28.00
Kitchen, Breadboard, Wooden, Round, 9 1/2 In.	20.00
Kitchen, Broom, Whisk, China Doll Handle, 7 1/2 In.	15.00
Kitchen, Bucket, Apple Butter, Brass	65.00
Kitchen, Bucket, Sugar, Blue Paint, Wooden Handle, Lid, 12 1/2 X 11 1/2 In.	30.00
Kitchen, Bucket, Sugar, Copper Rivet	38.50
Kitchen, Butter Crock, Grayish White Stoneware With Blue Decorations	55.00
Kitchen, Butter Pat, Crystal, Etch Design, Sunburst On Bottom, Set Of 12	30.00
Kitchen, Butter Print, Cow, Glass	15.00
Kitchen, Butter Print, Sheaf Of Wheat, Glass	12.00
Kitchen, Butter, Stamp, Ball Handle, 5 Concentric Circles, 3 5/8 X 2 3/4 In.	29.00
Kitchen, Butter, Stamp, Deep Sunflower, Edge Carving, Ball Handle, 4 X 4 In.	48.00
Kitchen, Canister Set, Blue & White, Germany, 8 Pieces	48.00
Kitchen, Canister Set, Tin, Blue, White, Windmills, 4 Large, 5 Small	35.00

Kitchen, Canister, Wooden, Tin Bound Top And Bottom, Dated 1858, Set Of 5	100.00
Kitchen, Cheese Press, Man Riding Horse, Wooden Pegged, 12 In.	90.00
Kitchen, Chopper, Crescent Shape, 2 Handles, 10 1/2 In.Blade	22.50
Kitchen, Chopper, Food, Single Blade With Wooden Handle	3.95
Kitchen, Churn, Blue, Dated 1879	65.00
Kitchen, Churn, Bulbous, Round Handle, Chocolate Glaze, 12 In.	47.00
Kitchen, Churn, Butter, Glass, 1 X 6 In.	25.00
Kitchen, Churn, Butter, Lapped Wooden Bands, Red Paint, Up And Down	135.00
Kitchen, Churn, Butter, Miniature, Maple, Turned, 4 In.	120.00
Kitchen, Churn, Butter, Tin, Dazey, Flywheel	37.50
Kitchen, Churn, Dazey, No.40, Homemade Strainer	25.00
Kitchen, Churn, Dazey, Tin Body, Maple Top, Cast-Iron Base & Gears, 2 Gallon	50.00
Kitchen, Churn, Dazey, 4 Paddle, Gallon	24.00
Kitchen, Churn, Fingered, Staved, Dasher	210.00
Kitchen, Churn, Glass, 3-Gallon	15.00
Kitchen, Churn, Metal Bands, 10 Gallon Cap	140.00
Kitchen, Churn, Metal Bands, 8 Gallon Cap	110.00
Kitchen, Churn, On Legs, Blue, Patented 1868, New Ipswich, N.H.	120.00
Kitchen, Churn, Red, Slosh Piggin, 18th Century	325.00
Kitchen, Coffee Grinder, see Coffee Grinder	
Kitchen, Colander, Mottled Gray, Round Base	18.00
Kitchen, Cookie Roller, Wooden, 1 Handle, 11 1/2 X 2 1/2 In.	15.00
Kitchen, Cookie Roller, Wooden, 2 Handled, 13 X 1 1/2 In.	21.00
Kitchen, Cork Squeezer, Cast Iron, Wooden Base, 98 Percent Paint, 1898	45.00
Kitchen, Crimper, Pastry, Ivory With Treen Handle, C.1850	19.00
Kitchen, Crimper, Pie, Brass, Marked Thuringia, 4 1/2 In.	14.00
Kitchen, Crimper, Pie, Wooden Turned Handle With Pewter Wheel	30.00
Kitchen, Crock, Butter, Butter On Front Stencil Pattern, Lid	65.00
Kitchen, Crock, Butter, Daisy, Dark Blue, Light Blue	55.00
Kitchen, Crumb Set, Chasing Of Bird, Foliage, Nickel, Marked, Two Piece	12.50
Kitchen, Cutter, Apple, Cast Iron, 4 1/2 In.	14.50
Kitchen, Cutter, Cabbage, Black Walnut, With Box, 10 X 36 In.	35.00
Kitchen, Cutter, Cabbage, Tin Blade, Pierced For Hanging	10.00
Kitchen, Cutter, Cookie, Cat, 4 In.	8.00
Kitchen, Cutter, Cookie, Chick, Tin, 3 In.	5.00
Kitchen, Cutter, Cookie, Duck Pattern, Tin, 3 1/4 X 4 1/4 In.	9.00
Kitchen, Cutter, Cookie, Heart, Handled, Tin, 2 In.	3.50
Kitchen, Cutter, Cookie, Horse, 4 In.	16.00
Kitchen, Cutter, Cookie, Lady With Scalloped Dress, Tin	15.00
Kitchen, Cutter, Cookie, Old Tin Cat, 4 In.	8.00
Kitchen, Cutter, Cookie, Rabbit, Tin	2.00
Kitchen, Cutter, Cookie, Robin Hood Flour, Set Of 3	6.50
Kitchen, Cutter, Cookie, Round Maple Leaf, Tin Strutted Veins, 4 In.	40.00
Kitchen, Cutter, Cookie, Spread-Winged American Eagle, Tin, 4 1/4 In.	32.00
Kitchen, Cutter, Kraut, Burl Walnut, 19th Century	225.00
Kitchen, Cutter, Kraut, Hand Dovetailed Box, 8 1/2 X 11 In.	22.50
Kitchen, Cutter, Slaw, Table Model	110.00
Kitchen, Cutter, Slaw, Walnut	8.00
Kitchen, Dipper, Gourd, Wooden Handle, 12 In.	75.00
Kitchen, Dipper, Ice Cream, Tin, Cone Shaped	12.50
Kitchen, Dipper, Wrought Iron, Handle Stamped 859, 12 3/4 In.	20.00
Kitchen, Dough Box, Wooden, Red	85.00
Kitchen, Dough Riser, Tin	22.50
Kitchen, Dough Riser, Tin, 2 Handles, Rim Raised Base, 14 In.	20.00
Kitchen, Dough Tray, Wood	50.00
Kitchen, Dryer, Clothers, Wall, Folds Down	12.00
Kitchen, Egg Basket, Wire, Round, 20 In.High	6.00
Kitchen, Egg Timer, Hourglass In Pine Frame	30.00
Kitchen, Egg Timer, Wood Frame, 3 1/2 In.	5.00
Kitchen, Eggbeater, Cast Iron & Tin, Marked Lyon	3.50
Kitchen, Eggbeater, Crockery, Mason City, Iowa	30.00
Kitchen, Eggbeater, Crockery, Wesson Oil	25.00
Kitchen, Eggbeater, Iron, Revolving	9.00
Kitchen, Eggbeater, Iron, 1908, Shaped Grip Handle	15.00
Kitchen, Eggbeater, Turbine, 1912	15.00

Kitchen, Flask, Miniature, Clear, Gold Leaf Lip & Neck, Crocheted Handle	12.00
Kitchen, Fluter, Iron, 2 Piece	35.00
Kitchen, Fly Catcher, Glass, Mid-1800s	125.00
Kitchen, Fork, Toasting, Brass & Iron, Collapsible, 19 In.	27.50
Kitchen, Freezer, Ice Cream, Miniature, Shepard's Lightning, 4 7/8 X 7 In.	35.00
Kitchen, Fryer, Bacon, July 24, 1869	27.50
Kitchen, Funnel, Milk, Screen Cover, 4 In.Diameter, 6 In.High	4.50
Kitchen, Grater, Cast-Iron Frame, 18th Century, 12 1/2 In.	65.00
Kitchen, Grater, Corn, Dated Feb.22, 1890	28.50
Kitchen, Grater, Nutmeg, Hand-Pierced Tin, 4 In.	25.00
Kitchen, Grater, Nutmeg, The Edgar, Sliding Box, Spring Loading, 1891	30.00
Kitchen, Grater, Vegetable, Tin & Iron, Table Mount Type	12.00
Kitchen, Griddle, Abelskiva, Iron	45.00
Kitchen, Grinder, Coffee, Iron, Arcade, Glass Container, Wall Type, 19 In.	45.00
Kitchen, Grinder, Coffee, Universal, No.0014, Table Clamps	20.00
Kitchen, Grinder, Herb, Tin, Cylindrical, Removable Pierced Basket	34.00
Kitchen, Grinder, Nutmeg, Brass Bowls	37.50
Kitchen, Grinder, Sausage, Cast Iron, Dated 1864	22.00 To 25.00
Kitchen, Grinder, Sausage, Shapleigh, Large, Cast Iron	10.00
Kitchen, Gun, Sausage, Wooden Pestle & Tin Casing, New England	12.50
Kitchen, Ice Tongs, Wooden Handles, Pair	6.00
Kitchen, Icebox, Golden Oak, Miniature	225.00
Kitchen, Icebox, Oak	350.00
Kitchen, Icebox, Oak, 6 X 6 Feet	300.00
Kitchen, Icebox, Pine	80.00
Kitchen, Icebox, Walnut, 2 Doors, 36 X 20 X 54 In.	400.00
Kitchen, Iron, Diamond Kerosene, With Accessories, Original Box	17.50
Kitchen, Iron, Fluting, Cast Iron, Crank Type With Brass Rollers, Crown, 1875	37.50
Kitchen, Iron, Fluting, Shepard Hardware Co., Buffalo, N.Y., 3 Piece	75.00
Kitchen, Iron, Gas, Blue Enamelware	5.00
Kitchen, Iron, Goffering, Queen Anne Hand-Wrought Legs & Feet, Arched	140.00
Kitchen, Iron, Pleating, With Holder, Signed Gophering	135.00
Kitchen, Iron, Tailor's, Cast Iron With Twisted Handle	15.00
Kitchen, Iron, Waffle, Cast Iron, Heart Shapes, C.1840	85.00
Kitchen, Iron, Waffle, For Fireplace, 22 In.	25.00
Kitchen, Iron, Waffle, Round Holder, Pivots, Griswold, Dated 1922	35.00
Kitchen, Jar, Etched Glass, Footed, Green, Pink Applied Flower Finial, 9 In.	20.00
Kitchen, Jar, Ginger, White Floral, Capped Lid, Chinese Export, 19th Century	135.00
Kitchen, Jug, Molasses, Brown, Saucer Spout, 2-Gallon	45.00
Kitchen, Juicer Press, Meat, Cast Iron	8.50
Kitchen, Juicer, Boat Shaped, Ceramic	25.00
Kitchen, Juicer, China, 2-Part, Victoria, Austria	35.00
Kitchen, Juicer, Figural, Bozo	40.00
Kitchen, Juicer, Figural, Pear, 3 Piece, China	40.00
Kitchen, Juicer, Lemon, Cast Iron With Porcelain Insert	16.50
Kitchen, Juicer, Lemon, Translucent Blue Opalescent Glass	35.00
Kitchen, Juicer, Lemon, Wooden With Brass Hinges, 13 In.	31.00
Kitchen, Juicer, Sunkist, Opalescent, 6 In.	10.00
Kitchen, Juicer, Wooden, Brass Hinges, 13 In.Folded	31.00
Kitchen, Kettle, Apple Butter, Cooper On Iron Stand, 15 Gallon	125.00
Kitchen, Kettle, Brass, 3 Ball Feet, 14 In.	65.00
Kitchen, Kettle, Butter, Copper Apple	75.00
Kitchen, Kettle, Copper, Handmade, Strap Handle, 12 X 12 In.	46.00
Kitchen, Kettle, Doughnut, Wrought-Iron Handle	28.00
Kitchen, Kettle, Spun Bell Metal, Molded Lip, Handle, 19th Century, 6 1/8 In.	225.00
Kitchen, Knife, Bread, Wooden Handle Carved Bread	24.00
Kitchen, Knife, Corn Cutting	4.50
Kitchen, Knife, Large Winchester	25.00
Kitchen, Ladder, Cheese	36.00
Kitchen, Ladle, Iron, Hand-Forged, Handle Ends In Curved Hook, 15 In.	35.00
Kitchen, Ladle, Maple Butter, Carved Crescent Moon, Star, Letter B On Back	30.00
Kitchen, Lamp, Tin, Applied Handle For Hanging, Burner & Chimney, 12 1/2 In.	45.00
Kitchen, Lid Lifter, Peninsular	7.00
Kitchen, Lifter, Pie, Wire, Wooden Handle	12.00
Kitchen, Loom Board, American Pine, 8 X 30 3/4 In.	195.00

Kitchen, **Masher**, Potato, Turned Handle	5.50
Kitchen, **Measure**, Food, Figural, Mr.Peanut	3.00
Kitchen, **Measure**, 2 Compartments, Reversible Metal Bands, Wooden	45.00
Kitchen, **Measure**, 2 Quart, Metal Bands, Wooden	30.00
Kitchen, **Measure**, 4 Quart, Metal Bands, Wooden	30.00
Kitchen, **Meat Cleaver**, Crescent-Shaped Blade, Brass Mountings, Large	45.00
Kitchen, **Mold**, Ice Cream, see Pewter, Mold, Ice Cream	
Kitchen, **Mold**, see also Pewter, Mold, Tin, Mold	
Kitchen, **Mold**, Butter, Deep Floral, 2 3/4 In.Diameter	35.00
Kitchen, **Mold**, Butter, Eagle, Hand-Carved, Wooden, Round	145.00
Kitchen, **Mold**, Butter, Eagle, Wooden	190.00
Kitchen, **Mold**, Butter, Fern, Flower, Scroll	25.00
Kitchen, **Mold**, Butter, Figural, Cow, Round	65.00
Kitchen, **Mold**, Butter, Hand-Carved Cow, 3 1/4 In.	135.00
Kitchen, **Mold**, Butter, Hand-Carved Strawberry & Leaf, 4 1/4 In.	45.00
Kitchen, **Mold**, Butter, Imprint Kelly, 3 X 5 In.	15.00
Kitchen, **Mold**, Butter, Intricately Carved, Depicts Cow With Sheaf Of Wheat	36.00
Kitchen, **Mold**, Butter, Pineapple & Leaves, Plunger Type	58.00
Kitchen, **Mold**, Butter, Plunger Type, Beaver Print, Half Pound	68.00
Kitchen, **Mold**, Butter, Plunger Type, Flower & Leaf Design, Round	35.00
Kitchen, **Mold**, Butter, Round Pineapple Design, Wooden	55.00
Kitchen, **Mold**, Butter, Round, Carved Leaf & Flower, Plunger, Lb.3 1/4 X 4 In.	50.00
Kitchen, **Mold**, Butter, Sheaf Of Wheat, Wooden	29.00
Kitchen, **Mold**, Butter, Snowflake	25.00
Kitchen, **Mold**, Butter, Square, 1 Pound Side, Brass Hinges	15.00
Kitchen, **Mold**, Butter, Square, 4 Flower Print, Brass Corner Hooks, Lb.	37.00
Kitchen, **Mold**, Butter, Strawberry, Hand-Carved	55.00
Kitchen, **Mold**, Butter, Swan, 2-Piece, Large	45.00
Kitchen, **Mold**, Butter, Tulip, Hand-Carved, Stylized, Wooden, 3 1/4 In.	155.00
Kitchen, **Mold**, Butter, 6 Petal Carvings	24.00
Kitchen, **Mold**, Butter, 6 Point Star, Wood, Miniature Size, 1 1/4 In.	7.00
Kitchen, **Mold**, Candle, see also Tin, Mold, Candle	
Kitchen, **Mold**, Candle, Bench, 10 Tubes In Pine Frame, Pewter	525.00
Kitchen, **Mold**, Candle, 24 Tube, Tin	120.00
Kitchen, **Mold**, Candle, 24 Tube, Tin, Red Wood Frame, 4 Hangers ....*Illus*	550.00
Kitchen, **Mold**, Candle, 6 Tube	22.00
Kitchen, **Mold**, Candy, Basket, Germany, 5 In.	20.00
Kitchen, **Mold**, Candy, Marzipan, Tin Plated, Germany, 3 X 3 In.	35.00
Kitchen, **Mold**, Candy, Rabbit	28.00
Kitchen, **Mold**, Candy, Santa, 20 In.	125.00
Kitchen, **Mold**, Chocolate, Bottle Shape, 4 In.	22.50
Kitchen, **Mold**, Chocolate, Chicken	35.00
Kitchen, **Mold**, Chocolate, Prancing Horse, Two Part, Tin, 4 1/2 X 4 1/2 In.	32.00
Kitchen, **Mold**, Chocolate, Santa Claus, Tin, Old Costume, Two Halves, 10 In.	45.00
Kitchen, **Mold**, Chocolate, Walter Baker	25.00
Kitchen, **Mold**, Chocolate, 5 Tennis Racket Prints, German, 4 X 9 In.	32.50
Kitchen, **Mold**, Cookie, Carved Figure Of Man, 2 X 5 1/2 In.	45.00
Kitchen, **Mold**, Cookie, Tulips, Cast Iron, Albany, New York Foundry Mark, 6 In.	65.00
Kitchen, **Mold**, Jelly, Copper Coated In, Ornamental Figure Of Squirrel On Top	45.00
Kitchen, **Mold**, Jelly, Tin Top, Oval, July 6, 1897, 3 1/2 In.	8.50

Kitchen, Mold, Candle, 24 Tube, Tin, Red Wood Frame, 4 Hangers

Kitchen, Mold, Maple Sugar, Pine, 81 Hole, 14 X 21 In. 68.00
Kitchen, Mold, Maple Sugar, Rectangular, Wooden, Carved, 2 X 7 X 26 In. 140.00
Kitchen, Mold, Maple Sugar, Round, Fluted, Flat Rim, 3 1/2 In., Set Of 6 .... 15.00
Kitchen, Mold, Maple, Sheaf Of Wheat, Border, Carved, Round Plunger 48.00
Kitchen, Mold, Pudding, Copper, Tin Coating, Oval, Rooster Top, 8 In. 45.00
Kitchen, Mold, Pudding, Curved, Ring For Hanging, Tin, 9 X 12 In. 50.00
Kitchen, Mold, Pudding, Ear Of Corn, Bunch Of Grapes, Tin, Copper, Pair 48.00
Kitchen, Mold, Pudding, Fish, Straight Body, Tin, Signed, 5 X 10 1/2 In. 44.00
Kitchen, Mold, Pudding, Tin, Melon-Shaped, 1 Quart 10.00
Kitchen, Mold, Pudding, Tin, Seashell 27.00
Kitchen, Mold, Tin, Quaker Oats 8.00
Kitchen, Nipper, Sugar, Wrought Iron, With Spring Piece, 1800s, 7 1/2 In. 85.00
Kitchen, Nutcracker, Brass, Man-In-Moon Design 50.00
Kitchen, Nutcracker, Wooden, Carved Bear Head, Glass Eyes 140.00
Kitchen, Opener, Bottle, Cast Iron, Model Of Bulldog's Head, 3 X 4 In. 10.50
Kitchen, Oven, Covered Wagon Cookstove, Lady's Head Insert 12.50
Kitchen, Paddle, Candle Dipping & Drying, Shaped Maple, Handle, 8 X 9 In. 40.00
Kitchen, Pan, Baking, 12 Rosette Baking Molds, Handled, 12 3/4 X 8 1/4 In. 25.00
Kitchen, Pan, Cake, Fry Ovenglass, 9 In. 12.00
Kitchen, Pan, Candy Mold, Baker's Chocolate, Logo Imprints On Bottom 65.00
Kitchen, Pan, Corn Muffin, 11 Molds, C.1862, 13 X 6 1/2 In. 25.00
Kitchen, Pan, Cornstick, Cast Iron, 7 Ear Mold .... 10.00 To 15.00
Kitchen, Pan, Fry, Long Handle, Wrought Iron, 47 1/2 X 12 3/4 In. 145.00
Kitchen, Pan, Milk Redware, Light Green Glaze Inside, 17 In. 120.00
Kitchen, Pan, Muffin, Heart Design 16.00
Kitchen, Pan, Muffin, 3 Cup, Cast Iron, 7 1/2 X 9 In. 8.00
Kitchen, Pan, Pie, 1877, 10 In. 7.50
Kitchen, Paper, Apple, Cast Iron, Turntable, Lockey & Howland, 1856 Patent 25.00
Kitchen, Parer, Apple, Cast Iron, Hudson Parer Co. 15.00
Kitchen, Parer, Apple, On Board, Amos Mosher, 1829, Pegged, 26 In. 185.00
Kitchen, Pastry Jigger, Wrought Iron, Scalloped, Turned Shaft, 18th Century 50.00
Kitchen, Peel, Pie, Paddle Shaped, Tapered End, Patina, 9 3/4 X 4 In. 25.00
Kitchen, Peeler, Apple, Cast Iron, Goodell Co., Antrim, N.H., May, 1898 .... 21.50
Kitchen, Peeler, Apple, Cast Iron, Reading Hardware Co., May 5, 1868 .... 28.00
Kitchen, Peeler, Apple, Cast Iron, Turntable, Lockey & Howland, 1856 .... 25.00
Kitchen, Peeler, Apple, Domestic, Cast Iron, Peels & Rejects, June 10, 1873 .... 35.00
Kitchen, Peeler, Apple, Floor Model, All Wood, C.1820, 32 In. 265.00
Kitchen, Peeler, Apple, Iron, Hudson, Patent 1882 .... 32.00
Kitchen, Peeler, Apple, Iron, Patented 1863 .... 20.00
Kitchen, Peeler, Apple, Iron, 8 Gears 30.00
Kitchen, Peeler, Apple, Keen Kutter, Cast Iron, Patent 1898, 5 Gears 27.50
Kitchen, Peeler, Apple, Mechanical, Table Clamp, Goodell Co., 1898 .... 35.00
Kitchen, Peeler, Apple, Turntable Clamp, Lockey & Howland, 1856 .... 35.00
Kitchen, Peeler, Apple, Wooden, Steel Blade, Handle, 10 In. 60.00
Kitchen, Peeler, Apple, Wooden, Wheel Like Wagon Wheel, Turns 2 In., 12 In. 135.00
Kitchen, Peeler, Apple, Wooden, 2 Wheel 140.00
Kitchen, Peeler, Potato, Hamlnite 22.00
Kitchen, Peeler, Wooden, Iron Prongs, Crank Handle, Pine Base, 12 In. 150.00
Kitchen, Pie Board, Slate 42.00
Kitchen, Pie Lifter, Hand-Forged Iron 25.00
Kitchen, Pie Rack, Tin, 11 In.Diameter, 5 In.High 15.00
Kitchen, Pitcher, Blue Diamond-Quilted Crimped Top & Reeded Handle, 9 In. 175.00
Kitchen, Pitcher, Flint Rockingham Glaze, Embossed Berry Spray, 6 1/2 In. 40.00
Kitchen, Pitcher, Milk, Sponge, Blue, Handled, 6 In. 65.00
Kitchen, Pitter, Cherry, Cast Iron, Enterprise 1883 .... 22.00
Kitchen, Pitter, Cherry, Cast Iron, Spring Type 12.00
Kitchen, Pitter, Cherry, Cast Iron, 4-Legged 31.50
Kitchen, Pitter, Cherry, Enterprise, Pat.1883 .... 18.00
Kitchen, Pitter, Cherry, New Standard 21.00
Kitchen, Pitter, Cherry, Rollman, No.3 .... 12.00
Kitchen, Plate, Eating, Maple, Round, Small, 6 X 6 1/2 In. 95.00
Kitchen, Plate, Hand-Wrought Iron, Scalloped Edge, 18th Century, 9 In. 125.00
Kitchen, Popcorn Popper, Solid Copper, Wood Handle, Hand Crank, 4 1/2 X 7 In. 22.50
Kitchen, Porringer, Hand-Wrought Iron, Handled, 5 1/2 In. 65.00
Kitchen, Pot, Bean, Cast Iron, 10 X 6 1/2 In. 15.00

Kitchen, Pot, Iron, Handle, Henrick & Co., Pint 30.00
Kitchen, Potato Masher, Tiger Maple, 11 In. 19.00
Kitchen, Potato Masher, Wooden .... 4.00 To 8.00
Kitchen, Potholder, Iron, Double 18.00
Kitchen, Raisin Seeder, Clamp On Bench, F.E.Tournier, Boston 15.00
Kitchen, Raisin Seeder, Wood & Wire, The Everett 26.00
Kitchen, Reamer, Wooden, Metal Clamp 23.00
Kitchen, Ricer, Potato, Iron, Dated 1887, 11 X 4 1/2 In. 15.00
Kitchen, Roaster, Bird, Wireware For Open Fireplace, Collapsible, C.1870 .... 24.50
Kitchen, Rolling Pin, Blown Amber Glass, 15 In. 60.00
Kitchen, Rolling Pin, Blown Glass, Stoddard, New Hampshire 60.00
Kitchen, Rolling Pin, Blown Opalescent Glass 25.00
Kitchen, Rolling Pin, Blue, Blown Glass 40.00
Kitchen, Rolling Pin, Clear Glass, Pink & White Decoration 120.00
Kitchen, Rolling Pin, Cookie, Carved Flower, Wooden Pin, Yoke, Handle 140.00
Kitchen, Rolling Pin, Cookie, Child's, Corrugated Wood 15.00
Kitchen, Rolling Pin, Cookie, Corrugated Grooves 9.00
Kitchen, Rolling Pin, Cookie, Wooden, 1 Handle Type 22.00
Kitchen, Rolling Pin, Cylinder Turns Separate, Curly Maple 38.00
Kitchen, Rolling Pin, Glass, Black, Spattered 50.00
Kitchen, Rolling Pin, Glass, Metal Closure 18.00
Kitchen, Rolling Pin, Glass, Tin Cap On One End 12.00
Kitchen, Rolling Pin, Hand Blown, Dark Blue, C.1890, 14 In. 45.00
Kitchen, Rolling Pin, Maple, Curly, Burl 120.00
Kitchen, Rolling Pin, Maple, 18 In. 15.00
Kitchen, Rolling Pin, Springerle, Hand-Carved, Yoke, Geometric Flower Design 130.00
Kitchen, Rolling Pin, Tiger Maple .... 33.00 To 45.00
Kitchen, Rolling Pin, Tiger Maple, Hand-Carved Ball Handles 22.00
Kitchen, Rolling Pin, Turned From One Piece, 5 In.Diameter, Center, 15 In. 25.00
Kitchen, Sausage Stuffer, Cast Iron, Enterprise, Patents 1888 & 1906 .... 25.00
Kitchen, Sausage Stuffer, Cast Iron, 1876 .... 35.00
Kitchen, Sausage Stuffer, Hanging, Tin & Wood 100.00
Kitchen, Scoop & Strainer, Maple Syrup, Tin 25.00
Kitchen, Scoop, Apple Butter, Maple, Hand-Hewn, One Piece Handle 75.00
Kitchen, Scoop, Candy, Aluminum 3.50
Kitchen, Scoop, Cheese, Ivory Handle, Silver Plate, Hallmark, Stilton 12.50
Kitchen, Scoop, Grain, Pine, One Piece, Miniature, 5 1/2 In. 9.00
Kitchen, Scoop, Hand Whittled, Deep 70.00
Kitchen, Scoop, Ice Cream, Heavy Nickel Over Brass, Wooden Handle 20.00
Kitchen, Scoop, Ice Cream, Pewter 18.00
Kitchen, Scraper, Dough, Wrought Iron 10.00
Kitchen, Sharpener, Knife, Hanging Wall Box, Pine, 18 In. 50.00
Kitchen, Sifter, Flour, Miniature, Salesman's Sample, 2 In. 25.00
Kitchen, Skillet, Cast Iron, 3 Footed, Handled 12.00
Kitchen, Spatula, Hand-Forged Iron 18.00
Kitchen, Spice Set, Round Tin Containing 6 Tin Containers Inside 26.00
Kitchen, Spice Set, Victorian Tole, Black Paint, 7 Piece 35.00
    Kitchen, Spinning Wheel, see Tool, Spinning Wheel
Kitchen, Spit-Jack, Reflector Stand, Drip Well In Stand, Iron, Early 1800s 850.00
Kitchen, Spoon Rack, Pennsylvania Dutch, 18 X 18 X 4 In. 45.00
Kitchen, Spoon, Cherry, Turned, Scribed, Shaped Handle, Finial, Wood, 6 1/2 In. ... 10.00
Kitchen, Spoon, Iron Forged, Handled, 18 1/2 In. 35.00
Kitchen, Sprinkler, Clothes, Figural, Chinaman, Sprinkle Plenty, Tin Cap 14.00
Kitchen, Squeezer, Lemon, Cast Iron 14.00
Kitchen, Squeezer, Lemon, Cast Iron With China Insert 16.00
Kitchen, Squeezer, Lemon, Iron, Hinged, Wooded Inserts, Patented, 10 3/4 In. 22.00
Kitchen, Squeezer, Lemon, Wooden 18.00
Kitchen, Squeezer, Mop 20.00
Kitchen, Stomper, Sauerkraut, Hand-Cut, 22 In. 8.50
Kitchen, Strainer, Blue Tones, Marked Germany, 2 Piece 18.50
Kitchen, Strainer, Porcelain, Gold Band, Pierced, Wooden Handle, 9 1/2 In. 28.00
Kitchen, Sugar Shaker, Tin 9.00
Kitchen, Teakettle, Brass & Copper, Dovetailed Side & Bottom, 6 In. 90.00
Kitchen, Teakettle, Cast Iron, Gooseneck Spout & Lid .... 15.00 To 25.00
Kitchen, Thermometer, Candy, German, Copper, Wooden Handle, 11 X 1 1/2 In. 18.25

Kitchen, Toast Rack, Ball Feet	15.00
Kitchen, Toast Rack, Silver Plating Over Nickel Silver, Decorated	40.00
Kitchen, Toast Rack, 4 Ball Feet, Center Handle, Holds 6 Toasts, Hallmarked	28.00
Kitchen, Toaster, Hand-Wrought	32.00
Kitchen, Toaster, Iron, Rotating Hearth, Penny Footed, 18th Century	200.00
Kitchen, Toaster, Or Small Game Broiler On Stand, Iron	225.00
Kitchen, Towel Holder, Original Box	4.00
Kitchen, Tray, Apple, Wooden, Red, Footed, Square, 10 In.	50.00
Kitchen, Tray, Old Wicker, Glass Bottom, 22 X 7 In.	15.00
Kitchen, Treadle, Butter Churner, Dog Shape, Large	300.00
Kitchen, Trivet, Combination Meat Fork & Adjustable Toaster, Iron	275.00
Kitchen, Wafer, People & Flowers Design, Iron, 18th Century	125.00
Kitchen, Warmer, Food, Child's, Animals	5.00
Kitchen, Washboard, Brass, Dovetailed, Sears Kenmore	12.00
Kitchen, Washboard, Cast Iron, Soap Pockets, 10 1/4 In.	38.00
Kitchen, Washboard, Wooden With Tin Scrubbing Surface	1.75
Kitchen, Washing Machine, Wooden	125.00
Kitchen, Wine Press, Cast Iron, 1895	15.00
Knowles, Taylor & Knowles, see KTK, Lotus Ware	
Koch, Bowl, Grapes, Louise, Bavaria Blank, 6 3/4 In.	32.50
Koch, Bowl, Water Scene, Purple & Green Grapes, Gold Scalloped Rim, 9 In.	45.00
Koch, Creamer, Apples	25.00
Koch, Dish, Berry	12.50
Koch, Jar, Jam, Apples & Cherry, Open Finial, Signed 4 1/2 In.	75.00
Koch, Plate, Apple	32.50
Koch, Plate, Apples, Leaves, Blossoms, Artist Signed, J & C Louise, Bavaria	35.00
Koch, Plate, Fruit, Apples, White Background, 7 5/8 In.	18.00
Koch, Plate, Fruit, Bavarian Peaches, White Background, Signed Louise, 8 In.	21.00
Koch, Plate, Fruit, Grapes, White Background, Signed Louise, 7 5/8 In.	22.50
Koch, Plate, Grape Clusters, Signed, 9 3/4 In.	35.00
Koch, Plate, Grapes, Brown Ground, J & C, Bavaria, Signed, 8 1/2 In.	24.00
Koch, Plate, Purple Grapes, Leaves & Stems, Gold, 6 3/4 In.	15.00
Korean Ware, Basket, Drip Glaze, 10 1/2 In.	215.00
Korean Ware, Dish, 10 Figures Looking Into Bowl, 9 X 2 1/4 In.	385.00
Korean Ware, Lamp Base, Children Playing, Glazed Blue, Green, Purple & Brown	195.00
Korean Ware, Tankard, 3 Applied Porcelain Figures, 12 1/2 In.	220.00
Korean Ware, Vase, Applied Native & Bird, 7 In.	75.00
Korean Ware, Vase, Black & Purple Glaze, 6 Figures, Signed, 12 In.High	265.00
Korean Ware, Vase, Canteen Shaped, Poured Porcelain Neck, 2 Figures, 9 In.	175.00
Korean Ware, Vase, Red, 3 Porcelain Figures, Poured Porcelain Border, 12 In.	165.00

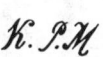

KPM is part of one of the marks used about 1723 by the Meissen Factory Konigliche Porzellan Manufaktur. Other firms using the letters include the Royal Manufactory of Berlin, Germany, that worked from 1832 to 1847. A factory in Scheibe, Germany, used the mark in 1928. The mark was also used in Waldenburg, Germany, and other German cities during the twentieth century.

KPM, Bowl, Floral, 13 In.	67.00
KPM, Cachepot, Pink On White, Hand-Painted Roses & Ferns, 6 1/4 In.	95.00
KPM, Compote, Figure On Base, Flared Top, Basket Design, 14 In., Pair	960.00
KPM, Creamer, Cow, White, Signed	22.00
KPM, Cup & Saucer, Demitasse, Fuchsia With Gold, German	8.50
KPM, Cup & Saucer, Demitasse, White, Red & Gold Trim, Blue Scepter Mark	29.00
KPM, Cup & Saucer, Multicolor Floral, Butterflies, Scepter Mark, 1870s	35.00
KPM, Cup & Saucer, Rust Florals, Blue Prunus, Gold Scrolled Handle, 1880	65.00
KPM, Gravy Boat & Underplate, Gold Interior	45.00
KPM, Painting, Lady On Beach, Frame With Velvet Insert, 14 X 18 In.	925.00
KPM, Painting, Ruth, Woman With Sheaf Of Wheat, Oil On Porcelain, 8 X 5 In.	425.00
KPM, Plaque, Liebesfruhling, Signed Knonllez, 9 X 11 In.	1250.00
KPM, Plaque, Lorelei, Signed Wagner, 5 X 7 In., 8 X 10 In.Frame	1050.00
KPM, Plaque, Mary & Child, Oval, Framed, 6 1/2 In.	625.00
KPM, Plaque, Spanish Lady, Vines, Deep Purple Grapes, 8 1/4 X 10 In.	1850.00
KPM, Plaque, The Beggar Boys, C.1850, 9 3/4 X 12 1/4 In.	1800.00
KPM, Plate, Cake, Handled, Pale Blue Rose Floral, Gilt Edge, 10 In.	65.00
KPM, Plate, Floral Bouquet Center, Gold Border, White, Marked, 5 In., Set Of 3	7.50

KPM, Plate, Floral Rim, White Center, Gold Trim, Open Handles, 10 1/2 In. 20.00
KPM, Plate, Floral Spray Center, Gold Rim, Open Handle, 10 In. 30.00
KPM, Sugar & Creamer & Teapot, Covered, Blue Underglaze, Germany 65.00
KPM, Sugar & Creamer, Poppies 16.00
KPM, Tea Set, Blue Morning Glories, Gold Band, Blue Scepter Mark, 24 Piece 550.00
KPM, Toilet Set, Flowers, Gilding, Pin Tray, 2 Soaps, 2 Powders, 2 Bottles 450.00
KPM, Tureen, Covered, Gold 45.00

      KT&K.
      CHINA
      KTK are the initials of the Knowles, Taylor and Knowles Company of
      East Liverpool, Ohio, founded by Isaac W.Knowles in 1853. They
      made Lotus Ware.

KTK Lotus Ware, see Lotus Ware
KTK, Perfume, Figural, Cat, Crown Stopper, 2 1/4 In. 10.00
KTK, Pitcher, Graniteware, 9 In. 22.50
KTK, Pitcher, Pewter Lid, 3 1/2 In. 88.00
KTK, Plate, Wall, Polychrome Dutch Scene, Edwin M.Knowles, 8 In. 25.00
Ku Klux Klan, Buckle, Brass, Belt, K.K.K., Oval, C.1926 .... 14.00
Ku Klux Klan, Sheet Music, Ku Klux Klan Forever, C.1925 .... 38.00

    Kutani ware is a Japanese porcelain made after the mid-seventeenth century.
    Most of the pieces found today are nineteenth century.
Kutani, Bowl, Blown-Out Bird, White, Applied Cobalt, Yellow, & Red Snake, Label 279.00
Kutani, Bowl, Chrysanthemums, 9 In. 75.00
Kutani, Bowl, Oriental Scenes, Scalloped Rim, 9 In. 35.00
Kutani, Bowl, Red, 8 1/2 X 2 1/2 In. 89.00
Kutani, Bowl, Red, 8 1/2 X 4 In. 89.00
Kutani, Bowl, Rice, Square Top, Spoon 37.00
Kutani, Burner, Incense, Shape Of House 210.00
Kutani, Creamer, Geisha Girl 17.00
Kutani, Figurine, Man Holding Scroll, Seated, Bisque Face & Hands, 12 In. 100.00
Kutani, Figurine, Oriental, Orange & White, Holding Peach, 11 In. 95.00
Kutani, Figurine, Standing Figure Holding Peach In Hand, Orange & White 95.00
Kutani, Ginger Jar, Cream & Light Blue, Butterflies, Birds, Gold, 7 1/2 In. 75.00
Kutani, Ginger Jar, Orange, Foo Dog Finial, 10 In. .... 62.50 To 75.00
Kutani, Jardiniere, Black & Orange Diamond, Lions' Heads For Feet & Handle 135.00
Kutani, Plate, Quail In The Grasses, 8 1/2 In. 60.00
Kutani, Plate, Quail In The Grasses, 9 1/2 In. 75.00
Kutani, Saki Bottle, Bamboo Leaves, Autumn Color, C.1900, 6 In. 30.00
Kutani, Saki Bottle, 6 Gold Panels, Oriental Figures, Calligraphy, 6 In., Set 30.00
Kutani, Sugar & Creamer, Blue 24.00
Kutani, Sugar & Creamer, Figures In Medallions, Gold Trim, Red Mark 35.00
Kutani, Tea Caddy, Covered, Allover Design, Gold Trim, Jeweled Florals, 4 In. 50.00
Kutani, Tea Set, Famille Decoration, Signed 125.00
Kutani, Tea Set, Scenic, Geishas, Blue, C.1890, 3 Piece 165.00
Kutani, Tea Strainer, Red & Gold, 2 Piece 22.00
Kutani, Teapot, Birds & Flowers, Individual 25.00
Kutani, Teapot, Bulbous, Porcelain Strainer Insert, Jeweled, 8 X 6 In. 60.00
Kutani, Teapot, Panels Of Scenes With Flowers & People, 4 1/2 X 8 1/2 In. 85.00
Kutani, Teapot, Winter Scene, Enameled Snows, Seascape, Waves, 4 Piece 225.00
Kutani, Vase, Bud, Floral, Gray Background, Bulbous, 3 1/2 In., Pair 30.00
Kutani, Vase, Figures On One Side, Scenic On Other, Signed, 7 In. 45.00
Kutani, Vase, Floral, Bird Panels, 2 Character Mark, C.1880, 9 1/2 In., Pair 200.00
Kutani, Vase, Kishihara, 2 1/2 In. 6.00
Lacquer, Box, Sewing, Oval, Chinese 25.00
Lacquer, Cabinet, Chinese, Rouge, Two Part, Inset Panels, C.1800 .... 1600.00
Lacquer, Figurine, Standing Buddha, Lotus Blossom Base, 22 In. 150.00
Lacquer, Lunch Box, 4 Part, Black & Gold, Japan, Late 19th Century 150.00
Lacquer, Panel, Relief Figure In Landscape, 24 X 13 In., Pair 70.00
Lacquer, Portrait, Chinese Shrine Panel, Buddhist Priest, C.1800, 24 1/2 In. 375.00
Lacquer, Screen, Twofold Table, Polychrome Panels, Japanese, 31 X 35 In. 120.00
Lacquer, Tea Caddy, Lotus Form, Incised Decoration, Soft Metal Inner Boxes 245.00
Lacquer, Vase, Korean Temple, Inlaid Mother-Of-Pearl, Phoenix Birds, 24 In. 50.00

LALIQUE
    Lalique glass was made by Rene Lalique in Paris, France, between
LALIQUE
    the 1890s and his death in 1945. The glass was molded, pressed, and

*engraved in Art Nouveau and Art Deco styles. Pieces were marked
with the signature, "R. Lalique." Lalique glass is still being made.
Pieces made after 1945 bear the mark "Lalique."*

Lalique, Ashtray, Frosted Love Birds On Clear Base, 4 X 2 In.	37.50
Lalique, Ashtray, Grasshoppers, Molded, Brown, Triangular, 1 1/8 In.	200.00
Lalique, Ashtray, Marinique, Stylized Flowers, 6 In.	100.00
Lalique, Ashtray, Owl, Frosted & Clear, Signed, 3 1/2 In.	95.00
Lalique, Atomizer, Sculptured Nudes, Signed, 5 In.	110.00
Lalique, Bell, Frosted Bird Top, Crystal, France, 7 In.	65.00
Lalique, Bookend, Winged Cherub, Frosted, Clear Base, 8 In., Pair	600.00
Lalique, Bottle, Cologne, Crescent & Stars On Stopper, Cobalt Blue, 6 1/2 In.	55.00
Lalique, Bottle, Cologne, Monkey Design, Blue Enamel, Frosted, 3 1/2 In.	210.00
Lalique, Bottle, Perfume, Art Deco Geometric Design, Tzigane, Corday, Paris	75.00
Lalique, Bottle, Perfume, Clear, Frosted Butterflies & Stopper, 2 1/4 In.	265.00
Lalique, Bottle, Perfume, Floral, Floral Stopper, 3 1/2 In.	85.00
Lalique, Bottle, Perfume, Flower Garlands, Floral Stopper, Cylindrical, 3 In.	75.00
Lalique, Bottle, Perfume, Impressed, Blue Wash Stopper	90.00
Lalique, Bottle, Perfume, Laurel Leaf Wreath Garland, Stopper, Frosted, 4 In.	25.00
Lalique, Bottle, Perfume, Nude, Cupid, & Grapes, Cupid On Stopper, 8 X 6 In.	125.00
Lalique, Bottle, Perfume, Nudes With Connecting Garlands, Brass Top, Signed	185.00
Lalique, Bottle, Perfume, Nudes With Garland Of Flowers, Gold Top, 6 1/4 In.	175.00
Lalique, Bottle, Perfume, Nudes, Green Wash, Gold Atomizer Top, 5 In.	200.00
Lalique, Bottle, Perfume, Tulip Stopper	175.00
Lalique, Bowl, Band Of Frosted Fruits In Relief, 7 1/2 In.	76.00
Lalique, Bowl, Berry, Swirling Fish, Controlled Bubbles, R.Lalique	250.00
Lalique, Bowl, Birds In Relief, Block Sign, 9 1/4 X 4 In.	150.00
Lalique, Bowl, Block Letters, Opal, Blue Beaded Circles, 8 In.	135.00
Lalique, Bowl, Caviar, Covered, Glass Beads On Rim, Signed	285.00
Lalique, Bowl, Center Bust Of Gentleman, Scarf, Hat, Leaves, Grapes, 7 7/8 In.	125.00
Lalique, Bowl, Clamshell, Opalescent, 8 In.	200.00
Lalique, Bowl, Clamshells In Relief, Opalescent, Signed, 8 X 3 In.	180.00
Lalique, Bowl, Clear & Frosted Birds, Script Signature, 4 3/4 X 4 1/2 In.	65.00
Lalique, Bowl, Clear, Frosted Leaf In Relief, Signed, 4 1/2 X 5 1/2 In.	59.00
Lalique, Bowl, Finger With Underplate, Trees And Florettes, Signed	95.00
Lalique, Bowl, Fishscale, Amber, Signed, 9 1/2 X 4 In.	425.00
Lalique, Bowl, Frosted White, Ornamental Designs, Oval, Signed, 5 1/2 X 18 In.	300.00
Lalique, Bowl, Fruit In Bottom, Frosted, Block Letters, Signed, 10 In.	95.00
Lalique, Bowl, Green, Raised Fish, Bulbous, R.Lalique, 7 1/2 In.	1500.00
Lalique, Bowl, Lily Pad, Yellow, 3 Iridescent Feet, Signed, 8 1/2 X 2 1/4 In.	325.00
Lalique, Bowl, Lily Pad, 3 Iridescent Feet, Yellow, Signed, 1/2 X 2 1/4 In.	325.00
Lalique, Bowl, Mistletoe In Relief, Opalescent, Signed, 6 1/4 In.	65.00
Lalique, Bowl, Mistletoe, Clear, Opalescent, 9 1/2 In.	225.00
Lalique, Bowl, Octagon Rimmed, 11 In.	70.00
Lalique, Bowl, Opalescent Blue, Beaded Circles, 8 In.	135.00
Lalique, Bowl, Petals Forming Scalloped Edge, Clear, 10 In.	235.00
Lalique, Bowl, Salad, Coupe Chicoree, Blue Opalescent, Dandelion Leaves	425.00
Lalique, Bowl, Salad, Zigzag, Molded, Underplate, Signed In Block Letters	175.00
Lalique, Bowl, Stylized Leaves, 8 In.	140.00
Lalique, Bowl, Sweet, Frosted & Clear, Signed Lalique, Script France, 4 In.	32.00
Lalique, Bowl, Thistle, Clear & Frosted, France, Script, 10 X 5 In.	175.00
Lalique, Bowl, 3 Morning Glories, Amber Stained & Opalescent, 8 1/2 In.	225.00
Lalique, Box Lid, Powder, Frosted Flowers & Leaves, 3 3/4 In.	90.00
Lalique, Box, Powder, Cupid On Cover, Round, Signed	175.00
Lalique, Box, Powder, D'Orsay, Floral Design, Round, 4 In.	200.00
Lalique, Box, Powder, Fleurs D'Amour Roger Et Gallet, Birds, Metal	85.00
Lalique, Box, Powder, Masks With Roses, Striated Sides	225.00
Lalique, Box, Powder, Smoke Blue, Roger	425.00
Lalique, Box, Powder, 3 Nudes, Floral Border	225.00
Lalique, Candlestick, Clear, Frosted Leaf Pattern, 2 In., Pair	225.00
Lalique, Candlestick, Frosted & Clear, Scroll Stem, Signed, 8 In.	95.00
Lalique, Candlestick, Frosted Leaf Design, 2 X 4 3/8 In., Pair	235.00
Lalique, Clock, Frosted, Sculpted Birds On Sides, Silver Face, 6 1/2 In.	375.00
Lalique, Clock, Pentagon Shape, Black Enamel, Art Deco, Block Signature	650.00
Lalique, Creamer, Lady With Flowing Hair, Green Mark	45.00
Lalique, Decanter, Bubble Design, 6 X 7 In.	95.00

Lalique, Decanter, Clear Optic Bottle, Small Stopper, Black Center	40.00
Lalique, Decanter, Geometric Lines, 3 Nudes In Center, Rectangular, R.Lalique	135.00
Lalique, Dish, Clear & Frosted Floral, Covered, Signed, 4 In.	75.00
Lalique, Dish, Fan Shape, Clear With Frosted Thistles, Signed	58.00
Lalique, Dish, Fruit, Cherry Design, Pale Yellow, 4 1/2 In.	30.00
Lalique, Ewer, Figural, Bacchus, Relief, Cire Perdue, Inscribed, 4-25-22, 9 In.	8000.00
Lalique, Figurine, Bird, Frosted, 1/2 Sphere Base, 5 In.	50.00
Lalique, Figurine, Madonna & Child, Wood Base, Block Signature, 14 In.	375.00
Lalique, Figurine, Man In 18th Century Costume, Script Signature, 5 1/2 In.	100.00
Lalique, Figurine, Nude Kneeling Among Wheat Sheaves, Art Deco, 8 In.	235.00
Lalique, Figurine, Nude Male, White, Frosted, Standing On Clear Base, 8 In.	250.00
Lalique, Figurine, Nude On Black Base, 3 1/2 In.	35.00
Lalique, Figurine, Spanish Dancer, Pleated Flaring Skirt, Art Nouveau, 12 In.	325.00
Lalique, Figurine, Squirrel, Opaline, Signed In Block Letters, 4 3/4 In.	195.00
Lalique, Flask, Scent, Leaves In High Releif, Domed, 2 1/2 In.	50.00
Lalique, Flip Glass, Clear, Round, Clusters Of Grapes, Signed, 5 1/2 X 5 In.	55.00
Lalique, Goblet, Blue Enameled Roosters On Stem, 5 3/4 In., Pair	125.00
Lalique, Goblet, Flat Stems, Blackberry Clusters, 5 1/2 In.	85.00
Lalique, Holder, Place Card, 2 X 1 3/4 In.	35.00
Lalique, Hood Ornament, Clear & Frosted Eagle's Head, 5 1/2 X 4 1/4 In.	575.00
Lalique, Hood Ornament, Dragonfly	750.00
Lalique, Hood Ornament, Eagle, C.1925, 5 3/4 In. *Illus*	650.00
Lalique, Hood Ornament, Eagle, Molded Signature, 4 In.	550.00
Lalique, Hood Ornament, Lady With Flowing Hair	95.00
Lalique, Hood Ornament, Rooster, Crouching, Raised Letters	350.00 To 400.00
Lalique, Hood Ornament, The Comet, Set In Car Metal	1200.00
Lalique, Inkwell, Geometric Art Deco Rim, Owl Shape, 3 1/2 X 5 3/4 In.	45.00
Lalique, Jar, Stylized Floral Cover, Tinted Brown, Raised Arches, 3 In.	95.00
Lalique, Jigger, Frosted Cherubs, Script Signature	50.00
Lalique, Lamp Base, Frosted, Stylized Triangular Leaves, 8 5/8 X 12 In.	400.00
Lalique, Lamp, Cherub Base, Block Signature, 9 In.	500.00
Lalique, Luminaire, School Of Fish, Bubbling Water, Silver Base, Electrified	2700.00
Lalique, Paperweight, Frosted Owl, Signed, 3 1/2 In.	55.00
Lalique, Plaque, Full Figure Nude In Relief, Amber, Signed, 9 X 9 In.	500.00
Lalique, Plaque, Love Birds & Blossoms On Tree Branches, Green, 7 X 10 In.	475.00
Lalique, Plate, Blue Opalescent Tone, Spiraling Circles Center, 12 In.	250.00
Lalique, Plate, Opalescent Blue, Expanding Hobnail Comet Design, 11 In.	125.00
Lalique, Plate, Wheat Raised All Around Back, Spoke-Like Fashion, Signed	125.00
Lalique, Platter, Frosted Stylized Leaves, 14 In.	225.00
Lalique, Sconce, Fountain Design, Silver Brackets, Signed, 36 X 20 In., Pair	5000.00
Lalique, Shade, Saint Vincent, Grapes & Scrolling Vines, Yellow Stain, 16 In.	700.00
Lalique, Shade, Topaz, Hanging, Allover Stylized Flowers	725.00
Lalique, Sugar Shaker, Raised Orange Egyptian Figures, Frosted, 5 1/4 In.	165.00
Lalique, Sweet Dish, Frosted Leaf Handles, Signed, Script France, Pair	30.00
Lalique, Toothpick, Cherubs, France	25.00
Lalique, Tray, Card, Nudes & Bird Recessed, Block Signature, 4 X 6 In.	32.50
Lalique, Tray, Clear, Etched Chrysanthemums, Clear, Signed, 15 In.	200.00
Lalique, Tray, Glass, Clear, Round, Bird In Center, 3 X 3 1/2 In.	45.00
Lalique, Tray, Pin, Oblong, Frosted Reclining Nudes, 6 X 3 1/2 In.	95.00
Lalique, Tray, Pin, Round, Frosted Bird On Pedestal In Center, Signed, 3 In.	65.00
Lalique, Trivet, Fish Ballet, Block Signature	250.00
Lalique, Tumbler, Clear, Frosted, & Blue Stain Decoration, Art Deco, 3 In.	73.50
Lalique, Vase, Art Deco, Diamond-Shaped Knobs, Amber Stain, Signed, 5 In.	105.00

Lalique, Hood Ornament, Eagle, C.1925, 5 3/4 In.

Lalique, Vase, Black Enamel, Molded, C.1925, 7 1/2 In.

Lalique, Vase, Art Deco, Opalescent, Broad Overlapping Petals, 5 1/2 In.	325.00
Lalique, Vase, Bacchantes, Smoke Color With Bronze, Block Signature	3465.00
Lalique, Vase, Band Of Florals In Relief At Rim, Opalescent Blue, 6 In.	165.00
Lalique, Vase, Bird Appliques, Block Signature, 20 In.	125.00
Lalique, Vase, Birds, Branches, Clear & Frosted, Signed, 6 In.	550.00
Lalique, Vase, Black Enamel, Molded, C.1925, 7 1/2 In. ...... *Illus*	950.00
Lalique, Vase, Blown Leaf Decoration, Flared Neck, Impressed, Signed, 7 In.	275.00
Lalique, Vase, Blown-Out Fish, Opalescent, 4 In.	155.00
Lalique, Vase, Blown-Out Thistles, Opalescent, 8 1/2 In.	295.00 To 300.00
Lalique, Vase, Blue Frosted, Relief Cranes, Art Nouveau, Signed, 7 1/4 In.	350.00
Lalique, Vase, Blue Wash, Birds & Leaves, 12 In.	600.00
Lalique, Vase, Blue, Deer Running Around Vase, 3 Panels, 7 In.	325.00
Lalique, Vase, Bulbous, Blown-Out Druids, 7 In.	225.00 To 425.00
Lalique, Vase, Cameo Leaves, Gray Shadings, 6 1/2 In.	295.00
Lalique, Vase, Clear, Brown Highlights, Thorn Handles With Flowers, 7 1/2 In.	225.00
Lalique, Vase, Cylindrical Shape, Roosters, Grass Sheaths, 6 In.	285.00
Lalique, Vase, Deep Forest Scene, Heavy Leaded Crystal, 13 In.	250.00
Lalique, Vase, Escargot, 6 X 7 In.	350.00
Lalique, Vase, Fern Pattern, R.Lalique, 4 1/2 In.	170.00
Lalique, Vase, Folded Leaves, Frost, Signed, 7 1/2 In.	95.00
Lalique, Vase, Fontaine, Rounded, Frosted Gray, Cut Free-Form Leaves, 11 In.	325.00
Lalique, Vase, Formosa, Amber Yellow, 8 X 8 In.	900.00
Lalique, Vase, Formosa, Gray, Cased, 7 In.	695.00
Lalique, Vase, Formosa, Swirling Fish, Opalescent, Signed, 6 1/2 In.	375.00
Lalique, Vase, Frosted & Clear, Molded Rows Of Cherries, Signed, 8 In.	475.00
Lalique, Vase, Frosted Opalescent, Band Of Roosters Under Foliage, 6 In.	265.00
Lalique, Vase, Frosted, Protruding Bubbles On Sides, 4 1/2 In.	150.00
Lalique, Vase, Frosted, Vertical Raised Sheaths Of Grass, 5 3/4 In.	140.00
Lalique, Vase, Graduated Tiers Of Fern Fronds, Green, Inscribed, No.7015	1300.00
Lalique, Vase, Gray Enamel Background, Opaque Gazelles In High Relief, 5 In.	750.00
Lalique, Vase, Green To Clear Raised Berries, Signed R.Lalique, 5 1/2 In.	175.00
Lalique, Vase, Gui, Rounded, Blue White, Raised Branches, 7 In.	195.00
Lalique, Vase, Horizontal Fish Design, Opaline Turquoise & Clear, 5 1/2 In.	500.00
Lalique, Vase, Light Blue Tint, Nude Figures, Block Signature, 8 1/2 In.	375.00
Lalique, Vase, Marigolds, Blue Stain, 6 X 5 In.	250.00
Lalique, Vase, Milk Pod Designs, Bulbous, Colorless, 6 1/2 In.	150.00
Lalique, Vase, Nude Woman Against Block Design, Signed R.Lalique, 9 1/2 In.	250.00
Lalique, Vase, Open Fan Design, Frosted Opaline, Signed, 7 1/2 In.	145.00
Lalique, Vase, Open Scroll Design In Handles, 6 X 12 In.	700.00
Lalique, Vase, Owl, Blue, Gold Trim, 6 In.	18.50
Lalique, Vase, Petals With Bluish Tinge Reflect From Vase, 5 In.	195.00
Lalique, Vase, Pierrefonds, Open Scroll Designed Handles, C.1927, 6 In.	700.00
Lalique, Vase, Rampillon, Triangular Protrusions, Patina Floral, 5 In.	200.00
Lalique, Vase, Red Flowers, Clear & Brown, Thorny Handles, 7 1/2 In.	225.00
Lalique, Vase, Roosters In Various Positions, Grass, Cylindrical, 3 In.	285.00
Lalique, Vase, Roosters, Grass, Cylindrical Shaped, 6 In.	270.00 To 285.00
Lalique, Vase, Serpent, Amber Body, Coiling Serpent, Molded, R.Lalique, 11 In.	4000.00
Lalique, Vase, Snails On Clear Frosted Ground, C.1890, 6 3/4 X 5 In.	300.00
Lalique, Vase, Thistle, Blue Opalescent, 11 In.	425.00
Lalique, Vase, Thistle, Blue Tinted, Signed, 10 In., Pair	700.00
Lalique, Vase, Tiers Of Stylized Ferns, Florets, Emerald Green, 7 In.	375.00
Lalique, Vase, White Opalescent, Paneled, Nudes, Script Signature, 9 In.	750.00

Lalique, Vase, 12 Parakeets, Cerulean Blue, Signed, 13 1/2 In. 1150.00
Lalique, Vase, 8 Nudes, Etched, Clear, Art Nouveau, Signed Script, 9 1/2 In. 325.00
Lalique, Wine, Nudes In Relief, Footed, Block Signature 55.00
Lamartine, Vase, Scenic, Birch Trees, Pond, Enameled, Pink Ground, 16 1/2 In. 645.00
    Lamp, see also Bradley & Hubbard, Lamp; Burmese, Lamp
Lamp, Akro Agate, White With Blue Swirls 48.00
Lamp, Aladdin, Alacite, Art Deco, Electric 35.00
Lamp, Aladdin, Alacite, World Lamp 225.00
Lamp, Aladdin, Blown Drape, Milk Glass Shade, Flint Glass, Rings, Chimney 145.00
Lamp, Aladdin, Brass, Model 12 .... 85.00
Lamp, Aladdin, Burner, Green Stem, Clear Font, Vertical Ribs 62.00
Lamp, Aladdin, Drape, Flint, Milk Glass Shade 145.00
Lamp, Aladdin, Electric, Chartreuse Decoration, 25 1/2 In.Pair 70.00
Lamp, Aladdin, Electric, Finial, Acorn Shape, Leaf Embossed G-186 .... 32.00
Lamp, Aladdin, Female Figure, Alacite, Pair 175.00
Lamp, Aladdin, Lady With Leopard, Art Deco, 14 In. 350.00
Lamp, Aladdin, Light Pink Milk Glass Drape 75.00
Lamp, Aladdin, No.B-60, Lincoln Drape, White .... 49.00 To 80.00
Lamp, Aladdin, No.B-75, Lincoln Drape, Ivory Alacite 72.00
Lamp, Aladdin, No.B-76, Lincoln Drape, Tall, Cobalt Blue 135.00
Lamp, Aladdin, No.B-90, White Moonstone Bowl, Black Moonstone Base 125.00
Lamp, Aladdin, No.B-92, Vertique, Green Moonstone 125.00
Lamp, Aladdin, No.B-95, Green White Moonstone, Bronze Base 70.00
Lamp, Aladdin, No.B-100, Venetian, Satin White, Alpha 60.00
Lamp, Aladdin, No.B-124, White Moonstone 85.00
Lamp, Aladdin, No.B-130, Orientale, Ivory, Rose 80.00
Lamp, Aladdin, No.B-133, Orientale, Silver Plate 82.00
Lamp, Aladdin, No.6, Brass Plated Frame, Brass Font, Hangs 30 In. 145.00
Lamp, Aladdin, Oil, Cathedral, Moonstone Green 85.00
Lamp, Aladdin, Oil, Moonstone Green, Cathedral 95.00
Lamp, Aladdin, Oil, Pink Moonstone, Ribbed Font, Glass Shade 65.00
Lamp, Aladdin, Urn, Alacite, Pair 100.00
Lamp, Aladdin, Vase, No.12 .... 65.00
Lamp, Aladdin, Washington Drape, Clear 50.00
Lamp, Alcohol, Glass, Cover, Wick, Miniature 16.00
Lamp, Alcohol, Ground Glass Cover, Small 12.50
Lamp, Angle, Milk White Shade, Embossed Silver & Brass 125.00
Lamp, Art Deco, Marble, Italian, Seductive Girl With Fan, Onyx Base, 13 In. 250.00
Lamp, Art Nouveau, Art Glass And Bronze, Octagonal Shade, 26 In. 130.00
Lamp, Art Nouveau, Clear, Glass Pedestal, 9 1/2 In. 55.00
Lamp, Art Nouveau, Girl, Metal, 24 In. 160.00
Lamp, Art Nouveau, Nude Woman On Sea Lion, 19 1/2 In.High 85.00
Lamp, Astral, Brass Column Marble Base, Cut Glass Shade, 16 1/2 In. 85.00
Lamp, Automobile Light, Kerosene, Adlake 17.00
Lamp, Banquet, Cupid In Stem, Brass Plated, Frosted Font, 25 In. 69.00
Lamp, Banquet, Marble Stem, Blue-Green Globe, Britannia Base, 31 In. 195.00
Lamp, Banquet, Oil, Brass, Electrified, 28 In. 198.00
Lamp, Banquet, Pale Pink Globe, 32 In. 375.00
Lamp, Banquet, Pink Marble-Like Font, Polished Brass Stemmed Base, 28 In. 150.00
Lamp, Banquet, Polished Brass, Flower Decorated Shade, 20 In. 95.00
Lamp, Banquet, Silver Plated & Onyx, 32 In. 375.00
Lamp, Base, Green Stippled Glass Panels, Brass Oil Font, Square, Iron 59.50
Lamp, Base, Wheeling Peachblow, Yellow To Cranberry, 9 In. 695.00
Lamp, Basket Of Fruit, Gold Fitted Handles, Tumbling Fruit Top 195.00
Lamp, Betty, Iron, 12 In. 65.00
Lamp, Betty, Strap Handle, Saucer Base, Tin, 6 3/4 In. 85.00
Lamp, Bisque, Raised Leaf Design, 17 In., Pair 400.00
Lamp, Black Amethyst, Electric, Octagonal, 24 In. 60.00
Lamp, Bracket, Brass Filler Cup, Clown Chimney, Beaded Top, El Dorado 59.50
Lamp, Bracket, Flint Glass Chimney, Beaded Top, 1/2 Pint, 10 3/4 In. 30.00
Lamp, Bracket, Moonstone, White 45.00
    Lamp, Bradley & Hubbard, see Bradley & Hubbard, Lamp
Lamp, Brass, Genie, Floral Shade 100.00
Lamp, Brass, Mayflower Shade 85.00
Lamp, Brass, Miniature, Shade, Beauty Night Lamp 42.00

Lamp, Brass, Student, Manhattan Brass, May 23, 1876	295.00
Lamp, Bronze Figural, Dated 1868, 12 In.	58.00
Lamp, Bronze, Chocolate, Birds In High Relief, Japanese	250.00
Lamp, Bronze, Figural, Dated 1868, 12 In.	58.00
Lamp, Bronze, Leaded Glass Shade, Caramel, Orange Striations, 7 X 18 In.	325.00
Lamp, Bronze, Merchants Standing On Oriental Carpet, Vienna, 10 In.	750.00
Lamp, Bronze, Peacock, Onyx Base, Blue, Amber, Green, & Clear Beads, 24 X 17 In.	750.00
Lamp, Bronze, Vienna, Carpet Seller, 20 1/2 In.	750.00
Lamp, Candle, Bisque, Skull-Head Wire Holder, Patent	125.00
Lamp, Candle, Milk Glass, Cape Cod Pattern	85.00
Lamp, Candle, Scalloped Socket, Hinged, Folding, Traveling, Tin, C.1870, 3 In.	75.00
Lamp, Canopy, Mica, Tin Center & Insert Support	10.00
Lamp, Carnival Glass, Oil, Zipper, Chimney, Marigold	285.00
Lamp, Carnival Glass, Red Regal, Iris, Gone With The Wind	9400.00
Lamp, Carnival Glass, Table, Sherman Hands, Marigold	295.00
Lamp, Carriage, Beveled Glass, 3 X 6 In., Pair	30.00
Lamp, Carriage, Nickel Brass Trim, Black, Candle Socket, 11 1/2 In.	35.00
Lamp, Cased Glass, Lavender, Camphor, Diamond Pattern	65.00
Lamp, Cased Glass, Pink, 28 1/2 In.	225.00
Lamp, Castle, Red Deer, Bohemian, 17 In.	275.00
Lamp, Ceiling, 4-Arm Light, Brass, 44 X 18 In.	165.00
Lamp, Chandelier, 6 Light, Adam Style, Silver Plate, 24 In.	230.00
Lamp, Children's, Batman	5.00
Lamp, Chinese Carved Green Quartz Urn, Carnelian, Ormolu, 26 In.	250.00
Lamp, Chinese, Slick Dragon, Gray Crackle, 10 X 4 In.	45.00
Lamp, Clambroth Base, Marriage, Signed & Dated, Ripley	375.00
Lamp, Clambroth, Blown, Miniature, 6 In.	40.00
Lamp, Clamp Chimney, Hinge Burner, Glass Stem, Carnival Glass Shade, Embossed	185.00
Lamp, Cloisonne, Opium, 4 1/2 In.	90.00
Lamp, Cobalt Blue, Miniature, Nutmeg	45.00
Lamp, Copper, Triple Angle, Embossed Reservoir	550.00
Lamp, Cosmos, see Cosmos, Lamp	
Lamp, Cranberry Glass, Miniature, Ribbed Shade & Base, 8 In.	365.00
Lamp, Crusie, Double, Double Reflectors, Tin, American	195.00
Lamp, Cut Glass, Diamond Point, Prism, Cane, Mushroom Shaped Shade, 15 1/2 In.	165.00
Lamp, Cut Glass, Globe Type Shade, 14 In.	300.00
Lamp, Cut Glass, Mushroom Shade, Prisms, 2 Lights, Harvard Pattern, 22 In.	1500.00
Lamp, Cut Glass, Pinwheel Pattern, 21 In.	1950.00
Lamp, Cut Glass, Prisms, Mushroom Shade, 2 Lights, 23 In.	950.00
Lamp, Cut Glass, Silver Platform Mirrored Base, 9 X 9 1/2 In.	775.00
Lamp, Cut Glass, Strawberry Shape Dome, Strawberry, Diamond & Fan, 21 In.	1200.00
Lamp, Cut Glass, Strawberry Shape, Heavy Harvard, 20 In.	1400.00
Lamp, Cut Glass, Strawberry, Harvard & Floral Hob Top, 19 X 9 In.	1195.00
Lamp, Depression Glass, Heart & Waffle	140.00
Lamp, Depression Glass, Southern Belle, Blue, Pair	32.50
Lamp, Desk With Swing Ashtray, Art Deco, Golfer Figure, Chrome, 13 1/2 In.	45.00
Lamp, Desk, Emeralite, Brass, Green Shade	65.00
Lamp, Dittmar Brunner, Marble Base, Brass	45.00
Lamp, Dome, Leaded, Brass Ceiling Fixture, 18 1/2 In.	450.00
Lamp, Dopey, W.D.Ent., 1938	35.00
Lamp, Double Betty, Iron	34.00
Lamp, Double Betty, Twisted Swivel Hook, Iron	70.00
Lamp, Dresden, 13 In.	225.00
Lamp, Driving, Dietz Union, Brass Bezel, Kerosene, Iron, 11 1/2 In.	59.50
Lamp, Duffner Kimberly, Floral, Purple Orchids, Draperly Glass, 30 In.	1950.00
Lamp, Fairy, Amethyst Glass, Signed, S.Clark, 4 3/4 In.	125.00
Lamp, Fairy, Amethyst, Clear To Amethyst Shaded Globe, S.Clark, 4 3/4 In.	150.00
Lamp, Fairy, Baccarat, Sapphire Blue, Embossed Sunburst, 4 X 5 1/2 In.	250.00
Lamp, Fairy, Blue Nailsea, Ruffled Matching Base	400.00
Lamp, Fairy, Brass Wire Mesh, Jewels, Scrolled Designs, Wooden Base, 4 In.	35.00
Lamp, Fairy, Burmese, see Burmese , Lamp, Fairy	
Lamp, Fairy, Burmese Shade, Clarke, Signed	150.00
Lamp, Fairy, Burmese, Clear Cricket Base	235.00
Lamp, Fairy, Burmese, Prunus Blossom, Decorated Base & Globe, 5 3/4 X 8 In.	650.00
Lamp, Fairy, Clarke Base, Blue Glass Shade, English Hobnail	55.00

Lamp, Fairy, Clarke Base, Blue Opalescent Ribbed Shade, 2 7/8 X 3 5/8 In.	68.00
Lamp, Fairy, Clarke Base, Diamond-Quilted Mother-Of-Pearl Satin Glass	175.00
Lamp, Fairy, Clarke Base, Shaded Globe From Clear To Amethyst, 4 3/4 In.	125.00
Lamp, Fairy, Clarke Base, Signed, Burmese, 5 In.	300.00
Lamp, Fairy, Clarke Clear Base, Amber Overshot Chinese Lantern, 4 5/8 In.	135.00
Lamp, Fairy, Clarke Clear Base, Mother-Of-Pearl Satin Glass, Ormolu Stand	195.00
Lamp, Fairy, Clarke Clear Base, Sapphire Blue, Dome Shade, 4 In.	95.00
Lamp, Fairy, Clarke Clear Base, Webb Burmese, Pink To Yellow, 2 7/8 In.	135.00
Lamp, Fairy, Clarke Cricklite Base, Blue Moire Glass, White Loopings, 7 In.	525.00
Lamp, Fairy, Clarke Pyramid Holder, Owl, Pink	115.00
Lamp, Fairy, Clarke, Cut Glass Holder And Cups	95.00
Lamp, Fairy, Clarke, Frosted Cranberry Verre Moire, Bowl Base, 4 5/8 In.	365.00
Lamp, Fairy, Coralene, Pink Satin Glass, Tulip Shape, Pyramid Base	350.00
Lamp, Fairy, Frosted Cranberry, Verre Moire, Bowl Base, White Loopings	365.00
Lamp, Fairy, Mother-Of-Pearl, Robin's-Egg Blue, 4 3/4 In.	235.00
Lamp, Fairy, Nailsea, Blue & White, Ruffled Base, Clarke Candle, 6 In.	325.00
Lamp, Fairy, Nailsea, Blue, Clarke Crystal Base, 5 1/2 In.	185.00
Lamp, Fairy, Overshot Crown, 1887, Queen Victoria's Jubilee	195.00
Lamp, Fairy, Reversible Base, Signed, 7 1/2 In.Diameter X 5 1/2 In. High	750.00
Lamp, Fairy, Ruffled Holder, 3 Piece	50.00
Lamp, Fairy, Smiling Monk, Blue Satin Castle	295.00
Lamp, Fairy, Webb Burmese, Burmese Bowl Base, Pink To Yellow, 5 1/4 In.	345.00
Lamp, Finger Hold, Chimney, Light Blue, Small	50.00
Lamp, Finger, Blown, Applied Handle, Flippant Rattail At End, Lavender, 3 In.	45.00
Lamp, Finger, Cranberry & Opalescent	150.00
Lamp, Finger, Pressed Glass, Bull's-Eye & Fan, Three Mold, Footed, 5 1/2 In.	75.00
Lamp, Flint, Whale Oil, Three Printie Block, Pair	175.00
Lamp, Flint, Whale Oil, 9 In.	65.00
Lamp, Float Light, Forest Green, Thoro 77	22.50
Lamp, Floor, Brass & Cloisonne, Bell Shape, C.1880, 69 In.	225.00
Lamp, Floor, Brass, Leaves, Parchment Shade, 70 In.	200.00
Lamp, Floor, Damascene Shade, Blue, Green, 10 In.Diameter	2250.00
Lamp, Floor, Fringe Of Glass Beads	1500.00
Lamp, Floral & Swag Filigree, Caramel To Purple, Shade, 27 In.	375.00
Lamp, Flowers, Figure, Ormolu Mount, 10 In.	125.00
Lamp, Fluid, Wick Pick, Saucer Base, Tin, 9 1/2 In.	95.00
Lamp, Frankart, 2 Nude Females Back To Back, Durand Gold Iridescent Globe	300.00
Lamp, French Porcelain, Group Of Lovers & Putti With Lute, 31 In.	30.00
Lamp, Fulper, Ballerina, Perfume, Pink	45.00
Lamp, Fulper, Night, Figural, Seated Lady Holding Hat In Hand	145.00
Lamp, Gas, White Metal, Indian Figure, 17 In.	75.00
Lamp, Gaslight Hanging Fixture, Original Shade	22.50
Lamp, Gaslight, Brass & Porcelain, Morning Glory Shape, European, 15 In., Pair	90.00
Lamp, Glass, Blown-Out Apple Blossom, Opalescent White, 16 In.	325.00
Lamp, Glass, Lovebird, Crystal, C.1923, 10 1/2 In.	100.00
Lamp, Glass, Owl, Shades Of Brown, C.1923, 8 1/2 In.	100.00
Lamp, Glass, Parrot, Blue & Brown Base, Red Combination, C.1923, 13 In.	100.00
Lamp, Globe, Cut Crystal, Jeweled, Brass Hanger, 15 In.Globe, 23 In.Hanger	700.00
Lamp, Gone With The Wind, Base Signed, P.L.B.& G.Company	600.00
Lamp, Gone With The Wind, Blown Pink Roses On Yellow, Metal Base, 20 In.	300.00
Lamp, Gone With The Wind, Cranberry Coin Spot, Miniature, 9 In.	95.00
Lamp, Gone With The Wind, Electrified, Animals On Base	575.00
Lamp, Gone With The Wind, Hand-Painted Iris On Brown, 23 In.	425.00
Lamp, Gone With The Wind, Hand-Painted, Aqua, White Blossoms	355.00
Lamp, Gone With The Wind, Kerosene, Satin Glass Globe & Base, 17 1/2 In.	150.00
Lamp, Gone With The Wind, Lavender, Pink Flowers, 13 In.	100.00
Lamp, Gone With The Wind, Lion Heads & Camels On Brown, 25 In.	550.00
Lamp, Gone With The Wind, Milk Glass, All Original	265.00
Lamp, Gone With The Wind, Milk Glass, Spider Web, Hand-Painted Floral, 18 In.	225.00
Lamp, Gone With The Wind, Mushroom Shade, Pink Roses, Electrified, 25 In.	225.00
Lamp, Gone With The Wind, Pink & White, Blue Flowers, 13 1/2 In.	250.00
Lamp, Gone With The Wind, Pink, White & Yellow Daisies	125.00
Lamp, Gone With The Wind, Red Satin Feather And Ball Pattern, Brass	500.00
Lamp, Gone With The Wind, Red Satin, 27 1/2 In.	650.00
Lamp, Gone With The Wind, Roses On Yellow, Ornate Metal Base, 20 In.	320.00

Lamp, Gone With The Wind, Umbrella Shade, Filigree Brass Base, 24 In.	275.00
Lamp, Gone With The Wind, Umbrella Shade, 1882-92, 11 X 20 In.	250.00
Lamp, Gone With The Wind, Violets	200.00
Lamp, Gone With The Wind, 3 Roses, Harp, Shade, Electrified, Pink, Green, 26 In.	79.00
Lamp, Grease, Open Heart Finial, Twisted Hanger, Wrought Iron	295.00
Lamp, Grease, Wrought Iron Tripod, 4 Wicks, Drip Pan, 18th Century, 20 In.	150.00
Lamp, Greek Key, Miniature	80.00
Lamp, Green Celadon, Teak Base, 17 In.	45.00
Lamp, Hall, Slag Glass	150.00
Lamp, Hand-Painted, Chrysanthemums, Red, White Enamel, Ornate Base, Large	325.00
Lamp, Hand, American Shield & Stars, Applied Handle	80.00
Lamp, Hand, Atterbury, Melon, Kerosene	25.00
Lamp, Hand, Flat Turkey Foot, Kerosene	28.00
Lamp, Hand, Formalin Base & Burner, Kerosene	25.00
Lamp, Hand, Heavy Cylinder, Tin, 6 1/2 In.	20.00
Lamp, Hand, Lomax, Kerosene	28.00
Lamp, Hand, Miniature, Green, Worded Nutmeg, 7 In.	45.00
Lamp, Hand, Pressed Glass, Plume	50.00
Lamp, Hand, Purple Slag Base & Stem, Clear Font, 11 1/2 In.	225.00
Lamp, Hand, Tin, With Chimney, 9 In.	10.00
Lamp, Hand, Whale Oil, Amethyst Base, Amber Swirl Font	110.00
Lamp, Handel, see Handel, Lamp	
Lamp, Hanging Hall, Cranberry Swirl, Ceiling Pull-Down Canopy	195.00
Lamp, Hanging Hall, Cranberry With Ornate Frame, Pull-Down Canopy	250.00
Lamp, Hanging Hall, Cut And Frosted Crystal, Smoked Shade, English, 22 In.	300.00
Lamp, Hanging Jeweled, 50 Jewels In Brass Filigree Pull-Down Canopy, 7 In.	295.00
Lamp, Hanging, Caramel, 6 Panel, 46 In.	275.00
Lamp, Hanging, Cast Iron, Ornate, Raises & Lowers On Chain, 14 In.White Shade	145.00
Lamp, Hanging, Country Store, Brass Font & Burner, 28 In.	185.00
Lamp, Hanging, Cranberry Glass, Swirled, Globe, 8 X 7 1/2 In.	210.00
Lamp, Hanging, Cranberry Swirl Globe, Brass Framing, 24 X 12 In.	175.00
Lamp, Hanging, Cut Crystal, 70 X 44 In.	900.00
Lamp, Hanging, Flowers & Bows, Caramel, White, Pink, Green, & Red, 22 1/2 In.	1350.00
Lamp, Hanging, Hall, Slag	150.00
Lamp, Hanging, Leaded, Geometric Pattern, 18 1/2 In., Diameter	450.00
Lamp, Hanging, Raises & Lowers On Chains, Counterweight, Shade, Font, Iron	145.00
Lamp, Hanging, Sandwich Peachblow, Pink To White, Embossed Diamond, 14 In.	450.00
Lamp, Hanging, Store, Brass Oil, Country Store, Milk Glass Smoke Bell, 14 In.	200.00
Lamp, Hanging, Store, Country, Tin Shade	225.00
Lamp, Hanging, Store, Floral Shade, Brass Font, 14 In.	125.00
Lamp, Hanging, Water Lilies, Pink, Green, Caramel Slag, 24 In.	1250.00
Lamp, Hanging, White Shade, Brass Font, 14 In.	185.00
Lamp, Hurricane, Crystal, Drops, Engraved Shades, Pair	125.00
Lamp, Iron Base, Girl, Dog, Etched Font, Brass Top, Green Overlay Shade, 22 In.	168.00
Lamp, Iron Base, Hunter For Stem, Etched Font, Brass Top, 17 In.	125.00
Lamp, Iron Footed Base, Font, Pink, Blue, Tree Scene, Matching Shade, Oil Pot	360.00
Lamp, Iron Hanging Spout, 4 Spouts & Pick	13.00
Lamp, Ivory, Carved, Animal Motif, 11 1/2 In.	395.00
Lamp, Jack-O-Lantern, Child's, Metal Bail, 4 In.	14.00
Lamp, Juno, Urn Style, Embossed Nickel, Green Overlay, Tam-O-Shanter Shade	165.00
Lamp, Kerosene, Blown Out Rose Metal Base, Home Sweet Home Chimney	69.00
Lamp, Kerosene, Burner, Cobalt Blue, Princess Feather	28.00
Lamp, Kerosene, Caramel, Red, Green, Stained Glass, 13 In.	395.00
Lamp, Kerosene, Cast Iron Base, Brass, Dated 1871	32.00
Lamp, Kerosene, Glass Base, Brass, Queen Mary Burner	32.00
Lamp, Kerosene, Glass Pedestal, Reverse Painting Of Girl's Face	75.00
Lamp, Kerosene, Glass Wall, Brass Bracket	40.00
Lamp, Kerosene, Glass, With Chimney	25.00
Lamp, Kerosene, Gone With The Wind, Green To Pink, Floral, Windmill, Ships	285.00
Lamp, Kerosene, Greek Key, Globe Shade, 18 In.	100.00
Lamp, Kerosene, Iron Base, Melon Pattern	42.00
Lamp, Kerosene, Pressed Glass, Columbian Coin	125.00
Lamp, Kerosene, Rose, Green Cabbage	65.00
Lamp, Kerosene, Scalloped, Folded Chimney Top, Pedestal, Burner	59.50
Lamp, Kerosene, Snowy Owl, Amber Glass Eyes, China, France, 15 In., Pair	325.00

Lamp, Kerosene, Sweetheart	125.00
Lamp, Kerosene, Table, Frosted Glass Paneled Font, Embossed Iron Base	48.00
Lamp, Kerosene, Tall Emerald Green, Square Base & Font	75.00
Lamp, Kerosene, White Base, Pale Pink To Deep Rose, 11 1/2 In.	795.00
Lamp, Lantern, Jewel, Skater's, Paneled Globe	40.00
Lamp, Lard Oil, Tin, Cylindrical	70.00
Lamp, Leaded Chocolate Glass, Filigree Border, Orange & Green Design	365.00
Lamp, Leaded Table, Green Leaves, White Daffodil Border, 18 X 21 In.	950.00
Lamp, Leaded, Table, Caramel Ground, Blue, Red, Green Border, 19 In.	900.00
Lamp, Liberty Bell, Sesquicentennial	35.00
Lamp, Library, Bristol Shade, Ceiling Canopy 3 Smoke Bell, 14 In.	195.00
Lamp, Little Buttercup, Cobalt, Glass Handle, Miniature	68.00
Lamp, Log Cabin, Clear, Brass Collar, C.1875, 2 3/4 X 3 1/8 In.	200.00
Lamp, London, Tin Reflector, 5 In.	50.00
Lamp, McKee, Clear Font And White Base	48.00
Lamp, Milk Glass, Christmas Tree, Miniature, 6 3/4 In.	95.00
Lamp, Milk Glass, Glow Lamp With Glass Wick Holder, Miniature	55.00
Lamp, Milk Glass, Gold Paint, Miniature	150.00
Lamp, Milk Glass, Hand-Painted, House Scene, Kerosene, Miniature, 4 In.	75.00
Lamp, Milk Glass, Kerosene, Hand-Painted Jonquils On Yellow, Chimney	65.00
Lamp, Milk Glass, Kerosene, Hand-Painted, Brass Base	65.00
Lamp, Milk Glass, Miniature, Basket Of Flowers	100.00
Lamp, Milk Glass, Miniature, Stippled Ground, Maroon Design	275.00
Lamp, Milk Glass, Nutmeg, Metal Handle, Miniature	50.00
Lamp, Milk Glass, Oil, Natural Color Embossed Shells, Matching Shade, 16 In.	140.00
Lamp, Milk Glass, Oil, White, Miniature, 6 In.High	80.00
Lamp, Milk Glass, Swan, Blue, Miniature	110.00
Lamp, Miller, Caramel Slag Panels, 24 In.	325.00
Lamp, Miller, Copper Base, Satin White Glass, Yellow Accent, 4 Jewels, 18 In.	500.00
Lamp, Miller, Obverse Painted, Cream & Green, Greek Key, 14 X 21 In.	400.00
Lamp, Miller, Tam O'shanter Shade, Art Nouveau, Beaded, Brass Base	300.00
Lamp, Miller, Triple Pulls, Base Green Patina Bulb, Bronze Foot, Signed	500.00
Lamp, Miner's, National Carbide, Powder Tin Cans, 13 X 8 1/2 In.	15.00

The S numbers refer to the book "Miniature Lamps" by Frank R. and Ruth E. Smith

Lamp, Miniature, All Milk Glass	130.00
Lamp, Miniature, Amethyst, Original Base, Burner, Marching Shade	135.00
Lamp, Miniature, Ball Shade, White Satin With Pink	145.00
Lamp, Miniature, Blue Band, Small Enamel Flowers	145.00
Lamp, Miniature, Clear Handled Base, Blue Shade, Smith No.48	95.00
Lamp, Miniature, Cobalt, Attached To Square Tin Saucer	68.00
Lamp, Miniature, Copper Base, Milk Glass Shade, The Acorn Manufacturing Co.	30.00
Lamp, Miniature, Cranberry Satin, Hand-Painted, Cased	255.00
Lamp, Miniature, Cresolene	35.00
Lamp, Miniature, Firefly, All Brass With Brass Reflector	45.00
Lamp, Miniature, Hand-Painted Basket Of Flowers	185.00
Lamp, Miniature, Hand-Painted Blue Base, Cherubs, Acorn Burner, 5 1/4 In.	145.00
Lamp, Miniature, Metal With Dragon Handle, 6 In.	75.00
Lamp, Miniature, Milk Glass, Elephant, Reclining	625.00
Lamp, Miniature, Mission, Milk Glass	110.00
Lamp, Miniature, Nutmeg, Cobalt Blue	62.00 To 65.00
Lamp, Miniature, Oil, Blue, Daisy, Bull's-Eye Foot & Shoulder, 5 In.	85.00
Lamp, Miniature, Pink Milk Glass, Cupid On Base, Birds On Shade, 10 1/2 In.	110.00
Lamp, Miniature, Pressed Glass, Moon & Star Variant, Amber, Font, Half Shade	135.00
Lamp, Miniature, Reclining Elephant, Milk Glass, Chimney & Globe	250.00
Lamp, Miniature, Red Bull's-Eye	40.00
Lamp, Miniature, Square Body & Matching Chimney	72.00
Lamp, Miniature, White, Colorful Open Flowers	135.00
Lamp, Mission, Oak, Green Slag	195.00
Lamp, Moe Bridges, Green, Caramel, Mottled Flowers, Blue Jewels, 24 X 22 In.	675.00
Lamp, Moe Bridges, Reverse Painted Shade, Signed, Metal Base	850.00
Lamp, Nelly Bly, Pink Band With Rose Decoration, Miniature	145.00
Lamp, Night, Figural, Dove, Glass Eyes, German, 6 1/2 In.	70.00
Lamp, Night, Figural, Terrier, Glass Eyes, German, 7 1/2 In.	70.00

Lamp, Night, Ruffled Cranberry Shade, Gold Designs, Brass Base, 16 In.	50.00
Lamp, Nippon, Deep Orchid Shading To Lavender, Filigree Brass Base, Large	110.00
Lamp, Nippon, Scenic, Windmill, Satin Matte Finish, 44 In.	85.00
Lamp, Nurse's Milk Warmer, Whale Oil Burner	150.00
Lamp, Nutmeg, Miniature, Cobalt	50.00
Lamp, Nutmeg, Miniature, Green	48.00
Lamp, Oil, Acorn Pattern Shade In Dark Green, Grecian Design Base	4500.00
Lamp, Oil, Apollo, Amber, 9 In.	135.00
Lamp, Oil, Brass, Art Nouveau, Glass Chimney & Shade	235.00
Lamp, Oil, Brass, Punchwork On Tab, C.19th Century, Flemish, 12 In.	110.00
Lamp, Oil, Coal, Milk Glass, Metal Base, Font	29.00
Lamp, Oil, Cobalt Blue Font, Brass Base, Frosted Ball Shade, Electrified	150.00
Lamp, Oil, Coolidge Drape, C.1880, 10 X 6 1/2 In.	65.00
Lamp, Oil, Finger, Cross Lens, Flat Base	30.00
Lamp, Oil, Finger, Cup & Saucer, Flat Base	32.00
Lamp, Oil, Finger, Dogtooth, Flat Base	26.00
Lamp, Oil, Finger, Floral, Footed, Flat Base	31.00
Lamp, Oil, Finger, Scroll, Applied Handle, Flat Base, 3 X 3 In.	25.00
Lamp, Oil, Finger, Whale, 3 1/2 X 4 3/4 In.	95.00
Lamp, Oil, Flat Chimney, Font Frosted, Embossed Base, July 2, 1872, 19 In.	210.00
Lamp, Oil, Green Glass, Applied Glass Handle, No.1 Burner With Chimney	45.00
Lamp, Oil, Icicle Font, Square, Marble	25.00
Lamp, Oil, King's Crown, Made From Saltshaker Mold, 10 In.	75.00
Lamp, Oil, Metal, Isinglass, 8 In.Metal Chimney, Marked Miller, C.1860	45.00
Lamp, Oil, Milk Glass, Embossed Shells, 8 In.Shade, 16 In.	140.00
Lamp, Oil, Miniature, Pale Custard Satin Glass, Embossed Floral Design	300.00
Lamp, Oil, Paneled Font, Emerald Green, Clear Stem With Beaded Base, 10 In.	38.50
Lamp, Oil, Pewter Base & Sapphire Blue Front, Kosmos & Brenner, 18 In.	65.00
Lamp, Oil, Riverside Panel, Emerald Green Font, 8 In.	75.00
Lamp, Oil, Riverside Panel, Green Font, Clear Stem & Base, 8 1/2 In.	85.00
Lamp, Oil, Russian, Blue Glass, 19th Century, 11 In., Pair	70.00
Lamp, Oil, Satin Glass, Red	250.00
Lamp, Oil, Sheldon Swirl, Vaseline Opalescent Font, Clear Stem	130.00
Lamp, Oil, Tin, 3 1/2 In.	40.00
Lamp, Opium, Pewter Base, 7 In.	75.00
Lamp, Oriental Wood Carving Of Old Sage, 23 In.	35.00
Lamp, Overlay, Blue Cut To Clear Pear Font, Gilt Decoration, Baroque Base	480.00
Lamp, Overlay, Ruby Cut To Clear Font, Opalescent Baroque Base	135.00
Lamp, Pairpoint, see Pairpoint, Lamp	
Lamp, Pairpoint, Reverse Painting, 22 X 16 3/4 In.	1000.00
Lamp, Panel, Caramel Shade, Signed, Miller, Small	150.00
Lamp, Paneled Shade, Blue To Sunset Shading, Tree Filigree, Signed, 15 In.	425.00
Lamp, Pate De Verre, Female Figures Holding Fruit, Signed, 9 In.	1450.00
Lamp, Peg, Cut Glass, Faceted, With Burners, Pair	95.00
Lamp, Peg, Satin Glass, Swirled Shade, Pink To Rose, Brass Base, 19 1/2 In.	375.00
Lamp, Perfume, Blue Scenic, Signed De Veau	175.00
Lamp, Perfume, Fulper, Pink, Signed, No.310	75.00
Lamp, Pickard Vase, Signed, Double Handles	235.00
Lamp, Porcelain, Baluster Shape Table, Floral & Tassel Decorations, Pair	250.00
Lamp, Porcelain, Miniature, Blue & Brown, Cherub Faces In Relief, 4 In., Pair	125.00
Lamp, Porcelain, Owl With Glass Eyes, German, Miniature	95.00
Lamp, Pressed Glass, Acanthus, Blue Font, Clambroth Stem & Base	750.00
Lamp, Pressed Glass, Almond Thumbprint, Whale Oil Burner	60.00
Lamp, Pressed Glass, Beaded Band, Clear Base, Green Font, 8 In.	82.50
Lamp, Pressed Glass, Beaded Oval & Scroll, Blue, 7 1/2 X 4 1/2 In.	195.00
Lamp, Pressed Glass, Beaded Wild Rose, Clear, Greentown, 8 In.	150.00
Lamp, Pressed Glass, Bellflower, Oil, Flint, Blue Marble Stem, Square Base	85.00
Lamp, Pressed Glass, Bird Ribbed Font, Tole Cone Top, Blue & Yellow Design	30.00
Lamp, Pressed Glass, Bull's-Eye Clear Font, Clambroth Baroque Base	125.00
Lamp, Pressed Glass, Bull's-Eye With Fleur-De-Lis, Flint, Whale Oil, 10 In.	110.00
Lamp, Pressed Glass, Bull's-Eye, Brass Connection Marble Base, 12 In.	65.00
Lamp, Pressed Glass, Bull's-Eye, Miniature	35.00
Lamp, Pressed Glass, Bull's-Eye, Red, Miniature	40.00
Lamp, Pressed Glass, Coin Dot, Cranberry, Ruffled Top Shade, Milk Glass Base	295.00
Lamp, Pressed Glass, Coolidge Drape, Blue Milk Glass, 10 In.	165.00

Lamp, Pressed Glass, Coolidge Drape, 9 In. 65.00
Lamp, Pressed Glass, Cosmos, Large 135.00
Lamp, Pressed Glass, Cosmos, Miniature, Painted 65.00
Lamp, Pressed Glass, Cosmos, Pink, Miniature 225.00
Lamp, Pressed Glass, Daisy & Button, Yellow, 8 X 4 1/2 In. 150.00
Lamp, Pressed Glass, Diamond Point, Amber, Kerosene, Pedestal, 9 In. 75.00
Lamp, Pressed Glass, Diamond Point, Ribbed Panel, Whale Oil, Pair 175.00
Lamp, Pressed Glass, Diamond Sawtooth & Sheath, Finger 43.00
Lamp, Pressed Glass, Excelsior, Whale Oil, Hand 65.00
Lamp, Pressed Glass, Fern & Shield, Oil, Brass Stem, Beige Marble Base, 10 In. 45.00
Lamp, Pressed Glass, Flute, Whale Oil, Amethyst, Octagonal, Flint 135.00
Lamp, Pressed Glass, Greek Key, Miniature 80.00
Lamp, Pressed Glass, Greek Key, 8 In. 55.00
Lamp, Pressed Glass, Hamilton With Leaf, Flint, 7 In. 100.00
Lamp, Pressed Glass, Horn Of Plenty, Emerald Green Font, White Opaline Base 140.00
Lamp, Pressed Glass, Leaf & Dart, Handle, 3 1/2 In. 38.50
Lamp, Pressed Glass, Lincoln Drape, Cobalt Blue, 9 1/2 In. 165.00
Lamp, Pressed Glass, Lincoln Drape, Frosted Shade, Miniature 45.00
Lamp, Pressed Glass, Lincoln Drape, Miniature .... 30.00 To 65.00
Lamp, Pressed Glass, Lincoln Drape, Ruby, Kerosene 250.00
Lamp, Pressed Glass, Moon & Star, Blue, Amber Pattern Bowl, Burner 125.00
Lamp, Pressed Glass, Moon & Star, Font, C.1820, 10 In. 110.00
Lamp, Pressed Glass, Moon & Star, Hand 85.00
Lamp, Pressed Glass, Moon & Star, Miniature 40.00
Lamp, Pressed Glass, Moon & Star, Whale Oil, Hand 65.00
Lamp, Pressed Glass, Optic, Blue, Miniature 150.00
Lamp, Pressed Glass, Peacock Feather, Blue, 7 In., Pair 195.00
Lamp, Pressed Glass, Peacock Feather, Blue, 10 In. 125.00
Lamp, Pressed Glass, Paneled Dogwood, 10 In. 50.00
Lamp, Pressed Glass, Peanut Pattern, Oil, Large Size 85.00
Lamp, Pressed Glass, Princess Feather, Clear, 8 In. 70.00
Lamp, Pressed Glass, Sweetheart, Emerald Green, Clear, Beaded Font, 10 In. 125.00
Lamp, Pressed Glass, Thumbprint, Oil, Marble Base, 9 1/2 In. 50.00
Lamp, Pressed Glass, Tulip & Star, Atterbury, Dated 1862 .... 245.00
Lamp, Pressed Glass, Turkey Foot, 10 In. 45.00
Lamp, Pressed Glass, Twelve Panel, Emerald Green, Oil, 8 5/8 In. 75.00
Lamp, Pressed Glass, Washington Font, Brass Stem, Marble Base 90.00
Lamp, Reverse Painted Shade, Hills, Trees, Water, Moon, Unsigned 380.00
Lamp, Reverse Painted, Czechoslovakian 135.00
Lamp, Ruby Heart-Shaped Stained Font, Brass Connector, Opaline Square Base 65.00
Lamp, Ruby Red, Hobnail, Brass Trimmed Shade, Clear Feet, 15 In. .... *Illus* 400.00
Lamp, Sandwich Overlay, Double Marble Base, Amethyst To Clear, 10 3/4 In. 395.00
Lamp, Sandwich, Acanthus Leaf, Square Base, Acid Finish, 12 In. 750.00
Lamp, Sandwich, Acanthus, Blue Font, Clambroth Stem & Base 750.00
Lamp, Sandwich, Amber Bowl, Sapphire Blue, 8 1/4 In. 100.00
Lamp, Sandwich, Blown Font, Stepped Base, 6 1/2 In. 70.00
Lamp, Sandwich, Double Cut Overlay, Blue, White, Clear, Flint, 13 In. 575.00
Lamp, Sandwich, Sparking, Pewter, Brass Spout & Cover, 4 In. 30.00
Lamp, Sandwich, Whale Oil, Sawtooth, Burner 110.00
Lamp, Sandwich, Wild Flower, Pear-Shaped Font, Brass Stem, 19 In. 175.00
    Lamp, Satin Glass, see Satin Glass, Lamp
Lamp, Satin Glass, Diamond-Quilted, Lavender 500.00

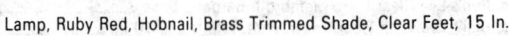

Lamp, Ruby Red, Hobnail, Brass Trimmed Shade, Clear Feet, 15 In.

Lamp, Schneider, Amber Bubbly, Signed	95.00
Lamp, Sewing, Kerosene, Dated 1875, Glass	27.50
Lamp, Shade, Hanging, 8 Panel, Green Slag, Tulips, Red Centers, Bronze Frame	385.00
Lamp, Slag, Caramel Panels, Numbered, 23 X 17 In.	190.00
Lamp, Spanish-American War, Embossed Admiral Dewey Flagship, Shell Font	175.00
Lamp, Stand, Regency Night Light, Clarke Blue & Ruby Holders, 7 In., Pair	190.00
Lamp, Star & Punty, Sandwich, Pewter Top, Pair, 9 In.	250.00
Lamp, Stillman Safety, Brass, Deep Saucer & Handle, Round, C.August 19, '02	45.00
Lamp, Store, Jeweler's, Green, Original Holder, Patent 1880	25.00
Lamp, Store, Welsbach, Smoke Catcher, Electrified, White With Gold Striping	185.00
Lamp, Street Light, 8 Panels, Mounting Hardware, 32 In.	150.00
Lamp, Student, Adjustable, C.1880, 21 1/2 In.	290.00
Lamp, Student, Brass Candle, Cut-Out Work, Jewels On Shade & Hammered Base	110.00
Lamp, Student, Double, Kerosene, Burnished Brass, Patent 1868, 19 In.	495.00
Lamp, Student, Fluted And Cased Satin Glass Shade, Pinkto Rose, 28 In.	300.00
Lamp, Table, Base Dolphins, Caramel Slag Shade, Art Nouveau	250.00
Lamp, Table, Blue, Rust, Gold Floral Panels, Black & Bronze Trims	450.00
Lamp, Table, Brass, Green Slag Glass Shade	125.00
Lamp, Table, Jefferson, Scenic, Green, 23 In.	550.00
Lamp, Table, Leaded, Floral Shade, Urn Type Base, 22 In.	950.00
Lamp, Table, Mission, Wooden, Double Globe, Green Slag Glass In Shades, 24 In.	175.00
Lamp, Table, Radio In Base, 1940s	35.00
Lamp, Teak, Chinese, Saddle Shape, Joined By Shelf, C.1880, 32 In., Pair	250.00
Lamp, Temple Lantern, Champleve, Pagoda Shape, Shade, Electrified, Pair	600.00
Lamp, Tiffany, see Tiffany, Lamp	
Lamp, Tiffany Type, Miniature, Pink With Yellow Swirls, 10 1/2 In.	110.00
Lamp, Tin, Miniature, Hanging, Cooley Bros., Good Clothes For Men & Boys	49.00
Lamp, Torchere, Floor, Italian Renaissance, Early 18th Century, 60 In., Pair	375.00
Lamp, Twilight, Miniature Candlestick, Beaded Fringe Shade	28.00
Lamp, Umbrella Shade, Red Roses On Beige Ground, Top & Bottom Lights	410.00
Lamp, Val St.Lambert, Table, Art Nouveau Crystal, 25 1/2 In.	140.00
Lamp, Val St.Lambert, Table, Art Nouveau Cyrstal, 25 1/2 In.	140.00
Lamp, Van Briggle, Seated Figure Of Woman, Blue, Maroon, Butterflies On Shade	165.00
Lamp, Vapo-Cresolene Vaporizer, Kerosene, Ornate, Small, 6 In.	43.00
Lamp, Vapo-Cresolene, Original Box	37.50
Lamp, Wall, Victorian, Lacy Iron Bracket	45.00

The McK numbers refer to the book, "American Glass, " by George and Helen McKearin.

Lamp, Whale Oil, Asphatum Petticoat, Double Burner, Handled, 4 3/4 In.	70.00
Lamp, Whale Oil, Blown Font, Pressed Base, Tin & Cork Drop Burner	90.00
Lamp, Whale Oil, Blown Font, 5-Step Base, Tin & Cork Burner, Pair	180.00
Lamp, Whale Oil, Blown Glass, McK 192-2, Pair	250.00
Lamp, Whale Oil, Blown Glass, Onion Font, Heavy Stem & Foot, 8 1/4 In.	110.00
Lamp, Whale Oil, Blown Onion Font, With Burner	60.00
Lamp, Whale Oil, Blown, McK G I-6, Pewter Collar & Burner, Small	80.00
Lamp, Whale Oil, Brass, Mid-19th Century, 22 1/2 In., Pair	85.00
Lamp, Whale Oil, Clear Waisted Loop Font, McK 288-58, 11 In.	165.00
Lamp, Whale Oil, Cone Shape, Tin, 4 1/4 In.Diameter	125.00
Lamp, Whale Oil, Figural, Bird, 5 In.	99.00
Lamp, Whale Oil, Heavy Loop, Flint, 9 1/2 In.	85.00
Lamp, Whale Oil, Light Bulb Font, 9 1/2 In.	85.00
Lamp, Whale Oil, Miniature, Inside Reflector, 3 Sided, Tin, 2 1/4 X 5 3/4 In.	150.00
Lamp, Whale Oil, Nurse's, Tole	15.00
Lamp, Whale Oil, Peg, Blown Onion Font, Tin & Cork Drop Burner, 3 1/2 In.	110.00
Lamp, Whale Oil, Pewter, R.Gleason Lemon Top, Knob Turns Spikes	375.00
Lamp, Whale Oil, Pressed Glass, Almond Thumbprint, Flint	60.00
Lamp, Whale Oil, Pressed Glass, Sawtooth, 11 1/4 In.	110.00
Lamp, Whale Oil, Star & Punty, Brass Column, Flint, 9 In.	115.00
Lamp, Whale Oil, Stem With Lemon-Shaped Reservoir, Tin, 8 1/2 In.	125.00
Lamp, Whale Oil, Tin, Patent 1842, 7 In.	75.00
Lamp, Whale Oil, Tin, Wagon Lantern, 8 In.	125.00
Lamp, 16 Panel, Light Caramel, 22 In.	225.00

Lantern, Candle, Candle Socket Lifts Out, Pan, Bail, Pierced Tin Hinged Lid 325.00
Lantern, Candle, Tin, Pierced 120.00
Lantern, Candle, 4 Panel Sides, Tin 20.00
Lantern, Marine, Dated 1868, 18 In., Pair 400.00
Lantern, Sport, Dietz, 7 3/4 In., Pair 65.00
Lantern, Watchman's, Bull's-Eye Glass Door, 2-Wick Sperm Oil Lamp Inside 55.00
Lantern, Whale Oil, Punched Tin, Glass 125.00
Lapis Lazuli, Figurine, Hoeti, Mineral Carved, 2 1/4 X 2 1/2 In. 275.00

Le Verre Francais cameo glass was made in France between 1920 and
1933 by the C. Schneider Factory. It is mottled and usually
decorated with floral designs, and bears the incised signature
Le Verre Francais.

Le Verre Francais, Bowl, Purple, Blue, Lemon, Orange, & Brown, 10 3/4 In. 450.00
Le Verre Francais, Bowl, Purple, Blue, Lemon, Orange, Brown, Art Deco, 11 In. 400.00
Le Verre Francais, Jardiniere, Cameo, Amethyst Floral Cut To Purple, 12 In. 200.00
Le Verre Francais, Lamp, Hanging, Orange On Lemon Yellow, Blue Border, 18 In. 650.00
Le Verre Francais, Pitcher, Lavender To Amethyst, Charder, 18 1/4 In. 495.00
Le Verre Francais, Vase, Art Deco, Cobalt, Orange, Gold, Bulbous, 7 1/2 In. 265.00
Le Verre Francais, Vase, Cameo Cut, Blue, Orange, Citrine, Tortoise, 7 In. 295.00
Le Verre Francais, Vase, Cameo Cut, Tortoise, Citrine, & Amber, Footed, 6 In. 425.00
Le Verre Francais, Vase, Cameo, Acid Etched, Blue, Orange, Candy Cane, 16 In. 450.00
Le Verre Francais, Vase, Cameo, Green, Brown, 9 1/2 X 5 In. 225.00
Le Verre Francais, Vase, Double-Handled 390.00
Le Verre Francais, Vase, Lavender Flowers On Mottled Pink, Signed Charder 700.00
Le Verre Francais, Vase, Stick, Red & Orange Tortoiseshell, Snails, 10 In. 525.00
Le Verre Francais, Vase, Tortoiseshell Flowers, Matte Red, Cameo, 18 In. 300.00
Le Verre Francais, Vase, Urn Shape, Cameo, Rose To Raspberry, Charder, 4 In. 215.00
Le Verre Francais, Vase, Wild Geese Tortoiseshell & Blue Marsh, 6 1/2 In. 700.00
Leather, Box, Cuff & Collar, Red Satin Lining, Stud In Silver Lid 25.00
Leather, Case, Sewing, Ornate, Engraved Brass Trim, Brass Footed, Mirror 38.00
Leather, Pouch, Powder & Shot, Shoulder Straps 26.00

Leeds pottery was made at Leeds, Yorkshire, England, from 1774 to 1878.
Most Leeds ware was not marked. Early Leeds pieces had distinctive
twisted handles with a greenish glaze on part of the creamy ware. Later ware
often had blue borders on the creamy pottery.

Leeds, Bowl, Ocher Decoration, Gaudy Blue, White, Yellow, 11 1/4 X 3 1/2 In. 250.00
Leeds, Charger, Bird In Tree, Sponged Foliage Center, Blue Feather Edge 85.00
Leeds, Creamer, Goat & Cherubs In Relief, Black Basalt, C.1795-1815 .... 92.00
Leeds, Cup & Saucer, Blue & White, Oriental Decoration, Handleless 25.00
Leeds, Plate, American Spread Eagle, Green Scalloped Edge, 10 In. 275.00
Leeds, Plate, Green Feather Edge, C.1810, 10 In. 24.00
Leeds, Plate, Soft Paste, Creamware, Open Edge, 9 1/2 In. 55.00
Leeds, Platter, Creamware, Loop Pattern Border, 18th Century, 12 In. 90.00
Leeds, Sugar, Blue Decoration, Large 95.00
Leeds, Sugar, Cover, Cobalt Leaves On Cream, Handled, 4 In. 25.00
Lefton, Creamer & Sugar, White With Gold Thistles, Set 8.00
Lefton, Dish, Candy, China, Blue Floral, 6 In. 7.00

LeqvAS   *Legras glass was made by August J. F. Legras in Saint-Denis,*
France, between 1864 and 1914. Cameo, acid cut, and enameled glass were
made.

Legras, Bowl, Cameo, Tan, Reddish Brown & Green Leaves, Caramel Cased, 3 In. 450.00
Legras, Cameo, Four Colors, 13 1/2 In. 475.00
Legras, Centerpiece, Floral, Gilt Border On Mouth, Oblong, Cased, Brown, Orange 650.00
Legras, Dish, Harbor Scene In Brown Cameo, Serpentine Top, 5 X 5 In. 345.00
Legras, Rose Bowl, Cameo Glass, Signed 475.00
Legras, Rose Bowl, Green Mottled, Orange, Red, Yellow & Black Enamel, 5 In. 80.00
Legras, Rose Bowl, Green, Stippled, Enameled Flowers, Stylus & Wheelcut, 5 In. 425.00
Legras, Tray, Frosted Gray, Amethyst Enamel, 4 3/4 X 2 3/4 X 2 In. 80.00
Legras, Tray, Red Cameo & Enamel Of Frosted Background, 4 3/4 X 2 3/4 In. 160.00
Legras, Vase, Blue, White, Smoke Background, Enamel Leaves, Signed, 8 In. 95.00
Legras, Vase, Bowl Shape, Blue & White Enamel Pattern, Leaves, Gray, 8 In. 125.00
Legras, Vase, Brown Leaves, Vines, Pods, Cut To Tan & Beige, 5 1/2 In. 325.00
Legras, Vase, Converted Into Lamp, Daisies, Orange, Yellow, Blue, 13 In. 190.00

Legras, Vase, Enamel & Acid Cut, Pink, Olive, Brown On Gray, 14 In., Pair	675.00
Legras, Vase, Enameled Winter Scene, Square, 7 1/2 In.	115.00
Legras, Vase, Enameled, 4 Scalloped Sides, Gold Shows Through Pines, 8 In.	185.00
Legras, Vase, Forest Scene, 15 3/4 In.	185.00
Legras, Vase, French Cameo, Scenic, Signed, 5 1/2 Inch	550.00
Legras, Vase, Frosted To Purple, Berries, Leaves, Cameo Signature, 15 5/8 In.	495.00
Legras, Vase, Geometric Art Deco Design, 5 In.	175.00
Legras, Vase, Grapes And Leaves, Gold, Signed, 4 1/2 X 3 1/2 In.	200.00
Legras, Vase, Green Acid Cut, Polished & Enameled Leaves, Signed Cameo, 8 In.	350.00
Legras, Vase, Green, Brown, Enamelware, Autumn Leaf, 4 1/2 In.	130.00
Legras, Vase, Harbor Scene, Sailboats, Amber, Green, 5 In.	345.00
Legras, Vase, Lake, Tree, Enameling, Purple, Green, Brown, 5 X 3 In.	220.00
Legras, Vase, Lakes, Mountains, Trees, Countryside, Cylindrical, 8 1/2 In.	175.00
Legras, Vase, Leaves, Bowl Shape, Blue, White, Gray, 8 In.	125.00
Legras, Vase, Miniature, Butterscotch, Floral, Cameo, 3 1/2 In.	250.00
Legras, Vase, Mulberry Colored Leaves & Berries, Frosted Ground, 10 In.	450.00
Legras, Vase, Olive Green & Brown Swirls, Raised Gold Grapes & Leaves, 4 In.	210.00
Legras, Vase, Pink, Olive, Browns On Gray, Enamel & Acid Cut, 14 In., Pair	675.00
Legras, Vase, Sailboats With City In Background, Cameo & Enamel, 7 1/2 In.	495.00
Legras, Vase, Scenic, Cameo & Enameled Trees, 6 1/4 In.	175.00
Legras, Vase, Scenic, Cameo, 8 In.	195.00
Legras, Vase, Scenic, Lakes, Mountains, Trees & Countryside, 8 1/2 In.	175.00
Legras, Vase, Scenic, Tree & Landscape, 14 In.	125.00
Legras, Vase, Wheel Cutting, Applied Handles, 4 Shades Of Green, 8 In.	450.00
Legras, Vase, White Frost, Red Enameling, Flowers & Foliage, 15 In.	300.00
Legras, Vase, White Frosted, Maroon Leaves & Flowers, 9 In.	350.00
Legras, Vase, Winter Scenic, Enameled, Square, 7 1/4 In.	115.00
Legras, Vase, Woodland Scene, Dog, Cameo Brick Red Cut To Pale Blue, 10 In.	595.00
Legras, Vase, 4 Casings, 3 Cuttings, Scenic, Trees, Water, Signed, 7 1/4 In.	400.00

Lenox china was made in Trenton, New Jersey, after 1906. The firm also makes a porcelain similar to Belleek.

Lenox, see also Ceramic Art Co.

Lenox, Ashtray, Gold Mark	12.00
Lenox, Bouillon Inserts, Sterling Silver Holder, Marked, Set Of 12	295.00
Lenox, Bouillon, Sterling Holders, Green Wreath Mark, Set Of 12	240.00
Lenox, Bowl & Underplate, Sterling Overlay Radials & Borders, 6 X 3 In.	45.00
Lenox, Bowl & Underplate, Sterling Overlay, Floral Shape, Ivory, Green Wreath	45.00
Lenox, Bowl, Blossom Shape, Geometric Sterling Overlay, Underplate, 6 X 3 In.	35.00
Lenox, Bowl, Gold Band, 1920, 3 X 1 3/4 In., Set Of 12	225.00
Lenox, Bowl, Ivory, Blossom Shape, Sterling Overlay, Underplate, 6 X 3 In.	45.00
Lenox, Bowl, 8 Petal, Dark Green Mark, 10 1/2 In.	30.00
Lenox, Box & Ashtray, Lenox Rose, Green Wreath Mark	45.00
Lenox, Box, Apple, Blossoms, Twig Handles, White, Green Mark	35.00
Lenox, Box, Knob, Green With Gold, Round, Green Mark, 5 X 4 In.	35.00
Lenox, Box, White Stylized Leaf Handle, Gray, 3 1/2 X 5 X 3 In.	32.00
Lenox, Candlestick, Belleek, Rose Floral, Silver Overlay, 5 In., Pair	65.00
Lenox, Candlestick, White Platinum Trim, Embossed 7, Gold Mark, 3 In., Pair	26.00
Lenox, Chocolate Pot, Applied, Sterling Florals, 10 3/4 In.	100.00
Lenox, Chocolate Pot, Art Nouveau Shape, White, Gold, Green Mark	60.00
Lenox, Chocolate Set, Belleek, Cream With Gold & Cobalt Bands, Tiffany Co.	395.00
Lenox, Chocolate Set, Cobalt Bands, Gold Handle, Cream, Belleek, 12 Piece	375.00
Lenox, Chocolate Set, Roses, Buds, Leaves, Gold Ground, Scallop Rims, 7 Piece	175.00
Lenox, Cigarette Set, Box & Ash Tray, Gold Handle, Green, Green Mark	35.00
Lenox, Coffee Set, Silver Overlay, 3 Piece	155.00
Lenox, Coffeepot, Short Spout, Ring Holder Cover, 1930s, Small	85.00
Lenox, Coffeepot, White, Gold Trim, Green Wreath Mark	55.00
Lenox, Compote, Fluted And Scalloped, Gray, Green Wreath Mark, 6 In.	75.00
Lenox, Compote, Ivory & Gray, Fluted And Scalloped, Green Wreath Mark, 6 In.	55.00
Lenox, Cornucopia, Lenox Rose Pattern, Green Wreath Mark	30.00
Lenox, Creamer, Belleek, Rose Garlands, Gold Rim, Handled, Palette Mark	30.00
Lenox, Creamer, Floral Decoration, Gold, Palette Mark, 6 In.	30.00
Lenox, Creamer, Green Leaf, Handled, Green Mark, 2 1/4 In.	22.00
Lenox, Cup & Saucer, Demitasse, Blue Band, Edged In Gold, 1919, 16 Piece	175.00
Lenox, Cup & Saucer, Demitasse, Sterling Saucer, Filigree Holders, Set Of 8	275.00

Lenox, **Cup,** Demitasse, Hammered Sterling Silver Inserts, Underplate	25.00
Lenox, **Cup,** Demitasse, White, Gold Trimmed Liners, Sterling Holders, Set Of 6	115.00
Lenox, **Demitasse Set,** Green Mark, Set Of 12	250.00
Lenox, **Demitasse,** Sterling Holders, Saucers, Set Of 6	115.00
Lenox, **Dessert Set,** Blue Floral, Pink Ribbon, Signed, 3 Piece Setting For 8	119.00
Lenox, **Dessert Set,** Meadowbrook, Fruit, Blue Border, Green Mark, C.1920's	100.00
Lenox, **Dish,** Candy, China	10.00
Lenox, **Dish,** Cheese & Cracker, 2 Part, Sterling Overlay, 10 3/4 In.	75.00
Lenox, **Dish,** Cracker & Cheese, Ming Pattern, Pedestal Cheese In Center	50.00
Lenox, **Dish,** Fluted, Dark Green Mark, 6 In.	18.00
Lenox, **Dish,** Scallop Shell, Green Mark, 6 In.	22.00
Lenox, **Dish,** Serving, Swirls, Curved Floral, Ivory, Green Mark, 10 1/2 In.	23.00
Lenox, **Dish,** Shell Shape, Ivory, Green Mark	28.00
Lenox, **Dish,** Swirls, Curved Floral, Ivory, Green Mark, 7 1/2 In.	16.00
Lenox, **Figurine,** Bird, Yellow, Green Wreath Mark, 3 1/2 In., Pair	25.00
Lenox, **Figurine,** Girl Dancing, 1937, 14 In.	235.00
Lenox, **Figurine,** Man's Head, Green Wreath, Magenta Glaze, Numbered, 9 1/2 In.	150.00
Lenox, **Figurine,** Schnauzer, Running	35.00
Lenox, **Figurine,** Swan, Green, Green Wreath Mark, 4 1/2 In.	27.00
Lenox, **Figurine,** Twin Winsome Girls In Party Dress, Painted	85.00
Lenox, **Figurine,** Woman In Plumed Hat, C.1931, Green Wreath, 9 In.	150.00
Lenox, **Figurine,** Woman's Profile, White, Green Wreath	40.00
Lenox, **Grinder,** Salt & Pepper, Gold Top & Band, 5 1/2 In.	23.00
Lenox, **Humidor,** Hanging Corn & Leaves On Tan, 5 1/2 In.	88.00
Lenox, **Humidor,** Tobacco, Brown Glaze, Black Signatures, Silver Overlay, CAC	295.00
Lenox, **Lamp,** Green, Raised Floral, Bronze Base, Green Mark, Pair	98.00
Lenox, **Lamp,** Oil, Golfing Scene, 3 1/2 In.	125.00
Lenox, **Lamp,** Torchere, Ivory, 11 3/4 In., Pair	95.00
Lenox, **Liners,** Demitasse, Sterling Holders & Saucers, Green Mark, Set Of 8	175.00
Lenox, **Mug,** Belleek, Handled, Ivory Palette Mark, 6 In.	28.00
Lenox, **Mug,** Belleek, Ivory, Palette Mark, 6 In.	30.00
Lenox, **Mug,** Miniature, Cobalt & Sterling Overlay, Bluefield, W.Va., 2 1/8 In.	55.00
Lenox, **Mug,** Tankard, Ears Of Corn, Belleek, Palette Mark	50.00
Lenox, **Mustard,** Footed, Silver Overlay, Sterling Ladle	38.00
Lenox, **Night-Light,** Leda & The Swan, White Matte Finish, Art Deco, C.1929	160.00
Lenox, **Pitcher,** Belleek, Art Deco Decoration, White, Pink, Blue, C.1920, Signed	135.00
Lenox, **Pitcher,** Bouquet, Pink With White Handle, Gold Mark, 5 1/2 In.	18.00
Lenox, **Pitcher,** Cider, Apples On Vine Decoration, Palette Mark, 6 X 8 1/2 In.	95.00
Lenox, **Pitcher,** Colonial, White Handle, Green, Green Mark, 5 In.	35.00
Lenox, **Pitcher,** Cream, Swirls & Beading, Green Mark, 6 X 4 3/4 In.	25.00
Lenox, **Pitcher,** Ivory With Gold Trim, 9 1/4 In.	32.00
Lenox, **Pitcher,** Lemonade, Red, Purple, Hyacinth, Foliage, Palette Mark, 1906	75.00
Lenox, **Pitcher,** White, Gold Trim, 9 1/2 In.	35.00
Lenox, **Plate,** Bread & Butter, Ming	6.50
Lenox, **Plate,** Cake, Enameled Birds & Floral, Gold Trim, Pedestal	45.00
Lenox, **Plate,** Cake, Ming, Handled	25.00
Lenox, **Plate,** Fish, Gold Rimmed, Hand-Painted Brook Trout, Seaweed, Signed	85.00
Lenox, **Plate,** Florida, 7 1/4 In., Set Of 4	30.00
Lenox, **Plate,** Hand-Painted Fish, Gold Border, E.A.Delan, C.1900, 9 In.	68.00
Lenox, **Plate,** Hand-Painted Florals Outlined In Gold	30.00
Lenox, **Plate,** Kent Hall, Columbia, 1932, Green Wreath, Blue	35.00
Lenox, **Plate,** Rose, Caribee, 6 1/4 In.	8.50
Lenox, **Plate,** Silver Swirled Floral On White, Silver Overlay, 4 1/2 In.	10.00
Lenox, **Plate,** Virginian, 8 1/4 In.	25.00
Lenox, **Plate,** Washington-Wakefield, Green Mark	20.00
Lenox, **Platter,** Ming, 10 X 14 In.	35.00
Lenox, **Pot,** Chocolate, Cream With Gold, Green Mark	45.00
Lenox, **Pot,** Honey, Yellow Iridescent, Gold Bees, Palette Mark	45.00
Lenox, **Pot,** Jam, Hand-Painted, Beehive, Bees, Factory Wreath L. Mark, C.1910	65.00
Lenox, **Pot,** Jam, Silver Overlay In Form Of Strawberries, Green Wreath Mark	60.00
Lenox, **Pot,** Jam, Strawberries On White, Silver Overlay, Green Wreath, 1910	75.00
Lenox, **Ramekin & Underplate,** Gold Band, 1916, Set Of 8	195.00
Lenox, **Rose Bowl,** Rosebuds & Leaves On Cream, CAC Palette Mark	39.00
Lenox, **Salt & Pepper,** Gold Farber Holder With Tray	30.00
Lenox, **Salt & Pepper,** RCA Victor Dogs	20.00

Lenox, Salt Dip, Roses, CAC	10.00
Lenox, Salt, Belleek	8.50
Lenox, Salt, Footed, Belleek	10.00
Lenox, Salt, Ivory, Gold, Sterling Silver Pierced Holders, Marked, 6 Piece	75.00
Lenox, Salt, Master	15.00
Lenox, Saucer, Demitasse, Salmon, White, Green Wreath Mark	20.00
Lenox, Sugar & Creamer, Hand-Painted, Pedestal, Pink, Roses, Raised Enamel	75.00
Lenox, Sugar & Creamer, Ribbed Shell Form, Enameled Gold Florals, 4 3/4 In.	185.00
Lenox, Sugar & Creamer, Silver Floral Overlay, Beige	110.00
Lenox, Sugar & Creamer, Sterling Overlay, Green Vase Mark	75.00
Lenox, Sugar & Creamer, Sterling Silver Overlay, Cobalt	75.00
Lenox, Sugar, Hexagonal, Gold Handles & Trim, Black Wreath	22.00
Lenox, Swan, Blue Wreath Mark, 4 1/2 X 3 1/4 In.	31.00
Lenox, Swan, Green, Green Wreath Mark, 4 1/2 In.	27.00
Lenox, Swan, Open, 2 In.	15.00
Lenox, Swan, Open, 4 In.	22.00
Lenox, Swan, Open, 5 In.	30.00
Lenox, Swan, Pink, Gold Trim, 4 In.	12.00
Lenox, Swan, 12 In.	75.00
Lenox, Tankard, Belleek, Oriental Lady Decoration, 7 1/4 In.	70.00
Lenox, Tankard, Enamel Bird Of Paradise, Palette Mark, Artist Signed, 15 In.	240.00
Lenox, Tea Set, Belleek, Gold Trim, Blue & Gold Design, 3 Piece	90.00
Lenox, Tea Set, Demitasse, Raised Orange & Green Florals, Signed, 9 Piece	95.00
Lenox, Tea Set, Gold Handles, Finials, Belleek, Made For Tiffany & Company	150.00
Lenox, Tea Set, Teapot, Sugar, Creamer, Insert, Silver Overlay, Green Mark	145.00
Lenox, Teapot, Flower Decoration, White Silver Overlay, 6 1/2 In.	62.00
Lenox, Teapot, Mystic Pattern, Green Mark	35.00
Lenox, Teapot, Pink, Green Mark	32.00
Lenox, Teapot, Silver Overlay On Antique White, 5 1/2 In.	39.00
Lenox, Teapot, Sterling Overlay, Floral, Blue, Green Wreath, 5 1/4 In.	75.00
Lenox, Toby Mug, William Penn Treaty, Indian Handle, 6 1/2 In.	110.00 To 150.00
Lenox, Toby Mug, William Penn, Natural Colors, 6 In.	265.00
Lenox, Toothpick, Platinum Trim, Green Wreath	18.00
Lenox, Tumbler, Ming	22.00
Lenox, Urn, Cream, Handled, Square Base, Green Wreath Mark, 5 1/2 In.	28.00
Lenox, Urn, Miniature, White With Silver Trim, Green Wreath Mark	15.00
Lenox, Vase, Belleek, Floral, 15 1/2 In.	160.00
Lenox, Vase, Belleek, Green With Pink Roses, 3 1/4 X 5 1/4 In.	26.00
Lenox, Vase, Belleek, Palette, Gold Grapes, Art Nouveau Design, 6 In.	80.00
Lenox, Vase, Belleek, Pearlized Green Blue, 6 Sided, Palette Mark, 10 1/4 In.	75.00
Lenox, Vase, Belleek, Water Lilies, Hand-Painted, 12 In.	95.00
Lenox, Vase, Belleek, Wine Luster & Pink Interior, Palette Marked, 8 1/2 In.	42.00
Lenox, Vase, Belleek, Woodpecker On Tree, Hand Painted, Palette Mark, 10 In.	100.00
Lenox, Vase, Black & White Stripe, Green Mark, 1727I47-B, 6 In.	40.00
Lenox, Vase, Blue Decoration, White, Green Mark, 10 1/2 In., Pair	65.00
Lenox, Vase, Brown, Tree Design In Silhouette Landscape, CAC, 15 1/2 In.	175.00
Lenox, Vase, Bud, Blue Border, Hand-Enameled Decoration, Green Wreath, 10 In.	38.00
Lenox, Vase, Bud, Gold Mark, 10 1/2 In.	20.00
Lenox, Vase, Bud, Gold Trimmed Rim, Palette Mark, 9 1/2 In.	35.00
Lenox, Vase, Cabbage, Wheat, White Trimmed, Gold, Green Mark, 12 X 6 In.	50.00
Lenox, Vase, Cobalt, Art Deco Designed Sterling Overlay, CAC, 4 1/4 In.	75.00
Lenox, Vase, Cream & Dark Green, Flared, 2 Handled, Green Mark, 6 In., Pair	80.00
Lenox, Vase, Enameled On Blue Border, Green Mark, 10 In.	35.00
Lenox, Vase, Figurine, Bird, Pink, Blue Mark, 6 1/2 In.	16.00
Lenox, Vase, Floral, Fluted Cone, Raised Foot, Green Wreath Mark, 7 1/2 In.	36.00
Lenox, Vase, Golden Grape Clusters, Red, Gold, Black Designs, Palette Mark	75.00
Lenox, Vase, Green Base, Ivory Top, Green Mark, 10 In.	95.00
Lenox, Vase, Green Palette Mark, Belleek	195.00
Lenox, Vase, Green With Cream, 2 Handled, Flared Top, 6 In., Pair	75.00
Lenox, Vase, Green, Crescent Shape, Open Both Ends, Circle Handle, Gold Trim	42.00
Lenox, Vase, Green, Flared, 7 In.	22.00
Lenox, Vase, Ivory, Urn Shape, Green Mark, 9 In., Pair	50.00
Lenox, Vase, Landscape Decoration, Trees On Tan Backbround, Palette Mark	90.00
Lenox, Vase, Meadowbrook, Green Mark, 10 In.	35.00
Lenox, Vase, Ovoid, Fluted, Floral And Leaf On Side, 8 X 4 1/2 In.	30.00

Lenox, Vase, Pastel Colors, Yellow Jonquils, Palette Mark, Belleek, 9 In. 85.00
Lenox, Vase, Pink, Red, White Roses, Gold Butterflies, Signed, 8 1/4 In. 125.00
Lenox, Vase, Pink, White Interior, Gold Band On Rim & Base, Green Mark, 7 In. 35.00
Lenox, Vase, Regal, Pink Base, White, Green Mark, 8 1/2 In. 35.00
Lenox, Vase, Regal, Pink With White Base, Gold Mark, 8 1/2 In. 30.00
Lenox, Vase, Sculptured Around, Scalloped Top, Green Mark, 8 1/2 In. 45.00
Lenox, Vase, White Fluted Stem, Bulbous, Pink, Green Wreath Mark, 7 1/2 In. 15.00
Lenox, Vase, White, Art Deco Black Lines, Green Mark, 9 1/2 In. 28.00
Leune, Vase, Blue Berries, Green & Rust Leaves, Frosted, Orange Collar, 10 In. 225.00
Libbey, Bottle, Cologne, Design, Signed, 6 In. 30.00
Libbey, Bottle, Cordial, Good Night, Pinched, 12 In. 54.00
Libbey, Bowl, Allover Cut, Signed, 8 In. 165.00
Libbey, Bowl, Columbia Variation, Low, 10 In. 325.00
Libbey, Bowl, Corinthian, Low, Signed, 8 X 1 3/4 In. 80.00
Libbey, Bowl, Finger, Ruffled Top, Pair 320.00
Libbey, Bowl, Rose, Corinthian, Blank, Signed, 6 1/2 X 7 1/2 In. 350.00
Libbey, Bowl, Salad, Oval, Eulalia 175.00
Libbey, Bowl, Sugar, Hobstar, Rayed Base, Notched Handles 45.00
Libbey, Candlestick, Copper Wheel, Floral, Stem, Foot, 10 In. 55.00
Libbey, Candlestick, Engraved Flowers, Leaves, Signed, Pair, 10 X 4 1/2 In. 225.00
Libbey, Candlestick, Rayed Base, Suspended Teardrop In Stem, 12 In. 150.00
Libbey, Carafe, Hobstars & Crosscut Diamonds, Signed, 7 In. 135.00
Libbey, Carafe, 32 Point Star Base, Signed, 8 1/2 In. 145.00
Libbey, Celery, Cream Opaque, Gold Enameled Leaves, 6 1/2 In. 165.00
Libbey, Celery, Silver Frame, 9 In. 60.00
Libbey, Cocktail, Giraffe Stem, Signed 95.00
Libbey, Compote, Colonna, Signed, 7 X 8 In. 210.00
Libbey, Cornucopia, Square Base, Signed, 9 1/4 In. 87.50
Libbey, Decanter, Single Star, C.1800, 10 In. 88.00
Libbey, Dish, Cut Glass, Hobstars, Sawtooth Rim, Signed, 7 In. 60.00
Libbey, Dish, Cut Holly, Shallow, Ruffled Rims, Saber Mark, Set Of 4, 6 1/2 In. 200.00
Libbey, Dish, Relish, Hobstar, Signed, 8 In. 85.00
Libbey, Goblet, Bear Stem, Signed 95.00
Libbey, Goblet, Cat Stem, Signed 125.00
Libbey, Hatchet, Amber, World's Fair, 1893, Washington, The Father Of Country 49.00
Libbey, Knife Rest, Large, 5 In. 55.00
Libbey, Plate, Fruit, Signed, 11 1/2 In. 255.00
Libbey, Salt, Flower Etched, Pedestal, Signed 35.00
Libbey, Saltshaker, Blue Satin Glass, Souvenir, Columbian Exhibition, 1893 .... 65.00
Libbey, Saltshaker, Reclining Egg, Marked Columbian Exhibition 1893, Signed 65.00
Libbey, Sugar & Creamer, Cut Glass, Signed 125.00
Libbey, Tazza, Signed, 5 3/4 In. 35.00
Libbey, Tumbler, Diamond & Fan, Signed 35.00
Libbey, Tumbler, Princess, Signed 35.00
Libbey, Tumbler, Spillane, Signed 35.00
Libbey, Tumbler, Wheel Cut Design, C.1950 .... 4.50
Libbey, Vase, Bull's-Eye, Star, Signed, 10 In. 100.00
Libbey, Vase, Heavy Sham, Full Leaded Clear Crystal, 6 1/2 In. 40.00
Libbey, Vase, Intaglio, 10 In. 195.00
Libbey, Vase, Lily Of The Valley, Flared Ruffled Edge, Signed, 4 In. 105.00
Libbey, Vase, Mums, Leaves, Stems, Teardrop Knobbed Stem, Rayed Base, 10 In. 185.00
Libbey, Vase, Trumpet, Intaglio Floral, Crosshatch, Bull's-Eyes, 10 In. 175.00
Libbey, Wine, Amberina 8.00
Libbey, Wine, Crystal, Frosted Gazelle Stem, Signed 85.00
    Lighting Devices, see Candleholder, Candlestick, Lamp, etc.

Lightning rod balls are collected for their variety of shape and color.
These glass balls were at the center of the rod that was attached to the
roof of a house or barn to avoid lightning damage.

Lightning Rod, Aluminum Arrow And Stand 20.00
Lightning Rod, Ball, Cobalt Blue 20.00
Lightning Rod, Ball, Earthen Beehive, White, Pair 18.50
Lightning Rod, Ball, Milk Glass, Blue .... 6.00 To 10.00
Lightning Rod, Ball, Milk Glass, White 95.00
Lightning Rod, Ball, White Milk Glass, Electra 8.00

*Limoges porcelain has been made in Limoges, France, since the
mid-nineteenth century. Fine porcelains were made by many factories,
including Haviland, Ahrenfeldt, Guerin, Pouyat, Elite, and others.*

Limoges, see also Haviland

Limoges, Basket, Gold Outlined Flowers, 1891-97, Marked, 7 X 4 1/2 In.	30.00
Limoges, Basket, Violets, Pansy, Liner, 6 In.	34.00
Limoges, Blotter, Ink, Gold Flowers, White	30.00
Limoges, Boat Scene, Rococo Gold Border, L.S. & S., 13 1/2 In.	235.00
Limoges, Bonbon, Hand-Painted, 4 1/2 In., Pair	18.00
Limoges, Bowl & Tray, Berry, Red Fruit, Gold Trim, Ruffled Edge	65.00
Limoges, Bowl, Cream, Sprays Of Violets, Gold Ruffled Edge, Duval, 10 In.	30.00
Limoges, Bowl, Floral On Cream, Signed M.Redon, 10 X 9 In.	15.00
Limoges, Bowl, Footed, Strawberries, Gold Trim, Signed, 7 In.	30.00
Limoges, Bowl, Fruit, Fruits, Green Leaves, Artist Signed, T & V Co.	85.00
Limoges, Bowl, Gold Border, Artist Signed, 9 1/2 In.	65.00
Limoges, Bowl, Grapes, Butterflies, 2 Handled, Gold, Blues, Signed, 9 1/2 In.	23.00
Limoges, Bowl, Hand-Painted Purple Berries, T & V, France, 9 In.	35.00
Limoges, Bowl, Hand-Painted Roses, 3 Gold Feet, 9 In.	39.50
Limoges, Bowl, Holly Design, Gold Trim, Green, Footed, 9 1/4 In.	75.00
Limoges, Bowl, Mayonnaise, Pink Flowers, 3 Gold Feet	40.00
Limoges, Bowl, Oyster, Artist, L.P.	65.00
Limoges, Bowl, Peaches, Scalloped, Green, 10 In.	35.00
Limoges, Bowl, Pink Clover & Leaves, D & C, 7 1/4 X 9 1/2 In.	11.00
Limoges, Bowl, Punch, Grapes In & Out, Gold Border, Footed, T & V, 11 In.	175.00
Limoges, Bowl, Punch, Interior & Exterior Decoration, Pedestal Base, 14 In.	225.00
Limoges, Bowl, Punch, Leaf & Fruit, 12 In.	150.00
Limoges, Bowl, Punch, Purple, Green & Red Grapes, Gold Trim, Pedestal, 16 In.	185.00
Limoges, Bowl, Punch, Rust, Purple, Grape Design, Silver Enameled Handle, Ladle	350.00
Limoges, Bowl, Rose & Gold, L.S.& S., 10 In.	18.00
Limoges, Bowl, Roses, Gold Trimmed Rim, Late 19th Century, 9 1/2 In.	40.00
Limoges, Bowl, Scalloped Top, Haviland, 10 In.	90.00
Limoges, Bowl, Scalloped, 10 In.	25.00
Limoges, Bowl, Violets, 3 Feet, Pale Green, T & V Mark, 8 In.	40.00
Limoges, Box, Enameled, Hinged, Signed Lepinois, 4 1/2 X 3 1/2 In.	225.00
Limoges, Box, Floral, Footed, Lid, Red Tones, 3 1/4 In.	97.50
Limoges, Box, Flowers, 4 Legs, Lid, 4 1/2 X 3 In.	20.00
Limoges, Box, Pate-Sur-Pate, Blue & White, Cupids On Lid, 7 X 4 1/2 In.	135.00
Limoges, Box, Pin, Round, 3 Gold Feet, 1 3/4 X 2 3/4 In.	30.00
Limoges, Box, Powder, Figural, Standing Elephant, Green, 6 1/4 In.	28.00
Limoges, Box, Powder, Figural, Standing Elephant, White, 6 1/4 In.	20.00
Limoges, Box, Powder, Pink & White	25.00
Limoges, Box, Red Roses & Green Leaf, Pale Green, Iridescent Interior, 8 In.	85.00
Limoges, Box, Soft Blue, Flowers On Hinged Cover, 3 1/2 X 3 X 2 In.	50.00
Limoges, Box, Square Base & Round Cover, Hand-Painted Floral, 4 In.	75.00
Limoges, Box, Trinket, Goulevre, France	32.00
Limoges, Box, Turtle, Footed, Lid, T & V Mark, 5 X 3 In.	30.00
Limoges, Butter, Engraved Gold Band, W.G.& Co., France, 3 In., Set Of 8	45.00
Limoges, Cachepot, Orange, Green & Floral Decoration, 5 1/2 In.	38.00
Limoges, Cachepot, Orange, Green, Blue Florals, Raynaud Et Cie, France, 5 In.	38.00
Limoges, Cake Set, Chateaudun Pattern, 7-Piece, T.Haviland	40.00
Limoges, Cake Set, Ivory, Flowers, 13 Piece	95.00
Limoges, Candlestick, Floral, A.Lanternier, 5 In., Pair	50.00
Limoges, Candlesticks, Cream & Rose Panels, Pair, 7 1/2 In.	35.00
Limoges, Celery, Bluebirds, Gold Rim & Handles, 12 3/4 In.	12.00
Limoges, Chamberstick, Green & Gold, Ornate Ring Handle	22.50
Limoges, Chamberstick, Hand-Painted Pink Roses, Leaf Shape, J.Pierre	30.00
Limoges, Chamberstick, Leaf Shaped, Hand-Painted Roses	18.00
Limoges, Charger, Pheasant, Scalloped Gold Edge, Artist Signed Dubois, 12 In.	95.00
Limoges, Chest, Jewel, Decorated In & Out, 12 X 8 In.	450.00
Limoges, Chocolate Pot & Underplate, Lavender, Violets, Gold Handle	115.00
Limoges, Chocolate Pot, Allover Gold Design, Cream Background, 7 1/2 In.	65.00
Limoges, Chocolate Pot, Blue Flowers, Gold Trim, GDA, 9 1/2 In.	32.00
Limoges, Chocolate Pot, Cream, Gold Trim, Fluted Shape, 8 3/4 In.	45.00
Limoges, Chocolate Pot, Floral, Gold Trim & Handle, Pink, Green, Wreath Mark	
Limoges, Chocolate Pot, Gold Handle, Bow, & Trim, 10 In.	50.00

Limoges, Chocolate Pot, Green Grapes, Outlined Gold, 11 In.	75.00
Limoges, Chocolate Pot, Green, Gold Trim, Handle, Bow, GDA Mark, 11 In.	65.00
Limoges, Chocolate Pot, Hand-Painted Roses, Gold Handle, Green Ground, 8 In.	59.00
Limoges, Chocolate Pot, Roses On White, Ornate Handle, Gold, Scalloped Base	42.00
Limoges, Chocolate Pot, White, Blue, Gold, & Moss Pink Rose Buds	48.00
Limoges, Chocolate Pot, White, Pink Flowers, T & V	28.00
Limoges, Chocolate Set, Blue, Pink Dogwood, Gold Handles, T & V, 11 Piece	185.00
Limoges, Chocolate Set, Roses, Gold Trim, 5 Piece	145.00
Limoges, Cider Set, Apples, Leaves, Green, Dated May 9, 1907, 6 Piece	295.00
Limoges, Coffeepot, Floral, Flow Blue Border, White, Lid, 10 X 6 In.	50.00
Limoges, Coffeepot, Pink Floral, Gold, White Ground, C.Ahrenfeldt, 9 In.	65.00
Limoges, Console Set, Blue, Gold Edging, Hand-Painted, Signed, 3 Piece	95.00
Limoges, Cracker Jar, Pink, White, & Yellow Roses, Gold Scrolls, Coronet	85.00
Limoges, Cup & Saucer, Chocolate, Carnations, Sponge Gold Trim, Set Of 6	38.00
Limoges, Cup & Saucer, Chocolate, Peach Pink, Napoleon	45.00
Limoges, Cup & Saucer, Demitasse, Mixed Bouquet, Butterflies, Set Of 4	60.00
Limoges, Cup & Saucer, Demitasse, White, Pink Flowers, Gold Leaves, Marked	35.00
Limoges, Cup & Saucer, Fluted & Scalloped, Gold Trim, Elite, Miniature	28.00
Limoges, Cup & Saucer, Garlands Of Roses, Gold Trim On Handle, Marked	9.00
Limoges, Cup & Saucer, Hand-Painted, Signed Luc	15.00
Limoges, Cup, Chocolate, Lidded, 2-Handled, White	10.00
Limoges, Cup, Nut, Handled, Set Of 8	48.00
Limoges, Dessert Set, Pink, Blue Leaves, Pink Flowers & Butterflies, 7 Piece	175.00
Limoges, Dish, Bouillon & Saucer, Pink Bands	45.00
Limoges, Dish, Covered, Roses, 5 In.	18.50
Limoges, Dish, Flowers, Gold Handles, Blue, Lid, 7 In.	30.00
Limoges, Dish, Pancake, Cover, Pink Carnations, Elite	47.50
Limoges, Dish, Pin, Gold Trim, Forget-Me-Nots, J.P.L.France, 5 1/2 In.	20.00
Limoges, Dish, Pin, Scalloped Roses	10.00
Limoges, Dish, Pink Roses, Oval, Handled, 7 1/2 In.	8.00
Limoges, Dish, Serving, Cheese, Signed M.W.C., 13 X 7 1/2 X 7 In.	145.00
Limoges, Dish, 3 Sectional, Hand-Painted, Raised Looped Handle, 12 In.	47.50
Limoges, Dresser Set, Flowers, Vines, Pale Green Background, 6 Pieces	150.00
Limoges, Dresser Set, Pale Blue, Pink Roses, Set Of 6	145.00
Limoges, Dresser Set, Tea Roses, Kidney Shaped, Pastels	92.00
Limoges, Eggcup, Face, Child's	10.00
Limoges, Ewer, Roses, Gold Tracery, 12 1/2 In.	129.00
Limoges, Figurine, Reclining Nude Figure, Bisque & Glaze, 1904, 12 In.	500.00
Limoges, Fish Set, Bronze Seaweed & Coral Decorated, Fish, 11 Piece	325.00
Limoges, Fish Set, Elite, Floral Rim, Gold Trim, Greens, Browns, Blues, 12 Piece	315.00
Limoges, Fish Set, Gold Trim, Scalloped Corners, 12 Pieces	240.00
Limoges, Fish Set, Gold-Edged, 15 Piece	650.00
Limoges, Fish Set, Green, Gold, Artist Signed, 12 Piece	353.00
Limoges, Flask, Book Shape, 7 In.	125.00
Limoges, Game Set, Duck, Grouse, Partridge, Roosters, Gold Border, 13 Piece	650.00
Limoges, Game Set, France, Gold Rims, 7 Piece	395.00
Limoges, Gravy Boat & Attached Saucer, Hand-Painted Violets, E.Lewis, T & V	45.00
Limoges, Gravy Boat & Attached Saucer, Violets, Leaf Shape, E.Lewis	25.00
Limoges, Hair Receiver, Signed & Dated	24.00
Limoges, Ice Cream Set, Cupid, 11 Piece	145.00
Limoges, Inkwell, Leaves, Scrolls, Floral, Tray, Attached Pot, Basin, Cover	65.00
Limoges, Jar & Underplate, Condensed Milk Server, Covered, 5 1/2 X 5 In.	39.00
Limoges, Jar, Biscuit, Hand-Painted, Lotus Blossoms, Gold Trim, Bamboo Handle	40.00
Limoges, Jar, Cracker, Gold Trim, Florals, H & Co., L.France	45.00
Limoges, Jar, Cracker, Swirl, Rib Shape, Raised Gold Floral, Foliage, Cream	65.00
Limoges, Jar, Cracker, White With Gold Specks, Floral Sprays	25.00
Limoges, Jar, Dresser, Cover, 2 1/2 X 3 In.	12.00
Limoges, Jar, Dresser, Portrait Lid, Pink, Cream, Gold Trim, T & V	38.00
Limoges, Jardiniere, Pink & Red Roses On Green, T & V, 11 1/2 X 8 1/2 In.	75.00
Limoges, Jug, Ears Of Corn Ring Handle, T. & V., Hand-Painted, 1 Qt.	50.00
Limoges, Mug, Bearded Monk Holding Glass Of Beer, Hand-Painted, 6 In.	125.00
Limoges, Mug, Birds, Yellow Grapes, Tankard Shape, Signed	36.00
Limoges, Mug, Cream, Brown Monk At Wine Cask, J.P.L., Timberlake, 5 1/2 In.	60.00
Limoges, Mug, Farmhouse With Haystacks, Hand-Painted	34.00
Limoges, Mug, Gold Handle, Leaping Elk, Mountains, Lake, Hand-Painted, Signed	50.00

Limoges, Mug, Grape Decoration, Blending Color, T & V, 5 3/4 In.	26.00
Limoges, Mug, Hand-Painted Grapes, 6 In.	32.00
Limoges, Mug, Pastel Colors, Yellow Violets, 3 1/2 In.	28.50
Limoges, Mug, Portrait, Tall Cavalier, Green, Tan Background, 5 In.	65.00
Limoges, Mug, Portrait, Tall Monk, Brown Background, 5 In.	65.00
Limoges, Mug, Scrollwork On Top & Base, Leaves & Grapes, J.P.L., 5 1/4 In.	65.00
Limoges, Mug, Shaving, Gold Borders, Black In Center, Name In Gold, T & V	30.00
Limoges, Mug, Tankard, Bough Handle, Twisted, Brown, Cream, Green, 5 1/4 In.	55.00
Limoges, Mug, Tankard, Brown, Cream, Artist Timberlake, 5 1/2 In.	55.00
Limoges, Mug, Tankard, Shades Of Green, Rust, Rose, 5 In.	55.00
Limoges, Nappy, Candy, Roses, Finger Loop Handle, Gold, Artist Signed	29.50
Limoges, Pitcher, Cider, Beaded Handle, Marked	58.00
Limoges, Pitcher, Cider, Blackberries, Leaves Circle Body, Beaded Handle, Mark	60.00
Limoges, Pitcher, Cider, Grapes, Gold Handle, Rim, Purple, Coronet Mark, Rancor	65.00
Limoges, Pitcher, Grapes & Berries, Pink Ground, Green Leaves, GDA, 8 In.	85.00
Limoges, Pitcher, Grapes, Red & Purple, Light & Dark Green Ground, Gold Trim	90.00
Limoges, Pitcher, Grapevine, Blue & Red Grapes, Gold Dragon Handle, 15 In.	200.00
Limoges, Pitcher, Lemonade, Green Background, Gold Bottom & Top, 12 In.	135.00
Limoges, Pitcher, Lemonade, Hand-Painted Lemons, Luster Finish, Signed, 6 In.	135.00
Limoges, Pitcher, Lemonade, Lemons, Blossoms, Leaves, Bulbous, 6 In.	97.50
Limoges, Pitcher, Lemonade, Red, Purple Grapes, Green Leaves, Gold Beading	85.00
Limoges, Pitcher, Pale Blue, Yellow Roses & Vines, Gold Beading, T & V, 12 In.	185.00
Limoges, Pitcher, Tankard, Floral, Handle, Blue-Green Glaze, Marked, 12 In.	165.00
Limoges, Pitcher, Yellow To Brown Background, Yellow Roses, T & V, 6 In.	32.00
Limoges, Plaque, Castle, Water & Florals, Rococo Border, Gold, 13 In.	175.00
Limoges, Plaque, Coronet, Flowers, Gold Rococo Border, Signed, 10 In.	49.00
Limoges, Plaque, Coronet, Flowers, Rococo Bird, Signed, 9 1/2 In.	65.00
Limoges, Plaque, Coronet, Gold Rococo Border, Purple & White Flowers, 10 In.	59.00
Limoges, Plaque, Game, Red-Breasted Birds, Signed Dubois, 12 3/4 In.	250.00
Limoges, Plaque, Game, Rococo Border, Cavaliers, Signed Bazanar, 15 1/2 In.	375.00
Limoges, Plaque, Game, Rococo Border, Fish, Signed De Nerval, 11 3/4 In.	150.00
Limoges, Plaque, Gold, Rococo Border, Dogs On 1, Horse On 1, Pair	450.00
Limoges, Plaque, Gold, Rococo Border, 2 Birds, Marras, 15 1/4 In.	350.00
Limoges, Plaque, Hand-Painted Castle Scene, 13 In., Pair	300.00
Limoges, Plaque, Marked T & V Limoges, 8 1/2 X 11 1/2 In.	950.00
Limoges, Plaque, Purple Flowers, Leaves, Gold, Signed, 12 In.	35.00
Limoges, Plaque, Red Poppies, Cream Ground, Gold Filigree Border, 15 X 9 In.	60.00
Limoges, Plaque, St.George Slaying The Dragon, Enameled, 10 X 15 In.	2500.00
Limoges, Plaque, Unicorn Tapestry, Gilt & Bronze Frame, 20th Century, 11 In.	650.00
Limoges, Plaque, 2 Women & Man, Outdoor Setting, Gold Rococo, 12 1/2 In.	175.00
Limoges, Plate Set, Oyster, 7 Piece	250.00
Limoges, Plate, Allover Hand-Painted, Signed Nellet, 10 In.	20.00
Limoges, Plate, Birds Over Water, Baroque Gold Border, Crown Mark, 10 In.	175.00
Limoges, Plate, Bouquets Of Roses, L.Bernadaud, 7 1/2 In.	35.00
Limoges, Plate, Cake, Floral Painted, Pierced Handles	25.00
Limoges, Plate, Cake, Gold Trim, Clematis Flowers, Green, Pink, White, Yellow	26.00
Limoges, Plate, Cake, Open Handled, Floral & Gold Trim, France, 10 In.	75.00
Limoges, Plate, Cake, Reticulated Handles, Double Elite Mark, 10 1/4 In.	24.00
Limoges, Plate, Cherub, C.1860, One Pink, One Blue, Pair, 8 In.	195.00
Limoges, Plate, Chop, Blackberries, Blossoms, Double Handled, Signed E, 14 In.	110.00
Limoges, Plate, Chop, Gold Band, Poppies, Coronet, 13 In.	67.50
Limoges, Plate, Cookie, Figural Leaf Shape, Stem Looping, Blanc Du Chine, Pair	15.00
Limoges, Plate, Coronet, Bird, Signed, Pair, 9 3/4 In.	167.00
Limoges, Plate, Coronet, Scrolled Gold Edge, 2 Fishes, J.Barin, 10 In.	70.00
Limoges, Plate, Coronet, Signed, 9 1/2 In.	65.00
Limoges, Plate, Cries Of London, 5 In.	9.00
Limoges, Plate, Cupid, Pink Luster, Signed Bailey, Dated 1893, 6 In.	22.50
Limoges, Plate, Dessert, Flowers, Set Of Six	20.00
Limoges, Plate, Drawing Room Scene, Man & Women, Rococo Edge, Dubois, 12 In.	250.00
Limoges, Plate, Enamel On Copper Decoration, Pink Flowers With Ruby, 4 In.	95.00
Limoges, Plate, Figural, 2 Ladies, Green & Blue Rim, Gold, Signed J.H.S.Syin	27.50
Limoges, Plate, Fish & Water Lilies, Gold Border, 9 1/2 In., Set Of 12	195.00
Limoges, Plate, Fish Swimming, 11 In.	50.00
Limoges, Plate, Fish, Brown On Cream, Hand-Painted, 8 1/2 In.	10.00
Limoges, Plate, Fish, Coronet, 8 In.	40.00

Limoges, Plate, Fish, Gold Borders, 5 In. 14.00
Limoges, Plate, Fish, Hand-Painted, Signed Rex, 9 In. 45.00
Limoges, Plate, Fish, Swimming, Enameled Floral, 9 1/2 In., Set Of 6 .... 90.00
Limoges, Plate, Fish, Swirling Water, Scalloped Gold Border, Coronet, 9 In. 40.00
Limoges, Plate, Fish, 2 Underwater Fish, Gold Rim, Colorful, Crown Mark, 11 In. 135.00
Limoges, Plate, Fishermen In Boat, Signed Duval, 10 In. 46.00
Limoges, Plate, Floral, Gold Border, Scenic, Hand-Painted, Signed, 10 1/2 In. 40.00
Limoges, Plate, Floral, J.P.L., Hand-Painted, 8 1/2 In. 15.00
Limoges, Plate, Floral, Signed Bailey, Dated 1892, 6 In. 14.50
Limoges, Plate, Fruit, Persimmons & Roses, Hand-Painted, Jasmin, 15 1/4 In. 550.00
Limoges, Plate, Fruit, Pomegranate, Roses, Signed, Jasmin, 15 1/4 In. 425.00
Limoges, Plate, Fruit, Red & Green Currants, Purple Grapes, 9 1/4 In., Pair 72.00
Limoges, Plate, Game Bird, Gold Border, Floral & Scenic, Hand-Painted, 9 In. 50.00
Limoges, Plate, Game Bird, Gold Rococo Border, Signed Rene, 10 In. 95.00
Limoges, Plate, Game Bird, Signed MAX, Scalloped Border, 10 In. 58.00
Limoges, Plate, Game Bird, Snipes, Gold Scalloped Embossed Border, 13 1/4 In. 265.00
Limoges, Plate, Game, Bass In Stream, Signed MAX, Coronet, 8 1/2 In. 45.00
Limoges, Plate, Game, Bird Looking Under Foliage, Rococo Edge, 11 3/4 In. 185.00
Limoges, Plate, Game, Bird On Turquoise, Rococo Scallop Gold Rim, 10 1/4 In. 60.00
Limoges, Plate, Game, Bird, Gold Rococo Border, Coronet, 9 1/2 In. 65.00
Limoges, Plate, Game, Birds, Trees, Log, Artist Signed, 10 In. 100.00
Limoges, Plate, Game, Duck, Lake Scene, Embossed, Signed MAX, Coronet, 10 In. 75.00
Limoges, Plate, Game, Flying Pheasant, Coronet, Signed Duval, 8 5/8 In. 40.00
Limoges, Plate, Game, Gilt Scallop Border, Coronet, L.Courder, 10 In. 200.00
Limoges, Plate, Game, Grouse On Green Ground, L.D.B.& Co., 12 In. 350.00
Limoges, Plate, Game, Hand-Painted, Progin, 10 In. 200.00
Limoges, Plate, Game, Hand-Painted, 10 3/4 In. 125.00
Limoges, Plate, Game, Mallard Drake, Signed MAX, 10 In. 65.00
Limoges, Plate, Game, Partridge In Bed Of Iris, 10 In. 65.00
Limoges, Plate, Game, Scalloped & Gilded, Grouse In Flight, 10 In. 80.00
Limoges, Plate, Game, Scalloped Border, Hand-Painted, Coronet, Signed, 10 In. 200.00
Limoges, Plate, Game, Standing Bird, Signed Max, 10 In. 42.50
Limoges, Plate, Game, Uneven Rococo Border, Signed, 15 1/4 In. 350.00
Limoges, Plate, Game, 2 Birds, Green & White, Rococo Edge, 15 1/2 In. 375.00
Limoges, Plate, Game, 2 Grouse, Green Background, Signed, 12 In. 275.00
Limoges, Plate, Game, 3 Cavaliers, Rococo Border, Signed Bazarad, 13 1/2 In. 185.00
Limoges, Plate, Gold & Rust Border, Cupid In Center, D & C, 9 In. 75.00
Limoges, Plate, Gold Baroque Border, Grapes & Floral, T.Golse, 12 In. 65.00
Limoges, Plate, Gold Border, Foliage, White Flowers, 6 In. 20.00
Limoges, Plate, Gold Decoration, T & V, 8 1/2 In. 35.00
Limoges, Plate, Gold Flowers On Peach, Yellow, Pink, & Blue, T & V, 8 1/4 In. 25.00
Limoges, Plate, Gold Leaf Border, Lady Among Flowers, 13 X 13 In. 295.00
Limoges, Plate, Goldfish Center, Light Blue, Scalloped Edge, 8 In. 60.00
Limoges, Plate, Grapes & Leaves, Pink, Yellow, Purple, Blue, Signed, 13 In. 100.00
Limoges, Plate, Hand-Painted Birds, Gold Border, 9 1/4 In. 36.00
Limoges, Plate, Hand-Painted Plums, Uneven Gold Rim, Signed, France, 7 In. 35.00
Limoges, Plate, Hand-Painted, Cupids On Light Blue Background, 8 3/4 In. 20.00
Limoges, Plate, Holly Berries & Leaves, Hand-Painted, 9 In. 10.00
Limoges, Plate, Monk Holding Cup, Coronet, Le Pic, 10 In. 60.00
Limoges, Plate, Mother & Child At Lake, Gold Rim, 6 In. 38.00
Limoges, Plate, Mums, Yellow Centers, Bee, Floral Rim, Artist Signed, 6 In. 22.00
Limoges, Plate, Oyster, Cobalt Blue, Gold Trim, Bird Scenes, H & Co., Set Of 6 .... 249.00
Limoges, Plate, Oyster, Floral Decoration, Gold Trim 45.00
Limoges, Plate, Oyster, Gold & White, Lanternier, C.1890, Set Of 10 .... 150.00
Limoges, Plate, Oyster, Shell Indentations, Scalloped Edge, Gold, Set Of 6 .... 150.00
Limoges, Plate, Oyster, White, Gold & Floral Designs, 8 In., Set Of 3 .... 50.00
Limoges, Plate, Pears, Grapes, Roses, Gold Rococo Edge, Royal, 8 1/2 In. 20.00
Limoges, Plate, Philadelphia, 8 1/2 In. 30.00
Limoges, Plate, Pink & Yellow Roses, Gold Band, Signed Luken, 12 1/2 In. 75.00
Limoges, Plate, Pink Rose, Green Trimmed Border, Gold Trimmed Edge, 10 In. 30.00
Limoges, Plate, Portrait Of Court Jester, Hand-Painted, 15 In. 295.00
Limoges, Plate, Portrait Of Marie Louise, Brown, Gold, 12 1/2 In. 75.00
Limoges, Plate, Portrait, Lady, Long Hair, Peach Ground, Signed Lolis, 9 In. 89.00
Limoges, Plate, Portrait, Seated Cavalier, Signed, Gold Rococo Border, 10 In. 225.00
Limoges, Plate, Red & Pink Poppies On Pale Green Background, 10 1/2 In. 30.00

Limoges, Plate, Red Currants, Green Leaves, Gold Rim, Signed Roby, 8 In.	40.00
Limoges, Plate, Rococo Border, DuBois, 12 1/2 In.	250.00
Limoges, Plate, Roses, Gold, Hand-Painted, T. & V., 8 In.	16.00
Limoges, Plate, Roses, Raised Gold Inside Border, White, Blue, Signed, 13 In.	100.00
Limoges, Plate, Roses, Violets, Gold, Marked T & V, 9 In.	14.00
Limoges, Plate, Serving, Wild Crab Apples, Foliage, Scalloped Gold Rim, 9 In.	50.00
Limoges, Plate, Shells & Seaweed, Scalloped Edge, 14 In.	60.00
Limoges, Plate, Souvenir, Philadelphia, 8 1/2 In.	30.00
Limoges, Plate, Teddy Roosevelt, 11 In., Artist Signed Lajourainie	375.00
Limoges, Plate, Wall, Cherub, Florals, Gold Banding & Edging, Signed, 6 In.	15.00
Limoges, Plate, Wall, T. & V., 14K Gold Border, Florals, 6 In.	14.00
Limoges, Plate, Woman Reading, Man With Mandolin, Gold Rococo Border, 12 In.	125.00
Limoges, Plate, 2 Swimming Fish, Hand-Painted, Pierced, Plusoye, 11 In.	50.00
Limoges, Platter, Fish, Brown & Gold, M.Redow, Limoges, France, 23 In.	85.00
Limoges, Platter, Fish, Sprigs Of Seaweed, Pale Gold, 22 X 8 In.	75.00
Limoges, Platter, Roses, Blue Rim, Pink, U.C.Mark, 13 X 9 In.	25.00
Limoges, Platter, Sandwich, Flower Decoration, 13 In.	35.00
Limoges, Powder Box & Hair Receiver, Artist Signed, 4 1/2 In.Diameter	48.00
Limoges, Ramekin & Underplate, Gold & Maroon Baroque Decoration	18.00
Limoges, Ramekin & Underplate, Pink & Lavender, Tiny Flowers, C.Arenfeldt	15.00
Limoges, Ramekin & Underplate, Swags Of Roses	5.00
Limoges, Ramekin, Elite, Silver Handled Holder	29.00
Limoges, Rose Bowl, Florals, Raised Gold Outlines, Hand-Painted	45.00
Limoges, Rose Bowl, Pink, Yellow, Red Roses, Gold Trim, J.P.	48.00
Limoges, Server, Dessert, Flowers, Gold, Center Handle, 11 X 6 In.	65.00
Limoges, Server, Pancake	68.00
Limoges, Spooner, Footed, Gold & Pink Roses, 4 1/2 In.	28.00
Limoges, Sugar & Creamer, Cover, Gold & Pink Flowers, Blue Mark, Gold Handles	48.00
Limoges, Sugar & Creamer, Open Sugar, Pitcher Type Creamer, Roses, Artist	28.00
Limoges, Sugar & Creamer, Tricorner Shape, Berries & Leaves, Old Abbey	55.00
Limoges, Sugar & Creamer, Violets, Gold Rim & Handle	34.00
Limoges, Tankard, Brown Matte Glaze, Hand-Painted, Drinking Monk, 6 In.	67.50
Limoges, Tankard, Elite, Birds On Tree, Flowers, Gold Handle & Scalloped Base	110.00
Limoges, Tankard, Grapes, Signed, Dated 1909, 11 1/2 In.	150.00
Limoges, Tankard, Hand-Painted, Beige, Purple Grapes, Gold Rim, Handle, 14 In.	220.00
Limoges, Tankard, Holly & Berry, Green & Yellow Background, 11 1/2 In.	175.00
Limoges, Tankard, Lemons, Dragon Handle, Gold Head & Feet, Pougat, 14 In.	275.00
Limoges, Tea Set, Blue Decoration, Yellow Roses On White, Gold, 15 Piece	165.00
Limoges, Tea Set, Gold Encrusted, Jesse Dean, 3 Piece	100.00
Limoges, Tea Set, Heavy Gold, Green Floral, 4 Piece	175.00
Limoges, Tea Set, Pink & Green, T. & V., France	50.00
Limoges, Tea Set, Silver Luster, Vegnaud, Rose Bands, Artist Signed, 3 Piece	89.50
Limoges, Tea Set, Sugar, Creamer & Teapot, Signed, 1910	60.00
Limoges, Tea Set, Pink & White Roses, Gold Handles, 16 Piece	125.00
Limoges, Teapot, Pale Green, Roses, Gold Ribbon Trim & Beading, 1896, T & V	85.00
Limoges, Teapot, White, Pink Roses, Gold Trim, Marked Coronet	23.00
Limoges, Toothpick, Roses, 8 Sided, Cream, Gold	16.00
Limoges, Tray, Calling Card, Hanging Dead Pheasant, Cobalt Blue Border, Gold	75.00
Limoges, Tray, Celery, Pastel Floral & Scroll Border, Signed	22.50
Limoges, Tray, Dresser, Gold Edge, Roses, Hand-Painted	40.00
Limoges, Tray, Dresser, Gold Rim, Blue Flowers, Green Leaves, Kidney Shape	40.00
Limoges, Tray, Dresser, Green, Pink Carnations, Hand-Painted	35.00
Limoges, Tray, Dresser, Roses, Leafage, Vines, Rectangular, Pink, Green, Brown	45.00
Limoges, Tray, Dresser, Roses, Rosebuds, Leaves, Scalloped, Gold, Rectangular	59.00
Limoges, Tray, Gold Design, Scalloped, Beige Satin, 16 X 9 X 2 In., 7 Piece	125.00
Limoges, Tray, Hand-Painted, Handled, E.Ladd, 16 In.	20.00
Limoges, Tray, Perfume, Pink & Gold Border, 11 1/2 X 9 In.	18.00
Limoges, Tray, Pin, Mums, Foliage, Gold, Pierced Handles, Gold Border, Signed	38.00
Limoges, Tray, Round, Marked T.V., 16 3/4 In.	115.00
Limoges, Tray, Water, Floral Bouquet, 13 1/2 In.Diameter	150.00
Limoges, Tray, Wine Cellar, Lady & Cavalier, Open Handles, 8 X 12 In.	175.00
Limoges, Tub, Butter, Gold Concentrics, 2 Gold Leaf Handles & Lid, Underplate	39.50
Limoges, Vase, Allover Irises, T. & V. Mark, 13 In.	150.00
Limoges, Vase, Birds Resting In Dark Gray Tree Branches, 11 X 4 In.	65.00
Limoges, Vase, Blue, Gold Gilded Top & Handles, M.Redon, France, 9 1/2 In.	95.00

Limoges, Vase, Bulbous, Garden Scene, Pastels, Game, 5 1/2 In.	550.00
Limoges, Vase, Enameled, Bulbous, Signed P.Bonnaud, 7 In.	225.00
Limoges, Vase, Floral, Gold Handles, Trim, & Foot, M.Redon, Limoges, 10 1/2 In.	50.00
Limoges, Vase, Gilded, Worcester-Like Pink, 5 In.	40.00
Limoges, Vase, Gold Applied Feet, Nude Painting, Double Mark, 10 1/2 In.	145.00
Limoges, Vase, Gold Handles, Scalloped Top, Gold Trim, 7 1/2 In.	95.00
Limoges, Vase, Green, Pink Tulips, Water Scenes, Gold Dragon Handles, 10 In.	150.00
Limoges, Vase, Hand-Painted, Signed T. & V., 10 In.	80.00
Limoges, Vase, Lady In Garden, Pastel Colors, Enameled, Bulbous, Gamet, 5 In.	550.00
Limoges, Vase, Ornate Handles, Artist Signed, 10 1/2 In.	120.00
Limoges, Vase, Ovoid Body, Gold Dragon Foot Handles, Signed, 8 In	95.00
Limoges, Vase, Pastel, Yellow Floral, Green Leaves, Gold Handle, 5 X 7 In.	42.50
Limoges, Vase, Peacock In Tree, 13 In.	165.00
Limoges, Vase, Pink Asters, Gold Trim, Fluted Gourd Shape, Signed, 7 In.	30.00
Limoges, Vase, Red & Yellow Rose Decoration, Hand-Painted, J.P.L., 5 X 7 In.	50.00
Limoges, Vase, Red Grapes, Signed Burgnett, 10 In.	149.00
Lindbergh, Bookend, Bronze, Full Face, Helmet & Goggles	15.00
Lindbergh, Box, Pencil, Spirit Of St.Louis	15.00
Lindbergh, Button, Welcome Lindy	12.00
Lindbergh, Figurine, Plaster, Bronze Color, Dated 1927, 14 In.	65.00

Lithophanes are porcelain pictures made by casting clay in layers of various thicknesses. When a piece is held to the light, a picture of light and shadow is seen through it. Most lithophanes date from the 1825 to 1875 period. A few are still being made.

Lithophane, Cup & Saucer, White, Oriental Figures & Scenery	20.00
Lithophane, Mug, Porcelain, Enamel Colors, Crown, Shamrocks, 2 1/2 In.	55.00
Lithophane, Plaque, Child In Cradle, 7 X 5 In.	110.00
Lithophane, Plaque, German Lady Holding Prayer Book, 7 3/4 X 6 1/4 In.	175.00
Lithophane, Plaque, Lovers Walking In Woods, Signed, 4 1/2 X 5 1/4 In.	55.00
Lithophane, Shade, 6 Panels, 4 HPM No.36, 37, 38, 2 PPM No.366, 367	385.00
Lithophane, Stein, Figural, Monk, 7 In.	245.00
Lithophane, Stein, Figural, Nun, 7 In.	250.00 To 275.00
Lithophane, Stein, Hand-Painted, Forest Scene, Lovers, German, 1/2 Liter	135.00
Lithophane, Stein, Woodland Scene Of Deer, Pewter Lid & Lift, Nude Base	62.50
Lithophane, Warmer, Tea, Brass Body, Reticulated Lid, Beaded, 4 Plaques	125.00
Lithophane, Warmer, Tea, 4 Scenic Panels, Nickel Plated Silver Holder, 5 In.	105.00
Lithyalin Glass, Vase, Signed, F.Egermann, C.1830, 2 1/2 X 3 1/4 In.	125.00
Lithyalin, Vase, Marbleized Agate To Amber, 11 Panels, 4 1/2 In.	225.00

Liverpool, England, has been the site of several pottery and porcelain factories from 1716 to 1785. Some earthenware was made with transfer decorations. Sadler and Green made print-decorated wares from 1756. Many of the pieces were made for the American market and featured patriotic emblems such as eagles, flags, and other special-interest motifs.

Liverpool, Jug, Black Transfer Creamware, Arms Of United States, 4 1/2 In.	525.00
Liverpool, Jug, Black Transfer Creamware, 3 Figures, Masonic Designs, 4 In.	200.00
Liverpool, Mug, Washington Map	325.00
Liverpool, Pitcher, Landing Of Lafayette, 12 In.	275.00
Liverpool, Tankard, Black Transfer Creamware, Shakespeare, C.1775, 5 In.	200.00
Locke Art, Goblet, Ivy Pattern	65.00
Locke Art, Salt Dip, Etched Sunflower, Footed, Signed, 2 7/8 In.	39.00
Locke Art, Tumbler, Clear, Intaglio Cut, Grape Leaf Pattern, Signed, 4 3/8 In.	60.00
Loebmeyer, Tumbler, Colonial Man, Scrolls & Floral, Faceted, Enameled, 4 In.	110.00

Loetz glass was made in Austria in the late nineteenth century. Many pieces are signed Loetz, Loetz-Austria, or Austria, and a pair of crossed arrows in a circle. Some unsigned pieces are confused with Tiffany glass.

Loetz, Atomizer, Blue, Green, Brown Iridescence, Austria, Signed, 5 In.	150.00
Loetz, Basket, Applied Threading, Iridescence, Signed, 7 In.	350.00
Loetz, Basket, Green Iridescent, Red Handle, 6 1/2 X 6 1/2 In.	225.00
Loetz, Bowl, Iridescent Amber, 3-Footed Circular Bronze Base, 13 In.	225.00
Loetz, Bowl, Reeding, Tricornered Rim, Iridescent Red, 3 X 4 In.	75.00
Loetz, Bowl, Reeding, Tricornered Top, Iridescent Red, Unsigned, 4 In.	70.00
Loetz, Box, Cameo Lid, Gold, Blue Florals, Signed, 10 In.	450.00

Loetz, Vase, Green, Blue, Signed, C.1900, 8 1/2 In.

Loetz, Compote, Green Iridescent, Metal Stand, 8 In.	145.00
Loetz, Compote, Purple Iridescent, Enameled Floral, Pewter Cherub Base, 9 In.	250.00
Loetz, Dish, Bonbon, Iridescent, Signed, 5 1/2 In.	300.00
Loetz, Dish, Fruit, Blue-Green Iridescence, Gold Highlights, 12 In.	225.00
Loetz, Inkwell, White & Maroon, Iridescent, Brass Lid, 2 1/8 In.	135.00
Loetz, Jar, Pickle, Blue & Purple, Iridescent, Threading, Silver Fittings	145.00
Loetz, Paperweight, Feather, Multicolored Iridescent, Blue, White, Signed	260.00
Loetz, Pitcher, White, Fine Pink Threading On Upper Half, 4 1/2 X 4 In.	120.00
Loetz, Rose Bowl, Blue Green, Brass Lattice Top	85.00
Loetz, Rose Bowl, Dark Blue & Green, Iridescent, Crisscross Threading, 4 In.	75.00
Loetz, Rose Bowl, Iridescent, Purple Veining, Polished Pontil, 2 1/2 X 4 In.	35.00
Loetz, Rose Bowl, Melon Ribbed, Green Iridescent, Flare Rim, 3 1/2 In.	150.00
Loetz, Sprinkler, Rose Water, Raindrop, Gold, Signed, 9 3/4 In.	400.00
Loetz, Urn, Miniature, Purple Blue, Silver Highlights, Iridescent, Pair	32.00
Loetz, Vase, Amber With Gold, Green, & Red Iridescence, 10 In.	150.00
Loetz, Vase, Aqua Swirled Design, Gold Enameled Floral, 10 In.	295.00
Loetz, Vase, Art Nouveau Flowers, Beaded Ring Base, Iridescent, 8 1/2 In.	145.00
Loetz, Vase, Blown-Out Tear Drops, Iridescent Colors, 10 In.	68.00
Loetz, Vase, Blue & Green Iridescent, Silver Overlay, 5 1/2 In.	165.00
Loetz, Vase, Blue Highlights, Pinched-In Sides, Bulbous Bottom, 9 1/4 In.	375.00
Loetz, Vase, Bud, Green & Gold Iridescent, Signed, 9 In.	85.00
Loetz, Vase, Deep Plum, Thick Ribbon Threading, Turquoise Iridescence, 4 In.	115.00
Loetz, Vase, Draped Iridescent, Amethyst, Austria, Signed, 10 X 7 In.	225.00
Loetz, Vase, Flower Form, Triangular, Green Iridescent To Burgundy Red, 9 In.	235.00
Loetz, Vase, Flowers In Relief, Rainbow Iridescence, Gourd Shape, 10 In.	185.00
Loetz, Vase, Golden With Silvery Iridescence, Bulbous, 9 X 7 In.	150.00
Loetz, Vase, Green & Blue, Iridescent, 7 In.	145.00
Loetz, Vase, Green At Bottom Shading To Red, Iridescent, 9 In.	125.00
Loetz, Vase, Green Iridescence, Dimpled, 7 1/2 X 7 In.	125.00
Loetz, Vase, Green Iridescent, Flared, Bronze Leaf Holder, 8 In.	100.00
Loetz, Vase, Green Pearlized, Leaf Decoration, 13 In.	145.00
Loetz, Vase, Green, Blue Iridescent Satin Spots, 3 1/2 X 3 3/4 In.	72.00
Loetz, Vase, Green, Blue, Signed, C.1900, 8 1/2 In. *Illus*	1250.00
Loetz, Vase, Green, Bulbous, Dimpled, Metal Collar, 7 In.	100.00
Loetz, Vase, Green, Iridescent, Dimpled, Ruffled, Textured, 7 1/2 X 7 1/2 In.	135.00
Loetz, Vase, Green, Purple Plums, Iridescent, 7 1/2 In.	95.00
Loetz, Vase, Iridescent Pink & Green, Mottling, 3 Handled, 5 In.	130.00
Loetz, Vase, Iridescent Silver On Indigo, 11 In.	175.00
Loetz, Vase, Iridescent, Applied Iridescent Green Grapes & Vines, 14 In.	148.00
Loetz, Vase, Iridescent, Swirl Silver Overlay, Austria, 4 1/2 In.	195.00
Loetz, Vase, Lavender, Aqua, Iridescent, Green, Rust Tracing, 7 X 7 1/4 In.	125.00
Loetz, Vase, Maroon, Cased, Iridescent, Green & White Pulled Design, 6 In.	125.00
Loetz, Vase, Mottled Green, Iridescent, 7 In., Pair	175.00
Loetz, Vase, Mottled Turquoise, Purple, Three Pinched Sides, 4 1/4 In.	95.00
Loetz, Vase, Multicolored Iridescence, 5 1/4 In.	80.00
Loetz, Vase, Orange, 2 Layers Of Red & Purple Cameo Carving, 7 1/4 In.	625.00
Loetz, Vase, Pastel Iridescence, Sterling Silver Overlay, Art Nouveau, 4 In.	125.00
Loetz, Vase, Peacock Blue & Green, Purple Iridescent, Pulled Lines, 3 3/4 In.	165.00
Loetz, Vase, Pinched At Neck, Green, Violet, Gold, Silver Overlay, 8 In.	225.00
Loetz, Vase, Pinched, Unsigned, 10 1/2 In.	110.00
Loetz, Vase, Pink Opalescent, 8 In.	70.00

Loetz, Vase, Pulled Iridescent Silver Over Olive, Square, 9 1/2 In. 350.00
Loetz, Vase, Purple, Turquoise, 4 1/4 X 3 In. 50.00
Loetz, Vase, Raindrop Pattern, Iridized, Stick Type, Blue, 12 In. 185.00
Loetz, Vase, Red & Green, Feathery Leaf Design, Square, Dimpled Base, 11 In. 285.00
Loetz, Vase, Reticulated Serpent Climbing, Blue, Green Iridescence, 8 1/2 In. 85.00
Loetz, Vase, Scrolls, Oil Streaks, Baluster, Salmon, Blue, Signed, C.1900, 15 In. 425.00
Loetz, Vase, Seashell, Gold, Blue Iridescence, Clear Pedestal, 7 In., Pair 500.00
Loetz, Vase, Shell, Mottled Shimmering Gold, Blue Iridescent, 7 In. 500.00
Loetz, Vase, Signed, C.1900, 9 1/2 In. .... *Illus* 500.00
Loetz, Vase, Spider, Web, Gold, Ivory, Purple, Green Iridescent, 6 1/2 In. 95.00
Loetz, Vase, Sterling Overlay, 5 In. 145.00
Loetz, Vase, Three Friar Vessels, 6 Twisted Handles, Signed, 5 3/4 In. 410.00
Loetz, Vase, Yellow, Cranberry & White Swirls, 9 In. 90.00
Lone Ranger, Belt, Etched Scenes, Safety Phrases, Glows In Dark 75.00
Lone Ranger, Figurine, Plastic, On Silver, With Box, 6 In. 29.00
Lone Ranger, Game, Target, 1930s 20.00
Lone Ranger, Glass, Dated 1938, Set Of 4 .... 24.00
Lone Ranger, Holder, Toothbrush, 1938 .... 12.00 To 35.00
Lone Ranger, Holster Set, Black Metal Dart Guns .... *Illus* 90.00
Lone Ranger, Knife, Silver Bullet 20.00
Lone Ranger, Lunch Box 5.00
Lone Ranger, Pinback, 1938 .... 7.00
Lone Ranger, Ring, Telescoping 33.00
Lone Ranger, Rocking Horse, Late 1930s 75.00
Longwy, Vase, Allover Enameled Florals, Fully Marked, 7 In. 85.00
Longwy, Vase, Blue, Cobalt Rim, Incised Designs, Enameled Florals, 8 X 14 In. 50.00
Longwy, Vase, Brown, Blue, White, & Yellow, Beaded, Footed, Metal Base, 10 In. 135.00
Longwy, Vase, Multicolored Enameled Florals, 7 In. 65.00

Lonhuda Pottery Company of Steubenville, Ohio, was organized in 1892 by William Long, W. H. Hunter, and Alfred Day. Brown underglaze slip decorated pottery was made. The firm closed in 1896.

Lonhuda, Vase, Black-Eyed Susans, 6 3/4 In. 135.00
Lonhuda, Vase, Flowers, Green, Orange, 8 In. 140.00

Lotus ware was made by the Knowles, Taylor & Knowles Company of East Liverpool, Ohio, from 1890 to 1900.

Lotus Ware, Bowl, Open Medallion Handles, Signed, 6 1/2 X 5 X 4 In. 210.00
Lotus Ware, Creamer, Bamboo Handle, Floral, Artist Signed, 6 1/2 In. 350.00
Lotus Ware, Creamer, Pink Net Design, Lotus Leaves & Blossoms 125.00
Lotus Ware, Creamer, Violet Decoration, Gold Trim, 4 In. 112.00
Lotus Ware, Fernery, Cloverleaf Shape, Ruffled Top, 4 Feet, Floral, 8 In. 185.00
Lotus Ware, Jar, Cover, Fishnet, Panels Of Purple Violets, 1894, Signed K.T.K. 450.00
Lotus Ware, Rose Bowl, Gold Fishnet, Florals, Beaded, K.T.K.4 1/2 In. 350.00
Lotus Ware, Rose Bowl, Hand-Painted Roses, Raised Gold Fishnet, Signed, 5 In. 375.00
Lotus Ware, Rose Bowl, K.T.K., Ruffled Rim, Gold Beaded, Pink Florals, 4 In. 450.00
Lotus Ware, Rose Bowl, K.T.K., White, Raised Pink Flowers, Gold Trim, Beaded 217.00
Lotus Ware, Rose Bowl, Leaves & Berries In High Relief, Gold, 4 In. 175.00
Lotus Ware, Rose Bowl, Pink & White Florals, Raised Gold Blossoms, 4 1/2 In. 500.00
Lotus Ware, Rose Bowl, Pink To Fuchsia Apple Blossoms, Ruffled Blue Collar 375.00
Lotus Ware, Sugar & Creamer, Gold Handles, Fishnet Design, Pink & Red 385.00

Loetz, Vase, Signed, C.1900, 9 1/2 In.

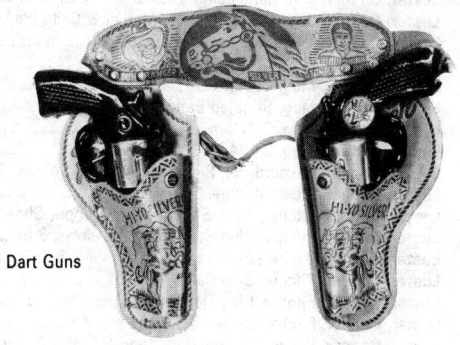

Lone Ranger, Holster Set, Black Metal Dart Guns

Lotus Ware, Tea Set, Raised Pink Blossoms With Gold, 4 Piece	600.00
Lotus Ware, Vase, K.T.K.Floral On Coral, Gold Winged Handles, 6 In.Diameter	385.00
Lotus Ware, Vase, White, Gold Net Pattern, Ball Feet, 8 X 5 In.	550.00

*Low art tiles were made by the J. and J.G. Low Art Tile Works
of Chelsea, Massachusetts, from 1877 to 1902. A variety of art and other
tiles were made.*

Low, Tile, Floral Design, Green, 3 In. Square	10.00
Low, Tile, Inlaid, Tiger Maple Box, Brown, 5 X 5 In.	30.00

*The Lowestoft factory in Suffolk, England, worked from 1757 to 1802.
They made many commemorative gift pieces and small dated, inscribed pieces of
soft paste porcelain.*

Lowestoft, see also Chinese Export

Lowestoft, Mug, Gold Rim, Oval Scroll Medallion, Handled, Initials, 2 1/2 In.	195.00
Loy-Nel-Art, see McCoy	
Lundberg, Vase, Swirled, Round, Flaring Neck, Blue, Gold On Dark Blue, 6 In.	75.00

*Luneville, a French faience factory, was established in 1731 by Jacques
Chambrette. It is best known for its fine biscuit figures and groups and
for large faience dogs and lions. The early pieces were unmarked. The
Terre de Lorraine of T.D.L.impression was used after 1766.*

Luneville, Bowl, Iridescent, Pine Cones & Leafage, K.& G., Low, 6 1/2 In.	65.00
Luneville, Plate, Fruit, Apples, Signed Obert, 9 In.	25.00

*Lusterware was meant to resemble copper, silver, or gold. It has been used
since the sixteenth century. Most of the luster found today was made during
the nineteenth century.*

Luster, Copper, Bowl, Blue Scroll Band, 5 1/2 X 3 In.	32.50
Luster, Copper, Bowl, Hand-Painted Red Roses On Dark Blue Band, 4 In.	40.00
Luster, Copper, Bowl, Tan Scroll Band, 4 3/4 X 2 1/2 In.	25.00
Luster, Copper, Butter Dish, Covered, Square, Anthony Shaw & Son	45.00
Luster, Copper, Chalice, Band Of Pink Luster, White Leaf Pattern, 4 1/4 In.	80.00
Luster, Copper, Compote, Blue Band, 4 3/4 In.	36.00
Luster, Copper, Creamer, Beaded, 3 1/8 In.	20.00
Luster, Copper, Creamer, Hand-Painted	30.00
Luster, Copper, Creamer, Mr.Pickwick Behind The Door, Bristol Kepple, Ridgway	26.00
Luster, Copper, Creamer, Raised Figs, Allerton Longton, England, 3 1/2 In.	25.00
Luster, Copper, Creamer, White, Sanded Band, 2 1/2 In.	22.00
Luster, Copper, Creamer, Yellow Band, Blue Dots, 2 1/2 In.	22.00
Luster, Copper, Creamer, 1 In.Black Band With Scroll	35.00
Luster, Copper, Cup & Saucer, Bellflower & Wheat	24.00
Luster, Copper, Dish, Pedestal, 2 X 2 1/2 In.	45.00
Luster, Copper, Egg, Duck, Blue, 5 Prisms, Hand-Painted Floral, 3 1/2 In.	125.00
Luster, Copper, Face Spout, Beading, Blue Band, Floral, 4 1/2 In.	65.00
Luster, Copper, Figural, Owl, Peaked Bonnet, Iridescent Blue, German, 5 In.	26.00
Luster, Copper, Jug, Blue Bank, 5 1/2 In.	43.00
Luster, Copper, Jug, Bulbous, Blue Band At Top, 5 1/2 In.	50.00

Luster, Copper, Jug, Hand-Painted Floral, 5 1/2 In. 50.00
Luster, Copper, Jug, Yellow Banded, Mother & Child Playing, C.1820, 6 1/2 In. 150.00
Luster, Copper, Mug, Blue Patterned Band, 2 1/2 In. 22.00
Luster, Copper, Mug, Child's, 2 1/4 In. 22.50
Luster, Copper, Mug, Cobalt Blue Band, Luster Floral Leafing 35.00
Luster, Copper, Mug, Stippled Band, 3 1/2 In. 10.00
Luster, Copper, Mug, 2 1/2 In. 35.00
Luster, Copper, Mug, 3 1/4 In. 45.00
Luster, Copper, Mustard Pot, Pink Band, Copper Specks, 2 In. 38.00
Luster, Copper, Mustard, Blue, 3 In. 45.00
Luster, Copper, Pitcher, Beak Spout, Raised Copper Sheep & Dog, C.1830, 7 In. 140.00
Luster, Copper, Pitcher, Blue Band, Copper Leaves, 3 In. 29.00
Luster, Copper, Pitcher, Blue Band, Copper Vine, 5 1/2 In. 65.00
Luster, Copper, Pitcher, Blue Band, 4 In. 27.00
Luster, Copper, Pitcher, Blue Flower Designed Band, 6 1/2 In. 95.00
Luster, Copper, Pitcher, Brown Sanded Band, 4 In. 28.00
Luster, Copper, Pitcher, Cream, Blue Band & Luster Decoration, 3 In. 35.00
Luster, Copper, Pitcher, Dancers In Relief, Blue Scrolls, 5 1/2 In. 77.00
Luster, Copper, Pitcher, Dancers, Blue Scrolls, 6 1/2 In. 75.00
Luster, Copper, Pitcher, Dancers, Blue, Marked Allerton, England, 6 1/2 In. 30.00
Luster, Copper, Pitcher, Dancing Couple, 7 In. 45.00
Luster, Copper, Pitcher, Dancing Figures Each Side, 5 In. 35.00
Luster, Copper, Pitcher, Dancing Girls, Blue Decoration, 6 In. 65.00
Luster, Copper, Pitcher, Decorated Green Band, 5 1/2 In. 40.00
Luster, Copper, Pitcher, Duckbilled Handle, Blue, White & Yellow, 6 In. 65.00
Luster, Copper, Pitcher, Figures Of Sultry Dancers, 7 In. 85.00
Luster, Copper, Pitcher, Floral Trim, Allertons-Longton, England, 6 In. 24.00
Luster, Copper, Pitcher, Hand-Painted Flowers, Diamond-Mold Base, 6 1/4 In. 75.00
Luster, Copper, Pitcher, Masked Spout, 5 1/2 In. 55.00
Luster, Copper, Pitcher, Milk, White Petals & Leaves On Purple Luster Band 75.00
Luster, Copper, Pitcher, Molded Deer Decoration, 6 1/2 In. 45.00
Luster, Copper, Pitcher, Pink Band, 6 In. 45.00
Luster, Copper, Pitcher, Pink, Green, Blue, & Yellow Enameling, 6 1/2 In. 100.00
Luster, Copper, Pitcher, Raised Children, Animals, Polychrome, Banded, 8 In. 65.00
Luster, Copper, Pitcher, Sand Band, 2 1/2 In. 20.00
Luster, Copper, Pitcher, Scroll Handle, Blue Band With Flowers, 4 In. 27.50
Luster, Copper, Pitcher, Scroll Handle, English, C.1820, 8 In. 155.00
Luster, Copper, Pitcher, Tan & Orange Bands, 8 In. 125.00
Luster, Copper, Pitcher, Thorn Handle, Blue Band, Gold Decoration, 8 In. 100.00
Luster, Copper, Pitcher, White Interior, 4 In. 45.00
Luster, Copper, Pitcher, Wide Blue Decoration, 6 In. 30.00
Luster, Copper, Pitcher, Yellow Band, 6 In. 44.00
Luster, Copper, Plate, Charles Allerton & Sons, C.1890 .... 10.00
Luster, Copper, Salt, Blue 15.00
Luster, Copper, Salt, Ivory Band, 2 1/4 X 3 In. 18.00
Luster, Copper, Shaving Mug, Scuttle, Left-Handed, Pink Flower 35.00
Luster, Copper, Sugar, House Pattern, 7 In. 75.00
Luster, Copper, Tea Leaf, see Ironstone, Tea Leaf
Luster, Copper, Vase, Blue Dragon, Z4829, 10 1/4 In. 265.00
Luster, Copper, Vase, Crown Devin, Deep Ruby, 6 1/4 In. 120.00
Luster, Fairyland, see Wedgwood, Fairyland Luster
Luster, Green, Chocolate Pot, Raised Classical Figures, German 45.00
Luster, Green, Touring Car, White Mice, German 45.00
Luster, Pearl, Sugar & Creamer, Gold Trim, Small 8.00
Luster, Pink & Copper, Canister Set, German 75.00
Luster, Pink, Bowl, Devon, Fieldings, Stroke-On-Trent, 10 1/2 In. 85.00
Luster, Pink, Butter, Decorative 37.00
Luster, Pink, Cake Plate, House Pattern 32.50
Luster, Pink, Chocolate Set, Gold Bleeding Heart, 13 Piece 175.00
Luster, Pink, Coffee Set, Child's, Ornate, Cats, 11 Piece 125.00
Luster, Pink, Creamer, Bubbles, Allerton, 5 1/2 In. 45.00
Luster, Pink, Creamer, Gold Decoration, 3 1/2 In. 15.00
Luster, Pink, Cup & Saucer, Carnation 20.00
Luster, Pink, Cup & Saucer, Deep Drinking Saucer, Scroll Work, Florals 45.00
Luster, Pink, Cup & Saucer, Faith & Hope Black Transfer, Charity On Saucer 40.00

Luster, Pink, Cup & Saucer, Faith & Hope On Cup, Charity On Saucer	40.00
Luster, Pink, Cup & Saucer, Flowers All Over	22.00
Luster, Pink, Cup & Saucer, Hand-Painted Floral	13.00
Luster, Pink, Cup & Saucer, Hand-Painted Landscape, House & Windmill	55.00
Luster, Pink, Cup & Saucer, Poppy	20.00
Luster, Pink, Cup & Saucer, Portrait, Lady, Heavy Gold	36.00
Luster, Pink, Cup & Saucer, Raised Florals To Front Of Cup, Gold Trim	11.50
Luster, Pink, Cup & Saucer, Rose Band, German, Large	10.00
Luster, Pink, Cup & Saucer, Sunderland	36.00
Luster, Pink, Goblet, Luster Band, House Design	90.00
Luster, Pink, Jug, Green Highlights, Foal & Cow, C.1820, 5 In.	180.00
Luster, Pink, Jug, Milk, Black Transfer, C.1800	42.00
Luster, Pink, Match Holder, Figural, Dog, Marked Japan	7.50
Luster, Pink, Mug, Child's, Strawberry Trim, 2 1/2 In.	38.00
Luster, Pink, Plate, Floral Decoration, C.1840, 6 In.	18.00
Luster, Pink, Plate, Floral, 6 In.	15.00
Luster, Pink, Plate, 8 In.	30.00
Luster, Pink, Saucer, Floral Decoration, C.1840, 6 In.	12.00
Luster, Pink, Sugar & Creamer, Allerton, England	31.00
Luster, Pink, Tea Set, School House	275.00
Luster, Pink, Teapot, Pink Band With Roses, Ornate Handle	85.00
Luster, Pink, Tumbler, Birthplace Of Daniel Webster, C.1880, Marked	14.50
Luster, Pink, Vase, Peabody, Kansas, Handled, 4 1/2 In.	15.00
Luster, Purple, Coffeepot, Peacock In Tree, Bavarian	42.00
Luster, Purple, Dresser Set, Scalloped Tray	28.00
Luster, Silver, Creamer, Ribbed, Copper Luster Inside, H.J.Wood, England	12.00
Luster, Silver, Cup & Saucer	10.00
Luster, Silver, Figurine, Belly Dancer, Larne	85.00
Luster, Silver, Goblet, Copper Luster Lining, C.1840	48.00
Luster, Silver, Jug, Dutch Children, Dark Green & Buff, Pewter Top, 7 In.	78.00
Luster, Silver, Sugar & Creamer, Rococo Design, C.1830	90.00
Luster, Silver, Sugar, Scalloped Top, Copper Luster Inside	8.00
Luster, Silver, Teapot, Acorn Finial, Footed, 7 1/2 In.	175.00
Luster, Silver, Teapot, Footed, Domed Lid, 10 In.	235.00
Luster, Silver, Teapot, Ribbed, Black Handle, Finial, Longport, England	17.00
Luster, Silver, Waste Bowl, Footed, Ribbed	50.00

Lustre Art Glass Company was founded in Long Island, New York, in 1920 by Conrad Vahlsing and Paul Frank. The company made lampshades and globes that are almost indistinguishable from those made by Quezal.

Lustre Art, Lamp, Pulled Feather Shade, Floral & Cherub Base, 14 In.	325.00
Lustre Art, Shade, Iridescent Calcite, Signed, Set Of 5	250.00
Lustre Art, Shade, Iridescent Fold Trumpet, Set Of 6	420.00
Lustre Art, Shade, No.282, Spider Web, Opalescent, Brown, Gold, Pair	225.00
Lustre Art, Shade, Opalescent Feather, Green Edge On Gold, Threading, Notched	95.00
Lustre Art, Shade, Pulled Feather, Set Of 3	300.00

Lustres are mantel decorations, or pedestal vases, with many hanging glass prisms. The name really refers to the prisms, and it is proper to refer to a single glass prism as a lustre. Either spelling, luster or lustre, is correct.

Lustres, European Cut Crystal, Electrified, 20th Century, 16 1/2 In., Pair	500.00
Lustres, Tulip Shape, White Overlay Cut To Green, Prisms, 10 In., Pair	700.00

Lutz glass was made in the 1870s by Nicholas Lutz at the Boston and Sandwich Company. He made a delicate and intricate threaded glass of several colors. Other similar wares are referred to as Lutz.

Lutz, Bottle, Cologne, Swirled Enameled Florals, Numbered, 5 In.	50.00
Lutz, Bowl & Underplate, Finger, Threaded & Quilted Amber Shaded To Rose	140.00
Lutz, Bowl, Covered Bonbon, Latticinio, Blown Finial, 6 X 5 In.	89.00
Lutz, Bowl, Finger & Underplate, Sandwich	75.00
Lutz, Bowl, Threaded, Clear, White & Gold Twists, 2 3/8 X 4 1/2 In.	85.00
Lutz, Compote, Pink, Green, Blue, & White Twists, Gold Filigree, Flared, 3 In.	42.50
Lutz, Creamer, Opaline, Cranberry Threading	95.00
Lutz, Dish, Latticinio Stripes, Goldstone, Scalloped	78.00

Lutz, Plate, Filigree Canes, Blue, White, Yellow, Orange, Gold, 6 1/2 In. 88.00

Petrus Regout established the De Sphinx pottery in Maastricht,
Holland in 1836. The firm was noted for its transfer-printed earthenware.
Maastricht, Chocolate Pot, Children Scene On 2 Sides, Dated 1914 .... 50.00
Maastricht, Plate, Blue & White, Marked, 9 In. 39.00
Maastricht, Plate, Blue & Yellow Stick Spatter, 9 In. 20.00
Maastricht, Plate, Flow Blue, Petrus Regout, Sphinx Mark, 9 1/2 In. 25.00
Maastricht, Plate, Game, Mallard Drake, 9 1/2 In. 32.50
Maastricht, Vase, Hand-Painted, Swirls, Yellow Flowers, Ferns, Sailing Boats 95.00

Maize glass, sold by the W.L.Libbey & Son Company of Toledo, Ohio,
was made by Joseph Locke in 1889. It is pressed glass formed like an ear
of corn. Most pieces were made for household use.
Maize, Bowl, Green Leaves, 9 In. 200.00
Maize, Castor, Pickle, Green Husks, Footed Frame 425.00
Maize, Celery, Green Leaves 95.00
Maize, Pitcher, Green Leaves, Libbey, 8 3/4 In. 300.00
Maize, Salt & Pepper, Libbey 110.00
Maize, Sugar Shaker, Libbey, Custard, Blue Leaves 140.00
Maize, Toothpick, Ivory, Blue Staining & Gold 275.00
Maize, Tumbler, Cream Opaque Background, Yellow Enamel & Gold, Libbey 195.00
Maize, Tumbler, Cream Opaque Ground, Blue Enameled Leaves, 4 1/2 In. 195.00

Majolica is any pottery glazed with a tin enamel. Most of the majolica
found today is decorated with leaves, shells, branches, and other natural shapes
and in natural colors. It was a popular nineteenth-century product.
Majolica, see also Wedgwood
Majolica, Ashtray, Man With Monocle Carrying Suitcase, Dogs 35.00
Majolica, Basket, Decorated, Orchid Lining, 8 X 8 1/2 In. 52.50
Majolica, Basket, Fruit, Pierced Oak Leaves, Turquoise, Green, 13 X 8 1/2 In. 45.00
Majolica, Bowl & Mug, Child's, Leaves, Waterlilies, Frogs 35.00
Majolica, Bowl, Fruit Center, Green, 8 1/2 In. 16.00
Majolica, Bowl, Maple-Leaf Shape, Raised Leaf Center, 10 In. 15.00
Majolica, Bowl, Salad, Footed, Serving Spoon & Fork, Wedgwood, 9 X 5 In. 195.00
Majolica, Bowl, Shell, Seaweed, Signed Etruscan, 8 In. 85.00
Majolica, Bowl, Sugar, Floral, Cable Decoration, Blue 27.50
Majolica, Bowl, Turned In Rim, Raised Florals, Blue, Yellow Centers, Green 31.50
Majolica, Bust, Lady With Plumed Hat, 19 In. 275.00
Majolica, Butter Pat 4.50
Majolica, Cake Set, 1 Large & 6 Small Plates, Red Flower Center, German 45.00
Majolica, Cake Stand, Etruscan, Tree Trunk, Footed Base, Leaf-Effect Top 50.00
Majolica, Candleholder, Girl With White Cat, Kate Greenaway, 6 1/2 In. 37.50
Majolica, Coffee Service, Marked A.Z., Nove, 16 Piece 72.50
Majolica, Compote, Etruscan, Leaf, 8 In. 65.00
Majolica, Compote, Green Leaves On Yellow Basket Weave 55.00
Majolica, Compote, Lavender Lined Shell, Dolphins On Seaweed Base, 11 In. 90.00
Majolica, Compote, Leaves, George Jones, Dec.23, 1871, Pair 125.00
Majolica, Creamer, Basket Weave Base, Green & Tan Flowers & Leaves, 4 In. 12.50
Majolica, Creamer, Etruscan, Albino, Orange Seaweed 24.00
Majolica, Creamer, Etruscan, Primrose, Green 35.00
Majolica, Creamer, Open Mouth Fish Forms Spout, Tail Handle 20.00
Majolica, Cup & Saucer, Etruscan, Bamboo 68.00
Majolica, Cup & Saucer, Etruscan, Shell & Seaweed Pattern 58.00
Majolica, Dish, Estruscan, Begonia Leaf, Green, Gold, & Pink, 9 In. 25.00
Majolica, Dish, Etruscan, Green, Blue, & Brown, Orchid Rim, Branch Handle, 9 In. 42.00
Majolica, Dish, Etruscan, Leaf, Smith & Hill, Handled, Pink, Green, 12 In. 55.00
Majolica, Dish, Feeding, Children Playing, Germany, 7 1/4 In. 25.00
Majolica, Dish, Leaf-Shaped, Etruscan, 9 In. .... 15.00 To 25.00
Majolica, Dish, Leaf, Etruscan, Pinks, Yellow, Green, Tan Handle, 12 X 9 In. 55.00
Majolica, Dish, Leaf, Pink Border, Signed Etruscan, 12 1/4 In. 35.00
Majolica, Dish, Sardine, Lavender Lining, With Cover And Underplate 125.00
Majolica, Figurine, Ape Holding Hat-Shaped Dish, Novelty 38.00
Majolica, Figurine, Etruscan, Black Cat, Mustard Colored Orb, Zodiac Signs 155.00
Majolica, Figurine, Monk, Standing Holding Tankard Under Arm, Planter, 9 In. 75.00

Majolica, Figurine, The Goat Herder, Pocket Vase, Green Blue Lining, Signed	62.50
Majolica, Jar, Drug, Blue & White, Spanish, Late 17th Century, 9 3/4 In., Pair	225.00
Majolica, Jar, Indian Tobacco, 7 In.	40.00
Majolica, Jar, Tobacco, Chinese Man, 4 In.	30.00
Majolica, Jar, Tobacco, Fox Head With Hat Cover, 1853, 5 1/2 In.	45.00
Majolica, Jar, Tobacco, Head, Green Turban, Veil, Pink Collar, 6 X 4 In.	75.00
Majolica, Jar, Tobacco, Indian Head	95.00
Majolica, Jar, Tobacco, Mariner, Dark Blue Hat, Bearded	40.00
Majolica, Jar, Tobacco, Negro Jockey, Pink & Yellow Cap, Green Bowtie	69.00
Majolica, Jar, Tobacco, Pink Hat, White Collar, 6 1/2 X 5 In.	70.00
Majolica, Jar, Tobacco, Pipe On Top	45.00
Majolica, Jar, Tobacco, Tiger, 4 In.	50.00
Majolica, Jardiniere, One Piece, Pedestal	115.00
Majolica, Jug, Lemonade, Etruscan, Seaweed & Shell	135.00
Majolica, Jug, Syrup, Pink Flower On Turquoise Basket Weave, Pewter Lid	32.00
Majolica, Match Holder, Brown, Dog Beside Barrel, Striker Plate	20.00
Majolica, Mug, Ferns On Brown, 2 Frogs Inside, 4 1/2 In.	65.00
Majolica, Mug, Spanish Grandee, Blue Coat, Yellow Trousers, Pink Inside, 6 In.	135.00
Majolica, Pitcher, Basket Weave Design, Cream Background, 6 In.	28.00
Majolica, Pitcher, Basket Weave, Yellow, Green Foliage, Purple Lining, 7 In.	24.00
Majolica, Pitcher, Corn Shape, Yellow & Green, Signed, 6 1/2 In.	40.00
Majolica, Pitcher, Corn, Purple Lining, 5 1/2 In.	22.00
Majolica, Pitcher, Corn, 4 1/4 In.	24.00
Majolica, Pitcher, Dolphin, Handled, 10 In.	52.00
Majolica, Pitcher, Ear Of Corn, Green Leaves, Green Handle, 4 1/2 In.	14.50
Majolica, Pitcher, Etruscan Shell, Seaweed, Pink Lined, 5 1/2 In.	85.00
Majolica, Pitcher, Etruscan, Hawthorne, 9 In.	80.00
Majolica, Pitcher, Etruscan, Shell & Seaweed Pattern, 4 In.	75.00
Majolica, Pitcher, Etruscan, Shell & Seaweed, Signed, 6 In.	125.00
Majolica, Pitcher, Etruscan, Thorn Pattern, 7 In.	85.00
Majolica, Pitcher, Figural, Owl, Browns & Greens, C.1880, 10 In.	75.00
Majolica, Pitcher, Fish On Yellow & Turquoise, Purple Interior, 6 1/2 In.	45.00
Majolica, Pitcher, Fish, Calder-Portugal, 1880's, 10 In.	45.00
Majolica, Pitcher, Leaves, Vine, Roses, Green, Pink, Brown, 9 In.	67.50
Majolica, Pitcher, Milk, Figural, Ear Of Corn, Yellow & Green, Purple Lining	35.00
Majolica, Pitcher, Roses & Ivy, 9 1/2 In.	85.00
Majolica, Pitcher, Tan Basket Weave, Green Leaves, Orchid Lined, 4 1/2 In.	28.00
Majolica, Pitcher, Triangular, Mauve Interior, 7 In.	22.00
Majolica, Pitcher, Water, Ham For Pocketbook	175.00
Majolica, Pitcher, Yellow Sunflowers, High Gloss, C.1880, 5 In.	20.00
Majolica, Planter, Embossed Cherubs, Magenta, Green, Brown, Large	95.00
Majolica, Planter, Wall, Hanging, Shape Of Nest, Robin, 11 1/2 In.	310.00
Majolica, Plate Set, Oyster, Minton, 19th Century, Set Of 6	275.00
Majolica, Plate, Asparagus, Green, White, Purple, Butter-Well Rim	20.00
Majolica, Plate, Begonia Leaf In Pink, White, Green, Brown, 8 In.	15.00
Majolica, Plate, Blue & White Snow Scene, Yellow Church, 8 In.	10.00
Majolica, Plate, Bread, Eat Thy Bread, Leaf Center, Green, Gold, Brown, 13 In.	38.00
Majolica, Plate, Brown Scroll Handles, Center Scene Of Shaggy Dog, 11 In.	30.00
Majolica, Plate, Etruscan, Cauliflower Pattern, 8 In.	20.00
Majolica, Plate, Etruscan, Cauliflower, 9 In.	35.00
Majolica, Plate, Etruscan, Cauliflower, 10 In.	40.00
Majolica, Plate, Etruscan, Grapes, Leaves, Light Blue, 6 1/2 In.	22.50
Majolica, Plate, Etruscan, Green, Brown & Yellow, 8 In.	18.00
Majolica, Plate, Etruscan, Leaf, 9 In.	38.00
Majolica, Plate, Etruscan, Overlapping Leaves, Rainbow Colors, 7 1/2 In.	18.00
Majolica, Plate, Etruscan, Shell & Seaweed Pattern, 8 3/4 In.	50.00
Majolica, Plate, Etruscan, Shell & Seaweed, 8 In.	75.00
Majolica, Plate, Etruscan, Starfish Shape	26.00
Majolica, Plate, Etruscan, Yellow Apples, Pink Strawberries, Signed, 9 In.	25.00
Majolica, Plate, Fern Leaves, Flowers On Branches, Fancy Border, 8 In.	18.00
Majolica, Plate, Girl Playing With Doll Center, Turquoise, 6 1/2 In.	15.00
Majolica, Plate, Greek Key Border, HBC & Co., Choisy Le Roi	17.00
Majolica, Plate, Greek Key Border, 9 In.	16.00
Majolica, Plate, Green & Raspberry Foxgloves & Leaves, Cobalt Blue, 8 In.	15.00
Majolica, Plate, Green Leaf Center, Basket Weave Edge, 7 3/4 In.	18.00

Majolica, Plate, Green Leaf In Center, Roman Key Border, 6 In.	8.00
Majolica, Plate, Hunting Scene, Brown Stag & Dog, Yellow Tortoiseshell, 11 In.	24.50
Majolica, Plate, Leaves & Flowers, Greek Key Border, 9 In.	18.00
Majolica, Plate, Maple Leaves Edged In Tan & Yellow, 7 3/4 In.	18.00
Majolica, Plate, Oyster, Incised, Register Mark, Signed, 19th Century, Set Of 6	290.00
Majolica, Plate, Pink, Gnomes, Aqua In Center, 7 1/2 In.	29.00
Majolica, Plate, Shell & Seaweed, 10 In.	35.00
Majolica, Platter, Etruscan, Leaf Shape, Pond Lilies, Signed, 12 X 9 1/2 In.	45.00
Majolica, Platter, Leaves On Pink & Blue, Yellow Border, 11 1/2 X 8 1/2 In.	32.00
Majolica, Platter, Oval, Blue, Butterflies, Flowers, Brown Sponge Back, 14 In.	65.00
Majolica, Platter, Shell & Seaweed, 13 In.	70.00
Majolica, Salt, Figural, Seated Man & Woman, Marked, 1867, Pair, 7 3/4 In.	400.00
Majolica, Sauce, Pebbled Blue Background, Butterfly, Fan Shaped, Set Of 4	25.00
Majolica, Sugar & Creamer, Etruscan, Cauliflower, Cover, Signed	100.00 To 135.00
Majolica, Sugar, Etruscan, Handled, Covered, 6 In.	75.00
Majolica, Syrup, Bird, Flower, Yellow	35.00
Majolica, Syrup, Etruscan, Bamboo Pattern	52.00 To 100.00
Majolica, Syrup, Etruscan, Sunflower	85.00 To 95.00
Majolica, Syrup, Shells & Seaweed On Gray-Green Ground, 6 In.	51.00
Majolica, Syrup, Sunflower Pattern, Pewter Top, Signed Etruscan, 8 1/4 In.	155.00
Majolica, Tazza, Apollo & Muses Scene, Late Renaissance Style, 11 1/4 In.	275.00
Majolica, Tea Set, Etruscan, Cauliflower, 3 Piece	95.00
Majolica, Tea Set, Etruscan, Yellow & Brown Bamboo Shaped Bodies, 3 Piece	75.00
Majolica, Teapot & Sugar Bowl, Etruscan, Basket Weave & Bamboo, Songbirds	40.00
Majolica, Teapot, Owl & Shell, Pink Lining, Tricornered, 8 In.	85.00
Majolica, Tile, Tea, Green Leaves, 5 1/2 In.	10.00
Majolica, Toby Mug, Red, Sailor, Seashell Border, English, C.1850, 10 In.	110.00
Majolica, Tray, Oval, Open Handles, 1871 Red Mark, 11 X 9 In.	65.00
Majolica, Tray, Oval, Seaweed Decoration, 12 X 9 In.	75.00
Majolica, Trivet, Metal Frame, 6 In. Square	7.00
Majolica, Vase, Boy On One, Girl On Other, Pair, 6 In.	18.00
Majolica, Vase, Multicolor Water Lily Decoration, Orchid Lining, 5 1/2 In.	30.00
Majolica, Vase, Pink Applied Roses, 14 1/2 In., 3 Piece	185.00
Majolica, Vase, Tree Trunk, Entwined Serpent, Orchid Lining, 5 1/2 In.	26.00
Majolica, Vase, Yellow, Sanded, Incised Sunflower Design, 6 1/4 In.	20.00
Malachite, Figurine, Buddha, 8 In.	110.00
Malachite, Jar, Powder, Nude On Cover, Rose Border, 4 1/2 In.	32.50

Marbles of glass were made during the nineteenth century. Venetian swirl, clear glass, sulfides, and marbles with frosted white animal figures embedded in the glass were popular. Handmade clay marbles were made in many places, but most of them came from the pottery factories of Ohio and Pennsylvania. Occasionally, real stone marbles of onyx, carnelian, or jasper can be found.

Marble, Carving, Bust, Young Woman In Turban, Italian, 19th Century, 14 In.	225.00
Marble, Carving, Lion, Monim, 24 In.	450.00
Marble, Comic, Annie & Sandy, Pair	45.00
Marble, Core Swirl, Solid, 2 In.	35.00
Marble, Core, Latticinio, Orange & Blue Swirled Striped, White, 19th Century	35.00
Marble, Onionskin Swirl, Set Of 3, 1 In.	15.00
Marble, Sulfide, Ball, Small Victorian Boy In Chair, Inside, 3 In.	25.00
Marble, Sulfide, Cow, 1 5/8 In.	27.50
Marble, Sulfide, Dog, Large	40.00
Marble, Sulfide, Lamb, Bubbles, 1 1/4 In.	60.00
Marble, Sulfide, Lion, 1 1/2 In.	45.00
Marble, Sulfide, Ram, 1 3/4 In.	52.50
Marble, Sulfide, Ram's Head, 1 1/2 In.	47.50
Marble, Sulfide, Rooster, 1 1/2 In.	50.00
Marble, Sulfide, Sitting Cat, 1 1/2 In.	45.00
Marble, Sulfide, Stag's Head, Hunter Sleeping With Gun	225.00
Marble, Sulfide, Standing Bear, 1 1/2 In.	47.50
Marble, Sulfide, Standing Dog, 2 In.	45.00
Marble, Sulfide, Woodpecker, 5 In.	75.00
Marble, Swirl, Blue, Red, Green, 2 In.	40.00
Marble, Swirl, Green, Yellow, Red Splatter, 2 1/2 In.	45.00
Marble, Swirl, Red, White & Blue Center Swirl, Yellow Outer Swirl, 5 3/4 In.	30.00

Marble, Swirl, White, Red, & Blue, 1 1/2 In.	27.00
Marble, Swirl, 2 1/2 In.	50.00
Marble, Swirl, 5 1/4 In.	15.00
Marble, Swirl, 5 1/2 In.	65.00

*The Marblehead Pottery was founded in 1905 as a rehabilitative program
for the patients of a Marblehead, Mass., sanitarium by
Dr. J. Hall. Two years later it was separated from the sanitarium, and
it continued operations until 1936. Many of the pieces were decorated with
marine motifs.*

Marblehead, Bowl, Blue-Gray Outside Shading To Lavender Inside, 6 In.	37.50
Marblehead, Bowl, Burnt Orange, Bulbous, 4 X 5 In.	18.00
Marblehead, Bowl, Green, Incised & Painted Design, Signed, 3 1/2 In.	235.00
Marblehead, Bowl, Low, Pink, Marked, 7 1/2 X 1 1/2 In.	17.00
Marblehead, Planter, Wall, Ribbed Design, Blue, 5 In.	30.00
Marblehead, Tea Set, Dark Matte Blue Finish, Artist Signed, 3 Piece	150.00
Marblehead, Tile, High Glaze With Ship Scene	90.00
Marblehead, Vase, Blue Matte, 9 In.	45.00
Marblehead, Vase, Blue, Stylized Leaf Design, Artist Signature, 3 3/4 In.	220.00
Marblehead, Vase, Brown Speckle, Matte Finish, 5 1/4 In.	35.00
Marblehead, Vase, Butterflies, Flowers, Dark Blue, 4 1/2 In.	325.00
Marblehead, Vase, Dark Blue, 4 In.	20.00
Marblehead, Vase, Dark Blue, 8 1/2 In.	28.00
Marblehead, Vase, Fan Shaped Branches, Foliage On Speckled Ground, 10 In.	425.00
Marblehead, Vase, Gray Exterior, Blue Interior, 7 In.	60.00
Marblehead, Vase, Green, Corset Shape, 4 1/2 In.	23.00
Marblehead, Vase, Hand-Decorated Yellow Roses, 3 1/2 In.	295.00
Marblehead, Vase, Incised Butterflies, Branches, Leaves, & Red Fruit, 5 In.	265.00
Marblehead, Vase, Rose, White Scenic, Black & Blue Detail, 4 1/4 In.	63.00
Marblehead, Vase, With Frog, Blue Bowl, Shallow, 8 In.	65.00
Marblehead, Wall Pocket, Dark Green Matte, 5 X 3 1/2 X 4 1/2 In.	30.00
Marilyn Monroe, Card, Theater Lobby, Film Marilyn	7.50
Marilyn Monroe, Tray, Tip, Nude	15.00
Marine, see Nautical	

*Martinware is a salt-glazed stoneware made by the Martin Brothers of
Middlesex, England, between 1873 and 1915. Many figural jugs and vases
were made.*

Martinware, Vase, Gourd Shape, Striated, Green Tints, 2 3/4 In.	110.00
Martinware, Vase, Gray, Raised Nailheads, Blue Leaves & Birds, 9 1/2 In.	200.00
Martinware, Vase, Signed, Dated, 1898, 9 In.	275.00

*Mary Gregory glass is identified by a characteristic white figure painted
on dark glass. It was made from 1870 to 1910. The name refers to any glass
decorated with a white silhouette figure and not just the Sandwich glass
originally painted by Miss Mary Gregory.*

Mary Gregory, Atomizer, Blue, White Enamel Barefoot Boy In Knee Pants, Hat	125.00
Mary Gregory, Basket, Applied Handle, White Boy Blowing Horn, 4 3/4 In.	87.00
Mary Gregory, Basket, Green, H, 1908 Engraved On Bottom, 4 In.	65.00
Mary Gregory, Bottle, Barber, Amethyst, Sandwich	100.00
Mary Gregory, Bottle, Barber, Boy & Flowers, Green	75.00
Mary Gregory, Bottle, Barber, Boy & Girl Playing Tennis, Cobalt, Stopper, Pair	350.00
Mary Gregory, Bottle, Barber, Cobalt Blue, White Enameled Tennis Boy, 7 In.	135.00
Mary Gregory, Bottle, Cologne, Clear, White Enameled Boy & Girl, 8 In., Pair	190.00
Mary Gregory, Bottle, Cologne, Steeple Stopper, Boy, Girl, Pair	190.00
Mary Gregory, Bottle, Perfume, Clear, White Boy, Flowers, Birds, Stopper	12.00
Mary Gregory, Bottle, Perfume, Clear, White Girl, Faceted Stopper, 4 In.	75.00
Mary Gregory, Bottle, Water, Clear, White Enameled Boy & Foliage, 7 1/2 In.	85.00
Mary Gregory, Bottle, Wine, Bulbous, White Girl, Lime Green, Stopper, 9 1/4 In.	165.00
Mary Gregory, Bowl, Berry, 2 Small Bowls, Tinted Faces, Clear	125.00
Mary Gregory, Bowl, Figure Of Girl, Tinted Face, White Foliage, Blown, 5 In.	30.00
Mary Gregory, Bowl, Finger, Cranberry, White Enameled Boy, 2 1/2 X 4 1/2 In.	65.00
Mary Gregory, Bowl, Girl Picking Flower, Tinted Face, White Trees, 3 1/4 In.	145.00
Mary Gregory, Box, Amethyst Glass, Girl, Paneled, Brass Hinged Rim, 3 1/4 In.	175.00
Mary Gregory, Box, Cobalt, Lady, Gold Filigree Berry & Leaf, Covered, Hinged	95.00

Mary Gregory, Box, Electric Blue, White Girl, Hinged, 3 X 3 In.	150.00
Mary Gregory, Box, Girl, Butterfly, Hinged, Round, Sapphire Blue, 3 1/2 In.	135.00
Mary Gregory, Box, Hinged, Amethyst, White Boy Figure, 4 In.	95.00
Mary Gregory, Box, Hinged, Cranberry, Brass, Little Boy, Gold Enamel, 3 In.	145.00
Mary Gregory, Box, Jewel, Hinged Top, Boy Holding Spray Of Flowers	225.00
Mary Gregory, Box, Pill, Hinged Cover, Amethyst, Enameled White Decoration	95.00
Mary Gregory, Box, Powder, Sapphire, Hinged	195.00
Mary Gregory, Box, Round, Girl With Butterfly, Lime Green, 4 X 3 1/2 In.	135.00
Mary Gregory, Box, Round, Hinged, Girl With Flowers, Sapphire Blue, 4 1/8 In.	275.00
Mary Gregory, Butter, Girl, Tinted, Lid	120.00
Mary Gregory, Castor, Pickle, Waffle, Silver Plate, Tongs	65.00
Mary Gregory, Creamer, Oliver, Spray Of Leaves, Amethyst To Clear	125.00
Mary Gregory, Cruet, Cherub, Green, White, Stopper, Large	135.00
Mary Gregory, Cruet, Cobalt Blue, Girl With Flower, Bubble Stopper, 8 1/2 In.	195.00
Mary Gregory, Cruet, Fern Green, White Girl & Boy Dancing, Foliage, 10 In.	175.00
Mary Gregory, Cruet, Girl Seated On Stump With Flowers, Boy, 10 In., Pair	375.00
Mary Gregory, Cruet, Wine, Bulbous, White Girl, Lilies Of Valley, Stopper	125.00
Mary Gregory, Decanter, Blue, White Enamel, Barefoot Boy In Knee Pants	125.00
Mary Gregory, Decanter, Boy, Tinted Face	135.00
Mary Gregory, Decanter, Clear, Bulbous, Inverted Thumbprint, Boy, Bird, Stopper	150.00
Mary Gregory, Decanter, Girl & Trees, 11 In.	34.00
Mary Gregory, Decanter, Girl, Lilies In Valley, White Enamel, 10 1/2 In.	98.00
Mary Gregory, Decanter, Pigeon Blood, Mushroom Stopper, Gold Trim, 7 1/4 In.	60.00
Mary Gregory, Decanter, Red, Mushroom Stopper, Gold Trim, Handle, 7 1/4 In.	65.00
Mary Gregory, Decanter, Wine Bottle, Young Girl, Foliage, Stopper, Green, 9 In.	165.00
Mary Gregory, Decanter, Wine, Boy	130.00
Mary Gregory, Dish, Pin, Cobalt Blue, Oval	140.00
Mary Gregory, Ewer, Cranberry, White Enameled Girl, 9 7/8 In.	145.00
Mary Gregory, Ewer, Emerald Green, 8 1/2 In.	60.00
Mary Gregory, Glass, Girl With Wheat In Hand, Flowers	90.00
Mary Gregory, Goblet, Boy	45.00
Mary Gregory, Goblet, Girl	45.00
Mary Gregory, Goblet, Sapphire Blue, 5 5/8 In.	69.00
Mary Gregory, Holder, Playing Cards, Clear Glass	48.00
Mary Gregory, Holder, Toothbrush, Little Girl Feeding Birds, Black Amethyst	110.00
Mary Gregory, Jar, Biscuit, Covered, Clear, Girl In White	138.00
Mary Gregory, Jar, Biscuit, Girl, Ornate Silver Plate, Lid, Gold, Electric Blue	150.00
Mary Gregory, Jar, Biscuit, White Cherub, Flashed Cranberry	135.00
Mary Gregory, Lamp Base, Oil, Blue, White Girl, 9 1/2 In.	135.00
Mary Gregory, Lamp, Black Amethyst, Font Removes To Form Vase	625.00
Mary Gregory, Lamp, Cranberry, White Enameled Girl Figures, 11 1/2 In., Pair	199.00
Mary Gregory, Lamp, Oil, Green Glass Oil Font, White Boy & Foliage, 8 In.	135.00
Mary Gregory, Lamp, Oil, White Enamel Girl & Scenery, Green, Opaque Blue, Pair	400.00
Mary Gregory, Mug, Boy, Honey Amber	87.00
Mary Gregory, Mug, Bulge Body, Applied Handle, Boy	120.00
Mary Gregory, Mug, Cranbbery, All White Boy & Foliage, Clear Applied Handle	75.00
Mary Gregory, Mug, Cranberry, Clear Applied Handle, 4 In.	65.00
Mary Gregory, Mug, Sapphire Blue, 3 3/4 In.	50.00
Mary Gregory, Mush Set, Child's, White Children, 2 Piece	78.00 To 85.00
Mary Gregory, Pitcher, Ale, 6 Pedestal Tumblers, Green, White Figures	425.00
Mary Gregory, Pitcher, Cranberry, 8 1/2 X 7 1/2 In.	75.00
Mary Gregory, Pitcher, Emerald Blue, Boy In White In Forest, 12 1/2 In.	118.00
Mary Gregory, Pitcher, Girl Chasing Butterfly, Dark Amber, 2 X 3 1/2 In.	125.00
Mary Gregory, Pitcher, Girl Picking Flowers, Hand-Painted, Blown, 11 1/2 In.	145.00
Mary Gregory, Pitcher, Miniature, Green	22.00
Mary Gregory, Pitcher, Tankard Shape, Blue Thumbprint, Ribbed Handle, Gold	165.00
Mary Gregory, Pitcher, Tankard, Emerald Blue, White Boy In Forest, 12 1/2 In.	118.00
Mary Gregory, Pitcher, Water, Boy Playing	85.00
Mary Gregory, Pitcher, Water, Cranberry	175.00
Mary Gregory, Pitcher, Water, Green	125.00
Mary Gregory, Pitcher, Water, Pink	135.00
Mary Gregory, Pitcher, Water, White Girl, Green	175.00
Mary Gregory, Rose Bowl, Clear, White Figure Of Little Girl	95.00
Mary Gregory, Rose Bowl, Emerald Green, All White Boy & Dove, 6 In.	150.00
Mary Gregory, Rose Bowl, Lime Green, Crimped Top, 5 In.	95.00

Mary Gregory, Rose Bowl, White On Amber, Scalloped Rim, 3 3/4 In. 115.00
Mary Gregory, Rose Bowl, Yellow, 2 1/4 X 2 1/4 In. 65.00
Mary Gregory, Sauce, Clear, Crimped Gold Edge, Tinted Girl's Face, 4 1/2 In. 65.00
Mary Gregory, Stein Lady, Maria Enzersdorf, Green Glass, Lid, Pewter, 5 In. 95.00
Mary Gregory, Sugar & Creamer, Tinted Girls, Covered Sugar 125.00
Mary Gregory, Tankard, Boy, Butterfly Net, Tinted Face, Sapphire Blue, 12 In. 250.00
Mary Gregory, Tree, Ring, Cobalt, Enameled Decoration 125.00
Mary Gregory, Tumbler, Amber, White Figures 35.00
Mary Gregory, Tumbler, Boy & Girl Facing, Paneled, 3 5/8 In., Pair 135.00
Mary Gregory, Tumbler, Boy & Girl, Blue, Pair 98.00
Mary Gregory, Tumbler, Cranberry, Inverted Thumbprint, Tinted Lady, 3 In. 85.00
Mary Gregory, Tumbler, Cranberry, White Girl Feeding Birds, 4 3/4 In. 85.00
Mary Gregory, Tumbler, Cranberry, 3 3/4 In. 35.00
Mary Gregory, Tumbler, Girl, Blue 43.00
Mary Gregory, Tumbler, Girl, Foliage, Gold Rim, Blue, White Enamel, 4 In. 75.00
Mary Gregory, Tumbler, Green, White Enamel Scene Of Boy, Gold Rim, 6 In. 70.00
Mary Gregory, Tumbler, Green, White Enameled Boy 28.00
Mary Gregory, Tumbler, Smoky Inverted Thumbprint, White Child 125.00
Mary Gregory, Vase, Amber, Girl & Foliage, Ruffled, 8 1/8 In. 80.00
Mary Gregory, Vase, Amethyst Glass, Angel Pursuing Butterfly, Bulbous, 3 In. 110.00
Mary Gregory, Vase, Black Amethyst, Girl, Boy With Horn, 11 In., Pair 265.00
Mary Gregory, Vase, Black Amethyst, 8 In. 65.00
Mary Gregory, Vase, Black Amethyst, 9 3/4 In. 150.00
Mary Gregory, Vase, Boy Shaking Apple Tree, Fluted, Gold Edge, Green, 7 In. 75.00
Mary Gregory, Vase, Boy With Horn, Ferns, Crimped Top, 12 1/2 X 4 1/2 In. 110.00
Mary Gregory, Vase, Bud, Figural, White, Boy & Girl, 4 3/4 In., Pair 168.00
Mary Gregory, Vase, Clear, Tinted Face, 7 1/2 In. 69.00
Mary Gregory, Vase, Clear, Trees, Girl Holding String Of Flowers, 5 In. 110.00
Mary Gregory, Vase, Cobalt, Clear Fluting, Little Girl In Meadow, 6 In. 125.00
Mary Gregory, Vase, Cobalt, White Enamel Floral, 9 1/2 In., Pair 150.00
Mary Gregory, Vase, Cobalt, White Girl, 10 1/2 In. 145.00
Mary Gregory, Vase, Crackle, Smokey, Boy With Bow & Arrow, 8 In. 45.00
Mary Gregory, Vase, Cranberry, Boy & Girl, Foliage, 8 1/2 X 4 In. 265.00
Mary Gregory, Vase, Cranberry, Gold Scrolling, White Figure, 14 In. .... 159.00 ←
Mary Gregory, Vase, Cranberry, White Enameled Boy, 6 7/8 X 3 3/8 In. 125.00
Mary Gregory, Vase, Cranberry, White Enameled Decoration, Square Shape, 3 In. 120.00
Mary Gregory, Vase, Cranberry, White Enameled Girl With Net, 7 1/2 In. 75.00
Mary Gregory, Vase, Cranberry, 6 3/4 In. 65.00
Mary Gregory, Vase, Girl Holding Flowers, 4 3/4 X 4 1/2 In. 65.00
Mary Gregory, Vase, Girl With Urn, Man Seated Drinking Water, Scalloped, Feet 210.00
Mary Gregory, Vase, Green, Boy With Horn, Ferns, 4 1/2 In. 110.00
Mary Gregory, Vase, Green, 12 In., Pair 225.00
Mary Gregory, Vase, Inverted Thumbprint, Amber, 5 1/2 In. 75.00
Mary Gregory, Vase, Lady, Lilies-Of-The-Valley, Ruffled, Green Satin Glass 135.00
Mary Gregory, Vase, Orange, Young Boy Carrying Flowers, 10 1/4 In. 125.00
Mary Gregory, Vase, Pink Spatter Cased In Clear, White Child Figure, 6 In. 115.00
Mary Gregory, Vase, Pink To White Frosted 65.00
Mary Gregory, Vase, Ribbed Inside, Subject Shooting Bow & Arrow, Green Rim 65.00
Mary Gregory, Vase, Rigaree Sides, Clear Glass, Tinted Face, 8 In. 79.00
Mary Gregory, Vase, Rigaree Sides, Green, 10 In. 75.00
Mary Gregory, Vase, Sapphire Blue, Girl & Foliage, Cylindrical, 9 5/8 In. 75.00
Mary Gregory, Vase, Sapphire Blue, Girl With Butterfly Net, Foliage, 9 In. 175.00
Mary Gregory, Vase, Stick, Amethyst, Crimped Top, 7 In. 95.00
Mary Gregory, Vase, White Boy & Trees, White, 5 X 4 3/4 In. 85.00
Mary Gregory, Vase, White Boy, Foliage, Green, 12 In. 60.00
Mary Gregory, Vase, White Girl & Foliage, Sapphire Blue, Handles, 11 In. 185.00
Mary Gregory, Vase, White Girl Holding Wreath, Trees, Snow, 5 X 4 3/4 In. 65.00
Mary Gregory, Water Set, Clear, White Enamel, 6 Tumblers, 3 Boys, 3 Girls 495.00
Mary Gregory, Water Set, Cranberry, Girl With Bird, Boy With Fish, 7 Piece 450.00
Mary Gregory, Wine, Amber, Girl, Tinted Face 35.00
Mary Gregory, Wine, Sapphire Blue, Girl, Tinted Face, Cone Shape 110.00
Mary Gregory, Wine, White Girl, Forget-Me-Not Spray, 5 1/4 In. 30.00

Masonic Shrine glassware was made from 1893 to 1917. It is occasionally
called Syrian Temple Shrine glassware. Most pieces are dated.

Masonic, Ashtray, Shrine Emblem, Metal, 6 1/4 In. 10.00
Masonic, Badge, Police Provost Guard, Murat 1941, Indianapolis 30.00
Masonic, Badge, Shrine Police, Harold Lloyd, Imperial Potentate 42.50
Masonic, Bowl, Triple Footed, Gold, 59 K.T.Pittsburgh Etched, 1898, 3 1/2 In. 55.00
Masonic, Champagne, Alligators & Bearded Man, 1910 .... 50.00
Masonic, Champagne, Louisville, Tobacco Leaf, 1909 .... 46.00 To 60.00
Masonic, Champagne, Man With Camera, 2 Buildings, 3 Swords Hold Bowl 145.00
Masonic, Champagne, Rochester, New York, 1911 .... 60.00 To 63.00
Masonic, Goblet, Syria Temple, Pittsburgh, 1899 .... 65.00
Masonic, Goblet, Washington, D.C., May, 1900 .... 42.00
Masonic, Match Holder, 1904 .... 20.00
Masonic, Mug, Syria Shrine & Niagara Falls, 1905, Enameled, 3 Handles 55.00
Masonic, Mug, Syria Temple, Atlantic City, 1904 .... 35.00 To 50.00
Masonic, Paper Clip, Figural, No.5263 .... 35.00
Masonic, Paperweight, Gold Crown With Red Cross Embossed, 1898 .... 55.00
Masonic, Penny, San Francisco, C.1910 .... 12.00
Masonic, Pin, Grand Lodge, South Dakota, 50 Year 20.00
Masonic, Pin, Past Master, Original Case, 1881 .... 85.00
Masonic, Pin, White Enamel On Crescent, 10K Gold 10.00
Masonic, Pin, 14K Gold, Past Master's, Rose Quartz Stone 150.00
Masonic, Plate, Lodge No.1234, China, 10 In. 10.00
Masonic, Plate, Man Driving Oxen, 64th Annual Conclave, 4 Emblems, C.1906 ...... 55.00
Masonic, Plate, Syria Shrine, May 1906, 6 In. 36.00
Masonic, Plate, York, Pa., 1904, Black & White 40.00
Masonic, Ring, Man's, 10 Karat Gold, Blue Stone, Square, Compass In Gold 37.00
Masonic, Sign, Bavaria, Black 18.00
Masonic, Trowel, Aluminum, Connecticut Lodge, C.1920 .... 12.50
Masonic, Tumbler, Man On Longhorn, Dallas, June 1898, 4 In. 70.00
Masonic, Tumbler, Woman In Tears, I Want To Be A Shriner, 1897 .... 85.00
Masonic, Vase, Paperweight Bottom, Symbols & Chicago, Dated 1892 .... 45.00
Masonic, Watch Fob, Medinah Temple, Chicago, 1907 .... 30.00
Masonic, Watch Fob, Shriner, Red Fez, Hands In Pockets, White Metal, 5 In. 12.00

*Massier pottery is iridescent French art pottery made by Clement
Massier in Golfe-Juane, France, in the late nineteenth and early
twentieth centuries. It is characterized by a metallic luster glaze.*
Massier, Vase, Clover, 2 Handles, Iridescent, 6 In. 145.00
    Match Holder, see also Iron, Match Holder, Store, Match Holder
Match Holder, Bisque, Old Man's Skull, Moving Lower Jaw, Japan 20.00
Match Holder, Black Boy Bust, Pottery, Bretby, England, 5 X 5 In. 22.00
Match Holder, Brass, Gott Mit Uns 15.00
Match Holder, China Dog In Man's Clothes, Brown Glaze, 4 1/2 In. 25.00
Match Holder, Cowboy Boots, Grand Rapids, Michigan, Bronze Metal 15.00
Match Holder, Crescent, Scratcher On Bottom, Tin, C.1870, 4 1/2 X 3 In. 8.50
Match Holder, Dog Dressed In Jacket, 2 1/2 X 4 In. 16.00
Match Holder, Eagle Emblem, Cast Iron 10.00
Match Holder, Embossed Deer, Metal, Pocket 10.50
Match Holder, Figural, Covered Well, Rope & Bucket, Lady Standing With Pail 125.00
Match Holder, Figural, Pig, Head Opens, Striker Tummy 15.00
Match Holder, Glass, Charlie Chaplin Standing By Barrel 35.00
Match Holder, Hanging, Brass, Double Pocket, 1883, 3 1/2 X 5 1/2 In. 17.00
Match Holder, Hanging, Clear Satchel 28.00
Match Holder, I'm Your Match, Silver Plate, Meriden, 2 1/2 In. 24.00
Match Holder, Judson Whiskey, Child Serving Father 20.00
Match Holder, Keg On Fence, Iron 20.00
Match Holder, Man On Chair, Smoke Comes From Mouth, Gilt, Metal, 6 In. 70.00
Match Holder, Olson's Electric Store, Tin 20.00
Match Holder, Red & Black, The Spot To Buy Oil, C.1900 .... 20.00
Match Holder, Strike On Back, Chef Holding Skillet, Blue & White, 3 3/4 In. 48.00
Match Holder, Table, 6 Footed, Slanted Sides, Cast Iron, 1 3/4 X 2 3/4 In. 29.50
Match Holder, The Spot To Buy Oil, C.1900 .... 20.00
Match Holder, Tin, Dockash Stove Factory, Scranton, Pa. 20.00
Match Holder, Tin, Hanging, Cresota Prize Bread Flour 37.00
Match Holder, Tole 19.00
    Match Safe, see also Silver, Sterling, Match Safe

Match Safe, Brass Skull, Jaw Opens, Striker Under Chin	135.00
Match Safe, Figural, Girl On Ledge	79.00
Match Safe, Figural, Pig Body	92.75
Match Safe, Figural, Stein Shape, Lady & Boy	73.00
Match Safe, Figural, W.C.Fields, Silver Plated Brass	190.00
Match Safe, Grant's Tomb On One Side, Brooklyn Bridge On Other	18.00
Match Safe, Hercules Powder, Celluloid Cover	35.00
Match Safe, High Button Shoe On Stand Shape, 4 X 5 1/2 In.	45.00
Match Safe, Pocket, Brass, Ornate Lettering	12.50
Match Safe, Pocket, Elephant On Cover	84.50
Match Safe, Pocket, Protruding Birds	43.00
Match Safe, Pocket, Tin, Striker On Bottom, 1 3/4 X 1 1/4 In.	7.50
Match Safe, Pottery, 2 Lovebirds	20.00
Match Safe, Raised Scrollwork Lid, Reclining Dog Finial, Iron, 3 1/4 In.	22.50
Match Safe, Silver Plate, Figural, Owl On Tree Branch, Meriden	115.00
Match Safe, Silver Plate, Man On Galloping Horse	21.00
Match Safe, Sterling Silver, Allegorical Figure	60.00
Match Safe, Sterling Silver, Raised Jester & Women	46.00
Match Safe, Wall, Twin Pocket, Embossed Star, C.1860	13.00

Matt Morgan opened an art pottery company in Cincinnati, Ohio, in 1883. It lasted in business for only a year, closing because of money problems.

Matt Morgan, Jug, Red, Gold Trim, Corn & Leaves, Handled, 7 In.	385.00

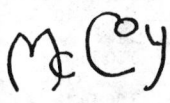

McCoy pottery is made in Roseville, Ohio. The J. W. McCoy Pottery was founded in 1899. It became the Brush McCoy Pottery Company in 1911. The name changed to the Brush Pottery in 1925. The Nelson McCoy Sanitary and Stoneware Company was founded in Roseville, Ohio, in 1910. This firm made art pottery after 1926. In 1933 it became the Nelson McCoy Pottery. Pieces marked McCoy were made by the Nelson McCoy Company.

McCoy, Bank, Seaman's Savings	8.00
McCoy, Basket, Green, Brown, Leaves, Raised Berries, High Handle, 10 X 9 In.	22.00
McCoy, Basket, Hanging, Chains	32.50
McCoy, Basket, Red Berries, 9 In.	15.00
McCoy, Basket, Tulip, 9 In.High	18.00
McCoy, Bucket, Ice	30.00
McCoy, Clock, Cuckoo, Wall Hanger, Brown, Green, Cream	18.00
McCoy, Cookie Jar, Apple, 1950-64	13.50 To 15.00
McCoy, Cookie Jar, Bananas, 1950-52	17.00 To 27.00
McCoy, Cookie Jar, Bear, No.22, White, 1943-45	21.00 To 32.00
McCoy, Cookie Jar, Black Circus Horse With Monkey On Back, 1962	50.00
McCoy, Cookie Jar, Chipmunk, 1959-62	30.00
McCoy, Cookie Jar, Clown Head, 1943-49	12.50 To 22.00
McCoy, Cookie Jar, Clown In Barrel, 1953-56	12.50
McCoy, Cookie Jar, Coal By Cat, 1967	15.00
McCoy, Cookie Jar, Coffee Grinder, 1961-64	12.50
McCoy, Cookie Jar, Coffee Mug, 1965	12.00 To 16.00
McCoy, Cookie Jar, Cook Stove, Black, 1963	15.00 To 17.00
McCoy, Cookie Jar, Cookie Cabin, 1957-60	20.00
McCoy, Cookie Jar, Country Stove, 1967	14.00
McCoy, Cookie Jar, Covered Wagon, 1959-62	24.00 To 32.00
McCoy, Cookie Jar, Dog On Basket Weave, 1956-57	12.50
McCoy, Cookie Jar, Drum, Red, 1959-60	12.00
McCoy, Cookie Jar, Dutch Boy, 1945	15.00
McCoy, Cookie Jar, Engine, 1963-64	20.00
McCoy, Cookie Jar, Freddy Gleep, 1974	9.00 To 12.00
McCoy, Cookie Jar, Hobby Horse, 1950	20.00 To 38.00
McCoy, Cookie Jar, Honey Bear, Tree, Green, Brown, 1953-55	10.00 To 25.00
McCoy, Cookie Jar, Indian Teepee, 1957-59	35.00
McCoy, Cookie Jar, Jack-O-Lantern, 1955	10.00
McCoy, Cookie Jar, Jug, 1967	17.00
McCoy, Cookie Jar, Kitten On Basket Weave, 1956-69	18.00
McCoy, Cookie Jar, Kookie Kettle, 1959-75	15.00
McCoy, Cookie Jar, Little Clown, 1945	24.00

McCoy, Cookie Jar, Lollipop, 9 In., 1958-60	18.00
McCoy, Cookie Jar, Mac Dog, 1967	17.00
McCoy, Cookie Jar, Mammy Cookies, 1948-57	12.50 To 30.00
McCoy, Cookie Jar, Mr. & Mrs. Owl, 1953-55, 10 3/4 In.	25.00 To 35.00
McCoy, Cookie Jar, Pears On Basket Weave, 1957	12.50
McCoy, Cookie Jar, Pineapple, 1955-57	12.00 To 18.00
McCoy, Cookie Jar, Rooster, 1955-57	17.00
McCoy, Cookie Jar, Sad Clown, 1970-71	12.50
McCoy, Cookie Jar, Snow Bear, 1965	25.00
McCoy, Cookie Jar, Touring Car, 1962-64	20.00
McCoy, Cookie Jar, Windmill, 1961	19.00
McCoy, Dish, Dog, To Man's Best Friend, His Dog, Brown, 1935	18.00
McCoy, Figurine, Wishing Well	4.00
McCoy, Figurine, Wishing Well, 1950	4.00
McCoy, Jardiniere, Brown Glaze, Pansies, 3 Feet, 5 X 6 1/2 In.	45.00
McCoy, Jardiniere, Pinecone, 6 1/2 In.	14.50
McCoy, Lamp, Cowboy Boots, Small, 1956	15.00
McCoy, Pitcher, Grape Pattern, Yellow	38.00
McCoy, Pitcher, Green, No Mark, 1953	8.00
McCoy, Pitcher, Yellow, Molded Grapes, 9 In.	22.50
McCoy, Pitcher, 100 Scotch Pipers	7.50
McCoy, Planter, Baby Buggy With Puppy, What About Me, 1955	6.00
McCoy, Planter, Bird, Green, Rectangular, 9 1/2 In.	8.00
McCoy, Planter, Birds In Nest, Green, 4 In., 1957	8.00
McCoy, Planter, Black Gondola With Pink Flowers, 1955	10.00
McCoy, Planter, Old Mill, 1953	9.00
McCoy, Planter, Pelican, Signed NM, 7 1/2 In., 1941	10.00
McCoy, Planter, Rooster, Gray, 1951	2.50
McCoy, Planter, Spinning Wheel, 1953	5.50 To 15.00
McCoy, Planter, Turtle, 1955	10.00
McCoy, Planter, Wishing Well, 1950	5.00 To 15.00
McCoy, Pot, Amish, Turquoise, Open	15.00
McCoy, Pot, Flower, Quilted, Leaves Circle Top & Drainer Base, Turquoise	6.50
McCoy, Punchbowl, Olympia, Brown Glaze, Tiger Lily, 13 X 13 X 6 In.	300.00
McCoy, Sugar & Creamer, Pinecone	10.00
McCoy, Tankard, Berries, 13 X 6 1/2 X 9 1/2 In.	225.00
McCoy, Tea Set, English Ivy, 3 Piece, 1950	30.00 To 35.00
McCoy, Tea Set, Pinecone, 3 Piece, 1946	15.00 To 27.00
McCoy, Turtle, Watering, 1950	14.00
McCoy, Vase, Apricot, Leaves & Berries Around Bottom, 7 In.	8.00
McCoy, Vase, Bird Of Paradise, Blue Handled, Hourglass Shape, 8 In.	5.00
McCoy, Vase, Butterfly, Green, 1956, 6 X 3 In.	6.00
McCoy, Vase, Glazed Yellow, Leaves Around Top, 8 1/2 In.	12.50
McCoy, Vase, Grapes, White, 14 In.	12.00
McCoy, Vase, Green, Handled, Ribbon Effect, 12 In.	15.00
McCoy, Vase, Green, 6 In.	6.00
McCoy, Vase, Loy-Nel, Brown, High Glaze, Blooming Irises, 9 In.	70.00
McCoy, Vase, Matte Green, Gold Vertical Bars On Front, 13 1/2 In.	18.00
McCoy, Vase, Pearly White, 9 In.	17.50
McCoy, Vase, Pink, Octagonal Applied Roses & Leaves, 6 In.	7.50
McCoy, Vase, Republican, 7 3/4 In.	14.00
McCoy, Vase, Rosewood, Embossed Florals On Chocolate Ground, 11 In.	95.00
McCoy, Vase, Standard Brown High Glaze, Jonquils, 9 1/2 In.	65.00 To 90.00
McCoy, Vase, Swan, Aqua, 1949, 9 1/2 In.	10.00
McCoy, Vase, Wheat Gold To Green, 8 In.	7.00
McCoy, Vase, White, Art Deco, Square, 9 1/4 In.	9.50
McCoy, Vase, White, Grapes & Leaves, 14 1/2 In.	16.00
McCoy, Vase, Yellow, Brown Branches & Leaves, 15 In.	32.00
McCoy, Wall Pocket, Bud, Single Lily, Hand-Painted, 1948, 8 In.	10.00
McCoy, Wall Pocket, Violin, 1957	9.00

The McKee name has been associated with various glass enterprises in the U.S. since 1836, including J. & F. McKee (1850), Bryce, McKee & Co. (1850-1854), McKee and Brothers (1865), and National Glass Co. (1899). In 1903 the McKee Glass Company was formed in Jeannette, Pennsylvania. It became McKee Division of the Thatcher Glass Co. in 1951, and was bought out by the Jeannette Corporation in 1961. Pressed glass, kitchenware, and tableware were produced.

McKee, Berry Bowl, Holly Berry Pattern, Custard, 11 In.	35.00
McKee, Bowl, Berry, Rainbow, Green, 9 1/4 In.	34.00
McKee, Bowl, Coach, Canary Color	98.00
McKee, Bowl, Figural, Coach, Amber	110.00
McKee, Bowl, Jade, Round, 10 1/2 In.	12.00
McKee, Candlestick, Double, Rock Crystal, Pair	16.50
McKee, Creamer, Laurel, French Ivory, Child's	12.00
McKee, Cup, Punch, Sunbeam	6.50
McKee, Dish, Lamb Cover, Milk Glass	50.00
McKee, Dish, Robin On Nest Cover, Vaseline, 4 1/2 In.	125.00
McKee, Dish, Turkey Cover, Split Rib Base	65.00
McKee, Glass, Bottoms Up, Opalescent Custard	25.00
McKee, Goblet, Rock Crystal, Red, 5 1/2 In.	25.00
McKee, Pitcher, Water, Snowflake & Sunburst	25.00
McKee, Punch Set, Custard, Cream & Black, 13 Piece	65.00
McKee, Punch Set, Sleigh Design, Custard, 7 Piece	45.00
McKee, Server, Cheese & Cracker, Red Crystal	65.00
McKee, Tom & Jerry Set, White, 13 Piece	23.50
McKee, Toothpick, Aztec, Marked Prescut	17.50
McKee, Tray, Pin, Milk Glass, Shape Of Entwined Leaves	18.50
McKee, Tumble-Up, Opalescent Green, Art Deco	32.00
McKee, Tumbler, Cobalt Blue, Gold Rim Gladiator	45.00
McKee, Tumbler, Custard, Signed	10.00
McKee, Tumbler, Gladiator, Cobalt Blue, Gold Rim	45.00
McKee, Tumbler, Whiskey, Bottoms Up, Art Deco, Green Opaque	29.00

Mechanical Bank, see Bank, Mechanical
Medicine, see Doctor

Meerschaum pipes and other carved pieces of meerschaum date from the nineteenth century to the present time.

Meerschaum, Cigar Holder, Carved Horse Design, Satin Lined Case	60.00
Meerschaum, Cigar Holder, Lady Of Evening Recling Top, Amber Stem, 3 1/2 In.	45.00
Meerschaum, Cigarette Holder, Carved, Owl On Branch	59.00
Meerschaum, Pipe, Antlered Deer, 14 1/2 In.	250.00
Meerschaum, Pipe, Art Nouveau Maiden, Case, 8 1/4 In. *Illus*	160.00
Meerschaum, Pipe, Boy, Old-Fashioned Costume, Holding Flower, Case	110.00
Meerschaum, Pipe, Cheroot, Acorn Cluster, Leather Case, 3 3/4 In *Illus*	60.00
Meerschaum, Pipe, Cheroot, Hunter And Dog, 4 3/4 In. *Illus*	80.00
Meerschaum, Pipe, Cheroot, Trumpet Form, Leather Case, 4 1/2 In. *Illus*	50.00
Meerschaum, Pipe, Cheroot, Winged Maiden, Leather Case, 5 1/2 In *Illus*	130.00
Meerschaum, Pipe, Devil, Leather Case, 4 In. *Illus*	160.00
Meerschaum, Pipe, Fu Man Chu	200.00
Meerschaum, Pipe, Hand Holds Ball, Leather Case, 4 3/4 In. *Illus*	70.00
Meerschaum, Pipe, Hand Holds Fruit, Amber Stem, Case, 3 3/4 In. *Illus*	70.00
Meerschaum, Pipe, Horse & Driver On Sulky, Leather Case, Amber Mouthpiece	115.00
Meerschaum, Pipe, Horse Head Bowl, Leather Case, 11 In. *Illus*	350.00
Meerschaum, Pipe, Horse Throwing Rider, Case, 9 In.	75.00
Meerschaum, Pipe, Horse With Driver On Racing Sulky, Amber Mouthpiece	115.00
Meerschaum, Pipe, Horse, Large	145.00
Meerschaum, Pipe, In Case, Nude Lady, Large	250.00
Meerschaum, Pipe, Man On Horse, Velvet Case, 14 X 10 In.	2500.00
Meerschaum, Pipe, Miniature, 2 Dogs Carved On Bowl, Case, 4 In.	65.00
Meerschaum, Pipe, Monk's Head, Amber Stem, Signed The Cloisters, 6 In.	35.00
Meerschaum, Pipe, Monkey Head, Glass Eyes, Open Mouth	150.00
Meerschaum, Pipe, Nude Lady, Arms Crossed Overhead, Flower-Shaped Bowl	225.00
Meerschaum, Pipe, Nude Maiden, 4 1/4 In. *Illus*	50.00
Meerschaum, Pipe, Ram Carved On Bowl, 24K Gold Rim, Leather Case	195.00
Meerschaum, Pipe, Smiling Monk, Case, 4 1/4 In. *Illus*	130.00
Meerschaum, Pipe, Smiling Monk, Leather Case, 3 In. *Illus*	100.00
Meerschaum, Pipe, Tiger's Head, Leather Case, 3 1/4 In. *Illus*	75.00
Meerschaum, Pipe, Turbaned Head Of Negro Woman, Amber Stem, Dated 1878, Case	62.00

Meerschaum, Pipe, Smiling Monk,
Leather Case, 3 In.

Meerschaum, Pipe, Smiling Monk,
Case, 4 1/4 In.

*(For All Descriptions,
See Page 313)*

Meerschaum, Pipe, Devil, Leather Case, 4 In.

Meerschaum, Pipe, Nude Maiden,
4 1/4 In.

Meerschaum, Pipe, Hand Holds Fruit,
Amber Stem, Case, 3 3/4 In.

Meerschaum, Pipe, Cheroot, Winged Maiden,
Leather Case, 5 1/2 In

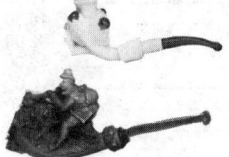

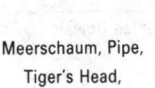

Meerschaum, Pipe, Art Nouveau
Maiden, Case, 8 1/4 In.

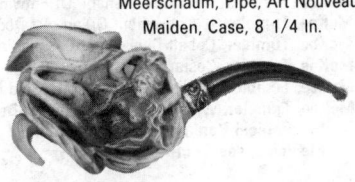

Meerschaum, Pipe,
Tiger's Head,
Leather Case, 3 1/4 In.

Meerschaum, Pipe, Cheroot,
Hunter And Dog, 4 3/4 In.

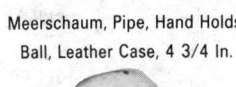

Meerschaum, Pipe,
Cheroot, Acorn Cluster,
Leather Case, 3 3/4 In

Meerschaum, Pipe, Hand Holds
Ball, Leather Case, 4 3/4 In.

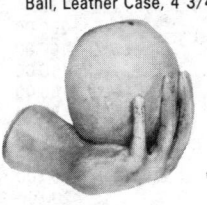

Meerschaum, Pipe, Horse Head Bowl,
Leather Case, 11 In.

Meerschaum, Pipe, Cheroot,
Trumpet Form, Leather Case, 4 1/2 In.

Meerschaum, Pipe, Two Dogs	110.00
Meerschaum, Pipe, White, Amberoid Stem	20.00

*Meissen is a town in Germany where porcelain has been made since 1710.
Any china made in that town can be called Meissen, although the famous
Meissen Factory made the finest porcelains of the area.*

Meissen, see also Dresden, Onion

Meissen, Basket, Handled, Applied Cherub & Lilacs, 7 X 4 In.	350.00
Meissen, Bottle, Scent, Silver Mount & Stopper, Hand-Painted Florals, 5 In.	250.00
Meissen, Bowl, Applied Floral, Rococo Border, Roses In Relief, C.1860, 12 In.	195.00
Meissen, Bowl, Birds Interior, Bees & Butter Exterior, Gold, Pedestal, 10 In.	195.00
Meissen, Bowl, Gilt Flowers, Leaves, Crossed Swords, 11 In.	115.00
Meissen, Bowl, Gold Luster & Pink, Roses Inside, 1845, 14 In.	225.00
Meissen, Bowl, Pink & Gold Interior, Long X Swords Mark, C.1848, 14 In.	219.00
Meissen, Box, Jewelry, Round, Crossed Swords Mark	20.00

Meissen, Box, Life Of Christ Scenes, Gilt-Metal Mounts, Cover, 19th Century	900.00
Meissen, Box, Patch, Allover Floral Decoration, 3 In.	150.00
Meissen, Butter, Covered, With Drainer, Blue Onion, Rose Finial	75.00
Meissen, Candelabra, 5-Branch, Angelica Kauffmann Type, 19 1/4 In., Pair	750.00
Meissen, Candelabra, 5-Branch, Figurines, Pair	1000.00
Meissen, Candlestick, Wheat Sheaf Pattern, Gilt Border, Baroque Form, Pair	2800.00
Meissen, Centerpiece, French Blue Ground, Gold, Flowers, Louis XVI	650.00
Meissen, Charger, Cobalt, Gold Trim Floral, Crossed Swords Mark, 11 In.	250.00
Meissen, Charger, Flower Decoration, Gold Leaf Border On White, 11 3/4 In.	115.00
Meissen, Compote, Gold & White Leaves, Berries, Crossed Sword, 5 In.	140.00
Meissen, Compote, Gold Edge, Floral, Butterflies & Insects, 6 3/4 X 8 1/2 In.	225.00
Meissen, Compote, Grape & Leaves, Sword Mark, 10 X 7 In.	195.00
Meissen, Compote, White, Gold Relief Floral, Crossed Swords Mark, 7 X 10 In.	175.00
Meissen, Cup & Saucer, Cobalt Blue, Romantic Couple, Bouquet Of Flowers, Mark	100.00
Meissen, Cup & Saucer, Demitasse, Colorful Bouquets, Crossed Swords Mark	22.00
Meissen, Cup & Saucer, Demitasse, Green, White	35.00
Meissen, Cup & Saucer, Demitasse, Pink, White	35.00
Meissen, Cup & Saucer, Gilt Wavy Rims, Vine Handles, Florals, 1815-60	50.00
Meissen, Cup & Saucer, Landscape, Figural Vignettes, Maroon & Gold Scrolls	75.00
Meissen, Dish, Cobalt Blue, Butterfly, Gold, Shallow, C.1924	24.00
Meissen, Dish, Honey, Crossed Swords	87.00
Meissen, Dish, Serving, Two-Tier, Figures Of Boys, White Glaze, 15 In., Pair	795.00
Meissen, Figurine, Begger Woman Playing Mandolin, Child, Crossed Sword, 4 In.	385.00
Meissen, Figurine, Bird On Tree Trunk, Crossed Swords Mark, Life Size	155.00
Meissen, Figurine, Boston Bull Dog, Crossed Swords Mark, 6 In.	335.00
Meissen, Figurine, Boy With Rake, Crossed Swords Under Glaze, 5 1/2 In.	225.00
Meissen, Figurine, Boy, Flower Basket, Blue Loin Cloth, Crossed Swords Mark	285.00
Meissen, Figurine, Cherub Cavalier With Walking Stick, 3 1/2 In.	125.00
Meissen, Figurine, Dog, Crossed Swords Mark, 5 1/2 In.	200.00
Meissen, Figurine, Eros, Inscribed In Pink Panel Je Les Enflamme, 5 1/4 In.	525.00
Meissen, Figurine, Gardener With Spade & Flower Bouquet, 5 1/4 In.	350.00
Meissen, Figurine, Gardener, Blue Crossed Swords, Dated 1710-1910	225.00
Meissen, Figurine, Gentleman Leaning On Walking Stick, Sword At Side, 7 In.	380.00
Meissen, Figurine, Goat, White, Bearded, Crossed Swords Mark, 5 3/4 In.	160.00
Meissen, Figurine, Hunting Dog In Tracking Position, 2 X 4 1/4 In.	125.00
Meissen, Figurine, Lady Relaxing At The Ball, Late 16th Century, 8 In.	375.00
Meissen, Figurine, Little Girl, Green Decorated Dress, Feeding Dog, 5 In.	325.00
Meissen, Figurine, Parrot, Crossed Swords Mark, 19th Century, 3 1/4 X 4 In.	175.00
Meissen, Figurine, Pug, Green Collar, Crossed Swords Mark, 6 In.	335.00
Meissen, Figurine, Scene Of Smell, 18th Century, 10 1/2 In.	290.00
Meissen, Figurine, Sheep Dog, Green Collar, Crossed Swords, 5 X 5 In.	225.00
Meissen, Figurine, Shepherd Boy, 7 1/2 In.	275.00
Meissen, Figurine, Short-Haired Hunting Dog In Tracking Position, 2 X 4 In.	135.00
Meissen, Figurine, Sitting Pug, Green Collar, Crossed Swords Mark, 6 1/2 In.	335.00
Meissen, Figurine, White Colt, Playful Position, 4 1/2 X 7 In.	55.00
Meissen, Handle, Umbrella, Cobalt Blue, 2 Medallions Of Flowers, Gold	75.00
Meissen, Knife, Dinner, Pistol Handled, Crossed Swords Mark	20.00
Meissen, Match Holder, Wall, Blue & White, Beehive Shape, Brass Base	60.00
Meissen, Pitcher, White, Entwined Dragon, Sterling Silver Lip, Bulbous, 6 In.	50.00
Meissen, Plate, Floral Bouquets, Gold Border, Blue Cross, Swords, 8 1/2 In.	25.00
Meissen, Plate, Florals & Courting Scenes In Quatrefoil Design, 8 In.	175.00
Meissen, Plate, Florals & Shore Scenes, Crossed Swords Mark, 7 In.	95.00
Meissen, Plate, Garden Scene With 2 Seated Figures, 9 In.	250.00
Meissen, Plate, Hand-Painted Maidens & Castle, Reticulated Rim, 10 In.	125.00
Meissen, Plate, Lattice Border, Medallions, Blue Flowers, Gold, Marked, 11 In.	85.00
Meissen, Plate, Leaf, Blue, Cobalt & Gold Leaves, Beading, 9 1/2 In.	125.00
Meissen, Plate, Pierced Edge, Latticework, Floral, 6 In., Set Of 8	200.00
Meissen, Plate, Pink & White, 9 1/2 In., Set Of 8	30.00
Meissen, Plate, White, Floral Medallions, Gold Outlined, Crossed Swords	85.00
Meissen, Plate, White, Floral, Crossed Swords Mark, 5 1/4 In.	95.00
Meissen, Platter, Embossed Florals, Gold Rim, Hand-Painted, C.1870, 15 In.	350.00
Meissen, Platter, Flowers In Fuchsia, Floral Border, Gold Rim, Marked, 19 In.	375.00
Meissen, Platter, Oval, Scattered Florals, Gold Trim, C.1860, 18 3/4 In.	350.00
Meissen, Sauceboat, Kakiemon, C.1740, 9 1/2 In. *Illus*	1400.00
Meissen, Statue, The Engagement, Ring Presented To Maiden, Crossed Swords	2000.00

Meissen, Sauceboat, Kakiemon, C.1740, 9 1/2 In.
(See Page 315)

Meissen, Swan, Crossed Swords, 6 In.	175.00
Meissen, Tea Caddy, Hand-Painted Floral Design	95.00
Meissen, Teapot, 4 Decorated Panels, 7 1/2 X 7 In.	175.00
Meissen, Tureen, Covered, Handles & Finial, Early 19th Century, 10 1/2 In.	228.00
Meissen, Urn, Pate-Sur-Pate Panels, Converted To Lamps, C.1880, 16 In., Pair	1750.00
Meissen, Vase, Cabinet, Hand-Painted Floral, Underglaze, Marked, 3 1/2 In.	30.00
Meissen, Vase, Gold Trim, Old Mark, 9 1/2 In.	190.00
Meissen, Vase, Orange Dragon Decoration, Flared, Gilt, Crossed Swords Mark	95.00
Meissen, Vase, White, Orange Dragon, Gilt Borders, Blue Crossed Swords, 5 In.	95.00

Mercury, or silvered, glass was first made in the 1850s. It lost favor for a while but became popular again about 1910. It looks like a piece of silver.

Mercury Glass, Bowl, 5 1/2 X 2 1/2 In.	35.00
Mercury Glass, Candlestick, 8 In.	15.00
Mercury Glass, Figurine, Birds, German, 5 In.	20.00
Mercury Glass, Figurine, Reindeer, German, 5 In.	15.00
Mercury Glass, Goblet, Grape Leaf, 5 3/4 In.	40.00
Mercury Glass, Goblet, 16-Panel Top, Birds, Berries, Leaves, Gold Washed	47.50
Mercury Glass, Lamp, White Flowers, Gold, 9 In., Pair	42.00
Mercury Glass, Vase, Bird Decoration, 8 In., Pair	55.00
Mercury Glass, Vase, Enamel Crane & Water Elements, Pair, 9 In.	35.00
Mercury Glass, Vase, Palm Tree Design, 9 1/2 In.	25.00
Mercury Glass, Vase, White Ferns, 4 In., Diameter	35.00
Mercury Glass, Vase, White Painted Stork, Tree & Grass, Pedestal, 10 In.	30.00
Metal, Bookends, Nudes In Flowing Draperies, Bronze Tints, Green, 7 In., Pair	35.00

Mettlach, Germany, is a city where the Villeroy and Boch factories worked. Steins from the firm are known as Mettlach steins. They date from about 1842. PUG means painted under glaze.

Mettlach, Beaker, No.1110, 1/4 Liter	65.00
Mettlach, Beaker, No.2327/1023, Man Playing Violin	45.00
Mettlach, Beaker, No.2327, 1/4 Liter, Girl Carrying Platter & Pitcher	55.00
Mettlach, Beaker, No.2327, 1/4 Liter, Minstrel Playing Flute	55.00
Mettlach, Beaker, No.2327, 1/4 Liter, Minstrel Playing Violin	55.00 To 80.00
Mettlach, Bowl, Punch.No.3037, Lid & Coaster	425.00
Mettlach, Chamber Pot, Ivory With Gold Rim	65.00
Mettlach, Charger, Spread-Winged Eagle Medallion, C.1880, 27 In.	700.00
Mettlach, Mug, No.1526, 1/4 Liter, Villeroy & Boch, Tan, 84/95 Mark	25.00
Mettlach, Mug, No.1526, 4/10 Liter	35.00
Mettlach, Mug, No.3095, Drink Hire's Root Beer, Boy Holding Mug	85.00
Mettlach, Pitcher, Cameo, Golf Players, 4 1/2 In.	110.00
Mettlach, Pitcher, Cupid, Tan & Silver Trim, 10 In.	75.00
Mettlach, Pitcher, Melon Shape, 3 Pewter Bands, Rivets, Green, Marked, 10 In.	89.50
Mettlach, Pitcher, No.1028, 3 Liter	275.00
Mettlach, Pitcher, No.2332-1031	350.00
Mettlach, Planter, No.2987, Terra Cotta & Green On White, Etched, 5 X 14 In.	150.00
Mettlach, Plaque, Cameo, Castlemark, 1809, Artist Signed, 18 In.	2480.00
Mettlach, Plaque, City Of Rothenburg, Green Mercury Mark, 12 1/2 In.	125.00
Mettlach, Plaque, Deer In Forest, Signed, 7 X 12 In.	250.00
Mettlach, Plaque, No.1025, 8 1/2 In.	125.00
Mettlach, Plaque, No.1044/dec.196, Stolxerfels, PUG, 12 In.	145.00
Mettlach, Plaque, No.1044/304, Seashore Scene, Mother & Children, 13 1/2 In.	200.00
Mettlach, Plaque, No.1044, Burghaus Kurbisch, 14 In.	165.00
Mettlach, Plaque, No.1044, Norwegian Fjord Scene, Ship, Boats, 13 1/2 In.	165.00
Mettlach, Plaque, No.1044, The Student Prince, 17 1/2 In.	495.00

Mettlach, Plaque, No.1048, Etched Castle, Horseman, King, & Ladies, 16 In.	750.00
Mettlach, Plaque, No.2195, Etched Castle On River	725.00
Mettlach, Plaque, No.2288, Etched, Quideness, 17 In.	725.00
Mettlach, Plaque, No.2361, Etched Castle Scene	550.00
Mettlach, Plaque, No.2621, Engraved Picture Of Boy Pouring, Marked, 7 1/2 In.	120.00
Mettlach, Plaque, No.2626, Cavalier Drinking Beer, Frintz Quidenus, 7 3/4 In.	139.00
Mettlach, Plaque, No.2875, Cameo, Two Women And Man, 18 In.	750.00
Mettlach, Plaque, No.3161, Medieval Soldiers Drinking On Cannon, 17 1/2 In.	875.00
Mettlach, Plaque, No.3165, Viking In Armor, Sword, Shield, Holding Maiden, Etch	875.00
Mettlach, Plaque, No.3181, Elks & Deer In Forest, 12 In.	125.00
Mettlach, Plaque, No.7036, Cameo, Harvest Scene, 17 1/2 In.	750.00
Mettlach, Plaque, No.7040, Cameo, 3 Mythological Figures Dancing, White, Green	1350.00
Mettlach, Stein, No.285, Coat Of Arms, Pewter Lid, 1/2 Liter	175.00
Mettlach, Stein, No.675, 1/2 Liter, Pewter Lid, Gray & Brown, Barrel Shape	185.00
Mettlach, Stein, No.812, 1 Liter, Hunting Scene, Signed	375.00
Mettlach, Stein, No.1028, Pouring, Raised Paste	395.00
Mettlach, Stein, No.1132, Egyptian Design, Pewter Lid, 1/2 Liter	390.00
Mettlach, Stein, No.1180, 1/2 Liter	235.00
Mettlach, Stein, No.1266, 1/4 Liter	200.00
Mettlach, Stein, No.1476, 1/2 Liter, Inlaid Lid	400.00
Mettlach, Stein, No.1526/1145, Embossed Woman, Pewter Cover, PUG, 1/2 Liter	165.00
Mettlach, Stein, No.1526, Coat Of Arms, K.Willmann Heidelberg, 1/2 Liter	175.00
Mettlach, Stein, No.1526, 3 Liter, PUG, Falstaff	400.00
Mettlach, Stein, No.1527, Liter, Etched	625.00
Mettlach, Stein, No.1527, 1/2 Liter, Etched	450.00
Mettlach, Stein, No.1638, Heidleberg, Etched	425.00
Mettlach, Stein, No.1641, Cavalier Smoking Pipe, Tapestry Style, 1/2 Liter	275.00
Mettlach, Stein, No.1734, 2 Liter	795.00
Mettlach, Stein, No.1739, 3 Liter	495.00
Mettlach, Stein, No.1740, Relief Molded, Pewter Lid, 1/4 Liter	165.00
Mettlach, Stein, No.1741, 1/2 Liter, Engraved	500.00
Mettlach, Stein, No.1786, St.Florian & The Dragon, 1 Liter	695.00
Mettlach, Stein, No.1786, 1/2 Liter	600.00
Mettlach, Stein, No.1794, 1/2 Liter, Etched	440.00
Mettlach, Stein, No.1809, 1/2 Liter	495.00
Mettlach, Stein, No.1909, Raised Paste, PUG	155.00
Mettlach, Stein, No.1932, 1/2 Liter, 2 Cavaliers Drinking, C.Warth	450.00
Mettlach, Stein, No.1959, 1/2 Liter, Etched	350.00
Mettlach, Stein, No.1997, Ehret 1866-91, Founder, Ruppert Brewery, 1/2 Liter	285.00
Mettlach, Stein, No.2001, Doctor's Books	550.00
Mettlach, Stein, No.2001, Lawyer's Books, Inlaid Lid, 1/2 Liter	370.00
Mettlach, Stein, No.2001K, Banker Book Stein	425.00

Mettlach, Stein, No.2038, 4 Liter, Black Forest

Mettlach, Stein, No.2025, 1/2 Liter, Etched	425.00
Mettlach, Stein, No.2035, 3/10 Liter	280.00
Mettlach, Stein, No.2038, 4 Liter, Black Forest *Illus*	3600.00
Mettlach, Stein, No.2057, 3/10 Liter, Inlaid Pewter Lid, Etch Of Revelers	275.00
Mettlach, Stein, No.2057, 1/2 Liter, Etched, Dancing Figures, Red Terra Cotta	285.00
Mettlach, Stein, No.2057, 3/10 Liter	250.00
Mettlach, Stein, No.2089, Inlaid Lid, Etched, Signed H.Schlitt	450.00
Mettlach, Stein, No.2089, 1/2 Liter, Angel Hands Stein To Man At Table	595.00
Mettlach, Stein, No.2090, 1/2 Liter, Husband Seated, Drinking, Cards, Dice	525.00
Mettlach, Stein, No.2097, Etched	500.00
Mettlach, Stein, No.2131, Knave With Violin, Girl, Man Dancing, Blue, 1/2 Liter	325.00

Mettlach, Stein, No.2182, Bowling, Relief, Castle Mark, 1/2 Liter 275.00
Mettlach, Stein, No.2182, 1/2 Liter, Relief, Pewter Lid 265.00
Mettlach, Stein, No.2183/953, 3 Liter, PUG, Bulbous, Dwarfs 495.00
Mettlach, Stein, No.2183, Chalet & Mountains, 2 1/2 Liter 425.00
Mettlach, Stein, No.2184/0996, 1/2 Liter, Dwarfs, PUG 225.00
Mettlach, Stein, No.2190, 1/2 Liter, Etched, Bicycles 650.00
Mettlach, Stein, No.2233, 1/2 Liter, Decorated Relief 250.00
Mettlach, Stein, No.2235, 1/2 Liter, Etched, Inlaid Lid .... 450.00 To 525.00
Mettlach, Stein, No.2249, 3/10 Liter, 3 Figures, Gray & Tan Relief 165.00
Mettlach, Stein, No.2271-955, 1/2 Liter 150.00
Mettlach, Stein, No.2311, Incised Nouveau Grains Pattern, 1/2 Liter 325.00
Mettlach, Stein, No.2350, 1 Liter, Cameo, Boar Hunting Scene, Signed Stahl 750.00
Mettlach, Stein, No.2382, Etched Thirsty Rider, 1/2 Liter .... 600.00 To 695.00
Mettlach, Stein, No.2388, 3 Liter, Cameo, Figures In Forest 1350.00
Mettlach, Stein, No.2520, Etched, Liter 575.00
Mettlach, Stein, No.2531, Etched Pewter Lid, Quidenus, 1/2 Liter 425.00
Mettlach, Stein, No.2580, 1/2 Liter, Knight In Armor, Castle, Signed Schlitt 800.00
Mettlach, Stein, No.2632, 1/2 Liter, Etched Bowling Scene .... 435.00 To 450.00
Mettlach, Stein, No.2635, Bicycle, Etched, Inlaid Lid, 1/2 Liter 625.00
Mettlach, Stein, No.2702, Art Nouveau, 1/2 Liter 340.00
Mettlach, Stein, No.2798, 1/2 Liter, Etched Bust Of Wagner, Opera Characters 475.00
Mettlach, Stein, No.2802, 1/2 Liter, Etched Art Nouveau Barley Swirls 245.00
Mettlach, Stein, No.2813, 1/2 Liter, Etched Inlay Lid 385.00
Mettlach, Stein, No.2829, 3 Liter 500.00
Mettlach, Stein, No.2892, Art Nouveau, 1/2 Liter 250.00
Mettlach, Stein, No.2958, 3 Liter, Etched 875.00
Mettlach, Stein, No.3070, Cameo Man With Stein & Monkey, 1/2 Liter 235.00
Mettlach, Stein, No.3087, Woman Holding Beer Stein, 1/2 Liter 375.00
Mettlach, Stein, No.3220, 1/2 Liter 400.00
Mettlach, Stein, Thristy Knight, No.2482, 1/2 Liter 500.00
Mettlach, Stein, Villeroy & Boch, 1/2 Liter 165.00
Mettlach, Teapot, No.2946, Art Nouveau, Castle Mark 165.00
Mettlach, Tile, Deer Resting In Woods, Wooden Frame, Signed, 13 X 7 In. 250.00
Mettlach, Toothpick, Honey Brown, Matte Blue, Beaded, High Gloss, 2 In. 10.00
Mettlach, Tumbler, No.428, 1/4 Liter 45.00
Mettlach, Tumbler, No.1167, 1/4 Liter 45.00
Mettlach, Tumbler, No.1191, 1/4 Liter 45.00
Mettlach, Tumbler, No.2327, Winged Mercury Stamp .... 45.00 To 60.00
Mettlach, Tumbler, No.2378, 1/4 Liter, Tan, Drinking Scene, 5 In. 75.00
Mettlach, Urn, Handle, Twisted Hissing Asps, Brown, Colored Fruit, 12 In. 400.00
Mettlach, Urn, No.362, Coral, Turquoise Jewels, 15 In. 295.00
Mettlach, Vase, Art Nouveau, Blue, Brown, Beige, Castle Mark VB, 14 1/2 In. 175.00
Mettlach, Vase, Blue & White, Impressed Castle Marks, 14 In. 108.00
Mettlach, Vase, Faenza, Beige Oak Leaves, Berries, Grapes, Fish, Magenta, Green 160.00
Mettlach, Vase, No.2915, Deep Blue & Ivory, Castle Mark, 14 In., Pair 550.00
Mettlach, Vase, Peasant Girl, Beading, Cylindrical, Castle Marked, 13 1/2 In. 850.00
Mickey Mouse, see Disneyana, Mickey Mouse

*Milk glass was named for its milky white color. It was first made in
England during the 1700s. The height of its popularity in the United
States was from 1870 to 1880. It is now correct to refer to some colored
glass as blue milk glass, black milk glass, etc. The letter B before the
numbers xx refers to the book "Milk Glass" by E. Belknap.*

Milk Glass, see also Cambridge, Cosmos

Milk Glass, Basket, Hobnail, Pink Interior, Amber Thorn Handle, 6 In. 135.00
Milk Glass, Bell, Liberty, Centennial, Shell Handled, 11 1/4 In. 275.00
Milk Glass, Bell, Smoke, Ruffled Edges, Blown, Hanging Loop, C.1880, 6 3/4 In. 20.00
Milk Glass, Bottle, Barber, Tonic, White, Floral Designs, Matching Stopper 68.00
Milk Glass, Bottle, Blown, Flint, Pontil, Marked Rum, 11 In. 20.00
Milk Glass, Bottle, Bulbous, Glossy, 9 1/2 In. 22.00
Milk Glass, Bottle, Cologne, Actress, Stopper, 11 In. 40.00
Milk Glass, Bottle, Figural, Kummel Bear 75.00
Milk Glass, Bottle, Figural, Sitting Bear 110.00
Milk Glass, Bottle, Green, Ivory Flowers, Atomizer Bulb, Round, 3 In. 45.00
Milk Glass, Bottle, Perfume, Swirl, Fenton 15.00

Milk Glass, Bottle, Pinch, Green Opaque	35.00
Milk Glass, Bottle, Raised Leaves On Base, Leaf Clustered Stopper, Pair	100.00
Milk Glass, Bowl & Mug, Davy Crockett, White With Red	10.00
Milk Glass, Bowl, Acanthus Leaves, Footed, 7 1/2 In.	10.00
Milk Glass, Bowl, Apple Blossom, Low Lattice, 9 In.	48.00
Milk Glass, Bowl, Covered, Tree Of Life, Blue	110.00
Milk Glass, Bowl, Embossed Daisy, Scalloped Edge, 8 X 4 1/2 In.	65.00
Milk Glass, Bowl, Forget-Me-Not Edge	3.50
Milk Glass, Bowl, Hobnail Exterior, Fluted & Crimped Edges, 4 1/2 In.	50.00
Milk Glass, Bowl, Lacy Edge, Crimped Edge, Square	38.00
Milk Glass, Bowl, Lacy Edge, 8 X 4 In.	40.00
Milk Glass, Bowl, Lacy Rim, 7 In.	30.00
Milk Glass, Bowl, Painted, Round Lacy Edge, Blue & Pink Daisies In Panels	85.00
Milk Glass, Bowl, Scroll & Eye, Blue, 7 In.	22.00
Milk Glass, Bowl, Square, Lacy Edge, Crimped, Square	38.00
Milk Glass, Bowl, White, Rock Crystal Design, 9 1/2 In.	15.00
Milk Glass, Box, Blue, Gold Floral & Scroll, Curved, Covered, 5 In.	22.00
Milk Glass, Box, Dresser, Scallops & Scrolls, Square, Covered, 5 In.	20.00
Milk Glass, Box, Dresser, Scroll Variant, Covered, 2 1/2 X 4 In.	15.00
Milk Glass, Box, Globe, White, 10 In.	26.00
Milk Glass, Box, Handkerchief, Marked Handkerchief	55.00
Milk Glass, Box, Plume In Gold, Pink Rose On Cover, Heart Shape, 3 1/4 In.	28.00
Milk Glass, Box, Powder, Flower On Top, 4 In.	4.50
Milk Glass, Box, Powder, Raised Pattern, Souvenir Sedan, Kansas, 5 In.	18.50
Milk Glass, Box, Powder, Yellow, Portrait In Raised Scroll On Lid, 5 In.	45.00
Milk Glass, Box, Raised Plume, Gold, Purple, Covered, 5 1/2 X 3 3/4 In.	30.00
Milk Glass, Box, Salt, Wooden Top	38.00
Milk Glass, Bread Platter, Diamond Grill	45.00
Milk Glass, Bucket, Ice, Black, Gold Rim, Enameled Flowers	34.00
Milk Glass, Butter, Beaded Swirl, Oval, Covered	25.00
Milk Glass, Butter, Blackberry, Covered	30.00
Milk Glass, Butter, Daisy, Covered	70.00
Milk Glass, Butter, Milled Edge Blackberry, Covered	35.00
Milk Glass, Butter, Sawtooth, Acorn Finial, Covered	85.00
Milk Glass, Butter, Scrolls, Green, Covered	110.00
Milk Glass, Butter, Square, Daisy & Button, Covered	115.00
Milk Glass, Cake Stand, Flowers	25.00
Milk Glass, Cake Stand, Ribbed Stem, 9 In.	25.00
Milk Glass, Cake Stand, Seaweed, Pink, Fenton	50.00
Milk Glass, Candleholder, Black	18.00
Milk Glass, Candlestick, Crucifix	12.00
Milk Glass, Candlestick, Crucifix, Off-White, Pair	35.00
Milk Glass, Candlestick, Mt.Vernon, Pair	35.00
Milk Glass, Candlestick, White With Blue Decoration, Pair	25.00
Milk Glass, Celery, Sawtooth, Short	20.00
Milk Glass, Coaster Set, Bridge, Heart And Club, Floral, Pair	12.00
Milk Glass, Compote, Atlas, Scalloped Edge, 7 3/4 X 7 3/4 In.	75.00
Milk Glass, Compote, Blue, Lacy Border, Daisy Center, Basket Weave Pedestal	125.00
Milk Glass, Compote, Dolphin, Shell Shape, 9 In.	25.00
Milk Glass, Compote, Hercules, Scalloped	88.00
Milk Glass, Compote, Jenny Lind, 8 X 7 1/2 In.	85.00
Milk Glass, Compote, Jewel Medallion, 6 In.	35.00
Milk Glass, Compote, Lattice, Basket Weave Stem, Blue, 7 In.	75.00
Milk Glass, Compote, Pedestaled Hobnail, Fluted & Crimped, Blue, 5 1/2 In.	50.00
Milk Glass, Compote, Rose & Thistle, Impressed Lion Rampant, England, 7 In.	26.00
Milk Glass, Compote, Sawtooth, 6 1/2 X 4 1/2 In.	22.50
Milk Glass, Compote, Scroll, Chartreuse, 6 Sided, 8 X 8 In.	175.00
Milk Glass, Compote, Scroll, Tall	60.00
Milk Glass, Compote, Strawberry, Covered	65.00
Milk Glass, Condiment Set, Forget-Me-Not, Miniature	55.00
Milk Glass, Condiment Set, Grapes, 3 Piece	55.00
Milk Glass, Condiment Set, White, English Hobnail, 4 Piece	35.00
Milk Glass, Cookie Jar, Hobnail, 1930s	10.00
Milk Glass, Creamer, Blackberry	20.00 To 80.00
Milk Glass, Creamer, Blue, Two Fruits, Lid, Chain Handle, Pedestal Base	15.00

Milk Glass, Creamer, Ceres	16.50
Milk Glass, Creamer, Child's, Alternating Blocks & Bars, Blue, 3 In.	23.00
Milk Glass, Creamer, Cornucopia Cover, White	30.00
Milk Glass, Creamer, Figural, Owl, Child's, Eyes	30.00 To 45.00
Milk Glass, Creamer, Flute & Crown, Lid, Paper Label	18.00
Milk Glass, Creamer, Green & White Marbleized	50.00
Milk Glass, Creamer, Melon, Leaf & Net, C.1878	20.00 To 45.00
Milk Glass, Creamer, Paneled Wheat	25.00
Milk Glass, Creamer, Rose & Thistle, English	22.00
Milk Glass, Creamer, Rose & Thistle, Impressed Lion Rampant, England	22.00
Milk Glass, Creamer, Sawtooth	20.00
Milk Glass, Creamer, Sawtooth, Pedestal Foot	39.00
Milk Glass, Creamer, Scalloped Rimmed Cover Turns To Become Sugar	35.00
Milk Glass, Creamer, Swan	65.00
Milk Glass, Creamer, Swimming Swan, Atterbury	45.00 To 50.00
Milk Glass, Cruet, Emerald Green, Empress, Stopper	150.00
Milk Glass, Cup & Saucer, Candlewick, Set Of 3	12.50
Milk Glass, Cup, Punch, Blue, Miniature	40.00
Milk Glass, Cup, Punch, Wild Rose, Miniature	18.00
Milk Glass, Cuspidor, Lady's, 6 Sided, Opalescent, 7 X 4 In.	56.00
Milk Glass, Decanter, Floral Decoration, Gold, Stopper, 10 1/2 In.	20.00
Milk Glass, Decanter, Grape Pattern, Stopper, Marked Italy, 14 In.	50.00
Milk Glass, Dish, American Hen Cover, 6 In.	65.00
Milk Glass, Dish, Battleship Maine Cover	45.00
Milk Glass, Dish, Boar's Head Cover, Atterbury, Dated 5/29/88	750.00
Milk Glass, Dish, Boat Cover	55.00
Milk Glass, Dish, Bonbon, Black, 2 Footed	10.00
Milk Glass, Dish, Butter, Little Lamb, Pinafores	100.00
Milk Glass, Dish, Camel Cover, White, 5 1/2 X 6 In.	115.00 To 125.00
Milk Glass, Dish, Cat Cover, Original Eyes	47.00
Milk Glass, Dish, Cat Head Cover, Ribbed Base, Blue, White, 5 1/2 In.	42.00
Milk Glass, Dish, Cat On Basket Cover, Dark Blue, White Head, 5 In.	75.00
Milk Glass, Dish, Cat On Drum Cover	35.00
Milk Glass, Dish, Chick & Eggs Cover, 1889	110.00
Milk Glass, Dish, Chick In Egg Cover, On Sleigh Base	55.00
Milk Glass, Dish, Chicks Cover, Basket Base, 3 X 4 1/4 In.	35.00
Milk Glass, Dish, Chicks Hatching From Eggs Cover, Basket Weave Base, 3 In.	45.00
Milk Glass, Dish, Clown Playing Banjo Cover, Pink Frosted	45.00
Milk Glass, Dish, Dewey Cover, Tile Base	45.00
Milk Glass, Dish, Dog Cover, Blue, White, Oval, 5 X 4 1/2 In.	45.00
Milk Glass, Dish, Dog Cover, Ribbed Base	45.00
Milk Glass, Dish, Dog Cover, White Head & Forelegs, Ribbed Base, Blue, 6 In.	65.00
Milk Glass, Dish, Duck Cover, Atterbury, Dated, 11 In.	162.50
Milk Glass, Dish, Eagle On Nest With 3 Chicks, Blue, 7 In. *Illus*	75.00
Milk Glass, Dish, Fish Cover, Fishtail Base, 8 1/2 X 4 3/4 X 3 In.	135.00
Milk Glass, Dish, Fish On Bottom, C.June 4, 1872, 9 1/2 X 6 1/8 In.	50.00
Milk Glass, Dish, Fish On Skiff Cover	35.00
Milk Glass, Dish, Hand & Dove Cover, White	58.00 To 110.00
Milk Glass, Dish, Hen Cover, Atterbury, Dated 1889	150.00
Milk Glass, Dish, Hen Cover, Basket Weave Base	40.00
Milk Glass, Dish, Hen Cover, Basket Weave Base, Blue	45.00
Milk Glass, Dish, Hen Cover, Basket Weave Nest, Brown Glass Eyes, 8 In.	85.00
Milk Glass, Dish, Hen Cover, Black, White Head	125.00
Milk Glass, Dish, Hen Cover, Black, 7 In.	65.00

Milk Glass, Dish, Eagle On Nest With 3 Chicks, Blue, 7 In.

Milk Glass, Dish, Hen Cover, Blue Head	28.00
Milk Glass, Dish, Hen Cover, Dark Blue	36.00
Milk Glass, Dish, Hen Cover, Nest Base, Black, 7 In.	65.00
Milk Glass, Dish, Hen Cover, Nest Base, Flecks Of Royal Blue, 7 1/2 In.	150.00
Milk Glass, Dish, Hen Cover, White, Lacy Nest, 7 In.	90.00
Milk Glass, Dish, Hen Cover, 5 In.	20.00
Milk Glass, Dish, Hen Cover, 6 In.	8.50
Milk Glass, Dish, Hen Cover, 7 In.	20.00
Milk Glass, Dish, Honey, Individual, Leaf Design, Flint	15.00
Milk Glass, Dish, Mother Eagle Cover, Westmoreland, C.1920	55.00
Milk Glass, Dish, Mule-Eared Rabbit Cover, Picket Fence Base, Gilding, 6 In.	20.00
Milk Glass, Dish, Oval, Blackberry, 8 1/2 X 5 1/4 In.	30.00
Milk Glass, Dish, Owl Cover, Blue, 5 In.	12.00
Milk Glass, Dish, Pink, Frosted, Clown Playing Banjo, Covered	45.00
Milk Glass, Dish, Rabbit Cover, Atterbury, 9 In.	145.00
Milk Glass, Dish, Rabbit Cover, Basket Weave Base, 4 3/4 In.	25.00
Milk Glass, Dish, Rabbit Cover, Nest With Eggs Base, Opalescent, 4 1/2 In.	40.00
Milk Glass, Dish, Rabbit Cover, Picket Fence Base, Traces Of Gilding	35.00
Milk Glass, Dish, Rabbit Cover, Red Eyes, Atterbury, 6 1/2 In.	110.00
Milk Glass, Dish, Robin On Nest Cover, Greentown	165.00
Milk Glass, Dish, Rooster Cover, On Nest, Blue, White Head	30.00
Milk Glass, Dish, Rooster Cover, Red Comb, Yellow Beak, 8 1/2 In.	75.00
Milk Glass, Dish, Santa In Sleigh Cover	65.00
Milk Glass, Dish, Swan Cover, Blue, 5 In.	12.00
Milk Glass, Dish, Swan Cover, Closed Neck	65.00
Milk Glass, Dish, Swan Cover, 5 In.	50.00
Milk Glass, Dish, Turtle Cover	90.00
Milk Glass, Dish, Uncle Sam On Battleship Cover, White	45.00 To 50.00
Milk Glass, Dresser Set, Floral, Embossed Ladies Heads, 3 Piece, Bottle, Tray	100.00
Milk Glass, Dresser Set, Hobnail, Pair Of Colognes, Covered Box	45.00
Milk Glass, Easter Egg, Gilt Cross, Flowers, Blown, 3 1/2 In.	9.00
Milk Glass, Egg, Blown, Pontil, Large	6.00
Milk Glass, Egg, Easter, Chick, 3 1/4 In.	8.50
Milk Glass, Egg, Easter, Floral, Easter Anthem Inscribed, 6 X 4 In.	42.50
Milk Glass, Egg, Goose, Blown	10.00
Milk Glass, Eggcup, Birch Leaf	24.00
Milk Glass, Eggnog Set, Red & Green, Jingle Bells, 7 Piece	14.00
Milk Glass, Epergne, Blue, Embossed Scrolling, 2 Piece, 14 In.	85.00
Milk Glass, Epergne, Blue, Victorian, Signed Portieux, 14 X 10 In.	89.00
Milk Glass, Figurine, Baby Bootie, Lemon Spatter	50.00
Milk Glass, Figurine, Bulldog, Seated, Gold Beaded, Rhinestone Eye, 2 1/2 In.	40.00
Milk Glass, Figurine, Dog Head, Blue, Ribbed Base	42.00
Milk Glass, Figurine, Elephant, Jade, Teak Stand, 3 1/2 X 4 In.	50.00
Milk Glass, Figurine, Frowning Cat On Rib Base	14.00
Milk Glass, Figurine, Pekingese Dog	200.00
Milk Glass, Goblet, Blackberry	27.00
Milk Glass, Goblet, Strawberry	25.00
Milk Glass, Guttate, Sugar Shaker, Pink, Glossy, Cased	120.00
Milk Glass, Guttate, Syrup, Pink, Glossy, Cased	145.00
Milk Glass, Guttate, Vase, Celery, Pink, Cased	85.00
Milk Glass, Hair Receiver, Thistle, Signed M	23.50
Milk Glass, Hamper, Car Cover, Greentown, 5 In.	385.00
Milk Glass, Hat, 2 In.	5.00
Milk Glass, Inkwell, Snail, Ornate Engraved Iron Disk, May 14, 1878	60.00
Milk Glass, Jar, Biscuit, Blue Flowers, Silver Lid, Handle	65.00
Milk Glass, Jar, Cracker, Covered, Coreopsis	110.00
Milk Glass, Jar, Owl, Tall	100.00
Milk Glass, Jar, Tobacco, Beaded Swirl, Scalloped Top, 4 1/2 In.	35.00
Milk Glass, Jug, Syrup, Beads, Arabesque Type Decoration Both Sides, 5 In.	24.00
Milk Glass, Jug, Syrup, Tree Of Life	40.00
Milk Glass, Kerosene Lamp, Scrolled Footed Metal Base, Font	55.00
Milk Glass, Lamp, see Lamp, Milk Glass	
Milk Glass, Lamp, Maltese Cross, C.1894, Miniature	150.00
Milk Glass, Lamp, Miniature, Roses, Chimney, 7 1/4 In.	95.00
Milk Glass, Lamp, Oil, Miniature, Painted, Cream, Pink, Gold, Scrolling, Floral	130.00

Milk Glass, Match Holder, English Hobnail, Hat	15.00
Milk Glass, Match Holder, Figural, Baby Mine, Frosted Elephant	45.00
Milk Glass, Match Holder, Hat, English Hobnail	10.00
Milk Glass, Match Holder, Paneled Rib	16.00
Milk Glass, Match Holder, Pretty Maid, Frosted & Clear	45.00
Milk Glass, Match Holder, Swan & Cattails	15.00 To 20.00
Milk Glass, Muffineer, Moss Rose, Hand-Painted, Eagle Glass & Mfg. Co.	55.00
Milk Glass, Mug, Blown, Applied Handle, Hand-Painted	20.00
Milk Glass, Mug, Child's, Beads In Relief, Blue, 1 3/4 In.	25.00
Milk Glass, Mug, Child's, Hobnail, 2 1/2 In.	15.00
Milk Glass, Mug, English, Raised Thistles, Shamrocks, Roses, Oak Leaves, 4 In.	32.50
Milk Glass, Mug, Gothic Arches & Roses	25.00
Milk Glass, Mug, Serenade, Greentown	27.50
Milk Glass, Mustard Pot, Blue, Swirled Body & Lid, Scallop Top	22.00
Milk Glass, Mustard, Bull's Head, Blue	200.00
Milk Glass, Mustard, Swan Cover	40.00
Milk Glass, Mustard, 3 Bears On Mountains In Relief, Westmoreland, Cover	135.00
Milk Glass, Napkin Ring, Raised Scroll Pattern, Beaded Edges	25.00
Milk Glass, Pepper, Raised Flowers, Swirling Leaves, Opalescent, 6 In.	18.00
Milk Glass, Pitcher, Bethlehem Star, 4 Glasses	27.50
Milk Glass, Pitcher, Blue Applied Handle, Fenton, 3 1/2 In.	12.00
Milk Glass, Pitcher, Cream, Figural, Swan	50.00
Milk Glass, Pitcher, Owl, Glass Eyes, 4 In.	40.00
Milk Glass, Pitcher, Syrup, Blue, Flower & Leaf, Original Top, 7 In.	32.00
Milk Glass, Pitcher, Water, Grape, Imperial	45.00
Milk Glass, Plate, Anchor & Yacht, 7 1/2 In.	15.00 To 18.00
Milk Glass, Plate, Angel Head Border, White, 9 In.	22.50
Milk Glass, Plate, Apple Blossom, Lattice Edge, 11 In.	40.00
Milk Glass, Plate, Arch Border, Blue, 10 In.	20.00
Milk Glass, Plate, Backward C, 9 In.	10.00
Milk Glass, Plate, Battleship Maine	25.00
Milk Glass, Plate, Black, H-Border	18.00
Milk Glass, Plate, Black, Pinwheel, 8 1/4 In.	12.00
Milk Glass, Plate, Black, Swirled Edge, Anchor & Floral, 8 1/4 In.	12.50
Milk Glass, Plate, Black, 6 3/4 In., Set Of 8	50.00
Milk Glass, Plate, Blue, Lattice Edge, 10 1/2 In.	65.00
Milk Glass, Plate, Blue, Peg Border, 9 In.	50.00
Milk Glass, Plate, Blue, Pinwheel Edge, 8 1/2 In.	50.00
Milk Glass, Plate, Bread, Give Us This Day	48.00
Milk Glass, Plate, Cake, Pink, Beaded Edge, 5 In.	13.00
Milk Glass, Plate, Cane, Apple Green	20.00
Milk Glass, Plate, Chartreuse Green, Basket Weave, 8 1/2 In.	50.00
Milk Glass, Plate, Columbus, 10 In.	35.00 To 40.00
Milk Glass, Plate, Cutout Eagles & Fleur-De-Lis Border, 1903, 7 In.	38.00
Milk Glass, Plate, Dark Blue, Angel Head, 9 In.	50.00
Milk Glass, Plate, Eagle & Flag, Dated 9-8-08	18.00
Milk Glass, Plate, Eagles & Flags, Dated 1903	18.00
Milk Glass, Plate, Eagles, Fleur-De-Lis	15.00
Milk Glass, Plate, Easter Chicks, Embossed, Original Paint	28.00
Milk Glass, Plate, Fish On Skiff	35.00
Milk Glass, Plate, Fleur-De-Lis, Open Edge, 7 In.	15.00
Milk Glass, Plate, Forget-Me-Not Border, 8 1/2 In.	12.50
Milk Glass, Plate, Gothic Border, Black, 7 1/2 In.	14.00
Milk Glass, Plate, Gothic, Black, 8 1/4 In.	12.00
Milk Glass, Plate, Hare & Clover Leaf	30.00
Milk Glass, Plate, Horseshoe Anchor, Painted Scene, Dec.10, 1901, 8 In.	52.00
Milk Glass, Plate, Indian Head	22.50
Milk Glass, Plate, Keyhole Border, Black, 9 1/4 In.	20.00
Milk Glass, Plate, Lacy Edge, 8 In.	12.00 To 15.00
Milk Glass, Plate, Lacy Open Edge, 7 In.	15.00
Milk Glass, Plate, Lattice Edge, Flower Center, Apple Blossoms, 10 1/2 In.	65.00
Milk Glass, Plate, Open Gothic, Open Edge, 8 In.	20.00
Milk Glass, Plate, Open Heart Border, 7 In.	12.00
Milk Glass, Plate, Owl Lovers, 7 1/2 In.	35.00
Milk Glass, Plate, Pinwheel Edge, Painted Flower Center, White, 10 1/2 In.	65.00

Milk Glass, Plate, Reticulated, 7 In.Diameter

Milk Glass, Plate, Rabbit	37.00
Milk Glass, Plate, Rabbit & Horseshoe	23.00
Milk Glass, Plate, Rabbit Chariot	28.00
Milk Glass, Plate, Reticulated, 7 In.Diameter .... *Illus*	12.00
Milk Glass, Plate, Retriever, White	70.00
Milk Glass, Plate, Rooster And Hen, No Easter Without Us	28.00
Milk Glass, Plate, Serenade, 6 In.	45.00
Milk Glass, Plate, Square, Black, 9 In.	15.00
Milk Glass, Plate, Stars & Stripes, Patented September 8, 1903, 7 1/2 In.	30.00
Milk Glass, Plate, Sunken Rabbit, 7 1/2 In.	35.00
Milk Glass, Plate, Three Bears, Reading, Smoking, 7 In.	28.00
Milk Glass, Plate, Three Kittens, Open Edge, Gilding, 7 In.	12.00
Milk Glass, Plate, Three Kittens, Open Edge, Gilding, 8 In.	15.00 To 20.00
Milk Glass, Plate, Triple Forget-Me-Not, Black, 8 1/4 In.	12.00
Milk Glass, Plate, Triple Forget-Me-Not, 8 1/2 In.	9.00
Milk Glass, Plate, Trumpet Vine, Lattice Edge, 11 In.	40.00
Milk Glass, Plate, Trumpet Vine, 9 Piece	30.00
Milk Glass, Plate, U.S.Battleship Maine	15.00
Milk Glass, Plate, Washington, Star Border	45.00 To 50.00
Milk Glass, Plate, Wicket Border, Black, 8 1/4 In.	12.00
Milk Glass, Plate, Wicket, 7 1/4 In.	12.50
Milk Glass, Plate, Woof Woof	35.00
Milk Glass, Plate, 2 Owls & Parrot, 7 1/2 In.	20.00
Milk Glass, Punch Bowl, Nursery Rhymes, Blue, Miniature	225.00
Milk Glass, Relish, Fish, Dated 1872	30.00
Milk Glass, Rolling Pin, Blown, Painted Scenes, For My Sister, C.1850	50.00
Milk Glass, Rolling Pin, Wooden Handles, Patented Imperial, Ohio	35.00
Milk Glass, Rolling Pin, Wooden Handles, 18 In.	30.00
Milk Glass, Rose Bowl, Pink Roses, Embossed Leaf Design	15.00
Milk Glass, Salt & Pepper, Beehive, C.1888	38.00
Milk Glass, Salt & Pepper, Billiken	150.00 To 200.00
Milk Glass, Salt & Pepper, Heart, White	29.00
Milk Glass, Salt & Pepper, Pansy, Bud, Scrolling, Design On 4 Panels, Pair	35.00
Milk Glass, Salt & Pepper, Pink Sunset	48.00
Milk Glass, Salt & Pepper, Refrigerator	12.00
Milk Glass, Salt & Pepper, Swirl & Bulge	12.00
Milk Glass, Salt, Blue Bulging Petal	17.00
Milk Glass, Salt, Blue Overlapping Shell	22.00
Milk Glass, Salt, Coat Of Mail	16.00
Milk Glass, Salt, Double Cord & Tassel, Blue	25.00
Milk Glass, Salt, Green Bulging Petal	20.00
Milk Glass, Salt, Master, Milled Edge Blackberry	15.00
Milk Glass, Salt, Rose Relief	17.00
Milk Glass, Salt, Sunset, Blue, Dithridge, 1894	15.00
Milk Glass, Salt, Swirl With Floral	7.00

The letter P before the numbers xx refers to the books
"333 Glass Saltshakers" and "Glass Saltshakers, 1, 000 Patterns" by
Arthur Peterson.

Milk Glass, Saltshaker, Blue Scroll & Net	19.00
Milk Glass, Saltshaker, Blue, Green Vine Border	23.00
Milk Glass, Saltshaker, Challinors No.20, Pair	26.00
Milk Glass, Saltshaker, Corn With Husk	37.50
Milk Glass, Saltshaker, Embossed Rabbits	19.50

Milk Glass, Saltshaker, Flower Assortment, Green Opaque	32.50
Milk Glass, Saltshaker, Hand-Painted Flowers, 4 In.	15.00
Milk Glass, Saltshaker, Opalescent Reverse Swirls	15.00
Milk Glass, Saltshaker, Overlapping Leaf, Blue	20.00
Milk Glass, Saltshaker, Pineapple, Blue	24.00
Milk Glass, Saltshaker, Pink Sunset	24.00
Milk Glass, Saltshaker, Scrolls, Diamonds, Green	14.00
Milk Glass, Saltshaker, Thistle & Leaves, Gold	25.00
Milk Glass, Sauce, Blackberry	9.00
Milk Glass, Sauce, Cherry, White	15.00
Milk Glass, Shaker, End-Of-Day, Pink & White On Clear	45.00
Milk Glass, Shoe, Blue	6.50
Milk Glass, Sleigh, Embossed Scrolls & Dots, 9 In.	35.00
Milk Glass, Spooner, Blackberry	20.00 To 37.50
Milk Glass, Spooner, Block & Fan	20.00
Milk Glass, Spooner, Cameo	25.00 To 65.00
Milk Glass, Spooner, Lacy Edge	15.00
Milk Glass, Spooner, Milled Edge Blackberry	25.00
Milk Glass, Spooner, Paneled Wheat, Scalloped Top	30.00
Milk Glass, Spooner, Shell Pattern	20.00
Milk Glass, Spooner, Stork, Blue	10.00
Milk Glass, Spooner, Versailles, Pink	24.00
Milk Glass, Stand, Banana, Openwork Around Edge & Base, 8 In.	55.00
Milk Glass, Stein, Knights, With Lid, Greentown	25.00
Milk Glass, Stein, Monk, Tan Portrait, 2 1/2 In.	18.00
Milk Glass, Sugar & Creamer, Blackberry Pattern	175.00
Milk Glass, Sugar & Creamer, Cherry And Grape, Numbered	25.00
Milk Glass, Sugar & Creamer, Cherry, Blue	20.00
Milk Glass, Sugar & Creamer, Cherry, White	24.00
Milk Glass, Sugar & Creamer, Crown	30.00
Milk Glass, Sugar & Creamer, Paneled Forget-Me-Nots, Both Crown Finial, Lid	60.00
Milk Glass, Sugar & Creamer, Twelve Panel	15.00 To 20.00
Milk Glass, Sugar Shaker, Atterbury Marble	20.00
Milk Glass, Sugar Shaker, Beaded Swirl, Ribbed	30.00
Milk Glass, Sugar Shaker, Floral Decoration	15.00
Milk Glass, Sugar Shaker, Forget-Me-Not, Pink	48.00
Milk Glass, Sugar Shaker, Hand-Painted Trumpet Flowers	26.00
Milk Glass, Sugar Shaker, Melligo	30.00 To 35.00
Milk Glass, Sugar Shaker, Royal Oak	55.00
Milk Glass, Sugar, Acorn, Open, Green Top	35.00
Milk Glass, Sugar, Blackberry, Covered	36.00
Milk Glass, Sugar, Cat-On-Hamper Cover, White, Greentown, 5 In.	345.00
Milk Glass, Sugar, Grape & Cherry, Cover	20.00
Milk Glass, Sugar, Milled Edge Blackberry, Covered	35.00
Milk Glass, Swan, Opalescent, Marked Meisenthal, 4 In.	10.00
Milk Glass, Syrup, Blue, Original Top, 7 In.	32.00
Milk Glass, Syrup, Bulge Bottom, Yellow Flower, Pansy	70.00
Milk Glass, Syrup, Catherine Ann	33.00
Milk Glass, Syrup, Catherine Ann, Gold	74.50
Milk Glass, Syrup, Enameled Blue & Pink, Cherries, Metal Top, 7 In.	25.00
Milk Glass, Syrup, Fishnet & Poppy, Colored Floral Base	148.00 To 195.00
Milk Glass, Syrup, French Primrose	25.00
Milk Glass, Syrup, Hand-Painted Floral, Applied Handle, Tin Top, 1887, 5 In.	30.00
Milk Glass, Syrup, Marked PresCut, Top Dated 1867	25.00
Milk Glass, Syrup, Tree Of Life, Metal Top, Blue	65.00
Milk Glass, Table Set, Basket Weave, Dated, Atterbury, 4 Piece	135.00
Milk Glass, Table Set, Tomato Pattern, Sugar, Creamer, Salt, Pepper, 4 Piece	36.00
Milk Glass, Table Set, Versailles, 4 Piece	225.00
Milk Glass, Tankard, Scroll, Jade Green, 11 1/2 In.	125.00
Milk Glass, Tankard, Scroll, White, 11 1/2 In.	100.00
Milk Glass, Toothpick, Blue, Horizontal Ribs	28.00
Milk Glass, Toothpick, Button Arches	20.00
Milk Glass, Toothpick, Good Luck, Clover	27.50
Milk Glass, Toothpick, Ribbed, Pastel Blue To Cream, Posies All Around	20.00
Milk Glass, Toothpick, Square, Ribbed, 4 Feet, 2 3/8 In.	10.00

Milk Glass, Toothpick, Tramp Shoe, White	15.00
Milk Glass, Top Hat, Pointed Hobnail, Band Of Milling Around Brim	16.50
Milk Glass, Top Hat, 2 1/2 In.	4.50
Milk Glass, Tray, Bread, Basket Weave	45.00
Milk Glass, Tray, Bread, Diamond Grill	25.00
Milk Glass, Tray, Pin, Heart Shaped, 5 X 4 In.	7.50
Milk Glass, Tray, Pin, Star Shape, Gilt, 5 1/2 In.	10.00
Milk Glass, Tray, Spoke-Like Wheel Decoration, Easter Greetings, Ornate Edge	25.00
Milk Glass, Tumbler, Louisiana Exposition, Numbered	15.00
Milk Glass, Tumbler, Scroll, Blue	37.50
Milk Glass, Tumbler, Scroll, Blue, 3 3/4 In.	35.00
Milk Glass, Tumbler, Scroll, White, 3 3/4 In.	25.00
Milk Glass, Tumbler, Single Rose	23.50
Milk Glass, Vase, Black, Urn Shape, 8 In.	18.00
Milk Glass, Vase, Bulbous, Gold Enameled Flowers & Beading, Miniature	35.00
Milk Glass, Vase, Flower, Irregular Fluted Edge, 10 In.Across, 3 1/2 In.High	18.00
Milk Glass, Vase, Frog Pulling Large Seashell, Lily Pad Base	45.00
Milk Glass, Vase, Hand Holding Flared, Scalloped Top, 6 1/2 In.	17.50
Milk Glass, Vase, Hand-Painted Flowers, Longmont, Colorado, Ribbed Base, 4 In.	10.00
Milk Glass, Vase, Hand, Blue, Victorian, 8 1/2 In.	39.00
Milk Glass, Vase, Hansel & Gretel	125.00
Milk Glass, Vase, Lithographed Stag Decoration, Opaque, 4 In.	22.00
Milk Glass, Vase, Poppy, 8 In.	35.00
Milk Glass, Vase, Scalloped Top, Rose, 4 In.	32.50
Milk Glass, Vase, Top Hat, Stars & Stripes, 4 In.	19.50
Milk Glass, Wine, Paneled Scroll	18.00

Millefiori means many flowers. It is a type of glasswork popular in paperweights. Many small flowerlike pieces of glass are grouped together to form a design.

Millefiori, see also Paperweight

Millefiori, Epergne, 3 Lilies In Bowl, Dated 1860	500.00
Millefiori, Lamp, Ball Shade, Nymphet Dancer, Marble Base	225.00
Millefiori, Paperweight, Green, 2 1/2 In.	25.00
Millefiori, Pitcher, Applied Handle, 2 3/4 In.	90.00
Millefiori, Vase, Blue, 6 In.	45.00
Millefiori, Vase, Green, Brown, White, 2 Handled, 7 In.	100.00
Millefiori, Vase, White, Green, & Yellow Paperweight Pastry Canes, 5 1/4 In.	80.00
Millefiori, Vase, 2-Handled, Green Background, 5 1/2 In.	90.00

Minton china has been made in the Staffordshire region of England from 1793 to the present. Many marks have been used; the one shown dates from c.1873 to 1911.

Minton, Bowl, Cabbage Leaf, Green & Ivory, 9 1/2 In.	95.00
Minton, Bowl, Underplate, Flower Sprigs, Diamond Date Mark, 3 X 5 1/2 In.	40.00
Minton, Bust, Prince Albert, Parian, Marked, 12 In.	175.00
Minton, Cup & Saucer, Demitasse, Floral Garland, Blue Border, 19th Century	22.00
Minton, Cup & Saucer, Pate-Sur-Pate, Four Panels, Signed	395.00
Minton, Dish, Salad, Blue & White, Marked, 9 In.	39.00
Minton, Dish, Sardine, Majolica, 1868, 8 1/4 X 7 1/4 In.	65.00
Minton, Dish, Steamer, Floral Scroll, Beading, Dated 1928, 8 1/2 In.	32.00
Minton, Dish, 3-Compartment, Handle, Impressed Mark, Clover Shape, 12 In.	55.00
Minton, Jar, Biscuit, Blue Willow, Silver Handle And Lid	150.00
Minton, Pitcher, Majolica, Left And Right Hand, Pair	75.00
Minton, Pitcher, White With Gold, Metal Pouring Lip, 6 In.	45.00
Minton, Plate, Basket Weave & Ribbon Rim, 9 In.	35.00
Minton, Plate, Castle Scene, 9 In.	75.00
Minton, Plate, Ganges Pattern, C.1881, Set Of 8	97.50
Minton, Plate, Scalloped, Turquoise Jeweled Center, Made For Tiffany, Pair	30.00
Minton, Plate, Tree Of Life, Impressed Marks, 8 In.	15.00
Minton, Platter, Black & White, Portrait Center, 1886, Holland, 15 1/2 In.	40.00
Minton, Platter, Chinese Key, 1867, Round, 12 In.	30.00
Minton, Platter, Dutch Boy & Girl, C.1875, 13 In.	30.00
Minton, Tea Set, Cobalt, Sepia, Gilt, C.1810, 23 Piece	550.00
Minton, Tea Set, Molded Parian, 1850, 6 Piece	250.00

Minton, Tile, Art Nouveau, Green & Cream, Pair	19.00
Minton, Tile, Bird On Tree Branch, Flowers, Grass, 1871, Square, 6 In.	20.00
Minton, Tile, Bird Roosting On Tree, Flowery Field, 1871, Mark, 6 In.	20.00
Minton, Tile, Black On White, Taming Of The Shrew, 6 X 6 In.	22.00
Minton, Tile, Blue & White, Oriental Vases, 1882, 6 In., Pair	30.00
Minton, Tile, Hollins, Blue & White, Girl Rowing Boat, Oriental Design	12.00
Minton, Tile, Victorian Girl Picking Flowers, 6 In.	20.00
Minton, Tray, Cheese, White, Footed, 15 In.Diameter	48.00
Minton, Tureen, Vegetable, Chinese Key, 1867, Oval, Covered, 10 In.	50.00
Minton, Vase, Majolica, Green, Gray, Blue, Tan Handles, 7 In., Pair	75.00
Minton, Vase, Pink & Green, Abstract Leaf Design, Art Nouveau, 6 In.	45.00
Minton, Vase, Pink, Beige, Gold Flowers, C.1875, 9 3/4 In.	195.00
Minton, Vase, Porcelain, Cinnabar, White Flower & Flying Insects, 7 1/4 In.	165.00
Minton, Vase, Turquoise, Apple Green Ribbon, Prunus Tree, Double Pillow Shape	125.00
Mirror, see Furniture, Mirror	

Mocha ware is an English-made product that was sold in America during the early 1800s. It is a heavy pottery with pale coffee and cream coloring. Designs of blue, brown, green, orange, or black or white were added to the pottery.

Mocha, Bowl, Blue & Tan, Earthworm Pattern Band, 6 1/2 In.	135.00
Mocha, Bowl, Blue Seaweed, 9 1/2 In.	85.00
Mocha, Bowl, Brown, Blue, 6 1/4 In. *Illus*	250.00
Mocha, Bowl, Earthworm Design, Brown, Orange, Tan, Creamware, 3 1/2 X 6 3/4 In.	175.00

Mocha, Bowl, Brown, Blue, 6 1/4 In.   Mocha, Bowl, Scroddled Brown,
Cream, Blue, 19th Century, 6 1/4 In.

Mocha, Bowl, Earthworm, Bands, Blue, Gray, White, 7 In.	85.00
Mocha, Bowl, Scroddled Brown, Cream, Blue, 19th Century, 6 1/4 In. *Illus*	225.00
Mocha, Bowl, Yellow Wear, Green Seaweed Pattern Above Top Band, 14 3/4 In.	200.00
Mocha, Jug, Feathering Seaplants, Green Striping, Tan, Blue, 5 In.	120.00
Mocha, Jug, Ocher Color, Seaplant Decoration, 5 X 1 1/4 In.	135.00
Mocha, Mug, Blue Stripe On Yellow, Sanded Exterior, 2 In.	35.00
Mocha, Mug, Dark Beige Band, Black Seaplant Designs, Blue & Black Stripes	95.00
Mocha, Mug, Earthworm, Bands, Yellow, Black, 3 1/2 In.	95.00
Mocha, Mug, Three Cream Bands	35.00
Mocha, Pitcher, Mug, Smoky Seaplants, Tan Band, Blue & Black Striping, 7 In.	145.00
Mocha, Pot, Chamber, Blue Seaweed Decoration, Yellowware, 5 1/2 X 9 In.	75.00
Mocha, Pot, Mustard, Brown, Amber, Powder Blue, 2 X 3 1/4 In.	65.00
Mocha, Salt, Pedestal, Blue & Black Bands	25.00
Mocha, Salt, Standing, Amber, Brown, 1 3/4 X 3 In.	40.00
Mocha, Sugar, Seaweed, Bands, Yellow, Black, Lid	125.00
Mocha, White Slip Band With Blue Seaplant Designs, Yellow Ware Body, 12 In.	110.00
Mold, Candle, see Kitchen, Mold, Candle; Tin, Mold, Candle	
Mold, Bullet, see Weapon, Mold, Bullet	
Mold, Ice Cream, see Pewter, Mold, Ice Cream	
Monart, Bowl, Green Swirls, Gold Flecks, Air Bubbles, Flared Top, 7 X 2 In.	45.00
Monart, Bowl, Orange & Brown, Scottish Cluthra, 2 1/4 X 4 5/8 In.	58.00
Monart, Vase, Green, Amber, Blue, Goldstone, 12 1/2 In.	125.00
Monart, Vase, Mottled Green, Brown, Yellow, & Blue, 9 1/2 X 7 In.	85.00
Mont Joye, see Mt.Joye	
Montieres, Vase, Art Nouveau, Luster On Luster, Enameled Florals, 9 1/2 In.	375.00

Moorcroft Pottery was founded in Burslem, England, in 1914 by William Moorcroft. The earlier wares are similar to those made today, but color and marking will help indicate the age.

Moorcroft, Ashtray, Sterling Mounts, Marked	60.00
Moorcroft, Bottle, Cologne, Poppies, Green Wreath Mark, 6 In.	65.00
Moorcroft, Bowl, Blue, Multicolor Flower Inside, 5 In.	30.00
Moorcroft, Bowl, Cobalt And Pansies Decoration, 4 In.	20.00
Moorcroft, Bowl, Cobalt With Peaches Interior, Grapes Exterior, 8 In.	40.00
Moorcroft, Bowl, Dark & Light Green, Scarlet & Red Dahlias In & Out, 6 In.	28.50
Moorcroft, Bowl, Floral On Olive Green, 6 1/4 X 3 In.	27.00
Moorcroft, Bowl, Green Glaze Over Tan, Floral, Embossed Border	135.00
Moorcroft, Bowl, Pomegranates Exterior, Berries Interior, Burslem, 9 X 4 In.	95.00
Moorcroft, Bowl, Pomegranates, Footed, Blue, Script Signature, 7 In.	95.00
Moorcroft, Bowl, Raised Florals On Plum Ground, 5 1/2 X 2 1/2 In.	45.00
Moorcroft, Bowl, Rose Background, Flowers In Center, 7 1/2 In.	85.00
Moorcroft, Bowl, Yellow Streaked With Green, Pansy Flowers Inside	32.00
Moorcroft, Bowl, 2-Handled, Pomegranates, Green Script Signature	68.50
Moorcroft, Box, Blooming Dahlias, Script Signature, Lidded, 3 1/2 X 5 In.	70.00
Moorcroft, Box, Blooming Jonquil, Lidded, Script Signature, 1 1/2 X 4 1/2 In.	65.00
Moorcroft, Box, Blue & Olive Green, Impressed Marked, Covered, 3 1/2 X 5 In.	38.00
Moorcroft, Box, Blue To Green, Yellow & Red Florals, Covered, 1919, 4 1/2 In.	65.00
Moorcroft, Box, Green Glaze, Floral, Round, Covered, 5 1/2 In.Diameter	38.00
Moorcroft, Box, Jonquils, Lidded, Script Signature, 4 1/2 X 4 In.	65.00
Moorcroft, Box, Yellow & Red Florals, Blue To Green Ground, 1919, 4 1/2 In.	48.00
Moorcroft, Butter Pat, Floral	10.00
Moorcroft, Candleholder, Cobalt, Fruit & Leaves, Green Signature, 7 1/2 In.	30.00
Moorcroft, Candlestick, Pansy Design, Blue, Signed, 9 In., Pair	85.00
Moorcroft, Candlestick, Yellow & Blue Flowers On Dark Blue, Burslem, 10 In.	70.00
Moorcroft, Compote, Cobalt Blue, Pansies, Tudric Pewter Foot, WM, 8 1/2 In.	95.00
Moorcroft, Compote, Mushrooms, Silver Overlay, Handled, Pedestaled, 7 In.	430.00
Moorcroft, Cup & Saucer, Grapes & Pomegranates, Green Script Signature	30.00
Moorcroft, Dish, Flower, Green, Blue, Red, Made In England, 3 In.	20.00
Moorcroft, Dish, Pansy Center, Blue, 4 1/4 In.	30.00
Moorcroft, Inkwell, Mushroom Design	125.00
Moorcroft, Jar, Blue, Pastel Orchid On Body & Lid, Signed, 5 1/4 In.	85.00
Moorcroft, Lighter, Cigarette, Paper Label	30.00
Moorcroft, Pitcher, Flambe, Berries & Leaves, 3 In.	110.00
Moorcroft, Plate, Poppies On Olive Green, Pierced To Hang, 8 1/2 In.	68.00
Moorcroft, Pot, Miniature Fern, Fruit, 2 1/2 In.High	75.00
Moorcroft, Potpourri, Reticulated Lid, Pedestal, Flamminian Line	160.00
Moorcroft, Sauce, Blue, Pansy, 4 1/4 In.	30.00
Moorcroft, Tea Set, Currants, Pomegranates, Foliage On Green, 1912, 5 Piece	210.00
Moorcroft, Tray & Candlestick, Dated 1912	350.00
Moorcroft, Tray, Card, Light Green, Blue Tulips, Leaves, Stems, Signed	65.00
Moorcroft, Vase, Apricots, Name Impressed & In Script, 5 1/2 In.	85.00
Moorcroft, Vase, Blooming Orchids, Script Signature, 12 In. 200.00 To	225.00
Moorcroft, Vase, Blue Background, Raised Embossed Leaves, 7 1/2 In.	36.00
Moorcroft, Vase, Blue Mark, Cobalt, 7 In.	48.00
Moorcroft, Vase, Blue With Pansy Design, Script Signature, 8 In. Pair	225.00
Moorcroft, Vase, Blue-Green Ground, Raspberries, 10 In.	75.00
Moorcroft, Vase, Blue, Pansies, Blue Signature, 4 1/2 In.	45.00
Moorcroft, Vase, Blue, Pomegranates, Bulbous, Green Signature, 8 In.	60.00
Moorcroft, Vase, Bowl Shaped, Flamminian, Green, Liberty & Co., Green Sign	65.00
Moorcroft, Vase, Cabinet, Floral, No.326468, C.1889, Macintyre, 3 1/2 In.	145.00
Moorcroft, Vase, Cobalt Blue, Flared Top, C.1925, 12 3/8 X 7 1/4 In.	195.00
Moorcroft, Vase, Cobalt Blue, Maroon Pansies, 9 1/4 In.	75.00
Moorcroft, Vase, Cobalt Blue, Pansies, Bulbous, 3 X 3 In.	42.50
Moorcroft, Vase, Cobalt Blue, Pansy Floral, Block Letters, Signed, 4 In.	27.50
Moorcroft, Vase, Cobalt Blue, Rouge, Green, Yellow Flowers, 7 In.	46.00
Moorcroft, Vase, Cobalt Fruit Luster, 3 1/2 In.	30.00
Moorcroft, Vase, Flambe, Baluster Shape, Script Signature, 9 In.	95.00
Moorcroft, Vase, Flambe, Bulbous, Tapering Neck, Script Signed, 9 In.	110.00
Moorcroft, Vase, Flamminian, Green, 6 In.	140.00
Moorcroft, Vase, Flamminian, Red, 5 1/2 In.	120.00
Moorcroft, Vase, Floral Decoration, Green Mark, 11 In.	98.00

Moorcroft, Vase, Florianware, Blue Flowers, Green Stems, Marked, 9 In.	350.00
Moorcroft, Vase, Green, Yellow Blue Flowers, Art Nouveau, Signed, 8 1/2 In.	110.00
Moorcroft, Vase, Incised Flowers, Blue, Miniature	14.00
Moorcroft, Vase, Iridescent, Yellow & Orange, Burslem, Block Signed, 11 In.	125.00
Moorcroft, Vase, Miniature, Blue, Incised Flowers	14.00
Moorcroft, Vase, Miniature, Green, Flower On Each Side, 2 In.	48.00
Moorcroft, Vase, Moonlight Blue, 4 In.	150.00
Moorcroft, Vase, Multicolor Flowers On White, Signed, 7 In.	90.00
Moorcroft, Vase, Pansy Design, Blue, Signed, 9 In.	135.00
Moorcroft, Vase, Purple & Rose Flowers, Blue Mark, England, 3 1/2 In.	45.00
Moorcroft, Vase, Red & Yellow Flowers, 4 1/2 In.	45.00
Moorcroft, Vase, Ruby Glaze, Cobalt Blue Peacock Feather Design, 12 1/4 In.	110.00
Moorcroft, Vase, Salt Glazed, Trees, Hills, 8 1/4 X 5 1/2 In.	325.00
Moorcroft, Vase, Spanish Pattern, Red Flowers, Green, Burslem, 10 1/4 In., Pair	450.00
Moorcroft, Vase, Swags Of Pink & Blue Florals, Green Bows, 1897-1913, 5 In.	165.00
Moorcroft, Vase, Tree Design, Orange, 8 1/2 In.	275.00
Moorcroft, Vase, Windswept Corn, C.1932, Double Handled, England, Signed	200.00
Moorcroft, Vase, Yellow, Fuchsia Flowers, Green Leaves, Signed, 8 1/2 In.	80.00

Moriage is used to identify Japanese pottery to which a raised overglaze decoration has been added. This relief ornamentation may be elaborate. The term applies to the style or technique.

Moriage, Bowl, Six Floral Panels, Intricate Slip Work	145.00
Moriage, Box, Cigarette, Ashtray, Dragon Decorated, Set, 1930s	22.00
Moriage, Cracker Jar, Melon Ribbed, Jeweling, Hand-Painted Flowers	98.00
Moriage, Ewer, Enamel Florals On Blue-Gray Bisque, 7 In.	125.00
Moriage, Ewer, Purple Orchids, Raised Enamel & White Slip Work, 10 In.	115.00
Moriage, Ewer, 4 Bouquets, Green, Pink, Beaded, Enameled & Slip, 4 In.	110.00
Moriage, Mug, Cartouches, Rose, Lavender, White, Green, Slip Lid, 5 1/2 In.	60.00
Moriage, Pitcher, Vase, Light & Dark Green, Magenta Flowers, 8 1/2 In.	65.00
Moriage, Plate Set, Raised Dragon Decoration, Pale Blue Mark, 6 Piece	75.00
Moriage, Server, Vegetable, Enameled, Red, Green, Blue Florals, 3 Piece	85.00
Moriage, Sugar & Creamer, Floral, Buildings On Reverse, Footed	115.00
Moriage, Sugar & Creamer, Green, Pastel Portrait Enameling, Signed	90.00
Moriage, Sugar & Creamer, Hand-Painted Roses, Matte Green Ground	125.00
Moriage, Sugar & Creamer, Heavy Pastel Slip With Floral Medallion	95.00
Moriage, Tea Set, Aqua Bisque Ground, Bird, Pinecones, 9 Piece	90.00
Moriage, Teapot, Greens, Reds, Blues, Beading, Enameled & Slip Work, 4 1/2 In.	79.00
Moriage, Toothpick, Light Green, Roses, Turquoise Beading, 6 Sided, Footed	28.00
Moriage, Urn, Dark Green, Heavy Enamel Beading, 2 Ornate Handles, 11 In.	135.00
Moriage, Vase, Brown, Gold Dragon Heads, 6 In., Pair	25.00
Moriage, Vase, Floral Medallions, Green, 2-Handled, 8 1/2 In.	115.00
Moriage, Vase, Florals, Brown, Nippon Mark, 13 1/2 In.	195.00
Moriage, Vase, Footed, Green Matte Finish, Handled, 13 In.	225.00
Moriage, Vase, Green, White Slip Work, Pedestaled, 12 In.	180.00
Moriage, Vase, Hour Glass Shape, Green With White Slip, 8 In.	95.00
Moriage, Vase, Jack-In-The-Pulpit, 10 In.	125.00
Moriage, Vase, Matte Finish, Magenta Beads In Flowers, 13 In.	225.00
Moriage, Vase, Outlined Florals, 3 Handled, 3 In.	35.00
Moriage, Vase, Pedestal, 4 Handled, Slip Over Dark Green	145.00
Moriage, Vase, Pink Shaded To Green, Purple & Yellow Florals, 9 In.	35.00
Moriage, Vase, Raised Flowers, Floral Medallion Center, 3-Handled, Pedestal	165.00
Moriage, Vase, Raised Tree Trunk & Leaves, Green M Mark, Nippon, 7 1/2 In.	95.00
Moriage, Vase, Roses, Beading, Hip Handles, Flare Top, 11 In.	135.00
Moriage, Vase, Tan & Brown, Purple Flowers, White Jeweling, EE, 12 1/2 In.	295.00

 Mosaic Tile Company of Zanesville, Ohio, was started by Karl Langenbeck and Herman Mueller in 1894. Many types of plain and ornamental tiles were made until 1959. The company closed in 1967.

Mosaic Tile Co., Ashtray, Dog, Dark Green	65.00
Mosaic Tile Co., Ashtray, Fox Terrier, Black & White Dog On Green	65.00
Mosaic Tile Co., Box, General Pershing	25.00
Mosaic Tile Co., Plaque, Classical Scene, Figures & Poem, 6 X 6 In.	65.00

Moser glass was made by Ludwig Moser and Sohne, a Bohemian glasshouse founded in 1857. Art Nouveau type glassware and iridescent glassware were made. The firm is still working.

Moser, Ashtray, Cameo Scenes Of Amazon Warriors, Amethyst, Signed, 5 1/2 In.	100.00
Moser, Ashtray, Gold Cameo Scenes Of Amazon Warriors, Amethyst, 5 1/2 In.	125.00
Moser, Atomizer, Amber, Gold Encrusted Graphic Cut Figures & Warriors, 9 In.	125.00
Moser, Bottle, Cologne, Amethyst, Yellow Garlands, Gold Trim, Karlsbad, 6 In.	110.00
Moser, Bottle, Malachite, Roses, Stopper, Polished Sides, 3 1/4 X 5 1/2 In.	40.00
Moser, Bottle, Perfume, Amethyst Glass, Gold Bands, Yellow Floral, 4 3/4 In.	75.00
Moser, Bottle, Perfume, Cranberry, Gold Ball Stopper, 5 In.	395.00
Moser, Bottle, Perfume, Gold & Enameling, Brass Stem, 8 In.	154.00
Moser, Bottle, Perfume, Oak Leaves, Acorns, Enamel Spray, Ball Stopper, 5 In.	430.00
Moser, Bowl, Alexandrite, Lavender, Large	85.00
Moser, Bowl, Amber, Cut & Faceted Loop, Etruscan Warriors, Gold Rim, 4 1/2 In.	185.00
Moser, Bowl, Amber, Enameled Water & Fish Scenes, Karlsbad, 7 1/2 In.	225.00
Moser, Bowl, Gold Top Trim, Cut Clear Bottom, 5 1/2 X 9 In.	115.00
Moser, Bowl, Gold Warriors Band, Black Amethyst, 4 1/2 X 10 1/2 In.	115.00
Moser, Bowl, Pale Amethyst, Large	75.00
Moser, Bowl, Punch, Amazon Warriors, Cameo Designs, Karlsbad	400.00
Moser, Bowl, Shaded Green, Intaglio Cut Flowers, Etched, 11 In.	225.00
Moser, Bowl, Warrior Band In Gold, Amber, Signed, 4 X 3 1/2 In.	235.00
Moser, Box, Cigarette, Raised Nude Girls On Lid, Green, Signed, 3 X 7 X 4 In.	125.00
Moser, Box, Cranberry Flashed, Enamel, Hinged Lid, Signed, 5 X 4 In.	145.00
Moser, Box, Etched Band Around Cover, Amber, Signed, 3 3/4 X 3 1/4 In.	125.00
Moser, Box, Patch, Ladies, Amber Glass With Enamel	135.00
Moser, Box, Powder, Amber, Etched Band On Cover Edge, 3 1/4 X 3 1/4 In.	120.00
Moser, Box, Powder, Gold Plated Rim, Cranberry, Signed, 4 X 3 1/2 In.	160.00
Moser, Box, Round, Gold & White, Signed, 4 In.	345.00
Moser, Box, Signed Karlsbad, Girl On Top, 4 In.	350.00
Moser, Champagne, Cobalt Panels, Gold Tracery, Signed, 4 1/2 In.	95.00
Moser, Coffee Set, Cranberry, Intaglio Cut With Gold, 8 In.Pot, 5 Piece	55.00
Moser, Compote, Windows, Alexandrite, Domed, Signed, 9 1/2 In.	250.00
Moser, Cordial, Amber Panels, Gold Tracery, Signed, 4 1/2 In.	55.00
Moser, Cruet, Cranberry, Enamel Acorns & Foliage, 6 In.	235.00
Moser, Cruet, Cranberry, Gold & Silver Enameling	170.00
Moser, Cup & Saucer, Cranberry Lid, Gold, Blown-Out Areas, Demitasse, Signed	125.00
Moser, Cup & Saucer, Green, Gold Leaves, Vines, & Floral, Footed	45.00
Moser, Cup, Punch, Cranberry, Acorns, Gold Foliage, Enameled Leaves, 2 1/8 In.	225.00
Moser, Cup, Punch, Enameled Oak Leaves, Applied Acorns, 2 1/8 In.	225.00
Moser, Decanter, Intaglio Cut Frosted Morning Glories, Signed, Stopper, 9 In.	145.00
Moser, Decanter, Overlay Cut To Cranberry, 15 In.	170.00
Moser, Decanter, Pinwheel, Pointed Stopper, 14 In.	95.00
Moser, Decanter, Ruby, Etched & Gold Enameld Birds & Flowers, 14 1/2 In.	95.00
Moser, Decanter, Ruby, Etched Floral Design, Signed, 12 In.	100.00
Moser, Decanter, Section Shaped Stopper & Base, Signed Alexandrite	250.00
Moser, Decanter, Winter Scene, Ruby, Carlsbad, 12 In.	60.00
Moser, Figurine, Malachite Glass Panther, 1 X 4 In.	35.00
Moser, Goblet, Amber Foot & Stem, Clear Bowl, 7 1/2 In., Six	225.00
Moser, Goblet, Amber, Gold Warrior's Band, 7 1/4 In.	75.00
Moser, Goblet, Cranberry, Gold & Leaf Decoration, Clear Top, Gold Rim	85.00
Moser, Goblet, Wine, Cut Floral, Leaves, Clear Stem, Purple, Set Of 8	295.00
Moser, Jar, Candy, Cranberry, Gold Enamel Flowers, Sterling Frame & Lid	185.00
Moser, Liqueur, Blue, Oak Leaves Enameled With Gold Foliage, 3 X 1 1/4 In.	100.00
Moser, Mug, Liqueur, Glass Handled, Applied Lustered Acorn, 2 1/8 In.	95.00
Moser, Perfume, Finger, Gold Enamel Dominating Brass Lid & Ring, Amber, 3 In.	135.00
Moser, Plate, Art Nouveau Enameled Lady With Harp, Cranberry, 7 1/2 In.	80.00
Moser, Plate, Green & Gold, Small	90.00
Moser, Plate, Vintage, Intaglio, Etched, Signed, 9 In.	75.00
Moser, Rose Bowl, Tic-Tac-Toe, White, 3 1/2 X 5 In.	225.00
Moser, Scent Bottle, Cut Glass, Amethyst, 3 In.	60.00
Moser, Spooner, Overlay Cut To Cranberry, Moser Label, 5 1/2 In.	89.00
Moser, Tumbler, Amber, Intaglio Cut, 4 3/4 In.	125.00
Moser, Tumbler, Blue	95.00
Moser, Tumbler, Floral, Gold Edge, Canberry Blue, Wine, 5 Piece	250.00
Moser, Vase, Amazon Warrior Scene, Gold Relief, 9 In.	315.00

Moser, Vase, Amber, Amazon Gold Border, Signed, 6 In.	85.00
Moser, Vase, Amber, Flared Rib Art Nouveau Design, Floral, Gold Rim, 18 In.	265.00
Moser, Vase, Amber, Ribbed, Enameled Art Nouveau, Floral, 16 In., Pair	550.00
Moser, Vase, Amber, 11 1/2 In.	245.00
Moser, Vase, Amethyst To Clear, Gold Design, White Frosted Top & Base, 19 In.	250.00
Moser, Vase, Amethyst, Acid Etch, Gold Band Warriors, Signed, 7 X 6 1/4 In.	350.00
Moser, Vase, Amethyst, Applied Lizard, Signed, 6 1/2 In.	375.00
Moser, Vase, Blue Wisteria, Green Leaves, Gold, Signed, 12 In.	130.00
Moser, Vase, Blue, Wishbone Feet, Gold Enameled Leaves, 5 5/8 X 2 5/8 In.	375.00
Moser, Vase, Bud, Shaded Green, Intaglio Cut Flowers, Etched, 5 In.	125.00
Moser, Vase, Cameo, Dark Amethyst, Glossy Floral, Karlsbad, 8 In.	275.00
Moser, Vase, Clear Crystal, Etched Maids In Forest, Silver Trim	65.00
Moser, Vase, Cobalt Blue, Acid Cut Elephants & Palms In Gold, 8 In.	325.00
Moser, Vase, Cobalt Blue, Pedestal Base, Gold Warrior Band, 8 In.	165.00
Moser, Vase, Cobalt Blue, 8 1/4 In.	225.00
Moser, Vase, Cranberry, Applied Grapes, Enameled, 18 In.	450.00
Moser, Vase, Cranberry, Enameled Floral, Gold Tracery, Applied Bees, 10 In.	275.00
Moser, Vase, Cranberry, Enameled Pink & Blue Florals, Gilt Leaves, 5 1/2 In.	110.00
Moser, Vase, Cranberry, Enameling & Applied Grapes, Pedestaled, 18 In.	395.00
Moser, Vase, Cranberry, Gold & Floral Decoration, Crimped, 6 1/2 In.	125.00
Moser, Vase, Cranberry, Gold Acorns, Leaves & Stems, Ovoid Shape, 5 1/2 In.	135.00
Moser, Vase, Cranberry, Pedestal, Raised Grapes, Enameled, 18 In.	650.00
Moser, Vase, Cranberry, Pink & Blue Flowers, Gold Leaves, 5 1/2 In.	110.00
Moser, Vase, Electric Blue, Gold Trim, Wishbone Feet, 5 5/8 In.	395.00
Moser, Vase, Enameled Cranberry, Applied Grapes, 18 In.	400.00
Moser, Vase, Enameled Pansies, Signed, 12 In.	185.00
Moser, Vase, Gold Elephants In Jungle, Cameo, 8 X 25 In.	120.00
Moser, Vase, Gold-Applied Greek Pattern, Glass, 5 In.	65.00
Moser, Vase, Green Jadeite, Nude Figures, Grape Clusters, Tapered, 8 In.	265.00
Moser, Vase, Green, Enameled Gold & Silver Flowers, Footed, 4-Sided, 4 1/2 In.	70.00
Moser, Vase, Green, Gold Top, Enameling, 16 1/2 X 8 In.	90.00
Moser, Vase, Light Red To Dark At Top, Decorated, 10 In.	92.50
Moser, Vase, Overlay Lusters, White Cut To Green, 8 1/2 In., Pair	175.00
Moser, Vase, Pastel Shaded Enamel, Fern Pattern, Moss Green Background, 9 In.	295.00
Moser, Vase, Peacock Sitting On Tree Limb, Rising Sun, Silver Rim, 12 In.	350.00
Moser, Vase, Pedestal, Wide Mouthed, Signed, 7 3/8 In.	165.00
Moser, Vase, Portrait, Hand-Painted, Green Glass, Gold Tracery, 7 1/2 In.	75.00
Moser, Vase, Prisms, Triangular, Luster Tops Scalloped, Cranberry, White, Pair	325.00
Moser, Vase, Purple, Circles, Teardrops, Roman Scenic Gold Border, 10 In.	75.00
Moser, Vase, Purple, 4 1/2 X 4 1/2 In.	110.00
Moser, Vase, Purple, 6 Panel, 6 In.	62.00
Moser, Vase, Round, Enameled Blue & Lavender Flowers, Purple Ground, 14 In.	145.00
Moser, Vase, Rubena, Gold Coin Bow, One Green Jewel In Each Bow	160.00
Moser, Vase, Square, 3 Gold Bands, Enameled Gold Trim, 11 1/2 In.	110.00
Moser, Vase, Trumpet, Cranberry, Applied Bees, 18 1/2 In.	285.00
Moser, Vase, Trumpet, Faceted Knob, Scalloped Foot, Cranberry & Gold Tracery	295.00
Moser, Vase, 2 Applied Fish And Enameled Seaweed, Signed	165.00
Moser, Vase, 3 Poses Of Raised Nude Girls Holding Grape Bunches, Cone Shape	265.00
Moser, Wine, Cobalt Overlay, Gold Enamel Design, 6 In.	85.00
Moser, Wine, Cranberry Overlay, Crystal, Gold Enamel, 6 In.	110.00
Moser, Wine, Enameled And Applied Acorns On Blue	175.00
Moser, Wine, Gold Decoration, Cranberry Ground, 8 1/2 In.	125.00
Moser, Wine, Rhine, Applied & Enameled Acorns On Blue Glass	150.00
Moser, Wine, Rhine, Blue, Two Applied Acorns	135.00
Moser, Wine, Sapphire Blue, Protruding Acorns	195.00

Moss rose china was made by many firms from 1808 to 1900. It refers to any china decorated with the moss rose flower.

Moss Rose, Bowl, Spill	38.00
Moss Rose, Coffeepot, 9 In.	68.00
Moss Rose, Mustard Pot	14.00
Moss Rose, Pitcher, Octagonal, Hand-Painted Spray, 5 1/2 In.	8.50
Moss Rose, Plate, Gold Band, Haviland, 7 1/2 In.	30.00
Moss Rose, Tea Set, Child's, 8 Piece	12.00
Moss Rose, Tureen, Covered, Handled, John Maddock & Sons, England, 7 In.	45.00

Moss Rose, Tureen, Covered, John Maddock & Sons, Black Mark, 7 X 9 In. 45.00
    Mother-of -Pearl, see also Pearl

> *Mother-of-pearl glass, or pearl satin glass, was first made in the 1850s in*
> *England and in Massachusetts. It was a special type of mold-blown satin*
> *glass with air bubbles in the glass, giving it a pearlized color.*

Mother-Of-Pearl, Basket, Diamond-Quilted, Ruffled, Pink, White, 6 X 3 In. 100.00
Mother-Of-Pearl, Bottle, Diamond-Quilted, Pink, 7 In. 72.00
Mother-Of-Pearl, Bowl, Rainbow, Satin, Folded Ruffle Top, 4 3/4 X 7 1/2 In. 925.00
Mother-Of-Pearl, Bowl, Satin Glass, Blue, Diamond-Quilted, 2 1/2 X 7 In. 225.00
Mother-Of-Pearl, Cheese Keeper, Floral, Gold Handle, Victoria, Austria 85.00
Mother-Of-Pearl, Ewer, Herringbone, 12 1/2 In. 500.00
Mother-Of-Pearl, Ewer, Pink To White, Herringbone, Spherical, 8 1/2 In. 325.00
Mother-Of-Pearl, Jar, Cracker, Quilted, Silver Cover & Bail 285.00
Mother-Of-Pearl, Pitcher, Blue, Diamond-Quilted, Satin Handle, 9 In. 360.00
Mother-Of-Pearl, Pitcher, Herringbone, Rainbow Colors 350.00
Mother-Of-Pearl, Pitcher, Rainbow, Coin Spot, Off-White Casing 675.00
Mother-Of-Pearl, Pitcher, Water, Raindrop Pattern, 7 In. 165.00
Mother-Of-Pearl, Pitcher, Water, Raindrop, Blue Satin, Camphor Handle, Lid 380.00
Mother-Of-Pearl, Rose Bowl, Daffodil Yellow 158.00
Mother-Of-Pearl, Rose Bowl, Diamond-Quilted, White Lining, 3 3/8 In. 210.00
Mother-Of-Pearl, Rose Bowl, Diamond-Quilted, 4 5/8 X 5 In. 275.00
Mother-Of-Pearl, Rose Bowl, Herringbone 110.00
Mother-Of-Pearl, Rose Bowl, 6-Crimp Top, Satin Glass, Quilted, 3 3/4 In. 295.00
    Mother-of-Pearl, Satin Glass, see also Satin Glass, Smith
    Brothers, Tiffany Glass, etc.
Mother-Of-Pearl, Tumbler, Diamond-Quilted, Pink, Cased 85.00
Mother-Of-Pearl, Tumbler, Diamond-Quilted, Rubena 152.00
Mother-Of-Pearl, Tumbler, Diamond-Quilted, Rubena, Decorated 185.00
Mother-Of-Pearl, Tumbler, Diamond-Quilted, White To Salmon .... 147.50 To 150.00
Mother-Of-Pearl, Vase, Apricot, Diamond-Quilted, Ruffled, Miniature, 5 In. 165.00
Mother-Of-Pearl, Vase, Blue Diamond-Quilted, 6 3/4 In. X 3 3/4 In.Diameter 258.00
Mother-Of-Pearl, Vase, Blue, Herringbone, 4 3/4 In. 75.00
Mother-Of-Pearl, Vase, Bulbous To Rounded Pedestal, Ruffled, Scallops, 8 In. 2150.00
Mother-Of-Pearl, Vase, Diamond-Quilted, Butterscotch, Ruffled Collar, 5 In. 110.00
Mother-Of-Pearl, Vase, Diamond-Quilted, Ruffled Top, 7 1/4 In. 195.00
Mother-Of-Pearl, Vase, Diamond-Quilted, Ruffled, Pink, White, 4 3/4 In. 140.00
Mother-Of-Pearl, Vase, Diamond-Quilted, Ruffled, 9 5/8 In. 195.00
Mother-Of-Pearl, Vase, Diamond-Quilted, 10 1/2 In. X 4 3/4 In. 175.00
Mother-Of-Pearl, Vase, Herringbone, Pink, Cased White, 7 1/2 In. 90.00
Mother-Of-Pearl, Vase, Pink, Herringbone, 7 In. 80.00
Mother-Of-Pearl, Vase, Quilted, Ruffled Top, Rose Shaded, 9 5/8 In. 195.00
    Moustache Cup, see Mustache Cup

> *Mont Joye is an enameled cameo glass made in the late nineteenth and the*
> *twentieth centuries by Saint-Hilaire Touvoir de Varraux and Co. of*
> *Pantin, France. This same company produced De Vez glass.*

Mt.Joye, Pitcher, Amethyst, Enameled Floral, Crystal Handle & Stopper, 14 In. 165.00
Mt.Joye, Pitcher, Light To Dark Green, Etched Iris, Enameling, 9 In. 165.00
Mt.Joye, Pitcher, Water, Blown, Cameo Iris Decoration, Green To Clear 150.00
Mt.Joye, Rose Bowl, Cameo Cut, Iris Decoration, 3 3/4 In. 185.00
Mt.Joye, Rose Bowl, Holly Leaves In Gold, Signed 225.00
Mt.Joye, Vase, Amethyst, Iris, Leaves, Gold Border With Iris Around, Pair 175.00
Mt.Joye, Vase, Cameo & Enamel Yellow, Purple, Floral, Acid Etched, 6 In. 235.00
Mt.Joye, Vase, Enameled Flowers, Ribbed, Clear To Amethyst, 7 1/2 In. 175.00
Mt.Joye, Vase, Enameled, Gold, Signed, 10 1/2 In. 250.00
Mt.Joye, Vase, Floral, Vertical Sided, Rounded X-Section, Ribbed Inside, 6 In. 250.00
Mt.Joye, Vase, Gold Leaf Flower In Relief, Frosted Green, 9 3/4 In. 265.00
Mt.Joye, Vase, Green, Etched, Gold Top, Enameled, 5 1/4 In. 175.00
Mt.Joye, Vase, Green, Gold Oak Leaves, Silver Acorns, 6 1/2 In. 295.00
Mt.Joye, Vase, Green, Orchid, 14 In. 145.00
Mt.Joye, Vase, Modified Rectangular Cross, Clear, Ribbed In, Floral, 6 1/2 In. 250.00
Mt.Joye, Vase, Mums, Green To Clear, Pastel, Signed, 11 In. 125.00

Mt.Joye, Vase, Pansy & Gold Leaf Decoration, Dimpled, 4 1/2 In.	200.00
Mt.Joye, Vase, Pink Spider Mums, Signed, 9 In.	240.00
Mt.Joye, Vase, Poppies, Leaves, Hammered, Gilt, Pink, Signed, C.1910, 16 In., Pair	450.00
Mt.Joye, Vase, Purple Iris, Frosted Body, Signed, 7 3/8 In.	225.00
Mt.Joye, Vase, Ribbed, Cameo & Yellow Enamel Florals, Signed, 6 1/2 In.	235.00
Mt.Joye, Vase, Vertical Sided, Ribbed, Frosted, Enameled Floral, Purple, Gold	250.00

 Mt.Washington Glass was made at the Mt.Washington Glass Co. located in New Bedford, Massachusetts. Many types of art glass were made there from 1850 to the 1890s.

Mt.Washington, see also Burmese, Crown Milano

Mt.Washington, Barrel, Biscuit, Melon Ribbed Ivory Satin, Florals, Silver Rim	295.00
Mt.Washington, Barrel, Light Blue, Scroll Flower Medallion	125.00
Mt.Washington, Basket, Swirled, Dimpled Cranberry To Opalescent, 7 3/4 In.	85.00
Mt.Washington, Biscuit Jar, Hand-Painted, Floral, Ornate, Impressed Lid, Gold	295.00
Mt.Washington, Biscuit Jar, Melon Ribbed, Art Nouveau, Silver Top	195.00
Mt.Washington, Biscuit Jar, White Opaque, Blue Flowers, Marked M.W.	165.00
Mt.Washington, Biscuit Jar, White, Opaque, Hand-Painted Blue Floral	225.00
Mt.Washington, Bowl, Burmese, Tricornered, Acid Finish	375.00
Mt.Washington, Bowl, Burmese, Tricornered, Salmon Pink To Yellow, 2 X 5 In.	210.00
Mt.Washington, Bowl, Burmese, Yellow Top, Vertical Stripes, 2 X 5 1/8 In.	195.00
Mt.Washington, Bowl, Floral, Protruded Panels, 15 In.	296.00
Mt.Washington, Bowl, Nasturtiums, Gold Outline Inside, Ruffled, 10 X 3 In.	85.00
Mt.Washington, Bowl, Quilted, Round Body, Oblong Top, Pink, Blue, 14 In.	340.00
Mt.Washington, Bowl, Rose, Peachblow, 4 1/4 In.	300.00
Mt.Washington, Bowl, Sugar, Squatty Shape, Blue Flowers, Green Ivy, Tendrils	65.00
Mt.Washington, Box, Biscuit, Silver Cover, Signed, Handle, 7 X 8 1/2 In.	295.00
Mt.Washington, Box, Dresser, Bronze Coloring, Enamel Leaves, Round, 4 In.	165.00
Mt.Washington, Box, Trinket, Frosted Green, Covered	40.00
Mt.Washington, Butter, Covered, Triple Cased Spatter Glass, 4 X 5 In.	65.00
Mt.Washington, Cookie Jar, Pairpoint, Blown-Out Panels, Pink Enamel Floral	160.00
Mt.Washington, Cracker Jar, Melon Ribbed, Opalescent, Floral Enamel	240.00
Mt.Washington, Cracker Jar, Melon Ribbed, Satin, Enameled Blue Flowers	95.00
Mt.Washington, Creamer, Alabaster Ware, Florals On White Satin	90.00
Mt.Washington, Cruet, Peachblow, Applied Rigaree	850.00
Mt.Washington, Cruet, Rose To Amber, Amberina, Ball Stopper, Blown Rib, 7 In.	225.00
Mt.Washington, Decanter, Brandy, Flat Sided, 9 X 5 In. 210.00 To	225.00
Mt.Washington, Figurine, Frog, Mushroom Flower, Flowers, Pink Bottom	160.00
Mt.Washington, Flower Frog, Mushroom, Enameled Decoration	165.00
Mt.Washington, Flower Frog, Opalescent, Trails Of Vines & Pink Flowers	95.00
Mt.Washington, Flower Frog, Varied Colored Flowers, Trailing Vines	160.00
Mt.Washington, Glass, Tavern, Lemonade, Fish Decoration, Green, Yellow	22.00
Mt.Washington, Hatpin Holder, Mushroom Shape, Beige Satin, Leaves In Enamel	175.00
Mt.Washington, Inkwell, Blue Swirl	135.00
Mt.Washington, Jar, Cracker, Melon Ribbed With Pansies	150.00
Mt.Washington, Lamp, Double Fairy, Burmese, Base And Holders Signed, 17 In.	1175.00
Mt.Washington, Lamp, Miniature, Floral Decoration, 6 1/4 In.	74.50
Mt.Washington, Muffineer, Egg Shape, Blue & White Flowers, Enamel, Pewter Lid	165.00
Mt.Washington, Mustard Pot, Flowers, Ribbed Barrel, Satin, Beige To Yellow	65.00
Mt.Washington, Mustard Pot, Flowers, Ribbed Barrel, Satin, Pink To Yellow	65.00
Mt.Washington, Mustard Pot, Ribbed, Leaf & Berry	65.00
Mt.Washington, Mustard, Burmese, Enameled, 3 In.	325.00
Mt.Washington, Mustard, Lily, Pewter Lid & Handle, White, Pink	45.00
Mt.Washington, Pitcher, Milk, Burmese, Yellow Handle, Pink Top, 7 1/2 In.	450.00
Mt.Washington, Pitcher, Verona, Lily Of The Valley, Shell Handle, 8 In.	90.00
Mt.Washington, Plate, Lusterless White Satin Glass, 12 1/4 In.	85.00
Mt.Washington, Plate, Ruffled, White, 10 In.	22.50
Mt.Washington, Rose Bowl, Peachblow, Satin Finish	575.00
Mt.Washington, Rose Bowl, Unfired Burmese, Ribbed & Swirled, Hand-Painted	185.00
Mt.Washington, Salt & Pepper, Blue Florals	51.00
Mt.Washington, Salt & Pepper, Egg Shaped, Silver Plated Footed Holder	185.00
Mt.Washington, Salt & Pepper, Figural, Pink, Yellow, Lidded	165.00
Mt.Washington, Salt & Pepper, Floral, Pewter Tops	55.00
Mt.Washington, Salt & Pepper, Lay-Down Egg, Pansy, New York In Gold	195.00
Mt.Washington, Salt & Pepper, Round, Forget-Me-Not, 2 In.Diameter	51.00

Mt.Washington, **Salt,** Glossy Pink, Blossom Decoration 15.00
Mt.Washington, **Salt,** Melon Shape, Decorated 55.00
Mt.Washington, **Salt,** Pairpoint Holder, Signed 140.00
Mt.Washington, **Salt,** Pale Blue, Blue Flowers, Red Centers, Pale Greeen Leaves 85.00
Mt.Washington, **Salt,** Tomato Shape, Peach Color, Pewter Lid, Enamel Flowers 50.00
Mt.Washington, **Saltshaker,** Apple Shape, Small 28.00
Mt.Washington, **Saltshaker,** Blue Violets 45.00
Mt.Washington, **Saltshaker,** Cockleshell, Pair 335.00
Mt.Washington, **Saltshaker,** Egg In Blossom Pattern, Pair 55.00
Mt.Washington, **Saltshaker,** Egg Shape, Enamel Flowers, Peach 40.00
Mt.Washington, **Saltshaker,** Egg Shape, Ivy Leaves 28.00
Mt.Washington, **Saltshaker,** Egg, Flat Sided, Coral To White, Yellow Flowers 55.00
Mt.Washington, **Saltshaker,** Enameled Tomato 58.00
Mt.Washington, **Saltshaker,** Fig, Florals On Yellow Ground 75.00
Mt.Washington, **Saltshaker,** Pepper, Figure Decorated, Pale Pink, Yellow, Pair 165.00
Mt.Washington, **Saltshaker,** Satin, Hand-Painted Floral, Acorn Shaped, 3 In. 40.00
Mt.Washington, **Sauce,** Burmese, Crimped Top, Mauve To Yellow, 4 1/2 In. 195.00
Mt.Washington, **Server,** Cake, Lava Glass 1150.00
Mt.Washington, **Spoon Holder,** Acid Finish, 4 1/4 X 2 5/8 In.Diameter 225.00
Mt.Washington, **Sugar & Creamer,** Pink Satin, Shell & Seaweed, Enameling 250.00
Mt.Washington, **Sugar Shaker,** Blue To White, Pink Flower, Tomato Shape 185.00
Mt.Washington, **Sugar Shaker,** Egg Shape, Floral, Leaves, White, Green, Pink 165.00
Mt.Washington, **Sugar Shaker,** Egg Shape, Florals, Burmese Color, 5 In. 152.00
Mt.Washington, **Sugar Shaker,** Egg Shape, Pewter Top, Signed, 4 1/2 In. 175.00
Mt.Washington, **Sugar Shaker,** Egg, White, Blue & White Dotted Floral 125.00
Mt.Washington, **Sugar Shaker,** Eggshell Satin, Pansies 150.00
Mt.Washington, **Sugar Shaker,** Eggshell, Yellow, Acid Finish 125.00
Mt.Washington, **Sugar Shaker,** Fig, Bark Finish, Flowers 250.00
Mt.Washington, **Sugar Shaker,** Fig, Florals On Pink Ground 200.00
Mt.Washington, **Sugar Shaker,** Green & Pink Leaf, Egg Shape, Pewter Top 110.00
Mt.Washington, **Sugar Shaker,** Opaque Pink Forget-Me-Not 75.00
Mt.Washington, **Sugar Shaker,** Pansies, Purple, White 275.00
Mt.Washington, **Sugar Shaker,** Pansy, Satin Egg Shape, Pewter Top, 4 1/2 In. 130.00
Mt.Washington, **Sugar Shaker,** Ribbed, Glossy, 6 5/8 In. 75.00
Mt.Washington, **Sugar Shaker,** Ribbed, Satin, 2 Piece Top, 5 3/4 In. 150.00
Mt.Washington, **Sugar Shaker,** Satin Finish, Ribbed Pillar 110.00
Mt.Washington, **Sugar Shaker,** Tomato Shape, Melon Sectioning, Calladiums 195.00
Mt.Washington, **Sugar Shaker,** Tomato, Blue & Cream, Purple & Red Flowers 200.00
Mt.Washington, **Sugar Shaker,** Tomato, White & Blue Dotted Floral 210.00
Mt.Washington, **Sugar Shaker,** White, Dotted Flowers, Egg Shape 120.00
Mt.Washington, **Tazza,** Orchid Top With Flowers, Knop Stem, Artist Signed 235.00
Mt.Washington, **Toothpick,** Burmese, Tricorn, Salmon, Yellow, 2 In. 225.00
Mt.Washington, **Toothpick,** Thorn Top, Enameled Red & Green Flowers 75.00
Mt.Washington, **Tumbler,** Amber, Thumbprint, Gold Design, Flower 107.00
Mt.Washington, **Tumbler,** Tavern Glass, Black Ship Decoration, 5 1/4 In. 27.00
Mt.Washington, **Vase,** Burmese, Acorns & Oak Leaves Outlined In Gold, 8 In. 575.00
Mt.Washington, **Vase,** Burmese, Mother-Of-Pearl Herringbone, Deep Rose, 5 In. 195.00
Mt.Washington, **Vase,** Burmese, Scalloped, Salmon Pink To Yellow, 5 In. 225.00
Mt.Washington, **Vase,** Colored Birds, 7 In. 270.00
Mt.Washington, **Vase,** Cranberry Overlay, Opaline, Fluted Tops, Pair, 7 3/4 In. 100.00
Mt.Washington, **Vase,** Diamond-Quilted, Blue Satin, 7 1/4 In. 145.00
Mt.Washington, **Vase,** Diamond-Quilted, Pink Satin, 7 1/4 In. 145.00
Mt.Washington, **Vase,** Enameled Flowers, 6 In. 59.00
Mt.Washington, **Vase,** Fish Swimming Among Weeds, Enamel, Two Handled, 7 In. 135.00
Mt.Washington, **Vase,** Floral, 7 In. 148.00
Mt.Washington, **Vase,** Hand-Painted Flower, Gold & Silver, Oriental, 8 In. 550.00
Mt.Washington, **Vase,** Jack, Enamel Apple Blossoms, White Satin, 9 1/4 In. 195.00
Mt.Washington, **Vase,** Lava Glass, Fluxs, Handles, 1870s, 4 In. 475.00
Mt.Washington, **Vase,** Lava Glass, Glossy Finish, Bulbous, 8 In. 1000.00
Mt.Washington, **Vase,** Raised Gold Leaf Design, Smith Bros., 6 In. 275.00
Mt.Washington, **Vase,** Rose Color, Sterling Holder, Strawberry Signed 85.00
Mt.Washington, **Vase,** Trumpet, Burmese, Tricornered Pedestal, 9 In. 300.00
Mt.Washington, **Vase,** Verona, Lily & Leaf Decoration, Gold Outline, 8 X 5 In. 80.00
Mt.Washington, **Vase,** Verona, Ribbed, Lily Of The Valley, Reeded Handle 200.00
Mt.Washington, **Vase,** Verona, Shasta Daisy, Gold Outline On Leaves, 11 X 7 In. 150.00

Muffineer, see also Cranberry, Muffineer

Muffineer, Guttate, Pink Cased Glass	125.00
Muffineer, Orange Flashed Glass, Gold Top, 6 1/2 In.	45.00

Muller Freres, French for Muller Brothers, made cameo and other art glass from the early 1900s to the late 1930s. Their factory was first located in Luneville and later moved to Croismaire, France.

Muller Freres, Cameo, Floral, Three Colors, 8 In.	550.00
Muller Freres, Cameo, Scenic, Three Colors, 5 3/4 In.	550.00
Muller Freres, Lamp Base, Dark Blue Mottling, Frosted Aqua Background, 8 In.	125.00
Muller Freres, Lamp Base, Frosted, Purple Mottling, Tripod Bronze Collar	180.00
Muller Freres, Lamp Shade, Brown, Yellow, Signed, 6 X 3 1/2 In.	65.00
Muller Freres, Lamp, Acid Cut, Three Colors, Table Lamp	997.00
Muller Freres, Lamp, Double French Hanging Table, 2 Shades, Orange, Black	975.00
Muller Freres, Shade, Luneville, Mottled Pink Green & Purple, Signed, Pair	105.00
Muller Freres, Shade, Purple, Red, Orange Mottling	58.00
Muller Freres, Vase, Cameo In Free Form Geometrics & Flowers, Smoke, 11 In.	600.00
Muller Freres, Vase, Cameo, Luneville, 8 Red Parrots, Blue, Yellow	625.00
Muller Freres, Vase, Cameo, Tree Landscape, River Bank, 3 Acid Cuttings, 3 In.	245.00
Muller Freres, Vase, Landscape, Cameo, Signed, 5 1/2 X 2 1/4 In.	265.00
Muller Freres, Vase, Luneville, Greens, Gold Mica Flecks, Glossy, 20 In.	495.00
Muller Freres, Vase, Luneville, Mauve, Mottled Pink, Red, Green, 7 In.	225.00
Muller Freres, Vase, Scenic Cutting, Tawny Colors, 15 In.	275.00
Muller Freres, Vase, Scenic, Cameo, Signed, 7 In.	249.00
Muncie, Vase, Fan Shaped, Green Over Rose, Marked, 5 1/4 In.	15.00
Muncie, Vase, Green & Pink Matte, 6 In.	9.00

Music, Guitar, see also Disneyana, Guitar

Music, Accordion, Inlaid Wood, Mother-Of-Pearl Keys, Brass Fittings	70.00
Music, Album, Barney Google	10.00
Music, Amberola, Edison, 30 Cylinder	175.00
Music, American Theatre Fotoplayer, Model 39	16000.00
Music, Automaton, Manivelle, 5 Figures, Marked Simon & Halbig	1395.00
Music, Automaton, Manivelle, 5 Figures, 2 Play Strings, 3 Dance, Crank, Marked	1395.00
Music, Automaton, 2 Tune Movement, Black Man Smokes Hookah When Activated	2495.00
Music, Band Organ Facade, 41 Lights, Screen Painting, 8 Ft X 92 In.	1995.00
Music, Banjo, Banjeaurine, 4 String, Mother-Of-Pearl, Signed Stewart	350.00
Music, Banjo, Bird's-Eye, Maple, Inlaid	65.00
Music, Banjo, Calvert Parker, New Hampshire	210.00
Music, Banjo, Mandolin, Walnut, Marked Mile, B & J., N.Y.	40.00
Music, Banjo, Orchestrella, Pearl Inlay Neck, Gretsch, 1926	165.00
Music, Banjo, Schoenhut, Wood, Marked, 21 In.	135.00
Music, Banjo, 4 String, Maple, Mother-Of-Pearl Inlay	65.00
Music, Booklet, Army Songs, 1918	5.00
Music, Box & Table, Plays 10 Tunes, Drum, 6 Bells, Castanet, Mandolin, Maple	4900.00
Music, Box, Bird In Cage, Gilded, Hanging	65.00
Music, Box, Bremond, 16 Note, 13 X 12 X 21 In.	2195.00
Music, Box, Burl Walnut, Brass, Pewter, Mother-Of-Pearl, Drawer, Large	4000.00
Music, Box, Bust Of Brahms, Wooden, 5 1/2 In.	12.00
Music, Box, Columbia, Inlaid Box, 10 Tunes	1200.00
Music, Box, Cylinder Type, 1 Tune, Wood Box, Thorens, 4 3/4 X 3 1/2 In.	55.00
Music, Box, Disc, Musical, Mira, Mahogany Case, 26 Discs, 18 In. .... *Illus*	4200.00
Music, Box, Disc, Musical, Polyphon, 24 Discs, Rosewood Case .... *Illus*	3750.00
Music, Box, Disc, Musical, Regina, Oak Case, 48 Discs, 27 In. .... *Illus*	4250.00
Music, Box, Disc, Symphonion, Hand Crank, Coin Operated, 18 Discs .... *Illus*	3500.00
Music, Box, Empress Concert Grand, Disc, Console, Coin Operated, 30 Discs	5000.00
Music, Box, Euphonia, Discs	17.50
Music, Box, Inlaid, 3 Bells, 9 Tunes, Swiss	1200.00
Music, Box, Japanese Lacquer, Round, 5 In.	25.00
Music, Box, Mermod Freres, Walnut Case, Slant Glass Top, 8 Tunes, C.1880-90	1500.00
Music, Box, Musical, Bells In Sight, Bird's Head Strikers, Clock .... *Illus*	1700.00
Music, Box, Musical, Mother-Of-Pearl, Interchangeable, Walnut .... *Illus*	1700.00
Music, Box, Oil Painted Decoration, Swiss, 33 X 15 X 8 In.	950.00
Music, Box, Olympia, Mahogany Case, Inlaid Lid, Double Comb	795.00
Music, Box, Paillard Sublime Harmonie, Cylinder, 12 X 15 X 47 In.	2300.00
Music, Box, Piccolo Zither, Mermod Freres, 10 Tunes, 9 1/2 X 27 X 7 In.	895.00

Music, Box, Disc, Musical, Polyphon,
24 Discs, Rosewood Case

Music, Box, Disc, Musical, Mira,
Mahogany Case, 26 Discs, 18 In.

Music, Box, Disc, Musical, Regina,
Oak Case, 48 Discs, 27 In.

Music, Box, Disc, Symphonion, Hand Crank,
Coin Operated, 18 Discs

Music, Box, Musical, Bells In Sight,
Bird's Head Strikers, Clock

Music, Box, Musical, Mother-Of-Pearl,
Interchangeable, Walnut

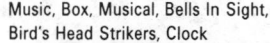

Music, Box, Polyphon, Serpentine Case, 8 1/2 In.	495.00
Music, Box, Polyphon, Walnut, 7 Discs	110.00
Music, Box, Regina, Disc, Solid Oak Case, Brass Parts, 27 Records, Coin Slot	2000.00
Music, Box, Regina, Oak Table Model, 17 15 1/2 In.Discs	1800.00
Music, Box, Regina, Orchestral, Mahogany Case, 27 In.	6000.00
Music, Box, Regina, Oriental Lacquer Finish, 8 In.Disks	995.00
Music, Box, Regina, Solid Oak, Custom Floor Model, 40 X 23 X 21 In.	2500.00
Music, Box, Regina, Table Model, Oak Cabinet, Serpentine Front, 10 Discs	2300.00
Music, Box, Regina, Table Top, 12 Discs	675.00
Music, Box, Regina, 14a, Coin Operated, Oak Case, 5 Cent Slot, 1895	1495.00
Music, Box, Reginaphone, 15 Discs, 15 1/2 In.	1995.00
Music, Box, Stella Double Comb, 10 Discs, Oak Case, Storage In Base	2295.00
Music, Box, Stella, Inlaid Case, 17 1/4 In.	3250.00
Music, Box, Stella, Single Comb	1495.00
Music, Box, Stella, Single Comb, Mahogany Case, 15 Discs, 14 In.	1795.00
Music, Box, Swiss, Carved, Girl Holding Basket Of Chicks, Thorens	45.00
Music, Box, Swiss, Cylinder, Carved, Ebonized & Gilt Wood Case, 6 Tunes, 13 In.	450.00
Music, Box, Swiss, Inlaid Burly Maple, Table, Drum, Bells, Castanet, 10 Tunes	6000.00
Music, Box, Swiss, Mahogany, 24 18 1/2 In.Discs, C.1900, 30 X 23 X 42 In.	1300.00
Music, Box, Swiss, Rosewood & Ebony Satin Case, 3 Cylinders, 7 X 13 In.	600.00
Music, Box, Swiss, Rosewood Inlaid Case, 13 In.Brass Cylinder	575.00
Music, Box, Swiss, 3 Bells, 9 Tunes, Inlaid	1200.00
Music, Box, Swiss, 6 Bells, Drum & Block, 10 Tunes, Cylinder, 12 X 31 X 31 In.	2295.00
Music, Calliope, Tangley, Restored	9000.00
Music, Chair, Child's, Carved, 27 In.	295.00
Music, Clarinet, Ebony, Marked Buffet, Paris, Leather Case	75.00
Music, Clarinet, Othello, Teak & Silver, Take Apart	50.00
Music, Flute, Wood, 1 Key, Conical Bore, C.Peloubet, N.Y., 1829	750.00
Music, Guitar, Martin, F-2, 1942	1000.00
Music, Guitar, National Triolan, 1929	350.00
Music, Harmonica, Hohner, Marine Band Harmonica, Original Box	10.00
Music, Harmonica, P.Pohl Germany	8.50
Music, Harmonica, Rolmonica, 17 Paper Rolls, Box	150.00
Music, Harmonica, The Engineer, Germany	10.00

Music, Horn, Metal, 11 Sides, Gilt Rim, Pink Roses, Blue, Stand

Music, Harmonica, Tin Case	12.00
Music, Harp, Old Grosjean, Angel Decoration	850.00
Music, Horn, Metal, 11 Sides, Gilt Rim, Pink Roses, Blue, Stand .... *Illus*	190.00
Music, Horn, Morning Glory For Old Phonograph	18.00 To 30.00
Music, Hurdy Gurdy, 7 Tunes, Mechanical Animals, Mulanari	3200.00
Music, Jazz Flutrombone, Improved Easy Slide	35.00
Music, Jukebox, Capehart, Oak Cabinet	295.00
Music, Jukebox, Chicago Coin Band Box	450.00
Music, Jukebox, Seeburg, Style A	3500.00
Music, Jukebox, Wurlitzer, Model 616, Wood Case	475.00
Music, Jukebox, Wurlitzer, Model 950	2000.00
Music, Jukebox, Wurlitzer, No.1015	2200.00
Music, Jukebox, Wurlitzer, No.41, Countertop	1000.00

Music, Jukebox, Wurlitzer, No.771	300.00
Music, Jukebox, Wurlitzer, 412	500.00
Music, Mandolin Guitar, Menzenbauer, Panama Model, 1915, Carton & Music	97.50
Music, Melodeon, Mason & Hamlin, Walnut Case, Folding Legs	625.00
Music, Melodeon, Pump, Rosewood, C.1870s	450.00
Music, Melodeon, 6 Octave, Rosewood, Ornate, Whitney & Slayton, Restored	1100.00
Music, Needle, Tin, Victor, Red	20.00
Music, Nickelodeon, Electrova, Rebuilt	3500.00
Music, Nickelodeon, Seeburg, C, Swan On The Lake	4995.00
Music, Nickelodeon, Wurlitzer, Violin Pipes, Rebuilt	5500.00
Music, Oboe, Gunter Korber, Berlin, 4 Ivory Rings, 2 Silver Keys, Baroque	280.00
Music, Orchestrion, Barrel, Piano, Mandolin, Drum, Cymbal, Xylophone, 7 Ft.5 In.	6500.00
Music, Orchestrion, Jazzband, Losche, C.1928	7995.00
Music, Organ & Piano, Player, 2 Keyboards, 99 Pipes, 20 Rolls, Reproduco	4500.00
Music, Organ, Aeolian, 46 Note, 26 In. X 5 Feet X 5 Feet, 2 In.	895.00
Music, Organ, Barrel, German, Oil Painting On Front, Coin Operated, 1852	1850.00
Music, Organ, Barrel, Hurdy-Gurdy Variety, Zimmermann Of Leipzig, Germany	1995.00
Music, Organ, Beckwith Pump, Oak	500.00
Music, Organ, Circus, Bruder, 42 Keys	9975.00
Music, Organ, Concert Roller, 10 Rolls, Restored	600.00
Music, Organ, Estey Reed, Oak, Large	500.00
Music, Organ, Gem Roller, 10 Rolls	350.00
Music, Organ, Hammond Aeolian Player, 1937, 2 Keyboard, 40 Rolls	6500.00
Music, Organ, Lakeside, Oak High Back, C.1904	850.00
Music, Organ, North Tonawanda Band, 48 Keys, Restored, Plays Wurlitzer Rolls	7000.00
Music, Organ, Paper Roll, One Roll, Clariona	325.00
Music, Organ, Player, North Tonawanda Bank, 48 Key, Plays 150 Wurlitzer Rolls	7000.00
Music, Organ, Player, Wilcox & White	1475.00
Music, Organ, Pump, Beckwith, Light Oak	500.00
Music, Organ, Pump, Esley, Oak Case	400.00
Music, Organ, Pump, Parlor, Mason & Hamlin	125.00
Music, Organ, Pump, Putnam, Walnut Case	700.00
Music, Organ, Pump, Rolltop Desk Combination, Cherry, Hugo Wertheim, C.1888	7500.00
Music, Organ, Pump, Story & Clark, 1886, Carved Mahogany, Beveled Mirrors	2500.00
Music, Organ, Pump, Walnut, Parlor Type	375.00
Music, Organ, Ruth Barrel, 145 Wood Pipes, Crank & Electric Motor	2450.00
Music, Organ, Seeburg, Mortuary	2800.00
Music, Organ, Street, Automaton, Handmade	225.00
Music, Organ, Street, Miniature, 6 Tunes, Barrel, Pipes, Molinari, 14 X 16 In.	2400.00
Music, Organ, Street, Molinari, Miniature Barrel, 14 X 16 In.	2400.00
Music, Organ, Wangerin Pipe, 5 Ranks, Player Mechanism	4500.00
Music, Organ, Wurlitzer, Double Tracker Band, 10 X 6 Ft.	10000.00
Music, Organ, Wurlitzer, Military Band, 2 Ranks Of Pipes, Early 1900s	7000.00
Music, Organ, 48 Key, North Tonawanda, Plays Wurlitzer 150 Rolls, Restored	7000.00

The Phonograph, invented by Thomas Edison in the 1880s, has been made by many firms.

Music, Phonograph, Cylinder Player, Junior, Trivet Base, Brass Bell Horn	385.00
Music, Phonograph, Cylinder, Floor Model, M-75, With 120 Cylinders	650.00
Music, Phonograph, Cylinder, Thomas A.Edison, Fireside, Cherry, Horn, Records	475.00
Music, Phonograph, Edison Amberola, Cylinder, Model No.30	275.00
Music, Phonograph, Edison Cylinder Player, Oak Case, Side Wind, 2 Cylinders	265.00
Music, Phonograph, Edison Floor Model, Diamond Disc, Model VU37	125.00
Music, Phonograph, Edison, Cylinder, Brass Horn	250.00
Music, Phonograph, Edison, Cylinder, Electric Motor, 14 In.Brass Bell Horn	300.00
Music, Phonograph, Edison, Cylinder, Portable, 12 Cylinder Records	295.00
Music, Phonograph, Edison, Cylinder, Table Model, Horn In Base, 6 Minute Play	175.00
Music, Phonograph, Edison, Disk Console, Oak Case, 1916, 75 Thick Records	175.00
Music, Phonograph, Edison, Standard, Brass Horn, 5 Cylinders	340.00
Music, Phonograph, Edison, Standard, C & H Reproducers, 20 Records	495.00
Music, Phonograph, Edison, Triumph E., Oak Horn	1600.00
Music, Phonograph, Genola, Child's	200.00
Music, Phonograph, Harmony Talking Machine, Table Model, Tulip Horn, Oak	350.00
Music, Phonograph, Harmony, 12 Records, 1 Foot Square X 7 In.High	100.00
Music, Phonograph, Home Edison, Morning Glory Horn, U/ Cylinder Records	350.00

Music, Phonograph, Model A, 1901, Standard Talking Machine Co., 11 In. 325.00
Music, Phonograph, Pathe, Disc, With Horn, Ornate 550.00
Music, Phonograph, Triumphone, Crank, Miniature 57.00
Music, Phonograph, Victor Talking Machine, Model VV90, Stand Up 140.00
Music, Phonograph, Victor, R Model, Wooden Arm, Horn 750.00
Music, Phonograph, Victor, 1914, Oak 67.50
Music, Photophone, Bronze Clip, Original Calendar 29.00
Music, Piano Roll, Duo-Art 7.00
Music, Piano, Ampico Grand, Wm.Knabe & Co., Model A-6E, Restored 5200.00
Music, Piano, Ampico Upright, Marshall & Wendell 2300.00
Music, Piano, Ampico, Chickering, 1927 .... 12000.00
Music, Piano, Baby Grand, Aeolian-Duo Art, Player 2100.00
Music, Piano, Barrel, French, 8 Tunes, 4 Ft.5 In. 1495.00
Music, Piano, Barrel, Vossen, Ornate Cabinet, 7 Ft.8 In. 2795.00
Music, Piano, Cabinet, Chickering Ampico, Everything Original, C.1927 .... 12000.00
Music, Piano, Duo-Art Grand, Steinway, Model XR, Finish H-1721, 1930s 9700.00
Music, Piano, Electric Upright, Duo-Art 1100.00
Music, Piano, Grand Player, Welte Mignon, Mehlin & Sons, Mahogany, 5 Ft. 5000.00
Music, Piano, Grand, Dubois, Bacon, Square, Rosewood 1000.00
Music, Piano, Grand, Lindeman & Sons, 3 Legs, Victorian Baroque, Rosewood 7500.00
Music, Piano, Grand, Square, Decker Bros.1863, Rosewood Finish, Hand-Carved 1000.00
Music, Piano, Grand, Wm.Knabe & Co., Ampico, Style A-GE, Mahogany, Restored 5100.00
Music, Piano, Harmonyphone, Street Piano, 10 Tune 1100.00
Music, Piano, Knabe, Louis XIV, Walnut, 1927, 5 Ft. 8 In. 9500.00
Music, Piano, Mechanical, 64 Note Pianotist Music, Blasius & Sons 995.00
Music, Piano, Player, Baby Grand, Ampico, Fisher, Case Refinished 2150.00
Music, Piano, Player, Gulbranson, Restored 1200.00
Music, Piano, Player, Mehlin & Sons, Mahogany, Welte Mignon, 5 Ft. 5000.00
Music, Piano, Player, Meldorf 425.00
Music, Piano, Player, Norris & Hyde, Upright, 60 Rolls 1150.00
Music, Piano, Player, Peerless A-Roll 3000.00
Music, Piano, Player, Peerless, Style D 1250.00
Music, Piano, Player, Stool, 60 Rolls, Norris & Hyde 950.00
Music, Piano, Player, Upright, Standard, Behr Bros. 800.00
Music, Piano, Player, Whitney, Cherry Mahogany, 1905 .... 2350.00
Music, Piano, Regina, Sublima, Moving Advertising Scene 3995.00
Music, Piano, Reproducer, Knabe, 1904, 5 Ft., 6 In. 4000.00
Music, Piano, Reproducing, Duo-Art, C.1930, 5 Ft.1 In. 3495.00
Music, Piano, Reproducing, Marshall & Wendell Ampico, Grand 3495.00
Music, Piano, Spinet, Bressler, Paris, Mahogany, French Empire, 67 X 33 In. 450.00
Music, Piano, Steinway Grand Duo-Art 7500.00
Music, Piano, Steinway Grand, Square, 1898, 80 X 40 X 38 In. 6500.00
Music, Piano, Steinway Verti-Grand, 1904, Restored 4000.00
Music, Piano, Steinway, Duo-Art Grand, Model XR, 1930 .... 9700.00
Music, Piano, Street, Harmonyphone 1150.00
Music, Piano, Upright, Ampico, J.& C.Fischer, Model A, 1925 .... 2200.00
Music, Piano, Upright, Ampico, Marshall & Wendell, Rebuilt And Refinished 3950.00
Music, Piano, Weber Aeolean Player, 6 Ft. 1800.00
Music, Piano, Weber, Grand, Ornate Carved Legs, Rosewood, C.1860 .... 1500.00
Music, Piano, Wurlitzer, Upright, Miniature, 4 1/4 X 4 1/4 In. 22.00
Music, Pianoforte, Mahogany & Satinwood Inlay, American Federal, N.Y., C.1835 .... 350.00
Music, Radio Horn, Music Master Wooden Gooseneck 30.00
Music, Radio, Atwater Kent, Wooden Model 48 .... 42.50
Music, Radio, Crosley, 2 Floating Tubes, Wooden Cased, 1914 .... 99.00
Music, Radio, Echophone, 5 Tubes, Model KS5 .... 10.00
Music, Radio, Phonograph, Brunswick, Model 460, 1924 .... 300.00
Music, Record Player, Edison, C.1906 .... 250.00
Music, Record, Astronaut Glenn, Friendship 7, Dated, 33 1/3 RPM 25.00
Music, Record, Edison, Thick, Set Of 5 .... 10.00
Music, Regina Music Box, Set Of 25 Discs, 20 3/4 In. 40.00
Music, Reginaphone, 15 Discs, Single Comb, Spindle Supported The Turntable 1995.00
Music, Reginaphone, 20 Discs, Mahogany, Style No.150, 15 1/2 In. 3495.00
Music, Roller Organ, Celestina, C.1870, Hand Crank, For Paper Rolls 350.00
Music, Saxophone, Old Vega, In Case, Pearl Finger Tabs 65.00
Music, Sheet, Al Jolson 4.00

Music, Sheet, Antler's March, 1900	6.50
Music, Sheet, Baseball Waltz, 1885	3.00
Music, Sheet, Bing Crosby	60.00
Music, Sheet, Blue Bell, Soldier Telling Sweetheart Goodbye On Cover, 1923	12.00
Music, Sheet, Charge Of The Light Brigade, 1896	7.00
Music, Sheet, Come Josephine In Your Flying Machine, Biplane On Cover	10.00
Music, Sheet, Daddy Long Legs, Mary Pickford On Cover, 1919	5.00
Music, Sheet, Down In Dixie, Stella	3.00
Music, Sheet, Lindbergh The Eagle Of The U.S.A.	10.00
Music, Sheet, Lindbergh, When Lindy Comes Home	8.00
Music, Sheet, Lump Of Sugar, Al Jolson	3.00
Music, Sheet, My Mammy, Al Jolson	3.00
Music, Sheet, Napoleon's Last Charge	10.00
Music, Sheet, Nation Mourns, Black & White Bust Of Lincoln On Cover	25.00
Music, Sheet, New York Minstrels Songster, 32 Pages	15.00
Music, Sheet, Ocean Roll, 1911	2.50
Music, Sheet, On The Mississippi, 1912	4.50
Music, Sheet, On The Old Fall River Line, 1913	12.50
Music, Sheet, Over There, Cohen, 1918	3.00
Music, Sheet, Signal From Mars	9.00
Music, Sheet, Somebody's Wrong, Sophie Tucker	3.00
Music, Sheet, Sunny Boy, Al Jolson	6.00
Music, Sheet, The Witch's Whirl	35.00
Music, Sheet, When That Midnight Choo-Choo Leaves For Alabam, 1912	8.50
Music, Sheet, Wizard Of Oz, Judy Garland, 1939	15.00
Music, Sheet, World's Exposition Grand March, 1890	5.00
Music, Sheet, 3 Little Words, Amos & Andy On Cover	10.00
Music, Stand, Iron, Forged	375.00
Music, Ukelin, International Musical Corporation	48.50
Music, Ukulele, Camp	35.00
Music, Violano-Virtuosos, Single, Mills, Restore, 12 Rolls	8900.00
Music, Violin, Label, G.A.Pfretzschner, N.A.Stadivarius, Anno 1716	300.00
Music, Violin, Ole Bull, Wooden Case	1750.00
Music, Zither, Bowed, Zaver Kerschersteiner, C.1900	500.00
Music, Zither, Franz Schwarzer, World's Fair, Austria, 1873	350.00

Mustache cups were popular from 1850 to 1900. A ledge of china or silver held the hair out of the liquid in the cup.

Mustache Cup & Saucer, Armorial	48.00
Mustache Cup & Saucer, Bone China Pumpkin Shape & Color, Pedestal Base	42.50
Mustache Cup & Saucer, Father, Gold Florals & Handles, Marked Germany	38.00
Mustache Cup & Saucer, Floral Design, Gold Trim Saucer	27.50
Mustache Cup & Saucer, Flow Blue, Staffordshire, Ironstone	52.00
Mustache Cup & Saucer, Gold And Roses, Left-Handed	85.00
Mustache Cup & Saucer, Hand-Painted, Noritake	25.00
Mustache Cup & Saucer, Owl & Florals, Hand-Painted	35.00
Mustache Cup & Saucer, Pansies, China	32.00
Mustache Cup & Saucer, Pink Luster, Forget-Me-Not, German	35.00
Mustache Cup & Saucer, Pink Roses, Gold, Embossed Rims	29.50
Mustache Cup & Saucer, Raspberry Luster, Victorian	25.00
Mustache Cup & Saucer, Red Roses, Blue	25.00
Mustache Cup & Saucer, Scalloped, Floral Inside & Out, Pink, Yellow, Lavender	27.50
Mustache Cup & Saucer, Silver Plate, Floral Engraving, Pairpoint	95.00
Mustache Cup & Saucer, Silver Plated, Engraved, Aurora	28.00
Mustache Cup & Saucer, Small Clusters Of Roses, Gilt Edging	40.00
Mustache Cup & Saucer, Violets & Green Leafings, Band Of Green On Saucer	31.50
Mustache Cup, Flowers, Gold Trim, Marked Germany	32.00
Mustache Cup, Hand-Painted, Flowers, Raised Lettering	24.50
Mustache Cup, Left-Handed, Nippon, 2 Lions In Relief, Green Wreath	200.00
Mustache Cup, Nippon, Egyptian Scenic, River, Trees, Sunset, Green M Mark	120.00
Mustache Cup, Pastel Blue Swirling To White, Gold, KPM	16.00
Mustache Cup, R.D.Bunnykins	17.00
Mustache Cup, Raised Flowers & Lettering, Love The Giver	12.50 To 18.50
Mustache Cup, Red Floral Wreath, Friendship's Gift	10.00
Mustache Cup, Rose Decoration	22.50

Mustache Cup, **Royal Crown**, Left-Handed, Hand-Painted	45.00
Mustache Cup, **Rs Prussia**, Bevel Mirror, Red Mark	95.00
Mustache Cup, **Sky Blue**, White Enameled Fish & Lily Pads, Gold Edging	35.00
Mustache Cup, **Think Of Me**, Raised Gold Coralene, Pink Flower, Green Fernery	37.00
Mustache Cup, **Violets**, Marked Bavaria	20.00
Mustache Cup, **White**, Black Sailing Ship, Gold Rim	10.00
Mustache Cup, **White**, Gold Flower, Remember Me	25.00
MZ Austria, **Bowl**, Signed ES, 1908, Gold Feet, 9 1/4 In.	100.00
MZ Austria, **Chocolate Pot**, Green, Blown Pink & White Roses, Gold Trim	65.00
MZ Austria, **Dish**, Gold Center Handle & Edge, Pastel Flowers, Signed, 11 In.	30.00
MZ Austria, **Plate**, Irregular Gold Edge, Signed ES, 6 In.	10.00
MZ Austria, **Plate**, Portrait, Josephine, Ladies & Napoleon Around Rim, 12 In.	145.00
MZ Austria, **Plate**, Portrait, Lady In Profile, Marked Constance, 8 In.	40.00
MZ Austria, **Plate**, Portrait, Lady With Long Hair, Marked Constance, 9 3/4 In.	40.00
MZ Austria, **Sugar & Creamer**, Eggshell Porcelain, Crown Mark	35.00
MZ Austria, **Sugar & Creamer**, Good Luck Symbols	25.00
MZ Austria, **Syrup & Underplate**, Enameled Roses	27.50
MZ Austria, **Syrup & Underplate**, Single Rose, Green Leaves, 6 Sided, Marked	28.50
MZ Austria, **Teapot**, Roses & Gold Trim	25.00

Nailsea glass was made in the Bristol District in England from 1788 to 1873. Many pieces were made with loopings of colored glass as decorations.

Nailsea, **Ball**, Witches, Red, White & Clear	45.00
Nailsea, **Barrel**, Biscuit, Blue	250.00
Nailsea, **Cruet**, Electric Blue & White, Applied Crystal Handle, Base, 8 In.	85.00
Nailsea, **Pitcher**, Ewer, Loops, White Clear Reeded Applied Handle, Blown, 6 In.	68.00
Nailsea, **Rolling Pin**, Red & Clear	80.00
Nailsea, **Rose Bowl**, Verre Moire, Blue, Frosted Loopings, 6 Crimp Top, 3 In.	145.00
Nailsea, **Shade**, Clear, White Loopings, Blue Threading, Ruffled, 6 In.	72.00
Nailsea, **Vase**, Blue & White, 10 In.	95.00
Nailsea, **Vase**, Gold, Yellow, White, 8 1/2 In.	125.00
Nailsea, **Vase**, Green & White Swirls On Clear, 6 1/4 In.	125.00
Nailsea, **Vase**, Squatty, Low, 8 In.Diameter	25.00

Nakara is a trade name for a white glassware made around 1900 that was decorated in pastel colors. It was made by the C. F. Monroe Company of Meriden, Connecticut.

Nakara, **Basket**, Pink Dogwood Blossoms On Blue, Brass Collar & Handle, 6 In.	165.00
Nakara, **Box**, Apricot, Winged Cherubs On Lid Tossing Fruit From Tree	222.50
Nakara, **Box**, Decorated Brass Mounts, Openwork Feet, Hinged, 4 In.Diameter	325.00
Nakara, **Box**, Decorated, 6 Sided, Hinged Cover, 3 3/4 In.	190.00
Nakara, **Box**, Floral, Dots, Panels, Cloverleaf, Mirror, Hinged, 2 3/4 In.	245.00
Nakara, **Box**, Green, Pink Flowers, Square, 6 In.	175.00
Nakara, **Box**, Jewel, Flowers, White Beading, Lavender, Lid, Signed, 5 In.	225.00
Nakara, **Box**, Jewel, Pink, Blue Florals, Swivel Mirror Inside, Hinged, 5 1/2 In.	215.00
Nakara, **Box**, Sage Green, Floral Design, Round, 4 1/2 In.	385.00
Nakara, **Box**, Star Shaped, Jeweled, Cover, Green, Pink	250.00
Nakara, **Box**, Tapestry Decoration, Hexagon, Footed, 3 In.	265.00
Nakara, **Box**, Trinket, Blue, Red & Yellow Floral, Ormolu Rim, 6 Sided, 2 X 4 In.	125.00
Nakara, **Box**, White, Ink, Maroon, 6 Sided, Beading, 4 1/2 In.	225.00
Nakara, **Box**, Yellow & Orange, Lavender Flowers, Beaded Lid, Oblong	390.00
Nakara, **Dish**, Dresser, Blue, 6 Sided	150.00
Nakara, **Dish**, Pink, Blue, Pink Blossoms, Signed, Hexagonal, 3 1/2 In.	75.00
Nakara, **Humidor**, Indian Portrait Decoration, Signed	395.00
Nakara, **Jar**, Tobacco, Portrait, Lion, Signed	375.00
Nakara, **Tray**, Dresser, Niagara Falls In Gold, Ormolu Collar & Handles, Pink	175.00
Nakara, **Tray**, Pin, Beaded Florals & Swirls, Ormolu Handles, C.F.M.Co.	150.00
Nakara, **Vase**, Ormolu Footed Base, Enameled Flowers, 14 In.	395.00

Nanking china is a blue-and-white porcelain made in China for export during the eighteenth century.

Nanking, **Dish**, Vegetable, Oval, Covered, C.1790	40.00

Napkin rings were popular from 1869 to about 1900.

Napkin Ring, **Alphabet Engraved All Around**, Sterling Silver	20.00

Napkin Ring, Bracelet Type, Sterling Silver 15.00
Napkin Ring, Capital, Washington, D.C. 15.00
Napkin Ring, Carved Snake, Ivory 18.50
Napkin Ring, Celluloid 3.00
Napkin Ring, Corset Shaped, Chased Leaves, Silver Plate, 1 3/4 In. 15.00
Napkin Ring, Cut Glass, Deeply Cut Geometric, 1 In.Wide 22.00
Napkin Ring, Figural, Bear On Platform 60.00
Napkin Ring, Figural, Billy Goat 125.00
Napkin Ring, Figural, Bird & Scottie, Celluloid 5.00
Napkin Ring, Figural, Bird Beside Ring On Leaf, Silver 85.00
Napkin Ring, Figural, Bird On Branch, Base Is Ornate Tablecloth 75.00
Napkin Ring, Figural, Bird On Each Side Of Base, Wings Spread, Touching Ring 46.00
Napkin Ring, Figural, Bird On Leaf 87.00
Napkin Ring, Figural, Bird On Top Ring, Tasseled Leaves, Reed & Barton 85.00
Napkin Ring, Figural, Birds, Leaves, Square Base, Gold Wash And Silver 95.00
Napkin Ring, Figural, Boy Offering Cracker To Dog, Kate Greenaway 75.00
Napkin Ring, Figural, Boy On Dolphin, Ring On Tail, Trident In Hand 53.50
Napkin Ring, Figural, Boy On Each Side, Middletown No.87 .... 75.00
Napkin Ring, Figural, Boy Pulling Ring, Bridgeport Silver Co., No.58 .... 150.00
Napkin Ring, Figural, Boy Pushing Ring, Pewter, Kate Greenaway 199.00
Napkin Ring, Figural, Boy Stealing Eggs 95.00
Napkin Ring, Figural, Boy With Cookie For Begging Dog 145.00
Napkin Ring, Figural, Boy, Foot In Air, Holding Ring On Shoulders 125.00
Napkin Ring, Figural, Boy's Bust On Round Base Holds Ring Over Head 60.00
Napkin Ring, Figural, Bulldog On Side, Silver Plate 40.00
Napkin Ring, Figural, Bushy-Tailed Dogs, Front Paws Resting On Round Ring 115.00
Napkin Ring, Figural, Butterflies, Meriden 160.00
Napkin Ring, Figural, Butterfly, 2 Oriental Fans Hold Up Napkin Ring 75.00
Napkin Ring, Figural, Cherub Carrying Engraved Ring, Barbour, Silver 135.00
Napkin Ring, Figural, Cherub Holding Vase 135.00
Napkin Ring, Figural, Cherub, Wishbone, Silver Plate 80.00
Napkin Ring, Figural, Chick Wishbone, Chicken Leg, Wilcox, Silver Plate 52.00
Napkin Ring, Figural, Clown Holding Hoop For Dog, 4 In. 76.00
Napkin Ring, Figural, Cupid With Ring On Back, Rogers & Bros., Silver 65.00
Napkin Ring, Figural, Dog In Doghouse 75.00
Napkin Ring, Figural, Dog Next To Barrel-Shaped Ring, Tufts 89.00
Napkin Ring, Figural, Dog On Platform 60.00
Napkin Ring, Figural, Dog Sitting Upon Shield, Stars, Stripes 70.00
Napkin Ring, Figural, Dog With Collar & Tassel On One Side, 2 1/2 In. 70.00
Napkin Ring, Figural, Easter Nest & Rabbit 25.00
Napkin Ring, Figural, Embossed Birds, Flowers, Plated 22.00
Napkin Ring, Figural, Fan, Pairpoint, Silver 140.00
Napkin Ring, Figural, Fans, Ball Foot, Butterfly, Meriden Silver Plate 85.00
Napkin Ring, Figural, Floral & Leaves Form Footed Base, Silver Plate 40.00
Napkin Ring, Figural, Flowers At Side 75.00
Napkin Ring, Figural, Footed Base Supports Salt, Pepper, Ring & Bird 175.00
Napkin Ring, Figural, Goat On Circular Base, Ring On Ball 144.00
Napkin Ring, Figural, Goat Standing Beside 6-Sided Ring 95.00
Napkin Ring, Figural, Goat, Whole Body, Rockford Silver Co. 73.00
Napkin Ring, Figural, Horse Pushing Ring On Stand, Silver Plate 40.00
Napkin Ring, Figural, Horseshoes Topped By Jockey Cap, Silver Plate 63.00
Napkin Ring, Figural, Hummingbird On Round Raised Base 80.00
Napkin Ring, Figural, Kneeling Cherub Chasing Bird, Wilcox Co. 75.00
Napkin Ring, Figural, Kookaburra, Ring On Branch, Stewart Dawson, EPNS ... 90.00
Napkin Ring, Figural, Lady's Fan, Engraved Mother, Marked Pairpoint Corp. ... 48.00
Napkin Ring, Figural, Leaf Base, Flower & Stem At Side, M.S.Co.No.298 .... 74.50
Napkin Ring, Figural, Leaf, Fluted Ring, Open Flower & Stem, M.S.Co. 75.00
Napkin Ring, Figural, Lily Bud On Pad, Meridan Silver Co. 25.00
Napkin Ring, Figural, Lily Pad, Victorian 75.00
Napkin Ring, Figural, Monkey Playing Horn, Imbricated Ring 150.00
Napkin Ring, Figural, Mouse Pushes Ring 45.00
Napkin Ring, Figural, On Back Of Pair Of Pointer Dogs, Webster Mfg.Co. 75.00
Napkin Ring, Figural, Owl, Silver Plate 17.50
Napkin Ring, Figural, Peacock Standing On Ring 144.00
Napkin Ring, Figural, Reindeer, Whole Body 218.00

Napkin Ring, Figural, Republican Elephant, Coolidge's Boyhood Home, Silver	15.00
Napkin Ring, Figural, Ring Base, Bird On Top, Dog Looking Up, Aurora S.P.Co.	95.00
Napkin Ring, Figural, Ring On Ornate Base Supported By Soldiers	75.00
Napkin Ring, Figural, Ring Sits On Wheelbarrow	65.00
Napkin Ring, Figural, Robin, Chain	55.00
Napkin Ring, Figural, Satchel	25.00
Napkin Ring, Figural, Setter, Ring On Head And Neck	150.00
Napkin Ring, Figural, Squirrel, Silver Plate	50.00
Napkin Ring, Figural, Stag, Decorated Ring On Back, Rectangular Base	149.50
Napkin Ring, Figural, Tulip At Side, Leaf Base, Meriden	47.00
Napkin Ring, Figural, Turtle, Ring On Back, Rogers	48.00
Napkin Ring, Figural, Two Boys Standing, Holding 4-Sided Lacy-Edged Ring	135.00
Napkin Ring, Figural, Two Cherries & Leaves On Ring	50.00
Napkin Ring, Figural, Two Cherubs Holding The Ring	85.00
Napkin Ring, Figural, Two Foxes, Eggs In Nest	165.00
Napkin Ring, Figural, Two Squirrels, Marked Hartford, Co.	75.00
Napkin Ring, Figural, Victorian Chair, Engraved, 1874	25.00
Napkin Ring, Figural, Water Lily Bud On Pad, Silver Plate, Meriden	25.00
Napkin Ring, Figural, Wooden Boy Sitting On Top Of Ring, Hand-Carved	12.00
Napkin Ring, Fish Biting His Tail, Pair	15.00
Napkin Ring, Floral Relief, Victorian, Hallmarked Sterling Silver, 1 1/4 In.	25.00
Napkin Ring, Fretwork Arch, Birds, Leaves, Gold Wash & Silver	95.00
Napkin Ring, Hammered Pewter, Agate-Type Stone	15.00
Napkin Ring, Ivory, Birds & Flowers	14.00
Napkin Ring, Ivory, Chain Of Elephants, Set Of 4	40.00
Napkin Ring, Ivory, Hand-Carved, Deer Family In Woodland	32.00
Napkin Ring, Ivory, Scrimshaw, Seal & Leaves	25.00
Napkin Ring, Miss., Santa Barbara, 1786, Mauchine	10.00
Napkin Ring, Monogrammed Gertrude, Silver Plate, 1 In.	12.00
Napkin Ring, Old Witch House & First Church, 1692, Metal	9.95
Napkin Ring, Pedestal, Animals In Filigree	30.00
Napkin Ring, Repousse Scenic, House, Trees Sterling Silver	45.00
Napkin Ring, Roses, Convex Shape, Gold Edging, Pastel Green, 2 In.	15.00
Napkin Ring, Scalloped Edge & Flowers	20.00
Napkin Ring, Silver Plate, Flower On Leaf	25.00
Napkin Ring, Silver Plate, Grape Design, Beaded Edges, Set Of 6	75.00
Napkin Ring, Silver, Inscription, 1861	5.50
Napkin Ring, Sterling Silver, Large, Wide, Victorian	22.50
Napkin Ring, Sterling Silver, Monogrammed, 2 In.	27.50
Napkin Ring, Sterling Silver, Wood & Hughes, Pair	95.00
Napkin Ring, Triangle, Wishbones, Beaded Eagle, Meriden	34.00

Nash glass was made in Corona, New York, by Arthur Nash and his sons after 1919. He worked at the Webb Factory in England and for the Tiffany Glassworks in the United States.

Nash, Candlestick, Blue Chintz On Crystal, Unsigned	55.00
Nash, Candlestick, Blue, Chintz, Signed	85.00
Nash, Candlestick, Curvaceous, Embossed, 4 1/2 In., Pair	395.00
Nash, Rose Bowl, Vertical Blue Stripes, Amber Opalescent	150.00
Nash, Vase, Bud, Gold, Pink, Lavender, Blue Highlights, Wafer Foot, 7 3/4 In.	248.50
Nash, Vase, Flared & Fluted, Indigo Iridescent, Flower Form, 7 X 7 In.	135.00
Nash, Vase, Lavender Highlights, Pedestal Foot, Gold, Signed Nash 532	395.00
Nautical, see also Scrimshaw	
Nautical, Anchor, Ship's, 600 Pounds	200.00
Nautical, Binacle, 8-Sided Mahogany Base, Brass Top, 54 In.	1200.00
Nautical, Boat, Model, Lead Ballast, Hand-Carved, C.1860, 12 1/2 X 4 1/4 In.	85.00
Nautical, Bottle, Antique Ship Inside	24.00
Nautical, Bowl, Queen Mary, Cunard Mark, 3 In.	5.00
Nautical, Chest, Seaman's, Early 19th Century, 28 X 18 X 19 1/2 In.	235.00
Nautical, Clock, Seth Thomas, Brass	110.00
Nautical, Compass, Brass Gimbals, Mahogany Box, 1873, 6 In.	225.00
Nautical, Compass, Brass, Mounted In Handled Mahogany Box, 1900, 8 1/2 In.	185.00
Nautical, Compass, Portable, Brass, Mahogany Box, C.1900, 8 1/2 In.	185.00
Nautical, Compass, Watercolor Decoration, Pine Box, 18th Century	120.00
Nautical, Compass, Wood Box, Lid, Marked Boston, Massachusetts, 5 X 5 In.	45.00

Nautical, Cowery Shell, Writing, Lord's Prayer 85.00
Nautical, Cup, Cunard Mark, Royal Doulton 7.50
Nautical, Desk, From S.S.Vermont II, C.1890 .... 850.00
Nautical, Engraving, Paddlewheel Steamer, Fall River Line, 9 1/2 X 12 In. 35.00
Nautical, Gauge, Panel, Brass & Brazilian Rosewood 38.00
Nautical, Horn, Boat, Tapering Trumpet Shape, Tin, 11 3/4 In. 16.00
Nautical, Horn, Fog, Ship's, E.A.Gill, Gloucester, Mass., 3 Brass Whistles 125.00
Nautical, Horn, Ship's, Brass, Steam Or Air 45.00
Nautical, Lantern, Brass, Flat Back, Octagonal Front, 15 In. 135.00
Nautical, Lantern, Ship's, Brass, Gyroscope Type 65.00
Nautical, Light, Anchor, Ship's, Solid Brass 225.00
Nautical, Light, Ship's, Brass, Port & Starboard, Pair, 12 In. 295.00
Nautical, Light, Ship's, Polished Steel & Brass, G & B Company, 22 1/2 In. 180.00
Nautical, Log Book, 1807, Dromo, 2 1/2 Year Voyage, Boston To Canton 350.00
Nautical, Net Float, Blown Glass 35.00
Nautical, Plate, I.D., Brass, 1925, 1 X 11 3/4 In. 25.00
Nautical, Porthole, Brass, Double Glass & Metal Storm Cover, 3 Dogs, 18 In. ... 200.00
Nautical, Porthole, Solid Brass 58.00
Nautical, Pump, All Wood, Dovetailed Corners, Brass Faucet, 36 In. 27.50
Nautical, Sextant, Dovetailed Box, Spencer Browning 325.00
Nautical, Sextant, Mahogany Dovetailed Box 240.00
Nautical, Shell, Carved, Chambered Nautilus, Dated 1845 .... 1500.00
Nautical, Ship Model, Fully Rigged, Cradle, 75 In.Long 850.00
Nautical, Ship's Wheel, Wood, Brass Fittings, 58 In.Diameter 325.00
Nautical, Steam Engine, 2 Horsepower, Brass Cylinder, Crated, 27 X 20 In. 475.00
Nautical, Stove, Ship's, Little Cod, Charles Fawcett Mfg.Co., Ltd. 150.00
Nautical, Sugar, Square, Queen Mary 5.00
Nautical, Telescope, Brass & Copper, 1 Pull, 19th Century, 3 In.Closed 25.00
Nautical, Telescope, Brass & Mahogany, Victorian, Pocket Size, One Pull, 6 In. . 20.00
Nautical, Telescope, Brass, Leather Case, 45 3/4 In.Opened 85.00
Nautical, Telescope, Brass, Leather Cover, Signed Spencer Browning, 40 In. 230.00
Nautical, Telescope, Brass, Spencer Browning, C.1820, 39 In. 88.00
Nautical, Telescope, Brass, Spencer Browning, Leather Cover, 38 In. 224.00
Nautical, Telescope, Brass, Sunshade Extended, 36 3/8 In.Opened 65.00
Nautical, Telescope, Brass, 4 Sections, John Bruce, Liverpool, 29 1/2 In. 75.00
Nautical, Telescope, Folding, Miniature, Brass 30.00
Nautical, Telescope, Octangular, 21 In.Open 110.00
Nautical, Telescope, Reflecting, C.1800 .... 820.00
Nautical, Thimble, Sailor's Palm, Brass 10.00
Nautical, Timepiece, Heavy Brass, Chelsea 165.00
Nautical, Transit, Surveyor's, Brass, Keuffel & Esser 295.00
Nautical, Wheel, Ship's, Brass Center, 32 In. 240.00
Nautical, Wheel, Ship's, Brass, Walnut Handles, Brass Caps 85.00
Nautical, Whistle, Ship's Distress, Leather, Wood, Brass 150.00
Nautical, Whistle, Steam, Brass 39.00
 Needlework, see Textile, Picture; Textile, Sampler

*Netsuke are small ivory, wood, metal, or porcelain pieces used as the button on
the end of a cord holding a Japanese money pouch. The earliest date from
the sixteenth century.*
Netsuke, Chicken In The Egg 50.00
Netsuke, Foo Dogs In Crouching Position, 1 3/4 X 2 1/4 In. 100.00
Netsuke, Ivory Kabuki Dancer, Revolving Face 50.00
Netsuke, Ivory, Bearded Old Man With Frog On Back, Signed, 2 In. 80.00
Netsuke, Ivory, Bearded Tortoise Man, Signed, 2 1/2 In. 65.00
Netsuke, Ivory, Man With Adze, Squirrel At Feet, Signed, 2 In. 45.00
Netsuke, Mask, Signed By Hiroyouri 65.00
Netsuke, Monkey Group, Mother & Child, Ivory, Inlaid Eye Pupils, 19th Century . 480.00
Netsuke, Monkey, Reclining Against Catfish, Ivory, Inlaid Brass Eyes 180.00
Netsuke, Monkeys, Hear No Evil, See No Evil, Speak No Evil, Signed By Sada ... 85.00
Netsuke, Mouse Charming Coiled Snake 75.00
Netsuke, Peach & Leaves, Green Jade, Signed 175.00
Netsuke, Rat, Signed 250.00
Netsuke, Revolving Face, Angry To Happy Expression, 2 In. 38.00
Netsuke, Revolving Face, Ivory 40.00

Netsuke, Sculptor, Reclining Against Tool Box, Ivory, Masaaki, 1 1/2 In.	420.00
Netsuke, Seated Man Holding Cloth Around Shoulders, Ivory, 1 3/8 In.	90.00
Netsuke, Snail On Egg Plant, Ivory, Signed, Mid-19th Century	350.00
Netsuke, Standing Figure, Revolved Face, Happy To Angry, 2 1/4 In.	35.00
Netsuke, Warrior Training Horse To Stand On Chess Board, Ivory, Signed	150.00
Netsuke, Woman In Costume, Ivory, 1 1/2 X 1 1/2 In.	50.00
Netsuke, Wrestlers, Black Belts & Hair, Ivory, Signed, 1 1/4 In.	150.00
New England Glass Co., Bottle, Cologne, Engraved Shoulders, Stopper	45.00
New England Glass Co., Bowl, Finger, Amberina, Ruby To Violet	82.00
New England Glass Co., Celery, Washington	89.50
New England Glass Co., Cup, Punch, Peachblow	395.00

New Geneva stoneware was made in New Geneva, Pennsylvania, between 1854 and 1900.

New Martinsville, see also Peachblow

New Martinsville, Basket, Black Amethyst, Dancing Girls, Handled, 9 In.	10.00
New Martinsville, Basket, Crystal, 9 In.	10.50
New Martinsville, Bookend, Horse, Clear, Pair	48.00
New Martinsville, Bowl, Console, Ruff Rim, 15 In.	12.00
New Martinsville, Bowl, Lace Edge, Black Glass Base, 12 In.	16.00
New Martinsville, Bowl, Peachblow, Sunburst, Ruffled, Crimped, Gold Iridescent	110.00
New Martinsville, Bowl, Sunglow, 5 In.	85.00
New Martinsville, Bowl, Swan Head, Crystal Heads, Cobalt	37.50
New Martinsville, Candelabra, Double, Clear Glass, 5 X 7 In., Pair	30.00
New Martinsville, Candleholder, Double, Etched Teardrop, Pair	26.00
New Martinsville, Chick, Baby	22.50
New Martinsville, Console Set, Green Swan, Swan Candleholders	49.50
New Martinsville, Cordial Set, Amber, 5 Piece	25.00
New Martinsville, Cup & Saucer, Janice, Ruby	6.00
New Martinsville, Dish, Cobalt, Swan Handle, 6 In.	12.00
New Martinsville, Dish, Powder, Amber, Covered	15.00
New Martinsville, Figurine, Bear, Crystal, 4 1/2 In.	30.00
New Martinsville, Figurine, Bear, 5 In.	28.50
New Martinsville, Figurine, Crystal Rooster, 7 1/2 In.	28.00
New Martinsville, Figurine, Elephant	50.00
New Martinsville, Figurine, Police Dog	30.00
New Martinsville, Figurine, Rooster, 7 1/2 In.	30.00
New Martinsville, Figurine, Seal, Large	35.00
New Martinsville, Figurine, Squirrel On Base, 6 In.	30.00
New Martinsville, Figurine, Squirrel On Rectangular Base	35.00
New Martinsville, Figurine, Swan, Green Body, Clear Neck, 12 In.	35.00
New Martinsville, Figurine, Swan, Wingspread, Green Body, Clear Neck, 12 In.	30.00
New Martinsville, Jar, Powder, Covered, Amber	11.00
New Martinsville, Pitcher, Lorraine, Ruby Stained	58.00
New Martinsville, Pitcher, Water, Leaf & Star, Ice Lip, 7 1/2 In.	28.50
New Martinsville, Plate, Janice, Ruby, 8 In.	7.50
New Martinsville, Refreshment Set, Ruby Oscar, 7 Piece	75.00
New Martinsville, Seal, Clear, 7 In.	45.00
New Martinsville, Seal, Frosted, 7 In.	47.50
New Martinsville, Sugar & Creamer, Janice, Ruby	12.00
New Martinsville, Sugar & Creamer, Radiance, Ruby	23.00
New Martinsville, Swan, Blue, Janice, 9 1/2 In.	24.50
New Martinsville, Swan, Cobalt Blue, Clear Neck, 5 In.	16.00
New Martinsville, Swan, Cobalt Neck, Janice, 9 1/2 In.	24.50
New Martinsville, Swan, Green Body, Clear Neck, 12 In.	35.00
New Martinsville, Swan, Heart Shape, Blue, 5 In.	12.50
New Martinsville, Swan, Janice, Clear, Red Neck, 3 1/2 In.	32.00
New Martinsville, Swan, Janice, Crystal & Cobalt, 9 1/2 In.	24.75
New Martinsville, Swan, Red, Heart Shape, 6 In.	22.00
New Martinsville, Tumbler, Red	8.00
New Martinsville, Water Set, Amber, Pitcher & 5 Tumblers, 6 Piece	150.00
New Martinsville, Wine Set, Decanter, Six Glasses, Ruby Moondrops	95.00

Newcomb Pottery was founded by Ellsworth and William Woodward at Sophie Newcomb College, New Orleans, Louisiana, in 1896. The work

continued through the 1940s. Pieces of this art pottery are marked with the
letter N inside the letter C.

Newcomb, Bowl, Aqua, Anne Francis Simpson, 3 1/4 X 6 In.	425.00
Newcomb, Bowl, Misty Green, White Blossoms, High Glaze, 8 In.	225.00
Newcomb, Bowl, 4 Handled, Blue, Geometric Design, Green, White Flower	325.00
Newcomb, Candlestick, 7 1/2 In.	295.00
Newcomb, Dish, Blue, Green, Floral, Signed, 8 X 2 In.	350.00
Newcomb, Mug, Floral Above Green Ground At Neck, Cream, Artist Signed SEW	550.00
Newcomb, Plate, Daisy Decoration, Green, Signed J.M. & A.F.S., 8 1/2 In.	225.00
Newcomb, Vase, Aqua, Moss Decoration, Signed, 6 1/4 In.	425.00
Newcomb, Vase, Blue Green, Incised Trees, High Glaze, 6 1/2 In.	650.00
Newcomb, Vase, Blue, Floral In Relief, Bulbous, Sadie Irvine, 3 1/2 In.	295.00
Newcomb, Vase, Blue, Yellow, & Green Floral Rim, H.B., 7 1/4 X 4 In.	345.00
Newcomb, Vase, Bud, High Glaze Floral, May Morel, 1910, 6 1/2 In.	275.00
Newcomb, Vase, Bud, Matte Green, NC & JM, 6 X 2 1/2 In.	85.00 To 100.00
Newcomb, Vase, Bud, Speckled Blue, Raised Pastel Floral, Sadie Irvine	295.00
Newcomb, Vase, Cypress, Blue, Signed JM, 8 In.	285.00
Newcomb, Vase, Flower, Rings At Throat, Blue-Gray, White, Signed, 7 In.	375.00
Newcomb, Vase, Green, Brown Drip Effect, High Gloss, Signed NC, 3 1/2 In.	145.00
Newcomb, Vase, Lavender, Leaves & Berries, Signed JM, 8 1/2 In.	325.00
Newcomb, Vase, Moss Decoration, Aqua Ground, Signed, 6 1/4 In.	425.00
Newcomb, Vase, Pink Floral On Blue, Signed, 8 X 3 1/2 In.	265.00
Newcomb, Vase, Scenic, Moon Through Trees, Heavy Relief, A.F.Simpson, 6 In.	275.00
Newcomb, Vase, Semi Gloss, Pink Flowers & Green Leaves, 6 X 6 1/2 In.	185.00
Newcomb, Vase, Stylized Leafage At Shoulder, Red Glaze, Signed, 10 In.	550.00
Newcomb, Vase, Tulip Shape, High Gloss, 9 X 6 1/2 In.	400.00

Newhall Porcelain Manufactory was started at Newhall, Shelton,
Staffordshire, England, in 1782. Simple decorated wares were made.
Between 1810 and 1825, the factory made a glassy bone porcelain marked with
the factory name.

Newhall, Plate, Center Bouquet, Single Floral Motifs At Intervals, 8 In.	225.00
Newhall, Tankard, Famille Rose Decoration, Girl At Window, 5 1/4 In.	175.00
Newhall, Tea Set, Oriental Pattern, 6 Piece	1250.00

Niloak Pottery (Kaolin spelled backwards) was made at the Hyten
Brothers Pottery in Benton, Arkansas, between 1909 and 1946.
Although the factory did make cast and molded wares, collectors are
most interested in the marbleized art pottery line.

Niloak, Ashtray, Swirl, Signed, 5 In.	28.00
Niloak, Bowl, Beige-Brown Blue Swirl, Blue & Beige Glaze Interior, 7 In.	30.00
Niloak, Bowl, Swirl, Marbleized, Footed, Glazed Interior, Beige, Blue, 7 X 3 In.	30.00
Niloak, Cornucopia, Embossed Feather, Green & Gold Glaze	12.50
Niloak, Creamer, Tan Streaked With Brownish Red, High Glaze	15.00
Niloak, Ewer, Blue Matte, 11 In.	14.00
Niloak, Ewer, Marbleized Swirls, 7 In.	28.50
Niloak, Ewer, Plum, Blue Shading, 17 In.	35.00
Niloak, Ewer, Shaded To Deep Rose, 7 In.	10.00
Niloak, Figurine, Dog, 4 In.	22.50
Niloak, Jug, Pink & Blue, Stoppered	18.00
Niloak, Lamp, Base, Marbleized, Unmarked, 6 1/2 X 5 1/2 In.	35.00
Niloak, Mug, Pink, Embossed Flowers	15.00
Niloak, Pitcher, Pink, Embossed Round Flowers, Marked, 7 In.	12.00
Niloak, Pitcher, Small	5.00
Niloak, Planter, Brown, Squirrel	12.50
Niloak, Planter, Dog, White Matte Finish, 4 1/2 In.	7.00
Niloak, Planter, Elephant, Beige, Green, Stamped Hywood, Pressed Mark, 4 In.	18.00
Niloak, Planter, Green Frog	12.50
Niloak, Planter, Kangaroo, White Matte Finish, 5 X 5 In.	12.50
Niloak, Planter, Parrot, Marked	20.00
Niloak, Planter, Rabbit, 5 In.	6.00
Niloak, Rose Bowl, Marble Swirl, 5 In.	12.50
Niloak, Sugar & Creamer, Brown With Yellow & Green	16.00
Niloak, Vase, Blue, Swirl, High Glaze, 4 1/2 In.	45.00
Niloak, Vase, Bud, Mission Ware, 8 In.	25.00

Niloak, Vase, Bud, 6 1/2 In. 40.00
Niloak, Vase, Bulbous Bottom, Narrow Top, Marbleized Swirls, 6 1/2 In. 37.00
Niloak, Vase, Cone Shape, Marbleized, 10 In. 58.00
Niloak, Vase, Cylindrical, Marbleized Brown, Aqua, Rouge Swirls, 8 In. 30.00
Niloak, Vase, Dusty Rose, Matte Glaze, Handles, 6 In. 15.00
Niloak, Vase, Hourglass Shape, Marbleized Brown, Tan, Blue, Cream, 5 1/2 In. 25.00
Niloak, Vase, Hywood, 3 1/2 In. 8.00
Niloak, Vase, Marbleized Swirls, Urn Shape, Signed, 8 In. 32.00
Niloak, Vase, Marbleized Swirls, 4 1/2 In. .... 18.00 To 24.00
Niloak, Vase, Marbleized Swirls, 5 In. .... 22.50 To 35.00
Niloak, Vase, Marbleized Swirls, 6 In. 22.50
Niloak, Vase, Marbleized Swirls, 8 In. 33.50
Niloak, Vase, Marbleized Swirls, 8 1/4 In. 28.00
Niloak, Vase, Marbleized, Blue Brown, Grayish Cream, Bulbous, 8 X 3 In. 40.00
Niloak, Vase, Marbleized, Hour Glass Shape, 6 1/2 In. 24.00
Niloak, Vase, Mauve, Five Holes, 7 In. 35.00
Niloak, Vase, Rose Color, Signed, 3 3/4 In. 12.00
Niloak, Vase, Rose Matte Finish, 6 In. 9.00
Niloak, Vase, Swirl, 9 1/2 X 3 3/4 In. 40.00
Niloak, Vase, Swirl, 10 1/2 X 5 1/2 X 2 In. 42.00

Nippon-marked porcelain was made in Japan after 1891.

Nippon, Ashtray, Country Scene, Raised Snow On Foliage 38.00
Nippon, Ashtray, Domino, Chess, & Checker, 4 In. 25.00
Nippon, Ashtray, Lake Scene, Hand-Painted, Leaf Shape, 4 1/2 In. 16.00
Nippon, Ashtray, Orange & Blue Floral, Brown Beaded Trim, Rising Sun Mark 33.00
Nippon, Ashtray, Queen Of Clubs, Poker Chips, Ball Shaped, Green W Mark 68.00
Nippon, Ashtray, Scenic, Hand-Painted, Green M In Wreath, 6 1/2 In. 40.00
Nippon, Ashtray, Scenic, Jeweled, 4 1/2 In. 45.00
Nippon, Ashtray, Tan To Brown, Pipe & Matches Center, Mk4, 5 In. 60.00
Nippon, Base, Hand-Painted, Mountains, Trees, 2 Handles, 10 In. 50.00
Nippon, Basket, Bird Decorated Gold Handle, 8 In. 27.00
Nippon, Basket, Blown-Out Plums, Leaves, Basket Weave, Bisque Finish, 6 In. 75.00
Nippon, Basket, Brown Pottery, Enameled Egyptian Figures, Gold M Mark 125.00
Nippon, Basket, Gold Cloisonne Of Butterflies On Blue Bisque, Green M, 7 In. 85.00
Nippon, Basket, Lavender, Green & Ocher Water Scene, Beaded & Jeweled, 4 In. 50.00
Nippon, Berry Set, Crimped, Blown Rim, Chestnuts, Leaves, Green Wreath Mark 65.00
Nippon, Berry Set, Figures, Iridescent, Hand-Painted, Pagoda Mark, 7 Piece 130.00
Nippon, Berry Set, Geisha Design, Red, Red Oriental Mark, 7 Piece 45.00
Nippon, Berry Set, Pink Roses & Gold Edge 40.00
Nippon, Berry Set, Raspberries & Flowers, Gold Trim, 7 Piece 78.00
Nippon, Berry Set, Red Roses On White & Gold, 7 Pieces 50.00
Nippon, Berry Set, Rising Sun, Mother-Of-Pearl Strawberries, Signed, 7 Piece 75.00
Nippon, Biscuit Jar, Orange, Blue Flowers, Gold, Matte Finish, Ruffled Base 75.00
Nippon, Biscuit Jar, Portrait, Cobalt, Footed 165.00
Nippon, Biscuit Jar, Raised Floral, Gold On Handles 60.00
Nippon, Biscuit Jar, Scenic & Raised Floral, 7 In. 65.00
Nippon, Bottle, Cologne, Stopper, Hand-Painted Violets, 4 1/2 In. 19.50
Nippon, Bottle, Perfume, Lavender Flowers, 6 Sides, Green M Mark, 5 1/4 In. 45.00
Nippon, Bottle, Perfume, Purple Flowers, Enameled Decoration, 5 In. 48.00
Nippon, Bottle, Saki, South Seas Scene, Square Shape, Pouring Spout, 7 1/4 In. 110.00
Nippon, Bouillon, Purple Violets On Saucer, Inside Cup, White 18.00
Nippon, Bowl, Berry, Floral, Gold Trim 17.50
Nippon, Bowl, Birds, Floral, Footed, 8 1/2 In. 50.00
Nippon, Bowl, Bisque, Pink Floral, Gold Edge, Beading, Open Handled, 7 In. 34.50
Nippon, Bowl, Black Scene Of Swans In Lake On Blue Ground, 4 Sided, 7 In. 65.00
Nippon, Bowl, Blackberries, Flowers, Gold Trim, Scalloped Rim, 1898, 7 1/4 In. 125.00
Nippon, Bowl, Blown-Out Brazil Nuts, Matte Finish, Green Leaf Mark, 7 In. 84.00
Nippon, Bowl, Blown-Out Peanuts, Acorns, Autumn Colors, Handled, 7 X 2 In. 55.00
Nippon, Bowl, Brazil Nuts, Bisque Finish, Jeweled Handles, M In Wreath, 8 In. 100.00
Nippon, Bowl, Castle Wooded Scene, Ball Footed, Beading, Bisque, Green Wreath 37.50
Nippon, Bowl, Cobalt & Gold, Floral, 1 In. 95.00
Nippon, Bowl, Cobalt, Floral & Gold, Blue Leaf Mark, Oval, 6 X 10 In. 46.00
Nippon, Bowl, Cobalt, Gold Beading, Rose Medallions, Petal Shaped, 10 In. 85.00
Nippon, Bowl, Coral & Blue Enameling, Rural Scene, Gilt Beading, 2 X 8 In. 85.00

Nippon, Bowl, Curled Edge, 3 Handled, Roses, Matte, 7 In.	55.00
Nippon, Bowl, Desert Scene, Camel & Rider, 7 1/2 In.	20.00
Nippon, Bowl, Encrusted Gold Roses & Scroll, Handled, 9 X 2 In.	35.00
Nippon, Bowl, Floral & Butterflies On White, Green Wreath Mark, 9 In.	36.00
Nippon, Bowl, Floral Border, Blue Rising Sun Mark, 7 In.	17.00
Nippon, Bowl, Floral Decoration, Black, 8 In.	35.00
Nippon, Bowl, Floral Design, Scalloped, Coral & Gold, 11 In.	75.00
Nippon, Bowl, Floral Insets In Pastel, Celery Green, Gold Rim, Handles, 3 In.	30.00
Nippon, Bowl, Floral Medallions, Green, Gold, 9 3/4 In.	38.00
Nippon, Bowl, Flowers, 10 In.	38.00
Nippon, Bowl, Fluted, Acorns, Earth Tones, M In Wreath, 7 In.	100.00
Nippon, Bowl, Fluted, Open Handled, 8 In.	20.00
Nippon, Bowl, Flying Duck, Water, Flowers, Open Handled, 6 In.	15.00
Nippon, Bowl, Footed, Apple Blossoms, 5 In.	15.00
Nippon, Bowl, Forest Scene, Raised Black Beading, Scalloped, 8 X 4 In.	140.00
Nippon, Bowl, Forest Scene, Raised Geometric Black Border, 6 1/4 In.	80.00
Nippon, Bowl, Fruit, Fruit In Center, Medallions, Gold, Handled, 10 In.	60.00
Nippon, Bowl, Gold Floral & Beaded Rim, White Floral, Trailing Leaves, 6 In.	30.00
Nippon, Bowl, Gold Handles, Swan, House, Trees, 9 In.	40.00
Nippon, Bowl, Gold On White, Gold Inside, Rim Beading, 4 Footed, Large, 5 In.	65.00
Nippon, Bowl, Gold Trim, Green M In Wreath, 6 1/4 In.	10.00
Nippon, Bowl, Gold, Ruffled Top, Cobalt, Coralene Floral, Gold, Signed, 7 In.	125.00
Nippon, Bowl, Handles, 3 Feet, Pink Floral, Pastel, Beaded, Marked, 4 In.	35.00
Nippon, Bowl, House, Lake, Sunset, Trees, Superior Mark, Signed, 6 X 4 3/4 In.	22.00
Nippon, Bowl, House, Trees, Flowers, Gold Trim, Oval, M In Wreath, 9 In.	45.00
Nippon, Bowl, Jeweled Border, Roses Center, Matte Finish, 9 1/2 In.	15.00
Nippon, Bowl, Jeweled, Cottage Scene, Trees, Lake, Boat, Sunset Colors, 9 In.	23.00
Nippon, Bowl, Leaf Handles, Green Wreath, 7 1/2 X 3 In.	89.00
Nippon, Bowl, Maroon, Green, Gold, Roses, 9 1/2 X 6 In.	28.00
Nippon, Bowl, Moriye, Jeweled, Heavy Gold, Marked, 10 1/2 In.	195.00
Nippon, Bowl, Moriye, 2-Handled, Nut & Leaf Design, Matte Finish, 9 In.	96.00
Nippon, Bowl, Nut, Acorns Molded In Relief, Hand-Painted Scene, Handle, 6 In.	19.00
Nippon, Bowl, Nut, Basket Weave & Blown-Out Black Walnuts, 7 1/2 In.	85.00
Nippon, Bowl, Nut, Four Raised Acorns, Handled, 6 1/2 In.	30.00
Nippon, Bowl, Octagon, Cobalt Blue, Applied Gold Trim, Lid & Saucer, 5 In.	58.00
Nippon, Bowl, Orange, Cobalt Gold, 10 In.	68.00
Nippon, Bowl, Pastel Pinks & Green Coralene Floral, Ruffled, Footed, 8 In.	145.00
Nippon, Bowl, Pierced Handle, Windmill Scene, Green Wreath, 6 1/2 In.	25.00
Nippon, Bowl, Pink & Green, Floral, Gold Trim, Footed, M In Wreath Mark, 5 In.	12.50
Nippon, Bowl, Pink Floral, Beaded Rim, 3 Gold Feet, M In Wreath, 4 3/4 In.	12.75
Nippon, Bowl, Pond Scene, Iris, Gold Trim, Beading, Green Wreath, 6 In.	40.00
Nippon, Bowl, Rose Bushes, Gold Trim, Matte Glaze, Handled, Maple Leaf, 5 In.	30.00
Nippon, Bowl, Roses, Green Background, Yellow, Pink, 10 In.	55.00
Nippon, Bowl, Roses, Scalloped Edge, Gold Beaded Band, Blue Leaf Mark, 6 In.	60.00
Nippon, Bowl, Ruffled Edge, Irises, Maroon Rim, Oval, Maple Leaf Mark, 8 In.	60.00
Nippon, Bowl, Scalloped, Floral, Gold, Beading, Hand-Painted, Blue M, 4 1/2 In.	85.00
Nippon, Bowl, Scenic, Green & Blue, Geese Flying, 8 1/2 In.	37.00
Nippon, Bowl, Shallow, Beaded Gold, M In Wreath, 6 1/4 In.	12.00
Nippon, Bowl, Shallow, Pierced Handles, Green M Mark, 9 1/2 In.	18.00
Nippon, Bowl, Shell Shape, Long, Green M Wreath Mark, Lake Scene, 7 1/4 In.	90.00
Nippon, Bowl, Square Fernery Painted Roses, Gold, 4 Feet, 5 1/2 In.	45.00
Nippon, Bowl, Sunset, Palms, Floral, 2 Handles, 6 1/2 X 7 In.	37.00
Nippon, Bowl, Three Blown-Out Peanuts, Brown Trim, Vines, 5 Cornered, 7 In.	72.00
Nippon, Bowl, Twig Handles, Molded, Matte Outside, Glazed Inside, 6 1/2 In.	60.00
Nippon, Bowl, Walnuts, Brown & Greens, Jeweled Handles, M In Wreath, 8 1/4 In.	55.00
Nippon, Bowl, White, Peanuts In Center, 2 Handled, Green Wreath Mark, 7 In.	45.00
Nippon, Bowl, White, Poppy & Gold Trim, Handles, M In Wreath, 8 In.	20.00
Nippon, Bowl, Yellow, Orange & White Floral Interior, Shaded Ground, 4 In.	33.00
Nippon, Box, Biscuit, Fruits, Leaves, Scroll Handles, Scallops, Gold, 10 X 7 In.	125.00
Nippon, Box, Button, Pink & Green Florals, Button Forms Finial, Stem Base	8.00
Nippon, Box, Cornflowers On Pale Blue, 6 Feet, 1 1/4 X 3 X 1 In.	16.00
Nippon, Box, Heart Shape, Scenic, Beaded Edge, Green Wreath Mark, Miniature	35.00
Nippon, Box, Horse Head Medallion Cover, Black & Brown On Cream, 5 X 2 In.	50.00
Nippon, Box, Lacquer, Scalloped Shape, 3 X 5 In.	14.00
Nippon, Box, Lady's Portrait, Gold, Covered, 5 In.	85.00

Nippon, Box, Oriental Scene, Cobalt, Green, Matte Finish, Round, Green Wreath 135.00
Nippon, Box, Powder, Bisque Finish, Snow Scene, Green M In Wreath 65.00
Nippon, Box, Powder, Raised Gold Florals, Footed, RC Mark 60.00
Nippon, Box, Trinket, Brown Floral, Gold Beading & Trim, Round, Marked, 3 In. 18.00
Nippon, Box, Trinket, Desert Scene, 3 Legged 25.00
Nippon, Box, Trinket, Floral, Gold Trim, Lid 23.00
Nippon, Box, Trinket, Flowers, Gold Trim, Round, Covered, 3 In. 19.00
Nippon, Box, Trinket, Hand-Painted House Scene, Heart Shape, Covered 22.00
Nippon, Breakfast Set, Child's, Clowns, Elephants, Seals, Red, Green Plaid Rim 50.00
Nippon, Burner, Incense, Foo Dog Finial, Black, Signed 28.00
Nippon, Butter Pat, Portland, Set Of 6 .... 30.00
Nippon, Butter, Blue & White Flying Dragon, Round, Covered 30.00
Nippon, Butter, Tub, Open With Insert, Violets 22.00
Nippon, Cake Set, Arab On Camel, Palm Trees, 6 Piece .... 82.00 To 98.00
Nippon, Cake Set, Black & Gold Raised Design, 6 Piece 35.00
Nippon, Cake Set, Greek Key Design, Flowers, 7 Piece 22.00
Nippon, Cake Set, Island, Tree, House Scene, Crown Mark, 7 Piece 30.00
Nippon, Cake Set, Scenic, Green M Wreath Mark, 7 Piece .... 68.00 To 75.00
Nippon, Cake Set, White & Gold, 7 Piece 28.00
Nippon, Candleholder, Footed, Scenic, 7 3/4 In. 40.00
Nippon, Candleholder, Scarabs, Egyptian Figures, Pair 65.00
Nippon, Candlestick, Geese In Flight, Column, Jeweled, Gold, Blue, 9 In., Pair 175.00
Nippon, Candlestick, Gold Floral, Pink Ground, Maple Leaf Mark, Pair, 9 In. 50.00
Nippon, Candlestick, Gray, Floral, Leaves, Gold Outlining, 8 1/2 In., Pair 95.00
Nippon, Candlestick, Hand-Painted, Violet, Beading 15.00
Nippon, Candlestick, Roses, Tinted Background, 6 1/4 In. 16.00
Nippon, Candlestick, White Porcelain, Beading, M In Green Wreath, Pair, 5 In. 54.00
Nippon, Candy Dish, Block, Flowers, Leaves, Pink, Green 15.00
Nippon, Casserole, White With Gold, Cover 28.00
Nippon, Celery Set, Daisy Border 40.00
Nippon, Celery Set, Green Wreath, Blue On White, Gold Trimmed 75.00
Nippon, Celery Set, Pink Flowers, Yellow Border Decoration, Mark, 6 Piece 28.00
Nippon, Celery Set, Pink Roses, Gold Border, 7 Piece 42.00
Nippon, Celery, Floral, Gold Border, Marked E.E., 9 In. 15.00
Nippon, Celery, Hand-Painted Violets, 5 Matching Individuals 95.00
Nippon, Celery, Open Handled, 5 Salts, Gold Beadwork, 12 In. 60.00
Nippon, Celery, Purple & Green, Maple Leaf Mark 50.00
Nippon, Celery, Sailboat, Gulls, Trees, White Enameling, Pierced Handles 30.00
Nippon, Celery, Two Robins, House, Pasture, Oblong, 13 In. 35.00
Nippon, Chamberstick, Violets, Gold Beading, Small 10.00
Nippon, Charger, Framed Dutch Scenic Center, Oriental Poppies, 11 In. 80.00
Nippon, Cheese, Rising Sun, Cover, 8 1/2 In. 25.00
Nippon, Chocolate Pot, Apple Blossoms, Cobalt Trim, Gold Beading, M In Wreath 145.00
Nippon, Chocolate Pot, Aqua, Flying Geese, Gold Trim & Handle, Pagoda Mark 80.00
Nippon, Chocolate Pot, Cobalt & Blue Panels, Gold Beading 40.00
Nippon, Chocolate Pot, Cobalt Blue, Gold Trim, Pink Flowers, Green Vines 55.00
Nippon, Chocolate Pot, Cobalt Handle, Gold Trim, Roses, Scalloped Top 38.00
Nippon, Chocolate Pot, Cobalt, Geisha Girl, Flowers 26.00
Nippon, Chocolate Pot, Flared, Raised Gold & Black Borders, 8 1/2 In. 135.00
Nippon, Chocolate Pot, Floral Band, 8 1/2 In. 39.00
Nippon, Chocolate Pot, Flowers & Leaves, Gold Outline, Spoke Mark 35.00
Nippon, Chocolate Pot, Geisha Girl' Decoration 45.00
Nippon, Chocolate Pot, Gold & Painted Violets 60.00
Nippon, Chocolate Pot, Panels Of Gold Wheat On Pale Yellow, Superior Mark 45.00
Nippon, Chocolate Pot, Pink Apple Blossom, Gold Beading, Blue Trim 145.00
Nippon, Chocolate Pot, Pink On White, Floral Dome, Gold 70.00
Nippon, Chocolate Pot, Red, Gold Paisley Overlay, Maple Leaf, Cover 150.00
Nippon, Chocolate Pot, Roses Outlined In Gold, Basket Weave, Maple Leaf 65.00
Nippon, Chocolate Pot, Set, Cream Band, Gold Beading 75.00
Nippon, Chocolate Pot, Stippled Gold Around Flowers, Hand-Painted, 11 In. 145.00
Nippon, Chocolate Pot, Trees, Lake, Swans In Foreground, Gold Handle, Green M 50.00
Nippon, Chocolate Pot, Zinnias, Cobalt, Gold Top, Handle, Blue Maple Leaf 50.00
Nippon, Chocolate Pot, 6 Sided, Flares To Top, Raised Decoration, 10 In. 145.00
Nippon, Chocolate Set, Blue & Red Flowers, Green Wreath Mark, 17 Piece 145.00
Nippon, Chocolate Set, Cobalt Blue, Heavy Gold Dragons, 5 Piece 57.50

Nippon, Chocolate Set, Country Scene, 13 Piece	175.00
Nippon, Chocolate Set, Flying Dragon, Flow Blue, 9 Piece	55.00
Nippon, Chocolate Set, Geisha Pattern, Red & Gold On White, 15 Piece	200.00
Nippon, Chocolate Set, Geisha, Red & Gold On White, 8 Piece	200.00
Nippon, Chocolate Set, Hand-Painted Border, 8 In. Pot, 4 Cups & Saucers	135.00
Nippon, Chocolate Set, Heavy Gold On White, 9 Piece	85.00
Nippon, Chocolate Set, Lavish Beaded Gold, Purple Pansies, 13 Piece	185.00
Nippon, Chocolate Set, Light Blue With White, Green Wreath Mark, 9 Piece	65.00
Nippon, Chocolate Set, Moriye Dragon, Green & Gray Matte, M Mark, 9 Piece	135.00
Nippon, Chocolate Set, Oriental Figures, Blue, Orange On White, 4 Piece	165.00
Nippon, Chocolate Set, Pale Green, Foliage, Flowers, Gold Trim, 6 Piece	80.00
Nippon, Chocolate Set, Pink & Purple Flowers, 5 Piece	75.00
Nippon, Chocolate Set, Pink & Yellow Roses, Marked Germany, 4 Piece	65.00
Nippon, Chocolate Set, Pink Roses, Gemoetric Green Trim, Gold Trim, 11 Piece	95.00
Nippon, Chocolate Set, Pink Roses, M In Wreath, 7 Piece	125.00
Nippon, Chocolate Set, Pink, Morning Glories, Gold Dots, 9 Piece	275.00
Nippon, Chocolate Set, Pitcher, 6 Cups, Saucers, White, Pink Roses, Gold Rim	95.00
Nippon, Chocolate Set, Purple Pansies, E-OH Mark, 5 Cups & Saucers	75.00
Nippon, Chocolate Set, Rising Sun, Pink, Blue, & Gold Trim, 8 Piece	69.00
Nippon, Chocolate Set, Rose Decoration, 5 Piece	60.00
Nippon, Chocolate Set, Roses, Gold Trim, Green Maple Leaf Mark, 9 Piece	95.00
Nippon, Chocolate Set, Sailboat, Windmill, Trees, Green, Brown, Orange, 4 Piece	85.00
Nippon, Chocolate Set, Scenic, 7 Piece	145.00
Nippon, Chocolate Set, Tree Limb, Blossoms, Bird, Green M In Wreath, 9 Piece	100.00
Nippon, Chocolate Set, White & Red Roses, Gold, 13 Piece	250.00
Nippon, Chocolate Set, White, Band Of Pastel Flowers, Gold Trim, 11 Piece	95.00
Nippon, Chocolate Set, White, Gold Floral & Leaves, Blue Spoke Mark, 16 Piece	195.00
Nippon, Chocolate Set, White, Gold Trim, Pink Roses, Rising Run Mark, 9 Piece	58.50
Nippon, Chocolate Set, White, Pink, Blue Flowers, Signed, 9 Piece	60.00
Nippon, Chocolate Set, Yellow Roses, Blue Ribbed To White, 9 Piece	110.00
Nippon, Cider Set, Roses, Scenery, 6 X 5 3/4 In., 4 Piece	95.00
Nippon, Coaster, Hand-Painted	3.50
Nippon, Coaster, Round Tray, Flowers On White, Set Of 5	50.00
Nippon, Compote, Art Deco, 4 In.	12.50
Nippon, Compote, Basket Of Fruit, Pedestal, Handled, Marked, 11 1/2 In.	90.00
Nippon, Compote, Floral And Gold Trim, 4 In.	12.50
Nippon, Compote, Grapes & Leaves, Gold Trim & Beading, M In Wreath, 6 In.	42.00
Nippon, Compote, Triangular Base, White Ground, Gold Scrolling, 6 In.	125.00
Nippon, Compote, Walnuts & Peanuts, Bisque Finish, Green M Mark, 7 3/4 In.	38.00
Nippon, Compote, Water Scene, Pink, Gray, Blue, Brown, 6 In.	65.00
Nippon, Compote, Wild Flowers, 2 Handles, 9 In.	18.00
Nippon, Condiment Set, Floral & Geometrics, 4 Piece	30.00
Nippon, Condiment Set, In Lacquer Box, Blue With White Cranes, Circular	58.00
Nippon, Condiment Set, Orange & Brown Foliage On White, 5 Piece	28.00
Nippon, Condiment Set, Small Roses, Gold, 3 Pieces & Spoon	16.00
Nippon, Container, Talcum, Roses, Green Noritake Mark	37.50
Nippon, Cookie Jar, Geraniums & Encrusted Gold, Beaded Trim, Cover	150.00
Nippon, Cookie Jar, Gold Flowers On Beige, Two Handled, Signed	50.00
Nippon, Cookie Jar, Hexagonal, Covered	115.00
Nippon, Corn Set, Gold Handles & Trim, 7 Piece	128.00
Nippon, Corn Set, Harvest Golds, Green, Hand-Painted Ears Of Corn, 7 Piece	150.00
Nippon, Cracker Jar, Brown Background, Gold	60.00
Nippon, Cracker Jar, Desert Scene, Camel & Rider, Bulbous, Ribbed, 3 Footed	90.00
Nippon, Cracker Jar, Floral & Gold, Double Handles	45.00
Nippon, Cracker Jar, Floral Gold Trim	60.00
Nippon, Cracker Jar, Footed, Covered, Green M Mark, 7 In.	150.00
Nippon, Cracker Jar, Green, Pastel Floral, Matte Finish, Jeweled Handles	65.00
Nippon, Cracker Jar, Melon Ribbed, Cobalt Blue, Gold Trim, Floral, 7 1/2 In.	135.00
Nippon, Cracker Jar, Melon Shaped Sections, Cobalt Blue, Gold, Floral, Footed	55.00
Nippon, Cracker Jar, Pink & Orange Roses, Gold Beading, Jewels, 7 In.	98.00
Nippon, Cracker Jar, Pink & Yellow Flowers, Melon Shape, 3 Footed, 7 In.	55.00
Nippon, Cracker Jar, Pink Flowers, Green & Gold Trim, 8 In.	75.00
Nippon, Cracker Jar, Red, Yellow, & Pink Roses, Gold Trim, Handled	95.00
Nippon, Cracker Jar, Roses, Gold Beading, Green Gray	75.00
Nippon, Cracker Jar, Scenic, Blue, Green, Gold, Pink, Blue Jewel Trim, Marked	155.00

Nippon, Cracker Jar, White With Gold Enameling 65.00
Nippon, Cracker Jar, White, Pinkish-White Roses, Greens, Browns, Handled, Mark 26.00
Nippon, Cracker Jar, 6-Sided Gold Trimmed Panels, Floral & Scenic 175.00
Nippon, Creamer, Blown-Out Child's Face 25.00
Nippon, Creamer, Child's, Blown-Out Doll Face, 3 In. 90.00
Nippon, Creamer, Gold Borders, White Porcelain, 2 1/4 In. 4.50
Nippon, Creamer, Gold On Cream, Underplate, Gold 45.00
Nippon, Cucumber Dish, Floral Border, Drain Insert, Gold, 10 1/2 In. 22.50
Nippon, Cup & Saucer, Beige, Tan, White & Pink Apple Blossoms, Gold Beading 20.00
Nippon, Cup & Saucer, Bluebirds, Pink Flowers On White, Set Of 4 .... 4.00
Nippon, Cup & Saucer, Demitasse, Cream Band, Gold Decoration 6.00
Nippon, Cup & Saucer, Forget-Me-Nots, Cream Border, Crown Mark 7.00
Nippon, Cup & Saucer, Landscape Scene 9.00
Nippon, Cup & Saucer, Mt.Fuji, Water Scene, Blue To Brown, Gold Dots 22.00
Nippon, Decanter, Captain's, Green, Purple Orchid, Slipwork, Moriye, 9 In. 185.00
Nippon, Demitasse Set, Row Of Flowers Banded Around Rims, White, 13 Piece 60.00
Nippon, Desk Set, Blue-Violet Color, 7 Piece 130.00
Nippon, Dish & Underplate, Cucumber, Red & Pink Roses, Gold 30.00
Nippon, Dish Set, Child's, Rising Sun, Service For 4 .... 75.00
Nippon, Dish, Arabic Boat Scene, Gold Trim, Matte Finish, Green M, 12 In. 35.00
Nippon, Dish, Asparagus, Yellow & Lavender On Green Leaf, 4 X 8 1/2 In. 18.00
Nippon, Dish, Basket Form, Handles, Blown-Out Nuts, Brown Tones, 7 1/2 In. 90.00
Nippon, Dish, Basket, Blown-Out Peanuts, Basket Weave, 4 1/2 In.Square 25.00
Nippon, Dish, Candy, Purple Flowers, Gold Trim, Pierced Edges 22.00
Nippon, Dish, Celery, Pink & Blue Flowers, Gold, Rising Sun Mark, 11 1/2 In. 16.00
Nippon, Dish, Celery, Pink Roses, Gold Edge & Handles, 12 1/2 In. 30.00
Nippon, Dish, Cheese & Cracker, Beaded, Raised Gold & Roses 22.00
Nippon, Dish, Cheese, Azalea, Domed Lid, 9 In. 38.00
Nippon, Dish, Cheese, Pink & Yellow Floral, Oblong Shape 39.00
Nippon, Dish, Cheese, Slanted, Birds On Lid, White, Blue 65.00
Nippon, Dish, Cheese, White, Yellow & Blue Butterfly, Slanted 32.00
Nippon, Dish, Cucumber, Flowers, Gold, Center Drain Insert 17.00
Nippon, Dish, Dip & Cracker, Floral Garlands, Gold, Sectioned, 9 1/2 In. 39.00
Nippon, Dish, Farmhouse, Wooded Shoreline, Beaded Edge, Matte, 4 X 4 1/2 In. 24.00
Nippon, Dish, Feeding, Child's, Animals On Inside, 6 1/2 In. 25.00
Nippon, Dish, Floral Motif, Open Handled, Green, Gold, 3 3/4 In., Pair 7.00
Nippon, Dish, Footed, Green & White, Scalloped Border, 6 1/2 X 8 In. 68.00
Nippon, Dish, Green & White, Beaded Jewels, Scalloped Borders, 6 1/2 X 8 In. 68.00
Nippon, Dish, Heart Shape, Brown, Jeweled Border, Indian Provile, 3 1/2 In. 45.00
Nippon, Dish, Island Scene, Ruffled Sides, Jeweled Edges, 7 1/2 In. 45.00
Nippon, Dish, Lake Scene, Gold Tracing & Beading, Oval, Maple Leaf, 7 1/4 In. 60.00
Nippon, Dish, Nut, Blown-Out, Black Walnuts, Green M In Wreath 65.00
Nippon, Dish, Nut, Footed, Painted Flowers, Blue Mark, 4 3/4 In. 8.00
Nippon, Dish, Nut, Gold Borders, Watermill Scene, Green Mark, Pair, 5 1/4 In. 25.00
Nippon, Dish, Oval, Gold Beading, ML Mark, 8 In. 26.00
Nippon, Dish, Pancake, Bird Knob, Gold Enameling 50.00
Nippon, Dish, Pancake, Red Poppies Outlined In Gold, Blue Maple Leaf Mark 45.00
Nippon, Dish, Pancake, White With Gold, 2 Piece 45.00
Nippon, Dish, Pastel Acorns & Leaves, Molded M In Wreath, 9 In. 85.00
Nippon, Dish, Pickle, Gold Beads & Roses, 7 3/4 X 4 1/2 In. 32.00
Nippon, Dish, Pickle, Gold Handles, 9 1/2 In. 38.00
Nippon, Dish, Pin, Lake Scene, Moriye, Green, Jewels, Maple Leaf, 6 X 3 In. 32.00
Nippon, Dish, Serving, Gold Flowers, C.1890, 8 X 11 In. 50.00
Nippon, Dish, Snack, Roses, Gold, Iridescent Background, Lid 35.00
Nippon, Dish, Square Ring, Lid, Gold Trim, Pink Roses, 4 Feet, Maple Leaf, 3 In. 32.00
Nippon, Dish, Windmill, Multicolor, Pastoral Scene, Matte, 6 In. 18.00
Nippon, Dish, 3 Blue Ball Feet, Blue, Maroon, Florals, Maple Leaf, 7 In. 42.00
Nippon, Dish, 6 Panel, Footed, Gold Trim 18.00
Nippon, Doll, Bisque, Molded Hair, Blonde, Molded Shoes & Socks, 7 In. 42.50
Nippon, Dresser Set, Scenic, 3 Piece 32.50
Nippon, Dresser Set, Tea Roses, Gold Trim, 3 Piece 95.00
Nippon, Dutch Shoe, White, Gold Ceramic, 4 X 2 In. 45.00
Nippon, Ewer, Brown Satin Finish, Pink Poppies, Maple Leaf Mark, 11 In. 112.00
Nippon, Ewer, Gold Enameling, Beading, Roses, White Background, Red, 4 In. 52.00
Nippon, Ewer, Moriye, Green, Moriage & Beads, 4 Floral Bouquets, 5 In. 120.00

Nippon, Ewer, Ornate, Gold, Cobalt, Pink, Yellow Roses, 10 1/2 In.	80.00
Nippon, Ewer, Pink Roses, Gold Beading, Blue Maple Leaf Mark, 4 In.	38.00
Nippon, Ewer, Pink Roses, Gold Beading, Cobalt, 8 In.	40.00
Nippon, Ewer, Rose Medallions, Gold Flowers & Leaves, Blue Wreath, 7 1/4 In.	125.00
Nippon, Ewer, Roses, Gold Beading, Overlay, Cobalt Border, Red, Yellow, 8 In.	165.00
Nippon, Ewer, Roses, Gold Trim, 5 In.	35.00
Nippon, Ewer, White, Pink & Red Roses, Gold Scrolling, Beaded, 10 1/2 In., Pair	250.00
Nippon, Fernery, Floral Medallions, Octagonal, 8 In.	35.00
Nippon, Fernery, Floral Patches, Allover Gold	28.00
Nippon, Fernery, Hand-Painted Bird, Crane Design	45.00
Nippon, Fernery, Moriye, Handled, 10 1/2 X 5 1/2 In.	125.00
Nippon, Fernery, Octagonal, Floral Medallions, 8 In.	38.00
Nippon, Figurine, Happy Fats, Boy & Girl, Bisque, 3 3/4 In., Pair	165.00
Nippon, Fruit Set, Poinsettias, 7 Piece	48.00
Nippon, Hair Receiver, Cobalt Blue, Gold Tracery, Blue Maple Leaf Mark, 5 In.	18.00
Nippon, Hair Receiver, Floral With Gold, Footed	13.00
Nippon, Hair Receiver, Gold Legs, Yellow & Blue Butterflies, M In Wreath	24.00
Nippon, Hair Receiver, Green, Flowers & Gold Trim, Leaf Mark, 5 1/4 In.	23.00
Nippon, Hair Receiver, Orchid Color, Beaded Flowers, Footed	35.00
Nippon, Hair Receiver, Pink Flowers, Green Leaves, 4 1/2 X 3 In.	27.50
Nippon, Hair Receiver, Roses, Gold, Marked	35.00
Nippon, Hair Receiver, Roses, Jewels, Green Ground, Blue Leaf Mark, 4 1/2 In.	55.00
Nippon, Hair Receiver, Scenic	45.00
Nippon, Hair Receiver, Scenic, Black & Gold, Footed, Green Wreath Mark	35.00
Nippon, Hair Receiver, 3 Curved Legs, Light Blue	38.00
Nippon, Hatpin Holder, Beaded & Floral, Attached Saucer	45.00
Nippon, Hatpin Holder, Beaded, Raised Gold & Roses	18.50
Nippon, Hatpin Holder, Birds, Blue Background	23.00
Nippon, Hatpin Holder, Bisque Finish, Desert Scene With Beading	22.00
Nippon, Hatpin Holder, Blue Roses, White	15.00
Nippon, Hatpin Holder, Flowers, Gold Trim, Attached Pin Tray Base, RC Mark	30.00
Nippon, Hatpin Holder, Gold Beading & Outline, Swags, Pink Roses, M In Wreath	25.00
Nippon, Hatpin Holder, Green, Violets & Gold, Vase Type	17.00
Nippon, Hatpin Holder, Pink & Green Floral On White, 5 In.	9.00
Nippon, Hatpin Holder, Scenic & Moriye, 4 In.	55.00
Nippon, Hatpin Holder, Violets, Gold Border, ML Mark	35.00
Nippon, Holder, Can, Condensed Milk, Hand-Painted Florals & Gold Decoration	20.00
Nippon, Hostess Set, Bisque, Scenic, Boxed, 7 Piece	65.00
Nippon, Humidor & Tray, Bull Moose, Green M Mark	110.00
Nippon, Humidor, American Indian In Canoe, Imperial Mark	169.00
Nippon, Humidor, Bisque Floral On Blending Brown, 6 Sided, EE, 6 3/4 In.	95.00
Nippon, Humidor, Bisque Scenic, Jeweled, Blue Leaf Mark, 5 X 5 1/2 In.	125.00
Nippon, Humidor, Blown-Out, Bulldog Smoking Pipe, Brown	400.00
Nippon, Humidor, Buck, Doe, Acorns, Green Wreath Mark	275.00
Nippon, Humidor, Cigarette Picture, Pipe On Lid, Match Holder, Green W Mark	85.00
Nippon, Humidor, Desert Scene, Camel, Riders, Palm Trees, Green M, Wreath Mark	230.00
Nippon, Humidor, Floral Designs, 5 In.	55.00
Nippon, Humidor, Flowers, Gold Beading, Imperial Mark, 6 1/2 X 5 In.	58.00
Nippon, Humidor, Green Body, Textured Car, Red, Brown, People, Blue, Lavender	295.00
Nippon, Humidor, Hand-Painted Art Nouveau, Jeweled, Maple Leaf Mark	185.00
Nippon, Humidor, Horse-Drawn Carriage, English Cottage, 6 In.	250.00
Nippon, Humidor, Hunting Dog Motif, 4 Curved Panels, 5 In.	235.00
Nippon, Humidor, Landscaping, Brown & Green Enameling, Green M Mark, 5 In.	95.00
Nippon, Humidor, Playing Cards, 2 Raised Matches On Lid, 4 1/2 In.	150.00
Nippon, Humidor, Red Sweet Peas On Lid, Gold Outlines	45.00
Nippon, Humidor, Riverbank Scene, Raised Decoration Around Rim, 6 3/4 In.	105.00
Nippon, Humidor, Standing Camels In Each Of 7 Panels, 5 In.	10.00
Nippon, Humidor, Trees & Water, Raised Paste, Blue Maple Leaf Mark, 5 In.	140.00
Nippon, Ice Cream Set, Green With Violets, M In Wreath, 7 Piece	50.00
Nippon, Inkwell, Scenic, Matte Finish	27.00
Nippon, Jam Set, Rising Sun, Pink Blue & Gold Trim	25.00
Nippon, Jam Set, 3 Pieces, Gold Beaded, Pink Roses, Green Leaves	43.00
Nippon, Jar, Covered, Pink, Yellow, Floral Border, Hand-Painted, 7 X 4 In.	50.00
Nippon, Jar, Jam, Underplate & Ladle, Blue Medallions, Gold Trim	24.00 To 25.00
Nippon, Jar, Jam, With Underplate, Coin Gold Side Handles, Daisies, M Wreath	43.50

Nippon, Jar, Jam, With Underplate, Pink Roses, Ladle, Gold Rims, M In Wreath 40.00
Nippon, Jar, Mustard, Lid, Hand-Painted 7.00
Nippon, Jar, Mustard, With Spoon, Gold Rim, Attached Plate, Green M In Wreath 18.00
Nippon, Jar, Pink Roses On Green Band, Lid 12.00
Nippon, Jar, Powder, Bands Of Red & Gold, Basket Of Flowers, 9 In. 70.00
Nippon, Jar, Powder, Covered, Pastel Rural Scenes, Signed, 6 In. 48.00
Nippon, Jar, Powder, Pink With Allover Gold Trim, Wreath Mark 27.00
Nippon, Jar, Puff, Windmill Scene, Beaded Trim, Signed, 7 1/4 In. 125.00
Nippon, Jar, Scent, Leaves, Tracings, Moriye, Pedestal Base, 5 In. 100.00
Nippon, Jar, Tiny Jewels, Gold On White, Covered, A Mark, 2 X 2 1/4 In. 12.00
Nippon, Jar, Tobacco, Tropical Shore With Boat, 5 In. 70.00
Nippon, Jar, Trinket, Round, Covered 8.00
Nippon, Jardiniere, Swans On Lake, Florals, Gold, Footed, 7 X 7 In. 35.00
Nippon, Jug, Bulldog On Front, Mottled Finish, Stopper 175.00
Nippon, Jug, Leaves & Acorns, Applied Branches, Maple Leaf, Stopper, 8 1/2 In. 125.00
Nippon, Jug, Stopper, Bisque Scene, Enamel Decoration, 4-Sided, Green M Wreath 275.00
Nippon, Jug, Water Scene, Bisque Finish, Green Wreath Mark, 5 In. 25.00
Nippon, Jug, Whiskey, Hand-Painted 225.00
Nippon, Jug, Wine, Garden Scene On Black Matte, Gold Overlay, 4 Sided, Green M 265.00
Nippon, Kitchen Set, Rising Sun, 4 1/2 In.Bowl, Saucer, Ladle 20.00
Nippon, Lamp, Finger, Cable, Emerald Green, Green W Mark 65.00
Nippon, Lemonade Set, Bird In Flight, Pink Roses, 7 Piece 80.00
Nippon, Lemonade Set, Bisque Scenic, E-OH Mark, 6 Piece 105.00
Nippon, Lemonade Set, Brown, Yellow, Hand-Painted, Signed, 7 Piece 110.00
Nippon, Lemonade Set, Bulbous, Grape, T In Wreath Mark, 6 Piece 50.00
Nippon, Lemonade Set, Hand-Painted, Marked E-OH Nippon, 5 Piece 125.00
Nippon, Lemonade Set, Purple Violets, Green Leaves, Gold Outlining, 7 Piece 150.00
Nippon, Lobster Set, Red Lobster On Green, Gold Floral Border, 6 Piece 225.00
Nippon, Luncheon Set, Rose Florals, Gold Border, Kidney Shape Tray, Marked 7.00
Nippon, Match Holder, Roses, Attached Heart-Shaped Tray, Striker, Marked 27.00
Nippon, Matchbox Holder, Attached Ashtray, Fatima Cigarettes 25.00
Nippon, Matchbox Holder, Hanging, Floral 25.00
Nippon, Mayonnaise Set, Beaded & Raised Gold With Roses 17.50
Nippon, Mayonnaise Set, Gold On White, Red M Mark, 3 Piece 26.00
Nippon, Mayonnaise, Floral, Beading, Attached Saucer 14.00
Nippon, Mayonnaise, Ladle, Underplate 12.00
Nippon, Mayonnaise, Pink Floral, Gold Trim, Jewels, Purple Mark, 7 1/2 X 2 In. 22.00
Nippon, Mug, Gray Bisque, Raised Dragons, Green M Mark 62.00
Nippon, Mug, Moriaga Dragon On Matte Finish, Gray, Beaded Trim, Green M 85.00
Nippon, Mustard Pot & Saucer, Bright Scene, Jeweled 22.00
Nippon, Mustard Pot & Saucer, Hand-Painted Floral With Gold, 5 In. 30.00
Nippon, Mustard Pot, Attached Tray, Gold, Double Handled, Marked 16.50
Nippon, Mustard Pot, Attached Underplate, Blue Border, Green Beading 22.00
Nippon, Mustard Pot, Floral With Gold, Attached Saucer, 5 In. 30.00
Nippon, Mustard Pot, Florals, Gold, Underplate, No.4 Mark 16.50
Nippon, Mustard Pot, Hand-Painted Violets, Green Crown Mark 12.50
Nippon, Mustard Pot, Scenic, Attached Tray, Covered, Green Wreath Mark 20.00
Nippon, Napkin Ring, Beaded Holly Design 45.00
Nippon, Napkin Ring, Floral & Gold .... 33.00 To 45.00
Nippon, Napkin Ring, Scenic, Green Wreath Mark .... 25.00 To 45.00
Nippon, Napkin Ring, Teahouse Scene, Royal Kaga Mark 25.00
Nippon, Napkin, Ring, Gold Beaded Rim, Pink Raised Dots, Roses, Centerpiece 35.00
Nippon, Nappy, Sailing Ships, Bisque Finish, Green Mark, 4 1/2 In. 25.00
Nippon, Nappy, Sailing Ships, Orange, Lilac Shading, 5 1/2 In. 14.00
Nippon, Nappy, Scenic, Ornamental Open Handles 16.00
Nippon, Nut Set, Bisque Finish Acorns, Autumn Colors, Green M, 7 Piece 95.00
Nippon, Nut Set, Flowered, Open Handles, 6 Piece 45.00
Nippon, Nut Set, Inside Rim Scenes, Gold Beaded, White, Footed, Signed, 6 Piece 75.00
Nippon, Nut Set, Lake Scene, Brown Beading, 7 Piece 45.00
Nippon, Nut Set, Pink Roses, Gold Bead Edge, M In Wreath, 7 Piece 45.00
Nippon, Nut Set, Scalloped, Red Flowers, Beaded Edge, Footed, 6 Piece 25.00
Nippon, Nut Set, Tea Roses, Hand-Painted, Gold, Peanut Shape, 7 Piece 55.00
Nippon, Pincushion Dish, Heart Shaped 50.00
Nippon, Pitcher Vase, Cobalt Blue, Pink Roses, & Gold, 9 In. 50.00
Nippon, Pitcher, Child's Blown-Out Face, 3 In. 35.00

Nippon, Pitcher, Floral, Gold & Yellow Trim, Covered, 5 In. 32.00
Nippon, Pitcher, Gold Filigree, White & Pink Mums On White, 11 In. 200.00
Nippon, Pitcher, Hand-Painted, Moriye Leaves, Maple Leaf Mark, 10 In. 125.00
Nippon, Pitcher, Lemonade, Ice Lip, Floral Decoration, White 45.00
Nippon, Pitcher, Lemonade, Zinnias, Butterflies, Gold Encrustations, 17 In. 400.00
Nippon, Pitcher, Moriye, Soft Green, Pink & Lavender Roses, 5 X 6 In. 45.00
Nippon, Pitcher, Pink & Yellow Roses, 8 1/4 In. 80.00
Nippon, Pitcher, Pink Cherries, Gold Beading, Green Maple Leaf, 5 1/2 In. 32.50
Nippon, Pitcher, Red Roses On Shades Of Green, Gilded Handle & Base, 7 In. 50.00
Nippon, Planter, Enamel Design On Green, House, Horse, Green Mark, Triangular 95.00
Nippon, Planter, Floral Design, Wreath Mark, 5 3/4 X 2 1/2 In. 46.00
Nippon, Planter, Gold Curved Feet, Orchids, Jeweled Gold Border 115.00
Nippon, Planter, Melon Ribbed, Six-Sided, Satin Finish, Blue, Flowers, Green M 95.00
Nippon, Planter, Six-Sided Bisque, Desert Scene, Beaded Trim 65.00
Nippon, Plaque, Arabian Village, Beaded Gold, Foo Dog Rim, Marked, 10 In. 125.00
Nippon, Plaque, Bird's-Eye View Of Castle On Rhine Scene, M Mark, 10 In. 60.00
Nippon, Plaque, Bisque Sailboat Scene, Beaded Trim, 7 1/2 In. 65.00
Nippon, Plaque, Bisque, House, Lake, Trees, Sunset, Green M In Wreath, 10 In. 85.00
Nippon, Plaque, Blown-Out Deer, Signed, 10 3/4 In. 275.00
Nippon, Plaque, Blown-Out Indian Hunter, Green M Mark, 10 1/2 In. 135.00
Nippon, Plaque, Blown-Out Indian Riding Horse, Aiming Gun In Forest, 11 In. 300.00
Nippon, Plaque, Blown-Out Indian Standing In Stream, Bird Over Back, Matte 450.00
Nippon, Plaque, Blown-Out Lion & Lioness, Matte Finish, Signed, 10 1/2 In. 350.00
Nippon, Plaque, Blown-Out Lions & Lioness, Green M In Wreath, 10 3/4 In. 450.00
Nippon, Plaque, Blown-Out Moose, Green M Mark, 10 1/2 In. .... 315.00 To 350.00
Nippon, Plaque, Blown-Out Stag, Green Mark, 10 1/2 In. 300.00
Nippon, Plaque, Blown-Out Stag, 10 3/4 In. 375.00
Nippon, Plaque, Country Cottage In Spring, Green M, Round, 10 In. 55.00
Nippon, Plaque, Countryside Scene, Bisque Finish, Enameled Beading, Pierced 165.00
Nippon, Plaque, Dutch Farm Scene, Green Mark, 10 In. 80.00
Nippon, Plaque, Flowers, White Beaded & Swirled Rim, 8 1/2 In. 55.00
Nippon, Plaque, Hanging, Shepherd Herding Flock, 10 In. 115.00
Nippon, Plaque, Horse Gazing Out Of Stable, Flowers, Beaded, 9 In. 95.00
Nippon, Plaque, Indian Portrait, Hand-Painted, Green M In Wreath Mark, 8 In. 110.00
Nippon, Plaque, Lake Scene, Cobalt Enamel Slip Work, 9 In. 100.00
Nippon, Plaque, Landscape Scene, Raised Enamel, Blue Maple Leaf, 9 In. 125.00
Nippon, Plaque, Man In Wagon On Beach, Pierced, 10 1/2 In. 95.00
Nippon, Plaque, Oriental Scene Of Trees & Ivy, Beige, Lavender, & Green, 9 In. 75.00
Nippon, Plaque, Ornate Gold Border, Red Roses, Scenic, 9 1/2 In. 22.50
Nippon, Plaque, Portrait, Indian, Green M Wreath, 7 3/4 In. 110.00
Nippon, Plaque, Roses, Enameled Border, Satin Finish, Blue M Mark, 10 In. 85.00
Nippon, Plaque, Scenic, Matte Finish, Gold Trim, Green M, 9 In. 35.00
Nippon, Plaque, Sgraffitto American Indian, 13 In. Diameter 250.00
Nippon, Plaque, Stag, Autumn Colors, Moriye Overlay, Acorns & Leaves 125.00
Nippon, Plaque, Standing Stag, Green Wreath Mark, 10 In. 95.00
Nippon, Plaque, Trees With Coralene Raised Decoration On Leaves, 9 1/2 In. 95.00
Nippon, Plaque, Wall, Bisque Finish, Egyptian Boat Scene, Enamel, Green M Mark 135.00
Nippon, Plaque, Water Scene, Pierced, Marked M, 10 In. 58.00
Nippon, Plate, Betty Boop, Marked, 6 In. 16.00
Nippon, Plate, Bisque, Lavender Wisteria, Gold Leaves, Beaded Border, 19 In. 145.00
Nippon, Plate, Black Enamel, Peacock In Magnolia Tree, 8 3/4 In. 55.00
Nippon, Plate, Blown-Out Swans, Gold Beading, 9 1/2 In. 65.00
Nippon, Plate, Blue Windmills, Boats, Water Scene On Rim, Old Blue Mark, 9 In. 32.00
Nippon, Plate, Bluebird, 7 1/2 In. 15.00
Nippon, Plate, Boat, Lake, Hills, & Palms, Beach, Gold Tracing & Trim, 11 In. 58.00
Nippon, Plate, Bronze Ground, Scene In Black, M In Wreath, 2 Handled, 8 In. 35.00
Nippon, Plate, Bust Portrait, Pale Yellow, Purple Luster, Gold Rim, 8 In. 20.00
Nippon, Plate, Butterflies & Flowers, Embossed Gold Leaves & Trim, 8 In. 25.00
Nippon, Plate, Cake, Bright Flowers, Gold Trim, Spoke Mark, 9 3/4 In. 28.00
Nippon, Plate, Cake, Flowers All Over, Hand-Painted 18.00
Nippon, Plate, Cake, Flying Swans, Green, Gold Rim, Jeweled, 7 1/2 In., Set Of 4 ...... 35.00
Nippon, Plate, Cake, Gold Flowers, C.1890, 10 In. 40.00
Nippon, Plate, Cake, Handle, Cream Band Outlined In Gold, Multifloral Band 22.50
Nippon, Plate, Cake, Oranges, Green Leaves 15.00
Nippon, Plate, Cake, Pink & Green, Roses, Blue Maple Leaf Mark, 6 1/4 In. 10.00

Nippon, Plate, Cake, Swimming Swans, Open Handled, 9 1/2 In.	12.00
Nippon, Plate, Cheese & Cracker, Purple Flowers, Gold, Green Wreath, 9 In.	25.00
Nippon, Plate, Deep Brown, Orange Poppies, Gold Scalloped Border, 11 In.	150.00
Nippon, Plate, Desert Scene Of Camel Riders, Palm Trees, Tents, Islam Border	85.00
Nippon, Plate, Embossed Child's Face, 6 1/2 In.	43.00
Nippon, Plate, Floral With Gold Trim, Marked JPL, 7 In.	10.00
Nippon, Plate, Gold Band, Pink Roses, RC Mark, 9 3/4 In.	12.00
Nippon, Plate, Gold Border, 7 1/2 In.	7.00
Nippon, Plate, Hand-Painted Rabbits, Field, Artist Signature, E.Poore	35.00
Nippon, Plate, Hand-Painted Swans, Pink Jewels, M In Green Wreath, 7 1/4 In.	45.00
Nippon, Plate, Independence Hall, 1907, 7 In.	9.00
Nippon, Plate, Indian, Full Headdress, Green Mark, 8 In.	165.00
Nippon, Plate, Lake Scene, Autumn Colors, Beaded Border, Leaf Mark, 10 In.	10.00
Nippon, Plate, Lake Scene, Green M Mark, 8 In.	10.00
Nippon, Plate, Moriye, Floral & Leaves, 9 In.	45.00
Nippon, Plate, Pastel Tones, Raised Lilacs, Bisque Finish, 10 1/4 In.	80.00
Nippon, Plate, Pink Floral Border, Green Crown Mark, Hand-Painted, 6 1/4 In.	3.00
Nippon, Plate, Portrait, Hand-Painted, Gold Beaded Rim, 11 In.	145.00
Nippon, Plate, Portrait, Lady, Head & Shoulders, Lilac In Hair, Beehive Mark	147.00
Nippon, Plate, Portrait, Signed In Gold Block Letters	145.00
Nippon, Plate, Pug Dog, All Around Raised Enameling, Matte, Brown, Green, 9 In.	145.00
Nippon, Plate, Purple Flowers, Raised Gold Leaves, Gold Trim, 8 1/2 In.	18.00
Nippon, Plate, Roses, Hand-Painted, Yellow, Signed K.Saito	12.00
Nippon, Plate, Scenic Bridge, 2 Houses, Trees, Path, Raised Decoration On Rim	70.00
Nippon, Plate, Scenic, Sunset, Pierced Handles, Green Wreath M, 9 1/2 In.	12.00
Nippon, Plate, Seascape Image, Windmill, Soft Pastel Colors, Signed, 10 In.	40.00
Nippon, Plate, Seascape With Sailboats, Soft Pastel Colors, 12 In.	45.00
Nippon, Plate, Windmill & Water, Pierced Handles, Matte, M Mark, 9 3/4 In.	50.00
Nippon, Plate, Windmill, Lavender, Gray, Brown & Blue, Matte, 6 1/4 In.	15.00
Nippon, Plate, Yellow Flowers, Pink Border, Hand-Painted, 6 1/2 In.	11.00
Nippon, Platter, Flying Turkey, Signed, 16 In.	35.00
Nippon, Platter, Red Florals, Blue & Yellow Florals, Butterflies, 13 X 10 In.	65.00
Nippon, Relish Set, Gold, Green, Red, White Flowers, 3 Piece	35.00
Nippon, Relish, Gold Handled, Blue Birds, Roses, Green Mark, 8 1/2 In.	13.00
Nippon, Relish, Gold, Cobalt, Pink Roses, Oval, 9 In.	18.00
Nippon, Relish, Peanut Plant Design, Green Leaf Mark, 8 In.	45.00
Nippon, Relish, Scenic, Profile Of Indian In Full Headdress On Handles	42.00
Nippon, Relish, Shore Scene, Windmill, Hand-Painted	10.00
Nippon, Ring Tree, Floral, Ornate	45.00
Nippon, Ring Tree, Geometric & Roses, Gold Handle, RC Mark	38.00
Nippon, Ring Tree, Green Band, Pink Roses, Gold Beading, Green Mark	15.00
Nippon, Ring Tree, Ships, Gold Hand Outstretched, Green Wreath Mark	37.50
Nippon, Rose Bowl, Red & White, Red Roses In Gold Medallions, RC, 4 1/2 In.	43.00
Nippon, Rose Bowl, Strawberry, Footed	50.00
Nippon, Rose Jar, Bisque Finish, Pink Primroses, Gold Pinecones, 5 1/2 In.	59.00
Nippon, Rose Jar, Pink Primroses, Gold Pinecones, Blue Maple Leaf Mark, 6 In.	58.00
Nippon, Rose Jar, Swirled Green, Scenic Band At Center, Green M, 5 1/2 In.	75.00
Nippon, Rose Jar, White Background, Violets, Green, White Beads	37.00
Nippon, Salt & Pepper, Floral On White	9.00
Nippon, Salt & Pepper, Gold Decoration	7.00
Nippon, Salt & Pepper, Gold Trim, Handled	25.00
Nippon, Salt & Pepper, Moriye Scenic Tree Design, Matte, 3 In.	25.00
Nippon, Salt & Pepper, Pink & Yellow Roses, Hand-Painted	12.00
Nippon, Salt & Pepper, Scenic, Beading, Cherry Blossom, 3 In.	12.00
Nippon, Salt & Pepper, Scenic, Mushroom Top	12.00
Nippon, Salt & Pepper, Ships On Sea With Sunset, Green, Wreath Mark	22.50
Nippon, Salt & Pepper, Square Base, Roses, Gold Banded, Hand-Painted	10.00
Nippon, Salt, Geometric Floral Rim, Pedestal, Red Wreath Mark, Set Of 4	25.00
Nippon, Salt, Pastoral Scene, Beaded, Matte	17.00
Nippon, Salt, Rising Sun Mark, Set Of 6	20.00
Nippon, Salt, Royal Kaga, Japanese Scenes, 3 In.	18.00
Nippon, Saltdip, Boat Shape, Pink & Red Rose, Embossed Handle, Set Of 6	20.00
Nippon, Sauce Set, Blue & Brown Grapes Border, Gold, 6 Piece	85.00
Nippon, Server, Cheese & Cracker, 2-Tiered, Pink Strawberries, Gold Beading	40.00
Nippon, Serving Set, Gold Vintage Band From Rim, 3 Piece	45.00

Nippon, Shaving Mug, Green Wreath Mark 65.00
Nippon, Spooner, Blossom Sprig On Tinted Background, Handled, 8 In. 48.00
Nippon, Stickpin Holder, Floral 33.00
Nippon, Sugar & Creamer, Azalea, Marked .... 22.00 To 25.00
Nippon, Sugar & Creamer, Blue Birds 50.00
Nippon, Sugar & Creamer, Blue Floral, Gold Key Border 29.00
Nippon, Sugar & Creamer, Blue Floral, Gold Trim, 1905 Mark 38.00
Nippon, Sugar & Creamer, Bluebirds, Gold Trim, Square Crown Mark 21.00
Nippon, Sugar & Creamer, Claw Feet, Ornate, RC Crown Mark, 5 In. 39.00
Nippon, Sugar & Creamer, Cover, Raised Gold Trim 30.00
Nippon, Sugar & Creamer, Covered, Pink Roses, Blue Butterfly, Leaf Mark 15.00
Nippon, Sugar & Creamer, Cream Background, Blue Shades, Green M Wreath Mark 47.00
Nippon, Sugar & Creamer, Dark Green Border, Gold Trim, Violets, Marked 65.00
Nippon, Sugar & Creamer, Farm & Water Scene, Signed, Green M In Wreath Mark ... 45.00
Nippon, Sugar & Creamer, Floral Medallions, Royal Dinran 35.00
Nippon, Sugar & Creamer, Flying Rooster Pattern 50.00
Nippon, Sugar & Creamer, Gold & Floral, Green Mark 22.50
Nippon, Sugar & Creamer, Green & Gold Ground, Jeweled, Blue Maple Leaf Mark ... 150.00
Nippon, Sugar & Creamer, Hand-Painted Dragon, Gray-Green Ground, Moriye 75.00
Nippon, Sugar & Creamer, Hand-Painted Flowers, Gold, Pink 42.00
Nippon, Sugar & Creamer, Hand-Painted, Blue Crown Mark 30.00
Nippon, Sugar & Creamer, Lace Gold Bands Enclosing Violet Clusters, Mark 20.00
Nippon, Sugar & Creamer, Moriye, Jewel-Eyed Dragon, Blue Pagoda Mark, Covered ... 75.00
Nippon, Sugar & Creamer, Oval, Colors, Gold Trim, Wreath Mark 37.50
Nippon, Sugar & Creamer, Pinecones, Leaves, Gold Trim, Green Wreath Mark 25.00
Nippon, Sugar & Creamer, Pink Roses, Blue & Yellow Square, Gold Trim 23.00
Nippon, Sugar & Creamer, Pumpkin Shape, Pink & Purple Roses, Green Leaves 28.00
Nippon, Sugar & Creamer, Rose Decoration, Gold 26.00
Nippon, Sugar & Creamer, Roses, Jeweling & Gold, Hand-Painted 45.00
Nippon, Sugar & Creamer, Roses, Pair 15.00
Nippon, Sugar & Creamer, Trees, Meadow, Gold Trim 48.00
Nippon, Sugar & Creamer, White, Gold Flowers 10.00
Nippon, Sugar & Creamer, White, Gold Geometrics, Greek Key Border, Maple Leaf ... 35.00
Nippon, Sugar & Creamer, 4 Colored Roses, Gold Trim & Beading, Green 7 .... 29.50
Nippon, Sugar Shaker, Cobalt, Gold Trim, White, Unmarked 30.00
Nippon, Sugar Shaker, Cream, Pink & Red Roses, Gold Decorated, Handled 40.00
Nippon, Sugar Shaker, Hand-Painted Violets, 3 1/2 In. 38.00
Nippon, Sugar Shaker, Poppies, Orange, Pink, Gold Bead, M In Wreath 45.00
Nippon, Sugar Shaker, Soft Pastel Floral, Green Mark, Hand-Painted 22.50
Nippon, Sugar Shaker, White, Floral Border, Handled 18.00
Nippon, Sugar Shaker, White, Raised Gold, Pastel Flowers, M In Wreath 26.00
Nippon, Sugar, Attached Tray, Roses & Web, Gilt & Beading, Two Handled 23.00
Nippon, Sugar, Covered, Pink Azaleas 9.00
Nippon, Sugar, Floral, Covered 15.00
Nippon, Sugar, Gold On Cobalt Border, Bisque, Florals, Blue Leaf, Plantation 45.00
Nippon, Syrup & Underplate, Dark Green, Red & Yellow Roses, Gold Beading 60.00
Nippon, Syrup & Underplate, Floral & Gold 23.00
Nippon, Syrup & Underplate, House Scene, Green, Yellow, Brown, M In Wreath 36.00
Nippon, Syrup & Underplate, Lake Scene, Black, Gold Accents & Trim, Marked 30.00
Nippon, Syrup & Underplate, Pink Flowers, Leaves, Moriaga Trim, Loop Handle 65.00
Nippon, Syrup & Underplate, Pink Roses, Gold Border 22.00
Nippon, Syrup & Underplate, White, Roses, Blue Bands, TN In Wreath 28.00
Nippon, Syrup & Underplate, 6 Sided, Gold Trim, Roses, M In Wreath 36.00
Nippon, Tankard, Flowers, Gold Trim, Royal Nippon 225.00
Nippon, Tankard, Flowers, 12 In. 50.00
Nippon, Tankard, Scenic, Sailboats, Beaded Borders, 11 In. 165.00
Nippon, Tea Caddy, 3 Sided, Nile River Scene, Raised Palm Trees, 6 In. 135.00
Nippon, Tea Set, Beige To Brown, Mauve, Swans On Lake, Gold Trim, 11 Piece ... 150.00
Nippon, Tea Set, Black Matte, Silver Deposit Dragon, Flowers, 3 Piece 175.00
Nippon, Tea Set, Child's, Dutch Decoration, 9 Piece 65.00
Nippon, Tea Set, Child's, Flowers, 20 Piece 45.00
Nippon, Tea Set, Child's, Teapot, Sugar, Creamer, 4 Plates, 5 Cups & Saucers 69.00
Nippon, Tea Set, Child's, 15 Piece 175.00
Nippon, Tea Set, Completely Gold With Black Flowers, 15 Pieces 165.00
Nippon, Tea Set, Floral, Melon Rib, Beads, Cobalt, Footed, Green, Red, 3 Piece ... 135.00

Nippon, Tea Set, Gold Luster, Hand-Painted Insects, Covers, 3 Piece 85.00
Nippon, Tea Set, Green Band, Pink Roses, Blue Rising Sun, 4 Piece 40.00
Nippon, Tea Set, Large Japanese Sampans, 3 Piece 48.00
Nippon, Tea Set, Large Moriye Dragons, 13 Piece 90.00
Nippon, Tea Set, Matte Floral, 3 Piece 175.00
Nippon, Tea Set, Oriental Scenic, Lithopane, Red Mark, 18 Piece 65.00
Nippon, Tea Set, Pink & Red Roses, Cobalt Blue Trim, Pagoda Mark, 15 Piece 68.00
Nippon, Tea Set, Raised Gold Designs, Signed R.C.Nippon, 16 Piece 250.00
Nippon, Tea Set, Red Trim, Geisha Koga 45.00
Nippon, Tea Set, Ribbed, Footed, Gold, 15 Piece 185.00
Nippon, Tea Set, Roses, Gold Work Raised, Signed RC, 14 Piece 250.00
Nippon, Tea Set, Sailboats On Lake, Gold Beaded Trim, Hand-Painted, 3 Piece 68.00
Nippon, Tea Set, Scenic, Paprika, Green, Gold, Hand-Painted, 3 Piece 150.00
Nippon, Tea Set, Sugar, Creamer, 4 Cups & Saucers, Gold Beading 105.00
Nippon, Tea Set, 19 Pieces, Black & White, Floral Ovals, Green Mark 95.00
Nippon, Tea Strainer, Cobalt & Gold Beading 39.00
Nippon, Tea Strainer, Flowers And Gold 28.00
Nippon, Tea Strainer, Gold, Cobalt, Ornate Trim, 2 Piece, Blue Leaf 39.00
Nippon, Tea Strainer, Undercup, Hand-Painted, White, Gold Trim, R.C. 28.00
Nippon, Tea Strainer, Undercup, Roses, Gold, Rising Sun, 3 1/2 In. 21.00
Nippon, Tea Strainer, Underplate, Ornate, Flowers, Gold, Cobalt 40.00
Nippon, Teapot, Azalea, Miniature, 2 1/2 In. 15.00
Nippon, Teapot, Blown-Out Face, 3 1/4 In.High 35.00
Nippon, Teapot, Footed, Large Pink Flowers All Over 22.00
Nippon, Teapot, Gold & Orange, Geishas, Blue Crown Mark 45.00
Nippon, Teapot, Hand-Painted Roses, Beaded Gold Swags, Signed 65.00
Nippon, Teapot, Heavy Raised Gold Decoration, 6 Sided, Blue Mark, 5 1/2 In. 22.00
Nippon, Teapot, Pink & Yellow Floral, Gold & Black Band On Pot & Lid, Mark 28.00
Nippon, Teapot, Raised Decoration, Gold Trim & Handle, M In Wreath, 4 1/2 In. 17.50
Nippon, Teapot, Sugar & Creamer, Pink Roses, Blue Mark 75.00
Nippon, Tile, Bird, Hand-Painted, Green Wreath, 6 In. 12.00
Nippon, Tile, Enameled Pink Flowers, Green Leaves 15.00
Nippon, Tile, Swan 23.00
Nippon, Tile, Windmill 23.00
Nippon, Tile, Windmill Scene, Footed 13.00
Nippon, Toothpick, Edged In Violets 15.00
Nippon, Toothpick, Egg Shape, 3 Ball Feet, Ship Decoration, Green M Mark 40.00
Nippon, Toothpick, Farm Scene, Beading, Yellow, Brown, Handled, Pair 40.00
Nippon, Toothpick, Gold Band, M 6.00
Nippon, Toothpick, Green Wreath, Slip Work 45.00
Nippon, Toothpick, Light Green, Roses, Beaded 30.00
Nippon, Toothpick, Pink Roses, Gold Beading, 2 Handles 35.00
Nippon, Toothpick, Roses, Raised Gold Decoration, 2 Handled 12.00
Nippon, Toothpick, Six-Sided, Footed, Green Wreath Mark 14.00
Nippon, Toothpick, Two-Handled, Roses, Gold Tracery, M In Wreath 13.00
Nippon, Tray & Box, Dresser, Desert Scene, Footed Box, Marked 54.00
Nippon, Tray, Bread, Allover Color, Gold Trim, 17 X 5 In. 14.00
Nippon, Tray, Celery, Desert Scene, Hand-Painted 48.00
Nippon, Tray, Cheese & Cracker, Magenta Mark 38.00
Nippon, Tray, Cookie, Pastel Floral, White, Gold Border, 14 X 6 X 7 In. 40.00
Nippon, Tray, Dresser, Desert Scene 20.00
Nippon, Tray, Dresser, White, Lavender Flowers, Gold Border 18.00
Nippon, Tray, Hors D'oeuvre, 2-Section, Flowers, Gold, Handled 33.00
Nippon, Tray, Pastel, Lake, Trees, Pink Roses, Gold & Beads, 7 X 10 In. 42.50
Nippon, Tray, Pin, Butterfly Shape, Hand-Painted, 5 1/4 X 3 1/2 In. 18.00
Nippon, Tray, Pink Iris, Gold Beading, Round, 12 In. 18.00
Nippon, Tray, Roses, Oval, 6 In. 10.00
Nippon, Tray, Scenic, Octagonal, 13 X 9 In. 70.00
Nippon, Trivet, Holland Scene, Blues, Girl, Umbrella, Dark Beading, 8 Sided 48.00
Nippon, Urn, Cobalt & Gold, 15 In. 225.00
Nippon, Urn, Country Scene, Ornate Gold, Heavy Jeweling, Covered, 14 In. 145.00
Nippon, Urn, Floral, Cobalt, Gold, 10 In. 95.00
Nippon, Urn, Scenic, Gold, Jeweled, 2 Handled, 5 1/2 In. 50.00
Nippon, Vase, Apple Blossoms, Gold Trim, M In Wreath, 10 In. 67.00
Nippon, Vase, Arab Scene, Matte Finish, 8 In. 95.00

Nippon, Vase, Arabian & Camel Scene, 4 3/4 In., Pair	35.00
Nippon, Vase, Basket, Black, Flowers, Green M, 7 1/2 In.	58.00
Nippon, Vase, Basket, Brown, Yellow Iris, Leaves, Artist Signed MK, Marked	125.00
Nippon, Vase, Basket, Enameled Owl Design	225.00
Nippon, Vase, Beaded Rim, Floral, Ivys, Shadow Forms, Gold, Pink, Matte, 4 In.	55.00
Nippon, Vase, Beaded, Gold Trimmed, 2 Plaques, Girl, Flowers, 18 3/4 In.	325.00
Nippon, Vase, Birch Trees At Water's Edge, Green Wreath Mark, 5 1/2 In.	40.00
Nippon, Vase, Bird & Floral, Gold Beading, Nishki, 12 In.	62.00
Nippon, Vase, Bird Decoration, 8 In., Pair	55.00
Nippon, Vase, Birds Of Paradise, Floral, Medallion, Gold Handle, 10 In.	110.00
Nippon, Vase, Birds, Turquoise & Gold, 2 Handled, Moriye, Marked, 8 1/2 In.	165.00
Nippon, Vase, Bisque Finish, Red Roses, Encrusted Gold & Beading Top, 10 In.	110.00
Nippon, Vase, Bisque Finish, 2 Handles, Green Wreath, 8 In.	85.00
Nippon, Vase, Bisque, Earthtones, Desert, Camel, Dark Tracing Beads, 5 1/2 In.	70.00
Nippon, Vase, Bisque, Lake, Boat, Jeweled Handles, M In Wreath, 5 1/2 In.	40.00
Nippon, Vase, Bisque, Pair, 8 1/2 In.	150.00
Nippon, Vase, Bisque, Tropical Scene, Gold Decorated Collar, 8 In.	33.00
Nippon, Vase, Black, Hand-Painted Scene, Gold Trim, L. & Co., 7 X 11 In., Pair	100.00
Nippon, Vase, Blue Highlighting Shoreline, Sky, Foliage, Maple Leaf, 4 1/2 In.	28.00
Nippon, Vase, Blue Jewels, 2 Handles, Imperial Mark, 10 1/2 In.	110.00
Nippon, Vase, Blue, Gold, & Green Decoration On Brown, Handled, 7 1/2 In.	30.00
Nippon, Vase, Bluebird, Robin, Pink & White Dogwoods, Green Mark, 14 In., Pair	375.00
Nippon, Vase, Boat Scenes In Oval Panels, White Ground, Gold Beading, 7 In.	65.00
Nippon, Vase, Brown Bisque Finish, 6 Raised Rosebuds, Cream Enamel, 9 In.	95.00
Nippon, Vase, Bulbous, Roses, Gold Trim, M In Wreath, 6 1/2 In.	35.00
Nippon, Vase, Bulbous, Scenic, Jeweled, Satin Finish, Green Mark, 7 In.	60.00
Nippon, Vase, Classic Ruins, Bisque, Gold Beaded Rim, Gold Handles, 6 In.	75.00
Nippon, Vase, Cobalt Blue Trim, Water Scene, Pink Floral Front, 5 In.	65.00
Nippon, Vase, Cobalt, Gold Florals, Blue Maple Leaf Mark	95.00
Nippon, Vase, Cobalt, Gold Trim, Medallions Of Sailing Ships, Green M, 9 In.	165.00
Nippon, Vase, Cobalt, Gold Trim, Red Poppies, Royal Kinran, 16 In.	175.00
Nippon, Vase, Cobalt, Lady In Garden Holding Flowers, Gold, 7 In.	150.00
Nippon, Vase, Colored, Gold Trim, 6 In.	37.50
Nippon, Vase, Coralene, Gold Figure Top, Pink, Yellow, Florals, 4 3/4 In.	125.00
Nippon, Vase, Coralene, Green, Blue & White Floral, 2 Handles, 9 In.	165.00
Nippon, Vase, Coralene, Maple Leaf Decoration, Gold Trim, Signed, 11 3/4 In.	155.00
Nippon, Vase, Coralene, 2 Handles, Floral On Green Background, Signed, 9 In.	150.00
Nippon, Vase, Coralene, 2 Handles, 4 3/4 In.	59.00
Nippon, Vase, Cottage By Lake, Brown Bead Border, Lima Mark No.39, 8 In., Pair	75.00
Nippon, Vase, Country Scene, Foliage, Gold & Beading, Urn Shape, Pagoda, 10 In.	89.00
Nippon, Vase, Cream, Hand-Painted Roses, In 4 Block Panels, Gold, 9 1/2 In.	85.00
Nippon, Vase, Daisies, Gold Handles, Acid Finish, Green Wreath, 12 1/2 In.	145.00
Nippon, Vase, Dark Green & Gold, Square, Art Nouveau, Green Wreath Mark, 7 In.	45.00
Nippon, Vase, Dark Green, Irises, 7 1/2 In.	45.00
Nippon, Vase, Deep Red, Gold, Encircled With Florals, 2 Handled, 9 In.	115.00
Nippon, Vase, Double Handles, Swans On Lake, 7 1/2 In.	235.00
Nippon, Vase, Dutch Sailing Scene, Windmills, Green M In Wreath, 8 In.	95.00
Nippon, Vase, Dutch Scene, 2 Handles, Green Wreath, 13 In.	145.00
Nippon, Vase, Ewer, Allover Floral, Handled, 6 In.	75.00
Nippon, Vase, Floral Decoration, Purple, Gold, 6 In.	15.00
Nippon, Vase, Floral, Beading, Red, Pink, Yellow, Gold, 12 In.	150.00
Nippon, Vase, Floral, Cream, Gold Beading, Double Handles, Marked, 10 In.	85.00
Nippon, Vase, Floral, Gold Beading & Trim, Curled Open, Handles, 11 In.	47.50
Nippon, Vase, Floral, Gold, Green Wreath Mark, 9 In.	65.00
Nippon, Vase, Floral, Hand-Painted, 5 1/2 In.	12.50
Nippon, Vase, Floral, Handled, Signed, 8 1/2 In.	45.00
Nippon, Vase, Floral, 2 Handles, Yellow, Gold, Pastel, Green Wreath Mark, 9 In.	135.00
Nippon, Vase, Flowers, Cobalt Blue, Gold Rim, Pink, Blue Maple Leaf Mark, 7 In.	68.00
Nippon, Vase, Flowers, Gold Handles, Brown, Yellow, Blue, Green W Mark, 4 In.	20.00
Nippon, Vase, Flowers, Leaves, 2 Handles, Brown, 9 In.	90.00
Nippon, Vase, Flowers, 2 Handles, Moriye, 8 In.	125.00
Nippon, Vase, Flying Geese, 10 1/2 In.	175.00
Nippon, Vase, Footed, Handled, Primitive Type House Scene, 5 1/2 In.	25.00
Nippon, Vase, Four Medallions, Red & Pink Roses, Gold, 7 1/2 In.	45.00
Nippon, Vase, Gold Beaded Floral, Double Handled, Green M Wreath Mark, 6 In.	40.00

Nippon, Vase, Gold Beading & Hand-Painted Roses, Handled, 10 In. 65.00
Nippon, Vase, Gold Beading, 6 Sided, Hand-Painted, 9 X 8 1/2 In. 189.00
Nippon, Vase, Gold Decorated, Raised Beading, Ostrich In Center, Cobalt, 8 In. 135.00
Nippon, Vase, Gold Elephant-Head Handles, Arab Woman On Camel, 6 In. 125.00
Nippon, Vase, Gold Floral Rim, Red & White Roses, Pastel Ground, 12 In. 185.00
Nippon, Vase, Gold Handles & Beading, Satin Finish, Roses, 5 1/2 In. 32.00
Nippon, Vase, Gold Relief, Pink & Green, Maple Leaf Mark, 5 1/2 In. 54.00
Nippon, Vase, Gray Bisque Background, Raised Flowers, Sunset, 6 1/2 In. 35.00
Nippon, Vase, Green & Pink Flowers, White Frosting, Moriye, 6 In. 135.00
Nippon, Vase, Green & White Enameled Bird, Raised Flowers, 2 Handles, Signed 65.00
Nippon, Vase, Green Shaded To Yellow, Water Lilies & Pads, Gold Rim, Pair 80.00
Nippon, Vase, Green, Blue & White Floral, Coralene, 2 Handled, 9 In. 165.00
Nippon, Vase, Green, Roses, House, Gold Trim, Green Wreath Mark, 6 1/2 In. 37.50
Nippon, Vase, Hand-Painted Florals, Beaded Base, 10 1/2 In. 100.00
Nippon, Vase, Hand-Painted Florals, Handled, 10 1/2 In. 100.00
Nippon, Vase, Hand-Painted Flowers, Large, Footed, 13 1/2 In. 125.00
Nippon, Vase, Hand-Painted Roses, Gold Enameled Flowers, Maple Leaf, 10 In. 95.00
Nippon, Vase, Hand-Painted Scene Of Farmhouse, Swan Handles, 10 1/2 In. 75.00
Nippon, Vase, Hand-Painted Scenic, 2 Handles, 9 X 6 In. 85.00
Nippon, Vase, Hand-Painted, Scenic, Gold & Pastel, M In Wreath, 12 In., Pair 200.00
Nippon, Vase, Handled, Black Background, Raised Gold Designs 45.00
Nippon, Vase, Handled, Footed, House, Tree & Water Scene, 8 In. 49.00
Nippon, Vase, Handled, House & Water Wheel Scene, Gold & Jeweled Top, 6 In. 33.00
Nippon, Vase, Handled, Moriye Dragon, Gray & White Background, 4 3/4 In. 22.00
Nippon, Vase, Harbor Scene, 11 In. 75.00
Nippon, Vase, House & Water Scene On White, Gold Handles, Green M Mark, 8 In. 38.00
Nippon, Vase, House On Lake Scene, Beading, Double Handled, 5 In., Pair 25.00
Nippon, Vase, House, Trees, Beading, Browns & Greens, Green M In Wreath, 6 In. 23.00
Nippon, Vase, House, Trees, Lake, Gold Handles, Glazed, M In Wreath, 5 1/2 In. 45.00
Nippon, Vase, House, Water Scene, Oval, 2 Handles, Green M In Wreath, 7 3/4 In. 38.00
Nippon, Vase, Jeweled, Beading, Mixed Colors, 18 In. 225.00
Nippon, Vase, Lady With Urn Of Flowers, Gold, Cobalt Blue, 2 Handles, 7 In. 265.00
Nippon, Vase, Lake Scene, 2 Handles, 6 In. 25.00
Nippon, Vase, Magenta & Green Flowers, Gold Handles, M In Wreath, 5 In. 27.50
Nippon, Vase, Man On Camel, Handle, 6 In. 65.00
Nippon, Vase, Maple Leaf, Seashore Scene, Diamond Shape, Yellow, Blue, 5 In. 25.00
Nippon, Vase, Matte Gray, Raised Pink Dragon, Green Wreath Mark, 6 1/4 In. 30.00
Nippon, Vase, Matte, Cream & Gold Handles, Geometrics, Turquoise, 13 1/2 In. 220.00
Nippon, Vase, Medallion Scenes, Floral Background, Handled, Gold, Maple Leaf 60.00
Nippon, Vase, Moriye, Butterflies & Floral, Cylindrical, 10 In. 45.00
Nippon, Vase, Moriye, Floral Medallion, Twisted & Turned Handles, 9 1/2 In. 145.00
Nippon, Vase, Moriye, Flying Bird, Hand-Painted Florals, Blue Leaf Mark, 9 In. 115.00
Nippon, Vase, Moriye, Green With White Slip, 8 1/4 In. 125.00
Nippon, Vase, Moriye, Green, Turquoise Enameled Beads, Urn Shaped, 8 1/4 In. 125.00
Nippon, Vase, Moriye, Green, White Slipwork, 12 In. 185.00
Nippon, Vase, Moriye, Greens & Beige, Floral, Beading, Urn Shape, 11 In. 145.00
Nippon, Vase, Moriye, Lavender Flowers, Butterfly, Pale Green & Brown, 9 In. 94.00
Nippon, Vase, Moriye, Leaf Mark, Handled, 6 In. 68.00
Nippon, Vase, Moriye, 2 Handles, Green Background, Brown, Yellow Floral, 6 In. 85.00
Nippon, Vase, Ornate Handle, Dark Green, Signed Royal Kinran, 10 In. 110.00
Nippon, Vase, Palm Tree Scene, 2 Handles, Blue Leaf Mark, 5 In. 25.00
Nippon, Vase, Pastel Scene, Trees, Water, Cranes, Setting Sun, Signed, 7 In. 38.00
Nippon, Vase, Pink & White Roses, Leaves, Matte Finish, Handled, Marked, 8 In. 55.00
Nippon, Vase, Pink Florals, Glazed, Base, 13 X 4 In. 35.00
Nippon, Vase, Pink Flowers, Green Leaves, Gold, 4 Feet, 6 1/4 In. 65.00
Nippon, Vase, Pink Iridescent, Gold Trim & Beading, 8 In. 50.00
Nippon, Vase, Pink Roses, Gold, Beading, Pedestal, M In Wreath, 5 1/2 In. 46.00
Nippon, Vase, Pink Roses, Green, Gold, 2 Handles, Maple Leaf Mark, 8 In. 95.00
Nippon, Vase, Pink, Red, & White Mums On Gray, Gold Handled, 9 1/2 In. 80.00
Nippon, Vase, Poinsettias, Gold Beading, 2 Handles, Blue Maple Leaf, 12 In. 65.00
Nippon, Vase, Poppies, Gold Trim, 12 In. 125.00
Nippon, Vase, Portrait Of Lady Wearing Crown, Ring Handles, Green M, 6 In. 185.00
Nippon, Vase, Portrait, Gold & Jewels, Leaf Mark, 6 In. 135.00
Nippon, Vase, Portrait, Lady, Two Handles, Bulbous, Pedestal, Gold, Cream, 8 In. 240.00

Nippon, Vase, Profile Portrait Of Indian In Full Headdress, 3 In. 59.00
Nippon, Vase, Raised Enamel, Gold Beading, Green, Yellow, Pink Iris, 8 In. 85.00
Nippon, Vase, Ram's-Head Handles, Fruit Trees, Lake Scene, Green M, 9 In. 119.00
Nippon, Vase, Red & Pink Flowers On Light Green, Gold Handled, 6 In., Pair 95.00
Nippon, Vase, Red & White Roses, Gold Jewels, Raised Work, Footed, 10 In., Pair 160.00
Nippon, Vase, Red & Yellow Roses Center, Raised Gold Beaded Border, 15 In. 225.00
Nippon, Vase, Red, Blue Flowers, Gold, 3 Paw Feet, 8 1/2 In. 95.00
Nippon, Vase, Red, Yellow Roses, Gold Beading, Blue Maple Leaf Mark, 7 1/2 In. 45.00
Nippon, Vase, Red, Yellow, & Pink Flowers, Gold, 10 In. 110.00
Nippon, Vase, Rose & Lavender Floral, Caning, Gold 4-Corner Shape, 8 1/2 In. 75.00
Nippon, Vase, Rose, Gold, 1896-1921, M In Wreath Mark, 6 1/2 In. 38.00
Nippon, Vase, Roses & Gold Beading, 6 Sided, 9 X 7 In. 145.00
Nippon, Vase, Roses & Heavy Gold Bands, Coralene Beading, Blue Leaf, 6 In. 250.00
Nippon, Vase, Roses On Mauve, Medallion & Slip, Maple Leaf, 10 1/2 In. 195.00
Nippon, Vase, Roses, Applied Handle, Pink, Brown Satin Finish, 11 1/2 In. 230.00
Nippon, Vase, Roses, Beading, Banding, Gold, Green Wreath, 6 1/2 In. 37.50
Nippon, Vase, Roses, Beading, Gold Trim, Handled, Maple Leaf Mark, 9 In. 65.00
Nippon, Vase, Roses, Bulbous, Matte, 2 Handles, Gold, Blue Wreath Mark, 7 In. 155.00
Nippon, Vase, Roses, Gold Beading, 2 Handles, Matte, Paste, Marked, 8 In. 170.00
Nippon, Vase, Roses, Gold Beading, 6 Sided, Bulbous, 7 X 6 In. 135.00
Nippon, Vase, Roses, Gold Handles, Satin Finish, Green M Mark, 10 1/2 In., Pair 135.00
Nippon, Vase, Roses, Ivy, Gold Handles, Beaded, Satin Finish, Marked, 7 In. 125.00
Nippon, Vase, Roses, Mauve, Double Handled, Slip & Bead Work, Bulbous, 10 In. 100.00
Nippon, Vase, Roses, Medallions, Bulbous, Red, Gold, 9 In. 145.00
Nippon, Vase, Roses, Tapestry, Jewels, Bulbous, Blue Maple Leaf, 8 In. 75.00
Nippon, Vase, Roses, Violets, Gold & White, Gold Handles, 10 1/2 In. 128.00
Nippon, Vase, Round, Mums On Brown, Etched Band, M In Green Wreath, 11 In. 95.00
Nippon, Vase, Royal, Gold Trim On Handle, 8 In. 45.00
Nippon, Vase, Satin Finish, Roses, Gold Handles, Green M Mark, 10 1/2 In., Pair 135.00
Nippon, Vase, Satin Finish, Tan Background, 10 In. 65.00
Nippon, Vase, Scenic Medallion, Iris, Beading, Gold, Handles, Mark, 6 In. 150.00
Nippon, Vase, Scenic Painting, Pastels, Gold Overlay, Cloverleaf Mark, 10 In. 125.00
Nippon, Vase, Scenic Tapestry, Blue Leaf Mark, 6 In. 215.00
Nippon, Vase, Scenic Tapestry, Cylindrical, 5 1/2 In. 255.00
Nippon, Vase, Scenic, Airplane, Green Wreath Mark, 4 1/2 In. 55.00
Nippon, Vase, Scenic, Double Handle, Footed, Art Nouveau, 7 3/4 In. 135.00
Nippon, Vase, Scenic, Hand-Painted, Matte Finish, Jeweled Handles, 9 1/2 In. 125.00
Nippon, Vase, Ship Motif, Hand-Painted, 9 1/2 In. 95.00
Nippon, Vase, Snow Scene, Beading Framing Scene, 7 And Wreath Mark, 10 In. 90.00
Nippon, Vase, Squat & Double Handled, Gold, Gray Matte 40.00
Nippon, Vase, Squatty, Beading & Jeweled Colors, Flowers, Fluted, 2 Handles 65.00
Nippon, Vase, Stag & Hounds In Woods, Raised Designed Edges, 6 1/2 X 5 In. 50.00
Nippon, Vase, Swan Scene Front & Back, Gold Handles, 23 3/4 In. 450.00
Nippon, Vase, Swans On Lake Medallions, Gold Handles, Cobalt, Green Wreath 85.00
Nippon, Vase, Tan, Rust, Red, Lavender Flowers, Handled, 7 In. 45.00
Nippon, Vase, Tapestry Handled, Footed, Royal Nishike Mark, 12 1/2 In. 385.00
Nippon, Vase, Tapestry, Fruits, Signed, 8 In. 350.00
Nippon, Vase, Tapestry, Scenic, 5 1/2 In. 255.00
Nippon, Vase, Tapestry, Women & Cherubs, Pastoral Ground, 9 1/2 In. 345.00
Nippon, Vase, Tapestry, 8 In. 300.00
Nippon, Vase, Trees & Flowers, Hand-Painted, 2 Handles, 7 1/2 In. 37.00
Nippon, Vase, Trees, Evergreen, Rocks, Bulbous, 7 1/2 In. 125.00
Nippon, Vase, Trees, Mountains, Moon, Flowers, Raised Gold, Square, 10 In. 75.00
Nippon, Vase, Trees, Water, Beaded, Jewels, 2 Handles, M Wreath, 6 In. 38.00
Nippon, Vase, Urn, Vines, Florals, Gold Rim, Handles, Royal Nishiki, 12 In. 60.00
Nippon, Vase, Warrior On Horse, Brown On Tan, Orange & Gold Trim, 11 In. 185.00
Nippon, Vase, White Red & Pink Roses, Gold Handles, Base & Top, 7 In. 95.00
Nippon, Vase, Winter Scene, White & Black Beading, Green M In Wreath, 6 In. 45.00
Nippon, Vase, Woodland Scene, Blue Maple Leaf Mark, 6 X 5 In. 125.00
Nippon, Vase, Woodland Scene, Gold, Blue, Jewels, 2 Handles, 10 1/2 In. 130.00
Nippon, Vase, Yellow & Pink Roses, Gold Trim, Green M In Wreath, 13 In. 155.00
Nippon, Vase, Yellow Satin Finish, Cobalt Raised Slipwork, Signed, 8 1/2 In. 95.00
Nippon, Vase, Yellow, 24K Gold Washed, Hand Beaded, Signed 75.00
Nippon, Warmer, Egg, Pink Roses, Blue Flowers, Gold Handle, Heats 4 Eggs 70.00

Nippon, Whimsey, White With Fold, Dutch Shoe, 4 X 2 In. 45.00

*Nodders or nodding figures, or pagods, are porcelain figures with heads and
hands that are attached to wires. Any slight movement causes the parts to
move up and down. They were made in many countries during the eighteenth and
nineteenth centuries.*

Nodder, Bisque, Full-Bellied Fellow, Dressed In Top Hat, Vest, 3 In. 75.00
Nodder, Negro Boy, Bisque 30.00
Nodder, Uncle Walt, Skeezix Character, Bisque 35.00
Nodder, Woodpecker, Top Is Saltshaker, German 16.00

*Noritake-marked porcelain was made in Japan after 1904 by Nippon Toki
Kaisha.*

Noritake, Ashtray, Figurine, Girl Clown Sitting 25.00
Noritake, Ashtray, Fox Hunters 7.50
Noritake, Ashtray, Head Of Indian Chief With Full Headdress 35.00
Noritake, Ashtray, Pinecones 35.00
Noritake, Basket, Azalea Pattern 65.00
Noritake, Basket, Flowers, White Ground, Gold Trim, Miniature, M In Wreath 10.00
Noritake, Basket, Geometric, Aqua Shades 26.00
Noritake, Basket, Gold Fleur-De-Lis & Handle, Scrolls, Feather, Marked, 6 In. 32.00
Noritake, Basket, Orange Luster, Gold Handle, Butterfly & Floral, 5 In. 22.00
Noritake, Basket, Tree In Meadow .... 58.00 To 60.00
Noritake, Berry Set, Raised Gold 60.00
Noritake, Bonbon, Turquoise With Gold, Oval, Handled, 7 In. 10.00
Noritake, Bowl, Black, Green, Gold, Octagon, 7 X 2 1/2 In. 15.00
Noritake, Bowl, Boat Shape, Lovebirds, Green Wreath, 10 1/2 X 6 1/2 In. 20.00
Noritake, Bowl, Candy, Footed, House & Scenery, 2 Handles 15.00
Noritake, Bowl, Floral, Handled, Green M In Wreath, 7 1/2 In. 18.00
Noritake, Bowl, Marbleized Brown, Yellow, & Beige, Coral & Blue Swirls, 8 In. 55.00
Noritake, Bowl, Nut, Walnut, Peanut, Underplate, Green M Mark 25.00
Noritake, Bowl, Peanut, Blown-Out, Basket Weave, Brown, 4 1/2 In. 12.00
Noritake, Bowl, Pedestal, Handles, Poppies, 7 In. 12.00
Noritake, Bowl, Punch, Cobalt, Encrusted Gold Trim, Gold Claw Feet, Spoke Mark 385.00
Noritake, Bowl, Shallow, Pierced Handles, Lake Scene, Green Wreath M, 9 In. 18.00
Noritake, Bowl, Shallow, Swan On River, Earth Colors, Green Mark, 9 In. 20.00
Noritake, Bowl, Shell Shape, Fruit, Azalea 165.00
Noritake, Bowl, Vegetable, Azalea, Covered, 10 In. 40.00
Noritake, Bowl, Vegetable, Oval, Azalea, 9 1/2 In. 18.00
Noritake, Bowl, Walnut Decoration Inside, Fluted Rim, Beige, Brown, Walnut 25.00
Noritake, Bowl, Waste, Azalea 37.00
Noritake, Bowl, 3-Footed, Pheasant Center, Blue & Gold Border 18.00
Noritake, Box, Rose, Gold Filigree, Ivory Lid With Gold Roses, M Wreath Mark 30.00
Noritake, Butter Tub, Azalea, With Tabs 25.00
Noritake, Cake Plate, Azalea 14.00
Noritake, Cake Set, Flower Design, 7 Piece 35.00
Noritake, Cake Set, Fruits, Ram's Heads, Horn Handles, Marked, 7 Piece 65.00
Noritake, Candleholder, Orange & Black, Green Wreath M, 8 1/2 In., Pair 20.00
Noritake, Celery, Azalea, 12 1/2 In. 22.00
Noritake, Celery, Blues, Floral, Red M In Wreath 12.00
Noritake, Celery, No.42200 .... 10.00
Noritake, Celery, Sailboats, Gold Rim, Pierce Handles, Artist Signed, 12 In. 35.00
Noritake, Chocolate Pot, Blue, Hand-Painted Birds & Flowers On Band, Quart 20.00
Noritake, Chocolate Pot, Cream & Gold, Flower Trim Top & Bottom 50.00
Noritake, Chocolate Pot, Hand-Painted Barn & Trees, 1 1/2 Quart 20.00
Noritake, Chocolate Set, Cream & White Bands, Roses, Gold Trim, 11 Piece 85.00
Noritake, Coffeepot, Azalea 325.00
Noritake, Compote, Azalea 35.00
Noritake, Condiment Set, Azalea 22.00
Noritake, Condiment Set, Tree In Meadow 17.50
Noritake, Cruet, Azalea .... 125.00 To 135.00
Noritake, Cup & Saucer, Azalea .... 7.50 To 15.00
Noritake, Cup & Saucer, Demitasse, Azalea 60.00
Noritake, Cup & Saucer, Demitasse, Pink, Blue Garland Flowers 8.50
Noritake, Cup & Saucer, Tree In Meadow 7.50
Noritake, Cup & Saucer, White, Gold Cornucopia Decoration 17.00
Noritake, Cup, Child's, Ding Dong Pussy In Well 13.00

Noritake, Cup, Custard, Scenic, Covered	16.50
Noritake, Dinner Set, Child's, 24 Piece	120.00
Noritake, Dinner Set, Sedan Pattern, 47 Piece	125.00
Noritake, Dish, Azalea, Cutout Handles, 10 In.	20.00
Noritake, Dish, Azalea, 8 Sided, Divided, 8 1/4 In.	25.00
Noritake, Dish, Basket, Blue Birds, Flowers, Handle Across Middle	35.00
Noritake, Dish, Bluebirds, Gold Flowers, Covered, 5 In.	12.00
Noritake, Dish, Butter, Covered, Roses With Gold Trim	25.00
Noritake, Dish, Candy, Covered, Azalea	175.00
Noritake, Dish, Cheese, Covered, Azalea	45.00
Noritake, Dish, Houses And Trees, Green Wreath, 6 In.	25.00
Noritake, Dish, Lemon, Azalea	12.00
Noritake, Dish, Openwork Handles, Marked M, 5 1/2 In.	3.00
Noritake, Dish, Pickle, Small House Scene, Green Wreath M, 6 In.	7.00
Noritake, Dish, 3 Floral Medallions, Gold, Beige, 5 In.	3.00
Noritake, Dish, 4 Divisions, Azalea, 10 In.	55.00
Noritake, Eggcup, Azalea, 3 1/8 In.	25.00
Noritake, Gravy Boat, Azalea	22.50 To 27.00
Noritake, Hatpin Holder, Camel Scene, Cobalt, Raised Gold, Gold Pierced Top	35.00
Noritake, Humidor, Blown-Out Owl, Orange, Black, White	250.00
Noritake, Humidor, Elk By River, Beaded Rim	65.00
Noritake, Humidor, Orange Luster, Owl, 7 X 5 1/2 In.	40.00
Noritake, Humidor, Painted House & Trees Scene, Square Opening, 6 1/4 In.	55.00
Noritake, Humidor, Scene With Trees, 5 1/2 In.	35.00
Noritake, Jam Set, Basket Handled, Red Wreath Mark, 3 Piece	9.00
Noritake, Jar, Jam, Azalea	58.00
Noritake, Luncheon Set, Azalea, 26 Piece	125.00
Noritake, Marmalade Set, No.42200, 3 Piece	18.00
Noritake, Match Holder, Scenic, Attached Ashtray	12.00
Noritake, Mayonnaise Set, Azalea, Two Parts	14.00
Noritake, Mayonnaise Set, Blue, Floral, Gold Trim, 4 Piece	14.00
Noritake, Mayonnaise With Ladle, Blue Band Top, Pearlized Center, Floral	20.00
Noritake, Mayonnaise, Azalea, Green Wreath Mark	15.00
Noritake, Mayonnaise, Blue & Gold, 2 Piece	14.50
Noritake, Mustard With Ladle, Cottage Scene, Covered	16.50
Noritake, Napkin Ring, Art Deco	16.00
Noritake, Napkin Ring, Scene Of Woman In Red Cloak, High Luster Finish	18.00
Noritake, Nappy, Azalea	10.00
Noritake, Nut Set, Hand-Painted, Chestnut Shaped Bowl, 5 Cups, C.1920	65.00
Noritake, Peach, Multicolor Scene, Silver Overlay Handles, 6 1/2 In.	18.00
Noritake, Pitcher, Sunbonnet Babies, White, Green, Blue Wreath Mark, 3 1/4 In.	30.00
Noritake, Pitcher, 8 Sided, Art Deco, Red Maple Leaf Mark, 6 In.	12.00
Noritake, Plaque, Desert Scene, Artist Signed, 10 In.	38.50
Noritake, Plate, Azalea, 7 1/2 In.	4.50 To 8.50
Noritake, Plate, Cake, Azalea	17.50
Noritake, Plate, Cake, Tree In Meadow	15.00
Noritake, Plate, Dinner, Azalea, 9 3/4 In.	12.00
Noritake, Plate, Dinner, Encrusted Gold Trim, M Mark, Set Of 5	45.00
Noritake, Plate, Parrot On Branch, Black Border With Gold Trim, 9 In. Square	30.00
Noritake, Plate, Tree In Meadow, 6 1/4 In.	3.50
Noritake, Plate, White With Gold Roses, M In Wreath, 6 1/2 In.	5.50
Noritake, Plate, 2 Peanuts, 7 1/2 In.	14.00
Noritake, Platter, Azalea, 14 In.	28.00 To 30.00
Noritake, Platter, Azalea, 16 In.	180.00 To 185.00
Noritake, Platter, Fleur, Gold Pattern, Oval, 13 1/4 In.	16.00
Noritake, Platter, Turkey, Azalea, 16 X 12 In.	285.00
Noritake, Pot, Jam, Tree In Meadow, Cover & Ladle	50.00
Noritake, Relish, Azalea Pattern, 4 Section, Handled, 9 In.	45.00
Noritake, Relish, Oval, Azalea	9.00
Noritake, Relish, Two Section, Azalea	20.00
Noritake, Salt & Pepper, Azalea, Bell Bottom, 3 1/2 In.	10.00
Noritake, Salt, Single With Top, Cottage On Lake	10.00
Noritake, Sauce, Azalea	9.00
Noritake, Saucer Set, Glenwood, Set Of 5	11.00
Noritake, Spooner, Azalea	40.00

Noritake, Spooner, Hand-Painted Fruit, Light Green, Gold Handles 30.00
Noritake, Strainer, Tea, Floral On Ivory, Gold Trim, Green, Black, Underplate 23.50
Noritake, Strawberry Set, Azalea 75.00
Noritake, Sugar & Creamer, Azalea, No.123, 2 1/2 In.High .... 55.00 To 65.00
Noritake, Sugar & Creamer, Azalea, Ruffled Edge 150.00
Noritake, Sugar & Creamer, Azalea, 3 5/8 In. .... 15.00 To 25.00
Noritake, Sugar & Creamer, Cream & Turquoise, Floral, Red Wreath Mark, 7 In. 30.00
Noritake, Sugar & Creamer, Green Wreath 25.00
Noritake, Sugar & Creamer, Ivory, Black, Gold Panels With Roses, Marked 22.00
Noritake, Sugar & Creamer, Lake, Trees, Boat, Lid, Green Wreath Mark 22.50
Noritake, Sugar & Creamer, Lanare 10.00
Noritake, Sugar & Creamer, Rhoda, No. 7542 .... 15.00
Noritake, Sugar & Creamer, Tree In Meadow 22.50
Noritake, Sugar Shaker & Syrup Pitcher, Azalea 58.00
Noritake, Sugar Shaker, Azalea, No.122 .... 40.00
Noritake, Sugar, Flamingo, Covered 8.00
Noritake, Sugar, Open, Azalea 30.00
Noritake, Syrup & Underplate, Azalea, Covered 38.00
Noritake, Syrup & Underplate, Yellow, Flowers, Gold Trim, M In Wreath 21.50
Noritake, Tea Set, Coral Luster, Gold Beading, Orange & Blue Zinnias, 5 Piece 47.50
Noritake, Tea Set, Decorate Gold On Black, 11 Piece 150.00
Noritake, Tea Set, Demitasse, Light Blue, Floral Band, Marked, 3 Piece 30.00
Noritake, Tea Set, Lucerne, No. 6880, 17 Piece 60.00
Noritake, Tea Set, Luster Band & Flowers, 8 Piece 13.00
Noritake, Teapot, Azalea 40.00
Noritake, Teapot, Scenic, Raised Enameling, Green Mark 15.00
Noritake, Teapot, Tree In Meadow 40.00
Noritake, Tile, Azalea, 6 In. .... 20.00 To 25.00
Noritake, Tile, Tree In Meadow 30.00
Noritake, Toothpick, Azalea .... 55.00 To 80.00
Noritake, Tray, Blue, Yellow, Dragon, Oval, Flared Edge, 12 X 6 In. 22.00
Noritake, Tray, Pin, Dog 6.00
Noritake, Vase, Cottage, Woodlands, Swans, Lake, Double Handle, 13 In. 75.00
Noritake, Vase, Fan Shape, Footed, Azalea .... 50.00 To 65.00
Noritake, Vase, Four Painted Scenes, Black & Gold Trim, Handled, 9 3/8 In. 60.00
Noritake, Vase, Lake Scene, Applied Block Threading, 5 In. 35.00
Noritake, Vase, Lake Scene, Handled, 5 1/2 In. 35.00
Noritake, Vase, Peach, Multicolor Scene, 2 Silver Overlay Handles, 6 1/2 In. 18.00
Noritake, Vase, Scenic, Marked, 9 In. 110.00
Noritake, Vase, Scenic, Wraps Around Front To Back, Twin Handled, 5 In., Pair 39.00
Noritake, Vase, Wall, Azalea, Hand-Painted, 7 In. 25.00
Noritake, Vase, Wreath, Green, Blue, Hand-Painted, Outdoor Scene, 10 1/2 In. 40.00

*The North Dakota School of Mines was established in 1892 at the
University of North Dakota.*
North Dakota School Of Mines, Bowl, Mauve, Mattson, 2 1/4 X 20 In. 26.50
North Dakota School Of Mines, Vase, Brown, Semiglossy, FLH 32.00

*Northwood Glass Company worked in Martins Ferry, Ohio, in the 1880s.
They marked some pieces with the letter N in a circle. Many pieces of
carnival glass were made by this company.*

Northwood, see also Carnival Glass; Custard Glass; Goofus Glass;
Pressed Glass
Northwood, Berry Bowl, Netted Oak, Goofus Gold, Signed 35.00
Northwood, Berry Set, Argonaut Shell, Gold Decoration, 7 Piece 495.00
Northwood, Berry Set, Cherry & Lattice, Gold And Red, 7 Piece 95.00
Northwood, Berry Set, Cherry Cluster, 5 Piece 75.00
Northwood, Berry Set, Intaglio Green Decoration, 7 Piece 395.00
Northwood, Berry Set, Jeweled Heart, White Opalescent, 11 Piece 98.00
Northwood, Berry Set, Louis XV, 7 Piece 355.00
Northwood, Berry Set, Sunburst On Hobstar, 7 Piece 100.00
Northwood, Berry Set, 5 Pieces, Teardrop Flower, Blue 160.00
Northwood, Bowl, Berry, Cherry & Cable, Signed, 8 1/2 In. 25.00
Northwood, Bowl, Berry, Cherry, Clear With Gold 9.00
Northwood, Bowl, Berry, Daisy & Fern, Cranberry, Small, Set Of 6 .... 120.00

Chalk and charcoal landscape on sandpaper. Taken from an engraving, c. 1840.

Mug and pitcher, English creamware, multicolored transfer decoration. "The Farmer's Arms," early nineteenth century.

Yarn sewn rug, 23″ by 49½″, extremely rare early homemade rug with interesting pattern, c. 1810–1840.

Floral bouquet. Reverse painting on glass backed with tinfoil, c. 1840.

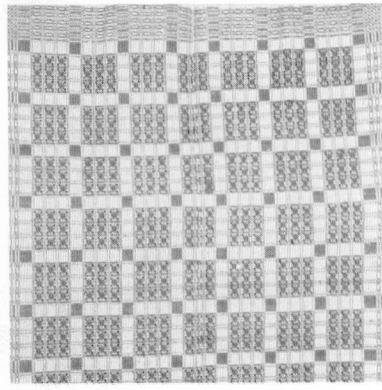

Handwoven wool and linen coverlet in white, indigo, and red, c. 1800.

Appliqué, quilted coverlet in the Whig Rose pattern, N.H., c. 1840.

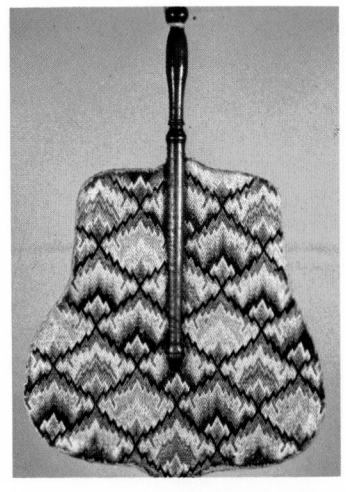

Bedspread, stenciled pattern on cotton muslin. Colors: green, yellow, red, and black. Mass., c. 1825.

Hand-held fire screen. Multicolored flame stitch needlework. Boston, Mass., area, late eighteenth century.

Handkerchief, copperplate print on cotton. Bible story of *Joseph and His Brethren,* c. 1830.

Handkerchiefs, copperplate print on cotton, red on white. Scenes taken from a child's book, c. 1830.

Carved wooden Cat's Head. Work of John H. Bellemy, Portsmouth, N.H., c. 1859.

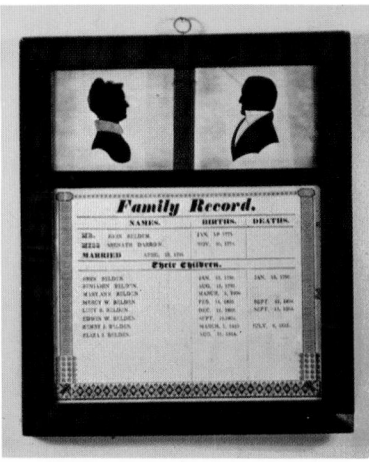

Theorem painting, watercolor on velvet. Towne family. Charlton, Mass., c. 1830.

Family record and silhouettes of the parents, c. 1815–1820.

English Mocha-ware washbowl and water pitcher. Bands of brown, tan, blue, and black on white, c. 1810–1840.

English creamware bowl, King's Rose freehand pattern. England, c. 1780.

English Staffordshire washbowl and pitcher. Dark blue transfer-printed floral decoration. Adams. England, c. 1810–1825.

English Staffordshire washbowl. Dark blue transfer print. "Lafayette at Franklin's Tomb." England, 1825–1830.

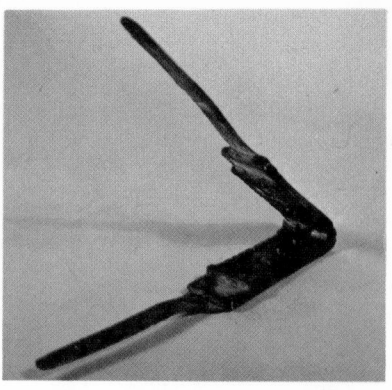

Brass bullet mold, iron handles. Late eighteenth-century.

Man's pocketbook, multicolored flame-stitch needlework. Mass., late eighteenth century.

Fan, ivory and paper. Printed French pastoral scene with hand-painted decoration. French, c. 1800.

Large tin gunpowder canister. Yellow on green, c. 1840.

Footed open salt and muffineer. English creamware, cobalt blue decoration, c. 1820.

Pillar and scroll mantel clock. Seth Thomas. Plymouth, Conn., c. 1816.

Pressed paper spectacle case with early spectacles, c. 1820. Metal spectacle case, c. 1850–1860.

Shell-shaped sweetmeat dish. Mason's Patent. Ironstone. England, c. 1820.

Large platter. Chinese Export Nanking ware, c. 1820–1840.

English pearl-ware punch pot. Blue Oriental transfer pattern, c. 1820.

English miniature creamware jelly mold, c. 1820.

English Pratt-ware pitcher. Molded decoration, hand painted, c. 1790–1810.

Large English Staffordshire mug, hand-painted transfer-printed decoration. *The real Cabinet of Friendship,* c. 1830.

English Delft fireplace tile. Manganese on white, c. 1760.

Green-glazed redware pottery inkwell and steinpot. The steinpot is
marked John Safford. Monmouth,
Me., c. 1845.

Cast-iron fireplace cooking kettle. Maker
Ellis Griffeth. Eighteen century.

Wooden-handled cork-
screw. English, late eighteenth century.

Cast-iron schoolhouse stove. Tun-
bridge, Vt., c. 1825.

Sheraton-style doll's bed, early
nineteenth century.

Northwood, Bowl, Berry, Geneva, Green, Small, Round	22.00
Northwood, Bowl, Berry, Grape & Gothic Arches, Green And Gold	20.00
Northwood, Bowl, Berry, Intaglio, Emerald Green, Gold	30.00
Northwood, Bowl, Berry, Inverted Fan & Feather, Green With Gold, Small	25.00
Northwood, Bowl, Berry, Paneled Cherry, Glass Signed, Set Of Four	32.00
Northwood, Bowl, Blue Opalescent, Ribbed Sprial, Fluted, 12 In.	26.00
Northwood, Bowl, Hat Shape, Blackberry, Clear, Opalescent, 6 In.	22.50
Northwood, Bowl, Jeweled Heart, Fluted, Blue, 10 In.	65.00
Northwood, Bowl, Master Berry, Geneva, Green, Oval	45.00
Northwood, Bowl, Netted Roses, Emerald Green, 9 In.	30.00
Northwood, Bowl, Paneled Cherry, 8 1/2 In.	35.00
Northwood, Bowl, Punch, Memphis, Clear, Signed	30.00
Northwood, Bowl, Red Cherries, Gold Trim, Signed, 4 1/2 In., Set Of 4	24.00
Northwood, Bowl, Ruffled, Lacy, Blue Opalescent, 9 In.	50.00
Northwood, Bowl, Star Of David & Flowers, Dark Amethyst, 6 1/4 In.	25.00
Northwood, Butter, Cherry Cable, Covered, Signed	55.00
Northwood, Butter, Covered, Green Feather	135.00
Northwood, Butter, Covered, Paneled Cherry	45.00
Northwood, Butter, Geneva, Green With Gold, Covered	95.00
Northwood, Butter, Jeweled Heart, Gold, Cover	60.00
Northwood, Candlestick, Grape & Cable, Aqua, Pair	30.00
Northwood, Castor, Pickle, Cranberry Insert, Gold, Enamel, Ornate, Footed	235.00
Northwood, Compote, Candy, Spool Of Threads, Crimped Rim, Opalescent, Clear	35.00
Northwood, Compote, Jelly, Apple Green & Gold Shell Pattern	37.00
Northwood, Compote, Jelly, Green	47.00
Northwood, Compote, Jelly, Leaf Medallion, Green	65.00
Northwood, Compote, Singing Bird, Covered, 7 X 25 In.	65.00
Northwood, Compote, Strawberry, Covered, Marked	35.00
Northwood, Creamer, American Beauty, Green With Gold	45.00
Northwood, Creamer, Breakfast, Grape & Cable	75.00
Northwood, Creamer, Cherry Lattice	20.00
Northwood, Creamer, Cherry Thumbprint, Gold Trim	45.00
Northwood, Creamer, Grape & Gothic Arches, Green And Gold	45.00
Northwood, Creamer, Green, Posy & Pod, Gold	73.00
Northwood, Creamer, Inverted Fan & Feather, Green & Gold	65.00
Northwood, Creamer, Iris, Clear Opalescent	59.00
Northwood, Creamer, Jeweled Heart, Clear With Gold	28.00
Northwood, Creamer, Leaf Medallion, Green And Gold	75.00
Northwood, Creamer, Scroll With Acanthus, Green And Gold, Enameled	45.00
Northwood, Cruet, Daisy & Fern, Clear To Opalescent	65.00
Northwood, Cruet, Fluted Scroll, Opalescent Vaseline With Flowers, Stopper	135.00
Northwood, Cup, Punch, Grape Vivid	20.00
Northwood, Decanter, Wine, Memphis, Stopper, 10 3/4 In.	175.00
Northwood, Dish, Bonbon, Water Lily & Cattail, White Opalescent, 7 X 3 In.	40.00
Northwood, Dish, Ice Cream, Grape & Cable, Footed	25.00
Northwood, Dish, Opalescent, White, Blue Leaf Design, Scalloped Rim, Signed	65.00
Northwood, Jar, Mustard, Wild Rose And Bowknot, Frosted, Pewter Lid And Spoon	45.00
Northwood, Jar, Powder, Fluted Scrolls, Emerald Green, Covered	45.00
Northwood, Jar, Sweetmeat, Rainbow Royal Ivy, White Casing, Silver Lid, 4 In.	110.00
Northwood, Jelly, Argonaut Shell	125.00
Northwood, Jelly, Feather, Amber Stained	55.00
Northwood, Jelly, Intaglio Green Decoration	130.00
Northwood, Pitcher, Argonaut Shell, Blue, Full Signature	350.00
Northwood, Pitcher, Pink, Yellow, White Casing, Clear Applied Handle, Small	75.00
Northwood, Pitcher, Water, Fan, Gold	225.00
Northwood, Pitcher, Water, Grape & Cable	100.00
Northwood, Pitcher, Water, Louis XV, Green & Gold	95.00
Northwood, Plate, Blue, Grape Stippled	165.00
Northwood, Salt & Pepper, Apple Blossom, Blue Band	25.00
Northwood, Salt & Pepper, Sawtooth Honeycomb, Amber	19.00
Northwood, Sauce, Emerald, Peach, Gold, Scalloped Rim, 4 1/2 In.	20.00
Northwood, Sauce, Fan, Cobalt Blue, Gold Trim	27.00
Northwood, Sauce, Louis XV, 5 In.	50.00
Northwood, Saucer, Grape & Cable, 7 In.	45.00
Northwood, Spooner, American Beauty, Green With Gold	28.00

Northwood, Spooner, Jeweled Heart, Clear With Gold	24.00
Northwood, Spooner, Leaf Medallion, Green And Gold	60.00
Northwood, Spooner, Opalescent, Drapery, Signed	50.00
Northwood, Spooner, Wild Bouquet, Opalescent	28.00
Northwood, Sugar, Covered, Emerald Green, Regal	28.00
Northwood, Sugar, Emerald Green, Opalescent Finial, Regal, Covered	60.00
Northwood, Sugar, Leaf Medallion, Amethyst, Open	45.00
Northwood, Sugar, Nestor Enamel & Gold Amethyst, Covered	75.00
Northwood, Sugar, Open, Cherry Lattice	20.00
Northwood, Sugar, Shaker, Rainbow	165.00
Northwood, Sugar, Wyeth, Covered, Large	35.00
Northwood, Syrup, Amber, Frosted Leaf, Flower	175.00
Northwood, Syrup, Blue Wildflower	142.00
Northwood, Table Set, Argonaut Shell, 4 Piece	340.00 To 595.00
Northwood, Table Set, Grape And Gothic Arch, Green With Gold, 4 Piece	240.00
Northwood, Table Set, Intaglio Green Decoration	495.00
Northwood, Table Set, Louis XV, Butter, Creamer, Spooner, 3 Piece	375.00
Northwood, Table Set, Peach, Green, Gold, 4 Piece	325.00
Northwood, Table Set, Swag With Brackets, Clear Opalescent, 4 Piece	240.00
Northwood, Town Pump & Trough Set, Blue Opalescent, Signed In Script	225.00
Northwood, Town Pump, Blue, Opalescent, Signed	95.00
Northwood, Tray, Condiment, Chrysanthemum Sprig, Green, Signed	85.00
Northwood, Tumbler, American Beauty, Green With Gold	18.00
Northwood, Tumbler, Belladonna, Enameled Flowers	10.00
Northwood, Tumbler, Cherry Thumbprint, Gold Trim	35.00
Northwood, Tumbler, Cobalt, Enameled Cherries, Iridescent	21.00
Northwood, Tumbler, Drapery, Clear Opalescent	32.50
Northwood, Tumbler, Drapery, Opalescent, Signed	38.00
Northwood, Tumbler, Emerald Green, Louis XV	18.00
Northwood, Tumbler, Enameled Flowers	95.00
Northwood, Tumbler, Grape & Thumbprint, Amethyst, Set Of 6	200.00
Northwood, Tumbler, Green, Peach, Gold	24.00
Northwood, Tumbler, Inverted Fan & Feather, Green With Gold	28.00
Northwood, Tumbler, Leaf Medallion, Amethyst	35.00
Northwood, Tumbler, Leaf Medallion, Green And Gold	30.00
Northwood, Tumbler, Leaf Umbrella, Light Green, Cased Satin	40.00
Northwood, Tumbler, Memphis, Green With Gold	15.00
Northwood, Tumbler, Oriental Poppy, Blue, Gold Flashed	22.00
Northwood, Tumbler, Painted Flowers, Green, Set Of 2	7.50
Northwood, Vase, Diamond Point, Purple, 10 In., Pair	60.00
Northwood, Vase, Feathers, Blue Opalescent, Signed, 10 In.	30.00
Northwood, Vase, Thin Rib, Emerald Green, 9 In.	48.00
Northwood, Vase, Tree Bark, Blue Opalescent, 12 In.	35.00 To 38.00
Northwood, Vase, White Opalescent, 10 In.	40.00
Northwood, Water Set, Cherry Lattice Pattern, Gold, Signed, 7 Piece	265.00
Northwood, Water Set, Cherry, Painted Cherries Trimmed In Gold, 7 Piece	179.00
Northwood, Water Set, Gold Rose, Pitcher, 6 Tumblers, Green, Gold, Signed N	325.00
Northwood, Water Set, Louis XV, Gold, 4 Piece	295.00
Northwood, Water Set, Memphis, Clear With Gold, 3 Piece	80.00
Northwood, Water Set, Memphis, Green, Gold, Signed N, Set Of 7	220.00
Northwood, Water Set, Wild Rose And Bowknot, Frosted, 7 Piece	135.00
Nuart, Shade, Amber, Iridescent, Set Of 4	65.00
Nuart, Shade, Carnival, Marigold, 4 1/2 In.	18.00
Nuart, Shade, Clambroth, Iridescent, Set Of 6	180.00
Nuart, Shade, Iridescent, Salmon Translucent Glass, Ribbed, Signed, 5 1/2 In.	60.00
Nuart, Shade, Marigold, Signed	25.00
Nuart, Shade, Pale, Translucent, Ribbed, Signed, 5 1/2 X 4 1/2 In.	50.00
Nuart, Shade, Ribbed, Iridescent, Signed On Fitter Rim, 5 5/8 In.	60.00
Nuart, Vase, Pontil, Iridescent, Signed, 7 1/2 In.	90.00

Nymphenburg, a German porcelain factory, was established at Neudeck-ob-der-Au in 1753 and moved to Nymphenburg in 1761. The company is still in existence. Modern marks include a shield superseded by a star or crown, and a crowned CT with a checkered shield.

Nymphenburg, Figurine, Booted Peruked Dandy Blows Horn, Green, Black, 1887	195.00

Nymphenburg, Group, Impetuous Lover, C.1756, 5 1/2 In.

Nymphenburg, Figurine, Stallion, Getting Up From Sitting, Impressed Mark	225.00
Nymphenburg, Figurine, Whippet, Crouching Position, 3 1/2 X 4 In.	85.00
Nymphenburg, Group, Impetuous Lover, C.1756, 5 1/2 In. .... *Illus*	7000.00

*Occupied Japan is the mark used on pieces of pottery and porcelain made
during the American occupation of Japan after World War II.
Collectors are now buying these pieces. The items were made for export to
the United States.*

Occupied Japan, Ashtray Set, Elephants, 5 Piece	12.00
Occupied Japan, Bank, Glass Pig	3.50
Occupied Japan, Basket, Coaster, Different Scenes, Artist Signed, 6 Coasters	35.00
Occupied Japan, Bell, Shape Of Chubby Chef, 3 1/4 In.	10.00
Occupied Japan, Binoculars, Prism, Pocket Size, Case, 6 X 15 In.	25.00
Occupied Japan, Bowl, 2 Cherubs On Edge, Pastel Colors, Heart Shaped	75.00
Occupied Japan, Box, Cherubs On Top, Metal, Wood Lining	25.00
Occupied Japan, Burner, Incense, Seated Oriental, 4 1/4 In.	10.00
Occupied Japan, Bust, Lady, Hat With Flower	5.00
Occupied Japan, Clock, Brown Bear, Pendulum, Weight Driven	60.00
Occupied Japan, Cocktail Set, Doll, Tin, Miniature	12.00
Occupied Japan, Coffee Set, Hand-Colored Flowers In Gold Panel, White Ground	20.00
Occupied Japan, Condiment Set, Hand-Painted, English Cottage Shapes, 6 Piece	15.00
Occupied Japan, Cookie Jar, Tomato, Wicker Handle, 6 X 7 In.	30.00
Occupied Japan, Cup & Saucer, Blue Luster Trim, Birds, Flowers, Red Lettering	5.50
Occupied Japan, Cup & Saucer, Child's, Hand-Painted Flowers	4.50
Occupied Japan, Cup & Saucer, Child's, Oriental Design	3.00
Occupied Japan, Cup & Saucer, Demitasse, Medallion With People, Gold Trim	12.00
Occupied Japan, Cup & Saucer, Demitasse, Set Of Four	14.00
Occupied Japan, Cup & Saucer, Dragon Design	4.00
Occupied Japan, Cup & Saucer, Evangeline Country, La.	10.00
Occupied Japan, Cup & Saucer, Pink, Flowers & Leaves, Translucent	5.00
Occupied Japan, Dessert Set, Floral, Blue Band, Gold Trim, MB, 25 Piece	66.00
Occupied Japan, Dessert Set, Floral, Gold Trim, MB In Wreath, Set Of 6	27.00
Occupied Japan, Dinner Set, Montana Rose, Service For 11, 97 Piece	282.00
Occupied Japan, Dish, Bisque Cherubs Supporting Boat, Lamore, 4 3/4 In., Pair	40.00
Occupied Japan, Dish, Girl With Flowered Skirt	10.00
Occupied Japan, Figurine, Andrea, Bisque, Pastoral, 4 7/8 In. .... 23.00 To	24.00
Occupied Japan, Figurine, Arabic, Bisque, Marked	7.00
Occupied Japan, Figurine, Bisque, Colonial Girl, Moriyama, 7 1/2 In.	12.00
Occupied Japan, Figurine, Bisque, Fancy Dressed Man, 10 1/4 In.	25.00
Occupied Japan, Figurine, Bisque, Pastoral, Hal-Sey, Pair, 11 1/2 In.	53.00
Occupied Japan, Figurine, Boy With Parrot, 4 In.	4.00
Occupied Japan, Figurine, Bride & Groom, 5 In.	10.50
Occupied Japan, Figurine, China, Girl In Fancy Costume With Violin, 10 In.	45.00
Occupied Japan, Figurine, Clown Riding Pig	13.00
Occupied Japan, Figurine, Colonial Couple Playing Flute & Mandolin, Pair	21.00
Occupied Japan, Figurine, Colonial Man & Woman, Cobalt Trim, 5 1/4 In., Pair	55.00
Occupied Japan, Figurine, Colonial Man & Woman, 8 1/2 In.	15.00
Occupied Japan, Figurine, Colonial Man, 10 In.	20.00
Occupied Japan, Figurine, Cowboy, 5 In.	6.00
Occupied Japan, Figurine, Dwarf Pulling Cart, 7 1/4 In.	25.00
Occupied Japan, Figurine, Elf With Drum, 5 3/4 In.	26.50

Occupied Japan, Figurine, Girl In Fancy Costume With Violin, 10 In.	45.00
Occupied Japan, Figurine, Girl In Oversized Shoes, 5 1/4 In.	8.00
Occupied Japan, Figurine, Girl With Apple, 2 Geese	30.00
Occupied Japan, Figurine, Girl With Parasol, Pastel Colors, Kate Greenaway	22.00
Occupied Japan, Figurine, Lady Bee With Umbrella	10.00
Occupied Japan, Figurine, Lady Sitting, Man Standing, 4 In.	15.00
Occupied Japan, Figurine, Little Girl & Cat, Marked	5.00
Occupied Japan, Figurine, Open Lady's Hand, Gold Band, Marked, 4 X 1 In.	2.00
Occupied Japan, Figurine, Oriental Boy, On Stomach, Feet Up	3.00
Occupied Japan, Figurine, Oriental Lady, 8 3/4 In.	15.00
Occupied Japan, Figurine, Oriental Man, 4 In.	3.00
Occupied Japan, Figurine, Pastoral, Bisque, Hal-Sey, 11 1/2 In., Pair	50.00
Occupied Japan, Figurine, Pastoral, Bisque, 4 1/2 In., Pair	55.00
Occupied Japan, Figurine, Piano Player, Two Piece	12.50
Occupied Japan, Figurine, Pink Angel On Blue & White Base, 3 In.	15.50
Occupied Japan, Figurine, Santa, 5 In.	10.00
Occupied Japan, Figurine, Seated Couple, 6 1/2 In.	18.00
Occupied Japan, Figurine, Shepherd Dog, 5 X 4 In.	8.00
Occupied Japan, Figurine, Ten Children Over 2 1/2 In. Lot, 7 In., Pair	14.00
Occupied Japan, Figurine, Wolf, Gray & White, 2 In.	3.00
Occupied Japan, Group, Colonial Couple, 3 1/2 In.	6.00
Occupied Japan, Inkwell, Cover Is Woman Holding Frame, Child's Head, 6 In.	48.00
Occupied Japan, Lamp, Boy & Girl, Bisque, 11 1/2 In., Pair	75.00
Occupied Japan, Lamp, Colonial Couple, Blue & White, Gold Trim, 11 In.	20.00
Occupied Japan, Lamp, Floral, Green, 11 1/2 In.	15.00
Occupied Japan, Lighter, Camel, Gilded Metal, 2 X 3 In.	10.00
Occupied Japan, Lighter, Cigarette, Table, Silver Plated	12.50
Occupied Japan, Lighter, Figural, Piano	8.00
Occupied Japan, Match Holder, Colonial Man & Woman Holding Baskets, Bisque	28.00
Occupied Japan, Mug, Barrel, Figural Handle	12.00
Occupied Japan, Mug, Cowgirl Handle, 5 In.	15.00
Occupied Japan, Mug, Douglas MacArthur	15.00
Occupied Japan, Pitcher, Hand-Painted, Tulips, 3 In.	4.00
Occupied Japan, Pitcher, Shape Of Woman With Hands In Apron, 6 1/2 In.	9.00
Occupied Japan, Planter, Donkey, 6 In.	15.00
Occupied Japan, Planter, Elephant With Howdah, Trunk Raised, 7 X 5 In.	12.00
Occupied Japan, Planter, Ribbed Bottom, Hand-Painted Flowers, 8 X 3 3/4 In.	8.00
Occupied Japan, Plaque, Chinese Man & Woman, Signed Yamska, Pair	10.00
Occupied Japan, Plate, Dalmatians, German Shepherds, Brown, 3 In.	5.00
Occupied Japan, Plate, Hand-Painted, Signed, 11 In.	30.00
Occupied Japan, Salt & Pepper, Hen & Rooster Nodders	12.50
Occupied Japan, Salt & Pepper, Indian Busts, 2 1/2 In.	6.50
Occupied Japan, Salt & Pepper, Peasant Boy & Girl	4.50
Occupied Japan, Saltshaker, Figural, Schoolgirl, 4 1/2 In.	7.50
Occupied Japan, Sewing Machine, Portable	25.00
Occupied Japan, Shoe, Metal Pincushion, 3 In.	8.50
Occupied Japan, Stein, German Design, 8 1/2 In.	50.00
Occupied Japan, Swan, Bisque, Open Back	10.00
Occupied Japan, Tea Set, Child's, Red, Yellow, Tan Birds, 17 Piece	27.00
Occupied Japan, Tea Set, Miniature, Floral, 11 Piece	17.50
Occupied Japan, Teapot, Applied Flowers & Insects, 3 In. Handle, 2 In. High	30.00
Occupied Japan, Teapot, Brown	15.00
Occupied Japan, Teapot, Dark Brown Glaze, Flowers & Beading, 5 1/4 In.	20.00
Occupied Japan, Teapot, Hand-Painted, Bouquets Of Violets, 5 In.	15.00
Occupied Japan, Toby Mug, Bird Shape, 2 3/4 In.	12.00
Occupied Japan, Toby Mug, Ole King Cole, Face Only, 4 In.	10.00
Occupied Japan, Toby Mug, Winking Bearded Man, Full Body King	10.00
Occupied Japan, Toby Mug, Winking Sailor, Squirrel Handle, 5 In.	12.00
Occupied Japan, Vase, Lacquer Over Metal, Gold Bamboo On Red, 6 In.	10.00
Occupied Japan, Vase, Oriental Man On Front, 3 1/2 In.	4.00
Occupied Japan, Vase, Oriental Woman, 3 In.	3.00
Occupied Japan, Vase, Wedgwood Type, 4 In.	6.50

G. E. OHR, BILOXI.   *Ohr pottery was made by George E. Ohr in Biloxi, Mississippi, between 1883 and 1918. The pieces were made of very thin clay and were twisted, folded and dented into odd, graceful shapes.*

Ohr, Chamber Pot, Yellow With Brown & Green Sponging, 2 In.	95.00
Ohr, Inkwell, Pottery Donkey Head, Green, High Glaze, 3 X 4 1/2 In.	200.00
Ohr, Mug, Puzzle, Bennington Type Glaze, Sunburst Handle	75.00
Ohr, Mug, Red Handle, Incised Toasting Inscription Center, 3-18-96, 3 1/4 In.	145.00
Ohr, Pitcher, Browns & Golds, Slight Blue Iridescence, 1906, 3 3/4 In.	195.00
Ohr, Pitcher, Tan Stoneware, 4 1/2 X 5 1/2 In.	85.00
Ohr, Vase, Crimped, Twisted, Light Brown High Glaze, Signed, 4 1/2 In.	125.00
Ohr, Vase, Light Green Underglaze, Hugh Luster Metallic Over, 8 1/2 In.	185.00

Old ivory china was made in Silesia, Germany, at the end of the nineteenth century. It is often marked with a crown and the word Silesia. The pattern numbers appear on the base of each piece.

Old Ivory, Berry Set, Crown Mark, 7 Piece	60.00
Old Ivory, Berry Set, Open Handled, 4 Small Bowls	95.00
Old Ivory, Bowl, Elysee, Pierced Handles, 9 1/2 In.	70.00
Old Ivory, Bowl, No.200, Oblong, 6 1/2 X 4 In.	40.00
Old Ivory, Cake Plate, Crown Mark, No.15	28.00
Old Ivory, Cake Plate, No.16, 10 In.	55.00
Old Ivory, Cake Plate, No.32	50.00
Old Ivory, Cake Plate, No.73	55.00
Old Ivory, Cake Plate, 10 Matching Plates, Crown Mark, No.75	120.00
Old Ivory, Cake Set, No.84, Set Of 7	115.00
Old Ivory, Cake Set, Open Handle Cakeplate, 5 Plates, 6 1/4 In.	110.00
Old Ivory, Celery	41.00
Old Ivory, Chocolate Pot, No.XIV	185.00
Old Ivory, Chocolate Pot, Pink Flowers, Gold, Crown Mark, Germany, 8 1/2 In.	68.00
Old Ivory, Creamer, No.16	35.00
Old Ivory, Creamer, No.84	40.00
Old Ivory, Cup & Saucer	33.50
Old Ivory, Cup & Saucer, Crown Mark, No.15	25.00
Old Ivory, Cup & Saucer, Demitasse, No.200	30.00
Old Ivory, Cup & Saucer, No.16	24.00
Old Ivory, Cup & Saucer, No.75	29.00
Old Ivory, Cup & Saucer, No.84	35.00
Old Ivory, Cup & Saucer, No.202	35.00
Old Ivory, Dessert Set, No.16, Silesia, C.1800, 9 Piece	200.00
Old Ivory, Dish, Candy, Crown Mark, No.75, 7 3/4 In.	22.00
Old Ivory, Dish, Relish, 6 1/2 In.	30.00
Old Ivory, Pitcher & Sugar, Covered Pitcher, No.84	110.00
Old Ivory, Plate, Chop	125.00
Old Ivory, Plate, No.12, Holly	30.00
Old Ivory, Plate, No.15, 6 1/2 In.	18.00
Old Ivory, Plate, No.15, 7 1/2 In.	20.00
Old Ivory, Plate, No.84, 6 In.	13.00
Old Ivory, Plate, No.123, 8 1/2 In.	35.00
Old Ivory, Plate, Poppies, Silesia, No.202 Mark, 8 1/2 In.	25.00
Old Ivory, Plate, Silesia, 6 In.	21.50
Old Ivory, Plate, 7 In.	25.00
Old Ivory, Plate, 8 1/4 In.	22.50
Old Ivory, Platter, 11 1/2 X 8 In.	75.00
Old Ivory, Relish, No.16, 8 1/4 In.	37.50
Old Ivory, Sauce, German Red Mark, 5 1/2 In.	15.00
Old Ivory, Sauce, 5 1/2 In.	17.00
Old Ivory, Sauce, 6 3/8 In.	19.00
Old Ivory, Sugar & Creamer, Breakfast	128.00
Old Ivory, Teapot, No.200, Covered	85.00
Old Ivory, Tray, Handled, Ohme, No.200, 8 1/2 X 5 In.	35.00

Onion, originally named "bulb pattern," is a white ware decorated with cobalt blue. Although it is commonly associated with Meissen, other companies made the pattern in the latter part of the nineteenth century.

Onion, Bowl, Blue, Flat, Meissen, 9 1/2 In.	68.00
Onion, Coffeepot, Blue, Finial Figural Rosebud, Meissen, 9 In.	125.00
Onion, Cup & Saucer, Crossed Swords, Meissen, Set Of 8	300.00

Onion, Cup & Saucer, Demitasse, Meissen, Pair	35.00
Onion, Cup & Saucer, Meissen	30.00
Onion, Dish, Sweetmeat, Meissen, Blue & White, Maiden Reclining, 7 X 12 In.	275.00
Onion, Eggcup, Meissen, Crossed Swords Mark	27.00
Onion, Feeder, Invalid, Meissen	14.00
Onion, Jar, Covered, Spice, Cinnamon, 3 In.	70.00
Onion, Knife Rest, Crossed Swords, Meissen	30.00
Onion, Knife, Fruit, Meissen, Set Of 6	55.00
Onion, Mug, Shaving, Meissen	45.00
Onion, Opener, Letter, Blue, Handled, Bohemia, 6 In.	20.00
Onion, Pitcher, Dark Blue, 3 Legs, Meissen, Crossed Swords Mark, 2 1/2 In.	35.00
Onion, Plate, Cauldon England, 7 1/2 In.	20.00
Onion, Plate, Cobalt Blue, England, Adderleys Ltd., 7 In.	8.00
Onion, Plate, Hot Water Warmer	125.00
Cnion, Plate, Meissen, 8 1/2 In.	30.00
Onion, Plate, Soup, Caldon, England, 7 1/2 In.	25.00
Onion, Platter, Meissen, C.1860, 9 1/2 In.	65.00
Onion, Rolling Pin, Porcelain, Blue & White, Maple Handle, 14 In.	80.00
Onion, Salt Box, Blue Decoration, Wooden Cover, Ceramic	55.00
Onion, Sugar, Covered, Meissen	45.00
Onion, Tea Set, Rosebud Finial, Teapot, Creamer, Sugar, Meissen	150.00

Opalescent glass is translucent glass that has the bluish-white tones of the opal gemstone. It is often found in pressed glassware made in Victorian times. Some dealers use the terms opaline and opalescent for any of the bluish-white translucent wares.

Opalescent, Basket, Applied Leaves & Flowers, Amber Twisted Handle, 8 In.	125.00
Opalescent, Basket, Bushel, Aqua	165.00
Opalescent, Basket, Glass, Blue	45.00
Opalescent, Basket, May Basket, 5 In.	45.00
Opalescent, Basket, Plated Frame, Vaseline, 5 In.	60.00
Opalescent, Basket, Shaded Blue To Opalescent, Applied Feet & Handle, 5 In.	50.00
Opalescent, Berry Bowl, Blue, Wreath & Shell, Small	22.50
Opalescent, Berry Bowl, Seaweed, White	50.00
Opalescent, Berry Set, Jeweled Heart	78.00
Opalescent, Berry Set, Jeweled Heart, White Fiery, 7 Piece	95.00
Opalescent, Berry Set, Shell, White, N, 7 Piece	175.00
Opalescent, Berry, Intaglio, Blue, Footed, Small	28.00
Opalescent, Berry, May Basket, Green, Ruffled, Small	22.00
Opalescent, Berry, Shell & Wreath, Vaseline, Small	25.00
Opalescent, Berry, Waterlily & Cattails, Amethyst, 8 In.	75.00
Opalescent, Bonbon, Threaded, Blue, White, Tri-Footed, Scalloped, 7 In.	25.00
Opalescent, Bowl & Underplate, Finger, Threaded, Pale Blue, 7 In.	95.00
Opalescent, Bowl, Basket Weave, Blue, 6 1/2 In.	8.00
Opalescent, Bowl, Berry, Clear, Seaweed Pattern, 9 X 3 In.	38.00
Opalescent, Bowl, Berry, Paneled Holly, White With Red & Green, Small	15.00
Opalescent, Bowl, Blossom & Palm, Fluted, Blue Opalescent, 9 In.	39.00
Opalescent, Bowl, Blue, Canterbury, 6 In.	19.50
Opalescent, Bowl, Blue, Canterbury, 8 3/4 In.	29.00
Opalescent, Bowl, Blue, Daisy & Fern	32.00
Opalescent, Bowl, Blue, Fan Pattern, 8 3/4 In.	20.00
Opalescent, Bowl, Blue, Open Fretwork, Footed, Signed N, 8 In.	75.00
Opalescent, Bowl, Blue, Pearl Flowers, Fluted, 3 Ball Feet, 9 In.	40.00
Opalescent, Bowl, Daisy & Fern, Blue, Ball Feet	38.00
Opalescent, Bowl, Dogwood Flowers, Deep Blue, Scalloped, 7 1/2 In.	35.00
Opalescent, Bowl, Green, Classical Border, 3 Open Feet, 8 1/2 In.	55.00
Opalescent, Bowl, Green, Many Loops, 6 1/2 In.	25.00
Opalescent, Bowl, Green, Ruby Rimmed, Footed, 8 In.	30.00
Opalescent, Bowl, Jefferson Wheel, Footed	25.00
Opalescent, Bowl, Lattice & Poinsettia, Ruffled, Footed, 8 3/4 In.	40.00
Opalescent, Bowl, Leaf Chalice, Blue To Opalescent	40.00
Opalescent, Bowl, Loops, Green, 6 1/2 In.	25.00
Opalescent, Bowl, Meander, Fluted, Green To Opalescent, 9 In.	25.00
Opalescent, Bowl, Palm & Scroll, Footed	28.00
Opalescent, Bowl, Pearl Flowers, White, 3 Footed	30.00

Opalescent, Bowl, Pink, Footed, 6 In.	24.50
Opalescent, Bowl, Rose, Blue, Pearls, Scales, Green Pedestal	35.00
Opalescent, Bowl, Ruffled Top, Hobnail, Aqua, 4 1/2 In.	65.00
Opalescent, Bowl, Ruffles & Rings, Footed, 9 In.	30.00
Opalescent, Bowl, Shell & Dots, Green	22.50
Opalescent, Bowl, Stripped, Ground Pontil, Blown, 4 1/4 X 7 1/4 In.	35.00
Opalescent, Bowl, Vintage, Blue, Footed	32.50
Opalescent, Bowl, Water Lily & Cattails, Blue Edge	15.00
Opalescent, Bowl, White Ruffled Top, Hobnail, 6 In.	70.00
Opalescent, Bowl, White, Pearl Flowers, 3 Footed	30.00
Opalescent, Bride's Bowl, Green Poinsettia, Ruffled Border, 10 1/2 In.	125.00
Opalescent, Butter, Crystal Base, Swirl, Cranberry	175.00
Opalescent, Butter, Shell & Wreath, Covered	195.00
Opalescent, Butter, Swag & Bracket	65.00
Opalescent, Candlestick, Basket Weave, Footed Base, Open Edge, Pair	28.00
Opalescent, Candlestick, Madonna & Child Stem, White, Tin Top, Pair	250.00
Opalescent, Candy, Argonaut Shell, Turned Up Sides, Vaseline Shades	32.00
Opalescent, Celery, Beatty Rib, White	23.00
Opalescent, Celery, Swirl, Crystal Base, Cranberry	95.00
Opalescent, Compote, Argonaut Shell, Blue, 8 X 3 3/4 In.	50.00
Opalescent, Compote, Green, Beaded Fleur-De-Lis, 4 1/2 X 8 In.	42.50
Opalescent, Compote, Intaglio, Canary, 5 1/2 In.	27.00
Opalescent, Compote, Intaglio, Fluted, Blue	15.00
Opalescent, Compote, Jade Stem, Silver Overlay On Bowl & Base, Signed	150.00
Opalescent, Compote, Jelly, Argonaut Shell, Blue	50.00
Opalescent, Compote, Jelly, Everglades, Blue	125.00
Opalescent, Compote, Jelly, Swag & Bracket	45.00
Opalescent, Compote, Star And Snail, White	15.00
Opalescent, Creamer, Alaska Blue	48.00
Opalescent, Creamer, Alaska, Clear To Opalescent	27.50
Opalescent, Creamer, Beatty Honeycomb, Blue	25.00
Opalescent, Creamer, Blue, Shell Pattern, Shell-Footed Standard	65.00
Opalescent, Creamer, Fan, Clear To Opalescent	25.00
Opalescent, Creamer, Fluted Scroll, Blue	65.00
Opalescent, Creamer, Fluted Scroll, Blue, Flower Band	75.00
Opalescent, Creamer, Hobnail, Paneled, Thumbprint	23.00
Opalescent, Creamer, Intaglio, Clear To Opalescent	12.00
Opalescent, Creamer, Jewel & Flower, Clear	45.00
Opalescent, Creamer, Jeweled Heart, Clear To Opalescent	25.00
Opalescent, Creamer, Scroll With Acanthus, White	28.00
Opalescent, Creamer, Shell & Wreath	175.00
Opalescent, Creamer, Swag With Brackets, Blue	42.00
Opalescent, Creamer, Tokyo, Clear To Opalescent	25.00
Opalescent, Creamer, Tokyo, White	32.00
Opalescent, Creamer, Water Lily & Cattails, Green	65.00
Opalescent, Cup & Saucer, Ribbed, Spiral, Blue	65.00
Opalescent, Cuspidor, Lady's, Clear White, Floral, Footed, 4 1/2 X 4 In.	65.00
Opalescent, Dish, Candy, Finecut & Roses, White	28.00
Opalescent, Dish, Candy, Green Jewel & Fan	25.00
Opalescent, Dish, Candy, Green, Grape Design, Fluted, 8 In.	30.00
Opalescent, Dish, Fluted Scrolls, Covered	40.00
Opalescent, Dish, Green, Pearl Flowers	25.00
Opalescent, Dish, Green, Roulette, Footed	25.00
Opalescent, Dish, Olive, Sea Spray, Handled, 1908, 5 1/2 In.	18.00
Opalescent, Dish, Puff, Blue Opalescent, Fluted Scroll	40.00
Opalescent, Dish, Rooster Cover, Milk White, Pedestal Base	35.00
Opalescent, Dish, Shell, 6 3/4 In.	13.00
Opalescent, Dish, Squirrel, Green	38.00
Opalescent, Dish, War Of Roses, Boat Shape, Blue	30.00
Opalescent, Epergne, Blue Opalescent, Side Lilies, Wide Panel, Ruffled Edge	25.00
Opalescent, Epergne, 3 Lily, Blue	225.00
Opalescent, Figurine, Swan, Pink, Burtles-Tate, C.1885	45.00
Opalescent, Flower Arranger, Blue, 5 X 7 In.	35.00
Opalescent, Glass, Blue Stripes, Cobalt Handles	30.00
Opalescent, Glass, Cocktail, Bottoms Up, Cream Nude Base To Rim	25.00

Opalescent, Goblet, Blown Flint, Pittsburgh, 4 3/4 In. 135.00
Opalescent, Jar, Cookie, White To Green, Roses, Silver Plated Cover 81.00
Opalescent, Jelly, Pump & Trough 135.00
Opalescent, Lattice, Ribbed, Salt, White 35.00
Opalescent, Mug, Arches & Rose 25.00
Opalescent, Pitcher & 5 Tumblers, Blue, Seaweed 170.00
Opalescent, Pitcher, Blue, Swirl, Ruffled Top, Hobbs Shape 145.00
Opalescent, Pitcher, Buttons And Braid, Blue 165.00
Opalescent, Pitcher, Coin Spot 65.00
Opalescent, Pitcher, Coin Spot, Bulbous, Ruffled Top 75.00
Opalescent, Pitcher, Coin Spot, Cranberry, Opalescent Spots, 6 In. 75.00
Opalescent, Pitcher, Coin Spot, Opalescent Spots, Ruffled, 10 1/2 In. 75.00
Opalescent, Pitcher, Drape, Bulbous, Ruffled Top 85.00
Opalescent, Pitcher, Milk, Blue, Bull's-Eye, Hobnail, Clear Feet .... *Illus* 67.50
Opalescent, Pitcher, Poinsettia, Bulbous, Ruffled Top, Blue 145.00
Opalescent, Pitcher, Water, Blue, Acorn & Leaf, 8 In. .... *Illus* 125.00
Opalescent, Pitcher, Water, Buttons & Braids, White Bulbous, Applied Handle 100.00
Opalescent, Pitcher, Water, Clear, White Swirls, Applied Handle, 9 1/2 In. 75.00
Opalescent, Pitcher, Water, Drapery, White 75.00
Opalescent, Pitcher, Water, Intaglio, Blue 235.00
Opalescent, Pitcher, Water, Scottish Moor, Clear Reeded Handle, White 95.00
Opalescent, Pitcher, Water, Swag With Brackets, Green 115.00
Opalescent, Pitcher, Water, White Swirl, Clear Applied Handle, 9 1/2 In. 45.00
Opalescent, Pitcher, Water, White, Honeycomb & Clover 45.00
Opalescent, Pitcher, Water, Windows, Handle, Pontil, Blue 130.00
Opalescent, Pitcher, Water, Windows, Square Top, Blue 185.00
Opalescent, Plate, Basket Weave, Blue, Open Rim, 7 1/2 In. 8.00
Opalescent, Plate, Blue, Flat-Footed, Tokyo, 8 1/4 In. 28.00
Opalescent, Plate, Blue, Optic, Signed & Numbered, C.1920, 9 In., Pair 425.00
Opalescent, Plate, Grapes & Cherries 27.50
Opalescent, Plate, Jeweled Heart, Blue, 9 In. 35.00
Opalescent, Receiver, Card, Fluted Scrolls 17.50
Opalescent, Rose Bowl, Blue 17.00
Opalescent, Rose Bowl, Fleur-De-Lis, Beaded, Clear To Opalescent 22.00
Opalescent, Rose Bowl, Inverted Fan, Feather, Blue 18.50
Opalescent, Rose Bowl, Ruffled, Beaded Swags, Green, Footed 38.00
Opalescent, Rose Bowl, Seaweed, Vaseline 48.00
Opalescent, Salt & Pepper, Hobnail, Blue 15.00
Opalescent, Salt, Shell & Wreath, Footed 39.00
Opalescent, Saltshaker, Blue, Ribbed, 3 In. 25.00

Opalescent, Pitcher, Milk, Blue, Bull's-Eye, Hobnail, Clear Feet

Opalescent, Pitcher, Water, Blue, Acorn & Leaf, 8 In.

Opalescent, Sauce, Alaska, Blue	25.00
Opalescent, Sauce, Drapery, White	15.00
Opalescent, Sauce, Intaglio, Ruffled, Small, Vaseline	25.00
Opalescent, Sauce, Swirl, Blue	15.00
Opalescent, Sauce, Tokyo	9.00
Opalescent, Sauce, Wild Bouquet, Blue	20.00
Opalescent, Server, Pink, Shell, Long End Turned Up, 7 1/2 X 2 3/4 In.	22.50
Opalescent, Shade, Gas, Blue, Raised Daisies, Beaded Chains, Jewels, 7 3/4 In.	85.00
Opalescent, Shade, Peach, Pastoral Scenes, 5 1/4 In.	49.00
Opalescent, Shade, Satinized White, Pink Cameo Cut Border Designs, Set Of 3	35.00
Opalescent, Spooner, Alaska, Blue	45.00
Opalescent, Spooner, Fluted Scroll, Blue	42.00 To 50.00
Opalescent, Spooner, Intaglio, Blue	65.00
Opalescent, Spooner, Shell & Wreath	85.00
Opalescent, Spooner, Tokyo, Green	95.00
Opalescent, Spooner, Water Lily & Cattails	55.00
Opalescent, Spooner, Water Lily & Cattails, Blue	32.50
Opalescent, Spooner, Wreath, Shell, Blue	85.00
Opalescent, Sugar & Creamer, Hobnail, Blue	45.00
Opalescent, Sugar & Creamer, Hobnail, Miniature	12.75
Opalescent, Sugar Shaker, Blue, Ribbed, Lattice, Lid	65.00
Opalescent, Sugar Shaker, Blue, Windows Swirl	95.00
Opalescent, Sugar Shaker, Daisy & Fern, Spiral Melon Rib, Original Top	45.00
Opalescent, Sugar, Beatty Honeycomb, Lid, Blue	60.00
Opalescent, Sugar, Blue, Swirling Maize, Covered	65.00
Opalescent, Sugar, Cover, Everglade, Blue, Gold	95.00
Opalescent, Sugar, Cover, Seaweed, Cranberry	120.00
Opalescent, Sugar, Covered, Tokyo, Green	120.00
Opalescent, Sugar, Scrolls, Fluted, Blue	45.00
Opalescent, Sugar, Shell & Wreath, Covered	195.00
Opalescent, Swan, Blue, 4 1/4 X 3 In.	15.00 To 15.50
Opalescent, Syrup, Beatty Swirl, Blue	275.00
Opalescent, Syrup, Canary, Reverse Swirl	215.00
Opalescent, Tankard, Ribbed Lattice, White	110.00
Opalescent, Tieback, Pewter Shank, Floral Design, Pair	40.00
Opalescent, Toothpick, Blue, Iris, Meander	55.00
Opalescent, Toothpick, Blue, Ribbed, Beatty	30.00
Opalescent, Toothpick, Overall Hobnail, H219	30.00
Opalescent, Toothpick, Overall Hobnail, White	18.00
Opalescent, Tray, Forget-Me-Not, Clover Shape, Pink, 6 In.	48.00
Opalescent, Tray, Water, Blue, Beatty Swirl	65.00
Opalescent, Tumbler, Argonaut Shell, Blue	55.00
Opalescent, Tumbler, Blue, Arabian Nights	55.00
Opalescent, Tumbler, Blue, Cattails & Water Lilies	22.50
Opalescent, Tumbler, Buttons & Braid, Blue	30.00 To 35.00
Opalescent, Tumbler, Drapery, White	22.00
Opalescent, Tumbler, Hobnail, Pink Cased, Sapphire Blue	35.00
Opalescent, Tumbler, Hobnail, 10 Row, White	58.00
Opalescent, Tumbler, Inverted Fan & Feather, Blue With Gold	65.00
Opalescent, Tumbler, Jefferson Drape	28.00
Opalescent, Tumbler, Jefferson Drape, Green	14.00
Opalescent, Tumbler, Jewel & Flower, Gold & Pink	30.00
Opalescent, Tumbler, Paneled Holly, White With Gold	22.00
Opalescent, Tumbler, Swirl, Blue	40.00
Opalescent, Tumbler, Water Lily & Cattails, Blue	22.00
Opalescent, Vase, Bars & Beads, Fluted, Blue	25.00
Opalescent, Vase, Beads & Bark, Green, 6 1/4 In.	35.00
Opalescent, Vase, Blue Twig, Blue, Rim Not Flared	25.00
Opalescent, Vase, Blue, Crimped, Paper Label, 3 1/2 In.	15.00
Opalescent, Vase, Blue, White Swirl, Cranberry Edge, 6 In.	55.00
Opalescent, Vase, Diamond Point, White Opalescent To Clear, 8 1/2 In.	14.00
Opalescent, Vase, Diamond-Quilted, Light Blue, Signed N, 10 In.	27.50
Opalescent, Vase, Diamond, Gilded Britannia Metal Holder, 11 3/4 In.	27.50
Opalescent, Vase, Emerald Green, Hobnail, Ruffled, Light Green Top, 4 1/2 In.	27.50
Opalescent, Vase, Fluted Bars And Beads, Footed, Green	22.00

Opalescent, Vase, Green, Feather Designs, Scallops, 11 In.	25.00
Opalescent, Vase, Heatherbloom, Green, 12 In.	20.00
Opalescent, Vase, Iris With Meander, Green, 12 In.	18.00
Opalescent, Vase, Jack-In-The-Pulpit, Pink, 9 1/4 In.	60.00
Opalescent, Vase, Jefferson Spool, Blue, 6 1/2 In.	45.00
Opalescent, Vase, Persian Type Enameled Pattern On Green, Hawkes, England	350.00
Opalescent, Vase, Pump & Trough	110.00
Opalescent, Vase, Rib, Blue, 11 In.	15.00
Opalescent, Vase, Rib, Green, 11 In.	16.00
Opalescent, Vase, Striped, 12 In.	20.00
Opalescent, Vase, Swirl, Blue, 12 In.	16.00
Opalescent, Vase, Thousand-Eye, Blue, 6 In.	35.00
Opalescent, Vase, Tree Trunk, Deep Blue, 11 In.	27.50
Opalescent, Vase, Water Lily Base, Stem Is Fish, Green, 11 In.	127.00
Opalescent, Vase, White, Ruffled, 10 In.	20.00
Opalescent, Vase, Yellow, Flared Top, 3 1/2 In.	42.50
Opalescent, Water Set, Arabian Nights, Blue, 7 Piece	395.00
Opalescent, Water Set, Jeweled Heart, Pitcher & 4 Tumblers	95.00

Opaline glass, or opal glass, was made in white, apple green, and other colors.
The glass had a matte surface and a lack of transparency. It was often
gilded or painted. It was a popular mid-nineteenth-century European
glassware.

Opaline Glass, Cigarette Urn, Tabletop	9.00
Opaline Glass, Salt, Silver Over Brass, Leaves, Inset, 4 Jadeite-Like Stones	25.00
Opaline, Bottle, Green, 8 In.	45.00
Opaline, Bowl, Finger, Green, Polished Base	45.00
Opaline, Bowl, Scalloped Edges, Ground Pontil, Czechoslovakia, 4 1/2 In.	50.00
Opaline, Cup & Saucer, French, 2 1/4 In.	22.50
Opaline, Dresser Set, Yellow Enamel Scroll, Gilt, 4 Piece	115.00
Opaline, Pitcher, Rose Colored, Optic Ribbing, Applied Reeded Handle, 8 In.	85.00
Opaline, Vase, Blue, Floral & Bird Design, 8 In.	65.00
Opaline, Vase, Figural, Peacock, Gold Trim, Hand-Painted Flowers, 9 1/2 In.	150.00
Opaline, Vase, Peacock, Tail Spread In Bas-Relief, Gold Trim, 9 1/2 In.	150.00
Opaline, Vase, White, Fluted Rim, 8 In.	30.00
Opera Glasses, French, Mother-Of-Pearl And Brass, Ornate, Handle Extends	68.00
Opera Glasses, French, Mother-Of-Pearl, La Reine, Leather Case	32.00
Opera Glasses, Mother-Of-Pearl & Gold Trim, Gold Brocaded Case, Paris	65.00
Opera Glasses, Telescopic Brass And Mother-Of-Pearl	50.00
Organ, see Music, Organ	
Ormolu, Box, French, Ivory Painting Of Young Woman, Signed, 5 1/2 X 7 X 5 In.	215.00
Orphan Annie, Ashtray, Annie & Sandy, Bisque, Painted & Glazed	25.00
Orphan Annie, Badge, Decoder, 1916	15.00
Orphan Annie, Decoder, 1940	15.00
Orphan Annie, Figurine, Annie & Sandy, 3 1/2 In., Pair	20.00
Orphan Annie, Game, Box	15.00
Orphan Annie, Glass, Plastic, 1930s	8.00
Orphan Annie, Holder, Toothbrush, Bisque, Annie & Sandy On Sofa	65.00
Orphan Annie, Mug, Beetleware	26.50
Orphan Annie, Mug, China	20.00
Orphan Annie, Pin, Secret Society	10.00
Orphan Annie, Plate	20.00
Orphan Annie, Puzzle, Radio, Original Mailing Carton	7.00
Orphan Annie, Salt & Pepper	15.00
Orphan Annie, Stove, Double Oven, 9 1/2 X 8 1/2 In.	45.00
Orphan Annie, Toy, Skipping Rope, Windup, Lehman, German, Original Box	225.00
Orphan Annie, Tumbler, Annie & Sandy	10.00
Orphan Annie, Vase, Wall Pocket, Annie & Sandy, Tapering To Base, Tan Trim	25.00
Orphan Annie, Watch, 1936	45.00

Orrefors Glassworks, located in the Swedish Province of Smaaland, was
established in 1916.

Orrefors, Bowl, Intarsia, Fish With Seaweed, Signed Graal	185.00
Orrefors, Vase, Crystal, Slightly Opaque, Signed & Numbered, 12 1/2 In.	70.00
Orrefors, Vase, Orange & Black Cut Design, 11 In.	300.00

Ott & Brewer Company operated the Etruria Pottery at Trenton, New Jersey, from 1863 to 1893. It was under the direction of William Bromley, Sr., from the Belleek factory at Belleek, Ireland, from 1883.

Ott & Brewer, Bowl, Cream, Gold Paste Design, 4 X 2 In.	98.00
Ott & Brewer, Card Tray, Belleek, Ruffled Edge, Floral, Butterfly, Square	175.00
Ott & Brewer, Coffeepot, Pink Quilted Bottom, Gold Dragon Head Spout	360.00
Ott & Brewer, Cracker Jar, Covered, Cobalt Ground, Gold Oriental Decoration	95.00
Ott & Brewer, Cup & Saucer, Belleek, Floral, Large Coffee Cup, Gold, Pastel	110.00
Ott & Brewer, Cup & Saucer, Demitasse, Fluted & Scalloped, Gold Trim	55.00
Ott & Brewer, Cup & Saucer, Demitasse, Fluted, Twig Strap Handle	50.00
Ott & Brewer, Cup & Saucer, Demitasse, Gold, White, Pebbly Surface	66.00
Ott & Brewer, Cup & Saucer, Demitasse, Tridacna, Gold Trim, Marked	57.50
Ott & Brewer, Cup, Cream, Raised Gold Designs	35.00
Ott & Brewer, Cup, Demitasse, Belleek, Gold Trim	18.00
Ott & Brewer, Cup, Gold Floral On White Seashell, Demitasse, Marked	110.00
Ott & Brewer, Cup, Wishbone Handle, Iridescent Yellow, Gold Edge	28.00
Ott & Brewer, Ewer, Belleek, Gold Floral On Cream, Twig Handle, Marked, 4 In.	295.00
Ott & Brewer, Pitcher & Tricorn Bowl, Belleek, Cream, Raised Gold Designs	145.00
Ott & Brewer, Platter, Spongeware, Blue, 10 X 13 1/2 In.	125.00
Ott & Brewer, Sugar & Creamer, Belleek, Gold Floral, Butterfly & Dragonfly	295.00
Ott & Brewer, Sugar, Gold Pastel, Palm Leaves, Dragonfly, Covered	120.00
Ott & Brewer, Teapot, Belleek, Gold Butterfly, Twig Handle, 8 In.	175.00

OWENS UTOPIAN

Owens Pottery was made in Zanesville, Ohio, from 1891 to 1928. The first art pottery was made after 1896. Utopian Ware, Cyrano, Navarre, Feroza, and Henri Deux were made. Pieces were usually marked with a form of the name Owens. About 1907 the firm began to make tile and gave up the art pottery wares.

Owens, Ewer, Utopian, Florals On Both Sides, Impressed Utopian, 5 1/2 In.	125.00
Owens, Jug, Left-Handed, Cherries & Leaves, Standard Glaze	65.00
Owens, Lamp Base, Utopian, Golden Shading Behind Large Yellow Tulips, 10 In.	50.00
Owens, Match Holder, Raised Flower	75.00
Owens, Mug, Brown, Leaves & Berries, Artist's Initials, 5 In.	78.50
Owens, Mug, Utopian, Cherry Decorated, Standard Glaze, T.S., 5 In.	95.00
Owens, Pitcher, Lotus, Crane, 7 1/2 In.	445.00
Owens, Pitcher, Tankard, Wild Rose Decoration, 12 In.	165.00
Owens, Tankard & 4 Mugs, Utopian, Currant Decoration, Artist Signed, 12 In.	450.00
Owens, Tankard Set, Cherries, Artist Signed, 5 Piece	385.00
Owens, Tankard, Brown Glaze, Yellow Florals, Green Leaves, Handled, 5 In.	70.00
Owens, Tankard, High Glaze Brown, Raised Yellow & Orange Pansies, 11 1/4 In.	165.00
Owens, Tankard, Utopian, Berry Pattern, Artist's Initials, Marked, 12 In.	135.00
Owens, Tankard, Utopian, Blackberries, Trailing Vines, Heubrick, 12 In.	150.00
Owens, Vase, Aborigine, Green, Marked 215, 4 3/4 In.	70.00
Owens, Vase, Aborigine, Green, 2-Handled, Marked 230, 4 1/2 In.	70.00
Owens, Vase, Aborigine, Matte Green Glaze, Marked 234, 4 3/4 In.	70.00
Owens, Vase, Autumn Colored Leaves, Hattie Eberlein, 6 1/2 In.	125.00
Owens, Vase, Bisque Tan Body, Indian Motif Light Brown, Black, 4 3/4 In.	78.00
Owens, Vase, Brown Glaze With Flowers, Artist Signed, 11 In.	170.00
Owens, Vase, Brown Glaze, Yellow Roses, Green Leaves, Handled, 5 In.	70.00
Owens, Vase, Fish, White & Gray Shading, Semi-Matte, Numbered, 12 1/2 In.	665.00
Owens, Vase, Floral Decoration, Utopian, 3 In.	60.00
Owens, Vase, Floral, Shaded White To Green, 7 In.	55.00
Owens, Vase, Lotus, Gray-Cream, Vine Of Fruit At Top, Signed Chilcote, 8 In.	200.00
Owens, Vase, Matte, Utopian Swirl, Artist Initialed TS, 4 1/2 In.	55.00
Owens, Vase, Metallic Luster Finish, Feroza, 6 X 5 In.	225.00
Owens, Vase, Nasturtiums, Brown Glaze, Owens In Block Mark, 10 In.	85.00
Owens, Vase, Orange Poppy On Browns, High Gloss, Marked, 10 1/2 In.	95.00
Owens, Vase, Pink Poppies On Blue To White, 7 3/4 In.	175.00
Owens, Vase, Red & Green Leaves, Red Berries, Dark Glaze, 12 1/4 In.	85.00
Owens, Vase, Semi-Matte Green, Gold Branch & Leaves, Red Cherries, 10 1/2 In.	200.00
Owens, Vase, Standard Glaze Floral, Twisted Shape, Signed, 3 In.	65.00
Owens, Vase, Twist, Brown Glaze, 4 In.	65.00
Owens, Vase, Utopian, Blooming Clover Decoration, Marked 232, 5 1/2 In.	85.00
Owens, Vase, Utopian, Brown Glaze, Rust & Green Leaves, Edith Bell, 5 In.	77.00

Owens, Vase, Utopian, Daffodils, 13 In.	125.00
Owens, Vase, Utopian, Orange Floral, Twisted Shape, Standard Glaze, 5 1/2 In.	55.00
Owens, Vase, Utopian, Twisted, Floral Decoration, Marked Utopian, 3 3/4 In.	95.00
Owens, Vase, Utopian, Yellow Roses, 2 Handles, 5 In.	70.00
Owens, Vase, Utopian, Yellow-Green To Amber, Yellow Pansies Scattered, 7 In.	65.00
Owens, Vase, Yellow & Orange Daisies, Standard Glaze, T.Steel, 11 In.	135.00
Owens, Water Set, Utopian, Currant Decoration, Marked & Signed, 5 Piece	450.00
Oyster Plate, 5 Section, Lavender, Gold, White, Scalloped, Weimar, Germany	20.00
Oyster Plate, 5 Well, Pastel Colors, German, Set Of 8	75.00
Painting On Porcelain, Dark Haired Lady, Wagner, Signed, 2 X 2 1/2 In.	275.00
Painting, Oil On Copper, Dutch, Men Playing Cards, 19th Century, 4 X 5 In.	60.00
Painting, Oil On Tin, Peasant Boys, Italian, 19th Century, 8 X 7 In.	70.00
Painting, On Enamel, Plaque, Marie Antoinette, Signed Vignet	295.00
Painting, On Ivory, Cavalier After Rubens, Green, Wood Frame, Miniature	150.00
Painting, On Ivory, Country Scene, Signed Wouverman, Framed, Oval, 3 3/4 In.	175.00
Painting, On Ivory, Head Of Neapolitan Man, C.1917, Owen Hughes, 3 X 4 In.	150.00
Painting, On Ivory, Lady Hamilton, Ivory Frame, 5 X 6 In.	135.00
Painting, On Ivory, Louis XVI, Ivory Frame, 5 X 6 In.	135.00
Painting, On Ivory, Lovers In Garden, Boudin, Inlaid Ivory Frame, 3 3/4 In.	175.00
Painting, On Ivory, Man, Woman, Miniature, French, 19th Century, 4 X 4 In., Pair	295.00
Painting, On Ivory, Marie Antoinette, Ivory Frame, 5 X 6 In.	135.00
Painting, On Ivory, Miniature, Man, C.1840	155.00
Painting, On Ivory, Napoleon & Troops, Vernet, Inlaid Ivory Frame, 3 3/4 In.	200.00
Painting, On Ivory, Old Woman With Cane, Wood Frame, Miniature	175.00
Painting, On Ivory, Victorian Lady, Beaded Brass Footed Frame, 3 1/2 In.	55.00
Painting, On Ivory, Woman Wearing Bonnet, Pastel, Red Velvet Frame, Signed	145.00
Painting, On Ivory, Young French Woman, Bronze Frame, Signed, 2 1/2 In.	100.00
Painting, On Ivory, Young Lady, White Gown, Wood Frame, Daffinger, 2 3/4 In.	110.00
Painting, On Porcelain, Lady, White Cap, Fur Trimmed Velvet Robe, Framed	95.00
Painting, On Porcelain, Madonna, Marked Firenze, 3 1/2 X 5 In.	200.00
Painting, On Porcelain, Marked Vestalin-Germany, 3 1/4 X 2 1/2 In.	165.00
Painting, On Porcelain, McKinley, Raised Gold Trim, M.E.Jillman, 4 X 5 In.	185.00
Painting, On Porcelain, Oval, Blue Madonna, 3 1/4 X 2 3/4 In.	60.00
Painting, On Porcelain, Renaissance Lady, 7 1/4 X 5 1/2 In.	285.00
Painting, On Porcelain, Seascape, Ship, Sweet Oak Frame, 3 1/4 In.	32.00
Painting, On Porcelain, Woman, Brooch, Numbered, 1 1/2 X 2 In.	75.00
Painting, On Porcelain, Young Girl, Gayhart, Oval, 7 X 5 1/2 In.	85.00
Painting, On Porcelain, Young Girl, Pastels, Wood Frame, 3 1/4 X 2 1/2 In.	85.00
Painting, On Silk, Bengal Tiger Mother & Young, Japanese, Signed, 14 1/2 In.	150.00
Painting, On Silk, Prince Of 4th Rank, Chinese, Kakemono, 19th Century, 38 In.	190.00
Painting, On Silk, Siamese Triptych, 25 X 72 In.	50.00
Painting, On Silk, Village Scene, Chinese, 18th Century, Signed, 41 X 21 In.	450.00
Painting, On Wood, Candlelight Girl, Brass Plated Frame, 10 1/2 X 7 In.	65.00
Painting, Reverse On Glass, Gold & Black, Garden Scene, 5 1/2 X 6 3/4 In.	8.50
Painting, Reverse On Glass, Old House, River, Bridge, Gold Frame, 10 In.	39.50
Painting, Reverse On Glass, Peasants & Emperor, Chinese, 19th Century, 19 In.	150.00
Painting, Reverse On Glass, Table Screen, Chinese, 4-Fold, 20 X 28 In.	70.00
Painting, Reverse On Glass, Titanic Going Down, Gold Leaf Frame, 22 X 38 In.	125.00
Painting, Reverse On Glass, White House, Mother-Of-Pearl Inlay, Frame, 11 In.	20.00

Pairpoint Corporation was a silver and glass firm founded in New Bedford, Massachusetts, in 1880.

Pairpoint, Basket, Cake, Floral Cutout Bail, 5 In.	35.00
Pairpoint, Basket, Ruby Glass Liner, Silver Plated Footed Fretwork, Signed	140.00
Pairpoint, Bottle, Perfume, Wilton Design, Engraved, Melon Shape, 7 In.	50.00
Pairpoint, Bowl, Compote, Ruby Glass, Clear Glass Ball In Stem, 6 X 6 In.	125.00
Pairpoint, Bowl, Cut, Bishop's Hat, Butterflies & Flowers	345.00
Pairpoint, Bowl, Fruit, Copper Wheel, Engraved Vintage, Olive Green, 7 In.	150.00
Pairpoint, Bowl, Fruit, Reverse Painted, Art Nouveau Base	175.00
Pairpoint, Bowl, Oval, Sawtooth, Silver Stand Held By 4 Cherubs	325.00
Pairpoint, Bowl, Sky Blue, Clear Swirled Pedestal, 6 X 14 In.	65.00
Pairpoint, Box, Covered, Leaf Shaped, Signed, 7 1/2 X 6 X 3 In.	300.00
Pairpoint, Box, Intaglio Flowers, Silver Mounted, 6 1/2 X 3 In.	175.00
Pairpoint, Box, Opal Glass Cover, Center Cartouche, Signed, 6 X 5 In.	150.00
Pairpoint, Box, Scrolls, Floral, Cloth Lined, Circular, White Porcelain, Signed	175.00

Pairpoint, Box, Silver Plate, Collar, Cuff's, Round	22.00
Pairpoint, Bride's Basket, Melon Rib, Cardinal Red, Deep, Signed	147.00
Pairpoint, Bride's Basket, Oval, Unusual Frame	25.00
Pairpoint, Bucket, Ice, Butterfly, Narcissus, Silver Plate Handle, Rim, Insert	85.00
Pairpoint, Burner, Incense, Silver Plated	22.00
Pairpoint, Butter, Flowers, Finial, Glass Insert, Dome Top, Nellie On Bottom	28.00
Pairpoint, Butter, Rose Pattern, Glass Insert & Knife, Covered	47.50
Pairpoint, Candelabra, 4 Branch, Eternal Flame Center, 13 In.	175.00
Pairpoint, Candleholder, Blue, Pair	110.00
Pairpoint, Candleholder, Clear Bubble Knop, Yellow	22.00
Pairpoint, Candlestick, Amber, Clear Ball Connector, Rolled-Over Top, Pair	55.00
Pairpoint, Candlestick, Bubble Balls In Stem, Bell Base, Pair, 11 1/2 In.	150.00
Pairpoint, Candlestick, Cobalt, 11 In., Pair	95.00
Pairpoint, Candlestick, Green, Festoons & Flowers, Urn Shaped Shank, 12 In.	58.00
Pairpoint, Candlestick, Intaglio, Vaseline, 10 1/4 In.	175.00
Pairpoint, Candlestick, Silver Plated, Art Nouveau Style, Pair	75.00
Pairpoint, Candy Dish, Bubble-Ball Connector, Bubble Egg Finial On Lid	150.00
Pairpoint, Castor, Pickle, Block Glass Insert	70.00
Pairpoint, Castor, Pickle, Cranberry, Silver Overlay	200.00
Pairpoint, Castor, Pickle, Pink Plush Unlined Satin Glass	350.00
Pairpoint, Castor, Pickle, Rubena To Cranberry, Frosted Insert, Signed Frame	235.00
Pairpoint, Castor, Pickle, Tongs, Cranberry	195.00
Pairpoint, Centerpiece, Silver Plate Holder, 3 Hoof Feet, Ram's Head, 6 In.	75.00
Pairpoint, Chalice, Clear Crystal, Etched Fernery, Blue Ribbon Stem, 7 In.	100.00
Pairpoint, Champagne, Tudor, Twisted Stems, 5 1/2 In.	20.00
Pairpoint, Cigarette Holder, Roses, Garlands, Bows, Urn Shaped, Silver Plate	10.00
Pairpoint, Compote, Amber, Pair, 7 1/2 In.	155.00
Pairpoint, Compote, Belvedere Pattern, Pair	65.00
Pairpoint, Compote, Bubble Ball In Stem, Footed, Shallow, Ruby Glass, 6 In.	125.00
Pairpoint, Compote, Clear Bubble-Ball Connector In Stem, Apple Green, 7 In.	75.00
Pairpoint, Compote, Cobalt Blue, Bubble Knop In Stem, 7 X 8 In.	120.00
Pairpoint, Compote, Cobalt, Bubble, 14 X 6 In.	150.00
Pairpoint, Compote, Controlled Bubble, Ruby Red, High Standard, 12 In.	95.00
Pairpoint, Compote, Etched Butterflies, Pedestal, Starred Base	125.00
Pairpoint, Compote, Etched Fernery & Leaves, Blue Ribbon Spiral, 7 In.	100.00
Pairpoint, Compote, Intaglio, Butterfly & Web	105.00
Pairpoint, Compote, Light Green, Slender Pedestal Foot, 6 In	100.00
Pairpoint, Compote, Ruby, Controlled Bubble Clear Glass Ball In Stem, 6 In.	125.00
Pairpoint, Compote, Vaseline, Bubble Connector Stem, Copper Wheel Vintage	78.00
Pairpoint, Cracker, Asters, Silver, Marked	325.00
Pairpoint, Cup, Silver Plate, Initialed & Dated 1900	6.00
Pairpoint, Dish, Oblong, Silver, Signed, 9 In.	32.50
Pairpoint, Epergne, Grapes & Leaves, 18 1/2 In.	300.00
Pairpoint, Finger Bowl & Underplate, Cobalt Blue	32.00
Pairpoint, Inkwell, Bubble Ball, 2 3/4 In.	30.00
Pairpoint, Jar, Cracker, Hand-Painted, Footed Metal Holder, 7 X 5 1/2 In.	235.00
Pairpoint, Lamp, Acid Finish Shade, Oak Leaves, Acorns, Art Nouveau Base, SB	950.00
Pairpoint, Lamp, Art Deco, Signed, 26 X 18 In.	2450.00
Pairpoint, Lamp, Base, Brass Tree Trunk, 9 In.	95.00
Pairpoint, Lamp, Blown Out, Roses, Hummingbird, Signed Base & Shade, 14 In.	1975.00
Pairpoint, Lamp, Boudoir, Puffy, Floral & Lattice, Silver Background, 8 In.	725.00
Pairpoint, Lamp, Boudoir, Shade And Base Signed	795.00
Pairpoint, Lamp, Butterfly, Signed, 8 In.	850.00
Pairpoint, Lamp, Candle, Puffy, Blown-Out Pansies, Wooden Base, 7 3/4 In.	250.00
Pairpoint, Lamp, Carlisle Shade, 9 In.Diameter, Floral Border, Signed	345.00
Pairpoint, Lamp, Desert Oasis, Palms, Camels, W.Macy, 23 In.	850.00
Pairpoint, Lamp, Desk, Raised Diamond, 24-Point Rayed, Domed Top, 7 In.	475.00
Pairpoint, Lamp, Floral Sprays On Tan, Black Speckled, Brass Base, 16 In.	800.00
Pairpoint, Lamp, Miniature, Round Globe, Signed, 12 In.	325.00
Pairpoint, Lamp, Puffy, Green, Red, 8 In.	750.00
Pairpoint, Lamp, Reverse Painted Venetian Harbor Scene, 16 In.	895.00
Pairpoint, Lamp, Reverse Painted, Scenic, Brass Filigreed Footed Base	685.00
Pairpoint, Lamp, Stylistic Floral & Scroll, Acid Finish, Brass Base, 17 In.	900.00
Pairpoint, Lamp, The Garden Of Allah, Signed Shade & Base, 22 In.High	2400.00
Pairpoint, Nut Set, Roses, Leaves & Vines, Marked, 7 Pieces	40.00

Pairpoint, Paperweight, Blue Swan Atop Crystal Bubbly Globe, Pedestal Base 27.00
Pairpoint, Paperweight, Shells, Faceting, Yellow Ground, Blue, 2 X 2 In. 35.00
Pairpoint, Pitcher, Aqua, 1 1/2 Quart, Inverted Thumbprint, Applied Handle 50.00
Pairpoint, Plate, Cake, Pedestal, Octagonal Shaped, 4 In. 38.00
Pairpoint, Plate, Cobalt Blue, Blown, 8 1/2 In., Set Of 12 .... 125.00
Pairpoint, Plate, Large Bowl Holder, Handled 40.00
Pairpoint, Salt & Pepper, Egg Shaped, Windmills, Ships, Blue On White, Pair 200.00
Pairpoint, Sconce, Florals & Pink Band On Shade, Signed, Pair 400.00
Pairpoint, Shade, Hurricane, Birch Trees, Greens & Yellow, Signed, Pair 350.00
Pairpoint, Sugar & Creamer, Raised Berries, Signed 25.00
Pairpoint, Sugar Shaker, Delft, Blue Decoration, 4 3/4 In. 175.00
Pairpoint, Tazza, Green To Clear Engraved Vintage, 7 1/2 X 8 In. 85.00
Pairpoint, Tazza, Green To Clear, Air Bubble In Stem, 7 1/2 X 8 In. 75.00
Pairpoint, Tazza, Intaglio Cut Daisy, Fan, Wheel, Clear, Amber Rim, 8 In. 70.00
Pairpoint, Tazza, Poppies, Glass Bowl, Silver Base, Signed, 6 X 8 In. 175.00
Pairpoint, Tazza, Ruby Glass, Clear Bubble Glass Ball Stem, 6 X 6 1/4 In. 125.00
Pairpoint, Toothpick, Adelaide, Amber 14.00
Pairpoint, Tray, Purple, Pink, White Flowers, Enameled, Gold Scrolls, 12 In. 110.00
Pairpoint, Urn, Bubble On Pedestal, Intaglio Cut, 13 In. 95.00
Pairpoint, Vase, Air Trap Connector, 12 In. 95.00
Pairpoint, Vase, Amethyst, Allover Copper Wheel Cutting 95.00
Pairpoint, Vase, Amethyst, Engraved, Chalice, Pair 400.00
Pairpoint, Vase, Bubble Ball Connector In Stem, Engraved, Polished, 13 In. 125.00
Pairpoint, Vase, Bud, Amber Iridescence, Sheffield Silver Base, 7 7/8 In. 265.00
Pairpoint, Vase, Cased Ruby Crystal Liner, Silver Plated Holder, 8 In. 48.00
Pairpoint, Vase, Cobalt Blue, Bubble Ball Stem, 12 In. 83.50
Pairpoint, Vase, Cornucopia, Ruby Red On Clear, 12 In. Tall 97.50
Pairpoint, Vase, Cranberry, Vintage Design, 12 In., Pair 475.00
Pairpoint, Vase, Engraved, Amethyst Trim, 14 In. 85.00
Pairpoint, Vase, Footed, Pierced Brass Holder, Signed 45.00
Pairpoint, Vase, Trumpet, 14 In. 25.00
  Paper, Book, see also Dick Tracy, Book; Disneyana, Book;
  Lone Ranger, Book; Store, Book; Gene Autry, Book; Kate
  Greenaway, Book; Kewpie, Book; Sunbonnet Babies, Book;
  World's Fair, Book
Paper, Almanac, Ayers, 1898 .... 3.00
Paper, Almanac, Kate Greenaway, 1887 .... 45.00
Paper, Almanac, Shaker, 1886 .... 12.00
Paper, Atlas, Rand McNally, 1896 .... 15.00
Paper, Book, Adventures Of Dick Tracy & Junior, 1933, Big Little Book 7.50
Paper, Book, Alice In Wonderland, Paramount Pictures, 1934, Big Little Book 7.00
Paper, Book, Alley Oop & Dinny In The Jungles Of Moo, Big Little Book 5.75
Paper, Book, Almanac, Illustrated, Frank Leslie, 1886 .... 15.00
Paper, Book, Almanac, 1888, Kate Greenaway 45.00
Paper, Book, Apple Mary, The Swindlers, Big Little Book 8.00
Paper, Book, Arizona Kid, 1936, Big Little Book 4.00
Paper, Book, Bambi, 1942, Walt Disney, Big Little Book 12.00
Paper, Book, Bambi's Children, 1943, Walt Disney, Big Little Book 13.00
Paper, Book, Beauties Of English Landscape, Gold-Leaf Edges, 1874 .... 32.50
Paper, Book, Blondie, Trace & Color, 6 In Box 7.50
Paper, Book, Buck Jones & Ride 'Em Cowboy, Big Little Book 4.00
Paper, Book, Buck Rogers & The Doom Comet, 1935, Big Little Book 14.50
Paper, Book, Buffalo Bill Plays A Lone Hand, 1936, Big Little Book 5.00
Paper, Book, Captain Easy, Behind Enemy Lines Lines, 1943, Big Little Book 12.00
Paper, Book, Captain Midnight's Trick & Riddle Book 14.00
Paper, Book, Child's, Country Stories, Jessie Wilcox Smith Illustrations 8.00
Paper, Book, Coloring, Mickey Mouse 3.50
Paper, Book, Comic, Tad's Dog, 1912 .... 17.50
Paper, Book, Cracker Jack Riddles, 32 Pages, C. 1915 .... 9.00
Paper, Book, Dan Dunn, Secret Operative 48, Big Little Book 5.00
Paper, Book, Dick Tracy & Yogee Yamma, Big Little Book 8.50
Paper, Book, Dick Tracy On Voodoo Island, Big Little Book 6.00
Paper, Book, Dick Tracy Out West, Big Little Book 5.50
Paper, Book, Dick Tracy Solves The Penfield Mystery, Big Little Book 10.00
Paper, Book, Donald Duck Says Such Luck, Big Little Book 5.00

Paper, Book, Ellery Queen, Murdered Millionaire, No.1472, Big Little Book	6.50
Paper, Book, Famous Actresses Of The Day In America, 1st Edition, C.1899	15.00
Paper, Book, Flash Gordon And The Red Sword Invaders, Big Little Book	31.00
Paper, Book, Flash Gordon, Perils Of Mongo, Big Little Book	12.50
Paper, Book, Flowers Of Friendship, Gift Book In Box, C.1913	6.50
Paper, Book, Gang Busters Smash Through, Big Little Book	8.50
Paper, Book, Gene Autry In Law Of The Range, Big Little Book	8.50
Paper, Book, Gene Autry Public Cowboy, No.1, 1938, Big Little Book	4.00
Paper, Book, Ghost Avenger, Big Little Book	10.00
Paper, Book, Gone With The Wind, Program From Original Showing	10.00
Paper, Book, Green Hornet Strikes, Big Little Book	15.00
Paper, Book, Harrison Cady Animal Book, Linen Like Finish, C.1928, Whitman	10.00
Paper, Book, Hawks Air Ace, 1938, Big Little Book	7.00
Paper, Book, Instruction, 1940 Lionel Train	5.00
Paper, Book, Jolly Tars, Illustrations, M.M.Jamieson Jr., Ernest Nister	7.50
Paper, Book, King Of The Royal Mounted, Great Jewel Mystery, Big Little Book	14.00
Paper, Book, Life Of P.T.Barnum, Autobiography, Illustrations, Sample Copy	30.00
Paper, Book, Little Orphan Annie In The Thieves' Den, Big Little Book	6.00
Paper, Book, Little Red Riding Hood, Pop-Up, Dated 1934	20.00
Paper, Book, Little Showman Series, Jumbo And The Countryman, Pop-Up	50.00
Paper, Book, Magazine And Daily Review, Ringling Bros., Barnum & Bailey, 1920	20.00
Paper, Book, Mandrake The Magician, 1941, Big Little Book	9.50
Paper, Book, Mechanical, Peeps Into Fairyland, Pop-Out Pictures, 11 X 14 In.	125.00
Paper, Book, Men Of The Mounted, Big Little Book	7.00
Paper, Book, Mickey Mouse And The Foreign Legion, Big Little Book	10.00
Paper, Book, Mickey Mouse In The World Of Tomorrow, Big Little Book	7.00
Paper, Book, Mickey Mouse, Bell Boy Detective, Big Little Book	10.00
Paper, Book, Moon Mullins, Kayo, Big Little Book	70.00
Paper, Book, Mother Goose Magic Window, Animated Nursery Rhymes, C.1943	12.00

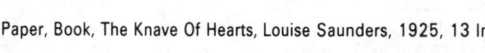

Paper, Book, The Knave Of Hearts, Louise Saunders, 1925, 13 In.

Paper, Book, Og, Son Of Fire, Big Little Book	8.00
Paper, Book, Overall Boys In Switzerland, 1916, Eulalie Osgood Grover	37.50
Paper, Book, Panama Canal, Official Handbook, Illustrated, Original Map, 1915	25.00
Paper, Book, Paper Toys For Children, Series, Baby Carriage, Lion Coffe Ad	5.00
Paper, Book, Pattern Cookbook, First Edition, Butterick Publishing Co.	20.00
Paper, Book, Perry Winkle & The Rinky Dinks, Big Little Book	12.00
Paper, Book, Poems, Old Voices, Black Dialect And Pictures, Howard Weeden	35.00
Paper, Book, Popeye In Quest Of Poopdeck Pappy, Big Little Book	5.00
Paper, Book, Prairie Bill, Big Little Book	7.00
Paper, Book, Puss-N-Boots, Pop-Up, C.1934	65.00
Paper, Book, Red Badge Of Courage, Crane, 1896, New York, D.Appleton & Co.	25.00
Paper, Book, Red Ryder And The Outlaw Of Painted Valley, Big Little Book	5.00
Paper, Book, Red Ryder, The Rimrock Killer, Big Little Book	6.00
Paper, Book, Roy Rogers, 1940s, Big Little Book	5.00
Paper, Book, Scrapbook, Roy Rogers, 120 Pages	10.00
Paper, Book, Skippy, Big Little Book	10.00

Paper, Book, Tarzan And The Ant Men, Big Little Book	21.00
Paper, Book, Tarzan And The Golden Lion, Big Little Book	21.00
Paper, Book, Tarzan's Revenge, 1938, Big Little Book	14.25
Paper, Book, Teenie Weenie, Under The Rose Bush, 1920s	24.00
Paper, Book, Terry & War In The Jungle, Big Little Book	25.00
Paper, Book, The Brownies Through The Union, Palmer Cox, 1895	20.00
Paper, Book, The Knave Of Hearts, Louise Saunders, 1925, 13 In. *Illus*	80.00
Paper, Book, The Lone Ranger Traps The Smugglers, Grosset & Dunlap, 1941	8.00
Paper, Book, The Oz Toy Book, Cutouts Of All Oz Characters, C.1915	35.00
Paper, Book, The Phantom, Sign Of Skull, Big Little Book	10.00
Paper, Book, Tom Mix, 1937, Hoard Of Montezuma, Big Little Book	7.00
Paper, Book, Useful Birds Of America, In Envelope, Church & Dwight Soda, 15	5.00
Paper, Book, 55 Japanese Prints On Rice Paper	30.00
Paper, Booklet, Jingle Jokes For Little Folks, Hires, 1901	22.00
Paper, Calendar, Marilyn Monroe, Pinup, 12 Pages	11.00
Paper, Calendar, 1892, Children Singing, Frances Brundage, Opens & Stands	25.00
Paper, Calendar, 1894, Hood's Sarsaparilla	16.00
Paper, Calendar, 1916, J.F.Milkman Millinery Co., Lady In Hat, Phyliss, 7 In.	8.50
Paper, Catalogue, Buster Brown, 1922 Brown Shoe Co.	18.00
Paper, Catalogue, Butterick Quarterly, 1919	8.00
Paper, Catalogue, Crusader Bikes, 1914	7.00
Paper, Catalogue, E.C.Meacham Arms Co., Bicycle, 1897	20.00
Paper, Catalogue, Gilbert Hall Of Science American Flyer Train, 1948	25.00
Paper, Catalogue, Lionel Train, 1929	35.00
Paper, Catalogue, Lionel, 1936-1961	250.00
Paper, Catalogue, Montgomery Ward, 1927	10.00
Paper, Catalogue, Piano, 1909, Frank L.Wing, N.Y., Information & Prices	45.00
Paper, Catalogue, Schoenhut, 1918, Toys	78.00
Paper, Catalogue, Victor Book Of The Opera, RCA, Illustrated, 1936	15.00
Paper, Directory, Troy, N.Y., 1864	50.00
Paper, Doll, A No.1 Chocolate Brownies, Wild West, Buffalo Bill, 1895	12.50
Paper, Doll, Annie Oakley, Uncut	7.00
Paper, Doll, Articulated Limbs, 2 Crepe-Paper Dresses, August 24, 1880, Pair	25.00
Paper, Doll, Aunt Jemima Doll Family, Original Envelope	25.00
Paper, Doll, Baby Sparkle Plenty, Uncut	4.50
Paper, Doll, Ballet Dolls, Whitman, 1957	5.00
Paper, Doll, Barbie & Ken, Cut Set, 1962	5.00
Paper, Doll, Betty Field, Uncut	12.00 To 17.50
Paper, Doll, Blondie Cutout Dolls, 1947, Whitman	12.50
Paper, Doll, Boston Herald, Lady With 26 Outfits	50.00
Paper, Doll, Bradley, Tru-Life, 1916	10.00
Paper, Doll, Captain Marvel, Envelope, 7 X 10 In.	12.00
Paper, Doll, Celebrity, Ziegfeld Follies, Gone With The Wind, 23 Different	125.00
Paper, Doll, Coronation Paper Dolls & Coloring Book, 1953, Saalfield	10.00
Paper, Doll, Curly Locks, Easel Stand, 2 Dolls, 5 Costumes, 6 Hats, 20 In.	48.00
Paper, Doll, Daisy Mae & Lil Abner, 1951, Saalfield	10.00
Paper, Doll, Dolly Dingle In Denmark, 3 Pages	20.00
Paper, Doll, Dolly Dingle In Holland, 3 Pages	20.00
Paper, Doll, Dolly Dingle In Sweden, 3 Pages	20.00
Paper, Doll, Dottie Darling, Pictorial Review, Sept., 1934	5.50
Paper, Doll, Dresses Worn By First Ladies Of White House, No.2164, 1937	35.00
Paper, Doll, Esther Williams, Uncut	12.00
Paper, Doll, Farbes, June 6, 1895, Uncut	10.00
Paper, Doll, Fern Bissel Rest, Let's Play Store, 1933	20.00
Paper, Doll, Flying Captain Marvel, 8 X 12 In.	4.00
Paper, Doll, Fontaine Fox Toonerville Town, Vaseline, Uncut	55.00
Paper, Doll, Frazee, Cut	10.50
Paper, Doll, Girl, 5 Costumes, C.1921	7.00
Paper, Doll, Jill & Brother, McCall, 1921, Uncut	7.00
Paper, Doll, Jolly Jane, 5 Costumes, 1923	7.00
Paper, Doll, Lettie Lane, Around The World, Russia	7.00
Paper, Doll, Little Miss Sunbeam, Set No.1 & No.2, With Dollhouse, Uncut	20.00
Paper, Doll, Mary Martin, Uncut	17.50
Paper, Doll, Mary Poppins, Uncut	4.50
Paper, Doll, Merrill, Liberty Belles, Uncut	17.50

Paper, Doll, Merrill, Soldiers & Sailors House Party, 1943, Uncut	17.50
Paper, Doll, Nagel, Cut	10.50
Paper, Doll, Nancy & Her Dolls, Saalfield, 1944	4.25
Paper, Doll, Nonesuch New England Mincemeat, German & Swiss Outfits	45.00
Paper, Doll, Parrish, Cut	10.50
Paper, Doll, Penny Dolls, Tom Thumb Series, McLoughlin	23.50
Paper, Doll, Post Cereal Zippo The Human Cannonball, Uncut, 1947	10.00
Paper, Doll, Queen Holden Books, Joan & Bobby	15.00
Paper, Doll, Queen Holden, Our Gang, 1931	30.00
Paper, Doll, Rabbit Family, McCall, 1920	7.00
Paper, Doll, Raphael Tuck, Four Dresses, Four Hats, Large	38.00
Paper, Doll, Sandy & Candy, Uncut	5.00
Paper, Doll, Sheet, Cloth, Uncut, Kellogg's Johnny Bear, Dated 1925	25.00
Paper, Doll, Susan Doll Book, Uncut	5.00
Paper, Doll, Teddy Bear, J.Ottman, 5 Outfits, 1910	300.00
Paper, Doll, Tom Corbett Space Cadet, Rocket Ships, Ray Guns	17.00
Paper, Doll, Tricia Nixon, Uncut	4.50
Paper, Doll, Twiggy, Uncut	4.50
Paper, Doll, Whitman, Pollyanna, 1941, Uncut	20.00
Paper, Doll, Whitman, Powers Models, 1942, Uncut	20.00
Paper, Encyclopedia, Dyke's Auto, 1233 Pages, Dust Jacket, 1926	16.00
Paper, Magazine, Burten's Follies Quarterly, May 1925 .... *Illus*	17.00
Paper, Magazine, Harper's Bound Weekly, 1903	160.00
Paper, Program, Ringling Bros.Circus, 1914, 9 1/2 X 7 In. .... *Illus*	11.00

Paper, Magazine, Burten's Follies Quarterly, May 1925

Paper, Program, Ringling Bros.Circus, 1914, 9 1/2 X 7 In.

Paper, Toy, The New Pretty Village, Floor Mat, 5 Houses, Figures, McLoughlin 75.00
  Paperweight, see also Baccarat, Paperweight; Gillinder, Paperweight;
  Masonic, Paperweight; Political Campaign, Paperweight;
  Rookwood, Paperweight; Shirley Temple, Paperweight;
  Store, Paperweight
Paperweight, Acorn Gas Ranges, Cast Iron 7.50
Paperweight, American, Magnum, Floral, 4 3/4 In. .... *Illus* 650.00
Paperweight, Apollo XI Moon Landing, Clear & Frosted, 1969 .... 20.00
Paperweight, Bacchus, Concentric Millefiori, 3 1/16 In. .... *Illus* 425.00
Paperweight, Bacchus, Concentric Millefiori, 3 7/16 In. .... *Illus* 475.00
Paperweight, Bacchus, Magnum Concentric Millefiori, 3 1/2 In. .... *Illus* 475.00
Paperweight, Bacchus, Magnum Concentric Millefiori, 3 1/2 In. .... *Illus* 450.00
Paperweight, Bacchus, Magnum Concentric Mushroom, 3 5/8 In. .... *Illus* 750.00
Paperweight, Bacchus, Scattered Millefiori, 3 1/8 In. .... *Illus* 475.00
Paperweight, Barker, Crystal, Poinsettias, Leaves, Faceted, 2 1/4 In. 115.00
Paperweight, Blown, 3 Groups Of Swirling Green & White Florals 35.00
Paperweight, Brass Bell, Liberty Foundry, St.Louis, Missouri, 3 In. 12.50
Paperweight, Brass, Crosby Brothers, Topeka, Kansas, Seal Of Kansas 12.50
Paperweight, Bronze, Kangaroo, 3 In. 95.00

Paperweight, American, Magnum,
Floral, 4 3/4 In.

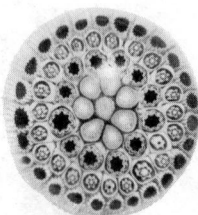

Paperweight, Bacchus,
Concentric Millefiori, 3 1/16 In.

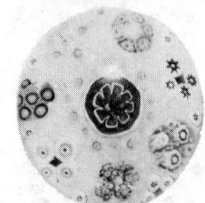

Paperweight, Bacchus, Magnum
Concentric Mushroom, 3 5/8 In.

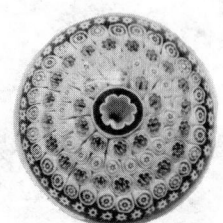

Paperweight, Bacchus,
Concentric Millefiori, 3 7/16 In.

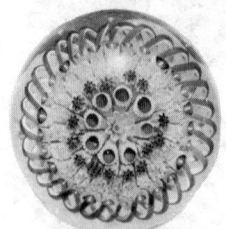

Paperweight, Bacchus,
Scattered Millefiori, 3 1/8 In.

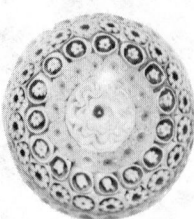

Paperweight, Bacchus, Magnum
Concentric Millefiori, 3 1/2 In.

Paperweight, Cast Iron, Pen & Pencil Holder	75.00
Paperweight, Century Of Progress, Glass Oblong	15.00
Paperweight, Chinese, Blue, Green, Red, Yellow Canes, 3 In.	35.00
Paperweight, Circular, Glass, Riverboat On Natchez, Red & White Bubbles	35.00
Paperweight, Clichy, Blue & White Swirl, Center Cane	500.00
Paperweight, Clichy, Swirl, 3 1/16 In. ....*Illus*	800.00
Paperweight, Clock, Amber, Octagonal, E.M.Welch, November 22, 1881	150.00
Paperweight, Coal Co., 1 3/4 In.	6.50
Paperweight, Cobalt Telephone, Hollow, 3 1/2 In.	20.00
Paperweight, Cobalt Telephone, Solid, 3 1/2 In.	30.00
Paperweight, Coca-Cola	15.00
Paperweight, Controlled Bubbles, Block, Round, C.1880, 3 In.	25.00
Paperweight, Cowboy Hat, Brass, Kansas City Dressed Beef	32.50
Paperweight, Cube, Cut Glass, Beveled Edges, Electric Blue, 1 3/4 In.	27.50
Paperweight, Dog, Signed Bennington	375.00
Paperweight, Don't Monkey With Anything On Desk, 3 Monkeys, Cody Memorial	10.50
Paperweight, Duro Water Pump & Tank, Metal, Wood, 3 X 4 1/2 In.	28.00
Paperweight, Figural, Horseshoe & Badge, Stone Arch Bridge	5.00
Paperweight, Figure, Porcelain, Painted, 3 1/8 In. ....*Illus*	425.00
Paperweight, Fort Dearborn, 1933 World's Fair	20.00
Paperweight, Frog, Male, Green, Yellow Eyes & Underside, 3 X 2 3/4 In.	40.00
Paperweight, Gainesville, Ga.	3.50
Paperweight, General John J.Pershing, 1917	25.00
Paperweight, Gilded Bronze Hand On Black Marble Base, Snake Entwined	67.00
Paperweight, Glass, Photo Insert, Ornate Soldier's Monument, 4 X 2 1/2 In.	10.00
Paperweight, Glass, Photo Of Scranton Steel & Iron Works, C.1890	18.00
Paperweight, God Bless Our Home, Odd Shape	20.00
Paperweight, Home Sweet Home To Mother, White Letters, Multicolor, Pontil	75.00
Paperweight, Horseman Doll Co., 60 Year Anniversary, Bronze, 1865-1925	25.00
Paperweight, Intaglio Cut Frosted Head Of Gibson Girl, U.S.Glass Co., 4 In.	65.00
Paperweight, Joe Barker, Crystal, Clear, Blooming Red Poinsettia, 2 1/4 In.	115.00
Paperweight, Joe Barker, Crystal, Clear, Red Poinsettia, Green Leaves, 2 In.	115.00

*Kaziun glass has been made by Charles Kaziun since 1942. His
paperweights have been gaining fame steadily. Most of his glass and all of
the paperweights are signed with a K designed cane worked into the design.
He makes buttons, earrings, perfume bottles, and paperweights.*

Paperweight, Livitamin, Cast Iron Anvil	8.50
Paperweight, McKinley, God's Way, No.356	25.00
Paperweight, McKinley, Music Hall, American Exposition, 4 X 2 In.	28.00
Paperweight, McKinley, Protection & Plenty, No.333	12.00

Paperweight, Clichy, Swirl, 3 1/16 In.

Paperweight, Figure, Porcelain, Painted, 3 1/8 In.

Paperweight, Memorial Hall, Frosted Except For Clear Top, 3 1/2 In.	150.00
Paperweight, Millefiori, Dated In Weight, C.1887	95.00
Paperweight, Miniature, Concentric Millefiori, Star Cut Base	150.00
Paperweight, Miniature, Latticinio Swirl, Central Complex Cane	150.00
Paperweight, Miniature, Millefiori Pattern, Star Cut Base, 19th Century	215.00
Paperweight, Mother-Of-Pearl, Gandhi On Black Glass Base, Flat	48.00
Paperweight, Multicolored Glass, Home Sweet Home, To Mother, 4 In.	75.00
Paperweight, Nailsea, Green, Pontil, 6 In.	40.00
Paperweight, National Cash Register, Iron, 3 In.	30.00
Paperweight, Pairpoint, see Pairpoint, Paperweight	
Paperweight, Patriotic Rose, Signed R.Hamon	145.00
Paperweight, Peach & Lily Rises To Top, Multicolor Spatter, Crimped, 4 In.	22.00
Paperweight, Pear, Iridescent, Black Base, 3 X 4 X 2 1/2 In.	140.00
Paperweight, Pears Soap	4.75
Paperweight, Pepsin Gum	15.00
Paperweight, Perthshire, Butterfly, Green Overlay, Signed, 2 In.	195.00
Paperweight, Pig, Sitting Position, Iron, 3 X 1 1/4 In.	16.00
Paperweight, Porcelain, Painted, 3 1/8 In. *Illus*	425.00
Paperweight, President William McKinley, Glass	16.50
Paperweight, President Wm.McKinley, 1892, Milk Glass Back, 4 X 2 1/2 In.	9.95
Paperweight, Rithner, White Spatter, Cut Candy Sticks, Mushroom Domed, C.1920	35.00
Paperweight, Rocks, Spires, Joseph Sabot In Script, 4 X 2 In.	20.00
Paperweight, Round, Advertising, Heppenstall	10.00
Paperweight, Royal Crown Cola, Metal, C.1938	4.50
Paperweight, Sand Dune	30.00
Paperweight, Scrambled, New England Glass Co.	28.00
Paperweight, Scranton Steel & Iron Works, C.1890	18.00
Paperweight, Sinclair Oil Co., Metal Model Of Dinosaur	6.50
Paperweight, Snow, Mark Twain's Home	7.00
Paperweight, St.Claire, Apple, Applied Glass Leaf & Stem, Signed	30.00
Paperweight, St.Louis Fair, Reverse Painting	30.00
Paperweight, Standing Bear, Bronze, Holding Black Marble Ball, 4 1/2 In.	45.00
Paperweight, Statue Of Liberty, Bronze	4.50
Paperweight, Sulfide, Faceted, Swan On Tortoise-Colored Base	95.00
Paperweight, Sulfide, Swan, Faceted Top	85.00
Paperweight, Tiger Lilies, Blown, Emerald Green	59.00
Paperweight, Victor Dog, Metal Plate On Marble	30.00
Paperweight, Victorian, Reverse Painting On Glass, C.1850-1890 *Illus*	65.00
Paperweight, White Friars, 1976 Bicentennial, Signed, Numbered, Box	155.00
Paperweight, Whittemore Bottle, Shape Of Perfume Bottle, Blue Rose Stopper	290.00
Paperweight, Winchester, C.1910	14.00
Paperweight, Woolworth Building, Bronze, Tallest Building In World	6.00
Paperweight, World's Columbian Expo 1893, Agricultural Building	19.00
Paperweight, Yellow & Pink Dahlia, Signed Lew Kaines, 2 In.	75.00
Paperweight, Yellowstone Park, Snow, Standing Bear	18.00
Paperweight, Ysart, Magnum Butterfly, 3 1/2 In. *Illus*	800.00
Paperweight, Ysart, Swimming Fish, Green & Red, Pebbled Sand Ground, 3 In.	240.00

Paperweight, Victorian, Reverse Painting On Glass, C.1850-1890

Paperweight, Ysart, Magnum Butterfly, 3 1/2 In.

Papier-mache is a decorative form made from paper mixed with glue, chalk, and other ingredients, then molded and baked. It becomes very hard and can be decorated. Boxes, trays, and furniture were made of papier-mache. Some of the early-nineteenth-century pieces were decorated with mother-of-pearl.

Papier-Mache, Basket, Ornate Brass Handle, Signed Jennens, 1860, 10 In.	110.00
Papier-Mache, Bottle Opener, Figural, Black Waiter, 5 In.	28.00
Papier-Mache, Bowl, Deep, C.1883, 17 In.	24.50
Papier-Mache, Box, Glove, Mother-Of-Pearl Inlaid Top, English	70.00
Papier-Mache, Box, Gold Honeycombing On Black, Geese In Flight, Dome Top	16.00
Papier-Mache, Box, Hinged, Oblong, Inlaid Mother-Of-Pearl On Lid, Queenstown	35.00
Papier-Mache, Box, Pencil, Painted Scene, Hinged Lid, 2 1/2 X 9 X 1 1/2 In.	20.00
Papier-Mache, Box, Snuff, Shoe Form, Yellow Floral, 18th Century, 3 1/4 In.	32.00
Papier-Mache, Box, Stationery, Painting After Landseer, C.1830	325.00
Papier-Mache, Case, Spectacle, Metal Inlaid Border, Central Ornament, 5 In.	15.00
Papier-Mache, Chicken, Folk Art, Life Size, Early 20th Century	95.00
Papier-Mache, Dog, 25 In.	75.00
Papier-Mache, Figurine, Beagle Hound, Glass Eyes, Bobbing Head, 3 X 7 In.	38.00
Papier-Mache, Nodder, Santa Claus	10.00
Papier-Mache, Snuffbox, Black, Pewter Trim	25.00
Papier-Mache, Snuffbox, Inlaid Mother-Of-Pearl Border, 2 X 3 X 1 In.	25.00
Papier-Mache, Snuffbox, Mother-Of-Pearl Inlay, Victorian, 2 1/2 X 1 In.	10.00
Papier-Mache, Snuffbox, With Pewter Trim	25.00
Papier-Mache, Snuffbox, 1 1/2 X 3 X 1 Inch	22.00
Papier-Mache, Spectacle Case, Border, Metal, Ornament, 5 Inch	15.00
Papier-Mache, Tray, Handled, Grape, 12 X 10 In.	128.00
Papier-Mache, Watch Stand, Brass Feet, Gilded Decoration, 4 X 7 In.	48.00
Parasol, see Umbrella	
Parasol, Black Silk, Wood Handle, 18 In.Diameter, 24 In.Long	25.00
Parasol, Folding, Carved Ivory Handle, Black Lace Over White Taffeta	40.00

Parian is a fine-grained, hard-paste porcelain named for the marble it resembles. It was first made in England in 1846 and gained in favor in the United States about 1860. Figures, tea sets, vases, and other items were made of Parian at many English and American factories.

Parian, Bust, General Robert E. Lee, 7 1/2 In.	115.00
Parian, Bust, George Stevenson, Wedgwood & Sons, 1858, E.W.Wyon Sculpt.	425.00
Parian, Bust, Oenone, Flowers & Leaves In Hair, 1860, 11 1/4 X 6 In.	485.00
Parian, Bust, Prince & Princess Of Wales, John Rose, 1863, 17 In., Pair	150.00
Parian, Bust, Princess Alexander & Prince Of Wales, Coalport, 14 In., Pair	150.00
Parian, Bust, Sir Walter Scott, Germany, No.1829016, 6 In.	30.00
Parian, Bust, Veiled Lady, 19th Century, 10 In.	35.00
Parian, Bust, Washington, 7 In.	32.00
Parian, Cheese Keeper, Shakespeare's House Form, Signed, Marked, Dated 1847	295.00
Parian, Creamer, Figural, Swan, Swan-Neck Handle, White & Blue	32.00
Parian, Ewer, Green & White Glaze, Raised Decoration, 8 1/2 In.	32.00
Parian, Figurine, Dorothea, John Bell, C.1868, 14 In.	275.00
Parian, Figurine, Fishnet Lady & Man Holding Basket Of Fish, 7 1/2 In., Pair	135.00
Parian, Figurine, Girl Kneeling In Prayer, 9 In.	51.00
Parian, Figurine, Girl With Bundle Of Wheat On Her Back, English, 7 3/4 In.	80.00
Parian, Figurine, Half Nude, Reclining	155.00
Parian, Figurine, Lady With Dove, 9 In.	85.00
Parian, Figurine, Man And Lady, Bennington, 11 In.	300.00
Parian, Figurine, Nude Riding Lioness, 5 1/2 In.	27.00
Parian, Figurine, Peacock, White, 9 In.	24.00
Parian, Figurine, Young Girl, Sitting In Chair, 9 1/2 In.	75.00
Parian, Jar, Cracker, Gold Washed Metal Fittings, 8 In.	145.00
Parian, Pitcher, Grapes, Leaves In Relief, Twig Handle, C.1848, 3 X 5 In.	45.00
Parian, Pitcher, Water, Cupids And Grapes	200.00
Parian, Ring Tree, Child's Hand, 4 In.	55.00
Parian, Vase, Boy & Girl Golfers, Pastel Shades, Gold Sticks, 4 1/2 In.	44.00
Parian, Vase, Hand Holding Flower, 6 In.	30.00
Parian, Vase, In Hand, Rings On 2 Fingers, Scene In Oval Vase, 1868, 9 In.	150.00
Parian, Vase, Light Blue, White Aventurine, Twig Handled, 8 In., Pair	84.00
Parian, Vase, Pastel Shades, 4 1/2 In.	44.00
Parian, Vase, White, Light Blue Background, 8 In.	84.00

Vieux Paris, or Old Paris, is porcelain ware that is known to have been made in Paris in the eighteenth or early nineteenth century but has no identifying manufacturer's mark.

Paris, Bowl, Attached Scalloped Plate, Pink Roses, 2 Handles, 4 1/2 In.	45.00
Paris, Console Set, Basketwork, Gilt Decorations, Early 1800s, 3 Piece	450.00
Paris, Cup & Saucer, Bisque Lions Masks In Handles, Scenic, Gold	35.00
Paris, Dessert Set, Cobalt & Gold, Multicolored Flowers, 1850, 5 Piece	55.00
Paris, Dessert Set, Gold, Floral, Medallions, Napoleon III, 11 Piece	325.00
Paris, Tazza, Hand-Painted, Artist Signed, Gold, 18th Century	75.00
Paris, Tray, Hand-Painted Flowers & Bird, Round, 11 In.	25.00
Paris, Vase, Porcelain, 5 In., Pair	150.00

Pate de verre is an ancient technique in which glass is made by blending and refining powdered glass of different colors into molds. The process was revived by French glassmakers, especially Galle, around the end of the nineteenth century.

Pate De Verre, Figurine, Duck, Blues & Greens, A.Walter, Berge, 5 In.	650.00
Pate De Verre, Inkwell, Blue, Red Fruit, Multicolor Giant Fly, Walter, Berge	1050.00
Pate De Verre, Paperweight, Beetle, Green & Yellow Foliage, Daum Nancy, 4 In.	875.00
Pate De Verre, Vase, Bottle Shape, Poppies, Pontil, Short Neck, Red, Gray, 6 In.	210.00
Pate De Verre, Vase, Lemon Yellow, Raised Floral Border, Fruit, 4 In.	495.00
Pate De Verre, Vase, Raised Flowers, Bunches Of Cherries, Yellow, 4 In.	425.00

Pate-sur-pate means paste on paste. The design was made by painting layers of slip on the ceramic piece until a relief decoration was formed. The method was developed at the Sevres factory in France about 1850. It became even more famous at the English Minton factory about 1870.

Pate-Sur-Pate, Plaque, Child Cutting Wheat, Cobalt Blue, Framed, 7 1/2 In.	225.00
Pate-Sur-Pate, Plaque, Nude Nymph, Blue Velvet, Gold Frame, 9 X 12 In.	350.00
Pate-Sur-Pate, Plate, 3 Miniature Panels On White, Signed, Marked, 3 X 1 In.	250.00
Pate-Sur-Pate, Vase, Climb Up A Golden Rope, 2 Cherubs, 2 Handles, 7 In.	450.00
Pate-Sur-Pate, Vase, Green, Oval Scene Of Maiden In White Relief, 6 In.	35.00
Pate-Sur-Pate, Vase, Portrait, Green & White	65.00
Patent Model, Cartridge Loading Device, Tin, Wood, 10 1/2 In. ....*Illus*	150.00
Patent Model, Hull Of Ship, Operating Rudder, Wood, 1876, 25 In. ....*Illus*	125.00
Patent Model, Inkstand, Grain Painted, Grapevine, Wood, 4 3/4 In ....*Illus*	125.00
Patent Model, Inkstand, Pincushion On Brass Base, Cup, Sponge ....*Illus*	50.00
Patent Model, Magic Lantern, Black Painted Tin, 1864, 13 In. ....*Illus*	70.00
Patent Model, Rotary Engine, Wood, T.E.Stewart, 1874, 12 In. ....*Illus*	100.00
Patent Model, Submarine, E.Bazin, No Tag ....*Illus*	300.00

Paul Revere pottery was made at several locations in and around Boston between 1906 and 1942. The pottery was operated as a settlement-house type of program for teen-aged girls. Many pieces were signed S.E.G. for Saturday Evening Girls. The firm concentrated on children's dishes and tiles. Decorations were outlined in black and filled in with color.

Patent Model, Cartridge Loading Device, Tin, Wood, 10 1/2 In.

Patent Model, Hull Of Ship, Operating Rudder, Wood, 1876, 25 In.

Patent Model, Inkstand, Grain Painted, Grapevine, Wood, 4 3/4 In

Patent Model, Inkstand, Pincushion On Brass Base, Cup, Sponge

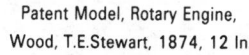

Patent Model, Magic Lantern, Black Painted Tin, 1864, 13 In.

Patent Model, Rotary Engine,
Wood, T.E.Stewart, 1874, 12 In.

Patent Model, Submarine, E.Bazin, No Tag

Paul Revere, Bowl, Green, Ring Foot, SEG, 10 In.	24.00
Paul Revere, Bowl, Squirrel Scene In Center, Artist Signed, May 1926	75.00
Paul Revere, Paperweight, Yellow, White Swan Swimming, 1914, Signed, 2 1/2 In.	68.00
Paul Revere, Pitcher, Aqua Glaze, Signed J., Dated 10-24, 4 1/4 In.	50.00
Paul Revere, Pitcher, Semi-Gloss Blue, White Top, 6 3/4 X 5 In.	48.00
Paul Revere, Plate, Brown, Signed SEG	20.00
Paul Revere, Pot, Flower, Blue, SEG, 4 1/2 In.	18.00
Paul Revere, Salt, Figural, Chick, Dark Blue, 2 3/4 X 3 1/4 In.	40.00
Paul Revere, Tile, Boat Scene, Artist Signed, Dated October, 1927	50.00
Paul Revere, Vase, Blue, High Glaze, 7 In.	20.00
Paul Revere, Vase, Bulbous, Pink, Signed, 5 1/2 In.	30.00
Paul Revere, Vase, Dark Blue With Black Speckles, 8 1/4 In.	32.00
Paul Revere, Vase, Incised Bands Of White Tulips, Blue, Green, Signed, Dated	225.00

Peachblow glass originated about 1883 at Hobbs, Brockunier and Company of Wheeling, West Virginia. It is a glass that shades from yellow to peach. It was lined in white. New England peachblow is a one-layer glass with a lining shading from red to white. Mt.Washington peachblow shades from pink to blue. Reproductions of peachblow have been made, but they are of a poor quality and can be detected.

Peachblow, see also Gunderson, Peachblow, Sewing Tool, Darner, Webb, Peachblow

Peachblow, Basket, Basket Weave Pattern, Two Handles, Marked	18.00
Peachblow, Basket, Bride's, New Martinsville	295.00
Peachblow, Bottle, Perfume, Webb, Acid Finish, Gold Butterfly, 4 3/4 In.	547.00
Peachblow, Bowl, Bride's, New Martinsville, Glossy Rose Pink, 10 1/4 In.	180.00
Peachblow, Bowl, Cambridge, Pink, Etched Floral, 8 Sided, Footed, 7 1/2 In.	48.00
Peachblow, Bowl, Crimped, Ruffled Edge, Footed, Signed Webb & Son, 11 In.	225.00
Peachblow, Bowl, Finger, New England, 5 X 2 1/2 In.	250.00
Peachblow, Bowl, Finger, Wheeling, Glossy, 4 1/2 In.	425.00
Peachblow, Bowl, Sandwich, White To Rose To White, New England, 7 X 3 1/2 In.	200.00
Peachblow, Bowl, Square, Ruffly Edge, Pearlized Finish, 6 1/2 In.	115.00
Peachblow, Cruet, Red To Yellow, Yellow Case, Frosted Handle & Stopper, Satin	650.00
Peachblow, Cruet, Wheeling, Glossy, C.1880, 6 1/2 In. ....*Illus*	275.00
Peachblow, Dish, New Martinsville, Square, 4 1/2 In.Diameter	108.00
Peachblow, Ewer, Applied Amber Handle, English, 7 In.	125.00
Peachblow, Ewer, English, Ruffled Top, Applied Amber Handle, Shading, 7 In.	80.00
Peachblow, Gunderson, see Gunderson, Peachblow	
Peachblow, Mustard, Wheeling	215.00

Peachblow, Cruet, Wheeling, Glossy, C.1880, 6 1/2 In.

Peachblow, Pear, Curved, Open Stem, Glossy, 5 In.	125.00 To 225.00
Peachblow, Pear, Pink To White, 5 1/4 X 2 1/4 In.	90.00
Peachblow, Pear, Stem, New England	115.00
Peachblow, Pear, Stem, Pink To White, 4 1/2 In.	195.00
Peachblow, Pitcher, Milk, Leaf On Front, Applied Handle, Webb	175.00
Peachblow, Pitcher, 6 1/2 In.	550.00
Peachblow, Rose Bowl, New England, Crimped Rim, 3 1/2 In.	500.00
Peachblow, Rose Bowl, New England, 3 In.Across X 2 3/4 In.High	325.00
Peachblow, Rose Bowl, Spherical Shaped, Wheeling, 3 In.Diameter	225.00
Peachblow, Swan, Cambridge, 2 1/2 In.	22.00
Peachblow, Toothpick, New England, Glossy, Square Top	375.00

Peachblow, Toothpick, New England, Light Yellow To Light Pink, Tricornered	295.00
Peachblow, Toothpick, Square Top, New England	345.00
Peachblow, Toothpick, Wheeling, Rose Shaded To Yellow, White Cased, Glossy	150.00
Peachblow, Tumbler, New England, Deep Raspberry Halfway Down, Glossy	325.00
Peachblow, Tumbler, New England, 2 1/2 In.	195.00
Peachblow, Tumbler, Wheeling, Glossy, 3 3/4 In.	325.00
Peachblow, Tumbler, Wheeling, Red Shaded To Yellow, White Lining, 3 7/8 In.	350.00
Peachblow, Vase, Amber Holder, Wheeling	1350.00
Peachblow, Vase, Bulbous, Gold, Red Mahogany, Wheeling, 9 X 5 In.	495.00
Peachblow, Vase, English, Pink To Rose, White Lining, Gold Floral, Signed	300.00
Peachblow, Vase, Gourd Shaped, Webb, 5 1/2 In.	75.00
Peachblow, Vase, Mt.Washington, Blue-Gray Bottom To Pink Top, 12 In.	950.00
Peachblow, Vase, New England, Blue & Purple Flowers, Green Leaves, 9 1/4 In.	300.00
Peachblow, Vase, New England, Jack-In-The-Pulpit, 5 In.	150.00
Peachblow, Vase, New England, Square Top, Rose To White, 5 In.	300.00
Peachblow, Vase, New England, Trumpet, Ruffled Top, Deep Coloring, 10 1/4 In.	450.00
Peachblow, Vase, Pink Floral, Yellow Leaves, Enameled, Ruffled, 10 1/2 In.	120.00
Peachblow, Vase, Rose To White, Gold & Brown Dragonfly, Floral, 8 In., Pair	850.00
Peachblow, Vase, Sandwich Glass, 5 1/4 In.	125.00
Peachblow, Vase, Stevens & Williams, Applied Decorations, 7 1/2 In.	650.00
Peachblow, Vase, Webb, Red To Rose, 8 X 3 In.	395.00
Peachblow, Vase, Wheeling, Acid Finish, Mahogany, 8 In.	685.00
Peachblow, Vase, Wheeling, Deep Mahogany To Peach, 15 In.	1350.00
Peachblow, Vase, Wheeling, Mahogany To Mustard, Bulbous Bottom, 9 In.	595.00
Peachblow, Vase, White Lining, Egg Shape, Crimped Top, 7 1/2 In.	200.00
Peachblow, Vase, Yellow To Mahogany Color, 3 In.	375.00
Peachblow, Water Set, C.1950, 5 Piece	155.00
Peachblow, Whiskey, New England	275.00
Pearl, Card Case, Calling, Hand-Carved, C.1900	25.00
Pearl, Chopsticks, Lacquered Case	15.00
Pearl, Cigarette Holder, Inlaid Coral	22.00
Pearl, Knife, Fruit, Twisted Handles, Set Of Six	34.50
Pearl, Needle Case, Quiver Shape, Silver Insert, Gold Mounts	58.00
Pearl, Nut Pick, Sterling Silver Bands, Handled, Set Of Six	55.00
Pearl, Opera Glasses, see Opera Glasses	
Pearl, Server, Cake, Handled, Sterling Silver Trim	18.00

Peking glass is a Chinese cameo glass of the eighteenth and nineteenth centuries.

Peking Glass, Bottle, Cobalt Floral Overlay On White, Cobalt Stopper, 4 In.	75.00
Peking Glass, Bottle, Snuff, Blue Cameo On White, Oriental Man, 4 1/2 In.	85.00
Peking Glass, Bottle, Snuff, Red Foliage On White, Double Gourd, 3 In.	285.00
Peking Glass, Bowl, Clear Body, Flared Ruby Rim, Straight Base, 3 X 7 In.	30.00
Peking Glass, Bowl, Deep Amethyst, Stand, 4 X 4 In.	36.00
Peking Glass, Bowl, Pale Green In, White Out, Children Playing, Enamel, 8 In.	150.00
Peking Glass, Bowl, Wheel Cut Red To White, 4 1/2 X 5 7/8 In.	850.00
Peking Glass, Jar, Urn Shape, Royal Blue On White, Cameo Cover, 5 3/4 In.	575.00
Peking Glass, Vase, Blue To Milky White, Flower On Back, 11 In.	200.00
Peking, Tray, Enamel, Oriental Lady, Scenery, 12 X 7 1/2 In.	110.00

Peloton glass is European glass with small threads of colored glass rolled onto the surface of clear or colored glass. It is sometimes called spaghetti, or shredded coconut glass.

Peloton, Bowl, Candy, Green, Dark Red Threading, Iridescent, Scalloped, 8 In.	185.00
Peloton, Cruet, Clear, White & Pink Threading, Clear Stopper	275.00
Peloton, Pitcher, Coral, Pink, Red, White, Yellow & Blue, Ribbed Handle	275.00
Peloton, Tumbler, Amber, Pink, Yellow, Green & White Fragments	110.00
Peloton, Vase, Black Amethyst, Embedded White Threadings, Floral, 7 In.	145.00
Peloton, Vase, Clear, Blue Threading, Bulbous Bottom, Straight Collared, 4 In.	55.00
Peloton, Vase, Cobalt Coconut Threads On Clear, Polished Bottom, 8 X 6 In.	72.00
Peloton, Vase, Opaque Black Amethyst, Embedded White Threads & Enamel, 7 In.	145.00
Pen, see Store, Pen	
Pencil, see Store, Pencil	
Pennsbury, Bowl, Fruit, Sweet Adeline, Oval, 11 3/4 X 8 In.	15.00
Pennsbury, Figurine, Bird, 3 1/4 X 7 In.	20.00

Pennsbury, Figurine, Rooster, 10 1/2 X 8 In. 42.00
Pennsbury, Mug, Here's Looking At You 12.00

Peters and Reed Pottery Company of Zanesville, Ohio, was founded by
John D. Peters and Adam Reed in 1897. Chromal, Landsun, Montene,
Pereco, and Persian are some of the art lines that were made until the
company closed in 1920.

Peters & Reed, see also Zane

Peters & Reed, Bowl & Frog, Zaneware, Blue Matte, 10 In. 18.00
Peters & Reed, Bowl, Pereco, Butterflies, Matte Green On Red Clay, 6 1/2 In. 10.00
Peters & Reed, Bowl, Pereco, Green, 10 1/2 X 2 In. 18.00
Peters & Reed, Bowl, Pereco, Green, 3 1/2 X 8 1/2 In. 24.00
Peters & Reed, Box, Window, Moss Aztec, 2 Ladies, Man With Harp, Ferrell 75.00
Peters & Reed, Cream, Glaze Drips, Zanesville Mark, 12 X 5 In. 80.00
Peters & Reed, Jug, Cavalier & Florals On Brown Glaze, 7 1/2 In. 75.00
Peters & Reed, Jug, Lion, Floral, 5 In. 45.00
Peters & Reed, Jug, 2 George Washington Portraits On Each Side, 10 1/2 In. 75.00
Peters & Reed, Mug, Cavalier, Brown Glaze, 5 1/2 In. 50.00
Peters & Reed, Mug, High Glaze, Sprigged On Floral, 5 3/4 In. 25.00
Peters & Reed, Vase, Aztec, 6 In. 22.00
Peters & Reed, Vase, Blue, Landsun Line, 5 In. 20.00
Peters & Reed, Vase, Cream, Brown & Green Glaze Drip Lines, Zaneware, 12 In. 80.00
Peters & Reed, Vase, Garlands, Montene, 11 In. 45.00
Peters & Reed, Vase, George Washington Profile, 7 1/2 In. 75.00
Peters & Reed, Vase, Lion Decoration, Handle, 5 In. 48.00
Peters & Reed, Vase, Moss Aztec, 8 In. 34.00
Peters & Reed, Vase, Moss Aztec, 10 3/4 In. 37.00
Peters & Reed, Vase, Moss Aztec, 14 1/2 In. 34.00
Peters & Reed, Vase, Oak Leaf Columns, Terra-Cotta, Green Background, 14 In. 75.00
Peters & Reed, Vase, Sheenware, 11 In. 35.00
Peters & Reed, Vase, Slip Floral Decoration, 11 In. 65.00
Peters & Reed, Vase, Sprigged Floral Decoration, 11 In. 55.00
Pewabic, Box, Bird Of Paradise Cover, Pink & High Luster Light Green, 4 In. 150.00
Pewabic, Vase, Golden Brown Textured Glaze, 11 X 6 In. 245.00
Pewabic, Vase, Matte Milk Chocolate Finish, Bulbous, Signed, 10 X 8 In. 155.00

Pewter is a metal alloy of tin and lead. Some of the pewter made after
about 1840 has a slightly different composition and is called Britannia
metal.

Pewter, Basin, Israel Trask, Beverly, Mass, 1810, 7 1/4 In. 475.00
Pewter, Basin, Woodbury Pewterers, 10 In. 80.00
Pewter, Beaker, Flaring Rim, American, 3 X 3 In. 35.00
Pewter, Bowl, Copper Washed, C.1900 .... 18.00
Pewter, Bowl, Kayserzinn, Open Shellfish Center, Art Nouveau, 9 1/2 X 4 In. 60.00
Pewter, Bowl, Octagonal, Enamel Rooster, Flower, Tree, Marked China, Set Of 4 ..... 40.00
Pewter, Bowl, Scalloped Edge, Crescent Mark, 1 1/4 X 9 3/4 In. 16.00
Pewter, Bowl, Stamped Made In London, 2 1/2 X 10 In. 95.00
Pewter, Box, Chinese, Set With Stones, Hinged, 4 In. 26.00
Pewter, Box, Dog Finial, Round, Chinese, 2 1/2 In. 22.50
Pewter, Box, Jewel, Raised Hunting Scenes, 6 In. 250.00
Pewter, Box, Oval, Hinged, Swirled, German, 3 1/4 X 2 1/4 In. 45.00
Pewter, Box, Pill, Raised Peacock, Round, 2 In. 16.00
Pewter, Candelabra, Brass Bobeches, Art Nouveau, Pair 50.00
Pewter, Candelabra, Scroll Legs, Leaves, Brass Candle Cup, Art Nouveau, Pair 225.00
Pewter, Candlestick, Baluster Shape, C.1800, 11 In., Pair 500.00
Pewter, Candlestick, Danish, 6 In., Pair 26.00
Pewter, Candlestick, French, 1750, Decorate, Pair, 9 1/2 In. 225.00
Pewter, Candlestick, Gleason, 7 1/2 In., Pair 165.00
Pewter, Candlestick, Russian Wolfhound Base, Mayflower Mark, Pair 45.00
Pewter, Candlestick, Saucer Base, Cincinnati, 10 In. 150.00
Pewter, Capstan, Cylindrical, English 65.00
Pewter, Castor Set, Revolving, Gothic, Blown Bottles, Center Post Handle 95.00
Pewter, Chamberstick, James Dixon & Sons, Sheffield, Pair 85.00
Pewter, Charger, American, Samuel Hamlin, Marked, 1767-1801, 13 1/2 In. 595.00
Pewter, Charger, English, 18th Century, 15 In. 125.00

Pewter, **Charger,** London, 15 In.	165.00
Pewter, **Charger,** Samuel Ellis English, C.1725-50, 15 In.	175.00
Pewter, **Charger,** Thomas Swanson, London, 1765, 16 1/2 In.	185.00
Pewter, **Charger,** Yates-London, Hammered Booge, Late 18th Century, 16 1/2 In.	395.00
Pewter, **Coffeepot,** Acorn Shape, Gooseneck Spout, Mono B, Marked New Amsterdam	45.00
Pewter, **Coffeepot,** Dutch, Black, Dark Floral, 18th Century, 16 1/2 In.	275.00
Pewter, **Coffeepot,** Embossed Flowers, White Porcelain Inserts, Kayserzinn	95.00
Pewter, **Coffeepot,** Enamel, C.1895 ....*Illus*	85.00
Pewter, **Coffeepot,** Enamel, Long Spout ....*Illus*	85.00
Pewter, **Coffeepot,** Gooseneck, Lacy Handle, Bulbous, 3 X 3 In.	20.00
Pewter, **Coffeepot,** H.Homan, American	225.00
Pewter, **Coffeepot,** Octagonal, James Dixon & Sons, C.1840, 14 In.	90.00
Pewter, **Coffeepot,** Patina, Copper Bottom, Leaf Finial	125.00
Pewter, **Coffeepot,** Plain, 4 X 6 In.	27.50
Pewter, **Coffeepot,** Roswell Gleason, C.1840	325.00
Pewter, **Coffeepot,** Shaw & Fisher, Sheffield, 9 1/2 In.	80.00
Pewter, **Coffeepot,** Sheets Rockford 1875, 8 1/2 In.	56.00
Pewter, **Communion Token,** Scottish, Early 19th Century	10.00
Pewter, **Compote,** Dolphin Stem, Rice	20.00
Pewter, **Compote,** Flagg & Homan	25.00
Pewter, **Compote,** 609 Rockford, Marked, 7 X 6 In.	35.00
Pewter, **Console Set,** Wilcox	32.00
Pewter, **Cup,** Chalice, Kayserzinn, No.4083, 7 In.	95.00
Pewter, **Cup,** Marriage, Engraved Band, Rogers Smith & Co., Conn., No.1502, Pair	25.00
Pewter, **Cup,** Measuring, Pint, James Yaks, C.1800, Fishtail Handle	98.00
Pewter, **Cup,** Salt, Footed, C.1750, 3 3/8 In.	185.00
Pewter, **Dish,** English, 12 1/4 In.	115.00
Pewter, **Dish,** Flowers & Leaves, 3 Section, Nekrassof, 13 1/2 In.	24.95
Pewter, **Dish,** Hammered, 18th Century, Townsend & Compton, 14 3/4 In.	100.00
Pewter, **Dish,** Hot Water, 9 1/2 In.	128.00

Pewter, Coffeepot, Enamel, C.1895

Pewter, Coffeepot, Enamel, Long Spout

Pewter, **Dish,** Leaf Form, Greenish-White Jade Handle, Brass Rim, Chinese, 5 In.	22.00
Pewter, **Dish,** Oval Meat, Watts & Harton, London, C.1810, 17 X 13 In.	375.00
Pewter, **Dish,** Pumpkin Feet, Fluted, Rectangular, Flagg & Homan	57.50
Pewter, **Dish,** Vegetable, Covered, W.S.Pewter, 9 X 11 In.	20.00
Pewter, **Dish,** Warming, Duck Form, Chinese, Mid-19th Century, 15 In.	110.00
Pewter, **Figurine,** Cherub Holding Card Salver, 4 In.	30.00
Pewter, **Flagon,** Wine, Decorative Band, Double-Domed Lid, C.1760	2250.00
Pewter, **Flagon,** 2 Chalices, Reed & Barton, C.1840	850.00
Pewter, **Flask,** Hip, To Thee, Raised Spider Web, Round	60.00
Pewter, **Foot Warmer,** Ring Handle, Oval, 7 X 11 1/2 In.	100.00
Pewter, **Funnel,** 6 In.	74.00
Pewter, **Goblet,** Footed, Marked Genuine Pewter, 7 In.	25.00
Pewter, **Goblet,** Queen City Silver Mark, Set Of 12	175.00
Pewter, **Holder,** For Car Vase	16.50
Pewter, **Inkstand,** Treasury, Double Lidded, English	195.00
Pewter, **Inkwell,** Bulldog With Pipe In Mouth	75.00
Pewter, **Inkwell,** Elephant's Head, Monkey Finial Porcelain Inset	125.00
Pewter, **Inkwell,** Kayserzinn, 4 People In Toboggan	245.00
Pewter, **Inkwell,** On Free-Form Platter, Kayserzinn, 10 1/2 In.	110.00
Pewter, **Inkwell,** Urn Shape, Sander On Tray, Dutch Mark, C.1870, 10 1/8 In.	225.00
Pewter, **Inkwell,** Whitcomb, K876, Hinge Cover	53.00

Pewter, Jug, Ale, Quart, C.1800, 8 In.	210.00
Pewter, Jug, Beverage, Poole, 7 1/4 X 8 1/2 In.	75.00
Pewter, Jug, Tudoric, Art Nouveau, Covered, 4 1/2 In.	35.00
Pewter, Jug, Wine, P.Seaton Cricketers Inn, Greenwich, C.1820, 3 1/2 In.	165.00
Pewter, Lamp, Camphene, 8 In.	230.00
Pewter, Lamp, Hand, Camphene, Twin Tube, 4 X 5 In.	155.00
Pewter, Lamp, Putnam, Signed, 9 In.	385.00
Pewter, Lamp, Whale Oil, Handle, Yale & Curtis, 3 1/2 In.	125.00
Pewter, Leaf, Nekrassof, 17 In.	30.00
Pewter, Lid, Corn Leaves Around Top, Allover Jewel-Like Pattern, Finial	78.00
Pewter, Match Holder, Standing Negro, Hand Polished	12.00
Pewter, Measure, Letters Around Top, Double Deciliter	35.00
Pewter, Measure, Set Of 5, Graduated, 1 3/4 To 4 1/4 In., French	175.00
Pewter, Mirror, Looking Glass, Chinese	85.00
Pewter, Mold, Chocolate, Elk, 2 Section, Hinged, 3 1/2 X 5 In.	28.00
Pewter, Mold, Ice Cream, Bell With Marriage On Interior	20.00
Pewter, Mold, Ice Cream, Chicken	15.00
Pewter, Mold, Ice Cream, Chicken On Nest	15.00
Pewter, Mold, Ice Cream, Dahlia	20.00
Pewter, Mold, Ice Cream, Eagle	35.00
Pewter, Mold, Ice Cream, Football, Hinged, 3 Part	13.50
Pewter, Mold, Ice Cream, Golfer	25.00
Pewter, Mold, Ice Cream, Heart	15.00
Pewter, Mold, Ice Cream, Heart & Cupid	20.00
Pewter, Mold, Ice Cream, Heart And Cupid With Arrow	25.00
Pewter, Mold, Ice Cream, Heart And 4-Leaf Clover	25.00
Pewter, Mold, Ice Cream, Hen	15.00
Pewter, Mold, Ice Cream, Hinged, Banana	22.50
Pewter, Mold, Ice Cream, Oval Ribbed Basket	25.00
Pewter, Mold, Ice Cream, Rabbit	15.00
Pewter, Mold, Ice Cream, Rose	20.00
Pewter, Mold, Ice Cream, Small Pumpkin, S & Co., 600	22.00
Pewter, Mold, Ice Cream, Strawberry	28.00
Pewter, Mold, Ice Cream, Strawberry, No.608 On Side	18.00
Pewter, Mold, Ice Cream, Three Little Pigs	35.00
Pewter, Mold, Ice Cream, Turkey	18.00 To 22.50
Pewter, Mold, Ice Cream, Walnut	20.00
Pewter, Mug, Gaskell & Chambers, Birmingham, Pint Size	110.00
Pewter, Mug, Gill & C.Wilson	85.00
Pewter, Mug, Handled, Whiskey, 2 In.	50.00
Pewter, Mug, James Yates, Early 19th Century, 4 1/2 In.	65.00
Pewter, Mug, James Yates, 1/2 Pint, English	55.00
Pewter, Mug, JB& Co., English, Pint	25.00
Pewter, Mug, Old Musty Ale-Bunker Hill Breweries, Etched, Glass Bottom, 4 In.	25.00
Pewter, Mug, Pint, Gaskell & Chambers, Birmington	90.00
Pewter, Napkin Ring, see Napkin Ring	
Pewter, Noggin, English, One Gill, C.1840	37.50
Pewter, Pitcher, American, Covered, 1 Gallon	425.00
Pewter, Pitcher, American, 2 Quart	37.50
Pewter, Pitcher, Brass Handle, China, 6 In.	25.00
Pewter, Pitcher, Covered, Roswell Gleason	350.00
Pewter, Pitcher, Freeman Porter, Westbrook, Maine, 1840	375.00
Pewter, Pitcher, Pairpoint, Signed, 8 1/2 In.	25.00
Pewter, Pitcher, Syrup, Lid, Marked Genuine Pewter	25.00
Pewter, Pitcher, Water, Cover, Daniel Curtiss, Albany, N.Y., 1824	950.00
Pewter, Pitcher, Water, Priscilla	40.00
Pewter, Planter, Squirrels Eating Acorns, Kayserzinn, Footed, 7 1/2 In.	65.00
Pewter, Plate, Beindorf Blockzinn, German, 9 In.	35.00
Pewter, Plate, Crowned Rose Touchmark, 9 In., Set Of 6	295.00
Pewter, Plate, English, 18th Century, 9 In.	80.00
Pewter, Plate, English, 8 3/4 In.	65.00
Pewter, Plate, Indian Chief Smoking Pipe, Raised, 4 In.	14.00
Pewter, Plate, Kayserzinn, Birds & Berry Sprig Border, No.4315, 10 In.	50.00
Pewter, Plate, Kayserzinn, Floral & Insects, Numbered, 10 In.	80.00

Pewter, Plate, Marked 36, 9 3/4 In.	75.00
Pewter, Plate, Townsend And Compton, Early 19th Century, 8 1/2 In.	65.00
Pewter, Plate, 3 Touch Marks, 2-Headed Griffin, Rampant Lion, S.W.Flixzinn	55.00
Pewter, Platter, Cock, Hen, Game Birds Center, Kayserzinn, No.4342, 16 1/2 In.	46.50
Pewter, Platter, Fish, Fish In Center, Kayserzinn, 21 X 10 In.	120.00
Pewter, Porringer, American, SG Reversed	250.00
Pewter, Porringer, Crown Handle, 5 In.	230.00
Pewter, Porringer, Crown Handle, 5 1/2 In.	165.00
Pewter, Porringer, Crown, Signed Stede, 4 In.	12.00
Pewter, Porringer, Handles, French, 6 In.	125.00
Pewter, Porringer, Stede, 8 1/2 In.	17.00
Pewter, Porringer, Tasting, Dome-Based, Heart & Crescent Handle, C.1800	375.00
Pewter, Porringer, 2 Handles, French, 6 In.	125.00
Pewter, Pot, Copper Bottom, 1860, Leaf Finial, Marked, 10 In.	95.00
Pewter, Pot, Signed Boardman, 12 In.	280.00
Pewter, Salt & Pepper, Shaped Like Beer Steins	5.00
Pewter, Salver, Bifid Loop Handle, Handle, Marked, 6 In.	39.00
Pewter, Server, Three Well, Applied Handles, 10 1/2 In.	50.00
Pewter, Spittoon, Ring-Handled, Josia Danforth	270.00
Pewter, Spoon, Wedding, Dutch	18.00
Pewter, Stein, Dated, 1774, 1830, & 1923, 1 Liter	275.00
Pewter, Stein, Engraved, Bottom Mark, 1820	3000.00
Pewter, Stein, Guild, Dated 1709, 15 In.	475.00
Pewter, Stein, Kayserzinn, Double Acorn, No.9911, 10 In.	95.00
Pewter, Sugar & Creamer, Incised, Open, 3 In.	15.00
Pewter, Syrup, Covered, H.H.Graves, Middletown, Conn., 1850	200.00
Pewter, Tankard, Embossed Grapes & Leaves, Handled, Signed Etain, 6 In.	45.00
Pewter, Tankard, Inscribed William, English, 1/2 Pint	75.00
Pewter, Tankard, Lidded, R.Yates, English, Quart	750.00
Pewter, Tankard, Threaded Ball Feet, Reed & Barton, C.1840, 6 X 8 In.	145.00
Pewter, Tea Set, Child's Ornate, 16 Piece	35.00
Pewter, Tea Set, Miniature, 15 Piece	65.00
Pewter, Teapot, Acorn Finial, American, T.D.& S.Boardman, C.1830, 5 1/2 In.	175.00
Pewter, Teapot, American, J.W.Cahill & Co.	200.00
Pewter, Teapot, Boardman Shape, 8 1/4 In.	95.00
Pewter, Teapot, C.1830, Allen Porter, Westbrook, Maine	100.00
Pewter, Teapot, Copper Bottom, Marked J.A. & Co., 9 1/2 In.	45.00
Pewter, Teapot, G.Richardson, Boston, Mass., 1818-1845, 7 In.	550.00
Pewter, Teapot, James Dixon & Sons, Sheffield, 5 1/2 In.	120.00
Pewter, Teapot, Lid, Rose Design, James Dixon & Sons, Sheffield	95.00
Pewter, Teapot, Melon Ribbed, Shaw & Fisher, Sheffield, 5 1/2 In. ... 100.00 To	125.00
Pewter, Teapot, Pear Shape, Decorated, Engraved, Footed, Thomas Otley & Sons	75.00
Pewter, Teapot, Smith & Co., Boston, C.1847	235.00
Pewter, Teapot, Umbrella Finale, Bulbous, American	45.00
Pewter, Teapot, Wood Handle & Finial, Schorhoff & Co.	18.00
Pewter, Teaspoon, Shell Design On Base Of Handle	12.95
Pewter, Tray, Bread, Fluted Ends, Flagg & Homan, C.1850	35.00
Pewter, Tray, Cheese, Pairpoint	35.00
Pewter, Tray, Condiment, Cut Inserts, Kayserzinn, 8 X 11 In.	80.00
Pewter, Tray, Embossed Wheat Edge, Game Birds Center, Kayserzinn, 16 1/4 In.	95.00
Pewter, Tray, Grape Bunches On Border, Handled	30.00
Pewter, Tray, Hammered, Long Leaf To Curled Handle, Nekrassoff, 17 In.	50.00
Pewter, Tray, Kayserzinn, Leaf Decoration Forms Art Nouveau Handle, Woman	85.00
Pewter, Tray, Pairpoint, Incised Tall Ship, Round, 13 1/2 In.	25.00
Pewter, Tumbler, Marked American Pewter, 5 1/4 In.	20.00
Pewter, Tureen & Underplate, Dutch, Mid-19th Century, 15 In.	110.00
Pewter, Vase, Corset-Shaped Bodies, Pair, 7 1/4 In.	65.00
Pewter, Vase, Imperial Zinn, Semifigural Woman In Relief, Art Nouveau, 9 In.	125.00
Pewter, Vase, Kayserzinn, Floral, Flared Top, Pedestal Base, No.4076	110.00
Pewter, Vase, Kayserzinn, 2 Naked Children Holding Fish, Art Nouveau, 10 In.	225.00
Pewter, Vase, Trumpet, Priscilla, No.4518, 14 1/4 In.	29.50
Pewter, Warmer, Foot, American, 12 X 7 In.	60.00
Pewter, Warmer, Foot, Salesman's Sample, Miniature, Oval, 2 1/4 X 1 1/2 In.	45.00
Pewter, Washstand Set, Underwater Scene, Kayserzinn Pewter, 6 Piece	425.00

Phoenix Bird, or flying Phoenix, is the name given to a blue and white chinaware made between 1900 and World War II. A variant is known as the Flying Turkey.

Phoenix Bird, Casserole, Lid, Red	35.00
Phoenix Bird, Cup & Saucer, Blue & White, Set Of 6	5.00
Phoenix Bird, Gravy Boat, With Separate Underplate	18.00
Phoenix Bird, Hair Receiver	18.00
Phoenix Bird, Jar, Ginger, Blue, Lid, 5 In.	85.00
Phoenix Bird, Jar, Mustard	12.00
Phoenix Bird, Platter, 12 X 8 In.	18.00
Phoenix Bird, Tea Strainer	45.00

Phoenix Glass Company was founded in 1880 in Pennsylvania. The firm made commercial products such as lampshades, bottles, glassware. Collectors today are interested in the sculptured glassware made by the company from the 1930s until the mid-1950s.

Phoenix, Ashtray, Raised Grasshoppers	12.00
Phoenix, Bowl, Caramel Goldfish, Water Lilies, 16 1/4 In.	150.00
Phoenix, Bowl, Console, Diving Girl, 10 In.	75.00
Phoenix, Bowl, Footed, Open Rose, Green, 10 X 5 In.	68.00
Phoenix, Bowl, Green Parrots, Purple Berries, Brown Branches, 9 1/2 X 32 In.	140.00
Phoenix, Bowl, Open Rose, Green, Footed, 10 X 5 In.	65.00 To 70.00
Phoenix, Bowl, Water Lilies Inside, Caramel Goldfish Outside, 16 1/4 In.	160.00
Phoenix, Bowl, White, Nasturtium, 11 1/2 In.	40.00
Phoenix, Box, Candy, Pearlized Flowers, Apricot Color, Covered, 7 1/2 X 4 In.	37.50
Phoenix, Box, Cigarette, Covered, Sculptured White Floral On Green, 4 3/8 In.	23.50
Phoenix, Box, Cigarette, Lid, White Flowers On Blue Background	55.00
Phoenix, Box, Cigarette, Sculptured White Floral On Sea Green, 4 3/8 In.	23.50
Phoenix, Box, Hummingbirds & Roses, Round, Green, Lid, 6 3/4 X 3 1/2 In.	60.00
Phoenix, Box, Hummingbirds & Roses, 6 3/4 X 3 1/2 In.	62.00
Phoenix, Candlestick, Hummingbirds & Orchids, Amethyst, Pair	125.00
Phoenix, Compote, Amber, Daffodils, 4 1/2 X 10 1/2 In.	45.00
Phoenix, Compote, Fish & Lilies, Amethyst, 6 In.	85.00
Phoenix, Compote, Lavender, Clear, Fish Decoration, 6 1/4 In.	20.00
Phoenix, Glass, Vase, Gold Dragonflies & Cattails On White Opaque, 6 In.	37.50
Phoenix, Lamp Base, Sculptured Leaves, Blue Matte, White	65.00
Phoenix, Lamp, Bluebell, Pair	40.00
Phoenix, Lamp, Glass, Blueberries & Leaves, Not Wired	35.00
Phoenix, Lamp, Night, Owl, 8 1/2 X 4 1/2 In.	150.00
Phoenix, Lamp, Trumpet Flowers, White, Blue	40.00
Phoenix, Lamp, White, Cream & Blue Floral, 15 In.	15.00
Phoenix, Lamp, White, Orange Honeysuckle, Green Leaves, 22 In.	85.00
Phoenix, Pitcher, Milk, Bird, Quart	49.00
Phoenix, Plate, Bubble Glass, Rainbow Effect, Blue, Pink, Green, 10 In.	35.00
Phoenix, Plate, Dancing Nudes, 8 1/4 In.	40.00
Phoenix, Plate, Dancing Nudes, 10 In.	65.00
Phoenix, Shade, Frosted, Clear Cutting, L Panels, 6 3/4 In., Pair	69.50
Phoenix, Snack Set, Tray With Sherbet, Molded Fruit	30.00
Phoenix, Urn, Dancing Nudes, White & Tan, 12 In.	135.00
Phoenix, Vase, Albatrosses, White, Satin Glass, 11 X 9 In.	85.00
Phoenix, Vase, Amber Frosted, Clear Vertical Ribbons, Flared Rim, 8 In.	45.00
Phoenix, Vase, Beige & Yellow, Pinecone, Bulbous, 7 In.	65.00
Phoenix, Vase, Bittersweet, Custard, 9 1/2 In.	65.00
Phoenix, Vase, Blown-Out Pink Flowers & Green Leaves, 6 1/2 In.	27.50
Phoenix, Vase, Blue Praying Mantis On White, 7 1/4 X 8 In.	85.00
Phoenix, Vase, Blue With White Leaves, 8 In.	35.00
Phoenix, Vase, Bluebells, White, 10 1/2 In.	72.00
Phoenix, Vase, Bluebirds & Flowers, Frosted White, 6 1/2 In.	50.00
Phoenix, Vase, Bluebirds, Flowers, Frosted White, Turquoise, 6 1/2 In.	45.00
Phoenix, Vase, Cameo Cut, 13 Seagulls, Pink, Blue, Oblong, 12 X 10 In.	165.00
Phoenix, Vase, Coral Dogwood, Brown Leaves, Matte Finish	95.00
Phoenix, Vase, Cream, White Bell Flowers, 6 In.	36.00
Phoenix, Vase, Dogwood Decoration In Green & Brown, 11 In.	75.00
Phoenix, Vase, Dogwood, Chartreuse, White Luster Flowers, 10 1/4 In.	85.00

Phoenix, Vase, Dogwood, White Flowers, Chartreuse, 10 1/4 In.	80.00
Phoenix, Vase, Dogwood, White Luster Flowers On Chartreuse, 10 1/4 In.	75.00
Phoenix, Vase, Fairy, Arcs & Flowers, Green, 7 1/2 In.	60.00
Phoenix, Vase, Fairy, Arcs & Flowers, Pale Green, 7 1/2 In.	58.00
Phoenix, Vase, Fan, Purple, Bubble, 4 1/2 In.	25.00
Phoenix, Vase, Fern & Leaves, White, 7 In.	50.00
Phoenix, Vase, Fern, Sculptured, 7 X 6 In.	50.00
Phoenix, Vase, Floral, Green Leaves, Yellow Ivory, Blue, 9 In.	80.00
Phoenix, Vase, Flowers & Leaves, White, Light Blue, 7 In.	55.00
Phoenix, Vase, Flying Geese, Blue, White, Paper Label, 11 In.	95.00
Phoenix, Vase, Flying Geese, Pink, Iridescent White, 9 In.	110.00
Phoenix, Vase, Foliage Around Birds On Tree, Rectangular Mouth, Purple, 7 In.	75.00
Phoenix, Vase, Freesia Fan, Raised Clear Floral, Blue, Frosted, 5 X 9 In.	55.00
Phoenix, Vase, Frost On White, 8 3/8 X 4 X 3 1/2 In.	33.00
Phoenix, Vase, Frosted Cream, Blown-Out Pink Flowers, 12 1/2 In.	60.00
Phoenix, Vase, Frosted White With Blue Birds & Flowers, 6 1/2 In.	50.00
Phoenix, Vase, Frosted, Grasshoppers, 8 1/2 In.	64.00
Phoenix, Vase, Goldfish, Rectangular, White, 9 In.	77.00 To 85.00
Phoenix, Vase, Grasshopper, Green, 8 X 7 1/2 In.	60.00
Phoenix, Vase, Grasshoppers On Vines, Pale Green Frosted, 5 1/4 X 8 In.	45.00
Phoenix, Vase, Grasshoppers, Frosted, 8 1/2 In.	64.00
Phoenix, Vase, Head Of Lady, Art Deco, Pearlized Creamy Iridescence, 10 In.	85.00
Phoenix, Vase, Leaves And Birds, White Matte Background, 5 3/4 In.	30.00
Phoenix, Vase, Lovebirds, Orange & Turquoise On White, Rectangular, 6 X 6 In.	37.00
Phoenix, Vase, Lovebirds, Orange & Turquoise On White, 6 1/4 X 3 1/2 In.	40.00
Phoenix, Vase, Lovebirds, White Rectangle, Orange, Turquoise	37.00
Phoenix, Vase, Madonna, Blue, 10 1/4 In.	80.00 To 95.00
Phoenix, Vase, Madonna, Raised Mother-Of-Pearl Head, 10 In.	75.00
Phoenix, Vase, Mums, Green Leaves, White, Yellow, 12 1/2 In.	95.00
Phoenix, Vase, Orange Dragonfly, Brown Foliage, White Background, 6 In.	44.00
Phoenix, Vase, Owls, 7 In.	115.00
Phoenix, Vase, Peach, Blown-Out Floral, 4 In.	32.50
Phoenix, Vase, Peony, Rose Flowers, Custard Ground, 12 In.	70.00
Phoenix, Vase, Pillow, Flying Geese, Iridescent Pearl, Pink Ground	110.00
Phoenix, Vase, Pillow, Flying Geese, Pearl, Blue Ground	100.00
Phoenix, Vase, Pinecones, Rose Bowl Shape, Creamy Yellow, 6 1/2 In.	55.00
Phoenix, Vase, Praying Mantis, Amethyst, 8 1/2 In.	65.00
Phoenix, Vase, Profile Of Madonna, 10 In.	125.00
Phoenix, Vase, Roses On Rose Background, 10 In.	74.00 To 85.00
Phoenix, Vase, Six Nudes, Satin, 11 1/2 In.	115.00
Phoenix, Vase, Star Flower, Paper Label, 7 In.	58.00
Phoenix, Vase, Star Flowers, Green, White, 6 1/2 In.Diameter	65.75
Phoenix, Vase, White Background, Raised Leaves, 11 1/4 In.	45.00
Phoenix, Vase, White Sea Gulls, Turquoise Ground, 11 In.	90.00
Phonograph, see Music, Phonograph	
Photography, Album, Celluloid Cover, Columbian Exposition	75.00
Photography, Album, Gold Plush, Beveled Mirror Cover, Norwegian Immigrant	55.00
Photography, Album, Red Velvet, Admiral Dewey, Celluloid Cover, 8 X 10 In.	45.00
Photography, Album, Victorian, Filled With Photos	25.00
Photography, Album, 13 Alaska Gold Mining Photos, 1898	110.00
Photography, Album, 200 Photos Pershing's Cavalry, Pancho Villa Uprising	38.00
Photography, Ambrotype, Case, Girl Holding Rose, Some In Hat, Cross Necklace	45.00
Photography, Ambrotype, Man Holding Baby	12.00
Photography, Ambrotype, 1/2 Plate, South Carolina Cavalrymen	106.00
Photography, Ambrotype, 1/9 Plate, Hand-Printed Lord's Prayer	22.50
Photography, Camera, Brownie Jr.No.620, 1930s	5.00
Photography, Camera, Cyclone Magazine, No.3, 12 Plates, 4 X 5 In.	50.00
Photography, Camera, Eastman Kodak, F.P.K.Automatic, Model 4074, 1905-06	55.00
Photography, Camera, Kodak, Autographic Special, Model A	15.00
Photography, Camera, Premo, Wood & Leather, Case, 1890	60.00
Photography, Camera, Premo, 1892, Case & Tripod, 5 X 7 In.	50.00
Photography, Camera, R.B.Graflex, 3 1/4 X 4 1/4 In.	75.00
Photography, Camera, Rochester Optical, Premo, 1891	85.00
Photography, Camera, Seneca, Folding Ingento, No.1, 1905	18.00

Photography, Carte De Visite, Abraham Lincoln

Photography, Camera, Studio, Brass & Wood, James W.Queen, Philadelphia 200.00
Photography, Camera, Unicum, Seroco Camera Co., 1891, 3 Film Slides, Case 70.00
Photography, Camera, Vitascope Movie 58.00
Photography, Camera, Wood, Brass, Tripod, Case, Plate Frames, Conley 750.00
Photography, Camera, Wooden, Leather Bellows, Glass Plate Holder, Case 20.00
Photography, Carte De Visite, Abraham Lincoln .... *Illus* 750.00
Photography, Carte De Visite, Bishop Baker 5.00
Photography, Carte De Visite, Brigham Young, Savage & Ottinger 20.00
Photography, Carte De Visite, Charles Sumner 4.00
Photography, Carte De Visite, City Hall, Salt Lake City, 1860s 20.00
Photography, Carte De Visite, Clark Foss 5.00
Photography, Carte De Visite, Dingman Soap, 1891, E.Leslie Photo, 7 X 12 In. 275.00
Photography, Carte De Visite, Eagle Gate & Schoolhouse, Salt Lake City 30.00
Photography, Carte De Visite, Edwin M.Stanton 8.00
Photography, Carte De Visite, Garibaldi 5.00
Photography, Carte De Visite, General Grant 10.00
Photography, Carte De Visite, General Thomas 8.00
Photography, Carte De Visite, George Smith, Mormons, 1860s, Salt Lake City 10.00
Photography, Carte De Visite, Governor Andrews 5.00
Photography, Carte De Visite, John Wilkes Booth 15.00
Photography, Carte De Visite, Lieutenant General U.S.Grant 8.00
Photography, Carte De Visite, Main Street, West Side, Salt Lake City 40.00
Photography, Carte De Visite, Major General Philip H.Sheridan 8.00
Photography, Carte De Visite, Major General W.T.Sherman 8.00
Photography, Carte De Visite, Mrs. Lincoln 8.00
Photography, Carte De Visite, Old Policeman 5.00
Photography, Carte De Visite, Samuel Chase 10.00
Photography, Carte De Visite, Theater, South End, Salt Lake City, 1860s 20.00
Photography, Carte De Visite, Washington Receiving Lincoln 18.00
Photography, Daguerreotype Case, Double, Quaker Lady & Man, 3 1/4 X 3 3/4 In 95.00
Photography, Daguerreotype Case, Gutta-Percha, Angel, Babies, Brown 68.00
Photography, Daguerreotype Case, Gutta-Percha, Basket Of Fruit 29.00
Photography, Daguerreotype Case, Gutta-Percha, Birds, Nest & Eggs 50.00
Photography, Daguerreotype Case, Gutta-Percha, Camp Scene, Young Man, Black 68.00
Photography, Daguerreotype Case, Gutta-Percha, Children Chasing Butterfly 30.00
Photography, Daguerreotype Case, Gutta-Percha, Country Life, 7 X 5 In. 125.00
Photography, Daguerreotype Case, Gutta-Percha, Double, Grill & Scroll, 3 In. 22.95
Photography, Daguerreotype Case, Gutta-Percha, Double, 6 1/4 X 3 3/4 In. 90.00
Photography, Daguerreotype Case, Gutta-Percha, Faithful Hound 40.00
Photography, Daguerreotype Case, Gutta-Percha, Little Girl, 2 X 2 1/2 In. 30.00
Photography, Daguerreotype Case, Gutta-Percha, Photograph Of Lady 90.00
Photography, Daguerreotype Case, Gutta-Percha, Proud Elk, Smith, 3 3/4 In. 42.00
Photography, Daguerreotype Case, Gutta-Percha, Scotch Highlander Hunter 55.00
Photography, Daguerreotype Case, Gutta-Percha, The Wheat Sheaves, 4 In. 80.00
Photography, Daguerreotype Case, Gutta-Percha, Wheat Sheaves, 4 X 4 7/8 In. 80.00
Photography, Daguerreotype Case, Gutta-Percha, 2 Little Girls 28.00
Photography, Daguerreotype Case, Leather, Deer Decoration 17.00
Photography, Daguerreotype Case, The Musicians, Signed 70.00
Photography, Daguerreotype Case, Victorian Medallion Decoration, 3 In. 20.00

Photography, Daguerreotype Case, Watch Case Style, Gold Filled Frame 75.00
Photography, Daguerreotype, Civil War Soldier In Uniform .... 70.00 To 73.00
Photography, Daguerreotype, Lady, Unusual Hairdo, Ornate Case, 3 1/2 X 2 In. 42.00
Photography, Daguerreotype, Sisters, 3 X 2 1/2 In. 33.50
Photography, Daguerreotype, Young Girls, Leather Case, 4 1/2 X 3 In. 20.00
Photography, Daguerreotype, Young Man, Leather Case, 4 1/2 X 3 In. 20.00
Photography, Daguerreotype, 1/2 Plate, Rattlesnake Hotel .... *Illus* 800.00
Photography, Daguerreotype, 1/4 Plate, Cemetery, Case, Seal .... *Illus* 225.00
Photography, Daguerreotype, 1/4 Plate, New England .... *Illus* 375.00
Photography, Daguerreotype, 1/4 Plate, Soldier, Lady, Fully Cased, C.1850 .... 375.00
Photography, Daguerreotype, 1/6 Plate, Baby In High Chair, Case 45.00
Photography, Daguerreotype, 1/6 Plate, Brother & Sister 14.00
Photography, Daguerreotype, 1/6 Plate, Mason, Case, C.1852 .... *Illus* 95.00
Photography, Daguerreotype, 1/6 Plate, Warren Hose Co. .... *Illus* 245.00
Photography, Daguerreotype, 1/6 Plate, Woman Next To Window .... *Illus* 600.00
Photography, Kitten In Basket, Sepia Color, C.1903, 5 X 7 1/2 In. 25.00
Photography, Lantern, Dark Room, Kerosene, Kodak 35.00
Photography, Lantern, Kerosene, Tin, C.1880 .... 22.50
Photography, Magic Lantern, Cased, 10 Slides 50.00
Photography, Magic Lantern, E.P.Co., Kerosene Lamp & 1 Slide, 8 X 3 In. 50.00
Photography, Magic Lantern, Mahogany, Brass, Wood Case, Pair .... *Illus* 1044.00
Photography, Magic Lantern, Miniature Kerosene Lamp Inside, 8 Slides 85.00
Photography, Meter, Print, With Box & Directions, Wynne's 30.00
Photography, Photograph, Boarding House, Dining Room For Workers, Food, Women 45.00
Photography, Photograph, Bottle Factory, Interior, Workers, C.1895 .... 25.00
Photography, Photograph, Factory, Young Boys Employed, C.1891 .... 25.00
Photography, Photograph, Highwheel Bike Rider, 1894, 13 X 21 In. 75.00
Photography, Photograph, Home Comfort Steel Ranges, Salesman, Buggy, 2 Horses 35.00
Photography, Photograph, Indian Chief, 5 X 7 In. 1750.00
Photography, Photograph, New York Garment Industry, Interior 25.00
Photography, Photograph, New York Jew, Early Bronx 20.00
Photography, Photograph, New York Tailor Shop 25.00
Photography, Photograph, Traveling Medicine Man, Dr.Baker Medicine Co. 25.00
Photography, Photograph, Women Reporter In Field, Tacoma Ledger, Tent, Stove 25.00
Photography, Projector, Keystone, Moviegraph Model 193W 22.00
Photography, Projector, Radiophone, With Old Bulbs 35.00
Photography, Projector, 35MM, Holmes, Model No.4585 .... 200.00
Photography, Scrapbook, Victorian, Yellow Cover, Birds, Butterflies, 96 Page 42.50

Photography, Daguerreotype, 1/2 Plate, Rattlesnake Hotel

Photography, Daguerreotype, 1/4 Plate, New England

Photography, Daguerreotype, 1/4 Plate, Cemetery, Case, Seal

Photography, Stereo, see Stereo

Photography, Tintype, C.W., Corporal Seated In Full Uniform, Tents, Flag	38.00
Photography, Tintype, Civil War Soldier, 1/4 Plate, Framed	67.00
Photography, Tintype, Fireman, Long Brass-Buttoned Coat	10.00
Photography, Tintype, Full Plate, Portrait Of Lady, Fully Colored	8.50
Photography, Tintype, I Boys In Sulky, Horse Wears Leather Flyguard	12.00
Photography, Tintype, Quaker Holding Wood Frame On Lap, 2 1/4 X 3 1/4 In.	30.00
Photography, Tintype, Seated Girl Holding Large Dog, 2 X 2 1/2 In.	8.00
Photography, Tintype, Whole Plate, Early Wilderness Home & Family, C.1870	150.00
Photography, Tintype, 1/6 Plate, Black Dandy	75.00
Photography, Tintype, 1/6 Plate, Girl On Beach, Gilt Frame	55.00
Photography, Tintype, 1/6 Plate, Horse, Buggy, Passengers, Fully Cased	75.00
Photography, Tintype, 1/9 Plate, Policeman In Half Case	20.00
Photography, Viewer, Mirroscope Lantern Slide	25.00

Piano, see Music, Piano

Piano Baby, Andrea, Open Jointed Arms, White & Pink Gown, Sitting	45.00
Piano Baby, Baby Lying On Back Holding Toes, Heubach, 8 In.	135.00
Piano Baby, Bisque, Laying Down, Pulling Off Sock, Impressed German, Number	125.00
Piano Baby, Blue Eyes, Blonde Hair, Blue Bow, Red Crown Mark, German, 6 In.	125.00
Piano Baby, Crawling, Bisque, Signed Heubach, 4 1/2 In.	60.00
Piano Baby, Crawling, Heubach, 6 1/2 In.	85.00
Piano Baby, Crawling, White, Aqua Trim, Heubach, 8 In.	165.00
Piano Baby, German, 8 In.	85.00
Piano Baby, Girl, Leg Crossed To Remove Sock, Pink Frock, Bonnet, 8 In.	275.00
Piano Baby, Girl, Sitting, Head Bent To Side, Upstretched Hands, 6 1/2 In.	75.00
Piano, Baby, Heubach, Sitting Beside A Holder For Matches, Marked	85.00
Piano Baby, Holding Baby, German, 12 In.	35.00

Photography, Daguerreotype, 1/6 Plate, Mason, Case, C.1852
(See Page 395)

Photography, Daguerreotype, 1/6 Plate, Warren Hose Co.
(See Page 395)

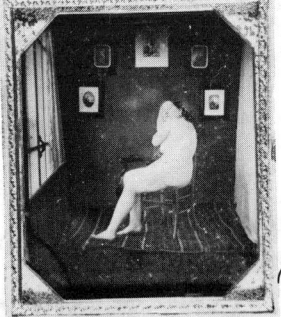

Photography, Daguerreotype, 1/6 Plate, Woman Next To Window
(See Page 395)

Piano Baby, Holding Cup, German, 12 In.	45.00
Piano Baby, Laying Prone, Propped Up On Pillow, Dog, Pacifier, 8 1/2 In.	175.00
Piano Baby, Lying On Back, White, Aqua Trim, Heubach, 8 1/2 In.	165.00
Piano Baby, On Tummy, Dog On Back, Dog Under Blanket, 10 X 5 In.	250.00
Piano Baby, On Tummy, Large Egg On Back, 8 In.	125.00
Piano Baby, Seated, Nude With Fly On Knee, Heubach, 5 1/4 In.	125.00
Piano Baby, Seated, Touching Toes, White, Aqua Trim, Heubach, 8 1/4 In.	165.00
Piano Baby, Sitting, German, 8 In.	85.00
Piano Baby, Sitting, Hand & Leg Up, Pink Dress, Plaster Of Paris, 11 In.	75.00

Pickard china was started in 1898 by Wilder Pickard. Hand-painted china was a featured product. The firm is still working in Antioch, Illinois.

Pickard, Bonbon, Ravenswood, Violets, Gold, Handled, Signed, 4 1/2 In.	35.00
Pickard, Bottle, Perfume, Gold, Green Shamrocks, 5 In.	48.00
Pickard, Bowl, Autumn Colors, Gooseberries, Leaves, Gold, 8 3/4 X 2 1/4 In.	55.00
Pickard, Bowl, Basket Of Roses, Gold Rim & Handles, Florence James, 9 1/2 In.	75.00
Pickard, Bowl, F.James, Rose Basket Design, Gold Rim & Handles, 9 1/2 In.	70.00
Pickard, Bowl, Floral, Fluted Edges, Gold Border, Footed, Koep, 6 In.	32.00
Pickard, Bowl, Gold Etched, Leaf Shape, 12 In.	25.00
Pickard, Bowl, Gold Flowered, Molded Handles, 6 In.	17.00
Pickard, Bowl, Gold, Lavender & Pansies, Artist Signed, 7 1/4 In.	42.00
Pickard, Bowl, Hand-Painted Orchard, Bisque, Handled, 1912 Mark, 7 In.	55.00
Pickard, Bowl, Hand-Painted Violets, Leaves, 1905-10 Mark, 7 3/4 In.	28.00
Pickard, Bowl, Hazelnuts, Gold Edge, Signed, 11 In.	115.00
Pickard, Bowl, Peaches, Leaves, Gold, 2 Handles, Beattich, 8 1/2 X 3 In.	110.00
Pickard, Bowl, Pinched, 3 Handled, Signed, 1894-1904	265.00
Pickard, Bowl, Pink Wild Roses, Footed, Gold Rim, Signed Teon, 10 In.	145.00
Pickard, Bowl, Poppies, N.McHord, 1905-10 Mark, 5 1/2 In.	55.00
Pickard, Bowl, Punch, Blackberries, White Flowers, Gold Band, Koenia, 12 In.	275.00
Pickard, Bowl, Punch, Rean, 1898, Gooseberries, Peachblow Shading, 9 3/8 In.	295.00
Pickard, Bowl, Scalloped Rim, Embossed Gold Flowers, Gold, 6 In.	50.00
Pickard, Bowl, Strawberries, Scalloped Gold Rim, C.Hohn, 1898 Mark, 5 3/4 In.	50.00
Pickard, Butter Tub & Underplate, Maple Leaf, Floral, Gold	48.00
Pickard, Candleholder, Gold Etched Floral, Limoges Blank, 1925, Marked, 9 In.	55.00
Pickard, Candlestick, Dutch Girl Decoration, Artist Signed, 9 1/2 In., Pair	195.00
Pickard, Charger, Stylized Tulips, Heavy Gold, F.C., 12 1/2 In.	125.00
Pickard, Chocolate Pot, Creamer, Covered Sugar, Signed, 1905-10	335.00
Pickard, Chocolate Pot, Green, Purple Violets, Gold, Signed Reury, 10 In.	125.00
Pickard, Chocolate Pot, Purple Floral, Iridescent, Red Ground, Rean, 11 In.	285.00
Pickard, Coffeepot, Chinese Enamel Design, Gold Trim, Red, White, Blue, Marked	95.00
Pickard, Coffeepot, Red, White, Blue, & Green, Chinese Enameling, Gold, 1930	95.00
Pickard, Coffee Set, Gasper, 1912, Venetian Renaissance, Cameos, Gold Stipple	375.00
Pickard, Creamer & Sugar, Tray, Gold	55.00
Pickard, Creamer, Gold Etched Floral, Rs Germany Blank, 1925, 4 1/2 In.	25.00
Pickard, Creamer, Grecian Shape, Gold, Miniature, 2 1/2 In.	15.00
Pickard, Creamer, Hand-Painted Flowers, Ovoid, Signed Gold Leaf, 2 X 4 In.	25.00
Pickard, Creamer, Metallic Grapes, Robert Hessler, 1905-10, 3 3/4 In.	75.00
Pickard, Creamer, Metallic Grapes, 1905-10 Mark, Signed R.H. Limoges Blank	70.00
Pickard, Cup & Saucer, Gold Decorated, Floral, Vertical Panels	38.00

Photography, Magic Lantern. Mahogany, Brass, Wood Case, Pair
(See Page 395)

Pickard, Decanter, Whiskey, & 4 Shot Glasses, Marked, Artist Signed	350.00
Pickard, Dish, Fruits Border, Oval, Handled, Signed Yeschak, 11 In.	75.00
Pickard, Dish, Leaf Shape, Gold Floral, Signed, 12 1/2 X 5 1/2 In.	35.00
Pickard, Dish, Oval, 8 1/2 X 4 1/2	50.00
Pickard, Dish, Pickle, Gold & Stippled Decoration, Pierced Handles, 8 1/2 In.	8.50
Pickard, Dish, Round, 2 Handled, Violets, 6 X 5 In.	38.50
Pickard, Ewer, Ornamental, Red Currants, Ivory Ground, Gold Top, 10 1/2 In.	275.00
Pickard, Gravy Boat, Tree Of Life, Gold Handles, Gold Rim, Attached Base	40.00
Pickard, Hair Receiver, Gold, Green Shamrocks	20.00
Pickard, Hair Receiver, Poppies, 2 Piece	78.00
Pickard, Hair Receiver, Stylized Lotus, Leaf Mark, C.1912	32.00
Pickard, Jar & Underplate, Jam, Gold, Band Of Plums, Raspberries, Handles	175.00
Pickard, Jar, Marmalade, Underplate, Gold Leaf, Hand-Painted Fruit, 6 1/2 In.	70.00
Pickard, Jug, Pond Lily, Gold Trim, 1912 Mark, 7 1/2 In.	150.00
Pickard, Mug, Oranges, Grapes On Gold, Green Background, 5 In.	30.00
Pickard, Mustard Jar, Dutch Girl, Rawlins, Leaf Mark, 3 1/4 In.	75.00
Pickard, Nappy, Violets, Leaves, Ring Handle, Gold, Triangular Shape, Signed	85.00
Pickard, Pickle, Open Handled, Orange, White, Rust, Floral, Gold, Signed, 9 In.	40.00
Pickard, Pitcher, Aura Argenta Linear, 2 Sided, Artist Signed, 8 1/4 In.	195.00
Pickard, Pitcher, Blaha, Red Currants, Paneled, Embossed, Gold Top, 1898, 10 In.	245.00
Pickard, Pitcher, Cider, Aura Argenta Linear, Signed, 1905-10	260.00
Pickard, Pitcher, Grapes & Vines, Gold & Black, Hessler, 1905-10, 6 In.	145.00
Pickard, Pitcher, Hand-Painted, Gold Handle, Lid, 6 1/2 In.	28.00
Pickard, Pitcher, Iris, Gold, Silver Trim, Blue Portions, 1905-10, 3 1/4 In.	45.00
Pickard, Pitcher, Lemonade, Art Deco	65.00
Pickard, Pitcher, Water, Red Poppy Decoration, Bulbous, Gold Trim, 1898, 8 In.	220.00
Pickard, Plate, American Wildflower, A.Cornyn, 1910-12, 9 In.	85.00
Pickard, Plate, Black Geometrics, Gold Rim, Hand-Painted, 6 In.	4.00
Pickard, Plate, Blue Border With Gold, Dots, Multicolor Pattern, 7 In.	25.00
Pickard, Plate, Cake, Floral & Gold, Open Handle, Maple Leaf Mark, 10 1/2 In.	34.00
Pickard, Plate, Cake, Gold Center, Fruits Around Banded Edge, Vokral, 10 In.	100.00
Pickard, Plate, Cake, Gold Open Handles, Landscape, Challinor, Gold Leaf Mark	135.00
Pickard, Plate, Cake, Lake Scene, Trees, Pink Roses, Gold, Challinor, 11 1/8 In.	135.00
Pickard, Plate, Cake, Scenic, Lake Surrounded By Trees, Challinor, 1912, 12 In.	150.00
Pickard, Plate, Cake, Scenic, Lake, Trees, Roses, E.Challinor, 1912, 11 1/8 In.	175.00
Pickard, Plate, Deep Green, Yellow Cherries, Floral, Enamel, 1905, 8 3/4 In.	80.00
Pickard, Plate, Etched Gold, Floral Border, 1912, 7 1/2 In.	15.00
Pickard, Plate, Floral Drapes, Gold White, 12 In.	27.50 To 40.00
Pickard, Plate, Flowers & Gold Banding, Gold Leaf Mark	45.00
Pickard, Plate, Flowers, Hand-Painted, Scalloped Rim, F.James, 1905, 8 1/2 In.	80.00
Pickard, Plate, Green, Yellow Cherries, Floral, Enameling, Lind, 1905, 8 3/4 In.	80.00
Pickard, Plate, Hand-Painted Floral, Gold Open Handle, Maple Leaf, 10 3/4 In.	35.00
Pickard, Plate, Hand-Painted, Gold Border, Signed, 8 1/2 In.	35.00
Pickard, Plate, Lake & Trees In Shades Of Blue, Challinor, 1912, 8 1/2 In.	115.00
Pickard, Plate, Lake & Trees Scene, Challinor, 12 5/8 In.	95.00
Pickard, Plate, Palm Trees, Grassy Path, Matte Finish, Gold Leaf Mark, Signed	165.00
Pickard, Plate, Peaches, Gold Trim, Signed, 1910-12 Mark, 8 3/4 In.	75.00
Pickard, Plate, Peaches, Green & Gold, Seidel, 1898, 8 1/2 In.	95.00
Pickard, Plate, Poinsettias, Gold Scalloped Edge, Signed Wight, 8 3/4 In.	69.50
Pickard, Plate, Poppies, Gold Trim, Signed, 9 1/2 In.	43.50
Pickard, Plate, Poppies, Green, Maroon Ground, Gold Handles, Leon, 1898, 13 In.	150.00
Pickard, Plate, Purple Grapes, Gold, Scalloped Rim, 1905, 8 1/2 In.	45.00
Pickard, Plate, Red Poppies On Cream, Gasper, 1905-10, 8 1/2 In.	55.00
Pickard, Plate, Sweet Clover & Bees, Gold Rim, Signed, 9 In.	50.00
Pickard, Plate, Water Lilies, Signed, 1918 Mark, 9 In.	78.00
Pickard, Plate, Wildflowers, Cornyn, 1910-12, 9 In.	85.00
Pickard, Plate, Yellow Buttercup Florals, Gold Scalloped Rim, 1905, 8 5/8 In.	45.00
Pickard, Plate, Yellow Floral & Leaves, Gold Border, Circle Mark, 8 1/2 In.	37.00
Pickard, Plate, 5 Red Flowers On Gold Border, 3 1/2 In.	32.00
Pickard, Platter, Peacock, On Wall, Artist Signed Vokral, 12 In.	220.00
Pickard, Platter, Scenic, Gold Border, 2 Handles, B.H., 7 In.	105.00
Pickard, Platter, Scenic, Gold Border, 2 Handles, E.Challinor, 10 In.	225.00
Pickard, Salt & Pepper, Gold All Over, 3 3/4 In.	25.00
Pickard, Salt & Pepper, Roses, Gold Trim, Hand-Painted	35.00
Pickard, Saltshaker, All Gold	9.00

Pickard, Sherbet, Chinese Decoration, Tolpin Signature, 3 X 4 In. 45.00
Pickard, Stein, Poinsettias, Gifford, Circle Mark, 7 In. 175.00
Pickard, Sugar & Creamer, Art Nouveau Design, Signed 65.00
Pickard, Sugar & Creamer, Bronze Tulips, Gold Outlined Foliage, Footed, Lind 85.00
Pickard, Sugar & Creamer, Dutch Girl, Signed Leaf Mark 155.00
Pickard, Sugar & Creamer, Gold .... 30.00 To 45.00
Pickard, Sugar & Creamer, Purple Grapes On Black, Gold, Pedestaled, Hess 95.00
Pickard, Sugar & Creamer, Tray, Lind, Bronze Tulips, Gold Bands, 11 1/2 In. 150.00
Pickard, Sugar & Creamer, Violets, Gold, Signed 90.00
Pickard, Sugar & Creamer, 24K Gold, Nippon Blanks 55.00
Pickard, Sugar, Covered, Gold 20.00
Pickard, Sugar, Daisy Pattern, Crow Foot On Bottom 25.00
Pickard, Sugar, Dutch Girl, Alex, 1912 .... 15.00
Pickard, Sugar, Gold, Band Of Garlands Of Pink Roses, Blue Bows, Lid, White 35.00
Pickard, Sugar Shaker, Garden Scene, Signed Vokral, C.1905, 3 In. 150.00
Pickard, Tea Set, Stippled Gold, Scalloped Top, 3 Piece 90.00
Pickard, Teapot, One Cup, Silver Overlay Floral On White, Miniature, C.1910 .... 45.00
Pickard, Tray, Bread, Gold Decorated Fruit, Yeschek, Leaf Mark, 10 1/2 In. 110.00
Pickard, Tray, Roses, Scalloped, 2 Handled, Hand-Painted, Challinor, 11 In. 40.00
Pickard, Tub & Underplate, Butter, Floral, Gold Trim, Covered, Maple Leaf Mark 50.00
Pickard, Tumbler, Silver Resist 25.00
Pickard, Urn, Gold, Embossed Floral Design, 2 Handled, 8 1/2 In. 36.75
Pickard, Vase, Deep Green, High Gloss Grape Leaves, Lind, C.1905, 6 In. 100.00
Pickard, Vase, Deserted Garden, Bulbous, J.Nessy, 1912, 8 In. 125.00
Pickard, Vase, Deserted Garden, J.Nessy, 1912, 7 3/4 In. 165.00
Pickard, Vase, Etched, Peacock Overlooking Lake, Flowers, Trees, Artist Signed 495.00
Pickard, Vase, Gold Band, Shaded Flowers And Green Leaves, 7 1/2 In. 85.00
Pickard, Vase, Gold Decorated, Floral, Vertical Panels, Scalloped, 7 In. 95.00
Pickard, Vase, Gold Decoration Outside, Green Inside, 6 In. 36.00
Pickard, Vase, Gold, 2 Handled, Urn Shape, 9 In. 36.00
Pickard, Vase, Grecian Style, 2 Handled, 8 In. 55.00
Pickard, Vase, Green, High Gloss Grape Leaves, Lind, 1905, 13 1/2 In. 100.00
Pickard, Vase, Landscape Scene, Gold Leaf Mark, Artist Signed, 8 In. 195.00
Pickard, Vase, Lind, 1905, Green, High Gloss Grape Leaves, 6 In. 115.00
Pickard, Vase, Multicolored Birds On Branch, Gold Shield Mark, 8 In. 110.00
Pickard, Vase, Pansies & Daisies, Pastel Ground, Signed, 1904-10, 5 1/4 In. 75.00
Pickard, Vase, Red Poppy, Two Handled, Artist Signed, Circle Mark, 6 1/4 In. 110.00
Pickard, Vase, Shamrocks, Singing Magic Harp, Green, Gold, Artist N., 8 1/2 In. 150.00
Pickard, Vase, Trees & Shrub Scene, Challinor, 9 1/2 In. 95.00
Pickard, Vase, Trees, Lake, Purple & Lavender, Bisque Finish, Challinor, 8 In. 225.00
Pickard, Vase, Tulips, Green Leaves, W.Lemke, 8 1/4 In. 95.00
Pickard, Vase, Violets, Trellis, 9 1/2 In. 120.00
Pickard, Vase, Water Lilies Band, Gold Background, Signed, 7 In. 165.00
Picture, see also Painting, Print
Picture Frame, see Furniture, Frame
Picture, Calligraphy, Signed C.D.Coffman, April 15, '97 .... 265.00
Picture, Etching, Lee Rail Under, Signed, Don Swann 13.00
Picture, Hand-Colored Birds & Angels, Wood-Grained Frame, Dated 1862 .... 86.00
Picture, Pen And Ink, Winsor McCay, Eagle, Wings Spread, 10 1/2 X 23 In. 300.00
Picture, Silhouette, Clifford Sisters, Mt.Vernon, New Hampshire, C.1830, Pair 175.00
Picture, Silhouette, Family, Signed Aug.Edouart 120.00
Picture, Silhouette, Gentleman & 2 Children, Costumes Picked Out With Gilt 750.00
Picture, Silhouette, Gilt Work & Frame, Pair, 5 3/4 X 7 3/4 In. .... Illus 40.00
Picture, Silhouette, Hollow Cut, Gutta-Percha Frame, 8-7-1855 .... Illus 100.00
Picture, Silhouette, Hollow Cut, Mary Fitch Bryant .... Illus 170.00
Picture, Silhouette, Hon.Edward Bradbury & Family, Augustin Edouart, 1844 .... 400.00
Picture, Silhouette, Ink, Gilt, Brass Frame, 4 3/4 In. .... Illus 45.00
Picture, Silhouette, Man, Rectangular Frame, Stamped W.King 165.00
Picture, Silhouette, Man, Reverse Painted On Glass, Silk Background, White 125.00
Picture, Silhouette, Man's Head, Pine Frame, 7 1/2 In. 65.00
Picture, Silhouette, Older Man, Oval Frame, Signed Doyle 160.00
Picture, Silhouette, On Fabric, Hollow Cut, Unframed .... Illus 35.00
Picture, Silhouette, On Fabric, Hollow Cut, Walnut Frame, Pair .... Illus 60.00
Picture, Silhouette, School Mistress & 4 Young Ladies, Augustin Edouart 1200.00
Picture, Silhouette, Woman, Oval Frame, Stamped Williams 175.00

Picture, Silhouette, Hollow Cut,
Gutta-Percha Frame, 8-7-1855
(See Page 399)

Picture, Silhouette, Hollow Cut, Mary Fitch Bryant
(See Page 399)

Picture, Silhouette, Gilt Work & Frame. Pair, 5 3/4 X 7 3/4 In.
(See Page 399)

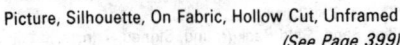

Picture, Silhouette, On Fabric, Hollow Cut, Unframed
(See Page 399)

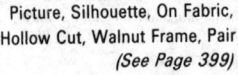

Picture, Silhouette, Ink, Gilt,
Brass Frame, 4 3/4 In.
(See Page 399)

Picture, Silhouette, On Fabric,
Hollow Cut, Walnut Frame, Pair
(See Page 399)

Picture, Silhouette, Young Boy, Hollow Cut, 3 1/4 X 4 In.	75.00
Picture, Silhouette, Young Girl, Gilt Frame, Signed P.Holmes, June 1840	120.00
Picture, Silhouette, Young Man, Round Frame, Stamped Museum	125.00
Picture, Silhouette, 4 People In Gray Washed Interior, Saml Metford, 1841	350.00
Picture, State Of Maine, Civil War Discharge, 1868	100.00
Picture, Stratoliner In Flight, Framed, 21 X 23 In.	12.00
Picture, Watercolor, Gibson Girl, Dated 1907, Signed, H.Fisher, 4 X 6 In.	65.00
Pigeon Blood, see Cranberry Glass, Ruby Glass	
Pilkington, Vase, Crystalline Glaze On Flambe Ground, Dated 1912	135.00
Pilkington, Vase, Gold Luster Animals, Purple Flowers, C.E.Cundall, 4 In.	350.00
Pilkington, Vase, Iridescent, Pinecone, Gladys Rodgers, 1913, 8 In.	195.00
Pilkington, Vase, Royal Lancastrian, Floral, Artist Signed, 8 1/2 X 2 In.	325.00
Pincushion Doll, Arms, Hutschenreuther, 4 In.	42.00
Pincushion Doll, Art Deco, Lady In Hat, Arms Away, 5 In.	175.00
Pincushion Doll, Bisque Arms, 5 1/2 In.	100.00
Pincushion Doll, Blonde, Fan, Red Line Eyes, 3 1/2 In.	20.00
Pincushion Doll, Blue Spanish Comb, Black Hair, Hand On Hip, German, 3 In.	10.00
Pincushion Doll, Bobbed Hair, Holds Rose, Japan, 3 In.	9.00
Pincushion Doll, Carmen, Luster Finish, Large, Germany, 4 In.	28.00
Pincushion Doll, China, On Whiskbroom	25.00
Pincushion Doll, Cloth Body, Composition Head, Red Satin Front, Hanging Type	15.00
Pincushion Doll, Clown Lady, 3 1/2 In.	15.00
Pincushion Doll, Composition Head, Cloth Body, Hanging Type, 8 1/2 In.	15.00
Pincushion Doll, Dutch Cap, Blonde Hair, Holding Cherries, Germany, 3 In.	18.00
Pincushion Doll, Extended Arms, Wide-Brim Hat, Germany, 2 1/2 In.	25.00
Pincushion Doll, Fancy Lady, Signed Goebel, 2 1/2 In.	35.00
Pincushion Doll, Flapper With Hat, German, 3 1/2 In.	18.00
Pincushion Doll, Flapper, Hands To Chest, Feather In Hair, 3 In.	20.00
Pincushion Doll, Flapper, Hands To Chest, Red & Blue Flowers In Hair, 3 In.	26.50
Pincushion Doll, Flapper, Hands To Waist, Beads In Hair, 2 3/4 In.	18.00
Pincushion Doll, Flapper, 5 In.	125.00
Pincushion Doll, German, Black Dress, Flapper Hair, Arms Away, Hand On Neck	25.00
Pincushion Doll, German, Blonde Hair, 3 3/4 In.	16.00
Pincushion Doll, German, Brunette, 3 In.	14.00
Pincushion Doll, German, Child, Blonde Hair, Yellow Cap & Blue Ribbons	24.00
Pincushion Doll, German, Child, Dutch Cap, Arms Extended, 2 1/2 In.	24.00
Pincushion Doll, German, Cloche Hat, Rose On Each Side, Hand Front & Back	25.00
Pincushion Doll, German, Lamp, Gray Pompadour, Arms Across Breast	28.00
Pincushion Doll, German, Open Arms, Brush Stroke Hair, Feathers On Top, Nude	75.00
Pincushion Doll, German, Spanish Hat, Yellow Shawl, 3 1/2 In.	25.00
Pincushion Doll, Germany, 3 In.	20.00
Pincushion Doll, Gray Hair, Pink Ribbon, Colonial Lady, 3 In.	13.50
Pincushion Doll, Hand On Breast, German, 3 In.	13.50
Pincushion Doll, Head, Signed Germany, Open Elbow, 3 In.	12.50
Pincushion Doll, Japan, Blue Suit, Blue Cloche Hat, Hands On Front, 2 1/2 In.	12.00
Pincushion Doll, Japan, Marie Antoinette Hair, 3 1/2 In.	12.00
Pincushion Doll, Low Neckline, Extended Arms With Fan, Germany, 3 3/4 In.	32.50
Pincushion Doll, Monkey, Brown, Bisque, German, 3 In.	25.00
Pincushion Doll, Nude, Gray Hair, 3 In.	25.00
Pincushion Doll, Porcelain, Colonial Lady, Gray Hair, Pink Ribbon, 3 In.	13.50
Pincushion Doll, With Base, 9 In.	35.00
Pincushion Doll, Woman, Hands To Breast, 1 Open Elbow, 4 In.	20.00
Pink Slag, see Slag, Pink	
Pinocchio, see Disneyana	
Pipe, see also Cloisonne, Pipe	
Pipe, Andrew Jackson, Clay	200.00
Pipe, French Briar, Amber Bowl, UJK Plated Band, Velvet Case	38.00
Pipe, Hand-Carved Leaping Stag, Forest Cabin, Burl Walnut	75.00
Pipe, Meerschaum, see Meerschaum, Pipe	
Pipe, Opium, Polished Bamboo & Silver, 23 In.	85.00
Pipe, Red Clay, Family Standing On Stem, Box	39.00
Pipe, Teddy Roosevelt, Rough Rider, 904, Briarwood, Initialed W.D.C.	75.00

Pirkenhammer is a porcelain manufactory started in 1802 by Friedrich Holke and J. G. List.

Pirkenhammer, Bowl, Green, Red Flowers, 6 In.Diameter	125.00
Pirkenhammer, Vase, Gold, Raised Decoration, 8 In.	75.00

Pisgah pottery pieces that are marked Pisgah Forest Pottery were made in North Carolina from 1926 until the present. Vases, teapots, jugs, candlesticks, and many other items were made.

Pisgah Forest, Jug, Brown Speckled Celadon, Handled, 1943, 4 3/4 In.	12.00
Pisgah Forest, Pitcher, Blue Glaze, Pink Lining, 8 In.	15.00
Pisgah Forest, Pitcher, Blue, Wine, C.1939, 2 1/4 In.	5.50
Pisgah Forest, Pitcher, Wine Color, 4 In.	19.00
Pisgah Forest, Pitcher, 3 1/2 In.	8.00
Pisgah Forest, Vase, Cream Glaze, Apricot Interior, 4 In.	12.00
Pisgah Forest, Vase, Cream, Apricot Interior, Raised Potter Mark, Signed, Pair	16.00
Pisgah Forest, Vase, Turquoise Crackle, Stephen, 1930, 4 1/2 X 6 1/2 In.	42.00
Pisgah, Sugar & Creamer, Miniature, Turquoise	15.00
Plate, see under special types such as ABC, Calendar, Christmas	
Plated Amberina, Bowl, 8 X 3 1/2 In.	5500.00
Plated Silver, see Silver Plate	

Plique a jour is an enameling process. The enamel was laid between thin raised metal lines and heated. The finished piece has transparent enamel held between the thin metal wires.

Political Campaign, Badge, President McKinley Hurrah Procession	45.00
Political Campaign, Balloting Box, Marbles For Blackballing	30.00
Political Campaign, Bandana, Benjamin Harrison, Silk, 20 X 19 In.	68.00
Political Campaign, Bandana, Red, White, Blue, We Want Roosevelt	7.00
Political Campaign, Bandana, Teddy Roosevelt, Red, Portrait, Slogan	40.00
Political Campaign, Bandana, Woodrow Wilson	15.00
Political Campaign, Bank, McGovern, Shriver	5.50
Political Campaign, Banner, Suffragette, Votes For Women, C.1919	3.50
Political Campaign, Banner, 1908, Hello Bill, Taft, Cloth	12.00
Political Campaign, Belt Buckle, LBJ	5.00
Political Campaign, Belt, Hoover & Victory, Leather	50.00
Political Campaign, Book, Abraham Lincoln Campaign Song Book, C.1860	45.00
Political Campaign, Book, Song, Garfield & Arthur, 1880, 24 Pages	25.00
Political Campaign, Box, Candy, McKinley, Chelsea, Mass., 7 1/2 In.	11.00
Political Campaign, Button, Al Smith, Bronze, Hat Shaped	10.00
Political Campaign, Button, All The Way With Adlai, 9 In.	8.00
Political Campaign, Button, Browder, Ford, Communist, Oval, 1940	25.00
Political Campaign, Button, Bryan, Kern	28.00
Political Campaign, Button, Bury Goldwater	.50
Political Campaign, Button, Carter Talks In Playboy	25.00
Political Campaign, Button, Clothing, Zachary Taylor, Raised Letters, Brass	28.00
Political Campaign, Button, Coolidge, Dawes	6.00
Political Campaign, Button, Dewey & Bricker	3.00
Political Campaign, Button, Dewey & Warren	3.00
Political Campaign, Button, Dewey, Creighton, Warren	3.00
Political Campaign, Button, Dick Nixon, Acrostic Of Dick	1.00
Political Campaign, Button, Embossed Flag, Bryan, Sewall	22.50
Political Campaign, Button, Garfield, Arthur	15.00
Political Campaign, Button, Goober Peas For Carter-Mondale	5.00
Political Campaign, Button, Harding, 5/8 In.	9.00
Political Campaign, Button, Harding, 7/8 In.	10.00
Political Campaign, Button, Hoover, Cooper, Black, 9/16 In.	16.00
Political Campaign, Button, Ike And Mamie, Picture	15.00
Political Campaign, Button, J.F.Kennedy, Inauguration Day, 1961, 3 1/2 In.	1.00
Political Campaign, Button, Johnson, Peace & Prosperity, Vote L.B.J. In '64	2.00
Political Campaign, Button, Landon & Knox, Elephant	3.00
Political Campaign, Button, Landon & Knox, Sunflower	3.00
Political Campaign, Button, Lemke, O'Brien, 1936	38.00
Political Campaign, Button, McKinley	8.00
Political Campaign, Button, McKinley, Hobart	10.00
Political Campaign, Button, McKinley, Roosevelt	10.00
Political Campaign, Button, Missouri Is Bayh Partisan	2.50
Political Campaign, Button, New Deal In Pennsylvania	5.00

Political Campaign, Button, Nixon & Lodge, Picture Of Elephant, Experience	.60
Political Campaign, Button, Nixon-Agnew, Jugate, Inauguration, 1969, 3 1/2 In.	7.50
Political Campaign, Button, Nixon, Flasher, I'm For Nixon, 1960	.75
Political Campaign, Button, No Third Term, Yellow And Black	3.00
Political Campaign, Button, Our Choice, Hiram W.Johnson For President	8.50
Political Campaign, Button, Rockefeller For President	.75
Political Campaign, Button, Roosevelt	8.00
Political Campaign, Button, Roosevelt, Truman, 1 1/2 In.	35.00
Political Campaign, Button, Speed Recovery, Re-Elect Hoover	5.00
Political Campaign, Button, Spiro In '76	2.50
Political Campaign, Button, St.Louisans For Carter-Mondale	5.00
Political Campaign, Button, Stevenson, Flasher, All The Way With Adlai	1.50
Political Campaign, Button, Stevenson, Picture Of G.I., I Like Stevenson	10.00
Political Campaign, Button, Taft	15.00
Political Campaign, Button, Votes For Women, 1915	5.00
Political Campaign, Button, Wendell Willkie, 1 3/4 In.	12.00
Political Campaign, Button, Willkie & McNary	3.00
Political Campaign, Button, Wilson	15.00
Political Campaign, Button, Wilson, Marshall, Black, White	45.00
Political Campaign, Button, Wilson, Marshall, Red, White, Blue	25.00
Political Campaign, Cane, President McKinley	52.00
Political Campaign, Card, Metamorphosis, Grant, Tilden, Tobacco Advertisement	30.00
Political Campaign, Catalogue, 1904, Roosevelt, Campaign Supplies	125.00
Political Campaign, Cigar, Nixon, 10 In.	9.50
Political Campaign, Cigarettes, Eisenhower, Unopened	15.00
Political Campaign, Coloring Book, Anti-Carter	2.00
Political Campaign, Cutter, Cigar, Souvenir, T.Roosevelt Bull Part, 1912	48.00
Political Campaign, Doll, Full Uniform Eisenhower	15.00
Political Campaign, Ferrotype, Lincoln, 1860, Metallic Frame, Brass Shell	160.00
Political Campaign, Flyer, Cleveland U.S. Blaine, Lithograph, 1888, 13 In.	35.00
Political Campaign, Hat, Straw, Wallace For President, Red, White, Blue Band	15.00
Political Campaign, Holder, Cigar, Wooden, Celluloid Picture, Gus A.Wenzel	15.00
Political Campaign, Inaugural Invitation, Nixon, Agnew, 1969	7.50
Political Campaign, Inaugural, Harry Truman, 1949	22.00
Political Campaign, Jugate, Bryan, Stevenson	15.00
Political Campaign, Jugate, Goldwater & Miller, 3 1/2 In.	.75
Political Campaign, Jugate, Kennedy & Johnson, Eagle	2.50
Political Campaign, Jugate, Kennedy & Johnson, My Choice For '60	1.50
Political Campaign, Jugate, McGovern & Shriver, Give Peace A Chance	35.00
Political Campaign, Jugate, Nixon & Lodge, Bunting Background	2.50
Political Campaign, Jugate, Nixon & Lodge, Eagle	2.50
Political Campaign, Jugate, Stevenson And Sparkman	8.00
Political Campaign, Kerchief, Teddy Roosevelt	9.50
Political Campaign, Lantern, Paper, Garfield & Arthur	65.00
Political Campaign, Lap Robe, Teddy Roosevelt, Rough Rider, 46 X 57 In.	150.00
Political Campaign, License Plate Attachment, Hope Of Our Country, Willkie	15.00
Political Campaign, License Plate, Townsend Plan, 1936, 13 X 4 1/4 In.	8.50
Political Campaign, Matchbook, Willkie	6.00
Political Campaign, Medal, Inaugural, John Kennedy, Lincoln On Reverse, 3 In.	18.00
Political Campaign, Medal, McKinley Inauguration, Red, White, Blue Ribbon	30.00
Political Campaign, Medal, Peach, President Wilson, Bronze Picture, 1918	15.00
Political Campaign, Menu, Dinner, Lincoln & Ike Prints, January, 1960	12.00
Political Campaign, Mug, Atlantic City, R.E.Delany, National Convention, 1911	35.00
Political Campaign, Mug, Robert Kennedy	7.00
Political Campaign, Necktie, Landon Portrait	20.00
Political Campaign, Pack Of Cigarettes, McGovern	12.50
Political Campaign, Paperweight, 1901, Pan American	20.00
Political Campaign, Peepview, President Garfield & Family, Ivory	45.00
Political Campaign, Pen, Nixon Now More Than Ever	4.00
Political Campaign, Pencil, Al Smith Head, Celluloid	22.50
Political Campaign, Pencil, Figural Head, Al Smith For President, 1928	22.00
Political Campaign, Pin, Anti-Roosevelt, 1944	3.50
Political Campaign, Pin, Brass Elephant Head, Willkie	18.50
Political Campaign, Pin, Dewey	
Political Campaign, Pin, Golden P.T.Boat, Figure Of Kennedy, 1 3/4 In.	6.50

Political Campaign, Pin, Harrison & Reid, 1892, Jugate, Cardboard, Tin Frame	160.00
Political Campaign, Pin, Ike With 5 Stars	15.00
Political Campaign, Pin, Lapel, Bull Moose, PTAP	10.00
Political Campaign, Pin, Lapel, Cox, Pewter	12.00
Political Campaign, Pin, Rooster, I Will Crow In November, Cox Campaign	25.00
Political Campaign, Pin, Tin, 1961, 1 1/4 In.	86.50
Political Campaign, Pin, 1844, Ashland Farmer Henry Clay	9.50
Political Campaign, Plate, Garfield	14.00
Political Campaign, Plate, McKinley Protection Of Plenty, Frosted, Gilt	24.00
Political Campaign, Plate, Nixon	12.00
Political Campaign, Portrait, Win With Wilson, Color, 1 1/4 In.	20.00
Political Campaign, Postcard, Our Choice, Taft & Sherman	8.00
Political Campaign, Poster, Harding & Coolidge, Eagle, Flag In Center, 16 In.	28.00
Political Campaign, Poster, Nixon, Watergate, Last Supper, 1973	15.00
Political Campaign, Ribbon, Cleveland-Hendricks, 1884, Silk, Floral, 6 In.	28.00
Political Campaign, Ribbon, J.F.Kennedy, Inauguration, Jan.20, 1961	.50
Political Campaign, Sealer, Wax, Board Of Elections	50.00
Political Campaign, Sewing Kit, Hoover & Curtis	7.50
Political Campaign, Sheet Music, Up Went McKinley, C.1895	18.00
Political Campaign, Slide, Theater, Hughes & Fairbanks, 1916	45.00
Political Campaign, Song, Al Smith, Sidewalks Of New York, 1928	12.00
Political Campaign, Spoon, Wm.J.Bryan, Poor Man's Candidate	6.00
Political Campaign, Standard Bearer, GOP, 10 Presidents, Taft & Sherman	95.00
Political Campaign, Stick, Walking, Bryan & Stevenson, Portraits, Flags	285.00
Political Campaign, Sticker, Bumper, J.F.Kennedy	3.00
Political Campaign, Teapot, Musical, Hail To The Chief, LBJ	45.00
Political Campaign, Thimble, Coolidge, Dawes	8.00
Political Campaign, Ticket, Democratic Convention, 1912	5.00
Political Campaign, Ticket, Republican National Convention, 1896	7.50
Political Campaign, Tie Tac, Eisenhower	3.00
Political Campaign, Tie Tac, Truman	1.00
Political Campaign, Toby Mug, Herbert Hoover, Syracuse China, 7 In.	85.00
Political Campaign, Token, James Buchanan, Picture	9.50
Political Campaign, Token, Winnfield S.Hancock For President	7.50
Political Campaign, Torch, Parade, Glass Ball Type, 1880 Letters On Front	47.50
Political Campaign, Torch, Peace 1865, Orange County, N.Y.	40.00
Political Campaign, Tray, Oval, William Jennings Bryan	22.00
Political Campaign, Tray, Taft, Sherman, Scallop Edge, Medallions, 10 1/2 In.	39.00
Political Campaign, U.S.Grant Peace, Green Maple Leaf	35.00
Political Campaign, Watch Fob, Mechanical, McKinley, Eagle Moves	65.00
Political Campaign, Watch Fob, Roosevelt & Johnson, 1912	27.00

Pomona glass is clear with a soft amber border decorated with pale blue or rose-colored flowers and leaves. The colors are very, very pale. The background of the glass is covered with a network of fine lines. It was made from 1885 to 1888 by the New England Glass Company.

Pomona, Bowl, Amber Stained Upper, 2nd Grind Clear Glass Below, 4 1/2 In.	75.00
Pomona, Bowl, Crimped Sides, Amber Stained, 4 1/2 X 2 1/4 In.	75.00
Pomona, Bowl, Finger, Honey Amber Stain, 2 1/2 X 5 1/2 In.	115.00
Pomona, Bowl, Finger, Strawflower, Ruffled	135.00
Pomona, Bowl, Finger, Thumbprint	50.00
Pomona, Bowl, Low, Crimped Sides, Amber, 4 1/2 X 2 1/4 In.	75.00
Pomona, Bowl, New England, Blueberry Pattern, Crimped Handle	98.00
Pomona, Bowl, New England, Cornflower Garland, Ruffled, 2nd Grind, 9 1/2 In.	450.00
Pomona, Bowl, Ruffled Rim, Amber And Clear, 2 1/4 X 4 In.	75.00
Pomona, Castor, Pickle, Cornflowers, 2nd Grind, Footed Frame	325.00
Pomona, Creamer, Ruffled Top, Applied Handle, 2nd Grind	135.00
Pomona, Cup, Punch, Blue Cornflowers	85.00
Pomona, Cup, Punch, 1st Grind, Amber Top, Acanthus Leaves, Amber Handle	115.00
Pomona, Pitcher, Cornflowers, 2nd Grind, 7 1/2 In.	265.00
Pomona, Pitcher, Pansy & Butterfly, Amber Handle, 2nd Grind, 8 1/2 In.	575.00
Pomona, Pitcher, Tankard, Pansy, Butterfly, Amber Handle, 2nd Grind, 8 1/4 In.	205.00
Pomona, Table Set, Midwestern, 4 Piece	185.00
Pomona, Toothpick, Diamond-Quilted	150.00
Pomona, Toothpick, Tapered, Applied Rigaree	85.00

Pomona, Tumbler, Blue Cornflower Design, 1st Grind .... 105.00 To 225.00
Pomona, Tumbler, Expanded Diamond, Amber Stain, 2nd Grind 67.00
Pomona, Tumbler, New England, Blue Cornflowers, Amber Rim, 1st Grind, 4 In. 103.00
Pomona, Tumbler, Pale Blue Cornflower, Amber Trim, 1st Grind 104.00
Pomona, Tumbler, Pansy & Butterfly .... 162.50 To 167.50
Pomona, Tumbler, Pansy & Butterfly, Applied Amber Handle, 2nd Grind 575.00
Pomona, Tumbler, 2nd Grind, Amber Stain 35.00
Pomona, Vase, Blue Cornflowers, Toed Base, 5 1/4 In. 175.00
Pomona, Vase, Celery, New England, Cornflower Pattern 240.00
Pomona, Vase, Raised Fish & Seaweed, Bulbous, 2nd Grind, 6 In. 150.00
Pontypool, see Tole
Popeye, Bank, Dime, 1956 .... 17.50
Popeye, Bank, Lithographed Tin, 1935, 1 3/4 X 2 1/4 X 3 1/2 In. 69.00
Popeye, Bank, Register, Dime, King Features, 1929 .... 17.50
Popeye, Book, Popeye And The Pirates, Movable Parts, 1945 .... 25.00
Popeye, Box, Pencil, 1934 .... 9.00
Popeye, Bubble Set, 1935 .... 8.00
Popeye, Doll, Bisque, 5 In. 50.00
Popeye, Doll, Popeye's Dog, Jeep, Wood, Jointed, 1936, 4 1/2 In. 66.00
Popeye, Doll, Wood, Carved & Painted, With Bowling Ball, 18 In. 135.00
Popeye, Figurine, With Bowling Ball, 18 In. 165.00
Popeye, Game, Pipe Toss, 1935 .... 20.00
Popeye, Pegboard, King Features, 1934, Complete 30.00
Popeye, Plate, Picture, I Yam So Strong Cause I Eats My Spinach, 7 1/2 In. 15.00
Popeye, Puzzle, Popeye The Juggler, 1929 .... 20.00
Popeye, Sparkler, Chein, 1959, Box 10.00
Popeye, Toy, Sweet Pea On Lap, 1929, Fisher Price, Pull, 7 1/2 X 9 1/2 In. 95.00
Popeye, Truck, Semi, Popeye Transit Co., 1950s 125.00
Porcelain, see also Copeland, Nippon, R.S.Prussia, etc.
Porcelain, Apothecary Mortar & Pestle, Blue Arrow Mark, Made In Germany 22.50
Porcelain, Barrel, Biscuit, Red Roses, Receded Handle, Dark Blue, 8 In. 49.00
Porcelain, Berry Set, Portrait, Austria, 6 Piece 75.00
Porcelain, Bone Dish, Crescent Shape, Floral Lei, Red Roses, Gold Rim, Marked 5.00
Porcelain, Bone Dish, Hand-Painted, Cupid, Set Of 4 .... 40.00
Porcelain, Bone Dish, Pink Carnation Decoration 2.50
Porcelain, Bookends, German, Deco Period Lady, White & Gold Trim 48.00
Porcelain, Boot, Lady's, Floral, German 18.00
Porcelain, Bowl, Austrian, 3 Children Playing, Ormolu Stand, 8 In. 85.00
Porcelain, Bowl, Blackberry Design, 3-Legged, AKD France, 9 1/2 In. 42.00
Porcelain, Bowl, Blue Geisha Girl, Deep, 9 In. 14.50
Porcelain, Bowl, Centerpiece, Rosebuds, Forget-Me-Nots, Pink, Red, Blue, 10 In. 22.50
Porcelain, Bowl, Famille Rose, Family Scene Medallion, Japanese, 9 1/2 In. 50.00
Porcelain, Bowl, Gold Gilding, Blue, Birds, Handled & Lidded, English, 6 In. 95.00
Porcelain, Bowl, Hand-Painted Flowers, Gold Trim, Moliere, Germany, 9 1/2 In. 49.00
Porcelain, Bowl, Oval Fruit, Open Handles, Florals, Altwasser, 12 3/4 In. 28.00
Porcelain, Bowl, Red Roses, German, 10 1/2 In. 34.00
Porcelain, Bowl, Rice, Marsh Grasses, Cobalt Blue Ring, Brown, Cream 25.00
Porcelain, Bowl, Rosebuds, Forget-Me-Nots, Scalloped, Gold, Pink, Red, 10 In. 22.50
Porcelain, Bowl, 4 Leaf Clovers, Good Luck, White, Square, German, 9 In. 22.00
Porcelain, Box, Dove, Russian Marks, 8 1/2 In. 150.00
Porcelain, Box, Floral Lid, Maroon & Gold Border, Fluted Edge, 4 X 2 X 2 In. 22.50
Porcelain, Box, Hairpin, Heart Shaped, Floral Bouquets, Lid, French 14.00
Porcelain, Box, Hand-Painted Roses, 4 X 5 In. 7.50
Porcelain, Box, Hinged, Cherubs, 3 X 3 In. 42.00
Porcelain, Box, Patch, Insect Shape, Orange, Brown, Black, 2 1/2 X 4 1/2 In. 85.00
Porcelain, Box, Patch, Multicolored Blossoms, Gold Tracery, Hinged Lid 37.50
Porcelain, Box, Patch, Painted, Ladies, German 85.00
Porcelain, Box, Patch, Shape Of Insect, Lidded Top, Fisher & Meig, 4 1/2 In. 85.00
Porcelain, Box, Pin, Figural, Pink Pig On Overstuffed Chair, Opens Behind 25.00
Porcelain, Box, Puff, Blue, Hand-Painted Roses & Scrolls On Lid, France 45.00
Porcelain, Box, Ram, Russian Marks, 8 1/2 In. 150.00
Porcelain, Box, Trinket, Roses, Gold Trimmed, Pagoda Shaped Top, Ribbed, 4 In. 5.00
Porcelain, Bust, Marie Antoinette, Biscuit Porcelain, Glass Case, 12 1/2 In. 150.00
Porcelain, Butter, Florals On Green, Pink Strainer, Round, Incised, Numbered 9.50
Porcelain, Butter, Hand-Painted Bird Of Paradise, German 6.00

Porcelain, **Butter,** Insert Strainer, Round, Pastel Blue, Green, Pink, Orange 9.50
Porcelain, **Caddy,** Tea, Hand-Painted Flowers, Carlsbad, Austria 29.00
Porcelain, **Cake Set,** Hand-Painted Flowers, German, 7 Piece 20.00
Porcelain, **Candlestick,** Chamber, Gold & Blue Floral Decoration 18.50
Porcelain, **Candlestick,** Dragons, Bats, Bandings, Pricket Type, 2 Part, Pair 1000.00
Porcelain, **Candlestick,** Shaped Like A Vase, Roses, 2 Handles, C.1880 .... 4.00
Porcelain, **Canister Set,** Floral, 4 Piece, Saltbox, 3 Peppers, Cinnamon, Nutmeg 45.00
Porcelain, **Canister Set,** White Luster, Gold Beading, German, 6 Piece 115.00
Porcelain, **Cap Stand,** 8 Sided, Chinese, C.1870, 11 In. 185.00
Porcelain, **Celery,** Roses, Green, German, Large 14.00
Porcelain, **Chocolate Pot,** Blue, Pink & Purple Roses, Gold Tracery, 10 In. 70.00
Porcelain, **Chocolate Pot,** Daisies, Roses, Cupid, Green Wreath With Cross Mark 38.00
Porcelain, **Chocolate Pot,** Red Geisha Girl 25.00
Porcelain, **Chocolate Pot,** Yellow Roses 33.00
Porcelain, **Chocolate Set,** Geisha Girl, 7 Piece 140.00
Porcelain, **Chocolate Set,** Gold Trim, Red Roses, White Ground, 9 Piece 135.00
Porcelain, **Chocolate Set,** Orange Border, 4 Cups & Saucers, 8 Piece, Geisha 75.00
Porcelain, **Coffee Set,** White, Gold, Finial, Ribbed, C.1840, French, 4 Piece 110.00
Porcelain, **Compote,** English Country Scene, Teal Blue, Gold Beading, 8 1/2 In. 27.50
Porcelain, **Compote,** White, Pedestal, Openwork, Basket Weave, 8 3/4 In. 35.00
Porcelain, **Creamer,** Chinese Oriental Figures, Water Scene, 5 In. 20.00
Porcelain, **Creamer,** Cow, Marked Czechoslovakia 10.00
Porcelain, **Creamer,** Figural Cow, White, Tan, Brown, C.1900 .... 27.00
Porcelain, **Creamer,** Figural, Cow, Brown & White, C.1890, 6 In. 45.00
Porcelain, **Creamer,** Figural, Cow, White, Black Upper Torso, Marked Germany 40.00
Porcelain, **Creamer,** German, Figural, Blue & White Cow, Scenic 40.00
Porcelain, **Creamer,** Mother-Of-Pearl Finish, Cat Handle, Czechoslovakia 8.00
Porcelain, **Creamer,** Old Mother Hubbard, Full Verse On Back, German 16.00
Porcelain, **Creamer,** Roses, Bouquets, Beaded, Handle, White, 5 In. 11.00
Porcelain, **Cup & Saucer,** Blue Flowering Vine, C.1800, Rauenstein 35.00
Porcelain, **Cup & Saucer,** Chocolate, Double Handle, Gold, Green Trim, Signed 15.00
Porcelain, **Cup & Saucer,** Demitasse, Gray Dragon, Yellow Lined, Hirode 7.50
Porcelain, **Cup & Saucer,** Flying Turkey, 3-Legged Cup, Oriental Writing 22.00
Porcelain, **Cup & Saucer,** German, Blue And White, Resembling Delft, Weimar 22.50
Porcelain, **Cup & Saucer,** Gold Leaf Cup & Handle, Petunias Interior, Gold 12.50
Porcelain, **Cup & Saucer,** Gray Dragon, Yellow Lining, Marked 15.00
Porcelain, **Cup & Saucer,** Hand-Painted, Roses, Pointed Panels, Gold, Japan 7.00
Porcelain, **Cup & Saucer,** Red Edge, Floral Center, Pair 22.50
Porcelain, **Cup & Saucer,** Thistle, Wishbone Handle, White, Blue, Green 8.50
Porcelain, **Cup & Saucer,** Thousand Faces, Japanese 18.00
Porcelain, **Cup & Saucer,** Victorian, A Present From Blackpool 20.00
Porcelain, **Cup,** Nut, Geisha Girl, Fluted, Footed 8.00
Porcelain, **Decanter,** Russian, Firebird Shape, Red, Gilt, Black, & White, 8 In. 95.00
Porcelain, **Desk Set,** Florals On White, Victoria Austria, 6 Piece 75.00
Porcelain, **Dish,** Basket, Crocuses, Handled, IPF Germany, 8 1/2 In. 20.00
Porcelain, **Dish,** Cheese, Slant Top, Hand-Painted, English, 6 X 7 1/2 In. 35.00
Porcelain, **Dish,** Divided, Round Dancing Ladies, Ivory, Gold 25.00
Porcelain, **Dish,** Double Leaf, Tree Handle, Pink & Gold, Luster, C.T., German 29.50
Porcelain, **Dish,** Double Shell, Flowers, Gold, RRM, Eagle Mark, 11 1/4 In. 32.00
Porcelain, **Dish,** Hand-Painted Landscape, View Of North Wales, Bloor Derby 150.00
Porcelain, **Dish,** Sauce, Blue & White, Oblong, 8 Ft. 30.00
Porcelain, **Egg,** Hand-Decorated, Opens To Hold Rings, Trinkets, 2 In., Pair 2.00
Porcelain, **Eggcup,** Lightweight, Unmarked 3.00
Porcelain, **Ewer,** Monk, 7 In., Pair 150.00
Porcelain, **Figurine,** Bird Rests On Brown Stump Pedestal, Molded Feathers 55.00
Porcelain, **Figurine,** Black, On Potty, White Nightshirt & Cap, Gold Trim 55.00
Porcelain, **Figurine,** Bluebird, Signed Cordey, 10 In. 40.00
Porcelain, **Figurine,** Boy Riding Red Carp, Chinese, 6 1/2 X 6 1/4 In. 110.00
Porcelain, **Figurine,** Brown & White Hunting Dog, 7 In. 20.00
Porcelain, **Figurine,** Cat, Sitting On Tails, Blue, 10 In., Pair 185.00
Porcelain, **Figurine,** Children Singing From Book, Marked, German, 3 1/2 In. 24.00
Porcelain, **Figurine,** Chinese Man, Impressed China Mark, 12 1/2 In. 65.00
Porcelain, **Figurine,** Cleopatra, Holding Snake Over Head, 8 1/2 In. 100.00
Porcelain, **Figurine,** Clown Pets Pony, Russian, S.Orlov In Cyrillic Lettering 45.00
Porcelain, **Figurine,** Eagle, Galluba & Hofman, 1889 .... 95.00

Porcelain, Figurine, Foxes, Two Standing Side By Side, 7 X 11 In.	195.00
Porcelain, Figurine, German, Girl In Bathing Suit, 1900, 8 In.	65.00
Porcelain, Figurine, Germany, Pig Driving Railroad Engine	38.00
Porcelain, Figurine, Girl In Knee-Length Swimsuit, Schierholz & Sohn, 8 In.	65.00
Porcelain, Figurine, Girl, Floral On Dress, Bisque, German, 16 In.	95.00
Porcelain, Figurine, Goddess With Harp, European, C.1880, 12 In.	175.00
Porcelain, Figurine, Gypsy Girl, Flower In Left Hand, 8 In.	35.00
Porcelain, Figurine, Lady, Pink & Green Enamel, Chinese, 5 1/2 In.	25.00
Porcelain, Figurine, Monkey Wearing Turquoise Decorated Robe, 6 In.	55.00
Porcelain, Figurine, Napoleon 3rd, Victorian	58.00
Porcelain, Figurine, Negro Baby, 19th Century, 2 1/2 In.	32.00
Porcelain, Figurine, Pekinese, Brown, 3 1/2 X 4 1/2 In.	44.00
Porcelain, Figurine, Tiger, Marked West Germany, 10 In.Long	9.00
Porcelain, Figurine, Victorian, Boy On Chair With Lute, 4 1/2 In.	20.00
Porcelain, Figurine, 2 Dachshunds, Stands Side-By-Side On Pedestal, German	35.00
Porcelain, Furniture, Living Room, Miniature, Gold Trim, 4 Piece	60.00
Porcelain, Furniture, Miniature, Hand-Painted Florals, Blue Enamel, 6 Piece	150.00
Porcelain, Group, Colts On White Base, German, Brown, White Base, 3 1/2 In.	25.00
Porcelain, Group, Louis XVI Lady In Carriage, Raustein, 19th Century, 9 In.	350.00
Porcelain, Hair Receiver, Chinese, Colorful Enameled Scene, 2 X 4 In.	17.50
Porcelain, Hair Receiver, Cream & Floral, Austria, Signed	9.00
Porcelain, Hair Receiver, Red Geisha Girl	8.50
Porcelain, Hatpin Holder, Austrian, Pink Violets	42.50
Porcelain, Hatpin Holder, White With Roses	18.00
Porcelain, Holder, Jam Jar, Hand-Painted Currants, Gold, Handled	45.00
Porcelain, Inkstand, Cupid, Schlaggenwald, C.1835	80.00
Porcelain, Inkstand, Garland Of Flowers, German Eagles, Flame Torch	125.00
Porcelain, Jam, Cover & Underplate, Hand-Painted	37.50
Porcelain, Jar, Cookie, Pig, 12 In.	15.00
Porcelain, Jar, Cracker, Oriental Geisha Girls, Pink, Blue, Rust	75.00
Porcelain, Jar, Ginger, Floral, Green & Gold, Bone China	25.00
Porcelain, Jar, Mustard, Hobnail Effect, Handled, Footed, Lid	7.50
Porcelain, Jar, Tobacco, Bird, Full Figure, 5 In.	45.00
Porcelain, Jar, Tobacco, Cat & Dog, Each	55.00
Porcelain, Jar, Tobacco, Dog, Blue & White, German	35.00
Porcelain, Jar, Tobacco, Figural, Dog, White With Blue Green, German, 5 1/2 In.	48.00
Porcelain, Jar, Tobacco, Figural, Policeman, Googlie Eyes, German, 9 In.	165.00
Porcelain, Jardiniere, Octagonal, Blue & White, Japanese, 10 In.	35.00
Porcelain, Knife Rest, Hand-Painted	33.00
Porcelain, Lunch Box, Green Bonsai Tree, Gold, 4 Tiers With Lid, C.1900	225.00
Porcelain, Match Holder, Figural, Potty Baby, Blue & White	35.00
Porcelain, Match Holder, Wall, Striker, Hand-Painted Floral, Dog Head, 7 In.	45.00
Porcelain, Match Holder, White, Gold Band, Czechoslovakia, 2 1/2 In.	12.00
Porcelain, Mirror, Hand, Beveled Glass, Apple Blossom Designs	18.50
Porcelain, Muffineer, Katani	60.00
Porcelain, Mug, Child's, White, Florals, Leaves, Gold Band & Handle, 2 1/8 In.	15.00
Porcelain, Mug, Child's, Windmill, Chicken, Child Scene, Austria	12.00
Porcelain, Mug, Hand-Painted Game Scenes, English	5.00
Porcelain, Mug, Miniature, Get It At Evan's, Black Letters, Beige, 1 1/4 In.	5.00
Porcelain, Napkin Ring, see Napkin Ring	
Porcelain, Pig, At Fence, Toothpick, Pink, 3 X 3 In.	28.00
Porcelain, Pig, At Tree Base, White, 4 X 3 In.	20.00
Porcelain, Pig, In Bathtub, Pink, 5 X 3 1/4 In.	40.00
Porcelain, Pigs, In Bushel Basket, One Peeking Out Hole	22.00
Porcelain, Pigs, In Purse With Red Seal	58.00
Porcelain, Pitcher, Austrian, Alhambra, Multicolored Designs	35.00 To 350.00
Porcelain, Pitcher, Birds, Flowers, Bulbous, No.473, Arzberg, 7 1/2 In.	25.00
Porcelain, Pitcher, Card Decoration, Matte Finish, Trophy, Erie, Pa., 1901	42.00
Porcelain, Pitcher, Cobalt Ground, Gold Trim, Lady In Garden, 11 1/2 In.	135.00
Porcelain, Pitcher, Dewey & Gridley	125.00
Porcelain, Pitcher, English, Pink, Floral Border, Set Of 3 Graduating Sizes	75.00
Porcelain, Pitcher, Figural, Elk	19.00
Porcelain, Pitcher, Oriental Ship Scenes, White, Signed Haynes, 11 1/4 In.	125.00
Porcelain, Pitcher, Swans, Czechoslovakian, 5 In.	8.00
Porcelain, Pitcher, Syrup, Rose, Gold, Flip Lid, Crescent China, England Mark	45.00

Porcelain, Pitcher, Vine, Dragon Handle, White With Gold, 9 In. 25.00
Porcelain, Planter, Wall, French, Musicians & Dancers, Gold Trim, 9 X 13 In. 85.00
Porcelain, Plaque, A Trooper, Mounted Soldier, Royal Horse Artillery, 7 In. 12.50
Porcelain, Plaque, Lady & Cherubs, Gesso Frame, Printenier, 5 X 6 In. 300.00
Porcelain, Plaque, Long-Haired Draped Ladies, Raised Gold, Signed, Pair 35.00
Porcelain, Plaque, Madonna, Gilt Frame, Russian, 4 X 3 In. 150.00
Porcelain, Plate, A Present From Fedimiletown, Rose, Lattice Rim, 243 On Rear 7.50
Porcelain, Plate, Austrian, Portrait, Scenic, Viking Warrior & Lady, 9 5/8 In. 75.00
Porcelain, Plate, Cake, Austrian, Portrait Of Lady In Colonial Dress 25.00
Porcelain, Plate, Cake, German, Blue, Stripe Chintz Flowers In Center, 10 In. 10.00
Porcelain, Plate, Enamel Colors, Signed, China, 8 3/4 In. 35.00
Porcelain, Plate, English Coach Scene, Imperial Crown China, 8 In. 60.00
Porcelain, Plate, Exotic Birds, Urns Of Flowers, Rust Red Trim, Set Of 16 .... 20.00
Porcelain, Plate, German Luster, Lattice Rim, Pears, 8 In. 15.00
Porcelain, Plate, German, Coral Roses, Blue Daisies, Pierced Border, 7 1/2 In. 7.50
Porcelain, Plate, Handkerchief, Hand-Painted, 8 In.Diameter 20.00
Porcelain, Plate, Holly Pattern Center, Light To Dark Green, 12 1/4 In. 95.00
Porcelain, Plate, Japanese Portrait, 8 1/2 X 9 In. 20.00
Porcelain, Plate, Napkin, Hand-Painted Clematis, H & Co., Square, 8 3/4 In. 20.00
Porcelain, Plate, Portrait, Brunette Profile, Gold, Florals, Austria, 7 5/8 In. 30.00
Porcelain, Plate, Portrait, Gold Tracery, Beehive, Austria, 9 1/2 In. 85.00
Porcelain, Plate, Portrait, Green With Gold Trim, German, 11 1/2 In. 95.00
Porcelain, Plate, Portrait, Red-Haired Woman, Cherry Blossoms, D&C, France 39.00
Porcelain, Plate, Portrait, St.Bernard, Rococo Border, Beehive Mark, Austria 67.50
Porcelain, Plate, 5 White Mice On Limb, Yellow Ocher Ground, Austria, Crown 10.00
Porcelain, Platter, Protruded Decoration, C.1863, Alcock, 17 In. 34.00
Porcelain, Portrait, German, Scenic, L.T.Johnson, 1893, 12 X 16 In. 425.00
Porcelain, Pot De Creme Set, Gold Trim, C.1820, France, 11 Piece 185.00
Porcelain, Punch Bowl & 3 Mugs, Beige, Cream, Rose, Chocolate Style Mugs 400.00
Porcelain, Ramekin & Underliner, Blue & Green Floral Border, 1900 Kpm Mark 70.00
Porcelain, Range, Kitchen, Robin's-Egg Blue, Majestic 395.00
Porcelain, Ring Tree, Hand, Attached Tray, Gold & Pink Flowers, German 22.00
Porcelain, Salt & Pepper, Wraparound Lakeside Cottage Scene, Pair 5.00
Porcelain, Shoe, Dutch Clog, Says Bunker Hill Monument, Charlestown, Mass. 7.50
Porcelain, Shoe, German, 2 Cupids Sitting On Rim, 6 1/2 X 8 1/2 In. 125.00
Porcelain, Shoe, Gilding & Floral, Cupids Sitting On Top, German, 6 1/2 In. 165.00
Porcelain, Shoe, On Porcelain Pillow, Two Cupids On Shoe, 9 X 5 1/2 In. 95.00
Porcelain, Shoe, Pink Lusterware, Whitefish Bay Resort, Milwaukee, 7 In. 32.50
Porcelain, Shoe, 2 Cupids Sitting On Top, Gilded & Floral, 6 1/2 In. 165.00
Porcelain, Slipper, Mottled Green, 8 Holes For Lacing, 4 3/4 In. 15.00
Porcelain, Spittoon, Lady's, Brown & Orange Floral 30.00
Porcelain, Sugar & Creamer, 4 Leaf Clovers & Card Suits, German 25.00
Porcelain, Tankard & 4 Mugs, Beige, Rose, Smith Phillips China 250.00
Porcelain, Tea Set, Child's, Bluebird, 12 Piece 15.00
Porcelain, Tea Set, Child's, Cat & Dog Color Scenes, 24 Piece 125.00
Porcelain, Tea Set, Child's, Circus Scene, 18 Piece 125.00
Porcelain, Tea Set, Child's, Floral Pattern, 12 Piece 15.00
Porcelain, Tea Set, Child's, Floral, 19 Piece 22.50
Porcelain, Tea Set, Child's, Gold, Colorful Decorations, German, 15 Piece 168.00
Porcelain, Tea Set, Child's, Happy Fats, 23 Piece 500.00
Porcelain, Tea Set, Child's, Rose Pattern, 27 Piece 35.00
Porcelain, Tea Set, Child's, Rosebuds & Leaves, Gold Trim, 15 Piece 48.00
Porcelain, Tea Set, Child's, Small Rosebuds, 23 Piece 80.00
Porcelain, Tea Set, Child's, White With Gold Flowers, C.1880, German, 15 Piece 85.00
Porcelain, Tea Set, Roses, Leaves, Tirscehnreuth P.T.Bavaria, 15 Piece 150.00
Porcelain, Tea Set, Russian, Floral, Eagle & Cyrillic Marks, 1900, 14 Piece 175.00
Porcelain, Tea Set, Toy, Purple Grapes, 11 Piece 148.00
Porcelain, Tea Set, 6 Cup & Saucers, Sugar, Creamer, Gold Etched Floral 40.00
Porcelain, Tea Strainer, Soft Peach, Gold & Forget-Me-Nots, Fits Over Cup 22.00
Porcelain, Tile, Chinese, Landscape Designs, Famille Rose Colors, Framed, Pair 450.00
Porcelain, Tile, Tea, Hand-Painted, Pink & Yellow Roses, Pink Luster Rim 25.00
Porcelain, Toothpick, White, Melon Section, Floral, Gold Edged, 2 3/8 In. 22.50
Porcelain, Tray, Dark Wine & Gold Border, Inside Scene, Austria, Signed 70.00
Porcelain, Tray, Dogwood Decorations, Gold Edge On Open Handles, 17 In. 32.00
Porcelain, Tray, Pin, Three Figural Pigs, 2 3/4 In. 28.00

Porcelain, Tray, Portrait Of Monk, Green To Cream, Germany, 9 3/4 X 6 3/4 In. 27.00
Porcelain, Trinket Box, Hinged Lid, Brass Mounts, Green Cover, Base & Border 38.00
Porcelain, Tureen, Covered, Round, Gilt Decorated, French, C.1890, 12 In. 130.00
Porcelain, Umbrella Stand, Cobalt Blue, Cream, Japanese, C.1900, Pair, 25 In. 675.00
Porcelain, Urn, French Ormolu, Blue Baluster Body, Painted Lady, 10 In. 80.00
Porcelain, Vase, Austria, Beige, Orange & Red Floral, Matte, 6 1/2 In., Pair 35.00
Porcelain, Vase, Bronze Mounted, Lid, Figural, Scenic, Signed, 13 1/4 In. 400.00
Porcelain, Vase, Chinese, Orchid, Orange & Green, Figural, 22 1/2 In. 1200.00
Porcelain, Vase, Chinese, Runny Cobalts, Russets, Greens, Yellow, C.1850, 5 In. 37.50
Porcelain, Vase, Chinese, Temple, Geisha Woman In Garden, 11 In., Pair 255.00
Porcelain, Vase, Cobalt Blue, Foo Dog Handles, Raised Enamel Scene, 8 In. 30.00
Porcelain, Vase, Cupid On Side, 7 1/2 In. 40.00
Porcelain, Vase, Elephant With Rider, Blue & Brown, Marked, 6 X 4 In. 28.00
Porcelain, Vase, Fish In Relief, Marked, Japanese, C.1850 .... 385.00
Porcelain, Vase, Floral Decoration, Gold Edging, Multicolor, 9 In. 65.00
Porcelain, Vase, Floral, Vignette Of Lovers, 2 Handled, Footed, 13 1/2 X 9 In. 149.00
Porcelain, Vase, German, Forget-Me-Nots & Roses Raised In Relief, 3 In. 22.00
Porcelain, Vase, German, Woman Gathering Water From Waterfall, 5 In. 65.00
Porcelain, Vase, Gray Dragon, 3 In. 15.00
Porcelain, Vase, Ivory, Floral Band, Wachtersbach, Germany, 9 1/2 In. 35.00
Porcelain, Vase, Japanese, Blue & White Brown Bands, 9 1/2 In. 65.00
Porcelain, Vase, Melon Boys, Golds, Browns, 14 In., Pair 150.00
Porcelain, Vase, Oriental, People In Medallions, Cobalt, Greens, Russets, 4 In. 39.00
Porcelain, Vase, Roses, Forget-Me-Not, Pink, Blue, 3 In. 7.50
Porcelain, Vase, Temple, Polychromed Warrior Scenes, Handled, 17 1/2 In., Pair 350.00
Porcelain, Vase, Trumpet Shape, Blue Underglaze, Japanese, Pair, 12 In. 95.00
Porcelain, Vase, Violet Holder, Coin Gold Handle, Hand-Painted Roses 28.50
Porcelain, Vase, 3 Faces, Brown & Orange, Gold Trim, Marked, 6 X 3 In. 20.00
Porcelain, Wall Plate, Lattice Edging, Cupid With Bowl & Arrow To Center 26.00
Porcelain, Wig Stand, Chinese, Celadon Ground, Bird Motif, 12 In. 55.00
Porcelain, Wine, Oriental, Band Of Russet, Character Legends On Sides, Mark 12.00

Postcards were first legally permitted in Austria on October 1, 1869.
The United States passed postal regulations allowing the card in 1873.
Most of the picture postcards collected today date from 1910.

Postcard, Album, 1876 .... 55.00
Postcard, Alphabet, Klein, F 10.00
Postcard, Cherry Smash, Washington 100.00
Postcard, Gene Autry 5.00
Postcard, Judy Garland 6.00
Postcard, Katzenjammers, Buster Brown, Set Of 4 Uncut Sheets 12.00
Postcard, Lone Ranger & Silver 8.00
Postcard, Signed Shirley Temple Agar, 1948 .... 10.00
Postcard, White House Coffee, Picture Of White House, Dated 1907 .... 15.00
Postcard, Yellowstone National Park, Original Box, Haynes, 50 In Set 12.50
    Potlid, see also Pratt
Potlid, Burgess's Genuine Anchovy Paste, Base, Shield, Coat Of Arms 44.50
Potlid, Cries Of London, Adams 30.00
Potlid, Shakespeare's House, Adams 30.00
Potlid, Uncle Toby 55.00
    Pottery, see also Buffalo Pottery, Staffordshire, Wedgwood, etc.
Pottery, Bank, Still, Fat Pig, Mottled Glaze, Brown, Yellow, Ohio, 7 X 3 1/4 In. 40.00
Pottery, Bottle, Bird, Wooden Perch, 7 In. 10.95
Pottery, Bowl, Alamo, Green & Gold High Glaze, Art Deco, 3 X 6 In. 10.00
Pottery, Bowl, Red Interior, Brown, Light Green Exterior, Walley, 7 1/4 In. 170.00
Pottery, Canister Set, Mother-Of-Pearl, Gold Band, 10 Piece 60.00
Pottery, Canister Set, Pearlized, Gold Letters, 28 Pieces With Covers, German 125.00
Pottery, Celery, Flower Bouquet, Luster Border, No.136, Green Mark In Circle 13.00
Pottery, Decanter, Dutch Girl Holding Bottle, Bols 15.00
Pottery, Dish, Feeding, Baby's, This Is The Maiden All Forlorn, German 25.00
Pottery, Figurine, Peasant Woman With Basket, Signed, 4 In. 25.00
Pottery, Jar, Dragon-Like Creature In Relief, Carved, Black, 5 1/2 In. 175.00
Pottery, Jar, Glazed Aqua, Gourd Shaped, Catalina Mark, 5 In. 12.00
Pottery, Jar, Tobacco, Figural, Head Of Arab 45.00
Pottery, Jar, Tobacco, Figural, Motorcyclist 165.00

Pottery, Jug, Blue Stenciling, Bolstein & Miller Wine & Liquor, 1 Gallon 47.50
Pottery, Jug, Miniature, Ballantine's Whiskey, 3 In. 6.00
Pottery, Jug, Miniature, Blue-Green, Pair 6.50
Pottery, Mug, Child's, Christmas, Gold Drawing Of Santa & Children, Germany 22.00
Pottery, Mug, Indian Portrait, Usona, Goodwin Pottery, Ohio 100.00
Pottery, Mug, Ladies In Garden On Cream Glaze, Frog In Bottom, 4 1/2 In. 120.00
Pottery, Mug, Portrait Of St.Bernard Dog, Taylor Smith Taylor 45.00
Pottery, Pitcher, Blue Glazed, Bulbous, 7 1/2 In. 35.00
Pottery, Pitcher, Columbian Art, Tankard, Tavern, Green, Marked M & W 135.00
Pottery, Pitcher, Madonna, Star Of David, Gold Flowers, Medallions, Glazed 45.00
Pottery, Pitcher, Shamrocks, Green Beer, Green, Quart, 7 1/2 In. 10.00
Pottery, Relish, Spatters, Leaves, Pods, Poppies, 1634, Carleton Ware, 6 3/4 In. 10.00
Pottery, Salt & Pepper, Scottish, 1830-40, Pair 95.00
Pottery, Spittoon, Animated Bottles & Barrels, English, C.1900 .... 55.00
Pottery, Tankard Set, Pewter Top, 5 Amber Stained Glasses, German 225.00
Pottery, Tobacco Jar, Figural, Chinaman 35.00
Pottery, Tobacco Jar, Figural, German Man With Alpine Hat 30.00
Pottery, Tobacco Jar, Figural, Horse On Barrel 42.00
Pottery, Toby Mug, Black Tricorn, Blue Coat, Red Mug, England, 9 In. 165.00
Pottery, Toby Mug, Woman Holding Bottle, Brown Glaze, 7 1/2 In. 80.00
Pottery, Vase, Light Blue Archings, Indigo Blue, 7 1/4 In. 27.00
Pottery, Vase, Scarab, Sun God Design, Relief, Matte Green, Bulbous, 8 In. 135.00
Pottery, Vase, Vontury, Hummingbird, Floral, Pastel, 1940s Studio Artist 95.00

PRATT FENTON . *Pratt ware means two different things. It was an early Staffordshire pottery, cream colored with colored decorations, made by Felix Pratt during the late eighteenth century. There was also Pratt ware made with transfer designs during the mid-nineteenth century in Fenton, England.*

Pratt, Cup & Saucer, Indian, C.1840, Handleless Cup 55.00
Pratt, Figurine, Autumn, 9 1/2 In. 175.00
Pratt, Jar, Mustard, Blue, Fox Hunt Scene, January 19, 1856, 4 In. 40.00
Pratt, Jar, Ointment, Transfer Print Of Hunting Scene, Blue, 4 1/2 In. 45.00
Pratt, Jar, Pomade, Sailing Vessels At Sea 55.00
Pratt, Jar, Pomade, The Chin Chew River Scene 75.00
Pratt, Jar, Street Scene, Signed Austin, 5 In. 47.50
Pratt, Jar, Uncle Toby 60.00
Pratt, Jug, Bacchanalians At Play, C.1860, 7 In. 65.00
Pratt, Mug, Women Doing Laundry In Stream, Turquoise Background 175.00
Pratt, Pitcher, Decoration In Gray, Black Background, 3 In. 25.00
Pratt, Pitcher, Dogs, Hunter & Grapes In Raised Relief, Lavender, 6 In. 140.00
Pratt, Pitcher, Glazed Green, White Raised Figures, 8 1/2 In. 40.00
Pratt, Pitcher, Wellington & Hill, High Relief, Brown, Blue, Orange, 6 In. 150.00
Pratt, Plate, Village Wedding, 1861, 8 1/2 In. 46.00
Pratt, Potlid, Alexandra Palace 1873 .... 80.00
Pratt, Potlid, Bear, Lion & Cock, Political Reference To Crimean War 85.00
Pratt, Potlid, Cavalier 57.00
Pratt, Potlid, Children Of Flora 140.00
Pratt, Potlid, Country Quarters, Horse, Goats, Cat, Barn, 4 5/8 In. 75.00
Pratt, Potlid, Cries Of London, Lavender, Primrose 45.00
Pratt, Potlid, Doctor Johnson 50.00
Pratt, Potlid, Fishmonger, Housewife & Children, 5 1/2 In. 75.00
Pratt, Potlid, Game Bag, Pomade Jar 62.50
Pratt, Potlid, Harbor Of Hong Kong 65.00
Pratt, Potlid, Little Red Riding Hood 75.00
Pratt, Potlid, Low Life 75.00
Pratt, Potlid, Master Of The Hounds, With Pot 85.00
Pratt, Potlid, Pegwell Bay, Bellevue Walnut Frame 90.00
Pratt, Potlid, Persuasion 80.00
Pratt, Potlid, Red Bull Inn 65.00
Pratt, Potlid, Red Bull Inn, Large 90.00
Pratt, Potlid, Residence Of Anne Hathaway 65.00
Pratt, Potlid, Room Where Shakespeare Was Born, Engraving On Base Of Lid 95.00
Pratt, Potlid, Sebastopol, Two Soldiers 75.00
Pratt, Potlid, Sir, Robert Peel, Wheat Ear Border 120.00
Pratt, Potlid, Soldiers & Ladies In Courtyard, Buildings, Oak 70.00

Pratt, Potlid, Uncle Toby, Jesse Austin 35.00
Pratt, Potlid, Village Wedding 80.00
Pratt, Potlid, War, Signed Austin 65.00
Pratt, Potlid, Wimbledon, July 1860, Queen Victoria's First Shot 70.00
Pratt, Potlid, Wolf & The Lamb 70.00
Pratt, Sauce, Lady With Falcon, Lovers, Purple Borders, Framed, 7 In., Pair 110.00
Pratt, Sugar & Creamer, Orange Red With Scene 85.00
Pratt, Tea Set, Old Greek, 3 Piece 270.00
Pratt, Teapot, Indian, C.1840, Flow Blue, 9 In. 225.00
Presidential China, Plate, Oyster, Rutherford B.Hayes, Eagle Stamp, Haviland 195.00

*Pressed glass was first made in the United States in the 1820s after the
invention of pressed-glass machines. Hundreds of patterns of pressed glass
were made in complete table settings. Although the Boston and Sandwich
Works was the most famous of the pressed glass factories, there were about
sixteen other factories making pressed glass from 1830 to 1850, and still more
from 1850 to 1900, when pressed glass reached its greatest popularity. It is
now being widely reproduced.*

Recessed Ovals with Block Band, see Recessed Ovals
Pressed Glass, A Good Boy, Mug 11.50
Pressed Glass, A Good Mother, Star Rosetted, Plate, Bread 32.00
Acanthus, see Ribbed Palm
Pressed Glass, Acanthus Leaf, Eggcup, Dated April 23, 1878 .... 48.00
Acme, see Butterfly & Spray
Pressed Glass, Acorn Band, Spooner 15.00
Pressed Glass, Acorn, Salt & Pepper, Pink 35.00
Pressed Glass, Acorn, Spooner 20.00
Pressed Glass, Acorn, Sugar Shaker, Pink With Enameling 135.00
Pressed Glass, Acorn, Sugar Shaker, Shaded Pink, Satin Finish 140.00
Pressed Glass, Actress, Bottle, Dresser, Milk Glass 36.00
Pressed Glass, Actress, Bowl, 6 X 1 3/4 In. 37.50
Pressed Glass, Actress, Bread Tray, Miss Neilson 75.00
Pressed Glass, Actress, Cake Stand, Frosted Base, 10 In. 85.00
Pressed Glass, Actress, Celery 75.00
Pressed Glass, Actress, Compote, Covered, Frosted, High Standard, 7 1/4 In. 48.00
Pressed Glass, Actress, Compote, Covered, 6 In. 70.00
Pressed Glass, Actress, Compote, Frosted & Clear, High Standard, 8 In. 92.50
Pressed Glass, Actress, Compote, Frosted, Covered, 7 In. 48.00
Pressed Glass, Actress, Compote, High Standard, Covered, 6 In.Diameter 70.00
Pressed Glass, Actress, Compote, High Standard, Covered, 8 In. 87.50
Pressed Glass, Actress, Creamer 58.00
Pressed Glass, Actress, Creamer, All Clear 55.00
Pressed Glass, Actress, Dish, Cheese 185.00
Pressed Glass, Actress, Dish, Pickle, Miss Neilson 45.00
Pressed Glass, Actress, Goblet 75.00
Pressed Glass, Actress, Goblet, Stemmed, 6 1/2 In. 65.00
Pressed Glass, Actress, Platter, Bread, Miss Neilson 45.00
Pressed Glass, Actress, Sauce, Footed 17.50
Pressed Glass, Actress, Spooner, Maud Granger And Mary Anderson 48.00
Pressed Glass, Actress, Sugar, Covered, Kate Claxton 75.00
Pressed Glass, Admiral Dewey, Pitcher, Water 55.00
Pressed Glass, Admiral Dewey, Tumbler 55.00
Pressed Glass, Adonis, Butter, Lid 10.00
Pressed Glass, Adonis, Compote, 7 3/4 In. .... 15.00 To 21.50
Pressed Glass, Adonis, Spooner, Scalloped Top 14.50
Pressed Glass, Adonis, Sugar 15.00
Pressed Glass, Akron Block, Goblet 16.25
Pressed Glass, Alabama, Bowl, Flat, 5 In. 15.00
Pressed Glass, Alabama, Celery 14.00
Pressed Glass, Alabama, Compote, Open, 5 In. 22.50
Pressed Glass, Alabama, Creamer, Large 27.50
Pressed Glass, Alabama, Cruet, Facet Stopper 39.50
Pressed Glass, Alabama, Cruet, Stopper 38.00
Pressed Glass, Alabama, Nappy, Handled 11.00
Pressed Glass, Alabama, Pitcher, Water 22.00

Pressed Glass, Arched Grape, Goblet

Pressed Glass, **Alabama,** Relish, Oval	18.00
Pressed Glass, **Alabama,** Toothpick, Clear	20.00
Pressed Glass, **Alaska,** Bowl, Berry, Green, Enameled Flowers	80.00 To 95.00
Pressed Glass, **Alaska,** Creamer	27.00
Pressed Glass, **Alaska,** Creamer, Vaseline, Opalescent	45.00
Pressed Glass, **Alaska,** Sauce, Clear, Opalescent	22.00
Pressed Glass, **Alaska,** Sauce, Green	24.00
Pressed Glass, **Alaska,** Spooner, Blue, Opalescent	45.00 To 55.00
Pressed Glass, **Alaska,** Spooner, Opalescent	45.00
Pressed Glass, **Alaska,** Spooner, Opalescent To Clear	27.00
Pressed Glass, **Alaska,** Spooner, Vaseline, Opalescent	50.00
Pressed Glass, **Alaska,** Spooner, White, Opalescent	40.00
Pressed Glass, **Alaska,** Sugar & Creamer, Blue, Opalescent, Covered	150.00
Pressed Glass, **Alexis,** Toothpick, Clear	15.00
Pressed Glass, **Alligator Scales With Spear Point,** Sugar, Fern Etching	21.00
Pressed Glass, **Alligator Scales,** Toothpick, Blue	40.00
Pressed Glass, **Almond Thumbprint,** Eggcup	12.50
Pressed Glass, **Almond Thumbprint,** Salt, Covered	48.00
Pressed Glass, **Almond Thumbprint,** Sugar, Flint	32.00
Pressed Glass, **Almond Thumbprint,** Sugar, Open	18.00
Pressed Glass, **Almond Thumbprint,** Wine	10.00
Pressed Glass, **Amazon,** Cordial, Ruby	35.00
Pressed Glass, **Amazon,** Creamer, Child's	15.00
Pressed Glass, **Amazon,** Dish, Lions Finial, Handles, Oval	15.00
Pressed Glass, **Amazon,** Spooner, Miniature	22.50
Pressed Glass, **Amazon,** Tumbler	15.00
Pressed Glass, **Amber Block,** Water Set, 7 Piece	195.00
Amberette, see Klondike	
Pressed Glass, **Amberette,** Plate, Bread, "Give Us This Day," Edge Turned Up	40.00
Pressed Glass, **Anderson,** Creamer	18.00
Pressed Glass, **Angel,** Candlestick, Child's, Pair	18.00
Pressed Glass, **Anthemion,** Pitcher, Water	37.50
Pressed Glass, **Anthemion,** Plate, Flared, 10 In.	21.00
Pressed Glass, **Anthemion,** Sugar & Creamer, Covered	30.00
Pressed Glass, **Apollo,** Pitcher, Water, Bulbous	27.50
Pressed Glass, **Apollo,** Sauce, Footed, Green	14.00
Pressed Glass, **Apple Blossom,** Pitcher, Water	18.50
Pressed Glass, **Apple Blossom,** Tumbler	15.00
Pressed Glass, **Arabesque,** Goblet	16.00
Pressed Glass, **Arch,** Salt, Master, Footed, Flint	14.00
Pressed Glass, **Arch,** Wine, Flint	29.50
Pressed Glass, **Arched Fleur-De-Lis,** Banana Stand	30.00
Pressed Glass, **Arched Grape,** Sauce, 4 In.	6.00
Pressed Glass, **Arched Leaf,** Spill, Flint	75.00
Pressed Glass, **Arched Leaf,** Spooner, Flint	75.00
Pressed Glass, **Arched Ovals,** Toothpick, Ruby Stained, Souvenir	22.00
Pressed Glass, **Arched Panel,** Pitcher, Water	30.00
Argonaut Shell, see Nautilus	
Pressed Glass, **Argus,** Champagne, Flint	50.00
Pressed Glass, **Argus,** Eggcup, Flint	16.00
Pressed Glass, **Argus,** Goblet	31.00
Pressed Glass, **Argus,** Goblet, Wine	37.50

Pressed Glass, **Argus,** Jar, Mustard, Hinged Lid, Reed & Barton Spoon	28.50
Pressed Glass, **Argus,** Spooner, Plain Rim, Flint	40.00
Pressed Glass, **Argus,** Tumbler, Whiskey, Flint	25.00
Pressed Glass, **Argus,** Wine, Flint	27.50
Pressed Glass, **Arrowhead In Oval,** Butter Base	12.00
Pressed Glass, **Arrowhead In Oval,** Table Set, Child's, 4 Piece	75.00
Pressed Glass, **Arrowhead In Oval,** Wine	12.00
Art Novo, see Dogwood	
Pressed Glass, **Art,** Banana Stand, Large	65.00
Pressed Glass, **Art,** Butter, Covered	18.50
Pressed Glass, **Art,** Celery	25.00
Pressed Glass, **Art,** Creamer	16.50 To 26.50
Pressed Glass, **Art,** Relish, 6 X 8 In.	20.00
Pressed Glass, **Art,** Spooner	20.00
Pressed Glass, **Art,** Stand, Banana	75.00
Pressed Glass, **Artichoke,** Butter, Frosted	60.00
Pressed Glass, **Artichoke,** Sugar Shaker, Pink Top	65.00
Pressed Glass, **Artichoke,** Sugar, 2-Handled, Open, Frosted	22.00
Pressed Glass, **Ashburton,** Champagne	95.00
Pressed Glass, **Ashburton,** Champagne, Flint, 5 5/8 In.	30.00
Pressed Glass, **Ashburton,** Claret, Flint	40.00 To 44.50
Pressed Glass, **Ashburton,** Claret, Flint, Large, 5 1/4 In.	75.00
Pressed Glass, **Ashburton,** Claret, Flint, Small, 4 1/4 In.	125.00
Pressed Glass, **Ashburton,** Cup, Punch, Footed, Flint	32.00
Pressed Glass, **Ashburton,** Decanter, Pint, Flint	65.00
Pressed Glass, **Ashburton,** Eggcup, Cut Flint	27.50
Pressed Glass, **Ashburton,** Eggcup, Flint	17.50 To 20.00
Pressed Glass, **Ashburton,** Eggcup, Knob Stem	18.00
Pressed Glass, **Ashburton,** Goblet	9.00
Pressed Glass, **Ashburton,** Goblet, Flint	25.00 To 35.00
Pressed Glass, **Ashburton,** Goblet, Semisquared, Flint	30.00
Pressed Glass, **Ashburton,** Sugar, Covered, Flint	85.00
Pressed Glass, **Ashburton,** Tumbler, Flint	55.00
Pressed Glass, **Ashburton,** Tumbler, Flint, 8 Oz.	65.00
Pressed Glass, **Ashburton,** Tumbler, Water	55.00
Pressed Glass, **Ashburton,** Whiskey, Flint	40.00
Pressed Glass, **Ashburton,** Whiskey, Handled, Flint	60.00 To 125.00
Pressed Glass, **Ashburton,** Wine	28.50
Pressed Glass, **Ashburton,** Wine, Flint	30.00 To 45.00
Pressed Glass, **Ashburton,** Wine, 4 1/2 In.	38.00
Pressed Glass, **Ashman,** Bread Tray, Motto	45.00
Pressed Glass, **Ashman,** Celery	21.50
Pressed Glass, **Ashman,** Compote, Covered, 7 In.	45.00
Pressed Glass, **Ashman,** Sugar, Covered, Etched	43.00
Pressed Glass, **Ashman,** Water Set, Ruby Stained, Etched, Fern, 7 Piece	280.00
Pressed Glass, **Atlanta,** Dish, Rectangular, 4 1/2 X 7 In.	22.00
Pressed Glass, **Atlanta,** Tumbler, Clear	32.00
Pressed Glass, **Atlas,** Cake Stand, 8 1/2 In.	20.00
Pressed Glass, **Atlas,** Goblet, Lady's, 5 1/2 X 2 3/4 In.	18.50

Pressed Glass, Arched Fleur-De-Lis, Sugar

Pressed Glass, Atlas, Mug 12.00
Pressed Glass, Atlas, Saltshaker 8.50
Pressed Glass, Atlas, Toothpick 12.00
Pressed Glass, Atlas, Wine 15.00
Pressed Glass, Aurora, Decanter, Original Stopper, Ruby Stained 80.00
Pressed Glass, Aurora, Pitcher, Tankard, Etched Floral, 9 1/2 In. 28.00
Pressed Glass, Aurora, Tray For Wine Set, Ruby Stained 30.00
Pressed Glass, Aurora, Tray, Water 10.00
Pressed Glass, Austrian, Creamer, Clear 12.00
Pressed Glass, Austrian, Goblet 25.00
Pressed Glass, Austrian, Goblet, Clear 23.00
Pressed Glass, Aztec, Tumbler 3.50
    Baby Thumbprint, see Dakota
Pressed Glass, Bakewell Block, Sugar, Flint 50.00
    Balder, see also Pennsylvania
Pressed Glass, Balder, Glass, Juice 8.50
Pressed Glass, Balder, Goblet .... 12.50 To 15.00
Pressed Glass, Balder, Tumbler, Ground Bottom 9.75
Pressed Glass, Balder, Wine .... 13.00 To 18.50
    Balky Mule, see Currier & Ives
Pressed Glass, Ball & Swirl, Compote, 6 3/4 In. 25.00
Pressed Glass, Ball & Swirl, Creamer .... 9.00 To 24.50
Pressed Glass, Ball & Swirl, Creamer, Pedestal Base 25.00
Pressed Glass, Ball & Swirl, Sauce, Footed 9.50
Pressed Glass, Ball & Swirl, Spoon Holder 25.00
Pressed Glass, Baltimore Pear, Butter 27.50
Pressed Glass, Baltimore Pear, Butter, Covered .... 35.00 To 45.00

Pressed Glass, Ashburton, Bottle, Amethyst, Tumbler Mold

Pressed Glass, Ashburton, Champagne, Presentation Piece

Pressed Glass, Baltimore Pear, Compote, High Standard, Covered, 7 In.	70.00
Pressed Glass, Baltimore Pear, Creamer	15.00
Pressed Glass, Baltimore Pear, Goblet	30.00
Pressed Glass, Baltimore Pear, Plate	25.00
Pressed Glass, Baltimore Pear, Plate, 9 In.	15.00
Pressed Glass, Baltimore Pear, Sugar & Creamer	14.00

Bamboo, see Broken Column
Banded Beaded Grape Medallion, see Beaded Grape Medallion,
Banded

Pressed Glass, Banded Buckle, Spooner	17.50
Pressed Glass, Banded Buckle, Spooner, Flint	22.00
Pressed Glass, Banded Buckle, Sugar, Open	15.00
Pressed Glass, Banded Flute, Salt & Pepper	30.00
Pressed Glass, Banded Grape, Dish, Honey	6.00

Banded Portland when flashed with pink is sometimes called Maiden
Blush

Pressed Glass, Banded Portland, Celery, Ruby & Clear	55.00
Pressed Glass, Banded Portland, Compote, 7 X 7 1/2 In.	38.00
Pressed Glass, Banded Portland, Cup, Punch, Yellow Flash	28.00
Pressed Glass, Banded Portland, Dish, Pickle, Oval, Green Stained Rim, 8 3/4 In.	22.50
Pressed Glass, Banded Portland, Pitcher, Water, Ruby & Clear	145.00
Pressed Glass, Banded Portland, Relish	30.00
Pressed Glass, Banded Portland, Relish Boat, 6 1/2 In.	12.50
Pressed Glass, Banded Portland, Sugar Shaker	30.00
Pressed Glass, Banded Portland, Toothpick	28.00
Pressed Glass, Banded Portland, Toothpick, Maiden's Blush Color	28.50
Pressed Glass, Banded Portland, Toothpick, Ruby Stained	24.00
Pressed Glass, Banded Portland, Vase, Pink Flashed, 6 In.	45.00

Banded Raindrop, see Candlewick

Pressed Glass, Banded Stippled Star Flower, Goblet	15.00

Other Banded patterns, see under name of basic pattern. e.g.: Banded
Honeycomb, see Honeycomb, Banded
Bar & Diamond, see Kokomo

Pressed Glass, Barberry, Celery, Footed	33.00
Pressed Glass, Barberry, Compote, Low, 8 In.	16.00
Pressed Glass, Barberry, Eggcup	15.00 To 22.50
Pressed Glass, Barberry, Eggcup, Oval Berry	16.00
Pressed Glass, Barberry, Goblet	16.00 To 23.50
Pressed Glass, Barberry, Pitcher, Water, Applied Handle	75.00
Pressed Glass, Barberry, Plate, 6 In.	22.50
Pressed Glass, Barberry, Sauce, Footed	7.00
Pressed Glass, Barberry, Sauce, Footed, 4 In.	6.50
Pressed Glass, Barberry, Sherbet, Footed	6.00
Pressed Glass, Barberry, Spooner	17.00 To 17.50
Pressed Glass, Barberry, Spooner, Oval Berries	19.50

Barley & Oats, see Wheat & Barley
Barley & Wheat, see Wheat & Barley

Pressed Glass, Barley, Butter	30.00
Pressed Glass, Barley, Cake Stand	16.00
Pressed Glass, Barley, Cake Stand, Clear To Purple, 8 X 9 In.	35.00
Pressed Glass, Barley, Cake Stand, Pedestal, 9 1/2 In.	29.00
Pressed Glass, Barley, Celery	16.00
Pressed Glass, Barley, Compote, Open	25.00
Pressed Glass, Barley, Compote, Open, 8 1/2 In.	33.00
Pressed Glass, Barley, Pitcher, Water, Applied Handle	56.00
Pressed Glass, Barley, Sauce, Footed, 4 In.	7.50
Pressed Glass, Barley, Sauce, 4 In.	4.50
Pressed Glass, Barley, Spooner	16.50
Pressed Glass, Barley, Sugar	13.00
Pressed Glass, Barley, Tray, Bread, Gray	22.00
Pressed Glass, Barred Forget-Me-Not, Compote, Covered, 7 In.	35.00
Pressed Glass, Barred Forget-Me-Not, Goblet	19.50
Pressed Glass, Barred Forget-Me-Not, Pitcher, Water, Canton, Ohio	50.00
Pressed Glass, Barred Forget-Me-Not, Sugar & Creamer	55.00
Pressed Glass, Barred Forget-Me-Not, Wine	18.75

Barred Ovals, see Banded Portland

Pressed Glass, Barred Star, Pitcher 25.00

Pressed Glass, Barrel Huber, Goblet, 2 1/2 X 1 1/8 In. 30.00

Barreled Block, see Red Block

Bartlett Pear, see Pear

Pressed Glass, Basket Weave, Pitcher, Blue 32.00

Pressed Glass, Basket Weave, Pitcher, Water, Vaseline 45.00

Pressed Glass, Basket Weave, Salt & Pepper, Basket Holder 22.00

Pressed Glass, Basket Weave, Tray, Water, Blue 35.00

Pressed Glass, Basket Weave, Water Set, Blue, 4 Piece 135.00

Pressed Glass, Battleship Maine, Plate, 5 1/2 In. 15.00

Pressed Glass, Bead & Scroll, Creamer, Enameled Pink & Green Flowers Top 15.00

Pressed Glass, Bead & Scroll, Saltshaker 10.00

Pressed Glass, Bead & Scroll, Table Set, Child's, 3 Piece 110.00

Pressed Glass, Bead & Scroll, Wine 14.00

Pressed Glass, Beaded Acorn Medallion, Goblet .... 19.00 To 30.00

Pressed Glass, Beaded Acorn With Leaf Band, Spooner, Flint 45.00

Pressed Glass, Beaded Acorn, Champagne 32.50

Pressed Glass, Beaded Acorn, Goblet 19.00

Pressed Glass, Beaded Band, Butter .... 22.50 To 26.00

Pressed Glass, Beaded Band, Pickle Castor, Tongs 50.00

Beaded Bull's-Eye & Drape, see also Alabama

Pressed Glass, Beaded Cable, Wine 14.00

Pressed Glass, Beaded Chain, Creamer 20.00

Pressed Glass, Beaded Dart Band, Goblet 15.00

Pressed Glass, Beaded Dewdrop, Bowl, Handled, 7 1/2 In. 17.50

Pressed Glass, Beaded Dewdrop, Butter, Covered 50.00

Pressed Glass, Beaded Dewdrop, Salt, Footed 22.50

Pressed Glass, Beaded Dewdrop, Sauce, 4 1/4 In. 9.50

Pressed Glass, Beaded Dewdrop, Wine .... 30.00 To 45.00

Pressed Glass, Beaded Drape, Rose Bowl, Green, Opalescent 22.50

Pressed Glass, Beaded Ellipse, Butter, Covered 33.00

Pressed Glass, Beaded Fan, Rose Bowl, Opalescent, Footed 23.00

Pressed Glass, Beaded Grape Medallion, Banded, Pitcher, Water, Applied Handle 65.00

Pressed Glass, Beaded Grape Medallion, Banded, Wine 20.00

Pressed Glass, Beaded Grape Medallion, Eggcup 16.50

Pressed Glass, Beaded Grape Medallion, Goblet 20.00

Pressed Glass, Beaded Grape Medallion, Goblet, 4 5/8 X 4 In. 20.00

Pressed Glass, Beaded Grape Medallion, Spooner .... 16.50 To 17.00

Pressed Glass, Beaded Grape Medallion, Spooner, Banded 30.00

Pressed Glass, Beaded Grape, Bowl, 8 In. 25.00

Pressed Glass, Beaded Grape Medallion, Dish, Covered

Pressed Glass, Beaded Grape, Toothpick, Green

Pressed Glass, Beaded Grape, Butter, Covered	45.00
Pressed Glass, Beaded Grape, Cake Stand, Emerald Green	70.00
Pressed Glass, Beaded Grape, Celery, Green, Flat	36.00
Pressed Glass, Beaded Grape, Compote, Shallow	45.00
Pressed Glass, Beaded Grape, Creamer, Green	70.00
Pressed Glass, Beaded Grape, Pitcher, Water, Green, Gold	85.00
Pressed Glass, Beaded Grape, Pitcher, Water, Green, Round	82.50
Pressed Glass, Beaded Grape, Sauce	8.00
Pressed Glass, Beaded Grape, Sauce, 4 In.Square	5.00
Pressed Glass, Beaded Grape, Spooner	18.00
Pressed Glass, Beaded Grape, Toothpick, Green	37.50
Pressed Glass, Beaded Grape, Wine, Clear	14.00
Pressed Glass, Beaded Heart, Saltshaker, Clear	16.00
Pressed Glass, Beaded Leaf, Bowl, Green, Opalescent	20.00
Pressed Glass, Beaded Loop, Cake Stand, 9 In.	25.00 To 28.50
Pressed Glass, Beaded Loop, Dish, Honey	5.50
Pressed Glass, Beaded Loop, Goblet	32.00 To 32.50
Pressed Glass, Beaded Loop, Relish	15.00
Pressed Glass, Beaded Loop, Vase	19.00
Beaded Medallion, see Beaded Mirror	
Pressed Glass, Beaded Mirror, Goblet	15.00
Pressed Glass, Beaded Oval & Scroll, Butter	23.50
Pressed Glass, Beaded Oval Window, Creamer	25.00
Pressed Glass, Beaded Oval Window, Sugar, Open	22.50
Pressed Glass, Beaded Panel & Sunburst, Cracker Jar, Covered	135.00
Pressed Glass, Beaded Panel & Sunburst, Cup, Punch	20.00
Pressed Glass, Beaded Raindrop, Butter	22.00
Pressed Glass, Beaded Rosette, Goblet	14.50
Pressed Glass, Beaded Rosette, Goblet, Findlay	18.00
Pressed Glass, Beaded Snowflake, Applied Handle With Thumbprint, 7 1/2 In.	30.00
Pressed Glass, Beaded Swag, Rose Bowl, Footed, Crimped Top	45.00
Pressed Glass, Beaded Swirl Variation, Butter, Miniature, Clear	25.00
Pressed Glass, Beaded Swirl Variation, Sugar, Miniature, Clear	20.00
Pressed Glass, Beaded Swirl With Disc Band, Tumbler	8.75
Pressed Glass, Beaded Swirl, Butter, Child's	50.00
Pressed Glass, Beaded Swirl, Butter, Child's, Clear, Covered	30.00
Pressed Glass, Beaded Swirl, Butter, Green And Gold	85.00
Pressed Glass, Beaded Swirl, Creamer	15.00
Pressed Glass, Beaded Swirl, Creamer, Green	20.00 To 69.50
Pressed Glass, Beaded Swirl, Cruet, Ruby Stained, Stopper	80.00
Pressed Glass, Beaded Swirl, Pitcher, Child's	25.00
Pressed Glass, Beaded Swirl, Sauce, Green	14.00
Pressed Glass, Beaded Swirl, Spooner	17.75
Pressed Glass, Beaded Swirl, Sugar, Miniature	25.00
Pressed Glass, Beaded Tulip, Goblet	28.00
Bearded Man, see Viking	
Pressed Glass, Beatty Honeycomb, Jar, Blue, Opalescent, Lid, 6 1/2 In.	85.00
Pressed Glass, Beatty Honeycomb, Toothpick, White Opalescent	32.00
Pressed Glass, Beatty Rib, Celery, Opalescent	26.00
Pressed Glass, Beatty Rib, Creamer, Blue, Opalescent	29.00 To 35.00
Pressed Glass, Beatty Rib, Creamer, Flint	25.00
Pressed Glass, Beatty Rib, Sauce, White	16.00
Pressed Glass, Beatty Rib, Sugar Shaker, White, Opalescent	33.00 To 40.00
Pressed Glass, Beatty Rib, Toothpick, Blue, Opalescent	30.00 To 32.00
Pressed Glass, Beatty Rib, Toothpick, Opalescent	20.00
Pressed Glass, Beatty Swirl, Celery, Opalescent	45.00
Pressed Glass, Beatty Swirl, Sauce, Blue, Opalescent	25.00
Pressed Glass, Beatty Swirl, Tumbler, Blue, Opalescent	45.00
Pressed Glass, Beautiful Lady, Bowl, 9 In.	9.00
Pressed Glass, Beautiful Lady, Cake Stand, Child's	25.00
Pressed Glass, Beautiful Lady, Pitcher, Milk	20.00
Pressed Glass, Beautiful Lady, Relish	8.50
Pressed Glass, Beautiful Lady, Wine	15.00
Pressed Glass, Beehive, Plate, Bread	40.00
Pressed Glass, Beehive, Plate, Green Border, Gold Trim, Lady Center, 13 In.	100.00

Pressed Glass, **Beehive**, Platter, Be Industrious, Leaf Handle 65.00
Pressed Glass, **Bellaire**, Cake Stand, Findlay, 10 In. 47.50
Pressed Glass, **Bellaire**, Cruet, Matching Stopper 15.00
Pressed Glass, **Belle**, Creamer 10.50
Pressed Glass, **Bellflower Single Vine**, Spooner 40.00
Pressed Glass, **Bellflower**, Bowl, Rayed Base, Oval, 9 X 6 In. 125.00
Pressed Glass, **Bellflower**, Butter, Covered, Flint .... 60.00 To 100.00
Pressed Glass, **Bellflower**, Castor Set, Flint, Pewter Stand, 6 Pieces 275.00
Pressed Glass, **Bellflower**, Champagne, Barrel Shape, Flint .... 65.00 To 100.00
Pressed Glass, **Bellflower**, Champagne, Flint, Knob Stem 110.00
Pressed Glass, **Bellflower**, Compote, Low Standard, 8 1/2 In. 22.00
Pressed Glass, **Bellflower**, Compote, Open, Scalloped Rim, Flint 60.00
Pressed Glass, **Bellflower**, Compote, Open, Scalloped Rim, Flint, 7 1/2 In. 50.00
Pressed Glass, **Bellflower**, Compote, Scalloped & Pointed Rim, 8 X 5 In. 45.00
Pressed Glass, **Bellflower**, Compote, Scalloped Rim, 8 X 5 In. 45.00
Pressed Glass, **Bellflower**, Compote, 8 In. 75.00
Pressed Glass, **Bellflower**, Decanter, Flange Top & Stopper 125.00
Pressed Glass, **Bellflower**, Decanter, Quart 115.00
Pressed Glass, **Bellflower**, Decanter, Ribbed, Double Vine, Rose Color, 12 In. 250.00
Pressed Glass, **Bellflower**, Decanter, Waffle Thumbprint, Stopper 120.00
Pressed Glass, **Bellflower**, Dish, Honey, Flint 10.00
Pressed Glass, **Bellflower**, Double Vine, Plate, Bread 15.00
Pressed Glass, **Bellflower**, Eggcup .... 23.00 To 26.00
Pressed Glass, **Bellflower**, Eggcup, Flared 25.00
Pressed Glass, **Bellflower**, Eggcup, Flint .... 20.00 To 25.00
Pressed Glass, **Bellflower**, Glass, Buttermilk 35.00
Pressed Glass, **Bellflower**, Goblet, Barrel Shape, Knob Stem, Flint 25.00
Pressed Glass, **Bellflower**, Goblet, Flint .... 22.00 To 30.00
Pressed Glass, **Bellflower**, Goblet, Knob Stem 40.00
Pressed Glass, **Bellflower**, Goblet, Knob Stem, Set Of 6 .... 240.00
Pressed Glass, **Bellflower**, Mug 9.50
Pressed Glass, **Bellflower**, Pitcher, Syrup, Hollow Applied Handle 225.00
Pressed Glass, **Bellflower**, Pitcher, Water 215.00
Pressed Glass, **Bellflower**, Pitcher, Water, Double Vine, Flint 185.00
Pressed Glass, **Bellflower**, Pitcher, Water, Flint 175.00
Pressed Glass, **Bellflower**, Plate, 6 In. 45.00
Pressed Glass, **Bellflower**, Salt, Flint 25.00
Pressed Glass, **Bellflower**, Salt, Flint, Footed, Scalloped Top 35.00
Pressed Glass, **Bellflower**, Salt, Master, Footed, Flint 20.00
Pressed Glass, **Bellflower**, Salt, Pedestal Dip, Single Vine, Flint 33.00
Pressed Glass, **Bellflower**, Sauce, Green Tint, 4 In. 75.00
Pressed Glass, **Bellflower**, Sauce, Scallop Edge, 4 In. 7.50
Pressed Glass, **Bellflower**, Sauce, 4 In. 7.00
Pressed Glass, **Bellflower**, Spooner, Double Vine, Flint .... 30.00 To 35.00
Pressed Glass, **Bellflower**, Spooner, Flint 27.00
Pressed Glass, **Bellflower**, Spooner, 3-Sided Vine, Flint 15.00
Pressed Glass, **Bellflower**, Sugar, Flint 87.50
Pressed Glass, **Bellflower**, Sugar, Flint, 4 1/2 In. 17.50
Pressed Glass, **Bellflower**, Sugar, Open, Flint .... 23.00 To 25.00
Pressed Glass, **Bellflower**, Sugar, Plain Band Around Top, 4 In. 22.50
Pressed Glass, **Bellflower**, Tumbler 85.00
Pressed Glass, **Bellflower**, Tumbler, Bar 65.00
Pressed Glass, **Bellflower**, Tumbler, Flint, 8 Oz. 65.00
Pressed Glass, **Bellflower**, Wine, Barrel Shape, Flint 75.00
Pressed Glass, **Bellflower**, Wine, Flint .... 55.00 To 75.00
Pressed Glass, **Bellflower**, Wine, Knob Stem 75.00
    Belted Worcester, see Worcester, Belted
    Bent Buckle, see New Hampshire
Pressed Glass, **Bent Buckle**, Sugar, Open 16.00
    Berkeley, see Blocked Arches
Pressed Glass, **Berlin**, Sugar, Open 12.00
Pressed Glass, **Bessemer Flute**, Goblet, Flint 25.00
Pressed Glass, **Bethlehem Star**, Compote, Covered, 4 1/2 In. 32.00
Pressed Glass, **Bethlehem Star**, Creamer 10.00
Pressed Glass, **Bethlehem Star**, Pitcher, Water 25.00

Pressed Glass, Beveled Diagonal Block, Celery 20.00
Pressed Glass, Beveled Diagonal Block, Spooner 12.50
Pressed Glass, Beveled Diamond & Star, Cracker Jar 29.00
Pressed Glass, Beveled Star, Spooner, Emerald Green 35.00
Pressed Glass, Bible, Platter, Bread 35.00
Pressed Glass, Bigler, Celery, Flint 39.00
Pressed Glass, Bigler, Champagne, Flint 57.50
Pressed Glass, Bigler, Decanter, Polished Pontil, Flint, 1 Quart 40.00
Pressed Glass, Bigler, Goblet, Flint .... 20.00 To 35.00
Pressed Glass, Bigler, Goblet, Flint, Polished Pontil 25.00
Pressed Glass, Bigler, Grooved, Tumbler, Footed, Flint 45.00
Pressed Glass, Bigler, Sauce 7.50
Pressed Glass, Bigler, Wine, Flint 48.00
Pressed Glass, Birch Leaf, Tumbler, Footed 18.00
Pressed Glass, Bird & Strawberry, Bowl, Large .... 37.00 To 37.50
Pressed Glass, Bird & Strawberry, Butter 65.00
Pressed Glass, Bird & Strawberry, Cake Stand, 9 In. 18.75
Pressed Glass, Bird & Strawberry, Compote, Covered, 6 In. 79.50
Pressed Glass, Bird & Strawberry, Compote, Lid, 6 1/2 In. 75.00
Pressed Glass, Bird & Strawberry, Cracker Jar, Ring Finial, 7 X 6 In. 225.00
Pressed Glass, Bird & Strawberry, Cup, Punch .... 9.50 To 35.00
Pressed Glass, Bird & Strawberry, Dish, Footed, 5 1/4 In. 30.00
Pressed Glass, Bird & Strawberry, Dish, Round, Footed, 5 1/2 In. 18.00
Pressed Glass, Bird & Strawberry, Pitcher, Water 145.00
Pressed Glass, Bird & Strawberry, Plate, Cake, Pedestal 29.00
Pressed Glass, Bird & Strawberry, Plate, Goofus, 12 In. 110.00
Pressed Glass, Bird & Strawberry, Sauce, Flat 10.00
Pressed Glass, Bird & Strawberry, Sauce, Footed .... 12.00 To 20.00
Pressed Glass, Bird & Strawberry, Sauce, 3 Legged 22.50
Pressed Glass, Bird & Strawberry, Tumbler 30.00
Pressed Glass, Bird & Strawberry, Tumbler, Clear 25.00
   Bird in Ring, see Butterfly & Fan
Pressed Glass, Bird, Relish, Blue, 10 1/2 X 2 1/2 In. 75.50
Pressed Glass, Birds & Wheat, Mug, 3 1/2 In. .... 20.50 To 21.50
Pressed Glass, Birds At Fountain, Goblet 28.00
Pressed Glass, Blackberry Band, Spooner 18.00
Pressed Glass, Blackberry, Creamer 25.00
Pressed Glass, Blackberry, Eggcup, Double 12.50
Pressed Glass, Blackberry, Goblet 20.00
Pressed Glass, Blackberry, Salt, White, Opaque, Footed 32.00
Pressed Glass, Blackberry, Sauce, White, Opaque, 4 In. 19.00
Pressed Glass, Blackberry, Spooner 22.00
Pressed Glass, Blaine, Plate 250.00
Pressed Glass, Bleeding Heart, Butter, Covered .... 40.00 To 45.00
Pressed Glass, Bleeding Heart, Cake Stand, Gallery Edge, 9 1/2 In. 42.00
Pressed Glass, Bleeding Heart, Cake Stand, 9 1/2 In. 47.50
Pressed Glass, Bleeding Heart, Compote, High Standard, 8 1/2 In. 24.00
Pressed Glass, Bleeding Heart, Compote, Low Standard, 8 1/2 In. 21.00
Pressed Glass, Bleeding Heart, Creamer, Applied Handle 48.00
Pressed Glass, Bleeding Heart, Eggcup .... 35.00 To 45.00

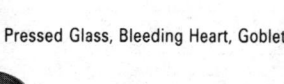

Pressed Glass, Bleeding Heart, Goblet

Pressed Glass, Bleeding Heart, Goblet .... 28.00 To 32.00
Pressed Glass, Bleeding Heart, Goblet, Knob Stem .... 25.00 To 27.50
Pressed Glass, Bleeding Heart, Relish, Pear Shape 25.00
Pressed Glass, Bleeding Heart, Sauce 3.50
Pressed Glass, Bleeding Heart, Sauce, 4 In. 12.00
Pressed Glass, Bleeding Heart, Spooner .... 16.50 To 20.00
Pressed Glass, Bleeding Heart, Sugar, Covered 37.50
Pressed Glass, Bleeding Heart, Sugar, Covered, Heart Finial 58.00
Pressed Glass, Bleeding Heart, Sugar, 5 In. 44.00
Pressed Glass, Bleeding Heart, Tumbler, Footed 30.00
Pressed Glass, Block & Circle, Goblet 14.00
Pressed Glass, Block & Fan, Bowl, Ice 22.00
Pressed Glass, Block & Fan, Bowl, 9 3/4 In. 14.50
Pressed Glass, Block & Fan, Cake Stand, 10 In. 23.50
Pressed Glass, Block & Fan, Celery 18.00
Pressed Glass, Block & Fan, Cracker Jar, Covered 37.50
Pressed Glass, Block & Fan, Cruet, Large 24.00
Pressed Glass, Block & Fan, Ice Bowl 28.00
Pressed Glass, Block & Fan, Pitcher, Water 25.00
Pressed Glass, Block & Fan, Saltshaker .... 13.50 To 14.50
Pressed Glass, Block & Fan, Sauce, Footed 8.00
Pressed Glass, Block & Fan, Sauce, Footed, 3 3/4 In. 6.00
Pressed Glass, Block & Fan, Sauce, Footed, 4 In. .... 4.50 To 7.50
Pressed Glass, Block & Fan, Wine .... 22.50 To 32.50
   Block & Finecut, see Finecut & Block
Pressed Glass, Block & Lattice, Bowl, 7 In. 40.00
Pressed Glass, Block & Lattice, Water Set, Amber Stain, 6 Piece 325.00
Pressed Glass, Block & Pleat, Celery 25.50
Pressed Glass, Block & Pleat, Goblet 10.00
Pressed Glass, Block & Rib, Bowl, Octagon, 8 In., Underplate, 11 In. 32.50
   Block & Star, see Valencia Waffle
Pressed Glass, Block & Thumbprint, Glass, Ale, Flint 28.00
Pressed Glass, Block & Thumbprint, Salt, Double 27.00
   Block with Stars, see Hanover
Pressed Glass, Block, Butter, Red, Covered 65.00
Pressed Glass, Block, Celery, Northwood 40.00
Pressed Glass, Block, Creamer, Red 40.00
Pressed Glass, Block, Dish, Banana, Clear 23.75
Pressed Glass, Block, Goblet, Red .... 15.00 To 25.00
Pressed Glass, Block, Pitcher, Water, Amber 95.00
Pressed Glass, Block, Spooner, Red .... 20.00 To 29.50
Pressed Glass, Block, Spooner, Red, Flashed, 2 Handles 42.50
Pressed Glass, Block, Sugar, Open, Clear, Violet Tinge 10.50
Pressed Glass, Block, Sugar, Red, Cover 32.50
Pressed Glass, Block, Sugar, Red, Handled, Covered 50.00
Pressed Glass, Block, Table Set, Red, 4 Piece 175.00
Pressed Glass, Block, Tumbler, Red 25.00
Pressed Glass, Block, Water Set, Ruby Stained, 7 Piece 265.00
   Blockade, see Diamond Block with Fan
Pressed Glass, Blocked Arches, Goblet 16.00
Pressed Glass, Blocked Arches, Pitcher, Water, Frosted & Clear 47.50
Pressed Glass, Blocked Arches, Pitcher, Water, Ruby Flashed, 9 In. 95.00
   Blockhouse, see Hanover
   Bluebird, see Bird & Strawberry
Pressed Glass, Bordered Ellipse, Mug, Ruby Stained, 3 In. 21.50
Pressed Glass, Bouquet, Creamer 20.00
Pressed Glass, Bouquet, Spooner, 2 Handled, Colored Design 37.50
Pressed Glass, Bow Tie, Cake Stand 35.00
Pressed Glass, Bow Tie, Cake Stand, 9 In.Diameter 45.00
Pressed Glass, Bow Tie, Compote, Open, 6 1/2 X 8 In. 40.00
Pressed Glass, Bow Tie, Jar, Jam, Covered 37.50
Pressed Glass, Bow Tie, Marmalade 24.00
Pressed Glass, Bow Tie, Pitcher, Clouded Glass Bottom, 6 1/2 In. 37.50
Pressed Glass, Box In Box, Sauce 13.50
   Bradford Blackberry, see Bradford Grape

Pressed Glass, Broken Column, Goblet

Pressed Glass, Buckle, Goblet

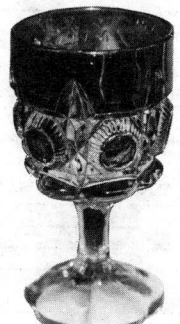

Pressed Glass, Bull's Eye & Daisy, Goblet

Pressed Glass, Bull's Eye & Diamond Point, Goblet, 7 In.

Pressed Glass, Bradford Grape, Champagne, Flint	57.50
Pressed Glass, Bradford Grape, Goblet, Flint	45.00
Pressed Glass, Bradford Grape, Tumbler, Flint	85.00
Pressed Glass, Bradford Grape, Wine, Flint	50.00
Pressed Glass, Brazen Shield, Sugar, Covered	20.00
Pressed Glass, Brazen Shield, Tumbler, Clear	12.00
Pressed Glass, Bridle Rosettes, Wine	9.00
Pressed Glass, Bringing Home The Cows, Pitcher	250.00
Pressed Glass, Britannic, Toothpick, Ruby Stained	35.00
Pressed Glass, Broad Flute, Bowl, Flint, 7 1/4 In.	12.00
Pressed Glass, Broad Flute, Bowl, Footed, Flint	23.00
Pressed Glass, Broad Flute, Compote, Flint, Low Standard, 9 In.	12.50
Pressed Glass, Broken Column, Basket, 14 X 11 X 6 In.	85.00
Pressed Glass, Broken Column, Berry Set, 7 Piece	65.00
Pressed Glass, Broken Column, Bowl, Flat, 9 In.	25.00
Pressed Glass, Broken Column, Cake Stand, 10 In.	45.00
Pressed Glass, Broken Column, Cake Stand, 10 1/4 In.	85.00
Pressed Glass, Broken Column, Cake Stand, 9 In.	45.00
Pressed Glass, Broken Column, Carafe, Water	45.00
Pressed Glass, Broken Column, Castor, Pickle, Original Frame	75.00
Pressed Glass, Broken Column, Celery	12.00 To 32.50
Pressed Glass, Broken Column, Compote, Fruit, Red Dots, 9 1/2 In.	135.00
Pressed Glass, Broken Column, Creamer	22.00 To 28.50
Pressed Glass, Broken Column, Creamer, Ruby Stained	47.50
Pressed Glass, Broken Column, Cruet, Original Stopper	45.00
Pressed Glass, Broken Column, Goblet	35.00
Pressed Glass, Broken Column, Jar, Marmalade, Covered	55.00
Pressed Glass, Broken Column, Plate, 8 In.	28.00
Pressed Glass, Broken Column, Salt & Pepper	45.00
Pressed Glass, Broken Column, Saltshaker	22.00
Pressed Glass, Broken Column, Sugar & Creamer & Spooner	95.00
Pressed Glass, Broken Column, Water Set, 5 Piece	155.00
Pressed Glass, Brooklyn Flute, Goblet, Flint	85.00

Pressed Glass, **Brooklyn**, Goblet, Flint .... 28.00 To 85.00
Pressed Glass, **Broughton**, Sauce 6.00
Pressed Glass, **Broughton**, Water Set, Child's, 7 Piece 70.00
  Bryce, see Ribbon Candy
Pressed Glass, **Bubble Lattice**, Celery, Satin Blue, Opalescent 60.00
Pressed Glass, **Buckingham**, Compote, Open, U.S.Glass, 1906, 7 In. 32.00
Pressed Glass, **Buckingham**, Cruet 15.00
Pressed Glass, **Buckingham**, Tumbler, Gold 12.00
Pressed Glass, **Buckle & Diamond**, Sauce, 4 1/4 In. 4.50
Pressed Glass, **Buckle & Star**, Compote, Low Standard, Open, 9 In. 15.00
Pressed Glass, **Buckle & Star**, Creamer 45.00
Pressed Glass, **Buckle & Star**, Goblet 22.50
Pressed Glass, **Buckle With English Hobnail**, Sugar & Creamer 10.00
Pressed Glass, **Buckle**, Butter, Covered 55.00
Pressed Glass, **Buckle**, Compote 25.00
Pressed Glass, **Buckle**, Eggcup .... 17.50 To 38.00
Pressed Glass, **Buckle**, Eggcup, Flint .... 21.00 To 26.00
Pressed Glass, **Buckle**, Goblet, Flint .... 30.00 To 35.00
Pressed Glass, **Buckle**, Sauce, Flint, 3 3/4 In. 7.50
Pressed Glass, **Buckle**, Sauce, 4 In. 6.00
Pressed Glass, **Buckle**, Spooner 18.00
Pressed Glass, **Buckle**, Sugar, Flint .... 22.50 To 47.50
Pressed Glass, **Budded Ivy**, Spooner .... 12.50 To 16.00
Pressed Glass, **Bulging Loops**, Toothpick, Ruby Stained 49.00
  Bull's-Eye & Fan, see Daisies in Oval Panels
  Bull's-Eye Variant, see Texas Bull's-Eye
Pressed Glass, **Bull's-Eye & Bar**, Wine, Flint 95.00
Pressed Glass, **Bull's-Eye & Broken Column**, Tumbler, Footed .... 35.00 To 45.00
Pressed Glass, **Bull's-Eye & Cube**, Spill, Flint 30.00
Pressed Glass, **Bull's-Eye & Daisy**, Fruit Bowl, Green Eyes 38.00
Pressed Glass, **Bull's-Eye & Daisy**, Goblet, Green Eyes 17.50
Pressed Glass, **Bull's-Eye & Daisy**, Goblet, Green Eyes, Gold Trim 12.50
Pressed Glass, **Bull's-Eye & Daisy**, Goblet, Purple Eyes 12.50
Pressed Glass, **Bull's-Eye & Daisy**, Nappy, Green Eyes 18.00
Pressed Glass, **Bull's-Eye & Daisy**, Tumbler, Gilt Eyes 11.00
Pressed Glass, **Bull's-Eye & Daisy**, Tumbler, Green Eyes 21.00
Pressed Glass, **Bull's-Eye & Daisy**, Wine, Purple Eyes 19.00
Pressed Glass, **Bull's-Eye & Diamond Point**, Dish, Honey, Flint 12.00
Pressed Glass, **Bull's-Eye & Diamond Point**, Goblet 20.00
Pressed Glass, **Bull's-Eye & Diamond Point**, Goblet, Flint 87.50
Pressed Glass, **Bull's-Eye & Diamond Point**, Sauce, 4 In. 12.50
Pressed Glass, **Bull's-Eye & Diamond Point**, Sugar, Flint, Covered 95.00
Pressed Glass, **Bull's-Eye & Prism**, Goblet, 5 1/2 In. 52.00
Pressed Glass, **Bull's-Eye & Scrolls**, Goblet 34.00
Pressed Glass, **Bull's-Eye & Sunburst**, Dish, Sauce 7.00
Pressed Glass, **Bull's-Eye & Waffle**, Goblet, Flint 40.00
  Bull's-Eye Band, see Reverse Torpedo
Pressed Glass, **Bull's-Eye With Fleur-De-Lis**, Decanter, Bar, Quart 125.00
Pressed Glass, **Bull's-Eye With Fleur-De-Lis**, Goblet, Flint .... 65.00 To 75.00
Pressed Glass, **Bull's-Eye With Fleur-De-Lis**, Salt, Flint 37.50
Pressed Glass, **Bull's-Eye**, Creamer, Hexagon 20.00
Pressed Glass, **Bull's-Eye**, Goblet, Flint 55.00
Pressed Glass, **Bull's-Eye**, Jar, Jam, Covered, Bulbous, Lid In Pattern 35.00
Pressed Glass, **Bull's-Eye**, Salt, Flint, Hexagonal 6.00
Pressed Glass, **Bull's-Eye**, Spooner, Flint 27.00
Pressed Glass, **Bull's-Eye**, Wine, Flint .... 32.50 To 45.00
Pressed Glass, **Bunker Hill**, Plate, Bread 45.00
Pressed Glass, **Butterfly & Fan**, Butter 25.00
Pressed Glass, **Butterfly & Fan**, Pitcher, Water 85.00
Pressed Glass, **Butterfly With Spray**, Mug, 2 1/2 In. .... 18.50 To 19.50
Pressed Glass, **Butterfly With Spray**, Mug, 3 1/4 In. 20.50
Pressed Glass, **Butterfly With Spray**, Spooner 26.50
Pressed Glass, **Button & Daisy**, Compote, 7 1/2 X 6 1/2 In. 32.50
Pressed Glass, **Button Arches**, Banana Boat, Green 15.00
Pressed Glass, **Button Arches**, Cake Stand 39.50

Pressed Glass, **Button Arches**, Pitcher, Ruby & Clear, Dated 1905, 3 3/4 In.	22.00
Pressed Glass, **Button Arches**, Pitcher, Ruby, Clear Base & Handle, 9 In.	75.00
Pressed Glass, **Button Arches**, Pitcher, Tankard, Gold Leaf Band, 11 In.	42.50
Pressed Glass, **Button Arches**, Toothpick, Ruby Flashed, Mother, 1906	21.00
Pressed Glass, **Button Band**, Bowl, Berry	35.00
Pressed Glass, **Button Panel**, Salt & Pepper	18.00
Pressed Glass, **Button Panel**, Sugar, Ruby Flashed, Covered	45.00
Pressed Glass, **Button**, Basket, Flare Top, Applied Handle, 12 In.	35.00
Pressed Glass, **Buttons & Bows**, Pitcher, Water, Apple Green	95.00
Pressed Glass, **Buttons And Braid**, Tumbler, Blue	35.00
Pressed Glass, **Buzzsaw**, Table Set, Child's, 4 Piece	85.00
Pressed Glass, **Cabbage Leaf**, Compote, Frosted Amber, Covered, 2 In.	50.00
Pressed Glass, **Cabbage Leaf**, Goblet	25.00
Pressed Glass, **Cabbage Rose**, Bowl, 7 1/2 In.	16.50
Pressed Glass, **Cabbage Rose**, Butter	35.00
Pressed Glass, **Cabbage Rose**, Butter, Covered	37.50 To 39.50
Pressed Glass, **Cabbage Rose**, Cake Stand	48.50
Pressed Glass, **Cabbage Rose**, Celery	37.50
Pressed Glass, **Cabbage Rose**, Champagne	29.50
Pressed Glass, **Cabbage Rose**, Compote, Covered, High Standard, 8 In.	70.00
Pressed Glass, **Cabbage Rose**, Compote, Covered, 8 In.	67.00 To 70.00
Pressed Glass, **Cabbage Rose**, Pitcher	40.00
Pressed Glass, **Cabbage Rose**, Spooner	12.00 To 22.00
Pressed Glass, **Cabbage Rose**, Sugar, Covered	37.00
Pressed Glass, **Cabbage Rose**, Tumbler	34.00 To 35.00
Pressed Glass, **Cabbage Rose**, Wine	28.00 To 32.50
Pressed Glass, **Cable With Fan**, Sauce, 4 In.	6.00
Pressed Glass, **Cable With Ring**, Sauce, Flint	8.00
Pressed Glass, **Cable With Ring**, Sugar, Flint	42.00
Pressed Glass, **Cable**, Bowl, 9 In.	28.00
Pressed Glass, **Cable**, Celery, Flint	85.00
Pressed Glass, **Cable**, Compote, Flint, Low Standard, 7 In.	45.00
Pressed Glass, **Cable**, Decanter, Bar, Quart	100.00
Pressed Glass, **Cable**, Decanter, Cable Stopper, Flint	225.00
Pressed Glass, **Cable**, Eggcup, Flint	37.50
Pressed Glass, **Cable**, Goblet	59.00
Pressed Glass, **Cable**, Goblet, Flint	45.00 To 55.00
Pressed Glass, **Cable**, Honey, Flint	9.50
Pressed Glass, **Cable**, Sauce, Flint	14.00
Pressed Glass, **Cable**, Sauce, 4 In.	7.50
Pressed Glass, **Cable**, Spooner, Flint, Shell Scalloped Top	30.00
Pressed Glass, **Cable**, Wine, Flint	35.00
Pressed Glass, **Cable**, Wine, Semiflint	20.00
Cameo, see Ceres	
Canadian Drape, see Garfield Drape	
Pressed Glass, **Canadian**, Plate, Scene In Extended Handles, 7 In.	32.50
Pressed Glass, **Canadian**, Plate, 10 In.	28.00
Pressed Glass, **Canadian**, Plate, 8 In.	20.00 To 24.00

Pressed Glass, Cabbage Rose, Mug

Pressed Glass, Canadian, Wine .... 20.00 To 25.00
Pressed Glass, Candlewick, Bowl, Footed, 7 In. 22.50
Pressed Glass, Candlewick, Butter 30.00
Pressed Glass, Candlewick, Creamer 12.50
Pressed Glass, Candlewick, Dish, Rectangular, 9 X 5 X 2 In. 22.50
Pressed Glass, Candlewick, Wine 22.00
    Candy Ribbon, see Ribbon Candy
Pressed Glass, Cane & Medallion, Creamer, 5 3/4 In. 20.00
Pressed Glass, Cane & Medallion, Sugar, 3 3/4 In. 15.00
Pressed Glass, Cane Column, Goblet 12.00
Pressed Glass, Cane Horseshoe, Pitcher, Water, Child's 21.00
Pressed Glass, Cane, Goblet .... 15.00 To 16.50
Pressed Glass, Cane, Goblet, Amber 27.00
Pressed Glass, Cane, Goblet, Apple Green 40.00
Pressed Glass, Cane, Goblet, Blue 32.00
Pressed Glass, Cane, Goblet, Green .... 25.00 To 27.00
Pressed Glass, Cane, Goblet, Vaseline 27.00
Pressed Glass, Cane, Kettle, Blue, Bail Handle, Footed 20.00
Pressed Glass, Cane, Pitcher, Water 22.00
Pressed Glass, Cane, Pitcher, Water, Blue 50.00
Pressed Glass, Cannonball, Butter 25.00
Pressed Glass, Cannonball, Butter, Etched, Covered 45.00
Pressed Glass, Cannonball, Butter, Pinwheel Cover 25.00
Pressed Glass, Cannonball, Goblet 17.50
Pressed Glass, Cannonball, Tumbler 17.50
Pressed Glass, Cape Cod, Compote, Covered, 11 In. 75.00
Pressed Glass, Cape Cod, Goblet 28.00
Pressed Glass, Capitol Building, Champagne 25.00
Pressed Glass, Capitol Building, Goblet .... 23.00 To 25.00
Pressed Glass, Cardinal Bird, Basket, Ruby Flashed Inlay 50.00
Pressed Glass, Cardinal Bird, Butter 60.00
Pressed Glass, Cardinal Bird, Creamer .... 35.00 To 36.50

Pressed Glass, Cable With Rings, Bowl, Footed

Pressed Glass, Cardinal Bird, Goblet .... 25.00 To 32.50
Pressed Glass, Cardinal Bird, Goblet, Clear 25.00
Pressed Glass, Cardinal, Goblet .... 28.00 To 30.00
    Carmen, see Paneled Diamond & Finecut
Pressed Glass, Cat's-Eye, Creamer 27.50
Pressed Glass, Cat's-Eye, Wine .... 13.50 To 17.00
Pressed Glass, Cathedral, Bowl, Blue, Crimped Edge, 7 In. 35.00
Pressed Glass, Cathedral, Bowl, Vaseline, 6 In. 30.00
Pressed Glass, Cathedral, Butter, Covered 27.00
Pressed Glass, Cathedral, Cake Stand, Amber 47.50
Pressed Glass, Cathedral, Cake Stand, Vaseline, 9 1/2 In. 55.00
Pressed Glass, Cathedral, Compote, Covered, High Standard, 7 In. 55.00
Pressed Glass, Cathedral, Compote, Ruby Stained, 9 X 6 1/2 In. 16.00
Pressed Glass, Cathedral, Creamer 24.50

Pressed Glass, Cable, Spooner

Pressed Glass, Canadian, Compote, Covered

Pressed Glass, Cathedral, Compote

Pressed Glass, **Cathedral,** Dish, Waved Rim, Blue, 6 In.	32.00
Pressed Glass, **Cathedral,** Goblet, Amber	39.75
Pressed Glass, **Cathedral,** Sugar, Pedestal, Covered	42.00
Pressed Glass, **Cathedral,** Wine, Clear	22.00
Pressed Glass, **Cattail & Water Lily,** Spooner, Clear, Opalescent	22.50
Pressed Glass, **Cattail & Water Lily,** Tumbler, Blue, Opalescent	25.00
Pressed Glass, **Cavitt,** Goblet	10.00 To 13.00
Pressed Glass, **Celery**	12.00
Pressed Glass, **Celtic Cross,** Celery, Etched	18.00
Pressed Glass, **Celtic Cross,** Spooner, Etched	15.00
Pressed Glass, **Celtic,** Tumbler, Gold Trim	3.00
Centennial, see also Liberty Bell, Washington Centennial	
Pressed Glass, **Centennial,** Champagne	43.00
Pressed Glass, **Centennial,** Goblet	32.50
Pressed Glass, **Centennial,** Vase, Hand, Frosted, Signed	18.00
Pressed Glass, **Ceres,** Compote	22.50
Pressed Glass, **Ceres,** Creamer	12.00 To 13.00
Pressed Glass, **Ceres,** Goblet	50.00
Pressed Glass, **Ceres,** Spooner	15.00
Pressed Glass, **Ceres,** Sugar, Open	12.00

Pressed Glass, Ceres, Bowl, Covered

Pressed Glass, Chain & Shield, Pitcher

Pressed Glass, Chicken, Jar, Mustard, Frosted, Covered

Pressed Glass, **Chain & Shield**, Compote, Low Standard, 6 In.	15.00
Pressed Glass, **Chain & Shield**, Creamer	17.50
Pressed Glass, **Chain & Shield**, Goblet	29.00
Pressed Glass, **Chain & Shield**, Plate, Bread	17.00
Pressed Glass, **Chain & Shield**, Plate, Bread, 12 In.	20.00
Chain With Diamonds, see Washington Centennial	
Pressed Glass, **Chain With Star**, Goblet	15.00 To 18.00
Pressed Glass, **Chain With Star**, Pitcher	23.00
Pressed Glass, **Chain With Star**, Relish	11.50
Pressed Glass, **Chain With Star**, Sugar	8.00
Pressed Glass, **Chain With Star**, Wine	18.00
Pressed Glass, **Chain**, Goblet	16.50 To 18.00
Pressed Glass, **Chain**, Spooner	20.00
Pressed Glass, **Chain**, Sugar, Covered	28.00
Pressed Glass, **Chain**, Wine	14.00 To 22.00
Pressed Glass, **Challinor**, Salt & Pepper, Blue	35.00
Pressed Glass, **Champion**, Cake Stand, 10 1/2 X 5 In.	19.00
Pressed Glass, **Champion**, Vase, Greentown, 8 1/2 In.	17.50
Chandelier, see also Crown Jewels	
Pressed Glass, **Checkerboard**, Celery	20.00
Pressed Glass, **Checkerboard**, Cruet	15.00
Pressed Glass, **Checkerboard**, Plate	15.00
Pressed Glass, **Checkerboard**, Wine, Flared	12.50
Pressed Glass, **Cherry**, Goblet	10.00
Pressed Glass, **Cherry**, Spooner	17.00 To 22.00
Pressed Glass, **Chestnut Oak**, Sugar	12.00
Pressed Glass, **Chicken**, Compote, Frosted, Low Standard, Covered, 7 1/2 In.	95.00
Pressed Glass, **Chimo**, Creamer, Child's	10.00
Pressed Glass, **Christmas**, Salt, Blue With Agitator	48.00
Pressed Glass, **Chrysanthemum Leaf**, Bowl, 9 In.	20.00
Pressed Glass, **Chrysanthemum Leaf**, Tumbler, Gold Trim	25.00
Pressed Glass, **Chrysanthemum**, Sugar Shaker, White, Opalescent	75.00
Pressed Glass, **Chrysanthemum**, Vase, Base Blue With White Speckling, Celery	55.00
Church Windows, see Tulip Petals	
Pressed Glass, **Circle**, Cake Stand, Frosted	30.00
Pressed Glass, **Circle**, Cake Stand, Frosted, 9 1/2 In.	35.00
Pressed Glass, **Circled Scroll**, Spooner, Blue, Opalescent	88.00

Pressed Glass, Classic Warrior, Plate 100.00
Pressed Glass, Classic Warrior, Plate, Signed 125.00
Pressed Glass, Classic, Compote, Covered, 9 X 7 3/8 In. 125.00
Pressed Glass, Classic, Compote, Log Feet, Covered, 8 In. 195.00
Pressed Glass, Classic, Compote, Low Standard, Covered, 8 In. 200.00
Pressed Glass, Classic, Creamer, Collared Base 110.00
Pressed Glass, Classic, Goblet .... 165.00 To 215.00
Pressed Glass, Classic, Pitcher, Water 250.00
Pressed Glass, Classic, Pitcher, Water, Open Log Feet, 10 In. 185.00
Pressed Glass, Classic, Plate, Warrior, Signed Jacobus 95.00
Pressed Glass, Classic, Sauce, 4 1/4 In. 10.00
Pressed Glass, Classic, Spooner 97.00
Pressed Glass, Clear & Diamond Panels, Goblet 10.00
Pressed Glass, Clear Circle, Compote, Jelly 18.00
Pressed Glass, Clear Circle, Compote, Scalloped Rim, Tall 32.00
Pressed Glass, Clear Diagonal Band, Creamer 26.50
Pressed Glass, Clear Panels With Cord Band, Creamer 7.00
Pressed Glass, Clear Panels With Cord Band, Wine 17.50
Pressed Glass, Cleat, Pitcher, Water, Flint 150.00
Pressed Glass, Clematis & Scroll, Salt & Pepper, Glass Frame With Handle 25.00
Pressed Glass, Clematis, Goblet 16.50
Pressed Glass, Cleveland, Plate 250.00
Pressed Glass, Clio, Plate, 10 1/4 In. 19.00
Pressed Glass, Clover, Creamer, Child's 15.00
Coin Spot, see Coin Spot Category
Pressed Glass, Colonial, Champagne 15.00
Pressed Glass, Colonial, Champagne, Flint 57.50
Pressed Glass, Colonial, Compote, Broken Column Stand, 8 X 10 In. 50.00
Pressed Glass, Colonial, Creamer, Child's 15.00
Pressed Glass, Colonial, Creamer, Flint 20.00
Pressed Glass, Colonial, Creamer, Sandwich, Flint, Applied Handle 20.00
Pressed Glass, Colonial, Spooner, Clear, Miniature 12.00
Pressed Glass, Colonial, Spooner, Cobalt, Miniature 22.00
Pressed Glass, Colonial, Sugar, Covered, Cambridge, Miniature 14.00
Pressed Glass, Colonial, Sugar, Covered, Child's 23.00
Pressed Glass, Colonial, Sugar, Flint, Covered 70.00
Pressed Glass, Colonial, Wine, Flint 52.50
Pressed Glass, Colorado, Bonbon, Footed, Blue, Gold Trim, 7 1/2 In. 43.00
Pressed Glass, Colorado, Bowl, Blue, 7 In. 37.50
Pressed Glass, Colorado, Bowl, Green And Gold, Ruffled, 8 In. 35.00

Pressed Glass, Circle & Ellipse, Vase, Canary, 7 1/4 In.

Pressed Glass, Classic, Compote, Covered

Pressed Glass, Colorado, Bowl, Round, Blue, 7 In.	37.50
Pressed Glass, Colorado, Bowl, Violet, Blue With Gold	38.00
Pressed Glass, Colorado, Butter Base, Emerald Green	35.00
Pressed Glass, Colorado, Butter, Blue	35.00
Pressed Glass, Colorado, Butter, Covered	85.00
Pressed Glass, Colorado, Creamer, Green, Small	23.00
Pressed Glass, Colorado, Creamer, Ruby, Liberty, N.Y.	22.00
Pressed Glass, Colorado, Creamer, Souvenir, Green	15.00
Pressed Glass, Colorado, Creamer, Souvenir, Green, 3 1/2 In.	21.50
Pressed Glass, Colorado, Cup	33.00
Pressed Glass, Colorado, Cup, Emerald	17.50 To 18.00
Pressed Glass, Colorado, Cup, Footed, Green, Gold Trim, Souvenir, Portland, 1905	23.00
Pressed Glass, Colorado, Dish, Footed, Gold Trim, Green, 5 In.	28.00
Pressed Glass, Colorado, Dish, Green, Square, Footed, 6 In.	16.50
Pressed Glass, Colorado, Dish, Green, 5 In.	10.00
Pressed Glass, Colorado, Dish, Tricornered, Footed, Green, Gold, 6 3/4 In.	32.00
Pressed Glass, Colorado, Dish, 4 Sides Turned, 5 1/2 In.	12.00
Pressed Glass, Colorado, Mug, Pat.1908	30.00
Pressed Glass, Colorado, Pitcher, Water, Emerald Green, 3 Feet	98.00
Pressed Glass, Colorado, Sauce, Blue	25.00
Pressed Glass, Colorado, Sauce, Footed, Green, 5 In.	33.00
Pressed Glass, Colorado, Sherbet, Emerald	16.00
Pressed Glass, Colorado, Sherbet, Individual, Footed	30.00
Pressed Glass, Colorado, Sugar & Creamer, Green	55.00
Pressed Glass, Colorado, Toothpick, Barrel Inkwell Shape, Blue	24.00 To 29.50
Pressed Glass, Colorado, Toothpick, Cobalt	21.00
Pressed Glass, Colorado, Vase, Blue, 14 1/2 In., Pair	135.00
Pressed Glass, Colorado, Wine	20.00
Pressed Glass, Colossus, Goblet	15.00
Pressed Glass, Columbia, Bowl, 9 In.	12.00
Pressed Glass, Columbia, Butter, Pink With Gold Trim, Covered	45.00
Pressed Glass, Columbia, Mug	10.00

Pressed Glass, Clover, Creamer, 3 1/2 In.

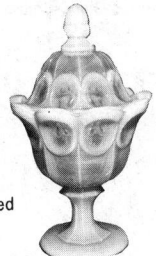

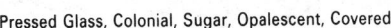

Pressed Glass, Colonial, Sugar, Opalescent, Covered

Pressed Glass, Clear Diagonal Band, Creamer

Pressed Glass, Columbia, Spooner 11.00
Pressed Glass, Columbia, Toothpick 15.00
Pressed Glass, Columbian Coin, Butter 115.00
Pressed Glass, Columbian Coin, Creamer 70.00
Pressed Glass, Columbian Coin, Creamer, Gilded 105.00
Pressed Glass, Columbian Coin, Salt & Pepper 65.00
Pressed Glass, Columbian Coin, Sauce, Bronzed Coins 125.00
Pressed Glass, Columbian Coin, Spooner 47.00
Pressed Glass, Columbian Coin, Sugar 95.00
Pressed Glass, Columbian Exposition, Goblet .... 12.00 To 15.00
Pressed Glass, Columbian Exposition, Mug 14.00
Pressed Glass, Columned Thumbprints, Bowl, Covered, 6 X 4 1/2 In. 25.00
Pressed Glass, Comet, Goblet 75.00
Pressed Glass, Comet, Goblet, Flint .... 50.00 To 65.00
 Compact, see Snail
Pressed Glass, Constitution, Plate, Bread 50.00
Pressed Glass, Container, Candy, Turkey Gobbler 75.00
Pressed Glass, Continental, Plate, Bread 40.00
Pressed Glass, Cord & Tassel, Goblet .... 15.00 To 22.50
Pressed Glass, Cord & Tassel, Spooner 27.00
Pressed Glass, Cord & Tassel, Wine 20.00
Pressed Glass, Cord Drapery, Berry Set, Clear, 7 Piece 80.00
Pressed Glass, Cord Drapery, Relish 22.50
Pressed Glass, Cord Drapery, Sauce, Set Of 4 .... 20.00
Pressed Glass, Cord Rosette, Goblet, Clear 35.00
Pressed Glass, Cordova, Toothpick 9.00
Pressed Glass, Corn, Vase, Blue, Opalescent 95.00
Pressed Glass, Corner Medallion, Creamer 26.00
Pressed Glass, Cornucopia, Champagne, 5 In. 95.00
Pressed Glass, Cornucopia, Pitcher, Water 28.00
Pressed Glass, Cornucopia, Plate, Flint, 6 In. 85.00
Pressed Glass, Cornucopia, Sugar, Flint 22.50
Pressed Glass, Cornucopia, Wine 14.50
 Pressed Glass, Cosmos, see also Cosmos, Vaseline Glass
Pressed Glass, Cosmos, Butter, Covered, Pink Band 195.00
Pressed Glass, Cosmos, Spooner 110.00
Pressed Glass, Cosmos, Tumbler, Pink Band 55.00
Pressed Glass, Cottage, Cake Stand 18.00
Pressed Glass, Cottage, Cake Stand, Electric Blue 68.00
Pressed Glass, Cottage, Cake Stand, High Standard 22.00
Pressed Glass, Cottage, Cake Stand, 9 In. 25.00
Pressed Glass, Cottage, Compote, Jelly, Green 28.00
Pressed Glass, Cottage, Creamer, 5 1/2 In. 12.00
Pressed Glass, Cottage, Goblet 14.50
Pressed Glass, Cottage, Pitcher, Water 45.00
Pressed Glass, Cottage, Plate, 6 In. 10.50
Pressed Glass, Cottage, Plate, 9 In. 15.00

Pressed Glass, Columbian Coin, Salt & Pepper

Pressed Glass, Cottage, Sauce, Green	10.00
Pressed Glass, Cottage, Syrup	37.50
Crane, see Stork	
Pressed Glass, Crazy Patch, Goblet	15.00
Pressed Glass, Crescent & Fan, Goblet	20.00
Crisscross, see Rexford	
Pressed Glass, Croesus, Berry Set, Gold Decorated, 7 Piece	350.00
Pressed Glass, Croesus, Berry Set, Green, Gold Trim, Set Of 7	110.00
Pressed Glass, Croesus, Bowl, Berry, Green, 8 X 4 In.	85.00
Pressed Glass, Croesus, Butter, Covered, Amethyst	145.00
Pressed Glass, Croesus, Butter, Emerald Green, Covered	125.00
Pressed Glass, Croesus, Creamer, Purple	60.00
Pressed Glass, Croesus, Cruet, Green, Ball Stopper, Small	50.00
Pressed Glass, Croesus, Dish, 3 Footed, 8 In.	22.50
Pressed Glass, Croesus, Pitcher, Green, Gold, 10 1/2 In.	175.00 To 195.00
Pressed Glass, Croesus, Pitcher, Water, Green	95.00
Pressed Glass, Croesus, Sauce, Footed, Purple	28.00
Pressed Glass, Croesus, Sauce, Purple	50.00
Pressed Glass, Croesus, Sauce, Purple, Gold Trim	45.00
Pressed Glass, Croesus, Sugar Shaker, Purple	40.00
Pressed Glass, Croesus, Sugar, Covered, Pear Shaped, 7 In.	110.00
Pressed Glass, Croesus, Tumbler, Amethyst, Gold	65.00
Pressed Glass, Croesus, Tumbler, Green	45.00
Pressed Glass, Croesus, Tumbler, Green With Gilt	29.00
Pressed Glass, Croesus, Tumbler, Purple, Gold	69.00 To 75.00
Crossbar & Finecut, see Ashman	
Pressed Glass, Crowfoot, Compote, 7 In.	25.00
Pressed Glass, Crowfoot, Creamer	22.50
Pressed Glass, Crowfoot, Goblet	26.00
Pressed Glass, Crowfoot, Lamp, 9 1/2 In.	40.00
Pressed Glass, Crowfoot, Sauce, 5 1/2 In.	6.50
Pressed Glass, Crowfoot, Spooner	15.00 To 22.50
Pressed Glass, Crowfoot, Sugar, Covered	40.00
Crown Jewels, see also Chandelier, Queen's Necklace	
Pressed Glass, Crying Baby, Plate, Bread	40.00
Pressed Glass, Crysanthemum Leaf, Creamer	33.00
Pressed Glass, Crystal Wedding, Creamer, Ruby Stained	65.00
Pressed Glass, Crystal Wedding, Sauce, Flat, 3 1/2 In.	8.50
Pressed Glass, Crystal Wedding, Spooner	22.00
Pressed Glass, Crystal Wedding, Spooner, Frosted	25.00
Pressed Glass, Crystal Wedding, Sugar, Covered, Frosted	40.00
Pressed Glass, Crystal, Butter, Covered, Frosted	30.00
Pressed Glass, Crystal, Creamer, Frosted	20.00
Pressed Glass, Crystal, Spooner, Frosted	30.00
Pressed Glass, Crystal, Spooner, Scalloped Rim	9.00
Pressed Glass, Crystal, Sugar, Covered, Frosted	30.00
Pressed Glass, Crystal, Table Set, Frosted, Ruby Stained, Gold, 4 Piece	285.00
Cube & Diamond, see Milton	
Cube & Fan, see Pineapple & Fan	
Pressed Glass, Cube, Goblet, Square Stem, Etched	14.00
Pressed Glass, Cupid & Venus, Bowl, Footed, Scalloped, 8 3/4 In.	26.00
Pressed Glass, Cupid & Venus, Bowl, 8 3/4 In.	25.00
Pressed Glass, Cupid & Venus, Butter, Covered	45.00
Pressed Glass, Cupid & Venus, Cake Plate, Metal Carrier	20.00
Pressed Glass, Cupid & Venus, Castor, Pickle, Silver Frame	65.00
Pressed Glass, Cupid & Venus, Celery	35.00 To 40.00
Pressed Glass, Cupid & Venus, Compote, High	30.00
Pressed Glass, Cupid & Venus, Compote, Low Standard, Covered	55.00
Pressed Glass, Cupid & Venus, Compote, Low Standard, 8 In.	14.50
Pressed Glass, Cupid & Venus, Compote, 7 In.	15.00
Pressed Glass, Cupid & Venus, Creamer	27.50
Pressed Glass, Cupid & Venus, Cruet	30.00
Pressed Glass, Cupid & Venus, Dish, Honey	5.00
Pressed Glass, Cupid & Venus, Dish, Oval, Large	26.00
Pressed Glass, Cupid & Venus, Goblet	35.00

Pressed Glass, Compote, Bellflower

Pressed Glass, Cupid & Venus, Jar, Jam, Covered	37.50
Pressed Glass, Cupid & Venus, Marmalade, Covered	38.00
Pressed Glass, Cupid & Venus, Mug, 2 1/4 In.	25.00
Pressed Glass, Cupid & Venus, Mug, 3 1/2 In.	25.00
Pressed Glass, Cupid & Venus, Pitcher, Milk	38.00 To 40.00
Pressed Glass, Cupid & Venus, Pitcher, Water	40.00 To 48.50
Pressed Glass, Cupid & Venus, Plate, Bread	25.00 To 27.00
Pressed Glass, Cupid & Venus, Plate, Bread, 11 In.	30.00
Pressed Glass, Cupid & Venus, Plate, 10 In.	30.00
Pressed Glass, Cupid & Venus, Plate, 10 1/2 In.	25.00
Pressed Glass, Cupid & Venus, Relish	18.00
Pressed Glass, Cupid & Venus, Sauce	7.50
Pressed Glass, Cupid & Venus, Sauce, Footed	4.00
Pressed Glass, Cupid & Venus, Sauce, Footed, 4 1/2 In.	7.00 To 10.00
Pressed Glass, Cupid & Venus, Spooner	22.00 To 29.00
Pressed Glass, Cupid & Venus, Sugar & Creamer	65.00
Pressed Glass, Cupid & Venus, Tumbler, Buttermilk	25.00
Pressed Glass, Cupid's Hunt, Sherbet	12.00
Pressed Glass, Cupid's Hunt, Tumbler	10.00
Pressed Glass, Curled Leaf, Goblet	22.00
Pressed Glass, Currant, Goblet	14.00 To 18.00
Pressed Glass, Currant, Spooner	18.50 To 21.00
Pressed Glass, Currier & Ives, Bowl, Boat Shaped	18.50
Pressed Glass, Currier & Ives, Bowl, Oval Footed	17.50
Pressed Glass, Currier & Ives, Cup & Saucer	25.00
Pressed Glass, Currier & Ives, Dish, Oval, 10 In.	30.00
Pressed Glass, Currier & Ives, Goblet	14.50 To 24.50
Pressed Glass, Currier & Ives, Mug, Amber	27.50
Pressed Glass, Currier & Ives, Pitcher, Milk	32.00
Pressed Glass, Currier & Ives, Pitcher, Water	20.00
Pressed Glass, Currier & Ives, Pitcher, Water, Deep Sapphire Blue, 9 In.	175.00
Pressed Glass, Currier & Ives, Pitcher, Water, Sapphire Blue, 9 In.	150.00
Pressed Glass, Currier & Ives, Plate, Bread, Scenic, Frosted Center	100.00
Pressed Glass, Currier & Ives, Sauce	9.00
Pressed Glass, Currier & Ives, Spooner	15.00
Pressed Glass, Currier & Ives, Syrup	42.50
Pressed Glass, Currier & Ives, Tray, Wine	35.00
Pressed Glass, Currier & Ives, Wine	12.50 To 14.00
Pressed Glass, Curtain Tieback, Goblet	10.00 To 14.00
Pressed Glass, Curtain, Cake Stand	10.00
Pressed Glass, Curtain, Cake Stand, 8 In.	20.00
Pressed Glass, Curtain, Compote, True Open	20.00
Pressed Glass, Curtain, Spooner	18.50
Pressed Glass, Curtain, Tumbler	13.50
Pressed Glass, Curtain, Water Set, Gold Trim, 5 Piece	125.00
Pressed Glass, Cut Ashburton, Wine, Flint	65.00
Pressed Glass, Cut Log, Bowl, Flat, 8 In.	15.00
Pressed Glass, Cut Log, Bowl, 7 1/4 In.	9.00
Pressed Glass, Cut Log, Bowl, 8 In.	16.00
Pressed Glass, Cut Log, Cake Stand, 9 In.	29.50
Pressed Glass, Cut Log, Celery	25.00
Pressed Glass, Cut Log, Compote, Covered, 8 X 5 1/4 In.	35.00
Pressed Glass, Cut Log, Compote, Covered, 9 X 6 1/4 In.	45.00

Pressed Glass, Cupid & Psyche, Creamer

Pressed Glass, Cupid & Venus, Plate, Bread

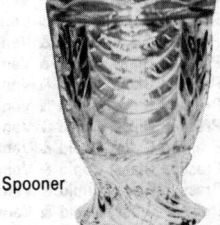

Pressed Glass, Curtain, Spooner

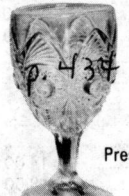

Pressed Glass, Daisies In Oval Panels, Goblet

Pressed Glass, Cut Log, Compote, Jelly, Square	35.00
Pressed Glass, Cut Log, Compote, Low Standard, 6 In.	16.00
Pressed Glass, Cut Log, Compote, 6 In.	23.50
Pressed Glass, Cut Log, Creamer	8.00
Pressed Glass, Cut Log, Creamer, Small	12.50
Pressed Glass, Cut Log, Creamer, 3 In.	15.00
Pressed Glass, Cut Log, Creamer, 5 In.	17.50
Pressed Glass, Cut Log, Cruet	35.00
Pressed Glass, Cut Log, Cruet, Original Stopper, Small	25.00
Pressed Glass, Cut Log, Dish, Designed Base & Ends, Rectangular, 8 X 5 In.	25.00
Pressed Glass, Cut Log, Dish, Oblong, 9 1/4 X 3 1/2 In.	10.00
Pressed Glass, Cut Log, Goblet	32.00
Pressed Glass, Cut Log, Mug	10.00 To 12.00
Pressed Glass, Cut Log, Nappy, Round Handle, 5 In.	18.50
Pressed Glass, Cut Log, Pitcher, Tankard, Applied Handle	55.00
Pressed Glass, Cut Log, Wine	18.00
Pressed Glass, Cut Log, Wine, Clear	18.00
Pressed Glass, Cyclone, Spooner	15.00
Pressed Glass, Daffodil, Syrup, White Opalescent	95.00
Pressed Glass, Dahlia With Petal, Wine, Green	22.00
Pressed Glass, Dahlia, Cake Stand, Blue, 9 1/2 In.	55.00
Pressed Glass, Dahlia, Champagne	47.50
Pressed Glass, Dahlia, Creamer	17.50
Pressed Glass, Dahlia, Dish, Double Handled, 9 In.	14.00
Pressed Glass, Dahlia, Eggcup, Double	29.50 To 45.00
Pressed Glass, Dahlia, Goblet	29.00
Pressed Glass, Dahlia, Goblet, Etched	12.00

Pressed Glass, Dahlia, Mug, 3 1/2 In.	35.00
Pressed Glass, Dahlia, Pitcher, Milk	28.00
Pressed Glass, Dahlia, Pitcher, Water	40.00 To 56.00
Pressed Glass, Dahlia, Plate, Cake	25.00
Pressed Glass, Dahlia, Relish, Handled, Clear & Stippled, 9 1/2 In.	14.00
Pressed Glass, Dahlia, Sauce, Footed, 4 In.	10.00
Pressed Glass, Dahlia, Sauce, 4 1/2 In.	6.00
Pressed Glass, Dahlia, Spooner	30.00
Pressed Glass, Dahlia, Stippled, Candlestick, 8 In.	15.00
Pressed Glass, Dahlia, Wine	30.00
Pressed Glass, Daisies In Oval Panels, Berry Set, Blue, Gold Trim, 4 Piece	88.50
Pressed Glass, Daisies In Oval Panels, Creamer, Small	65.00
Pressed Glass, Daisies In Oval Panels, Goblet	14.00
Pressed Glass, Daisies In Oval Panels, Nappy	8.00
Pressed Glass, Daisies In Oval Panels, Toothpick, Clear With Gold	15.00
Pressed Glass, Daisies In Oval Panels, Tumbler	7.00
Pressed Glass, Daisy & Block, Goblet	10.00
Daisy & Button, see also Paneled Daisy & Button	
Pressed Glass, Daisy & Button Band, Compote, Low Standard, Open, 9 In.	10.00
Pressed Glass, Daisy & Button With Almond Band, Goblet	14.00
Pressed Glass, Daisy & Button With Amber Panels, Pitcher, Water, 8 In.	150.00
Pressed Glass, Daisy & Button With Crossbar, Compote, Blue, Low Standard	14.00
Pressed Glass, Daisy & Button With Crossbar, Compote, Low, Blue	14.00
Pressed Glass, Daisy & Button With Crossbar, Goblet	12.50 To 35.00
Pressed Glass, Daisy & Button With Crossbar, Pitcher, Water	47.50
Pressed Glass, Daisy & Button With Crossbar, Platter, Bread, Amber	35.00
Pressed Glass, Daisy & Button With Crossbar, Sauce, Vaseline, 4 In.	7.50
Pressed Glass, Daisy & Button With Crossbar, Wine	18.00 To 21.00
Pressed Glass, Daisy & Button With Crossbar, Wine, Vaseline	25.00
Pressed Glass, Daisy & Button With Narcissus, Butter, Fuchsia, Covered	55.00
Pressed Glass, Daisy & Button With Narcissus, Decanter, Lavender Stained	22.00
Pressed Glass, Daisy & Button With Narcissus, Pitcher, Water, Fuchsia	55.00
Pressed Glass, Daisy & Button With Narcissus, Spooner, Fuchsia, 2 Handled	30.00
Pressed Glass, Daisy & Button With Narcissus, Wine	10.00
Daisy & Button with Oval Panels, see Hartley	
Pressed Glass, Daisy & Button With Rimmed Oval Panels, Cake Stand, 9 In.	23.50
Pressed Glass, Daisy & Button With Ruby Panels, Celery, Scalloped Rim, 7 In.	55.00
Pressed Glass, Daisy & Button With Thumbprint, Compote, Covered, Amber	70.00
Pressed Glass, Daisy & Button With Thumbprint, Pitcher, Water, Blue	50.00
Pressed Glass, Daisy & Button With Thumbprint, Sauce, Amber	6.00
Pressed Glass, Daisy & Button With V Ornament, Creamer, Amber	40.00
Pressed Glass, Daisy & Button With V Ornament, Cup, Punch, Aqua	25.00
Pressed Glass, Daisy & Button With V Ornament, Pitcher, Water	22.00
Pressed Glass, Daisy & Button With V Ornament, Toothpick, Amber	30.00
Pressed Glass, Daisy & Button, Basket, Amber, Oval, Small	65.00
Pressed Glass, Daisy & Button, Berry Set, Green, Clover Shape, 3 Piece	75.00
Pressed Glass, Daisy & Button, Boot With Spur, Clear	25.00
Pressed Glass, Daisy & Button, Bowl, Octagonal, 9 In.	10.00

Pressed Glass, Daisy Whorl With Diamond Band, Goblet

Pressed Glass, Daisy & Button With Thumbprint, Goblet

Pressed Glass, Daisy & Button, Bowl, Rose, 3 1/2 In.	35.00
Pressed Glass, Daisy & Button, Bowl, Silver Plated Frame, 10 In.	80.00
Pressed Glass, Daisy & Button, Bowl, Vaseline, 5 X 6 1/2 In.	55.00
Pressed Glass, Daisy & Button, Butter, Lid Is Handled Bell, Blue, 8 1/2 In.	225.00
Pressed Glass, Daisy & Button, Cake Stand, 9 X 6 1/2 In.	19.00
Pressed Glass, Daisy & Button, Canoe, Amber	25.00
Pressed Glass, Daisy & Button, Canoe, Vaseline	35.00
Pressed Glass, Daisy & Button, Compote, Covered, 8 In.	90.00
Pressed Glass, Daisy & Button, Compote, Octagonal, Open, 8 1/2 X 7 3/4 In.	50.00
Pressed Glass, Daisy & Button, Compote, Openwork Top Edge, Vaseline, 9 In.	38.00
Pressed Glass, Daisy & Button, Creamer, Amber Square, Applied Handle, Flint	20.00
Pressed Glass, Daisy & Button, Creamer, Amberette	87.50
Pressed Glass, Daisy & Button, Creamer, Child's, Pink Frosted	17.50
Pressed Glass, Daisy & Button, Creamer, Large	35.00
Pressed Glass, Daisy & Button, Dish, Square, 6 In.	19.00
Pressed Glass, Daisy & Button, Goblet, Flat Stem	23.50
Pressed Glass, Daisy & Button, Inkwell, Blue	45.00
Pressed Glass, Daisy & Button, Inkwell, Vaseline, Iron Holder & Ornate Lid	95.00
Pressed Glass, Daisy & Button, Match Holder, Blue, Double Compartment	32.00
Pressed Glass, Daisy & Button, Pitcher, Vaseline, Reed Handle, 9 1/2 In.	60.00
Pressed Glass, Daisy & Button, Pitcher, Water	25.00
Pressed Glass, Daisy & Button, Pitcher, Water, Amber	65.00
Pressed Glass, Daisy & Button, Pitcher, Water, Amberette, Amber Panel	145.00
Pressed Glass, Daisy & Button, Plate, Blue, Scalloped, 9 In.	20.00
Pressed Glass, Daisy & Button, Plate, Clear With Amber Button	20.00
Pressed Glass, Daisy & Button, Plate, Vaseline, Scalloped Edge	45.00
Pressed Glass, Daisy & Button, Salt & Pepper, Ring Handle Base	15.00
Pressed Glass, Daisy & Button, Sauce, Amber, Round	18.00
Pressed Glass, Daisy & Button, Sauce, Amber, Round, 4 1/2 In.	10.00
Pressed Glass, Daisy & Button, Sauce, Oval, 4 X 6 In.	7.50
Pressed Glass, Daisy & Button, Sauce, Pointed Sides, Amber	10.00
Pressed Glass, Daisy & Button, Sauce, Square, Amberina	125.00
Pressed Glass, Daisy & Button, Sauce, Vaseline, Triangular	14.00
Pressed Glass, Daisy & Button, Sauce, Vaseline, 4 In.Square	6.00
Pressed Glass, Daisy & Button, Shoe, Amber Bands, 5 1/2 In.	48.00
Pressed Glass, Daisy & Button, Slipper, Blue, 11 1/2 In.	175.00
Pressed Glass, Daisy & Button, Slipper, Canary, 11 1/2 In.	135.00
Pressed Glass, Daisy & Button, Slipper, Open, Amber	24.00
Pressed Glass, Daisy & Button, Spooner, Amber	24.00
Pressed Glass, Daisy & Button, Sugar, Tall	35.00
Pressed Glass, Daisy & Button, Toothpick, Cradle, Amber	55.00
Pressed Glass, Daisy & Button, Toothpick, Gyspy Kettle, Blue	20.00
Pressed Glass, Daisy & Button, Toothpick, Hat Form, Golden Amber, C.1885	22.50
Pressed Glass, Daisy & Button, Toothpick, Hat, Blue	30.00
Pressed Glass, Daisy & Button, Toothpick, Hat, Turquoise	28.00
Pressed Glass, Daisy & Button, Toothpick, Vaseline, Silver Metal Holder	32.00

Pressed Glass, Deer & Dog, Goblet

Pressed Glass, Delaware, Pitcher, Rose Color, 9 1/2 In.

Pressed Glass, Daisy & Button, Tub, Miniature, Blue 18.00
Pressed Glass, Daisy & Button, Tumbler 40.00
Pressed Glass, Daisy & Button, Tumbler, Amber 22.50
Pressed Glass, Daisy & Cube, Cruet, Stopper, Blue, 7 In. 65.00
Pressed Glass, Daisy & Feather, Wine 12.50
Pressed Glass, Daisy & Fern, Cruet, Opalescent, Clear Stopper & Handle 45.00
Pressed Glass, Daisy & Fern, Pitcher, Blue, Opalescent 110.00
Pressed Glass, Daisy & Fern, Pitcher, Water, Blue, Opalescent 85.00
Pressed Glass, Daisy & Fern, Pitcher, Water, White, Opalescent 65.00
Pressed Glass, Daisy & Fern, Saltshaker, Cranberry, Opalescent 85.00
Pressed Glass, Daisy & Fern, Shaker, Blue 75.00
Pressed Glass, Daisy & Fern, Syrup, Clear, Opalescent 58.00
Pressed Glass, Daisy & Fern, Syrup, Opalescent, Blue, W.Va. 125.00
Pressed Glass, Daisy & Fern, Water Set, Blue, Opalescent, 5 Piece 158.00
Pressed Glass, Daisy & Greek Key, Sauce, Blue, Opalescent 35.00
Pressed Glass, Daisy & Scroll, Bowl, 8 In. 18.00
Pressed Glass, Daisy & Scroll, Tumbler 14.00
Pressed Glass, Daisy In Diamond, Creamer, Child's 15.00
Pressed Glass, Daisy, Celery, Engraved Band 28.50
Pressed Glass, Dakota, Butter, Covered 38.50
Pressed Glass, Dakota, Butter, Covered, Etched, Piecrust Rim 65.00
Pressed Glass, Dakota, Butter, Covered, Etched, Thumbprint Edge 48.50
Pressed Glass, Dakota, Butter, Covered, Piecrust Edge 45.00
Pressed Glass, Dakota, Butter, Etched 47.50
Pressed Glass, Dakota, Cake Stand 20.00
Pressed Glass, Dakota, Celery, Etched .... 24.00 To 32.50
Pressed Glass, Dakota, Celery, Etched Fern & Berries 35.00
Pressed Glass, Dakota, Celery, Etched, Pedestal 45.00
Pressed Glass, Dakota, Celery, Flat 25.00
Pressed Glass, Dakota, Celery, Footed 20.00
Pressed Glass, Dakota, Celery, Pedestal, Etched Fern & Berry 45.00
Pressed Glass, Dakota, Compote, Covered, Child's .... 80.00 To 85.00
Pressed Glass, Dakota, Compote, Etched, 6 In. 34.00
Pressed Glass, Dakota, Compote, Etched, 7 3/4 X 8 In. 38.00
Pressed Glass, Dakota, Compote, Open, Etched Fern & Berry, High, 6 7/8 In. 27.50
Pressed Glass, Dakota, Compote, 7 In. 24.50
Pressed Glass, Dakota, Etched, Celery 16.50
Pressed Glass, Dakota, Goblet .... 17.00 To 18.50
Pressed Glass, Dakota, Goblet, Etched .... 17.50 To 32.50
Pressed Glass, Dakota, Goblet, Etched Berry 25.00
Pressed Glass, Dakota, Goblet, Etched Fern & Berry .... 23.00 To 35.00
Pressed Glass, Dakota, Goblet, Etched, Ruby Top 28.00
Pressed Glass, Dakota, Leaf & Berry, Goblet 23.00
Pressed Glass, Dakota, Pitcher, Water 45.00
Pressed Glass, Dakota, Pitcher, Water, Etched Fern & Berry 60.00
Pressed Glass, Dakota, Red Top, Etched 45.00
Pressed Glass, Dakota, Salt & Pepper, Pair 75.00
Pressed Glass, Dakota, Saltshaker, Etched, Pewter Lid 32.00
Pressed Glass, Dakota, Sauce, Footed 9.50
Pressed Glass, Dakota, Spooner .... 15.00 To 20.00
Pressed Glass, Dakota, Spooner, Pedestal, Etched 18.00
Pressed Glass, Dakota, Sugar, Covered 32.50
Pressed Glass, Dakota, Sugar, 4 1/16 In. 10.00
Pressed Glass, Dakota, Tumbler, Clear, Etched 18.00
Pressed Glass, Dakota, Tumbler, Etched Fern & Berry 38.50
Pressed Glass, Dakota, Tumbler, Ruby 45.00
Pressed Glass, Dakota, Tumbler, Water, Etched 38.50
Pressed Glass, Dakota, Vase, 5 In. 38.00
Pressed Glass, Dakota, Wine, Amethyst, 4 In. 13.50
Pressed Glass, Dakota, Wine, Etched 35.00
Pressed Glass, Dakota, Wine, Etched Fern & Berry 38.50
Pressed Glass, Dart & Ball, Mug, Cobalt Blue 20.00
Pressed Glass, Dart, Compote, Low Standard, Open, 9 In. 15.00
Pressed Glass, Dart, Creamer .... 22.00 To 22.50
Pressed Glass, Dart, Spooner 20.00

Pressed Glass, **Dart**, Sugar	28.00
Pressed Glass, **Dart**, Sugar & Creamer	52.00
Pressed Glass, **Dart**, Sugar, Covered	22.00
Pressed Glass, **Deer & Cow**, Mug, Miniature, Blue	27.00
Pressed Glass, **Deer & Doe With Lily Of The Valley**, Goblet, Signed	62.00
Pressed Glass, **Deer & Dog & Hunter**, Spooner, Etched	52.50
Pressed Glass, **Deer & Dog & Hunter**, Spooner, Etched, Footed	40.00
Pressed Glass, **Deer & Dog**, Bowl, U-Shaped	85.00
Pressed Glass, **Deer & Dog**, Celery, Gillinder	67.50
Pressed Glass, **Deer & Dog**, Goblet	50.00 To 75.00
Pressed Glass, **Deer & Dog**, Goblet, Etched	75.00
Pressed Glass, **Deer & Oak Tree**, Pitcher, Water	97.50
Pressed Glass, **Deer & Pine Tree**, Bread Tray, Amber	59.50
Pressed Glass, **Deer & Pine Tree**, Butter	57.50
Pressed Glass, **Deer & Pine Tree**, Goblet	35.00
Pressed Glass, **Deer & Pine Tree**, Mug	28.50
Pressed Glass, **Deer & Pine Tree**, Pitcher, Water	75.00 To 92.50
Pressed Glass, **Deer & Pine Tree**, Pitcher, Water, 8 1/2 In.	60.00
Pressed Glass, **Deer & Pine Tree**, Plate, Bread	30.00
Pressed Glass, **Deer & Pine Tree**, Platter, 13 X 8 In.	42.50
Pressed Glass, **Deer & Pine Tree**, Sauce, Footed, 3 1/2 X 4 1/2 In.	17.50
Pressed Glass, **Deer & Pine Tree**, Sugar	25.00
Pressed Glass, **Deer & Pine Tree**, Tray, Handles, 15 In.	135.00
Pressed Glass, **Deer & Pine Tree**, Tray, Raised Sides, Handled, 15 X 9 In.	45.00
Pressed Glass, **Deer & Pine Tree**, Tray, Water, 15 X 9 In.	75.00
Pressed Glass, **Delaware**, Banana Boat, Cranberry, Gold Trim	58.00
Pressed Glass, **Delaware**, Banana Boat, Green, Gold Trim	48.00
Pressed Glass, **Delaware**, Banana Boat, Oval, Green	60.00
Pressed Glass, **Delaware**, Banana Boat, Pink	75.00
Pressed Glass, **Delaware**, Basket, Bride's, Green, Footed Holder, 8 1/2 In.	155.00
Pressed Glass, **Delaware**, Berry Set, Cranberry & Gold, 6 Piece	165.00
Pressed Glass, **Delaware**, Berry Set, Cranberry Leaves & Flowers	95.00
Pressed Glass, **Delaware**, Berry Set, Gold On Green, 7 Piece	95.00
Pressed Glass, **Delaware**, Berry Set, Rose, Gold, 7 Piece	30.00
Pressed Glass, **Delaware**, Berry Set, 7 Piece	225.00
Pressed Glass, **Delaware**, Bowl, Bride's, Rose Color, Silver Holder, 8 1/2 In.	65.00
Pressed Glass, **Delaware**, Bowl, Fruit, Green	42.00
Pressed Glass, **Delaware**, Bowl, Green & Gilt, 8 In.	38.00
Pressed Glass, **Delaware**, Bowl, Green, Gold Trim, Octagon, 9 1/2 In.	36.00
Pressed Glass, **Delaware**, Bowl, Green, Gold, 8 1/2 In.	30.00
Pressed Glass, **Delaware**, Bowl, Oval, Cranberry, 11 X 7 In.	100.00
Pressed Glass, **Delaware**, Bowl, Ruffled, Green With Gold, 9 1/2 In.	35.00
Pressed Glass, **Delaware**, Compote, Green, Gold Decoration, 9 1/2 In.	85.00
Pressed Glass, **Delaware**, Creamer, Green	50.00
Pressed Glass, **Delaware**, Cruet, Green, Gold, Original Stopper	110.00
Pressed Glass, **Delaware**, Dish, Boat Shaped, Green	35.00
Pressed Glass, **Delaware**, Green, Banana Boat, 12 In.	75.00
Pressed Glass, **Delaware**, Jug, Claret, Green, Gold	100.00
Pressed Glass, **Delaware**, Pitcher, Water, Green	80.00
Pressed Glass, **Delaware**, Pitcher, Water, Green & Gold	85.00
Pressed Glass, **Delaware**, Pitcher, Water, Red	90.00
Pressed Glass, **Delaware**, Sauceboat, Cranberry Stain, Gold	97.50
Pressed Glass, **Delaware**, Shade, Gas, Cranberry & Gold, 5 In.	75.00
Pressed Glass, **Delaware**, Spooner, Green And Gold	85.00
Pressed Glass, **Delaware**, Spooner, Green, Gold Trim	50.00
Pressed Glass, **Delaware**, Sugar & Creamer, Clear	65.00
Pressed Glass, **Delaware**, Sugar & Creamer, Green, Open	80.00 To 125.00
Pressed Glass, **Delaware**, Table Set, Rose, 4 Piece	425.00
Pressed Glass, **Delaware**, Toothpick, Green And Gold	45.00
Pressed Glass, **Delaware**, Tumbler, Cranberry Pink, Gold	115.00
Pressed Glass, **Delaware**, Tumbler, Green	42.00
Pressed Glass, **Delaware**, Tumbler, Red, 3 3/4 In., Set Of Four	100.00
Pressed Glass, **Delaware**, Tumbler, Rose, Gold	40.00
Pressed Glass, **Delaware**, Vase, Cranberry Flashed Pleated Rim, Gold Floral	95.00
Pressed Glass, **Delaware**, Vase, Ruffled Rim, Clear Body, Gold Flowers, 10 In.	65.00

Pressed Glass, Diamond Cut With Leaf, Plate

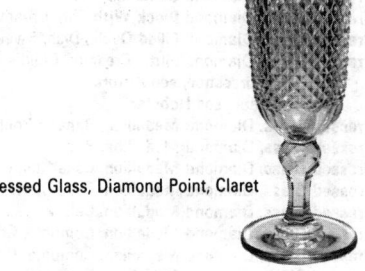

Pressed Glass, Diamond Point, Claret

Pressed Glass, **Delaware,** Water Set, Green, Gold	295.00
Pressed Glass, **Della Robbia,** Goblet	10.00
Pressed Glass, **Dew & Raindrop,** Bowl	38.00
Pressed Glass, **Dew & Raindrop,** Cordial	20.00
Pressed Glass, **Dew & Raindrop,** Cup, Punch	5.00
Pressed Glass, **Dewdrop With Sheaf Of Wheat,** Plate, Bread	30.00
Pressed Glass, **Dewdrop With Small Stars,** Goblet	12.00 To 13.00
Pressed Glass, **Dewdrop With Star,** Bowl, Footed, 6 In.	15.00
Pressed Glass, **Dewdrop With Star,** Bowl, Soup, 8 In.	10.00
Pressed Glass, **Dewdrop With Star,** Cake Stand, 9 1/2 In.	32.50
Pressed Glass, **Dewdrop With Star,** Goblet	15.00
Pressed Glass, **Dewdrop With Star,** Plate, 6 1/4 In.	14.00
Pressed Glass, **Dewdrop With Star,** Plate, 7 1/4 In.	15.00
Pressed Glass, **Dewdrop With Star,** Relish, 10 In.	10.00
Pressed Glass, **Dewdrop With Star,** Relish, 10 X 5 1/2 In.	12.00
Pressed Glass, **Dewdrop With Star,** Salt, Footed	15.00
Pressed Glass, **Dewdrop With Star,** Sauce, Flat, 5 1/4 In.	11.00
Pressed Glass, **Dewdrop With Star,** Sugar, Lid	30.00
Pressed Glass, **Dewdrop,** Mug, Handled, 3 1/2 In.	22.50
Dewey, see also Admiral Dewey	
Pressed Glass, **Dewey,** Butter, Amber	34.00
Pressed Glass, **Dewey,** Butter, Covered, Clear, C.1890	48.00
Pressed Glass, **Dewey,** Butter, Covered, Dark Amber, Small	45.00
Pressed Glass, **Dewey,** Cruet, Amber, Clear Stopper	75.00
Pressed Glass, **Dewey,** Cruet, Nile Green, Greentown	600.00
Pressed Glass, **Dewey,** Mug, Amber, 3 1/2 In.	65.00
Pressed Glass, **Dewey,** Mug, Canary, Greentown	50.00
Pressed Glass, **Dewey,** Mug, Green	60.00
Pressed Glass, **Dewey,** Pitcher	55.00
Pressed Glass, **Dewey,** Pitcher, Water	48.00 To 65.00
Pressed Glass, **Dewey,** Plate, 6 In.	15.00
Pressed Glass, **Diagonal Band & Fan,** Goblet	16.00
Pressed Glass, **Diagonal Band & Fan,** Plate, 7 In.	11.50
Pressed Glass, **Diagonal Band & Fan,** Sugar	12.00
Pressed Glass, **Diagonal Band & Fan,** Sugar, Open	15.00
Pressed Glass, **Diagonal Band,** Cake Stand, 9 In.	22.50
Pressed Glass, **Diagonal Band,** Creamer	14.00
Pressed Glass, **Diagonal Band,** Creamer, Clear	26.50
Pressed Glass, **Diagonal Band,** Dish, Clear, 11 1/2 X 9 In.	35.00
Pressed Glass, **Diagonal Band,** Goblet	15.00
Pressed Glass, **Diagonal Band,** Wine	14.00

Pressed Glass, Diagonal Block Band, Goblet 13.00
    Diamond, see Umbilicated Sawtooth
Pressed Glass, Diamond & Drape, Celery, English Flint 75.00
Pressed Glass, Diamond & Fleur-De-Lis, Bracket Lamp, Beaded, Font, Blown 59.50
    Diamond & Sunburst, see also Flattened Diamond & Sunburst
Pressed Glass, Diamond & Sunburst, Goblet 12.50
Pressed Glass, Diamond & Sunburst, Pitcher, Water, U.S.Glass No.15018 .... 25.00
Pressed Glass, Diamond & Sunburst, Table Set, Child's, 3 Piece 50.00
Pressed Glass, Diamond Band & Fan, Sauce, 4 In. 4.00
Pressed Glass, Diamond Band, Mug 20.00
Pressed Glass, Diamond Block With Fan, Creamer 18.50
Pressed Glass, Diamond Filled Ovals, Dish, Sweetmeat, Flint 37.50
Pressed Glass, Diamond Flute, Creamer, Child's 15.00
    Diamond Horseshoe, see Aurora
    Diamond Lace, see Hobstar
Pressed Glass, Diamond Medallion, Banana Boat, Footed 15.00
Pressed Glass, Diamond Medallion, Butter 23.00
Pressed Glass, Diamond Medallion, Cake Stand 15.00
Pressed Glass, Diamond Medallion, Cake Stand, Footed 18.00
Pressed Glass, Diamond Medallion, Celery 17.00
Pressed Glass, Diamond Medallion, Compote, Covered, High Standard, 8 In. 55.00
Pressed Glass, Diamond Medallion, Compote, Covered, 5 1/2 In. 28.00
Pressed Glass, Diamond Medallion, Compote, Covered, 9 X 6 In. 30.00
Pressed Glass, Diamond Medallion, Compote, High Standard, Covered, 8 In. 52.50
Pressed Glass, Diamond Medallion, Compote, 6 X 8 In. 20.00
Pressed Glass, Diamond Medallion, Plate, 10 In. .... 13.00 To 22.00
Pressed Glass, Diamond Medallion, Spooner 13.00
Pressed Glass, Diamond Medallion, Spooner, Scallop Top 16.00
Pressed Glass, Diamond Medallion, Sugar & Creamer 30.00
Pressed Glass, Diamond Panel, Spooner, Green 25.00
Pressed Glass, Diamond Panels, Butter, Miniature, Blue, Covered 40.00
Pressed Glass, Diamond Peg, Tumbler, Custard, Gold, Rose Decoration 65.00
    Diamond Point Discs, see Eyewinker
Pressed Glass, Diamond Point Loop, Bowl, Blue, Etched, 8 In. 25.00
Pressed Glass, Diamond Point Loop, Butter, Blue, Etched 10.00
Pressed Glass, Diamond Point Loop, Sauce, Blue, Etched, 4 In. 10.00
Pressed Glass, Diamond Point Loop, Spooner, Blue, Etched, 5 1/2 In. 22.00
Pressed Glass, Diamond Point With Flutes, Wine, Blue 20.00
Pressed Glass, Diamond Point With Leaf, Creamer 14.00
    Diamond Point with Panels, see Hinoto
Pressed Glass, Diamond Point, Champagne, Flint .... 75.00 To 87.50
Pressed Glass, Diamond Point, Claret, Flint 87.50
Pressed Glass, Diamond Point, Decanter, Stopper, Quart 80.00
Pressed Glass, Diamond Point, Eggcup, Flint 30.00
Pressed Glass, Diamond Point, Eggcup, Flint, Clambroth 125.00
Pressed Glass, Diamond Point, Goblet, Flint 30.00
Pressed Glass, Diamond Point, Goblet, Flint, Polished Pontil 34.00
Pressed Glass, Diamond Point, Tumbler 6.50
Pressed Glass, Diamond Point, Whiskey, Handled, Flint 95.00
Pressed Glass, Diamond Point, Wine, Flint 40.00
Pressed Glass, Diamond Prisms, Wine 10.00
Pressed Glass, Diamond Quilt With Stars, Goblet 12.50
Pressed Glass, Diamond Quilted, Goblet, Amethyst 35.00
Pressed Glass, Diamond Quilted, Goblet, Vaseline 29.00
Pressed Glass, Diamond Quilted, Sauce, Amethyst, Footed, 4 In. 12.50
Pressed Glass, Diamond Quilted, Sauce, Amethyst, 4 In. 7.50
Pressed Glass, Diamond Quilted, Sauce, Turquoise, Footed, 3 3/4 In. 6.50
Pressed Glass, Diamond Spearhead, Toothpick, Opalescent, Vaseline 40.00
    Diamond Swag, see Fandango
Pressed Glass, Diamond Thumbprint, Bowl, Footed, Flint, 9 1/4 In. 80.00
Pressed Glass, Diamond Thumbprint, Celery 185.00
Pressed Glass, Diamond Thumbprint, Celery, Flint 200.00
Pressed Glass, Diamond Thumbprint, Champagne, Flint, 5 1/4 In. 225.00
Pressed Glass, Diamond Thumbprint, Compote, Clear, Flint, 4 1/2 X 7 1/2 In. 75.00
Pressed Glass, Diamond Thumbprint, Compote, Flint, 4 1/2 X 7 1/2 In. 75.00

Pressed Glass, Diamond Thumbprint, Compote, Low, Scalloped Edge, Flint 85.00
Pressed Glass, Diamond Thumbprint, Goblet 392.00
Pressed Glass, Diamond Thumbprint, Pitcher, Water 225.00
Pressed Glass, Diamond With Double Fan, Pitcher, Water 25.00
Pressed Glass, Diamond With Double Fan, Sugar, Ruby & Clear 25.00
Pressed Glass, Diana, Salt & Pepper, Amber 47.50
Pressed Glass, Dickinson, Goblet, Flint 28.00
Pressed Glass, Dickinson, Sauce, Flint, 4 In. 14.50
Pressed Glass, Divided Block With Sunburst, Sauce, Clear, Ruby Stained 12.50
Pressed Glass, Divided Hearts, Eggcup, Flint 55.00
Pressed Glass, Dodomo, Compote, Jelly 12.00
Pressed Glass, Dog Finial, Compote, High Standard, Covered, 8 In. 115.00
    Dog on Drum, see Cat in Basket & Dog on Drum
Pressed Glass, Dolphin, Bowl, 2 Frosted Dolphins Holding Clear Bowl, 8 In. 95.00
Pressed Glass, Dolphin, Candlestick, Blue Top, Clambroth Base, Flint 450.00
Pressed Glass, Dolphin, Candlestick, Clambroth, Sandwich Flint 350.00
Pressed Glass, Dolphin, Compote, Opalescent 38.50
Pressed Glass, Dolphin, Sugar, Frosted, Covered 80.00
Pressed Glass, Dolphin, Sugar, Frosted, Dolphin Finial 125.00
    Doric, see Feather
Pressed Glass, Doric & Pansy, Cup & Saucer, Plate, Aqua, Child's 30.00
Pressed Glass, Double Beaded Band, Wine 13.00
Pressed Glass, Double Beetle Band, Goblet 13.00
Pressed Glass, Double Dahlia & Lens, Goblet, Green, Gold Rim & Leaves 28.50
Pressed Glass, Double Dahlia & Lens, Wine, Green 25.00
Pressed Glass, Double Leaf & Dart, Goblet 16.50
    Double Loop, see Double Loop & Dart
Pressed Glass, Double Loop & Dart, Goblet .... 13.00 To 15.00
Pressed Glass, Double Loop & Dart, Tumbler 14.00
Pressed Glass, Double Ribbon, Butter, Covered, Footed 38.00
Pressed Glass, Double Spear, Goblet 10.00
Pressed Glass, Double Spear, Sugar & Creamer 50.00
    Double Vine, see Bellflower, Double Vine
Pressed Glass, Double Wedding Ring, Goblet 18.50
Pressed Glass, Double Wedding Ring, Tumbler 36.50

Pressed Glass, Diamond Thumbprint, Decanter

Pressed Glass, Dolphin, Pitcher, Frosted

Pressed Glass, Egg In Sand, Goblet

Pressed Glass, Egyptian, Goblet

Pressed Glass, Drapery Band With Stars, Goblet	15.00
Pressed Glass, Drapery, Goblet	12.50 To 22.00
Pressed Glass, Drapery, Goblet, Bakewell Pears	14.50
Pressed Glass, Drapery, Sauce, Gold, Opalescent, Northwood	20.00
Pressed Glass, Drapery, Spooner	15.00 To 33.50
Pressed Glass, Drapery, Spooner, Opalescent, Northwood	40.00
Pressed Glass, Drapery, Sugar, Blue, Opalescent, Covered, Northwood	60.00
Pressed Glass, Drapery, Water Set, Clear, Northwood, 7 Piece	125.00
Pressed Glass, Drum, Butter, Covered	75.00
Pressed Glass, Drum, Mug, Child's, Gold Trim	12.50
Pressed Glass, Drum, Spooner	20.00
Pressed Glass, Drum, Spooner, Child's	45.00
Pressed Glass, Drum, Table Set, Miniature	225.00
Pressed Glass, Duchess Flute, Mustard, Covered	18.00
Pressed Glass, Duchess Flute, Spooner	20.00
Pressed Glass, Duchess Flute, Sugar & Creamer, Georgian Handles	45.00
Pressed Glass, Duchess Flute, Toothpick	12.00
Pressed Glass, Duck Cover, Dish, Frosted	75.00
Pressed Glass, Duck, Dish, Pond Base, Frosted, 7 In.	60.00
Pressed Glass, Duke, Goblet	12.00
Pressed Glass, Duquesne, Goblet	10.00
Dynast, see Radiant	
Pressed Glass, Eagle, Humidor, Blown In Mold	26.00
Pressed Glass, Eagle, Spooner, Bullet Emblem	125.00
Pressed Glass, Eagle, Sugar, Covered, Frosted, Etched	125.00
Earl, see Spirea Band	
Pressed Glass, Eastern Star, Cup & Saucer	12.50
Pressed Glass, Edgerton, Creamer	15.00
Pressed Glass, Effulgent Star, Goblet	32.50
Pressed Glass, Egg In Sand, Butter, Covered, Amber	55.00
Pressed Glass, Egg In Sand, Goblet	24.50 To 25.00
Pressed Glass, Egg In Sand, Pitcher, Milk	30.00
Pressed Glass, Egg In Sand, Spooner	14.00
Pressed Glass, Egyptian, Celery, 8 1/2 In.	45.00
Pressed Glass, Egyptian, Compote, Sphinx, Tall, Covered	80.00
Pressed Glass, Egyptian, Dish, Pickle	22.00
Pressed Glass, Egyptian, Goblet	30.00
Pressed Glass, Egyptian, Sauce, Footed	12.00
Pressed Glass, Egyptian, Sauce, Footed, 4 In.	7.50
Pressed Glass, Egyptian, Spooner	24.00 To 28.00
Pressed Glass, Egyptian, Sugar	20.00
Pressed Glass, Egyptian, Tray, Bread, Cleo	45.00
Pressed Glass, Eight-O-Eight, Compote, Open, Ruffled, 7 1/2 In.	73.50
Pressed Glass, Eight-O-Eight, Wine	20.00
Pressed Glass, Electric, Plate, Bread, Blue Basket Weave, Rope Handles, Dated	90.00
Pressed Glass, Elegance, Bowl, Punch, Child's	20.00
Pressed Glass, Elmino, Goblet, Etched	9.50
Pressed Glass, Empress, Creamer, Emerald Green And Gold	65.00
Pressed Glass, Empress, Cruet, Emerald Green, Gold Trim, Stopper	128.00
Pressed Glass, Empress, Salt & Pepper, Emerald Green, Gold Trim	68.00
Pressed Glass, Empress, Tray, Condiment, Emerald Green, Gold	165.00
English Hobnail Cross, see Klondike	
Pressed Glass, English Hobnail, Bottle, Perfume	12.00
Pressed Glass, English Hobnail, Condiment Set, Child's, 4 Piece	40.00
Pressed Glass, English Hobnail, Goblet	10.00 To 12.50
Pressed Glass, English Hobnail, Pitcher, Amber, Reeded & Applied Handle	30.00
Pressed Glass, Engraved Cow In Wreath, Goblet, Flint	85.00
Pressed Glass, Esther, Berry Set, Green, Gold, 5 Piece	160.00
Pressed Glass, Esther, Compote, Covered, Tall	45.00
Pressed Glass, Esther, Creamer, Emerald Green And Gold	55.00
Pressed Glass, Esther, Goblet	35.00
Pressed Glass, Esther, Sugar & Creamer, Small	22.00
Pressed Glass, Esther, Toothpick, Green, Gold	95.00
Pressed Glass, Esther, Tumbler, Green, Gold	45.00
Pressed Glass, Etched Angels, Creamer	19.00

Pressed Glass, Excelsior, Bottle, Bitters

Pressed Glass, Fern Burst, Goblet

Etched Band, see Dakota
Etched Dakota, see Dakota
Etched Fern, see Ashman
Etched patterns, see under main pattern, e.g.: Etched Dakota, see
Dakota

Pressed Glass, Etruscan, Goblet, Flint	30.00
Pressed Glass, Eugenie, Goblet, Flint	45.00
Pressed Glass, Eureka, Eggcup, Flint	16.50
Pressed Glass, Eureka, Goblet	10.00
Pressed Glass, Eureka, Goblet, Flint	22.50 To 25.00
Pressed Glass, Eureka, Platter, Oval	35.00
Pressed Glass, Everglades, Bowl, Banana, Opalescent, Gold	150.00
Pressed Glass, Excelsior With Maltese Cross, Whiskey	47.50
Pressed Glass, Excelsior With Maltese Cross, Whiskey, Flint	65.00
Pressed Glass, Excelsior, Candlestick, Flint	125.00
Pressed Glass, Excelsior, Castor Set	65.00
Pressed Glass, Excelsior, Champagne, Flint	55.00
Pressed Glass, Excelsior, Cordial, Flint	28.00
Pressed Glass, Excelsior, Eggcup	22.00
Pressed Glass, Excelsior, Goblet, Flint	37.50 To 55.00
Pressed Glass, Excelsior, Whiskey, 3 In.	47.00
Pressed Glass, Eyewinker & Fan, Vase, Green, Footed, 1885, 7 In.	75.00
Pressed Glass, Eyewinker, Berry Bowl, 9 In.	65.00
Pressed Glass, Eyewinker, Butter	49.50
Pressed Glass, Eyewinker, Cake Stand, 9 1/2 In.	65.00
Pressed Glass, Eyewinker, Compote, High Standard, Covered	60.00
Pressed Glass, Eyewinker, Goblet	35.00
Pressed Glass, Eyewinker, Plate, Square, Turned Up Sides, 8 3/4 In.	48.00
Pressed Glass, Eyewinker, Plate, 9 In.	22.50
Pressed Glass, Eyewinker, Salt & Pepper, Pewter Lids	45.00
Pressed Glass, Eyewinker, Sugar	17.00
Pressed Glass, Eyewinker, Syrup	75.00
Pressed Glass, Eyewinker, Table Set, 4 Piece	250.00
Pressed Glass, Eyewinker, Tray, Cookie, 10 In.	40.00
Pressed Glass, Faceted Flower, Pitcher, Water	25.00
Fagot, see Vera	
Pressed Glass, Falcon Strawberry, Creamer, Covered	35.00
Pressed Glass, Falcon Strawberry, Dish, Oval	15.00
Pressed Glass, Falcon Strawberry, Goblet	15.00 To 22.00
Pressed Glass, Falcon Strawberry, Sugar, Covered	35.00
Pressed Glass, Famous, Wine	16.00
Fan, see also Butterfly & Fan	
Pressed Glass, Fan With Diamond, Goblet	12.00 To 13.00
Pressed Glass, Fan, Butter, Emerald Green, Gold, Northwood	120.00
Pressed Glass, Fan, Gravy Boat, Blue Opalescent	35.00
Pressed Glass, Fan, Muffineer	38.00
Pressed Glass, Fan, Plate, Amber	22.00
Pressed Glass, Fancy Cut, Spooner	14.00
Pressed Glass, Fancy Loop, Bowl, Punch, Crimped, Base, 12 In.	90.00

Pressed Glass, **Fandango,** Bowl, 10 In. 30.00
Pressed Glass, **Feather & Arches,** Bowl, Punch, Child's 35.00
Pressed Glass, **Feather Duster,** Goblet 21.00
Pressed Glass, **Feather Duster,** Pitcher, Water, Green 42.50
Pressed Glass, **Feather Duster,** Tumbler 9.50
Pressed Glass, **Feather,** Bowl, Footed, 5 1/2 In. 17.50
Pressed Glass, **Feather,** Butter, Covered 39.50
Pressed Glass, **Feather,** Cake Stand .... 20.00 To 28.50
Pressed Glass, **Feather,** Cake Stand, 5 In. 25.00
Pressed Glass, **Feather,** Cake Stand, 7 1/2 X 4 1/2 In. 18.00
Pressed Glass, **Feather,** Cake Stand, 8 In. 19.50
Pressed Glass, **Feather,** Cake Stand, 8 1/4 In. .... 14.00 To 22.00
Pressed Glass, **Feather,** Celery 25.00
Pressed Glass, **Feather,** Compote, Covered, 3 X 7 In. 36.50
Pressed Glass, **Feather,** Compote, Jelly, 4 1/2 In. 12.50
Pressed Glass, **Feather,** Compote, Portland Glass Co., 9 In. 20.00
Pressed Glass, **Feather,** Cruet .... 30.00 To 42.50
Pressed Glass, **Feather,** Goblet .... 30.00 To 47.00
Pressed Glass, **Feather,** Nappy, Footed 24.50
Pressed Glass, **Feather,** Pitcher, Water .... 20.00 To 24.00
Pressed Glass, **Feather,** Sauce 6.00
Pressed Glass, **Feather,** Sauce, Flat 6.00
Pressed Glass, **Feather,** Sauce, 4 In. 5.00
Pressed Glass, **Feather,** Sugar, Covered 52.00
Pressed Glass, **Feather,** Vase, Green, Opalescent, 10 In. 52.50
Pressed Glass, **Feather,** Water Set, 7 Piece 140.00
Pressed Glass, **Feather,** Wine .... 25.00 To 35.00
Pressed Glass, **Feathered Points,** Pitcher, Water 16.00
Pressed Glass, **Fern Burst,** Goblet 15.00
Pressed Glass, **Fern Garland,** Cordial 14.00
Pressed Glass, **Fernland,** Butter, Child's, Covered 25.00
Pressed Glass, **Fernland,** Creamer 10.00
Pressed Glass, **Fernland,** Creamer, Clear, Miniature 15.00
Pressed Glass, **Fernland,** Spooner, Child's 15.00
Pressed Glass, **Fernland,** Sugar, Child's, Covered 25.00
   Festoon and Grape, see Grape and Festoon
Pressed Glass, **Festoon,** Bowl, Berry, 7 In. 14.50
Pressed Glass, **Festoon,** Bowl, Berry, 9 In. 18.50
Pressed Glass, **Festoon,** Bowl, Rectangular, 7 X 4 1/2 In. 22.50
Pressed Glass, **Festoon,** Bowl, Rectangular, 9 In. 15.00
Pressed Glass, **Festoon,** Bowl, 9 In. .... 15.00 To 21.00
Pressed Glass, **Festoon,** Cake Stand .... 25.00 To 37.50
Pressed Glass, **Festoon,** Cake Stand, 9 In. .... 22.00 To 23.00
Pressed Glass, **Festoon,** Compote, Open 35.00
Pressed Glass, **Festoon,** Creamer .... 21.00 To 23.00
Pressed Glass, **Festoon,** Pitcher, Water 45.00
Pressed Glass, **Festoon,** Sauce 5.50
Pressed Glass, **Festoon,** Spooner .... 18.00 To 19.50
Pressed Glass, **Festoon,** Sugar, Covered 45.00
Pressed Glass, **Festoon,** Tray, 10 In. 18.00
Pressed Glass, **Festoon,** Tumbler .... 14.50 To 28.00
Pressed Glass, **File,** Pitcher 42.00
Pressed Glass, **Fine Feather,** Salt & Pepper, Clear 20.00
Pressed Glass, **Fine Prism,** Champagne, Flint .... 30.00 To 42.50
Pressed Glass, **Fine Prism,** Wine, Flint 34.50
Pressed Glass, **Fine Rib With Cut Ovals,** Wine, Flint 95.00
Pressed Glass, **Fine Rib,** Celery, Flint 65.00
Pressed Glass, **Fine Rib,** Champagne, Flint 47.50
Pressed Glass, **Fine Rib,** Compote, Flint, 7 3/8 X 6 5/8 In. 50.00
Pressed Glass, **Fine Rib,** Creamer, Applied Handle 175.00
Pressed Glass, **Fine Rib,** Decanter, Bar, Quart 65.00
Pressed Glass, **Fine Rib,** Eggcup, Flint 32.50
Pressed Glass, **Fine Rib,** Goblet, Flint .... 25.00 To 35.00
Pressed Glass, **Fine Rib,** Spooner, Flint .... 20.00 To 55.00
Pressed Glass, **Fine Rib,** Tumbler, Miniature, Opalescent, Flint, 1 3/4 In. 45.00

Pressed Glass, Fine Rib With Cut Ovals, Cordial

Pressed Glass, Fine Rib, Whiskey, Flint	28.00
Pressed Glass, Fine Rib, Whiskey, Handled, Flint	75.00
Pressed Glass, Finecut & Block, Celery, Flat, Clear	38.00
Pressed Glass, Finecut & Block, Compote, Jelly, Pink	55.00
Pressed Glass, Finecut & Block, Compote, 7 1/2 In.	18.00
Pressed Glass, Finecut & Block, Cup, Punch	8.00 To 12.00
Pressed Glass, Finecut & Block, Goblet	12.50 To 22.50
Pressed Glass, Finecut & Block, Sauce, Collared, 4 In.	9.00
Pressed Glass, Finecut & Block, Sauce, Footed, 4 In.	10.00
Pressed Glass, Finecut & Block, Sauce, Footed, 4 1/2 In.	12.50
Pressed Glass, Finecut & Panel, Bowl, Blue, 7 In.	30.00
Pressed Glass, Finecut & Panel, Cruet, Apple Green	18.00
Pressed Glass, Finecut & Panel, Dish, Oblong	20.00
Pressed Glass, Finecut & Panel, Goblet	16.00
Pressed Glass, Finecut & Panel, Plate, Bread	12.00
Pressed Glass, Finecut & Panel, Plate, 6 In.	14.00
Pressed Glass, Finecut & Panel, Sauce, Blue	15.00
Pressed Glass, Finecut & Panel, Wine Set, Green, 7 Piece	135.00
Pressed Glass, Finecut & Panel, Wine, Blue	21.50
Pressed Glass, Finecut & Panel, Wine, Canary	14.00
Pressed Glass, Finecut & Rib, Baby Shoe, Amber	25.00
Finecut Medallion, see Austrian	
Pressed Glass, Finecut, Butter, Covered	26.75 To 30.00
Pressed Glass, Finecut, Butter, Pat, Amber, Set Of Six	30.00
Pressed Glass, Finecut, Cake Stand, Amber	40.00
Pressed Glass, Finecut, Creamer	24.00
Pressed Glass, Finecut, Goblet, Vaseline	35.00
Pressed Glass, Finecut, Syrup, Blue, 1883 Patent Pewter Lid	75.00
Pressed Glass, Fishscale, Berry Set, 6 Piece	42.00
Pressed Glass, Fishscale, Bowl, Covered, 7 3/4 X 9 1/2 In.	37.50
Pressed Glass, Fishscale, Butter	23.00
Pressed Glass, Fishscale, Cake Stand	22.50 To 25.00
Pressed Glass, Fishscale, Celery	19.00 To 24.00
Pressed Glass, Fishscale, Compote, Jelly	15.00
Pressed Glass, Fishscale, Goblet	25.00
Pressed Glass, Fishscale, Lamp Base, Finger, Clear	75.00
Pressed Glass, Fishscale, Pitcher, Milk	29.50
Pressed Glass, Fishscale, Pitcher, Water	32.00
Pressed Glass, Fishscale, Plate	26.50
Pressed Glass, Fishscale, Plate, 7 In.	16.00 To 21.00
Pressed Glass, Fishscale, Plate, 8 In.	28.50
Pressed Glass, Fishscale, Plate, 9 In. Square	26.00
Pressed Glass, Fishscale, Sauce	5.00 To 5.50
Pressed Glass, Fishscale, Sauce, 4 In.	6.00
Pressed Glass, Flamingo Habitat, Goblet	19.00
Pressed Glass, Flamingo Habitat, Pitcher, Etched Tankard, Applied Handle	45.00
Pressed Glass, Flamingo Habitat, Sugar & Creamer	45.00
Pressed Glass, Flamingo Habitat, Wine	25.00
Pressed Glass, Flamingo, Goblet	25.00
Pressed Glass, Flamingo, Goblet, Frosted	35.00
Pressed Glass, Flat Block, Cake Stand, Amber	60.00
Flat Diamond & Panel, see Lattice & Oval Panels	

Pressed Glass, **Flat Diamond**, Pitcher, Water, Amber	85.00
Pressed Glass, **Flat Panel**, Compote, Covered, High Standard, 7 X 12 In.	195.00
Pressed Glass, **Flattened Diamond & Sunburst**, Creamer, Child's	12.00 To 20.00
Pressed Glass, **Flattened Diamond & Sunburst**, Punch Set, Child's, 7 Piece	40.00
Pressed Glass, **Flattened Diamond & Sunburst**, Spooner, Double Handle	12.00
Pressed Glass, **Flattened Sawtooth**, Salt, Master	15.00
Pressed Glass, **Flattened Sawtooth**, Spill, Flint	24.00
Pressed Glass, **Fleur-De-Lis & Drape**, Compote, Covered, High Standard, 7 In.	42.00
Pressed Glass, **Fleur-De-Lis & Drape**, Spooner	14.50
Pressed Glass, **Fleur-De-Lis & Tassel**, Pitcher, Water, Green	45.00 To 47.50
Pressed Glass, **Fleur-De-Lis & Tassel**, Plate, Emerald Green, 8 I	21.00 To 26.00
Pressed Glass, **Fleur-De-Lis**, Ashtray, Etched Bottom, 2 In., Pair	3.50
Pressed Glass, **Fleur-De-Lis**, Banana Boat	25.00
Pressed Glass, **Fleur-De-Lis**, Cake Stand, 9 1/2 In.	23.50
Pressed Glass, **Fleur-De-Lis**, Dish, Candy, Pink, Divided, 7 In.	40.00
Pressed Glass, **Fleur-De-Lis**, Goblet	12.50 To 19.00
Pressed Glass, **Fleur-De-Lis**, Plate, Square, 7 1/4 In.	15.00
Pressed Glass, **Fleur-De-Lis**, Punch Set, Miniature, 7 Piece	55.00
Pressed Glass, **Fleur-De-Lis**, Rose Bowl, Clear, Opalescent, Footed	25.00
Pressed Glass, **Fleur-De-Lis**, Sauce, Blue	10.00
Pressed Glass, **Fleur-De-Lis**, Toothpick	15.00
Pressed Glass, **Fleur-De-Lis**, Toothpick, Clear, 3 7/8 In.	12.00
Pressed Glass, **Fleur-Di-Lis**, Sauce, Blue	10.00
Pressed Glass, **Fleur-De-Lis**, Wine	20.00
Pressed Glass, **Flora**, Cruet, Green, Gold	75.00
Pressed Glass, **Flora**, Spooner, Blue Opalescent	70.00
Pressed Glass, **Flora**, Water Set, Gold Trim, 6 Piece	90.00
Pressed Glass, **Floradora**, Spooner, Footed	45.00
Pressed Glass, **Floral Diamond**, Cruet, With Stopper	15.00
Pressed Glass, **Floral Oval With Bee**, Wine	9.50
Pressed Glass, **Floral Oval**, Celery	15.00
Pressed Glass, **Florette**, Butter Dish, Pink, Frosted Base & Finial	195.00
Pressed Glass, **Florette**, Salt & Pepper, Opaque Yellow Cased In Clear	42.00
Florida, see Herringbone	
Pressed Glass, **Flower & Hobstar**, Celery, Pedestal	9.50
Pressed Glass, **Flower & Leaf**, Syrup, Amber Stain	150.00
Pressed Glass, **Flower & Pleat**, Pitcher, Water	85.00
Pressed Glass, **Flower & Pleat**, Syrup	48.00
Pressed Glass, **Flower & Pleat**, Water Set, Clear & Frosted, 7 Piece	195.00
Pressed Glass, **Flower & Quill**, Butter	22.00
Pressed Glass, **Flower & Quill**, Creamer	12.00
Pressed Glass, **Flower & Quill**, Sugar	25.00
Pressed Glass, **Flower Band**, Frosted, Sauce, 4 In	14.50
Flower Flange, see Dewey	
Flower Paneled Cane, see Cane & Rosette	
Pressed Glass, **Flowerpot**, Compote, 7 X 7 In.	33.00
Pressed Glass, **Flowerpot**, Spooner	30.00
Pressed Glass, **Flowerpot**, Sugar	30.00
Pressed Glass, **Flute**, Berry Set, Miniature, 7 Piece	58.00
Pressed Glass, **Flute**, Berry Set, 5 Piece	15.00
Pressed Glass, **Flute**, Butter, Covered, Scalloped Rim, Miniature	18.00
Pressed Glass, **Flute**, Cake Stand	20.00
Pressed Glass, **Flute**, Eggcup, Knob Stem	15.00
Pressed Glass, **Flute**, Goblet	22.00
Pressed Glass, **Flute**, Goblet, Flint	14.00
Pressed Glass, **Flute**, Mug, Applied Crimped Handle, Flint	40.00
Pressed Glass, **Flute**, Pitcher	325.00
Pressed Glass, **Flute**, Pitcher, Water	15.00
Pressed Glass, **Flute**, Whiskey, Applied Handle	16.00
Pressed Glass, **Flute**, Whiskey, Deep Blue, Flint	60.00
Pressed Glass, **Flute**, Whiskey, 5 Sides, Applied Handle	17.50
Pressed Glass, **Flute**, Wine, Flared Rim, Polished Pontil, Flint	24.00
Pressed Glass, **Flute**, Wine, Flint	15.00
Pressed Glass, **Fluted Scrolls**, Creamer, Blue	45.00
Pressed Glass, **Fluted Scrolls**, Creamer, Green, Opalescent	75.00

Pressed Glass, Forget-Me-Not, Jar, Marmalade

Pressed Glass, Frosted Ribbon With Double Bands, Goblet

Pressed Glass, Frosted Eagle, Compote

Pressed Glass, Fluted Scrolls, Creamer, Opalescent	65.00
Pressed Glass, Fluted Scrolls, Dish, Candy, White, Opalescent, Footed	22.00
Pressed Glass, Fluted Scrolls, Sauce, Vaseline, Opalescent	24.50
Pressed Glass, Fluted Scrolls, Spooner, Blue, Opalescent	45.00
Pressed Glass, Fluted Scrolls, Spooner, Yellow, Opalescent	48.00
Pressed Glass, Fluted Scrolls, Sugar, Blue, Opalescent, Covered	75.00
Pressed Glass, Fluted Scrolls, Sugar, Vaseline, Covered	95.00
Flying Robin, see Hummingbird	
Pressed Glass, Forget-Me-Not In Scroll, Goblet	17.50
Pressed Glass, Forget-Me-Not In Scroll, Spooner	17.00
Forget-Me-Not in Snow, see Stippled Forget-Me-Not	
Pressed Glass, Forget-Me-Not, Jar, Mustard, Covered, Ribbed	20.00
Pressed Glass, Forget-Me-Not, Jar, Mustard, Pink, Top	47.50
Pressed Glass, Forget-Me-Not, Plate, Cake, Blue	20.00
Pressed Glass, Forget-Me-Not, Relish, Blue, Handled	28.00
Pressed Glass, Forget-Me-Not, Salt & Pepper, Milk Glass, Miniature	40.00
Pressed Glass, Forget-Me-Not, Sugar Shaker, Pink, Opaque, Covered	75.00
Pressed Glass, Four Petal, Bowl, Sugar, Lid	65.00
Pressed Glass, Fox & Crow, Pitcher, Water, Turning Purple	97.50
Pressed Glass, Frazier, Salt & Pepper, Cranberry Flashed, Enamel Flowers	38.00
Pressed Glass, Frost Crystal, Cup, Punch	7.00
Frosted patterns, see also under name of main pattern	
Pressed Glass, Frosted Circle, Cake Stand	30.00
Pressed Glass, Frosted Circle, Compote, High Standard, Covered, 6 In.	60.00
Pressed Glass, Frosted Circle, Spooner	17.00 To 22.00
Frosted Crane, see Frosted Stork	
Pressed Glass, Frosted Eagle, Sugar, Covered	175.00
Frosted Flower Band, see Flower Band, Frosted	
Pressed Glass, Frosted Leaf, Champagne, Flint	165.00
Pressed Glass, Frosted Leaf, Compote, High Standard, Pedestal, 8 In.	95.00
Pressed Glass, Frosted Leaf, Goblet	125.00
Pressed Glass, Frosted Leaf, Goblet, Lady's, Flint	95.00
Pressed Glass, Frosted Leaf, Goblet, 6 X 3 1/8 In.	45.00

Pressed Glass, Frosted Lion, Creamer .... 20.00 To 65.00
Pressed Glass, Frosted Lion, Dish, Cheese, Covered, Lion Finial 325.00
Pressed Glass, Frosted Lion, Eggcup 58.00
Pressed Glass, Frosted Pheasant, Dish, Oval, Covered, 8 In. 145.00
Pressed Glass, Frosted Ribbon, Celery 22.50
Pressed Glass, Frosted Ribbon, Compote, Open, High Standard 30.00
Pressed Glass, Frosted Ribbon, Compote, 5 1/4 In. 18.00
Pressed Glass, Frosted Ribbon, Goblet, Straight Sides 28.50
Pressed Glass, Frosted Ribbon, Sugar 67.50
Pressed Glass, Frosted Stork, Platter 55.00
Pressed Glass, Frosted Stork, Platter, Iowa City 45.00
Pressed Glass, Frosted Stork, Tray, Water 75.00
Frosted Waffle, see Hidalgo
Pressed Glass, Fuchsia, Plate, 10 In.Square 22.50
Pressed Glass, Gaelic, Cruet 10.00
Pressed Glass, Gaelic, Relish, Heart Shaped 14.00
Pressed Glass, Gaelic, Saltshaker 7.50
Pressed Glass, Gaelic, Toothpick 7.50
Pressed Glass, Gaelic, Tray, Condiment 9.00
Pressed Glass, Galaxy, Goblet 20.00
Pressed Glass, Galloway, Bowl, 10 In. 22.50
Pressed Glass, Galloway, Carafe 38.00
Pressed Glass, Galloway, Carafe, Water 33.50
Pressed Glass, Galloway, Creamer, Child's 10.00
Pressed Glass, Galloway, Cruet, Handled 17.00
Pressed Glass, Galloway, Cup, Punch 7.00
Pressed Glass, Galloway, Salt & Pepper 16.00
Pressed Glass, Galloway, Sherbet, Footed 12.00
Pressed Glass, Galloway, Syrup 15.00
Pressed Glass, Galloway, Toothpick 18.00
Pressed Glass, Galloway, Toothpick, Clear With Gold 18.00
Pressed Glass, Galloway, Vase, Emerald Green, Scalloped Rim, 10 In. 55.00
Pressed Glass, Galloway, Vase, 12 In. 15.00
Garden of Eden, see Lotus & Serpent
Pressed Glass, Garfield Drape, Cake Stand 35.00
Pressed Glass, Garfield Drape, Cake Stand, 10 In. 45.00
Pressed Glass, Garfield Drape, Creamer 22.50
Pressed Glass, Garfield Drape, Creamer, 5 1/2 In. 15.00
Pressed Glass, Garfield Drape, Goblet .... 25.00 To 27.00
Pressed Glass, Garfield Drape, Mug, Miniature, 2 1/4 In. 60.00
Pressed Glass, Garfield Drape, Pitcher, Water 50.00
Pressed Glass, Garfield Drape, Spooner 35.00
Pressed Glass, Geneva, Bowl, Emerald Green, Gold Footed, Oval, 8 1/2 In. 48.00
Pressed Glass, Geneva, Bowl, Fruit, Individual, Set Of 6 .... 300.00
Pressed Glass, Geneva, Pitcher, Water, Dark Green, Gold, Footed 155.00
Pressed Glass, Geneva, Spooner 125.00
Pressed Glass, Geneva, Tumbler, Clear 17.00
Pressed Glass, Geneva, Water Set, Green & Red, 7 Piece 450.00
Pressed Glass, George Washington, Platter, 1st In War, 1st In Peace, 12 In. 75.00
Pressed Glass, Georgia Gem, Cruet, Custard, Green, Stopper 95.00
Pressed Glass, Georgia, Sugar & Creamer, Ruby, Footed, 3 1/2 In. 6.50
Pressed Glass, Georgian, Compote, 6 1/4 X 9 3/4 In. 47.50
Pressed Glass, Giant Prism With Thumbprint Band, Celery, Flint 125.00
Pressed Glass, Giant Sawtooth, Eggcup, Covered 35.00
Pressed Glass, Giant Sawtooth, Goblet, Flint 85.00
Pressed Glass, Girl At Play, Plate, Bread 42.00
Pressed Glass, Girl With Fan, Goblet 48.00
Pressed Glass, Give Us This Day, Bread Tray, 8 1/2 X 13 In. 25.00
Pressed Glass, Gonterman Swirl, Dish, Berry, Amber, Opalescent 25.00
Pressed Glass, Gonterman Swirl, Pitcher, Water, 5 Tumblers, Amber Top 525.00
Pressed Glass, Gonterman Swirl, Spooner, Blue, White Opalescence 75.00
Pressed Glass, Gonterman Swirl, Syrup, Opalescent Base, Amber Top 250.00
Good Luck, see Horseshoe
Pressed Glass, Gooseberry, Creamer 32.00
Pressed Glass, Gooseberry, Goblet 21.00

Pressed Glass, Fruit Panels, Goblet

Pressed Glass, Frosted Stork, Goblet

Pressed Glass, **Gothic,** Celery, Arched Punties And Loops	95.00
Pressed Glass, **Gothic,** Dish, Rectangular, Lacy, Sandwich Flint, 7 In.	50.00
Pressed Glass, **Gothic,** Eggcup	40.00
Pressed Glass, **Gothic,** Eggcup, Flint	32.50
Pressed Glass, **Gothic,** Goblet	96.00
Pressed Glass, **Gothic,** Goblet, Flint	36.50 To 59.50
Pressed Glass, **Gothic,** Sugar, Flint	50.00
Pressed Glass, **Gothic,** Sugar, Flint, Covered	42.00
Pressed Glass, **Gothic,** Wine, Flint	85.00
Grace, see Butterfly & Fan	
Grand, see Diamond Medallion	
Pressed Glass, **Grant,** Soldier, Plate, Bread	30.00
Pressed Glass, **Grant,** Tray, Water, Square, 9 1/2 In.	27.50
Grape, see also Beaded Grape, Beaded Grape Medallion, Magnet &	
Grape, Magnet & Grape with Frosted Leaf, Paneled Grape, Paneled	
Grape Band	
Pressed Glass, **Grape & Cable,** Powder Dish	80.00
Pressed Glass, **Grape & Cable,** Whiskey, N	45.00
Pressed Glass, **Grape & Festoon With Shield,** Goblet	29.00 To 30.00
Pressed Glass, **Grape & Festoon With Shield,** Mug	21.50
Pressed Glass, **Grape & Festoon With Shield,** Mug, Miniature	25.00
Pressed Glass, **Grape & Festoon With Stippled Leaf,** Spooner	14.00
Pressed Glass, **Grape & Festoon,** Pitcher, Water, Applied Handle	54.00
Pressed Glass, **Grape & Festoon,** Spooner	30.00
Pressed Glass, **Grape Band,** Spooner	18.00 To 19.00
Pressed Glass, **Grape With Scroll Band,** Butter	25.00
Pressed Glass, **Grape With Scroll Medallion,** Creamer	18.50
Pressed Glass, **Grape,** Bowl, Banana, Purple Grapes, Gold Leaves, Northwood	36.00
Pressed Glass, **Grape,** Goblet, Opaque Custard	65.00
Pressed Glass, **Grape,** Plate, Bread	25.00
Pressed Glass, **Grape,** Tray, Dresser, Marigold, N	145.00
Pressed Glass, **Grapevine With Ovals,** Creamer, Child's, Blue	47.50
Pressed Glass, **Grapevine,** Tankard, 6 Tumblers	595.00
Pressed Glass, **Grasshopper With Insect,** Spooner	38.50
Pressed Glass, **Grasshopper,** Bowl, Covered, Footed	42.50
Pressed Glass, **Grasshopper,** Bowl, 3 Feet	12.00
Pressed Glass, **Grasshopper,** Butter, Etched, Covered	45.00
Pressed Glass, **Grasshopper,** Compote, Etched, Covered, 10 1/2 In.	55.00
Pressed Glass, **Grasshopper,** Creamer	10.00
Pressed Glass, **Grasshopper,** Creamer, Without Insect	11.00
Pressed Glass, **Grasshopper,** Goblet	30.00
Pressed Glass, **Grasshopper,** Pitcher, Water	45.00
Pressed Glass, **Grogan,** Goblet	10.00
Pressed Glass, **Grogan,** Pitcher, Water	22.00
Pressed Glass, **Guttate,** Syrup, White, Gold Trim, Metal Top, Dated 1881	100.00
Pressed Glass, **Gypsy Kettle,** Toothpick, Flashed	18.00
Pressed Glass, **Hairpin With Thumbprint,** Eggcup, Double, Flint	30.00
Pressed Glass, **Hairpin,** Cruet	20.00
Pressed Glass, **Hairpin,** Eggcup	20.00
Pressed Glass, **Hairpin,** Eggcup, Flint	18.50

Pressed Glass, Hairpin, Eggcup, Opalescent, White, Flint	39.00
Pressed Glass, Hairpin, Goblet, Flint	30.00
Pressed Glass, Hairpin, Goblet, Rayed Base, Flint	35.00
Pressed Glass, Hairpin, Sugar Base, Opalescent, White, Flint	23.00
Pressed Glass, Hairpin, Wine, Flint	24.00
Pressed Glass, Hairpin, Wine, Rayed Base, Flint	45.00
Pressed Glass, Hairpin, Wine, Rayed Base, 5 In.	25.00
Pressed Glass, Halley's Comet, Celery	27.00
Pressed Glass, Halley's Comet, Wine	18.50 To 20.00
Pressed Glass, Hamilton With Leaf, Whiskey, Flint	55.00
Pressed Glass, Hamilton, Compote, Flint, Footed, 5 X 7 In.	55.00
Pressed Glass, Hamilton, Eggcup	24.50
Pressed Glass, Hamilton, Eggcup, Flint	25.00
Pressed Glass, Hamilton, Goblet	25.00
Pressed Glass, Hamilton, Goblet, Flint	35.00 To 37.50
Pressed Glass, Hamilton, Spooner	15.00
Pressed Glass, Hamilton, Spooner, Flint	24.00
Pressed Glass, Hamilton, Sugar, Flint, 4 1/4 In.	22.50
Pressed Glass, Hamilton, Sugar, Open	20.00 To 25.00
Pressed Glass, Hanover, Goblet	14.75
Pressed Glass, Hartford, Celery	19.00
Pressed Glass, Hartley, Goblet	17.50
Pressed Glass, Harvard, Toothpick, Custard	30.00
Pressed Glass, Harvard, Toothpick, Ruby Stained	28.00
Pressed Glass, Hawaiian Lei, Bowl, Berry	12.00
Pressed Glass, Hawaiian Lei, Cake Stand, 9 3/4 In.	35.00
Pressed Glass, Hawaiian Lei, Creamer, Child's	15.00
Pressed Glass, Hawaiian Lei, Plate, 7 1/2 In.	10.00
Pressed Glass, Hawaiian Lei, Sugar, Open Bubble On Rim	24.00
Pressed Glass, Heart Stem, Creamer	25.00
Pressed Glass, Heart With Thumbprint, Banana Boat, Low	35.00
Pressed Glass, Heart With Thumbprint, Berry Set, 7 Piece	97.00
Pressed Glass, Heart With Thumbprint, Bowl, Berry, Ruffled Edge, Gold, 9 In.	24.50
Pressed Glass, Heart With Thumbprint, Bowl, Berry, 9 In.	32.50
Pressed Glass, Heart With Thumbprint, Bowl, Flared Serrated Edge, 7 1/4 In.	22.00
Pressed Glass, Heart With Thumbprint, Bucket, Ice	65.00
Pressed Glass, Heart With Thumbprint, Creamer	15.00 To 16.00
Pressed Glass, Heart With Thumbprint, Creamer ,	15.00 To 16.00
Pressed Glass, Heart With Thumbprint, Creamer, Individual	15.00
Pressed Glass, Heart With Thumbprint, Cup, Punch	13.50 To 21.50
Pressed Glass, Heart With Thumbprint, Dish, Banana, Oval	22.00
Pressed Glass, Heart With Thumbprint, Dish, Card, Gilt	15.00
Pressed Glass, Heart With Thumbprint, Dish, Turned-Up Sides, Gold, 8 In.	17.50
Pressed Glass, Heart With Thumbprint, Goblet	29.00
Pressed Glass, Heart With Thumbprint, Jelly Dish, Gold Trim	13.50
Pressed Glass, Heart With Thumbprint, Pitcher, Syrup	48.00
Pressed Glass, Heart With Thumbprint, Plate, Gilt, 6 1/2 In.	15.00
Pressed Glass, Heart With Thumbprint, Plate, 10 In.	35.00 To 39.50
Pressed Glass, Heart With Thumbprint, Plate, 12 In.	35.00
Pressed Glass, Heart With Thumbprint, Rose Bowl, 3 In.	20.00
Pressed Glass, Heart With Thumbprint, Rose Bowl, 4 1/2 In.	26.50
Pressed Glass, Heart With Thumbprint, Sauce, 4 1/2 In.	9.50
Pressed Glass, Heart With Thumbprint, Sugar & Creamer	20.00
Pressed Glass, Heart With Thumbprint, Sugar & Creamer, Gold	24.50
Pressed Glass, Heart With Thumbprint, Sugar & Creamer, Open	18.00
Pressed Glass, Heart With Thumbprint, Sugar, Individual	15.00
Pressed Glass, Heart With Thumbprint, Sugar, Individual, Gold Trim	14.50
Pressed Glass, Heart With Thumbprint, Tray, Card	11.50
Pressed Glass, Heart With Thumbprint, Tumbler	25.00
Pressed Glass, Heart With Thumbprint, Tumbler, Gold Trim	20.00
Pressed Glass, Heart With Thumbprint, Vase, 10 In.	19.00
Pressed Glass, Heart With Thumbprint, Vase, 5 1/8 In.	28.00
Pressed Glass, Heart With Thumbprint, Vase, 6 In.	12.50 To 15.00
Pressed Glass, Heart With Thumbprint, Wine	25.00
Pressed Glass, Heart, Goblet	17.00

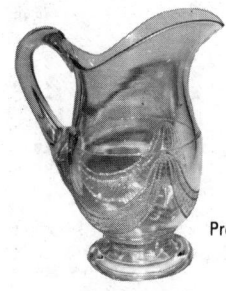

Pressed Glass, Garfield Drape, Pitcher, Water

Pressed Glass, Grape & Festoon, Cup

Pressed Glass, Grape & Festoon With Shield, Goblet

Pressed Glass, Hairpin, Goblet, Rayed Base

Pressed Glass, Hamilton, Compote

Pressed Glass, Harp, Spill

Hearts of Loch Laven, see Shuttle

Pressed Glass, Hercules Pillar, Goblet	25.00
Pressed Glass, Hercules Pillar, Jug, Syrup, Blue	95.00
Pressed Glass, Heron, Creamer	28.50
Pressed Glass, Heron, Marmalade, Covered	25.00
Pressed Glass, Heron, Sugar, Covered	35.00
Pressed Glass, Herringbone Band, Goblet	11.00
Pressed Glass, Herringbone Rib, Wine, Green	25.00
Pressed Glass, Herringbone, Bowl, Emerald Green, 8 In.	48.00
Pressed Glass, Herringbone, Creamer	20.00
Pressed Glass, Herringbone, Nappy, Gold & Ruby Panels	19.50
Pressed Glass, Herringbone, Pitcher, Water, Emerald Green	48.00
Pressed Glass, Herringbone, Relish, Green	20.00
Pressed Glass, Herringbone, Sauce, Emerald Green	8.00 To 15.00
Pressed Glass, Herringbone, Sauce, Emerald Green, 4 In.	9.50
Pressed Glass, Herringbone, Water Set, Green, 5 Piece	85.00
Pressed Glass, Hexagon Block, Spooner, Ruby Stained	35.00
Pressed Glass, Hexagon Block, Tankard, Leaf Etching, Amber Stained	115.00
Pressed Glass, Hexagon Block, Water Set, Bird Etchings, Ruby Stained	225.00
Pressed Glass, Hexagon Block, Water Set, Ruby & Clear, Fern Etching, 7 Piece	280.00
Pressed Glass, Hexagon Block, Water Set, Tankard Pitcher, Ruby Stained	260.00
Pressed Glass, Hexagonal Bull's-Eye, Cake Stand, 9 In.	27.00
Pressed Glass, Hey Diddle Diddle, Dish, Child's, 6 In.	31.00
Pressed Glass, Hickman, Cake Stand, 9 1/4 In.	19.50
Pressed Glass, Hickman, Condiment Set, 3 Piece	30.00
Pressed Glass, Hickman, Creamer	10.00
Pressed Glass, Hickman, Dish, Square, 4 1/2 In.	7.50
Pressed Glass, Hickman, Goblet	18.50 To 22.00
Pressed Glass, Hickman, Pepper Shaker, Original Top	9.50
Pressed Glass, Hickman, Sauce, Emerald Green	8.00
Pressed Glass, Hickman, Tray, Condiment, Tiny	12.00
Pressed Glass, Hidalgo, Celery, Frosted	15.00
Pressed Glass, Hidalgo, Creamer, Frosted With Cut Star	28.00
Pressed Glass, Hidalgo, Goblet, Etched	18.00
Pressed Glass, Higbee, Dish, Candy, Basket Shape	13.50
Pressed Glass, High Hob, Wine	14.00
Pressed Glass, Hinoto, Champagne, Flint	37.50
Pressed Glass, Hinoto, Goblet, Flint	35.00
Pressed Glass, Hinoto, Goblet, Sandwich	45.00

Hobnail & Bars, see Barred Hobnail

Pressed Glass, Hobnail With Line Band, Toothpick	7.00
Pressed Glass, Hobnail With Thumbprint, Creamer, Vaseline, Opalescent	45.00
Pressed Glass, Hobnail, Bowl, Cranberry, Opalescent, Fluted, 9 1/2 In.	30.00
Pressed Glass, Hobnail, Compote, Opalescent, Footed, 6 1/2 In.	47.00
Pressed Glass, Hobnail, Cornucopia, Opalescent, Vaseline, Pair	45.00
Pressed Glass, Hobnail, Creamer, Blue, Opalescent Scalloped Edge	35.00
Pressed Glass, Hobnail, Goblet, Fantop, Findlay	16.50
Pressed Glass, Hobnail, Jar, Mustard, Handled	8.00
Pressed Glass, Hobnail, Mug, Thumbprint	16.00
Pressed Glass, Hobnail, Pitcher, Water, Ruby Stained	55.00
Pressed Glass, Hobnail, Rose Bowl, Blue, Fluted, 4 1/2 In.	25.00
Pressed Glass, Hobnail, Rose Bowl, Cranberry, Fluted, 5 In.	25.00
Pressed Glass, Hobnail, Salt & Pepper, Pointed	10.00
Pressed Glass, Hobnail, Sauce, Amber, 4 In.Square	10.00
Pressed Glass, Hobnail, Spooner	11.50
Pressed Glass, Hobnail, Spooner, Ruffled	18.00
Pressed Glass, Hobnail, Sugar & Creamer, White, Opalescent	25.00
Pressed Glass, Hobnail, Sugar Shaker, Amber	58.00
Pressed Glass, Hobnail, Sugar Shaker, Original Top, Green	22.00
Pressed Glass, Hobnail, Sugar, Blue	35.00
Pressed Glass, Hobnail, Toothpick, Hat Shape, Blue	15.00
Pressed Glass, Hobnail, Toothpick, Opalescent	29.00

Pressed Glass, Hobnail, Toothpick, Sapphire Blue	45.00
Pressed Glass, Hobnail, Tray, Water, Amber, Fluted Edge	25.00
Pressed Glass, Hobnail, Tumbler, Water, Peacock Blue	25.00
Pressed Glass, Hobnail, Vase, Blue, Fan, Crimped Top, 6 1/2 In.	30.00
Pressed Glass, Hobnail, Vase, Bulbous, Fluted, 8 In.	30.00
Pressed Glass, Hobnail, Vase, Pink, Hat Shape, 4 1/2 In.	28.00
Pressed Glass, Hobnail, Wine	12.50
Pressed Glass, Hobstar, Creamer	20.00
Holbrook, see Pineapple & Fan	
Pressed Glass, Holly & Tassel, Creamer, English	35.00
Pressed Glass, Holly, Bowl, Ribbed, Cobalt Blue, 9 In.	50.00
Pressed Glass, Holly, Cake Stand, 9 1/4 In.	68.00
Pressed Glass, Holly, Compote, Covered, 8 In.	155.00
Pressed Glass, Home, Creamer	14.00
Honeycomb, see also Vernon Honeycomb	
Pressed Glass, Honeycomb & Clover, Bowl, Blue, Flat, Opalescent, 9 In.	22.50
Pressed Glass, Honeycomb With Diamond, Eggcup	6.50
Pressed Glass, Honeycomb With Flower Rim, Butter	37.50
Pressed Glass, Honeycomb With Pillar, Wine	14.00
Pressed Glass, Honeycomb, Compote, Flint, 5 1/2 X 8 In.	30.00
Pressed Glass, Honeycomb, Cordial, Flint, 4 1/2 In.	20.00
Pressed Glass, Honeycomb, Creamer, White, Opalescent	35.00
Pressed Glass, Honeycomb, Dish, Pedestal, Square, 10 X 5 In.	85.00
Pressed Glass, Honeycomb, Eggcup	10.00 To 12.00
Pressed Glass, Honeycomb, Goblet	5.00 To 15.00
Pressed Glass, Honeycomb, Goblet, Flint	22.50
Pressed Glass, Honeycomb, Pitcher, Water, Ruby Applied Handle	75.00
Pressed Glass, Honeycomb, Spooner, Flint, Clear	30.00
Pressed Glass, Honeycomb, Spooner, Flint, Clear Band	22.00
Pressed Glass, Honeycomb, Toothpick, White, 2 1/2 In.	40.00

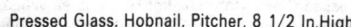

Pressed Glass, Hobnail, Pitcher, 8 1/2 In.High

Pressed Glass, Hobnail,
Tumbler, 4 1/2 In.High

Pressed Glass, Holly Band, Celery

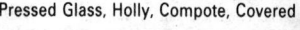

Pressed Glass, Holly, Compote, Covered

Pressed Glass, Honeycomb, Tumbler, Flower Rim 22.00
Pressed Glass, Honeycomb, Tumbler, Footed, Flint 25.00
Pressed Glass, Honeycomb, Wine .... 8.00 To 25.00
Pressed Glass, Honeycomb, Wine, Flint 20.00
Pressed Glass, Honeycomb, Wine, Flint, New York, 4 In. 45.00
Pressed Glass, Hops Band, Goblet .... 12.00 To 18.00
Pressed Glass, Horizontal Thread, Creamer 10.00
Pressed Glass, Horn Of Plenty, Bottle, Pepper Sauce 70.00
Pressed Glass, Horn Of Plenty, Celery 110.00
Pressed Glass, Horn Of Plenty, Compote, Flint, 8 In. 80.00
Pressed Glass, Horn Of Plenty, Compote, Open, Round, 7 In. 75.00
Pressed Glass, Horn Of Plenty, Compote, 6 X 6 In. 85.00
Pressed Glass, Horn Of Plenty, Compote, 8 X 7 1/2 In. 120.00
Pressed Glass, Horn Of Plenty, Decanter, Diamond Point Stopper, Quart Size 95.00
Pressed Glass, Horn Of Plenty, Decanter, Stopper, Quart 100.00
Pressed Glass, Horn Of Plenty, Eggcup 32.50
Pressed Glass, Horn Of Plenty, Eggcup, Flint 35.00
Pressed Glass, Horn Of Plenty, Goblet .... 52.50 To 75.00
Pressed Glass, Horn Of Plenty, Goblet, Flint .... 48.00 To 65.00
Pressed Glass, Horn Of Plenty, Pitcher, Applied Handle, 7 In. 125.00
Pressed Glass, Horn Of Plenty, Plate, Flint, 6 In. .... 45.00 To 85.00
Pressed Glass, Horn Of Plenty, Salt, Oval .... 35.00 To 75.00
Pressed Glass, Horn Of Plenty, Salt, Oval, Flint 75.00
Pressed Glass, Horn Of Plenty, Sauce, 4 1/2 In. 7.50
Pressed Glass, Horn Of Plenty, Spill, Flint 45.00
Pressed Glass, Horn Of Plenty, Spooner 65.00
Pressed Glass, Horn Of Plenty, Spooner, Flint 40.00
Pressed Glass, Horn Of Plenty, Sugar, Cover, Flint 110.00
Pressed Glass, Horn Of Plenty, Sugar, Covered 85.00
Pressed Glass, Horn Of Plenty, Sugar, Open, Flint 50.00
Pressed Glass, Horn Of Plenty, Tumbler, Flint 65.00
Pressed Glass, Horn Of Plenty, Tumbler, Whiskey 75.00
Pressed Glass, Horn Of Plenty, Whiskey, Handled, Flint 195.00
Pressed Glass, Horn Of Plenty, Wine 8.00
Pressed Glass, Horseshoe, Bowl, Blue, 9 In. 85.00
Pressed Glass, Horseshoe, Bread Tray, Horseshoe Handles .... 35.00 To 47.50
Pressed Glass, Horseshoe, Butter 40.00
Pressed Glass, Horseshoe, Cake Stand, 10 In. 65.00
Pressed Glass, Horseshoe, Cake Stand, 9 In. .... 30.00 To 38.00
Pressed Glass, Horseshoe, Celery 36.00
Pressed Glass, Horseshoe, Compote, Covered, High Standard, 7 In. 44.50
Pressed Glass, Horseshoe, Compote, Covered, Low Standard, 7 In. 55.00
Pressed Glass, Horseshoe, Creamer .... 26.50 To 32.00
Pressed Glass, Horseshoe, Goblet 25.00
Pressed Glass, Horseshoe, Goblet, Knob Stem 17.50
Pressed Glass, Horseshoe, Goblet, Plain Stem 22.00
Pressed Glass, Horseshoe, Pitcher, Milk, Sawtooth Applied Handle 65.00
Pressed Glass, Horseshoe, Plate, Bread, 9 X 13 In. 24.50
Pressed Glass, Horseshoe, Plate, Good Luck, 7 In. 42.50
Pressed Glass, Horseshoe, Plate, Good Luck, 10 In. 50.00
Pressed Glass, Horseshoe, Plate, 8 In. 32.00
Pressed Glass, Horseshoe, Platter, Double Handles, 15 X 10 In. 65.00
Pressed Glass, Horseshoe, Relish 12.50
Pressed Glass, Horseshoe, Relish, Oval, Handled, 9 In 18.50
Pressed Glass, Horseshoe, Sauce, Footed 7.50
Pressed Glass, Horseshoe, Sugar Shaker, Amber 75.00
Pressed Glass, Horseshoe, Tray, Bread 42.00
Pressed Glass, Horseshoe, Wine 150.00
Pressed Glass, Huber, Cordial, Flint, Barrel Shape, 4 In. 21.00
Pressed Glass, Huber, Creamer, Applied Crimped Handle, Flint 32.00
Pressed Glass, Huber, Eggcup, Flint 18.00
Pressed Glass, Huber, Goblet, Flint .... 17.00 To 18.50
Pressed Glass, Huber, Wine, Flint 18.50
    Huckle, see Feather Duster
Pressed Glass, Hummingbird, Creamer 30.00

Pressed Glass, Hummingbird, Goblet .... 20.00 To 35.00
Pressed Glass, Hummingbird, Goblet, Clear 25.00
Pressed Glass, Hummingbird, Pitcher, Water, Amber 54.00
Pressed Glass, Hummingbird, Sugar, Amber Cover 65.00
Pressed Glass, Humpty-Dumpty, Mug 14.00
Pressed Glass, Icicle With Loops, Goblet, Flint .... 25.00 To 28.00
Pressed Glass, Icicle With Star, Pitcher, Water 20.00
Pressed Glass, Icicle, Goblet, Fluted 27.50
Pressed Glass, Icicle, Pitcher, Water 28.00
Pressed Glass, Icicle, Sugar, Flint, Covered 35.00
  Ida, see Sheraton

Pressed Glass, Horn Of Plenty, Bowl

Pressed Glass, Horseshoe, Bowl, Covered, Stemmed

Pressed Glass, Horn Of Plenty, Tumbler, Whiskey

Pressed Glass, Idyll, Sauce, Green With Gold, 4 1/2 In. 20.00
Pressed Glass, Illinois, Toothpick 16.00
Pressed Glass, Indian Geometric, Goblet 16.00
  Indian Tree, see Sprig
  Indiana Swirl, see Feather
Pressed Glass, Intaglio, Butter, White, Opalescent, Covered 140.00
Pressed Glass, Intaglio, Compote, Jelly, Opalescent 18.00
Pressed Glass, Intaglio, Creamer, Clear, Opalescent 25.00
Pressed Glass, Interlocked Hearts, Butter 25.00
Pressed Glass, Interlocked Hearts, Wine 14.00
Pressed Glass, Inverted Fan & Feather, Bowl, Footed, Vaseline, 6 3/4 In. 65.00
Pressed Glass, Inverted Fan & Feather, Rose Bowl, White, Opalescent 45.00
Pressed Glass, Inverted Fan & Feather, Tumbler, Green, Gold Trim, Northwood 45.00
Pressed Glass, Inverted Fern, Butter, Flint 15.00
Pressed Glass, Inverted Fern, Eggcup .... 25.00 To 32.00
Pressed Glass, Inverted Fern, Eggcup, Flint .... 18.00 To 25.00
Pressed Glass, Inverted Fern, Goblet 35.00
Pressed Glass, Inverted Fern, Goblet, Flint .... 28.00 To 38.00
Pressed Glass, Inverted Fern, Spooner, Flint .... 28.00 To 30.00
Pressed Glass, Inverted Fern, Sugar, Covered, Flint 70.00
Pressed Glass, Inverted Fern, Sugar, Covered, Stemmed, Flint 75.00
Pressed Glass, Inverted Heart, Sauce, Flint 8.00
Pressed Glass, Inverted Hobnail Arches, Mug 13.50
Pressed Glass, Inverted Ovals, Wheelbarrow, Covered, Clear, Novelty 62.00
Pressed Glass, Inverted Strawberry, Bowl, Punch, Child's 40.00

Pressed Glass, Inverted Strawberry, Sugar, Covered	25.00
Pressed Glass, Inverted Strawberry, Tumbler	15.00
Pressed Glass, Inverted Strawberry, Water Set, Ice Green, 7 Piece	150.00
Pressed Glass, Inverted Thumbprint & Star, Goblet, Vaseline	35.00
Pressed Glass, Inverted Thumbprint, Amber	18.00
Pressed Glass, Inverted Thumbprint, Sauce, Footed, Blue	9.00
Pressed Glass, Inverted Thumbprint, Sugar, Covered, Amber	50.00
Pressed Glass, Inverted Thumbprint, Syrup, Blue	80.00
Pressed Glass, Inverted Thumbprint, Tumbler, Blue	26.00
Pressed Glass, Inverted Thumbprint, Whiskey, Vaseline	15.00
Pressed Glass, Ionia, Goblet	5.00
Pressed Glass, Ionia, Table Set, Covered Butter & Sugar With Creamer	90.00
Pressed Glass, Iowa, Salt, Gold Trim	22.00
Pressed Glass, Iowa, Saltshaker, With Gold	22.00
Pressed Glass, Iris & Herringbone, Bowl, Clear, Flared, Curved Lip, 9 1/2 In.	15.00
Pressed Glass, Iris & Herringbone, Bowl, Nut, Chrome Base & Nut Pick, 12 In.	30.00
Pressed Glass, Iris & Herringbone, Candlestick, Clear	6.00
Pressed Glass, Iris & Herringbone, Candlestick, Double, Pair	15.00
Pressed Glass, Iris & Herringbone, Goblet, Stemmed, Clear	12.00
Pressed Glass, Iris & Herringbone, Sugar & Creamer	12.00
Pressed Glass, Iris & Herringbone, Water Set, Frosted, Colored, 9 Piece	65.00
Pressed Glass, Iris & Herringbone, Wine	12.00
Pressed Glass, Iris With Meander, Compote, Jelly, Blue Opalescent	45.00
Pressed Glass, Iris With Meander, Pitcher, Water, Vaseline, Opalescent	225.00
Pressed Glass, Iris With Meander, Toothpick	20.00
Pressed Glass, Iris With Meander, Toothpick, Amethyst, Gold Decoration	40.00
Pressed Glass, Iris With Meander, Toothpick, Blue Opalescent	65.00 To 68.00
Pressed Glass, Iris With Meander, Toothpick, Green	45.00
Pressed Glass, Iris With Meander, Toothpick, Purple	40.00
Pressed Glass, Ivanhoe, Bowl, 9 In.	20.00
Pressed Glass, Ivanhoe, Compote, 5 X 7 In.	20.00
Pressed Glass, Ivy In Snow, Plate, Blue Leaves, 10 In.	40.00
Pressed Glass, Ivy In Snow, Relish	11.00
Pressed Glass, Ivy In Snow, Spooner	18.50
Pressed Glass, Ivy In Snow, Wine	15.00
Pressed Glass, Jackson, Bowl, Footed	20.00
Pressed Glass, Jacob's Ladder, Celery	20.00 To 30.00
Pressed Glass, Jacob's Ladder, Celery, Tall	36.00
Pressed Glass, Jacob's Ladder, Compote, Covered, 7 1/2 In.	70.00
Pressed Glass, Jacob's Ladder, Compote, High Standard, 7 In.	14.50
Pressed Glass, Jacob's Ladder, Compote, Low Standard, 9 1/3 In.	27.50
Pressed Glass, Jacob's Ladder, Creamer, Footed	38.00
Pressed Glass, Jacob's Ladder, Creamer, Pedestal	25.00 To 29.50
Pressed Glass, Jacob's Ladder, Dish, Honey	8.00 To 9.00
Pressed Glass, Jacob's Ladder, Pitcher, 7 1/2 In.	50.00
Pressed Glass, Jacob's Ladder, Plate, 6 In.	15.00
Pressed Glass, Jacob's Ladder, Relish, Oval	10.00
Pressed Glass, Jacob's Ladder, Salt, Master	22.00
Pressed Glass, Jacob's Ladder, Sauce	8.50
Pressed Glass, Jacob's Ladder, Sauce, 4 1/2 In.	7.50
Pressed Glass, Jacob's Ladder, Spooner	14.00
Pressed Glass, Japanese, Creamer	35.00
Pressed Glass, Jardiniere, Velmoss II, Blue, 5 In.	33.00
Jasper, see Late Buckle	
Pressed Glass, Jenny Lind, Tray, Bread	40.00
Pressed Glass, Jersey Swirl, Buttermilk	18.00
Pressed Glass, Jersey Swirl, Celery, Amber	25.00
Pressed Glass, Jersey Swirl, Plate, Amber, 10 In.	32.00
Pressed Glass, Jersey Swirl, Plate, 10 In.	18.00
Pressed Glass, Jersey Swirl, Plate, 6 1/4 In.	19.00
Pressed Glass, Jersey Swirl, Salt, Master, Spittoon Shape, Ruby Stained	40.00
Pressed Glass, Jersey Swirl, Sauce, Footed, 4 In.	6.00
Pressed Glass, Jewel & Dewdrop, Bowl, Flat	20.00
Pressed Glass, Jewel & Dewdrop, Compote, Open, 6 1/2 In.	29.50
Pressed Glass, Jewel & Dewdrop, Compote, 6 In.	16.00

Pressed Glass, Jewel & Dewdrop, Mug, Children's, 3 1/2 In., Set Of 8 .... 160.00
Pressed Glass, Jewel & Dewdrop, Sauce 11.00
Pressed Glass, Jewel & Dewdrop, Toothpick 26.00
Pressed Glass, Jewel & Dewdrop, Wine .... 25.00 To 45.00
Pressed Glass, Jewel & Fan, Relish, Green, Opalescent 23.50
    Jewel & Festoon, see Loop & Jewel
Pressed Glass, Jewel & Flower, Butter, Cranberry Stain, Opalescent, Covered 75.00
Pressed Glass, Jewel & Flower, Spooner, Clear To Opalescent 32.00
Pressed Glass, Jewel & Heart, Creamer, Clear, Opalescent 48.00
    Jewel Band, see Scalloped Tape
Pressed Glass, Jeweled Heart, Berry Set, Clear To White Opalescent, 5 Piece 75.00
Pressed Glass, Jeweled Heart, Berry Set, Opalescent, 7 Piece 125.00
Pressed Glass, Jeweled Heart, Creamer, Clear, Opalescent 25.00
Pressed Glass, Jeweled Heart, Creamer, Gold Jewels .... 28.50 To 36.50
Pressed Glass, Jeweled Heart, Tumbler, Green, Opalescent 55.00
Pressed Glass, Jeweled Heart, Tumbler, Opalescent 29.50

Pressed Glass, Iconoclast, Goblet

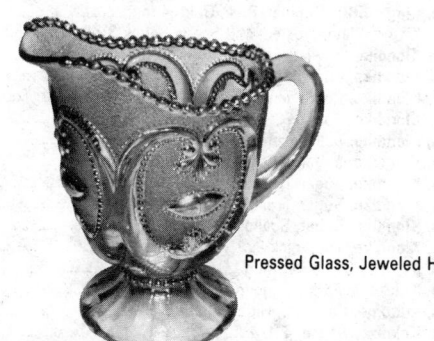

Pressed Glass, Jeweled Heart, Pitcher

Pressed Glass, Jeweled Moon & Star, Cake Stand, 10 1/2 In. 37.50
    Job's Tears, see Art
    Jubilee, see Hickman
Pressed Glass, Kalbach, Spooner, Ruffled Top 10.00
    Kamoni, see Balder
    Kansas, see Jewel & Dewdrop
Pressed Glass, Kentucky, Celery 17.50
Pressed Glass, Kentucky, Cruet 48.00
Pressed Glass, Kentucky, Dalzell, Celery 27.50
Pressed Glass, Kentucky, Wine, Green 21.00
Pressed Glass, Keystone Grape, Goblet 18.50
Pressed Glass, King's Crown, Butter, Covered 45.00
Pressed Glass, King's Crown, Celery 57.50
Pressed Glass, King's Crown, Champagne 14.50
Pressed Glass, King's Crown, Compote, High Standard, 5 In. 65.00
Pressed Glass, King's Crown, Creamer 35.00
Pressed Glass, King's Crown, Dish, Candy, Round, Handled 24.50
Pressed Glass, King's Crown, Goblet .... 12.00 To 20.00
Pressed Glass, King's Crown, Goblet, Green Eyes 20.00
Pressed Glass, King's Crown, Goblet, Souvenir, To My Mother, 1895, Ruby Stain 35.00
Pressed Glass, King's Crown, Jar, Covered Mustard 28.00
Pressed Glass, King's Crown, Sauce, Boat Shape, Set Of 6 .... 59.50
Pressed Glass, King's Crown, Toothpick 18.00
Pressed Glass, King's Crown, Tumbler, Ruby Thumbprint 30.00
Pressed Glass, King's Crown, Wine, Clear 10.00
Pressed Glass, King's 500, Cup, Custard, Cobalt Blue & Gold Trim 29.50

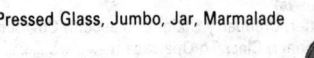

Pressed Glass, Jumbo, Jar, Marmalade

Pressed Glass, King's 500, Cup, Frosted And Clear, 3 In.	15.00
Pressed Glass, King's 500, Dish, Cobalt & Gold	29.50
Pressed Glass, King's 500, Tumbler, Blue, Gold, 4 In.	25.00
Pressed Glass, Kitten, Plate, Frosted, Mill Scene Below 3 Kittens	22.50
Pressed Glass, Klondike, Bowl, 8 Petaled, 10 In.	45.00
Pressed Glass, Klondike, Champagne, Frosted, With Amber Cross	425.00
Pressed Glass, Klondike, Condiment Set, Tray, Cruet, Salt, Pepper, Toothpick	1175.00
Pressed Glass, Klondike, Salt	95.00
Pressed Glass, Klondike, Saltshaker, Frosted And Amber	65.00
Pressed Glass, Klondike, Sugar & Creamer, Frost With Amber	395.00
Pressed Glass, Klondike, Sugar, Covered, 6 1/2 In.	75.00
Pressed Glass, Klondike, Sugar, Frosted With Amber Cross	132.50
Pressed Glass, Klondike, Sugar, Scalloped Rim	245.00
Pressed Glass, Klondike, Toothpick	235.00
Pressed Glass, Knights Of Labor, Mug	25.00
Pressed Glass, Knives & Forks, Eggcup	5.00
Pressed Glass, Kokomo, Compote, High Standard, 9 1/2 In.	12.50
Pressed Glass, Kokomo, Sauce, 4 1/4 In.	5.50
Pressed Glass, Kokomo, Wine	16.00
Lace, see Drapery	
Pressed Glass, Lacy Daisy, Berry Set, Child's, 8 Piece	65.00
Pressed Glass, Lacy Daisy, Berry Set, 5 Pieces	45.00
Pressed Glass, Lacy Medallion, Creamer, Emerald Green, Trimmed With Gold	15.00
Pressed Glass, Lacy Medallion, Pitcher, Emerald, Gold Trim, 2 1/4 In.	22.00
Pressed Glass, Lacy Medallion, Toothpick, Gold	17.50
Pressed Glass, Lacy Medallion, Tumbler, Mother, 1926, Emerald Green	25.00
Lacy Spiral, see Colossus	
Pressed Glass, Lamb, Creamer, Clear, Miniature	55.00
Pressed Glass, Laminated Petals, Claret, Flint	25.00
Pressed Glass, Lamp, see Lamp, Pressed Glass	
Pressed Glass, Late Block, Bowl, Master Berry	35.00
Pressed Glass, Late Buckle, Sauce, 4 In.	3.00
Pressed Glass, Late Thistle, Butter	25.00
Pressed Glass, Later Double Vine, Plate, Bread, 10 3/4 In.	18.00
Pressed Glass, Lattice & Oval Panels, Claret, Flint	165.00
Pressed Glass, Lattice & Oval Panels, Eggcup, Flint	13.00
Pressed Glass, Lattice & Oval Panels, Wine, Flint	50.00
Pressed Glass, Lattice Poinsettia, Bowl, Opalescent To Clear, 8 3/4 In.	40.00
Pressed Glass, Lattice With Ovals, Claret, Flint	65.00
Pressed Glass, Lattice With Ovals, Decanter, Stopper, Quart	150.00
Pressed Glass, Lattice With Ovals, Eggcup, Flint	59.50
Pressed Glass, Lattice With Ovals, Wine, Etched, Flint	75.00
Pressed Glass, Lattice, Goblet	15.00
Pressed Glass, Lattice, Plate, 6 In.	14.00
Pressed Glass, Leaf & Berry, Goblet	24.00
Pressed Glass, Leaf & Dart, Creamer, Applied Handle	45.00

Pressed Glass, Leaf & Dart, Eggcup	27.50
Pressed Glass, Leaf & Dart, Goblet	21.50
Pressed Glass, Leaf & Dart, Salt	22.50
Pressed Glass, Leaf & Dart, Tumbler, Footed	18.50 To 35.00
Pressed Glass, Leaf & Dart, Wine	15.00
Pressed Glass, Leaf & Flower, Bowl, Flower, Amber, 7 In.	52.00
Pressed Glass, Leaf & Flower, Butter, Amber Stained, Frosted, Covered	85.00
Pressed Glass, Leaf & Flower, Celery	75.00
Pressed Glass, Leaf & Flower, Creamer, Amber Stain	62.00
Pressed Glass, Leaf & Flower, Jug, Syrup, Frosted, Amber	150.00
Pressed Glass, Leaf & Flower, Pitcher, Amber Leaves & Flowers, 12 1/2 In.	50.00
Pressed Glass, Leaf & Flower, Salt & Pepper, Frosted	24.00
Pressed Glass, Leaf & Grape, Cup, Miniature	10.00
Pressed Glass, Leaf & Star, Hair Receiver	27.00
Pressed Glass, Leaf & Star, Sugar, Open, Scalloped Rim	15.00
Pressed Glass, Leaf & Star, Water Set, 7 Piece	110.00
Pressed Glass, Leaf Medallion, Berry Set, Northwood, 7 Piece	210.00
Pressed Glass, Leaf Medallion, Compote, Jelly, Cobalt Blue, Gold Trim	135.00
Pressed Glass, Leaf Medallion, Pitcher, Amethyst, Gold	165.00
Pressed Glass, Leaf Medallion, Sauce, Cobalt And Gold	25.00
Pressed Glass, Leaf Medallion, Tumbler, Amethyst	22.00
Pressed Glass, Leaf Medallion, Water Set, Cobalt Blue, Northwood, 7 Piece	225.00
Pressed Glass, Leaf Mold, Rose Bowl, Vaseline, Satin Spatter, 5 X 4 1/2 In.	175.00
Pressed Glass, Leaf Mold, Toothpick, Cased, Mica Fleck	125.00
Pressed Glass, Leaf Mold, Toothpick, Vaseline Spatter	95.00
Pressed Glass, Leaf Mold, Tumbler, Vaseline, Clear And Frosted	55.00
Pressed Glass, Leaf, Cake Stand, Emerald Green, 9 X 5 In.	33.00
Pressed Glass, Leaf, Goblet, Frosted, Lady's, Flint	95.00
Pressed Glass, Leaf, Pitcher, Water, Applied Handle, Flint	85.00
Pressed Glass, Leaf, Wine	18.50
Pressed Glass, Lee, Champagne, Flint	115.00
Lens & Star, see Star & Oval	
Leverne, see Star in Honeycomb	
Pressed Glass, Liberty Bell, Bowl, Fruit, Collared Base	65.00

Pressed Glass, Liberty Bell, Plate

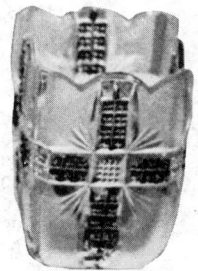

Pressed Glass, Klondike, Toothpick

Pressed Glass, Liberty Bell, Bread Plate 75.00
Pressed Glass, Liberty Bell, Butter 125.00
Pressed Glass, Liberty Bell, Butter, Covered .... 55.00 To 95.00
Pressed Glass, Liberty Bell, Butter, Covered, Miniature 135.00
Pressed Glass, Liberty Bell, Castor, Pickle 33.00
Pressed Glass, Liberty Bell, Compote, Low Standard, 7 7/8 In. 95.00
Pressed Glass, Liberty Bell, Compote, 8 In. 75.00
Pressed Glass, Liberty Bell, Creamer, Applied Rope Handle 120.00
Pressed Glass, Liberty Bell, Creamer, Miniature, Clear 75.00
Pressed Glass, Liberty Bell, Creamer, Reeded Handle 85.00
Pressed Glass, Liberty Bell, Goblet .... 25.00 To 45.00
Pressed Glass, Liberty Bell, Goblet, Knob Stem 42.50
Pressed Glass, Liberty Bell, Goblet, 1776-1876 .... 30.00
Pressed Glass, Liberty Bell, Mug, Miniature 95.00
Pressed Glass, Liberty Bell, Mug, Snake Handle, Clear 150.00
Pressed Glass, Liberty Bell, Mug, Snake Handled 250.00
Pressed Glass, Liberty Bell, Plate, Bread 60.00
Pressed Glass, Liberty Bell, Plate, Colonies On Rim, 8 In. 55.00
Pressed Glass, Liberty Bell, Plate, Dated, 6 1/4 In. 50.00
Pressed Glass, Liberty Bell, Plate, Twig Handles, States, 10 In. 80.00
Pressed Glass, Liberty Bell, Plate, 8 In. 55.00
Pressed Glass, Liberty Bell, Platter, Oval, Shell Handles, 7 X 11 3/4 In. 80.00
Pressed Glass, Liberty Bell, Platter, Signers 75.00
Pressed Glass, Liberty Bell, Platter, 13 X 9 1/2 In. 75.00
Pressed Glass, Liberty Bell, Relish 25.00
Pressed Glass, Liberty Bell, Salt Dip 27.50
Pressed Glass, Liberty Bell, Saltshaker 45.00
Pressed Glass, Liberty Bell, Sauce, Footed, 4 1/2 In. 27.50
Pressed Glass, Liberty Bell, Sauce, Footed, 4 3/4 In. 24.50
Pressed Glass, Liberty Bell, Sauce, 4 In. 20.00
Pressed Glass, Liberty Bell, Spooner .... 65.00 To 80.00
Pressed Glass, Liberty Bell, Sugar, Covered .... 50.00 To 110.00
Pressed Glass, Lightning, Bowl 8.50
Pressed Glass, Lightning, Tumbler 22.00
Pressed Glass, Lily Of The Valley, Butter, Clear, Footed 45.00
Pressed Glass, Lily Of The Valley, Celery, Etched, Flint 30.00
Pressed Glass, Lily Of The Valley, Creamer 40.00
Pressed Glass, Lily Of The Valley, Goblet, Etched .... 11.00 To 12.50
Pressed Glass, Lily Of The Valley, Pitcher, Milk 66.00
Pressed Glass, Lily Of The Valley, Pitcher, Milk, Applied Handle 68.00
Pressed Glass, Lily Of The Valley, Relish, Oval 14.00
Pressed Glass, Lily Of The Valley, Salt, Master, Footed 15.00
Pressed Glass, Lily Of The Valley, Spooner .... 20.00 To 26.00
Pressed Glass, Lily Of The Valley, Wine 37.50
Pressed Glass, Lincoln & Garfield, Mug, Martyrs 45.00
Pressed Glass, Lincoln Drape, Compote, Low Standard, Flint, 8 In. 45.00
Pressed Glass, Lincoln Drape, Eggcup .... 32.50 To 42.50
Pressed Glass, Lincoln Drape, Eggcup, Flint 37.50
Pressed Glass, Lincoln, Compote, 7 In. 165.00
Pressed Glass, Lined Ribs, Wine 12.00
Lion, see also Frosted Lion
Pressed Glass, Lion, Butter, Miniature, Clear 75.00
Pressed Glass, Lion, Celery .... 43.00 To 55.00
Pressed Glass, Lion, Celery, Frosted 110.00
Pressed Glass, Lion, Compote, Clear, Covered, 6 In.Square 40.00
Pressed Glass, Lion, Compote, Crouching Lion Oval Cover, 7 3/4 In. 85.00
Pressed Glass, Lion, Compote, Frosted Lion Base & Finial, 12 X 8 In. 125.00
Pressed Glass, Lion, Compote, Frosted, Clear Base, 8 1/2 X 4 1/2 In., Pair 160.00
Pressed Glass, Lion, Compote, Frosted, Covered, 11 In. 95.00
Pressed Glass, Lion, Compote, Frosted, Low Standard, Covered, 10 In. 120.00
Pressed Glass, Lion, Compote, Frosted, 7 In. 60.00
Pressed Glass, Lion, Compote, 6 In. 30.00
Pressed Glass, Lion, Creamer .... 20.00 To 75.00
Pressed Glass, Lion, Creamer, Child's 50.00
Pressed Glass, Lion, Creamer, Frosted Collar Base 31.50

Pressed Glass, Lincoln Drape, Compote, 8 In.

Pressed Glass, Lily Of The Valley, Etched, Goblet

Pressed Glass, Loop With Fisheye, Goblet

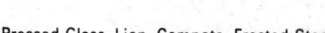

Pressed Glass, Lion, Compote, Frosted Stem

Pressed Glass, Lion, Cup & Saucer	55.00
Pressed Glass, Lion, Cup & Saucer, Miniature	50.00
Pressed Glass, Lion, Cup, Miniature	15.00
Pressed Glass, Lion, Cup, Miniature, Clear	25.00
Pressed Glass, Lion, Eggcup	40.00
Pressed Glass, Lion, Goblet, Frosted	47.50
Pressed Glass, Lion, Marmalade, Crouching Lion Cover	62.50
Pressed Glass, Lion, Pickle Jar, Frosted Border, Lion Cover	32.00
Pressed Glass, Lion, Plate, Bread, Give Us This Day	30.00
Pressed Glass, Lion, Sauce, Footed	15.00
Pressed Glass, Lion, Spooner	75.00
Pressed Glass, Lion, Sugar, Covered, Miniature	65.00
Pressed Glass, Lion, Sugar, Crouching Lion Cover	48.00 To 55.00
Pressed Glass, Lion, Sugar, Crouching Lion Cover, Frosted	55.00
Pressed Glass, Lion, Sugar, Frosted	20.00
Pressed Glass, Lion, Syrup, Frosted, Figural Angel With Horn, Pewter Cover	75.00
Pressed Glass, Lion, Table Set, Clear, 4 Piece	285.00
Pressed Glass, Lion's Head, Cake Stand, Square, 9 In.	37.50
Lion's Leg, see Alaska	
Pressed Glass, Little Lamb, Creamer, Miniature, Clear	50.00
Pressed Glass, Locket, Tumbler, Green, Northwood	18.00
Pressed Glass, Log Cabin, Creamer	165.00
Pressed Glass, Log, Sauce, 4 In.	5.00
Pressed Glass, Logan, Plate	250.00
Pressed Glass, Long Diamond, Butter, Child's, Covered	20.00
Pressed Glass, Long Diamond, Creamer	20.00

Pressed Glass, Long Diamond, Creamer, Child's 30.00
    Loop, see also Seneca Loop, Yuma Loop
Pressed Glass, Loop & Daisy, Saltshaker 45.00
Pressed Glass, Loop & Dart With Diamond Ornament, Goblet 20.00
Pressed Glass, Loop & Dart With Diamond Ornament, Sauce, 4 In. 4.50
Pressed Glass, Loop & Dart With Diamond Ornament, Sugar 22.50
Pressed Glass, Loop & Dart With Round Ornament, Compote, Flint, 8 In. 42.50
Pressed Glass, Loop & Dart With Round Ornament, Goblet, Flint 30.00
Pressed Glass, Loop & Dart With Round Ornament, Salt, Flint 22.00
Pressed Glass, Loop & Dart, Bowl, Oval, 6 X 9 In. 18.00
Pressed Glass, Loop & Dart, Creamer, Applied Handle, Flint 55.00
Pressed Glass, Loop & Dart, Eggcup .... 8.50 To 21.50
Pressed Glass, Loop & Dart, Spooner 12.00
Pressed Glass, Loop & Dart, Spooner, Round Ornament 45.00
Pressed Glass, Loop & Dart, Table Set, Flint, 4 Piece 130.00
Pressed Glass, Loop & Dart, Tumbler, Footed 18.00
Pressed Glass, Loop & Dart, Wine 16.50
Pressed Glass, Loop & Jewel, Spooner 18.00
Pressed Glass, Loop With Dewdrop, Creamer .... 15.00 To 30.00
Pressed Glass, Loop With Fisheye, Goblet 15.00
Pressed Glass, Loop With Prism Band, Goblet 17.50
    Loop with Stippled Panels, see Texas
Pressed Glass, Loop, Compote, Lyon & Co., 8 3/4 In. 23.00
Pressed Glass, Loop, Eggcup, Flint 22.50
Pressed Glass, Loop, Goblet 14.00
Pressed Glass, Loop, Goblet, Flint 20.50
Pressed Glass, Loop, Salt, Master, Without Foot, Flint 18.00
Pressed Glass, Loop, Spooner, Flint 20.00
Pressed Glass, Looped Band & Honeycomb, Goblet, Flint 24.00
Pressed Glass, Loops & Fans, Sauce 4.50
Pressed Glass, Lord's Supper, Plate, Bread 25.00
Pressed Glass, Lorne, Butter, Covered 18.00
Pressed Glass, Lotus & Serpent, Mug 35.00
Pressed Glass, Lotus & Serpent, Spooner 22.00
Pressed Glass, Lotus, Relish, 2 Handles 10.00
Pressed Glass, Louisiana Purchase, Tumbler 28.00
Pressed Glass, Louise, Sugar & Creamer, Covered 35.00
Pressed Glass, Loving Cup, Toothpick, 3-Handled 25.00
Pressed Glass, Magnet & Grape With Frosted Leaf, Eggcup, Flint 75.00
Pressed Glass, Magnet & Grape With Frosted Leaf, Spooner 35.00
Pressed Glass, Magnet & Grape With Frosted Leaf, Tumbler 95.00
Pressed Glass, Magnet & Grape With Stippled Leaf, Creamer, Applied Handle 42.00
Pressed Glass, Magnet & Grape With Stippled Leaf, Goblet 15.00
Pressed Glass, Magnet & Grape, Goblet, Plain 22.50
Pressed Glass, Magnet & Grape, Spooner, Flint, Clear 24.00
Pressed Glass, Magnolia, Cake Stand, Clear 35.00
Pressed Glass, Magnolia, Pitcher, Water, Clear .... 38.00 To 60.00

Pressed Glass, Maine, Syrup

Pressed Glass, Magnet & Grape With Stippled Leaf, Goblet

Pressed Glass, **Magnolia,** Spooner, Frosted	55.00
Pressed Glass, **Magnolia,** Sugar, Frosted, Covered	35.00
Pressed Glass, **Magnolia,** Tankard, Clear	65.00
Maiden Blush, see Banded Portland	
Pressed Glass, **Maine,** Bowl, Berry, 8 In.	25.00
Pressed Glass, **Maine,** Cake Stand	49.50
Pressed Glass, **Maine,** Cake Stand, 8 In.	25.00
Pressed Glass, **Maine,** Pitcher, Water	30.00
Pressed Glass, **Maine,** Spooner	17.50
Pressed Glass, **Majestic,** Pitcher, Water, Scalloped Top, Polished Bottom	17.00
Pressed Glass, **Majestic,** Tumbler	24.50
Pressed Glass, **Maltese Cross In Circles,** Platter, Bread	25.00
Pressed Glass, **Maltese Cross,** Salt, Embossed Boston 1865	6.00
Pressed Glass, **Manhattan,** Compote, Acorn Finial, 7 1/2 In.	35.00
Pressed Glass, **Manhattan,** Jar, Cracker, Ruby Stained	30.00
Pressed Glass, **Manhattan,** Plate, Clear & Gold, 10 1/2 In.	10.25 To 11.25
Pressed Glass, **Manhattan,** Punch Set, 16 Piece	180.00
Pressed Glass, **Manhattan,** Tumbler, Miniature	15.00
Pressed Glass, **Manhattan,** Wine, Stem, 4 1/2 In.	10.00
Pressed Glass, **Manting,** Goblet, Flint	35.00
Pressed Glass, **Many Loops,** Dish, Opalescent	32.50
Pressed Glass, **Maple Leaf Band,** Goblet	25.00
Pressed Glass, **Maple Leaf,** Chalice, Opalescent To Clear, N	40.00
Pressed Glass, **Maple Leaf,** Creamer, Canary Yellow	35.00
Pressed Glass, **Maple Leaf,** Creamer, Vaseline	45.00
Pressed Glass, **Maple Leaf,** Sauce, Leaf Shape, Vaseline	6.00
Pressed Glass, **Maple Leaf,** Tray, 11 In.	15.00
Pressed Glass, **Marquisette,** Butter	28.00
Pressed Glass, **Marquisette,** Celery	27.50
Pressed Glass, **Marquisette,** Goblet	26.00
Pressed Glass, **Marquisette,** Spooner	20.00
Pressed Glass, **Marsh Pink,** Cake Stand, 9 1/4 In.	42.50
Pressed Glass, **Marsh Pink,** Tray, Bread	25.00
Pressed Glass, **Martha's Tears,** Goblet	9.50
Pressed Glass, **Maryland,** Celery	20.00
Pressed Glass, **Maryland,** Compote, Jelly	10.00
Pressed Glass, **Maryland,** Creamer	10.00
Pressed Glass, **Mascotte,** Celery, Flint	24.00
Pressed Glass, **Mascotte,** Compote, Open, 8 1/4 In.	25.00
Pressed Glass, **Mascotte,** Creamer, Applied Handle	24.00
Pressed Glass, **Mascotte,** Goblet, Etched	25.00
Pressed Glass, **Mascotte,** Sauce, Etched, Footed, 4 In.	9.00
Pressed Glass, **Mascotte,** Tumbler	12.00
Pressed Glass, **Mascotte,** Wine	15.00
Pressed Glass, **Masonic,** Bowl, 8 In.	20.00
Pressed Glass, **Masonic,** Creamer	20.00
Pressed Glass, **Masonic,** Spooner	15.00
Pressed Glass, **Massachusetts,** Bottle, Bar	25.00
Pressed Glass, **Massachusetts,** Bowl, Berry, Square, 9 In.	20.00
Pressed Glass, **Massachusetts,** Cup, Punch	15.00
Pressed Glass, **Massachusetts,** Goblet	28.00 To 35.00
Pressed Glass, **Massachusetts,** Jug, Rum, Large	67.00
Pressed Glass, **Massachusetts,** Jug, Rum, Small	78.00
Pressed Glass, **Massachusetts,** Plate, Clear, Square, 8 In.	9.50
Pressed Glass, **Massachusetts,** Plate, Edges Turned Up, 8 1/4 In.	25.00
Pressed Glass, **Massachusetts,** Plate, Square, 8 In.	18.00
Pressed Glass, **Massachusetts,** Sugar, Covered	30.00
Pressed Glass, **Massachusetts,** Toothpick	75.00
Pressed Glass, **Massachusetts,** Vase, Trumpet, Cobalt Blue, 6 1/2 In.	28.00
Pressed Glass, **Massachusetts,** Vase, 6 3/4 In.	15.00
Pressed Glass, **Massachusetts,** Vase, 9 3/4 In.	20.00
Pressed Glass, **Massachusetts,** Whiskey	12.00
Pressed Glass, **Massachusetts,** Wine	35.00
Pressed Glass, **McCormick Reaper,** Bread Plate	85.00
Pressed Glass, **McKee,** Compote, Opaque Pink, 10 X 7 In.	25.00

Pressed Glass, McKinley, Mug, Clear, 3 1/2 In. 37.50
Pressed Glass, McKinley, Mug, Covered .... 39.00 To 55.00
Pressed Glass, McKinley, Plate, Protection & Plenty 16.50
Pressed Glass, McKinley, Tray, Bread, Oblong 27.50
Pressed Glass, Medallion Sunburst, Plate, 10 In. 13.00
Pressed Glass, Medallion Sunburst, Plate, 7 In.Square 12.50
Pressed Glass, Medallion Sunburst, Plate, 8 In. 8.00
Pressed Glass, Medallion Sunburst, Salt 5.50
Pressed Glass, Medallion Sunburst, Wine 11.00
Pressed Glass, Medallion, Creamer, Green Lacy 22.00
Pressed Glass, Medallion, Mug, Child's 25.00
Pressed Glass, Medallion, Pitcher, Water, Green 50.00
Pressed Glass, Melon, Sugar And Creamer 150.00
Pressed Glass, Melrose, Goblet 12.50
Pressed Glass, Melrose, Goblet, Etched 22.50
Pressed Glass, Melrose, Pitcher, Water 45.00
Pressed Glass, Melrose, Tray, Water 25.00
Pressed Glass, Melrose, Tumbler 11.00
Pressed Glass, Melrose, Wine, Greentown 16.50
Pressed Glass, Memphis, Butter, Covered, Green, Northwood 55.00
Pressed Glass, Memphis, Tumbler, Green 20.00
Pressed Glass, Memphis, Tumbler, Green, Northwood 15.00
Pressed Glass, Memphis, Water Set, Clear, Northwood, 7 Piece 200.00
Pressed Glass, Memphis, Water Set, Green, Gold, 6 Piece 185.00
Pressed Glass, Mephistopheles, Pitcher, Water, 4 Goblets 350.00
Pressed Glass, Mercury, Tieback, Etched, Pair 20.00
Pressed Glass, Michigan, Creamer, Child's 22.00
Pressed Glass, Michigan, Creamer, Individual, Yellow Stained, Enameled Flower 60.00
Pressed Glass, Michigan, Creamer, 3 In. 16.00
Pressed Glass, Michigan, Dish, Berry, Gold Decoration 8.00
Pressed Glass, Michigan, Goblet, Gold Trim .... 18.50 To 20.00
Pressed Glass, Michigan, Maiden's Blush Top, Gold Notches 22.50
Pressed Glass, Michigan, Mug 12.00
Pressed Glass, Michigan, Pitcher, Miniature .... 18.00 To 25.00
Pressed Glass, Michigan, Pitcher, Water 18.00
Pressed Glass, Michigan, Relish, Scalloped, Enameled 16.00
Pressed Glass, Michigan, Sugar, Open 20.00
Pressed Glass, Michigan, Table Set, Gold, Pink Stained, 4 Piece 185.00
Pressed Glass, Michigan, Toothpick, Yellow Stained 43.00
Pressed Glass, Michigan, Vase, 8 1/4 In. 25.00
Pressed Glass, Mikado Fan, Goblet 12.00
Pressed Glass, Millard, Saltshaker, Ruby Stained 20.00
Pressed Glass, Millard, Sauce, Footed, Ruby Stained 12.50
Pressed Glass, Milton, Cruet, Vinegar, Amber, Square Stopper, 6 In. 50.00
Pressed Glass, Milton, Goblet .... 13.50 To 18.50
Pressed Glass, Minerva, Butter .... 55.00 To 58.00
Pressed Glass, Minerva, Cake Stand, 9 In. .... 50.00 To 75.00
Pressed Glass, Minerva, Creamer 50.00
Pressed Glass, Minerva, Creamer, Footed 38.00
Pressed Glass, Minerva, Dish, Pickle, Love's Request 30.00
Pressed Glass, Minerva, Dish, Pickle, 7 In. 25.00
Pressed Glass, Minerva, Goblet .... 65.00 To 72.00
Pressed Glass, Minerva, Pitcher, Water, Slight Purple Tint 150.00
Pressed Glass, Minerva, Plate, 10 In. 39.50
Pressed Glass, Minerva, Platter, 13 X 9 In. 42.50
Pressed Glass, Minerva, Sauce, Footed, 4 In. .... 12.00 To 12.50
Pressed Glass, Minerva, Sugar 18.50
Pressed Glass, Minerva, Tray, Bread 48.00
Pressed Glass, Minnesota, Compote, Open, 9 3/4 In. 47.50
Pressed Glass, Minnesota, Compote, 9 In. 22.00
Pressed Glass, Minnesota, Cup 15.00
Pressed Glass, Minnesota, Mug, Gold Trim 10.00
Pressed Glass, Minnesota, Toothpick 25.00
Pressed Glass, Minnesota, Toothpick, 3-Handled 35.00
Pressed Glass, Minnesota, Tumbler 10.00

Pressed Glass, Moon & Star, Bowl, Covered, Footed

Pressed Glass, Mitered Diamond, Goblet

Pressed Glass, Mioton, Goblet	8.00
Pressed Glass, Mirror & Fan, Wine	10.00
Pressed Glass, Mirror, Champagne, Flint	32.50
Pressed Glass, Mirror, Compote, Flint, High Standard, 7 In.	75.00
Pressed Glass, Mirror, Goblet, Flint	26.50 To 30.00
Pressed Glass, Mirror, Wine, Flint	29.00
Pressed Glass, Missouri, Celery	23.50
Pressed Glass, Mitered Diamond, Salt & Pepper	18.00
Pressed Glass, Mitered Diamond, Tumbler, Amber	14.00 To 17.00
Pressed Glass, Mitered Oval, Goblet, Flint	25.00
Pressed Glass, Mitered Prisms, Cake Stand, 9 In.	29.50
Pressed Glass, Monkey On Tree Trunk, Toothpick, Blue	22.50
Pressed Glass, Monkey Under Tree, Mug	70.00
Pressed Glass, Monkey With Hat, Toothpick, Clear	38.50
Pressed Glass, Monkey, Bowl, Centerpiece	58.00
Pressed Glass, Monkey, Spooner, Vaseline	48.00
Pressed Glass, Monkey, Toothpick	45.00
Pressed Glass, Moon & Star, Bowl, Collared Base, 7 1/2 In.	22.50
Pressed Glass, Moon & Star, Bowl, 6 In.	12.00
Pressed Glass, Moon & Star, Cake Stand	14.00
Pressed Glass, Moon & Star, Compote	39.00
Pressed Glass, Moon & Star, Compote, Amber, Open	48.00
Pressed Glass, Moon & Star, Compote, Collared Base, Covered, 7 1/2 In.	50.00
Pressed Glass, Moon & Star, Compote, Low Standard, 6 In.	20.00 To 25.00
Pressed Glass, Moon & Star, Compote, Open, 8 In.	32.00
Pressed Glass, Moon & Star, Compote, 11 In.	60.00
Pressed Glass, Moon & Star, Compote, 8 In.	45.00
Pressed Glass, Moon & Star, Goblet	25.00
Pressed Glass, Moon & Star, Salt	11.50
Pressed Glass, Moon Drops, Punch Bowl, Stand, 5 Cups	100.00
Pressed Glass, Morning Glory, Champagne, Flint	135.00
Pressed Glass, Morning Glory, Compote, Flint	185.00
Pressed Glass, Morning Glory, Dish, Honey, Flint, 3 1/2 In.	45.00
Pressed Glass, Morning Glory, Eggcup, Flint	125.00
Pressed Glass, Morning Glory, Sauce, 4 In.	45.00
Pressed Glass, Morning Glory, Wine	110.00
Pressed Glass, Mt.Vernon, Butter, Clear, Covered	18.50
Pressed Glass, Mt.Vernon, Salt & Pepper, Clear	8.00
Pressed Glass, Nail, Goblet	21.50
Pressed Glass, Nail, Jug, Syrup, Etched	45.00
Pressed Glass, Nail, Pitcher, Water	55.00
Pressed Glass, Nailhead, Cake Stand, 10 1/2 In.	27.50
Pressed Glass, Nailhead, Cake Stand, 9 In.	16.50 To 17.00
Pressed Glass, Nailhead, Cake Stand, 9 1/2 In.	23.50
Pressed Glass, Nailhead, Celery, Flint	32.00

Pressed Glass, Nailhead, Compote, Covered, High Standard, 6 In. .... 34.00 To 35.00
Pressed Glass, Nailhead, Plate, 7 In.Square .... 15.00 To 17.50
Pressed Glass, Nailhead, Plate, 9 In. .... 14.00 To 18.00
Pressed Glass, Nailhead, Wine 20.00
Pressed Glass, Narcissus Spray, Butter 30.00
Pressed Glass, Narcissus Spray, Spoon Holder 18.00
Pressed Glass, Nautilus, Banana Boat 250.00
Pressed Glass, Nautilus, Bowl, Fruit, Individual 65.00
Pressed Glass, Nautilus, Compote, Custard Stem 165.00
Pressed Glass, Nelly Bly, Platter 76.50
Pressed Glass, Nelly, Goblet 10.00
Pressed Glass, Nevada, Celery 19.00
Pressed Glass, New England Centennial, Goblet 96.00
Pressed Glass, New England Pineapple, Champagne, Flint 95.00
Pressed Glass, New England Pineapple, Compote, Low Standard, 7 In. 75.00
Pressed Glass, New England Pineapple, Compote, Low Standard, 8 In. 85.00
Pressed Glass, New England Pineapple, Cordial, 4 X 1 7/8 In. 85.00
Pressed Glass, New England Pineapple, Eggcup 26.00
Pressed Glass, New England Pineapple, Goblet .... 35.00 To 45.00
Pressed Glass, New England Pineapple, Goblet, Lady's, Flint 55.00
Pressed Glass, New England Pineapple, Plate, Flint, 6 In. 95.00
Pressed Glass, New England Pineapple, Plate, 6 In. 85.00
Pressed Glass, New England Pineapple, Salt, Master, Flint 32.00
Pressed Glass, New England Pineapple, Spooner 45.00
Pressed Glass, New England Pineapple, Spooner, Flint 40.00
Pressed Glass, New England Pineapple, Tumbler, Whiskey 85.00
Pressed Glass, New Hampshire, Mug, Gold Trim 20.00
Pressed Glass, New Hampshire, Relish 8.50
Pressed Glass, New Hampshire, Sauce, Ruby Flashed 5.50
Pressed Glass, New Hampshire, Sugar, Covered, 8 In. 25.00
Pressed Glass, New Hampshire, Toothpick 19.50
Pressed Glass, New Hampshire, Tumbler, Clear, Gold Flashed 10.00
Pressed Glass, New Jersey Swirl, Spittoon 20.00
Pressed Glass, New Jersey, Carafe 60.00
Pressed Glass, New Jersey, Cruet 28.50
Pressed Glass, New Jersey, Goblet 26.50
Pressed Glass, New Jersey, Relish, Ruby Stained 24.50
Pressed Glass, New Jersey, Toothpick 12.00
Pressed Glass, New Jersey, Toothpick, Clear With Gold 16.00
Pressed Glass, New Jersey, Tumbler 12.00
Pressed Glass, New Jersey, Wine 28.00
Pressed Glass, New York Honeycomb, Celery, Flint 25.00
Pressed Glass, New York Honeycomb, Sugar, Open, Flint 20.00
Pressed Glass, New York State, Jar, Apothecary, Covered, 11 In. 100.00
Pressed Glass, Niagara Falls, Tray, Bread, Frosted & Clear 97.50
Pressed Glass, Notched Bars, Plate, Bread, Blue 45.00

Pressed Glass, New England Flute, Goblet

Pressed Glass, New England Pineapple, Pitcher

Pressed Glass, Nova Scotia Raspberry, Goblet 20.00
Pressed Glass, Nursery Rhymes, Bowl, Berry .... 8.50 To 12.00
Pressed Glass, Nursery Rhymes, Butter, Miniature 65.00
Pressed Glass, Nursery Rhymes, Creamer, Miniature, Clear 30.00
Pressed Glass, Nursery Rhymes, Cup, Punch 10.00
Pressed Glass, Nursery Rhymes, Cup, Punch, Milk Glass 22.00
Pressed Glass, Nursery Rhymes, Pitcher, Water, Miniature 65.00
Pressed Glass, Nursery Rhymes, Punch Set, Child's, Clear, 7 Piece 175.00
Pressed Glass, Nursery Rhymes, Sauce 16.50
Pressed Glass, Nursery Rhymes, Spooner 25.00
Pressed Glass, Nursery Rhymes, Table Set, Child's 175.00
Pressed Glass, Nursery Rhymes, Tumbler, Child's 20.00
Pressed Glass, O'Hara Loop, Compote, 8 1/2 In. 15.00
Pressed Glass, O'Hara Star, Saltshaker 12.00
Pressed Glass, Oak Leaf Band, Goblet 17.00
Pressed Glass, Oaken Bucket, Pitcher, Water 40.00
Pressed Glass, Oaken Bucket, Pitcher, Water, Amber 35.00
Pressed Glass, Oaken Bucket, Pitcher, Water, Amethyst 48.00
Pressed Glass, Oaken Bucket, Spooner, Vaseline 35.50
Pressed Glass, Oaken Bucket, Toothpick 10.00
Pressed Glass, Oasis, Goblet, Camel Caravan 45.00
Pressed Glass, Old Abe, Compote, Covered 195.00
Pressed Glass, Old State House, Philadelphia, Tray, Water 90.00
   One Hundred One, see One-O-One
Pressed Glass, One-O-One, Celery, 6 3/8 In. .... 17.00 To 25.00
Pressed Glass, One-O-One, Creamer, Footed 16.00
Pressed Glass, One-O-One, Plate 12.00
Pressed Glass, One-O-One, Sauce 10.00
   One-Thousand Eye, see Thousand Eye
Pressed Glass, Open Rose, Eggcup .... 16.00 To 18.50
Pressed Glass, Open Rose, Glass, Buttermilk 32.00
Pressed Glass, Open Rose, Goblet .... 14.50 To 22.50
Pressed Glass, Open Rose, Pitcher, Water, Applied Handle 165.00
Pressed Glass, Open Rose, Spooner 17.00
Pressed Glass, Open Rose, Sugar, Covered 49.50
Pressed Glass, Optic, Sugar Shaker, Cranberry Ring Neck 65.00
   Oregon, see also Beaded Loop
Pressed Glass, Oregon, Bowl, Flat, 8 In. 35.00
Pressed Glass, Oregon, Creamer 26.00
Pressed Glass, Oregon, Spooner 20.00
Pressed Glass, Oregon, Sugar, Covered, 1845 .... 175.00
Pressed Glass, Oriental Fan, Goblet 42.00
Pressed Glass, Oriental Poppy, Tumbler, Green, Northwood 35.00
   Orion, see Cathedral
   Oval Loop, see Question Mark
Pressed Glass, Oval Miter, Sweetmeat, Covered, 6 In. 49.50
Pressed Glass, Oval Panels, Goblet, Blue 22.00
Pressed Glass, Oval Shell & Tassel, Bowl, 13 X 5 1/2 In. 25.00
Pressed Glass, Oval Star, Butter 20.00
Pressed Glass, Oval Star, Butter, Child's 25.00
Pressed Glass, Oval Star, Butter, Child's, Covered .... 16.00 To 27.00
Pressed Glass, Oval Star, Butter, Covered 16.50
Pressed Glass, Oval Star, Creamer, Child's .... 15.00 To 20.00
Pressed Glass, Oval Star, Pitcher, Water 30.00
Pressed Glass, Oval Star, Spooner, Child's 19.00
Pressed Glass, Oval Star, Sugar, Cover, Child's .... 22.00 To 23.00
Pressed Glass, Oval Star, Sugar, Covered 14.50
Pressed Glass, Oval Star, Table Set, Miniature 75.00
Pressed Glass, Oval Star, Table Set, Miniature, 3 Piece 53.00
Pressed Glass, Oval Star, Table Set, 4 Piece 65.00
Pressed Glass, Oval Star, Tea Set, Miniature, 3 Piece 58.00
Pressed Glass, Oval Star, Water Set, Child's, 5 Piece 95.00
Pressed Glass, Oval Star, Water Set, Child's, 7 Piece .... 55.00 To 85.00
   Owl, see Bull's-Eye & Diamond Point
   Owl & Fan, see Parrot & Fan

Pressed Glass, Oval & Crossbar, Tumbler, Whiskey

Pressed Glass, Orange Peel, Goblet

Pressed Glass, Oval Miter, Salt, Footed

Pressed Glass, **Owl & Possum,** Goblet	45.00 To 100.00
Pressed Glass, **Owl & Pussycat,** Dish, Cheese, Domed	95.00 To 275.00
Pressed Glass, **Paddle Wheel,** Cruet	16.00
Pressed Glass, **Paisley,** Relish	9.00
Pressed Glass, **Paling,** Creamer	12.50
Pressed Glass, **Paling,** Goblet	12.00
Pressed Glass, **Paling,** Sugar	16.00
Pressed Glass, **Palm & Scroll,** Bowl, Blue, Opalescent, C.1905, 9 In.	45.00
Pressed Glass, **Palm & Scroll,** Bowl, Blue, Opalescent, 3 Footed, 9 In.	30.00
Pressed Glass, **Palm & Scroll,** Cake Stand, 6 3/4 In.	25.00
Pressed Glass, **Palm & Scroll,** Pitcher, Milk	24.00
Pressed Glass, **Palm & Scroll,** Saltshaker, Pair	25.00
Pressed Glass, **Palm & Scroll,** Table Set, 4 Piece	80.00
Pressed Glass, **Palm Beach,** Pitcher, Vaseline, Opalescent	225.00
Pressed Glass, **Palm Leaf Fan,** Banana Stand	35.00
Pressed Glass, **Palm Leaf Fan,** Cake Stand, 9 1/2 In	23.00 To 25.00
Pressed Glass, **Palm Leaf Fan,** Plate, 7 1/2 In.	9.00
Pressed Glass, **Palm Stub,** Goblet	10.00 To 15.00
Pressed Glass, **Palmette,** Cake Stand	32.00
Pressed Glass, **Palmette,** Compote, Open, 8 1/2 In.	27.50
Pressed Glass, **Palmette,** Relish, Scoop	14.00
Pressed Glass, **Palmette,** Salt, Master, Footed	15.00
Pressed Glass, **Palmette,** Sauce, 4 In.	4.50
Pressed Glass, **Palmette,** Sauce, 6 In.	15.00
Pressed Glass, **Palmette,** Spooner	20.00
Pressed Glass, **Palmette,** Tray, Bread	18.00
Pressed Glass, **Palmette,** Wine	25.00
Pressed Glass, **Panel & Star,** Dish, Bonbon	8.50
Pressed Glass, **Panel,** Lamp, Kerosene, Footed, Burner	12.50
Pressed Glass, **Paneled & Finecut,** Blue, Wine	35.00
Pressed Glass, **Paneled Acorn Band,** Champagne, Flint	50.00
Pressed Glass, **Paneled Apple Blossom,** Tumbler	13.50
Pressed Glass, **Paneled Bar,** Decanter, Applied Rigaree, Flint	50.00
Pressed Glass, **Paneled Bull's-Eye,** Goblet, Flint	27.50
Pressed Glass, **Paneled Cane,** Creamer	18.00
Pressed Glass, **Paneled Cane,** Pitcher, Milk, Vaseline, 6 1/8 In.	45.00
Pressed Glass, **Paneled Cherry,** Butter, Northwood	50.00
Pressed Glass, **Paneled Cherry,** Goblet	28.00
Pressed Glass, **Paneled Cherry,** Pitcher, Covered	37.50
Pressed Glass, **Paneled Cherry,** Sugar, Covered, Northwood	48.00
Paneled Daisy & Button, see also Daisy & Button with Amber Panels	
Pressed Glass, **Paneled Daisy & Button,** Bowl, Berry, Emerald Green, Oblong	42.50
Pressed Glass, **Paneled Daisy,** Bowl, Oval, 9 In.	15.00
Pressed Glass, **Paneled Daisy,** Compote, Covered, 8 In.	65.00
Pressed Glass, **Paneled Daisy,** Pitcher, Water	27.00

Pressed Glass, Paneled Daisy, Plate, 9 In.Square	22.00 To 25.00
Pressed Glass, Paneled Daisy, Relish, Teardrop	11.00
Pressed Glass, Paneled Dewdrop, Celery	17.50
Pressed Glass, Paneled Dewdrop, Cordial	18.50
Pressed Glass, Paneled Dewdrop, Sauce, 4 In.	4.50
Pressed Glass, Paneled Dewdrop, Spooner	13.00
Pressed Glass, Paneled Dewdrop, Wine	14.50
Pressed Glass, Paneled Diamond & Finecut, Berry Set, 9 Piece	75.00
Pressed Glass, Paneled Diamond Point, Goblet	11.00 To 13.00
Pressed Glass, Paneled Diamond, Wine	9.50
Pressed Glass, Paneled English Hobnail With Prisms, Butter, Gold Trim	35.00
Pressed Glass, Paneled English Hobnail, Goblet	12.50 To 17.00
Pressed Glass, Paneled Flowers, Goblet	17.50
Pressed Glass, Paneled Forget-Me-Not, Cake Stand, 9 1/2 In.	23.50 To 32.50
Pressed Glass, Paneled Forget-Me-Not, Celery	33.00 To 33.50
Pressed Glass, Paneled Forget-Me-Not, Compote, Covered	34.00
Pressed Glass, Paneled Forget-Me-Not, Compote, Covered, 6 X 9 1/2 In.	42.50
Pressed Glass, Paneled Forget-Me-Not, Compote, 7 In.	15.00
Pressed Glass, Paneled Forget-Me-Not, Relish	12.50
Pressed Glass, Paneled Grape Band, Goblet	15.00
Pressed Glass, Paneled Grape Band, Goblet, Flint	35.00
Pressed Glass, Paneled Grape With Thumbprint, Goblet	14.00
Pressed Glass, Paneled Grape, Sauce, 4 In.	6.00
Pressed Glass, Paneled Grape, Tumbler	24.00
Pressed Glass, Paneled Heather, Spooner	14.00
Pressed Glass, Paneled Heather, Sugar & Creamer, Gold Flashed, Footed	17.50
Pressed Glass, Paneled Heather, Water Set, Clear With Gold, 6 Piece	45.00
Pressed Glass, Paneled Heather, Wine	19.50
Pressed Glass, Paneled Herringbone, Tumbler, Green	20.00
Pressed Glass, Paneled Holly, Creamer, Northwood	42.00
Pressed Glass, Paneled Holly, Pitcher, Water	65.00
Pressed Glass, Paneled Holly, Tumbler, Green, Gold, Northwood	35.00
Pressed Glass, Paneled Honeycomb, Pitcher, Covered	12.00
Pressed Glass, Paneled Jewels, Goblet	14.00
Pressed Glass, Paneled Jewels, Goblet, Dark Amber	38.00
Pressed Glass, Paneled Jewels, Goblet, Light Amber	35.00
Pressed Glass, Paneled Nightshade, Wine	15.00
Pressed Glass, Paneled Ovals, Eggcup, Flint	35.00
Pressed Glass, Paneled Palm, Bowl	12.50
Pressed Glass, Paneled Palm, Pitcher, Water	27.50
Pressed Glass, Paneled Palm, Toothpick, Ruby Stained	30.00
Pressed Glass, Paneled Sprig, Sugar Shaker, Cranberry	120.00

Paneled Star & Button, see Sedan
Paneled Stippled Bowl, see Stippled Band

Pressed Glass, Paneled Diamond Cross

Pressed Glass, Paneled Diamond & Flowers, Goblet

Pressed Glass, Paneled Sunflower, Creamer 15.00
Pressed Glass, Paneled Sunflower, Spooner 9.00
Pressed Glass, Paneled Swan, Pitcher, Water 65.00
Pressed Glass, Paneled Thistle, Bowl, Honey, Square, Footed 12.00
Pressed Glass, Paneled Thistle, Dish, Honey, Covered, Marked 47.50
Pressed Glass, Paneled Thistle, Dish, Honey, Covered, Square 20.00
Pressed Glass, Paneled Thistle, Pitcher, Milk, 7 1/4 In. 28.50
Pressed Glass, Paneled Thistle, Plate, 7 1/2 In. 19.00
Pressed Glass, Paneled Thistle, Plate. 9 1/2 In. 22.50
Pressed Glass, Paneled Thistle, Relish, Unsigned 12.50
Pressed Glass, Paneled Thistle, Sauce, Flared, Marked, 4 3/4 In. 12.50
Pressed Glass, Paneled Thistle, Sauce, 4 1/2 In. 10.00
Pressed Glass, Paneled Thistle, Sugar & Creamer 32.50
Pressed Glass, Paneled Thistle, Sugar, Covered 35.00
Pressed Glass, Paneled Thistle, Sugar, Double Handle 20.00
Pressed Glass, Paneled Thistle, Vase, Footed, 9 In. 25.00
Pressed Glass, Paneled Thistle, Vase, 6 In. .... 6.50 To 28.00
Pressed Glass, Paneled Thistle, Wine .... 20.75 To 22.50
Pressed Glass, Paneled Wheat, Butter, Covered 45.00
Pressed Glass, Paneled Wild Daisy, Creamer 15.00
Pressed Glass, Paneled Wild Daisy, Spooner 13.00
Pressed Glass, Paneled 44, Relish, Green Flash 16.00
Pressed Glass, Paneled 44, Toothpick, Silver Decoration 33.00
Pressed Glass, Paneled, Goblet, Flint 25.00
Pressed Glass, Paneled, Stein, Pewter Top, Amber Jewel Star Inset, 1/2 Liter 45.00
Pressed Glass, Paneled, Toothpick, Silver Decoration 33.00
Pressed Glass, Paris, Compote, High 15.00
Pressed Glass, Parrot & Fan, Goblet 26.00
Pressed Glass, Parrot & Fan, Wine 35.00
Pressed Glass, Parrot, Goblet .... 20.00 To 63.00
Pressed Glass, Parrot, Wine 18.00
     Pattee Cross, see Broughton
Pressed Glass, Pavonia, Celery, Etched 25.00
Pressed Glass, Pavonia, Goblet, Etched .... 20.00 To 22.50
Pressed Glass, Pavonia, Pitcher, Tankard, Etched 35.00
Pressed Glass, Pavonia, Pitcher, Tankard, Ruby Stained, 11 In. 95.00
Pressed Glass, Pavonia, Tumbler .... 8.00 To 20.00
Pressed Glass, Pavonia, Wine 25.00
Pressed Glass, Pavonia, Wine, Pineapple Stem 25.00
Pressed Glass, Peacock Feather, Creamer .... 16.00 To 25.00
Pressed Glass, Peacock Feather, Cruet 22.00
Pressed Glass, Peacock Feather, Dish, 7 In. 21.00
Pressed Glass, Peacock Feather, Fruit Set, 7 Piece 48.00
Pressed Glass, Peacock Feather, Plate, 6 1/2 In. 45.00
Pressed Glass, Peacock Feather, Sugar, Covered 35.00
     Peacock's Eye, see Peacock Feather
Pressed Glass, Pear, Eggcup 18.50
Pressed Glass, Peerless, Eggcup 14.50
Pressed Glass, Peerless, Platter, Oval, Handled, 9 X 13 In. 15.00
     Pennsylvania, see also Balder
Pressed Glass, Pennsylvania, Butter 34.00
Pressed Glass, Pennsylvania, Butter, Child's, Covered 35.00
Pressed Glass, Pennsylvania, Butter, Covered 65.00
Pressed Glass, Pennsylvania, Cake Stand, 7 1/2 X 9 In. 22.50
Pressed Glass, Pennsylvania, Carafe, Water 15.00
Pressed Glass, Pennsylvania, Celery 20.00
Pressed Glass, Pennsylvania, Compote 15.00
Pressed Glass, Pennsylvania, Creamer 20.00
Pressed Glass, Pennsylvania, Creamer, Child's .... 15.00 To 25.00
Pressed Glass, Pennsylvania, Creamer, Gold 20.00
Pressed Glass, Pennsylvania, Goblet .... 15.00 To 38.00
Pressed Glass, Pennsylvania, Goblet, Clear 33.00
Pressed Glass, Pennsylvania, Spooner 20.00
Pressed Glass, Pennsylvania, Sugar, Child's, Covered 30.00
Pressed Glass, Pennsylvania, Syrup 38.00

Pressed Glass, Parrot & Fan, Goblet

Pressed Glass, Pennsylvania, Goblet

Pressed Glass, Pennsylvania, Table Set, 4 Piece	100.00
Pressed Glass, Pennsylvania, Tumbler, Whiskey	8.50
Pressed Glass, Pennsylvania, Water Set, 6 Tumblers & Carafe	90.00
Pressed Glass, Pennsylvania, Whiskey	7.50
Pressed Glass, Pennsylvania, Whiskey Taster, Emerald Green	18.00
Pressed Glass, Pennsylvania, Whiskey, Emerald Green, Gold	18.00
Pressed Glass, Pennsylvania, Wine	16.50 To 17.50
Pressed Glass, Pennsylvania, Wine, Clear, Gold	20.00
Pressed Glass, Pentagon, Cake Stand, 9 In.	35.00
Pressed Glass, Pentagon, Wine	13.50
Pressed Glass, Pentagon, Wine, Etched	17.00
Pressed Glass, Pequot, Butter	28.50
Pressed Glass, Perkins, Cake Stand, 3 In.	18.50
Pressed Glass, Perkins, Mug	18.00
Pressed Glass, Petal & Loop, Candlestick, Canary Yellow, Sandwich Flint, Pair	280.00
Pressed Glass, Petal & Loop, Compote, Sandwich, 9 X 11 1/4 In.	150.00
Pressed Glass, Philadelphia Centennial, Goblet	32.00
Pressed Glass, Phoenix, Compote, Orange, Goldfish, 7 In.	25.00
Pressed Glass, Picket, Compote, High Standard, 9 In.	38.00
Pressed Glass, Picket, Goblet	10.00
Pressed Glass, Picket, Goblet, Clear	36.00
Pressed Glass, Picket, Toothpick	14.00
Pressed Glass, Pigs In Corn, Goblet	115.00 To 225.00
Pillar & Bull's-Eye, see Thistle	
Pressed Glass, Pillar, Bottle, Bar, 8 In.	26.00
Pressed Glass, Pillar, Celery, Hand-Attached Stem & Base, 9 In.	45.00
Pressed Glass, Pillar, Celery, Pittsburgh, 9 3/4 In.	65.00
Pressed Glass, Pillar, Claret, Flint	29.50
Pressed Glass, Pillar, Compote, Low Stem, Bakewell & Pears, 8 In.	75.00
Pressed Glass, Pillar, Syrup, Frosted Pink Spatter	125.00
Pressed Glass, Pillar, Wine	45.00
Pressed Glass, Pillar, Wine, Findlay	20.00
Pressed Glass, Pillow & Sunburst, Wine	12.00
Pressed Glass, Pillow Encircled, Cruet, Enameled Flowers	30.00
Pressed Glass, Pillow Encircled, Sauce	13.50
Pressed Glass, Pillow Encircled, Tankard, Ruby	100.00
Pressed Glass, Pillow Encircled, Tumbler, Ruby Stained	18.50
Pressed Glass, Pillow Encircled, Tumbler, Ruby Stained, Flower Etching	15.00
Pinafore, see Actress	
Pressed Glass, Pineapple & Fan, Ice Bucket, Covered	39.50
Pressed Glass, Pineapple & Fan, Spooner	16.00
Pressed Glass, Pineapple & Fan, Toothpick	30.00
Pressed Glass, Pineapple, Bowl, Scalloped, 10 In.	14.00
Pressed Glass, Pineapple, Muffineer	36.00
Pressed Glass, Pinecone, Sugar Shaker, Pale Green	65.00

Pressed Glass, Pioneer, Compote, Covered, 1885, 12 1/2 In.	38.00
Pressed Glass, Pioneer's White Wing Flour, Platter, 9 X 12 In.	85.00
Pressed Glass, Pitcher, Royal Ivy, Frosted, Rubena	165.00
Pressed Glass, Pittsburgh Daisy, Bowl, Vegetable, Rectangular	20.00
Pressed Glass, Pittsburgh Fan, Goblet	12.00
Pressed Glass, Pittsburgh Flute, Tumbler, Bar, Purple, Flint	110.00
Pressed Glass, Pittsburgh, Candlestick, Canary, Opalescent, Dolphin, Pair	350.00
Plain Smocking, see Smocking	
Pressed Glass, Pleat & Bows, Toothpick, Blue Bows	40.00
Pressed Glass, Pleat & Panel, Cake Stand, Octagonal, High Standard, 8 1/2 In.	25.00
Pressed Glass, Pleat & Panel, Compote, Covered, High Standard, 8 In.	50.00
Pressed Glass, Pleat & Panel, Compote, Covered, Pink, Gold, Pedestal	35.00
Pressed Glass, Pleat & Panel, Compote, Low Standard, Covered, 7 In.	31.50
Pressed Glass, Pleat & Panel, Creamer	29.50
Pressed Glass, Pleat & Panel, Creamer, Blue	29.00
Pressed Glass, Pleat & Panel, Goblet	12.50 To 18.50
Pressed Glass, Pleat & Panel, Pitcher, Milk, 7 In.	28.00
Pressed Glass, Pleat & Panel, Plate, Bread	25.00
Pressed Glass, Pleat & Panel, Plate, Square, 7 In.	17.50
Pressed Glass, Pleat & Panel, Plate, 6 In.	14.50
Pressed Glass, Pleat & Panel, Sauce, Footed, 4 In.	9.50
Pressed Glass, Pleat & Panel, Tray, Large	45.00
Pressed Glass, Pleated Band, Sugar, Footed	9.00
Pressed Glass, Plume, Berry Set, 6 Piece	55.00
Pressed Glass, Plume, Butter, Covered	35.00
Pressed Glass, Plume, Cake Stand, 10 In.	32.00
Pressed Glass, Plume, Cake Stand, 9 In.	30.00
Pressed Glass, Plume, Compote, Flared, High Standard, 7 1/4 In.	27.00
Pressed Glass, Plume, Compote, Open, Scalloped Edge	30.00
Pressed Glass, Plume, Compote, 8 In.	20.00
Pressed Glass, Plume, Creamer	25.00
Pressed Glass, Plume, Goblet	22.00 To 25.00
Pressed Glass, Plume, Sauce, 4 In.	5.00
Pressed Glass, Plume, Sauce, 4 1/4 In.	8.00
Pressed Glass, Plume, Spooner	20.00
Pressed Glass, Pogo Stick, Cake Stand, Low Standard	15.00
Pressed Glass, Pogo Stick, Cruet, Stopper	18.50
Pressed Glass, Pointed Hobnail, Tray, Water, Blue, 11 1/2 In.	28.00
Pressed Glass, Pointed Jewel, Creamer	18.00
Pressed Glass, Pointed Jewel, Goblet	14.00
Pressed Glass, Pointed Jewel, Sugar, Covered, Findlay	35.00
Pressed Glass, Pointed Oval, Wine, Amber	12.00
Pointed Paneled Daisy & Button, see Queen	
Pointed Thumbprint, see Almond Thumbprint	
Pressed Glass, Polar Bear With Seals, Waste Bowl	60.00
Pressed Glass, Polar Bear, Bowl, Waste	28.00

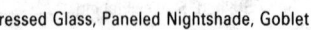

Pressed Glass, Paneled Nightshade, Goblet

Pressed Glass, Paneled Wheat, Compote, Covered, 7 1/2 In.

Pressed Glass, Polar Bear, Bowl, Waste, Frosted .... 50.00 To 65.00
Pressed Glass, Polar Bear, Goblet, Frosted 95.00
Pressed Glass, Polar Bear, Tray, With Seals 165.00
Pressed Glass, Pomona, Toothpick 75.00
Pressed Glass, Popcorn, Goblet .... 20.00 To 29.00
Pressed Glass, Popcorn, Wine 25.00
    Portland with Diamond Point Band, see Galloway, Virginia
Pressed Glass, Portland, Bowl, Covered, Slot For Spoon, 6 1/2 In. 35.00
Pressed Glass, Portland, Candlestick, Scalloped Base, 7 In., Pair 55.00
Pressed Glass, Portland, Creamer, Clear, Gold Tracing, Small 12.00
Pressed Glass, Portland, Creamer, Gold Flashing 13.50
Pressed Glass, Portland, Goblet .... 18.50 To 25.00
Pressed Glass, Portland, Jar, Silver Plated Cover, 5 1/2 In. 22.00
Pressed Glass, Portland, Pitcher, Water, Gold Panels 14.00
Pressed Glass, Portland, Relish, Blue Tree Of Life Insert, Silverplated 135.00
Pressed Glass, Portland, Sauce 6.00
Pressed Glass, Portland, Sauce, Snowdrop, Set Of 6, 6 In. 38.00
Pressed Glass, Portland, Sugar & Creamer, Gold Trim 38.00
Pressed Glass, Portland, Sugar & Creamer, Oval, 2 1/2 In. 20.00
Pressed Glass, Portland, Toothpick 14.50
Pressed Glass, Portland, Vase, Bud 15.00
    Potted Plant, see Flowerpot
Pressed Glass, Powder & Shot, Eggcup, Flint 52.00
Pressed Glass, Powder & Shot, Goblet 48.00
Pressed Glass, Powder & Shot, Goblet, Flint .... 44.00 To 48.50
Pressed Glass, Powder & Shot, Spooner .... 17.00 To 24.00
    Prayer Rug, see Horseshoe
Pressed Glass, President, Plate, Bread 50.00
Pressed Glass, Pressed Diamond, Celery, Amber 20.00
Pressed Glass, Pressed Diamond, Celery, Clear, 7 In. 22.00
Pressed Glass, Pressed Diamond, Cruet, Amber 45.00
Pressed Glass, Pressed Leaf, Spooner 10.00
Pressed Glass, Pretty Maid, Toothpick, Clear 39.00
Pressed Glass, Primrose, Butter 30.00
Pressed Glass, Primrose, Celery 16.00
Pressed Glass, Primrose, Creamer, Apple Green 45.00
Pressed Glass, Primrose, Dish, Pickle 11.00
Pressed Glass, Primrose, Plate, Amber, 2 Handled, 9 In. 30.00
Pressed Glass, Primrose, Plate, Amber, 6 In. 16.50
Pressed Glass, Primrose, Plate, Amber, 7 In. 16.50
Pressed Glass, Primrose, Plate, Blue, 6 In. 16.50
Pressed Glass, Primrose, Plate, 7 In. 13.00
Pressed Glass, Primrose, Sauce, Amber, Footed, 4 1/2 In. 12.50
Pressed Glass, Prince Albert, Pitcher, Water 35.00
    Princess Feather, see also Lacy Medallion
Pressed Glass, Princess Feather, Compote, Covered, High Standard, 8 In. 65.00
Pressed Glass, Princess Feather, Creamer, Applied Handle 55.00
Pressed Glass, Princess Feather, Creamer, Milk, Flint 28.00
Pressed Glass, Princess Feather, Eggcup 25.00
Pressed Glass, Princess Feather, Goblet 29.50
Pressed Glass, Princess Feather, Plate, 6 In. 22.50
Pressed Glass, Princess Feather, Plate, 7 In. 25.00
Pressed Glass, Princess Feather, Plate, 9 In. 35.00
Pressed Glass, Princess Feather, Sauce 8.00
Pressed Glass, Princess Feather, Spooner .... 18.50 To 19.00
Pressed Glass, Princess Feather, Sugar, Covered 55.00
Pressed Glass, Priscilla, Bowl, Flat, 7 In. 33.00
Pressed Glass, Priscilla, Cake Stand 45.00
Pressed Glass, Priscilla, Creamer 20.00
Pressed Glass, Priscilla, Plate, 9 In. 9.50
Pressed Glass, Priscilla, Rose Bowl, 4 1/2 In. 39.00
Pressed Glass, Priscilla, Tumbler 27.50
Pressed Glass, Priscilla, Tumbler, Findlay 22.00
Pressed Glass, Prism & Block Band, Goblet 20.00
Pressed Glass, Prism & Flattened Sawtooth, Spooner, Flint 36.00

Pressed Glass, Prism & Flute, Compote, 8 In.	15.00
Pressed Glass, Prism & Flute, Goblet	15.00
Pressed Glass, Prism & Flute, Sugar, Flint	45.00
Pressed Glass, Prism Arc, Wine	14.00
Pressed Glass, Prism With Ball & Button, Creamer	12.00
Pressed Glass, Prism With Diamond Point, Sugar, Cover	27.00
Pressed Glass, Prism With Loops, Goblet	9.50
Pressed Glass, Prism, Bracket Lamp, Brass Collar, Filler Cap, Burner, Chimney	30.00
Pressed Glass, Prism, Candleholder, 7 In., Pair	35.00
Pressed Glass, Prism, Compote, Flint	8.50
Pressed Glass, Prism, Compote, Flint, 7 1/2 In.	25.00
Pressed Glass, Prism, Eggcup, Flint	18.00
Pressed Glass, Prism, Goblet, Flint	22.50
Pressed Glass, Prism, Goblet, 6 X 3 3/8 In.	35.00
Pressed Glass, Prism, Plate, Flint, 7 3/4 In.	32.00
Pressed Glass, Prism, Spooner, Flint	17.00
Pressed Glass, Psyche & Cupid, Compote, Covered, 6 1/2 In.	43.75
Pressed Glass, Psyche & Cupid, Creamer	27.50
Pressed Glass, Psyche & Cupid, Pitcher, Water	55.00
Pressed Glass, Punty, Tumbler, Miniature, Deep Green, Flint	55.00
Pressed Glass, Quaker Lady, Bowl, Berry, Findlay, 6 1/4 In.	18.50
Pressed Glass, Quartered Block, Creamer	7.00
Pressed Glass, Quartered Block, Vase, 9 1/2 In.	12.50
Queen Anne, see Viking	
Pressed Glass, Queen, Cake Stand, Amber, 9 In.	42.50
Pressed Glass, Queen, Cake Stand, Blue	55.00
Pressed Glass, Queen, Goblet	15.00
Pressed Glass, Queen, Goblet, Amber	17.50
Pressed Glass, Queen's Necklace, Cruet, Matching Findlay Ring-Top Stopper	45.00
Pressed Glass, Queen's Necklace, Salt	22.00
Pressed Glass, Queen's Necklace, Wine	24.00
Pressed Glass, Question Mark, Celery	35.00
Pressed Glass, Question Mark, Cordial	16.00
Pressed Glass, Quilted Phlox, Sugar Shaker, Green, Opaque	65.00
Pressed Glass, Quixote, Cup, Punch	6.00
Pressed Glass, Quixote, Plate, 10 1/2 In.	11.50
Pressed Glass, Quixote, Wine	12.50
Pressed Glass, Racing Deer, Pitcher	95.00
Pressed Glass, Racing Deer, Pitcher, 9 In.	55.00
Pressed Glass, Radiant Daisy, Wine, Gold Trim	10.00
Pressed Glass, Radiant, Pitcher, Water, Galloway	40.00
Pressed Glass, Railroad Train, Bread Plate	65.00
Pressed Glass, Railroad Train, Platter	70.00
Pressed Glass, Rain & Dewdrop, Pitcher	20.00
Pressed Glass, Rainbow, Tumbler, Whiskey	17.00
Pressed Glass, Ramsay Grape, Dish, Cheese	45.00
Pressed Glass, Ray, Mug	12.00
Pressed Glass, Rayed Flower, Cup, Punch	6.00
Pressed Glass, Red Block, Pitcher, Water, Ruby	110.00

Pressed Glass, Pleat & Panel, Bowl

Pressed Glass, Pleat Band, Compote, Covered

Pressed Glass, **Red Block,** Spooner .... 28.00 To 50.00
Pressed Glass, **Red Block,** Spooner, Double Handled 30.00
Pressed Glass, **Red Block,** Sugar, Covered .... 39.00 To 42.00
Pressed Glass, **Red Block,** Sugar, Covered, Extra Flashing 63.00
Pressed Glass, **Red Block,** Tumbler .... 22.00 To 30.00
     Regal, see Paneled Forget-Me-Not
Pressed Glass, **Regal Block,** Wine Set, Gold Trim, 7 Piece 85.00
Pressed Glass, **Regal Block,** Wine, Gold 9.50
Pressed Glass, **Regal,** Creamer, Green, Opalescent 55.00
Pressed Glass, **Regal,** Pitcher, Water, Green, Opalescent 200.00
Pressed Glass, **Reticulated Cord,** Creamer 18.00
Pressed Glass, **Reverse Swirl,** Saltshaker, Vaseline 20.00
Pressed Glass, **Reverse Torpedo,** Banana Boat 95.00
Pressed Glass, **Reverse Torpedo,** Cake Stand 65.00
Pressed Glass, **Reverse Torpedo,** Celery, Etched 35.00
Pressed Glass, **Reverse Torpedo,** Dish, Jelly 18.00
Pressed Glass, **Reverse Torpedo,** Tumbler, Etched 15.00
Pressed Glass, **Reverse Torpedo,** Vase 35.00
Pressed Glass, **Rexford,** Bowl, 9 In. 13.00
Pressed Glass, **Rexford,** Cake Stand, 9 3/4 In. 17.00
Pressed Glass, **Rexford,** Spooner 14.00
Pressed Glass, **Rexford,** Wine 14.00
Pressed Glass, **Ribbed Acorn,** Compote, Scalloped Edge, Flint, 8 In. 45.00
Pressed Glass, **Ribbed Acorn,** Dish, Honey, Flint 13.00
Pressed Glass, **Ribbed Acorn,** Sauce, 4 In. 7.50
Pressed Glass, **Ribbed Bellflower,** Tumbler, 3 3/8 In. 50.00
Pressed Glass, **Ribbed Ellipse,** Celery 14.00
Pressed Glass, **Ribbed Forget-Me-Not,** Mug, Footed 15.00
Pressed Glass, **Ribbed Forget-Me-Not,** Table Set, Child's 80.00
Pressed Glass, **Ribbed Grape,** Compote, Flint, Bellflower Base, Low, 8 In. 87.50
Pressed Glass, **Ribbed Grape,** Plate, Flint, 6 In. .... 22.50 To 45.00
Pressed Glass, **Ribbed Grape,** Plate, 6 In. 25.00
Pressed Glass, **Ribbed Grape,** Sauce, Flint, 4 In. 12.50
Pressed Glass, **Ribbed Grape,** Sugar, Flint, Covered 85.00
Pressed Glass, **Ribbed Ivy,** Butter, Covered, Flint 95.00
Pressed Glass, **Ribbed Ivy,** Eggcup .... 24.00 To 27.50
Pressed Glass, **Ribbed Ivy,** Eggcup, Flint .... 20.00 To 22.00
Pressed Glass, **Ribbed Ivy,** Goblet, Flint 27.50
Pressed Glass, **Ribbed Ivy,** Salt, Covered 120.00
Pressed Glass, **Ribbed Ivy,** Sauce, 4 In. 10.50
Pressed Glass, **Ribbed Ivy,** Sauce, 4 In., Flint 12.00
Pressed Glass, **Ribbed Ivy,** Spooner, Flint .... 38.00 To 55.00
Pressed Glass, **Ribbed Ivy,** Whiskey 50.00
Pressed Glass, **Ribbed Ivy,** Whiskey, Flint .... 40.00 To 52.50
Pressed Glass, **Ribbed Lattice,** Blue, Opalescent 45.00
Pressed Glass, **Ribbed Lattice,** Sugar Shaker, Blue Opalescent 60.00
Pressed Glass, **Ribbed Lattice,** Toothpick, Cranberry Opalescent 60.00
     Ribbed Leaf, see Bellflower
     Ribbed Opal, see Beatty Rib
Pressed Glass, **Ribbed Palm,** Castor Set, Silver Plated Holder 75.00
Pressed Glass, **Ribbed Palm,** Eggcup 24.00
Pressed Glass, **Ribbed Palm,** Eggcup, Double, Flint 17.00
Pressed Glass, **Ribbed Palm,** Eggcup, Flint .... 22.50 To 24.50
Pressed Glass, **Ribbed Palm,** Goblet 22.50
Pressed Glass, **Ribbed Palm,** Goblet, Flint .... 23.00 To 38.50
Pressed Glass, **Ribbed Palm,** Pitcher, Flint, 8 1/2 In. 150.00
Pressed Glass, **Ribbed Palm,** Plate, Flint, 6 In. 48.50
Pressed Glass, **Ribbed Palm,** Sauce, Flint 6.00
Pressed Glass, **Ribbed Palm,** Sauce, 4 In. 9.50
Pressed Glass, **Ribbed Palm,** Spooner .... 30.00 To 40.00
Pressed Glass, **Ribbed Palm,** Sugar, Covered, Flint 52.50
Pressed Glass, **Ribbed Palm,** Wine, Flint 55.00
     Ribbed Pineapple, see Prism & Flattened Sawtooth
Pressed Glass, **Ribbed Scroll,** Sugar Shaker, White, Opaque 30.00

Pressed Glass, Primrose, Pitcher, 7 In.

Pressed Glass, Princess Feather, Spooner

Pressed Glass, Princess Feather, Tazza

Pressed Glass, Prism With Diamond Point, Salt, Master

Pressed Glass, **Ribbed Spiral**, Spooner, Blue Opalescent	50.00
Pressed Glass, **Ribbed Spiral**, Toothpick, Canary Opalescent	47.00
Pressed Glass, **Ribbed**, Creamer, Opalescent, Flint	25.00
Pressed Glass, **Ribbon Candy**, Butter, Covered	26.50
Pressed Glass, **Ribbon Candy**, Cake Stand, Child's	26.00
Pressed Glass, **Ribbon Candy**, Cake Stand, 8 1/4 In.	22.00
Pressed Glass, **Ribbon Candy**, Cake Stand, 9 1/2 In.	25.00
Pressed Glass, **Ribbon Candy**, Cocktail, Tall, Stemmed, Red	12.00
Pressed Glass, **Ribbon Candy**, Compote, 5 3/4 In.	18.00
Pressed Glass, **Ribbon Candy**, Doughnut Stand, Miniature, 7 In.	23.50
Pressed Glass, **Ribbon Candy**, Pitcher, Milk	28.00
Pressed Glass, **Ribbon Candy**, Spooner	13.50 To 15.00
Pressed Glass, **Ribbon Candy**, Spooner, Footed	25.00
Pressed Glass, **Ribbon Candy**, Sugar, Open	12.00
Pressed Glass, **Ribbon**, Cake Stand, Clear, 8 1/2 In.	26.00
Pressed Glass, **Ribbon**, Compote, Frosted, 8 1/4 In.	15.00
Pressed Glass, **Ribbon**, Compote, Silver Plated Frame, C.1850, 11 X 10 1/2 In.	95.00
Pressed Glass, **Ribbon**, Goblet, Frosted	24.00
Pressed Glass, **Ribbon**, Sauce, Footed, 3 3/4 In.	10.00
Pressed Glass, **Ribbon**, Sauce, 3 1/3 In. Square	6.00
Pressed Glass, **Ribbon**, Spooner	28.00
Pressed Glass, **Ribbon**, Sugar, Covered, Frosted	29.50
Ripple Band, see Ripple	
Pressed Glass, **Ripple**, Eggcup	15.00
Pressed Glass, **Ripple**, Spooner	15.00
Pressed Glass, **Ripple**, Wine	12.00
Pressed Glass, **Rising Sun**, Compote, Jelly, Scalloped Top Red Sun, 3 1/2 In.	11.00
Pressed Glass, **Robin Hood**, Butter	27.50
Rochelle, see Princess Feather	

Pressed Glass, Rock Crystal, Glass, Juice, 3 1/2 In.	4.00
Pressed Glass, Rock Crystal, Pitcher, Milk	27.00
Pressed Glass, Rock Of Ages, Platter, Milk Glass Center, 7 X 9 In.	125.00
Pressed Glass, Roman Key, Celery, Flint, Frosted, Pair	125.00
Pressed Glass, Roman Key, Compote, Flint, 7 In.	35.00
Pressed Glass, Roman Key, Compote, Frosted, 5 In.	30.00
Pressed Glass, Roman Key, Decanter, Flint	125.00
Pressed Glass, Roman Key, Frosted, Compote, Stemmed, 6 X 5 1/2 In., C.1880	45.00
Pressed Glass, Roman Key, Frosted, 4 In.	8.50
Pressed Glass, Roman Key, Goblet	15.00
Pressed Glass, Roman Key, Goblet, Flint	40.00
Pressed Glass, Roman Key, Goblet, Flint, Frosted	25.00
Pressed Glass, Roman Key, Sugar, Frosted, Open	20.00
Pressed Glass, Roman Key, Sugar, Open, Flint	20.00
Pressed Glass, Roman Key, Tumbler, Flint, Clear	39.50
Pressed Glass, Roman Key, Whiskey	75.00
Pressed Glass, Roman Rosette, Butter, Covered	35.00
Pressed Glass, Roman Rosette, Cake Stand	49.50
Pressed Glass, Roman Rosette, Compote, 4 1/2 In.	22.00
Pressed Glass, Roman Rosette, Creamer	13.50 To 25.00
Pressed Glass, Roman Rosette, Goblet	17.50
Pressed Glass, Roman Rosette, Plate, Bread	22.00
Pressed Glass, Roman Rosette, Platter	18.00
Pressed Glass, Roman Rosette, Platter, 8 1/2 X 11 In.	15.00
Pressed Glass, Roman Rosette, Salt	10.00
Pressed Glass, Roman Rosette, Salt & Pepper	17.00
Pressed Glass, Roman Rosette, Sugar	28.00
Pressed Glass, Roman Rosette, Sugar, Covered	35.00
Pressed Glass, Romeo, Goblet	14.50
Pressed Glass, Roosevelt Teddy Bears, Jar, Milk Glass Cover	40.00
Pressed Glass, Roosevelt Teddy Bears, Platter	67.50
Pressed Glass, Roosevelt Teddy Bears, Tray, Bread, Frosted Center, Bear Border	55.00
Pressed Glass, Roosevelt, Platter, Bread, Frosted Center	55.00
Pressed Glass, Rope & Thumbprint, Syrup	40.00
Rope Bands, see Clear Panels with Cord Band	
Pressed Glass, Rose Cameo, Tumbler, Green, Footed	10.00
Pressed Glass, Rose Delaware, Toothpick, Gold Trim	60.00
Pressed Glass, Rose In Snow, Compote, Covered, 8 In.	65.00
Pressed Glass, Rose In Snow, Compote, Open, 7 X 6 3/4 In.	34.00
Pressed Glass, Rose In Snow, Compote, Tall	22.00
Pressed Glass, Rose In Snow, Compote, 6 1/4 In.	50.00
Pressed Glass, Rose In Snow, Creamer, Square	30.00
Pressed Glass, Rose In Snow, Goblet, Blue	25.00
Pressed Glass, Rose In Snow, Goblet, Clear	29.00
Pressed Glass, Rose In Snow, Goblet, Vaseline	34.00
Pressed Glass, Rose In Snow, Pitcher, Water	75.00 To 125.00
Pressed Glass, Rose In Snow, Plate, 6 In.	17.50
Pressed Glass, Rose In Snow, Plate, 7 1/4 In.	27.50
Pressed Glass, Rose In Snow, Plate, 9 1/2 In.	15.00 To 20.00
Pressed Glass, Rose In Snow, Relish, Handled	18.00
Pressed Glass, Rose In Snow, Sauce	10.00
Pressed Glass, Rose In Snow, Sauce, 4 In.	3.00
Pressed Glass, Rose In Snow, Spooner	28.00
Pressed Glass, Rose In Snow, Tray, Bread	20.00
Pressed Glass, Rose In Snow, Tumbler, Handled	24.50
Pressed Glass, Rose Sprig, Cake Stand, Amber, Octagon, 9 In.	47.50
Pressed Glass, Rose Sprig, Cake Stand, Amber, 9 1/4 In.	45.00
Pressed Glass, Rose Sprig, Celery	22.50
Pressed Glass, Rose Sprig, Pitcher, Water	45.00
Pressed Glass, Rose Sprig, Plate, Blue, Handled, 6 1/2 In.Square	22.50
Pressed Glass, Rose Sprig, Sauce, Blue, 4 X 4 1/2 In.	13.50
Pressed Glass, Rose, Creamer, Gold, Green	55.00
Rosette Medallion, see Feather Duster	
Pressed Glass, Rosette With Palms, Cake Stand, 9 1/2 In.	25.00
Pressed Glass, Rosette With Palms, Celery	16.00

Pressed Glass, Rosette With Palms, Wine 16.00
Pressed Glass, Rosette, Butter 23.00
Pressed Glass, Rosette, Celery 17.50
Pressed Glass, Rosette, Goblet 22.00
Pressed Glass, Rosette, Mug, Blue 29.50
Pressed Glass, Rosette, Pitcher, 7 In. 30.00
Pressed Glass, Rosette, Plate, Handled, 9 In. 12.50
Pressed Glass, Rosette, Spooner 17.00
Pressed Glass, Rosette, Sugar, Covered 25.00
Pressed Glass, Royal Crystal, Compote, Open, 7 1/2 In. 21.50
Pressed Glass, Royal Crystal, Cruet, Clear 25.00
Pressed Glass, Royal Crystal, Sauce 9.00
Pressed Glass, Royal Crystal, Syrup, Clear 36.00
Pressed Glass, Royal Crystal, Table Set, Ruby & Clear, 4 Piece 225.00
Pressed Glass, Royal Crystal, Water Set, Ruby Stained, 4 Piece 245.00
Pressed Glass, Royal Crystal, Water Set, Ruby Stained, 4 Piece 265.00
Pressed Glass, Royal Ivy, Berry Set, Cranberry To Clear, 6 Piece 250.00
Pressed Glass, Royal Ivy, Bowl, Berry, Cranberry To Clear 135.00
Pressed Glass, Royal Ivy, Bowl, Cranberry To Clear 125.00
Pressed Glass, Royal Ivy, Bowl, Cranberry Top, Clear Bottom, Large 175.00
Pressed Glass, Royal Ivy, Creamer, Clear, Frosted 70.00
Pressed Glass, Royal Ivy, Creamer, Cranberry To Clear 140.00
Pressed Glass, Royal Ivy, Pitcher, Clear, Frosted, 5 In. 60.00
Pressed Glass, Royal Ivy, Pitcher, Cranberry To Clear 175.00
Pressed Glass, Royal Ivy, Pitcher, Water, Amber Spatter .... 275.00 To 300.00
Pressed Glass, Royal Ivy, Pitcher, Water, Cased Spatter, Northwood 300.00
Pressed Glass, Royal Ivy, Pitcher, Water, Clear, Frosted 235.00
Pressed Glass, Royal Ivy, Pitcher, Water, Cranberry To Clear 195.00
Pressed Glass, Royal Ivy, Pitcher, Water, Cranberry To Clear Frosted 200.00
Pressed Glass, Royal Ivy, Salt 34.00
Pressed Glass, Royal Ivy, Salt & Pepper, Cranberry To Clear 58.00
Pressed Glass, Royal Ivy, Sauce, Frosted 22.00
Pressed Glass, Royal Ivy, Sugar Shaker, Cranberry To Clear .... 110.00 To 125.00
Pressed Glass, Royal Ivy, Sugar Shaker, Frosted 39.00
Pressed Glass, Royal Ivy, Sugar, Clear, Frosted 50.00
Pressed Glass, Royal Ivy, Toothpick, Cranberry To Clear 65.00
Pressed Glass, Royal Ivy, Toothpick, Rainbow, Crackle 70.00
Pressed Glass, Royal Ivy, Tumbler, Cranberry To Clear, Frosted, 3 3/4 In. 65.00
Pressed Glass, Royal King, Wine, Souvenir, Ruby Stained 18.00
Pressed Glass, Royal Lace, Salt & Pepper, Green 65.00
Pressed Glass, Royal Lace, Salt & Pepper, Pink 24.00
Pressed Glass, Royal Oak, Butter, Cranberry To Clear, Frosted 210.00
Pressed Glass, Royal Oak, Creamer, Cranberry To Clear 120.00
Pressed Glass, Royal Oak, Jar, Clear And Frosted 30.00

Pressed Glass, Viking, Compote, Covered

Pressed Glass, Punty, Syrup, Opalescent

Pressed Glass, Royal Oak, Jar, Cranberry To Clear, Large 60.00
Pressed Glass, Royal Oak, Pitcher, Water, Cranberry To Clear 200.00
Pressed Glass, Royal Oak, Salt & Pepper, Cranberry To Clear, Frosted 85.00
Pressed Glass, Royal Oak, Sugar Shaker, Clear, Frosted 35.00
Pressed Glass, Royal Oak, Tumbler, Cranberry To Frosted, 3 3/4 In. 55.00
Pressed Glass, Royal, Compote, High Standard, Covered, 7 In. 37.50
　Ruby Rosette, see Pillow Encircled
　Ruby Thumbprint, see King's Crown
Pressed Glass, Ruffles & Rings, Bowl, Green, Opalescent, C.1905, 9 In. 45.00
Pressed Glass, Ruffles & Rings, Bowl, Opalescent, Clear, Footed, 9 In. 30.00
Pressed Glass, S Repeat, Pitcher, Water 65.00
Pressed Glass, S Repeat, Sugar, Apple Green, White & Gold Enamel Decoration 47.00
Pressed Glass, S Repeat, Tumbler, Amethyst 16.00
Pressed Glass, S Repeat, Water Set, Blue, 5 Piece 260.00
Pressed Glass, S Repeat, Wine, Gold Trim 20.00
　Sandwich Loop, see Hairpin
Pressed Glass, Sandwich Overshot, Pitcher, Water, Tankard 65.00
Pressed Glass, Sandwich Petal, Salt, Master, Flint 15.00
Pressed Glass, Sandwich Star, Goblet, Flint 350.00
Pressed Glass, Sandwich Star, Spill, Flint 65.00
Pressed Glass, Sandwich Star, Wine 250.00
Pressed Glass, Sandwich Tulip, Celery, Clear, Flint 45.00
Pressed Glass, Sandwich, Candlestick, Child's, Pontil 35.00
Pressed Glass, Sandwich, Dish, Oval, Deep, Flint, 8 X 6 In. 185.00
Pressed Glass, Santa Maria, Plate, 7 In. 15.00
Pressed Glass, Sawtooth & Star, Sauce, 4 In. 4.50
Pressed Glass, Sawtooth Circle, Salt, Footed, Flint 18.50
　Sawtooth with Panels, see Hinoto
Pressed Glass, Sawtooth, Butter, Covered 35.00
Pressed Glass, Sawtooth, Butter, Covered, Flint 85.00
Pressed Glass, Sawtooth, Celery, Knob Stem, 9 1/2 In. 32.00
Pressed Glass, Sawtooth, Champagne, Flint 60.00
Pressed Glass, Sawtooth, Champagne, Straight Side, Knob Stem 35.00
Pressed Glass, Sawtooth, Compote, Flint, Covered, Low Standard, 8 In. 125.00
Pressed Glass, Sawtooth, Compote, Flint, Knob Stem, 9 1/2 X 10 In. 75.00
Pressed Glass, Sawtooth, Compote, Flint, 7 1/2 In. 38.00
Pressed Glass, Sawtooth, Compote, Knob Stem, 9 1/2 X 10 In. 75.00
Pressed Glass, Sawtooth, Compote, Low Foot, Flint, 7 1/4 X 8 1/4 In. 65.00
Pressed Glass, Sawtooth, Creamer, Child's 20.00
Pressed Glass, Sawtooth, Creamer, Flint, Ovoid, Applied Handle 85.00
Pressed Glass, Sawtooth, Creamer, 6 In. 58.00
Pressed Glass, Sawtooth, Cruet, Applied Handle, Sawtooth & Acorn Stopper 125.00
Pressed Glass, Sawtooth, Dish, Honey, Flint, 3 1/2 In. 7.50
Pressed Glass, Sawtooth, Eggcup, Flint .... 12.50 To 35.00
Pressed Glass, Sawtooth, Goblet 10.00
Pressed Glass, Sawtooth, Pitcher, Milk, Applied Handle 65.00
Pressed Glass, Sawtooth, Salt, Covered 55.00
Pressed Glass, Sawtooth, Salt, Flint 29.50
Pressed Glass, Sawtooth, Salt, Flint, Fiery Opalescence 145.00
Pressed Glass, Sawtooth, Salt, Master, Footed, Flint 20.00
Pressed Glass, Sawtooth, Salt, Master, Footed, Opalescent, Flint 40.00
Pressed Glass, Sawtooth, Spooner 15.00
Pressed Glass, Sawtooth, Spooner, Flint .... 22.00 To 29.50
Pressed Glass, Sawtooth, Spooner, Miniature 14.00
Pressed Glass, Sawtooth, Spooner, Opaque White, Opalescent, Flint 24.00
Pressed Glass, Sawtooth, Sugar, Open, Opaque White, Opalescent, Flint 17.00
Pressed Glass, Sawtooth, Table Set, Flint, 4 Piece 120.00
Pressed Glass, Sawtooth, Table Set, Miniature, Flint, 4 Piece 90.00
Pressed Glass, Sawtooth, Tumbler, Flint, Footed 35.00
Pressed Glass, Sawtooth, Wine, Flint 52.50
Pressed Glass, Sawtooth, Wine, Knob Stem, Flint 22.50
Pressed Glass, Scallop & Bull's-Eye, Goblet, Amber 10.50
Pressed Glass, Scallop Shell, Pitcher, Water 25.00
Pressed Glass, Scalloped Diamond Point, Plate, 5 1/4 In. 8.00
Pressed Glass, Scalloped Diamond Point, Plate, 8 In. 10.00

Pressed Glass, Scalloped Tape, Compote, Hand Stem, Amber, 8 1/2 In. 27.00
Pressed Glass, Scalloped Tape, Creamer 16.00
Pressed Glass, Scarab, Champagne, Flint 85.00
Pressed Glass, Scroll With Acanthus, Compote, Jelly 45.00
Pressed Glass, Scroll With Cane Band, Celery, Amber Stain 70.00
Pressed Glass, Scroll With Cane Band, Toothpick, Ruby Stained 45.00
Pressed Glass, Scroll With Flowers, Cake Stand 28.00
Pressed Glass, Scroll With Flowers, Creamer 17.50
Pressed Glass, Scroll With Flowers, Goblet 27.00
Pressed Glass, Scroll With Flowers, Pitcher, Water 38.50
Pressed Glass, Scroll With Flowers, Sugar, Covered 25.00
Pressed Glass, Scroll, Celery 18.00
Pressed Glass, Scroll, Eggcup 15.00
Pressed Glass, Scroll, Goblet 16.50
Pressed Glass, Scroll, Sugar, Covered 22.00
Pressed Glass, Scrolled Spray, Sugar & Creamer, Blue 95.00
Pressed Glass, Seashell, Creamer 40.00
Pressed Glass, Sedan, Wine 12.00
Pressed Glass, Seed Pod, Pitcher, Green & Gold 125.00
Pressed Glass, Seneca Loop, Compote, Scalloped Rim, 4 X 6 1/2 X 8 In. 65.00

Pressed Glass, Rexford, Goblet

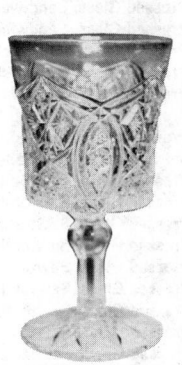

Pressed Glass, Sequoia, Tumbler, Etched 11.50
Pressed Glass, Serrated Prism, Cruet 16.00
Pressed Glass, Sexton Flute, Eggcup, Flint 13.50
Pressed Glass, Sheaf & Block, Pitcher, Water, Ruby Stained, 7 1/4 In. 50.00
Pressed Glass, Sheaf & Block, Wine 9.50
Pressed Glass, Sheaf Of Wheat, Pitcher 32.00
Pressed Glass, Sheaf Of Wheat, Platter 35.00
Pressed Glass, Shell & Jewel, Berry Set, 7 Piece .... 25.00 To 33.00
Pressed Glass, Shell & Jewel, Butter 29.50
Pressed Glass, Shell & Jewel, Pitcher, Water .... 20.00 To 25.00
Pressed Glass, Shell & Jewel, Pitcher, Water, Blue .... 69.50 To 75.00
Pressed Glass, Shell & Jewel, Pitcher, Water, Clear 39.00
Pressed Glass, Shell & Jewel, Sugar & Creamer 30.00
Pressed Glass, Shell & Jewel, Tumbler .... 14.00 To 14.50
Pressed Glass, Shell & Jewel, Tumbler, Blue 22.00
Pressed Glass, Shell & Jewel, Tumbler, Green 25.00
Pressed Glass, Shell & Jewel, Tumbler, Water 14.50
Pressed Glass, Shell & Jewel, Water Set, Green, 7 Piece 110.00
Pressed Glass, Shell & Tassel, Cake Stand, Square, 11 In. 55.00
Pressed Glass, Shell & Tassel, Cake Stand, Square, 8 In. 32.00
Pressed Glass, Shell & Tassel, Celery, Square .... 32.00 To 38.00
Pressed Glass, Shell & Tassel, Compote, Open, Large 25.00
Pressed Glass, Shell & Tassel, Compote, Open, 7 3/4 In. 30.00
Pressed Glass, Shell & Tassel, Compote, Open, 8 1/2 In. 35.00
Pressed Glass, Shell & Tassel, Compote, Square, High Standard, 7 X 7 1/2 In. 35.00
Pressed Glass, Shell & Tassel, Compote, Square, 7 1/4 X 8 In. 45.00
Pressed Glass, Shell & Tassel, Compote, 4 1/2 X 4 3/4 In. 48.00

Pressed Glass, Ribbon, Etched, Goblet

Pressed Glass, Roman Cross, Goblet

Pressed Glass, Robin, Mug, Blue

Pressed Glass, Shell & Tassel, Creamer	40.00
Pressed Glass, Shell & Tassel, Goblet	38.00
Pressed Glass, Shell & Tassel, Oblong, Plate, Bread	40.00
Pressed Glass, Shell & Tassel, Relish, Etched	45.00
Pressed Glass, Shell & Tassel, Relish, 8 X 5 1/4 In.	25.00
Pressed Glass, Shell & Tassel, Sauce, Footed, Square, 4 1/2 In.	10.50
Pressed Glass, Shell & Tassel, Sauce, Porringer Handles	11.50
Pressed Glass, Shell & Tassel, Sauce, 4 In.	4.50
Pressed Glass, Shell & Tassel, Sauce, 4 1/2 In.	7.50
Pressed Glass, Shell & Tassel, Sugar, Covered, Dog Finial, Round	65.00 To 85.00
Pressed Glass, Shell & Tassel, Tray, Oblong, 14 X 8 In.	57.50
Pressed Glass, Sheraton, Butter, Covered	32.50
Pressed Glass, Sheraton, Goblet	22.00
Pressed Glass, Sheraton, Pitcher, Milk	18.50
Pressed Glass, Sheraton, Pitcher, Water	14.75
Pressed Glass, Sheraton, Platter, Amber	23.50
Pressed Glass, Shield, Condiment Set, Miniature, Pewter Holder, 1876	45.00
Pressed Glass, Shield, Platter, Amethyst	150.00
Pressed Glass, Shield, Platter, Blue	125.00
Pressed Glass, Short Ribs, Goblet	17.50
Pressed Glass, Short Ribs, Wine	10.00
Short Teasel, see Teasel	
Pressed Glass, Shoshone, Cake Stand, Green	38.00
Pressed Glass, Shoshone, Cake Stand, 4 1/2 X 9 In.	22.00
Pressed Glass, Shoshone, Cruet	96.00
Pressed Glass, Shoshone, Cruet, Emerald Green, Stopper	95.00
Pressed Glass, Shoshone, Cruet, Faceted Stopper	18.00
Pressed Glass, Shoshone, Cup, Punch	8.00
Pressed Glass, Shoshone, Salt, Gold Trim	8.50
Pressed Glass, Shoshone, Spooner	16.00
Pressed Glass, Shoshone, Toothpick	12.50
Pressed Glass, Shoshone, Toothpick, Clear, Gold	15.00
Pressed Glass, Shovel, Goblet	10.00
Pressed Glass, Shrine, Bowl, Flat, 7 1/2 In.	20.00
Pressed Glass, Shrine, Butter	38.00
Pressed Glass, Shrine, Pitcher, Water	42.50 To 48.50
Pressed Glass, Shrine, Spconer	16.00
Pressed Glass, Shrine, Toothpick	30.00

Pressed Glass, **Shrine,** Tumbler, Lemonade 25.00
Pressed Glass, **Shuttle,** Cup, Punch 6.00
Pressed Glass, **Shuttle,** Pitcher, Water, Clear 22.00
Pressed Glass, **Shuttle,** Tumbler, Clear 8.00
Pressed Glass, **Shuttle,** Wine .... 10.00 To 13.50
Pressed Glass, **Signers,** Plate, Bread 50.00
Pressed Glass, **Singing Birds,** Creamer, N 37.00
Pressed Glass, **Single Rose,** Tumbler, Green 12.50
Pressed Glass, **Six Panel Finecut,** Goblet, Etched 22.50
Pressed Glass, **Six Panel Finecut,** Tumbler, Amber Stripes 27.50
Pressed Glass, **Slim Crystal,** Goblet, Flint 25.00
Pressed Glass, **Smocking,** Wine, Knob Stem, Flint 30.00
Pressed Glass, **Snail,** Butter, Covered .... 35.00 To 75.00
Pressed Glass, **Snail,** Jug, Syrup, Stopper 8.00
Pressed Glass, **Snail,** Pitcher, Water 50.00
Pressed Glass, **Snail,** Saltshaker 17.00
Pressed Glass, **Snail,** Sugar, Covered 59.00
Pressed Glass, **Snail,** Vase, 12 1/2 In. 28.00
Pressed Glass, **Snake Drape,** Goblet 15.00
Pressed Glass, **Snakeskin & Dot,** Compote, Covered, 12 1/2 In. 75.00
Pressed Glass, **Snakeskin & Dot,** Goblet 18.50
Pressed Glass, **Snakeskin,** Berry Set, Shell Shaped, 9 Pieces 45.00
Pressed Glass, **Snow Band,** Goblet 7.00
Pressed Glass, **Snow Bank,** Goblet 12.50
Pressed Glass, **Snowdrop,** Plate, 6 In. 5.00
Pressed Glass, **Snowdrop,** Sauce, Pear Shape 3.50
    Spanish American, see Admiral Dewey
    Spanish Coin, see Columbian Coin

Pressed Glass, Roman Rosette, Sugar & Creamer

Pressed Glass, Rose In Snow, Goblet

Pressed Glass, **Spear Point Band,** Compote, 4 3/4 In. 12.50
Pressed Glass, **Spear Point Band,** Tumbler 10.00
Pressed Glass, **Spear,** Butter 38.00
Pressed Glass, **Spirea Band,** Butter, Amber, Covered 34.00
Pressed Glass, **Spirea Band,** Cake Stand, Blue, 10 1/2 In. 55.00
Pressed Glass, **Spirea Band,** Compote, Covered, 7 1/4 In. 40.00
Pressed Glass, **Spirea Band,** Goblet, Amber .... 20.00 To 30.00
Pressed Glass, **Spirea Band,** Platter, Blue, 8 1/2 X 10 1/2 In. 18.00
Pressed Glass, **Spirea Band,** Relish, Amber, Handled 12.00
Pressed Glass, **Spirea Band,** Sauce, Amber, Footed 12.00
Pressed Glass, **Spirea Band,** Tray, Bread, Blue, 8 1/2 X 11 In. .... 22.00 To 22.50
Pressed Glass, **Spirea Band,** Wine, Blue .... 30.00 To 35.00
Pressed Glass, **Sprig,** Bowl, Master Berry, Blue 325.00
Pressed Glass, **Sprig,** Cake Stand, 8 In. 30.00
Pressed Glass, **Sprig,** Compote, Low, Open 18.00
Pressed Glass, **Sprig,** Goblet 20.00

Pressed Glass, Rose Sprig, Goblet

Pressed Glass, Royal, Butter, Covered

Pressed Glass, Sawtooth, Jar, Pomade

Pressed Glass, Sprig, Wine	22.00
Pressed Glass, Squared Star, Spooner	12.00
Pressed Glass, Squirrel With Nut, Pitcher, Water	96.00
Pressed Glass, Squirrel, Pitcher, Water	110.00 To 150.00
Pressed Glass, St.Louis Exposition, Tumbler, Louisiana Purchase, Buildings	22.50
Pressed Glass, Star & Dewdrop, Butter, Covered	45.00
Pressed Glass, Star & Feather, Plate, Amber, 7 In.	17.50
Pressed Glass, Star & Oval, Celery	20.00
Star & Punty, see Moon & Star	
Pressed Glass, Star Arches, Bowl, Miniature, Set Of 6	25.00
Pressed Glass, Star Arches, Bowl, Punch, Child's	18.00
Star Band, see also Bosworth	
Pressed Glass, Star Band, Goblet	15.00
Pressed Glass, Star Band, Sugar & Creamer	20.00
Pressed Glass, Star Galaxy, Goblet	29.00
Pressed Glass, Star In Bull's-Eye, Bowl, Gold Edge, 10 In.	16.00
Pressed Glass, Star In Bull's-Eye, Mug, Gold	7.50
Pressed Glass, Star In Bull's-Eye, Toothpick, Reversible, Gold Trim	14.50
Pressed Glass, Star In Bull's-Eye, Wine	10.00
Pressed Glass, Star In Honeycomb, Goblet	22.00
Pressed Glass, Star In Honeycomb, Wine	22.00
Pressed Glass, Star Medallion, Bowl, 6 In.	7.00
Pressed Glass, Star Medallion, Creamer	10.00
Pressed Glass, Star Medallion, Spooner	12.00
Pressed Glass, Star Of Bethlehem, Tumbler	24.50
Pressed Glass, Star Of David, Compote, Open, Footed, 8 X 5 1/2 In.	35.00
Pressed Glass, Star Rosetted, Goblet	15.00 To 20.00
Pressed Glass, Star Rosetted, Plate, Green, 7 In.	12.50
Pressed Glass, Star Rosetted, Platter, Good Mother, 10 1/2 In.	18.50 To 25.00
Pressed Glass, Star Rosetted, Relish, 6 In.	8.00
Pressed Glass, Star Rosetted, Relish, 9 In.	10.00 To 14.50

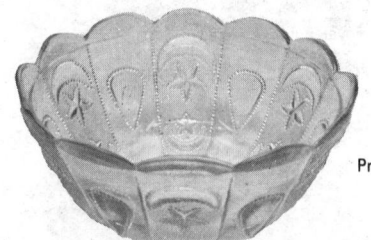

Pressed Glass, Shrine, Bowl

Pressed Glass, Star Rosetted, Spill, Flint	30.00
Pressed Glass, Star Rosetted, Spooner, Clear	15.00
Pressed Glass, Starred Block, Compote, Open, 7 In.	35.00
Pressed Glass, Starred Block, Spooner	20.00
Pressed Glass, Starred Block, Tumbler, Etched	18.00
Pressed Glass, Starred Cosmos, Butter	27.50
Pressed Glass, Stars & Bars, Butter, Footed, Etched	28.00
Pressed Glass, Stars & Bars, Cruet Set, Dark Amber	50.00
Pressed Glass, Stars & Bars, Cruet, Blue, Square Patterned Stopper	48.00
Pressed Glass, Stars & Bars, Cruet, Original Stopper, Amber, Findlay	65.00
Pressed Glass, Stars & Bars, Salt, Findlay	8.50
Pressed Glass, Stars & Bars, Tumbler, Cranberry, Opalescent	25.00
Pressed Glass, Stars & Stripes, Cordial	7.50
Pressed Glass, Stars & Stripes, Creamer, Clear	10.00
Pressed Glass, Stars & Stripes, Tumbler	32.50
Pressed Glass, States, Bowl, Emerald Green, Gold Rim, 4 X 5 1/2 In.	30.00
Pressed Glass, States, Bowl, Emerald Green, Round, Pulled-Out Top, 5 1/2 In.	30.00
Pressed Glass, States, Creamer	15.00
Pressed Glass, States, Toothpick, Flat	35.00
Pressed Glass, States, Tumbler	17.50
Pressed Glass, States, Wine, Flared, Gold Trim	16.00
Pressed Glass, Statue Of Liberty, Jar, 12 1/2 In.	72.00
Stayman, see Tidy	
Pressed Glass, Stedman, Champagne, Flint	27.50
Pressed Glass, Stedman, Eggcup, Flint	22.00
Pressed Glass, Stedman, Goblet	20.00
Pressed Glass, Stedman, Goblet, Barrel Shape, Flint	27.50
Pressed Glass, Stippled Arrow, Mug, Child's	10.00
Pressed Glass, Stippled Band, Goblet	12.00
Pressed Glass, Stippled Cherry, Pitcher, Water	30.00
Pressed Glass, Stippled Cherry, Tray, Bread, Our Daily Bread	25.00
Stippled Dahlia, see Dahlia	
Pressed Glass, Stippled Double Loop, Creamer	12.00
Pressed Glass, Stippled Fleur-De-Lis, Tumbler, Green	22.00
Pressed Glass, Stippled Forget-Me-Not, Cup, Findlay	15.00
Pressed Glass, Stippled Grape & Festoon, Celery, 1870	40.00
Pressed Glass, Stippled Grape & Festoon, Clear Leaf, Spooner	24.00 To 28.00
Pressed Glass, Stippled Grape & Festoon, Goblet	22.50
Pressed Glass, Stippled Grape & Festoon, Spooner	18.00
Pressed Glass, Stippled Grape & Festoon, Sugar & Creamer, Applied Handles	50.00
Pressed Glass, Stippled Ivy, Eggcup	20.00
Pressed Glass, Stippled Ivy, Spooner	32.00
Pressed Glass, Stippled Loop, Goblet	12.50
Pressed Glass, Stippled Magnet & Grape, Wine, Clear	22.00
Pressed Glass, Stippled Medallion, Eggcup, Flint	23.00
Stippled Paneled Flower, see Maine	
Pressed Glass, Stippled Sandburr, Dish, Pickle	8.00
Stippled Scroll, see Scroll	
Stippled Star Variant, see Stippled Sandburr	
Pressed Glass, Stippled Star, Spooner	15.00

Pressed Glass, Stork, Goblet, Clear, Frosted 55.00
Pressed Glass, Stork, Pitcher, Water, Fern & Cattails 50.00
Pressed Glass, Stork, Platter, Bread, Frosted, Pictorial Border 65.00
Pressed Glass, Stork, Spooner 30.00
Pressed Glass, Strawberry & Currant, Goblet .... 25.00 To 27.50
Pressed Glass, Strawberry & Greek Key, Tumbler 21.50
Pressed Glass, Strawberry, Butter, Covered 45.00
Pressed Glass, Strawberry, Celery, Flat, Oval, 10 X 5 In. 11.50
Pressed Glass, Strawberry, Goblet 22.00
Pressed Glass, Strawberry, Goblet, Northwood 24.75
Pressed Glass, Strawberry, Pitcher, Water, Applied Handles 75.00
Pressed Glass, Strigil, Card Tray, C.1880 .... 13.00
Pressed Glass, Sugar Shaker, Royal Ivy, Rubena .... 85.00 To 95.00
Pressed Glass, Sugar Shaker, Royal Oak, Rubena .... 95.00 To 175.00
Pressed Glass, Sunbeam, Toothpick 25.00
Pressed Glass, Sunbeam, Wine, Green 28.00
Pressed Glass, Sunburst & Teepee, Syrup, Findlay 40.00
Pressed Glass, Sunburst Variant, Tumbler, Ruby Stained 22.00
Pressed Glass, Sunburst, Bowl, Oval 10.00
Pressed Glass, Sunburst, Eggcup 11.00
Pressed Glass, Sunburst, Goblet 16.50
Pressed Glass, Sunburst, Plate, Cup, Amethyst 47.00
Pressed Glass, Sunburst, Plate, 8 In. 10.00
Pressed Glass, Sunburst, Salt, Master, Blue, Rectangular, Flint 45.00
Pressed Glass, Sunburst, Sauce 5.00
Pressed Glass, Sunk Daisy, Cracker Jar 30.00
Pressed Glass, Sunk Daisy, Wine .... 14.00 To 15.00
Pressed Glass, Sunk Diamond & Lattice, Pitcher, 8 3/4 In. 40.00
  Sunken Buttons, see Mitered Diamond

Pressed Glass, Squirrel, Creamer

Pressed Glass, Sunray, Cup, Green 12.00
  Sunrise, see Rising Sun
Pressed Glass, Sunset, Salt Shaker, Pink 18.00
Pressed Glass, Swag Block, Celery, Frosted 16.00
Pressed Glass, Swag With Brackets, Berry Bowl 85.00
Pressed Glass, Swag With Brackets, Compote, Jelly, Open, Green, 5 In. 97.50
Pressed Glass, Swag With Brackets, Creamer, Amethyst 55.00
Pressed Glass, Swan, Compote, Open, High Standard, 8 1/4 In. 41.50
Pressed Glass, Sweetheart, Butter 30.00
Pressed Glass, Sweetheart, Butter, Covered, Miniature 22.00
Pressed Glass, Sweetheart, Creamer, Miniature 30.00
Pressed Glass, Sweetheart, Table Set, Miniature, 4 Piece 60.00
Pressed Glass, Swirl & Ball, Mug 6.00
Pressed Glass, Swirl, Bowl, Finger, Blue, Opalescent 40.00
Pressed Glass, Swirl, Butter 20.00
Pressed Glass, Swirl, Celery, Footed 15.00
Pressed Glass, Swirl, Creamer, Child's 15.00
Pressed Glass, Swirl, Inkwell, Rayed Base, Metal Collar, 2 X 2 In. 12.50
Pressed Glass, Swirl, Pitcher, Water, Blue, Opalescent 85.00
Pressed Glass, Swirl, Spooner, Clear To Opalescent 30.00
Pressed Glass, Swirl, Toothpick, Blue Opalescent, Chrysanthemum Base 60.00
Pressed Glass, Swirl, Tumbler, Blue 14.00

Pressed Glass, Star & Dewdrop, Butter, Covered

Pressed Glass, Swirl, Tumbler, Blue Opalescent	25.00
Pressed Glass, Swirl, Water Set, Blue Opalescent, 7 Piece	135.00
Pressed Glass, Swirl, Water Set, Pink Amber, 7 Piece	495.00
Pressed Glass, Swirled Window, Sugar Shaker, Blue, Opalescent	110.00
Pressed Glass, Tackle Block, Goblet	35.00
Pressed Glass, Tackle Block, Goblet, Flint	28.00
Pressed Glass, Tacoma, Sauce, Ruby, 4 In.	15.00
Pressed Glass, Tacoma, Spooner, Ruby Stain	50.00
Tape Measure, see Shields	
Pressed Glass, Tappan, Creamer, Child's	15.00
Pressed Glass, Tappan, Spooner & Creamer, Miniature	14.00
Pressed Glass, Tappan, Sugar, Clear, Miniature	15.00
Pressed Glass, Tappan, Sugar, Covered, Child's	23.00
Pressed Glass, Tappan, Table Set, Miniature, Clear, 4 Piece	58.00
Pressed Glass, Teardrop & Tassel, Berry Set, Blue, Greentown, 6 Piece	135.00
Pressed Glass, Teardrop & Tassel, Butter, Blue, Greentown	55.00
Pressed Glass, Teardrop & Tassel, Pitcher, Water	55.00
Pressed Glass, Teardrop & Tassel, Tumbler	22.00
Teardrop & Thumbprint, see Teardrop	
Pressed Glass, Teardrop, Compote	15.00
Pressed Glass, Teardrop, Pitcher, Blue, Greentown	95.00
Pressed Glass, Teardrop, Sugar, Covered, Blue & Gold	45.00
Pressed Glass, Teasel, Celery	18.00
Pressed Glass, Teasel, Goblet	15.00
Pressed Glass, Teasel, Sauce, Footed, Gold, 5 1/4 In.	8.00
Pressed Glass, Teddy Roosevelt, Tray, Frosted, Profile Bust, Square Deal	85.00
Pressed Glass, Teepee, Cup, Punch	7.00
Pressed Glass, Teepee, Goblet	12.50
Pressed Glass, Teepee, Plate, 6 In.	6.00
Pressed Glass, Tennessee, Bowl, 8 In.	10.00
Pressed Glass, Tennessee, Cake Stand, 8 3/4 In.	36.75
Pressed Glass, Tennessee, Mug	18.00 To 22.00
Pressed Glass, Tennessee, Pitcher, Milk	37.00
Pressed Glass, Tennessee, Toothpick	35.00
Pressed Glass, Texas Bull's-Eye, Goblet	13.00 To 16.50
Pressed Glass, Texas Bull's-Eye, Tumbler	27.50
Pressed Glass, Texas Bull's-Eye, Tumbler, Footed	16.50
Pressed Glass, Texas Star, Bowl, Flat, 9 In.	55.00
Pressed Glass, Texas, Creamer	19.50
Pressed Glass, Texas, Creamer, Gold	16.00
Pressed Glass, Texas, Creamer, Gold Tracing, Small	8.00
Pressed Glass, Texas, Relish	18.00
Pressed Glass, Texas, Salt, Master, Footed	19.50
Pressed Glass, Texas, Sugar & Creamer, Gold Trim	18.00 To 20.00
Pressed Glass, Texas, Sugar, Open	9.50
Pressed Glass, Texas, Toothpick	14.50 To 35.00
Pressed Glass, Texas, Wine	15.00
Pressed Glass, Thistle, Bowl, Near Cut, 8 In.	18.00
Pressed Glass, Thistle, Compote, Open, 7 X 6 1/4 In.	27.00

Pressed Glass, Thistle, Decanter, Blown Matched Stopper, 7 1/2 In. 30.00
Pressed Glass, Thistle, Goblet .... 22.00 To 32.50
Pressed Glass, Thistle, Sugar, Nearcut 25.00
Pressed Glass, Thistle, Tumbler, Footed 26.00
Pressed Glass, Thistles, Candy Compote, Paneled Top, Faceted Knob, 8 In. 22.50
Pressed Glass, Thousand Eye, Bottle, Castor, With Top 15.00
Pressed Glass, Thousand Eye, Bottle, Cologne, Stopper, 6 1/2 In., Pair 33.00
Pressed Glass, Thousand Eye, Bowl, Opaque White, Footed, Richard & Hartley 70.00
Pressed Glass, Thousand Eye, Cake Stand, Amber, 12 In. 75.00
Pressed Glass, Thousand Eye, Cake Stand, Amber, 3 Knob Stem 28.00
Pressed Glass, Thousand Eye, Cake Stand, Amber, 3 Knob, 10 1/4 In. 47.50
Pressed Glass, Thousand Eye, Celery, 3 Knob, Amber 28.50
Pressed Glass, Thousand Eye, Compote, Jelly, Blue 28.00
Pressed Glass, Thousand Eye, Compote, Knob Stem, Low Standard, 8 In. 42.00
Pressed Glass, Thousand Eye, Compote, Open, Amber, 3 Knob, 9 In. 45.00

Pressed Glass, Strawberry, Creamer, 5 1/2 In.

Pressed Glass, Tandem Diamonds And Thumbprint, Goblet

Pressed Glass, Thousand Eye, Compote, Open, Low Standard, 8 In. 30.00
Pressed Glass, Thousand Eye, Compote, 7 In. 24.00
Pressed Glass, Thousand Eye, Creamer, Amber 38.00
Pressed Glass, Thousand Eye, Cruet, Dark Amber 55.00
Pressed Glass, Thousand Eye, Eggcup, Clear 35.00
Pressed Glass, Thousand Eye, Goblet, Blue 25.00
Pressed Glass, Thousand Eye, Mug, Amber 15.00
Pressed Glass, Thousand Eye, Mug, Amber, 2 1/2 In. 11.00
Pressed Glass, Thousand Eye, Mug, Blue, Large 25.00
Pressed Glass, Thousand Eye, Pitcher, Blue, Knob Stem 70.00
Pressed Glass, Thousand Eye, Pitcher, Water 32.00
Pressed Glass, Thousand Eye, Plate, Square, Light Amber, 10 In. 17.50
Pressed Glass, Thousand Eye, Plate, Square, 10 In. 18.50
Pressed Glass, Thousand Eye, Plate, Vaseline, Square, 8 In. 32.50
Pressed Glass, Thousand Eye, Salt & Pepper, Clear 25.00
Pressed Glass, Thousand Eye, Saltshaker, Clear 12.00
Pressed Glass, Thousand Eye, Sauce, Apple Green, Footed, 4 1/4 In. 12.50
Pressed Glass, Thousand Eye, Sauce, Footed, 3 1/2 In. 15.00
Pressed Glass, Thousand Eye, Spooner, Amber 30.00
Pressed Glass, Thousand Eye, Sugar 32.50
Pressed Glass, Thousand Eye, Sugar, Amber 35.00
Pressed Glass, Thousand Eye, Sugar, Knob Stem, 4 In. 15.00

Pressed Glass, Thousand Eye, Tumbler, Amber .... 13.50 To 24.00
Pressed Glass, Thousand Eye, Vase, Blue, Opalescent, 6 In. 35.00
Pressed Glass, Thousand Eye, Wine 12.00
Pressed Glass, Three Face, Cake Stand, 9 1/2 In. 82.50
Pressed Glass, Three Face, Champagne 125.00
Pressed Glass, Three Face, Compote, Beaded Rim, Open, 8 In. 75.00
Pressed Glass, Three Face, Compote, Covered, 7 1/2 X 8 In. 95.00
Pressed Glass, Three Face, Compote, 9 3/4 In. 105.00
Pressed Glass, Three Face, Goblet 60.00
Pressed Glass, Three Face, Goblet, Etched 75.00
Pressed Glass, Three Face, Pitcher, Milk, Head At Base Of Handle 175.00
Pressed Glass, Three Face, Sauce, Etched, Footed, 4 In. 12.50
Pressed Glass, Three Face, Sugar & Creamer 60.00
Pressed Glass, Three Face, Wine 125.00
    Three Graces, see also Three Face
Pressed Glass, Three Panel, Berry Set, Amber, 5 Footed Pieces 70.00
Pressed Glass, Three Panel, Bowl, Flared, 10 In. 14.50
Pressed Glass, Three Panel, Compote, Blue, Covered 39.00
Pressed Glass, Three Panel, Compote, Low, Clear 20.00
Pressed Glass, Three Panel, Spooner 17.50
Pressed Glass, Three Panel, Spooner, Vaseline 30.00
Pressed Glass, Three Panel, Sugar, Amber 30.00
Pressed Glass, Three Presidents, Bread Plate .... 40.00 To 55.00
Pressed Glass, Three Presidents, Platter, Clear Center 35.00
Pressed Glass, Three Presidents, Platter, Frosted, 10 X 12 1/2 In. 60.00
Pressed Glass, Three Presidents, Platter, In Remembrance, 12 In .... 53.00 To 65.00
Pressed Glass, Three Presidents, Platter, 10 1/2 In. 50.00
Pressed Glass, Three Shields, Dish, Golden Amber, Covered 135.00
    Three Sisters, see Three Face
Pressed Glass, Three Star Band, Goblet 18.00
Pressed Glass, Thumbprint, Bowl, Clear, Covered, 6 X 4 1/2 In. 25.00
Pressed Glass, Thumbprint, Celery, Ruby Stained 45.00
Pressed Glass, Thumbprint, Compote, Low, Flint 50.00
Pressed Glass, Thumbprint, Compote, 5 1/2 X 5 In. 40.00
Pressed Glass, Thumbprint, Decanter, Bar Lip 85.00
Pressed Glass, Thumbprint, Goblet, Flint 42.50
Pressed Glass, Thumbprint, Goblet, Knob Stem, Flint 40.00
Pressed Glass, Thumbprint, Goblet, Ruby 32.50
Pressed Glass, Thumbprint, Pitcher, Trefoil Top, Blue, Reeded Handle 85.00
Pressed Glass, Thumbprint, Sauce, Scallop Rim, 4 In. 12.50
Pressed Glass, Thumbprint, Spooner 48.00
Pressed Glass, Thumbprint, Spooner, 3 Legs, Scalloped Rim, Green 22.50
Pressed Glass, Thumbprint, Sugar & Creamer, Cobalt 27.50

Pressed Glass, Thistle, Goblet

Pressed Glass, Thumbprint, Toothpick, Ruby Stained	35.00
Pressed Glass, Thumbprint, Tumbler	50.00
Pressed Glass, Thumbprint, Tumbler, Rum, Flint	30.00
Pressed Glass, Thumbprint, Whiskey, Footed, Flint	35.00
Pressed Glass, Thumbprint, Wine, Flint	40.00 To 55.00
Pressed Glass, Thumbprint, Wine, Ruby Stained	25.00
Pressed Glass, Tidy, Creamer	10.00
Pressed Glass, Tidy, Goblet	17.50
Pressed Glass, Tiny Finecut, Wine	12.00
Pressed Glass, Tiny Lion, Celery	22.00
Pressed Glass, Tiny Lion, Celery, Engraved Cattails	34.00 To 36.00
Tobin, see Leaf & Star	
Pressed Glass, Tokyo, Bowl, Master Berry, Green	35.00
Pressed Glass, Tokyo, Butter, Green, Opalescent, Covered	165.00
Pressed Glass, Tokyo, Butter, Lid, Green, Opal	135.00
Pressed Glass, Tokyo, Compote, Jelly, Clear, Opalescent	18.00
Pressed Glass, Tokyo, Compote, Jelly, Flat	45.00
Pressed Glass, Tokyo, Creamer, Green, Opal	85.00
Pressed Glass, Tokyo, Dish, Blue, Opalescent, Flat, Footed, 8 1/4 In.	35.00
Pressed Glass, Tokyo, Pitcher, Water, Green, Opal	120.00
Pressed Glass, Toltec, Cruet	14.00
Tom Thumb, see Humpty-Dumpty	
Pressed Glass, Tong, Celery	60.00
Pressed Glass, Toothpick, Royal Ivy, Glossy, Rubena	55.00
Pressed Glass, Torpedo, Bowl, Flat, Straight Sides, 6 1/2 In.	20.00
Pressed Glass, Torpedo, Bowl, Open, 7 1/2 In.	22.00
Pressed Glass, Torpedo, Bowl, 9 1/4 In.	25.00
Pressed Glass, Torpedo, Cake Stand, 9 In.	42.00
Pressed Glass, Torpedo, Compote, Covered, 6 In.	65.00
Pressed Glass, Torpedo, Compote, Jelly	15.00 To 18.00
Pressed Glass, Torpedo, Pitcher, Milk, Ruby Stained, 9 1/2 In.	75.00
Pressed Glass, Torpedo, Pitcher, Milk, 8 1/4 In.	50.00
Pressed Glass, Torpedo, Pitcher, Water, 10 1/2 In.	62.50 To 85.00
Pressed Glass, Torpedo, Sauce, 4 In.	9.50
Pressed Glass, Torpedo, Syrup, Dated 1883	43.00
Pressed Glass, Torquay, Sugar, Covered, Ruby Stained	95.00
Pressed Glass, Transcontinental Railroad, Platter, 9 X 12 In.	75.00
Pressed Glass, Tree Of Life, Berry Set, 6 Piece	60.00
Pressed Glass, Tree Of Life, Celery, Flint	45.00
Pressed Glass, Tree Of Life, Compote, 8 In.	75.00
Pressed Glass, Tree Of Life, Dish, Ice Cream, Rectangular, Amber, Portland	37.50

Pressed Glass, Three Face, Bowl, Covered, Footed

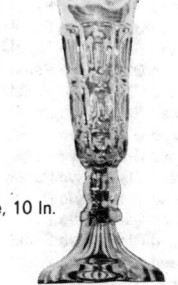

Pressed Glass, Three Printie, Vase, 10 In.

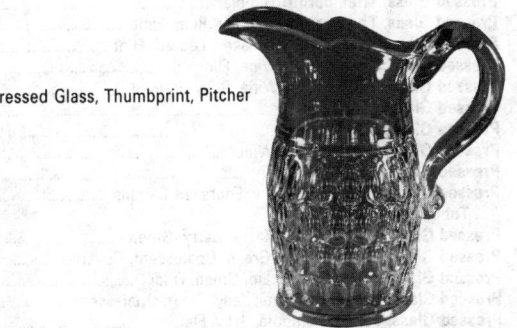

Pressed Glass, Thumbprint, Pitcher

Pressed Glass, Tree Of Life, Goblet	10.00
Pressed Glass, Tree Of Life, Plate, Portland, 6 1/4 In.	12.50
Pressed Glass, Tree Of Life, Sauce, Footed, Hand & Ball Stem	14.00
Pressed Glass, Triangular Prism, Goblet, Lady's, Flint	35.00
Pressed Glass, Triangular Prism, Spooner, Fling	26.00
Pressed Glass, Triple Triangle, Goblet, Ruby Flash	37.50
Pressed Glass, Triple Triangle, Sugar, Open, Ruby Flashed	30.00
Pressed Glass, Triple Triangle, Table Set, Ruby Stained, 4 Piece	245.00
Pressed Glass, Triple Triangle, Water Set, Ruby Stained, 7 Piece	225.00
Pressed Glass, Tropical Villa, Compote, Covered, High Standard, 8 In.	120.00
Pressed Glass, Truncated Cube, Toothpick, Ruby Stained	25.00 To 28.00
Pressed Glass, Tulip & Honeycomb, Bowl, Punch	17.50 To 18.00
Pressed Glass, Tulip & Honeycomb, Butter, Covered, Large	25.00
Pressed Glass, Tulip & Honeycomb, Creamer	14.50
Pressed Glass, Tulip & Honeycomb, Punch Bowl, Child's	15.00 To 18.00
Pressed Glass, Tulip & Honeycomb, Punch Set, Miniature, 5 Piece	50.00
Pressed Glass, Tulip & Honeycomb, Spooner	12.00 To 12.50
Pressed Glass, Tulip & Thumbprint, Spooner, Flint	30.00
Pressed Glass, Tulip Petals, Bowl, 10 3/4 In.	29.00
Pressed Glass, Tulip Petals, Cup, Punch	6.00
Pressed Glass, Tulip With Sawtooth, Celery, Flint	40.00
Pressed Glass, Tulip With Sawtooth, Compote, Flint, 10 In.	95.00
Pressed Glass, Tulip With Sawtooth, Goblet	18.00
Pressed Glass, Tulip With Sawtooth, Goblet, Knob Stem	22.00
Pressed Glass, Tulip With Sawtooth, Salt, Master	12.00
Pressed Glass, Tulip With Sawtooth, Spooner	28.50
Pressed Glass, Tulip With Sawtooth, Tumbler, Flint	45.00
Pressed Glass, Tulip With Sawtooth, Wine	32.00
Pressed Glass, Tulip, Tumbler, Footed, Flint	38.00
Pressed Glass, Twin Snowshoes, Creamer	15.00
Pressed Glass, Twinkle Star, Tumbler, 3 3/4 In.	25.00
Pressed Glass, Two Band, Spooner	16.00
Pressed Glass, Two Panel, Berry Set, Amber, 5 Piece	69.50
Pressed Glass, Two Panel, Bowl, Apple Green, Covered, 6 3/4 In.	45.00
Pressed Glass, Two Panel, Bowl, Collared, 8 X 6 1/2 In.	42.50
Pressed Glass, Two Panel, Bowl, Flat, Vaseline, 10 1/4 X 8 1/2 In.	37.50
Pressed Glass, Two Panel, Bowl, Waste	27.50
Pressed Glass, Two Panel, Bowl, Waste, Amber	25.00
Pressed Glass, Two Panel, Goblet	32.00
Pressed Glass, Two Panel, Goblet, Apple Green	25.00
Pressed Glass, Two Panel, Goblet, Blue	25.00 To 40.00
Pressed Glass, Two Panel, Pitcher, Water	42.50
Pressed Glass, Two Panel, Relish, Oval, 7 X 4 1/2 In.	5.75
Pressed Glass, Two Panel, Salt, Green	11.50
Pressed Glass, Two Panel, Salt, Individual	8.50
Pressed Glass, Two Panel, Salt, Master	18.50
Pressed Glass, Two Panel, Sauce	14.00

Pressed Glass, **Two Panel**, Spooner	28.00
Pressed Glass, **Two Panel**, Spooner, Amber	32.00
Pressed Glass, **Two Panel**, Sugar, Open	24.00
Pressed Glass, **Two Panel**, Wine, Apple Green	23.00
Pressed Glass, **Two Panel**, Wine, Canary, 4 In.	26.00
Pressed Glass, **Two-Panel**, Goblet, Vaseline	23.00
Pressed Glass, **U.S.Coin**, Bread Tray, Frosted Dollars & Halves, 1892	310.00
Pressed Glass, **U.S.Coin**, Butter	575.00
Pressed Glass, **U.S.Coin**, Compote, Covered, Dollar, Quarters & Dimes	550.00
Pressed Glass, **U.S.Coin**, Compote, Frosted, Covered, 7 1/2 In.	200.00
Pressed Glass, **U.S.Coin**, Compote, Quarters, Covered, 11 1/2 In.	450.00
Pressed Glass, **U.S.Coin**, Sugar, Open, Frosted	130.00
Pressed Glass, **U.S.Coin**, Toothpick	20.00
Pressed Glass, **U.S.Coin**, Tray, Half Dollars & Quarters, 7 X 10 In.	400.00
Pressed Glass, **U.S.Coin**, Tumbler, American Dollar In Base, Dated 1879	128.00
Pressed Glass, **U.S.Regal**, Toothpick	20.00
Pressed Glass, **Umbilicated Hobnail**, Spooner, Leaf & Berry Etching	25.00
Pressed Glass, **Umbilicated Sawtooth**, Cake Stand, Amber, 9 In.	28.00
Pressed Glass, **Umbilicated Sawtooth**, Plate, Flint, 6 In.	12.50
Pressed Glass, **Umbilicated Sawtooth**, Sauce, 4 In.	5.00
Pressed Glass, **Utah**, Tumbler, 3 3/4 In.	25.00
Pressed Glass, **Valencia Waffle**, Compote, Blue, Open, Footed, 8 In.	25.00
Pressed Glass, **Valencia Waffle**, Compote, Covered, High Stand, 7 In.Square	48.75
Pressed Glass, **Valencia Waffle**, Compote, Covered, Low, Amber, Square, 7 In.	65.00
Pressed Glass, **Valencia Waffle**, Goblet	15.00
Pressed Glass, **Valencia Waffle**, Pitcher, Water, Apple Green	85.00
Pressed Glass, **Valencia Waffle**, Spooner, Apple Green	40.00
Pressed Glass, **Valencia Waffle**, Syrup, Electric Blue	95.00
Pressed Glass, **Valencia Waffle**, Syrup, Green	90.00
Pressed Glass, **Vera**, Bowl, 5 In.	18.00
Pressed Glass, **Vermont**, Toothpick, Green, Gold	35.00
Pressed Glass, **Vermont**, Toothpick, Opalescent, 3-Footed	28.00
Pressed Glass, **Vernon Honeycomb**, Banded, Pitcher, Ale	18.00
Pressed Glass, **Vernon Honeycomb**, Goblet, Flint	22.00
Pressed Glass, **Victoria**, Celery, Pioneer	18.00
Pressed Glass, **Victoria**, Salt & Pepper, Clear, Frosted	15.00
Pressed Glass, **Viking**, Bowl, Footed, 9 In.	35.00
Pressed Glass, **Viking**, Butter	40.00
Pressed Glass, **Viking**, Butter, Covered	62.50
Pressed Glass, **Viking**, Celery	42.50 To 50.00
Pressed Glass, **Viking**, Compote, Covered	80.00
Pressed Glass, **Viking**, Compote, Low Standard, Covered, 8 1/2 In.	45.00
Pressed Glass, **Viking**, Creamer	20.00
Pressed Glass, **Viking**, Pitcher, Water	65.00 To 68.00
Pressed Glass, **Viking**, Sauce, Footed, 4 In.	18.50
Pressed Glass, **Viking**, Sauce, 4 In.	6.00 To 10.00

Pressed Glass, Tulip & Sawtooth, Decanter

Pressed Glass, Tree Of Life, Compote

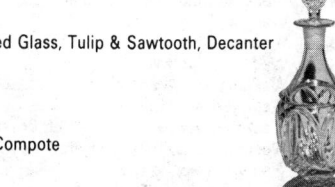

Pressed Glass, Viking, Spooner	24.50
Virginia, see also Galloway	
Pressed Glass, Virginia, Celery, U.S.Glass Co.	14.50
Pressed Glass, Virginia, Cup, Punch	7.00
Pressed Glass, Waffle & Thumbprint, Champagne, Flint	95.00
Pressed Glass, Waffle & Thumbprint, Claret, Flint	95.00
Pressed Glass, Waffle & Thumbprint, Compote, Flint, 6 1/2 In.	55.00
Pressed Glass, Waffle & Thumbprint, Compote, High Standard, Flint	95.00
Pressed Glass, Waffle & Thumbprint, Decanter, Patterned Stopper	67.50
Pressed Glass, Waffle & Thumbprint, Goblet, Bulb Stem	55.00
Pressed Glass, Waffle & Thumbprint, Spooner, Flint	45.00
Pressed Glass, Waffle, Celery, Scalloped & Flared Rim, Flint	85.00
Pressed Glass, Waffle, Champagne	65.00

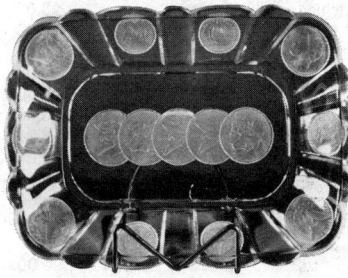

Pressed Glass, U.S.Coin, Plate, Bread

Pressed Glass, Waffle, Creamer	9.00
Pressed Glass, Waffle, Plate, Flint, 6 In.	35.00
Pressed Glass, Waffle, Salt, Master, Clambroth, Rectangular	45.00
Pressed Glass, Waffle, Sugar, Covered	70.00
Pressed Glass, Waffle, Tumbler, Flint	50.00
Pressed Glass, Warrior, Plate	175.00
Washboard, see Adonis	
Pressed Glass, Washington Centennial, Cake Stand, 11 1/2 In.	65.00 To 68.50
Pressed Glass, Washington Centennial, Celery	35.00
Pressed Glass, Washington Centennial, Dish, Relish, Claw Handles	22.00
Pressed Glass, Washington Centennial, Eggcup	37.50
Pressed Glass, Washington Centennial, Goblet	35.00
Pressed Glass, Washington Centennial, Pitcher, Water	70.00 To 85.00
Pressed Glass, Washington Centennial, Relish, Bear Handles	45.00
Pressed Glass, Washington Centennial, Spooner	39.00
Pressed Glass, Washington, Bread Tray, Frosted	85.00
Pressed Glass, Washington, Celery	65.00
Pressed Glass, Washington, Celery, Flint	65.00
Pressed Glass, Wedding Bells, Bowl, Gold, Clear	25.00
Pressed Glass, Wedding Ring, Bottle, Cologne	35.00
Pressed Glass, Wedding Ring, Goblet	55.00
Pressed Glass, Wedding Ring, Syrup, Tin & Pewter Top	70.00
Pressed Glass, Wedding Ring, Wine	18.00
Pressed Glass, Wedding Ring, Wine, Flint	40.00
Pressed Glass, Westmoreland, Goblet	12.00
Pressed Glass, Westmoreland, Jar, Pickle, With Cover	22.00
Pressed Glass, Westmoreland, Tumbler, Flared	12.50
Pressed Glass, Westward Ho, Berry Set, 10 Piece	245.00
Pressed Glass, Westward Ho, Celery	95.00
Pressed Glass, Westward Ho, Compote, Child's, Covered, 4 In.	75.00
Pressed Glass, Westward Ho, Compote, Covered, High Stand, 5 In.	185.00 To 225.00
Pressed Glass, Westward Ho, Compote, Covered, Low Stand, 5 In.	175.00
Pressed Glass, Westward Ho, Compote, Indian Finial, 11 1/2 In.	225.00

Pressed Glass, Westward Ho, Compote, Oval, Covered, 6 3/4 In.	120.00
Pressed Glass, Westward Ho, Compote, 6 In.	125.00
Pressed Glass, Westward Ho, Creamer	75.00
Pressed Glass, Westward Ho, Jar, Marmalade, Indian Finial	145.00
Pressed Glass, Westward Ho, Plate, Bread	65.00 To 90.00
Pressed Glass, Westward Ho, Platter, Bread, Frosted Deer Handles	85.00
Pressed Glass, Westward Ho, Platter, Deer & Antler, 9 X 13 In.	55.00
Pressed Glass, Westward Ho, Sauce, Footed, 4 In.	19.50 To 20.00
Pressed Glass, Westward Ho, Sugar & Creamer, Indian Finial, Frosted	249.00
Pressed Glass, Westward Ho, Sugar, Indian Finial, Covered	135.00
Pressed Glass, Westward Ho, Table Set, 4 Piece	425.00
Pressed Glass, Wheat & Barley, Bowl, Covered, 7 In.	28.00
Pressed Glass, Wheat & Barley, Butter	23.00
Pressed Glass, Wheat & Barley, Compote, Jelly	9.75
Pressed Glass, Wheat & Barley, Compote, Jelly, Amber	22.50
Pressed Glass, Wheat & Barley, Creamer	16.50
Pressed Glass, Wheat & Barley, Goblet	18.00
Pressed Glass, Wheat & Barley, Mug, Amber	20.00
Pressed Glass, Wheat & Barley, Plate, Handled, 9 In.	10.00
Pressed Glass, Wheat & Barley, Plate, 9 In.	14.50
Pressed Glass, Wheat & Barley, Spooner	20.00
Pressed Glass, Wheat & Barley, Sugar & Creamer, Covered	40.00
Pressed Glass, Wheat & Barley, Tumbler, Amber	22.50 To 25.00
Pressed Glass, Wheat Sheaf, Bowl, Punch	15.00
Pressed Glass, Wheat Sheaf, Goblet	25.00

Pressed Glass, Waffle & Thumbprint, Flip Glass

Pressed Glass, Washington Centennial, Relish Dish

Pressed Glass, Wheat Sheaf, Pitcher, Water	37.50
Pressed Glass, Wheat, Plate, Bread, Give Us Our Daily Bread, 10 In.	23.00
Pressed Glass, Wheeling Drape, Tumbler, Red, Flower Decoration	126.50
Pressed Glass, Whirligig, Butter, Covered, Child's	23.00
Pressed Glass, Whirligig, Creamer, Child's	13.50 To 15.00
Pressed Glass, Whirligig, Punch Set, Miniature, 7 Piece	50.00 To 60.00
Pressed Glass, Whirligig, Punch Set, 7 Piece	67.50
Pressed Glass, Whirligig, Spooner	7.00
Pressed Glass, Whirligig, Spooner, Child's	10.00
Pressed Glass, Wide Band, Goblet, Etched	6.00
Pressed Glass, Wild Bouquet, Creamer, Blue, Opalescent	58.00
Pressed Glass, Wild Bouquet, Creamer, Opalescent	32.00
Pressed Glass, Wild Bouquet, Sauce, Green, Opalescent	25.00
Pressed Glass, Wild Bouquet, Spooner, Blue, Opalescent	65.00
Pressed Glass, Wild Rose With Bowknot, Butter, Frosted	35.00
Pressed Glass, Wild Rose With Bowknot, Creamer, Frosted	18.00
Pressed Glass, Wild Rose With Scrolling, Creamer, Green, Gold Trim	50.00
Pressed Glass, Wild Rose With Scrolling, Spooner, Child's	50.00

Pressed Glass, **Wild Rose,** Bowl, Open Edge, Footed, Amethyst, N 45.00
Pressed Glass, **Wild Rose,** Cup, Punch, Milk Glass 18.00
Pressed Glass, **Wild Rose,** Table Set, Milk Glass 175.00
Pressed Glass, **Wildflower,** Cake Stand, Blue 45.00
Pressed Glass, **Wildflower,** Cake Stand, Vaseline, 10 1/2 In. 55.00
Pressed Glass, **Wildflower,** Cake Stand, 10 1/2 X 7 1/2 In. 24.00
Pressed Glass, **Wildflower,** Celery, 8 1/2 In. 28.00
Pressed Glass, **Wildflower,** Compote, Open, High Standard, 7 1/2 X 8 In. 23.50
Pressed Glass, **Wildflower,** Creamer 21.50
Pressed Glass, **Wildflower,** Creamer, Blue 37.50
Pressed Glass, **Wildflower,** Dish, Tricorner, Handled, Opalescent 42.50
Pressed Glass, **Wildflower,** Goblet 23.50
Pressed Glass, **Wildflower,** Goblet, Blue .... 28.00 To 38.50
Pressed Glass, **Wildflower,** Pitcher 35.00
Pressed Glass, **Wildflower,** Plate, Amber, 9 3/4 In. 25.00
Pressed Glass, **Wildflower,** Plate, Apple Green, 10 In.Square 24.00
Pressed Glass, **Wildflower,** Plate, 10 In.Square 12.50
Pressed Glass, **Wildflower,** Platter, Apple Green, 8 X 11 In. 25.00
Pressed Glass, **Wildflower,** Salt & Pepper, Pewter Tops 35.00
Pressed Glass, **Wildflower,** Salt, Blue 35.00
Pressed Glass, **Wildflower,** Salt, Master, Amber, Boat On Turtle's Back 40.00
Pressed Glass, **Wildflower,** Sauce, Amber 7.50
Pressed Glass, **Wildflower,** Sauce, Apple Green, 4 In. 7.50
Pressed Glass, **Wildflower,** Spooner 24.00
Pressed Glass, **Wildflower,** Table Set, Amber 125.00
Pressed Glass, **Wildflower,** Tray, Amber 32.00
Pressed Glass, **Wildflower,** Tray, Apple Green, Oval, 11 X 13 1/2 In. 35.00
Pressed Glass, **Wildflower,** Tumbler, Amber 22.00
Pressed Glass, **William & Mary,** Vase, Vaseline, Opalescent, 6 In. 48.00
Pressed Glass, **Willow Oak,** Bowl, Amber, Round, 7 In. 18.00

Pressed Glass, Wedding Ring, Syrup, Flint

Pressed Glass, Westward Ho, Compote, Covered, 7 3/4 In.

Pressed Glass, **Willow Oak,** Bowl, Waste 34.00
Pressed Glass, **Willow Oak,** Butter, Amber 27.50
Pressed Glass, **Willow Oak,** Cake Stand, Clear, 8 1/2 In. .... 15.00 To 18.00
Pressed Glass, **Willow Oak,** Cake Stand, 10 1/2 In. 32.50
Pressed Glass, **Willow Oak,** Celery 34.00
Pressed Glass, **Willow Oak,** Compote, Covered, 6 In. 32.50
Pressed Glass, **Willow Oak,** Compote, High Standard, Covered, 6 1/4 In. 23.00
Pressed Glass, **Willow Oak,** Compote, Open, 6 1/2 In. .... 26.50 To 27.50
Pressed Glass, **Willow Oak,** Compote, 7 3/4 In. 24.00
Pressed Glass, **Willow Oak,** Creamer 16.00
Pressed Glass, **Willow Oak,** Goblet .... 23.00 To 25.00
Pressed Glass, **Willow Oak,** Goblet, Amber .... 35.00 To 38.00
Pressed Glass, **Willow Oak,** Pitcher, Milk 30.00
Pressed Glass, **Willow Oak,** Pitcher, Water 32.00
Pressed Glass, **Willow Oak,** Plate, Amber, 7 In. 35.00
Pressed Glass, **Willow Oak,** Plate, Blue, Handled, 9 In. 35.00

Pressed Glass, Willow Oak, Sauce, Footed, Set Of 6	55.00
Pressed Glass, Willow Oak, Sugar, 3 3/4 In.	12.00
Pressed Glass, Willow Oak, Tray, 11 In.	12.50
Pressed Glass, Willow Oak, Tumbler	25.00
Pressed Glass, Windows, Salt & Pepper, White, Opalescent	38.00
Pressed Glass, Windows, Toothpick, Blue, Opalescent	60.00
Winona, see Barred Hobnail	
Wisconsin, see Beaded Dewdrop	
Pressed Glass, Wooden Pail, Creamer, Clear, Miniature	30.00
Pressed Glass, Worcester, Belted, Goblet	32.00
Pressed Glass, Worcester, Belted, Whiskey, Handled	12.50
Pressed Glass, Wreath & Shell, Salt, Vaseline, Opalescent	55.00
Pressed Glass, Wreath & Shell, Salt, White, Opalescent	40.00
Pressed Glass, Wyoming, Compote, Covered, High Standard, 6 1/2 In.	55.00
Pressed Glass, X-Ray, Berry Set, Emerald Green, Gold Trim, 7 Piece	85.00
Pressed Glass, X-Ray, Berry Set, Green, Gold Trim, 9 Piece	125.00
Pressed Glass, X-Ray, Bowl, Berry, Green, Gold, 8 In.	40.00
Pressed Glass, X-Ray, Creamer, Emerald Green And Gold	75.00
Pressed Glass, X-Ray, Dish, Berry, Green, Gold Decoration	12.00
Pressed Glass, X-Ray, Pitcher, Water, Green	75.00
Pressed Glass, X-Ray, Toothpick, Gold Trim	40.00
Yale, see Crow's-Foot	
Pressed Glass, Yoke Band, Goblet	9.75
Pressed Glass, Yoked Loop, Bowl, Footed, Flint, 8 In.	45.00
Pressed Glass, Yoked Loop, Goblet	18.00
Pressed Glass, Yoked Loop, Sugar, Covered, Flint	50.00
Pressed Glass, Yoked Loop, Sugar, Open, Flint	30.00
Pressed Glass, York Herringbone, Creamer	15.00
Pressed Glass, York Herringbone, Tumbler	15.00
Pressed Glass, Yuma Loop, Compote, Covered, 10 1/2 In.	40.00
Pressed Glass, Yuma Loop, Spooner	14.50
Pressed Glass, Zipper & Loops, Vase, Blue, Opalescent	40.00
Pressed Glass, Zipper, Pitcher, Water, Amber	65.00
Pressed Glass, Zipper, Spooner	15.00
Pressed Glass, 100 Leaved Ivy, Relish	9.00
100-Eye, see Hundred Eye	
101, see One-O-One	
1, 000-Eye, see Thousand Eye	
8-0-8, see Eight-O-Eight	

The size of the print is given, not the overall size with frame.
   Print, see also Store, Sign

Print, Audubon, Pigeon Hawks, Male & Female, Dated	185.00
Print, Audubon, Texan Skunk, Bowen, 1845, Framed, 30 X 36 In.	500.00
Print, Baillie, Soldiers' Return, 1847 Mexican War, Framed	45.00
Print, Christy, Gold Is Not All, 16 X 12 1/2 In.	15.00
Print, Christy, Lady Descending Stairs, Dated 1907, Oak Frame, 16 X 19 In.	18.00
Print, Christy, Sailing Close, 17 X 12 1/4 In.	18.00
Print, Currier, see Currier	
Print, Currier & Ives, see Currier & Ives	
Print, Fisher, Befriended, Gibson-Type Girl Holding Kitten	16.50
Print, Fisher, Greatest Moments Of A Girl's Life, Framed, 9 1/2 X 27 1/2 In.	55.00
Print, Flagg, You Can Lick Runaway Prices, Uncle Sam, 16 X 22 In.	75.00
Print, Godey, Twins, Cherry Carved Frame, 10 1/2 X 13 1/2 In., Pair	22.50
Print, Icart, Along The Quais, 1929, 6 X 12 1/2 In.	75.00
Print, Icart, Angry Buddha, Signed, Framed	475.00
Print, Icart, Apple Girl, Colored, 18 X 22 In, C.1930	20.00
Print, Icart, Autumn, Signed	90.00
Print, Icart, Follies, 1935, 25 X 15 1/2 In.	1375.00
Print, Icart, Girl In Crinoline, Uncut, Framed	450.00
Print, Icart, Kittens, Signed, 1925	395.00
Print, Icart, Laughing, Nude, 1930, Signed	600.00
Print, Icart, Lithograph Of Oil Tea Party, Framed And Matted	675.00
Print, Icart, Mardi Gras, Signed	625.00
Print, Icart, Place Vendome, Signed	125.00

Print, **Icart,** Spanish Dancer, Original Art Nouveau Frame, Signed 250.00
Print, **Icart,** Speed, Woman & Greyhounds, 14 1/2 X 22 1/2 In. 25.00
Print, **Icart,** Spring, Signed 90.00
Print, **Icart,** The Letter, Color, 18 X 22 In., C.1930 .... 20.00
Print, **Icart,** Venetian Nights, Art Nouveau Frame, Signed 600.00
Print, **Icart,** Waiting, 1927 .... 395.00
Print, **Icart,** Winter, Signed 175.00
Print, **Icart,** Wisteria, 1940 .... 850.00
Print, **Icart,** Youth, Artist's Proof, Original Art Nouveau Frame, Signed 650.00

Japanese prints are listed as follows: Print, Japanese, name of artist,
title or description, type, size. The following terms are used to denote type:
Tate-e is a vertical composition. Yoko-e is a horizontal composition.
The words Aiban, Chuban, Hosoban, Oban, and Koban denote size.
The sizes are 13 x 9 inches, 10 x 7 1/2 inches, 12 x 6 inches,
15 x 10 inches, and 7 x 4 1/2 inches respectively.

Print, **Japanese,** Haunobuga, Two Women Six Iris, 10 1/2 X 8 1/4 In. 225.00
Print, **Japanese,** Hiroshige, Villagers In Akabone On A Snowy Day 270.00
Print, **Japanese,** Hokusai, Snowy Morning In Koishikawas 120.00
Print, **Japanese,** Toyokuri, Kabuki Actor, C.1820 .... 325.00
Print, **Lithograph,** Courage Tobacco, Framed, Signed, 10 X 10 In. 45.00
Print, **Lithograph,** Hand Colored, A.F.Tair, 1863, 18 7/8 X 27 5/8 In. 325.00
Print, **Lithograph,** Hand Colored, Joshua Shaw, Dated 1829, 11 3/4 X 15 In. 175.00
Print, **Map,** Erie Canal, Profile, 1817, 43 X 10 In. 95.00
Print, **Map,** Northeastern States, Copperplate, J.Russel, 1795, 18 X 14 1/2 In. 90.00
Print, **Maxfield Parrish,** Dinkey Bird, Framed, 16 X 13 In. 45.00
Print, **Meyers,** The Silver-Cascade, Steel Engraving, New Hampshire, 5 X 7 In. 15.00
Print, **Nutting,** A Chair For John, Framed, 22 1/4 In. 63.00
Print, **Nutting,** All Sunshine, Matted & Framed, 16 1/2 X 13 1/2 In. 25.00
Print, **Nutting,** An Elaborate Dinner, Frame, 22 1/2 In. 65.00
Print, **Nutting,** Birthday Flowers, Framed, 6 1/4 X 4 3/4 In. 35.00
Print, **Nutting,** Coming Out Of Rosa, Framed, 12 1/2 X 10 1/2 In. 24.00
Print, **Nutting,** Fair Autumn, Frame, 15 In. 25.00
Print, **Nutting,** Garden Scene, 15 X 12 In. 5.00
Print, **Nutting,** Lady At Hearth, Framed, 10 In. 30.00
Print, **Nutting,** Lady Descending Stairs, Wood Frame, 9 3/4 X 7 3/4 In. 35.00
Print, **Nutting,** Sallying Of Sally 25.00
Print, **Nutting,** Swimming Pool, Framed, 18 1/2 X 15 1/2 In. 26.00
Print, **Nutting,** The Coming Out Of Rosa, 15 1/2 X 18 1/2 In. 45.00
Print, **Nutting,** Westmore Drive, Framed, 11 X 13 In. 18.00
Print, **Nutting,** Woman Tatting 35.00
Print, **Parrish,** Canyon, Framed, 16 X 13 In. 35.00
Print, **Parrish,** Cleopatra, Framed, Large 250.00
Print, **Parrish,** Collier's Cover, Framed 50.00
Print, **Parrish,** Dawn, Framed, 17 1/2 X 29 1/2 In. 110.00
Print, **Parrish,** Daybreak, Large, Framed .... 110.00 To 120.00
Print, **Parrish,** Garden Of Allah, Framed, 8 1/4 X 11 1/4 In. 22.50
Print, **Parrish,** Morning, Framed, 16 X 13 In. 31.00
Print, **Parrish,** Wild Geese, Framed 50.00
Print, **Prang,** Chromolithograph, Late Autumn In White Mts., Framed 100.00
Print, **Prang,** Cupid Awake, Parkinson 1897, Oval Tin Frame 11.00
Print, **Prang,** Lady With Infant, 1888, Framed 15.00
Print, **Rockwell,** Boy Scout, George Washington, 16 1/2 X 21 1/2 In. 99.00
Print, **Smirnoff,** Thoroughbred Dogs, Framed, Matte Stain 12.00
Print, **Stagecoach** Scene, Signed, 18 X 25 1/2 In. 35.00
Print, **Villagers In Akabane On A Snowy Day,** 8 1/2 X 13 In. .... *Illus* 270.00
Providential, Tile, Warrior's Head, Beige, Beaded Trim, 6 In. 32.00
    Purple Slag, see Slag, Purple
Purse, **Black Needlepoint,** Florals, Scroll Border, 15 X 11 1/2 In. 87.50
Purse, **Change,** Finger Ring Chain, Sterling Silver 27.00
Purse, **Leather,** Silver Embossed Picture Of Auto On Lid, 1910 .... 8.50
Purse, **Mesh,** England, Art Deco, 10 Signed Whiting & Davis, Set Of 40 .... 100.00
Purse, **Mesh,** Whiting & Davis .... 25.00 To 38.50
Purse, **Petitpoint,** Metal Clasp, Chain Handle 9.00

Print, Villagers In Akabane On A Snowy Day, 8 1/2 X 13 In.

Quezal

Quezal glass was made from 1901 to 1920 by Martin Bach, Sr. He made iridescent glass of the same type as Tiffany.

Quezal, Bowl & Underplate, Signed, 1 3/4 X 3 In.	285.00
Quezal, Bowl, Cloisonne Cover, Handled, Footed	200.00
Quezal, Bowl, Gold Iridescence, Pulled Feather Decoration, Signed Rim, 6 In.	295.00
Quezal, Bowl, Green & Gold Pulled Feather, Iridescent, Footed, 5 1/4 In.	410.00
Quezal, Bowl, Iridescent Gold & Pulled Feather, Signed, 6 In.	295.00
Quezal, Bowl, Rose, 6 Petals Turn Over At Top, Threading, Lily Pads, Signed	875.00
Quezal, Candlestick, Blue Iridescent, Script Signed, 10 1/2 In.	190.00 To 350.00
Quezal, Compote, Flower Shape, White Background, Signed, 5 1/2 In.	850.00
Quezal, Glass, Dimpled, Rainbow Iridescent, Signed, 3 In.	135.00
Quezal, Lamp, Amber Iridescent Glass, Stick Vase Base, Signed, 17 In.	575.00
Quezal, Lampshade, Barrel Shape, Amber, Caramel Inside, Signed, 4 X 4 In.	80.00
Quezal, Lampshade, Ruffles Gold Candle, Signed, 3 X 6 In.	120.00
Quezal, Plate, Iridescent, Signed, 4 1/2 In.	90.00
Quezal, Salt, Amber Irdescence To Purple At Base, 4 X 2 1/4 In.	235.00
Quezal, Salt, Blue Iridescence, Bronze	175.00
Quezal, Salt, Gold Iridescent, Round, Violet Interior, 1 X 2 3/4 In.	175.00
Quezal, Salt, Gold, Multicolor Rainbow Iridescence	120.00
Quezal, Salt, Gold, Multicolored Highlights, Ribbed	150.00
Quezal, Salt, Gold, Paneled, Signed	115.00
Quezal, Salt, Master, Amber & Purple Iridescent, Signed, 3 1/2 In.	125.00
Quezal, Shade, Autumnal Ives, Threading, Signed	85.00
Quezal, Shade, Bell Form, Creamy Opalescent, Gold Iridescence, Heart Forms	85.00
Quezal, Shade, Blue Feather, Hooked, Signed	175.00
Quezal, Shade, Decorated, Green Feather, Set Of Four	360.00
Quezal, Shade, Diamond-Quilted, Gold Iridescent, Set Of 3	275.00
Quezal, Shade, Gass, Gold Iridescent, Embossed Ribbing, 4 3/8 X 4 1/4 In.	75.00
Quezal, Shade, Gold Aurene, 5 1/2 In.	55.00
Quezal, Shade, Gold Autumn Leaves, Random Threading, Signed, 6 In.	85.00
Quezal, Shade, Gold Calcite, Feather	110.00
Quezal, Shade, Gold Diamond Quilted, Signed, 5 1/2 In.	120.00
Quezal, Shade, Gold Drape On White With Green Border, Iridescent, Set Of 5	600.00
Quezal, Shade, Gold Drape, Green Rim, Pink Iridescent, Signed, 5 Piece	600.00
Quezal, Shade, Gold Feather On Calcite, Signed	110.00
Quezal, Shade, Gold Feather On White Calcite Background	135.00
Quezal, Shade, Gold Feather, Gold Lined, Ruffled Edge, Bulbous	115.00
Quezal, Shade, Gold Feather, Green Border, Opalescent, Signed, Pair	175.00
Quezal, Shade, Gold Hearts On Opalescent, Gold Spider Webs, Shape No.40	95.00
Quezal, Shade, Gold King Tut, Bullet Shaped, 5 3/4 In.	245.00
Quezal, Shade, Gold Leaves On Opal, Allover Gold Threading, Signed, Pair	190.00
Quezal, Shade, Gold Pulled Feather On Opal, Gold Lining, 6 5/8 In., Signed	90.00
Quezal, Shade, Gold Ric Rac On Calcite, Signed, Pair	160.00
Quezal, Shade, Gold Spider Web, Notched Rims	95.00
Quezal, Shade, Gold Tortoise Shell, Opalescent, 4 1/2 X 3 In.	200.00
Quezal, Shade, Gold Zipper Pattern On Opal Glass, Signed On Rim	125.00
Quezal, Shade, Gold Zipper, White Pearl Interior, Signed	75.00
Quezal, Shade, Gold, Blue Iridescent Highlights, Ribbed	70.00

Quezal, Shade, Gold, White Feather, Green Border, Pair	165.00
Quezal, Shade, Gold, White Pulled Feather	75.00
Quezal, Shade, Green Feather On Gold Iridescent	115.00
Quezal, Shade, Green Feather On Gold, Signed, Set Of 4	440.00
Quezal, Shade, Green Feather On Opalescent Gold, Signed, Set Of 4	500.00
Quezal, Shade, Green Pulled Feathers, Bordered In Gold, 5 1/4 X 3 1/2 In.	165.00
Quezal, Shade, Hooked Feather, Blue, Signed, Pair	150.00
Quezal, Shade, Hooked Feather, Green, Gold Lined, 7 In., Pair	155.00
Quezal, Shade, Iridescent Green, Gold Leaf & Vine, 4 1/2 In.	130.00
Quezal, Shade, King Tut, Wavy Gold & White Bands, White Iridescent, Pair	115.00
Quezal, Shade, Miniature, Gold Lining, Green Feather, Gold Border On Calcite	95.00
Quezal, Shade, Mottled Deep Golden Amber, Purple Iridescence, 5 1/4 X 5 In.	90.00
Quezal, Shade, No.258, Yellow Feather, Signed	85.00
Quezal, Shade, Opalescent, Gold Bands & Lining, Ribbed	80.00
Quezal, Shade, Opalescent, Iridescent, Cream, Gold Pulled Feathers	90.00
Quezal, Shade, Opalescent, Snakeskin On Gold, Green Iridescent Bottom, Pair	325.00
Quezal, Shade, Optic Rib, Amber Iridescence, Scalloped, 6 X 4 1/2 In.	130.00
Quezal, Shade, Pink Feather, Flared Rim, Signed, 6 In.	110.00
Quezal, Shade, Ribbed, Gold Feather, Green Outline, Opalescent, 6 In., Pair	185.00
Quezal, Shade, Ribbed, Pumpkin, Heavy Cased Glass, 4 1/2 In.	95.00
Quezal, Shade, Threading With Leaf Design, Signed	100.00
Quezal, Shade, White Snakeskin On Gold Iridescent Rose Tones, Gold Lined	190.00
Quezal, Shade, White With Gold Ribbon, Gold Lining, Signed, Set Of 3	240.00
Quezal, Shade, White, Gold Threading, Green Leaves, Iridescent, 4 1/2 In., Pair	200.00
Quezal, Shade, White, Pulled Feather, Green Border On Gold Glass	120.00
Quezal, Shade, Yellow Feather, Green Edge On Opalescent Gold Lining, Pair	180.00
Quezal, Vase, Amber Iridescence, Spherical Neck, Globular Body, 4 1/2 In.	375.00
Quezal, Vase, Blue & Lavender, Signed, 14 In.	375.00
Quezal, Vase, Blue Iridescence, White Hearts, Pale Blue Vines, 12 In.	1250.00
Quezal, Vase, Dark Green, Iridescent, 6 1/2 In.	275.00
Quezal, Vase, Flared, Gold Iridescent, Signed, 10 In.	175.00
Quezal, Vase, Flower Form, Gold With White Pulled Feathers, 11 1/2 In.	1500.00
Quezal, Vase, Gold Iridescent, Bronze Art Nouveau Decorated Base, 12 In.	275.00
Quezal, Vase, Gold Iridescent, Bronze Snake Base, 1916, Signed, 12 In.	295.00
Quezal, Vase, Gold Iridescent, Flared Rim & Base, 10 In.	245.00
Quezal, Vase, Gold Top, Green Feathering, Gold On White Background, 5 In.	1150.00
Quezal, Vase, Gold With Purple & Blue Iridescent, Signed, 12 In.	850.00
Quezal, Vase, Gold, Flared Rim & Base, Signed, 10 In.	210.00
Quezal, Vase, Gold, Rainbow Effect, 10 In.	550.00
Quezal, Vase, Green Feather With Gold Outline, Gold Feather On Foot, 5 In.	875.00
Quezal, Vase, Iridescent, Globular Body, Signed Base, 4 1/2 In.	375.00
Quezal, Vase, Jack-In-The-Pulpit, Iridescent, Base Inscribed Quezal/2, 9 In.	1500.00
Quezal, Vase, Leaves To Midway, Gold, Opal Top, Forms Flower, Signed, 6 In.	1150.00
Quezal, Vase, Pink & Amber Iridescence, Trumpet Shaped, Flared Rim, 6 In.	525.00
Quezal, Vase, Rainbow, Iridescent, 12 In.	475.00
Quezal, Vase, Stick, Iridescent Orange, Petal-Form Rim, Signed, 10 1/2 In.	350.00
Quezal, Vase, Trumpet, Gold Luster, 15 In.	325.00
Quezal, Vase, White Pulled Feather, Gold, Signed, 11 1/2 In.	1175.00
Quilt, see Textile, Quilt	

Quimper pottery was made in Finistere, France, after 1900. Most of the pieces found today were made during the twentieth century. A Quimper factory has worked in France since the eighteenth century.

Quimper, Ashtray, Peasant & Foliage	10.00
Quimper, Bowl, Green, Man & Woman, Handled, 5 In., Pair	37.50
Quimper, Bowl, Peasant Decoration, Tab Handles, Signed, 5 1/2 In.	20.00
Quimper, Bowl, 2-Handled, Peasant Woman With Flowers, Signed	18.00
Quimper, Box, Figural, Peasant, Hat Shape, Covered	60.00
Quimper, Candlestick, Cream, Peasant Woman & Flowers, 8 In., Pair	40.00
Quimper, Candlestick, Man & Woman, Yellow, Glazed, HB, 8 1/2 In., Pair	135.00
Quimper, Creamer, Figural, Man With Pipe, 5 1/2 In.	35.00
Quimper, Creamer, Miniature	14.00
Quimper, Cup & Saucer, Octagonal, HR Quimper	18.00
Quimper, Dish, Black, Flowered Center	35.00
Quimper, Dish, Serving, 3-Part, 16 1/2 In.	55.00

Quimper, Eggcup, Flowers, Footed	10.00
Quimper, Inkwell, Double, Bagpipe Player, Signed	125.00
Quimper, Inkwell, Place For Pens, Figure, White, 2 Ink Pots, Signed	50.00
Quimper, Knife Rest, Peasant	18.00
Quimper, Pitcher, Breton Peasant Woman, 6 In.	30.00
Quimper, Pitcher, Breton Peasant, White, Redware Base, Signed P.B., 8 In.	130.00
Quimper, Pitcher, Figural, Floral, 4 1/2 In.	11.00
Quimper, Pitcher, Large, 9 In.	34.00
Quimper, Pitcher, Signed, 5 1/2 In.	30.00
Quimper, Planter, Cradle Shaped, 8 X 4 X 4 In.	45.00
Quimper, Plate, Bird Design, Yellow, 10 In.	22.00
Quimper, Plate, Coat Of Arms Center, 10 In.	50.00
Quimper, Plate, Signed Henriot, 8 1/2 In.	27.50
Quimper, Platter, Yellow, 8 Sided, HB Quimper, 10 1/2 In.	20.00
Quimper, Relish, Man & Woman, Spatter Edge, 3 Section, Handled, 16 1/2 In.	55.00
Quimper, Salt, Individual, Open, 3 3/4 In.	10.00
Quimper, Salt, Swan, Peasants, Center Ring Handle, Henriot	22.50
Quimper, Shoe, Signed, Pair	35.00
Quimper, Sugar & Creamer, Hexagonal, Peasants & Floral Decoration, White	28.50
Quimper, Teapot, Brown, Blue Gray Band Of Hearts, 6 1/4 In.	40.00
Quimper, Teapot, Pink, Breton, Man	35.00

*Radford pottery was made by Alfred Radford in Broadway, Virginia,
Tiffin and Zanesville, Ohio, and Clarksburg, West Virginia, from 1891
until 1912. Jasperware, Ruko, Thera, Radera, and Velvety Art Ware
were made.*

Radford, Vase, Jasperware, Blue Ground, 2 Cherubs Each Side, Marked 57, 5 In.	90.00
Radford, Vase, Jasperware, 4-Sided, Woman On Olive Ground, No.59, 4 In.	125.00
Radio, Angeulus, Cathedral Type Case	125.00
Radio, Crystal, Capped Copper Cylinder, Raised Tin Base, Earphones, 5 In.	35.00
Radio, Philco, Round	65.00
Railroad, Ashtray, Marked Clinchfield	5.00
Railroad, Ashtray, New York Central, 24K Gold Trim	22.00
Railroad, Ashtray, Penn.RR	5.00
Railroad, Ashtray, SOO Line, Cobalt	9.50
Railroad, Badge, Police Shield, Eagle Top, Erie RR	60.00
Railroad, Bell, Brass, 26 In.	400.00
Railroad, Bell, Locomotive, Brass, Hand-Actuated Or Hand-And-Air, 17 In.	690.00
Railroad, Bell, Locomotive, Brass, Hand-And-Air Actuated, 17 In.	695.00
Railroad, Bell, Rock Island, MoPac, Steam Locomotive, Brass, 12 In.	165.00
Railroad, Bell, Street Car Safety, Bronze, St.L.C.Co., 2 Hand Pulls	42.50
Railroad, Book Of Matches, U.P.Streamliner	1.00
Railroad, Book, Rules & Regulations, Oregon RR & Navigation Co., 1907	22.00
Railroad, Book, Telegraphers, Leather Bound, 1896	20.00
Railroad, Box, Ticket Agent's, 72 Cubbyholes, Colorado-Kansas Lines, Pine	65.00
Railroad, Box, Wall, Glass Door, Rules For Week Lettered On Front, 17 In.	22.00
Railroad, Button, Union Pacific, Set Of 5	5.00
Railroad, Calendar, Pennsylvania Railroad, 1956	15.00
Railroad, Calendar, 1939, Denver & Rio Grande	8.00
Railroad, Can, Water, Long Spout, 4 Gallon	10.00
Railroad, Can, Water, N.Y.C., 2 Gallon	12.00
Railroad, Can, Water, W.L.E., Gallon	10.00
Railroad, Card, Pullman, Dining Car In Opposite Direction, 5 X 7 In.	5.00
Railroad, Case, Filing, Tin, Hanlan, St.Louis, USA, MKT, 15 X 7 In., Set Of 4	65.00
Railroad, Clock, Heavy Brass, Steam-Gauge Shape, McGran	425.00
Railroad, Coffeepot, UPRR, Individual, Silver Metal	12.50
Railroad, Creamer, Baltimore & Ohio, Blue, Scenic, Dated 1857-1927	18.00
Railroad, Cup & Saucer, Baltimore & Ohio, Shenango China, Blue & White	14.00
Railroad, Cup, Chief Lines, Indian Chief 1 Side, Truck On Other	14.00
Railroad, Cuspidor, Pullman, Nickel-Plated Brass	85.00
Railroad, Fan, Burlington Route, 1880s, Routes & Train Stops	35.00
Railroad, Globe, D.L.S., Clear, Embossed, 3 1/4 In.	14.50
Railroad, Goblet, Union Pacific	7.50
Railroad, Gravy Boat, Blue China, B.& O.Railroad	12.00
Railroad, Headrest, Rio Grande	6.00

Railroad, Key, Brass, D.L. & W.D. 7.00
Railroad, Key, Steel With Brass, Rio Grande 17.50
Railroad, Key, Switch, Burlington Route, Brass 10.00
Railroad, Key, Switch, Penn Central, Brass 6.50
Railroad, Key, Telegraph 15.00
Railroad, Lamp, Cabin, Wall, P.R.R., Urbana 40.00
Railroad, Lamp, Caboose, Kerosene Type, Wall Hanger, Bracket, Shade & Chimney 58.00
Railroad, Lamp, Semaphore Signal, CStPM & O 37.00
Railroad, Lantern, Adlake D & H.R.R., Stenciled Globe 18.00
Railroad, Lantern, Adlake, Original Globe 44.00
Railroad, Lantern, Bell Bottom, Glass Wire Guard, Marked No.18 ..... 65.00
Railroad, Lantern, BMRR, Marked Frame & Globe 45.00
Railroad, Lantern, Boston & Maine-Dietz On Frame, Dietz, Vesta On Red Globe 37.00
Railroad, Lantern, Brakeman's, The Adams, Pennsylvania Lines, 5 In.Globe 35.00
Railroad, Lantern, C & O RR, Clear Globe, Raised Letters 55.00
Railroad, Lantern, C.& N.W. 38.00
Railroad, Lantern, Caboose, Pair 40.00
Railroad, Lantern, CRRNJ, Red Cast Globe 95.00
Railroad, Lantern, Dietz Vesta, N.Y.C., Globe Stenciled L.V.R.R. 22.00
Railroad, Lantern, Erie, Marked Frame & Globe 50.00
Railroad, Lantern, Hanlan Switch, Blue Globe 35.00
Railroad, Lantern, Kerosene, AT & SF, Adlake 35.00
Railroad, Lantern, Kerosene, Caboose, Brass Wall Bracket & Shade .. 42.00
Railroad, Lantern, LVRR, Marked Frame & Globe 50.00
Railroad, Lantern, N.Y.C., Bell Bottom 40.00
Railroad, Lantern, N.Y.C., Embossed Globe 55.00
Railroad, Lantern, N.Y.C.S., Etched Blue Globe 55.00
Railroad, Lantern, NoPac, Rock Island, 5 3/8 In. 50.00
Railroad, Lantern, NYC, Bell Bottom 40.00
Railroad, Lantern, Pennsylvania Railroad, Brass Top, Globe Bell Bottom 150.00
Railroad, Lantern, PRR, Bell Bottom 55.00
Railroad, Lantern, R.F.& P.R.R., Etched Globe 55.00
Railroad, Lantern, Red Globe, S.P.Co., 3 1/2 In. 35.00
Railroad, Lantern, Switch, CCC & S RRR Lens, 3 Reflectors, Electrified 120.00
Railroad, Lantern, W.M.Ry., Red Embossed Globe 55.00
Railroad, Light, Locomotive, Kerosene, Tin, C.1870, Stenciled, 27 X 17 In. 475.00
Railroad, Lock & Key, AT & SF, Adlake 15.00
Railroad, Lock & Key, B&O, Brass, Dayton Mfg.Co. 25.00
Railroad, Lock, OSY Of O, Adlake, Brass 15.00
Railroad, Lock, Switch, Iron, No Key, S.A.L 8.00
Railroad, Map, A.C.L.System, 1963, 3 X 4 In. 6.50
Railroad, Medal, Baltimore & Ohio, 1827-1927 .... 45.00
Railroad, Menu, Great Northern, Picture Of Indians, 1938 .... 7.50
Railroad, Mirror, Pocket, Iron Mountain RR 27.50
Railroad, Mold, Wooden Wheel For Handcar, WBIMCO 1915 In Brass, 14 1/2 In. 85.00
Railroad, Money Bag, Railway Express Agency, Gray Canvas 10.00
Railroad, Oilcan, B & O Railroad, Gallon 10.00
Railroad, Oiler, Copper, 30 In. 35.00
Railroad, Oiler, Long Spout, 12 In. 12.50
Railroad, Padlock, South Pacific RR, 6 Lever, Brass 14.00
Railroad, Pass, Conductor's, 1896 .... 12.50
Railroad, Pitcher, Cream, Centennial, Baltimore & Ohio R.R. 24.00
Railroad, Plate, Baltimore & Ohio, Blue & White, 1927, 6 3/4 In. 10.00
Railroad, Plate, Baltimore & Ohio, 8 In. 35.00
Railroad, Platter, New York Central, Buffalo Railroad China, 3 Pieces .. 58.00
Railroad, Poster, Union Pacific, Soldier Throwing Grenade, WW II 20.00
Railroad, Punch, Ticket, Conductor's 5.00
Railroad, Rack, Luggage, Iron 36.50
Railroad, Receiver, Phone, Head Band, Candlestick 75.00
Railroad, Saucer, U.P.Streamliner 5.00
Railroad, Sheet, Berth, Pullman Logo 18.00
Railroad, Shovel, Burlington Route, Cast Iron, For Coal Stove 18.50
Railroad, Sign, Missouri Pacific, Tin, C.1930s, 19 X 12 In. 50.00
Railroad, Sign, Railway Express Agency, Porcelain, Diamond Shaped, 8 In. .. 20.00
Railroad, Sign, Reverse Painting, Colored Waiting Room, 1932, 9 X 31 In. 90.00

Railroad, Sign, Reverse Painting, Rest Rooms, Whites, 1929, 4 X 12 In.	65.00
Railroad, Sign, Seaboard Coast Lines	30.00
Railroad, Spoon, Canadian Pacific	2.50
Railroad, Sugar & Creamer, Silver, Lid, Marked NY, NH & Hartford RR	62.00
Railroad, Switch Light, Bull's-Eyes, Green & Red, Electrified	98.00
Railroad, Teapot, Signed, 5 In.X 8 In.	35.00
Railroad, Telegraph Sounder, Morse, Used In N.K.P. Depot	85.00
Railroad, Ticket Punch	6.50
Railroad, Timetable, Nantasket Beach RR Co., 1881, Lithograph, Framed	14.00
Railroad, Timetable, Nickel Plate Railroad, 1893	7.50
Railroad, Timetable, Pennsylvania, 1944, October	2.50
Railroad, Timetable, St.Louis, 1888	15.00
Railroad, Torch, New York Central, Tin	10.00
Railroad, Tray, Oblong, Santa Fe R.R., Ancient Mimbreno Indian, 12 In.	25.00
Railroad, Uniform, United Pacific	25.00
Railroad, Watch, 23J, Waltham, Up & Down Indiana, YFG	295.00
Railroad, Whistle, Caboose, Steam Operated, Embossed Sherburne Co.	65.00
Railroad, Wine Glass, Stemware, Marked New York Central RR	15.00
Railroad, Wine, Stemware, Marked N.Y.Central	13.50
Rainbow, see Mother-of-Pearl, Satin Glass	

*The Red Wing Pottery of Red Wing, Minnesota, was a firm started in
1878. It was not until the 1920s that art pottery was made. It closed in
1967. Rumrill pottery was made for George Rumrill by the Red Wing
Pottery Company and other firms. It was sold in the 1930s.*

Red Wing, Bowl, Bobwhite, 5 1/2 In.	3.00
Red Wing, Bowl, Centerpiece, Deer Frog, Brown On Cream, 2 Piece	15.00
Red Wing, Bowl, Console, Deer Flower Holder, 15 In.	22.50
Red Wing, Bowl, High Glaze Green, Design Band, Shallow, 7 In.	7.00
Red Wing, Bowl, Sponge Daubed Decoration, Stoneware, 7 In.	45.00
Red Wing, Bowl, Stippled Brushware, Acorns, Leaves, 6 X 26 In.	36.00
Red Wing, Candlestick, Cream Color, Raised Leaf Design, 6 In., Pair	12.50
Red Wing, Canoe, 17 In.	25.00
Red Wing, Cookie Jar, Blue Monk, Marked	15.00
Red Wing, Cookie Jar, Dutch Girl, Blue	35.00
Red Wing, Cookie Jar, French Chef, Caramel Colored	16.50
Red Wing, Cookie Jar, Monk	20.00 To 22.00
Red Wing, Cooler, Water, Wire Handles, Union Stoneware Co., Red Wing, Minn.	95.00
Red Wing, Crock, With Lid, 10 Gallon	40.00
Red Wing, Dish, Figural, Pear, Orange	6.00
Red Wing, Dish, Fish, Lid	12.00
Red Wing, Dish, Hors D'oeuvre, Bobwhite	30.00
Red Wing, Figurine, Girl, Dutch, Yellow	15.00
Red Wing, Figurine, Monk, Yellow	18.00
Red Wing, Jar, Canning, One Quart	30.00
Red Wing, Mug, Beer, Brown	3.50
Red Wing, Pitcher, Ball-Shaped, Metallic, Splotched Glaze, Gray-Green, Tan	20.00
Red Wing, Pitcher, Car, Train, Cream Color, Blue Circle Mark, 9 In.	32.00
Red Wing, Pitcher, Green, 9 In.	20.00
Red Wing, Pitcher, Lady Figurines In Panels On Sides	35.00
Red Wing, Pitcher, Orange, 4 1/2 In.	7.00
Red Wing, Pitcher, Sponge Band, 7 1/2 In.	40.00
Red Wing, Pitcher, Water, Bobwhite, 12 In.	19.50
Red Wing, Place Setting, Bobwhite	8.50
Red Wing, Planter, Conch Shell	6.50
Red Wing, Planter, Hanging Violin	15.00
Red Wing, Plate, Bobwhite, 10 3/4 In.	3.50
Red Wing, Plate, Bobwhite, 6 1/2 In.	2.00
Red Wing, Plate, Dinner, Bobwhite	3.50
Red Wing, Pocket, Wall, Violin	15.00
Red Wing, Salt, Sponge Band Decoration, Grayline	10.00
Red Wing, Server, Tidbit, Brass Center Handle, 18 In.	8.50
Red Wing, Server, Tidbit, 11 In.	8.50
Red Wing, Spittoon, Glazed, 8 X 6 1/2 In.	10.00
Red Wing, Stand, Umbrella, Union Stoneware, 12 In.High	25.00

Red Wing, Teapot, Figural, Lady Atop Chicken, Cobalt	20.00
Red Wing, Teapot, Yellow, Globe With Rim, 4 Cup	15.00
Red Wing, Tray, Hors D'oeuvre, Bobwhite	27.50
Red Wing, Vase, Blue Satin Finish, Floral, Marked & Numbered, 10 In., Pair	25.00
Red Wing, Vase, Blue, Brown Panels, 2 Handled, 10 In.	35.00
Red Wing, Vase, Brown Exterior, Marigold Interior, Ruffled Top, 8 1/2 In.	30.00
Red Wing, Vase, Brown, Embossed Flowers & Leaves, Union Stone, 8 1/2 In.	25.00
Red Wing, Vase, Chartreuse & Gray, High Glaze, 7 X 5 3/4 X 2 1/2 In., Pair	30.00
Red Wing, Vase, Cream, Handled, 7 3/4 In.	6.00
Red Wing, Vase, Egyptian Design On Cream & Green, 2-Handled, 9 1/4 In.	20.00
Red Wing, Vase, Free Form, Half Cylinder, Chartreuse, Gray, 7 X 6 X 3 In., Pair	28.00
Red Wing, Vase, Glazed Chartreuse, 4 Sided, Molded Design On One, 8 1/2 In.	15.00
Red Wing, Vase, Gold, Green, Silver, 6 1/4 In.	20.00
Red Wing, Vase, Pussy Willows, Cylindrical, 8 In.	12.00
Red Wing, Vase, Stoneware, Incised, Grecian People, White, Green, Marked, 8 In.	20.00
Red Wing, Vase, Turquoise, Raised Cactus Decoration, 7 1/2 In.	12.00
Red Wing, Vase, Union Stoneware, Blue, Olive, 7 1/2 In.	45.00
Red Wing, Vase, Union Stoneware, Lions, 7 In.	35.00
Red Wing, Vase, Urn, Stalks Of Wheat, Brown, Green, Luster Glaze, Pink, 8 In.	30.00

Redware is a hard red stoneware that originated in the late 1600s and continues to be made. The term is also used to describe any common clay pottery that is reddish in color.

Redware, see also Kitchen, Koreanware

Redware, Bowl, Black & Yellow Slip, Tulip, 10 3/4 In.	*Illus*	450.00
Redware, Bowl, Mixing, Early 19th Century, 13 In.Diameter		135.00
Redware, Bowl, Mixing, Light Brown Glaze, 14 1/2 In.		50.00
Redware, Bowl, Slip Decoration, 11 1/2 In.	*Illus*	135.00
Redware, Butter Churn, Green Glaze, 19th Century, 18 1/2 In.	*Illus*	300.00
Redware, Creamer, Black, Brown, Speckled Glaze		28.00
Redware, Cup, Saki, Blue & White Slip Decoration		20.00
Redware, Cuspidor, Glazed, S.Bell & Son, 19th Century, 3 1/4 X 6 1/4 In.		225.00
Redware, Dish, Loaf, Slip Decoration, 14 1/2 In.	*Illus*	475.00
Redware, Dish, Piecrust Edge, Pennsylvania, 9 In.		55.00
Redware, Figurine, Dog, Sgraffito Detail		255.00
Redware, Figurine, Spaniel, Signed Solomon Bell, 8 3/4 In.	*Illus*	1000.00
Redware, Flowerpot, Yellow Splotches		85.00
Redware, Inkwell, Drip Glaze, 1 3/4 X 1 1/4 In.		60.00
Redware, Jug, Brown Glaze, Handled, Small Mouth, Miniature, 2 3/4 In.		38.00
Redware, Jug, Brown Glaze, Handled, 2 1/2 X 1 1/2 In.		40.00
Redware, Jug, Green-Red Mottling, Double Handled, 14 In.		135.00
Redware, Jug, Ovoid, Brown Glaze, High Round Handle		38.00
Redware, Jug, Pear Shaped, Small		65.00
Redware, Mold, Pudding, Turk's Head, Black Sponge Decoration, 6 1/2 In.		95.00
Redware, Mold, 8 In.		32.00
Redware, Mug, Flared Top, Brown Glaze	*Illus*	35.00
Redware, Pan, Milk, Middlebury		75.00
Redware, Pitcher, Handled, Overall Nouveau Sgraffito, Signed, 12 In.		445.00
Redware, Plate, Slip Decoration, 9 1/4 In.	*Illus*	105.00
Redware, Plate, Slip, Signed W.Smith, Womelsdorf, 8 In.		85.00
Redware, Vase, Chinese, Blue, Glazed, Incised 6 Character Reign Mark, 6 In.		49.00
Redware, Vase, Ohio Origin, 16 In.		75.00
Redwood, Mug, Brown Glaze, Indian In Headdress, Redwood In Oval, 5 1/2 In.		95.00
Rekston, Ewer, Morning Glories On Glossy Brown, Stockton, 9 1/2 In.		145.00

Reverse Painting, see Painting, Reverse on Glass

Richard, Atomizer, Black Cameo Scene On Orange, 14 1/2 In.	375.00
Richard, Atomizer, Black On Orange, Trees, Lake, Mountains, Castle, 14 In.	475.00
Richard, Atomizer, Pink & Maroon Flowers, Signed, 6 3/4 In.	175.00
Richard, Vase, Cameo, Orange, Purlish Brown Leaves, Signed Cameo, 6 1/2 In.	275.00
Richard, Vase, Cameo, Yellow, Brown Trees, Castles, Lake, 16 In.	950.00
Richard, Vase, French Cameo, Royal Blue, White, Signed, 3 3/4 Inch	195.00
Richard, Vase, French, Orchid & Leaves In Burgundy, Signed, 11 1/2 In.	395.00
Richard, Vase, Landscape, Frosted Orange, Acid Cut, Cameo, 3 1/8 In.	225.00
Richard, Vase, Orange, Cobalt Blue Floral, Cameo Glass, 6 1/2 In.	185.00
Richard, Vase, Yellow Satin Translucent, Navy Blue Floral, 5 7/8 X 2 3/8 In.	175.00

Redware, Bowl, Black & Yellow Slip, Tulip, 10 3/4 In.

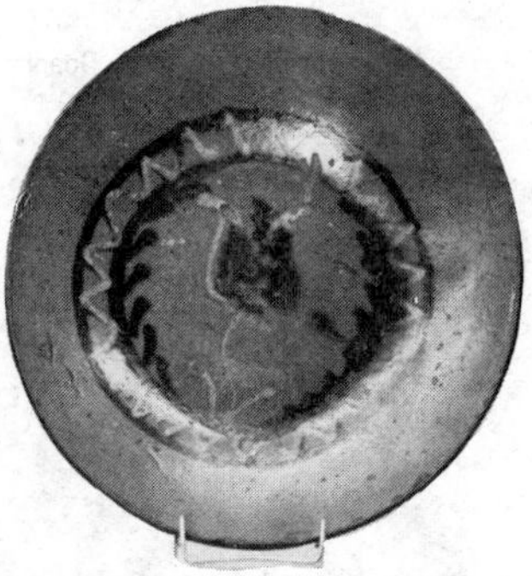

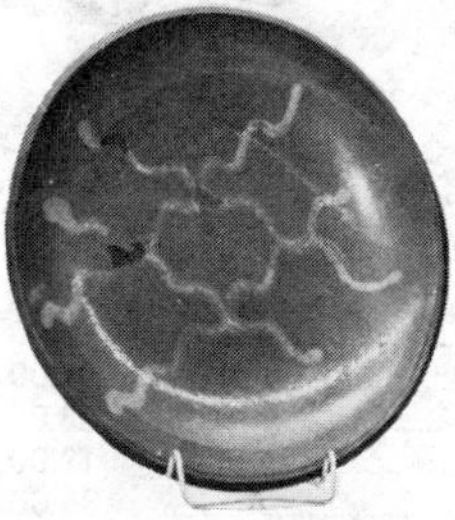

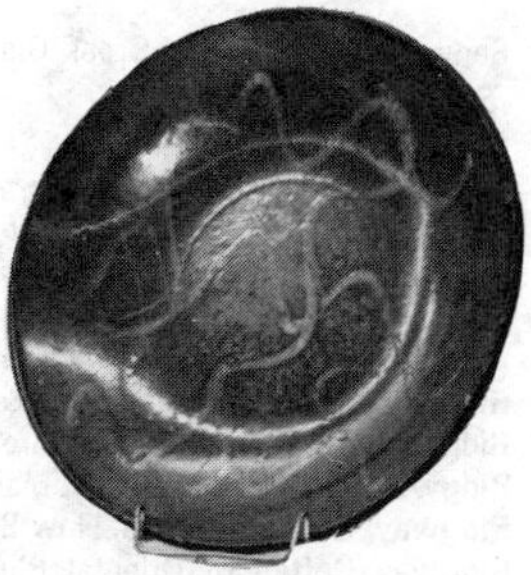

Redware, Plate, Slip, Signed W.Smith, Womelsdorf, 8 In.

Redware, Plate, Slip Decoration, 9 1/4 In.

Redware, Bowl, Slip Decoration, 11 1/2 In.

Redware, Dish, Loaf, Slip Decoration, 14 1/2 In.

Redware, Mug, Flared Top, Brown Glaze

Redware, Figurine, Spaniel, Signed Solomon Bell, 8 3/4 In.
(See Page 500)

Redware, Butter Churn, Green Glaze, 19th Century, 18 1/2 In.
(See Page 500)

Ridgway pottery has been made in the Staffordshire District in England since 1808 by a series of companies with the name Ridgway. The transfer-design dinner sets are the most widely known product. They are still being made.

Ridgway, Bowl, Coaching Days & Coaching Ways, Deep	20.00
Ridgway, Bowl, Coaching Days & Ways, Post Boys, Silver Luster Border, 9 In.	35.00
Ridgway, Bowl, Royal Vista Ware, 9 1/2 In.	38.00
Ridgway, Butter Pat, Willow, Marked	12.00
Ridgway, Coaching Days, Flow Blue, 10 1/2 In.	35.00
Ridgway, Coffeepot, Oriental, Blue, 7 In.	22.00
Ridgway, Creamer, Coaching Days & Ways 3 1/2 In.	10.00
Ridgway, Creamer, Giraffe, Brown, C.1840s	36.00
Ridgway, Cup & Saucer, Oriental, Light Blue	12.50
Ridgway, Cup, Coaching Days & Ways	10.00
Ridgway, Dish, Giraffe, Blue On White Stoneware, Aug.30, 1856, 10 In.	45.00
Ridgway, Dish, Giraffe, Brown & White, 1836, 10 1/4 In.	45.00
Ridgway, Dish, Vegetable, Covered, Delft Pattern	30.00
Ridgway, Jug, Coaching Days & Ways, Black On Gold Scene, 4 1/2 In.	65.00
Ridgway, Mug, Christmas Eve, Silver Trim & Handle, 4 1/2 In.	41.00
Ridgway, Mug, Coaching Days & Ways, 4 In.	21.00 To 25.00
Ridgway, Mug, Coaching Days, Silver Luster, Brown, 5 In.	32.00
Ridgway, Pitcher, Bulbous, Henry The Eighth & Abbot Of Reading, 4 In.	30.00
Ridgway, Pitcher, Green, Exotic Birds, Anchor Mark, C.1830, 6 In.	70.00
Ridgway, Pitcher, Wilkes Barre, Brown, 1840, 8 1/2 In.	165.00
Ridgway, Plaque, Royal Vistas, 9 1/2 In.	22.00
Ridgway, Plate, Bulldog, Silver Border, 9 In.	30.00
Ridgway, Plate, Cake, Royal Vista, Open-Eared, Moss Rose, Leaves, 10 1/2 In.	15.00
Ridgway, Plate, City Hall, N.Y., Deep Blue, 10 In.	150.00
Ridgway, Plate, Coaching Days & Coaching Ways, 9 In.	20.00
Ridgway, Plate, Dickens, Old Curiosity Shop, Cobalt Blue, 4 1/2 In.	15.00
Ridgway, Plate, Fairmount At Philadelphia, Spread Eagle	185.00
Ridgway, Plate, Insane Hospital, Boston, Dark Blue, 7 1/4 In.	175.00
Ridgway, Plate, Marmora, Brown, 9 In.	15.00
Ridgway, Plate, Royal Vistas, Venice	18.00
Ridgway, Plate, Senate House Cambridge, Blue, 7 In.	65.00
Ridgway, Plate, Soup, Octagon Church, Boston, 10 In.	185.00
Ridgway, Plate, The Rainbow, 10 In.	22.00
Ridgway, Plate, Venice, 10 In.	22.00
Ridgway, Platter, Blue, Molded Rose, Thistle Handles, 14 1/2 In.	48.00
Ridgway, Platter, Floral & Scroll Border, Blue Pantheon, 1842-44, 9 X 13 In.	38.00
Ridgway, Platter, Gold Banded, 8 1/2 X 13 1/2 In.	14.00
Ridgway, Platter, Pantheon Center, Floral & Scroll Border, 1942-44, 13 In.	38.00
Ridgway, Relish, Coaching Ways & Coaching Days, Caramel, 9 In.	22.00
Ridgway, Stein, Coaching Days, To A Snow Drift & Picking Up Mail, 12 1/2 In.	75.00
Ridgway, Tankard, Coaching Days, Salisbury Cathedral Scene, 4 1/4 In.	25.00

Ridgway, Tea Set, Maidenhair Fern, Child's, Green, 16 Piece 100.00

Riviera Ware was made by the Homer Laughlin Co. from 1938 to 1950. Plates were square and cup handles were squared.

Riviera Ware, Cup & Saucer, Yellow 3.00
Riviera Ware, Plate, Blue, 8 In. 2.50
Riviera Ware, Plate, Blue, 10 In. 4.00
Robj, Vase, Blue, Handled, 4 In. 12.00

Rockingham in the United States is a brown glazed pottery with a tortoiseshell-like glaze. It was made from 1840 to 1900 by many American potteries. The mottled brown Rockingham wares were first made in England at the Rockingham factory. Other wares were also made by the English firm.

Rockingham, Dessert Set, Apple Green & Gilt Decorations, C.1850, 7 Piece 150.00
Rockingham, Jug, Washington's Head In Raised Medallion, 6 In. 58.00
Rockingham, Pitcher, Batter, Flint Enameled, Yellow, Brown, 5 X 8 1/2 In. 35.00
Rockingham, Pitcher, Dead Game, Hound, Handled, C.1844, 9 1/2 In. 95.00
Rockingham, Plate, Pie, 9 1/2 In. 60.00
Rockingham, Teapot, Glazed, 1875, 5 1/4 In. 135.00
Rockingham, Toby Mug, Woman Holding Mug, Bottle In Other Hand, 7 1/2 In. 45.00
Rogers, see John Rogers

Rookwood pottery was made in Cincinnati, Ohio, from 1880 to 1960. All of this art pottery is marked, most with the famous flame mark. The R is reversed and placed back to back with the letter P. Flames surround the letters.

Rookwood, Ashtray, Bird, Spreading Wings, 15 Flames, Green, 7 In. 45.00
Rookwood, Ashtray, Figural, Bee, Triangular, Gold, Impressed Mark, 1927, 6 In. 20.00
Rookwood, Ashtray, Figural, Clown, Yellow, Black Glossy Finish, Signed, 6 In. 75.00
Rookwood, Ashtray, Figural, Pelican, 1933 .... 35.00
Rookwood, Ashtray, Fox, Cream, 1946 .... 40.00
Rookwood, Ashtray, Pelican, 1933 .... 35.00
Rookwood, Bookend, Babies Sitting On Books, Bronze Color, 1920, Pair 125.00
Rookwood, Bookend, Blue Elephant, 1921 .... 35.00
Rookwood, Bookend, Brass Owl, Expanding, Pair 22.00
Rookwood, Bookend, Buddha, Dark Green, Glazed, 1921, Pair 80.00
Rookwood, Bookend, Caramel, Blue Speckles, 1927, Numbered, 5 1/2 In. 100.00
Rookwood, Bookend, Dutch Boy & Girl, Brick Garden Wall, 1943, 5 In., Pair 115.00
Rookwood, Bookend, Dutch Boy & Girl, C.1929, Artist Signed, Pair 100.00
Rookwood, Bookend, Egyptian, Blue Drip Glaze, C.1921, Pair 135.00
Rookwood, Bookend, Elephant, Matte Tan, Cream, 1921, 6 X 7 In., Pair 115.00
Rookwood, Bookend, Elephant, White Matte Finish, 5 X 6 In., Pair 85.00
Rookwood, Bookend, Monk, Fox & Dove, High Glazed, 7 1/2 X 5 X 3 In., Pair 100.00
Rookwood, Bookend, Monkey, 1930, Pair 80.00
Rookwood, Bookend, Rook, Green Glaze, McMillan, Pair 95.00
Rookwood, Bookend, Seated Babies, Arms & Feet Braced, No.2447, C.1921, Pair 50.00
Rookwood, Bowl & Flower Frog, No.9641, Impressed Fish On Blue Green, 1922 .... 42.50
Rookwood, Bowl, Blue Outside, Red Inside, Handled, 1920, 10 In. 35.00
Rookwood, Bowl, Butterflies, 3 1/2 X 5 In. 135.00
Rookwood, Bowl, Conventional Raised Flower & Band, Rose, C.1921, 5 X 3 In. 55.00
Rookwood, Bowl, Floral, Inturned Rim, Extended Stems, Green Specks, Brown 45.00
Rookwood, Bowl, Gold Brush, Foliage, Sky, & Flying Birds, 1883, 4 1/2 In. 200.00
Rookwood, Bowl, Green To Blue Green, Vellum, Molded Rim Pattern, 9 1/4 In. 40.00
Rookwood, Bowl, Matte Green, Incised Geometric Design, 1904, 8 In. 20.00
Rookwood, Bowl, Mauve, Blue Interior, , Glazed Finish, C.1820, 8 In. 60.00
Rookwood, Bowl, Semigloss, Green, 2 X 4 In. 22.00
Rookwood, Bowl, Vellum, Floral, Margaret McDonald, 1920, 3 X 5 In. 155.00
Rookwood, Bowl, Vellum, Florals On Blue & Pink, 1920, 5 In. 95.00
Rookwood, Bowl, Vellum, Green To Blue-Green, Molded Design, 1910, 9 1/4 In. 38.00
Rookwood, Bowl, Vellum, Green To Blue-Green, 1910, 9 1/4 In. 45.00
Rookwood, Bowl, Vellum, Shaded Green, Molded Design, 1910, 9 1/4 In. 35.00
Rookwood, Box, Cigarette, Crown Tuscan 38.00
Rookwood, Bust, Madonna, White Face, Blue Veil, 9 1/4 In. 50.00
Rookwood, Candleholder, Blue, 1920, 7 In. 45.00
Rookwood, Candleholder, Handle On Back Of Windshield, Pin, 5 X 7 In. 45.00

Rookwood, Ewer, Water Lilies, A.M.V., 1896

Rookwood, Chocolate Pot, Water Lilies, E.Lincoln, 1899

Rookwood, Candleholder, Pink Satin, 5 X 3 In., Pair	35.00
Rookwood, Candleholder, Turquoise Matte Glaze, Art Deco, C.1920, Pair	42.00
Rookwood, Candlestick, Blossom Shaped Dripcatcher, Pink To Brown, 1918, 6 In.	38.00
Rookwood, Candlestick, High Glaze, Green, 4 1/4 In., Pair	35.00
Rookwood, Chocolate Pot, Brown, C.1885	275.00
Rookwood, Chocolate Pot, Water Lilies, E.Lincoln, 1899 .... Illus	275.00
Rookwood, Clock, Anniversary, 4 Columns, Blue Glaze, Round Face, Marked, 12 In.	250.00
Rookwood, Cockatoo, Chartreuse, Coffee Colors, 1943, Numbered, 9 1/2 In.	125.00
Rookwood, Creamer, Clover Decoration, Butterfly Handle, Brown Glaze, C.1899	145.00
Rookwood, Creamer, Dark Green Glaze, Bayberries, Signed, 1893	175.00
Rookwood, Creamer, Dark Green Glaze, Bayberry, 1893, Clotildo Zan Etta	195.00
Rookwood, Creamer, Flowers, Hand-Painted, 1881, 3 1/4 In.	275.00
Rookwood, Creamer, Mistletoe Decoration, 1898, Rose Fechheimer	185.00
Rookwood, Creamer, Pink Clover & Leaves, Amber To Light High Gloss, 1890	100.00
Rookwood, Creamer, Red Flowers, Fred Rothenbush, 1897, 3 1/2 In.	150.00
Rookwood, Dish, Cabbage Leaf, Green, 5 X 4 In.	18.00
Rookwood, Dish, Figural, Grapes & Leaf, 1938, 5 In.	35.00
Rookwood, Egg, Easter, High-Gloss Amber, Incised Clovers, 1885, 6 In.	325.00
Rookwood, Ewer, Apple Blossoms, Signed CCL, 1907, 6 In.	95.00
Rookwood, Ewer, Black Flying Swallow, Tan Background, Handled, 1884, 11 In.	695.00
Rookwood, Ewer, Blackbird, Leaves, Gold, White On Matt, 1884, 11 1/2 In.	750.00
Rookwood, Ewer, Blue Glaze, Roman Figures, Mother Nursing Child, 1946, 3 In.	60.00
Rookwood, Ewer, Brown To Yellow Standard Glaze, Flowers, 1894, C.S., 6 In.	225.00
Rookwood, Ewer, Brown, Yellow Flower, Standard Glaze, C.S., 1894, 6 In.	150.00
Rookwood, Ewer, Red Clover, Trefoil Lip, Signed C.C.L., 6 X 3 1/2 In.	185.00
Rookwood, Ewer, Silver Overlay, Red Clover, Leaves, AMV, 1891, 5 1/2 In.	1375.00
Rookwood, Ewer, Standard Glaze, Flowers, Signed LNL, 1897, 6 1/2 In.	95.00
Rookwood, Ewer, Violets, Leaves, Irene Bishop, 1902, 8 In.	345.00
Rookwood, Ewer, Water Lilies, A.M.V., 1896 .... Illus	200.00
Rookwood, Ewer, Yellow Violets, Brown Glaze, LNL, 7 In.	235.00
Rookwood, Figurine, Ballerina, High Glaze, Art Deco, L.Abel, 1931, 6 In.	95.00
Rookwood, Figurine, Bust Of Young Girl In Matte White, 8 X 8 In.	130.00
Rookwood, Figurine, Cat, Brown, 1911, 5 1/2 In.	250.00
Rookwood, Figurine, Dog, Tan & White On Green Base, 1945, 10 In.	225.00
Rookwood, Figurine, Donkey, White, Paper Label, C.1935, Louise Abel, 5 X 7 In.	145.00
Rookwood, Figurine, Elephant, Brown, Glossy, 4 1/4 X 3 1/2 In.	55.00
Rookwood, Figurine, Horse, Cherry Amber, 8 In.	125.00
Rookwood, Figurine, Monkey, 1929 Flame Mark, 3 3/4 In.	110.00
Rookwood, Figurine, Nude Girl Sitting On Oblong Base, Beige, Chocolate, 6 In.	65.00
Rookwood, Figurine, Pheasant, Blue Glaze, C.1947, 9 X 13 1/2 In.	90.00
Rookwood, Figurine, Rabbit, White, 1932, 3 1/2 In.	65.00
Rookwood, Figurine, Seated Nude, Creamy White Glaze, Louise Abel, 1928, 4 In.	95.00
Rookwood, Flowers, Slender Neck, Flared Top, C.1897, Artist Signed, 7 X 5 In.	225.00
Rookwood, Humidor, Pipes, Cigars, Matches, Glazed, 1900, Artist Signed	600.00
Rookwood, Inkwell, Dark Green Matte, Round Insert, Numbered	105.00
Rookwood, Inkwell, Thistle Bud Finial, Artist Signed, 5 1/4 X 3 In.	195.00
Rookwood, Jar, Art Nouveau Floral & Butterfly, Cover, 1919, 6 1/2 In.	165.00

Rookwood, Jar, Brown Glaze, Sallie Toohey, 1889, 5 In. 90.00
Rookwood, Jar, Powder, Ivory, Embossed Flowers On Lid, Dated, 5 In. 65.00
Rookwood, Jar, Vellum Finish, Covered, 1924, Signed LA, 10 In., Pair 800.00
Rookwood, Jardiniere, Matte Green, Incised, 1903, 8 1/2 X 9 In. 65.00
Rookwood, Jug, Birds In Tree & In Flight, Red Clay, Gold, 1882, A.R.V., 5 In. 995.00
Rookwood, Jug, Clear High Glaze With Butterfly, 1884, 4 3/4 In. 250.00
Rookwood, Jug, Crocus, Sterling Silver Overlay, A.R.Valentien, 9 In. 1500.00
Rookwood, Jug, Honey, Brown, Blue, Green, Gold Brush Strokes, 1885, Signed, 4 In. 350.00
Rookwood, Jug, Honey, Red Clay, Sgraffito Florals & Leaves, H.W., 5 In. 250.00
Rookwood, Jug, Honey, Strokes, Palm Leaves, Clouds, Birds, Brown, Blue, Signed 250.00
Rookwood, Mug, Barn Swallow, Valentien, 1896, Standard Glaze, 11 1/2 In. 550.00
Rookwood, Mug, Corn & Tassel, Shape No.587C, Artist MN, 1902 .... 185.00
Rookwood, Mug, Portrait, Wm.P.McDonald, 1894, Hairline .... Illus 600.00
Rookwood, Paperweight, Three-Mast Sailing Ship On Waves, Matte Blue, 4 In. 75.00
Rookwood, Pitcher, Baby's Breath Flowers, Leaves, 1899, C.A.B., 8 3/4 In. 85.00
Rookwood, Pitcher, Cherry Decoration, C.1899, Artist Signed, 5 1/4 In. 185.00
Rookwood, Pitcher, Figural Butterfly Handle, Standard Glaze, C.S., 1892, 3 In. 175.00
Rookwood, Pitcher, Green, High Glaze, 1946, 3 1/2 In. 22.00

Rookwood, Mug, Portrait, Wm.P.McDonald, 1894, Hairline

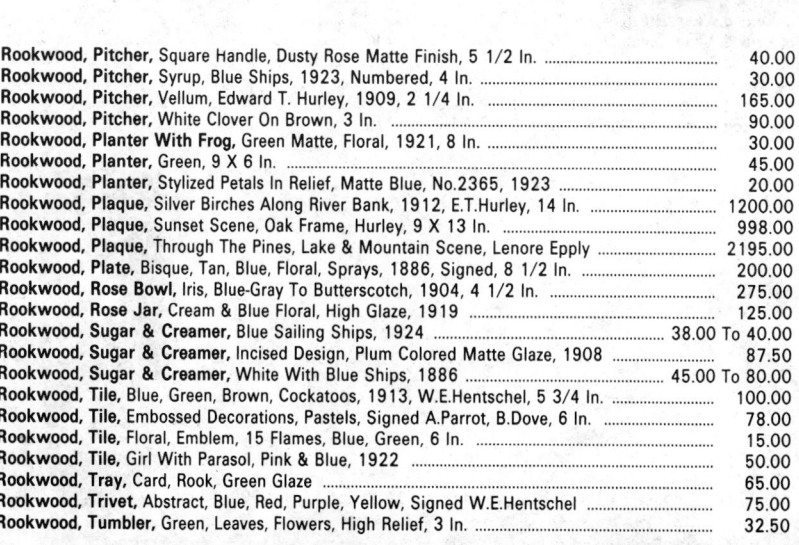

Rookwood, Vase, Birds Of Paradise, Flowers, S.A.X., 1916, 15 In.
(See Page 506)

Rookwood, Pitcher, Square Handle, Dusty Rose Matte Finish, 5 1/2 In. 40.00
Rookwood, Pitcher, Syrup, Blue Ships, 1923, Numbered, 4 In. 30.00
Rookwood, Pitcher, Vellum, Edward T. Hurley, 1909, 2 1/4 In. 165.00
Rookwood, Pitcher, White Clover On Brown, 3 In. 90.00
Rookwood, Planter With Frog, Green Matte, Floral, 1921, 8 In. 30.00
Rookwood, Planter, Green, 9 X 6 In. 45.00
Rookwood, Planter, Stylized Petals In Relief, Matte Blue, No.2365, 1923 .... 20.00
Rookwood, Plaque, Silver Birches Along River Bank, 1912, E.T.Hurley, 14 In. 1200.00
Rookwood, Plaque, Sunset Scene, Oak Frame, Hurley, 9 X 13 In. 998.00
Rookwood, Plaque, Through The Pines, Lake & Mountain Scene, Lenore Epply 2195.00
Rookwood, Plate, Bisque, Tan, Blue, Floral, Sprays, 1886, Signed, 8 1/2 In. 200.00
Rookwood, Rose Bowl, Iris, Blue-Gray To Butterscotch, 1904, 4 1/2 In. 275.00
Rookwood, Rose Jar, Cream & Blue Floral, High Glaze, 1919 .... 125.00
Rookwood, Sugar & Creamer, Blue Sailing Ships, 1924 .... 38.00 To 40.00
Rookwood, Sugar & Creamer, Incised Design, Plum Colored Matte Glaze, 1908 .... 87.50
Rookwood, Sugar & Creamer, White With Blue Ships, 1886 .... 45.00 To 80.00
Rookwood, Tile, Blue, Green, Brown, Cockatoos, 1913, W.E.Hentschel, 5 3/4 In. 100.00
Rookwood, Tile, Embossed Decorations, Pastels, Signed A.Parrot, B.Dove, 6 In. 78.00
Rookwood, Tile, Floral, Emblem, 15 Flames, Blue, Green, 6 In. 15.00
Rookwood, Tile, Girl With Parasol, Pink & Blue, 1922 .... 50.00
Rookwood, Tray, Card, Rook, Green Glaze 65.00
Rookwood, Trivet, Abstract, Blue, Red, Purple, Yellow, Signed W.E.Hentschel 75.00
Rookwood, Tumbler, Green, Leaves, Flowers, High Relief, 3 In. 32.50

Rookwood, Vase, Art Nouveau Decoration, 16 Flames, Blue Glaze, 9 In.	55.00
Rookwood, Vase, Birds Of Paradise, Flowers, S.A.X., 1916, 15 In. .... *Illus*	800.00
Rookwood, Vase, Bisque, Floral, Gold Neck, Laura Fry, 1887, Special, 8 In.	310.00
Rookwood, Vase, Blackeyed Susans, High Glaze Ground, 1904, 4 In.	165.00
Rookwood, Vase, Blooming Irises, Standard Glaze, Laura Lindeman, 1907, 6 In.	185.00
Rookwood, Vase, Blue Eggshell, 6 1/2 In., Pair	30.00
Rookwood, Vase, Blue Vellum, Leaves, Flowers, 1914, Sara Sax, 5 1/2 X 7 In.	90.00
Rookwood, Vase, Blue, Signed & Dated 1931, 6 1/4 In.	45.00
Rookwood, Vase, Brown Glaze, Blooming Daisies, 1901, Caroline Steinle, 6 In.	225.00
Rookwood, Vase, Brown To Orange, Dark Brown Leaves, Mary Norse, 1900, 10 In.	325.00
Rookwood, Vase, Brown, Yellow Clovers, E.Lincoln, 1898, 7 In.	195.00
Rookwood, Vase, Bud, Floral, Wax Matte, 1930, Pink, 7 In.	75.00
Rookwood, Vase, Bud, Flowers, Relief, Yellow, C.1928, 4 In.	22.00
Rookwood, Vase, Bud, Ivory Matte Glaze, Chocolate Glaze Interior, 1934, 6 In.	90.00
Rookwood, Vase, Bulbous, Carved And Incised Floral On Red, 1882, 8 In.	220.00
Rookwood, Vase, Bulbous, Leaf & Strawberry Molds, Pink, 5 In.	16.00
Rookwood, Vase, Bulbous, Mottled Green, Design At Top, 5 1/2 In.	28.00
Rookwood, Vase, Bulbous, Multicolored Drip Glaze, Katherine Jones, 4 1/2 In.	35.00
Rookwood, Vase, Burgundy To Olive, Matte Finish, 1911, Greek Key Trim, 8 In.	35.00
Rookwood, Vase, Butterfly Decoration, Footed, Blue Matte, C.1913, 6 In.	50.00
Rookwood, Vase, Butterfly Relief, High Glaze, Pale Blue, XIV 6457, 5 In.	25.00
Rookwood, Vase, Carmondale, 8 1/2 In.	245.00
Rookwood, Vase, Chestnuts, Leaves, Standard Glaze, No.892b, C.1901, 10 1/4 In.	240.00
Rookwood, Vase, Chrysanthemums, Stems, & Leaves, Handled, 1892, S.C., 8 1/2 In.	75.00
Rookwood, Vase, Cream, Raised African Gazelles, Foliage, Green Inside, 12 In.	200.00
Rookwood, Vase, Dancing Ladies, Blue Glaze, 9 1/4 X 5 1/2 In.	48.00
Rookwood, Vase, Deep Red, Gold Flecks, 1932, Cora Mundel, 3 In.	95.00
Rookwood, Vase, Egyptian Water Bottle, 3 Handles, Mottled, No.2428, 4 In.	38.00
Rookwood, Vase, Fish Swimming Under Water, E.T.H., 1909, 13 In. .... *Illus*	325.00
Rookwood, Vase, Floral Border, Light Blue Ground, Lorinda Epply, 1915, 6 In.	125.00
Rookwood, Vase, Floral Decoration, Matte Glaze, Signed Todd, 1914, 6 1/4 In.	70.00
Rookwood, Vase, Floral Wax Matte, C.1910, 6 In.	105.00
Rookwood, Vase, Floral Wax Matte, Sallie Coyne, Shape No.2307, 1930, 7 In.	150.00
Rookwood, Vase, Floral, Brown Glaze, Adeliza D.Sehon, 1899, 5 1/2 In.	175.00
Rookwood, Vase, Floral, Brown Shades, Standard Glaze, A.B.S., 1891, 7 In.	235.00
Rookwood, Vase, Floral, Molded, Blue Matte, Red, Signed CST, 1913, 6 In.	95.00
Rookwood, Vase, Floral, Sallie Toohey, 1904, 6 1/2 In.	145.00
Rookwood, Vase, Florals, Foliage, Iridescent, Sallie Toohey, 1894, 10 1/2 In.	150.00
Rookwood, Vase, Goldenrod, Standard Glaze, Josephine Zettel, 1898, 9 In.	225.00
Rookwood, Vase, Grape Clusters, Brown, High Glaze, 1904, 4 In.	157.00
Rookwood, Vase, Gray To Pink Glaze, 1920, 5 In.	62.00
Rookwood, Vase, Green Matte, No.2282, 1934, 5 1/2 In.	23.00
Rookwood, Vase, Green Matte, Raised Design, 1936, 6 In.	22.00
Rookwood, Vase, Green, Red Berries, Green Leaves, Signed, Impressed, 5 1/4 In.	75.00
Rookwood, Vase, Green, 1931, 6 In.	30.00
Rookwood, Vase, Greenish Blue, Floral Pattern On Top, No.2210, 7 1/4 In.	43.00
Rookwood, Vase, Handled, Blackbird & Black Foliage, Tan, 1884, 11 1/2 In.	750.00

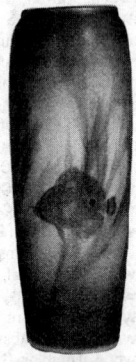

Rookwood, Vase, Fish Swimming Under Water, E.T.H., 1909, 13 In.

Rookwood, Vase, Pillow, Silver Overlay, 1892, Albert Valentien

Rookwood, Vase, High-Gloss Celadon, No.6567, 1944, 4 1/4 In.	21.50
Rookwood, Vase, High-Gloss Marbleized Lavender Glaze, 1905, 7 1/2 In.	30.00
Rookwood, Vase, Incised Conventional Decoration, Pink, 5 X 6 1/2 In.	75.00
Rookwood, Vase, Incised Leaves, Green, Handled, 1906, 7 X 5 In.	60.00
Rookwood, Vase, Iris Glaze, 1906, H.Van Horn, 6 In.	175.00
Rookwood, Vase, Iris, Daisies, Grapes, Yellow, Pink, Blue, Green, Beige, 9 In.	235.00
Rookwood, Vase, Iris, Glazed, Poppies, 1908, 9 In.	140.00
Rookwood, Vase, Iris, Sallie Coyne, 1907, 10 1/2 In.	425.00
Rookwood, Vase, Iris, Sallie Coyne, 1908, 9 In.	375.00
Rookwood, Vase, Landscape, Blue, Pastels, Signed, Number XLV 6866	175.00
Rookwood, Vase, Lavender Shades, Dated 1949, Rectangular, 4 Feet, No.6036	30.00
Rookwood, Vase, Leaf & Flower, Embossed, Matte, Dated XVI, Number 2167, 8 In.	55.00
Rookwood, Vase, Leaves, Glossy Brown, Bowling Pin Shape, LNL, 1900, 9 3/4 In.	225.00
Rookwood, Vase, Leaves, Standard Glaze, M.Mitchell, 1902, 4 X 4 In.	185.00
Rookwood, Vase, Lily Of The Valley, Drip At Base, Plum, Blue, No.2040D, 10 In.	135.00
Rookwood, Vase, Lily Of The Valley, Vellum, LNL VIII 949D, 8 3/4 In.	165.00
Rookwood, Vase, Lily Of The Valley, Vellum, Signed LNL, No.VII 949D, 9 In.	155.00
Rookwood, Vase, Male Golfer, 2nd Line Dickensware, 8 In.	200.00
Rookwood, Vase, Matte Blue-Green, Arrowheads, 1929, 8 1/2 In.	140.00
Rookwood, Vase, Matte Blue, Greek Key Trim, 1912, 4 In.	25.00
Rookwood, Vase, Matte Blue, Molded Red Flowers, 1913, 7 1/2 In.	95.00
Rookwood, Vase, Matte Glaze, Gray To Pink, Bamboo Leaves, 1920, 5 X 3 1/2 In.	62.00
Rookwood, Vase, Mistletoe, Deep Smoke To Light Gray, Iris Glaze, Signed, 5 In.	225.00
Rookwood, Vase, Mistletoe, Standard Glaze, Carrie Steinle, 1905, 7 1/2 In.	165.00
Rookwood, Vase, Molded Stylized Flowers, Blue Matte, No.2380, 6 In.	30.00
Rookwood, Vase, Molded Violets And Leaves, High Glaze, 1949, 4 In.	27.50
Rookwood, Vase, Muted Flowers, Pink, Iris Glaze, 1940, Artist Signed, 7 In.	180.00
Rookwood, Vase, Olive Green, Molded Flower In Light Green, C.1923, 5 3/4 In.	30.00
Rookwood, Vase, Ovoid, Blue, Geometric, 1927, E.Barrett, 6 X 4 1/2 In.	60.00
Rookwood, Vase, Pillow, Silver Overlay, 1892, Albert Valentien ....Illus	1350.00
Rookwood, Vase, Pink Mums & Pale Green Leaves, 7 X 5 1/2 In.	68.00
Rookwood, Vase, Pink Panels, 1927, 7 1/2 X 12 1/2 In.	25.00
Rookwood, Vase, Pink, Commercial, 1928, 6 In.	17.00
Rookwood, Vase, Raised Greek Key Band At Neck, Green, Blue, C.1900, 6 X 4 In.	85.00
Rookwood, Vase, Raised Leaf, Buff Panels, Brown, No.1823, C.1922, 7 In.	50.00
Rookwood, Vase, Raised Roses & Leaves, Green & Mustard Ground, 12 3/4 In.	350.00
Rookwood, Vase, Raised Roses & Leaves, Green & Mustard, 12 3/4 X 8 1/2 In.	325.00
Rookwood, Vase, Red, Hand-Painted, White Stork, Sallie Toohey, 4 1/2 In.	150.00
Rookwood, Vase, Rose, Floral, Matte Finish, 1923, K.Jones, 8 In.	225.00
Rookwood, Vase, Rose, Impressed Motif, Flame Mark XXVII, 5 In.	18.00
Rookwood, Vase, Sallie Toohey, 1894, 10 1/2 In.	175.00
Rookwood, Vase, Scenic Vellum, ETH, 1947, 8 In.	410.00
Rookwood, Vase, Scenic Vellum, Shirayamadani, 1911, Shape No.1655E, 8 1/4 In.	345.00
Rookwood, Vase, Sea Green Glaze Floral, Josephine E.Zettal, 8 1/2 In.	145.00
Rookwood, Vase, Sea Green, Clover, S.E.Coyne, 1902, 5 1/2 X 3 In.	275.00
Rookwood, Vase, Soft Green, Flared Base, 1927, 4 1/2 In.	29.00
Rookwood, Vase, Squatty, Pink Matte Finish, Floral Band, 1930, 4 In.	20.00
Rookwood, Vase, Standard Brown Glaze, Gold Grapes On Vine, 4 1/2 In.	160.00
Rookwood, Vase, Standard Glaze, Apple Blossoms, Hurley, 1898, 7 In.	170.00
Rookwood, Vase, Standard Glaze, Brown, Jonquils, 1898, Artist Signed, 5 In.	165.00
Rookwood, Vase, Standard Glaze, Pink, Molded, 1919, No.1890, 6 X 3 1/4 In.	40.00

Rookwood, Vase, White Flowers On Gray,
Dated, Signed, 12-15-1881

Rookwood, Vase, Vellum, Forest & Snow,
Ed Diers, 1924, 11 In.

Rookwood, Vase, Sunflowers & Foliage Molded Glaze, Blue Matte, 5 1/2 In.	49.00
Rookwood, Vase, Teal Blue, Flower Panels, Shape No.2380, 1928, 6 1/4 In.	22.00
Rookwood, Vase, Teal Blue, Marked & Numbered, 9 1/4 In.	60.00
Rookwood, Vase, Three Dragonflies, Vellum, 1905	115.00
Rookwood, Vase, Trumpet Top, Semigloss Blue-Gray, No.2736, 1923, 7 1/2 In.	32.00
Rookwood, Vase, Turquoise Crackle Glaze, Souvenir, Cincinnati, 1956	56.00
Rookwood, Vase, Vellum Glaze, Steel Blue, Molded, 1919, No.2091, 6 1/2 X 3 In.	30.00
Rookwood, Vase, Vellum, Blue Bird In Foliage, Hurley, 1908, 10 1/2 In.	385.00
Rookwood, Vase, Vellum, Carved Floral Top, Mustard Color, Sax, 1905, 4 1/2 In.	98.00
Rookwood, Vase, Vellum, Fish, LE, 1907, 5 In.	595.00
Rookwood, Vase, Vellum, Floral, Elizabeth Lincoln, 1910, 6 In.	140.00
Rookwood, Vase, Vellum, Forest & Snow, Ed Diers, 1924, 11 In. _Illus_	750.00
Rookwood, Vase, Vellum, Gold, 1928, 6 1/2 In.	45.00
Rookwood, Vase, Vellum, Lavender Chrysanthemums, Carrie Steinle, 1917, 9 In.	195.00
Rookwood, Vase, Vellum, Lily Of The Valley, Signed LNL, 1908	160.00
Rookwood, Vase, Vellum, Pastel Blue, Daisies In Pink Band, EGD, 5 3/4 In.	175.00
Rookwood, Vase, Vellum, Peacocks, Scenic Background, 1909, SS, 9 In.	585.00
Rookwood, Vase, Vellum, Purple, Incised Art Deco Green Painted Arrows, 9 In.	100.00
Rookwood, Vase, Vellum, Scenic, Blue, Gray, Salmon, 1913, Edward T.Hurley, 15 In.	350.00
Rookwood, Vase, Vera Tishler, Floral Design, 1923, 9 In.	145.00
Rookwood, Vase, Violets, Leaves, Swans In Center, Marked, 1904, 10 In., Pair	450.00
Rookwood, Vase, Wax Matte, Green, Brown, Red, Sallie Tooey, C.1905, 13 In.	185.00
Rookwood, Vase, Wax Matte, Red Floral, Blue Ground, 1923, 4 3/4 In.	115.00
Rookwood, Vase, White Flowers On Gray, Dated, Signed, 12-15-1881 _Illus_	700.00
Rookwood, Vase, Yellow Matte, Impressed Blossoms & Leaves, 1922, 10 1/2 In.	35.00
Rookwood, Vase, Yellow Roses, Foliage, Sallie Toohey, 10 1/2 In.	185.00

*Rosaline glass is a rose-colored jade glass that was made by the Steuben
Glass Works in Corning, New York.*

Rosaline, Vase, 8 In.	150.00

*Rose bowls were popular during the 1880s. Rose petals were kept in the open
bowl to add fragrance to a room. The glass bowls were made with crimped tops,
which kept the petals inside. Many types of Victorian art glass were made
into rose bowls.*

Rose Bowl, Apple Green, Pointed Hobs, 7 1/4 In.	35.00
Rose Bowl, Black Amethyst, Footed, Round Hobs, 5 1/4 X 14 1/2 In.	18.00
Rose Bowl, Emerald Green, Enameled Flowers With Gold, 7 In.	135.00
Rose Bowl, Enameled Gold & Jeweling On Turquoise, 3 Ball Feet	135.00
Rose Bowl, Iridescent, Puffed Panels, Lattice Brass Top, 5 1/2 In.	45.00
Rose Canton, Bowl, Four Panels Floral With Birds, 3 X 7 1/4 In.	95.00
Rose Canton, Charger, 16 In.	150.00
Rose Canton, Cup & Saucer, Covered	30.00
Rose Canton, Dish, Decorated With Figures, Birds & Flowers, 8 1/2 X 10 In.	165.00
Rose Canton, Ginger Jar, Medallions With Flowers & Insects, 5 In.	36.00
Rose Canton, Jug, Foo Dog Top, Gourd Shaped, 17 1/2 X 27 In.	1800.00
Rose Canton, Mug, Oriental Scene, 4 In.	400.00

Rose Canton, Plate, Octagon, 1920s, 7 In.	25.00
Rose Canton, Plate, Octagon, 1920s, 7 1/2 In.	30.00
Rose Canton, Plate, Square, 6 In.	30.00
Rose Canton, Plate, 19th Century, 8 1/2 In.	45.00
Rose Canton, Plate, 4 3/4 In.	20.00
Rose Canton, Plate, 9 1/2 In.	75.00
Rose Canton, Teapot, Decorated With Figures, Birds & Flowers	675.00

Rose Medallion china was made in China during the nineteenth and twentieth centuries. It is a distinctive design picturing people, flowers, birds, and butterflies. They are colored in greens, pinks, and other colors.

Rose Medallion, Bowl, Decorated Inside & Out, 9 In.	100.00
Rose Medallion, Bowl, Deep, 7 1/2 In.	48.00
Rose Medallion, Bowl, Inside & Out Decoration, 3 X 8 In.	65.00
Rose Medallion, Bowl, Lion, Decorated Inside & Out, 9 In.	100.00
Rose Medallion, Bowl, Oblong Fruit, Flared Rim, 6 3/4 X 8 3/4 In.	175.00
Rose Medallion, Bowl, Reticulated, 9 5/8 X 8 7/8 In.	328.00
Rose Medallion, Bowl, Round, 5 In.	48.00
Rose Medallion, Bowl, 1850, 11 In.	500.00
Rose Medallion, Box, Figures On Top, 2 Piece, 3 1/2 In.	35.00
Rose Medallion, Box, Octagon, Hand-Painted Oriental Scene, 2 1/2 X 1 1/4 In.	50.00
Rose Medallion, Box, Oval, People, Roses, Birds, Gold Trim, Covered, 5 1/4 In.	185.00
Rose Medallion, Box, 2 1/2 X 1 1/4 In.	50.00
Rose Medallion, Brush Holder, 6 In.	250.00
Rose Medallion, Candleholder, Marked China, 7 In., Pair	175.00
Rose Medallion, Candleholder, 9 In., Pair	325.00
Rose Medallion, Candlestick, Figures Of People, Flowers, 7 1/2 In., Pair	435.00
Rose Medallion, Charger, Enamel Colors, Made In China, 13 1/2 In.	115.00
Rose Medallion, Creamer, Bulbous	100.00
Rose Medallion, Cup & Saucer, Bouillon, Set Of 5	125.00
Rose Medallion, Cup & Saucer, Demitasse	28.50
Rose Medallion, Cup & Saucer, Handled	50.00
Rose Medallion, Cup & Saucer, Rests On Four Feet, C.1810	72.00
Rose Medallion, Cup & Saucer, 12 Sided Cup, C.1810	70.00
Rose Medallion, Cup, Handleless	20.00
Rose Medallion, Dish, Vegetable, Covered, 9 1/2 In.	150.00
Rose Medallion, Dish, Vegetable, Gold Acorns, Roses, Butterflies, 9 In.	255.00
Rose Medallion, Ladle, 4 3/4 In.	12.50
Rose Medallion, Mug, Strap Handle, 4 In.	90.00
Rose Medallion, Pitcher, Helmet, 5 In.	185.00
Rose Medallion, Plate, Birds, Butterflies, Floral, China, 8 In.	18.00
Rose Medallion, Plate, Butterflies, 10 1/2 In.	55.00
Rose Medallion, Plate, C.1820, 7 3/4 In.	75.00
Rose Medallion, Plate, Chop, Marked China, 12 In.	150.00
Rose Medallion, Plate, Fluted Edge, Round, 9 1/2 In.	50.00
Rose Medallion, Plate, Marked China In Box, 8 1/2 In., Pair	55.00
Rose Medallion, Plate, Panels Of People, Floral, Birds, Fruit, 1865, 9 In.	40.00
Rose Medallion, Plate, Soup, 9 1/2 In., Pair	175.00
Rose Medallion, Plate, White, Nine Colors, 8 1/2 In, Set Of 4	115.00
Rose Medallion, Plate, 8 1/2 In.	50.00
Rose Medallion, Plate, 9 1/2 In.	65.00
Rose Medallion, Platter, Child's, Vivid Colors, Gold Trim	50.00
Rose Medallion, Platter, Heavy, 12 X 15 In.	275.00
Rose Medallion, Platter, Helmet, 9 In.	175.00
Rose Medallion, Platter, 10 In.	100.00
Rose Medallion, Platter, 12 X 15 In.	275.00
Rose Medallion, Salt & Pepper, Oriental Faces, Flowers, China	27.50
Rose Medallion, Spoon, Rice	15.00
Rose Medallion, Sugar, Covered, Bulbous	125.00
Rose Medallion, Tea Set, Teapot With 2 Cups In Woven Basket	185.00
Rose Medallion, Tea Set, 4 Cups, China Mark	395.00
Rose Medallion, Teapot, Bell Shaped, 4 1/2 In.	95.00
Rose Medallion, Teapot, Cadagon	95.00
Rose Medallion, Teapot, Interior Scenes, Women, Floral, Birds, & Insects, 5 In.	125.00
Rose Medallion, Teapot, Matted Cover	45.00

Rose Medallion, Teapot, Muted Pastel Coloring, 6 In. 175.00
Rose Medallion, Teapot, Paneled, Original Handle, 5 1/2 In. 85.00
Rose Medallion, Teapot, Removable Wire Handles, Covered, 5 1/4 X 4 1/2 In. 110.00
Rose Medallion, Teapot, Scenes, Women, Floral, Birds, Insects, 5 X 4 In. 125.00
Rose Medallion, Teapot, Scenic Interior, Women, Birds, Insects, Floral, 5 In. 125.00
Rose Medallion, Teapot, Soft Pastel Coloring, 6 In. 180.00
Rose Medallion, Teapot, Wrapped Handles, Double Wire, 5 1/2 In. 98.50
Rose Medallion, Vase, Orange & Blue, 10 X 6 In. 35.00
Rose Medallion, Vase, Salamanders In Relief, Mid-19th Century, 12 1/2 In. 375.00
    Rose O'Neill, see Kewpie

*Rose Tapestry porcelain was made by the Royal Bayreuth Factory of
Germany during the late nineteenth century. The surface of the ware feels
like cloth.*

Rose Tapestry, Ashtray, Green Mark 90.00
Rose Tapestry, Basket, Blue Mark, Small 180.00
Rose Tapestry, Basket, Royal Bayreuth, Blue Mark, 5 X 5 1/2 In. 265.00
Rose Tapestry, Basket, Royal Bayreuth, Blue Mark, 6 1/2 X 6 In. 215.00
Rose Tapestry, Basket, Royal Bayreuth, Romantic Scene, Rope Handle, 4 3/8 In. 225.00
Rose Tapestry, Berry Bowl, Royal Bayreuth, Blue Mark 115.00
Rose Tapestry, Boudoir Clock, Royal Bayreuth, Roses, Signed, 4 1/4 In. 550.00
Rose Tapestry, Box, Lidded, Pink Roses, Royal Bayreuth 152.00
Rose Tapestry, Box, Lidded, Pink Roses, Royal Bayreuth, Small 152.50
Rose Tapestry, Box, Pin, Roses & White Daisies, Royal Bayreuth, 4 1/4 In. 185.00
Rose Tapestry, Box, Powder, Royal Bayreuth, Pink Roses, 3 Gold Feet, Blue Mark 175.00
Rose Tapestry, Box, Powder, Royal Bayreuth, Roses, Covered, Footed, 4 In. 185.00
Rose Tapestry, Box, Red Roses, Gold Trim, Royal Bayreuth, Blue Mark 325.00
Rose Tapestry, Box, Trinket, Kidney Shape, Large, Royal Bayreuth Blue Mark 245.00
Rose Tapestry, Chocolate Pot, 3 Color Roses, Royal Bayreuth, No Cover 750.00
Rose Tapestry, Chocolate Set, Two Cups Mismatched ....*Illus* 1900.00
Rose Tapestry, Clock 450.00
Rose Tapestry, Clock, Royal Bayreuth, White & Grays, Daisies, Blue Mark 350.00
Rose Tapestry, Creamer, Corset, Roses, Beaded Border, Blue Mark, 3 3/4 In. 155.00
Rose Tapestry, Creamer, Cows, Pinched Spout 175.00
Rose Tapestry, Creamer, Gold Trim, Signed, Royal Bayreuth 125.00
Rose Tapestry, Creamer, Maiden With Hat, Arm Around A Pony, 5 In. 120.00
Rose Tapestry, Creamer, Pinched Spout, Gold, Royal Bayreuth, 3 1/2 In. 135.00
Rose Tapestry, Creamer, Pink Roses, Corset, Blue Mark 140.00
Rose Tapestry, Creamer, Pink, Tea Roses, Green Leaves, Gold Handle, Blue Mark 155.00
Rose Tapestry, Creamer, Roses, Straight Shape, Pink 120.00
Rose Tapestry, Creamer, White Roses, Straight Side, Pink, Blue Mark 135.00
Rose Tapestry, Cup & Saucer, White, With Yellow & Pink Roses, Royal Bayreuth 115.00

Rose Tapestry, Chocolate Set, Two Cups Mismatched

Rose Tapestry, **Dish,** Collared Base, Ring Handle, 5 In. 185.00
Rose Tapestry, **Dish,** Leaf, Pink Roses, Royal Bayreuth, Blue Mark 122.50
Rose Tapestry, **Dish,** Leaf, Royal Bayreuth, Blue Mark, 5 X 4 In. 100.00
Rose Tapestry, **Dish,** Leaf, Royal Bayreuth, Pink Roses, Blue Mark 122.50
Rose Tapestry, **Dish,** Roses, Gold Handle, Royal Bayreuth, Blue Mark, 5 In. 135.00
Rose Tapestry, **Dresser Set,** Royal Bayreuth, Pink Roses, Blue Mark, 3 Piece 550.00
Rose Tapestry, **Dresser Tray,** Royal Bayreuth, Blue Mark 200.00
Rose Tapestry, **Egg,** Cockfight, Footed, Covered 190.00
Rose Tapestry, **Hair Receiver,** Footed .... 85.00 To 155.00
Rose Tapestry, **Hair Receiver,** Footed, Three Goats, Royal Bayreuth 85.00
Rose Tapestry, **Hair Receiver,** Red & Pink Roses, Royal Bayreuth, Blue Mark 175.00
Rose Tapestry, **Hair Receiver,** Royal Bayreuth, 3 Shades Of Rose .... 150.00 To 175.00
Rose Tapestry, **Hair Receiver,** Turkey Boy, Royal Bayreuth, Blue Mark 145.00
Rose Tapestry, **Hair Receiver,** Turkey Scene, Blue Mark, Royal Bayreuth 165.00
Rose Tapestry, **Hatpin Holder,** Openwork Base, Royal Bayreuth, Blue Mark 165.00
Rose Tapestry, **Hatpin Holder,** Royal Bayreuth, Yellow Roses 170.00
Rose Tapestry, **Hatpin Holder,** Royal Bayreuth, 3 Color Flowers, Footed, 4 In. 225.00
Rose Tapestry, **Hatpin Holder,** Royal Bayreuth, 3 Colored Roses, Gold Foot 185.00
Rose Tapestry, **Jar,** Powder, Pink & Yellow Roses, Round, Covered .... 150.00 To 174.00
Rose Tapestry, **Jar,** Powder, Royal Bayreuth, Lid, Footed 175.00
Rose Tapestry, **Nappy,** Royal Bayreuth, Clover Shaped 175.00
Rose Tapestry, **Pitcher,** Cream, Pink & Salmon Roses, Royal Bayreuth, 4 In. 155.00
Rose Tapestry, **Pitcher,** Milk, Roses, Large 170.00
Rose Tapestry, **Pitcher,** Milk, Royal Bayreuth, Pinch Spout, Blue Mark, 5 In. 185.00
Rose Tapestry, **Pitcher,** Pinch Spout, Royal Bayreuth, Blue Blue Mark, 4 In. 220.00
Rose Tapestry, **Pitcher,** Roses, Royal Bayreuth, Blue Mark, 3 1/4 In. 145.00
Rose Tapestry, **Pitcher,** Roses, Royal Bayreuth, Blue Mark, 4 5/8 In. 200.00
Rose Tapestry, **Pitcher,** Royal Bayreuth, Corset Shaped, 5 3/4 In. 275.00
Rose Tapestry, **Pitcher,** Royal Bayreuth, Pinch Spout, Gold, Blue Mark, 4 In. 220.00
Rose Tapestry, **Pitcher,** Royal Bayreuth, Roses, Blue Mark, 3 1/2 In. 135.00
Rose Tapestry, **Pitcher,** Royal Bayreuth, Roses, Corset Shaped, Blue Mark, 4 In. 185.00
Rose Tapestry, **Pitcher,** Royal Bayreuth, Roses, Daisies, Gold Trim, 3 1/2 In. 140.00
Rose Tapestry, **Pitcher,** Royal Bayreuth, Roses, 3 3/4 In. 120.00
Rose Tapestry, **Planter,** Bulbous Base, Gold Handles, Royal Bayreuth, 2 3/4 In. 175.00
Rose Tapestry, **Planter,** Gold Handles, Royal Bayreuth, Blue Mark, 3 X 3 In. 150.00
Rose Tapestry, **Planter,** Handled, Pink Roses, Blue Mark 205.00
Rose Tapestry, **Planter,** Royal Bayreuth, 2 Gold Handles, Blue Mark, 3 X 3 In. 150.00
Rose Tapestry, **Planter,** Royal Bayreuth, 3 Color Roses, Gold Handles, Insert 175.00
Rose Tapestry, **Planter,** Royal Bayreuth, 3 Color, Blue Mark, 3 X 3 1/2 In. 210.00
Rose Tapestry, **Plate,** Cake, Roses, Open Handled 245.00
Rose Tapestry, **Plate,** Cake, 10 In. 260.00
Rose Tapestry, **Plate,** Gold Beaded Scalloped Edge, Blue Mark, 8 1/2 In. 140.00
Rose Tapestry, **Plate,** Oval, Open Handles, 8 In. 160.00
Rose Tapestry, **Plate,** Royal Bayreuth, Blue Mark, 7 In. 195.00
Rose Tapestry, **Plate,** 3 Color Roses, Royal Bayreuth, Blue Mark, 8 1/4 In. 150.00
Rose Tapestry, **Relish,** Royal Bayreuth, Pink & White Roses, Open Handled, Blue 145.00
Rose Tapestry, **Salt & Pepper,** Royal Bayreuth, Pink Roses, Blue Mark 400.00
Rose Tapestry, **Saucer,** Demitasse, Royal Bayreuth, Blue Mark 75.00
Rose Tapestry, **Sugar & Creamer,** Cows & Grazing Scene, Royal Bayreuth 125.00
Rose Tapestry, **Sugar Shaker,** Hatpin Shape, Royal Bayreuth 225.00
Rose Tapestry, **Tea Set,** Teapot, Covered Sugar, Creamer, Blue Mark, 3 Piece 550.00
Rose Tapestry, **Tea Set,** 1 Cup Size Pot, Cream, Sugar, 3 Pieces 495.00
Rose Tapestry, **Tray,** Dresser, Royal Bayreuth, Blue Mark, 7 1/2 X 11 In. 200.00
Rose Tapestry, **Tray,** Dresser, Yellow Roses, Blue Mark, Royal Bayreuth, 9 In. 375.00
Rose Tapestry, **Tray,** Royal Bayreuth, Blue Mark, 8 X 11 In. .... 225.00 To 350.00
Rose Tapestry, **Tray,** Royal Bayreuth, Pink Roses, Blue Mark, 11 X 7 3/4 In. 215.00
Rose Tapestry, **Tumbler,** Barrel Shape, Signed Royal Bayreuth 368.00
Rose Tapestry, **Tumbler,** Royal Bayreuth, Bulbous Shape 368.00
Rose Tapestry, **Vase,** Girls Dancing, German, No.3105, 5 1/2 In., Pair 225.00
Rose Tapestry, **Vase,** Light Blue To White, Pink Flowers, 9 In. 55.00
Rose Tapestry, **Vase,** Pink Roses, Royal Bayreuth, Blue Mark, 5 In. 195.00
Rose Tapestry, **Vase,** Portrait, Royal Bayreuth, Bulbous, 8 In. 450.00
Rose Tapestry, **Vase,** Royal Bayreuth, 2 Polar Bears, Gold Handles, 6 In. 225.00
Rose Tapestry, **Vase,** Royal Bayreuth, 3 Color, Blue Mark, 5 1/2 In. 195.00
Rose Tapestry, **Vase,** Scenic, Gold Handles, Royal Bayreuth, 8 1/2 In. 185.00

MARKE

Rosenthal porcelain was established in Sels, Bavaria, in 1880. The German factory still continues to make fine-quality tableware and figurines.

Rosenthal, Barrel, Biscuit, Pate-Sur-Pate Floral Sprays, Celadon Background	110.00
Rosenthal, Bird, Gray, Tan, Yellow, On Pussy Willow, 5 1/2 In.	55.00
Rosenthal, Bowl, Blue Mottled Out, Orange Luster In, Butterflies, 6 X 3 In.	80.00
Rosenthal, Bowl, Windmill & People, Edge Forms 2 Handles, 10 In.	85.00
Rosenthal, Chocolate Pot, Portrait, Apricot, Brown	75.00
Rosenthal, Cookie Jar, Green, Apple Blossoms, Hand-Painted	95.00
Rosenthal, Cookie Jar, Pate-Sur-Pate, Green, White Raised Flowers, 7 In.	155.00
Rosenthal, Cup & Saucer, Bettina-Sommerbluten	7.50
Rosenthal, Dish, Relish, Signed	25.00
Rosenthal, Figurine, Begging Dachshund, 5 1/2 In.	55.00
Rosenthal, Figurine, Bird On Leafy Branch, C.1940, Artist Signed, 5 1/2 In.	55.00
Rosenthal, Figurine, Bird, Gray, Tan, & Yellow, Pussy Willow Branch, 5 1/2 In.	55.00
Rosenthal, Figurine, Bird, Leafy Branch, Yellow, Gray, Heidenreich, 5 1/2 In.	55.00
Rosenthal, Figurine, Cat, Green Mark, 5 In.	28.00
Rosenthal, Figurine, Colt, C.1946, 7 In.	80.00
Rosenthal, Figurine, Dachshund Puppy, Karner, 6 X 6 In.	85.00
Rosenthal, Figurine, Dachshund Puppy, Sitting, Karner, 6 1/2 X 7 In.	125.00
Rosenthal, Figurine, Dog On Hind Legs, 7 1/4 In.	85.00
Rosenthal, Figurine, Fish, Flat-Sided, Vertical On Seaweed Stand, 8 X 5 In.	75.00
Rosenthal, Figurine, Goat, Orange Glaze, 7 1/2 In.	145.00
Rosenthal, Figurine, Horse Standing On Hind Legs, Dapple Colored, 7 In.	75.00
Rosenthal, Figurine, Kitten, Lying On Tummy, White, Gray, Black, Pink Nose, Mark	50.00
Rosenthal, Figurine, Little Girl With Four Chicks, Signed Loze, 5 In.	55.00
Rosenthal, Figurine, Nude Child Riding Large Grasshopper, A.Caasmann, 4 In.	68.00
Rosenthal, Figurine, Nude Lady, Kneels, Brown Hair, Green Shirt, Artist Signed	165.00
Rosenthal, Figurine, Nude Woman Sitting, White, Signed L.F.G., 4 X 5 X 8 In.	85.00
Rosenthal, Figurine, Pigeon, Chest Fully Puffed, 6 X 6 1/2 In. .... 120.00 To 135.00	
Rosenthal, Figurine, Rabbit, 2 1/2 In.	30.00
Rosenthal, Figurine, Seals, Nuzzling, K.Himmelstoff, 3 1/2 X 4 X 3 In.	55.00
Rosenthal, Figurine, Singing Bird Perched On Pussy Willows, 5 1/2 In.	55.00
Rosenthal, Figurine, Sitting Dog, Scotty, Selb-Bavaria, 5 In.	125.00
Rosenthal, Figurine, Sitting Dog, Signed Selb-Bavaria, 5 1/2 X 7 1/2 In.	145.00
Rosenthal, Figurine, Wire-Haired Terrier, Sitting, Signed, 5 In.	110.00
Rosenthal, Figurine, Woman In Long Gown, Reaching To Clasp Angel's Hands	185.00
Rosenthal, Figurine, Yellow Bird On Pussy Willow Branch, Signed, 5 1/2 In.	55.00
Rosenthal, Goblet, Roses, Panel Stems, Intaglio, Signed, 6 In., Pair	45.00
Rosenthal, Plaque, Sitting Brown Rabbit, Albrecht Durer, 7 1/2 X 9 1/2 In.	235.00
Rosenthal, Plate, Austria & Eagle, Pink, Green Geometric, 6 In.	5.00
Rosenthal, Plate, Cake, Roses On White, Scalloped, Open Handle, 10 In.	27.00
Rosenthal, Plate, Claire, Hand-Painted Yellow Rose On Green, 9 1/2 In.	25.00
Rosenthal, Plate, Fruit, Embossed Gold Leaf Border, Fruits, 8 1/2 In.	30.00
Rosenthal, Plate, Hand-Painted Poinsettias, Gold Border, Fluted, Signed, 6 In.	12.00
Rosenthal, Plate, Oberammergau, 1922, Signed	195.00
Rosenthal, Plate, Snowball Design, 9 In., Pair	16.00
Rosenthal, Plate, The Prima Donna, Bavaria Gold, Cobalt Trim On White, 6 In.	90.00
Rosenthal, Plate, Wild Rose, Pink, 6 3/4 In., Pair	15.00
Rosenthal, Punch Bowl, Gold Handles, Gold, Artist Signed	165.00
Rosenthal, Ramekin, Hand-Painted, Floral, Gold Handles, Mint Green, Set Of 4	30.00
Rosenthal, Relish, Gooseberries, Hand-Painted, 12 In.	18.00
Rosenthal, Sculpture, Nude, Matte Finish, Signed, No.1734 LFG, 8 In.	100.00
Rosenthal, Sugar & Creamer, Ruffled, Pink Floral, Gold Trim	25.00
Rosenthal, Tray, Rosebuds, Sterling Silver Band, Beading, 4 1/8 In.	16.00
Rosenthal, Tureen, White, Raised Flowers & Leaves, Gold, 10 In.	50.00
Rosenthal, Vase, Black, Orchid Flower Swirling Around To Back, Gold, 5 In.	85.00
Rosenthal, Vase, Hand-Painted Landscape Around Top Border, Pearlized, 6 In.	18.50
Rosenthal, Vase, Panels, Hand-Painted Landscapes Around Top Border, 6 In.	22.50
Rosenthal, Vase, Russet Ground, White & Red Geraniums, 9 1/2 In.	55.00

Roseville Pottery Company was established in 1891 in Zanesville, Ohio. Many types of pottery were made, including flower vases.

Roseville, Ashtray, Artcraft, Blue Square Shape	25.00
Roseville, Ashtray, Bushberry, Blue	32.50
Roseville, Ashtray, Snowberry, Blue	20.00

Roseville, Basket, Apple Blossom, Boat Shape, Pink, 10 In.	32.00
Roseville, Basket, Apple Blossom, Pink, 10 In.	28.00
Roseville, Basket, Bittersweet, Rose, Gray, Numbered, 8 In.	24.00
Roseville, Basket, Bushberry, Blue, 10 In.	36.00
Roseville, Basket, Bushberry, Brown & Green, 8 In.	25.00
Roseville, Basket, Bushberry, Green, 8 1/2 X 9 In.	30.00 To 32.00
Roseville, Basket, Bushberry, 10 In.	40.00
Roseville, Basket, Clematis, Orange, 7 In.	22.00
Roseville, Basket, Freesia, Blue, 10 In.	30.00
Roseville, Basket, Freesia, Blue, 7 In.	26.00
Roseville, Basket, Freesia, Blue, 8 In.	18.00 To 28.00
Roseville, Basket, Freesia, Green, Handled, 8 In.	35.00
Roseville, Basket, Freesia, Green, 8 In.	30.00
Roseville, Basket, Gardenia, Gray, No.609, 10 In.	47.50
Roseville, Basket, Hanging, Columbine, Blue, With Chains, 6 In.	32.00
Roseville, Basket, Hanging, Dahlrose, Chains, Unmarked, 6 In.	35.00
Roseville, Basket, Hanging, Donatello, 6 1/2 X 31 In.	95.00
Roseville, Basket, Hanging, Foxglove, Pink, 5 In.	25.00
Roseville, Basket, Hanging, Matte Green, 6 In.	32.00
Roseville, Basket, Hanging, Normandy, 6 X 4 1/2 In.	85.00
Roseville, Basket, Hanging, Persian, Fully Marked, 11 In.	100.00
Roseville, Basket, Hanging, Zephyr Lily, Blue, 6 In.	28.00
Roseville, Basket, Imperial I, Cutout Handle, 6 X 7 In.	32.00
Roseville, Basket, Magnolia, Blue, No.384, 8 In.	22.00 To 38.00
Roseville, Basket, Magnolia, Blue, 7 In.	27.00
Roseville, Basket, Magnolia, Brown, 7 In.	22.00
Roseville, Basket, Magnolia, Brown, 12 In.	45.00
Roseville, Basket, Magnolia, Green, 13 X 9 1/2 In.	75.00
Roseville, Basket, Magnolia, Sideways Handle, No.386, 12 In.	38.00 To 45.00
Roseville, Basket, Mayfair, Green, 6 In.	28.00
Roseville, Basket, Ming Tree, White, Green, Brown Handle, 5 In.	20.00
Roseville, Basket, Peony, Pink, 10 In.	25.00 To 32.00
Roseville, Basket, Pinecone, Blue Boat, 10 In.	40.00
Roseville, Basket, Pinecone, Rustic, Brown, 10 In.	38.00
Roseville, Basket, Rozane, Cream White, 1917, 7 In.	35.00
Roseville, Basket, Rozane, Light Green, 9 In.	40.00
Roseville, Basket, Silhouette, Blue, 7 In.	35.00
Roseville, Basket, Silhouette, Burgundy, 6 1/2 In.	25.00
Roseville, Basket, Snowberry, Blue, Shape No.1BK, 7 In.	35.00
Roseville, Basket, Snowberry, Blue, 6 In.	25.00
Roseville, Basket, Snowberry, Pink, 7 In.	22.00
Roseville, Basket, Snowberry, Rose, 10 In.	28.00
Roseville, Basket, Water Lily, Pink & Green, 7 In.	35.00
Roseville, Basket, Water Lily, 10 In.	50.00
Roseville, Basket, White Rose, Green, 12 In.	41.00
Roseville, Basket, White Rose, Pink, 12 In.	39.00
Roseville, Basket, Windcraft, Blue, No.209, 10 In.	35.00
Roseville, Basket, Zephyr Lily, Brown & Green, Handled, 7 In.	25.00
Roseville, Beanpot, Raymor, No.195	16.00
Roseville, Bookend, Bittersweet, Pair	50.00
Roseville, Bookend, Clematis, Blue, Pair	40.00
Roseville, Bookend, Clematis, Matte Green, H & W, 5 1/4 In., Pair	30.00
Roseville, Bookend, Freesia, Pair	45.00
Roseville, Bookend, Gardenia, Open Books, No.659, Brown, Pair	28.00 To 50.00
Roseville, Bookend, Pinecone, Blue, Pair	40.00
Roseville, Bookend, Snowberry, Green, Pair	50.00
Roseville, Bookend, Snowberry, Matte Rose, H & W, 5 1/8 In., Pair	30.00
Roseville, Bowl, Apple Blossom, Brown, No.1361-6	12.00
Roseville, Bowl, Apple Blossom, Pink, 6 In.	30.00
Roseville, Bowl, Attached Candlestick, Thornapple, Brown	37.00
Roseville, Bowl, Bittersweet, Orange To Gray, 6 In.	15.00
Roseville, Bowl, Blackberry, 4 X 7 1/2 In.	34.00
Roseville, Bowl, Brown With Orange Floral, 9 In.	23.00
Roseville, Bowl, Carnelian, Blue, 10 In.	18.00
Roseville, Bowl, Carnelian, Marked RV, Blue, 6 1/2 In.	15.00

Roseville, Bowl, Columbine, Pink, 4 X 7 In. 30.00
Roseville, Bowl, Columbine, Pink, 12 In. 18.00
Roseville, Bowl, Centerpiece, Dogwood, Brown, No.449-10, 13 1/2 In. 29.00
Roseville, Bowl, Console, Cherry Blossom, 10 In. 32.00
Roseville, Bowl, Console, Ferella, Brown, 13 X 7 1/2 X 5 1/2 In. 100.00
Roseville, Bowl, Console, Freesia, Dark Green 30.00
Roseville, Bowl, Console, Frog, Rosecraft, Blue, 8 1/2 In. 19.00
Roseville, Bowl, Console, Jonquil, 12 1/2 In. 38.00
Roseville, Bowl, Console, Moderne, Blue, 10 In. 20.00
Roseville, Bowl, Console, Panel, Brown, 8 In. 26.00
Roseville, Bowl, Console, Pinecone, Brown, 12 In. 25.00
Roseville, Bowl, Console, Thornapple, Blue, 1930s, 4 3/4 X 11 1/2 In. 35.00
Roseville, Bowl, Console, Wisteria, Oblong, 12 In. 32.00
Roseville, Bowl, Dahlrose, Paper Label, 4 In. 15.00
Roseville, Bowl, Dahlrose, Two Handles, 10 In. .... 26.00 To 30.00
Roseville, Bowl, Dogwood 1, Marked RV, Glaze Bubble, 8 In. 26.00
Roseville, Bowl, Donatello, Footed, 5 1/2 X 12 In. 65.00
Roseville, Bowl, Donatello, Pedestal, 5 X 6 1/2 In. 45.00
Roseville, Bowl, Donatello, 7 1/2 In. 35.00
Roseville, Bowl, Florentine, Cascades Of Fruit, 9 In. 20.00
Roseville, Bowl, Florentine, Marked RV, 8 1/2 In. 21.00
Roseville, Bowl, Florentine, RV Mark, 7 1/2 In. 23.00
Roseville, Bowl, Florentine, Square Top, Handles, RV, 3 X 9 In. 24.00
Roseville, Bowl, Florentine, Tan & Green, 3 X 7 In. 20.00
Roseville, Bowl, Fruit, Flowers In Relief, Handled, 8 1/2 In. 35.00
Roseville, Bowl, Fuchsia, Brown, 3 1/2 In. 20.00
Roseville, Bowl, Fuchsia, Green, 4 X 6 In. 24.00
Roseville, Bowl, Geometric Decoration, Gray Bisque, Multicolor, 6 1/2 In. 20.00
Roseville, Bowl, Imperial, Pierced Handle, 7 In. 20.00
Roseville, Bowl, Ivory II, 3 1/2 X 6 1/2 In. 18.00
Roseville, Bowl, Jonquil, Handled, 8 In. 35.00
Roseville, Bowl, LaRose, Marked, 2 X 7 1/2 In. 25.00
Roseville, Bowl, Lily, Zephyr, Blue 12.00
Roseville, Bowl, Low, Florentine, Cascades Of Fruit, 1924-28, 9 In. 25.00
Roseville, Bowl, Magnolia, Rust, 4 X 6 In. 18.00
Roseville, Bowl, Moss, 6 In. 25.00
Roseville, Bowl, Mostique, Gray Background, 6 In. 10.00
Roseville, Bowl, Mostique, Gray Bisque, Glazed Geometrics, Shallow, 6 1/2 In. ... 20.00
Roseville, Bowl, Mostique, 3 In. 10.00
Roseville, Bowl, Mostique, 8 In. 18.00
Roseville, Bowl, Panel, Brown & Orange, UM Boxton, 4 X 7 In. 28.00
Roseville, Bowl, Panel, Dark Brown, Florals, 8 In. 24.00
Roseville, Bowl, Pinecone, Blue, Twig Handles, 6 1/2 X 8 In. 35.00
Roseville, Bowl, Pinecone, Green, 9 In. 45.00
Roseville, Bowl, Pinecone, Green, 11 X 6 In. 25.00
Roseville, Bowl, Rosecraft, Black, 2 1/2 X 8 1/2 In. 60.00
Roseville, Bowl, Rosecraft, Black, 6 1/2 X 3 1/2 In. 55.00
Roseville, Bowl, Rosecraft, Blue, Glossy, RV, 6 In. 18.00
Roseville, Bowl, Rosecraft, Hexagon, Blue, 1 1/2 In. 28.00
Roseville, Bowl, Thistle, Green, 5 1/2 In. 5.00
Roseville, Bowl, Tourmaline, Aqua Drizzles, 5 X 8 X 13 1/2 In. 60.00
Roseville, Bowl, Utility, Lily Of The Valley, 6 1/2 In. 30.00
Roseville, Bowl, Water Lily, Blue, No.663, 4 In. 12.00
Roseville, Bowl, White Rose, Green, 3 In. 15.00
Roseville, Bowl, Wisteria, Eared, Widest At Bottom, 4 X 6 In. 28.00
Roseville, Bowl, Wisteria, Mottled Brown & Blue, Purple Flowers, 6 X 4 In. 35.00
Roseville, Bowl, Wisteria, UM, 2 1/2 X 6 1/2 In. 18.00
Roseville, Candleholder, Burmese, Green, No.70B 125.00
Roseville, Candleholder, Carnelian 1 Drip, Dark To Light Blue, 3 In., Pair 16.00
Roseville, Candleholder, Carnelian, 11, Low, Blue On Beige, 1910, Pair 25.00
Roseville, Candleholder, Cremona, Green, Black, 4 1/2 In., Pair 26.00
Roseville, Candleholder, Dahlrose, 3 1/2 In., Pair 26.00
Roseville, Candleholder, Lily On Brown, Pair 16.00
Roseville, Candleholder, Pinecone, Brown, 5 In. 16.00
Roseville, Candleholder, Topeo, Red, 4 In. 24.00

Roseville, Candlestick, Baneda, Handles, 4 In. 7.00
Roseville, Candlestick, Bleeding Heart, Green, 4 1/2 In., Pair 30.00
Roseville, Candlestick, Carnelian, Pale Green, Pair 13.00
Roseville, Candlestick, Cosmos, Blue, No.1137, Pair 18.00
Roseville, Candlestick, Donatello, 6 1/2 In. 25.00
Roseville, Candlestick, La Rose, 4 In. 22.50
Roseville, Candlestick, Magnolia, Brown, No.1157, 5 In., Pair 18.00
Roseville, Candlestick, Panel, Dark Brown, 8 1/2 In. 55.00
Roseville, Candlestick, Pinecone, Blue, Pair 15.00
Roseville, Candlestick, Pinecone, Brown, 4 1/2 In., Pair 18.00
Roseville, Candlestick, Yellow, Crackle, Glaze, 6 In., Pair 19.00
Roseville, Console Set, Apple Blossom, 3 Piece 25.00
Roseville, Console Set, Bushberry, Blue, 4 Piece 63.00
Roseville, Console Set, Cremona, Green, 3 Piece 50.00
Roseville, Console Set, Dahlrose, 3 Piece 44.00
Roseville, Console Set, Peony, Deep Pink To Green, 4 Piece 45.00
Roseville, Console Set, Pink Bleeding Heart, 10 In. 30.00
Roseville, Console Set, Pink Snowberry, 3 Piece 50.00
Roseville, Console Set, White Rose, Pink, 3 Piece 36.00
Roseville, Cookie Jar, Clematis, Pink Flower, Green 47.50
Roseville, Cookie Jar, Magnolia, Green, Lid, 10 In. 45.00
Roseville, Cookie Jar, Water Lily, Blue 45.00
Roseville, Cookie Jar, Water Lily, Brown 70.00
Roseville, Cookie Jar, Water Lily, Pink To Green 65.00
Roseville, Cornucopia, Apple Blossom, No.321-6 .... 15.00
Roseville, Cornucopia, Bleeding Heart, Pink 10.00
Roseville, Cornucopia, Bushberry, Blue, 6 In. 11.00
Roseville, Cornucopia, Foxglove, Blue, No.163, 6 In. 22.00
Roseville, Cornucopia, Gardenia, Green, 6 In. 11.00
Roseville, Cornucopia, Peony, Yellow, 6 In. 18.00
Roseville, Cornucopia, Pinecone, Brown, No.126, 6 In. 22.00
Roseville, Cornucopia, Pinecone, 1932-37, Green, 8 In. 25.00
Roseville, Cornucopia, Snowberry, Green, 8 In., Pair 40.00
Roseville, Cornucopia, White Rose, Green, No.143, 6 In. 18.00
Roseville, Cracker Jar, Covered, Yellow & Pink Lilies, 2 Handled, 10 1/4 In. 75.00
Roseville, Creamer, Baby Bunting, Juvenile, Side Pouring, 3 In. 48.00
Roseville, Creamer, Two Bunnies, Creamware 15.00
Roseville, Cup, Coffee, Magnolia, Handle, Blue, Joseph Horne Sticker, 3 In. 25.00
Roseville, Cuspidor, Blue, High Glaze 125.00
Roseville, Dish, Baby, Chick Design 15.00
Roseville, Dish, Bittersweet, Brown, Yellow, Pedestal, 3 3/4 X 5 1/4 In. 35.00
Roseville, Dish, Candy, Pinecone, Leaf Shape, Brown, 2 X 7 In. 24.00
Roseville, Dish, Child's, Dog Design 27.00
Roseville, Dish, Florentine, Silver Sticker, 2 3/4 X 7 In. 28.00
Roseville, Dish, Nut, Foxglove, Blue, 10 1/2 X 6 In. 26.00
Roseville, Dish, Panel, 2 1/2 X 7 In. 24.00
Roseville, Dish, Pinecone, Green, Leaf Shaped, 7 In. 22.00
Roseville, Ewer, Clematis, Green, 10 1/2 In. 25.00
Roseville, Ewer, Clematis, Rust, 10 In. 35.00
Roseville, Ewer, Columbine, Pink, 7 In. 30.00
Roseville, Ewer, Columbine, Tan, 7 In. 19.50
Roseville, Ewer, Foxglove, Blue, 10 In. 32.00
Roseville, Ewer, Freesia, Blue, 6 In. 20.00
Roseville, Ewer, Freesia, Brown, 15 In. 55.00
Roseville, Ewer, Freesia, Green, Numbered, 15 1/2 In. 75.00
Roseville, Ewer, Freesia, Green, 6 In. 20.00
Roseville, Ewer, Magnolia, Green, Large, 15 In. 85.00
Roseville, Ewer, Mock Orange, 16 In. 60.00
Roseville, Ewer, Peony, Yellow, 6 In. 18.50
Roseville, Ewer, Poppy, 18 In., Pair 145.00
Roseville, Ewer, Zephyr Lily, Green, 10 In. 34.00
Roseville, Figurine, Elephant With Monkey On Back, Carved, 6 X 5 In. 35.00
Roseville, Flower, Bridge, Bushberry, Blue Double Bud 22.00
Roseville, Flower, Frog, Bushberry, Orange 22.50
Roseville, Flower, Frog, Donatello, 11 Holes 8.00

Roseville, Flowerpot, Bleeding Heart, Blue, Drain Hole In Bottom, 5 In. 25.00
Roseville, Flowerpot, Wincraft, Blue 18.00
Roseville, Jardiniere, Apple Blossom, Blue, Pedestal, 24 1/2 In. .... 150.00 To 160.00
Roseville, Jardiniere, Bushberry, Pedestal, 30 In. 265.00
Roseville, Jardiniere, Dahlrose, Trial, Glaze, Black, Blue, Beige, 6 1/2 In. 125.00
Roseville, Jardiniere, Dahlrose, 26 In. 33.00
Roseville, Jardiniere, Donatello, Cherubs, 6 In. 45.00
Roseville, Jardiniere, Donatello, 4 X 5 In. 34.00
Roseville, Jardiniere, Donatello, 8 X 10 1/2 In. 58.00
Roseville, Jardiniere, Earlam, No.515, 4 In. 25.00
Roseville, Jardiniere, Florentine, 8 X 9 In. 30.00
Roseville, Jardiniere, Freesia, Handled, Brown, No.463, 6 X 7 In. 18.00
Roseville, Jardiniere, Green, 4 In. 14.00
Roseville, Jardiniere, Imperial 1, Pedestal, 29 In. 250.00
Roseville, Jardiniere, Magnolia, Brown, No.665-4, 4 In. 18.00
Roseville, Jardiniere, Magnolia, Green, No.665, 3 In. 12.00
Roseville, Jardiniere, Moss, Peach & Feathery Green, No.290, 6 In. 36.00
Roseville, Jardiniere, Mostique, Gray Matte, Stylized Design, 8 X 10 In. 30.00
Roseville, Jardiniere, Nude Silhouette, Aqua, No.763, 8 In. 95.00
Roseville, Jardiniere, Pinecone, Blue, Footed, Square Base, 8 X 8 In. 30.00
Roseville, Jardiniere, Pinecone, Brown, Impressed Mark, 6 1/2 X 8 1/2 In. 45.00
Roseville, Jardiniere, Pinecone, Bulbous, Blue, Gold, 6 1/2 In. 19.00
Roseville, Jardiniere, Rosecraft Vintage, 6 X 6 3/4 In. 40.00
Roseville, Jardiniere, Rozane, Pedestal, 1917, 29 In. 275.00
Roseville, Jardiniere, Snowberry, Green, Pedestal, 26 In. 225.00
Roseville, Jardiniere, Teasel, Blue, 4 In. 17.00
Roseville, Jardiniere, Water Lily, 2 Handles, Tan To Brown, Yellow, Green 38.00
Roseville, Jardiniere, Zephyr Lily, Blue, 10 In. 55.00
Roseville, Lamp Base, Rozane Royal, Yellow Daffodils On Brown 145.00
Roseville, Lamp, Basket, Imperial 45.00
Roseville, Lamp, Cherry Blossom, Pink, 20 In. 55.00
Roseville, Lamp, Jonquil, 19 In. 45.00
Roseville, Lamp, Sunflower, Handles, 10 X 8 In. 65.00
Roseville, Mug, Decal Of 2 Children, Boat Near Water, Dutch Creamware 35.00
Roseville, Mug, Eagle On Globe 55.00
Roseville, Mug, Holland, 4 In., Pair 80.00
Roseville, Mug, Rozane, Cherries, Marked Rozane RPCO, 4 1/2 In. 90.00
Roseville, Pitcher, Cream, Green & Blue, The Bridge, 5 1/2 In. .... 30.00 To 75.00
Roseville, Pitcher, Cream, Green & Brown, The Cow, 7 1/2 In. .... 55.00 To 125.00
Roseville, Pitcher, Cream, Landscape, C.1915, 7 1/2 In. .... 45.00 To 115.00
Roseville, Pitcher, Creamware, Green Band, Chicks, 3 1/2 In. 15.00
Roseville, Pitcher, Dog With Sad Eyes 18.50
Roseville, Pitcher, Freesia, Green 45.00
Roseville, Pitcher, Fuschia, Ice Lip, Brown, 8 In. 65.00
Roseville, Pitcher, Juvenile, Rabbits, Matte Glaze, 4 In. 45.00
Roseville, Pitcher, Lemonade, Rozane, Portrait, Alfred Best, 9 In. .... Illus 400.00
Roseville, Pitcher, Pinecone, Ice Lip, Silver Sticker, Green, 8 X 7 In. 44.00
Roseville, Pitcher, Tankard, 2 Dutchmen In Decal, 11 1/2 In. .... 60.00 To 90.00
Roseville, Pitcher, The Tulip 32.00

Roseville, Pitcher, Lemonade, Rozane, Portrait, Alfred Best, 9 In

Roseville, Pitcher, Utility, Green Stripe, 6 In.	22.00
Roseville, Planter, Apple Blossom, Hanging	20.00
Roseville, Planter, Apple Blossom, Rose, Large	35.00
Roseville, Planter, Artwood, Wincraft, Green, No.1054, 8 1/2 In.	24.00
Roseville, Planter, Artwood, Yellow, 9 In.	21.00
Roseville, Planter, Bittersweet, Green, No.828, 10 In.	20.00
Roseville, Planter, Cosmos, Pink, Lavender, & White On Blue Matte, 1930, 5 In.	16.00
Roseville, Planter, Dahlrose, 30 In.	200.00
Roseville, Planter, Donatello, Glazed, 5 In.	25.00
Roseville, Planter, Donatello, 3 1/2 X 8 In.	22.00
Roseville, Planter, Jonquil, 4 X 6 In.	28.00
Roseville, Planter, Mayfair, Oblong, Beige, 8 In.	19.00
Roseville, Planter, Mostique, No.253, 3 1/2 X 7 In.	16.00
Roseville, Planter, Pinecone, Green, Oblong, Dividing Handle, 8 In.	20.00
Roseville, Planter, Rozane, Beige, Multicolor Florals, Snakeskin Design, 8 In.	45.00
Roseville, Planter, Snowberry, Pink	25.00
Roseville, Planter, Velmoss II, Green, 9 X 4 1/2 In.	30.00
Roseville, Planter, White Rose, Blue, 16 X 6 1/2 In.	28.00
Roseville, Planter, Wincraft, 12 In.	22.00
Roseville, Plate, Child's, Chicks	10.00 To 22.00
Roseville, Plate, Child's, Flat, Duck, 8 In.	28.00
Roseville, Plate, Child's, Santa Claus, Rolled Edge, 8 In.	115.00
Roseville, Plate, Donatello, 8 In.	130.00
Roseville, Platter, Raymor, Forest Green, 14 X 9 In.	18.00
Roseville, Pot, Magnolia, Green, 3 In.	10.00
Roseville, Rose Bowl, Donatello, 4 In.	32.50
Roseville, Shell, Conch, Water Lily, Brown	40.00
Roseville, Shell, Magnolia Pattern, Brown To Tan, Embossed Signature	35.00
Roseville, Sign, Display, Blue With Cream Lettering	60.00
Roseville, Smoker Set, One Piece, Dutch	65.00
Roseville, Spittoon, Blue, Gold, Cobalt, Embossed Tulips	125.00
Roseville, Sugar & Creamer, Mock Orange, Green	45.00
Roseville, Sugar & Creamer, Snowberry, Blue	15.00
Roseville, Sugar, Dutch Children, Lid	56.00
Roseville, Tankard & 4 Mugs, Elk	250.00
Roseville, Tankard, Creamware, Dutch Woman Holds Hand Of Girl & Boy, 11 In.	85.00
Roseville, Tankard, Moose Lodge, 11 1/2 In.	145.00
Roseville, Tankard, Rozane, Blackberries, 12 In.	105.00
Roseville, Tankard, Rozane, Cherries, Impressed RPCo., 10 1/2 In.	150.00
Roseville, Tea Set, Apple Blossom, Pink, 3 Piece	75.00
Roseville, Tea Set, Blue, Raised Flowers, 3 Piece	55.00
Roseville, Tea Set, Bushberry, Blue, 3 Piece	65.00
Roseville, Tea Set, Clematis, Burnt Orange, 3 Piece	58.00
Roseville, Tea Set, Clematis, Green, 3 Piece	55.00
Roseville, Tea Set, Freesia, 3 Piece	75.00
Roseville, Tea Set, No.371, Orange, 3 Piece	40.00
Roseville, Tea Set, Snowberry, Blue, 3 Piece	50.00
Roseville, Tea Set, Snowberry, Green, 3 Piece	70.00
Roseville, Tea Set, Snowberry, Pink, 3 Piece	65.00
Roseville, Tea Set, White Rose, Green, 3 Piece	70.00
Roseville, Tea Set, Windcraft, 3 Piece	55.00
Roseville, Teapot, Apple Blossom, Blue	35.00
Roseville, Teapot, Apple Blossom, Green	38.00 To 48.00
Roseville, Teapot, Black, 3 In.	90.00
Roseville, Teapot, Bushberry, Relief Mark, No.2-T	50.00
Roseville, Teapot, Clematis, Blue	50.00
Roseville, Teapot, Covered, Apple Blossom, Green	45.00
Roseville, Teapot, Dutch Creamware	55.00
Roseville, Teapot, Peony, No.3, Green	28.00
Roseville, Tray, Pinecone, 12 In.	18.00
Roseville, Tray, Snowberry, Pink, Green, Handled, 10 In.	30.00
Roseville, Tray, Snowberry, Pink, Leaf Shape, 12 In.	24.00 To 30.00
Roseville, Umbrella Stand, Florentine, Ivory, Green & Brown, 21 1/2 In.	175.00
Roseville, Umbrella Stand, Water Lily On Brown Gound, 2 Handles, 20 In.	120.00
Roseville, Urn, Azurine, 4 In.	26.00

Roseville, Urn, Cherry Blossom, 8 In. 75.00
Roseville, Urn, Gardenia, Green, No.689, 14 In. 85.00
Roseville, Urn, Gardenia, No.690, 16 In. 75.00
Roseville, Vase, Apple Blossom, Brown, No.381, 6 In. 12.00
Roseville, Vase, Apple Blossom, Green, 10 In. 12.50
Roseville, Vase, Aztec, 11 In. 185.00
Roseville, Vase, Baneda, Blue, 5 In. 15.00
Roseville, Vase, Baneda, Blue, 9 1/2 In. 45.00
Roseville, Vase, Baneda, Green, UM, 7 In. .... 30.00 To 32.00
Roseville, Vase, Baneda, Green, 2 Handles, 8 In. .... 30.00 To 35.00
Roseville, Vase, Baneda, Green, 4 1/2 In. 23.00
Roseville, Vase, Baneda, Green, 6 In. 40.00
Roseville, Vase, Baneda, Pink, Handled, 7 In. 32.00
Roseville, Vase, Baneda, Rose, Silver Sticker, 2 Handled, 4 1/4 X 4 In. 24.00
Roseville, Vase, Baneda, 6 In. 18.00
Roseville, Vase, Blackberry, Flowerpot Shape, 6 In. 19.00
Roseville, Vase, Blackberry, 2 Handles, RV Sticker, 5 In. .... 25.00 To 55.00
Roseville, Vase, Blackberry, 4 In. 45.00
Roseville, Vase, Blackberry, 5 In. 50.00
Roseville, Vase, Blackberry, 8 In. 59.00
Roseville, Vase, Bleeding Heart, Fancy Top, 15 In. 63.00
Roseville, Vase, Brown With Orange Melon Vine Design, 6 1/2 In. 45.00
Roseville, Vase, Bud, Apple Blossom, Blue, 7 In. 18.00
Roseville, Vase, Bud, Apple Blossom, Green, 7 In. 16.00
Roseville, Vase, Bud, Blue, 2 Handles, 5 In. 15.00
Roseville, Vase, Bud, Clematis, Reddish Brown, No.187, 7 In. 18.00
Roseville, Vase, Bud, Dogwood II, 9 In. 26.00
Roseville, Vase, Bud, Dogwood, 9 In. 20.00
Roseville, Vase, Bud, Florane, Marked R In Script, No.7978, Peach 14.00
Roseville, Vase, Bud, Freesia, Blue, No.195, 7 In. 16.00
Roseville, Vase, Bud, Jonquil, 7 In. 18.00
Roseville, Vase, Bud, Mock Orange, 6 In. 20.00
Roseville, Vase, Bud, Roma, 3 Sections, 6 In. 12.00
Roseville, Vase, Bud, Zephyr Lily, Brown, 6 In. 14.00
Roseville, Vase, Bushberry, Blue, Branch Handle, 14 In., Pair 165.00
Roseville, Vase, Bushberry, Blue, 4 In. 9.50
Roseville, Vase, Bushberry, Green, 4 In. 15.00
Roseville, Vase, Bushberry, Orange, Handled, 12 In. 30.00
Roseville, Vase, Bushberry, Rust, 2 Handled, 10 1/2 In. 28.00
Roseville, Vase, Bushberry, Terra-Cotta, No.31, 7 In. 25.00
Roseville, Vase, Carnelian II, Jar Shape, 1915, Green Drip On Blue, 6 In. 25.00
Roseville, Vase, Carnelian, Olive Drip, RV Mark, 15 1/2 X 5 1/2 In. 48.00
Roseville, Vase, Carnelian, Pink, 8 In. 18.00
Roseville, Vase, Caterpillar, Yellow, RRPCo., 7 In. 22.00
Roseville, Vase, Clematis, Blue, Flared Opening, Bulbous Base, 9 1/4 In. 18.50
Roseville, Vase, Clematis, Brown, 15 In. 60.00
Roseville, Vase, Clematis, Handled, Blue, No.107, 8 In. 18.00
Roseville, Vase, Clemena, Blue, Tulip Shaped, 8 In. 50.00
Roseville, Vase, Clemena, Brown, 2 Large Handles, Made Into Lamp, 8 In. 65.00
Roseville, Vase, Columbine, Blue No.27, 16 In. 75.00
Roseville, Vase, Columbine, Brown, 7 1/2 In. 15.00
Roseville, Vase, Columbine, Rose, No.16, 7 In. 22.00
Roseville, Vase, Conch Shell, Water Lily, Pink & Green, 16 1/2 In. 30.00
Roseville, Vase, Corinthian, Fruit Wreath Band, 6 In. 22.00
Roseville, Vase, Corinthian, Jardiniere, 8 X 11 In. 105.00
Roseville, Vase, Cornucopia, White Rose, No.143, Brown, Pair, 6 In. 18.00
Roseville, Vase, Cosmos, Brown, 9 In. 25.00
Roseville, Vase, Cremona, Pink, 10 In. 35.00
Roseville, Vase, Dahlrose, Brown, Square, 6 In. 17.00
Roseville, Vase, Dahlrose, Eared, Ivory Flowers, Pebbly Tan, 8 X 4 3/4 In. 27.00
Roseville, Vase, Dahlrose, Eared, Tapered, 9 In. 22.00
Roseville, Vase, Dahlrose, Jug Shape, Eared, Large, Florals, 8 In. 25.00
Roseville, Vase, Dahlrose, Pedestal, UM, 16 X 7 In. 75.00
Roseville, Vase, Dahlrose, Square, 10 In. 17.50

Roseville, Vase, Dahlrose, Vertical Sided, 2 Ears, 1924-28, 6 In. .... 20.00 To 25.00
Roseville, Vase, Dahlrose, 8 In. 18.00
Roseville, Vase, Dawn, Light Yellow, No.315, 4 In. 30.00
Roseville, Vase, Dogwood II, 10 In. 38.00
Roseville, Vase, Dogwood, Green, No.2, 12 In. 35.00
Roseville, Vase, Dogwood, Green, Raised White Floral, C.1918, 8 1/2 In. 30.00
Roseville, Vase, Donatello, Cylinder, 12 In. 48.00
Roseville, Vase, Donatello, Cylindrical, 8 X 2 1/4 In. 18.00
Roseville, Vase, Donatello, Double, Cherubs, 4 1/2 X 7 1/2 In. .... 24.00 To 29.00
Roseville, Vase, Donatello, 9 3/4 In. 42.00
Roseville, Vase, Double Bud, Lustre, Blue, RV Mark 22.00
Roseville, Vase, Double Bud, Rosecraft, Vintage Brown 38.00
Roseville, Vase, Earlam, 2 Handled, No.517, 5 1/2 In. 35.00
Roseville, Vase, Egyptian, Ivory Tint, No.E-68, 15 1/2 In. 245.00
Roseville, Vase, Etruscan, Blue, Orange Interior, 6 1/4 X 5 In. 30.00
Roseville, Vase, Falline, Handles, Brown, 6 In. 52.00
Roseville, Vase, Floor, Apple Blossom, Branch Handles, 18 In. 95.00
Roseville, Vase, Florane, Marked RV, 6 1/4 In. 25.00
Roseville, Vase, Florentine, Double Bud, 6 In. 19.00
Roseville, Vase, Florentine, Marked RV, 8 In. 27.00
Roseville, Vase, Florentine, RV, 10 1/2 In. 28.00
Roseville, Vase, Florentine, 8 1/2 In. 14.00
Roseville, Vase, Forest, 15 In. 125.00
Roseville, Vase, Foxglove, Green, No.42, 4 In. 16.00
Roseville, Vase, Freesia Green, Handled, 7 In. 22.00
Roseville, Vase, Freesia, Blue, 2 Handled, 9 1/2 In. 28.00
Roseville, Vase, Freesia, Blue, 7 1/2 In. 15.00
Roseville, Vase, Freesia, Green, Shoulder Handles, 15 1/2 In. 70.00
Roseville, Vase, Fuchsia, Blue, Light-Bulb Shape, 2 Handles, 6 In., Pair 60.00
Roseville, Vase, Fuchsia, Blue, 10 In. 28.00
Roseville, Vase, Fuchsia, Blue, 2 Handled, 8 1/4 X 7 1/2 X 3 In. 34.00
Roseville, Vase, Fuchsia, Brown, 6 In. .... 18.00 To 28.00
Roseville, Vase, Futura, Beehive, Leaf Design, Made Into Lamp, 9 In. 55.00
Roseville, Vase, Futura, Brown, 5 In. 24.00
Roseville, Vase, Futura, Matte Turquoise & Coral, Square, Twisted, 6 In. 33.00
Roseville, Vase, Futura, Stacked, Green, 12 In. 29.50
Roseville, Vase, Gardenia, Tan Ground, 8 In. 18.00
Roseville, Vase, Gardenia, Tan, 10 In. 18.00
Roseville, Vase, Grapes, Green & Red Leaves, Brown Glaze, Ferrell, 12 In. 300.00
Roseville, Vase, Horn Of Plenty, Green, 8 In. 23.00
Roseville, Vase, Iris, Blue, 7 In. 35.00
Roseville, Vase, Ivory, Ball, 4 In. 14.00
Roseville, Vase, Ixia, Blue, 3 1/4 In. 15.00
Roseville, Vase, Ixia, Green, 12 In. 60.00
Roseville, Vase, Ixia, Pink, Impressed 864, 12 In. 40.00
Roseville, Vase, Ixia, Pink, 8 In., Pair .... 22.00 To 25.00
Roseville, Vase, Ixia, 10 In. 26.00
Roseville, Vase, Jonquil, 2 Handled, 7 1/2 In. 35.00
Roseville, Vase, Laurel, Green, 2 Handles, 7 1/4 X 3 1/2 In. .... 30.00 To 35.00
Roseville, Vase, Laurel, Green, 6 In. 29.00
Roseville, Vase, Laurel, Green, 8 1/2 In. 48.00
Roseville, Vase, Laurel, Paper Label, Green, 8 1/2 X 7 In. 28.00
Roseville, Vase, Laurel, Yellow, 2 Handles, 8 In. 40.00
Roseville, Vase, Lilies, Blue With Yellow, Handles, 15 In. 65.00
Roseville, Vase, Lotus, Blue & Cream, 10 In. 75.00
Roseville, Vase, Lotus, Blue, 10 In. 115.00
Roseville, Vase, Lotus, Green, 10 In. 115.00
Roseville, Vase, Lotus, Turquoise On Cream, 10 In. 85.00
Roseville, Vase, Luffa, Brown, 6 In. .... 22.50 To 25.00
Roseville, Vase, Luffa, Brown, 8 In. .... 30.00 To 37.00
Roseville, Vase, Luffa, Green, Unmarked, 6 In. 20.00
Roseville, Vase, Luffa, Green, 7 In. 24.00
Roseville, Vase, Magnolia, Blue, 9 In. 25.00
Roseville, Vase, Magnolia, Brown, Side-Handled, 8 1/4 X 10 In. 45.00

Roseville, Vase, Mayfair, Brown Outside, Tan Inside, 8 In. 14.00
Roseville, Vase, Ming Tree, Blue, Low & Long, No.568, 8 In. 18.00
Roseville, Vase, Ming Tree, Blue, 10 In. 39.00
Roseville, Vase, Ming Tree, Blue, 8 In. 20.00
Roseville, Vase, Mock Orange, Green, 12 In. 35.00
Roseville, Vase, Moderne, Beige, 7 1/2 X 3 1/2 In. 22.00
Roseville, Vase, Moderne, Blue, 7 In. 18.00
Roseville, Vase, Mongol, Red, 5 In. 425.00
Roseville, Vase, Monticello, Blue, 2 Handled, 8 1/2 X 3 3/4 In. 39.00
Roseville, Vase, Monticello, Brown, Handled, Footed, 10 1/4 In. 45.00
Roseville, Vase, Monticello, Brown, 8 1/2 In. 45.00
Roseville, Vase, Moss, Blue, 12 In. 40.00
Roseville, Vase, Moss, 16 In. 22.00
Roseville, Vase, Mostique, Arrowheads, 7 In. 16.00
Roseville, Vase, Mostique, Gray Matte Finish, 10 In. 35.00
Roseville, Vase, Mostique, Marked RV, 6 In. 18.00
Roseville, Vase, Mostique, UM, 10 X 5 1/2 In. 35.00
Roseville, Vase, Mostique, 12 1/2 In. 25.00
Roseville, Vase, Mostique, 6 In. 24.00
Roseville, Vase, New Hampshire Vintage, Bulbous, 8 In. 145.00
Roseville, Vase, Olive, Orange Floral, RV Mark, 6 In. 20.00
Roseville, Vase, Orian, Blue, 14 In. 75.00
Roseville, Vase, Orian, Blue, 6 In. 30.00
Roseville, Vase, Orian, Red, 12 1/2 In. 95.00
Roseville, Vase, Pauleo, Blue & Veined Glaze, Narrow, Satiny Sheen, 12 In. 375.00
Roseville, Vase, Pear Shape, Coppertone, 7 1/2 In. 24.00
Roseville, Vase, Peony, Handles, 6 In. 16.00
Roseville, Vase, Pinecone, Blue, No.112, 7 In. 25.00
Roseville, Vase, Pinecone, Blue, 8 In. 20.00
Roseville, Vase, Pinecone, Brown, Twig Ears, Blue, 1931, 9 X 6 In. 30.00
Roseville, Vase, Pinecone, Brown, 6 In. 32.00
Roseville, Vase, Pinecone, Green, Footed, Handled, 10 In. 45.00
Roseville, Vase, Pinecone, Green, No.711, 10 1/4 X 8 1/2 In. 55.00
Roseville, Vase, Pinecone, Green, 10 1/2 In. 37.50
Roseville, Vase, Pinecone, Green, 8 1/2 In. 12.50
Roseville, Vase, Pinecone, Handled, Green, No.709, 10 In. 42.00
Roseville, Vase, Pinecone, 5 In. 18.00
Roseville, Vase, Pinecone, 9 X 6 1/2 In. 20.00
Roseville, Vase, Poppy, Pink, 7 In. 20.00
Roseville, Vase, Poppy, 2 Handled, 4 In. 22.00
Roseville, Vase, Primrose, Blue, Marked, 760, 6 In. 15.00
Roseville, Vase, Rose Blossoms, Green, 2 Handled, 6 In., Pair 18.00
Roseville, Vase, Rosecraft, Blue, 6 X 2 1/4 In. 25.00
Roseville, Vase, Rosecraft, Vintage, 8 1/2 In. 37.00
Roseville, Vase, Rozane Light, Orchid & Gray, Artist Signed, 8 In. 195.00
Roseville, Vase, Rozane, Aztec, 8 In. 175.00
Roseville, Vase, Rozane, Blended, Greens, Browns, 4 In. 40.00
Roseville, Vase, Rozane, Clover, Gray Shades, Artist Signed, 10 In. 110.00
Roseville, Vase, Rozane, Cylinder Shape, 11 1/2 In. 125.00
Roseville, Vase, Rozane, Egyptian, Handles, 6 1/2 In. 160.00
Roseville, Vase, Rozane, Pedestal, 1917, 5 1/4 X 7 In. 40.00
Roseville, Vase, Rozane, Royal Light, Clover, Green, Artist Signed, 6 1/2 In. 150.00
Roseville, Vase, Rozane, Woodland, Poppies, 6 1/2 In. 160.00
Roseville, Vase, Rozane, 4 In. 125.00
Roseville, Vase, Rusco, Salmon, 8 In. 45.00
Roseville, Vase, Silhouette, Nude In Panel, Red, Art Deco, 8 1/4 In. 125.00
Roseville, Vase, Snowberry, Blue, 7 In. 15.00
Roseville, Vase, Snowberry, Green, No.1FH, 6 In. 20.00
Roseville, Vase, Snowberry, Green, 10 In. 20.00
Roseville, Vase, Snowberry, Green, 7 1/2 In. 12.00
Roseville, Vase, Sunflower, Blue, 5 In. 48.00
Roseville, Vase, Sunflower, Eared, 4 Flowers On Pebbly Green Ground, 5 In. 40.00
Roseville, Vase, Sunflower, Green To Brown Ground, Eared, 5 In. 32.00
Roseville, Vase, Sunflower, Green, 8 In. 40.00
Roseville, Vase, Teasel, No.883, 7 In. 20.00

Roseville, Vase, Teasel, 6 In. 22.50
Roseville, Vase, Thornapple, Brown, Eared, No.810, 1930, 6 In. .... 19.00 To 21.00
Roseville, Vase, Thornapple, Eared, 1932-37, 6 In. 26.00
Roseville, Vase, Thornapple, Rose, Art Deco, 6 1/4 In. 20.00
Roseville, Vase, Topeo, Glossy Shaded Amber, 6 1/4 In. 35.00
Roseville, Vase, Triple Bud, Dahlrose, Sticker 25.00
Roseville, Vase, Tulip, Clemana, Blue, 8 In. 50.00
Roseville, Vase, Tuscany, Gray, 8 In. 18.00
Roseville, Vase, Tuscany, Hexagonal, Fancy Handles, 6 In. 24.00
Roseville, Vase, Tuscany, Pink, Green Handles, Rectangular, 7 In. 24.00
Roseville, Vase, Tuscany, Pink, 5 X 6 In. 25.00
Roseville, Vase, Tuscany, Rectangular X-Section, Green Leaf Handles, 7 In. 24.00
Roseville, Vase, Velmoss II, Blue, 6 In. 18.00
Roseville, Vase, Wall, Tuscany, Pink, 8 1/2 In. 16.00
Roseville, Vase, Wall, Vertical Bar Handles, 8 In. 16.00
Roseville, Vase, Water Lily, Blue & Green, 8 In. 17.00
Roseville, Vase, Water Lily, Blue, Handles, 14 In. 35.00
Roseville, Vase, Water Lily, Blue, Handles, 6 In. .... 8.50 To 18.00
Roseville, Vase, White Rose, Blue, 6 In. 15.00
Roseville, Vase, White Rose, Pink, No.146, 6 In. .... 20.00 To 22.00
Roseville, Vase, White Rose, Tan, 7 In. 22.00
Roseville, Vase, White Rose, 2 Handled, 6 In. 25.00
Roseville, Vase, White With Green Berries & Leaves, 5 3/4 X 8 1/2 In. 28.00
Roseville, Vase, Wincraft, Green & Brown, 10 X 6 1/2 In. 12.00
Roseville, Vase, Wincraft, No.241, 6 In. 15.00
Roseville, Vase, Wisteria, Handles, 4 1/2 X 7 In. 25.00
Roseville, Vase, Wisteria, 10 In. 60.00
Roseville, Vase, Wisteria, 2 Handled, Squatty, 4 1/2 In. 40.00
Roseville, Vase, Wisteria, 5 X 6 In. 35.00
Roseville, Vase, Zephyr Lily, Blue, No.141, 15 In. 70.00
Roseville, Vase, 2 Handles, Earlam, 7 1/4 X 8 1/2 X 4 3/4 In. 45.00
Roseville, Wall Pocket & Basket, Hanging, Corinthian, Blue RV 90.00
Roseville, Wall Pocket, Apple Blossom, Blue 15.00
Roseville, Wall Pocket, Blue Freesia, RV 15.00
Roseville, Wall Pocket, Carnelian, Pink, Green Drip 23.00
Roseville, Wall Pocket, Clematis, Green, 1295, 8 In. 22.00
Roseville, Wall Pocket, Corinthian, 8 In. 32.00
Roseville, Wall Pocket, Donatello, 10 In. .... 25.00 To 40.00
Roseville, Wall Pocket, Freesia, Blue, 8 In. 22.00
Roseville, Wall Pocket, Freesia, 8 In. 28.00
Roseville, Wall Pocket, Rosecraft, Yellow, 10 In. 28.00
Roseville, Wall Pocket, Snowberry, Blue, Pair 35.00
Roseville, Wall Pocket, Sunflower 55.00
Roseville, Wall Pocket, Tuscany, Side Handles, 8 In. 23.00
Roseville, Water Set, Magnolia, Green, 7 Piece 180.00
Roseville, Window Box, Pinecone, Green 30.00
Rosewood, Chair, Peking, Carved, 19th Century 600.00
Rosewood, Figurine, Oriental Man, Carved, 7 In. 35.00
Rosewood, Table, Peking, Carved Apron, Square, 18th Century, 30 X 30 In. 1500.00

Rowland and Marsellus Company is a mark which appears on historical
Staffordshire dating from the late nineteenth and early twentieth centuries.
Rowland and Marsellus is believed to be the British Anchor Pottery
Co. of Longton, England. Many American views were made.

Rowland & Marsellus, Creamer, Plymouth, Pilgrim, Blue 15.00
Rowland & Marsellus, Plate, Albany, N.Y., Dark Blue Rolled Rim .... 24.00 To 28.00
Rowland & Marsellus, Plate, Horseshoe Curve Center 28.00
Rowland & Marsellus, Plate, Indianapolis, Blue, Roll Rim, 10 In. 34.00
Rowland & Marsellus, Plate, Landing Of Hendrick Hudson, Rolled Edge, Blue 25.00
Rowland & Marsellus, Plate, New York City, Dark Blue Rolled Edge 27.00
Rowland & Marsellus, Plate, New York City, Rolled Edge, Dark Blue 25.00
Rowland & Marsellus, Plate, New York State, Blue, Roll Rim, 10 In. 34.00
Rowland & Marsellus, Plate, Old Boston Church, 9 3/4 In. 22.50
Rowland & Marsellus, Plate, Portland, Oregon, Dark Blue, 10 In. 27.00
Rowland & Marsellus, Plate, Syracuse, New York, Indian Head In Medallion 27.00

Rowland & Marsellus, Plate, T.Roosevelt Portrait, Rolled Edge 55.00
Rowland & Marsellus, Plate, White House, Washington, D.C., Blue, White, 10 In. 18.00
Roy Rogers, Badge, Deputy, Tin Star, 1950 .... 3.50 To 5.00
Roy Rogers, Box, Lunch 8.00
Roy Rogers, Card, Movie Lobby, 11 X 14 In. 9.00
Roy Rogers, Guitar, Adult Size, Original Case, Large 125.00
Roy Rogers, Gun, Tuck-A-Way, Cap, Original Package 20.00
Roy Rogers, Harmonica 10.00
Roy Rogers, Hat, Quick-Shooter 15.00
Roy Rogers, Lariat, Rodeo 10.00
Roy Rogers, Mug, Figural, Plastic 5.00
Roy Rogers, Photograpy, Roy & Trigger 6.00
Roy Rogers, Pistol, Cap, Miniature, On Store Card 3.00
Roy Rogers, Thermos, Roy & Dale 5.00
Roy Rogers, Toby Mug, Plastic 8.00
Royal Austria, Plate, Cake, Pink Roses, Blue Egg, 10 3/4 In. 65.00
Royal Austria, Plate, Gold Edge, Violets & Roses 14.00
Royal Austria, Platter, White, Green Leaves, Pink Flower Border 25.00
Royal Austria, Salt Dip, White, Gilt Rims, Set Of Five 10.00
Royal Austrian, Bowl, Iris, Brown Ground, Beaded Goldleaf Scallop, 9 In. 60.00

Royal Bayreuth porcelain was made in Germany during the late nineteenth and twentieth centuries. Many types of wares were made.

Royal Bayreuth, see also Old Ivory, Rose Tapestry, Sand Babies
Royal Berlin, see also KPM

Royal Bayreuth, Ashtray, Black Corinthian, Blue Mark .... 45.00 To 49.00
Royal Bayreuth, Ashtray, Eagle, Blue Mark 35.00
Royal Bayreuth, Ashtray, Maiden, 2 Baskets, Blue Mark 40.00
Royal Bayreuth, Ashtray, Mountain Goat, Signed 140.00
Royal Bayreuth, Ashtray, Pearlized 25.00
Royal Bayreuth, Ashtray, White Ground, Art Deco Outline, Gold, Black, Red Mark 12.50
Royal Bayreuth, Bonbon, Rooster & Hen Scene, Finger Handle, Blue Mark 20.00
Royal Bayreuth, Bowl, Berry, Angels & Flowers, 10 1/2 In. 150.00
Royal Bayreuth, Bowl, Berry, Blown-Out Orchids, Gold, Pink Roses, Blue Mark 45.00
Royal Bayreuth, Bowl, Berry, Cupids, 10 In. 165.00
Royal Bayreuth, Bowl, Corinthian, 2 Handled, Lid, Red, Black, Black Mark, 6 In. 135.00
Royal Bayreuth, Bowl, Floral, 10 In. 50.00
Royal Bayreuth, Bowl, Pansy Flower, Deep Raspberry Color, Ruffled, 5 3/4 In. 45.00
Royal Bayreuth, Bowl, Poppy, Blue Mark, 3 X 6 In. 35.00
Royal Bayreuth, Bowl, Salad, Figural, Tomatoes 50.00
Royal Bayreuth, Bowl, Satin Finish, Blown-Out Grape, Blue Mark, 9 1/4 In. 125.00
Royal Bayreuth, Bowl, Shell Shaped, Mother-Of-Pearl, Blue Mark 110.00
Royal Bayreuth, Bowl, 2 Peasants, Signed, 3 3/4 In. 108.00
Royal Bayreuth, Box, Card, Green, 3 Storks 46.00
Royal Bayreuth, Box, Card, Green, 3 Storks, Blue Mark 36.00
Royal Bayreuth, Box, Cows, Sunset Colors, Covered, Blue Mark 49.00

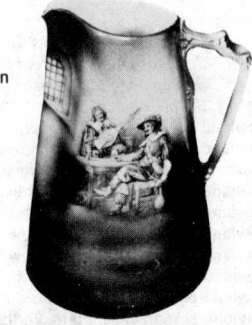

Royal Bayreuth, Milk Pitcher, Cavalier, Signed Dixon

Royal Bayreuth, Box, Hairpin, 2 Cows, Scenic Ground, Covered, Blue Mark	60.00
Royal Bayreuth, Box, Hunting Scene, Club Shape	40.00
Royal Bayreuth, Box, Lurex, Shell Shape, Covered	48.00
Royal Bayreuth, Box, Patch, Sheep Cover, Blue Mark, 2 1/2 In.	125.00
Royal Bayreuth, Box, Pin, Rose Tapestry, Oval, Cover	135.00
Royal Bayreuth, Box, Powder, Tapestry Cover, Roses, 3 Footed, Gold Feet, 5 In.	200.00
Royal Bayreuth, Box, Rose Tapestry, Cover, Three Colors, Blue Mark, 6 1/2 In.	135.00
Royal Bayreuth, Box, Tomato, Covered, Signed, Small	48.00
Royal Bayreuth, Box, Trinket, Red Rose, Lid	225.00
Royal Bayreuth, Bread & Milk Set, Little Jack Horner, Blue Mark, 3 Piece	145.00
Royal Bayreuth, Candleholder, Clown, Match Holder, Red, Blue Mark, 6 3/4 In.	165.00
Royal Bayreuth, Candleholder, Handle On Back, Signed The Rivals, Black Mark	125.00
Royal Bayreuth, Candlestick, Corinthian, Blue Mark	60.00
Royal Bayreuth, Candlestick, Dutch Girl With Basket, Dog On Leash, Mark, Pair	57.50
Royal Bayreuth, Candlestick, Jack & Jill, Blue Mark, 4 1/4 In.	75.00
Royal Bayreuth, Candy, Black Corinthian, Two Handles, Blue, Marigold	49.00
Royal Bayreuth, Celery, Brittany Girls, Blue Mark, 8 In.	45.00
Royal Bayreuth, Celery, Lobster	95.00
Royal Bayreuth, Chamberstick, Corinthian, Orange, Blue Mark, 5 1/2 In.	28.00
Royal Bayreuth, Chamberstick, Red Poppy Figural Handle	110.00
Royal Bayreuth, Chocolate Set, Flowers, Pink, Gold, Blue Mark	200.00
Royal Bayreuth, Chocolate Set, Pink Flowers, Gold, 9 Piece	275.00
Royal Bayreuth, Cigar & Match Holder, Huntsman, Footed, Blue Mark, 2 3/4 In.	35.00
Royal Bayreuth, Cigar Holder, Hunt Scene, Round, Opening On Side For Ashes	85.00
Royal Bayreuth, Clock, Hand-Painted, Orange & White Flowers	160.00
Royal Bayreuth, Compote, Goats, 4 1/4 In.	85.00
Royal Bayreuth, Cracker Jar, Tomato, Blue Mark	110.00
Royal Bayreuth, Cracker, Jar, Lobster, Signed	200.00
Royal Bayreuth, Creamer, Alligator	120.00 To 125.00
Royal Bayreuth, Creamer, Alligator, Black Mark	95.00 To 110.00
Royal Bayreuth, Creamer, Alligator, Blue Mark	60.00 To 135.00
Royal Bayreuth, Creamer, Apple	78.00
Royal Bayreuth, Creamer, Apple, Black Mark	45.00 To 50.00
Royal Bayreuth, Creamer, Apple, Blue Mark	40.00 To 85.00
Royal Bayreuth, Creamer, Bird Of Paradise	125.00
Royal Bayreuth, Creamer, Black Cat	65.00 To 80.00
Royal Bayreuth, Creamer, Black Cat, Blue Mark	72.00
Royal Bayreuth, Creamer, Black Cat, Red Interior	70.00
Royal Bayreuth, Creamer, Black Mountain Goat, Horns Form Handle	125.00
Royal Bayreuth, Creamer, Black Water Buffalo, Blue Mark	90.00
Royal Bayreuth, Creamer, Black Water Buffalo, Red Tusks, Blue Mark, 3 1/2 In.	42.00
Royal Bayreuth, Creamer, Brittany Girl, Flared Rim, Blue Mark	69.00
Royal Bayreuth, Creamer, Bulbous, Boy With Scythe, Chickens, 5 In.	60.00
Royal Bayreuth, Creamer, Bull	110.00
Royal Bayreuth, Creamer, Bull, Blue Mark	85.00
Royal Bayreuth, Creamer, Butterfly, Blue Mark	100.00 To 110.00
Royal Bayreuth, Creamer, Cat	85.00
Royal Bayreuth, Creamer, Cat Handle	115.00
Royal Bayreuth, Creamer, Cat, Gray, Blue Mark	55.00
Royal Bayreuth, Creamer, Cattle, Farmhouse, Blue Mark, 3 In.	37.50
Royal Bayreuth, Creamer, Cavalier Scene, Blue Mark	50.00 To 57.00
Royal Bayreuth, Creamer, Clown, Blue Mark	95.00 To 105.00
Royal Bayreuth, Creamer, Clown, Red	85.00
Royal Bayreuth, Creamer, Clown, Red, Blue Mark	95.00
Royal Bayreuth, Creamer, Coachman, Blue Mark, 4 1/2 In.	110.00 To 115.00
Royal Bayreuth, Creamer, Conch Shell	30.00
Royal Bayreuth, Creamer, Conch Shell, Pearlized, Blue Mark	65.00 To 74.00
Royal Bayreuth, Creamer, Corinthian	42.00
Royal Bayreuth, Creamer, Corinthian, Black, Grecian Figures, Greek Key	35.00
Royal Bayreuth, Creamer, Corinthian, Gold & Black Greek Key, Grecian Figures	40.00
Royal Bayreuth, Creamer, Corinthian, Grecian Figures, Gold & Black Greek Key	32.00
Royal Bayreuth, Creamer, Corinthian, Orange	32.00
Royal Bayreuth, Creamer, Cow	85.00
Royal Bayreuth, Creamer, Cows In Meadow, Blue Mark	55.00
Royal Bayreuth, Creamer, Cows, Puckered Spout, Flared Base, Signed, 3 1/2 In.	87.00

Royal Bayreuth, Creamer, Crow, Blue Mark 75.00
Royal Bayreuth, Creamer, Crow, Orange Beak, Blue Mark, 4 1/2 In. .... 65.00 To 90.00
Royal Bayreuth, Creamer, Crow, 4 3/4 In. .... 40.00 To 82.00
Royal Bayreuth, Creamer, Dachshund, Marked 135.00
Royal Bayreuth, Creamer, Dark Gray, Sailboat, Men, Blue Mark 45.00
Royal Bayreuth, Creamer, Devil & Cards, Blue Mark, 4 In. .... 40.00 To 75.00
Royal Bayreuth, Creamer, Devil & Cards, Green Mark 95.00
Royal Bayreuth, Creamer, Devil & Cards, 4 3/4 In. 95.00
Royal Bayreuth, Creamer, Duck 40.00
Royal Bayreuth, Creamer, Duck, Marblehead On Handle, Blue Mark 85.00
Royal Bayreuth, Creamer, Dutch Scene 52.50
Royal Bayreuth, Creamer, Eagle 120.00
Royal Bayreuth, Creamer, Eagle, Gray, Brown, Signed, Blue Mark 105.00
Royal Bayreuth, Creamer, Elk, Black Mark 40.00
Royal Bayreuth, Creamer, Elk, Blue Mark, 4 1/4 In. .... 42.00 To 65.00
Royal Bayreuth, Creamer, Elk, C.1910, Blue Mark, 5 In. 55.00
Royal Bayreuth, Creamer, Fish 115.00
Royal Bayreuth, Creamer, Fish Head, Blue Mark, 4 1/4 In. .... 65.00 To 85.00
Royal Bayreuth, Creamer, Floral, Pinched Spout, Blue Mark 16.00
Royal Bayreuth, Creamer, Flowers, Ribbons, Pink, Blue, Slender, Blue Mark 45.00
Royal Bayreuth, Creamer, Frog, Blue Mark .... 67.50 To 75.00
Royal Bayreuth, Creamer, Frog, Orange 85.00
Royal Bayreuth, Creamer, Frog, Red, Black Mark, 2 1/2 In. 85.00
Royal Bayreuth, Creamer, Frog, Red, Blue Mark .... 85.00 To 95.00
Royal Bayreuth, Creamer, Geranium Flower, Blue Mark 125.00
Royal Bayreuth, Creamer, Girl & Dog 65.00
Royal Bayreuth, Creamer, Girl Holding Dog On Leash, Blue Mark, 4 In. 45.00
Royal Bayreuth, Creamer, Girl In White Dress & Hat, Holding Dog, Blue Mark 75.00
Royal Bayreuth, Creamer, Goats, Pinched Spout, Green 50.00
Royal Bayreuth, Creamer, Grapes, Iridescent, Lavender 65.00
Royal Bayreuth, Creamer, Grapes, Pearlized, Iridescent 85.00
Royal Bayreuth, Creamer, Grapes, Purple 58.00
Royal Bayreuth, Creamer, Honey Bear, Black Mark 80.00
Royal Bayreuth, Creamer, Ibex 90.00
Royal Bayreuth, Creamer, Jack & Beanstalk 52.00
Royal Bayreuth, Creamer, Jack & Jill, Blue Mark, 4 In. .... 65.00 To 75.00
Royal Bayreuth, Creamer, Leaf, Lobster Decorated, Handle, Blue Mark 45.00
Royal Bayreuth, Creamer, Lemon, Blue Mark 45.00
Royal Bayreuth, Creamer, Lemon, Green Twig Handle, Leaf 75.00
Royal Bayreuth, Creamer, Little Boy Blue, Scuttle Shape, Blue Mark 60.00
Royal Bayreuth, Creamer, Lobster 65.00
Royal Bayreuth, Creamer, Lobster With Leaf, Handle 20.00
Royal Bayreuth, Creamer, Lobster, Green Mark 25.00
Royal Bayreuth, Creamer, Lobster, Green Mark, 4 In. 40.00
Royal Bayreuth, Creamer, Man In The Mountain, Black Mark 70.00
Royal Bayreuth, Creamer, Man In The Mountain, Brown, Gray 87.00
Royal Bayreuth, Creamer, Man In The Mountain, Green Mark, 4 In. 70.00
Royal Bayreuth, Creamer, Man In The Mountain, Yellow, Brown 87.00
Royal Bayreuth, Creamer, Milkmaid 120.00
Royal Bayreuth, Creamer, Monkey, Green, Blue Mark 85.00
Royal Bayreuth, Creamer, Monkey, Green, Marked 120.00
Royal Bayreuth, Creamer, Moose, Blue Mark 55.00
Royal Bayreuth, Creamer, Moosehead, Blue Mark, 5 1/2 In. 54.00
Royal Bayreuth, Creamer, Mountain Goat, Blue Mark 125.00
Royal Bayreuth, Creamer, Mountain Goat, Blue Mark, 4 In. 60.00
Royal Bayreuth, Creamer, Murex Shell, Low Profile, Blue Mark 48.00
Royal Bayreuth, Creamer, Oak Leaf, Green, Blue Mark 75.00
Royal Bayreuth, Creamer, Oak Leaf, Twig Handle, Black Mark 65.00
Royal Bayreuth, Creamer, Orange, Blue Mark 45.00
Royal Bayreuth, Creamer, Orange, Daisy, Leaf, Twig Trim, Signed 85.00
Royal Bayreuth, Creamer, Orange, Signed 85.00
Royal Bayreuth, Creamer, Owl, Blue Mark 150.00
Royal Bayreuth, Creamer, Oyster Shell 75.00
Royal Bayreuth, Creamer, Oyster Shell, Signed 65.00

Royal Bayreuth, Creamer, Pansy, Green Mark	85.00
Royal Bayreuth, Creamer, Parakeet, Blue Mark	135.00
Royal Bayreuth, Creamer, Parrot	65.00
Royal Bayreuth, Creamer, Parrot, Blue Mark	35.00
Royal Bayreuth, Creamer, Pearl & Pink Luster, Puffed Sides, 2 X 5 In.	35.00
Royal Bayreuth, Creamer, Peasants With Horses, Scenic, Signed, 4 In.	160.00
Royal Bayreuth, Creamer, Polar Bears, Pinched Spout, Brown & Green	60.00
Royal Bayreuth, Creamer, Poppy, Blue Mark, 6 X 2 In.	45.00
Royal Bayreuth, Creamer, Red Devil	75.00
Royal Bayreuth, Creamer, Robin	40.00
Royal Bayreuth, Creamer, Roses, Pink, Yellow, Green, Black Mark, 4 In.	90.00
Royal Bayreuth, Creamer, Roses, Yellow And Pink, Blue Mark	55.00
Royal Bayreuth, Creamer, Saint Bernard, Blue Mark	120.00
Royal Bayreuth, Creamer, Scene With Sheep	65.00
Royal Bayreuth, Creamer, Seal, Blue Mark	135.00
Royal Bayreuth, Creamer, Sheep, Shepherdess, Blue Mark, 3 In.	37.50
Royal Bayreuth, Creamer, Shell	35.00
Royal Bayreuth, Creamer, Shell With Coral Handle, Blue Mark	30.00
Royal Bayreuth, Creamer, Shell With Lobster Handle	65.00
Royal Bayreuth, Creamer, Shell With Lobster Handle, Blue Mark	35.00
Royal Bayreuth, Creamer, St.Bernard	115.00
Royal Bayreuth, Creamer, Standing Trout, Blue Mark	95.00
Royal Bayreuth, Creamer, Strawberry	78.00
Royal Bayreuth, Creamer, Strawberry, Blue Mark	85.00
Royal Bayreuth, Creamer, Strawberry, Signed, 4 In.	75.00
Royal Bayreuth, Creamer, To Bed By Candlelight, Pinched Spout, Blue Mark	65.00
Royal Bayreuth, Creamer, Tomato	25.00
Royal Bayreuth, Creamer, Tomato, Blue Mark	28.00
Royal Bayreuth, Creamer, Tomato, Footed, Vine Handle	45.00
Royal Bayreuth, Creamer, Tomato, Red & Green, Blue Mark, 4 In.	50.00
Royal Bayreuth, Creamer, Tomato, Red Mark	25.00
Royal Bayreuth, Creamer, Turtle, Black Mark	150.00
Royal Bayreuth, Creamer, Verse, Little Bo-Peep, Blue Mark	85.00
Royal Bayreuth, Creamer, Water Buffalo, Black & White, Blue Mark	95.00
Royal Bayreuth, Creamer, Water Buffalo, Black, Blue Mark, Red Trim	105.00
Royal Bayreuth, Creamer, Water Buffalo, Black, Red Horns	47.00
Royal Bayreuth, Creamer, Water Buffalo, Black, Red, Blue Mark	55.00
Royal Bayreuth, Creamer, Water Buffalo, Blue Mark	105.00 To 120.00
Royal Bayreuth, Creamer, Water Buffalo, Brown, White, Marked	95.00
Royal Bayreuth, Cup & Saucer, Deer Scene, Blue Mark	25.00
Royal Bayreuth, Cup & Saucer, Demitasse, Elk Head Cup, Green Leaf Saucer	75.00
Royal Bayreuth, Cup & Saucer, Demitasse, Peacock Inside Cup & On Saucer	50.00
Royal Bayreuth, Cup & Saucer, Jack & Jill	50.00
Royal Bayreuth, Cup & Saucer, Pink Roses, Gold Band	25.00
Royal Bayreuth, Cup & Saucer, Poppy, Blue Mark	60.00 To 85.00
Royal Bayreuth, Dish, Candy, Handled, Black Corinthian, Blue Mark	45.00
Royal Bayreuth, Dish, Child's, Jack & The Beanstalk, Blue Mark	45.00
Royal Bayreuth, Dish, Child's, Little Miss Muffet	65.00
Royal Bayreuth, Dish, Child's, Ring Around Rosie, Blue Mark	66.00
Royal Bayreuth, Dish, Clown, Hands Clasped Together, Red	150.00

Royal Bayreuth, Dresser Tray, Man Fishing
(See Page 526)

Royal Bayreuth, **Dish,** Donkey & Boy, Footed, Blue Mark, 5 1/2 In.	65.00
Royal Bayreuth, **Dish,** Jack & Beanstalk, Heart Shaped, Blue Mark	55.00
Royal Bayreuth, **Dish,** Leaf, Handled, Blue Mark, 6 1/2 In.	20.00
Royal Bayreuth, **Dish,** Lettuce	35.00
Royal Bayreuth, **Dish,** Nut, 4 Feet, Openwork In Gold, Satin Finish	50.00
Royal Bayreuth, **Dish,** Rectangular, White, Pink, Yellow Roses, Blue Mark	210.00
Royal Bayreuth, **Dish,** Tomato On Green Leaf, Covered, Blue Mark, 3 Piece	55.00
Royal Bayreuth, **Dish,** Tomato, Blue Mark	30.00
Royal Bayreuth, **Dish,** Trinket, Oval, Lid, Black Mark	145.00
Royal Bayreuth, **Dresser Set,** Roses On Blue, Blue Mark, 2 Piece	125.00
Royal Bayreuth, **Dresser Tray,** Man Fishing _Illus_	165.00
Royal Bayreuth, **Ewer,** Pastoral Scene, Sheep, Rams, Pasture, Trees, 4 1/4 In.	45.00
Royal Bayreuth, **Figurine,** Alligator	115.00
Royal Bayreuth, **Figurine,** Apple, Small	28.00
Royal Bayreuth, **Figurine,** Crow, Blue Mark	75.00
Royal Bayreuth, **Figurine,** Horseback Rider & Peasant On Wheel Cart	87.00
Royal Bayreuth, **Gravy Boat,** Attached Dish, U.S.Zone, Germany	15.00
Royal Bayreuth, **Hair Receiver & Powder Dish,** Footed, Blue Mark	125.00
Royal Bayreuth, **Hair Receiver,** Footed, Fall Colors, Hunter & Turkeys	85.00
Royal Bayreuth, **Hair Receiver,** Hunting Scene, Footed, Blue Mark	85.00
Royal Bayreuth, **Hair Receiver,** Ivory, Black Mark	50.00
Royal Bayreuth, **Hair Receiver,** Yellow Roses, Blue Mark	60.00
Royal Bayreuth, **Hatpin Holder,** Base Scene Of Mules & Small Boy, Blue Mark	75.00
Royal Bayreuth, **Hatpin Holder,** Bell Ringer, Blue Mark	225.00
Royal Bayreuth, **Hatpin Holder,** Hunt Scene, Blue Mark	75.00
Royal Bayreuth, **Hatpin Holder,** Owl, Blue Mark	250.00
Royal Bayreuth, **Hatpin Holder,** Penguins, Raised Decoration	75.00
Royal Bayreuth, **Hatpin Holder,** Pink, Yellow Roses, Gold Trim, Blue Mark	250.00
Royal Bayreuth, **Hatpin Holder,** Red & Green Poppy, Black Mark	95.00
Royal Bayreuth, **Hatpin Holder,** Red Poppy	145.00
Royal Bayreuth, **Hatpin Holder,** Red Poppy, Blue Mark	135.00
Royal Bayreuth, **Holder,** String, Wall Type, Rooster, Blue Mark	110.00
Royal Bayreuth, **Humidor,** Eagle, Signed	125.00
Royal Bayreuth, **Humidor,** Legal Advice, Dark Green, 5 In.	90.00
Royal Bayreuth, **Humidor,** Pink Roses, Gold Overlay Base & Lid, Gold Handles	225.00
Royal Bayreuth, **Jar,** Jam, Covered, Spoon, Satin Finish, Blown-Out Grape	95.00
Royal Bayreuth, **Jar,** Mustard Apple, Leaf Cover Spoon	50.00
Royal Bayreuth, **Jar,** Mustard, Orange Lobster Head, Ladle, 4 X 4 In.	60.00
Royal Bayreuth, **Jar,** Powder, Little Children, Green Background, 3 1/4 X 3 In.	65.00
Royal Bayreuth, **Jar,** Powder, Oyster & Pearl, Mother-Of-Pearl, Signed	75.00
Royal Bayreuth, **Jar,** Powder, Rose Colors, Footed	175.00
Royal Bayreuth, **Jar,** Powder, Yellow Roses, Gold Feet, Blue Mark 65.00 To	70.00
Royal Bayreuth, **Jug,** Black Crow, Signed, 5 In.	65.00
Royal Bayreuth, **Marmalade,** Figural, Grape, Bavaria, 6 1/4 In.	50.00
Royal Bayreuth, **Marmalade,** Lobster Cover, Large	48.00
Royal Bayreuth, **Match Holder,** Clown, Pearlized, Blue Mark, 5 X 3 1/4 In.	125.00
Royal Bayreuth, **Match Holder,** Floral	65.00
Royal Bayreuth, **Match Holder,** Hanging, Devil & Cards, Green Mark	135.00
Royal Bayreuth, **Match Holder,** Hanging, Little Jack Horner, Red Suit, Marked	75.00
Royal Bayreuth, **Match Holder,** Hanging, Penguin, Blue Mark	85.00
Royal Bayreuth, **Match Holder,** Hanging, Red Clown	145.00
Royal Bayreuth, **Match Holder,** Pearlized Clown, Blue Mark	140.00
Royal Bayreuth, **Match Holder,** Poppy, Unsigned	68.00
Royal Bayreuth, **Match Holder,** Red Devil Holding Cards, Striker At Base, Mark	150.00
Royal Bayreuth, **Mayonnaise,** Tomato	35.00
Royal Bayreuth, **Milk Pitcher,** Alligator, Black Mark	150.00
Royal Bayreuth, **Milk Pitcher,** Cavaliers, Signed Dixon _Illus_	130.00
Royal Bayreuth, **Mug,** Clown, Child's	108.00
Royal Bayreuth, **Mug,** Cows In Pasture, 4 3/4 In.	50.00
Royal Bayreuth, **Mug,** Devil & Cards, Signed	45.00
Royal Bayreuth, **Mug,** Elk, 5 3/4 In.	150.00
Royal Bayreuth, **Mug,** Green, Ye Little Bottel, Blue Mark	75.00
Royal Bayreuth, **Mug,** Sunbonnet, Blue Mark	85.00
Royal Bayreuth, **Mug,** Yellow With Drinking Scene At Top, Green, Set Of 4	440.00
Royal Bayreuth, **Mustard,** Apple, With Spoon	75.00
Royal Bayreuth, **Mustard,** Murex, Covered, With Spoon	65.00

Royal Bayreuth, Mustard, Red Poppy 85.00
Royal Bayreuth, Mustard, Tomato 35.00
Royal Bayreuth, Mustard, Tomato, Blue Mark, Three Piece 40.00
Royal Bayreuth, Nappy, Children Sliding Down Hill, Blue Mark, 4 In. 60.00
Royal Bayreuth, Nappy, Leaf, Apple Blossoms, Blue Mark 20.00
Royal Bayreuth, Nappy, Poppy, Blue Mark 35.00
Royal Bayreuth, Nappy, Swans On Lake, Oval, Handled, Blue Mark 32.00
Royal Bayreuth, Nut Set, 3 Mountain Goats, 7 Piece 135.00
Royal Bayreuth, Pin Tray, Corinthian, Classical Figure, Heart Shape, Marked 48.00
Royal Bayreuth, Pin Tray, Pale Pink, White Roses, Blue Mark, 6 1/4 In. 32.50
Royal Bayreuth, Pitcher, Art Nouveau Lady, 4 1/2 In. 55.00
Royal Bayreuth, Pitcher, Black, Greek Figures, Hand-Painted, 6 X 3 In. 125.00
Royal Bayreuth, Pitcher, Brittany Girl, Blue Mark, 4 3/4 In. 95.00
Royal Bayreuth, Pitcher, Brown & Pink, Drinking Scene, Blue Mark, 3 1/2 In. 70.00
Royal Bayreuth, Pitcher, Cavalier Drinking Scene, 6 In. 75.00
Royal Bayreuth, Pitcher, Cobalt Blue, Roses, Blue Mark, 4 In. 68.00
Royal Bayreuth, Pitcher, Colonial Lady, Brown, 3 3/4 In. 35.00
Royal Bayreuth, Pitcher, Girls & Sheep, Blue Mark, 3 In. 21.00
Royal Bayreuth, Pitcher, Hunt Scene, Blue Mark, 3 1/2 In. 65.00
Royal Bayreuth, Pitcher, Lobster, Blue Mark, 5 In. 65.00
Royal Bayreuth, Pitcher, Lobster, 4 In. 45.00
Royal Bayreuth, Pitcher, Lobster, 4 1/2 In. 60.00
Royal Bayreuth, Pitcher, Milk, Alligator, Signed 150.00
Royal Bayreuth, Pitcher, Milk, Babes In Woods, Blue Mark 50.00
Royal Bayreuth, Pitcher, Milk, Dachshund .... 150.00 To 155.00
Royal Bayreuth, Pitcher, Milk, Devil & Cards, Green Mark 160.00
Royal Bayreuth, Pitcher, Milk, Fish Head, Black Mark 125.00
Royal Bayreuth, Pitcher, Milk, Goat Scene, Blue Mark, 4 1/2 X 4 1/2 In. 60.00
Royal Bayreuth, Pitcher, Milk, Pink Morning Glory, Melon, Blue Mark, 5 In. 135.00
Royal Bayreuth, Pitcher, Milk, Snow Babies On Sled, Black Mark, 6 In. 250.00
Royal Bayreuth, Pitcher, Milk, St.Bernard 125.00
Royal Bayreuth, Pitcher, Mountain Goat, Brown, Gray, Pink, Blue Mark, 4 In. 210.00
Royal Bayreuth, Pitcher, Opalescent Shell, Twisted Handle 100.00
Royal Bayreuth, Pitcher, Pastoral Scene, Blue Mark, 5 In. 60.00
Royal Bayreuth, Pitcher, Poppy, Red, 4 1/2 In. 65.00
Royal Bayreuth, Pitcher, Portrait Of A Woman, Pinched Spout, 5 3/4 In. 95.00
Royal Bayreuth, Pitcher, Red Bottom, Cavaliers, Mandolin, Blue Mark, 7 1/2 In. 125.00
Royal Bayreuth, Pitcher, Stag, Blue Mark, 4 1/4 In. 65.00
Royal Bayreuth, Pitcher, Stork On Yellow Background, Black Mark, 7 1/2 In. 80.00
Royal Bayreuth, Pitcher, Water, Beetle, Black Mark 335.00
Royal Bayreuth, Pitcher, Water, Lobster 155.00
Royal Bayreuth, Pitcher, Water, Lobster, Signed 175.00
Royal Bayreuth, Pitcher, Water, Yellow, Clown 305.00
Royal Bayreuth, Pitcher, 3 Fishermen, Boat, Clouds, Waves, Black, Blue Mark 70.00
Royal Bayreuth, Pitcher, 3 Greek Figures, Leaves & Cones In Corners 95.00
Royal Bayreuth, Plate, Arab, Horses, In Desert, 10 In. 65.00
Royal Bayreuth, Plate, Cake, Oak Leaf, Blue Mark, 8 In. 65.00
Royal Bayreuth, Plate, Cavaliers, Dixon, Blue Mark, 10 In. 125.00
Royal Bayreuth, Plate, Dutch Children, 6 In. 30.00
Royal Bayreuth, Plate, Farmer, Leghorns, Trees, Blue Mark, 9 In. 82.00
Royal Bayreuth, Plate, Girl And Dog, 9 In. 135.00
Royal Bayreuth, Plate, Green, Jack & Jill, Blue Mark, 10 1/2 In. 100.00
Royal Bayreuth, Plate, Jack & Jill, Open Handles, Green, Blue Mark, 10 1/2 In. 90.00
Royal Bayreuth, Plate, Lettuce, Ring Handled, Blue Mark, 6 In. 20.00
Royal Bayreuth, Plate, Man With Shotgun, Dog, Country Scene, 10 1/2 In. 75.00
Royal Bayreuth, Plate, Man, Turkeys, Violet Sunset Over Mountains, 6 In. 25.00
Royal Bayreuth, Plate, Nursery Rhyme, Jack The Giant Killer, Blue Mark, 6 In. 45.00
Royal Bayreuth, Plate, Oak Leaf, Satin Finish, 8 1/2 In. 75.00
Royal Bayreuth, Plate, Pastoral Scene, Man With Turkeys, Blue Mark, 6 1/2 In. 35.00
Royal Bayreuth, Plate, Pastoral With Sheep 40.00
Royal Bayreuth, Plate, Pastoral, Sheep, Blue Mark 40.00
Royal Bayreuth, Plate, Pink Roses, Scalloped Edge, Blue Mark, 9 1/4 In. 120.00
Royal Bayreuth, Plate, Poppy, Red, 8 1/4 In. 25.00
Royal Bayreuth, Plate, Tomato, Cover, Blue Mark, 7 1/2 In. 35.00
Royal Bayreuth, Plate, Tomato, Handled, Cover, Blue Mark, 7 In. 60.00
Royal Bayreuth, Plate, Tomato, Set Of Six 50.00

Royal Bayreuth, Shoes, Brown Rust High Top, Pair

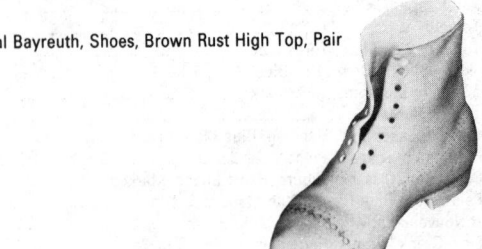
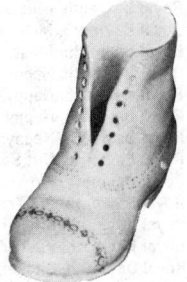

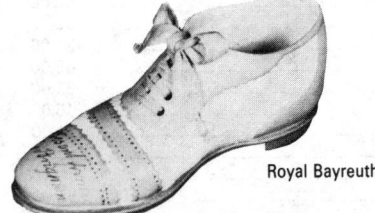

Royal Bayreuth, Shoe, Present From New Brighton Written

Royal Bayreuth, Plate, White Flowers, Handled, Blue Mark, 5 1/2 In.	18.00
Royal Bayreuth, Powder Box, Tapestry, Lady Leans On Horse, Puffy Hat & Dress	185.00
Royal Bayreuth, Relish, Jack-In-The-Beanstalk, Blue Mark, 8 X 4 1/4 X 2 In.	75.00
Royal Bayreuth, Relish, Lobster Over Leaf, Curved Tail Forms Handle, 6 In.	34.00
Royal Bayreuth, Rose Bowl, Floral, Gold Overlay	45.00
Royal Bayreuth, Rose Bowl, Little Jack Horner, Full Verse, Blue Mark, 4 In.	65.00
Royal Bayreuth, Rose Bowl, Little Miss Muffet, Insert, Black Mark	125.00
Royal Bayreuth, Rose Bowl, Little Miss Muffet, Insert, Blue Mark	125.00
Royal Bayreuth, Rose Bowl, Pastel Flowers, Reticulated & Footed	85.00
Royal Bayreuth, Salt & Pepper, Figural, Elk, Pair	75.00
Royal Bayreuth, Salt & Pepper, Figural, Red Lobster, Unmarked	28.50
Royal Bayreuth, Salt & Pepper, Grape, Blue Mark	60.00
Royal Bayreuth, Salt & Pepper, Tomato, Small Leaf	15.00
Royal Bayreuth, Shaving Mug, Elk	225.00
Royal Bayreuth, Shell, Orange To Pink, Covered, Blue Mark, 3 1/2 In.	45.00
Royal Bayreuth, Shoe, High Top, Blue Mark	45.00
Royal Bayreuth, Shoe, Man's White Oxford, Silk Lace	65.00
Royal Bayreuth, Shoe, Present From New Brighton Written *Illus*	60.00
Royal Bayreuth, Shoe, Woman's High Button, Black	110.00
Royal Bayreuth, Shoe, 2-Tone Tan, Laces, Back Strap, Black Mark	100.00
Royal Bayreuth, Shoes, Brown Rust High Top, Pair *Illus*	60.00
Royal Bayreuth, Stein, Elk, Blue Mark, 5 3/4 In.	175.00
Royal Bayreuth, Sugar & Creamer, Black Corinthian, Blue Mark	60.00
Royal Bayreuth, Sugar & Creamer, Corinthian, Classical Figures On Black	65.00
Royal Bayreuth, Sugar & Creamer, Grape, Blown	125.00
Royal Bayreuth, Sugar & Creamer, Grapes & Leaves, Black Mark	175.00
Royal Bayreuth, Sugar & Creamer, Lid, Lobster	55.00
Royal Bayreuth, Sugar & Creamer, Tomato, Blue Mark	85.00
Royal Bayreuth, Sugar & Creamer, Tomato, Covered Sugar, 2nd Mark, 3 In.	85.00
Royal Bayreuth, Sugar, Cover, Tomato, Blue Mark	12.50
Royal Bayreuth, Sugar, Cover, 2 Handled, Hand-Painted Roses, Gold	150.00
Royal Bayreuth, Sugar, Covered, Tomato, 2 1/2 X 3 In.	38.00
Royal Bayreuth, Sugar, Grape, Covered, Blue Mark	38.00
Royal Bayreuth, Sugar, Man & Woman On Horseback, Riding Hounds, Blue Mark	45.00
Royal Bayreuth, Sugar, Purple Grapes, Covered	65.00
Royal Bayreuth, Sugar, Ring Around The Rosie, Covered, Blue Mark	75.00
Royal Bayreuth, Sugar, Tomato, Blue Mark, 4 In.	35.00 To 48.50
Royal Bayreuth, Sugar, Tomato, Cover, Marked	30.00

Royal Bayreuth, Tea Set, Large Tomato, Blue Mark, 3 Piece .... 110.00 To 135.00
Royal Bayreuth, Tea Set, Tomato, Teapot, Creamer, Sugar, Black Mark 95.00
Royal Bayreuth, Tea Set, Tomato, 3 Piece .... 120.00 To 150.00
Royal Bayreuth, Teapot, Little Bo Peep, Covered, Blue Mark, 5 In. 95.00
Royal Bayreuth, Teapot, Tomato, Blue Mark 100.00
Royal Bayreuth, Teapot, Tomato, Blue Mark, Footed 125.00
Royal Bayreuth, Tobacco, Corinthian 175.00
Royal Bayreuth, Toothpick, Brittany Girl, 3-Handled 75.00
Royal Bayreuth, Toothpick, Coachman 140.00
Royal Bayreuth, Toothpick, Corinthian 49.00
Royal Bayreuth, Toothpick, Devil & Cards 110.00
Royal Bayreuth, Toothpick, Elk 75.00
Royal Bayreuth, Toothpick, Elk, Green Mark 55.00
Royal Bayreuth, Toothpick, Hunt Scene, 3-Handled, Blue Mark 58.00
Royal Bayreuth, Toothpick, Musicians, 4 Corner 65.00
Royal Bayreuth, Toothpick, Peach Roses, Lavender Handles, 3-Handled 65.00
Royal Bayreuth, Toothpick, Roses, German US Zone 12.00
Royal Bayreuth, Toothpick, Scenic, Green & Tan, Double Handles, Blue Mark 65.00
Royal Bayreuth, Toothpick, 3-Handled, Turkey Hunt Scene 85.00
Royal Bayreuth, Tray, Devil & Cards, Blue Mark, 10 X 7 1/4 In. 225.00
Royal Bayreuth, Tray, Jack & Jill Decoration, Ruffled, 7 X 10 In. 140.00
Royal Bayreuth, Tumbler, Girl & Dog 75.00
Royal Bayreuth, Vase, Allover Scenic, Mountain Rams, Black Mark, 4 In. 48.00
Royal Bayreuth, Vase, Arab Scene, Blue Mark, Handled, 4 In. 49.00
Royal Bayreuth, Vase, Black, Orange Interior, Greek Shield, Crown, Lion, Signed 165.00
Royal Bayreuth, Vase, Blue, Ginger Jar Shape, 9 In. 120.00
Royal Bayreuth, Vase, Boy With Turkeys, Blue Mark, 4 1/4 In. 45.00
Royal Bayreuth, Vase, Castle, Mountain Scene Around Top, Yellow, 6 1/4 In. 42.00
Royal Bayreuth, Vase, Cavaliers Drinking, Signed Dixon, Black Mark, 4 In. 65.00
Royal Bayreuth, Vase, Cavaliers, Tavern Scene, Blue Mark, 5 1/2 In. 50.00
Royal Bayreuth, Vase, Corinthian, Black, Red Lining, Unsigned, 4 1/2 In. 27.00
Royal Bayreuth, Vase, Dutch Boy & Girl, Blue Mark, 6 In. 25.00
Royal Bayreuth, Vase, Dutch Homes Village, Lady Foreground, 4 1/2 In. 15.00
Royal Bayreuth, Vase, Farmer, Horses, 3 Ornate Handles, 5 1/2 In. 85.00
Royal Bayreuth, Vase, Green, Buck, Doe & Fawn, 2 Handled, Blue Mark, 3 1/2 In. 65.00
Royal Bayreuth, Vase, Hand-Painted Pastoral Scene, 3 1/4 In. 65.00
Royal Bayreuth, Vase, Horses, Peasants, Trumpet Shell Base, Signed 112.00
Royal Bayreuth, Vase, Hunt Scene, 3 Handles, Signed, 2 1/2 In.High 45.00
Royal Bayreuth, Vase, Hunter & Dog Scene, Gourd Shaped, Blue Mark, 7 In. 150.00
Royal Bayreuth, Vase, Hunter, Five Dogs, Blue Mark, 4 In. 65.00
Royal Bayreuth, Vase, Lady Carrying Basket Along Shore, Blue Mark, 2 3/4 In. 40.00
Royal Bayreuth, Vase, Lady In Evening Dress, 3 3/4 In. 55.00
Royal Bayreuth, Vase, Lady, Ship Background, 3 3/4 In. 55.00
Royal Bayreuth, Vase, Peasant With Donkeys, Saucer Base, Knob Stem, Signed 187.00
Royal Bayreuth, Vase, Portrait, Babes In Woods, 4 5/8 In. 105.00
Royal Bayreuth, Vase, Portrait, Blue Mark, 4 In. 65.00
Royal Bayreuth, Vase, Portrait, Dutch Boy & Girl, Urn Shape, Silver Rim, 4 In. 53.00
Royal Bayreuth, Vase, Sailing Scene, Orange Beading, Blue Mark, 6 1/2 In. 75.00
Royal Bayreuth, Vase, Scenic, Black Mark, 3 3/4 In. 30.00
Royal Bayreuth, Vase, Scenic, Signed, 4 1/2 In. 122.00
Royal Bayreuth, Vase, Sheep Scene, Yellow Band, Handled, Blue Mark, 5 1/2 In. 55.00
Royal Bayreuth, Vase, Six Cows In Pasture, Signed, 8 In. 195.00
Royal Bayreuth, Vase, Sterling Top, Green Mark, 4 In. 40.00
Royal Bayreuth, Vase, Sterling Top, Tropical Birds, Blue Mark, 3 3/4 In. 30.00
Royal Bayreuth, Vase, 2 Birds, Sterling Silver Rim, C.1917, Blue Mark, 4 In. 45.00
Royal Bayreuth, Vase, 3 Dutch Children, 3 1/4 In. 55.00
Royal Berlin, Figurine, Boy Carrying Lamb Over Shoulder, White, 4 1/4 In. 90.00
Royal Berlin, Figurine, Young Boy With Lamb Over Shoulder, 4 1/4 In. 90.00

 Royal Bonn is the nineteenth century trade name for the Bonn China Manufactory established in 1755 at Bonn, Germany. A general line of porcelain dishes was made.

Royal Bonn, see also Flow Blue
Royal Bonn, Bowl, Punch, Blue & White, 3 Dutch Landscapes, 9 1/4 In. 150.00
Royal Bonn, Bowl, Punch, Footed, Blue & White, Dutch Landscapes, 17 In. 150.00

Royal Bonn, Case, Clock, Ansonia	275.00
Royal Bonn, Clock, Blue, Yellow, Flowers, Signed LaHuym, 10 1/2 X 8 In.	250.00
Royal Bonn, Clock, Boy & Girl Country Scene, Royal Blue Background, 13 In.	275.00
Royal Bonn, Compote, Ships In Port, Pedestal Base, 9 1/4 In.	40.00
Royal Bonn, Ewer, Flowers & Cartouche	89.00
Royal Bonn, Ewer, Pansies, 10 In.	110.00
Royal Bonn, Ewer, Parrot On Tree Branches, Hand-Painted, 12 In.	75.00
Royal Bonn, Ewer, Persian Style, Gilt Accent, 8 In.	80.00
Royal Bonn, Jardiniere, Hand-Painted Violets & Poppies	175.00
Royal Bonn, Pitcher, Green, Natural Colored Orchids, 5 In.	25.00
Royal Bonn, Plaque, Dimpled Woman, Fruit Border, Blue, Pierced To Hang, 14 In.	140.00
Royal Bonn, Salad Set, Hand-Painted Pastels, Servers With Porcelain Handles	225.00
Royal Bonn, Vase, Blue Yellow Florals On Burgundy Cobalt, Bulbous, 5 In.	25.00
Royal Bonn, Vase, Bulbous, Hand-Painted, 7 1/2 In.	32.00
Royal Bonn, Vase, Castle Scene On White, Bulbous, 12 In.	95.00
Royal Bonn, Vase, Cavalier, Gold Beaded Top & Rim, Gold Leaf Base, 5 3/4 In.	85.00
Royal Bonn, Vase, Cows Scene, Gold Trim, Handled, Sticher, 12 X 4 3/4 In.	195.00
Royal Bonn, Vase, Floral Bouquets, 10 1/2 In., Pair	75.00
Royal Bonn, Vase, Floral, Signed, 15 X 12 In.	210.00
Royal Bonn, Vase, Floral, 15 In.	75.00
Royal Bonn, Vase, Flowers, Bluebirds, Gold Trim, 10 In., Pair	100.00
Royal Bonn, Vase, Gold & Floral, 13 1/2 In.	119.00
Royal Bonn, Vase, Hand-Painted Flowers, Handled, 10 1/2 In.	90.00
Royal Bonn, Vase, Light Green, Flowers, Gold Trim, Signed, Numbered, 6 1/2 In.	39.00
Royal Bonn, Vase, Old Dutch, Bulbous, 10 In.	30.00
Royal Bonn, Vase, Pastel Colors Scene, Art Nouveau Handles, Footed, 18 In.	185.00
Royal Bonn, Vase, Portrait, Lady, Picking Flowers In Field, Gold Trim, 8 In.	175.00
Royal Bonn, Vase, Portrait, Woman, Gold & Green, 2 Handled, Signed, 6 In.	168.00
Royal Bonn, Vase, Portrait, Woman, Gold, Green, Yellow, Artist Signed, 5 3/4 In.	75.00
Royal Bonn, Vase, Roses, Olive Green Background, Bulbous, 11 X 11 In.	159.00
Royal Bonn, Vase, Roses, Signed, 13 In.	95.00
Royal Bonn, Vase, Roses, 15 X 12 In.	225.00
Royal Bonn, Vase, Scenic, Orchids, Gold, High Gloss Enamel Overlay, 9 In.	95.00
Royal Bonn, Vase, Seascape, Signed, 11 In.	185.00
Royal Bonn, Vase, Signed, Green, Orchids, Gold, 10 In.	95.00
Royal Bonn, Vase, Tapestry, Garden Gate Scene, Florals, Bulbous, 5 In.	97.00
Royal Bonn, Vase, Two Handles, Green Blue, Gold, Wine, 12 1/4 In.	85.00
Royal Bonn, Vase, White, Hand-Painted Cow Medallion, Signed Sticher, 12 In.	195.00
Royal Bonn, Vase, White, Leaf Design, Signed, 13 1/2 In.	125.00
Royal Bonn, Vase, Yellow & Pink Roses, 5 1/2 In.	24.00

Royal Copenhagen porcelain and pottery has been made in Denmark since 1772. It is still being made. One of their most famous wares is the Christmas Plate Series.

Royal Copenhagen, see also Collector, Plate, Royal Copenhagen

Royal Copenhagen, Ashtray, Figural, Crab	55.00
Royal Copenhagen, Charger, Light Brown, Stylized Leaf, Crouching Monkey, KF	35.00
Royal Copenhagen, Coffeepot, Blue Flower Finial, Marked & Numbered	110.00
Royal Copenhagen, Coffeepot, Cobalt Flowers, Knob, Blue Nut	40.00
Royal Copenhagen, Dish, Square Shape, Green & Gray, Gold, 3 X 6 In.	35.00
Royal Copenhagen, Dish, Square, 4 In.	27.00
Royal Copenhagen, Figurine, Birds, Two Lover Birds On Leafy Perch, 5 In.	65.00
Royal Copenhagen, Figurine, Boy & Girl, 17 1/2 X 9 In.	650.00
Royal Copenhagen, Figurine, Boy On Ground, Reading, No.1669, 8 In.	125.00
Royal Copenhagen, Figurine, Boy With Bag Of Stones, 6 1/2 In.	60.00
Royal Copenhagen, Figurine, Boy With Horn, No.3989, 4 1/4 In.	55.00
Royal Copenhagen, Figurine, Cat, Gray, White Tilted Head, 5 1/2 In.	60.00
Royal Copenhagen, Figurine, Elephant Vocalizing, No.2998, 4 1/2 In.	52.00
Royal Copenhagen, Figurine, Girl Lifting Skirt, No.694, 9 1/2 In.	125.00
Royal Copenhagen, Figurine, Girl Seated On Floor Holding Doll, 5 In.	85.00
Royal Copenhagen, Figurine, Girl With Goose, No.527, 9 1/2 In.	95.00 To 145.00
Royal Copenhagen, Figurine, Goose Girl, Artist Signed, Numbered, 7 1/2 In.	75.00
Royal Copenhagen, Figurine, Man Walking, 1903, 6 1/2 In.	38.00
Royal Copenhagen, Figurine, Penguin, 4 1/2 In.	38.00
Royal Copenhagen, Figurine, Polar Bear, Head Down, Shaded Whites, 3 1/2 In.	40.00

Royal Copenhagen, Figurine, Puppies Playing, 2 1/2 X 4 In.	70.00
Royal Copenhagen, Figurine, Puppy Trying To Catch His Tail In Mouth, 5 In.	45.00
Royal Copenhagen, Figurine, Resting Faun, Signed OP, Paper Sticker, No.756	50.00
Royal Copenhagen, Figurine, Robin, Standing, One Foot On Berries, 8 In.	78.00
Royal Copenhagen, Figurine, Sandman, Young Man With Umbrella, 7 In.	90.00
Royal Copenhagen, Figurine, Sandman, Young Man With Umbrellas, No.1129	95.00
Royal Copenhagen, Figurine, Satyr Riding Butting Goat, 1898-1921, 8 1/4 In.	195.00
Royal Copenhagen, Figurine, School Boy, Valise And Coat, 7 In.	75.00
Royal Copenhagen, Figurine, Squirrel, 3 1/2 In.	25.00
Royal Copenhagen, Figurine, Swan, No.755	45.00
Royal Copenhagen, Figurine, Terrier, 5 X 4 In.	58.00
Royal Copenhagen, Figurine, Two Puppies Wrestling, 3 X 4 X 2 In.	55.00
Royal Copenhagen, Figurine, Wee Willie Winkie, 7 In.	75.00
Royal Copenhagen, Figurine, Woman Leading Goose, Marked Danmark 528, 6 In.	145.00
Royal Copenhagen, Figurine, Young Girl Seated, Holding Doll, 5 In.	90.00
Royal Copenhagen, Ginger Jar, Butterflies, Old Mark	65.00
Royal Copenhagen, Holder, Flower, Girl & Boy, Signed, Marked, Pair	95.00
Royal Copenhagen, Inkwell, Triangular Tray, Leaf, Berry On Tray	65.00
Royal Copenhagen, Jar, Cover, Figural Relief, Milkmaid Finial, White, 9 In.	65.00
Royal Copenhagen, Plate, Fruit Center, Salmon Pink Border, 8 In.	25.00
Royal Copenhagen, Tile, Tea, Blue & White	18.50
Royal Copenhagen, Tray, Green Crackle Glaze, Gold Edge, 8 1/4 In.	35.00
Royal Copenhagen, Vase, Blue Chrysanthemums, C.1900, 9 1/2 In.	130.00
Royal Copenhagen, Vase, Floral Design, 1923 Mark, 7 1/2 In.	55.00
Royal Copenhagen, Vase, Flowers, Crackle Glaze, Green & White, 5 In.	30.00
Royal Copenhagen, Vase, Gray, Gold & Green Floral, Bulbous, C.F.T., 5 1/2 In.	35.00
Royal Copenhagen, Vase, Krouberg Castle, C.1920, 8 1/2 In.	48.00
Royal Copenhagen, Vase, Pale Blue, Artist Signed, C.1920's, 7 1/2 In.	35.00
Royal Copenhagen, Vase, Reticulated Daisies Form Top, Raised Stems To Base	195.00
Royal Copenhagen, Vase, Sailboat, 7 In.	38.00
Royal Copenhagen, Vase, Scenic, 9 X 6 In., Pair	275.00

Royal Crown Derby Company, Ltd., was established in England in 1876.
Royal Crown Derby, see also Crown Derby, Derby

Royal Crown Derby, Bowl, Gold Rim, White Background, 1810, 2 1/2 In.	75.00
Royal Crown Derby, Box, Powder, Covered, Hand-Painted, 5 1/2 X 4 1/2 In.	45.00
Royal Crown Derby, Box, Trinket, Colonial Couple On Lid	18.00
Royal Crown Derby, Coffee Set, Wilmot, Blue & White, 19th Century, 15 Piece	85.00
Royal Crown Derby, Cup & Saucer, Rust, Gold, Blue, 1800-25	50.00
Royal Crown Derby, Dish, Mask Comedy Handles, Gold Beading	95.00
Royal Crown Derby, Plate, Dessert, Golden Pheasant Design, Set Of 6	150.00
Royal Crown Derby, Plate, Green, White Medallions, Floral, Gold Trim, 9 In.	40.00
Royal Crown Derby, Plate, Imari Pattern No.2451, Square, 9 1/4 In.	85.00
Royal Crown Derby, Pot, Covered, Miniature, 1911, 2 1/2 In.	54.00
Royal Crown Derby, Vase, Blue, Overlay Design, Cream Panels, Gold, 9 In.	250.00

Royal Doulton was the name used on pottery made after 1902 by Doulton & Co., in Lambeth and Burslem, England. The Doulton factory was founded in 1815. Their wares are still being made.

Royal Doulton, Ash Bowl, Parson Brown	95.00
Royal Doulton, Ash Bowl, Sairey Gamp, A Mark	60.00
Royal Doulton, Ashtray, English Beer Advertisement, C.1900, 4 1/2 In.	20.00
Royal Doulton, Barrel, Biscuit, Coaching Days, Metal Collar, Bail, Lid, Motif	130.00
Royal Doulton, Belvedere Pattern, Service For 12	500.00
Royal Doulton, Bottle, Sandman, A Mark	32.50
Royal Doulton, Bowl, Battle Of Hastings, Bayeux Tapestry, 3 1/2 In.	50.00
Royal Doulton, Bowl, Blue Stoneware, Tan Border, C.1900, 4 1/2 X 4 In.	28.00
Royal Doulton, Bowl, Cotswold Shepherd, Flanged, 10 In.	55.00
Royal Doulton, Bowl, Country Scene, Gold Scalloped Foot, Signed, 9 In.	100.00
Royal Doulton, Bowl, Dickensware, Mr.Pickwick, Noke, 8 1/2 X 8 1/2 In.	115.00
Royal Doulton, Bowl, Dickensware, Tony Weller, 2 1/4 X 9 1/2 In.	75.00
Royal Doulton, Bowl, Gaffer, C.1923, 9 X 3 In.	37.50
Royal Doulton, Bowl, Golfers, 6 1/2 In.	35.00
Royal Doulton, Bowl, Golfers, 9 1/4 In.	75.00
Royal Doulton, Bowl, Octagonal, Handled, 6 1/2 X 8 In.	25.00

Royal Doulton, Bowl, Oliver Asks For More, 8 Inch	80.00
Royal Doulton, Box, Bill Sikes, Square, Covered, 1 3/4 X 3 1/2 In.	45.00
Royal Doulton, Box, Cigarette, Covered, Golfers	75.00
Royal Doulton, Box, Mr. Pickwick, Square, Covered, 3 1/4 X 3 1/2 In.	55.00
Royal Doulton, Breakfast Set, Action Bunnies Riding 1880s Train, 3 Piece	25.00
Royal Doulton, Bust, Mr. Pickwick, Miniature	40.00 To 54.00
Royal Doulton, Bust, Tony Weller, Miniature	40.00
Royal Doulton, Candlestick, Dickensware, Captain Cuttles, 6 1/2 In.	85.00
Royal Doulton, Candlestick, Micawber & Pickwick, 6 1/2 In., Pair	95.00
Royal Doulton, Candlestick, Welsh Ladies, Pair	95.00
Royal Doulton, Chamberstick, Sailboat Decoration	45.00
Royal Doulton, Chamberstick, Witches, Handle, Yellow, Brown	75.00
Royal Doulton, Chamberstick, Woodland, Handle, Green, Tan	87.50

*Character jugs are modeled of the head and shoulders of the subject. They
were made in four sizes large - 5 1/4 to 7 inches, small - 3 1/4 to 4 inches,
miniature - 2 1/4 to 2 1/2 inches, and tiny - 1 1/4 inches. Toby mugs depict
a full-seated figure.*

Royal Doulton, Character Jug, 'Arriet, Marked A, 1 1/4 In.	65.00
Royal Doulton, Character Jug, 'Arriet, 2 1/2 In.	50.00
Royal Doulton, Character Jug, 'Arriet, 6 1/2 In.	95.00
Royal Doulton, Character Jug, 'Arry, 1 1/4 In.	75.00
Royal Doulton, Character Jug, Auld Mac, Marked A, 6 In.	55.00
Royal Doulton, Character Jug, Auld Mac, 1 1/4 In.	65.00
Royal Doulton, Character Jug, Auld Mac, 6 In.	48.00
Royal Doulton, Character Jug, Bacchus, 2 1/2 In.	14.00
Royal Doulton, Character Jug, Bacchus, 6 In.	22.50
Royal Doulton, Character Jug, Beefeater, GR Raised On Handle, 6 1/4 In.	60.00
Royal Doulton, Character Jug, Captain Hook, 3 1/2 In.	150.00
Royal Doulton, Character Jug, Cardinal, A Mark, 2 1/4 In.	37.50
Royal Doulton, Character Jug, Cardinal, 1 1/4 In.	70.00
Royal Doulton, Character Jug, Cardinal, 6 In.	87.50
Royal Doulton, Character Jug, Cavalier, 3 1/2 In.	55.00
Royal Doulton, Character Jug, Cavalier, 6 1/2 In.	80.00
Royal Doulton, Character Jug, Dick Turpin, Marked A, Large, 6 In.	93.00
Royal Doulton, Character Jug, Dick Turpin, 2 1/2 In.	37.50
Royal Doulton, Character Jug, Dick Whittington, 6 In.	310.00
Royal Doulton, Character Jug, Don Quixote, 2 1/2 In.	14.00
Royal Doulton, Character Jug, Falstaff & Bardolph, 7 In.	90.00
Royal Doulton, Character Jug, Falstaff, 6 In.	22.50
Royal Doulton, Character Jug, Farmer John, 6 In.	95.00
Royal Doulton, Character Jug, Fat Boy, 1 1/4 In.	63.00 To 85.00
Royal Doulton, Character Jug, Fat Boy, 2 1/4 In.	30.00
Royal Doulton, Character Jug, Gardener, 2 1/2 In.	14.00
Royal Doulton, Character Jug, Gladiator, Small, 3 1/2 In.	195.00
Royal Doulton, Character Jug, Gladiator, 3 1/2 In.	235.00
Royal Doulton, Character Jug, Gladiator, 6 In.	300.00 To 325.00
Royal Doulton, Character Jug, Gone Away, 2 1/2 In.	14.00
Royal Doulton, Character Jug, Granny, Marked A, 6 In.	110.00
Royal Doulton, Character Jug, Granny, Marked A, 6 1/4 In.	65.00
Royal Doulton, Character Jug, Gulliver, 2 1/4 In.	225.00
Royal Doulton, Character Jug, Gulliver, 6 In.	325.00
Royal Doulton, Character Jug, Henry Morgan, 2 1/2 In.	14.00
Royal Doulton, Character Jug, Jarge, 3 1/2 In.	130.00
Royal Doulton, Character Jug, John Peel, Marked A, 2 1/4 In.	30.50 To 55.00
Royal Doulton, Character Jug, John Peel, 2 1/4 In.	37.50 To 40.00
Royal Doulton, Character Jug, John Peel, 6 In.	80.50
Royal Doulton, Character Jug, Lawyer, 6 In.	22.50
Royal Doulton, Character Jug, Lobster Man, 2 1/2 In.	14.00
Royal Doulton, Character Jug, Long John Silver, 2 1/2 In.	14.00
Royal Doulton, Character Jug, Lord Nelson, 6 In.	192.00
Royal Doulton, Character Jug, Lumberjack, 2 1/2 In.	14.00
Royal Doulton, Character Jug, Mephistopheles, 6 In.	800.00
Royal Doulton, Character Jug, Merlin, 3 1/2 In.	13.50
Royal Doulton, Character Jug, Mr.Micawber, Marked A, 2 1/4 In.	45.00

Royal Doulton, Character Jug, Mr. Micawber, 1 1/4 In.	75.00
Royal Doulton, Character Jug, Mr. Micawber, 2 1/4 In.	32.00
Royal Doulton, Character Jug, Mr. Pickwick, 1 1/4 In.	80.00
Royal Doulton, Character Jug, Neptune, 2 1/2 In.	14.00
Royal Doulton, Character Jug, Old Charley, Marked A, 3 1/2 In.	40.00
Royal Doulton, Character Jug, Old Charley, Marked A, 5 1/4 In.	55.00 To 60.00
Royal Doulton, Character Jug, Old Charley, 1 1/4 In.	65.00 To 80.00
Royal Doulton, Character Jug, Old Charley, 2 1/2 In.	14.00
Royal Doulton, Character Jug, Old Charley, 3 1/2 In.	33.00
Royal Doulton, Character Jug, Old Salt, 3 1/2 In.	13.50
Royal Doulton, Character Jug, Paddy, Marked A, 3 1/2 In.	50.00
Royal Doulton, Character Jug, Paddy, 1 1/4 In.	56.00 To 95.00
Royal Doulton, Character Jug, Parson Brown, Marked A, 6 In.	90.00
Royal Doulton, Character Jug, Parson Brown, 3 1/2 In.	45.00
Royal Doulton, Character Jug, Porthos, 2 1/4 In.	10.95
Royal Doulton, Character Jug, Punch & Judy, 6 In.	350.00
Royal Doulton, Character Jug, Regency Beau, 3 1/2 In.	255.00
Royal Doulton, Character Jug, Rip Van Winkle, 2 1/2 In.	14.00
Royal Doulton, Character Jug, Robin Hood, 2 1/4 In.	10.95
Royal Doulton, Character Jug, Robin Hood, 6 In.	115.00
Royal Doulton, Character Jug, Sairey Gamp, Marked A, 3 1/2 In.	35.50
Royal Doulton, Character Jug, Sairey Gamp, Marked A, 6 In.	55.00
Royal Doulton, Character Jug, Sairey Gamp, 1 1/4 In.	75.00
Royal Doulton, Character Jug, Sairey Gamp, 3 1/2 In.	50.00
Royal Doulton, Character Jug, Sam Johnson, 1 1/4 In.	35.00
Royal Doulton, Character Jug, Sam Weller, 1 1/4 In.	75.00
Royal Doulton, Character Jug, Sam Weller, 2 1/2 In.	37.50
Royal Doulton, Character Jug, Scaramouche, 3 1/2 In.	255.00
Royal Doulton, Character Jug, Simon The Cellarer, Marked A, 6 In.	90.00
Royal Doulton, Character Jug, Simple Simon, 6 In.	325.00
Royal Doulton, Character Jug, Smuggler, 2 1/2 In.	14.00
Royal Doulton, Character Jug, St.George, 4 In.	42.50
Royal Doulton, Character Jug, St.George, 6 In.	87.50
Royal Doulton, Character Jug, Tam O'Shanter, 2 1/2 In.	14.00
Royal Doulton, Character Jug, Tam O'Shanter, 6 In.	25.00
Royal Doulton, Character Jug, Tony Weller, 2 1/2 In.	40.00
Royal Doulton, Character Jug, Town Crier, 6 In.	87.50
Royal Doulton, Character Jug, Ugly Duchess, Marked A, 7 In.	85.00
Royal Doulton, Character Jug, Uncle Tom Cobbleigh, Large	170.00
Royal Doulton, Character Jug, Vicar Of Bray, Marked A, 6 In.	120.00 To 125.00
Royal Doulton, Character Jug, Viking, 3 1/2 In.	40.00
Royal Doulton, Charger, Automobile Series, Itch Yer On Guvenor, 12 5/8 In.	195.00
Royal Doulton, Creamer, Dutch Children, Black Lion & Crown Mark, 4 1/2 In.	45.00
Royal Doulton, Creamer, The Cardinal, 4 In.	75.00
Royal Doulton, Cup & Saucer, Bunnykins, Signed Barbara Vernon	15.00
Royal Doulton, Cup & Saucer, Bunnykins, Vernon	45.00
Royal Doulton, Cup & Saucer, Coaching Days	20.00 To 25.00
Royal Doulton, Cup & Saucer, Colonial Scene	30.00
Royal Doulton, Cup & Saucer, Dickensware Demitasse	75.00
Royal Doulton, Cup & Saucer, Fat Boy	47.50
Royal Doulton, Cup & Saucer, Indian Tree Pattern	18.00
Royal Doulton, Cup & Saucer, Robin Hood & Maid Marian, Colors On Cream	40.00
Royal Doulton, Cup, Baby, Lambeth Walk, Barbara Vernon	38.00
Royal Doulton, Cup, Commemorative, Loving, Mayflower, Black	200.00
Royal Doulton, Decanter, Bell Shape, Brown Stoneware, Bell, 10 1/2 In.	40.00
Royal Doulton, Demitasse Set, Old Leeds, Set Of 4	40.00
Royal Doulton, Demitasse, Ivory, Gray Band, Gold Vine, Gold Trim On Cup, 6 Set	90.00
Royal Doulton, Dinner Set, Arcadia, 12 Place Settings	360.00
Royal Doulton, Dish, Child's, Bunnykins, Santa	40.00
Royal Doulton, Dish, Child's, Bunnykins, Signed, 7 In.	22.50
Royal Doulton, Dish, Feeding, Sir Roger De Coverly	38.00
Royal Doulton, Dish, The Arrival Of The Unknown Princess, 8 In.	58.00
Royal Doulton, Figurine, Abdullah, HN 2104, 6 1/4 In.	500.00
Royal Doulton, Figurine, Adrienne, HN 2152, Purple, 7 5/8 In.	65.00
Royal Doulton, Figurine, Annette, HN 1471	300.00

Royal Doulton, Figurine, Autumn Breezes, Black, HN 2747, 7 1/2 In. 195.00
Royal Doulton, Figurine, Autumn Breezes, Pink, HN 1911, 7 1/2 In. 65.00
Royal Doulton, Figurine, Autumn Breezes, Red, HN 1934, 7 1/2 In. 55.00
Royal Doulton, Figurine, Ballad Seller, HN 2266, 7 3/4 In. 115.00
Royal Doulton, Figurine, Balloon Man, HN 1954, 7 1/2 In. .... 65.00 To 95.00
Royal Doulton, Figurine, Balloon Seller With Child, HN 583, 9 In. 375.00
Royal Doulton, Figurine, Beachcomber, HN 2487, 6 1/2 In. 85.00
Royal Doulton, Figurine, Biddu, HN 1513, 5 1/2 In. .... 125.00 To 150.00
Royal Doulton, Figurine, Biddy Penny Farthing, HN 1843, 8 3/8 In. 65.00
Royal Doulton, Figurine, Bisque Porcelain, Nude, 4 3/4 In. 225.00
Royal Doulton, Figurine, Black Cat, K12, 2 3/4 In. 18.00
Royal Doulton, Figurine, Blithe Morning, HN 2021, Pink, 7 In. .... 125.00 To 130.00
Royal Doulton, Figurine, Blithe Morning, Red, HN 2065, 7 In. 95.00
Royal Doulton, Figurine, Bluebeard, HN 2105, 10 5/8 In. 112.50
Royal Doulton, Figurine, Bride, HN 2166, 8 1/2 In. .... 65.00 To 90.00
Royal Doulton, Figurine, Bulldog, British Flag Back, 4 In. 115.00
Royal Doulton, Figurine, Camellia, HN 2222, 7 3/4 In. 170.00
Royal Doulton, Figurine, Captain Cuttle, Standing, 4 In. .... 35.00 To 70.00
Royal Doulton, Figurine, Carolyn, HN 2112, 7 In. 185.00
Royal Doulton, Figurine, Carpet Seller, HN 1464, 9 1/4 In. .... 165.00 To 185.00
Royal Doulton, Figurine, Cat, Flambe, 4 3/4 In. .... 25.00 To 35.00
Royal Doulton, Figurine, Celeste, HN 2237, 7 In. .... 135.00 To 145.00
Royal Doulton, Figurine, Cellist, HN 2226, 8 1/4 In. 250.00
Royal Doulton, Figurine, Chloe, HN 1765, 6 In. 167.00
Royal Doulton, Figurine, Christmas Morn, HN 1992, 7 In. 110.00
Royal Doulton, Figurine, Cobbler, HN 1706, 7 1/2 In. 185.00
Royal Doulton, Figurine, Cocker Spaniel, HN 1037, 3 1/2 In. 55.00
Royal Doulton, Figurine, Cocker Spaniel, K9, 2 1/2 In. 18.00
Royal Doulton, Figurine, Columbine, HN 2185, 7 1/4 In. 170.00
Royal Doulton, Figurine, Creeping Fox, Flambe, 29 B, 1 In. 20.00
Royal Doulton, Figurine, Curly Knob, HN 1627, 6 1/4 In. .... 225.00 To 250.00
Royal Doulton, Figurine, Daffy Down Dilly, HN 1712, 8 1/4 In. 130.00
Royal Doulton, Figurine, Dancing Eyes, HN 1543 .... 165.00
Royal Doulton, Figurine, Daphne, HN 2268, 8 1/2 In. 90.00
Royal Doulton, Figurine, Darling, HN 1319, 7 1/2 In. 80.00
Royal Doulton, Figurine, Dawn, HN 1858, 10 In. 425.00
Royal Doulton, Figurine, Debutante, HN 2210, 5 In. 185.00
Royal Doulton, Figurine, Delight, HN 1772, 7 In. .... 105.00 To 125.00
Royal Doulton, Figurine, Diana, Blue, No.1716, 5 3/4 In. 165.00
Royal Doulton, Figurine, Dorcas, 7 In. 150.00
Royal Doulton, Figurine, Easter Day, Lavender, HN 1976 .... 200.00
Royal Doulton, Figurine, Easter Day, 7 1/4 In. 170.00
Royal Doulton, Figurine, English Setter, Black & White, HN 1051, 3 3/4 In. 45.00
Royal Doulton, Figurine, Fat Boy, HN 1893, C.1939, 7 1/2 In. 195.00
Royal Doulton, Figurine, Fat Boy, 4 In. 18.00
Royal Doulton, Figurine, First Steps, HN 2242, 6 3/4 In. 250.00
Royal Doulton, Figurine, Flora, HN 2349, 7 3/4 In. 115.00
Royal Doulton, Figurine, Flower Seller's Children, HN 1342, 7 In. 200.00
Royal Doulton, Figurine, Forest Glade Giselle, HN 2140, 7 1/4 In. 210.00
Royal Doulton, Figurine, Fox, Flambe, 4 1/2 In. 42.00
Royal Doulton, Figurine, Gaffer, HN 2053, 7 1/2 In. 185.00
Royal Doulton, Figurine, Garbe Seal, No.249, 8 In. 195.00
Royal Doulton, Figurine, Gay Morning, HN 2135, 7 In. 170.00
Royal Doulton, Figurine, Good Morning, HN 2671, 8 In. 75.00
Royal Doulton, Figurine, Gossips, HN 2025, 5 1/2 In. 250.00
Royal Doulton, Figurine, Greta, HN 1485, 5 1/2 In. 135.00
Royal Doulton, Figurine, Harlequin & Columbine, Pair, 7 1/4 In. 240.00
Royal Doulton, Figurine, Her Ladyship, HN 1977, 7 In. 250.00
Royal Doulton, Figurine, Huntsman, HN 2492, 8 In. 62.50
Royal Doulton, Figurine, Invitation, HN 217C, 5 1/2 In. 115.00
Royal Doulton, Figurine, Irene, HN 1621, 6 3/4 In. 175.00
Royal Doulton, Figurine, Jean, 7 1/4 In. 180.00
Royal Doulton, Figurine, Jersey Milkmaid, HN 2057, 6 1/4 In. 165.00
Royal Doulton, Figurine, Lady Charmian, Pink, HN 1949, 8 In. 125.00
Royal Doulton, Figurine, Laird, HN 2361, 8 In. 55.00

Royal Doulton, Figurine, Lilac Time, HN 2137, 7 1/2 In. 185.00
Royal Doulton, Figurine, Lily, HN 1798, 5 1/4 In. 70.00
Royal Doulton, Figurine, Linda, Red Dress, Green Hat, HN 2106, 5 In. 55.00
Royal Doulton, Figurine, Lion On Rock, No.2641, 12 X 11 1/2 In. 420.00
Royal Doulton, Figurine, Little Bridesmaid, Green Dress, C.1934 .... 90.00
Royal Doulton, Figurine, Little Bridesmaid, HN 1433, 5 In. 93.00
Royal Doulton, Figurine, Margaret, HN 198987 1/4 In. 185.00
Royal Doulton, Figurine, Margery, HN 1413, 10 1/4 In. 275.00
Royal Doulton, Figurine, Marie, HN 1370, 4 1/2 In. 48.00
Royal Doulton, Figurine, Market Day, HN 1991, 7 1/4 In. 200.00
Royal Doulton, Figurine, Maureen, HN 1770, 7 1/2 In. 175.00
Royal Doulton, Figurine, Maureen, Pink, 7 1/2 In. .... 140.00 To 160.00
Royal Doulton, Figurine, Mendicant, Early Script, C.1942, HN 1365, 8 1/2 In. 150.00
Royal Doulton, Figurine, Midinette, HN 2090, 7 In. 250.00
Royal Doulton, Figurine, Midsummer Noon, 4 1/2 In. 180.00
Royal Doulton, Figurine, Milkmaid, HN 2057, 6 3/4 In. 45.00
Royal Doulton, Figurine, Minuet, HN 2019, White, 7 1/4 In. .... 175.00 To 200.00
Royal Doulton, Figurine, Monica, HN 1467, 4 In. .... 53.00 To 85.00
Royal Doulton, Figurine, Mr.Pickwick, HN 2099, 7 1/2 In. 185.00
Royal Doulton, Figurine, My Love, HN 2339, 6 1/2 In. 65.00
Royal Doulton, Figurine, Nell Gwyn, HN 1887, 6 1/2 In. 300.00
Royal Doulton, Figurine, Old Balloon Seller, HN 1315, 7 In. .... 60.00 To 70.00
Royal Doulton, Figurine, Old Meg, HN 2494, 8 In. 87.50
Royal Doulton, Figurine, Old Mother Hubbard, HN 2314, 7 1/2 In. 140.00
Royal Doulton, Figurine, Olga, HN 2463, 8 1/4 In. 95.00
Royal Doulton, Figurine, One That Got Away, HN 2153 .... 135.00
Royal Doulton, Figurine, Owl, Flambe, 12 In. 250.00
Royal Doulton, Figurine, Paisley Shawl, HN 1987, 9 In. 75.00
Royal Doulton, Figurine, Pantalettes, HN 1362, 8 In. 185.00
Royal Doulton, Figurine, Parisian, HN 2445, 8 In. 100.00
Royal Doulton, Figurine, Pearly Boy & Pearly Girl, Pair, 5 1/2 In. 250.00
Royal Doulton, Figurine, Pearly Boy, HN 1432, Pearly Girl, Pair, 5 1/2 In. 250.00
Royal Doulton, Figurine, Pekingese, Champion Biddee Of Field, 3 1/8 In. 25.00
Royal Doulton, Figurine, Penelope, HN 1901, 6 1/2 In. 190.00
Royal Doulton, Figurine, Penguin, Flambe, 6 In. .... 27.50 To 28.00
Royal Doulton, Figurine, Pensive Moments, HN 2704, 4 7/8 In. 55.00
Royal Doulton, Figurine, Poacher, HN 2043, 6 1/8 In. .... 47.00 To 180.00
Royal Doulton, Figurine, Polka, HN 2156, 7 1/2 In. .... 175.00 To 225.00
Royal Doulton, Figurine, Polly Peachum 215.00
Royal Doulton, Figurine, Priscilla, HN 1337, 8 In. 250.00
Royal Doulton, Figurine, Queen Elizabeth At Old Moreton, 10 1/2 In. 35.00
Royal Doulton, Figurine, Red & White Setter, Bird In Mouth, 3 1/2 In. 60.00
Royal Doulton, Figurine, River Boy, HN 2128, 4 In. 55.00
Royal Doulton, Figurine, Rose, Blue & Lavender, HN 1416, 4 5/8 In. 85.00
Royal Doulton, Figurine, Rose, HN 1368, Pink, 4 5/8 In. .... 25.00 To 38.00
Royal Doulton, Figurine, Sabbath Morn, HN 1982, 7 1/4 In. 185.00
Royal Doulton, Figurine, Sea Harvest, HN 2257, 7 1/8 In. 85.00
Royal Doulton, Figurine, She Loves Me Not, HN 2045, 5 1/2 In. 80.00
Royal Doulton, Figurine, She Loves Me Not, Pair, 5 1/2 In. 150.00
Royal Doulton, Figurine, Shepherd, HN 1975, 8 3/4 In. .... 110.00 To 135.00
Royal Doulton, Figurine, Siamese Cat, Laying Down, 3 3/4 In. 29.00
Royal Doulton, Figurine, Southern Belle, HN 2229, 7 1/2 In. 65.00
Royal Doulton, Figurine, Spring Flowers, HN 1807, 7 1/4 In. 175.00
Royal Doulton, Figurine, Spring Morning, HN 1922, 7 1/4 In. 145.00
Royal Doulton, Figurine, Spring Morning, Pink, 7 1/4 In. 130.00
Royal Doulton, Figurine, Summer, Winter, Autumn, Spring, Set 1200.00
Royal Doulton, Figurine, Susan, HN 2056, 6 3/4 In. 175.00
Royal Doulton, Figurine, Suzette, HN 2026, 7 1/2 In. 265.00
Royal Doulton, Figurine, Sweet And Twenty 155.00
Royal Doulton, Figurine, Sweet Anne, Green, HN 1318, 7 In. 155.00
Royal Doulton, Figurine, Sweet Anne, 7 In. 140.00
Royal Doulton, Figurine, Sweeting, HN 1935, 6 In. 75.00
Royal Doulton, Figurine, Tall Story, HN 2248, 6 1/4 In. 125.00
Royal Doulton, Figurine, Tiger, Flambe, No.809, 6 In. 210.00
Royal Doulton, Figurine, Tinker Bell, HN 1677, 4 3/4 In. .... 25.00 To 48.00

Royal Doulton, Figurine, Tinsmith, HN 2146, 6 1/2 In.	250.00
Royal Doulton, Figurine, Tip Of Hill, No.1849, Pink	75.00
Royal Doulton, Figurine, Tootles, HN 1680, 4 3/4 In.	40.00
Royal Doulton, Figurine, Town Crier, HN 2119, 8 1/2 In.	95.00
Royal Doulton, Figurine, Toymaker, HN 2250, 6 1/4 In.	200.00
Royal Doulton, Figurine, Vanity, HN 2475, 5 1/4 In.	30.00
Royal Doulton, Figurine, Veronica, HN 1517, 8 In.	195.00 To 275.00
Royal Doulton, Figurine, Victorian Lady, HN 728, 8in.	195.00
Royal Doulton, Figurine, Viking, HN 2375, 8 3/4 In.	40.00
Royal Doulton, Figurine, Vivienne, HN 2073, 8 In.	165.00 To 180.00
Royal Doulton, Figurine, Walking Duck, Flambe	20.00
Royal Doulton, Figurine, Wardrobe Mistress, HN 2145, 5 3/4 In.	350.00
Royal Doulton, Figurine, Wayfarer, HN 2362, 5 1/4 In.	85.00
Royal Doulton, Figurine, Wee Willie Winkie, HN 2050, 5 1/4 In.	135.00
Royal Doulton, Flask, Mr.Pickwick, Cream Color, Signed Noke, 9 In.	135.00
Royal Doulton, Foot Warmer, C.1905, For Carriage Or Open Car, 12 In.	65.00
Royal Doulton, Jar, Tobacco, Convalescent Homes, Cobalt Blue Lid & Borders	52.00
Royal Doulton, Jar, Tobacco, Stirrup, Cup, Health Unto His Majesty, Blue, White	65.00
Royal Doulton, Jardiniere, Blue, Green, & Browns, Raised Floral, 6 1/2 X 8 In.	110.00
Royal Doulton, Jug, Blue & Green, 8 Standing Polar Bears, 5 In.	85.00
Royal Doulton, Jug, Dewar's Whiskey, The Watchman	85.00
Royal Doulton, Jug, Dewar's, Bonnie Prince Charlie	94.00
Royal Doulton, Jug, Dickens, 14 Characters, Noke & Fenton, 11 X 8 In.	775.00
Royal Doulton, Jug, Dickens, 1936	750.00
Royal Doulton, Jug, Dickensware, Barnaby Rudge, Squared Shape, 6 5/8 In.	75.00
Royal Doulton, Jug, Golfing Scene, Brown Glazed Kingsware, 1902-22, 9 In.	135.00
Royal Doulton, Jug, Golfing, Applied White Vignettes On Buff	225.00
Royal Doulton, Jug, Master Of Fox Hunt, 1930, 13 In.	475.00
Royal Doulton, Jug, Nelson, Stoneware	180.00
Royal Doulton, Jug, The Pickwick Papers, 4 X 5 X 5 1/2 In.	100.00
Royal Doulton, Lighter, Long John Silver	60.00
Royal Doulton, Lighter, Poacher	75.00
Royal Doulton, Loving Cup, Coronation, 2000 Limited Edition, May 1937, 11 In.	485.00
Royal Doulton, Luncheon Set, Coaching Days, 42 Piece	650.00
Royal Doulton, Mask, Wall, Jester	375.00
Royal Doulton, Mug, Auto Scene And Portrait, Signed, 5 1/2 In.	100.00
Royal Doulton, Mug, Bunnykins	25.00
Royal Doulton, Mug, Dickensware, Sam Weller, 2 Handles, 4 In.	65.00
Royal Doulton, Mug, Dr.Johnson At The Cheshire Cheese, 4 1/2 In.	25.00
Royal Doulton, Mug, Harvest Scene, Black Transfer With Red & Green, Small	50.00
Royal Doulton, Mug, Lord Nelson Memorial, Relief Portrait, 2-Handled	250.00
Royal Doulton, Mug, Mr.Pickwick, White, Small	85.00
Royal Doulton, Mug, Tankard, Mr.Micawber, Dickensware	85.00
Royal Doulton, Mush Set & Plate, Child's, C.1906	55.00
Royal Doulton, Pin Tray, Robin Hood, Life In Sherwood Forest, 5 In.	24.00
Royal Doulton, Pitcher & Mug, Nursery Rhyme, Blue Figures & Rhymes	60.00
Royal Doulton, Pitcher, Angular, Multicolored Geometrics, 3 1/2 X 5 In.	38.00
Royal Doulton, Pitcher, Arabian Nights, Ali Baba, Serpent Handle	69.00
Royal Doulton, Pitcher, Babes In Woods, Signed, 9 In.	215.00
Royal Doulton, Pitcher, Battle Of Hastings, Bayeux Tapestry, 7 1/4 In.	65.00
Royal Doulton, Pitcher, Bayeux Tapestry, Bulbous, 6 In.	85.00
Royal Doulton, Pitcher, Canterbury Tales, Scene Of Martyrdom, 8 In.	95.00
Royal Doulton, Pitcher, Cream, Sailing Ships, Brown Band Trim, 10 1/2 In.	50.00
Royal Doulton, Pitcher, Dancing Girls, Flow Blue On Beige, Morrison, 8 In.	95.00
Royal Doulton, Pitcher, Dickensware, Fagin, 7 In.	155.00
Royal Doulton, Pitcher, Dickensware, Mr.Pickwick, 7 3/4 In.	78.00
Royal Doulton, Pitcher, Dickensware, Oliver Twist, Square	90.00
Royal Doulton, Pitcher, Dickensware, Sairey Gamp, 10 In.	135.00
Royal Doulton, Pitcher, Dickensware, Sam Weller, Signed Noke, 6 1/2 In.	115.00
Royal Doulton, Pitcher, Dickensware, Square, Pecksniff, 6 1/2 In.	125.00
Royal Doulton, Pitcher, Drake	550.00
Royal Doulton, Pitcher, Falconer, 7 1/2 In.	75.00
Royal Doulton, Pitcher, Flow Blue, Eglinton Tournament, 3 3/4 In.	26.50
Royal Doulton, Pitcher, Flowers On Blue, Brown Handle, 5 In.	35.00
Royal Doulton, Pitcher, Gondoliers, Venice Scene, Marked, 8 In.	77.00 To 80.00

Royal Doulton, Pitcher, Guy Fawkes 400.00
Royal Doulton, Pitcher, John Peel 400.00
Royal Doulton, Pitcher, Low, Gaffers Scene, 4 1/2 X 5 1/2 In. 95.00
Royal Doulton, Pitcher, Old Curiosity Shop, 5 1/2 In. .... 75.00 To 85.00
Royal Doulton, Pitcher, Old London 165.00
Royal Doulton, Pitcher, Oliver Asks For More 85.00
Royal Doulton, Pitcher, Oliver Twist 100.00
Royal Doulton, Pitcher, Pickwick Papers, Square 125.00
Royal Doulton, Pitcher, Pied Piper 750.00
Royal Doulton, Pitcher, Pied Piper, 1933, Large 350.00
Royal Doulton, Pitcher, Pinch Spout, Dark Blue Flowers, 7 1/2 In. 50.00
Royal Doulton, Pitcher, Queen Elizabeth In Relief, 6 1/2 In. 80.00
Royal Doulton, Pitcher, Red Golds, Greens, Scenic, Sheep Grazing, 3 3/4 In. 22.50
Royal Doulton, Pitcher, Regency Coach 550.00
Royal Doulton, Pitcher, Shakespeare, 1933 .... 450.00
Royal Doulton, Pitcher, Sydney Carton, 10 In. 135.00
Royal Doulton, Pitcher, Tan & Brown, White Applied Figures 79.00
Royal Doulton, Pitcher, Toby Philpot In Relief, Signed, 8 5/8 X 7 1/2 In. 120.00
Royal Doulton, Pitcher, Treasure Island 550.00
Royal Doulton, Plaque, Babe-In-The-Wood, 11 X 14 In. 245.00
Royal Doulton, Plaque, Coaching Days, Changing Horses, Cream, Green, Pierced 125.00
Royal Doulton, Plate, Baby, Hushabye Baby Scene 35.00
Royal Doulton, Plate, Bobbie Burns, I Have A Wife, 6 1/2 In. 18.00
Royal Doulton, Plate, Book Worm, 10 In. 40.00
Royal Doulton, Plate, Canterbury Pilgrims On Horseback, Cream, 10 1/2 In. 45.00
Royal Doulton, Plate, Castle Scene, 10 1/2 In. 33.00
Royal Doulton, Plate, Chop, Blue Leaf Border, Cream, 10 In. 85.00
Royal Doulton, Plate, Coaching Scene, 7 1/2 In. 10.00
Royal Doulton, Plate, Coaching Scene, 8 1/4 In. 20.00
Royal Doulton, Plate, Congressional Library, Flow Blue, 10 In. 31.50
Royal Doulton, Plate, Dickensware, Alfred Jingle, 10 In. 50.00
Royal Doulton, Plate, Dickensware, Barkis Against Street Scene, 10 1/4 In. 45.00
Royal Doulton, Plate, Dickensware, Barnaby Rudge, 6 1/2 In. 37.50
Royal Doulton, Plate, Dickensware, Barnaby Rudge, 10 In. 50.00
Royal Doulton, Plate, Dickensware, Bill Sykes, 10 In. 45.00
Royal Doulton, Plate, Dickensware, Captain Cuttle, 10 1/2 In. .... 48.00 To 50.00
Royal Doulton, Plate, Dickensware, Captain Cuttle, 6 1/2 In. 37.50
Royal Doulton, Plate, Dickensware, Little Nell, 10 In. 60.00
Royal Doulton, Plate, Dickensware, Mr.Pickwick, Railroad Station, 10 1/2 In. 35.00
Royal Doulton, Plate, Dickensware, Mr.Squeers, Square, 8 In. 50.00
Royal Doulton, Plate, Dickensware, Sairey Gamp, 10 In. 45.00
Royal Doulton, Plate, Dickensware, Sam Weller, Signed Noke, 10 In. 34.00
Royal Doulton, Plate, Dickensware, Sam Weller, 5 1/2 In. 37.50
Royal Doulton, Plate, Dickensware, Tony Weller, 10 In. 45.00
Royal Doulton, Plate, Dog, Rococo Wood Frame, 13 3/4 In. 165.00
Royal Doulton, Plate, Falconer, C.1900, 10 1/2 In. 45.00
Royal Doulton, Plate, Farm Girl Working In Garden, 10 1/2 In. 29.00
Royal Doulton, Plate, Game, Gold Border & Design, Nelson 52.50
Royal Doulton, Plate, General Lee On Horse, May 1911, 7 In. 40.00
Royal Doulton, Plate, Golfers, 10 In. 55.00
Royal Doulton, Plate, Hyde Park Hotel, Oval, 5 1/4 X 3 1/2 In. 10.00
Royal Doulton, Plate, Jackdaw Of Rheims, 2 Monks, 6 1/2 In. 28.00
Royal Doulton, Plate, Jester, C.1900, 10 1/2 In. 45.00
Royal Doulton, Plate, Jester, Lanterns & Foliage Border, 10 1/2 In. 60.00
Royal Doulton, Plate, Mayor, C.1900, 10 1/2 In. 45.00
Royal Doulton, Plate, Mr.Pickwick, 4 In. 25.00
Royal Doulton, Plate, Mr.Piggily's Store, Bunnykins, Signed B.Vernon, 8 In. 20.00
Royal Doulton, Plate, Mr.Squeers, Made In England, 8 In. 50.00
Royal Doulton, Plate, Nothing Venture, Nothing Gain, Hunting Dog In Woods 35.00
Royal Doulton, Plate, Old English Coaching Scenes, 5 1/4 In. 18.00
Royal Doulton, Plate, Old English Coaching Scenes, 10 In. 45.00
Royal Doulton, Plate, Old English Inns, Leather Bottle, 10 In. .... 22.00 To 32.50
Royal Doulton, Plate, Parson, C.1900, 10 1/2 In. 45.00
Royal Doulton, Plate, Robin Hood, 8 3/4 In. 38.00
Royal Doulton, Plate, Romeo & Juliet, Blue & White 32.00

Royal Doulton, Plate, Romeo, Beige Pastel Color, 8 In. 50.00
Royal Doulton, Plate, Sailing Vessels, 10 1/4 In. 30.00
Royal Doulton, Plate, Scenic, 1902 Mark, 10 1/2 In. 45.00
Royal Doulton, Plate, Shakespeare, Blue, White, 10 1/2 In. 42.00
Royal Doulton, Plate, Shakespeare, Portia, Brown To Yellow Ground, Pre-1936 .... 55.00
Royal Doulton, Plate, Shakespeare, Romeo, 10 In. 45.00
Royal Doulton, Plate, Spanish Armada, Blue And White, 10 1/2 In. 35.00
Royal Doulton, Plate, Squire, 10 In. 35.00
Royal Doulton, Plate, Tavern Scene, 10 1/2 In. 30.00
Royal Doulton, Plate, Tea, Norfolk, Blue & White Scenes Of Norfolk 8.00
Royal Doulton, Plate, U.S.Capitol, Blue & White, 10 In. 32.00
Royal Doulton, Plate, Watteau, 9 In. 24.00
Royal Doulton, Plate, White House 20.00
Royal Doulton, Plate, 12-Sided, Blue With Florals, Parrots, C.1912, 10 1/4 In. 25.00
Royal Doulton, Rose Bowl, Flowers, Speckled, Dark Blue, Tan, Artist Signed 65.00
Royal Doulton, Smoke Set, Playing Card Design, 5 Piece, England 35.00
Royal Doulton, Soup & Underplate, Fox Hunting Scene, Set Of 4 .... 125.00
Royal Doulton, Stand, Teapot, The Artful Dodger 45.00
Royal Doulton, Sugar & Creamer, Jackdaw Of Rheims, Miniature 65.00
Royal Doulton, Sugar, Dickensware, Fat Boy Scenes On Handle, 3 X 4 1/4 In. 75.00
Royal Doulton, Tankard, Dickensware Old Curiosity Shop, Marked, 5 1/2 In. 115.00
Royal Doulton, Tankard, Dickensware, Fagin, D2973 Series, 5 3/4 In. 70.00
Royal Doulton, Tankard, Dickensware, Oliver Twist, 6 In. 110.00
Royal Doulton, Teapot, Blue & Gold Decoration, Artist Initialed F.J. 90.00
Royal Doulton, Teapot, Old Charlie 250.00
Royal Doulton, Tile, Scenes Of South & Loose, Pair, 5 1/2 X 6 1/4 In. 90.00
Royal Doulton, Tile, Tea, Life In The Forest Of Sherwood 22.00
Royal Doulton, Tile, Tea, Old Woman With Kitten Indoors 25.00
Royal Doulton, Tobacco Jar, Uncle Toby, Stoneware 60.00
Royal Doulton, Toby Mug, Best Is Not Too Good, 4 1/2 In. .... 175.00 To 250.00
Royal Doulton, Toby Mug, Churchill, Large, 9 In. 24.50
Royal Doulton, Toby Mug, Churchill, Medium, 5 1/2 In. 18.75
Royal Doulton, Toby Mug, Double XX, Full Seated, 6 1/2 In. 295.00
Royal Doulton, Toby Mug, Falstaff, 5 1/4 In. 18.00
Royal Doulton, Toby Mug, Falstaff, 8 1/2 In. 29.00
Royal Doulton, Toby Mug, Happy John, 5 1/2 In. 18.00
Royal Doulton, Toby Mug, Happy John, 9 In. .... 24.50 To 29.00
Royal Doulton, Toby Mug, Hearty Good Fellow, 1820, 9 In. 116.00
Royal Doulton, Toby Mug, Herbert Hoover, No.337, 7 In. 85.00
Royal Doulton, Toby Mug, Honest Measure, 4 1/2 In. 18.00
Royal Doulton, Toby Mug, Huntsman, Browns 115.00
Royal Doulton, Toby Mug, Huntsman, 7 3/4 In. 24.50
Royal Doulton, Toby Mug, John Peel, 3 1/2 In. 63.00
Royal Doulton, Toby Mug, Jolly Toby, 6 1/4 In. .... 14.95 To 18.00
Royal Doulton, Toby Mug, Man Smoking Cigar, Cliff Cornell, 9 1/4 In. 275.00
Royal Doulton, Toby Mug, Mr.Micawber, A Mark, 4 1/2 In. 140.00
Royal Doulton, Toby Mug, Old Charley, Full Seated, 5 1/2 In. 165.00
Royal Doulton, Toby Mug, Old Charley, Full Seated, 8 1/2 In. 175.00
Royal Doulton, Toothpick, Old Charley, 1940s 50.00
Royal Doulton, Toothpick, Sairey Gamp, 3 In. .... 45.00 To 75.00
Royal Doulton, Tray, Dickensware, Fat Boy, 3 1/2 X 5 1/2 In. 50.00
Royal Doulton, Tray, Dickensware, Fat Boy, 4 X 5 1/2 In. 58.00
Royal Doulton, Tray, Dickensware, Poor Jo, 11 X 5 In. 52.00
Royal Doulton, Vase, Art Nouveau Flowers, Stoneware, 14 1/4 In. 150.00
Royal Doulton, Vase, Babes In The Woods, Delft Blue, White, 10 In., Pair 400.00
Royal Doulton, Vase, Blue & Light Brown, 4 1/2 In. 30.00
Royal Doulton, Vase, Blue Children, Numbered, 10 In., Pair 400.00
Royal Doulton, Vase, Blue, Brown Scrollwork, George Tinworth, 8 In. 210.00
Royal Doulton, Vase, Boat Scene, Gold Handles & Trim, H.Allen, 5 7/8 In. 150.00
Royal Doulton, Vase, C.1874, Signed Arthur Barlow, 7 In. 175.00
Royal Doulton, Vase, Cavalier, Here's A Health Unto His Majesty, 13 In. 175.00
Royal Doulton, Vase, Coaching Scene, 4 1/4 In. 32.00
Royal Doulton, Vase, Cows & Horses, Gray, Olive Leaf Borders, Hannah Barlow 265.00
Royal Doulton, Vase, Cream, Young Man, Trees, Hills, Bulbous, Crown Mark, 10 In. 125.00
Royal Doulton, Vase, Delft Blue & White, Girls & Dog, 8 1/2 In. 125.00

Royal Doulton, Vase, Dickensware, Square, Tony Weller, Marked, 8 In. 120.00
Royal Doulton, Vase, Dickensware, Tony Weller, Noke, Small Handles, 4 1/2 In. 65.00
Royal Doulton, Vase, Dickensware, Tony Weller, 3 1/8 In. 48.00
Royal Doulton, Vase, Flambe, Blue, Gold, Red, No.1619, 11 3/4 In. 115.00
Royal Doulton, Vase, Flambe, Camel, Miniature 60.00
Royal Doulton, Vase, Flambe, Flowers, Castle, C.1905, 7 In. 150.00
Royal Doulton, Vase, Flambe, Forest Scene, Woodcut Of Deer, 11 1/2 In. 150.00
Royal Doulton, Vase, Flambe, Gourd Shaped, 6 In. 40.00
Royal Doulton, Vase, Flambe, Tapered, Veined, 8 1/2 In. 135.00
Royal Doulton, Vase, Flambe, Veined Sung, HN 1605, 5 In. 30.00
Royal Doulton, Vase, Flambe, Veined Sung, HN 1606, 4 1/2 In. 30.00
Royal Doulton, Vase, Flambe, Veined Sung, HN 1613, 7 In. 42.00
Royal Doulton, Vase, Flambe, Veined Sung, HN 1614, 6 In. 38.00
Royal Doulton, Vase, Flambe, Woodcut Scene Of People Walking In Woods, 6 In. 52.00
Royal Doulton, Vase, Flambe, 2 1/2 In. 50.00
Royal Doulton, Vase, Floral, Blue, White, Pink, Green, Brown, Signed, 12 In. 98.00
Royal Doulton, Vase, Flow Blue Daffodils, Gold Trim, 11 In. 89.00
Royal Doulton, Vase, Fruits, Blue, Signed, 10 X 5 In. 95.00
Royal Doulton, Vase, Gibson Girl, Is A Caddie Always Necessary, 5 X 4 In. 65.00
Royal Doulton, Vase, Girl Playing Guitar, No.6100, Blue, Beige 195.00
Royal Doulton, Vase, Gold Floral On Blue & Gray, Art Deco, W.B., 6 In. 135.00
Royal Doulton, Vase, Horses, Cows, Field, Raised Border, Beading, Signed, 17 In. 425.00
Royal Doulton, Vase, Mottled Blue, Brown Ribs, Artist, Frank Pope, 6 In. 60.00
Royal Doulton, Vase, Portrait, Cobalt, White, Blue Chrysanthemums, 7 1/4 In. 175.00
Royal Doulton, Vase, Rouge Flambe, Bulbous, Coach, Horses, 10 In. 120.00
Royal Doulton, Vase, Scenic Woodcut, 4 1/2 In. 32.00
Royal Doulton, Vase, Sir Roger De Coverly, 5 1/2 In. 55.00
Royal Doulton, Vase, Slater, Brown Tapestry, 11 In. 85.00
Royal Doulton, Vase, Spill, Fagin 45.00
Royal Doulton, Vase, Square, Tony Weller, 8 In. 120.00
Royal Doulton, Vase, Stoneware, Art Nouveau Mermaid, Francis Pope, 13 In. 250.00
Royal Doulton, Vase, Sung, Noke & Fred Moore, 6 In. 175.00
Royal Doulton, Vase, Tapestry, Gold Clock, White Enamel Flowers, Slaters Pat. 159.00
Royal Doulton, Vase, Trumpet, George Tinworth, Blue, 3 Mice At Base, C.1885 .... 325.00
Royal Doulton, Vase, Veined Sung, 7 1/2 In. 42.00
Royal Doulton, Vase, Veined, Sung, Woodcut, Flambe, No.1606 .... 27.50
Royal Doulton, Vase, Veined, Sung, Woodcut, Flambe, No.1617 .... 140.00
Royal Doulton, Vase, Welsh Ladies, Signed Noke, 5 3/4 In. 37.50
Royal Doulton, Wall Pocket, Raised Brown Owl On Front 55.00

Royal Dux is a porcelain made by Duxer Porzellanmanufaktur, a factory established in 1860 in Dux, Bohemia (now Czechoslovakia). Reproductions are being made.

Royal Dux, Bowl, Girl Standing On Rim Holding Goose, Shell Center, 11 In. 275.00
Royal Dux, Centerpiece, Girl In Dress Supports Seashell On Back, Waves, Mark 325.00
Royal Dux, Chess Set, Royal Blue & Gold, 32 Piece 275.00
Royal Dux, Compote, Maiden Draped Across Shell, Art Nouveau, Pink Triangle 295.00
Royal Dux, Figurine, Boy At Well, C.1935, 24 In. 260.00
Royal Dux, Figurine, Dog Dressed In Pastel Men's Clothes, Stands, 5 1/4 In. 35.00
Royal Dux, Figurine, Elephant, 5 X 8 In. 30.00
Royal Dux, Figurine, Fisherman & Wife, Pink Triangle Mark, 21 In., Pair 525.00
Royal Dux, Figurine, Fishermen Bringing In The Catch, Brown Tones, 18 In. 975.00
Royal Dux, Figurine, Girl Looking Over Shell 195.00
Royal Dux, Figurine, Girl On Conch Shell, Pink Mark In Triangle, 8 X 8 In. 195.00
Royal Dux, Figurine, Girl On Shell, Signed 270.00
Royal Dux, Figurine, Hunting Dog, Oval Base, Pink Triangle, 15 X 8 In., Pair 175.00
Royal Dux, Figurine, Hunting Theme, Pink Diamond Mark, 16 X 18 1/4 In. 450.00
Royal Dux, Figurine, Lady Playing Mandolin, Art Nouveau, 18 X 6 3/4 In. 265.00
Royal Dux, Figurine, Man & Woman, Cobalt Blue Costumes, Art Deco, 12 In. 175.00
Royal Dux, Figurine, Man With Bull, Pink Triangle Mark, 13 In. .... 695.00 To 750.00
Royal Dux, Figurine, Pheasant, High Glaze, Pink Triangle Mark, 7 In. 65.00
Royal Dux, Figurine, Seated Dog, Bowtie, 5 1/2 In. 115.00
Royal Dux, Figurine, Stone Cutter, Sledge, Green Loincloth, Chisel, Wall 135.00
Royal Dux, Figurine, The Wildcat, Marbleized Base, Pink Mark, 5 X 11 In. 145.00
Royal Dux, Figurine, Women Wearing Working Class Clothes, Fancy Apron, 5 In. 35.00

Royal Flemish, Vase, Geese, C.1895, 14 1/4 In.

Royal Dux, Group, Bird Dogs, Pink Triangle Mark, 11 X 8 In. 65.00
Royal Dux, Group, Boy & Girl, Pastel, Gilt Trim, Pink Triangle, 5 1/2 In. 80.00
Royal Dux, Vase, Applied Apricot, Roses, Olive Ground, 2 Handled, Signed, 5 In. 32.00
Royal Dux, Vase, Applied Grapes, Pink Triangle Mark, 11 1/2 In., Pair 145.00
Royal Dux, Vase, Embossed Fruit, Triangle Mark, 15 In. 135.00
Royal Dux, Vase, Flowers & Leaves, Signed, Triangle Mark, 9 In. 130.00
Royal Dux, Vase, Fruit & Vine, Pink Triangle, Handled, 19 In., Pair 365.00
Royal Dux, Vase, Molded Cherries, Handles, Pink Triangle, 11 1/2 In., Pair 165.00
Royal Dux, Vase, Raised Fruit & Leaves, 4 In. 8.50
Royal Dux, Vase, Venus & Conch Shell, Green, Mauve, Cream, 11 In. 300.00

Royal Flemish glass was made during the late 1880s in New Bedford,
Massachusetts, by the Mt.Washington Glass Works. It is a colored
satin glass decorated in dark colors with gold designs.
Royal Flemish, Box, Dresser, Satin Lining, Gold Scroll 875.00
Royal Flemish, Cookie Jar 1650.00
Royal Flemish, Jar, Silver Lid & Handle, 7 In. 1150.00
Royal Flemish, Jardiniere, Parrots & Cockatoo, Multicolor 1095.00
Royal Flemish, Vase, Coin Design, 11 1/2 In. 1950.00
Royal Flemish, Vase, Coin Design, 11 1/4 In. 1800.00
Royal Flemish, Vase, Geese, C.1895, 14 1/4 In. .... *Illus* 3800.00
   Royal Ivy, see Northwood
Royal Munich, Chocolate Pot, Pale & Dark Green, Pink, Roses, Gold Trim 75.00
Royal Munich, Dish, Hand-Painted Roses, Oval, Handles, 8 In. 14.00
Royal Munich, Pitcher, Milk, Pink, Yellow, Red Roses, Hand-Painted, 8 In. 145.00
Royal Munich, Plate, Grouse In A Field, Gold Rococo Border, Blue Mark, 10 In. 40.00
Royal Munich, Sugar, Covered, Pale & Dark Green, Roses, Gold Trim, Oblong 35.00
   Royal Oak, see Pressed Glass

Royal Rudolstadt, a German faience factory, was established in Thuringia,
Germany, in 1721. Hard paste porcelain was made by E.Bohne after 1854.
Late nineteenth- and early twentieth-century pieces are most commonly found
today. The later mark is a shield with the letters RW inside superseded by
a crown and the words Royal Rudolstadt.
   Royal Rudolstadt, see also Kewpie
Royal Rudolstadt, Banana Dish, Reverse Torpedo, 9 In. 93.00
Royal Rudolstadt, Basket, Floral, Gold Handle, Rust, Cream, 5 X 3 X 4 In. 37.50
Royal Rudolstadt, Bowl, Berry, Blackberries, Gray, Blue, Gold, 13 In. 35.00
Royal Rudolstadt, Bowl, Pink & Yellow Floral, 3 Gold Ball Feet, 6 1/2 In. 30.00
Royal Rudolstadt, Bowl, Pink & Yellow Roses, Gold Rim, F.Hahn, 7 In. 25.00
Royal Rudolstadt, Bowl, Roses, Double Handle, Yellow, 6 1/2 X 2 1/2 In. 22.00
Royal Rudolstadt, Bowl, Roses, Gold Rim, White, Yellow, Red, Pink, Signed, 10 In. 45.00
Royal Rudolstadt, Bowl, Roses, Pink, Prussia, Artist Signed, 9 1/2 In. 65.00
Royal Rudolstadt, Bowl, Shell Shape, Gold Turned Handle, 10 1/2 In. 85.00
Royal Rudolstadt, Box, Powder, Covered, Pink Roses 18.00
Royal Rudolstadt, Box, Powder, Pink Roses On Pale Background, Covered 18.00
Royal Rudolstadt, Celery, Yellow And Red Roses, Raised Star On Bottom 45.00
Royal Rudolstadt, Cup & Saucer, Floral, Pedestal, Signed 37.50
Royal Rudolstadt, Cup & Saucer, Flowers, Pastel 22.00
Royal Rudolstadt, Dish, Cheese, Cream, Pink, Yellow, Orange, Roses, Small 30.00

Royal Rudolstadt, Dish, Feeding, 7 Action Kewpies, Signed Rose O'Neill 125.00
Royal Rudolstadt, Dish, Hen Cover, 19th Century, 8 In. 115.00
Royal Rudolstadt, Dish, Pierced Handle, Leaves & Grapes, Gold Border 45.00
Royal Rudolstadt, Dresser Set, Florals On Blue-Mauve Background, Signed 85.00
Royal Rudolstadt, Ewer, Floral, Scalloped, Gold Handle, Blue, Yellow, 7 In. 59.00
Royal Rudolstadt, Ewer, Flowers On Cream, Satin Finish, 10 In. 45.00
Royal Rudolstadt, Figurine, Boy In Toga Holding Mallet & Chisel, 16 1/2 In. 250.00
Royal Rudolstadt, Jar, Jam, Holly & Berries, Spoon & Lid, 4 In. 35.00
Royal Rudolstadt, Pitcher, Beige, Floral, Blown Roses At Neck, 10 In. 69.00
Royal Rudolstadt, Pitcher, Ewer, Signed Hahn, 12 In. 85.00
Royal Rudolstadt, Plate, Bread, Gold Handles, Signed, 12 In. 32.50
Royal Rudolstadt, Plate, Cake, Roses, 10 In. 35.00
Royal Rudolstadt, Plate, Cream, Yellow Roses, Gold Trim, 8 1/2 In., Set Of 6 .... 180.00
Royal Rudolstadt, Plate, Hand-Painted, Gold Rim 27.50
Royal Rudolstadt, Plate, Hand-Painted, Red Tulips, 8 1/4 In. .... 12.00 To 17.00
Royal Rudolstadt, Plate, Hand-Painted, Roses, Pastel, 8 1/2 In. 12.50
Royal Rudolstadt, Plate, Holly Berry, Signed, 6 In. 25.00
Royal Rudolstadt, Plate, Ivory, Gold, Yellow Roses, Holly, 6 In. 12.50
Royal Rudolstadt, Plate, Leaf Decoration, Signed, 6 In. 25.00
Royal Rudolstadt, Plate, Pastel, Flowers, Gold Border, 8 1/2 In. 14.50
Royal Rudolstadt, Plate, Pink & Pastel Roses, Floral Border, 8 1/2 In. 35.00
Royal Rudolstadt, Plate, Roses, Gold Border, Pink, Cream, 8 1/2 In. 17.50
Royal Rudolstadt, Plate, Roses, 3 Pink, Signed, 8 In. 27.50
Royal Rudolstadt, Plate, Roses, 4 Wild, Signed, 8 1/2 In. 30.00
Royal Rudolstadt, Plate, White Rose, 3 In Center, 6 On Gold Rim, Signed, 8 In. 32.50
Royal Rudolstadt, Sugar & Creamer, Gold Handles & Bands, Blue Flowers 60.00
Royal Rudolstadt, Sugar & Creamer, Roses, Gold Rim, White, Signed 57.50
Royal Rudolstadt, Teapot, Daisies On Ivory Ground, Rose Finial, Relief 110.00
Royal Rudolstadt, Tray, Dresser, Leaf Shape, Signed, 9 In. 32.50
Royal Rudolstadt, Vase, Beige, Floral, Gold Filigree Handles, 10 In., Pair 150.00
Royal Rudolstadt, Vase, Cream, Pink & Gold Floral, Gold Vine Handle, 9 In. 60.00
Royal Rudolstadt, Vase, Cream, Pink Florals, 2 Gold Handles, 5 1/2 In. 9.50
Royal Rudolstadt, Vase, Dolphin Spout, Gold Dolphin Handles, 13 1/2 In. 175.00
Royal Rudolstadt, Vase, Morning Glories, Gold Outlined Leaves, Gold Handle 40.00
Royal Rudolstadt, Vase, Prussia, Bluebird, 2 Handled, 7 In. 56.00
Royal Saxe, Dish, Fuchsia Leaf, Green, Gold, Dancing Ladies, Flowers, 11 In. 20.00
Royal Saxe, Plate, Portrait, Sitting Bull, 6 1/2 In. 20.00

> *Royal Vienna was established in Vienna by Claude Innocentius du*
> *Paquier in 1719. The factory closed in 1865. Since then, various German*
> *and Austrian factories have reproduced Royal Vienna wares, complete with*
> *the original beehive mark.*

Royal Vienna, see also Beehive
Royal Vienna, Basket, Ming Tree, White, 12 1/2 In. 65.00
Royal Vienna, Bowl, Mythological Scene, Enamel Beading, Beehive, 9 X 13 In. 49.00
Royal Vienna, Bowl, Portrait, Gold Trim, Handles, Blue, Beehive Mark, 5 In. 60.00
Royal Vienna, Box, Jewel, Footed, Hand-Painted Love Scene Lid, Brass, Ornate 63.00
Royal Vienna, Box, Jewel, Love Scene, Brass Trimming, Footed, 3 X 3 X 3 In. 63.00
Royal Vienna, Box, Powder, Blue, Hand-Painted Boy & Girl 80.00
Royal Vienna, Box, Powder, Pink & Green, Hand-Painted Cherubs 65.00
Royal Vienna, Chocolate Pot, Portrait Of Lady In Pink Gown, Vettori, Marked 150.00
Royal Vienna, Coffeepot, Dice Players, Cobalt, Beehive Mark, 7 In. 100.00
Royal Vienna, Coffeepot, Lady With Flowers, Cobalt & Gold Trim, 12 In. 200.00
Royal Vienna, Coffepot, Cobalt Blue, Dice Players, Gold Handle, Beehive Mark 110.00
Royal Vienna, Cup & Saucer, Chocolate, Mother-Of-Pearl, Classic Scene 38.00
Royal Vienna, Cup & Saucer, Cobalt Blue, Raised Gold, Portrait Of Girl 75.00
Royal Vienna, Cup & Saucer, Demitasse, Cobalt & Gold, Seminude Lady, Signed 95.00
Royal Vienna, Cup & Saucer, Demitasse, Magenta & Green, Pearlized, Gold Trim 24.00
Royal Vienna, Cup & Saucer, Demitasse, Portrait, Young Woman & Cupid, Gold 145.00
Royal Vienna, Cup & Saucer, Demitasse, Seminude Woman, Cobalt Blue & Gold 95.00
Royal Vienna, Cup & Saucer, Portrait, Pedestal, Beehive Mark 65.00
Royal Vienna, Cup & Saucer, Reticulated, Beehive Mark 35.00
Royal Vienna, Jar, Portrait Medallion, Woman & Shepherd, Cobalt, Pre-1820 .... 135.00
Royal Vienna, Jar, Sleeping Maiden, Winged Cherub, Beading, Beehive, 12 In. 125.00
Royal Vienna, Planter, Landscape 40.00

Royal Vienna, Plate, Ariadne, Seminude Nymph On Rocks, Raised Gold, Wagner	275.00
Royal Vienna, Plate, Beautiful Maiden, Gold Border, Beehive Mark, 9 In.	95.00
Royal Vienna, Plate, Classical Portrait, Red Beehive Mark, Signed, 8 1/2 In.	75.00
Royal Vienna, Plate, Classical Scene, Woman By Lake, Cherub Center, 9 1/2 In.	175.00
Royal Vienna, Plate, Diana & Eros, Matted With Velvet, Frame, Beehive, Signed	295.00
Royal Vienna, Plate, Garden Scene, Cherub, Signed Kauffmann, 12 X 13 In.	325.00
Royal Vienna, Plate, Gypsy Girl, 1906, Wagner, 10 In.	20.00
Royal Vienna, Plate, Hanging, Gold Leaf Border, 14 X 9 1/2 In.	275.00
Royal Vienna, Plate, Hillside Scene, Cobalt Border & Gold, Beehive, 9 1/2 In.	145.00
Royal Vienna, Plate, Lady With Cupids In Garden, Cobalt Border, Gold, 8 In.	275.00
Royal Vienna, Plate, Painted Lady, Overglazed, Amiciatia Mark, 20 In.	210.00
Royal Vienna, Plate, Portrait, Brunette, Gold Trim, Amorosa, 9 1/2 In.	100.00
Royal Vienna, Plate, Portrait, Daphne, Maroon Border, Raised Gold, Beehive	300.00
Royal Vienna, Plate, Portrait, Lady Pompadour & Lovers, Pink Luster, Beehive	36.00
Royal Vienna, Plate, Portrait, Ornate, Wagner	400.00
Royal Vienna, Plate, Portrait, Ruth, Beaded Raised Border, Signed Wagner	425.00
Royal Vienna, Plate, Red Border, Gold Scroll, Beehive Mark, 14 In.	265.00
Royal Vienna, Plate, Scenes In Border, Red, Lilac, Yellow, Beehive, 14 In.	285.00
Royal Vienna, Plate, Woman, Ornate Gold Border, Wagner, 9 1/2 In.	350.00
Royal Vienna, Plate, 3 Nymphs & Cupid, Dark Green, Gold Borders, 9 1/2 In.	125.00
Royal Vienna, Stein, Tollins, Painting On Lid, Beehive Under Glaze, 1/2 Liter	995.00
Royal Vienna, Sugar Shaker, Satin Finish, Art Nouveau Shape	40.00
Royal Vienna, Tureen, Flying Cherubs, Gold Handles, Beehive Mark, 9 In.	300.00
Royal Vienna, Urn, Classical Scene, Blue Beehive Mark, 15 1/4 In.	275.00
Royal Vienna, Urn, Cobalt, Gold Trim, Beehive Mark Under Glaze, 3 1/2 In.	310.00
Royal Vienna, Urn, Covered, Pedestal, Raised Decoration, Purple & Red, 9 In.	95.00
Royal Vienna, Urn, Covered, Portait Woman & Angels, Beading, Handles, 10 In.	225.00
Royal Vienna, Urn, Medallion Of 3 Women, Handles, Red, Gold, Blue Beehive Sign	125.00
Royal Vienna, Urn, Medallion, 3 Heroic Figures, Beehive Mark, 11 1/2 X 4 In.	165.00
Royal Vienna, Urn, Portrait Of Lady In Yellow Gown, Gold Trim, 10 1/2 In.	150.00
Royal Vienna, Urn, Signed Portrait Center, Cobalt Blue, Gold, Beehive, 7 In.	225.00
Royal Vienna, Urn, Sleeping Lady & Cupid, Red & Green, Gold & Beading, 13 In.	115.00
Royal Vienna, Vase, Cupid In Chariot, 3 Women, Beehive, P.Max, 10 1/2 In.	145.00
Royal Vienna, Vase, Enameled Floral Decoration, 11 In.	125.00
Royal Vienna, Vase, Floral On Cream, Signed, 10 1/2 In.	85.00
Royal Vienna, Vase, Florals & Gilding On Lemon Yellow, Covered, 4 1/2 In.	285.00
Royal Vienna, Vase, Medallions Of Women & Cupids, Gold, Handled, 9 In.	125.00
Royal Vienna, Vase, Portrait Of Girl, Wagner, 4 1/2 In.	275.00
Royal Vienna, Vase, Portrait, Aqua & White, Gold Handles, 12 In.	125.00
Royal Vienna, Vase, Portrait, Cobalt Blue, 10 In.	150.00
Royal Vienna, Vase, Portrait, Flossie, 8 In.	110.00
Royal Vienna, Vase, Portrait, Girl, Bared Torso, Blue Jewels, Handles, Signed	395.00
Royal Vienna, Vase, Portrait, Nude Woman, Cupids, Raised Gold, Red, Beehive	325.00
Royal Vienna, Vase, Portrait, Ustana, Maroon, Wagner, C.1850, 9 1/2 In.	365.00
Royal Vienna, Vase, Portrait, Wagner, 3 In.	135.00
Royal Vienna, Vase, Seated Woman, Light Blue & Cream, Gold Trim, 16 In.	150.00
Royal Vienna, Vase, Urn, Beehive Under Glaze, Artist Signed, 16 1/2 In.	195.00

Royal Worcester porcelain was made in the later period of Worcester pottery, which was originally established in 1751. The Royal Worcester trade name has been used by Worcester Royal Porcelain Company, Ltd., since 1862.

Royal Worcester, Barrel, Biscuit, Cream, Floral, Gold Washed Lid & Rim, 6 In.	160.00
Royal Worcester, Basket, Beige Satin, Floral Sprays, 1903, Handled, 5 3/4 In.	175.00
Royal Worcester, Basket, Cream & Tan, Basket Weave, Pinched Sides, 7 X 5 In.	82.00
Royal Worcester, Basket, Sewing, Woven With Wicker Look, Floral Inside, Gilt	145.00
Royal Worcester, Bottle, Perfume, Bird, 3 In.	40.00
Royal Worcester, Bowl, Apples & Blackberries, Shell Shaped Handle, 7 1/4 In.	175.00
Royal Worcester, Bowl, Fruit Center, Gold Outside, Purple Mark, 7 In.	90.00
Royal Worcester, Bowl, Satin Finish, Florals, Gold Trim, 3 1/2 In.	75.00
Royal Worcester, Candlesnuffer, Hat Shaped, Yellow Band, Feather, 3 In.	35.00
Royal Worcester, Candlesnuffer, Monk, Purple Mark, 4 1/2 In.	45.00
Royal Worcester, Candlesnuffer, Nun, Purple Mark, C.1921	55.00
Royal Worcester, Candlesnuffer, The Cook, Purple Mark, C.1908	115.00

Royal Worcester, Candlestick, Turquoise, Beige, Brown, & Gold, Hadley, 6 In. 85.00
Royal Worcester, Charger, Oriental Design, Red & Green Pagodas, People, 1916 ..... 65.00
Royal Worcester, Chocolate Pot, Apple Green, Florals, Gold Handle & Finial 275.00
Royal Worcester, Chocolate Pot, Beige Satin Finish, Dated 1894, 8 3/4 In. 275.00
Royal Worcester, Chocolate Pot, Floral, Bamboo, 7 1/4 In. ..... 165.00 To 185.00
Royal Worcester, Chocolate Pot, Green, Gold Finial, Floral, Purple Mark, 9 In. 275.00
Royal Worcester, Cracker Jar, Bark Pattern, 5 1/2 X 6 1/4 In. 175.00
Royal Worcester, Creamer, Cream, Lavender Flowers, Gold Trim, No.125349, 3 In. 75.00
Royal Worcester, Creamer, English, C.1885, 4W & Crown, 5 1/2 In. 48.00
Royal Worcester, Creamer, English, C.1885, 4W & Crown, 6 X 12 In. 55.00
Royal Worcester, Creamer, Floral Decoration, Beige Satin Finish, C.1899 ..... 95.00
Royal Worcester, Creamer, Yellow, Flower Band, Twig Handle, 3 1/2 In. 40.00
Royal Worcester, Cup & Saucer, Demitasse, C.1890 Mark, Set Of 12 ..... 125.00
Royal Worcester, Cup & Saucer, Demitasse, Dunrobin, Pink, Green, Floral Sprigs 27.50
Royal Worcester, Cup & Saucer, Demitasse, Enamel Colors, Purple Mark 17.50
Royal Worcester, Cup & Saucer, Demitasse, Floral 38.50
Royal Worcester, Cup & Saucer, Demitasse, Gold Handle, Purple Mark 85.00
Royal Worcester, Cup & Saucer, Demitasse, Pink Floral, Gold Band, 1886 ..... 45.00
Royal Worcester, Cup & Saucer, Demitasse, Pink Flower Swag, Blue Bows 20.00
Royal Worcester, Cup & Saucer, Demitasse, White, Pink Floral & Foliage, 1886 ..... 45.00
Royal Worcester, Cup & Saucer, Roses, Leaves, Hand-Painted In & Out 39.50
Royal Worcester, Dish, Shell On 3 Shell Feet, Floral 45.00
Royal Worcester, Egg Coddler, Blackberry Pattern 9.00
Royal Worcester, Ewer, Beige, Enameled Bird On Branch, Serpent Handle, 6 In. 75.00
Royal Worcester, Ewer, Beige, Raised Gold & Pink Scroll Work, 1891, 6 1/2 In. 130.00
Royal Worcester, Ewer, Bulbous, Gold Border, Enameled, C.1887, 13 1/4 In. 275.00
Royal Worcester, Ewer, Butterflies And Flowers, Dated 1884, 9 In. 225.00
Royal Worcester, Ewer, Cane Shape, Gold Flowers, No.37112, 7 1/2 In. 75.00
Royal Worcester, Ewer, Cream, Bouquet, Gold Front & Back, C.1908, 10 In. 200.00
Royal Worcester, Ewer, Cream, Flowers, Gold Trim, RD 19115 1094, 5 1/4 In. 100.00
Royal Worcester, Ewer, Dragon Handle, White Glaze, Relief Scales, 12 In. 180.00
Royal Worcester, Ewer, Floral Handle, 12 In. 225.00
Royal Worcester, Ewer, Floral, Green Flowers, Light Beige Yellow Background 125.00
Royal Worcester, Ewer, Gold Lizard Handle, Purple Mark, 9 In. 225.00
Royal Worcester, Ewer, Pink, Green, & Gold On Ivory, Flowers & Leaves, 14 In. 235.00
Royal Worcester, Ewer, Raised Gold Windflowers & Leaves, Gilt Handle, 7 In. 165.00
Royal Worcester, Ewer, Twisted Tree Roots Shaped Handle, Gilt, C.1889, 7 In. 225.00
Royal Worcester, Ewer, Violets, Hand-Painted, C.1890, 7 1/2 In. 129.00
Royal Worcester, Ewer, Yellow, Serpent Handle, Green Mark, 1887, 7 1/2 In. 125.00
Royal Worcester, Figurine, A Woodland Dance, No.3073, F.G.Doughty, 4 In. 85.00
Royal Worcester, Figurine, Boy In Green Overcoat, Brown Cap, 6 1/4 In. 45.00
Royal Worcester, Figurine, Bridesmaid, F.Doughty, 8 1/2 In. 110.00
Royal Worcester, Figurine, Burma, F.Doughty, 5 In. 60.00
Royal Worcester, Figurine, Chopsticks, China, Doughty 95.00
Royal Worcester, Figurine, Columbine, Pink Mark, Numbered, Doris Linder, 7 In. 175.00
Royal Worcester, Figurine, Dancing Waves, No.3225, F.G.Doughty, 9 In. 90.00
Royal Worcester, Figurine, Dancing Waves, Young Girl, Blue Wave Base 80.00
Royal Worcester, Figurine, Dolphin, Shell On Tail, Beige, Gold Trim, 4 In. 75.00
Royal Worcester, Figurine, First Dance, Auburgine Dress 60.00
Royal Worcester, Figurine, First Dance, Green, F.Doughty, 8 In. 80.00
Royal Worcester, Figurine, Fish, Red Hind, Signed R.Vankuyult, 5 1/2 X 5 In. 90.00
Royal Worcester, Figurine, Friday Boy ..... 79.00 To 80.00
Royal Worcester, Figurine, Friday's Child, No.3261, Blue Mark, Red No.832593 ..... 75.00
Royal Worcester, Figurine, Girl With Lamp, 9 In. 135.00
Royal Worcester, Figurine, Girl, Thursday's Child, 7 1/2 In. 65.00
Royal Worcester, Figurine, Grandmother's Dress, F.Doughty, 6 1/2 ..... 60.00 To 70.00
Royal Worcester, Figurine, Hunting Dog Sitting, 7 1/2 In. ..... 145.00 To 160.00
Royal Worcester, Figurine, Joy & Sorrow, James Hadley, 10 1/2 In., Pair 450.00
Royal Worcester, Figurine, Joy & Sorrow, James Hadley, 10 1/2 In., Pair 500.00
Royal Worcester, Figurine, Joy & Sorrow, James Hadley, 19 1/2 In., Pair 450.00
Royal Worcester, Figurine, Joy & Sorrow, 10 1/2 In., Pair 450.00
Royal Worcester, Figurine, June Lady, Pink Dress, Bouquet Of Flowers, 1931 ..... 85.00
Royal Worcester, Figurine, Little Girl, No.J075, Blonde, Blue Dress, Flowers 85.00
Royal Worcester, Figurine, Monday's Child Is Fair Of Face, No.3519, Marked 50.00
Royal Worcester, Figurine, Mother Machree, Fortune Teller ..... 85.00 To 115.00

Royal Worcester, Figurine, Mother Machree, No.2324, F.G.Doughty, Red Mark	100.00
Royal Worcester, Figurine, Parakeet And Boy In Red	65.00
Royal Worcester, Figurine, Parakeet Boy, Green, F.Doughty, 7 1/2 In.	60.00
Royal Worcester, Figurine, Parakeet, Doughty	100.00
Royal Worcester, Figurine, Peter Pan, No.3011, F.Gernes, 8 In.	110.00
Royal Worcester, Figurine, Peter Pan, Pink, F.Gertner, Numbered, 8 1/2 In.	150.00
Royal Worcester, Figurine, Polly Put The Kettle On, No.3303, 6 In.	45.00
Royal Worcester, Figurine, Saturday's Child, Knitting, Cat, 5 1/2 In.	55.00
Royal Worcester, Figurine, Scotsman, Applied Register Mark, 1882	60.00
Royal Worcester, Figurine, Sea Breeze	95.00
Royal Worcester, Figurine, Sitting Hound, 7 In.	145.00
Royal Worcester, Figurine, Woman, Oriental, Holding Fan, Purple Mark, 7 In.	210.00
Royal Worcester, Figurine, Young Boy, Greece, F.G.Doughty, 5 1/2 In.	125.00
Royal Worcester, Figurine, Young Girl Carrying Brass Teapot, 6 In.	45.00
Royal Worcester, Jar, Creamware, Melon Ribbed, Floral, Purple Mark, 6 1/2 In.	128.00
Royal Worcester, Jar, Mustard, Potato Shape	25.00
Royal Worcester, Jar, Pilgrim, Floral, Leaves, Butterflies, 2 Handled, 8 In.	325.00
Royal Worcester, Jar, Rose, Lid, Cream, Hand-Painted Butterfly, Flowers, 5 In.	155.00
Royal Worcester, Jug, Embossed Branches, Flowers, Gold On Cream, 1887, 8 In.	115.00
Royal Worcester, Jug, Floral Decoration, Purple Mark	78.00 To 95.00
Royal Worcester, Jug, Floral Over Scale, Lizard Handle, Magenta, Gold, 11 In.	250.00
Royal Worcester, Jug, Floral, Beige Satin Finish, Roman Gold Reeded Handle	175.00
Royal Worcester, Jug, White, Cabbage Leaf, 1931, 8 In.	86.00
Royal Worcester, Mug, Miniature, Floral, 1 1/2 In.	60.00
Royal Worcester, Nappy, Shell Shape, Purple Mark, 5 In.	35.00
Royal Worcester, Pitcher, Beige, Flowers, Gold Trim, Flat Back, 1890, 5 In.	85.00
Royal Worcester, Pitcher, Beige, Flowers, Handled, Flat Back, 10 In.	85.00
Royal Worcester, Pitcher, Cabbage Leaf, White, C.1920, 8 In.	45.00
Royal Worcester, Pitcher, Classical, Gold Reed Handle, Multicolored Flowers	150.00
Royal Worcester, Pitcher, Cream Color, Multicolor Floral, Gilt Handle, 1890	105.00
Royal Worcester, Pitcher, Cream To Pink, Basket Weave, Green & Gold, 6 In.	159.00
Royal Worcester, Pitcher, Dragon Forms Handle, Signed, 11 1/2 In.	399.00
Royal Worcester, Pitcher, Floral On Beige, Helmet Shape, 8 In.	140.00
Royal Worcester, Pitcher, Florals, Curved Spout, Purple Mark, 5 1/2 In.	85.00
Royal Worcester, Pitcher, Full Masque Spout, Gadrooning, Signed, 9 3/4 In.	350.00
Royal Worcester, Pitcher, Gilt Handle, Hand-Painted, Dated 1890, 6 In.	115.00
Royal Worcester, Pitcher, Glazed Molded Design, 3 1/2 In.	20.00
Royal Worcester, Pitcher, Gold & Silver Floral, Green Mark, C.1890, 9 In.	225.00
Royal Worcester, Pitcher, Gold To Green, Iridescent Leaves, C.1895, 7 In.	210.00
Royal Worcester, Pitcher, Gold Twig Handle, Hand-Painted, 5 In.	95.00
Royal Worcester, Pitcher, J.F.Kennedy Memorial, Mask Spout, Picture, Seal	125.00
Royal Worcester, Pitcher, King Neptune Head, Purple Mark, 8 In.	165.00
Royal Worcester, Pitcher, Milk, Cabbage Leaf, Burnished Gold To Rose, 7 In.	175.00
Royal Worcester, Pitcher, Palm Leaf, Bulbous, Man With Hat Spout, 5 In.	55.00
Royal Worcester, Pitcher, Raised Tree Of Life, No.121932, Gold, Violet Mark	95.00
Royal Worcester, Pitcher, Ram's-Head Handle, Floral, Purple Mark, 8 1/2 In.	225.00
Royal Worcester, Pitcher, Satin Finish, Florals, Gold Trim, 7 In.	130.00
Royal Worcester, Pitcher, Serpentine, Aqua, Gold Snake, Ornate Handle, 12 In.	379.00
Royal Worcester, Pitcher, Water, Oriental, Elephant Handles	125.00 To 150.00
Royal Worcester, Pitcher, White Satiny Background, Powder Horn Shape, 9 In.	95.00
Royal Worcester, Pitcher, Wild Flowers On Cream, Gilt Handle, 1891, 7 1/2 In.	145.00
Royal Worcester, Pitcher, Winged Dragon Shaped Handle, Floral, 8 In.	75.00
Royal Worcester, Plate, Blue & White Blossoms, Gold Trim, C.1883, 8 In.	14.00
Royal Worcester, Plate, Blue & White Florals, C.1883, 8 In.	14.50
Royal Worcester, Plate, Cream With Wild Flowers, Fluted Edge, 6 In., Set Of 6	650.00
Royal Worcester, Plate, Floral, Butterfly, Cream, Scalloped, Purple Mark, 9 In.	75.00
Royal Worcester, Plate, Flowers, Gold, 8 In.	20.00
Royal Worcester, Plate, Hand-Painted Decoration, Purple Mark, 12 1/2 In.	65.00
Royal Worcester, Plate, Magenta Leaves, Floral Background, Signed, 9 In.	31.00
Royal Worcester, Plate, The Blind Earl, 8 In.	75.00
Royal Worcester, Plate, 2 Birds, Butterfly, Floral, Raised Enamel, Purple Mark	32.00
Royal Worcester, Platter, Blue Willow, 17 In.	75.00
Royal Worcester, Pot, Bamboo Handle & Lid Holder, Ivory, 2 Cup	95.00
Royal Worcester, Pot, Mustard, Miniature, C.1923, 2 In.	39.00
Royal Worcester, Rose Bowl, Hand-Painted, Footed, BK, 1888	35.00

Royal Worcester, Sugar & Creamer, Leaf Shaped, White, Signed	40.00
Royal Worcester, Swan & Nautilus Shell, Faience, Multicolored, 9 In.	225.00
Royal Worcester, Tazza, Beige & Green, Pedestal, Reticulated Cover, 1903	160.00
Royal Worcester, Tea Caddy, Fernery Decoration, Gilded, Green Mark, 4 1/2 In.	65.00
Royal Worcester, Tea Set, Butterflies & Flowers, C.1880, 8 Piece	750.00
Royal Worcester, Tea Set, Sugar, Creamer, Teapot, Signed, 1879 Mark	275.00
Royal Worcester, Toby, Black Hat, Trousers, Orange Coat, Purple Mark, 4 In.	65.00
Royal Worcester, Toothpick, Hand-Painted Birds	75.00
Royal Worcester, Tray, Oriental Designs, C.1880	85.00
Royal Worcester, Tray, Oriental Scene, Blue On White Glaze, C.1883	200.00
Royal Worcester, Tub, Flower Trim, Beige, Gold Trim, 2 X 3 In.	80.00
Royal Worcester, Urn, Double-Handled, Floral Decoration, 6 1/2 In.	150.00
Royal Worcester, Vase, Bamboo, Ivory, Gold, Raised Gold Leaves, 6 In., Pair	270.00
Royal Worcester, Vase, Banjo, Seaweeds In Gold, Green, Red Brown, 2 Handles	155.00
Royal Worcester, Vase, Beige, Gold Overlay Flowers, Leaves, C.1884, 6 3/4 In.	187.00
Royal Worcester, Vase, Bird, Brown, Orange, Gold, Dated 1912, 3 3/8 X 3 1/4 In.	88.00
Royal Worcester, Vase, Cream, Hand-Painted Flowers, Purple Mark, 10 In.	180.00
Royal Worcester, Vase, Creamy Beige, Floral, Gold Tracing, C.1887, 9 1/4 In.	185.00
Royal Worcester, Vase, Dogwood Blossoms, Gold Trim, C.1892, Marked, 6 1/2 In.	110.00
Royal Worcester, Vase, Floral, Beige Satin Finish, Gold Handles & Trim, 1907	225.00
Royal Worcester, Vase, Floral, Cylinder, Reticulated Bases, 10 1/2 In., Pair	400.00
Royal Worcester, Vase, Flowers, 1892, 6 1/2 In.	105.00
Royal Worcester, Vase, Fruits, Berries, Flowers, Satin Cream Ground, 10 In.	185.00
Royal Worcester, Vase, Gold & Silver Design, Snake Handles, C.1870, 9 In.	250.00
Royal Worcester, Vase, Gold Lizard Handle, C.1880, 7 In.	250.00
Royal Worcester, Vase, Heart Shape, Dated 1909, 4 In.	65.00
Royal Worcester, Vase, Highland Cattle Scenes, Artist Signed, 16 In.	950.00
Royal Worcester, Vase, Lighthouse Scene, Gold Trim, Handled, E.Salter, 14 In.	120.00
Royal Worcester, Vase, Marked Sabrina Ware, 6 1/2 In.	59.00
Royal Worcester, Vase, Pastel Colors, Peacocks, Glazed, A.Watkins, 5 1/2 In.	149.00
Royal Worcester, Vase, Pate-Sur-Pate, Reticulated Neck, 6 In.	300.00
Royal Worcester, Vase, Pedestal, Marked, 1899, 11 1/2 In.	225.00
Royal Worcester, Vase, Robin Decorated, Ruffled Top, 3 In.	95.00
Royal Worcester, Vase, Satin Finish, Green Trim, 11 1/2 In., Gold Trim, 1889	218.00
Royal Worcester, Vase, Signed, Dated 1901, Satin Finish, 11 In.	205.00
Royal Worcester, Vase, Water Lilies, Hand-Painted, 17 X 9 In., Pair	850.00
Royal Worcester, Vase, White, Shell Shape, Branch Coral Base, 6 1/4 In.	150.00
Royal Worcester, Vase, 2 Cows In Field, Cloud, Purple Mark, Signed, 10 In.	375.00
Royal Worcester, Wall Pocket, Gold Fringe Draperies, Teardrop Bowl, Pair	200.00
Royal Worcester, Wall Pocket, Wild Orchid, Beige, Gold, Brown, C.1883, 9 In.	225.00

*Roycroft products were made by the Roycrofter community of East Aurora,
New York, in the late nineteenth and early twentieth centuries. The
community was founded by Elbert Hubbard. The products included furniture,
metalware, leatherwork, and jewelry.*

Roycroft, Ashtray, Hammered Copper, 2 Handles, 6 3/4 In.	36.00
Roycroft, Ashtray, Hammered Copper, 2 Handles, 8 1/2 In.	35.00
Roycroft, Ashtray, Individual, Plated Copper, 4 Pieces	28.00
Roycroft, Book, Elbert Hubbard Scrapbook, Cloth Bound	9.00
Roycroft, Bookend, Copper, 3 1/2 In.	27.00
Roycroft, Bookend, Hammered Bronze, Cockatoo Decoration, Signed	35.00 To 70.00
Roycroft, Bookend, Hammered Copper, Floral, 5 1/2 In.	25.00
Roycroft, Bookends, Copper, 9 In., Pair	27.50
Roycroft, Chamberstick, Hammered Copper, 3 1/4 X 4 1/2 In., Pair	50.00
Roycroft, Desk Set, Art Deco, Metal With Bronze Finish, Waterbury Clock, Set	75.00
Roycroft, Jug, Brown, High Glaze, 6 In.	22.50
Roycroft, Jug, Honey, Brown Glaze, 5 1/2 In.	20.00
Roycroft, Tray, Applied Handles, Hammered Copper, 15 X 6 In.	45.00
Rozenburg, Planter, Blue, Green, Gold, Rust Batik Design, 5 X 5 3/4 In.	225.00
Rozenburg, Vase, Blue, Green, Gold, Rust Batik Design, Bulbous, 4 X 5 1/2 In.	185.00
RRP Co., Vase, Bulb Bottom, Flared Ruffled Top, Fans, 8 In.	15.00

*RS Germany porcelain was made at the factory of Rheinhold Schlegelmilch
after 1869 in Tillowitz, Germany. It was sold both decorated and
undecorated.*

RS Germany, Ashtray, Figural, Gold Pipe, Spade 48.00
RS Germany, Ashtray, Pink Roses, Leaves, 3 Rests, 4 1/2 X 1 1/4 In. 18.50
RS Germany, Ashtray, Pink Roses, Round, Green Mark, 4 1/4 X 1 1/2 In. 20.00
RS Germany, Basket, Gold On Gold, 5 In. 35.00
RS Germany, Basket, Orange Luster, Black Trim, Blue Mark, 7 In. 10.00
RS Germany, Berry Bowl, Gold Rim, Pink Roses, 5 1/4 In. 8.50
RS Germany, Berry Bowl, House In Woods, Greens, 24 Mark, 6 In., 4 Piece 95.00
RS Germany, Berry Bowl, Roses Decoration, 9 1/2 In. 35.00
RS Germany, Berry Set, Green & Beige, Daisies, Leaves, 6 Piece 58.00
RS Germany, Berry Set, 4 Calla Lilies, Shadow Flowers, Gold Rim, Dish, 4 Piece 35.00
RS Germany, Biscuit Jar, Floral Decoration, Handled 50.00
RS Germany, Bottle, Cologne, Pearlized 18.00
RS Germany, Bowl, Apple Blossom Branches, Pink, Black, 8 1/2 In. 50.00
RS Germany, Bowl, Berry, Shades Of Green, White Day Lily, 5 1/4 In., Set Of 6 .... 30.00
RS Germany, Bowl, Farmhouse, Lady, Yoked Oxen, 10 In. 42.00
RS Germany, Bowl, Floral Decoration, Signed Steeple Mark, 10 In. 75.00
RS Germany, Bowl, Floral, Green To Beige, Green Mark, 10 X 2 3/4 In. 60.00
RS Germany, Bowl, Floral, Open, Hand-Painted, 2 In. 12.00
RS Germany, Bowl, Green, Pink Tulips, Green Mark, 9 1/2 In. 19.50
RS Germany, Bowl, Large Poppies, Ruffled, 11 In. 40.00
RS Germany, Bowl, Luster, Silver Deposit Handles, Floral, Blue Mark, 6 In. 28.50
RS Germany, Bowl, Mountains, Land, Lake, Yellow Poppy, Coral Rose, Mark, 8 In. 50.00
RS Germany, Bowl, Multicolored Flowers, Footed, 2 Handles, Oval, 9 X 6 1/2 In. 35.00
RS Germany, Bowl, Orange Luster Flat Border, White Leaves, 6 1/4 In. 12.00
RS Germany, Bowl, Pennsylvania Dutch Flowers, 2 Horse Heads In Base, 9 In. 50.00
RS Germany, Bowl, Pink Carnations, Blue Ground, 6 1/2 In. 13.00
RS Germany, Bowl, Pink Peonies, White Snowball, Brown, 18 Mark, 10 In. 45.00
RS Germany, Bowl, Salmon-Colored Sweet Peas, Shaded Green Ground, 6 In. 45.00
RS Germany, Bowl, Scenic, Brown, Shallow, Green Mark, 10 In. 85.00
RS Germany, Bowl, Silvery Gray, Pink & Brown, Dark To Light Poppies, 10 In. 42.00
RS Germany, Bowl, Sugar, Covered, Cotton Plant 35.00
RS Germany, Bowl, Whipped Cream, Ladle & Underplate, Sugar & Creamer 90.00
RS Germany, Bowl, White Roses, Orchids, Green Ivy Shadows, Scalloped, 6 In. 35.00
RS Germany, Bowl, White Roses, Peach Centers, Gold Rim, Red Mark, 9 1/4 In. 30.00
RS Germany, Bowl, White Tulips, Gray & Green Shading, 6 In. 37.50
RS Germany, Box, Roses, Cover, Square, Pink, Brown, 3 In. 24.00
RS Germany, Cake Set, Brown, Orange Flowers, 7 Piece 65.00
RS Germany, Cake Set, Green & Tan Shades, Carnations, Green Mark, 7 Piece 125.00
RS Germany, Cake Set, Platter With Cut For Handles, 7 Piece 95.00
RS Germany, Candlestick, Art Nouveau, 6 In. 25.00
RS Germany, Candlestick, Parrot, Red Mark, 6 In. 75.00
RS Germany, Candy, Semiblown Flowers On Edge, 3 Footed, Steeple Mark, 4 In. 20.00
RS Germany, Celery, Blue Flowers, Green Mark, 11 In. 22.00
RS Germany, Celery, Clematis Blossoms, Green Leaves, 12 1/2 X 6 In. 32.00
RS Germany, Celery, Clematis On Pastel Ground, 12 1/2 X 9 In. 36.00
RS Germany, Celery, Flowers, 14 X 7 In. 35.00
RS Germany, Celery, Salmon & White Poppy, 2-Handled 42.00
RS Germany, Celery, 2-Handled, Beaded Edge, Pastel Flowers On Green, 13 In. 38.00
RS Germany, Chocolate Pot, Art Nouveau Florals, 9 1/2 In. 85.00
RS Germany, Chocolate Pot, Floral, Gold Trim 38.00
RS Germany, Chocolate Pot, Tan, Yellow Roses, Satin Finish, Green Mark 78.00
RS Germany, Chocolate Set, Flowers, Green & Ivory Background, 13 Piece 85.00
RS Germany, Chocolate Set, Pastel Floral, Gold, 9 Piece 195.00
RS Germany, Chocolate Set, Roses, Pot, Sugar, Creamer, Cup, Saucer, 11 Piece 275.00
RS Germany, Coffeepot, Cover, Carnations On Cream Ground, 9 In.High 75.00
RS Germany, Cracker Jar, Acorns & Oak Leaves, Covered 35.00
RS Germany, Cracker Jar, Pastel Flowers On Cream 59.00
RS Germany, Cracker Jar, Pink & White Roses, Green Leaves, Gold Trim, 9 In. 115.00
RS Germany, Cracker Jar, Tulips, Handles, Blue Mark 65.00
RS Germany, Creamer, Bird's Head Spout, Green Mark 48.00
RS Germany, Creamer, Covered, Gooseberries, Blossoms, Leaves, Blue Mark, 4 In. ... 22.00
RS Germany, Creamer, Flower Decoration, Brown Star, Wing Mark 14.00
RS Germany, Creamer, Hand-Painted, Poppy Decoration, Marked, 5 In. 10.00
RS Germany, Creamer, Red Poppies, Signed 29.00
RS Germany, Cruet, Pink Rose, 3 3/4 In. 45.00

RS Germany, Cup & Saucer, Acorns, Oak Leaves, Demitasse 25.00
RS Germany, Cup & Saucer, Demitasse, Portrait, Pedestal 40.00
RS Germany, Cup & Saucer, Jonquils, Pussy Willows, Green, Salmon, Set Of 5 .... 62.50
RS Germany, Cup, Demitasse, Poppy, Tinted Ground, Gold 22.00
RS Germany, Dark Green, Pinkish White Lilies, Gold Border 16.00
RS Germany, Dish, Berry, Green Background, Apricot & Pink Flower, Set Of 6 .... 62.00
RS Germany, Dish, Boat Shape, Pink, Floral, Gold Tracery, 7 In. 40.00
RS Germany, Dish, Candy, Marked Reinhold Schlegelmilch, 7 1/4 In. 12.00
RS Germany, Dish, Footed, Scalloped, White, Pink, Red Roses, 7 In. 45.00
RS Germany, Dish, Hand-Painted Yellow Rose, Handles, 4 1/2 In. 8.00
RS Germany, Dish, Sailboat On Lake, Windmill, Gold Rim, Green Mark, 8 In. 75.00
RS Germany, Dish, Sauce, Water Lilies, Roses 12.00
RS Germany, Dish, White, Pink, Red Roses, Footed, Scalloped, Green Mark, 7 In. 45.00
RS Germany, Dresser Set, Green, Roses, Yellow, Pink, & White, Luster, 4 Piece 48.00
RS Germany, Dresser Set, Light Green, White Camellias, Gold Trim, 3 Piece 69.00
RS Germany, Gravy Boat & Underplate, Pale Green, Pink Apple Blossoms, 1912 .... 35.00
RS Germany, Gravy Boat, White Dogwood Blossoms, Green, Underplate, 24 Mark 35.00
RS Germany, Green & Silver Luster, White Flowers, Green Mark 12.00
RS Germany, Hair Receiver, Cottage Scene, Green Mark 110.00
RS Germany, Hair Receiver, Cream & Beige, White Floral, Green Mark 20.00
RS Germany, Hair Receiver, Floral, Gold Trim, Hand-Painted 18.50
RS Germany, Hair Receiver, Florals On Beige 22.00
RS Germany, Hatpin Holder, Pale Green, Pink Roses, Green Mark, 7 In. 35.00
RS Germany, Hatpin Holder, Raised Blue Florals, White 35.00
RS Germany, Hatpin Holder, Rose Decoration 32.00
RS Germany, Hatpin Holder, Violets, Blue Mark, Signed 22.50
RS Germany, Hatpin Holder, White With Gold Bands, Large Size 20.00
RS Germany, Holder, Toothbrush, Hanging 28.00
RS Germany, Inkwell, Roses, Yellow, Green Ground, Square, Blue Mark, 1913 .... 40.00
RS Germany, Jar, Jam, Orchids, Mauve Luster Background, Lid, Blue Mark 28.00
RS Germany, Jar, Mustard, White & Pink Rose, 24 Mark 20.00
RS Germany, Jar, Powder, Light To Dark Green, Pink Roses 27.00
RS Germany, Jelly Set, 18K Gold, Signed, 3 Pieces 40.00
RS Germany, Match, Floral, Diamond Shape, Strike On Bottom, Gold Steeple Mark 35.00
RS Germany, Mayonnaise Set, Under Liner, Ladle 45.00
RS Germany, Mug, Pink & White Poppies, Gold Band With Fleur-De-Lis, Footed 15.00
RS Germany, Mug, Shaving, Pink Roses, Soft Beige To Cream 110.00
RS Germany, Mustard Pot, Fancy Molded, Red Steeple Mark 40.00
RS Germany, Mustard Pot, Large Snowballs, Gold Trim, Black Mark 32.00
RS Germany, Mustard Pot, Pink Roses, Shaded Leaves 32.00
RS Germany, Mustard, Covered, Cotton Plant, Tapestry Border 28.00
RS Germany, Pancake Set, All Gold, Artist Signed, Eagon, C.1928, 8 In., 3 Piece 55.00
RS Germany, Pitcher, Cider, Orange Roses, Round Brown Leaves, Silesia, 6 In. 60.00
RS Germany, Pitcher, Lemonade, Florals 65.00
RS Germany, Pitcher, Milk, Snowballs, Gold Trim, Gold Flowers, No.18 Mark 120.00
RS Germany, Pitcher, Syrup, Shaded Blue Asters & Foliage, Covered 30.00
RS Germany, Plate, Apricot & Yellow Roses, 8 1/2 In. 20.00
RS Germany, Plate, Beaded Rim, Pastel Coloring, White & Pink Flowers, 6 In. 15.00
RS Germany, Plate, Cake, Blue Flowers, Green Background, Open Ends, 10 3/4 In. 19.00
RS Germany, Plate, Cake, Calla Lilies On Eggshell, Scalloped Gold Rim, Handle 30.00
RS Germany, Plate, Cake, Coral, Lavender, & Pink Flowers, Satin Finish, 12 In. 55.00
RS Germany, Plate, Cake, Flowers On Tan, Scalloped Gold Rim, Handle, Pierced 18.00
RS Germany, Plate, Cake, Petunias On White, Green, Tan, Green Mark, 9 3/4 In. 25.00
RS Germany, Plate, Cake, Pink Peonies On White, Green, Blue Mark, 9 1/2 In. 18.00
RS Germany, Plate, Calla Lily, 8 In. 22.00
RS Germany, Plate, Chop, Art Nouveau Border, Matte, Gold, No.17, 12 3/4 In. 50.00
RS Germany, Plate, Chop, Pink To Red Roses, Gold Bank, 11 In. 47.50
RS Germany, Plate, Gold Beaded Rim, 6 Pieces, 6 In. 45.00
RS Germany, Plate, Hand-Painted, Artist Signed, 6 1/2 In. 14.00
RS Germany, Plate, Ivory, Salmon, Gold, Roses, Apple Form, 3 Open Handles, 8 In. 45.00
RS Germany, Plate, Lilies, Art Nouveau, 8 In. 24.00
RS Germany, Plate, Lily Motif, Schlegelmilch, 7 In. 12.00
RS Germany, Plate, Luster, 3 Open Handles, Pinecones, Gold Rim, Blue Mark 24.50
RS Germany, Plate, Maidens In Forest, Orange Border, Gold Trim, Mark No.29 .... 30.00
RS Germany, Plate, Pastel Floral, 8 1/2 In. 32.00

RS Germany, Plate, Pastel Green & Deep Green, White Azaleas, Gold Border	35.00
RS Germany, Plate, Pink Flowers, Gray Shading, 8 1/2 In.	35.00
RS Germany, Plate, Red & White Tulips, Gold Decorated Border, 11 In.	40.00
RS Germany, Plate, Set, Luncheon, Tulips, Beige, White, Pink, Green, Blue Mark	65.00
RS Germany, Plate, Soft Green, White Blossoms, 8 1/4 In.	19.50
RS Germany, Plate, Wild Roses, Gilding, 8 In.	15.00
RS Germany, Plate, Yellow & White Flowers, Blue Mark, 8 1/4 In.	15.00
RS Germany, Plate, Yellow, Sprays Of Pink Flowers & Buds, Leaves, 6 1/8 In.	10.00
RS Germany, Relish, Calla Lily, Open Handles, 8 In.	25.00
RS Germany, Relish, Dogwood, Green Background Handle	23.00
RS Germany, Relish, Flowers, Green, Yellow	27.00
RS Germany, Relish, Gold Rim, Gold Iris & Leaves, Green Mark, 8 3/4 X 4 In.	20.00
RS Germany, Relish, Lilies Reflecting On Water, Open Handle, Black Mark	45.00
RS Germany, Relish, Orchids, Blue Mark, 9 In.	18.00
RS Germany, Salt & Pepper, Pink Roses, Green Mark	50.00
RS Germany, Saltshaker, Hand-Painted	26.00
RS Germany, Sauce, Double Open Handle, Gold Edge, 5 1/4 In.	7.50
RS Germany, Sauce, Green, Beige On White, Calla Lily Center, Blue Mark, 5 In.	70.00
RS Germany, Sauce, Oval, One Open Handle, 5 1/2 In.	7.50
RS Germany, Sauce, Tray With Apricot Roses, Green Leaves, Gold Rim, Blue Mark	26.00
RS Germany, Sauce, View Of Windmill At Lake's Edge, Gold, Green Mark	40.00
RS Germany, Server, Candy, Floral, Center Handle, White, Green, 8 In.	31.00
RS Germany, Server, Cheese & Cracker, Soft Green, Hand-Painted Pink Roses	48.00
RS Germany, Spooner, Hand-Painted Floral, Enclosed Handles, Flat	18.00
RS Germany, Sugar & Creamer, Blue, Wild Roses, Gold Rim, Covered	29.00
RS Germany, Sugar & Creamer, Burnt Orange, White Bell Type Flowers, 6 Sided	28.00
RS Germany, Sugar & Creamer, Gold Decoration, Pickard Stamped, Blue Mark	65.00
RS Germany, Sugar & Creamer, Gold Embossed Florals, Covered	60.00
RS Germany, Sugar & Creamer, Green To Beige, Dogwood Flowers	55.00
RS Germany, Sugar & Creamer, Ivory, Salmon, Gold, Roses	60.00
RS Germany, Sugar & Creamer, Pastel Flowers, Green Mark	25.00
RS Germany, Sugar & Creamer, Pinkish Gray, Flowers, Gold Trim, Satin Finish	45.00
RS Germany, Sugar & Creamer, Roses, Leaves, Gold Handle & Finial, Brown, Pink	42.00
RS Germany, Sugar & Creamer, Roses, Leaves, Gold Rim & Handles, Blue Mark	42.00
RS Germany, Sugar & Creamer, Straw Basket Of Flowers	75.00
RS Germany, Sugar & Creamer, White, Orchid Band Top, Pink Flowers, Blue Mark	44.00
RS Germany, Sugar & Creamer, White, Purple Violets, Blue Mark	38.00
RS Germany, Sugar Shaker, Pink Roses, Shaded Background	35.00
RS Germany, Sugar, Beige-Pink Roses, Leaves, Luster Finish	14.00
RS Germany, Sugar, Blue Luster With Pink Peonies, Covered	17.00
RS Germany, Sugar, Covered, Flowers, Gold Trim, Signed	39.00
RS Germany, Sugar, Gold Finial & Handles, Covered	10.00
RS Germany, Sugar, Shaded Green, Pink Roses, 2 Handles, Covered, Green Mark	25.00
RS Germany, Syrup & Underplate, Golden Iris Outlined With Gold, Green Mark	27.50
RS Germany, Tankard, Rosebud Handle, Red Steeple Mark, 14 In.	225.00
RS Germany, Tea Set, Child's, Teapot, Creamer, 2 Cups, Saucers, Floral	60.00
RS Germany, Toothbrush Holder, Wall Type, Floral	35.00
RS Germany, Toothpick, Basket Of Roses, 2-Handled	35.00
RS Germany, Toothpick, Blue Forget-Me-Nots, 2-Handled	35.00
RS Germany, Toothpick, Floral, Gold, 2-Handled	50.00
RS Germany, Toothpick, Floral, 3-Handled, Green Mark	57.00
RS Germany, Toothpick, Three Coin Gold Handles, Pink Roses, Artist Signed	28.00
RS Germany, Toothpick, 2-Handled, Pink Floral, Blue Mark	47.00
RS Germany, Toothpick, 3-Handled, Coin Gold Handles	39.00
RS Germany, Toothpick, 3-Handled, Roses, Gold, Marked	45.00
RS Germany, Tray, Bread, Floating Lilies Decoration, Open, Handled	50.00
RS Germany, Tray, Celery, Bluish Pink, Pink & Yellow Roses, Gold Trim, 10 In.	16.50
RS Germany, Tray, Celery, Pierce-Handled, Cottage Scene, Blue Mark, 13 In.	55.00
RS Germany, Tray, Dresser, Pink Roses, Green Leaves, 3 Mark, 8 X 11 In.	30.00
RS Germany, Tray, Dresser, Satin Colors, Tulips, 12 X 8 In.	35.00
RS Germany, Tray, Gold, Floral, Open Handles, 7 X 11 1/2 In.	42.50
RS Germany, Tray, Oval, Open Handles, Gold Border, Blue Mark, 7 In.	40.00
RS Germany, Tray, Red & White Tulip, Shaded Leaves, Gold Trim, Signed, 11 In.	45.00
RS Germany, Tray, Serving, Green Poppy Plant, 24 Mark, 14 1/2 X 15 1/2 In.	150.00
RS Germany, Vase, Bud, Apple Green, Outline Of Castle, Green Mark, 8 In.	95.00

RS Germany, Vase, Bud, Copper Luster, Gold Trim, Artist Signed, 6 1/2 In.	18.00
RS Germany, Vase, Camellias, 2 Handles, Cylinder Shape, Yellow, White, Green	22.00
RS Germany, Vase, Camels, 4 1/2 In.	64.00
RS Germany, Vase, Green, Easter Lily, Ornate Handles, 5 1/2 In.	30.00
RS Germany, Vase, Green, Orange Poppies, Green Mark, 5 3/4 In.	29.50
RS Germany, Vase, Hand-Painted White Roses On Apricot, Urn Handles, 10 In.	64.00
RS Germany, Vase, Lavender Iris, Green Leaves, Pale Blue, Gold Rim, 5 3/4 In.	45.00
RS Germany, Vase, Scenic, Gondolas On Lake, Burnt Orange Trim, Handles, 6 In.	111.00
RS Germany, Vase, Scenic, Windmill & Man, 4 In.	75.00
RS Germany, Vase, Seashore Scene, Gold Handles, Blue Mark, 5 In.	28.00
RS Germany, Vase, White With Gold Trim, 18 Mark, 4 1/2 In.	30.00
RS Poland, Sugar & Creamer, Flowered	30.00
RS Poland, Tray, Dresser, Handled, Pink & White Flowers	30.00
RS Poland, Tray, Dresser, Pink Floral, Open Handles	42.00
RS Poland, Vase, Floral, Handled, 11 In.	137.50
RS Poland, Vase, Gold Handles, Pink Floral, Green Leaves, Red Mark, Pair	145.00
RS Poland, Vase, Satin Finish, Roses, Gold Border & Wreaths, 7 In.	85.00
RS Poland, Vase, Satin, Floral, Red Mark	125.00

 RS Prussia porcelain was made at the factory of Rheinhold Schlegelmilch after 1869 in Tillowitz, Germany. The porcelain was sold decorated or undecorated.

RS Prussia, Ashtray, Tea Roses, Gold Trim, Square, Red Mark, 4 1/2 In.	95.00
RS Prussia, Basket, Ivory, Green, & Pink, Rose, 7 1/4 X 5 X 3 1/2 In.	300.00
RS Prussia, Berry Bowl, Floral, Gold Trim, White, Green	85.00
RS Prussia, Berry Set, Bouquet, Scalloped, Gold Leaves, Red Mark, 6 Piece	190.00
RS Prussia, Berry Set, Dark To Light Green, Yellow & White Daisies, 6 Piece	48.50
RS Prussia, Berry Set, Floral, Red Mark, 9 Piece	275.00
RS Prussia, Berry Set, Gold, Blue To Green, White Background, Floral, 7 Piece	275.00
RS Prussia, Berry Set, Green Shades, Pink Roses, Snowballs, Red Mark, 7 Piece	350.00
RS Prussia, Berry Set, Mixed Floral On Dark Green Embossed Panels, 6 Piece	225.00
RS Prussia, Berry Set, Patina Green To White, Lilies, Florals, Gold, 6 Piece	115.00
RS Prussia, Berry Set, Pearlized, Pink & White Floral, Red Mark, 7 Piece	175.00
RS Prussia, Berry Set, Wild Roses On Beige To Blue, Red Mark, 5 Piece	175.00
RS Prussia, Bowl, Basket Style, Red Mark	165.00
RS Prussia, Bowl, Beige & Pink Roses, Red Mark, 11 In.	125.00
RS Prussia, Bowl, Berry, Blown-Out Iris Form, Gold Trim, Red Mark	85.00
RS Prussia, Bowl, Berry, Floral Leaf & Berry Rim, Red Mark, 10 1/2 In.	120.00
RS Prussia, Bowl, Berry, Mill Scene	37.50
RS Prussia, Bowl, Berry, Pink, Red Roses, White Daisies, Green, Red Mark, 9 In.	40.00
RS Prussia, Bowl, Berry, Satin Finish, Open Carnations, Ruffled Edges, Four	95.00
RS Prussia, Bowl, Blown-Out Fans On Border, Roses Center, 9 In.	98.00
RS Prussia, Bowl, Blown-Out Iris & Roses, 3-Footed, Red Mark, 5 1/2 In.	58.00
RS Prussia, Bowl, Blown-Out Irises, Pink Floral Center, Red Mark, 9 3/4 In.	135.00
RS Prussia, Bowl, Blown-Out Medallion, 10 1/2 In.	145.00
RS Prussia, Bowl, Blown-Out Pink Flowers, Gold Trim, Red Mark, 9 1/2 In.	240.00
RS Prussia, Bowl, Blue-Green On White, Freesias, Scalloped Edge, 10 1/2 In.	100.00
RS Prussia, Bowl, Castle Scene, Gold Trim, Beige Background, 10 1/2 In.	285.00
RS Prussia, Bowl, Classical Portrait, Man, 3 Ladies, 2 Babies, Marked, 14 In.	185.00
RS Prussia, Bowl, Cobalt, Roses, Red Mark, 10 In.	395.00
RS Prussia, Bowl, Colorful Roses, Red Mark, 9 In.	95.00
RS Prussia, Bowl, Cottage Scene, 11 In.	195.00
RS Prussia, Bowl, Cracker, Calla Lilies, Gold, Hand-Painted, Signed	145.00
RS Prussia, Bowl, Dark Green, Pink Camellias, 13 X 9 In.	115.00
RS Prussia, Bowl, Decorated Green Border, Flowers, 6 In.	58.00
RS Prussia, Bowl, Diana The Huntress, 11 In. *Illus*	1700.00
RS Prussia, Bowl, Earthtones, Lilies, 10 In.	145.00
RS Prussia, Bowl, Easter Lilies, Gold Trim, Red Mark, 11 In.	135.00
RS Prussia, Bowl, Floral Basket, Pink & Yellow, Green Background, 11 In.	135.00
RS Prussia, Bowl, Floral Pattern, Pierced Handles, Signed, Marked, 9 In.	97.50
RS Prussia, Bowl, Floral, Scalloped, 3-Footed, White, Gold, 6 1/2 X 2 1/2 In.	50.00
RS Prussia, Bowl, Flowers, Everted Squiggly Rim, Indents, Yellow, Red, Red Mark	75.00
RS Prussia, Bowl, Green Luster, White Carnations, Gold Stems, Red Mark, 9 In.	60.00
RS Prussia, Bowl, Green, White, Roses, Fluted, Scroll Rim, Red Mark, 10 1/2 In.	100.00
RS Prussia, Bowl, Hearts, Flowers, Yellow, Turquoise Fern, Gold, Red Mark, 8 In.	90.00

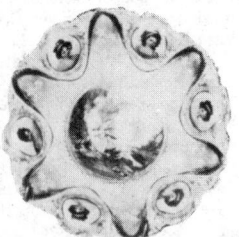

RS Prussia, Bowl, Diana The Huntress, 11 In.

(See Page 549)

RS Prussia, Bowl, Jewels Around Border, Roses, Red Mark, 9 3/8 In.	150.00
RS Prussia, Bowl, Jewels, Gold, Burgundy, Florals, Shamrock & Bud Border	75.00
RS Prussia, Bowl, Leaf, Roses, Tiffany Colors, Red Mark, 9 In.	185.00
RS Prussia, Bowl, Lilies, Red Mark, 10 In.	145.00
RS Prussia, Bowl, Lily Of The Valley, 10 In.	152.00
RS Prussia, Bowl, Man In Mountain, Icicle Sides, Red Mark, 10 1/2 In.	875.00
RS Prussia, Bowl, Man In Mountain, 10 1/2 In.	775.00
RS Prussia, Bowl, Master Nut, Dogwood, Footed, Red Mark, 6 In.	50.00
RS Prussia, Bowl, Medallion Border, Wicker Basket Of Flowers Center, 11 In.	175.0C
RS Prussia, Bowl, Mill Scene, 10 1/2 In.	450.00
RS Prussia, Bowl, Mixed Floral, Green, Gold Finish, Scalloped, 8 1/2 X 2 In.	120.00
RS Prussia, Bowl, Molded Shell, Red, Yellow Florals, Red Mark, 5 X 1 In.	35.00
RS Prussia, Bowl, Pearlized, Christmas Rose, Red Mark, 11 In.	185.00
RS Prussia, Bowl, Pearlized, Roses, Flowers, Gold Raised Dots, Red Mark, 10 In.	75.00
RS Prussia, Bowl, Pears, Grapes, Plums, Fancy Rim, 10 1/2 In.	145.00
RS Prussia, Bowl, Pink & Red Floral, 10 In.	195.00
RS Prussia, Bowl, Pink & White Roses On Shades Of Green, Red Mark, 7 1/2 In.	70.00
RS Prussia, Bowl, Pink Iridescent, Pink Roses, Red Mark, 11 1/2 In.	120.00
RS Prussia, Bowl, Pink Roses, Daffodil Blown-Out Edge, Red Mark, 10 1/2 In.	165.00
RS Prussia, Bowl, Pink Roses, Green & Gold Trim, Red Mark, 10 1/2 In.	95.00
RS Prussia, Bowl, Pink Roses, Green, Beige, 9 In.	50.00
RS Prussia, Bowl, Pink Roses, Ruffled Edges, Red Mark, 11 In.	85.00
RS Prussia, Bowl, Pink Roses, Scalloped Green & Gold Trim, Red Mark, 5 In.	25.00
RS Prussia, Bowl, Poppies, Scalloped Edges, Pink, Blown Out, Red Mark, 10 In.	230.00
RS Prussia, Bowl, Puffed Out Flowers, Gold, Roses, Long, Shallow, 6 In.	90.00
RS Prussia, Bowl, Raised Decoration, Roses, Beaded Center, Red Mark, 11 In.	70.00
RS Prussia, Bowl, Red Mark, 5 1/4 In.Diameter	25.00
RS Prussia, Bowl, Reflecting Lily Pad, Red Mark, 11 In.	155.00
RS Prussia, Bowl, Roses & Daisies, Raised Design, Gold Trim, Red Mark, 9 In.	135.00
RS Prussia, Bowl, Roses Center, 5 Panels, Gold, Red Mark, 8 1/2 In.	125.00
RS Prussia, Bowl, Roses, Blown-Out Edge, Gold, Pink, Yellow, Red Mark, 7 In.	70.00
RS Prussia, Bowl, Roses, Blown-Out Flowers, 8 In.	135.00
RS Prussia, Bowl, Roses, Buds, Paneled, Scalloped Rim, Gold, Pink, White, 10 In.	95.00
RS Prussia, Bowl, Roses, Gold Outlined Leaves, Pink, Green, Red Mark, 11 In.	80.00
RS Prussia, Bowl, Roses, Lilacs, 3-Footed, Pink, Blue, White, 6 In.	65.00
RS Prussia, Bowl, Roses, Puffed Out Poppies On Rim, Pink, 8 In.	125.00
RS Prussia, Bowl, Roses, Water Lilies, Scalloped, Beaded, Red Mark, 11 In.	150.00
RS Prussia, Bowl, Roses, 5 Medallions, Gold-Tipped Flowers, Mark, 10 In.	70.00
RS Prussia, Bowl, Sailing Ships In Harbor, Jeweled Border, Red Mark, 10 In.	630.00
RS Prussia, Bowl, Satin Finish Floral, Art Nouveau, Handled, Red Mark, 6 In.	86.00
RS Prussia, Bowl, Scalloped, Roses Inside & Out, Pedestal, Red Mark	140.00
RS Prussia, Bowl, Schooner, Red Mark, 8 In.	625.00
RS Prussia, Bowl, Shell Shape, Cream To Green, Poinsettias, 10 1/4 In.	135.00
RS Prussia, Bowl, Shell Shape, Red & Cream Florals, 10 In.	75.00
RS Prussia, Bowl, Stag, Flowers, 9 In.	50.00
RS Prussia, Bowl, Swans & Bluebirds, Red Mark, 9 1/2 In.	485.00
RS Prussia, Bowl, Swans & Flying Blue Bird, Footed, Red Mark, 6 1/2 In.	225.00
RS Prussia, Bowl, Swans & Lilies, Red Mark, 9 In.	425.00
RS Prussia, Bowl, Swans, Red Mark, 10 1/2 In.	190.00
RS Prussia, Bowl, White Blossoms, Gold Centers, Gold Scalloped Edge, 10 In.	35.00
RS Prussia, Bowl, Yellow Rose, White & Gold Crimped Edge, Red Mark, 11 In.	95.00

RS Prussia, Bowl, Yellow Roses, Scalloped, Red Mark, 11 In. 130.00
RS Prussia, Box, Leaf Shaped, Swans, Stream Between Pine Trees, 5 X 3 In. 95.00
RS Prussia, Butter, Pink & Yellow Roses, Raised Enamel 350.00
RS Prussia, Candy Dish, Water Lily & Pads, 3-Footed, Marked 160.00
RS Prussia, Card Holder, Calling, Flowers, Lavender 60.00
RS Prussia, Celery, Blown Iris Mold, Colorful Floral, 12 In. 75.00
RS Prussia, Celery, Blue & Shaded Border 22.50
RS Prussia, Celery, Cream Ground, Pink & Peach Roses & Daisies, Red Mark 85.00
RS Prussia, Celery, Floral, Red Star, 6 1/2 X 13 1/2 In. 95.00
RS Prussia, Celery, Heart Shape, Embossed, Gold Flower Forms, Red Mark, 12 In. 80.00
RS Prussia, Celery, Lebrum Medallion Floral Center, Red Border, 14 In. 750.00
RS Prussia, Celery, Luster, Open Handled, Marked, 12 1/2 In. 195.00
RS Prussia, Celery, Open Handled, Scalloped, Green, Lavender, Red Roses, 12 In. 75.00
RS Prussia, Celery, Pastel Colors, Roses, Red Mark, 12 In. 85.00
RS Prussia, Celery, Poppies, Red Mark, 13 1/2 X 6 1/2 In. 95.00
RS Prussia, Celery, Roses Design, 9 1/2 In. 39.00
RS Prussia, Celery, Roses, Open Handles, White To Green, Red Mark, 12 In. 115.00
RS Prussia, Celery, Roses, 13 In. 69.00
RS Prussia, Celery, Swans, Pond, Arches, Evergreens, Handles, Blue, White, 13 In. 295.00
RS Prussia, Celery, Tea Roses On Ivory To Aqua, Handled, Red Mark 80.00
RS Prussia, Chocolate Pot, Bouquets, Handle, Blown-Out Berries, 13 In. 225.00
RS Prussia, Chocolate Pot, Bulbous Top, Red Mark 75.00
RS Prussia, Chocolate Pot, Cream, Multicolored Flowers, Blown-Out Bottom 175.00
RS Prussia, Chocolate Pot, Floral, Pearl Satin, Blown-Out Body, Red Mark 275.00
RS Prussia, Chocolate Pot, Floral, Red Mark 190.00
RS Prussia, Chocolate Pot, Flowers, Leaves, Gold, Brown, Green, Pink, 10 In. 110.00
RS Prussia, Chocolate Pot, Green, Roses, Luster, Ornate Handle, 8 1/4 In. 135.00
RS Prussia, Chocolate Pot, Hand-Painted Roses & Leaves, Marked, 10 In. 89.00
RS Prussia, Chocolate Pot, Iridized Green With Leaf Pattern, Gold Tracery 135.00
RS Prussia, Chocolate Pot, Peach, Roses, Green Leaves 140.00
RS Prussia, Chocolate Pot, Pond Lilies & Roses, Aqua Color 150.00
RS Prussia, Chocolate Pot, Roses, Blown-Out Top, Gold, Blue, Yellow, Red Mark 165.00
RS Prussia, Chocolate Pot, Roses, Ornate Gold Handle, Red Mark 165.00
RS Prussia, Chocolate Pot, Spring Seasons 185.00
RS Prussia, Chocolate Pot, Strawberry Flowers, Ornate, Red Mark, 10 1/2 In. 135.00
RS Prussia, Chocolate Pot, Swans & Evergreens, 8 Feet, Red Mark, 10 1/2 In. 375.00
RS Prussia, Chocolate Pot, Swans, Gold, Beige, Brown, Blue Water, Lily Pads 250.00
RS Prussia, Chocolate Pot, Swans, Red Mark 125.00
RS Prussia, Chocolate Pot, 3 Swans, No Mark 350.00
RS Prussia, Chocolate Set, Flowers, Pedestaled Cups, Red Mark, 7 Piece 700.00
RS Prussia, Chocolate Set, Pearlized, Green Leaf Base, Roses, 5 Piece 325.00
RS Prussia, Chocolate Set, Pink & White Poppies, Red Mark, 5 Piece 225.00
RS Prussia, Chocolate Set, Pink Roses, 11 Piece 175.00
RS Prussia, Chocolate Set, Roses, Leaves, Green, White, Ivory, Red Mark, 9 Piece 100.00
RS Prussia, Chocolate Set, Roses, Pearlized Finish, Petaled Base, Handled 325.00
RS Prussia, Compote, Green Leaves, White Berries, Red Star, 4 X 7 In. 125.00
RS Prussia, Cookie Jar, Shaded Green & Ivory, Red Mark 175.00
RS Prussia, Cracker Jar, Bulbous, White & Lavender Flowers, Gold Trim 125.00
RS Prussia, Cracker Jar, Cerise, Yellow Blown Carnations, Flower Finial 250.00
RS Prussia, Cracker Jar, Cream & Light Brown Satin, White Hydrangeas, 5 In. 85.00
RS Prussia, Cracker Jar, Eggshell, Pink & White Carnations, Red Mark 175.00
RS Prussia, Cracker Jar, Floral, Blown-Out & Molded Irises, Satin Finish 175.00
RS Prussia, Cracker Jar, Floral, Squatty, 2 Handled, Steeple Mark 135.00
RS Prussia, Cracker Jar, Green & White Floral, Touches Of Lavender 95.00
RS Prussia, Cracker Jar, Lily Of The Valley, Bulbous, Red Mark 185.00
RS Prussia, Cracker Jar, Mother-Of-Pearl White, Melon Ribbed, Floral, Marked 200.00
RS Prussia, Cracker Jar, Pearlized Pink Roses, Petal Pedestal, Leaf Handles 200.00
RS Prussia, Cracker Jar, Roses, Gold Trim, Footed, Blown-Out Bottom, Red Mark 275.00
RS Prussia, Cracker Jar, White, Pink, Gold, Flowers, Scallops, Footed, 6 1/2 In. 130.00
RS Prussia, Cracker Jar, 3-Color Roses On Pale & Dark Green, Red Mark, 6 In. 135.00
RS Prussia, Creamer & Spooner, Whites & Greens, Roses, Red Mark 65.00
RS Prussia, Creamer, Blown-Out Flowers, Pink & Yellow, Pansies, Red Mark 75.00
RS Prussia, Creamer, Breakfast, Castle Scene, Unmarked 95.00
RS Prussia, Creamer, Castle Scene, Molded Boyd, Blown-Out Floral Spout 275.00
RS Prussia, Creamer, Floral Bouquet, Gold Tracery, Pedestal, Pink, Green, Mark 70.00

RS Prussia, **Creamer**, Floral, Pedestal, Square Base	44.00
RS Prussia, **Creamer**, Flower-Petals Form, White Roses, Footed	20.00
RS Prussia, **Creamer**, Ornate Roses, Indented Collar, Red Mark	46.00
RS Prussia, **Creamer**, Pale Blue, Roses, Alternating Petal, Gold Trim, 3 In.	42.00
RS Prussia, **Creamer**, White & Green, Dark Pink Roses, Ornate Handle, Footed	40.00
RS Prussia, **Creamer**, White Shading, Cream Pastel Roses, Red Mark	55.00
RS Prussia, **Creamer**, Woman Raised With Blown-Out Floral, Raised Star Base	64.00
RS Prussia, **Cup & Saucer**, Berries, Green Leaves, Red Mark	60.00
RS Prussia, **Cup & Saucer**, Chocolate, Calla Lily, White, Gold, Red Mark	40.00
RS Prussia, **Cup & Saucer**, Chocolate, Cottage Scene, Red Mark	78.00
RS Prussia, **Cup & Saucer**, Chocolate, Strawberry Flowers, Red Mark	25.00
RS Prussia, **Cup & Saucer**, Demitasse, Pedestal, Satin Finish, Swan	95.00
RS Prussia, **Cup & Saucer**, Demitasse, Satin Finish, Floral	65.00
RS Prussia, **Cup & Saucer**, Duck, Chocolate, Red Mark	47.50
RS Prussia, **Cup & Saucer**, Floral, Hexagon Shape, Signed	45.00
RS Prussia, **Cup & Saucer**, Floral, Pedestal, Signed	45.00
RS Prussia, **Cup & Saucer**, Floral, 4-Footed, Luster Finish, Signed	65.00
RS Prussia, **Cup & Saucer**, Footed, White Flowers On Green Luster, Red Mark	45.00
RS Prussia, **Cup & Saucer**, Gold Trim, Embossed Feet, Floral, Shadow Forms, Mark	75.00
RS Prussia, **Cup & Saucer**, Green Ribbed, Pink Poppies, Gold Trim, Red Mark	35.00
RS Prussia, **Cup & Saucer**, Green, White Flowers, Red Star	55.00
RS Prussia, **Cup & Saucer**, Hand-Painted Flowers, Red Mark	90.00
RS Prussia, **Cup & Saucer**, Mother-Of-Pearl Roses, Gold Set, Mini-Footed	52.00
RS Prussia, **Cup & Saucer**, Red Roses, Chain Of Garland, Footed, Red Mark	28.00
RS Prussia, **Cup**, Chocolate, Ball Feet, Winter Season, Red Mark	175.00
RS Prussia, **Cup**, Chocolate, Lily Of The Valley, Signed	27.50
RS Prussia, **Cup**, Floral, Blue & White, Red Mark	20.00
RS Prussia, **Dish**, Berry, Peacock, Gold, Red Mark, 6 In.	95.00
RS Prussia, **Dish**, Berry, Satin Finish, Tiffany Edge, Red Mark, 5 1/2 In.	395.00
RS Prussia, **Dish**, Candy, Footed, Green, White Flowers, 6 In.	35.00
RS Prussia, **Dish**, Candy, Reflections Of Water Lilies, Three Feet, Red Mark	132.00
RS Prussia, **Dish**, Candy, Roses, Scalloped Edge, Footed, Red Mark	60.00
RS Prussia, **Dish**, Covered Sweetmeat, Bulbous, Pearlized Florals, Red Mark	135.00
RS Prussia, **Dish**, Floral, Open Handled, Red Mark, 12 X 6 In.	125.00
RS Prussia, **Dish**, Green, Flowers, Gold Trim, Handled, Covered, 8 In.	165.00
RS Prussia, **Dish**, Lily, Red Mark, 9 1/2 X 4 1/2 In.	55.00
RS Prussia, **Dish**, Open Flower Shape, Pink Florals, Green, Red Mark, 6 In.	55.00
RS Prussia, **Dish**, Relish, Roses In Oranges, Gold	69.50
RS Prussia, **Dish**, Roses, Gold Leaf Rim, Pink, 3 Green Shades, Red Mark, 5 In.	45.00
RS Prussia, **Dish**, Roses, Ruffled, Beaded, Gold Border, 3 Footed, Red Mark, 6 In.	60.00
RS Prussia, **Dish**, Sauce, Pink & Yellow Tulips, Red Mark, 5 In.	15.00
RS Prussia, **Ferner**, Forest, Swans, Blue, Green, Satin Finish, Red Mark, 6 In.	375.00
RS Prussia, **Fernery**, Pearlized Finish, Pink & White Roses, Red Mark, 10 In.	250.00
RS Prussia, **Fernery**, Pink & White Roses, Scalloped, Round, Red Mark, 10 In.	250.00
RS Prussia, **Fernery**, Pink Roses, Scalloped Edge, Round, Red Mark, 10 In.	265.00
RS Prussia, **Fernery**, Scalloped, Pink Roses, Applied Gold, Red Mark, 10 In.	265.00
RS Prussia, **Gravy Boat & Attached Underplate**, Pearlized, Roses, Red Mark	195.00
RS Prussia, **Gravy Boat & Underplate**, Scallops, Gold Pastels, Floral, Red Mark	95.00
RS Prussia, **Hair Receiver**, Bluebirds, Cottage Scene, Hexagon, Red Mark, 5 In.	265.00
RS Prussia, **Hair Receiver**, Cream To Tan, Roses, Leaves, Lid & Base	28.00
RS Prussia, **Hair Receiver**, Footed, Petal Shape Cover, Red Mark	98.00
RS Prussia, **Hair Receiver**, Footed, Red Roses, Green & Lavender, Red Mark	55.00
RS Prussia, **Hair Receiver**, Gold Scrolls, Pond Lilies, Beaded & Scalloped	95.00
RS Prussia, **Hair Receiver**, Gold, Pale Green, Gray, Red Mark	75.00
RS Prussia, **Hair Receiver**, Green & Gold, Oval	85.00
RS Prussia, **Hair Receiver**, Green Springs, Flowers, Gold Stippling, Footed	85.00
RS Prussia, **Hair Receiver**, Petaled Cover, Light Blue, Pink Roses, Gold Trim	125.00
RS Prussia, **Hair Receiver**, Pink Roses, Green & Yellow, Red Mark	85.00
RS Prussia, **Hair Receiver**, Yellow Roses, Green Leaves	65.00
RS Prussia, **Hatpin Holder**, Floral Decoration, 3-Footed, Red Mark, 4 1/2 In.	25.00
RS Prussia, **Hatpin Holder**, Floral, Footed, Hexagon Shape, Signed	95.00
RS Prussia, **Hatpin Holder**, Floral, Gilt Scrolls, Footed, Attached Tray	145.00
RS Prussia, **Hatpin Holder**, Hanging Basket Of Flowers	95.00
RS Prussia, **Hatpin Holder**, Hanging, Floral Basket Decorated, Red Mark	165.00
RS Prussia, **Hatpin Holder**, Maple Leaf Decoration	85.00

RS Prussia, Hatpin Holder, Pink Roses, Gold Trim, White, Footed, Red Mark	95.00
RS Prussia, Hatpin Holder, Pink Roses, White & Green Background, Footed, Mark	40.00
RS Prussia, Hatpin Holder, Roses & Gold, Red Mark, 5 3/4 In.	110.00
RS Prussia, Hatpin Holder, White & Pink Water Lilies, Blue Water, 6 Feet	110.00
RS Prussia, Hatpin Holder, 3 Handled, Pink Flowers, Leaves, Gold Rim, 4 In.	85.00
RS Prussia, Jar, Cookie, Melon Shape, Red Mark	265.00
RS Prussia, Jar, Lid, Open Finial, Gold Trim, 4 Feet, Red Mark, 5 1/2 In.	95.00
RS Prussia, Jar, Lid, Scalloped Top, Red Mark, 5 1/2 In.	95.00
RS Prussia, Muffineer, Lilies, Red Mark	100.00
RS Prussia, Mug, Blown-Out Purple Iris, Satinized, Red Mark	110.00
RS Prussia, Mush Set, Fancy Loop-Handled Creamer, 3 Piece	45.00
RS Prussia, Mustache Cup, Blown-Out Leaves, Multicolor Floral, Leaf Handle	135.00
RS Prussia, Mustache Cup, Garlands, Pink Roses, Gold Applied Handle & Rim	165.00
RS Prussia, Mustard Pot, Florals, Gold, Lid	22.50
RS Prussia, Mustard Pot, Green, Pink Roses, Red Mark	165.00
RS Prussia, Mustard Pot, Lily Finial On Lid, Roses, Red, Green Trim, Spoon	150.00
RS Prussia, Mustard Pot, Rose Decoration, Red Star Mark, 3 3/4 In.	65.00
RS Prussia, Mustard Pot, Spoon, White Flowers, Cream With Gold Bands	65.00
RS Prussia, Mustard Pot, Swirl Background, Luster, Red Mark	75.00
RS Prussia, Pitcher, Lemonade, Pink Roses, Greens, Red Mark, 11 1/4 In.	185.00
RS Prussia, Pitcher, Milk, Pale Pink, Peach & White Roses, 6 In.	135.00
RS Prussia, Pitcher, Milk, Swans On Blue Water	245.00
RS Prussia, Pitcher, Syrup, Floral, Red Mark	100.00
RS Prussia, Planter, Deep Green, Red Roses, Jeweled, Embossed, Footed, 7 In.	125.00
RS Prussia, Planter, Footed, Jeweled, Green, Red Roses, Red Mark, 7 In.	125.00
RS Prussia, Planter, Jeweled, Embossed, Deep Green, Red Roses, Red Mark	115.00
RS Prussia, Planter, Poppies Inside And Out	60.00
RS Prussia, Plaque, Bust Portrait, No.30 Mark, 12 In.	325.00
RS Prussia, Plaque, Red Roses, 13 In.	45.00
RS Prussia, Plate, Apple Blossoms, Red Mark, 8 1/2 In.	60.00
RS Prussia, Plate, Bluebird Medallions, Gold Trim, Red Mark, 11 3/4 In.	275.00
RS Prussia, Plate, Bread, Open Handled, 11 In.	90.00
RS Prussia, Plate, Bread, Red Roses, Raised Orchids	130.00
RS Prussia, Plate, Cake, Aqua Flowers, Red Mark, Pair	175.00
RS Prussia, Plate, Cake, Cluster Of Fruits In Center, Handled, Red Mark, 9 In.	180.00
RS Prussia, Plate, Cake, Floral, Gold Trim, White, Green, Large	85.00
RS Prussia, Plate, Cake, Floral, Open Handle, Pink, Red Mark, 11 In.	80.00
RS Prussia, Plate, Cake, Floral, Turquoise Edge, Pastel Cream, Lavender, Gold	85.00
RS Prussia, Plate, Cake, Matte Finish, Gold Leaf, Red Mark, 7 1/2 In.	78.00
RS Prussia, Plate, Cake, Mill Scene, Brown, Gold, Open Handles, Red Mark, 10 In.	490.00
RS Prussia, Plate, Cake, Pastel Green Border, Inverted Floral, Gold Trim	35.00
RS Prussia, Plate, Cake, Roses, Daisies, Open Handled, Red Mark, 10 1/4 In.	125.00
RS Prussia, Plate, Cake, Roses, Molded Maple Leaf Rim, Open Handle, Green, Sign	90.00
RS Prussia, Plate, Cake, Snowballs, Roses, Red Mark, 11 In.	145.00
RS Prussia, Plate, Cake, Snowballs, Tan Shades, 10 Fans Divide Rim, 10 In.	60.00
RS Prussia, Plate, Cake, 2 Handled, Carnations, Raised Gold Trim, Scalloped	115.00
RS Prussia, Plate, Castle & Mill, 8 1/2 In.	450.00
RS Prussia, Plate, Chop, Roses, 13 In.	49.00
RS Prussia, Plate, Cloud Effect, Floral, 10 3/4 In.	125.00
RS Prussia, Plate, Dogwood On Cream, Blue, Gold Leaf Border, Oblong, Red Mark	60.00
RS Prussia, Plate, Embossed Shells, Pink, Gold, Pansies, Red Mark, 8 1/2 In.	90.00
RS Prussia, Plate, Farmyard, Scene With Roosters & Hens, 8 In.	625.00
RS Prussia, Plate, Fleur-De-Lis, Gold, Ecru, Turquoise, Red Mark, 11 1/2 In.	100.00
RS Prussia, Plate, Floral	95.00
RS Prussia, Plate, Floral, Blue Tones With Tans, 12 In.	150.00
RS Prussia, Plate, Floral, Gold Panels, Roses, Daisies, Foliage, Pastels, 10 In.	70.00
RS Prussia, Plate, Floral, Luster, Signed, 6 In.	32.50
RS Prussia, Plate, Floral, Open Handled, Red Mark, 10 In.	125.00
RS Prussia, Plate, Floral, Open Handled, Red Mark, 10 1/4 In.	110.00
RS Prussia, Plate, Floral, Pierced Handles, Red Mark, 9 1/2 In.	125.00
RS Prussia, Plate, Floral, Signed, 8 1/2 In., Set Of 3	57.50
RS Prussia, Plate, Flow Blue, G.M.Steeple Mark, 11 In.	155.00
RS Prussia, Plate, Flowers Reflected In Water, Red Mark, 8 1/2 In.	63.00
RS Prussia, Plate, Fruit, Turquoise, Blown-Out Floral, Red Mark, 10 1/2 In.	90.00
RS Prussia, Plate, Garlands Of Roses, Cream & Green, Red Mark, 10 1/2 In.	135.00

RS Prussia, Plate, Gold Figure Work, Floral, 11 1/4 In. 140.00
RS Prussia, Plate, Gold Flowers, Custard Ground, Hand-Painted, 8 1/2 In. 55.00
RS Prussia, Plate, Gold On Deep Embossed Edge, Red Star, 11 In.Wide 225.00
RS Prussia, Plate, Leaf, Green, Roses, Gold-Trimmed Leaves, Red Mark, 11 In. 265.00
RS Prussia, Plate, Leaf, Satin Finish, Pink Roses, Red Mark, 10 In. 185.00
RS Prussia, Plate, Lily Of The Valley, Satin, Red Mark, 7 In. 49.00
RS Prussia, Plate, Lily Of The Valley, Satin, Red Mark, 9 In. 89.00
RS Prussia, Plate, Mill Scene, Decorated Edge, Red Mark, 8 In. 475.00
RS Prussia, Plate, Mill, Signed UM, 8 1/2 In. 195.00
RS Prussia, Plate, Narcissus, Gold Trim, Scalloped, Red Mark, 6 In. 55.00
RS Prussia, Plate, Old Man Mountain, Red Mark 425.00
RS Prussia, Plate, Open Handle, Red Mark, 10 In. 60.00
RS Prussia, Plate, Pearlized Finish, Pink Roses, Red Mark, 8 In. 85.00
RS Prussia, Plate, Petal Shape, Gold Band, Green, Roses, Red Mark, 8 1/2 In. 85.00
RS Prussia, Plate, Pierced Handles, Scalloped, Gold, Lilies, Red Mark, 8 In. 60.00
RS Prussia, Plate, Pink & Yellow Mums, 10 In. 75.00
RS Prussia, Plate, Portrait Of Lady, Red & Gold Border, Winter, Summer, Pair 200.00
RS Prussia, Plate, Raised Ovals, Gold Outline, Red Mark, 11 In. 137.00
RS Prussia, Plate, Roses, Daisies, Draped, Ruffled Petal Between, 8 1/2 In. 75.00
RS Prussia, Plate, Roses, Scalloped, Open Handles, Satin Finish, 10 In. 65.00
RS Prussia, Plate, Scalloped Gold Edge, Pink Roses, 2 Handled, 9 1/2 In. 95.00
RS Prussia, Plate, Scalloped, Brown Mill Scene, 6 In. 50.00
RS Prussia, Plate, Scalloped, Iridescent, Pebbly Border, Green Pink Roses 40.00
RS Prussia, Plate, Scalloped, Peach Roses, Leaves, 9 In. 40.00
RS Prussia, Plate, Scenic, Masted Schooner, Pearlized, 7 1/2 In., Pair 800.00
RS Prussia, Plate, Ships, Quiet Cove, 10 In. 725.00
RS Prussia, Plate, Snowbird, Beaded Edge, Gold Scrollwork, Red Mark, 8 In. 1375.00
RS Prussia, Plate, Snowbird, Beaded Edge, Gold Scrollwork, 8 1/2 In. 1375.00
RS Prussia, Plate, Swans, Trees, Lake & Stream, 12 1/4 X 6 In. 235.00
RS Prussia, Plate, White Gloss, Pink Roses, Green & White Leaves, 11 In. 110.00
RS Prussia, Platter, Open Handles, Scalloped Rim, Red Mark, 10 In. 385.00
RS Prussia, Relish, Dogwood Pattern, Open Handles, Scalloped, Red Mark 40.00
RS Prussia, Relish, Floral, Pierced Handles 65.00
RS Prussia, Relish, Gold, White Flowers, Red Mark, 3 X 8 In. 30.00
RS Prussia, Relish, Green, Lavender & White Floral, Red Mark 25.00
RS Prussia, Relish, Pink Roses, Satin Finish, Pierced Handles, 9 1/2 In. 45.00
RS Prussia, Relish, Poppies, Gold Border, Pink, White, Red Mark, 10 X 4 In. 30.00
RS Prussia, Relish, Reflecting Water Lilies, Jeweled, 10 In. 48.00
RS Prussia, Relish, Strawberry Flower, Red Mark, 7 X 4 In. 20.00
RS Prussia, Relish, Yellow, Roses & Lily Of The Valley, Gold Trim, Red Mark 40.00
RS Prussia, Shoe, Floral, Red Mark, 3 1/2 X 2 1/2 In. 295.00
RS Prussia, Sugar & Creamer, Covered, Satin Finish, Pink Roses, Red Mark 50.00
RS Prussia, Sugar & Creamer, Floral, Footed, Hex Shape, Gold, Signed 147.00
RS Prussia, Sugar & Creamer, Floral, Garland Of Tiny Roses Around Rims 125.00
RS Prussia, Sugar & Creamer, Green & Yellow, Pansy, Ribbon Handle, Pedestaled 70.00
RS Prussia, Sugar & Creamer, Green Festooning, Gold Trim, Pedestal, Red Mark 165.00
RS Prussia, Sugar & Creamer, Green, Roses, Gold Tracery, Blown Top, Red Mark 120.00
RS Prussia, Sugar & Creamer, Iridescent Mauve & Floral, Applied Legs, Gold 135.00
RS Prussia, Sugar & Creamer, Pale Green, Purple & White Floral, Red Mark 127.00
RS Prussia, Sugar & Creamer, Petal Feet, Flower Finial, Pansies, Unmarked 70.00
RS Prussia, Sugar & Creamer, Roses In Basket, Scalloped Pedestal, Emblem 135.00
RS Prussia, Sugar & Creamer, Roses, Fruits, Signed, Red Mark, Green Wreath 155.00
RS Prussia, Sugar & Creamer, Roses, Gold Trim, Luster Finish, Lid, Red Mark 60.00
RS Prussia, Sugar & Creamer, Roses, Pedestal, Green, Red Mark .... 70.00 To 150.00
RS Prussia, Sugar & Creamer, Satin Finish, Swans 275.00
RS Prussia, Sugar & Creamer, Satin Pedestal, Green, White 200.00
RS Prussia, Sugar & Creamer, Shaded Green, Pink Roses, Gold, Pedestal 165.00
RS Prussia, Sugar & Creamer, Sheepherder & Bluebirds 650.00
RS Prussia, Sugar & Creamer, White, Pink Roses, Pedestaled, Red Mark 90.00
RS Prussia, Sugar & Creamer, White, Purple, Red & Pink Roses, Red Mark 110.00
RS Prussia, Sugar & Creamer, Yellow Roses, Ruffled, Green To Pink, Red Mark 90.00
RS Prussia, Sugar Shaker, Butterfly Decoration 90.00
RS Prussia, Sugar Shaker, Cream, Tan & Green Shading, Poppies, Red Mark 125.00
RS Prussia, Sugar Shaker, Floral, Red Mark 75.00
RS Prussia, Sugar Shaker, Flowers, Iridescent Strawberries, Red Mark, 3 In. 115.00

RS Prussia, Toothpick

RS Prussia, Sugar Shaker, Lilies, Red Mark	135.00
RS Prussia, Sugar Shaker, White & Green, Roses, Gold Trim, Red Mark	75.00
RS Prussia, Sugar, Blossoms, White, Green, Lavender, 4 In.	45.00
RS Prussia, Sugar, Calla Lily, Lid, Artist Signed, Red Mark	65.00
RS Prussia, Sugar, Dogwood Pattern, Scalloped Top, Red Mark	45.00
RS Prussia, Sugar, Green, White Floral, Gold Stems, Scalloped Edge	45.00
RS Prussia, Sugar, Lily Decoration, Covered, Signed, Red Mark	65.00
RS Prussia, Sugar, Pink Roses, Gold Stems, Covered, Pedestal, Red Mark	35.00
RS Prussia, Sugar, Rose-Colored Flowers, Fluted, Red Mark	35.00
RS Prussia, Sugar, Roses, Gold Trim, Handled, Covered, Red Mark, 4 In.	35.00
RS Prussia, Sugar, White Roses On White & Yellow, Lid	65.00
RS Prussia, Sugar, Winter Season, Red Mark	195.00
RS Prussia, Syrup With Underplate, Red Mark	55.00
RS Prussia, Syrup, Pansies, Orchids, Blown, Yellow To Green, Lid, Underplate	62.00
RS Prussia, Tankard, Ecru, Lavender Flowers, Red Mark, 11 1/2 In.	425.00
RS Prussia, Tankard, Pink & Yellow Roses, 6 Sided, Red Mark, 10 X 5 In.	265.00
RS Prussia, Tea Set, Chrysanthemums, Gold, 3 Piece	225.00
RS Prussia, Tea Set, Dogwood, Leaves, Gold Trim, White, Tan, Green, Red Mark, 3	150.00
RS Prussia, Tea Set, Pale Green, Rose Decoration, 3 Piece	295.00
RS Prussia, Tea Set, Roses, Pink, Yellow, Blue On Cream, Red Mark, 3 Piece	125.00
RS Prussia, Tea Strainer, Salmon & White Roses, Footed, Red Mark	75.00
RS Prussia, Teapot & Sugar, Roses, Ruffled Ribbon On Sides, Red Mark	175.00
RS Prussia, Teapot, Bisque, Pink Tea Roses, Square Pedestal, Red Mark	165.00
RS Prussia, Teapot, Gold Trim With Pink Roses, Red Mark, 5 3/4 X 8 In.	145.00
RS Prussia, Teapot, White Flowers, Gray-Green Leaves, Luster, Red Mark	85.00
RS Prussia, Toothpick *Illus*	105.00
RS Prussia, Toothpick, Floral, Green Shading, Gold Trim, 3 Handles, Red Mark	175.00
RS Prussia, Toothpick, Green, Roses, Signed, 4 Feet	60.00
RS Prussia, Toothpick, Roses, 2 Handled, Pink, White, Red Mark	85.00
RS Prussia, Toothpick, Trees, Duck, Handled, Red Mark	240.00
RS Prussia, Toothpick, 2 Handled, Red Mark	120.00
RS Prussia, Tray, Bread, Bright Green Luster, White Dogwood, Red Mark	115.00
RS Prussia, Tray, Bread, Red Roses, White Snowballs, Gold & White Edge, 12 In.	95.00
RS Prussia, Tray, Bread, Snowbird, Icicle Molded Edge, 13 1/2 X 7 In.	125.00
RS Prussia, Tray, Bread, Tulip Decoration, Gold Trim, Satin, Red Mark, 11 In.	95.00
RS Prussia, Tray, Bread, 3 Swan Reflecting Lily, Icicle Mold, Blue Shades	225.00
RS Prussia, Tray, Card, 6 Swans In Lake, Scallop Gold Rim, Gold Scroll Trim	120.00
RS Prussia, Tray, Dresser, Basket Of Flowers, Lavender	125.00
RS Prussia, Tray, Dresser, Multicolor Floral, Gold Beading, Red Mark, 7 In.	90.00
RS Prussia, Tray, Dresser, Roses, Gold Rim, Red, White, Oval Shape, Signed	75.00
RS Prussia, Tray, Dresser, Tulips, Green Background, White, Red Mark	75.00
RS Prussia, Tray, Dresser, White, Lilies In Center, Red Mark	110.00
RS Prussia, Tray, Floral Group In Center, Blown Out In Corners, Gold Trim	95.00
RS Prussia, Tray, Floral, Open Handled, Red Mark, 12 X 6 In.	95.00
RS Prussia, Tray, Floral, Red Mark, 8 X 11 In.	95.00
RS Prussia, Tray, Oval, Gold Tracery, Crown With B., Signed, 10 In.	35.00
RS Prussia, Tray, Perfume, Cherubs, Red Mark, 6 X 7 1/2 In.	185.00
RS Prussia, Tray, Pink Roses With Green, Yellow, Gold Floral, 6 X 4 In.	36.00
RS Prussia, Tray, Relish, Burnt Oranges, Golds, Rose Colors, Roses, Gold Trim	75.00
RS Prussia, Tray, Relish, Castle, Brown	375.00
RS Prussia, Tray, Relish, Fleur-De-Lis, Roses, Snow Balls, Scalloped, Red Mark	85.00

RS Prussia, Tray, Relish, Shaded Burnt Yellow, Violets, Red Mark	58.00
RS Prussia, Tray, Rose Decoration, 11 In.	80.00
RS Prussia, Tray, Roses & Snow Balls, Fleur-De-Lis Edge, Red Mark, 12 In.	85.00
RS Prussia, Tray, Satin, Gold Rim, Gold Speckle, Red Mark, 11 3/4 X 7 5/8 In.	125.00
RS Prussia, Tray, Swans & Water Lilies Scene, Red Mark, 11 1/2 X 7 1/2 In.	275.00
RS Prussia, Tray, Tin, Blue, Roses, Blown Plume Edge, Red Mark, 14 In.	120.00
RS Prussia, Tray, White & Yellow Flowers, Dark Leaves, Red Mark, Signed, 9 In.	115.00
RS Prussia, Tray, White Apple Blossoms, Open Handle, Oval, 12 3/4 In.	95.00
RS Prussia, Tumble-Up, Pink & Yellow Roses, Red Mark	200.00
RS Prussia, Vase, Bird Of Paradise ....*Illus*	425.00
RS Prussia, Vase, Brown, Mill Scene, 4 In.	115.00
RS Prussia, Vase, Bust Portrait, No.30 Mark, 8 1/2 In.	550.00
RS Prussia, Vase, Castle Scene, Bulbous, Red Mark, 4 1/2 In.	280.00
RS Prussia, Vase, Cupids, Red Mark, 9 In.	425.00
RS Prussia, Vase, Floral, Gold Handles, Red Mark, 8 3/4 In.	125.00
RS Prussia, Vase, Floral, Roses, Pink, Brown, Blue, Red Mark, 7 1/2 In.	125.00
RS Prussia, Vase, Florals, Cream To Dusky Green, 5 In.	70.00
RS Prussia, Vase, Melon Boys Shooting Dice, Handles, Red Mark, 9 In.	250.00
RS Prussia, Vase, Melon Boys, 6 In.	500.00
RS Prussia, Vase, Mill Scene, R.S.Suhl, Red Mark, Handled, 4 In.	265.00
RS Prussia, Vase, Mill Scene, Suhl, Red Mark, Lidded, 3 1/2 X 5 In.	385.00
RS Prussia, Vase, Peacock & Golden Pheasant, Gold Trim, Red Mark, 4 In.	300.00
RS Prussia, Vase, Peacock, 7 In.	550.00
RS Prussia, Vase, Pearlized Jewels, Gold Handles, Flowers, Red Mark, 10 In.	250.00
RS Prussia, Vase, Pheasant, 3 1/2 In.	70.00
RS Prussia, Vase, Pheasants, 4 1/2 In.	150.00
RS Prussia, Vase, Pink Roses, Cream To Dusky Green, 9 In.	105.00
RS Prussia, Vase, Poppies, Art Nouveau, 2 Handles, Red Mark, 9 In.	85.00
RS Prussia, Vase, Poppies, 2 Handled, Art Nouveau, 9 In.	95.00
RS Prussia, Vase, Portrait, Spring Scenic, Cobalt & Gold Trim, Handled, 7 In.	600.00
RS Prussia, Vase, Red & Pink Poppies, Gold Leaves, Satin Finish, 9 3/4 In.	145.00
RS Prussia, Vase, Roses, Satin Finish, Red Mark, 4 1/2 In.	145.00

*R.S.Tillowitz porcelain factory was started at Tillowitz near Silesia
in 1869 by Rheinhold Schlegelmilch. Table services and ornamental pieces
were made.*

RS Tillowitz, Cake Set, Large Plate, Six Small Plates, Signed	225.00
RS Tillowitz, Dessert Set, 5 Piece, Orange & White Flowers, Gold Trim	50.00
RS Tillowitz, Flower Holder, Violet Decoration, Reticulated Gold Top, Marked	195.00
RS Tillowitz, Jar, Cracker, Pink Roses, Gold Garlands, 6 X 4 In.	65.00
RS Tillowitz, Tray, Candy, Hand-Painted, Lilies On Green, Gold, 8 1/2 In.	35.00
RS Tillowitz, Tray, Pin, Pickard Gold, Red Mark, 5 1/2 X 3 1/2 In.	48.00
RS Tillowitz, Vase, Flowers, Bulbous, 6 In.	20.00
RS Tillowitz, Vase, Orange, Epos With Globe Mark, Art Nouveau, 7 1/2 In.	45.00
RS Tillowtiz, Fernery, White, Gold & Green Floral Border, 8 1/2 In.	30.00

*Rubena Verde is a Victorian glassware that was shaded from red to green.
It was first made by Hobbs, Brockunier and Company of Wheeling,
West Virginia, about 1890.*

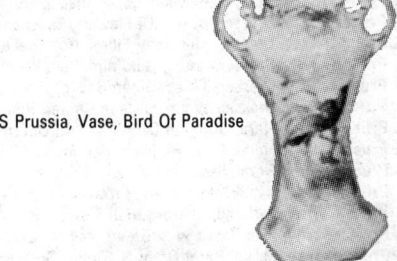

RS Prussia, Vase, Bird Of Paradise

Rubena Verde, Basket, Cranberry Petals, Pointed Handle, 6 1/2 X 6 In. 75.00
Rubena Verde, Bowl, Enameled Daisies & Flowers, 4 1/2 X 8 X 5 In. 140.00
Rubena Verde, Cruet 165.00
Rubena Verde, Dish, Crackle Glass, Red To Vaseline, Metal Base, 6 1/4 In. 110.00
Rubena Verde, Epergne, Bowl & Trumpet, Cranberry, Ruffled, Crimped 150.00
Rubena Verde, Pitcher, Corset Shape, Scalloped Top, Lacy Enamel 175.00
Rubena Verde, Pitcher, Inverted Thumbprint, Applied Green Handle, 9 In. 125.00
Rubena Verde, Pitcher, Lemonade, Hobnail 295.00
Rubena Verde, Pitcher, Water, Inverted Thumbprint, 8 In. 275.00
Rubena Verde, Shade, Shell Pattern, Ruffled Top, 9 1/2 X 9 1/2 In. 198.00
Rubena Verde, Tumbler, Cranberry Shaded To Vaseline, 10 Row Hobnail 165.00
Rubena Verde, Tumbler, Thumbprint .... 65.00 To 102.00
Rubena Verde, Underplate, Ruffled Edge, Threaded 48.00
Rubena Verde, Vase, Bulbous, Pink & White Enameled Flowers, 4 1/2 In. 85.00
Rubena Verde, Vase, Cranberry To Light Green, Paneled Optic, Enameled Floral 85.00
Rubena Verde, Vase, Daisies, Gold Leaf Tracery, Rib, Ruffled, Pink, White, 6 In. 140.00
Rubena Verde, Vase, Enameled Flowers, Gold, 9 1/2 In. 30.00
Rubena Verde, Vase, Flower Decoration, Deep Coloring, 8 In. 295.00
Rubena Verde, Vase, Pinched Sides, 12 1/2 In. 95.00
Rubena Verde, Vase, Ruffled, Blown, Green Bulbous Base & Neck, Opalescent 85.00
Rubena Verde, Vase, Small Enameled Flowers, 6 1/2 In. 235.00

*Rubena is a glassware that shades from red to clear. It was first made by
George Duncan and Sons of Pittsburgh, Pennsylvania, about 1885.*
Rubena, see also Pressed Glass, Royal Ivy Pressed Glass, Royal Oak
Rubena, Bottle, Cologne, Cranberry To Clear, White & Blue Enameled Flowers 75.00
Rubena, Bottle, Cologne, Pear Shaped, Florals, Scrolls, Red Jewel In Gold Cap 65.00
Rubena, Bottle, Perfume, Enameling, Flared Top Filigree Around Center 85.00
Rubena, Bottle, Perfume, Square, 2 1/2 X 4 1/2 In. 30.00
Rubena, Bottle, Shell Feet, Enameled Decoration, Stopper 69.00
Rubena, Bowl, Honeycomb, Signed Cambridge 89.00
Rubena, Bucket, Ice, Clear & Frosted, Polar Bear, 1885, 6 3/4 X 5 1/4 In. 125.00
Rubena, Castor, Pickle, Coralene Decorations, Footed Frame 325.00
Rubena, Castor, Pickle, Inverted Thumbprint Enameled Insert, Pear Shape 285.00
Rubena, Castor, Pickle, Vase-Shaped Insert, Footed Frame 225.00
Rubena, Condiment Set, Salt, Pepper, Mustard, Silver Plated Holder, Panel Cut 125.00
Rubena, Creamer, Hobnail, Applied Clear Handle, Bulbous, Small, 4 In. 160.00
Rubena, Epergne, 1 Tall Lily, 3 Small, 3 Crystal Canes 295.00
Rubena, Goblet, Applied Decoration, Teardrop Stem, Mellon-Ribbed Bowl 18.00
Rubena, Jug, Syrup, Cranberry To Clear, Nickel Plated Metal Top, 6 In. 68.00
Rubena, Lampshade, Etched, Scalloped Base, Hobnail 27.50
Rubena, Mustard Pot, 10 Panels, Plated Hinged Top, 3 In. 35.00
Rubena, Pitcher, Cranberry Shading To Clear, Reeded Handle, 8 In. 135.00
Rubena, Pitcher, Inverted Thumbprint, Tricorn Top, 1880s, 9 In. 150.00
Rubena, Pitcher, Water, Diamond, Cut Band, Rayed Bottom, Applied Handle, 9 In. 150.00
Rubena, Pitcher, Water, Inverted Thumbprint, Tricorn Top, 1880s, 9 In. 150.00
Rubena, Pitcher, Water, Raspberry Color, Clear Handle 140.00
Rubena, Pitcher, Water, 4 Tumblers, Reverse Thumbprint, Hand-Painted 250.00
Rubena, Rose Bowl, Cranberry Shaded To Clear, Crimped Top, 5 1/8 In. 110.00
Rubena, Saltshaker, Little Apple 19.00
Rubena, Saltshaker, 4 Enameled Flower Sprigs 35.00
Rubena, Shaker, Pepper Sauce, 10 Panels, Plated Top, 3 In. 35.00
Rubena, Sugar Shaker, Medallion Sprig 125.00
Rubena, Syrup, Coin Spot, Ring Neck 110.00
Rubena, Tumbler, Inverted Thumbprint 20.00
Rubena, Tumbler, Opalescent Swirl .... 35.00 To 60.50
Rubena, Tumbler, Thumbprint, Etched 93.50
Rubena, Vase, Blown, Gold, 10 In. 110.00
Rubena, Vase, Blown, Ground Pontil, Applied Base, 10 In. 32.00
Rubena, Vase, Flared Top, Bulbous, 3 3/4 In. 35.00
Rubena, Vase, Flared, Ribbed Top, Gold Filigree Enamel, Bulbous Base, 12 In. 40.00
Rubena, Vase, Hand Blown, Gold Trim, Enamel Decoration, 10 In. 95.00
Rubena, Vase, Jack-In-The-Pulpit, 9 In. 28.00
Rubena, Vase, Ribbed, Petal Shaped Rim, Applied Petal Feet, 7 X 5 In. 125.00

Rubena, Vase, Ruffled Top, Enameled Gold, Blue, & White Decoration, 10 In.	95.00
Rubena, Vase, Sterling Rim, 8 In.	35.00
Rubena, Vase, Swirl, Clear Glass Applied Feet, Flared Top, 7 X 5 In.	50.00
Rubena, Vase, Swirled, Sterling Rim, 8 In.	30.00
Rubena, Water Set, Reverse Thumbprint, Hand-Painted Daisies, 5 Piece	275.00

Ruby glass is a dark red color. It was a Victorian and twentieth-century ware. The name means many different types of red glass.

Ruby Glass, see also Cranberry Glass

Ruby Glass, Berry Set, Roanoke	110.00
Ruby Glass, Berry Set, Round, 7 Piece	15.00
Ruby Glass, Bottle, Perfume, Clear Flashed Flutes, Peacock Pan, Stopper, 4 In.	25.00
Ruby Glass, Bowl & Underplate, Dolphin Handled	45.00
Ruby Glass, Bowl, Master Berry, Ellipses	16.00
Ruby Glass, Bowl, Punch, Matching Stand, 10 In.	38.00
Ruby Glass, Box, Jewelry, Brass & Copper Engraved Trim, C.1820	255.00
Ruby Glass, Butter, Metal Lid	110.00
Ruby Glass, Canoe, Beaver Dam, Wisconsin, Stain	25.00
Ruby Glass, Carafe, Dolphin Stopper	125.00
Ruby Glass, Celery, Thumbprint	40.00
Ruby Glass, Compote, Hexagon Block, 7 In.	75.00
Ruby Glass, Compote, Ruby Thumbprint, Jelly	45.00
Ruby Glass, Creamer, Individual, Souvenir, To My Mother, 1892	28.00
Ruby Glass, Creamer, Ladder With Diamond	37.50
Ruby Glass, Creamer, Petaled Medallion With Etching	35.00
Ruby Glass, Creamer, Souvenir, Mother, Atlantic City, 1903	50.00
Ruby Glass, Creamer, Souvenir, Mother, 1898, Atlantic City	45.00
Ruby Glass, Creamer, Souvenir, Mrs.Barker, Atlantic City, 1907	50.00
Ruby Glass, Creamer, St.Paul, Minnesota	15.00
Ruby Glass, Cup, Clear Handle, Lula, 1898	10.00
Ruby Glass, Decanter, Aurora, Original Stopper	85.00
Ruby Glass, Decanter, Flowers, Arches, Decorated Stopper, 8 1/2 In.	45.00
Ruby Glass, Decanter, 6 Footed Glasses	30.00
Ruby Glass, Dish, Berry, Ruby Thumbprint, Etching Of Small Berries	18.00
Ruby Glass, Glow Lamp, Shade, Base, Dated 1895, 4 3/8 X 4 In.	110.00
Ruby Glass, Goblet, Etched Swirl Band	10.00
Ruby Glass, Goblet, Short Paneled	18.50
Ruby Glass, Goblet, Souvenir, Scranton, Pa.	24.00
Ruby Glass, Goblet, Souvenir, Utica, N.Y.	24.00
Ruby Glass, Goblet, Thumbprint With Etching	45.00
Ruby Glass, Jar, Covered, Dated 1873, Flashed & Clear, 9 In.	85.00
Ruby Glass, Mug, Calamity Jane, 1905, Button Arches, Handled, Stain	15.00
Ruby Glass, Mug, Child's, Ruby, Beatrice, 1906, Stain	17.00
Ruby Glass, Mug, Souvenir, Duluth	20.00
Ruby Glass, Mug, Souvenir, Frosted Band, Helen Petoskey, 1904	18.00
Ruby Glass, Mug, Souvenir, Lancaster, O., 1903	10.00
Ruby Glass, Mug, Souvenir, Maude, 1910	22.00
Ruby Glass, Mug, Souvenir, Portland, Oregon, 1905	16.00
Ruby Glass, Mug, Souvenir, Rapid City, Michigan, Button & Arches	20.00
Ruby Glass, Mug, Souvenir, World's Fair, 1893, Applied Handle, 4 In.	30.00
Ruby Glass, Pitcher, Souvenir, Button Arches, H.W.Wheeler, 1939, 2 1/2 In.	19.00
Ruby Glass, Pitcher, Souvenir, Mother, Button & Arches	100.00
Ruby Glass, Pitcher, Souvenir, Toledo, Ohio, 4 In.	19.00
Ruby Glass, Pitcher, Thumbprint, Reeded Handle	75.00
Ruby Glass, Punch Set, 14 Piece	60.00
Ruby Glass, Saltshaker, Crosshatched, Dundee, Minnesota, Stain	15.00
Ruby Glass, Saltshaker, Ruby To Clear, Button Arches, Schuyler Lake, N.Y.	12.50
Ruby Glass, Sauce, Nail Footed	39.50
Ruby Glass, Sauce, Thumbprint, 4 In.	15.00
Ruby Glass, Sauce, Truncated Cube	15.00
Ruby Glass, Spooner, Idaho, 1937, Footed, 4 X 2 In.	15.00
Ruby Glass, Spooner, Snail	45.00
Ruby Glass, Sugar, Button Arches, Covered, Frosted Band	55.00
Ruby Glass, Sugar, Triple Triangle, Covered	65.00
Ruby Glass, Tankard, Pavonia, 12 In.	84.50

Ruby Glass, Tumbler, Cut To Clear

Ruby Glass, Toothpick, Button & Arches	15.00
Ruby Glass, Toothpick, Button & Arches, Sarah Winslow, 1906	19.00
Ruby Glass, Toothpick, Signed Father, 1906	13.50
Ruby Glass, Toothpick, Souvenir, Chancellor, S.D., Gold Trimmed	14.50
Ruby Glass, Toothpick, Souvenir, Edgerly, N.D., Gold Trimmed	14.50
Ruby Glass, Toothpick, Souvenir, Fayette, Iowa	13.00
Ruby Glass, Toothpick, Souvenir, Hearts	20.00
Ruby Glass, Toothpick, Souvenir, Lancaster, Ohio, 1903	10.00
Ruby Glass, Toothpick, Souvenir, Mackinac Island, Michigan, 1898	22.00
Ruby Glass, Toothpick, St.Paul, Coal Scuttle	17.00
Ruby Glass, Toothpick, Thumbprint	25.00
Ruby Glass, Toothpick, Zipper Slash, Inscribed Ellen, Stain	25.00
Ruby Glass, Tray, Pin, Clear & Ruby, Compliments Omaha Crockery Co.	15.00
Ruby Glass, Tray, Pin, Souvenir Quenemo, Kansas, Oval	18.50
Ruby Glass, Tray, Pin, Souvenir, St.Louis	7.50
Ruby Glass, Tumbler, Block & Lattice	28.00
Ruby Glass, Tumbler, Button & Arches, B.P.O.E.	40.00
Ruby Glass, Tumbler, Cut To Clear .... Illus	20.00
Ruby Glass, Tumbler, High Hobnail	15.00
Ruby Glass, Tumbler, Thumbprint	25.00
Ruby Glass, Vase, Bulbous, 3 1/2 In.	3.00
Ruby Glass, Vase, Figural, Hand, Daisy & Button, Scalloped Top, 6 1/4 In.	75.00
Ruby Glass, Vase, Souvenir, Silver Lake, 6 In.	20.00
Ruby Glass, Vase, 14 Panel, Cut Top, Brass Base, 8 1/2 X 21 In.	125.00
Ruby Glass, Vase, 14 Panels, Gold Florals & Leaves, Brass Lion's-Paw Base	95.00
Ruby Glass, Water Set, Red Block, 7 Piece	265.00
Ruby Glass, Whiskey, Souvenir, Rhode Island, Scalloped Daisy, 2 In.	14.50
Ruby Glass, Wine, Souvenir, Cassville, Wisconsin	23.00
Ruby Glass, Wine, Sunken Honeycomb	29.00
Ruby Glass, Wine, Thumbprint, Hot Springs, 1892	28.00
Ruby Glass, Wine, Thumbprint, Souvenir, Hot Springs, 1892	28.00
Rudolstadt, Berry Set, Bowl, 12 Sauces, Fern Pattern, Green, Germany	35.00
Rudolstadt, Bowl, Pink Daisies, Signed Beyer, 9 3/4 In.	45.00
Rudolstadt, Bowl, 3 Gold Ball Feet, Yellow & Pink Roses, 6 1/2 In.	30.00
Rudolstadt, Bust, Woman, Art Nouveau, No.5730	159.00
Rudolstadt, Cup & Saucer, Game Scene, Crown Mark	55.00
Rudolstadt, Figurine, Bathing Beauty, Net & Fringe Suit, 13 In.	575.00
Rudolstadt, Figurine, Boy & Girl, Beige, 11 In.	85.00
Rudolstadt, Hatpin Holder, Violets Decoration, Prussia	42.00
Rudolstadt, Humidor, Figural, Indian In Full Headdress, Pastel Bisque	150.00
Rudolstadt, Pitcher, Floral, Gold Handle & Trim, Melon Shape, 9 In.	65.00
Rudolstadt, Pitcher, Flower Sprays, Gold Handles, Entwined Neck, 11 In.	125.00
Rudolstadt, Plate, Children's, Happy Fats, Germany, Marked, 6 In.	15.00 To 45.00
Rudolstadt, Plate, Roses, Thuringer, Signed	20.00
Rudolstadt, Saucer, Happy Fats	12.00
Rudolstadt, Vase, Floral Decoration, Double Handles, Signed, 8 1/4 In.	75.00

Rudolstadt, Vase, Floral, Creamy Background, Pinched Neck, Gold Handles 40.00
Rudolstadt, Vase, Floral, Multicolor, Creamy Background, 7 X 4 X 2 In. 40.00
    Rug, see Textile, Rug

Rumrill Pottery was designed by George Rumrill of Little Rock,
Arkansas. From 1930 to 1933, it was produced by the Red Wing
Pottery of Red Wing, Minnesota. In 1938 production was transferred
to the Shawnee Pottery, Zanesville, Ohio.
Rumrill, Figurine, Dove, Original Sticker 7.00
Rumrill, Pitcher, Red 8.00
Rumrill, Pitcher, Water, Bulbous, Green, Marked 16.00
Rumrill, Vase, Green 5.00
Ruskin, Candlestick, Iridescent, C.1923, Signed, 6 1/2 In., Pair 98.00
Ruskin, Cup & Saucer, Iridescent Green, Set Of 6 .... 150.00
Ruskin, Jar, Cinnamon, Lavender Iridescent, Pierced Floral, Covered, 6 1/2 In. 150.00
Sabino, Blotter, Roll Type, Cluster Of Flags, Sabino, France, High Relief 125.00
Sabino, Bottle, Perfume, Dancing Nudes, 6 1/2 In. 55.00
Sabino, Bottle, Perfume, 5 Nudes, Pineapple Stopper, 6 In. 45.00
Sabino, Dish, Snail Shell, 2 X 3 3/4 In. .... 37.00 To 44.00
Sabino, Figurine, Barn Owl, Frosted, Perched On Stump, 4 1/2 In. 55.00
Sabino, Figurine, Butterfly, Open Wings, Signed, 2 3/4 In. 22.00
Sabino, Figurine, Butterfly, 6 In. X 4 1/2 In. .... 60.00 To 95.00
Sabino, Figurine, Cat, Signed, 2 In. .... 17.00 To 19.00
Sabino, Figurine, Cupid, 2 In. .... 15.80 To 17.00
Sabino, Figurine, Dragonfly, Signed, 6 In. .... 65.00 To 73.00
Sabino, Figurine, Draped Nude, 7 3/4 In. 155.00
Sabino, Figurine, Elephant, Signed, 2 3/8 In. 17.00
Sabino, Figurine, Fish, 2 In. 25.00
Sabino, Figurine, Frosted Owl On Stump, 4 1/2 In. .... 55.00 To 60.00
Sabino, Figurine, Hen, 3 1/2 In. 26.00
Sabino, Figurine, Leaping Gazelle, 7 X 4 1/2 In. .... 55.00 To 62.00
Sabino, Figurine, Madonna, 3 In. .... 21.00 To 25.00
Sabino, Figurine, Mouse, Signed, 3 In. .... 39.00 To 50.00
Sabino, Figurine, Owl, 4 1/2 In. .... 49.00 To 54.00
Sabino, Figurine, Pekingese Dog, 3 1/2 X 2 3/4 In. 85.00
Sabino, Figurine, Pekingese, Begging, Signed, 2 In. .... 17.50 To 25.00
Sabino, Figurine, Rabbit, Signed, 1 1/4 X 2 In. 22.00
Sabino, Figurine, Rooster, 3 3/4 In. 27.00
Sabino, Figurine, Scotty, Signed, 3 X 1/2 X 4 3/4 In. 45.00
Sabino, Figurine, Snail, Signed, 3 In. .... 18.00 To 19.00
Sabino, Figurine, Squirrel, 3 In. 26.00
Sabino, Figurine, Swan, Signed, 1 3/4 In. 17.00
Sabino, Figurine, Three Birds In Flight, Signed, 5 1/2 In. 125.00
Sabino, Knife Rest, Duck 17.50
Sabino, Plate, Colorful Oyster And Clamshells, Paris, 6 In. 65.00
Sabino, Plate, Goldfish, Opalescent, 9 1/2 In. 100.00
Sabino, Vase, Beehive, Large 119.00
Sabino, Vase, Parrots In Relief, Clear & Frosted, Green Staining, 8 1/4 In. 85.00

Salopian ware was made by the Caughley Factory of England during the
eighteenth century. The early pieces were in blue and white with some colored
decorations. Many of the pieces called Salopian are elaborate
color-transfer decorated tablewares made during the late nineteenth century.
Salopian, see also Caughley
Salt & Pepper, see Pressed Glass, Porcelain, etc.

Salt glaze is a hard, shiny glaze that was developed for pottery during the
eighteenth century. It is still being made.
Salt Glaze, Bowl, Blue White, Wedding Band Pattern, 11 In. 55.00
Salt Glaze, Crock, Cobalt Sunflower, Eared, 4 Gallon, J.Burger, Jr., 7 X 7 In. 65.00
Salt Glaze, Crock, Covered, Embossed Blue & Gray, Daisy, 10 In. 50.00
Salt Glaze, Figurine, Boy With Accordion & Dog, 4 In. 12.00
Salt Glaze, Jug, Cream, Blue Basket Weave Bottom, England 18.00
Salt Glaze, Jug, Gray, Cobalt Impressed Wm.Radam's Microbe Killer Co., 1885 .... 39.00
Salt Glaze, Jug, The Gypsies, White, By Alcock, 1830, 8 3/4 In. 145.00

Salt Glaze, Pitcher, Blue & Gray, 9 X 8 In.	115.00
Salt Glaze, Pitcher, Buttermilk, Barleycorn, 1856, 2 Quart	65.00
Salt Glaze, Pitcher, Dated 1842, Embossed Holly & Scrolls, 3 Graduated	135.00
Salt Glaze, Pitcher, Fawn Deer, 8 X 5 1/2 In.	65.00
Salt Glaze, Pitcher, Parlor Scene On Both Sides, Pewter Lid	86.00
Salt Glaze, Pitcher, Pewter Lid, Parlor Scene	86.00
Salt Glaze, Pitcher, The Gleaners, Registry Mark, England, C.1858, 10 1/2 In.	100.00
Salt Glaze, Teapot, Birds Flying Among Trees, Registration Mark	175.00
Salt Glaze, Teapot, Blue And White Decoration	18.50
Sampler, see Textile, Sampler	

Samson and Company, a French firm specializing in the reproduction of collectible wares of many countries and periods, was founded in Paris in the early nineteenth century. Chelsea, Meissen, Famille Verte, and Oriental Lowestoft are some of the wares that have been reproduced by the company. The company uses a variety of marks to distinguish its reproductions. It is still in operation.

Samson, Bottle, Cologne, Rose Pompadour	45.00
Samson, Figurine, Cockatoo, Yellow On White, Blue Underglaze Mark, 18 In.	275.00
Samson, Salt, Enamel Decoration Inside & Out, Chinese Export Style	37.00
Sand Babies, Creamer, Royal Bayreuth, Black Mark, 4 In.	85.00
Sand Babies, Pitcher, Royal Bayreuth, Blue Mark, 4 1/4 In.	85.00

Sandwich glass is any one of the myriad types of glass made by the Boston and Sandwich Glass Works in Sandwich, Massachusetts, between 1825 and 1888. It is often very difficult to be sure whether a piece was really made at the Sandwich factory because so many types were made there and similar pieces were made at other glass factories. The McK numbers refer to the book "American Glass" by George P. and Helen McKearin.

Sandwich Glass, see also Pressed Glass, etc.
Sandwich Glass, Cup Plate, see Cup Plate

Sandwich Glass, Basket, Pink Cased, Ruffled Edge, Amber Thorn Handle & Trim	125.00
Sandwich Glass, Bottle, Scent, Opalescent, Flint	30.00
Sandwich Glass, Bottle, Vinegar, Blown, Original Stopper, 7 In., Pair	125.00
Sandwich Glass, Bottle, Vinegar, Blue, Tam-O-Shanter Stopper	150.00
Sandwich Glass, Bowl, Lacy, Oak Leaf, 9 1/4 In.	165.00
Sandwich Glass, Bowl, Lacy, Princess Feather, 7 1/2 In.	38.00
Sandwich Glass, Bowl, Oval, Horn Of Plenty, 8 X 5 1/2 In.	150.00
Sandwich Glass, Bowl, Plume Oval, Lacy, Double Acorn, 8 1/2 In.	75.00
Sandwich Glass, Bowl, Princess Feather, Lacy, Silvery Brilliance, 8 1/2 In.	125.00
Sandwich Glass, Bowl, Roman Rosette, 6 In.	56.00
Sandwich Glass, Bowl, Sapphire Blue Loop, 5 1/2 In.	375.00
Sandwich Glass, Bowl, Scalloped, Lacy, Midwestern, 9 X 6 1/2 In.	100.00
Sandwich Glass, Bowl, Tulip & Acanthus Leaf, Lacy, 5 1/2 In.	35.00
Sandwich Glass, Cake Stand, Blown-Molded Top, Pressed Base	225.00
Sandwich Glass, Cake Stand, Clear, Blown Molded Top	225.00
Sandwich Glass, Candlestick, Camphor, Petal Top, 7 In.	38.00
Sandwich Glass, Candlestick, Canary Dolphin, Double Step Base, Pair	875.00
Sandwich Glass, Candlestick, Clambroth, Dolphin, Flint	30.00
Sandwich Glass, Candlestick, Clambroth, Sanded Finish, Pair, 7 1/4 In.	165.00
Sandwich Glass, Candlestick, Crucifix, Opalescent, Flint, 12 1/2 In.	55.00
Sandwich Glass, Candlestick, Crucifix, 10 In., Pair	95.00
Sandwich Glass, Candlestick, Dolphin, Clambroth	325.00
Sandwich Glass, Candlestick, Dolphin, Double Base, Canary Yellow	250.00
Sandwich Glass, Candlestick, Dolphin, Double Pedestal Base, Flint, 10 In.	195.00
Sandwich Glass, Candlestick, Dolphin, Opaque White Base, Blue Petal Socket	475.00
Sandwich Glass, Candlestick, Dolphin, Stepped Pedestal	150.00
Sandwich Glass, Candlestick, Figural, Canary, Dolphin, Double Step Base, Pair	875.00
Sandwich Glass, Candlestick, Opaque White Hexagon Base, Top Blue, 10 In.	300.00
Sandwich Glass, Candlestick, Peacock's-Eye Socket, Paw Foot Base, Pair	775.00
Sandwich Glass, Candlestick, Petal & Loop, Vaseline, 7 In., Pair	250.00
Sandwich Glass, Candlestick, Petal Socket, Hexagon Base, Amethyst, Pair	900.00
Sandwich Glass, Celery, Ivy, Flint	110.00
Sandwich Glass, Chamberstick, Broad Rib, Applied Loop Handle, Jade Green	450.00
Sandwich Glass, Champagne, Diamond Thumbprint, Flint, 5 1/4 In.	200.00

Sandwich Glass, Compote, Leaf, Leaf Patterned Pedestal, 8 In.	125.00
Sandwich Glass, Compote, Tulip Top, Loop Base, Large	150.00
Sandwich Glass, Cordial, Diamond Thumbprint, Flint, 4 1/4 In.	195.00
Sandwich Glass, Creamer, Miniature, Lacy, 1 1/4 In.	95.00
Sandwich Glass, Creamer, Opaque, Silver-Blue	750.00
Sandwich Glass, Creamer, Waffle, Applied Tooled Handle, 6 1/4 In.	85.00
Sandwich Glass, Decanter, Diamond Thumbprint, Flint, Quart, 10 1/2 In.	135.00
Sandwich Glass, Dish, Butter, Covered, Twig Handle, Signed, 1918	225.00
Sandwich Glass, Dish, Cheese, Blow Dome, Cut Tear Drop Finial, C.1870	95.00
Sandwich Glass, Dish, Frosted Pheasant, Oval, Covered	165.00
Sandwich Glass, Dish, Sauce, Stippled Rays, Lacy, Clear	10.00
Sandwich Glass, Drawer Pull, Rosette Decoration, Set	65.00
Sandwich Glass, Drawer Pull, 6 Petal, Flint, 2 1/4 In., Set Of 3	18.00
Sandwich Glass, Finger Bowl, Greek Key, 4 3/4 In.	15.00
Sandwich Glass, Goblet, Grape Band Variant	25.00
Sandwich Glass, Holder, Spill, Star, Flint	60.00
Sandwich Glass, Holder, String, Applied Cobalt Blue Rim, Collar	135.00
Sandwich Glass, Honey, Lacy	10.00
Sandwich Glass, Jar, Apothecary, Cover, Berry Finial, 14 In.	45.00
Sandwich Glass, Jar, Cover, Overlay, Cut To Clear, Dark Green, 6 X 3 1/2 In.	150.00
Sandwich Glass, Jar, Covered, Dark Green, Cut To Clear, 6 X 3 1/2 In.	125.00
Sandwich Glass, Jar, Pomade, Black Amethyst, 3 3/4 In.	95.00
Sandwich Glass, Jar, Pomade, Pewter Cover, Fiery Opalescent, Circular	125.00
Sandwich Glass, Jar, Salve, Cobalt & Pewter Lid	110.00
Sandwich Glass, Knob, Pewter Shank, Blown, Set Of 4	32.00
Sandwich Glass, Lamp, see Lamp	
Sandwich Glass, Lamp, Bull's-Eye, Brass Stem, Marble Base	80.00
Sandwich Glass, Lamp, Pressed, Blown, Stepped Base, 6 1/2 In.	70.00
Sandwich Glass, Lamp, Pressed, Tulip Font, Column Base, 12 In.	165.00
Sandwich Glass, Lamp, Whale Oil, Stepped Base, 2 Eagles Engraved On Font	450.00
Sandwich Glass, Master Salt, Lime Green, Scalloped Footed Base, Finecut	35.00
Sandwich Glass, Mug, Fighting Cats, Miniature, 2 1/8 In.	25.00
Sandwich Glass, Pitcher, Bladder, Overshot, White, Proof, 11 1/2 In.	165.00
Sandwich Glass, Pitcher, Blue, Amber Applied Handle, Bulbous Body	165.00
Sandwich Glass, Pitcher, Blue, Applied Amber Handle, 7 In.	95.00
Sandwich Glass, Pitcher, Miniature, Overshot, 4 1/2 In.	45.00
Sandwich Glass, Pitcher, Spun Rope Handle, Raspberry Buttons	195.00
Sandwich Glass, Pitcher, Water, Thumbprint, Royal Blue, Rope Handle	142.00
Sandwich Glass, Pitcher, Water, Thumbprint, Sapphire Blue, 8 1/2 X 6 1/2 In.	165.00
Sandwich Glass, Plate, Cake, Beehive, Ring, Flint, Beehives, Thistles, Stars	165.00
Sandwich Glass, Plate, Hairpin, 6 In.	120.00
Sandwich Glass, Plate, Lacy, Miniature, Concentric Rings, 2 1/2 In.	85.00
Sandwich Glass, Plate, Lacy, Shell Pattern, 6 In.	32.00
Sandwich Glass, Plate, Toddy, Grapevine With Harp, 4 1/2 In.	25.00
Sandwich Glass, Plate, Toddy, Peacock's-Eye With Scroll, 5 In.	40.00
Sandwich Glass, Plate, Toddy, Scotch Plaid	85.00
Sandwich Glass, Plate, Yellow, Horn Of Plenty, 6 In.	450.00
Sandwich Glass, Rose Bowl, Melon, Ribbed, Rubena, 5 In.	195.00
Sandwich Glass, Salt, Chariot Race	65.00
Sandwich Glass, Salt, Cover, Acorn Finial, Opaque White Sawtooth	225.00
Sandwich Glass, Salt, Flattened Diamond, 2 1/2 In.	8.00
Sandwich Glass, Salt, Geometric, Waffle Base, Amber, 3 1/4 X 2 1/2 In.	95.00
Sandwich Glass, Salt, Lacy, Flint	65.00 To 120.00
Sandwich Glass, Sauce, Lacy, Peacock's-Eye, 4 1/4 In.	20.00
Sandwich Glass, Sauce, Lacy, Princess Feather, 4 1/2 In.	15.00
Sandwich Glass, Sauce, Princess Feather, 5 1/2 In.	60.00
Sandwich Glass, Sauce, Stippled Bull's-Eye	35.00
Sandwich Glass, Saucer, Child-Size, Lacy, Blue	75.00
Sandwich Glass, Spooner, Star	30.00
Sandwich Glass, Sugar & Creamer, Individual, Oval	39.50
Sandwich Glass, Sugar, Covered, Diamond Thumbprint	145.00
Sandwich Glass, Sugar, Covered, Gothic, Flint	150.00
Sandwich Glass, Tieback, Amethyst, Pair	25.00
Sandwich Glass, Tieback, Opalescent, 4 1/2 In., Pair	75.00
Sandwich Glass, Tumbler, Water, Diamond Thumbprint, Flint, 3 In.	125.00

Sandwich Glass, Tureen, Miniature, Cover, Canary, Lacy, Paneled Undertray	775.00
Sandwich Glass, Vase, Canary Yellow, Satin Swirl, 8 In.	150.00
Sandwich Glass, Vase, Canary, Flared Rim, Blown, Footed, 6 1/2 In.	275.00
Sandwich Glass, Vase, Clear, Marble Base	125.00
Sandwich Glass, Vase, Loop, Amethyst, 6 1/4 In., Pair	1250.00
Sandwich Glass, Vase, Multicolor Spangled Glass, Flint, 10 1/2 In.	60.00
Sandwich Glass, Vase, Opaque Blue, Gold Decoration, Ruffled Rim, Pair	135.00
Sandwich Glass, Vase, Stick, Lacy Socket, Waterfall Base, 5 1/4 In.	175.00
Sandwich Glass, Vase, Swirl, Canary Yellow, Satin, 8 In.	150.00
Sandwich Glass, Vase, Trumpet, Emerald Green, Blown, Expanded Ribbed, Ruffled	325.00
Sandwich Glass, Vase, Victorian, Ruffled Rim, Gold, Opaque Blue, Pair	135.00
Sanwich Glass, Bowl, Peacock's-Eye, Rayed, 6 In.	45.00

Sarreguemines   *Sarreguemines pottery was first made in Lorraine, France, about 1770.*
Most of the pieces found today date from the late nineteenth century.

Sarreguemines, see also Kate Greenaway

Sarreguemines, Jar, Covered, Country Scene, 3 3/4 X 3 1/2 In.	15.00
Sarreguemines, Jug, Character, 8 1/2 In.	100.00
Sarreguemines, Pitcher, Owl, Rose Glazed Interior, 7 1/2 In.	45.00
Sarreguemines, Plate, Childrens' Scene	22.50
Sarreguemines, Plate, Courting Scene	22.50
Sarreguemines, Plate, Music, Ch.Lecocq, La Fille De Mme.Angot, 8 1/2 In.	22.00
Sarreguemines, Toby Mug, Double Headed, 8 1/2 In.	45.00

Satin glass is a late-nineteenth-century art glass. It has a dull finish
that is caused by a hydrofluoric acid vapor treatment. Satin glass was made
in many colors and sometimes had applied decorations.

Satin Glass, Atomizer, Decorated, Pink	95.00
Satin Glass, Basket, Camphor Glass Handle, Gold Enamel Floral, Rose, 8 In.	250.00
Satin Glass, Basket, Cased Butterscotch Over White, Frosted Edge, 5 In.	65.00
Satin Glass, Basket, Handled, 11 In.	55.00
Satin Glass, Basket, Light Blue, 8 In.	65.00
Satin Glass, Basket, Ribbon, Yellow-Green, 6 In.	50.00
Satin Glass, Basket, White Daisies, 10 In.	75.00
Satin Glass, Basket, White To Rose Pink, Braid Handle, 6 X 7 1/2 In.	225.00
Satin Glass, Basket, White, Blue Lined, Hobnail, Applied Handle, 6 1/8 In.	105.00
Satin Glass, Biscuit Barrel, Flowers, Silver Bail & Lid, Blue, White	125.00
Satin Glass, Biscuit, Jar, Enameled Posies On 4 Panels, Silver Plate Collar	125.00
Satin Glass, Biscuit, Jar, Painted Flowers, Silver Rim, Bail & Lid	85.00
Satin Glass, Biscuit, Jar, Red, Beaded Drape	138.00
Satin Glass, Biscuit, Jar, Tufted Puffy Design, Silver Top, Pink	175.00
Satin Glass, Bottle, Barber, Pink, Stopper	85.00
Satin Glass, Bottle, Perfume, Pink, Tapered, 5 1/2 In.	12.00
Satin Glass, Bottle, Perfume, Spray, Pink, Paris Ribbon, 7 X 3 In.	15.00
Satin Glass, Bowl, Blue, White Ribbon Candy Trim, 8 In.	95.00
Satin Glass, Bowl, Candy, Mother-Of-Pearl, Butterscotch Raindrop	150.00
Satin Glass, Bowl, Diamond-Quilted, Blue, Crimped Sides, 5 1/2 X 3 1/2 In.	110.00
Satin Glass, Bowl, Diamond-Quilted, Mother-Of-Pearl, Folded Sides, 6 In.	110.00
Satin Glass, Bowl, Embossed Swans, Footed, Scalloped, 13 1/2 In.	45.00
Satin Glass, Bowl, Pink & White End-Of-Day, Rounded Panels, 6 1/2 In.	90.00
Satin Glass, Bowl, Pink Overlay, Satin Finish, 11 1/2 In.Diameter	245.00
Satin Glass, Bowl, Rose Mother-Of-Pearl, Ruffled Edge, 5 1/2 In.	95.00
Satin Glass, Bowl, Rose To Pink, White Lining, Crimped Top, 4 In.	60.00
Satin Glass, Bowl, Rose, Blue Over White, 9 X 4 In.	70.00
Satin Glass, Box, Cobalt, Gold & White Enameling, Hinged	57.50
Satin Glass, Box, Powder, Pink Nudes	9.50
Satin Glass, Bride's Basket, Blue, Enameled, Ruffled, Triangular, 7 In.	67.00
Satin Glass, Bride's Basket, Deep Rose, Pleated Rim, Oblong, 9 1/4 X 7 In.	395.00
Satin Glass, Bride's Bowl, Blue, Applied Multicolor Floral, 4 1/4 X 9 In.	195.00
Satin Glass, Butter, Blown-Out Diamond-Quilted Top, Frosted Finial Bottom	250.00
Satin Glass, Candlestick, Black, 7 1/2 In.	25.00
Satin Glass, Castor, Pickle, Cream Color, Floral Decoration	200.00
Satin Glass, Castor, Pickle, Fireglow, Beige Decorations, Fancy Frame	225.00
Satin Glass, Castor, Pickle, Red, Bulbous Insert, Footed Frame	225.00
Satin Glass, Celery, Bubble Lattice, Blue	60.00

Satin Glass, Compote, Black, Twisted Stem, 7 In.	22.00
Satin Glass, Compote, Rose Shading To White, Hallmarked Pedestal, 7 1/2 In.	155.00
Satin Glass, Console Set, Deep Pink, Quilted Center, 3 Piece	49.00
Satin Glass, Cookie Jar, Beaded Drape, Dark Red, Silver Plate Bail & Cover	185.00
Satin Glass, Cookie Jar, Glossy White Cased, Floral, Silver Cover, 6 3/4 In.	155.00
Satin Glass, Cracker Jar, Blue, Bead, Drape, Silver Rim, Bail, Lid	235.00
Satin Glass, Cracker Jar, Cream, Enameled Panels, Silver Plated Collar	168.00
Satin Glass, Cracker Jar, Cream, Enameled Posies, Silver Plated Fittings	135.00
Satin Glass, Cracker Jar, Daisy, Pink, Ornate Silver Top	275.00
Satin Glass, Cracker Jar, Diamond-Quilted, Pink	125.00
Satin Glass, Cracker Jar, Florette, Bird Finial, Bail Handle, Lid, Apricot	155.00
Satin Glass, Cracker Jar, Florette, Pink, Cased, Silver Cover	90.00
Satin Glass, Cracker Jar, Florette, Red, Silver Rim, Cover, & Bail	150.00
Satin Glass, Cracker Jar, Pink Tufted, Silver Plated Top	160.00
Satin Glass, Cracker Jar, Pink, Cover, Florette	230.00
Satin Glass, Cracker Jar, Pink, Daisy, Silver Lid, Sears Label	250.00
Satin Glass, Cracker Jar, Roses, Van Bergh Top & Bail, Green, White, Pink	95.00
Satin Glass, Dish, Berry, White Cut Bottom, Yellow Clear Scalloped Rim	15.00
Satin Glass, Dish, Hen, Covered, Green	18.00
Satin Glass, Dish, Sweet Meat, Silver Holder, Victorian, Covered	200.00
Satin Glass, Dish, White, Blue, Cased, Ruffled, 9 1/2 In.	85.00
Satin Glass, Egg, Green, Diamond-Quilted, Gold Stand, 5 In.	45.00
Satin Glass, Epergne, 1 Lily, Gold Wash Cherub Holder	195.00
Satin Glass, Ewer, Blue Overlay, Flowers, Frosted Handles, 9 3/4 In., Pair	175.00
Satin Glass, Ewer, Butterfly & Flowers, Blue Enamel, 9 X 6 In.	95.00
Satin Glass, Ewer, Cased, Floral, Blue, 9 1/2 In.	85.00
Satin Glass, Ewer, Dark To Light Blue, Clear Handle, Floral, 9 In., Pair	325.00
Satin Glass, Ewer, Floral Design, Pink, 10 In., Pair	145.00
Satin Glass, Ewer, Mother-Of-Pearl, Apricot To White Herringbone, 9 In.	300.00
Satin Glass, Ewer, Mother-Of-Pearl, Cerulean Blue, Crystal Thread, 12 1/2 In.	500.00
Satin Glass, Ewer, Pastel Green, Enameled Floral, Gold Stems, 9 1/2 In., Pair	245.00
Satin Glass, Ewer, Peach Overlay, Blue Enameled Flowers, 8 1/2 In.	95.00
Satin Glass, Ewer, Pink To Rose Swirl, Frosted Handle, White Cased Interior	55.00
Satin Glass, Ewer, Robin Blue, Camphor Satin Twisted Rope Handle, 10 In.	80.00
Satin Glass, Jar, Powder, Pink, Elephant Finial, 6 1/2 In.	45.00
Satin Glass, Jar, Sweetmeat, Beaded Coralene, 5 In.	225.00
Satin Glass, Jar, Tobacco, Detailed Boar, Pig On Lid, 9 X 9 In.	125.00
Satin Glass, Lamp Base, Gone With The Wind, Red, Kerosene Font, Medallions	120.00
Satin Glass, Lamp Base, Pink, Raindrop, Miniature	42.00
Satin Glass, Lamp Base, Red, Ripple Pattern, Miniature	50.00
Satin Glass, Lamp, Beaded Drape, Pink, Miniature	265.00
Satin Glass, Lamp, Desk, Blue, Quilted, Swirl Base, 19 In.	250.00
Satin Glass, Lamp, Fairy, Apple Green, Embossed Swirl, Clarke Base, 3 1/2 In.	95.00
Satin Glass, Lamp, Fairy, Castle, Blue	295.00
Satin Glass, Lamp, Fairy, Deep Pink, Cut Velvet Honeycomb, Clear Base, 5 In.	198.00
Satin Glass, Lamp, Lavender, Diamond Pattern, Miniature	550.00
Satin Glass, Lamp, Miniature, Melon Ribbed Ball Shade, Font Nutmeg Burner	95.00
Satin Glass, Lamp, Miniature, Plume Pattern, Pink, Chimney	125.00
Satin Glass, Lamp, Mottled Base, Miniature	195.00
Satin Glass, Lamp, Pansy, Ball Shade, Melon Ribbed Base, Pink, Miniature	350.00
Satin Glass, Lamp, Peg, Blue, Rolled Gilt Base	350.00
Satin Glass, Lamp, Pink Mottled, Miniature	55.00
Satin Glass, Lamp, Red, Drape, Miniature	275.00
Satin Glass, Lamp, Red, Miniature	195.00
Satin Glass, Lamp, Rose To Pink, Cased, Miniature	395.00
Satin Glass, Lamp, Tulip Shade, Miniature	125.00
Satin Glass, Lamp, Turquoise, Opalescent, Flint Base, 9 In.	275.00
Satin Glass, Pin Tray, 4 X 8 1/2 In.	8.50
Satin Glass, Pitcher, Diamond-Quilted, Blue Mother Of Pearl Camphor Handle	195.00
Satin Glass, Pitcher, Diamond-Quilted, Camphor Handle, Pink	350.00
Satin Glass, Pitcher, Gray-Green, Blue Circles, Applied Handle, 9 In.	35.00
Satin Glass, Pitcher, Mother-Of-Pearl, Blue To White, Ruffled, 8 3/4 In.	295.00
Satin Glass, Pitcher, Pink To Raspberry, Polished Pontil, 7 1/2 In. X 5 In.	155.00
Satin Glass, Pitcher, Pink, Guttate, 5 In.	85.00
Satin Glass, Pitcher, Pink, Swirl, Bulbous, Applied Handle, 6 1/2 In.	48.00

Satin Glass, Pitcher, Rainbow Mother-Of-Pearl, Camphor Handle, 5 1/2 In. 750.00
Satin Glass, Pitcher, Rose Mother-Of-Pearl, Peacock's-Eye, Thorn Handle 350.00
Satin Glass, Pitcher, Water, Blue, Mother-Of-Pearl, Raindrop 400.00
Satin Glass, Pitcher, Water, Blue, Mother-Of-Pearl, Satin Thorn Handle 360.00
Satin Glass, Pitcher, Water, Florette, Camphor Handle, Pink 275.00
Satin Glass, Pitcher, Water, Florette, Frosted Applied Handle 195.00
Satin Glass, Pitcher, Water, Florette, Pink, Bulbous, Frosted Handle, 7 In. 200.00
Satin Glass, Pitcher, Water, Mother-Of-Pearl, Blue Raindrop 390.00
Satin Glass, Rose Bowl, Blue Cased, White Lined, Crimped Top, Blown, 4 In. 65.00
Satin Glass, Rose Bowl, Blue Overlay, Frosted Handles, Bird, 6 In. 135.00
Satin Glass, Rose Bowl, Blue To White, White Cased, Gold Enameling, 17 In. 75.00
Satin Glass, Rose Bowl, Blue To White, 4 1/2 X 13 1/2 In. 32.00
Satin Glass, Rose Bowl, Blue, Cased, Enameled Florals 45.00
Satin Glass, Rose Bowl, Blue, Diamond-Quilted, Mother-Of-Pearl, 3 1/2 In. 85.00
Satin Glass, Rose Bowl, Blue, Diamond-Quilted, White Lining, Crimp Top, 3 In. 145.00
Satin Glass, Rose Bowl, Blue, Enamel Flowers, Medium Size 75.00
Satin Glass, Rose Bowl, Butterfly, Flowers, Blue, 4-Crimp Top, 5 1/8 In. 135.00
Satin Glass, Rose Bowl, Crimped, Ribbon, Mother-Of-Pearl, Lining, Brown, 5 In. 295.00
Satin Glass, Rose Bowl, Deep Coral Fading To Pale Pink, 4 X 4 In. 75.00
Satin Glass, Rose Bowl, Deep To Light Blue, Shell Design, 5 In. 65.00
Satin Glass, Rose Bowl, Diamond-Quilted, Deep Rose, 3 1/4 In. 165.00
Satin Glass, Rose Bowl, Enameled Pink & Blue Wildflowers, 5 X 2 1/2 In. 158.00
Satin Glass, Rose Bowl, Fluted Rim, Fan Design, Blue & White, 4 1/2 In. 65.00
Satin Glass, Rose Bowl, Frosted Soft Pink To Apricot Base, 6 In. 38.00
Satin Glass, Rose Bowl, Lemon Shading To White At Base 65.00
Satin Glass, Rose Bowl, Light To Dark Pink, Pinched Scalloped Top, 6 In. 45.00
Satin Glass, Rose Bowl, Mother-Of-Pearl, Blue, Crimped Edges, 4 In. 295.00
Satin Glass, Rose Bowl, Pink, Crimped Top, 3 1/2 X 4 In. 35.00
Satin Glass, Rose Bowl, Pink, Shell & Seaweed, 3 1/2 X 4 3/4 In. 65.00
Satin Glass, Rose Bowl, Robin's-Egg Blue, Enameled Flowers 75.00
Satin Glass, Rose Bowl, Rose To Pink, Flowers, Gold Leaves, Crimped, 4 In. 95.00
Satin Glass, Rose Bowl, Ruffled Collar Turned Inward, Victorian, Yellow 55.00
Satin Glass, Rose Bowl, Seashell, Blue, Gold & White Enameling, 4 X 4 In. 150.00
Satin Glass, Rose Bowl, Shell & Seaweed, Light Yellow To Gold, 5 X 6 1/2 In. 235.00
Satin Glass, Rose Bowl, Shell & Seaweed, Pink, 3 1/2 In. 65.00
Satin Glass, Rose Bowl, Shell & Seaweed, Yellow 75.00
Satin Glass, Rose Bowl, Shell Design, Enamel Flowers, 5 1/2 In., Diameter 165.00
Satin Glass, Rose Bowl, Shell, Yellow To White, 3 3/4 In. 65.00
Satin Glass, Salt & Pepper, Diamond-Quilted, Pink 225.00
Satin Glass, Salt & Pepper, Hand-Painted, Melon Ribbed 85.00
Satin Glass, Salt & Pepper, White With Florals, Melon Ribbed 50.00
Satin Glass, Saltshaker, Cranberry 85.00
Satin Glass, Saltshaker, Green 18.00
Satin Glass, Shade, Miniature, Blue 55.00
Satin Glass, Shade, Pink, 5 1/4 X 7 1/2 In. 48.00
Satin Glass, Shade, Shaped Like Rose, Pink, Set Of 2 .... 100.00
Satin Glass, Sugar Shaker, Guttate, Pink .... 122.00 To 135.00
Satin Glass, Sugar Shaker, Pillar, Pink Spatter 75.00
Satin Glass, Sugar, Red, Beaded Drape, Silver Plated, Covered, Handled 138.00
Satin Glass, Syrup, Cone, Pink 150.00
Satin Glass, Toothpick, Enameled Floral, Raspberry, Flair & Ruffle Top 75.00
Satin Glass, Toothpick, Pastel Blue, Cream, & Pink, Enameled Posies, 2 1/2 In. 85.00
Satin Glass, Toothpick, Pastel, Enameled Posies 40.00
Satin Glass, Toothpick, White To Pink, Swirled Beaded Top, Daisies, Enameled 100.00
Satin Glass, Tumbler, Diamond-Quilted, Pink 75.00
Satin Glass, Vase, Apricot To Pink, Mother Of Pearl, Diamond-Quilted, 6 In. 90.00
Satin Glass, Vase, Blossom Shape, Blue To White, Florals In Enamel, 11 In. 80.00
Satin Glass, Vase, Blown Poppies, Black, Bulbous, 8 In. 38.00
Satin Glass, Vase, Blue Cased, Blossom-Shaped Top, Enameled Florals, 11 In. 80.00
Satin Glass, Vase, Blue Overlay, White Lined, Frosted Foot, Floral, Pair 185.00
Satin Glass, Vase, Blue-Gray, Windmill Scene, 6 1/2 In. 42.00
Satin Glass, Vase, Blue, Cased, Enameled Floral, Applied Frosted Edge, 10 In. 125.00
Satin Glass, Vase, Blue, Diamond-Quilted, Crimped, Ruffled Top, 5 1/2 In. 70.00
Satin Glass, Vase, Blue, Mother-Of-Pearl, Teardrop Pattern, 7 In., Pair 225.00
Satin Glass, Vase, Blue, Yellow Coralene Seaweed, Bulbous, 8 1/2 In. 350.00

Satin Glass, Vase, Rose, Fluted, Pink, White, Pewter Holder, 9 In.

Satin Glass, Vase, Bud, Black, Crimped Top, Pair	35.00
Satin Glass, Vase, Bud, Mother-Of-Pearl, Bridal White, 5 1/2 In., Pair	135.00
Satin Glass, Vase, Cased, Bulbous Melon Body, Pink To Peach, Enameled, 10 In.	125.00
Satin Glass, Vase, Cut Velvet Stem, Blue, 6 In.	140.00
Satin Glass, Vase, Deep To Light Teal Blue, White Lining, 10 In.	135.00
Satin Glass, Vase, Diamond-Quilted, Mother-Of-Pearl, 10 1/2 In., Pair	325.00
Satin Glass, Vase, Diamond-Quilted, Pink, 6 1/4 In.	145.00
Satin Glass, Vase, Diamond-Quilted, Ruffled Rim, Rose, White, Cased, 8 In.	85.00
Satin Glass, Vase, Diamond-Quilted, Ruffled Top, 6 1/4 In.	135.00
Satin Glass, Vase, Enameled Bird & Flowers, Green	26.00
Satin Glass, Vase, Enameled Hummingbird, Bulbous Base, 5 In.	45.00
Satin Glass, Vase, Floral, Enameled, Footed, 10 In., Pair	128.00
Satin Glass, Vase, Floral, Raised Gold Outline, Leaves, Vines, Dimpled, 11 In.	300.00
Satin Glass, Vase, Herringbone, Mother-Of-Pearl French Blue, 8 In.	250.00
Satin Glass, Vase, Herringbone, Mother-Of-Pearl, Blue, White Lined, 5 In.	125.00
Satin Glass, Vase, Herringbone, Mother-Of-Pearl, Light To Dark Blue, 7 In.	190.00
Satin Glass, Vase, Light Blue To Bluish White, Blossom Shape, Floral, 11 In.	80.00
Satin Glass, Vase, Light Blue, Ruffled Top, 6 In., Pair	125.00
Satin Glass, Vase, Lime Green, Gold Enamel, Cranberry Inside, Cased, 7 In.	195.00
Satin Glass, Vase, Melon Rib, White Lining, Raindrop Pattern, 20 X 8 In.	285.00
Satin Glass, Vase, Mother-Of-Pearl, Diamond Pattern, Blue, 6 1/2 In., Pair	500.00
Satin Glass, Vase, Mother-Of-Pearl, Diamond-Quilted, Crimped, Ruffled, 8 In.	125.00
Satin Glass, Vase, Mother-Of-Pearl, Flower-Like Ruffled Top, 3 1/2 In.	340.00
Satin Glass, Vase, Mother-Of-Pearl, Peach, Applied Frosted Binding, 5 In.	190.00
Satin Glass, Vase, Mother-Of-Pearl, Serpent Rigaree	165.00
Satin Glass, Vase, Mother-Of-Pearl, Yellow, Camphor Feet, 6 In.	125.00
Satin Glass, Vase, Pale Blue Cased In Darker Blue, Ruffled Top, 6 1/2 In.	85.00
Satin Glass, Vase, Pink, Diamond-Quilted, Polished Pontil, 6 In.	145.00
Satin Glass, Vase, Pink, Mother-Of-Pearl, Quilted, 10 1/2 In.	225.00
Satin Glass, Vase, Pinkish White To Deep Pink Top, 5 1/4 In.	100.00
Satin Glass, Vase, Popcorn Pattern, Cranberry To Light, 8-Crimp Top, 8 In.	325.00
Satin Glass, Vase, Rainbow, Quilted, Mother-Of-Pearl, 6 In.	595.00 To 825.00
Satin Glass, Vase, Raindrops, Blue, 10 In.	88.00
Satin Glass, Vase, Raspberry To White, Cased, Applied Trim, 6 3/4 In.	45.00
Satin Glass, Vase, Raspberry, Diamond-Quilted, 10 X 5 In.	89.00
Satin Glass, Vase, Ribbon, Turned Down Ruffled Top, Yellow Stripes, 6 In.	95.00
Satin Glass, Vase, Rose, Flared, Scalloped, Mother-Of-Pearl, Chartreuse, Green	195.00
Satin Glass, Vase, Rose, Fluted, Pink, White, Pewter Holder, 9 In. ...... *Illus*	87.50
Satin Glass, Vase, Ruffled Cranberry Cased Top, White, 8 In.	38.00
Satin Glass, Vase, Ruffled Top Edge, Pedestal Foot, 14 3/4 In.	395.00
Satin Glass, Vase, Ruffled Top, Peachblow Colors From Pink To Rose, 10 In.	85.00
Satin Glass, Vase, Ruffled, Ribbed, Mother-Of-Pearl, Blue, Herringbone, 6 In.	160.00
Satin Glass, Vase, Salmon Pink Bottom To Raspberry Ruffled Top, 13 In.	175.00
Satin Glass, Vase, Salmon To Raspberry, Ruffled Top, Diamond Pattern, 13 In.	175.00
Satin Glass, Vase, Seaweed, Cased White, 5 3/8 In.	395.00
Satin Glass, Vase, Shaded Pink Overlay, White & Lavender Flower, 10 In., Pair	175.00
Satin Glass, Vase, Swirl, Mother-Of-Pearl, Rose To Pink, Bulbous, 5 In.	185.00
Satin Glass, Vase, Trumpet, Ribbed, Satin, Ruffled, Silver Plated Holder, 8 In.	99.00
Satin Glass, Vase, Tulip, Opalescent, Stourbridge Green To Blue, 6 1/2 In.	160.00
Satin Glass, Vase, Vaseline Honeycomb, 7 Footed, Pinched Inward, 4-Loop Top	99.00
Satin Glass, Vase, White To Yellow, Applied Coralene Seaweed, 4 In.	150.00

Satin Glass, Vase, White, Melon Ribbed, Blue, Pink, Gold Floral, 7 1/2 In. 150.00
Satin Glass, Vase, Yellow To White, Herringbone, Ruffled, White Lined, 5 In. 122.00
Satin Glass, Vase, Yellow To White, Jack-In-The-Pulpit, 6 In. 50.00
Satin Glass, Water Set, Blue, 7 Piece 85.00
Satin Glass, Water Set, Diamond-Quilted, Yellow, Mother-Of-Pearl, 4 Piece 460.00
    Satin Glass, Webb, see Webb

> *Satsuma is a Japanese pottery with a distinctive creamy beige crackled*
> *glaze. Most of the pieces were decorated with blue, red, green, orange, or gold.*
> *Almost all the Satsuma found today was made after 1860. Japanese faces*
> *are often a part of the decorative scheme.*

Satsuma, Berry Set, Flowers, Figures, Diapered Border, Gold, 5 Piece 135.00
Satsuma, Bottle, Figural, Meiji, C.1885, 5 In. 125.00
Satsuma, Bottle, Sake, Beige Background, Orange, Green, Gold, 5 Matching Cups 55.00
Satsuma, Bowl, Flowers, Signed By Artist, 4 1/2 In. 72.00
Satsuma, Bowl, Kwannon With Arats, 5 In. 150.00
Satsuma, Bowl, Sugar, Ivory Lid 75.00
Satsuma, Bowl, 6 People In Middle Of Bowl, Beaded Border, C.1850, Gold, 4 In. 450.00
Satsuma, Box, Dresser, Swirl, Florals, Butterflies, Enamels, Gold Trim, 5 In. 85.00
Satsuma, Box, Flower, Butterflies, Gold, Melon Shape, Covered, 1840, 3 X 5 In. 220.00
Satsuma, Box, 3 Women In Garden Cover, Flowers, Scrolls, Creamy Glaze, 5 In. 175.00
Satsuma, Brush Pot, Dragon, Scale, Oriental Figures 110.00
Satsuma, Brush Pot, Oriental Figures, 6 3/8 In. 90.00
Satsuma, Buckle, Commemorative, Opening Of Panama Canal, Hexagon, Marked, Pair 185.00
Satsuma, Buckle, Silver Mounting, Birds, Leaves, Mountains, 3 1/4 In. 135.00
Satsuma, Burner, Incense, Gold Decorated, Faces, 2 Handles, 3 Footed, 5 X 6 In. 22.50
Satsuma, Button, Hand-Painted, Scalloped, Four Women, 3/4 In. 27.50
Satsuma, Button, Oriental Mother & Child, 1 In. 20.00
Satsuma, Chocolate Set, Warriors, Late 19th Century, 9 Piece 160.00
Satsuma, Chocolate Set, Warriors, 13 Piece 285.00
Satsuma, Coffeepot, Demitasse, Portrait & Scenic Medallions, 8 In. 125.00
Satsuma, Coffeepot, Figures, Flower Finial, Signed 100.00
Satsuma, Coffeepot, Yokohama, Floral, Female Figures On Bride, Gold, 7 1/4 In. 125.00
Satsuma, Covered Urn, Oriental Decoration 35.00
Satsuma, Cup & Saucer, Black, Gods' Heads, Imperial Mark 50.00
Satsuma, Cup & Saucer, Floral, Meiji, C.1880 .... 45.00
Satsuma, Cup & Saucer, Flowers, Green Handle 25.00
Satsuma, Cup & Saucer, Hexagonal 55.00
Satsuma, Cup & Saucer, People Motif, Pastels, 14K Gold, Signed 10.00
Satsuma, Cup & Saucer, Polychrome Chrysanthemum 35.00
Satsuma, Dish, Men's Faces, Gold Trim, Footed, Imperial Mark, 1 1/4 X 4 In. 75.00
Satsuma, Figurine, Elephant, Gold, Late 19th Century, Signed, 7 X 9 In. 975.00
Satsuma, Figurine, Hotei, 8 X 7 In. 160.00
Satsuma, Figurine, Wrestler, Open Mouth, Pierced Eyes, Beaded, C.1915, 7 In. 125.00
Satsuma, Ginger Jar, Cover, War Lords, 1860 .... 75.00
Satsuma, Ginger Jar, 4 Panels, Figures, Mountains, Gold Outlined, 5 In. 105.00
Satsuma, Jar, Medallions, Dog Finial, Figural Handles, Gold, 3 Legged, 18 In. 250.00
Satsuma, Jar, Tobacco, Children At Play, 5 1/2 In. 75.00
Satsuma, Lamp, Painted Figures & Landscape, Brown, Orange, Gold 225.00
Satsuma, Lamp, Three Faces, Brass Base 50.00
Satsuma, Lunch Set, Multicolor Flowers, Bird, Butterfly, C.1850, 14 Piece 275.00
Satsuma, Pitcher & Sugar, Paneled, Flowers, Oriental Figures, Gold Outline 50.00
Satsuma, Pitcher, Bees, Hives, Butterflies, C.1865, 5 1/2 In. 265.00
Satsuma, Pitcher, Dragon Design, 12 1/2 In. 125.00
Satsuma, Plaque, Pastels & Gold, 6 In. .... 25.00 To 40.00
Satsuma, Plate, Oriental Figures Pulling Flower Cart, Gold Border, 7 1/8 In. 168.00
Satsuma, Plate, Various Insects, 9 In. 75.00
Satsuma, Saucer, Thousand Face 15.00
Satsuma, Sugar & Creamer, Warrior Scene, Footed, Melon Ribbed 50.00
Satsuma, Sugar, Children Encrusted In Gold, Covered, Pagoda Mark 14.00
Satsuma, Sugar, Foo Dog Handles 250.00
Satsuma, Tankard, Raised Beaded Dragon Design, Brown, Taisho Period, Signed 105.00
Satsuma, Tea Set, Aqua & Beige Panels, Gold Trim & Bamboo Handles, 3 Piece 155.00
Satsuma, Tea Set, Bird Bamboo Design, Gold Outlined, Red-Gold Mark, 21 Piece 220.00
Satsuma, Tea Set, Blue On Off-White, 19th Century, 11 Piece 350.00
Satsuma, Tea Set, Covered Pot, Sugar, Creamer, 6 Cups & Saucers 190.00

Satsuma, Tea Set, Dragon Decorated, Dragon-Mouth Spouts, C.1926, 3 Piece	65.00
Satsuma, Tea Set, Gold Painted Scenes Of The Orient, Gold Handles, 30 Piece	140.00
Satsuma, Tea Set, Gold, Blue On Beige, Late 9th Century, 11 Piece	350.00
Satsuma, Tea Set, Hand-Painted, Enameled, Flowers, C.1920, 15 Piece	200.00
Satsuma, Tea Set, Multicolor Flowers, Gold, Cobalt, Crackle, 15 Piece	185.00
Satsuma, Tea Set, Raised Gold & Beaded Male & Female, 14 Piece	75.00
Satsuma, Tea Set, Teapot, Creamer, Sugar, 6 Cups & Saucers, 6 Plates	375.00
Satsuma, Tea Set, Thousand Face, Dragon Handles & Spouts, 21 Piece	1250.00
Satsuma, Tea Set, Warrior's Head Decorated, Dragon Head Finial, 14 Piece	250.00
Satsuma, Teapot, Crackle Background, Brocade & Floral Sprays	65.00
Satsuma, Teapot, Gold Encrusted Children, Pagoda Mark	28.00
Satsuma, Teapot, Oriental Ladies Around Sides, Reed Handle, Orange	35.00
Satsuma, Tray, Ornate Decoration, 6-Sided, Marked Royal Satsuma, 3 3/4 In.	105.00
Satsuma, Umbrella Stand, 28 In.	1000.00
Satsuma, Urn, Handled, Raised Figures	50.00
Satsuma, Vase, Beige, Scene On Front, Flowers On Back, 12 In.	65.00
Satsuma, Vase, Blue Birds On Hawthorn Branch, 16 X 8 In.	135.00
Satsuma, Vase, Blue With Red, White, & Gold Flowers, 7 1/2 In., Pair	95.00
Satsuma, Vase, Cobalt Blue, Gilt Floral, Medallions, 3 Figures, Landscape	90.00
Satsuma, Vase, Cobalt Blue, Gilt, 2 Hand-Painted Panels, 7 1/2 In.	120.00
Satsuma, Vase, Crackle Ivory, Beaded Figures, 19 In.	195.00
Satsuma, Vase, Decorated Ivory, White, Gilt, Blue & Red, Hexagonal, 12 In.	160.00
Satsuma, Vase, Deep Blue And Black, Figural, 4 In.	24.00
Satsuma, Vase, Dragon Handles, 7 Panels, Different Poets & His Poem, 6 In.	475.00
Satsuma, Vase, Egrets, Bush-Tailed Turtles, Black, White, Gold, 4 3/4 In.	385.00
Satsuma, Vase, Elongated Neck, Intricate, Character Signed, 6 In.	165.00
Satsuma, Vase, Emperor & Empress, Gold Jewel Robes, Cobalt, 4 In.	95.00
Satsuma, Vase, Enamel Rooster & Hen, 12 In.	110.00
Satsuma, Vase, Enameled Birds On Branches, Hawthorn, 15 In.	135.00
Satsuma, Vase, Enameled Birds, 15 In.	145.00
Satsuma, Vase, Faces Of 15 Immortals, Dragon, Cross Above, Ovoid, 5 In.	125.00
Satsuma, Vase, Figures & Flowers, Royal Blue, Signed, 12 In., Pair	100.00
Satsuma, Vase, Figures, Gold Dog Handles, Gold Trim, 7 In.	50.00
Satsuma, Vase, Figures, Protruding Dragon's Head, Gold, C.1930, 6 In.	45.00
Satsuma, Vase, Five Figures, Enameled Floral, Late 19th Century, 13 In.	75.00
Satsuma, Vase, Floral Panels Alternating With Women, 3 3/4 In.	75.00
Satsuma, Vase, Floral, Multicolored, Hens & Roosters, 7 1/2 In.	175.00
Satsuma, Vase, Flowers, Butterflies, Narrow Neck, Bulbous, Gold, Teak Stand	55.00
Satsuma, Vase, Flowers, 8 Sided, Round Neck, Cream, Oriental Signature, 6 In.	95.00
Satsuma, Vase, Gold Background, 4 Panels Depicting Japanese Life, 6 In.	225.00
Satsuma, Vase, Gold Bird Under Golden Moon, Green Background, C.1910	145.00
Satsuma, Vase, Gold Scenic On Blue, Geishas, C.1875, 7 1/2 In., Pair	160.00
Satsuma, Vase, Gold Trim, Miniature, 3 In., Pair	135.00
Satsuma, Vase, Gold, Heads Of 15 Immortals, Dragon, 5 X 2 1/4 In.	125.00
Satsuma, Vase, Japanese Actor, Seated Man On Reverse Side, 6 In.	125.00
Satsuma, Vase, Japanese Princess, Light Green, Gold Slip, 9 In.	185.00
Satsuma, Vase, Kimono Clad Beauty Figures, Florals, Dragon Handles, 10 In.	81.50
Satsuma, Vase, Landscape, Dark Blue Field, Base & Neck, 3 3/4 In.	95.00
Satsuma, Vase, Man & Woman, Beading, 7 In.	25.00
Satsuma, Vase, Maroon, Flowers, Birds, Gold Dragon's Head Handles, 28 In.	1000.00
Satsuma, Vase, Men's Faces, Gold Trim, Handle, Footed, Imperial Mark, 4 3/4 In.	125.00
Satsuma, Vase, Mirrored, Cobalt Bordered Scenes, 10 1/2 In., Pair	175.00
Satsuma, Vase, Moriye Handles, Enamel Stippled Body, 16 1/4 In.	116.00
Satsuma, Vase, Nine Three Dimensional Quails, Field Scene	95.00
Satsuma, Vase, Ornate With Gold, C.1895, 10 In.	37.50
Satsuma, Vase, Overall Gold Scrolls, Teak Stand, 10 1/4 In.	125.00
Satsuma, Vase, Panels, Warriors, Japanese Women, Raised Gold, 7 3/8 In., Pair	275.00
Satsuma, Vase, Raised Figures & Landscape, Gilt, Cylindrical, C.1905, 10 In.	70.00
Satsuma, Vase, Red, White, & Gold Flowers On Blue, 7 1/2 In., Pair	95.00
Satsuma, Vase, Rooster & Hen, Bamboo Plants, 6 1/2 In., Pair	300.00
Satsuma, Vase, Roosters & Hens, Flowers, Gold Trim, 4 5/8 In.	210.00
Satsuma, Vase, Rust, Brown, & Gold, Male Figures, 6 1/2 In., Pair	65.00
Satsuma, Vase, Samurai Warrior, Warriors On Foot & Mounted, 4 Dragons	100.00
Satsuma, Vase, Scholars & Students On Sides, 12 1/4 In.	225.00
Satsuma, Vase, Stick, Bird In Flight, Prunus Tree, 3 1/2 In.	125.00

Satsuma, Vase, Stick, Imperial, Miniature, Bird In Flight, Apple Blossoms, Pink 125.00
Satsuma, Vase, Thousand Face, Cylindrical, Signed, 7 1/4 X 5 In. 170.00
Satsuma, Vase, Warlords, Cobalt, Yellow & Orange Raised Enameling, 13 In. 60.00
Satsuma, Vase, Warriors & Ladies On Foo Dog, 8 In. 175.00
Satsuma, Vase, Warriors With Dragon, Signed, C.1900, 10 In. 145.00
Satsuma, Vase, 2 Panels, 5 Warriors, 3 Students, Raised Enamel & Gold, 12 In. 350.00
Satsuma, Vase, 3 Warlords On Front, Dragon Reverse, Gold Trim, 18 1/2 In. 1100.00
Satsuma, Vase, 6 People On Each Side, Gold Trim, Imperial, 3 1/2 In. 115.00
Scale, Apothecary, Dram Weights In Case 35.00
Scale, Apothecary, Pine Case, Glass In Lid, Henry Troemner, 13 1/2 In. 150.00
Scale, Arcade, Mills, 1920, 6 Feet 200.00
Scale, Balance, Country, Counter Type, Brass Pan, Red Paint 50.00
Scale, Beam, Wooden & Glass Case, Marble Base, Weights, 9 X 16 In. 139.00
Scale, Brass, Collar Base, 12 X 16 In. 23.00
Scale, Brass, Rope Turned Standard & Adjustment Lever, 19 1/2 In. 125.00
Scale, Candy, Brass Pan, C.1898, 14 1/2 X 18 In. 115.00
Scale, Candy, Computing Scale Co., Dayton, Ohio, 1906, Brass Pan 115.00
Scale, Candy, May 26, 1915, Pelouze Mfg.Co. 40.00
Scale, Dairy, Hanson, Model 60, 7 1/2 In. Round, 60 Lb. Capacity 10.00
Scale, Drugstore, Cent Weight, Date, Fate 175.00
Scale, Gold, Hold In Hand, Brass Beam, Pans, Chains, 7 1/2 X 3 1/2 In. 18.00
Scale, Hamilton, White Porcelain, 1 Cent Slot, 36 In. 60.00
Scale, Hanging Meat, Brass, Iron, 600 Pound Capacity 70.00
Scale, Hanging, Brass, Bottom Tray Brass & Porcelain, 1906, Weighs 30 Lbs. 165.00
Scale, Hanging, Steel Face, Marked In Kilos And Pounds, 18 In. 25.00
Scale, Hardware, Cast Iron, 25 Lbs., Platforms 11 In. 45.00
Scale, Henry Troemner, Phila. Brass Pans, 20 X 8 In., 5 Weights 159.00
Scale, Metric, Brass Face, Patented May 12, 1925 .... 35.00
Scale, Pharmaceutical, Dr.Fitch's Prescription, In Box 12.00
Scale, Photography, With Weights 65.00
Scale, Pill Measuring Porcelain Tile, 30 Graduations, C.1875 .... 45.00
Scale, Postal, English, Full Set Of Weights, Mahogany Base, 16 X 12 X 8 In. 435.00
Scale, Postal, German, Brass & Iron 29.50
Scale, Postal, Pelouze, 16 In. 40.00
Scale, Prescription, Brass, Wooden Base With Drawer, Weights, 12 In. 75.00
Scale, Railway Express Agency Diamond, Red Pan, 69 Pounds 50.00
Scale, Weight, Horoscope, Floor Model, Enameled 85.00

Schneider   *Schneider Glassworks was founded in 1903 at Epinay-sur-Seine, France,
by Charles and Ernest Schneider. Art glass was made between 1903 and
1930. The company still produces clear crystal glass.*

Schneider, Bowl & Underplate, Tango Orange To Mottled Clear & White, 6 In. 165.00
Schneider, Bowl, Mottled Blue Or Red, Etched Signature, 4 1/2 In. 40.00
Schneider, Bowl, Mottled Pedestal, Signed, 8 X 8 In. 155.00
Schneider, Bowl, 5 Mottled Colors, Marbleized Finish, Pedestal, 8 X 8 In. 225.00
Schneider, Compote, Amethyst Stem To Mottled Orange Bowl, 7 X 6 In. 145.00
Schneider, Compote, Amethyst Stem To Mottled Orange, Cobalt Blue Edge, 8 In. 145.00
Schneider, Compote, Cameo, Yellow, Black Foot, Panels, Frosty Finish, 5 1/4 In. 195.00
Schneider, Compote, Mottled Orange, Lavender, Yellow Knob, Paneled, 10 In. 225.00
Schneider, Creamer, Ornate Spout & Handle, Signed, 6 In. 215.00
Schneider, Dish, Fiddleback Cuttings, Frosted, Bell Form, C.1925, 5 In. 120.00
Schneider, Dish, Orange Flame, Black Metal Holder, Acanthus Leaves, 5 In. 250.00
Schneider, Ewer, Applied Amethyst Handle, Signed, 6 3/8 In. 175.00
Schneider, Ewer, Maroon To Mottled Rose, Satin Finish, Frosted Handle 195.00
Schneider, Ewer, Mauve To Blue, Amethyst Applied Handle, Signed, 6 3/8 In. 200.00
Schneider, Ewer, Orange, Cobalt Blue Mottling, Purple Applied Handle, 6 In. 195.00
Schneider, Plate, Cobalt & Orange, Stemmed, Signed, 15 X 4 3/4 In. 225.00
Schneider, Plate, Dark Blue, Yellow Center, 8 In. 55.00
Schneider, Plate, Red, Blue Mottling, Ovington, N.Y., Signed, 15 In. 120.00
Schneider, Vase, Amethyst To Clear, Mottled, 8 In. 90.00
Schneider, Vase, Cherry Red With Deep Mottled Blue, Bulbous, 6 In. 195.00
Schneider, Vase, Green-Brown To Rose, Stemmed, 11 In. 95.00
Schneider, Vase, Light Orange To Burnt Orange, Ribbed, Conical, 8 X 7 In. 225.00
Schneider, Vase, Pink Frosted, Cluthra Bubbles, Ovoid, 7 In. 89.00
Schneider, Vase, Pink, Brown, Mauve, Yellow, Baluster Shape, 14 In. 80.00

Scrimshaw, Pan Bone, 2 Polychromed Figures, 8 1/2 X 6 1/2 In.

Scrimshaw, Whale's Tooth, Eagle, Sailing Ship On Reverse, 9 In.

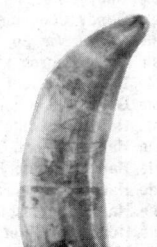

Scrimshaw, Whale's Tooth, Praying Woman, Eagle Reverse, 6 In.

Schneider, Vase, Pink, Brown, Mauve, Yellow, Urn Shape, Signed, 14 X 9 In.	400.00
Schneider, Vase, Pink, Mauve, Yellow, & Brown, Tapered, Baluster, Footed, 14 In.	125.00
Schneider, Vase, Shades Of Purple, 8 1/4 In.	275.00
Schneider, Vase, Tapered, Baluster, Blotches Of Pink, Brown, Yellow, 14 In.	125.00

Scrimshaw is bone or ivory or whale's teeth carved by sailors and others for entertainment during the sailing-ship days. Some scrimshaw was carved as early as 1800.

Scrimshaw, see also Nautical

Scrimshaw, Caribou Antler	150.00
Scrimshaw, Corset Busk, Engraved Eagle, Ships, & Stars, 8 1/4 In.	130.00
Scrimshaw, Knife & Sheath, 7 1/2 In.	95.00
Scrimshaw, Pan Bone, 2 Polychromed Figures, 8 1/2 X 6 1/2 In. ....*Illus*	650.00
Scrimshaw, Salt & Pepper, Polar Bear, 1 3/4 In.	65.00
Scrimshaw, Snuffbox, Sailing Scene, Brass Lid, 19th Century	225.00
Scrimshaw, Whale's Tooth, Eagle, Sailing Ship On Reverse, 9 In. ....*Illus*	550.00
Scrimshaw, Whale's Tooth, Emancipation Of The Slaves, 8 In.	550.00
Scrimshaw, Whale's Tooth, Engraved Crossed Harpoons, American, 6 In.	100.00
Scrimshaw, Whale's Tooth, Praying Woman, Eagle Reverse, 6 In. ....*Illus*	230.00

Scuttle Mug, see Shaving Mug, Scuttle

SEG, see Paul Revere Pottery

Sevres porcelain has been made in Sevres, France, since 1769. Many copies of the famous ware have been made. The name originally referred to the works of the Royal Factory. The name now includes any of the wares made in the town of Sevres, France.

Sevres, Bottle, Scent, Scrolled Stopper, 6 1/2 In.	150.00
Sevres, Bowl, Footed Fruit, Celeste, C.1848, Cherubs, Flowers, 9 3/8 In.	325.00
Sevres, Bowl, Fruit, Multicolor Roses, Ormolu Beading, Handled, 13 X 5 In.	400.00
Sevres, Box, Heart Shape, Florals On White, Shell Clasp, 3 1/4 X 1 1/2 In.	95.00
Sevres, Box, Hinged, C.1771, Signed, 5 X 5 In.	250.00
Sevres, Box, Jewel, French, Rose, White, Gold, Signed	385.00
Sevres, Box, Plum, Gold Beaded Rim, Floral, Round, Signed, 1 1/4 X 1 3/4 In.	100.00
Sevres, Box, Round, Plum Color, Floral Decoration, 1 3/4 X 1 1/4 In.	75.00
Sevres, Bust, Marie Antoinette, Bisque, Gilt Bronze Base, 31 In.High	1200.00

Sevres, Cup & Saucer, Cobalt, Florals Encircled In Gold, Courtyard Scene 175.00
Sevres, Cup & Saucer, Master, Medallions, Louis Philippe Monogram 175.00
Sevres, Cup & Saucer, Portrait, Elizabeth Petrovna, Empress Of Russia, 1840 .... 175.00
Sevres, Dish, Oval, Center Crest, Cherubs, Gold Trim, Yellow Band, Signed 55.00
Sevres, Figurine, Boy With Duck, Parian, C.1890, 6 In. 100.00
Sevres, Figurine, Girl With Book, Blonde Hair, Gold Trim, 15 In. 175.00
Sevres, Group, La Dame Aux Camelias, White Porcelain, 1906, 14 In. 175.00
Sevres, Inkstand, Porcelain, C.1804-09, Red Mark 300.00
Sevres, Knife Rest, Crystal, Leather Case, Pair 40.00
Sevres, Lamp, Romantic Scene, Floral, Ram's Head, Rings, Gold, 31 In. 750.00
Sevres, Plate, Birds In Landscape, Raised Gilded Swag Decoration, 9 1/2 In. 75.00
Sevres, Plate, Blue, 3 Reserves, Flowers, Gold Tracery, 7 In. 57.50
Sevres, Plate, Cherubs, Floral Border, Gold Scalloped Edge, 1848, 9 1/4 In. 59.00
Sevres, Plate, Duchesse, Signed Debue, Chateau De St.Cloud, 9 1/2 In. 75.00
Sevres, Plate, Flowers On Border, 1800's, 9 In.Pair 50.00
Sevres, Plate, Open Lacy Edged In Silver, Portrait, Louis XV, 9 In. 95.00
Sevres, Plate, Pink & Red Roses, Thomas, 7 In. 35.00
Sevres, Plate, Portrait, Cobalt Blue Scalloped Border, Gold & Blue Designs 145.00
Sevres, Plate, Portrait, Duchesse De Burgoyne, Gold Over White, 9 1/2 In. 110.00
Sevres, Plate, Portrait, Gold Design, 9 1/2 In. 225.00
Sevres, Plate, Portrait, Hand-Painted, Gold Tracery, Floral Border, 9 1/2 In. 115.00
Sevres, Plate, Portrait, Marie Leczinska & Donna Bourgogne, 9 In., Pair 295.00
Sevres, Plate, Portrait, Mme De Montespan, Gold Border, C.1840, 9 1/2 In. 60.00
Sevres, Plate, Portrait, Mme Du Barry, Gold Border, C.1840, 10 In .... 60.00 To 125.00
Sevres, Plate, Soup, Crest Of King Louis Philippe, Dated 1846, 9 1/2 In. 85.00
Sevres, Rose Bowl, Lady, Birds & Flowers, Bronze Handles, E.Dabon, 10 1/2 In. 395.00
Sevres, Tray, Floral Bouquet, Pastel Shades, Gilt Scroll, Floral Border, 1767 .... 1200.00
Sevres, Urn, Blue & Gilt, Pastoral Scene, Signed Fragona, C.1840, Pair 1200.00
Sevres, Urn, Covered, Bronze Mounting, Man & Woman Painting, Artist Signed 250.00
Sevres, Urn, Covered, Footing, Handles, Finial, Floral, Scene, Portrait, Marked 265.00
Sevres, Urn, Girl With Dove, Girl With Bow & Arrows, Purple, Pink Floral, Pair 350.00
Sevres, Urn, Lake Scene, Enamel, Dragon Handles, Bronze Top, 10 1/4 In. 150.00
Sevres, Urn, Man & Woman, Scenic Landscape, Lion On Each Side, 19 In. 425.00
Sevres, Urn, Mounted In Bronze, Cavalier & Lady, Blue, Orange Lilies, 12 In. 275.00
Sevres, Urn, Portrait Medallion, Ram's-Head Handles, Covered, 13 In. 365.00
Sevres, Urn, Portrait, Bronze Base & Mounts, Covered, Signed, 12 In. 275.00
Sevres, Vase, Blue-Green High Glaze, Bronze Trim, 7 In. 75.00
Sevres, Vase, Courting Scene, Royal Blue & Gilded, P & A, 19 1/2 In., Pair 850.00
Sevres, Vase, Floral Decoration, Cupids, Bronze Base & Handles, Zieu, 10 In. 175.00
Sevres, Vase, Flowers, Leaves, Cobalt Blue, Gold, Paris, 28 In. 700.00
Sevres, Vase, Gold Fleur-De-Lis On Cobalt, 1904, 6 In. 65.00

*Sewer tile figures were made by workers in the sewer tile factories in the
Ohio area during the late nineteenth and early twentieth centuries.*
Sewer Tile, Bird, 6 In. 55.00
Sewer Tile, Little Man, 8 In. 375.00
Sewer Tile, Tree-Stump Planter, 22 In. 150.00
    Sewing Tool, see also Pincushion Doll
Sewing Tool, Basket, Covered, Victorian, 7 1/4 X 3 1/2 In. 8.50
Sewing Tool, Basket, Wicker, 10 In. 15.00
Sewing Tool, Basket, Yarn, Oval, Handled, 9 X 12 In. 22.00
Sewing Tool, Bird, Hand-Forged Iron, Clamp On, Heart Shaped, 18th Century 140.00
Sewing Tool, Bird, Nickel Plated Brass, 1853, Pair 125.00
Sewing Tool, Bird, Patented February 15, 1853 .... 50.00
Sewing Tool, Bird, Silver Plated Brass Clamp, 2 Green Velvet Pincushions 60.00
Sewing Tool, Box, Brass Knobs, Spindle On Top, Victorian, 8 1/2 X 7 1/2 In. 60.00
Sewing Tool, Box, Coffee Grinder Shape, Spool Drawer, Mid-Victorian 35.00
Sewing Tool, Box, I Drawer, Pedestaled, Mushroom Shape, 5 1/2 X 7 1/2 In. 65.00
Sewing Tool, Box, Inlaid, Victorian 58.00
Sewing Tool, Box, Pin Hinge, Double Lid, 1840 .... 75.00
Sewing Tool, Box, Sewing, 2 Tiered, 15 Spindles, Victorian, 7 X 10 In. 75.00
Sewing Tool, Box, Thread, Walnut, 2 Drawer, 14 X 26 X 7 1/2 In. 65.00
Sewing Tool, Box, 2 Drawer, Pincushion On Top, 6 Spool Spindle, C.1880 .... 55.00
Sewing Tool, Caddy, Pincushion Top, Spool Spindles, Kenola Lake, N.Y. 10.00

Sewing Tool, Case, Needle, Carved Ivory, 2-Part, Cylindrical, 3 In.	28.00
Sewing Tool, Case, Pin, Turned Wood, Crescent Brass & Pin Company	4.50
Sewing Tool, Case, Thimble, Acorn Shape, Carved Bone, Bone Thimble	30.00
Sewing Tool, Clamp, Carved Ivory, Velvet Pincushion, 1 1/4 X 2 In.	45.00
Sewing Tool, Darner & Needle Holder, Ashbrop, Germany	8.50
Sewing Tool, Darner, Bottle Green, Blown Glass	26.00
Sewing Tool, Darner, Double Ended, Wood	4.50
Sewing Tool, Darner, Ebony, Sterling Handle	12.00
Sewing Tool, Darner, Ivory, French, C.1850	28.00
Sewing Tool, Darner, Maple, Round, Handled, 2 In.	5.00
Sewing Tool, Darner, Mushroom Shape, Blown	25.00
Sewing Tool, Darner, Peachblow, Open End	125.00
Sewing Tool, Darner, Sock, Pearlized	7.00
Sewing Tool, Darner, Stocking, Blown Glass, Green	48.00
Sewing Tool, Darning Egg & Needlecase, The Columbian	22.00
Sewing Tool, Darning Egg, Custard Glass, Footed	15.00
Sewing Tool, Finger, Spinning Wheel, Lignum Vitae Wood	12.50
Sewing Tool, Hoop, Embroidery, Wooden	3.00
Sewing Tool, Kit, Sewing, Metal, Lydia Pinkham	6.00
Sewing Tool, Machine, Miniature, Cast Iron, Gold Stenciling, Bavaria	37.50
Sewing Tool, Machine, New Home, Patented 1911-12	95.00
Sewing Tool, Machine, Singer, C.1887	240.00
Sewing Tool, Machine, Singer, Walnut, 2 Drawers Each Side	125.00
Sewing Tool, Machine, Wilcox & Gibbs, Dated 1857-60	20.00
Sewing Tool, Machine, Wilcox & Gibbs, 1875, 9 In.High	25.00
Sewing Tool, Marker, Fitted Box, Ink & Instructions, Gorham Linen Marker	12.50
Sewing Tool, Mold, Shoulder Pad, C.1880, Carved Of A Single Stock Of Wood	15.00
Sewing Tool, Needle Holder, Lacquer, Inlaid Ivory, Oriental Scene	25.00
Sewing Tool, Needle Holder, Parasol, Ivory	24.00
Sewing Tool, Needle Holder, Pedestaled, Rotating Carousel, 3 In.	16.50
Sewing Tool, Needle Holder, Rolling Pin Shape, Celluloid	12.00
Sewing Tool, Needle Roll, Beaded, Velvet & Silk	22.00
Sewing Tool, Pin Holder, Papier-Mache, Pearl Floral, Round	40.00
Sewing Tool, Pincushion, see also Pincushion Doll,	
Sewing Tool, Pincushion, Crescent Brass & Pin Co., Wood Case	10.00
Sewing Tool, Pincushion, Negro Bisque Boy Kneeling	9.00
Sewing Tool, Pincushion, Pedestal Base, Ivory	35.00
Sewing Tool, Pincushion, Ribbon Trim, C.1900, 8 In.Diameter	3.50
Sewing Tool, Pincushion, Satin Apple, Leaves, Red, Yellow, Green, 3 X 3 In.	12.00
Sewing Tool, Pincushion, Turreted Castle, Miniature, Lift Top, 6 1/2 In.	39.50
Sewing Tool, Rug Stitcher, Hand-Held, Crank Operated, Singer	75.00
Sewing Tool, Scissors, Button Hole, Marked Ideal	9.50
Sewing Tool, Scissors, Embroidery, Peacock Decoration, Sterling Silver	18.00
Sewing Tool, Scissors, Stork, Engraved, Steel Mark	15.00
Sewing Tool, Sewing Bird, Brass, 1873	125.00
Sewing Tool, Shears, Tailor's, Store, Sign, Du Bois Budweiser, Tin, 4 X 5 In.	6.00
Sewing Tool, Shuttle, Tatting	3.00
Sewing Tool, Spool Holder, Miniature, Victorian, 4 In.	15.00
Sewing Tool, Spool Holder, Pincushion On Top, C.1880s, 6 1/2 In.Diameter	30.00
Sewing Tool, Spool Holder, Pincushion On Top, 12 X 11 X 3 In.	60.00
Sewing Tool, Spool Holder, Shaped Like A Candlestand, Brown, 19th Century	85.00
Sewing Tool, Spool Holder, 3 Divided Drawers, 12 1/2 X 9 X 21 In.	65.00
Sewing Tool, Spool, Carved Mother-Of-Pearl, Ivory	3.00
Sewing Tool, Stand, Mahogany & Sterling Banded, Sterling Needle Basket, 5 In.	30.00
Sewing Tool, Table, Basket, Hinged Top, Bamboo Legshelf, 19 X 17 X 7 In.	75.00
Sewing Tool, Tape Measure, Acorn, Vegetable, Ivory With Ivory Trim	15.00
Sewing Tool, Tape Measure, Brass House, Water Wheel Turns Tape	75.00
Sewing Tool, Tape Measure, Celluloid Basket Of Flowers	25.00
Sewing Tool, Tape Measure, Celluloid Clipper Ship	39.00
Sewing Tool, Tape Measure, Cloth, Our Native Herbs, 36 In.	8.50
Sewing Tool, Tape Measure, Colored Celluloid Policeman, Billyclub Tape Pull	45.00
Sewing Tool, Tape Measure, Daddy's Picture, Celluloid, C.1900	5.00
Sewing Tool, Tape Measure, Electric Lustre Starch, 36 In.	3.50
Sewing Tool, Tape Measure, Fab	5.00
Sewing Tool, Tape Measure, Favorite Stoves & Ranges, Celluloid	16.75

Sewing Tool, Tape Measure, Figural, Apple 7.00
Sewing Tool, Tape Measure, Figural, Dutch Girl On Brick Block 30.00
Sewing Tool, Tape Measure, Figural, Pig, Patented 1896 .... 37.50
Sewing Tool, Tape Measure, Figural, Silver Plated Straw Hat 46.00
Sewing Tool, Tape Measure, First National Bank, Celluloid 8.00
Sewing Tool, Tape Measure, Gold Metal Nutshell, Squirrel Pull Tab, C.1930 .... 7.50
Sewing Tool, Tape Measure, Kelvinator Dealer, Springfield, Missouri 6.00
Sewing Tool, Tape Measure, Lydia Pinkham 9.00
Sewing Tool, Tape Measure, Wallace Furniture, Music Department, Celluloid 17.00
Sewing Tool, Thimble Holder, Egg Shaped, Enameled Over Metal, Germany 14.50
Sewing Tool, Thimble Holder, Maple, 3 Tiered, 19 Spools, 8 1/2 In. 125.00
Sewing Tool, Thimble, Beaded Edge, Sterling 20.00
Sewing Tool, Thimble, Blue Delft Windmill Scene, Holland 5.00
Sewing Tool, Thimble, Brass, Embossed Stars, Large 5.00
Sewing Tool, Thimble, Celluloid, Kasco Dog Ration 2.00
Sewing Tool, Thimble, Chased Fancy Border, Sterling Silver 18.00
Sewing Tool, Thimble, China, Hand-Painted Flowers 16.00
Sewing Tool, Thimble, Danish Enameled Scene, Sterling 50.00
Sewing Tool, Thimble, Dog Beside Pewter Top Hat Which Holds Silver Thimble 54.00
Sewing Tool, Thimble, English Raised Band Design, Carnelian Top, Silver 25.00
Sewing Tool, Thimble, Fancy Mexican, Sterling 8.00
Sewing Tool, Thimble, Gold, Scrolled Border 35.00
Sewing Tool, Thimble, Gold, Wide Band Of Leaves & Berries, Leather Case 75.00
Sewing Tool, Thimble, Gold, 14K, Engraved Castle Scene 34.00
Sewing Tool, Thimble, Gold, 14K, Size 7, Ornate Scroll Rim, 1912 .... 35.00
Sewing Tool, Thimble, Ivory 15.00
Sewing Tool, Thimble, Mexican Applied Wire Decoration 42.50
Sewing Tool, Thimble, Navajo, Sterling Silver, 6 Turquoise 24.00
Sewing Tool, Thimble, Porcelain, Floral Design 4.00
Sewing Tool, Thimble, Porcelain, Floral, Chinese Export 4.00
Sewing Tool, Thimble, Porcelain, Hand-Painted Flowers 7.50
Sewing Tool, Thimble, Priscilla, Scroll, Sterling Silver 20.00
Sewing Tool, Thimble, Prudential Life Insurance Advertisement 7.00
Sewing Tool, Thimble, Silver, Gold Engraved Band 40.00
Sewing Tool, Thimble, Silver, Raised Tudor Roses, English 23.00
Sewing Tool, Thimble, Sterling Silver, Dated 1881 .... 10.00
Sewing Tool, Thimble, Sterling Silver, Grape & Leaf In High Relief, 1907 .... 20.00
Sewing Tool, Thimble, Sterling Silver, Overlayed Band Of Gold, Scrolling 25.00
Sewing Tool, Thimble, Sterling Silver, Scenic 22.00
Sewing Tool, Thimble, Sterling Silver, Scroll Rim, Marked 6.00
Sewing Tool, Thimble, Sterling Silver, Thomas Brogan, Size 8 .... 16.50
Sewing Tool, Thimble, Sterling Silver, 1/4 In.Turquoise Colored Band 5.00
Sewing Tool, Thimble, Sterling, Lighthouse Scene 35.00
Sewing Tool, Thimble, Sterling, Raised Scrolls 16.00
Sewing Tool, Thread & Thimble Holder, Carousel, C.1870, 7 X 10 X 3 3/4 In. 69.00
Sewing Tool, Thread & Thimble Holder, 2 Tiered, 5 In.Diameter 32.00
Sewing Tool, Thread Caddy, Pincushion Top, Holds 18-24 Spools 30.00
Sewing Tool, Winder, Silk, Sterling Silver 12.00
Sewing Tool, Winder, Thread, Mother-Of-Pearl 2.50
Sewing Tool, Winder, Yarn, Hand-Hewn, 4 Legged Base 48.00
Sewing Tool, Winder, Yarn, New Holland, Pennsylvania 225.00
Sewing Tool, Winder, Yarn, 38 In. 125.00
Sewing Tool, 6 Spool Caddy, Carousel Pincushion, Drawer, 5 1/2 X 8 In. 42.50
Shaker, Basket, Double Handle, 7 1/2 In. 95.00
Shaker, Basket, Swivel Handle, 16 In. 110.00
Shaker, Bookmark, White Daisies On Blue Silk, Early 1800s 80.00
Shaker, Box, Black & Gold Decoration, 7 1/2 In., P.B. 175.00
Shaker, Box, Carrying, Oval, 11 In. 125.00
Shaker, Box, Hymnal, Hinged Panel Cover, Blue-Green Paint, 37 X 8 In. 450.00
Shaker, Box, Oval, Name Pepper On Top, 5 1/8 In. 38.00
Shaker, Box, Oval, 6 1/2 In. 28.00
Shaker, Box, Oval, 7 1/2 In. 85.00
Shaker, Box, Oval, 9 In. 95.00
Shaker, Box, Paper, Round, Green, Small 30.00
Shaker, Box, Pincushion, Painted, 5 In. .... *Illus* 165.00

Shaker, Box, Pincushion, Painted, 5 In.
(See Page 573)

Shaker, Box, Round, Covered, Blue	39.00
Shaker, Box, Sewing, Laminated Top, 3 Finger, Lined, 8 In.	225.00
Shaker, Box, Sewing, 3 Fingers On Bottom, One On Top, 10 X 6 X 4 In.	115.00
Shaker, Box, Woven Poplar, 12 1/2 In.	75.00
Shaker, Brush, Dusting	50.00
Shaker, Bucket, Green, Small	85.00
Shaker, Bucket, Interwoven Laps, Dark Green, Covered, 9 1/2 In.	78.00
Shaker, Bucket, Sugar, 2 Quart	35.00
Shaker, Bucket, Wine Cooler, Legs, Maple Finish, 27 In.High, 50 In.Diameter	100.00
Shaker, Bucket, Wooden, Blue, Handle & Lid, 10 In.	74.00
Shaker, Comb, Hair Scrubbing, Wooden Teeth, Round, 1 1/4 X 2 1/4 In.	19.00
Shaker, Comb, Round Shampoo	25.00
Shaker, Doll, Pen Wiper	65.00
Shaker, Furniture, see Furniture	
Shaker, Hanger, Garment, Signed, Enfield, Connecticut	50.00
Shaker, Measure, Tin, Quart	45.00
Shaker, Pan, Dust, Tin	35.00
Shaker, Pegboard	160.00
Shaker, Piggin, Geometric Design On Handle, Blue-Gray Paint	235.00
Shaker, Rack, Drying	175.00
Shaker, Sander, Ink, Yellow Paint, 3 1/2 In.	58.00

Shaving mugs were popular from 1860 to 1900. Many types were made, including occupational mugs featuring pictures of the man's job. There were scuttle mugs, silver-plated mugs, glass-lined mugs, and others.

Shaving Mug, Advertising William Shaving Soaps, U.S. Flags, 46 Stars, Rest	95.00
Shaving Mug, Black & Gold, T.V. Limoges, France	28.00
Shaving Mug, Blue Forget-Me-Not-Gold Trim, Haviland	25.00
Shaving Mug, Cigar Maker's, Name John Brunce	85.00
Shaving Mug, Cobalt Blue, Orange Tree	45.00
Shaving Mug, Copper Luster, Narrow Green Band, Wide Multicolored Band	65.00
Shaving Mug, Deer's Head, Remember Me	10.00
Shaving Mug, Farmer Plowing	75.00
Shaving Mug, Floral And Gold, Z.S.& Co., Bavaria	25.00
Shaving Mug, Floral Engraving, Brush Rest, Handle, Silver Plate, Pre-1912	28.00
Shaving Mug, Floral Wreath, Gold Trim, Soap Shelf, Marked, September 20, 1876	10.00
Shaving Mug, Floral, Soap Shelf	16.00
Shaving Mug, George Washington, Glass	15.00
Shaving Mug, Golden Knight, Shaving Soap, Glass	34.50
Shaving Mug, Horseshoe, 4 Leaf Clover, Limoges, C.W.Fingar	45.00
Shaving Mug, Ironstone, Shaw, Tea Leaf	40.00
Shaving Mug, Large Flower, Black Band, Marked T. & V., France	24.00
Shaving Mug, Limoges, Roses, Snyder, T. & V.	45.00
Shaving Mug, Milk Glass, White, Straight Sides, Applied Handle	15.00
Shaving Mug, Moriye Trim, Autumn Colors	65.00
Shaving Mug, Nippon, Scenic, Brown Trim, Green Mark	85.00
Shaving Mug, Occupational, Bakers Working	125.00
Shaving Mug, Occupational, Barbershop Singing Quartet	100.00
Shaving Mug, Occupational, Bartender, Bar Scene	70.00
Shaving Mug, Occupational, Bicyclist	135.00

Shaving Mug, Occupational, Black Window Wagon, 2 Horses, Driver, Black Drapes	50.00
Shaving Mug, Occupational, Bricklayer, Man Building Small Bridge	55.00
Shaving Mug, Occupational, Butcher & Customer	90.00
Shaving Mug, Occupational, Butcher Shop, Koken Stamp	25.00
Shaving Mug, Occupational, Butcher, Steer Head And Tools	110.00
Shaving Mug, Occupational, Cigars, Ivy & Berries At Top, John Brunce	85.00
Shaving Mug, Occupational, Cloth Dyer, Man Dipping Cloth In Dye Barrel	125.00
Shaving Mug, Occupational, Doctor's Bag, W.C.Barker	100.00
Shaving Mug, Occupational, Dray Wagon, Kern Mark	50.00
Shaving Mug, Occupational, Dray Wagon, Name, Driver, Horses, Logs	100.00
Shaving Mug, Occupational, Druggist, B.T.Cantwell	80.00
Shaving Mug, Occupational, Druggist, Yellow, Mortar & Pestal, Name In Gold	90.00
Shaving Mug, Occupational, Farmer With Hoe	175.00
Shaving Mug, Occupational, Farmer, Gold Name	175.00
Shaving Mug, Occupational, Fishermen	110.00
Shaving Mug, Occupational, Grocer Wagon	45.00
Shaving Mug, Occupational, Horse-Drawn Hansom Cab, Signed	135.00
Shaving Mug, Occupational, Horse-Drawn Hearse	140.00
Shaving Mug, Occupational, Horse-Drawn Streetcar	120.00
Shaving Mug, Occupational, Hunter With Dog, Dog Pointing, Bird, Gold Name	165.00
Shaving Mug, Occupational, Hunter, Gun, Dog, Birds	85.00
Shaving Mug, Occupational, Lamplighter, Sportsman	85.00
Shaving Mug, Occupational, Lawyer, Justice For All	45.00
Shaving Mug, Occupational, Locomotive & Tender, E.E. & W.R.R.	125.00
Shaving Mug, Occupational, Locomotive With Name	92.00
Shaving Mug, Occupational, Mortician, W.Dyer	410.00
Shaving Mug, Occupational, Photographer Taking Lady's Picture	225.00
Shaving Mug, Occupational, Photographers	350.00
Shaving Mug, Occupational, Railroad Engine, Wood Burner, Name, Gold, Signed	165.00
Shaving Mug, Occupational, Railroad Engineer, Steam Engine, Coal Car	125.00
Shaving Mug, Occupational, Railroad Handcar	75.00
Shaving Mug, Occupational, Railroad Scene	45.00
Shaving Mug, Occupational, Saloon Keeper, Barroom, Barman Drawing Beer	145.00
Shaving Mug, Occupational, Tailor Sewing Pants	125.00
Shaving Mug, Occupational, Theatrical Drape, Name, Gold	115.00
Shaving Mug, Occupational, Violinist, E.Sonderman	95.00
Shaving Mug, Opaque, Embossed Washington Head	35.00
Shaving Mug, Ornate Design, Orange Gold, Green Flowers, German	12.50
Shaving Mug, Patriotic, Flying Eagle On Flag	45.00
Shaving Mug, Pearl Luster, Rose Decoration, Gold Trim, Brush	22.00
Shaving Mug, Red Roses, Germany	20.00
Shaving Mug, Rockingham, Toby Figures On Each Side	85.00
Shaving Mug, Rose & Buds, Stems, Leaves, A Present On Front, Gold Rim, 4 In.	20.00
Shaving Mug, RS Prussia, Pink Floral, Satin, Red Mark	135.00 To 165.00
Shaving Mug, RS Prussia, Rose Decoration, Red Star	80.00
Shaving Mug, Scuttle With Soap Holder, Floral, Yellow To Green, Austria	35.00
Shaving Mug, Scuttle, Floral, Vienna	45.00
Shaving Mug, Scuttle, Flower Decoration, 1870	45.00
Shaving Mug, Scuttle, Ironstone, Floral	25.00
Shaving Mug, Scuttle, Old Foley, James Kent, England, Gold Rim, Roses	24.00
Shaving Mug, Scuttle, Purple & Orange Flowers, Green Foliage	35.00
Shaving Mug, Scuttle, Roses On Both Sides	30.00
Shaving Mug, Scuttle, Soft Green Around Multicolored Flowers, 4 In.	42.00
Shaving Mug, Scuttle, Victorian, Green Shaded To White, Raised Scroll Border	225.00
Shaving Mug, Scuttle, Wedding Band China, 1880s	20.00
Shaving Mug, Silver Plate, Milk Glass Liner, Victorian, 3 1/2 In.	38.00
Shaving Mug, Silver Plate, Reed And Barton	40.00
Shaving Mug, Silver, Pairpoint, Insert	40.00
Shaving Mug, Tea Leaf, Luster	35.00
Shaving Mug, Vipenta, Gold Bands	30.00
Shaving Mug, W.R.Morton, Gold	35.00
Shaving Mug, White, Blue, Pink Roses, Soap Shelf	17.50
Shaving Mug, Witch's Head	225.00

Shawnee pottery was made in Zanesville, Ohio, from 1935 until 1961.
Shawnee also produced pottery for George Rumrill during the late 1930s.

Shawnee, Bowl, Corn, Oval, 6 In.	4.50
Shawnee, Bowl, Dessert, Corn	15.00
Shawnee, Bowl, Ice Cream, Corn	13.00
Shawnee, Bowl, Vegetable, Corn	22.00
Shawnee, Butter, Covered, Corn Queen Line	12.50 To 20.00
Shawnee, Casserole, Corn, Large, No.74	20.00 To 25.00
Shawnee, Casserole, Corn, Small	20.00
Shawnee, Cookie Jar, Basket Of Fruit	12.00 To 16.00
Shawnee, Cookie Jar, Corn, No.66	25.00 To 28.00
Shawnee, Cookie Jar, Dutch Girl	12.50
Shawnee, Cookie Jar, Mugsy Dog	15.00 To 20.00
Shawnee, Cookie Jar, Owl	18.00
Shawnee, Cookie Jar, Pig	18.00
Shawnee, Cookie Jar, Puss & Boots	12.00
Shawnee, Cookie Jar, Smiley Pig Boy	15.00
Shawnee, Cookie Jar, Smiley The Pig	23.00
Shawnee, Cookie Jar, Winnie	20.00
Shawnee, Cookie Jar, Winnie With Bank Top	25.00
Shawnee, Corn Holder, Corn	10.00
Shawnee, Creamer, Corn, No.70	9.00
Shawnee, Creamer, Puss In Boots	9.00
Shawnee, Cup, Corn, No.90	6.50 To 12.00
Shawnee, Figurine, Corn Queen	50.00
Shawnee, Pitcher, Chicken, Charliclear	12.00
Shawnee, Pitcher, Colored Fruit On Cream, Ice Lip	12.00
Shawnee, Pitcher, Elephant	9.00
Shawnee, Pitcher, Figural, Little Bo Peep	8.00
Shawnee, Pitcher, Figural, Pig, Mustard Color	10.00
Shawnee, Pitcher, Fruit	10.00
Shawnee, Pitcher, Little Bo Peep	18.00
Shawnee, Pitcher, Little Boy Blue	15.00
Shawnee, Pitcher, Milk, Bo Peep	15.00
Shawnee, Pitcher, Milk, Figural, Smiling Pig	6.00
Shawnee, Pitcher, Smiley, 2 Quart	15.00
Shawnee, Pitcher, Water, Smiley Farmer, Pig	15.00 To 18.00
Shawnee, Planter, Figural, Deer, Yellow & Green, Pair	15.00
Shawnee, Planter, Woman's Head, Oriental	10.00
Shawnee, Plate, Bo Peep	25.00
Shawnee, Plate, Bread & Butter, Corn	12.00
Shawnee, Plate, Corn, 10 In.	9.50 To 12.00
Shawnee, Plate, Luncheon, Corn	10.00
Shawnee, Salt & Pepper, Corn, Large	15.00
Shawnee, Salt & Pepper, Figural, Flower Pot	5.00
Shawnee, Salt & Pepper, Figural, Winnie & Pig Boy	70.00
Shawnee, Salt & Pepper, Puss In Boots, 3 1/4 In., Pair	3.50
Shawnee, Saucer, Corn	10.00
Shawnee, Sugar & Creamer, Corn	15.00
Shawnee, Sugar Bowl, Corn	12.00
Shawnee, Teapot, Corn	25.00
Shawnee, Teapot, Granny Anne	18.00
Shawnee, Teapot, Tom The Piper's Son	13.50 To 14.50
Shawnee, Vase, Figural, Rooster	7.00
Shawnee, Vase, Pink, Cameo Label, Large	6.00
Shawsheen, Vase, Green, 3 Handles, 7 1/2 X 7 X 4 1/4 In.	225.00

Sheffield, see Silver, Sheffield
Ship, see Nautical

*Shirley Temple dishes, blue glassware, and any other souvenir-type objects
with her name and picture are now collected.*

Shirley Temple, Book, Captain January & Little Colonel	7.00
Shirley Temple, Book, How I Raised Shirley Temple, Book By Mother	24.00
Shirley Temple, Book, Littlest Rebel, Famous Movie Edition, 1939	12.00
Shirley Temple, Book, Paper Doll, Uncut	5.00
Shirley Temple, Book, Pastime, 1935	15.00
Shirley Temple, Book, Rebecca Of Sunnybrook Farm	6.00

Shirley Temple, Book, ST & Spirit Of Dragonwood 12.00
Shirley Temple, Book, Susannah Of The Mounties 7.00
Shirley Temple, Book, The Little Colonel .... 5.00 To 8.00
Shirley Temple, Bowl, Cereal, Portrait .... 15.00 To 25.00
Shirley Temple, Breakfast Set, Bowl, Mug, Pitcher 45.00
Shirley Temple, Button, Pinback, Pink, Blue & White, 1 1/4 In. 1.75
Shirley Temple, Card, Lobby, Bright Eyes 25.00
Shirley Temple, Card, Poster, Shirley 35.00
Shirley Temple, Cards, Playing, 1930s, Deck 25.00
Shirley Temple, Creamer, Portrait 15.00
Shirley Temple, Cross, Sterling, 1950s 20.00
Shirley Temple, Doll Carriage, Wicker, Tin Picture Of Shirley 325.00
Shirley Temple, Doll, Composition Body, Ideal Mark, 18 In. 135.00
Shirley Temple, Doll, Composition Body, Polka-Dot Dress, 17 In. 125.00
Shirley Temple, Doll, Composition Body, Signed, 18 In. 125.00
Shirley Temple, Doll, Composition Body, Signed, 21 In. 100.00
Shirley Temple, Doll, Composition, Original Dress, 15 In. 85.00
Shirley Temple, Doll, Flirty Eyes 75.00
Shirley Temple, Doll, Flirty Eyes, Composition, 27 In. .... 185.00 To 225.00
Shirley Temple, Doll, Ideal, Composition Body, 16 In. 85.00
Shirley Temple, Doll, MIB, 1973 .... 15.00
Shirley Temple, Doll, Original Clothes, 18 In. 110.00
Shirley Temple, Doll, Original Dress, 13 In. 120.00
Shirley Temple, Doll, Vinyl, Heidi Dress, 36 In. 450.00
Shirley Temple, Doll, Vinyl, 15 In. .... 27.50 To 45.00
Shirley Temple, Doll, 1972 Ideal, 17 In. 20.00
Shirley Temple, Figurine, Bisque, Wearing Overalls, Hands On Hip, Sager, 5 In. 25.00
Shirley Temple, Mirror, Pocket, Blue & Pink, Shirley & Her Doll 2.50
Shirley Temple, Mirror, Pocket, Round, Shirley Temple's Picture, 2 1/4 In. 5.00
Shirley Temple, Mirror, Pocket, Shirley As Heidi, 1938 .... 3.50
Shirley Temple, Movie Ad, Little Princess, S.E.Post, 1939, 10 X 12 In. 10.00
Shirley Temple, Mug & Pitcher, Cobalt Blue Glass 50.00
Shirley Temple, Mug, Cobalt Blue .... 35.00 To 45.00
Shirley Temple, Paper Doll, Stand Up, 2 Ft., Original Box 75.00
Shirley Temple, Paperweight, Glass, 2 1/2 X 4 1/2 In. 14.00
Shirley Temple, Picture, To My Friend, Framed, Signed, 5 1/4 X 7 1/4 In. 15.00
Shirley Temple, Postcards, Unused, Shirley Inset 3.50
Shirley Temple, Poster, 18 X 44 In. 10.00
Shirley Temple, Salt, Bisque, 4 1/2 In. 22.50
Shirley Temple, Salt, Figural, Baby Take A Bow, Brown Dress, Flock, 6 1/2 In. 45.00
Shirley Temple, Sign, Cardboard, Shirley, 25 In. 25.00
Shirley Temple, Statue, Chalk, Carnival Prize 35.00
Shirley Temple, Trunk, Doll's 45.00
Silesia, Basket, Oval, Hand-Painted, Crown Mark, 7 X 11 In. 22.00
Silesia, Bowl, Rose Center, Wide Rose Border, 6 X 2 In., Set Of 4 .... 56.00
Silesia, Hair Receiver, Florals, Hand-Painted, P.K. 19.00
Silesia, Plate, Bird In Center, 8 1/2 In. 32.50
Silesia, Plate, Bread, Give Us This Day, Gold Letters, Roses, 9 1/2 In. 12.50
Silesia, Plate, Cake, Holly, Gold Rim, 10 In. 15.00
Silesia, Plate, Tea Rose Border, 7 1/2 In. 3.00
Silesia, Plate, White Lilies, Green Ground, Gold Rim, C.T.Altwasser, 8 1/4 In. 15.00
Silesia, Sugar, Covered, Pink Roses, Gold Tracery, 4 1/2 In. 22.50
Silesia, Tray, Floral, Hand-Painted, Round, H.M.Busse, 6 1/4 In. 22.50
Silesia, Vase, Gold, Purple, & Green On Cream, Art Deco Design, 6 1/2 In. 32.00
   Silhouette, see Picture, Silhouette

Silver deposit glass was made during the late nineteenth and early twentieth
centuries. Solid sterling silver was applied to the glass by a chemical
method so that a cutout design of silver metal appeared against a clear or
colored glass. It is sometimes called silver overlay.

Silver Deposit, Base, Bud, Bulbous Base, Pink Porcelain Body, 4 1/2 In. 35.00
Silver Deposit, Bottle, Birds & Bamboo Decoration, Pinched, 4 In. 95.00
Silver Deposit, Bottle, Perfume, Green Glass, 3 1/2 In. 65.00
Silver Deposit, Bowl, Grapes, Vines, Paneled Crystal Body, 11 In. 22.00

Silver Deposit, Compote, Cobalt, Lilies Of The Valley, 7 1/2 In.	35.00
Silver Deposit, Cordial Set, Florals With Bands, 6 Piece	22.00
Silver Deposit, Decanter Set, Stylized Leaves, Bands, C.1890, 5 Piece	135.00
Silver Deposit, Decanter, Etched Fish Design, 11 In.	22.00
Silver Deposit, Decanter, Starcut Base, Allover Design, 8 In.	75.00
Silver Deposit, Decanter, Wild Roses, Leaves, Cut Stopper, 11 1/2 In.	235.00
Silver Deposit, Dish, Cherries, Grapes, 7 In.	45.00
Silver Deposit, Dish, Fruit, Green, Ruffled Rim, 4 X 4 X 10 In.	30.00
Silver Deposit, Dish, Scalloped Silver Rim & Handles, 8 In.	15.00
Silver Deposit, Pitcher, Emerald Green, Flowers, 8 In.	37.00
Silver Deposit, Pitcher, Flowers & Leaves, Cut Sunburst Bottom, Handle	45.00
Silver Deposit, Pitcher, Water, Art Nouveau, Iris, Lilies, Butterflies, 10 In.	45.00
Silver Deposit, Sugar & Creamer	14.00
Silver Deposit, Sugar & Creamer, Bonbon Dish	34.00
Silver Deposit, Tray, Cake, 25th Anniversary, 2 Handles, 13 In.	25.00
Silver Deposit, Tray, Fan Shaped Center Handle, 11 In.	18.00
Silver Deposit, Vase, Amethyst, Large Handles From Middle To Base, 8 In.	28.00
Silver Deposit, Vase, Brown & Green, 4 1/4 In.	95.00
Silver Deposit, Vase, Bud, Boat Scene, Emerald Green, 4 1/2 In.	15.00
Silver Deposit, Vase, Cobalt, 6 In.	15.00
Silver Deposit, Vase, Floral Decoration, Silver Rims, 9 In.	275.00
Silver Deposit, Vase, Green Glass, 3 In.	85.00
Silver Deposit, Vase, Green, Persian Scene In Medallion, Rose Design	38.50
Silver Deposit, Vase, Green, Satin Finish, 4 In.	20.00 To 22.00
Silver Deposit, Vase, Sterling, Green, 14 In.	195.00
Silver Deposit, Vase, Vertical Optic, Green, Polished Pontil, 8 In.	35.00
Silver Plate, see also Silver, Sheffield	
Silver Plate, Ashtray, Clip Onto The Dinner Plate, Ornate	6.00
Silver Plate, Basket, Cake, Butterflies, Handled, Victorian, Reed & Barton	65.00
Silver Plate, Basket, Cake, Floral Border, Meriden, C.1885, 7 In.	35.00
Silver Plate, Basket, Cake, Octagonal Pedestal, Curved Bail, Rogers & Smith	45.00
Silver Plate, Basket, Fluted, Ribbing, Decorated Handle, Footed, Victorian	18.50
Silver Plate, Basket, Handled, Repousse Flowers, 5 1/2 In.	20.00
Silver Plate, Basket, Oval Ribbed, Meriden Britannia Co.	48.00
Silver Plate, Bell, Dutch Girl, Czechoslovakia	25.00
Silver Plate, Bowl, Grape Trim, Footed, 7 1/2 In.	40.00
Silver Plate, Bowl, Nut, 2 Squirrels, Engraved Flowers, Scalloped, 9 In.	75.00
Silver Plate, Bowl, Squirrel On Side Branch, 2 In.	19.50
Silver Plate, Box, Jewel, Pinecones & Branches, Silk Lining, 3 1/2 In.	25.00
Silver Plate, Box, Stud, Gold Wash Interior, Stud Figural Top	15.00
Silver Plate, Brush, Butterfly & Flowers, Art Nouveau	10.00
Silver Plate, Bucket, Champagne, Footed	65.00
Silver Plate, Bucket, Champagne, Ram's Head In Relief, 8 1/2 In., Pair	60.00
Silver Plate, Bucket, Ice, Glass Lined, Paul Revere, Rogers	35.00
Silver Plate, Butter Dish, Footed Base, Domed Lid, Melon Shaped Finial	35.00
Silver Plate, Butter Dish, Silver, Scales Sign, No.4999, Marked Meriden Co.	30.00
Silver Plate, Butter, Dome Cover, Liner, Cut Flowers, Victorian	39.00
Silver Plate, Butter, Embossed Edge Baluster Finial, Meriden	35.00
Silver Plate, Butter, Ornate Revolving Lid	40.00
Silver Plate, Butter, Tub, Drainer, Leaf Handles	30.00
Silver Plate, Butter, Victorian, Stand, Simpson, Hall, Miller & Co., 14 In.	60.00
Silver Plate, Cake Stand, Victorian, Pedestal	10.00
Silver Plate, Candelabra, 3 Light, Converts To Single, On Copper, 18 In., Pair	150.00
Silver Plate, Candleholder, Attached Snuffer, Owl For Matches, 7 In.	90.00
Silver Plate, Candlestick, Protruded Applications, Sheffield, 12 In., Pair	87.00
Silver Plate, Casserole, Covered, Victorian, Meriden Silver Co., 1869, Ornate	71.50
Silver Plate, Caster Stand, 5 Bottles, Marked Near Cut	65.00
Silver Plate, Castor, see also Castor	
Silver Plate, Celery, Leaves, Berries, Birds, Etched, Rabbit Handles, Frame	45.00
Silver Plate, Cigar Cutter, Penknife Type	14.50
Silver Plate, Coffeepot, Grape Clusters On Finial, Handle, Spout	35.00
Silver, Plate, Coffeepot, Hinged Cover, Footed, Reed & Barton, 8 1/2 In.	75.00
Silver Plate, Compact, Name Eleanor	25.00
Silver Plate, Cooler, Champagne, Hallmarked, Footed, 2 Handles, 13 X 11 In.	125.00
Silver Plate, Cooler, Wine, 2 Goblets, Porcelain Lined, Reed & Barton, 20 In.	600.00

Silver Plate, Cracker Jar, English, Bail & Lid, Pink & Red Roses	39.50
Silver Plate, Dish, Butter, Etched Floral Decoration	22.50
Silver Plate, Dish, Butter, Lid & Insert, Stand With Handle	22.50
Silver Plate, Dish, Candy, Figural, Peacock, Footed With Foliage	45.00
Silver Plate, Dish, Revolving Hot Water Lazy Susan, 6 Pieces, 17 In.	450.00
Silver Plate, Dish, Serving, Covered, Removable Double Compartment, Sheffield	25.00
Silver Plate, Figurine, Standing Horse, Signed J.B., 5 1/2 X 4 3/4 In.	60.00
Silver Plate, Flask, Fern, Winding Ribbon, Chained Top, Cylinder Shape, 6 In.	42.00
Silver Plate, Flask, Hip, Hammered, E.P.N.S., 8 In.	14.00
Silver Plate, Flask, Hip, Meridan International, Front Design, Initials	30.00
Silver Plate, Flask, Pocket, Art Deco Girl In Black	22.50
Silver Plate, Food Pusher, Roger & Son, Scrolled Handle	10.00
Silver Plate, Fork, Serving, Ornate, 3 Tined, Columbia, 7 1/2 In.	18.00
Silver Plate, Holder, Bottle, Grape, Sheffield On Copper, 3 In.	40.00
Silver Plate, Humidor, Clear Octagon Jar, Sterling Lid, 9 In.	42.00
Silver Plate, Humidor, Horse & Rider On Top, Derby, 1900	125.00
Silver Plate, Inkwell, Figural Golf Ball, Green Liner, Marked J.B.	12.00
Silver Plate, Juicer, Lemon	25.00
Silver Plate, Knife Rest, Figural, Greyhound	25.00
Silver Plate, Knife Rest, Figural, Nude Cupid On Each End, Meriden	30.00
Silver Plate, Knife Rest, Figural, Rabbit, English	21.00
Silver Plate, Knife Rest, Spread-Wing Cockatoos, 2 1/2 X 5 In.	29.00
Silver Plate, Knife, Butter, Border Decoration, 1881 Rogers, 1910	4.00
Silver Plate, Knife, Pocket, Engraved Holly Leaves & Berries, 2 Blades, 3 In.	20.00
Silver Plate, Ladle, Gravy, Border Decoration	3.00
Silver Plate, Match Safe, Boar's Head, Embossed, Hinged Base Striker, 3 In.	35.00
Silver Plate, Match Safe, Figural, W.C.Fields, Brass	190.00
Silver Plate, Measure, Whiskey, Figural, Bull, Bear, Lewis & Son, N.Y.	18.00
Silver Plate, Mirror, Butterfly & Flowers, Art Nouveau	12.00
Silver Plate, Mug, Shaving, Brush Rest, Poole Silver Co., C.1893	14.95
Silver Plate, Mustache Cup, see Mustache Cup	
Silver Plate, Napkin Ring, see Napkin Ring	
Silver Plate, Pitcher, Ice Water, Ornate, Monogram 881, Derby Silver Co.	170.00
Silver Plate, Pitcher, Ice Water, Tilting With Goblet, Racine Silver Co.	275.00
Silver Plate, Pitcher, Syrup, Repousse Floral, Flip Lid, Wilcox, 5 1/2 In.	32.00
Silver Plate, Pitcher, Water, Floral Engraving, Sheffield, 13 In.	115.00
Silver Plate, Planter, White Stoneware Liner, Lattice & Flower Designs	25.00
Silver Plate, Plaque, Bas Relief Scene, Men At Leisure, Continental, 15 In.	80.00
Silver Plate, Reed & Barton, Urn, Coffee, Bone Handle	195.00
Silver Plate, Rocker, Blotter, German Tavern & Courting Scenes, German	18.00
Silver Plate, Shears, C.1863, J.Prime	100.00
Silver Plate, Shears, Grape, Entwined Grapes & Leaves	35.00
Silver Plate, Shoehorn, 11 In.	20.00
Silver Plate, Spoon Ends, English Hallmark, 5 1/2 In.	8.50
Silver Plate, Spoon, Little Red Riding Hood, Child's	10.00
Silver Plate, Spoon, Souvenir, see Souvenir, Spoon, Silver Plate	
Silver Plate, Spooner, Barrel Shape, Ornate Handles, 6 In.	28.00
Silver Plate, Spooner, Basket Shape, Floral Design, Meriden Co., 8 1/4 In.	55.00
Silver Plate, Spooner, Egyptian Heads On Handles, 1871	35.00
Silver Plate, Spooner, Homan Mfg.Co., 1920s, 3 1/2 In.	10.00
Silver Plate, Spooner, 12 Hooks, Bird Finial, Scenic Band	75.00
Silver Plate, Stand, Fruit, Reed & Barton, Embossed Band, Handle, 7 X 9 In.	45.00
Silver Plate, Sugar Shaker, Classic Design, 5 In.	25.00
Silver Plate, Sugar Shaker, Reed & Barton, 1898	38.00
Silver Plate, Sugar, Scoop, Coal Scoop Type	25.00
Silver Plate, Sugar, Shell, Ornate, Towle, Dated 1884	12.50
Silver Plate, Syrup, Decorative Handle, Hinged Lid, 5 In.	15.00
Silver Plate, Syrup, Hinged Lid, Beacon Silver Co., 5 1/2 In.	15.00
Silver Plate, Syrup, Pat.1878	24.00
Silver Plate, Table Set, Napkin Rings, Salt & Pepper Shakers, Dish, Caddy	30.00
Silver Plate, Tankard, Icewater, Reed, Barton, Holder, Cupid Finial, C.1854	125.00
Silver Plate, Tea Caddy, French Repousse	35.00
Silver Plate, Tea Caddy, Octagonal	18.00
Silver Plate, Tea Service, Wilcox, C.1865, 6 Piece	625.00
Silver Plate, Tea Set, Ebony Handles, Rogers, 3 Piece	79.00

Silver Plate, Teapot, Stand With Burner, Gorham	70.00
Silver Plate, Toast Rack, Ball Feet, Heart Shaped Handle, 6 In.	35.00
Silver Plate, Toast Rack, Tray, E.P.N.S., 5 X 5 In.	22.00
Silver Plate, Tongs, Sugar, Sailboat & Concentrics Embossed	4.50
Silver Plate, Toothpick, see Toothpick	
Silver Plate, Toothpick, Attached Bulldog, Glass Eyes	55.00
Silver Plate, Toothpick, Owl On A Branch	55.00
Silver Plate, Tray, Bread, Applied 1/2 In., Loop Trim, Marked Colonial	18.00
Silver Plate, Tray, Card, Scallop Edge, Engraved Owl	45.00
Silver Plate, Tray, Card, Squirrel On Rim, Engraved Birds	32.00
Silver Plate, Tray, Grape & Vine Border, Chased Interior, On Copper, 29 In.	100.00
Silver Plate, Tray, Scroll Feet, Open Handles, Shell Corners, Gadroon, 20 In.	225.00
Silver Plate, Tray, Victorian, Gorham, Grapes & Leaf Border, 30 In.	275.00
Silver Plate, Tray, 2 Handles, Footed, Shell, Rococo Border, On Copper, 29 In.	90.00
Silver Plate, Tureen, Lid & Ladle, Pedestal Base, Gadroon Rim, 9 In.	68.00
Silver Plate, Urn, Chinese, Applied Plated Flowers, Stand, 7 In., Pair	65.00
Silver Plate, Vase, Victorian, Raised Flowers	30.00
Silver Sterling, Figurine, Elk, Walking, 4 X 5 In.	180.00
Silver, American, see also Tiffany Silver, Silver, Sterling	
Silver, American Ladle, Coin, A.H. DeWitt, Columbus, Georgia	250.00
Silver, American, Bell, Ivory Handle, Gorham, Silver Over Bronze, No.042	140.00
Silver, American, Bell, Tea, Engraving, Gorham, Silver Over Bronze, 4 1/2 In.	95.00
Silver, American, Bone Holder, Silver Thumbscrew, Geo.Sharp, Phila., C.1845	250.00
Silver, American, Bowl, Applied Sterling On Border, Whiting, 11 1/4 In.	325.00
Silver, American, Bowl, Berry, Lily, Gold Washed, Initial E, Whiting	43.00
Silver, American, Bowl, Bread, Oval, Gorham, 10 X 7 1/2 In.	245.00
Silver, American, Bowl, Centerpiece, Bas Relief Greek God, Gorham, 11 In.	180.00
Silver, American, Bowl, Clusters Of Fruit On Flange, Wallace, 11 X 2 In.	75.00
Silver, American, Bowl, Footed, Caldwell, Philadelphia, 1836-42, 5 In.	45.00
Silver, American, Bowl, Plate & Mug, T.B.Starr, C.1900, Plate 8 In.Diameter	170.00
Silver, American, Box, Soap, CC Monogram, Oval, Gorham, Sterling	45.00
Silver, American, Brush, Clothes, Unger Brothers, Rococo	22.00
Silver, American, Brush, Military, Unger Brothers	25.00
Silver, American, Buckle, Rosettes, Scroll, Double Tined, Arched, 2 1/4 X 3 In.	75.00
Silver, American, Butter Pat, Rose, Gorham, Set Of 12	120.00
Silver, American, Butter, Covered, Lincoln & Foss, Boston, 1829, Coin	425.00
Silver, American, Candelabra, Art Nouveau, 3 Light, Boardman, 11 1/2 In., Pair	475.00
Silver, American, Candlesnuffer, Bell Top, Gorham, 6 In.	16.00
Silver, American, Candlestick, Fluted Corinthian Column, Gorham, A8207, 10 In.	57.00
Silver, American, Candlestick, Raised Flowers, Wallace, 3 1/2 In., Pair	24.00
Silver, American, Carving Set, Florentine, F.N.Whiting	30.00
Silver, American, Case With Chain, Card, Lady's, Bright Cut, Whiting, 1887	40.00
Silver, American, Chocolate Pot, Repousse, Dominic & Haff, C.1903, 9 In.	225.00
Silver, American, Clip, Paper, Ornate, Gorham	65.00
Silver, American, Coffee Set, Adams Pattern, Gorham, 4 Piece	950.00
Silver, American, Coffee Set, Adams, Classic Lines, Gorham, 4 Piece	600.00
Silver, American, Coffeepot, Pineapple Finial, Monogram, Gorham	130.00
Silver, American, Coffeepot, Repousse, Dominic & Haff, C.1903, 10 In.	300.00
Silver, American, Compote, Verre De Soie Intaglio Cut Top, Gorham, 4 X 6 In.	95.00
Silver, American, Cup, Gorham, Beaded Rim & Bottom, C.1848, Coin	150.00
Silver, American, Cup, Octagonal W.Tucker, San Francisco, C.1850, Coin	450.00
Silver, American, Cup, Ornate Handles, Newburyport Silver Co., 1905-14	42.00
Silver, American, Cup, Palmer & Batchelder, Boston, Beaded Rim & Bottom, Coin	150.00
Silver, American, Cup, R.Hill & Bros. Beaded Rim & Bottom, Coin	150.00
Silver, American, Cutter, Sugar Cube, Howard Sterling Co., 5 In.	30.00
Silver, American, Dish, Candy Lily Pads, Relief, Art Nouveau, Kerr, 6 1/2 In.	35.00
Silver, American, Dish, Mint, Footed, Black Starr & Frost	20.00
Silver, American, Dish, Nut, Art Deco, Cartier	125.00
Silver, American, Dish, Serving, Removable Handle, Black Starr And Frost	285.00
Silver, American, Ewer, Bulbous Body, Inscription, 19th Century, 16 In.	850.00
Silver, American, Fish Slice, Lowell & Senter, Coin	125.00
Silver, American, Flatware, Le Conn Fleurs, 19th Century, Reed & Barton	2490.00
Silver, American, Flatware, Towle's Old Brocade, 84 Pieces	840.00
Silver, American, Fork & Spoon, Salad, Gorham, Milan, 10 1/2 In.	125.00
Silver, American, Fork, Dinner, Kings Pattern, Bailey & Kitchen, Coin	25.00

Silver, American, Fork, Grape Pattern, Fenno & Hale, C.1850, Coin 20.00
Silver, American, Fork, Pastry Server, J.B.Knowles Apollo, C.1892 .... 35.00
Silver, American, Fork, Pickle, S.Kirk & Son, 5 1/2 In. 19.95
Silver, American, Fork, Serving, Hoyt, Badger & Dillon, New York, C.1850, Coin 175.00
Silver, American, Glass, Wine, Kirk, Set Of 10, 4 1/2 In. 300.00
Silver, American, Goblet, Renaissance Revival Chasing, Gorham, C.1865, Coin 175.00
Silver, American, Goblet, Wallis, Set Of 12 .... 450.00
Silver, American, Gold Washed Interior, Inscribed, 1859, Gade & Willis 130.00
Silver, American, Jar, Cover, Lid, Repousse Base, Floral, Gorham, 3 X 4 In. 135.00
Silver, American, Kettle, Tilting, Repousse, Dominic & Haff, C.1903, 73 Oz. 400.00
Silver, American, Knife, Butter Serving, J.Moulton, Newburyport, Mass., Coin 24.95
Silver, American, Knife, Butter, Engraved, Daniel Low, Salem, Mass., C.1850, Coin 13.75
Silver, American, Knife, Butter, Initialed, Newell Harding, Boston, C.1850, Coin 12.75
Silver, American, Knife, Butter, Large, Ch.Maynard, C.1840, Coin 19.95
Silver, American, Knife, Butter, Large, Farrington & Hunewell, C.1835-50, Coin 19.75
Silver, American, Knife, Butter, Olive Pattern, Bigelow Bros.& Kennard, Coin 20.00
Silver, American, Knife, Butter, Ornate Scene Of House On Blade, Coin 35.00
Silver, American, Knife, Cheese Serving, Joseph Seymour & Co., Utica, N.Y. 16.95
Silver, American, Knife, Fish, Hand-Engraved Fish, C.1850, Unmarked 150.00
Silver, American, Knife, Ice Cream, Medallion, Serrated Edge, Wood & Hughes 115.00
Silver, American, Knife, Luncheon, Flat Handle & Blade, E.L.D.Set Of 6, Coin 68.00
Silver, American, Knife, Pie, Etruscan, Gorham, 9 1/2 In. 35.00
Silver, American, Ladle, A.S.Devondorf, Coin, 6 1/2 In. 30.00
Silver, American, Ladle, Claret, Grape, Dominick & Haff, 13 In. 85.00
Silver, American, Ladle, Coin, C.1840, 6 In. 15.00
Silver, American, Ladle, Cream, Straight Handle, G.Fitts, Coin, 5 1/2 In. 25.00
Silver, American, Ladle, Face At Top, Pierced, Gorham, 1868, 9 3/4 X 5 1/2 In. 129.00
Silver, American, Ladle, Gold-Washed Bowl, Repousse Floral, Gorham, 4 1/2 In. 35.00
Silver, American, Ladle, Gravy, Oval Twist, Whiting 45.00
Silver, American, Ladle, Gravy, Palmer & Bachelder, Boston, C.1850, Coin 26.75
Silver, American, Ladle, Gravy, Stieff Rose 40.00
Silver, American, Ladle, Gravy, Whitney & Hoyt, N.Y., C.1840, Coin, 6 1/4 In. 35.00
Silver, American, Ladle, Mayonnaise, L.P.Coe, N.Y., N.Y., 1820-25 .... 25.00
Silver, American, Ladle, Mustard, Gold-Washed Bowl, T.Steele & Son, Hartford 18.00
Silver, American, Ladle, Mustard, N.E.Crittenden, Cleveland, Ohio, C.1830, 4 In. 20.00
Silver, American, Ladle, Mustard, Pear & Bacall, Fiddle Tip Handle, Coin 20.00
Silver, American, Ladle, Oyster, A.Fellow R.I., C.1826 .... 95.00
Silver, American, Ladle, Pear-Shaped Bowl, Gold Washed, Stag Head Handle, Coin 85.00
Silver, American, Ladle, Punch, Arabesque, Whiting 150.00
Silver, American, Ladle, Punch, Brown, Palmer, & Dwight, C.1850, Coin, 13 In. 135.00
Silver, American, Ladle, Punch, J.E.Caldwill, Pennsylvania 160.00
Silver, American, Ladle, Punch, Medallion, Twist Handle, Duhme, Cincinnati, Coin 300.00
Silver, American, Ladle, Sauce, Initialed, Benjamin C.Frobisher, C.1820, Coin 24.75
Silver, American, Ladle, Sauce, Theophilus Bradbury, C.1815, Coin 55.00
Silver, American, Ladle, Soup, Chamberlain & Smith, Scalloped, Coin 225.00
Silver, American, Ladle, Soup, Curved, Kentucky, Bettrolf & Son, Coin 125.00
Silver, American, Ladle, Soup, Duhme, Coin, Massive 225.00
Silver, American, Ladle, Soup, J.P.Mood & Son 475.00
Silver, American, Ladle, Soup, James P.Barnes, Louisville, 1869, Coin 100.00
Silver, American, Ladle, Soup, Lady Washington, Fluted Bowl, Gorham, Sterling 135.00
Silver, American, Ladle, Soup, Mayflower, S.Kirk & Son 225.00
Silver, American, Ladle, Soup, Medallion, Wood & Hughes, 12 1/2 In. 250.00
Silver, American, Ladle, Soup, Samuel C.Brown, Albany, N.Y., 1830's, 13 1/2 In. 225.00
Silver, American, Ladle, Soup, Wm.Faber & Son, Philadelphia, Pa., C.1837, Coin 195.00
Silver, American, Letter Opener, Black, Starr & Frost, Art Nouveau Handle 245.00
Silver, American, Letter Opener, Kirk 10.00
Silver, American, Match Safe, Woman & Flowers, Art Nouveau, Gorham 75.00
Silver, American, Mirror, Hand, Art Nouveau, Unger Bros. 125.00
Silver, American, Mug, Lizzie From Mother, July 29, 1858, Coin 50.00
Silver, American, Mug, Lows, Ball & Co., Boston 130.00
Silver, American, Mug, Shaving, Unger Bros. 125.00
Silver, American, Mug, Wood & Hughes, New York City, 1888, 3 1/2 In. 44.95
Silver, American, Pie Server, Threaded Oval, Engraved Blade, Coin, 10 In. 55.00
Silver, American, Pitcher, Bigelow Bros. & Kennard, Boston, 1825-40, 9 In. 850.00
Silver, American, Pitcher, Milk, Jones, Shreve, Brown & Co., Coin, 9 In. 375.00

Silver, American, Pitcher, Water, Ornate Handle, Gorham, Coin, C.1855	675.00
Silver, American, Pitcher, Water, Wm.Forbes, C.1820, Coin, 10 In.	695.00
Silver, American, Plate, Blown-Out Water Lilies, Wallace, 10 1/2 In.	100.00
Silver, American, Ruler, Flowers In Relief On Edge, S.Kirk & Son, 12 In.	125.00
Silver, American, Salt Shovel, C.1850, Coin, 3 In.	24.50
Silver, American, Salt, Master, Repousse, Handled, Bailey & Co.	39.00
Silver, American, Salt, Medallion, Open, 1850 Mark, Gorham, 2 1/4 In., Pair	175.00
Silver, American, Salt, Ram's Head Feet, Gorham 1850, 2 1/2 In., Pair	225.00
Silver, American, Salt, Shaker, Individual, 8 Sided, Cartier, Set Of 8	56.00
Silver, American, Scoop, Cheese, Boas & Newhard, C.1825, Coin	19.75
Silver, American, Server, Asparagus, Fessenden Bros., Coin	175.00
Silver, American, Server, Gold-Washed Bowl, Wood & Hughes	45.00
Silver, American, Server, Oyster, Floral Pattern, Unger Bros.	90.00
Silver, American, Server, Tomato, Twisted Handle, Bailey & Co., Philadelphia	90.00
Silver, American, Serving, Fork, Engraving & Raised Fruit Design, C.1850, Coin	19.75
Silver, American, Shears, Grape	38.00
Silver, American, Shell, Sugar, Farrington & Hunnewell, Boston, C.1835, Coin	13.75
Silver, American, Snuffbox, Zachariah Brigden, Boston, C.1743, Coin, 3 1/2 In.	700.00
Silver, American, Spoon, Baby Webster Co., Stork Handle, Birth Record, Clock	15.00
Silver, American, Spoon, Berry, Gold Washed Bowl, Lily, Whiting	115.00
Silver, American, Spoon, Bonbon, Enameled Bowl, Great Seal U.S., Gorham	75.00
Silver, American, Spoon, Bonbon, Pierced, Gorham, Luxembourg	28.00
Silver, American, Spoon, Bright Cut, John W.Gethen, Philadelphia, C.1785, Coin	45.00
Silver, American, Spoon, Dessert, Adrian Holmes, C.1801-49, Coin	12.95
Silver, American, Spoon, Dessert, Bows, Ball & Co., C.1840, Coin	13.00
Silver, American, Spoon, Dessert, H.V.A.X., C.1850, Coin	13.00
Silver, American, Spoon, Dessert, J.E.Brown, Baltimore, C.1816, Coin	15.95
Silver, American, Spoon, Dessert, John Price, Lancaster, PA, 1810, Coin	45.00
Silver, American, Spoon, Dessert, N.Harding, C.1850, Coin	12.95
Silver, American, Spoon, Dessert, Ordway, Initial Cab, C.1816, Coin	12.95
Silver, American, Spoon, Dessert, Straight Fiddle Tip Handle, Pair, Coin	28.00
Silver, American, Spoon, Dessert, W.L.Knox, C.1850, Coin	9.75
Silver, American, Spoon, Dessert, Wm.Walker, C.1816, Coin	12.95
Silver, American, Spoon, J.Moulton, Newburyport, Massachusets, J.B.Noyes, Coin	35.00
Silver, American, Spoon, Master Salt, A.Cutler, Boston, C.1820, Coin	12.50
Silver, American, Spoon, Master Salt, Currier & Trott, Boston, C.1836, Coin	9.95
Silver, American, Spoon, Master Salt, Farrington & Hunnewell, Boston, C.1835	9.95
Silver, American, Spoon, Master Salt, L.Studley, Coin	15.00
Silver, American, Spoon, Mustard, Lander, 5 3/8 In.	27.00
Silver, American, Spoon, Salt, Coffin Back, Abel Moulton, C.1810, Coin	45.00
Silver, American, Spoon, Salt, Currier & Trott, Boston, C.1836, Coin	9.95
Silver, American, Spoon, Salt, E.Benjamin & Co., New Haven, Coin	18.00
Silver, American, Spoon, Salt, Master, A.Culter, Engraved M.Swain, C.1820, Coin	12.50
Silver, American, Spoon, Salt, Master, Chantilly, Gorham	16.50
Silver, American, Spoon, Salt, Robert Wilson, C.1803-25, Coin	35.00
Silver, American, Spoon, Serving, C.E.Butler, Coin	25.00
Silver, American, Spoon, Serving, E.Burr, Pair, 9 1/2 In.	225.00
Silver, American, Spoon, Serving, E.Shaw, Coin	18.00
Silver, American, Spoon, Serving, Farrington & Honeywell, Coin, 9 1/2 In.	22.00
Silver, American, Spoon, Serving, George Appleton, C.1850, Coin	15.00
Silver, American, Spoon, Serving, George III, Whiting, C.1891, Pair	30.00
Silver, American, Spoon, Serving, Jones, Lows & Ball, Coin, Pair	40.00
Silver, American, Spoon, Serving, Large, George Appleton, C.1850, Coin	14.95
Silver, American, Spoon, Serving, Large, J.Moulton, C.1835-50, Coin	29.95
Silver, American, Spoon, Serving, Large, Lows Ball & Co., C.1840, Fiddle Thread	14.95
Silver, American, Spoon, Serving, Large, SG Beers, C.1835-50, Coin	14.95
Silver, American, Spoon, Serving, Large, Wm.Walker, C.1816, Coin	14.95
Silver, American, Spoon, Serving, Lily, Gold Washed, Whiting, 7 3/4 In.	65.00
Silver, American, Spoon, Serving, Shell Shape, Gold-Washed Bowl, Bailey & Co.	55.00
Silver, American, Spoon, Serving, W.Pitkin, East Hartford, Conn., C.1825, Coin	14.95
Silver, American, Spoon, Shell, Sugar, Jones, Shreve, Brown & Co., C.1854, Coin	19.95
Silver, American, Spoon, Soup, Fiddle Tip Handle, S.Semkin, Coin, 13 In.	135.00
Silver, American, Spoon, Zodiac, Taurus, Gorham, 6 In.	40.00
Silver, American, Strainer, Footed Tea, N.Harding, Boston, Coin, 6 In.	68.00
Silver, American, Sugar & Creamer, Applied Sterling Floral Decoration, Kerr	250.00

Silver, American, Sugar & Creamer, Art Nouveau, Bailey, Banks, & Biddle 75.00
Silver, American, Sugar & Creamer, Cover, Gorham, C.1850, Coin 150.00
Silver, American, Sugar & Creamer, Gilt Lined, Webster Company 27.50
Silver, American, Sugar Shaker, Liberty Browne & William Seal, Philadelphia 800.00
Silver, American, Sugar Shaker, Ornate, Jas.Tufts, Boston 25.00
Silver, American, Sugar Shell, Farrington & Hunnewell, Boston, C.1835, Coin 13.75
Silver, American, Sugar Shell, Fiddle Tip Handle, Monogram, Jones, Ball & Co. 15.00
Silver, American, Sugar Shell, J.Moulton, Bright Cut, Scalloped Bowl 50.00
Silver, American, Sugar Shell, La Contessa, Reed & Barton, 1897 .... 22.00
Silver, American, Sugar Shell, N.Harding & Co., C.1850, Coin 19.75
Silver, American, Sugar Shovel, Chapin, Coin, 6 1/2 In. 15.00
Silver, American, Sugar, Shell, C.1830-50, Coin 24.95
Silver, American, Tablespoon, E.Whiton, Boston, C.1835, Coin 14.95
Silver, American, Tablespoon, Engraved, Baltimore, P.Eltonhead, E.M.R., Coin 30.00
Silver, American, Tablespoon, Fiddle Handle, Elias Davis, Boston, C.1810, Coin 18.00
Silver, American, Tablespoon, Fiddle, Wm.B.Durgin, Concord, N.H., C.1870, Coin 30.00
Silver, American, Tablespoon, Fiddleback, G.H.Gibbs, Coin, 8 1/2 In., Pair 20.00
Silver, American, Tablespoon, Gorham, C.1832, Coin 25.00
Silver, American, Tablespoon, Greenbury Gaither, Washington, D.C., C.1830, Coin 50.00
Silver, American, Tablespoon, J.Clarico, Norfolk, Va., Coin 65.00
Silver, American, Tablespoon, J.Conning, Mobile, Ala., C.1830, Coin 75.00
Silver, American, Tablespoon, J.H.Hollister, Oswego, N.Y., C.1840, Coin 14.95
Silver, American, Tablespoon, Medallion, F.A.Durgin, St.Louis 45.00
Silver, American, Tablespoon, N.Harding, C.1850, Coin 13.00
Silver, American, Tablespoon, N.Harding, C.1866, Coin 25.00
Silver, American, Tablespoon, Norris & Co., Mid-1880s, Coin 19.50

Silver, American, Tea Set, Wm.B.North & Co., C.1830, 4 Piece

Silver, American, Tablespoon, R. & W.Wilson, Straight Fiddle Handle, Pair 38.00
Silver, American, Tablespoon, Reverse Tip, A.C.Benedict, N.Y., C.1830, Coin 25.00
Silver, American, Tablespoon, Sheaf Of Wheat, J.B.Jones, Coin 95.00
Silver, American, Tablespoon, Theophilus Bradbury, C.1815, Coin 18.00
Silver, American, Tablespoon, Wavy End, B.H.Smith & Co., C.1836, Coin 85.00
Silver, American, Tablespoon, Wm.Mitchell, Jr., Richmond, Va. 75.00
Silver, American, Tea Caddy, Black Starr & Co. 175.00
Silver, American, Tea Set, Engraved Design, Gorham Mfg. Co., 3 Piece 295.00
Silver, American, Tea Set, Oval Shapes, Gorham, C.1900, 4 Piece 465.00
Silver, American, Tea Set, Raised Leaf, Beaded Rims, Gorham, 5 Piece 925.00
Silver, American, Tea Set, Wm.B.North & Co., C.1830, 4 Piece .... Illus 1550.00
Silver, American, Teapot, Greek Key Border, Ivory Insulator, Gorham, C.1925 .... 225.00
Silver, American, Teapot, Round, Butterfly Finial, Gorham, C.1850, Coin 150.00
Silver, American, Teaspoon, A.Logan, C.1805, Set Of Four, Coin 48.00
Silver, American, Teaspoon, B.Cleveland, Newark, N.J., Coin 32.00
Silver, American, Teaspoon, Bancroft Woodcock, Set Of 5, C.1780 .... 250.00
Silver, American, Teaspoon, Basket Of Flowers, S.Piggot, Coin 35.00
Silver, American, Teaspoon, Blackman & Warner, Coin 7.50
Silver, American, Teaspoon, Brackett, Boston, 1840, Coin 6.00
Silver, American, Teaspoon, Coffin Back, Van, Keene, N.H., Coin 28.00
Silver, American, Teaspoon, Coffin Handle, Engraved, Hohn LeRdux, Coin 30.00

Silver, American, Teaspoon, Cornell, Providence, R.I., Bright Cut, C.1780, Coin	48.00
Silver, American, Teaspoon, Currier & Trott, Boston, Coin	10.00
Silver, American, Teaspoon, D.Becker & Co., Engraved A.C.Loomis, Set Of 3	26.95
Silver, American, Teaspoon, Damon & Wentworth, C.1835, Set Of 5, Coin	42.00
Silver, American, Teaspoon, Ebenezer Moulton, C.1790, Coin, Pair	40.00
Silver, American, Teaspoon, Engraved Clara, C.1800, Pearson, NYC, Coin, 3	27.00
Silver, American, Teaspoon, F & D Kinsey, Ohio & Kentucky, F.E.W., Coin, Pair	30.00
Silver, American, Teaspoon, Fiddleback, Seth E.Brown On Back, Coin	15.00
Silver, American, Teaspoon, Gary & Co., Co.1815-20, Coin, Set Of 5	44.95
Silver, American, Teaspoon, Henry Bayeaux, C.1801-12, Coin, Set Of 3	26.95
Silver, American, Teaspoon, J.B.Jones, C.1810-20, Coin, Set Of 4	39.95
Silver, American, Teaspoon, J.Monroe, C.1810, Coin	8.00
Silver, American, Teaspoon, Jabez Gorham & Son, Providence, R.I., Coin	15.00
Silver, American, Teaspoon, Joshua Lowe, C.1828, Coin	9.95
Silver, American, Teaspoon, Kitts, Coin	30.00
Silver, American, Teaspoon, Lily Pattern, Monogram L, Whiting	18.50
Silver, American, Teaspoon, Lows, Ball & Co., C.1840, Coin	7.95
Silver, American, Teaspoon, Lows, Ball & Co., Set Of 6, Coin	45.00
Silver, American, Teaspoon, Macauly, Charleston, South Carolina	110.00
Silver, American, Teaspoon, Monroe & DeFrieze, Coin	13.00
Silver, American, Teaspoon, N.Harding, Boston, 1850, Coin	20.00
Silver, American, Teaspoon, Old Virginia, Reed & Barton	10.00
Silver, American, Teaspoon, Pear & Bacall, Boston, 1850, Coin	35.00
Silver, American, Teaspoon, Raised Drop On Back Of Bowl, A.Jacobs, Coin, Pair	30.00
Silver, American, Teaspoon, Rounded End, W.Pitkin, Coin	6.00
Silver, American, Teaspoon, S.Chapin, Connecticut, 1800, Coin	7.50
Silver, American, Teaspoon, Seymore, Connecticut, 1843, Coin	6.00
Silver, American, Teaspoon, Sheaf Of Wheat, Coin	30.00
Silver, American, Teaspoon, Twisted Handle, Ouhme & Co., C.1860	16.00
Silver, American, Teaspoon, W.Gennet, Coin	12.50
Silver, American, Teaspoon, W.P.& H Stanton, 1840-50, Coin, Set Of 6	70.00
Silver, American, Teaspoon, W.W.W.In Shield, Dated 1880, Coin	14.00
Silver, American, Teaspoon, William Moulton, Newburyport, Mass., 1771, Coin	75.00
Silver, American, Teaspoon, Wm.I.Pitkin, Coin	12.50
Silver, American, Tomato Server, Twisted Handle, Engraved, Bailey & Co., Coin	90.00
Silver, American, Tong, Ice, Grecian, Gorham, 10 1/2 In.	115.00
Silver, American, Tong, Sugar, Violet, Whiting, 5 In.	40.00
Silver, American, Tongs, American Eagle Touchmark, C.1820, Coin	34.75
Silver, American, Tongs, Basket Of Flowers, D.Cohen, Shell Grips, Coin	145.00
Silver, American, Tongs, Basket Of Flowers, John P.Grott & Sons, Coin	85.00
Silver, American, Tongs, Farrington & Huntington, 1835-50	28.00
Silver, American, Tongs, Garson & Hall, Albany, N.Y., C.1810, Coin	85.00
Silver, American, Tongs, Shubael Starrs, C.1803-28, Coin, 6 1/4 In.	65.00
Silver, American, Tongs, Straight Fiddle Bow & Sides, Coin, Pair, 6 In.	40.00
Silver, American, Vase, Medallion, Gorham, Coin, 7 1/2 In.	225.00
Silver, American, Whisk Broom, Lover's Dream, Unger Bros.	75.00
Silver, American, Winged Cherub, Albert Coles & Co., Initialed	10.00
Silver, Bowl, American, Greek Key, Beaded Border, Gale & Son, C.1860, 5 1/2 In.	235.00
Silver, Canadian, Sugar Shell, Medallion, C.1830	55.00

Silver, Dutch, Corkscrew, C.1740, 4 1/2 In.

Silver, Chinese, Egg Set, Fiddle Thread, Shell Pattern, 17 Piece	775.00
Silver, Chinese, Strainer, Tea, Carved Jade Handle, 4 In.	125.00
Silver, Danish, Mirror, Hand, Child's, Scene In Relief, 5 1/4 In.	20.00
Silver, Danish, Muffineer, Pear Shape, Domed Top, Embossed, Beaded, 6 1/2 In.	48.00
Silver, Danish, Sifter, Sugar, Grape Cluster Finial, Jensen, 6 In.	325.00
Silver, Dutch, Basket, Reticulated & Repousse, Handle, 3 Cupids In Bowl	50.00
Silver, Dutch, Corkscrew, C.1740, 4 1/2 In. _____ Illus	500.00
Silver, Dutch, Pianoforte, Miniature, Top Opens, 800	135.00
Silver, Dutch, Tea Set & Tray, Repousse Scenes Of Villagers	450.00
Silver, English, Bowl, Punch, Georgian, Orlando Jackson, Lond., 1771, 7 In.	3500.00
Silver, English, Bowl, Sauce, Georgian, 1763, Horse Hoof, Claw Feet	450.00
Silver, English, Box, Card, Birmingham, 1904, 4 X 3 1/4 X 2/3 In.	98.00
Silver, English, Box, Snuff, Rectangular, Cover, C.1720, 2 7/8 In.Long	200.00
Silver, English, Candelabra, 3-Arm, C.1790, Sheffield, 27 In., Pair	975.00
Silver, English, Candlestick, Corinthian Column, Tho.Law, C.1760, Signed, Pair	350.00
Silver, English, Candlestick, 19th Century, Hallmarked, 11 In., Pair	245.00
Silver, English, Castor, Sugar, Paneled, Raised Ribbon, Birmingham, 1913, 8 In.	110.00
Silver, English, Cup, Crespin Fuller, London, 1810, Gold-Washed Interior	300.00
Silver, English, Cup, Pedestal, Drapery Ornamentation, Benjamin Laver, 1888	225.00
Silver, English, Fork, Pickle, Ladder Style Top, Hallmark, 3 Time	15.00
Silver, English, Hallmarks, C.1910	11.00
Silver, English, Inkwell, Glass Insert, 3 1/2 In.	24.00
Silver, English, Knife, Butter, Wm.Chawner, London, 1826, Kings Pattern	42.00
Silver, English, Label, Georgian, John Robinson, C.1792, Claret & Hock, Pair	85.00
Silver, English, Ladle, Gravy, Richard Crossley, 1792	150.00
Silver, English, Ladle, Gravy, W.J., London 1823, 2 1/2 Oz.	65.00
Silver, English, Ladle, Soup, Geo.III, Hallmarked	325.00
Silver, English, Platter, Gadroon Border, 1785-86, Signed, 16 1/2 In.	450.00
Silver, English, Platter, Rococo Shape, Gadroon Border, 18th Century, 12 In.	450.00
Silver, English, Salt, Master, Urn Shape, Peter, Wm.& Ann Bateman, 1801, Pair	400.00
Silver, English, Scoop, Marrow, Double End, Hallmarked John Wren, 1777, 9 In.	250.00
Silver, English, Scoop, Marrow, Peter And Ann Bateman, 1809	90.00
Silver, English, Serving Spoon, Griffin Crest, Hallmarked, 8 1/4 In.	45.00
Silver, English, Sifter, Urn Shaped, Georgian, C.1814, 3 3/4 In.	195.00
Silver, English, Skewer, Meat, Wm.Sumner, London, 1804	135.00
Silver, English, Skewer, Peter And Ann Bateman, 1791	125.00
Silver, English, Spoon, Berry, Trifid, James Wilks, London, 1726, Rat Tail	150.00
Silver, English, Spoon, Berry, Vermeil Bowl, Hester Bateman, 1781, Pair	200.00
Silver, English, Spoon, Berry, Vermeil, Bright Cut Decorations, Pair	100.00
Silver, English, Spoon, Dessert, Fiddle Handle, Wm.Eley, 1845, Set Of 10	200.00
Silver, English, Spoon, Dressing, London, 1788	245.00
Silver, English, Spoon, Serving, Fiddle Handle, William Bateman, 1835, Pair	125.00
Silver, English, Spoon, Serving, Hallmarked, Vines & Grapes, 2 Piece, 9 In.	95.00
Silver, English, Spoon, Serving, Hester Bateman, London, 1784, Pair	250.00
Silver, English, Spoon, Serving, M.E.& M.E., London 1826, 11 1/2 In., Pair	210.00
Silver, English, Spoon, Serving, Repousse Fluted Bowl, John Wren, 1791, 8 In.	125.00
Silver, English, Spoon, Serving, Thomas Wallis, London, 1807-8, Pair	110.00
Silver, English, Spoon, Soup, Fiddle Handle, C.1810, Set Of 6	200.00
Silver, English, Spoon, Stuffing, Hallmarked Edinburgh, 1869, Pair	175.00
Silver, English, Table Set, Demitasse, Creamer, Sugar, Spoon, Hester Pate, 1910	80.00
Silver, English, Tablespoon, Hester Bateman, London, 1777, Marked, Pair	125.00
Silver, English, Tea Set, Georgian, Floral Pattern, 4 Pieces	2200.00
Silver, English, Teaspoon, Marked Peter, Ann, Wm., Bateman, 1803	35.00
Silver, English, Tongs, Sugar, Cut Decoration, Hester Bateman, 1784-85	150.00
Silver, English, Tongs, Sugar, Figural, Stork, Infant In Cavity Of Body	75.00
Silver, English, Tongs, Sugar, Georgian, Samuel Hennel, 1802-1903	48.00
Silver, English, Tongs, Sugar, Hallmarked London, 1860, T.S.	50.00
Silver, English, Tongs, Sugar, Lizards Form Base, Infant In Cavity, C.1750	75.00
Silver, English, Turkey Cover, Beaded Bottom, Decorated Handle, Hallmarks	210.00
Silver, English, Vinaigrette, Birmingham, 1813, 1 X 2/3 In.	185.00
Silver, English, Vinaigrette, Engraved, Gilt Pierced, Joseph Willmore, 2 In.	140.00
Silver, English, Wine Caddy, Figure 8 Shape, Ornate, Gargoyles, 1863, 2 Bottle	40.00
Silver, English, Wine Cooler, Urn Shape, Repousse Decoration, 12 In.	70.00
Silver, English, Wine Cooler, 20th Century, 9 1/2 In., Pair	100.00
Silver, English, Wine Label, Port, S.Hennel, London 1818	130.00

Silver, English, Wine Spout, London, W.A.	60.00
Silver, French, Box, Snuff, Vermeille Inside, Relief Picture On Lid	96.00
Silver, French, Caddy, Tea, Squatty Casket Shape, Ball Feet, 18th Century	395.00
Silver, German, Brush, Clothes, Art Nouveau	7.50
Silver, German, Ladle, C.1840, 4 3/8 X 8 1/2 In.	130.00
Silver, German, Letter Poener, Art Nouveau Repousse Disign	55.00
Silver, Irish, Jug, Hot Beverage, Charles Townsend, C.1776, 11 3/4 In.	3000.00
Silver, Irish, Spoon, Dessert, Dublin, C.1800	38.00
Silver, Irish, Spoon, Serving, Fiddle Handle, Samuel Neville, Dublin, 1804, Pair	120.00
Silver, Mexican, Candelabra, 5 Holders, Signed A Torres Vega, 12 In.	250.00
Silver, Mexican, Centerpiece, Footed, Scalloped Border, 13 In.	150.00
Silver, Mexican, Coffee & Tea Service, 7 Piece, Early 20th Century	1300.00
Silver, Mexican, Tea & Coffee Set, Miniature, Green & Pink Stones, 17 Piece	35.00
Silver, Mexican, Tray, Repousse, Gadroon Border, 21 In.	175.00
Silver, Persian, Tray, Copper Footed, Chased Hunting Scene, 19 1/2 In.	250.00
Silver, Peruvian, Candelabra, 2-Light, Repousse, 8 1/2 In., Pair	150.00
Silver, Peruvian, Centerpiece, Separate Pierced Frog, Hammered, Perez, C.1800	225.00
Silver, Peruvian, Platter, Oval, 19th Century, 20 In.	180.00
Silver, Peruvian, Tray, Serving, Two Handles, Gadroon Border, 28 In.	135.00
Silver, Portuguese, Candlestick, Decorated, 5 In., Set Of 6	6000.00
Silver, Russian, see also Faberge	
Silver, Russian, Beaker, Engraved Design, Full Marks, 1 3/4 In.	25.00
Silver, Russian, Beaker, Landscape & Floral Scenes, 2 1/2 In.	75.00
Silver, Russian, Beaker, Star Of David & Floral, 2 1/2 In.	75.00
Silver, Russian, Belt, Lady's, Niello, Large Buckle With Sabre Catch, 84 HC	185.00
Silver, Russian, Box, Cigar, M.Ivanov, St.Petersburg, 6 3/8 In. .... *Illus*	1600.00
Silver, Russian, Box, Cigar, Parcel-Gilt, E.K.Mark, 1887, 7 X 2 In .... *Illus*	1500.00
Silver, Russian, Box, Cigar, Scene Inside Fancy Border, Marked, 1888	125.00
Silver, Russian, Box, Cigarette, Alexander Muchin, 1889, 3 5/8 In .... *Illus*	1100.00

Silver, Russian, Box, Cigar, M.Ivanov, St.Petersburg, 6 3/8 In.

Silver, Russian, Box, Cigar, Parcel-Gilt, E.K.Mark, 1887, 7 X 2 In.

Silver, Russian, Box, Cigarette, Alexander Muchin, 1889, 3 5/8 In.

Silver, Russian, Box, Cigarette, Gilt Interior, 1873, 3 1/4 In.

Silver, Russian, Box, Cigarette, Moscow, C.1880, 3 5/8 X 3/4 In.

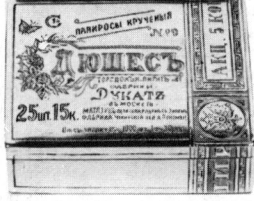

Silver, Russian, Box, Cigarette, Parcel-Gilt, 1889, 3 5/8 X 2 In.

Silver, Russian, Box, Cigarette, Gilt Interior, 1873, 3 1/4 In. *Illus*	1200.00
Silver, Russian, Box, Cigarette, Gold-Washed Interior, Hallmarked, 4 1/4 In.	225.00
Silver, Russian, Box, Cigarette, Moscow, C.1880, 3 5/8 X 3/4 In. *Illus*	1000.00
Silver, Russian, Box, Cigarette, Parcel-Gilt, 1889, 3 5/8 X 2 In. *Illus*	1100.00
Silver, Russian, Box, Sugar, Engraved Decoration, A.Turczynski, 1864	500.00
Silver, Russian, Case, Cigarette, Building Scene, Dated 1888	125.00
Silver, Russian, Case, Cigarette, Niello Farm Scene, Hallmarked, 3 1/2 X 2 In.	135.00
Silver, Russian, Cup, Engraved Floral, Pedestal, Hallmarked, 5 1/2 In.	65.00
Silver, Russian, Cup, Etched, Handled, Marked 84, 1 3/4 X 1 1/4 In.	96.00
Silver, Russian, Cup, Vodka, Chased Floral, Gilt Inside, Kokoshnik, Kiev Region	50.00
Silver, Russian, Cup, Wine, Floral, Impressed Kokoshnik, 2 1/2 In.	50.00
Silver, Russian, Cutter, Cigar, Bulldog With Ruby Eyes, Oak Leaves & Acorns	500.00
Silver, Russian, Enameled Pastel Colors, Hallmarked & Maker's Mark	235.00
Silver, Russian, Goblet, Scroll Work, 4 In.	90.00
Silver, Russian, Jigger, Etched, Marked 84, 2 1/8 X 1 7/8 In.	30.00
Silver, Russian, Money Holder, Enameled, Hallmarked	300.00
Silver, Russian, Money Holder, With Enamel, Fully Hallmarked	300.00
Silver, Russian, Salt, Etched, Dated 1884	47.00
Silver, Russian, Spoon, Caviar, Enamel	255.00
Silver, Russian, Spoon, Serving, Dated 1876, 9 In.	55.00
Silver, Russian, Spoon, Serving, Marked 84, 1876, 9 In.	55.00
Silver, Russian, Sugar & Creamer, Miniature, Marked 84	50.00
Silver, Russian, Tablespoon, Hallmarked, AC, 1872, 8 1/2 In.	32.00
Silver, Russian, Teaspoon, Matte Finish With Gold Etching	55.00
Silver, Russian, Teaspoon, Twisted Handle, Pair	88.00
Silver, Russian, Wine Cup, Engraved & Hallmarked	35.00
Silver, Russian, Wine Cup, Engraved, Church, Hallmarks, 2 In.	38.00
Silver, Sheffield, see also Silver Plate	
Silver, Sheffield, Candlestick, Bobeche, Fluted Oval Base, 12 In., Pair	248.00
Silver, Sheffield, Candlestick, Gadroon Border, Matthew Boulton, 10 In., Pair	325.00
Silver, Sheffield, Candlestick, Georgian, Round Bases, Pair	125.00
Silver, Sheffield, Fish Set, Bone Handles, Boxed, C.1897, 2 Piece	60.00
Silver, Sheffield, Inkstand, 2 Cut Glass Wells, Beehive Pattern, C.1800	58.00
Silver, Sheffield, Spoon, Salt, William Moulton, 1772	35.00
Silver, Sheffield, Tea Set, William & George Sessions, 3 Piece	195.00
Silver, Sheffield, Tray, Silver On Copper, Grapes & Leaves In Relief, 12 In.	35.00

Sterling silver is made with 925 parts of silver out of 1, 000 parts of metal.
The word sterling is a quality guarantee used in the United States after
about 1860.

Silver, Sterling, Napkin Ring, see Napkin Ring
Silver, Sterling, see also Silver, American; Silver, English; etc.

Silver, Sterling, Ashtray, Golf	14.00
Silver, Sterling, Ashtray, Two Cigar Rests, 4 1/4 In.	45.00
Silver, Sterling, Baby, Stork, Curved Handle, Birth Record In Bowl, 10/25/16	25.00
Silver, Sterling, Barn Owl, Vermeil Work, Paperweight Eyes, 6 1/4 In.	300.00
Silver, Sterling, Basket, Black Starr & Frost, Cutout & Relief, 12 1/2 In.	275.00
Silver, Sterling, Basket, Bread, Oval, Pierced Border, Handled, 5 1/8 X 1 1/4 In.	65.00
Silver, Sterling, Basket, Candy, Pierced Sides, Handle, 5 1/8 X 1 1/4 In.	35.00
Silver, Sterling, Basket, Sugar, Cobalt Liner, Ornately Pierced, Footed, 3 In.	42.00
Silver, Sterling, Bell, Dinner, 3 Panels Of Embossed Floral Work, 3 1/4 In.	45.00
Silver, Sterling, Belt, 11 Links Repousse, Female Heads, Flowing Hair, Marked	650.00
Silver, Sterling, Bookmark, Pearl Handle, Birmingham, 1897-98, 1 3/4 In.	35.00
Silver, Sterling, Bottle Opener, Art Nouveau	10.00
Silver, Sterling, Bottle Opener, Ornate Flowered Handle	7.95
Silver, Sterling, Bottle, Perfume, Cranberry Overlay, Stopper, 3 1/2 In.	65.00
Silver, Sterling, Bottle, Perfume, Purse Size	12.00
Silver, Sterling, Bottle, Perfume, Yellow Enamel, 1 3/4 In.	25.00
Silver, Sterling, Bowl, Console, Overlay Ships On Green Rolled Edge, 11 In.	60.00
Silver, Sterling, Bowl, Cutout Rim, Gadroon Edge, Pedestal, 8 1/4 In.	25.00
Silver, Sterling, Bowl, Strawberries Surround Rim, Art Nouveau, 12 1/2 In.	225.00
Silver, Sterling, Box, Match, Embossed Decoration	27.50
Silver, Sterling, Box, Powder, Victorian Reticule, Enamel Cover, 1 X 1/2 In.	28.00
Silver, Sterling, Box, Stamp	55.00
Silver, Sterling, Brush, Clothes, Art Nouveau	15.00
Silver, Sterling, Brush, Crumb, Art Nouveau, 10 In.	12.50
Silver, Sterling, Brush, Hair, Art Nouveau, 9 1/4 In.	125.00
Silver, Sterling, Brush, Shaving, 1895	35.00
Silver, Sterling, Buckle, Satin Finish, Floral, Kerr Mark	45.00
Silver, Sterling, Buckle, Shoe, Pair	12.00
Silver, Sterling, Butterpick, Chippendale Pattern	18.00
Silver, Sterling, Buttonhook, Art Nouveau	22.50
Silver, Sterling, Buttonhook, Handled, Ornate	20.00
Silver, Sterling, Buttonhook, Ornate Flowered Handle, 8 In.	9.50
Silver, Sterling, Caddy, Tea, 8 Ribs, 4 1/2 In.	60.00
Silver, Sterling, Candelabra, 3 Light, 11 1/4 In., Pair	30.00
Silver, Sterling, Candelabrum, 3 Cup, Rosepoint Pattern, 6 X 12 In.	75.00
Silver, Sterling, Candleholder, Engraved Glass Shades, Pair	125.00
Silver, Sterling, Candlestick, Miniature, Turned Pedestal, Heavy Base, 3 In.	20.00
Silver, Sterling, Card, Case, Ornate	50.00
Silver, Sterling, Case, Card, Engraved, Flip Open, 2 X 3 In.	30.00
Silver, Sterling, Case, Card, Hammered, Cartouche For Monogram	52.00
Silver, Sterling, Case, Cigar, Chased Design, 3-Part, 5 In.	65.00
Silver, Sterling, Case, Cigarette, Art Deco	25.00
Silver, Sterling, Case, Cigarette, Flip Top, Gilt Initial	20.00
Silver, Sterling, Case, Cigarette, Gold Washed, R.B.Company	32.50
Silver, Sterling, Case, Cigarette, Initialed JMAW	10.00
Silver, Sterling, Case, Cigarette, Initials CRP	10.00
Silver, Sterling, Case, Cigarette, Lady's, Compact, Gold-Washed Interior	20.00
Silver, Sterling, Case, Cigarette, Ornate, Deeply Carved, 3 X 4 In.	35.00
Silver, Sterling, Case, Cigarette, R.Blackinton & Co., 1925	20.00
Silver, Sterling, Case, Cigarette, 4 Sections, Chased Design, 950, 6 In.	55.00
Silver, Sterling, Case, Lipstick, Engraved Floral, Numbered	20.00
Silver, Sterling, Case, Single Cigar, Gold-Washed Inside, Box	65.00
Silver, Sterling, Chocolate Pot, Hammered, Floral Design On Top, 10 1/2 In.	265.00
Silver, Sterling, Cigar Case, Chased Design, Three Parts, 5 In.	65.00
Silver, Sterling, Cigar, Cutter, Ornate Dragon With Woman's Breasts, 6 In.	80.00
Silver, Sterling, Cigar, Cutter, Pocket, Salem Witch In Relief, Dated 1902	25.00
Silver, Sterling, Cigar, Cutter, Pocket, Slide Type, 1902, P.B.H.	14.00
Silver, Sterling, Cigarette Case, Symmetrically Designed, 3.5 Oz.	20.00
Silver, Sterling, Cigarette Holder, Chalice-Type, Hobstars, File, Fans, Gem	55.00

Silver, Sterling, Coffee Set, Also Tea, Square Footed, 1899, Schultz, 5 Pieces 1450.00
Silver, Sterling, Coin Carrier, Nickels, Dimes, Quarters, Lid Snaps Shut, Chain 35.00
Silver, Sterling, Comb, Baby, Art Nouveau 15.00
Silver, Sterling, Compote, Flower Edge Around Top, 3 X 6 1/2 In. 12.50
Silver, Sterling, Compote, Handled, Engraved Vera, 1924 .... 45.00
Silver, Sterling, Corn Holder 6.00
Silver, Sterling, Creamer, Cow, Embossed Insect On Lid, 2 1/2 X 5 In. 145.00
Silver, Sterling, Creamer, Cow, Embossed Insect On Lid, 4 1/2 X 7 In. 195.00
Silver, Sterling, Crumber, Decorated Handle, 14 In. 18.00
Silver, Sterling, Cup & Saucer, Demitasse, C.1880 .... 25.00
Silver, Sterling, Cup, Baby, Mama & Papa To Their Son, German Script 65.00
Silver, Sterling, Cup, Inlaid Stone Work, Maker Greif, 4 1/2 X 6 In. 240.00
Silver, Sterling, Cup, Wedding, Woman Wearing Hoop Skirt, Dutch, 4 1/2 In. 85.00
Silver, Sterling, Cup, Wedding, Woman Wearing Hoop Skirt, 5 1/4 In. 110.00
Silver, Sterling, Curling Iron, Miniature, Mother-Of-Pearl Button, 6 In. 30.00
Silver, Sterling, Decanter, Shape Of Pheasant 250.00
Silver, Sterling, Desk Set, Russian Rock Crystal, 2 Inkpots, Domed 1150.00
Silver, Sterling, Dish, Candy, Pedestal, Basket Weave Edge, 2 1/2 X 5 7/8 In. 25.00
Silver, Sterling, Dish, Nut, Floral, 1903, 3 1/2 X 2 3/4 In. 15.00
Silver, Sterling, Dish, Olive, 4 Lobe, 4 Legs 58.50
Silver, Sterling, Dish, Porridge, Pierced-Work Handle, Engraved, 5 1/2 In. 75.00
Silver, Sterling, Dish, Seder, Star Of David, Judaic Inscriptions, 6 1/2 In. 100.00
Silver, Sterling, Dish, Vegetable, Lid, Gorham, C.1870, 18 1/4 In. ....*Illus* 1500.00

Silver, Sterling, Dish, Vegetable, Lid, Gorham, C.1870, 18 1/4 In.

Silver, Sterling, Dresser Set, 10 Pieces, Includes 3 Jars With Sterling Tops 145.00
Silver, Sterling, Eraser, Ink, Chased Handle, Steel Blade 12.00
Silver, Sterling, Figural, Donkey, Standing, 2 1/2 X 2 1/2 In. 58.00
Silver, Sterling, Figural, Fox, Running, 1 1/2 X 4 1/2 In. 95.00
Silver, Sterling, Figural, Owl, Barn, Standing, 3 In. 75.00
Silver, Sterling, Figural, Pheasant, Standing, 2 X 2 1/2 In. 55.00
Silver, Sterling, Figurine, Bulldog, 2 1/2 X 4 1/2 In. 13.00
Silver, Sterling, Figurine, Carved Ivory Hands, Face, Stones, 6 1/2 In. 225.00
Silver, Sterling, Figurine, Colonial Man Pulling Cart With Pig, 2 3/4 In. 45.00
Silver, Sterling, Figurine, Horse, One Leg In Raised Position, 4 1/2 In. 210.00
Silver, Sterling, Figurine, Horse, Prancing, 4 1/2 X 5 1/2 In. 285.00
Silver, Sterling, Figurine, Knight, Embossed Decoration, Ivory Face, 5 1/2 In. 170.00
Silver, Sterling, Figurine, Nativity Set, Set Of 7 .... 75.00
Silver, Sterling, Figurine, Owl, Vermeil Work, Paperweight Eyes, 6 1/4 In. 300.00
Silver, Sterling, Figurine, Prancing Horse, 4 1/2 X 5 1/2 In. 235.00
Silver, Sterling, Figurine, Queen, Ivory Face & Hands, Inlaid Stones, 7 In. 225.00
Silver, Sterling, Figurine, Two Mallard Ducks, 5 X 5 In. 290.00
Silver, Sterling, Figurine, Walking Puma, 2 1/4 X 3 1/2 In. 90.00
Silver, Sterling, Figurine, Whole Body Lion, 5 In. 134.00
Silver, Sterling, Flask, Lift-Up Screw-On Top, C.A.Vanderbilt 85.00
Silver, Sterling, Fork, Baby's, Cutout Rabbit Skipping Rope Handle, 3 1/2 In. 15.00
Silver, Sterling, Fork, Lemon, Flower Design Handle, 5 1/8 In. 9.95
Silver, Sterling, Fork, Oyster, Floral Enamel Handle, C.1900 .... 25.00
Silver, Sterling, Fork, Pickle, Pearl Handle 15.00

Silver, Sterling, Fork, Serving, Windmill, Turning Blades, C.1898, 11 In.	38.00
Silver, Sterling, Fork, 2 Tine, Twisted Shaft, Lacy Flower Ferrule, Stag, 6 In.	15.00
Silver, Sterling, Frame, Bun Feet, Art Nouveau Flowers, Oval, 10 In.	12.00
Silver, Sterling, Frame, Cutout, Handles, Holds White Ramekins	265.00
Silver, Sterling, Frame, Oval, Easel Type Ball Feet, 4 X 6 In.	30.00
Silver, Sterling, Glove Stretcher, Fancy	12.00
Silver, Sterling, Hairbrush, Full-Figure Woman Handle, Art Nouveau, 9 1/2 In.	125.00
Silver, Sterling, Holder, Lipstick And Hairpin, Silver Chain	12.00
Silver, Sterling, Holder, Sugar Cube, Handles, Footed, 6 In.	20.00
Silver, Sterling, Horse In Raised Position, 4 1/2 X 5 1/2 In.	210.00
Silver, Sterling, Knife, Caviar, Mother-Of-Pearl, Shell, Blade	24.00
Silver, Sterling, Knife, Fruit, Lady On Handle	15.00
Silver, Sterling, Knife, Fruit, Sterling Blades, Set Of 5	90.00
Silver, Sterling, Knife, Pocket, Art Nouveau Lady, 1 Blade	25.00
Silver, Sterling, Knife, Pocket, Flowing Hair Maiden Both Sides, 2 Blades	35.00
Silver, Sterling, Knight, Ivory Face, Embossed Decoration, 10 1/2 In.	495.00
Silver, Sterling, Ladle, Mustard, Flower Handle, 5 In.	11.95
Silver, Sterling, Ladle, Soup, Regent, C.1901	90.00
Silver, Sterling, Letter Opener, Mother-Of-Pearl Blade	25.00
Silver, Sterling, Letter Opener, Openwork Handle, Flower Design, 5 3/4 In.	9.95
Silver, Sterling, Lighter, Wick & Chained Cover, 3 1/2 In.	55.00
Silver, Sterling, Lorgnette, French, Lacy Openwork Case, Hallmarked, 2 3/4 In.	25.00
Silver, Sterling, Lorngette, Sterling Rope Chain	47.50
Silver, Sterling, Manicure Set, Beveled Glass Mirror, Fitted Case, 7 Piece	85.00
Silver, Sterling, Match Safe, Enameled, Dartmouth Seal, High Relief Flower	28.00
Silver, Sterling, Match Safe, Man, Girl, Fish Amid Waves, Art Nouveau	40.00
Silver, Sterling, Match Safe, Mythological Figures	45.00
Silver, Sterling, Match Safe, Ornate Floral Sprays In Relief	30.00
Silver, Sterling, Match Safe, Ornate Relief Boat Decoration	42.00
Silver, Sterling, Match Safe, Pocket, Engraved Flowers, 1 X 2 3/8 In.	14.00
Silver, Sterling, Match Safe, Ship And Anchor Relief	42.00
Silver, Sterling, Menorah, Judaic Lions & Star Of David	395.00
Silver, Sterling, Mirror, Hand, Beveled Glass, Raised Flowers	26.35
Silver, Sterling, Mirror, Hand, Dolphin On Front, Georg Jensen	125.00
Silver, Sterling, Mirror, Hand, Dresser, Art Nouveau	125.00
Silver, Sterling, Mirror, Hand, Embossed Lady & Flowers, Art Noveau	85.00
Silver, Sterling, Mirror, Hand, Initial JBM	22.00
Silver, Sterling, Mirror, Hand, Raised Decoration	25.00
Silver, Sterling, Mirror, Plateau, Cutout Lattices, 15 In.	45.00
Silver, Sterling, Money Clip, Dollar Sign, Hayward	8.00
Silver, Sterling, Muffineer, Feather, Domed Lid, Pierced, 5 1/2 In.	75.00
Silver, Sterling, Muffineer, Square Base, 7 In.	150.00
Silver, Sterling, Mug, Child's, Figural Clown Handle	28.00
Silver, Sterling, Nail File, Large	8.00
Silver, Sterling, Nail File, Ornate Handle	6.00
Silver, Sterling, Nail Set, Nail File, Buttonhook, Scissors, Cuticle Knife	38.50
Silver, Sterling, Napkin Ring, Child's, Nursery Rhyme Motifs Encircle Band	50.00
Silver, Sterling, Nut Cup, Gold-Wash Figural, Lily On Pad, Case, 6	95.00
Silver, Sterling, Nut Set, Master Bowl & 12 Individuals	85.00
Silver, Sterling, Pencil, Loop For Chain, 4 In.	8.95
Silver, Sterling, Penholder, Repousse Flower & Leaf Design, 6 1/4 In.	24.00
Silver, Sterling, Perfume, Overlay, Stopper, 4 In.	40.00
Silver, Sterling, Pick, Olive, Initialed S, 5 3/4 In.	12.50
Silver, Sterling, Pitcher, Water, Ebony Handle, 1940's, Georg Jensen	450.00
Silver, Sterling, Pitcher, Water, 16 Troy Oz., 8 1/2 In.	175.00
Silver, Sterling, Plate, Butter, Square, Gadroon Rim, 3 In.	10.00
Silver, Sterling, Pot, Rouge, Hinged Lid, Mirror Inside, Wear On Chain	22.00
Silver, Sterling, Pusher, Fancy Pierced Figural Decoration, Twisted Handle	18.50
Silver, Sterling, Pusher, Flowers On Handle	19.50
Silver, Sterling, Rattle, Baby, Double Baby Face, Ruffled Bonnet, 1 3/4 In.	85.00
Silver, Sterling, Rattle, Bell-Shaped, Blue Enameled, Baby	45.00
Silver, Sterling, Rattle, Figural, Mother-Of-Pearl Handle, 1 3/4 In.	85.00
Silver, Sterling, Rocker, Blotter, Bead & Scroll, 3 5/8 In.	22.00
Silver, Sterling, Salt & Pepper, Champagne Bottles, Small	15.00

Silver, Sterling, Salt & Pepper, Chinese Umbrella Shape On Platform Shoes	22.00
Silver, Sterling, Salt & Pepper, Jensen, 2 In.	150.00
Silver, Sterling, Salt, Cobalt Liners, With Spoon	16.00
Silver, Sterling, Salt, Figural, Swan, Movable Wings, Long Neck, Crystal Base	45.00
Silver, Sterling, Salt, Master, Bright Cut, Fluted Design, Pair	28.00
Silver, Sterling, Scoop, Cheese, Napoleon, Enameling On Handle	35.00
Silver, Sterling, Seal, Monogrammed	25.00
Silver, Sterling, Sealer, Letter, Initialed E.B.M., 4 1/2 In.	10.00
Silver, Sterling, Sealer, Wax, Engraved, 4 In.	30.00
Silver, Sterling, Sealer, Wax, Ornate Handle	15.00
Silver, Sterling, Server, Asparagus, Plain Pattern, Whiting	54.00
Silver, Sterling, Server, Cheese Cake, Embellished Handle, Schneider	19.00
Silver, Sterling, Shakers, Artichoke Shape, 1 1/2 In.	60.00
Silver, Sterling, Sharpener, Knife, 1878	30.00
Silver, Sterling, Shears, Grape, Grapes & Leaves, Ornate	32.00
Silver, Sterling, Shears, Grape, 6 1/4 In.	49.00
Silver, Sterling, Shoehorn, Floral, Handled	9.00
Silver, Sterling, Shoehorn, Flowers & Scrolls On Handle, 6 3/4 In.	7.95
Silver, Sterling, Shoehorn, Handled, Gorham, 7 5/8 In.	45.00
Silver, Sterling, Shoehorn, Repousse Angel Handle	18.00
Silver, Sterling, Soap Dish, Ornate Cover	55.00
Silver, Sterling, Spoon, Apostle, Dated 1891, 8 In.	45.00
Silver, Sterling, Spoon, Apostle, Figure On End Of Handle, 5 In.	35.00
Silver, Sterling, Spoon, Baby, Curled, Floral Trim, May 4, '09	14.00
Silver, Sterling, Spoon, Baby's, Curled Handle	12.00
Silver, Sterling, Spoon, Baby's, Navajo, Small Turquoise Stone	12.00
Silver, Sterling, Spoon, Baby's, Raised Figure, Jack Squirrel	15.00
Silver, Sterling, Spoon, Berry, Double Headed Passon, Shell Design, Set Of 12	120.00
Silver, Sterling, Spoon, Bonbon, Gold Wash, Pierced Bowl, Beaded-Edge Handle	13.95
Silver, Sterling, Spoon, Demitasse, Kabuki Dancers, Gold Wash Bowls, Pair	24.00
Silver, Sterling, Spoon, Demitasse, Ornate Handle, Hallmarked, 1900, Set Of 8	35.00
Silver, Sterling, Spoon, Grapefruit, Versailles, Gold Washed, 1893	19.00
Silver, Sterling, Spoon, Medicine, Folding For Traveling, Hinged	38.00
Silver, Sterling, Spoon, Nut, Open Design Bowl, Child's Head On Handle	14.95
Silver, Sterling, Spoon, Serving, Cut Glass Handle, 11 1/2 In.	135.00
Silver, Sterling, Spoon, Souvenir, see Souvenir, Spoon, Sterling	
Silver, Sterling, Tea Caddy, and various porcelain categories	
Silver, Sterling, Spoon, Sugar Sifter, Apostle, Hallmarks, 1899, 5 In.	18.00
Silver, Sterling, Stand, Pocket Watch, Engraved Floral, Monogrammed	65.00
Silver, Sterling, Stretcher, Glove, Art Nouveau	30.00
Silver, Sterling, Stretcher, Glove, Floral	35.00
Silver, Sterling, Tea & Coffee Set, Philip Oriel, Lion's Head Design, 5 Piece	1200.00
Silver, Sterling, Tea Ball, Chain & Ring	22.50
Silver, Sterling, Tea Set, Graylock Concord, 5 Piece	550.00
Silver, Sterling, Tea Set, Lion's Head, Philip Oriel, 6 Piece	2150.00
Silver, Sterling, Tea Set, 1893, Birmingham, 4 Piece	675.00
Silver, Sterling, Tea, Strainer, Ebony Handle	17.00
Silver, Sterling, Tea, Strainer, Flower Form, Art Nouveau	25.00
Silver, Sterling, Tea, Strainer, Heart Shaped, Wood Handle	15.00
Silver, Sterling, Teaball, Embossed, Watrous Manufacturing Company	37.50
Silver, Sterling, Teapot Spout Strainer	14.95
Silver, Sterling, Teaspoon, Baby's Head In Bowl, Leaf & Floral Handle	8.00
Silver, Sterling, Teaspoon, Buttercup, Dated 1899	12.00
Silver, Sterling, Teaspoons, Buttercup, 1899	9.00
Silver, Sterling, Thimble, see Sewing Tool, Thimble, Sterling	
Silver, Sterling, Thimble, Open Top	12.50
Silver, Sterling, Thimble, Scenic Border	20.00
Silver, Sterling, Toilet Set, Ornate, 4 Piece	48.00
Silver, Sterling, Toothpick, Crystal Liner, Pierced	18.00
Silver, Sterling, Tray, Card, Oval, Dated 1860, 6 X 4 3/4 X 7/8 In.	195.00
Silver, Sterling, Tray, Oval, Hand Hammered, Hallmarked, 12 X 18 In.	600.00
Silver, Sterling, Tray, Pin, Souvenir, The Piers, Hamilton Beach, 4 3/4 In.	17.00
Silver, Sterling, Tray, Rectangle, Open Cutwork, Handled, 7 Troy Oz., 9 X 6 In.	85.00
Silver, Sterling, Tray, Sandwich, Decorated Border, 10 In.	60.00

Silver, Sterling, Tray, Serving, Mahogany Insert, Hallmarked 1889, 17 X 23 In.	165.00
Silver, Sterling, Tumbler, Black Leather Case, Velvet Lined, Pair	38.00
Silver, Sterling, Vanity Set, 7 Pieces	49.00
Silver, Sterling, Vase, Bell Shape, Ruffled Rim, 13 In.	48.00
Silver, Sterling, Vase, Trumpet Shape, Etching, 10 In.	30.00
Silver, Sterling, Vinaigrette, Cut Glass Insert, Chain Attachment	40.00
Silver, Sterling, Wax Sealer, Victorian	12.00
Silver, Tiffany, Knife, Cake, Winthrop, 11 1/4 In.	95.00
Silveria, Vase, Creen Dripped Glass, 6 In.	385.00

Sinclaire cut glass was made by H.P.Sinclaire and Company of Corning, New York, between 1905 and 1929. Pieces were made of crystal as well as amber, blue, green, or ruby. Only a small percentage of Sinclaire glass is marked.

Sinclaire, Bowl, Centerpiece, Pansies Pattern, 13 1/2 In.	360.00
Sinclaire, Bowl, Etched Flowers Allover, Amber, Signed, 12 X 4 In.	50.00
Sinclaire, Bowl, Pale Green, Turned-Down Rim, Signed, 3 1/2 X 11 1/2 In.	55.00
Sinclaire, Bowl, Turned-Down Rim, Centerpiece, Green, Signed, 11 1/2 X 4 In.	50.00
Sinclaire, Candlestick, Amber Swirled Stem, Signed, 10 In., Pair	250.00
Sinclaire, Candlestick, Flutes & Panels Cutting, 8 Prisms, 9 In., Pair	250.00
Sinclaire, Compote, Amber	50.00
Sinclaire, Compote, Engraved, Floral Drapes, Cut To Clear, Blue Overlay Rim	150.00
Sinclaire, Dish, Candy, Handled, Floral Intaglio Cut	25.00
Sinclaire, Plate, Bread, Flowers & Vine	25.00
Sinclaire, Plate, Cake, Green, Pedestal	49.00
Sinclaire, Plate, Purple, 8 In., Set Of 6	150.00
Sinclaire, Platter, Ice Cream, Hobstars, Signed, Large	375.00
Sinclaire, Relish, Rectangular, Cane Pattern, 4 3/8 X 11 In.	195.00
Sinclaire, Tumbler, Copper, Wheel Cut, Etched	37.50
Sinclaire, Tumbler, Floral Cut & Etched	45.00
Sinclaire, Vase, Bud, Blue, Signed, 7 1/2 In.	65.00
Sinclaire, Vase, Intaglio Clematis, Leaves & Florals, Cylindrical, 14 In.	125.00
Sinclaire, Vase, Pedestal, Engraved Mums & Ferns, 7 In.	55.00
Sinclaire, Vase, Rose, 10 3/4 X 8 1/4 In.	275.00
Sinclaire, Vase, Trumpet, Flutes & Panels, Signed, 10 In.	35.00
Sitzendorf, Chamberstick, Figurine, 13 1/2 In.	485.00
Sitzendorf, Figurine, Ballet Dancer, C.1860, 13 In.	300.00
Sitzendorf, Figurine, Barefoot Boy With Flowers, 4 1/2 In.	69.00
Sitzendorf, Vase, Figural, Pair	185.00

Slag glass is streaked with several colors. There were many types made from about 1880. Pink slag was an American Victorian product of unknown origin. Purple and blue slag were made in American and English factories. Red slag is a very late Victorian product. Other colors are known, but are of less importance to the collector. The numbers B-xx refer to the book "Milk Glass" by E. Belknap.

Slag, Blue, Creamer, Light Panels	20.00
Slag, Blue, Dish, Fish, 8 3/4 In.	140.00
Slag, Blue, Jar, Atterbury, Original Top	85.00
Slag, Blue, Vase, Draped Nudes, 8 In.	65.00
Slag, Blue, Vase, Fan, Fluted, 8 In.	48.50
Slag, Blue, Vase, Peacocks, 8 In.	69.00
Slag, Bowl, Red & Orange, Opaque, Black Glass Stand, 9 1/2 In.	35.00
Slag, Bowl, Red, 5 X 3 In.	55.00
Slag, Caramel, see Chocolate Glass	
Slag, Caramel, Cruet, Leaf	160.00
Slag, Green & Yellow, Shade, Hanging, Grape Motif, 21 In.	675.00
Slag, Green, Basket, Sowerly Glass Works, 19th Century, 3 3/4 In., Pair	65.00
Slag, Green, Bottle, Talc, Powder	28.00
Slag, Green, Bowl, Spaced Rib	35.00
Slag, Green, Dish, Deep, Open Scalloped Edge, 11 1/2 X 7 In.	45.00
Slag, Green, Dish, Herringbone	15.00
Slag, Green, Match Holder, Rooster	20.00
Slag, Green, Pitcher, Windmill, Frosted	22.00

Slag, Green, Toothpick, Witch's Head 35.00
Slag, Green, Vase, Imperial, 10 In., Pair 45.00
Slag, Green, Wine Set 125.00
Slag, Pink, Bowl, Footed, Fan & Feather, Scalloped Edge, 2 1/2 In. 575.00
Slag, Pink, Cruet, Inverted Fan & Feather, Stopper, 6 1/2 In. 975.00
Slag, Pink, Cup, Punch, Inverted Fan & Feather, 4 Feet, 2 3/8 In. .... 245.00 To 350.00
Slag, Pink, Dish, Sauce, Feather & Fan .... 195.00 To 225.00
Slag, Pink, Pitcher, Water, Inverted Fern & Feather, 8 In. 895.00
Slag, Pink, Salt & Pepper, Inverted Fan & Feather 295.00
Slag, Pink, Saltshaker, Owl's Head, Ground Top, 2 1/2 X 2 1/4 In. 450.00
Slag, Pink, Toothpick, Inverted Fan & Feather .... 350.00 To 395.00
Slag, Pink, Tumbler, Inverted Fan & Feather .... 250.00 To 275.00
Slag, Purple, Boot With Spurs, 3 1/2 In. 40.00
Slag, Purple, Bowl, Acanthus Leaf, 10 X 4 1/2 In. 95.00
Slag, Purple, Bowl, Acanthus, Dated 85.00
Slag, Purple, Bowl, Dart Bar, 8 In. 38.00
Slag, Purple, Bowl, Dated April 23, 1878, 9 In. 85.00
Slag, Purple, Bowl, Pressed Leaf Pattern, 1878, Notched Rim Flares To 10 In. 185.00
Slag, Purple, Bowl, Raindrop 35.00
Slag, Purple, Box, Rooster Cover 40.00
Slag, Purple, Butter, Flower & Panel, Challinor & Taylor 85.00
Slag, Purple, Cake Stand, 5 3/4 X 9 In. 62.00
Slag, Purple, Candy, Crimped Edge 20.00
Slag, Purple, Castor, Pickle, Frame 375.00
Slag, Purple, Celery, Fluted, 9 In. .... 55.00 To 75.00
Slag, Purple, Celery, Jeweled, Star Medallion, Challinor & Taylor, 9 In. 90.00
Slag, Purple, Compote, Jelly, Scroll With Acanthus 40.00
Slag, Purple, Compote, Ribbon Edge, 5 In. 95.00
Slag, Purple, Compote, Threaded Bowl 45.00
Slag, Purple, Creamer, Acorns, England 75.00
Slag, Purple, Creamer, Scroll, Leaves & Fruit, 4 1/2 In. 95.00
Slag, Purple, Creamer, Sunflower .... 20.00 To 30.00
Slag, Purple, Cruet, Scroll With Acanthus 165.00
Slag, Purple, Dish, Eagle Cover 40.00
Slag, Purple, Dish, Honey 35.00
Slag, Purple, Dish, Log, Swan 24.00
Slag, Purple, Dish, Ruffled Edge, Low 25.00
Slag, Purple, Dish, Soap 55.00
Slag, Purple, Dish, Soap, Rectangular 42.00
Slag, Purple, Dish, Winged Scroll Cover 35.00
Slag, Purple, Match Holder, Flowers, Rectangular 28.00
Slag, Purple, Match Holder, 4 Feet, 3 In. .... 25.00 To 50.00
Slag, Purple, Mustard Pot, Bull's Head 95.00
Slag, Purple, Pitcher, Milk, Fish, Tail Handle, 1882 .... 55.00
Slag, Purple, Pitcher, Water, Dart Bar 65.00
Slag, Purple, Plate, Closed Lattice Edge, Marbling, 10 1/4 In. 39.00
Slag, Purple, Plate, Lattice Border, Challinor & Taylor, 10 1/4 In. 55.00
Slag, Purple, Plate, Lattice Edge, 10 In. 95.00
Slag, Purple, Plate, Open Edge, 10 In. 110.00
Slag, Purple, Platter, Tam O'shanter 125.00
Slag, Purple, Spoon Holder, Embossed Leaf & Bead Design, 4 In. 38.00
Slag, Purple, Spooner, English, Pierced Border, Raised Heart & Diamond 48.00
Slag, Purple, Spooner, Flower Panel 63.00
Slag, Purple, Spooner, Oval Medallion 38.00
Slag, Purple, Spooner, Scroll With Acanthus, Pastel 65.00
Slag, Purple, Stand, Cake, Dart Bar, 11 In. 75.00
Slag, Purple, Stand, Cake, Ringed Foot, 9 In. 55.00
Slag, Purple, Sugar & Creamer, Oval-Beaded Medallion 150.00
Slag, Purple, Sugar, Individual 28.50
Slag, Purple, Toothpick, Scroll With Acanthus 95.00
Slag, Purple, Tumbler, 10 Panel 42.00
Slag, Purple, Vase, Branches On Sides 40.00
Slag, Purple, Vase, Embossed Grapes With Leaves, Leaf Pedestal, 6 In. 47.00
Slag, Purple, Vase, Miniature, Embossed Leaf Decoration, 3 1/2 In. 22.00

Slag, Red-Orange, Candlestick, 3 In., Pair 35.00
Slag, Red, Bowl, Black Attached Base, 10 1/2 In. 65.00
Slag, Red, Bowl, Citizens Mutual Trust Co., Wheeling, West Virginia, 1924 .... 79.00
Slag, Red, Bowl, Console, Flared, Applied Black Amethyst Foot 45.00
Slag, Red, Bowl, 8 X 2 1/2 In. 65.00
Slag, Red, Console Set, 3 Pieces 90.00
Slag, Red, Pitcher, Windmill 17.00
Slag, Red, Vase, Fan, 8 In. 95.00
Slag, Red, Vase, Peacock, Allover Floral, 7 1/2 In. 75.00
Slag, Rose, Vase, 6 1/2 In., Pair 140.00
Slag, Yellow, Mug, Peacock & Heron 35.00

Sleepy Eye pottery was made to be given away with the flour products of
the Sleepy Eye Milling Co., Sleepy Eye, Minnesota, from about 1893
to 1952. It is a heavy stoneware with blue decorations, usually the famous
profile of an Indian.
Sleepy Eye, Bowl, Salt .... 135.00 To 170.00
Sleepy Eye, Cookbook 115.00
Sleepy Eye, Creamer, Blue & White .... 85.00 To 115.00
Sleepy Eye, Crock, Butter 175.00
Sleepy Eye, Jar, Butter, Indian Head, Flemish Blue On Gray, Signed 233.00
Sleepy Eye, Mug, Blue & White 125.00
Sleepy Eye, Mug, Gray Blue, 4 1/2 In. .... 125.00 To 165.00
Sleepy Eye, Mug, Signed Monmouth 90.00
Sleepy Eye, Pitcher, Blue & White, Blue Rim, 1 Gal. 130.00
Sleepy Eye, Pitcher, Blue On Cream, 4 In. 95.00
Sleepy Eye, Pitcher, Blue, White, Blue Top Edge, 8 In. 125.00
Sleepy Eye, Pitcher, Cobalt & White, 9 In., 3/4 Gallon .... 125.00 To 160.00
Sleepy Eye, Pitcher, Cobalt Blue On Cream, 4 In. 65.00
Sleepy Eye, Pitcher, Gray, 4 In. 85.00
Sleepy Eye, Pitcher, Indian Head On Handle, Cobalt Blue On Cream, 8 1/2 In. 130.00
Sleepy Eye, Pitcher, Milk, 5 1/2 In. 95.00
Sleepy Eye, Postcard, Pipe Of Peace 50.00
Sleepy Eye, Stein, Blue & Gray 195.00
Sleepy Eye, Sugar, Cobalt & White, Campfire Scene 195.00
Sleepy Eye, Teaspoon .... 115.00 To 125.00
Sleepy Eye, Vase, Cattails, Dragonfly, Frog, 8 1/2 In. 100.00
Sleepy Eye, Vase, Cobalt & White, Cattails On Both Sides 175.00
Sleepy Eye, Vase, Cylinder, Blue & Gray, Signed, 8 1/2 In. .... 90.00 To 145.00
Sleepy Eye, Vase, Cylindrical, 8 3/4 X 4 In. 155.00
Sleepy Eye, Vase, Flemish Blue On Gray, Marked, 9 In. 175.00

Slip is a thin mixture of clay and water, about the consistency of sour cream,
that is applied to the pottery for decoration.
Slipware, Pitcher, Yellow Slip On Red Clay, Early 19th Century, 8 In. 80.00
Slipware, Plate, Pie, Decorated, 8 In.Diameter 125.00
Slipware, Plate, Pie, Managanese, Triangular Geometric Border, Black, 8 In. 140.00
    Slot Machine, see Store, Machine

Smith Brothers glass was made after 1878. The owners had worked for the
Mt.Washington Glass Company in New Bedford, Massachusetts, for
seven years before going into their own shop. Some of the designs were
similar.
Smith Brothers, Bowl, Burmese Colored Ground, Floral, Melon Ribbed, 3 In. 185.00
Smith Brothers, Bowl, Salad, Floral, Melon Ribbed, Silver Plate Collar 290.00
Smith Brothers, Box, Melon Ribbed, White, Blue Flowers, 2 3/4 X 4 1/4 In. 85.00
Smith Brothers, Box, Pink To White, Blue Floral, Covered, 3 3/4 In. 165.00
Smith Brothers, Cracker Jar, Ground, Daisies, Signed, 4 1/2 X 6 1/2 In. 265.00
Smith Brothers, Creamer, Melon Ribbed, Biscuit Color, Pansies, Metal Collar 150.00
Smith Brothers, Creamer, Pansies, Signed 250.00
Smith Brothers, Egg Shaker, White To Pale Yellow, Enamel Berries, 4 1/2 In. 110.00
Smith Brothers, Figurine, Owl, Frosted, 3 3/4 In. 12.00
Smith Brothers, Holder, Vase Insert, Deer In Forest, Silver Plate, 8 In. 85.00

Smith Brothers, Jar, Jam, Purple & Magenta Violets On Ivory, Signed 290.00
Smith Brothers, Jar, Mustard, Barrel Shape, Tan, Hand-Painted Butterfly, Top 45.00
Smith Brothers, Jar, Sweetmeat, Gold Outlined Floral & Leaves, Melon-Ribbed 425.00
Smith Brothers, Owl, Frosted, 3 3/4 In. 12.00
Smith Brothers, Plate, Santa Maria, Dated 1893, World's Fair, 6 1/2 In. 175.00
Smith Brothers, Salt, Melon Ribbed, Blue, Decorated 45.00
Smith Brothers, Salt, Yellow & Blue Floral, Melon Ribbed, Gold Beading 35.00
Smith Brothers, Sugar & Creamer, Silver Tops, Pansy Decoration, 3 In. 295.00
Smith Brothers, Sugar Shaker, Cabin Scene 125.00
Smith Brothers, Sugar Shaker, Leaves, Cattails, Heron Standing, 2 Parts, 5 In. 88.00
Smith Brothers, Sugar Shaker, Log Cabin, Opaque, Hand-Painted, Pewter Top 85.00
Smith Brothers, Sugar Shaker, Satin Glass, Melon, Silver-Plated Top, 5 In. 165.00
Smith Brothers, Swan, Clear, 7 In. 13.00
Smith Brothers, Swan, Open Back, Clear, 7 In. 13.00
Smith Brothers, Vase, Cylinder, Opaque, White Heron, Tan Background, 6 1/2 In. 125.00
Smith Brothers, Vase, Double Ring, Opaque, Hand-Painted Heron, Silver Holder 118.00
Smith Brothers, Vase, Glossy Violets, White Dotted Top, 3 Sided, 4 1/2 In. 190.00
Smith Brothers, Vase, Opalescent, Bird & Flower, Meriden Base, 8 In., Pair 300.00
Smith Brothers, Vase, Peach Ground, Hand-Painted Bird, Opaque, 5 3/4 In. 60.00
Smith Brothers, Vase, Robin With Trees And Leaves 150.00
Smith Brothers, Vase, White, Pink & Purple Violets, 3 1/2 In. 170.00
Snow Babies, Admiral Peary & Admiral Cook Embracing World 100.00
Snow Babies, Attached Pair 60.00
Snow Babies, Babies On Sled 55.00
Snow Babies, Baby On Bear, 3 In. 55.00
Snow Babies, Baby On Log, 1 1/4 In. 50.00
Snow Babies, Baby On Polar Bear 55.00
Snow Babies, Baby On Red Sled, Molded Suit & Cap, 1 3/4 In. .... 30.00 To 45.00
Snow Babies, Baby On Reindeer, 2 3/4 In. 75.00
Snow Babies, Baby On Sled, 3 In. 30.00
Snow Babies, Baby On Snowball, 2 1/2 In. 45.00
Snow Babies, Baby Riding Polar Bear 36.00
Snow Babies, Baby Seated, Arms Outstretched, 2 In. 78.00
Snow Babies, Baby Seated, Miniature, Bisque, Marked Japan, 1 In. 10.00
Snow Babies, Baby Seated, One Arm Up, Other Down, 3 In. 168.00
Snow Babies, Baby Seated, 2 1/4 In. 75.00
Snow Babies, Baby Sliding On Snowy Rock, Open Pocket Beside Baby 31.50
Snow Babies, Baby Sliding, 1 In. 27.00
Snow Babies, Baby Standing Beside Seal Balancing Ball 30.00
Snow Babies, Baby With Hole For Pin, 1 In. 27.00
Snow Babies, Baby, Seated, 1 1/4 In. 45.00
Snow Babies, Bear, Upright, 2 1/2 In. 65.00
Snow Babies, Bear, 1 1/2 In. 45.00
Snow Babies, Boy Skier, 3 In. 65.00
Snow Babies, Candleholder, Royal Bayreuth, Handle, Black Mark 169.00
Snow Babies, Child Holding Accordion, 2 In. 65.00
Snow Babies, Children On Sled 55.00
Snow Babies, Creamer, Royal Bayreuth, Blue Mark, 2 1/2 In. 85.00
Snow Babies, Dish, Royal Bayreuth, Oval, Covered 125.00
Snow Babies, Elf, Seated, 1 1/4 In. 35.00
Snow Babies, Frozen Charlotte, 2 1/2 In. 30.00
Snow Babies, House, English Estate, Snow On Roof, Tower, 1 1/2 X 1 1/2 In. 50.00
Snow Babies, Monkey 75.00
Snow Babies, Paperweight, Snow Baby 47.50
Snow Babies, Pitcher, Royal Bayreuth, Double Handled, Blue Mark, 3 3/4 In. 85.00
Snow Babies, Polar Bear, Red Eyes, 1 In. 30.00
Snow Babies, Santa On Sled, Arms Outstretched 45.00
Snow Babies, Snowman, 1 3/4 In. 65.00
Snow Babies, Tumbler, 3 In. 50.00
Snow Babies, Two Babies, One Pushing Other On Sled 37.00
Snow Babies, Vase, Bulbous, Royal Bayreuth, Blue Mark, 7 In. 165.00
    Snuff Bottle, see Bottle, Snuff
Snuff Bottle, Jade Agate, Pear Shape, Fruit Stem Enamel Top, 2 1/2 In., Pair 55.00
Snuffbox, Black Lacquer, Mother-Of-Pearl Inlay 35.00

Snuffbox, Boat Shape, Inlaid Mahogany, 1 1/2 X 4 X 1 In.	24.00
Snuffbox, Celluloid, Inlaid Pewter Design	15.00
Snuffbox, Faience, Silver Mounted, Cloverleaf Shape, V.Perrin, 2 1/2 In.	125.00
Snuffbox, Hand-Painted Flowers, Brass Mounts, C.1890, German, 2 1/4 In.	35.00
Snuffbox, Horn & Silver	46.00
Snuffbox, Horn, 2-Color	35.00
Snuffbox, Miner's, Oval, Brass, Dated 1891	28.00
Snuffbox, Round, Hinged, Signed 1860, Tin	13.50
Snuffbox, Silver, Lift-Off Lid, Dutch, 19th Century	35.00
Snuffbox, Sterling Silver, English, 1895, 2 1/2 X 1 1/2 In.	55.00

*Soapstone is a mineral that was used for foot warmers or griddles because of
its heat-retaining properties. Soapstone was carved in many countries
in the nineteenth and twentieth centuries.*

Soapstone, Ashtray, Fluted Edges, Lotus Stems, China	10.00
Soapstone, Bookend, Bird & Flowers, Pair	35.00
Soapstone, Bookend, Bird & Tree, 5 1/2 In., Pair	45.00
Soapstone, Bookend, Carved Flower Bowl & Mums, 5 X 4 In., Pair	75.00
Soapstone, Bookend, Carved Mums & Foliage, Marked China, 4 X 5 In., Pair	75.00
Soapstone, Bookend, Chinese, 4 X 5 In.	48.00
Soapstone, Carving, Foliage & Watering Pool, 7 1/2 X 6 1/2 In.	110.00
Soapstone, Figurine, Altar Goddess, C.1830, Chinese, 3 3/4 In.	45.00
Soapstone, Figurine, Buddha, Carved, Soapstone Base, 5 In.	25.00
Soapstone, Figurine, Buddha, Footed, Carved, 4 X 3 In.	25.00
Soapstone, Figurine, Buddha, Light Green, 4 1/2 In.	35.00
Soapstone, Figurine, Carving Of Deity, Mottled Blue, Marbleized Base, 10 In.	65.00
Soapstone, Figurine, Chinese Village, 5 1/2 X 10 1/2 In.	65.00
Soapstone, Figurine, Foo Dog, Late 19th Century, 4 In., Pair	80.00
Soapstone, Figurine, Foo Dog, Pedestal, Green, 19th Century, 2 1/2 In., Pair	23.00
Soapstone, Figurine, Horse, 2 1/2 X 1 3/4 In.	8.00
Soapstone, Figurine, Semireclining Lady Holding Basket, Chinese, 3 1/4 In.	22.00
Soapstone, Figurine, Water Buffalo, Lying Side By Side, Teakwood Base	125.00
Soapstone, Foo Dog, Black, Chinese, 2 3/4 In.	25.00
Soapstone, Foot Warmer, Iron Handle, Pair	35.00
Soapstone, Foot Warmer, With Bail	12.50
Soapstone, Muffwarmer, Child's, Black Seal For Muff, L.A.Q.Initialed	45.00
Soapstone, Statue, Man Holding Kumquat, Pair	200.00
Soapstone, Urn, Carved Foo Dog, Elephant Head, Raised Legs, C.1850, 14 In.	300.00
Soapstone, Vase, Daisies, China, 9 In.	75.00
Soapstone, Vase, Elaborate Piercing, 9 In.	55.00
Soapstone, Vase, Filigree Flower & Leaves, Amber, Carved, 7 In.	60.00
Soapstone, Vase, Floral, 8 3/4 In.	75.00
Soapstone, Vase, Monkey & Bird, 6 In.	32.00
Soapstone, Vase, Monkeys, Boars, Crows, China Mark, 8 In.	45.00
Soapstone, Vase, Piercing, 9 In.	50.00
Soapstone, Vase, Vine, Leaves, Berries, 3 1/2 X 4 1/2 In.	12.00 To 15.00
Soft Paste, Cup & Saucer, Handleless, Off-White, Bittersweet, 18th Century	45.00
Soft Paste, Cup & Saucer, King's Rose	125.00
Soft Paste, Jug, Sailing Vessel, American Flag, 8 1/4 In.	250.00
Soft Paste, Mug, Blind Man's Bluff	38.00
Soft Paste, Mug, Child's, Grandma's Tales, Verse	49.50
Soft Paste, Mug, Child's, Grandmamma's Tales, Verse & Scene In Mulberry	35.00
Soft Paste, Plate, Blue, Openwork Edge, Impressed Mark B, 8 X 10 In.	87.50
Soft Paste, Plate, Octagon, Luster Trim, Bishop Of Heliopolis, C.1840, 7 In.	32.00
Soft Paste, Plate, Sailing Vessel, American Flag, 9 1/8 In.	250.00
Soft Paste, Plate, Spiral Border, Pink Luster, 5 1/4 In.	45.00
Soft Paste, Sugar, Queen's Rose, Covered	155.00
Soft Paste, Tea Set, Canary Luster, 16 Piece	2500.00
Soft Paste, Teapot, Queen's Rose	185.00
Soft Paste, Teapot, Strawberry	155.00
Soft Paste, The Bishop Of Helipolis, Color Transfer, Daisy Border, 7 In.	32.00
Souvenir, see also Napkin Ring	
Souvenir, Ashtray With Matchbox Holder, Hotel Muehleback, Iron & Nickel	20.00
Souvenir, Ashtray, Armce Road Supply, Topeka, Kansas	18.50

Souvenir, Ashtray, Elks Lodge, Yellow & Brown Stoneware	16.50
Souvenir, Ashtray, Hotel Baltimore, Kansas City, Missouri, Silver Plate	22.50
Souvenir, Ashtray, Jamestown, Virginia, Camphor Glass Base	12.00
Souvenir, Ashtray, R.M.S.Sylvania, Picture Of Ship, China	9.50
Souvenir, Badge, BPOE 1922, Brass Convention	8.00
Souvenir, Badge, Grant's Monument, April 27, 1897, Red, White, & Blue	20.00
Souvenir, Bell, Bronze, California, Buckin' Bronco Handle	20.00
Souvenir, Binoculars, Jockey Club, Paris, Leather Cover	15.00
Souvenir, Bookmark, Home Sweet Home, 200th Anniversary, Woven Silk, 11 In.	42.00
Souvenir, Bookmark, Woven Silk, Warner Mfg.Co., Home Sweet Home, 11 In.	42.00
Souvenir, Bottle & Pen Holder, Ink, Use Only Carter's Ink	10.50
Souvenir, Box, Covered, U.S.Capitol, Washington, Mauchline, Chas.Baum, 2 In.	20.00
Souvenir, Box, Jewel, Capitol, Washingon, D.C., Pink Satin, German Silver	18.50
Souvenir, Case, Stamp, With Chain, Elk's, Sterling Silver	9.00
Souvenir, Casket, Jewelry, Brass Trim, Niagara Falls	22.00
Souvenir, Creamer, Custard Glass, Masonic Temple, Chicago	35.00
Souvenir, Creamer, Lexington, Massachusetts, Trolley Car	9.00
Souvenir, Cufflinks, G.A.R., Gold, Pearl Background, Nov.1875	20.50
Souvenir, Cup, Child's, Remember Me, Pink, Blue, Gold	12.00
Souvenir, Cup, Gold, Machinery Building, St.Louis	22.00
Souvenir, Cup, Punch, Colorado, Applied Handle, C.1913	15.00
Souvenir, Dish, Nut, Main St., Newport, Vermont, Black Transfer, 1 1/2 X 4 In.	7.50
Souvenir, Figurine, Whale, Massachusetts, Copper, 4 3/4 In.	12.00
Souvenir, Flask, Lady's, New Year's Eve, Hotel Statler, N.Y., 1924, Sterling	35.00
Souvenir, G.A.R., Photograph, Virginia City, Montana, 1880	10.00
Souvenir, Goblet, Indiana St.Fair Premium, 1857, Coin, 3 3/4 Oz.	225.00
Souvenir, Goblet, McKeesport, Pa., Ruby & Clear	12.00
Souvenir, Inkwell, Shape Of Building, Columbia Exposition, 1893, Libbey	48.00
Souvenir, Jar, Apothecary, Statue Of Liberty	85.00
Souvenir, Jug, Carnegie Public Library, East Liverpool, Ohio	3.50
Souvenir, Jug, Lake George 1893, Redware, Ovoid, 2 1/2 In.	18.00
Souvenir, Knife, Dinner, Elks	6.50
Souvenir, Letter Opener, Memphis Confederate Veterans Reunion, 1909	20.00
Souvenir, Locket, Gold Filled, Blue Enamel, Pictures Washington, D.C., 1880	35.00
Souvenir, Lucky Penny, Mormon Temple, 1947, Salt Lake City	7.50
Souvenir, Mug, Colorado, Green And Gold, Wilber	18.00
Souvenir, Mug, Dallas, Wis., Glazed Beige Stoneware, 3 1/2 In.	5.00
Souvenir, Mug, Detroit, Gray Crockery, Decorated	40.00
Souvenir, Mug, Hanover, Pa., 1969, Wooden Handle, Clear Glass	8.50
Souvenir, Mug, Mary, Coney Island, 1906	15.00
Souvenir, Painting, Reverse On Glass, Cunard Lines, 6 1/2 X 6 1/2 In.	28.00
Souvenir, Pen, Fountain, Swan, Gold Filled, New York	35.00
Souvenir, Pencil, Baseball Bat, 100th Anniversary, New York Yankee, June, 1939	15.00
Souvenir, Pillbox, Scene Of Capitol At Washington, D.C.	19.00
Souvenir, Pillow, Hot Springs, South Dakota, Leather, Fringed	22.50
Souvenir, Pillow, Leather, Fringed, Hot Springs, South Dakota	22.50
Souvenir, Pin, St.Louis Fair, Brass, Heart Shape, Enamel Lettering	8.00
Souvenir, Pincushion, Slipper, Silver Plated, Woolworth Building Embossed	9.00
Souvenir, Pitcher, Central Park, Davenport, Iowa, Cream, Brown, 3 3/4 In.	15.00
Souvenir, Pitcher, Lake St.Catherine, Vermont, 3 1/2 In.	5.00
Souvenir, Pitcher, Trenton, N.J., 1907, 3 In.	18.50
Souvenir, Pitcher, Water, Cobalt, White & Gold China, Scene In Canada, 5 In.	8.00
Souvenir, Plate, Bathing Beauty, Collinsville, Connecticut, 7 1/2 In.	10.00
Souvenir, Plate, Blue, 75th Anniversary Orphan Asylum Brooklyn, 1833-1908	20.00
Souvenir, Plate, Bonesteel, South Dakota, 7 In.	7.50
Souvenir, Plate, BPOE, 7 5/8 In.	11.00
Souvenir, Plate, Bread, Oval, Lillian Neilson	42.00
Souvenir, Plate, Campaign, Teddy Roosevelt, Teddy Bears	65.00
Souvenir, Plate, Charles Lindbergh	15.00
Souvenir, Plate, F.E.E., Brown, Gold Edges, Warner Keffer China Co.	35.00
Souvenir, Plate, Gettysburg, 1863-1913, Blue White, Lee, Meade, 7 1/2 In.	15.00
Souvenir, Plate, Glens Falls, New York	14.00
Souvenir, Plate, Historical Buildings, Parks, Copper, Tampa, Florida	4.00
Souvenir, Plate, Historical, Pink, View Near Conway, N.H., 9 In.	50.00

Souvenir, Plate, International Silver Company, TWA In Globe, 9 In.	12.50
Souvenir, Plate, Memorial, Milton S.Hershey, 1953	45.00
Souvenir, Plate, Milbank, South Dakota, Red & Yellow Roses, 8 1/2 In.	7.50
Souvenir, Plate, Milk Glass, BPOE, 1907, 7 In.	18.50
Souvenir, Plate, Nazi Swastika, German Eagle, Bavaria, 9 In.	95.00
Souvenir, Plate, New York City, 1968, China, Decorated	10.00
Souvenir, Plate, New York, Ribbon Laced, 5 3/4 In.	10.00
Souvenir, Plate, Niagara Falls, R & M, 10 1/4 In.	30.00
Souvenir, Plate, Pennsylvania Turnpike, Brown, Vennon Kiln	6.50
Souvenir, Plate, Tin, Philadelphia, 1907, BPOE	20.00
Souvenir, Pocketknife, Babe Ruth, Baseball Bat, Yankee Stadium, 1927	2.00
Souvenir, Pocketknife, Firemen's Fund Insurance, Reverse Figure, 1911	42.50
Souvenir, Pocketknife, New York City, Celluloid Handle, 2 Blades	12.50
Souvenir, Program, Buffalo Bill's Wild West Show, 1895	22.00
Souvenir, Sign, Cardboard, Columbia Exposition, 10 X 12 In.	50.00
Souvenir, Spoon, Silver Plate, Adams	3.00
Souvenir, Spoon, Silver Plate, Baby Jane, Oneida	4.00
Souvenir, Spoon, Silver Plate, Birth Of Israel	4.00
Souvenir, Spoon, Silver Plate, Buffalo, Merry Christmas, 1897	6.50
Souvenir, Spoon, Silver Plate, Buffalo, Twisted Handle	5.00
Souvenir, Spoon, Silver Plate, Carlsbad Caverns	3.00
Souvenir, Spoon, Silver Plate, Christmas Symbols Front & Back	22.00
Souvenir, Spoon, Silver Plate, Christopher Columbus, Santa Maria On Back	25.00
Souvenir, Spoon, Silver Plate, Eisenhower	3.00
Souvenir, Spoon, Silver Plate, Flagship Olympia, Dewey, U.S.Shield	12.00
Souvenir, Spoon, Silver Plate, G.A.R.Convention, Buffalo, N.Y., 1871	25.00
Souvenir, Spoon, Silver Plate, Gene & Gleen, Quaker Earlybirds	8.00
Souvenir, Spoon, Silver Plate, Huckleberry Hound	5.50
Souvenir, Spoon, Silver Plate, Ice Cream Soda, May 2, 1899	4.00
Souvenir, Spoon, Silver Plate, Iron Maiden, Nuremberg, Germany, Plain Bowl	20.00
Souvenir, Spoon, Silver Plate, Kukla	15.00
Souvenir, Spoon, Silver Plate, Lone Ranger	5.00
Souvenir, Spoon, Silver Plate, Mary Pickford	8.00
Souvenir, Spoon, Silver Plate, Mary Poppins	4.00 To 5.00
Souvenir, Spoon, Silver Plate, Massachusetts	4.00
Souvenir, Spoon, Silver Plate, Muncie, Ind., 1899	18.50
Souvenir, Spoon, Silver Plate, Round Oak Stove, Doe Wah Jack	65.00
Souvenir, Spoon, Silver Plate, Thomas Meighan	8.00
Souvenir, Spoon, Silver Plate, Towle's Log Cabin, Stem In Shape Of Log	8.00
Souvenir, Spoon, Silver Plate, Yogi Bear	5.00
Souvenir, Spoon, Sterling Silver, Alaska Yukon Exposition, Seattle In Bowl	35.00
Souvenir, Spoon, Sterling Silver, Alaska, Sea, Mountain Scene, Gold Wash Bowl	62.00
Souvenir, Spoon, Sterling Silver, Alaska, Totem Pole Handle, Demitasse	18.00
Souvenir, Spoon, Sterling Silver, Annapolis, City Seal	17.00
Souvenir, Spoon, Sterling Silver, Arkansas, Arlington Hotel, Hot Springs	19.00
Souvenir, Spoon, Sterling Silver, Arkansas, State Capitol, Little Rock	22.00
Souvenir, Spoon, Sterling Silver, Atlantic City	12.00
Souvenir, Spoon, Sterling Silver, Auburn, California, Teddy Bear Top	47.50
Souvenir, Spoon, Sterling Silver, Baltimore, Washington Monument	15.00
Souvenir, Spoon, Sterling Silver, Berkshire Inn, Great Barrington, Mass.	15.00
Souvenir, Spoon, Sterling Silver, Bethlehem, N.H., Gold Wash Bowl, Demitasse	8.00
Souvenir, Spoon, Sterling Silver, Birmingham, Plain Bowl	16.00
Souvenir, Spoon, Sterling Silver, Boston, GAR	8.50
Souvenir, Spoon, Sterling Silver, Boston, Old Square Church, Demitasse	15.00
Souvenir, Spoon, Sterling Silver, Boston, Old State House, Demitasse	11.00
Souvenir, Spoon, Sterling Silver, Boston, Public Library, Gold Bowl	15.00
Souvenir, Spoon, Sterling Silver, Boston, Trinity Church, Demitasse	8.00
Souvenir, Spoon, Sterling Silver, Bronco Buster	85.00
Souvenir, Spoon, Sterling Silver, California, E.Pluribus Unum, Eagle	14.00
Souvenir, Spoon, Sterling Silver, California, Los Angeles, Gold Wash Bowl	17.00
Souvenir, Spoon, Sterling Silver, Capitol Bldg., Albany N.Y., Indian Top	25.00
Souvenir, Spoon, Sterling Silver, Capitol Dome, 4 1/4 In.	20.00
Souvenir, Spoon, Sterling Silver, Capitol Dome, 5 7/8 In.	37.00
Souvenir, Spoon, Sterling Silver, Century Of Progress, Chicago	10.00

Souvenir, Spoon, Sterling Silver, Chamberlin, South Dakota, Poppies 9.00
Souvenir, Spoon, Sterling Silver, Champlain, Quebec In Bowl, 6 In. 85.00
Souvenir, Spoon, Sterling Silver, Charter Oak, Demitasse 20.00
Souvenir, Spoon, Sterling Silver, Charter Oak, Orange Bowl, 5 7/8 In. 75.00
Souvenir, Spoon, Sterling Silver, Chicago Fair, Electrical Bldg. 12.50
Souvenir, Spoon, Sterling Silver, Chicago Handle, Fort Dearborn 1830 Bowl 17.50
Souvenir, Spoon, Sterling Silver, Chief Seattle, 5 1/4 In. 25.00
Souvenir, Spoon, Sterling Silver, Christmas, Demitasse 32.00
Souvenir, Spoon, Sterling Silver, Christopher Columbus, 6 In. 45.00
Souvenir, Spoon, Sterling Silver, City Hall, Los Angeles 11.95
Souvenir, Spoon, Sterling Silver, Colorado, Sugar Beet, Foliage On Handle 19.95
Souvenir, Spoon, Sterling Silver, Colosseum, Rome, Enameled Handle 10.00
Souvenir, Spoon, Sterling Silver, Columbian Exposition, 1892, Columbus 18.00
Souvenir, Spoon, Sterling Silver, Columbus, Santa Maria In Bowl, Embossed 12.50
Souvenir, Spoon, Sterling Silver, Congressional Library, Demitasse 8.00
Souvenir, Spoon, Sterling Silver, Cutouts, Las Vegas, Nevada 9.00
Souvenir, Spoon, Sterling Silver, Deep Copper Indian Face 28.00
Souvenir, Spoon, Sterling Silver, Detroit Skyline, The Heart Of Detroit 65.00
Souvenir, Spoon, Sterling Silver, Easter, 5 1/2 In. 58.00
Souvenir, Spoon, Sterling Silver, Edinburgh, Scotland, Demitasse 10.00
Souvenir, Spoon, Sterling Silver, Figural, College Girl 32.00
Souvenir, Spoon, Sterling Silver, Florida, Black Boy Handle, Pat.1892 .... 24.95
Souvenir, Spoon, Sterling Silver, Georgia, Plain Bowl 17.00
Souvenir, Spoon, Sterling Silver, Gertrude, 1896 .... 8.50
Souvenir, Spoon, Sterling Silver, Girl Graduate, 5 7/8 In. 58.00
Souvenir, Spoon, Sterling Silver, Girl Holding Racquet, Marion, 1904 .... 35.00
Souvenir, Spoon, Sterling Silver, Gorham, Los Angeles, Fruit Bowl, Demitasse 12.00
Souvenir, Spoon, Sterling Silver, Green Bay, Wisconsin 10.00
Souvenir, Spoon, Sterling Silver, Hartford, Plain Bowl 17.00
Souvenir, Spoon, Sterling Silver, Havana, Columbus Memorial, Enameled 55.00
Souvenir, Spoon, Sterling Silver, Honolulu, Man, Demitasse 15.00
Souvenir, Spoon, Sterling Silver, Hospital For The Insane, Cherokee, Iowa 15.00
Souvenir, Spoon, Sterling Silver, Idaho, Pocatello In Bowl 7.00
Souvenir, Spoon, Sterling Silver, Illinois, Chicago Engraved In Bowl 14.00
Souvenir, Spoon, Sterling Silver, Indian 62.00
Souvenir, Spoon, Sterling Silver, Indian On Warpath, New Union Station, Mo. 40.00
Souvenir, Spoon, Sterling Silver, Indian Totem Pole, Alaska, Demitasse 7.95
Souvenir, Spoon, Sterling Silver, Indian, Globe Of World, Dowagiac, Mich. 55.00
Souvenir, Spoon, Sterling Silver, Indian, San Miguel Church, 4 1/2 In. 42.00
Souvenir, Spoon, Sterling Silver, Indian, 5 7/8 In. 28.00
Souvenir, Spoon, Sterling Silver, Indiana State, Dated December 25, 1902 .... 12.00
Souvenir, Spoon, Sterling Silver, Indiana, West Baden Springs Hotel In Bowl 14.00
Souvenir, Spoon, Sterling Silver, Jefferson Davis 85.00
Souvenir, Spoon, Sterling Silver, John Whitter Home, Amesbury 22.50
Souvenir, Spoon, Sterling Silver, Justice Figure, Court House, Jefferson, Wis. 30.00
Souvenir, Spoon, Sterling Silver, Kansas City, Convention Hall, Embossed Bowl 19.00
Souvenir, Spoon, Sterling Silver, Kentucky, Louisville In Bowl 16.00
Souvenir, Spoon, Sterling Silver, Knickerbocker, Spain 20.00
Souvenir, Spoon, Sterling Silver, LaGrande, Oregon, Demitasse 15.00
Souvenir, Spoon, Sterling Silver, LaPorte, Indiana, Floral Handle 8.00
Souvenir, Spoon, Sterling Silver, Land Of Evangeline, Gold Wash, Demitasse 15.00
Souvenir, Spoon, Sterling Silver, Lenape, Penn Treaty 45.00
Souvenir, Spoon, Sterling Silver, Lewis & Clark 1905 Exposition, Portland 37.50
Souvenir, Spoon, Sterling Silver, Los Angeles Harbor & Breakwater, 1928 .... 11.95
Souvenir, Spoon, Sterling Silver, Louisiana Exposition, Wagon Train Handle 28.00
Souvenir, Spoon, Sterling Silver, Louisiana Purchase, Covered Wagon Handle 29.00
Souvenir, Spoon, Sterling Silver, Louisville, Daniel Boone, Demitasse 12.00
Souvenir, Spoon, Sterling Silver, Mary & Her Lamb Cutout Handle, Wilcox Co. 12.00
Souvenir, Spoon, Sterling Silver, Masonic Sword, 4 1/4 In. 42.00
Souvenir, Spoon, Sterling Silver, Masonic, Denver In Bowl 12.00
Souvenir, Spoon, Sterling Silver, Matador 85.00
Souvenir, Spoon, Sterling Silver, Mexico, Man, Burro, Enameled Flag 55.00
Souvenir, Spoon, Sterling Silver, Michelsen Commemorative, FrlX On Front 35.00
Souvenir, Spoon, Sterling Silver, Michigan, Soldier's Monument, Battle Creek 14.00

Souvenir, Spoon, Sterling Silver, Mid-Winter Exposition, 1894, Demitasse 15.50
Souvenir, Spoon, Sterling Silver, Milwaukee Indian, Waupaca, Wis., Bowl 42.00
Souvenir, Spoon, Sterling Silver, Miner, Full Figure, 5 1/2 In. 45.00
Souvenir, Spoon, Sterling Silver, Miner's, California, Gold Bowl 25.00
Souvenir, Spoon, Sterling Silver, Mining Gold With Pail Of Gold Handle 37.50
Souvenir, Spoon, Sterling Silver, Minnesota, Gold Wash Bowl 14.00
Souvenir, Spoon, Sterling Silver, Minnesota, Old Fort Nelling, 1820 In Bowl 15.00
Souvenir, Spoon, Sterling Silver, Missouri, Convention Hall, Kansas City 14.00
Souvenir, Spoon, Sterling Silver, Missouri, Letters Forming Handle, 5 1/2 In. 28.00
Souvenir, Spoon, Sterling Silver, Montana, Miles City, Charging Buffalo 22.00
Souvenir, Spoon, Sterling Silver, Mount Clemens, Ornate Handle 8.00
Souvenir, Spoon, Sterling Silver, Mount Vernon, Demitasse 15.00
Souvenir, Spoon, Sterling Silver, Mt.Hood, Engraved, Fish-Shaped Handle 17.00
Souvenir, Spoon, Sterling Silver, Natatorium, Boise, Idaho 15.00
Souvenir, Spoon, Sterling Silver, New York State Capitol, Albany, N.Y. 18.00
Souvenir, Spoon, Sterling Silver, New York, Metropolitan Bldg., Landmarks 55.00
Souvenir, Spoon, Sterling Silver, Newburgh, Washington's Headquarters, 6 In. 32.00
Souvenir, Spoon, Sterling Silver, Newbury, Vermont, Demitasse 7.00
Souvenir, Spoon, Sterling Silver, Newport, R.I., Indian Figure, Demitasse 9.95
Souvenir, Spoon, Sterling Silver, North Dakota, Grand Forks Gold Wash Bowl 18.00
Souvenir, Spoon, Sterling Silver, Nude Indian Girl 25.00
Souvenir, Spoon, Sterling Silver, Ohio, Garfield Memorial, Cleveland 16.00
Souvenir, Spoon, Sterling Silver, Old Town Mill, 1650, New London, Demitasse 11.00
Souvenir, Spoon, Sterling Silver, Our Martyred Presidents, 1901, Demitasse 8.00
Souvenir, Spoon, Sterling Silver, Palmyra, Floral Handle 8.00
Souvenir, Spoon, Sterling Silver, Pan American Exposition, 1901, Demitasse 15.00
Souvenir, Spoon, Sterling Silver, Pan-Am Exposition, 5 1/2 In. .... 22.00 To 24.00
Souvenir, Spoon, Sterling Silver, Panama Pacific Exposition, 1915 .... 10.00
Souvenir, Spoon, Sterling Silver, Pipestone, Minnesota 8.50
Souvenir, Spoon, Sterling Silver, Pittsburgh 7.50
Souvenir, Spoon, Sterling Silver, Pittsburgh Skyline, Carnegie Library 65.00
Souvenir, Spoon, Sterling Silver, Pittsburgh, Plain Back, Demitasse 35.00
Souvenir, Spoon, Sterling Silver, Plymouth Rock 15.00
Souvenir, Spoon, Sterling Silver, Portland, Oregon 15.50
Souvenir, Spoon, Sterling Silver, Post Office, San Francisco In Bowl 19.50
Souvenir, Spoon, Sterling Silver, Public Library, Rockford, Ill. 15.00
Souvenir, Spoon, Sterling Silver, Rip Van Winkle 25.00
Souvenir, Spoon, Sterling Silver, Rochester, 1896 .... 12.00
Souvenir, Spoon, Sterling Silver, Russian Neillo, Dated 1852, 6 1/4 In. 125.00
Souvenir, Spoon, Sterling Silver, S.A.Douglas Birthplace, Vermont, Demitasse 15.00
Souvenir, Spoon, Sterling Silver, Salem Witch, Demitasse 40.00
Souvenir, Spoon, Sterling Silver, Salem Witch, Orange Bowl, 5 1/4 In. 75.00
Souvenir, Spoon, Sterling Silver, Salem Witch, 5 7/8 In. 115.00
Souvenir, Spoon, Sterling Silver, San Francisco Exposition, Demitasse 15.00
Souvenir, Spoon, Sterling Silver, San Gabriel Mission, Angel Gabriel Handle 24.95
Souvenir, Spoon, Sterling Silver, San Gabriel Mission, California, 1771 .... 12.00
Souvenir, Spoon, Sterling Silver, Santa Fe, N.M., Gilt Bowl, 2 Children, Horse 15.00
Souvenir, Spoon, Sterling Silver, Seattle World's Fair, Demitasse 12.00
Souvenir, Spoon, Sterling Silver, Shabbona, The White Man's Friend 120.00
Souvenir, Spoon, Sterling Silver, Southern Pines Hotel, Southern Pines, N.C. 15.00
Souvenir, Spoon, Sterling Silver, Spoon, Demitasse, Figural Indian 14.00
Souvenir, Spoon, Sterling Silver, Spoon, Demitasse, Newbury, Vermont 7.00
Souvenir, Spoon, Sterling Silver, Spoon, Figural, Indian Chief, Paye & Bader 36.00
Souvenir, Spoon, Sterling Silver, St.Louis On Horse, Union Station Bowl 21.00
Souvenir, Spoon, Sterling Silver, St.Peter, Minn., Large 12.00
Souvenir, Spoon, Sterling Silver, Standing Stag, Adirondack, Plain Bowl 38.00
Souvenir, Spoon, Sterling Silver, Surveyor's Symbol On Handle, 1888 .... 15.00
Souvenir, Spoon, Sterling Silver, Tacoma, Wash., Indian & Headdress Handle 23.00
Souvenir, Spoon, Sterling Silver, The Balsams, Dixville Notch, Demitasse 10.00
Souvenir, Spoon, Sterling Silver, The New Cliff House, San Francisco, Roses 17.95
Souvenir, Spoon, Sterling Silver, Thermopolis, Wyo., Gold Bowl, Ornate Handle 16.75
Souvenir, Spoon, Sterling Silver, Toledo, Ohio, Frog With Cigar, River Scene 55.00
Souvenir, Spoon, Sterling Silver, Toronto, Beaver Handle, 1893, 4 1/2 In. 25.00
Souvenir, Spoon, Sterling Silver, Turtle, Northpoint, Baltimore, Demitasse 55.00

Souvenir, Spoon, Sterling Silver, Virginia, 5 In.	17.00
Souvenir, Spoon, Sterling Silver, Washington Monument Handle	20.00
Souvenir, Spoon, Sterling Silver, Washington State, Demitasse	8.00
Souvenir, Spoon, Sterling Silver, Washington, D.C., Capitol Handle	20.00
Souvenir, Spoon, Sterling Silver, Washington, Mt.Rainier, Seattle	14.00
Souvenir, Spoon, Sterling Silver, West Virginia, Wood County Court House	28.00
Souvenir, Spoon, Sterling Silver, Wichita	12.00
Souvenir, Spoon, Sterling Silver, Winnewissa Falls, Pipestone, Minn.	15.00
Souvenir, Spoon, Sterling Silver, Wisconsin Dells, Wild Rose On Handle	12.00
Souvenir, Spoon, Sterling Silver, Wisconsin State, Madison In Bowl	11.00
Souvenir, Spoon, Sterling Silver, World's Fair, Chicago, 1892, Demitasse	11.00
Souvenir, Spoon, Sterling Silver, Zodiac, Feb., Wallace, 5 7/8 In.	30.00
Souvenir, Spoon, Sterling Silver, Zodiac, July, Gorham, 5 7/8 In.	30.00
Souvenir, Spoon, Sterling Silver, Zodiac, July, Watson, 5 In.	25.00
Souvenir, Spoon, Sterling Silver, 1st SW Baptist Church, Gold Wash	12.95
Souvenir, Spoon, Sterling Silver, 1698-1898, Washington Square	11.00
Souvenir, Spoon, Sterling Silver, 1775 Concord, Oct.10, 1891	15.00
Souvenir, Spoon, Sterling Silver, 1904, St.Louis World's Fair	10.00
Souvenir, Spoon, Sterling Silver, 1933 Chicago Fair, Large	15.00
Souvenir, Stein, Elks Motto, Temple, Detroit Michigan, Made In Germany	55.00
Souvenir, Sugar, Aqua, Lily Pad, New York State, 4 3/4 In.	850.00
Souvenir, Tape Measure, Lydia Pinkham	15.00
Souvenir, Teapot, Niagara Falls, Gold Trim, Royal Winton, England	240.00
Souvenir, Token, Century Of Progress 1933, Hoover Exposition, Brass	6.50
Souvenir, Toothbrush Holder, Skippy, Bisque	22.00
Souvenir, Toothpick, Diagonal Drape, Glass, Signed Laura, 1894	15.00
Souvenir, Toothpick, Green Glass Hat, Webster, Wisconsin, 2 X 3 1/2 In.	16.00
Souvenir, Toothpick, Jefferson Glass Co., Ring & Beads, Gold Trim	12.50
Souvenir, Tray, Iowa City, Pressed Glass, Be Industrious, Frosted Center	80.00
Souvenir, Tray, Serving, Tin, White House, F.D.R. Picture	45.00
Souvenir, Tray, Tip, United Spanish War Veterans Grand Military Ball, 1934	20.00

Spangle glass is multicolored glass made from odds and ends of colored glass rods. It includes metallic flakes of mica covered with gold, silver, nickel, or copper. Spangle glass is usually cased with a thin layer of clear glass over the multicolored layer.

Spangle Glass, see also Vasa Murrhina

Spangle Glass, Basket, Blue, Silver Mica Flecks, Applied Reeded Handle	90.00
Spangle Glass, Basket, Cased, Ruffled Edge, Clear Applied Handle, 7 In.	115.00
Spangle Glass, Bowl, Cranberry, Pink, Greens, Crimped Rim, 7 1/2 In., Pair	90.00
Spangle Glass, Epergne, 3 Trumpets, Swirled, Scalloped Bowl, 26 In.	165.00
Spangle Glass, Lamp, Hurricane, Globe, Turquoise Blue Specks, Gold, Pink, 8 In.	75.00
Spangle Glass, Pitcher, Drape, Pink	85.00
Spangle Glass, Vase, Aqua, Mica & Gold Flakes, 4 1/2 In.	30.00
Spangle Glass, Vase, Aquamarine, Silver Mica Flecks, Thorn Handle, 7 1/4 In.	150.00
Spangle Glass, Vase, Beige, Multicolored, Gold Mica, Cased Lining, 4 In.	38.00
Spangle Glass, Vase, Cased, Rigaree Center & Neck, Blue, Yellow, 6 1/2 In.	45.00
Spangle Glass, Vase, Pink, Cobalt, Chartreuse, Mica Flecks, Rigaree, English	48.00
Spangle Glass, Vase, Pink, Silver Mica Flakes In Clear Glass, 7 1/2 In.	45.00
Spangle Glass, Vase, Striped Pink, Yellow, Blue, & Silver Mica, Footed, 9 In.	65.00

Spanish lace is a Victorian glass pattern that seems to have white lace on a colored background. Blue, yellow, cranberry, and clear glass was made with this distinctive white pattern.

Spanish Lace, Bowl, Finger, Blue	38.00
Spanish Lace, Bowl, Ruffled Turned-Down Rim, Canary Yellow, C.1895, 7 In.	50.00
Spanish Lace, Celery, Ruffled Rim, Canary Yellow, 6 In.	37.00 To 45.00
Spanish Lace, Cruet & Stopper, Applied Clear Handle, Clear To Opalescent	45.00
Spanish Lace, Cruet, Blue Fern, 6 In.	55.00
Spanish Lace, Cruet, Clear Cut Stopper, Applied Handle, Cranberry, 7 1/2 In.	125.00
Spanish Lace, Lamp, Cranberry, Milk Glass Step Column Base, 27 In.	275.00
Spanish Lace, Lemonade Set, Vaseline Color, Daisy & Fern, 5 Piece	250.00
Spanish Lace, Pitcher, Blue, Poinsettias, Applied Handle, 14 In.	125.00
Spanish Lace, Pitcher, Syrup, Bulbous, Pewter Lid, White, 6 1/2 In.	125.00

Spanish Lace, Pitcher, Syrup, Pewter Top, Signed Victoria, 7 1/2 In.	72.00
Spanish Lace, Pitcher, Water, Cobalt	90.00
Spanish Lace, Rose Bowl, Blue	55.00
Spanish Lace, Rose Bowl, Blue Opalescent	37.00
Spanish Lace, Rose Bowl, Crimped Rim, Clear To Opalescent, 4 In.	40.00
Spanish Lace, Sugar Shaker, Blue Opalescent	120.00
Spanish Lace, Sugar Shaker, Vaseline, Opalescent	85.00
Spanish Lace, Syrup, White On Clear, Opalescent, Pewter Lid, 7 In.	79.00
Spanish Lace, Tumbler, Blue	24.50 To 30.00
Spanish Lace, Tumbler, Smoke	100.00
Spanish Lace, Tumbler, Yellow	28.50
Spanish Lace, Vase, Blue & White, Ruffled Top, Bulbous Base	23.00
Spanish Lace, Water Set, Blue, Daisy, Fern, 7 Piece	185.00
Spanish Lace, Water Set, Opalescent, Blue, 7 Piece	250.00

Spatter glass is a multicolored glass made from many small pieces of different colored glass.

Spatter Glass, Barrel, Biscuit, Blue & Yellow, Silver Rim, Cover, & Handle	75.00
Spatter Glass, Barrel, Biscuit, Triple Cased, Silver Rim & Cover, C.Bros.	65.00
Spatter Glass, Basket, Blue With Pink, Yellow, & White Spatters, 5 1/4 In.	52.00
Spatter Glass, Basket, Blue, Red, Purple, & White, Rope Twist Handle, 9 1/2 In.	69.00
Spatter Glass, Basket, Clear Applied Handle & Feet, 6 In.	65.00
Spatter Glass, Basket, Pink & White, Cased With White, Applied Handle, 7 In.	95.00
Spatter Glass, Basket, Rainbow, Cased, Clear Thorn Handle, 5 1/2 In.	145.00
Spatter Glass, Basket, Red, Green, & Blue Spatters, Twisted Rope Handle, 9 In.	75.00
Spatter Glass, Bowl, Blue & White On Clear, Blown Mold, Scalloped Rim, 9 In.	35.00
Spatter Glass, Bowl, Pink, White, Clear, Deep, 9 In.	50.00
Spatter Glass, Bowl, Rose, Crimped Opalescent Rims, Rolled Over, Blue	45.00
Spatter Glass, Butter, Cranberry, Clear Ruffle & Finial	65.00
Spatter Glass, Butter, Triple Cased, Clear Applied Ruffled Rim, Covered	65.00
Spatter Glass, Cruet, Vinegar, Blue & White, Clear Applied Handle, 6 3/4 In.	125.00
Spatter Glass, Cup & Saucer, Tea, Red & Green	75.00
Spatter Glass, Decanter, Cranberry & White, Crystal Stopper, 12 In.	52.00
Spatter Glass, Hat, Blue & White, Blown, 3 In.	35.00
Spatter Glass, Muffineer, Cranberry	57.00
Spatter Glass, Pitcher, Clover Top, Reeded Handle	175.00
Spatter Glass, Rose Bowl, Pink & Yellow, Crimped Rim	48.00
Spatter Glass, Sugar Shaker, Leaf Umbrella, Cranberry & White	165.00
Spatter Glass, Sugar Shaker, Pink & White	65.00
Spatter Glass, Sugar Shaker, Ring Neck, Cranberry	65.00
Spatter Glass, Sugar Shaker, Ring Neck, Deep Pink	48.00
Spatter Glass, Tumbler, Baby Thumbprint, Lime Green & White	22.00
Spatter Glass, Tumbler, Column Pattern, Pink & White	15.00
Spatter Glass, Vase, Blue & Deep Blood Red Spatterings, Paneled, 9 1/4 In.	50.00
Spatter Glass, Vase, Blue, White, & Clear, 8 X 4 In.	150.00
Spatter Glass, Vase, Bud, Yellow, Cased, 7 1/2 In.	28.00
Spatter Glass, Vase, Bulbous Base, Pinched & Ribbed Sides, 4 1/2 In.	35.00
Spatter Glass, Vase, Bulbous, Ruffled, Pinks & Greens, 5 1/2 In., Pair	45.00
Spatter Glass, Vase, Burgundy & White Spatter, Cased, Gourd Shaped, 6 In.	69.00
Spatter Glass, Vase, Orange, Red, & Yellow Spatter, 8 1/4 In.	78.50
Spatter Glass, Vase, Rainbow, Cased, Melon Ribbed, Flared Neck, 6 In., Pair	67.50
Spatter Glass, Vase, Red On Pink, Ruffle Rim, Globular, 5 In.	24.00
Spatter Glass, Vase, Victorian, Cobalt Blue, Corset Shaped, Gold Mica	65.00
Spatter Glass, Vaseline, Inverted Thumbprint, 1885 Period, 6 1/4 In.	87.50

Spatterware is a creamware or soft-paste dinnerware decorated with spatter designs. The earliest pieces were made during the late eighteenth century, but most of the wares found today were made from 1800 to 1850. The spatterware dishes were made in the Staffordshire District of England for sale on the American market.

Spatterware, see also Spongeware

Spatterware, Bowl, Red Stick Spatter, Flowers, Blue Swags, 8 1/2 X 6 In.	20.00
Spatterware, Bowl, Ruffled Edge, Eagle Decoration, 13 In.	195.00
Spatterware, Bowl, Tea, Blue	25.00

Spatterware, Creamer, Peafowl, Blue Spatter	225.00
Spatterware, Creamer, Red Bud Cluster On Blue, 4 In.	75.00
Spatterware, Crock, Good Luck, 7 1/2 In.	48.00
Spatterware, Cup & Saucer, Blue Spatter, Peafowl	155.00 To 160.00
Spatterware, Cup & Saucer, Handleless, Blue With Acorn Pattern	125.00
Spatterware, Cup & Saucer, Red, Blue Flower	135.00
Spatterware, Cup & Saucer, Red, Small Dot Pattern	95.00
Spatterware, Cup, Handleless, Green, Peafowl, 3 In.	95.00
Spatterware, Cup, Tea, Pink & White, Handleless	25.00
Spatterware, Dish, Large Dot, Dark Blue, 7 1/4 In.	85.00
Spatterware, Jar, Tobacco, Covered	145.00
Spatterware, Jug, Blue Spatter, Handled, 6 1/2 In.	24.00
Spatterware, Pitcher, Bulbous, Pink & White, 9 1/2 In.	150.00
Spatterware, Pitcher, Mark Under Handle, 8 In.	115.00
Spatterware, Plate, Blue, Eagle & American Shield Center, 7 1/2 In.	75.00
Spatterware, Plate, Peafowl, Red Spatter, 9 1/4 In.	225.00 To 250.00
Spatterware, Plate, Purple Holly Berry, 8 1/2 In.	135.00 To 175.00
Spatterware, Plate, Red & Green Bull's-Eye, Rainbow, 9 1/2 In.	150.00
Spatterware, Plate, Red With Chinese Man In Brown, 6 1/2 In.	75.00
Spatterware, Platter, Blue, Oriental Garden Scene, Peacock On Fountain	60.00
Spatterware, Platter, Cut Corners, Castle In Center, 8 X 10 1/2 In.	345.00
Spatterware, Platter, Green & Purple Holly Leaf, Elsmore & Foster, 13 In.	150.00
Spatterware, Platter, Trees, Peacock On Fountain, Blue Border Spatter, 11 In.	195.00
Spatterware, Sugar, Blue, Adams Rose Decoration, Covered	130.00
Spatterware, Sugar, Blue, Covered	77.00 To 85.00
Spatterware, Sugar, Covered, Blue, 5 1/2 In.	99.00
Spatterware, Sugarshaker, Pink And White	45.00
Spatterware, Tea Bowl & Saucer, Miniature, Red & Green	190.00
Spatterware, Tea Bowl & Saucer, Peafowl, Blue	230.00
Spelter, Figurine, Musicians, Mandolin, Flute, 17 In., Pair	95.00
Spelter, Inkwell, Elephant	75.00

Spinning Wheel, see Tool, Spinning Wheel

Spode pottery, porcelain, and bone china were made by the Stoke-on-Trent Factory of England founded by Josiah Spode about 1770. The firm became Copeland and Garrett from 1833 to 1847, then W.T.Copeland or W.T.Copeland and Sons until the present time. The word Spode appears on many pieces made by the Copeland Factory. Most collectors include all the wares under the more familiar name of Spode.

Spode, see also Copeland

Spode, Bowl, Punch, Stone China, Famille Rose, C.1821, 15 1/2 In.	275.00
Spode, Bowl, White Classical Figures On Green Ground, 3 3/4 In.	65.00
Spode, Creamer, Aster	16.00
Spode, Cup & Saucer, Bell Shape, C.1820	148.00
Spode, Cup & Saucer, Blue Willow Decoration, 1784	65.00
Spode, Cup & Saucer, Cabbage Leaf, C.1829	85.00
Spode, Cup & Saucer, Handleless, Blue Willow, After 1784	65.00
Spode, Cup & Saucer, White Geometric, Gray, Bone China	16.00
Spode, Cup, Victoria Pattern	4.00
Spode, Dessert Set, Landscape Decoration, Early 19th Century, 15 Piece	110.00
Spode, Dish, Red & Pink Florals On White, C.1805, 10 1/2 In., Oblong	50.00
Spode, Dish, Relish, Mandarin Pattern, 5 1/2 X 3 1/2 In.	10.00
Spode, Figurine, Shepherd Boy & Girl, 1933, Pair	150.00
Spode, Pitcher, Blue Italian Scene, C.1900	59.00
Spode, Pitcher, Jasperware, Football Players In Relief, 6 1/4 In.	95.00
Spode, Pitcher, Water, Cameo, Winston Churchill, 7 1/2 In.	75.00
Spode, Plate, Blackbird Pattern, 7 1/2 In.	18.00
Spode, Plate, British Flowers II, Medium To Dark Blue, C.1850, 10 In.	60.00
Spode, Plate, Chop, Reynolds	30.00
Spode, Plate, Game, Wild Duck, Cobalt Blue, 10 1/4 In.	65.00
Spode, Plate, Girl At The Well, Blue & White, C.1830	45.00
Spode, Plate, Green & White Floral On Light Green, 1703-1805, Hexagonal	36.00
Spode, Plate, Imari Decoration, C.1840, 7 In.	128.00
Spode, Pot, Hot Water, With Cover, 12 Classical White Figures On Green, 8 In.	150.00

Spode, Sauceboat, Tobacco Leaf, 4 X 5 3/4 In.	32.50
Spode, Teapot, Rosso Antico Enamel, 1784-1805	120.00

Spongeware is very similar to spatterware in appearance. The designs were applied to the ware by daubing the color. Many dealers do not differentiate between the two wares and use the names interchangeably.

Spongeware, Bowl, Blue & Brown On Buff, 4 X 6 1/2 In.	50.00
Spongeware, Bowl, Blue & Rust On Beige, 9 In.	37.00
Spongeware, Bowl, Blue On White, 13 X 4 1/2 In.	27.50
Spongeware, Bowl, Blue On White, 8 In.	30.00
Spongeware, Bowl, Blue-Green Sponge, Cream Ground, Rolled Rim, 7 1/2 In.	45.00
Spongeware, Bowl, Blue, Flat Rim, 10 X 3 1/4 In.	80.00
Spongeware, Bowl, Blue, Orange On Cream, Large	30.00
Spongeware, Bowl, Blue, Wire Bail, Covered, 10 In.	95.00
Spongeware, Bowl, Brown & Cream, 5 In.	14.00
Spongeware, Bowl, Cereal, Brown Daubing On Tan	18.00
Spongeware, Bowl, Dark Green On Yellow, 14 In.	260.00
Spongeware, Bowl, Mixing, Blue, Taupe On Tan, 10 1/4 In.	46.00
Spongeware, Bowl, Mixing, Blue, 9 In.	55.00
Spongeware, Bowl, Multicolored, 9 In.	45.00
Spongeware, Bowl, Salt, Blue & Brown On Gray, 7 X 4 1/4 In.	36.00
Spongeware, Bowl, Salt, Cobalt & Brown On Gray, 7 X 4 In.	36.00
Spongeware, Bowl, Waste, Dark Blue	85.00
Spongeware, Bowl, 3 X 9 In.	48.00
Spongeware, Bowl, 8 1/2 In.	65.00
Spongeware, Cookie Jar, Bulbous, Wooden Lid, Green, Brown On Cream, 6 In.	35.00
Spongeware, Cookie Jar, Multicolor Banded, Covered	25.00
Spongeware, Crock, Butter, Covered, Blue Trim, 4 1/2 In.	35.00
Spongeware, Crock, Butter, Covered, Wooden Lid, 2 Lb., Green, Brown On Cream	38.00
Spongeware, Cup & Saucer, Handleless, Double Ogee Shape Cup	95.00
Spongeware, Dish, Baking, Blue Sponge On White, 9 1/2 X 8 X 2 1/2 In.	58.00
Spongeware, Dish, Pie	28.00
Spongeware, Jug, Blue, Yellow, 1 Gallon	125.00
Spongeware, Jug, Raspberry Sponge On Creamware, Mohawk Liquor, Handled, 1 Qt.	35.00
Spongeware, Jug, Vinegar, Green Sponge Color	39.00
Spongeware, Mug, Blue & White, Burford Porcelain	67.00
Spongeware, Pan, Dish, Blue & White, 12 1/2 X 3 1/2 In.	12.50
Spongeware, Pitcher, Blue & Rust On Beige, 9 In.	38.00
Spongeware, Pitcher, Blue On Buff, 4 1/2 In.	12.00
Spongeware, Pitcher, Blue, 9 In.	95.00
Spongeware, Pitcher, Chocolate Glaze, 8 In.	18.00
Spongeware, Pitcher, Green, Brown On Cream, Barrel, Bulbous, 7 1/2 In.	35.00
Spongeware, Pitcher, Rose, Blue, 9 In.	110.00
Spongeware, Pitcher, 5 In. *Illus*	25.00

Spongeware, Pitcher, 5 In.

Staffordshire, Creamer, Ashworth Bros., 4 In.

Spongeware, Plate, Cake, Blue, International Pottery, 10 1/2 In. 125.00
Spongeware, Plate, Dark Blue, 9 1/2 In. 75.00
Spongeware, Plate, Holly Berry, Spatter, 9 3/4 In. 55.00
Spongeware, Plate, Soup, Mottled Blue, Scalloped Edge, 9 1/4 In. 75.00
Spongeware, Platter, Blue, 11 3/4 X 8 In. 60.00
Spongeware, Platter, Turtle Top, Blues, 14 X 10 1/2 In. 70.00
Spongeware, Safe, Cheese, Cockscomb Decoration 30.00
Spongeware, Spittoon, Blue With Blue Bands, 5 1/4 X 7 1/2 In. 65.00
Spongeware, Spittoon, 3 Bands, Blue, White 45.00
Spongeware, Tea Bowl & Saucer, Blue 75.00

*Staffordshire is a district in England where pottery and porcelain have
been made since the 1900s. Thousands of types of pottery and porcelain have
been made in the hundreds of factories that worked in the area. Some of the
most famous factories have been listed separately. See Royal Doulton,
Royal Worcester, Spode, Wedgwood, and others.*

Staffordshire, see also Flow Blue, Ridgway

Staffordshire, Bank, Cottage, Ann Hathaway's Cottage Inscribed On Base 45.00
Staffordshire, Bank, English Style House, Dated 1932 .... 85.00
Staffordshire, Bowl, Lavender, Royal Sketches, Latin Motto, C.1835, 10 1/4 In. 45.00
Staffordshire, Bowl, Purple With Green, Yellow, Blue Underglaze, C.1840 .... 22.00
Staffordshire, Bowl, Soup, Harvard College, Enoch Wood & Sons, Purple, 10 In. 100.00
Staffordshire, Bowl, Stag Chased By Hounds Scene, Dark Blue, 6 1/2 In. 125.00
Staffordshire, Bowl, Vegetable, Covered, Asiatic Plant, Mulberry 65.00
Staffordshire, Bowl, Vegetable, English Scenery, Medium Blue, Enoch Wood 45.00
Staffordshire, Bowl, Vegetable, Open, Jeddo, Mulberry, Wm.Adams, C.1845 .... 20.00
Staffordshire, Bowl, Waste, Jeddo, Mulberry, Wm.Adams, C.1845, 5 1/2 In. 30.00
Staffordshire, Bust, John Wesley, 12 In. 85.00
Staffordshire, Cocoa Pot, Childs 13.50
Staffordshire, Condiment Set, Gaudy Welsh Designed Shaker, 2 Open Salts 95.00
Staffordshire, Cottage, Pastille Burner, 3 Story Tudor, 7 In. 65.00
Staffordshire, Creamer & Sugar, Child's, Water Hen, Pink, C.1860 .... 24.00
Staffordshire, Creamer, Ashworth Bros., 4 In. .... *Illus*   33.00
Staffordshire, Creamer, Corean, Mulberry, Podmore & Walker, C.1850 .... 75.00
Staffordshire, Creamer, Cow, Iron Red Sponge Decoration, Gold Horns, 5 In. 75.00
Staffordshire, Creamer, Cow, Lid, White, Rust Spots, Green Base, 4 X 6 1/2 In. 95.00
Staffordshire, Creamer, Cow, White With Brown, 5 In. 75.00
Staffordshire, Creamer, Little Meg, Child's Server 32.00
Staffordshire, Creamer, Lorne, Green 70.00
Staffordshire, Creamer, Pelew, Mulberry, C.1850, E.Challinor 75.00
Staffordshire, Creamer, Stag Chased By Hounds Scene, Dark Blue 225.00
Staffordshire, Creamer, Washington Vase, Mulberry, Podmore & Walker 75.00
Staffordshire, Cup & Saucer, American Eagle On Urn, Deep Blue 250.00
Staffordshire, Cup & Saucer, Child's, Brown Stag 10.00
Staffordshire, Cup & Saucer, Corea, Handleless, J.Clemtson, Mulberry 36.00
Staffordshire, Cup & Saucer, Hand-Painted Magenta Florals, 19th Century 15.00
Staffordshire, Cup & Saucer, Indian Tree, Hand-Painted, Gilded 25.00
Staffordshire, Cup & Saucer, Jeddo, Mulberry, Handleless, Wm.Adams, C.1845 .... 30.00
Staffordshire, Cup & Saucer, Natural Bridge, Virginia, Purple 5.00
Staffordshire, Cup & Saucer, Pink, Handleless, Gazelle, Adams 38.00
Staffordshire, Cup & Saucer, Rose Floral, Gold Rims, Marked England 17.00
Staffordshire, Cup & Saucer, Wilkes-Barre And Troy N.Y., Light Blue 75.00
Staffordshire, Cup Plate, Constitution Tyrants' Foe, Brown 110.00
Staffordshire, Cup Plate, Cottage In The Woods, Trefoil Border 140.00
Staffordshire, Cup Plate, Deep Blue, Franklin Flying Kite, 2 In. 85.00
Staffordshire, Cup Plate, Flow Mulberry, Cypress 18.00
Staffordshire, Cup Plate, Franklin Flying Kite, Blue, 19th Century, 2 In. 85.00
Staffordshire, Cup Plate, Light Blue, Marked Blantyre, J.& G.Alcock 15.00
Staffordshire, Cup Plate, Urn, Pink, Mayer 16.00
Staffordshire, Cup Plate, Willow 25.00
Staffordshire, Cup, Handleless, Floral, Mulberry, Sponged Inside Rim 32.50
Staffordshire, Dinner Service, Doll's, Pearlware, C.1810, 20 Pieces 275.00
Staffordshire, Dish, Dove & Blue Jay On Cover, 7 1/2 X 6 In. 250.00
Staffordshire, Dish, Fruit, Hindoo Pagoda, Deep Blue, Openwork, Hall, 12 In. 250.00

Staffordshire, Dish, Hen Cover, Basket Weave Base, Orange, 6 1/2 In.	135.00
Staffordshire, Dish, Hen Cover, Nest Base, White, 9 In.	125.00
Staffordshire, Dish, Soap, Etruscan Vase, Mulberry, Covered, 5 1/2 X 4 In.	45.00
Staffordshire, Dish, Vegetable, Blue, Cottage Fishing Scene, Dome Lid, 12 In.	210.00
Staffordshire, Figurine, Attached Ladies' Boots, White, Blue Laces, 2 1/2 In.	35.00
Staffordshire, Figurine, Baker & Wife, 13 1/2 In.	48.00
Staffordshire, Figurine, Boy With Horn, Flat Back, 12 X 8 In.	65.00
Staffordshire, Figurine, Cat, Beige Glaze, Molded Fur, Black Eyes, 10 In., Pair	75.00
Staffordshire, Figurine, Cat, Black & White, Orange Base, 7 1/2 In., Pair	80.00
Staffordshire, Figurine, Cobbler's Wife, C.1830	45.00
Staffordshire, Figurine, Colonial Costumed Man, 7 1/2 In.	22.00
Staffordshire, Figurine, Dog On Pillow, Basket In Mouth, 3 In.	15.00
Staffordshire, Figurine, Dog With Basket Of Flowers, 10 In.	55.00
Staffordshire, Figurine, Dog With Luster Chain, 11 1/2 In.	55.00
Staffordshire, Figurine, Dog, Black & White, Chain Around Neck, 9 In., Pair	85.00
Staffordshire, Figurine, Dog, Girl On Back, Colorful, Marked, 5 3/4 In.	65.00
Staffordshire, Figurine, Dog, Mongrel Seated, Orange-Rust, C.1850, 13 1/2 In.	68.00
Staffordshire, Figurine, Dog, One Black, One White, 9 1/2 In., Pair	65.00
Staffordshire, Figurine, Dog, Pekinese, Cobalt Base, 8 In., Pair	175.00
Staffordshire, Figurine, Dog, Poodle, Cream, Gold Collar, 9 1/2 In., Pair	150.00
Staffordshire, Figurine, Dog, Poodle, Fur-Textured Bodies, 12 In., Pair	135.00
Staffordshire, Figurine, Dog, Poodle, White, Pink Chin, 3 X 3 1/2 In.	36.00
Staffordshire, Figurine, Dog, Poodle, White, Sitting, 3 In., Pair	32.50
Staffordshire, Figurine, Dog, Poodle, 6 In., Pair	37.50
Staffordshire, Figurine, Dog, Sitting, White, Gold Luster Design, 13 In., Pair	125.00
Staffordshire, Figurine, Dog, Spaniel Seated, Cream, Brown Spots, 13 In., Pair	115.00
Staffordshire, Figurine, Dog, Spaniel Seated, Rust & White, 4 In.	35.00
Staffordshire, Figurine, Dog, Spaniel Seated, Taupe, Black, Glass Eyes, Pair	165.00
Staffordshire, Figurine, Dog, Spaniel, Black & White, 7 In., Pair	125.00
Staffordshire, Figurine, Dog, Spaniel, Glass Eyes, Hand-Painted, 11 In.	60.00
Staffordshire, Figurine, Dog, Spaniel, Glass Eyes, 11 In., Pair	95.00 To 120.00
Staffordshire, Figurine, Dog, Spaniel, Glass Eyes, 19th Century, 10 1/2 In.	35.00
Staffordshire, Figurine, Dog, Spaniel, Off White, Gold Chains, 13 In., Pair	225.00
Staffordshire, Figurine, Dog, Spaniel, Red Spots, Gold Lock, Collar, 3 1/4 In.	29.00
Staffordshire, Figurine, Dog, Spaniel, Reddish-Tan, Glass Eyes, 10 1/2 In.	120.00
Staffordshire, Figurine, Dog, Spaniel, Rust On White, C.1850, 10 1/2 In., Pair	95.00
Staffordshire, Figurine, Dog, Spaniel, White, Gold Markings, 9 In., Pair	100.00
Staffordshire, Figurine, Dog, Spaniel, White, Red Markings, 10 3/4 In., Pair	125.00
Staffordshire, Figurine, Dog, Whippet Seated, Tan, Blue Collar, 5 1/2 In.	55.00
Staffordshire, Figurine, Dog, Whippet With Hare, Brown On Cobalt, 11 In.	58.00
Staffordshire, Figurine, Dog, Whippet, 4 In.	42.00
Staffordshire, Figurine, Dog, White, Gold Markings, Pair, 12 1/4 In.	110.00
Staffordshire, Figurine, Edward VII, Prince Of Wales, 16 1/2 In.	145.00
Staffordshire, Figurine, Farmer, White, Orange, Gold, Holding Jug	75.00
Staffordshire, Figurine, German Tailor & Wife Riding Goats, 12 1/2 In., Pair	175.00
Staffordshire, Figurine, Girl & Boy With Flower Baskets, White & Gold, 7 In.	28.00
Staffordshire, Figurine, Huntsman & Dog, 14 In.	70.00
Staffordshire, Figurine, King Charles Spaniel, Flow Blue Base, 8 In., Pair	115.00
Staffordshire, Figurine, Lady Holding Dog, Nodding Head, Gold Trim, 7 In.	65.00
Staffordshire, Figurine, Lamb On Base, White, 3 1/2 X 2 1/2 In.	35.00
Staffordshire, Figurine, Leopard, Ocher, Reddish Brown, C.1800, 8 1/2 In., Pair	1100.00
Staffordshire, Figurine, Lion Slayer, 17 In.	120.00
Staffordshire, Figurine, Lion, Brown & Tan, Glass Eyes, Lying Position, Pair	130.00
Staffordshire, Figurine, Napoleon On Horse, 7 In.	75.00
Staffordshire, Figurine, Old Woman, Purple Muff, Cane, Soft Paste, 7 1/2 In.	65.00
Staffordshire, Figurine, Pebbly Sheep Standing Near Tree Trunk	95.00
Staffordshire, Figurine, Princess Victoria & Prince Arthur, 7 1/8 In., Pair	150.00
Staffordshire, Figurine, Red Riding Hood & Wolf, 6 In.	21.00
Staffordshire, Figurine, Returning Home, Man & Woman On Horse, 8 In.High	60.00
Staffordshire, Figurine, Robin Hood, Little John & Dog	65.00
Staffordshire, Figurine, Samuel & Eli, 11 1/4 In.	225.00
Staffordshire, Figurine, Scot & Maid, 12 1/2 In.	65.00
Staffordshire, Figurine, Scotch Lassie, Tambourine, Turquoise, Gold, Parian	65.00
Staffordshire, Figurine, Shepherd Girl Holding Flowers, 7 1/2 In.	85.00

Staffordshire, Figurine, Toby, Hardy Good Fellow 95.00
Staffordshire, Figurine, Tony Weller, Hand-Painted, 5 3/4 In. 24.00
Staffordshire, Figurine, Turk, 1820's, 5 In. 165.00
Staffordshire, Figurine, Uncle Tom & Eva, 9 3/4 In. 225.00
Staffordshire, Figurine, Victoria, Seated, Blue & Gold Gown, Green Crown 175.00
Staffordshire, Figurine, White Hen On Brown Nest 85.00
Staffordshire, Gravy Boat, Rhine Pattern, Brown Transfer, C.1850, 9 In. 35.00
Staffordshire, Group, Boy & Girl On Tree Stump, Basket Of Eggs, Pedestal 55.00
Staffordshire, Group, Equestrian, Returning Home, Man & Woman On Horse, 8 In. 60.00
Staffordshire, Group, Lovers Embracing, Reddish-Brown Hair, 8 1/2 In. 55.00
Staffordshire, Group, Musicians, Lady & Man, Flatback, 17 In. 85.00
Staffordshire, Group, Tam O'Shanter & Sooter Johnny, C.1850, 12 1/2 In. 125.00
Staffordshire, Inkwell, Figural, Bear, Well In Mouth, 4 1/2 In. 125.00
Staffordshire, Inkwell, Figural, Whippet, Cobalt Base, 6 1/2 X 4 3/4 In. 110.00
Staffordshire, Jardiniere, Blue, White, Cattle Scenery, Adams & Co., 7 1/2 In. 65.00
Staffordshire, Jug, John Wesley 150.00
Staffordshire, Jug, Masonic, Transfer Printed, C.1800, 8 1/2 In. 500.00
Staffordshire, Jug, Tulip Tree, Double Twisted Twig Handle, C.1860, 9 In. 50.00
Staffordshire, Lamp, Fairy, Shape Of Bunny Rabbit 55.00
Staffordshire, Mug, Alphabet Series, 4 Children Riding An Early Bike 46.00
Staffordshire, Mug, Alphabet, Y & Z, Pink, Yellow, Green, Children's Scenes 60.00
Staffordshire, Mug, Blowing Bubbles, Children, Basket Of Laundry 50.00
Staffordshire, Mug, Corean, Handled, Hand-Painted, 2 3/4 In. 45.00
Staffordshire, Mug, Dragons Transfer On White, 2 1/2 In. 28.00
Staffordshire, Mug, Franklin Maxims 85.00
Staffordshire, Mug, Frog, Drinking Scene In Relief, Yellow & Brown 195.00
Staffordshire, Mug, Green Transfer On Beige, The Seasons-June, Rhyme 35.00
Staffordshire, Mug, Handled, Floral, Marked 30.00
Staffordshire, Mug, Huntsman, 3 1/2 In. 32.00
Staffordshire, Mug, Pink Luster, Cottage Decoration, Applied Handle 28.00
Staffordshire, Mug, Railroad, Blue, Engine Pilot Pulling 4-Car Train, 1850 .... 325.00
Staffordshire, Mug, Shuttlecock 52.00
Staffordshire, Mug, Tam O'Shanter, Multicolored, 2 Scenes, Tavern, Demons 110.00
Staffordshire, Mug, Top Whipping, Children Playing, 2 1/2 In. 38.00
Staffordshire, Mug, Wooden Bowls & Spoons, Peddler Scene 70.00
Staffordshire, Pepper Pot, Basket Of Flowers, Blue 85.00
Staffordshire, Pitcher, Battle Scene, Soldiers, Warriors, Pink, 5 7/8 In. 65.00
Staffordshire, Pitcher, Cherubs, Roses, Grapes, Gold Luster, 6 3/4 In. 48.00
Staffordshire, Pitcher, Continental Cathedral, Black On White, T.Shirley 30.00
Staffordshire, Pitcher, Dark Blue, Deer In Medallions, 7 In. 150.00
Staffordshire, Pitcher, Dog, 10 In. 70.00
Staffordshire, Pitcher, Franklin Flying A Kite, Transfer, 10 In. 110.00
Staffordshire, Pitcher, Martyred President Garfield, Portrait, 10 In. 110.00
Staffordshire, Pitcher, Milk, Aurora, Brown, White, 8 In. 45.00
Staffordshire, Pitcher, Milk, Columbia, Blue & White, Clementson & Young 150.00
Staffordshire, Pitcher, Oriental, Blue & White, C.1940, 10 In. 150.00
Staffordshire, Pitcher, Pink Luster, House, 2 1/4 In. 28.00
Staffordshire, Pitcher, Sepia Transfer, Franklin Flying A Kite 110.00
Staffordshire, Plaque, Reverend John Wesley, C.1839 .... 95.00
Staffordshire, Plaque, Sandland Ware, Watteau Scene, 4 In., Pair 15.00
Staffordshire, Plate, Adams Palestine, Purple, 10 1/2 In. 38.00
Staffordshire, Plate, American Marine, Brown, 9 1/4 In. 32.50
Staffordshire, Plate, Arms Of New York, Thomas Mayer, 10 In. 750.00
Staffordshire, Plate, At Richmond, Virginia, Black, White, Jackson, 7 In. 95.00
Staffordshire, Plate, Aurora, Brown, White, 9 1/2 In. 10.00
Staffordshire, Plate, Bank Of U.S., Philadelphia, Eagle Border, Stubbs, 10 In. 300.00
Staffordshire, Plate, Bank Of U.S.Philadelphia, Stubbs, 10 In. 300.00
Staffordshire, Plate, Beggars Children, 8 1/2 In. 48.00
Staffordshire, Plate, Black Print Of Man On Horse, Deep Pink, Green, 8 In. 35.00
Staffordshire, Plate, Black Transfer, William Penn's Treaty, 8 1/2 In. 42.50
Staffordshire, Plate, Black, Ornate Ship Border, Edwards, C.1840, 9 In. 40.00
Staffordshire, Plate, Blue & White, Taft & Sherman, R & M, 10 In. 28.00
Staffordshire, Plate, Blue, Flowers & Dove, 7 1/2 In. 12.00
Staffordshire, Plate, Blue, White, Historic Williamsburg, Virginia, Wren Bldg. 35.00

Staffordshire, Plate, Bosphorus, Lavender On White, R.Hall, 10 1/3 In.	18.00
Staffordshire, Plate, Bosphorus, Mulberry, 10 In.	25.00
Staffordshire, Plate, Boston Mails, Edwards, C.1840, 8 In.	40.00
Staffordshire, Plate, Boston State House, Dark Blue, Enoch Wood, 7 1/2 In.	125.00
Staffordshire, Plate, Brown, Ornate Ship Border, Edwards, C.1840, 8 In.	35.00
Staffordshire, Plate, Caledonia, Adams, Purple, 10 1/2 In.	45.00
Staffordshire, Plate, Caledonia, Purple, Adams, 10 1/2 In.	48.00
Staffordshire, Plate, Caledonia, Scotch Deer Hunting Scene, Purple, Adams	39.00
Staffordshire, Plate, Canova, Black, 6 In.	20.00
Staffordshire, Plate, Canova, Pink, T.Mayer, 9 1/4 In.	22.50
Staffordshire, Plate, Canova, T.Mayer, Pink, 9 1/4 In.	22.00
Staffordshire, Plate, Capitol In Washington, Shell Border, 7 1/4 In.	275.00
Staffordshire, Plate, Castle Garden, Battery, New York, Blue, Shell Border	110.00
Staffordshire, Plate, Catskill Moss, Narrows, Fort Hamilton, N.Y., Light Blue	45.00
Staffordshire, Plate, Child's Golliwog	10.00
Staffordshire, Plate, Chinese Pastime, C.1840, 7 3/4 In.	28.00
Staffordshire, Plate, Christmas Eve, Wilkie, Dark Blue, 9 In.	135.00
Staffordshire, Plate, City Of Albany, New York, Shell Border, 10 In.	200.00
Staffordshire, Plate, Clyde Scenery, Jackson's Warranted, Purple, 10 In.	30.00
Staffordshire, Plate, Columbia Shape, Plain, Clementson, 7 1/4 In.	6.00
Staffordshire, Plate, Corean, Mulberry, 7 In.	20.00
Staffordshire, Plate, Corean, Mulberry, 8 In.	30.00
Staffordshire, Plate, Corean, Mulberry, 10 In.	35.00
Staffordshire, Plate, Corinthia, Blue, Ironstone, Challinor, 9 In.	19.50
Staffordshire, Plate, Corinthia, Challinor, Blue, 9 In.	18.50
Staffordshire, Plate, Culzeon Castle, Ayrshire, Medium Blue, Wood, 8 1/2 In.	35.00
Staffordshire, Plate, Cup, Sandy Hill, Hudson River, Clews, Light Blue	50.00
Staffordshire, Plate, Cup, Women In Archery Game, Blue	18.00
Staffordshire, Plate, Dam & Waterworks, Philadelphia, 10 In.	195.00
Staffordshire, Plate, Damascus, Blue, C.1840, 8 In.	24.00
Staffordshire, Plate, Dr.Syntax Disputing His Bill	95.00
Staffordshire, Plate, Drury Lane Theatre, London, Blue, Tans, 9 In.	59.00
Staffordshire, Plate, European Lions, Conway Bridge, J R Lavender, 10 In.	35.00
Staffordshire, Plate, Excelsior, Purple, Ironstone, G.Woolscroft, 9 1/2 In.	55.00
Staffordshire, Plate, Fairmount Near Philadelphia, Stubbs, 10 In.	200.00
Staffordshire, Plate, Falls Of Montmorency, Quebec, Dark Blue, Wood, 8 1/2 In.	210.00
Staffordshire, Plate, Floral Center, Light Blue Trim, Wood & Sons, 8 In.	22.00
Staffordshire, Plate, Fountain Scenery, Pink, Scalloped, 10 In.	16.00 To 24.00
Staffordshire, Plate, Friburg, Blue, Davenport, C.1845, 7 1/2 In.	18.00
Staffordshire, Plate, Fruit, Blue, Pear, 7 3/4 In.	12.00
Staffordshire, Plate, Heath Italian Villas, Pink, 10 In.	16.00 To 24.00
Staffordshire, Plate, Hoboken, N.J., Eagle Border, Stubbs, 7 7/8 In.	185.00
Staffordshire, Plate, Holland's Carrara, Mulberry	20.00
Staffordshire, Plate, Hudson River, Purple, Sandy Hill, 8 In.	83.00
Staffordshire, Plate, Hudson, Brown, White, 10 1/2 In.	45.00
Staffordshire, Plate, Independence Hall, 10 In.	18.00
Staffordshire, Plate, Insane Hospital, Boston, Dark Blue, Ridgway, 7 1/4 In.	175.00
Staffordshire, Plate, Iris, Set Of 5 Plates	55.00
Staffordshire, Plate, Italian Buildings, Blue, R.Hall, 10 In.	20.00
Staffordshire, Plate, Italian Buildings, 7 In.	12.00
Staffordshire, Plate, Italian Scene, Stubbs, Pre-1850, 6 1/2 In.	35.00
Staffordshire, Plate, Italy, Lavender, Chas.Meigh & Sons, C.1851, 9 1/2 In.	32.00
Staffordshire, Plate, Jeddo, Mulberry, Wm.Adams, C.1845, 9 1/2 In.	12.00
Staffordshire, Plate, Junction Of Ticonderoga And Hudson River, 6 1/2 In.	60.00
Staffordshire, Plate, King's Cottage, Windsor Park, C.1820, 7 1/4 In.	20.00
Staffordshire, Plate, Landing Of The Pilgrims, Blue, Enoch Wood, 10 In.	125.00
Staffordshire, Plate, Lincoln Memorial, Purple, White	35.00
Staffordshire, Plate, Lisbon, Brown, Edge, Malkin & Co., 9 1/4 In.	12.00
Staffordshire, Plate, Llanarth Court, Monmouthshire, Hall, Blue, 10 In.	55.00
Staffordshire, Plate, Lozere, Blue, Challinor, 7 1/2 In.	10.00
Staffordshire, Plate, Marine Hospital, Louisville, Kentucky	275.00 To 400.00
Staffordshire, Plate, McDonough's Victory, Shell Border, 10 In.	300.00
Staffordshire, Plate, Medina, Blue, 7 1/2 In.	14.00
Staffordshire, Plate, Meredith, N.H., Blue, 9 1/4 In.	45.00

Staffordshire, Plate, Neptune, J & G Alcock, 7 1/2 In. 27.50
Staffordshire, Plate, New York City Hall, Blue 175.00
Staffordshire, Plate, Palestine, Willow Tree, Stevenson, 7 3/8 In. 35.00
Staffordshire, Plate, Park Scene, Animals In Field, Brown, C.1840, 10 In. 28.00
Staffordshire, Plate, Park Theater, New York, Dark Blue, 10 1/4 In. 250.00
Staffordshire, Plate, Pekin, Multicolor, C.1880, 9 In. 20.00
Staffordshire, Plate, Pennsylvania, Deep Purple, Knight Elkins 33.00
Staffordshire, Plate, Perthshire, 10 In. 42.00
Staffordshire, Plate, Ponte Rotto, Medium Dark Blue, C.1825, 10 In. 38.00
Staffordshire, Plate, Priory, Cobridge, John Alcock, 10 1/2 In. 12.00
Staffordshire, Plate, Provincetown, Massachusetts, Blue, R.& M.Co., 10 1/2 In. 50.00
Staffordshire, Plate, Purple Sirius, Pink, 9 In. 18.00
Staffordshire, Plate, Purple Sirius, Pink, 10 In. 12.00
Staffordshire, Plate, Rapids Above Hadley Falls, Clews, Purple, 7 In. 55.00
Staffordshire, Plate, Regents Park, Adams, Blue 75.00
Staffordshire, Plate, Riley, 10 In. 42.00
Staffordshire, Plate, Service, Pink & Green, Set Of 12 .... 95.00
Staffordshire, Plate, Shannondale Springs, Va., Adams, Pink, 8 In. 68.00
Staffordshire, Plate, Soup, Camel Pattern, Rogers, Pre-1850, 9 1/2 In. 55.00
Staffordshire, Plate, Soup, Harvard College, E.W.& Sons Celtic China, 10 In. 130.00
Staffordshire, Plate, Soup, Wm.Penn's Treaty, Black, 10 1/2 In. 120.00
Staffordshire, Plate, Spotted Deer, Ruins, Floral Border, Pre-1850, 9 1/2 In. 48.00
Staffordshire, Plate, St.Catherine's Hall, Guilford, Clews In Circle, 10 In. 75.00
Staffordshire, Plate, Stamboul, Purple, 9 In. 10.00
Staffordshire, Plate, States, Dark Blue, Clews, 8 In. .... 175.00 To 275.00
Staffordshire, Plate, States, With Fishermen, Blue, 10 1/4 In. 250.00
Staffordshire, Plate, Tear For Poland, Floral Scalloped Border, Dark Pink 55.00
Staffordshire, Plate, Texan, Brown, Marked J.B., 8 1/4 In. 42.00
Staffordshire, Plate, Teymouth Castle, 10 In. 42.00
Staffordshire, Plate, Toddy, E.Challinor & Co., 5 1/4 In. 25.00
Staffordshire, Plate, Toddy, Hudson River, Clews, Light Blue 60.00
Staffordshire, Plate, Transylvania University, Lexington, Shell Border, 9 In. 250.00
Staffordshire, Plate, View Near Conway, N.H., Pink, Adams, 9 In. .... 65.00 To 75.00
Staffordshire, Plate, View Of St.Paul's Church Yard, Initialed, 10 3/8 In. 39.00
Staffordshire, Plate, View Trenton Falls, Shell Border, 6 1/4 In. 250.00
Staffordshire, Plate, Waterworks, Phila, Purple, 9 In. 83.00
Staffordshire, Plate, William Penn's Treaty, Brown, Godwin, 10 3/4 In. 68.00
Staffordshire, Plate, Winter View, Pittsfield, Mass., Dark Blue, 10 1/2 In. 200.00
Staffordshire, Plate, Wistow Hall, Leicestershire, Dark Blue, Hall, 9 In. 95.00
Staffordshire, Plate, Women In Field, Raised Floral & Ribbon In Pink, Green 35.00
Staffordshire, Plate, Woodlands, Near Philadelphia, Dark Blue, 6 1/2 In. 145.00
Staffordshire, Plate, Zoological, Deer Hunting, Deep Blue, Wood, 10 1/4 In. 79.00
Staffordshire, Platter, American Villa, Dark Blue, 9 1/2 In. 165.00
Staffordshire, Platter, Aurora, Brown, White, 13 1/2 In. 35.00
Staffordshire, Platter, Blue, Bristol With Anchor, 16 1/4 X 12 In. 148.00
Staffordshire, Platter, Caledonia, Soft Pink, Glazed, Adams, 17 In. 150.00
Staffordshire, Platter, Capitol In Washington, D.C., Blue, 21 X 15 In. 950.00
Staffordshire, Platter, Chinese Scene, Rectangular, Challinor, 10 3/4 In. 20.00
Staffordshire, Platter, Dark Blue, Davenport Mark, C.1810, 10 1/4 X 9 1/4 In. 45.00
Staffordshire, Platter, Davenport, Blue, 20 X 3/4 X 15 1/4 In. 150.00
Staffordshire, Platter, Fisherman, With Fishbowl Border, Blue, 17 In. 85.00
Staffordshire, Platter, Hudson, Black, White, 12 In. 125.00
Staffordshire, Platter, Jeddo, Mulberry, Wm.Adams, C.1845, 11 X 8 In. 15.00
Staffordshire, Platter, Kenmount House, Deep Blue, 16 1/2 In. 260.00
Staffordshire, Platter, Melbourne, 18 X 14 1/2 In. 40.00
Staffordshire, Platter, Minerva, Podmore & Walker, Mulberry, C.1849, 12 In. 55.00
Staffordshire, Platter, Miniature, Octagonal, Numbered, C.1810, 10 X 7 1/4 In. 32.00
Staffordshire, Platter, Near Fishkill, Light Blue, 10 In. 60.00
Staffordshire, Platter, Patna On Ganges, Dark Blue, I.Hall & Sons, 14 1/2 In. 110.00
Staffordshire, Platter, Rhone Scene, Mulberry, TJpJ Mayer, C.1845, 16 In. 100.00
Staffordshire, Platter, State House, Boston, 14 1/2 In. 525.00
Staffordshire, Platter, Tyrolean, Green, 14 3/4 In. 78.00
Staffordshire, Platter, View Of Newburg, New York, Mulberry, C.1844, 18 In. 385.00
Staffordshire, Platter, Warwick Vase, Green, 17 In. 85.00

Staffordshire, **Platter,** Washington Vase, Mulberry, 13 1/2 In.	65.00
Staffordshire, **Quill Holder,** Dog Each Side, Flower Holder, 5 1/2 X 5 In.	34.50
Staffordshire, **Salt & Pepper,** Toby Mugs, Prestopans Pottery, Scotland, 1830	95.00
Staffordshire, **Saucer,** Log Cabin, Green, 4 In.	25.00
Staffordshire, **Soup,** Mulberry, Hyson, J.Clementson, C.1845, 9 In.	15.00
Staffordshire, **Sugar & Creamer,** Bombay, Blue, Enoch And Ralph Wood	125.00
Staffordshire, **Sugar,** Abbey Ruins, R.Mayer, Dark Pink	40.00
Staffordshire, **Sugar,** Basket Of Flowers, Dark Blue, Covered	90.00
Staffordshire, **Sugar,** Countess, Black On White, C.1890, Covered, 6 1/2 In.	15.00
Staffordshire, **Sugar,** Pink, Floral, Diapered Decoration, 7 1/2 In.	42.00
Staffordshire, **Sugar,** Ribbed, Dome Lid, Grapes, C.1860, W & E Corn	350.00
Staffordshire, **Sugar,** Stag Chased By Hounds Scene, Dark Blue	175.00
Staffordshire, **Sugar,** Swiss Scene, Brown, Octagonal, C.1850	32.00
Staffordshire, **Tea Set,** Child's, Brown & White, Victorian Girl, Pets, 12 Piece	57.00
Staffordshire, **Tea Set,** Child's, Rural Scenes In Brown, 19 Piece	200.00
Staffordshire, **Teapot & Sugar Bowl,** Black, White	100.00
Staffordshire, **Teapot,** Blue, White Floral, Dome Lid, 12 In.	125.00
Staffordshire, **Teapot,** Canova	35.00
Staffordshire, **Teapot,** Jeddo, Mulberry, Wm.Adams, C.1845, 9 In.	90.00
Staffordshire, **Teapot,** Lafayette At Franklin's Tomb, Wood	475.00
Staffordshire, **Teapot,** Manilla, Pink, White	265.00
Staffordshire, **Teapot,** Pagoda Shape, Washington, Pink	110.00
Staffordshire, **Teapot,** Stag Chased By Hounds Scene, Dark Blue	275.00
Staffordshire, **Teapot,** Swan	34.00
Staffordshire, **Toby Mug,** Colonel, 3 1/2 In.	20.00
Staffordshire, **Toby Mug,** Nicholas Nickleby, 5 1/2 In.	20.00
Staffordshire, **Toby Mug,** Scotty, Shorter & Son	45.00
Staffordshire, **Toby Snuff Taker,** Free Standing With Removable Hat, 14 In.	135.00
Staffordshire, **Toothpick,** Child With Flower, Rabbit	35.00
Staffordshire, **Tureen,** Sauce, Brown, Covered, Rural Scene, C.1840	40.00
Staffordshire, **Vase,** Crown, Miniature, Cobalt Blue, Floral, 3 In.	54.00
Staffordshire, **Vase,** Double Flaring Handles, Miniature, 2 1/2 In., Pair	32.00
Staffordshire, **Vase,** Dove, Pink Applied Flowers, 5 X 5 In.	18.00
Staffordshire, **Vase,** Figural, Lady With Vase At Side, 13 1/2 In.	85.00
Staffordshire, **Vase,** Spill, Cow And Calf	85.00
Staffordshire, **Vase,** Spill, Robin Hood, Black & Gold Highlights, 14 1/2 In.	95.00
Staffordshire, **Wash Set,** Blue Floral, 2 Piece	150.00
Staffordshire, **Watch Holder,** 11 X 6 In.	75.00
Stained Glass, see Windowpane	

*Stangl pottery was organized in 1929, succeeding the
Fulper Pottery Company. Stangl porcelain birds are popular
collectibles.*

Stangl, **Bird,** Bird Of Paradise, 5 In.	28.00
Stangl, **Bird,** Black Body, Red Breast, Yellow Wings, No.3402s, Signed	27.00
Stangl, **Bird,** Black Head, Blue Wings & Tail, Leaf Base, No.3811	50.00
Stangl, **Bird,** Blue & Yellow, Signed ESF, 5 In.	19.00
Stangl, **Bird,** Blue Jay	34.00
Stangl, **Bird,** Blue Jay, Artist Signed, 5 In.	38.00
Stangl, **Bird,** Blue Jay, 3 In.	18.50
Stangl, **Bird,** Blue Lovebirds On Branch, No.3582, Signed ES, 7 X 7 In.	60.00
Stangl, **Bird,** Bluebird On Leaves & Berries, No.3456, Signed E.S., 4 In.	28.00
Stangl, **Bird,** Bluebird, Baby, No.5594, Signed MD, 3 In.	12.00
Stangl, **Bird,** Bluebird, No.3276, 5 1/2 In.	39.00
Stangl, **Bird,** Bluebird, 5 In.	22.00
Stangl, **Bird,** Brown Wren, No.34018, Signed MWF, 4 1/4 In.	21.00
Stangl, **Bird,** Cardinal On Stump, No.3444, 6 1/2 In.	55.00
Stangl, **Bird,** Cardinal, Gray Back, No.3594, Signed BM	30.00
Stangl, **Bird,** Cardinal, Gray Back, No.3596, Signed EF	30.00
Stangl, **Bird,** Chickadee, No.597, 4 1/2 X 3 1/2 In.	20.00
Stangl, **Bird,** Cockatoo, No.3405, 6 1/2 In.	20.00 To 30.00
Stangl, **Bird,** Cockatoo, No.3405, 7 In.	44.00
Stangl, **Bird,** Cockatoo, No.3405, 77 On Bottom, 6 In.	18.00

Sampler, needlework on linen. Levena Comins. Charlton, Mass., 1813.

Child's brass cannon mounted on a wooden carriage, c. 1835.

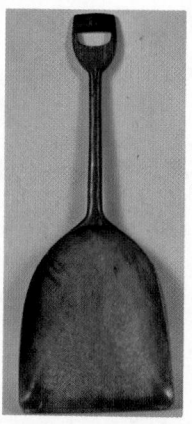

Wooden grain shovel. Single piece of wood. New England, c. 1840.

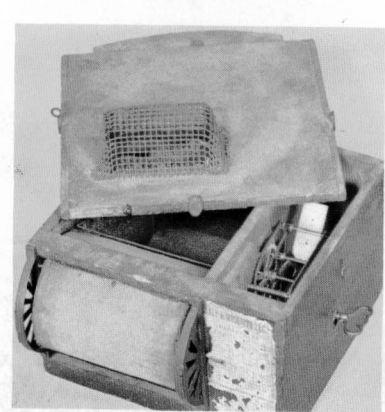

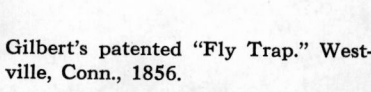

Fireplace bellows. Stenciled decoration. New England, c. 1825.

Gilbert's patented "Fly Trap." Westville, Conn., 1856.

Flax spinning wheel, late eighteenth century.

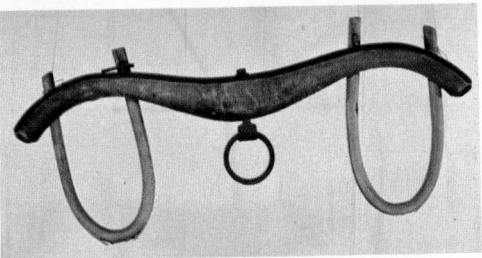

Ox yoke with ring for wagon tongue. New England, c. 1840.

"Tenderness," Ralph Wood. English Staffordshire, c. 1790.

Tall-case clock. Simon Willard. Roxbury, Mass., c. 1810. Miniature grandfather clock. Peter Cushing. Braintree, Mass., c. 1815.

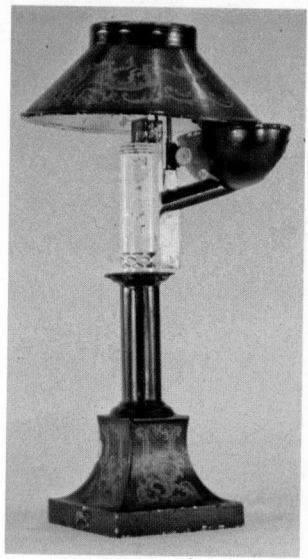

Argand-type lamp. Rumford
patent. English, early nineteenth century.

Girandole clock. "L. Curtis Patent."
Concord, Mass., c. 1815.

Argand-type mantel lamp. Whale oil.
English, c. 1830.

Large apple peeler mounted on a bench
with seat. Late eighteenth century.

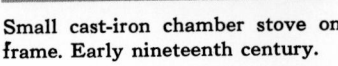

Small cast-iron chamber stove on frame. Early nineteenth century.

Hanging knife box with unusual cut-out decoration. Eighteenth century.

Sheet music cover. "Pulaski Quick Step" by James Hooton. Boston, 1836.

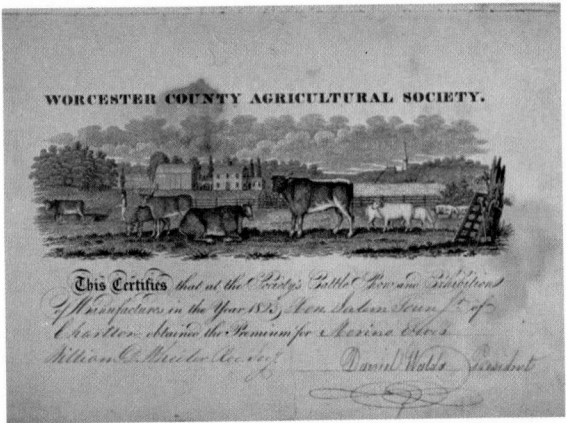

Award to Salem Towne, Jr., for his Merino ewes from the Worcester County Agricultural Society, 1825.

Militia snare drum. Made by Abner Stevens. Pittsfield, Mass., c. 1815.

Unusual belt or tape loom mounted on stand. New England, c. 1760.

"The Double Game of Modern Dominoes." Published by Richard H. Pease. Albany, N.Y., c. 1841–1846.

Sticking tommy wrought-iron candle holder. Multiposition arrangement, c. 1800.

Wooden burl sugar bowl, late eighteenth century.

Hitchcock-type stenciled decorated chairs, c.
1825.

Transitional chair. Chip-
pendale back and William
and Mary base, c. 1780.

Corner chair, belonged to Governor
Roger Wolcott, Conn., c. 1770.

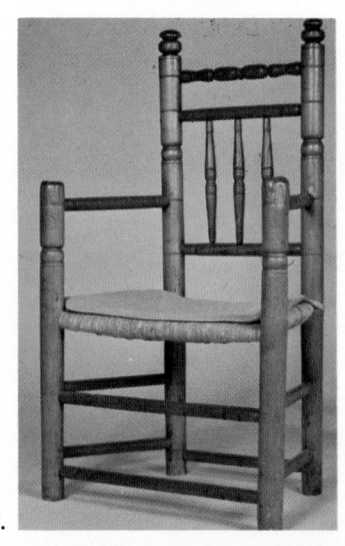

Carver-type chair, c. 1650.

Loop-back Windsor chair. Label of Charles Cotton, chairmaker, c. 1800.

Miniature child's desk, c. 1740–1760.

Stenciled decorated footstool, c. 1830.

Maple Queen Anne-style tea table, c. 1760.

Bedside stand, country Chippendale style, c. 1800.

Sheraton-style card table. N.H., c. 1790.

Bedside stand, painted curly maple. Dated 1818. Camden, Me.

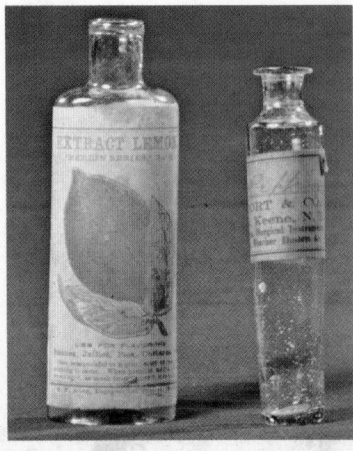

Extract bottle, clear free-blown glass. Early nineteenth century. Label for Dr. Hartshorn, Berlin, Mass. Extract lemon. Medicine vial, free-blown aqua-colored glass. New England, early nineteenth century Labeled "Oil Peppermint," Keene, N.H.

Stangl, Bird, Cockatoo, No.3580, Cream, Yellow Crest, Impressed Mark, 9 In. 75.00
Stangl, Bird, Cockatoo, Pink, Signed & Numbered, 5 In. 40.00
Stangl, Bird, Double Bluebird, 8 In. 65.00
Stangl, Bird, Double Cockatoo, No.3405d, 9 1/2 In. 65.00
Stangl, Bird, Double Hummingbirds, Flowers, 9 1/2 X 9 In. 135.00
Stangl, Bird, Double Parrots, Blue, 10 1/4 In. 58.00
Stangl, Bird, Finch, Yellow & Black, 4 X 11 In. 75.00
Stangl, Bird, Flying Duck, 9 In. 95.00
Stangl, Bird, Flying Goose, No.3432, 10 In. 65.00
Stangl, Bird, Hen, Brown & Yellow, No.3446 .... 45.00
Stangl, Bird, Hummingbird, Branch, Taking Nectar From Flower, No.3827 .... 50.00
Stangl, Bird, Hummingbird, No.3629, Raised Wings, Signed, 6 1/2 X 6 In. 45.00
Stangl, Bird, Hummingbird, No.3634, Signed MLF, 3 3/4 In. 24.00
Stangl, Bird, Hummingbird, Red Flower, Green Foliage, Marked, 9 X 10 In. 80.00
Stangl, Bird, Indigo Bunting, No.3589 .... 30.00
Stangl, Bird, Kentucky Warbler, No.3598, 6 In. 10.00
Stangl, Bird, Kingfisher, Black, Oval, Signed YRF, 4 1/2 In. 25.00
Stangl, Bird, Lovebird, No.3400, 4 1/2 In. 16.50
Stangl, Bird, Nuthatch, No.3593, 2 1/2 In. 10.00
Stangl, Bird, Oriole, No.3402, 3 1/4 In. .... 10.00 To 24.00
Stangl, Bird, Parakeet, No.3596, 5 In. 30.00
Stangl, Bird, Parrot, No.3589, 5 1/2 In. 30.00
Stangl, Bird, Prothonotary Warbler, No.3447, 5 In. 38.00
Stangl, Bird, Ringneck Peasant, WK, 17 In. 50.00
Stangl, Bird, Rooster & Hen, California Blues, Artist Signed, 9 In., Pair 75.00
Stangl, Bird, Titmouse, No.3592, 2 1/2 In. 10.00
Stangl, Bird, Warbler, No.3583, Artist Initialed 29.00
Stangl, Bird, Wilson Warbler, No.3597, 3 In. .... 24.00 To 27.50
Stangl, Bird, Wren, No.3401, 3 1/2 In. 10.00
Stangl, Bird, Wren, Signed DM, 5 In. 17.50
Stangl, Blue Jay, No.3456, 5 In. 30.00
Stangl, Bluebird, No.3456, Raspberries, Leaves, Black Oval, Signed ES, 4 In. 25.00
Stangl, Bowl, Six Petaled Shaped, 1 3/4 In. 15.00
Stangl, Box, Cigarette, Turquoise Bottom, White Floral Lid 10.00
Stangl, Cruet, Tiger Lily 10.00
Stangl, Pitcher, Green Glaze, 6 In. 12.00
Stangl, Plate, Fishes, Mustard Color, Signed M.B. 8.00
Stangl, Vase, Blue, No.1878-M 10.00
Stangl, Vase, Urn Shape, Handle, Black Gold Stamped On Bottom, 11 In. 50.00
Stangl, Warmer, Candle, Gray & Green 8.00

Star Holly is a milk glass type of glass made by the Imperial Glass
Company of Bellaire, Ohio, in 1957. The pieces were made to look like
Wedgwood jasperware. White holly leaves appear against colored borders of
blue, green, or rust. It is marked on the bottom of every piece.
Star Holly, Plate, Blue, 10 In. 65.00
Star Holly, Sherbet, Green 95.00

Steins have been used for over 500 years. They have been made of ivory,
porcelain, stoneware, faience, silver, pewter, wood, or glass in sizes up to nine
gallons. Although some were made by Meissen, Capo-Di-Monte, and other
famous factories, most were made in Germany. The words Geschutz or
Musterschutz on a stein are the German for patented or registered design,
not company names.
Stein, A.T.1373, Beige, Green Scenes, Homes & Family, 11 1/2 In. 45.00
Stein, Bismarck, Musterschutz, Porcelain, Radish Top, 1 1/2 Liter 375.00
Stein, Bohemian Glass, Ruby Cut To Clear, 15 Square Panels, Pewter Lid, 1831 .... 70.00
Stein, Brass Gnome Carrying Beer Barrel, Paneled, Blown, Etched 65.00
Stein, Butcher, Bayreuth Crown & Shield, 1/2 Liter 155.00
Stein, Cameo Court Scene, Pewter Lid, Impressed Star & RM, 20 1/2 Liter 298.00
Stein, Character, Figures, Elk Finial, German Writing, T.X.Mark, 14 In. 225.00
Stein, Character, Red Devil With Anchor Mark 700.00
Stein, Character, Skull On Book, Beige Bisque, Lid Inset, Pewter Thumbrest 345.00

Stein, Ivory, Carved, Battle Scene, 19th Century, 13 3/4 In.

Stein, Ivory, Carved, French, 19th Century, 25 In.

Stein, Ivory, Carved, French, Late 19th Century, 24 3/4 In.

Stein, Cherub Scene, German, Black Glaze, White, Pewter Lid, 6 In.	95.00
Stein, Crystal, Raised Flowers & Lions' Heads On Lid	40.00
Stein, Cut Glass, Nailhead, English Hobnail, Rayed Base, Pewter Lid, 10 In.	400.00
Stein, Cut Glass, Panel Cut Body, Pewter Lid, Bowling Pins, 1919, 5 1/4 In.	40.00
Stein, Cut Glass, Pewter Lid, Bowling Pins, 1919, 5 1/4 In.	40.00
Stein, Drinking Scene In Relief, Made In Germany, 11 1/2 In.	59.00
Stein, Ecru, Child Holding Bible, Pewter Monk Finial, 4 Liter, Marked V	388.00
Stein, Figures In 3 Panels, Branch Double Handle, German, 8 Liter	145.00
Stein, German Officer's Beaker, Imperial Eagle, 1/4 Liter	85.00
Stein, German, Der Sontagsjager, Raised Scene, Impressed Cross, 16 1/4 In.	95.00
Stein, German, Europa, 1/2 Liter	26.00
Stein, German, Hunting Scene, Finialed Pewter Lid, Numbered, 9 1/2 In.	75.00
Stein, Germany, Hussar Regiment, 1894, Pewter Lid, Crest, 1/2 Liter	215.00
Stein, Germany, Presentation, 1895, Pewter Lid, 1/2 Liter	185.00
Stein, Glass With Pewter Thumbrest & Cover, Painted Glass Insert, 7 1/4 In.	68.00
Stein, Glass, Ceramic Inlay Lid, Floral Design	48.00
Stein, Glass, Cut X And Circle Design, Pedestal Base, Steeple Lid	45.00
Stein, Glass, Early, 1/2 Liter, Flat Pewter Lid, Impressed Circles	35.00
Stein, Gray & Blue, Pewter Lid, German, 3 In.	25.00
Stein, Hunter, Dog, Forest, Pewter Lid, Gesetzlich Gesehutzt, No.7693, 10 In.	90.00
Stein, Ivory, Carved, Battle Scene, 19th Century, 13 3/4 In. ....Illus	2000.00
Stein, Ivory, Carved, French, 19th Century, 25 In. ....Illus	5250.00
Stein, Ivory, Carved, French, Late 19th Century, 24 3/4 In. ....Illus	7000.00
Stein, Lithophane Base, Cooper	125.00
Stein, Lithophane Base, Domestic Scene, Raised City Scene On Body, Liter	135.00
Stein, Lithophane Base, League Of Wheelers, 1/2 Liter	265.00
Stein, Lithophane Base, Monk, 7 In.	250.00
Stein, Lithophane Base, Mountain Climber, Alpine Scene On Body, 3/10 Liter	115.00
Stein, Lithophane Base, Munich Maid, Hofbrau Haus, 1/2 Liter	175.00
Stein, Lithophane Base, Nun, 7 In.	250.00
Stein, Lithophane Base, Peasants Kissing, Aum Andenken, Pewter Lid, 8 1/2 In.	145.00
Stein, Locomotive Engineer, Hand-Painted, German, 9 1/2 In.	200.00
Stein, Mettlach, see Mettlach, Stein	
Stein, Monk, Pewter Collar & Thumb Lift, Black Robe, 6 1/2 In.	125.00
Stein, Monk, Pot Hole Under Chin, J.Reinemann, Munchen, 4 1/2 In.	95.00
Stein, Munich Maid Decoration, 1/4 Liter	30.00
Stein, Munich Maid, German, Cream Glaze, Pewter Lid, Impressed DW, 6 In.	85.00
Stein, Musterschutz, Berlin Bear, 1/2 Liter	800.00

Stein, Musterschutz, Bismark Civilian, 1/2 Liter	500.00 To 650.00
Stein, Musterschutz, Caroline Bismark, 1/2 Liter	550.00
Stein, Musterschutz, Cat With Hangover, 1/2 Liter	550.00
Stein, Musterschutz, Drunken Monkey, 1/2 Liter	450.00
Stein, Musterschutz, Father John, 1 Liter	1500.00
Stein, Musterschutz, Hops Lady, 1/2 Liter	650.00
Stein, Musterschutz, Indian Chief, 1/2 Liter	850.00
Stein, Musterschutz, Indian, 1/4 Liter	450.00
Stein, Musterschutz, Jolly Boy	650.00
Stein, Musterschutz, Judge, 1/2 Liter	650.00
Stein, Musterschutz, L.A.W., League Of American Wheelers, Bicycle Lithophane	350.00
Stein, Musterschutz, Miniature, Cameo Of Officer & Lady, 1 1/2 In.	20.00
Stein, Musterschutz, Pig, 1/2 Liter	375.00
Stein, Musterschutz, Pixie	850.00
Stein, Musterschutz, Satan, 1/2 Liter	800.00
Stein, Musterschutz, Satan, 1/4 Liter	400.00
Stein, Musterschutz, Sea Captain, 1/2 Liter	850.00
Stein, Musterschutz, Singing Pig	350.00
Stein, Musterschutz, Target Lady, 1/2 Liter	650.00
Stein, Musterschutz, Turkish Man, 1/2 Liter	800.00
Stein, Musterschutz, Umbrella, 1/2 Liter	800.00
Stein, Musterschutz, Van Maltke, 1/2 Liter	850.00
Stein, Pewter Base, Glass Thumbprint, Decorated Top With Cherub, 1 Liter	68.00
Stein, Pressed Glass, Brauerei Sandler Kulmback, Keeper Of Cellar On Lid	40.00
Stein, Pressed Glass, 1901 On Lid, Eagle Tilt Lift	45.00
Stein, Puss In Boots, Germany	35.00
Stein, Red-Haired Girl In Cover, German War, 1911-13	175.00
Stein, Regimental, 1st Fuss Art.Regt.Van Bathmer, 1901., Pewter Lid	215.00
Stein, Satan Character, Bisque, 1/4 Liter	495.00
Stein, Schlitz Beer, Ceramic	13.30
Stein, Soldier & Horse Finial, 5 Panel Scenes, Esk, 1897, Germany, 1/2 Liter	275.00
Stein, Stoneware, Battling Warriors In Relief, Pewter Steeple Lid, 1 Liter	80.00
Stein, Stoneware, Bowlers In Relief In White On Blue, Pewter Lid, 1/2 Liter	38.00
Stein, Stoneware, Cobalt & Gray, Pewter Lid, German Phrase, 1/2 Liter	65.00
Stein, Thirsty Knight, Marked 954, Germany, JWR, 1/2 Liter	450.00
Stein, Wedding Party, Cupids Playing Music, 1 Liter	150.00

*Stereo cards that were made for stereopticon viewers became popular after
1840. Two almost identical pictures were mounted on a stiff cardboard backing
so that, when viewed through a stereoscope, a three-dimensional picture could be
seen.*

Stereo, Card, Indians, 11	38.00
Stereo, Card, Japan, 100	25.00
Stereo, Card, San Francisco Earthquake, 1906, 23	50.00
Stereo, Card, Sears & Roebuck, 47	50.00
Stereo, Card, Sears Roebuck, 50	35.00
Stereo, Card, Siege Of Port Arthur, 1904, 100	40.00
Stereo, Card, Underwood, 1901	20.00
Stereo, Card, Views Of France, 87	22.00
Stereo, Card, World War I, Keystone, 97	35.00
Stereo, Card, WWII Scenes, 39	45.00
Stereo, Viewer, Sculptoscope, 2 Cent Operated, Colorful Views	345.00

*Stereoscopes, or stereopticons, were used for viewing the stereo cards. The
hand viewer was invented by Oliver Wendell Holmes, although more
complicated table models were used before his was placed in
production in 1859.*

Stereoscope, Metal Hood, 55 Cards	45.00
Stereoscope, Table Model, Walnut	750.00
Stereoscope, Walnut With Aluminum Eye Shield, 20 Views	25.00
Stereoscope, 70 View Cards	45.00
Sterling Silver, see Silver, Sterling	
Sterling Silver, Purse, Victorian, Leather Lined, 4 1/2 X 2 1/2 In.	45.00

Steuben glass was made at the Steuben Glass Works of Corning, New York. The factory, founded by Frederick Carder and T.C.Hawkes, Sr., was purchased by the Corning Glass Company. They continued to make glass called Steuben. Many types of art glass were made at Steuben. The firm is still producing glass of exceptional quality.

Steuben, see also Aurene

Steuben, **Ashtray**, Clear, Script Signature, 5 3/4 In.	50.00
Steuben, **Atomizer**, Aqua Aurene, Threaded Brass Fitting, 8 In.	80.00
Steuben, **Atomizer**, Blue Aurene, Gold Metal Top	215.00
Steuben, **Atomizer**, DeVilbiss, Honey Iridescent, Blue & Lavender Highlights	135.00
Steuben, **Atomizer**, DeVilbiss, Mesh Bulb, Black & Gold Rings, Clear Crystal	85.00
Steuben, **Atomizer**, Gold Aurene, Net Bag With Gold Metal Top	155.00
Steuben, **Basket**, Dark Flemish Blue, Buttoned Handles, 8 1/2 X 6 1/2 In.	155.00
Steuben, **Basket**, Verre De Soie, Swirled, Ribbed, Ruffled, Thorn Handle, 10 In.	155.00
Steuben, **Bell**, Signed Diamond Point On Clapper, 4 1/2 X 2 3/4 In.	125.00
Steuben, **Bookend**, Clear, Unicorns, Art Deco, Signed, Pair	275.00
Steuben, **Bottle**, Perfume, Aurene, Iridescent, 3 1/2 In.	312.00
Steuben, **Bottle**, Perfume, Black & Gold Rings, Stopper, 6 1/2 In.	60.00
Steuben, **Bottle**, Perfume, Black Jade	225.00
Steuben, **Bottle**, Perfume, Clear, Green Machine Threading, Floral, 4 1/2 In.	75.00
Steuben, **Bottle**, Perfume, DeVilbiss, Black & Gold Rings, Clear Crystal	75.00
Steuben, **Bottle**, Perfume, Green Jade, Alabaster, Flower Stopper, 23 In., Pair	750.00
Steuben, **Bottle**, Perfume, Verre De Soie, Blue Flame Stopper, 4 1/2 In.	150.00
Steuben, **Bottle**, Perfume, Verre De Soie, Blue Stopper, 6 In.	125.00
Steuben, **Bowl & Underplate**, Finger, Aurene, Gold, Calcite, 6 In.	187.00
Steuben, **Bowl & Underplate**, Finger, Selenium Red	175.00
Steuben, **Bowl**, Amethyst, Fleur-De-Lis, 11 3/4 In.	125.00
Steuben, **Bowl**, Amethyst, Fleur-Di-Lis Mark, 11 1/2 In.	125.00
Steuben, **Bowl**, Aurene And Calacite, Iridescent, Turned-Down Rim, 14 In.	300.00
Steuben, **Bowl**, Blue Aurene Lining, Calcite, 3 1/4 X 5 3/4 In.	300.00
Steuben, **Bowl**, Blue Aurene, Iridescent, Urn Shape, 6 1/2 In.	1350.00
Steuben, **Bowl**, Blue Aurene, Numbered 2852, Signed, 9 In.	345.00
Steuben, **Bowl**, Blue To Clear, Flared, Cut Base, Signed, 13 1/4 In.	87.00
Steuben, **Bowl**, Blue, Aurene, Signed, 2 In.	310.00
Steuben, **Bowl**, Bristol Yellow, Turned-Down Top, Ribbed Body, 13 1/2 In.	95.00
Steuben, **Bowl**, Butterfly, Iridescent Lining, Blue, Calcite, 3 X 5 3/4 In.	300.00
Steuben, **Bowl**, Calcite, Blue, 8 X 2 1/2 In.	395.00
Steuben, **Bowl**, Calcite, Gold Iridescent, Amethyst, 10 X 2 1/2 In.	225.00
Steuben, **Bowl**, Centerpiece, Blue Green, Ribbed, 4 X 10 1/4 In.	65.00
Steuben, **Bowl**, Centerpiece, Dark Amethyst, Pedestal Base, Turned Rim, 13 In.	65.00
Steuben, **Bowl**, Centerpiece, Ribbed, Dark Amethyst, Scalloped Rim, 13 In.	75.00
Steuben, **Bowl**, Centerpiece, Rosaline, 12 1/4 X 5 In.	275.00
Steuben, **Bowl**, Centerpiece, Topaz, Celeste Blue Edge, Signed, 10 1/4 In.	75.00
Steuben, **Bowl**, Centerpiece, Topaz, Celeste Blue Rim & Foot, 9 3/4 X 4 1/2 In.	75.00
Steuben, **Bowl**, Cobalt Blue, Flaring Mouth, Polished Pontil, 12 X 3 In.	190.00
Steuben, **Bowl**, Cobalt, Rolled-Down Edge, Signed & Numbered, 3 X 12 In.	120.00
Steuben, **Bowl**, Controlled Bubbles, Rolled Rim, Green, Signed, 5 X 7 In.	160.00
Steuben, **Bowl**, Crystal, Paneled, Emerald Green Top, Amber Base, Oblong, Signed	275.00
Steuben, **Bowl**, Dark Amethyst, Footed, 11 1/2 X 3 1/2 In.	70.00
Steuben, **Bowl**, Dark Amethyst, Turned Down Rim, 13 X 1 3/4 In.	55.00
Steuben, **Bowl**, Dark Green, Shape No.1984, 4 3/4 X 2 5/8 In.	25.00
Steuben, **Bowl**, Deep Blue To Deep Pink, Calcite Underside, 10 X 3 In.	300.00
Steuben, **Bowl**, Emerald Green Shaded To Clear, 7 3/4 In.	135.00
Steuben, **Bowl**, Emerald Green, Diagonal Swirl, Flare Top, 5 1/2 In.	95.00
Steuben, **Bowl**, Etched Amber Trim, White, 11 1/2 X 4 1/4 In.	110.00
Steuben, **Bowl**, Finger And Underplate	50.00
Steuben, **Bowl**, Finger, Aurene, Gold	225.00
Steuben, **Bowl**, Finger, Gold Aurene On Calcite, 2 In.	65.00
Steuben, **Bowl**, Finger, Pink Opalescent, Green Base, Oriental Poppy, Signed	350.00
Steuben, **Bowl**, Flint, White, 4 1/2 X 15 In.	225.00
Steuben, **Bowl**, Flower, Blue Aurene, 3 Legged, No.2586, Round, 2 1/2 In.	485.00
Steuben, **Bowl**, Fluted, Oval, Signed In Script, 5 X 9 X 5 1/2 In.	150.00
Steuben, **Bowl**, Fluted, Script Signature, 5 X 9 X 5 1/2 In.	150.00
Steuben, **Bowl**, Gold Aurene On Calcite, Signed, 7 X 2 In.	195.00

Steuben, Bowl, Gold Aurene, Calcite, 10 In.	250.00
Steuben, Bowl, Green Jade, Signed, 8 X 4 In.	85.00
Steuben, Bowl, Green, Signed, 10 X 3 1/2 In.	35.00
Steuben, Bowl, Iridescent Gold, Amethyst Inside, White Calcite On Obverse	350.00
Steuben, Bowl, Ivorene, Bulbous, 10 X 7 1/2 In.	390.00
Steuben, Bowl, Ivorene, Pearly Highlights, 2 1/4 X 5 1/2 In.	55.00
Steuben, Bowl, Jade Green, Raised Base, Signed, 4 X 11 1/2 In.	185.00
Steuben, Bowl, No.3200, Topaz, Blue Rim, Signed, 8 1/4 X 3 In.	55.00
Steuben, Bowl, Pansy, Deep Rose, Rosaline, Turned Over Rim, Alabaster Base	90.00
Steuben, Bowl, Pedestal, 7 1/2 In.	80.00
Steuben, Bowl, Pink Opalescent Stripes, Iridescent, Oriental Poppy, 11 In.	750.00
Steuben, Bowl, Ribbed, Marina Blue, No.3200, Signed, 10 1/4 X 4 In.	55.00
Steuben, Bowl, Rosaline With Alabaster Finial, Unsigned	85.00
Steuben, Bowl, Scalloped Edge, Pomona Green Wafer On Foot, 2 3/4 X 5 In.	35.00
Steuben, Bowl, Swirl, Amber, 11 In.	90.00
Steuben, Bowl, Topaz With Flemish Blue Rim, Signed, 8 In.	55.00
Steuben, Bowl, White Calcite, Everted Rim, Honey Amber, 10 1/2 X 2 1/2 In.	350.00
Steuben, Box, Puff, Cranberry, Diagonal Swirl, Cerise Ruby, 6 1/2 In.	150.00
Steuben, Bucket, Ice, French Blue Bands At Top, Amber, Marked, 6 1/2 In.	155.00
Steuben, Bucket, Ice, Light Pink Amber, 2 Applied French Blue Bands At Top	155.00
Steuben, Cake Stand, Pedestal, Celeste Blue, Flare Top, 2 1/4 X 10 In.	87.00
Steuben, Candleholder, Futuristic, Topaz, 6 1/2 In.	45.00
Steuben, Candlestick, Black, 10 In., Pair	295.00
Steuben, Candlestick, Cintra Threading, Prunts, Lavender, 12 In., Pair	225.00
Steuben, Candlestick, Clear Crystal, Moonlight Tone, Wheel Stem, 3 1/2 In.	23.00
Steuben, Candlestick, Clear, Script Signature, 5 In., Pair	125.00
Steuben, Candlestick, Dark Amethyst, Topaz Stem, 10 In.	135.00
Steuben, Candlestick, Emerald Green, Signed, 12 In., Pair	120.00
Steuben, Candlestick, Jade Green Over Alabaster, Greek Figures, 15 In., Pair	600.00
Steuben, Candlestick, Signed In Script, 5 In., Pair	125.00
Steuben, Candlestick, Selenium Red, F.Carder, Steuben, 10 In., Pair	395.00
Steuben, Candlestick, Topaz, Rolled Under Edge, Numbered, 10 In., Pair	140.00
Steuben, Candlestick, Yellow-Green, Signed, 8 1/4 In., Pair	95.00
Steuben, Centerpiece, Amethyst, Bowl Shape, No.6001, 11 1/2 X 3 1/2 In.	55.00
Steuben, Centerpiece, Aurene, Rounded, Flated Top, Calcite & Gold, 12 In.	275.00
Steuben, Centerpiece, Double Line Pillars, Pedestal Base, 6 1/2 X 7 1/2 In.	225.00
Steuben, Champagne, Topaz Twisted Stem, Celeste Blue Bowl, 4 1/2 In.	55.00
Steuben, Compote, Blue Calcite, Open, 6 In.	550.00
Steuben, Compote, Calcite, Satin Iridescence, Top Cups In, 8 1/4 In.	475.00
Steuben, Compote, Cintra, Orange, Blue Edge, Stem, Base, Orange Prunts, 7 In.	950.00
Steuben, Compote, Clear, Diamond-Quilted, Twisted Stem, Red Threading, 7 In.	75.00
Steuben, Compote, Green Crystal, Topaz Swirled Stem, 10 In.	125.00
Steuben, Compote, Oriental Jade, Twisted Opalescent Stem, 7 X 7 In.	850.00
Steuben, Compote, Rosaline, Alabaster Pedestal, 3 1/4 X 6 In.	85.00
Steuben, Compote, Topaz, 5 X 2 1/2 In.	27.50
Steuben, Compote, White Jade, Black Edging, Footed Circular Base, 7 3/4 In.	175.00
Steuben, Console Set, Amethyst & Emerald Green, F.Carder, Venetian, 5 Piece	995.00
Steuben, Console Set, Candleholders, 5 X 4 In., Bowl, 12 X 4 1/2 In.	350.00
Steuben, Console Set, Selenium Red, Fruit Pattern, Carders, 3 Piece	950.00
Steuben, Console Set, Threaded, Bubbly, Avocado Green, 3 Piece	185.00
Steuben, Console Set, Topaz, 3 Piece	230.00
Steuben, Console Set, Venetian Style, Celeste Blue, Wafer Joined, Ribbed	400.00
Steuben, Cornucopia, Amber, Green Pedestal, Signed, 8 In.	95.00
Steuben, Cornucopia, Crystal, Script Signed, 5 1/2 In.	35.00
Steuben, Cup & Saucer, Alabaster Handle, Rosaline	125.00
Steuben, Cup & Saucer, Blue Jade, Alabaster Handle	175.00
Steuben, Cup & Saucer, Green Jade, Alabaster Ring Handle	115.00
Steuben, Cup & Saucer, Rosaline, Alabaster Handle	145.00
Steuben, Cuspidor, Calcite & Gold Aurene, 7 1/4 X 3 1/4 In.	130.00
Steuben, Darner, Calcite	185.00
Steuben, Decanter, Baluster Shape, Signed, 11 In., Pair	175.00
Steuben, Decanter, Black Crystal, Ribbed, Syrian Shape, 13 In., Pair	375.00
Steuben, Dessert, Threaded Circle, Footed, Black, Signed	30.00
Steuben, Dish, Aurene, Ruffled, Diagonal Swirl, Ribbing, Signed, 7 1/2 In.	125.00

Steuben, Dish, Calcite, Amber Iridescent Crackle Glass Rim, 6 1/4 In.	200.00
Steuben, Dish, Calcite, Amber Iridescent Interior, 5 3/4 In.	175.00
Steuben, Dish, Calcite, Amber Iridescent, Shallow Sloping, 6 1/4 In.	115.00
Steuben, Dish, Nut, Aurene, Ruffled Lip, Signed	185.00
Steuben, Dish, Nut, Ruffled Lip, Aurene, Haviland & Co., Paper Label	185.00
Steuben, Ewer, Rosalene, Strawberries & Cream, Alabaster Handle, 7 1/4 In.	500.00
Steuben, Fairy Lamp, Frosted Yellow, Verre Moire, 4 3/4 In.	165.00
Steuben, Figurine, Fish, C.1930, Pair	750.00
Steuben, Figurine, Grotesque, Wisteria Color, Shape No.7307, 6 In.	175.00
Steuben, Figurine, Pheasant, Signed, 11 In.	650.00
Steuben, Figurine, Quan Yen In Matching Flower Block, Lavender	300.00
Steuben, Figurines, Pheasant, Cut Glass, 11 In., Pair	1500.00
Steuben, Flower Pot, Jade Green, No.1669	75.00
Steuben, Glass, Shot, Blue Aurene, No.2759, Signed, 6 In.	145.00
Steuben, Glass, Shot, Pinched Gold Aurene, No.2739, Signed	145.00
Steuben, Goblet, Controlled Bubbles, Ribbed Sides, Green, Signed, 6 In.	75.00
Steuben, Goblet, Deep Red To Clear Cut, Flower Form, 10 In.	250.00
Steuben, Goblet, Engraved, Amber, Signed, 8 In.	55.00
Steuben, Goblet, Fleur-De-Lis, Green, Square Wafer Cut Foot, Intaglio Cut	256.00
Steuben, Goblet, French Blue, Reeded Bowls, Optic Twist Stem, Signed	95.00
Steuben, Goblet, Opal Stem & Foot, Oriental Poppy, 8 1/4 X 3 3/4 In.	225.00
Steuben, Goblet, Oriental Poppy, Opalescent Stem & Foot, Signed, 8 1/4 In.	225.00
Steuben, Goblet, Rosaline, Opalescent, Twisted White Stem	325.00
Steuben, Goblet, Rosaline, Pink Intaglio Cut To White, Grapes, 8 1/2 In.	305.00
Steuben, Goblet, Selenium Red, Double Ball Stem, Pedestal Base, 6 3/4 In.	57.00
Steuben, Goblet, Selenium Red, Pedestal, Signed, 4 3/8 In.	45.00
Steuben, Goblet, Trapped Bubbles, Green Threading, No.6359	30.00
Steuben, Goblet, Water, Rosaline, Alabaster Braided Stem	135.00
Steuben, Goblet, Water, Twisted Lavender Cintra Stem, Opalescent Top	135.00
Steuben, Goblet, Wheat Pattern, No.6220, Signed	100.00
Steuben, Jar, Bathroom, Covered, Burnt Amber, Black Threading, 4 Sided	90.00
Steuben, Jar, Candy, Covered, Vaseline Color, Ball Knob, Pomona, 9 1/2 In.	135.00
Steuben, Ladle, Red & Silver Glass, Whimsey	295.00
Steuben, Lamp Base, Acid Cut Back, Floral, Yellow Jade, Silver Mounts, 20 In.	375.00
Steuben, Lamp, Amber Iridescent Shade, Optic Rib, Bronze Stand, O & S N.Y.	175.00
Steuben, Lamp, Amber Iridescent Shade, Optic Rib, Bronze Stand, 6 1/4 In.	225.00
Steuben, Lamp, Aurene, Gold Iridescence, Stretch Edge	495.00
Steuben, Lamp, Gold Ruby Cased Over Yellow, Gold Plated Fixture	2000.00
Steuben, Lamp, Green Cluthra, Chang Decoration, Acid Cut Back	800.00
Steuben, Lamp, Green Jade, Alabaster Base, 4 Hanging Prisms On Shade, 23 In.	425.00
Steuben, Lamp, Peacock Feather Design, Signed Quezal	900.00
Steuben, Mug, Beer, Engraved & Etched, Thumb Rest, Set Of 4	160.00
Steuben, Mug, Green Jade, Applied Black Glass Handle, Fleur-De-Lis Signed	85.00
Steuben, Nappy, Topaz, Applied Handle, Celeste Blue Feet, 5 In.	75.00
Steuben, Paperweight, Apple, Clear, Signed	70.00
Steuben, Paperweight, Teardrop, Signed	225.00
Steuben, Parfait, Amber, Engraved, Signed, 6 In.	85.00
Steuben, Parfait, Green Jade & Alabaster, 4 1/2 In.	45.00
Steuben, Pitcher, Lemonade, Ribbed, Green Jade, Alabaster Handle	450.00
Steuben, Pitcher, Water, Jade With Alabaster Handle, Swirl Pattern, 9 1/4 In.	235.00
Steuben, Plate, Amethyst, Etched Border, Signed Fleur-De-Lis, 8 1/2 In.	250.00
Steuben, Plate, Cake, Black With Applied White Rim, 20 In.	225.00
Steuben, Plate, Clear-Quilted, Black Threading, Signed, 8 1/2 In.	20.00
Steuben, Plate, Intaglio, Audubon Series	550.00
Steuben, Plate, Jade Green, Depressed Center, 8 1/2 In.	40.00
Steuben, Plate, Jade To Alabaster, York Pattern, Fleur-Di-Lis, Signed, 6 In.	75.00
Steuben, Plate, Monogram, Jade Green, 8 In.	30.00
Steuben, Plate, No.5, Green, 8 1/2 In., Set Of Four	48.00
Steuben, Plate, Pomona Green, 8 1/2 In.	25.00
Steuben, Plate, Ribbed Amethyst, Signed F.Carder, Steuben, 6 In.	95.00
Steuben, Plate, Rosaline, 8 1/2 In.	30.00
Steuben, Plate, Topaz, Etched Border, 8 1/2 In.	67.00
Steuben, Plate, Verre De Soie, Stretched Edge, 9 1/2 In.	28.00
Steuben, Plate, Verre De Soie, 27 1/2 In.	27.00

Steuben, Vase, Acid Cutback, C.1920, 12 In.

Steuben, Rose Bowl, Calcite & Gold Aurene, 6 1/4 In.	115.00
Steuben, Rose Bowl, Etched Lilies & Leaves, Stained Green, 6 In.	115.00
Steuben, Salt & Pepper, Sterling Lid, Open Salt	75.00
Steuben, Salt, Blue Aurene, Signed	375.00
Steuben, Salt, Gold Aurene On Calcite, Signed	275.00
Steuben, Salt, Gold Aurene, Pedestal	275.00
Steuben, Salt, Light Blue Jade, Alabaster Foot	345.00
Steuben, Sconce, Gold Aurene Shade, Brackets, Signed, Pair	285.00
Steuben, Shade, Amber, Pink & Lilac High-Lights, Ribbed, Scalloped	110.00
Steuben, Shade, Aurene, Gold Applied Rickrack Band	175.00
Steuben, Shade, Aurene, Green, Platinum Feather, Signed	270.00
Steuben, Shade, Drag Loop Dome, Green, Gold Lined, 6 In.	230.00
Steuben, Shade, Gold Aurene, Signed, 5 1/2 X 7 In.	155.00
Steuben, Shade, Gold Aurene, Signed, 6 In.	250.00
Steuben, Shade, Gold Drape & Hooked Border, Signed	150.00
Steuben, Shade, Gold Fishnet On Calcite, Signed, Set Of 3	450.00
Steuben, Shade, Gold Leaf & Vine	95.00
Steuben, Shade, Gold Leaf & Vine On Calcite, Calcite Lined, Ruffled, Set Of 3	450.00
Steuben, Shade, Gold, Alternating Wide & Narrow Ribs, Scalloped, 5 In.	75.00
Steuben, Shade, Green Feather, Gold Edge On Opalescent, Scalloped Edge	90.00
Steuben, Shade, King Tut, Green On Opalescent, Calcite Lining, 4 5/8 In.	160.00
Steuben, Shade, King Tut, Green On Opalescent, Fleur-De-Lis Mark, 4 5/8 In.	160.00
Steuben, Shade, Loop Dome On Calcite, Signed	320.00
Steuben, Shade, Medallions, Swags, Ribbons, Acid Etch, Fishbowl, Calcite, 16 In.	95.00
Steuben, Shade, Pearly Iridescence, Gold Feathering, 5 3/4 In.	82.50
Steuben, Shade, Yellow Feathering On White Ivorene, Signed	95.00
Steuben, Shades, Blue Feather On Calcite, Signed Set Of 4, 6 In.	950.00
Steuben, Sherbet & Plate, Gold Calcite	130.00 To 185.00
Steuben, Sherbet & Underplate, Calcite	150.00
Steuben, Sherbet & Underplate, Gold Aurene, Calcite, Gold Paper Label	215.00
Steuben, Sherbet, Calcite, Amber Interior, Footed, 3 3/4 In.	125.00
Steuben, Sherbet, Cerise Reeding, Paneled, Footed, 4 X 3 1/2 In.	35.00
Steuben, Sherbet, Clear, Cerise Threading Around Bowl, Signed, 4 X 3 1/2 In.	40.00
Steuben, Sherbet, Rosaline, Matching Underplate, 5 In.	105.00
Steuben, Stein, Engraved, Etched, Thumb Rest, Signed, Set Of 4	175.00
Steuben, Tray, 8 Sided, Signed In Diamond Point, 11 3/4 In.	115.00
Steuben, Tumbler, Amethyst, Ribbed, Flared Top, 6 1/2 In.	28.00
Steuben, Tumbler, Calcite, Iridescent, Slightly Flaring Top, 5 In.	125.00
Steuben, Tumbler, Floral Engraving, Flared Rim, Signed	95.00
Steuben, Tumbler, Iced Tea, Cobalt Color, Flared Tops, 6 In., Pair	55.00
Steuben, Tumbler, Lemonade, Clear, Green Decoration, Matsu-No-Ke, 6 In.	135.00
Steuben, Tumbler, Lemonade, Topaz, Clear Foot, 4 5/8 In.	25.00
Steuben, Tumbler, Reeded In Pomona Green, Fleur-De-Lis, Crystal, 5 In.	50.00
Steuben, Tumbler, Reeding, Curved Sides, Fleur-De-Lis, Green, Signed	55.00
Steuben, Urn, Clear, Grecian	95.00
Steuben, Urn, Ivorene, Handled, Signed, 12 In.	165.00
Steuben, Urn, Light Blue Jade, Flint White Foot, 9 1/2 In.	1050.00
Steuben, Vase, Acid Cutback, C.1920, 12 In. Illus	950.00

Steuben, Vase, Alabaster, Double Gourd, Signed, 6 In. 135.00
Steuben, Vase, Amber, Optic Ribbed, Everted Lip, Signed, Footed Base, 8 In. 135.00
Steuben, Vase, Amber, Signed, Metal Pedestal Roycroft Signed Base, 6 In. 95.00
Steuben, Vase, Amethyst, 10 In. 425.00
Steuben, Vase, Applied Spaghetti Bands, Emerald Green, Signed, 7 3/4 In. 105.00
Steuben, Vase, Aurene Bud, Wafer Base, Flare, Mirror Finish, Highlights, 12 In. 295.00
Steuben, Vase, Aurene, Amber Iridescence, Footed, 3 Applied Handles 750.00
Steuben, Vase, Aurene, Applied Prunts, 6 In. 95.00
Steuben, Vase, Aurene, Gold & Green, Purple 300.00
Steuben, Vase, Aurene, Gold, Chalice Shape, 10 In. 325.00
Steuben, Vase, Base Turns Inward, Flares Out To Ruffle Top, 8 1/2 In. 275.00
Steuben, Vase, Blue Aurene, Flared Top, Purple Highlights, Signed, 5 1/4 In. 300.00
Steuben, Vase, Blue Aurene, Footed, 3 Applied Handles, 6 In. 750.00
Steuben, Vase, Blue Aurene, Iridescent, 3 1/2 In., Pair 950.00
Steuben, Vase, Blue Aurene, Scenic, Colorful, 3-Prong Tree Trunk, Signed 750.00
Steuben, Vase, Blue, Inverted Lamp Shade Shape, Signed, 5 1/2 In. 325.00
Steuben, Vase, Blue, Signed, 12 In. 750.00
Steuben, Vase, Bristol Yellow, Ball-Wheel Stem, 11 In. 110.00
Steuben, Vase, Bubbly, Severely Ruffled, 4 Sided Top, Signed, 8 3/4 In. 115.00
Steuben, Vase, Clear Amber, Optic Rib, Footed, Signed Fleur-De-Lis, 8 In. 135.00
Steuben, Vase, Clear Amber, Optic Rib, Inverted Lip, Footed, Signed, 8 In. 90.00
Steuben, Vase, Clear, Diamond-Optic Crystal, Blue Top Threading, Signed, 6 In. 67.00
Steuben, Vase, Clear, Loop Handles, Signed, 7 In. 70.00
Steuben, Vase, Cluthra, Black & White, Bubbles, 6 In. 350.00
Steuben, Vase, Cluthra, Classic Shape, Purple, Signed, 8 1/2 In. 475.00
Steuben, Vase, Cluthra, Dark Amethyst, Signed, 6 In. 675.00
Steuben, Vase, Cluthra, Lavender, Purple, Signed, 8 1/2 In. 475.00
Steuben, Vase, Cluthra, Raspberry, Rose Bowl Shape, Bubbles, 5 X 7 In. 350.00
Steuben, Vase, Cornucopia, Crystal, No.7579 .... 35.00
Steuben, Vase, Crystal, Chalice Shaped Base, 9 In. 115.00
Steuben, Vase, Diamond-Quilted Clear Crystal, Cranberry Threaded Top, 10 In. 325.00
Steuben, Vase, Double Prong, Cluthra, Appled Pedestal, 10 1/4 In. 545.00
Steuben, Vase, Fan, Blue & Amber, 7 X 6 In. .... 185.00 To 195.00
Steuben, Vase, Fan, Green & Amber, 9 X 7 In. 185.00
Steuben, Vase, Fan, Green Jade, Alabaster Foot, Stem, 5 3/4 In. 95.00
Steuben, Vase, Fan, Green Jade, Alabaster Pedestal, 6 In. 120.00
Steuben, Vase, Fan, Ribbed, Bristol Yellow, Signed, 11 In. 110.00
Steuben, Vase, Fan, Selenium Red, Ribbed, 8 In. 130.00
Steuben, Vase, Flare Top, Cylindrical, Paper Label, Topaz, 8 In. 45.00
Steuben, Vase, French Blue, Controlled Bubble, Red Reeding, 7 1/2 In. 100.00
Steuben, Vase, Gold Aurene, Glossy Caramel, Signed, 7 In. 375.00
Steuben, Vase, Gold Iridescence, Aurene, 5 In.High 375.00
Steuben, Vase, Gold, Signed, 11 1/2 In. 550.00
Steuben, Vase, Green Base, Bristol Yellow Top, Hexagonal, Signed, 8 1/4 In. 120.00
Steuben, Vase, Green Feather Decoration, Gold Aurene, No.219b, Signed, 8 In. 600.00
Steuben, Vase, Green Iridescent, Handled, Footed, 6 In. 125.00
Steuben, Vase, Green Jade & Alabaster, Oriental Motif, Trumpet, 12 In. 700.00
Steuben, Vase, Green Jade, Alabaster Foot, 5 In.High 125.00
Steuben, Vase, Green Jade, Alabaster Foot, 6 In. 125.00
Steuben, Vase, Green Jade, Swirl, Alabaster Base, Signed & Numbered, 9 1/4 In. 175.00
Steuben, Vase, Green Jade, 5 In. 375.00
Steuben, Vase, Green Jade, 8 In. 135.00
Steuben, Vase, Green Oriental Jade, Corset Shape, Script Signed 750.00
Steuben, Vase, Green, Acid Etched Dragons, Hawkes, 8 1/4 In. 180.00
Steuben, Vase, Green, Blue, Gold Threading, 9 X 6 In. 120.00
Steuben, Vase, Green, Diagonal Swirl, Signed & Numbered, 10 1/4 In. 60.00
Steuben, Vase, Green, Signed, 12 1/2 X 9 In. 295.00
Steuben, Vase, Grotesque, Cerise Ruby To Clear, Signed, 9 In. 260.00
Steuben, Vase, Handles, Opalescent, One Signed, 7 3/4 In., Pair 650.00
Steuben, Vase, Ivorene, Applied M Shaped Handles, Signed 10 In. 375.00
Steuben, Vase, Ivorene, Tri-Lily & Trumpet Shape, 12 In. 575.00
Steuben, Vase, Ivorene, Tri-Lily, 12 In. 695.00
Steuben, Vase, Ivory, Black Base, Bell Shape, 9 In. 175.00
Steuben, Vase, Ivory, Numbered, 6 In. 55.00

Steuben, Vase, Ivory, Ribbed Urn Body, Flared, 5 1/4 In.	200.00
Steuben, Vase, Jade Green & Alabaster, Signed, 11 In., No6287	200.00
Steuben, Vase, Jade Green, Flowerpot Shape, Numbered, 7 In.	75.00
Steuben, Vase, Jade, Alabaster Base, Fleur-De-Lis Mark	265.00
Steuben, Vase, Jade, Alabaster Handles, Signed, 9 1/2 In.	425.00
Steuben, Vase, Jade, Green, Alabaster Foot, 5 In.High	125.00
Steuben, Vase, Jade, Ribbing, Signed & Numbered, 10 In.	380.00
Steuben, Vase, Lampshade, Inverted, Ribbed, Footed, Peacock Blue, 5 1/2 In.	325.00
Steuben, Vase, Light Amber, Parfait Shape, Signed, 8 In.	85.00
Steuben, Vase, Marina Blue, Applied Clear Handles With Rigaree	95.00 To 100.00
Steuben, Vase, Maroon To Clear Crystal, Raised Diagonal Swirl, 7 In.	105.00
Steuben, Vase, Moonlight Color, Engraved Vintage Top, Cone Shape, 7 In.	125.00
Steuben, Vase, No.6817, Diamond & Optic, Blue Threaded Underside, 6 In.	65.00
Steuben, Vase, Ovoid Form, White Feathering, Calcite Interior, 8 1/2 In.	375.00
Steuben, Vase, Peacock Blue, Iridescent, Inverted Lampshade Type, 5 1/2 In.	325.00
Steuben, Vase, Pomona Green, Air Bubbles, Reeding, 9 In.	138.00
Steuben, Vase, Ribbed, Wisteria, Signed, 6 In.	150.00
Steuben, Vase, Rosaline Jade, Cone Shape, Alabaster Base, 7 In.	235.00
Steuben, Vase, Rosaline, Alabaster, Shape No.3143, 10 In.	210.00
Steuben, Vase, Rose Color, Lily-Shaped Mouth, Selenium, 6 In.	190.00
Steuben, Vase, Ruby, Fan, Ribbed, 8 In.	130.00
Steuben, Vase, Selenium Red Aurene, Lily-Shaped Mouth, 4 1/4 X 6 In.	170.00
Steuben, Vase, Shaded Rose To Crystal, Pedestaled, FDL, 9 In.	195.00
Steuben, Vase, Silverene, Green, 10 In.	275.00
Steuben, Vase, Spaghetti Bands, Applied Prunts, Moonlight, 7 1/2 In.	150.00
Steuben, Vase, Stick, Green Jade, Stem Flaring To Form Top, Footed, 7 3/4 In.	350.00
Steuben, Vase, Swirled, Green, Signed, 8 In.	85.00
Steuben, Vase, Topaz Crystal, Loving Cup Shape, 7 1/2 In.	90.00
Steuben, Vase, Topaz With Flemish Blue Rim, Footed, Signed, 7 X 5 1/2 In.	80.00
Steuben, Vase, Topaz, Signed, 6 1/2 In.	40.00
Steuben, Vase, Trumpet, Applied Decoration, 8 In.	75.00
Steuben, Vase, Trumpet, Ivorene Exterior, Aurene Interior, Iridescent, 5 In.	145.00
Steuben, Vase, Trumpet, Jade Lacy Curlicues Cut To Alabaster, Set Of 3	250.00
Steuben, Vase, Urn, Bristol Yellow, Diagonal Swirls, 7 In.	125.00
Steuben, Vase, Urn, Celeste Blue, Diagonal Swirls, 7 In.	120.00
Steuben, Vase, Urn, Green, Diagonal Swirls, 7 In.	110.00
Steuben, Vase, Urn, Purple, Crystal Pedestal, 4 7/8 In.	100.00
Steuben, Vase, Wisteria, Paneled, 5 1/4 In.	95.00
Steuben, Whiskey Glass, Reeded In Pomona Green, Signed, Fleur-De-Lis	25.00
Steuben, Wine, Blue Ribbed Crystal, Clear Stem, 4 1/2 In., Set Of 4	125.00
Steuben, Wine, Cobalt Blue, Signed & Numbered	125.00
Steuben, Wine, Crystal, Dark Green Reeding, 6 In., Pair	60.00
Steuben, Wine, French Blue Bubbly Glass With Reeding, 5 3/4 In., Signed, Pair	65.00
Steuben, Wine, Green Jade, Alabaster Stem & Base	100.00
Steuben, Wine, Selenium Red, Intaglio Cut Fleur-De-Lis, 4 5/8 In.	145.00
Steuben, Wine, Twisted Stem, Aurene	165.00

Stevengraphs are woven pictures made like ribbons. They were manufactured by Thomas Stevens of Coventry, England, and became popular in 1862.

Stevengraph, Bookmark, Centennial, 1776-1876, George Washington's Bust	80.00
Stevengraph, Bookmark, For A Good Girl	80.00
Stevengraph, Bookmark, Hebrew Letters, English Translation, Signed T.Stevens	50.00
Stevengraph, Bookmark, Home Sweet Home	35.00
Stevengraph, Bookmark, Landing Of Columbus, Red, White, Blue	75.00 To 100.00
Stevengraph, Bookmark, New Year's Gift	34.00
Stevengraph, Bookmark, Norwich, Connecticut, 1659-1909	29.00
Stevengraph, Bookmark, Shakespeare	45.00
Stevengraph, Bookmark, Verse, Signed Moore	40.00
Stevengraph, Bookmark, World's Columbian Exposition, Welcome To All Nations	65.00
Stevengraph, Bookmark, World's Industrial & Cotton Centennial Exposition	75.00
Stevengraph, Bookmark, 1776-1876 Centennial, George Washington	75.00
Stevengraph, Handel Festival Crystal Palace, Signed, June 1862	30.00
Stevengraph, Lusitania, Woven, Bright Colors	45.00
Stevengraph, Moses In Bullrushes, Signed	65.00

Stevengraph, Original 13 Colonies, C.1876 .... 175.00
Stevengraph, W.E.Gladstone, Signed 60.00

Stevens & Williams of Stourbridge, England, made many types of glass,
including layered, etched, cameo, and art glass, between the 1830s and
the 1930s. Some pieces are signed S and W.

Stevens & Williams, Basket, Green Jade, Alabaster Handle, Leaf & Berries 175.00
Stevens & Williams, Bottle, Scent, Intaglio Cut, Golden Interior 750.00
Stevens & Williams, Bowl, Flower, Pearlized Waffle, Drape Over, 7 In. 50.00
Stevens & Williams, Bowl, Ice Blue, Brass Footed Ormolu Ring, 10 In. 250.00
Stevens & Williams, Compote, Gold Decoration, 8 X 10 In. 525.00
Stevens & Williams, Dish, Candy, Rosaline & Alabaster, 4 1/2 X 5 In. 295.00
Stevens & Williams, Epergne, Fluted Bowl, Single Lily, Burmese Pink, 9 In. 175.00
Stevens & Williams, Finger Bowl & Underplate, Blue 125.00
Stevens & Williams, Pitcher, Milk, Amber Thorn Handle, Peachblow Pink, 8 In. 95.00
Stevens & Williams, Pitcher, Water, Apricot To Clear, Opalescent, 9 In. 175.00
Stevens & Williams, Rose Bowl, Blue, Diamond-Quilted, Satin Finish, 4 In. 145.00
Stevens & Williams, Rose Bowl, Iridescent, Green Applique Flowers, 5 1/4 In. 135.00
Stevens & Williams, Salt, Moss Agate, 1 1/2 X 2 1/2 In. 225.00
Stevens & Williams, Spittoon, Lady's, 9 In. 90.00
Stevens & Williams, Tumbler & Underplate, Salmon Jade, Shading, 6 1/2 In. 38.00
Stevens & Williams, Tumbler, Cased, Light Yellow, Gold Mica, Footed 75.00
Stevens & Williams, Vase, Amber, Blue Trim, Applied Floral, 12 1/8 In. 195.00
Stevens & Williams, Vase, Cased Blown, Applied Floral, 6 1/2 In. 185.00
Stevens & Williams, Vase, Cased Pink Glass, Swirled, Candy Stripes, 8 In. 275.00
Stevens & Williams, Vase, Clear, Green & Blue Peacock's Eyes, 3 3/4 X 4 In. 115.00
Stevens & Williams, Vase, Cream Over Pink, 3 Colored Rigaree, 7 In. 160.00
Stevens & Williams, Vase, Cream, Amber Foot, Vines, Red Cherries, 6 In. 135.00
Stevens & Williams, Vase, Crystal, 2-Tone Green Peacock Eyes, 3 1/2 X 4 In. 135.00
Stevens & Williams, Vase, Dark To Light Blue, Alabaster Foot, 9 1/2 In. 115.00
Stevens & Williams, Vase, Emerald Green, Expanded Diamond Pattern, 6 1/4 In. 95.00
Stevens & Williams, Vase, Glass, Amber, Enamel, Fish, 4 1/2 In. 57.00
Stevens & Williams, Vase, Intaglio Cut, Fan-Shaped, Marked, 3 1/4 X 5 1/4 In. 48.00
Stevens & Williams, Vase, Miniature, Blue & Amber, 3 1/2 In. 39.00
Stevens & Williams, Vase, Red With White Floral, Signed, 5 1/4 In. 1700.00
Stevens & Williams, Vase, Rose & Amber Leaves & Branches, Opalescent, 8 In. 125.00
Stevens & Williams, Vase, Topaz & Blue, Applied Gold Foliage, 8 1/2 In. 115.00
Stevens & Williams, Vase, White, Morning Glory, Frosted Blue Cameo, 8 In. 1400.00
Stiegel Type, Bottle, Scent, Flint, Blown Glass, 20 Swirled Ribs 35.00
Stiegel Type, Bottle, Scent, Swirled, Clear 35.00
Stiegel Type, Bottle, Soda Lime, Gilt Shoulder Decoration, 8 In. 45.00
Stiegel Type, Creamer, Blue, Applied Crimped Handle 325.00
Stiegel Type, Flip, Molded Panels, Engraved Leaf Band, C.1770, 6 1/2 In. 75.00
Stiegel Type, Funnel, Expanded Ribbed, 9 In. 150.00
Stiegel Type, Rummer 85.00
Stiegel Type, Salt, Cobalt Blue, Expanded Diamond, Unfooted, Flint 225.00
Stiegel Type, Salt, Cobalt, Ogee Shape, Footed, Flint 150.00
Stiegel Type, Salt, Footed, Clear, 11 Diamond, 3 In. 60.00
Stiegel Type, Tumbler, Bubbly, Engraved Basket Of Flowers, 6 In. 85.00
Stiegel Type, Tumbler, Enameled Flowers On Upper Half 75.00
Stiegel Type, Tumbler, Gold Scroll Decoration, 6-Sided, 5 1/4 In. 35.00
Stiegel Type, Vigil Light, 13 Diamond, Clear, Flint 60.00
Stiegel Type, Wine, Folded Foot 85.00
Stitzendorf, Group, Two Dancing Girls, 5 In. 60.00

Stoneware is a coarse glazed and fired potter's ware that is used to make
crocks, jugs, etc.

Stoneware, Bean Pot, Scroll Printing, Friend's, Pint 5.00
Stoneware, Bowl, Dark Wheat Color, 3 Nesting 20.00
Stoneware, Bowl, Mixing, Blue 6.50
Stoneware, Bowl, Pumpkinware, 10 X 6 In. 17.00
Stoneware, Chicken Feeder 5.00
Stoneware, Churn, Blue Figure, 6 Gallon, Lyons, New York, Fisher & Co. 140.00
Stoneware, Churn, Butter, Cobalt Blue Florals, Gray, Earred Handles, 15 In. 85.00

Stoneware, Crock,
Salt Glazed, Cobalt Bird,
American, 13 In.

Stoneware, Crock,
Cobalt Hen,
19th Century, 11 1/2 In.

Stoneware, Jug, Salt Glazed,
Cobalt Bird, 19th Century, 16 In.

Stoneware, Jug, Salt Glazed,
Cobalt Bird, 19th Century, 16 1/2 In.
(See Page 622)

Stoneware, Churn, Cream & Brown	15.00
Stoneware, Churn, Cobalt Flower, Seymour, Bosworth, Hartford, 4 Gallon, 12 In.	185.00
Stoneware, Crock, A.P.Donogho, 1 Gallon	28.00
Stoneware, Crock, A.P.Donogho, 2 Gallon	40.00
Stoneware, Crock, Beige Glaze, Tapers At Top	40.00
Stoneware, Crock, Bird, Norton, 1 1/2 Gallon	195.00
Stoneware, Crock, Bird, 4 Gallon	90.00
Stoneware, Crock, Blue & Gray, Blue Scroll Decoration, Remmey, Pa., 4 X 6 In.	195.00
Stoneware, Crock, Blue & Gray, Chicken Picking Corn, 2 Gallon	250.00
Stoneware, Crock, Blue Floral, Spring Valley, Pennsylvania, 1 1/2 Gallon	55.00
Stoneware, Crock, Blue Flower & Leaf, Hart, Sherburne, 2 Gallon	65.00
Stoneware, Crock, Blue Hen Pecking Corn, Buff Tone, 2 Gallon	125.00
Stoneware, Crock, Blue, Fort Edwards, New York, 3 Gallon	57.00
Stoneware, Crock, Bluebird, 8 Gallon	95.00
Stoneware, Crock, Burbank & Douglas, Portland, Maine, 4 Gallon	60.00
Stoneware, Crock, Butter, Blue & Gray, Hunting Scene, 4 1/2 X 7 1/4 In.	65.00
Stoneware, Crock, Butter, Blue, Peace Mark With Lid	45.00
Stoneware, Crock, Butter, Lid, Blue Cows	55.00
Stoneware, Crock, Canning, Donagho	35.00
Stoneware, Crock, Churn, Small Mouth, Double Flower, Leaves, Tall	120.00
Stoneware, Crock, Cobalt Bird, 3 Gallon	155.00
Stoneware, Crock, Cobalt Blue Flower, Whites, Utica, C.1875, 1 Gallon	69.00
Stoneware, Crock, Cobalt Bluebird On Tree Stump, Blue Weeds, 1865, 2 Gallon	155.00
Stoneware, Crock, Cobalt Brushed Leaves, E.S.& B., New Brighton, Pa., 5 Gallon	65.00
Stoneware, Crock, Cobalt Chicken Pecking Corn, C.1875, 3 Gallon	140.00
Stoneware, Crock, Cobalt Hen, 19th Century, 11 1/2 In. .... *Illus*	350.00
Stoneware, Crock, Cobalt Orchid, N.A.White & Son, Utica, New York, 3 Gallon	95.00
Stoneware, Crock, Floral, Cobalt Crossed, Signed, Handled, 1 1/2 Gallon	85.00
Stoneware, Crock, J.W.Penney, Boyntonville, New York, Blue Flower, 3 Gallon	85.00
Stoneware, Crock, N.Y.Stoneware Co., Fort Edward, 3 Gallon	135.00
Stoneware, Crock, Ovoid, Decorated Around Ears, 9 In.	38.00
Stoneware, Crock, Pear-Shape, Blue Splash, Handled, 12 X 10 In.	65.00
Stoneware, Crock, Pickle, Blue Flower & Scroll, 9 In., Diam., 15 1/2 In.	150.00
Stoneware, Crock, Salt Glazed, Cobalt Bird, American, 13 In. .... *Illus*	300.00
Stoneware, Crock, Singing Doves, Blue No.3, S.Hart, Fulton, C.1860, 3 Gallon	335.00
Stoneware, Crock, Stenciled Cobalt Eagle, Brown Bros.Huntington, 2 Gallon	135.00
Stoneware, Crock, T.P.Repptert, Blue Stripes, 1/2 Gallon	32.00
Stoneware, Crock, Three Stamped Swans, 3 Gallon	135.00
Stoneware, Crock, Tulip, Blue, Utica, White's, 1 Gallon	68.00
Stoneware, Crock, Tulips, Wm.E.Warner, West Troy, New York, 3 Gallon	95.00
Stoneware, Crock, W.E.Warner, Brushed Double Tulip, Eared, 3 Gallon	95.00
Stoneware, Crock, Whites Utica, Flowers, Leaves, 1 Gallon	95.00
Stoneware, Crock, Whites Utica, Heart Shaped Leaves, 5 Gallon	150.00
Stoneware, Crock, Wide Mouth, Blue Chicken Pecking Corn, 3 Gallon	280.00
Stoneware, Crock, Wide Mouth, Eared, Daisies, Leaves, Lyons, N.Y., 3 Gallon	65.00

Stoneware, Crock, Wide Mouth, Paddle Bird On Stump, 4 Gallon 250.00
Stoneware, Decanter, Bell's Whiskey, Brown, 19 1/2 In. 45.00
Stoneware, Drainer, Cheese, Flowerpot Shape, Footed, Pierced, Glazed, 9 1/4 In. 150.00
Stoneware, Flask, Tea, Lies On Side, Handle Opposite Flat Side, Gray Glaze 95.00
Stoneware, Foot Warmer, Cream, Incised Bovancroft Pottery, Glasgow 27.00
Stoneware, Inkwell, Gray, Incised Band, 3 Quill Holes, 4 1/4 X 2 1/4 In. 67.00
Stoneware, Inkwell, Marked DM 26 .... 475.00
Stoneware, Inkwell, Three Quill Holders, Gray, 4 1/4 X 2 1/4 In. 67.00
Stoneware, Jar, A.P.Donagho, 1 Gallon 17.00
Stoneware, Jar, Apple Butter, Brown, White Bottom, Bail Handle, Lid Lock, 9 In. 15.00
Stoneware, Jar, Brown Yellow, Orange Peel Type Salt Glaze, C.1880, 15 1/2 In. 60.00
Stoneware, Jar, Earred, Stenciled Tiger, F.T.Wrightson & Son, 3 Gallon 95.00
Stoneware, Jar, Earred, 5 Cobalt Leaves, Burger, Rochester, New York, 2 Gallon 135.00
Stoneware, Jar, Ice Water, Blue Flowers, Brass Spigot, 2 Gallon, 15 In. 195.00
Stoneware, Jar, Ovoid, Blue Handles, Goodwin, Webster, C.1820, 1 Gallon 59.00
Stoneware, Jar, Ovoid, Two-Tone Glaze, Sea Serpent, Boston, C.1797, 2 Gallon 75.00
Stoneware, Jar, Salt, Blue To Light Blue 65.00
Stoneware, Jar, Sloping Shoulders, C.1880, 3 Gallon 20.00
Stoneware, Jar, Tobacco, German, Gray, Cobalt Blue Trim, 6 X 10 In. 75.00
Stoneware, Jardiniere, Western Stoneware, Monmouth, 4 X 8 In. 20.00
Stoneware, Jug, A.Hartz, Gloversville, N.Y., Brown, 2 Gallon 45.00
Stoneware, Jug, A.K.Ballard, Burlington, Vermont, 2 Gallon 50.00
Stoneware, Jug, Batter, Bulbous, Ear Handle At Base, Wire Bail, Gray, 10 In. 50.00
Stoneware, Jug, Batter, Bulbous, Wire Bail, Brown Glaze, Gray, 10 X 6 1/2 In. 55.00
Stoneware, Jug, Bird, 2 Gallon 80.00
Stoneware, Jug, Blue Lettering, Hallenbeck Bros., 3 Gallon 57.00
Stoneware, Jug, Blue Pomegranate, H.Weston, Honesdale, Pa., C.1888, 2 Gallon 85.00
Stoneware, Jug, Blue Spatter, Handled, Miniature 14.00
Stoneware, Jug, Bluebird, Fort Edward Pottery Company, 2 Gallon 175.00
Stoneware, Jug, Bluebird, Fort Edward, N.Y., Blue, Gray, 1 Gallon 130.00
Stoneware, Jug, Brown & Gray With Cobalt Blue, 4 Gallon 45.00
Stoneware, Jug, Brown, Pear Shape, 18th Century, 3 Gallon 125.00
Stoneware, Jug, C.Meigh, Julius Caesar Embossed, 1839, 5 3/4 X 3 1/2 In. 85.00
Stoneware, Jug, Chick Feeder, Balteldes Feed Co., Blue Insignia 45.00
Stoneware, Jug, Cobalt Blue Dragonfly, J.Fisher, Lyons, N.Y., C.1882, 13 In. 60.00
Stoneware, Jug, Cobalt Blue Flamingo Bird On Stump, Whites, Utica, 1 Gallon 150.00
Stoneware, Jug, Cobalt Blue Singing Doves, S.Hart Fulton, C.1840-76, 12 In. 325.00
Stoneware, Jug, Cobalt Inscription, Ft.Edward Stoneware Co., 5 Gallon 95.00
Stoneware, Jug, Cobalt Lettering, Registered, O'Toole Distilling Co., 3 Qt. 35.00
Stoneware, Jug, E & L P Norton, Bennington, Vermont, Blue-Gray, 2 Gallon 69.00
Stoneware, Jug, Floral, 2 Gallon 75.00
Stoneware, Jug, Gray Glaze, Blue Flower, 15 In. 35.00
Stoneware, Jug, Handled, Blue, 2 Marked Lyons, 2 Gallon 95.00
Stoneware, Jug, High Relief Figures, Silver Rim, Turner, C.1800, 10 In. 350.00
Stoneware, Jug, Impressed Applied Decoration, 1890, 7 In. 30.00
Stoneware, Jug, Incised Bird On Branch, Cobalt Blue Filled, 1815, 14 In. 1500.00
Stoneware, Jug, J.W.Smith, 2 Gallon 42.00
Stoneware, Jug, Landlord's Caution In Verse, 1889, 10 In. 150.00
Stoneware, Jug, Marked Hart, Fulton, 2 Gallon 95.00
Stoneware, Jug, Mead & Co., 2 Gallon 55.00
Stoneware, Jug, Miniature, Compliments I.W.Harper, Nelson, Kentucky 22.00
Stoneware, Jug, Molasses, Cup Pour Spout, Brown, 2 Gallon 45.00
Stoneware, Jug, Motto, Eat Drink & Be Merry 29.00
Stoneware, Jug, Motto, If You Try Me Once You'll Try Me Again 29.00
Stoneware, Jug, Natural Foliage, 1890, 8 In. 35.00
Stoneware, Jug, Ovoid, Blue Crolius Rosette Stamp, Ringed Neck, 12 In. 135.00
Stoneware, Jug, Ovoid, Cobalt Flower, T.Harrington Lyons, C.1850, 2 Gallon 135.00
Stoneware, Jug, Parrot On Stump, Cobalt Slip, 1 Gallon 105.00
Stoneware, Jug, Salt Glazed, Cobalt Bird, 19th Century, 16 In. .... *Illus* 250.00
Stoneware, Jug, Salt Glazed, Cobalt Bird, 19th Century, 16 1/2 In. .... *Illus* 475.00
Stoneware, Jug, Spice, Blue On Gray, Small, Round, Cork, 4 In. 23.00
Stoneware, Jug, Tan, Blue Flower, Seymour Brothers, C.1870, 2 Gallon 59.00
Stoneware, Jug, Tan, Cobalt-Blue Design, Geddes, N.Y., C.1883, 14 In. 66.00
Stoneware, Jug, Three Sterling Figures, Musical, 10 In. 125.00
Stoneware, Jug, Whiskey, O'Keef's Pure Malt Whiskey, Oswego, N.Y. 20.00

Stoneware, Jug, Whits Binghamton, Flower, Leaves, 1 Gallon 80.00
Stoneware, Jug, Wreath Of Thistles, The Kintore Scotch Whiskey, 2 Quart 17.00
Stoneware, Mold, Pudding 20.00
Stoneware, Mortar & Pestle, White, 10 In. 45.00
Stoneware, Mortar & Pestle, 10 Lbs., Diameter, 10 In. 40.00
Stoneware, Mug, Blue Glaze, Mining Scene, Miners' Rootbeer 29.00
Stoneware, Mug, Blue, C.N.Y.Pottery, Utica, N.Y., 5 In. 35.00
Stoneware, Mug, Blue, Embossed Lady & Building, Akron, Ohio 75.00
Stoneware, Mug, Century Of Progress, Nude Lady Handle, C.1933, 6 1/2 In. 45.00
Stoneware, Mug, Cider, Blue Trim, 19th Century 14.00
Stoneware, Mug, Golfers, B & G 40.00
Stoneware, Mug, Miniature, Cobalt Blue On Gray, Raised Mirth Expression 8.50
Stoneware, Mug, Miniature, Petroleum Across Front, Gold Handle, White, 3 In. 6.50
Stoneware, Mug, Root Beer, Embossed, Blue, Miners 24.00
Stoneware, Mug, Schlitz Brewing Co., Milwaukee, 2 Lines Of German, Blue, Tan 35.00
Stoneware, Pan, Milk, Glazed, Leafed Flowers, C.1845, 5 X 11 1/4 In. 175.00
Stoneware, Pitcher, Batter, Brown, Yellow Glaze, Bail Handle, Wood Grips 55.00
Stoneware, Pitcher, Batter, Cobalt Blue, Embossed Monks 45.00
Stoneware, Pitcher, Blue & Gray, Cherry Band, 9 In. 45.00
Stoneware, Pitcher, Blue Spiral Cobalt, Marked Burger & Lang-Rochester 125.00
Stoneware, Pitcher, Brown, Ovenproof, Harcrest, 6 In. 12.00
Stoneware, Pitcher, Buttermilk, Grape Pattern, Blue 40.00
Stoneware, Pitcher, Canterbury Bells, Bulbous, Glazed, C.1890, 7 In. 35.00
Stoneware, Pitcher, Chamber, Mulberry, Beatrice Pattern, Turnstall, 11 In. 45.00
Stoneware, Pitcher, Cobalt Incised Leaves & Stems, C.1820-50, 12 In. 125.00
Stoneware, Pitcher, Cobalt Random Design, C.1870, 1 Gallon 145.00
Stoneware, Pitcher, Green Glaze, Grapes & Bark Decoration, 2 1/2 Quarts 20.00
Stoneware, Pitcher, Milk, Basket Weave, Embossed Grapes & Leaves, 9 1/2 In. 45.00
Stoneware, Pitcher, Milk, Brown Glaze, Albany, New York, 5 3/4 In. 40.00
Stoneware, Pitcher, Milk, Dutch Girl Kissing Boy, Windmill Scene, 7 X 6 In. 60.00
Stoneware, Pitcher, Syrup, Handled, Bulbous, Outside Spout, Brown Glaze, 5 In. 75.00
Stoneware, Pitcher, 2-Quart Milk, Brownish Purple Glaze, Zigzag Border 45.00
Stoneware, Planter, Strawberry, Tree Trunk Form, Leaves, Bark, 1865, 11 In. 225.00
Stoneware, Platter, Blue Peasant, Floral Border, C.1840, Meigh, 6 X 8 In. 20.00
Stoneware, Pot, Crocus, Handled, Circle Of Pierced Holes, Tan, 3 X 5 1/2 In. 28.00
Stoneware, Rolling Pin, Light Yellow, Wooden Handles, 8 X 3 In. 50.00
Stoneware, Rolling Pin, Orange Banded 55.00
Stoneware, Salt, Apricot Pattern, Hanging, B & G 45.00
Stoneware, Soap Dish, Flowers, Cobalt & Gray, Bennington Type, 4 1/2 In. 27.50
Stoneware, Spittoon, Cobalt Decoration 165.00
Stoneware, Spittoon, Pastel Colored 15.00
Stoneware, Syrup, Gray, Vertical Markings, Pewter Lid, Bennett, 6 1/2 In. 85.00
Stoneware, Teapot, Oriental, Embossed Dragons, Inside Strainer 60.00
Stoneware, Tureen, Covered, Ladle, Ivory, Green, J.C.Meakin, Pair 28.00
Stoneware, Urn, Cobalt Decoration, Brown-Gray Patina, 12 1/2 In. 155.00
Stoneware, Water Cooler, 4 Gallon, N.Clark & Co., Lyons, C.1822-52, 14 In. 450.00
Stoneware, Water Set, Buff, Blue Trim, Incised Buckeye, 5 Piece 75.00
      Store, see also Card, Advertising Coffee Grinder, Scale
Store, , Mirror, Pershing, Flags Of Allies, 3 In. 20.00
Store, Album, Leather-Like, Old Victorian Pictures, Antebellum 40.00
Store, Anvil, Jeweler's, Cast Iron 20.00
Store, Ashtray, Aunt Jemima Cast Iron Frypan, 6 In. 7.00
Store, Ashtray, B.F.Goodrich, Shoe Heel, Extra Soft Rubber Heels 17.50
Store, Ashtray, Black Rubber, Crystal Center, Mohawk Rubber Co. 5.50
Store, Ashtray, Black Sandman Figures, Marked Royal Doulton, Green Mark 6.00
Store, Ashtray, Coor's, Ceramic 5.00
Store, Ashtray, Figural, Standing Colt In Center, 2 1/2 In. 12.50
Store, Ashtray, Firestone, Clear Insert In Rubber Tire Shape 6.50
Store, Ashtray, French Line, Green Glass 5.00
Store, Ashtray, Glass, John Deere, Nebraska 6.00
Store, Ashtray, Goodrich Silvertown, Green Glass, 6 1/2 In. 17.00
Store, Ashtray, Lemp Brewing, Tin 10.00
Store, Ashtray, Levasoy Need Polishing, 4 3/4 In. 9.50
Store, Ashtray, Mr.Peanut, 50th Anniversary 15.00

Store, Ashtray, Players Navy Mixture, Copper, Embossed Sailor, 5 1/4 In. 20.00
Store, Ashtray, Remington Arms, Oval, Smoked Glass, 150th Anniversary, Large 12.50
Store, Ashtray, White Trucks, Chrome Mascot 5.00
Store, Back Bar & Counter, Tobacco Store, Cherry, Maple, 15 Feet X 7 Feet 900.00
Store, Back Bar, 2 Mirrors, Display Case, Marble Top, Clock, Brass Feet 3800.00
Store, Bag, Anheuser-Busch 5.50
Store, Bag, Tobacco, Piedmont, C.1908, 2 X 3 In. 5.00
Store, Bar & Back Bar, Oak, Marble Top, Beveled Mirror, Brass Fittings 3500.00
Store, Bar, Barber, Marble, Oak Base & Drawers, Marble Framed Mirror, 4 Ft. 295.00
Store, Barber Pole, Wood, Old Paint, 7 Ft.4 In. 750.00
Store, Barrel Cover, Cracker, Wooden, Hinged, Patented 1877, 19 In. 45.00
Store, Barrel, Flour, Interlocking Wood Hoops, C.1870, 26 In. 85.00
Store, Barrel, Planter's 165.00
Store, Basket, Picnic, Kidney Shaped, One End Opening 75.00
Store, Beer Tray Set, Strohs, Bohemian, Detroit, Waiter Carries Tray, Bottles 300.00
Store, Bill Spindle, National Cash Register, 6 In. 8.50
Store, Bin, Aunt Lydia, Threads, 8 1/2 X 9 3/4 X 11 1/4 In. 35.00
Store, Bin, Barber's, Match, Different Races Of People, Dated 1870 .... 125.00
Store, Bin, Beacon Coffee, Red & Gold, Tin, 13 X 12 X 13 In. 59.00
Store, Bin, Cremo Cigar, Tin, 14 X 6 X 6 In. 68.00
Store, Bin, Grain, Old Paint 125.00
Store, Bin, Greggs Tea, Roll Top 70.00
Store, Bin, Leverings Coffee, With Gold Lettering, 18 X 18 X 14 In. 40.00
Store, Bin, Mitchell's Original Kidney Plasters, Crawer, Counter Top 45.00
Store, Bin, Monadnock Coffee 45.00
Store, Bin, Norian's Dear Heart, Pistachio Nuts, 25 Lb. 30.00
Store, Bin, Perfection Java, G.Thalheimer, Syracuse, N.Y., Roll-Back Lid, Red 160.00
Store, Bin, Rice's Seeds, 1939, Collapsible Front Tin, Advertisement 75.00
Store, Bin, Slant Top, Hinged Cover, Porcelain Knob, 13 1/4 X 12 3/4 In. 30.00
Store, Bin, Sure Shot Tobacco 175.00
Store, Bin, Sweet Burley Red Tobacco 36.00
Store, Bin, Tobacco, Game Fine Cut 175.00
Store, Bin, Zanzibar Brand Seasoning, 10 Pounds, 1924, 8 1/2 X 11 In. 115.00
Store, Biscuit Baker, Knapp Monarch 32.00
Store, Booklet, Accordion Advertising, Remington Arms Company, 1931 .... 35.00
Store, Bookmark, Heinz, Pickle Shaped 4.00
Store, Bootjack, see also Iron, Bootjack
Store, Bottle, see Bottle
Store, Bottle Opener, Parrot 17.50
Store, Bowl, Display, Trowbridge Original Chocolate Chips, China, Pedestal 100.00
Store, Bowl, Willow Pattern, Schweppes Tonic Water On Border, 4 1/2 In. 15.00
Store, Box, Bait, Tin, Lettering, 3 X 3 1/2 In. 12.00
Store, Box, Barbour's Linen Thread, Lithograph On Cardboard, C.1880 .... 5.00
Store, Box, Bicycle Tire Plugs, Tin, Small 4.00
Store, Box, Biscuit, Tin, Huston's, Hinged Cover, 8 1/2 X 9 X 10 In. 18.00
Store, Box, Cake, Schepp's, Tin 65.00
Store, Box, Candle, Red Varnish 22.00
Store, Box, Carborundum Niagara Scythe Stones, Wood, 12 X 8 In. 16.00
Store, Box, CB, Goodrich Yankee Pure Rubber Bands 2.50
Store, Box, CB, Nyal Relief Of Indigestion, Gas Pains, Dyspepsia Lettered 3.50
Store, Box, Chiclets Gum, Glass Cover, 13 X 8 In. 18.00
Store, Box, Chocolate, Palmer Cox Brownies, Runkles, 8 X 10 In. 32.00
Store, Box, Cigar, MapaCuba Havana, Holds 50 Cigars, Tin, 4 1/2 X 5 In. 65.00
Store, Box, Cigar, Quintessa 3.00
Store, Box, Collar Stud, Shape Of Collar, Yellow, Gold Stud On Lid, Initialed 10.00
Store, Box, Counter Display, Beech-Nut Chewing Gum 32.00
Store, Box, Cracker, Beech-Nut, Mohawk Valley Scene, 12 X 11 In. 18.00
Store, Box, Cracker, Pine Grain, Painted, Sliding Lid, 20 X 12 X 9 In. 36.00
Store, Box, Cutex Five Minute Set, Tin, 4 3/8 X 3 1/4 In. 5.00
Store, Box, Daisy Fly Killer, Daisies & Skeleton, Tin 25.00
Store, Box, Display, Ferry's Seeds, Oak, Dovetailed, Hinged Lid, 9 1/2 X 6 In. 75.00
Store, Box, Dovetailed Wooden, Atlas Powder Co. 5.00
Store, Box, Dunlap Seed 12.50
Store, Box, Durkee's Spices, Elephants, Howdah, Label 65.00

Store, Box, Ferry's Seeds, Dovetailed, Hinged Lid, 9 1/2 X 6 1/2 X 3 3/4 In. 15.00
Store, Box, Goldthread Herb, Cardboard, Cure-All Drug 6.00
Store, Box, Harmonica, F.A.Bohm's Violin 5.00
Store, Box, Hiawatha Tobacco, Picture Of Hiawatha, Tin 30.00
Store, Box, Ice, Tin, Counter Top, 16 X 11 X 11 In. 50.00
Store, Box, Jack & Jill Jungle Jinks, California Perfume Co. 48.00
Store, Box, Johnston Candy Co., Cameo, Celluloid, 8 1/2 X 5 1/2 In. 15.00
Store, Box, Karonol For Burns, Tin, 3 X 3 1/2 In. 9.00
Store, Box, MacDonalds Atlas Compound, Cardboard, 2 X 3 In. 3.00
Store, Box, Mandeville & King Seed 25.00
Store, Box, Match, Hinkel Brewing Co., Albany, N.Y., 1892, Hinged, 2 X 3 In. 30.00
Store, Box, Mustard, Sailboat, Flowers, Slades, 12 X 18 In. 55.00
Store, Box, Mustard, World Lighting, Gold, Ardenter, 12 X 18 In. 55.00
Store, Box, Needle, Round, Revolving, Size Indicator 37.50
Store, Box, Old Briar Tobacco, Tin 8.00
Store, Box, Pencil, Form Of Closed Umbrella, Wood, 12 1/2 In. 35.00
Store, Box, Pencil, Wooden 3.00
Store, Box, Philips Seed, Vegetable Label, 5 1/2 X 12 X 28 In. 55.00
Store, Box, Powder, La Lete 2.00
Store, Box, Powder, Three Scotty, Pink Painted Lining 15.00
Store, Box, Prince Albert Tobacco, Christmas Design With Santa, Tin 20.00
Store, Box, Putnam Dye, Wooden 55.00
Store, Box, Razor, Wilkinson Chrome, C.1930s 12.00
Store, Box, Rutland Cracker, Wooden, Paper Label Inside Lid, 21 X 11 X 14 In. 35.00
Store, Box, Salt, Diamond Crystal Shaker, Shaker Lady On Front, Red, 1 Pound 30.00
Store, Box, Salt, Wood Cover, German, Blue & White 40.50
Store, Box, Seed, Hiram Sibley Co., Picture Inside Lid, Walnut, 12 X 7 In. 25.00
Store, Box, Seed, Mandeville & King, Oak, Brett Pansies Lithograph 25.00
Store, Box, Shadow, Budweiser, Draft Horse 65.00
Store, Box, Shippin, Ohio Blue Tip Match, 25 X 17 X 11 In. 15.00
Store, Box, Silverware Polishing, Square Nails 49.00
Store, Box, Sir Walter Raleigh Tobacco, Christmas Design 20.00
Store, Box, Thread, Clark's, Arched Top, 7 1/2 X 3 1/2 X 2 In. 35.00
Store, Box, Tin, Glycerole Shoes, Hinged Lock & Key, New York, 13 X 6 3/4 In. 75.00
Store, Box, Tobacco, Zig Zag Cigarette Papers, C.1910 ...... 2.50
Store, Box, Tool, Kellog Toasted Corn Flake Co., Open & Close, Wood 22.50
Store, Box, Vaseline Camphor Ice, Tin, 1 3/8 Ounce 3.00
Store, Brush, Clothes, Figural, Boston Terrier, Dog's Head Handle, Porcelain 10.00
Store, Brush, Clothes, Schiff & Co.State Bank, 1892-1922, 3 1/2 In. 16.00
Store, Bucket, Armour Veribest Peanut Butter, Nursery Rhymes, Tin, With Lid 45.00
Store, Butcher Block, Solid Maple, Dove-Tailed Jointed, Turned Legs 350.00
Store, Butter Chips, Rowley's Company, Silver Soldered, 11 Pieces, 3 7/8 In. 27.50
Store, Button, Esso, Merry Christmas, Picture Of Santa 12.00
Store, Button, Lapel, Elk's Tooth In 14K Gold Setting 6.00
Store, Button, Tom Mix Floto Circus 10.00
Store, Button, Wallace Company, Poughkeepsie, N.Y., Santa Claus 7.00
    Store, Buttonhook, see also Art Nouveau, Buttonhook; Brass,
    Buttonhook
Store, Buttonhook, Jockey, Amber Colored Head 45.00
Store, Buttonhook, Stag Handle, Pair 12.50
Store, Cabinet, Barber's Glass Sterilizer, Nickel Plated, Brass, Doorframe 29.00
Store, Cabinet, Cheese, Country, Oak, Revolving Slide-Out Tray, 18 X 20 In. 235.00
Store, Cabinet, Clark's O.N.T.Steel, Wood Grained, 3 Glass Front Drawers 42.50
Store, Cabinet, Diamond Dye, Children With Balloon 350.00
Store, Cabinet, Diamond Dye, Court Jester 425.00
Store, Cabinet, Diamond Dye, Evolution Of Woman 295.00
Store, Cabinet, Diamond Dye, Fairy, Children, Tin Front, Large 675.00
Store, Cabinet, Diamond Dye, Washer Woman 395.00
Store, Cabinet, Diamond Dye, Woman Washing Clothes 200.00
Store, Cabinet, Dr.Daniels' Veterinary Medicine, With Medicines 220.00
Store, Cabinet, Dr.Daniels', Tin, Man With Medicines 325.00
Store, Cabinet, Dr.Frost's Homeopathic Remedies, Oak, Tin Front 325.00
Store, Cabinet, Dr.Lesures, Horse With Head Through Porthole 675.00
Store, Cabinet, Hardware, Nut & Bolt, 80 Drawers, Pine, Porcelain Pulls, 5 Ft. 650.00

Store, Cabinet, Hardware, Nut & Bolts, 80 Drawers, Lazy Susan Style	550.00
Store, Cabinet, Humphrey, Listing Products, Tin	135.00
Store, Cabinet, Humphrey's Remedies, 34 Drawers, Blue Tin Front	400.00
Store, Cabinet, Needle, Oak, 3-Drawer	85.00
Store, Cabinet, Oak, 4 Drawer, Brass Pulls, 48 Brass Label Dispensers	125.00
Store, Cabinet, Perfection Dye	25.00
Store, Cabinet, Ribbon, Walnut, Glass Sections	525.00
Store, Cabinet, Screw, 72 Drawer, Dark Oak, Octagonal, Brass Label Holders	675.00
Store, Cabinet, Screw, 72 Drawer, Imprinted Drawers	850.00
Store, Cabinet, Screw, 72 Drawer, Octagonal	900.00
Store, Cabinet, Shoe, Oak, Stacking Type, 4 X 6 Ft.	250.00
Store, Cabinet, Silk, Oak, 20 Drawer	650.00
Store, Cabinet, Spool, Brook's, 4 Drawer, Oak	310.00
Store, Cabinet, Spool, Clark, Revolving	375.00
Store, Cabinet, Spool, J & P Coats, Oak, 6-Drawer, Decals, Brass Pulls	250.00
Store, Cabinet, Spool, J & P Coats, Walnut, 2-Drawer, Brass Knobs	275.00
Store, Cabinet, Spool, J.P.Coats, Rotating	375.00
Store, Cabinet, Spool, Revolving, Victorian, Mirrored	425.00
Store, Cabinet, Spool, Roll-Top Front, Lift Top, Oak, J.P.Coats	350.00
Store, Cabinet, Spool, Star Brand, Oak, 6 Drawers	125.00
Store, Cabinet, Spool, Star Twist, 4 Glass Front Pullout Drawers, Metal	75.00
Store, Cabinet, Spool, Thomas Russel, 4 Drawer, Walnut, Lift Top	280.00
Store, Cabinet, Spool, Wooden, 3 Drawers, J & P Coats	65.00
Store, Cabinet, Spool, 4-Drawer, Oak	190.00
Store, Cabinet, Thread, 5-Drawer, Coats & Clark, 18 X 15 In.	240.00
Store, Cabinet, Thread, 5-Drawer, Star Thread, 18 X 15 In.	240.00
Store, Cake Box, Schepps's, 16 X 11 1/2 X 14 In.	145.00
Store, Calendar Of Favorites, 17 3/4 X 13 1/2 In.	35.00
Store, Calendar, Brown Bros.Co., Picture Of 2 Girls, 1891, 7 X 11 In.	10.00
Store, Calendar, Coupon, Hood's Sarsaparilla, Pretty Girl, 4 1/2 X 7 In.	5.00
Store, Calendar, Prints, Currier & Ives	2.50
Store, Calendar, Prints, Hintermeister	2.50
Store, Calendar, 1894, Scott's Emulsion	10.00
Store, Calendar, 1904, Du Pont, Battle Scene On Spanish American Warship	245.00
Store, Calendar, 1905, Dr.Pepper, January Through June, Bluebirds	500.00
Store, Calendar, 1905, Elgin Watch Co., 4 Pages, Maud Humphrey	135.00
Store, Calendar, 1906, Metropolitan Life Insurance, Babyhood To Motherhood	25.00
Store, Calendar, 1909, Fighters, C.Twelvetrees, 17 3/4 X 13 1/2 In.	35.00
Store, Calendar, 1909, Grand Union Tea, 18 X 13 In.	15.00
Store, Calendar, 1910 Calendar Of Indoor Girls, 17 3/4 X 13 1/2 In.	35.00
Store, Calendar, 1910, Children, Animals, Katherine Pyle, 18 X 13 1/2 In.	35.00
Store, Calendar, 1912, Buster Brown Shoe Co., White House Queen	175.00
Store, Calendar, 1912, Chetopa, Kansas, Ice & Bottling Works	8.50
Store, Calendar, 1912, Du Pont, Minora, Winner Of National Field Trial	175.00
Store, Calendar, 1917, Hood's Sarsaparilla	2.00
Store, Calendar, 1922, Great American Insurance Co., Lincoln, 7 In.	4.00
Store, Calendar, 1929, Iceman & Maid	7.50
Store, Calendar, 1930, Snow Scene	5.00
Store, Calendar, 1931, Edison Mazda, Maxfield Parrish, 38 1/2 X 18 1/2 In.	29.00
Store, Calendar, 1938, Snow Scene	5.00
Store, Calendar, 1939, Boy & Dogs	5.00
Store, Can, Cavalier Cigarettes, 100, Oval	6.00
Store, Can, Fort Western Coffee	35.00
Store, Can, Gluek's Pilsener Pale Beer, Cone Top	35.00
Store, Can, Gunpowder, Du Pont Superfine, Dated 1924, 6 1/2 In.	15.00
Store, Can, Gunpowder, DuPont, Two Dogs	28.00
Store, Can, Gunpowder, Old Mathewson FFFF, Label	12.00
Store, Can, Hire's Syrup, Tin Tag On Handle, 1 Gallon	25.00
Store, Can, MacLarens Peanut Butter, 1 Lb.	15.00
Store, Can, Milk, Carnation, Tin, 25 Lbs.	27.50
Store, Can, Miller Select Beer, Punch Top	10.00
Store, Can, Mop, Kleen-O	2.00
Store, Can, Norian's Dear Brand Pistachio Nuts, Lithograph Girl, 25 Lb.	35.00
Store, Can, Old Reliable Brand Blended Coffee, Tin, 25 Lb.	35.00

Store, Can, Parke's Gold Camel Tea, Lithograph Of Japanese Ladies 15.00
Store, Can, Planters Peanuts, 10 Lbs. 39.00
Store, Can, Rainier Special Export, Cone 6.00
Store, Can, Richelieu Crystal Ginger, Hinged Lid, 6 1/4 X 1 In. 10.00
Store, Can, Shortening, Swift Jewel, 4 Lb. 5.00
Store, Can, Sunshine Biscuit, Martini Crackers 12.00
Store, Can, Thos.Wood Coffee, Lithograph Of Boston, Wooden Knob, 6 1/2 In. 15.00
Store, Can, Tiger Tobacco, Heavy Cardboard, Red, Tin Top 85.00
Store, Can, Tin Trash, Swinging Top, Drive A Buick, 3 1/2 In. 24.00
Store, Canister, Brundage, Tin, Nuts, 10 Lb. 37.50
Store, Canister, Cigar, LaPalina, Gold Tone 3.50
Store, Canister, Dixie Queen Plug Cut 70.00
Store, Canister, Gunpowder Tea, Roll Top, Woman's Head On Front, 14 X 12 In. 90.00
Store, Canister, Havana Cadet Cigars, Picture Of Soldier, 5 1/2 X 5 In. 28.00
Store, Canister, Old Chum Tobacco 11.00
Store, Canister, Pickaninny, Tin, Nuts, 10 Lb. 70.00
Store, Canister, Ramon's, White Figures, 8 1/2 In. 45.00
Store, Canister, Rum Maple Tobacco 15.00
Store, Canister, Spice, Original Japanning, Set Of 5, 3 In. 22.50
Store, Canister, Stag Tobacco, 5 X 5 X 6 In. 24.00
Store, Canister, Sweet Cuba Tobacco, 8 X 10 1/2 In. 39.50
Store, Canister, Sweet Mist Tobacco 85.00
Store, Canister, Tanaline For Simple Tanning, Tin, 3 Pound, 8 1/2 In. 12.00
Store, Canister, Tea, Deer On Front, 2 High Wheel Bikes On Sides, 20 X 19 In. 100.00
Store, Canister, Tuxedo Tobacco 12.00
    Store, Card, see Card
Store, Card, Advertising, Story, Piedmont Cigarette, Rip Van Winkle, Set Of 10 .... 100.00
Store, Card, Playing, Edison Mazda, Maxfield Parrish, Venetian Lamplighter 9.00
Store, Carriage, Tin, Cracker Jack 5.00
Store, Carrier, Egg, Wooden, Marked Humpty Dumpty, Held 24 Dozen 24.50
Store, Cart, Grocery, Wicker 65.00
Store, Case, Counter Display, Oak, Secret Release Cash Drawer, 53 X 23 In. 300.00
Store, Case, Cushman's Bread, Oak, Advertising On Side Glasses, 19 X 23 In. 110.00
Store, Case, Display, Beaded Oak Trim, 8 Ft. X 3 1/2 In. 145.00
Store, Case, Display, Counter Top, Walnut Frame, 27 X 42 In. 125.00
Store, Case, Display, Counter, Tin, Ingersoll 38.00
Store, Case, Display, De Nobili, Glass Top 40.00
Store, Case, Display, Dr.Myers Remedies, Wood & Glass, Sign On Front, 27 In. 255.00
Store, Case, Display, Metal, Kodak, Ed Sullivan Face 15.00
Store, Case, Display, P.Lorillard & Co., Double Door, 1760-1883 .... 450.00
Store, Case, Gum, California Fruit Curved Glass Fronts 175.00
Store, Case, Hardware Store Bank Case, 68 Framed Glass Openings, Oak, 54 In. 400.00
Store, Case, Sewing, Figural, Dog, Velour Over Metal, Hinged, 1920's 35.00
Store, Cash Register, Brass, Model 313, Small 450.00
Store, Cash Register, Brass, National, Marble Ledge, 16 X 15 X 17 In. 295.00
Store, Cash Register, Michigan Candy Store, Brass Plated 395.00
Store, Cash Register, National Cash, Fancy, Brass 350.00
Store, Cash Register, National, Brass, Crank, Model 455, Single Drawer 1200.00
Store, Cash Register, National, Brass, 6 Drawers, Oak Cabinet, Model No.562 .... 950.00
Store, Cash Register, National, Burnished And Lacquered 550.00
Store, Cash Register, National, Model 216, Brass 425.00
Store, Cash Register, National, Model 332, Brass 450.00
Store, Cash Register, National, Model 711 .... 100.00
Store, Cash Register, National, No.1413851, Brass, C.1914 .... 175.00
Store, Cash Register, National, Solid Brass, Small, 1912 .... 450.00
Store, Cash Register, National, 8-Drawer, Oak, C.1925, 76 X 34 In. 425.00
Store, Cash Register, Weights, Cast Iron 35.00
Store, Cash Register, 4 Key, Cast Iron, C.1894 .... 275.00
Store, Chair, Barber, Child's, Porcelain 350.00
Store, Chair, Barber, Walnut, Footrest, Carved Dog's Heads On Arms 350.00
Store, Chair, Barber, Wooden, Pair 250.00
Store, Chair, Barber, 1920 .... 90.00
Store, Chair, Folding, Piedmont Cigarettes On Enameled Backrest 60.00
Store, Chair, Shoeshine, Metal 100.00

Store, **Change Receiver & Tray,** Baby Ruth Gum, Glass, 8 X 6 In. 35.00
Store, **Change Receiver,** Cuticura Hand Cream, Glass 20.00
Store, **Change Receiver,** Don Digs Cigars, Glass 20.00
Store, **Charm,** Mr.Peanut 2.50
Store, **Chest,** Printer's, 25 Drawer, Oak, 2200 Divisions, 44 In. 1000.00
Store, **Chicken Snatcher,** Iron, Wood Handle, Fogelsville, Pa., Poultry Auction 15.00
Store, **Chopper,** Nut, Planters, C.1938 .... 35.00
Store, **Churn,** Dazey, Glass, Gallon 22.00
Store, **Cigar Mold,** Wooden, 20 Unit, Miller, Dobrue, Peters Mfg., Co., 1914 .... 35.00
Store, **Clamp,** Glue, 2 Bars, Wooden, Stamped Albany & Susquehanna Railroad 25.00
Store, **Clicker,** Buster Brown Shoes, Shape Of Shoe 12.50
Store, **Clicker,** Satisfaction Coffee, 1910 .... 10.00
Store, **Clip,** Money, First Social Security Card, C.1935, 2 In. 12.00
Store, **Clipboard,** Brass, Perpetual Calendar, Midwest Life, 4 3/4 X 8 1/2 In. 17.50
Store, **Clipboard,** Steel, Miller's Mutual Insurance Company, 1881 .... 12.50
Store, **Clipboard,** The National Fire Group, 53th Anniversary, 1888-1938 .... 15.00
Store, **Clock,** Bulova Electric, Wooden Case, 16 X 18 In. 55.00
Store, **Clock,** Burger Bohemian Beer, Oak, Electric, Vase You Efer In Zinzinati 250.00
Store, **Clock,** Coronet Brandy, Plastic Figure Inside 12.50
Store, **Clock,** Duquesne Beer 25.00
Store, **Clock,** Ever-Ready Shaving, C.1905 .... 675.00
Store, **Clock,** Garfield Tea & Syrup, Seth Thomas 900.00
Store, **Clock,** Mr.Boston Liquors In Shape Of A Bottle, Advertising 225.00
Store, **Clock,** Orange Crush 20.00
Store, **Clock,** Pabst Beer 35.00
Store, **Clock,** Pepsi, Say Pepsi Please 29.00
Store, **Clock,** Tetley Tea, Electric, Tin, 1930s, 14 1/2 In. 67.50
Store, **Clock,** Use Dickey's Indian Blood & Liver Pills, Waterbury, C.1890 .... 585.00
Store, **Clock,** Wall, Tin With Delft Blue & White Decoration, Home Coal Co. 45.00
Store, **Clock,** 7-Up 20.00
Store, **Clothespin,** Bone Hand-Carved 31.25
Store, **Coaster,** Wooden Wagon, Lettering, White's 35.00
Store, **Coffee Bin,** Stenciled Pinkerton Oriental Coffee, Red, Wood 165.00
   Store, **Coffee Grinder, see Coffee Grinder**
Store, **Comb,** Gleen Durling Motorcycle Headquarters, Toledo, Celluloid 8.50
Store, **Comb,** Hair, Wooden, Arched Top, Ladies, 5 1/2 X 2 1/2 In. 30.00
Store, **Comb,** Tortoiseshell Cutout, 7 X 7 In. 35.00
Store, **Condiment Set,** Hotpoint Range, White Milk Glass, 5 In., 4 Piece 35.00
Store, **Corkscrew,** Champion, Clamps On Bar, Used In Saloons, Patent 1898 .... 97.50
Store, **Corkscrew,** Whiskey, Peebles 20.00
Store, **Corn Drier,** 21 Prong, 29 In. 22.50
Store, **Counter,** Oak Beam, 10 Ft. 450.00
Store, **Counter,** Oak, Marble Top, White Vitrolite Insets 200.00
Store, **Counter,** Oak, 4 Ft. 150.00
Store, **Counter,** Wall, 21 Drawers, 12 Ft., 23 X 32 In. 250.00
Store, **Creamer,** Kellogg Cereal 4.00
Store, **Creamer,** Post Cereal, Measure, Red, 2 3/4 In. 6.00
Store, **Crock,** Butter, Domser's Creamery, Utica, N.Y. 10.00
Store, **Crock,** Peanut Butter On Front, Gray, Covered, 13 X 11 In. 65.00
Store, **Cuff Links,** Delco Battery, Shape Of Battery 8.50
Store, **Cup,** Folding, Cyclists, Picture Of Tandem Bicycle 45.00
Store, **Cup,** Measuring, Pink, Kelloggs 4.50
Store, **Cutouts,** Tin, DeLaval, Cow & Calf 30.00
Store, **Cutter,** Cheese, Hand-Wrought 30.00
Store, **Cutter,** Cigar, Barrel Shape, Smoke Marblehead, 5 Cents 175.00
Store, **Cutter,** Cigar, Bronze, Reclining Nude, Table Model, Signed, 6 In. 85.00
Store, **Cutter,** Cigar, Counter, Peter Shuyler, Red 100.00
Store, **Cutter,** Cigar, Double Pump 145.00
Store, **Cutter,** Cigar, Mandolin Shape, For Watch Chain, 2 In. 25.00
Store, **Cutter,** Cigar, Mechanical, Spring Wound 125.00

Store, Cutter, Cigar, Single Pump	125.00
Store, Cutter, Cookie, Planters Peanuts	10.00
Store, Cutter, Tobacco, Brass Handled, Counter Top, C.1860, 3 1/4 In.	45.00
Store, Cutter, Tobacco, Brown Mule	40.00
Store, Cutter, Tobacco, Carved Wood, Green Hat, Coat, Red Pants, Vest, 9 In.	150.00
Store, Cutter, Tobacco, Counter Top, Iron, Embossed Enterprise 1885	25.00
Store, Cutter, Tobacco, Cut Plug, Peace And Good Will, 9 In.	19.50
Store, Cutter, Tobacco, Cutter	38.00
Store, Cutter, Tobacco, John Finzer & Bros., Five Bros.Tobacco Works	39.00
Store, Cutter, Tobacco, Loullards Tomahawk	50.00
Store, Cutter, Tobacco, Spearhead, R.J.Sorg Co.	60.00
Store, Cutter, Tobacco, Star, Save The Tags, Enterprise, 1885	42.00
Store, Cutter, Tobacco, The Prize Cutter By S.Lee	35.00
Store, Cutter, Tobacco, Workman's Label, Small	20.00
Store, Desk, Counter Top, Pine, Slant Lift, Cubby Hole Section, 18 X 19 In.	90.00
Store, Dish, Counter Display, Lutton's Cough Drops, Log Cabin, Roof Cover	45.00
Store, Dish, Soap, Cast Iron, Laxton's	10.00
Store, Dispenser, Alka Seltzer	48.00
Store, Dispenser, Anheuser-Busch, 5 Cent Crock, Cordley & Hayes, 1919	210.00
Store, Dispenser, Armour's Vigoral, 16 Flared China Glasses	600.00
Store, Dispenser, Buckeye Root Beer Tree Trunk, China	350.00
Store, Dispenser, Candy Machine, 2 Cent Shute	35.00
Store, Dispenser, Clark's Teaberry Gum, Vaseline Glass	33.00
Store, Dispenser, Diamond Match, 2 For 1 Cent, White Metal, 7 X 13 In.	65.00
Store, Dispenser, Gem Razor Blade, Man, Little Boy, Beveled Mirror, Tin	125.00
Store, Dispenser, Hire's Root Beer With Pump	225.00
Store, Dispenser, Hire's Root Beer, Hourglass	210.00 To 350.00
Store, Dispenser, Hunter's Milk Glass Base	65.00
Store, Dispenser, Lash's Orangeade, Orange On Top	165.00
Store, Dispenser, Mission Orange Syrup, Orange, Black, 13 X 27 In.	125.00
Store, Dispenser, Orange Crush Beverage, Ice Insert, McKee Glass Co.	95.00
Store, Dispenser, Orange Crush, Ceramic, 10 In.	150.00
Store, Dispenser, Orange Crush, Paddles Spin To Blend, 15 1/2 In.	325.00
Store, Dispenser, Orange Crush, Ward's, Ceramic, Orange Shape, 10 In.	165.00
Store, Dispenser, Orange, Lemon, Lime, Figural, With Pumps, Set Of 3	750.00
Store, Dispenser, Paper, Counter Top	26.00
Store, Dispenser, Ruby Red Cherry Smash	75.00
Store, Dispenser, Smith Brothers, Cough Drop, Tin, 12 In.	48.00
Store, Dispenser, Soda Fountain, Richardson.Maid Of Honor, 4 Spigots, 33 In.	285.00
Store, Dispenser, Syrup, Mission Real Fruit Juice, Pink Glass	55.00
Store, Dispenser, Syrup, Ward's, Orange Crush, Pump	150.00 To 165.00
Store, Dispenser, Tin, Sunset Soap Dyes, 24 Open Sections, 13 X 20 X 7 In.	45.00
Store, Dispenser, Vinegar, Barrel, Base, Heinz	275.00
Store, Dispenser, Ward's Orange Crush, Ceramic, Orange, 10 In.	150.00
Store, Dispenser, Ward's, Orange, Lemon, Lime	1050.00
Store, Dispenser, Water, Lion's Head Handles	150.00
Store, Dispenser, Wrapping Paper, Cast Iron, Fancy	10.00
Store, Display Case, Lifesavers, Slant Top, 10 X 11 X 8 In.	45.00
Store, Display Case, Tung-Sol Auto Bulbs, 18 In.	19.00
Store, Display Case, Umbrella, Oak, Glass Sides & Top	300.00
Store, Display Case, Wilson Biscuits, Wood	20.00
Store, Display, Arm & Hammer, Cardboard, 1930s Woman, 21 X 50 In.	55.00
Store, Display, Bonnie B Hair Net, C.1930	160.00
Store, Display, Coor's Malted Milk, White Ironstone, Tin Lid, 7 X 8 In.	47.00
Store, Display, Detmer Woolen, Opens Up, 20s Panorama	75.00
Store, Display, Goebbal's Bean, Chalkware, Rooster In Top Hat	8.00
Store, Display, Gruen Guild Watch, Plaster, Copper Stained	30.00
Store, Display, Kraft Cheese, 5 Shelf, Original Advertising	40.00
Store, Display, Laymon's Kwality, Cascara-Quinine, Cardboard, For Colds	15.00
Store, Display, Lighted Knickerbocker Beer Sign With Clock, 40 X 15 In.	45.00

Store, Display, Mechanical, Roy Rogers, Revolving Lasso, 24 In.

Store, **Display,** Mechanical, Roy Rogers, Revolving Lasso, 24 In. .... *Illus*	99.00
Store, **Display,** Sunshine Bisquit, 5 Shelves, 5 Feet	200.00
Store, **Doll,** Cracker Jack Boy	10.00
Store, **Doll,** Cream Of Wheat, Cloth	45.00
Store, **Doll,** Kellogg's Daddy Bear, Uncut Cloth, Dated 1926 .... 25.00 To 40.00	
Store, **Doll,** Kellogg's Johnny Bear, Uncut Cloth, Dated 1925	25.00
Store, **Doll,** Kellogg's, Stuffed Rag, Goldilocks, Papa, & Mama Bear	150.00
Store, **Doll,** Lotta Light, Uncut Cloth, Mazda Light Co.	22.50
Store, **Doll,** Mannikin, McCalls, Patterns, Material, 1942	35.00
Store, **Doll,** Mannikin, Singer Sewing Machine, 1949, Patterns, Material	40.00
Store, **Doll,** Mr.Peanut, Cloth, 21 In.	20.00
Store, **Doll,** Paper, Hood's Sarsaparilla, 5 Dolls & Clothes, Copyright 1894	35.00
Store, **Doll,** Planters Peanuts	7.00
Store, **Doll,** Rastus, Cream Of Wheat	30.00
Store, **Doll,** Scarecrow, Purina Cereal	10.00
Store, **Doll,** Stuffed, Mr.Peanut, 21 In.	9.00
Store, **Door,** Push, Ex-Lax, Plastic, Pair	15.00
Store, **Drawer Pull,** Apothecary, Porcelain, 1800s, Set Of 24	135.00
Store, **Drawer Pull,** Sandwich Canary, Pair	35.00
Store, **Drawer,** Cash, Pine & Oak, Nashua, 4 Compartments, 18 X 16 1/2 In.	80.00
Store, **Duster,** Ostrich Feather, Turned Wooden Handle, Victorian	8.50
Store, **Fan,** Ceiling, Single Speed, 110 Volts	125.00
Store, **Fan,** Ceiling, Westinghouse, Wood Blade .... 158.00 To 175.00	
Store, **Fan,** Desk, 1920s	30.00
Store, **Fan,** Hand, Folding, Bissell's Carpet Sweeper, Opens To 15 In.Span	10.00
Store, **Fan,** Star Brand Shoes	3.50
Store, **Feeder,** Chicken, Ki-Rec	32.00
Store, **Figure,** Countertop, Iroquois Club Cigars, Plaster	350.00
Store, **Figurine,** Horse, White Horse Whiskey, Metal, 8 In.	15.00
Store, **Figurine,** Victor, Nipper Dog, Chalk, 4 In.	15.00
Store, **Flyswatter,** Daisy	4.50
Store, **Foot Warmer,** Hearts	95.00
Store, **Foot Warmer,** Soapstone Insert On Top, Pierced	68.00
Store, **Fork & Spoon,** Mr.Peanut Handles	14.00
Store, **Fork,** Pickle, Heinz 57, Silver Plated Pickle	15.00
Store, **Funnel,** Copper, Offset Shape, 2 1/4 X 5 In.	7.50
Store, **Funnel,** Used To Put Water In Steam Engine	25.00
Store, **Glass,** Measuring, Reads J.E.Simas Prescription Druggist, Haverhill	7.00
Store, **Grinder,** Sausage, Pegs & Inside Knives, Cast Iron	16.00
Store, **Gum Machine, see Store, Machine, Gum ball**	
Store, **Halter,** Horse, Hand-Braided	60.00
Store, **Halter,** Horse, Leather, Brass U.S.Military Rosettes	12.50
Store, **Holder,** Paper, Buster Brown Vacation Days, 1946, 2 1/2 In.	15.00
Store, **Holder,** Paper, Fancy Iron, Claw Feet	28.50
Store, **Holder,** Paper, Metal & Celluloid, Bottle Of Milk, Townsend West Dairy	14.00
Store, **Holder,** Pencil, Umbrella Shaped, Child's, Silvery Handle	9.00
Store, **Holder,** Straw, 10 In.	35.00
Store, **Holder,** String, Applied Cobalt Blue Rim & Collar	135.00

Store, Holder, String, Aunt Jemima	12.50
Store, Holder, String, Brass, Raised Design, Lift Off Top	15.75
Store, Holder, String, Cast Iron, Lacy Openwork	22.00
Store, Holder, String, Cast Iron, 6 1/2 In.Ball	28.00
Store, Holder, String, Ceiling, Mechanical	37.50
Store, Holder, String, Cone, Cast Iron	8.00
Store, Holder, String, Glass, Beehive, Tin Closure, 4 3/4 In.	30.00
Store, Horseshoe, Brass, Simmons Liver Regulator, Take In Time, 5 1/4 In.	75.00
Store, Humidor, Brigg's Lorillard, Wooden, Aged In Wood, 7 1/4 X 17 In.	20.00
Store, Humidor, Wooden Barrel, Briggs Tobacco, 7 In.	15.00
Store, Humidor, 2 Figural Hunting Dogs Stand On Hinged Lid, Sections, Feet	115.00
Store, Ice Shaver, Cast Iron, Wrightsville Hardware Co., Pennsylvania, 8 In.	25.00
Store, Jar, Beick's Candy, Large, Ornate	45.00
Store, Jar, Borden's Condensed Milk, 8-Sided, Tin & Milk Glass Cover, 4 In.	8.95
Store, Jar, Burma Shave	3.50
Store, Jar, Candy Stick, Glass	15.00
Store, Jar, Candy, Footed, Bulbous, Glass Cover, 10 In.	28.00
Store, Jar, Candy, Lid, Round, Large	7.00
Store, Jar, Candy, Necco, Art Deco	9.00
Store, Jar, Cigar, Cover, La Palina Cigar Since 1896, 7 X 6 In.	50.00
Store, Jar, Cigar, La Fendrich, Full	18.00
Store, Jar, Cover, Amber, Wan-Eta Cocoa, Boston	7.00
Store, Jar, David 1 For 1 Cent Old Homestead Fudge, Lid, 7 X 8 1/2 In.	35.00
Store, Jar, Dr.Ramon's, Doctor Etched In White	25.00
Store, Jar, Glass, Straight Sides, Tin Top, 10 1/2 In.	40.00
Store, Jar, Jumbo Peanut Butter, 3 In.	10.00
Store, Jar, Lance, Glass Lid, 12 1/2 In.	25.00
Store, Jar, Minter's Log Cabin Fudge, 10 X 7 In.	35.00
Store, Jar, Pickle, Little River	35.00
Store, Jar, Planters Peanuts, Eight-Sided	68.00
Store, Jar, Planters Peanuts, Embossed, Lid	35.00
Store, Jar, Planters Peanuts, Fishbowl Lid	45.00
Store, Jar, Planters Peanuts, Large Fishbowl	68.00
Store, Jar, Planters Peanuts, Leap Year 1940	41.00
Store, Jar, Planters Peanuts, Original Cover, 8-Sided, Full Label	55.00
Store, Jar, Planters Peanuts, Peanut Handle, Hexagonal	75.00
Store, Jar, Planters Peanuts, Peanut On Four Corners, With Label, 11 In.	60.00
Store, Jar, Planters Peanuts, Streamline	39.00
Store, Jar, Planters Peanuts, 10 In.	50.00
Store, Jar, Planters, Seal, Peanut On Lid, Octagon	100.00
Store, Jar, Prince Albert, Glass	20.00
Store, Jar, Squirrel Brand, Picture Of Squirrel	32.00
Store, Jar, Storage, Cover, Incised Decoration On Shoulder, Brown Glaze, 8 In.	29.00
Store, Jar, Sweetmeat, Victorian, Bird In Flight, Foliage, Gold, Black Amethyst	25.00
Store, Jar, Tobacco, Boar, 12 Panels, Blue, 9 X 6 In.	150.00
Store, Jar, Tobacco, Versailles	40.00
Store, Jar, Toms Peanut Butter Sandwiches, Large	25.00
Store, Jar, U.S.Nut Co., Lynn, Massachusetts, Slant Front, Round	25.00
Store, Jug, Glass With Spigot, Kentucky Straight Bourbon Whiskey, 1 Gallon	15.00
Store, Jug, H.A.Johnson, Headquarters Soda & Extracts Supplies, Boston, Pair	62.00
Store, Jug, Hire's Root Beer, Mechanical Stopper, Cast Iron, Pint	85.00
Store, Jug, N.R.Bianchi Wines, Liquors, Calumet, Mich., Gallon Whiskey	34.50
Store, Jug, Tri-Pure, 5 Gallon, 1929	17.50
Store, Keg, Walter's Beer, Pueblo, Colorado	39.00
Store, Knife, Crooked, American Indian, Leather Belt Sheath, State Of Maine	68.00
Store, Knife, Indian, Crooked, Carving	40.00
Store, Knife, Key Chain, Try Country Club Beer	12.50
Store, Knife, Pocket, Buffalo Bill	1.15
Store, Knife, Pocket, Dakin Implement, Missouri, John Deere	17.50
Store, Knife, Pocket, Davy Crockett	1.15
Store, Knife, Pocket, Figural, Lady's Leg, High Button Shoe, Utica Club Beer	12.00
Store, Knife, Pocket, Graybar, Silver Plate	8.00
Store, Knife, Purina, 3 Blade, Checkerboard Handle, 3 3/8 In.	12.50
Store, Knob, Beer, Edelweiss Beer	8.50

Store, Label, Cigar Box, Bang Up

Store, Label, Cigar Box, Capt.Noah, 1884

Store, Label, Citrus, Good Will

Store, Label, Citrus, Fancia

Store, Knob, Tap, Lucky Lager		11.50
Store, Label, Bottle, Druggist's, Original Box, Red, Gold, Black, Set		35.00
Store, Label, Cigar Box, Bang Up	*Illus*	1.50
Store, Label, Cigar Box, Capt.Noah, 1884	*Illus*	1.50
Store, Label, Citrus, Fancia	*Illus*	1.00
Store, Label, Citrus, Good Will	*Illus*	1.00
Store, Label, Citrus, Justice	*Illus*	1.00
Store, Label, Citrus, Marc Antony	*Illus*	1.00
Store, Label, Citrus, Paula	*Illus*	1.00
Store, Label, Citrus, Ramona	*Illus*	1.00

Store, Label, Citrus, Justice

Store, Label, Citrus, Marc Antony

Store, Label, Citrus, Paula

Store, Label, Citrus, Ramona

Store, Lifter, Stove Lid, Coil Spring	3.00
Store, Light, Bar, Mountain Stream, Coors On Tap, 15 X 10 In.	25.00
Store, Lighter, Cigar & Tobacco, Midland Jump Spark	225.00
Store, Lighter, Cigar, Brass, Gas Counter Model	175.00
Store, Lighter, Cigar, Cylinder, Bowers Sure Fire	3.50
Store, Lighter, Cigar, 2 Cape Cod Lighters Both Sides, Ruby Globe, 11 In.	195.00
Store, Lighter, Cigarette, One-Arm-Bandit, Works, 5 In.	48.00
Store, Lighter, Cigarette, Royal Crown, R.C.Cola, Bottle Shape, Nickel, Brass	5.00
Store, Lighter, Counselor Cigar, Green Glass Font, White Ball Shade	185.00
Store, Lunch Box, Aladdin, The Walton's, With Thermos	7.50

Store, Lunch Box, Blue Tiger Tobacco	32.00
Store, Lunch Box, Bonanza, Tin	10.00
Store, Lunch Box, Central Union Tobacco	15.00 To 36.50
Store, Lunch Box, Dixie Kid	165.00
Store, Lunch Box, Dixie Queen Tobacco	36.00
Store, Lunch Box, Eagle Tobacco, Green	35.00
Store, Lunch Box, Fashion Cut Plug Tobacco	60.00
Store, Lunch Box, George Washington	15.00 To 23.00
Store, Lunch Box, George Washington Cut, Latch & Handle	4.50
Store, Lunch Box, H-O Tobacco	17.50
Store, Lunch Box, Handbag Tobacco, Shape Of Handbag	38.00
Store, Lunch Box, Huntley Palmer, Art Nouveau Decoration	45.00
Store, Lunch Box, King Koal Stripped Tobacco	30.00
Store, Lunch Box, Laredo	20.00
Store, Lunch Box, Lorillard's Tiger Chewing Tobacco, Double Handle	22.00
Store, Lunch Box, Lorillard's Tobacco, Brown	25.00
Store, Lunch Box, Mayo's	20.00
Store, Lunch Box, Mayo's Cut Plug Tobacco, Blue	10.00
Store, Lunch Box, Mayo's Cut Plug, Black & Gold, 8 X 5 X 4 In.	12.50
Store, Lunch Box, Mayo's Cut Plug, Latch & Handle	20.00
Store, Lunch Box, Ojibua Tobacco, 10 Lb.	40.00
Store, Lunch Box, Paterson's Seal, Basket Weave	18.00
Store, Lunch Box, Pedro	65.00
Store, Lunch Box, Peter Rabbit On Parade	48.00
Store, Lunch Box, Quick Draw McGraw, With Thermos	7.50
Store, Lunch Box, Red Tiger Tobacco, Tin, 8 X 10 X 5 1/2 In.	30.00
Store, Lunch Box, Red Tiger, Large	14.00
Store, Lunch Box, Richmond Club	30.00
Store, Lunch Box, Skookum Cut Plug, Picture Of Apple, Tin	40.00
Store, Lunch Box, Tiger Tobacco, Blue Large	35.00
Store, Lunch Box, Tiger Tobacco, Cardboard	20.00
Store, Lunch Box, Tom Corbett, 1950s	10.00
Store, Lunch Box, U.S. Marine Tobacco, Sailor	35.00
Store, Lunch Box, Union Leader Cut Plug, Red With Eagle	14.00
Store, Lunch Box, Union Leader Tobacco, With Poinsettia	22.50
Store, Lunch Box, Union Leader, Eagle, 1910 Stamp	25.00
Store, Lunch Box, Winner Tobacco, Race Cars	45.00 To 65.00
Store, Lunch Box, Worker's Cut Plug, Alligator Grain	30.00
Store, Machine, A.B.T.Challenger Game	175.00
Store, Machine, Admiral Dewey, Small Penny Wooden Case	150.00
Store, Machine, Arcade, Exhibit Magic Finger	995.00
Store, Machine, Arcade, Exhibit Model, Card Vendor	650.00
Store, Machine, Arcade, Harvard 5 Cent Medallion Stamper	1500.00
Store, Machine, Arcade, Iron Mutoscope	1295.00
Store, Machine, Arcade, Medallion Stamper, Harvard, 5 Cent Slot	1500.00
Store, Machine, Arcade, Mercury Grip, Floor Model	100.00
Store, Machine, Arcade, Penny Slot, 30 Photos Of Movie Stars	250.00
Store, Machine, Arcade, Tin Mutoscope	450.00
Store, Machine, Bingo, 1 Cent Slot, 1930s	90.00
Store, Machine, Bookmatch Vendor, Two For 1 Cent Decal, C.1930s	100.00
Store, Machine, Caille, Five Cent Slot, 1935	295.00
Store, Machine, Challenger Shooting Gallery, Coin Operated	125.00
Store, Machine, Coin-Operated, Gypsy Palm Card Reader, Oak, 72 X 18 In.	675.00
Store, Machine, Coontown Shooting Gallery, C.1900	65.00
Store, Machine, Cretor's 1906 Popcorn Wagon, Restored	6500.00
Store, Machine, Cretor's 1922 Sidewalk Popcorn & Peanut Booth, 10 X 3 Ft.	6500.00
Store, Machine, Dale Jet Gun, 5 Cent Slot, 6 Ft.	125.00
Store, Machine, Deuces Wild, Walnut Cabinet, Colorful Poker, C.1930s	350.00
Store, Machine, Digger, Exhibit Supply, With Ship	650.00
Store, Machine, Dr.Scholl's Arch Fitting	20.00
Store, Machine, Drop 10 Cent In Slot For Zeno Collar Button *Illus*	500.00
Store, Machine, Fortune & Weight, 4 Lucky Slot, Mechanical	245.00
Store, Machine, Fortune Telling, Peerless, Grandma	600.00
Store, Machine, Gambling, Evans, Dice Wheel, 15 1/2 In.	195.00

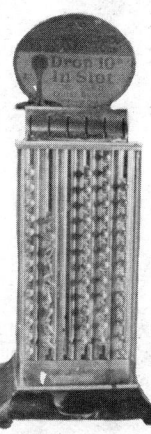

Store, Machine, Drop 10 Cent In Slot For Zeno Collar Button

Store, Machine, Gambling, Four Jacks, Front Has 4 Jackpots	250.00
Store, Machine, Gambling, Wizard Token Payout Clock	975.00
Store, Machine, Game, Pollard Penny Arcade Race, Natives Climbing Trees	950.00
Store, Machine, Genco Fortune Teller, Gypsy Woman, Crystal Ball, 6 Ft.	400.00
Store, Machine, Girly, On Stand, Coin Operated	150.00
Store, Machine, Gum Ball & 5 Reel Poker, ACE, Miniature, Coin Operated	300.00
Store, Machine, Gum Ball, A.B.C., Coin Operated, Cast Iron & Plexiglass	200.00
Store, Machine, Gum Ball, Automatic Clerk, 5 Cent Slot	300.00
Store, Machine, Gum Ball, Black Baker Boy, Manikin Vendor Co.	1300.00
Store, Machine, Gum Ball, Cigarette Reels, IMP Miniature	200.00
Store, Machine, Gum Ball, Columbus, Star Imprint, 1925	85.00
Store, Machine, Gum Ball, Daval 21, Hold And Draw Blackjack, C.1930s	350.00
Store, Machine, Gum Ball, Daval, 5 Cent Slot, Awards Free Games	165.00
Store, Machine, Gum Ball, Football, CVI, Multi-Vendor	135.00
Store, Machine, Gum Ball, Ford, Glass Dome, Ford Logo & Decals, C.1916	200.00
Store, Machine, Gum Ball, Gambling, Ad-Lee, Cast Iron	90.00
Store, Machine, Gum Ball, Shooting Gallery, Penny From Gun Shoots Ducks	150.00
Store, Machine, Gum Ball, What Will You Be, Drops Into Window, Fortune, Coin	575.00
Store, Machine, Gum, Chlorophyll, Victor, Wooden	30.00
Store, Machine, Gum, Dial Flavor, Flat	20.00
Store, Machine, Gum, Glass, Automatic Clerk, 5 Cent Slot	300.00
Store, Machine, Gum, National Self-Service Gum & Mints, 6 Slots, 8 X 15 In.	85.00
Store, Machine, Gum, Policeman Inside, Pulver	175.00
Store, Machine, Gum, Wooden Case, Pulver	135.00
Store, Machine, Hershey's Chocolate, Coin Operated, 1930s	150.00
Store, Machine, Hit A Homer, Nickel Drop, Baseball Background	200.00
Store, Machine, Holly Grip Tester, Stand	125.00
Store, Machine, I Never Lose, Penny Drop, 1930s	125.00
Store, Machine, Imperial Puritan, Cash Register Shape, Gargoyles, Marque, Coin	1200.00
Store, Machine, Jigger Pinball, Walnut Counter Model, Coin Operated	400.00
Store, Machine, Kingrey Popcorn Wagon, 1900-1910, Original Condition	6000.00
Store, Machine, Kola-Pepsin Gum & Chocolate, Pulver	500.00
Store, Machine, Little Perfection, Quartered Oak, Iron, Coin Operated	975.00
Store, Machine, Matchbox Vendor, Rosebud Decal, Iron, Metal, Coin Operated	150.00
Store, Machine, Matchbox Vendor, 4 Column, Iron & Oak, Coin Operated	375.00
Store, Machine, Mills, Oak, Drop Card On Legs	650.00
Store, Machine, Mills, One Cent Slot	295.00
Store, Machine, Mills, Slot, Gooseneck	900.00
Store, Machine, Mills, 5 Cent Puritan Trade Stimulator	450.00
Store, Machine, Mints, Side Vendor, Aluminum With All Quality Mints On Flag	200.00
Store, Machine, Movie, Mickey Mouse & Donald Duck, Ten Cent Clot	195.00

Store, Machine, The Best 5 Cent Cigar

Store, Machine, Zeno Chewing Gum, Drop One Cent In Slot

Store, Machine, Mutoscope With Stand	235.00
Store, Machine, Over The Top, Pinball, World War I Theme, 3 Solonoid Kickers	500.00
Store, Machine, Peanut, Northwestern, Porcelain Cover & Base, One Cent Slot	50.00
Store, Machine, Pencil Vendor & Engraver, Cast Iron, 5 Cent Slot, C.1925	550.00
Store, Machine, Photoscope On Stand	250.00
Store, Machine, Pill, Walnut & Brass, 2-Piece, 7 1/2 X 12 In.	65.00
Store, Machine, Pinball, Gottlieb, Baffle Ball	225.00
Store, Machine, Pinball, Gottlieb, Spot Pool	160.00
Store, Machine, Pinball, Rockola World's Fair Jigsaw	400.00
Store, Machine, Pinball, Skyrocket, Wooden Rail	200.00
Store, Machine, Pinball, Three Deuces, Wooden Rail	300.00
Store, Machine, Pulver Kola Pepsin Gum & Chocolate Machine	500.00
Store, Machine, Puritan Baby Vender, Buckley Mfg.Co., Penny, Working	215.00
Store, Machine, Puritan Trade Stimulator, 5 Cent Slot	450.00
Store, Machine, Race Around The World, Mutoscope, Oak, 6 Ft.9 In.	1500.00
Store, Machine, Scale, Mills Standard, One Cent Slot	275.00
Store, Machine, Shock, Advance Manufacturing, C.1916, Coin Operated	375.00
Store, Machine, Side Vendor, Early Slot, Gum On Front, Iron, Coin Operated	500.00
Store, Machine, Slot, Brown Cherry, Starburst Design, Golden Oak Sides, 1937	750.00
Store, Machine, Slot, Mills Novelty Co., 1910	375.00
Store, Machine, Slot, Watling	450.00
Store, Machine, Stamp Vendor, Visible Mechanism, Glass Sides, Coin Operated	300.00
Store, Machine, Stamp, Shaped Like Ships Telegraph, Anderson Die Co., Iron	350.00
Store, Machine, Target Practice, Penny Drop, Nickeled Cast Iron, C.1910	875.00
Store, Machine, The Best 5 Cent Cigar .... *Illus*	1750.00
Store, Machine, Titan Gumball, 38 In.	125.00
Store, Machine, Vending, Hot Nut, Standard, 5 Cent, Red Glass Dome Like Peanut	68.00
Store, Machine, Vending, Peanut, Red Top, Light-Up, Nation Wide Vending Co.	65.00
Store, Machine, Vending, Spin It Horse Race, Boston Baked Bean, 5 Cent Slot	125.00
Store, Machine, Vendor, Spin It, Horse Race, Nickel Slot	85.00
Store, Machine, Vest Pocket Basketball, Cast Marque, Coin Operated, 1930s	375.00
Store, Machine, Vikinor Hot Nut Vendor, Side Vendor For Cups, Coin Operated	150.00
Store, Machine, Whiting Sculptoscope, Improved Trigger Model, Coin Operated	500.00
Store, Machine, Whiting Sculptoscope, 2 Views, Instruction Card, Iron, Metal	475.00
Store, Machine, World Series, Pinball, Revolving Bases, Scores, Coin Operated	750.00
Store, Machine, Zeno Chewing Gum, Drop One Cent In Slot .... *Illus*	425.00
Store, Machine, 1920 Cretor's Theatre Upright Popcorn & Peanut Machine	1200.00
Store, Mail Box, U.S.Post Office, 36 Pigeon Holes, 56 X 23 In.	575.00

Store, Marking Machine, Ticket, Jr.Monarch 100.00
Store, Match Holder, DeLaval, Tin 45.00
Store, Match Holder, Figural, Hat, Rosebuds, Striker At Base 12.00
Store, Match Holder, Juicy Fruit Gum 32.00
Store, Match Holder, Sharples Separator, Woman Holding Separator, Tin 90.00
Store, Match Holder, Snowflake Bread 20.00
Store, Match Holder, Victor Coffee 10.00
Store, Match Safe, Anheuser-Busch, Dated 1899, Eagle Logo, St.Louis, Mo. 37.50
Store, Match Safe, Hercules Powder, Celluloid Cover 35.00
Store, Match Safe, Inland Printing Co., Spokane, Wash., Celluloid Cover 35.00
Store, Match Safe, United Brewery Workmen Against Prohibition 35.00
Store, Measure, Grain, Half-Moon Shape, Wooden, 15 X 7 1/2 X 1 In. 30.00
Store, Mirror With Thermometer, John Deere, 8 X 9 In. 35.00
Store, Mirror, Advertising, 1920s Girl In Hillcrest Coat 23.00
Store, Mirror, Andy Gump For President 15.00
Store, Mirror, Angelus Marshmallows, 2 Cherubs, Pocket 25.00
Store, Mirror, Anheuser-Busch Ginger Ale 26.00
Store, Mirror, Becky's Flower Shop, Frankfort, Kentucky 8.50
Store, Mirror, Berry Brothers Toy Wagon, Dog Pulling Children 55.00
Store, Mirror, Buster Brown, Tige, Shoes 65.00
Store, Mirror, Calox 12.50
Store, Mirror, Carmen Complexion Powder 17.00
Store, Mirror, Cascarets Laxative, Angel Sitting On Pot 28.00
Store, Mirror, Cracker Jack 22.00
Store, Mirror, Dentist, Miniature, For Looking Into Mouth, Marked 4.00
Store, Mirror, Diamond Saw Stamping Works, 2 In.Diameter 12.50
Store, Mirror, Dockash Stoves 12.50
Store, Mirror, Dutch-Java Coffee, Dutch Boy & Girl Kissing 35.00
Store, Mirror, Face With Nature's Remedy Tablet On Tongue 28.50
Store, Mirror, Garland Stoves & Ranges, The World's Best, 1 3/4 In. 17.50
Store, Mirror, Gooch's Sarsaparilla For Blood & Liver, Wood Frame, 15 In. ... 125.00
Store, Mirror, Holeproof Hosiery 12.50
Store, Mirror, Horse, White Horse Whiskey, Ceramic 22.50
Store, Mirror, Kist Beverage, Red Kissed, 12 In. 25.00
Store, Mirror, Knights & Ladies Of Security Insurance 10.00
Store, Mirror, La Compagnie Paquet Limitee, Quebec, Cadeau De Santa Claus ... 30.00
Store, Mirror, Mascot Tobacco 18.00
Store, Mirror, Mascot Tobacco, Bulldog 12.00
Store, Mirror, Maude Hillman Co., Traveling Theatrical Troupe 12.00
Store, Mirror, Mennen's Violet Talcum Toilet Powder, Violets & Trade Mark ... 14.00
Store, Mirror, Nash Automobile, 6 X 11 In. 10.00
Store, Mirror, Nude Girl Trying On Brotherhood Overalls 65.00
Store, Mirror, Old Reliable Coffee 15.00
Store, Mirror, Pocket, Continental Cubes 45.00
Store, Mirror, Queen Quality Shoes, Victorian In Long White Dress 28.00
Store, Mirror, Red Seal Lye Soap 12.00
Store, Mirror, Rhodes Casino, R.I. 5.00
Store, Mirror, Sailor Boy On Burning Deck, Good Mother's Bread, 1910 ...... 45.00
Store, Mirror, San Pedro Cigars, Victorian Brunette 28.00
Store, Mirror, Security Life Insurance 23.50
Store, Mirror, Southern Bell 3.50
Store, Mirror, Spiegel's Ice Cream, Devil Picture 45.00
Store, Mirror, Standard Oil Co. 16.50
Store, Mirror, Style Shoe Shop, Beautiful Blonde 28.00
Store, Mirror, Terre Haute Brewing Co., Nude, Arm Around Bottle 75.00
Store, Mirror, Union Made Cigars 15.00
Store, Mirror, United Motors, Shows Car 11.00
Store, Mirror, Young-Love Elevator, Old Grain Elevator 13.50
    Store, Mold, see also Pewter, Mold; Tin, Mold
Store, Mold, Butter, Wood, Swan 50.00
Store, Mold, Candy, Bride & Groom 45.00
Store, Mold, Candy, Chicken 20.00
Store, Mold, Candy, Lamb 20.00
Store, Mold, Candy, Rabbit & Cart 20.00

Store, Mold, Candy, Rabbits 24.00
Store, Mold, Candy, Sitting Rabbit .... 15.00 To 20.00
Store, Mold, Candy, Swan 25.00
Store, Mold, Candy, Turkey 20.00
Store, Mold, Chocolate, Bugs Bunnies, Set Of 3 .... 24.00
Store, Mold, Hat, Hardwood 14.00
    Store, Mold, Ice Cream, see Pewter, Mold, Ice Cream
Store, Mold, Ice Cream, Apple, Pewter, 2 1/2 In. 30.00
Store, Mold, Iron 45.00
Store, Mold, Lead Soldiers, 2 Part, Cast Iron, Marching Cadets, 3 1/4 In. 45.00
Store, Mold, Soap, Plunger Type, Wooden 18.00
Store, Money Changer, Brandt Automatic Cashier, Pat.1921 .... 135.00
Store, Money Clip, 2-Blade Knife, Standard Milling Co., Boy Fishing 14.00
Store, Mortar & Pestle, Cast Iron, Urn Shape, Footed, 5 3/4 In. 39.00
Store, Mortar & Pestle, Glass, 8 Oz. 20.00
Store, Mortar & Pestle, Porcelain, Shallow, Pouring Lip, 9 In. 25.00
Store, Mug, Baby's, Planter's Peanuts, Silver Plate 35.00
Store, Mug, Brown Pottery, Bovox Makes Real Strength, 4 In. 19.00
Store, Mug, Buckeye Root Beer 15.00
Store, Mug, Child's, Uncle Wiggily Wants His Ovaltine, 1924 .... 48.00
Store, Mug, Cream Of Wheat, Rastus, 1930s 25.00
Store, Mug, Drink Hires Root Beer, Child In Color Under Glaze 60.00
Store, Mug, Glass, Pinch Waist, Moxie, 5 1/4 In. 18.00
Store, Mug, Ovaltine, Uncle Wiggily 22.00
Store, Mug, Root Beer, Men Drinking 35.00
Store, Mug, Tivoli Brewing Co., Copper, Brass Handle 15.00
Store, Mug, Today I Am A Little Dear, Today I Am A Little Stinker Obverse 45.00
Store, Mug, XXX Root Beer 5.00
Store, Nut Set, Lithograph, Mr.Peanut, Tin, 5 Piece 16.00
Store, Nut Set, 5 Pieces, Mr.Peanut 6.50
Store, Oil, Vinegar, Salt & Pepper, Ceramic, Aunt Jemima 14.00
Store, Opener, Bottle, Apollo Beer, Rochester, N.Y. 4.00
Store, Opener, Bottle, Blatz Beer, Wooden, Bottle Shaped 10.00
Store, Opener, Bottle, Brass, Nude Girl, 4 3/8 In. 18.00
Store, Opener, Bottle, Coors Steel 4.00
Store, Opener, Bottle, Drunk With Top Hat & Tails 10.00
Store, Opener, Bottle, Figural, Leg, Gay-Ola 7.50
Store, Opener, Bottle, Figurine Holding Guitar 6.00
Store, Opener, Bottle, Golden Glow Beer 4.00
Store, Opener, Bottle, Muelbach 2.00
Store, Opener, Bottle, Nudes, Utica Club 7.00
Store, Opener, Bottle, Old Crow Whiskey, Bottle Shape 9.00
Store, Opener, Bottle, Peerless, Wood Handle 3.50
Store, Opener, Bottle, Rooster Head, Cast Iron, 5 In. 15.00
Store, Opener, Bottle, Shape Of Boot, Miami, Arizona 10.00
Store, Opener, Bottle, White Rock 7.00
Store, Opener, Bottle, Wild Animals, Bengal Tiger Charging, Benson's Farm 2.00
Store, Opener, Bottle, Wood, Bottle Shape, Fehrs 9.00
Store, Opener, Can, Wall, Dazey 25.00
Store, Opener, Can, Wood Handle 3.00
Store, Opener, Letter, Carved Handle, One Handle Is Plain, 8 In., Pair 10.00
Store, Opener, Letter, Uneeda Biscuit 7.50
Store, Opener, Transom, Maple Handle, Brass Window Hook, Shaker, 35 1/2 In. 22.50
Store, Package, Cardboard, Tower Brand Powdered Rosin, Yellow & Black Label 7.00
Store, Package, Yellow Lily Root, Nuphar Advena, Apothecarist's 4.00
Store, Paddle, Rolling Butter Into Balls, Pair 12.50
Store, Pail, American Royal, Kansas City, 1/2 Gallon 7.50
Store, Pail, Berry, Penobscot Indian, Bark 145.00
Store, Pail, Big Sister Peanut Butter, Witches 50.00
Store, Pail, Blue, Purity Brand Sugar Butter, 3 3/4 X 4 1/2 In. 22.00
Store, Pail, Blue Sultana Peanut Butter, Super Size 45.00
Store, Pail, Buffalo Brand Peanut Butter 15.00
Store, Pail, Buffalo Peanut Butter .... 25.00 To 38.00

Store, **Pail,** Credo Peanut Butter, 1 Lb. 12.00
Store, **Pail,** F.F.Adams & Co., Milwaukee, Tobacco, 1943 Stamp, Paper Label 12.00
Store, **Pail,** Finest Peanut Butter 10.00
Store, **Pail,** Golden Rod Coffee 20.00
Store, **Pail,** Home Comfort Tobacco 22.50
Store, **Pail,** Home Rendered Lard, Mann's, Freeport, Illinois, 10 Pound 16.00
Store, **Pail,** Honey, Bees, Roses, 6 In. 4.50
Store, **Pail,** Jackie Coogan Kid Kandy, Cop Chasing Kid, 3 1/2 In. 85.00
Store, **Pail,** Jones, Pure Lard, Ft.Atkinson, Wisconsin, 4 Pound 16.00
Store, **Pail,** Mayo's Milk 115.00
Store, **Pail,** Monadnock Peanut Butter 45.00
Store, **Pail,** Monarch Peanut Butter 20.00
Store, **Pail,** Monarch Teenie Weenie Peanut Butter, 1926 .... 60.00
Store, **Pail,** Monkey On Lid, Recipes On Backschepp's Coconut, 1 Pound 60.00
Store, **Pail,** Morning Glory Coffee, 5 X 4 In. 30.00
Store, **Pail,** Mosemann's, Cartoon Characters, Peanut Butter 25.00
Store, **Pail,** Naphey's Lard, 1876, 2 In. 20.00
Store, **Pail,** Nigger Hair 75.00
Store, **Pail,** Ontario Peanut Butter .... 10.00 To 55.00
Store, **Pail,** Oscar Meyer, Pure Pork Sausage, Lard, Gold, Blue, 5 Pound 16.00
Store, **Pail,** Ox Heart Peanut Butter 45.00
Store, **Pail,** Patterson's Seal Cut Plug, Basket Weave, Tobacco 18.00
Store, **Pail,** Pickanninny Brand Peanut Butter, 1 Pound 20.00
Store, **Pail,** Queen Of Hearts Candy 65.00
Store, **Pail,** Shield, Pure Lard, Silver & Blue, Armour & Co., 4 Pound 16.00
Store, **Pail,** Squirrel Peanut Butter, 10 Lb. 50.00
Store, **Pail,** Sultana Peanut Butter, Tin 8.50
Store, **Pail,** Swift's Selected Pork Chops, Tin, Bail Handle 12.50
Store, **Pail,** Tobacco, Blue Tiger, Tiger Face On Each End 62.00
Store, **Pail,** Toyland Peanut Butter, Tin, 2 Pound 15.00
Store, **Pail,** Union Leader, Gold Letters, Red, Tobacco 32.00
Store, **Paper Clip,** Copper, Keystone Elevator Grain Company 14.00
Store, **Paperweight, see Paperweight**
Store, **Pen & Pencil,** Swan, 14K 200.00
Store, **Pen,** Dip, Sterling Silver Overlay, Place For Initial, Waterman's 45.00
Store, **Pen,** Glass, Oakland Jordan Marmon Autos 15.00
Store, **Pen,** Ivory Handle 27.50
Store, **Pen,** Pearl Handle 27.50
Store, **Pen,** Pencil, 14K Gold, Velour Lined Leather Case, Sheaffer, 5 In. 75.00
Store, **Pencil,** Mechanical, Planters Peanuts 6.00
Store, **Pencil,** Mr.Peanut Floating In Water On Top, Mechanical 6.50
Store, **Penknife,** Drink Pepsi-Cola, 5 Cents 25.00
Store, **Pennant,** Planter's Brand Salted Peanuts, C.1909, 10 X 16 In. 32.00
Store, **Pennant,** Theodora Cigars, Felt 15.00
Store, **Pin,** Gene Autry, Sunbeam Bread 3.00
Store, **Pin,** Heinz Pickle 2.00
Store, **Pin,** Lapel, John Dough, Raised On Fleischmann's Yeast, Oval 6.50
Store, **Pin,** Mr.Peanut, Plastic, 1 1/2 In. 50.00
Store, **Pin,** Tray, Compliments Montgomery Ward Co., Tin 18.50
Store, **Pin,** Tray, 2 Long Feathered Birds 7.00
Store, **Pin,** Wichita Port Huron Thresher Co.Best Machinery, Shock Wheat 18.50
Store, **Pipeholder,** Tin Clay 5.00
Store, **Pitcher,** Canadian Club, White, Woman Holding Bottle 8.00
Store, **Pitcher,** Flow Blue, Crawford Cooking Ranges, Small 75.00
Store, **Pitcher,** Hiram Walker's Ten High, White, McCoy 10.00
Store, **Pitcher,** Johnnie Walker Black Label Scotch Whiskey 6.50
Store, **Pitcher,** Walker's Deluxe Bourbon, Gray, 1931 Cord On Front 8.00
Store, **Pitcher,** Water, Seagram 7 Crown 4.00
Store, **Pitcher,** Wing Saffron Ware, Advertising 35.00
Store, **Pitcher,** 4 Steins, Khorassan, Leisy Brewery Co. 300.00
Store, **Plaque,** Goodyear, Zeppelin, Factory, 10 Years Friendly Relations, 1931 .... 95.00
Store, **Plaque,** Sailing Schooner, Sunshine Biscuits, 12 1/2 In. 10.00
Store, **Plate,** Beard Furniture, Pawtucket, R.I., Roses, Tin 15.00

Store, Plate, Borden's Dairy, Elsie The Cow	8.00
Store, Plate, C.D.Kenny, Santa	47.50
Store, Plate, Carnival Glass, Grape & Cable, Green, Advertisement On Back	135.00
Store, Plate, Child's, C.G.McMillen, Pickering, Mo., Dutch Girl	16.00
Store, Plate, Coors, Thermo-Porcelain, 9 3/4 In.	8.00
Store, Plate, Cushman Furniture Co., Attleboro, Mass, Flow Blue, States, 9 In.	45.00
Store, Plate, Fred Krug Brewing Co., 50th Anniversary, 1859-1909	95.00
Store, Plate, Pioneer Flour, Elf Hand-Painted, 1927	25.00
Store, Platter, Picture Of Turkey, West Memphis, Ark.	15.00
Store, Pole, Barber, Leaded Glass & Porcelain, Koken, 32 In.	450.00
Store, Pole, Barber, Wood, Red, White, Blue, 7 Ft.	1000.00
Store, Polish, Metal, G.W.Hoffman U.S.	2.00
Store, Polish, Shoe, Howdy Doody	8.50
Store, Post Office Front, Cashier Window, 36 Letter Boxes Each Side, Oak	450.00
Store, Post Office, Oak, Complete, 7 Feet X 8 In. X 47 In.	625.00
Store, Post Office, 120 Bronze Doors, 3 Feet, 9 In. X 4 Feet, 6 In.	465.00
Store, Post Office, 50 Boxes, All Wood, Double Combination Doors	275.00
Store, Poster, Ammunition, Winchester, Lady Hunter, 1915	300.00
Store, Poster, Barnum & Bailey Circus, Famous Founders Of Greatest Show	95.00
Store, Poster, Bugler Cigarette Tobacco, 16 1/2 X 15 In.	20.00
Store, Poster, Catcher Rough Cut Tobacco, 19 X 14 In.	20.00
Store, Poster, Circus, Barnum & Bailey French Tour Of 1900, 20 X 30 In.	100.00
Store, Poster, Circus, Elephant, , 1940, 6 1/2 Feet High X 10 1/2 Feet Wide	40.00
Store, Poster, Circus, Rhinoceros, 1940, 6 1/2 Feet High X 10 1/2 Feet Wide	40.00
Store, Poster, Eberhardt & Obert, Shows Brewery In Allegheny, Pennsylvania	350.00
Store, Poster, English, Carnival, English, 1940, 30 X 40 In.	25.00
Store, Poster, Farm Auction, 1885	15.00
Store, Poster, Golden Grain Burley Blend Tobacco, 20 X 14 In.	20.00
Store, Poster, Heinz Spaghetti, Chef With Can, 11 X 21 In.	38.00
Store, Poster, Hercules Powder, Metal Rims, C.1918, 26 X 20 In.	125.00
Store, Poster, Humphrey Bogart, Morgan Lithograph, 1930, 27 X 41 In.	45.00
Store, Poster, Kool, 15 Cent Pack, 10 X 15 In.	12.00
Store, Poster, Men Wanted, Recruiting, 1897, 40 X 30 In.	80.00
Store, Poster, Movie, The Bad One, Starring Dolores Del Rio, 1930	30.00
Store, Poster, Post Toasties Tin String Holder, C.1920	95.00
Store, Poster, Quick Shot, King Powder Co., Slain Duck Falling, 1880s	275.00
Store, Poster, Red Indian Cut Plug Tobacco, Indian, C.1900, 22 X 28 In.	125.00
Store, Poster, Sante Fe, Olympic Games Of 1932, Los Angeles, Indians Running	85.00
Store, Poster, Smoke Avalon, 18 X 12 In.	12.00
Store, Poster, Winchester Arms, 1904, Hunter With 1895 Carbine, 16 X 19 In.	85.00
Store, Pot Holder, Wall, Figural, Negro Aunt Jemima	4.00
Store, Pot, Bean, Brown & Cream Stoneware, Miniature, Heinz, 1/2 Pint	6.50
Store, Pot, Mustard, Colonial, Curved Shaped Handle, 3 1/2 X 2 1/2 In.	15.00
Store, Press, Cork, Enterprise	65.00
Store, Print, Fairy Soap Advertising, Fairy Tales, 1897	55.00
Store, Prize Wheel Barrow, Cracker Jack, Tin	17.00
Store, Punch Board, Shirley Temple, Little Colonel Doll Prize Picture	24.00
Store, Puzzle, Angelus Campfire Marshmallows, 1930s, 6 3/4 X 9 3/4 In.	34.00
Store, Puzzle, Kellogg's, Lithograph On Wood, Cut Out Edges, Heinz	50.00
Store, Puzzle, Valley City Milling Company, C.1870, 16 1/2 X 10 1/2 In.	15.00
Store, Puzzle, Victor Talking Machine, Record, Stars	35.00
Store, Rack, Display, Candy, Necco, 5 Cent	45.00
Store, Rack, Display, National Biscuit Co., Oak, 4 Shelf, Large	325.00
Store, Rack, Folds, Tin & Wire Prongs, Queen Anne Fresh Nuts, 5 Cents, 16 In.	25.00
Store, Rack, Meat, Carved Snowflake Motif On Front, 9 Handwrought Hooks, Pine	87.00
Store, Rattle, Baby's, Manru Coffee Can, Tin	10.00
Store, Razor Hone, Diamond King, Case	17.50
Store, Razor, Brass, Durham	2.50
Store, Razor, Brass, Eveready	3.00
Store, Razor, Hone, Keen Kutter, Original Tin Case	7.50
Store, Razor, Straight Edge	12.00
Store, Razor, Straight Edge, Red Imp	15.00
Store, Razor, Straight, Art Noveau Design, Ivory Handle, Head Of Girl	12.95
Store, Razor, Straight, Black Handle, Busts Of Washington & Jefferson	9.95

Store, Razor, Straight, Miniature, Steel, White Plastic Handle, 1 1/4 To 2 In.	12.50
Store, Razor, Straight, Queen 1865	8.00
Store, Razor, Straight, Sheffield, Corn Razor	7.00
Store, Razor, Straight, Simmons Hardware	3.50
Store, Razor, 1893 Columbian Exposition, In Case	35.00
Store, Reamer, Custard, Sunkist	35.00
Store, Reamer, Opaque, Yellow, Green	12.00
Store, Receiver, Card, Victorian, Girl, Cornucopia, Holds 3 Water Lilies	115.00
Store, Register, Account, Wood, Brass Trim, Stenciling, McCaskey	65.00
Store, Ring, Child's, Advertising American Airlines, Brass	7.50
Store, Roller, Cigarette, Axton Fisher Tobacco Co., Pat.1919	12.00
Store, Ruler, Eat Luxury Bread	2.00
Store, Ruler, German Coal Heater, Wooden	5.00
Store, Ruler, Wooden, Planters Five Cent Bag	3.50
Store, Ruler, Zeno Advertisement, 12 In.	4.00
Store, Sack, Flour, Mark Twain, 1920s, 24 X 13 In.	10.00
Store, Sack, Sunshine Flour, Cloth	2.00
Store, Salt & Pepper, Aunt Jemima & Mose	7.00
Store, Salt & Pepper, Aunt Jemima, 3 1/2 In.	2.00
Store, Salt & Pepper, Budweiser Beer, Amber, Beer Bottle Shape, 4 In.	5.50
Store, Salt & Pepper, Campbell Kids	12.00
Store, Salt & Pepper, Coors Beer, 3 1/2 In.	5.00
Store, Salt & Pepper, Felix The Cat	25.00
Store, Salt & Pepper, G.E.Refrigerator	13.00
Store, Salt & Pepper, Greyhound Bus	7.00
Store, Salt & Pepper, His Master's Voice, Dogs	9.00 To 12.00
Store, Salt & Pepper, Mr.Peanut, Plastic	4.00
Store, Sausage Press, Enterprise No.25, Cast Iron, Table Model, 18 In.	60.00
Store, Scissors, Sewing, Stork Figural Handle	7.00
Store, Scissors, Wick Trimming, Kerosene Lamp Wick	12.50
Store, Scoop, Cranberry, Small	55.00
Store, Scoop, Ice Cream, Cone Shape, All Metal	12.00
Store, Scoop, Ice Cream, Cone Shape, Brass	16.00
Store, Scoop, Lyons Best Flour, Tin	10.00
Store, Scoop, Melon Ball, Wood Handle	2.00
Store, Scoop, Metal, Large	3.50
Store, Scoop, Penny Candy, Aluminum, Germany	6.00
Store, Scraper, Foam, Rogers Williams Brewing Co.	18.00
Store, Scraper, Tin, Sharples Tubular Cream Separator, Beautiful Lady	16.00
Store, Seal, Wax, Black Handle, R	6.00
Store, Seed Spreader, Hang Over Chest, Turn Handle	17.00
Store, Seeder, Rest Metal Against Tummy, Fill Bag, Turn Crank, Seeds Come Out	28.00
Store, Separator, Cream, Tubular, Separator Stick	24.50
Store, Shaker, Alice-In-Wonderland's Tweedledum, C.1950, Marked, 5 In.	15.00
Store, Sharpener, Knife, Brass Fittings, Floor Model, Kent Co., London	325.00
Store, Sharpener, Lead Pencil, Shape Of A Zeppelin, Green Paint	25.00
Store, Sharpener, Lead Pencil, Walter Baker, Lady With Booklet	300.00
Store, Sharpener, Pencil, Alarm Clock	16.00
Store, Sharpener, Pencil, Baker's Chocolates, Chocolate Lady, 2 In.	11.00
Store, Sharpener, Razor Blade, Red Glass	6.00
Store, Sharpener, Scissors, Diamond Cutlery Co.	2.50
Store, Sharpener, Spee-D-Hone, Curtiss Candy Co., Sharpens Double Edge Razor	5.00
Store, Shaver, Soap, Make Your Own Fels Naptha Soap Chips	10.00
Store, Shoe, Button-Up, Child	15.00
Store, Shoe, Hi-Button, Southern Girl	35.00
Store, Shoe, Wooden, Heineken Beer	6.00
Store, Shot Glass, Whiskey, From West Coast, Set Of 100	2000.00
Store, Shuttle, Tatting, Lydia Pinkham, Celluloid	16.00
Store, Sieve, Miniature, Bentwood, Double Screen, C.1850, 5 1/2 In.	22.50
Store, Sign, A.B.C.Bohemian Beer, St.Louis, Bulldog, Tin, 22 X 18 In.	265.00
Store, Sign, A.N.P.Marshmallows, Oval, Tin, 3 1/2 X 4 3/4 In.	5.00
Store, Sign, Adams Tutti Frutti Gum, Lady On Grass, Paper Under Glass, 1900	450.00
Store, Sign, American Express Company, 2 Sided, Right Angled, C.1900	50.00
Store, Sign, Amos-N-Andy On Rexall, Tin, C.1930, 34 X 16 In.	75.00

Store, Sign, Aranac Ginger Ale, Tin, 1920s, 6 X 11 In. 10.00
Store, Sign, Armour Star Ham, Tin, 16 X 24 In. .... *Illus* 150.00
Store, Sign, Baby Ruth Gum, Tin, Embossed, C.1930, 26 X 10 In. 35.00
Store, Sign, Baker's Chocolate, La Belle Chocolatiere, Tin 400.00
Store, Sign, Baltimore Star, Tin, 1930s, 10 X 13 In. 8.00
Store, Sign, Barber, Curved Enamel, 14 1/2 X 27 In. 22.50
Store, Sign, Barber, Williams Shaving Soap, Barber Shaving Man, 21 X 26 In. 175.00
Store, Sign, Barbershop, Porcelain, Red, White, & Blue, 21 X 12 In. 58.00
Store, Sign, Beer, Shape Of Bottle, Old Colony Brewing Co. 38.00
Store, Sign, Beer, Wine & Iron, Bottle, Stands On Wood Legs 125.00
Store, Sign, Beeswing Gold Leaf Cavendish Tobacco, Tin, 3 X 4 1/2 In. 12.50
Store, Sign, Ben Hur Cigars, Roman Chariot Race, Tin, C.1900, 19 X 27 In. 225.00
Store, Sign, Bengal Cigars, Paper Litho, C.1910, 31 X 17 In. 75.00
Store, Sign, Bevv The Beverage & The All Year Round Soft Drink, 6 X 10 In. 20.00
Store, Sign, Birchola Soda, Tin, 13 X 20 In. 10.00
Store, Sign, Birchola Soda, Tin, 9 1/2 X 28 In. 10.00
Store, Sign, Bire-Ley's, Cardboard, 1949, 19 X 33 In. 12.00
Store, Sign, Bire-Ley's, Tin, 1948, 14 X 36 In. 10.00
Store, Sign, Blatz Beer, Man With Beer Mug & Clock, Lights Up, Metal 35.00
Store, Sign, Boston Herald, Boy With Newspaper, Tin 24.00
Store, Sign, Brass, Simmons Liver Regulator Cure 32.50
Store, Sign, Brookfield Rye, Tin, C.1907, 32 X 23 In. 650.00
Store, Sign, Buckeye Beer, Tin, 1930s, 7 X 17 In. 40.00
Store, Sign, Budweiser Beer, Heavy Paper Poster, C.1926, 18 X 40 In. 25.00
Store, Sign, Budweiser, Custer's Last Fight, Cardboard, Self-Framed 55.00
Store, Sign, Budweiser, Custer's Last Fight, Tin, 45 X 35 In. 350.00
Store, Sign, Buffalo Brewery, Sacramento, California, Multicolor, 17 X 22 In. 3.50
Store, Sign, Buffalo Brewery, Still Life, Bottles, Tin, 28 X 22 In. 150.00
Store, Sign, Bull Of The Woods, Cardboard, 1930s, 18 X 12 In. 40.00
Store, Sign, Burke's Superior Ale, Thermometer In Center, Tin, 8 1/4 In. 22.50
Store, Sign, Buster Brown Bread, Wood Frame, Embossed Tin, C.1920, 22 X 30 In. 150.00
Store, Sign, Buster Brown Shoes, Buster & Tige, Plaster Of Paris 55.00
Store, Sign, Buster Brown, Tige, Advertising Bread, Tin, 20 X 27 In. 125.00
Store, Sign, Call For Philip Morris, Picture Of Johnny, Tin, 20 X 35 In. 38.50
Store, Sign, Carling's Beer, 9 Pints Of The Law, Cardboard .... 30.00 To 35.00
Store, Sign, Carling's, 9 Pints Of The Law, Tin .... 45.00 To 50.00
Store, Sign, Carnation Milk, Girl Holding Flowers, Tin, 14 1/2 X 17 1/2 In. 75.00
Store, Sign, Carter's Ink, Tin, Self-Framed, Kaufmann & Strauss Co., 1900 .... 325.00
Store, Sign, Cetacolor, Cloth, 1910, 25 X 36 In. 40.00
Store, Sign, Cherry Smash, Embossed, Tin, 9 1/4 X 5 In. 65.00
Store, Sign, Chesterfield, Thermometer, Tin, 5 3/4 X 13 1/2 In. 15.00
Store, Sign, Chief Paints, Tin, 1940s, 12 X 22 In. 12.00
Store, Sign, Cigars, Convex Glass Circles Spell Cigars, Electric, Metal 750.00
Store, Sign, Clabber Girl Baking Powder, Tin, C.1940s, 12 X 30 In. 12.00
Store, Sign, Clarion Ranges & Stoves, Tin, Embossed, 6 1/2 X 19 In. 48.00
Store, Sign, Cobbler's Front Door, Hand-Painted, C.1850, 14 X 20 In. 125.00
Store, Sign, Coleman's Mustard, Dog Paintings, Tin, 8 1/2 X 5 1/4 X 5 1/4 In. 45.00
Store, Sign, Cook's Beer, Self-Framed, Tin, 1930s, 17 X 13 In. 65.00
Store, Sign, Cook's Beer, Tin, C.1940, 14 X 27 In. 8.00
Store, Sign, Corner, Du Bois Beer, 1900s 225.00
Store, Sign, Cream Of Kentucky Whiskey, Paper Under Glass, Wood Frame, 1900 .... 175.00
Store, Sign, Crescent Watch Cases, Lettering 14 Gold, 14 X 20 In. 220.00
Store, Sign, Crosley Radio, Master Of Mass Production, 16 1/2 In. 65.00
Store, Sign, Crown Ice Cream, Tin, Embossed, C.1920, 32 X 23 In. 90.00
Store, Sign, Curved Porcelain, Crown Furnaces & Globe Ranges, 13 X 18 In. 95.00
Store, Sign, Dairy Made Ice Cream, Wood Framed Tin, 1920s, 32 X 27 In. 200.00
Store, Sign, Dead Stock, Embossed, Tin, 1930s, 10 X 13 In. 12.00
Store, Sign, DeLaval Cream Separators, Picture Milkmaid & Farm, Tin 400.00
Store, Sign, DeLaval, Mother, Child On Farm, Separator, Tin, 24 X 36 In. 285.00
Store, Sign, Devilish Good, Tin, 1910, 8 X 10 In. 45.00
Store, Sign, Diamant's Shoe Repair, Rangeley, Maine 700.00
Store, Sign, Diamond Cords, Paper Poster, C.1920, 29 X 25 In. 60.00
Store, Sign, Did You Say 10 Cents, Tobacco, 15 X 6 In. 25.00

Store, Sign, Armour Star Ham, Tin, 16 X 24 In.

Store, **Sign,** Double Orange, Signed Rolf Armstrong, Tin, 1930s, 21 X 21 In.	30.00
Store, **Sign,** Doughboy Prophylactic, Sanger Pro-Tek-Tubes, Prescription 10000	30.00
Store, **Sign,** Dr.Baxter's Mandrake Bitters Tabs, Tin, 3 X 2 In.	15.00
Store, **Sign,** Dr.Blumer's, Tin, 1915, 4 X 24 In.	12.00
Store, **Sign,** Dr.Draker's Cough Remedy, Tin, Child's Picture	100.00
Store, **Sign,** Drink Nehi Quality Beverages, Inner Gold Frame, 6 1/2 X 7 In.	7.50
Store, **Sign,** Du Bois Beer, Corner Vitrolite & Copper, C.1900	250.00
Store, **Sign,** Du Bois Budweiser, Tin, 1930s, 18 In.	25.00
Store, **Sign,** Du Pont Powder, Troopers Hunting Buffalo, 1900, 13 X 8 1/2 In.	55.00
Store, **Sign,** Du Pont Red Cross Dynamite, Tree Blowing Apart, 12 X 23 In.	160.00
Store, **Sign,** Du Pont Smokeless Shotgun Powder, Hunter, Dog, Game	125.00
Store, **Sign,** Du Pont, Generations Have Used Du Pont Gunpowder, 23 X 33 In.	235.00
Store, **Sign,** Ebbert Wagons, In Shade Of Apple Tree, 1906, Tin, 36 X 24 In.	125.00
Store, **Sign,** Egyptienne Straights Cigarette, Woman's Face, Red Ground, 17 In.	145.00
Store, **Sign,** Elgin Watch, Tom Sawyer Type Little Boy, 1889, Paper, Framed	275.00
Store, **Sign,** Elgin, Father Time Holding Elgin, 15 X 21 In.	55.00
Store, **Sign,** Ethyl Logo, Porcelain, 8 In.Diameter	12.00
Store, **Sign,** Everybody Loves To Get Kist, Tin	25.00
Store, **Sign,** F.W.Cook Beer, Steamboat Wharf Scene, Tin, 23 X 30 In.	50.00
Store, **Sign,** Fairy Soap, Maud Humphrey, Kitty's Bath Lithograph, 15 X 21 In.	100.00
Store, **Sign,** Falstaff Lamp, Medieval Scene, Round, 1910, 24 In.	250.00
Store, **Sign,** Falstaff Lamp, The Home Of Falstaff, Tin	125.00
Store, **Sign,** Faust Beer, Anheuser-Busch, Faust With Sword, St.Louis, 10 Cents	300.00
Store, **Sign,** Fehr Malt Tonic, Woman With Cherubs	260.00
Store, **Sign,** Figural, Sundae Glass, Wooden	100.00
Store, **Sign,** Fiske Tires, Framed, 1930s, 31 X 26 In.	100.00
Store, **Sign,** Fleischmann's, Wood Framed Tin, C.1910, 15 X 40 In.	150.00
Store, **Sign,** Four Brothers High Standard Paint, Tin & Porcelain, 2 Sided	27.50
Store, **Sign,** Free Sewing Machine, Embossed Tin, C.1920, 11 X 21 In.	125.00
Store, **Sign,** Frostie Root Beer, Bottle Cap Shape	17.50
Store, **Sign,** Frostie Root Beer, Tin, Round, 12 In.	15.00
Store, **Sign,** Gas While You Wait & Dr.Pepper Sold Here, Tin, 18 X 40 In.	55.00
Store, **Sign,** Gem Razors, Man & Baby Sitting On Razor, Tin	95.00
Store, **Sign,** Genesee Beer, Reverse On Glass, Framed, 13 X 17 In.	30.00
Store, **Sign,** German Laundry, 2-Sided Porcelain, 1920s, 10 X 21 In.	75.00
Store, **Sign,** Glass, Colored Waiting Room, N.C. & St.L.R.R., 9 X 31 In.	85.00
Store, **Sign,** Gluek, Milk Glass Corner Sign	275.00
Store, **Sign,** Gold Metal Flour, Oilcloth, C.1905, 28 X 41 In.	15.00
Store, **Sign,** Golden Wedding Whiskey, Men Drinking By Fireplace, Tin, C.1915	65.00
Store, **Sign,** Golden Wedding Whiskey, 2 Men At Hearth, Tin, 20 X 13 In.	50.00
Store, **Sign,** Goldyrock, Tin, 1930s, 10 X 20 In.	12.00
Store, **Sign,** Grant's Whiskey, Tin, C.1915, 13 X 10 In.	60.00
Store, **Sign,** Grape-Nuts, Girl, St.Bernard, Tin, Lithograph, 31 In. 350.00 To	525.00
Store, **Sign,** Grape-Ola, Tin, 1920s, 16 X 22 In.	60.00
Store, **Sign,** Green River Whiskey, Cardboard, Self-Framed, 19 X 24 In.	65.00
Store, **Sign,** Green River Whiskey, Negro, Horse, Cardboard, Framed, 1899, 32 In.	185.00
Store, **Sign,** Green River Whiskey, Tin, 21 X 31 In.	575.00
Store, **Sign,** Greyhound Bus, Colored Seated In Rear, 1929, 4 1/2 X 11 In.	50.00
Store, **Sign,** Greyhound Bus, Colored Seated In Rear, 5 X 4 3/4 In.	42.50
Store, **Sign,** Haberdasher's, Tin, Iron, Early 19th Century	650.00

Store, Sign, Have Your Hat Cleaned, Shoes Shined, Tin, 1920, 18 In. 225.00
Store, Sign, Helmar Tobacco, Porcelain, 1920s, 24 X 15 In. 120.00
Store, Sign, Henrietta Cigar, Tin, 9 X 13 1/2 In. 50.00
Store, Sign, Hi-Plane Tobacco, Single Engine Monoplane, Tin 45.00
Store, Sign, Highland Ale, Reverse On Glass 30.00
Store, Sign, Hoffman Brewing, Flowers & Beer Glass 25.00
Store, Sign, Houk Wire Wheel Co., Buffalo, N.Y., Canvas, Signed, WW1 Era 435.00
Store, Sign, Howard Furnaces, Curved Tin, Wood Corner, C.1920, 20 X 18 In. 60.00
Store, Sign, Hunt Clue Shoe, Tin, Large 95.00
Store, Sign, Illinois Watch Co., Railroad Brakeman, Oil Can, Looking At Watch 250.00
Store, Sign, Insurance Co., Reverse Painting, Gold Leaf Lettering, Framed 20.00
Store, Sign, J & P Coats, Cardboard, 24 X 18 In. 125.00
Store, Sign, J.I.Case Threshing Machine, Brass, 30 X 5 In. 60.00
Store, Sign, John Deere, Tractor, Cardboard, C.1920, 26 X 22 In. 60.00
Store, Sign, Karo, Corn Girl, Motto, Yellow, Blue, 11 3/4 X 23 1/4 In. 30.00
Store, Sign, Kayo, Chalk Board, Tin, 1930s, 26 X 13 In. .... 10.00 To 15.00
Store, Sign, Kelly Axe, Stagecoach, Dated 1881, S.W.Price, 23 X 17 In. 275.00
Store, Sign, Kemp's Root Beer, Tin, 1920s, 13 X 20 In. 18.00
Store, Sign, Kemp's, Root Beer, Tin, 1920s, 9 X 20 In. 15.00
Store, Sign, Kist Soda Blackboard 7.50
Store, Sign, Knox Gelatin, Mammy With White Child, Signed, Canvas, 1901 .... 50.00
Store, Sign, L & M Cigarettes, 1950, 12 X 17 1/2 In. .... 6.00 To 60.00
Store, Sign, La Preferencia Cigar, Paper Lithograph, Wood Frame, C.1910 .... 225.00
Store, Sign, Lion Lamp, Framed, 1900, 30 X 22 In. 125.00
Store, Sign, Lionel, A Lifetime Of Ralroading, Historic RR Scenes, 22 In. 35.00
Store, Sign, Loose Wiles Chocolates, Cutout Of 1900 Vassar Graduate, 36 In. 600.00
Store, Sign, Lowenbrau Beer, Man In Swiss Alps, 32 In. 20.00
Store, Sign, Lowney's Chocolates, Girl, 1905, Tin, Self-Framed, 15 X 19 In. 125.00
Store, Sign, Lucky Strike Cigarettes, C.1950, 15 In. 17.00
Store, Sign, Lucky Strike, Green, Cardboard, 28 X 36 In. 75.00
Store, Sign, Lucky Teter, C.1940, 42 X 26 In. 15.00
Store, Sign, Luxor Cigarette, Hootchy Kootchy Dancer Smoking, 1910, Paper 165.00
Store, Sign, Marden Reliable Shoe House, Black On Yellow, 10 X 14 In. 22.50
Store, Sign, Mayo's Plug, Cock Of The Walk, Porcelain, 13 X 7 In. .... 42.00 To 50.00
Store, Sign, Mayo's Plug, Giant Rooster, Canvas, 24 X 40 In. 65.00
Store, Sign, Merita Bread, Tin, C.1940s, 36 X 23 In. 110.00
Store, Sign, Miller's Beer, Light-Up 15.00
Store, Sign, Miller's Beer, Porcelain, Half-Round, 14 X 24 In. 95.00
Store, Sign, Miller's High Life Brew, Woman In Moon, Tin, 11 X 17 In. 95.00
Store, Sign, Minard's Liniment, Children .... 10.00 To 15.00
Store, Sign, Mission Orange, 14 In. 15.00
Store, Sign, Mobil Gas, Flying Horse, Porcelain Shield 35.00
Store, Sign, Mogul Cigarettes, Oval, Arab Warrior, Tin, 20 X 24 In. 350.00
Store, Sign, Monticello Whiskey, Tin, Self-Frame, Jefferson Home, 37 X 28 In. 200.00
Store, Sign, Morton's Salt, Paper Poster, 1930s, 34 X 22 In. 75.00
Store, Sign, Mother's Oats, Lithograph Of Child Wearing Tiger Skin, C.1901 .... 85.00
Store, Sign, Moxie, 2-Sided, 17 In. 35.00
Store, Sign, Mrs.A.M.Hidden-Dressmaker, Tin, C.1870, 13 1/2 X 20 In. 35.00
Store, Sign, Mule Hide Products, Mule's Head, Tin 15.00
Store, Sign, Mule Hide Roofs, Not A Kick In A Million Feet, Tin, 13 1/2 In. 15.00
Store, Sign, Murad Cigarette, Paper, Frame, C.1905, 24 X 31 In. 250.00
Store, Sign, Murphy's Ale, Reverse On Glass, 16 X 7 In. 35.00
Store, Sign, Nash, Authorized Service, Porcelain, 2-Sided, 36 X 22 In. 125.00
Store, Sign, Nectar Tea, Porcelain, C.1920, 10 X 16 In. 30.00
Store, Sign, Nehi, Cardboard, C.1928, 22 X 14 In. 20.00
Store, Sign, Nehi, Cardboard, 1920s, 13 X 21 In. 12.00
Store, Sign, Nehi, Heavy Paper, C.1927, 18 X 40 In. 25.00
Store, Sign, Nehi, Self-Framed, Tin, C.1930, 15 X 40 In. 45.00
Store, Sign, New Seasons Formosa Oolong, C.1895, 10 X 12 In. 11.50
Store, Sign, No Smoking, Porcelain, Texaco, 4 X 23 In. 12.00
Store, Sign, Nude Holding Bottle Of Brookfield Rye, C.1900, Tin, Self-Framed 550.00
Store, Sign, O-So-Grape Blackboard 11.00
Store, Sign, Oh Boy Gum, Tin, 1930s, 12 X 5 In. 30.00
Store, Sign, Oh Boy Gum, Tin, 7 1/2 X 15 1/2 In. 20.00

Store, Sign, Old Overholt Whiskey, Canvas, Wood Frame, Dated 1913, 38 X 26 In. 200.00
Store, Sign, Old Settler, Cardboard, C.1930s, 9 X 12 In. 8.00
Store, Sign, Omar Cigarettes, 20 For 15 Cents, Picture Of Pack, Tin 35.00
Store, Sign, Pabst Beer, Oyster Cherubs 70.00
Store, Sign, Pabst Blue Ribbon Beer, Bottle, Glass, Cheese, C.1915, Tin 30.00
Store, Sign, Palmer's Root Beer, Porcelain, 1920s 35.00
Store, Sign, Palmer's, Porcelain, Curved, C.1920, 13 X 19 In. 35.00
Store, Sign, Paul Jones Whiskey, Temptation Of St.Anthony, Tin 425.00
Store, Sign, Pawn Shop Balls, French, Brass, Size Of Large Duck Egg, Set 3 .... 40.00
Store, Sign, Peach Whip, Tin, 1920s, 9 X 19 In. 15.00
Store, Sign, Pepsi-Cola, Tin, 12 X 36 In. 19.00
Store, Sign, Philip Morris, Tin, 1940s, 12 X 22 In. 18.00
Store, Sign, Photographers, Self-Framed Pine, C.1880, 13 1/2 X 68 1/2 In. 75.00
Store, Sign, Pickwick Ale, Horses, Tin, Wood Frame, 6 X 24 In. 35.00
Store, Sign, Piedmont Cigarettes, Brunette, Large Hat, 1908, Paper Board 145.00
Store, Sign, Piedmont Cigarettes, Washington's Return To Mt.Vernon, C.1900 .... 325.00
Store, Sign, Pierce-Arrow Cycles, 1898, 41 X 84 In. 400.00
Store, Sign, Pistol-Packin Cowgirl Carving Walk-Over Shoes On Tree, 30 In. 75.00
Store, Sign, Prince's Spaghetti, Tin, 1940s, 9 X 22 In. 9.00
Store, Sign, Public, Round, Blue, Heavy Metal, 19 X 20 In. 30.00
Store, Sign, Public, Round, Blue, Heavy Metal, 11 X 13 In. 20.00
Store, Sign, Quick Lunch, Coca-Cola And Sandwich, C.1940, 12 X 17 In. 7.50
Store, Sign, R.E.A., Porcelain On Tin, 12 In.Square .... 29.00 To 35.00
Store, Sign, RCA Victor, Steel, 2-Sided, 12 X 19 In. 25.00
Store, Sign, Red Cross Stoves, Oak Frame, Reverse On Glass, 2 X 32 In. 150.00
Store, Sign, Red Goose Shoes, Tin, Embossed, C.1930, 14 X 20 In. 16.00
Store, Sign, Red Horse Chewing Tobacco, Cardboard, 1930s, 16 X 12 In. 50.00
Store, Sign, Red Wing, Mottled Beige, 5 In. X 3 1/4 In. 35.00
Store, Sign, Regulate Traffic On Vermont Covered Bridge 95.00
Store, Sign, Rheingold Beer, Miss Rheingold 10.00
Store, Sign, Rose O'Neill Kewpie Eating Quaker Ice Cream, Tin, 20 X 14 In. 95.00
Store, Sign, Royal Crown Cola, Tin, Red & White, 19 X 7 In. 7.00
Store, Sign, RugGrip, Girl Slipping On Carpet, Cardboard, 24 X 36 In. 25.00
Store, Sign, Ruppert, Mugs Toasting, Laminated 32.00
Store, Sign, Sacony, We Sell Sacony Motor Gasoline, Porcelain, 20 X 24 In. 50.00
Store, Sign, Safe Deposit & Trust Co., Black & Red On White, Oval 17.50
Store, Sign, Sanger's Capsules, 3 1/2 X 6 In. 20.00
Store, Sign, Sapolin Paint, Lincoln, Washington & T.Roosevelt, 14 X 21 In. 40.00
Store, Sign, Saratoga Bell & The Bathtub, 2 Fingers In Hole For Legs 6.50
Store, Sign, Satin Skin Powder, Lithograph, Dated 1903, 42 X 36 In. 35.00
Store, Sign, Schlitz Beer, Man, Woman Drinks, In Barn Waiting For Blacksmith ... 550.00
Store, Sign, Schmidt Brewing Co., Big Game, Oil Painting, Otto Bremer, 24 In. ... 1200.00
Store, Sign, Schrafft's Chocolates, Beautiful Girl, Heavy Cardboard 45.00
Store, Sign, Seeded, Please Keep Off, Metal, 9 X 14 In. 3.50
Store, Sign, Sensation Tobacco, Lithograph Of Greek God Holding Back Dogs ... 130.00
Store, Sign, Sherwood Pure Rye, Frame, Reverse Glass, 24 X 45 In. 400.00
Store, Sign, Shredded Wheat, Rin Tin Tin Offer, Cardboard 5.00
Store, Sign, Silvertop Beer, Reverse Painted, Wooden Frame, Hangs Or Stands .. 25.00
Store, Sign, Sinclair, Porcelain 12.00
Store, Sign, Singer, 2 Sided, Porcelain, Circa 1910, 24 X 16 In. .... 200.00 To 225.00
Store, Sign, Smiling Sun, 24 In. 15.00
Store, Sign, Smith & Wesson Revolvers, Paper, Framed, C.1930, 26 X 20 In. 110.00
Store, Sign, South Bend Watches, 1920s, Watch In Block Of Ice, Tin 50.00
Store, Sign, Sunny Brook Whiskey, Inspector With 2 Bottles Of Whiskey, Tin ... 95.00
Store, Sign, Sweet Caporal, Paper, C.1915, 30 X 18 In. 125.00
Store, Sign, Sweets Super Fine Candies 10 Cents, 19 X 7 In. 7.00
Store, Sign, Target Tobacco, Man & Pocket Tin, Dated 1931, Tin, 56 X 30 In. 45.00
Store, Sign, Texaco Fire Chief, Porcelain, 12 X 18 In. 16.00
Store, Sign, Texaco Sky Chief, Porcelain, 12 X 18 In. 12.00
Store, Sign, Texas Cattle Barbwire, Tin 6.00
Store, Sign, Texas Hog Barbwire, 10 X 15 In. 5.00
Store, Sign, That Good Gulf Gasoline, Porcelain, 11 In.Diameter 15.00
Store, Sign, Titan Tractor, Tin, 20 X 14 In. 35.00
Store, Sign, Trolley, 2-Sided, Porcelain, 1920s 200.00

Store, Sign, True Fruit Beverage, Tin, Still Life Fruit, Cherub, 38 X 25 In. 95.00
Store, Sign, True Fruit Soft Drink, Still Life, Self-Framed, Tin, C.1900 .... 95.00
Store, Sign, Turkish Trophies, Embossed Frame, C.1920, 36 X 27 In. 275.00
Store, Sign, Turnbull's Scotch Whiskey, C.1890, Tin, 12 X 18 In. .... 30.00 To 80.00
Store, Sign, Tuttles Elixir For Man & Beast, Tin, 20 X 5 In. 48.00
Store, Sign, Uncle Rube 5c Cigar, Cardboard, C.1910, 26 X 22 In. 85.00
Store, Sign, Uncle Tom's Cabin, 1900, 20 X 28 In. 90.00
Store, Sign, Union Leader Smoking Tobacco, Shape Of Pocket Tin, Tin 36.00
Store, Sign, Union Stamps, Tin, 1920s, 9 X 12 In. 5.00
Store, Sign, Valley Forge Beer, 2-Sided, Tin 45.00
Store, Sign, Van Houten Cocoa, Cardboard, Framed, C.1900, 33 X 22 In. 225.00
Store, Sign, Velvet Tobacco, Men, Boy, Dog, Tin 300.00
Store, Sign, Velvet Tobacco, Velvet Joe, Boy & Dog, 1910, 25 X 31 In. 325.00
Store, Sign, Velvet Tobacco, Velvet Joe, Man & Dog, C.1915, Tin, Framed 275.00
Store, Sign, Virginia Dare Wine, Tin, Wood Frame, C.1910, 36 X 46 In. 575.00
Store, Sign, Virginia Dare, Tin, 1930s, 9 X 24 In. 10.00
Store, Sign, Watch, Jeweler's Window Dummy, All Gilt 25.00
Store, Sign, Weed Gasoline, Shows Tire, Chains, Price Changer, Tin 98.00
Store, Sign, Wells Fargo & Co. Express, Yellow, Blue, Red, 14 X 14 In. 100.00
Store, Sign, Wild Root, Barber Shop, Tin, 13 X 39 In. 12.00
Store, Sign, Winchester, Hunters In Woods, 1954 .... 45.00
Store, Sign, Winchester, Pocket Catalog, Guns & Ammo., 1922 .... 6.00
Store, Sign, Wiss Shears, Tin, Embossed, C.1915, 12 X 15 In. 55.00
Store, Sign, X-Ray, Cardboard, C.1905, 5 X 13 In. 5.00
Store, Sign, Zubelda Cigarettes, Framed, 1920s, 20 X 13 In. 60.00
Store, Sign, 7-Up 9.00
Store, Slicer, Cheese, Dunn 100.00
Store, Slides, Swift's Ham, Signed Maxfield Parrish 30.00
Store, Spoon, Measuring, Phillips Milk Of Magnesia, Glass 15.00
Store, Stand, Plant, Wicker, 3 Splayed Legs, 22 1/4 In. 27.50
Store, Staple Puller, Fencing Tool, Boss 5.00
Store, Statue, Green River Whiskey, Old Negro & Mule 79.00
Store, Statue, Miller High Life Girl, 1930 .... 28.00
Store, Stereoscope, see Stereoscope
Store, Stickpin, Fox River Butter Co., Lady With Pail Of Milk 12.50
Store, Stool, Elevator Operator's Brass, Nickel Plated, Foldaway 35.00
Store, Strop, Razor, Wooden Handle, Highland Falls, N.Y., 1884 .... 7.50
Store, Syringe, Velvet-Lined Box, Needle & Glass Vial 27.00
Store, Table, Display, National Bisquit Company, Oak, 30 In.High 135.00
Store, Tape Measure, see Sewing Tool, Tape Measure
Store, Tea Caddy, Tao Tea Balls 5.00
Store, Teapot, Lipton Tea, Ceramic, Citron-Yellow Body 26.00
Store, Teapot, Lipton Tea, Green 9.50
Store, Thermometer, Black Boy, Dated 1949 .... 6.00
Store, Thermometer, Camel Cigarette 16.00
Store, Thermometer, Hills Bros., Porcelain 100.00
Store, Thermometer, Hornung's White Rock, C.1910, 7 Inch Round 25.00
Store, Thermometer, Lash's Bitters, Wooden .... 47.50 To 110.00
Store, Thermometer, Lehigh Coal, Wooden, 11 1/2 In. 15.00
Store, Thermometer, Mail Pouch .... 45.00 To 50.00
Store, Thermometer, Mail Pouch Tobacco, 39 In. 25.00
Store, Thermometer, Mission Orange, Tin, 17 In. 12.00
Store, Thermometer, Mr.Westwind Figure, Enamel Cover, 4 1/2 X 3 In. 12.00
Store, Thermometer, Negro Boy, 1949 .... 6.00
Store, Thermometer, Orange Crush, Tin, C.1940, 27 In. 40.00
Store, Thermometer, Pabst Blue Ribbon, Tin, 20 In. 10.00
Store, Thermometer, Prestone, Porcelain 12.50
Store, Thermometer, Red Seal Dry Battery, Porcelain, 26 In. 65.00
Store, Thermometer, Royal Crown Cola, Embossed, 13 In. 5.00
Store, Thermometer, Royal Crown, Red, 25 In. 10.00
Store, Thermometer, Stackpole Motor Transport Co., Tin, Red, White 12.50
Store, Thermometer, Sun-Crest Soda, 7 X 16 In. 8.00
Store, Thimble, Advertising, Flour, Metal 2.50
Store, Tie Pin, International Tailoring Company, New York 12.50

Store, Tie Pin, Priscilla Says, Your Credit Is Good At The New England	12.50
Store, Tin, A & P Allspice, Paper Label	3.00
Store, Tin, A & P Cinnamon, Paper Label	3.00
Store, Tin, A & P Pepper, Paper Label	3.00
Store, Tin, A & P Spice Mills Pure Ground Pepper, Paper Label	4.00
Store, Tin, Adams Honey Chewing Gum, Ginna & Co.	26.00
Store, Tin, Air Ship Tobacco, Pocket	250.00
Store, Tin, American Navy Tobacco	20.00
Store, Tin, Belfast Cut Plug, Dark Green, 7 Oz.	10.00
Store, Tin, Between The Acts Cigars	4.00
Store, Tin, Biscuit, Cupboard, 2 Simulated Glass Doors, Filled With Dishes	86.00
Store, Tin, Black Beauty Stove Polish, Pictures A Horse, Lithograph, 4 In.	4.50
Store, Tin, Black Cough Drops, 5 Pound Can, 5 1/4 X 7 1/2 In.	38.00
Store, Tin, Blue Boy Fruits, Bow, Cherries, Cover, 30 Pound	45.00
Store, Tin, Boston Blend Coffee	10.00
Store, Tin, Briggs Tobacco	10.00
Store, Tin, Buffalo Peanut Butter, 1 Pound	22.00
Store, Tin, Bugler, Pocket	2.50
Store, Tin, Bunker Hill Coffee	20.00
Store, Tin, Butterfly Talcum	15.00
Store, Tin, Calumet Baking Powder, Lithograph, 12 Ounces	6.50
Store, Tin, Camel Tobacco Base, Fertilizer, Camel & Pyramids	22.50
Store, Tin, Campbell's Coffee, Bail Handle, Yellow, Red Label, 4 Pound	35.00
Store, Tin, Campbell's Coffee, Desert Scene, 1920, 4 Pound	45.00
Store, Tin, Campfire Marshmallow Tin, 5 Pound Size	22.00
Store, Tin, Can, Mayo Cut Plug, Cover	99.00
Store, Tin, Capital, 10 Lb.	28.00
Store, Tin, Central Union Tobacco, Pocket	20.00
Store, Tin, Chesterfield Cigarettes, Flat Fifties	5.25
Store, Tin, Chickadee Talc	10.00
Store, Tin, Cinco Handy Tobacco Humidor, Lithograph, 5 In.Square	21.00
Store, Tin, Climax Peanut Butter, 1 Pound	37.00
Store, Tin, Coffee, Counter, Stenciled	100.00
Store, Tin, Colonial Dame Coffee	35.00
Store, Tin, Coors, Malted Milk, 25 Lb., Blue On White	50.00
Store, Tin, Cough Lozenge, Flowers, Butterflies, 9 X 5 1/2 X 5 1/2 In.	32.00
Store, Tin, Cream Dove Nuts, Blue, 10 Lb.	50.00
Store, Tin, Cream Dove Salted Peanuts, Blue, Yellow, Round, 8 1/2 X 10 In.	25.00
Store, Tin, Cremo Cigars, 7 X 8 1/2 X 6 In.	42.50
Store, Tin, Culture Tobacco, Pocket	15.00
Store, Tin, Daisy Fly Killer, Pocket	9.50
Store, Tin, Dan Patch Cut Plug, Red & Yellow, 3 X 3 3/4 X 6 In.	32.00
Store, Tin, DeVoe's Sweet Smoke, 4 1/4 In.	8.00
Store, Tin, Dial Tobacco, Pocket	14.00
Store, Tin, Dill's Best Tobacco, Pocket, Free Sample	25.00
Store, Tin, Dillings Turkish Jellies & Gumdrops, 25 Lb., Turkish Lady	45.00
Store, Tin, Dr.J.O.Aldrich Lung Salve, 1906, Bath N.Y., 3 1/2 In.	3.00
Store, Tin, Dr.John's Educator Crackers, 5 X 5 1/2 In.	21.00
Store, Tin, Druckers Revelation Tooth Powder, Pocket, Sample	4.50
Store, Tin, Duco Tobacco	25.00
Store, Tin, Dutch Masters Cigars, Small, Flat	3.50
Store, Tin, E.I.Du Pont Powder Co., Round, 4 In.	27.00
Store, Tin, Edgeworth Tobacco	12.00
Store, Tin, Edgeworth Tobacco, 2 X 4 1/4 X 3 In.	5.00
Store, Tin, Egyptian Bouquet Talcum	35.00
Store, Tin, Epicure Tobacco, Pocket	35.00
Store, Tin, Epicure, Pocket	25.00
Store, Tin, Eve Cube Cut Tobacco, Nude Ladies, Pocket	85.00
Store, Tin, Famous Cake Box Mixture, Tobacco	18.00
Store, Tin, Flavignys Ala Violette Anise Candy	5.00
Store, Tin, Four-Packet, Nabisco Saltines, 14 Oz.	7.50
Store, Tin, Friends Smoking Tobacco	10.00
Store, Tin, George Washington Tobacco Can, Flag Blue, Red Letters	24.00
Store, Tin, Glebeas Adoration, Spider Web, Lady, Aqua & Gold	11.00

Store, Tin, Glendora, Coffee, Round	4.50
Store, Tin, Glicks Crispy Fluffs	20.00
Store, Tin, Gold Label Baking Powder	3.50
Store, Tin, Grand Union Tea Co., 3 Lithograph Sides, Horse & Wagon	37.00
Store, Tin, Great American Pepper, Parrot On Reverse, Green, Lithograph	7.50
Store, Tin, Hacks White Hudson & Co., Cough Drops, Oval, 10 In.	25.00
Store, Tin, Half & Half, Pocket-Size, 1 Pound	1.00
Store, Tin, Handmade Tobacco	22.50
Store, Tin, Harper's XL Lemon Sugar	5.00
Store, Tin, Hash Brown, Tri-Cut Tobacco, Water Pipe	30.00
Store, Tin, Heinz 57 Variety, Large	12.00
Store, Tin, Heinz, Green Pickle, Red, Black, Gold, 1 Gallon	37.00
Store, Tin, Hemstreet's Sweet Pea Talcum	15.00
Store, Tin, Herb, Parke Davis & Co., Green, Red Label, 9 X 5 In.	15.00
Store, Tin, Hi Plane Tobacco, Pocket	15.00
Store, Tin, High Lindens 1 Pound Coffee	8.00
Store, Tin, Holland House Coffee Lithograph, C.1920	5.00
Store, Tin, Hudson Bay, Round	12.50
Store, Tin, Humo Tin Cigar Box, Wood Grain, Gold Letters, Blue	14.00
Store, Tin, Huntley & Palmer Biscuit, Toy Soldier	75.00
Store, Tin, Huntley & Palmer Biscuits, 8 Bound Books With Strap, 6 1/4 In.	90.00
Store, Tin, Huntley & Palmer Cecil Aldin Scenes, Square, 9 In.	22.50
Store, Tin, Huntley & Palmer, Covered Urn, Applied Silver Handles	60.00
Store, Tin, Huntley & Palmer, Dresden Copy, 9 1/2 X 8 3/4 In.	44.00
Store, Tin, Huntley & Palmer, Satchel, Caramel Leather Finish	65.00
Store, Tin, Huntley & Palmer, Set Of 8 Books	25.00
Store, Tin, Huntley & Palmer, Single Book, 9 3/4 X 7 X 1 1/2 In.	55.00
Store, Tin, Huntley & Palmer, World Globe	20.00
Store, Tin, Huntley & Palmer, World Globe, Ball Feet, Hinged Lid, C.1900	120.00
Store, Tin, Huyler's, Cocoa	15.00
Store, Tin, Iona Cocao, Indian	5.00
Store, Tin, J.G.Dill, 1910, Pocket	6.00
Store, Tin, J.W.Wright Tobacco, The Pride Of Virginia, 3 X 4 1/2 In.	15.00
Store, Tin, Jaynees Sample Powder	6.50
Store, Tin, LaBara Bath Powder, Art Deco Lady With Mask	32.00
Store, Tin, LaFendrich, 10 Cigar, Pocket	10.00
Store, Tin, Landmark Cut Plug Label, Bail Handle, 1 Pound	15.00
Store, Tin, Lard, Kettle Rendered, Swift Premium, 50 Pound	5.00
Store, Tin, LaResta, Cigar, 3 1/2 X 7 1/2 In.Square	15.00
Store, Tin, Lipton Tea, Negroes Picking Tea Leaves On 4 Sides, 3 Pound Size	48.00
Store, Tin, Log Cabin Syrup Tin, 26 Oz.	22.00
Store, Tin, Log Cabin Syrup, Woman Inside Flipping Pancake, Boy Carries Logs	35.00
Store, Tin, Loose-Wiles, Octagonal, Picture Trylon Perisphere	25.00
Store, Tin, Loose-Wiles, Ships, Octagon	8.50
Store, Tin, Lord Salisbury Turkish Cigarettes, Flat 100s	8.50
Store, Tin, Louis Sherry Candy, Large Size	6.00
Store, Tin, Louis Sherry Candy, Small Size	4.00
Store, Tin, Mammy's Coffee	10.00
Store, Tin, Maryland Club Mixture, Hinged Lid, 4 X 2 1/2 In.	17.00
Store, Tin, Matador Tobacco	25.00
Store, Tin, Materia Medica Specimen, Glass Window On Top, Yellow, 2 1/4 In.	11.00
Store, Tin, Melachrino Egyptian Cigarettes, 1910 Stamp, 5 3/4 X 2 In.	10.00
Store, Tin, Mennen Barated Talcum	7.50
Store, Tin, Mennen Violet, Art Deco Pink & Green Stripes & Flowers	8.00
Store, Tin, Murad, Pocket	18.00
Store, Tin, Nigger Hair, Smoking Tobacco, Bail Handle, C.1878	95.00
Store, Tin, North Cut Plug, Oval Top, 4 X 6 In.	175.00
Store, Tin, Nut House Nuts, House, Ship, 1 Pound	28.00
Store, Tin, Old Colony Tobacco, Silver	57.50
Store, Tin, Old Gold Cigarettes, Pocket	8.00
Store, Tin, Old Judge	10.00
Store, Tin, Omar Cigarettes, Turkish Blend Light, Blue, Gold, Flat	12.00
Store, Tin, Orange Richmond Club Tobacco, 2 X 3 X 4 In.	13.00
Store, Tin, Patterson Lucky Strike, Flat, Pocket	12.00

Store, Tin, Peacock Blue Ink, Gold, Peacocks 30.00
Store, Tin, Pearson's Red Top Snuff 5.00
Store, Tin, Penn's Tobacco 25.00
Store, Tin, Pepsi-Cola Syrup, 1920s 30.00
Store, Tin, Peter Rabbit, Round 26.00
Store, Tin, Peter Rabbit, Talcum 22.50
Store, Tin, Petrings Coffee 12.50
Store, Tin, Phillies Tin Tobacco, 5 Word Grain, 50 Cigars, C.1925 .... 22.00
Store, Tin, Pickininny Peanut Butter, 1 Pound 65.00
Store, Tin, Pipe Major Tobacco, Butler Bringing Pipe To Gentleman, Pocket 60.00
Store, Tin, Piper Heidsieck Chewing Tobacco, Champagne Flavor, Small 15.00
Store, Tin, Planters Peanuts, Blue Label, Red Peanut Banner, 10 Pound Size 42.00
Store, Tin, Player's Navy Cut Cigaretts, 4 X 3 X 1 1/2 In. 15.00
Store, Tin, Pom Pom Quality Operat Cigars, 100s, C.1927 .... 7.00
Store, Tin, Pompeian Fragrance, Purple & Gold Lettering 7.00
Store, Tin, Prince Albert Tobacco, Pocket, 1926 .... 1.50
Store, Tin, Purity Rolled Oats 6.00
Store, Tin, Rajah Ground Nutmeg, Paper Label 3.50
Store, Tin, Red Apple Embossed On Poppins Green, Cigar, 5 1/2 X 3 1/4 In. 30.00
Store, Tin, Red J.Tobacco 50.00
Store, Tin, Red Man, 15 X 15 In. 8.00
Store, Tin, Revelation, Pocket 15.00
Store, Tin, Roly-Poly Tobacco, Dutchman, Mayo 425.00
Store, Tin, Roly-Poly Tobacco, Mammy, Mayo .... 265.00 To 325.00
Store, Tin, Roly-Poly Tobacco, Man From Scotland Yard, Mayo 850.00
Store, Tin, Roly-Poly Tobacco, Red Indian 285.00
Store, Tin, Roly-Poly Tobacco, Satisfied Customer, Mayo 475.00
Store, Tin, Roly-Poly Tobacco, Singing Waiter 290.00
Store, Tin, Roly-Poly Tobacco, Store Keeper, Mayo .... 246.00 To 375.00
Store, Tin, San Telmo Cigars, Square, Upright 13.50
Store, Tin, Sante Cheese 9.00
Store, Tin, Shedds Peanut Butter, 5 Pounds 14.00
Store, Tin, Sir Walter Raleigh, Pocket 2.50
Store, Tin, Snow Peak Ice Cream Freezer Label, Directions For Ice Cream 45.00
Store, Tin, Somnola Peanut Oil, Peanut Pictures, 9 X 14 In. 22.00
Store, Tin, Squibb's Bath Toilet Powder, Naked Venus, Tindeco 49.00
Store, Tin, Squirrel Brand Peanuts, Ten Pound 85.00
Store, Tin, Stag Tobacco, 5 X 5 X 6 In. 35.00
Store, Tin, Sultana Pepper Label, Sultan, His Lady, Little Black Boy 4.50
Store, Tin, Sunny South Peanut, Black Lady, 1 Pound 35.00
Store, Tin, Sunshine, Hexagonal, Bicentennial Theme 15.00
Store, Tin, Sunshine, Patriotic Scenes, Octagonal Shape 15.00
Store, Tin, Superb Baking Powder, Paper Label 3.50
Store, Tin, Sweet Burley, Hinged Top 6.00
Store, Tin, Sweet Cuba Tobacco, Green, Round 25.00
Store, Tin, Sweet Cuba, Counter, Yellow 65.00
Store, Tin, Sweet Cuba, Slant Bin, Green 60.00
Store, Tin, Sweet Georgia Brown Pomade, 1930s, Sample 2.00
Store, Tin, Swift Premium Kettle Rendered Lard, 50 Lb. 5.00
Store, Tin, Target Cigarettes 14.00
Store, Tin, Three States Mixture 9.00
Store, Tin, Tootsie Roll 5 Cents, 12 1/2 X 10 1/2 In. 75.00
Store, Tin, True Blue, Tobacco 15.00
Store, Tin, Tuxedo Tobacco, With Contents 5.00
Store, Tin, Tuxedo, Round 20.00
Store, Tin, Two Belles Cigars 10.00
Store, Tin, Uncle Daniel Fine Cut, Round Tin, 1 Pound, Red Box 35.00
Store, Tin, Uncle Daniel Tobacco 65.00
Store, Tin, Uncle Sam Shoe Polish, 1930 .... 25.00
Store, Tin, Uncle Sam Tobacco, Pocket 12.00
Store, Tin, Uneeda, Graham Cracker, 1 Lb., 3 Oz. .... .50
Store, Tin, Union Leader Cut Plug Eagle, Gold Letters, Bittersweet 12.00
Store, Tin, Union Leader, Tobacco, Uncle Sam, C.1917 .... 17.50
Store, Tin, Velvet Tobacco, Free Sample, Picture Of Pipe 40.00

Store, Tin, Velvet Tobacco, Short, Pocket	6.00
Store, Tin, Velvet, The Smoothest Smoking Tobacco	25.00
Store, Tin, Victor Hugo Cigars, Flat	2.50
Store, Tin, Virginia Brand Tobacco	7.50
Store, Tin, Waltham, Pictures Factory	6.00
Store, Tin, Wan-Eta Cocoa, Boston Jar, Round Zinc Top, Amber	8.50
Store, Tin, Ward's Violet, Gold & Pink Embossed Flowers	11.00
Store, Tin, Watkins Egyptian Bouquet Talcum	22.00
Store, Tin, Watkins Pure Ground Cinnamon, Lithograph	4.00
Store, Tin, Webster Cigar, Daniel Webster Picture, 1920s	20.00
Store, Tin, Weightman, Pharmaceutical, Factory, Powers, Philadelphia, 1880	15.00
Store, Tin, Whip Tobacco, Man & Horse, Pocket	35.00
Store, Tin, Whitman's Instaneous Chocolate, Oval, 1906, 4 1/2 In.	4.50
Store, Tin, Whitman's Prestige Chocolates	6.00
Store, Tin, Willoughby Taylor Tobacco, Pocket	25.00
Store, Tin, Woolworth Co., Santa Claus, 4 In.	25.00
Store, Tin, Worker's Cut Plug Tobacco	20.00
Store, Tin, Yankee Boy Tobacco	70.00
Store, Tin, Yankee Doodle Flake, Spirit Of 1776	250.00
Store, Tin, Yuban Coffee, Rectangular	4.50
Store, Token, Wingens 5 Cents Cigar	3.50
Store, Toothpaste, Cherry, Ironstone Container	25.00
Store, Tray, Anheuser-Busch, A & Eagle, Brass Note, 6 1/2 X 4 1/2 In.	23.00
Store, Tray, Anheuser-Busch, Factory Scene, Oval, Tin	375.00
Store, Tray, Anheuser-Busch, Oval, Woman With Cherubs, 1895, 16 In.	225.00
Store, Tray, Billy Baxter, Big Red Bird, 1920s	35.00
Store, Tray, Blatz, Rectangle, Students Drinking	65.00
Store, Tray, Brownie Ice Cream, 10 1/2 X 13 1/4 In.	50.00
Store, Tray, Budweiser, Foxhunters, Hound, Shadow Of Fox By Fireplace, C.1915	95.00
Store, Tray, Budweiser, St.Louis Levee In 1870s, 1914	75.00 To 95.00
Store, Tray, Carnation Milk, Girl With Flowers, 1905	47.00
Store, Tray, Christian Feigenspan Brewery, Signed Asti	28.00
Store, Tray, Coors Beer, Pre-Prohibition, Mountain	85.00
Store, Tray, Coors, Red & White Metal, Bavarian Lion, 13 In.	4.00
Store, Tray, Dawes, Porcelain, Horse	20.00
Store, Tray, Dobler Brewing Co., Portrait Of Lady, Signed Asti	15.00
Store, Tray, Dobler P.O.N.	25.00
Store, Tray, Dow Old Stock Ale, Pre-Prohibition, Porcelain	85.00
Store, Tray, Dr.Pepper, Red Roses	127.00
Store, Tray, Duesseldorfer Beer, Baby Holding Bottle, C.1906	225.00
Store, Tray, E & J Burke	15.00
Store, Tray, Fehr's Beer, Lovers Embracing, 1910	125.00
Store, Tray, Feigenspan Beer, Asti, Pretty Woman	35.00
Store, Tray, Fidelio Beer, 18th Century Men In Tavern Drinking, 1936	75.00
Store, Tray, George Ehret's Hells Brewing Co., Nude Woman In Flowing White	125.00
Store, Tray, Goebel, Blue Tones, 2 Dutch Girls, Sailing Ships, Water	65.00
Store, Tray, Gunther, Couple At Table	32.00
Store, Tray, Haberle Brewery Congress Beer, Shonk Lithograph, 12 In.	60.00
Store, Tray, Hampden, Handsome Waiter	25.00
Store, Tray, Hanley Bulldog	35.00
Store, Tray, Hires Root Beer Pictures Brunette, C.1910	85.00
Store, Tray, Hires, Child Holding Mug, Tin, 13 In.	65.00
Store, Tray, Jersey Creme, Red & Green, Girl In Plumed Hat, 12 In.	60.00
Store, Tray, Johnny Walker Whiskey, Embossed Copper, 13 1/2 In.	60.00
Store, Tray, Johnny Walker, Copper, 13 1/2 In.	55.00
Store, Tray, Kewpie, Ice Cream, Rectangular	135.00
Store, Tray, Kewpies Eating Ice Cream, Ice Cream Co.	50.00
Store, Tray, King Of Beers, Bow Tie	15.00
Store, Tray, King-Cola, 1911, American Art Works, 10 X 13 In.	45.00
Store, Tray, Knickerbocker	20.00
Store, Tray, Labatt's Ale, 13 1/2 In.	65.00
Store, Tray, Lithia Well Water, Girl With Flowers In Hair, C.1900	65.00
Store, Tray, McSorley's Beer, Man Playing Solitaire, 1935	35.00

Store, Tray, Millers High Life Beer, Round, Girl On Moon .... 15.00 To 50.00
Store, Tray, NuGrape 40.00
Store, Tray, Olympia, Cavalier 75.00
Store, Tray, Orange Julep, Bathing Beauty On Beach, 1920s 45.00
Store, Tray, Pabst Beer, Bicentennial, 1776-1976, Tin 12.00
Store, Tray, Pepsi-Cola, Oval 500.00
Store, Tray, Pepsi-Cola, Oval, 1900 .... 375.00
Store, Tray, Pepsi-Cola, Victorian Girl, C.1900, 11 X 13 In. 575.00
Store, Tray, Pure Milk Co. Ice Cream, Milk Bottle As Tall As Building, 1900 .... 125.00
Store, Tray, Rainier Beer, Seattle Brewing Co., Dated 1913 .... 100.00
Store, Tray, Rainier Beer, Seattle, Washington, C.1915, 13 In. 185.00
Store, Tray, Remember The Maine, Shonk Litho, 12 In. 75.00
Store, Tray, Scheidt's Valley Forge 25.00
Store, Tray, Schlitz Brewing Co., Girl On World Globe 10.00
Store, Tray, Semon's Ice Cream, Mother And Children, 1915 .... 85.00
Store, Tray, Stegmaier 25.00
Store, Tray, Tip, A-1 Pilsner Beer, Tin 2.00
Store, Tray, Tip, Bromo Seltzer 33.00
Store, Tray, Tip, Centennial Beer, Seminude On Cliff Pointing To Bottle 38.00
Store, Tray, Tip, Clark's Teaberry Gum 12.50
Store, Tray, Tip, Cleveland And Buffalo, Oval 70.00
Store, Tray, Tip, Columbus Brewing Company 65.00
Store, Tray, Tip, Cottolene Shortening, Negroes Picking Cotton 45.00
Store, Tray, Tip, Day & Night Tobacco, Pretty Girl In Low-Cut Dress, 1910 .... 36.00
Store, Tray, Tip, DeLaval 40.00
Store, Tray, Tip, DeLaval Cream Separator, Mother, Child, C.1900 .... 55.00
Store, Tray, Tip, Evervess Sparkling Water, Picture Of Parrot 6.00
Store, Tray, Tip, Grain Belt Beers 20.00
Store, Tray, Tip, Gypsy Hosiery, Gypsy Camp, Girl Dancing, C.1900 .... 46.00
Store, Tray, Tip, Hupfel Brewing Corp., Gold Embossed Red Design 35.00
Store, Tray, Tip, Hupfel, Raised 25.00
Store, Tray, Tip, Hyroller Whiskey, Man In Top Hat, Early 1900s .... 6.00 To 35.00
Store, Tray, Tip, Iroquois Brewery, Indian Chief, C.1910 .... 55.00
Store, Tray, Tip, Kenny Shoes, G.Washington, 1910 .... 36.00
Store, Tray, Tip, King's Beer, Barmaid Holding Bottle 37.00
Store, Tray, Tip, King's Pure Malt, Oval, Lithographed, 4 1/2 X 6 In. 39.50
Store, Tray, Tip, Kings Pure Malt 18.00
Store, Tray, Tip, Meuhlebach Pilsener Beer, 1941 .... 18.00
Store, Tray, Tip, Miller Beer, Ducks Landing In Marsh, 1940s 20.00
Store, Tray, Tip, Miller's, Coach Scene 6.00
Store, Tray, Tip, Monticello 45.00
Store, Tray, Tip, Moxie Girl With Glass, C.1900 .... 40.00 To 50.00
Store, Tray, Tip, Prudential Life Insurance 4.50
Store, Tray, Tip, Pulver Cocoa, Girl With Box Of Cocoa 45.00
Store, Tray, Tip, Quick Meal, New Born Chicks After Bee 30.00
Store, Tray, Tip, Quick Ranges, Baby Chicks 45.00
Store, Tray, Tip, Ruppert Beer, Art Deco, 4 1/4 In. 11.00
Store, Tray, Tip, Sears Roebuck, Oval, Factory 35.00
Store, Tray, Tip, Sears Roebuck, Picture Of Factory 35.00
Store, Tray, Tip, Stegmaier Brewing Co., Wilkes-Barre, Pa., Hand & 4 Bottles 12.50
Store, Tray, Tip, Telling's, Boy & Girl Eating Ice Cream From Barrel, C.1900 .... 65.00
Store, Tray, Tip, Welsbach Gas Mantles, 4 In. 18.00
Store, Tray, Tip, White Rock .... 35.00 To 45.00
Store, Tray, Tip, World's Fair, 1904 .... 14.00
Store, Tray, Wagner's Beer, Dutch Girl Carrying Basket, 1930s 75.00
Store, Tray, Weinhardt Beer, Portland, Eagle, C.1900 .... 175.00
Store, Tray, Williamson Milling Co., Clay Center, Kansas, Metal, 11 In. 25.00
Store, Tray, Wooden Shoe Beer, Two Children Carrying Basket, 1910 .... 95.00
Store, Tub, Kerosene, Brass Faucet, Wire Bail, Kerosene Oil Stencil, 13 In. 27.50
Store, Tumbler, Shot, Etched, Advertising 8.00
Store, Vacuum, Star, Hand Operated, Red Cylinder .... *Illus* 104.50
Store, Whip, Blacksnake, 10 Feet 24.50
Store, Whisk Broom, Leather Holder, Marked Steamer Robert Fulton 12.00

Store, Vacuum,
Star, Hand Operated, Red Cylinder
(See Page 651)

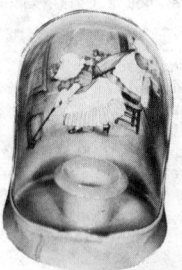

Sunbonnet Babies,
Candleholder With Shield

Sunbonnet Babies, Dresser Tray

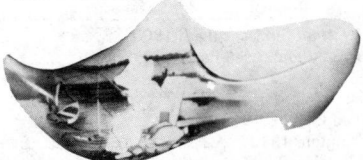

Sunbonnet Babies, Dutch Shoe

Store, Whistle, Wood, Red Goose Shoes	5.00
Stove, see Fire, Stove	
Strawberry, see Soft Paste	
Stretch Glass, Bottle, Iridescent, Stopper With Cork, 8 1/4 In.	10.00
Stretch Glass, Bowl, Blue Iridescent, Footed, 8 3/4 In.	45.00
Stretch Glass, Bowl, Blue, Flared, 9 1/2 In.	20.00
Stretch Glass, Bowl, Blue, Iridescent, 12 3/4 X 3 In.	27.50
Stretch Glass, Bowl, Blue, Square Feet, 8 1/2 In.	15.00
Stretch Glass, Bowl, Clear, Iridescent, 9 In.	12.50
Stretch Glass, Bowl, Console, Raised Base, Yellow, 9 In.	25.00
Stretch Glass, Bowl, Cupped, Vaseline Iridescent, 9 X 4 In.	35.00
Stretch Glass, Bowl, Flower, Vaseline Color, 8 In.	55.00
Stretch Glass, Bowl, Gold Edging, Blue, Opaque, 13 In.	48.00
Stretch Glass, Bowl, Green, Flared, 9 1/2 In.	20.00
Stretch Glass, Bowl, Green, 7 In.	25.00
Stretch Glass, Bowl, Green, 9 1/2 In.	22.00
Stretch Glass, Bowl, Imperial, Pink, Dome Foot, 11 In.	45.00
Stretch Glass, Bowl, Iridescent, Footed, 11 X 4 1/4 In.	20.00
Stretch Glass, Bowl, Iridescent, White, 3-Footed, In-Turned Rim, 8 In.	28.00
Stretch Glass, Bowl, Marigold, 11 X 3 3/4 In.	16.00
Stretch Glass, Bowl, Paneled, Smoke Blue, 8 1/4 In.	25.00
Stretch Glass, Bowl, Sapphire Blue, 5 X 10 1/2 In.	45.00
Stretch Glass, Bowl, Smoke Blue, Paneled, 8 1/4 In.	23.00
Stretch Glass, Bowl, White, Iridescent, Footed, Molded, Turned In Rim, 9 In.	28.00
Stretch Glass, Bowl, White, 12 In.	30.00
Stretch Glass, Candleholder, Cobalt, 8 3/4 In., Pair	35.00

Stretch Glass, Candlestick, Blue, 3 1/2 In.Pair	23.00
Stretch Glass, Candlestick, Green, 9 3/4 In.	15.00
Stretch Glass, Candlestick, Sapphire Blue, 8 1/4 In., Pair	30.00
Stretch Glass, Compote, Blue Iridescent, Twig Design Foot, 4 In.	27.50
Stretch Glass, Compote, Green, Covered, 6 In.	18.00
Stretch Glass, Console Set, Blue, 4 Piece	95.00
Stretch Glass, Console Set, Pink, Turned Edge Bowl, Pair Candlesticks	30.00
Stretch Glass, Dish, Candy, Covered, Opaque Custard, Iridescent, 5 1/2 In.	90.00
Stretch Glass, Dish, Candy, Mint Green, Covered	32.50
Stretch Glass, Mayonnaise, Underplate, Iridescent, White	35.00
Stretch Glass, Plate, Blue, 8 In.	12.00
Stretch Glass, Plate, Blue, 12 In.	25.00
Stretch Glass, Plate, Iridescent, 7 1/2 In.	15.00
Stretch Glass, Server, Center Handle, Vaseline, 9 1/2 In.	18.00
Stretch Glass, Server, Lemon, Yellow Iridescent, 4 1/2 In.	22.00
Stretch Glass, Tumble-Up, Green Iridescent	30.00
Stretch Glass, Vase, Bud, Blue, 9 3/4 In.	19.00
Stretch Glass, Vase, Fan, Blue, Green, Iridescent, 9 1/2 In.	130.00
Stretch Glass, Vase, Wall, Blue, Wrought Iron Holder	25.00

Sunbonnet Babies were first introduced in 1902 in the Sunbonnet Babies Primer. The stories were by Eulalie Osgood Grover, illustrated by Bertha Corbett. The children's faces were completely hidden by the sunbonnets, and had been pictured in black and white before this time. The color pictures in the book were immediately successful. The Royal Bayreuth China Company made a full line of children's dishes decorated with the Sunbonnet Babies.

Sunbonnet Babies, Bonbon, Spade-Shaped, Finger Grip, Babies Fishing	185.00
Sunbonnet Babies, Book, ABC, 1929	30.00
Sunbonnet Babies, Book, In Holland, 1915, Eulalie Osgood Grover	30.00
Sunbonnet Babies, Book, In Mother Goose Land, C.1936	25.00 To 40.00
Sunbonnet Babies, Book, Sunbonnet Babies In Italy, Hardbound, C.1922	50.00
Sunbonnet Babies, Book, The Sunbonnet Babies Book, First Edition, C.1902	75.00
Sunbonnet Babies, Book, 1902, Eulalie Osgood Grover	32.50
Sunbonnet Babies, Bottle, Doll	6.00
Sunbonnet Babies, Bowl, Sugar, Cover, Sweeping	120.00
Sunbonnet Babies, Bowl, Wednesday, Mending, Royal Bayreuth, Blue Mark, 8 In.	125.00
Sunbonnet Babies, Box	32.50
Sunbonnet Babies, Box, Wood	35.00
Sunbonnet Babies, Candleholder With Shield *Illus*	350.00
Sunbonnet Babies, Candleholder, Royal Bayreuth, Ring-Type Grip	175.00
Sunbonnet Babies, Candlestick, Cape Cod, Sewing, Royal Bayreuth, Blue Mark	285.00
Sunbonnet Babies, Card, Postal, Days Of The Week, Complete Set	35.00
Sunbonnet Babies, Chamberstick, Cleaning, Saucer Type, Handle	185.00 To 215.00
Sunbonnet Babies, Chamberstick, Handle, Royal Bayreuth	185.00
Sunbonnet Babies, Chamberstick, Washing, Saucer Type, Handle, Green Tones	215.00
Sunbonnet Babies, Creamer, Mopping & Cleaning, Royal Bayreuth, Blue Mark	135.00
Sunbonnet Babies, Cup & Saucer, Large	75.00
Sunbonnet Babies, Cup & Tray, German	55.00
Sunbonnet Babies, Cup, Child's, Marked Germany	35.00
Sunbonnet Babies, Cup, Reading & Knitting At Tea Table	21.50
Sunbonnet Babies, Dish, Diamond Shape, Babies Washing, BM Royal Bayreuth	65.00
Sunbonnet Babies, Dish, Feeding, Roseville, Signed	30.00
Sunbonnet Babies, Dish, Nut, Royal Bayreuth	100.00
Sunbonnet Babies, Dish, Ruffled, Sewing, 4 1/2 In.	55.00
Sunbonnet Babies, Doorstop, Girl, Iron, 6 In.	22.00
Sunbonnet Babies, Doorstop, Iron, Painted Blue Dress & Bonnet, 6 In.	30.00
Sunbonnet Babies, Dresser Tray *Illus*	160.00
Sunbonnet Babies, Dutch Shoe *Illus*	325.00
Sunbonnet Babies, Mug, Hand-Painted	7.00
Sunbonnet Babies, Nappy, Fishing, Royal Bayreuth, Blue Mark, Handled, 6 In.	180.00
Sunbonnet Babies, Paperweight, Twins Holding Dolls	35.00
Sunbonnet Babies, Picture, Original Frame, 7 Days Of Week, 25 X 7 1/4 In.	70.00

Sunbonnet Babies, Pitcher, Royal Bayreuth, Cleaning House, Blue Mark, 3 In.	110.00
Sunbonnet Babies, Plate, Babies Ironing, Open Handled, 10 In.	135.00
Sunbonnet Babies, Plate, Cake, Washing Clothes, Slotted Handles, 10 1/2 In.	250.00
Sunbonnet Babies, Plate, Fishing, Blue Mark, Royal Bayreuth, 6 1/2 In.	75.00
Sunbonnet Babies, Plate, Ironing, Royal Bayreuth	62.00
Sunbonnet Babies, Plate, Marked Dresden	15.00
Sunbonnet Babies, Plate, Mending, Royal Bayreuth, 7 1/2 In.	70.00
Sunbonnet Babies, Plate, Royal Bayreuth, Open Handle, 10 1/2 In.	195.00
Sunbonnet Babies, Plate, Sunbonnet Girl & Overall Boy Kissing, 7 In.	23.00
Sunbonnet Babies, Plate, Sweeping, 6 In.	95.00
Sunbonnet Babies, Plate, Washing & Hanging Clothes, Royal Bayreuth, 7 In.	71.00
Sunbonnet Babies, Plate, Washing & Ironing, Royal Bayreuth, Blue Mark	75.00
Sunbonnet Babies, Plate, Washing, Royal Bayreuth, Blue Mark, 8 1/2 In.	115.00
Sunbonnet Babies, Plate, Washing, Royal Bayreuth, Blue Mark, 9 In.	150.00
Sunbonnet Babies, Platter, Royal Bayreuth, Box	75.00
Sunbonnet Babies, Postcard, Day Of Week, Ullman, Set Of 7	65.00 To 75.00
Sunbonnet Babies, Relish, Children Sledding Down Hill, Royal Bayreuth, 8 In.	100.00
Sunbonnet Babies, Relish, Royal Bayreuth, Handled, Blue Mark, 8 X 4 In.	225.00
Sunbonnet Babies, Saucer, Ironing, 5 1/2 In.	55.00
Sunbonnet Babies, Sugar & Creamer, Ironing & Washing	285.00
Sunbonnet Babies, Teapot, Cleaning	245.00
Sunbonnet Babies, Tray, Babies Sorting Laundry & Washing, 10 X 7 1/2 In.	185.00
Sunbonnet Babies, Tray, Washing Clothes, 9 1/2 X 7 In.	250.00
Sunbonnet Babies, Vase, Royal Bayreuth, 4 1/4 In.	135.00

Sunderland luster is a name given to a characteristic pink luster made by Leeds, Newcastle, and other English firms during the nineteenth century. The luster glaze is metallic and glossy and sometimes appears to have bubbles as a decoration.

Sunderland, Box, Molded Rock Formations, Dove Perched On Top, Pink Luster	75.00
Sunderland, Cup & Saucer, Cloud, Allerton	55.00
Sunderland, Cup & Saucer, Pink Luster, Mottled	38.00 To 42.50
Sunderland, Cup & Saucer, Pink Luster, Wishbone Handle	18.00
Sunderland, Cup & Saucer, Ships, Luster	28.00
Sunderland, Mug, 3-Masted Ship, Poem, Double Handle, 8 1/2 X 5 In.	165.00
Sunderland, Mustard, Pink Splash Luster, Copper Luster Trim & Interior	68.00
Sunderland, Pitcher, Luster, Sailor's Farewell, 1/2 Gallon, C.1820	165.00
Sunderland, Pitcher, Milk, Cloud, Sailing Ship, The Sailor's Tear Lettered	145.00
Sunderland, Pitcher, Pink, Splash Design, May Peace & Plenty, Ship, 5 1/2 In.	165.00
Sunderland, Plaque, Prepare To Meet Thy God, Angel, Luster, 6 1/2 In.	135.00
Sunderland, Toby Mug, Copper	325.00
Superman, Button, 1940s	20.00
Superman, Card, Playing, 1966	6.00
Superman, Frog Feet, Kiddie Paddlers, 1940s, Boxed	46.00
Swansea, Figurine, Tulip Girl, 5 In.	38.00
Sword, see Weapon, Sword	
Syracuse, Dinner Set, Service For 8, Governor Clinton	235.00
Taffeta Glass, see Carnival Glass	
Tapestry, Porcelain, see Rose Tapestry	
Tea Leaf, see Ironstone, Tea Leaf	

Teco pottery is the art pottery line made by the Terra Cotta Tile Works of Terra Cotta, Illinois. The company was founded by William D.Gates in 1881. The Teco line was first made in 1902 and continued into the 1920s. It included over 500 designs, made in a variety of colors and glazes.

Teco, Bowl, Deep Blues, Greens, Tans, & Grays, Glossy, Art Nouveau, Signed	45.00
Teco, Bowl, Green, 3 1/2 X 3 1/2 In.	15.00
Teco, Candlestick, Green, 15 1/2 In.	65.00
Teco, Mug, Gray Matte, Quilted Design, 6 In.	45.00
Teco, Mug, Green Matte, Braided Design, 6 In.	49.00
Teco, Pocket, Wall, Green Matte, Art Deco Design Molded, 5 3/8 X 6 1/2 In.	49.00
Teco, Vase, Blue, 8 1/2 X 4 In.	95.00
Teco, Vase, Full Body, Embossed Floral Design, Green Porous Glaze, 9 In.	90.00

Teco, Vase, Green, 8 In.	35.00
Teco, Vase, Matte Green, Reticulated, 3 Footed, 9 In.	95.00
Telephone, Bell, Brass Receiver, Hand Crank To Ring, 27 In.	127.50
Telephone, Bell, Brass Receiver, Two Story, 27 X 7 In.	127.00
Telephone, Booth, Cathedral Style, Oak, Double Panel	900.00
Telephone, Bracket, Wall, Scissors Type For Candlestick	24.00
Telephone, Candlestick, Brass	135.00
Telephone, Candlestick, Brass Dial, 1921	69.00
Telephone, Candlestick, Brass, Oak Ringer Box, Black Enameled, 1915	135.00
Telephone, Candlestick, Chicago Telephone, Elkhart, Indiana	75.00
Telephone, Candlestick, Dial & Bell Ring Box, Brass	130.00
Telephone, Candlestick, Ericsson, Brass, Black, Original Dial, 1920s	178.00
Telephone, Candlestick, Monarch	75.00
Telephone, Candlestick, 1910	50.00
Telephone, Cathedral Top, Wall, Folding Shelf, Oak	120.00
Telephone, Connecticut, No Dial Candlestick, Brass	240.00
Telephone, Kellogg, Candlestick	80.00
Telephone, Stromberg Carlson, Oak	125.00
Telephone, Switchboard, Hotel Telephone, Oak, Full Size	245.00
Telephone, Switchboard, 16 Holes	25.00
Telephone, Wall, Golden Oak, Hand Crank, 2 Bells, 7 1/2 X 8 1/2 X 11 In.	148.00
Telephone, Wall, Oak, World's Fair Model	185.00
Television, Hallicraftor's, 7 In.Screen	100.00

 *Teplitz refers to art pottery manufactured by a number of companies in the Teplitz-Turn area of Bohemia during the late nineteenth and early twentieth centuries. The Amphora Porcelain Works and the Alexandra Works were two of these companies.*

Teplitz, Bowl, Amphora, Child In Court Dress, Ball, Blue, Gold, 7 1/2 In.	165.00
Teplitz, Bowl, Amphora, Face Design	45.00
Teplitz, Bust, French Dandy, Yellow, Peach, Blue, Lavender, Green, & Pink, 20 In.	450.00
Teplitz, Bust, Man's, French Dandy, Yellow, Blue, Lavender, Green, Pink, Beige	450.00
Teplitz, Creamer, Hand-Painted, 4 1/4 In.	25.00
Teplitz, Ewer, Floral, Swirl, Butterflies, Twig Handle, Gold, Blue, Purple, Beige	75.00
Teplitz, Ewer, Gold Dolphin Handle	65.00
Teplitz, Ewer, Orange, Black, Mosaic, Amphora, 8 1/2 In.	79.00
Teplitz, Figurine, Eagle, Perched On Base, Black Perch, Marked, Numbered, 8 In.	90.00
Teplitz, Planter, Amphora, Art Nouveau Faces, 10 X 6 1/2 In.	95.00
Teplitz, Planter, Statue, Girl & 6 Sheep, Terra Cotta, Amphora, 10 X 10 In.	190.00
Teplitz, Rose Bowl, Ivory, Pink Pansies, Green Leaves Outlined In Gold, 5 In.	55.00
Teplitz, Vase, Amphora, Blown-Out Lion, Palm Trees, Beige, Brown Tones, 11 In.	140.00
Teplitz, Vase, Amphora, Gold & Brown, Yellow Roses, 7 In.	47.50
Teplitz, Vase, Amphora, Iridescent Glaze, Roses, Winding Vine, 10 1/2 In.	75.00
Teplitz, Vase, Amphora, Purple Iridescent, Applied Gold Berries, 7 1/4 In.	52.00
Teplitz, Vase, Applied Leaves, Stem & Fruit, 2 Handled, Amphora, 12 In.	150.00
Teplitz, Vase, Applied Leaves, Stems, Blue Plums, Gold Trim, Handled, 12 In.	180.00
Teplitz, Vase, Art Nouveau, Birds, Leaves.Floral, Colorful, 2 Amphora Handles	110.00
Teplitz, Vase, Beige, Hand-Painted Gold & Red Carnations, 5 1/2 In., Pair	25.00
Teplitz, Vase, Bisque Background, Gold, Enamel Accents, 12 In.	275.00
Teplitz, Vase, Blown-Out Gold & Blue Iridescent Birds, Amphora, 7 In.	33.00
Teplitz, Vase, Dark Blue, Iridescent, Applied Gold Berries, Amphora, 8 In.	65.00
Teplitz, Vase, Dashing Cavalier, Gray Matte Finish, 3 Handled, 10 In.	55.00
Teplitz, Vase, Elite, Roses, Applied Leaves, Mottled Green, Amphora	45.00
Teplitz, Vase, Emerald Green, Gold Gilding, 9 In.	150.00
Teplitz, Vase, Enameled Leaves, Roses, Gold Reticulated Top, Signed, 6 In.	65.00
Teplitz, Vase, Figure, Man Playing Instrument, Marked Stellman, 4 1/2 In.	50.00
Teplitz, Vase, Friendship, Pink Roses, Blues, Greens, Amphora, Signed, 12 In.	235.00
Teplitz, Vase, Gold Cobwebs & Jewels, Amphora	80.00
Teplitz, Vase, Gold Flowers, 4 Handles, Amphora, 13 1/2 X 4 In.	67.00
Teplitz, Vase, Gold Handles, Narrow Neck, Matte Ground, Florals, 12 In.	145.00
Teplitz, Vase, Green & Gold, Serpent Handles, Gold, Amphora, 9 In.	65.00
Teplitz, Vase, Green, Varied Shades Of Green Thistles & Leaves, Footed, 9 In.	150.00
Teplitz, Vase, Hand-Painted Man Playing Instrument, Green Ground, 4 1/2 In.	55.00
Teplitz, Vase, Iridescent Rooster On Matte Green, Gold, Stellmacher, 5 In.	115.00

Teplitz, Vase, Spider Web,
Woman, Amphora, C.1920, 14 1/4 In.

Teplitz, Vase, Woman's Head,
Amphora, C.1920, 11 3/4 In.

Teplitz, Vase, Sea Monster,
Amphora, C.1920, 11 3/4 In.

Teplitz, Vase, Iridescent, Applied Berries, Signed, Amphora, 8 In.	68.00
Teplitz, Vase, Iridescent, Applied Cluster Grapes & Leaves, Handled, Amphora	48.00
Teplitz, Vase, Light Blue, Pink Roses, 4 Handles, Amphora, 8 In.	65.00
Teplitz, Vase, Lily Lip, Stem Handle, Base, Lavender, Green, Beige, Art Nouveau	110.00
Teplitz, Vase, Nude Full Figure Of Maiden, Art Nouveau, Amphora, 10 1/2 In.	195.00
Teplitz, Vase, Portrait, Art Nouveau Woman, Flowing Hair, 5 1/2 X 5 1/2 In.	240.00
Teplitz, Vase, Portrait, Gibson Girl, Hand-Painted, Enameled, 4 X 5 In.	65.00
Teplitz, Vase, Portrait, Gibston Girl, Enameled Floral, 4 X 5 In.	58.00
Teplitz, Vase, Portrait, Woman With Flowing Hair, Art Nouveau, 5 1/2 In.	240.00
Teplitz, Vase, Raised Acorns & Spider Webs, Jeweled Centers, 5 1/2 X 11 In.	165.00
Teplitz, Vase, Rose Decorated, Austria Mark, 13 In.	125.00
Teplitz, Vase, Sea Monster, Amphora, C.1920, 11 3/4 In. .... *Illus*	400.00
Teplitz, Vase, Spider Web, Woman, Amphora, C.1920, 14 1/4 In. .... *Illus*	950.00
Teplitz, Vase, Woman's Head, Amphora, C.1920, 11 3/4 In. .... *Illus*	750.00
Terra-Cotta, Bodhisattva, Diety On Pedestal, Lotus Leaves, Gilded, Red	155.00
Terra-Cotta, Plaque, Shepherdess With Nest Of Cupids, 1850-60, P.Ipsen	175.00
Terra-Cotta, Tea Set, Classical Scenes, White, 3 Piece	375.00
Terra-Cotta, Teapot, Raised Blossoms, Yellow & Green Bamboo, China, 3 X 3 In.	15.00
Terra-Cotta, Teapot, Yi-Hsing, Flowers In Relief, Lion Lid, 3 1/2 In.	20.00
Terra-Cotta, Vase, Dragon Decorated, 6 In., Pair	50.00

*Textile includes all types of table linens and household linens such as
coverlets, quilts, fabrics, etc.*

Textile, see also World's Fair items

Textile, Bedspread, Crocheted, Cream, Medallion Pattern, 94 X 110 In.	200.00
Textile, Bedspread, Crocheted, Petal Flower, Light Cream, 96 X 110 In.	225.00
Textile, Bedspread, Hand-Crocheted, Double Size, Early 1900s	150.00
Textile, Bedspread, Knitted, Early 1900s, Twin Size, Signed & Dated, Pair	200.00
Textile, Bedspread, Old Rose Damask, Fringe	30.00
Textile, Bedspread, Popcorn Stitch Crocheted, 78 X 90 In.	80.00
Textile, Bedspread, Turkish, Silk, Silver Metallic Embroidery, 70 X 98 In.	200.00
Textile, Berlin Work, Signed Mary Anne Moore, 1842, Framed	150.00
Textile, Blanket Cover, White, Russian Linen, 98 X 84 In.	15.00
Textile, Bonnet, Checkered Gingham, Button On Brim	25.00
Textile, Bonnet, Silk, Black, All Fur Edged	18.00
Textile, Bookmark, Silk, Spanish American War, 8 Line Verse	12.00
Textile, Bookmark, Woven Silk, Warner Mfg.Co., Home Sweet Home, 11 In.	35.00
Textile, Cape, Georgette, Gatsby, Long, Black, Heavily Fringed	37.00

Textile, Coverlet, Jacquard, Blue,
White, Signed, Dec.18, 1834

Textile, Dress, Flapper,
Pink Chiffon, Beadwork
Birds, C.1925

Textile, Coat, Black Silk

Textile, Dress, Pink Striped

Textile, Gown, Victorian,
Taffeta, Brown Silk, C.1895

Textile, Coat, Black Silk .... *Illus*	37.50
Textile, Coat, Embroidered Mongolian Mandarin, Horse Hoof Cuff, Silk	150.00

Linen or wool coverlets were made during the nineteenth century. Most of the coverlets date from 1800 to 1850. Four types were made, the double woven, jacquard, summer and winter, and overshot.

Textile, Coverlet, Black & White Stylized Flowers & Birds, Ohio, 1839	300.00
Textile, Coverlet, Boston Town Design	90.00
Textile, Coverlet, Heilbronn, Dated 1840	170.00
Textile, Coverlet, Homespun, Blue, Long Fringe, 3/4 Bed Size	145.00
Textile, Coverlet, Jacquard, Blue, White, Signed, Dec.18, 1834 .... *Illus*	1500.00
Textile, Coverlet, Jacquard, 80 Repeats Of Oak Leaf Design	375.00
Textile, Coverlet, Knox County, Ohio, 1851, Eagles, Churches, 93 1/2 X 75 In. ...	275.00
Textile, Coverlet, Memorial Hall, Centennial, 1876, Signed, Dated	275.00
Textile, Coverlet, Overshot In Red And Mustard	195.00
Textile, Coverlet, Red And Cream	295.00
Textile, Coverlet, Woven, Fliehr & Boettger, Millerstown, Lehigh Co., C.1860	295.00
Textile, Coverlet, 1893 Columbian Exposition, Red, White	145.00
Textile, Dress, Child's, Plaid, Red Trim, Tan Chintz Lined, C.1840	30.00
Textile, Dress, Evening, Flapper Style, Lavender, White Beading, 1920, Size 38 ...	80.00
Textile, Dress, Flapper, Pink Chiffon, Beadwork Birds, C.1925 .... *Illus*	50.00
Textile, Dress, Pink Striped .... *Illus*	37.50
Textile, Dress, Silk Chiffon, C.1910	40.00
Textile, Dress, Sleeveless, Beaded & Sequin, Black	50.00
Textile, Embroidery, Chinese, Silk, Dragon, Dogs, Flowers, 37 X 27 In.	250.00
Textile, Embroidery, Foo Dog, Silver Thread, Sequins On Red Silk, Framed, Pair	100.00
Textile, Flag, American, 46 Stars, Authentic Silk, 7 1/2 X 11 1/4 In.	6.00
Textile, Gown, Victorian, Taffeta, Brown Silk, C.1895 .... *Illus*	27.50

Textile, Hat, Military Dress, Gold Braided, Mounted

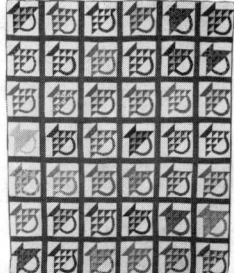

Textile, Quilt, Calico, Flower Basket,
Maroon, White, Multicolor

Textile, Quilt, Crazy, Patchwork,
Satin, Velvet, Maryland, 1890

Textile, Handkerchief, Blarney Castle, St.Louis Exposition, 1904	25.00
Textile, Handkerchief, Dewey, Hero Of Manila, 17 X 18 In.	20.00
Textile, Handkerchief, 1776-1876, Memorial Hall Art Gallery, Eagle	59.00
Textile, Hat, Beaver, Leather Case	80.00
Textile, Hat, Military Dress, Gold Braided, Mounted .... *Illus*	50.00
Textile, Hooked Chairback Cover, 13 1/2 X 12 1/2 In.	10.00
Textile, Lap Robe, Carriage, Horse-Head Design	6.00
Textile, Needlepoint Picture, European, Windmill, Animals, 1869, 24 X 30 In.	100.00
Textile, Needlepoint, Man With Rifle & Dog, Victorian, Framed, 16 X 19 In.	110.00
Textile, Picture, Embroidered Silk Chinese Pheasants, Carved Teakwood Frame	30.00
Textile, Pillow, Opium, White With Flowers, Singapore	55.00
Textile, Purse, Perfume, Paneled Green, Mushroom Screw Cap, Coralene Co.	12.50
Textile, Quilt, Amish Print, C.1880, Ohio Star, 76 X 68 In.	145.00
Textile, Quilt, Blue & White Star Design	70.00
Textile, Quilt, Blue & White, Double Irish Chain	145.00
Textile, Quilt, Bride's, All White Trapunto, Laurel Wreaths & Doves, C.1835	1200.00
Textile, Quilt, Calico, Flower Basket, Maroon, White, Multicolor .... *Illus*	400.00
Textile, Quilt, Churndash, Red & White, All Handstitched	135.00
Textile, Quilt, Crazy, Patchwork, Satin, Velvet, Maryland, 1890 .... *Illus*	550.00
Textile, Quilt, Crazy, Signed & Dated	125.00
Textile, Quilt, Crib, Child's, Pink, Bowtie Variation	38.00
Textile, Quilt, Crib, Log Cabin, Reds, Blues, Grays, 30 X 30 In.	58.00
Textile, Quilt, Crib, Sunburst Pattern, Rush Light, 4 X 4 In.	145.00
Textile, Quilt, Double Irish Chain, Red & White, Queen Size, Hand Quilted	100.00
Textile, Quilt, Double Wedding Ring, Double Bed Size, 1937	135.00
Textile, Quilt, Double Wedding Ring, Scalloped Edge, C.1930, 72 X 48 In.	75.00
Textile, Quilt, Double, 9 Patch Block, Red & Blue On White, C.1930	100.00
Textile, Quilt, Flower Basket, Friendship Quilt, 78 X 78 In.	400.00
Textile, Quilt, Friendship, Red, Black, & White, Snowflake, 77 X 78 In.	125.00
Textile, Quilt, Friendship, 60 Signed Names, C.1850, 74 X 82 1/2 In.	150.00
Textile, Quilt, Log Cabin	275.00
Textile, Quilt, Log Cabin, Brown & White Paisley, Red Gingham	125.00

Textile, Rug, Hooked, Blue, Gray, Brown, C.1920, 32 3/4 X 46 In.

Textile, Quilt, Log Cabin, Wool	66.00
Textile, Quilt, Log Cabin, 19th Century, Lined, 60 X 60 In.	85.00
Textile, Quilt, Looks Like Wagon Wheel	125.00
Textile, Quilt, Nine Patch, Pink, Black & White Squares, 82 X 80 In.	80.00
Textile, Quilt, Octagonal Design, Early 1900s, Double Size	85.00
Textile, Quilt, Red Flowers, Green Leaves & Trellis Border, 80 1/2 X 84 In.	950.00
Textile, Quilt, Red, White, And Blue Double Irish Chain	75.00
Textile, Quilt, Sunbonnet Baby, White Ground, Colored Dolls, Full Size	125.00
Textile, Quilt, Top, Log Cabin, Purple & Black Satin	65.00
Textile, Quilt, Wedding Ring, Double, Yellow	175.00
Textile, Ribbon, Arlington Mills, Columbus Sighting America, Woven In Silk	95.00
Textile, Ribbon, Arlington Mills, Woven In Silk, Oak Frame, Columbus	125.00
Textile, Robe, Chinese, Silk, Gold & Black	12.00
Textile, Robe, Sleigh, Horsehead Design, 45 X 60 In.	135.00
Textile, Rug On Homespun, Waldoboro, Dark Ground, Floral, 23 X 54 In.	385.00
Textile, Rug, Chinese, Green & Lilac, 9 X 12 In.	1450.00
Textile, Rug, Hand-Hooked, Pink Lion, American Shield Brackets, 34 X 65 In.	675.00
Textile, Rug, Hooked, Blue, Gray, Brown, C.1920, 32 3/4 X 46 In. ....Illus	500.00
Textile, Rug, Hooked, Geometric Design, 36 X 38 In.	40.00
Textile, Rug, Hooked, Horse, Hansom Cab, Gray, Green, Folk Art, 18 1/2 X 30 In.	140.00
Textile, Rug, Hooked, Late 19th Century, Bold Color	65.00
Textile, Rug, Hooked, Maple Sugarin In Vermont, Earthy Colors, 36 X 27 In.	95.00
Textile, Rug, Hooked, Red Shades, Dark Gray Scroll, 30 X 50 In.	65.00
Textile, Rug, Hooked, Scotty Wagging Tail, 23 X 35 In.	145.00
Textile, Rug, Hooked, Shades Of Red With Dark Gray Scroll, 30 X 50 In.	65.00
Textile, Rug, Navajo, Red & Tan, 37 X 22 In.	55.00
Textile, Rug, Needlepoint, Red & Pink Roses, Green Leaves, Navy Ground, 20 In.	48.00
Textile, Rug, Oriental, Beluchi, Red, Birds Design, 32 X 55 In.	175.00
Textile, Rug, Oriental, Hand-Knotted, Small	85.00
Textile, Rug, Oriental, Tan, Cobalt Border, Ruby Florals, Chinese, 2 X 4 Ft.	165.00
Textile, Rug, Persian, Dark Red, Blue, Brown, & Beige, 3 1/2 X 6 1/2 Ft.	250.00
Textile, Rug, Shades Of Gray, Tan, Black, 29 X 39 1/2 In.	35.00
Textile, Rug, Tabriz, Signed, Royal Blue, Ivory Medallion, 8 X 11 Ft.	1500.00
Textile, Rug, Waldoboro, Homespun, Dark Background, Floral, 23 X 54 In.	385.00

Samplers were made in the United States during the early 1700s. The best examples were made from 1790 to 1840. Long narrow samplers are usually older than the square ones. Early samplers just had stitching or alphabets. The later examples had numerals, borders, and pictorial decorations. Those with mottoes are mid-Victorian.

Textile, Sampler, Alphabet, Brown, Green, Black, Yellow Silk, Hand Woven Linen	23.00
Textile, Sampler, Alphabet, Faded, American, Dated 1812, 10 1/2 X 8 1/2 In.	125.00
Textile, Sampler, Alphabet, Florals, Signed, Dated 1787, 10 X 13 In.	650.00
Textile, Sampler, Alphabet, Numbers, Signed, Dated 1818, Framed, 17 X 18 In.	135.00
Textile, Sampler, Alphabet, Verse, Scene, 1871, Framed, 19 X 21 In.	110.00
Textile, Sampler, Animals, Birds, Trees, House, Alphabet, Martha Porder, 1843	225.00
Textile, Sampler, C.1804, Signed, 18 X 19 1/2 In.	325.00
Textile, Sampler, Castle, Strawberry Border, Mary Jackson, 1851, 18 X 20 In.	185.00

Textile, Sampler, Dated 1819, Mahogany Frame, 12 X 13 In.	125.00
Textile, Sampler, Elizabeth Rolston, 1837, Grapevine Border, Scene, Alphabet	275.00
Textile, Sampler, Eve Phillips, 1827, Birds, Alphabet, Verse, 21 X 7 In.	185.00
Textile, Sampler, House, Trees, Birds, Muted Colors, 1816, 15 1/2 X 21 In.	210.00
Textile, Sampler, Houses & Flowers, Verse, Alphabet, 1819, 8 X 12 1/2 In.	280.00
Textile, Sampler, In Walnut Frame, Dated 1849, 22 In.	145.00
Textile, Sampler, Lancaster County, Signed Elizabeth Musselman, 1836	225.00
Textile, Sampler, Lion, Crown, Hearts, Floral, Alphabet, 1771, Ann Mingey, 10 In.	265.00
Textile, Sampler, Map Of England	55.00
Textile, Sampler, Martha Jordon, Mar.3, 1829, House, Birds, Strawberry, Framed	225.00
Textile, Sampler, Mary Ann Fry, Nov.8, 1827, 6 3/4 X 12 1/2 In.	60.00
Textile, Sampler, Mary Hopkins, Detail, Design, Color, Small, Unframed	70.00
Textile, Sampler, Mary Hughes, Aged 9, Dated 1822, 15 1/2 X 19 1/2 In.	250.00
Textile, Sampler, Pennsylvania Dutch, 1818	225.00
Textile, Sampler, Quaker, West Town Style, Dated 1828, Framed, 6 X 6 In.	75.00
Textile, Sampler, Sally Doolittle, Oxford, NH, Framed, 1808, 12 1/4 X 12 In.	250.00
Textile, Sampler, Strawberry Border, Verse, Baskets Of Flowers, 17 X 19 In.	185.00
Textile, Sampler, Young Girl, Age 8, 1812, 13 X 12 1/2 In.	45.00
Textile, Sampler, 1814, Framed, 16 X 9 In.	75.00
Textile, Sampler, 6-Line Verse, House, Trees, Birds, Earth Colors, 1827, 17 In.	225.00
Textile, Scarf, Linen, 4 In.Crochet Lace Ends, 17 X 62 In.	4.00
Textile, Scarf, Piano Cover, Felt Floral	12.50
Textile, Shawl, Coverlet, Paisley, 60 X 120 In.	62.00
Textile, Shawl, Embroidered, Open Tail Peacocks, Macrame Fringe	300.00
Textile, Shawl, Paisley, 5 X 10 Feet	55.00
Textile, Shawl, Spanish, Embroidered Florals, Fringed	75.00
Textile, Spats, Gray, Pair	4.50
Textile, Tablecloth, Battenberg Lace, 67 In.Diameter	15.00
Textile, Tablecloth, Battenberg Lace, Scalloped Edge, 88 In.Square	118.00
Textile, Tablecloth, Crochet, C.1870, 45 X 50 In.	35.00
Textile, Tablecloth, Hand Crochet, 79 X 69 In.	65.00
Textile, Tablecloth, Linen Damask, 50 X 72 In.	18.00
Textile, Tablecloth, Linen Damask, 56 X 72 In.	20.00
Textile, Tablecloth, Linen Damask, 72 X 82 In.	35.00
Textile, Tablecloth, Linen Satin Damask, 2 X 2 1/2 Yards	20.00
Textile, Tablecloth, Linen, Damask, Patterned, 54 X 54 In.	12.00
Textile, Tablecloth, Quaker Lace, Countess Egyptian Pattern, 72 X 90 In.	75.00
Textile, Tapestry, Century Of Progress, 1933, 42 X 25 In.	45.00
Textile, Tapestry, Courtyard Scene, Troubador & Ladies, 19 X 36 In.	35.00
Textile, Tapestry, French Court Scene, 56 X 19 1/4 In.	45.00
Textile, Tapestry, Lindbergh, Atlantic Flight, 54 X 19 1/2 In.	50.00 To 125.00
Textile, Tapestry, Machine, Belgium, Mountains, C.1880, 13 X 6 In.	100.00
Textile, Towel, Crewel Work, 1837	395.00
Textile, Wall Hanging, Chinese Brocade, Dragon Medallions, Silk, 61 X 53 In.	200.00
Textile, Wall Hanging, Chinese Mythical Figures, Animals, 6 X 2 1/2 Ft.	150.00
Thermometer, James A.Stacey & Son, Lumber, Windsor, Vermont, Yellow	15.00

Tiffany pieces made of all combinations of materials.

Tiffany Bronze, Ashtray, Scalloped Edge, Dore, 4 1/4 X 1 1/2 In.	65.00
Tiffany Bronze, Bookend, Buddha, Dark Patina, Tiffany Studios, Pair	215.00
Tiffany Bronze, Bowl, Dore, No.1708, 9 In.	50.00 To 55.00
Tiffany Bronze, Box, Cigarette, Gilded, Ship Medallion, No.135 Favrile	65.00
Tiffany Bronze, Box, Pine Needle Design, Hinged, Dore, 8 X 8 In.	265.00
Tiffany Bronze, Candlestick, Globular Top, Amber Glass Inserts, 11 In.	225.00
Tiffany Bronze, Candlestick, Scalloped & Rayed Foot, 17 In.	350.00
Tiffany Bronze, Card Receiver, Dore, 8 In.	60.00
Tiffany Bronze, Compote, Dore, Geometric Design, Pedestal Base, 6 In.	125.00
Tiffany Bronze, Desk Set, Stylized Mythical Animals, Stone Setting, 7 Piece	695.00
Tiffany Bronze, Dore, Round, 15 In.	135.00
Tiffany Bronze, Figurine, Cat Playing With Doll, Miniature, 3 1/2 In.	135.00
Tiffany Bronze, Figurine, Gold Dore Lion, No.932, 5 In.	400.00
Tiffany Bronze, Figurine, Stalking Lion, Miniature	135.00
Tiffany Bronze, Frame, Easel Type, Sailboat Decoration, 6 1/2 X 6 1/2 In.	150.00
Tiffany Bronze, Lamp Base, Table, Gold Dore Finish, No.676	1000.00

Tiffany Bronze, Lamp, Desk, Chinese Design, Dore, Signed B.S., 416	600.00
Tiffany Bronze, Lamp, Hammertone & Smooth Finish, Curved Stick, 6 In.	350.00
Tiffany Bronze, Lantern, Blown, Scroll Arm, Ovoid, Elongated, Electrical	2500.00
Tiffany Bronze, Letter Rack, Chinese Pattern, 3-Compartment, 12 X 8 In.	225.00
Tiffany Bronze, Paperweight, Bulldog, Signed & Numbered	250.00 To 350.00
Tiffany Bronze, Paperweight, Bulldog, Tiffany Studio	95.00
Tiffany Bronze, Paperweight, Dog	250.00
Tiffany Bronze, Paperweight, Irish Setter, 3 1/2 In.	225.00 To 275.00
Tiffany Bronze, Pen Tray, Green Slag, 3 X 10 In.	110.00
Tiffany Bronze, Pen Tray, Zodiac	75.00
Tiffany Bronze, Pen Wiper, Dore	95.00
Tiffany Bronze, Platter, Round, 12 In.	85.00
Tiffany Bronze, Scissors, Desk, No.1837, Dore	210.00
Tiffany Bronze, Tray, Serving, Raised Border, Dore, 12 In.	75.00

Tiffany glass was made by Louis Comfort Tiffany, the American glass designer who worked from about 1879 to 1933. His work included iridescent glass, art nouveau styles of design, and original contemporary styles. He was also noted for his stained glass windows, his unusual lamps, bronze work, pottery, and silver.

Tiffany Glass, Basket, Bread, Pierced Sides, 12 1/2 X 7 1/2 In.	495.00
Tiffany Glass, Bonbon, Flower Form, Peacock Blue, Signed & Numbered	550.00
Tiffany Glass, Bonbon, Peacock Blue, 4 1/2 In.	525.00
Tiffany Glass, Bottle, Cologne, Gold, Stopper, 5 3/4 In.	325.00
Tiffany Glass, Bottle, Perfume, Iridescent, Stopper, Signed 1055-4166, 6 In.	375.00
Tiffany Glass, Bottle, Travel, Fluted Crystal, Pair, 7 In.And 6 3/4 In.	100.00
Tiffany Glass, Bowl, Amber, Bell Shaped, 4 3/8 In.High	150.00
Tiffany Glass, Bowl, Blue, Iridescent, Signed, 2 1/2 X 7 In.	350.00
Tiffany Glass, Bowl, Blue, L.C.Tiffany Favrile, 10 X 4 In.	695.00
Tiffany Glass, Bowl, Blue, Scalloped Edge, L.C.T.Favrile, 4 In.	350.00
Tiffany Glass, Bowl, Blue, 10 In.	895.00
Tiffany Glass, Bowl, Centerpiece, Yellow Green Pastel, Footed, 12 1/2 In.	600.00
Tiffany Glass, Bowl, Diatreta, Blue, 3 1/4 In.	6500.00
Tiffany Glass, Bowl, Finger, Underplate, Gold Iridescent, Blue Highlights	300.00
Tiffany Glass, Bowl, Finger, Underplate, Gold Stretch Iridescent, 6 1/2 In.	300.00
Tiffany Glass, Bowl, Finger, Underplate, Gold, Signed L.C.T.Favrile	295.00
Tiffany Glass, Bowl, Finger, With Plate, Iridescent, LCT	225.00 To 295.00
Tiffany Glass, Bowl, Gold Iridescent, L.C.Tiffany, Favrile, 12 1/4 In.	795.00
Tiffany Glass, Bowl, Gold Iridescent, Signed 1404 LCT Favrile	550.00
Tiffany Glass, Bowl, Gold, Amethyst & Platinum, 2 X 9 In.	445.00 To 525.00
Tiffany Glass, Bowl, Gold, Diamond Optic, Signed, No.7520n, 5 3/4 In.	210.00
Tiffany Glass, Bowl, Gold, Rainbow Iridescence, Fluted, L.C.T., 4 3/4 In.	425.00
Tiffany Glass, Bowl, Gold, Swirled Prunts, LCT & Numbered, 2 1/2 In.	325.00
Tiffany Glass, Bowl, Green, Blossom Shape, Luster, L.C.T.Favrile, 6 X 2 In.	350.00
Tiffany Glass, Bowl, Iridescent Gold, Ribbed, L.C.Tiffany Favrile, 7 In.	300.00
Tiffany Glass, Bowl, Iridescent, Purple, Gold, Favrile, 2508k, 9 1/2 In.	225.00
Tiffany Glass, Bowl, Lily Form, Green, L.C.T., Favrile, 6 X 2 In.	200.00
Tiffany Glass, Bowl, Morning-Glory Blue, Faint Ribbing, Favrile, 7 1/4 In.	650.00
Tiffany Glass, Bowl, Paneled, Serpentine Rim, Blue, Signed, 14 In.	245.00
Tiffany Glass, Bowl, Pastel Green, Domed Foot, Opalescent Laurel Leaf	575.00
Tiffany Glass, Bowl, Purple, Gold, Iridescent, Favrile, 2508k, 9 1/2 In.	225.00
Tiffany Glass, Bowl, Ribbed, Light Amber, Lavender & Blue Iridescent, 6 In.	265.00
Tiffany Glass, Bowl, Ribbed, Pink Gold, Scalloped, Iridescent, 3 X 8 In.	350.00
Tiffany Glass, Bowl, Ruffled, Gold Iridescent, Scalloped & Crimped, 4 1/2 In.	210.00
Tiffany Glass, Bowl, Scalloped, Favrile, Signed, Numbered, Labeled, 4 X 3 In.	225.00
Tiffany Glass, Bowl, Scalloped, Ribbed, Amber Iridescent, Signed, 8 In.	175.00
Tiffany Glass, Bowl, Spiral Ribbed, Blue, 7 In.	295.00
Tiffany Glass, Bowl, Swirled, Ribbed, Blue, Silver Highlights, 6 1/2 In.	495.00
Tiffany Glass, Candlestick, Flared Collar, Swirled & Ribbed, 7 In., Pair	695.00
Tiffany Glass, Candlestick, Gold, Amethyst & Platinum, Swirled, 7 In., Pair	750.00
Tiffany Glass, Candlestick, Gold, Iridescent Blue, Purple & Red, 8 In.	275.00
Tiffany Glass, Candlestick, Gold, Ribbed Swirl Stem, 8 1/4 In., Pair	850.00
Tiffany Glass, Candlestick, Gold, Signed & Paper Label, 7 In.	595.00
Tiffany Glass, Champagne, Gold, Iridescent, L.C.T.Favrile, 7 In., Set Of 6	2100.00

Tiffany Glass, Compote, Blue Maple Leaves, Intaglio Cut, Footed, 6 X 2 In.	975.00
Tiffany Glass, Compote, Blue, Favrile, 4 1/2 X 6 1/2 In.	725.00
Tiffany Glass, Compote, Fluted Rim, Gold Iridescent, Favrile	450.00
Tiffany Glass, Compote, Gold Florescent, Lavender, Scalloped Top, 6 1/2 In.	295.00
Tiffany Glass, Compote, Gold Luster & Highlights, Rippled Edge, 6 X 6 In.	325.00
Tiffany Glass, Compote, Gold, Blue & Lavender Iridescence, 6 1/2 In., Pair	950.00
Tiffany Glass, Compote, Gold, Blue Iridescent, Fluted, 6 X 6 In.	295.00
Tiffany Glass, Compote, Gold, Mirror Finish, Signed, 9 1/2 X 6 1/2 In.	575.00
Tiffany Glass, Compote, Iridescent, Stemmed, Signed, 4 In., 6 3/8 In.Diam.	425.00
Tiffany Glass, Compote, Pastel, Green Iridescent Stretch, Opalescent Rays	440.00
Tiffany Glass, Compote, Peacock Blue, Signed, 1 1/4 X 6 In.	525.00 To 550.00
Tiffany Glass, Console Set, Green, Intaglio Dragonfly, L.C.Tiffany, Favrile	1650.00
Tiffany Glass, Cordial Set, Gold Iridescence, Engraved Decoration, 5 Piece	1250.00
Tiffany Glass, Creamer, Blue, Corset Shape, Signed, 4 1/4 In.	365.00 To 395.00
Tiffany Glass, Cup, Loving, Green Leaves On Gold, 3 Handles, 5 In.	950.00
Tiffany Glass, Cup, Punch, Gold Iridescence, Applied Lily Pads, Handled	275.00
Tiffany Glass, Decanter Set, Tantalus, Cut & Polished, Signed, With Holder	595.00
Tiffany Glass, Dish, Blue, Triangular, Iridescent, Handle, 4 1/4 In.	750.00
Tiffany Glass, Dish, Candy, Flower Form, Peacock Blue, Signed & Numbered	525.00
Tiffany Glass, Dish, Fluted, Gold, Signed, 4 X 1 1/2 In.	145.00
Tiffany Glass, Dish, Nut, Blue-Gold Iridescence, Ruffled, 2 5/8 In., Set Of 6	750.00
Tiffany Glass, Dish, Nut, Gold Iridescent, Signed, 4 In.Diameter X 1 7/8 In.	550.00
Tiffany Glass, Dish, Nut, Gold, Blue, Scalloped, 3 In.	125.00
Tiffany Glass, Dish, Nut, Gold, Green Inside Border, Ivory Outside, 4 In.	450.00
Tiffany Glass, Dish, Nut, Individual, Iridescent, Ruffled, Signed L.C.T.	111.00
Tiffany Glass, Dish, Nut, Ruffled, Gold, Signed, 4 In.	175.00
Tiffany Glass, Dish, Salt, Gold Iridescent, Fluted, 2 1/2 In., Pair	115.00
Tiffany Glass, Flower, Frog, Blue Iridescent, Lily Pads & Vines, 10 1/2 In.	950.00
Tiffany Glass, Goblet, Lemon-Green Opalescent, Opal Stem & Foot, 8 In.	135.00
Tiffany Glass, Goblet, Opalescent Blue Cup, Pale Green Stem & Base, 9 In.	300.00
Tiffany Glass, Goblet, Turquoise Opalescence, Stemmed, Signed & Numbered	325.00
Tiffany Glass, Juice, Lily Pad, Signed, Numbered, Labeled	275.00
Tiffany Glass, Lamp, Desk, Cased, Brown, Iridescent, Domed Shade, L.C.T.Favrile	1350.00
Tiffany Glass, Liqueur, Blue Gold, Pinched Sides, 1 7/8 In.	135.00
Tiffany Glass, Master Salt, Gold & Blue, Signed	120.00
Tiffany Glass, Mug, Green Zigzag, Iridescent, Handled, 2 1/2 X 3 1/2 In.	375.00
Tiffany Glass, Night-Light, Brass Finial, Wood Stand, Signed D.Q.	650.00
Tiffany Glass, Paperweight, Narcissus Design, Bulbous, 12 In.	6500.00
Tiffany Glass, Parfait, Pastel, LCT Favrile, 6 1/2 In.	195.00
Tiffany Glass, Parfait, Pedestal Foot, Opalescent Feather, 5 1/8 In.	295.00
Tiffany Glass, Parfait, Pink, White Feathering, Slightly Flared, Green Foot	225.00
Tiffany Glass, Pitcher, Milk, Gold, Iridescent, 6 1/2 In.	265.00
Tiffany Glass, Pitcher, Milk, Iridescent, Numbered, Signed, 5 1/4 In.	485.00
Tiffany Glass, Plate, Aqua Pastel, 8 In.	250.00 To 280.00
Tiffany Glass, Plate, Iridescent, Scalloped, LCT, 6 3/4 In.	140.00
Tiffany Glass, Plate, Lavender Pastel, Signed, 8 1/2 In.	185.00
Tiffany Glass, Plate, Lavender Pastel, Signed, 9 In.	175.00
Tiffany Glass, Plate, Pink Pastel, White Feathering, Opalescent	235.00 To 275.00
Tiffany Glass, Plate, Pink, Onion Skin Effect, Opalescent & Iridescent	195.00
Tiffany Glass, Plate, Scalloped, Favrile, Signed, Numbered, 6 1/2 In.	210.00
Tiffany Glass, Punch, Gold, Intaglio Cut Grapes & Leaves, Signed, 3 1/2 In.	225.00
Tiffany Glass, Rose Bowl, Gold Iridescent, Green Random Leaf & Vine, Signed	525.00
Tiffany Glass, Salt & Pepper, Floral Design, 6 1/2 In.	275.00
Tiffany Glass, Salt Dip, Iridescent Gold, Open, Signed, 2 1/4 In.	115.00
Tiffany Glass, Salt, Blue, Pedestaled, Favrile, Signed, Numbered	145.00
Tiffany Glass, Salt, Crenated Rim, Scalloped, Gold Iridescent, Signed, 3 In.	95.00
Tiffany Glass, Salt, Favrile, Tapered Body, Wide Mouth, Everted Rim, Set Of 6	135.00
Tiffany Glass, Salt, Fluted Rims, Gold Iridescent, Pair	110.00
Tiffany Glass, Salt, Gold Luster, Purple, Scallops, Signed, 2 3/4 X 1 In.	90.00
Tiffany Glass, Salt, Gold Iridescent, Ruffled, Blue Highlights, 1 1/8 In.	145.00
Tiffany Glass, Salt, Gold Iridescent, Signed LCT Favrile	98.00
Tiffany Glass, Salt, Gold, Blue Iridescence, Ruffled, 3 In.	125.00
Tiffany Glass, Salt, Gold, Blue, Ruffled Edge, Signed, 4 In.	110.00 To 150.00
Tiffany Glass, Salt, Gold, Ruffled Top, Signed L.C.T.6303, 2 1/2 In.	120.00

Tiffany Glass, Salt, Gold, Swirled, Bumps, Signed 125.00
Tiffany Glass, Salt, Green Iridescent, 1 1/4 X 3 In. 175.00
Tiffany Glass, Salt, Kettle Shape, Gold Footed, Signed, 1 3/4 X 2 1/4 In. 125.00
Tiffany Glass, Salt, Master, Ruffled Rim, 4 1/2 In. 145.00
Tiffany Glass, Salt, Master, Scalloped, Wide Mouth, Signed, 5 In. 375.00
Tiffany Glass, Salt, Platinum & Blue, Ruffled, 2 1/2 In. 115.00
Tiffany Glass, Salt, Rattail Pattern, Gold, Blue Iridescence 115.00
Tiffany Glass, Salt, Ruffled Top, L.C.T.Favrile, 2 1/2 In. 95.00
Tiffany Glass, Salt, Scalloped Rim, Favrile, Signed LCT, 2 3/4 X 1 In. 95.00
Tiffany Glass, Salt, Snaketrack, Blue, Signed 146.00
Tiffany Glass, Shade, Candle Lamp, Gold, Pair 375.00
Tiffany Glass, Shade, Damascene, Band Of Peacocks Design, Signed, 10 In. 1500.00
Tiffany Glass, Shade, Gas, Gold, Signed 150.00
Tiffany Glass, Shade, Gold Aurene, Signed, 3 In. 125.00
Tiffany Glass, Shade, Gold Flame, Blue Highlights, Opal Reactive, Signed 350.00
Tiffany Glass, Shade, Gold Iridescent, Signed & Numbered, 5 In. 205.00
Tiffany Glass, Shade, Gold, Signed Fitter, Gold Mirror Finish, Favrile, 4 In. 175.00
Tiffany Glass, Shade, Hanging, Red, Green, Caramel, 18 In. 1200.00
Tiffany Glass, Shade, King Tut Pattern, Gold Iridescent, 4 3/4 X 4 1/4 In. 275.00
Tiffany Glass, Shade, No.295, Amber, Gold Damascene, Signed 275.00
Tiffany Glass, Shade, Pastel Striped, White On White, Signed, Bell Shape 150.00
Tiffany Glass, Shade, Stalactite, Gold Feather, Green Iridescent, 10 3/4 In. 345.00
Tiffany Glass, Sherbet, Gold Iridescent, Colonial Pattern, Favrile, 3 1/2 In. 135.00
Tiffany Glass, Sherbet, Gold, Etched Grapes & Leaves, L.C.T., 3 1/2 In. 175.00
Tiffany Glass, Sherbet, Quilted, Gold, Pink Highlights, Pedestal, Signed, Pair 395.00
Tiffany Glass, Tazza, Gadroon Rim, Vase Shaped Stem, Blue, 19 In. 324.00
Tiffany Glass, Tile, Iridescent, Green, Cream, L.C.T.& Co., 1881, 3 In., Pair 75.00
Tiffany Glass, Toothpick, Gold Iridescent, Urn Shape, Pinched Sides, 2 In. 145.00
Tiffany Glass, Toothpick, Gold, Pinched Sides, Signed, 1 1/2 In. 130.00
Tiffany Glass, Toothpick, Gold, 4 Sided, Dimpled, Signed & Numbered 115.00
Tiffany Glass, Toothpick, Handled, Blue, Signed 148.00
Tiffany Glass, Toothpick, Platinum Finish, 4 Pinched Sides, L.C.T. 205.00
Tiffany Glass, Toothpick, Twisted Prunts, LCT Favrile, 2 1/2 In. 150.00
Tiffany Glass, Tumbler, Faceted Bottom, Platinum Swirls & Waves Top, 3 In. 195.00
Tiffany Glass, Tumbler, Faceted Panels, Platinum Swirls, Fold, Signed 95.00
Tiffany Glass, Tumbler, Favrile Gold Iridescent, Signed L.C.T. 160.00
Tiffany Glass, Tumbler, Gold Plated, Signed 220.00
Tiffany Glass, Tumbler, Juice, Gold, Cut Panels, Cut Like Jewels, Signed 225.00
Tiffany Glass, Urn, Gold, Iridescent, Handled, L.C.T. Favrile, 3 1/4 In. 325.00
Tiffany Glass, Vase, Alabaster, Gold Luster Fcathering, L.C.Tiffany, 8 In. 700.00
Tiffany Glass, Vase, Alabaster, Gold Luster Leaf Decoration, Signed, 10 In. 650.00
Tiffany Glass, Vase, Aqua Top, Dark Green & Gold Feathering, 18 In. 2250.00
Tiffany Glass, Vase, Black, Blue Iridescence, Blue Pulled Feathers, 7 1/2 In. 1850.00
Tiffany Glass, Vase, Blue Iridescent, Fully Signed, 10 1/2 In. 675.00
Tiffany Glass, Vase, Blue Iridescent, Ribbed & Dimpled, Signed, 4 3/4 In. 475.00
Tiffany Glass, Vase, Blue Luster, 9 1/4 In. 875.00
Tiffany Glass, Vase, Blue Straited To Gold Iridescent, Favrile, 11 1/4 In. 1600.00
Tiffany Glass, Vase, Blue, Signed, 10 In. 650.00
Tiffany Glass, Vase, Blue, Signed, 4 3/4 In. 475.00
Tiffany Glass, Vase, Bronze Pinecone Stem, Trumpet Form, Signed, 12 In. 325.00
Tiffany Glass, Vase, Bud, Amber Iridescence, Blue Highlights, 11 3/4 In. 425.00
Tiffany Glass, Vase, Bud, Amber Iridescence, Bronze Base Plate, LCT, 13 In. 500.00
Tiffany Glass, Vase, Bud, Flower Form, Gold, Green Heart, Favrile, 6 In. 595.00
Tiffany Glass, Vase, Bud, Gold Iridescent, Bronze Base, 13 In. 500.00
Tiffany Glass, Vase, Bud, Gold With Ivy Decoration, 6 In. 550.00
Tiffany Glass, Vase, Bud, Gold, Pedestaled Foot, Hexagon Shape, Signed, 7 In. 325.00
Tiffany Glass, Vase, Bud, Green Iridescent, Gold Feather, Signed, 10 1/4 In. 875.00
Tiffany Glass, Vase, Bud, Ivy Decoration, Signed & Numbered, 6 In. 550.00
Tiffany Glass, Vase, Bud, Opalescent, Pink Pulled Feather Decoration, 6 In. 375.00
Tiffany Glass, Vase, Bud, Yellow, White Ribs, Ruffled Rim, 9 1/2 In. 250.00
Tiffany Glass, Vase, Butterfly, Fan, Ruffled, Iridescent, 2 X 6 In., Signed 695.00
Tiffany Glass, Vase, Cylindrical, Round Base, Red, Amber, 1899, 13 In. 300.00
Tiffany Glass, Vase, Deep Blue To Greenish Top, Signed, L.C.Tiffany, 8 In. 495.00
Tiffany Glass, Vase, Drawn Feather, Metal Base, Fully Signed, 14 In. 1250.00

Tiffany Glass, Vase, Etched Dragonfly, Insect, Gold Iridescent, 4 3/4 In. 325.00
Tiffany Glass, Vase, Floral Form, Amber Iridescent, L.C.T., 3174, 8 In. 950.00
Tiffany Glass, Vase, Floriform, Gold, 4 In. 350.00
Tiffany Glass, Vase, Flower Form, Gold, Green Ivy Decoration, Signed, 9 In. 595.00
Tiffany Glass, Vase, Flower Form, Green Pulled Feathers, Opalescent, 14 In. 1950.00
Tiffany Glass, Vase, Flower Form, No.8917 LCT.Favrile, 4 1/2 X 5 In. 450.00
Tiffany Glass, Vase, Flower Form, Paper Label, 15 In. 1575.00
Tiffany Glass, Vase, Flower Form, 14 In. 2500.00
Tiffany Glass, Vase, Freeform, Gold, 7373c, Signed, 4 1/4 In. 275.00
Tiffany Glass, Vase, Gold & Lavender, Free Form, L.C.T., No.5349, 3 1/2 In. 350.00
Tiffany Glass, Vase, Gold Iridescence, Green Cameo Carved Leaves, 8 In. 475.00
Tiffany Glass, Vase, Gold Iridescent, Free Form, Signed & Numbered, 4 In. 350.00
Tiffany Glass, Vase, Gold Iridescent, Green Lily Pads, Signed, 4 In. 125.00
Tiffany Glass, Vase, Gold Iridescent, L.C.T. & Numbered, 3 In. 220.00
Tiffany Glass, Vase, Gold Iridescent, Ribbed, Green & Blue Highlights, 3 In. 275.00
Tiffany Glass, Vase, Gold Iridescent, Signed, 2 3/4 In. 155.00
Tiffany Glass, Vase, Gold Iridescent, Swirled Body, Flared Top, 2 1/4 In. 175.00
Tiffany Glass, Vase, Gold Iridescent, 11 1/2 In. 500.00
Tiffany Glass, Vase, Gold Millefiore, Iridescent, 4 3/4 In. 1600.00
Tiffany Glass, Vase, Gold Pedestal, Hexagon, Pink & Purple, Signed, 7 In. 325.00
Tiffany Glass, Vase, Gold, Blue Highlights, Pinched Circles, 3 In. 185.00
Tiffany Glass, Vase, Gold, Flower Form, Signed, 9 In. 475.00
Tiffany Glass, Vase, Gold, Green Ivy Decoration, L.C.T.Favrile, 9 In.High 595.00
Tiffany Glass, Vase, Gold, Iridescent, Flower Form, Signed Bronze Base, 12 In. 400.00
Tiffany Glass, Vase, Gold, Iridescent, Twisted Stem, Favrile, 7 1/4 In. 485.00
Tiffany Glass, Vase, Gold, Pedestal, Hexagon Top, Signed & Numbered, 7 In. 325.00
Tiffany Glass, Vase, Gold, Pulled Up Handles, Applied Foot, Signed, 3 1/2 In. 250.00
Tiffany Glass, Vase, Gold, Ribbed, L.C.T. Favrile, No.3848c, 3 1/2 In. 195.00
Tiffany Glass, Vase, Gold, 2 Free Form Handles, Applied Foot, 3 1/2 In. 250.00
Tiffany Glass, Vase, Gourd Shaped Base, Pinches, 9 X 6 1/4 In. 950.00
Tiffany Glass, Vase, Gourd Shaped, Deep Amber Iridescence, 9 In. 950.00
Tiffany Glass, Vase, Grecian Urn Shape, Pulled Handles, Signed, 2 1/4 In. 235.00
Tiffany Glass, Vase, Green Feather, Platinum Iridescent, Number, Signed, 4 In. 625.00
Tiffany Glass, Vase, Green Iridescent, Gold Feather Decoration, Signed 875.00
Tiffany Glass, Vase, Green Iridescent, Silver & Green Ribbon Patterns, 2 In. 525.00
Tiffany Glass, Vase, Green Lily Pads & Vines, Bulbous Bottom, Signed, 6 In. 675.00
Tiffany Glass, Vase, Iridescent Amber, Floriform, C.1906, Numbered, 15 1/4 In. 1050.00
Tiffany Glass, Vase, Iridescent Blue, Black Heart Shaped Leaves, 11 In. 950.00
Tiffany Glass, Vase, Iridescent Gold, Green Inlaid Hearts And Vines, 15 In. 1250.00
Tiffany Glass, Vase, Iridescent Green, Gold Iridescent Leaf & Vine, 7 In. 675.00
Tiffany Glass, Vase, Leaf & Bud, Gourd Shape, 1892, Signed, 7 In. 2400.00
Tiffany Glass, Vase, Lily, White, Yellow Pulled Feathers, Signed, 10 1/4 In. 500.00
Tiffany Glass, Vase, Miniature, Gold Iridescent, Pinched Handles, 2 7/8 In. 425.00
Tiffany Glass, Vase, Miniature, Gold, Turned In Mouth, Signed, 2 In. 175.00
Tiffany Glass, Vase, Miniature, Green Iridescent, Handled, Signed, 2 In. 425.00
Tiffany Glass, Vase, Onion, 10 In. 8500.00
Tiffany Glass, Vase, Opalescent, Lavender, Tall, Sherbet Shape, 7 1/4 In. 485.00
Tiffany Glass, Vase, Opalescent, Signed, Paper Sticker 650.00
Tiffany Glass, Vase, Opaque, White, Faint Iridescent, LCT 9770b, 2 In. 375.00
Tiffany Glass, Vase, Optic Rib, Fold Luster, Signed, 10 In. 575.00
Tiffany Glass, Vase, Ovoid Shape, Flared Rim, Signed, L.C.T. Y3397, 2 1/2 In. 240.00
Tiffany Glass, Vase, Pulled Into 4 Sections, Gold Iridescent, 5 1/2 In. 535.00
Tiffany Glass, Vase, Red, Blue Iridescent, White Lined, Orange Crackle, 8 In. 87.00
Tiffany Glass, Vase, Red, Gold Iridescence, Red Swirl At Shoulder, 7 1/2 In. 2250.00
Tiffany Glass, Vase, Ribbed, Floriform, Gold, Signed L.C.T.Tiffany, 14 In. 550.00
Tiffany Glass, Vase, Ruffled Rim, Spherical, Footed, Inscribed 325.00
Tiffany Glass, Vase, Striated Feather Devices Over Border Of Arches, 8 In. 550.00
Tiffany Glass, Vase, Triple Hollow Stem, Gold, Signed, 9 1/2 In. 650.00
Tiffany Glass, Vase, Trumpet, Blue, Bronze Candlestick Base, Signed, Pair 3000.00
Tiffany Glass, Vase, Trumpet, Gold With Blue Hues, Base, Signed, 12 In. 350.00
Tiffany Glass, Vase, Trumpet, Gold, Green Cameo Leaves, Signed, 19 In. 1200.00
Tiffany Glass, Vase, Trumpet, Yellow Pastel, Bronze Holder, LCT, 17 In. 425.00
Tiffany Glass, Vase, Urn Shape, 3 Handles, Aquamarine, Signed, 1904, 9 In. 500.00
Tiffany Glass, Vase, Yellow Pastel, Pedestal Base, 10 In. 110.00

Tiffany Glass, Vase, Yellow, Gold, Pink Highlights, Pinched, Signed, 8 In.	350.00
Tiffany Glass, Vase, Zipper, Bulbous, Dimpled Sides, Favrile, 8 1/2 In.	1200.00
Tiffany Glass, Whiskey, Gold Iridescent, Dimpled Sides, 1 7/8 In.	145.00
Tiffany Glass, Whiskey, Gold Iridescent, Pinched Sides, Signed	125.00
Tiffany Glass, Wine, Gold Iridescent, Amber, Signed L.C.T., 6 In.	150.00 To 160.00
Tiffany Glass, Wine, Gold, 7 In.	275.00
Tiffany Glass, Wine, Pastel Green Iridescent, Stemmed, L.C.T.Favrile, 4 In.	295.00
Tiffany Glass, Wine, Pastel Green, Iridescent, Intaglio Cut Cherries, 4 In.	235.00
Tiffany Glass, Wine, Pink Striped Opalescent Optic Rib Top, Luster, Signed	345.00
Tiffany Glass, Wine, Twisted Stem, Signed, 6 In., Set Of 6	900.00
Tiffany Glass, 3 Curled Feet, Scalloped, Cone Shape, 9 X 5 In.	525.00
Tiffany Pottery, Vase, Brown & White, High Glaze, 5 1/2 In.	250.00
Tiffany Pottery, Vase, Trumpet, Vine In Relief, Green Glaze, Signed, 12 In.	575.00
Tiffany Silver, Bowl, Footed, 13 X 8 In.	600.00
Tiffany Silver, Bowl, Repousse, Footed, 5 1/2 In.	120.00
Tiffany Silver, Bowl, Scalloped Edge, Sterling, 2 In.Deep	115.00
Tiffany Silver, Bowl, Scroll Border, 4 Feet, C.1902-07, 7 1/4 In.	145.00
Tiffany Silver, Bowl, Strawberries In Relief Edging, 6 1/4 In., Pair	165.00
Tiffany Silver, Box, Hammered, 7 1/4 X 3 1/2 In.	155.00
Tiffany Silver, Box, Patch, Ornate Top Design In Relief, 1 7/8 In., Pair	150.00
Tiffany Silver, Box, Pill, Cylindrical, Sterling, 2 In.	25.00
Tiffany Silver, Box, Powder, 14K Gold Clasp, 3 Sapphires, 1940, 2 In.Square	225.00
Tiffany Silver, Brush, Hair, Embossed Flowers & Leaves, Sterling	40.00
Tiffany Silver, Brush, Hair, Men's, Sterling, Pair	43.00
Tiffany Silver, Candlesnuffer, Matching Tray, Art Nouveau Scissors, Marked	135.00
Tiffany Silver, Case, Eyeglass, Ornate, Raised Floral Sprays, Signed	45.00
Tiffany Silver, Clock, Traveling, Folding, Art Deco, 8 Day, 3 In.	200.00
Tiffany Silver, Coffee Set, No.1749a, 1926 In Script, 3 Piece	200.00
Tiffany Silver, Coffeepot, Black Handle & Finial, 30 Oz.	485.00
Tiffany Silver, Compact & Lipstick, Sterling, 14K Gold, Deco Period	185.00
Tiffany Silver, Compact, Chain Handle, Engraved Decoration	75.00
Tiffany Silver, Compote, Footed, 5 Ounce	60.00
Tiffany Silver, Compote, Pedestal Base, Pierced Gallery, 15 Oz., 8 1/2 In.	95.00
Tiffany Silver, Compote, Repousse Rims, Footed, 7 In.	195.00
Tiffany Silver, Cup & Salver, Handled Cup 6 3/4, Square Salver, 6 3/4 In.	268.00
Tiffany Silver, Cup, Loving, Ribbed, Repousse Handles, Sterling, C.1905, 9 In.	175.00
Tiffany Silver, Cup, Loving, 2 Handled, 1905, 9 In.	175.00
Tiffany Silver, Dish, Chrysanthemum, Gadrooning Cover, Oval, 1899, 11 In.	225.00
Tiffany Silver, Dish, Leaf Shape, 6 X 4 1/8 In.	75.00
Tiffany Silver, Dresser Set, Hand Chased, Monogrammed JTW, 7 Piece	695.00
Tiffany Silver, Fork & Spoon, Grape Pattern, Lap Over Edge, Sterling	165.00
Tiffany Silver, Fork & Spoon, Salad, Chrysanthemum	195.00
Tiffany Silver, Fork, Cold Meat, Queen Anne	25.00
Tiffany Silver, Fork, English Kings, Vermeil Sterling, C.1887, Set Of 10	350.00
Tiffany Silver, Fork, Little Girl Dancing On Flowered Handle, 6 1/4 In.	20.00
Tiffany Silver, Fork, Serving, English King, Initialed	60.00
Tiffany Silver, Frame, Picture, Engraved Paris, 1910, 7 1/2 In.	95.00
Tiffany Silver, Knife, Butter, Audubon	55.00
Tiffany Silver, Ladle, Scalloped, No.188SM, 12 In.	200.00
Tiffany Silver, Mug, 3 Handled, Engraved, Paris, 1911, 5 X 3 1/2 In.	125.00
Tiffany Silver, Pitcher, Embossed Band, Covered, 10 X 8 In.	95.00
Tiffany Silver, Plate, Cake, Etched Border, 8 1/2 In.	140.00
Tiffany Silver, Quiche Server, Flemish, Serrated Edge, Initialed	85.00
Tiffany Silver, Salt & Pepper, Scrolled Design On Base, Footed	70.00
Tiffany Silver, Scoop, Cheese, Colonial, Initialed	65.00
Tiffany Silver, Server, Tomato, Round, Ornately Pierced Blade, 1905	58.00
Tiffany Silver, Serving Set, Spoon & Fork	180.00
Tiffany Silver, Shears, Grape, Tiffany & Co., C.1852, 7 In.	60.00
Tiffany Silver, Spoon, Ice, Beckman, Round, Scalloped, Etched Bowl	85.00
Tiffany Silver, Spoon, Jockey-Cap Caddy	100.00
Tiffany Silver, Spoon, Olive, Richelieu	33.00
Tiffany Silver, Spoon, Serving, Olympian	90.00
Tiffany Silver, Spoon, Serving, Persian, Initialed	90.00
Tiffany Silver, Spoon, Serving, Sterling, Set Of 4	120.00

Tiffany Silver, Spoon, Souvenir, Statue Of Liberty 24.95
Tiffany Silver, Spoon, Squirrel At Tip, Leaves Below 85.00
Tiffany Silver, Spoon, Stuffing, Flemish, Initialed 75.00
Tiffany Silver, Spoon, Tea, Sterling, Decorated Handle Front & Back, 1884 .... 22.50
Tiffany Silver, Sugar Shell, Broom Corn 38.00
Tiffany Silver, Tablespoon, Wave Edge, Shell & Coral, G.T.M. 32.00
Tiffany Silver, Tazza, Repousse On Rims, Tiffany & Co., 9 In. 250.00
Tiffany Silver, Tazza, Sterling, Pierced Rim, Repousse, 8 X 4 In. 259.00
Tiffany Silver, Teaspoon, Beekman 10.00
Tiffany Silver, Tongs, Sugar, Broom Corn 45.00
Tiffany Silver, Tray, Gallery, Footed, Sterling, Round, 18 In. 900.00
Tiffany Silver, Tray, Heart Shaped, 5 In. 55.00
Tiffany Silver, Tray, Round, 22 1/2 In. 700.00
Tiffany Silver, Tray, Sterling, 32 Troy Oz., Signed, 16 X 11 3/4 In. 475.00
Tiffany Silver, Tray, 18 In., 54 Ounce 500.00
Tiffany Silver, Tray, 33 Oz. 280.00
Tiffany Silver, Tub, Ice, Baroque Floral, 2 Handles, Sterling, 4 1/2 X 6 In. 125.00
Tiffany Silver, Tumbler, Cocktail, Sterling, Initialed EJM, 3 In.Set Of 12 .... 300.00
Tiffany Silver, Vase, Trumpet, Signed, 20 In. 250.00
Tiffany Silver, Vial, Perfume, Cane, Sterling Cap, 6 In. 75.00
Tiffany Silver, Vinaigrette 65.00
Tiffany, Blotter, Ends, Russian Medallion, 12 In., Pair 145.00
Tiffany, Blotter, Ends, Zodiac, Signed, 19 In. 75.00
Tiffany, Bookend, Zodiac, Gold Dore, Signed, Pair 225.00
Tiffany, Bowl, Dore, Abalone Inserts, Bronze, Floral Border, 9 In. 90.00
Tiffany, Bowl, Favrile, Iridescent, Brass Plinth, Marked, 11 1/4 X 2 1/2 In. 750.00
Tiffany, Bowl, Glass, In Bronze Holder, 2 1/2 X 6 In. 350.00
Tiffany, Bowl, Glass, Stretch, Bronze Holder, Signed & Numbered, 6 In. 350.00
Tiffany, Box, Abalone, Cedar Lined, Signed & Numbered, 6 3/4 X 4 3/4 In. 225.00
Tiffany, Box, Cigar, Grape Vine, Green Slag, Key, 9 X 7 X 3 In. 325.00
Tiffany, Box, Round, Covered, Signed M & Union Square, 3 3/4 In. 65.00
Tiffany, Box, Stamp, Brass With Gold Wash, Art Nouveau, No.1184 .... 55.00
Tiffany, Box, Stamp, Venetian Decoration, Insert Divided 160.00
Tiffany, Box, Utility, Gold, Abalone, Bronze, Tiffany Studios, N.Y. 195.00
Tiffany, Box, Utility, Graduate, 5 1/2 X 3 1/2 X 1 1/8 In. 120.00
Tiffany, Calendar Stand, Pine Needle Pattern, Green Slag Glass 75.00
Tiffany, Calendar, American Indian, Insert, Green Patina, Signed, Numbered 95.00
Tiffany, Calendar, Desk, Pine Needle, 6 X 4 In. 85.00
Tiffany, Candlestick, Green Blown Glass Top, Dark Patina, 18 In. 385.00
Tiffany, Candlestick, Morning Glory Shape, Stretch Top, Aqua, Opalescent, Pair 300.00
Tiffany, Case, Spectacle, Attaching Chain, Coin Silver Openwork, Plush, Signed 98.00
Tiffany, Clip, Paper, Pine Needle, Green Glass, Green Patina 75.00
Tiffany, Clock, American Indian Pattern, Bronze, 4 1/2 X 5 1/2 In. 675.00
Tiffany, Clock, Carriage, Bronze, Tiffany & Co., 6 In. 425.00
Tiffany, Clock, Mantel, Pine Needle On Slag Glass, Bronze, 10 1/4 In. 1000.00
Tiffany, Clock, Wall, French Brass Rib Band Decorated, Case, 15 X 10 In. 950.00
Tiffany, Compote, Gold, Signed, 11 1/2 In. 650.00
Tiffany, Compote, Green Iridescent Stretch Over Opalescent Rays, Signed 425.00
Tiffany, Compote, Miniature, Gold, Iridescence, Signed L.C.T., 3 X 4 In. 350.00
Tiffany, Creamer, Handle, Deep Blue, LCT Favrile, Signed, 4 In. 425.00
Tiffany, Cup, Punch, Carved, Cameo, Red Grapes, Green Leaves, Signed, Numbered .. 675.00
Tiffany, Cup, Punch, Seven Applied Lily Pads, Signed 250.00
Tiffany, Desk Set, Chinese Pattern, Green Patina, 7 Piece 900.00
Tiffany, Desk Set, Chinese Pattern, Green Patina, 8 Piece 1150.00
Tiffany, Desk Set, Spider Web Pattern, 4 Blotter Corners, 5 Piece 550.00
Tiffany, Desk Set, Zodiac, Signed, 7 Piece 800.00
Tiffany, Dish, On Pedestal, Diamond-Quilted, Engraved Leaves, Signed, 8 In. 525.00
Tiffany, Flask, Half Pink, Polished Glass, Silver Plate Cap & Lid 20.00
Tiffany, Frame, Abalone Inlay, Bronze, Art Nouveau, No.1179, 4 X 5 1/2 In. 135.00
Tiffany, Frame, Calendar, Zodiac Pattern, Bronze, 8 1/2 X 7 1/4 In. 110.00
Tiffany, Frame, Chinese Pattern, Green Patina 225.00
Tiffany, Frame, Picture, Spider Web Gold Dore, Bronze, 12 X 14 In. 450.00
Tiffany, Frame, Picture, Zodiac, Bronze, Gold Dore, 12 X 14 In. 300.00
Tiffany, Furnace, Deep Red & Pink, Enameled, 3 X 3 In.Box 245.00

Tiffany, Glass, Compote, Gold, Favrile, 6 In. 475.00
Tiffany, Ink Set, Adams, Bronze, Dore Finish, 3 Piece 325.00
Tiffany, Ink Set, Zodiac, Numbered, 3 Piece 495.00
Tiffany, Inkstand, Zodiac, Signed Tiffany Studios, New York, No.1072, 7 In. 375.00
Tiffany, Inkwell, Brown Patina, Bronze, Signed, Large Zodiac No.1072 .... 195.00
Tiffany, Inkwell, Caramel, Spider, Metal 140.00
Tiffany, Inkwell, Cobweb, Bronze, Large, Signed 187.00
Tiffany, Inkwell, Dore, Bronze, Glass Encased, 7 1/2 In. 265.00
Tiffany, Inkwell, Grapevine, Verdigris Finish, Square 195.00
Tiffany, Inkwell, Green Slag Lined, No.845 .... 90.00
Tiffany, Inkwell, Indiana Pattern No.1183 .... 135.00
Tiffany, Inkwell, Modeled Design, Dark Patina, Signed 135.00
Tiffany, Inkwell, Pine Needle, Caramel Glass, Dore Patina, 6 1/2 In. 420.00
Tiffany, Inkwell, Pine Needle, Green Glass, Patina, 3 1/2 In. .... 130.00 To 420.00
Tiffany, Inkwell, Spanish, Dragons, Dore, Bronze, Signed In Bronze, 6 In. 550.00
Tiffany, Inkwell, Square, Pine Needle Design, Green Marble Glass Inserts, 4 In. 175.00
Tiffany, Inkwell, Zodiac, Hexagon Shape, Dore Finish, 6 1/2 In. 225.00
Tiffany, Knife, Dinner, Old Blade, King, 10 1/2 In. 15.00
Tiffany, Lamp, Acorn Shade, 21 In.Diameter 3850.00
Tiffany, Lamp, Acorn, Dark Patina Base, Signed Top & Bottom 2250.00
Tiffany, Lamp, Acorn, Signed, 19 In. 575.00
Tiffany, Lamp, Apple Blossom, Leaded, Green Shadings, Bronze Base, 21 In. 6000.00
Tiffany, Lamp, Arrowroot, Finial, Shade Signed, 1899-1920, 25 X 21 In. 7000.00
Tiffany, Lamp, Autumn Decoration, Bronze Tree Trunk Base, 20 In. 995.00
Tiffany, Lamp, Candle, Bronze Bamboo Base, Shade, Green To Turquoise To Green 675.00
Tiffany, Lamp, Candle, Gold Favrile Shade, Signed 1065.00
Tiffany, Lamp, Candle, Gold Iridescent Base & Shade, Signed 675.00
Tiffany, Lamp, Candle, Gold Iridescent, Base & Shade Signed, 16 In. 975.00
Tiffany, Lamp, Decorated, Shade, Signed, Numbered 1850.00
Tiffany, Lamp, Desk, Green Shade, 7 In., Green Patina Base, 14 1/2 In. 1025.00
Tiffany, Lamp, Desk, Liberty Bell, Favrile Gold Iridescent Glass Ball, 14 In. 1800.00
Tiffany, Lamp, Desk, Miniature Iridescent Scarab Shade, Signed, 8 3/4 In. 3500.00
Tiffany, Lamp, Desk, Zodiac, Turtle Back Tile, Amber Iridescent, Harp Support 1800.00
Tiffany, Lamp, Dragonfly, Mauve, Leaded, Bronze, Base, 25 In. 1300.00
Tiffany, Lamp, Electrified, Green Feather Shades 225.00
Tiffany, Lamp, Fabrique, 12 Bronze Panel Edges, Bronze Base, 24 In. 4200.00
Tiffany, Lamp, Floor, Swirled Fishnet In Gold & Yellow Harp Base, 56 In. 1950.00
Tiffany, Lamp, Gold Iridescent, Blue Highlights, 11 1/2 In. 625.00
Tiffany, Lamp, Gold Iridescent, Dore Bronze Signed Harp Base, 14 In. 875.00
Tiffany, Lamp, Golden Roses Clustered Shade, Bronze Border Base, 21 In. 9500.00
Tiffany, Lamp, Gone With The Wind, Red Favrile Globe, Bronze Base, 21 In. 1800.00
Tiffany, Lamp, Green & Gold Pomegranate, Mottled Glass, Signed, 19 X 16 In. 2950.00
Tiffany, Lamp, Harp, Dore Base, Signed Gold Iridescent Shade, 21 In. 1100.00
Tiffany, Lamp, Ivy Leaf, Leaded, Green & White, Bronze Base, 24 In. 2500.00
Tiffany, Lamp, Leaded Nautilus Shade, Bronze Mermaid Base, Signed, 16 In. 7500.00
Tiffany, Lamp, Lily, Ten Light, Amber Iridescent, Shade Inscribed, 21 In. 6000.00
Tiffany, Lamp, Lily, Ten Light, Signed, 1899-1920, 20 In. 5750.00
Tiffany, Lamp, Lotus, Bell Shaped Leaded Shade, Quadrangular Glass, 21 In. 6500.00
Tiffany, Lamp, Multicolored Glass Shade, Encircled By Red Bohemian Beads 3000.00
Tiffany, Lamp, Oil, Red Tones, 10 1/2 In. 475.00
Tiffany, Lamp, Oil, White Shade, Base Signed 985.00
Tiffany, Lamp, Rose Petal, Leaded, Favrile Cypriote Glass, Dore Base, 19 In. 8500.00
Tiffany, Lamp, Student, Double, Green Signed Damascene Shades, Base Signed 3200.00
Tiffany, Lamp, Student, Wavy, Harp Support, Salmon Shade, Amber Iridescence 1000.00
Tiffany, Lamp, Table, Harp, Damascene Shade, Signed, 7 In. 1150.00
Tiffany, Lamp, Table, Jeweled Dogwood, Leaded Shade, Pink Blossoms, 23 In. 8500.00
Tiffany, Lamp, Table, Kapa Shell, Dome, Bronze Arms, Base, Shade Swivels, 13 In. 675.00
Tiffany, Lamp, Turtle Back Desk, Leaded, Gold Iridescent, Bronze Base, 21 In. 3600.00
Tiffany, Lamp, Turtle Back Desk, Swivel, Zodiac Signs, Bronze Base, 14 1/2 In. 2250.00
Tiffany, Lamp, Turtle Back, Green To Yellow, Iridescent, Bronze Base, 22 In. 1700.00
Tiffany, Lamp, Twisted Rib, Scallops, Iridescent Green, Gold, Electric, 15 In. 950.00
Tiffany, Lamp, Tyler, Swirls On Leaded Glass Shade, Orange With Blue, 25 In. 6500.00
Tiffany, Lamp, 18-Branch Lily, Bronze Base, Favrile, 22 In. 2000.00
Tiffany, Lamp, 6 Leaded Panels, Metal Overlay, Shade & Base Signed, No.539 .... 1500.00

Tiffany, Lamp, 6 Light Lily Base, Candelabra Type, 22 In.	975.00
Tiffany, Letter File, Abalone, Signed & Numbered	130.00
Tiffany, Letter Opener, Bookmark Pattern	105.00
Tiffany, Magnifying Glass, Zodiac, Bronze, 9 X 4 In.	225.00
Tiffany, Magnifying Glass, Zodiac, Brown Patina, Signed & Numbered	225.00
Tiffany, Medal, Victory, Gold Iridescent, Bronze Mounted, C.1918, Signed	550.00
Tiffany, Pad, Memo, Gold, Bronze, Abalone, 1923, Tiffany Studios	195.00
Tiffany, Paper Clip, Grape Pattern, Green Slag Glass	75.00
Tiffany, Paperweight, Thermometer Ball, Sterling Back & Base, Marked, Number	138.00
Tiffany, Paperweight, Turtle Back, Gold Dore Bronze Mounting, 4 Squat Legs	650.00
Tiffany, Parfait, Gold With Blue, Signed L.C.T.Favrile, 3 1/2 In.	165.00
Tiffany, Pedestal, Miniature, Ribbed, Square Lip, Dated, Signed, 2 In.	175.00
Tiffany, Pen Holder, Easel Type, Dore, Bronze, Abalone Discs, 5 In.	150.00
Tiffany, Pen Tray, Green Slag & Bronze, 3 X 10 In.	110.00
Tiffany, Pen Tray, Russian Pattern, Blue Enamel, Signed And Numbered	100.00
Tiffany, Pen Tray, Zodiac, Gilt Bronze, Stamped & Numbered 100, 10 In.	190.00
Tiffany, Planter, Chocolate, Gold Dore, Grape Pattern, Signed, 11 In.	125.00
Tiffany, Planter, Gold Dore, Grape Pattern, Chocolate Glass, Signed 11 In.	125.00
Tiffany, Rack, Letter, Pine Needle, Chocolate Glass, Bronze, Dore	210.00
Tiffany, Rack, 2-Sided Letter, Grape Pattern, Green Slag Glass, 6 1/4 In.	150.00
Tiffany, Reading Glass, Zodiac, Signed	200.00
Tiffany, Rocker Blotter, Russian Pattern, Blue & Enamel, Signed, Numbered	75.00
Tiffany, Salt Dip, Iridescent Gold, Open, Signed, 2 1/4 In.	115.00
Tiffany, Salt, Iridescent Gold, Signed L.C.T., 2 1/4 In.	115.00
Tiffany, Salt, Scalloped Rim, Favrile, Signed LCT, 2 3/4 X 1 In.	95.00
Tiffany, Shade, Tulip Hanger, 16 Panel Triple Bend, Beaded Fringe, Green	400.00
Tiffany, Silver, Teapot On Lampstand, C.1850, 12 3/8 In. _Illus_	1100.00
Tiffany, Silver, Teaspoon, St.James	20.00
Tiffany, Silver, Tongs, Sugar, Broom Corn	55.00
Tiffany, Silver, Tray, Pin, 10 X 1 X 3 3/4 In.	45.00
Tiffany, Sugar & Creamer, Bat's Wing Fluting, Gadroon Rim, Wave Edge Handle	225.00
Tiffany, Tankard, Glass, Sterling Silver Top & Lid, Signed 12 1/2 In.	450.00
Tiffany, Tile, Pitted Outer Surface, Geometrics, Blue Iridescent, 4 Piece	175.00
Tiffany, Toothpick, Applied Lily Pad Decoration, Signed	165.00
Tiffany, Toothpick, Dimpled, Gold, Signed	135.00
Tiffany, Toothpick, Gold Iridescent, Dimpled Sides, Signed LCT, 2 In.	185.00
Tiffany, Tray, Zodiac, Attached Inkwell, Bronze, Brown Patina, 10 X 11 In.	495.00
Tiffany, Vase, Bud, Gold Iridescent, Tapered, Bronze Base Plate, Signed LCT	500.00
Tiffany, Vase, Gold Flame Decoration, Glass, Bronze Holder, L.C.T., 13 In.	285.00
Tiffany, Vase, Green Leaf On Gold Iridescence, Glass, Bronze Holder, 15 In.	410.00
Tiffany, Wallet, Men's, Black Leather, 14K Gold Rim All Around, Signed	75.00
Tiffany, Wax Sealer, Glass, Bronze Dore Grapevine, White Glass, 3 1/4 In.	65.00

Tiffin Glass Company of Tiffin, Ohio, was a subsidiary of the United States Glass Co.of Pittsburgh, Pa. Black satin glass, made by the company between 1923 and 1926, is very popular among collectors. Other types were also made.

Tiffin, Basket, Amberina, 6 In.	28.00
Tiffin, Bowl, Black, Coralene Poppies In Red, Leaves, 7 1/2 In.	50.00 To 65.00

Tiffany, Silver, Teapot On Lampstand, C.1850, 12 3/8 In.

Tiffin, Bowl, Black, Painted Poppies, Low 15.00
Tiffin, Bowl, Green Satin, 9 1/4 In. 26.00
Tiffin, Bowl, Ice Blue Satin, 9 1/4 In. 26.00
Tiffin, Candleholder, Green, 10 In., Pair 38.00
Tiffin, Compote, Black, Enameled, 7 In. 28.00
Tiffin, Compote, Dolphin Handles, Black 42.00
Tiffin, Console Set, Black Satin, 8 1/2 In.Candlesticks, 3 Piece 48.00
Tiffin, Dish, 3 Compartment, Cherokee Rose, Round, 6 1/2 In. 16.00
Tiffin, Flower Float, Chartreuse, Doe Inserted, 14 1/2 In. 70.00
Tiffin, Jar, Black, Flowers, Lid, Red, Yellow, White, Coralene, 8 X 5 In. .. 95.00
Tiffin, Rose Bowl, Black, Blown-Out Poppies, 5 1/2 X 6 In. 25.00
Tiffin, Vase, Black Amethyst, Blown-Out Flowers, Bulbous, 8 1/2 In. 50.00
Tiffin, Vase, Black Amethyst, 5 In. 20.00
Tiffin, Vase, Black Satin, Coralene Flowers & Leaves, 8 In. 40.00
Tiffin, Vase, Black, Yellow & Orange Coralene Flowers, 9 In. 45.00
Tiffin, Vase, Pink Satin, Raised Poppies, 5 1/2 In. 20.00
Tiffin, Vase, Poppy, Black Amethyst, 5 In. 25.00
Tiffin, Vase, Satin Glass, Frosted, Iris Raised Design, 10 In. 47.50
Tiffin, Wine, Cherokee Rose, 6 1/4 In. 12.95
    Tile, see listing by company name
Tile, Anheuser-Busch, Ceramic Clay, Reddish Color, 8 X 1 1/4 In. 95.00
Tile, August, Picture, Blue, White 65.00
Tile, Boy's Face, Blue 30.00
Tile, December, Shepherd & Flock, Maw & Co. 32.00
Tile, Dog Pictures, Marked Wheeling, 6 In., Pair 25.00
Tile, February, Farmer Planting, Maw & Co. 32.00
Tile, Flowers, Brown, Green Glaze, Victorian, 6 X 6 In. 50.00
Tile, Franklin, Oval, Full Figure, Franklin Pottery, Landsale, Pa., 5 1/2 In. ... 42.00
Tile, German Shepherd, Mosaic Tile Company, Marked, 9 1/4 X 8 In. 45.00
Tile, Henry Ward Beecher, 1882-88, Olive Green 45.00
Tile, Occupational, Minton, Pair 30.00
Tile, Pink & Purple Tulips, Wheelock, Germany 22.50
Tile, Polychrome Delft, Warrior With Sword 32.50
Tile, Portrait, Gibson Girl Type, Green 30.00
Tile, Queen Victoria, Round, Green, Minton, Hollins & Co., 7 In. 35.00
Tile, Tea, Floral Decoration 12.50
Tile, Tea, Flower Center, Raised Design Around, China 12.50
Tile, Three Crown Pink Roses 16.50
   Tin, see also Store
   Tin, Mold, Chocolate, see also Store, Mold, Chocolate
Tin, Baby Rattle, Raised Decoration, Whistle In Handle, Mallet Shape, 5 In. ... 15.00
Tin, Basket, Folding Handle, Victorian, C.1890 .... 12.50
Tin, Box, Candy, Lithographed, Parlor Courting Scene, 4 3/4 X 6 In. 5.00
Tin, Box, Candy, Rudolph Valentino Picture, 3 1/2 X 8 In. 25.00
Tin, Box, Chalk, With Lid 2.50
Tin, Box, Cigar, Green Turtle 100.00
Tin, Box, Document, Original Striping 12.50
Tin, Box, Document, 8 1/2 X 4 3/4 In. 13.50
Tin, Box, Love Letter, Key 12.00
Tin, Box, Pill, Oval, Flowers 25.00
Tin, Box, Spice, 6 Round Containers Inside, 9 X 6 In. 32.50
Tin, Box, Tinder, Oval, Gilt Scroll Border, Eagle On Cover, Oval 60.00
Tin, Bucket, Berry, Child's 12.00
Tin, Cage, Squirrel, Exerciser, House, Glass & Mesh Windows, Folk Art, 21 In. ... 125.00
Tin, Cage, Squirrel, Gold Stenciling, Green, C.1850 .... 140.00
Tin, Cage, Squirrel, Punched & Pierced, Revolving Drum 120.00
Tin, Can, Milk, Cover & Bail Handle 9.50
Tin, Can, Oil Lamp Filler, Glass Insert 38.00
Tin, Can, Oil, Cobbler 12.00
Tin, Can, Watering, 5 In. High, 2 3/4 Diameter 8.00
Tin, Can, Whale Oil Filler 27.00
Tin, Candleholder, Christmas Tree, Marked Germany, Set Of 24 .... 15.00
Tin, Candleholder, Push-Up, Decorated 28.00

Tin, Lamp, Betty,
Strap Handle,
Saucer Base,
6 3/4 In.

Tin, Strainer, Cheese Mold,
Strap Handles, Tin, Large

Tin, Lamp, Fluid,
Wick Pick,
Saucer Base,
9 1/2 In.

Tin, Teapot,
Gooseneck Spout,
Brass Knob,
19th Century

Tin, Teapot,
Straight Spout,
Circular Tin Lid Handle

Tin, Candlesticks, Ecclesiastical,
19th Century, 13 5/8 In., Pair

Tin, Candlesticks, Ecclesiastical, 19th Century, 13 5/8 In., Pair ....*Illus*	325.00
Tin, Case, Comb & Mirror, 2 Matchholders	12.50
Tin, Case, Comb, Wall, Floral & Deer	15.00
Tin, Case, Granny Glasses, 1872-74	5.00
Tin, Coal Bucket	5.00
Tin, Coffee Mill, One Drawer, Black, Square, C.1905, 5 X 6 In.	23.00
Tin, Coffeepot, Chubby, Side Spout, Tipping Handle, 10 1/2 In.	48.00
Tin, Coffeepot, Pewter Handle, Copper Base	75.00
Tin, Coffeepot, Pierced, Punched, Candlesocket In Bottom, Folk Art, 8 1/2 In.	160.00
Tin, Coffeepot, Scroll Handle, Chained Snout Cap, 7 In.	85.00
Tin, Container, Packers Tar Soap, Bar Of Soap In Container	6.00
Tin, Cradle, A-Frame Tinware Support, Tinker's Art	250.00
Tin, Creamer, Helmet Shape, Pewter Handle, 4 1/2 In.	19.95
Tin, Cup, Spit, Japanned	15.00
Tin, Cutter, Cookie, Child's, 11 In Round Tin Box, 4 1/4 X 3 1/2 In.	50.00
Tin, Dipper, Farm	16.00
Tin, Filler Can, Whale Oil, Japanned	45.00
Tin, Foot Warmer With Tray, Pierced, Brass Handle, 13 1/2 In.Square	145.00
Tin, Foot Warmer, Heart Design, Pierced	70.00
Tin, Foot Warmer, Miniature, Pierced	55.00
Tin, Foot Warmer, Punched, Walnut Frame, Turned Corner Posts	75.00
Tin, Grater, Nutmeg, Hand Crank	12.50
Tin, Grater, Nutmeg, 5 In.	6.00
Tin, Grinder, Nutmeg, Wood Stomper, Clamp On Table	29.00
Tin, Holder, Paintbrush, Lapped & Rolled Edges, Shaker, 1 Quart	45.00
Tin, Holder, Skewer, 3 Skewers, C.1850, 9 In.	140.00
Tin, Lamp, Betty, Strap Handle, Saucer Base, 6 3/4 In. ....*Illus*	85.00

Tin, Lamp, Fat	125.00
Tin, Lamp, Fluid, Wick Pick, Saucer Base, 9 1/2 In. ....*Illus*	95.00
Tin, Lamp, Miner's	20.00
Tin, Lamp, Miners', Sunshine	12.00
Tin, Lantern, Candle, 3 Glass Sides, Arched Top, Wire Bail	175.00
Tin, Lantern, Pierced, Connecticut, 15 In.	235.00
Tin, Lantern, Ribbed Globe, Perko Wonder Junior, 6 1/2 In.	23.00
Tin, Lantern, Skater's, 6 In.	25.00
Tin, Lantern, Skater's, 7 In.	12.50
Tin, Match Holder, Fleur-De-Lis Hanger, Fluted Edge	45.00
Tin, Match, Safe, Crimp Shell Shape, Arched Top, Slant Side Pocket, 7 X 4 In.	40.00
Tin, Matchbox, Wall Mounted, Embossed Dragons	10.00
Tin, Mold, Candle, 12 Tube	41.00 To 65.00
Tin, Mold, Candle, 6 Tube	35.00
Tin, Mold, Candy, Easter Egg, Pair, 4 In.	17.00
Tin, Mold, Chocolate, Turkey, Hinged Top, 2 Side Clamps, 3 1/2 X 3 3/4 In.	23.00
Tin, Mold, Food, Fish, 12 In.	35.00
Tin, Mold, Food, Parrot, Hinged, 8 In.	35.00
Tin, Mold, Ice Cream, 3 Tiered, Victorian, C.1880, 1/2 Gallon	75.00
Tin, Mold, Pudding, Rose Bud, Copper Bottom, C.1850, 4 X 5 1/4 In.	85.00
Tin, Mold, Strawberry, Oval, 5 X 7 X 2 1/4 In.	16.50
Tin, Pan, Teddy Roosevelt Bust Center, 8 In.	15.00
Tin, Picker, Blueberry, 13 X 8 In.	25.00
Tin, Pie, Pan, Fluted, 7 In.	10.00
Tin, Pipe Case, Frank Jones Brewing Co., Clay Pipe	35.00
Tin, Pitcher, Miniature, Iron Red Paint, C.1780, 2 In.	85.00
Tin, Pitcher, Seam Lapping, Lipped, 9 In.	12.00
Tin, Plate, Colored Baseball Scene, 10 In.	48.00
Tin, Plate, Pheasants, Baret Ware, 10 In.	3.00
Tin, Punched, Border Design, Oval Tin Teapot, Pennsylvania	350.00
Tin, Rattle, Baby, Whistle, Handle Is Whistle, Bottom Is Drumshape, Alphabet	45.00
Tin, Santa Tin, Decorated	22.00
Tin, Scale, Oval Tray, C.1898	13.50
Tin, Sconce, Crimped Top, 1790, 10 In.	185.00
Tin, Seeder, Handcrank, Goodell Mfg., Co., C.1890, 11 X 12 X 14 In.	21.00
Tin, Snuffer, Candle, Scissors Type, Wick Pick, 1892	12.50
Tin, Soap Saver	7.00
Tin, Spice Chest, 24 Drawer	85.00
Tin, Strainer, Cheese Mold, Strap Handles, Tin, Large ....*Illus*	40.00
Tin, Teapot, Gooseneck Spout, Brass Knob, 19th Century ....*Illus*	75.00
Tin, Teapot, Miniature, Strap Handle, C.1850, 5 In.	125.00
Tin, Teapot, Pewter Handle, Hinged Cover, C.1862, 2 Cup	45.00
Tin, Teapot, Straight Spout, Circular Tin Lid Handle ....*Illus*	30.00
Tin, Torch, Parade, Swinging	18.00

Tobacco, Tin, see Store, Tin

Toby mugs have been made since the seventeenth century.
Toby Mug, see also Royal Doulton, Toby Mug; Staffordshire,
   Toby Mug

Tole, Boiler, Ham	65.00
Tole, Box, Asphaltum Decoration, C.1825, 4 X 2 3/4 X 2 5/8 In.	48.00
Tole, Box, Candle, Cylinder, 19 In.	95.00
Tole, Box, Collar	25.00
Tole, Box, Deed, Original Decoration	85.00
Tole, Box, Deed, Smoke Grained, 5 X 8 In.	50.00
Tole, Box, Document	60.00 To 195.00
Tole, Box, Snuff, Oval, 2 1/2 In.	22.00
Tole, Box, Spice, 6 Individual Spices, Decorated	65.00
Tole, Can, Cream, Brown With Red Fruit, 2 1/2 Gallon	45.00
Tole, Canister, Tea, Decorated	75.00

Tole, Canister, Tea, Tin, Yellow Decoration, 8 1/4 In. .... *Illus*	200.00
Tole, Coffin Tray, Floral, Tin, Red, Yellow, Green, 8 1/4 In. .... *Illus*	270.00
Tole, Coffin Tray, Tulip & Floral, Crystallized Center, Tin .... *Illus*	130.00
Tole, Cream Pitcher, Floral, Tin, Red, Yellow, Green, 4 1/8 In. .... *Illus*	180.00
Tole, Egg Poacher, Covered, Early 19th Century, Footed	98.00
Tole, Fan, Anniversary Present, 19th Century, Pennsylvania, Large	150.00
Tole, Horn, Blue, Yellow Striping, Wooden Mouthpiece, Sander, 3 1/4 X 3 In.	32.00
Tole, Horn, Dinner	22.00
Tole, Horn, Fishmonger's, Wooden Mouthpiece, Blue Paint	12.00
Tole, Lantern, Nurse's, Decorated	40.00
Tole, Match Holder, Wall, Green, Stenciling, Hinged Lid With Striker	26.00
Tole, Mug, Floral, Tin, Red, Yellow, Green, 4 3/8 In. .... *Illus*	8.50
Tole, Mug, Floral, Tin, Red, Yellow, Green, 4 3/8 In. .... *Illus*	65.00

Tole, Mug, Floral, Tin,
Red, Yellow, Green, 4 3/8 In.

Tole, Coffin Tray, Floral, Tin, Red,
Yellow, Green, 8 1/4 In.

Tole, Cream Pitcher, Floral, Tin,
Red, Yellow, Green, 4 1/8 In.

Tole, Mug, Floral, Tin,
Red, Yellow, Green, 4 3/8 In.

Tole, Coffin Tray, Tulip & Floral,
Crystallized Center, Tin

Tole, Sugar Bowl, Yellow Band
Leaf, Floral, Tin

Tole, Teapot, Floral, Tin, Red, 8 1/2 In.

Tole, Canister, Tea, Tin, Yellow Decoration, 8 1/4 In.

Tole, Pot, Pennsylvania, Gooseneck, Red, Green & Yellow 550.00
Tole, Sander, Blue Paint With Yellow, 3 1/4 X 3 In. 32.00
Tole, Stand, Umbrella, Green, Orange Poppies 60.00
Tole, Sugar Bowl, Yellow Band, Leaf, Floral, Tin .... *Illus* 210.00
Tole, Tea Caddy, Oval Cylinder Shape, Blue, Green, Yellow & Red, Floral, Lid 14.50
Tole, Tea Caddy, Pennsylvania, Oval, Yellow & Green Decoration On Red 195.00
Tole, Teapot, Floral, Tin, Red, 8 1/2 In. .... *Illus* 450.00
Tole, Tray, Fruit Decoration, Rectangular, 10 X 7 1/2 In. 55.00
Tole, Tray, Octagonal, Red Flowers, Yellow, Green, 9 X 6 In. 465.00
Tole, Tray, Snuffer, Oil Paint & Gilt Decoration 65.00
Tom Mix, Badge, Ralston, Genuine Gold Ore, Post Cereal 8.75
Tom Mix, Book, Paint, 1935 .... 15.00
Tom Mix, Magnifying Glass & Compass .... 28.00 To 30.00
Tom Mix, Periscope, Ralston Straight Shooters 11.00
Tom Mix, Pocket Knife, Ralston 22.00
Tom Mix, Telegraph Signal Set, Ralston, Original Box 24.00
      Tool, see also Iron, Kitchen, Store, Tin, Wooden
Tool, Adze, Barrel Maker's 20.00
Tool, Adze, Bowlmaker's 64.00
Tool, Adze, Cooper's 20.00
Tool, Adze, Cooper's, Signed H.Sorby 40.00
Tool, Adze, Curved Bowl, Hand-Forged, Small 45.00
Tool, Adze, Foot, Carpenter's 12.50
Tool, Adze, Wheelwright's, 3 In.Blade, 7 In. 45.00
Tool, Auger, Beam, Wood Handle, 1 In.Bit, 48 In.Long 37.50
Tool, Auger, Bung Hole, Wooden, Handled 19.00
Tool, Auger, Fruit, Iron Spiral Screw, Wooden T Handle, 1886, 15 1/2 In. 65.00
Tool, Auger, Ice, Hand-Forged, 40 In. 18.50
Tool, Auger, Nose, 1 1/2 In. 27.50
Tool, Auger, Spoon, 2 1/2 In. 45.00
Tool, Ax Blade, Keen Kutter 7.50
Tool, Ax Head, Trade, Hand-Forged, C.1750 .... 65.00
Tool, Ax, Broad 35.00
Tool, Ax, Broad, Glasstown, Pa., 12 In.Wide Blade 60.00
Tool, Ax, Broad, Goosewing 70.00
Tool, Ax, Broad, Pointed 26.00
Tool, Ax, Brush 16.00
Tool, Ax, Cooper's, Broad, With Original Hickory Handle 35.00
Tool, Ax, Double Bit, Deeply Embossed, Black Raven, Kelly Axe & Tool Works 42.50
Tool, Ax, Early Shape, Blade, 5 1/2 In. 32.00
Tool, Ax, Felling 37.50
Tool, Ax, Fireman's, Original Haft, Doe Foot 22.50
Tool, Ax, Goosewing, Blacksmith Made, 17th Century, Signed, 12 In. 195.00
Tool, Ax, Hewing, L.Douglas, 8 In.Blade 25.00
Tool, Ax, Side, Cooper's, Signed M.Gregg 45.00
Tool, Ax, Steel Cutting, Blacksmith's, Hand-Forged 17.50
Tool, Ax, Stone, Dark Green Granite, 3/4 In.Groove, Indian, 3 3/4 In. 30.00
Tool, Ax, Stone, Light Green Granite, 3/4 In.Groove, Indian, 3 1/4 In. 20.00
Tool, Ax, Stone, Light Green Granite, 3/4 In.Groove, Indian, 4 In. 30.00
Tool, Ax, Trade, Brass Tack Design On Handle 275.00
Tool, Ax, Trade, Hudson Bay, Wood Handle 25.00
Tool, Ax, Twibill 300.00
Tool, Bee Smoker, Woodman 22.50
Tool, Bench, Cobbler's, 21 X 48 In. 395.00
Tool, Bevel, Brass Body, Patented 1867 .... 45.00
Tool, Bit Brace, Carriage Maker, Brass Screw & Ferrule, 11 In. 15.00
Tool, Bit Brace, Maple, American, 14 1/2 In. 100.00
Tool, Block Pulley 12.00
Tool, Blowtorch, Brass, Copper Trim, Ashton Manufacturing Company 22.50
Tool, Borer, Bung Hole, Crocker's, Pat.1866 .... 55.00
Tool, Borer, Hand-Operated Barn Timber 55.00
Tool, Box, Farrier, Set Of 8, 116 Hand-Forged Hoof Nails, 11 1/4 X 15 In. 85.00
Tool, Box, Mitre, Pat.1889 .... 25.00
Tool, Box, Tractor, Cast Iron, Richard Manufacturing Company 12.50

Tool, Brace, Birdcage Bit	400.00
Tool, Brace, Bit, Wooden, Brass Fittings	75.00
Tool, Brace, Brass Plated, Marked, C.1850	185.00
Tool, Brace, Carpenter	35.00
Tool, Brace, Chairmaker's, Iron Spring Release, C.1800	175.00
Tool, Brace, Rosewood Handle, Pair	17.00
Tool, Brace, Sheffield Bit, James Lee	100.00
Tool, Brace, Sheffield Type, Refinished	85.00
Tool, Brace, Sheffield, Brass Throat	65.00
Tool, Brace, Wooden Bit	140.00
Tool, Branding Iron, Lazy T-C, Hand-Forged, 3 1/4 X 5 In.	45.00
Tool, Branding, Set Of 10, 20 To 25 In.	65.00
Tool, Caliper, Double	85.00
Tool, Caliper, Iron, 24 In.	60.00
Tool, Caliper, Lady's Legs, 4 In.	12.00
Tool, Caliper, Log, J.Humphrey, Humphrey Decimal, C.1884	40.00
Tool, Caliper, Nose, Iron & Brass, Blunt, 12 In.	35.00
Tool, Can, Oil, Brass, 5 3/4 In.	9.00
Tool, Carousel, Nail, Cobbler, Cast Iron, 8 Pocket	40.00
Tool, Carrier, Splayed Sides	18.00
Tool, Chest, Wood Carver's With 60 Tools	400.00
Tool, Chisel, Clapboard, Marked J.S.4 In.	37.50
Tool, Chisel, Ice, Wooden Handle, 3 1/2 In.Blade, 17 In.	30.00
Tool, Chisel, Marked Buck Brothers, 2 In.Blade, 15 1/2 In.	13.00
Tool, Chisel, Mortise, Wooden Handle, 16 1/2 In.	10.00
Tool, Chopper, Food, Keen Kutter	18.00
Tool, Churn, Rotating On Platform, Star, Large	85.00
Tool, Clamp, Binder's, Mid-19th Century, 3 Feet	75.00
Tool, Comb, Curry, Wood Frame, Picture Of Horse, Watson Mfg.Co., Massachusetts	6.50
Tool, Comb, Flax, Wooden Toothed, Lollipop Shaped Handle, 13 X 3 1/2 In.	50.00
Tool, Compass, Centimeters, German	18.50
Tool, Compass, Surveyor's, Keuffel And Esser, C.1926	135.00
Tool, Cooper, Draw Shave, Crozes, Howell Planes	20.00
Tool, Cork Remover	15.00
Tool, Cork, Shaper, Enterprise Manufacturing Company, C.1857	36.00
Tool, Counter, Wood Mill, Clock Face For Count Of Lumber, C.1900	25.00
Tool, Croze, Cooper's, Hand-Forged Blade	60.00
Tool, Croze, Oak, Miniature, Wood, Iron Blade, 5 1/2 X 2 1/2 In.	165.00
Tool, Croze, Shafted, Adjustable, Sawtooth Blade, 18th Century, 20 In.	65.00
Tool, Divider, Wooden, Cabinet Maker, Opens To 16 In.	75.00
Tool, Doctor, see Doctor	
Tool, Drafting, Leather Case, Brass Trim, Set Of 12, Germany	30.00
Tool, Drawknife, Coachmaker's	40.00
Tool, Drawknife, Deep Gutter	50.00
Tool, Drawknife, Roby & Co., Cast Steel, 6 In.Blade	18.00
Tool, Drawknife, 16 In.Blade	17.50
Tool, Drawshave, Shipwright, 14 In.Blade, 22 In.	25.00
Tool, Drawshave, Wash & Company, Cast Steel, 18 In.	14.50
Tool, Drill, Adjustable, Chair Maker's	47.50
Tool, Drill, Bow	90.00
Tool, Drill, Chest, Brass Stock & Handle	175.00
Tool, Engraver's, Metal, Wooden Handles, Brass Ferrules, Cork Holder, 22	89.00
Tool, Flail, Wood & Tied Together With Thongs	12.00
Tool, Froe, Cooper's, Handle, 9 In.Blade	36.00
Tool, Froe, Curved, 9 In.	65.00
Tool, Froe, To Split A Block Of Wood Into Shingles, Hand-Forged	35.00
Tool, Gauge, Retractable Brass Scale, Rosewood, Brass Trim	27.50
Tool, Gauge, Schader Tire, Brass, Nickel Plated, Pair	5.00
Tool, Glass Cutter, Iron, 5 In.	4.00
Tool, Grafting Froe, Steel, Curved Blade, 9 1/4 In.	15.00
Tool, Hammer, Double Claw, Break Between Upper & Lower Claws	105.00
Tool, Hammer, Log Marking, Hammer Head 12 In.	45.00
Tool, Hammer, Prison, Stone	6.50
Tool, Hammer, Shaker, J.NIBB, 2 5/8 In.Long Head	55.00

Tool, Hay Harpoon, C.1850, 51 In. 8.50
Tool, Hayknife, Miniature, Hand-Forged, 27 In. 55.00
Tool, Heater, Chick, Single Glass Peep Hole, Tin, Kerosene 15.00
Tool, Hoe, Manure, 49 In. 17.50
Tool, Iron, Branding, Complete Numerals, 2 1/4 In., Set Of 9, 9 In. 65.00
Tool, Iron, Branding, Loop Handle, 17 In. 16.50
Tool, Iron, Calking, Shipwright, Hand-Forged 20.00
Tool, Iron, Docking, To Square Off Horse's Tail, Hand-Forged, 27 In. 49.50
Tool, Iron, Flagging, Hand-Forged, Cooper, 14 1/2 In. 20.00
Tool, Iron, Moulding, Rattail Ending, 1/4 In.Blade 15.00
Tool, Jack, Wagon, C.1890, Lever Action, 25 In. 24.50
Tool, Jagging Wheel Set, Form Of Gull In Flight, Ring, Walrus With Ships, 3 .... 400.00
Tool, Jointer, Bailey Victor No.7 .... 95.00
Tool, Knife, Belly, Cooper's, 6 In.Blade, 14 1/2 In. 30.00
Tool, Knife, Blubber, Whaler, 18 1/2 In. 35.00
Tool, Knife, Carpet, Newcomb Loom Company 12.50
Tool, Knife, Cooper's Chamfer, Signed H.Robbins 70.00
Tool, Knife, Dehairing, Tanner, 15 In.Curved Blade, 25 In. 25.00
Tool, Knife, Paring, Hoof, Rattail Loop 14.50
Tool, Knife, Whittler, Camillus, No.26 .... 22.00
Tool, Last, Shoe, Flat Set Into Wooden Base, 9 1/4 In.Diameter 15.00
Tool, Lathe, Machinist's, Table Top, Steel & Brass 140.00
Tool, Lathe, Rung, Chair Maker, Removable Legs 75.00
Tool, Level, Brass Hardware On Ends, Early Wood, Stanley 32.00
Tool, Level, Brass-Bound, Miller's Falls 75.00
Tool, Level, Carpenter's, Brass Edges & Ends, Marked Goodell Pratt, 26 In. 65.00
Tool, Level, Davis & Cook, Watertown, N.Y.Maple, 1886 .... 30.00
Tool, Level, Pocket, Dated June 23, 1896 .... 12.50
Tool, Level, Surveyor's, Case, Tripod, Inter-Focusing, Bausch & Lomb 375.00
Tool, Level, Wood, Stanley, 36 In. 30.00
Tool, Level, 72 Mahogany, Brassbound, 1862, Stanley 48.00
Tool, Lift, Wagon, Advertising On Jack, Wood & Cast Iron, C.1880, 48 In. 65.00
Tool, Machine, Dynamite Blasting, Maple, Brass Plaque, Lion No.3, Aetna Powder .. 75.00
Tool, Mallet, Carpenter, Gray Paint 14.00
Tool, Measure, Boxwood, Brass Rope, Kerby & Bro., N.Y., 6 In. 45.00
Tool, Measure, Caliper Type For Measuring Logs, Large 52.50
Tool, Measure, Cast Iron, Reads Right To Left, 24 In. 22.50
Tool, Measuring Stick, Brassbound, For Interior Carpentry, Pair 30.00
Tool, Measuring Wheel, Wheelwright's, Iron 35.00
Tool, Miter Jack, Mahogany 95.00
Tool, Mold, Boot, Upper Part Of Boot, Maple, 12 In. 6.00
Tool, Monkey Wrench, Winchester 15.00
Tool, Mortar, Pestle, Burl, Mid-19th Century, 5 X 4 In. 100.00
Tool, Nail Puller, Dated 1892 .... 18.00
Tool, Niddy Noddy, Oak, 19th Century 38.00
Tool, Padlock, Heart Shaped, Yale 3.00
Tool, Padlock, Railroad Type, No Key 7.50
Tool, Peel, Forged, Iron, 37 In. 45.00
Tool, Pincer, Farrier, Maud S, C.1905 .... 10.00
Tool, Pipecutter, Brass, Imperial, Marked, 6 In. 22.50
Tool, Pistol Grip, For Leather Worker, Rosewood, Brass Trim 35.00
Tool, Plane, Block, Cooper's 20.00
Tool, Plane, Brass Bullnose 140.00
Tool, Plane, Carpenter, Wooden 20.00
Tool, Plane, Coachmaker's Plow 150.00
Tool, Plane, Combination, Siegley 105.00
Tool, Plane, Compass, Stanley No.50 .... 40.00
Tool, Plane, Cooper's 47.50
Tool, Plane, Cooper's Sun 55.00
Tool, Plane, Cooper's, Howell 44.00
Tool, Plane, Curly Birch Plow 95.00
Tool, Plane, D.R.Barton, 1882 .... 12.50
Tool, Plane, Double Coachmaker's, Unique T-Handled, Brass & Maple 275.00
Tool, Plane, Filletster, Fancy 20.00

Tool, Plane, Fishrod-Maker, Beech, 19th Century	165.00
Tool, Plane, Floor, Stanley No.74	350.00
Tool, Plane, Hollowing, Ohio Tool Company, C.1885	12.50
Tool, Plane, James Cam Blade, 18th Century	130.00
Tool, Plane, Lignum Vitae Jointer, 28 In.	75.00
Tool, Plane, Miller's Patent Plow	110.00
Tool, Plane, Plow, Tote Handle, Brass Trim, Beech & Boxwood, C.1860	135.00
Tool, Plane, Rabbet, England, 1 1/2 In.	14.50
Tool, Plane, Rounder, Oak, 19th Century	52.00
Tool, Plane, Scraper, Stanley	25.00
Tool, Plane, Shouldering, Rhinoceros Horn, Ebony Infill & Steel Sole	225.00
Tool, Plane, Small Beech Horn, 5 1/2 In.	85.00
Tool, Plane, Smoothing Jack, Iron, 16 In.	12.50
Tool, Plane, Smoothing, Open Jack Handle, 19 1/2 In.	12.50
Tool, Plane, Smoothing, Swedish	20.00
Tool, Plane, Stair Rail, Small	35.00
Tool, Plane, Steel Panel, Brass Blade Cap, Norris-London, 14 1/2 In., Sole	210.00
Tool, Plane, Steel Panel, Brass Blade Cap, 7 1/2 In., Sole	185.00
Tool, Plane, Tongue, Ivory Inserts	37.50
Tool, Plane, Wood, Adjustable, Liberty Bell, C.1877, 20 In.	35.00
Tool, Planter, Corn, Tube Type With Shoulder Bag	14.50
Tool, Plumb & Level, Brass Plated	22.50
Tool, Plum Bob, Solid Brass, 5 1/2 In.	22.50
Tool, Potato Planter, Hand Handled, Lever Measures Distance	40.00
Tool, Press, Cork, Cast Iron, Nut-Cracker Style, 3 Cork Spaces, Design	39.00
Tool, Pump, Boat, Tin	9.00
Tool, Punch, Shingle	42.50
Tool, Ratchet, Set, 1916, Original Wood Case	65.00
Tool, Reed Splitter, Basket, Miniature, Brass Push-Down Lever, Shaker, 5 In.	39.50
Tool, Reel, Surveyor, Handles For Winding, 1 Brass Ferrule, 7 3/4 X 18 In.	8.50
Tool, Ripper, Slater, Hand-Forged	18.50
Tool, Roller, Furrow, Hand-Pegged & Mortised, C.1790	59.00
Tool, Rope Winder, Wood	22.50
Tool, Rule, Folding, Boxwood, Brass Trim, Stanley	10.00
Tool, Rule, Folding, Boxwood, Lufkin No.372	12.50
Tool, Rule, Folding, Ivory	32.00
Tool, Rule, Gas, Measuring Liquid Gas, Maple, 6 Feet	12.50
Tool, Rule, Log, Walnut, Brass Tips, Marked	15.00
Tool, Sander, Ink, Wooden, 2 3/4 In.	28.00
Tool, Saw, Belt-Driven, Barnes-Rockwell, Illinois, 1876	550.00
Tool, Saw, Bow, From Chairshop, Small	62.50
Tool, Saw, Circular, Cutting Soapstone, 9 1/4 In.	12.00
Tool, Saw, Early Hack Or Bone, Rosewood Handle	50.00
Tool, Saw, Ice, Bolt & Wedge Construction, Wooden Handle, 64 In.	45.00
Tool, Saw, Jog, Narrow Blade, Portable	40.00
Tool, Saw, No.2 Velocipede Foot-Operated Fret, Drill Attachment, Barnes, 1872	150.00
Tool, Saw, Stair, Brass Screws, 6 In.Blade	23.00
Tool, Scissors, Maple, 13 In.	30.00
Tool, Scissors, Remington, 10 1/2 In.	12.50
Tool, Scorp, Cooper's, Long Handle To Reach Into Barrel	35.00
Tool, Scorp, Saddle Seat, Used To Hollow Out Winsor Chair Seats	50.00
Tool, Scorp, Wooden Handle	22.50
Tool, Scraper, Cabinet, Reverse Side Serrated	18.50
Tool, Screwdriver, Hand-Wrought Iron, Twisted Shaft, Loop Handle	20.00
Tool, Scriber, Carpenter's, Black Walnut	12.50
Tool, Seeder, One Horse	65.00
Tool, Separator, Cream, DeLaval	65.00
Tool, Shaver, Carriage Maker's	40.00
Tool, Shaver, Shingle, Large	41.00
Tool, Shaver, Spoke, Cooper's, Flat	100.00
Tool, Shaver, Tanner, Wood Handles, 36 In.	25.00
Tool, Shears, Blacksmith Forged, Bench Mounted	15.00
Tool, Shears, Sailmaker's, Brass Holding Nut, 13 In.	35.00

Tool, Shears, Sheep	3.50
Tool, Shears, Tinsmith, Hand-Forged, 27 In.	60.00
Tool, Sheller, Corn, John Deere, Large, Standing	80.00
Tool, Sheller, Pea, Heavy Duty	45.00
Tool, Shovel, Apple Mill	110.00
Tool, Shovel, Grain, Green Paint	38.00
Tool, Shovel, Grain, Maple, One Piece	125.00
Tool, Shovel, Grain, Straight Handle	52.50
Tool, Shovel, Oven, Dutch	24.00
Tool, Slick	25.00
Tool, Slick, Shipwright, Metal, 52 In.	55.00
Tool, Smoother, Cement, 2 Handled	6.50
Tool, Spinning Wheel, Flax, Small	167.50
Tool, Spinning Wheel, Visiting, Signed, 24 In.Diameter Wheel, 36 In.High	450.00
Tool, Spinning Wheel, Yellow, Wooden	235.00
Tool, Spokeshave, Brass	55.00
Tool, Spokeshave, Maple & Brass, Bagshaw & Fiel	24.00
Tool, Square, Try, Brass, 4 1/2 In.	9.50
Tool, Stand, Shoe, Cobbler, C.1800, 26 1/2 In.	19.50
Tool, Stencil, Letter, Brass, Set Of 65, 2 X 3 In.	50.00
Tool, Stone, Facing Tool, Heavy	20.00
Tool, Stove, Tinker, Bail Handle, Tin, 10 In.	45.00
Tool, Tape Loom, Wooden	325.00
Tool, Taps & Dies, Cabinet Maker's, Set Of 16 Pieces, 14 1/2 X 9 3/4 In.	1200.00
Tool, Taps & Dies, Screw Box, Hand-Forged Screws	55.00
Tool, Telegraph Key & Sounder, Brass	32.00
Tool, Template, Curly Maple, Brass And Tin	16.00
Tool, Thumbscrew, Rare Whalebone, Marking Gauge, 6 In.	275.00
Tool, Tongs, Blacksmith's Iron, 20 In., Pair	29.00
Tool, Tongs, Fancy Forged Iron, 14 In.	28.50
Tool, Tongs, Log Pulling, Iron, B.I.Co.	18.00
Tool, Tongs, Pipe, Iron, 10 In.	32.00
Tool, Toy Chest, Oak Case, Paper Label, Tools	30.00
Tool, Trap, Bear, Newhouse No.15	160.00
Tool, Trap, Bear, 49 In.	125.00
Tool, Trap, Beaver, Double Spring	45.00
Tool, Trap, Bobcat, Interlocking Teeth	50.00
Tool, Trap, Fox, Hand-Wrought, C.1880	50.00
Tool, Trap, Mouse, Pine, Old Nails, Arch Top, 7 X 7 X 14 In.	22.50
Tool, Trap, Mouse, The Delusion, Label Intact	38.00
Tool, Trap, Mouse, The Delusion, Tin, C.1877	50.00
Tool, Trap, Wolf, Forged, 24 In.	35.00
Tool, Traveler, Wrought Iron	55.00
Tool, Trencher, Carved Of A Tree Trunk, Pre-1860, 11 X 18 X 6 In.	45.00
Tool, Trencher, Wooden, Birch, Boat Shape, Handled, 1878, 7 In.	78.00
Tool, Trivet, Colt, Iron, C.1920	19.00
Tool, Twichel	52.50
Tool, Vise, Blacksmith's	37.50
Tool, Vise, Blacksmith's, 4 1/2 In.Jaws, 40 In.	45.00
Tool, Vise, Blacksmith's, Horseshoe Caulking, Foot Operated, 41 1/2 In.	100.00
Tool, Vise, Hand-Forged, 42 Pounds	45.00
Tool, Vise, Wooden, Handmade, 15 X 10 In.	19.00
Tool, Watchmaker's Bench, Rolltop, Foot Wheel & Transmission, Oak	550.00
Tool, Watchmaker's Staking Set, Under Glass Dome	175.00
Tool, Wedge, Handle	20.00
Tool, Winder, Bobbin, Bench Clamp, Hand Winder, C.1880	24.50
Tool, Winder, Yarn, Maple, Carved Decoration	150.00
Tool, Witchet, Hand-Forged Nuts, Bolts & Plate	65.00
Tool, Work Horse, Wooden, Hand-Carved, C.1900	38.00
Tool, Wrench, Monkey, Wooden Handles, Small	3.50
Tool, Wrench, 1917	2.00
Tool, Yarn Holder, Hand-Painted Roses, Mauchline, 11 In.	15.00
Tool, Yarn Holder, Woven, Colorful Top	17.50

Tool, Yarn Winder, Primitive, Handmade, Wooden Pegged, 17 X 26 In. 150.00
Tool, Yoke, 4 Single, Hand-Hewn 28.00

Toothpick holders are sometimes called toothpicks by collectors. The
variously shaped containers made to hold the small wooden toothpicks are of
glass, china, or metal. Most of the toothpicks are Victorian.

Toothpick, see also other categories such as Bisque, Slag, etc.

Toothpick, Alert Dog 225.00
Toothpick, Banded Portland, Clear And Gold 15.00
Toothpick, Barrel Shape, Delft, Marked, Pair 16.00
Toothpick, Bathing Tub, Blue 55.00
Toothpick, Beaded Dewdrop, Opalescent, Souvenir, Wisconsin 5.00
Toothpick, Beaded Edge, Gold Wash Interior, Footed, Silver Plate 18.00
Toothpick, Beaded Grape 45.00
Toothpick, Beatty Honeycomb, White Opal 27.50
Toothpick, Beatty Ribbed Opalescent 32.50
Toothpick, Bird In Tree Stump, Amber 35.00
Toothpick, Blue Wedgwood 5.00
Toothpick, Bulging Loops, Pink Cased 40.00
Toothpick, Burmese, 2 1/2 In. 200.00
Toothpick, Buttons & Arches, Ruby Flash 12.00
Toothpick, Cactus, Blue, Opaque 40.00
Toothpick, Cactus, Chocolate 48.50
Toothpick, Cat Lying On Back Holding Daisy & Button Holder, Glass 35.00
Toothpick, Cherub, Clear 22.00
Toothpick, Chick On Wishbone, Silver Plate, 2 In. 28.00
Toothpick, Chick, Silver Plate 23.00
Toothpick, Chicken With Egg, Silver Plate 55.00
Toothpick, Chrysanthemum, White Opal Spiral .... 45.00 To 58.00
Toothpick, Cigars Tied With Ribbon, Emblem, Wheeling, W.Virgina, Amber 22.50
Toothpick, Clambroth, Souvenir, Endicott, New York 15.00
Toothpick, Clear, Beading In Swirl, Circle Dot Rim 10.00
Toothpick, Colorado, Blue 35.00
Toothpick, Colorado, Green 38.50
Toothpick, Colorado, Green, 1907 .... 20.00
Toothpick, Colorado, Souvenir, North Vasselboro, Maine 15.00
Toothpick, Colorado, Violet Bowl 25.00
Toothpick, Cordova 15.00
Toothpick, Croesus, Amethyst 75.00
Toothpick, Cupid Sitting On Half An Egg On Floral Embossed Saucer 26.00
Toothpick, Custard, Harvard Souvenir, Foxcroft, Maine 20.00
Toothpick, Custard, Harvard, Orange, Massachusetts 22.00
Toothpick, Custard, Harvard, Souvenir, Crescent Park, R.I. 20.00
Toothpick, Custard, Ring And Beads, Souvenir, North Haven, Maine 20.00
Toothpick, Daisy & Button, Amber, Metal Rims 18.00
Toothpick, Daisy & Button, Blue, Metal Rims 18.50
Toothpick, Daisy & Button, Square Footed, 3 In. 18.50
Toothpick, Daisy & Button, V Ornament, Blue 20.00
Toothpick, Delaware, Gold, Green 42.50
Toothpick, Diamond Point Center, Ribbed Top & Bottom, Clear 10.00
Toothpick, Diamonds, Amber Anvil 14.00
Toothpick, Dog With Glass Eyes, Silver Plate, 2 1/8 X 2 In. 45.00
Toothpick, Dolphin Stem, Blue 55.00
Toothpick, Eggshell, Wishbone, Chick, Silver Plated 17.50
Toothpick, Elephant's Head, Purple Slag 85.00
Toothpick, Elk, Royal Bayreuth 60.00
Toothpick, Finecut, Clear Hat 18.00
Toothpick, Fleur-De-Lis 18.00
Toothpick, Floradora, Gold, Pink, Clear 55.00
Toothpick, Florette, Clear 25.00
Toothpick, Florette, Yellow 40.00
Toothpick, Flower Flange, 3 Bracket Feet, Amber 22.50
Toothpick, Forget-Me-Nots, 6 Sided, Gold Rim, Yellow, Blue, Crown Mark, Austria 25.00
Toothpick, Frog & Snail 40.00

Toothpick, Frosted Elephant, Baby Mine In Base	36.00
Toothpick, Gaelic	17.00
Toothpick, Green Bunny With Basket, Glass	35.00
Toothpick, Green, Frankoma	5.00
Toothpick, Harvard, Lizzie Petoskey, 1899, Ruby Flashed Souvenir	24.00
Toothpick, Hat, Daisy & Button, Deep Purple	10.00
Toothpick, Hat, Porcelain, Rural Scene	17.00
Toothpick, Head Of Indian, Face, Feathers, Silver Plated	95.00
Toothpick, Heart Band, Souvenir Of Niagara Falls, Ruby Flashed	24.00
Toothpick, Heisey Custard, Ring Band, St.Cloud, Minnesota	25.00
Toothpick, Hobnail, Amber	17.00
Toothpick, Hobnail, Blue	18.50
Toothpick, Hobnail, Footed, Blue Opalescent	35.00
Toothpick, Hobnail, White Opal	20.00
Toothpick, Hound, Tufts, Silver Plate	30.00
Toothpick, Iris With Meanders, Green	32.00
Toothpick, Jewel & Dewdrop, Kansas	25.00
Toothpick, Kettle Shape, White Satin, Raised Decoration	18.00
Toothpick, Kettle, Green And White Slag	48.00
Toothpick, Kewpie	33.00 To 39.00
Toothpick, Lacy Medallion, Gold, Green	20.00
Toothpick, Lacy Medallion, Souvenir, Madison, Maine	15.00
Toothpick, Leaf Etching, King's Crown	32.00
Toothpick, Lignum Vitae, Albino Colorations, Grained, Pedestal, 3 1/4 In.	19.00
Toothpick, Maiden Blush, New Hampshire	25.00
Toothpick, Melon Sectioned White With Florals, Gold, 2 3/8 In.	22.50
Toothpick, Millefiori, Overall Flowers, Flared Rim	75.00
Toothpick, Monkey With Hat, Frosted	40.00
Toothpick, Monkeys On Tree Trunk, Amber	34.00
Toothpick, Mt.Washington, Tri-Cornered, Satin Finish	185.00
Toothpick, One-O-One, Opaque White	20.00
Toothpick, One-O-One, Pink	55.00
Toothpick, Overall Hobnail, White	18.00
Toothpick, Owl, Silver Plate	85.00
Toothpick, Parian, Girl On Rabbit Hutch Holding Bunny	34.00
Toothpick, Pennsylvania, Clear And Gold	12.50
Toothpick, Petticoat, Hat Shape	18.00
Toothpick, Pig, Pink, Open Mark	12.25
Toothpick, Pigs, Pink, German, 2 In.	58.00
Toothpick, Pineapple And Fan, Heisey	28.00
Toothpick, Pink, Camphor Glass	22.00
Toothpick, Pomona, Tri-Cornered	85.00
Toothpick, Porcupine, Silver Plate	37.00
Toothpick, Portland	14.00
Toothpick, Punch, Toby Mug, 2 1/2 In.	20.00
Toothpick, Rabbit In Tree	21.00
Toothpick, Reeded Basket, Blue Milk Glass, Oval, Handled, C.1885, 4 In.	45.00
Toothpick, Ribbed Opal	26.00 To 35.00
Toothpick, Ribbed Spiral Canary Opalescent	48.00
Toothpick, Ribbed, Opalescent White, Beatty	30.00
Toothpick, Riding Boot, Cobalt Blue	15.00
Toothpick, Royal Co-Ops, Flashed Red	22.50
Toothpick, Royal Ivy, Frosted & Clear	25.00
Toothpick, Ruby Thumbprint	17.00
Toothpick, Ruby Thumbprint, Atlantic City 1894	20.00
Toothpick, Ruby Thumbprint, World's Fair 1893, Winnie	24.00
Toothpick, Saddle Blanket, Silver Plate	27.00
Toothpick, Saddle On Barrel, Amber	28.00
Toothpick, Satin Glass, Cased, Rose Shading To White	65.00
Toothpick, Scalloped Panel, Green	20.00
Toothpick, Shamrock Souvenir, Green	19.00
Toothpick, Shoe On Stand, Amber	35.00
Toothpick, Shoe, Daisy & Button, Miller's Department Store On Sole	37.50
Toothpick, Shoshone	15.00

Toothpick, Soapstone, 3 Monkeys	12.00
Toothpick, Souvenir, Green, Gold, Colorado	25.00
Toothpick, Spittoon, Metal	3.00
Toothpick, Squirrel, Tree Stump	27.50
Toothpick, Stogie City, Amber	22.50
Toothpick, Strippled, Daisy & Button, Amber	25.00
Toothpick, Sunbeam, Clear	12.00
Toothpick, Sunbeam, Green	25.00
Toothpick, Swag & Bracket, Green	25.00
Toothpick, Swag With Brackets, Amethyst, Gold	30.00
Toothpick, Tapered Block Pattern, Fostoria	40.00
Toothpick, Texas	15.00
Toothpick, Thousand Eye, Vaseline	48.00
Toothpick, Three Monkeys, Soapstone	25.00
Toothpick, Town Pump & Trough, James Tufts, Silver Plate	48.00
Toothpick, Urn With Handles, Take Your Pick Engraved On Side	18.00
Toothpick, Utility Boot, Amber	37.00
Toothpick, Vermont, Gold , Reen	30.00 To 50.00
Toothpick, Vulcan, Amber, McKee	18.00
Toothpick, Webster's Dictionary, Glass	22.00
Toothpick, York Herringbone, Ruby Stained	25.00
Tortoise, Binoculars, Art Decoration	15.00

Tortoiseshell glass was made during the 1800s and after by the Sandwich Glass Works of Massachusetts and some firms in Germany. Tortoiseshell glass has been reproduced.

Tortoiseshell Glass, Bowl, Finger	45.00
Tortoiseshell Glass, Box, Powder, With Hair Receiver, Scalloped Edged Lids	15.00
Tortoiseshell Glass, Candy Container, Egg Shaped, 4 Amethyst Feet, Lid	75.00
Tortoiseshell Glass, Celery, Cream, Red-Brown Combing, 7 In.	135.00
Tortoiseshell Glass, Pitcher, Amber Reeded Handle, Cream Spatter Panels	225.00
Tortoiseshell Glass, Pitcher, Applied Green Handle, 1 1/4 In.	15.00
Tortoiseshell Glass, Rose Bowl, Applied Clear Rigaree At Collar	85.00
Tortoiseshell Glass, Vase, 9 In.	55.00
Tortoiseshell, Box, Hinged, 7 X 3 3/4 X 1/2 In.	45.00
Tortoiseshell, Button, Souvenir, 1876 Art Gallery, Inlaid Silver, 1 1/4 In.	38.00
Tortoiseshell, Card Case, Mother-Of-Pearl Floral Design	50.00
Tortoiseshell, Card Case, Silver Inlay Of Flowers, 4 1/2 X 2 1/2 In.	68.00
Tortoiseshell, Card Case, Silver, Flowers, 4 1/2 X 2 1/2 In.	68.00
Tortoiseshell, Case, Cigar, Empress Eugenie In Oval On Cover, C.1860	50.00
Tortoiseshell, Case, Cigarette, Wide Silver Border, 3 1/2 X 3 1/4 In.	25.00
Tortoiseshell, Comb, Curved, Large, C.1840, 5 X 7 In.	25.00
Tortoiseshell, Comb, 3 Prongs, Rounded Top, 6 1/2 In.	27.00
Tortoiseshell, Comb, 5 Prongs, Triangular Lattice Work Center, 8 1/2 In.	44.00
Tortoiseshell, Desk Set, Scalloped Corners, 4 Piece	200.00
Tortoiseshell, Figurine, Turtle, Carved, 3 In.	30.00
Tortoiseshell, Holder, Brush, Victorian, Looped To Hang By Blue Ribbon	12.00
Tortoiseshell, Razor, Straight, John Hiller & Co.Box	10.00
Tortoiseshell, Stretcher, Glove	22.50
Toy, see also Card, Disneyana, Doll, Game, Marble, Orphan Annie	
Toy, Adam, Lehmann, Patented 1913, Windup	225.00
Toy, Air-E-Go-Round, 3 Planes Fly Around Tower, Reeves, Milford, Conn.	125.00
Toy, Airplane, Hubley, Grumman Aircraft Carrier, Folding Wings, Metal, 10 In.	35.00
Toy, Airplane, Metal, Made In U.S.A., 1 1/2 X 2 1/2 In.	9.00
Toy, Airplane, Tin, Friction, Fire Comes From Tail, Japan	5.00
Toy, Airplane, Tin, Windup, Driver, Spiral Stand With Ball Weight, WW I	45.00
Toy, Airplane, Tootsietoy, UX214, 4 In.	35.00
Toy, Airplane, Whirligig, 2 Engine	35.00
Toy, Akro Agate, Pitcher & Cup, Green	20.00
Toy, Alligator, Native Boy Riding, Tin, Windup, Chein, 15 In.	45.00
Toy, Ambulance, Schuco, Garage & Track, Boxed	65.00
Toy, Amos-N-Andy, Pair, Marx	500.00
Toy, Amos-N-Andy, Windup, Tin	135.00

Toy, Animal Barber, Windup	25.00
Toy, Atomic Cape Canaveral Missile Base, Marx, Tin	25.00
Toy, Auto Race Marble Game, Brownies, 1910, Tin	10.00
Toy, Auto With Driver, Windup, Tin, Lehmann	60.00
Toy, Auto, Arcade, 5 In.	85.00
Toy, Automobile, Motor Kutsche, Lehmann, German, With Box	265.00
Toy, Automobile, 4 Door Sedan, Cast Iron, 6 1/2 X 2 1/4 X 3 1/4 In.	160.00
Toy, B.O.Plenty & Sparkle, Marx	100.00
Toy, B.O.Plenty, Windup	32.00
Toy, Baby Haymaker, Pat.1916, 4 Piece Metal Farm Set, Original Box	45.00
Toy, Baby, Crawling, Windup, Metal, 14 In.	300.00
Toy, Badge, Sheriff's, Frontier Town, New York	2.00
Toy, Balking Mule, Lehmann, Tin, Windup	95.00
Toy, Balky Mule, Marx, Windup	28.00
Toy, Ball, Leather, Red, White, Child's	15.00
Toy, Band, Clown, Tin, Red, Blue, Gold Clowns On White Bench, Marked, 7 X 9 In.	240.00
Toy, Barn & Animals, Fiberboard	10.00
Toy, Barnacle Bill, Windup	65.00
Toy, Bartender, Battery Operated, 1950s, MIB	27.00
Toy, Baseball Machine, Coin Operated, Oak Rails, 1950s	350.00
Toy, Bat, Baseball, Miniature, Louisville Slugger	10.00
Toy, Bathtub, Hat Shaped, Tin, 7 In.	17.00
Toy, Bathtub, Sink, Toilet, Tootsie	20.00
Toy, Batmobile, 1st Edition, Battery Operated	20.00
Toy, Battleship & Submarine, Schoenhut	65.00
Toy, Battleship, Tin, 7 In.	25.00
Toy, Battleship, Tin, 11 In.	15.00
Toy, Battleship, Tootsietoy, Cast Metal, 6 In.	10.00
Toy, Bear, Chein, Tin, Windup	8.50
Toy, Bear, Chein, Windup, 4 3/4 In.	12.00
Toy, Bear, Feeding Baby Bear, Battery Operated	50.00
Toy, Bear, Gray, Fur-Like Body, Glass Eyes, Windup, Occupied Japan	22.00
Toy, Bear, Hump-Backed, Straw Stuffed	95.00
Toy, Bear, Keywind, Japan	8.00
Toy, Bear, Pouring Soda, Battery Operated	16.00
Toy, Bear, Straw Filled, Bulb Eyes, 22 In.	75.00
Toy, Bear, Windup	8.00
Toy, Beatles, Figures, 2 In.	14.00
Toy, Bed, Tootsietoy, Pink, 2 X 3 1/2 In.	8.00
Toy, Beetle, Goes Forward, Turns, German, 1910, Tin, Windup	55.00
Toy, Beetle, Lehmann, Boxed	68.00
Toy, Bicycle, see Bicycle	
Toy, Bicycle, Child's, High Wheel, 53 In.	1150.00
Toy, Bird Cage, Miniature, Floor Stand, Quilted Cage Cover, Victorian, 3 In.	15.00
Toy, Bird In Cage, Windup, German, 3 1/2 In.	13.00
Toy, Bird, Hangs From String, Propeller Movement, German, Hand-Painted, 1900	95.00
Toy, Blimp, USN Los Angeles, Tootsietoy	19.00
Toy, Block, Schoenhut, Letters On Individual People, Alphies	275.00
Toy, Block, Wooden, Lithographed, Handmade Pine Tray, Set Of 24	60.00
Toy, Blocks, Animals & Alphabets, Wooden, 33 Piece	10.00
Toy, Blocks, Bing Arto Stove, Dated 1915, Wooden Box	25.00
Toy, Blocks, Building, In Original Box, Schoenhut	42.00
Toy, Blocks, Building, Stone, Richter's, C.1880s, 18 Piece, Box, Instructions	15.00
Toy, Blocks, Crandall's, Set Of 48, 6 1/2 X 10 X 2 In.	17.50
Toy, Blocks, Levering's Coffee, Lithographed Animals On Back, Set Of 4	5.00
Toy, Blocks, Lithographed, 6 Scenes, Set Of 12, 5 X 7 In.	60.00
Toy, Blocks, Musical Cardboard, Animals, Box With Instructions	8.00
Toy, Blocks, Picture Puzzle, 6 Sides, 6 Pictures, Victorian Children, C.1880	85.00
Toy, Blocks, Picture, Box, C.1890s, Set	28.00
Toy, Blocks, Santa Claus Puzzle, McLaughlin Bros., 1882, Set Of 20	150.00
Toy, Blocks, Scenes, Letters, Set Of 20	19.00
Toy, Board, Checker, Inlaid Mother Of Pearl, Framed, 7 In.Square	55.00
Toy, Boat, Chein, Windup, Tin	10.00
Toy, Boat, Gun, Penny Toy, German, 9 1/2 In.	125.00

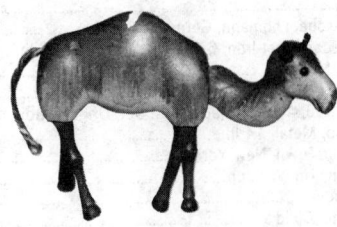

Toy, Camel, Schoenhut, 11 X 7 In.

Toy, Boat, Paddlewheel, Tin, Windup, C.1900, 8 In.	125.00
Toy, Boat, Racing, Bing, American Flag, Hand-Painted, 1900	350.00
Toy, Boat, Tin, Kanter's Sand Boat, Blue & White, 12 X 3 1/2 In.	15.00
Toy, Bobsled, Miniature, 2 Runner, Walnut, Dovetailed Braces, 3 1/2 X 5 In.	28.00
Toy, Book, Hillside Farm, Uncut, 1900	10.00
Toy, Book, Paint, Pinocchio	15.00
Toy, Box, Music, Tin, Parading Dogs, Circus, 5 In.	25.00
Toy, Box, Wooden, Multicolored Lithograph Of Circus, Large, C.1910	250.00
Toy, Boy & Girl On Seesaw, Gibbs, 1903, Hand-Painted	65.00
Toy, Boy On Scooter, Tin & Celluloid, Occupied Japan	15.00
Toy, Boy With Balls, C.1910, German, Windup	250.00
Toy, Broom, Child's, Stuffed Black Mammy Doll On Handle	38.00
Toy, Brown Bear, Glass Eyes, Schoenhut	200.00
Toy, Brownie Tracing, Glass Surface	25.00
Toy, Bucking Horse & Rider, Tin, Windup	12.00
Toy, Buggy, Doll, Wicker, C.1910, Wooden Wheels, Large	85.00 To 95.00
Toy, Buggy, Male Driver, Female Passenger, Horse, Cast Iron, 9 1/2 In.	30.00
Toy, Bugs Bunny, 1940s	29.00
Toy, Bull, Pull, Boston, Manufactured By Frantz	22.50
Toy, Bulldog, Celluloid Eyes, Steiff	15.00
Toy, Bulldozer, MT Japan, See-Through Engine, Tin Driver, Battery Operated	40.00
Toy, Bunny On Tricycle, Tin, Friction	4.00
Toy, Bureau, Doll, Mirror & Teardrop Pulls	35.00
Toy, Bus, Double Deck, 7 3/4 In.	35.00
Toy, Bus, Driver, Arcade, 1930, Cast Iron	85.00
Toy, Bus, Fageol, Arcade, Cast Iron, 12 1/2 In.	92.50
Toy, Bus, Greyhound, Kingsbury	60.00
Toy, Bus, Greyhound, Windup, Tin, Rubber Wheels, Kinsbury Toys Co., 18 In.	48.00
Toy, Bus, Interstate, Windup, Double Decker, Driver, Tin, Green, Yellow, Strauss	195.00
Toy, Bus, Jackie Gleason's Honeymoon Bus, 1955	40.00
Toy, Bus, School, Tin, Hubley, 9 In.	20.00
Toy, Bus, Swedish Seto, 1928, 10 1/2 In.	225.00
Toy, Busy Mike, Chein, Seesaw	10.00
Toy, Butter And Egg Man, Tin, Windup, Marx	100.00 To 125.00
Toy, Cab, Yellow, Friction, Marx, 1949, 12 In.	30.00
Toy, Cabinet, Child's, Kitchen, Paint, Porcelain, Hoosier	175.00
Toy, Cabinet, Kitchen, Tin, 10 X 8 In.	30.00
Toy, Caboose, Red, W. & W. R.R., France, Incised X	125.00
Toy, Caboose, Union Pacific, Tin, Yellow & Brown	9.00
Toy, Camel, Schoenhut, 11 X 7 In. .... Illus	175.00
Toy, Camel, Steiff	10.00
Toy, Camera, Teddy Camera, Tin, Box.1900	65.00
Toy, Cannon, Cap Firing, Metal, Mechanical, England, 1930s, 8 In.	15.00
Toy, Cannon, Cap, 4 In.	25.00
Toy, Cannon, Lever & Plunger Shoots Corks, Tin	14.00

Toy, Cannon, Tin, G.M.Cie-Wurtemberg, Green, Black Trim, 23 X 10 3/4 X 10 In. 65.00
Toy, Cap Exploder, Cannibal Headlarge 1200.00
Toy, Car, Animated Bump & Go Hot Rod, Tin 5.00
Toy, Car, Army Staff, Siren & Lights, Windup, Marx, 1949, 12 In. 35.00
Toy, Car, Auburn Toy Racer, Red, Silver, Black 16.00
Toy, Car, Box, Railroad, Lithographed Soldiers, Tin, Green, Red, Gilt, 3 X 2 In. 12.00
Toy, Car, Cadillac, Forward & Reverse, Headlight, Battery Operated 40.00
Toy, Car, Captain Marvel Lightning Racing, Box 300.00
Toy, Car, Charlie McCarthy, Car, Marx 95.00
Toy, Car, Convertible, Tootsietoy 8.50
Toy, Car, Convertible, Windup, Marx, 12 In. 35.00
Toy, Car, Coo Coo 15.00
Toy, Car, Dodge Charger, Battery, Roof Machine Guns 45.00
Toy, Car, Ford Fairlane, Friction, Tin, Boxed 12.50
Toy, Car, Ford V-8, 2 Piece, 4 In. 50.00
Toy, Car, French Hansom Cab, Tin 385.00
Toy, Car, Hubley Kiddie, Cast Iron & Tin 5.00
Toy, Car, Iron, Kilgore, Passengers, 3 1/2 In. 35.00
Toy, Car, Kingsbury Trolly, 14 In. 150.00
Toy, Car, Lehmann, Oho, 1903 .... 85.00
Toy, Car, Lionel Pullman, Opening Door, Light, 12 In. 50.00
Toy, Car, Marx Racing, Tin, Windup 20.00
Toy, Car, Meat Market, Metal, Keywind 25.00
Toy, Car, Model A Coupe, Iron Arcade 30.00
Toy, Car, Model T Ford, Black, Cast Iron, Made In U.S.A., 5 X 2 1/2 In. 75.00
Toy, Car, Model T Ford, Black, Cast Iron, 8 X 4 1/2 In. 50.00
Toy, Car, Model T Ford, Windup, C.1920 .... 65.00
Toy, Car, Moko Lesney, Gray Wheels, Two-Tone 20.00
Toy, Car, Packard, Sport Coupe, Potmetal, 2 1/2 In. 9.50
Toy, Car, Passenger, Railroad, Dated 1914, Cast Iron, 5 5/8 In. 30.00
Toy, Car, Pedal, 1920s 150.00
Toy, Car, Pepsi-Cola Car, 1961 Ford, Friction 7.50
Toy, Car, Racing, Green, Fin-Backed, Driver, 9 In. 45.00
Toy, Car, Rubber Race, White Rubber Tires, 7 In. 7.50
Toy, Car, Sedan, Tootsietoy, Separate Grill 20.00
Toy, Car, Sedan, Windup, Tin, 1920's, Marked TMC, 5 In. 45.00
Toy, Car, Station Wagon, Tootsietoy 8.50
Toy, Car, Two-Door Touring Sedan, Tin, 5 In. 10.00
Toy, Carousel, Aeronautical With Tail-First Airplanes, C.1910 .... 1200.00
Toy, Carousel, Clockwork Motor, Velvet, Jeweled Canopy, C.1895, 17 In. 1275.00
Toy, Carousel, Nonpareil, 3 Horses With Riders, Crank, Lithographed 65.00
Toy, Carpenter Upright Ladder Wagon, 1880, 26 In. 500.00
Toy, Carpet Balls, Plaid Glaze Ceramic, C.1830 .... 35.00
Toy, Carriage, Doll, Black Wood, Oil Cloth Hood, Wire Wheels, 1890, 18 X 9 In. 65.00
Toy, Carriage, Doll, Lacy Filigree Metal Umbrella Top, 5 1/4 X 5 1/2 In. 49.50
Toy, Carriage, Horseless, 1915, Cast Iron, 6 3/4 In. 75.00
Toy, Carriage, Women Playing With Dog, Lehmann, German, 1908 .... 305.00
Toy, Cart, German Butcher Boy, Lithographed, C.1912 .... 110.00
Toy, Cart, Goat Express, Cast Iron, 8 In. 25.00
Toy, Castle, Moat, Swim Water Toy, Tin, Windup, German, 13 X 9 In. 150.00
Toy, Castle, Wood, Painted, Moveable Drawbridge 45.00
Toy, Cat Playing Nursemaid To Mouse Cage On Wheels, German, C.1910 .... 180.00
Toy, Cat, Chases Rat, Hand-Painted, German, 1910, Tin, Windup 85.00
Toy, Cat, Plush Covered, With Voice, Glass Eyes, Windup, 1920s 60.00
Toy, Cat, Roll Over, Marx, Windup 35.00
Toy, Chair, Andirondack Twig, 6 1/4 In. 14.00
Toy, Chair, Doll's, Split Willow Branches 15.00
Toy, Chair, Tootsietoy, Pair 12.00
Toy, Charlie Chaplin, Tips Hat, Mechanical, Tin, 1920s 48.00
Toy, Charlie The Chimp With Hula Hoop, Windup 16.00
Toy, Charlie Weaver, Bartender, Battery Operated .... 18.50 To 30.00
Toy, Chemistry, Wood Box, Brass Handles, Gilbert Toys, 21 1/2 In. 25.00
Toy, Chess Set, Original Wooden Box, Finished Boxwood Pieces, 2 In. King 35.00
Toy, Chicken, Windup, Tin 6.00

Toy, Church, Furnishings, Handmade, 59 In.

Toy, Chimp, Musical Jolly, Battery Operated	40.00
Toy, China Closet, Doll, 14 X 8 In.	35.00
Toy, Church, Furnishings, Handmade, 59 In. .... *Illus*	200.00
Toy, Circus Alligator, Schoenhut, Glass Eyes	270.00
Toy, Circus Wagon, 2 Horse, Cast Iron, C.1900, 14 In. .... *Illus*	125.00
Toy, Circus White Horse, Schoenhut, Glass Eyes	95.00
Toy, Circus, 5 Bandsmen & Driver	75.00
Toy, Climbing Monkey, Tin, German	25.00
Toy, Clock, Grandfather, Dollhouse, Paper Face, 1930, 5 In.	12.00
Toy, Clown In Rollover Car, C.1927, German, 10 In.	85.00
Toy, Clown Musicians, Painted, Musical Base, German, 12 In.	295.00
Toy, Clown On Donkey, Push Toy, Iron, C.1880	225.00
Toy, Clown On Goat, C.1890, Windup, 8 1/2 X 7 In.	350.00
Toy, Clown Playing Accordion, Lithographed, 3 X 5 3/4 In.	54.00
Toy, Clown Riding Cart Pulled By Balking Mule, Lehmann, Tin, Windup	65.00
Toy, Clown Riding Donkey, Mechanical, 2-Wheeled, Cast Iron, Wood Handle, 1890s	275.00
Toy, Clown, Blowing Ball, Battery Operated	25.00
Toy, Clown, Emmett Kelly, C.1950, 18 In.	22.50
Toy, Clown, Schoenhut .... 35.00 To 50.00	
Toy, Clown, Walks On Hands, Chein	15.00
Toy, Coach, Coronation, Coach & Horses In Gilt, Moveable Back Wheels	45.00
Toy, Coal Car, Iron, No.152 On Sides	9.95
Toy, Coal Wagon, Cast Iron, Horse & Driver, 6 In.	25.00
Toy, Coffee Grinder, Miniature, 2 Wheel, 1 In.	6.50
Toy, Construction Set, Zeppelin, Metalcraft, St.Louis, Book & Box, 18 In.	85.00
Toy, Costume, Chief Thunderbird	18.00
Toy, Couch, Victorian Fainting, Doll's, 16 X 6 1/2 In.	48.00
Toy, Coupe T, Iron, 4 In.	38.00
Toy, Cow, Calfskin, Moos When Head Is Turned, Wooden Platform	85.00
Toy, Cow, On Wooden Dovetailed Base, Papier-Mache, Wooden Wheels, 12 X 9 In.	225.00
Toy, Cowboy Set, Composition, Elastolin, German, 6 Figures	25.00
Toy, Cowboy, Guns, Drawn, Windup, 7 1/2 In.	45.00
Toy, Cowboy, Tin Windup, Twirls Lasso, Japan, 8 In.	22.00
Toy, Cracker Jack, Barney Google	12.00
Toy, Cracker Jack, Wagon, Lithograph	4.00
Toy, Cracker Jack, Wagon, Pull	4.50
Toy, Cracker Jack, Whistle, Tin	3.00
Toy, Cradle, Doll, Homemade	8.50
Toy, Cradle, Doll, Pegged, White And Red Paint, 24 X 12 X 10 In.	125.00
Toy, Cradle, Doll, Wooden, 7 X 19 In.	40.00
Toy, Cradle, Doll's, Gray Paint	36.00
Toy, Cradle, Doll's, Painted And Grained, C.1838, 23 In.	265.00
Toy, Cradle, Wood, 11 In.	15.00
Toy, Crane, Sand, Operator, Scoop Drops Sand, Tin, 14 1/2 X 5 1/2 In.	139.00
Toy, Crapshooter, Cragstan, Battery Operated, Original Box	20.00
Toy, Crayons, Tom Sawyer, Large, 1932	15.00
Toy, Creamer, Sugar, Spooner, Butter Base & Punchbowl, Diamond & Sunburst	117.00
Toy, Croquet, Table, C.1880, Victorian	22.50
Toy, Cyclist Clown, Remote Control, Battery Operated	25.00
Toy, Dancer On A Stick, Wooden, Charlie McCarthy	28.00

Toy, Dancing Black Man On Round Base, Crank Handle, C.1915, 8 In. 60.00
Toy, Dancing Couple, Celluloid, Keywind, Occupied Japan 26.50
Toy, Dancing Couple, Tango, Painted Tin, German, C.1908 .... 225.00
Toy, Dancing Man, Tin, Jointed, Red, White, & Blue 150.00
Toy, Dancing Merry Chimp, Battery Operated 25.00
Toy, Dancing Sam, Windup 20.00
Toy, Decoder, Captain Midnight's Secret Squadron, 1946 .... 29.00
Toy, Destroyer, Tootsietoy, Cast Metal, 4 1/2 In. 8.50
Toy, Diddy Cyclist, Large 150.00
Toy, Dining Room Set, Tootsietoy, 7 Pieces 50.00
Toy, Dining Set, Doll's, Hutch, Table, 4 Chairs, Velvet Seats, 1930s 25.00
Toy, Dining Table, Chairs, Desk, Doll 25.00
Toy, Dish, Child's, Girl Holding Spoon, Enamel, Sweden 15.00
Toy, Dog House, Metal, St.Bernard Dog, 1 3/4 X 1 1/2 X 1 5/8 In. 28.00
Toy, Dog, Chalkware 2.50
Toy, Dog, Flipo, Louis Marx, N.Y., Key Wind, 3 3/4 In. 30.00
Toy, Dog, Glass Eyes, Marked Steiff, 9 X 8 In. 32.50
Toy, Dog, Mechanical, Old German, 8 X 10 In. 75.00
Toy, Dog, Peppy The Porky Pup, Battery Operated 30.00
Toy, Dog, Waling, Windup, Lehmann, German 285.00
Toy, Dog, Windup 8.50
Toy, Doll, see Doll
Toy, Doll's Bed, Wooden, Folding, Patchwork Coverlet 28.00
Toy, Dollhouse, Church, Opens, 2 Rooms Furnished, Electrified, Handmade 925.00
Toy, Dollhouse, Eight Rooms, 1915, 3 Feet X 4 Feet X 44 In. 850.00
Toy, Dollhouse, English, 1910, Triangular, Wired, 22 X 21 X 11 In. 200.00
Toy, Dollhouse, Georgian Baby House, 6 Rooms, Center Hall, Stairs, Electrified 1000.00
Toy, Dollhouse, Metal, Tootsie, By Marked, 1920 .... 4.50
Toy, Dollhouse, Suburban, 5 Rooms & Furniture, Original Box 50.00
Toy, Dollhouse, Swedish, 3 Rooms, Staircase, Ornate & Colorful, 19 X 17 In. 125.00
Toy, Dollhouse, 2 Rooms, Handcarved Door, Wainscoting, Removeable Top 295.00
Toy, Dollhouse, 4 Rooms & Hall, Front Porch, C.1900, 30 X 27 X 25 In. 450.00
Toy, Dollhouse, 44 Pieces Of Furniture, 4 Room, 1925, China Dolls 375.00
Toy, Dominoes, Ivory & Ebony, Wooden Box 17.50
Toy, Donald Duck Duet, Marx 170.00
Toy, Donkey With Woman Sidesaddle, Pull, Cast Iron 125.00
Toy, Donkey, Glass Eyes, Schoenhut .... 85.00 To 175.00
Toy, Donkey, Windup, Tin, Full Color, 6 X 6 In. 25.00
Toy, Drum & Sticks, C.1917, 7 In.Diameter 22.50
Toy, Drum Major, Wolverine, No.27, 13 In. 50.00
Toy, Drummer Boy, Marx 125.00
Toy, Duck, Chein, Tin, Windup 8.50
Toy, Duck, Friction, Hand-Painted, 8 In. 65.00
Toy, Duck, Pulls Cart With 3 Baby Ducks, Windup, Tin, Lehmann, 1903 .... 50.00
Toy, Duck, Tin, Windup 35.00
Toy, Duck, Yellow, Mechanical 11.00
Toy, Dump Truck, Tootsietoy, 5 1/4 In. 15.00
Toy, Electric Highway, Marx, 1949 .... 40.00
Toy, Elephant On Wheeled Platform, C.1870 .... 37.50
Toy, Elephant, Plush Covered, Windup 4.50
Toy, Elephant, Schoenhut, Paste Eyes 45.00
Toy, Elephant, Segmented Body, Wood 19.00
Toy, Engine, Bing Lionel, Cast Iron, Electric, No.027 .... 135.00
Toy, Erector Set, A.C.Gilbert Co., 1938 Instruction Book 35.00
Toy, Erector Set, Gilbert No.3, Wooden Box, 2 Manual Instructions 37.50
Toy, Erector Set, Gilbert, Electric Motor, 6 1/2 In. 28.00
Toy, Erector Set, Hundreds Of Pieces, 1913 .... 75.00
Toy, Erector Set, Structo, 1908 .... 20.00
Toy, Erector Set, The Rocket Launcher, Metal Case, Manual 18.00
Toy, Express, Lehmann, Patented 1913, Windup 125.00
Toy, Farm Implement Disc 25.00
Toy, Felix The Cat, Wood, Jointed, Sullivan 1925 .... 45.00
Toy, Felix, Walking, Wood & Papier-Mache, Schoenhut, 1924, 5 1/4 In. 200.00
Toy, Ferdinand The Bull, Windup, Mar Toy 25.00
Toy, Ferdinand, Marx, Tin, Windup 40.00

Toy, Fire Engine House, No Fire Pumper, Iron, Ives, C.1890, 16 In.

Toy, Golfer, Knickers, Putting Green,
Golf Club, Wood, Schoenhut

Toy, Fire Pumper,
Toledo Metal Wheel Co.,
Pedal Car, Red, 59 In.

Toy, Golfer, Skirt, Putting Green,
Golf Club, Wood, Schoenhut

Toy, Ferris Wheel, Tin		28.00
Toy, Ferris Wheel, Windup, Bell, J.Chein		45.00
Toy, Ferris Wheel, 3 Boys, 6 1/2 In.Diameter, 5 In.		25.00
Toy, Fire Chief, Lights, Windup, Marx, 12 In.		35.00
Toy, Fire Engine House, No Fire Pumper, Iron, Ives, C.1890, 16 In.	*Illus*	550.00
Toy, Fire Engine, Pumper, Cast Iron, 3 Horse Drawn, 10 In.		135.00
Toy, Fire Engine, Pumper, Cast Metal, C.1925, 4 1/4 In.		12.50
Toy, Fire Fighters, Negro Children With Boxing Gloves, Windup Marx, Boxed		75.00
Toy, Fire Pumper, Toledo Metal Wheel Co., Pedal Car, Red, 59 In.	*Illus*	325.00
Toy, Fire Truck, Pumper, Cast Iron, 14 1/2 In.		145.00
Toy, Fire Wagon, Carpenter Roller Bed, 1880, 26 In.		500.00
Toy, Fire Wagon, Driver, Horses, Iron, 12 In.		165.00
Toy, Fire Wagon, 2 Drivers, 3 Horses, Ladders, 21 In.		160.00
Toy, Fire Wagon, 3 Horse, Cast Iron, 13 1/2 In.	*Illus*	125.00
Toy, Fireman, Climbs Ladder, Tin, Windup		30.00
Toy, Flour Sifter, Child's, Tin, Wooden Knob		14.00
Toy, Flute, 6 Hole, Marked U.S.A., 11 In.		6.50
Toy, Food, Grinder, Regal Cast Iron, Miniature		15.00
Toy, Fortune Dispenser, The Planet, Metal, Penny Operated		27.00
Toy, Frankenstein, Tin, Windup		40.00
Toy, Frypan, 3 Footed, Side Handle, Iron, 3 1/4 In.		4.95
Toy, Furniture, Dollhouse, Hand-Painted Floral, Porcelain, 3 Piece		50.00
Toy, Furniture, Dollhouse, Schoenhut, 4 Piece Set		20.00
Toy, Furniture, Dollhouse, Sideboard, Tea Wagon, Hinged Cabinet Chair, Table		45.00
Toy, Furniture, Dollhouse, Wicker, Settee, Chair, Table		20.00
Toy, Fuzzy Rabbit, Mechanical, 8 In.		25.00
Toy, G.I.Joe & Pups, Windup		35.00
Toy, Game, see Game		
Toy, Game, Atkins Real Baseball Game, Tin, 1915		150.00
Toy, Game, Brownie Auto Race, With Cars		24.00
Toy, Game, College Baseball, Early 1900s, Parker		25.00
Toy, Game, Dutch Boy And Girl Ten Pins, Parker Bros., 1921		50.00
Toy, Game, Humpty Dumpty, Transogram, Boxed With Instructions		6.50

Toy, Game, Katzenjammer Kids	10.00
Toy, Game, Liberty Block Game, 1918, Original Box, Complete	15.50
Toy, Game, Mr.Potato	5.00
Toy, Game, Pinball, Lindstrom Atlas	20.00
Toy, Game, Pinball, Wooden	5.00
Toy, Game, Place Quintuplets In Carriage	12.50
Toy, Game, Radio Game, Milton Bradley	26.00
Toy, Game, Rainbow Puzzle, C.1890	12.50
Toy, Game, Skeezix, In Original Box	5.00
Toy, Game, Snap, Milton Bradley	25.00
Toy, Game, Spirit Of St.Louis, No.951, Metalcraft, Extra Box & Parts	95.00
Toy, Game, Telegraph Messenger, C.1895	12.50
Toy, Game, The Ferris Wheel Puzzle Ball Rolling Game, Box, 1894	32.00
Toy, Game, Three Little Pigs, Walt Disney, 1933	50.00
Toy, Game, Wooden Croquet Set, 4 Balls	15.00
Toy, Game, 48 States Block Game, 1918, Original Box, Complete	14.00
Toy, Garage, Bing, 2 Windup Cars, 6 1/2 X 8 In.	260.00
Toy, George Washington Riding Horse, Windup, 1914	250.00
Toy, GI Joe & K-9 Pups, Tin, Unique Art, Windup	38.00
Toy, Giraffe, Keywind, Japan	8.00
Toy, Glass Carrier, Painted Tin Lithograph, 4 Glasses & Pitcher	55.00
Toy, Go Cart, Original Paint, Decorative, Pre-Civil War	575.00
Toy, Goat, Schoenhut, 7 In. ...... *Illus*	95.00
Toy, Golfer, Knickers, Putting Green, Golf Club, Wood, Schoenhut ...... *Illus*	175.00
Toy, Golfer, Skirt, Putting Green, Golf Club, Wood, Schoenhut ...... *Illus*	300.00
Toy, Golfer Set, Schoenhut, 12 Piece Including Golfer	325.00
Toy, Goose, Moves On Wheels, Wings Flutter, Sound, German, 1900, Tin	225.00
Toy, Goose, Windup, Painted, Tin, Louis Marx, July 8, 1924	25.00
Toy, Graf Zeppelin, Strauss, 1930s, Tin, Windup, 17 In.	125.00
Toy, Graf Zeppelin, Tin, Pull, 25 In.	150.00
Toy, Gun, see also Buck Rogers, Gun; Roy Rogers, Gun; Gene Autry, Gun	
Toy, Gun, Big Bang Deck, Boxed	25.00
Toy, Gun, Cap Pistol, Single Shot, Marked Pluck, 3 1/2 In.	16.75
Toy, Gun, Cap The Eagle, Cast Iron, Dated June 17, 1890	35.00
Toy, Gun, Cap, Buffalo Bill, Cast Iron, 1923, 11 1/2 In.	60.00
Toy, Gun, Cap, Bulldogs, 1923	12.00
Toy, Gun, Cap, Cast Iron, Leather Holster	16.00
Toy, Gun, Cap, Gene Autry, Kenton	20.00
Toy, Gun, Cap, Hubley Pal, Pot Metal, 5 In.	6.00
Toy, Gun, Cap, Hubley Repeater, Pet	22.50
Toy, Gun, Cap, Kilgore Whizzer, Crank Operated	47.50
Toy, Gun, Cap, Kilgore, Iron, Six Shooter Automatic	12.50
Toy, Gun, Cap, Nigger Head	130.00
Toy, Gun, Cap, Single Shot, Iron, 3 1/2 In.	16.75
Toy, Gun, Cap, 6-Shot, Pat.Jan.22, 1895, 7 1/4 In.	165.00
Toy, Gun, Davey Crockett, Box	9.00
Toy, Gun, Double Barrel Shot Gun, A.H. Fox, Spring Load	150.00
Toy, Gun, Machine, Tin, Wooden Stock, Hage Mfg.Co.	15.00
Toy, Hammock, Doll's, Standing, 1905, 20 In.	22.50
Toy, Hammock, Miniature, Canvas, 21 X 10 X 10 In.	45.00
Toy, Handcar, Lionel, Donald, Pluto, 1935	350.00

Toy, Goat, Schoenhut, 7 In.

Toy, Santa And Sleigh, Cast Iron, C.1900
(See Page 692)

Toy, Circus Wagon, 2 Horse, Cast Iron,
C.1900, 14 In. *(See Page 684)*

Toy, Hook And Ladder, 2 Horse, Cast Iron, 20 In.

Toy, Fire Wagon, 3 Horse, Cast Iron, 13 1/2 In.
(See Page 686)

Toy, Handcar, Marx, Popeye, 1930s	65.00
Toy, Handcuffs, Releases To Either Shackle, C.1930	4.50
Toy, Happy Ham, Pull, Wooden	25.00
Toy, Happy Hooligan, Lithographed Tin, Windup, Chein, C.1932	130.00
Toy, Harley Davidson Motorcycle, Tin, Rubber Tires, 9 In.	15.00
Toy, Hen, Flaps Wings & Squawks, Push, Tin	22.50
Toy, Henry On Elephant, Borgfeldt, Celluloid Windup, Henry & Black Boy	175.00
Toy, Highway Henry, Windup	275.00
Toy, Hobby Horse, Metal Rocker, Glass Eyes, C.1880	185.00
Toy, Honeymoon Express, Marx, Windup, Tin	68.00
Toy, Hook & Ladder Truck, 3 Horse Drawn, Iron, Hubley, 27 3/4 In. *Illus*	175.00
Toy, Hook And Ladder, 2 Horse, Cast Iron, 20 In. *Illus*	150.00
Toy, Horn, Tin, Side Handle, 9 3/4 In.	5.95
Toy, Horse & Wagon, Mail, Cast Iron, 4 X 9 In.	85.00
Toy, Horse On Treadmill, Model For Life-Sized Working Device	2000.00
Toy, Horse On Wheels, Dapple Gray, German, C.1870, 12 1/2 In.	90.00
Toy, Horse-Pull, Dapple-Gray, German, 13 1/4 X 12 1/2 In.	125.00
Toy, Horse, Carousel, Glass Eyes, Mounted, Pine	875.00
Toy, Horse, Carousel, Velvet Seat, Glass Eyes, Carved Wood, C.1870, Maine	950.00
Toy, Horse, Felt, Pull, 19 In.	115.00
Toy, Horse, Lead, Miniature, White & Gray Paint, 2 Riders, Set Of 4, 1 1/2 In.	10.00
Toy, Horse, Schoenhut	65.00
Toy, Horse, Stuffed, On Wheels	95.00
Toy, Horse, Tin, Running, Flying Mane, Tail, On Wooden Tramp, 4 1/2 X 5 In.	58.00
Toy, Horse, Tin, With Rider, Tin Platform, Cast Iron Wheels, 11 In.	75.00
Toy, Hose Reel With Driver, 3 Horse, Iron, Hubley, C.1906, 19 In. *Illus*	250.00
Toy, Hose Reel, 1 Horse, Driver, Phoenix, Iron, Ives, 15 In. *Illus*	225.00
Toy, Hutch, Princess Patti, Ideal, Yellow & White	25.00
Toy, Hutch, Wood, 11 X 20 In.	25.00
Toy, Ice Skates, Tiger Curly Maple, Pair	150.00
Toy, Ice Skates, Wood, Forged, Acorn Tip Blades, C.1830	59.50
Toy, Ice Wagon, Iron	125.00
Toy, Iron, Child's, Leather Handle	19.00
Toy, Iron, Swan, 2 3/4 In.	20.00
Toy, Iron, Victorian, Full Figure Swan, Iron, 2 1/2 X 1 3/4 In.	15.00
Toy, Iron, Waffle, Stover, Cast Iron, Miniature	42.50
Toy, Iron, Wood Handle	12.50
Toy, Ives Hygeia Ice Wagon, 1890, 19 1/2 In.	750.00
Toy, Jazzobo Jim Jigger	125.00
Toy, Jockey & Horse, Cast Iron, Push	60.00
Toy, Jumbo The Angry Elephant, Shakes Head, Japan, 3 X 5 1/2 In.	12.00

Toy, Jumping Jack, Jointed, , 1876	29.50
Toy, Jumping Jeep, Marx	25.00
Toy, Jungle Boy, Marx, Windup, Tin, Original Box	12.50
Toy, Katzenjammer, Board Game	12.50
Toy, Kazoo, Marked Kirchnof, Tin	3.50
Toy, Kiddy Cyclist, Windup, Tin, Unique Art, Box	50.00 To 85.00
Toy, Kitchen Set, Tootsietoy, 7 Piece, Original Box	60.00
Toy, Komikal Kop, Windup, Louis Marx	75.00
Toy, Ladder, Schoenhut	4.00
Toy, Lady With Cart, Tin, French, C.1910	62.50
Toy, Lamb, Bellringer, Carved, Pulltoy, C.1890, 4 X 4 In.	69.50
Toy, Lamb, Platform, Pull, Cast Iron Wheels, Glass Eyes, 3 1/2 X 11 In.	105.00
Toy, Lamb, Pull, Carved, Bellringer, C.1890, 9 X 3 1/2 In.	69.50
Toy, Lamb, Wool Covered, Glass Eyes, C.1880, 6 1/2 X 9 X 3 1/2 In.	105.00
Toy, Lead Fox Hunt Set, C.1910, Set Of 32	125.00
Toy, Leopard, Schoenhut, Glass Eyes	245.00
Toy, Li'l Abner Band, Tin, Mechanical Windup	85.00 To 145.00
Toy, Library Table, Doll, Tootsie, Toy, Marked	8.00
Toy, Lincoln Tunnel, Tin, Windup, Unique Art Co., 24 In.	50.00
Toy, Lion Tamer, Schoenhut	95.00
Toy, Little Red Hen, Mechanical, Clucks & Lays Eggs, 1920s	25.00
Toy, Lizard, Tin & Wood, Windup	50.00
Toy, Llama, Steiff	10.00
Toy, Locomotive & 2 Cattle Cars, Cast Iron, Pull, 29 In.	115.00
Toy, Locomotive, Battery Operated, Overland Express	10.00
Toy, Locomotive, With Coal Car, Cast Iron, 5 1/4 In.	32.50
Toy, Lone Ranger, Marx	125.00
Toy, Lunch Box, Walt Disney School Bus & Fire Fighter	8.00
Toy, Mama Kangaroo, Windup	10.00

Toy, Hook & Ladder Truck, 3 Horse Drawn, Iron, Hubley, 27 3/4 In

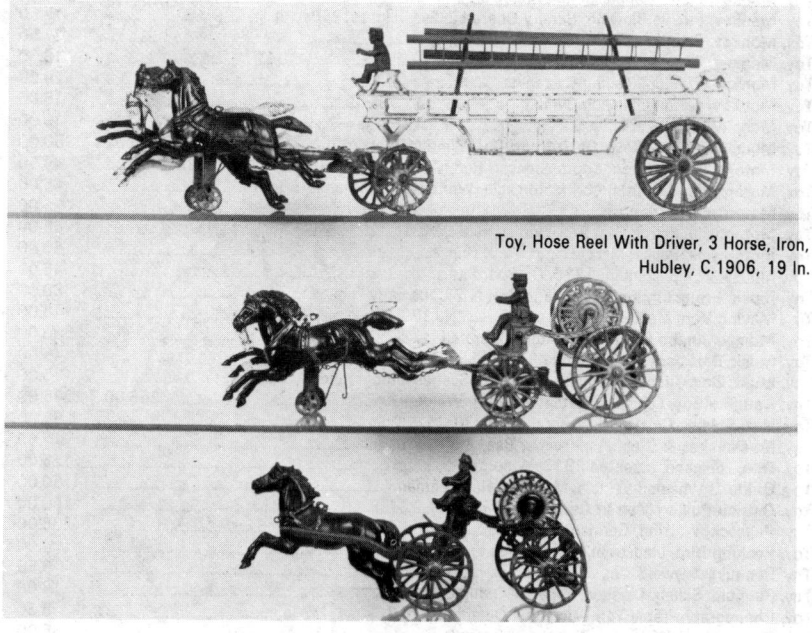

Toy, Hose Reel With Driver, 3 Horse, Iron,
Hubley, C.1906, 19 In.

Toy, Hose Reel, 1 Horse, Driver, Phoenix, Iron, Ives, 15 In.

Toy, Moon Mullins & Kayo On A Hand Car, Windup, Marx, 6 In.

Toy, Mammy, Tin, Windup	15.00
Toy, Man On Flying Trapeze, Wyandotte, Tin, Windup	18.00
Toy, Man, Flips Celluloid Girl In Air, Shuco, German, Windup, Tin	75.00
Toy, Marionette, Hazelle, Boxed	37.50
Toy, Men Mystery Game, Bradley, 1936	15.00
Toy, Mickey Mouse, see Disneyana	
Toy, Mickey Mouse Express, Marx	200.00
Toy, Mickey Mouse Merry Makers, Marx	500.00
Toy, Microscope, Gilbert, 1939	11.00
Toy, Military Transport, Marx, With Cannon	30.00
Toy, Milk Wagon & Horse, Borden's, Says Buy War Bonds & Stamps, Wooden	48.00
Toy, Miss Muffet	12.00
Toy, Mistah Sunshine, Mechanical, Composition Head, Key Wind, Original Box	125.00
Toy, Mobile Oil Flying Horse, 4 X 5 In., Tin	8.00
Toy, Monkey On Cycle, Tin & Celluloid, Windup, Occupied Japan	12.00
Toy, Monkey, Blows Bubbles, Tin, Windup	45.00
Toy, Monkey, Bubble Blowing, Battery Operated, Eyes Light, 1950s, 11 In.	17.00
Toy, Monkey, Climbing, Zippo Marx	27.50
Toy, Monkey, Crapshooting, Cragstan, Mechanical	16.00
Toy, Monkey, Windup, Playing Castanets	20.00
Toy, Monkey, Windup, Playing Cymbal	15.00
Toy, Moon Mullins	13.00
Toy, Moon Mullins & Kayo On A Hand Car, Windup, Marx, 6 In. .... *Illus*	250.00
Toy, Motorcycle, Cast Iron, Cop & Sidecar, Red, White Rubber Wheels, 4 In.	44.50
Toy, Motorcycle, Cast Iron, Cop Motorcycle, White Rubber Wheels, 5 In.	46.00
Toy, Motorcycle, Harley, Iron	25.00
Toy, Motorcycle, Patrol, Cast Iron, Hubley, Red	55.00
Toy, Motorcycle, Police, Marx, Tin, 8 1/2 X 6 In.	60.00
Toy, Mouse, Wood, Jointed, 1926, On Board	45.00
Toy, Movie Projector, Keystone, Hand Crank, 2 Cans Early Film	60.00
Toy, Moving Van, Moko Lesney, Gray Wheels, No.17	18.00
Toy, Mumbo Jumbo Drummer, Battery Operated	30.00
Toy, Music Box, Jack & Jill, Blonde Boy On Lid, Crank, Plays Tune, Blue, 3 In.	45.00
Toy, Music Box, Tin Horse Pulling Wagon, 4 Scenes Lithographed	125.00
Toy, Naughty Boy, Lehmann, Patented 1903, Windup	205.00 To 275.00
Toy, Nazi Soldier, Clockwork Motorcycle, 1930s, 5 1/2 In.	85.00
Toy, Noisemaker & Clappers, Krueger Beer & Ale, Wooden	7.50
Toy, Oho, Lehmann, Patented 1913, Windup	125.00
Toy, Onkle, 3 Wheeled Vehicle, Man Tips Hat, Lehmann	150.00
Toy, Ostrich Pulling Man In Cart, Lehmann, Tin	250.00
Toy, Peacock, Walking, German EBO	235.00
Toy, Pecking Bird, Lindstrom, Tin, Windup	4.00
Toy, Penguin, Keywind, Tin, J.Chein & Co.	9.50
Toy, Penguin, Skiing, Leashed, Japan, Windup	18.00
Toy, Phonograph, Table Top, Miniature, Outside Horn, 3/4 X 1 1/2 In.	8.50
Toy, Phonograph, Wolverine Zilotone, 5 Records	135.00
Toy, Piano Stool, Schoenhut	30.00
Toy, Piano, Baby Grand, Schoenhut	75.00
Toy, Piano, Bliss, 18 Keyboard, 19 X 16 1/2 X 10 In.	92.00
Toy, Piano, Grand, Oak, C.1920s, Japan	25.00

Toy, Piano, Schoenhut, Baby Grand, 1940s	18.00
Toy, Piano, Schoenhut, White, Upright	55.00
Toy, Piano, Schoenhut, 14 Keys, 1900, 15 X 10 1/2 X 8 1/2 In.	48.00
Toy, Piano, Schoenhut, 19 X 13 In.	85.00
Toy, Piano, Schoenhut, 20 In.	35.00
Toy, Piano, Schoenhut, 30 Keys, 10 X 18 X 20 In.	16.50
Toy, Piano, 17 Key, Upright, 18 1/2 X 8 1/2 X 11 1/4 In.	62.00
Toy, Piano, 17 Keys, Schoenhut, 17 1/2 X 11 1/2 X 8 1/4 In.	86.00
Toy, Picnic Bunny, Battery Operated, Boxed	35.00
Toy, Pig, Battery Operated	16.00
Toy, Pig, Dancing, Checkered Overalls, J.Chein, Tin, Windup	11.50
Toy, Pig, Windup, Tin, Flip Ears, 4 1/4 X 2 1/4 In.	12.00
Toy, Pin, Orphan Annie	15.00
Toy, Pinocchio, Marx, Windup, Tin	55.00 To 125.00
Toy, Pipe, Bubble, Howdy Doody	15.00
Toy, Pipe, Bubble, Tin, C.1860	10.00
Toy, Pistol, Buck Rogers, 25th Century, 1930s	35.00
Toy, Pistol, Pair, C.1914, 3 In.	6.00
Toy, Pistol, Tin Windup, WWI Camouflage, Shoots Sparks	9.00
Toy, Pistol, Tin, Red Ranger, Wyandotte	8.50
Toy, Pistol, Water, All Metal	7.00
Toy, Pitcher, Small China, Circus Animals & Clowns	15.00
Toy, Plane, Navy Aircraft Carrier Fighter, Folding Wings, Hubley, 9 1/2 In.	27.00
Toy, Platform, Circus Animal, Schoenhut, Wood	5.00
Toy, Plow, Twin Plow Blades, Cast Iron, 6 X 3 1/4 X 2 1/4 In.	24.50
Toy, Pluto, Marx, Windup	30.00
Toy, Pony Blimp, On Wheels, 1930s, Cast Iron, 6 In.	65.00
Toy, Pony Cart, Wood, Tin, Lithograph Of Horse, 18 In.	55.00
Toy, Poodle, Schoenhut	110.00
Toy, Popeye & Parrot Cage	50.00
Toy, Popeye In Barrel, Tin Windup	50.00
Toy, Popeye, Windup, Stand Up Punching Bag	250.00
Toy, Porky Pig, Marx, Windup, 1949	50.00
Toy, Projector, Kodascope Model No.40	45.00
Toy, Pug Dog, Chubby, Victorian, Iron Wheels, 1890	60.00
Toy, Pull, Wooden, Jumping Frog	2.50
Toy, Pump, Simple Simon, Ohio Art Co., 12 In.	18.00
Toy, Punch Cup, Whirlgig, 2 Pieces	18.00
Toy, Punchbowl, Tulip & Honeycomb	25.00
Toy, Puppet, Hand, Elf With Beard, Steiff	25.00
Toy, Puppet, Horse, Carved Legs Move At Both Joints, Head Pivots, 10 In.	20.00
Toy, Puppet, Indonesian Stick, Wooden Carved Head, Cloth Body, 2 1/2 In.	60.00
Toy, Puppet, Peter Pan, C.1960	12.00
Toy, Puppet, Santa Claus, Steiff	10.00
Toy, Puzzle, Brownie Scroll, Signed P.Cox, 1894, McLoughlin, 2 In Box	75.00
Toy, Puzzle, Fire Engine, Old 999 Railroad Train, McLoughlin, 1910	75.00
Toy, Puzzle, Fireman, Milton Bradley	15.00
Toy, Puzzle, Hood's Sarsaparilla, Complete With Instructions	47.00
Toy, Puzzle, Horse Blanket, Lithographed Color Box	7.50
Toy, Puzzle, Sliced Birds, C.1910, Selchow & Righter, Complete	22.00
Toy, Puzzle, 20 Mule Team Boraxo, 1933	25.00
Toy, Rabbit, Bisque, Japanese, 2 3/4 In.	7.50
Toy, Rabbit, Metal, Windup, Movements, Tin Eyes, Nose & Feet, Dressed, 9 In.	85.00
Toy, Rabbit, Squeak Toy	175.00
Toy, Rabbit, Windup, Old Plastic, 9 In.	12.00
Toy, Racetrack, Windup, Jeu De Course M.J. & Co., 9 X 9 In.	140.00
Toy, Railroad Signal Set, Semaphore, Signal, Marx, Original Box	7.00
Toy, Range, Electric, Western Electric, 11 X 14 1/2 In.	60.00
Toy, Rap & Tap In A Friendly Scrap, Windup, 1921	49.50
Toy, Rattle, A.B.C's Around Top, Fingerhold On Handle, Drum Shape	8.00
Toy, Rattle, Baby, Wooden, Carved, Round Ball Inside, 1780, 4 1/2 X 1 1/2 In.	25.00
Toy, Rattle, Carved Bone, Silver Bells & Whistle, C.1830	75.00
Toy, Rattle, Ivory, C.1860, 2 1/2 In.	19.00
Toy, Rattle, Silver, 5 Bells, Ivory Teething Ring	35.00
Toy, Rattle, Tin	10.00

Toy, Record Player, Lid Opens, Tootsie, Marked	9.00
Toy, Red Cap Porter, Marx	125.00
Toy, Reduced Clown, Schoenhut	35.00
Toy, Refrigerator, Pretty Maid, Louis Marx, 3 X 4 1/2 In.	15.00
Toy, Rhino, Schoenhut, Glass Eyes	290.00
Toy, Rifle, Buck Jones, Daisy Air, Compass & Sundial	25.00
Toy, Ringmaster, Schoenhut, 7 In.	95.00
Toy, Rocker, Kilgore	25.00
Toy, Rocker, Pine, 14 In.	15.00
Toy, Rocking Horse, Calfhide Covering, Amber Eyes, Leather Harness, Saddle	400.00
Toy, Rocking Horse, Mottled Body, Red Runners, 1902	350.00
Toy, Rocking Horse, Straw Stuffed, Wooden Platform With Wheels, Rockers	350.00
Toy, Rocking, Horse, Child's Dandy	165.00
Toy, Rocking, Horse, 34 1/2 X 29 In.	225.00
Toy, Roller, Cookie, Grooved Roller Surface, One Piece	22.00
Toy, Roller, Cookie, Mother's Little Helper, Wood, 11 In.	18.50
Toy, Roly-Poly, Chauffeur On Wheels, Composition	50.00
Toy, Rookie Pilot, Marx	90.00
Toy, Rug, Needlepoint, Miniature, 3 1/2 In.Diameter	12.50
Toy, Saddle, Pony, Leather, Miniature	75.00
Toy, Sand, Sunny Andy Fun Fair	40.00
Toy, Sandy Dog, Marx	115.00
Toy, Santa And Sleigh, Cast Iron, C.1900 .... Illus	70.00
Toy, Santa Claus, On Tricycle, Windup, Tin, 4 X 3 3/4 In.	15.00
Toy, Santa Claus, Walks, Chein, 1920s, Tin, Windup	68.00
Toy, Santa On Sled, Pulled By A Reindeer, Windup	22.50
Toy, Santa On Tricycle, Lithographed Tin Cycle, Plastic Santa, 4 In.	17.00
Toy, Santa, Bell Tinkles, Santa Goes Around, Windup	25.00
Toy, Sausage Mill, Works	9.50
Toy, Saxopone, Tin, Brass Plated, 8 Notes, 20 In.	7.50
Toy, Scale, Cast Iron, 2 Piece, Red Paint, 2 X 4 1/2 In.	10.00
Toy, Scale, Iron, Miniature	38.50
Toy, Scooter, Space, With Astronaut, Battery Operated, Boxed	25.00
Toy, Sewing Machine, Betsy Ross, Metal, U.S. .... 14.00 To 25.00	
Toy, Sewing Machine, Child's, Cast Iron, Bavaria, 4 1/2 X 8 X 7 In.	37.50
Toy, Sewing Machine, Germany, Box With Lithograph, 4 X 1 3/4 X 4 In.	24.50
Toy, Sewing Machine, Germany, Stenciled	22.00
Toy, Sewing Machine, M	45.00
Toy, Sewing Machine, Red Riding Hood	35.00
Toy, Sewing Machine, Singer, Miniature, Cast Metal, On Stand, 1 1/4 In.	5.00
Toy, Sewing Machine, Tin, Germany	12.00
Toy, Sewing Machine, U.S.Zone, Germany	15.00
Toy, Sewing Machine, 1940s, German	13.50
Toy, Shark, Chein, Tin, Windup	4.50
Toy, Singing Bird, Wings Flag, Tin, German	25.00
Toy, Sink, Bathroom, Pedestal.Tootsietoy, 1920	4.50
Toy, Sink, Wolverine, Original Box	8.00

Toy, Sleigh, Red Painted, Full Size

Toy, Skate, Ice, Metal, Winslow's National Club, Pair	12.00
Toy, Skate, Ice, Steel With Leather Straps, Clamp Onto Shoes, 1890, Pair	12.50
Toy, Skates, Ice, Clamp On, Pair	2.50
Toy, Skates, Ice, 1880's, Pair	6.00
Toy, Skates, 4 Wheels Down Middle, C.1880	17.50
Toy, Skillet, Iron, 3 Short Feet, Handle, 2 3/4 In.	8.00
Toy, Slate, Little Folks, 1860	20.00
Toy, Slate, School, Bound, Wooden, Child's	10.50
Toy, Sled, Child's, Red Paint, Black Decoration, Reindeer, 19th Century, 36 In.	85.00
Toy, Sled, Doll, Cast Iron Runners, C.1800, 14 In.	65.00
Toy, Sled, Doll's, Victorian, Metal Runners, Curling In Front, Side Grips	42.50
Toy, Sled, Doll's, Wood, C.1890, 11 X 5 1/4 X 3 In.	45.00
Toy, Sled, Flexible Flyer	30.00
Toy, Sled, Log, Curled Wooden Front Runners, Slatted Top, Wood, 36 In.	45.00
Toy, Sled, Push, Wooden, Green Upholstery, Brass Runners, Stenciling, C.1890	275.00
Toy, Sleigh, Hubley Single Horse, 1911, 17 In.	400.00
Toy, Sleigh, Red Painted, Full Size .... Illus	230.00
Toy, Sleigh, 1906 Hubley, Horse, Driver, Iron	275.00
Toy, Slide, Lantern, Woodburner Train, C.1860, 1 1/4 X 4 1/2 In.	4.00
Toy, Slot Machine & Chips, Schoenhut	20.00
Toy, Snowshoe, Handmade, Original Webbing, Wooden, C.1880, Pair	45.00
Toy, Soldier, Britain's Coldstream Guards, Original Box	50.00
Toy, Soldier, Child's Whistle, C.1920, 14 In.	25.00
Toy, Soldier, Lead, Roman, Marked England, Set Of 6	24.00
Toy, Soldier, On Horseback, Wooden, C.1890, 2 1/2 In.	4.50
Toy, Soldier, Spiked Helmet, German, Set Of 6, C.1895, 1 3/4 In.	15.00
Toy, Soldier, Wooden, Lithographed, Stand, C.1893, Set Of 10	85.00
Toy, Soldiers, Tin, British Navy, Heinrischsen, 20 Pcs., Original Box	200.00
Toy, Space Ship, Friction	6.00
Toy, Spinner, Boy & Girls On Horses	20.00
Toy, Squeak, Bird In Cage With Bellows Underneath, 6 1/2 In.	150.00
Toy, Squirrel, Furry, Windup	20.00
Toy, Stagecoach, Yellow, Potmetal, 2 Horses, France	14.00
Toy, Steam Gun Boat, Carpet Toy, Hess, 1910, 5 1/2 In.	65.00
Toy, Steam Shovel, Iron, 2 In.	10.00
Toy, Steam Shovel, Keystone	65.00
Toy, Steam Shovel, Tractor Treads, Buddy L	225.00
Toy, Steam Shovel, 1930	15.00
Toy, Steamboat, Side Wheel, Pull, Cast Iron, 1903, 5 1/2 In.	135.00
Toy, Steamroller, Windup, Marx, 1930, 9 In.	35.00
Toy, Stool, Kitchen, Miniature, Carved Legs, 1 In.Round, 1 1/2 In.High	5.00
Toy, Stove, Cast Iron, Miniature	11.00
Toy, Stove, Child's, Black Cast Iron, Chrome Trim, Buck's, 22 X 22 In.	450.00
Toy, Stove, Child's, Sheet Metal, Black, White, 4 Burners, C.1925	200.00
Toy, Stove, Cook, Eagle, Iron, 3 Lids, 2 Kettle, 5 1/2 X 4 1/2 In.	60.00
Toy, Stove, Covers, Venting Pipe, Trays, Cast Iron, 11 X 11 X 6 In.	115.00
Toy, Stove, Crescent, 9 X 10 X 4 In.	55.00
Toy, Stove, Eagle, Nickel Plated, Cast Iron, 16 X 13 In.	275.00
Toy, Stove, Electric, Oven, Empire, June 17, 1924, Green	50.00
Toy, Stove, Iron, Salesman Sample, Royal	150.00
Toy, Stove, Tin & Cast Iron, 4 Lids, 5 X 5 X 3 1/2 In.	34.00
Toy, Stove, Tin, Claw Feet	16.50
Toy, Stroller, Doll, Wicker, Two Wheel	45.00
Toy, Sugar & Creamer, Borden's Elsie	10.00
Toy, Sugar & Creamer, Child's, Lid, Westmoreland Glass, Thumbelina Pattern	35.00
Toy, Surrey, Stanley, Horses, Driver & Passengers, Canopy, 1940s, Cast Iron	75.00
Toy, Sweeper, Vacuum, Battery Operated, Campbell Kid	18.00
Toy, Sweeping Mammy, Windup, Lindstrom	40.00
Toy, Swing, Doll's, Pre-1900	35.00
Toy, Table, Bedside, Tootsietoy, Marked	3.00
Toy, Table, Iron, 2 X 3 1/8 X 2 1/4 In.	9.95
Toy, Tank, Roll-Over, Marx	10.00
Toy, Tank, Tumbling Army, Windup, Marx, 4 In.	15.00
Toy, Tanker, Tin, Orange, Hafner, 6 In.	9.00
Toy, Taxi, Amos 'n' Andy, Tin	225.00

Toy, Taxi, Arcade Cast Iron, 1923, No Driver	255.00
Toy, Tea Set, Blue Willow	50.00
Toy, Tea Set, Flowers, Blue Trim, Germany, 14 Piece	39.50
Toy, Teapot, Child's, Miniature, C.1800, 2 3/4 In.	125.00
Toy, Teddy Bear, Arms, Legs & Head Move, C.1912, 19 In.	55.00
Toy, Teddy Bear, In Night Shirt, Black Button Eyes, 8 1/2 In.	22.50
Toy, Teddy Bear, Plush, 14 In.	47.50
Toy, Teddy Bear, Straw Filled, Jointed	55.00
Toy, Teddy Bear, Swivel Head, Straw Filled, 24 In.	35.00
Toy, Teddy Bear, Tail Moves The Head, German	25.00
Toy, Teddy Bear, White, Glass Eyes, 1930s, 10 1/2 In.	37.00
Toy, Teddy Bear, 16 In.	75.00
Toy, Teeter-Totter, Uncle Sam, C.1912	75.00
Toy, Telephone, French Buddy Phone, Tin	35.00
Toy, The Wonder Cyclist, Windup, Bell, Marx, C.1930, 8 3/4 In. ..... *Illus*	180.00
Toy, Tiddly Winks, Peter Pan	10.00
Toy, Tiger, Schoenhut, Pasted Eyes	75.00
Toy, Tiger, Schoenhut, 7 In. ..... *Illus*	170.00
Toy, Tinkertoy In Case, 1914	15.00
Toy, Tinkertoy, Set With Instructions, 1920	13.00

Toy, Tiger, Schoenhut, 7 In.

Toy, The Wonder Cyclist, Windup, Bell, Marx, C.1930, 8 3/4 In.

Toy, Tinkertoy, 1913, In Case	11.00
Toy, Tombo, Negro Dances On Box, Strauss, 1918, Tin, Windup	115.00
Toy, Toonerville Trolley, Premium Box Prize, 2 In.	250.00
Toy, Toonerville Trolley, Windup, Fontaine Fox, 1922, German, Regular Wheels	265.00
Toy, Toonerville Trolley, Windup, Fontaine Fox, 1922, German, Train Wheels	425.00
Toy, Tootsietoy Midgets, 8 In Box	18.00
Toy, Top, Schoenhut, Wood & Metal	5.00
Toy, Top, 1918	5.00
Toy, Toss Ball, Leather, Red, White, Blue, Early 1800's	25.00
Toy, Tractor, Allis-Chalmers, Cast Iron, Rubber Tires, 7 In.	40.00
Toy, Tractor, Arcade Cast Iron, Farmall, Black Rubber Tires, 6 3/4 In.	120.00
Toy, Tractor, Arcade, Cast Iron Allis-Chalmers & Hay Wagon, 12 1/2 In.	65.00
Toy, Tractor, Contractor's Dump Wagon, Iron Wheels, 14 1/2 In.	110.00
Toy, Tractor, Iron Arcade	30.00
Toy, Tractor, Lugged Wheels, Driver, Arcade	42.50
Toy, Train Set, Gilbert American Flyer, C.1949	40.00
Toy, Train Set, Lionel, No.1065, Transformer, Tracks, Accessories, 2 Cars	18.00
Toy, Train Set, Lionel, No.33, Standard Gauge, 2 Cars	275.00
Toy, Train Set, Schoenhut, Wooden, Large, 5 Piece	195.00
Toy, Train Set, Windup, Overland Flyer, Hafner Mfg.Co., 1920s, 3 Piece	99.50
Toy, Train Set, Windup, Tin, German	65.00
Toy, Train, Engine, Iron, 7 In.	35.00
Toy, Train, Four Pieces, Pull, Ives	300.00
Toy, Train, Honeymoon Express, Marx, 1920	40.00
Toy, Train, Honeymoon Express, Tin Windup, Marx	100.00

Toy, Train, Lighting Express 175.00
Toy, Train, Lionel Wartime Freight, Fiber Board, 1943, 250 Pieces 90.00
Toy, Train, Lionel, O Gauge, 1940, Engine No.204, Accessories 125.00
Toy, Train, Metal, Miniature, 5 Pieces 7.00
Toy, Train, Overland Flyer, Sunshine Special, Track, Original Box, 1915 .... 145.00
Toy, Train, Pullman Car, Bogota, 6 In., Tin 8.00
Toy, Train, Pullman Car, Tin, Montclair, 6 In. 8.00
Toy, Train, Shuttle, Cragstan 40.00
Toy, Train, Steam Model 2500.00
Toy, Train, Tootsietoy, 1929 Model A 28.00
Toy, Train, 3 Cars, Tracks, Key Wind, Marx 25.00
Toy, Train, 5 Cars, S.T.N.Co., 1912 Special 250.00
Toy, Transmitter, Receiver, Remco Caravelle 25.00
Toy, Trapeze Girl, Celluloid Girl, Metal Trapeze, Keywind, 7 In. 27.00
Toy, Tray, Child's, Tole, Circus Design 70.00
Toy, Tri-Plane, Girard, Tin Litho, 1923, Box 125.00
Toy, Tricycle, Tin, Windup, Celluloid Teddy Bear 9.50
Toy, Trolley, Broadway-270, Extended Rod, Chein, Tin, 8 1/2 In. 35.00
Toy, Trolley, Car, Tin, Powell & Mason, Conductor & People 35.00
Toy, Trolley, Chein Lithograph, Tin, Broadway, 8 In. 85.00
Toy, Trolley, Toonerville, Fontaine Fox, 1922 .... 225.00 To 400.00
Toy, Trolley, Windup, Tin, Toonerville 265.00
Toy, Trolly Car, Rapid Transit Company, Windup, American, 8 1/2 In. 81.00
Toy, Truck With Driver, Tin, Windup, Marx, 10 1/2 In. 26.50
Toy, Truck, Advertising, Good Humor Ice Cream, Thin Lithophane, Box, 4 1/2 In. 25.00
Toy, Truck, Arctic Ice Cream, Kilgore, Cast Iron, 8 In. 225.00
Toy, Truck, C.I.Mack, Bell Telephone Embossed Sides, Hubley, 4 In. 50.00
Toy, Truck, Champion, Wrecker, 1930, Cast Iron, 8 In. 95.00
Toy, Truck, Coal Dump, Wyandotte, 11 1/2 In. 12.00
Toy, Truck, Dump, Buddy L, 15 In. 30.00
Toy, Truck, Dump, Doors Open, Paint, Decals, Buddy L 125.00
Toy, Truck, Dump, Mack Champion 165.00
Toy, Truck, Dump, Metal, Son-Ny By Dayton Toy & Specialty, 1920s 120.00
Toy, Truck, Finnegan The Baggage Man, Windup, Unique Art 25.00
Toy, Truck, Fire, Hubley Fox, 1934 .... 750.00
Toy, Truck, Fire, With Driver, Cast Iron 49.50
Toy, Truck, Gulf Oil Tanker, Friction 9.50
Toy, Truck, Hubley, Cast Iron Pickup, 5 In. 20.00
Toy, Truck, Jaegar Cement Mixer, Marked Kenton, 5 1/2 In. 135.00
Toy, Truck, Loader, Keystone, Complete 125.00
Toy, Truck, Loony Firetruck, Wood, Pull Toy, Firemen Move Heads, Bell Rings 14.50
Toy, Truck, Mack Dump, Open Cab, 15 1/2 In. 68.00
Toy, Truck, Mack, Cast Iron, Original Paint, 4 1/4 In. 30.00
Toy, Truck, Mars Royal Van Co., Windup, Tin 125.00
Toy, Truck, Metal Craft St.Louis, 1931, 11 In. 75.00
Toy, Truck, Milk, Barclay, Slush Mold, 3 1/2 In.Long 8.00
Toy, Truck, Panel, Champion, 1934, 7 1/2 In. 75.00
Toy, Truck, Pennsylvania Railroad, 6 1/2 In. 5.00
Toy, Truck, Ready Mix Concrete 35.00
Toy, Truck, Red Rubber, 4 1/2 In. 8.00
Toy, Truck, Sand, Marx, Tin, 1930s, 10 In. 30.00
Toy, Truck, Standard Oil, Key Wind, Strauss, 10 In. 135.00
Toy, Truck, Structo Dump 10.00
Toy, Truck, Sun Rubber Company, 5 3/4 In. 12.00
Toy, Truck, Texaco, Tootsietoy 10.00
Toy, Truck, Tootsietoy, Panel, Dairy Graham 75.00
Toy, Truck, U.S.Army Motor Unit, 2 Unit, Cannon At Rear On Caisson 115.00
Toy, Truck, Van, With Driver, Tin, Windup, Marx, 10 In. 28.50
Toy, Truck, Water Tower, Paint, Label, Keystone, 32 In. 95.00
     Toy, Trunk, see Trunk
Toy, Turtle, Bell, Cast Iron 55.00
Toy, Tut-Tut, Lehmann, Patented 1903, Windup 235.00
Toy, Twist Dancer, Windup 10.00
Toy, Typewriter, Marx 25.00
Toy, Typewriter, Punch Type 18.00

Toy, Typewriter, Simplex, Model R, Early 1900s, Original Box	65.00
Toy, Typewriter, Tin, Dial, Marx, Box	79.00
Toy, Uncle Sam Working Cash Register, Tin, C.1930	35.00
Toy, Uncle Wiggily Crazy Car, Mark	150.00 To 185.00
Toy, Unicycle, Lithographed, Push Toy, 4 1/2 X 3 In.	16.50
Toy, Victrola, Child's, General Phonograph, Elyria, Ohio, 1 Record	150.00
Toy, Wagon & 2 Horses, Cast Iron, 12 In.	38.00
Toy, Wagon, Bear Cage, Overland Circus	150.00
Toy, Wagon, Buffalo Carriage, 1890	450.00
Toy, Wagon, Carpenter Fire Patrol, 1880, 17 In.	700.00
Toy, Wagon, Coach, Metal, Red, Black, Yellow, Driver, 2 Passengers, 2 Horses	40.00
Toy, Wagon, Doll Size, Wooden, Small	65.00
Toy, Wagon, Doll's, Wooden Bentwood Wheels, 20 1/2 In.	42.50
Toy, Wagon, Horse Drawn, Tin, C.1870	57.50
Toy, Wagon, Hubley Log Wagon, 2 Oxen, 1906	600.00
Toy, Wagon, Ice, Cast Iron	95.00
Toy, Wagon, Ice, Horse Drawn, Cast Iron	17.50
Toy, Wagon, Red Racer, Wood, 43 X 29 In.	52.00
Toy, Wagon, Spring Seat, Horses, Driver, Arcade, Rubber Tires, 11 1/4 X 5 In.	135.00
Toy, Wagon, Studebaker, Junior Farm, Wooden, Full Size .... *Illus*	670.00
Toy, Wagon, Tin, Full Color, Wood Wheels, 1930, U.S., 3 X 9 X 2 In.	15.00
Toy, Wagon, Toy Town Dairy Wagon, Marx, Windup	35.00
Toy, Washboard, Crystal	25.00
Toy, Washer, Tin, Mickey Mouse	25.00
Toy, Washer, With Wringer, Pink & Blue Tin, Wolverine Deluxe, 12 1/2 In.	13.00
Toy, Washer, Wringer, 4 Piece	15.00
Toy, Washing Machine, Copper, Mechanical, 1 Gallon	175.00
Toy, Washing Machine, Tin, Lithographed Dutch Scene	10.50
Toy, Wheelbarrow, All Wooden, Pennsylvania Dutch, 29 1/2 X 10 X 8 3/4 In.	55.00
Toy, Wheelbarrow, Kilgore, Cast Iron	10.00

Toy, Wagon, Studebaker, Junior Farm, Wooden, Full Size

Toy, Whistle, Bull's-Eye Rifle	3.50
Toy, Whistle, Decoder, Captain Midnight, 1947	39.00
Toy, Whistle, Figural, Soldier, Child's, C.1920, 14 In.	25.00
Toy, Whistle, Penny Toy, 3 Animated Airplanes, French	175.00
Toy, Windmill, Mac Old Dutch, Tin	45.00
Toy, Window, Toy Show Window, Rockwell	24.50
Toy, Windup Plush Squirrel, Hops, Fur Tail, Occupied Japan	27.00
Toy, Windup, Man Pushing Wheelbarrow, Tin	65.00
Toy, Wonder Cyclist, Windup, Bell, Marx, C.1930, 8 3/4 In.	180.00
Toy, Wooden Alphabet, Letters Travel Around Hexagonal Board, Dated 1886	10.00
Toy, Woolly Dog, Windup, Hops, 5 In.	12.00
Toy, Work Shop, Miniature, Coin Operated, Oak, 1907, 36 X 30 X 18 In.	250.00
Toy, Wrecker, Sheet Metal, 1930s, Buddy L	75.00
Toy, Wringer, Little Princess	22.50
Toy, Yacht, Windup, Painted	50.00
Toy, Zeppelin, C/2, Original Paint, 5 In.	30.00
Toy, Zeppelin, Tootsietoy, Los Angeles	45.00 To 50.00

*Tramp Art is a form of folk art made since the Civil War. It is
usually made from chip-carved cigar boxes.*

Tramp Art, Box, Brass Fittings, Claw Feet	55.00
Tramp Art, Box, Covered, 11 X 6 In.	35.00
Tramp Art, Box, Hearts With Velvet Background, 6 1/2 X 11 X 5 In.	40.00
Tramp Art, Box, Jewelry, Heart On Cover	45.00
Tramp Art, Box, Milk, Tin Insert, Dated 1896, Wood Burned	58.00
Tramp Art, Chest, Footed, 15 X 22 X 10 In.	90.00
Tramp Art, Frame, 19 X 17 In.	65.00
Tramp Art, Mirror, 24 In.	60.00
Tramp Art, Shade, Lamp, Brass, Pierced, Miniature, 3 1/2 X 4 In., Pair	29.50
Tramp Art, Shelf, Hanging Double, Carved Tulips, Leaves, Fleur-De-Lis	70.00
Trap, see Tool, Trap	
Trap, Mouse, Wooden, Peerless	52.00

Treen are small wooden objects such as mugs, spoons, and bowls. The term is early English but is used in the United States in many areas.

Treen, Bowl, Footed, Bleached, 5 X 4 In.	32.00
Treen, Box, Jedburgh Aldsey, 2 1/2 In. .... *Illus*	15.00
Treen, Cordial	18.50
Treen, Eggcup	10.00

Treen, Box, Jedburgh Aldsey, 2 1/2 In.

Trivets are now used to hold hot dishes. Most of the late nineteenth and early twentieth century trivets were made to hold hot irons. Iron or brass reproductions are being made of many of the old styles.

Trivet, Brass, Footed, Horseshoe Shape, Good Luck	35.00
Trivet, Brass, George Washington, 4 X 9 1/2 In.	42.00
Trivet, China, Violets, Round, 6 In.	5.50
Trivet, Floral, Overlay, Sterling Silver, Signed, 6 In.	45.00
Trivet, George Washington, Handled, C.1918	50.00
Trivet, Iron, Broom Design	10.00
Trunk, Doll, Tin, Inner Tray	42.00
Trunk, Doll's, Paper Covered, Inside Tray, 10 X 6 X 4 In.	19.50
Trunk, Jenny Lind, Small, Leather Bound	8.50
Trunk, Miniature, Cotterpin Hinges, C.1800, 6 X 3 1/8 In.	150.00
Trunk, Pine, Small Dome, C.1830, 8 X 8 1/2 X 15 In.	28.00
Trunk, Wood, Dome Top, Pine, Hand-Forged Nails, 31 X 14 X 13 1/2 In.	125.00
Tuthill, Vase, Bud, Cut & Etched, Wafer Foot, Signed, 8 In.	109.00
Typewriter, Blickensdefer, Original Wood Case, 1890-98	85.00
Typewriter, Corona, Folding, 1910	125.00
Umbrella, Handle, Hand-Carved Dragon Head With Ball In Mouth	20.00
Umbrella, Parasol, Floral, Eagles, Shields, Ships, Ropes, Silk Shade, Handle	200.00
Umbrella, Parasol, With Wire, Fringe, Sequins, Ornate, 10 In.	28.00
Union Porcelain Works, Pitcher, Chinaman, Gambler, Marked, 10 In.	1150.00
Union Porcelain Works, Pitcher, Gargoyle Handle, Ice Lip, 8 In.	1350.00
University City, Vase, Classical, Mottled Brown Glaze, Marked UP, 7 In.	395.00
University City, Vase, Dark Blue Glaze, 4 Sided, Marked U.C.	295.00

Val St.Lambert *Val St.Lambert Cristalleries of Belgium was founded by Messieurs Kemlin and Lelievre in 1825. The company is still in operation.*

Val St.Lambert, Bottle, Perfume, Cameo Cut, Cranberry Florals, Signed, 6 In.	145.00
Val St.Lambert, Box, Bust Of Mother Holding Baby, C.1900, Green, 4 1/2 In.	65.00
Val St.Lambert, Box, Green Glass, Mother & Baby On Lid, C.1900, 4 1/2 In.	65.00
Val St.Lambert, Box, Green, Bust Of Mother & Baby, 1900, 4 1/2 X 2 In.	55.00
Val St.Lambert, Box, Powder, Magenta Color Decoration, Clear Background	225.00
Val St.Lambert, Cameo Carved Red Florals, Amber Ground, Signed, 5 In.	275.00
Val St.Lambert, Candelabra, Footed, Frosted, Pair	140.00
Val St.Lambert, Candlestick, Frosted And Painted, C.1890, Pair	48.00
Val St.Lambert, Candlestick, Gray, Frosted, Flowers On Base, C.1900, Pair	80.00
Val St.Lambert, Candy, Panel Cut All Over, Crystal Cover, Signed	30.00
Val St.Lambert, Dish, Cameo Cover, Cranberry Frosted Floral, 3 1/2 In.	150.00
Val St.Lambert, Dish, Candy, Clear Crystal, Paneled Cut Top, Covered	40.00
Val St.Lambert, Emerald Green Overlay Cut To Clear, Trumpet, 9 In.	155.00
Val St.Lambert, Epergne, Pressed Pattern, 14 In.	25.00
Val St.Lambert, Goblet, Green Frosted Top, Clear Stem & Base, Acid-Cut Back	95.00
Val St.Lambert, Vase, Cameo Carved Blue Florals, Clear Frosted, 6 In.	225.00
Val St.Lambert, Vase, Cameo, Acid-Cut Scroll On Front, Signed, 6 1/2 In.	210.00
Val St.Lambert, Vase, Cameo, Scroll In Acid Cut In Front, Signed, 6 1/2 In.	135.00
Val St.Lambert, Vase, Cobalt Blue Encasing, Copper Foil, Cut Roses, 10 In.	300.00
Val St.Lambert, Vase, Cranberry, Cut To Clear, Signed, 6 In.	80.00
Val St.Lambert, Vase, Trumpet, Emerald Green Overlay Cut To Clear, 9 In.	155.00
Val St.Lambert, Wine Set, 13 In.Crystal Decanter, 6 Bell-Shape Wines	145.00
Vallerystahl, Bowl, Turquoise, Milk Glass, Pedestal Foot, 9 In.	45.00
Vallerystahl, Box, Shape Of Frog, Grass Green, Signed	75.00
Vallerystahl, Dish, Covered, Figural Pear, Milk Glass	45.00
Vallerystahl, Dish, Covered, Rabbit, Signed	80.00
Vallerystahl, Dish, Dolphin Feet, Sea Shell Finial, White Milk Glass, 6 In.	85.00
Vallerystahl, Dish, Lid, Dolphin Feet, Shell Finial, Shells, 6 1/5 X 5 1/2 In.	85.00
Vallerystahl, Dish, Setter Dog Cover, Made In France	135.00
Vallerystahl, Jar, White, Clock Base, Knob Finial, Covered, 5 In.	75.00
Vallerystahl, Plate, Floral, Blue Aqua, Salad Size, Signed, Set Of 11	50.00
Vallerystahl, Salt, Hen Cover, Blue	47.50
Vallerystahl, Salt, Hen On Nest, Green	12.50
Vallerystahl, Salt, 2 Hens On Basket, Milk Glass, Pair	90.00
Vallerystahl, Vase, Cameo, Amber, Gold Lined Daffodils In Relief, 11 1/2 In.	385.00

 Van Briggle Pottery was made by Artus Van Briggle in Colorado Springs, Colorado, after 1901. Mr.Van Briggle had been a decorator at the Rookwood Pottery of Cincinnati, Ohio, and he died in 1904. His wares were original and had modeled relief decorations with a soft dull glaze.

Van Briggle, Ashtray, Diamond Shape, Red	12.50
Van Briggle, Ashtray, Figural, Indian Maiden, Persian Rose	60.00
Van Briggle, Ashtray, Owl, 5 1/2 X 4 In.	20.00
Van Briggle, Bookend, Owl, Blue-Green Shading To Maroon, Pair	60.00
Van Briggle, Bookend, Owl, Turquoise, Pair	40.00
Van Briggle, Boot, Signed, 2 3/4 In.	9.50
Van Briggle, Bowl & Frog, Stylized Dragonfly, 9 In.Diameter	47.50
Van Briggle, Bowl, Blue & Turquoise, Raised Leaves, 3 1/4 In.	35.00
Van Briggle, Bowl, Blue, Petal, 6 In.	18.50
Van Briggle, Bowl, Deep Blue, Flower Frog Consisting Of 3 Frogs, 9 In.	38.00
Van Briggle, Bowl, Ming Blue, Dated 1915, 8 In.	45.00
Van Briggle, Bowl, Molded Heart-Shaped Leaves, Blue, 1920, 6 X 3 1/4 In.	55.00
Van Briggle, Bowl, Persian Rose, Scalloped, 4 1/2 X 7 3/4 In.	20.00
Van Briggle, Bowl, Persian Rose, 7 1/2 X 2 5/8 In.	24.00
Van Briggle, Bowl, Tulips, Purple, Marked Colorado Springs, 5 X 5 1/4 In.	27.00
Van Briggle, Bowl, Turquoise, 9 3/4 In.	32.00
Van Briggle, Bowl, USA, Turquoise, 9 3/4 In.	35.00
Van Briggle, Candlestick, Maroon To Blue Glaze, 10 In., Pair	75.00
Van Briggle, Candlestick, Mulberry, Pair	25.00
Van Briggle, Candlestick, Persian Rose, Green, Pair	12.00
Van Briggle, Candlestick, Persian Rose, Raised, Blue, 6 1/2 In., Pair	14.00
Van Briggle, Conch, Figural, Blue, 9 In.	18.00
Van Briggle, Console Set, Persian Rose, 3 Piece	40.00
Van Briggle, Cup & Saucer, Light Blue, 1916-17	30.00
Van Briggle, Ewer, Turquoise Blue, Handle, 9 In.	25.00

Van Briggle, Figurine, Colt, 6 1/2 In.	28.00
Van Briggle, Figurine, Hat, Aqua, 2 In.	10.00
Van Briggle, Figurine, Hopi Indian Maiden, Turquoise	65.00
Van Briggle, Figurine, Seated Nude Holding Shell, 7 1/2 In.	70.00
Van Briggle, Lamp Base, Turquoise, Ming, Hectagonal Feet, 1922-29, 10 In.	75.00
Van Briggle, Lamp Base, Turquoise, 13 In., Pair	65.00
Van Briggle, Paperweight, Indian Head, Brown & Green	35.00
Van Briggle, Paperweight, Mule Lying Down, Ming Blue, 4 X 4 3/4 In.	38.00
Van Briggle, Pitcher, Persian Rose, 3 In.	30.00
Van Briggle, Planter, Blue & Green, Art Nouveau Design, 2 X 3 In.	35.00
Van Briggle, Planter, Seashell, Maroon	30.00
Van Briggle, Plaque, Head Of Indian A-Ya-Ni, Big Buffalo, Oval	50.00
Van Briggle, Plaque, Head Of Indian Maiden So-Ya-Zhe, Little Star, Oval	50.00
Van Briggle, Plate, Maroon, Turquoise, 4 Swirling Birds, Art Nouveau, 6 In.	25.00
Van Briggle, Tea Set, 3 Piece Set, Turquoise Matte	75.00
Van Briggle, Vase, Blue-Gray Stoneware Finish, 1935, 4 In.	100.00
Van Briggle, Vase, Blue-Green, Raised Swirled Designs, 7 1/2 In.	30.00
Van Briggle, Vase, Bowling Pin Shape, Blossoms, Green, Beige, 1922-29, 6 1/2 In.	30.00
Van Briggle, Vase, Brown & Green, Three Sculptured Indian Heads, 11 In.	100.00
Van Briggle, Vase, Conch Shell, Turquoise, Ming, Colorado Springs, 9 In.	20.00
Van Briggle, Vase, Corset Shape, Jonquils In Relief, 1919-22, 8 1/2 In.	38.00
Van Briggle, Vase, Cranberry, Leaves, 1915, 5 1/2 In.	45.00
Van Briggle, Vase, Dated 1920, P.N.838, 6 In.	28.00
Van Briggle, Vase, Dragonflies, Blue, C.1919-20, Marked, 6 1/2 X 2 In.	26.00
Van Briggle, Vase, Dragonfly, Brown And Blue Gray Glaze, 1910, 4 3/4 In.	35.00
Van Briggle, Vase, Dragonfly, Persian Rose, 3 X 4 1/2 In.	30.00
Van Briggle, Vase, Dragonfly, Purple To Blue, 10 In.	75.00
Van Briggle, Vase, Green, Swirled Leaves, Bottle Shaped, AA Mark, 11 In.	35.00
Van Briggle, Vase, Green, Tulips, 5 In.	12.50
Van Briggle, Vase, Horn Shape, 5 In.	17.00
Van Briggle, Vase, Jonquil, Blue, 10 In.	35.00
Van Briggle, Vase, Lampshade, Maroon, 9 In.	25.00
Van Briggle, Vase, Leaf, Blue, Pierced, AA Mark, 4 In.	35.00
Van Briggle, Vase, Lorelei, Turquoise, 10 1/2 In.	85.00
Van Briggle, Vase, Maroon & Blue, Molded, 1919, AA, 9 In.	45.00
Van Briggle, Vase, Maroon & Dark Blue, Bulbous, U.S.A., 4 In.	15.00
Van Briggle, Vase, Maroon To Blue, 5 1/2 In.	18.00
Van Briggle, Vase, Maroon, Dark Blue Matte, 13 In.	35.00
Van Briggle, Vase, Maroon, Indian Heads, 12 In.	95.00 To 125.00
Van Briggle, Vase, Ming Blue, 4 1/2 In.	18.00
Van Briggle, Vase, Ming, Blue Relief Design, Art Nouveau, 10 In.	45.00
Van Briggle, Vase, Molded Arrowhead Leaves, Blue-Black Glaze, 5 X 9 3/4 In.	150.00
Van Briggle, Vase, Molded Flowers, Long Stems, Blue, 1920, 7 1/4 In.	55.00
Van Briggle, Vase, Molded Leaf, Aqua, 5 In.	20.00
Van Briggle, Vase, Molded Leaves & Buds, Turquoise Ming Glaze, 8 In.	28.00
Van Briggle, Vase, Molded Nouveau, Marked, 4 1/2 In.	24.50
Van Briggle, Vase, Mulberry, Clover Pattern, 6 1/2 In.	22.50
Van Briggle, Vase, Mulberry, Numbered & Dated, 1920, 6 In.	33.00
Van Briggle, Vase, Persian Rose, Diagonal Overlapping Lotus, Marked, 6 In.	55.00
Van Briggle, Vase, Persian Rose, 3 1/2 In.	22.00
Van Briggle, Vase, Persian Rose, 4 1/2 In.	22.00
Van Briggle, Vase, Persian, Rose To Blue, Leaf & Bud Design, 5 In.	15.00
Van Briggle, Vase, Plum, Numbered, Dated 1920, 6 In.	30.00
Van Briggle, Vase, Raised Swirled Design, Blue Green Ground, 7 1/2 In.	35.00
Van Briggle, Vase, Raised Tulips, Turquoise, 5 1/4 In.	14.00
Van Briggle, Vase, Sea Foam Top, Green, Signed, 5 1/2 In.	20.00
Van Briggle, Vase, Shell, 4 X 8 3/4 In.	17.00
Van Briggle, Vase, Swirl, Open Handles, Blue Over Turquoise, 7 X 7 1/2 In.	45.00
Van Briggle, Vase, Swirl, Turquoise, Blue-Green, 8 In.	30.00
Van Briggle, Vase, Turquoise Stylized Flowers, 10 X 9 In.	50.00
Van Briggle, Vase, Turquoise, Raised Leaf, 4 1/2 In.	15.00

*Vasa Murrhina is the name of a glassware made by the Vasa Murrhina
Art Glass Company of Sandwich, Massachusetts, about 1884. The
glassware was transparent and was embedded with small pieces of colored glass*

and metallic flakes. Some of the pieces were cased. The same type of glass was made in England. Collectors often confuse Vasa Murrhina glass with aventurine, spatter, or spangle glass. There is much confusion about what actually was made by the Vasa Murrhina Factory.

Vasa Murrhina, see also Spangle Glass

Vasa Murrhina, Basket, Blown, 10 Pointed Rim, Red, Thorn Handle	200.00
Vasa Murrhina, Basket, Cranberry To Clear, Clear Twisted V Handle, 10 In.	150.00
Vasa Murrhina, Basket, Ribbed Handle, Gold Flakes Inside	250.00
Vasa Murrhina, Bowl, Metallic Flakes, Ruffled Rim, Clear Edge, Cased Glass	125.00
Vasa Murrhina, Bowl, Rose, White, Silver, Rose, 4 1/2 X 5 1/2 In.	85.00
Vasa Murrhina, Dish, Cheese, Amber, Pink, Spangle	225.00
Vasa Murrhina, Ewer, White Case, Blue With Mica Flared Top, 6 In.	52.00
Vasa Murrhina, Jar, Apothecary, Pink, Silver Mica	70.00
Vasa Murrhina, Pitcher, Cranberry & Custard Spatterings, Bulbous, 7 1/4 In.	110.00
Vasa Murrhina, Pitcher, Melon Ribbed, Mica Flecks, Applied Handle, Pink, White	65.00
Vasa Murrhina, Pitcher, Pink & White, Green Mica Flecks, Melon Ribbed	65.00
Vasa Murrhina, Pitcher, Water, Pink, Mica Flakes	155.00
Vasa Murrhina, Rose Bowl, Blue, Overlay Glass, 3 3/4 In. X 3 1/2 In.	88.00
Vasa Murrhina, Rose Bowl, Blue, White Lining, 8-Crimp Top, 3 1/4 In.	88.00
Vasa Murrhina, Rose Bowl, Crimped, Spangled, Cranberry & White Spatter, 3 In.	88.00
Vasa Murrhina, Rose Bowl, Deep Rose, Coral-Like Pattern, 3 1/2 X 3 1/2 In.	88.00
Vasa Murrhina, Rose Bowl, Leaf Mold, Cranberry Spatter, Northwood	65.00
Vasa Murrhina, Syrup, Leaf Mold	275.00
Vasa Murrhina, Tumbler, Pink Opaque, Mica Flakes, 3 1/2 In.	42.00
Vasa Murrhina, Tumbler, Pink, White, & Blue, Mica Flecks	48.50
Vasa Murrhina, Vase, Applied Leaf Handle, Gold Flecks, Amber, 7 1/2 In.	57.50
Vasa Murrhina, Vase, Aquamarine, Ruffled Top, Silver Spattering, 7 1/4 In.	250.00
Vasa Murrhina, Vase, Aquamarine, Silver Spatterings, Cased & Blown, 7 1/4 In.	150.00
Vasa Murrhina, Vase, Blue, Mica Flaking, Clear Applied Handle, 6 1/2 In., Pair	110.00
Vasa Murrhina, Vase, Clear Crystal, Thorn Handles, Cased, Blown, 7 1/4 In.	85.00
Vasa Murrhina, Vase, Cranberry, Gold Flecks, Beige Bubbles & Swirls, 10 In.	75.00
Vasa Murrhina, Vase, Entwining Rigaree Gold Mica, 8 In.	87.50
Vasa Murrhina, Vase, Footed, Applied Wishbone Feet, Pink, 6 1/4 In.	110.00
Vasa Murrhina, Vase, Gold Flecked In Amethyst, 6 1/2 In.	40.00
Vasa Murrhina, Vase, Gold Flecks, Amber With White Interior, 8 In.	75.00
Vasa Murrhina, Vase, Pink Overlay, Ruffled Top, Mica Flakes, 7 1/2 In.	65.00
Vasa Murrhina, Vase, Pink To Deep Rose, Swirled Mica Flakes, 6 1/2 In.	68.00

Vasart is the signature used on a late type of art glass made by the Streathearn Glass Company of Scotland.

Vasart, Basket, Hand-Blown, Pinkish Gray To Green, 4 1/2 X 5 1/4 X 4 In.	35.00
Vasart, Basket, Lavender Mottled, White, Signed, 3 X 5 X 3 In.	34.00
Vasart, Bowl, Blue, Rolled-Over Scalloped Top, 5 X 3 In.	48.00
Vasart, Bowl, Clear, Orange & Black Swirls, Semifooted, 9 In.	35.00
Vasart, Bowl, Cylindrical, Flaring Rim, Gray To Blue, Signed, 3 X 4 In.	22.00
Vasart, Bowl, Cylindrical, Flaring Rim, Mottled Gray-Blue, 2 1/2 X 3 1/2 In.	22.00
Vasart, Bowl, Flaring, Semifooted, Clear, Swirled Orange & Black, 9 In.	35.00
Vasart, Bowl, Footed, Increasing Diameter To Top, Orange To Black, Signed	45.00
Vasart, Bowl, Large Handles, Mottled Pink To Green, 4 1/2 X 6 X 2 1/2 In.	45.00
Vasart, Bowl, Low, Pastel Blue To Pink, Undulating Rim, 5 In.	20.00
Vasart, Bowl, Mottled Gray To Blue, Cylindrical, Flared Rim, 3 1/2 In.	22.00
Vasart, Bowl, Mottled Orange Mixed With Black, Semifooted, 7 1/2 In.	45.00
Vasart, Bowl, Mottled Pink To Green At Top, Handles, 4 1/2 X 6 X 2 1/2 In.	45.00
Vasart, Bowl, Orange, 3 7/8 X 8 1/2 In.	40.00
Vasart, Bowl, Semifooted, Mottled, Orange To Black, 3 1/2 X 7 1/2 In.	45.00
Vasart, Bowl, Swirled Orange & Black In Clear Glass, 3 X 9 In.	35.00
Vasart, Hat, Derby Shaped, Mottled Light Green & White, 3 X 4 X 2 1/4 In.	35.00
Vasart, Toothpick, Hat, Mottled Deep Pink, Mottled Dark Blue Brim, 2 1/2 In.	48.00
Vasart, Tray, Crimped Rim, Mottled Blue To Cerise, Signed, 4 X 12 In.	24.00

Vaseline glass is a greenish yellow glassware resembling petroleum jelly. Some vaseline glass is still being made in old and new styles. Pressed glass of the 1870s was often made of vaseline-colored glass. The old glass was made with uranium, but the reproductions are being colored in a different way. See Pressed Glass for more information about patterns that were also made of vaseline-colored glass.

Vaseline Glass, **Baby Bootee**	28.00
Vaseline Glass, **Basket**, Old Man Winter, Opalescent, Twisted Handle, 7 1/2 In.	95.00
Vaseline Glass, **Basket**, 6 1/2 In.High	52.00
Vaseline Glass, **Berry Set**, Maple Leaf, Footed Bowl	70.00
Vaseline Glass, **Berry Set**, Petticoat, Gold	175.00
Vaseline Glass, **Berry Set**, Scalloped Border, 3 Feet On Each Of 5 Pieces	225.00
Vaseline Glass, **Berry Set**, Two Panel, 7 Pieces	60.00
Vaseline Glass, **Biscuit Jar**, Diamond Band, 34 Rib Cuts, Star Base Plate	125.00
Vaseline Glass, **Bottle**, Barber, Swirled, Opalescent	45.00
Vaseline Glass, **Bottle**, Perfume, Footed, Mushroom Stopper, Art Deco, 8 In.	15.00
Vaseline Glass, **Bottle**, Wine, Diamond-Quilted, Faceted Stopper, 14 7/8 In.	118.00
Vaseline Glass, **Bowl & Candlestick**, Yellow, Pair	45.00
Vaseline Glass, **Bowl**, Berry, Master, Birchleaf	45.00
Vaseline Glass, **Bowl**, Bouillon, Plain Pattern, Wide Rim, 9 In.	75.00
Vaseline Glass, **Bowl**, Daisy & Button, Cloverleaf	26.50
Vaseline Glass, **Bowl**, Daisy & Button, Paneled, 8 1/2 In.	18.50
Vaseline Glass, **Bowl**, Daisy & Button, Tricornered, 9 In.	35.00
Vaseline Glass, **Bowl**, Finger, Fluted, Ruffled Top, 2 X 3 1/2 In.	17.50
Vaseline Glass, **Bowl**, Finger, Palm Beach, Opalescent, Set Of 8	275.00
Vaseline Glass, **Bowl**, Fruit, Rolled Edge & Paneled, 12 In.	18.00
Vaseline Glass, **Bowl**, Hobnail, Crimped Rim, Ruby Stained, Pontil, 8 X 3 In.	24.00
Vaseline Glass, **Bowl**, Imperial Jewels, Green, 8 In.	10.00
Vaseline Glass, **Bowl**, Petticoat	22.00
Vaseline Glass, **Bowl**, Ruby Stained, 7 1/2 X 3 1/4 In.	25.00
Vaseline Glass, **Bowl**, Wild Flower, Square, C.1874-98, 7 3/4 In.	24.00
Vaseline Glass, **Box**, Powder, Covered, Panel Cut, Gold Decoration, 4 1/2 In.	74.00
Vaseline Glass, **Butter Pat**, Finecut, Set Of 6	28.00
Vaseline Glass, **Cake Stand**, Cathedral, 9 1/2 In.	38.00
Vaseline Glass, **Candleholder**, Art Deco, 7 In., Pair	40.00
Vaseline Glass, **Candleholder**, Cornucopia, Hobnail	22.50
Vaseline Glass, **Candlestick**, Cactus, Opalescent, Pair	45.00
Vaseline Glass, **Candlestick**, 1-Step Dolphin, Pair	425.00
Vaseline Glass, **Candlestick**, 8 In., Pair	30.00
Vaseline Glass, **Castor**, Pickle, Enameled Swirl, Footed Frame, Lid & Tongs	165.00
Vaseline Glass, **Compote**, Blown, Blue Base, 7 In.	45.00
Vaseline Glass, **Compote**, Cactus, Opalescent	45.00 To 65.00
Vaseline Glass, **Compote**, Carnations, Ruffled, Marigold	7.00
Vaseline Glass, **Compote**, Chippendale, Opalescent, 5 3/4 X 5 In.	32.00
Vaseline Glass, **Compote**, Shell Shape, 6 In.	20.00
Vaseline Glass, **Creamer**, Daisy In Diamond, Miniature	24.00
Vaseline Glass, **Creamer**, Fluted Scrolls, Opalescent	80.00
Vaseline Glass, **Creamer**, Fluted, Scrolls, Footed, Opalescent	40.00
Vaseline Glass, **Creamer**, Maple Leaf, Footed, Oval	49.00
Vaseline Glass, **Creamer**, Rose Sprig	47.50
Vaseline Glass, **Creamer**, Three Panels	35.00
Vaseline Glass, **Cruet**, Daisy & Button	85.00
Vaseline Glass, **Cruet**, Gold Band	85.00
Vaseline Glass, **Cruet**, Opal, Fluted Scroll	120.00
Vaseline Glass, **Dish Butter**, Fluted, Scrolls, Opalescent	125.00
Vaseline Glass, **Dish**, Butter, Diamond-Quilted	45.00
Vaseline Glass, **Dish**, Butter, Wreathed Cherry, Covered	45.00
Vaseline Glass, **Dish**, Candy, Hobnail, 4 1/2 X 6 In.	15.75
Vaseline Glass, **Dish**, Candy, Opalescent, Ruffled, Beaded, Footed	27.00
Vaseline Glass, **Dish**, Candy, Starburst In Bottom, 4 Compartment, 8 In.	24.00
Vaseline Glass, **Dish**, Candy, Swag & Bracket, Opalescent, Footed	24.50
Vaseline Glass, **Dish**, Dove Cover, Basket Weave Base, McKee	100.00
Vaseline Glass, **Dish**, Ruffled, Opalescent, 5 1/2 In.	15.00
Vaseline Glass, **Epergne**, Lily, Opalescent Ribbons	190.00
Vaseline Glass, **Epergne**, Reeded, Overlay, 16 In.	200.00
Vaseline Glass, **Epergne**, Single Lily, Paneled Star, Pewter Rim, 14 In.	5.00
Vaseline Glass, **Epergne**, 3 Lily, Turquoise Threading, Ruffled Bowl, 23 In.	325.00
Vaseline Glass, **Goblet**, Cathedral	42.00

Vaseline Glass, Goblet, Daisy & Button, Thumbprint Panels, Opalescent	32.50
Vaseline Glass, Goblet, Three Panel	34.00
Vaseline Glass, Goblet, Two Panel	24.00
Vaseline Glass, Gum, Stand, Teaberry	22.00
Vaseline Glass, Hatchet, World's Fair, Libbey Glass, 1893	92.50
Vaseline Glass, Jar, Candy, Cactus, Opalescent	125.00
Vaseline Glass, Jug, Pewter Mountings, Foot, & Handle, 12 X 4 1/4 In.	165.00
Vaseline Glass, Match Holder, Daisy & Button, High Hat	25.00
Vaseline Glass, Mug, Child's, ABC With Girl At Christmas Tree, Boy At Desk	40.00
Vaseline Glass, Mug, Child's, Chick And Pugs	25.00
Vaseline Glass, Mug, Child's, Gold Band Trim, Scalloped Feet	18.50
Vaseline Glass, Mug, Daisy & Button, Ruffled Top Celery	22.00
Vaseline Glass, Nappy, Cactus, Opalescent	25.00
Vaseline Glass, Pitcher, Daisy & Button, Panels, Wishbone Handle, 5 1/2 In.	20.00
Vaseline Glass, Pitcher, Leaf & Mold, Spatter Frosted	285.00
Vaseline Glass, Pitcher, Water, Engraved Floral Design, Opalescent	80.00
Vaseline Glass, Pitcher, Water, Opalescent, Engraved Florals	80.00
Vaseline Glass, Pitcher, Water, Paneled Forget-Me-Not	32.50
Vaseline Glass, Pitcher, Water, Patterned	48.00
Vaseline Glass, Plate, Imperial Jewels, 8 In.	5.00
Vaseline Glass, Rose Bowl, Hobnail, Scalloped Top, Footed, 4 X 4 1/2 In.	35.00
Vaseline Glass, Rose Bowl, Souvenir, Palm Beach	60.00
Vaseline Glass, Salt, Christmas, Dated Top With Agitator	45.00
Vaseline Glass, Salt, Opalescent Pattern, Silver Plated Basket Holder, 3 In.	45.00
Vaseline Glass, Sauce, Opalescent, Iris, Meander	24.00
Vaseline Glass, Sconce, Wall, Candle, Clambroth, Pair	45.00 To 60.00
Vaseline Glass, Shade, Gas, Flared, Ruffled Vertical Opalescent Stripes	45.00
Vaseline Glass, Shade, Gas, Hobnail, Ruffled Rim, 8 1/2 X 6 1/2 In.	135.00
Vaseline Glass, Sherbet, Spider Web Pattern, Stemmed	12.00
Vaseline Glass, Shoe, Cat On Top, Hobnail, 3 X 5 In.	15.75
Vaseline Glass, Shoe, Daisy, Button, Small	12.00
Vaseline Glass, Spooner, Alaska Enameled Flower	59.00
Vaseline Glass, Sugar & Creamer, Cactus, Opalescent	80.00
Vaseline Glass, Sugar & Creamer, Maple Leaf Pattern	110.00
Vaseline Glass, Sugar, Opalescent Flowers And Fernery	50.00
Vaseline Glass, Syrup, Leaf Mold	260.00
Vaseline Glass, Table Set, Petticoat, 4 Piece	285.00
Vaseline Glass, Toothpick, Bathing Tub	39.00
Vaseline Glass, Toothpick, Boot	18.00
Vaseline Glass, Toothpick, Gold Band	28.00
Vaseline Glass, Toothpick, Leaf Mold, Spatter Frosted	85.00
Vaseline Glass, Toothpick, Opalescent, Overall Hobnail	58.00
Vaseline Glass, Toothpick, Spearhead, Opal, Diamond	55.00
Vaseline Glass, Town Pump And Trough, Opalescent, Northwood	95.00 To 135.00
Vaseline Glass, Tray, Daisy & Button, Scalloped, Fan Handles, 8 X 13 X 2 In.	85.00
Vaseline Glass, Tray, Lemon	25.00
Vaseline Glass, Tray, Sandwich, Fleur-De-Lis Handle, 11 1/2 In.	18.00
Vaseline Glass, Tray, Snack, Center Handle	35.00
Vaseline Glass, Trough, Water, Opalescent, Novelty	50.00
Vaseline Glass, Tumbler, Diamond Cut, 4 1/2 In.	15.00
Vaseline Glass, Vase, Automobile Bud, Daisy & Button Banded Top, 8 1/2 In.	100.00
Vaseline Glass, Vase, Cactus, Opalescent, 7 In.	50.00
Vaseline Glass, Vase, Car, Daisy & Button	20.00
Vaseline Glass, Vase, Chrysanthemum, Swirl Base, Bottle Shape, 8 3/4 In.	65.00
Vaseline Glass, Vase, Fluted Edge, 5 3/4 In.	65.00
Vaseline Glass, Vase, Opalescent, Ruffled, 9 In.	23.00
Vaseline Glass, Vase, Opalescent, Thomas Webb, 3 1/2 In.	95.00
Vaseline Glass, Vase, Ruffled Top, Tapers To 2 3/8 In. Base, 5 1/2 X 5 In.	20.00
Vaseline Glass, Vase, Trumpet, Fluted, Opalescent, Silver Leaf & Twigs Base	25.00
Vaseline Glass, Water Set, Rib, Pitcher, Applied Handle, 2 Tumblers	35.00
Vaseline Glass, Water Set, 8 In. Pitcher With Reed Handle, 7 Piece	95.00
Vaseline Glass, Wine, Chadwick	24.00
Vaseline Glass, Wine, Finecut & Panel	22.00
Vaseline, Glass, Creamer, Opalescent, Alaska	60.00
Vaseline, Glass, Pitcher, Clear Handle, 3 3/4 In.High	12.00

Vaseline, Glass, Shade, Raised Swirl Stripes, Opalescent, Ruffled Rim, 8 In. 95.00

Venetian glass has been made near Venice, Italy, from the thirteenth to the twentieth century. Thin colored glass with applied decorations is favored although many other types have been made.

Venetian Glass, Applied Rigaree, Ball Stem, Handled, 3 3/4 In. Diameter 75.00
Venetian Glass, Basket, Clear, 10 1/2 X 8 X 5 1/2 In. .... 150.00 To 175.00
Venetian Glass, Bottle, Scent, Applied Decoration To Top, 9 1/2 In., Pair 140.00
Venetian Glass, Bottle, Scent, Dark Blue, Gold Mica Ribbons, Gold Footed 125.00
Venetian Glass, Candlestick, Clear, Gold Wash, Red Trimmed Rims, 12 In., Pair 96.00
Venetian Glass, Candlestick, Gold Mica Flecks, Cobalt Trim, Pair 150.00
Venetian Glass, Champagne, Gold Mica Flecks, Cobalt Trim, Serpent Amber Stem 50.00
Venetian Glass, Compote, Blue, White Appliques, Murano, 7 1/2 X 7 1/2 In. 65.00
Venetian Glass, Compote, Gold Ruby, Diamond-Quilted, Dolphins, Gold Flecks 75.00
Venetian Glass, Ewer, Opalescent Swirl, Applied Cranberry Rigaree, 9 1/2 In. 200.00
Venetian Glass, Goblet, Gold Mica Flecks, Cobalt Trim, Serpent Amber Stem 55.00
Venetian Glass, Salt, Swan, Pair 35.00
Venetian Glass, Vase, White, Gilt Outlined Ruffles, Gilt Dolphin Stem, 10 In. 40.00

Verlys glass was made in France after 1931. Verlys was also made in the United States. The glass is either blown or molded. The American glass is signed with a diamond-point-scratched name, but the French pieces are marked with a molded signature.

Verlys, Bowl, Blue, Maple Leaf Decoration, Footed, 8 1/2 X 2 3/4 In. 165.00
Verlys, Bowl, Center, Tassel Pattern, Frosted & Clear, 11 3/4 In. 58.00
Verlys, Bowl, Console, Spreading To Fans Toward Rims, 6 Petal Feet, 12 In. 110.00
Verlys, Bowl, Crystal Etched Butterfly, Acid Etched, Signed, 3 X 13 3/4 In. 95.00
Verlys, Bowl, Dragonfly, Art Glass, Signed, 13 5/8 In. 80.00
Verlys, Bowl, Dusty Rose Wild Ducks, 13 1/2 In. 88.00
Verlys, Bowl, Flying Birds, Ocean & Fish, 13 1/2 In. 95.00
Verlys, Bowl, Footed, Directoire Blue, Pinecone, Signed, 6 In. 95.00
Verlys, Bowl, Four Frosted Poppies & Leaves, Script Signature, 13 1/2 In. 89.50
Verlys, Bowl, French, Thistle, Frosted Brown Wash, 8 1/2 In. 105.00
Verlys, Bowl, Frosted & Clear Lily Pads, Signed, 13 3/4 In. 100.00
Verlys, Bowl, Frosted Birds, 4 1/2 In. 45.00
Verlys, Bowl, Frosted Lotus Blossom, Lily Pad Feet, 13 1/2 In., Shallow 95.00
Verlys, Bowl, Frosted Poppies & Leaves, Signed, 13 1/2 X 2 3/4 In. 89.00
Verlys, Bowl, Frosted, Pond Lilies, Script Signature, 14 In. 100.00
Verlys, Bowl, Frosted, Tassel Script Signature, 11 3/4 X 2 3/4 In. 85.00
Verlys, Bowl, Fruit, Dragons In High Relief, 14 In. 68.00
Verlys, Bowl, Orchid, Crystal Etched, 14 X 1 3/8 In. 60.00
Verlys, Bowl, Pinecone, Frosted And Clear, Signed, Small 24.00
Verlys, Bowl, Poppies, Signed, 13 In. 45.00
Verlys, Bowl, Poppy, Signed, 13 3/4 In. 50.00
Verlys, Bowl, Tassel, Crystal Etched, 11 3/4 X 3 In. .... 95.00 To 125.00
Verlys, Bowl, Water Lilies, Frosted, 13 3/4 In. 150.00
Verlys, Bowl, Wild Ducks, Frosted, 13 1/2 In. 150.00
Verlys, Box, Horse Decoration, Signed, 3 3/4 X 5 In. 35.00
Verlys, Candlestick, Heisey, 3 In. 102.00
Verlys, Charger, Frosted, Large Orchids In Relief, Signed, 14 In. 145.00
Verlys, Charger, Orchid Design, Frosted & Clear, Round Script Signed, 14 In. 110.00
Verlys, Plaque, Madonna Of The Roses, Frosted, Clear, Script Signed, 5 1/2 In. 115.00
Verlys, Plate, Dragonfly Decoration, Frosted, Signed, 13 1/2 In. 95.00
Verlys, Plate, Frosted Design, Heisey, 11 1/2 In. 100.00
Verlys, Rose Bowl, Crystal, Etched, Script Signature 73.00
Verlys, Vase, Berries Molded In High Relief, Flower Frog Insert, 6 1/2 In. 119.00
Verlys, Vase, Dance Of The Nudes, 8 1/2 In. 135.00
Verlys, Vase, Frosted Sunflowers, Signed, 9 In. 135.00
Verlys, Vase, Icicle Pattern, 8 In. 60.00
Verlys, Vase, Lovebirds, Fan Shape, 4 1/2 In. 45.00
Verlys, Vase, Lovebirds, Half-Moon Shape, Frosted & Clear, 6 1/2 In. 55.00
Verlys, Vase, Mandarin, Crystal Etched, 5 1/16 X 9 1/2 In. 250.00
Verlys, Vase, Oriental Scenes In Relief On Clear Ground, 9 1/2 In. 145.00
Verlys, Vase, Seasons, Autumn, Spring, Intaglio Cut, Heisey, 8 1/4 In. 234.00

Verlys, Vase, Sunflower In Relief, Frosted On Clear, Signed, 9 In.	180.00
Verlys, Vase, Swimming Fish, Seahorse Handles, 7 In.	37.00
Verlys, Vase, Tassel, Signed	87.00
Verlys, Vase, Thistle, Frosted, Clear Convex Panels, Signed, 12 1/2 In.	275.00
Verlys, Vase, Two Seasons, Signed, Dated, 9 In.	90.00

Verre de soie glass was first made by Frederick Carder at the Steuben Glass Works from about 1905 to 1930. It is an iridescent glass of soft white or very, very pale green. The name means glass of silk, and it does resemble silk. Other factories have made verre de soie, and some of the English examples were made of different colors. Verre de soie is an art glass and is not related to the iridescent pressed white carnival glass mistakenly called by its name.

Verre De Soie, see also Steuben

Verre De Soie, Bowl, Finger, Engraved, Hawkes	55.00
Verre De Soie, Bowl, Floral Engraving, Numbered, Steuben, 8 In.Diameter	135.00
Verre De Soie, Bowl, Footed, Applied Rim, Steuben, 8 3/4 In.	80.00
Verre De Soie, Bowl, Steuben, 10 In.	45.00
Verre De Soie, Bowl, Steuben, 12 In.	68.00
Verre De Soie, Compote, Acid Etched, Sterling Silver Base, 4 1/4 X 6 In.	75.00
Verre De Soie, Compote, Ball Stem, Rolled Over Top, 7 X 10 3/4 In.	90.00
Verre De Soie, Compote, Copper Wheel Engraved Garlands, & Floral, Steuben	175.00
Verre De Soie, Compote, Engraved By Hawkes, Florals, Steuben, 7 In.	175.00
Verre De Soie, Compote, Footed Engraved Garland & Floral, Signed	175.00
Verre De Soie, Cruet, Hawkes Engraved, Steuben, 8 3/4 In.	225.00
Verre De Soie, Pitcher, Handle To Spout, 9 3/4 In.	100.00
Verre De Soie, Salt, Pedestal, Steuben	55.00
Verre De Soie, Shade, Steuben	25.00
Verre De Soie, Sherbet, Steuben	30.00
Verre De Soie, Sugar & Creamer, Iridescent, Flowers & Vines, Silver Pedestal	165.00
Verre De Soie, Sugar, Green, Double Handled	30.00
Verre De Soie, Vase, Green Reeded, Steuben, 4 In.	85.00
Verre De Soie, Vase, Nouveau Irises & Blades, Blown, 14 In.	150.00
Verre De Soie, Vase, Overturned, Shimmering, 4 1/2 In.	45.00
Verre De Soie, Vase, Three Handles, Polished Pontil, Greenish Variety, 7 In.	125.00
Verre De Soie, Vase, 3 Handled Silky Green, 7 1/8 In.	125.00

Vienna Art plates were round metal serving trays produced around the turn of the century. The designs, copied from Royal Vienna porcelain plates, usually featured a portrait of a lady encircled by a wide, ornate border. Many were used as advertising or promotional items and were produced in Coshocton, Ohio by J. F. Meek's Tuscarora Advertising Co., and H. D. Beach's Standard Advertising Co.

Vienna Art, see also Coca-Cola

Vienna Art, Plate, Grand Lodge, 1907, Philadelphia	45.00
Vienna Art, Plate, Gypsy Girl, Signed Wagner, Tin, 10 In.	20.00
Vienna Art, Plate, Lady In Grecian Gown By Urns, Tin, 10 In.	38.00
Vienna Art, Plate, Maiden, Fountain, Flowers, February 21, 1905	15.50
Vienna Art, Plate, Mathie Brewing Co.On Back	40.00
Vienna Art, Plate, Moose In Water Pursued By Hunter In Canoe, Tin, 10 In.	18.00
Vienna Art, Plate, Portland Oregon, 1912, 48th Grand Lodge Reunion	40.00
Vienna Art, Plate, Portrait Of Child, Fruit & Flower Border, Hanging, 10 In.	25.00
Vienna Art, Plate, Rose & Gold, Maiden, Cupid	15.50

Villeroy & Boch Pottery of Mettlach, Germany, was founded in 1841. The firm made many types of pottery, including the famous Mettlach steins.

Villeroy & Boch, see also Mettlach

Villeroy & Boch, Butter, Covered, No.332, Tan & Green, Raised Designs	95.00
Villeroy & Boch, Butter, Green & Tan Design In Relief, Tower Mark	65.00
Villeroy & Boch, Butter, Tan & Green Raised Designs, Covered	95.00
Villeroy & Boch, Cup, Yorkshire, 2 Handled	25.00
Villeroy & Boch, Dish, Serving, Vine & Floral, Green, Blue, 19th Century, 9 In.	50.00
Villeroy & Boch, Jug, Syrup, Light Blue Onion Pattern, Lidded, Handle, 4 In.	35.00
Villeroy & Boch, Pitcher, Beige, Tan, & Pink, C.1809, 9 In.	85.00

Warwick, Vase, Seagulls, Gold Rim, Marked Narcis, No.1 .... 30.00
Warwick, Vase, Trumpet Style, Clusters Of Cherries, Brown Tones, 11 1/2 In. 35.00
Warwick, Water Set, Portrait, 7 Piece 495.00

Watch fobs were worn on watch chains. They were popular during Victorian times and after.

Watch Fob, Allis-Chalmers Bulldozer, Gold Plated 30.00
Watch Fob, Angelic Figure, Embossed Florals & Leaves, Brass 29.00
Watch Fob, Banigan Rubbers 17.25
Watch Fob, Baseball, Man At Bat 15.00
Watch Fob, Bear Holding Log Map, California Star, I Love You On Bottom 40.00
Watch Fob, Boston Bulldog, Glass Eyes 7.50
Watch Fob, Brockton Fair, Charles Howard President, 1913 .... 14.00
Watch Fob, Cat, D-M 6.75
Watch Fob, Cherry Smash, Porcelain Front 75.00
Watch Fob, Cigar Cutter, Ornate, Devoe, 1st American Paint Maker, 1754-1909 .... 35.00
Watch Fob, Cox-Roosevelt, 1920, White Metal 75.00
Watch Fob, Crown Shaped, Gold Filled 12.50
Watch Fob, Dog's Head, Old Reliable, Always Ready, John McDonald Paint 32.50
Watch Fob, Dr.Pepper, Louisiana Purchase Exposition 60.00
Watch Fob, Eagle On Ball 40.00
Watch Fob, Eagle, Independence Day, 1918 .... 31.50
Watch Fob, Elk's Tooth, Gold Top With Elk Head 40.00
Watch Fob, Elk's Tooth, Ruby Eye, 1 1/4 In. 55.00
Watch Fob, Embossed Soldiers Firing Guns, National Guard War Maneuvers 12.50
Watch Fob, Erie Foundry Company 16.75
Watch Fob, Farmers & Merchants Insurance, Deer Head 28.50
Watch Fob, G.A.R., Brass, Detroit, 1891, Large 12.50
Watch Fob, Germer Stoves 27.25
Watch Fob, Grays Tonic, Horse Head Inside Letter G 17.00
Watch Fob, Green River Whiskey .... 7.50 To 15.00
Watch Fob, Groundhog, Punxutawney, Pennsylvania 10.00
Watch Fob, Herriott Shoe Polish, St.Louis, Black & Tan Dog 30.00
Watch Fob, Home Comfort Ranges, 1934-36, St.Louis, Mo., Brass, Good Luck 6.00
Watch Fob, Horseshoe & 4 Leaf Clover, Hamamoto Bicycle Shop, Honolulu 32.50
Watch Fob, Hutchinson, Kan., 1850, Plain With Elk Insignia 12.00
Watch Fob, If Shod With Wells Shoes, You Are Well Shod, Best On Earth 35.00
Watch Fob, Independent Order Of Vikings, Enameled 12.00
Watch Fob, Indianapolis, Initials, Sterling Silver 17.50
Watch Fob, J.F.K., On Leather 3.75
Watch Fob, Kellogg's Toasted Corn Flakes 32.50
Watch Fob, Kit Carson, Denver Colorado, Pioneer Monument 12.50
Watch Fob, Little Giant Crane & Shovel, Brass & Porcelain 27.50
Watch Fob, Lunkenheimer Regrinding Gate, Valve In Man's Hand 27.50
Watch Fob, Martin Vise Stand 18.75
Watch Fob, Massey Ferguson Tractor Pulling Farm Wagon 40.00
Watch Fob, McCormick Deering Farm Machines, Porcelain 15.00
Watch Fob, Monkey Wrench, Gold Filled 15.00
Watch Fob, Old Dutch Cleanser, Porcelain, Little Dutch Girl 37.50
Watch Fob, Ottawa, 1920 .... 15.00
Watch Fob, Owl On Tree Stump, Be Wise 25.00
Watch Fob, Pan American Exposition, Buffalo, New York, 1901, Lucky Penny 20.00
Watch Fob, Panama-Pacific Exposition, 1915, Brass 18.00
Watch Fob, Paul Revere Life Insurance Co., Worcester, Mass., Aluminum 7.50
Watch Fob, Political, Presidental Campaign, Bryan & Kern-1908 .... 24.00
Watch Fob, Rock Island 75th Anniversary, 1852-1922 .... 37.50
Watch Fob, Saxon Automobile 45.00
Watch Fob, Sesquicentennial, 1776-1926, Enamel, Golden Fob 20.00
Watch Fob, Silver With Raised Letters 15.00
Watch Fob, Stark Trees Bear Fruit, Tin 20.00
Watch Fob, Strap, Beaded, White With Gold, Blue, Yellow & Red Beads 9.00
Watch Fob, Sundial Shape, CE lettered, Leather Strap, Brass 10.00
Watch Fob, Sundial Shape, EASB lettered, Copper 6.00
Watch Fob, Techheimer Uniforms, Letter Carriers 27.50

Watch Fob, The Buffalo Calf Shoe, For The Man Who Works, Buffalo Emblem	26.50
Watch Fob, The National Sportsman	13.25
Watch Fob, U.S.Flag, With Strap, Enameled	5.95
Watch Fob, War Maneuvers, Spartan, Wisconsin, 1912	18.00
Watch Fob, Weatherbird Shoes, Rooster Crowing Atop Weather Vane	37.50
Watch Fob, Williams Buffett, 23 Quincy Street, Ornate	18.50
Watch Fob, Wisconsin Well Drillers Assoc., 1927	24.75
Watch Fob, World Globe, Via Panama, 1915	24.00
Watch Fob, 14K Gold, 9 Point Diamond, Double-Headed Eagle	175.00
Watch Fob, 14K Playing Cards, Enameled, 6 On Gold Loops	198.00
Watch, see also Gene Autry, Watch; Disneyana, Watch; Hopalong	
Cassidy, Watch; Roy Rogers, Watch	
Watch, Agassiz, 18K Gold Open Face Case, Key Wind, 4 Jewel	77.50
Watch, American Waltham Co., Bartlett Model, Civil War Presentation, Silver	350.00
Watch, American Waltham Co., No.2446614, Copper Case, Key Wind	85.00
Watch, American Waltham, Open Face, Gold Half Moons On Dial, 7 Jewel, Size 6	75.00
Watch, American Watch Co., No.614142, Brass Hunting Case, Key Wind, Size 18	95.00
Watch, Auburndale, 2326, 1/8th Jump Second Timer, Size 18	350.00
Watch, Aurora, Engraved Gold Hunting Case, White Enamel Dial	225.00
Watch, B.W.Raymond, Railroad, Yellow Gold Filled Open Case, 21 Jewel	110.00
Watch, B.W.Raymond, Railroad, 16-21, Yellow Gold Fill	110.00
Watch, B.W.Raymond, 21 Jewel, Size 16	110.00
Watch, Ball Official Railroad Standard, Base Metal Case, 19 Jewel	110.00
Watch, Ball Official Railroad Standard, Yellow Filled Gold Case, 21 Jewel	125.00
Watch, Ball, Railroad, Yellow Gold Filled Case, 17 Jewel	125.00
Watch, Ball, Silveroid Keystone Case, 17 Jewel	125.00
Watch, Ball, Yellow Gold Filled Case, 19 Jewel	165.00
Watch, Ball, Yellow Gold Filled Open Face Case, 21 Jewel	160.00
Watch, Brighton, Lady's, 14K Gold Hunting Case, Bird, Florals, Lever Set	145.00
Watch, Bunn Special, Railroad, Yellow Gold Filled Case	145.00
Watch, Bunn Special, Railroad, 60 Hour, Yellow Gold Filled Case, 21 Jewel	160.00
Watch, Bunn Special, Yellow Gold Railroad Case, Engraved, 24 Jewel	475.00
Watch, Bunn, Special, 16-21, White	125.00
Watch, Burlington Special, Yellow Gold Filled Case, 19 Jewel	125.00
Watch, Burlington, Gold Filled Open Face Case, 21 Jewel	47.50
Watch, Burlington, Montgomery Dial, 21 Jewel	145.00
Watch, Carriage, Nickel Plated Open Face Case, 2 1/4 X 1 In.	65.00
Watch, Cinderella	40.00
Watch, Columbia, Gold Filled Hunting Case, Bird Designs, Pouch	85.00
Watch, Columbia, 18-7, Silveroid Open Face	70.00
Watch, Columbus King, 23 Jewel, Size 16	850.00
Watch, Columbus Railway King, Fancy Hunting Case, 15 Jewel, Size 18	285.00
Watch, Dudley, Masonic, 18K Gold Open Face Case	1295.00
Watch, E.Howard Co., White Gold-Filled Case, Open Face, 21 Jewel	105.00
Watch, E.Howard, Pocket, Large 18K Case	675.00
Watch, E.Howard, 145 Gold Hunting Case, Engraved Scene, 15 Jewel	310.00
Watch, E.T.Brainerd, London, 14K Yellow Gold Filled Hunting Case, Key Wind	300.00
Watch, Elgin National Watch Co., Gold Hunting Case	275.00
Watch, Elgin, B.W.Raymond, Base Case, 21 Jewel	120.00
Watch, Elgin, B.W.Raymond, Yellow Gold Filled Open Face Case, 16 Jewel, R.R.	92.50
Watch, Elgin, B.W.Raymond, 14K Gold Hunting Case, Engraved	250.00
Watch, Elgin, Engraved Hunting Case, Yellow Gold-Filled	70.00
Watch, Elgin, Father Time, Railroad, Size 16	110.00
Watch, Elgin, Father Time, Time Zone Red Hand, Yellow Gold Filled Case	175.00
Watch, Elgin, Father Time, Yellow Gold Filled Case, 21 Jewel	125.00
Watch, Elgin, Father Time, Yellow Gold Filled Case, 21 Jewel, Size 16	115.00
Watch, Elgin, G.M.Wheeler, Hunting Case, Yellow Gold Filled, 17 Jewel	100.00
Watch, Elgin, Glass Back Case, Stem Wind, 21 Jewel, Size 16	240.00
Watch, Elgin, Glass Shipping Case	3.25
Watch, Elgin, Gold Filled Hunting Case, Engraved, 15 Jewel	72.50
Watch, Elgin, Gold Filled Hunting Case, Engraved, 7 Jewel	52.50
Watch, Elgin, Gold Filled Hunting Case, 17 Jewel	67.50
Watch, Elgin, Gold Filled Hunting Case, 7 Jewel	77.50
Watch, Elgin, Gold Filled Open Face Case, 17 Jewel	42.50
Watch, Elgin, Hunting Case, Size 6, 15 Jewel, 1894	130.00

Watch, Elgin, Hunting Case, 15 Jewel	135.00
Watch, Elgin, Hunting Case, 7 Jewel	130.00
Watch, Elgin, No.658, Railroad, Silver Case, 21 Jewel	150.00
Watch, Elgin, No.987777, Metal Open Face Case, 4 Jewel Swing-Out Movement	45.00
Watch, Elgin, Open Face, Hinged Case, Key Wind	65.00
Watch, Elgin, Presentation Model, Open Face, Pocket, Gold Case	270.00
Watch, Elgin, Railroad, B.W.Raymond	120.00
Watch, Elgin, Silver Open Face Case, Inlaid Gold Horse, 7 Jewel, Size 18	100.00
Watch, Elgin, Silver Open Face Case, 7 Jewel, Size 18	65.00
Watch, Elgin, Silverine Open Face Case, Key Wind, 7 Jewel	47.50
Watch, Elgin, Sterling Hunting Case, 0-7	80.00
Watch, Elgin, Veritas, Railroad, Yellow Gold Filled Case, 21 Jewel	155.00
Watch, Elgin, Veritas, Yellow Gold Filled Case, 23 Jewel, Size 18	210.00
Watch, Elgin, Yellow Gold Filled Case, B.W.Raymond, 21 Jewel	135.00
Watch, Elgin, Yellow Gold Filled Hunting Case, 17 Jewel, Size 16	75.00
Watch, Elgin, 10K Gold Hunting Case, 15 Jewel	145.00
Watch, Elgin, 14K Gold Engraved Case, Open Face, 17 Jewel, 2 In.	125.00
Watch, English, Charles Caddgan, Pair Case, Engraved Silver, C.1813	275.00
Watch, English, Silver Open Face Case, Key Wind, Crested, 7 Jewel, C.1860	52.50
Watch, English, William Crayton, Pair Case, Repousse Gold, Hallmarked 1771	1400.00
Watch, Fob, Strap Type, Enameled U.S.Flag	5.95
Watch, Hamilton, Ball, Yellow Gold Filled Case, Railroad, 21 Jewel	155.00
Watch, Hamilton, Hunting Case, 17 Jewel	135.00
Watch, Hamilton, Model 910, Gold Filled Open Face Case, 17 Jewel	42.50
Watch, Hamilton, Model 912, White Gold, Open Face Case, 17 Jewel	47.50 To 52.50
Watch, Hamilton, No.950B, Yellow Gold Filled Case, 23 Jewel	325.00
Watch, Hamilton, No.992, Gold Filled Case, 21 Jewel, Size 16	92.00
Watch, Hamilton, No.992, Yellow Gold Filled Case, Railroad, 21 Jewel	115.00
Watch, Hamilton, No.992, Yellow Gold Filled Open Face Case, 21 Jewel, R.R.	92.50
Watch, Hamilton, No.992B, Montgomery Dial, Yellow Gold Fill, 21 Jewel	140.00
Watch, Hamilton, No.992B, Yellow Gold Filled Case, Railroad, 21 Jewel	170.00
Watch, Hamilton, Railroad, Model 974	55.00
Watch, Hamilton, Railroad, Sterling Silver Case	125.00
Watch, Hamilton, Railroad, 940-18-21, Yellow Case	95.00
Watch, Hamilton, Railroad, 992B, White Case	125.00
Watch, Hamilton, Silver Open Face Case, 21 Jewel, Size 18	100.00
Watch, Hamilton, Sweep Second, 22 Jewel	125.00
Watch, Hamilton, Yellow Gold Filled Open Face, 17 Jewel, Size 18	100.00
Watch, Hamilton, 14K Gold Hunting Case, Engraved Deer's Head, 17 Jewel	250.00
Watch, Hamilton, 992, Gold Filled Open Face Case, Railroad, 21 Jewel	80.00
Watch, Hamilton, 992, White Gold Filled Open Face, Railroad, 21 Jewel, Size 16	110.00
Watch, Hampden, Champion, Duber, Keystone Gold Filled Open Face Case	40.00
Watch, Hampden, Engraved Gold Hands	60.00
Watch, Hampden, Hayward, Coin Silver Hunting Case, 15 Jewel	62.50
Watch, Hampden, Molly Stark, Gold Filled Open Face Case, 7 Jewel	37.50
Watch, Hampden, No.1357070, Engraved Gold & Silver Open Face Case, Size 16	45.00
Watch, Hampden, Railway Special, Sterling Silver Open Face Case, 21 Jewel	115.00
Watch, Hampden, Silver Hunting Case, Key Wind, 15 Jewel, Size 18	100.00
Watch, Hampden, Yellow Gold Filled Hunting Case, Size 18	95.00
Watch, Hampden, Yellow Gold Hunting Case, 17 Jewel	75.00
Watch, Hampden, 7 Jewel, Hunting Case	135.00
Watch, Hampton-Springfield, No.249229, German Silver Case	100.00
Watch, Henry Beguelin, Lady's, Key Wind, 18K Gold Hunting Case, Florals	195.00
Watch, Henry Lavalette, 18K Gold, Hunting Case	495.00
Watch, Howard No.11, Yellow Gold Filled Case, Chronometer, 21 Jewel	265.00
Watch, Howard, No.11, Railroad Chronometer, Yellow Gold Fill, 21 Jewel	225.00
Watch, Howard, No.1359578, White Gold Open Face Case, 17 Jewel	130.00
Watch, Howard, No.207748, Silver Open Face Case, 17 Jewel, Size 18	135.00
Watch, Howard, No.48235, Coin Silver Open Face Case, 17 Jewel	250.00
Watch, Howard, Pat.05, Yellow Gold Filled Railroad Case, 17 Jewel	140.00
Watch, Howard, Series O, Yellow Gold Filled Case, 23 Jewel	450.00
Watch, Howard, Series 11, Chronometer, Yellow Gold Filled Case, 21 Jewel	265.00
Watch, Howard, Yellow Gold Filled Case, 19 Jewel	250.00
Watch, Hudson, Time & Alarm	37.50
Watch, Hunting Case, Coin Silver, Key Wind, Fusee Movement	90.00

Watch, Illinois West Penn Special, Gold Filled Hunting Case, 17 Jewel	77.50
Watch, Illinois, A.Lincoln, Lever Set, 5 Positions, 21 Jewel	185.00
Watch, Illinois, Bunn Special, Base Case, 30 Hour, 21 Jewel	115.00
Watch, Illinois, Bunn Special, Elinvar, 60 Hour, 21 Jewel	295.00
Watch, Illinois, Bunn Special, Gold Filled Open Face Case, 2x Jewel, Size 18	100.00
Watch, Illinois, Bunn Special, Gold Filled Open Face Case, 21 Jewel	92.50
Watch, Illinois, Bunn Special, Silverine Open Face Case, No.1383527	110.00
Watch, Illinois, Bunn Special, Yellow Gold Filled Case, 23 Jewel	250.00
Watch, Illinois, Bunn Special, Yellow Gold Filled Case, 60 Hour	140.00 To 195.00
Watch, Illinois, Bunn Special, Yellow Gold Filled Open Face Case	100.00 To 475.00
Watch, Illinois, Bunn Special, Yellow Gold-Filled Case, 60 Hour, 21 Jewel	125.00
Watch, Illinois, Bunn Special, 21 Jewel, Size 18	150.00
Watch, Illinois, Bunn Special, 30 Hour, 23 Jewel	130.00
Watch, Illinois, Bunn Special, 60 Hour, Yellow Gold Filled Case, 21 Jewel	140.00
Watch, Illinois, Columbia, Coin Silver Hinged Case, Size 18	90.00
Watch, Illinois, Hunting Case, Starburst Rays, 17 Jewel	140.00
Watch, Illinois, Keywind & Key Set, Coin Silver Case	115.00
Watch, Illinois, No.3363917, Open Face, A.Lincoln Railroad, 21 Jewel, Size 16	90.00
Watch, Illinois, Open Face, Hinged Case, White, 18-7	70.00
Watch, Illinois, Railroad, , 30 Hour	115.00
Watch, Illinois, Railroad, Sangamo	135.00
Watch, Illinois, Railroad, Train On Reverse Side, Springfield, 17 Jewels	225.00
Watch, Illinois, Railroad, 19 Jewels	80.00
Watch, Illinois, Railroad, 60 Hour	140.00
Watch, Illinois, Sagamo, Yellow Gold Filled Case, 23 Jewel	325.00
Watch, Illinois, Victor Railroad, Yellow Gold Filled Case, 21 Jewel	125.00
Watch, J.J.Tobias & Co., Sterling Hunt Case, Key Wind, Railroad Timekeeper	125.00
Watch, Key Wind, Open Face, Silverene Case, 7 Jewel, C.1884	70.00
Watch, Little Abner, Animated	125.00
Watch, Longines, Silver Open Face Case, 21 Jewel, Size 18	75.00
Watch, Longines, Wrist, 28 Diamonds, Black Band, 14K Gold	120.00
Watch, Manhattan, Yellow Gold Filled Decorated Case, Size 18	135.00
Watch, Marion Watch Co.Brass Hunting Case, Railroad, Engraved, 15 Jewel	77.50
Watch, Metropole, Gold Filled Open Face Case, Moose Emblem, 17 Jewel	92.50
Watch, New York Standard, Engraved Hunting Case, 6-7	60.00
Watch, New York Watch Co., Springfield, Mass., No.24593, Silveroid Case	250.00
Watch, Omega, Silver Open Face Case, 21 Jewel, Size 20	75.00
Watch, Patek Philippe, Platinum, Original Box	950.00
Watch, Patek Philippe, 18K Gold Hunting Case, 1903 Presentation	750.00
Watch, Pendant, Sterling Silver, Light Blue Enamel, Lady's, Open Face, Small	125.00
Watch, Pocket, Gold Handle, Ring To Hang On Chain, 3 In.	10.00
Watch, Pocket, Hamilton, 21 Jewel, Open Face, Engraved Case, 1 3/4 In.	145.00
Watch, Pocket, Lady's, 14K, Case Engraved With Birds, Floral, Swiss	150.00
Watch, Pocket, Waltham, Size 12, Open Face, White Gold Case, Dated 1921	75.00
Watch, R.Roskell London, Silver, Ben Franklin On Face, Key Wind, C.1798	1200.00
Watch, Railroad King, Allover Decorated Case, Barrel Bridge, 17 Jewel	250.00
Watch, Repeater, Hunting Case, Gold, 1/4 Hour	1500.00
Watch, Rockford, Coin Silver Case, Key Wind, 15 Jewel, C.1876	100.00
Watch, Rockford, Winnebago, Yellow Gold Filled Case, 17 Jewel	225.00
Watch, Rockford, 18-15, Silveroid Open Face	65.00
Watch, Rockford, 18-15, Yellow Gold Hunter, 3 Color Dial	175.00
Watch, Sangamo, Yellow Gold Filled Open Face Case, 21 Jewel	175.00
Watch, Santa Fe Special, Yellow Gold Filled Case, 21 Jewel	165.00
Watch, Santa Fe Special, Yellow Gold Railroad Case, 17 Jewel	325.00
Watch, Sears Roebuck, Silveroid Hunting Case, 17 Jewel, Size 16	100.00
Watch, Seth Thomas, Coin Silver Hunting Case, 7 Jewel	77.50
Watch, Seth Thomas, Lady's, 1896	300.00
Watch, Seth Thomas, Silver Hunting Case, Pat.Dec.6, 1887, Size 16	85.00
Watch, South Bend, Model 229, Gold Filled Open Face Case, 21 Jewel	87.50
Watch, South Bend, Model 429, White Gold Filled Open Face Case, 19 Jewel	57.50
Watch, South Bend, No.305, Yellow Gold Filled Case, Fancy Dial, 15 Jewel	150.00
Watch, South Bend, 12-19, Green Gold Filled Case	65.00
Watch, South Bend, 16-19, Glass Back	85.00
Watch, Standard Watch Co., Gold Filled Hunting Case, 7 Jewel	72.50
Watch, Standard Watch Co., No.5944, Silver Hunting Case, Engraved, 15 Jewel	87.50

Watch, Swiss, Cylinder, Small Pendant, Engraved Case, 1825	85.00
Watch, Swiss, Cylinder, Sterling, Gold Bezels, 10-8	35.00
Watch, Swiss, Cylinder, 0-8, Sterling, Open Face Pendant	40.00
Watch, Swiss, Gold Bezels, St.Anthony On Back, 10-15	40.00
Watch, Swiss, Gold Engraved Case, Key Wind, L.S.Perret Muller, C.1850	250.00
Watch, Swiss, Henry Bequelin, Silver Hunting Case, Key Wind, 15 Jewel	62.50
Watch, Swiss, Lapel, 14K Pink Gold, 17 Jewels, Art Deco	50.00
Watch, Swiss, 14K Gold Hunting Case, 17 Jewel	155.00
Watch, Swiss, 14K Gold Open Face Engraved Case, Lady's, 10 Jewel	62.50
Watch, Swiss, 16-7, White Case, K.W.K.S.	30.00
Watch, Swiss, 18K Gold Case, Key Wind, Open Face, Dated 1870	175.00
Watch, Swiss, 18K Gold Open Face Case, Center Seconds Movement, 11 Jewel	210.00
Watch, Waltham, Ball, Yellow Gold Filled Case, 17 Jewel, Size 16	140.00
Watch, Waltham, Bridge Model, 21 Jewel, Size 12	400.00
Watch, Waltham, Gold Filled Hunting Case, Lady's, 15 Jewel	87.50
Watch, Waltham, Gold Filled Hunting Case, Lady's, 7 Jewel	72.50
Watch, Waltham, Gold Filled Hunting Case, Village Scene, 7 Jewel	82.50
Watch, Waltham, Gold Filled Hunting Case, 17 Jewel	67.50
Watch, Waltham, Hunter Case Engraved, Marked 14 Karat, 1 5/8 In.	235.00
Watch, Waltham, Key Wind, Key Set, 15 Jewel, Dated Front Cover, C.1876	450.00
Watch, Waltham, Key Wind, 1858	120.00 To 135.00
Watch, Waltham, Lady's, Gold Filled Hunting Case, 11 Jewel	85.00
Watch, Waltham, Model 645, Glass Back	95.00
Watch, Waltham, P.S.Bartlett, 18K Gold Hunting Case, Key Wind, Lapel Pin	280.00
Watch, Waltham, Pocket, Gold Face, 18 Jewels, 1 3/4 In.Diameter	195.00
Watch, Waltham, Pocket, 23 Jewel, Indicator Dial	150.00
Watch, Waltham, Railroad, No.645, Yellow Gold Filled Case, 21 Jewel	145.00
Watch, Waltham, Railroad, Yellow Gold Filled Case, 21 Jewel, Size 16	100.00
Watch, Waltham, Riverside Maximus, Double Back, Open Face, 23 Jewel, Size 16	330.00
Watch, Waltham, Riverside Maximus, 14K Wadsworth Case, 21 Jewel, Size 12	250.00
Watch, Waltham, Riverside, Grade 1621, Engraved Train, Open Face, 21 Jewel	105.00
Watch, Waltham, Riverside, 14K Gold Hinged Colonial Case, 19 Jewel	120.00
Watch, Waltham, Riverside, 14K Open Face Case, 17 Jewel	130.00
Watch, Waltham, Riverside, 21 Jewel, Size 16	105.00
Watch, Waltham, Silver Hunting Case, 7 Jewel, Size 18	85.00
Watch, Waltham, Silver Open Face Case, 7 Jewel, Size 18	65.00
Watch, Waltham, Vanguard, Montgomery Dial, Yellow Gold Filled Case, 23 Jewel	165.00
Watch, Waltham, Vanguard, Railroad, Gold Fillled Open Face Case, 23 Jewel	130.00
Watch, Waltham, Vanguard, Yellow Gold Filled Case, Lever Set, 19 Jewel	175.00
Watch, Waltham, Vanguard, Yellow Gold Filled Railroad Case, Premier, 23 Jewel	135.00
Watch, Waltham, White Gold Filled Open Face Case, 15 Jewel	42.50
Watch, Waltham, White Gold Filled Open Face Case, 7 Jewel	42.50
Watch, Waltham, Yellow Gold Filled Case, 23 Jewel	325.00
Watch, Waltham, 14K Gold Hunting Case	325.00
Watch, Waltham, 14K Gold Hunting Case, Engraved Lakeview Cartouches	250.00
Watch, Wittnauer, R.G.P. Case, 12-15	45.00
Watch, Wrist, Cinderella, Gold Colored Bank	15.00
Watch, Wrist, Lady's, 20 Diamonds, Gold Filled Mesh Band, 14K Gold	50.00
Watch, Wrist, Spiro Agnew, Original	250.00

Waterford type glass resembles the famous glass made in the Waterford
Glass Works in Ireland. It is a clear glass that was often cut for
decoration. Modern glass is still being made in Waterford, Ireland.

Waterford, Compote, 11 In.	185.00
Waterford, Flask, Lady's Whiskey, Cylinder Shape, Waffle Cut, Sterling Top	110.00
Waterford, Jar, Diamond Pattern, Sterling Base, Covered, 13 In.	175.00
Waterford, Wine Set, Decanter, 13 In., & 4 Goblets, Signed, Lismore	95.00

WAVE CREST WARE   *Wave Crest glass is a white glassware manufactured by the Pairpoint Manufacturing Company of New Bedford, Massachusetts, and some French factories. It was then decorated by the C.F.Monroe Company of Meriden, Connecticut. The glass was painted in pastel colors and decorated with flowers. The name Wave Crest was used after 1898.*

Wave Crest, Barrel, Biscuit, Egg Crate, Enameled Birds, 7 1/2 In.	365.00
Wave Crest, Barrel, Biscuit, Green, Pink Daisies, Pewter Handle & Cover	170.00

Wave Crest, Basket, Ormolu Rim & Handle, Enameled, Signed, 6 1/2 In.Diameter	215.00
Wave Crest, Blotter, Rolling, Ormolu & Embossed Scrolling	275.00
Wave Crest, Bottle, Cologne, Stopper, Signed, 8 In.	200.00
Wave Crest, Bowl, Dresser, Swirl Red & Blue Floral, Ormolu Handles, 7 In.	155.00
Wave Crest, Bowl, Flowers, Green To White, Signed, 7 1/2 In.	175.00
Wave Crest, Bowl, Flowers, Hand-Painted, Gilt Rim, Marked, 3 1/4 In.	115.00
Wave Crest, Bowl, Swirl Pattern, Blue And White Flowers, 7 In.	315.00
Wave Crest, Bowl, Trinket, Pink, Ormolu Handles, Enameled, Red Banner, 6 In.	165.00
Wave Crest, Box, Blown & Pinched, Green, Brass Rim, Signed, 4 1/2 X 3 In.	375.00
Wave Crest, Box, Blue & Yellow, Cherubs, Raised Scrolls, Round, Hinged, 5 In.	400.00
Wave Crest, Box, Blue Daisies, 4 Embossed Panels, Mirror In Lid, 5 In.	167.50
Wave Crest, Box, Blue Floral, Ormolu Feet, 5 In.	140.00
Wave Crest, Box, Blue To White Flowered Top, Signed, 4 1/2 In.	315.00
Wave Crest, Box, Blue, Ivory, Daisies, Embossed Scrolls, Hinged, 5 1/2 X 3 In.	200.00
Wave Crest, Box, Brass Collar, Blown-Out Design, Flowers, Open, Signed, 3 In.	65.00
Wave Crest, Box, Brass Ormolu Feet, Collar, Blue, Pink, Floral, Red Banner Mark	110.00
Wave Crest, Box, Cherub, Fishnet Over Shoulder, Carries Fish, Signed	450.00
Wave Crest, Box, Cigar, Floral On Pink Tinted Ivory Glass, Hinged, 6 In.	200.00
Wave Crest, Box, Cigarette, Hand-Painted Flowers, Raised Shell Design, Yellow	195.00
Wave Crest, Box, Collar & Cuffs, Puffy, Floral, Hand-Painted, 7 X 7 In.	425.00
Wave Crest, Box, Collar, Embossed Flowers	395.00
Wave Crest, Box, Covered, Lined, Brass Frame	225.00
Wave Crest, Box, Cream Daisies, Covered, 3 In.	160.00
Wave Crest, Box, Cream, Hand-Painted Daisies, Hinged, 3 1/2 In.	130.00
Wave Crest, Box, Double Shell, Aqua, Blossoms, Signed, 3 In.	155.00
Wave Crest, Box, Dresser, Pastel Yellow Posies, Swirls, Hinged, 5 In.	145.00
Wave Crest, Box, Egg Crate Pattern, Blue Flowers	175.00
Wave Crest, Box, Floral, Dots, Scroll, Pink, White, Blue, Black Mark, 4 X 5 In.	260.00
Wave Crest, Box, Floral, Double Shell, Hinged, Red Banner Mark, 2 1/2 In.	125.00
Wave Crest, Box, Floral, Swirled, Hinged Cover, 5 In.Diameter	135.00
Wave Crest, Box, Gold Ormolu Trim, Flowers, Blown-Out Design, 2 1/4 In.	75.00
Wave Crest, Box, Gold Silk Lining, Hand-Painted Daisy On Swirled Top, 5 In.	125.00
Wave Crest, Box, Hand-Painted Asters On Satin Ground, Brass Rim, 8 1/2 In.	425.00
Wave Crest, Box, Helms Swirl, Gold Flowers, Ruby Jewel Center, Hinged	245.00
Wave Crest, Box, Hinged, Blue Flowers, Green Foliage, 4 1/2 In.	175.00
Wave Crest, Box, Hinged, Dainty Flowers, Covered, Signed, 3 1/2 In.	206.00
Wave Crest, Box, Hinged, Embossed Shell, Blue Floral, Pink Banner Mark, 3 In.	245.00
Wave Crest, Box, Hinged, Raised Swirls, Satin Lining, 7 In.Square	325.00
Wave Crest, Box, Hinged, Red Banner, 3 In.	135.00
Wave Crest, Box, Hinged, Satin Lining, Enamel Floral Decoration, Signed, 4 In.	225.00
Wave Crest, Box, Jewel, Brass Trim, Blue Lining, Signed, 3 In.	95.00
Wave Crest, Box, Jewel, Floral, Swirl, Hand-Painted, Silk Lining, 3 In.	65.00
Wave Crest, Box, Jewel, Hinged Lid, Hand-Painted Daisies, Cream, 3 In.	130.00
Wave Crest, Box, Jewel, Hinged, Enameled, Blue & White Asters, 7 In.Wide	425.00
Wave Crest, Box, Jewel, Hinged, Helm Swirl, Original Label, 5 1/2 X 4 In.	255.00
Wave Crest, Box, Jewel, Hinged, Pink, Raised Beading, 5 1/2 In.	165.00
Wave Crest, Box, Jewel, Hinged, Puffy Flowers, Square, 6 In.	400.00
Wave Crest, Box, Jewel, Pale Pink, Floral, Hinged, 3 X 3 In.	125.00
Wave Crest, Box, Jewel, White, Blue, Pink Flowers On Cream Swirl, 7 X 4 In.	300.00
Wave Crest, Box, Lid, Puffed Out Pansy, No Lining, 5 In.	265.00
Wave Crest, Box, Light Blue To White, Flowered, 4 1/2 In.	315.00
Wave Crest, Box, Mill Scene, Covered, 5 In.	295.00
Wave Crest, Box, Open, Swirl, Florals, Blue Lining, Ormolu Handles, Signed	85.00
Wave Crest, Box, Ormolu Mounted In Frame, 4 Ornate Legs, Cream, Flowers	385.00
Wave Crest, Box, Pale Blue, Pink Floral, Brass Ormolu Rim & Feet, 2 X 6 In.	145.00
Wave Crest, Box, Pale Blue, Swirl, Pink Floral, Ormolu Neck & Handles, Signed	140.00
Wave Crest, Box, Pin, Floral, Handled, Open, Red Banner Mark, 6 In.Diameter	165.00
Wave Crest, Box, Pin, Floral, Round Swirled Body	45.00
Wave Crest, Box, Pink Satin Lining, Raised Scrolls, Cherubs, Hinged, 5 In.	400.00
Wave Crest, Box, Pink Shell, Floral, Lid, Banner Signature, 3 X 4 In.	215.00
Wave Crest, Box, Pink, Ormolu Legs, Cupid Cover, 4 X 3 1/2 In.	129.00
Wave Crest, Box, Powder, Milk Glass Floral In Relief, Blue & White Floral	275.00
Wave Crest, Box, Powder, Milk Glass Floral, Hand-Painted Floral, Brass Rim	275.00
Wave Crest, Box, Powder, Open, Scroll Design, 5 In.	35.00
Wave Crest, Box, Powder, Swirled, Flowers, Hinged, 3 In.	110.00

Wave Crest, Box, Powder, 5 1/2 In.Diameter	235.00
Wave Crest, Box, Puffy & Scrolling, Pearl White, Floral, 5 1/2 X 26 In.	550.00
Wave Crest, Box, Raised Shell, Floral, Round, Covered, Signed, 16 In.	142.00
Wave Crest, Box, Ring, Open, Blue, White Floral, Oval, Signed, 4 X 3 In.	45.00
Wave Crest, Box, Shell Puffs & Bluebells, Red Banner Mark, 3 1/2 In.	175.00
Wave Crest, Box, Shiny Finish, Blown-Out Pansy, Diamond Base, 3 X 4 1/2 In.	200.00
Wave Crest, Box, Spray Flowers, Silk Lining, Lid, Round, Blue, Signed	210.00
Wave Crest, Box, Swirl Pattern, Blue And White Flowers, 3 In.	115.00
Wave Crest, Box, Swirl Pattern, Blue And White Flowers, 5 In.	205.00
Wave Crest, Box, Swirled White, Gold Flowers, Jewel Center, Hinged, Signed	245.00
Wave Crest, Box, Swirled, Floral Sprays, Covered, 3 In.	135.00
Wave Crest, Box, Tobacco, 6 In.Square X 4 1/4 In.Tall	325.00
Wave Crest, Box, Trinket, Diagonal Swirls, Magenta, Aqua Raised Decoration	50.00
Wave Crest, Box, Trinket, Egg Crate, Ormolu Rims, Silk Lining, Flowers On Top	150.00
Wave Crest, Box, Trinket, Hinged	110.00
Wave Crest, Box, Trinket, Pink Flowers, Blue Background, Open, Signed	95.00
Wave Crest, Burner, Incense, Enameled Daisies, Pink Scrolls, Ormolu Base	150.00
Wave Crest, Casket, Floral Decoration, Hinged, Lid, Signed, 9 In.	198.00
Wave Crest, Cookie Jar, Pink, Embossed Flowers	150.00
Wave Crest, Cracker Jar, Floral, Metal Lid & Handle, 6 In.	295.00
Wave Crest, Cracker Jar, Puffy, Apple Blossom	150.00
Wave Crest, Cracker Jar, Sky Blue, Rococo Embossing, Floral, Silver Plated	135.00
Wave Crest, Cup, Punch, Diamond-Quilted, Fuchsia, Amberina	80.00
Wave Crest, Dish, Dresser, Floral, Brass Rim, Pink, 3 1/4 In.	60.00
Wave Crest, Dish, Dresser, Floral, Brass Rim, Pink, 5 1/2 In.	110.00
Wave Crest, Dish, Dresser, Lavender & Blue Floral, Banner Mark, 7 In.	200.00
Wave Crest, Dish, Open, Swirl Pattern, Pink And White Flowers, 3 In.	60.00
Wave Crest, Dish, Open, Swirl Pattern, Pink And White Flowers, 7 In.	145.00
Wave Crest, Dish, Pin, Open, Ormolu Rim, Signed, 4 In.Diameter	98.00
Wave Crest, Dish, Pin, Ormolu Mounted, Blue Flowers, Handles, Red Banner	65.00
Wave Crest, Dish, Pin, Swirled White, Pastel Flowers, Metal Rim & Handles	65.00
Wave Crest, Dish, Pink Floral, Ornate Ormolu Handle & Trim, Signed, 4 3/4 In.	95.00
Wave Crest, Dish, Swirls, Florals, Dore On Ormolu Rim, Signed, Footed	125.00
Wave Crest, Dish, Vanity Mirror, Signed	325.00
Wave Crest, Ferner, Brass Collar, 8 X 4 In.	185.00
Wave Crest, Flask, Red Flowers On Blue Gray Embossed Ground	95.00
Wave Crest, Hatpin Holder, Floral, White, Pink, Red, Signed	95.00
Wave Crest, Holder, Calling Card, Blue, Puffy Cream Panel, 4 Sides, Floral	200.00
Wave Crest, Humidor, Blue, Garlands Of Pink Roses, Banner Mark, Hinged Top	335.00
Wave Crest, Humidor, Cigars On Front In Raised Iridescent Purple, Key	300.00
Wave Crest, Humidor, Cream To Pink, Blue Flowers, Sterling Cover, 4 X 6 In.	275.00
Wave Crest, Jar, Brass Rim, Hand-Painted, Marked, 1 3/8 X 3 In.	125.00
Wave Crest, Jar, Cigar, Raised Scrolls, Key Lock, Signed, 6 In.	345.00
Wave Crest, Jar, Cracker, Blue & Pink, Enameled Flowers, Resilvered Lid	135.00
Wave Crest, Jar, Cracker, Embossed Medallion, Floral Center	165.00
Wave Crest, Jar, Cracker, Embossed With Flowers	135.00
Wave Crest, Jar, Cracker, Enameled Flowers, Lid	190.00
Wave Crest, Jar, Cracker, Pink & Yellow Roses On Front	275.00
Wave Crest, Jar, Dresser, White, Pink Painted Floral, Covered, 4 1/4 X 3 In.	195.00
Wave Crest, Jar, Flowers, Ormolu Handles, Brass, Signed, Small	65.00
Wave Crest, Jar, Open, Brass Ormolu Handles, Hand-Painted Flowers, Small	75.00
Wave Crest, Jar, Ring, Water Scenic On Cream Baroque, Hinged, 4 In.	265.00
Wave Crest, Jardiniere, Blue Floral, Cherub Head, Gold Traced Rim, 8 X 10 In.	325.00
Wave Crest, Lamp, Gone With The Wind, 22 In.	495.00
Wave Crest, Letter Holder, Blue Flowers, Signed	250.00
Wave Crest, Letter Holder, Brass Collar, Used For A Planter	95.00
Wave Crest, Muffineer, Flowers, Metal Top With Ornamental Decoration, 3 In.	85.00
Wave Crest, Pink, Orange, & Yellow Petal Flowers, Shell Swirls, 4 5/8 In.	120.00
Wave Crest, Pitcher, Syrup, Erie Twist	195.00
Wave Crest, Planter, Marshmallow Body, Pink Sprays, Beading, Brass Rim, 8 In.	155.00
Wave Crest, Salt & Pepper, Hand-Painted Floral, Pewter Tops	85.00
Wave Crest, Salt & Pepper, Raised Pink Swirls, Blue Flowers, Pair	110.00
Wave Crest, Salt & Pepper, Raised Swirls, Flowers, Pink, Blue, Pair	110.00
Wave Crest, Salt & Pepper, Scroll Work, Flower Decoration	100.00
Wave Crest, Salt & Pepper, Swirl, Hand-Painted Floral, Pewter Lids	95.00

Wave Crest, Salt & Pepper, Twist, Flowers, Footed, Pink, White, Silver Plate	115.00
Wave Crest, Salt & Pepper, Violets	150.00
Wave Crest, Salt, Daisies, Pansies On Yellow Ground, Pair	75.00
Wave Crest, Salt, Erie Twist, Pink Satin, Enamel Floral, Double Collared Top	42.50
Wave Crest, Sugar & Creamer, Blue Apple Blossoms, Twisted Handle & Finial	145.00
Wave Crest, Sugar & Creamer, Swirls, Blue, Pink	325.00
Wave Crest, Sugar Shaker, Flowers & Leaves	250.00
Wave Crest, Sugar Shaker, Hand-Painted Flowers, Paneled, Satin	95.00
Wave Crest, Vase, Blue, Pink Roses, Ormolu Gold Metal Collar, 7 1/2 In.	250.00
Wave Crest, Vase, Bud, Footed, Daisies On Ivory To Yellow, Signed	185.00
Wave Crest, Vase, Clear & Frosted, Blue Strawflowers, Ormulu Rim, Feet, 14 In.	475.00
Wave Crest, Vase, Dark Green Free-Form Design, Floral, Beaded Trim, 8 1/4 In.	225.00
Wave Crest, Vase, Floral, Raised Swirls, Metal Handles & Pedestal, 14 In.	210.00
Wave Crest, Vase, Forget-Me-Not Decoration, Blue, 5 In.High	130.00
Wave Crest, Vase, Ormolu Feet, 9 In.	200.00
Wave Crest, Vase, Ormulu Base, Trifooted, White Beaded, Green Swirls, Floral	345.00
Wave Crest, Vase, Pink Floral, Cobalt Accents, Ormolu Mount, 9 In.	175.00
Wave Crest, Vase, Pink Floral, Ormolu Mounts & Base, Signed, 11 In.	400.00
Wave Crest, Vase, Pink Floral, Ormulu Mounts, Footed, 11 In.	400.00
Wave Crest, Vase, Red On Green Color With Flowers, Signed, 12 In.	575.00
Wave Crest, Vase, Transparent, Enameling, Ormolu, 15 In.	395.00
Wave Crest, Wig Holder, White, Hand-Painted Flowers, Brass Ormolu Frame	475.00
Weapon, Ax, War, Indian, Comanche, Wm.T.Wood & Co., Iron	58.00
Weapon, Bayonet, Plug-Type, Revolution	60.00
Weapon, Bayonet, Wood Handle, 14 In.	7.00
Weapon, Box, Ammammo, Wood, Winchester New Rival Black Powder Shells, C.1873	20.00
Weapon, Broadsword, Austrian, C.1820	85.00
Weapon, Cannon Ball, Confederate, For Ship Cannon	10.50
Weapon, Dagger, Dress, Nazi Labor Corps, Stag Grip With Sheath	230.00
Weapon, Gun, BB, Iron & Wood, Embossed Buffalo, Wolves, 1883, 27 1/2 In.	230.00
Weapon, Gun, Navy Carbine, Sharpes & Hankins, C.1869	275.00
Weapon, Gun, Percussion, C.Sharpes, Civil War, 1858	450.00
Weapon, Gun, 12 Gauge, Zulu Country For Elephant Hunting, 51 In.	125.00
Weapon, Handgun, D.W.M.Luger, World War I	450.00
Weapon, Handgun, Remington, Single Shot Pistol, Engraved, Gold Plated Grips	235.00
Weapon, Handgun, Smith & Wesson, Model 2, Tip-Up Revolver, Civil War Era	125.00
Weapon, Horn, Powder, Bullet Lead Throat, July 3, 1839	295.00
Weapon, Indian, Kukri, Napal, 1820, Ivory Inlay	55.00
Weapon, Knife, see also Store, Knife	
Weapon, Knife, Brass Cap, Hand Guard, Horn, Pewter Rings, Revolution, 14 In.	45.00
Weapon, Knife, Fighting, Indian, Handmade, Horn Grips, 10 In.	38.00
Weapon, Knife, Hunting, Boxwood Handle, Engstrom	15.00
Weapon, Knife, Hunting, Leather Sheath, Marked Cattaraugus, 6 In.Blade	22.50
Weapon, Knife, Pocket, Pearl Handle, IXL Sheffield, England, 4 Blades	20.00
Weapon, Knife, Pocket, Pearl Handle, 5 1/2 In.	15.00
Weapon, Knife, Pocket, Remington, No.R1863	70.00
Weapon, Knife, Pocket, Remington, R7364, 3 Blade With Scissors	32.00
Weapon, Knife, Pocket, Robeson, No.642214	30.00
Weapon, Knife, Pocket, Solingen, Germany, Emblem	65.00
Weapon, Knife, Pocket, U.S.Navy, Antler Horn Handle, Sheffield, C.1880, 1 Blade	75.00
Weapon, Knife, Pocket, Woman's Name On Handle, C.December 6, 1901, 2 3/4 In.	200.00
Weapon, Knife, Pocket, 2 Blade, Corkscrew, Yellow Gold Filled	48.00
Weapon, Knife, Remington Arms, No.R1123, Bone Handle, Bullet-Shaped Shield	300.00
Weapon, Knife, Remington, Unused, Initialed F.A.M., 2 5/8 In.	27.00
Weapon, Knife, Trench, Brass Handle, Steel Blade, United States, 1918	19.95
Weapon, Knife, World War II, Remember Pearl Harbor	3.00
Weapon, Knife, 2 Blade, Long Beach, California, Girl On Beach	27.50
Weapon, Knuckles, Fighting, Metal	6.50
Weapon, Pistol, Boot, C.1850, 5 1/2 In.	85.00
Weapon, Pistol, Caplock, Single Shop, Belgian, Union Troops, Civil War, 6 In.	45.00
Weapon, Pistol, Percussion, Allen & Wheelock, Barrel 8 In.	120.00
Weapon, Pistol, Russian Flintlock, Cossack, 1800, Brass Butt	375.00
Weapon, Pistol, Single Shot, Caplock, Belgian, 6 In.	45.00
Weapon, Revolver & Badge, Miniature, Buntline Colt, Claremore, Oklahoma	8.00
Weapon, Revolver, 1879 Blue Jacket, Nickeled, Engraved	37.00

Weapon, Rifle, Air, Pump Action, Daisy, Scrolled Decoration, 34 In. 10.00
Weapon, Rifle, Boy's, 1886 Quackenbush 40.00
Weapon, Rifle, Carbine, Burnside, 4th Model, Civil War 225.00
Weapon, Rifle, Colt, Model 22 Caliber, 1890 .... 295.00
Weapon, Rifle, Kentucky, 27 Silver Inlays, Patch Box 1100.00
Weapon, Rifle, Smith, Carbine, Civil War 400.00
Weapon, Rifle, Springfield, .45-70, Bayonet & Scabbard, 1886 .... 180.00
Weapon, Rifle, Winchester, Single Shot, 1902 Model, 22 Caliber 65.00
Weapon, Saber, Cavalry, With Scabbard, 1861 .... 90.00
Weapon, Shotgun, Holland And Holland, Original Case 6900.00
Weapon, Shotgun, With Scope, Holland & Holland 1300.00
Weapon, Sword & Scabbard, Etched Blade, Imperial German Army 75.00
Weapon, Sword & Scabbard, Prussian, C.1800 .... 55.00
Weapon, Sword Cane, American, 28 In. 125.00
Weapon, Sword, Civil War Officer, 1860 .... 75.00
Weapon, Sword, Civil War, Emerson & Silver, Trenton, N.J., 1862 .... 125.00
Weapon, Sword, Eagle Head, Ivory Handle, Gold & Blue, Engraved Inlaid Motifs 135.00
Weapon, Sword, Engraved U.S., Emerson & Silver, Trenton, N.J. On Blade 200.00
Weapon, Sword, KKK, Scabbard, 36 In. 125.00
Weapon, Sword, Knights Of Malta, Fancy, Chamois Cover 235.00
Weapon, Sword, Lion's Head With Garnet Eyes, Swastika, German 160.00
Weapon, Sword, Lizard Sheath, 2 Attached Knives, NW Africa, C.1910 .... 125.00
Weapon, Sword, Ornate Brass Hilt, Ribbed Wooden Handle, Scabbard, 37 In. 42.00
Weapon, Sword, Samurai, Old Blade, 2 Holes In Tang 175.00
Weapon, Sword, Shashga Cossack, Silver & Gold, Red & Black Leather Scabbard 275.00
Weapon, Sword, Toledo, Spanish, 1880 .... 75.00
Weapon, Sword, U.S.Eagle, Hilted, Bone Grips, Scabbard, 1812 .... 135.00
Weather Vane, Angel Gabriel, Rod Standard, Sheet Metal, Yellow ....*Illus* 550.00
Weather Vane, Bull, Burnished Copper, Gold Paint, C.1800, 15 X 21 In. 850.00
Weather Vane, Codfish, Carved Wood, American, 19th Century ....*Illus* 1300.00
Weather Vane, Copper Cow, 27 In. 375.00
Weather Vane, Cow, Copper, Full Figure, Cast Head, Green Patina, 18 X 29 In. 500.00
Weather Vane, Cow, Molded Copper, Holes In Body, 15 In.High ....*Illus* 550.00
Weather Vane, Dove, Wings Raised, Perched Upon An Orb, Copper, Brass, Tin 900.00
Weather Vane, Goose, Copper, 43 In.Long Arrow 1550.00
Weather Vane, Horse, Cast Iron, Tin Tail, Mid-19th Century, 39 X 26 In. 4000.00

Weather Vane, Codfish, Carved Wood, American, 19th Century

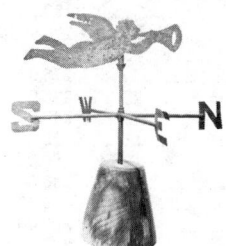

Weather Vane, Angel Gabriel, Rod Standard, Sheet Metal, Yellow

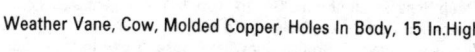

Weather Vane, Cow, Molded Copper, Holes In Body, 15 In.High

Weather Vane, Horse, Copper, Zinc Head, Gilding, Directionals

Weather Vane, Whale, Carved Wood, Eyes In Relief, 9 In.High

Weather Vane, Horse, Copper, Zinc Head, Gilding, Directionals .... *Illus*	1100.00
Weather Vane, Horse, Running, With Standard	500.00
Weather Vane, Locomotive, Sheet Iron, C.1870, 15 X 20 In.	800.00
Weather Vane, Rooster, Copper, Iron Talons, 21 X 21 In.	495.00
Weather Vane, Rooster, Copper, Original Gilding, On Standard, 24 1/2 In.	550.00
Weather Vane, Rooster, Hollow, Copper Rod, Blue Ball	115.00
Weather Vane, Spread Wings, Repousse, Copper, C.1850, 30 X 26 In.	1000.00
Weather Vane, Whale, Carved Wood, Eyes In Relief, 9 In.High .... *Illus*	575.00

Webb glass was made by Thomas Webb & Sons of Stourbridge, England.
Many types of art and cameo glass were made by them during the Victorian
era. The factory is still producing glass.

Webb Burmese, Bowl, Pinched Neck, Flared Top, Signed, 3 1/4 X 2 1/2 In.	275.00
Webb Burmese, Bride's Basket, Ruffled Bowl, Silver Holder, Straw Mark, 9 In.	60.00
Webb Burmese, Bride's Basket, Ruffled Edge, Silver-Plated Holder, 9 In.	140.00
Webb Burmese, Dish, Nut, Mt.Washington, Footed, 4 X 2 1/2 In.	350.00
Webb Burmese, Ewer, Applied Yellow Handles, 10 1/2 In.	950.00
Webb Burmese, Fairy Lamp, Marked Clarke, 5 3/4 In.	235.00
Webb Burmese, Jar, Sweetmeat, Butterfly & Blossoms, Brass Rim & Cover, 5 In.	695.00
Webb Burmese, Jar, Sweetmeat, Butterfly & Blossoms, Signed, 5 In.	750.00
Webb Burmese, Lamp, Fairy, Bowl Base, Marked Clarke, 6 1/2 X 4 1/4 In.	595.00
Webb Burmese, Lamp, Fairy, Clarke Clear Base, Dome Shade, 3 3/4 X 3 In.	135.00
Webb Burmese, Lamp, Fairy, Decorated, Queensware Burmese, 6 1/2 In.	1150.00
Webb Burmese, Lamp, Fairy, Miniature	225.00
Webb Burmese, Lamp, Fairy, Mt.Washington, Glossy, Clarke Signed Base	350.00
Webb Burmese, Lamp, Fairy, Ormolu Holder, Marked Clarke, 7 3/4 In.	275.00
Webb Burmese, Rose Bowl, Green Ivy Leaves, Acid Finish, Crimp Top, 2 1/2 In.	295.00
Webb Burmese, Rose Bowl, Queensware, Ruffled Top, Signed, 6 1/4 X 2 1/2 In.	310.00
Webb Burmese, Rose Bowl, 8 Crimped Top, Satin, Salmon To Yellow, 2 1/4 In.	225.00
Webb Burmese, Toothpick, Diamond Quilted, 2 5/8 In.	250.00
Webb Burmese, Vase, Bulbous, Glossy, Floral, Pink To Yellow Shading, 2 1/2 In.	245.00
Webb Burmese, Vase, Bulbous, 6 Sided Collar, Floral, Lemon To Rose, 2 1/2 In.	215.00
Webb Burmese, Vase, Enamel Decoration, Bulbous, 6 Sided Top, 3 X 3 1/4 In.	300.00
Webb Burmese, Vase, Flared, Ruffled, Acid Finish, Salmon Pink, Yellow, 3 In.	235.00
Webb Burmese, Vase, Flower Petal Top, Salmon, Pink, Yellow, Impressed Mark	245.00
Webb Burmese, Vase, Jack-In-The-Pulpit	950.00
Webb Burmese, Vase, Lemon To Rose, Floral, 6-Sided Collar, Bulbous, 2 1/2 In.	198.00
Webb Burmese, Vase, Pink To Yellow, Flower Petal Top, Acid Finish, 4 In.	245.00
Webb Burmese, Vase, Semiacid Finish, 2 5/8 In.	250.00
Webb Burmese, Vase, Stick, Ivy Leaves, 7 1/2 In.	385.00
Webb Burmese, Vase, 7 Petal Top, Bulbous, Acid Finish, 3 1/4 In.	315.00
Webb Peachblow, Celery, Deep Rose To Light Pink, Square Top, 5 1/2 In.	200.00
Webb Peachblow, Creamer, Applied Decoration & Handle, 4 In. .... 325.00 To	550.00
Webb Peachblow, Lamp, Fairy, Glass Jewels, Bronze Snowflake Base, 5 5/8 In.	750.00
Webb Peachblow, Pitcher, Applied Leaf With Vine Handle, 6 In.	175.00
Webb Peachblow, Pitcher, Cherry Red To Pink, Gold Decoration, Handle, 9 In.	400.00
Webb Peachblow, Pitcher, Enameled Flowers, Berries & Bumblebee, 9 In.	475.00
Webb Peachblow, Vase, Birds & Flowers, Basket Weave Cutting, 6 1/2 In.	450.00
Webb Peachblow, Vase, Butterfly & Blossoms On Rose To Pink, 5 1/2 In.	325.00

Item	Price
Webb Peachblow, Vase, Cased, Shaded To Deep Raspberry, 4 3/4 In.	125.00
Webb Peachblow, Vase, Cherry Red To Deep Pink, Glassy, 3 1/2 In.	185.00
Webb Peachblow, Vase, Coralene Decoration, 5 In.	230.00
Webb Peachblow, Vase, Coralene, Green, Turquoise, Blue, Yellow, 8 3/4 In.	350.00
Webb Peachblow, Vase, Enamel Decoration, Butterflies, Flowers, 9 In.	750.00
Webb Peachblow, Vase, Floral, Leaves, Gold Trim, Wishbone Feet, 6 X 4 In.	275.00
Webb Peachblow, Vase, Footed, 6 3/8 X 4 1/4 In.	275.00
Webb Peachblow, Vase, Pink To Deep Cherry Red, Cream Lining, 7 In.	310.00
Webb Peachblow, Vase, Propeller Marked, 8 1/4 X 3 3/4 In.	295.00
Webb Peachblow, Vase, Satin Glass, Cased, Butterfly, Rose, White, Signed	415.00
Webb Peachblow, Vase, Shaded To Deep Raspberry, 4 3/4 In.	117.00
Webb Peachblow, Vase, Shades To Raspberry At Top, 5 1/4 In.	90.00
Webb, Bottle, Perfume, Creamy White Satin, Coin Gold Flowers, 4 1/2 In.	195.00
Webb, Bottle, Perfume, Cut White To Red On Chartreuse Body, Cameo, 6 In.	1350.00
Webb, Bottle, Perfume, Ivory, Cameo, Signed, 4 1/2 In.	925.00
Webb, Bowl, Amber, Coin Gold Butterfly, Leaves, Stems, Fluted, 5 1/2 In.	150.00
Webb, Bowl, Amber, 9 In.	70.00
Webb, Bowl, Blown Crystal, Swirl Effect, Signed, 4 1/4 In.	12.00
Webb, Bowl, Blue Lining, Coin Gold Decoration, 2 1/8 In. X 3 3/4 In.Diam.	300.00
Webb, Bowl, Bronze, Dark Green Iridescence, 5 1/2 X 6 In.	85.00
Webb, Bowl, Burmese, Butterfly & Flowers, Gold, Log, 4 In.	550.00
Webb, Bowl, Cut Crystal, Shallow, 8 In., Signed, England	40.00
Webb, Bowl, Intaglio, Footed, 4 X 5 3/4 In.	795.00
Webb, Bowl, Satin, Pink Shading, Crimped, Signed, 10 In.	225.00 To 240.00
Webb, Candle Holder, Round Paperweight, Controlled Bubbles, Signed	37.50
Webb, Center Bowl, Blown, Ribbed, Flares, Amber, Signed, 8 X 4 X 5 In.	65.00
Webb, Compote, Ruffled, Cased, Mounted In Silver, Blue With White Casing	150.00
Webb, Dish, Bride's, Glossy Cased Glass, Raspberry To Pink, Yellow Enameling	375.00
Webb, Dish, Bride's, Silver Holder, Shades Of Rose	325.00
Webb, Dish, Nut, Corbett	25.00
Webb, Goblet, Stemware, Signed, Set Of 7	60.00
Webb, Matchstrike, Paperweight Design, Webb, England, Signed	45.00
Webb, Muffineer, Diamond Quilt Satin Glass, Coralene Floral, 5 1/2 In.	295.00
Webb, Pitcher, Satin Glass, Light To Dark Pink, Ruffled Top, 5 1/2 In.	150.00
Webb, Rose Bowl, Cameo, White, Raspberry, Rose Cutting, Metal Spot, 2 1/4 In.	575.00
Webb, Rose Bowl, Queensware, Leaves Around 6 Scalloped Top, Signed, Small	448.00
Webb, Salt & Pepper, Melon Ribbed, Silver Plated Holder	97.50
Webb, Salt Dip, Rose Color, Threaded Design, Berry Pontil	48.00
Webb, Salt, Green Glass, Ornate Jeweled Holder	250.00
Webb, Salt, Master, Rose Colored, Threaded Design, Berry Pontil	48.00
Webb, Sugar & Creamer, Cream Color, Pink Enameled Butterflies, Gold Edge	130.00
Webb, Urn, White & Gold, Turquoise Enamel, Butterfly Signature, Covered	450.00
Webb, Vase, Amber Glass, Water Lilies Etched, 9 3/4 In.	225.00
Webb, Vase, Azure Blue Satin, Teardrop Pattern, Mother-Of-Pearl, 10 In.	135.00
Webb, Vase, Blown Iris Flowers, Frosted, Lavender, 9 In.	125.00
Webb, Vase, Blue Overlay Satin Glass, Signed, 4 3, /8 In.	265.00
Webb, Vase, Bronze Glass, Silver Overlay Daffodil, 4 3/4 In.	55.00
Webb, Vase, Bud, Pale Pink Thistles, Silver Stand, Cameo, 7 1/4 In.	345.00
Webb, Vase, Butterflies, Flowers, Peachblow, Gold Decoration, 10 In.	375.00
Webb, Vase, Cameo On Mother-Of-Pearl Satin Glass, Floral Cutting, 10 In.	2650.00
Webb, Vase, Cameo Signed, Citron, Carved Floral Front & Back, 5 1/4 In.	675.00
Webb, Vase, Cameo, Floral, Butterfly, Miniature, 1 3/4 In.	800.00
Webb, Vase, Cameo, Green On Clear, Signed, 9 In.	575.00
Webb, Vase, Carved Leaves On Twisting Stems, Butterfly, Cameo, 7 In.	1800.00
Webb, Vase, Cased Raspberry, Amber Crimped Edge, Flowers, 10 1/2 In.	275.00
Webb, Vase, Cased White & Pink, Amber, Cranberry Overlay, Acorns, 12 In.	325.00
Webb, Vase, Coin Gold Decorated, Pedestal Foot, Signed, 3 7/8 In.	425.00
Webb, Vase, Cranberry & White, Floral Decoration, Cameo, 5 In.	1200.00
Webb, Vase, Deep Pink To White, Mother-Of-Pearl, Draped Pattern, 5 1/2 In.	175.00
Webb, Vase, Diamond-Quilted Mother-Of-Pearl, Satin, Blue To White, 7 In.	210.00
Webb, Vase, Gold Decoration, Ruffled Top, Pink To White, 7 X 5 In.	130.00
Webb, Vase, Gourd-Type Satin, Chartreuse, Ribbon, Floral, Signed WEBB MOP	875.00
Webb, Vase, Green & Pink Cased Glass, Veining, Enamel Decoration, 6 In.	325.00
Webb, Vase, Hand-Painted Poppies On Cream, Signed, 7 In.	125.00
Webb, Vase, Lemon-Lime, Floral, Carving, Cameo, 5 1/4 In.	775.00

Webb, Vase, Mother-Of-Pearl, Shaded To Pink, Ruffled Top, 6 In. 160.00
Webb, Vase, Pink To Rose Satin, Diamond-Quilted Mother-Of-Pearl, 4 1/2 In. 175.00
Webb, Vase, Pink, Lace Enamel, White Lining, 10 X 6 In. 319.00
Webb, Vase, Red, White Floral & Seedlings, Flowing Leafage, 4 1/2 In. 1500.00
Webb, Vase, Rose Cased Over Blue, Propeller Signed 375.00
Webb, Vase, Rouge Flambe, Enameled Butterflies & Dragons, 6 In. 550.00
Webb, Vase, Satin Glass, Olive Green, White Lining, Enameled Floral, Miniature 195.00
Webb, Vase, Stick, Cameo, Ivory, Bulbous Base, Signed, 8 1/4 In. 1500.00
Webb, Vase, White On Citron With Butterfly, 4 1/2 In. 1200.00
Webb, Vase, White, Gold Enameled Decoration & Butterfly, 7 3/4 In. 165.00
Webb, Vase, Yellow, White Floral, Cameo, 5 In. 850.00
Webb, Water Set, Rainbow Diamond-Quilted, Mother-Of-Pearl, 3 Piece 2500.00
Webb, Wine, Conical Shape, Gold Edge, Signed, 3 In., Set Of 12 .... 120.00

WEDGWOOD

Wedgwood pottery has been made at the famous Wedgwood Factory in England since 1759. A large variety of wares has been made, including the well-known jasperware, basalt, creamware, and even a limited amount of porcelain.

Wedgwood, Ashtray, Club Shaped, Green 14.00
Wedgwood, Ashtray, Jasper, Terra-Cotta, 1957, 4 1/4 In. 38.00
Wedgwood, Ashtray, Terra-Cotta & Black, Round, 7 In. 58.00
Wedgwood, Barometer, Lilac Jasperware, Ram's Head & Floral Plate, 9 1/4 In. 325.00
Wedgwood, Barrel, Biscuit Jasper, Blue, C.1820 .... 150.00
Wedgwood, Barrel, Biscuit, Acorn Finial On Lid, England, C.1897, 7 In. 175.00
Wedgwood, Barrel, Biscuit, Black, White 125.00
Wedgwood, Barrel, Biscuit, Blue & White, 6 In. 95.00
Wedgwood, Barrel, Biscuit, Blue Jasper, Handle, Bail, England, 6 In. 90.00
Wedgwood, Barrel, Biscuit, Caneware, C.1810, 8 In.Diameter 90.00
Wedgwood, Barrel, Biscuit, Classical Figures, Marked, 10 In. 195.00
Wedgwood, Barrel, Biscuit, Classical White Figures, Bulbous, Handle, Lid 75.00
Wedgwood, Barrel, Biscuit, Green, Lilac, White, Wedgwood Only 1250.00
Wedgwood, Barrel, Biscuit, Hunting Scene, Blue & White, 6 1/2 X 5 1/4 In. 135.00
Wedgwood, Barrel, Biscuit, Hunting Scene, Silver Plate Lid, Marked England 150.00
Wedgwood, Barrel, Biscuit, Jasperware, Acorn, Leaves, 7 X 5 1/2 In. 295.00
Wedgwood, Barrel, Biscuit, Jasperware, Classic Figures, England 92.00
Wedgwood, Barrel, Biscuit, Jasperware, Lilac, Plated Top, Ball Feet, 6 In. 210.00
Wedgwood, Barrel, Biscuit, Lid & Bail Handle, Silver Plate, C.1850 .... 150.00
Wedgwood, Barrel, Biscuit, Light Blue, Acorn Finial On Cover 170.00
Wedgwood, Barrel, Biscuit, Light Blue, White & Yellow, Silver Plate Trim 700.00
Wedgwood, Barrel, Biscuit, Light Blue, White, Silver Lid & Feet 130.00
Wedgwood, Barrel, Biscuit, Sage Green, Dancing Hours, 1906, 7 1/2 In. 450.00
Wedgwood, Barrel, Biscuit, Silver Lid, Bail Handle, 6 3/4 In. 120.00
Wedgwood, Barrel, Biscuit, White Classical Figures, Dark Blue, Ball Feet 123.00
Wedgwood, Barrel, Biscuit, Yellow & Black With White Relief 600.00
Wedgwood, Barrel, Biscuit, Yellow, Black, White 575.00
Wedgwood, Barrel, Biscut, Green Footed, Jasperware Cover, Base, Plate, 8 In. 275.00
Wedgwood, Barrel, Cookie, Lilac, White Figures, Silver Plated Cover, Footed 295.00
Wedgwood, Barrel, Cracker, Blue, White, Classic Figures, Plated Lid, 7 1/2 In. 138.50
Wedgwood, Basket, Creamware, Woven, C.1860, Pair 220.00
Wedgwood, Basket, Porcelain, Blue & White Harbor, Boat Scene, 6 X 4 1/4 In. 80.00
Wedgwood, Bookslide, Laburnum Wood, Pierced Brass Mountings, Jasper Plaques 295.00
Wedgwood, Bottle, Cologne, Green, Classic Figures, Wedgwood, England, 7 1/2 In. 135.00
Wedgwood, Bowl, Basalt, Turned In Rim, 12 In. 120.00
Wedgwood, Bowl, Basalt, 9 X 5 1/4 In. 125.00
Wedgwood, Bowl, Classical Figures, Blue, Straight-Sided, 2 X 4 1/4 In. 46.00
Wedgwood, Bowl, Creamware, Shell Shape, Bird & Flower Design, C.1875 .... 58.00
Wedgwood, Bowl, Drabware, Blue Floral Trim, 7 1/2 In. 125.00
Wedgwood, Bowl, Dragon, Footed, Ribbed, No.Z4929, 6 In. 275.00
Wedgwood, Bowl, Fairland Luster Hexagon, 5 Birds On Blue, 6 3/8 In. 460.00
Wedgwood, Bowl, Fairyland Luster, Angel's, Black Luster, Yellow & White 1100.00
Wedgwood, Bowl, Fairyland Luster, Butterflies In & Out, Octagonal, 7 In. 275.00
Wedgwood, Bowl, Fairyland Luster, Butterfly, 9 In. 295.00
Wedgwood, Bowl, Fairyland Luster, Butterscotch, Butterflies, 2 1/4 X 4 In. 195.00
Wedgwood, Bowl, Fairyland Luster, Daventry, Purple Panels, Chinese Design 1450.00
Wedgwood, Bowl, Fairyland Luster, Elves In Branches, Blue, Green Inside, 4 In. 575.00
Wedgwood, Bowl, Fairyland Luster, Firbolgs, Thumbelina Frog, 3 1/2 In. 160.00

Wedgwood, Bowl, Fairyland Luster, Fish On Outside, Ship Inside 98.00
Wedgwood, Bowl, Fairyland Luster, Hummingbirds, Flying Geese Border, 4 In. 150.00
Wedgwood, Bowl, Fairyland Luster, Man, Camel, Dragons, Z4829, Portland 125.00
Wedgwood, Bowl, Fairyland Luster, Octagon, Pearlized, Butterflies, 4 In. 65.00
Wedgwood, Bowl, Fairyland Luster, Woodland Bridge, Numbered, 8 1/4 In. 1500.00
Wedgwood, Bowl, Fairyland Luster, Woodland Elves, Landscaping, 11 In. 1950.00
Wedgwood, Bowl, Fairyland, Persian Border, Blue, Flaming Wheel Design, 8 In. 1200.00
Wedgwood, Bowl, Footed, Red, Blue-Green Inside, Gold Lined Butterfly, 2 In. 120.00
Wedgwood, Bowl, Hummingbird Luster, Octagonal, Z5294 Portland Vase Mark 225.00
Wedgwood, Bowl, Hummingbird Luster, Z5294 Portland Vase Mark, 2 1/4 In. 165.00
Wedgwood, Bowl, Jasperware, 5 X 2 1/2 In. 135.00
Wedgwood, Bowl, Orange, Creamware Body, Reticulated, Covered, 1917, 6 In. 225.00
Wedgwood, Bowl, Salad, Dark Blue Jasperware, Wedgwood Only 295.00
Wedgwood, Bowl, Sauce With Fitted Underplate, Queensware, C.1774 .... 185.00
Wedgwood, Bowl, Ships & Flowers, C.1880, 8 1/2 In. 45.00
Wedgwood, Bowl, Terra-Cotta, 5 In. 55.00
Wedgwood, Bowl, 3 Color, C.1865, 10 1/2 X 3 3/4 In. 700.00
Wedgwood, Box, Blue Jasperware, Grape Motif In White, Round, 5 In. 45.00
Wedgwood, Box, Cobalt, White Jasper, Scalloped, England, 5 In. 50.00
Wedgwood, Box, Covered, Jasperware, Dark Blue, Classical Figure Lid, 3 1/2 In. 75.00
Wedgwood, Box, Covered, Round, Jasperware, Dark Blue, 1 X 3 1/2 In. 75.00
Wedgwood, Box, Dark Blue, Round, Covered, Wedgwood, England, 3 X 3 In. 65.00
Wedgwood, Box, Heart Shaped, White, Green & Lilac, 4 1/4 X 3 1/2 In. 545.00
Wedgwood, Box, Jasper, Dark Blue, Classical Figures, Heart Shaped, Lidded 48.00
Wedgwood, Box, Jasper, Green Relief, Square, 4 X 4 In. 175.00
Wedgwood, Box, Jasper, Lilac, Rectangular, 1961, 3 1/2 In. 80.00
Wedgwood, Box, Jasper, Lilac, Round, 1961, 1 1/2 In. 60.00
Wedgwood, Box, Jasper, Lilac, 1961, 4 In. 100.00
Wedgwood, Box, Jasperware, Dark Blue Scalloped, 4 1/2 In. 95.00
Wedgwood, Box, Lilac, Square, 4 X 4 In. 85.00
Wedgwood, Box, Pomade, Covered, Dark Blue Jasperware, Wedgwood Only, 3 In. 75.00
Wedgwood, Box, Round, England Only, 3 X 2 3/4 In. 45.00
Wedgwood, Box, Sardine, Waves & Seaweed Border, Blue & Aqua, Majolica Cover 150.00
Wedgwood, Box, Terra-Cotta, 4 In. 25.00
Wedgwood, Bust, Byron, Basalt, 9 In. 875.00
Wedgwood, Bust, Churchill, Creamware, Glazed, 8 In. 25.00
Wedgwood, Bust, E.W.Lyon, Burns, 14 In. 295.00
Wedgwood, Bust, Mercury, Basalt, 1810, 18 In. 950.00
Wedgwood, Bust, Milton, Parian, Signed E W Wyon, C.1860, 14 1/2 In. 650.00
Wedgwood, Butter, Blue & White, Floral Lining In & Out 19.75
Wedgwood, Cachepot, Cobalt, White Jasper, Classic Figures, England, 3 1/2 In. 55.00
Wedgwood, Caddy, Tea, Light Green, Classical Figures, C.1850-60 .... 250.00
Wedgwood, Candlestick, Basalt With Capri Enamel Decorations, 5 3/4 In. 195.00
Wedgwood, Candlestick, Crimson, Allegorical Figures, 8 1/2 In. .... 575.00 To 625.00
Wedgwood, Candlestick, Dark Blue, Marked Wedgwood M.I.E., 5 In. 75.00
Wedgwood, Candlestick, Enamel Lion Crest, Black Basalt, Wedgwood Only, 5 In. 145.00
Wedgwood, Candlestick, Enameled Floral, Basalt, C.1870, 7 1/2 In. 185.00
Wedgwood, Candlestick, Floral, Basalt, 7 1/2 In. 195.00
Wedgwood, Candlestick, Green Jasper Swirl, 6 In., Pair 95.00
Wedgwood, Candlestick, Green Jasper, Wedgwood Only, 7 1/2 In., Pair 110.00
Wedgwood, Candlestick, Jasper, Classical Figures & Design, 5 In., Pair 104.00
Wedgwood, Candlestick, Jasper, White Reliefs, Blue, Marked, 6 1/2 In., Pair 195.00
Wedgwood, Candlestick, Jasperware, Light Blue, Marked, Pair, 6 1/2 In. 195.00
Wedgwood, Candlestick, Jasperware, Rosso & Black, 7 In. 205.00
Wedgwood, Candlestick, Miniature, Dark Blue, White 145.00
Wedgwood, Candlestick, Queensware, White, Raised Grapes, 9 3/4 In., Pair 110.00
Wedgwood, Candlestick, Sacrifice Relief, Basalt, C.1900, 11 In.Pair 290.00
Wedgwood, Candy, Cover, Blue & Red Flowers, Portland Vase Mark, 2 X 4 1/2 In. 50.00
Wedgwood, Clock, Blue & White Jasper, Domed Top, Dancing Figures, 6 1/2 In. 450.00
Wedgwood, Clock, Blue And White, Decorative, 6 1/4 X 5 1/2 In. 375.00
Wedgwood, Coffee Can With Saucer, Fruit, Flowers, Rams' Heads, C.1810 .... 500.00
Wedgwood, Coffeepot, Basalt, Enameled Flowers, 5 In. 275.00
Wedgwood, Compote, Figural, Ram's Head With Grapes, 3 1/3 X 6 In. 175.00
Wedgwood, Compote, Green Majolica, Wedgwood Only, 13 X 8 In. 75.00
Wedgwood, Compote, Majolica, Green, Sunflower Center, 17 X 12 X 4 In. 60.00
Wedgwood, Compote, Stoneware, Pagoda Pattern, Gold Edges, 1820s 110.00

Wedgwood, Cookie Jar, Cover, Dark Blue Decorated Inside Cover, 8 1/2 In.	450.00
Wedgwood, Cracker Jar, Blue, Plated Silver Cover, England, 6 X 6 In.	75.00
Wedgwood, Cracker Jar, Jasper, 3 Button Feet, Lid, Swing Handle, Silver Plate	85.00
Wedgwood, Cracker Jar, Jasperware, Dark Blue	145.00
Wedgwood, Creamer & Sugar, Covered	150.00
Wedgwood, Creamer, Basalt Decorated, C.1840, 2 7/8 In.	60.00
Wedgwood, Creamer, Basalt, Shamrock & Harp	50.00
Wedgwood, Creamer, Blue & White, 5 1/4 In.	30.00
Wedgwood, Creamer, Bulbous, Made In England, 3 1/2 In.	35.00
Wedgwood, Creamer, Bust Of Lady, Frilly Hat, Light Green, Rope Handle, Grapes	45.00
Wedgwood, Creamer, Caneware, Hawthorn, C.1810, 2 1/2 In.	145.00
Wedgwood, Creamer, Dark Blue & White, 5 1/4 In.	30.00
Wedgwood, Creamer, Dark Blue Jasper, Miniature, England	125.00
Wedgwood, Creamer, Dark Blue, Trees, Woman & Child Reading, England, 3 1/2 In.	30.00
Wedgwood, Creamer, Green Jasper, C.1871	105.00
Wedgwood, Creamer, Green, 3 3/4 In.	125.00
Wedgwood, Creamer, Impressed Hound Handle, Hunt Scene	24.50
Wedgwood, Creamer, Jasperware, England, Twisted Handle, 4 1/2 In.	40.00
Wedgwood, Creamer, Victorian Design, Green, Silver Plated Mount, 2 1/8 In.	85.00
Wedgwood, Creamer, Yellow, Black Relief, Made In England	245.00
Wedgwood, Cuff Links, Black Caesar On White Jasper, Sterling Silver Mount	15.00
Wedgwood, Cup & Saucer, Deer, Blue & White, 1901	22.00
Wedgwood, Cup & Saucer, Demitasse, Basalt	19.50
Wedgwood, Cup & Saucer, Flow Blue, Wedgwood Only	27.00
Wedgwood, Cup & Saucer, Glazed Drabware, White Vintage Relief	65.00
Wedgwood, Cup & Saucer, Gold Luster	55.00
Wedgwood, Cup & Saucer, Jasper, Lilac, 1961	95.00
Wedgwood, Cup & Saucer, Jasperware, Classic, Light Blue, 1858	15.00
Wedgwood, Cup & Saucer, Jasperware, Lilac	145.00
Wedgwood, Cup & Saucer, Miniature, Dark Blue, Heraldic Emblem	145.00
Wedgwood, Cup & Saucer, Pearlware, Blue Floral & Leaves, Gilt Outlined	65.00
Wedgwood, Cup, Blue, White & Orchid, 2 1/2 X 2 1/2 In.	475.00
Wedgwood, Cup, Dragons, 3 Handled, 2 In.	225.00
Wedgwood, Decanter, Figural, Sandeman, Moonstone-White, Black Marked, 11 In.	15.00
Wedgwood, Dessert Set, Cobalt Blue, Gold On White, Octagon Shape, 15 Piece	300.00
Wedgwood, Dessert Set, Moonlight Luster, Pink, Etruria, 4 Piece	85.00
Wedgwood, Dish, Basket Weave, Pierced Rim, Pre-1860, 7 1/2 In.	28.00
Wedgwood, Dish, Candy, Red & Blue Flowers, Covered, Portland Vase Mark	60.00
Wedgwood, Dish, Cheese, Cobalt Blue, Lid, Signed M.I.E., 9 X 4 In.	225.00
Wedgwood, Dish, Cheese, Covered, Stilton, Green Jasper, 1878, 11 3/4 In.	285.00
Wedgwood, Dish, Cheese, Dark Blue Jasper, Base, Wedgwood Only, 8 3/4 In.	175.00
Wedgwood, Dish, Cheese, Jasperware, Dark Blue, England, 11 1/2 In.Base	250.00
Wedgwood, Dish, Game, Caneware, Liner, 6 X 10 In.	250.00
Wedgwood, Dish, Game, Liner, Large	350.00
Wedgwood, Dish, Heart Shape, Classical Figures, Blue, Dated 1951	15.00
Wedgwood, Dish, Ice Cream, Footed, Cream Color, Signed Patrician	9.00
Wedgwood, Dish, Nut, Animal Luster, Z482 Portland Vase Mark, 1 X 3 In.	85.00
Wedgwood, Dish, Pin, Blue, Lady In Center, 4 1/4 In.	7.50
Wedgwood, Dish, Reindeer In Show Scene, C.1876, 5 In.	38.00
Wedgwood, Dish, Terra-Cotta, White Jasper, 4 X 5 In.Square	35.00
Wedgwood, Ewer, Wine, Basalt, C.1840, 17 1/2 In.	850.00
Wedgwood, Fairyland Luster, Bowl, Firbolgs & Thumbelina, No.Z5247, 4 In.	600.00
Wedgwood, Fairyland Luster, Dragon, Pearl Design Inside, Mottled Blue, 3 In.	90.00
Wedgwood, Figurine, Deer, Basalt, Crouching On Ground, Signed J.Skeaping	250.00
Wedgwood, Figurine, Fawn, Black Basalt, J.Skeaping, 7 1/2 X 6 1/2 In.	390.00
Wedgwood, Figurine, Kangaroo, Creamware, Skeaping	225.00
Wedgwood, Figurine, Lion, Basalt, 6 1/2 In.	890.00
Wedgwood, Figurine, Raven, Basalt, C.1915	675.00
Wedgwood, Figurine, Sphinx, Basalt, C.1805, 6 X 3 3/4 In., Pair	1700.00
Wedgwood, Flower Holder & Tray, Porcupine, Basalt, Signed, 11 X 7 In.	750.00
Wedgwood, Ginger Jar, Covered, Sycamore Tree Design, 10 In.	2400.00
Wedgwood, Ginger Jar, Fairyland Luster, Black, Green & Red Figures	1850.00
Wedgwood, Goblet, Diced, Three Colors, Jasper	1150.00
Wedgwood, Gravy Boat, Cathay	35.00

Wedgwood, Green Acanthus Leaves, Lilac Lilies Of The Valley, 8 In. 725.00
Wedgwood, Hatpin Holder, Green, Raised Cupid, Pink, Yellow & Blue, 1920 .... 37.50
Wedgwood, Jam, Classical Decoration, White On Green, Lid, Jasperware 67.00
Wedgwood, Jar, Cobalt, White Horse Hunt Scene, Tunstall, England, 4 In. 165.00
Wedgwood, Jar, Ginger, Fairyland Luster, Black, Green & Red, Landscape 1850.00
Wedgwood, Jar, Jam, Blue, White Classic Figures, Plated Lid & Spoon, 3 In. 115.00
Wedgwood, Jar, Mustard, Yellow, Black 275.00
Wedgwood, Jardiniere, Blue Jasper, 6 1/2 X 7 1/4 In. 165.00
Wedgwood, Jardiniere, Classical Figures, 2 Piece, Deep Blue 295.00
Wedgwood, Jardiniere, Crimson, 7 1/8 X 8 In. 900.00
Wedgwood, Jasperware, Creamer & Sugar, Gray, Green, White 55.00
Wedgwood, Jug, Ale, Cambridge, Redware, 1871, Engine-Turned Decoration, 5 In. 75.00
Wedgwood, Jug, Ale, Terra-Cotta, Winged Figures, Bird, Pinched Spout, Dated 175.00
Wedgwood, Jug, Ale, Terra-Cotta, 1871, 7 1/4 In. 75.00
Wedgwood, Jug, Blue & White Classical Figures, Signed Adams, 6 X 16 1/2 In. 90.00
Wedgwood, Jug, Blue & White Jasper, Classical Ladies, Wedgwood, 7 X 5 1/4 In. 125.00
Wedgwood, Jug, Dark Green, Sacrifice Scene, Wedgwood, England, 6 In. 135.00
Wedgwood, Jug, Doric, Light Blue & White, 1866, 8 1/2 In. 300.00
Wedgwood, Jug, Dutch, Jasperware, Crimson, 4 In.High .... 50.00 To 500.00
Wedgwood, Jug, Green Jasper, Busts Of Washington & Franklin, England 85.00
Wedgwood, Jug, Green Jasper, Washington, Franklin Medallions, Wedgwood Only 125.00
Wedgwood, Jug, Jasperware, Blue, Twisted Rope Handle, 5 In. 135.00
Wedgwood, Jug, Jasperware, Crimson, Orange, 6 In. 650.00
Wedgwood, Jug, Jasperware, Raised White Leaves, Raised Figures, 6 1/2 In. 150.00
Wedgwood, Jug, Jasperware, White On Blue, Wedgwood Only, 6 1/2 In. 150.00
Wedgwood, Jug, Liqueur, Olive Green, Classic Figures, England, 7 1/4 In. 185.00
Wedgwood, Jug, Milk, Caneware, Glazed, Hunt Scene In Relief, C.1810-20, 5 In. 175.00
Wedgwood, Jug, Milk, Crimson, Wedgwood, England, 6 1/2 In. 950.00
Wedgwood, Jug, Milk, Doric, Marbleized Orange, Tan, & Brown, 7 In. 115.00
Wedgwood, Jug, Miniature, Jasperware, Blue, White Classical Scene 148.00
Wedgwood, Jug, Pale Blue & White Jasper, Marked, 8 In. 180.00
Wedgwood, Jug, Stoneware, Blue & White, C.1810, 5 In. 145.00
Wedgwood, Jug, Syrup, Cattail, Leaves, Pewter Top With Snake, Deep Blue, 7 In. 130.00
Wedgwood, Jug, Syrup, Jasperware, White Classical Figures, Spring Lid, C.1880 .... 235.00
Wedgwood, Jug, Syrup, Rosso, Pewter Lid, Doric Head Design, 7 1/2 In. 195.00
Wedgwood, Jug, White Stoneware, C.1820, 8 1/2 In. 290.00
Wedgwood, Lamp, Jasper, 16 In. 12.00
Wedgwood, Lamp, Oil, Rosso Antico, Late 18th Century 425.00
Wedgwood, Lighter, Black Basalt, Grape & Leaf Cameo, England 20.00
Wedgwood, Lighter, Cigarette, Black Basalt, Grape & Leaf Cameo, England 20.00
Wedgwood, Lighter, Cigarette, Grape & Leaf Cameo, Black Basalt 20.00
Wedgwood, Lighter, Table, Jasper, Green 22.00
Wedgwood, Luncheon Set, Trentham Pattern, 1922, 40 Piece 200.00
Wedgwood, Match Holder, Jasperware, Blue, 2 1/2 In. 90.00
Wedgwood, Match Holder, Jasperware, 3 Inch 68.00
Wedgwood, Matchbox, Dark Blue Jasper, Covered, Classic Figure, Wedgwood Only 45.00
Wedgwood, Matchbox, Jasperware, Dark Blue, Pegasus 38.00
Wedgwood, Matchbox, Striker Lid, Dark Blue, Wedgwood, England 85.00
Wedgwood, Matchbox, White Classical Figure, Yellow, Oval, England 195.00
Wedgwood, Medallion, Benjamin Franklin 200.00
Wedgwood, Medallion, John Wesley, C.1795, 4 X 3 In. 255.00
Wedgwood, Medallion, Ulysses, Blue Jasper, 3 1/4 In. 50.00
Wedgwood, Mug, Commemorative, Elkington & Co., Ltd., Jasperware, Silver Rim 125.00
Wedgwood, Mug, Pearlware, Gold Band, Wedgwood Only 35.00
Wedgwood, Mug, Tankard, Majolica, Figural Egyptian Face Handle, 6 In. 250.00
Wedgwood, Paperweight, Caduceus, Black, White Jasper 35.00
Wedgwood, Pitcher, Berries & Leaves In Copper Relief On Cream, 6 3/4 In. 45.00
Wedgwood, Pitcher, Blue Jasper, Classical Decoration, C.1858, 6 3/4 In. 60.00
Wedgwood, Pitcher, Blue, Silver Plated Top, 8 1/2 In. 175.00
Wedgwood, Pitcher, Caneware, Grape & Vine Pattern On Body, 8 In. 275.00
Wedgwood, Pitcher, Charles Dickens Memorial, Creamware, 1879, 8 In. 200.00
Wedgwood, Pitcher, Classical Figures, Rope Handle, Dark Blue, Signed, 8 In. 175.00
Wedgwood, Pitcher, Commemorative, Roger Williams, 1875 Providence, R.I., Brown 75.00
Wedgwood, Pitcher, Copper Luster, Hunt, Dog Handle, 5 1/2 In. 90.00

Wedgwood, Pitcher, Crimson, Rope Handle, Made In England, 3 1/2 In.	550.00
Wedgwood, Pitcher, Crimson, Rope Handle, 3 1/2 In.	550.00
Wedgwood, Pitcher, Crimson, 5 1/4 In.	750.00
Wedgwood, Pitcher, Dark Blue Jasper, Wedgwood Only, 2 1/2 In.	110.00
Wedgwood, Pitcher, Dark Blue Jasperware, England Only, 8 In.	85.00
Wedgwood, Pitcher, Dark Blue, White Figures Around Jasper, 5 In.	85.00
Wedgwood, Pitcher, Dark Blue, White Figures, Twisted Handle, 8 1/2 In.	175.00
Wedgwood, Pitcher, Etruria, Blue, High Gloss, White Classical Figures, 4 In.	35.00
Wedgwood, Pitcher, Etruria, Landscape, Blue & White, Signed, 4 1/4 In.	36.50
Wedgwood, Pitcher, Ferrara Purple, White, Luster Handle & Bandings, 4 1/2 In.	75.00
Wedgwood, Pitcher, Jasper, Classical, Plate, Lid, Grape Leaf Border, 7 In.	160.00
Wedgwood, Pitcher, Jasper, Washington And Lincoln In Medallions, 8 1/2 In.	595.00
Wedgwood, Pitcher, Jasperware, Classical Scene, Blue & White, 4 In.	85.00
Wedgwood, Pitcher, Jasperware, Crimson, Twisted Rop Handle, 3 3/4 In.	425.00
Wedgwood, Pitcher, Light Blue, Marked Wedgwood, C.1900, 3 7/8 In.	65.00
Wedgwood, Pitcher, Lilac, Impressed XDG, 8 1/2 In.	200.00
Wedgwood, Pitcher, Milk, Blue Classical Figures, Bulbous, 5 1/2 In.	100.00
Wedgwood, Pitcher, Mr.Pickwick, The Two Wellers, Creamware, 5 X 4 1/4 In.	45.00
Wedgwood, Pitcher, Queensware, Blue, Grape Band Top, Grecian Girls, 6 1/2 In.	100.00
Wedgwood, Pitcher, Rope Handle, Crimson, 3 3/4 In.	375.00
Wedgwood, Pitcher, Syrup, Pewter Top, Dark Blue, White, Jasper	110.00
Wedgwood, Pitcher, Tea Leaf Luster, 2 Quart	18.00
Wedgwood, Pitcher, Terra-Cotta, White Jasper, 5 In.	165.00
Wedgwood, Pitcher, Water, Blue, White Classic Figures, Bulbous, England	175.00
Wedgwood, Planter, Bird's Nest, Robin Guarding Contents, 11 1/2 In.	288.00
Wedgwood, Planter, Terra-Cotta, Dated '59, Initials, F.R., 4 3/4 X 4 1/2 In.	265.00
Wedgwood, Plaque, Basalt & White, 3 Plaques In One Frame	95.00
Wedgwood, Plaque, Basalt, Framed, Female Dancing, 5 X 3 3/4 In.	145.00
Wedgwood, Plaque, Basalt, Framed, 10 X 8 1/2 In.	118.00
Wedgwood, Plaque, Dancing Hours, Blue & White, Black Frame, 18 X 6 In.	1250.00
Wedgwood, Plaque, Jasperware, Green, England, 7 1/2 X 5 1/2 In., Pair	175.00
Wedgwood, Plaque, Jasperware, Light Blue, Oval, Wedgwood, England, 8 X 6 In.	125.00
Wedgwood, Plaque, King Edward VII, Green, 5 1/4 In.	125.00
Wedgwood, Plaque, President Kennedy Bust Center, 4 1/2 In.	20.00
Wedgwood, Plaque, Wall, Ormolu, Hand-Painted Head Of Elk	395.00
Wedgwood, Plate, Bicentennial, 5 Color, 9 In.	950.00
Wedgwood, Plate, Birds & Fans Front, Brown, Blue, Black Border, 9 In.	33.00
Wedgwood, Plate, Birth Of American Flag, 1899, Blue, White, 9 In.	25.00
Wedgwood, Plate, Bone China, Mottled Design, Hand-Painted Chinese Scene, 10 In.	45.00
Wedgwood, Plate, Boston Buildings, Blue, White, 1900, 9 1/4 In.	30.00
Wedgwood, Plate, Bunker Hill Monument, 1899, Blue, White, 9 In.	25.00
Wedgwood, Plate, Cadet Chapel West Point, C.1930, Pink	12.00
Wedgwood, Plate, Calendar, September, Polychrome, 10 In.	85.00
Wedgwood, Plate, Cobalt Scene Of Albany, 1814, 9 1/4 In.	35.00
Wedgwood, Plate, Columbia Exposition, Machinery Building, Etruria, England	18.00
Wedgwood, Plate, Creamware, Be Always As Merry As Ever You Can, 10 In.	125.00
Wedgwood, Plate, Creamware, Life's A Grind And Woman's Unkind, 10 In.	125.00
Wedgwood, Plate, Creamware, Proverb & Children, 1878	45.00
Wedgwood, Plate, Creamware, Tree Branch & Flowers, C.1873, Wedgwood HHB	35.00
Wedgwood, Plate, Deer In Snow, Vulture, Verse On Back, 1876, 5 In.	40.00
Wedgwood, Plate, Dinner, Hedge Rose	8.00
Wedgwood, Plate, Etruria, Cerise Ground, White Relief Garlands, Scalloped	35.00
Wedgwood, Plate, Etruria, Floral, 8 In.	3.00
Wedgwood, Plate, Etruria, Water Lily, 20th Century, 10 1/2 In.	15.00
Wedgwood, Plate, Faneuil Hall, 1899, 9 In.	30.00
Wedgwood, Plate, Ferrara, Purple, 9 In.	75.00
Wedgwood, Plate, Fox Hunt, Cross-Country, 9 1/4 In.	25.00
Wedgwood, Plate, Green, Classical Scene, Made In England, 6 1/2 In.	6.00
Wedgwood, Plate, Green, Raised Branches & Leaves, Glazed, 8 1/4 In.	38.00
Wedgwood, Plate, Hand-Painted, Silver & Umber, Silver Border, Set Of 6	32.00
Wedgwood, Plate, Harbor Scene, 9 In.	25.00
Wedgwood, Plate, Harvard University, Widener Library, 1927	18.00
Wedgwood, Plate, Hunting Dogs With Spots, Grass, Gold, Blue, Marked, 9 In.	175.00
Wedgwood, Plate, Independence Hall, Blue, 9 In.	25.00
Wedgwood, Plate, Ivanhoe, Relating Her Story To Cedric, 8 3/4 In.	30.00

Wedgwood, Plate, Ivanhoe, Wamba, Gurth The Swineherd, Etruria, 10 In.	45.00
Wedgwood, Plate, Jasperware, Classic, Light Blue, 1858, 6 1/2 In.	7.00
Wedgwood, Plate, Jasperware, Lilac, Classical Figures, Floral, 6 3/4 In.	65.00
Wedgwood, Plate, Jasperware, 3 Graces Centered, Dark Blue, 9 1/2 In.	75.00
Wedgwood, Plate, John Hancock House, 9 In.	30.00
Wedgwood, Plate, Kruger National Park	28.00
Wedgwood, Plate, Lee's Home In Virginia	11.00
Wedgwood, Plate, Lilac, White Relief, 9 In.	95.00
Wedgwood, Plate, Lincoln, Springfield Buildings, 10 In.	35.00
Wedgwood, Plate, Majolica, Dancing Cherubs, Email Ombrant, 8 3/4 In.	100.00
Wedgwood, Plate, Majolica, Green, Grape & Leaf Border	30.00
Wedgwood, Plate, Majolica, Green, Grapes & Leaf Border, 11 1/2 X 8 In.	50.00
Wedgwood, Plate, Majolica, Harvest, Footed, 13 In.	225.00
Wedgwood, Plate, Majolica, Yellow & Red Daisies, White Background, 7 In.	20.00
Wedgwood, Plate, Mandarin, 9 In.	30.00
Wedgwood, Plate, Massachusetts Institute Of Technology, 12 In.	100.00
Wedgwood, Plate, Moonluster, Lily Tray Shape, 10 In.	300.00
Wedgwood, Plate, Moonluster, Shell Shape, 9 In.	300.00
Wedgwood, Plate, Mutual Benefit Life Insurance Co., Rose Color	45.00
Wedgwood, Plate, Niagara Falls, 9 In.	30.00
Wedgwood, Plate, Old Albany, Cobalt, Charles Company	15.00
Wedgwood, Plate, Old Capitol Building, Albany, New York, 9 In.	28.00
Wedgwood, Plate, Old London Views, British War Relief Society, 1941, 10 Piece	420.00
Wedgwood, Plate, Old Mill At Newport Rhode Island, 10 In.	28.00
Wedgwood, Plate, Old State House, Boston, 1899, Blue, White, 10 In.	25.00
Wedgwood, Plate, Oriental Flowers, Earthenware, Blue Rim, C.1820	75.00
Wedgwood, Plate, Oyster, Majolica, Shell & Seaweed, 9 In.	58.00
Wedgwood, Plate, Paul Revere's Ride, 1899, Blue, White, 9 In.	25.00
Wedgwood, Plate, Piranesi, Sepia On White, C.1935, Boston Charity, 10 1/2 In.	15.00
Wedgwood, Plate, Queensware, High Gloss, 6 1/4 In.	10.00
Wedgwood, Plate, Return Of The Mayflower, 9 In.	28.00
Wedgwood, Plate, Royal Palms, Bahamas, Cobalt Blue & Apricot Border	28.00
Wedgwood, Plate, Sailing Boat, Sepia Tones, 11 In.	19.00
Wedgwood, Plate, Sailing Vessels, 11 In., Set Of 4	75.00
Wedgwood, Plate, Scene Of Albany, Cobalt, 9 1/4 In.	35.00
Wedgwood, Plate, Square, English Hunt Scene, 8 1/2 In.	10.00
Wedgwood, Plate, St.Paul's School, Mulberry	12.00
Wedgwood, Plate, State House Boston, Blue & White, 1895	20.00
Wedgwood, Plate, Three Colors, Jasper	950.00
Wedgwood, Plate, Trophy, Light Blue	375.00
Wedgwood, Plate, Wadsworth Longfellow Home, Blue, White, 10 In.	30.00
Wedgwood, Plate, Washington Elm, 9 In.	30.00
Wedgwood, Plate, Washington's Headquarters, 1775, 9 In.	22.00
Wedgwood, Plate, White, Gold Net Design, Cobalt Border, 9 In.	10.00
Wedgwood, Plate, White House, 1899, Blue, White, 9 In.	25.00
Wedgwood, Plate, Yale College & Old College Fence, Blue, 9 In.	12.00
Wedgwood, Platter, Asiatic Pheasants, 13 X 16 In.	75.00
Wedgwood, Platter, Asiatic Pheasants, 16 In.	50.00
Wedgwood, Platter, Cows, 17 In.	160.00
Wedgwood, Platter, Fish, Dark Blue On White, 11 1/2 X 23 1/2 In.	42.00
Wedgwood, Platter, Lily Of The Valley, 15 In.	40.00
Wedgwood, Platter, Onion, 11 In.	55.00
Wedgwood, Platter, Rowena Granting A Safe Escort To Rebecca & Her Father	75.00
Wedgwood, Pot, Bulb, Jasperware, Blue & White	145.00
Wedgwood, Pot, Jam, Black Jasper, White Classic Figures, Silver Plated Rim	125.00
Wedgwood, Pot, Mustard, Covered, Creamware, Red, Orange, Yellow, Blue, 3 3/4 In.	95.00
Wedgwood, Pot, Posy, Jasper, Lilac, 1961	75.00
Wedgwood, Pot, Posy, Jasperware, Lilac, 3 1/2 X 3 1/2 In.	100.00
Wedgwood, Potpourri, Whiteware, Blue Relief, Wedgwood Only, 3 X 4 4/4 In.	195.00
Wedgwood, Relish, Floral Decoration	42.00
Wedgwood, Salt & Pepper, Floral, Marked	75.00
Wedgwood, Salt & Pepper, Terra-Cotta	200.00
Wedgwood, Salt Dip, Dark Blue Jasper, Silver Rim	60.00
Wedgwood, Salt, Blue, 2 1/4 In.	65.00
Wedgwood, Salt, Dark Blue Jasper, Silver Plated Rim, Wedgwood, England	53.00

Wedgwood, Salt, Jasper, Brown	22.00
Wedgwood, Soup, Queensware, Livingston, C.1896	25.00
Wedgwood, Spittoon, Lady's, Basalt, Engine Turned	150.00
Wedgwood, Sugar & Creamer, Basalt	125.00
Wedgwood, Sugar & Creamer, Jasperware, Green & White	40.00
Wedgwood, Sugar & Creamer, Raised Decoration On Blue, Gold Handles, M Mark	145.00
Wedgwood, Sugar, Jasper, Blue, 3 In.	50.00
Wedgwood, Sugar, Yellow, Black Relief, Made In England	275.00
Wedgwood, Syrup, Classic Figures, Rope Handle, Plated Lid, Wedgwood Only	150.00
Wedgwood, Syrup, Classical, Ivory Finial & Handle	185.00
Wedgwood, Syrup, Pewter Lid, Crimson, Wedgwood, England, 4 In.	325.00
Wedgwood, Tankard, Dip, Jasperware, Blue, Classical Scenes, Pre-1858, 6 3/4 In.	65.00
Wedgwood, Tea Caddy, Sage Green, White Decorative Relief, C.1850	240.00
Wedgwood, Tea Set, Basalt, Widow Finial, 3 Piece	145.00
Wedgwood, Tea Set, Blue & White Jasper, Made In England, 3 Pieces	250.00
Wedgwood, Tea Set, Jasperware Coated With Silver On Copper, 3 Piece	850.00
Wedgwood, Tea Set, Jasperware, Blue & White, Royal Crest, 1937, 3 Piece	595.00
Wedgwood, Tea Set, Jasperware, Dark Blue, Classical Figures, 3 Piece	225.00
Wedgwood, Tea Set, Jasperware, England, 3 Piece Set	195.00
Wedgwood, Teapot, Basalt, Widow Finial, 3 1/2 X 7 In.	225.00
Wedgwood, Teapot, Black Basalt, Capri Enameled Flowers, 7 In.	75.00
Wedgwood, Teapot, Blue, Wedgwood England Mark	100.00
Wedgwood, Teapot, Caneware, Basket Weave Design, C.1820, 6 In.	285.00
Wedgwood, Teapot, Caneware, Basket Weave, Wheat Finial, Glazed	175.00
Wedgwood, Teapot, Caneware, Blue, 10 X 4 1/2 In.	325.00
Wedgwood, Teapot, Creamware, Basket Weave, Sheaf Of Wheat Finial	190.00
Wedgwood, Teapot, Crimson, 9 1/2 X 5 In.	1050.00
Wedgwood, Teapot, Dark Blue Jasper, Miniature, England	225.00
Wedgwood, Teapot, Dark Blue, Wedgwood Only, 7 In.	155.00
Wedgwood, Teapot, Drabware, Arabesque Pattern, Spaniel Finial, C.1850	185.00
Wedgwood, Teapot, Jasperware, Classic, Light Blue, 1858, 7 In.	48.00
Wedgwood, Teapot, Pale Green, Classical Figures, 4 1/2 X 6 In.	75.00
Wedgwood, Teapot, Smear Glaze, Spaniel Finial, Wedgwood Only	295.00
Wedgwood, Teapot, Terra-Cotta, Enameled Florals, Capri Glaze, Wedgwood Only	375.00
Wedgwood, Teapot, White Allegorical Figures, Dark Blue	70.00
Wedgwood, Tile, Calendar, Etruria, 1892	35.00
Wedgwood, Tile, Calendar, John Hancock House, Boston, 1900, 29 In.	45.00
Wedgwood, Tile, Calendar, 1903, Cambridge Home Of James Russell Lowell	65.00
Wedgwood, Tile, Calendar, 1907, Harvard Stadium	55.00
Wedgwood, Tile, Calendar, 1909, Harvard Medical School	50.00
Wedgwood, Tile, Calendar, 1910, Mayflower Arriving	55.00
Wedgwood, Tile, Calendar, 1916, Massachusetts Institute Of Technology	65.00
Wedgwood, Tile, Calendar, 1917, U.S.Navy Yard, Boston	45.00
Wedgwood, Tile, Calendar, 1926, Coolidge Homestead	29.50
Wedgwood, Tile, Calendar, 1929, House Of Seven Gables	100.00
Wedgwood, Tile, January, Two Young Ladies, Blue	45.00
Wedgwood, Tile, November, Wood Frame, Blue, White	55.00
Wedgwood, Tile, Paris Exposition, 1900, 3 X 7 In.	50.00
Wedgwood, Tile, Portrait, Head Of Young Child, Marked Josiah Wedgwood & Sons	40.00
Wedgwood, Tile, Windmill On Nantucket Island, Etruria, Blue & White	30.00
Wedgwood, Tobacco Jar, Blue, White, Washington & Franklin On Body	220.00
Wedgwood, Tobacco Jar, Dark Blue & White, Insert, 5 In.	190.00
Wedgwood, Tobacco Jar, Dark Blue Jasperware, England, 5 In.	129.00
Wedgwood, Tobacco Jar, Jasperware, Raised White Figures, Panels, Mistletoe	78.00
Wedgwood, Toby Jug, Portly Gent, Tricorn Hat, Book, Bell, Creamware, 6 In.	115.00
Wedgwood, Toby Jug, Preacher, 776/3, 4 1/2 In.	75.00
Wedgwood, Toby Jug, Professor, 7 In.	100.00
Wedgwood, Toby Jug, Schoolmaster, 765/1, 7 1/4 In.	125.00
Wedgwood, Toby Jug, Town Crier, 7 In.	125.00
Wedgwood, Toothpick, Classical Decoration, White On Green, Lid, Jasperware	60.00
Wedgwood, Toothpick, Dark Blue, Wedgwood, England, 2 1/2 In.	40.00
Wedgwood, Tray, Majolica, Green, Grape & Leaf Border, 11 X 8 1/2 In.	49.00
Wedgwood, Tray, Pin, Jasperware, Blue, Heart Shaped, 4 In.Across	54.00
Wedgwood, Tray, Pin, Terra-Cotta	25.00
Wedgwood, Tray, Pin, White Mythological Figures, White Leaf Border, Basalt	45.00

Wedgwood, Tray, Sage Green, White Relief, Leaf & Acorn, Venus Scenes, C.1850 .... 225.00
Wedgwood, Tray, Terra-Cotta, Diamond Shape, England 44.00
Wedgwood, Tree, Ring, Jasper, Dark Blue, White 110.00
Wedgwood, Trembulese, Cover & Saucer, White, C.1800, 5 1/2 In. 335.00
Wedgwood, Trivet, Tea, Terra-Cotta, White Jasper, 6 In. 65.00
Wedgwood, Urn, Etruscan, Blue & White, Covered, C.1800, 11 1/2 In. 700.00
Wedgwood, Urn, Etruscan, Detailed, Pale Blue, White, 19th Century, 14 In. 550.00
Wedgwood, Vase, Birds & Flowers, Gold Designs On Blue, Covered, 11 In. 335.00
Wedgwood, Vase, Black Jasper, Portland, Wedgwood, England, 4 In. 300.00
Wedgwood, Vase, Blue, White Relief, Jasperware, Made In England, 5 In. 45.00
Wedgwood, Vase, Bluebells, Leaves, Black, White, 5 3/4 In. 125.00
Wedgwood, Vase, Bud, Brown, Golden Dragon, 5 1/4 In. 195.00
Wedgwood, Vase, Bud, Jasper, Blue, 5 In. 35.00
Wedgwood, Vase, Chinese Style, 4 X 9 In. 190.00
Wedgwood, Vase, Cupids, Blue, Marked, 5 In., Pair 125.00
Wedgwood, Vase, Dragon Luster, Blue & Gold, 9 In. 345.00
Wedgwood, Vase, Dragon Luster, Blue, Numbered, 8 3/4 In. 250.00
Wedgwood, Vase, Fairyland Luster, Blue Luster, Fairies On Ropes, 10 1/2 In. 1850.00
Wedgwood, Vase, Fairyland Luster, Blue, Gold Dragon, 8 X 5 In. 350.00
Wedgwood, Vase, Fairyland Luster, Blue, Gold Dragons, 9 In. 450.00
Wedgwood, Vase, Fairyland Luster, Dragon, 8 In. 300.00
Wedgwood, Vase, Fairyland Luster, Gold Dragon, Blue, 9 X 5 1/2 In. 395.00
Wedgwood, Vase, Fairyland Luster, Red, Dragon Decoration, 8 1/2 In. 575.00
Wedgwood, Vase, Fairyland Luster, Red, Dragon, Butterflies, 8 1/2 In. 575.00
Wedgwood, Vase, Grapes, Green Ivy Handles, Gold, Brown, White Purple, 11 In. 215.00
Wedgwood, Vase, Hummingbird Luster, Blue, 9 In. 425.00
Wedgwood, Vase, Hummingbird Luster, Mottle Flame Luster Inside, 5 In. 195.00
Wedgwood, Vase, Jasper, Dark Blue, 4 In. 50.00
Wedgwood, Vase, Jasper, Flower Holder In Top, Reliefs, Blue, White, Marked 45.00
Wedgwood, Vase, Luster, Hummingbird, Flying Geese, Mottled Blue, Orange, 5 In. 235.00
Wedgwood, Vase, Luster, Hummingbirds, Marked & Z5294, 4 1/4 In. 245.00
Wedgwood, Vase, Oriental Luster, Blue, Brown, Gold, Green, & Burgundy, 8 1/2 In. 325.00
Wedgwood, Vase, Portland, Blue, Decorated Bottom, 10 In. 1200.00
Wedgwood, Vase, Portland, Dark Blue, White Figures, 2 Handled, 9 In. 650.00
Wedgwood, Vase, Portland, Pale Blue, England, 7 3/4 In. 300.00
Wedgwood, Vase, Portland, White Corded Handles, Mask Face, C.1850, 6 In. 540.00
Wedgwood, Vase, Queensware, Pink Raised Border, C.1933, 12 In. 55.00
Wedgwood, Vase, Spill, Basalt, Swag & Lily Decoration 165.00
Wedgwood, Vase, Spill, Enamel, Flowers, Rosso Antico, Wedgwood Only, 3 1/2 In. 135.00
Wedgwood, Vase, Spill, Jasperware, Dark Blue, Acanthus Leaves, 5 1/2 In. 110.00
Wedgwood, Vase, Spill, Miniature, Blue, White, & Lilac, 3 In. 475.00
Wedgwood, Vase, Square Top, Blue & Gold Fish, 7 1/2 In. 285.00
Wedgwood, Vase, Urn Shaped, Gold Handled, Bone China, C.1880 .... 175.00
Wedgwood, Vase, White Stoneware, C.1840, 4 1/2 In., Pair 450.00
Wedgwood, Vase, 4 White Cupid Figures, Dark Blue, England, 5 1/4 In. 43.00
Wedgwood, Waste Bowl, Crimson, Made In England, 4 1/2 In. 490.00
Wedgwood, Waste Bowl, Crimson, 4 1/2 In. 490.00
Wedgwood, Water Set, Playing Cards, Gilding, 4 Piece 275.00

WELLER Weller pottery was first made in 1873 in Fultonham, Ohio. The firm moved to Zanesville, Ohio, in 1882. Art wares were first made in 1893. Hundreds of lines of pottery were made including Louwelsa, Eocean, Dickens, and Sicardo before the pottery closed in 1948.

Weller, Basket, Acorn, Browns & Greens, Twig Handle 35.00
Weller, Basket, Light Blue, White Flower, Signed, 8 1/2 In. 25.00
Weller, Basket, Wild Rose, Blue Green, 6 In. 22.00
Weller, Basket, Woodcraft, Acorn, Twig Handle, Clear Mold, 9 1/2 In. 95.00
Weller, Basket, Woodcraft, Hanging, Owls, 10 X 5 In. 75.00
Weller, Bowl, Blues & Greens, Red Dogwood Flowers, Tree Branches, 12 In. 65.00
Weller, Bowl, Bulb, White With Vertical Black Stripes 35.00
Weller, Bowl, Cattails, Fish & Frog In Center, Relief Decoration 65.00
Weller, Bowl, Child's, Cereal, 5 1/2 X 2 1/4 In. 18.00
Weller, Bowl, Console, Azalea, Footed 25.00
Weller, Bowl, Console, Oak Leaf, Blue, Green Leaves, 12 In. 22.00

Weller, Bowl, Coppertone, Square Handles, 8 1/2 In.	30.00
Weller, Bowl, Floral, Bulbous, Silver Metal Band, 9 X 4 In.	145.00
Weller, Bowl, Flower, Branch Handle, Dogwood Flower Trim, 6 In.	18.50 To 22.50
Weller, Bowl, Flower, Matte Green, Holes For Holding Flowers, 2 1/2 X 8 In.	20.00
Weller, Bowl, Glendale, Bird On Nest, Round, Small Opening, 4 In.	50.00
Weller, Bowl, Hudson, Floral Decoration, 4 1/2 X 6 In.	58.00 To 60.00
Weller, Bowl, Indian, 2 1/2 X 4 1/2 In.	27.00
Weller, Bowl, Louwelsa, Floral, Silver Rim, Bulbous, 3 1/2 In.	125.00
Weller, Bowl, Malvern, Reddish Brown And Green, 9 In.	18.00
Weller, Bowl, Marbleized, Impressed Mark, 9 1/2 In.	50.00
Weller, Bowl, Mixing, Tan With Brown Bands, 8 In.	12.00
Weller, Bowl, Oak Leaf, 12 In.	22.00
Weller, Bowl, Roma, Floral Buds, Brown, 5 X 7 In.	42.00
Weller, Bowl, Woodcraft, Squirrel, 4 Legs, 7 In.	45.00 To 55.00
Weller, Candelabra, Wood Rose, Matte Green To Peach, Pair	35.00
Weller, Candleholder, Brown Glaze Decorated, 2 Handled, Signed	38.00
Weller, Candleholder, Matte Blue, Lobbed, 2 1/2 In., Pair	18.00
Weller, Candlestick, Barcelona, 2 X 5 1/4 In., Pair	18.50 To 50.00
Weller, Candlestick, Blue Drapery, 7 1/2 In.	14.00
Weller, Candlestick, Blue Drapery, 9 In., Pair	30.00
Weller, Candlestick, Gloria, 2 1/2 In., Pair	15.00
Weller, Candlestick, Louwelsa, Floral, Handle, 5 In.	73.00
Weller, Candlestick, Louwelsa, Pansies, 9 In.	75.00
Weller, Candlestick, Malvern, 2 X 5 1/4 In., Pair	50.00
Weller, Candlestick, Roma, Impressed Mark, 8 In., Pair	26.00
Weller, Candlestick, Triple Green Cornucopia	12.95
Weller, Casserole, Pink Luster, Covered, Marked, 7 In.	12.00
Weller, Centerpiece, Pumilla, 4 X 9 In.	26.00
Weller, Chamberstick, Lily Pad	12.00
Weller, Chamberstick, Louwelsa, Clover, M.Mitchell, 7 1/2 In.	85.00
Weller, Clock, Louwelsa, Orange Flower Design, Artist MH, 86 In.	445.00
Weller, Clock, Louwelsa, Roses	575.00
Weller, Compote, Noval, Ivory, Molded Fruit, 7 In.	33.00
Weller, Console Set, Flowers, Branches, Birds, Nest, Eggs, Relief	180.00
Weller, Console Set, Kingfisher, 4 Piece	95.00
Weller, Console Set, Orange Luster, 4 Piece	75.00
Weller, Console Set, White Rose, Pink, 3 Piece	36.00
Weller, Console Set, Wild Rose Pattern	40.00
Weller, Cookie Jar, Woodcraft, Oak Leaves & Squirrel Handle, 8 1/2 In.	68.00
Weller, Cornucopia, Green With White Flowers	27.50
Weller, Cornucopia, Ivoris, Script Mark, 6 1/2 In.	14.00
Weller, Dish, Nut, Squirrels On Side, Signed, 5 1/2 In.	32.50 To 40.00
Weller, Ewer, Louwelsa, Poppy Decoration, Artist MD, 6 In.	97.50
Weller, Ewer, Louwelsa, Yellow Rose, 5 In.	100.00
Weller, Figurine, Art Deco Woman, Lavonia, Pockets To Hold Flowers, 11 In.	95.00
Weller, Figurine, Frog, Coppertone, Cream Water Lily In Arms, 3 1/2 In.	60.00
Weller, Figurine, Frog, Coppertone, Fountain	95.00
Weller, Figurine, Frog, On Lily Pad, 5 1/4 In.	42.00
Weller, Figurine, Hanging Squirrel	250.00
Weller, Figurine, Rabbit, Woodcraft, 7 1/2 In.	400.00
Weller, Figurine, Squirrel, Eating Nut, 12 X 11 In.	45.00
Weller, Figurine, Turtle, Coppertone, Weller Pottery In Script, 4 1/2 In.	52.50
Weller, Flower Frog, Bluebird, Black Beak, Forest Tree Trunk, 6 In.	45.00
Weller, Flower Frog, Fisher Boy On Rock, Green Glaze, Muskota	25.00
Weller, Flower Frog, Fishing Boy, Figural	65.00
Weller, Flower Frog, Pale Green, Glazed, Impressed Weller	5.00
Weller, Flower Frog, Starfish	19.50
Weller, Flower Frog, Swan, Muskota, 6 In.	28.00
Weller, Flower Frog, 8 Holes, Rose Pink, 3 1/4 In.	15.00
Weller, Flowerpot, Bonito, Ink Stamp	21.00
Weller, Jardiniere, Dancing Figures, Cream On Blue, Trees, Floral Band, 9 In.	125.00
Weller, Jardiniere, Dickens Ware, Amber Cherries, Amber Inside	125.00
Weller, Jardiniere, Dickens Ware, White, Yellow Asters On Green, MM, 8 In.	225.00
Weller, Jardiniere, Forest, 5 1/2 In.	70.00
Weller, Jardiniere, Forest, 6 In.	25.00

Weller, Jardiniere, Ivory On Knifewood, 9 X 11 In.	65.00
Weller, Jardiniere, Louwelsa, Brown Glaze, Yellow Flowers, V.Adams, 8 1/2 In.	170.00
Weller, Jardiniere, Louwelsa, Orange & Yellow Pansies, Green Ground, 7 In.	65.00
Weller, Jardiniere, Louwelsa, Yellow Pansies On Dark Brown, M.G., 8 3/4 In.	110.00
Weller, Jardiniere, Water Lilies & Pads, Matte Green, Footed, 9 1/2 In.	85.00
Weller, Jug, Dickens Ware, Sgraffito Portrait Of Stag, Numbered, 6 3/4 In.	145.00
Weller, Jug, Louwelsa, Blackberries, Signed, Squat	82.00
Weller, Jug, Louwelsa, Brown Glaze, Cherry Cluster, Handled, 8 In.	75.00
Weller, Jug, Louwelsa, Brown Glaze, Floral, Signed FR, 5 1/4 In.	85.00
Weller, Jug, Louwelsa, Cherry & Leaf Decoration, Handled, 6 In.	75.00
Weller, Jug, Louwelsa, Smiling Monk, Olive Green Shaded To Rust	350.00
Weller, Lamp Base, Ducks Walking, Sloped Round Base, Green, Ocher, Red, 7 In.	325.00
Weller, Lamp Base, Roma, Chain Of Roses On Beige, 12 In.	55.00
Weller, Lamp Base, Turada, Blue Glaze, Slip Decoration, Signed	145.00
Weller, Lamp Base, Woodcraft, Fish, Crane	210.00
Weller, Lamp, Dickens Ware, Blue Glaze, Leaves On Base, H.Mitchell, 13 In.	365.00
Weller, Lamp, Dickens Ware, Green, Sparrows, Pines, Abel, 1st Line, 30 X 13 In.	400.00
Weller, Lamp, Gone With The Wind, Yellow & Orange Florals On Glaze	250.00
Weller, Lamp, Lasa, Signed	60.00
Weller, Lamp, Oil, Dickens Ware, Cherry Decoration, Artist Initials	285.00
Weller, Mug, Dickens Ware, Deer's Head, Signed A, 6 In.	175.00
Weller, Mug, Dickens Ware, Indian Portrait, Handled, 5 1/2 In.	450.00
Weller, Mug, Etna, Grapes, 6 In.	59.00
Weller, Mug, Floretta, Clusters Of Grapes, Initialed	45.00
Weller, Mug, Incised Lady Golfer, Brown Skirt, White Blouse, Green Hat, Bushes	225.00
Weller, Mug, Ivory Pattern, 5 In., Set Of 5	100.00
Weller, Mug, Louwelsa, Birds, Flared Bottom, Artist E.Abel, 6 In.	795.00
Weller, Mug, Louwelsa, Blue Grapes, Artwork, Marked, Incised M, 6 In.	70.00
Weller, Mug, Louwelsa, Ear Of Corn, Burnt-Out Spot On Handle, 4 3/4 In.	90.00
Weller, Mug, Louwelsa, Silver Overlay, Dyker Meadow Golf Club, 1899, Brown	375.00
Weller, Mug, Pink Carnations Against Shaded Gray Background, 5 1/2 In.	62.00
Weller, Mug, Souevo, Indian Design, Marked, 4 1/2 In.	95.00
Weller, Mug, Woodcraft, 3 Foxes Decoration, 6 In.	125.00
Weller, Pitcher Vase, Squat Handle, White Flower, Green, Artist Signed, 7 In.	37.50
Weller, Pitcher, Basket Weave, Cream, 4 In.	10.00
Weller, Pitcher, Coppertone, Fish Handle, Lily Pad Under Spout, 7 1/2 In.	400.00
Weller, Pitcher, Eocean, Berries, Shades Of Green, 7 In.	68.00
Weller, Pitcher, Hunter, Sgraffito Fish, Undulating Blank, Spout, Signed	325.00
Weller, Pitcher, Kitchen Gem, Incised, Tan, Brown, 7 X 8 In.	40.00
Weller, Pitcher, Louwelsa, Straight Sided, Cherries, Signed WH, 4 In.	95.00
Weller, Pitcher, Ribbed, Rose To Blue To Yellow, Marked, 8 1/4 In.	48.00
Weller, Pitcher, Ribbed, Tall Rose To Blue To Yellow, 8 1/2 In.	48.00
Weller, Pitcher, Wild Rose, Tan, 12 In.	35.00
Weller, Pitcher, Yellow Jonquils On Green, 9 1/2 In.	22.00
Weller, Planter, Classic, 11 In.	15.00
Weller, Planter, Rabbit & Duck, Green, 7 In.	60.00
Weller, Planter, Roma, Liner, 4 X 12 In.	40.00
Weller, Planter, Swan, White, 6 In.	24.00
Weller, Planter, Woodcraft, Foxes, 5 X 7 1/2 In.	95.00
Weller, Planter, Woodcraft, Log, Handle, 4 Feet, Marked, 9 1/2 In.	22.00 To 32.50
Weller, Planter, Woodcraft, Tub Shape, Floral Decoration, Large	32.00
Weller, Plaque, Art Nouveau, Lincoln, 5 In.	85.00
Weller, Plaque, Bluebird	225.00
Weller, Plaque, Dutch Windmills, Trees, Picket Fence, Cobalt Squeezebag	435.00
Weller, Plaque, Old Indian Smoking Pipe	75.00
Weller, Plate, Burntwood, Birds, 9 In.	65.00
Weller, Plate, Child's, Rabbit & Blue Bird Border, 7 In.	17.00
Weller, Plate, Child's, With Ducks, 7 In.	22.00
Weller, Plate, Ivory, Washington Bust In Bottom, St.Louis, 1904, 5 In.	24.00
Weller, Plate, Portrait, St.Bernard, Weller Ware Sticker, 13 1/2 In.	475.00
Weller, Powder Jar, Luster, Yellow, 5 In.	24.00
Weller, Rose Bowl, Louwelsa, Floral, 3 Footed	58.00
Weller, Spittoon, Green High Glass, Early Mark	75.00
Weller, Tankard, Dickens Ware, Bust, Dashing Cavalier, Glazed, 12 In.	795.00
Weller, Tankard, Etna, Chrysanthemums, 10 1/4 In.	120.00

Weller, Tankard, Louwelsa, Cherries, Brown	65.00
Weller, Tankard, Louwelsa, Chrysanthemums, Signed A.Hendricks, 12 In.	95.00
Weller, Teapot, Pierre, 6 1/2 In.	10.00
Weller, Towel Bar, Bluebirds	400.00
Weller, Tray, Marbleized, 9 1/2 In.	40.00
Weller, Umbrella Stand, Ardsley	185.00
Weller, Umbrella Stand, Ivory, 19 In.	140.00
Weller, Umbrella Stand, Ivory, 20 In.	78.00
Weller, Vase, Art Nouveau, Woman, 8 In.	55.00
Weller, Vase, Art Nouveau, 13 In.	70.00
Weller, Vase, Aurelian, Grapes, Madge Hurst, 11 In.	140.00
Weller, Vase, Aurelian, Pillow, Floral, Artist Signed, 6 1/2 In.	155.00
Weller, Vase, Aurelian, 4 Footed Pillow, C.Minnie Terry, 6 1/2 X 5 In.	250.00
Weller, Vase, Baldwin, Apples, 2 Handled, 10 X 8 1/2 In.	125.00
Weller, Vase, Baldwin, Bud, Brown, Unmarked, 9 In.	23.00
Weller, Vase, Baldwin, Short Neck, 7 1/4 In.High	38.00
Weller, Vase, Bearded Iris, Timberlake, Hudson, 10 In.	135.00
Weller, Vase, Blackberry, High Glaze, Signed, 10 1/2 In.	65.00
Weller, Vase, Blossom Shape, Orange, Yellow, Green, Initials NC, 5 X 5 In.	35.00
Weller, Vase, Blown-Out Apples At Bottom, Peach Color, 7 In.	26.00
Weller, Vase, Blue Drapery, 8 In.	22.00
Weller, Vase, Blue Ware, Dancer, 9 1/2 In.	65.00
Weller, Vase, Blue Ware, Dancing Ladies, 10 In.	125.00
Weller, Vase, Blue Ware, Dancing Women, 10 In.	79.00
Weller, Vase, Blue, Decorated, Slip Painted Flowers, 8 In.	65.00
Weller, Vase, Blue, Figures, 10 In.	65.00
Weller, Vase, Blue, White Flowers, Horn Shape, 6 1/2 In.	8.00 To 16.00
Weller, Vase, Bo-Marblo, Paper Label, 9 1/2 In.	45.00
Weller, Vase, Bonita, Bluebells On Ivory, Marked Under Glaze, 4 1/2 In.	28.00
Weller, Vase, Bonita, 2 Handle, 8 X 5 1/4 In.	36.00
Weller, Vase, Bud, Etna, Raised Yellow, Pink, Blue Flowers, Gray To Black	43.00
Weller, Vase, Bud, Turned Top, Pansies, Standard Glaze, 8 In.	70.00
Weller, Vase, Bulbous, Twisted Ears, Silvertone, 9 In.	60.00
Weller, Vase, Burnt Wood, Birds, Flowers, Trees, 12 In.	125.00
Weller, Vase, Burnt Wood, Floral & Leaf, 5 In.	27.00
Weller, Vase, Burnt Wood, Signed, 8 In.	12.50
Weller, Vase, Cameo, Blue With White Flowers, 6 1/2 In.	16.00 To 20.00
Weller, Vase, Cameo, White Rose, Peach, 6 1/2 In.	25.00
Weller, Vase, Chase, Blue, 11 1/2 In.	135.00
Weller, Vase, Chase, Fox Hunter On Horse Jumping, Dog, 7 1/2 X 4 In.	125.00
Weller, Vase, Chengtu, Marked, 7 3/4 X 3 1/2 In.	25.00
Weller, Vase, Chengtu, 16 X 7 1/2 In.	70.00
Weller, Vase, Chengtu, 6 Sided, Paper Label, 9 In.	105.00
Weller, Vase, Claywood, Floral, 9 In.	24.00
Weller, Vase, Clinton Ivory	25.00
Weller, Vase, Cobalt Shaded, Daisies, 4 Footed, M.P.R., 8 In.	79.00
Weller, Vase, Coppertone, Frog Handles, Lily Pad Design	135.00
Weller, Vase, Coppertone, Incised Mark, 6 1/2 In.	45.00
Weller, Vase, Coppertone, Pear Shaped, 7 In.	38.00
Weller, Vase, Coppertone, 2 Handled, 8 1/2 X 6 In.	42.00
Weller, Vase, Cornish, Blue, Marked, 5 X 7 In.	12.00
Weller, Vase, Cornish, Script Mark, Brown, 5 In.	23.00
Weller, Vase, Darsie, Blue, 7 3/4 In.	22.00
Weller, Vase, Decorated Line, Blue, 8 1/4 In.	75.00
Weller, Vase, Dickens Ware, Black, Golfer, 2 Handled, 11 In.	145.00
Weller, Vase, Dickens Ware, Blackbird Decoration _Illus_	375.00
Weller, Vase, Dickens Ware, Boy Golfer, 2 Handled, 11 1/4 In.	215.00
Weller, Vase, Dickens Ware, Children Playing Football, 9 In.	495.00
Weller, Vase, Dickens Ware, Colorful Troubadour Plays Guitar, E.L.P., 12 In.	795.00
Weller, Vase, Dickens Ware, Embossed Berry Bush, Brown & Multicolored, 10 In.	295.00
Weller, Vase, Dickens Ware, Girl With Book On Bench, 3 Knights, A.S., 14 In.	1095.00
Weller, Vase, Dickens Ware, Gladiator, 2nd Period	275.00
Weller, Vase, Dickens Ware, Indian, Signed Diego Narango, 11 In.	850.00
Weller, Vase, Dickens Ware, Lady Golfer, Bulbous, 9 In.	295.00
Weller, Vase, Dickens Ware, Large Fish On 3 Sides, Triangular, L.M., 7 In.	395.00

Weller, Vase, Dickens Ware, Blackbird Decoration
(See Page 728)

Weller, Vase, Dickens Ware, Male Golfer, Numbered, 7 1/2 In.	295.00
Weller, Vase, Dickens Ware, Male Golfer, Trees, Fairway, Artist Initial, 9 In.	395.00
Weller, Vase, Dickens Ware, Monk At Table, Marked Dickens Ware, 7 1/2 In.	215.00
Weller, Vase, Dickens Ware, Monk Holding Stein, 3-Sided, 6 1/2 In.	215.00
Weller, Vase, Dickens Ware, Monk, Aqua Glaze, 16 In.	275.00
Weller, Vase, Dickens Ware, Monk, Matte, Iris Slip-Side Decoration, 6 In.	175.00
Weller, Vase, Dickens Ware, Old Man Fishing, 16 In.	675.00
Weller, Vase, Drapery, Blue, Raised Red Rose Buds, Fluted Sides, 7 In.	25.00
Weller, Vase, Eclair, 3 Roses Around Top, High Gloss, 8 In.	30.00
Weller, Vase, Eocean, Red, Purple Starflowers, Artist MP, 9 1/2 In.	20.00
Weller, Vase, Eocean, Rose, Handles, Gray, Pink Ivory, Rose Blossom, Bud	115.00
Weller, Vase, Eocean, Wild Geese In Flight, Green To Pinkish White, 10 In.	895.00
Weller, Vase, Etna, Blown-Out Grapes On Gray Shaded Ground, 14 In.	95.00
Weller, Vase, Etna, Blown-Out Roses, Signed	85.00
Weller, Vase, Etna, Pink Floral, Impressed Mark, 6 In.	75.00
Weller, Vase, Etna, Pink Mums On Gray Shaded Ground, 17 In.	165.00 To 175.00
Weller, Vase, Etna, Roses, 14 In.	120.00
Weller, Vase, Etna, Sunflower, 6 In.	30.00
Weller, Vase, Etna, 5 Pink Roses On Vine, 8 1/2 In.	75.00
Weller, Vase, Figural, Green, Frog Holding Water Lily, 4 X 4 In.	55.00
Weller, Vase, Floor, Atlantic, Creamware, 4 Panels Of Grape Clusters, 17 In.	135.00
Weller, Vase, Floor, Aurelian, Grape Clusters, Ferrell, 17 1/2 X 8 1/2 In.	320.00
Weller, Vase, Floral, Handled, 8 In.	45.00
Weller, Vase, Floral, Iris Glaze, Pink, 6 In.	30.00
Weller, Vase, Floretta, Berries, Fluted Top, Bulbous, 2 Open Handles, 5 In.	44.00
Weller, Vase, Floretta, Flowers, Urn Shape, High Glaze, 4 3/5 In.	55.00
Weller, Vase, Floretta, Grapes & Vines, Fluted Top, Bulbous, 8 X 9 In.	135.00
Weller, Vase, Floretta, Raised Red & Green Floral On Brown, 4 1/2 In.	35.00
Weller, Vase, Floretta, Raised Strawberries, Signed, 11 1/2 In.	75.00
Weller, Vase, Flowers In Relief, Pastel Blue, 8 In.	45.00
Weller, Vase, Forest, 8 In.	45.00
Weller, Vase, Gray To Cream, Floral, Red & Blue Accents, 7 1/4 X 4 1/2 In.	60.00
Weller, Vase, Green With Water Lilies, Double Vase, 10 In.	65.00
Weller, Vase, Hudson, Allover Floral, Leffler, 12 In.High	245.00
Weller, Vase, Hudson, Blue To Green, 15 In.	95.00
Weller, Vase, Hudson, Blue, Iris Decoration, Pillsbury, 7 In.	95.00
Weller, Vase, Hudson, Cone Shaped, White, Floral, 7 X 7 In.	48.00
Weller, Vase, Hudson, Floral, Blue, 8 In.	85.00
Weller, Vase, Hudson, Floral, Signed Pillsbury, 11 In.	125.00
Weller, Vase, Hudson, Florals On Gray Background, 11 In.	35.00
Weller, Vase, Hudson, Fruit Decoration, 6 1/2 In.	65.00
Weller, Vase, Hudson, Gray Pink To White To Gray Pink, Chrysanthemums, 18 In.	195.00
Weller, Vase, Hudson, Gray To Cream, Lilies Of The Valley, 7 In.	55.00
Weller, Vase, Hudson, Gray To Mauve, Magnolia Blossom, Bud, Drilled For Lamp	32.00
Weller, Vase, Hudson, Lavender To Gray-Green, White Florals, 7 In.	85.00
Weller, Vase, Hudson, Ovoid, Gray To Cream, Painted Florals, 7 1/4 In.	65.00
Weller, Vase, Hudson, Red Florals On Cream To Gray Ground, 11 In.	65.00
Weller, Vase, Hudson, Shaded Blue Gray, Pink Underglaze Flowers, 5 1/2 In.	37.50
Weller, Vase, Hudson, Watercolor Phlox, Gray, Cream, Signed C.Leffler	245.00
Weller, Vase, Hudson, White Florals On Lavender To Gray-Green, 7 In.	65.00
Weller, Vase, Hudson, 6 Flying Geese, Gray, Pink, Yellow, Cream, Signed, 12 In.	375.00
Weller, Vase, Hunting Scene, Tan Ground, Weller Pottery In Script, 7 1/2 In.	190.00
Weller, Vase, Lamar, Palm Trees Decoration, 7 In.	150.00

Weller, Vase, Lamar, Palm Trees, 9 In.	165.00
Weller, Vase, Lasa Bud, Signed, 6 1/2 In.	115.00
Weller, Vase, Lasa, Gold, Magenta, 12 In.	120.00
Weller, Vase, Lasa, Holed For Lamp, Marked Lasa, 15 1/2 In.	190.00
Weller, Vase, Lasa, Mountain, Lake, Palms, Gold, 10 In.	250.00
Weller, Vase, Lasa, Palm Tree, Castle, 4 In.	75.00
Weller, Vase, Lasa, Palm Trees In Maritime Setting, Signed, 2 X 1 X 6 In.	115.00
Weller, Vase, Lasa, Pine Trees, Iridescent, 5 1/4 In.	108.00
Weller, Vase, Lasa, Scenic Magenta, 4 1/2 In.	140.00
Weller, Vase, Lasa, Scenic, Signed, 11 1/4 In.	195.00
Weller, Vase, Lasa, Sunset On Beach, Palm Trees, Signed, 9 In.	325.00
Weller, Vase, Lasa, 11 In.	250.00
Weller, Vase, Louwelsa, Acorns, Footed, 4 3/4 X 5 1/2 X 3 1/4 In.	60.00
Weller, Vase, Louwelsa, Berries & Leaves, Cylindrical, Flared Opening, 13 In.	170.00
Weller, Vase, Louwelsa, Blue To White, Florals, Levi J.Burgess, 14 1/2 In.	200.00
Weller, Vase, Louwelsa, Blue, Floral, 7 In.	325.00
Weller, Vase, Louwelsa, Brown & Green Glaze, Yellow Flowers, 11 1/2 In.	95.00
Weller, Vase, Louwelsa, Brown Glaze, Pansies, Lizzie Perone, 8 1/4 In.	70.00
Weller, Vase, Louwelsa, Bud, Jug Shaped, Pansies, Green Stems MP, 6 In.	95.00
Weller, Vase, Louwelsa, Candlestick Shape, Floral, 6 In.	63.00
Weller, Vase, Louwelsa, Carnations, High Glaze, Eugene Roberts, 8 1/4 In.	120.00
Weller, Vase, Louwelsa, Christmas Holly, Signed, 7 In.	325.00
Weller, Vase, Louwelsa, Cobalt, Blackberries, A.H., 10 In.	350.00
Weller, Vase, Louwelsa, Dark Brown, Nasturtiums, Bulbous, 5 In.	71.00
Weller, Vase, Louwelsa, Floral, Bulbous, Artist Signed, 6 In.	110.00
Weller, Vase, Louwelsa, Fluted Rim, Spider Mum Art Work, 7 X 9 In.	50.00
Weller, Vase, Louwelsa, Gourd Shape, Floral, Gray Shading, 5 1/2 In.	95.00
Weller, Vase, Louwelsa, Grapes, Vine, Red, Purple, Brown, Green, Signed Ferrell	350.00
Weller, Vase, Louwelsa, Gray, 7 In.	45.00
Weller, Vase, Louwelsa, Holly Leaves & Berries, 7 In.	325.00
Weller, Vase, Louwelsa, Honeysuckle, Artist Signed, 5 1/2 In.	80.00
Weller, Vase, Louwelsa, Impressed Full Circle Medallion, 7 In.	125.00
Weller, Vase, Louwelsa, Indian, Marked, Artist Signed _____ Illus	900.00

Weller, Vase, Louwelsa, Indian, Marked, Artist Signed
(See Page 730)

Weller, Vase, Louwelsa, Iris On Brown Glaze, 7 In.High	75.00
Weller, Vase, Louwelsa, Nasturtiums, Marked, 6 In.	40.00
Weller, Vase, Louwelsa, Open Rose, Brown Glaze	82.00
Weller, Vase, Louwelsa, Palm Leaves, 4 1/2 In.	35.00
Weller, Vase, Louwelsa, Pansies, 4 1/4 X 4 X 2 1/2 In.	52.00
Weller, Vase, Louwelsa, Pillow Shape, Hearts, Mistletoe, Artist, L.B., 5 In.	125.00
Weller, Vase, Louwelsa, Pillow, Berries, Flowers, Leaves, 10 1/2 In.	195.00
Weller, Vase, Louwelsa, Pillow, Marked, 5 X 6 1/2 In.	65.00
Weller, Vase, Louwelsa, Portrait, Red Cloud Sioux Indian, Karl Kappes, 11 In.	3000.00
Weller, Vase, Louwelsa, Yellow Daffodil, Brown & Green Glaze, 7 1/4 In.	85.00
Weller, Vase, Luxor Line, High Glaze, Iridescent, 9 1/2 In.	30.00
Weller, Vase, Marbleized Green & Coppertone, Weller Incised In Script, 7 In.	30.00
Weller, Vase, Marengo, Scenic, Pink & Cranberry, 8 In.	70.00
Weller, Vase, Marvo, Bulbous, Green, 7 In.	21.00 To 24.00
Weller, Vase, Marvo, Tan On Green, 10 X 4 1/2 In.	18.00
Weller, Vase, Matte Green Dripped On Orange, 8 1/2 In.	70.00

Weller, Vase, Matte Green, Handled, 11 In. 15.00
Weller, Vase, Matte Green, Indian, 9 3/4 In. 35.00
Weller, Vase, Matte Green, 4 Raised Feet, 3 1/2 In. 15.00
Weller, Vase, Matte Green, 4 1/2 In. 16.00
Weller, Vase, Melrose, Cherries & Leaves, 9 In. 60.00
Weller, Vase, Oakleaf, Browntone, 6 1/2 In. 15.00
Weller, Vase, Paragon, Script Mark, Red, 4 1/2 In. 35.00
Weller, Vase, Patra, Blossom Shape, Orange Peel Finial, Green Trim, Signed 35.00
Weller, Vase, Patria, Orange, Yellow, & Green, Blossom Shape, 5 In. 35.00
Weller, Vase, Pink Large Floral, Blue, Green, Red, Yellow, 10 In. 35.00
Weller, Vase, Purple Luster, 7 In. 12.00
Weller, Vase, Rhead, Green, High Glaze, Owl & Moon Incised, 6 In. 275.00
Weller, Vase, Roma, Double Stick, Bud, 8 1/2 In. 12.00
Weller, Vase, Roma, 5 Openings, 8 X 8 In. 30.00
Weller, Vase, Roses, Etched, Matte Finish, 8 In. 65.00
Weller, Vase, Sicardo, Blue Lavender, Silver Green Stemmed Floral, Mark 185.00
Weller, Vase, Sicardo, Clover Design, Iridescent, 4 1/4 In. 192.00
Weller, Vase, Sicardo, Gold & Wine Floral, 5 1/2 In. 275.00
Weller, Vase, Sicardo, Gold Luster Foliage On Purple Luster, 4 1/2 In. 150.00
Weller, Vase, Sicardo, Iridescent Stars, Signed Sicardo & Weller, 4 In. 160.00
Weller, Vase, Sicardo, Iridescent, Signed, 6 1/2 In. .... 200.00 To 260.00
Weller, Vase, Sicardo, Leaf & Berry, Bulbous, Iridescent, Blue, 5 In. 235.00
Weller, Vase, Sicardo, Metallic Green, Rose, Berries, Leaves, 6 In. 225.00
Weller, Vase, Sicardo, Peacock Feather, 14 In. 595.00
Weller, Vase, Sicardo, Pink Lavender Ground, Silvery Flowers, 7 3/8 In. 175.00
Weller, Vase, Sicardo, Swirled Bowl 225.00
Weller, Vase, Silvertone, Ink Weller Ware Mark, 6 X 5 1/2 In. 55.00
Weller, Vase, Silvertone, Yellow Mums, 2 Handled, 6 1/2 In. 45.00
Weller, Vase, Souevo, Indian Design, 5 X 7 In. 75.00
Weller, Vase, Sunflower, Open Handles, 5 In. 32.00
Weller, Vase, Swirls, Green To Blue Iridescent, No.5323, Signed, 6 In. 300.00
Weller, Vase, Wall, Squirrel, 9 1/4 In. 30.00
Weller, Vase, Wheat Emblem, Pink, Green 45.00
Weller, Vase, Wild Rose, Handled, 6 1/2 In. 12.00
Weller, Vase, Wild Rose, No.22-4, 9 1/2 In. 20.00
Weller, Vase, Wild Rose, Pink, 7 In. .... 8.00 To 18.00
Weller, Vase, Woodcraft, Bud, Double, Two Cats Perched On Fence, 7 1/2 X 7 In. 145.00
Weller, Vase, Woodcraft, Double Tree Trunk, 7 1/2 X 8 1/2 In. 30.00
Weller, Vase, Woodcraft, Foxes, Twig Top, 5 X 7 In. 40.00
Weller, Vase, Woodcraft, Owl, 13 In. 125.00
Weller, Vase, Woodcraft, Tree Trunk, 9 In. 45.00
Weller, Vase, Woodcraft, 5 Openings, Impressed Weller, 10 1/2 In. 34.00
Weller, Vase, Woodline, 10 1/2 In. 60.00
Weller, Vase, Woodrose, 6 1/2 In. 23.50
Weller, Wall Pocket, Glendale, 4 Birds 65.00
Weller, Wall Pocket, Roma, 7 In. 20.00
Weller, Wall Pocket, Sydonia, Double, Blue 21.00
Weller, Wall Pocket, Woodcraft, Full Squirrel Figure, 9 In. 60.00
Weller, Woodcraft, Candlestick, Tan, Tree Trunk, Small Apples, 8 1/2 In. 16.50
Wheelock, Chocolate Pot, 4 Cup & Saucer, Floral, Pink, Green & Gold 400.00
Wheelock, Dish, Candy, White Flowers On Green, Signed, Vienna, 8 X 7 In. 25.00
Whieldon, Rooster, 4 In. 195.00
   Willow, see Blue Willow
Windowpane, Beveled Glass, 23 X 27 In. 750.00
Windowpane, Double Hung, Blue & Amber, Blue Jewels, 27 1/2 X 74 In. 700.00
Windowpane, Flower, Vase, Amber Beveled Glass, 44 X 89 In. 1750.00
Windowpane, Flowered, Blue Jewels, Amber Jewels, 56 X 86 In. 2250.00
Windowpane, Gilt Edge Whiskey, Leaded Glass, 33 X 43 In., Pair 1500.00
Windowpane, Iris, Purple, Green & Orange Leaves, 34 X 34 In. 450.00
Windowpane, Peasant Girl, 20 X 69 In. 700.00
Windowpane, Saloon, Advertising, Red Letters, Matching Window Included 1500.00
Windowpane, Saloon, Red Letters, 36 X 40 In. 400.00
Windowpane, Sandwich Glass, Amber, Leaf Design, 4 In.Square 19.00
Windowpane, Sandwich Glass, Blue, Concentric Circle Design, 5 3/4 In.Square 24.00

Windowpane, Stag Elk, 1903, 44 X 90 In.	1500.00
Windowpane, Stained Glass, Tulip Decoration, 44 X 19 In.	135.00
Windowpane, Theater Lobby, Colorful, 3 Baskets Of Oranges, 42 X 71 In.	1250.00
Wood Carving, Bear, Sitting Up, Glass Eyes, 17 In.	375.00
Wood Carving, Black Pig, Standing, Teakwood, 2 1/4 In.	4.00
Wood Carving, Bookend, Dragons, Brass, Pair	40.00
Wood Carving, Bookend, Duck's Head, 12 X 7 In., Pair	59.00
Wood Carving, Buddha, Kneeling, Indo-Chinese, Gilt Tracings, 24 In.	70.00
Wood Carving, Dog, Black, Glass Eyes, 4 X 3 In.	10.00
Wood Carving, Figurine, Turtle, 5 X 3 In.	12.00
Wood Carving, Fisherman, Ivory Eyes & Teeth, Cherry, Pair	550.00
Wood Carving, Fisherman, Oriental Cherry Carvings, 14 In., Pair	550.00
Wood Carving, Indian, Cigar Store, 44 In.	1250.00
Wood Carving, Lion, 17 X 11 In.	35.00
Wood Carving, Mask, Water Buffalo Form, African	40.00
Wood Carving, Match Holder, Barrel Shape, One Piece, 2 1/4 X 1 1/2 In.	12.00
Wood Carving, Nude Black Woman, Gay 90's Trade Figure, 63 In.	2500.00
Wood Carving, Nude Girl, 33 1/2 In.	250.00
Wood Carving, Owl, Sitting On Stump, Glass Eyes, 3 In.	28.00
Wood Carving, Pipe Rack, Bear Playing Flute, 6 X 11 In.	36.00
Wood Carving, Plate, Bread, Raised Flowers, German Wording	37.50
Wood Carving, Robin, Put On Wooden Base, Life-Size	35.00
Wood Carving, Rooster, Painted, 12 1/2 In.	85.00
Wood Carving, Russian Man & Woman, Polychrome, Pair	90.00
Wood Carving, 2 Huntsmen Descending Rocky Cliff, Swiss, 31 In.	250.00
Wooden, see also Kitchen, Store, Tool	
Wooden, Carousel Horse, see Carousel, Horse	
Wooden, Barrel, Cider, Birch Hoops, Center Bung Wooden Spigot, 22 1/2 In.	35.00
Wooden, Bellows, Oak	55.00
Wooden, Bellows, Oak, Small	35.00
Wooden, Birdcage, 10 1/2 In.Square, 12 1/2 In.High	33.00
Wooden, Board, Cheese, Bird Print, 12 In.	48.50

Wooden, Bobbin, 12 In.

Wooden, Bobbin, 12 In. ..... *Illus*	3.00
Wooden, Bootjack, Arched Top, Pegged Construction, 6 1/2 X 24 1/2 In.	16.00
Wooden, Bootjack, Bird's-Eye Maple, Scalloped, 12 1/4 In.	25.00
Wooden, Bootjack, Hand-Hewn, Hole For Hanging, 15 In.	6.50
Wooden, Bootjack, Signed B.E.True, Pine	18.00
Wooden, Bottle, Cliquot Club, 39 In.	150.00
Wooden, Bowl, Burl, Cereal Size	55.00
Wooden, Bowl, Burl, Ear Handle For Hanging, 8 In.	40.00
Wooden, Bowl, Burl, Flared Rim, 17 In.	300.00
Wooden, Bowl, Chopping, Red Exterior, 6 X 22 1/2 In.	150.00
Wooden, Bowl, Hand-Carved Burl, 2 1/2 X 6 3/4 In.	100.00
Wooden, Bowl, Hand-Carved Burl, 3 1/4 X 9 1/2 In.	150.00
Wooden, Bowl, Hand-Carved Burl, 5 1/4 X 12 In.	200.00
Wooden, Bowl, Light Green Paint, 10 In.	35.00
Wooden, Bowl, Maple Sugar, Wire Bail, Finial On Cover, Round	195.00
Wooden, Bowl, Natural Finish, Chestnut, 9 In.	23.00
Wooden, Bowl, Red Paint Outside, Patina Inside, Hand-Hewn, 21 In.Diameter	85.00
Wooden, Bowl, 2 Turnings At Base, Turned Collar, 16 X 16 In.	400.00
Wooden, Box, Ammunition, Brass Hinges, Stenciled, 9 1/2 X 9 1/2 X 14 1/2 In.	20.00

Wooden, Box, Bird's-Eye Maple, C.1830, 6 1/4 X 8 X 4 3/4 In. 75.00
Wooden, Box, Burl, Covered, Matching Scoop, 4 1/2 X 3 1/4 In. 285.00
Wooden, Box, Burl, Lidded, Butterfly Hinge, 7 X 5 X 4 1/2 In. 140.00
Wooden, Box, Butter, Pine, Bentwood Handle Locks When Lifted, 12 X 7 In. 75.00
Wooden, Box, Butter, Walnut, 5 Removable Shelves, Sliding Front Panels, 21 In. 150.00
Wooden, Box, Candle, Beveled Top, Square Nails, Red, 11 1/2 X 5 In. 65.00
Wooden, Box, Candle, Blue, 9 1/2 X 20 X 6 In. 100.00
Wooden, Box, Candle, Chip Carved, Pennsylvania, Dated 1789, 3 X 10 In. 325.00
Wooden, Box, Candle, Pine, Beveled Slide, Square Nailed, 13 X 8 X 10 In. 68.00
Wooden, Box, Candle, Pine, Red, Dovetailed, Hanging, Open, 13 1/4 In.Long 130.00
Wooden, Box, Candle, Pine, Slide Top, Finger Depression, 13 X 8 X 10 In. 68.00
Wooden, Box, Cheese, 2 X 3 X 9 In. 1.75
Wooden, Box, Church Collection, Turned Handle, Dovetailed, 5 In.Square 31.50
Wooden, Box, Dark Stain, Mixed Woods, Ivory Escutcheon, Lock & Key 45.00
Wooden, Box, Glove, Burnt, Art Nouveau 16.50
Wooden, Box, Jewelry, Rosewood 110.00
Wooden, Box, Knife, Pine, Slant Sides, Scalloped, Center Open Handle 25.00
Wooden, Box, Knife, 18th Century Sheraton, Inlaid Decoration 175.00
Wooden, Box, Lacquerware Hinged Top, C.1860, 3 3/4 X 2 1/2 X 1 In. 10.00
Wooden, Box, Pantry, Dark Green, Round Buttonhole Hoop 95.00
Wooden, Box, Pantry, Laps In Natural Finish, Copper Nails, 4 3/4 In. 25.00
Wooden, Box, Rosewood, Mother-Of-Pearl Inlay, Red Velvet Compartments 175.00
Wooden, Box, Russian, Village Scene Painted On Cover, Signed Inside Lid 25.00
Wooden, Box, Stereopticon Card, Walnut, Slotted, Brass Fittings, 9 X 14 In. 65.00
Wooden, Box, Storage, Covered, Green 65.00
Wooden, Box, Tea, Tin-Lined, Outside Papered With Tea Pickers, Japan, 15 In. 45.00
Wooden, Box, Turned Handle, Dovetailing On Corners 29.50
Wooden, Box, 2 Fingered, Wooden Pegs, Oval, Covered 75.00
Wooden, Bread Board, I Piece, With Edge, 20 X 24 In. 45.00
Wooden, Bride's Box, Bentwood, Clover, C.1825, 8 3/4 X 18 3/4 In. 475.00
Wooden, Broom, Hearth, Birch Splint, American 160.00
Wooden, Bucket, Sugar, Covered, Carved Handle & Pegs, Copper Nails 45.00
Wooden, Bucket, Water, Bentwood Handle, Wooden Pegs 27.50
Wooden, Bucket, Water, Wooden Handles, Hoops, Lid 160.00
Wooden, Bucket, Well, Iron Bands, Chain, Oak, 8 X 12 In. 65.00
Wooden, Butter Paddle, Burl, Hand-Carved, 8 In. 125.00
Wooden, Cabinet, Cherry, 8 Drawer 90.00
Wooden, Cabinet, Medicine, Oak 50.00
Wooden, Candlestick, Oak, Turnings, 10 1/4 In., Pair 15.00
Wooden, Candlestick, Spiral, Brass Drip Tray, 8 In., Pair 25.00
Wooden, Canteen, C.18th Century 120.00
Wooden, Case, Carrying, R.C.Cola 12.00
Wooden, Case, Jewel, Easel Mirror In Top, 3 Drawers, Chinese, C.1800, 10 In. 100.00
Wooden, Case, Watercolorist, With Fittings, Mahogany, C.1800 .... 285.00
Wooden, Chest, Blanket, Dark Blue Paint, Square Nails, 13 X 28 1/2 In. 85.00
Wooden, Chest, Dower, Turnip Feet, C.1750, 25 1/2 X 13 X 14 1/2 In. 185.00
Wooden, Chest, Folk Art Decorated, Brown & Yellow Paint, 7 X 10 1/2 In. 65.00
Wooden, Chest, Money, Korean, Fall Front, Brass Mounts, C.1890, 18 In. 200.00
Wooden, Chest, Money, Korean, Fall Front, Brass Mounts, C.1890, 19 In. 175.00
Wooden, Chest, Rice, Korean, Hinged Drop Front, Iron Mounts, C.1850, 24 In. 150.00
Wooden, Chest, Tool, Walnut, 4 Pine Trays, Lock & Key, Brass Escutcheon 125.00
Wooden, Coffin, Child's, Oak 60.00
Wooden, Cream Skimmer, Maple Burl, Handled, 2 3/4 X 3 3/4 In. 220.00
Wooden, Curd Breaker, Pine, Original Red Paint 90.00
Wooden, Desk Set, 3 Inkwell Inserts, Pressed Glass Tray For Pens 100.00
Wooden, Dish, Inlaid Brass Center, Carved Border & Center 7.50
Wooden, Eggcup, Albino Wood, Hand-Turned 12.50
Wooden, Firkin, Red, Covered, 1 Piece Base, 1 Piece Lid 235.00
Wooden, Firkin, Wooden Hoops & Handle 60.00
Wooden, Fork, Hay, 3 Tine 36.00
Wooden, Fork, 4 Tines, Signed M.B.Young 75.00
Wooden, Frame, Walnut, Miniature, 3 X 3 1/2 In., Pair 35.00
Wooden, Grater, Paper Label, Carved 1898, 20 X 4 In. 37.00
Wooden, Hat Stretcher 8.50
Wooden, Hatchel, Cover, Chip Carved, Handmade Nails, 23 X 5 X 5 In. 29.00

Wooden, Hay Fork, Tines Pegged, 22 1/2 X 51 In.	125.00
Wooden, Humidor, Mother-Of-Pearl Inlay	100.00
Wooden, Inkwell, Traveling, 2 In.	30.00
Wooden, Keg, Barrel-Shaped Rum, Iron Hoops, C.1770	150.00
Wooden, Keg, Rum Or Water, Staved Construction, Carved Sides	135.00
Wooden, Keg, Rum, Handle, Blue, No Stopper	45.00
Wooden, Keg, Rum, 8 In.	42.00
Wooden, Keller, Wooden Hoops	245.00
Wooden, Key, Bed, Handmade, For Tightening Rope Beds	18.00
Wooden, Lemon Squeezer, Chestnut, 10 1/2 In.	25.00
Wooden, Letter, D, 5 In. ....Illus	9.50
Wooden, Mattress Roller, Resembles Giant Rolling Pin, 5 X 28 In.	65.00

Wooden, Letter, D, 5 In.

Wooden, Mold, Maple Sugar, Square, 2 Part	150.00
Wooden, Mortar & Pestle, Bulging Base, 5 Scooped Steps, 3 X 7 In.	50.00
Wooden, Mortar, American, Footed, Bird's-Eye & Tiger, 5 3/4 X 5 1/4 In.	145.00
Wooden, Mug, 5 Iron Bands, Inscribed & Dated 1905, Scroll Handle	57.50
Wooden, Nutcracker, Carved Friar's Head With Cowl	34.00
Wooden, Nutcracker, Carved Head Of Bulldog, 19th Century, 9 In.	52.00
Wooden, Nutcracker, Woman's Head	35.00
Wooden, Paddle, Butter	8.00
Wooden, Pail, Sap, Maple, Wood Stave, C.1880, 2 1/2 Gallon	4.00
Wooden, Piggin	105.00
Wooden, Plate, Eating, 9 In.	130.00
Wooden, Rattle, Baby's, Turned Shaft With 5 Captive Rings, 5 3/4 In.	19.00
Wooden, Roasting Jack, C.1750	900.00
Wooden, Shoes, Large, Pair	30.00
Wooden, Shovel, Barn, C.1890, 36 In.	37.50
Wooden, Sleigh, Swan Shape, Restored	700.00
Wooden, Spice Rack, Knobs, Metal Name Plates, 7 Drawer, 9 X 11 1/2 In.	20.00
Wooden, Spoon, Carved, Oriental, 13 1/4 In.	35.00
Wooden, Stretcher, Sweater, Child's	25.00
Wooden, Sugar, Bulbous, Bail, Painesville, Ohio, 3 X 3 1/4 In.	195.00
Wooden, Tea Caddy, Rosewood, C.1845	165.00
Wooden, Timer, Music, Cased	3.50
Wooden, Tongs, Laundry, Scissor Shape, Open Handles, Copper Rivet, 12 1/2 In.	30.00
Wooden, Tray, Knife, Pine & Chestnut, Dovetailed Corners	27.00
Wooden, Tray, Knife, Walnut, Canted Sides, 2 Sections, Handled, 12 3/4 X 8 In.	16.00
Wooden, Tray, Walnut Veneer, Federal Period, 11 1/2 X 18 1/2 In.	2000.00
Wooden, Trencher, Maple, Round, 6 In.	125.00
Wooden, Vase, Burl, Turned Ovoid, Flared Lip	75.00
Wooden, Vase, Carved Teak, Birds, Pinecones, 11 In.	65.00
Wooden, Walker, Child's Lawn Ball, 44 Pieces Of Wood, Victorian, No Nails	150.00
Wooden, Wall Pocket, For Magazines, Carved	22.00
Wooden, Washboard, War Model, Marked, 8 1/2 X 18 In.	13.00
Wooden, Washing Machine, Rapid Washing Machine, Shear & Co., Table Top, 1910	99.00
Wooden, Whiffletree, Iron Hooks At Opposite Ends	7.50
Wooden, Winder, Yarn, Adjustable Squirrel Cage Swift	175.00
Wooden, Winder, Yarn, Walnut	69.50
Worcester, see also Royal Worcester	
Worcester, Barrel, Silver Plate Cover, White, Pink, Locke, 1895, 8 1/2 X 19 In.	100.00

Worcester, Bowl, Blossom Finial, Covered, Crescent Mark, Dr.Wall Period, 5 In. 195.00
Worcester, Bowl, Blue & White, Chinese, Crescent, Dr.Wall, 4 1/2 In. 195.00
Worcester, Bowl, Flowers & Insects, C.1770-80, Crescent Mark, 6 1/2 In. 125.00
Worcester, Bowl, Shell, Footed, Grainger, 4 1/2 X 4 In. 35.00
Worcester, Cake Stand, Daffodil, Yellow, Gold Trim, Scalloped Rim, 10 1/2 In. 65.00
Worcester, Figurine, Fox, 7 1/2 In. 95.00
Worcester, Figurine, Pug Dog, Chamberlain, Green Plinth, 3 X 2 1/2 In., Pair 225.00
Worcester, Jar, Chinese Decoration, Cover, Blue, White, Dr.Wall 225.00
Worcester, Jug, No, 1714, Purple Mark, 6 1/2 In. 140.00
Worcester, Pitcher, Cream, White, Gilt, Cobalt Bands, 4 1/2 In. 155.00
Worcester, Pitcher, Fluted White, Gilt Floral, Cobalt Bands, 4 1/2 In. 155.00
Worcester, Plate, Dessert, Royal Lily, Dr.Wall Period, 7 1/2 In. 145.00
Worcester, Plate, Heraldic Lion, Cobalt & Yellow, Chamberlain, 9 In. 28.00
Worcester, Plate, Ivory, Flowers, Scalloped Edge, C.1889, Set Of 8 .... 110.00
Worcester, Syrup, Basket Weave, Leaves & Acorns, Pewter Top, Incised, 8 In. 47.00
Worcester, Teapot, Oblong, Blue Underglaze, Royal Lily, 7 In. 340.00
Worcester, Thimble, Porcelain 15.00
Worcester, Tureen & Underplate, Soup, Blue, Gold, & White, Elephant Handles 295.00
Worcester, Vase, Hand-Painted Peacock, Locke, Signed Bach, 4 X 2 1/2 In. 88.00
Worcester, Vase, Reticulated, 3 Feet, 6 In. 275.00
Worcester, Vase, White & Pink, 6 1/2 In. 90.00
World War I, Belt Buckle, Gott Mit Uns, German 18.00
World War I, Bugle, Brass, U.S.Regulation 32.00
World War I, Calendar, 1917, Woman, Flag, Army, Framed 100.00
World War I, Cannon, Iron, Shoots Carbine Gas 22.50
World War I, Dish, Cheese, Flags, Miniature, 1914 .... 15.00
World War I, Figurine Set, Lead Soldiers, Set Of 54 .... 65.00
World War I, Paperweight, Metal, Marechal Foch Train, Armistice, 1918, 3 In. 17.00
World War I, Poster, Boys Come Over Here, You're Wanted, 40 X 51 In. 55.00
World War I, Poster, Fight Or Buy Bonds 40.00
World War I, Poster, Howard Chandler Christy, Fight Or Buy Bonds 75.00
World War I, Poster, Keep Him Free, 30 X 20 In. 35.00
World War I, Poster, Make Every Minute Count For Pershing, 28 X 22 In. 15.00
World War I, Poster, Uncle Sam, I Want You For The U.S.Army, Flagg, 38 In. 165.00
World War I, Silk, The Farewell, Square, 17 In. 11.00
World War I, Toy, Cannon, Lead 2.50
World War II, Badge, Nazi Luftwaffe Pilot's 12.00
World War II, Banner, American Eagle, 2 Flags, Large V, 23 X 17 In. 10.00
World War II, Buckle, Belt, Brass 1.00
World War II, Buckle, Belt, Luftwaffe Flyer's, Bird & Nazi Emblem 50.00
World War II, Cap, Luftwaffe African Campaign, Slouch Type, Brown 30.00
World War II, Cap, Nazi Luftwaffe Officer's Dress 55.00
World War II, Card, Playing, Caricatures By A.Bernal, Set Of 56 .... 125.00
World War II, Case, Cigarette, Nazi Flag Colors, Swastika 50.00
World War II, Dagger, Nazi SS, Black Hilt & Scabbard, Eagle & Swastika 250.00
World War II, Flag, Nazi, 5 X 9 In. 50.00
World War II, Flag, Surrender, Prisoner In Africa's, Cross In Center 75.00
World War II, Hat, Nazi SS General 150.00
World War II, Helmet, Doughboy 7.50
World War II, Helmet, Nazi Pith, Insignia & Strap 40.00
World War II, Knife & Case, Nazi Officer's 125.00
World War II, Knife & Case, Nazi Youth Gestapo 45.00
World War II, Knife, Remember Pearl Harbor, Victory 3.00
World War II, Pin, Uncle Sam Hanging Hitler 17.00
World War II, Poster, Fisher Bodies 15.00
World War II, Poster, Hitler, Monkey 5.00
World War II, Poster, Keep America Free 15.00
World War II, Poster, Uncle Sam, Organ Grinder 5.00
World War II, Range Finder, Hand, Navy 15.00
World War II, Ration Book, Leatherette Folder 5.00
World War II, Sword & Scabbard, Nazi Army Officer's, Eagle & Swastika 120.00
    World's Fair, see also Coca-Cola items; Copper, Ashtray; Milk
    Glass items; Souvenir, Spoon
World's Fair, Album, 1904 St.Louis In A Nut Shell, Egg Shape, Photos 38.00
World's Fair, Ashtray, Century Of Progress, Chrysler, Copper 7.00

World's Fair, Ashtray, Copper, 1940	5.00
World's Fair, Ashtray, 1926 Sesquicentennial, Philadelphia, Pewter	12.00
World's Fair, Bank, Esso, Glass, 1939, 5 1/2 In.	25.00
World's Fair, Bank, Flat Dime, Dated 1964-65	8.00
World's Fair, Banner, Gold & White Woven Silk, Columbian Expo, 10 X 12 In.	25.00
World's Fair, Basket, Columbian Exposition, Lead, Wicker Basket Shape	11.00
World's Fair, Bell, Columbian, Glass, 1893	95.00
World's Fair, Booklet, 1904 At St.Louis	10.00
World's Fair, Bottle, Perfume, Columbian Exposition, Blue, 1893	22.00
World's Fair, Bottle, Vinegar, Opaque, 1939	10.00
World's Fair, Box, Cigarette, Soviet Pavilion, 1939	6.00
World's Fair, Box, Hairpin, Columbian Exposition, Footed, Silver Plated, 1893	8.00
World's Fair, Box, Hairpin, Columbian Exposition, Silver Plate, 4 In., 1893	12.00
World's Fair, Box, Jewel, Columbian Exposition, Beveled Glass Top, Footed	55.00
World's Fair, Box, Pill, Columbian Fair, Landing Of Columbus, 1492-1892	46.50
World's Fair, Bracelet, Century Of Progress, 1933	4.00
World's Fair, Bracelet, 1933 Chicago	12.00
World's Fair, Bracelet, 1934	6.00
World's Fair, Buckle, Belt, Century Of Progress, Chicago, Nickel Silver, 1933	18.50
World's Fair, Button, Celluloid, With Picture, 1939	4.00
World's Fair, Charm, Columbian Exposition, Chicago, Sterling Silver Pig, 1893	34.00
World's Fair, Compact, Century Of Progress, Chicago, 1933	15.00
World's Fair, Compact, Chicago, Boxed	12.00
World's Fair, Cup, Collapsible, St.Louis, 1904	15.00
World's Fair, Cup, Folding, Aluminum, St.Louis, 1904	8.00
World's Fair, Cup, 1904, Green, 3 Legged, Colorado Design	25.00
World's Fair, Cup, 3-Legged, Pressed Glass, Colorado, Green, 1904	35.00
World's Fair, Ewer, Satin Glass, Blue On Pink Enamel, 19 In.	85.00
World's Fair, Fan, St.Louis, Education Building	45.00
World's Fair, Figurine, Dutch Boy & Girl Carrying Bucket, Pair, 1933	15.00
World's Fair, Handkerchief, Columbian Exposition, 1893, 18 In.	20.00
World's Fair, Handkerchief, 1939	5.00
World's Fair, Hatchet, Amethyst Glass, 1893, 6 In.	30.00
World's Fair, Hatchet, Glass, Embossed World's Fair 1893	15.00
World's Fair, Hatchet, Glass, 1893	12.00
World's Fair, Hatchet, Libbey, 1893, 8 In.	45.00
World's Fair, Hatchet, St.Louis, 1904	25.00
World's Fair, Horn, St.Louis, Carved Cow Horn	12.50
World's Fair, Kerchief, Pan American Exposition, 20 In.	45.00
World's Fair, Knife, Peephole, St.Louis Scene, 1904	1200.00
World's Fair, Match Holder, Cotton States Exposition, Metal, 1895	19.00
World's Fair, Match Holder, Figural, Frog, Frosted, 1893, 5 In.	100.00
World's Fair, Matchbox Holder, St.Louis Exposition, Metal, 1904, 4 In.	30.00
World's Fair, Mug, Pan American Exposition, Stoneware, Gray, Blue, Utica	48.00
World's Fair, Paperweight, Illuminated Lady, Columbian Exposition	43.00
World's Fair, Paperweight, Pan American Exposition, Picture, 1901	20.00
World's Fair, Paperweight, 1904 Exposition, Administration Building	20.00
World's Fair, Peep Show, 1939	35.00
World's Fair, Pen, Quill, World's Columbian Exposition, Chicago, 1893	18.50
World's Fair, Penny, Lucky Penny, Century Of Progress, 1938	4.00
World's Fair, Pin, N.Y.World's Fair, Opening For Photo	12.50
World's Fair, Pitcher, New York, Hand-Painted, Blue, Green, Cream, 1939, 7 In.	40.00
World's Fair, Plate, St.Louis, Festival & Cascade Garden, Clear, 1904	10.00
World's Fair, Plate, St.Louis, Festival Hall & Cascade Gardens, 1904, 7 In.	14.00
World's Fair, Postcard, Fold-Out, Stand-Up Views, Columbian Exposition	17.00
World's Fair, Postcard, Hold To Light, St.Louis Fair, 1904	18.00
World's Fair, Postcard, St.Louis, Samuel Cupples, 1904	7.50
World's Fair, Program, 1940, Billy Rose Aquacade	4.50
World's Fair, Purse, Child's, Metal, Chicago World's Fair	12.50
World's Fair, Salt & Pepper, Trylon & Perisphere, 1939	8.00
World's Fair, Saltshaker, Egg, Columbian Exposition, 1893, Milk Glass	35.00
World's Fair, Scarf, Columbian Exp.Chicago, Orange, Machinery Hall, 1893	19.95
World's Fair, Spoon Set, 1939, Set Of 12	35.00
World's Fair, Spoon, Pan American Exposition, Sterling Silver	24.00
World's Fair, Spoon, Sterling Silver, 1892	24.00

World's Fair, Spoon, W.Rogers, 1936	6.00
World's Fair, Stickpin, Pan American Exposition, 2 Hemispheres Connect, 1904	17.50
World's Fair, Sugar & Creamer, King's Crown, William Law, 1893	35.00
World's Fair, Sugar, Creamer, Pitcher, 1939	15.00
World's Fair, Thimble, Columbian Exposition, Fair Buildings, Sterling Silver	52.00
World's Fair, Tie Clip, Metal, New York, 1939	3.00
World's Fair, Tin, Coffee, Jamestown Exposition, White House Coffee, 1907	8.95
World's Fair, Toby Jug, George Washington, 1939, 5 1/2 In.	24.00
World's Fair, Toby Mugs, Miniature, Martha & George Washington, 1939, Pair	19.00
World's Fair, Toothpick, Columbian Exposition, Columbus-Vespucius, Glass	26.00
World's Fair, Toothpick, Saxon & William Law, Flashed Red, 1893	22.00
World's Fair, Tray, Change, Raised Buffalo, Pan American, 1901, 4 In.	12.00
World's Fair, Tray, Pin, Chicago, 1933	7.50
World's Fair, Tray, Seattle	5.00
World's Fair, Tray, Tip, St.Louis, Blonde Girl Eating Junket	47.50
World's Fair, Tray, Unisphere, Rectangular, 1965, 8 X 10 1/2 In.	7.00
World's Fair, Tray, Unisphere, Round, 1965, 8 In.	4.00
World's Fair, Trophy, Car Racing, St.Louis World's Fair	60.00
World's Fair, Tumbler, Draped Swirl, Ruby Flashed, 1893	27.00
World's Fair, Tumbler, Louisiana Exposition, Milk Glass, Tall	14.00
World's Fair, Tumbler, St.Louis, White Milk Glass, 1904	13.00
World's Fair, Tureen, White, Gold & Aqua Border, Paris Expo, 1867, 15 X 12 In.	195.00
World's Fair, Vase, Cranberry Glass, New York, 1940, 3 3/4 In.	10.00
World's Fair, Vase, New York, Cranberry Flash, Gold Trim, 1940, 4 In.	8.50
World's Fair, Watch Fob, 1940	4.50
Yellowware, Coffeepot, Lighthouse, Tall	120.00
Yellowware, Mold, Ear Of Corn	15.00
Yellowware, Mold, Pudding, Grape	38.00
Yellowware, Pan, Milk, 12 In.	30.00
Yellowware, Plate, Pie, Sharpe's Warranted	25.00

Zane Pottery was founded in 1921 by Adam, Reed, and McClelland in South Zanesville, Ohio. It was sold in 1941.

Zane, see also Peters & Reed

Zane, Bowl, Landsun, Blended Blue Matte Glaze, 8 In.	9.00
Zane, Pot, Hanging, Raised Floral, Green, Glazed Interior, 2 1/2 X 6 In.	9.00
Zane, Vase, Garland, Glaze, 6 1/2 In.	40.00
Zane, Vase, Slip Painted Iris, 15 In.	75.00

Zanesville Art Pottery was founded in 1900 by David Schmidt in Zanesville, Ohio. The firm made faience, umbrella stands, jardinieres, and pedestals. It worked until 1962.

Zanesville, Jardiniere, Forest, 5 1/2 In.	34.00 To 35.00
Zanesville, Jug, Whiskey, Floral Decoration, Brown Glaze.LaMoro, 5 1/2 In.	95.00
Zanesville, Tankard, Standard Glaze, Floral, La Moro, N.C., 13 1/2 In.	175.00
Zanesville, Vase, Pansies, Molded Leaves, Glazed, Handled, La Moro, 6 X 8 In.	185.00
Zs Bavaria, Plate, Violets In Basket, Gold Rococo Rim, 9 1/2 In.	34.00

Zsolnay pottery was made in Hungary after 1862, and was characterized by Persian, Art Nouveau, or Hungarian motifs.

Zsolnay, Bowl, Lobster Decoration, Rectangular, Signed, 7 X 3 In.	165.00
Zsolnay, Cup & Saucer, Beige, Enameled Florals	48.00
Zsolnay, Cup & Saucer, Demitasse, Gold & Purple Luster, Impressed Mark	25.00
Zsolnay, Cup & Saucer, Enameled Florals On Beige, Large	48.00
Zsolnay, Figurine, Crested Bird	15.00
Zsolnay, Figurine, Deer	85.00
Zsolnay, Figurine, Girl, Iridescent Green, Prior To WWI, Artist Signature	75.00
Zsolnay, Figurine, Goat With Baby, Green, Gold Iridescent, Simko, 5 1/2 In.	80.00
Zsolnay, Figurine, Little Girl Sitting Beside A Lamb, 3 X 3 1/2 In.	90.00
Zsolnay, Figurine, Nude Woman, Iridescent, Art Nouveau, 5 1/2 X 10 In.	325.00
Zsolnay, Figurine, Owl, Art Deco, 6 In.	35.00
Zsolnay, Figurine, Pair Of Goats	85.00
Zsolnay, Figurine, Sitting Fox, Green	62.00
Zsolnay, Group, Goat & Kid, Green, Gold, Iridescent	110.00
Zsolnay, Jug, Art Deco Floral, 2 Handled, Footed, 5 1/2 In.	28.00

Zsolnay, Jug, Whistling, Cream, Green, Gold, Turquoise, Mauve Raised Designs 125.00
Zsolnay, Jug, Whistling, Ivory, Floral, Green, Gold, Turquoise, & Rose, 6 1/4 In. 125.00
Zsolnay, Pitcher, Puzzle, Church Mark, 8 1/2 In. 149.00
Zsolnay, Teapot, Multicolored, Signed 175.00
Zsolnay, Vase, Blown-Out Reticulated Puffs, Loopings On Handle 200.00
Zsolnay, Vase, Cream, Blown-Out Pink, Blue, & Yellow Decoration, 6 In. 145.00
Zsolnay, Vase, Green, Gold Iridescent, 5 Medallions With Masks, Cabinet Size 95.00
Zsolnay, Vase, Green, Gold, Purple Iridescent, 4 Handles, 6 1/2 In. 185.00
Zsolnay, Vase, Iridescent Gold, Green, Purple Luster, 4 Handles, 6 1/2 In. 185.00
Zsolnay, Vase, Iridescent, Green, Blues, Brown, Orchids, Gold, 4 Handled, 9 In. 165.00
Zsolnay, Vase, Woman Figure, Gold & Green Iridescent, Art Nouveau, 9 1/2 In. 275.00
Zsolnay, Vase, Yellow And Brown, Signed, 13 In. 475.00